P9-DNM-876

The
Merriam-
Webster
Dictionary

# The Merriam-Webster Dictionary

Merriam-Webster, Incorporated
Springfield, Massachusetts

## A GENUINE MERRIAM-WEBSTER

The name *Webster* alone is no guarantee of excellence. It is used by a number of publishers and may serve mainly to mislead an unwary buyer.

*Merriam-Webster*™ is the name you should look for when you consider the purchase of dictionaries or other fine reference books. It carries the reputation of a company that has been publishing since 1831 and is your assurance of quality and authority.

Copyright © 2016 by Merriam-Webster, Incorporated

ISBN 978-0-87779-295-6

MADE IN THE UNITED STATES OF AMERICA

2nd Printing   Quad Graphics   Martinsburg, WV   March 2016

# PREFACE

This new edition of *The Merriam-Webster Dictionary* is the seventh in a line of Merriam-Webster paperback dictionaries which began in 1947. It is based on and preserves the best aspects of preceding editions, but it now includes the most important recent vocabulary that was added to *Merriam=Webster's Collegiate Dictionary, Eleventh Edition* over the past decade. Throughout the dictionary, over 8,000 usage examples, including 1,000 that are newly added for this edition, illustrate meanings and help to clarify definitions. All the new material has been based on examples of actual use found in the Merriam-Webster citation files and in edited texts online.

The nearly 65,000 entries and more than 75,000 definitions in this dictionary give coverage to the most frequently used words in the language. The heart of the dictionary is the A-Z vocabulary section, where readers will find information about meaning, spelling, pronunciation, etymology, and synonyms. This section is followed by others that users have long found useful: the section Foreign Words and Phrases covers words and phrases from other languages that often occur in English texts but have not become part of the English vocabulary; the section Biographical Names identifies individuals from history and contemporary culture, as well as biblical, legendary, and mythological characters; the section Geographical Names identifies places of importance in the United States and the world, along with current population figures.

*The Merriam-Webster Dictionary* has been created by a company that has been publishing dictionaries for more than 150 years and continues to maintain an in-house staff of experienced lexicographers. For this edition, the primary editing of the main A-Z vocabulary section and the Foreign Words and Phrases was done by Senior Editor James G. Lowe. Daniel J. Hopkins edited the Geographical Names, and Michael G. Belanger edited the Biographical Names. Specialist editors included Adrienne M. Scholz for cross=reference, Joshua S. Guenter for pronunciation, James L. Rader for etymology, and Joan I. Narmontas for life science. Data entry and data-file processing were handled by Daniel B. Brandon. Susan L. Brady acted as production editor, guiding the book through its typesetting stages, assisted by Emily A. Vezina. Proofreaders included Tasha Martino Bigelow, Serenity H. Carr, Ilya A. Davidovich, Allison M. DeJordy, Joanne M. Despres, Benjamin T. Korzec, Maria A.

Sansalone, Neil S. Serven, Mark A. Stevens, Paul S. Wood, and Judy Yeh, as well as some of the other editors mentioned above. All the editors join in the hope that users will find *The Merriam-Webster Dictionary* to be a concise, handy, and reliable guide to the English language of today.

# EXPLANATORY NOTES

The dictionary contains so much information, that it is necessary to condense much of it to accommodate the limitations of the printed page. This section provides information on the conventions used throughout the dictionary, from the styling of entries and pronunciation to how we present information on usage and meaning. An understanding of the information contained in these notes will make the dictionary both easier and more rewarding to use.

## ENTRIES

A boldface letter or a combination of such letters, including punctuation marks and diacritics where needed, that is set flush with the left-hand margin of each column of type is a main entry. The main entry may consist of letters set solid, of letters joined by a hyphen or a diagonal, or of letters separated by one or more spaces:

**alone** . . . *adj*
**avant–garde** . . . *n*
**and/or** . . . *conj*
**assembly language** *n*
**av·a·lanche** . . . *n*

The material in lightface type that follows each main entry on the same line and on succeeding indented lines presents information about the main entry.

The main entries follow one another in alphabetical order letter by letter: *bill of attainder* follows *billion; Day of Atonement* follows *daylight saving time*. Those containing an Arabic numeral are alphabetized as if the numeral were spelled out: *4-H* comes between *fourfold* and *Four Hundred; 3-D* comes between *three* and *three-dimensional*. Those that often begin with the abbreviation *St.* in common usage have the abbreviation spelled out: *Saint Valentine's Day*. Main entries that begin with *Mc* are alphabetized just as they are spelled.

A pair of guide words is printed at the top of each page. These indicate that the entries falling alphabetically between the words at the top of the outer column of each page are found on that page.

The guide words are the first and last main entries printed on the page:

**archway • armadillo**

When one main entry has exactly the same written form as another, the two are distinguished by superscript numerals preceding each word:

¹**melt** . . . *vb*
²**melt** *n*
¹**pine** . . . *n*
²**pine** *vb*

Full words come before parts of words made up of the same letters; solid compounds come before hyphenated compounds; hyphenated compounds come before open compounds; and lowercase entries come before those with an initial capital:

²**super** *n*
**super-** . . . *prefix*
**run·down** . . . *n*
**run–down** . . . *adj*
**run down** *vb*
**dutch** . . . *adv*
**Dutch** . . . *n*

The centered dots within entry words indicate division points at which a hyphen may be put at the end of a line of print or writing. Thus the noun *cap·puc·ci·no* may be ended on one line and continued on the next in this manner:

*cap-*

*puccino*

*cappuc-*

*cino*

*cappucci-*

*no*

Centered dots are not shown after a single initial letter or before a single terminal letter because typesetters seldom cut off a single letter:

**abyss** . . . *n*
**flighty** . . . *adj*
**idea** . . . *n*

Nor are they usually shown at the second and succeeding homographs unless they differ among themselves:

¹**sig·nal** . . . *n*
²**signal** *vb*
³**signal** *adj*
*but*
¹**min·ute** . . . *n*
²**mi·nute** . . . *adj*

There are acceptable alternative end-of-line divisions just as there are acceptable variant spellings and pronunciations, but no more than one division is shown for any entry in this dictionary.

A double hyphen at the end of a line in this dictionary (as in the definition at **cod**) stands for a hyphen that is retained when the word is written as a unit on one line. This kind of fixed hyphen is always represented in boldface words in this dictionary with an en dash, longer than an ordinary hyphen.

When a main entry is followed by the word *or* and another spelling, the two spellings are equal variants. Both are standard, and either one may be used according to personal inclination:

**ocher** *or* **ochre**

If two variants joined by *or* are out of alphabetical order, they remain equal variants. The one printed first is, however, slightly more common than the second:

¹**plow** *or* **plough**

When another spelling is joined to the main entry by the word *also*, the spelling after *also* is a secondary variant and occurs less frequently than the first:

**ab·sinthe** *also* **ab·sinth**

Secondary variants belong to standard usage and may be used according to personal inclination. Once the word *also* is used to signal a secondary variant, all following secondary variants are joined by *or*:

²**wool·ly** *also* **wool·ie** *or* **wooly**

Variants whose spelling puts them alphabetically more than a column away from the main entry are entered at their own alphabetical places as well as at the applicable main entry:

²**gage** *var of* GAUGE
. . .
¹**gauge** *also* **gage**
²**gauge** *also* **gage**

Variants having a usage label appear only at their own alphabetical places:

**me·tre** . . . *chiefly Brit var of* METER

To show all the stylings that are found for English compounds would require space that can be better used for other information. So this dictionary limits itself to a single styling for a compound:

**peace·mak·er**
**pell–mell**
**boom box**

When a compound is widely used and one styling predominates, that styling is shown. When a compound is uncommon or when the evidence indicates that two or three stylings are approximately equal in frequency, the styling shown is based on the comparison of other similar compounds.

A main entry may be followed by one or more derivatives or by a homograph with a different functional label. These are run-on entries. Each is introduced by a long dash and each has a functional label. They are not defined, however, since their meanings are readily understood from the meaning of the root word:

> **fear·less** . . . *adj* . . . — **fear·less·ly** *adv* — **fear·less·ness** *n*
> **hic·cup** . . . *n* . . . — **hiccup** *vb*

A main entry may be followed by one or more phrases containing the entry word or an inflected form of it. These are also run-on entries. Each is introduced by a long dash but there is no functional label. They are, however, defined since their meanings are more than the sum of the meanings of their elements:

> **¹set** . . . *vb* . . . — **set sail** : . . .

**¹hand** . . . *n* . . . — **at hand** : . . .

Defined phrases of this sort are run on at the entry defining the first major word in the phrase. When there are variants, however, the run-on appears at the entry defining the first major invariable word in the phrase:

> **¹seed** . . . *n* . . . — **go to seed** *or* **run to seed** 1 : . . .

Boldface words that appear within parentheses (as **co·ca** at **co·caine** and **jet engine** and **jet propulsion** at **jet–propelled**) are run-in entries.

Attention is called to the definition of *vocabulary entry* on page 810. The term *dictionary entry* includes all vocabulary entries as well as all boldface entries in the back sections headed "Foreign Words & Phrases," "Biographical Names," and "Geographical Names."

---

# PRONUNCIATION

The matter between a pair of reversed slashes \ \ following the entry word indicates the pronunciation. The symbols used are explained in the chart at the end of this section.

A hyphen is used in the pronunciation to show syllabic division. These hyphens sometimes coincide with the centered dots in the entry word that indicate end-of-line division:

> **ab·sen·tee** \ˌab-sən-ˈtē\

Sometimes they do not:

> **met·ric** \ˈme-trik\

A high-set mark ˈ indicates major (primary) stress or accent; a low-set mark ˌ indicates minor (secondary) stress or accent:

> **heart·beat** \ˈhärt-ˌbēt\

The stress mark stands at the beginning of the syllable that receives the stress.

A syllable with neither a high-set mark nor a low-set mark is unstressed:

> **¹struc·ture** \ˈstrək-chər\

The presence of variant pronunciations indicates that not all educated speakers pronounce words the same way. A second-place variant is not to be regarded as less acceptable than the pronunciation that is given first. It may, in fact, be used by as many educated speakers as the first variant, but the requirements of the printed page are such that one must precede the other:

> **apri·cot** \ˈa-prə-ˌkät, ˈā-\
> **fore·head** \ˈfȯr-əd, ˈfȯr-ˌhed\

Symbols enclosed by parentheses represent elements that are present in the pronunciation of some speakers but are absent from the pronunciation of other speakers, or elements that are present in some but absent from other utterances of the same speaker:

> **¹om·ni·bus** \ˈäm-ni-(ˌ)bəs\
> **ad·di·tion·al** \ə-ˈdish-(ə-)nəl\

Thus, the above parentheses indicate that some people say \ˈäm-ni-ˌbəs\ and others say \ˈäm-ni-bəs\; some \ə-ˈdish-ə-nəl\, others \ə-ˈdish-nəl\.

When a main entry has less than a full pronunciation, the missing part is to be supplied from a pronunciation in a preceding entry or within the same pair of reversed slashes:

> **cham·pi·on·ship** \-,ship\
> **pa·la·ver** \pə-'la-vər, -'lä-\

The pronunciation of the first three syllables of *championship* is found at the main entry *champion*. The hyphens before and after \'lä\ in the pronunciation of *palaver* indicate that both the first and the last parts of the pronunciation are to be taken from the immediately preceding pronunciation.

In general, no pronunciation is indicated for open compounds consisting of two or more English words that have own-place entry:

> **witch doctor** *n*

Only the first entry in a sequence of numbered homographs is given a pronunciation if their pronunciations are the same:

> ¹**re·ward** \ri-'wȯrd\ *vb*
> ²**reward** *n*

The absent but implied pronunciation of derivatives and compounds run on after a main entry is a combination of the pronunciation at the main entry and the pronunciation of the other element as given at its alphabetical place in the vocabulary:

> — **quick·ness** *n*
> — **hold with**

Thus, the pronunciation of *quickness* is the sum of the pronunciations given at *quick* and *-ness;* that of *hold with*, the sum of the pronunciations of the two elements that make up the phrase.

## FUNCTIONAL LABELS

An italic label indicating a part of speech or another functional classification follows the pronunciation or, if no pronunciation is given, the main entry. The eight traditional parts of speech are indicated as follows:

> **bold** . . . *adj*
> **forth·with** . . . *adv*
> ¹**but** . . . *conj*
> **ge·sund·heit** . . . *interj*
> **bo·le·ro** . . . *n*
> ²**un·der** . . . *prep*
> ¹**it** . . . *pron*
> **slap** . . . *vb*

Other italicized labels used to indicate functional classifications that are not traditional parts of speech include:

> **AT** *abbr*
> **self-** *comb form*
> **un-** . . . *prefix*
> **-ial** *adj suffix*
> ²**-ly** *adv suffix*
> ²**-er** . . . *n suffix*
> **-ize** *vb suffix*
> **Fe** *symbol*
> **may** . . . *verbal auxiliary*

Functional labels are sometimes combined:

> **afloat** . . . *adj or adv*

## INFLECTED FORMS

## NOUNS

The plurals of nouns are shown in this dictionary when suffixation brings about a change of final *-y* to *-i-*, when the noun ends in a consonant plus *-o* or in *-ey*, when the noun ends in *-oo*, when the noun has an irregular plural or an uninflected plural or a foreign plural, when the noun is a compound that pluralizes any element but the last, when a final consonant is doubled, when the noun has variant plurals, and when it is believed that the dictionary user might have reasonable doubts about the spelling of the plural or when the plural is spelled in a way contrary to what is expected:

²spy *n, pl* spies
si·lo     *n, pl* silos
val·ley . . . *n, pl* valleys
²shampoo *n, pl* shampoos
mouse . . . *n, pl* mice
moose . . . *n, pl* moose
cri·te·ri·on . . . *n, pl* -ria
son–in–law . . . *n, pl* sons–in–law
¹quiz . . . *n, pl* quiz·zes
¹fish . . . *n, pl* fish *or* fish·es
pi . . . *n, pl* pis
³dry *n, pl* drys

Cutback inflected forms are used when
the noun has three or more syllables:

ame·ni·ty . . . *n, pl* -ties

The plurals of nouns are usually not
shown when the base word is unchanged
by suffixation, when the noun is a compound whose second element is readily
recognizable as a regular free form entered at its own place, or when the noun
is unlikely to occur in the plural.

night . . . *n*
fore·foot . . . *n*
mo·nog·a·my . . . *n*

Nouns that are plural in form and that
are regularly construed as plural are
labeled *n pl*:

munch·ies . . . *n pl*

Nouns that are plural in form but that
are not always construed as plurals
are appropriately labeled:

lo·gis·tics . . . *n sing or pl*

# VERBS

The principal parts of verbs are shown
in this dictionary when suffixation
brings about a doubling of a final consonant or an elision of a final -e or a
change of final -y to -i-, when final -c
changes to -ck in suffixation, when the
verb ends in -ey, when the inflection is irregular, when there are variant inflected forms, and when it is believed that the dictionary user
might have reasonable doubts about
the spelling of an inflected form or
when the inflected form is spelled in a
way contrary to what is expected:

²snag *vb* snagged; snag·ging
¹move . . . *vb* moved; mov·ing
¹cry . . . *vb* cried; cry·ing
¹frol·ic . . . *vb* frol·icked; frol·ick·ing
¹sur·vey . . . *vb* sur·veyed; sur-
vey·ing
¹drive . . . *vb* drove . . . driv·en . . .
driv·ing
²bus *vb* bused *or* bussed; bus·ing
*or* bus·sing
²visa *vb* vi·saed . . . vi·sa·ing
²chagrin *vb* cha·grined . . . cha-
grin·ing

The principal parts of a regularly inflected verb are shown when it is desirable to indicate the pronunciation
of one of the inflected forms:

learn . . . *vb* learned \ˈlərnd, ˈlərnt\;
learn·ing

¹al·ter \ˈȯl-tər\ *vb* al·tered; al·ter-
ing \-t(ə-)riŋ\

Cutback inflected forms are usually
used when the verb has three or more
syllables, when it is a two-syllable
word that ends in -l and has variant
spellings, and when it is a compound
whose second element is readily recognized as an irregular verb:

elim·i·nate . . . *vb* -nat·ed; -nat·ing
²quarrel *vb* -reled *or* -relled; -rel-
ing *or* -rel·ling
¹re·take . . . *vb* -took . . . -tak·en . . .
-tak·ing

The principal parts of verbs are usually not shown when the base word is
unchanged by suffixation or when the
verb is a compound whose second
element is readily recognizable as a
regular free form entered at its own
place:

¹jump . . . *vb*
pre·judge . . . *vb*

Another inflected form of English
verbs is the third person singular of
the present tense, which is regularly
formed by the addition of -s or -es to
the base form of the verb. This inflected form is not shown except at a
handful of entries (as *have* and *do*) for
which it is in some way unusual.

## ADJECTIVES & ADVERBS

The comparative and superlative forms of adjectives and adverbs are shown in this dictionary when suffixation brings about a doubling of a final consonant or an elision of a final -e or a change of final -y to -i-, when the word ends in -ey, when the inflection is irregular, and when there are variant inflected forms:

¹red . . . adj red·der; red·dest
¹tame . . . adj tam·er; tam·est
¹kind·ly . . . adj kind·li·er; -est
hors·ey also horsy . . . adj hors·i·er; -est
¹good . . . adj bet·ter . . . best
¹far . . . adv far·ther . . . or fur·ther . . . far·thest or fur·thest

The superlative forms of adjectives and adverbs of two or more syllables are usually cut back:

³fancy adj fan·ci·er; -est
¹ear·ly . . . adv ear·li·er; -est

The comparative and superlative forms of regularly inflected adjectives and adverbs are shown when it is desirable to indicate the pronunciation of the inflected forms:

¹young \'yəŋ\ adj youn·ger \'yəŋ-gər\; youn·gest \'yəŋ-gəst\

The inclusion of inflected forms in -er and -est at adjective and adverb entries means nothing more about the use of more and most with these adjectives and adverbs than that their comparative and superlative degrees may be expressed in either way: lazier or more lazy; laziest or most lazy.

At a few adjective entries only the superlative form is shown:

²mere adj, superlative mer·est

The absence of the comparative form indicates that there is no evidence of its use.

The comparative and superlative forms of adjectives and adverbs are usually not shown when the base word is unchanged by suffixation, when the inflected forms of the word are identical with those of a preceding homograph, or when the word is a compound whose second element is readily recognizable as a regular free form entered at its own place:

¹near . . . adv
³good adv
un·wor·thy . . . adj

Inflected forms are not shown at undefined run-ons.

## CAPITALIZATION

Most entries in this dictionary begin with a lowercase letter. A few of these have an italicized label often cap, which indicates that the word is as likely to be capitalized as not and that it is as acceptable with an uppercase initial as it is with one in lowercase. Some entries begin with an uppercase letter, which indicates that the word is usually capitalized. The absence of an initial capital or of an often cap label indicates that the word is not ordinarily capitalized:

salm·on . . . n
gar·gan·tuan . . . adj, often cap
Mo·hawk . . . n

The capitalization of entries that are open or hyphenated compounds is similarly indicated by the form of the entry or by an italicized label:

dry goods . . . n pl
french fry n, often cap 1st F
un–Amer·i·can . . . adj
Par·kin·son's disease . . . n
lazy Su·san . . . n
Jack Frost n

A word that is capitalized in some senses and lowercase in others shows variations from the form of the main entry by the use of italicized labels at the appropriate senses:

Trin·i·ty . . . n . . . 2 not cap
To·ry . . . n . . . 3 often not cap
ti·tan . . . n 1 cap
re·nais·sance . . . n . . . 1 cap . . . 2 often cap

## ETYMOLOGY

This dictionary gives the etymologies for a number of the vocabulary entries. These etymologies are inside square brackets preceding the definition. Meanings given in roman type within these brackets are not definitions of the entry, but are meanings of the Middle English, Old English, or non-English words within the brackets.

The etymology gives the language from which words borrowed into English have come. It also gives the form of the word in that language or a representation of the word in our alphabet if the form in that language differs from that in English:

> **phi·lo·den·dron** . . . [NL, tr. Gk. neut. of *philodendros* loving trees . . . ]
> ¹**sav·age** . . . [ME, fr. AF *salvage*, *savage*, fr. LL *salvaticus*, alter.

of L *silvaticus* of the woods, wild . . . ]

An etymology beginning with the name of a language (including ME or OE) and not giving the foreign (or Middle English or Old English) form indicates that this form is the same as the form of the entry word:

> **le·gume** . . . [F]
> ¹**jour·ney** . . . [ME, fr. OF . . . ]

An etymology beginning with the name of a language (including ME or OE) and not giving the foreign (or Middle English or Old English) meaning indicates that this meaning is the same as the meaning expressed in the first definition in the entry:

> **ug·ly** . . . *adj* . . . [ME, fr. ON *uggligr* . . . ] **1** : FRIGHTFUL, DIRE

## USAGE

Three types of status labels are used in this dictionary—temporal, regional, and stylistic—to signal that a word or a sense of a word is not part of the standard vocabulary of English.

The temporal label *obs* for "obsolete" means that there is no evidence of use since 1755:

> ³**post** *n* **1** *obs*

The label *obs* is a comment on the word being defined. When a thing, as distinguished from the word used to designate it, is obsolete, appropriate orientation is usually given in the definition:

> **cat·a·pult** . . . *n* **1** : an ancient military machine for hurling missiles

The temporal label *archaic* means that a word or sense once in common use is found today only sporadically or in special contexts:

> ¹**mete** . . . *vb* . . . **1** *archaic*
> ¹**thou** . . . *pron, archaic*

A word or sense limited in use to a specific region of the U.S. has an appropriate label. The adverb *chiefly*

precedes a label when the word has some currency outside the specified region, and a double label is used to indicate considerable currency in each of two specific regions:

> ²**wash** *n* . . . **8** *West*
> **do·gie** . . . *n, chiefly West*
> **crul·ler** . . . *n* . . . **2** *Northern & Midland*

Words current in all regions of the U.S. have no label.

A word or sense limited in use to one of the other countries of the English-speaking world has an appropriate regional label:

> **chem·ist** . . . *n* . . . **2** *Brit*
> **loch** . . . *n, Scot*
> ²**wireless** *n* . . . **2** *chiefly Brit*

The label *dial* for "dialect" indicates that the pattern of use of a word or sense is too complex for summary labeling: it usually includes several regional varieties of American English or of American and British English:

> ²**mind** *vb* **1** *chiefly dial*

The stylistic label *slang* is used with words or senses that are especially appropriate in contexts of extreme informality:

> **³can** . . . *vb* . . . 2 *slang*
> **²grand** *n* . . . *slang*

There is no satisfactory objective test for slang, especially with reference to a word out of context. No word, in fact, is invariably slang, and many standard words can be given slang applications.

The stylistic labels *offensive* and *disparaging* are used for those words or senses that in common use are intended to hurt or that are likely to give offense even when they are used without such an intent:

> **dumb** . . . *adj* 1 *often offensive*
> **half–breed** . . . *n, often disparaging*

Definitions are sometimes followed by verbal illustrations that show a typical use of the word in context. These illustrations are enclosed in angle brackets, and the word being illustrated is usually replaced by a lightface swung dash. The swung dash stands for the boldface entry word, and it may be followed by an italicized suffix:

> **¹jump** . . . *vb* . . . 5 . . . ⟨∼ town⟩
> **all–around** . . . *adj* 1 . . . ⟨best ∼ performance⟩
> **¹can·on** . . . *n* . . . 3 . . . ⟨the ∼s of good taste⟩
> **en·joy** . . . *vb* . . . 2 . . . ⟨∼ed the concert⟩

The swung dash is not used when the form of the boldface entry word is changed in suffixation, and it is not used for open compounds:

> **²deal** *vb* . . . 2 . . . ⟨*dealt* him a blow⟩
> **drum up** *vb* 1 . . . ⟨*drum up* business⟩

Definitions are sometimes followed by usage notes that give supplementary information about such matters as idiom, syntax, and semantic relationship. A usage note is introduced by a lightface dash:

> **²cry** *n* . . . 5 . . . — usu. used in the phrase *a far cry*
> **²drum** *vb* . . . 4 . . . — usu. used with *out*
> **¹jaw** . . . *n* . . . 2 . . . — usu. used in pl.
> **¹ada·gio** . . . *adv or adj* . . . — used as a direction in music
> **hajji** . . . *n* . . . — often used as a title

Sometimes a usage note is used in place of a definition. Some function words (as conjunctions and prepositions) have chiefly grammatical meaning and little or no lexical meaning; most interjections express feelings but are otherwise untranslatable into lexical meaning; and some other words (as honorific titles) are more amenable to comment than to definition:

> **or** . . . *conj* — used as a function word to indicate an alternative
> **¹at** . . . *prep* 1 — used to indicate a point in time or space
> **auf Wie·der·seh·en** . . . *interj* . . . — used to express farewell
> **sir** . . . *n* . . . 2 — used as a usu. respectful form of address

## SENSE DIVISION

A boldface colon is used in this dictionary to introduce a definition:

> **equine** . . . *adj* . . . : of or relating to the horse

It is also used to separate two or more definitions of a single sense:

> **no·ti·fy** . . . *vb* . . . 1 : to give notice of : report the occurrence of

Boldface Arabic numerals separate the senses of a word that has more than one sense:

> **add** . . . *vb* 1 : to join to something else so as to increase in number or amount 2 : to say further . . . 3 : to combine (numbers) into one sum

A particular semantic relationship between senses is sometimes suggested by the use of one of the two italic sense dividers *esp* or *also*.

The sense divider *esp* (for *especially*) is used to introduce the most common meaning included in the more general preceding definition:

**crys·tal** . . . *n* . . . **2** : something resembling crystal (as in transparency); *esp* : a clear colorless glass of superior quality

The sense divider *also* is used to introduce a meaning related to the preceding sense by an easily understood extension of that sense:

**chi·na** . . . *n* : porcelain ware; *also* : domestic pottery in general

The order of senses is historical: the sense known to have been first used in English is entered first. This is not to be taken to mean, however, that each sense of a multisense word developed from the immediately preceding sense. It is altogether possible that sense 1 of a word has given rise to sense 2 and sense 2 to sense 3, but frequently sense 2 and sense 3 may have developed independently of one another from sense 1.

When an italicized label follows a boldface numeral, the label applies only to that specific numbered sense. It does not apply to any other boldface numbered senses:

**craft** . . . *n* . . . **3** *pl usu* **craft**
¹**fa·ther** . . . *n* . . . **2** *cap* . . . **5** *often cap*
**dul·ci·mer** . . . *n* . . . **2** *or* **dul·ci·more** \-ˌmȯr\
²**lift** *n* . . . **5** *chiefly Brit*

At *craft* the *pl* label applies to sense 3 but to none of the other numbered senses. At *father* the *cap* label applies only to sense 2 and the *often cap* label only to sense 5. At *dulcimer* the variant spelling and pronunciation apply only to sense 2, and the *chiefly Brit* label at *lift* applies only to sense 5.

# CROSS-REFERENCE

Four different kinds of cross-references are used in this dictionary: directional, synonymous, cognate, and inflectional. In each instance the cross-reference is readily recognized by the lightface small capitals in which it is printed.

A cross-reference following a lightface dash and beginning with *see* is a directional cross-reference. It directs the dictionary user to look elsewhere for further information:

**eu·ro** . . . *n* . . . — see MONEY table

A cross-reference following a boldface colon is a synonymous cross-reference. It may stand alone as the only definition for an entry or for a sense of an entry; it may follow an analytical definition; it may be one of two or more synonymous cross-references separated by commas:

**pa·pa** . . . *n* : FATHER
¹**par·tic·u·lar** . . . *adj* . . . **4** : attentive to details : PRECISE
²**main** *adj* **1** : CHIEF, PRINCIPAL
¹**fig·ure** . . . *n* . . . **6** : SHAPE, FORM, OUTLINE

A synonymous cross-reference indicates that an entry, a definition at the entry, or a specific sense at the entry cross-referred to can be substituted as a definition for the entry or the sense in which the cross-reference appears.

A cross-reference following an italic *var of* ("variant of") is a cognate cross-reference:

**pick·a·back** . . . *var of* PIGGYBACK

Occasionally a cognate cross-reference has a limiting label preceding *var of* as an indication that the variant is not standard American English:

**aero·plane** . . . *chiefly Brit var of* AIRPLANE

A cross-reference following an italic label that identifies an entry as an inflected form (as of a noun or verb) is an inflectional cross-reference:

**calves** *pl of* CALF
**woven** *past part of* WEAVE

Inflectional cross-references appear only when the inflected form falls at least a column away from the entry cross-referred to.

## SYNONYMS

A bold italic *Synonyms* preceded by a small black diamond figure near the end of an entry introduces words that are synonymous with the word being defined:

> **alone** . . . *adj* . . . ♦ *Synonyms* LONE-
> LY, LONESOME, LONE, SOLITARY

Synonyms are not definitions although they may often be substituted for each other in context.

## COMBINING FORMS, PREFIXES, & SUFFIXES

An entry that begins or ends with a hyphen is a word element that forms part of an English compound:

> **-wise** . . . *adv comb form* . . . ⟨slant-
> *wise*⟩
> **ex-** . . . *prefix* . . . **2** . . . ⟨*ex*-pres-
> ident⟩
> **-let** *n suffix* **1** . . . ⟨book*let*⟩

Combining forms, prefixes, and suffixes are entered in this dictionary for two reasons: to make understandable the meaning of many undefined run-ons and to make recognizable the meaningful elements of words that are not entered in the dictionary.

## LISTS OF UNDEFINED WORDS

Many words that begin with the prefixes or combining forms *anti-, in-, non-, over-, re-, self-, semi-, sub-, super-,* and *un-* are self-explanatory combinations of the prefix or combining form and a word entered elsewhere in the dictionary, and they are listed undefined at the bottom of the page or spread on which they would normally appear if defined.

## ABBREVIATIONS & SYMBOLS

Abbreviations and symbols for chemical elements are included as main entries in the vocabulary:

> **RSVP** *abbr* . . . please reply
> **Ca** *symbol* calcium

Abbreviations have been normalized to one form. In practice, however, there is considerable variation in the use of periods and in capitalization (as *vhf, v.h.f., VHF,* and *V.H.F.* for the entry **VHF**), and stylings other than those given in this dictionary are often acceptable.

# ABBREVIATIONS IN THIS WORK

| | | | |
|---|---|---|---|
| *ab* | about | *masc* | masculine |
| *abbr* | abbreviation | *MD* | Middle Dutch |
| *abl* | ablative | *ME* | Middle English |
| *acc* | accusative | *MexSp* | Mexican Spanish |
| *A.D.* | anno Domini | *MF* | Middle French |
| *adj* | adjective | *MGk* | Middle Greek |
| *adv* | adverb | *mi* | miles |
| *alter* | alteration | *ML* | Medieval Latin |
| *Am, Amer* | American | *modif* | modification |
| *AmerF* | American French | *MS* | manuscript |
| *AmerInd* | American Indian | *Mt* | Mount |
| *AmerSp* | American Spanish | *n* | noun |
| *Ar* | Arabic | *neut* | neuter |
| *Aram* | Aramaic | *NewEng* | New England |
| *B.C.* | before Christ | *NGk* | New Greek |
| *Brit* | British | *NHeb* | New Hebrew |
| *C* | Celsius | *NL* | New Latin |
| *ca* | circa | *No* | North |
| *Calif* | California | *Norw* | Norwegian |
| *Canad* | Canadian | *n pl* | noun plural |
| *CanF* | Canadian French | *obs* | obsolete |
| *cap* | capital, capitalized | *OE* | Old English |
| *Celt* | Celtic | *OF* | Old French |
| *cen* | central | *OIt* | Old Italian |
| *cent* | century | *ON* | Old Norse |
| *Chin* | Chinese | *OPer* | Old Persian |
| *comb* | combining | *orig* | originally |
| *compar* | comparative | *part* | participle |
| *conj* | conjunction | *Per* | Persian |
| *D* | Dutch | *perh* | perhaps |
| *Dan* | Danish | *Pg* | Portuguese |
| *dat* | dative | *pl* | plural |
| *deriv* | derivative | *Pol* | Polish |
| *dial* | dialect | *pp* | past participle |
| *dim* | diminutive | *prep* | preposition |
| *E* | English | *pres* | present, president |
| *Egypt* | Egyptian | *prob* | probably |
| *Eng* | English | *pron* | pronoun, pronunciation |
| *esp* | especially | *prp* | present participle |
| *est* | estimated | *pseud* | pseudonym |
| *F* | Fahrenheit, French | *r* | reigned |
| *fem* | feminine | *Russ* | Russian |
| *fl* | flourished | *Sc* | Scotch, Scots |
| *fr* | from | *Scand* | Scandinavian |
| *ft* | feet | *ScGael* | Scottish Gaelic |
| *G, Ger* | German | *Scot* | Scottish |
| *Gk* | Greek | *sing* | singular |
| *Gmc* | Germanic | *Skt* | Sanskrit |
| *Heb* | Hebrew | *Slav* | Slavic |
| *Hung* | Hungarian | *So* | South |
| *Icel* | Icelandic | *Sp, Span* | Spanish |
| *imit* | imitative | *St* | Saint |
| *imper* | imperative | *superl* | superlative |
| *interj* | interjection | *Sw* | Swedish |
| *Ir* | Irish | *syn* | synonym, synonymy |
| *irreg* | irregular | *trans* | translation |
| *It, Ital* | Italian | *Turk* | Turkish |
| *Jp* | Japanese | *US* | United States |
| *K* | Kelvin | *USSR* | Union of Soviet Socialist |
| *km* | kilometers | | Republics |
| *L* | Latin | *usu* | usually |
| *LaF* | Louisiana French | *var* | variant |
| *LG* | Low German | *vb* | verb |
| *LGk* | Late Greek | *vi* | verb intransitive |
| *LHeb* | Late Hebrew | *VL* | Vulgar Latin |
| *lit* | literally | *vt* | verb transitive |
| *LL* | Late Latin | *W* | Welsh |
| *m* | meters | | |

# PRONUNCIATION SYMBOLS

| | |
|---|---|
| ə | abut, collect, suppose |
| ˈə, ˌə | humdrum |
| ə | (in ᵊl, ᵊn) battle, cotton; (in lᵊ, mᵊ, rᵊ) French table, prisme, titre |
| ər | operation, further |
| a | map, patch |
| ā | day, fate |
| ä | bother, cot, father |
| är | car, heart |
| aù | now, out |
| b | baby, rib |
| ch | chin, catch |
| d | did, adder |
| e | set, red |
| er | bare, fair |
| ē | beat, easy |
| f | fifty, cuff |
| g | go, big |
| h | hat, ahead |
| hw | whale |
| i | tip, banish |
| ir | near, deer |
| ī | site, buy |
| j | job, edge |
| k | kin, cook |
| ḵ | German Bach, Scots loch |
| l | lily, cool |
| m | murmur, dim |
| n | nine, own |
| ⁿ | indicates that a preceding vowel is pronounced through both nose and mouth, as in French bon \bōⁿ\ |
| ŋ | sing, singer, finger, ink |
| ō | bone, hollow |
| ȯ | saw |
| ȯr | boar, port |
| œ | French bœuf, feu, German Hölle, Höhle |

| | |
|---|---|
| ȯi | toy |
| p | pepper, lip |
| r | rarity |
| s | source, less |
| sh | shy, mission |
| t | tie, attack |
| th | thin, ether |
| t͟h | then, either |
| ü | boot, few \ˈfyü\ |
| ù | put, pure \ˈpyùr\ |
| ùr | boor, tour |
| ṳe | French rue, German füllen, fühlen |
| v | vivid, give |
| w | we, away |
| y | yard, cue \ˈkyü\ |
| ʸ | indicates that a preceding \l\, \n\, or \w\ is modified by having the tongue approximate the position for \y\, as in French digne \dēnʸ\ |
| z | zone, raise |
| zh | vision, pleasure |
| \ | slant line used in pairs to mark the beginning and end of a transcription: \ˈpen\ |
| ˈ | mark at the beginning of a syllable that has primary (strongest) stress: \ˈshə-fəl-ˌbȯrd\ |
| ˌ | mark at the beginning of a syllable that has secondary (next‐strongest) stress: \ˈshə-fəl-ˌbȯrd\ |
| - | mark of a syllable division in pronunciations (the mark of end‐of-line division in boldface entries is a centered dot •) |
| ( ) | indicate that what is symbolized between sometimes occurs and sometimes does not occur in the pronunciation of the word: bakery \ˈbā-k(ə-)rē\ = \ˈbā-kə-rē, ˈbā-krē\ |

**¹a** \'ā\ *n, pl* **a's** *or* **as** \'āz\ *often cap* **1** : the 1st letter of the English alphabet **2** : a grade rating a student's work as superior

**²a** \ə, (')ā\ *indefinite article* : ONE, SOME — used to indicate an unspecified or unidentified individual ⟨there's ~ man outside⟩

**³a** *abbr, often cap* **1** absent **2** acre **3** alto **4** answer **5** are **6** area

**AA** *abbr* **1** Alcoholics Anonymous **2** antiaircraft **3** associate in arts

**AAA** *abbr* American Automobile Association

**A and M** *abbr* agricultural and mechanical

**A and R** *abbr* artists and repertory

**aard·vark** \'ärd-,värk\ *n* [obs. Afrikaans, fr. Afrikaans *aard* earth + *vark* pig] : a large burrowing African mammal that feeds on ants and termites with its long sticky tongue

**¹ab** \'ab\ *n* : an abdominal muscle

**²ab** *abbr* about

**AB** *abbr* **1** able-bodied seaman **2** airman basic **3** [NL *artium baccalaureus*] bachelor of arts

**ABA** *abbr* American Bar Association

**aback** \ə-'bak\ *adv* : by surprise ⟨taken ~⟩

**aba·cus** \'a-bə-kəs, ə-'ba-\ *n, pl* **aba·ci** \-,sī, -,kē\ *or* **aba·cus·es** : an instrument for making calculations by sliding counters along rods or grooves

**abaft** \ə-'baft\ *prep* : to the rear of

**²abaft** *adv* : toward or at the stern : AFT

**ab·a·lo·ne** \,a-bə-'lō-nē, 'a-bə-,\ *n* : any of a genus of large edible sea mollusks with a flattened slightly spiral shell with holes along the edge

**¹aban·don** \ə-'ban-dən\ *vb* [ME *abandounen*, fr. AF *abanduner*, fr. (*mettre*) *a bandun* to hand over, put in someone's control] : to give up completely : FORSAKE, DESERT — **aban·don·ment** *n*

**²abandon** *n* : a thorough yielding to natural impulses; *esp* : EXUBERANCE

**aban·doned** \ə-'ban-dənd\ *adj* : morally unrestrained ♦ *Synonyms* PROFLIGATE, DISSOLUTE, REPROBATE

**abase** \ə-'bās\ *vb* **abased**; **abas·ing** : HUMBLE, DEGRADE — **abase·ment** *n*

**abash** \ə-'bash\ *vb* : to destroy the composure of : EMBARRASS — **abash·ment** *n*

**abate** \ə-'bāt\ *vb* **abat·ed**; **abat·ing** **1** : to put an end to ⟨~ a nuisance⟩ **2** : to decrease in amount, number, or degree

**abate·ment** \ə-'bāt-mənt\ *n* **1** : DECREASE **2** : an amount abated; *esp* : a deduction from a tax

**ab·at·toir** \'a-bə-,twär\ *n* [F] : SLAUGHTERHOUSE

**ab·ba·cy** \'a-bə-sē\ *n, pl* **-cies** : the office or term of office of an abbot or abbess

**ab·bé** \a-'bā, 'a-,\ *n* : a member of the French secular clergy — used as a title

**ab·bess** \'a-bəs\ *n* : the superior of a convent for nuns

**ab·bey** \'a-bē\ *n, pl* **abbeys** **1** : MONASTERY **2** : CONVENT **3** : an abbey church

**ab·bot** \'a-bət\ *n* [ME *abbod*, fr. OE, fr. LL *abbat-, abbas*, fr. LGk *abbas*, fr. Aramaic *abbā* father] : the superior of a monastery for men

**abbr** *abbr* abbreviation

**ab·bre·vi·ate** \ə-'brē-vē-,āt\ *vb* **-at·ed**; **-at·ing** : SHORTEN, CURTAIL; *esp* : to reduce to an abbreviation

**ab·bre·vi·a·tion** \ə-,brē-vē-'ā-shən\ *n* **1** : the act or result of abbreviating **2** : a shortened form of a word or phrase used for brevity esp. in writing

**¹ABC** \ā-(,)bē-'sē\ *n, pl* **ABC's** *or* **ABCs** \-'sēz\ **1** : ALPHABET — usu. used in pl. **2** : RUDIMENTS — usu. used in pl.

**²ABC** *abbr* American Broadcasting Company

**Ab·di·as** \ab-'dī-əs\ *n* : OBADIAH

**ab·di·cate** \'ab-di-,kāt\ *vb* **-cat·ed**; **-cat·ing** : to give up (as a throne) formally — **ab·di·ca·tion** \,ab-di-'kā-shən\ *n*

**ab·do·men** \'ab-də-mən, ab-'dō-\ *n* **1** : the cavity in or area of the body between the chest and the pelvis **2** : the part of the body posterior to the thorax in an arthropod — **ab·dom·i·nal** \ab-'dä-mə-n°l\ *adj* — **ab·dom·i·nal·ly** *adv*

**ab·duct** \ab-'dəkt\ *vb* : to take away (a person) by force : KIDNAP — **ab·duc·tion** \-'dək-shən\ *n* — **ab·duc·tor** \-tər\ *n*

**abeam** \ə-'bēm\ *adv or adj* : on a line at right angles to a ship's keel

**abed** \ə-'bed\ *adv or adj* : in bed

**Abe·na·ki** \,a-bə-'nä-kē\ *also* **Ab·na·ki** \ab-'nä-kē\ *n, pl* **Abenaki** *or* **Abenakis** *also* **Abnaki** *or* **Abnakis** : a member of a group of American Indian peoples of northern New England and southern Quebec

**ab·er·ra·tion** \,a-bə-'rā-shən\ *n* **1** : deviation esp. from a moral standard or normal state **2** : failure of a mirror or lens to produce exact point-to-point correspondence between an object and its image **3** : unsoundness of mind : DERANGEMENT — **ab·er·rant** \a-'ber-ənt\ *adj*

**abet** \ə-'bet\ *vb* **abet·ted**; **abet·ting** [ME *abetten*, fr. AF *abeter*, fr. *beter* to bait] **1** : INCITE, ENCOURAGE **2** : to assist or support in the achievement of a purpose ⟨~ a fugitive⟩ — **abet·tor** *or* **abet·ter** \-'be-tər\ *n*

**abey·ance** \ə-'bā-əns\ *n* : a condition of suspended activity — **abey·ant** \-ənt\ *adj*

**ab·hor** \ab-'hòr, ab-\ *vb* **ab·horred**; **ab·hor·ring** [ME *abhorren*, fr. L *abhorrēre*, fr. *ab-* + *horrēre* to shudder] : LOATHE, DETEST — **ab·hor·rence** \-əns\ *n*

**ab·hor·rent** \-ənt\ *adj* : LOATHSOME, DETESTABLE ⟨~ crimes⟩

**abide** \ə-'bīd\ *vb* **abode** \-'bōd\ *or* **abid·ed**; **abid·ing** **1** : BEAR, ENDURE **2** : DWELL, REMAIN, LAST — **abide by** : to conform or acquiesce to ⟨*abide by* the law⟩

**abil·i·ty** \ə-'bi-lə-tē\ *n, pl* **-ties** : the quality of being able : POWER, SKILL

**-ability** *also* **-ibility** *n suffix* : capacity, fitness, or tendency to act or be acted on in a (specified) way ⟨flamm*ability*⟩

**ab·ject** \'ab-,jekt, ab-'jekt\ *adj* : low in spirit, hope, or state ⟨~ poverty⟩ — **ab·jec·tion** \ab-'jek-shən\ *n* — **ab·ject·ly** *adv* — **ab·ject·ness** *n*

**ab·jure** \ab-'jùr\ *vb* **ab·jured; ab·jur·ing** **1** : to renounce solemnly : RECANT **2** : to abstain from — **ab·ju·ra·tion** \,ab-jə-'rā-shən\ *n*

**abl** *abbr* ablative

**ab·late** \a-'blāt\ *vb* **ab·lat·ed; ab·lat·ing** : to remove or become removed esp. by cutting, abrading, or vaporizing

**ab·la·tion** \a-'blā-shən\ *n* **1** : surgical cutting and removal **2** : loss of a part (as the outside of a nose cone) by melting or vaporization

**ab·la·tive** \'ab-lə-tiv\ *adj* : of, relating to, or constituting a grammatical case (as in Latin) expressing typically the relation of separation and source — **ablative** *n*

**ablaze** \ə-'blāz\ *adj or adv* : being on fire : BLAZING

**able** \'ā-bəl\ *adj* **abler** \-b(ə-)lər\; **ablest** \-b(ə-)ləst\ [ME, fr. AF, fr. L *habilis* apt, fr. *habēre* to hold, possess] **1** : having sufficient power, skill, or resources to accomplish an object **2** : marked by skill or efficiency — **ably** \-blē\ *adv*

**-able** *also* **-ible** *adj suffix* **1** : capable of, fit for, or worthy of (being so acted upon or toward) ⟨break*able*⟩ ⟨collect*ible*⟩ **2** : tending, given, or liable to ⟨knowledge*able*⟩ ⟨perish*able*⟩

**able–bod·ied** \,ā-bəl-'bä-dēd\ *adj* : having a sound strong body

**abloom** \ə-'blüm\ *adj* : BLOOMING

**ab·lu·tion** \ə-'blü-shən, a-\ *n* : the washing of one's body or part of it

**ABM** \,ā-(,)bē-'em\ *n, pl* **ABM's** *or* **ABMs** : ANTIBALLISTIC MISSILE

**Abnaki** *var of* ABENAKI

**ab·ne·gate** \'ab-ni-,gāt\ *vb* **-gat·ed; -gat·ing** **1** : DENY, RENOUNCE **2** : SURRENDER, RELINQUISH ⟨~ her powers⟩ — **ab·ne·ga·tion** \,ab-ni-'gā-shən\ *n*

**ab·nor·mal** \ab-'nòr-məl\ *adj* : deviating from the normal or average — **ab·nor·mal·i·ty** \,ab-nòr-'ma-lə-tē\ *n* — **ab·nor·mal·ly** *adv*

**¹aboard** \ə-'bòrd\ *adv* **1** : ALONGSIDE **2** : on, onto, or within a car, ship, or aircraft **3** : in or into a group or association ⟨welcome new workers ~⟩

**²aboard** *prep* : ON, ONTO, WITHIN

**abode** \ə-'bōd\ *n* **1** : STAY, SOJOURN **2** : HOME, RESIDENCE

**abol·ish** \ə-'bä-lish\ *vb* : to do away with : ANNUL ⟨~ slavery⟩ — **ab·o·li·tion** \,a-bə-'li-shən\ *n*

**ab·o·li·tion·ism** \,a-bə-'li-shə-,ni-zəm\ *n* : advocacy of the abolition of slavery — **ab·o·li·tion·ist** \-'li-sh(ə-)nist\ *n or adj*

**A–bomb** \'ā-,bäm\ *n* : ATOMIC BOMB — **A–bomb** *vb*

**abom·i·na·ble** \ə-'bä-mə-nə-bəl\ *adj* : causing disgust or hatred : DETESTABLE

**abominable snow·man** \-'snō-mən, -,man\ *n, often cap A&S* : a mysterious creature with human or apelike characteristics reported to exist in the high Himalayas

**abom·i·nate** \ə-'bä-mə-,nāt\ *vb* **-nat·ed; -nat·ing** [L *abominari*, lit., to deprecate as an ill omen, fr. *ab-* away + *omen* omen] : to hate or loathe intensely

**abom·i·na·tion** \ə-,bä-mə-'nā-shən\ *n* **1** : something abominable **2** : extreme disgust or hatred : LOATHING

**ab·orig·i·nal** \,a-bə-'ri-jə-nəl\ *adj* : ORIGINAL, INDIGENOUS, PRIMITIVE

**ab·orig·i·ne** \,a-bə-'ri-jə-nē\ *n* : a member of the original race of inhabitants of a region : NATIVE

**aborn·ing** \ə-'bòr-niŋ\ *adv* : while being born or produced

**¹abort** \ə-'bòrt\ *vb* **1** : to cause or undergo abortion **2** : to terminate prematurely ⟨~ a spaceflight⟩ — **abor·tive** \-'bòr-tiv\ *adj*

**²abort** *n* : the premature termination of a mission or of a procedure relating to an aircraft or spacecraft

**abor·tion** \ə-'bòr-shən\ *n* : the spontaneous or induced termination of a pregnancy after, accompanied by, resulting in, or closely followed by the death of the embryo or fetus

**abor·tion·ist** \-sh(ə-)nist\ *n* : one who induces abortions

**abound** \ə-'baùnd\ *vb* **1** : to be plentiful : TEEM **2** : to be fully supplied

**¹about** \ə-'baùt\ *adv* **1** : reasonably close to; *also* : on the verge of ⟨~ to join the army⟩ **2** : on all sides : NEARBY

**²about** *prep* **1** : on every side of **2** : near to **3** : CONCERNING

**about–face** \-'fās\ *n* : a reversal of direction or attitude — **about–face** *vb*

**¹above** \ə-'bəv\ *adv* **1** : in the sky; *also* : in or to heaven **2** : in or to a higher place; *also* : higher on the same page or on a preceding page

**²above** *prep* **1** : in or to a higher place than : OVER ⟨storm clouds ~ the bay⟩ **2** : superior to ⟨he thought her far ~ him⟩ **3** : more than : EXCEEDING **4** : as distinct from ⟨~ the noise⟩

**above·board** \-,bòrd\ *adv or adj* : without concealment or deception : OPENLY

**abp** *abbr* archbishop

**abr** *abbr* abridged; abridgment

**ab·ra·ca·dab·ra** \,a-brə-kə-'da-brə\ *n* **1** : a magical charm or incantation against calamity **2** : GIBBERISH

**abrade** \ə-'brād\ *vb* **abrad·ed; abrad·ing** **1** : to wear away by friction **2** : to wear down in spirit : IRRITATE — **abra·sion** \-'brā-zhən\ *n*

**¹abra·sive** \ə-'brā-siv\ *n* : a substance (as pumice) for abrading, smoothing, or polishing

**²abrasive** *adj* : tending to abrade : causing irritation ⟨~ relationships⟩ — **abra·sive·ly** *adv* — **abra·sive·ness** *n*

**abreast** \ə-'brest\ *adv or adj* **1** : side by side **2** : up to a standard or level esp. of knowledge ⟨kept ~ of the news⟩

**abridge** \ə-'brij\ vb **abridged; abridg-ing** [ME abregen, fr. AF abreger, fr. LL abbreviare, fr. L ad to + brevis short] 1 : to lessen in length or extent : SHORTEN — **abridg·ment** or **abridge·ment** n

**abroad** \ə-'brȯd\ adv or adj 1 : over a wide area 2 : away from one's home 3 : outside one's country

**ab·ro·gate** \'a-brə-ˌgāt\ vb **-gat·ed; -gat-ing** : ANNUL, REVOKE — **ab·ro·ga·tion** \ˌa-brə-'gā-shən\ n

**abrupt** \ə-'brəpt\ adj 1 : broken or as if broken off 2 : SUDDEN, HASTY ⟨an ~ turn⟩ 3 : so quick as to seem rude ⟨an ~ reply⟩ 4 : DISCONNECTED 5 : STEEP — **abrupt·ly** adv

**abs** abbr absolute

**ab·scess** \'ab-ˌses\ n, pl **ab·cess·es** [L abscessus, lit., act of going away, fr. abscedere to go away, fr. abs-, ab- away + cedere to go] : a localized collection of pus surrounded by inflamed tissue — **ab·scessed** \-ˌsest\ adj

**ab·scis·sa** \ab-'si-sə\ n, pl **abscissas** also **ab·scis·sae** \-'si-(ˌ)sē\ : the horizontal coordinate of a point in a plane coordinate system obtained by measuring parallel to the x-axis

**ab·scis·sion** \ab-'si-zhən\ n 1 : the act or process of cutting off 2 : the natural separation of flowers, fruits, or leaves from plants — **ab·scise** \ab-'sīz\ vb

**ab·scond** \ab-'skänd\ vb : to depart secretly and hide oneself

**ab·sence** \'ab-səns\ n 1 : the state or time of being absent 2 : WANT, LACK 3 : INATTENTION ⟨~ of mind⟩

¹**ab·sent** \'ab-sənt\ adj 1 : not present 2 : LACKING 3 : INATTENTIVE

²**ab·sent** \ab-'sent\ vb : to keep (oneself) away

³**ab·sent** \'ab-sənt\ prep : in the absence of : WITHOUT

**ab·sen·tee** \ˌab-sən-'tē\ n : one that is absent or keeps away

**absentee ballot** n : a ballot submitted (as by mail) in advance of an election by a voter who is unable to be present at the polls

**ab·sen·tee·ism** \ˌab-sən-'tē-ˌi-zəm\ n : chronic absence (as from work or school)

**ab·sent·mind·ed** \ˌab-sənt-'mīn-dəd\ adj : unaware of one's surroundings or actions : INATTENTIVE — **ab·sent·mind-ed·ly** adv — **ab·sent·mind·ed·ness** n

**ab·sinthe** also **ab·sinth** \'ab-ˌsinth\ n [F] : a liqueur flavored esp. with wormwood and anise

**ab·so·lute** \'ab-sə-ˌlüt, ˌab-sə-'lüt\ adj 1 : free from imperfection or mixture 2 : free from control, restriction, or qualification ⟨~ power⟩ 3 : lacking grammatical connection with any other word in a sentence ⟨~ construction⟩ 4 : POSITIVE ⟨~ proof⟩ 5 : relating to the fundamental units of length, mass, and time 6 : FUNDAMENTAL, ULTIMATE ⟨~ knowledge⟩ — **ab·so·lute·ly** adv

**absolute pitch** n 1 : the position of a tone in a standard scale independently determined by its rate of vibration 2 : the ability to sing a note asked for or to name a note heard

**absolute value** n : a nonnegative number equal to a given real number with any negative sign removed

**absolute zero** n : a theoretical temperature marked by a complete absence of heat and motion and equivalent to exactly -273.15°C or -459.67°F

**ab·so·lu·tion** \ˌab-sə-'lü-shən\ n : the act of absolving; esp : a remission of sins pronounced by a priest in the sacrament of reconciliation

**ab·so·lut·ism** \'ab-sə-ˌlü-ˌti-zəm\ n 1 : the theory that a ruler or government should have unlimited power 2 : government by an absolute ruler or authority

**ab·solve** \ab-'zälv, -'sälv\ vb **ab·solved; ab·solv·ing** : to set free from an obligation or the consequences of guilt

**ab·sorb** \ab-'sȯrb, -'zȯrb\ vb 1 : to take in and make part of an existent whole 2 : to suck up or take in in the manner of a sponge 3 : to engage (one's attention) : ENGROSS 4 : to receive without recoil or echo ⟨a ceiling that ~s sound⟩ 5 : ASSUME, BEAR ⟨~ all costs⟩ 6 : to transform (radiant energy) into a different form esp. with a resulting rise in temperature — **ab·sorb·ing** adj — **ab·sorb-ing·ly** adv

**ab·sor·bent** also **ab·sor·bant** \ab-'sȯr-bant, -'zȯr-\ adj : able to absorb ⟨~ cotton⟩ — **ab·sor·ben·cy** \-bən-sē\ n — absorbent also absorbant n

**ab·sorp·tion** \ab-'sȯrp-shən, -'zȯrp-\ n 1 : a process of absorbing or being absorbed 2 : concentration of attention ⟨~ in his work⟩ — **ab·sorp·tive** \-tiv\ adj

**ab·stain** \ab-'stān\ vb : to refrain from an action or practice — **ab·stain·er** n

**ab·sten·tion** \-'sten-chən\ n

**ab·ste·mi·ous** \ab-'stē-mē-əs\ adj : sparing in use of food or drink : TEMPERATE — **ab·ste·mi·ous·ly** adv — **ab·ste·mi-ous·ness** n

**ab·sti·nence** \'ab-stə-nəns\ n : voluntary refraining esp. from eating certain foods, drinking liquor, or engaging in sexual intercourse — **ab·sti·nent** \-nənt\ adj

**abstr** abbr abstract

¹**ab·stract** \ab-'strakt, 'ab-ˌstrakt\ adj 1 : considered apart from a particular instance 2 : expressing a quality apart from an object ⟨whiteness is an ~ word⟩ 3 : having only intrinsic form with little or no pictorial representation ⟨~ painting⟩ — **ab·stract·ly** adv — **ab·stract-ness** n

²**ab·stract** \'ab-ˌstrakt; 2 also ab-'strakt\ n 1 : a written summary 2 : an abstract thing or state

³**ab·stract** \ab-'strakt, 'ab-ˌstrakt; 2 usu 'ab-ˌstrakt\ vb 1 : REMOVE, SEPARATE 2 : to make an abstract of : SUMMARIZE 3 : to draw away the attention of 4 : STEAL — **ab·stract·ed·ly** \ab-'strak-təd-lē, 'ab-ˌstrak-\ adv

**abstract expressionism** n : art that expresses the artist's attitudes and emotions through abstract forms — **abstract expressionist** n

**ab·strac·tion** \ab-'strak-shən\ *n* **1** : the act of abstracting : the state of being abstracted **2** : an abstract idea **3** : an abstract work of art

**ab·struse** \ab-'strüs\ *adj* : hard to understand : RECONDITE — **ab·struse·ly** *adv* — **ab·struse·ness** *n*

**ab·surd** \əb-'sərd, -'zərd\ *adj* [MF *absurde,* fr. L *absurdus,* fr. *ab-* from + *surdus* deaf, stupid] : RIDICULOUS, UNREASONABLE — **ab·sur·di·ty** \-'sər-də-tē, -'zər-\ *n* — **ab·surd·ly** *adv*

**abun·dant** \ə-'bən-dənt\ *adj* [ME, fr. AF, fr. L *abundant-, abundans,* prp. of *abundare* to abound, fr. *ab-* from + *unda* wave] : more than enough : amply sufficient ◆ *Synonyms* COPIOUS, PLENTIFUL, AMPLE, BOUNTIFUL — **abun·dance** \-dəns\ *n* — **abun·dant·ly** *adv*

**¹abuse** \ə-'byüs\ *n* **1** : a corrupt practice **2** : MISUSE ⟨drug ∼⟩ **3** : coarse and insulting speech ⟨verbal ∼⟩ **4** : MISTREATMENT ⟨child ∼⟩

**²abuse** \ə-'byüz\ *vb* **abused; abus·ing** **1** : to put to a wrong use : MISUSE **2** : to use excessively ⟨∼ alcohol⟩ **3** : MISTREAT **4** : to attack in words : REVILE — **abus·er** *n* — **abu·sive** \ə-'byü-siv\ *adj* — **abu·sive·ly** *adv* — **abu·sive·ness** *n*

**abut** \ə-'bət\ *vb* **abut·ted; abut·ting** : to touch along a border : border on

**abut·ment** \ə-'bət-mənt\ *n* : the part of a structure (as a bridge) that supports weight or withstands lateral pressure

**abut·ter** \ə-'bə-tər\ *n* : one that abuts; *esp* : the owner of a contiguous property

**abuzz** \ə-'bəz\ *adj* : filled or resounding with activity or excitement ⟨an office ∼ with rumors⟩

**abys·mal** \ə-'biz-məl\ *adj* **1** : immeasurably deep : BOTTOMLESS **2** : absolutely wretched ⟨∼ living conditions of the poor⟩ — **abys·mal·ly** *adv*

**abyss** \ə-'bis\ *n* **1** : the bottomless pit in old accounts of the universe **2** : an immeasurable depth

**abys·sal** \ə-'bi-səl\ *adj* : of or relating to the bottom waters of the ocean depths

**ac** *abbr* account

**-ac** *n suffix* : one affected with ⟨hypochondri*ac*⟩

**Ac** *symbol* actinium

**AC** *abbr* **1** air-conditioning **2** alternating current **3** [L *ante Christum*] before Christ **4** [L *ante cibum*] before meals **5** area code

**aca·cia** \ə-'kā-shə\ *n* : any of a genus of leguminous trees or shrubs with round white or yellow flower clusters and often feathery leaves

**acad** *abbr* academic; academy

**ac·a·deme** \'a-kə-ˌdēm, ˌa-kə-'\ *n* : SCHOOL; *also* : academic environment

**¹ac·a·dem·ic** \ˌa-kə-'de-mik\ *n* : a person who is academic in background, outlook, or methods

**²academic** *adj* **1** : of, relating to, or associated with schools or colleges **2** : literary or general rather than technical **3** : theoretical rather than practical — **ac·a·dem·i·cal·ly** \-mi-k(ə-)lē\ *adv*

**ac·a·de·mi·cian** \ˌa-kə-də-'mi-shən, ə-ˌka-də-\ *n* **1** : a member of a society of scholars or artists **2** : ACADEMIC

**ac·a·dem·i·cism** \ˌa-kə-'de-mə-ˌsi-zəm\ *also* **acad·e·mism** \ə-'ka-də-ˌmi-zəm\ *n* **1** : a formal academic quality **2** : purely speculative thinking

**acad·e·my** \ə-'ka-də-mē\ *n, pl* **-mies** [Gk *Akadēmeia,* school of philosophy founded by Plato, fr. *Akadēmeia,* gymnasium where Plato taught, fr. *Akadēmos* Greek mythological hero] **1** : a school above the elementary level; *esp* : a private high school **2** : a society of scholars or artists

**acan·thus** \ə-'kan-thəs\ *n, pl* **acanthus** **1** : any of a genus of prickly herbs of the Mediterranean region **2** : an ornamentation (as on a column) representing the leaves of the acanthus

**a cap·pel·la** *also* **a ca·pel·la** \ˌä-kə-'pe-lə\ *adv or adj* [It *a cappella* in chapel style] : without instrumental accompaniment

**acc** *abbr* accusative

**ac·cede** \ak-'sēd\ *vb* **ac·ced·ed; ac·ced·ing** **1** : to become a party to an agreement **2** : to express approval **3** : to enter upon an office ◆ *Synonyms* AGREE, ACQUIESCE, ASSENT, CONSENT, SUBSCRIBE

**ac·cel·er·ate** \ik-'se-lə-ˌrāt, ak-\ *vb* **-at·ed; -at·ing** **1** : to bring about earlier **2** : to speed up : QUICKEN — **ac·cel·er·a·tion** \-ˌse-lə-'rā-shən\ *n*

**ac·cel·er·a·tor** \ik-'se-lə-ˌrā-tər, ak-\ *n* **1** : one that accelerates **2** : a pedal for controlling the speed of a motor-vehicle engine **3** : an apparatus for imparting high velocities to charged particles

**ac·cel·er·om·e·ter** \ik-ˌse-lə-'rä-mə-tər, ak-\ *n* : an instrument for measuring acceleration or vibrations

**¹ac·cent** \'ak-ˌsent, ak-'sent\ *vb* : to give stress to : EMPHASIZE

**²ac·cent** \'ak-ˌsent\ *n* **1** : prominence given to one syllable of a word esp. by stress **2** : a distinctive manner of pronunciation ⟨a foreign ∼⟩ **3** : a mark (as ´, `, ˆ) over a vowel used usu. to indicate a difference in pronunciation from a vowel not so marked — **ac·cen·tu·al** \ak-'sen-chə-wəl\ *adj*

**ac·cen·tu·ate** \ak-'sen-chə-ˌwāt\ *vb* **-at·ed; -at·ing** : STRESS, EMPHASIZE — **ac·cen·tu·a·tion** \-ˌsen-chə-'wā-shən\ *n*

**ac·cept** \ik-'sept, ak-\ *vb* **1** : to receive willingly **2** : to agree to **3** : to assume an obligation to pay

**ac·cept·able** \ik-'sep-tə-bəl\ *adj* : capable or worthy of being accepted — **ac·cept·abil·i·ty** \ik-ˌsep-tə-'bi-lə-tē, ak-\ *n*

**ac·cep·tance** \ik-'sep-təns, ak-\ *n* **1** : the act of accepting **2** : the state of being accepted or acceptable **3** : an accepted bill of exchange

**ac·cep·ta·tion** \ˌak-ˌsep-'tā-shən\ *n* : the generally understood meaning of a word

**¹ac·cess** \'ak-ˌses\ *n* **1** : capacity to enter or approach **2** : a way of approach : ENTRANCE

²**access** *vb* : to get at : gain access to

**ac·ces·si·ble** \ik-'ses-sə-bəl, ak-, ek-\ *adj* **1** : capable of being reached ⟨~ by train⟩ **2** : capable of being used or seen ⟨~ archives⟩ **3** : capable of being understood ⟨an ~ film⟩ — **ac·ces·si·bil·i·ty** \-ˌse-sə-'bi-lə-tē\ *n*

**ac·ces·sion** \ik-'se-shən, ak-\ *n* **1** : increase by something added **2** : something added **3** : the act of coming to a high office or position

**ac·ces·so·ry** *also* **ac·ces·sa·ry** \ik-' se-sə-rē, ak-\ *n, pl* **-ries 1** : a person who though not present abets or assists in the commission of an offense **2** : something helpful but not essential ♦ **Synonyms** APPURTENANCE, ADJUNCT, APPENDAGE, APPENDIX — **accessory** *adj*

**ac·ci·dent** \'ak-sə-dənt\ *n* **1** : an event occurring by chance or unintentionally **2** : CHANCE ⟨met by ~⟩ **3** : a nonessential property

¹**ac·ci·den·tal** \ˌak-sə-'den-tᵊl\ *adj* **1** : happening unexpectedly or by chance **2** : happening without intent or through carelessness ♦ **Synonyms** CASUAL, FORTUITOUS, INCIDENTAL, CHANCE — **ac·ci·den·tal·ly** \-'den-tᵊl-ē\ *also* **ac·ci·dent·ly** \-'dent-lē\ *adv*

²**accidental** *n* : a musical note foreign to a key indicated by a signature

**ac·claim** \ə-'klām\ *vb* **1** : to give strong approval or praise to **2** : to declare by acclamation ♦ **Synonyms** EXTOL, LAUD, COMMEND, HAIL — **acclaim** *n*

**ac·cla·ma·tion** \ˌa-klə-'mā-shən\ *n* **1** : loud eager applause **2** : an overwhelming affirmative vote by shouting or applause rather than by ballot

**ac·cli·mate** \'a-klə-ˌmāt, ə-'klī-mət\ *vb* **-mat·ed; -mat·ing** : to accustom or become accustomed to a new climate or situation — **ac·cli·ma·tion** \ˌa-klə-'mā-shən, -ˌklī-\ *n*

**ac·cli·ma·tise** *Brit var of* ACCLIMATIZE

**ac·cli·ma·tize** \ə-'klī-mə-ˌtīz\ *vb* **-tized; -tiz·ing** : ACCLIMATE — **ac·cli·ma·ti·za·tion** \ˌklī-mə-tə-'zā-shən\ *n*

**ac·cliv·i·ty** \ə-'kli-və-tē\ *n, pl* **-ties** : an ascending slope

**ac·co·lade** \'a-kə-ˌlād\ *n* [F, fr. *accoler* to embrace, ultim. fr. L *ad-* to + *collum* neck] : an expression of praise : AWARD

**ac·com·mo·date** \ə-'kä-mə-ˌdāt\ *vb* **-dat·ed; -dat·ing 1** : to make fit or suitable : ADAPT, ADJUST **2** : HARMONIZE, RECONCILE **3** : to provide with something needed **4** : to hold without crowding **5** : to undergo visual accommodation

**ac·com·mo·dat·ing** *adj* : OBLIGING

**ac·com·mo·da·tion** \ə-ˌkä-mə-'dā-shən\ *n* **1** : something supplied to satisfy a need; *esp* : LODGINGS — usu. used in pl. **2** : the act of accommodating : ADJUSTMENT **3** : the automatic adjustment of the eye for seeing at different distances

**ac·com·pa·ni·ment** \ə-'kəm-pə-nē-mənt, -'kəmp-nē-\ *n* : something that accompanies another; *esp* : subordinate music to support a principal voice or instrument

**ac·com·pa·ny** \-nē\ *vb* **-nied; -ny·ing 1** : to go or occur with : ATTEND **2** : to play

an accompaniment for — **ac·com·pa·nist** \-nist\ *n*

**ac·com·plice** \ə-'käm-pləs, -'kəm-\ *n* : an associate in wrongdoing

**ac·com·plish** \ə-'kam-plish, -'kəm-\ *vb* : to bring to completion ♦ **Synonyms** ACHIEVE, EFFECT, EXECUTE, PERFORM — **ac·com·plish·er** *n*

**ac·com·plished** \-plisht\ *adj* **1** : EXPERT, SKILLED ⟨an ~ pianist⟩ **2** : established beyond doubt ⟨an ~ fact⟩

**ac·com·plish·ment** \ə-'käm-plish-mənt, -'kəm-\ *n* **1** : COMPLETION **2** : something completed or effected **3** : an acquired excellence or skill

¹**ac·cord** \ə-'kȯrd\ *vb* [ME, fr. AF *acorder*, fr. VL *accordare*, fr. L *ad-* to + *cord-, cor* heart] **1** : GRANT, CONCEDE **2** : AGREE, HARMONIZE ⟨his interpretation does not ~ with the facts⟩ — **ac·cor·dant** \-'kȯr-dᵊnt\ *adj*

²**accord** *n* **1** : AGREEMENT, HARMONY **2** : willingness to act ⟨gave of their own ~⟩

**ac·cor·dance** \ə-'kȯr-dᵊns\ *n* **1** : ACCORD **2** : the act of granting

**ac·cord·ing·ly** \ə-'kȯr-diŋ-lē\ *adv* **1** : in accordance **2** : CONSEQUENTLY, SO

**according to** *prep* **1** : in conformity with ⟨paid *according to* ability⟩ **2** : as stated or attested by ⟨*according to* you⟩

¹**ac·cor·di·on** \ə-'kȯr-dē-ən\ *n* [G *Akkordion*, fr. *Akkord* chord] : a portable keyboard instrument with a bellows and reeds — **ac·cor·di·on·ist** \-ə-nist\ *n*

²**accordion** *adj* : folding like the bellows of an accordion ⟨~ pleats⟩

**ac·cost** \ə-'kȯst\ *vb* [MF *accoster*, ultim. fr. L *ad-* to + *costa* rib, side] : to approach and speak to esp. aggressively

¹**ac·count** \ə-'kau̇nt\ *n* **1** : a statement of business transactions **2** : a formal business arrangement for regular dealings or services **3** : a statement of reasons, causes, or motives **4** : VALUE, IMPORTANCE ⟨his opinion is of little ~⟩ **5** : a sum of money deposited in a bank and subject to withdrawal by the depositor — **on account of** : BECAUSE OF — **on no account** : under no circumstances — **on one's own account** : on one's own behalf

²**account** *vb* **1** : CONSIDER ⟨I ~ him lucky⟩ **2** : to give an explanation ⟨~ for the money you spent⟩ — used with *for*

**ac·count·able** \ə-'kau̇n-tə-bəl\ *adj* **1** : ANSWERABLE, RESPONSIBLE **2** : EXPLICABLE — **ac·count·abil·i·ty** \-ˌkau̇n-tə-'bi-lə-tē\ *n*

**ac·coun·tant** \ə-'kau̇n-tᵊnt\ *n* : a person skilled in accounting — **ac·coun·tan·cy** \-tᵊn-sē\ *n*

**account executive** *n* : a business executive in charge of a client's account

**ac·count·ing** \ə-'kau̇n-tiŋ\ *n* : the art or system of keeping and analyzing financial records

**ac·cou·tre** *or* **ac·cou·ter** \ə-'kü-tər\ *vb* **-cou·tred** *or* **-cou·tered; -cou·tring** *or* **-cou·ter·ing** \-'kü-t(ə-)riŋ\ : EQUIP, OUTFIT ⟨the knights were *accoutred* for battle⟩

**ac·cou·tre·ment** *or* **ac·cou·ter·ment**

\ə-'kü-trə-mənt, -'kü-tər-\ n [F] **1** : an accessory item — usu. used in pl. **2** : an identifying characteristic

**ac·cred·it** \ə-'kre-dət\ vb **1** : to endorse or approve officially **2** : CREDIT — **ac·cred·i·ta·tion** \-,kre-də-'tā-shən\ n

**ac·cre·tion** \ə-'krē-shən\ n **1** : growth or enlargement esp. by addition from without **2** : a product of accretion

**accretion disk** n : a disk of usu. gaseous matter surrounding and gradually accumulating onto a massive celestial object

**ac·crue** \ə-'krü\ vb **ac·crued; ac·cru·ing 1** : to come by way of increase **2** : to be added by periodic growth — **ac·cru·al** \-əl-\ n

**acct** abbr account; accountant

**ac·cul·tur·a·tion** \ə-,kəl-chə-'rā-shən\ n : cultural modification of an individual or group by borrowing and adapting traits from another culture

**ac·cu·mu·late** \ə-'kyü-myə-,lāt\ vb **-lat·ed; -lat·ing** [L accumulare, fr. ad- to + cumulare to heap up] : to heap or pile up ◆ **Synonyms** AMASS, GATHER, COLLECT, STOCKPILE — **ac·cu·mu·la·tion** \-,kyü-myə-'lā-shən\ n — **ac·cu·mu·la·tive** \-'kyü-myə-lə-tiv\ adj — **ac·cu·mu·la·tor** \-'kyü-myə-,lā-tər\ n

**ac·cu·rate** \'a-kyə-rət\ adj : free from error : EXACT, PRECISE — **ac·cu·ra·cy** \-rə-sē\ n — **ac·cu·rate·ly** adv — **ac·cu·rate·ness** n

**ac·cursed** \ə-'kərst, -'kər-səd\ or **ac·curst** \ə-'kərst\ adj **1** : being under a curse **2** : DAMNABLE, EXECRABLE

**ac·cus·al** \ə-'kyü-zəl\ n : ACCUSATION

**ac·cu·sa·tive** \ə-'kyü-zə-tiv\ adj : of, relating to, or being a grammatical case marking the direct object of a verb or the object of a preposition — **accusative** n

**ac·cu·sa·to·ry** \ə-'kyü-zə-,tȯr-ē\ adj : expressing accusation ⟨an ~ tone⟩

**ac·cuse** \ə-'kyüz\ vb **ac·cused; ac·cus·ing** : to charge with an offense : BLAME — **ac·cu·sa·tion** \,a-kyə-'zā-shən\ n — **ac·cus·er** n

**ac·cused** \ə-'kyüzd\ n, pl **accused** : the defendant in a criminal case

**ac·cus·tom** \ə-'kəs-təm\ vb : to make familiar through use or experience

**ac·cus·tomed** \ə-'kəs-təmd\ adj : USUAL, CUSTOMARY ⟨with ~ grace⟩; also : being in the habit ⟨~ed to winning⟩

**¹ace** \'ās\ n [ME as a die face marked with one spot, fr. AF, fr. L, unit, a copper coin] **1** : a playing card bearing a single large pip in its center **2** : a point (as in tennis) won on a serve that goes untouched **3** : a golf score of one stroke on a hole **4** : a combat pilot who has downed five or more enemy planes **5** : one that excels **6** : the best pitcher on a baseball team

**²ace** vb **aced; ac·ing 1** : to score an ace against (an opponent) or on (a golf hole) **2** : to defeat decisively **3** : to perform extremely well in or on ⟨aced the quiz⟩

**³ace** adj : of first rank or quality

**ACE in·hib·i·tor** \,ā-,sē-'ē-in-'hi-bə-tər,

\'ās-\ n : any of a group of drugs that lower blood pressure by relaxing the arteries

**acer·bic** \ə-'sər-bik, a-\ adj : acid in temper, mood, or tone ⟨~ wit⟩

**acer·bi·ty** \ə-'sər-bə-tē\ n, pl **-ties** : SOURNESS, BITTERNESS

**acet·amin·o·phen** \ə-,sē-tə-'mi-nə-fən\ n : a crystalline compound used in chemical synthesis and in medicine to relieve pain and fever

**ac·e·tate** \'a-sə-,tāt\ n **1** : a salt or ester of acetic acid **2** : a textile fiber made from cellulose and acetic acid; also : a fabric or plastic made of this fiber

**ace·tic acid** \ə-'sē-tik-\ n : a colorless pungent liquid acid that is the chief acid of vinegar and is used esp. in making chemical compounds

**ac·e·tone** \'a-sə-,tōn\ n : a volatile flammable fragrant liquid compound used in making other chemical compounds and as a solvent

**ace·tyl·cho·line** \ə-,sē-t³l-'kō-,lēn\ n : a compound that is released at nerve endings of the autonomic nervous system and is active in the transmission of nerve impulses

**acet·y·lene** \ə-'se-t³l-ən, -t³l-,ēn\ n : a colorless flammable gas used as a fuel (as in welding and soldering)

**ace·tyl·sal·i·cyl·ic acid** \ə-'sē-t³l-,sa-lə-,si-lik-\ n : ASPIRIN 1

**ache** \'āk\ vb **ached; ach·ing 1** : to suffer a usu. dull persistent pain ⟨an aching back⟩ **2** : LONG, YEARN ⟨aching to go home⟩ — **ache** n — **ach·ing·ly** \'ā-kiŋ-lē\ adv

**achieve** \ə-'chēv\ vb **achieved; achiev·ing** [ME acheven, fr. AF achever to finish, fr. a- to (fr. L ad-) + chef end, head, fr. L caput] : to gain by work or effort ◆ **Synonyms** ACCOMPLISH, ATTAIN, REALIZE — **achiev·able** \-'chē-və-bəl\ adj — **achieve·ment** n — **achiev·er** n

**Achil·les' heel** \ə-,ki-lēz-\ n [fr. the story that the Greek warrior Achilles was vulnerable only in the heel] : a vulnerable point

**Achil·les tendon** \ə-,ki-lēz-\ n : the tendon joining the muscles in the calf of the leg to the bone of the heel

**ach·ro·mat·ic** \,a-krə-'ma-tik\ adj : giving an image almost free from extraneous colors ⟨~ lens⟩

**achy** \'ā-kē\ adj **ach·i·er; ach·i·est** : afflicted with aches — **ach·i·ness** n

**¹ac·id** \'a-səd\ adj **1** : sour or biting to the taste; also : sharp or sour in manner **2** : of or relating to an acid — **acid·i·ty** \ə-'si-də-tē\ n — **acid·ly** adv

**²acid** n **1** : a sour substance **2** : a usu. water-soluble chemical compound that has a sour taste, reacts with a base to form a salt, and reddens litmus **3** : LSD — **acid·ic** \ə-'si-dik\ adj

**acid·i·fy** \ə-'si-də-,fī\ vb **-fied; -fy·ing 1** : to make or become acid **2** : to change into an acid — **acid·i·fi·ca·tion** \-,si-də-fə-'kā-shən\ n

**ac·i·do·sis** \,a-sə-'dō-səs\ n, pl **-do·ses** \-,sēz\ : an abnormal state of reduced alkalinity of the blood and body tissues

**acid precipitation** *n* : precipitation with above normal acidity that is caused esp. by atmospheric pollutants

**acid rain** *n* : acid precipitation in the form of rain

**acid test** *n* : a severe or crucial test

**ac·id·u·lous** \ə-'si-jə-ləs\ *adj* : somewhat acid or harsh in taste or manner

**ack** *abbr* acknowledge; acknowledgment

**ac·knowl·edge** \ik-'nä-lij, ak-\ *vb* **-edged; -edg·ing** **1** : to recognize the rights or authority of **2** : to admit as true **3** : to express thanks for; *also* : to report receipt of ⟨~ a letter⟩ **4** : to recognize as valid — **ac·knowl·edg·ment** *or* **ac·knowl·edge·ment** *n*

**ACL** \ā-ˌsē-'el\ *n* : ANTERIOR CRUCIATE LIGAMENT

**ACLU** *abbr* American Civil Liberties Union

**ac·me** \'ak-mē\ *n* [Gk *akmē*] : the highest point

**ac·ne** \'ak-nē\ *n* [Gk *aknē*, MS var. of *akmē*, lit., point] : a skin disorder marked by inflammation of skin glands and hair follicles and by pimple formation esp. on the face

**ac·o·lyte** \'a-kə-ˌlīt\ *n* **1** : one who assists a member of the clergy in a liturgical service **2** : FOLLOWER

**ac·o·nite** \'a-kə-ˌnīt\ *n* **1** : MONKSHOOD **2** : the dried root of a common Eurasian monkshood used formerly as a drug

**acorn** \'ā-ˌkȯrn, -kərn\ *n* : the nut of the oak

**acorn squash** *n* : an acorn-shaped dark green winter squash with a ridged surface and yellow to orange flesh

**acous·tic** \ə-'kü-stik\ *or* **acous·ti·cal** \-sti-kəl\ *adj* **1** : of or relating to the sense or organs of hearing, to sound, or to the science of sounds **2** : deadening sound ⟨~ tile⟩ **3** : operated by or utilizing sound waves **4** : having a sound that is not electronically modified ⟨~ guitar⟩ — **acous·ti·cal·ly** \-k(ə-)lē\ *adv*

**acous·tics** \ə-'kü-stiks\ *n sing or pl* **1** : the science of sound **2** : the qualities in a room that make it easy or hard for a person in it to hear distinctly

**ac·quaint** \ə-'kwānt\ *vb* [ME, ultim. fr. L *ad-* + *cognoscere* to know] **1** : to cause to know personally **2** : INFORM

**ac·quain·tance** \ə-'kwān-tᵊns\ *n* **1** : personal knowledge **2** : a person with whom one is acquainted — **ac·quain·tance·ship** *n*

**acquaintance rape** *n* : rape committed by someone known to the victim

**ac·qui·esce** \ˌa-kwē-'es\ *vb* **-esced; -esc·ing** : to accept, comply, or submit without open opposition ♦ *Synonyms* CONSENT, AGREE, ASSENT, ACCEDE — **ac·qui·es·cence** \-'e-sᵊns\ *n* — **ac·qui·es·cent** \-sᵊnt\ *adj* — **ac·qui·es·cent·ly** *adv*

**ac·quire** \ə-'kwī-(ə)r\ *vb* **ac·quired; ac·quir·ing** : to gain possession of : GET — **ac·quir·able** \-'kwī-rə-bəl\ *adj*

**acquired** *adj* **1** : gained by or as a result of effort or experience **2** : caused by environmental forces and not passed from parent to offspring in the genes ⟨~ characteristics⟩

**acquired immune deficiency syndrome** *n* : AIDS

**acquired immunodeficiency syndrome** *n* : AIDS

**ac·quire·ment** \ə-'kwī-(ə)r-mənt\ *n* **1** : ATTAINMENT, ACCOMPLISHMENT **2** : the act of acquiring

**ac·qui·si·tion** \ˌa-kwə-'zi-shən\ *n* **1** : ACQUIREMENT **2** : something acquired

**ac·quis·i·tive** \ə-'kwi-zə-tiv\ *adj* : eager to acquire : GREEDY — **ac·quis·i·tive·ly** *adv* — **ac·quis·i·tive·ness** *n*

**ac·quit** \ə-'kwit\ *vb* **ac·quit·ted; ac·quit·ting** **1** : to pronounce not guilty **2** : to conduct (oneself) usu. satisfactorily — **ac·quit·tal** \-'kwi-tᵊl\ *n*

**acre** \'ā-kər\ *n* **1** *pl* : LANDS, ESTATE **2** — see WEIGHT table

**acre·age** \'ā-k(ə-)rij\ *n* : area in acres

**ac·rid** \'a-krəd\ *adj* **1** : sharp and biting in taste or odor **2** : deeply bitter : CAUSTIC — **ac·rid·i·ty** \a-'kri-də-tē\ *n* — **ac·rid·ly** *adv* — **ac·rid·ness** *n*

**ac·ri·mo·ny** \'a-krə-ˌmō-nē\ *n, pl* **-nies** : harsh or biting sharpness of language or feeling — **ac·ri·mo·ni·ous** \ˌa-krə-'mō-nē-əs\ *adj* — **ac·ri·mo·ni·ous·ly** *adv* — **ac·ri·mo·ni·ous·ness** *n*

**ac·ro·bat** \'a-krə-ˌbat\ *n* [F *acrobate*, fr. Gk *akrobatēs*, fr. *akros* topmost + *bainein* to go] : a performer of gymnastic feats — **ac·ro·bat·ic** \ˌa-krə-'ba-tik\ *adj* — **ac·ro·bat·i·cal·ly** \-ti-k(ə-)lē\ *adv*

**ac·ro·bat·ics** \ˌa-krə-'ba-tiks\ *n sing or pl* : the performance of an acrobat

**ac·ro·nym** \'a-krə-ˌnim\ *n* : a word (as *radar*) or abbreviation (as *FBI*) formed from the initial letter or letters of each of the successive parts or major parts of a compound term

**ac·ro·pho·bia** \ˌa-krə-'fō-bē-ə\ *n* : abnormal dread of being in a high place : fear of heights

**acrop·o·lis** \ə-'krä-pə-ləs\ *n* [Gk *akropolis*, fr. *akros* topmost + *polis* city] : the upper fortified part of an ancient Greek city

¹**across** \ə-'krȯs\ *adv* **1** : to or on the opposite side **2** : so as to be understandable ⟨get the point ~⟩

²**across** *prep* **1** : to or on the opposite side of ⟨ran ~ the street⟩ **2** : on so as to cross or pass at an angle ⟨a log ~ the road⟩

**across-the-board** *adj* **1** : placed to win if a competitor wins, places, or shows ⟨an ~ bet⟩ **2** : including all classes or categories ⟨an ~ wage increase⟩

**acros·tic** \ə-'krȯs-tik\ *n* : a composition usu. in verse in which the initial or final letters of the lines taken in order form a word or phrase — **acrostic** *adj*

**acryl·ic** \ə-'kri-lik\ *n* **1** : ACRYLIC RESIN **2** : a paint in which the vehicle is acrylic resin **3** : a quick-drying synthetic textile fiber

**acrylic resin** *n* : a glassy thermoplastic used for cast and molded parts or as coatings and adhesives

¹**act** \'akt\ *n* **1** : a thing done : DEED **2** : STATUTE, DECREE **3** : a main division of a play; *also* : an item on a variety program

**4** : an instance of insincere behavior : PRETENSE

**²act** *vb* **1** : to perform by action esp. on the stage; *also* : FEIGN, SIMULATE, PRETEND **2** : to take action **3** : to conduct oneself : BEHAVE **4** : to perform a specified function **5** : to produce an effect

**³act** *abbr* **1** active **2** actual

**ACT** *abbr* Australian Capital Territory

**actg** *abbr* acting

**ACTH** \ā-(ˌ)sē-(ˌ)tē-ˈāch\ *n* : a protein hormone of the pituitary gland that stimulates the adrenal cortex

**act·ing** \ˈak-tiŋ\ *adj* : doing duty temporarily or for another ⟨~ president⟩

**ac·tin·i·um** \ak-ˈti-nē-əm\ *n* : a radioactive metallic chemical element

**ac·tion** \ˈak-shən\ *n* **1** : a legal proceeding **2** : the manner or method of performing **3** : ACTIVITY **4** : ACT, DEED **5** : the accomplishment of a thing usu. over a period of time, in stages, or with the possibility of repetition **6** *pl* : CONDUCT **7** : COMBAT, BATTLE **8** : the events of a literary plot **9** : an operating mechanism ⟨the ~ of a gun⟩; *also* : the way it operates ⟨stiff ~⟩

**ac·tion·able** \ˈak-sh(ə-)nə-bəl\ *adj* : affording ground for an action or suit at law — **ac·tion·ably** \-blē\ *adv*

**ac·ti·vate** \ˈak-tə-ˌvāt\ *vb* **-vat·ed; -vat·ing** **1** : to spur into action; *also* : to make active, reactive, or radioactive **2** : to treat (as carbon) so as to improve adsorptive properties **3** : to set up (a military unit) formally; *also* : to call to active duty — **ac·ti·va·tion** \ˌak-tə-ˈvā-shən\ *n* — **ac·ti·va·tor** \ˈak-tə-ˌvā-tər\ *n*

**ac·tive** \ˈak-tiv\ *adj* **1** : causing or involving action or change **2** : asserting that the grammatical subject performs the action represented by the verb ⟨~ voice⟩ **3** : BRISK, LIVELY **4** : erupting or likely to erupt ⟨~ volcano⟩ **5** : presently in operation or use **6** : tending to progress or to cause degeneration ⟨~ tuberculosis⟩ — **active** *n* — **ac·tive·ly** *adv* — **ac·tive·ness** *n*

**ac·tive–ma·trix** \ˈak-tiv-ˌmā-triks\ *adj* : of, relating to, or being an LCD in which each pixel is individually controlled

**ac·tive·wear** \ˈak-tiv-ˌwer\ *n* : clothing designed for recreation or informal wear

**ac·tiv·ism** \ˈak-ti-ˌvi-zəm\ *n* : a doctrine or practice that emphasizes vigorous action for political ends — **ac·tiv·ist** \-vist\ *n or adj*

**ac·tiv·i·ty** \ak-ˈti-və-tē\ *n, pl* **-ties** **1** : the quality or state of being active **2** : forceful or energetic action **3** : an occupation in which one is engaged

**ac·tor** \ˈak-tər\ *n* : a person who acts in a play or motion picture

**ac·tress** \ˈak-trəs\ *n* : a woman who is an actor

**Acts** \ˈakts\ *or* **Acts of the Apostles** *n* — see BIBLE table

**ac·tu·al** \ˈak-chə-wəl, -shə-\ *adj* : really existing : REAL — **ac·tu·al·i·ty** \ˌak-chə-ˈwa-lə-tē, -shə-\ *n* — **ac·tu·al·i·za·tion** \ˌak-chə-wə-lə-ˈzā-shən, -shə-\ *n* — **ac·tu·al·ize** \ˈak-chə-wə-ˌlīz, -shə-\ *vb*

**ac·tu·al·ly** \ˈak-chə-wə-lē, -shə-\ *adv* : in fact or in truth : REALLY

**ac·tu·ary** \ˈak-chə-ˌwer-ē, -shə-\ *n, pl* **-ar·ies** : a person who calculates insurance risks and premiums — **ac·tu·ar·i·al** \ˌak-chə-ˈwer-ē-əl, -shə-\ *adj*

**ac·tu·ate** \ˈak-chə-ˌwāt\ *vb* **-at·ed; -at·ing** **1** : to put into action **2** : to move to action — **ac·tu·a·tion** \ˌak-chə-ˈwā-shən, -shə-\ *n* — **ac·tu·a·tor** \ˈak-chə-ˌwā-tər, -shə-\ *n*

**act up** *vb* **1** : MISBEHAVE **2** : to function improperly

**acu·ity** \ə-ˈkyü-ə-tē\ *n, pl* **-ities** : keenness of perception

**acu·men** \ə-ˈkyü-mən\ *n* : mental keenness and penetration ♦ **Synonyms** DISCERNMENT, INSIGHT, PERCIPIENCE, PERSPICACITY

**acu·pres·sure** \ˈa-kyü-ˌpre-shər\ *n* : a finger massage of those points on the body stimulated in acupuncture

**acu·punc·ture** \-ˌpəŋk-chər\ *n* : an orig. Chinese practice of inserting thin needles through the skin at specific points esp. to cure disease or relieve pain — **acu·punc·tur·ist** \ˌa-kyü-ˈpəŋk-chə-rist\ *n*

**acute** \ə-ˈkyüt\ *adj* **acut·er; acut·est** [ME, fr. L *acutus*, pp. of *acuere* to sharpen, fr. *acus* needle] **1** : SHARP, POINTED **2** : containing less than 90 degrees ⟨an ~ angle⟩ **3** : sharply perceptive; *esp* : mentally keen **4** : SEVERE ⟨~ distress⟩; *also* : having a sudden onset, sharp rise, and short duration ⟨~ inflammation⟩ **5** : of, marked by, or being an accent mark having the form ´ — **acute·ly** *adv* — **acute·ness** *n*

**acy·clo·vir** \(ˌ)ā-ˈsī-klō-ˌvir\ *n* : a drug used esp. to treat the genital form of herpes simplex

**ad** \ˈad\ *n* : ADVERTISEMENT

**AD** *abbr* **1** after date **2** [L *anno Domini*] in the year of our Lord — often printed in small capitals and often punctuated **3** assistant director **4** athletic director

**ad·age** \ˈa-dij\ *n* : an old familiar saying : PROVERB, MAXIM

**¹ada·gio** \ə-ˈdä-j(ē-ˌ)ō, -zh(ē-ˌ)ō\ *adv or adj* [It] : at a slow tempo — used as a direction in music

**²adagio** *n, pl* **-gios** **1** : an adagio movement **2** : a ballet duet or trio displaying feats of lifting and balancing

**¹ad·a·mant** \ˈa-də-mənt, -ˌmant\ *n* [ME, fr. AF, fr. L *adamant-, adamas* hardest metal, diamond, fr. Gk] : a stone believed to be impenetrably hard — **ad·a·man·tine** \ˌa-də-ˈman-ˌtēn, -ˌtīn\ *adj*

**²adamant** *adj* : very determined : INFLEXIBLE, UNYIELDING — **ad·a·man·cy** \ˈa-də-mən-sē\ *n* — **ad·a·mant·ly** *adv*

**Ad·am's apple** \ˈa-dəmz-\ *n* : the projection in front of the neck formed by the largest cartilage of the larynx

**adapt** \ə-ˈdapt\ *vb* **1** : to make suitable or fit (as for a new use or for a different situation) **2** : to adjust to environmental conditions ♦ **Synonyms** ADJUST, ACCOMMODATE, CONFORM — **adapt·abil·i·ty**

\ə-‚dap-tə-ˈbi-lə-tē\ n — **adapt·able** adj — **ad·ap·ta·tion** \‚a-‚dap-ˈtā-shən\ n — **ad·ap·ta·tion·al** \-sh(ə-)nəl\ adj — **adap·tive** \ə-ˈdap-tiv\ adj — **ad·ap·tiv·i·ty** \‚a-‚dap-ˈti-və-tē\ n

**adapt·er** also **adap·tor** \ə-ˈdap-tər\ n : **1** : one that adapts **2** : a device for connecting two dissimilar parts of an apparatus **3** : an attachment for adapting apparatus for uses not orig. intended

**adaptive optics** n sing or pl : a telescopic system that improves image resolution by compensating for distortions from atmospheric turbulence

**ADC** abbr **1** aide-de-camp **2** Aid to Dependent Children

**add** \ˈad\ vb **1** : to join to something else so as to increase in number or amount **2** : to say further ⟨let me ~ this⟩ **3** : to combine (numbers) into one sum

**ADD** abbr attention deficit disorder

**ad·dend** \ˈa-‚dend\ n : a number to be added to another

**ad·den·dum** \ə-ˈden-dəm\ n, pl **-da** \-də\ [L] : something added; esp : a supplement to a book

**¹ad·der** \ˈa-dər\ n [ME, alter. (by false division of a naddre) of naddre, fr. OE nǣddre] **1** : a poisonous European viper or a related snake **2** : any of various harmless No. American snakes (as the hognose snake)

**²add·er** \ˈa-dər\ n : one that adds; esp : a device that performs addition

**¹ad·dict** \ə-ˈdikt\ vb **1** : to devote or surrender (oneself) to something habitually or excessively **2** : to cause addiction to a substance in (as a person) — **ad·dic·tive** \-ˈdik-tiv\ adj

**²ad·dict** \ˈa-(‚)dikt\ n : one who is addicted esp. to a substance

**ad·dic·tion** \ə-ˈdik-shən\ n **1** : the quality or state of being addicted **2** : compulsive need for and use of a habit-forming substance (as heroin, nicotine, or alcohol) characterized by well-defined physiological symptoms upon withdrawal; also : persistent compulsive use of a substance known by the user to be harmful

**ad·di·tion** \ə-ˈdi-shən\ n **1** : the act or process of adding; also : something added **2** : the operation of combining numbers to obtain their sum ♦ **Synonyms** ACCRETION, INCREMENT, ACCESSION, AUGMENTATION

**ad·di·tion·al** \ə-ˈdi-sh(ə-)nəl\ adj : coming by way of addition : ADDED, EXTRA

**ad·di·tion·al·ly** \ə-ˈdi-sh(ə-)nə-lē\ adv : in or by way of addition : FURTHERMORE

**¹ad·di·tive** \ˈa-də-tiv\ adj **1** : of, relating to, or characterized by addition **2** : produced by addition — **ad·di·tiv·i·ty** \‚a-də-ˈti-və-tē\ n

**²additive** n : a substance added to another in small quantities to effect a desired change in properties ⟨food ~s⟩

**ad·dle** \ˈa-dᵊl\ vb **ad·dled; ad·dling 1** : to throw into confusion : MUDDLE **2** : to become rotten ⟨addled eggs⟩

**addn** abbr addition

**addnl** abbr additional

**add-on** \ˈad-‚ȯn, -‚än\ n : something (as a feature or accessory) added esp. as an enhancement

**¹ad·dress** \ə-ˈdres\ vb **1** : to direct the attention of (oneself) **2** : to direct one's remarks to : deliver an address to **3** : to mark directions for delivery on **4** : to identify (as a memory location) by an address

**²ad·dress** \ə-ˈdres, ˈa-‚dres\ n **1** : skillful management **2** : a formal speech : LECTURE **3** : the place where a person or organization may be communicated with **4** : the directions for delivery placed on mail; also : the designation of a computer account from which one can send or receive e-mail **5** : a location (as in a computer's memory) where particular data is stored; also : URL

**ad·dress·ee** \‚a-‚dre-ˈsē, ə-‚dre-ˈsē\ n : one to whom something is addressed

**ad·duce** \ə-ˈdüs, -ˈdyüs\ vb **ad·duced; ad·duc·ing** : to offer as argument, reason, or proof ♦ **Synonyms** ADVANCE, ALLEGE, CITE, SUBMIT — **ad·duc·er** n

**-ade** n suffix **1** : act : action ⟨blockade⟩ **2** : product; esp : sweet drink ⟨limeade⟩

**ad·e·nine** \ˈa-də-‚nēn\ n : a purine base that codes genetic information in the molecular chain of DNA and RNA

**ad·e·noid** \ˈa-də-‚nȯid, ˈad-‚nȯid\ n : an enlarged mass of tissue near the opening of the nose into the throat — usu. used in pl. — **adenoid** or **ad·e·noi·dal** \‚a-də-ˈnȯi-dᵊl\ adj

**aden·o·sine  tri·phos·phate** \ə-ˈde-nə-‚sēn-trī-ˈfäs-‚fāt\ n : ATP

**ad·e·no·vi·rus** \‚a-də-nō-ˈvī-rəs\ n : any of a family of viruses causing infections of the respiratory tract, conjunctiva, and gastrointestinal tract

**¹ad·ept** \ˈa-‚dept\ n : EXPERT

**²adept** \ə-ˈdept\ adj : highly skilled : EXPERT — **adept·ly** adv — **adept·ness** n

**ad·e·quate** \ˈa-di-kwət\ adj : equal to or sufficient for a specific requirement — **ad·e·qua·cy** \-kwə-sē\ n — **ad·e·quate·ly** adv — **ad·e·quate·ness** n

**ad·here** \ad-ˈhir\ vb **ad·hered; ad·her·ing 1** : to give support : maintain loyalty **2** : to stick fast : CLING — **ad·her·ence** \-ˈhir-əns\ n — **ad·her·ent** \-ənt\ adj or n

**ad·he·sion** \ad-ˈhē-zhən\ n **1** : the act or state of adhering **2** : the union of bodily tissues abnormally grown together after inflammation; also : the newly formed uniting tissue **3** : the molecular attraction between the surfaces of bodies in contact

**¹ad·he·sive** \-ˈhē-siv, -ziv\ adj **1** : tending to adhere : STICKY **2** : prepared for adhering

**²adhesive** n : an adhesive substance

**adhesive tape** n : tape coated on one side with an adhesive mixture; esp : one used for covering wounds

**¹ad hoc** \ˈad-ˈhäk, -ˈhōk\ adv [L, for this] : for the case at hand apart from other applications

**²ad hoc** adj : concerned with or formed for a particular purpose ⟨an ad hoc committee⟩ ⟨ad hoc solutions⟩

**adi·a·bat·ic** \‚a-dē-ə-ˈba-tik\ adj : occurring

without loss or gain of heat — **adi·a·bat·i·cal·ly** \-ti-k(ə-)lē\ *adv*

**adieu** \ə-'dü, -'dyü\ *n, pl* **adieus** *or* **adieux** \ə-'düz, -'dyüz\ : FAREWELL — often used interjectionally

**ad in·fi·ni·tum** \,ad-,in-fə-'nī-təm\ *adv or adj* : without end or limit

**ad in·ter·im** \ad-'in-tə-rəm, -,rim\ *adv* : for the intervening time — **ad interim** *adj*

**adi·os** \,a-dē-'ōs, ,ä-\ *interj* [Sp *adiós*, lit., to God] — used to express farewell

**adi·pose** \'a-də-,pōs\ *adj* : of or relating to animal fat : FATTY

**adj** *abbr* 1 adjective 2 adjutant

**ad·ja·cent** \ə-'jā-sᵊnt\ *adj* : situated near or next ◆ **Synonyms** ADJOINING, CONTIGUOUS, ABUTTING, JUXTAPOSED, CONTERMINOUS — **ad·ja·cent·ly** *adv*

**ad·jec·tive** \'a-jik-tiv\ *n* : a word that typically serves as a modifier of a noun — **ad·jec·ti·val** \,a-jik-'tī-vəl\ *adj* — **ad·jec·ti·val·ly** *adv*

**ad·join** \ə-'jȯin\ *vb* : to be situated next to

**ad·join·ing** *adj* : touching or bounding at a point or line \⟨∼ rooms⟩

**ad·journ** \ə-'jərn\ *vb* 1 : to suspend indefinitely or until a stated time 2 : to transfer to another place — **ad·journment** *n*

**ad·judge** \ə-'jəj\ *vb* **ad·judged; ad·judg·ing** 1 : JUDGE, ADJUDICATE 2 : to hold or pronounce to be : DEEM 3 : to award by judicial decision

**ad·ju·di·cate** \ə-'jü-di-,kāt\ *vb* **-cat·ed; -cat·ing** : to settle judicially — **ad·ju·di·ca·tion** \ə-,jü-di-'kā-shən\ *n*

**ad·junct** \'a-,jəŋkt\ *n* : something joined or added to another but not essentially a part of it ◆ **Synonyms** APPENDAGE, APPURTENANCE, ACCESSORY, APPENDIX — **adjunct** *adj*

**ad·jure** \ə-'jur\ *vb* **ad·jured; ad·jur·ing** : to command solemnly : urge earnestly ◆ **Synonyms** BEG, BESEECH, IMPLORE — **ad·ju·ra·tion** \,a-jə-'rā-shən\ *n*

**ad·just** \ə-'jəst\ *vb* 1 : to bring to agreement : SETTLE 2 : to cause to conform : ADAPT, FIT 3 : REGULATE ⟨∼ a watch⟩ — **ad·just·able** *adj* — **ad·just·er** *also* **ad·jus·tor** \ə-'jəs-tər\ *n* — **ad·just·ment** \ə-'jəst-mənt\ *n*

**ad·ju·tant** \'a-jə-tənt\ *n* : one who assists; *esp* : an officer who assists a commanding officer by handling correspondence and keeping records

**ad·ju·vant** \'a-jə-vənt\ *n* : one that helps or facilitates; *esp* : something that enhances the effectiveness of medical treatment — **adjuvant** *adj*

¹**ad–lib** \'ad-'lib\ *vb* **ad–libbed; ad–lib·bing** : IMPROVISE — **ad–lib** *n*

²**ad–lib** *adj* : spoken, composed, or performed without preparation

**ad lib** \'ad-'lib\ *adv* [NL *ad libitum*] 1 : at one's pleasure 2 : without limit

**adm** *abbr* administration; administrative

**ADM** *abbr* admiral

**ad·man** \'ad-,man\ *n* : one who writes, solicits, or places advertisements

**admin** *abbr* administration; administrative

**ad·min·is·ter** \əd-'mi-nə-stər\ *vb* 1 : MANAGE, SUPERINTEND 2 : to mete out : DISPENSE ⟨∼ punishment⟩ 3 : to give ritually or remedially ⟨∼ quinine for malaria⟩ 4 : to perform the office of administrator — **ad·min·is·tra·ble** \-strə-bəl\ *adj* — **ad·min·is·trant** \-strənt\ *n*

**ad·min·is·tra·tion** \əd-,mi-nə-'strā-shən\ *n* 1 : the act or process of administering 2 : MANAGEMENT 3 : the officials directing the government of a country 4 : the term of office of an administrative officer or body — **ad·min·is·tra·tive** \əd-'mi-nə-,strā-tiv\ *adj* — **ad·min·is·tra·tive·ly** *adv*

**ad·min·is·tra·tor** \əd-'mi-nə-,strā-tər\ *n* : one that administers; *esp* : one who settles an intestate estate

**ad·mi·ra·ble** \'ad-m(ə-)rə-bəl\ *adj* : worthy of admiration : EXCELLENT — **ad·mi·ra·bil·i·ty** \,ad-m(ə-)rə-'bi-lə-tē\ *n* — **ad·mi·ra·ble·ness** *n* — **ad·mi·ra·bly** \-blē\ *adv*

**ad·mi·ral** \'ad-m(ə-)rəl\ *n* [ME, ultim. fr. Ar *amīr-al-* commander of the (as in *amīr-al-baḥr* commander of the sea)] : a commissioned officer in the navy ranking next below a fleet admiral

**ad·mi·ral·ty** \'ad-m(ə-)rəl-tē\ *n* 1 *cap* : a British government department formerly having authority over naval affairs 2 : the court having jurisdiction over questions of maritime law

**ad·mire** \əd-'mī(-ə)r\ *vb* **ad·mired; ad·mir·ing** [MF *admirer*, fr. L *admirari*, fr. *ad-* to + *mirari* to wonder] : to regard with high esteem — **ad·mi·ra·tion** \,ad-mə-'rā-shən\ *n* — **ad·mir·er** *n* — **ad·mir·ing·ly** \-'mī-riŋ-lē\ *adv*

**ad·mis·si·ble** \əd-'mi-sə-bəl\ *adj* : that can be or is worthy to be admitted or allowed : ALLOWABLE ⟨∼ evidence⟩ — **ad·mis·si·bil·i·ty** \-,mi-sə-'bi-lə-tē\ *n*

**ad·mis·sion** \əd-'mi-shən\ *n* 1 : the act of admitting 2 : the privilege of being admitted 3 : a fee paid for admission 4 : the granting of an argument 5 : the acknowledgment of a fact

**ad·mit** \əd-'mit\ *vb* **ad·mit·ted; ad·mit·ting** 1 : PERMIT, ALLOW 2 : to recognize as genuine or valid 3 : to allow to enter ⟨*admitted* to the club⟩ 4 : to accept into a hospital as an inpatient

**ad·mit·tance** \əd-'mi-tᵊns\ *n* : the act or process of admitting : permission to enter

**ad·mit·ted·ly** \əd-'mi-təd-lē\ *adv* 1 : as has been or must be admitted 2 : it must be admitted

**ad·mix** \ad-'miks\ *vb* : to mix in

**ad·mix·ture** \ad-'miks-chər\ *n* 1 : something added in mixing 2 : MIXTURE

**ad·mon·ish** \əd-'mä-nish\ *vb* : to warn gently : reprove with a warning ◆ **Synonyms** CHIDE, REPROACH, REBUKE, REPRIMAND, REPROVE — **ad·mon·ish·er** *n* — **ad·mon·ish·ing·ly** *adv* — **ad·mon·ish·ment** *n* — **ad·mo·ni·tion** \,ad-mə-'ni-shən\ *n* — **ad·mon·i·to·ry** \ad-'mä-nə-,tȯr-ē\ *adj*

**ad nau·se·am** \ad-'nȯ-zē-əm\ *adv* [L] : to a sickening or excessive degree

**ado** \ə-'dü\ *n* **1** : heightened fuss or concern **2** : TROUBLE

**ado·be** \ə-'dō-bē\ *n* **1** : sun-dried brick; *also* : clay for making such bricks **2** : a structure made of adobe bricks

**ad·o·les·cence** \ˌa-də-'le-s⁹ns\ *n* : the process or period of growth between childhood and maturity — **ad·o·les·cent** \-s⁹nt\ *adj or n*

**adopt** \ə-'däpt\ *vb* **1** : to take (a child of other parents) as one's own child **2** : to take up and practice as one's own **3** : to accept formally and put into effect — **adopt·able** \-'däp-tə-bəl\ *adj* — **adopt·er** *n* — **adop·tion** \-'däp-shən\ *n*

**adop·tive** \ə-'däp-tiv\ *adj* : made or acquired by adoption ⟨the ~ father⟩ — **adop·tive·ly** *adv*

**ador·able** \ə-'dór-ə-bəl\ *adj* **1** : worthy of adoration **2** : extremely charming ⟨an ~ child⟩ — **ador·able·ness** *n* — **ador·ably** \-blē\ *adv*

**adore** \ə-'dór\ *vb* **adored; ador·ing** [ME *adouren*, fr. AF *aurer, adourer*, fr. L *adorare*, fr. *ad-* to + *orare* to speak, pray] **1** : WORSHIP **2** : to regard with loving admiration ⟨~s his wife⟩ **3** : to be extremely fond of ⟨~s pecan pie⟩ — **ado·ra·tion** \ˌa-də-'rā-shən\ *n*

**adorn** \ə-'dórn\ *vb* : to enhance the appearance of esp. with ornaments ⟨blouses ~ed with sequins⟩ — **adorn·ment** *n*

**ad·re·nal** \ə-'drē-n⁹l\ *adj* : of, relating to, or being a pair of endocrine organs (**adrenal glands**) that are located near the kidneys and produce several hormones and esp. epinephrine

**adren·a·line** \ə-'dre-nə-lən\ *n* : EPINEPHRINE

**adrift** \ə-'drift\ *adv or adj* **1** : afloat without motive power or moorings **2** : without guidance or purpose

**adroit** \ə-'dróit\ *adj* [F, fr. OF, fr. *a-* to + *droit* right] **1** : dexterous with one's hands **2** : SHREWD, RESOURCEFUL
♦ **Synonyms** CANNY, CLEVER, CUNNING, INGENIOUS — **adroit·ly** *adv* — **adroit·ness** *n*

**ad·sorb** \ad-'sórb, -'zórb\ *vb* : to take up (as molecules of gases) and hold on the surface of a solid or liquid — **ad·sorp·tion** \-'sórp-shən, -'zórp-\ *n*

**ad·u·la·tion** \ˌa-jə-'lā-shən\ *n* : excessive admiration or flattery — **ad·u·late** \'a-jə-ˌlāt\ *vb* — **ad·u·la·tor** \-ˌlā-tər\ *n* — **ad·u·la·to·ry** \-lə-ˌtór-ē\ *adj*

**¹adult** \ə-'dəlt, 'a-ˌ\ *adj* [L *adultus*, pp. of *adolescere* to grow up, fr. *ad-* to + *alescere* to grow] : fully developed and mature — **adult·hood** *n*

**²adult** *n* : one that is adult; *esp* : a human being after an age (as 18) specified by law

**adul·ter·ant** \ə-'dəl-tə-rənt\ *n* : something used to adulterate another

**adul·ter·ate** \ə-'dəl-tə-ˌrāt\ *vb* **-at·ed; -at·ing** [L *adulterare*, fr. *ad-* to + *alter* other] : to make impure by mixing in a foreign or inferior substance — **adul·ter·a·tion** \-ˌdəl-tə-'rā-shən\ *n*

**adul·tery** \ə-'dəl-t(ə-)rē\ *n, pl* **-ter·ies** : sexual unfaithfulness of a married person — **adul·ter·er** \-tər-ər\ *n* — **adul·-**

**ter·ess** \-t(ə-)rəs\ *also* **adul·tress** \-trəs\ *n* — **adul·ter·ous** \-t(ə-)rəs\ *adj*

**ad·um·brate** \'a-dəm-ˌbrāt\ *vb* **-brat·ed; -brat·ing** **1** : to foreshadow vaguely : INTIMATE **2** : to suggest or disclose partially **3** : SHADE, OBSCURE — **ad·um·bra·tion** \ˌa-dəm-'brā-shən\ *n*

**adv** *abbr* **1** adverb **2** advertisement

**ad va·lor·em** \ˌad-və-'lór-əm\ *adj* [L, according to the value] : imposed at a percentage of the value ⟨an *ad valorem* tax⟩

**¹ad·vance** \əd-'vans\ *vb* **ad·vanced; ad·vanc·ing** **1** : to assist the progress of ⟨~ a cause⟩ **2** : to bring or move forward ⟨~ a pawn⟩ **3** : to promote in rank **4** : to make earlier in time **5** : PROPOSE **6** : LEND **7** : to raise in rate : INCREASE — **ad·vance·ment** *n*

**²advance** *n* **1** : a forward movement **2** : IMPROVEMENT **3** : a rise esp. in price or value **4** : OFFER — **in advance** : BEFOREHAND

**³advance** *adj* : made, sent, or furnished ahead of time ⟨~ payment⟩

**ad·van·tage** \əd-'van-tij\ *n* **1** : superiority of position **2** : BENEFIT, GAIN **3** : the 1st point won in tennis after deuce — **ad·van·ta·geous** \ˌad-ˌvan-'tā-jəs\ *adj* — **ad·van·ta·geous·ly** *adv*

**ad·vent** \'ad-ˌvent\ *n* **1** *cap* : a penitential period beginning four Sundays before Christmas **2** *cap* : the coming of Christ **3** : a coming into being or use

**ad·ven·ti·tious** \ˌad-vən-'ti-shəs\ *adj* **1** : ACCIDENTAL, INCIDENTAL **2** : arising or occurring sporadically or in other than the usual location ⟨~ buds⟩ — **ad·ven·ti·tious·ly** *adv*

**¹ad·ven·ture** \əd-'ven-chər\ *n* **1** : a risky undertaking **2** : a remarkable and exciting experience — **ad·ven·tur·ous** \-ch(ə-)rəs\ *adj*

**²adventure** *vb* **-ven·tured; -ven·tur·ing** \-'ven-ch(ə-)riŋ\ **1** : RISK, HAZARD ⟨~ their capital in foreign trade⟩ **2** : to engage in adventure

**ad·ven·tur·er** \əd-'ven-ch(ə-)rər\ *n* **1** : a person who engages in new and risky undertakings **2** : a person who follows a military career for adventure or profit **3** : a person who tries to gain wealth by questionable means

**ad·ven·ture·some** \əd-'ven-chər-səm\ *adj* : inclined to take risks

**ad·ven·tur·ess** \əd-'ven-ch(ə-)rəs\ *n* : a female adventurer

**ad·verb** \'ad-ˌvərb\ *n* : a word that typically serves as a modifier of a verb, an adjective, or another adverb — **ad·ver·bi·al** \ad-'vər-bē-əl\ *adj* — **ad·ver·bi·al·ly** *adv*

**¹ad·ver·sary** \'ad-vər-ˌser-ē\ *n, pl* **-sar·ies** : FOE

**²adversary** *adj* : involving antagonistic parties or interests

**ad·verse** \ad-'vərs, 'ad-ˌvərs\ *adj* **1** : acting against or in a contrary direction ⟨~ winds⟩ **2** : UNFAVORABLE ⟨~ criticism⟩ — **ad·verse·ly** *adv*

**ad·ver·si·ty** \ad-'vər-sə-tē\ *n, pl* **-ties** : serious difficulty : MISFORTUNE

**ad·vert** \ad-'vərt\ *vb* : REFER ⟨∼ to a previous remark⟩

**ad·ver·tise** \'ad-vər-₁tīz\ *vb* -**tised**; -**tis·ing** 1 : INFORM, NOTIFY 2 : to call public attention to esp. in order to sell — **ad·ver·tis·er** *n*

**ad·ver·tise·ment** \₁ad-vər-'tīz-mənt; əd-'vər-təs-mənt\ *n* 1 : the act of advertising 2 : a public notice intended to advertise something

**ad·ver·tis·ing** \'ad-vər-₁tī-ziŋ\ *n* : the business of preparing advertisements

**ad·vice** \əd-'vīs\ *n* 1 : recommendation with regard to a course of action : COUNSEL 2 : INFORMATION, REPORT

**ad·vis·able** \əd-'vī-zə-bəl\ *adj* : proper to be done : EXPEDIENT ⟨∼ to stay fit⟩ — **ad·vis·abil·i·ty** \-₁vī-zə-'bi-lə-tē\ *n*

**ad·vise** \əd-'vīz\ *vb* **ad·vised**; **ad·vis·ing** 1 : to give advice to : COUNSEL 2 : INFORM, NOTIFY 3 : CONSULT, CONFER ⟨∼ with your friends⟩ — **ad·vis·er** *also* **ad·vi·sor** \-'vī-zər\ *n*

**ad·vised** \əd-'vīzd\ *adj* : thought out : CONSIDERED ⟨well-*advised*⟩ — **ad·vis·ed·ly** \-'vī-zəd-lē\ *adv*

**ad·vise·ment** \əd-'vīz-mənt\ *n* 1 : careful consideration ⟨take the matter under ∼⟩ 2 : the act of advising

**ad·vi·so·ry** \əd-'vī-zə-rē\ *adj* 1 : having or exercising power to advise 2 : containing or giving advice

¹**ad·vo·cate** \'ad-və-kət, -₁kāt\ *n* [ultim. fr. L *advocare* to summon, fr. *ad-* to + *vocare* to call] 1 : one who pleads another's cause 2 : one who argues or pleads for a cause or proposal — **ad·vo·ca·cy** \-və-kə-sē\ *n*

²**ad·vo·cate** \-₁kāt\ *vb* -**cat·ed**; -**cat·ing** : to plead in favor of — **ad·vo·ca·tion** \₁ad-və-'kā-shən\ *n*

**advt** *abbr* advertisement

**adze** *also* **adz** \'adz\ *n* : a tool with a curved blade set at right angles to the handle that is used in shaping wood

**AEC** *abbr* Atomic Energy Commission

**ae·gis** \'ē-jəs\ *n* 1 : SHIELD, PROTECTION ⟨under the ∼ of the constitution⟩ 2 : PATRONAGE, SPONSORSHIP ⟨under the ∼ of the museum⟩

**ae·o·li·an harp** \ē-'ō-lē-ən-\ *n* : a box with strings that produce musical sounds when the wind blows on them

**ae·on** *or* **eon** \'ē-ən, -₁än\ *n* : an indefinitely long time : AGE

**aer·ate** \'er-₁āt\ *vb* **aer·at·ed**; **aer·at·ing** 1 : to supply, impregnate, or combine with a gas and esp. air 2 : to supply (blood) with oxygen by respiration — **aer·a·tion** \₁er-'ā-shən\ *n* — **aer·a·tor** \'er-₁ā-tər\ *n*

¹**ae·ri·al** \'er-ē-əl\ *adj* 1 : inhabiting, occurring in, or done in the air 2 : AIRY 3 : of or relating to aircraft

²**aer·i·al** \'er-ē-əl\ *n* : ANTENNA 2

**ae·ri·al·ist** \'er-ē-ə-list\ *n* : a performer of feats above the ground esp. on a trapeze

**ae·rie** \'er-ē, 'ir-ē\ *n* : a highly placed nest (as of an eagle)

**aer·o·bat·ics** \₁er-ə-'ba-tiks\ *n sing or pl* : spectacular flying feats and maneuvers

**aer·o·bic** \₁er-'rō-bik\ *adj* 1 : living or active only in the presence of oxygen ⟨∼ bacteria⟩ 2 : involving or increasing oxygen consumption; *also* : of or relating to aerobics — **aer·o·bi·cal·ly** \-bi-k(ə-)lē\ *adv*

**aer·o·bics** \-biks\ *n sing or pl* : strenuous exercises that produce a marked temporary increase in respiration and heart rate; *also* : a system of physical conditioning involving these

**aero·drome** \'er-ə-₁drōm\ *n, chiefly Brit* : AIRPORT

**aero·dy·nam·ics** \₁er-ō-dī-'na-miks\ *n* : the science dealing with the forces acting on bodies in motion in a gas (as air) — **aero·dy·nam·ic** \-mik\ *also* **aero·dy·nam·i·cal** \-mi-kəl\ *adj* — **aero·dy·nam·i·cal·ly** \-mi-k(ə-)lē\ *adv*

**aero·naut** \'er-ə-₁nȯt\ *n* [F *aéronaute*, ultim. fr. Gk *aēr* air + *nautēs* sailor] : one who operates or travels in an airship or balloon

**aero·nau·tics** \₁er-ə-'nȯ-tiks\ *n* : the science of aircraft operation — **aero·nau·ti·cal** \-ti-kəl\ *also* **aero·nau·tic** \-tik\ *adj*

**aero·pho·bia** \₁er-ō-'fō-bē-ə\ *n* : fear or strong dislike of flying

**aero·plane** \'er-ə-₁plān\ *chiefly Brit var of* AIRPLANE

**aero·sol** \'er-ə-₁säl, -₁sȯl\ *n* 1 : a suspension of fine solid or liquid particles in a gas; *also, pl* : the particles themselves 2 : a substance (as an insecticide) dispensed from a pressurized container as an aerosol

**aero·space** \'er-ō-₁spās\ *n* : the earth's atmosphere and the space beyond — **aerospace** *adj*

**aery** \'er-ē\ *adj* **aer·i·er**; -**est** : having an aerial quality : ETHEREAL ⟨∼ visions⟩

**aes·thete** *also* **es·thete** \'es-₁thēt\ *n* : a person having or affecting sensitivity to beauty esp. in art

**aes·thet·ic** *also* **es·thet·ic** \es-'the-tik\ *adj* 1 : of or relating to aesthetics : ARTISTIC 2 : appreciative of the beautiful — **aes·thet·i·cal·ly** *also* **es·thet·i·cal·ly** \-ti-k(ə-)lē\ *adv*

**aes·thet·ics** *also* **es·thet·ics** \-tiks\ *n* : a branch of philosophy dealing with the nature, creation, and appreciation of beauty

**ae·ti·ol·o·gy** *chiefly Brit var of* ETIOLOGY

**AF** *abbr* 1 air force 2 audio frequency

¹**afar** \ə-'fär\ *adv* : from, at, or to a great distance

²**afar** *n* : a great distance

**AFB** *abbr* air force base

**AFC** *abbr* 1 American Football Conference 2 automatic frequency control

**AFDC** *abbr* Aid to Families with Dependent Children

**af·fa·ble** \'a-fə-bəl\ *adj* : courteous and agreeable in conversation — **af·fa·bil·i·ty** \₁a-fə-'bi-lə-tē\ *n* — **af·fa·bly** \'a-fə-blē\ *adv*

**af·fair** \ə-'fer\ *n* [ME *afere*, fr. AF fr. *afaire*, fr. *a faire* to do] 1 : something that relates to or involves one : CONCERN 2 : a romantic or sexual attachment of limited duration

¹**af·fect** \ə-'fekt, a-\ vb **1** : to be fond of using or wearing **2** : to pretend that an attitude or behavior is genuine

²**affect** vb : to produce an effect on : INFLUENCE

³**affect** \'a-ˌfekt\ n : EMOTION; also : an observable display of emotion ⟨an expressionless ~⟩

**af·fec·ta·tion** \ˌa-ˌfek-'tā-shən\ n : an attitude or behavior that is assumed by a person but not genuinely felt

**af·fect·ed** \ə-'fek-təd\ adj **1** : given to or marked by affectation **2** : artificially assumed to impress others — **af·fect·ed·ly** adv

**af·fect·ing** \ə-'fek-tiŋ\ adj : arousing pity, sympathy, or sorrow ⟨an ~ story⟩ — **af·fect·ing·ly** adv

**af·fec·tion** \ə-'fek-shən\ n : tender attachment — **af·fec·tion·ate** \-sh(ə-)nət\ adj — **af·fec·tion·ate·ly** adv

**af·fec·tive** \a-'fek-tiv\ adj : relating to, influencing, or expressing an emotion or feeling : EMOTIONAL ⟨an ~ disorder⟩

**af·fer·ent** \'a-fə-rənt, -ˌfer-ənt\ adj : bearing or conducting inward toward a more central part and esp. a nerve center (as the central nervous system)

**af·fi·ance** \ə-'fī-əns\ vb **-anced; -anc·ing** : to promise oneself or another in marriage

**af·fi·da·vit** \ˌa-fə-'dā-vət\ n [ML, he has made an oath] : a sworn statement in writing

¹**af·fil·i·ate** \ə-'fi-lē-ˌāt\ vb **-at·ed; -at·ing** : to associate as a member or branch — **af·fil·i·a·tion** \-ˌfi-lē-'ā-shən\ n

²**af·fil·i·ate** \ə-'fi-lē-ət\ n : an affiliated person or organization

**af·fin·i·ty** \ə-'fi-nə-tē\ n, pl **-ties 1** : KINSHIP, RELATIONSHIP **2** : attractive force : ATTRACTION, SYMPATHY

**affinity card** n : a credit card issued in affiliation with an organization (as a charity or an airline) the use of which benefits the organization or possessor of the card

**af·firm** \ə-'fərm\ vb **1** : CONFIRM **2** : to assert positively **3** : to make a solemn and formal declaration or assertion in place of an oath ♦ *Synonyms* AVER, AVOW, AVOUCH, DECLARE, ASSERT — **af·fir·ma·tion** \ˌa-fər-'mā-shən\ n

¹**af·fir·ma·tive** \ə-'fər-mə-tiv\ adj : asserting that the fact is so : POSITIVE

²**affirmative** n **1** : an expression of affirmation or assent **2** : the side that upholds the proposition stated in a debate

**affirmative action** n : an active effort to improve the employment or educational opportunities of members of minority groups and women

¹**af·fix** \ə-'fiks\ vb : ATTACH, ADD

²**af·fix** \'a-ˌfiks\ n : one or more sounds or letters attached to the beginning or end of a word that produce a derivative word or an inflectional form

**af·fla·tus** \ə-'flā-təs\ n : divine inspiration

**af·flict** \ə-'flikt\ vb : to cause pain and distress to ♦ *Synonyms* RACK, TRY, TORMENT, TORTURE — **af·flic·tion** \-'flik-shən\ n

**af·flic·tive** \ə-'flik-tiv\ adj : causing affliction : DISTRESSING ⟨~ emotions⟩ — **af·flic·tive·ly** adv

**af·flu·ence** \'a-ˌflü-ən(t)s, a-'flü-\ n : abundant supply; also : WEALTH, RICHES — **af·flu·ent** \-ənt\ adj

**af·ford** \ə-'förd\ vb **1** : to manage to bear or bear the cost of without serious harm or loss **2** : PROVIDE, FURNISH ⟨the roof ~ed a fine view⟩

**af·for·es·ta·tion** \ə-ˌför-ə-'stā-shən\ n : the act or process of establishing a forest — **af·for·est** \ə-'för-əst, -'fär-\ vb

**af·fray** \ə-'frā\ n : FIGHT, FRAY

**af·fright** \ə-'frīt\ vb, archaic : FRIGHTEN, ALARM — **affright** n

**af·front** \ə-'frənt\ vb **1** : INSULT **2** : CONFRONT ⟨~ death⟩ — **affront** n

**af·ghan** \'af-ˌgan\ n **1** cap : a native or inhabitant of Afghanistan **2** : a blanket or shawl of colored wool knitted or crocheted in sections — **Afghan** or **Afghani** \af-'ga-nē, -'gä-\ adj

**Afghan hound** n : any of a breed of tall slim swift hunting dogs with a coat of silky thick hair and a long silky top-knot

**af·gha·ni** \af-'ga-nē\ n — see MONEY table

**afi·cio·na·do** \ə-ˌfi-sh(ē-)ə-'nä-dō, -sē-ə-\ n, pl **-dos** [Sp, fr. pp. of *aficionar* to inspire affection] : DEVOTEE, FAN

**afield** \ə-'fēld\ adv or adj **1** : to, in, or on the field **2** : away from home **3** : out of the way : ASTRAY

**afire** \ə-'fī(-ə)r\ adj or adv : being on fire : BURNING

**AFL** abbr American Football League

**aflame** \ə-'flām\ adj or adv : FLAMING

**AFL–CIO** abbr American Federation of Labor and Congress of Industrial Organizations

**afloat** \ə-'flōt\ adj or adv **1** : borne on or as if on the water **2** : CIRCULATING ⟨rumors were ~⟩ **3** : ADRIFT

**aflut·ter** \ə-'flə-tər\ adj **1** : FLUTTERING **2** : nervously excited ⟨~ at the news⟩

**afoot** \ə-'fut\ adv or adj **1** : on foot **2** : in action : in progress

**afore·men·tioned** \ə-'för-'men-chənd\ adj : mentioned previously

**afore·said** \-ˌsed\ adj : said or named before

**afore·thought** \-ˌthȯt\ adj : planned beforehand : PREMEDITATED ⟨with malice ~⟩

**a for·ti·o·ri** \ˌä-ˌför-tē-'ȯr-ē\ adv [NL, lit., from the stronger (argument)] : with even greater reason

**afoul of** \ə-'faȯl-əv\ prep **1** : in or into conflict with **2** : in or into collision or entanglement with

**Afr** abbr Africa; African

**afraid** \ə-'frād\ adj **1** : FRIGHTENED, FEARFUL **2** : filled with concern or regret ⟨~ I won't be able to go⟩

**A–frame** \'ā-ˌfrām\ n : a building having triangular front and rear walls with the roof reaching to the ground

**afresh** \ə-'fresh\ adv : ANEW, AGAIN

**Af·ri·can** \'a-fri-kən\ n **1** : a native or inhabitant of Africa **2** : a person of African ancestry — **African** adj

**Af·ri·can—Amer·i·can** \-ə-'mer-ə-kən\ n : an American of African and esp. of black African descent — **African—American** adj

**Af·ri·can·ized bee** \'a-frə-kə-ˌnīzd-\ n : a highly aggressive hybrid honeybee accidentally produced from Brazilian and African stocks that has spread from So. America into Mexico and the southern U.S.

**Africanized honeybee** n : AFRICANIZED BEE

**African violet** n : a tropical African plant widely grown indoors for its velvety fleshy leaves and showy purple, pink, or white flowers

**Af·ri·kaans** \ˌa-fri-'käns\ n : a language developed from 17th century Dutch that is one of the official languages of the Republic of So. Africa

**Af·ro** \'a-(ˌ)frō\ n, pl **Afros** : a hairstyle of tight curls in a full evenly rounded shape

**Af·ro—Amer·i·can** \ˌa-frō-ə-'mer-ə-kən\ n : AFRICAN-AMERICAN — **Afro—American** adj

**aft** \'aft\ adv : near, toward, or in the stern of a ship or the tail of an aircraft

**AFT** abbr American Federation of Teachers

¹**af·ter** \'af-tər\ adv : AFTERWARD, SUBSEQUENTLY

²**after** prep **1** : behind in place **2** : later than ⟨~ dinner⟩ **3** : in pursuit or search of ⟨he's ~ your job⟩

³**after** conj : following the time when ⟨we will come ~ we make plans⟩

⁴**after** adj **1** : LATER ⟨in ~ years⟩ **2** : located toward the rear

**af·ter·birth** \'af-tər-ˌbərth\ n : the placenta and membranes of the fetus that are expelled after childbirth

**af·ter·burn·er** \-ˌbər-nər\ n : a device incorporated in the tail pipe of a turbojet engine for injecting fuel into the hot exhaust gases and burning it to provide extra thrust

**af·ter·care** \-ˌker\ n : the care, nursing, or treatment of a convalescent patient

**af·ter·deck** \-ˌdek\ n : the rear half of the deck of a ship

**af·ter·ef·fect** \-ə-ˌfekt\ n : an effect that follows its cause after an interval

**af·ter·glow** \-ˌglō\ n : a glow remaining where a light has disappeared

**af·ter·im·age** \-ˌim-ij\ n : a usu. visual sensation continuing after the stimulus causing it has ended

**af·ter·life** \-ˌlīf\ n : an existence after death

**af·ter·math** \-ˌmath\ n **1** : a second-growth crop esp. of hay **2** : CONSEQUENCES, EFFECTS ♦ Synonyms AFTEREFFECT, UPSHOT, RESULT, OUTCOME

**af·ter·noon** \ˌaf-tər-'nün\ n : the time between noon and evening

**af·ter·shave** \'af-tər-ˌshāv\ n : a usu. scented lotion for the face after shaving

**af·ter·taste** \-ˌtāst\ n : a sensation (as of flavor) continuing after the stimulus causing it has ended

**af·ter·tax** \'af-tər-ˌtaks\ adj : remaining after payment of taxes and esp. of income tax ⟨an ~ profit⟩

**af·ter·thought** \-ˌthȯt\ n : an idea occurring later

**af·ter·ward** \-wərd\ or **af·ter·wards** \-wərdz\ adv : at a later time

**Ag** symbol [L argentum] silver

**AG** abbr **1** adjutant general **2** attorney general

**again** \ə-'gen, -'gin\ adv **1** : once more : ANEW ⟨come see us ~⟩ **2** : on the other hand ⟨we may, and ~ we may not⟩ **3** : in addition : BESIDES

**against** \ə-'genst\ prep **1** : in opposition to **2** : directly opposite to : FACING **3** : as defense from **4** : so as to touch or strike ⟨threw him ~ the wall⟩; also : TOUCHING

¹**aga·pe** \ä-'gä-pā, 'ä-gə-ˌpā\ n [LL, fr. Gk agapē, lit., love] : unselfish unconditional love for another

²**agape** \ə-'gāp\ adj or adv : having the mouth open in wonder or surprise : GAPING

**agar** \'ä-ˌgär\ n **1** : a jellylike substance extracted from a red alga and used esp. as a gelling and stabilizing agent in foods **2** : a culture medium containing agar

**agar—agar** \ˌä-ˌgär-'ä-ˌgär\ n : AGAR

**ag·ate** \'a-gət\ n **1** : a striped or clouded quartz **2** : a playing marble of agate or of glass

**aga·ve** \ə-'gä-vē\ n : any of a genus of spiny-leaved plants (as a century plant) related to the amaryllis

**agcy** abbr agency

¹**age** \'āj\ n **1** : the length of time during which a being or thing has lived or existed **2** : the time of life at which some particular qualification is achieved; esp : MAJORITY **3** : the latter part of life **4** : a long time **5** : a period in history

²**age** vb **aged; ag·ing** or **age·ing 1** : to grow old or cause to grow old **2** : to become or cause to become mature or mellow

**-age** n suffix **1** : aggregate : collection ⟨trackage⟩ **2** : action : process ⟨haulage⟩ **3** : cumulative result of ⟨breakage⟩ **4** : rate of ⟨dosage⟩ **5** : house or place of ⟨orphanage⟩ **6** : state : rank ⟨vassalage⟩ **7** : fee : charge ⟨postage⟩

**aged** \'ā-jəd for 1; 'ājd for 2\ adj **1** : of advanced age **2** : having attained a specified age ⟨a man ~ 40 years⟩

**age·ism** \'ā-ji-zəm\ n : discrimination against persons of a particular age and esp. the elderly — **age·ist** \-jist\ n

**age·less** \'āj-ləs\ adj **1** : not growing old or showing the effects of age **2** : TIMELESS, ETERNAL ⟨~ truths⟩

**agen·cy** \'ā-jən-sē\ n, pl **-cies 1** : one through which something is accomplished : INSTRUMENTALITY **2** : the office or function of an agent **3** : an establishment doing business for another **4** : an administrative division (as of a government) ♦ Synonyms MEANS, MEDIUM, VEHICLE

**agen·da** \ə-'jen-də\ n : a list of things to be done : PROGRAM

**agent** \'ā-jənt\ n **1** : one that acts **2**

: MEANS, INSTRUMENT **3** : a person acting or doing business for another **4** : a computer program designed to automate certain tasks (as gathering information online) ◆ *Synonyms* ATTORNEY, DEPUTY, PROXY, DELEGATE

**Agent Orange** *n* : an herbicide widely used in the Vietnam War that is composed of 2,4-D and 2,4,5-T and contains a toxic contaminant

**agent pro·vo·ca·teur** \ä-ˌzhäⁿ-prō-ˌvä-kə-ˈtər, ˈä-jȯnt\ *n, pl* **agents provocateurs** \ˈä-ˌzhäⁿ-prō-ˌvä-ə-ˈtər, ˈä-jȯnts-prō-\ [F] : a person hired to infiltrate a group and incite its members to illegal action

**age of consent** : the age at which one is legally competent to give consent esp. to marriage or to sexual intercourse

**age–old** \ˈäj-ˈōld\ *adj* : having existed for ages : ANCIENT

**ag·er·a·tum** \ˌa-jə-ˈrä-təm\ *n, pl* **-tum** *also* **-tums** : any of a genus of tropical American plants that are related to the daisies and have small showy heads of usu. blue or white flowers

**age spots** *n pl* : benign flat spots of dark pigmentation on the skin occurring esp. among older people

**Ag·ge·us** \a-ˈgē-əs\ *n* : HAGGAI

¹**ag·glom·er·ate** \ə-ˈglä-mə-ˌrāt\ *vb* **-at·ed; -at·ing** [L *agglomerare* to heap up, join, fr. *ad-* to + *glomer-, glomus* ball) : to gather into a mass : CLUSTER — **ag·glom·er·a·tion** \-ˌglä-mə-ˈrā-shən\ *n*

²**ag·glom·er·ate** \-rət\ *n* : rock composed of volcanic fragments

**ag·glu·ti·nate** \ə-ˈglü-tᵊn-ˌāt\ *vb* **-nat·ed; -nat·ing** **1** : to cause to adhere : gather into a group or mass **2** : to cause (as red blood cells or bacteria) to collect into clumps — **ag·glu·ti·na·tion** \-ˌglü-tᵊn-ˈā-shən\ *n*

**ag·gran·dise** *Brit var of* AGGRANDIZE

**ag·gran·dize** \ə-ˈgran-ˌdīz, ˈa-grən-\ *vb* **-dized; -diz·ing** : to make great or greater ⟨~ an estate⟩ — **ag·gran·dize·ment** \ə-ˈgran-dəz-mənt, -ˌdīz-; ˌa-grən-ˈdīz-\ *n*

**ag·gra·vate** \ˈa-grə-ˌvāt\ *vb* **-vat·ed; -vat·ing** **1** : to make more severe : INTENSIFY **2** : IRRITATE — **ag·gra·va·tion** \ˌa-grə-ˈvā-shən\ *n*

¹**ag·gre·gate** \ˈa-gri-gət\ *adj* : formed by the gathering of units into one mass

²**ag·gre·gate** \-ˌgāt\ *vb* **-gat·ed; -gat·ing** : to collect into one mass

³**ag·gre·gate** \-gət\ *n* : a mass or body of units or parts somewhat loosely associated with one another; *also* : the whole amount

**ag·gre·ga·tion** \ˌa-gri-ˈgā-shən\ *n* **1** : a group, body, or mass composed of many distinct parts **2** : the collecting of units or parts into a mass or whole

**ag·gres·sion** \ə-ˈgre-shən\ *n* **1** : an unprovoked attack **2** : the practice of making attacks **3** : hostile, injurious, or destructive behavior or outlook esp. when caused by frustration — **ag·gres·sor** \-ˈgre-sər\ *n*

**ag·gres·sive** \ə-ˈgre-siv\ *adj* **1** : tending toward or exhibiting aggression; *esp*

: marked by combative readiness **2** : marked by driving energy or initiative : ENTERPRISING **3** : more intensive or comprehensive esp. in dosage or extent — **ag·gres·sive·ly** *adv* — **ag·gres·sive·ness** *n*

**ag·grieve** \ə-ˈgrēv\ *vb* **ag·grieved; ag·griev·ing** **1** : to cause grief to **2** : to inflict injury on : WRONG

**ag·gro** \ˈa-ˌgrō\ *adj* : aggressive or aggressively daring in style or manner ⟨~ music⟩ ⟨~ surfing⟩

**aghast** \ə-ˈgast\ *adj* : struck with amazement or horror

**ag·ile** \ˈa-jəl\ *adj* : able to move quickly and easily — **ag·ile·ly** *adv* — **agil·i·ty** \ə-ˈji-lə-tē\ *n*

**ag·i·ta** \ˈa-jə-tə\ *n* [southern It dial. pron. of It *acido*, lit., heartburn, acid] : a feeling of agitation or anxiety

**ag·i·tate** \ˈa-jə-ˌtāt\ *vb* **-tat·ed; -tat·ing** **1** : to move with an irregular rapid motion **2** : to stir up : EXCITE **3** : to discuss earnestly **4** : to attempt to arouse public feeling — **ag·i·ta·tion** \ˌa-jə-ˈtā-shən\ *n* — **ag·i·ta·tor** \ˈa-jə-ˌtā-tər\ *n*

**ag·it·prop** \ˈa-jət-ˌpräp\ *n* [Russ] : political propaganda promulgated esp. through the arts

**agleam** \ə-ˈglēm\ *adj* : GLEAMING ⟨eyes ~ with tears⟩

**aglit·ter** \ə-ˈgli-tər\ *adj* : GLITTERING

**aglow** \ə-ˈglō\ *adj* : GLOWING

**ag·nos·tic** \ag-ˈnäs-tik\ *adj* [Gk *agnōstos* unknown, unknowable, fr. *a-* un- + *gnōstos* known] : of or relating to the belief that the existence of any ultimate reality (as God) is unknown and prob. unknowable — **agnostic** *n* — **ag·nos·ti·cism** \-ˈnäs-tə-ˌsi-zəm\ *n*

**ago** \ə-ˈgō\ *adj or adv* : earlier than the present time ⟨10 years ~⟩

**agog** \ə-ˈgäg\ *adj* [MF *en gogues* in mirth] : full of excitement : EAGER

**a-go-go** \ä-ˈgō-ˌgō\ *adj* [*Whisky à Gogo*, café and disco in Paris, France, fr. F *à gogo* galore] : GO-GO

**ag·o·nise** *Brit var of* AGONIZE

**ag·o·nize** \ˈa-gə-ˌnīz\ *vb* **-nized; -niz·ing** : to suffer or cause to suffer agony — **ag·o·niz·ing·ly** *adv*

**ag·o·ny** \ˈa-gə-nē\ *n, pl* **-nies** [ME *agonie*, fr. L *agonia*, fr. Gk *agōnia* struggle, anguish, fr. *agōn* gathering, contest for a prize] : extreme pain of mind or body ◆ *Synonyms* SUFFERING, DISTRESS, MISERY

**ago·ra** \ä-gə-ˈrä\ *n, pl* **ago·rot** \-ˈrōt\ — see *shekel* at MONEY table

**ag·o·ra·pho·bia** \ˌa-gə-rə-ˈfō-bē-ə\ *n* : abnormal fear of being in a helpless, embarrassing, or inescapable situation characterized esp. by avoidance of open or public places — **ag·o·ra·pho·bic** \-ˈfō-bik, -ˈfä-\ *adj or n*

**agr** *abbr* agricultural; agriculture

**agrar·i·an** \ə-ˈgrer-ē-ən\ *adj* **1** : of or relating to land or its ownership ⟨~ reforms⟩ **2** : of or relating to farmers or farming interests — **agrarian** *n* — **agrar·i·an·ism** *n*

**agree** \ə-ˈgrē\ *vb* **agreed; agree·ing** **1**

: ADMIT, CONCEDE ⟨∼s that he was wrong⟩ **2** : to be similar : CORRESPOND ⟨both copies ∼⟩ **3** : to express agreement or approval **4** : to be in harmony **5** : to settle by common consent **6** : to be fitting or healthful : SUIT ⟨this climate ∼s with her⟩

**agree·able** \ə-'grē-ə-bəl\ *adj* **1** : PLEASING, PLEASANT ⟨an ∼ fragrance⟩ **2** : ready to consent ⟨I'm ∼ to their proposal⟩ **3** : being in harmony : CONSONANT — **agree·able·ness** *n* — **agree·ably** \-blē\ *adv*

**agree·ment** \ə-'grē-mənt\ *n* **1** : harmony of opinion or action **2** : mutual understanding or arrangement; *also* : a document containing such an arrangement

**ag·ri·busi·ness** \'a-grə-ˌbiz-nəs, -nəz\ *n* : an industry engaged in the manufacture and sale of farm equipment and supplies and in the production, processing, storage, and sale of farm commodities

**agric** *abbr* agricultural; agriculture

**ag·ri·cul·ture** \'a-gri-ˌkəl-chər\ *n* : FARMING, HUSBANDRY — **ag·ri·cul·tur·al** \ˌa-gri-'kəl-ch(ə-)rəl\ *adj* — **ag·ri·cul·tur·ist** \-ch(ə-)rist\ *or* **ag·ri·cul·tur·al·ist** \-ch(ə-)rə-list\ *n*

**agron·o·my** \ə-'grä-nə-mē\ *n* : a branch of agriculture that deals with the raising of crops and the care of the soil — **agro·nom·ic** \ˌa-grə-'nä-mik\ *adj* — **agron·o·mist** \ə-'grä-nə-mist\ *n*

**aground** \ə-'graünd\ *adv or adj* : on or onto the bottom or shore ⟨ran ∼⟩

**agt** *abbr* agent

**ague** \'ā-gyü\ *n* : a fever (as malaria) with recurrent chills and sweating

**ahead** \ə-'hed\ *adv or adj* **1** : in or toward the front **2** : into or for the future ⟨plan ∼⟩ **3** : in or toward a more advantageous position

**ahead of** *prep* **1** : in front or advance of **2** : in excess of : ABOVE

**ahoy** \ə-'hói\ *interj* — used in hailing ⟨ship ∼⟩

**AI** *abbr* artificial intelligence

¹**aid** \'ād\ *vb* : to provide with what is useful in achieving an end : ASSIST

²**aid** *n* **1** : ASSISTANCE **2** : ASSISTANT

**AID** *abbr* Agency for International Development

**aide** \'ād\ *n* : a person who acts as an assistant; *esp* : a military officer assisting a superior

**aide–de–camp** \ˌād-di-'kamp, -'kän\ *n, pl* **aides–de–camp** \ˌādz-di-\ [F] : AIDE

**AIDS** \'ādz\ *n* [*acquired immunodeficiency syndrome*] : a serious disease of the human immune system that is characterized by severe reduction in the numbers of helper T cells and increased vulnerability to life-threatening illnesses and that is caused by infection with HIV commonly transmitted in infected blood esp. during illicit intravenous drug use and in bodily secretions (as semen) during sexual intercourse

**AIDS–related complex** *n* : a group of symptoms (as fever, weight loss, and lymphadenopathy) that is associated with the presence of antibodies to HIV and is

followed by the development of AIDS in a certain proportion of cases

**AIDS virus** *n* : HIV

**ai·grette** \ā-'gret, 'ā-,\ *n* [F, plume, egret] : a plume or decorative tuft for the head

**ail** \'āl\ *vb* **1** : to be the matter with : TROUBLE **2** : to be unwell

**ai·lan·thus** \ā-'lan-thəs\ *n* : any of a genus of Asian trees or shrubs with pinnate leaves and ill-scented greenish flowers; *esp* : TREE OF HEAVEN

**ai·le·ron** \'ā-lə-ˌrän\ *n* : a movable part of an airplane wing used in banking

**ail·ment** \'āl-mənt\ *n* : a bodily disorder

¹**aim** \'ām\ *vb* [ME, fr. AF *aesmer & esmer*; AF *aesmer*, fr. *a-* to (fr. L *ad-*) + *esmer* to estimate, fr. L *aestimare*] **1** : to point a weapon at an object **2** : to direct one's efforts : ASPIRE **3** : to direct to or toward a specified object or goal

²**aim** *n* **1** : the pointing of a weapon at an object **2** : the ability to hit a target **3** : OBJECT, PURPOSE ⟨my ∼ is to win⟩ — **aim·less** \-ləs\ *adj* — **aim·less·ly** *adv* — **aim·less·ness** *n*

**AIM** *abbr* American Indian Movement

**ain't** \'ānt\ **1** : are not **2** : is not **3** : am not — though disapproved by many and more common in less educated speech, used in both speech and writing to catch attention and to gain emphasis

**Ai·nu** \'ī-nü\ *n, pl* **Ainu** *or* **Ainus** **1** : a member of an indigenous people of northern Japan **2** : the language of the Ainu people

¹**air** \'er\ *n* **1** : the gaseous mixture surrounding the earth **2** : a light breeze **3** : MELODY, TUNE **4** : the outward appearance of a person or thing : MANNER **5** : an artificial manner **6** : COMPRESSED AIR ⟨∼ sprayer⟩ **7** : AIRCRAFT ⟨traveled by ∼⟩ **8** : AVIATION ⟨∼ safety⟩ **9** : the medium of transmission of radio waves; *also* : RADIO, TELEVISION

²**air** *vb* **1** : to expose to the air ⟨∼ clothes⟩ **2** : to expose to public view **3** : to broadcast on radio or television

**air bag** *n* : a bag designed to inflate automatically to protect automobile occupants in case of collision

**air·boat** \'er-ˌbōt\ *n* : a shallow-draft boat driven by an airplane propeller

**air·borne** \-ˌbórn\ *adj* : done or being in the air

**air brake** *n* **1** : a brake operated by a piston driven by compressed air **2** : a surface projected into the airflow to lower an airplane's speed

**air·brush** \'er-ˌbrəsh\ *n* : a device for applying a fine spray (as of paint) by compressed air — **airbrush** *vb*

**air con·di·tion·er** \ˌer-kən-'dish-(ə-)nər\ *n* : an apparatus for filtering air and controlling its humidity and temperature — **air–con·di·tion** \-'di-shən\ *vb*

**air·craft** \'er-ˌkraft\ *n, pl* **aircraft** : a vehicle for traveling through the air

**aircraft carrier** *n* : a warship with a deck on which airplanes are launched and landed

**air·drop** \'er-ˌdräp\ *n* : delivery of cargo

or personnel by parachute from an airplane in flight — **air-drop** vb

**Aire-dale terrier** \'er-,dāl-\ n : any of a breed of large terriers with a hard wiry coat

**air-fare** \'er-,fer\ n : fare for travel by airplane

**air-field** \-,fēld\ n : AIRPORT

**air-flow** \-,flō\ n : the motion of air relative to a body in it

**air-foil** \-,fȯi(-ə)l\ n : an airplane surface designed to produce reaction forces from the air through which it moves

**air force** n : the military organization of a nation for air warfare

**air-frame** \'er-,frām\ n : the structure of an aircraft, rocket, or missile without the power plant; also : AIRCRAFT

**air-freight** \-'frāt\ n : freight transport by aircraft in volume; also : the charge for this service

**air gun** n **1** : a gun operated by compressed air **2** : a hand tool that works by compressed air; esp : AIRBRUSH

**air-head** \'er-,hed\ n : a mindless or stupid person

**air lane** n : AIRWAY 1

**air-lift** \'er-,lift\ n : transportation (as of supplies or passengers) by aircraft — **air-lift** vb

**air-line** \-,līn\ n : a transportation system using airplanes

**air-lin-er** \-,lī-nər\ n : a large passenger airplane operated by an airline

**air lock** n : an airtight chamber separating areas of different pressure

**air-mail** \'er-,māl\ n : the system of transporting mail by aircraft; also : mail so transported — **airmail** vb

**air-man** \-mən\ n **1** : AVIATOR, PILOT **2** : an enlisted person in the air force ranking next below an airman first class

**airman basic** n : an enlisted person of the lowest rank in the air force

**airman first class** n : an enlisted person in the air force ranking next below a senior airman

**air mass** n : a large horizontally homogeneous body of air

**air-mo-bile** \'er-,mō-bəl, -,bēl\ adj : of, relating to, or being a military unit whose members are transported to combat areas usu. by helicopter

**air-plane** \-,plān\ n : a powered heavier-than-air aircraft that has fixed wings from which it derives lift

**air-play** \-,plā\ n : the playing of a musical recording on the air by a radio station

**air pocket** n : a condition of the atmosphere (as a local downdraft) that causes an airplane to drop suddenly

**air police** n : the military police of an air force

**air-port** \'er-,pȯrt\ n : a place from which aircraft operate that usu. has paved runways and a terminal

**air rage** n : an airline passenger's uncontrolled anger that is usu. expressed in aggressive or violent behavior

**air raid** n : an attack by armed airplanes on a surface target

**air-ship** \'er-,ship\ n : a lighter-than-air

aircraft having propulsion and steering systems

**air-sick** \-,sik\ adj : affected with motion sickness associated with flying — **air-sick-ness** n

**air-space** \-,spās\ n : the space above a nation and under its jurisdiction

**air-speed** \-,spēd\ n : the speed of an object (as an airplane) with relation to the surrounding air

**air-strip** \-,strip\ n : a runway without normal airport facilities

**air-tight** \'er-'tīt\ adj **1** : so tightly sealed that no air can enter or escape **2** : leaving no opening for attack

**air-to-air** adj : launched from one airplane in flight at another; also : involving aircraft in flight

**air-waves** \'er-,wāvz\ n pl : AIR 9

**air-way** \-,wā\ n **1** : a regular route for airplanes **2** : AIRLINE

**air-wor-thy** \-,wər-thē\ adj : fit for operation in the air ⟨an ∼ plane⟩ — **air-wor-thi-ness** n

**airy** \'er-ē\ adj **air-i-er**; **-est 1** : LOFTY ⟨∼ perches⟩ **2** : lacking in reality : EMPTY **3** : DELICATE **4** : BREEZY

**aisle** \'ī(-ə)l\ n [ME ile, fr. AF ele, lit., wing, fr. L ala] **1** : the side of a church nave separated by piers from the nave proper **2** : a passage between sections of seats

**ajar** \ə-'jär\ adj or adv : partly open

**AK** abbr Alaska

**aka** abbr also known as

**AKC** abbr American Kennel Club

**akim-bo** \ə-'kim-bō\ adj or adv : having the hand on the hip and the elbow turned outward

**akin** \ə-'kin\ adj **1** : related by blood **2** : similar in kind

**Al** symbol aluminum

**AL** abbr **1** Alabama **2** American League **3** American Legion

**¹-al** adj suffix : of, relating to, or characterized by ⟨directional⟩

**²-al** n suffix : action : process ⟨rehearsal⟩

**Ala** abbr Alabama

**al-a-bas-ter** \'a-lə-,bas-tər\ n **1** : a compact fine-textured usu. white and translucent gypsum often carved into objects (as vases) **2** : a hard translucent calcite

**à la carte** \,a-lə-'kärt, ,ä-\ adv or adj [F] : with a separate price for each item on the menu

**alac-ri-ty** \ə-'la-krə-tē\ n : cheerful readiness : BRISKNESS

**à la mode** \,a-lə-'mōd, ,ä-\ adj [F, according to the fashion] **1** : FASHIONABLE, STYLISH **2** : topped with ice cream

**¹alarm** \ə-'lärm\ also **ala-rum** \ə-'lär-əm, -'ler-\ n [ME alarme, fr. MF, fr. OIt all'arme, lit., to arms] **1** : a warning signal or device **2** : the terror caused by sudden danger

**²alarm** also **alarum** vb **1** : to warn of danger **2** : FRIGHTEN

**alarm-ist** \ə-'lär-mist\ n : a person who alarms others esp. needlessly

**alas** \ə-'las\ interj — used to express unhappiness, pity, or concern

**al-ba-core** \'al-bə-,kȯr\ n, pl **-core** or

**-cores** : a large tuna that is a source of canned tuna

**Al·ba·nian** \al-'bā-nē-ən\ *n* : a native or inhabitant of Albania

**al·ba·tross** \'al-bə-ˌtròs, -ˌträs\ *n, pl* **-tross** *or* **-tross·es** : any of a family of large web-footed seabirds

**al·be·do** \al-'bē-(ˌ)dō\ *n, pl* **-dos** : the fraction of incident radiation that is reflected by a body or surface

**al·be·it** \òl-'bē-ət, al-\ *conj* : even though : ALTHOUGH

**al·bi·no** \al-'bī-nō\ *n, pl* **-nos** : a person or animal lacking coloring matter in the skin, hair, and eyes — **al·bi·nism** \'al-bə-ˌni-zəm\ *n*

**al·bum** \'al-bəm\ *n* **1** : a book with blank pages used for making a collection (as of stamps or photographs) **2** : one or more recordings (as on tape or disk) produced as a single unit

**al·bu·men** \al-'byü-mən\ *n* **1** : the white of an egg **2** : ALBUMIN

**al·bu·min** \al-'byü-mən\ *n* : any of numerous water-soluble proteins of blood, milk, egg white, and plant and animal tissues

**al·bu·min·ous** \al-'byü-mə-nəs\ *adj* : containing or resembling albumen or albumin

**al·bu·ter·ol** \al-'byü-tə-ˌròl, -ˌrōl\ *n* : a drug used as an aerosol or in tablet form to treat asthma

**alc** *abbr* alcohol

**al·cal·de** \al-'käl-dē\ *n* : the chief administrative and judicial officer of a Spanish or Spanish-American town

**al·ca·zar** \al-'kä-zər, -'ka-\ *n* [Sp *alcázar*, fr. Ar *al-qaṣr* the castle] : a Spanish fortress or palace

**al·che·my** \'al-kə-mē\ *n* : medieval chemistry chiefly concerned with efforts to turn base metals into gold — **al·che·mist** \'al-kə-mist\ *n*

**al·co·hol** \'al-kə-ˌhòl\ *n* [NL, fr. ML, powdered antimony, fr. Sp, fr. Ar *al-kuḥul* the powdered antimony] **1** : a colorless flammable liquid that is the intoxicating agent in fermented and distilled liquors **2** : any of various carbon compounds similar to alcohol **3** : beverages containing alcohol

**¹al·co·hol·ic** \ˌal-kə-'hò-lik, -'hä-\ *adj* **1** : of, relating to, caused by, or containing alcohol **2** : affected with alcoholism — **al·co·hol·i·cal·ly** \-li-k(ə-)lē\ *adv*

**²alcoholic** *n* : a person affected with alcoholism

**al·co·hol·ism** \'al-kə-ˌhò-ˌli-zəm\ *n* : continued excessive and usu. uncontrollable use of alcoholic drinks; *also* : a complex chronic psychological and nutritional disorder associated with such use

**al·cove** \'al-ˌkōv\ *n* **1** : a nook or small recess opening off a larger room **2** : a niche or arched opening (as in a wall)

**ald** *abbr* alderman

**al·der** \'òl-dər\ *n* : any of a genus of trees or shrubs related to the birches and growing in wet areas

**al·der·man** \'òl-dər-mən\ *n* : a member of a city legislative body

**ale** \'āl\ *n* : an alcoholic beverage brewed from malt and hops that is usu. more bitter than beer

**ale·a·tor·ic** \ˌā-lē-ə-'tòr-ik\ *adj* : characterized by chance or random elements ⟨~ music⟩

**ale·a·to·ry** \'ā-lē-ə-ˌtòr-ē\ *adj* : ALEATORIC

**alee** \ə-'lē\ *adv* : on or toward the lee

**ale·house** \'āl-ˌhaüs\ *n* : a place where ale is sold to be drunk on the premises

**¹alert** \ə-'lərt\ *adj* [It *all'erta*, lit., on the ascent] **1** : watchful against danger **2** : quick to perceive and act — **alert·ly** *adv* — **alert·ness** *n*

**²alert** *n* **1** : ALARM 1 **2** : the period during which an alert is in effect

**³alert** *vb* **1** : WARN **2** : to make aware of

**Aleut** \ˌa-lē-'üt, ə-'lüt\ *n* **1** : a member of a people of the Aleutian and Shumagin islands and the western part of Alaska Peninsula **2** : the language of the Aleuts

**ale·wife** \'āl-ˌwīf\ *n, pl* **ale·wives** \-ˌwīvz\ : a food fish related to the herring that is abundant esp. along the Atlantic coast

**Al·ex·an·dri·an** \ˌa-lig-'zan-drē-ən\ *adj* **1** : HELLENISTIC **2** : of or relating to Alexander the Great

**al·ex·an·drine** \-'zan-drən\ *n, often cap* : a line of six iambic feet

**al·fal·fa** \al-'fal-fə\ *n* : a leguminous plant widely grown for hay and forage

**al·fres·co** \al-'fres-kō\ *adj or adv* [It] : taking place in the open air

**alg** *abbr* algebra

**al·ga** \'al-gə\ *n, pl* **al·gae** \'al-(ˌ)jē\ : any of a group of lower plants having chlorophyll but no vascular system and including seaweeds and related freshwater plants — **al·gal** \-gəl\ *adj*

**al·ge·bra** \'al-jə-brə\ *n* [ML, fr. Ar *al-jabr*] : a generalization of arithmetic in which letters representing numbers are combined according to the rules of arithmetic — **al·ge·bra·ic** \ˌal-jə-'brā-ik\ *adj* — **al·ge·bra·i·cal·ly** \-'brā-ə-k(ə-)lē\ *adv*

**Al·gon·qui·an** \al-'gän-kwē-ən, -'gän-\ *or* **Al·gon·quin** \-'kwən\ *n* **1** *usu* Algonquin : a member of an American Indian people of the Ottawa River valley **2** *usu* Algonquian : a family of American Indian languages of eastern and central No. America

**al·go·rithm** \'al-gə-ˌri-thəm\ *n* : a procedure for solving a problem esp. in mathematics or computing — **al·go·rith·mic** \ˌal-gə-'rith-mik\ *adj* — **al·go·rith·mi·cal·ly** \-'mi-k(ə-)lē\ *adv*

**¹ali·as** \'ā-lē-əs, 'āl-yəs\ *adv* [L, otherwise, fr. *alius* other] : otherwise called

**²alias** *n* : an assumed name

**¹al·i·bi** \'a-lə-ˌbī\ *n* [L, elsewhere, fr. *alius* other] **1** : a plea offered by an accused person of not having been at the scene of an offense **2** : an excuse (as for failure)

**²alibi** *vb* **-bied; -bi·ing** **1** : to furnish an excuse for **2** : to offer an excuse

**¹ali·as** \'ā-lē-əs, 'āl-yəs\ *adv* [L, otherwise, fr. *alius* other] : otherwise called

**alien** *n* **1** : a foreign-born resident who has not been naturalized **2** : EXTRATERRESTRIAL

**alien·able** \'āl-yə-nə-bəl, 'ā-lē-ə-nə-\ *adj* : transferable to the ownership of another ⟨~ property⟩

**alien·ate** \'ā-lē-ə-ˌnāt, 'āl yə-\ *vb* **-at·ed; -at·ing 1** : to make hostile : ESTRANGE **2** : to transfer (property) to another — **alien·ation** \ˌā-lē-ə-'nā-shən, ˌāl-yə-\ *n*

**alien·ist** \'ā-lē-ə-nist, 'al-yə-\ *n* : PSYCHIATRIST

**¹alight** \ə-'līt\ *vb* **alight·ed** *also* **alit** \ə-'lit\; **alight·ing 1** : to get down (as from a vehicle) **2** : to come to rest from the air
 ♦ *Synonyms* SETTLE, LAND, PERCH

**²alight** *adj* : lighted up

**align** *also* **aline** \ə-'līn\ *vb* **1** : to bring into line **2** : to array on the side of or against a cause — **align·er** *n* — **alignment** *also* **aline·ment** *n*

**¹alike** \ə 'līk\ *adv* : EQUALLY ⟨denounced by teachers and students ~⟩

**²alike** *adj* : LIKE ⟨~ in their beliefs⟩
 ♦ *Synonyms* AKIN, ANALOGOUS, SIMILAR, COMPARABLE

**al·i·ment** \'a-lə-mənt\ *n* : NOURISHMENT **1** — **aliment** *vb*

**al·i·men·ta·ry** \ˌa-lə-'men-t(ə-)rē\ *adj* : of, relating to, or functioning in nourishment or nutrition

**alimentary canal** *n* : the tube that extends from the mouth to the anus and functions in the digestion and absorption of food and the elimination of residues

**al·i·mo·ny** \'a-lə-ˌmō-nē\ *n*, *pl* **-nies** [L *alimonia* sustenance, fr. *alere* to nourish] : an allowance made to one spouse by the other for support pending or after legal separation or divorce

**A-line** \'ā-ˌlīn\ *adj* : having a flared bottom and a close fitting top ⟨an ~ skirt⟩

**alive** \ə-'līv\ *adj* **1** : having life **2** : being in force or operation **3** : SENSITIVE ⟨~ to the danger⟩ **4** : ALERT, BRISK **5** : ANIMATED ⟨streets ~ with traffic⟩ — **alive·ness** *n*

**alk** *abbr* alkaline

**al·ka·li** \'al-kə-ˌlī\ *n*, *pl* **-lies** *or* **-lis 1** : a substance (as a hydroxide) that has a bitter taste and neutralizes acids **2** : a mixture of salts in the soil of some dry regions in such amount as to make ordinary farming impossible — **al·ka·line** \-kə-lən, -ˌlīn\ *adj* — **al·ka·lin·i·ty** \ˌal-kə-'li-nə-tē\ *n*

**al·ka·loid** \'al-kə-ˌlȯid\ *n* : any of various usu. basic and bitter organic compounds found esp. in seed plants

**al·kane** \'al-ˌkān\ *n* : a hydrocarbon in which each carbon atom is bonded to 4 other atoms

**al·kyd** \'al-kəd\ *n* : any of numerous synthetic resins used esp. for protective coatings and in paint

**¹all** \'ȯl\ *adj* **1** : the whole of ⟨sat up ~ night⟩ **2** : every member of **3** : EVERY ⟨~ manner of problems⟩ **4** : any whatever ⟨beyond ~ doubt⟩ **5** : nothing but ⟨~ ears⟩ **6** : being more than one person or thing ⟨who ~ is coming⟩

**²all** *adv* **1** : WHOLLY ⟨sat ~ alone⟩ **2** : selected as the best — used in combination ⟨*all*-state champs⟩ **3** : so much ⟨~ the

better for it⟩ **4** : for each side ⟨the score is two ~⟩

**³all** *pron sing or pl* **1** : the whole number, quantity, or amount ⟨~ of it is gone⟩ **2** : EVERYBODY, EVERYTHING ⟨~ are members⟩ ⟨that is ~⟩

**⁴all** *n* : the whole of one's resources ⟨gave his ~⟩

**Al·lah** \'ä-lə, 'a-; 'ä-ˌlä, ä-'lä\ *n* [Ar *allāh*] : GOD **1** — used in Islam

**all along** *adv* : all the time ⟨knew it *all along*⟩

**all-Amer·i·can** \ˌȯl-ə-'mer-ə-kən\ *adj* **1** : selected as the best in the U.S. **2** : composed wholly of American elements **3** : typical of the U.S. — **all-American** *n*

**all-around** \ˌȯl-ə-'raund\ *adj* **1** : considered in all aspects ⟨best ~ performance⟩ **2** : competent in many fields : VERSATILE ⟨an ~ athlete⟩

**al·lay** \ə-'lā\ *vb* **1** : ALLEVIATE **2** : CALM
 ♦ *Synonyms* LIGHTEN, RELIEVE, EASE, ASSUAGE

**all clear** *n* : a signal that a danger has passed

**al·lege** \ə-'lej\ *vb* **al·leged; al·leg·ing 1** : to assert without proof **2** : to offer as a reason — **al·le·ga·tion** \ˌa-li-'gā-shən\ *n* — **al·leged** \ə-'lejd, -'le-jəd\ *adj* — **al·leg·ed·ly** \ə-'le-jəd-lē\ *adv*

**al·le·giance** \ə-'lē-jəns\ *n* **1** : loyalty owed by a citizen to a government **2** : loyalty to a person or cause

**al·le·go·ry** \'a-lə-ˌgȯr-ē\ *n*, *pl* **-ries** : the expression through symbolism of truths or generalizations about human experience — **al·le·gor·i·cal** \ˌa-lə-'gȯr-i-kəl\ *adj* — **al·le·gor·i·cal·ly** \-k(ə-)lē\ *adv*

**¹al·le·gro** \ə-'le-grō, -'lā-\ *n*, *pl* **-gros** : an allegro movement

**²allegro** *adv or adj* [It, merry] : at a brisk lively tempo — used as a direction in music

**al·lele** \ə-'lēl\ *n* : any of the alternative forms of a gene that may occur at a given site on a chromosome — **al·le·lic** \-'lē-lik, -'le-\ *adj*

**al·le·lu·ia** \ˌa-lə-'lü-yə\ *interj* : HALLELUJAH

**Al·len wrench** \'a-lən-\ *n* [*Allen* Manufacturing Company, Hartford, Conn.] : an L-shaped hexagonal metal bar of which either end fits the socket of a screw or bolt

**al·ler·gen** \'a-lər-jən\ *n* : something that causes allergy — **al·ler·gen·ic** \ˌa-lər-'je-nik\ *adj*

**al·ler·gist** \'a-lər-jist\ *n* : a specialist in allergies

**al·ler·gy** \'a-lər-jē\ *n*, *pl* **-gies** [G *Allergie*, fr. Gk *allos* other + *ergon* work] : exaggerated or abnormal reaction (as by sneezing) to substances or situations harmless to most people — **al·ler·gic** \ə-'lər-jik\ *adj*

**al·le·vi·ate** \ə-'lē-vē-ˌāt\ *vb* **-at·ed; -at·ing** : RELIEVE, LESSEN ⟨~ pain⟩ ♦ *Synonyms* LIGHTEN, MITIGATE, ALLAY — **al·le·vi·a·tion** \ə-ˌlē-vē-'ā-shən\ *n*

**al·ley** \'a-lē\ *n*, *pl* **alleys 1** : a garden or park walk **2** : a place for bowling **3** : a narrow passageway esp. between buildings

**al·ley-oop** \\,a-lē-'yüp\ *n* : a basketball play in which a player catches a pass above the basket and immediately dunks the ball

**al·ley·way** \'a-lē-,wā\ *n* : ALLEY 3

**all–fired** \'ol-,fī(-ə)rd\ *adv* : EXTREMELY, EXCESSIVELY ⟨~ stubborn⟩

**All·hal·lows** \ol-'ha-lōz\ *n, pl* **Allhallows** : ALL SAINTS' DAY

**all hours** *n pl* : a very late time ⟨stayed up until *all hours*⟩

**al·li·ance** \ə-'lī-əns\ *n* : a union to promote common interests ♦ **Synonyms** LEAGUE, COALITION, CONFEDERACY, FEDERATION

**al·li·ga·tor** \'a-lə-,gā-tər\ *n* [Sp *el lagarto* the lizard] : either of two large short-legged reptiles resembling crocodiles but having a shorter and broader snout

**alligator pear** *n* : AVOCADO

**al·lit·er·ate** \ə-'li-tə-,rāt\ *vb* **-at·ed; -at·ing 1** : to form an alliteration **2** : to arrange so as to make alliteration

**al·lit·er·a·tion** \ə-,li-tə-'rā-shən\ *n* : the repetition of initial sounds in adjacent words or syllables — **al·lit·er·a·tive** \-'li-tə-,rā-tiv\ *adj*

**al·lo·cate** \'a-lə-,kāt\ *vb* **-cat·ed; -cat·ing** : ALLOT, ASSIGN — **al·lo·ca·tion** \,a-lə-'kā-shən\ *n*

**al·lot** \ə-'lät\ *vb* **al·lot·ted; al·lot·ting** : to distribute as a share ♦ **Synonyms** ASSIGN, APPORTION, ALLOCATE — **al·lot·ment** *n*

**all–out** \'ol-'aut\ *adj* : made with maximum effort

**¹all over** *adv* : EVERYWHERE

**²all over** *prep* **1** : in eagerly affectionate, attentive, or aggressive pursuit **2** : in or into a state marked by excessive criticism

**al·low** \ə-'lau\ *vb* **1** : to assign as a share ⟨~ time for rest⟩ **2** : to count as a deduction **3** : to make allowance ⟨~ for expansion⟩ **4** : ADMIT, CONCEDE ⟨~ed that the situation was serious⟩ **5** : PERMIT ⟨~s the dog to roam⟩ — **al·low·able** *adj*

**al·low·ance** \-əns\ *n* **1** : an allotted share **2** : money given regularly for expenses **3** : a taking into account of extenuating circumstances

**al·loy** \'a-,lói, ə-'lói\ *n* **1** : a substance composed of metals melted together **2** : an admixture that lessens value — **al·loy** \ə-'lói, 'a-,lói\ *vb*

**all right** *adv* **1** — used interjectionally esp. to express agreement or resignation or to indicate the resumption of a discussion ⟨*all right*, let's go⟩ **2** : beyond doubt **3** : SATISFACTORILY ⟨does *all right* in school⟩ — **all right** *adj*

**All Saints' Day** *n* : a Christian feast on November 1 in honor of all the saints

**All Souls' Day** *n* : a day of prayer observed by some Christian churches on November 2 for the souls of the faithful departed

**all·spice** \'ol-,spīs\ *n* : the berry of a West Indian tree related to the European myrtle; *also* : the mildly pungent and aromatic spice made from it

**all–star** \'ol-,stär\ *n* : a member of a team of star performers — **all–star** *adj*

**all–ter·rain vehicle** *n* : a small motor vehicle with three or four wheels for use on a wide range of terrain

**all told** *adv* : with everything or everyone counted ⟨expecting eight guests *all told*⟩

**al·lude** \ə-'lüd\ *vb* **al·lud·ed; al·lud·ing** [L *alludere*, lit., to play with] : to refer indirectly — **al·lu·sion** \-'lü-zhən\ *n* — **al·lu·sive** \-'lü-siv\ *adj* — **al·lu·sive·ly** *adv* — **al·lu·sive·ness** *n*

**al·lure** \ə-'lur\ *vb* **al·lured; al·lur·ing** : to attract by something desirable — **allure** *n* — **al·lur·ing·ly** *adv*

**al·lu·vi·um** \ə-'lü-vē-əm\ *n, pl* **-vi·ums** or **-via** \-vē-ə\ : soil material (as clay) deposited by running water — **al·lu·vi·al** \-vē-əl\ *adj or n*

**all–wheel** \'ol-'wēl\ *adj* : acting independently on or by means of all four wheels of a vehicle

**al·ly** \ə-'lī, 'a-,lī\ *vb* **al·lied; al·ly·ing** : to enter into an alliance — **al·ly** \'a-,lī, ə-'lī\ *n*

**-ally** *adv suffix* : ²-LY ⟨specific*ally*⟩

**al·ma ma·ter** \,al-mə-'mä-tər\ *n* [L, fostering mother] **1** : an educational institute that one has attended **2** : the song or hymn of an alma mater

**al·ma·nac** \'ol-mə-,nak, 'al-\ *n* **1** : a publication esp. of astronomical and meteorological data **2** : a usu. annual publication of miscellaneous information

**al·man·dite** \'al-mən-,dīt\ *n* : a deep red garnet

**al·mighty** \ol-'mī-tē\ *adj* **1** *often cap* : having absolute power over all ⟨*Almighty* God⟩ **2** : relatively unlimited in power — **al·might·i·ness** *n*

**Almighty** *n* : GOD 1

**al·mond** \'ä-mənd, 'a-; 'al-\ *n* : a small tree related to the peach; *also* : the edible nutlike kernel of its fruit

**al·mo·ner** \'al-mə-nər, 'ä-mə-\ *n* : a person who distributes alms

**al·most** \'ol-,mōst, ol-'mōst\ *adv* : very nearly but not exactly

**alms** \'ämz, 'älmz\ *n, pl* **alms** [ME *almesse*, *almes*, fr. OE *ælmesse*, *ælms*, fr. L *eleemosyna* alms, fr. Gk *eleēmosynē* pity, alms, fr. *eleēmōn* merciful, fr. *eleos* pity] : something given freely to relieve the poor

**alms·house** \-,haus\ *n* : POORHOUSE

**al·oe** \'a-lō\ *n* **1** : any of a large genus of succulent chiefly southern African plants related to the lilies **2** *pl* : the dried juice of the leaves of an aloe used esp. formerly as a laxative

**aloe vera** \-'ver-ə, -'vir-\ *n* : an aloe with leaves that yield a jellylike emollient extract used esp. in cosmetics; *also* : this extract

**aloft** \ə-'loft\ *adv* **1** : high in the air **2** : in flight

**alo·ha** \ə-'lō-ə, ä-'lō-hä\ *interj* [Hawaiian] — used to greet or bid farewell

**alone** \ə-'lōn\ *adj* **1** : separated from others **2** : not including anyone or anything else : ONLY ⟨she ∼ knows why⟩ ♦ **Syn·onyms** LONELY, LONESOME, LONE, SOLITARY — **alone** *adv*

¹**along** \ə-'lȯŋ\ *prep* 1 : in a line matching the direction of ⟨sail – the coast⟩ 2 : at a point on or during ⟨stopped ∼ the way⟩

²**along** *adv* 1 : FORWARD, ON ⟨move ∼⟩ 2 : as a companion ⟨bring her ∼⟩ 3 : at an advanced point ⟨plans are far ∼⟩

**along·shore** \ə-'lȯŋ-'shȯr\ *adv or adj* : along the shore or coast ⟨walked ∼⟩

¹**along·side** \-ˌsīd\ *adv* : along or by the side

²**alongside** *prep* 1 : along or by the side of 2 : in association with

**alongside of** *prep* : ALONGSIDE

**aloof** \ə-'lüf\ *adj* : removed or distant physically or emotionally — **aloof·ly** *adv* — **aloof·ness** *n*

**al·o·pe·cia** \ˌa-lə-'pē-sh(ē-)ə\ *n* : BALDNESS

**aloud** \ə-'laůd\ *adv* : with the speaking voice ⟨read ∼⟩

**alp** \'alp\ *n* : a high rugged mountain

**al·pac·a** \al-'pa-kə\ *n* : a domesticated mammal esp. of Peru that is prob. descended from the vicuña; *also* : its woolly hair or a thin cloth made from this hair

**al·pha** \'al-fə\ *n* 1 : the 1st letter of the Greek alphabet — A or α 2 : something first

**al·pha·bet** \'al-fə-ˌbet\ *n* : the set of letters or characters used in writing a language

**al·pha·bet·i·cal** \ˌal-fə-'be-ti-kəl\ *or* **al·pha·bet·ic** \-'be-tik\ *adj* 1 : arranged in the order of the letters of the alphabet 2 : of or employing an alphabet — **al·pha·bet·i·cal·ly** \-ti-k(ə-)lē\ *adv*

**al·pha·bet·ize** \'al-fə-bə-ˌtīz\ *vb* **-ized; -iz·ing** : to arrange in alphabetical order — **al·pha·bet·iz·er** *n*

**al·pha·nu·mer·ic** \ˌal-fə-nů-'mer-ik, -nyů-\ *adj* : consisting of letters and numbers and often other symbols ⟨an ∼ code⟩; *also* : being a character in an alphanumeric system

**alpha particle** *n* : a positively charged particle identical with the nucleus of a helium atom that is ejected at high speed in certain radioactive transformations

**alpha rhythm** *n* : ALPHA WAVE

**alpha wave** *n* : an electrical rhythm of the brain often associated with a state of wakeful relaxation

**Al·pine** \'al-ˌpīn\ *adj* 1 : relating to, located in, or resembling the Alps *often not cap* : of, relating to, or growing on upland slopes above timberline 3 : of or relating to competitive ski events consisting of slalom and downhill racing

**al·ready** \ȯl-'re-dē\ *adv* : by this time : PREVIOUSLY

**al·right** \ȯl-'rīt\ *adv* : ALL RIGHT

**al·so** \'ȯl-sō\ *adv* : in addition : TOO

**al·so–ran** \-ˌran\ *n* 1 : a horse or dog that finishes out of the money in a race 2 : a contestant that does not win

**alt** *abbr* 1 alternate 2 altitude

**Alta** *abbr* Alberta

**al·tar** \'ȯl-tər\ *n* 1 : a structure on which sacrifices are offered or incense is burned 2 : a table used as a center of ritual or worship

**altar server** *n* : a boy or girl who assists the celebrant at a church service

¹**al·ter** \'ȯl-tər\ *vb* **al·tered; al·ter·ing** \-t(ə-)riŋ\ 1 : to make or become different 2 : CASTRATE, SPAY — **al·ter·able** \'ȯl-tə-rə-bəl\ *adj* — **al·ter·a·tion** \ˌȯl-tə-'rā-shən\ *n*

²**alter** *abbr* alteration

**al·ter·ca·tion** \ˌȯl-tər-'kā-shən\ *n* : a noisy or angry dispute

**alter ego** \ˌȯl-tər-'ē-gō\ *n* [L, lit., second I] : a second self; *esp* : a trusted friend

**al·ter·i·ty** \ȯl-'ter-ə-tē\ *n* : the quality or state of being radically alien to the conscious self or a particular cultural orientation

¹**al·ter·nate** \'ȯl-tər-nət, 'al-\ *adj* 1 : arranged or succeeding by turns 2 : every other 3 : being an alternative ⟨an ∼ route⟩ — **al·ter·nate·ly** *adv*

²**al·ter·nate** \-ˌnāt\ *vb* **-nat·ed; -nat·ing** : to occur or cause to occur by turns — **al·ter·na·tion** \ˌȯl-tər-'nā-shən, ˌal-\ *n*

³**alternate** *n* : SUBSTITUTE

**alternating current** *n* : an electric current that reverses its direction at regular intervals

**al·ter·na·tive** \ȯl-'tər-nə-tiv, al-\ *adj* 1 : offering a choice ⟨several ∼ plans⟩ 2 : different from the usual or conventional — **alternative** *n*

**alternative medicine** *n* : any of various systems of healing (as homeopathy) not typically practiced in conventional Western medicine

**al·ter·na·tor** \'ȯl-tər-ˌnā-tər, 'al-\ *n* : an electric generator for producing alternating current

**al·though** *also* **al·tho** \ȯl-'thō\ *conj* : in spite of the fact that : even though

**al·tim·e·ter** \al-'ti-mə-tər, 'al-tə-ˌmē-tər\ *n* : an instrument for measuring altitude

**al·ti·tude** \'al-tə-ˌtüd, -ˌtyüd\ *n* 1 : angular distance above the horizon 2 : vertical distance : HEIGHT 3 : the perpendicular distance in a geometric figure from the vertex to the base, from the vertex of an angle to the side opposite, or from the base to a parallel side or face

**al·to** \'al-tō\ *n, pl* **altos** [It, lit., high, fr. L *altus*] : the lower female voice part in a 4-part chorus; *also* : a singer having this voice or part

¹**al·to·geth·er** \ˌȯl-tə-'ge-thər\ *adv* 1 : WHOLLY ⟨stopped raining ∼⟩ 2 : in all ⟨spent $100 ∼⟩ 3 : on the whole ⟨∼ their efforts were successful⟩

²**altogether** *n* : NUDE ⟨posed in the ∼⟩

**al·tru·ism** \'al-trü-ˌi-zəm\ *n* [F *altruisme*, fr. *autrui* other people, fr. OF, oblique case form of *autre* other, fr. L *alter*] : unselfish interest in the welfare of others — **al·tru·ist** \-ist\ *n* — **al·tru·is·tic** \ˌal-trü-'is-tik\ *adj* — **al·tru·is·ti·cal·ly** \-ti-k(ə-)lē\ *adv*

**al·um** \'a-ləm\ *n* : either of two colorless crystalline aluminum-containing compounds used esp. as an emetic or as an astringent and styptic

**alu·mi·na** \ə-ˈlü-mə-nə\ n : the oxide of aluminum occurring in nature as corundum and in bauxite

**al·u·min·i·um** \ˌal-yə-ˈmi-nē-əm\ n, chiefly Brit : ALUMINUM

**alu·mi·nize** \ə-ˈlü-mə-ˌnīz\ vb -nized; -niz·ing : to treat with aluminum

**alu·mi·num** \ə-ˈlü-mə-nəm\ n : a silver-white malleable ductile light metallic element that is the most abundant metal in the earth's crust

**aluminum oxide** n : ALUMINA

**alum·na** \ə-ˈləm-nə\ n, pl **-nae** \-(ˌ)nē\ : a woman graduate or former student of a college or school

**alum·nus** \ə-ˈləm-nəs\ n, pl **-ni** \-ˌnī\ [L, foster son, pupil, fr. alere to nourish] : a graduate or former student of a college or school

**al·ways** \ˈȯl-wēz, -wəz, -(ˌ)wāz\ adv **1** : at all times : INVARIABLY **2** : FOREVER

**Alz·hei·mer's disease** \ˈälts-hī-mərz-, ˈalts-\ n : a degenerative brain disease of unknown cause that is characterized esp. by progressive mental deterioration and memory loss

**am** pres 1st sing of BE

**¹Am** abbr America; American

**²Am** symbol americium

**¹AM** \ˈā-ˌem\ n : a broadcasting system using amplitude modulation; also : a radio receiver for broadcasts made by such a system

**²AM** abbr **1** ante meridiem — often not cap. and often punctuated **2** [NL artium magister] master of arts

**AMA** abbr American Medical Association

**amah** \ˈä-(ˌ)mä\ n : a female servant in eastern Asia; esp : a Chinese nurse

**amain** \ə-ˈmān\ adv, archaic : with full force or speed

**amal·gam** \ə-ˈmal-gəm\ n **1** : an alloy of mercury with another metal used in making dental cements **2** : a mixture of different elements

**amal·gam·ate** \ə-ˈmal-gə-ˌmāt\ vb **-at·ed; -at·ing** : to unite or merge into one body — **amal·gam·ation** \-ˌmal-gə-ˈmā-shən\ n

**aman·u·en·sis** \ə-ˌman-yə-ˈwen-səs\ n, pl **-en·ses** \-ˌsēz\ : one employed to write from dictation or to copy what another has written : SECRETARY

**am·a·ranth** \ˈa-mə-ˌranth\ n **1** : any of a large genus of coarse herbs sometimes grown for their showy flowers **2** : a flower that never fades

**am·a·ran·thine** \ˌa-mə-ˈran-thən, -ˌthīn\ adj **1** : relating to or resembling an amaranth **2** : UNDYING

**am·a·ryl·lis** \ˌa-mə-ˈri-ləs\ n : any of various plants related to the lilies; esp : an autumn-flowering South African bulbous herb widely grown for its large showy red to whitish flowers

**amass** \ə-ˈmas\ vb : ACCUMULATE

**am·a·teur** \ˈa-mə-(ˌ)tər, -ˌtür, -ˌtyür, -ˌchür, -chər\ n [F, fr. L amator lover, fr. amare to love] **1** : a person who engages in a pursuit for pleasure and not as a profession **2** : a person who is not expert — **am·a·teur·ish** \ˌa-mə-ˈtər-ish, -ˈtür-,

-ˈtyür-, -ˈchür-, -ˈchər-\ adj — **am·a·teur·ism** \ˈa-mə-(ˌ)tər-i-zəm, -ˌtür-, -ˌtyür-, -ˌchür-, -ˌchər-\ n

**am·a·tive** \ˈa-mə-tiv\ adj : indicative of love : AMOROUS — **am·a·tive·ly** adv — **am·a·tive·ness** n

**am·a·to·ry** \ˈa-mə-ˌtȯr-ē\ adj : of or expressing sexual love

**amaze** \ə-ˈmāz\ vb **amazed; amaz·ing** : to fill with wonder : ASTOUND ♦ **Synonyms** ASTONISH, SURPRISE, DUMBFOUND — **amaze·ment** n — **amaz·ing·ly** adv

**am·a·zon** \ˈa-mə-ˌzän, -zən\ n **1** cap : a member of a race of female warriors of Greek mythology **2** : a tall strong often masculine woman — **am·a·zo·ni·an** \ˌa-mə-ˈzō-nē-ən\ adj, often cap

**amb** abbr ambassador

**am·bas·sa·dor** \am-ˈba-sə-dər\ n : a representative esp. of a government — **am·bas·sa·do·ri·al** \-ˌba-sə-ˈdȯr-ē-əl\ adj — **am·bas·sa·dor·ship** n

**am·ber** \ˈam-bər\ n : a yellowish or brownish fossil resin used esp. for ornamental objects; also : the color of this resin

**am·ber·gris** \ˈam-bər-ˌgris, -ˌgrēs\ n : a waxy substance from the sperm whale used in making perfumes

**am·bi·dex·trous** \ˌam-bi-ˈdek-strəs\ adj : using both hands with equal ease — **am·bi·dex·trous·ly** adv

**am·bi·ence** or **am·bi·ance** \ˈam-bē-əns, äⁿ-ˈbyäⁿs\ n : a pervading atmosphere

**¹am·bi·ent** \ˈam-bē-ənt\ adj : existing on all sides

**²ambient** n : music intended to serve as an unobtrusive accompaniment to other activities

**am·big·u·ous** \am-ˈbi-gyə-wəs\ adj : capable of being understood in more than one way — **am·bi·gu·i·ty** \ˌam-bə-ˈgyü-ə-tē\ n — **am·big·u·ous·ly** adv

**am·bi·tion** \am-ˈbi-shən\ n [ME, fr. MF or L; MF, fr. L ambition-, ambitio, lit., act of soliciting for votes, fr. ambire to go around] : eager desire for success or power

**am·bi·tious** \-shəs\ adj : characterized by ambition — **am·bi·tious·ly** adv — **am·bi·tious·ness** n

**am·biv·a·lence** \am-ˈbi-və-ləns\ n : simultaneous attraction toward and repulsion from a person, object, or action — **am·biv·a·lent** \-lənt\ adj

**¹am·ble** \ˈam-bəl\ vb **am·bled; am·bling** \-b(ə-)liŋ\ : to go at an amble

**²amble** n : an easy gait esp. of a horse

**am·bro·sia** \am-ˈbrō-zh(ē-)ə\ n : the food of the Greek and Roman gods — **am·bro·sial** \-zh(ē-)əl\ adj

**am·bu·lance** \ˈam-byə-ləns\ n : a vehicle equipped for carrying the injured or sick

**am·bu·lant** \ˈam-byə-lənt\ adj : AMBULATORY

**¹am·bu·la·to·ry** \ˈam-byə-lə-ˌtȯr-ē\ adj **1** : of, relating to, or adapted to walking **2** : able to walk or move about

**²ambulatory** n, pl **-ries** : a sheltered place (as in a cloister) for walking

**am·bus·cade** \ˈam-bə-ˌskād\ n : AMBUSH

**am·bush** \'am-ˌbu̇sh\ *n* : a trap in which concealed persons wait to attack by surprise — **ambush** *vb*

**amdt** *abbr* amendment

**ameba, ameboid** *var of* AMOEBA, AMOEBOID

**ame·lio·rate** \ə-ˈmēl-yə-ˌrāt\ *vb* **-rat·ed; -rat·ing** : to make or grow better : IMPROVE — **ame·lio·ra·tion** \-ˌmēl-yə-ˈrā-shən\ *n*

**amen** \(ˌ)ā-ˈmen, (ˌ)ä-\ *interj* — used esp. at the end of prayers to affirm or express approval

**ame·na·ble** \ə-ˈmē-nə-bəl, -ˈme-\ *adj* 1 : ANSWERABLE ⟨~ to the law⟩ 2 : agreeable to something asked for

**amend** \ə-ˈmend\ *vb* 1 : to change for the better : IMPROVE 2 : to alter formally in phraseology — **amend·able** \-ˈmen-də-bəl\ *adj*

**amend·ment** \ə-ˈmend-mənt\ *n* 1 : correction of faults 2 : the process of amending a parliamentary motion or a constitution; *also* : the alteration so proposed or made

**amends** \ə-ˈmendz\ *n sing or pl* : compensation for injury or loss

**ame·ni·ty** \ə-ˈme-nə-tē, -ˈmē-\ *n, pl* **-ties** 1 : AGREEABLENESS 2 : a gesture observed in social relationships 3 : something that serves as a comfort or convenience

**Amer** *abbr* America; American

**amerce** \ə-ˈmərs\ *vb* **amerced; amerc·ing** 1 : to penalize by a fine determined by the court 2 : PUNISH — **amerce·ment** *n*

**Amer·i·ca·na** \ə-ˌmer-ə-ˈka-nə, -ˈkä-\ *n pl* : materials concerning or characteristic of America, its civilization, or its culture

**American Indian** *n* : a member of any of the aboriginal peoples of No. and So. America except the Eskimos

**Amer·i·can·ism** \ə-ˈmer-ə-kə-ˌni-zəm\ *n* 1 : a characteristic feature of English as used in the U.S. 2 : attachment or loyalty to the traditions, interests, or ideals of the U.S. 3 : a custom or trait peculiar to the U.S. or to Americans

**Amer·i·can·ize** \ə-ˈmer-ə-kə-ˌnīz\ *vb* : to make or become American — **Amer·i·can·i·za·tion** \ə-ˌmer-ə-kə-nə-ˈzā-shən\ *n*

**Amer·i·can·ness** \ə-ˈmer-ə-kən-nəs\ *n* : the quality or state of being American

**American plan** *n* : a hotel plan whereby the daily rates cover the cost of room and three meals

**American Sign Language** *n* : a sign language for the deaf in which meaning is conveyed by a system of hand gestures and placement

**amer·i·ci·um** \ˌam-ə-ˈrish-ē-əm, -ˈris-\ *n* : a radioactive metallic chemical element produced artificially from plutonium

**AmerInd** *abbr* American Indian

**Am·er·in·di·an** \ˌa-mə-ˈrin-dē-ən\ *n* : AMERICAN INDIAN — **Amerindian** *adj*

**am·e·thyst** \ˈa-mə-thəst\ *n* [ME *amatiste*, fr. AF & L; AF, fr. L *amethystus*, fr. Gk *amethystos*, lit., remedy against drunkenness, fr. *a-* not + *methyein* to be drunk, fr.

*methy* wine] : a gemstone consisting of clear purple or bluish-violet quartz

**ami·a·ble** \ˈā-mē-ə-bəl\ *adj* 1 : AGREEABLE ⟨an ~ comedy⟩ 2 : having a friendly and sociable disposition — **ami·a·bil·i·ty** \ˌā-mē-ə-ˈbi-lə-tē\ *n* — **ami·a·ble·ness** *n* — **ami·a·bly** \ˈā-mē-ə-blē\ *adv*

**am·i·ca·ble** \ˈa-mi-kə-bəl\ *adj* : FRIENDLY, PEACEABLE ⟨an ~ settlement of differences⟩ — **am·i·ca·bil·i·ty** \ˌa-mi-kə-ˈbi-lə-tē\ *n* — **am·i·ca·bly** \ˈa-mi-kə-blē\ *adv*

**amid** \ə-ˈmid\ *or* **amidst** \-ˈmidst\ *prep* : in or into the middle of : AMONG

**amid·ships** \ə-ˈmid-ˌships\ *adv* : in or near the middle of a ship

**ami·no acid** \ə-ˈmē-nō-\ *n* : any of numerous nitrogen-containing acids that include some which are used by cells to build proteins

**amir** *var of* EMIR

**¹amiss** \ə-ˈmis\ *adv* 1 : WRONGLY 2 : ASTRAY ⟨something had gone ~⟩ 3 : IMPERFECTLY

**²amiss** *adj* 1 : WRONG 2 : out of place

**am·i·ty** \ˈa-mə-tē\ *n, pl* **-ties** : FRIENDSHIP; *esp* : friendly relations between nations

**am·me·ter** \ˈa-ˌmē-tər\ *n* : an instrument for measuring electric current esp. in amperes

**am·mo** \ˈa-mō\ *n* : AMMUNITION

**am·mo·nia** \ə-ˈmō-nyə\ *n* [NL, fr. L *sal ammoniacus* sal ammoniac (ammonium chloride), lit., salt of Ammon, fr. Gk *ammōniakos* of Ammon, fr. *Ammōn* Ammon, an Egyptian god near one of whose temples it was extracted] 1 : a colorless gaseous compound of nitrogen and hydrogen used in refrigeration and in the making of fertilizers and explosives 2 : a solution (**ammonia water**) of ammonia in water

**am·mo·ni·um** \ə-ˈmō-nē-əm\ *n* : an ion or chemical group derived from ammonia by combination with hydrogen

**ammonium chloride** *n* : a white crystalline volatile salt used in batteries and as an expectorant

**am·mu·ni·tion** \ˌam-yə-ˈni-shən\ *n* 1 : projectiles fired from guns 2 : explosive items used in war 3 : material for use in attack or defense

**Amn** *abbr* airman

**am·ne·sia** \am-ˈnē-zhə\ *n* 1 : abnormal loss of memory 2 : the selective overlooking of events or acts not favorable to one's purpose — **am·ne·si·ac** \-zhē-ˌak, -zē-\ *or* **am·ne·sic** \-zik, -sik\ *adj or n*

**am·nes·ty** \ˈam-nə-stē\ *n, pl* **-ties** : an act granting a pardon to a group of individuals — **amnesty** *vb*

**am·nio·cen·te·sis** \ˌam-nē-ō-ˌsen-ˈtē-səs\ *n, pl* **-te·ses** \-ˌsēz\ : the surgical insertion of a hollow needle through the abdominal wall and uterus of a pregnant female esp. to obtain fluid used to check the fetus for chromosomal abnormality and to determine sex

**am·ni·ot·ic fluid** \ˌam-nē-ˈä-tik-\ *n* : the

watery fluid in which the embryo or fetus is immersed

**amoe·ba** also **ame·ba** \ə-'mē-bə\ n, pl **-bas** or **-bae** \-(ˌ)bē\ : any of various tiny one-celled protozoans that lack permanent cell organs and occur esp. in water and soil — **amoe·bic** \-bik\ adj

**amoe·boid** also **ame·boid** \-ˌbȯid\ adj : resembling an amoeba esp. in moving or readily changing shape

**amok** \ə-'mək, -'mäk\ or **amuck** \-'mək\ adv : in a violent, frenzied, or uncontrolled manner ⟨run ~⟩

**among** \ə-'məŋ\ also **amongst** \-'məŋst\ prep **1** : in or through the midst of **2** : in the number, class, or company of **3** : in shares to each of **4** : by common action of

**amon·til·la·do** \ə-ˌmän-tə-'lä-dō\ n, pl **-dos** [Sp] : a medium dry sherry

**amor·al** \ā-'mȯr-əl\ adj **1** : neither moral nor immoral; esp : being outside the sphere to which moral judgments apply **2** : lacking moral sensibility — **amor·al·ly** adv

**am·o·rous** \'a-mə-rəs\ adj **1** : inclined to love **2** : being in love **3** : of or indicative of love — **am·o·rous·ly** adv — **am·o·rous·ness** n

**amor·phous** \ə-'mȯr-fəs\ adj **1** : SHAPELESS, FORMLESS **2** : not crystallized

**amor·tize** \'a-mər-ˌtīz, ə-'mȯr-\ vb **-tized; -tiz·ing** : to extinguish (as a mortgage) usu. by payment on the principal at the time of each periodic interest payment — **amor·ti·za·tion** \ˌa-mər-tə-'zā-shən, ə-ˌmȯr-\ n

**Amos** \'ā-məs\ — see BIBLE table

**¹amount** \ə-'maúnt\ vb **1** : to be equivalent **2** : to reach a total : add up

**²amount** n **1** : the total number or quantity **2** : a principal sum plus the interest on it

**amour** \ə-'múr, ä-, a-\ n **1** : a love affair esp. when illicit **2** : LOVER

**amour pro·pre** \ˌa-ˌmúr-'prȯpr³, ä-, -'prȯpr³\ n [F] : SELF-ESTEEM

**¹amp** \'amp\ n **1** : AMPERE **2** : AMPLIFIER; also : a unit consisting of an electronic amplifier and a loudspeaker

**²amp** vb : EXCITE, ENERGIZE ⟨tried to ~ up the crowd⟩

**am·per·age** \'am-p(ə-)rij\ n : the strength of a current of electricity expressed in amperes

**am·pere** \'am-ˌpir\ n : a unit of electric current equivalent to a steady current produced by one volt applied across a resistance of one ohm

**am·per·sand** \'am-pər-ˌsand\ n [alter. of and per se and, spoken form of the phrase & per se and, lit., (the character) & by itself (stands for the word) and] : a character & used for the word and

**am·phet·amine** \am-'fe-tə-ˌmēn, -mən\ n : a compound or one of its derivatives that stimulates the central nervous system and is used esp. to treat hyperactive children and to suppress appetite

**am·phib·i·an** \am-'fi-bē-ən\ n **1** : an amphibious organism; esp : any of a class of vertebrate animals (as frogs and salamanders) intermediate between fishes and reptiles **2** : an airplane that can land on and take off from either land or water

**am·phib·i·ous** \am-'fi-bē-əs\ adj [Gk amphibios, lit., living a double life, fr. amphi- + bios mode of life] **1** : able to live both on land and in water **2** : adapted for both land and water **3** : made by joint action of land, sea, and air forces invading from the sea; also : trained for such action

**am·phi·bole** \'am-fə-ˌbōl\ n : any of a group of rock-forming minerals of similar crystal structure

**am·phi·the·ater** \'am-fə-ˌthē-ə-tər\ n **1** : an oval or circular structure with rising tiers of seats around an arena **2** : a very large auditorium

**am·pho·ra** \'am-fə-rə\ n, pl **-rae** \-ˌrē\ or **-ras** : an ancient Greek jar or vase with two handles that rise almost to the level of the mouth

**am·ple** \'am-pəl\ adj **am·pler** \-plər\; **am·plest** \-pləst\ **1** : LARGE, CAPACIOUS **2** : enough to satisfy : ABUNDANT — **am·ply** \-plē\ adv

**am·pli·fy** \'am-plə-ˌfī\ vb **-fied; -fy·ing** **1** : to expand by extended treatment **2** : to increase in magnitude or strength; also : to make louder — **am·pli·fi·ca·tion** \ˌam-plə-fə-kā-shən\ n — **am·pli·fi·er** \'am-plə-ˌfī(-ə)r\ n

**am·pli·tude** \-ˌtüd, -ˌtyüd\ n **1** : ample extent : FULLNESS **2** : the extent of a vibratory movement (as of a pendulum) **3** : the height or depth of an oscillation (as of an alternating current or a radio wave) compared to its average value

**amplitude modulation** n : modulation of the amplitude of a radio carrier wave in accordance with the strength of the signal; also : a broadcasting system using such modulation

**am·poule** or **am·pule** also **am·pul** \'am-ˌpyül, -ˌpül\ n : a small sealed bulbous glass vessel used to hold a solution for hypodermic injection

**am·pu·tate** \'am-pyə-ˌtāt\ vb **-tat·ed; -tat·ing** : to cut off ⟨~ a leg⟩ — **am·pu·ta·tion** \ˌam-pyə-'tā-shən\ n

**am·pu·tee** \ˌam-pyə-'tē\ n : one who has had a limb amputated

**AMSLAN** abbr American Sign Language

**amt** abbr amount

**amuck** var of AMOK

**am·u·let** \'am-yə-lət\ n : an ornament worn as a charm against evil

**amuse** \ə-'myüz\ vb **amused; amus·ing** : to entertain in a light or playful manner : DIVERT — **amuse·ment** n — **amus·ing** adj — **amus·ing·ly** adv

**amusement park** n : a commercially operated park having various devices (as a roller coaster) for entertainment and booths for selling refreshments

**AM·VETS** \'am-ˌvets\ abbr American Veterans (of World War II)

**am·y·lase** \'a-mə-ˌlās, -ˌlāz\ n : any of several enzymes that accelerate the breakdown of starch and glycogen

**an** \ən, (')an\ indefinite article : A — used

before words beginning with a vowel sound

¹**-an** *or* **-ian** *also* **-ean** *n suffix* **1** : one that belongs to ⟨American⟩ ⟨crustacean⟩ **2** : one skilled in or specializing in ⟨phonetician⟩

²**-an** *or* **-ian** *also* **-ean** *adj suffix* **1** : of or belonging to ⟨American⟩ **2** : characteristic of : resembling ⟨Mozartean⟩

**AN** *abbr* airman (Navy)

**an·a·bol·ic steroid** \ˌa-nə-ˈbä-lik-\ *n* : any of a group of synthetic steroid hormones sometimes abused by athletes in training to increase the size and strength of their muscles

**anach·ro·nism** \ə-ˈna-krə-ˌni-zəm\ *n* **1** : the error of placing a person or thing in the wrong period **2** : one that is chronologically out of place — **anach·ro·nis·tic** \-ˌna-krə-ˈnis-tik\ *adj* — **anach·ro·nous** \-ˈna-krə-nəs\ *adj*

**an·a·con·da** \ˌa-nə-ˈkän-də\ *n* : a large So. American snake that suffocates and kills its prey by constriction

**anad·ro·mous** \ə-ˈna-drə-məs\ *adj* : ascending rivers from the sea for breeding ⟨shad are ∼⟩

**anae·mia, anae·mic** *chiefly Brit var of* ANEMIA, ANEMIC

**an·aer·obe** \ˈa-nə-ˌrōb\ *n* : an anaerobic organism

**an·aer·o·bic** \ˌa-nə-ˈrō-bik\ *adj* : living, active, occurring, or existing in the absence of free oxygen

**an·aes·the·sia, an·aes·thet·ic** *chiefly Brit var of* ANESTHESIA, ANESTHETIC

**ana·gram** \ˈa-nə-ˌgram\ *n* : a word or phrase made by transposing the letters of another word or phrase

¹**anal** \ˈā-nᵊl\ *adj* **1** : of, relating to, situated near, or involving the anus **2** : of, relating to, or characterized by the stage of psychosexual development in psychoanalytic theory during which one is concerned esp. with feces **3** : of, relating to, or characterized by personality traits (as frugality and neatness) considered typical of fixation at the anal stage of development — **anal·ly** *adv*

²**anal** *abbr* **1** analogy **2** analysis; analytic

**an·al·ge·sia** \ˌa-nᵊl-ˈjē-zhə\ *n* : insensibility to pain — **an·al·ge·sic** \-ˈjē-zik, -sik\ *adj*

**an·al·ge·sic** \-ˈjē-zik, -sik\ *n* : an agent for producing analgesia

**analog computer** *n* : a computer that operates with numbers represented by directly measurable quantities (as voltages)

**anal·o·gous** \ə-ˈna-lə-gəs\ *adj* : similar in one or more respects — **anal·o·gous·ly** *adv*

**an·a·logue** *or* **an·a·log** \ˈa-nə-ˌlȯg, -ˌläg\ *n* **1** : something that is analogous to something else **2** : an organ similar in function to one of another animal or plant but different in structure or origin

**anal·o·gy** \ə-ˈna-lə-jē\ *n, pl* **-gies** **1** : inference that if two or more things agree in some respects they will probably agree in others **2** : a likeness in one or more ways between things otherwise unlike —

**an·a·log·i·cal** \ˌa-nə-ˈlä-ji-kəl\ *adj* — **an·a·log·i·cal·ly** \-k(ə-)lē\ *adv*

**anal–re·ten·tive** \ˈā-nᵊl-ri-ˈten-tiv\ *adj* : ANAL 3

**an·a·lyse** *chiefly Brit var of* ANALYZE

**anal·y·sis** \ə-ˈna-lə-səs\ *n, pl* **-y·ses** \-ˌsēz\ [NL, fr. Gk, fr. *analyein* to break up, fr. *ana-* up + *lyein* to loosen] **1** : separation of a thing into the parts or elements of which it is composed **2** : an examination of a thing to determine its parts or elements; *also* : a statement showing the results of such an examination **3** : PSYCHOANALYSIS — **an·a·lyst** \ˈa-nə-list\ *n* — **an·a·lyt·ic** \ˌa-nə-ˈli-tik\ *or* **an·a·lyt·i·cal** \-ti-kəl\ *adj* — **an·a·lyt·i·cal·ly** *adv*

**an·a·lyte** \ˈa-nə-ˌlīt\ *n* : a chemical substance that is the subject of chemical analysis

**an·a·lyze** \ˈa-nə-ˌlīz\ *vb* **-lyzed; -lyz·ing** : to make an analysis of

**an·a·pest** \ˈa-nə-ˌpest\ *n* : a metrical foot of two unaccented syllables followed by one accented syllable — **an·a·pes·tic** \ˌa-nə-ˈpes-tik\ *adj or n*

**an·ar·chism** \ˈa-nər-ˌki-zəm\ *n* : the theory that all government is undesirable — **an·ar·chist** \-kist\ *n or adj* — **an·ar·chis·tic** \ˌa-nər-ˈkis-tik\ *adj*

**an·ar·chy** \ˈa-nər-kē\ *n* **1** : a social structure without government or law and order **2** : utter confusion — **an·ar·chic** \a-ˈnär-kik\ *adj* — **an·ar·chi·cal·ly** \-ki-k(ə-)lē\ *adv*

**anas·to·mo·sis** \ə-ˌnas-tə-ˈmō-səs\ *n, pl* **-mo·ses** \-ˌsēz\ **1** : the union of parts or branches (as of blood vessels) **2** : NETWORK

**anat** *abbr* anatomical; anatomy

**anath·e·ma** \ə-ˈna-thə-mə\ *n* **1** : a solemn curse **2** : a person or thing accursed; *also* : one intensely disliked

**anath·e·ma·tize** \-ˌtīz\ *vb* **-tized; -tiz·ing** : to pronounce an anathema against : CURSE

**anat·o·mise** *Brit var of* ANATOMIZE

**anat·o·mize** \ə-ˈna-tə-ˌmīz\ *vb* **-mized; -miz·ing** : to dissect so as to examine the structure and parts; *also* : ANALYZE

**anat·o·my** \ə-ˈna-tə-mē\ *n, pl* **-mies** [LL *anatomia* dissection, fr. Gk *anatomē*, fr. *anatemnein* to dissect, fr. *ana-* up + *temnein* to cut] **1** : a branch of science dealing with the structure of organisms **2** : structural makeup esp. of an organism or any of its parts **3** : a separating into parts for detailed study : ANALYSIS — **an·a·tom·i·cal** \ˌa-nə-ˈtä-mi-kəl\ *or* **an·a·tom·ic** \-mik\ *adj* — **an·a·tom·i·cal·ly** \-mi-k(ə-)lē\ *adv* — **anat·o·mist** \ə-ˈna-tə-mist\ *n*

**anc** *abbr* ancient

**-ance** *n suffix* **1** : action or process ⟨furtherance⟩ : instance of an action or process ⟨performance⟩ **2** : quality or state : instance of a quality or state ⟨protuberance⟩ **3** : amount or degree ⟨conductance⟩

**an·ces·tor** \ˈan-ˌses-tər\ *n* [ME *ancestre*, fr. AF, fr. L *antecessor* predecessor, fr. *antecedere* to go before, fr. *ante-* before +

*cedere* to go] : one from whom an individual is descended

**an·ces·tress** \'an-₁ses-trəs\ *n* : a female ancestor

**an·ces·try** \'an-₁ses-trē\ *n* **1** : line of descent : LINEAGE **2** : ANCESTORS — **an·ces·tral** \an-'ses-trəl\ *adj*

**an·cho** \'än-chō\ *n, pl* **anchos** : a poblano chili pepper esp. when mature and dried to a reddish black

**¹an·chor** \'aŋ-kər\ *n* **1** : a heavy metal device attached to a ship that catches hold of the bottom and holds the ship in place **2** : something that serves to hold an object firmly **3** : ANCHORPERSON **4** : a large store that attracts customers and other businesses to a shopping mall

**²anchor** *vb* : to hold or become held in place by or as if by an anchor

**an·chor·age** \'aŋ-k(ə-)rij\ *n* : a place suitable for ships to anchor

**an·cho·rite** \'aŋ-kə-₁rīt\ *n* : HERMIT

**an·chor·man** \'aŋ-kər-₁man\ *n* **1** : the member of a team who competes last **2** : an anchorperson who is a man

**an·chor·per·son** \-₁pər-sən\ *n* : a broadcaster who reads the news and introduces the reports of other broadcasters

**an·chor·wom·an** \-₁wu̇-mən\ *n* **1** : a woman who competes last **2** : an anchorperson who is a woman

**an·cho·vy** \'an-₁chō-vē, an-'chō-\ *n, pl* **-vies** *or* **-vy** : any of a family of small herringlike fishes often used as food

**an·cien ré·gime** \äⁿs-yaⁿ-rā-'zhēm\ *n* **1** : the political and social system of France before the Revolution of 1789 **2** : a system no longer prevailing

**¹an·cient** \'ān-shənt\ *adj* **1** : having existed for many years ⟨~ customs⟩ **2** : belonging to times long past; *esp* : belonging to the period before the Middle Ages

**²ancient** *n* **1** : an aged person **2** *pl* : the peoples of ancient Greece and Rome; *esp* : the classical authors of Greece and Rome

**an·cil·lary** \'an-sə-₁ler-ē\ *adj* **1** : SUBORDINATE, SUBSIDIARY ⟨a factory's ~ plants⟩ **2** : AUXILIARY, SUPPLEMENTARY ⟨~ evidence⟩ — **ancillary** *n*

**-ancy** *n suffix* : quality or state ⟨flamboyancy⟩

**and** \ənd, (')and\ *conj* **1** — used to indicate connection or addition esp. of items within the same class or type or to join words or phrases of the same grammatical rank or function **2** — used to join one finite verb to another so that together they are equivalent to an infinitive of purpose ⟨come ~ see me⟩

**¹an·dan·te** \än-'dän-₁tā, -'tē\ *adv or adj* [It, lit., going, prp. of *andare* to go] : moderately slow — used as a direction in music

**²andante** *n* : an andante movement

**and·iron** \'an-₁dī(-ə)rn\ *n* : one of a pair of metal supports for firewood in a fireplace

**and/or** \'and-'ȯr\ *conj* — used to indicate that either *and* or *or* may apply ⟨men ~ women means men *and* women or men *or* women⟩

**an·dro·gen** \'an-drə-jən\ *n* : a male sex hormone (as testosterone)

**an·drog·y·nous** \an-'drä-jə-nəs\ *adj* **1** : having the characteristics of both male and female **2** : suitable for either sex ⟨~ clothing⟩ — **an·drog·y·ny** \-nē\ *n*

**an·droid** \'an-₁droid\ *n* : a mobile robot usu. with a human form

**an·ec·dot·al** \₁a-nik-'dō-t⁹l\ *adj* **1** : relating to or consisting of anecdotes **2** : based on reports of an unscientific nature — **an·ec·dot·al·ly** *adv*

**an·ec·dote** \'a-nik-₁dōt\ *n, pl* **-dotes** *also* **-dota** \₁a-nik-'dō-tə\ [F, fr. Gk *anekdota* unpublished items, fr. *a-* not + *ekdidonai* to publish] : a brief story of an interesting, amusing, or biographical incident

**ane·mia** \ə-'nē-mē-ə\ *n* **1** : a condition in which blood is deficient in quantity, in red blood cells, or in hemoglobin and which is marked by pallor, weakness, and irregular heart action **2** : lack of vitality — **ane·mic** \-'nē-mik\ *adj*

**an·e·mom·e·ter** \₁a-nə-'mä-mə-tər\ *n* : an instrument for measuring the force or speed of the wind

**anem·o·ne** \ə-'ne-mə-nē\ *n* : any of a large genus of herbs related to the buttercups that have showy flowers without petals but with conspicuous often colored sepals

**anent** \ə-'nent\ *prep* : CONCERNING

**an·es·the·sia** \₁a-nəs-'thē-zhə\ *n* : loss of bodily sensation

**an·es·the·si·ol·o·gy** \-₁thē-zē-'ä-lə-jē\ *n* : a branch of medical science dealing with anesthesia and anesthetics — **an·es·the·si·ol·o·gist** \-jist\ *n*

**¹an·es·thet·ic** \₁a-nəs-'the-tik\ *adj* : of, relating to, or capable of producing anesthesia

**²anesthetic** *n* : an agent that produces anesthesia

**anes·the·tist** \ə-'nes-thə-tist\ *n* : one who administers anesthetics

**anes·the·tize** \ə-'nes-thə-₁tīz\ *vb* **-tized; -tiz·ing** : to subject to anesthesia

**anew** \ə-'nü, -'nyü\ *adv* **1** : over again ⟨begin ~⟩ **2** : in a new form ⟨this film tells the story ~⟩

**an·gel** \'ān-jəl\ *n* [ME, fr. OE *engel* & AF *angele*, both fr. L *angelus*, fr. Gk *angelos*, lit., messenger] **1** : a spiritual being superior to man **2** : an attendant spirit **3** : a winged figure of human form in art **4** : MESSENGER, HARBINGER ⟨~ of death⟩ **5** : a person held to resemble an angel **6** : a financial backer — **an·gel·ic** \an-'je-lik\ *or* **an·gel·i·cal** \-li-kəl\ *adj* — **an·gel·i·cal·ly** \-k(ə-)lē\ *adv*

**an·gel·fish** \'ān-jəl-₁fish\ *n* : any of several brightly colored tropical fishes that are flattened from side to side

**an·gel·i·ca** \an-'je-li-kə\ *n* : a biennial herb related to the carrot whose roots and fruit furnish a flavoring oil

**¹an·ger** \'aŋ-gər\ *vb* : to make angry

**²anger** *n* [ME, affliction, anger, fr. ON *angr* grief] : a strong feeling of displeasure ♦ **Synonyms** WRATH, IRE, RAGE, FURY, INDIGNATION

**an·gi·na** \an-'jī-nə\ *n* : a disorder (as of the heart) marked by attacks of intense pain; *esp* : ANGINA PECTORIS — **an·gi·nal** \an-'jī-nᵊl\ *adj*

**angina pec·to·ris** \-'pek-t(ə-)rəs\ *n* : a heart disease marked by brief attacks of sharp chest pain caused by deficient oxygenation of heart muscles

**an·gio·gen·e·sis** \an-jē-ō-'je-nə-səs\ *n* : the formation of blood vessels — **an·gio·gen·ic** \-'je-nik\ *adj*

**an·gio·gram** \'an-jē-ə-,gram\ *n* : a radiograph made by angiography

**an·gi·og·ra·phy** \,an-jē-'ä-grə-fē\ *n* : the use of radiography to make blood vessels visible after injection of a substance opaque to radiation

**an·gio·plas·ty** \'an-jē-ə-,plas-tē\ *n* : surgical repair of a blood vessel esp. by using an inflatable catheter to unblock arteries clogged by atherosclerotic deposits

**an·gio·sperm** \-,spərm\ *n* : FLOWERING PLANT

¹**an·gle** \'aŋ-gəl\ *n* **1** : a sharp projecting corner **2** : the figure formed by the meeting of two lines in a point **3** : a point of view **4** : a special technique or plan : GIMMICK — **an·gled** *adj*

²**angle** *vb* **an·gled; an·gling** \-g(ə-)liŋ\ : to turn, move, or direct at an angle

³**angle** *vb* **an·gled; an·gling** \-g(ə-)liŋ\ : to fish with a hook and line — **an·gler** \-glər\ *n* — **an·gling** \-gliŋ\ *n*

**an·gle·worm** \'aŋ-gəl-,wərm\ *n* : EARTHWORM

**An·gli·can** \'aŋ-gli-kən\ *adj* **1** : of or relating to the established episcopal Church of England **2** : of or relating to England or the English nation — **Anglican** *n* — **An·gli·can·ism** \-kə-,ni-zəm\ *n*

**an·gli·cize** \'aŋ-glə-,sīz\ *vb* **-cized; -cizing** *often cap* **1** : to make English (as in habits, speech, character, or outlook) **2** : to borrow (a foreign word or phrase) into English without changing form or spelling and sometimes without changing pronunciation — **an·gli·ci·za·tion** \,aŋ-glə-sə-'zā-shən\ *n, often cap*

**An·glo** \'aŋ-glō\ *n, pl* **Anglos** : a non-Hispanic white inhabitant of the U.S.; *esp* : one of English origin and descent

**An·glo·cen·tric** \,aŋ-glō-'sen-trik\ *adj* : centered on or favoring England or things English

**An·glo-French** \,aŋ-glō-'french\ *n* : the French language used in medieval England

**An·glo·phile** \'aŋ-glə-,fī(-ə)l\ *also* **An·glo·phil** \-,fil\ *n* : one who greatly admires England and things English

**An·glo·phobe** \'aŋ-glə-,fōb\ *n* : one who is averse to England and things English

**An·glo-Sax·on** \,aŋ-glō-'sak-sən\ *n* **1** : a member of any of the Germanic peoples who invaded England in the 5th century A.D. **2** : a member of the English people **3** : Old English — **Anglo-Saxon** *adj*

**an·go·ra** \aŋ-'gȯr-ə, an-\ *n* **1** : yarn or cloth made from the hair of an Angora goat or rabbit **2** *cap* : any of a breed of cats, goats, or rabbits with a long silky coat

**an·gry** \'aŋ-grē\ *adj* **an·gri·er; -est** : feeling or showing anger ♦ **Synonyms** ENRAGED, WRATHFUL, IRATE, INDIGNANT, MAD — **an·gri·ly** \-grə-lē\ *adv*

**angst** \'äŋst\ *n* [G] : a feeling of anxiety

**ang·strom** \'aŋ-strəm\ *n* : a unit of length equal to one ten-billionth of a meter

**an·guish** \'aŋ-gwish\ *n* : extreme pain or distress esp. of mind — **an·guished** \-gwisht\ *adj*

**an·gu·lar** \'aŋ-gyə-lər\ *adj* **1** : sharp-cornered **2** : having one or more angles **3** : being thin and bony — **an·gu·lar·i·ty** \,aŋ-gyə-'ler-ə-tē\ *n*

**An·gus** \'aŋ-gəs\ *n* : any of a breed of usu. black hornless beef cattle originating in Scotland

**an·hy·drous** \an-'hī-drəs\ *adj* : free from water

**an·i·line** \'a-nᵊl-ən\ *n* : an oily poisonous liquid used in making dyes, medicines, and explosives

**an·i·mad·vert** \,a-nə-,mad-'vərt\ *vb* : to remark critically : express censure — **an·i·mad·ver·sion** \-'vər-zhən\ *n*

¹**an·i·mal** \'a-nə-məl\ *n* **1** : any of a kingdom of living things typically differing from plants in capacity for active movement, in rapid response to stimulation, and in lack of cellulose cell walls **2** : a lower animal as distinguished from human beings; *also* : MAMMAL

²**animal** *adj* **1** : of, relating to, or derived from animals **2** : of or relating to the physical as distinguished from the mental or spiritual ♦ **Synonyms** CARNAL, FLESHLY, SENSUAL

**an·i·mal·cule** \,a-nə-'mal-kyül\ *n* : a tiny animal usu. invisible to the naked eye

¹**an·i·mate** \'a-nə-mət\ *adj* : having life

²**an·i·mate** \-,māt\ *vb* **-mat·ed; -mat·ing** **1** : to impart life to **2** : to give spirit and vigor to **3** : to make appear to move ⟨~ a cartoon for motion pictures⟩ — **an·i·mat·ed** *adj* — **an·i·mat·ed·ly** *adv*

**an·i·ma·tion** \,a-nə-'mā-shən\ *n* **1** : VIVACITY, LIVELINESS **2** : a motion picture made from a series of drawings simulating motions by means of slight progressive changes

**an·i·ma·tron·ic** \,a-nə-mə-'trä-nik\ *adj* : of, relating to, or being an electrically animated mechanical figure (as a puppet)

**an·i·mism** \'a-nə-,mi-zəm\ *n* : attribution of conscious life to objects in and phenomena of nature or to inanimate objects — **an·i·mist** \-mist\ *n* — **an·i·mis·tic** \,a-nə-'mis-tik\ *adj*

**an·i·mos·i·ty** \,a-nə-'mä-sə-tē\ *n, pl* **-ties** : ILL WILL, RESENTMENT

**an·i·mus** \'a-nə-məs\ *n* : deep-seated resentment and hostility

**an·ion** \'a-,nī-ən, -,nī-,än\ *n* : a negatively charged ion

**an·ise** \'a-nəs\ *n* : an herb related to the carrot with aromatic seeds (**aniseed** \-sēd\) used in flavoring

**an·is·ette** \,a-nə-'set, -'zet\ *n* [F] : a usu. colorless sweet liqueur flavored with aniseed

**ankh** \\'äŋk\ *n* : a cross having a loop for its upper vertical arm and serving esp. in ancient Egypt as an emblem of life

**an·kle** \\'aŋ-kəl\ *n* : the joint or region between the foot and the leg

**an·kle·bone** \\'aŋ-kəl-,bōn\ *n* : the bone that in human beings bears the weight of the body and with the tibia and fibula forms the ankle joint

**an·klet** \\'aŋ-klət\ *n* **1** : something (as an ornament) worn around the ankle **2** : a short sock reaching slightly above the ankle

**ann** *abbr* **1** annals **2** annual

**an·nals** \\'a-nəlz\ *n pl* **1** : a record of events in chronological order **2** : historical records — **an·nal·ist** \-nəl-ist\ *n*

**an·neal** \ə-'nēl\ *vb* **1** : to make (as glass or steel) less brittle by heating and then cooling **2** : STRENGTHEN, TOUGHEN

**1an·nex** \ə-'neks, 'a-,neks\ *vb* **1** : to attach as an addition **2** : to incorporate (as a territory) within a political domain — **an·nex·a·tion** \,a-,nek-'sā-shən\ *n*

**2an·nex** \'a-,neks, -niks\ *n* : a subsidiary or supplementary structure

**an·nexe** *chiefly Brit var of* ANNEX

**an·ni·hi·late** \ə-'nī-ə-,lāt\ *vb* **-lat·ed; -lat·ing** : to destroy completely — **an·ni·hi·la·tion** \-,nī-ə-'lā-shən\ *n*

**an·ni·ver·sa·ry** \,a-nə-'vər-sə-rē\ *n, pl* **-ries** : the annual return of the date of a notable event and esp. a wedding

**an·no Do·mi·ni** \,a-nō-'dä-mə-nē, -'dō-, -,nī\ *adv, often cap A* [ML, in the year of the Lord] — used to indicate that a time division falls within the Christian era

**an·no·tate** \'a-nə-,tāt\ *vb* **-tat·ed; -tat·ing** : to furnish with notes — **an·no·ta·tion** \,a-nə-'tā-shən\ *n* — **an·no·ta·tor** \'a-nə-,tā-tər\ *n*

**an·nounce** \ə-'naúns\ *vb* **an·nounced; an·nounc·ing 1** : to make known publicly **2** : to give notice of the arrival or presence of — **an·nounce·ment** *n*

**an·nounc·er** \ə-'naún-sər\ *n* : a person who introduces radio or television programs, makes commercial announcements, or gives station identification

**an·noy** \ə-'nói\ *vb* : to disturb or irritate esp. by repeated acts : VEX ♦ **Synonyms** IRK, BOTHER, PESTER, TEASE, HARASS — **an·noy·ing·ly** *adv*

**an·noy·ance** \ə-'nói-əns\ *n* **1** : the act of annoying **2** : the state of being annoyed **3** : NUISANCE ⟨the delay was a minor ~⟩

**1an·nu·al** \'an-yə-wəl\ *adj* **1** : covering the period of a year ⟨~ rainfall⟩ **2** : occurring once a year : YEARLY **3** : completing the life cycle in one growing season ⟨~ plants⟩ — **an·nu·al·ly** *adv*

**2annual** *n* **1** : a publication appearing once a year **2** : an annual plant

**annual ring** *n* : the layer of wood produced by a single year's growth of a woody plant

**an·nu·i·tant** \ə-'nü-ə-tənt, -'nyü-\ *n* : a beneficiary of an annuity

**an·nu·i·ty** \ə-'nü-ə-tē, -'nyü-\ *n, pl* **-i·ties** : an amount payable annually; *also* : the right to receive such a payment

**an·nul** \ə-'nəl\ *vb* **an·nulled; an·nul·ling** : to make legally void — **an·nul·ment** *n*

**an·nu·lar** \'an-yə-lər\ *adj* : ring-shaped

**an·nun·ci·ate** \ə-'nən-sē-,āt\ *vb* **-at·ed; -at·ing** : ANNOUNCE

**an·nun·ci·a·tion** \ə-,nən-sē-'ā-shən\ *n* **1** *cap* : March 25 observed as a church festival commemorating the announcement of the Incarnation **2** : ANNOUNCEMENT

**an·nun·ci·a·tor** \ə-'nən-sē-,ā-tər\ *n* : one that annunciates; *specif* : a usu. electrically controlled signal board or indicator

**an·ode** \'a-,nōd\ *n* **1** : the positive electrode of an electrolytic cell **2** : the negative terminal of a battery **3** : the electron-collecting electrode of an electron tube — **an·od·ic** \a-'nä-dik\ *also* **an·od·al** \-'nō-dªl\ *adj*

**an·od·ize** \'a-nə-,dīz\ *vb* **-ized; -iz·ing** : to subject (a metal) to electrolytic action as the anode of a cell in order to coat with a protective or decorative film

**an·o·dyne** \'a-nə-,dīn\ *n* : something that relieves pain : a soothing agent

**anoint** \ə-'nóint\ *vb* **1** : to apply oil to esp. as a sacred rite **2** : CONSECRATE — **anoint·ment** *n*

**anom·a·lous** \ə-'nä-mə-ləs\ *adj* : deviating from a general rule : ABNORMAL

**anom·a·ly** \ə-'nä-mə-lē\ *n, pl* **-lies** : something anomalous : IRREGULARITY

**1anon** \ə-'nän\ *adv* : SOON

**2anon** *abbr* anonymous; anonymously

**anon·y·mous** \ə-'nä-ə-məs\ *adj* : of unknown or undeclared origin or authorship — **ano·nym·i·ty** \,a-nə-'ni-mə-tē\ *n* — **anon·y·mous·ly** *adv*

**anoph·e·les** \ə-'nä-fə-,lēz\ *n* [NL, genus name, fr. Gk *anōphelēs* useless, fr. *a-* not + *ophelos* advantage, help] : any of a genus of mosquitoes that includes all mosquitoes which transmit malaria to human beings

**an·o·rec·tic** \,a-nə-'rek-tik\ *adj* : ANOREXIC — **anorectic** *n*

**an·orex·ia** \,a-nə-'rek-sē-ə\ *n* **1** : loss of appetite esp. when prolonged **2** : ANOREXIA NERVOSA

**anorexia ner·vo·sa** \-,nər-'vō-sə\ *n* : a serious disorder in eating behavior marked esp. by a pathological fear of weight gain leading to faulty eating patterns, malnutrition, and usu. excessive weight loss

**an·orex·ic** \,a-nə-'rek-sik\ *adj* **1** : lacking or causing loss of appetite **2** : affected with or as if with anorexia nervosa — **anorexic** *n*

**1an·oth·er** \ə-'nə-thər\ *adj* **1** : some other ⟨do it ~ time⟩ **2** : being one in addition : one more ⟨~ piece of pie⟩

**2another** *pron* **1** : an additional one : one more **2** : one that is different from the first or present one

**ans** *abbr* answer

**1an·swer** \'an-sər\ *n* **1** : something spoken or written in reply to a question **2** : a solution of a problem

**2answer** *vb* **1** : to speak or write in reply to **2** : to be responsible **3** : to be adequate — **an·swer·er** *n*

**an·swer·able** \'an-sə-rə-bəl\ *adj* **1** : subject to taking blame or responsibility **2** : capable of being refuted

**answering machine** *n* : a machine that receives telephone calls by playing a recorded message and usu. by recording messages from callers

**answering service** *n* : a commercial service that answers telephone calls for its clients

**¹ant** \'ant\ *n* : any of a family of small social insects related to the bees and living in communities usu. in earth or wood

**²ant** *abbr* antonym

**Ant** *abbr* Antarctica

**ant-** — see ANTI-

**¹-ant** *n suffix* **1** : one that performs or promotes (a specified action) ⟨coolant⟩ **2** : thing that is acted upon (in a specified manner) ⟨inhalant⟩

**²-ant** *adj suffix* **1** : performing (a specified action) or being (in a specified condition) ⟨propellant⟩ **2** : promoting (a specified action or process) ⟨expectorant⟩

**ant·ac·id** \ant-'a-səd\ *n* : an agent that counteracts acidity — **antacid** *adj*

**an·tag·o·nism** \an-'ta-gə-ni-zəm\ *n* **1** : active opposition or hostility **2** : opposition in physiological action — **an·tag·o·nis·tic** \-,ta-gə-'nis-tik\ *adj*

**an·tag·o·nist** \-nist\ *n* : ADVERSARY, OPPONENT

**an·tag·o·nize** \an-'ta-gə-,nīz\ *vb* **-nized; -niz·ing** : to provoke the hostility of

**ant·arc·tic** \ant-'ärk-tik, -'är-tik\ *adj, often cap* : of or relating to the south pole or the region near it

**antarctic circle** *n, often cap A&C* : the parallel of latitude that is approximately 66½ degrees south of the equator

**¹an·te** \'an-tē\ *n* : a poker stake put up before the deal to build the pot; *also* : an amount paid : PRICE

**²ante** *vb* **an·ted; an·te·ing 1** : to put up (an ante) **2** : PAY

**ant·eat·er** \'ant-,ē-tər\ *n* : any of several mammals (as an aardvark) that feed mostly on ants or termites

**an·te·bel·lum** \,an-ti-'be-ləm\ *adj* : existing before a war; *esp* : existing before the U.S. Civil War of 1861-65

**an·te·ced·ent** \,an-tə-'sē-dᵊnt\ *n* **1** : a noun, pronoun, phrase, or clause referred to by a personal or relative pronoun **2** : a preceding event or cause **3** *pl* : the significant conditions of one's earlier life **4** *pl* : ANCESTORS — **antecedent** *adj*

**an·te·cham·ber** \'an-ti-,chām-bər\ *n* : ANTEROOM

**an·te·date** \'an-ti-,dāt\ *vb* **1** : to date (a paper) as of an earlier day than that on which the actual writing or signing is done **2** : to precede in time

**an·te·di·lu·vi·an** \,an-ti-də-'lü-vē-ən, -dī-\ *adj* **1** : of the period before the biblical flood **2** : ANTIQUATED, OUT-OF-DATE

**an·te·lope** \'an-tə-,lōp\ *n, pl* **-lope** *or* **-lopes** [ME, fabulous heraldic beast, prob. fr. MF *antelop* savage animal with sawlike horns, fr. ML *anthalopus*, fr. LGk *antholops*] : any of various deerlike ruminant mammals that chiefly inhabit Africa and have a slender build and horns extending upward and backward **2** : PRONGHORN

**an·te me·ri·di·em** \'an ti-ma-'ri-dē-əm\ *adj* [L] : being before noon

**an·ten·na** \an-'te-nə\ *n, pl* **-nae** \-(,)nē\ *or* **-nas** [ML, fr. L, sail yard] **1** : one of the long slender paired segmented sensory organs on the head of an arthropod (as an insect or crab) **2** *pl usu* **-nas** : a metallic device (as a rod or wire) for sending out or receiving radio waves

**an·te·pe·nult** \,an-ti-'pē-,nəlt\ *also* **an·te·pen·ul·ti·ma** \-pi-'nəl-tə-mə\ *n* : the 3d syllable of a word counting from the end — **an·te·pen·ul·ti·mate** \-pi'-nəl-tə-mət\ *adj or n*

**an·te·ri·or** \an-'tir-ē-ər\ *adj* **1** : situated before or toward the front **2** : situated near or nearer to the head **3** : coming before in time ♦ **Synonyms** PRECEDING, PREVIOUS, PRIOR, ANTECEDENT

**anterior cruciate ligament** *n* : a cross-shaped ligament of the knee that connects the tibia and femur

**an·te·room** \'an-ti-,rüm, -,rum\ *n* : a room forming the entrance to another and often used as a waiting room

**an·them** \'an-thəm\ *n* **1** : a sacred vocal composition **2** : a song or hymn of praise or gladness

**an·ther** \'an-thər\ *n* : the part of a stamen of a seed plant that produces and contains pollen

**ant·hill** \'ant-,hil\ *n* : a mound thrown up by ants or termites in digging their nest

**an·thol·o·gy** \an-'thä-lə-jē\ *n, pl* **-gies** [NL *anthologia* collection of epigrams, fr. MGk, fr. Gk, flower gathering, fr. *anthos* flower + *logia* collecting, fr. *legein* to gather] : a collection of literary selections — **an·thol·o·gist** \-jist\ *n* — **an·thol·o·gize** \-,jīz\ *vb*

**an·thra·cite** \'an-thrə-,sīt\ *n* : a hard glossy coal that burns without much smoke

**an·thrax** \'an-,thraks\ *n* : an infectious and usu. fatal bacterial disease of warm-blooded animals (as cattle and sheep) that is transmissible to humans; *also* : a bacterium causing anthrax

**an·thro·po·cen·tric** \,an-thrə-pə-'sen-trik\ *adj* : interpreting or regarding the world in terms of human values and experiences

**an·thro·poid** \'an-thrə-,pȯid\ *n* **1** : any of several large tailless apes (as a gorilla) **2** : a person resembling an ape — **anthropoid** *adj*

**an·thro·pol·o·gy** \,an-thrə-'pä-lə-jē\ *n* : the science of human beings and esp. of their physical characteristics, their origin and ancestry, their environment and social relations, and their culture — **an·thro·po·log·i·cal** \-pə-'lä-ji-kəl\ *adj* — **an·thro·pol·o·gist** \-'pä-lə-jist\ *n*

**an·thro·po·mor·phism** \,an-thrə-pə-'mȯr-,fi-zəm\ *n* : an interpretation of what is not human or personal in terms of human or personal characteristics

: HUMANIZATION — **an·thro·po·mor·phic** \-fik\ *adj*

**an·ti** \'an-,tī, -tē\ *n, pl* **antis** : one who is opposed

**anti-** \,an-ti, -tē, -,tī\ *or* **ant-** *or* **anth-** *prefix* **1** : opposite in kind, position, or action **2** : opposing : hostile toward **3** : counteractive **4** : preventive of : curative of

**an·ti·abor·tion** \,an-tē-ə-'bȯr-shən, ,an-,tī-\ *adj* : opposed to abortion — **an·ti·abor·tion·ist** \-shə-nist\ *n*

**an·ti·bal·lis·tic missile** \,an-ti-bə-'lis-tik-, ,an-,tī-\ *n* : a missile for intercepting and destroying ballistic missiles

**an·ti·bi·ot·ic** \-,bī-'ä-tik, -bē-\ *n* : a substance produced by or derived by chemical alteration of a substance produced by a microorganism (as a fungus or bacterium) that in dilute solution inhibits or kills another microorganism — **antibiotic** *adj*

**an·ti·body** \'an-ti-,bä-dē\ *n* : any of a large number of proteins of high molecular weight produced normally by specialized B cells after stimulation by an antigen and acting specifically against the antigen in an immune response

**¹an·tic** \'an-tik\ *n* [It *antico* ancient thing or person, fr. *antico* ancient, fr. L *antiquus*] : an often wildly playful or funny act or action

**²antic** *adj* **1** *archaic* : GROTESQUE **2** : PLAYFUL

**an·ti·can·cer** \,an-ti-'kan-sər, ,an-,tī-\ *adj* : used against or tending to arrest or prevent cancer ⟨~ drugs⟩

**An·ti·christ** \'an-ti-,krīst\ *n* **1** : one who denies or opposes Christ **2** : a false Christ

**an·tic·i·pate** \an-'ti-sə-,pāt\ *vb* **-pat·ed; -pat·ing 1** : to foresee and provide for beforehand ⟨~s problems⟩ **2** : to look forward to — **an·tic·i·pa·tion** \-,ti-sə-'pā-shən\ *n* — **an·tic·i·pa·to·ry** \-'ti-sə-pə-,tȯr-ē\ *adj*

**an·ti·cli·max** \,an-ti-'klī-,maks\ *n* : something (as the ending of a story) that is strikingly less important or dramatic than expected — **an·ti·cli·mac·tic** \-klī-'mak-tik\ *adj*

**an·ti·cline** \'an-ti-,klīn\ *n* : an arch of layers of rock in the earth's crust

**an·ti·co·ag·u·lant** \,an-ti-kō-'a-gyə-lənt\ *n* : a substance that hinders the clotting of blood — **anticoagulant** *adj*

**an·ti·cy·clone** \,an-ti-'sī-,klōn\ *n* : a system of winds that rotates about a center of high atmospheric pressure — **an·ti·cy·clon·ic** \-sī-'klä-nik\ *adj*

**an·ti·de·pres·sant** \,an-ti-di-'pres-°nt, ,an-,tī-\ *n* : a drug used to relieve psychic depression — **antidepressant** *adj*

**an·ti·dote** \'an-ti-,dōt\ *n* : a remedy to counteract the effects of poison

**an·ti·drug** \'an-,tī-,drəg\ *adj* : acting against or opposing illicit drugs

**an·ti·fer·til·i·ty** \,an-ti-fər-'ti-lə-tē\ *adj* : tending to reduce or destroy fertility : CONTRACEPTIVE ⟨~ agents⟩

**an·ti·freeze** \'an-ti-,frēz\ *n* : a substance added to a liquid to lower its freezing temperature

**an·ti·fun·gal** \,an-tē-'fən-gəl, ,an-,tī-\ *n* : FUNGICIDE — **antifungal** *adj*

**an·ti·gen** \'an-ti-jən\ *n* : any substance (as a toxin) foreign to the body that induces an immune response — **an·ti·gen·ic** \,an-ti-'je-nik\ *adj* — **an·ti·ge·nic·i·ty** \-jə-'ni-sə-tē\ *n*

**an·ti·grav·i·ty** \,an-ti-'gra-və-tē, ,an-,tī-\ *adj* : reducing or canceling the effect of gravity

**an·ti·he·ro** \'an-ti-,hē-rō, 'an-,tī-\ *n* : a protagonist who is notably lacking in heroic qualities (as courage)

**an·ti·his·ta·mine** \,an-ti-'his-tə-,mēn, ,an-,tī-, -mən\ *n* : any of various drugs used in treating allergies and colds — **antihistamine** *adj*

**an·ti·hy·per·ten·sive** \-,hī-pər-'ten-siv\ *n* : a substance that is effective against high blood pressure — **antihypertensive** *adj*

**an·ti·in·flam·ma·to·ry** \-in-'fla-mə-,tȯr-ē\ *adj* : counteracting inflammation — **anti–inflammatory** *n*

**an·ti·in·tel·lec·tu·al** \-,in-tə-'lek-chə-wəl\ *adj* : opposing or hostile to intellectuals or to an intellectual view or approach

**an·ti·lock** \'an-ti-,läk, 'an-,tī-\ *adj* : being a braking system designed to prevent the wheels from locking

**an·ti·log·a·rithm** \,an-ti-'lȯ-gə-,ri-thəm, ,an-,tī-, -'lä-\ *n* : the number corresponding to a given logarithm ⟨if the logarithm in base *x* of *a* equals *b* then the antilogarithm in base *x* of *b* equals *a*⟩

**an·ti·ma·cas·sar** \,an-ti-mə-'ka-sər\ *n* : a cover to protect the back or arms of furniture

**an·ti·mat·ter** \'an-ti-,ma-tər, 'an-,tī-\ *n* : matter composed of antiparticles

**an·ti·mo·ny** \'an-tə-,mō-nē\ *n* : a brittle silvery white metallic chemical element used esp. in alloys

**an·ti·neu·tron** \,an-ti-'nü-,trän, ,an-,tī-, -'nyü-\ *n* : the antiparticle of the neutron

**an·ti·no·mi·an** \,an-ti-'nō-mē-ən\ *n* : one who denies the validity of moral laws

**an·tin·o·my** \an-'ti-nə-mē\ *n, pl* **-mies** : a contradiction between two seemingly true statements

**an·ti·nov·el** \'an-ti-,nä-vəl, 'an-,tī-\ *n* : a work of fiction that lacks all or most of the traditional features of the novel

**an·ti·nu·cle·ar** \,an-ti-'nü-klē-ər, -'nyü-\ *adj* : opposing the use or production of nuclear power

---

| | | | |
|---|---|---|---|
| antiaging | antibacterial | anticommunist | anti-imperialism |
| anti-AIDS | anticapitalist | antidemocratic | anti-imperialist |
| antiaircraft | anti-Catholic | antidiscrimination | antiknock |
| antialcohol | anticholesterol | antiestablishment | antilabor |
| anti-American | anticlerical | antifascist | antimalarial |
| antianxiety | anticolonial | antigovernment | antimicrobial |
| antiapartheid | anticommunism | anti-HIV | antinausea |

**an·ti·ox·i·dant** \,an-tē-'äk-sə-dənt, ,an-
,tī-\ *n* : a substance that inhibits oxidation — **antioxidant** *adj*

**an·ti·par·ti·cle** \'an-ti-,pär-ti-kəl, 'an-,tī-\
*n* : a subatomic particle identical to another subatomic particle in mass but opposite to it in electric and magnetic properties

**an·ti·pas·to** \,an-ti-'pas-tō, ,än-ti-'päs-\ *n*,
*pl* -**ti** \-(,)tē\ : any of various typically Italian hors d'oeuvres

**an·tip·a·thy** \an-'ti-pə-thē\ *n*, *pl* -**thies** 1
: settled aversion or dislike 2 : an object
of aversion — **an·ti·pa·thet·ic** \,an-ti-pə-
'the-tik\ *adj*

**an·ti·per·son·nel** \,an-ti-,pər-sə-'nel, ,an-
,tī-\ *adj* : designed for use against military
personnel 〈~ mine〉

**an·ti·per·spi·rant** \-'pər-spə-rənt\ *n* : a
preparation used to reduce perspiration

**an·tiph·o·nal** \an-'ti-fə-n°l\ *adj* : performed by two alternating groups — **an·
tiph·o·nal·ly** *adv*

**an·ti·pode** \'an-tə-,pōd\ *n*, *pl* **an·tip·o·
des** \an-'ti-pə-,dēz\ [ME *antipodes*, pl.,
persons dwelling at opposite points on the
globe, fr. L, fr. Gk, fr. pl. of *antipod-*, *an-
tipous* with feet opposite, fr. *anti-* against
+ *pod-*, *pous* foot] : the parts of the earth
diametrically opposite — usu. used in pl.
— **an·tip·o·dal** \an-'ti-pə-d°l\ *adj* — **an·
tip·o·de·an** \(,)an-,ti-pə-'dē-ən\ *adj*

**an·ti·pol·lu·tion** \,an-ti-pə-'lü-shən\ *adj*
: designed to prevent, reduce, or eliminate pollution 〈~ laws〉

**an·ti·pope** \'an-ti-,pōp\ *n* : one elected or
claiming to be pope in opposition to the
pope canonically chosen

**an·ti·pro·ton** \,an-ti-'prō-,tän\ *n* : the antiparticle of the proton

**an·ti·psy·chot·ic** \,an-tē-sī-'kä-tik\ *adj*
: any of the powerful tranquilizers used
to treat psychosis — **antipsychotic** *adj*

**an·ti·quar·i·an** \,an-tə-'kwer-ē-ən\ *adj* 1
: of or relating to antiquities 2 : dealing
in old books — **antiquarian** *n* — **an·ti·
quar·i·an·ism** *n*

**an·ti·quary** \'an-tə-,kwer-ē\ *n*, *pl* -**quar·
ies** : a person who collects or studies antiquities

**an·ti·quat·ed** \'an-tə-,kwā-təd\ *adj* : OUT-
OF-DATE, OLD-FASHIONED

**¹an·tique** \an-'tēk\ *n* : an object made in a
bygone period

**²antique** *adj* 1 : belonging to antiquity 2
: OLD-FASHIONED 3 : of a bygone style
or period

**³antique** *vb* -**tiqued**; -**tiqu·ing** 1 : to finish or refinish in antique style : give an
appearance of age to 2 : to shop around
for antiques — **an·tiqu·er** *n*

**an·tiq·ui·ty** \an-'ti-kwə-tē\ *n*, *pl* -**ties** 1
: ancient times 2 : great age 3 *pl* : relics
of ancient times 4 *pl* : matters relating to
ancient culture

**an·ti·ret·ro·vi·ral** \,an-tē-'re-trō-,vī-rəl,
,an-tī-\ *adj* : effective against retroviruses 〈~ drugs〉 — **antiretroviral** *n*

**antis** *pl of* ANTI

**an·ti·Sem·i·tism** \,an-ti-'se-mə-,ti-zəm,
,an-,tī-\ *n* : hostility toward Jews as a religious or social minority — **an·ti·Sem·
ite** \-'se-,mīt\ *n* — **an·ti·Se·mit·ic** \-sə-
'mi-tik\ *adj*

**an·ti·sep·tic** \,an-tə-'sep-tik\ *adj* 1 : killing or checking the growth of germs that
cause decay or infection 2 : scrupulously
clean : ASEPTIC 3 : coldly impersonal 〈an
~ greeting〉 — **antiseptic** *n* — **an·ti·
sep·ti·cal·ly** *adv*

**an·ti·se·rum** \'an-ti-,sir-əm, 'an-,tī-\ *n* : a
serum containing antibodies

**an·ti·so·cial** \,an-ti-'sō-shəl\ *adj* 1 : disliking the society of others 2 : contrary
or hostile to the well-being of society
〈crime is ~〉; *esp* : deviating sharply
from the social norm — **an·ti·so·cial·ly**
*adv*

**an·tith·e·sis** \an-'ti-thə-səs\ *n*, *pl* -**e·ses**
\-,sēz\ 1 : the opposition or contrast of
ideas 2 : the direct opposite

**an·ti·thet·i·cal** \,an-tə-'the-ti-kəl\ *also* **an·
ti·thet·ic** \-'the-tik\ *adj* : constituting or
marked by antithesis — **an·ti·thet·i·cal·
ly** \-ti-k(ə-)lē\ *adv*

**an·ti·tox·in** \,an-ti-'täk-sən\ *n* : an antibody that is able to neutralize a particular toxin or disease-causing agent; *also*
: an antiserum containing an antitoxin

**an·ti·trust** \,an-ti-'trəst\ *adj* : of or relating to legislation against trusts; *also*
: consisting of laws to protect trade and
commerce from unlawful restraints and
monopolies or unfair business practices

**an·ti·ven·in** \-'ve-nən\ *n* : an antitoxin to
a venom; *also* : a serum containing such
antitoxin

**ant·ler** \'ant-lər\ *n* [ME *aunteler*, fr. AF
*antiler*, fr. VL \**anteocularis* located before the eye, fr. L *ante-* before + *oculus*
eye] : one of the paired deciduous solid
bone processes on the head of a deer; *also*
: a branch of this — **ant·lered** \-lərd\ *adj*

**ant lion** *n* : any of various insects having
a long-jawed larva that digs a conical pit
in which it lies in wait for insects (as ants)
on which it feeds

**an·to·nym** \'an-tə-,nim\ *n* : a word of opposite meaning

**ant·sy** \'ant-sē\ *adj* 1 : RESTLESS, IMPA-
TIENT 〈~ children〉 2 : APPREHENSIVE
〈~ investors〉

**anus** \'ā-nəs\ *n* [L] : the lower or posteri-
or opening of the alimentary canal

**an·vil** \'an-vəl\ *n* 1 : a heavy iron block
on which metal is shaped 2 : INCUS

**anx·i·ety** \aŋ-'zī-ə-tē\ *n*, *pl* -**et·ies** 1
: painful uneasiness of mind usu. over an
anticipated ill 2 : abnormal apprehension and fear often accompanied by
physiological signs (as sweating and increased pulse), by doubt about the nature
and reality of the threat itself, and by
self-doubt

**anx·ious** \'aŋk-shəs\ *adj* 1 : uneasy in
mind : WORRIED 〈~ parents〉 2 : ear-

---

antipoverty          antistatic          antitank          antiviral
antislavery          antisubmarine       antitumor         antiwar
antispasmodic

nestly wishing : EAGER ⟨~ to leave⟩ — **anx·ious·ly** *adv*

**¹any** \'e-nē\ *adj* **1** : one chosen at random **2** : of whatever number or quantity

**²any** *pron* **1** : any one or ones ⟨take ~ of the books you like⟩ **2** : any amount ⟨~ of the money not used is to be returned⟩

**³any** *adv* : to any extent or degree : AT ALL ⟨could not walk ~ farther⟩

**any·body** \-,bä-dē, -bə-dē\ *pron* : ANYONE

**any·how** \-,haù\ *adv* **1** : in any way **2** : NEVERTHELESS; *also* : in any case

**any·more** \,e-nē-'mòr\ *adv* **1** : any longer ⟨won't bother you ~⟩ **2** : at the present time

**any·one** \'e-nē-(,)wən\ *pron* : any person

**any·place** \-,plās\ *adv* : ANYWHERE 1

**any·thing** \-,thiŋ\ *pron* : any thing whatever

**any·time** \'e-nē-,tīm\ *adv* : at any time whatever

**any·way** \-,wā\ *adv* : ANYHOW

**any·where** \-,hwer\ *adv* **1** : in or to any place **2** : to any extent ⟨not ~ near done⟩

**any·wise** \-,wīz\ *adv* : in any way whatever

**A–OK** \,ā-ō-'kā\ *adv or adj* : very definitely OK

**A1** \'ā-'wən\ *adj* : of the finest quality

**aor·ta** \ā-'òr-tə\ *n, pl* **-tas** *or* **-tae** \-tē\ : the main artery that carries blood from the heart — **aor·tic** \-tik\ *adj*

**ap** *abbr* **1** apostle **2** apothecaries'

**AP** *abbr* **1** American plan **2** Associated Press

**apace** \ə-'pās\ *adv* : SWIFTLY

**Apache** \ə-'pa-chē\ *n, pl* **Apache** *or* **Apach·es** \-'pa-chēz, -'pa-shəz\ : a member of an American Indian people of the southwestern U.S.; *also* : any of the languages of the Apache people — **Apach·e·an** \ə-'pa-chē-ən\ *adj or n*

**apanage** *var of* APPANAGE

**apart** \ə-'pärt\ *adv* **1** : separately in place or time **2** : ASIDE **3** : in two or more parts : to pieces

**apart·heid** \ə-'pär-,tāt, -,tīt\ *n* [Afrikaans] : a policy of racial segregation formerly practiced in the Republic of So. Africa

**apart·ment** \ə-'pärt-mənt\ *n* : a room or set of rooms occupied as a dwelling; *also* : a building divided into individual dwelling units

**ap·a·thy** \'a-pə-thē\ *n* **1** : lack of emotion **2** : lack of interest : INDIFFERENCE — **ap·a·thet·ic** \,a-pə-'the-tik\ *adj* — **ap·a·thet·i·cal·ly** \-ti-k(ə-)lē\ *adv*

**ap·a·tite** \'a-pə-,tīt\ *n* : any of a group of minerals that are phosphates of calcium and occur esp. in phosphate rock and in bones and teeth

**apato·sau·rus** \ə-,pa-tə-'sòr-əs\ *n* : BRONTOSAURUS

**APB** *abbr* all points bulletin

**¹ape** \'āp\ *n* **1** : any of the larger tailless primates (as a baboon or gorilla); *also* : MONKEY **2** : MIMIC, IMITATOR; *also* : a large uncouth person

**²ape** *vb* **aped; ap·ing** : IMITATE, MIMIC

**ape–man** \'āp-,man\ *n* : a primate inter-mediate in character between Homo sapiens and the higher apes

**aper·çu** \,a-pər-'sü, *n, pl* **aperçus** \-'süz\ : an immediate impression; *esp* : INSIGHT

**aper·i·tif** \ä-,per-ə-'tēf\ *n* : an alcoholic drink taken as an appetizer

**ap·er·ture** \'a-pər-,chùr, -chər\ *n* : OPENING, HOLE

**apex** \'ā-,peks\ *n, pl* **apex·es** *or* **api·ces** \'ā-pə-,sēz, 'a-\ : the highest point : PEAK

**apha·sia** \ə-'fā-zh(ē-)ə\ *n* : loss or impairment of the power to use or comprehend words — **apha·sic** \-zik\ *adj or n*

**aph·elion** \a-'fēl-yən\ *n, pl* **-elia** \-yə\ [NL, fr. *apo-* away from + Gk *hēlios* sun] : the point in an object's orbit most distant from the sun

**aphid** \'ā-fəd\ *n* : any of numerous small insects that suck the juices of plants

**aphis** \'ā-fəs, 'a-\ *n, pl* **aphi·des** \-fə-,dēz\ : APHID

**aph·o·rism** \'a-fə-,ri-zəm\ *n* : a short saying stating a general truth : MAXIM — **aph·o·ris·tic** \,a-fə-'ris-tik\ *adj*

**aph·ro·di·si·ac** \,a-frə-'di-zē-,ak, -'dē-zē-\ *n* : an agent that excites sexual desire — **aphrodisiac** *adj*

**api·ary** \'ā-pē-,er-ē\ *n, pl* **-ar·ies** : a place where bees are kept — **api·a·rist** \'pē-ə-rist\ *n*

**api·cal** \'ā-pi-kəl, 'a-\ *adj* : of, relating to, or situated at an apex — **api·cal·ly** \-k(ə-)lē\ *adv*

**apiece** \ə-'pēs\ *adv* : for each one

**aplen·ty** \ə-'plen-tē\ *adj* : being in plenty or abundance

**aplomb** \ə-'pläm, -'pləm\ *n* [F, lit., perpendicularity, fr. MF, fr. *a plomb*, lit., according to the plummet] : complete composure or self-assurance

**APO** *abbr* army post office

**Apoc** *abbr* **1** Apocalypse **2** Apocrypha

**apoc·a·lypse** \ə-'pä-kə-,lips\ *n* **1** : a writing prophesying a cataclysm in which evil forces are destroyed **2** *cap* — see BIBLE table — **apoc·a·lyp·tic** \-,pä-kə-'lip-tik\ *also* **apoc·a·lyp·ti·cal** \-ti-kəl\ *adj*

**Apoc·ry·pha** \ə-'pä-krə-fə\ *n* **1** *not cap* : writings of dubious authenticity **2** : books included in the Septuagint and Vulgate but excluded from the Jewish and Protestant canons of the Old Testament — see BIBLE table **3** : early Christian writings not included in the New Testament

**apoc·ry·phal** \-fəl\ *adj* **1** : not canonical : SPURIOUS **2** *often cap* : of or resembling the Apocrypha — **apoc·ry·phal·ly** *adv* — **apoc·ry·phal·ness** *n*

**apo·gee** \'a-pə-(,)jē\ *n* [F *apogée*, fr. NL *apogaeum*, fr. Gk *apogaion*, fr. *apo* away from + *gē, gaia* earth] : the point at which an orbiting object is farthest from the body being orbited

**apo·lit·i·cal** \,ā-pə-'li-ti-kəl\ *adj* **1** : having an aversion for or no interest in political affairs **2** : having no political significance — **apo·lit·i·cal·ly** \-k(ə-)lē\ *adv*

**apol·o·get·ic** \ə-,pä-lə-'je-tik\ *adj* : expressing apology — **apol·o·get·i·cal·ly** \-ti-k(ə-)lē\ *adv*

**apo·lo·gia** \,a-pə-'lō-j(ē-)ə\ *n* : APOLOGY;

*esp* : an argument in support or justification

**apol·o·gise** *Brit var of* APOLOGIZE

**apol·o·gize** \ə-'pä-lə-ˌjīz\ *vb* **-gized; -gizing** : to make an apology : express regret — **apol·o·gist** \-jist\ *n*

**apol·o·gy** \ə-'pä-lə-jē\ *n, pl* **-gies** 1 : a formal justification : DEFENSE 2 : an expression of regret for a wrong

**ap·o·plexy** \'a-pə-ˌplek-sē\ *n* : STROKE 3 — **ap·o·plec·tic** \ˌa-pə-'plek-tik\ *adj*

**ap·o·pto·sis** \ˌa-pəp-'tō-səs, -pə-'tō-\ *n, pl* **-pto·ses** \-ˌsēz\ : a genetically directed process of cell self-destruction

**aport** \ə-'pȯrt\ *adv* : on or toward the left side of a ship

**apos·ta·sy** \ə-'päs-tə-sē\ *n, pl* **-sies** : a renunciation or abandonment of a former loyalty (as to a religion) — **apos·tate** \ə-'päs-ˌtāt, -tət\ *adj or n*

**a pos·te·ri·o·ri** \ˌä-pō-ˌstir-ē-'ȯr-ē\ *adj* [L, lit., from the latter] : relating to or derived by reasoning from observed facts — **a posteriori** *adv*

**apos·tle** \ə-'pä-səl\ *n* 1 : one of the group composed of Jesus' 12 original disciples and Paul 2 : the first prominent missionary to a region or group 3 : a person who initiates or first advocates a great reform — **apos·tle·ship** *n*

**ap·os·tol·ic** \ˌa-pə-'stä-lik\ *adj* 1 : of or relating to an apostle or to the New Testament apostles 2 : of or relating to a succession of spiritual authority from the apostles 3 : PAPAL ⟨~ authority⟩

¹**apos·tro·phe** \ə-'päs-trə-(ˌ)fē\ *n* : the rhetorical addressing of a usu. absent person or a usu. personified thing (as in "O grave, where is thy victory?")

²**apostrophe** *n* : a punctuation mark used esp. to indicate the possessive case or the omission of a letter or figure

**apos·tro·phise** *Brit var of* APOSTROPHIZE

**apos·tro·phize** \ə-'päs-trə-ˌfīz\ *vb* **-phized; -phiz·ing** : to address as if present or capable of understanding

**apothecaries' weight** *n* : a system of weights based on the troy pound and ounce and used chiefly by pharmacists — see WEIGHT table

**apoth·e·cary** \ə-'pä-thə-ˌker-ē\ *n, pl* **-car·ies** [ME *apothecarie*, fr. ML *apothecarius*, fr. LL, shopkeeper, fr. L *apotheca* storehouse, fr. Gk *apothēkē*, fr. *apotithenai* to put away] : DRUGGIST

**ap·o·thegm** \'a-pə-ˌthem\ *n* : APHORISM

**apo·the·o·sis** \ə-ˌpä-thē-'ō-səs, ˌa-pə-'thē-ə-səs\ *n, pl* **-o·ses** \-ˌsēz\ 1 : DEIFICATION 2 : the perfect example

¹**app** \'ap\ *n* : APPLICATION 6

²**app** *abbr* 1 apparatus 2 appendix

**ap·pall** *also* **ap·pal** \ə-'pȯl\ *vb* **ap·palled; ap·pall·ing** : to overcome with horror : DISMAY

**Ap·pa·loo·sa** \ˌa-pə-'lü-sə\ *n* : any of a breed of saddle horses developed in western No. America and usu. having a white or solid-colored coat with small spots

**ap·pa·nage** *also* **a·pa·nage** \'a-pə-nij\ *n* 1 : provision (as a grant of land) made by a sovereign or legislative body for depen-

dent members of the royal family 2 : a rightful adjunct

**ap·pa·ra·tus** \ˌa-pə-'ra-təs, -'rä-\ *n, pl* **-tus·es** *or* **-tus** [L] 1 : a set of materials or equipment for a particular use 2 : a complex machine or device : MECHANISM 3 : the organization of a political party or underground movement

¹**ap·par·el** \ə-'per-əl\ *vb* **-eled** *or* **-elled; -el·ing** *or* **-el·ling** 1 : CLOTHE 2 : ADORN

²**apparel** *n* : CLOTHING, DRESS

**ap·par·ent** \ə-'per-ənt\ *adj* 1 : open to view : VISIBLE 2 : EVIDENT, OBVIOUS 3 : appearing as real or true : SEEMING

**ap·par·ent·ly** \-lē\ *adv* : it seems apparent

**ap·pa·ri·tion** \ˌa-pə-'ri-shən\ *n* : a supernatural appearance : GHOST

¹**ap·peal** \ə-'pēl\ *vb* 1 : to take steps to have (a case) reheard in a higher court 2 : to plead for help, corroboration, or decision 3 : to arouse a sympathetic response — **appeal** *n*

**ap·pear** \ə-'pir\ *vb* 1 : to become visible 2 : to come formally before an authority 3 : SEEM 4 : to become evident 5 : to come before the public

**ap·pear·ance** \ə-'pir-əns\ *n* 1 : outward aspect : LOOK 2 : the act of appearing 3 : PHENOMENON

**ap·pease** \ə-'pēz\ *vb* **ap·peased; ap·peas·ing** 1 : to cause to subside : ALLAY 2 : PACIFY, CONCILIATE; *esp* : to buy off by concessions — **ap·pease·ment** *n* — **ap·peas·able** \-'pē-zə-bəl\ *adj*

**ap·pel·lant** \ə-'pe-lənt\ *n* : one who appeals esp. from a judicial decision

**ap·pel·late** \ə-'pe-lət\ *adj* : having power to review decisions of a lower court

**ap·pel·la·tion** \ˌa-pə-'lā-shən\ *n* : NAME, DESIGNATION

**ap·pel·lee** \ˌa-pə-'lē\ *n* : one against whom an appeal is taken

**ap·pend** \ə-'pend\ *vb* : to attach esp. as something additional : AFFIX

**ap·pend·age** \ə-'pen-dij\ *n* 1 : something appended to a principal or greater thing 2 : a projecting part (as an antenna) of an animal or plant body; *esp* : an arm, leg, or similar part ♦ **Synonyms** ACCESSORY, ADJUNCT, APPENDIX, APPURTENANCE

**ap·pen·dec·to·my** \ˌa-pən-'dek-tə-mē\ *n, pl* **-mies** : surgical removal of the intestinal appendix

**ap·pen·di·ci·tis** \ə-ˌpen-də-'sī-təs\ *n* : inflammation of the intestinal appendix

**ap·pen·dix** \ə-'pen-diks\ *n, pl* **-dix·es** *or* **-di·ces** \-də-ˌsēz\ [L] 1 : supplementary matter added at the end of a book 2 : a narrow blind tube usu. about three or four inches long that extends from the cecum in the lower right-hand part of the abdomen

**ap·per·tain** \ˌa-pər-'tān\ *vb* : to belong as a rightful part or privilege

**ap·pe·tis·er, ap·pe·tis·ing** *Brit var of* APPETIZER, APPETIZING

**ap·pe·tite** \'a-pə-ˌtīt\ *n* [ME *apetit*, fr. AF, fr. L *appetitus*, fr. *appetere* to strive after, fr. *ad-* to + *petere* to go to] 1 : natural desire for satisfying some want or need esp. for food 2 : TASTE, PREFERENCE ⟨an ~ for adventure⟩

**ap·pe·tiz·er** \'a-pə-ˌtī-zər\ *n* : a food or drink taken just before a meal to stimulate the appetite

**ap·pe·tiz·ing** \-ziŋ\ *adj* : tempting to the appetite — **ap·pe·tiz·ing·ly** *adv*

**appl** *abbr* applied

**ap·plaud** \ə-'plȯd\ *vb* : to show approval esp. by clapping

**ap·plause** \ə-'plȯz\ *n* : approval publicly expressed (as by clapping)

**ap·ple** \'a-pəl\ *n* : a rounded fruit with firm white flesh and a seedy core; *also* : a tree that bears this fruit

**ap·ple·jack** \-ˌjak\ *n* : a liquor distilled from fermented cider

**ap·plet** \'a-plət\ *n* : a short computer program esp. for performing a simple specific task

**ap·pli·ance** \ə-'plī-əns\ *n* **1** : INSTRUMENT, DEVICE **2** : a piece of household equipment (as a stove or toaster) operated by gas or electricity

**ap·pli·ca·ble** \'a-pli-kə-bəl, ə-'pli-kə-\ *adj* : capable of being applied : RELEVANT — **ap·pli·ca·bil·i·ty** \ˌa-pli-kə-'bi-lə-tē, ə-ˌpli-kə-\ *n*

**ap·pli·cant** \'a-pli-kənt\ *n* : one who applies ⟨a job ~⟩

**ap·pli·ca·tion** \ˌa-plə-'kā-shən\ *n* **1** : the act of applying **2** : assiduous attention **3** : REQUEST; *also* : a form used in making a request **4** : something placed or spread on a surface **5** : capacity for use **6** : a program (as a word processor) that performs one of a computer's major tasks

**ap·pli·ca·tor** \'a-plə-ˌkā-tər\ *n* : a device for applying a substance (as medicine or polish)

**ap·plied** \ə-'plīd\ *adj* : put to practical use ⟨~ art⟩

**ap·pli·qué** \ˌa-plə-'kā\ *n* [F] : a fabric decoration cut out and fastened to a larger piece of material — **appliqué** *vb*

**ap·ply** \ə-'plī\ *vb* **ap·plied; ap·ply·ing 1** : to put to practical use **2** : to place in contact : put or spread on a surface **3** : to employ with close attention **4** : to have reference or connection **5** : to submit a request

**ap·point** \ə-'pȯint\ *vb* **1** : to fix or set officially ⟨~ a day for trial⟩ **2** : to name officially **3** : to fit out : EQUIP

**ap·poin·tee** \ə-ˌpȯin-'tē, ˌa-\ *n* : a person appointed

**ap·point·ive** \ə-'pȯin-tiv\ *adj* : subject to appointment

**ap·point·ment** \ə-'pȯint-mənt\ *n* **1** : the act of appointing **2** : an arrangement for a meeting **3** *pl* : FURNISHINGS, EQUIPMENT **4** : a nonelective office or position

**ap·por·tion** \ə-'pȯr-shən\ *vb* : to distribute proportionately : ALLOT — **ap·por·tion·ment** *n*

**ap·po·site** \'a-pə-zət\ *adj* : APPROPRIATE, RELEVANT ⟨an ~ quotation⟩ — **ap·po·site·ly** *adv* — **ap·po·site·ness** *n*

**ap·po·si·tion** \ˌa-pə-'zi-shən\ *n* : a grammatical construction in which a noun or pronoun is followed by another that has the same referent (as *the poet* and *Burns* in "a biography of the poet Burns")

**ap·pos·i·tive** \ə-'pä-zə-tiv, a-\ *adj* : of, relating to, or standing in grammatical apposition — **appositive** *n*

**ap·praise** \ə-'prāz\ *vb* **ap·praised; ap·prais·ing** : to set a value on — **ap·prais·al** \-'prā-zəl\ *n* — **ap·prais·er** *n*

**ap·pre·cia·ble** \ə-'prē-shə-bəl\ *adj* : large enough to be recognized and measured — **ap·pre·cia·bly** *adv*

**ap·pre·ci·ate** \ə-'prē-shē-ˌāt\ *vb* **-at·ed; -at·ing 1** : to value justly **2** : to be aware of **3** : to be grateful for **4** : to increase in value — **ap·pre·ci·a·tion** \-ˌprē-shē-'ā-shən\ *n*

**ap·pre·cia·tive** \ə-'prē-shə-tiv, -shē-ˌāt-\ *adj* : having or showing appreciation — **ap·pre·cia·tive·ly** *adv*

**ap·pre·hend** \ˌa-pri-'hend\ *vb* **1** : ARREST **2** : to become aware of **3** : to look forward to with dread **4** : UNDERSTAND — **ap·pre·hen·sion** \-'hen-chən\ *n*

**ap·pre·hen·sive** \-'hen-siv\ *adj* : viewing the future with anxiety — **ap·pre·hen·sive·ly** *adv* — **ap·pre·hen·sive·ness** *n*

¹**ap·pren·tice** \ə-'pren-təs\ *n* **1** : a person learning a craft under a skilled worker **2** : BEGINNER — **ap·pren·tice·ship** *n*

²**apprentice** *vb* **-ticed; -tic·ing** : to bind or set at work as an apprentice

**ap·prise** \ə-'prīz\ *vb* **ap·prised; ap·pris·ing** : INFORM ⟨*apprised* him of his rights⟩

**ap·proach** \ə-'prōch\ *vb* **1** : to move nearer to ⟨~ the bench⟩ **2** : to be almost the same as **3** : to make advances to esp. for the purpose of creating a desired result **4** : to take preliminary steps toward ⟨~ the subject carefully⟩ — **approach** *n* — **ap·proach·able** *adj*

**ap·pro·ba·tion** \ˌa-prə-'bā-shən\ *n* : APPROVAL

¹**ap·pro·pri·ate** \ə-'prō-prē-ˌāt\ *vb* **-at·ed; -at·ing 1** : to take possession of **2** : to set apart for a particular use

²**ap·pro·pri·ate** \ə-'prō-prē-ət\ *adj* : fitted to a purpose or use : SUITABLE ♦ *Synonyms* PROPER, FIT, APT, BEFITTING — **ap·pro·pri·ate·ly** *adv* — **ap·pro·pri·ate·ness** *n*

**ap·pro·pri·a·tion** \ə-ˌprō-prē-'ā-shən\ *n* : something (as money) set aside for formal action for a specific use

**ap·prov·al** \ə-'prü-vəl\ *n* : an act of approving — **on approval** : subject to a prospective buyer's acceptance or refusal

**ap·prove** \ə-'prüv\ *vb* **ap·proved; ap·prov·ing 1** : to have or express a favorable opinion of **2** : to accept as satisfactory : RATIFY ⟨~ the treaty⟩

**approx** *abbr* approximate; approximately

¹**ap·prox·i·mate** \ə-'präk-sə-mət\ *adj* : nearly correct or exact ⟨an ~ count⟩ — **ap·prox·i·mate·ly** *adv*

²**ap·prox·i·mate** \-ˌmāt\ *vb* **-mat·ed; -mat·ing** : to come or bring near or close — **ap·prox·i·ma·tion** \ə-ˌpräk-sə-'mā-shən\ *n*

**appt** *abbr* appoint; appointed; appointment

**ap·pur·te·nance** \ə-'pərt-nəns, -'pər-tə-nəns\ *n* : something that belongs to or goes with another thing ♦ *Synonyms* ACCESSORY, ADJUNCT, APPENDAGE, AP-

PENDIX — **ap·pur·te·nant** \ə-ˈpərt-nənt, -ˈpərt-ə-nənt\ *adj*

**Apr** *abbr* April

**APR** *abbr* annual percentage rate

**apri·cot** \ˈa-prə-ˌkät, ˈä-\ *n* [alter. of earlier *abrecock*, ultim. fr. Ar *al-birqūq*, ultim. fr. L (*persicum*) *praecox*, lit., early-ripening (peach)] : an oval orange-colored fruit resembling the related peach and plum in flavor; *also* : a tree bearing apricots

**April** \ˈā-prəl\ *n* [ME, fr. AF & L; AF *avrill*, fr. L *Aprilis*] : the 4th month of the year

**a pri·o·ri** \ˌä-prē-ˈȯr-ē\ *adj* [L, from the former] **1** : characterized by or derived by reasoning from self-evident propositions **2** : independent of experience — **a priori** *adv*

**apron** \ˈā-prən\ *n* [ME, alter. (fr. misdivision of *a napron*) of *napron*, fr. MF *naperon*, dim. of *nape* cloth, modif. of L *mappa* napkin] **1** : a garment tied over the front of the body to protect the clothes **2** : a paved area for parking or handling airplanes — **aproned** *adj*

**¹ap·ro·pos** \ˌa-prə-ˈpō, ˈa-prə-ˌpō\ *adv* [F *à propos*, lit., to the purpose] **1** : OPPORTUNELY **2** : in passing : INCIDENTALLY

**²apropos** *adj* : being to the point

**apropos of** *prep* : with regard to

**apse** \ˈaps\ *n* : a projecting usu. semicircular and vaulted part of a building (as a church)

**¹apt** \ˈapt\ *adj* **1** : well adapted : SUITABLE **2** : having an habitual tendency : LIKELY **3** : quick to learn — **apt·ly** *adv* — **apt·ness** \ˈapt-nəs\ *n*

**²apt** *abbr* **1** apartment **2** aptitude

**ap·ti·tude** \ˈap-tə-ˌtüd, -ˌtyüd\ *n* **1** : natural ability : TALENT **2** : capacity for learning **3** : APPROPRIATENESS

**aqua** \ˈa-kwə, ˈä-\ *n* : a light greenish blue color

**aqua·cul·ture** \ˈa-kwə-ˌkəl-chər, ˈä-\ *n* : the cultivation of aquatic organisms (as fish or shellfish) for human use esp. as food — **aqua·cul·tur·ist** \-chə-rist\ *n*

**aqua·ma·rine** \ˌa-kwə-mə-ˈrēn, ˌä-\ *n* **1** : a bluish green gem **2** : a pale blue to light greenish blue

**aqua·naut** \ˈa-kwə-ˌnȯt, ˈä-\ *n* : a person who lives in an underwater shelter for an extended period

**aqua·plane** \-ˌplān\ *n* : a board towed behind a motorboat and ridden by a person standing on it — **aquaplane** *vb*

**aqua re·gia** \ˌa-kwə-ˈrē-j(ē-)ə\ *n* [NL, lit., royal water] : a mixture of nitric and hydrochloric acids that dissolves gold or platinum

**aquar·i·um** \ə-ˈkwer-ē-əm\ *n, pl* **-i·ums** or **-ia** \-ē-ə\ **1** : a container (as a glass tank) in which living aquatic animals or plants are kept **2** : a place where aquatic animals and plants are kept and shown

**Aquar·i·us** \ə-ˈkwer-ē-əs\ *n* [L, lit., water carrier] **1** : a zodiacal constellation between Capricorn and Pisces usu. pictured as a man pouring water **2** : the 11th sign of the zodiac in astrology; *also* : one born under this sign

**¹aquat·ic** \ə-ˈkwä-tik, -ˈkwa-\ *adj* **1** : growing or living in or frequenting water **2** : performed in or on water

**²aquatic** *n* : an aquatic animal or plant

**aqua·vit** \ˈä-kwə-ˌvēt\ *n* : a clear liquor flavored with caraway seeds

**aqua vi·tae** \ˌa-kwə-ˈvī-tē, ˌä-\ *n* [ME, fr. ML, lit., water of life] : a strong alcoholic liquor (as brandy)

**aq·ue·duct** \ˈa-kwə-ˌdəkt\ *n* **1** : a conduit for carrying running water **2** : a structure carrying a canal over a river or hollow **3** : a passage in a bodily part

**aque·ous** \ˈā-kwē-əs, ˈa-\ *adj* **1** : WATERY **2** : made of, by, or with water

**aqueous humor** *n* : a clear fluid occupying the space between the lens and the cornea of the eye

**aqui·fer** \ˈa-kwə-fər, ˈä-\ *n* : a water-bearing stratum of permeable rock, sand, or gravel

**aq·ui·line** \ˈa-kwə-ˌlīn, -lən\ *adj* **1** : of or resembling an eagle **2** : hooked like an eagle's beak ⟨an ~ nose⟩

**ar** *abbr* arrival; arrive

**Ar** *symbol* argon

**AR** *abbr* Arkansas

**-ar** *adj suffix* : of or relating to ⟨molecular⟩ : being ⟨spectacular⟩ : resembling ⟨oracular⟩

**Ar·ab** \ˈa-rəb\ *n* **1** : a member of a Semitic people of the Arabian peninsula in southwestern Asia **2** : a member of an Arabic-speaking people — **Arab** *adj* — **Ara·bi·an** \ə-ˈrā-bē-ən\ *adj or n*

**ar·a·besque** \ˌa-rə-ˈbesk\ *n* : a design of interlacing lines forming figures of flowers, foliage, and sometimes animals — **arabesque** *adj*

**¹Ar·a·bic** \ˈa-rə-bik\ *n* : a Semitic language of southwestern Asia and northern Africa

**²Arabic** *adj* **1** : of or relating to the Arabs, Arabic, or the Arabian peninsula in southwestern Asia **2** : expressed in or making use of Arabic numerals

**Arabic numeral** *n* : any of the number symbols 0, 1, 2, 3, 4, 5, 6, 7, 8, 9

**ar·a·ble** \ˈa-rə-bəl\ *adj* : fit for or used for the growing of crops ⟨~ land⟩

**arach·nid** \ə-ˈrak-nəd\ *n* : any of a class of usu. 8-legged arthropods comprising the spiders, scorpions, mites, and ticks — **arachnid** *adj*

**Ar·a·ma·ic** \ˌa-rə-ˈmā-ik\ *n* : an ancient Semitic language

**ar·a·mid** \ˈa-rə-məd, -ˌmid\ *n* : any of several light but very strong heat-resistant synthetic materials used esp. in textiles and plastics

**Arap·a·ho** *or* **Arap·a·hoe** \ə-ˈra-pə-ˌhō\ *n, pl* **-ho** *or* **-hos** *or* **-hoe** *or* **-hoes** : a member of an American Indian people of the western U.S.

**ar·bi·ter** \ˈär-bə-tər\ *n* : one having power to decide : JUDGE

**ar·bi·trage** \ˈär-bə-ˌträzh\ *n* [F, fr. MF, arbitration] : the purchase and sale of the same or equivalent securities in different markets in order to profit from price discrepancies

**ar·bi·tra·geur** \ˌär-bə-(ˌ)trä-ˈzhər\ *or* **ar·bi-**

**trag·er** \\är-bə-ˌträ-zhər\ *n* : one who practices arbitrage

**ar·bit·ra·ment** \är-ˈbi-trə-mənt\ *n* **1** : the act of deciding a dispute **2** : the judgment given by an arbitrator

**ar·bi·trary** \ˈär-bə-ˌtrer-ē\ *adj* **1** : AUTOCRATIC, DESPOTIC **2** : determined by will or caprice : selected at random — **ar·bi·trari·ly** \ˌär-bə-ˈtrer-ə-lē\ *adv* — **ar·bi·trari·ness** \ˈär-bə-ˌtrer-ē-nəs\ *n*

**ar·bi·trate** \ˈär-bə-ˌtrāt\ *vb* **-trat·ed; -trat·ing** **1** : to act as arbitrator **2** : to act on as arbitrator **3** : to submit for decision to an arbitrator — **ar·bi·tra·tion** \ˌär-bə-ˈträ-shən\ *n*

**ar·bi·tra·tor** \ˈär-bə-ˌträ-tər\ *n* : one chosen to settle differences between two parties in a controversy

**ar·bor** \ˈär-bər\ *n* [ME *erber, herber* garden, fr. AF, fr. *herbe* herb, grass] : a shelter formed of or covered with vines or branches

**ar·bo·re·al** \är-ˈbȯr-ē-əl\ *adj* **1** : of, relating to, or resembling a tree **2** : living in trees ⟨~ monkeys⟩

**ar·bo·re·tum** \ˌär-bə-ˈrē-təm\ *n, pl* **-re·tums** *or* **-re·ta** \-tə\ [L, plantation of trees, fr. *arbor* tree] : a place where trees and plants are grown for scientific and educational purposes

**ar·bor·vi·tae** \ˌär-bər-ˈvī-tē\ *n* : any of various evergreen trees and shrubs with scalelike leaves that are related to the cypresses

**ar·bour** *chiefly Brit var of* ARBOR

**ar·bu·tus** \är-ˈbyü-təs\ *n* : TRAILING ARBUTUS

**¹arc** \ˈärk\ *n* **1** : a sustained luminous discharge of electricity (as between two electrodes) **2** : a continuous portion of a curved line (as part of the circumference of a circle)

**²arc** *vb* **arced** \ˈärkt\; **arc·ing** \ˈär-kiŋ\ : to form an electric arc

**ARC** *abbr* **1** AIDS-related complex **2** American Red Cross

**ar·cade** \är-ˈkād\ *n* **1** : an arched or covered passageway; *esp* : one lined with shops **2** : a row of arches with their supporting columns **3** : an amusement center having coin-operated games

**ar·cane** \är-ˈkān\ *adj* : SECRET, MYSTERIOUS

**¹arch** \ˈärch\ *n* **1** : a curved structure spanning an opening (as a door) **2** : something resembling an arch : ARCHWAY

**²arch** *vb* **1** : to cover with an arch **2** : to form or bend into an arch

**³arch** *adj* **1** : CHIEF, EMINENT ⟨my ~ enemy⟩ **2** : ROGUISH, MISCHIEVOUS; *also* : deliberately playful or impudent ⟨~ comments⟩ — **arch·ly** *adv* — **arch·ness** *n*

**⁴arch** *abbr* architect; architectural; architecture

**ar·chae·ol·o·gy** *or* **ar·che·ol·o·gy** \ˌär-kē-ˈä-lə-jē\ *n* : the study of past human life as revealed by relics left by ancient peoples — **ar·chae·o·log·i·cal** \-ə-ˈlä-ji-kəl\ *adj* — **ar·chae·ol·o·gist** \-ˈä-lə-jist\ *n*

**ar·cha·ic** \är-ˈkā-ik\ *adj* **1** : having the characteristics of the language of the past and surviving chiefly in specialized uses ⟨~ words⟩ **2** : belonging to an earlier time : ANTIQUATED — **ar·cha·i·cal·ly** \-i-k(ə-)lē\ *adv*

**arch·an·gel** \ˈär-ˌkān-jəl\ *n* : a chief angel

**arch·bish·op** \ärch-ˈbi-shəp\ *n* : a bishop of high rank

**arch·bish·op·ric** \-shə-(ˌ)prik\ *n* : the jurisdiction or office of an archbishop

**arch·con·ser·va·tive** \(ˌ)ärch-kən-ˈsər-və-tiv\ *n* : an extreme conservative — **archconservative** *adj*

**arch·dea·con** \-ˈdē-kən\ *n* : a church official who assists a diocesan bishop in ceremonial or administrative functions

**arch·di·o·cese** \-ˈdī-ə-səs, -ˌsēz\ *n* : the diocese of an archbishop

**arch·duke** \-ˈdük, -ˈdyük\ *n* **1** : a sovereign prince **2** : a prince of the imperial family of Austria

**Ar·che·an** \är-ˈkē-ən\ *adj* : of, relating to, or being the earliest eon of geologic history — **Archean** *n*

**arch·en·e·my** \ˌärch-ˈe-nə-mē\ *n, pl* **-mies** : a principal enemy

**Ar·cheo·zo·ic** \ˌär-kē-ə-ˈzō-ik\ *adj* : ARCHEAN — **Archeozoic** *n*

**ar·chery** \ˈär-chə-rē\ *n* : the art or practice of shooting with bow and arrows — **ar·cher** \ˈär-chər\ *n*

**ar·che·type** \ˈär-ki-ˌtīp\ *n* : the original pattern or model of all things of the same type — **ar·che·typ·al** \ˌär-kə-ˈtī-pəl\ *adj*

**arch·fiend** \ˈärch-ˈfēnd\ *n* : a chief fiend; *esp* : SATAN

**ar·chi·epis·co·pal** \ˌär-kē-ə-ˈpis-kə-pəl\ *adj* : of or relating to an archbishop

**ar·chi·man·drite** \ˌär-kə-ˈman-ˌdrīt\ *n* : a dignitary in an Eastern church ranking below a bishop

**ar·chi·pel·a·go** \ˌär-kə-ˈpe-lə-ˌgō, ˌär-chə-\ *n, pl* **-goes** *or* **-gos** : a group of islands

**ar·chi·tect** \ˈär-kə-ˌtekt\ *n* **1** : a person who plans buildings and oversees their construction **2** : a person who designs and guides a plan or undertaking

**ar·chi·tec·ture** \ˈär-kə-ˌtek-chər\ *n* **1** : the art or science of planning and building structures **2** : a method or style of building **3** : the manner in which the elements (as of a design) or components (of a computer) are arranged or organized — **ar·chi·tec·tur·al** \ˌär-kə-ˈtek-chə-rəl, -ˈtek-shrəl\ *adj* — **ar·chi·tec·tur·al·ly** *adv*

**ar·chi·trave** \ˈär-kə-ˌtrāv\ *n* : the supporting horizontal member just above the columns in a building in the classical style of architecture

**ar·chive** \ˈär-ˌkīv\ *n* **1** : a place for keeping public records; *also* : public records — often used in pl. **2** : a repository esp. of information

**ar·chi·vist** \ˈär-kə-vist, -ˌkī-\ *n* : a person in charge of archives

**ar·chon** \ˈär-ˌkän, -kən\ *n* : a chief magistrate of ancient Athens

**arch·ri·val** \ˈärch-ˈrī-vəl\ *n* : a principal rival

**arch·way** \\'ärch-,wā\\ *n* : a passageway under an arch; *also* : an arch over a passage

**arc lamp** *n* : a gas-filled electric lamp that produces light when a current arcs between incandescent electrodes

¹**arc·tic** \\'ärk-tik, 'är-tik\\ *adj* [ME *artik*, fr. L *arcticus*, fr. Gk *arktikos*, fr. *arktos* bear, Ursa Major, north] **1** *often cap* : of or relating to the north pole or the region near it **2** : FRIGID

²**arc·tic** \\'är-tik, 'ärk-tik\\ *n* : a rubber overshoe that reaches to the ankle or above

**arctic circle** *n, often cap A&C* : the parallel of latitude that is approximately 66½ degrees north of the equator

**-ard** *also* **-art** *n suffix* : one that is characterized by performing some action, possessing some quality, or being associated with some thing esp. conspicuously or excessively ⟨brag*art*⟩ ⟨dull*ard*⟩

**ar·dent** \\'är-d²nt\\ *adj* **1** : characterized by warmth of feeling : PASSIONATE **2** : FIERY, HOT ⟨an ~ sun⟩ **3** : GLOWING ⟨~ eyes⟩ — **ar·dent·ly** *adv*

**ar·dor** \\'är-dər\\ *n* **1** : warmth of feeling : ZEAL **2** : sexual excitement

**ar·dour** *chiefly Brit var of* ARDOR

**ar·du·ous** \\'är-jə-wəs, -dyù-wəs\\ *adj* : DIFFICULT, LABORIOUS — **ar·du·ous·ly** *adv* — **ar·du·ous·ness** *n*

¹**are** *pres 2d sing or pres pl of* BE

²**are** \\'er\\ *n* — see METRIC SYSTEM table

**ar·ea** \\'er-ē-ə\\ *n* **1** : a flat surface or space **2** : the amount of surface included (as within the lines of a geometric figure) **3** : range or extent of some thing or concept : FIELD **4** : REGION

**area code** *n* : a usu. 3-digit number that identifies each telephone service area in a country (as the U.S. or Canada)

**are·na** \\ə-'rē-nə\\ *n* [L *harena, arena* sand, sandy place] **1** : an enclosed area used for public entertainment **2** : a sphere of activity or competition

**ar·gen·tite** \\'är-jən-,tīt\\ *n* : a dark gray or black mineral of metallic luster that is an important ore of silver

**ar·gon** \\'är-,gän\\ *n* [Gk, neut. of *argos* idle, lazy, fr. *a*- not + *ergon* work; fr. its relative inertness] : a colorless odorless gaseous chemical element found in the air and used for filling electric lamps

**ar·go·sy** \\'är-gə-sē\\ *n, pl* **-sies** **1** : a large merchant ship **2** : FLEET

**ar·got** \\'är-got, -,gō\\ *n* : the language of a particular group or class

**ar·gu·able** \\'är-gyü-ə-bəl\\ *adj* : open to argument, dispute, or question

**ar·gu·ably** \\'är-gyü-(ə-)blē\\ *adv* : as may be argued or shown by argument

**ar·gue** \\'är-gyü\\ *vb* **ar·gued; ar·gu·ing** **1** : to give reasons for or against something **2** : to contend in words : DISPUTE ⟨*argued* about money⟩ **3** : DEBATE **4** : to persuade by giving reasons

**ar·gu·ment** \\'är-gyə-mənt\\ *n* **1** : a reason offered in proof **2** : discourse intended to persuade **3** : QUARREL

**ar·gu·men·ta·tion** \\,är-gyə-mən-'tā-shən\\ *n* : the art of formal discussion

**ar·gu·men·ta·tive** \\,är-gyə-'men-tə-tiv\\ *adj* : inclined to argue

**ar·gyle** *also* **ar·gyll** \\'är-,gī(-ə)l\\ *n, often cap* : a geometric knitting pattern of varicolored diamonds on a single background color; *also* : a sock knit in this pattern

**aria** \\'är-ē-ə\\ *n* : an accompanied elaborate vocal solo forming part of a larger work

**ari·a·ry** \\,ä-rē-'ä-rē\\ *n, plural* **ariary** — see MONEY table

**ar·id** \\'a-rəd\\ *adj* : very dry; *esp* : having insufficient rainfall to support agriculture — **arid·i·ty** \\ə-'ri-də-tē\\ *n*

**Ar·ies** \\'er-,ēz, -ē-,ēz\\ *n* [L, lit., ram] **1** : a zodiacal constellation between Pisces and Taurus pictured as a ram **2** : the 1st sign of the zodiac in astrology; *also* : one born under this sign

**aright** \\ə-'rīt\\ *adv* : RIGHT, CORRECTLY

**arise** \\ə-'rīz\\ *vb* **arose** \\-'rōz\\; **aris·en** \\-'ri-z²n\\; **aris·ing** \\-'rī-ziŋ\\ **1** : to get up **2** : ORIGINATE **3** : ASCEND ♦ *Synonyms* RISE, DERIVE, SPRING, ISSUE

**ar·is·toc·ra·cy** \\,a-rə-'stä-krə-sē\\ *n, pl* **-cies** **1** : government by a noble or privileged class; *also* : a state so governed **2** : the governing class of an aristocracy **3** : UPPER CLASS — **aris·to·crat** \\ə-'ris-tə-,krat\\ *n* — **aris·to·crat·ic** \\ə-,ris-tə-'kra-tik\\ *adj*

**arith** *abbr* arithmetic; arithmetical

**arith·me·tic** \\ə-'rith-mə-,tik\\ *n* **1** : a branch of mathematics that deals with computations usu. with nonnegative real numbers **2** : COMPUTATION, CALCULATION — **ar·ith·met·ic** \\,er-ith-'me-tik\\ *or* **ar·ith·met·i·cal** \\-ti-kəl\\ *adj* — **ar·ith·met·i·cal·ly** \\-ti-k(ə-)lē\\ *adv* — **arith·me·ti·cian** \\ə-,rith-mə-'ti-shən\\ *n*

**arithmetic mean** *n* : the sum of a set of numbers divided by the number of numbers in the set

**Ariz** *abbr* Arizona

**ark** \\'ärk\\ *n* **1** : a boat held to resemble that of Noah's at the time of the Flood **2** : the sacred chest in a synagogue representing to Hebrews the presence of God; *also* : the repository for the scrolls of the Torah

**Ark** *abbr* Arkansas

¹**arm** \\'ärm\\ *n* [ME, fr. OE *earm*] **1** : a human upper limb and esp. the part between the shoulder and wrist; *also* : a corresponding limb of a 2-footed vertebrate **2** : something resembling an arm in shape or position ⟨an ~ of a chair⟩ ⟨the eight ~s of an octopus⟩ **3** : POWER, MIGHT ⟨the ~ of the law⟩ — **armed** \\'ärmd\\ *adj* — **arm·less** *adj*

²**arm** *vb* [ME, fr. AF *armer*, fr. L *armare*, fr. *arma* weapons, tools] : to furnish with weapons

³**arm** *n* **1** : WEAPON **2** : a branch of the military forces **3** *pl* : the hereditary heraldic devices of a family

**ar·ma·da** \\är-'mä-də, -'mā-\\ *n* : a fleet of warships

**ar·ma·dil·lo** \\,är-mə-'di-lō\\ *n, pl* **-los** [Sp, fr. dim. of *armado* armed one] : any of several small burrowing mammals with the head and body protected by an armor of bony plates

**Ar·ma·ged·don** \ˌär-mə-ˈge-d³n\ n : a final conclusive battle between the forces of good and evil; *also* : the site or time of this

**ar·ma·ment** \ˈär-mə-mənt\ n 1 : military strength 2 : arms and equipment (as of a tank or combat unit) 3 : the process of preparing for war

**ar·ma·ture** \ˈär-mə-ˌchúr, -chər\ n 1 : a protective covering or structure (as the spines of a cactus) 2 : the rotating part of an electric generator or motor; *also* : the movable part in an electromagnetic device (as a loudspeaker)

**arm·chair** \ˈärm-ˌcher\ n : a chair with armrests

**armed forces** n pl : the combined military, naval, and air forces of a nation

**Ar·me·nian** \är-ˈmē-nē-ən\ n 1 : a native or inhabitant of Armenia 2 : the Indo-European language of the Armenians

**arm·ful** \ˈärm-ˌfúl\ n, pl **armfuls** or **arms·ful** \ˈärmz-ˌfúl\ : as much as the arm or arms can hold

**arm·hole** \ˈärm-ˌhōl\ n : an opening for the arm in a garment

**ar·mi·stice** \ˈär-mə-stəs\ n : temporary suspension of hostilities by mutual agreement : TRUCE

**arm·let** \ˈärm-lət\ n : a band worn around the upper arm

**ar·mor** \ˈär-mər\ n 1 : protective covering 2 : armored forces and vehicles — **ar·mored** \-mərd\ adj

**ar·mor·er** \ˈär-mər-ər\ n 1 : a person who makes arms and armor 2 : a person who services firearms

**ar·mo·ri·al** \är-ˈmór-ē-əl\ adj : of or bearing heraldic arms

**ar·mory** \ˈär-mə-rē\ n, pl **ar·mor·ies** 1 : a place where arms are stored 2 : a factory where arms are made

**ar·mour, ar·moury** chiefly Brit var of ARMOR, ARMORY

**arm·pit** \ˈärm-ˌpit\ n : the hollow under the junction of the arm and shoulder

**arm·rest** \-ˌrest\ n : a support for the arm

**ar·my** \ˈär-mē\ n, pl **armies** 1 : a body of men organized for war 2 often cap : the complete military organization of a country for land warfare 3 : a great number 4 : a body of persons organized to advance a cause

**army ant** n : any of various nomadic social ants

**ar·my·worm** \ˈär-mē-ˌwərm\ n : any of numerous moths whose larvae move about destroying crops

**aro·ma** \ə-ˈrō-mə\ n : a usu. pleasing odor : FRAGRANCE — **ar·o·mat·ic** \ˌar-ə-ˈma-tik\ adj

**aro·ma·ther·a·py** \ə-ˌrō-mə-ˈther-ə-pē\ n : massage with a preparation of fragrant oils extracted from herbs, flowers, and fruits

**arose** past of ARISE

¹**around** \ə-ˈraúnd\ adv 1 : in a circle or in circumference ⟨a tree five feet ∼⟩ 2 : in or along a circuit ⟨the road goes ∼

by the lake⟩ 3 : on all sides ⟨nothing for miles ∼⟩ 4 : NEARBY ⟨wait ∼ awhile⟩ 5 : from one place to another ⟨travels ∼ on business⟩ 6 : in an opposite direction ⟨turn ∼⟩ 7 — used with some verbs to indicate continued action ⟨joking ∼⟩ 8 : APPROXIMATELY ⟨cost ∼ $5⟩

²**around** prep 1 : SURROUNDING ⟨trees ∼ the house⟩ 2 : to or on another side of ⟨∼ the corner⟩ 3 : NEAR ⟨stayed right ∼ home⟩ 4 : along the circuit of ⟨go ∼ the world⟩

**arouse** \ə-ˈraúz\ vb **aroused**; **arous·ing** 1 : to awaken from sleep 2 : to stir up : EXCITE — **arous·al** \-ˈraú-zəl\ n

**ar·peg·gio** \är-ˈpe-jē-ˌō, -ˈpe-jō\ n, pl **-gios** [It fr. arpeggiare to play on the harp, fr. arpa harp] : a chord whose notes are performed in succession and not simultaneously

**arr** abbr 1 arranged 2 arrival; arrive

**ar·raign** \ə-ˈrān\ vb 1 : to call before a court to answer to an indictment 2 : to accuse of wrong or imperfection — **ar·raign·ment** n

**ar·range** \ə-ˈrānj\ vb **ar·ranged**; **ar·rang·ing** 1 : to put in order 2 : PLAN ⟨∼ an interview⟩ 3 : to adapt (a musical composition) to voices or instruments other than those for which it was orig. written 4 : to come to an agreement about : SETTLE ⟨∼ a business deal⟩ — **ar·range·ment** n — **ar·rang·er** n

**ar·rant** \ˈa-rənt\ adj : being notoriously without moderation : EXTREME

**ar·ras** \ˈa-rəs\ n, pl **arras** 1 : TAPESTRY 2 : a wall hanging or screen of tapestry

¹**ar·ray** \ə-ˈrā\ vb 1 : to dress esp. splendidly 2 : to arrange in order (as in an array)

²**array** n 1 : a regular arrangement 2 : rich apparel 3 : a large or varied group

**ar·rears** \ə-ˈrirz\ n pl 1 : a state of being behind in the discharge of obligations ⟨in ∼ with the rent⟩ 2 : overdue debts

¹**ar·rest** \ə-ˈrest\ vb 1 : STOP, CHECK 2 : to take into legal custody

²**arrest** n 1 : the act of stopping; *also* : the state of being stopped 2 : the taking into custody by legal authority

**ar·rhyth·mia** \ā-ˈrith-mē-ə\ n : an alteration of the heartbeat's rhythm

**ar·riv·al** \ə-ˈrī-vəl\ n 1 : the act of arriving 2 : one that arrives

**ar·rive** \ə-ˈrīv\ vb **ar·rived**; **ar·riv·ing** 1 : to reach a destination 2 : to make an appearance ⟨the guests have arrived⟩ 3 : to attain success

**ar·ro·gant** \ˈer-ə-gənt\ adj : offensively exaggerating one's own importance — **ar·ro·gance** \-gəns\ n — **ar·ro·gant·ly** adv

**ar·ro·gate** \-ˌgāt\ vb **-gat·ed**; **-gat·ing** : to claim or seize without justification as one's right — **ar·ro·ga·tion** \ˌar-ə-ˈgā-shən\ n

**ar·row** \ˈer-ō\ n 1 : a missile shot from a bow and usu. having a slender shaft, a pointed head, and feathers at the butt 2 : a pointed mark used to indicate direction

**ar·row·head** \'er-ō-,hed\ n : the pointed end of an arrow

**ar·row·root** \-,rüt, -,růt\ n : an edible starch from the roots of any of several tropical American plants; also : a plant yielding arrowroot

**ar·royo** \ə-'rȯi-ə, -ō\ n, pl **-roy·os** [Sp] 1 : a watercourse in a dry region 2 : a water-carved gully or channel

**ar·se·nal** \'ärs-nəl, 'är-sə-nəl\ n [ultim. fr. Ar dār sinā'a house of manufacture] 1 : a place for making and storing arms and military equipment 2 : STORE, REPERTOIRE ⟨an ~ of tools⟩

**ar·se·nic** \'ärs-nik, 'är-sə-nik\ n 1 : a solid brittle poisonous chemical element of grayish metallic luster 2 : a very poisonous oxygen compound of arsenic used in making insecticides

**ar·son** \'är-sᵊn\ n : the willful or malicious burning of property — **ar·son·ist** \-ist\ n

¹**art** \'ärt\ n 1 : skill acquired by experience or study 2 : a branch of learning; esp : one of the humanities 3 : an occupation requiring knowledge or skill 4 : the use of skill and imagination in the production of things of beauty; also : works so produced 5 : ARTFULNESS

²**art** adj : produced as an artistic effort ⟨an ~ film⟩

³**art** abbr 1 article 2 artificial 3 artillery

**-art** — see -ARD

**ar·te·fact** chiefly Brit var of ARTIFACT

**ar·te·ri·al** \är-'tir-ē-əl\ adj 1 : of or relating to an artery; also : relating to or being the oxygenated blood found in most arteries 2 : of, relating to, or being a route for through traffic

**ar·te·ri·ole** \är-'tir-ē-,ōl\ n : any of the small terminal branches of an artery that ends in capillaries — **ar·te·ri·o·lar** \-,tir-ē-'ō-lər\ adj

**ar·te·rio·scle·ro·sis** \är-,tir-ē-ō-sklə-'rō-səs\ n : a chronic disease in which arterial walls are abnormally thickened and hardened — **ar·te·rio·scle·rot·ic** \-'rä-tik\ adj or n

**ar·tery** \'är-tə-rē\ n, pl **-ter·ies** 1 : one of the tubular vessels that carry blood from the heart 2 : a main channel of transportation or communication

**ar·te·sian well** \är-'tē-zhən-\ n : a well from which the water flows to the surface by natural pressure; also : a deep well

**art·ful** \'ärt-fəl\ adj 1 : performed with, showing, or using art or skill 2 : CRAFTY — **art·ful·ly** adv — **art·ful·ness** n

**ar·thri·tis** \är-'thrīt-əs\ n, pl **-thri·ti·des** \-'thrit-ə-,dēz\ : inflammation of the joints — **ar·thrit·ic** \-'thrit-ik\ adj or n

**ar·thro·pod** \'är-thrə-,päd\ n : any of a phylum of invertebrate animals comprising those (as insects, spiders, or crabs) with segmented bodies and jointed limbs — **arthropod** adj

**ar·thros·co·py** \är-'thräs-kə-pē\ n, pl **-pies** : visual examination of the interior of a joint (as the knee) with a special surgical instrument; also : surgery on a joint using arthroscopy — **ar·thro·scope** \'är-

thrə-,skōp\ n — **ar·thro·scop·ic** \,är-thrə-'skä-pik\ adj

**ar·ti·choke** \'är-tə-,chōk\ n [It dial. articiocco, ultim. fr. Ar al-khurshūf] : a tall thistlelike herb related to the daisies; also : its edible flower head

**ar·ti·cle** \'är-ti-kəl\ n [ME, fr. AF, fr. L articulus joint, division, dim. of artus joint, limb] 1 : a distinct part of a written document 2 : a nonfictional prose composition forming an independent part of a publication 3 : a word (as an, the) used with a noun to limit or give definiteness to its application 4 : a member of a class of things; esp : COMMODITY

**ar·tic·u·lar** \är-'ti-kyə-lər\ adj : of or relating to a joint ⟨~ cartilage⟩

¹**ar·tic·u·late** \är-'ti-kyə-lət\ adj 1 : divided into meaningful parts : INTELLIGIBLE 2 : able to speak; also : expressing oneself readily and effectively ⟨an ~ orator⟩ 3 : JOINTED — **ar·tic·u·late·ly** adv — **ar·tic·u·late·ness** n

²**ar·tic·u·late** \-,lāt\ vb **-lat·ed; -lat·ing** 1 : to utter distinctly 2 : to unite by or as if by joints — **ar·tic·u·la·tion** \-,ti-kyə-'lā-shən\ n

**ar·ti·fact** \'är-tə-,fakt\ n : something made or modified by humans usu. for a purpose; esp : an object remaining from another time or culture ⟨prehistoric ~s⟩

**ar·ti·fice** \'är-tə-fəs\ n 1 : TRICK; also : TRICKERY 2 : an ingenious device; also : INGENUITY

**ar·ti·fic·er** \är-'ti-fə-sər, 'är-tə-fə-sər\ n : a skilled worker

**ar·ti·fi·cial** \,är-tə-'fi-shəl\ adj 1 : produced by art rather than nature; also : made by humans to imitate nature 2 : not genuine : FEIGNED — **ar·ti·fi·ci·al·i·ty** \-,fi-shē-'a-lə-tē\ n — **ar·ti·fi·cial·ly** adv — **ar·ti·fi·cial·ness** n

**artificial insemination** n : introduction of semen into the uterus or oviduct by other than natural means

**artificial intelligence** n : the capability of a machine and esp. a computer to imitate intelligent human behavior

**artificial respiration** n : the rhythmic forcing of air into and out of the lungs of a person whose breathing has stopped

**ar·til·lery** \är-'ti-lə-rē\ n, pl **-ler·ies** 1 : crew-served mounted firearms (as guns) 2 : a branch of the army armed with artillery — **ar·til·ler·ist** \-rist\ n

**ar·ti·san** \'är-tə-zən, -sən\ n : a worker who practices a trade or handicraft

**art·ist** \'är-tist\ n 1 : one who practices an art; esp : one who creates objects of beauty 2 : ARTISTE

**ar·tiste** \är-'tēst\ n : a skilled public performer

**ar·tis·tic** \är-'tis-tik\ adj : showing taste and skill — **ar·tis·ti·cal·ly** \-ti-k(ə-)lē\ adv

**art·ist·ry** \'är-tə-strē\ n : artistic quality or ability

**art·less** \'ärt-ləs\ adj 1 : lacking art or skill 2 : free from artificiality : NATURAL

**3** : free from guile : SINCERE — **art·less·ly** adv — **art·less·ness** n

**art nou·veau** \ˌär-nü-ˈvō, ˌärt-\ n, often cap A&N [F, lit., new art] : a late 19th century design style characterized by sinuous lines and leaf-shaped forms

**art·work** \ˈärt-ˌwərk\ n : an artistic production or work

**arty** \ˈär-tē\ adj **art·i·er; -est** : showily or pretentiously artistic — **art·i·ly** \ˈär-tə-lē\ adv — **art·i·ness** n

**aru·gu·la** \ə-ˈrü-gə-lə\ n : a yellowish-flowered herb related to the mustards with edible leaves used esp. in salads

**ar·um** \ˈa-rəm\ n : any of a family of plants (as the jack-in-the-pulpit or a skunk cabbage) with flowers in a fleshy enclosed spike

**ARV** abbr American Revised Version

¹**-ary** n suffix : thing or person belonging to or connected with ⟨function*ary*⟩

²**-ary** adj suffix : of, relating to, or connected with ⟨budget*ary*⟩

**Ary·an** \ˈa-rē-ən, ˈer-ē-; ˈär-yən\ adj **1** : INDO-EUROPEAN **2** : NORDIC — **Aryan** n

¹**as** \əz, (ˌ)az\ adv **1** : to the same degree or amount : EQUALLY ⟨∼ green as grass⟩ **2** : for instance ⟨various trees, ∼ oak or pine⟩ **3** : when considered in a specified relation ⟨my opinion ∼ distinguished from his⟩

²**as** conj **1** : in the same amount or degree in which ⟨green ∼ grass⟩ **2** : in the same way that ⟨farmed ∼ his father before him had farmed⟩ **3** : WHILE, WHEN ⟨spoke to me ∼ I was leaving⟩ **4** : THOUGH ⟨improbable ∼ it seems⟩ **5** : SINCE, BECAUSE ⟨∼ I'm not wanted, I'll go⟩ **6** : that the result is ⟨so guilty ∼ to leave no doubt⟩

³**as** pron **1** : THAT — used after same or such ⟨it's the same price ∼ before⟩ **2** : a fact that ⟨he's rich, ∼ you know⟩

⁴**as** prep : in the capacity or character of ⟨this will serve ∼ a substitute⟩

**As** symbol arsenic

**AS** abbr **1** American Samoa **2** Anglo-Saxon **3** associate in science

**asa·fet·i·da** or **asa·foe·ti·da** \ˌa-sə-ˈfe-tə-dē, -ˈfē-\ n : an ill-smelling plant gum formerly used in medicine

**ASAP** abbr as soon as possible

**as·bes·tos** \as-ˈbes-təs, az-\ n : a noncombustible grayish mineral that occurs in fibrous form and has been used as a fireproof material

**as·cend** \ə-ˈsend\ vb **1** : to move upward : MOUNT, CLIMB **2** : to succeed to : OCCUPY ⟨∼ed the throne⟩

**as·cen·dan·cy** also **as·cen·den·cy** \ə-ˈsen-dən-sē\ n : controlling influence : DOMINATION

¹**as·cen·dant** also **as·cen·dent** \ə-ˈsen-dənt\ n : a dominant position

²**ascendant** also **ascendent** adj **1** : moving upward **2** : DOMINANT

**as·cen·sion** \ə-ˈsen-chən\ n : the act or process of ascending

**Ascension Day** n : the Thursday 40 days after Easter observed in commemoration of Christ's ascension into heaven

**as·cent** \ə-ˈsent\ n **1** : the act of mounting upward : CLIMB **2** : degree of upward slope

**as·cer·tain** \ˌa-sər-ˈtān\ vb : to learn with certainty — **as·cer·tain·able** adj

**as·cet·ic** \ə-ˈse-tik\ adj : practicing self-denial esp. for spiritual reasons : AUSTERE — **ascetic** n — **as·cet·i·cism** \-ˈse-tə-ˌsi-zəm\ n

**ASCII** \ˈas-kē\ n [American Standard Code for Information Interchange] : a computer code for representing alphanumeric information

**ascor·bic acid** \ə-ˈskor-bik-\ n : VITAMIN C

**as·cot** \ˈas-kət, -ˌkät\ n [Ascot Heath, racetrack near Ascot, England] : a broad neck scarf that is looped under the chin

**as·cribe** \ə-ˈskrīb\ vb **as·cribed; as·crib·ing** : to refer to a supposed cause, source, or author : ATTRIBUTE — **as·crib·able** adj — **as·crip·tion** \-ˈskrip-shən\ n

**asep·tic** \ā-ˈsep-tik\ adj : free or freed from disease-causing germs

**asex·u·al** \ā-ˈsek-shə-wəl\ adj **1** : lacking sex or functional sex organs **2** : occurring or formed without the production and union of two kinds of gametes ⟨∼ reproduction⟩ **3** : devoid of sexuality — **asex·u·al·ly** adv

**as for** prep : with regard to : CONCERNING ⟨as for the others, they were late⟩

¹**ash** \ˈash\ n **1** : any of a genus of trees related to the olive and having winged seeds and bark with grooves and ridges **2** : the tough elastic wood of an ash

²**ash** n **1** : the solid matter left when material is burned **2** : fine mineral particles from a volcano **3** pl : the remains of the dead human body after cremation or disintegration

**ashamed** \ə-ˈshāmd\ adj **1** : feeling shame **2** : restrained by anticipation of shame ⟨∼ to say anything⟩ — **asham·ed·ly** \-ˈshā-məd-lē\ adv

**ash·en** \ˈa-shən\ adj : resembling ashes (as in color); esp : deadly pale

**ash·lar** \ˈash-lər\ n : hewn or squared stone; also : masonry of such stone

**ashore** \ə-ˈshor\ adv : on or to the shore

**as how** conj : THAT ⟨allowed as how she was glad to be here⟩

**ash·ram** \ˈash-rəm\ n : a religious retreat esp. of a Hindu sage

**ash·tray** \ˈash-ˌtrā\ n : a receptacle for tobacco ashes

**Ash Wednesday** n : the 1st day of Lent

**ashy** \ˈa-shē\ adj **ash·i·er; -est** : ASHEN

**Asian** \ˈā-zhən\ adj : of, relating to, or characteristic of the continent of Asia or its people — **Asian** n

¹**aside** \ə-ˈsīd\ adv **1** : to or toward the side **2** : out of the way : AWAY ⟨putting ∼ savings⟩

²**aside** n : an actor's words heard by the audience but supposedly not by other characters on stage

**aside from** prep **1** : BESIDES ⟨aside from being pretty, she's intelligent⟩ **2** : with the exception of ⟨aside from one D his grades are excellent⟩

**as if** conj **1** : as it would be if ⟨it's as if

nothing had changed⟩ **2** : as one would if ⟨he acts *as if* he'd never been away⟩ **3** : THAT ⟨it seems *as if* nothing ever happens around here⟩

**as·i·nine** \'a-sə-ˌnīn\ *adj* [L *asininus*, fr. *asinus* ass] : STUPID, FOOLISH — **as·i·nin·i·ty** \ˌa-sə-'ni-nə-tē\ *n*

**ask** \'ask\ *vb* **asked** \'askt\; **ask·ing** **1** : to call on for an answer ⟨she ~ed him about his trip⟩ **2** : UTTER ⟨~ a question⟩ **3** : to make a request of ⟨~ him for help⟩ **4** : to make a request for ⟨~ help of her⟩ **5** : to set as a price ⟨~ed $800 for the car⟩ **6** : INVITE

**askance** \ə-'skans\ *adv* **1** : with a side glance **2** : with distrust

**askew** \ə-'skyü\ *adv or adj* : out of line : AWRY

**ASL** *abbr* American Sign Language

**¹aslant** \ə-'slant\ *adv or adj* : in a slanting direction

**²aslant** *prep* : over or across in a slanting direction

**asleep** \ə-'slēp\ *adv or adj* **1** : in or into a state of sleep **2** : DEAD **3** : NUMB **4** : INACTIVE

**as long as** *conj* **1** : provided that ⟨do as you like *as long as* you get home on time⟩ **2** : INASMUCH AS, SINCE ⟨*as long as* you're up, turn on the light⟩

**aso·cial** \(ˌ)ā-'sō-shəl\ *adj* : ANTISOCIAL

**as of** *prep* : AT, DURING, FROM, ON ⟨takes effect *as of* July 1⟩

**asp** \'asp\ *n* : a small poisonous African snake

**as·par·a·gus** \ə-'sper-ə-gəs\ *n* : a tall branching perennial herb related to the lilies; *also* : its edible young stalks

**as·par·tame** \'as-pər-ˌtām, ə-'spär-\ *n* : a crystalline low-calorie sweetener

**ASPCA** *abbr* American Society for the Prevention of Cruelty to Animals

**as·pect** \'as-ˌpekt\ *n* **1** : a position facing a particular direction **2** : APPEARANCE, LOOK **3** : PHASE

**as·pen** \'as-pən\ *n* : any of several poplars with leaves that flutter in the slightest breeze

**as per** \'az-ˌpər\ *prep* : in accordance with ⟨*as per* instructions⟩

**as·per·i·ty** \a-'sper-ə-tē\ *n, pl* **-ties** **1** : ROUGHNESS **2** : harshness of temper

**as·per·sion** \ə-'spər-zhən\ *n* : a slanderous or defamatory remark

**as·phalt** \'as-ˌfolt\ *also* **as·phal·tum** \as-'fol-təm\ *n* : a dark substance found in natural beds or obtained as a residue in petroleum refining and used esp. in paving streets

**asphalt jungle** *n* : a big city or a specified part of a big city

**as·pho·del** \'as-fə-ˌdel\ *n* : any of several Old World herbs related to the lilies and bearing flowers in long erect spikes

**as·phyx·ia** \as-'fik-sē-ə\ *n* : a lack of oxygen or excess of carbon dioxide in the body that results in unconsciousness and often death and is usu. caused by interruption of breathing

**as·phyx·i·ate** \-sē-ˌāt\ *vb* **-at·ed; -at·ing** : SUFFOCATE — **as·phyx·i·a·tion** \-ˌfik-sē-'ā-shən\ *n*

**as·pic** \'as-ˌpik\ *n* [F, lit., asp] : a savory meat jelly

**as·pi·rant** \'as-pə-rənt, ə-'spī-rənt\ *n* : one who aspires ⟨a presidential ~⟩ ♦ *Synonyms* CANDIDATE, SEEKER

**¹as·pi·rate** \'as-pə-rət\ *n* **1** : an independent sound \h\ or a character (as the letter *h*) representing it **2** : a consonant having aspiration as its final component

**²as·pi·rate** \'as-pə-ˌrāt\ *vb* **-rat·ed; -rat·ing** : to draw, remove, or take up or into by suction

**as·pi·ra·tion** \ˌas-pə-'rā-shən\ *n* **1** : the pronunciation or addition of an aspirate; *also* : the aspirate or its symbol **2** : a drawing of something in, out, up, or through by or as if by suction **3** : a strong desire to achieve something noble; *also* : an object of this desire

**as·pire** \ə-'spī(-ə)r\ *vb* **as·pired; as·pir·ing** **1** : to seek to attain or accomplish a particular goal **2** : to rise aloft

**as·pi·rin** \'as-pə-rən\ *n, pl* **aspirin** or **as·pi·rins** **1** : a white crystalline drug used to relieve pain and fever **2** : a tablet of aspirin

**as regards** *also* **as respects** *prep* : in regard to : with respect to

**ass** \'as\ *n* **1** : any of several long-eared mammals smaller than the related horses; *esp* : one of Africa ancestral to the donkey **2** : a stupid person

**as·sail** \ə-'sāl\ *vb* : to attack violently — **as·sail·able** *adj* — **as·sail·ant** *n*

**as·sas·sin** \ə-'sa-sᵊn\ *n* [ML *assassinus*, fr. Ar *ḥashshāshīn*, pl. of *ḥashshāsh* worthless person, lit., hashish-user, fr. *ḥashīsh* hashish] : a murderer esp. for hire or fanatical reasons

**as·sas·si·nate** \ə-'sa-sə-ˌnāt\ *vb* **-nat·ed; -nat·ing** : to murder by sudden or secret attack — **as·sas·si·na·tion** \-ˌsa-sə-'nā-shən\ *n*

**as·sault** \ə-'solt\ *n* **1** : a violent attack **2** : an unlawful attempt or threat to do harm to another — **assault** *vb* — **as·sault·ive** \ə-'sol-tiv\ *adj*

**assault rifle** *n* : a military automatic rifle with a large-capacity magazine

**¹as·say** \'aˌsā, a-'sā\ *n* : analysis to determine the quantity of one or more components present in a sample (as of an ore or drug)

**²as·say** \a-'sā, 'aˌsā\ *vb* **1** : TRY, ATTEMPT **2** : to subject (as an ore or drug) to an assay **3** : JUDGE 3

**as·sem·blage** \ə-'sem-blij, *3 & 4 also* ˌas-ˌäm-'bläzh\ *n* **1** : a collection of persons or things : GATHERING **2** : the act of assembling **3** : an artistic composition made from scraps, junk, and odds and ends **4** : the art of making assemblages

**as·sem·ble** \ə-'sem-bəl\ *vb* **-bled; -bling** **1** : to collect into one place : CONGREGATE **2** : to fit together the parts of **3** : to meet together : CONVENE

**as·sem·bly** \ə-'sem-blē\ *n, pl* **-blies** **1** : a gathering of persons : MEETING **2** *cap* : a legislative body; *esp* : the lower house of a legislature **3** : a signal for troops to assemble **4** : the fitting together of parts (as of a machine)

**assembly language** *n* : a computer language consisting of mnemonic codes corresponding to machine-language instructions

**as·sem·bly–line** \ə-'sem-blē-ˌlīn\ *adj* : made by or as if by an assembly line; *esp* : lacking originality or creativity

**assembly line** *n* : an arrangement of machines, equipment, and workers in which work passes from operation to operation in a direct line

**as·sem·bly·man** \ə-'sem-blē-mən\ *n* : a member of a legislative assembly

**as·sem·bly·wom·an** \-ˌwu̇-mən\ *n* : a woman who is a member of a legislative assembly

**as·sent** \ə-'sent\ *vb* : AGREE, CONCUR — **assent** *n*

**as·sert** \ə-'sərt\ *vb* 1 : to state positively 2 : to demonstrate the existence of ◆ **Synonyms** DECLARE, AFFIRM, PROTEST, AVOW, CLAIM — **as·ser·tive** \-'sər-tiv\ *adj* — **as·ser·tive·ly** *adv* — **as·ser·tive·ness** *n*

**as·ser·tion** \ə-'sər-shən\ *n* : a positive statement

**as·sess** \ə-'ses\ *vb* 1 : to fix the rate or amount of 2 : to impose (as a tax) at a specified rate 3 : to evaluate for taxation — **as·sess·ment** *n* — **as·ses·sor** \-'se-sər\ *n*

**as·set** \'a-ˌset\ *n* 1 *pl* : the entire property of a person or company that may be used to pay debts 2 : ADVANTAGE, RESOURCE ⟨my wit is my chief ∼⟩

**as·sev·er·ate** \ə-'se-və-ˌrāt\ *vb* **-at·ed; -at·ing** : to assert earnestly — **as·sev·er·a·tion** \-ˌse-və-'rā-shən\ *n*

**as·sid·u·ous** \ə-'si-jə-wəs\ *adj* : steadily attentive : DILIGENT — **as·si·du·i·ty** \ˌa-sə-'dü-ə-tē, -'dyü-\ *n* — **as·sid·u·ous·ly** *adv* — **as·sid·u·ous·ness** *n*

**as·sign** \ə-'sīn\ *vb* 1 : to transfer (property) to another 2 : to appoint to or as a duty ⟨∼ a lesson⟩ 3 : FIX, SPECIFY ⟨∼ a limit⟩ 4 : ASCRIBE ⟨∼ a reason⟩ — **sign·able** *adj*

**as·sig·na·tion** \ˌa-sig-'nā-shən\ *n* : an appointment for a meeting; *esp* : TRYST

**assigned risk** *n* : a poor risk (as an accident-prone motorist) that an insurance company is forced to insure by state law

**as·sign·ment** \ə-'sīn-mənt\ *n* 1 : the act of assigning 2 : something assigned

**as·sim·i·late** \ə-'si-mə-ˌlāt\ *vb* **-lat·ed; -lat·ing** 1 : to take up and absorb as nourishment; *also* : to absorb into a cultural tradition 2 : COMPREHEND 3 : to make or become similar — **as·sim·i·la·tion** \-ˌsi-mə-'lā-shən\ *n*

**¹as·sist** \ə-'sist\ *vb* : HELP, AID ⟨∼ed the injured⟩ — **as·sis·tance** \-'sis-təns\ *n*

**²assist** *n* 1 : an act of assistance 2 : the action of a player who enables a teammate to make a putout (as in baseball) or score a goal (as in hockey or basketball)

**as·sis·tant** \ə-'sis-tənt\ *n* : a person who assists : HELPER

**as·sis·ted living** \ə-'sīs-təd-\ *n* : a system of housing and limited care for senior citizens who need assistance with daily activities but do not require care in a nursing home

**as·sis·tive** \ə-'sis-tiv\ *adj* : providing aid or assistance ⟨∼ technology⟩

**as·size** \ə-'sīz\ *n* [ME *assise*, fr. AF, session, legal action, fr. *asseer, asseoir* to seat, fr. VL *assedēre*, fr. L *assidēre* to sit beside] 1 : a judicial inquest 2 *pl* : the former regular sessions of superior courts in English counties

**assn** *abbr* association

**assoc** *abbr* associate; associated; association

**¹as·so·ci·ate** \ə-'sō-shē-ˌāt, -sē-\ *vb* **-at·ed; -at·ing** 1 : to join in companionship or partnership 2 : to connect in thought

**²as·so·ciate** \-shē-ət, -sē-; -shət\ *n* 1 : a fellow worker : PARTNER 2 : COMPANION 3 *often cap* : a degree conferred esp. by a junior college ⟨∼ in arts⟩ — **associate** *adj*

**as·so·ci·a·tion** \ə-ˌsō-shē-'ā-shən, -sē-\ *n* 1 : the act of associating 2 : an organization of persons : SOCIETY

**as·so·cia·tive** \ə-'sō-shē-ˌā-tiv, -sē-; -shə-tiv\ *adj* 1 : of, relating to, or involved in association esp. of ideas or images 2 : of, having, or being the property of producing the same mathematical value regardless of how an expression's elements are grouped as long as their order is the same

**as·so·nance** \'a-sə-nəns\ *n* : repetition of vowels esp. as an alternative to rhyme in verse — **as·so·nant** \-nənt\ *adj or n*

**as soon as** *conj* : immediately at or shortly after the time that ⟨we'll start *as soon as* they arrive⟩

**as·sort** \ə-'sȯrt\ *vb* 1 : to distribute into like groups : CLASSIFY 2 : HARMONIZE

**as·sort·ed** \-'sȯr-təd\ *adj* : consisting of various kinds

**as·sort·ment** \-'sȯrt-mənt\ *n* : a collection of assorted things or persons

**asst** *abbr* assistant

**as·suage** \ə-'swāj\ *vb* **as·suaged; as·suag·ing** 1 : to make (as pain or grief) less : EASE 2 : SATISFY ◆ **Synonyms** ALLEVIATE, RELIEVE, LIGHTEN, MITIGATE

**as·sume** \ə-'süm\ *vb* **as·sumed; as·sum·ing** 1 : to take upon oneself 2 : to pretend to have or be 3 : to take as granted or true though not proved

**as·sump·tion** \ə-'səmp-shən\ *n* 1 : the taking up of a person into heaven 2 *cap* : August 15 observed in commemoration of the Assumption of the Virgin Mary 3 : a taking upon oneself 4 : PRETENSION 5 : SUPPOSITION

**as·sur·ance** \ə-'shu̇r-əns\ *n* 1 : PLEDGE 2 *chiefly Brit* : INSURANCE 3 : SECURITY 4 : SELF-CONFIDENCE; *also* : AUDACITY

**as·sure** \ə-'shu̇r\ *vb* **as·sured; as·sur·ing** 1 : INSURE 2 : to give confidence to 3 : to state confidently to 4 : to make certain the coming or attainment of

**as·sured** \ə-'shu̇rd\ *n, pl* **assured** *or* **assureds** : INSURED

**as·ta·tine** \'as-tə-ˌtēn\ *n* : an unstable radioactive chemical element

**as·ter** \'as-tər\ *n* : any of various mostly fall-blooming leafy-stemmed composite herbs with daisylike purple, white, pink, or yellow flower heads

**as·ter·isk** \'as-tə-,risk\ n [L asteriscus, fr. Gk asteriskos, lit., little star, dim. of astēr star] : a character * used as a reference mark or as an indication of the omission of letters or words

**astern** \ə-'stərn\ adv or adj 1 : in, at, or toward the stern 2 : BACKWARD

**as·ter·oid** \'as-tə-,rȯid\ n : any of the numerous small celestial bodies found esp. between Mars and Jupiter

**asth·ma** \'az-mə\ n : a chronic lung disorder marked by recurrent episodes of labored breathing, a feeling of tightness in the chest, and coughing — **asth·mat·ic** \az-'ma-tik\ adj or n

**as though** conj : AS IF

**astig·ma·tism** \ə-'stig-mə-,ti-zəm\ n : a defect in a lens or an eye causing improper focusing and blurred vision — **as·tig·mat·ic** \as-tig-'ma-tik\ adj

**astir** \ə-'stər\ adj 1 : being in action : MOVING 2 : being out of bed

**as to** prep 1 : ABOUT, CONCERNING ⟨uncertain as to what went on⟩ 2 : ACCORDING TO ⟨graded as to size⟩

**as·ton·ish** \ə-'stä-nish\ vb : to strike with sudden and esp. great wonder : AMAZE — **as·ton·ish·ing·ly** adv — **as·ton·ish·ment** n

**as·tound** \ə-'staȯnd\ vb : to fill with bewilderment or wonder — **as·tound·ing·ly** adv

**¹astrad·dle** \ə-'stra-d²l\ adv : on or above and extending onto both sides

**²astraddle** prep : ASTRIDE

**as·tra·khan** \'as-trə-kən, -,kan\ n, often cap 1 : karakul of Russian origin 2 : a cloth with a usu. wool, curled, and looped pile resembling karakul

**as·tral** \'as-trəl\ adj : of, relating to, or coming from the stars

**astray** \ə-'strā\ adv or adj 1 : off the right path or route 2 : into error

**¹astride** \ə-'strīd\ adv 1 : with one leg on each side 2 : with legs apart

**²astride** prep : with one leg on each side of

**¹as·trin·gent** \ə-'strin-jənt\ adj : able or tending to shrink body tissues — **as·trin·gen·cy** \-jən-sē\ n

**²astringent** n : an astringent agent or substance

**astrol** abbr astrologer; astrology

**as·tro·labe** \'as-trə-,lāb\ n : an instrument formerly used for observing the positions of celestial bodies

**as·trol·o·gy** \ə-'strä-lə-jē\ n : divination based on the supposed influence of the stars upon human events — **as·trol·o·ger** \-jər\ n — **as·tro·log·i·cal** \,as-trə-'lä-ji-kəl\ adj — **as·tro·log·i·cal·ly** \-kə-lē\ adv

**astron** abbr astronomer; astronomy

**as·tro·naut** \'as-trə-,nȯt\ n : a traveler in a spacecraft

**as·tro·nau·tics** \as-trə-'nȯ-tiks\ n : the science of the construction and operation of spacecraft — **as·tro·nau·tic** \-tik\ or **as·tro·nau·ti·cal** \-ti-kəl\ adj

**as·tro·nom·i·cal** \,as-trə-'nä-mi-kəl\ also **as·tro·nom·ic** \-mik\ adj 1 : of or relating to astronomy 2 : extremely large ⟨an ~ amount of money⟩

**astronomical unit** n : a unit of length used in astronomy equal to the mean distance of the earth from the sun or about 93 million miles (150 million kilometers)

**as·tron·o·my** \ə-'strä-nə-mē\ n, pl -mies : the science of objects and matter beyond the earth's atmosphere — **as·tron·o·mer** \-mər\ n

**as·tro·phys·ics** \,as-trə-'fi-ziks\ n : astronomy dealing esp. with the physical properties and dynamic processes of celestial objects — **as·tro·phys·i·cal** \-zi-kəl\ adj — **as·tro·phys·i·cist** \-'fi-zə-sist\ n

**as·tute** \ə-'stüt, -'styüt, a-\ adj [L astutus, fr. astus craft] : shrewdly discerning; also : WILY ⟨an ~ lawyer⟩ — **as·tute·ly** adv — **as·tute·ness** n

**asun·der** \ə-'sən-dər\ adv or adj 1 : into separate pieces ⟨torn ~⟩ 2 : separated in position from each other

**ASV** abbr American Standard Version

**¹as well as** conj : and in addition : and moreover ⟨brave as well as loyal⟩

**²as well as** prep : in addition to : BESIDES ⟨the coach, as well as the team, is ready⟩

**asy·lum** \ə-'sī-ləm\ n [ME, fr. L, fr. Gk asylon, neut. of asylos inviolable, fr. a- not + sylon right of seizure] 1 : a place of refuge 2 : protection given to esp. political fugitives 3 : an institution for the care of the needy or sick and esp. of the insane

**asym·met·ri·cal** \,ā-sə-'me-tri-kəl\ or **asym·met·ric** \-trik\ adj : not symmetrical — **asym·met·ri·cal·ly** \-tri-kə-lē\ adv — **asym·me·try** \(,)ā-'si-mə-trē\ n

**asymp·tom·at·ic** \,ā-,simp-tə-'ma-tik\ adj : presenting no symptoms of disease ⟨an ~ infection⟩

**as·ymp·tote** \'a-səmp-,tōt\ n : a straight line that is approached ever more closely by a curve that never coincides with it — **as·ymp·tot·ic** \,a-səmp-'tä-tik\ adj — **as·ymp·tot·i·cal·ly** \-ti-k(ə-)lē\ adv

**¹at** \ət, (')at\ prep 1 — used to indicate a point in time or space ⟨be here ~ 3 o'clock⟩ 2 — used to indicate a goal ⟨swung ~ the ball⟩ 3 — used to indicate position or condition ⟨~ rest⟩ 4 — used to indicate means, cause, or manner ⟨sold ~ auction⟩

**²at** \'ät\ n, pl at also att — see kip at MONEY table

**At** symbol astatine

**AT** abbr automatic transmission

**at all** adv : in any way : in any circumstances ⟨not at all likely⟩

**at·a·vism** \'a-tə-,vi-zəm\ n : appearance in an individual of a character typical of an ancestral form; also : such an individual or character — **at·a·vis·tic** \,a-tə-'vis-tik\ adj

**atax·ia** \ə-'tak-sē-ə\ n : an inability to coordinate muscular movements

**ate** past of EAT

**¹-ate** n suffix 1 : one acted upon (in a specified way) ⟨distillate⟩ 2 : chemical compound or complex derived from a (specified) compound or element ⟨ace-tate⟩

²-ate n suffix 1 : office : function : rank : group of persons holding a (specified) office or rank ⟨episcopate⟩ 2 : state : dominion : jurisdiction ⟨emirate⟩

³-ate adj suffix 1 : acted on (in a specified way) : being in a (specified) state ⟨temperate⟩ ⟨degenerate⟩ 2 : marked by having ⟨vertebrate⟩

⁴-ate vb suffix : cause to be modified or affected by ⟨pollinate⟩ : cause to become ⟨activate⟩ : furnish with ⟨aerate⟩

ate·lier \ˌa-tᵊl-ˈyā\ n 1 : an artist's or designer's studio 2 : WORKSHOP

athe·ist \ˈā-thē-ist\ n : one who denies the existence of God — athe·ism \-ˌi-zəm\ n — athe·is·tic \ˌā-thē-ˈis-tik\ adj

ath·e·nae·um or ath·e·ne·um \ˌa-thə-ˈnē-əm\ n : LIBRARY 1

ath·ero·scle·ro·sis \ˌa-thə-rō-sklə-ˈrō-səs\ n : arteriosclerosis characterized by the deposition of fatty substances in and the hardening of the inner layer of the arteries — ath·ero·scle·rot·ic \-ˈrä-tik\ adj

athirst \ə-ˈthərst\ adj 1 archaic : THIRSTY 2 : EAGER, LONGING

ath·lete \ˈath-ˌlēt\ n [ME, fr. L athleta, fr. Gk athlētēs, fr. athlein to contend for a prize, fr. athlon prize, contest] : a person who is trained to compete in athletics

athlete's foot n : ringworm of the feet

ath·let·ic \ath-ˈle-tik\ adj 1 : of or relating to athletes or athletics 2 : VIGOROUS, ACTIVE 3 : STURDY, MUSCULAR — ath·let·i·cal·ly \-ti-kə-lē\ adv — ath·let·i·cism \-tə-ˌsi-zəm\ n

ath·let·ics \ath-ˈle-tiks\ n sing or pl : exercises and games requiring physical skill, strength, and endurance

athletic supporter n : an elastic pouch used to support the male genitals and worn esp. during athletic activity

¹athwart \ə-ˈthwórt\ prep 1 : ACROSS 2 : in opposition to

²athwart adv : obliquely across

atilt \ə-ˈtilt\ adv or adj 1 : in a tilted position 2 : with lance in hand

-ation n suffix : action or process ⟨flirtation⟩ : something connected with an action or process ⟨discoloration⟩

Atl abbr Atlantic

at–large \ˈat-ˈlärj\ adj : of or being a political representative who is elected to serve an entire area rather than one of its subdivisions

at·las \ˈat-ləs\ n : a book of maps

atm abbr atmosphere; atmospheric

ATM n : a computerized electronic machine that performs basic banking functions

at·mo·sphere \ˈat-mə-ˌsfir\ n 1 : the gaseous envelope of a celestial body; esp : the mass of air surrounding the earth 2 : a surrounding influence 3 : a unit of pressure equal to the pressure of air at sea level or about 14.7 pounds per square inch (10 newtons per square centimeter) 4 : an intriguing or singular tone, effect, or appeal — at·mo·spher·ic \ˌat-mə-

ˈsfir-ik, -ˈsfer-\ adj — at·mo·spher·i·cal·ly \-i-k(ə-)lē\ adv

at·mo·sphe·rics \ˌat-mə-ˈsfir-iks, -ˈsfer-\ n pl : radio noise from atmospheric electrical phenomena

atoll \ˈa-ˌtól, -ˌtäl, ˈā-\ n : a coral island consisting of a reef surrounding a lagoon

at·om \ˈa-təm\ n [ME, fr. L atomus, fr. Gk atomos, fr. atomos indivisible, fr. a- not + temnein to cut] 1 : a tiny particle : BIT 2 : the smallest particle of a chemical element that can exist alone or in combination

atom·ic \ə-ˈtä-mik\ adj 1 : of or relating to atoms; also : NUCLEAR 2 ⟨∼ energy⟩ 2 : extremely small

atomic bomb n : a very destructive bomb utilizing the energy released by splitting the atom

atomic clock n : a very precise clock regulated by the natural vibration of atoms or molecules (as of cesium)

atomic number n : the number of protons in the nucleus of an element

atomic weight n : the mass of one atom of an element

at·om·ise, at·om·is·er Brit var of ATOMIZE, ATOMIZER

at·om·ize \ˈa-tə-ˌmīz\ vb -ized; -iz·ing : to reduce to minute particles

at·om·iz·er \ˈa-tə-ˌmī-zər\ n : a device for dispensing a liquid (as perfume) as a mist

atom smasher n : ACCELERATOR 3

aton·al \ā-ˈtō-nᵊl\ adj : marked by avoidance of traditional musical tonality — ato·nal·i·ty \ˌā-tō-ˈna-lə-tē\ n — aton·al·ly \ā-ˈtō-nə-lē\ adv

atone \ə-ˈtōn\ vb atoned; aton·ing 1 : to make amends 2 : EXPIATE ⟨∼ for sins⟩

atone·ment \ə-ˈtōn-mənt\ n 1 : the reconciliation of God and mankind through the death of Jesus Christ 2 : reparation for an offense : SATISFACTION

¹atop \ə-ˈtäp\ adv or adj : on, to, or at the top

²atop prep : on top of

ATP \ˌā-ˌtē-ˈpē\ n [adenosine triphosphate] : a compound that occurs widely in living tissue and supplies energy for many cellular processes by undergoing enzymatic hydrolysis

atri·um \ˈā-trē-əm\ n, pl atria \-trē-ə\ also atri·ums 1 : the central room of a Roman house; also : an open patio or court in the center of a building (as a hotel) 2 : an anatomical cavity or passage; esp : one of the chambers of the heart that receives blood from the veins — atri·al \-əl\ adj

atro·cious \ə-ˈtrō-shəs\ adj 1 : savagely brutal, cruel, or wicked 2 : very bad : ABOMINABLE — atro·cious·ly adv — atro·cious·ness n

atroc·i·ty \ə-ˈträ-sə-tē\ n, pl -ties 1 : ATROCIOUSNESS 2 : an atrocious act or object ⟨the atrocities of war⟩

at·ro·phy \ˈa-trə-fē\ n, pl -phies : decrease in size or wasting away of a bodily part or tissue — atrophy vb

**at·ro·pine** \'a-trə-ˌpēn\ n : a drug from belladonna and related plants used esp. to relieve spasms and to dilate the pupil of the eye

**¹att** var of AT

**²att** abbr 1 attached 2 attention 3 attorney

**at·tach** \ə-'tach\ vb 1 : to seize legally in order to force payment of a debt 2 : to bind by personal ties 3 : FASTEN, CONNECT 4 : to be fastened or connected

**at·ta·ché** \ˌa-tə-'shā, ˌa-ˌta-, ˌə-ˌta-\ n [F] : a technical expert on the diplomatic staff of an ambassador

**at·ta·ché case** \ə-'ta-shā-, ˌa-tə-'shā-\ n : a small thin suitcase used esp. for carrying business papers; also : BRIEFCASE

**at·tach·ment** \ə-'tach-mənt\ n 1 : legal seizure of property 2 : connection by ties of affection and regard 3 : a device attached to a machine or implement 4 : a connection by which one thing is attached to another

**¹at·tack** \ə-'tak\ vb 1 : to set upon with force or words : ASSAIL, ASSAULT 2 : to set to work on

**²attack** n 1 : an offensive action 2 : a fit of sickness 3 : a scoring action in a game

**³attack** adj : designed, planned, or used for a military attack

**at·tain** \ə-'tān\ vb 1 : ACHIEVE, ACCOMPLISH 2 : to arrive at : REACH — **at·tain·abil·i·ty** \-ˌtā-nə-'bi-lə-tē\ n — **at·tain·able** adj

**at·tain·der** \ə-'tān-dər\ n : extinction of the civil rights of a person upon sentence of death or outlawry

**at·tain·ment** \ə-'tān-mənt\ n 1 : the act of attaining 2 : ACCOMPLISHMENT

**at·tar** \'a-tər\ n [Pers ʿaṭir perfumed, fr. Ar, fr. ʿiṭr perfume] : a fragrant floral oil

**at·tempt** \ə-'tempt\ vb : to make an effort toward : TRY — **attempt** n

**at·tend** \ə-'tend\ vb 1 : to look after : TEND 2 : to be present with 3 : to be present at 4 : to apply oneself 5 : to pay attention 6 : to direct one's attention

**at·ten·dance** \ə-'ten-dəns\ n 1 : the act or fact of attending 2 : the number of persons present; also : the number of times a person attends

**¹at·ten·dant** \ə-'ten-dənt\ n : one that attends another to render a service

**²attendant** adj : ACCOMPANYING ⟨∼ circumstances⟩

**at·ten·tion** \ə-'ten-chən\ n 1 : the act or state of applying the mind to an object 2 : CONSIDERATION 3 : an act of courtesy 4 : a position of readiness assumed on command by a soldier — **at·ten·tive** \-'ten-tiv\ adj — **at·ten·tive·ly** adv — **at·ten·tive·ness** n

**attention deficit disorder** n : a behavioral syndrome esp. of children that is marked by hyperactivity, impulsive behavior, and inattention

**attention-deficit/hyperactivity disorder** n : ATTENTION DEFICIT DISORDER

**attention span** n : the length of time during which one is able to concentrate or remain interested

**at·ten·u·ate** \ə-'ten-yə-ˌwāt\ vb **-at·ed;** **-at·ing** 1 : to make or become thin 2 : WEAKEN ⟨sorrows ∼ with time⟩ — **attenuate** \-wət\ adj — **at·ten·u·a·tion** \-ˌten-yə-'wā-shən\ n

**at·test** \ə-'test\ vb 1 : to certify as genuine by signing as a witness 2 : MANIFEST ⟨her record ∼s her integrity⟩ 3 : TESTIFY ⟨∼ to a belief⟩ — **at·tes·ta·tion** \ˌa-ˌtes-'tā-shən\ n

**at·tic** \'a-tik\ n : the space or room in a building immediately below the roof

**¹at·tire** \ə-'tī(-ə)r\ vb **at·tired; at·tir·ing** : to put garments on : DRESS, ARRAY

**²attire** n : DRESS, CLOTHES

**at·ti·tude** \'a-tə-ˌtüd, -ˌtyüd\ n 1 : POSTURE 2 : a mental position or feeling with regard to a fact or state 3 : the position of something in relation to something else 4 : a negative or hostile state of mind 5 : a cocky or arrogant manner

**at·ti·tu·di·nise** Brit var of ATTITUDINIZE

**at·ti·tu·di·nize** \ˌa-tə-'tü-də-ˌnīz, -'tyü-\ vb **-nized; -niz·ing** : to assume an affected mental attitude : POSE

**attn** abbr attention

**at·tor·ney** \ə-'tər-nē\ n, pl **-neys** : a legal agent qualified to act for persons in legal proceedings

**attorney general** n, pl **attorneys general** or **attorney generals** : the chief legal representative and adviser of a nation or state

**at·tract** \ə-'trakt\ vb 1 : to draw to or toward oneself : cause to approach 2 : to draw by emotional or aesthetic appeal ♦ **Synonyms** CHARM, FASCINATE, ALLURE, CAPTIVATE, ENCHANT — **at·trac·tive** \-'trak-tiv\ adj — **at·trac·tive·ly** adv — **at·trac·tive·ness** n

**at·trac·tant** \ə-'trak-tənt\ n : a substance (as a pheromone) that attracts specific animals (as insects)

**at·trac·tion** \ə-'trak-shən\ n 1 : the act or power of attracting; esp : personal charm 2 : an attractive quality, object, or feature 3 : a force tending to draw particles together

**attrib** abbr attributive

**¹at·tri·bute** \'a-trə-ˌbyüt\ n 1 : an inherent characteristic 2 : a word ascribing a quality; esp : ADJECTIVE

**²at·trib·ute** \ə-'tri-ˌbyüt, -byət\ vb **-ut·ed; -ut·ing** 1 : to explain as to cause or origin ⟨∼ the illness to fatigue⟩ 2 : to regard as a characteristic ♦ **Synonyms** ASCRIBE, CREDIT, CHARGE, IMPUTE — **at·trib·ut·able** adj — **at·tri·bu·tion** \ˌa-trə-'byü-shən\ n

**at·trib·u·tive** \ə-'trib-yə-tiv\ adj : joined directly to a modified noun without a linking verb ⟨red in red hair is an ∼ adjective⟩ — **attributive** n — **at·trib·u·tive·ly** adv

**at·tri·tion** \ə-'tri-shən\ n 1 : the act of wearing away by or as if by rubbing 2 : a reduction in numbers as a result of resignation, retirement, or death

**at·tune** \ə-'tün, -'tyün\ vb : to bring into harmony : TUNE — **at·tune·ment** n

**atty** abbr attorney

**ATV** \ˌā-ˌtē-'vē\ n : ALL-TERRAIN VEHICLE

**atyp·i·cal** \ā-'ti-pi-kəl\ adj : not typical : IRREGULAR — **atyp·i·cal·ly** \-k(ə-)lē\ adv

**Au** symbol [L aurum] gold

**au·burn** \'ȯ-bərn\ adj : reddish brown — auburn n

**au cou·rant** \ˌō-ku̇-'rä<sup>n</sup>\ adj [F, lit., in the current] : UP-TO-DATE, STYLISH

¹**auc·tion** \'ȯk-shən\ n [L auction-, auctio, fr. augēre to increase] : public sale of property to the highest bidder

²**auction** vb **auc·tioned; auc·tion·ing** \-shə-niŋ\ : to sell at auction

**auc·tion·eer** \ˌȯk-shə-'nir\ n : an agent who conducts an auction

**aud** abbr audit; auditor

**au·da·cious** \ȯ-'dā-shəs\ adj 1 : DARING, BOLD 2 : INSOLENT — **au·da·cious·ly** adv — **au·da·cious·ness** n — **au·dac·i·ty** \-'da-sə-tē\ n

¹**au·di·ble** \'ȯ-də-bəl\ adj : capable of being heard — **au·di·bil·i·ty** \ˌȯ-də-'bi-lə-tē\ n — **au·di·bly** \'ȯ-də-blē\ adv

²**audible** n : a play called at the line of scrimmage — **audible** vb

**au·di·ence** \'ȯ-dē-əns\ n 1 : a formal interview 2 : an opportunity of being heard 3 : an assembly of listeners or spectators

¹**au·dio** \'ȯ-dē-ˌō\ adj 1 : of or relating to frequencies (as of radio waves) corresponding to those of audible sound waves 2 : of or relating to sound or its reproduction and esp. high-fidelity reproduction 3 : relating to or used in the transmission or reception of sound

²**audio** n 1 : the transmission, reception, or reproduction of sound 2 : the section of television or motion-picture equipment that deals with sound

**au·di·ol·o·gy** \ˌȯ-dē-'ä-lə-jē\ n : a branch of science dealing with hearing and esp. with the treatment of individuals having trouble with hearing — **au·di·o·log·i·cal** \-ə-'lä-ji-kəl\ adj — **au·di·ol·o·gist** \-'ä-lə-jist\ n

**au·dio·phile** \'ȯ-dē-ō-ˌfi(-ə)l\ n : one who is enthusiastic about high-fidelity sound reproduction

**au·dio·tape** \'ȯ-dē-ō-ˌtāp\ n : a tape recording of sound

**au·dio·vi·su·al** \ˌȯ-dē-ō-'vi-zhə-wəl\ adj : of, relating to, or making use of both hearing and sight

**au·dio·vi·su·als** \-wəlz\ n pl : audiovisual teaching materials (as videotapes)

¹**au·dit** \'ȯ-dət\ n : a formal examination and verification of financial accounts

²**audit** vb 1 : to perform an audit on or for 2 : to attend (a course) without expecting formal credit

¹**au·di·tion** \ȯ-'di-shən\ n 1 : HEARING 2 : a trial performance to appraise an entertainer's merits

²**audition** vb **-tioned; -tion·ing** \-'di-shə-niŋ\ : to give an audition to; also : to give a trial performance

**au·di·tor** \'ȯ-də-tər\ n 1 : LISTENER 2 : a person who audits

**au·di·to·ri·um** \ˌȯ-də-'tȯr-ē-əm\ n, pl **-ri·ums** or **-ria** \-rē-ə\ 1 : the part of a public building where an audience sits 2 : a hall or building used for public gatherings

**au·di·to·ry** \'ȯ-də-ˌtȯr-ē\ adj : of or relating to hearing or to the sense or organs of hearing ⟨∼ stimuli⟩

**auditory tube** n : EUSTACHIAN TUBE

**auf Wie·der·seh·en** \au̇f-'vē-dər-ˌzān\ interj [G] — used to express farewell

**Aug** abbr August

**au·ger** \'ȯ-gər\ n : a tool for boring

**aught** \'ȯt, 'ät\ n : ZERO, CIPHER

**aug·ment** \ȯg-'ment\ vb : ENLARGE, INCREASE — **aug·men·ta·tion** \ˌȯg-mən-'tā-shən\ n

**au gra·tin** \ō-'gra-t<sup>ə</sup>n, ȯ-, -'grä-\ adj [F, lit., with the burnt scrapings from the pan] : covered with bread crumbs or grated cheese and browned

¹**au·gur** \'ȯ-gər\ n : DIVINER, SOOTHSAYER

²**augur** vb 1 : to foretell esp. from omens 2 : to give promise of ⟨the decision doesn't ∼ well⟩

**au·gu·ry** \'ȯ-gyə-rē, -gə-\ n, pl **-ries** 1 : divination from omens 2 : OMEN, PORTENT

**au·gust** \ȯ-'gəst\ adj : marked by majestic dignity or grandeur — **au·gust·ly** adv — **au·gust·ness** n

**Au·gust** \'ȯ-gəst\ n [ME, fr. OE, fr. L Augustus, fr. Augustus Caesar] : the 8th month of the year

**au jus** \ō-'zhü, -'zhüs, -'jüs; ō-zhœ\ adj [F] : served in the juice obtained from roasting

**auk** \'ȯk\ n : any of several stocky black-and-white diving seabirds that breed in colder parts of the northern hemisphere

**auld** \'ȯl, 'ȯld, 'äl, 'äld\ adj, chiefly Scot : OLD

**aunt** \'ant, 'änt\ n 1 : the sister of one's father or mother 2 : the wife of one's uncle

**aunt·ie** \'an-tē, 'än-\ n : AUNT

**au pair** \ō-'per\ n [F, on even terms] : a usu. young foreign person who does domestic work for a family in return for room and board and to learn the family's language

**au·ra** \'ȯr-ə\ n 1 : a distinctive atmosphere surrounding a given source 2 : a luminous radiation

**au·ral** \'ȯr-əl\ adj : of or relating to the ear or to the sense of hearing

**aurar** pl of EYRIR

**au·re·ole** \'ȯr-ē-ˌōl\ or **au·re·o·la** \ȯ-'rē-ə-lə\ n : HALO, NIMBUS

**au re·voir** \ˌō-rə-'vwär\ n [F, lit., till seeing again] : GOOD-BYE

**au·ri·cle** \'ȯr-i-kəl\ n : an atrium of the heart

**au·ric·u·lar** \ȯ-'ri-kyə-lər\ adj 1 : told privately ⟨∼ confession⟩ 2 : known or recognized by the sense of hearing

**au·ro·ra** \ə-'rȯr-ə\ n, pl **auroras** or **au·ro·rae** \-(ˌ)ē\ : a luminous phenomenon of streamers or arches of light appearing in the upper atmosphere esp. of a planet's polar regions — **au·ro·ral** \-əl\ adj

**aurora aus·tra·lis** \-ȯ-'strā-ləs\ n : an aurora that occurs in earth's southern hemisphere

**aurora bo·re·al·is** \-ˌbȯr-ē-ˈa-ləs\ *n* : an aurora that occurs in earth's northern hemisphere

**AUS** *abbr* Army of the United States

**aus·pice** \ˈȯ-spəs\ *n, pl* **aus·pic·es** \-spə-səz, -ˌsēz\ [L *auspicium*, fr. *auspic-, auspex* diviner by birds, fr. *avis* bird + *specere* to look, look at] **1** : observation of birds by an augur **2** *pl* : kindly patronage and protection **3** : a prophetic sign or omen

**aus·pi·cious** \ȯ-ˈspi-shəs\ *adj* **1** : promising success : PROPITIOUS **2** : FORTUNATE, PROSPEROUS ⟨an ∼ year⟩ — **aus·pi·cious·ly** *adv* — **aus·pi·cious·ness** *n*

**aus·tere** \ȯ-ˈstir\ *adj* **1** : STERN, SEVERE, STRICT ⟨∼ Puritans⟩ **2** : markedly simple ⟨an ∼ lifestyle⟩ **3** : UNADORNED ⟨∼ furnishings⟩ — **aus·tere·ly** *adv* — **aus·ter·i·ty** \-ˈster-ə-tē\ *n*

**aus·tral** \ˈȯs-trəl\ *adj* : SOUTHERN

**Aus·tro·ne·sian** \ˌȯs-trə-ˈnē-zhən\ *adj* : of, relating to, or constituting a family of languages spoken in the area extending from Madagascar eastward through the Malay Peninsula to Hawaii and Easter Island

**auth** *abbr* **1** authentic **2** author **3** authorized

**au·then·tic** \ə-ˈthen-tik, ȯ-\ *adj* : GENUINE, REAL — **au·then·ti·cal·ly** \-ti-k(ə-)lē\ *adv* — **au·then·tic·i·ty** \-ˌthen-ˈti-sə-tē\ *n*

**au·then·ti·cate** \ə-ˈthen-ti-ˌkāt, ȯ-\ *vb* **-cat·ed; -cat·ing** : to prove genuine — **au·then·ti·ca·tion** \-ˌthen-ti-ˈkā-shən\ *n*

**au·thor** \ˈȯ-thər\ *n* [ME *auctour*, fr. AF *auctor, autor*, fr. L *auctor* originator, author, fr. *augēre* to increase] **1** : one that originates or creates **2** : one that writes or composes a literary work

**au·thor·ess** \ˈȯ-thə-rəs\ *n* : a woman author

**au·tho·ri·za·tion, au·tho·rise** *Brit var of* AUTHORIZATION, AUTHORIZE

**au·thor·i·tar·i·an** \ə-ˌthär-ə-ˈter-ē-ən, ə-, -ˌthȯr-\ *adj* **1** : characterized by or favoring the principle of blind obedience to authority **2** : characterized by or favoring concentration of political power in an authority not responsible to the people — **authoritarian** *n*

**au·thor·i·ta·tive** \ə-ˈthär-ə-ˌtā-tiv, ȯ-, -ˈthȯr-\ *adj* : supported by, proceeding from, or being an authority — **au·thor·i·ta·tive·ly** *adv* — **au·thor·i·ta·tive·ness** *n*

**au·thor·i·ty** \ə-ˈthär-ə-tē, ȯ-, -ˈthȯr-\ *n, pl* **-ties 1** : a citation used in support of a statement or in defense of an action; *also* : the source of such a citation **2** : one appealed to as an expert **3** : power to influence thought or behavior **4** : freedom granted : RIGHT **5** : persons in command; *esp* : GOVERNMENT **6** : convincing force

**au·tho·rize** \ˈȯ-thə-ˌrīz\ *vb* **-rized; -riz·ing 1** : SANCTION ⟨custom *authorized* by time⟩ **2** : to give legal power to — **au·tho·ri·za·tion** \ˌȯ-thə-rə-ˈzā-shən\ *n*

**au·thor·ship** \ˈȯ-thər-ˌship\ *n* **1** : the state of being an author **2** : the source of a piece of writing, music, or art

**au·tism** \ˈȯ-ˌti-zəm\ *n* : a disorder that appears by age three and is characterized esp. by impaired ability to communicate with others and form normal social relationships and by repetitive patterns of behavior — **au·tis·tic** \ȯ-ˈtis-tik\ *adj*

**¹au·to** \ˈȯ-tō\ *n, pl* **autos** : AUTOMOBILE

**²auto** *abbr* automatic

**au·to·bahn** \ˈȯ-tō-ˌbän, ˈau̇-\ *n* : a German, Swiss, or Austrian expressway

**au·to·bi·og·ra·phy** \ˌȯ-tə-bī-ˈä-grə-fē\ *n* : the biography of a person narrated by that person — **au·to·bi·og·ra·pher** \-fər\ *n* — **au·to·bi·o·graph·i·cal** \-ˌbī-ə-ˈgra-fi-kəl\ *adj* — **au·to·bi·o·graph·i·cal·ly** \-k(ə-)lē\ *adv*

**au·toch·tho·nous** \ȯ-ˈtäk-thə-nəs\ *adj* : INDIGENOUS, NATIVE ⟨an ∼ people⟩

**au·to·clave** \ˈȯ-tō-ˌklāv\ *n* : an apparatus (as for sterilizing) using superheated high-pressure steam

**au·toc·ra·cy** \ȯ-ˈtä-krə-sē\ *n, pl* **-cies** : government by one person having unlimited power — **au·to·crat** \ˈȯ-tə-ˌkrat\ *n* — **au·to·crat·ic** \ˌȯ-tə-ˈkra-tik\ *adj* — **au·to·crat·i·cal·ly** \-ti-k(ə-)lē\ *adv*

**¹au·to·graph** \ˈȯ-tə-ˌgraf\ *n* **1** : an original manuscript **2** : a person's signature written by hand

**²autograph** *vb* : to write one's signature on

**au·to·im·mune** \ˌȯ-tō-i-ˈmyün\ *adj* : of, relating to, or caused by antibodies or lymphocytes that attack molecules, cells, or tissues of the organism producing them ⟨∼ diseases⟩ — **au·to·im·mu·ni·ty** \-i-ˈmyü-nə-tē\ *n*

**au·to·mate** \ˈȯ-tə-ˌmat\ *vb* **-mat·ed; -mat·ing 1** : to operate automatically using mechanical or electronic devices **2** : to convert to automatic operation — **au·to·ma·tion** \ȯ-tə-ˈmā-shən\ *n*

**automated teller machine** *n* : ATM

**¹au·to·mat·ic** \ˌȯ-tə-ˈma-tik\ *adj* **1** : INVOLUNTARY **2** : made so that certain parts act in a desired manner at the proper time : SELF-ACTING ⟨an ∼ transmission⟩ — **au·to·mat·i·cal·ly** \-ti-k(ə-)lē\ *adv*

**²automatic** *n* : an automatic device; *esp* : an automatic firearm

**automatic teller** *n* : ATM

**automatic teller machine** *n* : ATM

**au·tom·a·ton** \ȯ-ˈtä-mə-tən, -ˌtän\ *n, pl* **-atons** *or* **-a·ta** \-ə-tə, -ˌtä\ **1** : an automatic machine; *esp* : ROBOT **2** : an individual who acts mechanically

**au·to·mo·bile** \ˈȯ-tə-mō-ˌbēl, ˌȯ-tə-mə-ˈbēl\ *n* : a usu. 4-wheeled automotive vehicle for passenger transportation

**au·to·mo·tive** \ˌȯ-tə-ˈmō-tiv\ *adj* **1** : of or relating to automobiles, trucks, or buses **2** : SELF-PROPELLED

**au·to·nom·ic nervous system** \ˌȯ-tə-ˈnä-mik-\ *n* : a part of the vertebrate nervous system that governs involuntary actions and that consists of the sympathetic nervous system and the parasympathetic nervous system

**au·ton·o·mous** \ȯ-'tä-nə-məs\ *adj* : having the right or power of self-government — **au·ton·o·mous·ly** *adv* — **au·ton·o·my** \-mē\ *n*

**au·top·sy** \'ȯ-ˌtäp-sē, 'ȯ-təp-\ *n, pl* **-sies** [Gk *autopsia* act of seeing with one's own eyes, fr. *autos* self + *opsis* sight] : examination of a dead body usu. with dissection sufficient to determine the cause of death or extent of change produced by disease — **autopsy** *vb*

**au·tumn** \'ȯ-təm\ *n* : the season between summer and winter — **au·tum·nal** \ȯ-'təm-nəl\ *adj*

**aux** *abbr* auxiliary

**¹aux·il·ia·ry** \ȯg-'zil-yə-rē, -'zi-lə-rē\ *adj* 1 : providing help 2 : functioning in a subsidiary capacity 3 : accompanying a verb form to express person, number, mood, or tense ⟨∼ verbs⟩

**²auxiliary** *n, pl* **-ries** 1 : an auxiliary person, group, or device 2 : an auxiliary verb

**aux·in** \'ȯk-sən\ *n* : a plant hormone that stimulates growth in length

**av** *abbr* 1 avenue 2 average 3 avoirdupois

**AV** *abbr* 1 ad valorem 2 audiovisual 3 Authorized Version

**¹avail** \ə-'vāl\ *vb* : to be of use or advantage : HELP, BENEFIT

**²avail** *n* : USE ⟨effort was of no ∼⟩

**avail·able** \ə-'vā-lə-bəl\ *adj* 1 : USABLE ⟨∼ resources⟩ 2 : ACCESSIBLE ⟨∼ in any drugstore⟩ — **avail·abil·i·ty** \-ˌvā-lə-'bi-lə-tē\ *n*

**av·a·lanche** \'a-və-ˌlanch\ *n* : a mass of snow, ice, earth, or rock sliding down a mountainside

**avant–garde** \ˌä-ˌvän-'gärd, ˌa-ˌvänt-\ *n* [F, vanguard] : those esp. in the arts who create or apply new or experimental ideas and techniques — **avant–garde** *adj*

**av·a·rice** \'a-və-rəs\ *n* : excessive desire for wealth : GREED — **av·a·ri·cious** \ˌa-və-'ri-shəs\ *adj*

**avast** \ə-'vast\ *vb imper* — a nautical command to stop or cease

**av·a·tar** \'a-və-ˌtär\ *n* [Skt *avatāra* descent] : INCARNATION

**avaunt** \ə-'vȯnt\ *adv* : AWAY, HENCE

**avdp** *abbr* avoirdupois

**ave** *abbr* avenue

**Ave Ma·ria** \ˌä-ˌvā-mə-'rē-ə\ *n* : HAIL MARY 1

**avenge** \ə-'venj\ *vb* **avenged; aveng·ing** : to take vengeance for — **aveng·er** *n*

**av·e·nue** \'a-və-ˌnü, -ˌnyü\ *n* 1 : a way or route to a place or goal : PATH 2 : a broad street

**aver** \ə-'vər\ *vb* **averred; aver·ring** : ALLEGE, ASSERT; *also* : DECLARE

**¹av·er·age** \'a-və-rij, 'a-vrij\ *n* [earlier, proportionally distributed charge for damage at sea, modif. of MF *avarie* damage to ship or cargo, fr. It *avaria*, fr. Ar '*awārīyah* damaged merchandise] 1 : ARITHMETIC MEAN 2 : a ratio of suc-

cessful tries to total tries esp. in athletics ⟨batting ∼ of .303⟩

**²average** *adj* 1 : equaling or approximating an arithmetic mean 2 : being about midway between extremes 3 : not out of the ordinary : COMMON

**³average** *vb* **av·er·aged; av·er·ag·ing** 1 : to be at or come to an average 2 : to be, do, or get usually 3 : to find the average of

**averse** \ə-'vərs\ *adj* : having an active feeling of dislike or reluctance ⟨∼ to exercise⟩

**aver·sion** \ə-'vər-zhən\ *n* 1 : a feeling of repugnance for something with a desire to avoid it 2 : something decidedly disliked

**avert** \ə-'vərt\ *vb* 1 : to turn aside or away ⟨∼ the eyes⟩ 2 : to ward off

**avg** *abbr* average

**avi·an** \'ā-vē-ən\ *adj* [L *avis* bird] : of, relating to, or derived from birds

**avi·ary** \'ā-vē-ˌer-ē\ *n, pl* **-ar·ies** : a place for keeping birds confined

**avi·a·tion** \ˌā-vē-'ā-shən, ˌa-\ *n* 1 : the operation of heavier-than-air aircraft 2 : aircraft manufacture, development, and design

**avi·a·tor** \'ā-vē-ˌā-tər, 'a-\ *n* : an airplane pilot

**avi·a·trix** \ˌā-vē-'ā-triks, ˌa-\ *n, pl* **-trix·es** \-trik-səz\ *or* **-tri·ces** \-trə-ˌsēz\ : a woman airplane pilot

**av·id** \'a-vəd\ *adj* 1 : craving eagerly : GREEDY 2 : enthusiastic in pursuit of an interest — **avid·i·ty** \ə-'vi-də-tē, a-\ *n* — **av·id·ly** *adv* — **av·id·ness** *n*

**avi·on·ics** \ˌā-vē-'ä-niks, ˌa-\ *n pl* : electronics designed for use in aerospace vehicles — **avi·on·ic** \-nik\ *adj*

**avo** \'a-(ˌ)vü\ *n, pl* **avos** — see *pataca* at MONEY table

**av·o·ca·do** \ˌa-və-'kä-dō, ˌä-\ *n, pl* **-dos** *also* **-does** [modif. of Sp *aguacate*, fr. Nahuatl *āhuacatl*, avocado, testicle] : a pulpy green- to purple-skinned nutty=flavored fruit of a tropical American tree; *also* : this tree

**avo·ca·tion** \ˌa-və-'kā-shən\ *n* : HOBBY

**av·o·cet** \'a-və-ˌset\ *n* : any of several long-legged shorebirds with webbed feet and slender upward-curving bills

**avoid** \ə-'vȯid\ *vb* 1 : to keep away from : SHUN 2 : to prevent the occurrence of 3 : to refrain from — **avoid·able** *adj* — **avoid·ably** *adv* — **avoid·ance** \ə-'vȯi-dəns\ *n*

**av·oir·du·pois** \ˌa-vər-də-'pȯiz\ *n* [ME *avoir de pois* goods sold by weight, fr. AF, lit., goods of weight] 1 : AVOIRDUPOIS WEIGHT 2 : WEIGHT, HEAVINESS; *esp* : personal weight

**avoirdupois weight** *n* : a system of weights based on a pound of 16 ounces and an ounce of 16 drams (28 grams) — see WEIGHT table

**avouch** \ə-'vauch\ *vb* 1 : to declare positively 2 : to vouch for

**avow** \ə-'vau\ *vb* : to declare openly — **avow·al** \-'vau(-ə)l\ *n*

**avun·cu·lar** \ə-'vən-kyə-lər\ *adj* : of, relating to, or resembling an uncle

**await** \ə-'wāt\ *vb* : to wait for : EXPECT

**¹awake** \ə-'wāk\ *vb* awoke \-'wōk\ *also* awaked \-'wākt\; awo·ken \-'wōkən\ *or* awaked *also* awoke; awak·ing : to bring back to consciousness : wake up

**²awake** *adj* : not asleep; *also* : ALERT

**awak·en** \ə-'wā-kən\ *vb* awak·ened; awak·en·ing \-'wā-kə-niŋ\ : AWAKE

**¹award** \ə-'word\ *vb* **1** : to give by judicial decision ⟨~ damages⟩ **2** : to give in recognition of merit or achievement

**²award** *n* **1** : a final decision : JUDGMENT **2** : something awarded : PRIZE

**aware** \ə-'wer\ *adj* : having perception or knowledge : CONSCIOUS, INFORMED — **aware·ness** *n*

**awash** \ə-'wȯsh, -'wäsh\ *adj* **1** : washed by waves or tide **2** : AFLOAT : FLOODED ⟨the street was ~ after the storm⟩

**¹away** \ə-'wā\ *adv* **1** : from this or that place ⟨go ~⟩ **2** : out of the way **3** : in another direction ⟨turn ~⟩ **4** : out of existence ⟨fade ~⟩ **5** : from one's possession ⟨give ~⟩ **6** : without interruption ⟨chatter ~⟩ **7** : at a distance in space or time ⟨far ~⟩ ⟨~ back in 1910⟩

**²away** *adj* **1** : ABSENT **2** : distant in space or time ⟨a lake 10 miles ~⟩

**¹awe** \'ȯ\ *n* **1** : profound and reverent dread of the supernatural **2** : respectful fear inspired by authority

**²awe** *vb* **awed; aw·ing** : to inspire with awe

**aweigh** \ə-'wā\ *adj* : just clear of the bottom ⟨anchors ~⟩

**awe·some** \'ȯ-səm\ *adj* **1** : expressive of awe ⟨~ tribute⟩ **2** : inspiring awe

**awe·struck** \-,strək\ *also* **awe·strick·en** \-,stri-kən\ *adj* : filled with awe

**aw·ful** \'ȯ-fəl\ *adj* **1** : inspiring awe **2** : extremely disagreeable **3** : very great ⟨an ~ lot of money⟩ — **aw·ful·ly** *adv*

**awhile** \ə-'hwīl\ *adv* : for a while

**awhirl** \ə-'hwərl\ *adj* : being in a whirl

**awk·ward** \'ȯ-kwərd\ *adj* **1** : CLUMSY ⟨~ with needle and thread⟩ **2** : UNGRACEFUL ⟨~ writing⟩ **3** : difficult to explain : EMBARRASSING **4** : difficult to deal with — **awk·ward·ly** *adv* — **awk·ward·ness** *n*

**awl** \'ȯl\ *n* : a pointed instrument for making small holes

**aw·ning** \'ȯ-niŋ\ *n* : a rooflike cover (as of canvas) extended over or in front of a place as a shelter

**AWOL** \'ā-,wȯl, ,ā-,də-bəl-yü-,ō-'el\ *n* : a person who is absent without leave — **AWOL** *adj or adv*

**awry** \ə-'rī\ *adv or adj* **1** : ASKEW ⟨with hair ~⟩ **2** : AMISS ⟨their plans went ~⟩

**ax** *or* **axe** \'aks\ *n* : a chopping or cutting tool with an edged head fitted parallel to a handle

**ax·i·al** \'ak-sē-əl\ *adj* **1** : of, relating to, or functioning as an axis **2** : situated around, in the direction of, on, or along an axis — **ax·i·al·ly** *adv*

**ax·i·om** \'ak-sē-əm\ *n* [L *axioma*, fr. Gk *axiōma*, lit., something worthy, fr. *axioun* to think worthy, fr. *axios* worthy] **1** : a statement generally accepted as true : MAXIM **2** : a proposition regarded as a self-evident truth — **ax·i·om·at·ic** \,ak-sē-ə-'ma-tik\ *adj* — **ax·i·om·at·i·cal·ly** \-ti-k(ə-)lē\ *adv*

**ax·is** \'ak-səs\ *n, pl* **ax·es** \-,sēz\ **1** : a straight line around which a body rotates **2** : a straight line or structure with respect to which a body or figure is symmetrical **3** : one of the reference lines of a system of coordinates **4** : an alliance between major powers

**ax·le** \'ak-səl\ *n* : a shaft on which a wheel revolves

**ax·on** \'ak-,sän\ *n* : the long thin usu. unbranched part of a nerve cell that usu. conducts impulses away from the cell body

**ayah** \'ī-ə\ *n* [Hindi & Urdu *āyā*, fr. Pg *aia*, fr. L *avia* grandmother] : a nurse or maid native to India

**aya·tol·lah** \,ī-ə-'tō-lə\ *n* [Pers *āyatollāh*, lit., sign of God, fr. Ar *aya* sign, miracle + *allāh* God] : an Islamic religious leader used as a title of respect

**¹aye** *also* **ay** \'ā\ *adv* : ALWAYS, EVER

**²aye** *also* **ay** \'ī\ *adv* : YES

**³aye** *also* **ay** \'ī\ *n, pl* **ayes** : an affirmative vote

**AZ** *abbr* Arizona

**aza·lea** \ə-'zāl-yə\ *n* : any of numerous rhododendrons with funnel-shaped blossoms and usu. deciduous leaves

**az·i·do·thy·mi·dine** \ə-,zī-dō-'thī-mə-,dēn\ *n* : AZT

**az·i·muth** \'a-zə-məth\ *n* : horizontal direction expressed as an angular distance from a fixed point

**AZT** \,ā-(,)zē-'tē\ *n* : an antiviral drug used to treat AIDS

**Az·tec** \'az-,tek\ *n* : a member of a Nahuatl-speaking people that founded the Mexican empire and were conquered by Hernan Cortes in 1519 — **Az·tec·an** *adj*

**azure** \'a-zhər\ *n* : the blue of the clear sky — **azure** *adj*

¹b \'bē\ *n, pl* **b's** *or* **bs** \'bēz\ *often cap* **1** : the 2d letter of the English alphabet **2** : a grade rating a student's work as good

²b *abbr, often cap* **1** bachelor **2** bass **3** bishop **4** book **5** born

**B** *symbol* boron

**Ba** *symbol* barium

**BA** *abbr* **1** bachelor of arts **2** batting average

**bab·ble** \'ba-bəl\ *vb* **bab·bled; bab·bling 1** : to talk enthusiastically or excessively **2** : to utter meaningless sounds — **bab·ble** *n* — **bab·bler** \-b(ə-)lər\ *n*

**babe** \'bāb\ *n* **1** : BABY **2** *slang* : GIRL, WOMAN

**ba·bel** \'bā-bəl, 'ba-\ *n, often cap* [fr. the Tower of *Babel*, Gen 11:4–9] : a place or scene of noise and confusion; *also* : a confused sound ♦ **Synonyms** HUBBUB, RACKET, DIN, UPROAR, CLAMOR

**ba·boon** \ba-'bün\ *n* [ME *babewin*, fr. MF *babouin*, fr. *baboue* grimace] : any of several large apes of Asia and Africa with doglike muzzles

**ba·bush·ka** \bə-'büsh-kə, -'bush-\ *n* [Russ, grandmother, dim. of *baba* old woman] : a kerchief for the head

¹**ba·by** \'bā-bē\ *n, pl* **babies 1** : a very young child : INFANT **2** : the youngest or smallest of a group **3** : a childish person — **baby** *adj* — **ba·by·hood** *n* — **ba·by·ish** *adj*

²**baby** *vb* **ba·bied; ba·by·ing** : to tend or treat often with excessive care

**baby boom** *n* : a marked rise in birthrate — **baby boom·er** \-'bü-mər\ *n*

**baby's breath** *n* : any of a genus of herbs that are related to the pinks and have small delicate flowers

**ba·by·sit** \'bā-bē-ˌsit\ *vb* **-sat** \-ˌsat\; **-sit·ting** : to care for children usu. during a short absence of the parents — **ba·by·sit·ter** *n*

**bac·ca·lau·re·ate** \ˌba-kə-'lȯr-ē-ət\ *n* **1** : the degree of bachelor conferred by colleges and universities **2** : a sermon delivered to a graduating class

**bac·ca·rat** \ˌbä-kə-'rä, ˌba-\ *n* : a card game in which three hands are dealt and players may bet either or both hands against the dealer's

**bac·cha·nal** \'ba-kə-nᵊl, ˌba-kə-'nal, ˌbä-kə-'näl\ *n* **1** : ORGY **2** : REVELER

**bac·cha·na·lia** \ˌba-kə-'nāl-yə\ *n, pl* **bacchanalia** : a drunken orgy — **bac·cha·na·lian** \-'nāl-yən\ *adj or n*

**bach·e·lor** \'bach-lər, 'ba-chə-lər\ *n* **1** : a person who has received the usu. lowest degree conferred by a 4-year college **2** : an unmarried man — **bach·e·lor·hood** *n*

**bach·e·lor·ette** \ˌbach-lə-'ret, ˌba-chə-\ *n* : a young unmarried woman

**bachelor's button** *n* : a European plant related to the daisies and having usu. blue, pink, or white flower heads

**ba·cil·lus** \bə-'si-ləs\ *n, pl* **-li** \-ˌlī\ [NL, fr. ML, small staff, dim. of L *baculus* staff] : any of a genus of rod-shaped bacteria; *also* : a disease-producing bacterium — **bac·il·lary** \'ba-sə-ˌler-ē\ *adj*

¹**back** \'bak\ *n* **1** : the rear or dorsal part of the human body; *also* : the corresponding part of a lower animal **2** : the part or surface opposite the front **3** : a player in the backfield in football — **back·less** \-ləs\ *adj*

²**back** *adv* **1** : to, toward, or at the rear **2** : AGO **3** : so as to be restrained or delayed **4** : to, toward, or in a former place or state **5** : in return or reply

³**back** *adj* **1** : located at or in the back; *also* : REMOTE **2** : OVERDUE ⟨~ rent⟩ **3** : moving or operating backward **4** : not current ⟨~ issues of a magazine⟩

⁴**back** *vb* **1** : SUPPORT, UPHOLD **2** : to go or cause to go backward or in reverse **3** : to furnish with a back : form the back of — **back·er** *n*

**back·ache** \'bak-ˌāk\ *n* : a pain in the lower back

**back–bench·er** \-'ben-chər\ *n* : a rank-and-file member of a British legislature

**back·bite** \-ˌbīt\ *vb* **-bit** \-ˌbit\; **-bit·ten** \-ˌbi-tᵊn\; **-bit·ing** \-ˌbī-tiŋ\ : to say mean or spiteful things about someone who is absent — **back·bit·er** *n*

**back·board** \-ˌbȯrd\ *n* : a board placed at or serving as the back of something

**back·bone** \-ˌbōn\ *n* **1** : the bony column in the back of a vertebrate that is the chief support of the trunk and consists of a jointed series of vertebrae enclosing and protecting the spinal cord **2** : firm resolute character **3** : the primary high-speed hardware and transmission lines of a telecommunication network

**back·drop** \'bak-ˌdräp\ *n* : a painted cloth hung across the rear of a stage

**back·field** \-ˌfēld\ *n* : the football players whose positions are behind the line

¹**back·fire** \-ˌfī(-ə)r\ *n* : a loud noise caused by the improperly timed explosion of fuel in the cylinder of an internal combustion engine

²**backfire** *vb* **1** : to make or undergo a backfire **2** : to have a result opposite to what was intended

**back·flip** \-ˌflip\ *n* : a backward somersault esp. in the air

**back·gam·mon** \'bak-ˌga-mən\ *n* : a game played with pieces on a double board in which the moves are determined by throwing dice

**back·ground** \'bak-ˌgraùnd\ *n* **1** : the scenery behind something **2** : the setting within which something takes place; *also* : the sum of a person's experience, training, and understanding

**back·hand** \'bak-ˌhand\ *n* : a stroke (as in tennis) made with the back of the hand

turned in the direction of movement; *also*
: the side on which such a stroke is made
— **back·hand** *vb*

**back·hand·ed** \'bak-'han-dəd\ *adj* 1 : IN-
DIRECT, DEVIOUS; *esp* : SARCASTIC (a ~
compliment) 2 : using or made with a
backhand (a ~ catch)

**back·hoe** \'bak-,hō\ *n* : an excavating
machine having a bucket that is drawn
toward the machine

**back·ing** \'ba-kiŋ\ *n* 1 : something forming a back 2 : SUPPORT, AID (needed financial ~); *also* : a body of supporters

**back·lash** \'bak-,lash\ *n* 1 : a sudden violent backward movement or reaction 2
: a strong adverse reaction

¹**back·log** \-,lóg, -,läg\ *n* 1 : a large log at
the back of a hearth fire 2 : an accumulation of tasks unperformed or materials
not processed

²**backlog** *vb* : to accumulate in reserve

**back of** *prep* : BEHIND

**back order** *n* : a business order yet to be
fulfilled because stock is unavailable —
**back–order** *vb*

**back out** *vb* : to withdraw esp. from a
commitment or contest

¹**back·pack** \'bak-,pak\ *n* : a camping
pack supported by an aluminum frame
and carried on the back

²**backpack** *vb* : to hike with a backpack —
**back·pack·er** *n*

**back·ped·al** \'bak-,pe-dᵊl\ *vb* : RETREAT

**back·rest** \-,rest\ *n* : a rest for the back

**back·side** \-,sīd\ *n* : BUTTOCKS

**back·slap** \-,slap\ *vb* : to display excessive
cordiality — **back·slap·per** *n*

**back·slide** \-,slīd\ *vb* **-slid** \-,slid\; **-slid**
*or* **-slid·den** \-,sli-dᵊn\; **-slid·ing** \-,slī-
diŋ\ : to lapse morally or in religious
practice — **back·slid·er** *n*

**back·space** \-,spās\ *vb* : to move back a
space in a text with the press of a key —
**backspace** *n*

**back·spin** \-,spin\ *n* : a backward rotary
motion of a ball

¹**back·stage** \'bak-'stāj\ *adj* 1 : relating to
or occurring in the area behind a stage 2
: of or relating to the private lives of theater people 3 : of or relating to the inner
working or operation

²**back·stage** \'bak-'stāj\ *adv* 1 : in or to a
backstage area 2 : SECRETLY (worked
~ to gain support)

**back·stairs** \-,sterz\ *adj* : SECRET, FUR-
TIVE; *also* : SORDID, SCANDALOUS

¹**back·stop** \-,stäp\ *n* : something serving
as a stop behind something else; *esp* : a
screen or fence to keep a ball from leaving the field of play

²**backstop** *vb* 1 : SUPPORT 2 : to serve as
a backstop to

**back·sto·ry** \-,stȯr-ē\ *n* : a story that tells
what led up to the main story or plot (as
of a film)

**back·stretch** \'bak-'strech\ *n* : the side opposite the homestretch on a racecourse

**back·stroke** \-,strōk\ *n* : a swimming
stroke executed on the back — **back·
strok·er** \-,strō-kər\ *n*

**back talk** *n* : impudent, insolent, or argumentative replies

**back·track** \'bak-,trak\ *vb* 1 : to retrace
one's course 2 : to reverse a position or
stand

**back·up** \-,əp\ *n* 1 : one that serves as a
substitute or alternative 2 : a copy of
computer data — **back up** *vb*

¹**back·ward** \'bak-wərd\ *or* **back·wards**
\-wərdz\ *adv* 1 : toward the back 2
: with the back foremost (ride ~) 3 : in
a reverse or contrary direction or way
(count ~) 4 : toward the past; *also* : toward a worse state

²**backward** *adj* 1 : directed, turned, or
done backward 2 : DIFFIDENT, SHY 3
: slow in development or learning —
**back·ward·ly** *adv* — **back·ward·ness** *n*

**back·wash** \'bak-,wȯsh, -,wäsh\ *n* : a
backward flow or movement (as of water
or air) produced by a propelling force (as
the motion of oars)

**back·wa·ter** \-,wȯ-tər, -,wä-\ *n* 1 : water
held or turned back in its course 2 : an
isolated or backward place or condition

**back·woods** \-'wu̇dz\ *n pl* 1 : wooded or
partly cleared areas far from cities 2 : a
remote or isolated place

**ba·con** \'bā-kən\ *n* : salted and smoked
meat from the sides or back of a pig

**bacteria** *pl of* BACTERIUM

**bac·te·ri·cid·al** \bak-,tir-ə-'sī-dᵊl\ *adj*
: destroying bacteria — **bac·te·ri·cide**
\-'tir-ə-,sīd\ *n*

**bac·te·ri·ol·o·gy** \bak-,tir-e-'ä-lə-jē\ *n* 1
: a science dealing with bacteria 2 : bacterial life and phenomena — **bac·te·ri·o·
log·ic** \-ə-'lä-jik\ *or* **bac·te·ri·o·log·i·cal**
\-ə-'lä-ji-kəl\ *adj* — **bac·te·ri·ol·o·gist**
\-'ä-lə-jist\ *n*

**bac·te·rio·phage** \bak-'tir-ē-ə-,fāj\ *n*
: any of various viruses that attack specific bacteria

**bac·te·ri·um** \bak-'tir-ē-əm\ *n, pl* **-ria** \-ē-
ə\ [NL, fr. Gk *baktērion* staff] : any of a
group of single-celled microorganisms
including some that cause disease and
others that are valued esp. for their
chemical effects (as fermentation) —
**bac·te·ri·al** \-ē-əl\ *adj*

**bad** \'bad\ *adj* **worse** \'wərs\; **worst**
\'wərst\ 1 : below standard : POOR; *also*
: UNFAVORABLE (a ~ report) 2
: SPOILED, DECAYED 3 : WICKED; *also*
: not well-behaved : NAUGHTY 4 : DIS-
AGREEABLE (a ~ taste); *also* : HARM-
FUL 5 : DEFECTIVE, FAULTY (~ wiring);
*also* : not valid (a ~ check) 6 : UN-
WELL, ILL 7 : SORRY, REGRETFUL (feels
~ about forgetting to call) ♦ **Syn-
onyms** EVIL, WRONG, IMMORAL, INIQUI-
TOUS — **bad·ly** *adv* — **bad·ness** *n*

**bade** *past and past part of* BID

**badge** \'baj\ *n* : a device or token usu.
worn as a sign of status

¹**bad·ger** \'ba-jər\ *n* : any of several sturdy
burrowing mammals with long claws on
their forefeet

²**badger** *vb* : to harass or annoy persistently

**ba·di·nage** \,ba-də-'näzh\ *n* [F] : playful
talk back and forth : BANTER

**bad·land** \'bad-,land\ *n* : a region marked
by intricate erosional sculpturing and
scanty vegetation — usu. used in pl.

# badminton • balboa

**52**

**bad·min·ton** \'bad-,mi-t⁵n, -,min-t⁵n\ *n* : a court game played with light rackets and a shuttlecock volleyed over a net

**bad–mouth** \'bad-,maúth\ *vb* : to criticize severely

**Bae·de·ker** \'bā-di-kər, 'be-\ *n* : GUIDEBOOK

¹**baf·fle** \'ba-fəl\ *vb* **baf·fled; baf·fling** \-f(ə-)liŋ\ 1 : FRUSTRATE, THWART, FOIL; *also* : PERPLEX — **baf·fle·ment** *n*

²**baffle** *n* : a device (as a wall or screen) to deflect, check, or regulate flow (as of liquid or sound) — **baf·fled** \'ba-fəld\ *adj*

¹**bag** \'bag\ *n* 1 : a flexible usu. closable container (as for storing or carrying) 2 : something that bulges and sags like a bag ⟨∼s under the eyes⟩

²**bag** *vb* **bagged; bag·ging** 1 : DISTEND, BULGE 2 : to put in a bag 3 : to get possession of; *esp* : to take in hunting ♦ **Synonyms** TRAP, SNARE, CATCH, CAPTURE, COLLAR

**ba·gasse** \bə-'gas\ *n* [F] : plant residue (as of sugarcane) left after a product (as juice) has been extracted

**bag·a·telle** \,ba-gə-'tel\ *n* [F] : TRIFLE 1

**ba·gel** \'bā-gəl\ *n* [Yiddish beygl] : a firm doughnut-shaped roll usu. made by boiling and then baking

**bag·gage** \'ba-gij\ *n* 1 : the traveling bags and personal belongings of a traveler : LUGGAGE 2 : intangible things that get in the way ⟨emotional ∼⟩

**bag·gies** \'ba-gēz\ *n pl* : baggy pants or shorts

**bag·gy** \'ba-gē\ *adj* **bag·gi·er; -est** : puffed out or hanging like a bag ⟨a ∼ sweater⟩ — **bag·gi·ly** \-gə-lē\ *adv* — **bag·gi·ness** \-gē-nəs\ *n*

**bag·man** \'bag-mən\ *n* : a person who collects or distributes illicitly gained money on behalf of another

**ba·gnio** \'ban-yō\ *n, pl* **bagnios** [It *bagno*, lit., public bath] : BROTHEL

**bag of waters** : a double-walled fluid-filled sac that encloses and protects the fetus in the womb and that breaks releasing its fluid during the process of birth

**bag·pipe** \'bag-,pīp\ *n* : a musical wind instrument consisting of a bag, a tube with valves, and sounding pipes — often used in pl. — **bag·pip·er** \-,pī-pər\ *n*

**ba·guette** \ba-'get\ *n* [F, lit., rod] 1 : a gem having the shape of a narrow rectangle; *also* : the shape itself 2 : a long thin loaf of French bread

**baht** \'bät\ *n, pl* **baht** *also* **bahts** — see MONEY table

¹**bail** \'bāl\ *n* : a container for ladling water out of a boat

²**bail** *vb* : to dip and throw out water from a boat — **bail·er** *n*

³**bail** *n* : security given to guarantee a prisoner's appearance when legally required; *also* : one giving such security or the release secured

⁴**bail** *vb* : to release under bail; *also* : to procure the release of by giving bail — **bail·able** \'bā-lə-bəl\ *adj*

⁵**bail** *n* : the arched handle (as of a pail or kettle)

**bai·liff** \'bā-ləf\ *n* 1 : an aide of a British sheriff who serves writs and makes arrests; *also* : a minor officer of a U.S. court 2 : an estate or farm manager esp. in Britain : STEWARD

**bai·li·wick** \'bā-li-,wik\ *n* : one's special province or domain ♦ **Synonyms** TERRITORY, FIELD, SPHERE

**bail·out** \'bā-,laút\ *n* : a rescue from financial distress

**bairn** \'bern\ *n, chiefly Scot* : CHILD

¹**bait** \'bāt\ *vb* 1 : to persecute by continued attacks 2 : to harass with dogs usu. for sport ⟨∼ a bear⟩ 3 : to furnish (as a hook) with bait 4 : ALLURE, ENTICE 5 : to give food and drink to (as an animal) ♦ **Synonyms** BADGER, HECKLE, HOUND

²**bait** *n* 1 : a lure for catching animals (as fish) 2 : LURE, TEMPTATION ♦ **Synonyms** SNARE, TRAP, DECOY, COME-ON, ENTICEMENT

**bait·fish** \'bāt-,fish\ *n* : a small fish that attracts and is a food source for a larger fish; *also* : a fish used for bait

**bai·za** \'bī-(,)zä\ *n, pl* **baiza** *or* **baizas** — see *rial* at MONEY table

**baize** \'bāz\ *n* : a coarse feltlike fabric

¹**bake** \'bāk\ *vb* **baked; bak·ing** 1 : to cook or become cooked in dry heat esp. in an oven 2 : to dry and harden by heat ⟨∼ bricks⟩ — **bak·er** *n*

²**bake** *n* : a social gathering featuring baked food

**baker's dozen** *n* : THIRTEEN

**bak·ery** \'bā-k(ə-)rē\ *n, pl* **-er·ies** : a place for baking or selling baked goods

**bake sale** *n* : a fund-raising event at which usu. homemade foods are sold

**bake·shop** \'bāk-,shäp\ *n* : BAKERY

**bake·ware** \-,wer\ *n* : dishes used for baking and serving food

**baking powder** *n* : a powder that consists of a carbonate, an acid, and a starch and that makes the dough rise in baking cakes and biscuits

**baking soda** *n* : SODIUM BICARBONATE

**bak·sheesh** \'bak-,shēsh\ *n* : payment (as a tip or bribe) to expedite service

**bal** *abbr* balance

**bal·a·lai·ka** \,ba-lə-'lī-kə\ *n* [Russ] : a triangular 3-stringed instrument of Russian origin played by plucking or strumming

¹**bal·ance** \'ba-ləns\ *n* [ME, fr. AF, fr. VL *bilancia*, fr. LL *bilanc-, bilanx* having two scalepans, fr. L *bi* two + *lanc-, lanx* plate] 1 : a weighing device : SCALE 2 : a weight, force, or influence counteracting the effect of another 3 : an oscillating wheel used to regulate a timepiece 4 : a state of equilibrium 5 : REMAINDER, REST; *esp* : an amount in excess esp. on the credit side of an account — **bal·anced** \-lənst\ *adj*

²**balance** *vb* **bal·anced; bal·anc·ing** 1 : to compute the balance of an account 2 : to arrange so that one set of elements equals another; *also* : to equal or equalize in weight, number, or proportions 3 : WEIGH 4 : to bring or come to a state or position of balance; *also* : to bring into harmony or proportion

**bal·boa** \bal-'bō-ə\ *n* — see MONEY table

**bal·brig·gan** \bal-ʹbri-gən\ n : a knitted cotton fabric used esp. for underwear

**bal·co·ny** \ʹbal-kə-nē\ n, pl **-nies** 1 : a platform projecting from the side of a building and enclosed by a railing 2 : a gallery inside a building

**bald** \ʹbȯld\ adj 1 : lacking a natural or usual covering (as of hair) 2 : UN-ADORNED, PLAIN \the ~ truth\ ♦ **Synonyms** BARE, BARREN, NAKED, NUDE — **bald·ly** adv — **bald·ness** n

**bal·da·chin** \ʹbȯl-də-kən, ʹbal-\ or **bal·da·chi·no** \ˌbal-də-ʹkē-nō\ n, pl **-chins** or **-chinos** : a canopylike structure over an altar

**bald cypress** n : either of two coniferous trees of southern U.S. swamps; also : their hard red wood

**bald eagle** n : a large brown eagle of No. America that when mature has white head and neck feathers and a white tail

**bal·der·dash** \ʹbȯl-dər-ˌdash\ n : NONSENSE

**bald·ing** \ʹbȯl-diŋ\ adj : becoming bald

**bal·dric** \ʹbȯl-drik\ n : a belt worn over the shoulder to carry a sword or bugle

¹**bale** \ʹbāl\ n : a large or closely packed bundle

²**bale** vb **baled; bal·ing** : to pack in a bale — **bal·er** n

**ba·leen** \bə-ʹlēn\ n : a horny substance attached in plates to the upper jaw of some large whales (baleen whales)

**bale·ful** \ʹbāl-fəl\ adj : DEADLY, HARMFUL; also : OMINOUS ♦ **Synonyms** SINISTER, MALEFIC, MALEFICENT, MALIGN

¹**balk** \ʹbȯk\ n 1 : HINDRANCE, CHECK, SETBACK 2 : an illegal motion of the pitcher in baseball while in position

²**balk** vb 1 : BLOCK, THWART 2 : to stop short and refuse to go on 3 : to commit a balk in sports ♦ **Synonyms** FRUSTRATE, BAFFLE, FOIL, THWART — **balky** \ʹbȯ-kē\ adj

¹**ball** \ʹbȯl\ n 1 : a rounded body or mass (as an object used in a game or as a missile); also : a roundish protuberant part of the body \the ~ of the foot\ 2 : a game played with a ball 3 : a pitched baseball that misses the strike zone and is not swung at by the batter 4 : a hit or thrown ball in various games \foul ~\ — **on the ball** : COMPETENT, KNOWLEDGEABLE, ALERT

²**ball** vb : to form into a ball

³**ball** n : a large formal dance

**bal·lad** \ʹba-ləd\ n 1 : a narrative poem of strongly marked rhythm suitable for singing 2 : a simple song : AIR 3 : a slow romantic song

**bal·lad·eer** \ˌba-lə-ʹdir\ n : a singer of ballads

¹**bal·last** \ʹba-ləst\ n 1 : heavy material used to stabilize a ship or control a balloon's ascent 2 : crushed stone laid in a railroad bed or used in making concrete

²**ballast** vb : to provide with ballast ♦ **Synonyms** BALANCE, STABILIZE, STEADY

**ball bearing** n : a bearing in which the revolving part turns upon steel balls that roll easily in a groove; also : one of the balls in such a bearing

**ball·car·ri·er** \ʹbȯl-ˌker-ē-ər\ n : the football player carrying the ball in an offensive play

**ball·er** \ʹbȯ-lər\ n : an implement for shaping food into a ball \melon ~\

**bal·le·ri·na** \ˌba-lə-ʹrē-nə\ n : a female ballet dancer

**bal·let** \ba-ʹlā, ba-ʹlā\ n 1 : dancing in which fixed poses and steps are combined with light flowing movements often to convey a story; also : a theatrical art form using ballet dancing 2 : a company of ballet dancers

**bal·let·o·mane** \ba-ʹle-tə-ˌmān\ n : a devotee of ballet

**bal·lis·tic missile** \bə-ʹlis-tik-\ n : a missile that is guided during ascent and that falls freely during descent

**bal·lis·tics** \-tiks\ n sing or pl 1 : the science of the motion of projectiles (as bullets) in flight 2 : the flight characteristics of a projectile — **ballistic** adj

**ball of fire** : an unusually energetic person

¹**bal·loon** \bə-ʹlün\ n 1 : a bag filled with gas or heated air so as to rise and float in the atmosphere usu. carrying a suspended load 2 : an inflatable bag used as a toy or decoration — **bal·loon·ist** n

²**balloon** vb 1 : to swell or puff out 2 : to travel in a balloon 3 : to increase rapidly

**bal·lot** \ʹba-lət\ n [It ballotta small ball used in secret voting, fr. It dial., dim. of balla ball] 1 : a piece of paper used to cast a vote 2 : the action or a system of voting; also : the right to vote

²**ballot** vb : to decide by ballot : VOTE

**ball·park** \ʹbȯl-ˌpark\ n : a park in which ball games are played

²**ballpark** adj : approximately correct \~ estimate\

**ball·point** \ʹbȯl-ˌpȯint\ n : a pen whose writing point is a small rotating metal ball that inks itself from an inner container

**ball·room** \ʹbȯl-ˌrüm, -ˌrum\ n : a large room for dances

**ballroom dance** n : any of various dances (as the tango, two-step, and waltz) in which couples perform set moves

**bal·ly·hoo** \ʹba-lē-ˌhü\ n, pl **-hoos** : extravagant statements and claims made for publicity — **ballyhoo** vb

**balm** \ʹbäm, ʹbälm\ n 1 : a fragrant healing or soothing lotion or ointment 2 : any of several spicy fragrant herbs of the mint family 3 : something that comforts or soothes

**balmy** \ʹbä-mē, ʹbäl-\ adj **balm·i·er; -est** 1 : gently soothing : MILD 2 : FOOLISH, ABSURD ♦ **Synonyms** SOFT, BLAND, MILD, GENTLE — **balm·i·ness** n

**ba·lo·ney** \bə-ʹlō-nē\ n : NONSENSE

**bal·sa** \ʹbȯl-sə\ n : the extremely light strong wood of a tropical American tree; also : the tree

**bal·sam** \ʹbȯl-səm\ n 1 : a fragrant aromatic and usu. resinous substance oozing from various plants; also : a preparation containing or smelling like balsam 2 : a balsam-yielding tree (as balsam fir) 3 : a common garden ornamental plant — **bal·sam·ic** \bȯl-ʹsa-mik\ adj

**balsam fir** *n* : a resinous No. American evergreen tree that is widely used for pulpwood and as a Christmas tree

**balsamic vinegar** *n* : an aged Italian vinegar made from white grapes

**Balt** \\'bȯlt\ *n* : a native or inhabitant of Lithuania, Latvia, or Estonia

**Bal·ti·more oriole** \\'bȯl-tə-ˌmȯr-\ *n* : a common American oriole in which the male is brightly colored with orange, black, and white

**bal·us·ter** \\'ba-lə-stər\ *n* [F *balustre*, fr. It *balaustro*, fr. *balaustra* wild pomegranate flower, fr. L *balaustium;* fr. its shape] : an upright support for a rail (as of a staircase)

**bal·us·trade** \\'ba-lə-ˌstrād\ *n* : a row of balusters topped by a rail

**bam·boo** \bam-ˈbü\ *n, pl* **bamboos** : any of various woody mostly tall tropical grasses including some with strong hollow stems used for building, furniture, or utensils

**bamboo curtain** *n, often cap B&C* : a political, military, and ideological barrier in eastern Asia

**bam·boo·zle** \bam-ˈbü-zəl\ *vb* **-boo·zled; -boo·zling** : TRICK, HOODWINK

¹**ban** \\'ban\ *vb* **banned; ban·ning** : PROHIBIT, FORBID

²**ban** *n* 1 : CURSE 2 : a legal or formal prohibition ⟨a ~ on beef imports⟩

³**ban** \\'bän\ *n, pl* **ba·ni** \\'bä-nē\ — see *leu* at MONEY table

**ba·nal** \bə-ˈnäl, -ˈnal; ˈbā-nᵊl\ *adj* [F] : COMMONPLACE, TRITE ⟨~ remarks⟩ — **ba·nal·i·ty** \bā-ˈna-lə-tē\ *n*

**ba·nana** \bə-ˈna-nə\ *n* : a treelike tropical plant bearing thick clusters of yellow or reddish finger-shaped fruit; *also* : this fruit

¹**band** \\'band\ *n* 1 : something that binds, ties, or goes around 2 : a strip or stripe that can be distinguished (as by color or texture) from nearby matter 3 : a range of wavelengths (as in radio)

²**band** *vb* 1 : to tie up, finish, or enclose with a band 2 : to gather together or unite esp. for some common end — **band·er** *n*

³**band** *n* : a group of persons, animals, or things; *esp* : a group of musicians organized for playing together

¹**ban·dage** \\'ban-dij\ *n* : a strip of material used esp. in dressing wounds

²**bandage** *vb* **ban·daged; ban·dag·ing** : to dress or cover with a bandage

**Band–Aid** \\'ban-ˌdād\ *adj* : offering, making use of, or serving as a temporary or expedient remedy or solution

**ban·dan·na** *or* **ban·dana** \ban-ˈda-nə\ *n* : a large colored figured handkerchief

**B and B** *abbr* bed-and-breakfast

**band·box** \\'band-ˌbäks\ *n* : a usu. cylindrical box for carrying clothing

**band·ed** \\'ban-dəd\ *adj* : having or marked with bands

**ban·de·role** *or* **ban·de·rol** \\'ban-də-ˌrōl\ *n* : a long narrow forked flag or streamer

**ban·dit** \\'ban-dət\ *n* [It *bandito*, fr. *bandire* to banish] 1 *pl also* **ban·dit·ti** \ban-ˈdi-tē\ : an outlaw who lives by plunder;

*esp* : a member of a band of marauders 2 : ROBBER — **ban·dit·ry** \\'ban-də-trē\ *n*

**ban·do·lier** *or* **ban·do·leer** \ˌban-də-ˈlir\ *n* : a belt slung over the shoulder esp. to carry ammunition

**band saw** *n* : a saw in the form of an endless steel belt running over pulleys

**band·stand** \\'band-ˌstand\ *n* : a usu. roofed platform on which a band or orchestra performs outdoors

**b and w** *abbr* black and white

**band·wag·on** \\'band-ˌwa-gən\ *n* 1 : a wagon carrying musicians in a parade 2 : a movement that attracts growing support ⟨a political ~⟩

**band·width** \-ˈwidth\ *n* : the capacity for data transfer of an electronic communication system

¹**ban·dy** \\'ban-dē\ *vb* **ban·died; ban·dy·ing** 1 : to exchange (as blows or quips) esp. in rapid succession 2 : to use in a glib or offhand way

²**bandy** *adj* : curved outward ⟨~ legs⟩

**bane** \\'bān\ *n* 1 : POISON 2 : WOE, HARM; *also* : a source of this — **bane·ful** *adj*

¹**bang** \\'baŋ\ *vb* 1 : BUMP ⟨fell and ~ed his knee⟩ 2 : to strike, thrust, or move usu. with a loud noise

²**bang** *n* 1 : a resounding blow 2 : a sudden loud noise

³**bang** *adv* : DIRECTLY, RIGHT ⟨ran ~ up against more trouble⟩

⁴**bang** *n* : a fringe of hair cut short (as across the forehead) — usu. used in pl.

⁵**bang** *vb* : to cut (as hair) to produce bangs

**ban·gle** \\'baŋ-gəl\ *n* 1 : BRACELET 2 : a loose-hanging ornament

**bang–up** \\'baŋ-ˌəp\ *adj* : FIRST-RATE, EXCELLENT ⟨a ~ job⟩

**bani** *pl of* ³BAN

**ban·ish** \\'ba-nish\ *vb* 1 : to require by authority to leave a country 2 : to drive out : EXPEL ♦ **Synonyms** EXILE, OSTRACIZE, DEPORT, RELEGATE — **ban·ish·ment** *n*

**ban·is·ter** \\'ba-nə-stər\ *n* 1 : a handrail with its supporting posts 2 : HANDRAIL 3 : BALUSTER

**ban·jo** \\'ban-ˌjō\ *n, pl* **banjos** *also* **banjoes** : a musical instrument with a long neck, a drumlike body, and usu. five strings — **ban·jo·ist** \-ist\ *n*

¹**bank** \\'baŋk\ *n* 1 : a piled-up mass (as of cloud or earth) 2 : an undersea elevation 3 : rising ground bordering a lake, river, or sea 4 : the sideways slope of a surface along a curve or of a vehicle as it rounds a curve

²**bank** *vb* 1 : to form a bank about 2 : to cover (as a fire) with fuel to keep inactive 3 : to build (a curve) with the roadbed or track inclined laterally upward from the inside edge 4 : to pile or heap in a bank; *also* : to arrange in a tier 5 : to incline (an airplane) laterally

³**bank** *n* [ME, fr. MF or It; MF *banque*, fr. It *banca*, lit., bench, of Gmc origin] 1 : an establishment concerned esp. with the custody, loan, exchange, or issue of money, the extension of credit, and the transmission of funds 2 : a stock of or a

place for holding something in reserve ⟨a blood ∼⟩

**⁴bank** vb **1** : to conduct the business of a bank **2** : to deposit money or have an account in a bank — **bank·er** n — **bank·ing** n

**⁵bank** n : a group of objects arranged close together (as in a row or tier) ⟨a ∼ of file drawers⟩

**bank·book** \'baŋk-ˌbůk\ n : the depositor's book in which a bank records deposits and withdrawals

**bank·card** \-ˌkärd\ n : a card (as a credit card or an ATM card) issued by a bank

**bank·note** \-ˌnōt\ n : a promissory note issued by a bank and circulating as money

**bank·roll** \-ˌrōl\ n : supply of money : FUNDS

**¹bank·rupt** \'baŋk-(ˌ)rəpt\ n [modif. of MF banqueroute bankruptcy, fr. It bancarotta, fr. banca bank + rotta broken] : an insolvent person; esp : one whose property is turned over by court action to a trustee to be handled for the benefit of his creditors — **bankrupt** vb

**²bankrupt** adj **1** : reduced to financial ruin; esp : legally declared a bankrupt **2** : wholly lacking in or deprived of some essential ⟨morally ∼⟩ — **bank·rupt·cy** \'baŋk-(ˌ)rəpt-sē\ n

**¹ban·ner** \'ba-nər\ n **1** : a piece of cloth attached to a staff and used by a leader as his standard **2** : FLAG **3** : an advertisement that runs usu. across the top of a Web page

**²banner** adj : distinguished from all others esp. in excellence ⟨a ∼ year⟩

**ban·nock** \'ba-nək\ n : a flat oatmeal or barley cake usu. cooked on a griddle

**banns** \'banz\ n pl : public announcement esp. in church of a proposed marriage

**ban·quet** \'baŋ-kwət\ n [MF, fr. It banchetto, fr. dim. of banca bench] : a ceremonial dinner — **banquet** vb

**ban·quette** \baŋ-'ket\ n : a long upholstered bench esp. along a wall

**ban·shee** \'ban-shē\ n [Ir bean sídhe & ScGael bean sith, lit., woman of fairyland] : a female spirit in Gaelic folklore whose wailing warns a family that one of them will soon die

**ban·tam** \'ban-təm\ n **1** : any of numerous small domestic fowls that are often miniatures of standard breeds **2** : a small but pugnacious person

**¹ban·ter** \'ban-tər\ vb : to speak to in a witty and teasing manner

**²banter** n : good-natured witty joking

**Ban·tu** \'ban-ˌtü\ n, pl Bantu or Bantus **1** : a group of languages spoken in central and southern Africa **2** : a member of a group of African peoples who speak Bantu

**ban·yan** \'ban-yən\ n : a large tropical Asian tree whose aerial roots grow downward to the ground and form new trunks

**ban·zai** \bän-'zī\ n : a Japanese cheer or cry of triumph

**bao·bab** \'baů-ˌbab, 'bā-ə-\ n : a tropical African tree with short swollen trunk and sour edible fruits resembling gourds

**bap·tism** \'bap-ˌti-zəm\ n **1** : a Christian sacrament signifying spiritual rebirth and symbolized by the ritual use of water **2** : an act of baptizing — **bap·tis·mal** \bap-'tiz-məl\ adj

**baptismal name** n : GIVEN NAME

**Bap·tist** \'bap-tist\ n : a member of any of several Protestant denominations emphasizing baptism by immersion of believers only

**bap·tis·tery** or **bap·tis·try** \'bap-tə-strē\ n, pl **-ter·ies** or **-tries** : a place esp. in a church used for baptism

**bap·tize** \bap-'tīz, 'bap-ˌtīz\ vb **bap·tized**; **bap·tiz·ing** [ME, fr. AF baptiser, fr. L baptizare, fr. Gk baptizein to dip, baptize, fr. baptein to dip] **1** : to administer baptism to; also : CHRISTEN **2** : to purify esp. by an ordeal

**¹bar** \'bär\ n **1** : a long narrow piece of material (as wood or metal) used esp. for a lever, fastening, or support **2** : BARRIER, OBSTACLE **3** : the railing in a law court at which prisoners are stationed; also : the legal profession or the whole body of lawyers **4** : a stripe, band, or line much longer than wide **5** : a counter at which food or esp. drink is served; also : BARROOM **6** : a vertical line across the musical staff

**²bar** vb **barred**; **bar·ring** **1** : to fasten, confine, or obstruct with or as if with a bar or bars **2** : to mark with bars : STRIPE **3** : to shut up or keep out : EXCLUDE **4** : FORBID, PREVENT

**³bar** prep : EXCEPT ⟨the most popular actor, ∼ none⟩

**⁴bar** abbr barometer; barometric

**Bar** abbr Baruch

**barb** \'bärb\ n **1** : a sharp projection extending backward (as from the point of an arrow) **2** : a biting critical remark — **barbed** \'bärbd\ adj — **barb·less** \'bärb-ləs\ adj

**bar·bar·ian** \bär-'ber-ē-ən\ adj **1** : of, relating to, or being a land, culture, or people alien to another's **2** : lacking refinement, learning, or artistic or literary culture — **barbarian** n — **bar·bar·i·an·ism** \-ē-ə-ˌni-zəm\ n

**bar·bar·ic** \bär-'ber-ik\ adj **1** : BARBARIAN ⟨∼ tribes⟩ **2** : marked by a lack of restraint : WILD ⟨∼ attacks⟩ **3** : PRIMITIVE, UNSOPHISTICATED

**bar·ba·rism** \'bär-bə-ˌri-zəm\ n **1** : the social condition of barbarians; also : the use or display of barbarian or barbarous acts, attitudes, or ideas **2** : a word or expression that offends standards of correctness or purity

**bar·ba·rous** \'bär-bə-rəs\ adj **1** : lacking culture or refinement **2** : using linguistic barbarisms **3** : mercilessly harsh or cruel — **bar·bar·i·ty** \bär-'ber-ə-tē\ n — **bar·ba·rous·ly** adv — **bar·ba·rous·ness** n

**¹bar·be·cue** \'bär-bi-ˌkyü\ vb **-cued**; **-cu·ing** **1** : to cook on a rack or revolving spit over or before a source of heat **2** : to cook in a highly seasoned vinegar sauce

²**barbecue** *n* : a social gathering at which barbecued food is served

**bar·bell** \'bär-,bel\ *n* : a bar with adjustable weights attached to each end used for exercise and in weight-lifting competition

**bar·ber** \'bär-bər\ *n* [ME, fr. AF *barboor*, fr. *barbe* beard, fr. L *barba*] : one whose business is cutting and dressing hair and shaving and trimming beards

**bar·ber·ry** \'bär-,ber-ē\ *n* : any of a genus of spiny shrubs bearing yellow flowers and oblong red berries

**bar·bi·tu·rate** \bär-'bi-chə-rət\ *n* : any of various compounds (as a salt or ester) formed from an organic acid (**bar·bi·tu·ric acid** \,bär-bə-'túr-ik-, -'tyúr-\); *esp* : one used as a sedative or hypnotic

**bar·ca·role** *or* **bar·ca·rolle** \'bär-kə-,rōl\ *n* : a Venetian boat song characterized by a beat suggesting a rowing rhythm; *also* : a piece of music imitating this

**bar chart** *n* : BAR GRAPH

**bar code** *n* : a set of printed and variously spaced bars and sometimes numerals that is designed to be scanned to provide information about the object it labels — **bar·cod·ed** \'bär-,kō-dəd\ *adj* — **bar coding** *n*

**bard** \'bärd\ *n* : POET

¹**bare** \'ber\ *adj* **bar·er; bar·est** **1** : NAKED **2** : UNCONCEALED, EXPOSED **3** : EMPTY ⟨the cupboard was ∼⟩ **4** : leaving nothing to spare : MERE **5** : PLAIN, UNADORNED ⟨the ∼ facts⟩ ♦ *Synonyms* NUDE, BALD — **bare·ness** *n*

²**bare** *vb* **bared; bar·ing** : to make or lay bare : UNCOVER

**bare·back** \-,bak\ *or* **bare·backed** \-'bakt\ *adv or adj* : without a saddle

**bare·faced** \-'fāst\ *adj* **1** : having the face uncovered; *esp* : BEARDLESS **2** : not concealed : OPEN ⟨a ∼ lie⟩ — **bare·faced·ly** \-'fā-səd-lē, -'fāst-lē\ *adv*

**bare·foot** \-,fút\ *or* **bare·foot·ed** \-'fú-təd\ *adv or adj* : with bare feet

**bare·hand·ed** \-'han-dəd\ *adv or adj* **1** : without gloves **2** : without tools or weapons ⟨∼ fighting⟩

**bare·head·ed** \-'he-dəd\ *adv or adj* : without a hat

**bare·ly** \'ber-lē\ *adv* **1** : PLAINLY, MEAGERLY ⟨a ∼ furnished room⟩ **2** : by a narrow margin : only just ⟨∼ enough money⟩

**bar·fly** \'bär-,flī\ *n* : a drinker who frequents bars

¹**bar·gain** \'bär-gən\ *n* **1** : AGREEMENT **2** : an advantageous purchase **3** : a transaction, situation, or event regarded in the light of its results

²**bargain** *vb* **1** : to negotiate over the terms of an agreement; *also* : to come to terms **2** : BARTER

**bar·gain–base·ment** \'bär-gən-'bās-mənt\ *adj* : markedly inexpensive

¹**barge** \'bärj\ *n* **1** : a broad flat-bottomed boat usu. moved by towing **2** : a motorboat supplied to a flagship (as for an admiral) **3** : a ceremonial boat elegantly furnished — **barge·man** \-mən\ *n*

²**barge** *vb* **barged; barg·ing** **1** : to carry by barge **2** : to move or thrust oneself clumsily or rudely

**bar graph** *n* : a graphic technique for comparing amounts by rectangles whose lengths are proportional to the amounts they represent

**ba·ris·ta** \bə-'rēs-tə\ *n* : a person who makes and serves coffee to the public

**bari·tone** \'ber-ə-,tōn\ *n* [F *baryton* or It *baritono*, fr. Gk *barytonos* deep sounding, fr. *barys* heavy + *tonos* tone] : a male voice between bass and tenor; *also* : a man with such a voice

**bar·i·um** \'ber-ē-əm\ *n* : a silver-white metallic chemical element that occurs only in combination

¹**bark** \'bärk\ *vb* **1** : to make the short loud cry of a dog **2** : to speak or utter in a curt loud tone : SNAP

²**bark** *n* : the sound made by a barking dog

³**bark** *n* : the tough corky outer covering of a woody stem or root

⁴**bark** *vb* **1** : to strip the bark from **2** : to rub the skin from : ABRADE

⁵**bark** *n* : a ship of three or more masts with the aft mast fore-and-aft rigged and the others square-rigged

**bar·keep** \'bär-,kēp\ *also* **bar·keep·er** \-,kē-pər\ *n* : BARTENDER

**bark·er** \'bär-kər\ *n* : a person who stands at the entrance esp. to a show and tries to attract customers to it

**bar·ley** \'bär-lē\ *n* : a cereal grass with seeds used as food and in making malt liquors; *also* : its seed

**bar mitz·vah** \bär-'mits-və\ *n, often cap* *B&M* [Heb *bar miṣwāh*, lit., son of the (divine) law] **1** : a Jewish boy who at about 13 years of age assumes religious responsibilities **2** : the ceremony recognizing a boy as a bar mitzvah

**barn** \'bärn\ *n* [ME *bern*, fr. OE *berærn*, fr. *bere* barley + *ærn* house, store] : a building used esp. for storing hay and grain and for housing livestock or farm equipment

**bar·na·cle** \'bär-ni-kəl\ *n* : any of numerous small marine crustaceans free-swimming when young but permanently fixed (as to rocks, whales, or ships) when adult

**barn·storm** \'bärn-,stórm\ *vb* : to travel through the country making brief stops to entertain (as with shows or flying stunts) or to campaign for political office

**barn·yard** \-,yärd\ *n* : a usu. fenced area adjoining a barn

**baro·graph** \'ber-ə-,graf\ *n* : a recording barometer

**ba·rom·e·ter** \bə-'räm-ə-tər\ *n* : an instrument for measuring atmospheric pressure — **baro·met·ric** \,bar-ə-'me-trik\ *adj*

**bar·on** \'ber-ən\ *n* : a member of the lowest grade of the British peerage — **ba·ro·ni·al** \bə-'rō-nē-əl\ *adj* — **bar·ony** \'ber-ə-nē\ *n*

**bar·on·age** \'ber-ə-nij\ *n* : PEERAGE

**bar·on·ess** \'ber-ə-nəs\ *n* **1** : the wife or widow of a baron **2** : a woman holding a baronial title in her own right

**bar·on·et** \'ber-ə-nət\ *n* : a man holding a

rank of honor below a baron but above a knight — **bar·on·et·cy** \-sē\ *n*

**ba·roque** \bə-'rōk, -'räk\ *adj* : marked by the use of complex forms, bold ornamentation, and the juxtapositioning of contrasting elements

**ba·rouche** \bə-'rüsh\ *n* [G *Barutsche,* fr. It *biroccio,* ultim. fr. LL *birotus* two-wheeled, fr. L *bi-* two + *rota* wheel] : a 4-wheeled carriage with a high driver's seat in front and a folding top

**bar·racks** \'ber-əks\ *n sing or pl* : a building or group of buildings for lodging soldiers

**bar·ra·cu·da** \ber-ə-'kü-də\ *n, pl* **-da** *or* **-das** : any of several large slender predaceous sea fishes including some used for food

**bar·rage** \bə-'räzh, -'räj\ *n* : a heavy concentration of fire (as of artillery)

**barred** \'bärd\ *adj* : STRIPED

**¹bar·rel** \'ber-əl\ *n* **1** : a round bulging cask with flat ends of equal diameter **2** : the amount contained in a barrel **3** : a cylindrical or tubular part ⟨gun ∼⟩ — **bar·reled** \-əld\ *adj*

**²barrel** *vb* **-reled** *or* **-relled; -rel·ing** *or* **-rel·ling** **1** : to pack in a barrel **2** : to travel at high speed

**bar·rel·head** \-ˌhed\ *n* : the flat end of a barrel — **on the barrelhead** : asking for or granting no credit ⟨paid cash *on the barrelhead*⟩

**barrel roll** *n* : an airplane maneuver in which a complete revolution about the longitudinal axis is made

**¹bar·ren** \'ber-ən\ *adj* **1** : STERILE, UNFRUITFUL **2** : unproductive of results ⟨a ∼ scheme⟩ **3** : lacking interest or charm **4** : lacking inspiration or ideas — **bar·ren·ness** \-nəs\ *n*

**²barren** *n* : a tract of barren land

**bar·rette** \bä-'ret, bə-\ *n* : a clasp or bar for holding the hair in place

**¹bar·ri·cade** \'ber-ə-ˌkād, ber-ə-'kād\ *vb* **-cad·ed; -cad·ing** : to block, obstruct, or fortify with a barricade

**²barricade** *n* [F, fr. MF, fr. *barriquer* to barricade, fr. *barrique* barrel] **1** : a hastily thrown-up obstruction or fortification **2** : BARRIER, OBSTACLE

**bar·ri·er** \'ber-ē-ər\ *n* : something that separates, demarcates, or serves as a barricade ⟨racial ∼s⟩

**barrier island** *n* : a long broad sandy island lying parallel to a shore

**barrier reef** *n* : a coral reef roughly parallel to a shore and separated from it usu. by a lagoon

**bar·ring** \'bär-iŋ\ *prep* : excluding by exception : EXCEPTING

**bar·rio** \'bär-ē-ˌō, 'ber-\ *n, pl* **-ri·os** **1** : a district of a city or town in a Spanish-speaking country **2** : a Spanish-speaking quarter in a U.S. city

**bar·ris·ter** \'ber-ə-stər\ *n* : a British counselor admitted to plead in the higher courts

**bar·room** \'bär-ˌrüm, -ˌru̇m\ *n* : a room or establishment whose main feature is a bar for the sale of liquor

**¹bar·row** \'ber-ō\ *n* : a large burial mound of earth and stones

**²barrow** *n* **1** : WHEELBARROW **2** : a cart with a boxlike body and two shafts for pushing it

**Bart** *abbr* baronet

**bar·tend·er** \'bär-ˌten-dər\ *n* : a person who serves liquor at a bar

**bar·ter** \'bär-tər\ *vb* : to trade by exchange of goods — **barter** *n* — **bar·ter·er** *n*

**Ba·ruch** \'bär-ˌük, bə-'rük\ *n* — see BIBLE table

**bas·al** \'bā-səl\ *adj* **1** : situated at or forming the base **2** : BASIC

**basal metabolism** *n* : the turnover of energy in a fasting and resting organism using energy solely to maintain vital cellular activity, respiration, and circulation as measured by the rate at which heat is given off

**ba·salt** \bə-'sȯlt, 'bā-ˌsȯlt\ *n* : a dark fine-grained igneous rock — **ba·sal·tic** \bə-'sȯl-tik\ *adj*

**¹base** \'bās\ *n, pl* **bas·es** \'bā-səz\ **1** : BOTTOM, FOUNDATION **2** : a side or face on which a geometrical figure stands; *also* : the length of a base **3** : a main ingredient or fundamental part **4** : the point of beginning an act or operation **5** : a place on which a force depends for supplies **6** : a number (as 5 in 5⁷) that is raised to a power; *esp* : a number that when raised to a power equal to the logarithm of a number yields the number itself ⟨the logarithm of 100 to ∼ 10 is 2 since 10² = 100⟩ **7** : the number of units in a given digit's place of a number system that is required to give the numeral 1 in the next higher place ⟨the decimal system uses a ∼ of 10⟩; *also* : such a system using an indicated base ⟨convert from ∼ 10 to ∼ 2⟩ **8** : any of the four stations at the corners of a baseball diamond **9** : a chemical compound (as lime or ammonia) that reacts with an acid to form a salt, has a bitter taste, and turns litmus blue ♦ *Synonyms* BASIS, GROUND, GROUNDWORK, FOOTING, FOUNDATION — **base·less** *adj*

**²base** *vb* **based; bas·ing** **1** : to form or serve as a base for **2** : ESTABLISH

**³base** *adj* **1** : of low value and inferior quality : DEBASED, ALLOYED **2** : CONTEMPTIBLE, IGNOBLE ⟨∼ motives⟩ **3** : MENIAL, DEGRADING ♦ *Synonyms* LOW, VILE, DESPICABLE, WRETCHED — **base·ly** *adv* — **base·ness** *n*

**base·ball** \'bās-ˌbȯl\ *n* : a game played with a bat and ball by two teams on a field with four bases arranged in a diamond; *also* : the ball used in this game

**baseball cap** *n* : a cap of the kind worn by baseball players that has a rounded crown and a long visor

**base·board** \-ˌbȯrd\ *n* : a line of boards or molding covering the joint of a wall and the adjoining floor

**base·born** \-'bȯrn\ *adj* **1** : MEAN, IGNOBLE **2** : of humble birth **3** : of illegitimate birth

**base exchange** *n* : a post exchange at a naval or air force base

**base hit** *n* : a hit in baseball that enables the batter to reach base safely with no error made and no base runner forced out

**BASE jumping** \'bās-\ *n* [*building, antenna, span, earth*] : the activity of parachuting from a high structure or cliff

**base-line** \'bās-,līn\ *n* 1 : a line serving as a basis esp. to calculate or locate something 2 : the area within which a baseball player must keep when running between bases

**base-ment** \-mənt\ *n* 1 : the part of a building that is wholly or partly below ground level 2 : the lowest or fundamental part of something

**base on balls** : an advance to first base given to a baseball player who receives four balls

**base runner** *n* : a baseball player who is on base or is attempting to reach a base

¹**bash** \'bash\ *vb* 1 : to strike violently : HIT 2 : to smash by a blow 3 : to attack physically or verbally

²**bash** *n* 1 : a heavy blow 2 : a festive social gathering : PARTY

**bash-ful** \'bash-fəl\ *adj* : inclined to shrink from public attention — **bash-ful-ly** \-fə-lē\ *adv* — **bash-ful-ness** *n*

**ba-sic** \'bā-sik\ *adj* 1 : of, relating to, or forming the base or essence : FUNDAMENTAL 2 : concerned with fundamental scientific principles : not applied 3 : of, relating to, or having the character of a chemical base ♦ *Synonyms* UNDERLYING, BASAL, PRIMARY — **ba-sic-i-ty** \bā-'si-sə-tē\ *n*

**BA-SIC** \'bā-sik\ *n* [*Beginner's All-purpose Symbolic Instruction Code*] : a simplified language for programming a computer

**ba-si-cal-ly** \'bā-si-k(ə-)lē\ *adv* 1 : at a basic level 2 : for the most part 3 : in a basic manner

**ba-sil** \'bā-zəl, 'bā-, -səl\ *n* : any of several mints with fragrant leaves used in cooking; *also* : the leaves

**ba-sil-i-ca** \bə-'si-li-kə, -'zi-\ *n* [L, fr. Gk *basilikē*, fr. fem. of *basilikos* royal, fr. *basileus* king] 1 : an early Christian church building consisting of nave and aisles with clerestory and apse 2 : a Roman Catholic church given ceremonial privileges

**bas-i-lisk** \'ba-sə-,lisk, 'ba-zə-\ *n* [ME, fr. L *basiliscus*, fr. Gk *basiliskos*, fr. dim. of *basileus* king] : a legendary reptile with fatal breath and glance

**ba-sin** \'bā-s³n\ *n* 1 : an open usu. circular vessel with sloping sides for holding liquid (as water) 2 : a hollow or enclosed place containing water; *also* : the region drained by a river

**ba-sis** \'bā-səs\ *n, pl* **ba-ses** \-,sēz\ 1 : FOUNDATION, BASE 2 : a fundamental principle

**bask** \'bask\ *vb* 1 : to expose oneself to comfortable heat 2 : to enjoy something warmly comforting ⟨~ing in his friends' admiration⟩

**bas-ket** \'bas-kət\ *n* : a container made of woven material (as twigs or grasses); *also* : any of various lightweight usu. wood containers — **bas-ket-ful** *n*

**bas-ket-ball** \-,bȯl\ *n* : a game played on a court by two teams who try to throw an inflated ball through a raised goal; *also* : the ball used in this game — **bas-ket-ball-er** \-,bȯ-lər\ *n*

**basket case** *n* 1 : a person who has all four limbs amputated 2 : a person who is mentally incapacitated or worn out (as from nervous tension)

**basket weave** *n* : a textile weave resembling the checkered pattern of a plaited basket

**bas-ma-ti rice** \,bäz-'mä-tē-\ *n* : an aromatic long-grain rice originating in southern Asia

**bas mitzvah** *var of* BAT MITZVAH

**Basque** \'bask\ *n* 1 : a member of a people inhabiting a region bordering on the Bay of Biscay in northern Spain and southwestern France 2 : the language of the Basque people — **Basque** *adj*

**bas-re-lief** \,bä-ri-'lēf\ *n* [F] : a sculpture in relief with the design raised very slightly from the background

¹**bass** \'bas\ *n, pl* **bass** *or* **bass-es** : any of numerous sport and food bony fishes (as a striped bass)

²**bass** \'bās\ *adj* : of low pitch

³**bass** \'bās\ *n* 1 : a deep sound or tone 2 : the lower half of the musical pitch range 3 : the lowest part in a 4-part chorus; *also* : a singer having this voice or part

**bas-set hound** \'ba-sət-\ *n* : any of an old breed of short-legged hunting dogs of French origin having long ears and a short smooth coat

**bas-si-net** \,ba-sə-'net\ *n* : a baby's bed that resembles a basket and often has a hood over one end

**bas-so** \'ba-sō, 'bä-\ *n, pl* **bassos** *or* **bas-si** \'bä-,sē\ [It] : a bass singer

**bas-soon** \bə-'sün\ *n* : a musical wind instrument lower in pitch than the oboe

**bass-wood** \'bas-,wu̇d\ *n* : any of several New World lindens or their wood

**bast** \'bast\ *n* : BAST FIBER

¹**bas-tard** \'bas-tərd\ *n* 1 : an illegitimate child 2 : an offensive or disagreeable person

²**bastard** *adj* 1 : ILLEGITIMATE 2 : of an inferior or nontypical kind, size, or form; *also* : SPURIOUS — **bas-tardy** *n*

**bas-tard-ise** *Brit var of* BASTARDIZE

**bas-tard-ize** \'bas-tər-,dīz\ *vb* **-ized; -iz-ing** : to reduce from a higher to a lower state : DEBASE

¹**baste** \'bāst\ *vb* **bast-ed; bast-ing** : to sew with long stitches so as to keep temporarily in place

²**baste** *vb* **bast-ed; bast-ing** : to moisten (as meat) at intervals with liquid while cooking

**bast fiber** *n* : a strong woody plant fiber obtained chiefly from phloem and used esp. in making ropes

**bas-ti-na-do** \,bas-tə-'nā-dō, -'nä-\ *or* **bas-ti-nade** \,bas-tə-'nād, -'näd\ *n, pl* **-na-does** *or* **-nades** 1 : a blow or beating esp. with a stick **2** : a punishment consisting of beating the soles of the feet

**bas·tion** \'bas-chən\ *n* : a projecting part of a fortification; *also* : a fortified position

**¹bat** \'bat\ *n* **1** : a stout stick : CLUB **2** : a sharp blow **3** : an implement (as of wood) used to hit a ball (as in baseball) **4** : a turn at batting — usu. used in the phrase *at bat*

**²bat** *vb* **bat·ted; bat·ting** : to hit with or as if with a bat

**³bat** *n* : any of an order of night-flying mammals with forelimbs modified to form wings

**⁴bat** *vb* **bat·ted; bat·ting** : WINK, BLINK

**batch** \'bach\ *n* **1** : a quantity (as of bread) baked at one time **2** : a quantity of material for use at one time or produced at one operation

**bate** \'bāt\ *vb* **bat·ed; bat·ing** : MODERATE, REDUCE ⟨he *bated* his breath⟩

**bath** \'bath, 'bȧth\ *n, pl* **baths** \'bathz, 'baths, 'bȧthz, 'bȧths\ **1** : a washing of the body **2** : water for washing the body **3** : a liquid in which objects are immersed so that it can act on them **4** : BATHROOM **5** : a financial loss ⟨took a ∼ in the market⟩

**bathe** \'bāth\ *vb* **bathed; bath·ing 1** : to wash in liquid and esp. water; *also* : to apply water or a medicated liquid to ⟨*bathed* her eyes⟩ **2** : to take a bath; *also* : to take a swim **3** : to wash along, over, or against so as to wet **4** : to suffuse with or as if with light — **bath·er** *n*

**bath·house** \'bath-ˌhaủs, 'bȧth-\ *n* **1** : a building equipped for bathing **2** : a building containing dressing rooms for bathers

**bathing suit** *n* : SWIMSUIT

**ba·thos** \'bā-ˌthäs\ *n* [Gk, lit., depth] **1** : the sudden appearance of the commonplace in otherwise elevated matter or style **2** : insincere or overdone pathos — **ba·thet·ic** \bə-'the-tik\ *adj*

**bath·robe** \'bath-ˌrōb, 'bȧth-\ *n* : a loose often absorbent robe worn before and after bathing or as a dressing gown

**bath·room** \-ˌrüm, -ˌrủm\ *n* : a room containing a bathtub or shower and usu. a sink and toilet

**bath·tub** \-ˌtəb\ *n* : a usu. fixed tub for bathing

**ba·tik** \bə-'tēk, 'ba-tik\ *n* [Javanese *baṭik*] **1** : an Indonesian method of hand-printing textiles by coating with wax the parts not to be dyed; *also* : a design so executed **2** : a fabric printed by batik

**ba·tiste** \bə-'tēst\ *n* : a fine sheer fabric of plain weave

**bat·man** \'bat-mən\ *n* : an orderly of a British military officer

**bat mitz·vah** \bät-'mits-və\ *also* **bas mitzvah** \bäs-\ *n, often cap B&M* [Heb *bath miṣwāh*, lit., daughter of the (divine) law] **1** : a Jewish girl who at 12 or more years of age assumes religious responsibilities **2** : the ceremony recognizing a girl as a bat mitzvah

**ba·ton** \bə-'tän\ *n* : STAFF, ROD; *esp* : a

stick with which the leader directs an orchestra or band

**bats·man** \'bats-mən\ *n* : a batter esp. in cricket

**bat·tal·ion** \bə-'tal-yən\ *n* **1** : a large body of troops organized to act together : ARMY **2** : a military unit composed of a headquarters and two or more units (as companies)

**¹bat·ten** \'ba-tᵊn\ *vb* **1** : to grow or make fat **2** : THRIVE

**²batten** *n* : a strip of wood used esp. to seal or strengthen a joint

**³batten** *vb* : to fasten with or as if with battens

**¹bat·ter** \'ba-tər\ *vb* : to beat or damage with repeated blows

**²batter** *n* : a soft mixture (as for cake) basically of flour and liquid

**³batter** *n* : one that bats; *esp* : the player whose turn it is to bat

**battering ram** *n* **1** : an ancient military machine for battering down walls **2** : a heavy metal bar with handles used to batter down doors

**bat·tery** \'ba-tə-rē\ *n, pl* **-ter·ies 1** : BEATING; *esp* : unlawful beating or use of force on a person **2** : a grouping of artillery pieces for tactical purposes; *also* : the guns of a warship **3** : a group of electric cells for furnishing electric current; *also* : a single electric cell ⟨a flashlight ∼⟩ **4** : a number of similar items grouped or used as a unit ⟨a ∼ of tests⟩ **5** : the pitcher and catcher of a baseball team

**bat·ting** \'ba-tiŋ\ *n* : layers or sheets of cotton or wool (as for lining quilts)

**batting cage** *n* : a screen around the back and sides of the home plate area to stop baseballs during practice

**¹bat·tle** \'ba-tᵊl\ *n* [ME *batel*, fr. AF *bataille* battle, battalion, fr. LL *battalia* combat, alter. of *battualia* fencing exercises, fr. L *battuere* to beat] : a general military engagement; *also* : an extended contest or controversy

**²battle** *vb* **bat·tled; bat·tling** : to engage in battle : CONTEND, FIGHT

**bat·tle-ax** *or* **battle-axe** \'ba-tᵊl-ˌaks\ *n* **1** : a long-handled ax formerly used as a weapon **2** : a quarrelsome domineering woman

**battle fatigue** *n* : COMBAT FATIGUE

**bat·tle·field** \'ba-tᵊl-ˌfēld\ *n* : a place where a battle is fought

**bat·tle·ment** \-mənt\ *n* : a decorative or defensive parapet on top of a wall

**bat·tle·ship** \-ˌship\ *n* : a warship of the most heavily armed and armored class

**bat·tle·wag·on** \-ˌwa-gən\ *n* : BATTLESHIP

**bat·ty** \'ba-tē\ *adj* **bat·ti·er; -est** : CRAZY, FOOLISH

**bau·ble** \'bȯ-bəl\ *n* : TRINKET

**baud** \'bȯd, *Brit* 'bȯd\ *n, pl* **baud** *also* **bauds** : a unit of data transmission speed

**baulk** *chiefly Brit var of* BALK

**baux·ite** \'bȯk-ˌsīt\ *n* : a clayey mixture that is the chief ore of aluminum

**bawd** \'bȯd\ *n* **1** : MADAM **2 2** : PROSTITUTE

**bawdy** \'bȯ-dē\ adj **bawd·i·er; -est** — OB-SCENE, LEWD — **bawd·i·ly** \'bȯ-də-lē\ adv — **bawd·i·ness** \-dē-nəs\ n

**¹bawl** \'bȯl\ vb : to cry or cry out loudly; also : to scold harshly

**²bawl** n : a long loud cry : BELLOW

**¹bay** \'bā\ adj : reddish brown

**²bay** n 1 : a bay-colored animal 2 : a reddish brown color

**³bay** n 1 : a section or compartment of a building or vehicle 2 : a compartment projecting outward from the wall of a building and containing a window (**bay window**)

**⁴bay** vb : to bark with deep long tones

**⁵bay** n 1 : the position of one unable to escape and forced to face danger 2 : a baying of dogs

**⁶bay** n : an inlet of a body of water (as the sea) usu. smaller than a gulf

**⁷bay** n : LAUREL; also : a shrub or tree resembling the laurel

**bay·ber·ry** \'bā-,ber-ē\ n : a hardy deciduous shrub of coastal eastern No. America bearing small hard berries coated with a white wax used for candles; also : its fruit

**bay leaf** n : the dried leaf of the European laurel used in cooking

**¹bay·o·net** \'bā-ə-nət, ,bā-ə-'net\ n : a daggerlike weapon made to fit on the muzzle end of a rifle

**²bayonet** vb **-net·ed** also **-net·ted; -net·ing** also **-net·ting** : to use or stab with a bayonet

**bay·ou** \'bī-yü, -ō\ n [Louisiana French, fr. Choctaw bayuk] : a marshy or sluggish body of water

**bay rum** n : a fragrant liquid used esp. as a cologne or after-shave lotion

**ba·zaar** \bə-'zär\ n 1 : a group of shops : MARKETPLACE 2 : a fair for the sale of articles usu. for charity

**ba·zoo·ka** \bə-'zü-kə\ n [bazooka (a crude musical instrument made of pipes and a funnel)] : a weapon consisting of a tube that launches an explosive rocket able to pierce armor

**¹BB** \'bē-(,)bē\ n : a small round shot pellet

**²BB** abbr base on balls

**BBB** abbr Better Business Bureau

**BBC** abbr British Broadcasting Corporation

**bbl** abbr barrel; barrels

**BC** abbr 1 before Christ — often printed in small capitals and often punctuated 2 British Columbia

**B cell** n [bone-marrow-derived cell] : any of the lymphocytes that secrete antibodies when mature

**B complex** n : VITAMIN B COMPLEX

**bd** abbr 1 board 2 bound

**bdl** or **bdle** abbr bundle

**bdrm** abbr bedroom

**be** \'bē\ vb, past 1st & 3d sing **was** \'wəz, 'wäz\; 2d sing **were** \'wər\; pl **were**; past subjunctive **were**; past part **been** \'bin\; pres part **be·ing** \'bē-in\; pres 1st sing **am** \əm, 'am\; 2d sing **are** \ər, 'är\; 3d sing **is** \'iz, əz\; pl **are**; pres subjunctive **be** 1 : to equal in meaning or symbolically (God is love); also : to have a specified qualification or relationship (leaves are green)

(this fish is a trout) 2 : to have objective existence (I think, therefore I am); also : to have or occupy a particular place (here is your pen) 3 : to take place : OCCUR (the meeting is tonight) 4 — used with the past participle of transitive verbs as a passive voice auxiliary (the door was opened) 5 — used as the auxiliary of the present participle in expressing continuous action (he is sleeping) 6 — used as an auxiliary with the past participle of some intransitive verbs to form archaic perfect tenses 7 — used as an auxiliary with to and the infinitive to express futurity, prearrangement, or obligation (you are to come when called)

**Be** symbol beryllium

**¹beach** \'bēch\ n : a sandy or gravelly part of the shore of an ocean or lake

**²beach** vb : to run or drive ashore

**beach buggy** n : DUNE BUGGY

**beach·comb·er** \'bēch-,kō-mər\ n : a person who searches along a shore for something of use or value

**beach·head** \'bēch-,hed\ n : a small area on an enemy-held shore occupied in the initial stages of an invasion

**bea·con** \'bē-kən\ n 1 : a signal fire 2 : a guiding or warning signal (as a lighthouse) 3 : a radio transmitter emitting signals for guidance of aircraft

**¹bead** \'bēd\ n [ME bede prayer, prayer bead, fr. OE bed, gebed prayer] 1 pl : a series of prayers and meditations made with a rosary 2 : a small piece of material pierced for threading on a line (as in a rosary) 3 : a small globular body 4 : a narrow projecting rim or band — **bead·ing** n — **beady** adj

**²bead** vb : to form into a bead

**bea·dle** \'bē-dᵊl\ n : a usu. English parish officer whose duties include keeping order in church

**bea·gle** \'bē-gəl\ n : a small short-legged smooth-coated hound

**beak** \'bēk\ n : the bill of a bird and esp. of a bird of prey; also : a pointed projecting part — **beaked** \'bēkt\ adj

**bea·ker** \'bē-kər\ n 1 : a large widemouthed drinking cup 2 : a widemouthed thin-walled laboratory vessel

**¹beam** \'bēm\ n 1 : a large long piece of timber or metal 2 : the bar of a balance from which the scales hang 3 : the breadth of a ship at its widest part 4 : a ray or shaft of light 5 : a collection of nearly parallel rays (as X-rays) or particles (as electrons) 6 : a constant radio signal transmitted for the guidance of pilots; also : the course indicated by this signal

**²beam** vb 1 : to send out light 2 : BROADCAST 3 : to transmit (data) electronically 4 : to smile with joy

**¹bean** \'bēn\ n : the edible seed borne in pods by some leguminous plants; also : a plant or a pod bearing beans

**²bean** vb : to strike on the head with an object

**bean·bag** \'bēn-,bag\ n : a cloth bag partially filled typically with dried beans and used as a toy

**bean·ball** \\'bēn-ˌból\\ n : a pitch thrown at a batter's head

**bean curd** n : TOFU

**bean·ie** \\'bē-nē\\ n : a small round tight-fitting skullcap

**beano** \\'bē-nō\\ n, pl **beanos** : BINGO

**¹bear** \\'ber\\ n, pl **bears 1** or pl **bear** : any of a family of large heavy mammals with shaggy hair and small tails **2** : a gruff or sullen person **3** : one who sells (as securities) in expectation of a price decline — **bear·ish** adj

**²bear** vb **bore** \\'bór\\; **borne** \\'bórn\\ also **born** \\'bórn\\; **bear·ing 1** : to carry **2** : to be equipped with **3** : to give as testimony 〈~ witness to the facts of the case〉 **4** : to give birth to; also : PRODUCE, YIELD 〈a tree that ~s regularly〉 **5** : ENDURE, SUSTAIN 〈~ pain〉 〈bore the weight on piles〉; also : to exert pressure or influence **6** : to go in an indicated direction 〈~ to the right〉 — **bear·able** adj — **bear·er** n

**¹beard** \\'bird\\ n **1** : the hair that grows on the face of a man **2** : a growth of bristly hairs (as on a goat's chin) — **beard·ed** \\'bir-dəd\\ adj — **beard·less** adj

**²beard** vb : to confront boldly

**bear·ing** n **1** : manner of carrying oneself : COMPORTMENT **2** : a supporting object, purpose, or point **3** : a machine part in which another part (as an axle or pin) turns **4** : an emblem in a coat of arms **5** : the direction or position of one point with respect to another or to the compass; also : a determination of position **6** pl : comprehension of one's situation **7** : connection with or influence on something; also : SIGNIFICANCE

**bear market** n : a market in which securities or commodities are persistently declining in value

**bear·skin** \\'ber-ˌskin\\ n : an article (as a hat) made of the skin of a bear

**beast** \\'bēst\\ n **1** : ANIMAL 1; esp : a 4-footed mammal **2** : a contemptible person

**¹beast·ly** \\'bēst-lē\\ adj **beast·li·er; -est 1** : BESTIAL **2** : ABOMINABLE, DISAGREEABLE — **beast·li·ness** \\-nəs\\ n

**²beastly** adv : VERY 〈a ~ cold day〉

**¹beat** \\'bēt\\ vb **beat; beat·en** \\'bē-t³n\\ or **beat; beat·ing 1** : to strike repeatedly **2** : TREAD **3** : to affect or alter by beating 〈~ metal into sheets〉 **4** : to sound (as an alarm) on a drum **5** : OVERCOME 〈~ his opponent〉; also : SURPASS 〈a meal hard to ~〉 **6** : to act or arrive before 〈~ his brother home〉 **7** : THROB — **beat·er** n

**²beat** n **1** : a single stroke or blow esp. of a series; also : PULSATION **2** : a rhythmic stress in poetry or music or the rhythmic effect of these **3** : a regularly traversed course

**³beat** adj **1** : EXHAUSTED **2** : of or relating to beatniks

**⁴beat** n : BEATNIK

**be·atif·ic** \\ˌbē-ə-'ti-fik\\ adj : giving or indicative of great joy or bliss

**be·at·i·fy** \\bē-'a-tə-ˌfī\\ vb **-fied; -fy·ing 1** : to make supremely happy **2** : to declare to have attained the blessedness of heav-en and authorize the title "Blessed" for — **be·at·i·fi·ca·tion** \\ˌ-ˌa-tə-fə-'kā-shən\\ n

**be·at·i·tude** \\bē-'a-tə-ˌtüd, -ˌtyüd\\ n **1** : a state of utmost bliss **2** : any of the declarations made in the Sermon on the Mount (Mt 5:3–12) beginning "Blessed are"

**beat·nik** \\'bēt-nik\\ n : a usu. young and artistic person who rejects the mores of established society

**beau** \\'bō\\ n, pl **beaux** \\'bōz\\ or **beaus** [F, fr. beau beautiful, fr. L bellus pretty] **1** : a man of fashion : DANDY **2** : SUITOR, LOVER

**beau geste** \\bō-'zhest\\ n, pl **beaux gestes** or **beau gestes** \\bō-'zhest\\ [F] : a graceful or magnanimous gesture

**beau ideal** \\ˌbō-ī-'dē(-ə)l\\ n, pl **beau ideals** [F] : the perfect type or model

**Beau·jo·lais** \\ˌbō-zho-'lā\\ n : a light fruity red wine

**beau monde** \\bō-'mänd, -'mōⁿd\\ n, pl **beau mondes** \\-'mänz, -'mändz\\ or **beaux mondes** \\bō-'mōⁿd\\ [F] : the world of high society and fashion

**beau·te·ous** \\'byü-tē-əs\\ adj : BEAUTIFUL — **beau·te·ous·ly** adv

**beau·ti·cian** \\byü-'ti-shən\\ n : COSMETOLOGIST

**beau·ti·ful** \\'byü-ti-fəl\\ adj : characterized by beauty : LOVELY ♦ **Synonyms** PRETTY, FAIR, COMELY — **beau·ti·ful·ly** \\-f(ə-)lē\\ adv

**beautiful people** n pl, often cap B&P : wealthy or famous people whose lifestyle is usu. expensive and well-publicized

**beau·ti·fy** \\'byü-tə-ˌfī\\ vb **-fied; -fy·ing** : to make more beautiful — **beau·ti·fi·ca·tion** \\ˌbyü-tə-fə-'kā-shən\\ n — **beau·ti·fi·er** n

**beau·ty** \\'byü-tē\\ n, pl **beauties** : qualities that give pleasure to the senses or exalt the mind : LOVELINESS; also : something having such qualities

**beauty shop** n : an establishment where hairdressing, facials, and manicures are done

**beaux arts** \\bō-'zär\\ n pl [F] : FINE ARTS

**bea·ver** \\'bē-vər\\ n, pl **beavers** : a large fur-bearing herbivorous rodent that builds dams and underwater houses of mud and sticks; also : its fur

**be·calm** \\bi-'käm, -'kälm\\ vb : to keep (as a ship) motionless by lack of wind

**be·cause** \\bi-'kóz, -'kəz\\ conj : for the reason that 〈ran away ~ they were afraid〉

**because of** prep : by reason of

**beck** \\'bek\\ n : a beckoning gesture; also : SUMMONS

**beck·on** \\'be-kən\\ vb : to summon or signal esp. by a nod or gesture; also : ATTRACT

**be·cloud** \\bi-'klaúd\\ vb : OBSCURE

**be·come** \\bi-'kəm\\ vb **-came** \\-'kām\\; **-come; -com·ing 1** : to come to be 〈~ tired〉 **2** : to suit or be suitable to 〈her dress ~s her〉

**becoming** adj : SUITABLE, FIT; also : ATTRACTIVE — **be·com·ing·ly** adv

**¹bed** \\'bed\\ n **1** : an article of furniture to

sleep on **2** : a plot of ground prepared for plants **3** : FOUNDATION, BOTTOM ⟨the ocean ∼⟩ **4** : LAYER, STRATUM ⟨a ∼ of rice⟩

²**bed** vb **bed·ded**; **bed·ding 1** : to put or go to bed **2** : to fix in a foundation : EMBED **3** : to plant in beds **4** : to lay or lie flat or in layers

**bed–and–breakfast** n : an establishment offering lodging and breakfast

**be·daub** \bi-'dòb\ vb : SMEAR

**be·daz·zle** \bi-'da-zəl\ vb : to confuse by or as if by a strong light; also : FASCINATE — **be·daz·zle·ment** n

**bed·bug** \'bed-,bəg\ n : a wingless bloodsucking bug infesting houses and esp. beds

**bed·clothes** \'bed-,klōthz\ n pl : materials for making up a bed

**bed·ding** \'be-diŋ\ n **1** : BEDCLOTHES **2** : FOUNDATION ⟨straw ∼⟩

**be·deck** \bi-'dek\ vb : ADORN

**be·dev·il** \bi-'de-vəl\ vb **1** : HARASS, TORMENT **2** : CONFUSE, MUDDLE

**be·dew** \bi-'dü, -'dyü\ vb : to wet with or as if with dew

**bed·fast** \'bed-,fast\ adj : BEDRIDDEN

**bed·fel·low** \-,fe-lō\ n **1** : one sharing the bed of another **2** : a close associate : ALLY ⟨politics makes strange ∼s⟩

**be·di·zen** \bi-'dī-z²n, -'di-\ vb : to dress or adorn with showy or vulgar finery

**bed·lam** \'bed-ləm\ n [Bedlam, popular name for the Hospital of St. Mary of Bethlehem, London, an insane asylum, fr. ME Bedlem Bethlehem] **1** often cap : an insane asylum **2** : a scene of uproar and confusion ⟨∼ in the court⟩

**bed·ou·in** also **bed·u·in** \'be-də-wən\ n, pl **bedouin** or **bedouins** also **beduin** or **beduins** often cap [ME Bedoyne, fr. MF bedoïn, fr. Ar badawī desert dweller] : a nomadic Arab of the Arabian, Syrian, or northern African deserts

**bed·pan** \'bed-,pan\ n : a shallow vessel used by a bedridden person for urination or defecation

**bed·post** \-,pōst\ n : the post of a bed

**be·drag·gled** \bi-'dra-gəld\ adj : soiled and disordered as if by being drenched

**bed·rid·den** \'bed-,ri-d²n\ adj : kept in bed by illness or weakness

¹**bed·rock** \-'räk\ n : the solid rock underlying surface materials (as soil)

²**bedrock** adj : solidly fundamental, basic, or reliable ⟨traditional ∼ values⟩

**bed·roll** \'bed-,rōl\ n : bedding rolled up for carrying

**bed·room** \-,rüm, -,rùm\ n : a room containing a bed and used esp. for sleeping

**bed·side** \-,sīd\ n : the place beside a bed esp. of a sick or dying person

**bed·sore** \-,sór\ n : an ulceration of tissue deprived of adequate blood supply by prolonged pressure

**bed·spread** \-,spred\ n : a usu. ornamental cloth cover for a bed

**bed·stead** \-,sted\ n : the framework of a bed

**bed·time** \-,tīm\ n : time for going to bed

**bed–wet·ting** \-,we-tiŋ\ n : involuntary

discharge of urine esp. in bed during sleep — **bed–wet·ter** n

¹**bee** \'bē\ n : any of numerous 4-winged insects (as honeybees or bumblebees) that feed on nectar and pollen and that sometimes produce honey or have a painful sting

²**bee** n : a gathering of people for a specific purpose ⟨a quilting ∼⟩

**beech** \'bēch\ n, pl **beech·es** or **beech** : any of a genus of hardwood trees with smooth gray bark and small sweet triangular nuts; also : its wood — **beech·en** \'bē-chən\ adj

**beech·nut** \'bēch-,nət\ n : the nut of a beech

¹**beef** \'bēf\ n, pl **beefs** \'bēfs\ or **beeves** \'bēvz\ **1** : the flesh of a steer, cow, or bull; also : the dressed carcass of a beef animal **2** : a steer, cow, or bull esp. when fattened for food **3** : MUSCLE, BRAWN **4** pl **beefs** : COMPLAINT

²**beef** vb **1** : STRENGTHEN — usu. used with up ⟨∼ed up security⟩ **2** : COMPLAIN

**beef·eat·er** \'bē-,fē-tər\ n : a yeoman of the guard of an English monarch

**beef·steak** \-,stāk\ n : a slice of beef suitable for broiling or frying

**beefy** \'bē-fē\ adj **beef·i·er; -est** : THICKSET, BRAWNY ⟨a ∼ wrestler⟩

**bee·hive** \'bē-,hīv\ n : HIVE 1, HIVE 3

**bee·keep·er** \-,kē-pər\ n : a person who raises bees — **bee·keep·ing** n

**bee·line** \-,līn\ n : a straight direct course

**been** past part of BE

**beep·er** \'bē-pər\ n : PAGER; esp : one that beeps

**beer** \'bir\ n : an alcoholic beverage brewed from malt and hops — **beery** adj

**beer belly** n : POTBELLY

**bees·wax** \'bēz-,waks\ n : WAX 1

**beet** \'bēt\ n : a garden plant with edible leaves and a thick sweet root used as a vegetable, as a source of sugar, or as forage; also : its root

¹**bee·tle** \'bē-t²l\ n : any of an order of insects having four wings of which the stiff outer pair covers the membranous inner pair when not in flight

²**beetle** vb **bee·tled; bee·tling** : to jut out : PROJECT

**be·fall** \bi-'fól\ vb **-fell** \-'fel\; **-fall·en** \-'fó-lən\ : to happen to : OCCUR

**be·fit** \bi-'fit\ vb : to be suitable to

**be·fog** \bi-'fòg, -'fäg\ vb : OBSCURE; also : CONFUSE ⟨drink befogged his senses⟩

¹**be·fore** \bi-'fór\ adv or adj **1** : in front **2** : EARLIER

²**before** prep **1** : in front of ⟨stood ∼ him⟩ **2** : earlier than ⟨got there ∼ me⟩ **3** : in a more important category than ⟨put quality ∼ quantity⟩

³**before** conj **1** : earlier than the time that ⟨he got here ∼ I did⟩ **2** : more willingly than ⟨she'd starve ∼ she'd steal⟩

**be·fore·hand** \bi-'fór-,hand\ adv or adj : in advance

**be·foul** \bi-'faù(-ə)l\ vb : SOIL

**be·friend** \bi-'frend\ vb : to act as friend to

**be·fud·dle** \bi-'fə-dᵊl\ *vb* : MUDDLE, CONFUSE

**beg** \'beg\ *vb* **begged; beg·ging** **1** : to ask as a charity; *also* : ENTREAT **2** : EVADE; *also* : assume as established, settled, or proved ⟨~ the question⟩

**be·get** \bi-'get\ *vb* **-got** \-'gät\; **-got·ten** \-'gä-tᵊn\ *or* **-got; -get·ting** : to become the father of : SIRE

**¹beg·gar** \'be-gər\ *n* : one that begs; *esp* : a person who begs as a way of life

**²beggar** *vb* : IMPOVERISH

**beg·gar·ly** \'be-gər-lē\ *adj* **1** : contemptibly mean or inadequate **2** : marked by unrelieved poverty ⟨a ~ life⟩

**beg·gary** \'be-gə-rē\ *n* : extreme poverty

**be·gin** \bi-'gin\ *vb* **be·gan** \-'gan\; **be·gun** \-'gən\; **be·gin·ning** **1** : to do the first part of an action : COMMENCE **2** : to come into being : ARISE; *also* : FOUND ⟨he *began* the movement⟩ **3** : ORIGINATE, INVENT — **be·gin·ner** *n*

**beg off** *vb* : to ask to be excused from something

**be·gone** \bi-'gȯn\ *vb* : to go away : DEPART — used esp. in the imperative

**be·go·nia** \bi-'gō-nyə\ *n* : any of a genus of tropical herbs widely grown for their showy leaves and waxy flowers

**be·grime** \bi-'grīm\ *vb* **be·grimed; be·grim·ing** : to make dirty

**be·grudge** \bi-'grəj\ *vb* **1** : to give or concede reluctantly **2** : to be reluctant to grant or allow — **be·grudg·ing·ly** \-'grə-jiŋ-lē\ *adv*

**be·guile** \bi-'gī(-ə)l\ *vb* **be·guiled; be·guil·ing** **1** : DECEIVE **2** : to while away ⟨*beguiled* sorrow with music⟩ **3** : to engage the interest of by guile

**be·guine** \bi-'gēn\ *n* [AmerF *béguine*, fr. F *béguin* flirtation] : a vigorous popular dance of the islands of Saint Lucia and Martinique

**be·gum** \'bā-gəm, 'bē-\ *n* : a Muslim woman of high rank

**be·half** \bi-'haf, -'häf\ *n* : BENEFIT, SUPPORT, DEFENSE ⟨argued in their ~⟩

**be·have** \bi-'hāv\ *vb* **be·haved; be·hav·ing** **1** : to bear, comport, or conduct oneself in a particular and esp. a proper way **2** : to act, function, or react in a particular way

**be·hav·ior** \bi-'hā-vyər\ *n* : way of behaving; *esp* : personal conduct — **be·hav·ior·al** \-vyə-rəl\ *adj* — **be·hav·ior·al·ly** \-rə-lē\ *adv*

**be·hav·ior·ism** \bi-'hā-vyə-ˌri-zəm\ *n* : a school of psychology concerned with the objective evidence of behavior without reference to conscious experience

**be·hav·ior·ist** \bi-'hā-vyə-rist\ *n* **1** : a person who supports behaviorism **2** : a person who studies behavior

**be·hav·iour, be·hav·iour·ism** *chiefly Brit var of* BEHAVIOR, BEHAVIORISM

**be·head** \bi-'hed\ *vb* : to cut off the head of

**be·he·moth** \bi-'hē-məth, 'bē-ə-ˌmäth\ *n* : a huge powerful animal described in Job 40:15–24; *also* : something of monstrous size or power

**be·hest** \bi-'hest\ *n* **1** : COMMAND **2** : an urgent prompting

**¹be·hind** \bi-'hīnd\ *adv or adj* **1** : BACK, BACKWARD ⟨look ~⟩ **2** : LATE, SLOW

**²behind** *prep* **1** : in or to a place or situation in back of or to the rear of ⟨look ~ you⟩ ⟨the staff stayed ~ the troops⟩ **2** : inferior to (as in rank) : BELOW ⟨three games ~ the first-place team⟩ **3** : in support of : SUPPORTING ⟨we're ~ you all the way⟩

**be·hind·hand** \bi-'hīnd-ˌhand\ *adj* : being in arrears ♦ *Synonyms* TARDY, LATE, OVERDUE, BELATED

**be·hold** \bi-'hōld\ *vb* **-held** \-'held\; **-hold·ing** **1** : to have in sight : SEE **2** — used imperatively to direct the attention ♦ *Synonyms* VIEW, OBSERVE, NOTICE, ESPY — **be·hold·er** *n*

**be·hold·en** \bi-'hōl-dən\ *adj* : OBLIGATED, INDEBTED

**be·hoove** \bi-'hüv\ *vb* **be·hooved; be·hoov·ing** : to be necessary, proper, or advantageous for

**be·hove** *chiefly Brit var of* BEHOOVE

**beige** \'bāzh\ *n* : a pale dull yellowish brown — **beige** *adj*

**be·ing** \'bē-iŋ\ *n* **1** : EXISTENCE; *also* : LIFE **2** : the qualities or constitution of an existent thing **3** : a living thing; *esp* : PERSON

**be·la·bor** \bi-'lā-bər\ *vb* : to assail (as with words) tiresomely or at length

**be·la·bour** *chiefly Brit var of* BELABOR

**be·lat·ed** \bi-'lā-təd\ *adj* : DELAYED, LATE ⟨~ birthday wishes⟩

**be·lay** \bi-'lā\ *vb* **1** : to wind (a rope) around a pin or cleat in order to hold secure **2** : QUIT, STOP — used in the imperative

**belch** \'belch\ *vb* **1** : to expel (gas) from the stomach through the mouth **2** : to gush forth ⟨a volcano ~*ing* lava⟩ — **belch** *n*

**bel·dam** *or* **bel·dame** \'bel-dəm\ *n* [ME *beldam* grandmother, fr. AF *bel* beautiful + ME *dam* lady, mother] : an old woman

**be·lea·guer** \bi-'lē-gər\ *vb* **1** : BESIEGE **2** : HARASS ⟨~ed parents⟩

**bel·fry** \'bel-frē\ *n, pl* **belfries** : a tower for a bell (as on a church); *also* : the part of the tower in which the bell hangs

**Belg** *abbr* Belgian; Belgium

**Bel·gian endive** \'bel-jən\ *n* : the blanched shoot of chicory

**Belgian waffle** *n* : a waffle having large depressions and usu. topped with fruit and whipped cream

**be·lie** \bi-'lī\ *vb* **-lied; -ly·ing** **1** : MISREPRESENT **2** : to show (something) to be false **3** : to run counter to

**be·lief** \bə-'lēf\ *n* **1** : CONFIDENCE, TRUST **2** : something (as a tenet or creed) believed ♦ *Synonyms* CONVICTION, OPINION, PERSUASION, SENTIMENT

**be·lieve** \bə-'lēv\ *vb* **be·lieved; be·liev·ing** **1** : to have religious convictions **2** : to have a firm conviction about something : accept as true **3** : to hold as an opinion : SUPPOSE — **be·liev·able** \-'lē-və-bəl\ *adj* — **be·liev·ably** \-blē\ *adv* — **be·liev·er** *n*

**be·like** \bi-'līk\ *adv, archaic* : PROBABLY

**be·lit·tle** \bi-'li-t³l\ *vb* -**lit·tled**; -**lit·tling** : to make seem little or less; *also* : DISPARAGE ⟨*belittled* his opponent⟩

¹**bell** \'bel\ *n* **1** : a hollow metallic device that makes a ringing sound when struck **2** : the sounding or stroke of a bell (as on shipboard to tell the time); *also* : time so indicated **3** : something with the flared form of a typical bell

²**bell** *vb* : to provide with a bell

**bel·la·don·na** \be-lə-'dä-nə\ *n* [It, lit., beautiful lady] : a medicinal extract (as atropine) from a poisonous European herb related to the potato; *also* : this herb

**bell–bot·toms** \'bel-'bä-təmz\ *n pl* : pants with wide flaring bottoms — **bell–bottom** *adj*

**bell·boy** \'bel-,bȯi\ *n* : BELLHOP

**belle** \'bel\ *n* : an attractive and popular girl or woman

**belles let·tres** \bel-'letr³\ *n pl* [F] : literature that is an end in itself and not practical or purely informative — **bel·le·tris·tic** \be-lə-'tris-tik\ *adj*

**bell·hop** \'bel-,häp\ *n* : a hotel or club employee who takes guests to rooms, carries luggage, and runs errands

**bel·li·cose** \'be-li-,kōs\ *adj* : WARLIKE, PUGNACIOUS ♦ **Synonyms** BELLIGERENT, QUARRELSOME, COMBATIVE, CONTENTIOUS — **bel·li·cos·i·ty** \,be-li-'kä-sə-tē\ *n*

**bel·lig·er·en·cy** \bə-'li-jə-rən-sē\ *n* **1** : the status of a nation engaged in war **2** : BELLIGERENCE, TRUCULENCE

**bel·lig·er·ent** \-rənt\ *adj* **1** : waging war **2** : aggressively self-assertive ♦ **Synonyms** BELLICOSE, PUGNACIOUS, COMBATIVE, CONTENTIOUS, WARLIKE — **bel·lig·er·ence** \-rəns\ *n* — **belligerent** *n* — **bel·lig·er·ent·ly** *adv*

**bel·low** \'be-lō\ *vb* **1** : to make the deep hollow sound characteristic of a bull **2** : to shout in a deep voice — **bellow** *n*

**bel·lows** \-lōz, -ləz\ *n sing or pl* : a closed device with sides that can be spread apart and then pressed together to draw in air and expel it through a tube

**bell·weth·er** \'bel-'we-thər, -,we-\ *n* : one that takes the lead or initiative; *also* : an indicator of trends

¹**bel·ly** \'be-lē\ *n, pl* **bellies** [ME *bely* bellows, belly, fr. OE *belg* bag, skin] **1** : ABDOMEN 1; *also* : POTBELLY **2** : the underpart of an animal's body

²**belly** *vb* **bel·lied**; **bel·ly·ing** : BULGE

¹**bel·ly·ache** \'be-lē-,āk\ *n* : pain in the abdomen : STOMACHACHE

²**bellyache** *vb* : COMPLAIN

**belly button** *n* : the human navel

**belly dance** *n* : a usu. solo dance emphasizing movement of the belly — **belly dance** *vb* — **belly dancer** *n*

**belly laugh** *n* : a deep hearty laugh

**be·long** \bi-'lȯŋ\ *vb* **1** : to be suitable or appropriate; *also* : to be properly situated ⟨shoes ~ in the closet⟩ **2** : to be the property ⟨this ~s to me⟩; *also* : to be attached (as through birth or membership) ⟨~ to a club⟩ **3** : to form an attribute or part ⟨this wheel ~s to the cart⟩ **4** : to be

classified ⟨whales ~ among the mammals⟩

**be·long·ings** \-'lȯŋ-iŋz\ *n pl* : GOODS, EFFECTS, POSSESSIONS

**be·loved** \bi-'ləvd, -'lə-vəd\ *adj* : dearly loved — **beloved** *n*

¹**be·low** \bi-'lō\ *adv* **1** : in or to a lower place or rank **2** : on earth **3** : in hell

²**below** *prep* **1** : lower than ⟨~ sea level⟩ **2** : inferior to (as in rank)

**be·low·decks** \bi-,lō-'deks, -'lō-,deks\ *adv* : inside the superstructure of a boat or down to a lower deck

¹**belt** \'belt\ *n* **1** : a strip (as of leather) worn about the waist **2** : a flexible continuous band to communicate motion or convey material **3** : a region marked by some distinctive feature; *esp* : one suited to a particular crop

²**belt** *vb* **1** : to encircle or secure with a belt **2** : to beat with or as if with a belt **3** : to mark with an encircling band **4** : to sing loudly

³**belt** *n* **1** : a jarring blow : WHACK **2** : DRINK ⟨a ~ of whiskey⟩

**belt·er** \'bel-tər\ *n* : a singer with a powerful voice

**belt–tightening** *n* : a reduction in spending

**belt·way** \'belt-,wā\ *n* : a highway around a city

**be·lu·ga** \bə-'lü-gə\ *n* [Russ] **1** : a large white sturgeon of the Black Sea, Caspian Sea, and their tributaries that is a source of caviar; *also* : caviar from beluga roe **2** : a whale of arctic and subarctic waters that is white when mature

**bel·ve·dere** \'bel-və-,dir\ *n* [It, lit., beautiful view] : a structure (as a summerhouse) designed to command a view

**be·mire** \bi-'mī(-ə)r\ *vb* : to cover or soil with or sink in mire

**be·moan** \bi-'mōn\ *vb* : LAMENT, DEPLORE ♦ **Synonyms** BEWAIL, GRIEVE, MOAN, WEEP

**be·muse** \bi-'myüz\ *vb* : BEWILDER, CONFUSE

¹**bench** \'bench\ *n* **1** : a long seat for two or more persons **2** : the seat of a judge in court; *also* : the office or dignity of a judge : COURT; *also* : JUDGES **3** : a table for holding work and tools ⟨a carpenter's ~⟩

²**bench** \'bench\ *vb* **1** : to furnish with benches **2** : to seat on a bench **3** : to remove from or keep out of a game

¹**bench·mark** \'bench-,märk\ *n* **1** *usu* **bench mark** : a mark on a permanent object serving as an elevation reference in topographical surveys **2** : a point of reference for measurement; *also* : STANDARD

²**benchmark** *vb* : to study (as a competitor's business practices) in order to improve one's own performance

**bench press** *n* : an exercise in which a weight is raised by a person lying on a bench — **bench–press** *vb*

**bench warrant** *n* : a warrant issued by a presiding judge or by a court against a person guilty of contempt or indicted for a crime

**¹bend** \'bend\ *vb* **bent** \'bent\; **bend·ing** **1** : to draw (as a bow) taut **2** : to curve or cause a change of shape in ⟨∼ a bar⟩ **3** : to make fast : SECURE **4** : DEFLECT **5** : to turn in a certain direction ⟨bent his steps toward town⟩ **6** : APPLY ⟨bent themselves to the task⟩ **7** : SUBDUE **8** : to curve downward **9** : YIELD, SUBMIT

**²bend** *n* **1** : an act or process of bending **2** : something bent; *esp* : CURVE **3** *pl* : a painful and sometimes fatal disorder caused by release of gas bubbles in the tissues upon too rapid decrease in air pressure after a stay in a compressed atmosphere

**³bend** *n* : a knot by which a rope is fastened (as to another rope)

**bend·er** \'ben-dər\ *n* : SPREE ⟨hangover after a weekend ∼⟩

**¹be·neath** \bi-'nēth\ *adv* : BELOW ⟨the mountains and the town ∼⟩ ◆ *Synonyms* UNDER, UNDERNEATH

**²beneath** *prep* **1** : BELOW, UNDER ⟨stood ∼ a tree⟩ **2** : unworthy of ⟨considered such behavior ∼ her⟩ **3** : concealed by ⟨a warm heart ∼ a gruff manner⟩

**bene·dic·tion** \ˌbe-nə-'dik-shən\ *n* : the invocation of a blessing esp. at the close of a public worship service

**ben·e·fac·tion** \-'fak-shən\ *n* : a charitable donation ◆ *Synonyms* CONTRIBUTION, ALMS, BENEFICENCE, OFFERING

**ben·e·fac·tor** \'ben-ə-ˌfak-tər\ *n* : one that confers a benefit and esp. a benefaction

**ben·e·fac·tress** \-ˌfak-trəs\ *n* : a woman who is a benefactor

**ben·e·fice** \'be-nə-fəs\ *n* : an ecclesiastical office to which the revenue from an endowment is attached

**be·nef·i·cence** \bə-'ne-fə-səns\ *n* **1** : beneficent quality **2** : BENEFACTION

**be·nef·i·cent** \-sənt\ *adj* : doing or producing good (as by acts of kindness or charity); *also* : BENEFICIAL

**ben·e·fi·cial** \ˌbe-nə-'fi-shəl\ *adj* : being of benefit or help : HELPFUL ◆ *Synonyms* ADVANTAGEOUS, PROFITABLE, FAVORABLE, PROPITIOUS — **ben·e·fi·cial·ly** *adv*

**ben·e·fi·cia·ry** \ˌbe-nə-'fi-shē-ˌer-ē, -'fi-shə-rē\ *n, pl* **-ries** : one that receives a benefit (as the income of a trust or the proceeds of an insurance)

**¹ben·e·fit** \'be-nə-ˌfit\ *n* **1** : ADVANTAGE ⟨the ∼s of exercise⟩ **2** : useful aid : HELP; *also* : material aid or service provided or due (as in sickness or unemployment) as a right in addition to regular pay **3** : a performance or event to raise funds

**²benefit** *vb* **-fit·ed** \-ˌfi-təd\ *also* **-fit·ted**; **-fit·ing** *also* **-fit·ting** **1** : to be useful or profitable to **2** : to receive benefit

**be·nev·o·lence** \bə-'ne-və-ləns\ *n* **1** : charitable nature **2** : an act of kindness : CHARITY — **be·nev·o·lent** \-lənt\ *adj* — **be·nev·o·lent·ly** *adv*

**be·night·ed** \bi-'nī-təd\ *adj* **1** : overtaken by darkness or night **2** : living in ignorance

**be·nign** \bi-'nīn\ *adj* [ME *benigne*, fr. AF, fr. L *benignus*] **1** : of a gentle disposition;

*also* : showing kindness **2** : of a mild kind; *esp* : not malignant ⟨∼ tumors⟩ ◆ *Synonyms* BENIGNANT, KIND, KINDLY, GOOD-HEARTED — **be·nig·ni·ty** \-'rig-nə-tē\ *n* — **be·nign·ly** *adv*

**be·nig·nant** \-'nig-nənt\ *adj* : BENIGN **1** ◆ *Synonyms* KIND, KINDLY, GOOD-HEARTED

**ben·i·son** \'be-nə-sən, -zən\ *n* : BLESSING, BENEDICTION

**¹bent** \'bent\ *n* **1** : strong inclination or interest; *also* : TALENT **2** : power of endurance ◆ *Synonyms* TALENT, APTITUDE, GIFT, FLAIR, KNACK, GENIUS

**²bent** *adj* **1** : changed by bending : CROOKED ⟨∼ branches⟩ **2** : strongly inclined : DETERMINED ⟨∼ on going⟩

**bent grass** *n* : any of a genus of stiff velvety grasses used esp. for lawns and pastures

**ben·thic** \'ben-thik\ *adj* : of, relating to, or occurring at the bottom of a body of water

**ben·ton·ite** \'ben-tə-ˌnīt\ *n* : an absorptive clay used esp. as a filler (as in paper)

**bent·wood** \'bent-ˌwud\ *adj* : made of wood bent into shape ⟨a ∼ rocker⟩

**be·numb** \bi-'nəm\ *vb* **1** : DULL, DEADEN **2** : to make numb esp. by cold

**ben·zene** \'ben-ˌzēn\ *n* : a colorless volatile flammable liquid hydrocarbon used in organic synthesis and as a solvent —
**ben·ze·noid** \-zə-ˌnȯid\ *adj or n*

**ben·zine** \'ben-ˌzēn\ *n* : any of various flammable petroleum distillates used as solvents or as motor fuels

**ben·zo·ate** \'ben-zə-ˌwāt\ *n* : a salt or ester of benzoic acid

**ben·zo·ic acid** \ben-ˌzō-ik-\ *n* : a white crystalline acid used as a preservative and antiseptic and in synthesizing chemicals

**ben·zo·in** \'ben-zə-wən, -ˌzȯin\ *n* : a balsamic resin from trees of southern Asia used esp. in medicine and perfumes

**be·queath** \bi-'kwēth, -'kwēth\ *vb* [ME *bequethen*, fr. OE *becwethan*, fr. *be-* + *cwethan* to say] **1** : to leave by will **2** : to hand down

**be·quest** \bi-'kwest\ *n* **1** : the action of bequeathing **2** : something bequeathed : LEGACY

**be·rate** \-'rāt\ *vb* : to scold harshly

**Ber·ber** \'bər-bər\ *n* : a member of any of various peoples living in northern Africa west of Tripoli

**ber·ceuse** \ber-'sœz, -'süz\ *n, pl* **ber·ceuses** \same *or* -'sœz-əz\ [F, fr. *bercer* to rock] **1** : LULLABY **2** : a musical composition that resembles a lullaby

**¹be·reaved** \bi-'rēvd\ *adj* : suffering the death of a loved one ⟨her ∼ parents⟩ — **be·reave·ment** *n*

**²bereaved** *n, pl* **bereaved** : one who is bereaved

**be·reft** \-'reft\ *adj* **1** : deprived of or lacking something — usu. used with *of* **2** : BEREAVED ⟨a ∼ mother⟩

**be·ret** \bə-'rā\ *n* : a round soft cap with no visor

**berg** \'bərg\ *n* : ICEBERG

**beri·beri** \ˌber-ē-'ber-ē\ *n* : a deficiency

disease marked by weakness, wasting, and nerve damage and caused by lack of thiamine

**berke·li·um** \'bər-klē-əm\ *n* : an artificially produced radioactive chemical element

**berm** \'bərm\ *n* : a narrow shelf or path at the top or bottom of a slope; *also* : a mound or bank of earth

**Bermuda grass** *n* : a creeping grass often used for lawns and pastures

**Ber·mu·das** \bər-'myü-dəz\ *n pl* : BERMUDA SHORTS

**Bermuda shorts** *n pl* : knee-length walking shorts

**ber·ry** \'ber-ē\ *n, pl* **berries 1** : a small pulpy fruit (as a strawberry) **2** : a simple fruit (as a grape, tomato, or cucumber) with the wall of the ripened ovary thick and pulpy **3** : the dry seed of some plants (as coffee)

**ber·serk** \bər-'sərk, -'zərk\ *adj* [ON *berserkr* warrior frenzied in battle, prob. fr. *ber-* bear + *serkr* shirt] : FRENZIED, CRAZED ⟨~ behavior⟩ — **berserk** *adv*

**¹berth** \'bərth\ *n* **1** : adequate distance esp. for a ship to maneuver **2** : the place where a ship is anchored or a vehicle rests **3** : ACCOMMODATIONS **4** : JOB, POSITION ♦ *Synonyms* POST, SITUATION, OFFICE, APPOINTMENT

**²berth** *vb* **1** : to bring or come into a berth **2** : to allot a berth to

**ber·yl** \'ber-əl\ *n* : a hard silicate mineral occurring as colorless hexagonal crystals when pure

**be·ryl·li·um** \bə-'ri-lē-əm\ *n* : a light strong metallic chemical element used as a hardener in alloys

**be·seech** \bi-'sēch\ *vb* **-sought** \-'sȯt\ *or* **-seeched; -seech·ing** : to beg urgently : ENTREAT ♦ *Synonyms* IMPLORE, PLEAD, SUPPLICATE, IMPORTUNE

**be·seem** \bi-'sēm\ *vb, archaic* : BEFIT

**be·set** \-'set\ *vb* **-set; -set·ting 1** : TROUBLE, HARASS ⟨the ills that ~ humanity⟩ **2** : ASSAIL ⟨~ by wild dogs⟩; *also* : SURROUND

**be·set·ting** *adj* : persistently present

**¹be·side** \bi-'sīd\ *prep* **1** : by the side of ⟨sit ~ me⟩ **2** : BESIDES **3** : not relevant to ⟨~ the point⟩

**²beside** *adv, archaic* : BESIDES

**¹be·sides** \bi-'sīdz\ *prep* **1** : other than ⟨no one ~ us⟩ **2** : together with

**²besides** *adv* **1** : as well : ALSO **2** : MOREOVER

**be·siege** \bi-'sēj\ *vb* : to lay siege to; *also* : to press with requests — **be·sieg·er** *n*

**be·smear** \-'smir\ *vb* : SMEAR

**be·smirch** \-'smərch\ *vb* : SMIRCH, SOIL

**be·som** \'bē-zəm\ *n* : BROOM

**be·sot** \bi-'sät\ *vb* **be·sot·ted; be·sot·ting 1** : INFATUATE ⟨*besotted* lovers⟩ **2** : to make dull esp. by drinking

**be·spat·ter** \-'spa-tər\ *vb* : SPATTER

**be·speak** \bi-'spēk\ *vb* **-spoke** \-'spōk\; **-spo·ken** \-'spō-kən\; **-speak·ing 1** : PREARRANGE **2** : ADDRESS **3** : REQUEST **4** : INDICATE, SIGNIFY ⟨her new album ~s her talent⟩ **5** : FORETELL

**be·sprin·kle** \-'spriŋ-kəl\ *vb* : SPRINKLE

**¹best** \'best\ *adj, superlative of* GOOD **1** : excelling all others **2** : most productive (as of good or satisfaction) ⟨the ~ thing to do⟩ **3** : LARGEST, MOST

**²best** *adv, superlative of* WELL **1** : in the best way **2** : MOST

**³best** *n* : something that is best

**⁴best** *vb* : to get the better of : OUTDO

**bes·tial** \'bes-chəl\ *adj* **1** : of or relating to beasts **2** : resembling a beast esp. in brutality or lack of intelligence

**bes·ti·al·i·ty** \ˌbes-chē-'a-lə-tē, ˌbēs-\ *n, pl* **-ties 1** : the condition or status of a lower animal **2** : display or gratification of bestial traits or impulses **3** : sexual relations between a human being and a lower animal

**bes·ti·ary** \'bes-chē-ˌer-ē\ *n, pl* **-ar·ies** : a medieval allegorical or moralizing work on the appearance and habits of animals

**be·stir** \bi-'stər\ *vb* : to rouse to action

**best man** *n* : the principal groomsman at a wedding

**be·stow** \bi-'stō\ *vb* **1** : PUT, PLACE, STOW **2** : to present as a gift — **be·stow·al** *n* — **be·stow·er** *n*

**be·stride** \bi-'strīd\ *vb* **-strode** \-'strōd\; **-strid·den** \-'stri-dᵊn\; **-strid·ing** : to ride, sit, or stand astride

**¹bet** \'bet\ *n* **1** : something that is wagered, risked, or pledged usu. between two parties on the outcome of a contest; *also* : the making of such a bet **2** : OPTION ⟨the back road is your best ~⟩

**²bet** *vb* **bet** *also* **bet·ted; bet·ting 1** : to stake on the outcome of an issue or a contest ⟨~ $2 on the race⟩ **2** : to make a bet with **3** : to lay a bet

**³bet** *abbr* between

**be·ta** \'bā-tə\ *n* **1** : the 2d letter of the Greek alphabet — B or β **2** : a nearly complete form of a new product (as software)

**beta–block·er** \-ˌblä-kər\ *n* : any of a group of drugs that decrease the rate and force of heart contractions and lower high blood pressure

**be·ta–car·o·tene** \-'ker-ə-ˌtēn\ *n* : an isomer of carotene found in dark green and dark yellow vegetables and fruits

**be·take** \bi-'tāk\ *vb* **-took** \-'tük\; **-tak·en** \-'tā-kən\; **-tak·ing** : to cause (oneself) to go

**beta particle** *n* : a high-speed electron; *esp* : one emitted by a radioactive nucleus

**beta ray** *n* **1** : BETA PARTICLE **2** : a stream of beta particles

**beta test** *n* : a field test of the beta version of a product esp. by outside testers and prior to commercial release — **beta test** *vb*

**be·tel** \'bē-tᵊl\ *n* : a climbing pepper of southern Asia whose leaves are chewed together with lime and betel nut as a stimulant

**betel nut** *n* : the astringent seed of an Asian palm that is chewed with betel leaves

**bête noire** \ˌbet-'nwär, ˌbät-\ *n, pl* **bêtes noires** \*same or* -'nwärz\ [F, lit., black beast] : a person or thing strongly disliked or avoided

**beth·el** \'be-thəl\ n [Heb *bēth'ēl* house of God] : a place of worship esp. for seamen

**be·tide** \bi-'tīd\ vb : to happen to

**be·times** \bi-'tīmz\ adv : in good time : EARLY ♦ *Synonyms* SOON, SEASONABLY, TIMELY

**be·to·ken** \bi-'tō-kən\ vb 1 : PRESAGE 2 : to give evidence of ♦ *Synonyms* INDICATE, ATTEST, BESPEAK, TESTIFY

**be·tray** \bi-'trā\ vb 1 : to lead astray; *esp* : SEDUCE 2 : to deliver to an enemy 3 : ABANDON 4 : to prove unfaithful to 5 : to reveal unintentionally; *also* : SHOW, INDICATE ♦ *Synonyms* MISLEAD, DELUDE, DECEIVE, BEGUILE — **be·tray·al** n — **be·tray·er** n

**be·troth** \bi-'trōth, -'trŏth, -'trōth\ vb : to promise to marry — **be·troth·al** n

**be·trothed** n : the person to whom one is betrothed

¹**bet·ter** \'be-tər\ adj, comparative of GOOD 1 : greater than half 2 : improved in health 3 : more attractive, favorable, or commendable 4 : more advantageous or effective ⟨a ∼ solution⟩ 5 : improved in accuracy or performance

²**better** vb 1 : to make or become better 2 : SURPASS, EXCEL

³**better** adv, comparative of WELL 1 : in a superior manner 2 : to a higher or greater degree; *also* : MORE

⁴**better** n 1 : something better; *also* : a superior esp. in merit or rank 2 : ADVANTAGE ⟨got the ∼ of his opponent⟩

⁵**better** verbal auxiliary : had better ⟨you ∼ hurry⟩

**better half** n : SPOUSE

**bet·ter·ment** \'be-tər-mənt\ n : IMPROVEMENT

**bet·tor** or **bet·ter** \'be-tər\ n : one that bets

¹**be·tween** \bi-'twēn\ prep 1 : by the common action of ⟨earned $10,000 ∼ the two of them⟩ 2 : in the interval separating ⟨an alley ∼ two buildings⟩; *also* : in intermediate relation to 3 : in point of comparison of ⟨choose ∼ two cars⟩

²**between** adv : in an intervening space or interval

**be·twixt** \bi-'twikst\ adv or prep : BETWEEN

¹**bev·el** \'be-vəl\ n 1 : a device for adjusting the slant of the surfaces of a piece of work 2 : the angle or slant that one surface or line makes with another when not at right angles

²**bevel** vb **-eled** or **-elled; -el·ing** or **-el·ling** 1 : to cut or shape to a bevel 2 : INCLINE, SLANT

**bev·er·age** \'bev-rij\ n : a drinkable liquid

**bevy** \'be-vē\ n, pl **bev·ies** 1 : a large group or collection 2 : a group of animals and esp. quail

**be·wail** \bi-'wāl\ vb : LAMENT ♦ *Synonyms* DEPLORE, BEMOAN, GRIEVE, MOAN, WEEP

**be·ware** \-'wer\ vb : to be on one's guard : be wary of

**be·wil·der** \bi-'wil-dər\ vb : PERPLEX, CONFUSE ♦ *Synonyms* MYSTIFY, DISTRACT, PUZZLE — **be·wil·der·ment** n

**be·witch** \-'wich\ vb 1 : to affect by witchcraft 2 : CHARM, FASCINATE ♦ *Synonyms* ENCHANT, ATTRACT, CAPTIVATE — **be·witch·ment** n

**bey** \'bā\ n 1 : a former Turkish provincial governor 2 : the former native ruler of Tunis or Tunisia

¹**be·yond** \bē-'änd\ adv 1 : FARTHER ⟨extends to the river and ∼⟩ 2 : BESIDES

²**beyond** prep 1 : on or to the farther side of 2 : out of the reach or sphere of 3 : BESIDES

**be·zel** \'bē-zəl, 'be-\ n 1 : a rim that holds a transparent covering (as on a watch) 2 : the faceted part of a cut gem that rises above the setting

**bf** abbr boldface

**BFF** abbr best friends forever

**BG** or **B Gen** abbr brigadier general

**Bh** symbol bohrium

**bhang** \'baŋ\ n [Hindi *bhāṅg*] : HEMP; *also* : a mildly intoxicating preparation made from hemp leaves

**Bi** symbol bismuth

**BIA** abbr Bureau of Indian Affairs

**bi·an·nu·al** \(,)bī-'an-yə-wəl\ adj : occurring twice a year — **bi·an·nu·al·ly** adv

¹**bi·as** \'bī-əs\ n 1 : a line diagonal to the grain of a fabric 2 : PREJUDICE, BENT

²**bias** adv : on the bias : DIAGONALLY

³**bias** vb **bi·ased** or **bi·assed; bi·as·ing** or **bi·as·sing** : PREJUDICE

**bi·ath·lon** \bī-'ath-lən, -,län\ n : a composite athletic contest consisting of cross-country skiing and target shooting with a rifle

¹**bib** \'bib\ n : a cloth or plastic shield tied under the chin to protect the clothes while eating

²**bib** abbr Bible; biblical

**bi·be·lot** \'bē-bə-,lō\ n, pl **bibelots** \same or -,lōz\ : a small household ornament or decorative object

**bi·ble** \'bī-bəl\ n [ME, fr. OF, fr. ML *biblia*, fr. Gk, pl. of *biblion* book, dim. of *byblos* papyrus, book, fr. *Byblos*, ancient Phoenician city from which papyrus was exported] 1 cap : the sacred scriptures of Christians comprising the Old and New Testaments 2 cap : the sacred scriptures of Judaism; *also* : those of some other religion 3 : a publication that is considered authoritative for its subject — **bib·li·cal** \'bi-bli-kəl\ adj

☞ the BIBLE table is on page 68

**bib·li·og·ra·phy** \,bi-blē-'ä-grə-fē\ n, pl **-phies** 1 : the history or description of writings or publications 2 : a list of writings (as on a subject or of an author) — **bib·li·og·ra·pher** \-fər\ n — **bib·li·o·graph·ic** \-ə-'gra-fik\ also **bib·li·o·graph·i·cal** \-fi-kəl\ adj

**bib·lio·phile** \'bi-blē-ə-,fī(-ə)l\ n : a lover of books

**bib·u·lous** \'bi-byə-ləs\ adj 1 : highly absorbent 2 : fond of alcoholic beverages

**bi·cam·er·al** \'bī-'ka-mə-rəl\ adj : having or consisting of two legislative branches

**bicarb** \(,)bī-'kärb, 'bī-,\ n : SODIUM BICARBONATE

**bi·car·bon·ate** \(,)bī-'kär-bə-,nāt, -nət\ n : an acid carbonate

# BOOKS OF THE BIBLE

## JEWISH SCRIPTURE

| LAW | PROPHETS | | WRITINGS |
|-----|----------|---|----------|
| Genesis | Joshua | Obadiah | Psalms |
| Exodus | Judges | Jonah | Proverbs |
| Leviticus | 1 & 2 Samuel | Micah | Job |
| Numbers | 1 & 2 Kings | Nahum | Song of Songs |
| Deuteronomy | Isaiah | Habakkuk | Ruth |
| | Jeremiah | Zephaniah | Lamentations |
| | Ezekiel | Haggai | Ecclesiastes |
| | Hosea | Zechariah | Esther |
| | Joel | Malachi | Daniel |
| | Amos | | Ezra |
| | | | Nehemiah |
| | | | 1 & 2 Chronicles |

## CHRISTIAN CANON——OLD TESTAMENT

| ROMAN CATHOLIC | PROTESTANT | ROMAN CATHOLIC | PROTESTANT |
|----------------|------------|----------------|------------|
| Genesis | Genesis | Wisdom | |
| Exodus | Exodus | Sirach | |
| Leviticus | Leviticus | Isaiah | Isaiah |
| Numbers | Numbers | Jeremiah | Jeremiah |
| Deuteronomy | Deuteronomy | Lamentations | Lamentations |
| Joshua | Joshua | Baruch | |
| Judges | Judges | Ezekiel | Ezekiel |
| Ruth | Ruth | Daniel | Daniel |
| 1 & 2 Samuel | 1 & 2 Samuel | Hosea | Hosea |
| 1 & 2 Kings | 1 & 2 Kings | Joel | Joel |
| 1 & 2 Chronicles | 1 & 2 Chronicles | Amos | Amos |
| Ezra | Ezra | Obadiah | Obadiah |
| Nehemiah | Nehemiah | Jonah | Jonah |
| Tobit | | Micah | Micah |
| Judith | | Nahum | Nahum |
| Esther | Esther | Habakkuk | Habakkuk |
| Job | Job | Zephaniah | Zephaniah |
| Psalms | Psalms | Haggai | Haggai |
| Proverbs | Proverbs | Zechariah | Zechariah |
| Ecclesiastes | Ecclesiastes | Malachi | Malachi |
| Song of Songs | Song of Solomon | 1 & 2 Maccabees | |

## PROTESTANT APOCRYPHA

| | |
|---|---|
| 1 & 2 Esdras | Baruch |
| Tobit | Prayer of Azariah and the Song |
| Judith | of the Three Holy Children |
| Additions to Esther | Susanna |
| Wisdom of Solomon | Bel and the Dragon |
| Ecclesiasticus or the Wisdom of Jesus | The Prayer of Manasses |
| Son of Sirach | 1 & 2 Maccabees |

## CHRISTIAN CANON——NEW TESTAMENT

| | | |
|---|---|---|
| Matthew | Ephesians | James |
| Mark | Philippians | 1 & 2 Peter |
| Luke | Colossians | 1, 2, 3 John |
| John | 1 & 2 Thessalonians | Jude |
| Acts of the Apostles | 1 & 2 Timothy | Revelation *or* |
| Romans | Titus | Apocalypse |
| 1 & 2 Corinthians | Philemon | |
| Galatians | Hebrews | |

**bicarbonate of soda** : SODIUM BICARBONATE

**bi·cen·te·na·ry** \ˌbī-sen-'te-nə-rē, bī-'sen-tᵊn ˌer-ē\ n : BICENTENNIAL — **bicentenary** adj

**bi·cen·ten·ni·al** \ˌbī-sen-'te-nē-əl\ n : a 200th anniversary or its celebration — **bicentennial** adj

**bi·ceps** \'bī-ˌseps\ n, pl **biceps** also **biceps·es** [NL, fr. L, two-headed, fr. bitwo + caput head] : a muscle (as in the front of the upper arm) having two points of origin

**¹bick·er** \'bi-kər\ n : ALTERCATION

**²bicker** vb : to engage in a petty quarrel

**bi·coast·al** \bī-'kōs-tᵊl\ adj : living or working on both the east and west coasts of the U.S.

**bi·con·cave** \ˌbī-(ˌ)kän-'kāv, (ˌ)bī-'kän-ˌkāv\ adj : concave on both sides

**bi·con·vex** \ˌbī-(ˌ)kän-'veks, (ˌ)bī-'kän-ˌveks\ adj : convex on both sides

**bi·cus·pid** \bī-'kəs-pəd\ n : PREMOLAR

**¹bi·cy·cle** \'bī-ˌsi-kəl\ n : a light 2-wheeled vehicle with a saddle, pedals, and handlebars for steering

**²bicycle** vb **-cy·cled; -cy·cling** \-ˌsi-k(ə-)liŋ, -ˌsī-\ : to ride a bicycle — **bi·cy·cler** \-k(ə-)lər\ n — **bi·cy·clist** \-k(ə-)list\ n

**¹bid** \'bid\ vb **bade** \'bad, 'bād\ or **bid; bid·den** \'bi-dᵊn\ or **bid** also **bade; bid·ding** 1 : COMMAND, ORDER 2 : INVITE 3 : to give expression to ⟨bade a tearful farewell⟩ 4 : to make a bid : OFFER — **bid·der** n

**²bid** n 1 : the act of one who bids; also : an offer for something 2 : INVITATION 3 : an announcement in a card game of what a player proposes to accomplish 4 : an attempt to win or gain ⟨a ~ for mayor⟩

**bid·da·ble** \'bi-də-bəl\ adj 1 : OBEDIENT, DOCILE 2 : capable of being bid

**bid·dy** \'bi-dē\ n, pl **biddies** : HEN; also : a young chicken

**bide** \'bīd\ vb **bode** \'bōd\ or **bid·ed; bided; bid·ing** 1 : to wait for 2 : WAIT, TARRY 3 : DWELL

**bi·det** \bi-'dā\ n : a bathroom fixture used esp. for bathing the external genitals and the anal region

**bi·di·rec·tion·al** \ˌbī-də-'rek-sh(ə-)nəl\ adj : involving, moving, or taking place in two usu. opposite directions — **bi·di·rection·al·ly** adv

**bi·en·ni·al** \bī-'e-nē-əl\ adj 1 : taking place once in two years 2 : lasting two years 3 : producing leaves the first year and fruiting and dying the second year — **biennial** n — **bi·en·ni·al·ly** adv

**bi·en·ni·um** \bī-'e-nē-əm\ n, pl **-niums** or **-nia** \-ə\ [L, fr. bi- two + annus year] : a period of two years

**bier** \'bir\ n : a stand bearing a coffin or corpse

**bi·fo·cal** \'bī-ˌfō-kəl\ adj : having two focal lengths

**bifocals** \-kəlz\ n pl : eyeglasses with lenses that have one part that corrects for near vision and one for distant vision

**bi·fold** \'bī-ˌfōld\ adj : designed to fold twice ⟨~ doors⟩

**bi·fur·cate** \'bī-fər-ˌkāt, bī-'fər-\ vb **-cat·ed; -cat·ing** : to divide into two branches or parts — **bi·fur·ca·tion** \ˌbī-fər-'kā-shən\ n

**big** \'big\ adj **big·ger; big·gest** 1 : large in size, amount, or scope 2 : PREGNANT; also : SWELLING 3 : IMPORTANT, IMPOSING 4 : NOBLE, GENEROUS 5 : POPULAR — **big·ness** n — **big on** : strongly favoring or liking

**big·a·my** \'bi-gə-mē\ n : the act of marrying one person while still legally married to another — **big·a·mist** \-mist\ n — **big·a·mous** \-məs\ adj

**big bang theory** n : a theory in astronomy: the universe originated in an explosion (**big bang**) from a single point of nearly infinite energy density

**big brother** n 1 : an older brother 2 : a man who befriends a delinquent or friendless boy 3 cap both Bs : the leader of an authoritarian state or movement

**big cheese** n : ³BOSS

**big crunch** n : a hypothetical event in which all matter in the universe collapses to a single point of nearly infinite energy density

**Big Dipper** n : the seven principal stars of Ursa Major in a form resembling a dipper

**big·foot** \'big-ˌfut\ n : SASQUATCH

**big·horn sheep** \'big-ˌhȯrn\ n : a wild sheep of mountainous western No. America

**bight** \'bīt\ n 1 : a curve in a coast; also : the bay formed by such a curve 2 : a slack part in a rope

**big-name** \'big-'nām\ adj : widely popular ⟨a ~ performer⟩ — **big name** n

**big·ot** \'bi-gət\ n : one who regards or treats members of a group with hatred and intolerance ♦ Synonyms FANATIC, ENTHUSIAST, ZEALOT — **big·ot·ed** \-gə-təd\ adj — **big·ot·ry** \-trē\ n

**big screen** n : the motion picture medium as contrasted to television

**big shot** \'big-ˌshät\ n : an important person

**big time** \-ˌtīm\ n 1 : a high-paying vaudeville circuit requiring only two performances a day 2 : the top rank of an activity or enterprise — **big-tim·er** n

**big top** n 1 : the main tent of a circus 2 : CIRCUS

**big·wig** \'big-ˌwig\ n : BIG SHOT

**bike** \'bīk\ n 1 : BICYCLE 2 : MOTORCYCLE

**bik·er** n : MOTORCYCLIST; esp : one who is a member of an organized gang

**bike·way** \'bīk-ˌwā\ n : a thoroughfare for bicycles

**bi·ki·ni** \bə-'kē-nē\ n [F, fr. Bikini, atoll in the Marshall Islands] : a woman's brief 2-piece bathing suit

**bi·lat·er·al** \bī-'la-tə-rəl\ adj 1 : having or involving two sides 2 : affecting reciprocally two sides or parties — **bi·lat·er·al·ism** \-tə-rə-ˌli-zəm\ n — **bi·lat·er·al·ly** adv

**bile** \'bī(-ə)l\ n 1 : a bitter greenish fluid secreted by the liver that aids in the digestion of fats 2 : an ill-humored mood

**bilge** \'bilj\ n 1 : the part of a ship that

lies between the bottom and the point where the sides go straight up **2** : stale or worthless remarks or ideas

**bi·lin·gual** \bī-'liŋ-gwəl\ *adj* : expressed in, knowing, or using two languages

**bil·ious** \'bil-yəs\ *adj* **1** : marked by or suffering from disordered liver function **2** : IRRITABLE, ILL-TEMPERED ⟨a ~ disposition⟩ — **bil·ious·ness** *n*

**bilk** \'bilk\ *vb* : CHEAT, SWINDLE

**¹bill** \'bil\ *n* : the jaws of a bird together with their horny covering; *also* : a mouthpart (as of a turtle) resembling these — **billed** \'bild\ *adj*

**²bill** *vb* : to caress fondly

**³bill** *n* **1** : an itemized statement of particulars; *also* : INVOICE **2** : a written document or note **3** : a printed advertisement (as a poster) announcing an event **4** : a draft of a law presented to a legislature for enactment **5** : a written statement of a legal wrong suffered or of some breach of law **6** : a piece of paper money

**⁴bill** *vb* **1** : to enter in or prepare a bill; *also* : to submit a bill or account to **2** : to advertise by bills or posters

**bill·board** \-,bórd\ *n* : a flat surface on which advertising bills are posted

**¹bil·let** \'bil-lət\ *n* **1** : an order requiring a person to provide lodging for a soldier; *also* : quarters assigned by or as if by such an order **2** : POSITION, APPOINTMENT

**²billet** *vb* : to assign lodging to by billet

**bil·let–doux** \,bil-ā-'dü\ *n, pl* **billets–doux** \*same or* -'düz\ [F *billet doux*, lit., sweet letter] : a love letter

**bill·fold** \'bil-,fōld\ *n* : WALLET

**bil·liards** \'bil-yərdz\ *n* : any of several games played on an oblong table by driving balls against each other or into pockets with a cue

**bil·lings·gate** \'bi-liŋz-,gāt, *Brit usu* -git\ *n* [*Billingsgate*, old gate and fish market, London, England] : coarsely abusive language

**bil·lion** \'bil-yən\ *n* **1** : a thousand millions **2** *Brit* : a million millions — **billion** *adj* — **bil·lionth** \-yənth\ *adj or n*

**bill of attainder** : a legislative act that imposes punishment without a trial

**bill of health** : a usu. favorable report following an examination

**bill of sale** : a legal document transferring ownership of goods

**¹bil·low** \'bi-lō\ *n* **1** : WAVE; *esp* : a great wave **2** : a rolling mass (as of fog or flame) like a great wave — **bil·lowy** \'bi-lə-wē\ *adj*

**²billow** *vb* : to rise and roll in waves; *also* : to swell out ⟨~*ing* sails⟩

**bil·ly** \'bi-lē\ *n, pl* **billies** : BILLY CLUB

**billy club** *n* : a heavy usu. wooden club; *esp* : a police officer's club

**bil·ly goat** \'bil-lē-\ *n* : a male goat

**bi·met·al** \'bī-,me-t⁹l\ *adj* : BIMETALLIC — **bimetal** *n*

**bi·me·tal·lic** \,bī-mə-'ta-lik\ *adj* : made of two different metals — often used of devices having a bonded expansive part — **bimetallic** *n*

**bi·met·al·lism** \bī-'me-t⁹l-,i-zəm\ *n* : the

use of two metals at fixed ratios to form a standard of value for a monetary system

**¹bi·month·ly** \bī-'mənth-lē\ *adj* **1** : occurring every two months **2** : occurring twice a month : SEMIMONTHLY — **bimonthly** *adv*

**²bimonthly** *n* : a bimonthly publication

**bin** \'bin\ *n* : a box, crib, or enclosure used for storage

**bi·na·ry** \'bī-nə-rē, -,ner-ē\ *adj* **1** : consisting of two things or parts **2** : relating to, being, or belonging to a system of numbers having 2 as its base ⟨the ~ digits 0 and 1⟩ **3** : involving a choice between or condition of two alternatives only (as on-off, yes-no) — **binary** *n*

**binary star** : a system of two stars revolving around each other

**binary system** *n* : BINARY STAR

**bin·au·ral** \bī-'nòr-əl\ *adj* : of or relating to sound reproduction involving the use of two separated microphones and two transmission channels to achieve a stereophonic effect

**bind** \'bīnd\ *vb* **bound** \'baùnd\; **binding 1** : TIE; *also* : to restrain as if by tying **2** : to put under an obligation; *also* : to constrain with legal authority **3** : BANDAGE **4** : to unite into a mass **5** : to compel as if by a pledge ⟨a handshake ~s the deal⟩ **6** : to strengthen or decorate with a band **7** : to fasten together and enclose in a cover ⟨~ books⟩ **8** : to exert a tying, restraining, or compelling effect — **binder** *n*

**bind·ing** \'bīn-diŋ\ *n* : something (as a ski fastening, a cover, or an edging fabric) used to bind

**bin·dle** \'bin-d⁹l\ *n* : a bundle of clothes or bedding

**¹binge** \'binj\ *n* **1** : SPREE **2** : an act of excessive consumption (as of food)

**²binge** *vb* **binged; binge·ing** *or* **bing·ing** : to go on a binge — **bing·er** *n*

**bin·go** \'biŋ-gō\ *n, pl* **bingos** : a game of chance played with cards having numbered squares corresponding to numbered balls drawn at random and won by covering five squares in a row

**bin·na·cle** \'bi-ni-kəl\ *n* [alter. of ME *bitakle*, fr. Pg or Sp; Pg *bitácola* & Sp *bitácula*, fr. L *habitaculum* dwelling place, fr. *habitare* to inhabit] : a container holding a ship's compass

**¹bin·oc·u·lar** \bī-'nä-kyə-lər, bə-\ *adj* : of, relating to, or adapted to the use of both eyes — **bin·oc·u·lar·ly** *adv*

**²bin·oc·u·lar** \bə-'nä-kyə-lər, bī-\ *n* **1** : a binocular optical instrument (as a microscope) **2** : a hand-held optical instrument composed of two telescopes and a focusing device — usu. used in pl.

**bi·no·mi·al** \bī-'nō-mē-əl\ *n* **1** : a mathematical expression consisting of two terms connected by the sign plus (+) or minus (−) **2** : a biological species name consisting of two terms — **binomial** *adj*

**bio·chem·is·try** \,bī-ō-'ke-mə-strē\ *n* : chemistry that deals with the chemical compounds and processes occurring in living things — **bio·chem·i·cal** \-mi-kəl\

*adj or n*    **bio·chem·i·cal·ly** \-k(ə-)lē\ *adv* — **bio·chem·ist** \-mist\ *n*

**bio·de·grad·able** \-di-'grā-də-bəl\ *adj* : capable of being broken down esp. into innocuous products by the actions of living things (as microorganisms) ⟨a ~ detergent⟩ — **bio·de·grad·abil·i·ty** \-grā-də-'bi-lə-tē\ *n* — **bio·deg·ra·da·tion** \-,de-grə-'dā-shən\ *n* — **bio·de·grade** \-di-'grād\ *vb*

**bio·di·ver·si·ty** \-də-'vər-sə-tē, -dī-\ *n* : biological diversity in an environment as indicated by numbers of different species of plants and animals

**bio·en·gi·neer·ing** \-,en-jə-'nir-iŋ\ *n* 1 : the application of engineering principles to medicine and biology 2 : GENETIC ENGINEERING

**bio·eth·ics** \-'e-thiks\ *n* : the ethics of biological research and its applications esp. in medicine — **bio·eth·i·cal** \-'e-thi-kəl\ *adj* — **bio·eth·i·cist** \-'e-thə-sist\ *n*

**bio·feed·back** \-'fēd-,bak\ *n* : the technique of making unconscious or involuntary bodily processes (as heartbeats or brain waves) perceptible to the senses (as by use of an oscilloscope) in order to manipulate them by conscious mental control

**biog** *abbr* biographer; biographical; biography

**bio·ge·og·ra·phy** \,bī-ō-jē-'ä-grə-fē\ *n* : a science that deals with the geographical distribution of plants and animals — **bio·ge·og·ra·pher** *n*

**bi·og·ra·phy** \bī-'ä-grə-fē, bē-\ *n, pl* **-phies** : a written history of a person's life; *also* : such writings in general — **bi·og·ra·pher** *n* — **bio·graph·i·cal** \,bī-ə-'gra-fi-kəl\ *also* **bio·graph·ic** \-fik\ *adj*

**bio·in·for·mat·ics** \,bī-ō-in-fər-'ma-tiks\ *n* : the storage, classification, and analysis of biological information using computers

**biol** *abbr* biologic; biological; biologist; biology

**bi·o·log·i·cal** \,bī-ə-'lä-ji-kəl\ *also* **bio·log·ic** \-jik\ *adj* 1 : of, relating to, or produced by biology or life and living processes 2 : connected by direct genetic relationship rather than by adoption or marriage ⟨her ~ father⟩ — **bi·o·log·i·cal·ly** \-ji-k(ə-)lē\ *adv*

**biological clock** *n* : an inherent timing mechanism in a living system that is inferred to exist in order to explain the timing of various physiological and behavioral states and processes

**biological warfare** *n* : warfare in which harmful living organisms (**biological weapons**) are used against an enemy esp. to cause large-scale death or disease

**bi·ol·o·gy** \bī-'ä-lə-jē\ *n* [G *Biologie,* fr. Gk *bios* mode of life + *logos* word, discourse] 1 : a science that deals with living beings and life processes 2 : the life processes of an organism or group — **bi·ol·o·gist** \bī-'ä-lə-jist\ *n*

**bio·mass** \'bī-ō-,mas\ *n* 1 : the amount of living matter (as in a unit area) 2 : plant materials and animal waste used esp. as fuel

**bio·med·i·cal** \,bī-ō-'me-di-kəl\ *adj* : of, relating to, or involving biological, medical, and physical science

**bi·on·ic** \bī-'ä-nik\ *adj* : having normal biological capability or performance enhanced by or as if by electronic or mechanical devices

**bio·phys·ics** \,bī-ō-'fi-ziks\ *n* : a branch of science concerned with the application of physical principles and methods to biological problems — **bio·phys·i·cal** \-zi-kəl\ *adj* — **bio·phys·i·cist** \-'fi-zə-sist\ *n*

**bio·pic** \'bī-ō-,pik\ *n* : a biographical movie

**bi·op·sy** \'bī-,äp-sē\ *n, pl* **-sies** : the removal of tissue, cells, or fluids from the living body for examination

**bio·rhythm** \'bī-ō-,ri-thəm\ *n* : an innately determined rhythmic biological process (as sleep); *also* : the internal mechanism controlling such a process

**bio·sci·ence** \-'sī-əns\ *n* : BIOLOGY 1; *also* : LIFE SCIENCE

**bio·sphere** \'bī-ə-,sfir\ *n* 1 : the part of the world in which life can exist 2 : living organisms together with their environment

**bio·tech** \'bī-ō-,tek\ *n* : BIOTECHNOLOGY

**bio·tech·nol·o·gy** \,bī-ō-tek-'nä-lə-jē\ *n* : the manipulation (as through genetic engineering) of living organisms to produce useful products; *also* : biological science so applied

**bio·ter·ror·ism** \-'ter-ər-,i-zəm\ *n* : terrorism involving the use of biological weapons — **bio·ter·ror·ist** \-ist\ *adj or n*

**bi·ot·ic** \bī-'ä-tik\ *adj* : of, relating to, or caused by living organisms

**bi·o·tin** \'bī-ə-tən\ *n* : a vitamin of the vitamin B complex found esp. in yeast, liver, and egg yolk and active in growth promotion

**bi·o·tite** \'bī-ə-,tīt\ *n* : a dark mica containing iron, magnesium, potassium, and aluminum

**bi·par·ti·san** \bī-'pär-tə-zən\ *adj* : marked by or involving cooperation, agreement, and compromise between two major political parties — **bi·par·ti·san·ship** \-,ship\ *n*

**bi·par·tite** \-'pär-,tīt\ *adj* 1 : being in two parts 2 : shared by two parties ⟨~ treaty⟩

**bi·ped** \'bī-,ped\ *n* : a 2-footed animal — **bi·ped·al** \(,)bī-'pe-dᵊl\ *adj*

**bi·plane** \'bī-,plān\ *n* : an aircraft with two wings placed one above the other

**bi·po·lar** \bī-'po-lər\ *adj* : having or involving the use of two poles — **bi·po·lar·i·ty** \,bī-pō-'ler-ə-tē\ *n*

**bipolar disorder** *n* : any of several psychological disorders of mood characterized usu. by alternating episodes of depression and mania

**bi·ra·cial** \bī-'rā-shəl\ *adj* : of, relating to, or involving members of two races

¹**birch** \'bərch\ *n* 1 : any of a genus of mostly short-lived deciduous shrubs and trees with membranous outer bark and pale close-grained wood; *also* : this wood 2 : a birch rod or bundle of twigs for flogging — **birch** *or* **birch·en** \'bər-chən\ *adj*

²**birch** *vb* : WHIP, FLOG

¹**bird** \'bərd\ *n* : any of a class of warm-blooded egg-laying vertebrates having the body feathered and the forelimbs modified to form wings

²**bird** *vb* : to observe or identify wild birds in their native habitat — **bird·er** *n*

**bird·bath** \'bərd-ˌbath, -ˌbäth\ *n* : a usu. ornamental basin set up for birds to bathe in

**bird·house** \-ˌhau̇s\ *n* : an artificial nesting place for birds; *also* : AVIARY

**bird·ie** \'bər-dē\ *n* : a score of one under par on a hole in golf

**bird·lime** \-ˌlīm\ *n* : a sticky substance smeared on twigs to snare small birds

**bird of paradise** : any of numerous brilliantly colored plumed birds of the New Guinea area

**bird of prey** : a carnivorous bird that feeds wholly or chiefly on carrion or on meat taken by hunting

**bird·seed** \'bərd-ˌsēd\ *n* : a mixture of small seeds (as of hemp or millet) used for feeding birds

**bird's-eye** \'bərdz-ˌī\ *adj* **1** : marked with spots resembling birds' eyes ⟨~ maple⟩ **2** : seen from above as if by a flying bird ⟨~ view⟩; *also* : CURSORY

**bi·ret·ta** \bə-'re-tə\ *n* : a square cap with three ridges on top worn esp. by Roman Catholic clergymen

**birr** \'bir, 'bər\ *n, pl* **birr** — see MONEY table

¹**birth** \'bərth\ *n* **1** : the act or fact of being born or of bringing forth young **2** : LINEAGE, DESCENT **3** : ORIGIN, BEGINNING — **birth** *vb*

²**birth** *adj* : BIOLOGICAL 2 ⟨~ parents⟩

**birth canal** : the channel formed by the cervix, vagina, and vulva through which the fetus passes during birth

**birth control** *n* : control of the number of children born esp. by preventing or lessening the frequency of conception

**birth·day** \'bərth-ˌdā\ *n* : the day or anniversary of one's birth

**birth defect** *n* : a physical or biochemical defect present at birth and inherited or environmentally induced

**birth·mark** \'bərth-ˌmärk\ *n* : an unusual mark or blemish on the skin at birth

**birth·place** \-ˌplās\ *n* : place of birth or origin

**birth·rate** \-ˌrāt\ *n* : the number of births per number of individuals in a given area or group during a given time

**birth·right** \-ˌrīt\ *n* : a right, privilege, or possession to which one is entitled by birth ♦ *Synonyms* LEGACY, PATRIMONY, HERITAGE, INHERITANCE

**birth·stone** \-ˌstōn\ *n* : a gemstone associated symbolically with the month of one's birth

**bis·cuit** \'bis-kət\ *n* [ME *bisquite*, fr. AF *besquit*, fr. (*pain*) *besquit* twice-cooked bread] **1** : a crisp flat cake; *esp, Brit* : CRACKER 2 **2** : a small quick bread made from dough that has been rolled and cut or dropped from a spoon

**bi·sect** \'bī-ˌsekt\ *vb* : to divide into two usu. equal parts; *also* : CROSS, INTERSECT — **bi·sec·tion** \'bī-ˌsek-shən\ *n* — **bi·sec·tor** \-tər\ *n*

**bi·sex·u·al** \bī-'sek-shə-wəl\ *adj* **1** : possessing characters of or having sexual desire for both sexes **2** : of, relating to, or involving both sexes — **bisexual** *n* — **bi·sex·u·al·i·ty** \ˌbī-ˌsek-shə-'wal-ə-tē\ *n*

**bish·op** \'bi-shəp\ *n* [ME *bisshop*, fr. OE *bisceop*, fr. LL *episcopus*, fr. Gk *episkopos*, lit., overseer, fr. *epi-* on, over + *skeptesthai* to look] **1** : a member of the clergy ranking above a priest and typically governing a diocese **2** : any of various Protestant church officials who superintend other clergy **3** : a chess piece that can move diagonally across any number of adjoining unoccupied squares

**bish·op·ric** \'bi-shə-prik\ *n* **1** : DIOCESE **2** : the office of bishop

**bis·muth** \'biz-məth\ *n* : a heavy brittle grayish white metallic chemical element used in alloys and medicine

**bi·son** \'bī-sᵊn, -zᵊn\ *n, pl* **bison** : BUFFALO 2

**bisque** \'bisk\ *n* : a thick cream soup

**bis·tro** \'bēs-trō, 'bis-\ *n, pl* **bistros** [F] **1** : a small or unpretentious restaurant **2** : BAR; *also* : NIGHTCLUB

¹**bit** \'bit\ *n* **1** : the biting or cutting edge or part of a tool **2** : the part of a bridle that is placed in a horse's mouth

²**bit** *n* **1** : a morsel of food; *also* : a small piece or quantity of something **2** : a small coin; *also* : a unit of value equal to 12½ cents **3** : something small or trivial **4** : an indefinite usu. small degree or extent ⟨a ~ tired⟩

³**bit** *n* [*b*inary dig*it*] : a unit of computer information equivalent to the result of a choice between two alternatives; *also* : its physical representation

¹**bitch** \'bich\ *n* **1** : a female canine; *esp* : a female dog **2** : a malicious, spiteful, or overbearing woman

²**bitch** *vb* : COMPLAIN

¹**bite** \'bīt\ *vb* **bit** \'bit\; **bit·ten** \'bi-tᵊn\ *also* **bit**; **bit·ing** \'bī-tiŋ\ **1** : to grip with teeth or jaws; *also* : to wound or sting with or as if with fangs **2** : to cut or pierce with or as if with an edged instrument **3** : to cause to smart or sting **4** : CORRODE **5** : to take bait

²**bite** *n* **1** : the act or manner of biting **2** : FOOD **3** : a wound made by biting; *also* : a penetrating effect

**bite-size** \'bīt-ˌsīz\ *adj* **1** : of a size that can be eaten in one bite **2** : being or made small or brief esp. so as to be easily manageable

**biting** *adj* : SHARP, CUTTING

**bit-map** \'bit-ˌmap\ *n* : an array of binary data representing a bitmapped image or display

**bit-mapped** \'bit-ˌmapt\ *adj* : of, relating to, or being a digital image or display for which an array of binary data specifies the value of each pixel

**bit·ter** \'bi-tər\ *adj* **1** : being or inducing the one of the basic taste sensations that is acrid, astringent, or disagreeable and is suggestive of hops **2** : marked by intensity or severity (as of distress or hatred)

3 : extremely harsh or cruel — **bit·ter·ly** *adv* — **bit·ter·ness** *n*

**bit·tern** \'bi-tərn\ *n* : any of various small or medium-sized herons

**bit·ters** \'bi-tərz\ *n sing or pl* : a usu. alcoholic solution of bitter and often aromatic plant products used in mixing drinks and as a mild tonic

¹**bit·ter·sweet** \'bi-tər-ˌswēt\ *n* **1** : a poisonous nightshade with purple flowers and reddish berries **2** : a woody vine with yellow capsules that open when ripe to show scarlet seed covers

²**bittersweet** *adj* : being at once both bitter and sweet

**bi·tu·mi·nous coal** \bə-ˈtü-mə-nəs-, bī-, -ˈtyü-\ *n* : a coal that when heated yields considerable volatile waste matter

**bi·valve** \'bī-ˌvalv\ *n* : any of a class of mollusks (as clams or scallops) of two separate parts that open and shut — **bivalve** *adj*

¹**biv·ouac** \'bi-və-ˌwak\ *n* [F, fr. LG *bi-wacht*, fr. *bi* at + *wacht* guard] : a temporary encampment or shelter

²**bivouac** *vb* **-ouacked; -ouack·ing** : to form a bivouac : CAMP

¹**bi·week·ly** \bī-ˈwē-klē\ *adj* **1** : occurring twice a week **2** : occurring every two weeks : FORTNIGHTLY — **biweekly** *adv*

²**biweekly** *n* : a biweekly publication

**bi·year·ly** \-ˈyir-lē\ *adj* **1** : BIANNUAL **2** : BIENNIAL

**bi·zarre** \bə-ˈzär\ *adj* : ODD, ECCENTRIC, FANTASTIC ⟨∼ costumes⟩ — **bi·zarre·ly** *adv*

**bi·zar·ro** \bə-ˈzär-ō\ *adj* : characterized by a bizarre, fantastic, or unconventional approach ⟨∼ horror movies⟩

**bk** *abbr* **1** bank **2** book

**Bk** *symbol* berkelium

**bkg** *abbr* banking

**bkgd** *abbr* background

**bks** *abbr* barracks

**bkt** *abbr* **1** basket **2** bracket

**bl** *abbr* **1** bale **2** barrel **3** blue

**blab** \'blab\ *vb* **blabbed; blab·bing** : TATTLE, GOSSIP

¹**black** \'blak\ *adj* **1** : of the color black; *also* : very dark **2** : SWARTHY **3** : of or relating to various groups of dark-skinned people **4** : of or relating to the African-American people or their culture **5** : SOILED, DIRTY **6** : lacking light ⟨a ∼ night⟩ **7** : WICKED, EVIL ⟨∼ magic⟩ **8** : DISMAL, GLOOMY ⟨a ∼ outlook⟩ **9** : SULLEN ⟨a ∼ mood⟩ — **black·ish** *adj* — **black·ly** *adv* — **black·ness** *n*

²**black** *n* **1** : a black pigment or dye; *also* : something (as clothing) that is black **2** : the characteristic color of soot or coal **3** : a person of a dark-skinned race **4** : AFRICAN-AMERICAN

³**black** *vb* : BLACKEN

**black·a·moor** \'bla-kə-ˌmùr\ *n* : a dark-skinned person

**black-and-blue** \ˌbla-kən-ˈblü\ *adj* : darkly discolored from blood effused by bruising

**black-and-white** \ˌbla-kən-ˈhwīt\ : SQUAD CAR

**black·ball** \'blak-ˌbȯl\ *vb* **1** : to vote against; *esp* : to exclude from membership by casting a negative vote **2** : OSTRACIZE — **black·ball** *n*

**black bass** *n* : any of several freshwater sunfishes native to eastern and central No. America

**black bear** *n* : a usu. black-furred bear of No. American forests

¹**black belt** \'blak-ˌbelt\ *n, often cap both Bs* : an area densely populated by blacks

²**black belt** \-ˈbelt\ *n* : one who holds the rating of expert (as in judo or karate); *also* : the rating itself

**black·ber·ry** \-ˌber-ē\ *n* : the usu. black or purple juicy but seedy edible fruit of various brambles; *also* : a plant bearing this fruit

**black·bird** \-ˌbərd\ *n* : any of various birds (as the red-winged blackbird) of which the male is largely or wholly black

**black·board** \-ˌbȯrd\ *n* : a smooth usu. dark surface used for writing or drawing on with chalk

**black·body** \-ˈbä-dē\ *n* : a body or surface that completely absorbs incident radiation with no reflection

**black box** *n* **1** : a usu. complicated electronic device whose components and workings are unknown or mysterious to the user **2** : a device used in aircraft to record cockpit conversations and flight data

**black death** *n* : an epidemic of bacterial plague and esp. bubonic plague that spread rapidly in Europe and Asia in the 14th century

**black·en** \'bla-kən\ *vb* **black·ened; black·en·ing 1** : to make or become black **2** : DEFAME, SULLY ⟨∼ed her reputation⟩

**black·ened** *adj* : coated with spices and quickly seared in a very hot skillet ⟨∼ swordfish⟩

**black eye** *n* : a discoloration of the skin around the eye from bruising

**black-eyed Su·san** \ˌblak-ˌīd-ˈsü-zᵊn\ *n* : a coarse No. American plant that is related to the daisies and has deep yellow to orange flower heads with dark conical centers

**Black·foot** \'blak-ˌfùt\ *n, pl* **Black·feet** *or* **Blackfoot** : a member of an American Indian people of Montana, Alberta, and Saskatchewan

**black·guard** \'bla-gərd, -ˌgärd\ *n* : SCOUNDREL, RASCAL

**black·head** \'blak-ˌhed\ *n* : a small usu. dark oily mass plugging the outlet of a skin gland

**black hole** *n* : a celestial object with a gravitational field so strong that light cannot escape from it

**black·ing** \'bla-kiŋ\ *n* : a substance applied to something to make it black

¹**black·jack** \'blak-ˌjak\ *n* **1** : a leather-covered club with a flexible handle **2** : a card game in which the object is to be dealt cards having a higher count than the dealer but not exceeding 21

²**blackjack** *vb* : to hit with or as if with a blackjack

**black light** *n* : invisible ultraviolet light

**black·list** \'blak-,list\ n : a list of persons who are disapproved of and are to be punished or boycotted — **blacklist** vb

**black·mail** \'blak-,māl\ n : extortion by threats esp. of public exposure; also : something so extorted — **blackmail** vb — **black·mail·er** n

**black market** n : illicit trade in goods; also : a place where such trade is carried on

**Black Mass** n : a travesty of the Christian Mass ascribed to worshipers of Satan

**Black Muslim** n : a member of a chiefly black group that professes Islamic religious belief

**black nationalist** n, often cap B&N : a member of a group of militant blacks who advocate separatism from whites and the formation of self-governing black communities — **black nationalism** n, often cap B&N

**black–on–black** adj : involving a black person against another black person ⟨∼ crime⟩

**black·out** \'blak-,aut\ n 1 : a period of darkness due to electrical power failure 2 : a transitory loss or dulling of vision or consciousness 3 : the prohibition or restriction of the telecasting of a sports event — **black out** vb

**black pepper** n : a spice that consists of the dried berry of a pepper plant ground with the black husk still on

**black power** n : the mobilization of the political and economic power of black Americans esp. to compel respect for their rights and improve their condition

**black sheep** n : a member of a group who is disreputable or not regarded favorably

**black·smith** \'blak-,smith\ n : a smith who forges iron — **black·smith·ing** n

**black·strap molasses** \'blak-,strap-\ n : a thick dark molasses obtained from successive processing of raw sugar

**black·thorn** \-,thȯrn\ n : a European thorny plum

**black–tie** \'blak-'tī\ adj : characterized by or requiring semiformal evening clothes consisting of a usu. black tie and tuxedo for men and a formal dress for women

**black·top** \'blak-,täp\ n : a dark tarry material (as asphalt) used esp. for surfacing roads — **blacktop** vb

**black widow** n : a venomous New World spider having the female black with an hourglass-shaped red mark on the underside of the abdomen

**blad·der** \'bla-dər\ n : a sac in which liquid or gas is stored; esp : one in a vertebrate into which urine passes from the kidneys

¹**blade** \'blād\ n 1 : a leaf of a plant and esp. of a grass; also : the flat part of a leaf as distinguished from its stalk 2 : something (as the flat part of an oar or an arm of a propeller) resembling the blade of a leaf 3 : the cutting part of an instrument or tool 4 : SWORD; also : SWORDSMAN 5 : a dashing fellow ⟨a gay ∼⟩ 6 : the runner of an ice skate — **blad·ed** \'blā-dəd\ adj

²**blade** vb **blad·ed; blad·ing** : to skate on in-line skates — **blad·er** \'blā-dər\ n

**blain** \'blān\ n : an inflammatory swelling or sore

¹**blame** \'blām\ vb **blamed; blam·ing** [ME, fr. AF blamer, blasmer, fr. L blasphemare to blaspheme, fr. Gk blasphēmein] 1 : to find fault with 2 : to hold responsible or responsible for ♦ **Synonyms** CENSURE, DENOUNCE, CONDEMN, CRITICIZE — **blam·able** adj

²**blame** n 1 : CENSURE, REPROOF 2 : responsibility for fault or error ♦ **Synonyms** GUILT, FAULT, CULPABILITY, ONUS — **blame·less** adj — **blame·less·ly** adv — **blame·less·ness** n

**blame·wor·thy** \-,wər-thē\ adj : deserving blame — **blame·wor·thi·ness** n

**blanch** \'blanch\ vb : to make or become white or pale ⟨fear ∼ed her cheeks⟩

**blanc·mange** \blə-'mänj, -'mäⁿzh\ n : a dessert made from gelatin or a starchy substance and milk usu. sweetened and flavored

**bland** \'bland\ adj 1 : smooth in manner : SUAVE ⟨a ∼ smile⟩ 2 : gently soothing ⟨a ∼ diet⟩; also : INSIPID ♦ **Synonyms** GENTLE, MILD, SOFT, BALMY — **bland·ly** adv — **bland·ness** n

**blan·dish·ment** \'blan-dish-mənt\ n : flattering or coaxing speech or action : CAJOLERY

¹**blank** \'blaŋk\ adj 1 : showing or causing an appearance of dazed dismay; also : EXPRESSIONLESS 2 : free from writing or marks; also : having spaces to be filled in 3 : DULL, EMPTY ⟨∼ moments⟩ 4 : ABSOLUTE, DOWNRIGHT ⟨a ∼ refusal⟩ 5 : not shaped in final form — **blank·ly** adv — **blank·ness** n

²**blank** n 1 : an empty space 2 : a form with spaces for the entry of data 3 : an unfinished form (as of a key) 4 : a cartridge with propellant and a seal but no projectile

³**blank** vb 1 : to cover or close up : OBSCURE 2 : to keep from scoring

**blank check** n 1 : a signed check with the amount unspecified 2 : complete freedom of action

¹**blan·ket** \'blaŋ-kət\ n 1 : a heavy woven often woolen covering 2 : a covering layer ⟨a ∼ of snow⟩

²**blanket** vb : to cover with a blanket

³**blanket** adj : covering a group or class ⟨∼ insurance⟩; also : applicable in all instances ⟨∼ rules⟩

**blank verse** n : unrhymed iambic pentameter

**blare** \'bler\ vb **blared; blar·ing** : to sound loud and harsh; also : to proclaim loudly — **blare** n

**blar·ney** \'blär-nē\ n [Blarney stone, a stone in Blarney Castle, near Cork, Ireland, held to bestow skill in flattery on those who kiss it] : skillful flattery : BLANDISHMENT

**bla·sé** \blä-'zā\ adj [F] : apathetic to pleasure or excitement as a result of excessive indulgence; also : SOPHISTICATED

**blas·pheme** \blas-'fēm, 'blas-,\ vb **blasphemed; blas·phem·ing** 1 : to speak of or address with irreverence **2** : to utter blasphemy — **blas·phem·er** *n*

**blas·phe·my** \'blas-fə-mē\ *n, pl* **-mies 1** : the act of expressing lack of reverence for God **2** : irreverence toward something considered sacred — **blas·phe·mous** \-məs\ *adj*

¹**blast** \'blast\ *n* **1** : a violent gust of wind; *also* : its effect **2** : sound made by a wind instrument **3** : a current of air forced at high pressure through a hole in a furnace (**blast furnace**) **4** : a sudden withering esp. of plants : BLIGHT **5** : EXPLOSION; *also* : the shock wave of an explosion

²**blast** *vb* : to shatter by or as if by an explosive

**blast off** *vb* : TAKE OFF 4 — used esp. of rocket-propelled vehicles — **blast-off** \'blast-ˌȯf\ *n*

**bla·tant** \'bla-tᵊnt\ *adj* : offensively obtrusive : vulgarly showy ◆ *Synonyms* VOCIFEROUS, BOISTEROUS, CLAMOROUS, OBSTREPEROUS — **bla·tan·cy** \-tᵊn-sē\ *n* — **bla·tant·ly** *adv*

**blath·er** \'bla-thər\ *vb* : to talk foolishly at length — **blather** *n*

**blath·er·skite** \'bla-thər-ˌskīt\ *n* : a person who blathers

¹**blaze** \'blāz\ *n* **1** : FIRE **2** : intense direct light accompanied by heat **3** : something (as a dazzling display or sudden outburst) suggesting fire ⟨a ∼ of autumn leaves⟩ ◆ *Synonyms* GLARE, GLOW, FLAME

²**blaze** *vb* **blazed; blaz·ing 1** : to burn brightly; *also* : to flare up **2** : to be conspicuously bright : GLITTER

³**blaze** *vb* **blazed; blaz·ing** : to make public or conspicuous

⁴**blaze** *n* **1** : a white stripe on the face of an animal **2** : a trail marker; *esp* : one made on a tree

⁵**blaze** *vb* **blazed; blaz·ing** : to mark (as a tree or trail) with blazes

**blaze orange** *n* : a very bright orange used in clothing for visibility

**blaz·er** \'blā-zər\ *n* : a sports jacket often with notched collar and pockets that are stitched on

¹**bla·zon** \'blā-zᵊn\ *n* **1** : COAT OF ARMS **2** : ostentatious display

²**blazon** *vb* **1** : to publish widely : PROCLAIM **2** : DECK, ADORN

**bldg** *abbr* building

**bldr** *abbr* builder

¹**bleach** \'blēch\ *vb* : WHITEN, BLANCH

²**bleach** *n* : a preparation used in bleaching

**bleach·ers** \'blē-chərz\ *n sing or pl* : a usu. uncovered stand of tiered seats for spectators

**bleak** \'blēk\ *adj* **1** : desolately barren and often windswept **2** : lacking warm or cheering qualities ⟨the future looks ∼⟩ — **bleak·ly** *adv* — **bleak·ness** *n*

**blear** \'blir\ *adj* : dim with water or tears ⟨∼ eyes⟩

**bleary** \'blir-ē\ *adj* **1** : dull or dimmed esp. from fatigue or sleep **2** : poorly outlined or defined ⟨a ∼ view⟩

**bleat** \'blēt\ *n* : the cry of a sheep or goat or a sound like it — **bleat** *vb*

**bleed** \'blēd\ *vb* **bled** \'bled\; **bleed·ing 1** : to lose or shed blood **2** : to be wounded; *also* : to feel pain or distress **3** : to flow or ooze from a wounded surface; *also* : to draw fluid from ⟨∼ a tire⟩ **4** : to extort money from

**bleed·er** \'blē-dər\ *n* : one that bleeds; *esp* : HEMOPHILIAC

**bleeding heart** *n* **1** : a garden plant related to the poppies that has usu. deep pink or white drooping heart-shaped flowers **2** : a person who shows extravagant sympathy esp. for an object of alleged persecution

¹**blem·ish** \'ble-mish\ *vb* : to spoil by a flaw : MAR

²**blemish** *n* : a noticeable flaw

**blench** \'blench\ *vb* [ME, to deceive, blench, fr. OE *blencan* to deceive] : FLINCH, QUAIL ◆ *Synonyms* SHRINK, RECOIL, WINCE, START

²**blench** *vb* : to grow or make pale

**blend** \'blend\ *vb* **blend·ed; blend·ing 1** : to mix thoroughly **2** : to prepare (as coffee) by mixing different varieties **3** : to combine into an integrated whole **4** : HARMONIZE ◆ *Synonyms* FUSE, MERGE, MINGLE, COALESCE — **blend·er** *n*

²**blend** *n* : a product of blending ◆ *Synonyms* COMPOUND, COMPOSITE, ALLOY, MIXTURE

**blended family** *n* : a family that includes children of a previous marriage of one spouse or both

**bless** \'bles\ *vb* **blessed** \'blest\ *also* **blest** \'blest\; **bless·ing** [ME, fr. OE *blētsian*, fr. *blōd* blood; fr. the use of blood in consecration] **1** : to consecrate by religious rite or word **2** : to sanctify with the sign of the cross **3** : to invoke divine care for **4** : PRAISE, GLORIFY **5** : to confer happiness upon

**bless·ed** \'ble-səd\ *also* **blest** \'blest\ *adj* **1** : HOLY **2** : BEATIFIED **3** : DELIGHTFUL ⟨∼ relief from the heat⟩ — **bless·ed·ly** *adv* — **bless·ed·ness** *n*

**bless·ing** \'ble-siŋ\ *n* **1** : the act or words of one who blesses; *also* : APPROVAL **2** : a thing conducive to happiness ⟨count your ∼s⟩ **3** : grace said at a meal

**blew** *past of* BLOW

¹**blight** \'blīt\ *n* **1** : a plant disease or injury marked esp. by withering and death of parts; *also* : an organism causing blight **2** : an impairing or frustrating influence; *also* : a deteriorated condition ⟨urban ∼⟩

²**blight** *vb* : to affect with or suffer from blight

**blimp** \'blimp\ *n* : an airship that maintains its form by pressure of contained gas

¹**blind** \'blīnd\ *adj* **1** : lacking or grossly deficient in ability to see; *also* : intended for blind persons **2** : not based on reason, evidence, or knowledge ⟨∼ faith⟩ **3** : not intelligently controlled or directed ⟨∼ chance⟩ **4** : performed solely by using aircraft instruments ⟨a ∼ landing⟩ **5** : hard to discern or make out : HIDDEN ⟨a ∼ seam⟩ **6** : lacking an opening or

outlet ⟨a ~ alley⟩ — **blind·ly** adv — **blind·ness** \'blīnd-nəs\ n

²**blind** vb **1** : to make blind **2** : DAZZLE **3** : DARKEN; also : HIDE

³**blind** n **1** : something (as a shutter) to hinder vision or keep out light **2** : a place of concealment **3** : SUBTERFUGE

**blind date** n : a date between persons who have not previously met; also : either of these persons

**blind·er** \'blīn-dər\ n : either of two flaps on a horse's bridle to prevent it from seeing to the side

**blind·fold** \'blīnd-,fōld\ vb : to cover the eyes of with or as if with a bandage — **blindfold** n

¹**blink** \'bliŋk\ vb **1** : WINK **3** : TWINKLE **3** : EVADE, IGNORE **4** : YIELD, GIVE IN

²**blink** n **1** : GLIMMER, SPARKLE **2** : a usu. involuntary shutting and opening of the eye

**blink·er** \'bliŋ-kər\ n : a blinking light used as a signal

**blin·tze** \'blint-sə\ or **blintz** \'blints\ n [Yiddish blintse] : a thin rolled pancake with a filling usu. of cream cheese

**blip** \'blip\ n **1** : a spot on a radar screen **2** : ABERRATION **1**

**bliss** \'blis\ n : complete happiness : JOY ♦ **Synonyms** BEATITUDE, BLESSEDNESS — **bliss·ful** \-fəl\ adj — **bliss·ful·ly** adv

¹**blis·ter** \'blis-tər\ n **1** : a raised area of skin containing watery fluid; also : an agent that causes blisters **2** : something (as a raised spot in paint) suggesting a blister **3** : a disease of plants marked by large raised patches on the leaves

²**blister** vb : to develop a blister; also : to cause blisters

**blithe** \'blīth, 'blīth\ adj **blith·er; blith·est** : happily lighthearted ♦ **Synonyms** MERRY, JOVIAL, JOLLY, JOCUND — **blithe·ly** adv — **blithe·some** \-səm\ adj

**blitz** \'blits\ n **1** : an intensive series of air raids **2** : a fast intensive campaign **3** : a rush of the passer by the defensive linebackers in football — **blitz** vb

**blitz·krieg** \-,krēg\ n [G, fr. Blitz lightning + Krieg war] : a sudden violent enemy attack

**bliz·zard** \'bli-zərd\ n : a long severe snowstorm

**blk** abbr **1** black **2** block

**bloat** \'blōt\ vb : to swell by or as if by filling with water or air

**blob** \'bläb\ n : a small lump or drop of a thick consistency

**bloc** \'bläk\ n [F, lit., block] : a combination of individuals or groups (as nations) working for a common purpose

¹**block** \'bläk\ n **1** : a solid piece of substantial material (as wood or stone) **2** : HINDRANCE, OBSTRUCTION; also : interruption of normal function of body or mind ⟨heart ~⟩ **3** : a frame enclosing one or more pulleys and having a hook or strap by which it may be attached **4** : a piece of material with a hand-cut design on its surface from which copies are to be made **5** : a large building divided into separate units (as apartments or offices) **6** : a row of houses or shops **7** : a city square; also : the distance along one of the sides of such a square **8** : a quantity of things considered as a unit ⟨a ~ of seats⟩

²**block** vb **1** : OBSTRUCT, CHECK **2** : to outline roughly ⟨~ out a design⟩ **3** : to provide or support with a block ♦ **Synonyms** BAR, IMPEDE, HINDER, OBSTRUCT — **block·er** n

**block·ade** \blä-'kād\ n : the isolation of a place usu. by troops or ships — **blockade** vb — **block·ad·er** n

**block·age** \'blä-kij\ n : an act or instance of obstructing : the state of being blocked

**block·bust·er** \'bläk-,bəs-tər\ n : one that is very large, successful, expensive, or extravagant ⟨a ~ movie⟩

**block·head** \'bläk-,hed\ n : DOLT, DUNCE

**block·house** \-,haus\ n : a small strong building used as a shelter (as from enemy fire) or observation post

**blog** \'blóg, 'bläg\ n [short for Weblog] : a website containing one's reflections, opinions, and comments; also : the contents of such a site — **blog** vb — **blog·ger** n

¹**blond** or **blonde** \'bländ\ adj : fair in complexion; also : of a light or bleached color ⟨~ mahogany⟩ — **blond·ish** \'blän-dish\ adj

²**blond** or **blonde** n : a person having blond hair

**blood** \'bləd\ n **1** : a usu. red liquid that circulates in the heart, arteries, and veins of animals **2** : LIFEBLOOD; also : LIFE **3** : LINEAGE, STOCK **4** : KINSHIP; also : KINDRED **5** : the taking of life **6** : TEMPER, PASSION **7** : DANDY **1** — **blood·less** adj — **bloody** adj

**blood·bath** \'bləd-,bath, -,bäth\ n : MASSACRE

**blood count** n : the determination of the number of blood cells in a specific volume of blood; also : the number of cells so determined

**blood·cur·dling** \'bləd-kərd-liŋ, -,kər-dªl-iŋ\ adj : arousing fright or horror

**blood·ed** \'blə-dəd\ adj **1** : having blood of a specified kind ⟨warm-blooded animals⟩ **2** : entirely or largely purebred ⟨~ horses⟩

**blood group** n : one of the classes into which human beings can be separated by the presence or absence in their blood of specific antigens

**blood·hound** \'bləd-,haund\ n : any of a breed of large powerful hounds with long drooping ears, a wrinkled face, and keen sense of smell

**blood·let·ting** \-,le-tiŋ\ n **1** : PHLEBOTOMY **2** : BLOODSHED

**blood·line** \-,līn\ n : a sequence of direct ancestors esp. in a pedigree

**blood·lust** \-,ləst\ n : desire for bloodshed

**blood·mo·bile** \-mō-,bēl\ n : a motor vehicle equipped for collecting blood from donors

**blood poisoning** n : invasion of the bloodstream by virulent microorganisms from a focus of infection accompanied esp. by chills, fever, and prostration

**blood pressure** *n* : pressure of the blood on the walls of the blood vessels and esp. arteries

**blood·root** \'bləd-ˌrüt, -ˌru̇t\ *n* : a plant related to the poppy that has a red root and sap, a solitary leaf, and a white flower in early spring

**blood·shed** \-ˌshed\ *n* : wounding or taking of life : CARNAGE, SLAUGHTER

**blood·shot** \-ˌshät\ *adj* : inflamed to redness ⟨~ eyes⟩

**blood·stain** \-ˌstān\ *n* : a discoloration caused by blood — **blood·stained** \-ˌstānd\ *adj*

**blood·stone** \-ˌstōn\ *n* : a green quartz sprinkled with red spots

**blood·stream** \-ˌstrēm\ *n* : the flowing blood in a circulatory system

**blood·suck·er** \-ˌsə-kər\ *n* : an animal that sucks blood; *esp* : LEECH — **blood·suck·ing** *adj*

**blood test** *n* : a test of the blood (as to detect disease-causing agents)

**blood thinner** *n* : a drug used to prevent the clotting of blood

**blood·thirsty** \'bləd-ˌthər-stē\ *adj* : eager to shed blood — **blood·thirst·i·ly** \-ˌthər-stə-lē\ *adv* — **blood·thirst·i·ness** \-stē-nəs\ *n*

**blood type** *n* : BLOOD GROUP — **blood-typ·ing** *n*

**blood vessel** *n* : a vessel (as a vein or artery) in which blood circulates in the body

**Bloody Mary** \-'mer-ē\ *n, pl* **Bloody Marys** : a drink made essentially of vodka and tomato juice

¹**bloom** \'blüm\ *n* **1** : FLOWER 1; *also* : flowers or amount of flowers (as of a plant) **2** : the period or state of flowering **3** : a state or time of beauty and vigor **4** : a powdery coating esp. on fruits and leaves **5** : rosy color; *also* : an appearance of freshness or health **bloomy** *adj*

²**bloom** *vb* **1** : to produce or yield flowers **2** : MATURE **3** : to glow esp. with healthy color ♦ **Synonyms** FLOWER, BLOSSOM

**bloo·mers** \'blü-mərz\ *n pl* [Amelia *Bloomer* †1894 Am. reformer] : a woman's garment of short loose pants gathered at the knee

**bloop·er** \'blü-pər\ *n* **1** : a fly ball hit barely beyond a baseball infield **2** : an embarrassing public blunder

¹**blos·som** \'blä-səm\ *n* **1** : the flower of a plant **2** : the period or state of flowering

²**blossom** *vb* : FLOWER, BLOOM

¹**blot** \'blät\ *n* **1** : SPOT, STAIN ⟨ink ~s⟩ **2** : BLEMISH ♦ **Synonyms** STIGMA, BRAND, SLUR

²**blot** *vb* **blot·ted; blot·ting 1** : SPOT, STAIN **2** : OBSCURE, ECLIPSE ⟨~ out the sun⟩ **3** *obs* : MAR; *esp* : DISGRACE **4** : to dry or remove with or as if with an absorbing material **5** : to make a blot

**blotch** \'bläch\ *n* : a usu. large and irregular spot or mark (as of ink or color) — **blotch** *vb* — **blotchy** *adj*

**blot·ter** \'blä-tər\ *n* **1** : a piece of blotting paper **2** : a book for preliminary records (as of sales or arrests)

**blot·ting paper** *n* : a spongy paper used to absorb ink

**blouse** \'blau̇s, 'blau̇z\ *n* **1** : a loose outer garment like a smock **2** : a usu. loose garment reaching from the neck to about the waist

¹**blow** \'blō\ *vb* **blew** \'blü\; **blown** \'blōn\; **blow·ing 1** : to be in motion; *esp* : to move forcibly ⟨the wind *blew*⟩ **2** : to send forth a current of gas (as air) **3** : to act on with a current of gas or vapor; *esp* : to drive with such a current : to clear with a current of air **5** : to sound or cause to sound ⟨~ a horn⟩ **6** : PANT, GASP; *also* : to expel moist air in breathing ⟨the whale *blew*⟩ **7** : BOAST; *also* : BLUSTER **8** : ERUPT, EXPLODE **9** : MELT — used of an electrical fuse **10** : to shape or form by blown or injected air ⟨~ glass⟩ **11** : to shatter or destroy by or as if by explosion **12** : to make breathless by exertion **13** : to spend recklessly **14** : BOTCH ⟨*blew* her lines⟩ — **blow·er** *n*

²**blow** *n* **1** : a usu. strong blowing of air : GALE **2** : BOASTING, BRAG **3** : an act or instance of blowing

³**blow** *vb* **blew** \'blü\; **blown** \'blōn\; **blow·ing** : FLOWER, BLOOM

⁴**blow** *n* **1** : a forcible stroke ⟨a ~ to the head⟩ **2** : COMBAT ⟨come to ~s⟩ **3** : a severe and usu. unexpected calamity

**blow-by-blow** *adj* : minutely detailed ⟨~ account⟩

**blow-dry** \-ˌdrī\ *vb* : to dry and usu. style hair with a blow-dryer

**blow-dryer** \-ˌdrī-(-ə)r\ *n* : a hand-held hair dryer

**blow·fly** \'blō-ˌflī\ *n* : any of a family of dipteran flies (as a bluebottle) that deposit their eggs or maggots on meat or in wounds

**blow·gun** \-ˌgən\ *n* : a tube from which an arrow or a dart may be shot by the force of the breath

**blow·out** \'blō-ˌau̇t\ *n* **1** : a bursting of something (as a tire) because of pressure of the contents (as air) **2** : a depression created by the wind in sand or soil

**blow·sy** *also* **blow·zy** \'blau̇-zē\ *adj* : DISHEVELED, SLOVENLY

**blow·torch** \'blō-ˌtȯrch\ *n* : a small portable burner whose flame is made hotter by a blast of air or oxygen

**blow·up** \'blō-ˌəp\ *n* **1** : EXPLOSION **2** : an outburst of temper **3** : a photographic enlargement

**blowy** \'blō-ē\ *adj* : WINDY

**BLT** \ˌbē-ˌel-'tē\ *n* : a bacon, lettuce, and tomato sandwich

¹**blub·ber** \'blə-bər\ *vb* : to cry noisily

²**blubber** *n* **1** : the fat of large sea mammals (as whales) **2** : a noisy crying

¹**blud·geon** \'blə-jən\ *n* : a short often loaded club

²**bludgeon** *vb* : to strike with or as if with a bludgeon

¹**blue** \'blü\ *adj* **blu·er; blu·est** [ME, fr. AF *blef, blew,* of Gmc origin] **1** : of the color blue; *also* : BLUISH **2** : MELANCHOLY; *also* : DEPRESSING **3** : PURITANICAL **4** : INDECENT **5** : tending to support

Democratic candidates ⟨~ states⟩ —
**blue·ness** n

²**blue** n 1 : a color between green and violet in the spectrum : the color of the clear daytime sky 2 : something (as clothing or the sky) that is blue

**blue baby** n : a baby with bluish skin due to faulty circulation caused by a heart defect

**blue·bell** \-ˌbel\ n : any of various plants with blue bell-shaped flowers

**blue·ber·ry** \ˈblü-ˌber-ē, -bə-rē\ n : the edible blue or blackish berry of various shrubs of the heath family; *also* : one of these shrubs

**blue·bird** \-ˌbərd\ n : any of three small No. American thrushes that are blue above and reddish-brown or pale blue below

**blue·bon·net** \ˈblü-ˌbä-nət\ n : either of two low-growing annual lupines of Texas with silky foliage and blue flowers

**blue·bot·tle** \ˈblü-ˌbä-tᵊl\ n : any of several blowflies with iridescent blue bodies or abdomens

**blue cheese** n : cheese having veins of greenish-blue mold

**blue·col·lar** \ˈblü-ˈkä-lər\ adj : of, relating to, or being the class of workers whose duties call for work clothes

**blue·fish** \-ˌfish\ n : a marine sport and food fish that is bluish above and silvery below

**blue·grass** \-ˌgras\ n 1 : KENTUCKY BLUEGRASS 2 : country music played on stringed instruments having free improvisation and close harmonies

**blue jay** \-ˌjā\ n : a crested bright blue No. American jay

**blue jeans** n pl : pants usu. made of blue denim

**blue·nose** \ˈblü-ˌnōz\ n : a person who advocates a rigorous moral code

**blue·point** \-ˌpóint\ n : a small oyster typically from the south shore of Long Island, New York

**blue·print** \-ˌprint\ n 1 : a photographic print in white on a blue ground used esp. for copying mechanical drawings and architects' plans 2 : a detailed plan of action — **blueprint** vb

**blues** \ˈblüz\ n pl 1 : MELANCHOLY 2 : music in a style marked by recurrent minor intervals and melancholy lyrics

**blue screen** n : a technique in which a subject is filmed in front of a blue background so as to allow the creation of a composite with other footage

**blue·stock·ing** \ˈblü-ˌstä-kiŋ\ n : a woman having intellectual interests

**blu·et** \ˈblü-ət\ n : a low No. American herb with dainty bluish flowers

**blue whale** n : a very large baleen whale that may reach a weight of 150 tons (135 metric tons) and a length of 100 feet (30 meters)

¹**bluff** \ˈbləf\ adj 1 : having a broad flattened front 2 : rising steeply with a broad flat front 3 : OUTSPOKEN, FRANK
♦ **Synonyms** ABRUPT, BLUNT, BRUSQUE, CURT, GRUFF

²**bluff** n : a high steep bank : CLIFF

³**bluff** vb : to frighten or deceive by pretense or a mere show of strength

⁴**bluff** n : an act or instance of bluffing; *also* : one who bluffs

**blu·ing** or **blue·ing** \ˈblü-iŋ\ n : a preparation used in laundering to counteract yellowing of white fabrics

**blu·ish** \ˈblü-ish\ adj : somewhat blue

¹**blun·der** \ˈblən-dər\ vb 1 : to move clumsily or unsteadily 2 : to make a stupid or needless mistake

²**blunder** n : an avoidable and usu. serious mistake

**blun·der·buss** \ˈblən-dər-ˌbəs\ n [obs. D *donderbus*, fr. D *donder* thunder + obs. D *bus* gun] : an obsolete short-barreled firearm with a flaring muzzle

¹**blunt** \ˈblənt\ adj 1 : not sharp : DULL 2 : lacking in tact : BLUFF ⟨~ criticism⟩
♦ **Synonyms** BRUSQUE, CURT, GRUFF, ABRUPT, CRUSTY — **blunt·ly** adv — **blunt·ness** n

²**blunt** vb : to make or become dull

**blur** \ˈblər\ n 1 : a smear or stain that obscures 2 : something vaguely perceived; *esp* : something moving too quickly to be clearly perceived — **blur·ry** \-ē\ adj

²**blur** vb blurred; blur·ring : DIM, CLOUD, OBSCURE ⟨*blurred* vision⟩

**blurb** \ˈblərb\ n : a short publicity notice (as on a book jacket)

**blurt** \ˈblərt\ vb : to utter suddenly and impulsively

**blush** \ˈbləsh\ n 1 : a reddening of the face (as from modesty or confusion) : FLUSH 2 : a cosmetic used to tint the face pink — **blush** vb — **blush·ful** adj

**blus·ter** \ˈbləs-tər\ vb 1 : to blow in stormy noisy gusts 2 : to talk or act with noisy swaggering threats — **bluster** n — **blus·tery** \-tə-rē\ adj

**blvd** abbr boulevard

**B lymphocyte** n : B CELL

**BM** abbr bowel movement

**B movie** n : a cheaply produced motion picture

**BO** abbr 1 best offer 2 body odor 3 box office 4 branch office

**boa** \ˈbō-ə\ n 1 : a large snake (as the **boa con·stric·tor** \-kən-ˈstrik-tər\ or the related anaconda) that suffocates and kills its prey by constriction 2 : a fluffy scarf usu. of fur or feathers

**boar** \ˈbór\ n : a male swine; *also* : WILD BOAR

¹**board** \ˈbórd\ n 1 : the side of a ship 2 : a thin flat length of sawed lumber; *also* : material (as cardboard) or a piece of material formed as a thin flat firm sheet 3 pl : STAGE 1 4 : a table spread with a meal; *also* : daily meals esp. when furnished for pay 5 : a table at which a council or magistrates sit 6 : a group or association of persons organized for a special responsibility (as the management of a business or institution); *also* : an organized commercial exchange 7 : a sheet of insulating material carrying circuit elements and inserted in an electronic device 8 : BULLETIN BOARD

²**board** vb 1 : to go or put aboard ⟨~ a

boat〉 **2** : to cover with boards **3** : to provide or be provided with meals and often lodging — **board·er** n

**board game** n : a game of strategy (as checkers or chess) played by moving pieces on a board

**board·ing·house** \'bȯr-diŋ-,haùs\ n : a house at which persons are boarded

**board·walk** \'bȯrd-,wȯk\ n : a promenade (as of planking) along a beach

**boast** \'bōst\ vb **1** : to praise oneself **2** : to mention or assert with excessive pride **3** : to prize as a possession; also : HAVE 〈the house ∼s a fireplace〉 — **boast** n — **boast·ful** \-fəl\ adj — **boast·ful·ly** adv

**boat** \'bōt\ n : a small vessel for travel on water; also : SHIP — **boat** vb

**boat·er** \'bō-tər\ n **1** : one that travels in a boat **2** : a stiff straw hat

**boat·man** \'bōt-mən\ n : a man who operates, works on, or deals in boats

**boat people** n pl : refugees fleeing by boat

**boat·swain** or **bo·sun** \'bō-s³n\ n : a subordinate officer of a ship in charge of the hull and related equipment

¹**bob** \'bäb\ vb **bobbed**; **bob·bing 1** : to move up and down jerkily or repeatedly **2** : to emerge, arise, or appear suddenly or unexpectedly

²**bob** n : a bobbing movement

³**bob** n **1** : a knob, knot, twist, or curl esp. of ribbons, yarn, or hair **2** : a short haircut of a woman or child **3** : FLOAT 2 **4** : a weight hanging from a line

⁴**bob** vb **bobbed**; **bob·bing** : to cut hair in a bob

⁵**bob** n, pl **bob** slang Brit : SHILLING

**bob·bin** \'bä-bən\ n : a cylinder or spindle for holding or dispensing thread (as in a sewing machine)

**bob·ble** \'bä-bəl\ vb **bob·bled**; **bob·bling 1** : to move up and down quickly or repeatedly **2** : FUMBLE 〈the catcher bobbled the ball〉 — **bobble** n

**bob·by** \'bä-bē\ n, pl **bobbies** [Bobby, nickname for Sir Robert Peel, who organized the London police force] Brit : a police officer

**bobby pin** n : a flat wire hairpin with prongs that press close together

**bob·cat** \'bäb-,kat\ n : a small usu. rusty-colored No. American lynx

**bob·o·link** \'bä-bə-,liŋk\ n : an American migratory songbird related to the meadowlarks

**bob·sled** \'bäb-,sled\ n **1** : a short sled usu. used as one of a joined pair **2** : a racing sled with two pairs of runners, a steering wheel, and a hand brake — **bobsled** vb

**bob·white** \(,)bäb-'hwīt\ n : any of a genus of quail; esp : a popular game bird of eastern and central No. America

**boc·cie** or **boc·ci** or **boc·ce** \'bä-chē\ n : Italian lawn bowling played on a long narrow court

**bock** \'bäk\ n : a strong dark beer usu. sold in early spring

**bod** \'bäd\ n : BODY

¹**bode** \'bōd\ vb **bod·ed**; **bod·ing** : to indicate by signs : PRESAGE

²**bode** past of BIDE

**bo·de·ga** \bō-'dā-gə\ n [Sp, fr. L apotheca storehouse] : a usu. small store specializing in Hispanic groceries

**bod·ice** \'bä-dəs\ n [alter. of bodies, pl. of body] : the usu. close-fitting part of a dress above the waist

**bodi·less** \'bä-di-ləs\ adj : lacking a body or material form

¹**bodi·ly** \'bä-d³l-ē\ adj : of or relating to the body 〈∼ contact〉 〈∼ organs〉

²**bodily** adv **1** : in the flesh **2** : as a whole 〈lifted the crate up ∼〉

**bod·kin** \'bäd-kən\ n **1** : DAGGER **2** : a pointed implement for punching holes in cloth **3** : a blunt needle for drawing tape or ribbon through a loop or hem

**body** \'bä-dē\ n, pl **bod·ies 1** : the physical whole of a living or dead organism; also : the trunk or main mass of an organism as distinguished from its appendages **2** : a human being : PERSON **3** : the main part of something **4** : a mass of matter distinct from other masses **5** : GROUP 〈the student ∼〉 **6** : VISCOSITY, FIRMNESS **7** : richness of flavor — used esp. of wines — **bod·ied** \-dēd\ adj

**body·build·ing** \'bä-dē-,bil-diŋ\ n : the developing of the body through exercise and diet — **body·build·er** \-dər\ n

**body English** n : bodily motions made in a usu. unconscious effort to influence the movement of a propelled object (as a ball)

**body·guard** \'bä-dē-,gärd\ n : a personal guard; also : RETINUE

**body language** n : movements (as with the hands) or posture used as a means of communication

**body stocking** n : a sheer close-fitting one-piece garment for the torso that often has sleeves and legs

**body·work** \'bä-dē-,wərk\ n : the making or repairing of vehicle bodies

**Boer** \'bȯr, 'bùr\ n [D, lit., farmer] : a South African of Dutch or Huguenot descent

¹**bog** \'bäg, 'bȯg\ n : wet, spongy, poorly drained, and usu. acid ground — **bog·gy** adj

²**bog** vb **bogged**; **bog·ging** : to sink into or as if into a bog

**bo·gey** also **bo·gie** or **bo·gy** \'bù-gē, 'bō- for 1; 'bō- for 2\ n, pl **bogeys** also **bo·gies 1** : SPECTER, HOBGOBLIN; also : a source of fear or annoyance **2** : a score of one over par on a hole in golf

**bo·gey·man** \'bù-gē-,man, 'bō-, 'bù-\ n : an imaginary monster used in threatening children

**bog·gle** \'bä-gəl\ vb **bog·gled**; **bog·gling** : to overwhelm or be overwhelmed with fright or amazement

**bo·gus** \'bō-gəs\ adj : SPURIOUS, SHAM

**Bo·he·mi·an** \bō-'hē-mē-ən\ n **1** : a native or inhabitant of Bohemia **2** often not cap : VAGABOND, WANDERER **3** often not cap : a person (as a writer or artist) living an unconventional life — **bohemian** adj, often cap

**bohr·i·um** \'bòr-ē-əm\ n : an artificially produced radioactive chemical element

¹**boil** \'bòi(-ə)l\ n : an inflamed swelling on the skin containing pus

²**boil** vb 1 : to heat or become heated to a temperature (**boil·ing point**) at which vapor is formed and rises in bubbles ⟨water ∼s and changes to steam⟩; also : to act on or be acted on by a boiling liquid ⟨∼ eggs⟩ 2 : to be in a state of seething agitation

³**boil** n 1 : the act or state of boiling 2 : a boiled dish (as of seafood) 3 : a gathering where boiled food is served

**boil·er** \'bòi-lər\ n 1 : a container in which something is boiled 2 : a strong vessel used in making steam 3 : a tank holding hot water

**boil·er·mak·er** \'bòi-lər-ˌmā-kər\ n : whiskey with a beer chaser

**bois·ter·ous** \'bòi-st(ə-)rəs\ adj : noisily turbulent or exuberant — **bois·ter·ous·ly** adv

**bok choy** \'bäk-ˌchòi\ n : a Chinese vegetable related to the mustards that forms a loose head of green leaves with long thick white stalks

**bo·la** \'bō-lə\ or **bo·las** \-ləs\ n, pl **bolas** \-ləz\ also **bo·las·es** [AmerSp bolas, fr. Sp bola ball] : a cord with weights attached to the ends for hurling at and entangling an animal

**bold** \'bōld\ adj 1 : COURAGEOUS, INTREPID 2 : IMPUDENT 3 : STEEP ⟨∼ cliffs⟩ 4 : ADVENTUROUS, FREE ⟨a ∼ thinker⟩ ♦ **Synonyms** DAUNTLESS, BRAVE, VALIANT — **bold·ly** adv — **bold·ness** \'bōld-nəs\ n

**bold·face** \'bōld-ˌfās\ n : a heavy-faced type; also : printing in boldface — **bold·faced** \-ˈfāst\ adj

**bole** \'bōl\ n : the trunk of a tree

**bo·le·ro** \bə-'ler-ō\ n, pl **-ros** 1 : a Spanish dance or its music 2 : a short loose jacket open at the front

**bo·li·var** \bə-'lē-ˌvär, 'bä-lə-vər\ n, pl **-va·res** \ˌbä-lə-'vär-ˌās, ˌbō-\ or **-vars** — see MONEY table

**Bo·liv·i·an** \bə-'li-vē-ən\ n : a native or inhabitant of Bolivia — **Bolivian** adj

**bo·li·vi·a·no** \bə-ˌli-vē-'ä-(ˌ)nō\ n, pl **-nos** — see MONEY table

**boll** \'bōl\ n : a seed pod (as of cotton)

**boll weevil** n : a small usu. grayish or brown weevil that infests the cotton plant both as a larva and as an adult

**boll·worm** \'bōl-ˌwərm\ n : any of several moths and esp. the corn earworm whose larvae feed on cotton bolls

**bo·lo·gna** \bə-'lō-nē\ n [short for Bologna sausage, fr. Bologna, Italy] : a large smoked sausage of beef, veal, and pork

**Bol·she·vik** \'bōl-shə-ˌvik\ n, pl **Bolsheviks** also **Bol·she·vi·ki** \ˌbōl-shə-'vi-kē\ [Russ bol'shevik, fr. bol'shiĭ larger] 1 : a member of the party that seized power in Russia in the revolution of November 1917 2 : COMMUNIST — **Bolshevik** adj

**bol·she·vism** \'bōl-shə-ˌvi-zəm\ n, often cap : the doctrine or program of the Bolsheviks advocating violent overthrow of capitalism

¹**bol·ster** \'bōl-stər\ n : a long pillow or cushion

²**bolster** vb : to support with or as if with a bolster; also : REINFORCE

¹**bolt** \'bōlt\ n 1 : a missile (as an arrow) for a crossbow or catapult 2 : a flash of lightning : THUNDERBOLT 3 : a sliding bar used to fasten a door 4 : a roll of cloth or wallpaper of specified length 5 : a rod with a head at one end and a screw thread at the other used with a nut to fasten objects together 6 : a metal cylinder that drives the cartridge into the chamber of a firearm

²**bolt** vb 1 : to move suddenly (as in fright or hurry) : START, DASH 2 : to break away (as from association) ⟨∼ from a political platform⟩ 3 : to produce seed prematurely 4 : to secure or fasten with a bolt 5 : to swallow hastily or without chewing

³**bolt** n : an act of bolting

**bo·lus** \'bō-ləs\ n, pl **bo·lus·es** 1 : a large pill 2 : a soft mass of chewed food

¹**bomb** \'bäm\ n 1 : a fused explosive device designed to detonate under specified conditions (as impact) 2 : an aerosol or foam dispenser (as of insecticide or hair spray) : SPRAY CAN 3 : FAILURE, FLOP 4 : a long pass, shot, or hit

²**bomb** vb 1 : to attack with bombs 2 : FAIL ⟨∼ed at the audition⟩

**bom·bard** \bäm-'bärd\ vb 1 : to attack esp. with artillery or bombers 2 : to assail persistently 3 : to subject to the impact of rapidly moving particles (as electrons) — **bom·bard·ment** n

**bom·bar·dier** \ˌbäm-bər-'dir\ n : a bomber-crew member who releases the bombs

**bom·bast** \'bäm-ˌbast\ n [ME, cotton padding, fr. MF bombace, fr. ML bombax cotton, alter. of L bombyx silkworm, silk, fr. Gk] : pretentious wordy speech or writing — **bom·bas·tic** \bäm-'bas-tik\ adj — **bom·bas·ti·cal·ly** \-ti-k(ə-)lē\ adv

**bom·ba·zine** \ˌbäm-bə-'zēn\ n 1 : a twilled fabric with silk warp and worsted filling 2 : a silk fabric in twill weave dyed black

**bomb·er** \'bä-mər\ n : one that bombs; esp : an airplane for dropping bombs

**bomb·proof** \'bäm-ˌprüf\ adj : safe against the explosive force of bombs

**bomb·shell** \'bäm-ˌshel\ n 1 : BOMB 1 2 : one that stuns, amazes, or completely upsets

**bona fide** \'bō-nə-ˌfīd, 'bä-; ˌbō-nə-'fī-dē, -də\ adj [L, in good faith] 1 : made in good faith ⟨a bona fide agreement⟩ 2 : GENUINE, REAL ⟨a bona fide bargain⟩

**bo·nan·za** \bə-'nan-zə\ n [Sp, lit., calm sea, fr. ML bonacia, alter. of L malacia, fr. Gk malakia, lit., softness, fr. malakos soft] 1 : something yielding a rich return 2 : a spectacular event

**bon·bon** \'bän-ˌbän\ n : a candy with a creamy center and a soft covering (as of chocolate)

¹**bond** \'bänd\ n 1 : FETTER 2 : a binding or uniting force or tie ⟨∼s of friendship⟩ 3 : an agreement or obligation often made binding by a pledge of money or

goods **4** : a person who acts as surety for another **5** : an interest-bearing certificate of public or private indebtedness **6** : the state of goods subject to supervision pending payment of taxes or duties due

²**bond** vb **1** : to assure payment of duties or taxes on (goods) by giving a bond **2** : to insure against losses caused by the acts of ⟨~ a bank teller⟩ **3** : to make or become firmly united as if by bonds ⟨~ iron to copper⟩ **4** : to form a close relationship ⟨~ed with her stepmother⟩

**bond·age** \'bän-dij\ n : SLAVERY, SERVITUDE

**bond·hold·er** \'bänd-ˌhōl-dər\ n : one that owns a government or corporation bond

**bond·ing** \'bän-diŋ\ n **1** : the formation of a close personal relationship esp. through frequent or constant association **2** : the attaching of a material (as porcelain) to a tooth surface esp. for cosmetic purposes

**bond·man** \'bänd-mən\ n : SLAVE, SERF

¹**bonds·man** \'bändz-mən\ n : SURETY 3

²**bondsman** var of BONDMAN

**bond·wom·an** \'bänd-ˌwu̇-mən\ n : a female slave or serf

¹**bone** \'bōn\ n **1** : a hard largely calcareous tissue forming most of the skeleton of a vertebrate animal; also : one of the pieces of bone making up a vertebrate skeleton **2** : a hard animal substance (as ivory or baleen) similar to true bone **3** : something made of bone — **bone·less** adj — bony also **bon·ey** \'bō-nē\ adj

²**bone** vb **boned**; **bon·ing** : to free from bones ⟨~ a chicken⟩

**bone black** n : the black carbon residue from calcined bones used esp. as a pigment

**bone marrow** n : MARROW

**bone·meal** \'bōn-ˌmēl\ n : crushed or ground bone used esp. as fertilizer or feed

**bon·er** \'bō-nər\ n : a stupid and ridiculous blunder

**bone up** vb **1** : CRAM 3 **2** : to refresh one's memory ⟨boned up on the speech before giving it⟩

**bon·fire** \'bän-ˌfī(-ə)r\ n [ME bonefire a fire of bones, fr. bon bone + fire] : a large fire built in the open air

**bon·go** \'bäŋ-gō\ n, pl **bongos** also **bongoes** [AmerSp bongó] : one of a pair of small tuned drums played with the hands

**bon·ho·mie** \ˌbä-nə-'mē\ n [F bonhomie, fr. bonhomme good-natured man, fr. bon good + homme man] : good-natured easy friendliness

**bo·ni·to** \bə-'nē-tō\ n, pl **-tos** or **-to** : any of several medium-sized tunas

**bon mot** \bōⁿ-'mō\ n, pl **bons mots** \same\ or **bon mots** \same\ [F, lit., good word] : a clever remark

**bon·net** \'bä-nət\ n : a covering (as a cap) for the head; esp : a hat for a woman or infant tied under the chin

**bon·ny** \'bä-nē\ adj **bon·ni·er**; **-est** chiefly Brit : ATTRACTIVE, FAIR; also : FINE, EXCELLENT

**bon·sai** \bōn-'sī, 'bän-ˌ\ n, pl **bonsai** [Jp]

: a potted plant (as a tree) dwarfed and trained to an artistic shape; also : the art of growing such a plant

**bo·nus** \'bō-nəs\ n : something in addition to what is expected

**bon vi·vant** \ˌbän-vē-'vänt, ˌbōⁿ-vē-'väⁿ\ n, pl **bons vivants** \ˌbän-vē-'vänts, ˌbōⁿ-vē-'väⁿ\ or **bon vivants** \same\ [F, lit., good liver] : a person having cultivated, refined, and sociable tastes esp. in food and drink

**bon voy·age** \ˌbōⁿ-, vȯi-'äzh, ˌbän-; ˌbōⁿ-ˌvwä-'yäzh\ n : FAREWELL — often used as an interjection

**bony fish** n : any of a class of fishes (as eels or sturgeons) with a bony rather than a cartilaginous skeleton

**bonze** \'bänz\ n : a Buddhist monk

**boo** \'bü\ n, pl **boos** : a shout of disapproval or contempt — **boo** vb

**boo·by** \'bü-bē\ n, pl **boobies** : an awkward foolish person : DOPE

**booby hatch** n : a psychiatric hospital

**booby prize** n : an award for the poorest performance in a contest

**booby trap** n : a trap for the unwary; esp : a concealed explosive device set to go off when some harmless-looking object is touched — **booby–trap** vb

**boo·dle** \'bü-dᵊl\ n **1** : bribe money **2** : a large amount of money

¹**book** \'bu̇k\ n **1** : a set of sheets bound into a volume **2** : a long written or printed narrative or record **3** : a major division of a long literary work **4** cap : BIBLE — in one's book : in one's own opinion

²**book** vb **1** : to engage, reserve, or schedule by or as if by writing in a book ⟨~ seats on a plane⟩ **2** : to enter charges against in a police register

**book·case** \-ˌkās\ n : a piece of furniture consisting of shelves to hold books

**book·end** \-ˌend\ n : a support to hold up a row of books

**book·ie** \'bu̇-kē\ n : BOOKMAKER

**book·ish** \'bu̇-kish\ adj **1** : fond of books and reading **2** : inclined to rely unduly on book knowledge

**book·keep·er** \'bu̇k-ˌkē-pər\ n : a person who records the accounts or transactions of a business — **book·keep·ing** n

**book·let** \'bu̇k-lət\ n : PAMPHLET

**book·mak·er** \'bu̇k-ˌmā-kər\ n : a person who determines odds and receives and pays off bets — **book·mak·ing** n

**book·mark** \-ˌmärk\ or **book·mark·er** \-ˌmär-kər\ n **1** : a marker for finding a place in a book **2** : a shortcut to a previously viewed location (as a website) on a computer — **bookmark** vb

**book·mo·bile** \'bu̇k-mō-ˌbēl\ n : a truck that serves as a traveling library

**book·plate** \'bu̇k-ˌplāt\ n : a label pasted in a book to show who owns it

**book·sell·er** \'bu̇k-ˌse-lər\ n : one that sells books; esp : the proprietor of a bookstore

**book·shelf** \-ˌshelf\ n : a shelf for books

**book·worm** \'bu̇k-ˌwərm\ n : a person unusually devoted to reading and study

¹**boom** \'büm\ vb **1** : to make a deep hollow sound : RESOUND **2** : to grow or

cause to grow rapidly esp. in number, value, esteem, or importance

²**boom** n 1 : a booming sound or cry 2 : a rapid expansion or increase esp. of economic activity

³**boom** n [D, tree, beam] 1 : a long spar used to extend the bottom of a sail 2 : a line of floating timbers used to obstruct passage or catch floating objects 3 : a beam projecting from the upright pole of a derrick to support or guide the object lifted 4 : a long usu. horizontal supporting arm (as for a microphone)

**boom box** n : a large portable radio and often tape or CD player

**boo·mer·ang** \'bü-mə-ˌraŋ\ n [Dharuk (an Australian aboriginal language) bumarin²] : a bent or angular club that can be so thrown as to return near the starting point

**boom·ing** \'bü-miŋ\ adj 1 : making a loud deep sound ⟨a ∼ voice⟩ 2 : powerfully executed ⟨a ∼ serve⟩

¹**boon** \'bün\ n [ME bone prayer, request, the favor requested, fr. ON bōn request] : BENEFIT, BLESSING ♦ **Synonyms** FAVOR, GIFT, LARGESS, PRESENT

²**boon** adj [ME bon, fr. AF, good] : CONVIVIAL ⟨a ∼ companion⟩

**boon·docks** \'bün-ˌdäks\ n pl [Tagalog (language of the Philippines) bundok mountain] 1 : rough country filled with dense brush 2 : a rural area

**boon·dog·gle** \'bün-ˌdä-gəl, -ˌdȯ-\ n : a useless or wasteful project or activity

**boor** \'bu̇r\ n 1 : YOKEL 2 : a rude or insensitive person ♦ **Synonyms** CHURL, LOUT, CLOWN, CLODHOPPER — **boor·ish** adj

**boost** \'bu̇st\ vb 1 : to push up from below 2 : INCREASE, RAISE ⟨∼ prices⟩ 3 : AID, PROMOTE ⟨voted a bonus to ∼ morale⟩ — **boost** n — **boost·er** n

¹**boot** \'büt\ n, chiefly dial : something to equalize a trade — **to boot** : BESIDES

²**boot** vb, archaic : AVAIL, PROFIT

³**boot** n 1 : a covering for the foot and leg 2 : a protective sheath (as of a flower) 3 Brit : an automobile trunk 4 : KICK; also : a discharge from employment 5 : a navy or marine corps trainee

⁴**boot** vb 1 : KICK 2 : to eject or discharge summarily 3 : to load or become loaded into a computer from a disk 4 : to start or become ready for use esp. by booting a program ⟨∼ up the computer⟩

**boot·black** \'büt-ˌblak\ n : a person who shines shoes

**boot camp** n 1 : a navy or marine corps training camp 2 : a facility with a rigorous disciplinary program for young offenders

**boo·tee** or **boo·tie** \'bü-tē\ n : an infant's knitted or crocheted sock

**booth** \'büth\ n, pl **booths** \'bü̇thz, 'bü̇ths\ 1 : a small enclosed stall (as at a fair) 2 : a small enclosure giving privacy for a person ⟨voting ∼⟩ ⟨telephone ∼⟩ 3 : a restaurant accommodation having a table between backed benches

**boot·leg** \'büt-ˌleg\ vb : to make, trans-

port, or sell (as liquor) illegally — **boot·leg** adj or n — **boot·leg·ger** n

**boot·less** \'büt-ləs\ adj : USELESS ⟨their efforts were ∼⟩ ♦ **Synonyms** FUTILE, VAIN, ABORTIVE, FRUITLESS — **boot·less·ly** adv — **boot·less·ness** n

¹**boo·ty** \'bü-tē\ n, pl **booties** : PLUNDER, SPOIL

²**booty** also **boo·tie** \'bü-tē\ n, pl **booties** slang : BUTTOCKS

¹**booze** \'büz\ vb **boozed; booz·ing** : to drink liquor to excess — **booz·er** n

²**booze** n : intoxicating liquor — **boozy** adj

**bop** \'bäp\ vb **bopped; bop·ping** : HIT, SOCK — **bop** n

**BOQ** abbr bachelor officers' quarters

**bor** abbr borough

**bo·rate** \'bȯr-ˌāt\ n : a salt or ester of boric acid

**bo·rax** \'bȯr-ˌaks\ n : a crystalline borate of sodium that occurs as a mineral and is used as a flux and cleanser

**bor·del·lo** \bȯr-'de-lō\ n, pl **-los** [It] : BROTHEL

¹**bor·der** \'bȯr-dər\ n 1 : EDGE, MARGIN 2 : BOUNDARY, FRONTIER ♦ **Synonyms** RIM, BRIM, BRINK, FRINGE, PERIMETER

²**border** vb **bor·dered; bor·der·ing** 1 : to put a border on 2 : ADJOIN 3 : VERGE

**border collie** n, often cap B : any of a British breed of medium-sized long-haired sheepdogs

**bor·der·land** \'bȯr-dər-ˌland\ n 1 : territory at or near a border 2 : an outlying or intermediate region often not clearly defined

**bor·der·line** \-ˌlīn\ adj : being in an intermediate position or state; esp : not quite up to what is standard or expected ⟨∼ intelligence⟩

¹**bore** \'bȯr\ vb **bored; bor·ing** 1 : to make a hole in with or as if with a drill 2 : to make (as a well) by boring or digging away material ♦ **Synonyms** PERFORATE, DRILL, PRICK, PUNCTURE — **bor·er** n

²**bore** n 1 : a hole made by or as if by boring 2 : a cylindrical cavity 3 : the diameter of a hole or tube; esp : the interior diameter of a gun barrel or engine cylinder

³**bore** past of BEAR

⁴**bore** n : a tidal flood with a high abrupt front

⁵**bore** n : one that causes boredom

⁶**bore** vb **bored; bor·ing** : to weary with tedious dullness

**bo·re·al** \'bȯr-ē-əl\ adj : of, relating to, or located in northern regions

**bore·dom** \'bȯr-dəm\ n : the condition of being bored

**bo·ric acid** \'bȯr-ik-\ n : a white crystalline weak acid that contains boron and is used esp. as an antiseptic

**born** \'bȯrn\ adj 1 : brought into life by birth 2 : NATIVE ⟨American-born⟩ 3 : having special natural abilities or character from birth ⟨a ∼ leader⟩

**born–again** adj : having experienced a revival of a personal faith or conviction ⟨a ∼ believer⟩ ⟨a ∼ liberal⟩

**borne** *past part of* BEAR

**bo·ron** \ˈbȯr-ˌän\ *n* : a chemical element that occurs in nature only in combination (as in borax)

**bor·ough** \ˈbər-ō\ *n* [ME *burgh*, fr. OE *burg* fortified town] **1** : a British town that sends one or more members to Parliament; *also* : an incorporated British urban area **2** : an incorporated town or village in some U.S. states; *also* : any of the five political divisions of New York City **3** : a civil division of the state of Alaska corresponding to a county in most other states

**bor·row** \ˈbär-ō\ *vb* **1** : to take or receive (something) temporarily and with intent to return ⟨*~ed* my car⟩ **2** : to take into possession or use from another source : DERIVE, APPROPRIATE ⟨*~* a metaphor⟩

**borscht** \ˈbȯrsht\ *or* **borsch** \ˈbȯrsh\ *n* [Yiddish *borsht* & Ukrainian & Russ *borshch*] : a soup made mainly from beets

**bosh** \ˈbäsh\ *n* [Turk *boş* empty] : foolish talk or action : NONSENSE

**bosky** \ˈbäs-kē\ *adj* : covered with trees or shrubs

**¹bos·om** \ˈbu̇z-əm, ˈbüz-\ *n* **1** : the front of the human chest; *esp* : the female breasts **2** : the seat of secret thoughts and feelings **3** : the part of a garment covering the breast — **bos·omed** \-zəmd\ *adj*

**²bosom** *adj* : CLOSE, INTIMATE

**¹boss** \ˈbäs, ˈbȯs\ *n* : a knoblike ornament : STUD

**²boss** *vb* : to ornament with bosses

**³boss** \ˈbȯs\ *n* **1** : one (as a foreman or manager) exercising control or supervision **2** : a politician who controls votes or dictates policies — **bossy** *adj*

**⁴boss** \ˈbȯs\ *vb* : to act as or in the manner of a boss

**bosun** *var of* BOATSWAIN

**bot** *abbr* **1** botanical; botanist; botany **2** robot

**bot·a·ny** \ˈbä-tə-nē, ˈbät-nē\ *n, pl* **-nies** **1** : a branch of biology dealing with plants and plant life **2** : plant life (as of a given region); *also* : the biology of a plant or plant group — **bo·tan·i·cal** \bə-ˈta-ni-kəl\ *adj or n* — **bo·tan·i·cal·ly** \-k(ə-)lē\ *adv* — **bot·a·nist** *n* — **bot·a·nize** \ˈbät-ə-ˌnīz\ *vb*

**botch** \ˈbäch\ *vb* : to foul up hopelessly : BUNGLE — **botch** *n*

**¹both** \ˈbōth\ *pron* : both ones : the one as well as the other

**²both** *conj* — used as a function word to indicate and stress the inclusion of each of two or more things specified by coordinated words, phrases, or clauses ⟨*~* New York and London⟩

**³both** *adj* : being the two : including the one and the other ⟨went to *~* museums⟩

**both·er** \ˈbä-thər\ *vb* : PESTER, TROUBLE ⟨was *~ed* by bees⟩ **2** : to concern oneself : make an effort ⟨didn't *~* asking⟩ ♦ *Synonyms* VEX, ANNOY, IRK, PROVOKE — **bother** *n* — **both·er·some** \-səm\ *adj*

**¹bot·tle** \ˈbä-tᵊl\ *n* **1** : a container (as of glass) with a narrow neck and usu. no

handles **2** : the quantity held by a bottle **3** : intoxicating liquor

**²bottle** *vb* **bot·tled; bot·tling** **1** : to confine as if in a bottle : RESTRAIN ⟨*bottled* up his anger⟩ **2** : to put into a bottle

**bot·tle·neck** \ˈbä-tᵊl-ˌnek\ *n* **1** : a narrow passage or point of congestion **2** : something that obstructs or impedes

**¹bot·tom** \ˈbä-təm\ *n* **1** : an under or supporting surface; *also* : BUTTOCKS **2** : the surface on which a body of water lies **3** : the lowest part or place; *also* : an inferior position ⟨start at the *~*⟩ **4** : BOTTOMLAND **5** : BASIS, SOURCE ⟨get to the *~* of this mystery⟩ **6** : a quark with a charge of −⅓ and a measured energy of approximately 5 billion electron volts

**bottom** *adj* — **bot·tom·less** *adj*

**²bottom** *vb* **1** : to furnish with a bottom **2** : to reach the bottom **3** : to reach a point where a decline is halted or reversed — usu. used with *out*

**bot·tom·land** \ˈbä-təm-ˌland\ *n* : low land along a river

**bottom line** *n* **1** : the essential point : CRUX **2** : the final result : OUTCOME

**bot·u·lism** \ˈbä-chə-ˌli-zəm\ *n* : an acute paralytic disease caused by a bacterial toxin (**bot·u·li·num toxin** \ˌbä-chə-ˈli-nəm-\) esp. in tainted food

**bou·doir** \ˈbü-ˌdwär, ˈbu̇-, -ˌbü-ˈ, ˌbu̇-ˈ\ *n* [F, fr. *bouder* to pout] : a woman's dressing room or bedroom

**bouf·fant** \bü-ˈfänt, ˈbü-ˌfänt\ *adj* [F] : puffed out ⟨*~* hairdos⟩

**bough** \ˈbau̇\ *n* : a usu. large or main branch of a tree

**bought** *past and past part of* BUY

**bouil·la·baisse** \ˌbü-yə-ˈbäs\ *n* [F] : a highly seasoned fish stew made with at least two kinds of fish

**bouil·lon** \ˈbu̇-ˌyän; ˈbül-ˌyän, ˈbu̇l-ˌyän, -yən\ *n* : a clear soup made usu. from beef

**boul·der** *also* **bowl·der** \ˈbōl-dər\ *n* : a large detached rounded or worn mass of rock — **boul·dered** \-dərd\ *adj*

**bou·le·vard** \ˈbu̇-lə-ˌvärd, ˈbü-\ *n* [F, modif. of MD *bolwerc* bulwark] : a broad often landscaped thoroughfare

**bounce** \ˈbau̇ns\ *vb* **bounced; bounc·ing** **1** : to cause to rebound ⟨*~* a ball⟩ **2** : to rebound after striking **3** : to issue (a check) from an account with insufficient funds — **bounce** *n* — **bouncy** \ˈbau̇n-sē\ *adj*

**bounc·er** \ˈbau̇n-sər\ *n* : a person employed in a public place to remove disorderly persons

**¹bound** \ˈbau̇nd\ *adj* : intending to go ⟨*homeward ~*⟩

**²bound** *n* : LIMIT, BOUNDARY — **bound·less** *adj* — **bound·less·ness** *n*

**³bound** *vb* **1** : to set limits to **2** : to form the boundary of **3** : to name the boundaries of

**⁴bound** *past and past part of* BIND

**⁵bound** *adj* **1** : constrained by or as if by bonds : CONFINED, OBLIGED ⟨was duty *~* to help⟩ **2** : enclosed in a binding or cover **3** : RESOLVED, DETERMINED; *also* : SURE

**⁶bound** n 1 : LEAP, JUMP 2 : REBOUND, BOUNCE

**⁷bound** vb : SPRING, BOUNCE

**bound·ary** \'baun-drē\ n, pl **-aries** : something that marks or fixes a limit or extent (as of territory) ♦ *Synonyms* BORDER, FRONTIER, MARCH

**bound·en** \'baun-dən\ adj : BINDING ⟨our ~ duty⟩

**boun·te·ous** \'baun-tē-əs\ adj 1 : GENEROUS 2 : ABUNDANT — **boun·te·ous·ly** adv — **boun·te·ous·ness** n

**boun·ti·ful** \'baun-ti-fəl\ adj 1 : giving freely 2 : PLENTIFUL — **boun·ti·ful·ly** adv — **boun·ti·ful·ness** n

**boun·ty** \'baun-tē\ n, pl **bounties** [ME *bounte* goodness, fr. AF *bunté*, fr. L *bonitas*, fr. *bonus* good] 1 : GENEROSITY 2 : something given liberally 3 : a reward, premium, or subsidy given usu. for doing something

**bou·quet** \bō-'kā, bü-\ n [F, fr. MF, thicket, bunch of flowers, fr. OF (dial. of Normandy and Picardy) *bosquet* thicket, fr. *bosc* forest] 1 : flowers picked and fastened together in a bunch 2 : a distinctive aroma (as of wine) ♦ *Synonyms* SCENT, FRAGRANCE, PERFUME, REDOLENCE

**bour·bon** \'bər-bən\ n : a whiskey distilled from a corn mash

**bour·geois** \'burzh-,wä, burzh-'wä\ n, pl **bourgeois** \*same or* -,wäz, -'wäz\ [MF, fr. OF *burgeis* townsman, fr. *burc, borg* town, fr. L *burgus* fortified place; of Gmc origin] : a middle-class person — **bourgeois** adj

**bour·geoi·sie** \,burzh-,wä-'zē\ n : a social order dominated by bourgeois

**bourne** *also* **bourn** \'bōrn, 'burn\ n : BOUNDARY; *also* : DESTINATION

**bourse** \'burs\ n : a European stock exchange

**bout** \'baut\ n 1 : CONTEST, MATCH 2 : OUTBREAK, ATTACK ⟨a ~ of measles⟩

**bou·tique** \bü-'tēk\ n : a small fashionable specialty shop

**bou·ton·niere** \,bü-t²n-'iər\ n : a flower or bouquet worn in a buttonhole

**¹bo·vine** \'bō-,vīn, -,vēn\ adj 1 : of or relating to bovines 2 : having qualities (as placidity or dullness) characteristic of oxen or cows

**²bovine** n : any of a group of mammals including oxen, buffalo, and their close relatives

**bovine spon·gi·form encephalopathy** \-'spän-ji-,fȯrm-\ n : MAD COW DISEASE

**¹bow** \'baù\ vb 1 : SUBMIT, YIELD 2 : to bend the head or body (as in submission, courtesy, or assent) 3 : DEBUT ⟨the play ~s next month⟩

**²bow** n : an act or posture of bowing

**³bow** \'bō\ n 1 : BEND, ARCH; *esp* : RAINBOW 2 : a weapon for shooting arrows; *also* : ARCHER 3 : a knot formed by doubling a line into two or more loops 4 : a wooden rod strung with horsehairs for playing an instrument of the violin family

**⁴bow** \'bō\ vb 1 : BEND, CURVE 2 : to play (an instrument) with a bow

**⁵bow** \'baù\ n : the forward part of a ship — **bow** adj

**bowd·ler·ise** *Brit var of* BOWDLERIZE

**bowd·ler·ize** \'bōd-lə-,rīz, 'baùd-\ vb **-ized; -iz·ing** : to expurgate by omitting parts considered vulgar

**bow·el** \'baù(-ə)l\ n 1 : INTESTINE; *also* : one of the divisions of the intestine — usu. used in pl. 2 pl : the inmost parts ⟨the ~s of the earth⟩

**bow·er** \'baù(-ə)r\ n : a shelter of boughs or vines : ARBOR

**¹bowl** \'bōl\ n 1 : a concave vessel used to hold liquids 2 : a drinking vessel 3 : a bowl-shaped part or structure — **bowl·ful** \-,fùl\ n

**²bowl** n 1 : a ball for rolling on a level surface in bowling 2 : a cast of the ball in bowling

**³bowl** vb 1 : to play a game of bowling; *also* : to roll a ball in bowling 2 : to travel (as in a vehicle) rapidly and smoothly 3 : to strike or knock down with a moving object

**bowlder** *var of* BOULDER

**bow·legged** \'bō-,le-gəd\ adj : having legs that bow outward at or below the knee — **bow·leg** \'bō-,leg\ n

**¹bowl·er** \'bō-lər\ n : a person who bowls

**²bowl·er** \'bō-lər\ n : DERBY 3

**bow·line** \'bō-lən, -,līn\ n : a knot used to form a loop that neither slips nor jams

**bowl·ing** \'bō-liŋ\ n : any of various games in which balls are rolled on a green or alley at an object or a group of objects

**bow·man** \'bō-mən\ n : ARCHER

**bow·sprit** \'baù-,sprit\ n : a spar projecting forward from the prow of a ship

**bow·string** \'bō-,striŋ\ n : the cord connecting the two ends of a shooting bow

**¹box** \'bäks\ n, pl **box** *or* **box·es** : an evergreen shrub or small tree used esp. for hedges

**²box** n 1 : a rigid typically rectangular receptacle often with a cover; *also* : the quantity held by a box 2 : a small compartment (as for a group of theater patrons); *also* : a boxlike receptacle or division 3 : a usu. rectangular space demarcated for a particular purpose ⟨the batter's ~⟩ 4 : a difficult situation : PREDICAMENT — **boxy** \'bäk-sē\ adj

**³box** vb : to enclose in or as if in a box

**⁴box** n : a punch or slap esp. on the ear

**⁵box** vb 1 : to strike with the hand 2 : to engage in boxing with

**box·car** \'bäks-,kär\ n : a roofed freight car usu. with sliding doors in the sides

**box cutter** n : a small cutting tool with a retractable razor blade

**¹box·er** \'bäk-sər\ n 1 : a person who engages in boxing 2 pl : BOXER SHORTS

**²boxer** n : any of a German breed of compact medium-sized dogs with a short usu. fawn or brindled coat

**boxer shorts** n pl : men's loose-fitting shorts worn as underwear

**box·ing** \'bäk-siŋ\ n : the sport of fighting with the fists

**box office** n : an office (as in a theater) where admission tickets are sold

**box turtle** *n* : any of several No. American land turtles able to withdraw completely into their shell

**box·wood** \'bäks-ˌwu̇d\ *n* : the tough hard wood of the box; *also* : a box tree or shrub

**boy** \'bȯi\ *n* **1** : a male child : YOUTH **2** : SON — **boy·hood** \-ˌhu̇d\ *n* — **boy·ish** *adj* — **boy·ish·ly** *adv* — **boy·ish·ness** *n*

**boy·cott** \'bȯi-ˌkät\ *vb* [Charles C. *Boycott* †1897 Eng. land agent in Ireland who was ostracized for refusing to reduce rents] : to refrain from having any dealings with — **boycott** *n*

**boy·friend** \'bȯi-ˌfrend\ *n* **1** : a male friend **2** : a frequent or regular male companion in a romantic relationship

**Boy Scout** *n* : a member of any of various national scouting programs (as the Boy Scouts of America)

**boy·sen·ber·ry** \'bȯi-zəⁿ-ˌber-ē, 'bȯis-ᵊn-\ *n* : a large reddish-black fruit with a raspberry flavor; *also* : the hybrid bramble bearing it developed by crossing blackberries and raspberries

**bo·zo** \'bō-ˌzō\ *n, pl* **bozos** : a foolish or incompetent person

**bp** *abbr* **1** bishop **2** birthplace

**BP** *abbr* **1** batting practice **2** blood pressure **3** boiling point

**bpl** *abbr* birthplace

**BPOE** *abbr* Benevolent and Protective Order of Elks

**br** *abbr* **1** branch **2** brass **3** brown

**¹Br** *abbr* Britain; British

**²Br** *symbol* bromine

**BR** *abbr* bedroom

**bra** \'brä\ *n* : BRASSIERE

**¹brace** \'brās\ *vb* **braced; brac·ing 1** *archaic* : to make fast : BIND **2** : to tighten preparatory to use; *also* : to get ready for : prepare oneself **3** : INVIGORATE **4** : to furnish or support with a brace; *also* : STRENGTHEN **5** : to set firmly **6** : to gain courage or confidence

**²brace** *n, pl* **brac·es 1** *or pl* **brace** : two of a kind ⟨a ~ of dogs⟩ **2** : a crank-shaped device for turning a bit **3** : something (as a tie, prop, or clamp) that distributes, directs, or resists pressure or weight **4** *pl* : SUSPENDERS **5** : an appliance for supporting a body part (as the shoulders) **6** *pl* : a dental appliance used to exert pressure to straighten misaligned teeth **7** : one of two marks { } used to connect words or items to be considered together

**brace·let** \'brā-slət\ *n* [ME, fr. MF, dim. of *bras* arm, fr. L *bracchium*, fr. Gk *brachiōn*] : an ornamental band or chain worn around the wrist

**bra·ce·ro** \brä-'ser-ō\ *n, pl* **-ros** : a Mexican laborer admitted to the U.S. esp. for seasonal farm work

**brack·en** \'bra-kən\ *n* : a large coarse fern; *also* : a growth of such ferns

**¹brack·et** \'bra-kət\ *n* **1** : a projecting framework or arm designed to support weight; *also* : a shelf on such framework **2** : one of a pair of punctuation marks [ ] used esp. to enclose interpolated matter **3** : a continuous section of a series; *esp* : one of a graded series of income groups

**²bracket** *vb* **1** : to furnish or fasten with brackets **2** : to place within brackets; *also* : to separate or group with or as if with brackets

**brack·ish** \'bra-kish\ *adj* : somewhat salty — **brack·ish·ness** *n*

**bract** \'brakt\ *n* : an often modified leaf on or at the base of a flower stalk

**brad** \'brad\ *n* : a slender nail with a small head

**brae** \'brā\ *n, chiefly Scot* : a hillside esp. along a river

**brag** \'brag\ *vb* **bragged; brag·ging** : to talk or assert boastfully — **brag·ger** *n*

**brag·ga·do·cio** \ˌbra-gə-'dō-shē-ˌō, -sē-, -chē-\ *n, pl* **-cios 1** : BRAGGART, BOASTER **2** : empty boasting **3** : arrogant pretension : COCKINESS

**brag·gart** \'bra-gərt\ *n* : one who brags

**Brah·man** *or* **Brah·min** \'brä-mən *for 1*; 'brä-, 'brä-, 'bra- *for 2*\ *n* **1** : a Hindu of the highest caste traditionally assigned to the priesthood **2** : any of a breed of large vigorous humped cattle developed in the southern U.S. from Indian stock **3** *usu* **Brahmin** : a person of high social standing and cultivated intellect and taste

**Brah·man·ism** \'brä-mə-ˌni-zəm\ *n* : orthodox Hinduism

**¹braid** \'brād\ *vb* **1** : to form (strands) into a braid : PLAIT; *also* : to make from braids **2** : to ornament with braid

**²braid** *n* **1** : a length of braided hair **2** : a cord or ribbon of three or more interwoven strands; *esp* : a narrow ornamental one

**braille** \'brāl\ *n, often cap* : a system of writing for the blind that uses characters made up of raised dots

**¹brain** \'brān\ *n* **1** : the part of the vertebrate central nervous system enclosed in the skull and continuous with the spinal cord that is composed of neurons and supporting structures and is the center of thought and nervous system control; *also* : a centralized mass of nerve tissue in an invertebrate **2** : INTELLECT, INTELLIGENCE — often used in *pl*. — **brained** \'brānd\ *adj* — **brain·less** *adj* — **brainy** *adj*

**²brain** *vb* **1** : to kill by smashing the skull **2** : to hit on the head

**brain·child** \'brān-ˌchī(-ə)ld\ *n* : a product of one's creative imagination

**brain death** *n* : final cessation of activity in the central nervous system esp. as indicated by a flat electroencephalogram — **brain–dead** \-ˌded\ *adj*

**brain drain** *n* : the departure of educated or professional people from one country, sector, or field to another usu. for better pay or living conditions

**brain·storm** \-ˌstȯrm\ *n* : a sudden inspiration or idea — **brainstorm** *vb*

**brain·teas·er** \-ˌtē-zər\ *n* : a challenging puzzle

**brain·wash·ing** \'brān-ˌwȯ-shiŋ, -ˌwä-\ *n* **1** : a forcible indoctrination to induce someone to give up basic political, social, or religious beliefs and attitudes and to accept contrasting regimented ideas **2**

: persuasion by propaganda or salesmanship — **brain·wash** vb

**brain wave** n **1** : BRAINSTORM **2** : rhythmic fluctuations of voltage between parts of the brain; also : a current produced by brain waves

**braise** \'brāz\ vb **braised; brais·ing** : to cook slowly in fat and little moisture in a closed pot

**¹brake** \'brāk\ n : a common bracken fern

**²brake** n : rough or wet land heavily overgrown (as with thickets or reeds)

**³brake** n : a device for slowing or stopping motion esp. by friction — **brake·less** adj

**⁴brake** vb **braked; brak·ing 1** : to slow or stop by or as if by a brake **2** : to apply a brake

**brake·man** \'brāk-mən\ n : a train crew member who inspects the train and assists the conductor

**bram·ble** \'bram-bəl\ n : any of a large genus of prickly shrubs (as a blackberry) related to the roses; also : any rough prickly shrub or vine — **bram·bly** \-b(ə-)lē\ adj

**bran** \'bran\ n : the edible broken husks of cereal grain sifted from flour or meal

**¹branch** \'branch\ n [ME, fr. AF branche, fr. LL branca paw] **1** : a natural subdivision (as a bough or twig) of a plant stem **2** : a division (as of an antler or a river) related to a whole like a plant branch to its stem **3** : a discrete element of a complex system ⟨the executive ∼⟩; esp : a division of a family descended from one ancestor — **branched** \'brancht\ adj

**²branch** vb **1** : to develop branches **2** : DIVERGE **3** : to extend activities ⟨the business is ∼ing out⟩

**¹brand** \'brand\ n **1** : a piece of charred or burning wood **2** : a mark made (as by burning) usu. to identify; also : a mark of disgrace : STIGMA **3** : a class of goods identified as the product of a particular firm or producer **4** : a distinctive kind ⟨my own ∼ of humor⟩

**²brand** vb **1** : to mark with a brand **2** : STIGMATIZE ⟨was ∼ed a traitor⟩

**bran·dish** \'bran-dish\ vb : to shake or wave menacingly ⟨∼ a knife⟩ ♦ **Synonyms** FLOURISH, FLASH, FLAUNT

**brand–new** \'bran-'nü, -'nyü\ adj : conspicuously new and unused

**bran·dy** \'bran-dē\ n, pl **brandies** [short for brandywine, fr. D brandewijn, fr. MD brantwijn, fr. brant distilled + wijn wine] : a liquor distilled from wine or fermented fruit juice — **brandy** vb

**brash** \'brash\ adj **1** : IMPETUOUS, AUDACIOUS **2** : aggressively self-assertive — **brash·ly** adv — **brash·ness** n

**brass** \'bras\ n **1** : an alloy of copper and zinc; also : an object of brass **2** : brazen self-assurance **3** : persons of high rank (as in the military) — **brassy** adj

**bras·siere** \brə-'zir\ n : a woman's close-fitting undergarment designed to support the breasts

**brat** \'brat\ n : an ill-behaved child — **brat·ti·ness** n — **brat·ty** adj

**bra·va·do** \brə-'vä-dō\ n, pl **-does** or

**-dos 1** : blustering swaggering conduct **2** : a show of bravery

**¹brave** \'brāv\ adj **brav·er; brav·est** [MF, fr. It & Sp bravo courageous, wild, prob. fr. L barbarus barbarous] **1** : showing courage **2** : EXCELLENT, SPLENDID ♦ **Synonyms** BOLD, INTREPID, COURAGEOUS, VALIANT — **brave·ly** adv

**²brave** vb **braved; brav·ing** : to face or endure bravely

**³brave** n : an American Indian warrior

**brav·ery** \'brā-və-rē\ n, pl **-er·ies** : COURAGE

**bra·vo** \'brä-vō\ n, pl **bravos** : a shout of approval — often used as an interjection in applauding

**bra·vu·ra** \brə-'vyùr-ə, -'vùr-\ n **1** : a florid brilliant musical style **2** : self-assured brilliant performance — **bravura** adj

**brawl** \'bròl\ n : a noisy quarrel ♦ **Synonyms** FRACAS, ROW, RUMPUS, SCRAP, FRAY, MELEE — **brawl** vb — **brawl·er** n

**brawn** \'brón\ n **1** : strong muscles; also : muscular strength — **brawn·i·ness** n — **brawny** adj

**bray** \'brā\ n : the characteristic harsh cry of a donkey — **bray** vb

**braze** \'brāz\ vb **brazed; braz·ing** : to solder with an alloy (as brass) that melts at a lower temperature than the metals being joined — **braz·er** n

**¹bra·zen** \'brā-z⁰n\ adj **1** : made of brass **2** : sounding harsh and loud **3** : of the color of brass **4** : marked by contemptuous boldness ⟨a ∼ rebuff⟩ — **bra·zen·ly** adv — **bra·zen·ness** n

**²brazen** vb : to face boldly or defiantly

**bra·zier** \'brā-zhər\ n : a worker in brass

**²brazier** n **1** : a vessel holding burning coals (as for heating) **2** : a device on which food is grilled

**Bra·zil nut** \brə-'zil-\ n : a triangular oily edible nut borne in large capsules by a tall So. American tree; also : the tree

**¹breach** \'brēch\ n **1** : a breaking of a law, obligation, tie (as of friendship), or standard (as of conduct) **2** : an interruption or opening made by or as if by breaking through ♦ **Synonyms** VIOLATION, TRANSGRESSION, INFRINGEMENT, TRESPASS

**²breach** vb **1** : to make a breach in ⟨the army ∼ed the castle wall⟩ **2** : to leap out of water ⟨whales ∼ing⟩

**¹bread** \'bred\ n **1** : baked food made basically of flour or meal **2** : FOOD

**²bread** vb : to cover with bread crumbs

**bread·bas·ket** \'bred-,bas-kət\ n : a major cereal-producing region

**bread·fruit** \-,früt\ n : a round usu. seedless fruit resembling bread in color and texture when baked; also : a tall tropical tree related to the mulberry and bearing breadfruit

**bread·stuff** \-,stəf\ n : GRAIN, FLOUR

**breadth** \'bredth, 'bretth\ n **1** : WIDTH **2** : comprehensive quality : SCOPE ⟨her ∼ of knowledge⟩

**bread·win·ner** \'bred-,wi-nər\ n : a member of a family whose wages supply its livelihood

¹**break** \'brāk\ vb **broke** \'brōk\; **bro·ken** \'brō-kən\; **break·ing** **1** : to separate into parts usu. suddenly or violently; also : to render inoperable ⟨broke his watch⟩ **2** : TRANSGRESS ⟨~ a law⟩ **3** : to force a way into, out of, or through **4** : to disrupt the order or unity of ⟨~ ranks⟩ ⟨~ up a gang⟩; also : to bring to submission or helplessness **5** : EXCEED, SURPASS ⟨~ a record⟩ **6** : RUIN **7** : to make known ⟨~ the bad news⟩ **8** : HALT, INTERRUPT; also : to act or change abruptly (as a course or activity) **9** : to come esp. suddenly into being or notice ⟨as day ~s⟩ **10** : to fail under stress **11** : HAPPEN, DEVELOP ⟨report news as it ~s⟩ — **break·able** adj or n — **break into** **1** : to begin with a sudden throwing off of restraint ⟨broke into tears⟩ **2** : to make entry or entrance into ⟨break into show business⟩

²**break** n **1** : an act of breaking **2** : a result of breaking; esp : an interruption of continuity ⟨coffee ~⟩ ⟨a ~ for the commercial⟩ **3** : a stroke of luck

**break·age** \'brā-kij\ n **1** : loss due to things broken **2** : the action of breaking **3** : articles or amount broken

**break·down** \'brāk-ˌdaún\ n **1** : functional failure; esp : a physical, mental, or nervous collapse **2** : DISINTEGRATION **3** : DECOMPOSITION **4** : ANALYSIS, CLASSIFICATION — **break down** vb

**break·er** \'brā-kər\ n **1** : one that breaks **2** : a wave that breaks into foam (as against the shore)

**break·fast** \'brek-fəst\ n : the first meal of the day — **breakfast** vb

**break in** vb **1** : to enter a building by force **2** : INTERRUPT; also : INTRUDE **3** : TRAIN ⟨break in new employees⟩ — **break-in** \'brāk-ˌin\ n

**break·neck** \'brāk-ˌnek\ adj : very fast or dangerous ⟨~ speed⟩

**break out** vb **1** : to develop or erupt suddenly or with force **2** : to develop a skin rash

**break·through** \'brāk-ˌthrü\ n **1** : an act or instance of breaking through an obstruction or defensive line **2** : a sudden advance in knowledge or technique ⟨a scientific ~⟩

**break·up** \-ˌəp\ n **1** : DISSOLUTION **2** : a division into smaller units — **break up** vb

**break·wa·ter** \'brāk-ˌwȯ-tər, -ˌwä-\ n : a structure protecting a harbor or beach from the force of waves

**bream** \'brim, 'brēm\ n, pl **bream** or **breams** : any of various small freshwater sunfishes

**breast** \'brest\ n **1** : either of the pair of mammary glands extending from the front of the chest esp. in pubescent and adult human females **2** : the front part of the body between the neck and the abdomen **3** : the seat of emotion and thought

**breast·bone** \'brest-ˌbōn\ n : STERNUM

**breast-feed** \-ˌfēd\ vb : to feed (a baby) from a mother's breast

**breast·plate** \-ˌplāt\ n : a metal plate of armor for the breast

**breast·stroke** \-ˌströk\ n : a swimming stroke executed by extending both arms forward and then sweeping them back with palms out while kicking backward and outward with both legs

**breast·work** \-ˌwərk\ n : a temporary fortification

**breath** \'breth\ n **1** : the act or power of breathing **2** : a slight breeze **3** : air inhaled or exhaled in breathing **4** : spoken sound **5** : SPIRIT — **breath·less** adj — **breath·less·ly** adv — **breath·less·ness** n — **breathy** \'bre-thē\ adj

**breathe** \'brēth\ vb **breathed**; **breath·ing** **1** : to inhale and exhale **2** : LIVE **3** : to halt for rest **4** : to utter softly or secretly — **breath·able** adj

**breath·er** \'brē-thər\ n **1** : one that breathes **2** : a short rest

**breath·tak·ing** \'breth-ˌtā-kiŋ\ adj **1** : making one out of breath **2** : EXCITING, THRILLING ⟨~ beauty⟩ — **breath·tak·ing·ly** adv

**brec·cia** \'bre-chē-ə, -chə\ n : a rock composed of sharp fragments held in fine-grained material

**breech** \'brēch\ n **1** pl \usu 'bri-chəz\ : pants ending near the knee **2** : BUTTOCKS, RUMP **3** : the part of a firearm at the rear of the barrel

¹**breed** \'brēd\ vb **bred** \'bred\; **breed·ing** **1** : BEGET; also : ORIGINATE **2** : to propagate sexually; also : MATE **3** : BRING UP, NURTURE **4** : to produce (fissionable material) from material that is not fissionable ♦ **Synonyms** GENERATE, REPRODUCE, PROCREATE, PROPAGATE — **breed·er** n

²**breed** n **1** : a strain of similar and presumably related plants or animals usu. developed in domestication **2** : KIND, SORT, CLASS

**breeding** n **1** : ANCESTRY **2** : training in polite social interaction **3** : sexual propagation of plants or animals

¹**breeze** \'brēz\ n **1** : a light wind **2** : CINCH, SNAP — **breeze·less** adj

²**breeze** vb **breezed**; **breez·ing** : to progress quickly and easily

**breeze·way** \'brēz-ˌwā\ n : a roofed open passage connecting two buildings (as a house and garage)

**breezy** \'brē-zē\ adj **1** : swept by breezes **2** : briskly informal ⟨~ prose⟩ — **breez·i·ly** \'brē-zə-lē\ adv — **breez·i·ness** \-zē-nəs\ n

**breth·ren** \'breth-rən, 'bre-thə-; 'bre-thərn\ pl of BROTHER — used esp. in formal or solemn address

**Brethren** n pl : members of one of several Protestant denominations originating chiefly in a German religious movement and stressing personal religious experience

**bre·via·ry** \'brē-vyə-rē, -vē-ˌer-ē\ n, pl **-ries** often cap : a book of prayers, hymns, psalms, and readings used by Roman Catholic priests

**brev·i·ty** \'bre-və-tē\ n, pl **-ties** **1** : shortness or conciseness of expression **2** : shortness of duration

**brew** \'brü\ vb **1** : to prepare (as beer) by

steeping, boiling, and fermenting **2** : to prepare (as tea) by steeping in hot water — **brew** *n* — **brew·er** *n* — **brew·ery** \ˈbrü-ə-rē, ˈbrů-(-ə)r-ē\ *n*

¹**bri·ar** *also* **bri·er** \ˈbrī-ər\ *n* : a plant (as a bramble or rose) with a thorny or prickly usu. woody stem; *also* : a mass or twig of these — **bri·ary** \ˈbrī-ər-ē\ *adj*

²**briar** *n* : a tobacco pipe made from the root or stem of a European heath

¹**bribe** \ˈbrīb\ *n* [ME, morsel given to a beggar, bribe, fr. AF, morsel] : something (as money or a favor) given or promised to a person to influence conduct

²**bribe** *vb* **bribed; brib·ing** : to influence by offering a bribe — **brib·able** *adj* — **brib·er** *n* — **brib·ery** \ˈbrī-bə-rē\ *n*

**bric–a–brac** \ˈbri-kə-ˌbrak\ *n pl* [F] : small ornamental articles

¹**brick** \ˈbrik\ *n* : a block molded from moist clay and hardened by heat used esp. for building

²**brick** *vb* : to close, cover, or pave with bricks

**brick·bat** \ˈbrik-ˌbat\ *n* **1** : a piece of a hard material (as a brick) esp. when thrown as a missile **2** : an uncomplimentary remark

**brick·lay·er** \ˈbrik-ˌlā-ər\ *n* : a person who builds or paves with bricks — **brick·lay·ing** *n*

¹**brid·al** \ˈbrī-dᵊl\ *n* [ME *bridale*, fr. OE *brȳdealu*, fr. *brȳd* bride + *ealu* ale] : **MARRIAGE, WEDDING**

²**bridal** *adj* : of or relating to a bride or a wedding

**bride** \ˈbrīd\ *n* : a woman just married or about to be married

**bride·groom** \ˈbrīd-ˌgrüm, -ˌgrům\ *n* : a man just married or about to be married

**brides·maid** \ˈbrīdz-ˌmād\ *n* : a woman who attends a bride at her wedding

¹**bridge** \ˈbrij\ *n* **1** : a structure built over a depression or obstacle for use as a passageway **2** : something (as the upper part of the nose) resembling a bridge in form or function **3** : a curved piece raising the strings of a musical instrument **4** : the forward part of a ship's superstructure from which it is navigated **5** : an artificial replacement for missing teeth

²**bridge** *vb* **bridged; bridg·ing** : to build a bridge over — **bridge·able** *adj*

³**bridge** *n* : a card game for four players developed from whist

**bridge·head** \-ˌhed\ *n* : an advanced position seized in enemy territory

**bridge·work** \-ˌwərk\ *n* : dental bridges

¹**bri·dle** \ˈbrī-dᵊl\ *n* **1** : headgear with which a horse is controlled **2** : **CURB, RESTRAINT**

²**bridle** *vb* **bri·dled; bri·dling** **1** : to put a bridle on; *also* : to restrain with or as if with a bridle **2** : to show hostility or scorn usu. by tossing the head

**Brie** \ˈbrē\ *n* : a soft cheese with a whitish rind and a pale yellow interior

¹**brief** \ˈbrēf\ *adj* **1** : short in duration or extent **2** : **CONCISE**; *also* : **CURT** — **brief·ly** *adv* — **brief·ness** *n*

²**brief** *n* **1** : a concise statement or document; *esp* : one summarizing a law cli-

ent's case or a legal argument **2** *pl* : short snug underpants

³**brief** *vb* : to give final instructions or essential information to

**brief·case** \ˈbrēf-ˌkās\ *n* : a flat flexible case for carrying papers

**brier** *var of* BRIAR

¹**brig** \ˈbrig\ *n* : a 2-masted square-rigged sailing ship

²**brig** *n* : the place of confinement for offenders on a naval ship

³**brig** *abbr* brigade

**bri·gade** \bri-ˈgād\ *n* **1** : a military unit composed of a headquarters, one or more units of infantry or armored forces, and supporting units **2** : a group organized for a particular purpose (as fire fighting)

**brig·a·dier general** \ˈbri-gə-ˌdir-\ *n* : a commissioned officer (as in the army) ranking next below a major general

**brig·and** \ˈbri-gənd\ *n* : **BANDIT** — **brig·and·age** \-gən-dij\ *n*

**brig·an·tine** \ˈbri-gən-ˌtēn\ *n* : a 2-masted square-rigged ship with a fore-and-aft mainsail

**Brig Gen** *abbr* brigadier general

**bright** \ˈbrīt\ *adj* **1** : **SHINING, RADIANT** **2** : **ILLUSTRIOUS, GLORIOUS** **3** : **INTELLIGENT, CLEVER**; *also* : **LIVELY, CHEERFUL** ⟨a ~ smile⟩ ♦ **Synonyms** BRILLIANT, LUSTROUS, BEAMING — **bright** *adv* — **bright·ly** *adv* — **bright·ness** *n*

**bright·en** \ˈbrī-tᵊn\ *vb* : to make or become bright or brighter ⟨the good news ~ed her mood⟩ — **bright·en·er** *n*

¹**bril·liant** \ˈbril-yənt\ *adj* [F *brillant*, prp. of *briller* to shine, fr. It *brillare*] **1** : very bright **2** : **STRIKING, DISTINCTIVE** **3** : very intelligent ⟨a ~ idea⟩ ♦ **Synonyms** RADIANT, LUSTROUS, BEAMING, LUCID, BRIGHT, LAMBENT — **bril·liance** \-yəns\ *n* — **bril·lian·cy** \-yən-sē\ *n* — **bril·liant·ly** *adv*

²**brilliant** *n* : a gem cut in a particular form with many facets

¹**brim** \ˈbrim\ *n* : **EDGE, RIM** ♦ **Synonyms** BRINK, BORDER, VERGE, FRINGE — **brim·less** *adj*

²**brim** *vb* **brimmed; brim·ming** : to be or become full often to overflowing

**brim·ful** \-ˈfúl\ *adj* : full to the brim

**brim·stone** \ˈbrim-ˌstōn\ *n* : **SULFUR**

**brin·dled** \ˈbrin-dᵊld\ *adj* : having dark streaks or flecks on a gray or tawny ground ⟨a ~ Great Dane⟩

**brine** \ˈbrīn\ *n* **1** : water saturated with salt **2** : **OCEAN** — **brin·i·ness** *n* — **briny** \ˈbrī-nē\ *adj*

**bring** \ˈbriŋ\ *vb* **brought** \ˈbrót\; **bring·ing** \ˈbriŋ-iŋ\ **1** : to cause to come with one **2** : **INDUCE, PERSUADE, LEAD** **3** : **PRODUCE, EFFECT** **4** : to sell for ⟨~ a good price⟩ — **bring·er** *n*

**bring about** *vb* : to cause to take place

**bring up** *vb* **1** : to give a parent's fostering care to **2** : to come or bring to a sudden halt **3** : to call to notice

**brink** \ˈbriŋk\ *n* **1** : an edge at the top of a steep place **2** : the point of onset

**brio** \ˈbrē-ō\ *n* : **VIVACITY, SPIRIT**

**bri·quette** *or* **bri·quet** \bri-ˈket\ *n* : a

compacted often brick-shaped mass of fine material ⟨a charcoal ~⟩

**bris** *also* **briss** \'bris\ *n* : the Jewish rite of circumcision

**brisk** \'brisk\ *adj* **1** : ALERT, LIVELY **2** : INVIGORATING ⟨~ weather⟩ **3** : highly active ⟨a ~ business⟩ ♦ *Synonyms* AGILE, SPRY, NIMBLE — **brisk·ly** *adv* — **brisk·ness** *n*

**bris·ket** \'bris-kət\ *n* : the breast or lower chest of a quadruped; *also* : a cut of beef from the brisket

**bris·ling** \'briz-liŋ, 'bris-\ *n* : SPRAT 1

**¹bris·tle** \'bri-səl\ *n* : a short stiff coarse hair — **bris·tle·like** \'bri-səl-,līk\ *adj* — **bris·tly** *adj*

**²bristle** *vb* **bris·tled; bris·tling 1** : to stand stiffly erect **2** : to show angry defiance ⟨bristled at the charges⟩ **3** : to appear as if covered with bristles

**Brit** *abbr* Britain; British

**Bri·tan·nic** \bri-'ta-nik\ *adj* : BRITISH

**britch·es** \'bri-chəz\ *n pl* : BREECHES, TROUSERS

**Brit·ish** \'bri-tish\ *n pl* : the people of Great Britain or the Commonwealth — **British** *adj* — **Brit·ish·ness** *n*

**British thermal unit** *n* : the quantity of heat needed to raise the temperature of one pound of water one degree Fahrenheit

**Brit·on** \'bri-t°n\ *n* **1** : a member of a people inhabiting Britain before the Anglo-Saxon invasion **2** : a native or inhabitant of Great Britain

**brit·tle** \'bri-t°l\ *adj* **brit·tler; brit·tlest** : easily broken : FRAGILE ♦ *Synonyms* CRISP, CRUMBLY, FRIABLE — **brit·tle·ness** *n*

**bro** \'brō\ *n, pl* **bros 1** : BROTHER 1 **2** : SOUL BROTHER

**¹broach** \'brōch\ *n* : a pointed tool

**²broach** *vb* **1** : to pierce (as a cask) in order to draw the contents **2** : to open up (a subject) for discussion

**broad** \'brōd\ *adj* **1** : WIDE **2** : SPACIOUS ⟨the ~ plains⟩ **3** : CLEAR, OPEN ⟨~ daylight⟩ **4** : OBVIOUS ⟨a ~ hint⟩ **5** : COARSE, CRUDE ⟨~ stories⟩ **6** : tolerant in outlook **7** : GENERAL ⟨a ~ rule⟩ **8** : dealing with essential points — **broad·ly** *adv* — **broad·ness** *n*

**broad·band** \'brōd-,band\ *n* : a system of high-speed telecommunication in which a frequency range is divided into multiple independent channels for simultaneous transmission of signals

**¹broad·cast** \'brōd-,kast\ *vb* **broadcast** *also* **broad·cast·ed; broad·cast·ing 1** : to scatter or sow broadcast **2** : to make widely known **3** : to transmit a broadcast — **broad·cast·er** *n*

**²broadcast** *adv* : to or over a wide area

**³broadcast** *n* **1** : the transmission of sound or images by radio or television **2** : a single radio or television program

**broad·cloth** \-,klȯth\ *n* **1** : a smooth dense woolen cloth **2** : a fine soft cloth of cotton, silk, or synthetic fiber

**broad·en** \'brȯ-d°n\ *vb* : WIDEN

**broad·loom** \-,lüm\ *adj* : woven on a wide loom esp. in a solid color

**broad–mind·ed** \-'mīn-dəd\ *adj* : tolerant of varied opinions — **broad–mind·ed·ly** *adv* — **broad–mind·ed·ness** *n*

**¹broad·side** \-,sīd\ *n* **1** : a sheet of paper printed usu. on one side (as an advertisement) **2** : all of the guns on one side of a ship; *also* : their simultaneous firing **3** : a volley of abuse or denunciation

**²broadside** *adv* **1** : with one side forward : SIDEWAYS **2** : from the side ⟨the car was hit ~⟩

**broad–spectrum** *adj* : effective against a wide range of organisms ⟨~ antibiotics⟩

**broad·sword** \'brȯd-,sȯrd\ *n* : a broad-bladed sword

**broad·tail** \-,tāl\ *n* : a karakul esp. with flat and wavy fur

**bro·cade** \brō-'kād\ *n* : a usu. silk fabric with a raised design

**broc·co·li** \'brä-kə-lē\ *n* [It, pl. of *broccolo* flowering top of a cabbage, dim. of *brocco* small nail, sprout, fr. L *broccus* projecting] : the stems and immature usu. green or purple flower heads of either of two garden vegetable plants closely related to the cabbage; *also* : either of the plants

**bro·chette** \brō-'shet\ *n* : SKEWER

**bro·chure** \brō-'shùr\ *n* [F, fr. *brocher* to sew, fr. MF, to prick, fr. OF *brochier*, fr. *broche* pointed tool] : PAMPHLET, BOOKLET

**bro·gan** \'brō-gən, brō-'gan\ *n* : a heavy shoe

**brogue** \'brōg\ *n* : a dialect or regional pronunciation; *esp* : an Irish accent

**broil** \'brȯi(-ə)l\ *vb* : to cook by exposure to radiant heat : GRILL — **broil** *n*

**broil·er** \'brȯi-lər\ *n* **1** : a utensil for broiling **2** : a young chicken fit for broiling

**broil·ing** \'brȯi-(ə)liŋ\ *adj* : extremely hot ⟨a ~ sun⟩

**¹broke** \'brōk\ *past of* BREAK

**²broke** *adj* : PENNILESS

**¹bro·ken** \'brō-kən\ *past part of* BREAK

**²broken** *adj* **1** : SHATTERED ⟨~ glass⟩ **2** : having gaps or breaks : INTERRUPTED, DISRUPTED **3** : SUBDUED, CRUSHED ⟨a ~ spirit⟩ **4** : BANKRUPT **5** : imperfectly spoken ⟨~ English⟩ — **bro·ken·ly** *adv*

**bro·ken·heart·ed** \,brō-kən-'här-təd\ *adj* : overcome by grief or despair

**bro·ker** \'brō-kər\ *n* : an agent who negotiates contracts of purchase and sale — **broker** *vb*

**bro·ker·age** \'brō-kə-rij\ *n* **1** : the business of a broker **2** : the fee or commission charged by a broker

**bro·mance** \'brō-,man(t)s\ *n* [blend of *bro* and *romance*] : a close nonsexual friendship between men — **bro·man·tic** \brō-'man-tik\ *adj*

**bro·me·li·ad** \brō-'mē-lē-,ad\ *n* : any of several tropical American ornamental plants related to the pineapple that usu. grow on trees

**bro·mide** \'brō-,mīd\ *n* : a compound of bromine and another element or chemical group including some (as potassium bromide) used as sedatives

**bro·mid·ic** \brō-'mi-dik\ *adj* : TRITE, UN-ORIGINAL

**bro·mine** \'brō-‚mēn\ *n* [F *brome* from bromine, fr. Gk *brōmos* stink] : a deep red liquid corrosive chemical element that gives off an irritating vapor

**bronc** \'bräŋk\ *n* : an unbroken or partly broken range horse of western No. America; *also* : MUSTANG

**bron·chi·al** \'bräŋ-kē-əl\ *adj* : of, relating to, or affecting the bronchi or their branches

**bron·chi·tis** \brän-'kī-təs, bräŋ-\ *n´* : inflammation of the bronchi and their branches — **bron·chit·ic** \-'ki-tik\ *adj*

**bron·chus** \'bräŋ-kəs\ *n, pl* **bron·chi** \'bräŋ-‚kī, -‚kē\ : either of the main divisions of the trachea each leading to a lung

**bron·co** \'bräŋ-kō\ *n, pl* **broncos** [Mex-Sp, fr. Sp, rough, wild] : BRONC

**bron·to·sau·rus** \‚brän-tə-'sȯr-əs\ *also* **bron·to·saur** \'brän-tə-‚sȯr\ *n* [NL, fr. Gk *brontē* thunder + *sauros* lizard] : any of a genus of large 4-footed sauropod dinosaurs of the Jurassic

**Bronx cheer** \'bräŋks-\ *n* : RASPBERRY 2

¹**bronze** \'bränz\ *vb* **bronzed; bronz·ing** : to give the appearance of bronze to

²**bronze** *n* **1** : an alloy of copper and tin and sometimes other elements; *also* : something shaped from it **2** : a yellowish brown color — **bronzy** \'brän-zē\ *adj*

**brooch** \'brōch, 'brüch\ *n* : an ornamental clasp or pin

¹**brood** \'brüd\ *n* : a family of young animals or children and esp. of birds

²**brood** *adj* : kept for breeding ⟨a ~ mare⟩

³**brood** *vb* **1** : to sit on eggs to hatch them; *also* : to shelter (hatched young) with the wings **2** : to think anxiously or gloomily about something — **brood·ing·ly** *adv*

**brood·er** \'brü-dər\ *n* **1** : one that broods **2** : a heated structure for raising young birds

¹**brook** \'brúk\ *n* : a small natural stream

²**brook** *vb* : TOLERATE, BEAR ⟨would ~ no interference with his plan⟩

**brook·let** \'brúk-lət\ *n* : a small brook

**brook trout** *n* : a common speckled coldwater char of No. America

**broom** \'brüm, 'brúm\ *n* **1** : any of several shrubs of the legume family with long slender branches and usu. yellow flowers **2** : an implement with a long handle (**broom·stick** \-‚stik\) used for sweeping

**broth** \'brȯth\ *n, pl* **broths** \'brȯths, 'brȯthz\ **1** : liquid in which meat or sometimes vegetable food has been cooked **2** : a fluid culture medium

**broth·el** \'brä-thəl, 'brȯ-\ *n* : a house of prostitution

**broth·er** \'brə-thər\ *n, pl* **brothers** *also* **breth·ren** \'breth-rən, 'bre-thə-; 'bre-thərn\ **1** : a male having one or both parents in common with another individual **2** : a man who is a religious but not a priest **3** : KINSMAN; *also* : SOUL BROTHER — **broth·er·li·ness** \-lē-nəs\ *n* — **broth·er·ly** *adj*

**broth·er·hood** \'brə-thər-‚húd\ *n* **1** : the state of being brothers or a brother **2** : ASSOCIATION, FRATERNITY **3** : the whole body of persons in a business or profession ⟨the medical ~⟩

**broth·er—in—law** \'brə-thə-rən-‚lȯ, 'brə-thərn-‚lȯ\ *n, pl* **brothers—in—law** \'brə-thər-zən-\ : the brother of one's spouse; *also* : the husband of one's sister or of one's spouse's sister

**brougham** \'brü-(ə)m, 'brō-(ə)m\ *n* : a light closed horse-drawn carriage with the driver outside in front

**brought** *past and past part of* BRING

**brou·ha·ha** \'brü-‚hä-‚hä\ *n* : HUBBUB, UPROAR

**brow** \'braú\ *n* **1** : the eyebrow or the ridge on which it grows; *also* : FOREHEAD **2** : the projecting upper part of a steep place

**brow·beat** \'braú-‚bēt\ *vb* **-beat; -beat·en** \-'bē-t³n\ *or* **-beat; -beat·ing** : to intimidate by sternness or arrogance

¹**brown** \'braún\ *adj* : of the color brown; *also* : of dark or tanned complexion

²**brown** *n* : a color like that of coffee or chocolate that is a blend of red and yellow darkened by black — **brown·ish** *adj*

³**brown** *vb* : to make or become brown

**brown bag·ging** \-'ba-giŋ\ *n* : the practice of carrying one's lunch usu. in a brown bag — **brown bag·ger** *n*

**brown bear** *n* : any of various large typically brown-furred bears including the grizzly bear

**brown·ie** \'braú-nē\ *n* **1** : a legendary cheerful elf who performs good deeds at night **2** *cap* : a member of a program of the Girl Scouts for girls in the first through third grades **3** : a small square or rectangle of chocolate cake

**brown·nose** \'braún-‚nōz\ *vb* : to ingratiate oneself with — **brownnose** *n*

**brown·out** \'braú-‚naút\ *n* : a period of reduced voltage of electricity caused esp. by high demand and resulting in reduced illumination

**brown rice** *n* : hulled but unpolished rice that retains most of the bran layers

**brown·stone** \'braún-‚stōn\ *n* : a dwelling faced with reddish-brown sandstone

¹**browse** \'braúz\ *vb* **browsed; brows·ing** **1** : to feed on browse; *also* : GRAZE **2** : to read or look over something in a casual way **3** : to access (a network) with a browser

²**browse** *n* : tender shoots, twigs, and leaves fit for food for cattle

**brows·er** \'braú-zər\ *n* : a computer program for accessing sites or information on a network (as the World Wide Web)

**bru·in** \'brü-ən\ *n* : BEAR

¹**bruise** \'brüz\ *vb* **bruised; bruis·ing** **1** : to inflict a bruise on; *also* : to become bruised **2** : to break down (as leaves or berries) by pounding

²**bruise** *n* : a surface injury to flesh : CONTUSION

**bruis·er** \'brü-zər\ *n* : a big husky man

**bruit** \'brüt\ *vb* : to make widely known by common report ⟨word of his dismissal was ~ed about⟩

**brunch** \\'brənch\ *n* : a meal that combines a late breakfast and an early lunch

**bru·net** *or* **bru·nette** \brü-'net\ *adj* [F *brunet*, masc., *brunette*, fem., *brownish*, fr. OF, fr. *brun* brown, of Gmc origin] : having brown or black hair and usu. a relatively dark complexion — **brunet** *or* **brunette** *n*

**brunt** \\'brənt\ *n* : the main shock, force, or stress esp. of an attack; *also* : the greater burden

**bru·schel·la** \brü-'she-tə, -'ske-\ *n* : an appetizer of grilled bread with toppings

¹**brush** \\'brəsh\ *n* 1 : BRUSHWOOD 2 : scrub vegetation or land covered with it

²**brush** *n* 1 : a device composed of bristles set in a handle and used esp. for cleaning or painting 2 : a bushy tail (as of a fox) 3 : an electrical conductor that makes contact between a stationary and a moving part (as of a motor) 4 : a quick light touch in passing

³**brush** *vb* 1 : to treat (as in cleaning or painting) with a brush : to remove with or as if with a brush; *also* : to dismiss in an offhand manner 3 : to touch gently in passing

⁴**brush** *n* : SKIRMISH ⟨a ~ with the law⟩
♦ **Synonyms** ENCOUNTER, RUN-IN

**brush fire** *n* 1 : a fire involving low-growing plants 2 : a minor conflict or crisis

**brush–off** \\'brəsh-,of\ *n* : a curt offhand dismissal

**brush up** *vb* : to renew one's skill

**brush·wood** \\'brəsh-,wud\ *n* 1 : small branches of wood esp. when cut 2 : a thicket of shrubs and small trees

**brusque** \\'brəsk\ *adj* [F *brusque*, fr. It *brusco*, fr. ML *bruscus* a plant with stiff twigs used for brooms] : CURT, BLUNT, ABRUPT ⟨a ~ answer⟩ ♦ **Synonyms** GRUFF, BLUFF, CRUSTY, SHORT — **brusque·ly** *adv*

**brus·sels sprout** \'brəs-əlz-\ *n, often cap B* : one of the edible green heads borne on the stalk of a plant closely related to the cabbage; *also, pl* : this plant

**bru·tal** \\'brü-t³l\ *adj* 1 : befitting a brute : UNFEELING, CRUEL 2 : HARSH, SEVERE ⟨~ weather⟩ 3 : unpleasantly accurate ⟨a ~ depiction of war⟩ — **bru·tal·i·ty** \brü-'ta-lə-tē\ *n*   **bru·tal·ly** *adv*

**bru·tal·ise** *Brit var of* BRUTALIZE

**bru·tal·ize** \\'brü-t³l-,īz\ *vb* -**ized**; -**iz·ing** 1 : to make brutal 2 : to treat brutally

¹**brute** \\'brüt\ *adj* [ME, fr. MF *brut* rough, fr. L *brutus* brutish, lit., heavy] 1 : of or relating to beasts 2 : BRUTAL 3 : UNREASONING; *also* : purely physical ⟨~ strength⟩

²**brute** *n* 1 : BEAST 1 2 : a brutal person

**brut·ish** \\'brü-tish\ *adj* 1 : BRUTE 1 2 : strongly sensual; *also* : showing little intelligence

**BS** *abbr* bachelor of science

**BSA** *abbr* Boy Scouts of America

**bskt** *abbr* basket

**Bt** *abbr* baronet

**btry** *abbr* battery

**Btu** *abbr* British thermal unit

**bu** *abbr* bushel

¹**bub·ble** \\'bə-bəl\ *n* 1 : a globule of gas in a liquid 2 : a thin film of liquid filled with gas 3 : something lacking firmness or solidity — **bub·bly** *adj*

²**bubble** *vb* **bub·bled**; **bub·bling** : to form, rise in, or give off bubbles

**bub·kes** \\'bəp-kəs, 'bup-\ *n pl* [Yiddish] : the least amount ⟨didn't win ~⟩

**bu·bo** \\'bü-bō, 'byü-\ *n, pl* **buboes** : an inflammatory swelling of a lymph gland

**bu·bon·ic plague** \bü-'bä-nik-, byü-\ *n* : plague caused by a bacterium transmitted to human beings by flea bites and marked esp. by chills and fever and by buboes usu. in the groin

**buc·ca·neer** \,bə-kə-'nir\ *n* : PIRATE

¹**buck** \\'bək\ *n, pl* **bucks** 1 *or pl* **buck** : a male animal (as a deer or antelope) 2 : DANDY 3 : DOLLAR

²**buck** *vb* 1 : to spring with an arching leap ⟨a ~ing horse⟩ 2 : to charge against something; *also* : to strive for advancement sometimes without regard to ethical behavior

**buck·board** \-,bord\ *n* : a 4-wheeled horse-drawn wagon with a floor of long springy boards

**buck·et** \\'bə-kət\ *n* 1 : PAIL 2 : an object resembling a bucket in collecting, scooping, or carrying something ⟨a tractor's ~⟩ — **buck·et·ful** *n*

**bucket list** *n* [from *kick the bucket* (to die)] : a list of things one has not done before but wants to do before dying

**bucket seat** *n* : a low separate seat for one person (as in an automobile)

**buck·eye** \\'bə-,kī\ *n* : any of various trees or shrubs related to the horse chestnut; *also* : the large nutlike seed of such a shrub or tree

**buck fever** *n* : nervous excitement of an inexperienced hunter at the sight of game

¹**buck·le** \\'bə-kəl\ *n* : a clasp (as on a belt) for two loose ends

²**buckle** *vb* **buck·led**; **buck·ling** 1 : to fasten with a buckle 2 : to apply oneself with vigor 3 : to crumple up : BEND, COLLAPSE

³**buckle** *n* : BEND, FOLD, KINK

**buck·ler** \\'bə-klər\ *n* : SHIELD

**buck·ram** \\'bə-krəm\ *n* : a coarse stiff cloth used esp. for binding books

**buck·saw** \\'bək-,so\ *n* : a saw set in a usu. H-shaped frame for sawing wood

**buck·shot** \\'bək-,shät\ *n* : lead shot that is from .24 to .33 inch (about 6.1 to 8.4 millimeters) in diameter

**buck·skin** \-,skin\ *n* 1 : the skin of a buck 2 : a soft usu. suede-finished leather — **buckskin** *adj*

**buck·tooth** \-'tüth\ *n* : a large protruding front tooth — **buck–toothed** \-'tütht\ *adj*

**buck·wheat** \-,hwēt\ *n* : either of two plants grown for their triangular seeds which are used as a cereal grain; *also* : these seeds

**bu·col·ic** \byü-'kä-lik\ *adj* [L *bucolicus*, fr. Gk *boukolikos*, fr. *boukolos* cowherd] : PASTORAL, RURAL ⟨a ~ countryside⟩

¹**bud** \\'bəd\ *n* 1 : an undeveloped plant shoot (as of a leaf or a flower); *also* : a

partly opened flower **2** : an asexual reproductive structure that detaches from the parent and forms a new individual **3** : something not yet fully developed ⟨nipped in the ∼⟩

²**bud** *vb* **bud·ded; bud·ding 1** : to form or put forth buds; *also* : to reproduce by asexual buds **2** : to be or develop like a bud **3** : to reproduce a desired variety (as of peach) by inserting a bud in a plant of a different variety

**Bud·dhism** \ˈbü-ˌdi-zəm, ˈbù-\ *n* : a religion of eastern and central Asia growing out of the teachings of Gautama Buddha — **Bud·dhist** \ˈbü-dist, ˈbù-\ *n or adj*

**bud·dy** \ˈbə-dē\ *n, pl* **buddies 1** : COMPANION; *also* : FRIEND **2** : FELLOW

**budge** \ˈbəj\ *vb* **budged; budg·ing** : MOVE, SHIFT; *also* : YIELD

**bud·ger·i·gar** \ˈbə-jə-rē-ˌgar\ *n* : a small brightly colored Australian parrot often kept as a pet

¹**bud·get** \ˈbə-jət\ *n* [ME *bowgette*, fr. MF *bougette*, dim. of *bouge* leather bag, fr. L *bulga*] **1** : STOCK, SUPPLY **2** : a financial report containing estimates of income and expenses; *also* : a plan for coordinating income and expenses **3** : the amount of money available for a particular use — **bud·get·ary** \ˈbə-jə-ˌter-ē\ *adj*

²**budget** *vb* **1** : to allow for in a budget **2** : to draw up a budget

³**budget** *adj* : INEXPENSIVE

**bud·gie** \ˈbə-jē\ *n* : BUDGERIGAR

¹**buff** \ˈbəf\ *n* **1** : a yellow to orange yellow color **2** : FAN, ENTHUSIAST

²**buff** *adj* : of the color buff

³**buff** *vb* : POLISH, SHINE

**buf·fa·lo** \ˈbə-fə-ˌlō\ *n, pl* **-lo** *or* **-loes** *also* **-los 1** : WATER BUFFALO **2** : a large shaggy-maned No. American wild bovine mammal that has short horns and heavy forequarters with a large muscular hump

**buffalo soldier** *n* : an African-American soldier serving in the western U.S. after the Civil War

¹**buf·fer** \ˈbə-fər\ *n* : something or someone that protects or shields (as from physical damage or a financial blow)

²**buffer** *n* : one that buffs

¹**buf·fet** \ˈbə-fət\ *n* : BLOW, SLAP

²**buffet** *vb* **1** : to strike with the hand; *also* : to pound repeatedly **2** : to struggle against or on ◆ **Synonyms** BEAT, BATTER, DRUB, PUMMEL, THRASH

³**buf·fet** \(ˌ)bə-ˈfā, bü-\ *n* **1** : SIDEBOARD **2** : a counter for refreshments; *also* : a meal at which people serve themselves informally

**buff leather** *n* : a strong supple oil-tanned leather

**buf·foon** \(ˌ)bə-ˈfün\ *n* [MF *bouffon*, fr. It *buffone*] : CLOWN **2** — **buf·foon·ery** \-ˈfü-nə-rē\ *n* — **buf·foon·ish** \-ˈfü-nish\ *adj*

¹**bug** \ˈbəg\ *n* **1** : an insect or other creeping or crawling invertebrate animal; *esp* : an insect pest (as the cockroach or bedbug **2** : any of an order of insects with sucking mouthparts and incomplete metamorphosis that includes many plant pests **3** : an unexpected flaw or imperfec-

tion ⟨a ∼ in a computer program⟩ **4** : a disease-producing germ; *also* : a disease caused by it **5** : a concealed listening device — **bug·gy** \ˈbə-gē\ *adj*

²**bug** *vb* **bugged; bug·ging 1** : BOTHER, ANNOY **2** : to plant a concealed microphone in

³**bug** *vb* **bugged; bug·ging** *of the eyes* : PROTRUDE, BULGE

**bug·a·boo** \ˈbə-gə-ˌbü\ *n, pl* **-boos** : BOGEY 1

**bug·bear** \ˈbəg-ˌber\ *n* : BOGEY 1; *also* : a source of dread

**bug·gy** \ˈbə-gē\ *n, pl* **buggies** : a light horse-drawn carriage; *also* : a carriage for a baby

**bu·gle** \ˈbyü-gəl\ *n* [ME, buffalo, instrument made of buffalo horn, bugle, fr. AF, fr. L *buculus*, dim. of *bos* head of cattle] : a valveless brass instrument resembling a trumpet and used esp. for military calls — **bu·gler** *n*

**bug out** *vb* **1** : to flee in panic **2** : to depart in a hurry

¹**build** \ˈbild\ *vb* **built** \ˈbilt\; **build·ing 1** : to form or have formed by ordering and uniting materials ⟨∼ a house⟩; *also* : to bring into being or develop ⟨∼ an argument on facts⟩ **3** : INCREASE, ENLARGE; *also* : ENHANCE **4** : to engage in building — **build·er** *n*

²**build** *n* : form or mode of structure; *esp* : PHYSIQUE

**build·ing** \ˈbil-diŋ\ *n* **1** : a usu. roofed and walled structure (as a house) for permanent use **2** : the art or business of constructing buildings

**build-up** \ˈbild-ˌəp\ *n* : the act or process of building up; *also* : something produced by this

**built-in** \ˈbilt-ˈin\ *adj* **1** : forming an integral part of a structure **2** : INHERENT

**bulb** \ˈbəlb\ *n* **1** : an underground resting stage of a plant (as a lily or an onion) consisting of a short stem base bearing one or more buds enclosed in overlapping leaves; *also* : a fleshy plant structure (as a tuber) resembling a bulb **2** : a plant having or growing from a bulb **3** : a rounded more or less bulb-shaped object or part (as for an electric lamp) — **bul·bous** \ˈbəl-bəs\ *adj*

¹**bulge** \ˈbəlj\ *vb* **bulged; bulg·ing** : to become or cause to become protuberant

²**bulge** *n* : a swelling projecting part

**bu·li·mia** \bü-ˈlē-mē-ə, byü-, -ˈli-\ *n* **1** : an abnormal and constant craving for food **2** : a serious eating disorder chiefly of females that is characterized by compulsive overeating usu. followed by self-induced vomiting or laxative or diuretic abuse — **bu·lim·ic** \-ˈlē-mik, -ˈli-\ *adj or n*

¹**bulk** \ˈbəlk\ *n* **1** : MAGNITUDE, VOLUME **2** : material that forms a mass in the intestine; *esp* : FIBER 2 **3** : a large mass **4** : the major portion

²**bulk** *vb* **1** : to cause to swell or bulge **2** : to appear as a factor : LOOM

**bulk·head** \ˈbəlk-ˌhed\ *n* **1** : a partition separating compartments **2** : a structure built to cover a shaft or a cellar stairway

**bulky** \'bəl-kē\ *adj* **bulk·i·er; -est** : having bulk; *esp* : being large and unwieldy

¹**bull** \'bùl\ *n* **1** : a male bovine animal; *also* : a usu. adult male of various large animals (as the moose, elephant, or whale) **2** : one who buys securities or commodities in expectation of a price increase — **bull·ish** *adj*

²**bull** *adj* **1** : of, relating to, or suggestive of a bull : MALE **2** : large of its kind ⟨a ~ lathe⟩

³**bull** *n* [ME *bulle,* fr. ML *bulla,* fr. L, bubble, amulet] **1** : a papal letter **2** : DECREE

⁴**bull** *n, slang* : NONSENSE

⁵**bull** *abbr* bulletin

¹**bull·dog** \'bùl-,dóg\ *n* : any of a breed of compact muscular short-haired dogs of English origin

²**bulldog** *vb* : to throw (a steer) by seizing the horns and twisting the neck

**bull·doze** \-,dōz\ *vb* **1** : to move, clear, or level with a tractor-driven machine (**bull·doz·er**) having a broad blade for pushing **2** : to force as if by using a bulldozer

**bul·let** \'bùl-ət\ *n* [MF *boulette* small ball & *boulet* missile, dims. of *boule* ball, fr. L *bulla* bubble] : a missile to be shot from a firearm

**bul·le·tin** \'bù-lə-t³n\ *n* **1** : a brief public report intended for immediate release on a matter of public interest **2** : a periodical publication (as of a college)

**bulletin board** *n* **1** : a board for posting notices **2** : a public forum on a computer network in which users write or read messages or download files

**bul·let·proof** \'bù-lət-,prüf\ *adj* **1** : impenetrable to bullets **2** : not subject to correction, alteration, or modification **3** : INVINCIBLE

**bull·fight** \'bùl-,fīt\ *n* : a spectacle in which people ceremonially fight with and usu. kill bulls in an arena — **bull·fight·er** *n*

**bull·frog** \-,fróg, -,fräg\ *n* : a large deep-voiced frog

**bull·head** \-,hed\ *n* : any of several common large-headed freshwater catfishes of the U.S.

**bull·head·ed** \-'he-dəd\ *adj* : stupidly stubborn : HEADSTRONG

**bul·lion** \'bùl-yən\ *n* : gold or silver esp. in bars or ingots

**bull market** *n* : a market in which securities or commodities are persistently rising in value

**bull·ock** \'bù-lək\ *n* : a young bull; *also* : STEER

**bull pen** *n* : a place on a baseball field where pitchers warm up; *also* : the relief pitchers of a baseball team

**bull session** *n* : an informal discussion

**bull's-eye** \'bùlz-,ī\ *n, pl* **bull's-eyes** : the center of a target; *also* : a shot that hits the bull's-eye

¹**bul·ly** \'bù-lē\ *n, pl* **bullies** : a person habitually cruel to others who are weaker

²**bully** *adj* : EXCELLENT, FIRST-RATE — often used interjectionally ⟨~ for you⟩

³**bully** *vb* **bul·lied; bul·ly·ing** : to behave as a bully toward : DOMINEER ♦ *Syn-*

*onyms* BROWBEAT, INTIMIDATE, HECTOR

**bul·rush** \'bùl-,rəsh\ *n* : any of several large rushes or sedges of wetlands

**bul·wark** \'bùl-(,)wərk, -,wòrk; 'bəl-(,)wərk\ *n* **1** : a wall-like defensive structure **2** : a strong support or protection

¹**bum** \'bəm\ *adj* **1** : of poor quality ⟨~ advice⟩ **2** : disabled by damage or injury ⟨a ~ knee⟩

²**bum** *vb* **bummed; bum·ming 1** : to spend time unemployed and wandering; *also* : LOAF **2** : to obtain by begging

³**bum** *n* **1** : LOAFER **2** : one whose time is devoted to a recreational activity ⟨a ski ~⟩ **3** : TRAMP 1

**bum·ble** \'bəm-bəl\ *vb* **bum·bled; bumbling 1** : to speak in a stuttering and faltering manner **2** : to proceed unsteadily **3** : BUNGLE

**bum·ble·bee** \'bəm-bəl-,bē\ *n* : any of numerous large hairy social bees

**bum·mer** \'bə-mər\ *n* **1** : an unpleasant experience **2** : FAILURE

¹**bump** \'bəmp\ *n* **1** : a local bulge; *esp* : a swelling of tissue **2** : a sudden forceful blow or impact — **bumpy** *adj*

²**bump** *vb* **1** : to strike or knock forcibly; *also* : to move by or as if by bumping **2** : to collide with

¹**bum·per** \'bəm-pər\ *n* **1** : a cup or glass filled to the brim **2** : something unusually large — **bumper** *adj*

²**bump·er** \'bəm-pər\ *n* : a device for absorbing shock or preventing damage; *esp* : a usu. metal bar at either end of an automobile

**bump·kin** \'bəmp-kən\ *n* : an awkward and unsophisticated country person

**bump·tious** \'bəmp-shəs\ *adj* : obtusely and often noisily self-assertive

**bun** \'bən\ *n* : a sweet or plain round roll

¹**bunch** \'bənch\ *n* **1** : SWELLING **2** : CLUSTER, GROUP — **bunchy** *adj*

²**bunch** *vb* : to form into a group or bunch

**bun·co** *or* **bun·ko** \'bəŋ-kō\ *n, pl* **buncos** *or* **bunkos** : a swindling scheme — **bunco** *vb*

¹**bun·dle** \'bən-d³l\ *n* **1** : several items bunched and fastened together; *also* : something wrapped for carrying **2** : a considerable amount : LOT **3** : a small band of mostly parallel nerve or muscle fibers **4** : a package offering related products or services at a single price

²**bundle** *vb* **bun·dled; bun·dling** : to gather or tie in a bundle

**bundling** *n* : a former custom of a courting couple's occupying the same bed without undressing

**bung** \'bəŋ\ *n* : the stopper in the bunghole of a cask

**bun·ga·low** \'bəŋ-gə-,lō\ *n* [Hindi & Urdu *banglā,* lit., (house) in the Bengal style] : a one-storied house with a low-pitched roof

**bun·gee cord** \'bən-jē-\ *n* : a long elastic cord used esp. as a fastening or shock-absorbing device

**bungee jump** *vb* : to jump from a height while attached to a bungee cord — **bungee jumper** *n*

**bung·hole** \'bəŋ-ˌhōl\ *n* : a hole for emptying or filling a cask

**bun·gle** \'bəŋ-gəl\ *vb* **bun·gled; bun·gling** : to do badly : BOTCH — **bungle** *n* — **bun·gler** *n*

**bun·ion** \'bən-yən\ *n* : an inflamed swelling of the first joint of the big toe

¹**bunk** \'bəŋk\ *n* : BED; *esp* : a built-in bed that is often one of a tier

²**bunk** *n* : BUNKUM, NONSENSE

**bunk bed** *n* : one of two single beds usu. placed one above the other

**bun·ker** \'bəŋ-kər\ *n* **1** : a bin or compartment for storage (as for coal on a ship) **2** : a protective embankment or dugout **3** : a sand trap or embankment constituting a hazard on a golf course

**bun·kum** *or* **bun·combe** \'bəŋ-kəm\ *n* [*Buncombe* County, N.C.; fr. a remark made by its congressman, who defended an irrelevant speech by claiming that he was speaking to Buncombe] : insincere or foolish talk

**bun·ny** \'bə-nē\ *n, pl* **-nies** : RABBIT

**bunny slope** *n* : a gentle incline used by novice skiers

**Bun·sen burner** \'bən-sən-\ *n* : a gas burner usu. consisting of a straight tube with air holes at the bottom

¹**bunt** \'bənt\ *vb* **1** : ¹BUTT **2** : to push or tap a baseball lightly without swinging the bat

²**bunt** *n* : an act or instance of bunting; *also* : a bunted ball

¹**bun·ting** \'bən-tiŋ\ *n* : any of numerous small stout-billed finches

²**bunting** *n* : a thin fabric used esp. for flags; *also* : FLAGS

¹**buoy** \'bü-ē, 'bȯi\ *n* **1** : a floating object anchored in water to mark something (as a channel) **2** : a float consisting of a ring of buoyant material to support a person who has fallen into the water

²**buoy** *vb* **1** : to mark by a buoy **2** : to keep afloat **3** : to raise the spirits of

**buoy·an·cy** \'bȯi-ən-sē, 'bü-yən-\ *n* **1** : the tendency of a body to float or rise when submerged in a fluid **2** : the power of a fluid to exert an upward force on a body placed in it **3** : resilience of spirit — **buoy·ant** \-ənt, -yənt\ *adj*

¹**bur** *var of* BURR

²**bur** *abbr* bureau

**burbs** \'bərbz\ *n pl* : SUBURBS

¹**bur·den** \'bər-dᵊn\ *n* **1** : LOAD; *also* : CARE, RESPONSIBILITY **2** : something oppressive : ENCUMBRANCE ⟨the tax ∼⟩ **3** : CARGO; *also* : capacity for cargo

²**burden** *vb* : LOAD, OPPRESS ⟨∼ed with guilt⟩ — **bur·den·some** \-səm\ *adj*

³**burden** *n* **1** : REFRAIN, CHORUS **2** : a main theme or idea : GIST

**bur·dock** \'bər-ˌdäk\ *n* : any of a genus of coarse composite herbs with globe-shaped flower heads surrounded by prickly bracts

**bu·reau** \'byúr-ō\ *n, pl* **bureaus** *also* **bu·reaux** \-ōz\ [F, desk, cloth covering for desks, fr. OF *burel* woolen cloth, ultim. fr. L *burra* shaggy cloth] **1** : a chest of drawers **2** : an administrative unit (as of a government department) **3** : a branch of a publication or wire service in an important news center

**bu·reau·cra·cy** \byú-'rä-krə-sē\ *n, pl* **-cies 1** : a body of appointive government officials **2** : government marked by specialization of functions under fixed rules and a hierarchy of authority; *also* : an unwieldy administrative system burdened with excessive complexity and lack of flexibility — **bu·reau·crat** \'byúr-ə-ˌkrat\ *n* — **bu·reau·crat·ic** \ˌbyúr-ə-'kra-tik\ *adj*

**bur·geon** \'bər-jən\ *vb* : to put forth fresh growth (as from buds) : grow vigorously : FLOURISH

**burgh** \'bər-ō\ *n* : a Scottish town

**bur·gher** \'bər-gər\ *n* **1** : TOWNSMAN **2** : a prosperous solid citizen

**bur·glary** \'bər-glə-rē\ *n, pl* **-glar·ies** : forcible entry into a building esp. at night with the intent to commit a crime (as theft) — **bur·glar** \-glər\ *n* — **bur·glar·ize** \'bər-glə-ˌrīz\ *vb*

**bur·gle** \'bər-gəl\ *vb* **bur·gled; bur·gling** : to commit burglary on

**bur·go·mas·ter** \'bər-gə-ˌmas-tər\ *n* : the chief magistrate of a town in some European countries

**bur·gun·dy** \'bər-gən-dē\ *n, pl* **-dies** *often cap* **1** : a red or white table wine from the Burgundy region of France **2** : a blended red wine

**buri·al** \'ber-ē-əl\ *n* : the act or process of burying

**bur·ka** *or* **bur·qa** \'búr-kə\ *n* : a loose garment that covers the face and body and is worn in public by certain Muslim women

**burl** \'bərl\ *n* : a hard woody often flattened hemispherical outgrowth on a tree

**bur·lap** \'bər-ˌlap\ *n* : a coarse fabric usu. of jute or hemp used esp. for bags

¹**bur·lesque** \(ˌ)bər-'lesk\ *n* [*burlesque*, adj., comic, droll, fr. F, fr. It *burlesco*, fr. *burla* joke, fr. Sp] **1** : a witty or derisive literary or dramatic imitative work **2** : broadly humorous theatrical entertainment consisting of several items (as songs, skits, or dances)

²**burlesque** *vb* **bur·lesqued; bur·lesqu·ing** : to make ludicrous by burlesque ♦ *Synonyms* CARICATURE, PARODY, TRAVESTY

**bur·ly** \'bər-lē\ *adj* **bur·li·er; -est** : strongly and heavily built : HUSKY ♦ *Synonyms* MUSCULAR, BRAWNY, BEEFY, HEFTY

¹**burn** \'bərn\ *vb* **burned** \'bərnd, 'bərnt\ *or* **burnt** \'bərnt\; **burn·ing 1** : to be on fire **2** : to feel or look as if on fire **3** : to alter or become altered by or as if by the action of fire or heat **4** : to use as fuel ⟨∼ coal⟩; *also* : to destroy by fire ⟨∼ trash⟩ **5** : to cause or make by fire ⟨∼ a hole⟩; *also* : to affect as if by heat **6** : to record digital data or music on (an optical disk) using a laser ⟨∼ a CD⟩

²**burn** *n* : an injury or effect produced by or as if by burning

**burn·er** \'bər-nər\ *n* : the part of a fuel-burning or heat-producing device where the flame or heat is produced

**bur·nish** \'bər-nish\ *vb* : to make shiny

esp. by rubbing : POLISH — **bur·nish·er** *n* — **bur·nish·ing** *adj or n*

**bur·noose** *or* **bur·nous** \(ˌ)bər-ˈnüs\ *n* : a hooded cloak worn esp. by Arabs

**burn·out** \ˈbərn-ˌau̇t\ *n* **1** : the cessation of operation of a jet or rocket engine **2** : exhaustion of one's physical or emotional strength; *also* : a person suffering from burnout

**burp** \ˈbərp\ *n* : an act of belching — **burp** *vb*

**burp gun** *n* : a small submachine gun

**burr** \ˈbər\ *n* **1** *usu* **bur** : a rough or prickly envelope of a fruit; *also* : a plant that bears burs **2** : roughness left in cutting or shaping metal **3** : a trilled \r\ as used by some speakers in northern England and Scotland **4** : WHIR — **bur·ry** *adj*

**bur·ri·to** \bə-ˈrē-tō\ *n* [AmerSp, fr. Sp, little donkey, dim. of *burro*] : a flour tortilla rolled around a filling and baked

**bur·ro** \ˈbər-ō, ˈbu̇r-\ *n, pl* **burros** [Sp] : a usu. small donkey

¹**bur·row** \ˈbər-ō\ *n* : a hole in the ground made by an animal (as a rabbit)

²**burrow** *vb* **1** : to form by tunneling; *also* : to make a burrow **2** : to progress by or as if by digging — **bur·row·er** *n*

**bur·sar** \ˈbər-sər\ *n* : a treasurer esp. of a college

**bur·si·tis** \(ˌ)bər-ˈsī-təs\ *n* : inflammation of the serous sac (**bur·sa** \ˈbər-sə\) of a joint (as the elbow or shoulder)

¹**burst** \ˈbərst\ *vb* **burst** *or* **burst·ed**; **burst·ing** **1** : to fly apart or into pieces **2** : to show one's feelings suddenly; *also* : PLUNGE ⟨~ into song⟩ **3** : to enter or emerge suddenly : SPRING **4** : to be filled to the breaking point

²**burst** *n* **1** : a sudden outbreak : SPURT : EXPLOSION **3** : result of bursting

**bury** \ˈber-ē\ *vb* **bur·ied**; **bury·ing 1** : to deposit in the earth; *also* : to inter with funeral ceremonies **2** : CONCEAL, HIDE **3** : SUBMERGE, ENGROSS — usu. used with *in* ⟨*buried* himself in work⟩

¹**bus** \ˈbəs\ *n, pl* **bus·es** *also* **bus·ses** [short for *omnibus*, fr. F, fr. L, for all, dat. pl. of *omnis* all] : a large motor vehicle for carrying passengers

²**bus** *vb* **bused** *or* **bussed**; **bus·ing** *or* **bus·sing 1** : to travel or transport by bus **2** : to work as a busboy

³**bus** *abbr* business

**bus·boy** \ˈbəs-ˌbȯi\ *n* : a waiter's helper

**bus·by** \ˈbəz-bē\ *n, pl* **busbies** : a military full-dress fur hat

**bush** \ˈbu̇sh\ *n* **1** : SHRUB **2** : rough uncleared country **3** : a thick tuft ⟨a ~ of hair⟩ — **bushy** *adj*

**bushed** \ˈbu̇sht\ *adj* : TIRED, EXHAUSTED

**bush·el** \ˈbu̇-shəl\ *n* — see WEIGHT table

**bush·ing** \ˈbu̇-shiŋ\ *n* : a usu. removable cylindrical lining for an opening of a mechanical part to limit the size of the opening, resist wear, or serve as a guide

**bush·mas·ter** \ˈbu̇sh-ˌmas-tər\ *n* : a large venomous pit viper of Central and So. America

**bush·whack** \-ˌhwak\ *vb* **1** : AMBUSH **2** : to clear a path through esp. by chopping

down bushes and branches — **bush·whack·er** *n*

**busi·ness** \ˈbiz-nəs, -nəz\ *n* **1** : OCCUPATION; *also* : TASK, MISSION **2** : a commercial or industrial enterprise; *also* : TRADE ⟨~ is good⟩ **3** : AFFAIR, MATTER **4** : personal concern

**busi·ness·man** \-ˌman\ *n* : a man engaged in business esp. as an executive

**busi·ness·per·son** \-ˌpər-sᵊn\ *n* : a businessman or businesswoman

**busi·ness·wom·an** \-ˌwu̇-mən\ *n* : a woman engaged in business esp. as an executive

**bus·kin** \ˈbəs-kən\ *n* **1** : a laced boot reaching halfway to the knee **2** : tragic drama

**buss** \ˈbəs\ *n* : KISS — **buss** *vb*

¹**bust** \ˈbəst\ *n* [F *buste*, fr. It *busto*, fr. L *bustum* tomb] **1** : sculpture representing the upper part of the human figure **2** : the part of the human torso between the neck and the waist; *esp* : the breasts of a woman

²**bust** *vb* **bust·ed** *also* **bust**; **bust·ing 1** : BREAK, SMASH; *also* : BURST **2** : to ruin financially **3** : TAME **4** : DEMOTE **5** *slang* : ARREST; *also* : RAID

³**bust** *n* **1** : a drinking session **2** : a complete failure : FLOP **3** : a business depression **4** : PUNCH, SOCK **5** *slang* : a police raid; *also* : ARREST

¹**bus·tle** \ˈbə-səl\ *vb* **bus·tled**; **bus·tling** : to move or work in a brisk busy manner

²**bustle** *n* : briskly energetic activity

³**bustle** *n* : a pad or frame worn to support the fullness at the back of a woman's skirt

¹**busy** \ˈbi-zē\ *adj* **busi·er; -est 1** : engaged in action : not idle **2** : being in use ⟨~ telephones⟩ **3** : full of activity ⟨~ streets⟩ **4** : full of distracting detail ⟨a ~ design⟩ — **busi·ly** \ˈbi-zə-lē\ *adv*

²**busy** *vb* **bus·ied**; **busy·ing** : to make or keep busy : OCCUPY

**busy·body** \ˈbi-zē-ˌbä-dē\ *n* : MEDDLER

**busy·work** \-ˌwərk\ *n* : work that appears productive but only keeps one occupied

¹**but** \ˈbət\ *conj* **1** : except for the fact ⟨would have protested ~ that he was afraid⟩ **2** : THAT ⟨there's no doubt ~ he won⟩ **3** : without the certainty that ⟨never rains ~ it pours⟩ **4** : on the contrary ⟨not one, ~ two job offers⟩ **5** : YET ⟨poor ~ proud⟩ **6** : with the exception of ⟨none ~ the strongest attempt it⟩

²**but** *prep* : other than : EXCEPT ⟨this letter is nothing ~ an insult⟩; *also* : with the exception of ⟨no one here ~ me⟩

**bu·tane** \ˈbyü-ˌtān\ *n* : either of two gaseous hydrocarbons used as a fuel

**butch** \ˈbu̇ch\ *adj* : notably masculine in appearance or manner

¹**butch·er** \ˈbu̇-chər\ *n* [ME *bocher*, fr. AF, fr. *buc* he-goat] **1** : one who slaughters animals or dresses their flesh; *also* : a dealer in meat **2** : one that kills brutally or needlessly **3** : one that botches — **butch·ery** \-chə-rē\ *n*

²**butcher** *vb* **1** : to slaughter and dress for meat ⟨~ hogs⟩ **2** : to kill barbarously **3**

: BOTCH ⟨the band ~ed my favorite song⟩

**but·ler** \'bət-lər\ n [ME buteler, fr. AF butiller, † fr. OF botele bottle] : the chief male servant of a household

¹**butt** \'bət\ vb : to strike with the head or horns

²**butt** n : a blow or thrust with the head or horns

³**butt** n : a large cask

⁴**butt** n 1 : TARGET 2 : an object of abuse or ridicule ⟨the ~ of everyone's jokes⟩

⁵**butt** n 1 : BUTTOCKS 2 : a large, thicker, or bottom end of something

⁶**butt** vb 1 : ABUT — used with on or against 2 : to place or join edge to edge without overlapping

**butte** \'byüt\ n : an isolated steep hill

¹**but·ter** \'bə-tər\ n [ME, fr. OE butere, fr. L butyrum butter, fr. Gk boutyron, fr. bous cow + tyros cheese] 1 : a solid edible emulsion of fat obtained from cream by churning 2 : a substance resembling butter — **but·tery** adj

²**butter** vb : to spread with or as if with butter ⟨~ed toast⟩

**but·ter-and-eggs** \,bə-tər-ᵊn-'egz\ n sing or pl : a common perennial herb related to the snapdragon that has showy yellow and orange flowers

**butter bean** n 1 : LIMA BEAN 2 : WAX BEAN 3 : a green shell bean

**but·ter·cream** \'bə-tər-,krēm\ n : a sweet butter-based mixture used esp. as a filling or frosting

**but·ter·cup** \'bə-tər-,kəp\ n : any of a genus of herbs having usu. yellow flowers with five petals and sepals

**but·ter·fat** \-,fat\ n : the natural fat of milk and chief constituent of butter

**but·ter·fin·gered** \-,fiŋ-gərd\ adj : likely to let things fall or slip through the fingers — **but·ter·fin·gers** \-gərz\ n sing or pl

**but·ter·fly** \-,flī\ n : any of a group of slender day-flying insects with broad often brightly-colored wings

**but·ter·milk** \-,milk\ n : the liquid remaining after butter is churned

**but·ter·nut** \-,nət\ n : the sweet egg-shaped nut of an American tree related to the walnut; also : this tree

**butternut squash** n : a smooth buff-colored cylindrical winter squash

**but·ter·scotch** \-,skäch\ n : a candy made from brown sugar, corn syrup, and water; also : the flavor of such candy

**but·tock** \'bə-tək\ n 1 : the back of a hip that forms one of the fleshy parts on which a person sits 2 pl : the seat of the body : RUMP

¹**but·ton** \'bə-tᵊn\ n 1 : a small knob secured to an article (as of clothing) and used as a fastener by passing it through a buttonhole or loop 2 : something that resembles a button 3 : PUSH BUTTON 4 : a hidden sensitivity that can be manipulated to produce a desired response 5 : a usu. box-shaped computer icon that initiates a software function

²**button** vb : to close or fasten with or as if with buttons

¹**but·ton·hole** \'bə-tᵊn-,hōl\ n : a slit or loop for a button to pass through

²**buttonhole** vb : to detain in conversation by or as if by holding on to the outer garments of

¹**but·tress** \'bə-trəs\ n [ME butres, fr. AF (arche) boteraz thrusting (arch), ultim. fr. buter to thrust] 1 : a projecting structure to support a wall 2 : PROP, SUPPORT

²**buttress** vb : PROP, SUPPORT

**bu·tut** \bü-'tüt\ n, pl bututs or butut — see dalasi at MONEY table

**bux·om** \'bək-səm\ adj : healthily plump; esp : full-bosomed

¹**buy** \'bī\ vb bought \'bȯt\; buy·ing 1 : to obtain for a price : PURCHASE; also : BRIBE 2 : to accept as true — **buy·er** n

²**buy** n 1 : PURCHASE 1, 2 2 : an exceptional value : BARGAIN

¹**buzz** \'bəz\ vb 1 : to make a buzz 2 : to fly fast and close to

²**buzz** n 1 : a low humming sound 2 : RUMOR, GOSSIP

**buz·zard** \'bə-zərd\ n : any of various usu. large birds of prey and esp. the turkey vulture

**buzz·er** \'bə-zər\ n : a device that signals with a buzzing sound

**buzz saw** n : CIRCULAR SAW

**buzz·word** \'bəz-,wərd\ n : a ↑voguish word or phrase often from technical jargon

**BVM** abbr Blessed Virgin Mary

**BWI** abbr British West Indies

**bx** abbr box

**BX** abbr base exchange

¹**by** \'bī\ prep 1 : NEAR ⟨stood ~ the window⟩ 2 : through or through the medium of : VIA ⟨left ~ the door⟩ 3 : PAST ⟨drove ~ the house⟩ 4 : DURING, AT ⟨studied ~ night⟩ 5 : no later than ⟨get here ~ 3 p.m.⟩ 6 : through the means or direct agency of ⟨~ force⟩ 7 : in conformity with; also : ACCORDING TO ⟨did it ~ the book⟩ 8 : with respect to ⟨a doctor ~ profession⟩ 9 : to the amount or extent of ⟨won ~ a nose⟩ 10 — used to express relationship in multiplication, in division, and in measurements ⟨divide a ~ b⟩ ⟨multiply ~ 6⟩ ⟨15 feet ~ 20 feet⟩

²**by** \'bī\ adv 1 : near at hand; also : IN ⟨stop ~⟩ 2 : PAST ⟨saw him go ~⟩ 3 : ASIDE, APART ⟨put some money ~⟩

**bye** \'bī\ n : a position of a participant in a tournament who advances to the next round without playing

**by-elec·tion** also **bye–election** \'bī-ə-,lek-shən\ n : a special election held between regular elections in order to fill a vacancy

**by·gone** \'bī-,gȯn\ adj : gone by : PAST — **bygone** n

**by·law** also **bye·law** \'bī-,lȯ\ n : a rule adopted by an organization for managing its internal affairs

**by–line** \'bī-,līn\ n : a line at the beginning of a news story or magazine article giving the writer's name

**BYO** abbr bring your own

**BYOB** abbr bring your own beer; bring your own booze; bring your own bottle

¹**by·pass** \'bī-,pas\ n : a passage to one

side or around a blocked or congested area; *also* : a surgical procedure establishing this ⟨a coronary ∼⟩

²**bypass** *vb* : to avoid by means of a bypass

**by·path** \-ˌpath, -ˌpäth\ *n* : BYWAY

**by·play** \ˈbī-ˌplā\ *n* : action engaged in on the side (as of a stage) while the main action proceeds

**by–prod·uct** \-ˌprä-(ˌ)dəkt\ *n* : a sometimes unexpected product or result produced in addition to the main product or result

**by·stand·er** \-ˌsfan-dər\ *n* : one present but not participating ♦ *Synonyms* ON-LOOKER, WITNESS, SPECTATOR, EYEWITNESS

**byte** \ˈbīt\ *n* : a unit of computer information consisting of a group of 8 bits

**by·way** \ˈbī-ˌwā\ *n* 1 : a little-traveled side road 2 : a secondary aspect

**by·word** \-ˌwərd\ *n* 1 : PROVERB 2 : one that is noteworthy or notorious

**Byz·an·tine** \ˈbiz-ᵊn-ˌtēn, ˈbī-, -ˌtīn; bə-ˈzan-, bī-\ *adj* 1 : of, relating to, or characteristic of the ancient city of Byzantium or the Byzantine Empire 2 *often not cap* : intricately involved and often devious

¹**c** \ˈsē\ *n, pl* **c's** *or* **cs** \ˈsēz\ *often cap* 1 : the 3d letter of the English alphabet 2 *slang* : a sum of $100 3 : a grade rating a student's work as fair

²**c** *abbr, often cap* 1 calorie 2 carat 3 Celsius 4 cent 5 centigrade 6 centimeter 7 century 8 chapter 9 circa 10 cocaine 11 copyright

**C** *symbol* carbon

**ca** *abbr* circa

**Ca** *symbol* calcium

**CA** *abbr* 1 California 2 chartered accountant 3 chief accountant 4 chronological age

**cab** \ˈkab\ *n* 1 : a light closed horse-drawn carriage 2 : TAXICAB 3 : the covered compartment for the engineer and controls of a locomotive; *also* : a similar compartment (as on a truck) — **cab** *vb*

**CAB** *abbr* Civil Aeronautics Board

**ca·bal** \kə-ˈbäl, -ˈbal\ *n* [F *cabale*, fr. ML *cabbala* cabala, fr. Heb *qabbālāh*, lit., received (lore)] 1 : a secret group of plotters or political conspirators 2 : CLUB, GROUP ⟨a ∼ of artists⟩

**cabala** *var of* KABBALAH

**ca·bana** \kə-ˈban-yə, -ˈba-nə\ *n* : a shelter at a beach or swimming pool

**cab·a·ret** \ˌka-bə-ˈrā\ *n* : NIGHTCLUB

**cab·bage** \ˈka-bij\ *n* [ME *caboche*, fr. MF dial., lit., head, noggin] : a vegetable related to the mustard with a dense head of leaves

**cab·bie** *or* **cab·by** \ˈka-bē\ *n, pl* **cabbies** : a driver of a cab

**cab·er·net sau·vi·gnon** \ˌka-bər-ˈnā-sō-vē-ˈnyōⁿ\ *n* : a dry red wine made from a single variety of black grape

**cab·in** \ˈka-bən\ *n* 1 : a private room on a ship; *also* : a compartment below deck on a boat for passengers or crew 2 : an aircraft or spacecraft compartment for passengers, crew, or cargo 3 : a small simple one-story house

**cabin boy** *n* : a boy working as a servant on a ship

**cabin class** *n* : a class of accommodations on a passenger ship superior to tourist class and inferior to first class

**cabin cruiser** *n* : CRUISER 3

**cab·i·net** \ˈkab-nit\ *n* 1 : a case or cupboard for holding or displaying articles 2 : the advisory council of a head of state (as a president or sovereign)

**cab·i·net·mak·er** \-ˌmā-kər\ *n* : a woodworker who makes fine furniture — **cab·i·net·mak·ing** *n*

**cab·i·net·work** \-ˌwərk\ *n* : the finished work of a cabinetmaker

¹**ca·ble** \ˈkā-bəl\ *n* 1 : a very strong rope, wire, or chain 2 : a bundle of insulated wires usu. twisted around a central core 3 : CABLEGRAM 4 : CABLE TELEVISION

²**cable** *vb* **ca·bled; ca·bling** : to telegraph by cable

**cable car** *n* : a vehicle moved by an endless cable

**ca·ble·cast** \ˈkā-bəl-ˌkast\ *n* : a cable television transmission — **cablecast** *vb*

**ca·ble·gram** \ˈkā-bəl-ˌgram\ *n* : a message sent by a submarine telegraph cable

**cable modem** *n* : a modem for connecting a computer to a network over a cable television line

**cable television** *n* : a system of television reception in which signals from distant stations are sent by cable to the receivers of paying subscribers

**cab·o·chon** \ˈka-bə-ˌshän\ *n* : a gem or bead cut in convex form and highly polished but not given facets; *also* : this style of cutting — **cabochon** *adv*

**ca·boose** \kə-ˈbüs\ *n* : a car usu. at the rear of a freight train for the use of the train crew and railroad workers

**cab·ri·o·let** \ˌka-brē-ə-ˈlā\ *n* [F] 1 : a light 2-wheeled one-horse carriage 2 : a convertible coupe

**cab·stand** \ˈkab-ˌstand\ *n* : a place where cabs wait for passengers

**ca·cao** \kə-ˈkaù, -ˈkā-ō\ *n, pl* **cacaos** [Sp, fr. Nahuatl *cacahuatl*] : a So. American tree whose seeds (**cacao beans**) are the source of cocoa and chocolate; *also* : its dried fatty seeds

**cac·cia·to·re** \ˌkä-chə-ˈtōr-ē\ *adj* [It] : cooked with tomatoes and herbs ⟨chicken ∼⟩

**cache** \'kash\ *n* [F] : a hiding place esp. for preserving provisions; *also* : something hidden or stored in a cache — **cache** *vb*

**ca·chet** \ka-'shā\ *n* [F] **1** : a seal used esp. as a mark of official approval **2** : a feature or quality conferring prestige; *also* : PRESTIGE **3** : a design, inscription, or advertisement printed or stamped on mail

**cack·le** \'ka-kəl\ *vb* **cack·led; cack·ling** **1** : to make the sharp broken cry characteristic of a hen **2** : to laugh or chatter noisily — **cackle** *n* — **cack·ler** *n*

**ca·coph·o·ny** \ka-'kä-fə-nē\ *n, pl* **-nies** : harsh or discordant sound — **ca·coph·o·nous** \-nəs\ *adj*

**cac·tus** \'kak-təs\ *n, pl* **cac·ti** \-ˌtī\ *or* **cac·tus·es** *also* **cactus** : any of a large family of drought-resistant flowering plants with succulent stems and with leaves replaced by scales or prickles

**cad** \'kad\ *n* : a man who deliberately disregards another's feelings — **cad·dish** \'ka-dish\ *adj* — **cad·dish·ly** *adv* — **cad·dish·ness** *n*

**ca·dav·er** \kə-'da-vər\ *n* : a dead body

**ca·dav·er·ous** \kə-'da-və-rəs\ *adj* : suggesting a corpse esp. in gauntness or pallor ♦ *Synonyms* WASTED, EMACIATED, GAUNT — **ca·dav·er·ous·ly** *adv*

**cad·die** *or* **cad·dy** \'ka-dē\ *n, pl* **caddies** [Sc, errand boy, modif. of F *cadet* military cadet] : a person who assists a golfer esp. by carrying the clubs — **caddie** *or* **caddy** *vb*

**cad·dy** \'ka-dē\ *n, pl* **caddies** [Malay *kati* a unit of weight] : a small box, can, or chest; *esp* : one to keep tea in

**ca·dence** \'kād-ᵊns\ *n* : the measure or beat of a rhythmical flow : RHYTHM — **ca·denced** \-ᵊnst\ *adj*

**ca·den·za** \kə-'den-zə\ *n* [It] : a brilliant sometimes improvised passage usu. toward the close of a musical composition

**ca·det** \kə-'det\ *n* [F, fr. Occitan (Gascony) *capdet* chief, fr. L *capitellum*, fr. L *caput* head] **1** : a younger son or brother **2** : a student in a service academy

**Ca·dette** \kə-'det\ *n* : a member of a Girl Scout program for girls in sixth through ninth grades

**cadge** \'kaj\ *vb* **cadged; cadg·ing** : SPONGE, BEG ⟨~ a free meal⟩ — **cadg·er** *n*

**cad·mi·um** \'kad-mē-əm\ *n* : a bluish-white metallic chemical element used esp. in protective platings

**cad·re** \'ka-ˌdrā, 'kä-, -drē\ *n* [F] **1** : FRAMEWORK **2** : a central unit esp. of trained personnel able to assume control and train others **3** : a group of indoctrinated leaders active in promoting the interests of a revolutionary party

**ca·du·ceus** \kə-'dü-sē-əs, -'dyü-, -shəs\ *n, pl* **-cei** \-sē-ˌī\ [L] **1** : the staff of a herald; *esp* : æ representation of a staff with two entwined snakes and two wings at the top **2** : an insignia bearing a caduceus and symbolizing a physician

**cae·cum** *var of* CECUM

**Cae·sar** \'sē-zər\ *n* **1** : any of the Roman emperors succeeding Augustus Caesar — used as a title **2** *often not cap* : a powerful ruler : AUTOCRAT, DICTATOR; *also* : the civil or temporal power

**caesarean** *also* **caesarian** *var of* CESAREAN

**cae·si·um** *chiefly Brit var of* CESIUM

**cae·su·ra** \si-'zhür-ə\ *n, pl* **-suras** *or* **-su·rae** \-'zhür-(ˌ)ē\ : a break in the flow of sound usu. in the middle of a line of verse

**ca·fé** \ka-'fā\ *n* [F, lit., coffee] **1** : RESTAURANT **2** : BARROOM **3** : NIGHTCLUB

**ca·fé au lait** \(ˌ)ka-ˌfā-ō-'lā\ *n* : coffee with hot milk in about equal parts

**caf·e·te·ria** \ˌka-fə-'tir-ē-ə\ *n* [AmerSp *cafetería* coffeehouse] : a restaurant in which the customers serve themselves or are served at a counter

**caf·fein·at·ed** \'ka-fə-ˌnā-təd\ *adj* **1** : stimulated by or as if by caffeine **2** : containing caffeine

**caf·feine** \ka-'fēn, 'ka-ˌfēn\ *n* : a stimulating alkaloid found esp. in coffee and tea

**caf·fe lat·te** \ˌka-fā-'lä-tā\ *n* [It] : espresso mixed with hot or steamed milk

**caf·tan** \kaf-'tan, 'kaf-ˌtan\ *n* [Russ *kaftan*, fr. Turk. fr. Pers *qaftān*] : an ankle-length garment with long sleeves worn in countries of the eastern Mediterranean

**¹cage** \'kāj\ *n* **1** : an openwork enclosure for confining an animal **2** : something resembling a cage

**²cage** *vb* **caged; cag·ing** : to put or keep in or as if in a cage

**ca·gey** *also* **ca·gy** \'kā-jē\ *adj* **ca·gi·er; -est** : wary of being trapped or deceived : SHREWD ⟨a ~ dealer⟩ — **ca·gi·ly** \-jə-lē\ *adv* — **ca·gi·ness** \-jē-nəs\ *n*

**CAGS** *abbr* Certificate of Advanced Graduate Study

**ca·hoot** \kə-'hüt\ *n* : PARTNERSHIP, LEAGUE — usu. used in pl. ⟨officials in ~s with the underworld⟩

**cai·man** *also* **cayman** \'kā-mən; kā-'man, kī-\ *n* : any of several Central and So. American reptiles closely related to alligators and crocodiles

**cairn** \'karn\ *n* : a heap of stones serving as a memorial or a landmark

**cais·son** \'kā-ˌsän, 'käs-ᵊn\ *n* **1** : a usu. 2-wheeled vehicle for artillery ammunition **2** : a watertight chamber used in underwater construction work or as a foundation

**caisson disease** *n* : ²BEND 3

**cai·tiff** \'kā-təf\ *adj* [ME *caitif*, fr. AF *caitif, chaitif* wretched, despicable, fr. L *captivus* captive] : being base, cowardly, or despicable — **caitiff** *n*

**ca·jole** \kə-'jōl\ *vb* **ca·joled; ca·jol·ing** [F *cajoler*] : to persuade or coax esp. with flattery or false promises — **ca·jole·ment** *n* — **ca·jol·ery** \-'jō-lə-rē\ *n*

**Ca·jun** \'kā-jən\ *n* : a Louisianian descended from French-speaking immigrants from Acadia (Nova Scotia) — **Cajun** *adj*

**¹cake** \'kāk\ *n* **1** : a baked or fried bread-like food usu. in a small flat shape **2** : a sweet baked food made from batter or dough usu. containing flour, sugar, shortening, and a leaven (as baking powder) **3**

: a hardened or compacted substance ⟨~ of soap⟩ **4** : something easily done ⟨the quiz was ~⟩

³**cake** *vb* **caked; cak·ing 1** : ENCRUST **2** : to form or harden into a cake

**cake·walk** \'kāk-ˌwok\ *n* **1** : a stage dance typically involving a high prance with backward tilt **2** : a one-sided contest or an easy task

**cal** *abbr* **1** calendar **2** caliber

**Cal** *abbr* **1** California **2** calorie

**cal·a·bash** \'ka-lə-ˌbash\ *n* : the fruit of a gourd; *also* : a utensil made from its hard shell

**cal·a·boose** \'ka-lə-ˌbüs\ *n* [Sp *calabozo* dungeon] : JAIL

**ca·la·di·um** \kə-'lā-de-əm\ *n* : any of a genus of tropical American ornamental plants related to the arums

**cal·a·mari** \ˌkä-lə-'mär-ē\ *n* [It] : squid used as food

**cal·a·mine** \'ka-lə-ˌmīn\ *n* : a lotion of oxides of zinc and iron

**ca·lam·i·ty** \kə-'la-mə-tē\ *n, pl* **-ties 1** : great distress or misfortune **2** : an event causing great harm or loss and affliction : DISASTER ⟨an economic ~⟩ — **ca·lam·i·tous** \-təs\ *adj* — **ca·lam·i·tous·ly** *adv* — **ca·lam·i·tous·ness** *n*

**calc** *abbr* calculate; calculated

**cal·car·e·ous** \kal-'kar-ē-əs\ *adj* : resembling calcium carbonate in hardness; *also* : containing calcium or calcium carbonate

**cal·cif·er·ous** \kal-'si-fə-rəs\ *adj* : producing or containing calcium carbonate

**cal·ci·fy** \'kal-sə-ˌfī\ *vb* **-fied; -fy·ing** : to make or become calcareous — **cal·ci·fi·ca·tion** \ˌkal-sə-fə-'kā-shən\ *n*

**cal·ci·mine** \'kal-sə-ˌmīn\ *n* : a thin water paint used esp. on plastered surfaces — **calcimine** *vb*

**cal·cine** \kal-'sīn\ *vb* **calcined; cal·cin·ing** : to heat to a high temperature but without fusing to drive off volatile matter and often to reduce to powder — **cal·ci·na·tion** \ˌkal-sə-'nā-shən\ *n*

**cal·cite** \'kal-ˌsīt\ *n* : a crystalline mineral consisting of calcium carbonate — **cal·cit·ic** \kal-'si-tik\ *adj*

**cal·ci·um** \'kal-sē-əm\ *n* : a silver-white soft metallic chemical element occurring only in combination

**calcium carbonate** *n* : a substance found in nature as limestone and marble and in plant ashes, bones, and shells

**cal·cu·late** \'kal-kyə-ˌlāt\ *vb* **-lat·ed; -lat·ing** [L *calculare*, fr. *calculus* pebble (used in reckoning)] **1** : to determine by mathematical processes : COMPUTE **2** : to reckon by exercise of practical judgment : ESTIMATE **3** : to design or adapt for a purpose **4** : COUNT, RELY — **cal·cu·la·ble** \-lə-bəl\ *adj* — **cal·cu·la·tor** \-ˌlā-tər\ *n*

**cal·cu·lat·ed** \-ˌlā-təd\ *adj* **1** : undertaken after estimating the chance of success or failure ⟨a ~ risk⟩ **2** : planned purposefully : DELIBERATE ⟨a ~ strategy⟩

**cal·cu·lat·ing** \-ˌlā-tiŋ\ *adj* : marked by shrewd consideration esp. of self-interest — **cal·cu·lat·ing·ly** *adv*

**cal·cu·la·tion** \ˌkal-kyə-'lā-shən\ *n* **1** : the process or an act of calculating **2** : the result of an act of calculating **3** : studied care; *also* : cold heartless planning to promote self-interest

**cal·cu·lus** \'kal-kyə-ləs\ *n, pl* **-li** \-ˌlī\ *also* **-lus·es** [L, pebble (used in reckoning)] **1** : a method of computation or calculation in a special notation (as of logic) **2** : a branch of mathematics concerned with the rate of change of functions and with methods of finding lengths, areas, and volumes **3** : a concretion usu. of mineral salts esp. in hollow organs or ducts

**cal·de·ra** \kal-'der-ə, kȯl-, -'dir-\ *n* [Sp, lit., cauldron] : a large crater usu. formed by the collapse of a volcanic cone

**cal·dron** *var of* CAULDRON

¹**cal·en·dar** \'ka-lən-dər\ *n* **1** : an arrangement of time into days, weeks, months, and years; *also* : a sheet or folder containing such an arrangement for a period : an orderly list

²**calendar** *vb* : to enter in a calendar

¹**cal·en·der** \'ka-lən-dər\ *vb* : to press (as cloth or paper) between rollers or plates so as to make smooth or glossy or to thin into sheets

²**calender** *n* : a machine for calendering

**ca·lends** \'ka-ləndz, 'kā-\ *n sing or pl* : the first day of the ancient Roman month

**ca·len·du·la** \kə-'len-jə-lə\ *n* : any of a genus of yellow-flowered herbs related to the daisies

¹**calf** \'kaf, 'káf\ *n, pl* **calves** \'kavz, 'kávz\ **1** : the young of the domestic cow; *also* : the young of various large mammals (as the elephant or whale) **2** : CALFSKIN

²**calf** *n, pl* **calves** \'kavz, 'kávz\ : the fleshy back of the leg below the knee

**calf·skin** \'kaf-ˌskin, 'káf-\ *n* : leather made of the skin of a calf

**cal·i·ber** *or* **cal·i·bre** \'ka-lə-bər\ *n* [MF *calibre*, fr. It *calibro*, fr. Ar *qālib* shoemaker's last] **1** : degree of mental capacity, excellence, or importance **2** : the diameter of a projectile **3** : the diameter of the bore of a gun

**cal·i·brate** \'ka-lə-ˌbrāt\ *vb* **-brat·ed; -brat·ing** : to adjust precisely

**cal·i·bra·tion** \ˌka-lə-'brā-shən\ *n* : a set of graduated marks indicating values or positions — usu. used in pl.

**cal·i·co** \'ka-li-ˌkō\ *n, pl* **-coes** *or* **-cos 1** : printed cotton fabric **2** : a mottled or spotted animal — **calico** *adj*

**Calif** *abbr* California

**Cal·i·for·nia poppy** \ˌka-lə-'fȯr-nyə-\ *n* : a widely cultivated herb with usu. yellow or orange flowers that is related to the poppies

**cal·i·for·ni·um** \ˌka-lə-'fȯr-nē-əm\ *n* : an artificially prepared radioactive chemical element

**cal·i·per** \'ka-lə-pər\ *n* **1** : any of various instruments having two arms, legs, or jaws used esp. to measure diameter or thickness — usu. used in pl. **2** : a device for pressing a frictional material against the sides of a rotating wheel or disk

**ca·liph** \'kā-ləf, 'ka-\ *n* : a successor of

Muhammad as head of Islam — used as a title — **ca·liph·ate** \-lə-,fāt, -fət\ *n*

**cal·is·then·ics** \,ka-ləs-'the-niks\ *n sing or pl* [Gk *kalos* beautiful + *sthenos* strength] : bodily exercises usu. done without apparatus — **cal·is·then·ic** *adj*

**calk** \'kòk\ *var of* CAULK

¹**call** \'kòl\ *vb* 1 : SHOUT, CRY; *also* : to utter a characteristic note or cry 2 : to utter in a loud clear voice ⟨~ed out my name⟩ 3 : to announce authoritatively 4 : SUMMON ⟨was ~ed to testify⟩ 5 : to make a request or demand ⟨~ for an investigation⟩ 6 : to halt (as a baseball game) because of unsuitable conditions 7 : to demand payment of (a loan); *also* : to demand surrender of (as a bond) for redemption 8 : to get or try to get in communication by telephone 9 : to make a brief visit 10 : to speak of or address by name : give a name to 11 : to estimate or consider for practical purposes ⟨~ it ten miles⟩ 12 : to temporarily transfer control of computer processing to (as a subroutine or procedure) — **call·er** *n*

²**call** *n* 1 : SHOUT 2 : the cry of an animal (as a bird) 3 : a request or a command to come or assemble : INVITATION, SUMMONS 4 : DEMAND, CLAIM; *also* : REQUEST 5 : a brief usu. formal visit 6 : an act of calling on the telephone 7 : DECISION ⟨a tough ~⟩ 8 : a temporary transfer of control of computer processing to a particular set of instructions

**cal·la lily** \'ka-lə-\ *n* : a plant related to the arums and grown for its large white lilylike bract that surrounds a fleshy spike of small yellow flowers

**call·back** \'kòl-,bak\ *n* : a calling back; *esp* : RECALL 5

**call·board** \-,bòrd\ *n* : a board for posting notices (as of rehearsal calls)

**call down** *vb* : REPRIMAND

**call girl** *n* : a prostitute with whom appointments are made by phone

**cal·lig·ra·phy** \kə-'li-grə-fē\ *n* : artistic or elegant handwriting; *also* : the art of producing such writing — **cal·lig·ra·pher** \-fər\ *n* — **cal·li·graph·ic** \,ka-lə-'graf-ik\ *adj*

**call–in** \'kòl-,in\ *adj* : allowing listeners to engage in broadcast telephone conversations ⟨a ~ show⟩

**call in** *vb* 1 : to order to return or be returned 2 : to summon to one's aid 3 : to report by telephone

**call·ing** \'kò-liŋ\ *n* 1 : a strong inner impulse toward a particular course of action 2 : the activity in which one customarily engages as an occupation

**cal·li·ope** \kə-'lī-ə-(,)pē, 'ka-lē-,ōp\ *n* [fr. *Calliope*, chief of the Muses, fr. L, fr. Gk *Kalliopē*] : a keyboard musical instrument similar to an organ and made up of a series of whistles

**cal·li·per** *chiefly Brit var of* CALIPER

**call number** *n* : a combination of characters assigned to a library book to indicate its place on a shelf

**call off** *vb* : CANCEL ⟨*called off* the trip⟩

**cal·los·i·ty** \ka-'lä-sə-tē\ *n, pl* **-ties** 1

: the quality or state of being callous 2 : CALLUS 1

¹**cal·lous** \'ka-ləs\ *adj* 1 : being thickened and hardened ⟨~ skin⟩ 2 : feeling no emotion or sympathy — **cal·lous·ly** *adv* — **cal·lous·ness** *n*

²**callous** *vb* : to make callous

**cal·low** \'ka-lō\ *adj* [ME *calu* bald, fr. OE] : lacking adult sophistication ⟨a ~ youth⟩ — **cal·low·ness** *n*

**call–up** \'kò-,ləp\ *n* : an order to report for active military service

**call up** *vb* : to summon for active military duty

**cal·lus** \'ka-ləs\ *n* 1 : a callous area on skin or bark 2 : tissue that is converted into bone in the healing of a bone fracture — **callus** *vb*

**call–waiting** *n* : a telephone service by which during a call in progress an incoming call is signaled (as by a click)

¹**calm** \'käm, 'kälm\ *n* 1 : a period or a condition free from storms, high winds, or rough water 2 : complete or almost complete absence of wind 3 : a state of tranquillity

²**calm** *vb* : to make or become calm

³**calm** *adj* : marked by calm : STILL, UNRUFFLED — **calm·ly** *adv* — **calm·ness** *n*

**cal·o·mel** \'ka-lə-məl, -,mel\ *n* : a chloride of mercury used esp. as a fungicide

**ca·lor·ic** \kə-'lòr-ik\ *adj* 1 : of or relating to heat 2 : of, relating to, or containing calories — **ca·lor·i·cal·ly** \-i-k(ə-)lē\ *adv*

**cal·o·rie** *also* **cal·o·ry** \'ka-lə-rē\ *n, pl* **-ries** : a unit for measuring heat; *esp* : one for measuring the value of foods for producing heat and energy in the human body equivalent to the amount of heat required to raise the temperature of one kilogram of water one degree Celsius

**cal·o·rim·e·ter** \,ka-lə-'ri-mə-tər\ *n* : an apparatus for measuring quantities of heat — **cal·o·rim·e·try** \-trē\ *n*

**cal·u·met** \'kal-yə-,met, -mət\ *n* : an American Indian ceremonial pipe

**ca·lum·ni·ate** \kə-'ləm-nē-,āt\ *vb* **-at·ed; -at·ing** : to make false and malicious statements about ♦ *Synonyms* DEFAME, MALIGN, LIBEL, SLANDER, TRADUCE — **ca·lum·ni·a·tion** \-,ləm-nē-'ā-shən\ *n* — **ca·lum·ni·a·tor** \-'ləm-nē-,ā-tər\ *n*

**cal·um·ny** \'ka-ləm-nē\ *n, pl* **-nies** : false and malicious accusation — **ca·lum·ni·ous** \kə-'ləm-nē-əs\ *adj*

**calve** \'kav, 'kàv\ *vb* **calved; calv·ing** : to give birth to a calf

**calves** *pl of* CALF

**Cal·vin·ism** \'kal-və-,ni-zəm\ *n* : the theological system of John Calvin and his followers — **Cal·vin·ist** \-nist\ *n or adj* — **Cal·vin·is·tic** \,kal-və-'nis-tik\ *adj*

**ca·lyp·so** \kə-'lip-sō\ *n, pl* **-sos** : a style of music originating in the British West Indies and having lyrics that usu. satirize local personalities and events

**ca·lyx** \'kā-liks, 'ka-\ *n, pl* **ca·lyx·es** *or* **ca·ly·ces** \'kā-lə-,sēz, 'ka-\ : the usu. green or leaflike outer part of a flower consisting of sepals

**cal·zo·ne** \kal-'zōn, -'zō-nē\ *n* : a baked or fried turnover of pizza dough stuffed with cheese and various fillings

**¹cam** \'kam\ *n* : a rotating or sliding piece in a mechanical linkage by which rotary motion is transformed into linear motion or vice versa

**²cam** *n* : CAMERA

**ca·ma·ra·de·rie** \ˌkäm-'rä-də-rē, ˌkam-, -'ra-\ *n* [F] : friendly feeling and goodwill among comrades

**cam·bi·um** \'kam-bē-əm\ *n, pl* **-bi·ums** *or* **-bia** \-bē-ə\ : a thin cellular layer between xylem and phloem of most higher plants from which new tissues develop — **cam·bi·al** \-əl\ *adj*

**Cam·bri·an** \'kam-brē-ən, 'käm-\ *adj* : of, relating to, or being the earliest period of the Paleozoic era — **Cambrian** *n*

**cam·bric** \'kām-brik\ *n* : a fine thin white linen or cotton fabric

**cam·cord·er** \'kam-ˌkȯr-dər\ *n* : a small portable combined camera and VCR

**came** *past of* COME

**cam·el** \'ka-məl\ *n* : either of two large hoofed cud-chewing mammals used esp. in desert regions of Asia and Africa for carrying and riding

**camel hair** *also* **camel's hair** *n* **1** : the hair of a camel or a substitute for it **2** : cloth made of camel hair or of camel hair and wool

**ca·mel·lia** \kə-'mēl-yə\ *n* : any of a genus of shrubs and trees related to the tea plant and grown in warm regions and greenhouses for their showy roselike flowers

**Cam·em·bert** \'ka-məm-ˌber\ *n* : a soft cheese with a grayish rind and yellow interior

**cam·eo** \'ka-mē-ˌō\ *n, pl* **-eos** **1** : a gem carved in relief; *also* : a small medallion with a profiled head in relief **2** : a brief appearance esp. by a well-known actor in a play or movie

**cam·era** \'kam-rə, 'ka-mər-ə\ *n* : a device with a lightproof chamber fitted with a lens through which the image of an object is projected onto a surface for recording (as on film) or for conversion into electrical signals (as for television broadcast) — **cam·era·man** \-ˌman, -mən\ *n* — **cam·era·wom·an** *n*

**cam·i·sole** \'ka-mə-ˌsōl\ *n* : a short sleeveless garment for women

**camomile** *var of* CHAMOMILE

**cam·ou·flage** \'ka-mə-ˌfläzh, -ˌfläj\ *n* [F] **1** : the disguising of military equipment with paint, nets, or foliage; *also* : the disguise itself **2** : deceptive behavior — **camouflage** *vb*

**¹camp** \'kamp\ *n* **1** : a place where tents or buildings are erected for usu. temporary shelter **2** : a collection of tents or other shelters **3** : a program offering recreational activities (as boating and hiking) for a limited time ⟨summer ~⟩ **4** : a body of persons encamped **5** : a training session for athletes outside of the regular season — **camp·ground** \-ˌgrau̇nd\ *n* — **camp·site** \-ˌsīt\ *n*

**²camp** *vb* **1** : to make or occupy a camp **2** : to live in a camp or outdoors

**³camp** *n* **1** : exaggerated effeminate mannerisms **2** : something so outrageous, inappropriate, or theatrical as to be considered amusing — **camp** *adj* — **camp·i·ly** \'kam-pə-lē\ *adv* — **camp·i·ness** \-pē-nəs\ *n* — **campy** \-pē\ *adj*

**⁴camp** *vb* : to engage in camp : exhibit the qualities of camp

**cam·paign** \kam-'pān\ *n* **1** : a series of military operations forming one distinct stage in a war **2** : a series of activities designed to bring about a particular result ⟨advertising ~⟩ — **campaign** *vb* — **cam·paign·er** *n*

**cam·pa·ni·le** \ˌkam-pə-'nē-lē\ *n, pl* **-ni·les** *or* **-ni·li** \-'nē-lē\ : a usu. freestanding bell tower

**cam·pa·nol·o·gy** \ˌkam-pə-'nä-lə-jē\ *n* : the art of bell ringing — **cam·pa·nol·o·gist** \-jist\ *n*

**camp·er** \'kam-pər\ *n* **1** : one who camps **2** : a portable dwelling (as a specially equipped vehicle) for use during casual travel and camping

**Camp Fire Girl** *n* : a member of a national organization of girls from ages 5 to 18

**camp follower** *n* **1** : a civilian (as a prostitute) who follows a military unit to attend or exploit its personnel **2** : a follower of a group who is not an adherent; *esp* : a politician who joins a movement solely for personal gain

**cam·phor** \'kam-fər\ *n* : a gummy volatile aromatic compound obtained from an evergreen Asian tree (**camphor tree**) and used esp. in medicine

**camp meeting** *n* : a series of evangelistic meetings usu. held outdoors

**camp·o·ree** \ˌkam-pə-'rē\ *n* : a gathering of Boy Scouts or Girl Scouts from a given geographic area

**cam·pus** \'kam-pəs\ *n* [L, plain] : the grounds and buildings of a college or school; *also* : grounds resembling a campus ⟨hospital ~⟩

**cam·shaft** \'kam-ˌshaft\ *n* : a shaft to which a cam is fastened

**¹can** \kən, 'kan\ *vb, past* **could** \kəd, 'ku̇d\; *pres sing & pl* **can** **1** : be able to **2** : may perhaps ⟨~ he still be alive⟩ **3** : be permitted by conscience or feeling to ⟨you ~ hardly blame her⟩ **4** : have permission to ⟨you ~ go now⟩

**²can** \'kan\ *n* : a usu. cylindrical container or receptacle ⟨garbage ~⟩ ⟨coffee ~⟩ **2** : JAIL **3** : TOILET

**³can** \'kan\ *vb* **canned; can·ning** **1** : to put in a can : preserve by sealing in airtight cans or jars **2** *slang* : to discharge from employment **3** *slang* : to put a stop or an end to — **can·ner** *n*

**Can** *or* **Canad** *abbr* Canada; Canadian

**Can·a·da goose** \'ka-nə-də-\ *n* : a common wild goose of No. America

**ca·naille** \kə-'nī, -'näl\ *n* [F, fr. It *canaglia*, fr. *cane* dog] : RABBLE, RIFFRAFF

**ca·nal** \kə-'nal\ *n* **1** : a tubular passage in the body : DUCT **2** : an artificial waterway (as for boats or irrigation)

**can·a·lize** \'kan-ºl-,īz\ *vb* **-lized; -liz·ing**
**1** : to provide with a canal or make into or like a channel **2** : to provide with an outlet; *esp* : to direct into preferred channels — **ca·nal·i·za·tion** \,kan-ºl-ə-'zā-shən\ *n*

**can·a·pé** \'ka-nə-pē, -,pā\ *n* [F, lit., sofa, fr. ML *canopeum, canapeum* mosquito net] : a piece of bread or toast or a cracker topped with a savory food

**ca·nard** \kə-'närd\ *n* : a false or unfounded report, story or belief

**ca·nary** \kə-'ner-ē\ *n, pl* **ca·nar·ies** [fr. the *Canary* islands] **1** : a usu. sweet wine similar to Madeira **2** : a usu. yellow or greenish finch often kept in a cage as a pet

**ca·nas·ta** \kə-'nas-tə\ *n* [Sp, lit., basket] : rummy played with two full decks of cards plus four jokers

**canc** *abbr* canceled

**can·can** \'kan-,kan\ *n* : a woman's dance of French origin characterized by high kicking

**¹can·cel** \'kan-səl\ *vb* **-celed** *or* **-celled; -cel·ing** *or* **-cel·ling** [ME *cancellen,* fr. AF *canceller, chanceler,* fr. LL *cancellare,* fr. L, to make like a lattice, fr. *cancelli* lattice] **1** : to destroy the force or validity of : ANNUL **2** : to match in force or effect : OFFSET **3** : to cross out : DELETE **4** : to remove (a common divisor) from a numerator and denominator; *also* : to remove (equivalents) on opposite sides of an equation or account **5** : to mark (a postage stamp or check) so that it cannot be reused **6** : to neutralize each other's strength or effect — **can·cel·la·tion** \,kan-sə-'lā-shən\ *n* — **can·cel·er** *or* **can·cel·ler** *n*

**²cancel** *n* **1** : CANCELLATION **2** : a deleted part

**can·cer** \'kan-sər\ *n* [L, lit., crab] **1** *cap* : a zodiacal constellation between Gemini and Leo usu. pictured as a crab **2** *cap* : the 4th sign of the zodiac in astrology; *also* : one born under this sign **3** : a malignant tumor that tends to spread in the body; *also* : an abnormal state marked by such tumors **4** : a malignant evil that spreads destructively — **can·cer·ous** \-sə-rəs\ *adj* — **can·cer·ous·ly** *adv*

**can·de·la·bra** \,kan-də-'lä-brə, -'la-\ *n* : an ornamental branched candlestick or lamp with several lights

**can·de·la·brum** \-brəm\ *n, pl* **-bra** *also* **-brums** : CANDELABRA

**can·did** \'kan-dəd\ *adj* **1** : FRANK, STRAIGHTFORWARD ⟨a ~ critique⟩ **2** : relating to photography of subjects acting naturally or spontaneously without being posed — **can·did·ly** *adv* — **can·did·ness** *n*

**can·di·da·cy** \'kan-də-də-sē\ *n, pl* **-cies** : the state of being a candidate

**can·di·date** \'kan-də-,dāt, 'kan-ə-, -dət\ *n* [L *candidatus,* fr. *candidatus* clothed in white, fr. *candidus* white; fr. the white toga worn by office seekers in ancient Rome] : one who seeks or is proposed for an office, honor, or membership ⟨a ~ for governor⟩

**can·di·da·ture** \'kan-də-də-,chùr, 'ka-nə-\ *n, chiefly Brit* : CANDIDACY

**can·died** \'kan-dēd\ *adj* : preserved in or encrusted with sugar

**¹can·dle** \'kan-dºl\ *n* : a usu. slender mass of tallow or wax molded around a wick that is burned to give light

**²candle** *vb* **can·dled; can·dling** : to examine (as eggs) by holding between the eye and a light — **can·dler** *n*

**can·dle·light** \'kan-dºl-,līt\ *n* **1** : the light of a candle; *also* : any soft artificial light **2** : the time when candles are lit : TWILIGHT

**can·dle·lit** \-,lit\ *adj* : illuminated by candlelight ⟨a ~ dinner⟩

**Can·dle·mas** \'kan-dºl-məs\ *n* : February 2 observed as a church festival in commemoration of the presentation of Christ in the temple

**can·dle·stick** \-,stik\ *n* : a holder with a socket for a candle

**can·dle·wick** \-,wik\ *n* : a soft cotton yarn; *also* : embroidery made with this yarn usu. in tufts

**can·dor** \'kan-dər\ *n* : FRANKNESS, OUTSPOKENNESS

**can·dour** *chiefly Brit var of* CANDOR

**C and W** *abbr* country and western

**¹can·dy** \'kan-dē\ *n, pl* **candies** [ME *sugre candy,* fr. MF *sucre candi,* fr. OF *sucre* sugar + Ar *qandī* candied, fr. *qand* crystallized sugar] **1** : a confection made from sugar often with flavoring and filling **2** : something that appeals in a light or frivolous way

**²candy** *vb* **can·died; can·dy·ing** : to encrust in sugar often by cooking in a syrup

**candy strip·er** \-'strī-pər\ *n* : a teenage volunteer worker at a hospital

**¹cane** \'kān\ *n* **1** : a slender hollow or pithy stem (as of a reed or bramble) **2** : a tall woody grass or reed (as sugarcane or sorghum) **3** : a walking stick; *also* : a rod for flogging

**²cane** *vb* **caned; can·ing 1** : to beat with a cane **2** : to weave or make with cane — **can·er** *n*

**cane·brake** \'kān-,brāk\ *n* : a thicket of cane

**¹ca·nine** \'kā-,nīn\ *n* **1** : a pointed tooth between the outer incisor and the first premolar **2** : a canine mammal (as a domestic dog)

**²canine** *adj* [L *caninus,* fr. *canis* dog] : of or relating to dogs or to the family to which they belong

**can·is·ter** \'ka-nə-stər\ *n* : an often cylindrical container

**can·ker** \'kaŋ-kər\ *n* : a spreading sore that eats into tissue — **can·ker·ous** \-kə-rəs\ *adj*

**can·ker·worm** \-,wərm\ *n* : either of two moths and esp. their larvae that are pests of fruit and shade trees

**can·na** \'ka-nə\ *n* : any of a genus of tropical herbs with large leaves and racemes of bright-colored flowers

**can·na·bis** \'ka-nə-bəs\ *n* : any of the psychoactive preparations (as marijuana) or chemicals (as THC) derived from hemp; *also* : HEMP

**canned** \'kand\ *adj* : prepared in standardized form for general use or wide distribution ⟨~ music⟩

**can·nery** \'ka-nə-rē\ *n, pl* **-ner·ies** : a factory for the canning of foods

**can·ni·bal** \'ka-nə-bəl\ *n* [NL *Canibalis* a member of a Caribbean Indian people, fr. Sp *Caníbal*] : one that eats the flesh of its own kind — **can·ni·bal·ism** \-bə-ˌli-zəm\ *n* — **can·ni·bal·is·tic** \-bə-'lis-tik\ *adj*

**can·ni·bal·ise** *Brit var of* CANNIBALIZE

**can·ni·bal·ize** \'ka-nə-bə-ˌlīz\ *vb* **-ized; -iz·ing** **1** : to take usable parts from (as an inoperative machine) to construct or repair another machine **2** : to practice cannibalism

**can·non** \'ka-nən\ *n, pl* **cannons** *or* **cannon** [ME *canon*, fr. AF, fr. It *cannone*, lit., large tube, fr. *canna* reed, tube, fr. L *canna* reed] : a large heavy gun; *esp* : one mounted on a carriage

**can·non·ade** \ˌka-nə-'nād\ *n* : a heavy fire of artillery — **cannonade** *vb*

**can·non·ball** \'ka-nən-ˌbȯl\ *n* : a usu. round solid missile for a cannon

**can·non·eer** \ˌka-nə-'nir\ *n* : an artillery gunner

**can·not** \'ka-ˌnät; kə-'nät\ : can not — **cannot but** : to be unable to do otherwise than ⟨we *cannot but* wonder why⟩

**can·nu·la** \'kan-yə-lə\ *n, pl* **-las** *or* **-lae** \-ˌlē\ : a small tube for insertion into a body cavity or into a duct or vessel

**can·ny** \'ka-nē\ *adj* **can·ni·er; -est** : PRUDENT, SHREWD — **can·ni·ly** \'kan-ᵊl-ē\ *adv* — **can·ni·ness** \'ka-nē-nəs\ *n*

**ca·noe** \kə-'nü\ *n* : a light narrow boat with sharp ends and curved sides that is usu. propelled by paddles — **canoe** *vb* — **ca·noe·ist** *n*

**ca·no·la** \kə-'nō-lə\ *n* : a rape plant producing seeds that are low in a toxic acid and yield an edible oil (**canola oil**) high in monounsaturated fatty acids; *also* : this oil

**¹can·on** \'ka-nən\ *n* **1** : a regulation decreed by a church council; *also* : a provision of canon law **2** : an official or authoritative list (as of works of literature) **3** : an accepted principle ⟨the ~s of good taste⟩

**²canon** *n* : a member of the clergy on the staff of a cathedral

**ca·non·i·cal** \kə-'nä-ni-kəl\ *adj* **1** : of, relating to, or forming a canon **2** : conforming to a general rule or acceptable procedure : ORTHODOX **3** : of or relating to a canon of a cathedral — **ca·non·i·cal·ly** \-k(ə-)lē\ *adv*

**can·on·ize** \'ka-nə-ˌnīz\ *vb* **can·on·ized** \-ˌnīzd\; **can·on·iz·ing** **1** : to declare (a deceased person) an officially recognized saint **2** : GLORIFY, EXALT — **can·on·i·za·tion** \ˌka-nə-nə-'zā-shən\ *n*

**canon law** *n* : the law governing a church

**can·o·py** \'ka-nə-pē\ *n, pl* **-pies** [ME *canope*, fr. ML *canopeum* mosquito net, fr. L *conopeum*, fr. Gk *kōnōpion*, fr. *kōnōps* mosquito] **1** : an overhanging cover, shelter, or shade **2** : the uppermost spreading layer of a forest **3** : a transparent cover for an airplane cockpit **4** : the fabric part of a parachute — **can·opy** *vb*

**¹cant** \'kant\ *vb* : to give a slant to

**²cant** *n* **1** : an oblique or slanting surface **2** : TILT, SLANT

**³cant** *vb* **1** : to beg in a whining manner **2** : to talk hypocritically

**⁴cant** *n* **1** : the special idiom of a profession or trade : JARGON **2** : insincere speech; *esp* : insincerely pious words or statements

**Cant** *abbr* Canticle of Canticles

**can·ta·bi·le** \kän-'tä-bə-ˌlä\ *adv or adj* [It] : in a singing manner — used as a direction in music

**can·ta·loupe** *also* **can·ta·loup** \'kant-ᵊl-ˌōp\ *n* : MUSKMELON; *esp* : one with orange flesh and rough skin

**can·tan·ker·ous** \kan-'taŋ-kə-rəs\ *adj* : difficult to deal with : ILL-NATURED ⟨a ~ mule⟩ — **can·tan·ker·ous·ly** *adv* — **can·tan·ker·ous·ness** *n*

**can·ta·ta** \kən-'tä-tə\ *n* [It] : a choral composition usu. sung to instrumental accompaniment

**can·teen** \kan-'tēn\ *n* [F *cantine* bottle case, canteen (store), fr. It *cantina* wine cellar] **1** : a flask for carrying liquids **2** : a place of recreation and entertainment for military personnel **3** : a small cafeteria or counter at which snacks are served

**can·ter** \'kan-tər\ *n* : a horse's 3-beat gait resembling but smoother and slower than a gallop — **canter** *vb*

**Can·ter·bury bell** \'kant-ər-ˌber-ē-\ *n* : any of several plants related to the bluebell that are cultivated for their showy flowers

**can·ti·cle** \'kan-ti-kəl\ *n* : SONG; *esp* : any of several liturgical songs taken from the Bible

**Canticle of Canticles** *n* : SONG OF SONGS

**¹can·ti·le·ver** \'kant-ᵊl-ˌē-vər\ *n* : a projecting beam or structure supported only at one end; *also* : either of a pair of such structures projecting toward each other so that when joined they form a bridge

**²cantilever** *vb* **1** : to support by a cantilever ⟨a ~ed shelf⟩ **2** : to build as a cantilever **3** : to project as a cantilever

**can·tle** \'kant-ᵊl\ *n* : the upwardly projecting rear part of a saddle

**can·to** \'kan-ˌtō\ *n, pl* **cantos** [It, fr. L *cantus* song] : one of the major divisions of a long poem

**can·ton** \'kant-ᵊn, 'kan-ˌtän\ *n* : a small territorial division of a country; *esp* : one of the political divisions of Switzerland — **can·ton·al** \'kant-ᵊn-əl, kan-'tän-ᵊl\ *adj*

**can·ton·ment** \kan-'tōn-mənt, -'tän-\ *n* : usu. temporary quarters for troops

**can·tor** \'kan-tər\ *n* **1** : a choir leader **2** : a synagogue official who sings liturgical music and leads the congregation in prayer

**can·vas** *also* **can·vass** \'kan-vəs\ *n* **1** : a strong cloth formerly much used for making tents and sails **2** : a set of sails **3** : a group of tents **4** : a piece of cloth prepared as a surface for a painting; *also* : a painting on this surface **5** : the canvas-covered floor of a boxing or wrestling ring

**can·vas·back** \'kan-vəs-ˌbak\ n : a No. American wild duck with red head and gray back

¹**can·vass** also **can·vas** \'kan-vəs\ vb **can·vassed; can·vas·sing** : to go through (a district) or to (persons) to solicit votes or orders for goods or to determine public opinion or sentiment — **can·vass·er** n

²**canvass** n : an act or instance of canvassing

**can·yon** \'kan-yən\ n : a deep narrow valley with high steep sides

¹**cap** \'kap\ n 1 : a covering for the head esp. with a visor and no brim; also : something resembling such a covering esp. on a tip, knob or end ⟨a bottle ~⟩ 2 : a container holding an explosive charge (as for a toy gun) 3 : an upper limit (as on expenditures)

²**cap** vb **capped; cap·ping** 1 : to provide or protect with a cap 2 : to form a cap over : CROWN ⟨snow-*capped* mountains⟩ 3 : OUTDO, SURPASS 4 : to bring to a conclusion ⟨~ off dinner with coffee⟩

³**cap** abbr 1 capacity 2 capital 3 capitalize; capitalized

**CAP** abbr Civil Air Patrol

**ca·pa·ble** \'kā-pə-bəl\ adj : having ability, capacity, or power to do something : ABLE, COMPETENT — **ca·pa·bil·i·ty** \ˌkā-pə-'bi-lə-tē\ n — **ca·pa·bly** adv

**ca·pa·cious** \kə-'pā-shəs\ adj : able to contain much — **ca·pa·cious·ly** adv — **ca·pa·cious·ness** n

**ca·pac·i·tance** \kə-'pa-sə-təns\ n : the property of an electric nonconductor that permits the storage of energy

**ca·pac·i·tor** \kə-'pa-sə-tər\ n : an electronic device for temporary storage of electrical energy

¹**ca·pac·i·ty** \kə-'pa-sə-tē\ n, pl **-ties** 1 : legal qualification or fitness ⟨~ to stand trial⟩ 2 : the ability to contain, receive, or accommodate ⟨seating ~⟩ 3 : the maximum amount or number that can be contained — see METRIC SYSTEM table, WEIGHT table 4 : ABILITY 5 : position or character assigned or assumed

²**capacity** adj : equaling maximum capacity ⟨a ~ crowd⟩

**cap–a–pie** or **cap–à–pie** \ˌka-pə-'pē\ adv [MF] : from head to foot : at all points

**ca·par·i·son** \kə-'par-ə-sən\ n 1 : an ornamental covering for a horse 2 : TRAPPINGS, ADORNMENT — **caparison** vb

¹**cape** \'kāp\ n 1 : a point of land jutting out into water 2 often cap : CAPE COD COTTAGE

²**cape** n : a sleeveless garment hanging from the neck over the shoulders — **caped** adj

**Cape Cod cottage** \'kāp-'käd-\ n : a compact rectangular dwelling of one or one-and-a-half stories usu. with a steep gable roof

¹**ca·per** \'kā-pər\ n : the greenish flower bud or young berry of a Mediterranean shrub pickled for use as a relish; also : this shrub

²**caper** vb **ca·pered; ca·per·ing** : to leap about in a playful manner

³**caper** n 1 : a frolicsome leap 2 : a capricious escapade 3 : an illegal or questionable act

**cape·skin** \'kāp-ˌskin\ n : a light flexible leather made from sheepskins

**cap·ful** \'kap-ˌfu̇l\ n, pl **cap·fuls** also **caps·ful** \'kaps-\ : as much as a cap will hold

**cap·il·lar·i·ty** \ˌka-pə-'lar-ə-tē\ n, pl **-ties** : the action by which the surface of a liquid where it is in contact with a solid (as in a slender tube) is raised or lowered depending on the relative attraction of the molecules of the liquid for each other and for those of the solid

¹**cap·il·lary** \'ka-pə-ˌler-ē\ adj 1 : resembling a hair 2 : having a very small bore ⟨~ tube⟩ 3 : of or relating to capillaries or to capillarity

²**capillary** n, pl **-lar·ies** : any of the tiny thin-walled blood vessels that carry blood between the smallest arteries and their corresponding veins

¹**cap·i·tal** \'ka-pə-t°l\ n : the top part or piece of an architectural column

²**capital** adj 1 : conforming to the series A, B, C rather than a, b, c ⟨~ letters⟩ ⟨~ G⟩ 2 : punishable by death ⟨a ~ crime⟩ 3 : most serious ⟨a ~ error⟩ 4 : first in importance or position : CHIEF; also : being the seat of government ⟨the ~ city⟩ 5 : of or relating to capital ⟨~ expenditures⟩; esp : relating to or being assets that add to the long-term net worth of a corporation 6 : FIRST-RATE, EXCELLENT

³**capital** n 1 : accumulated wealth esp. as used to produce more wealth 2 : the total face value of shares of stock issued by a company 3 : persons holding capital 4 : ADVANTAGE, GAIN 5 : a letter larger than the ordinary small letter and often different in form 6 : the capital city of a state, province or country; also : a city preeminent in some activity ⟨the fashion ~⟩

**capital gain** n : the increase in value of an asset (as stock or real estate) between the time it is bought and the time it is sold

**capital goods** n pl : machinery, tools, factories, and commodities used in the production of goods

**cap·i·tal·ise** Brit var of CAPITALIZE

**cap·i·tal·ism** \'ka-pət-°l-ˌi-zəm\ n : an economic system characterized by private or corporate ownership of capital goods and by prices, production, and distribution of goods that are determined mainly by competition in a free market

¹**cap·i·tal·ist** \-ist\ n 1 : a person who has capital esp. invested in business 2 : a person of great wealth : PLUTOCRAT 3 : a believer in capitalism

²**capitalist** or **cap·i·tal·is·tic** \ˌka-pət-°l-'is-tik\ adj 1 : owning capital 2 : practicing or advocating capitalism 3 : marked by capitalism — **cap·i·tal·is·ti·cal·ly** \-ti-k(ə-)lē\ adv

**cap·i·tal·iza·tion** \ˌka-pət-°l-ə-'zā-shən\ n 1 : the act or process of capitalizing 2

: the total amount of money used as capital in a business

**cap·i·tal·ize** \'ka-pət-ᵊl-ˌīz\ vb **-ized; -iz·ing 1** : to write or print with an initial capital or in capitals **2** : to convert into or use as capital **3** : to supply capital for **4** : to gain by turning something to advantage : PROFIT

**cap·i·tal·ly** \'ka-pət-ᵊl-ē\ adv : ADMIRABLY, EXCELLENTLY

**cap·i·ta·tion** \ˌka-pə-'tā-shən\ n : a direct uniform tax levied on each person

**cap·i·tol** \'ka-pət-ᵊl\ n : the building in which a legislature holds its sessions

**ca·pit·u·late** \kə-'pi-chə-ˌlāt\ vb **-lat·ed; -lat·ing 1** : to surrender esp. on conditions agreed upon **2** : to cease resisting : ACQUIESCE ♦ *Synonyms* SUBMIT, YIELD, SUCCUMB, CAVE, DEFER — **ca·pit·u·la·tion** \-ˌpi-chə-'lā-shən\ n

**cap·let** \'ka-plət\ n : a capsule-shaped medicinal tablet

**ca·pon** \'kā-ˌpän, -pən\ n : a castrated male chicken

**cap·puc·ci·no** \ˌka-pə-'chē-nō, ˌkä-\ n [It, lit., Capuchin; fr. the likeness of its color to that of a Capuchin's habit] : espresso mixed with foamy hot milk or cream and often flavored with cinnamon

**ca·pric·cio** \kə-'prē-chē-ˌō, -chō\ n, pl **-cios** [It, lit., whim, prank] : an instrumental piece in free form usu. lively in tempo and brilliant in style

**ca·price** \kə-'prēs\ n [F, fr. It *capriccio*] **1** : a sudden whim or fancy **2** : an inclination to do things impulsively : CAPRICCIO — **ca·pri·cious** \-'pri-shəs\ adj — **ca·pri·cious·ly** adv — **ca·pri·cious·ness** n

**Cap·ri·corn** \'ka-pri-ˌkȯrn\ n **1** : a zodiacal constellation between Sagittarius and Aquarius usu. pictured as a goat **2** : the 10th sign of the zodiac in astrology; also : one born under this sign

**cap·ri·ole** \'ka-prē-ˌōl\ n : ³CAPER 1; also : an upward leap of a horse with a backward kick at the height of the leap — **capriole** vb

**caps** abbr **1** capitals **2** capsule

**cap·sa·i·cin** \kap-'sā-ə-sən\ n : a colorless compound found in various capsicums that gives hot peppers their hotness

**cap·si·cum** \'kap-si-kəm\ n : PEPPER 2

**cap·size** \'kap-ˌsīz, kap-'sīz\ vb **cap·sized; cap·siz·ing** : UPSET, OVERTURN

**cap·stan** \'kap-stən, -ˌstan\ n **1** : a machine for moving or raising heavy weights that consists of a vertical drum which can be rotated and around which cable is turned **2** : a rotating shaft that drives recorder tape

**cap·su·lar** \'kap-sə-lər\ adj : of, relating to, or resembling a capsule

**cap·su·lat·ed** \-ˌlā-təd\ adj : enclosed in a capsule

**¹cap·sule** \'kap-səl, -sül\ n **1** : a membrane or sac enclosing a body part (as of a joint) **2** : a case bearing spores or seeds **3** : a shell usu. of gelatin that is used for packaging something (as a drug); also : such a shell together with its contents **4**

: a small pressurized compartment or vehicle (as for space flight)

**²capsule** adj **1** : very brief ⟨a ~ biography⟩ **2** : very compact ⟨a ~ camera⟩

**Capt** abbr captain

**¹cap·tain** \'kap-tən\ n **1** : a commander of a body of troops **2** : a commissioned officer in the army, air force, or marine corps ranking next below a major **3** : an officer in charge of a ship **4** : a commissioned officer in the navy ranking next below a rear admiral or a commodore **5** : a leader of a side or team **6** : a dominant figure — **cap·tain·cy** n

**²captain** vb : to be captain of : LEAD

**cap·tion** \'kap-shən\ n **1** : a heading esp. of an article or document : TITLE **2** : the explanatory matter accompanying an illustration **3** : a motion-picture subtitle — **cap·tion** vb

**cap·tious** \'kap-shəs\ adj : marked by an inclination to find fault — **cap·tious·ly** adv — **cap·tious·ness** n

**cap·ti·vate** \'kap-tə-ˌvāt\ vb **-vat·ed; -vat·ing** : to attract and hold irresistibly by some special charm or art — **cap·ti·va·tion** \ˌkap-tə-'vā-shən\ n — **cap·ti·va·tor** \'kap-tə-ˌvā-tər\ n

**cap·tive** \'kap-tiv\ adj **1** : made prisoner esp. in war **2** : kept within bounds : CONFINED **3** : held under control — **captive** n — **cap·tiv·i·ty** \kap-'ti-və-tē\ n

**cap·tor** \'kap-tər\ n : one that captures

**¹cap·ture** \'kap-chər\ n **1** : the act of capturing **2** : one that has been captured

**²capture** vb **cap·tured; cap·tur·ing 1** : to take captive : WIN, GAIN ⟨~ the crown⟩ **2** : to preserve in a relatively permanent form ⟨~ the moment on film⟩

**Ca·pu·chin** \'ka-pyə-shən\ n : a member of an austere branch of the order of St. Francis of Assisi engaged in missionary work and preaching

**car** \'kär\ n **1** : a vehicle moving on wheels **2** : the compartment of an elevator **3** : the part of a balloon or airship that carries passengers or equipment

**car·a·cole** \'kar-ə-ˌkōl\ n : a half turn to right or left executed by a mounted horse — **caracole** vb

**car·a·cul** \'kar-ə-ˌkəl\ n : the pelt of a karakul lamb after the curl begins to loosen

**ca·rafe** \kə-'raf, -'räf\ n **1** : a bottle with a flaring lip used esp. to hold wine **2** : a usu. glass pitcher for pouring coffee

**car·am·bo·la** \ˌkar-əm-'bō-lə\ n **1** : a 5-angled green to yellow edible tropical fruit of star-shaped cross section **2** : a tropical Asian tree widely cultivated for carambolas

**car·a·mel** \'kar-ə-məl, 'kär-məl\ n **1** : an amorphous substance obtained by heating sugar and used for flavoring and coloring **2** : a firm chewy candy

**car·a·pace** \'kar-ə-ˌpās\ n : a protective case or shell on the back of some animals (as turtles or crabs)

**¹carat** var of KARAT

**²car·at** \'kar-ət\ n : a unit of weight for precious stones equal to 200 milligrams

**car·a·van** \'kar-ə-ˌvan\ n **1** : a group of

travelers journeying together through desert or hostile regions **2** : a group of vehicles traveling in a file

**car·a·van·sa·ry** \ˌkar-ə-ˈvan-sə-rē\ *or* **car·a·van·se·rai** \-sə-ˌrī\ *n, pl* **-ries** *or* **-rais** *or* **-rai** [Pers *kārvānsarāī*, fr. *kārvān* caravan + *sarāī* palace, inn] **1** : an inn in eastern countries where caravans rest at night **2** : HOTEL, INN

**car·a·vel** \ˈkar-ə-ˌvel\ *n* : a small 15th and 16th century ship with a broad bow, high narrow poop, and usu. three masts

**car·a·way** \ˈkar-ə-ˌwā\ *n* : an aromatic herb related to the carrot with fruits (**caraway seed**) used in seasoning and medicine; *also* : its fruit

**car·bide** \ˈkär-ˌbīd\ *n* : a compound of carbon with another element

**car·bine** \ˈkär-ˌbēn, -ˌbīn\ *n* : a short-barreled lightweight rifle

**car·bo·hy·drate** \ˌkär-bō-ˈhī-ˌdrāt, -drət\ *n* : any of various compounds composed of carbon, hydrogen, and oxygen (as sugars and starches)

**car·bol·ic acid** \kär-ˈbä-lik-\ *n* : PHENOL

**car·bon** \ˈkär-bən\ *n* **1** : a nonmetallic chemical element occurring in nature esp. as diamond and graphite and as a constituent of coal, petroleum, and limestone **2** : a sheet of carbon paper; *also* : CARBON COPY 1 — **car·bon·less** \-ləs\ *adj*

**car·bo·na·ceous** \ˌkär-bə-ˈnā-shəs\ *adj* : relating to, containing, or composed of carbon

[1]**car·bon·ate** \ˈkär-bə-ˌnāt, -nət\ *n* : a salt or ester of carbonic acid

[2]**car·bon·ate** \-ˌnāt\ *vb* **-at·ed; -at·ing** : to combine or infuse with carbon dioxide ⟨*carbonated* beverages⟩ — **car·bon·ation** \ˌkär-bə-ˈnā-shən\ *n*

**carbon black** *n* : any of various black substances consisting chiefly of carbon and used esp. as pigments

**carbon copy** *n* **1** : a copy made by carbon paper **2** : DUPLICATE

**carbon dating** *n* : the determination of the age of old material (as an archaeological specimen) by its content of carbon 14

**carbon dioxide** *n* : a heavy colorless gas that does not support combustion and is formed in animal respiration and in the combustion and decomposition of organic substances

**carbon footprint** *n* : the amount of carbon dioxide emitted by something in a given period

**carbon 14** *n* : a heavy radioactive form of carbon used esp. in dating old materials (as archaeological specimens)

**car·bon·ic acid** \kär-ˈbä-nik-\ *n* : a weak acid that decomposes readily into water and carbon dioxide

**car·bon·if·er·ous** \ˌkär-bə-ˈni-fə-rəs\ *adj* **1** : producing or containing carbon or coal **2** *cap* : of, relating to, or being the period of the Paleozoic era between the Devonian and the Permian — **Carboniferous** *n*

**carbon monoxide** *n* : a colorless odorless very poisonous gas formed by the incomplete burning of carbon

**carbon paper** *n* : a thin paper coated with a pigment and used for making copies

**carbon tet·ra·chlo·ride** \-ˌte-trə-ˈklōr-ˌīd\ *n* : a colorless nonflammable toxic liquid used esp. as a solvent

**carbon 12** *n* : the most abundant isotope of carbon having a nucleus of 6 protons and 6 neutrons and used as a standard for measurements of atomic weight

**car·boy** \ˈkär-ˌbói\ *n* [Pers *qarāba*, fr. Ar *qarrāba* demijohn] : a large container for liquids

**car·bun·cle** \ˈkär-ˌbən-kəl\ *n* : a painful inflammation of the skin and underlying tissue that discharges pus from several openings

**car·bu·re·tor** \ˈkär-bə-ˌrā-tər, -byə-\ *n* : an apparatus for premixing vaporized fuel and air and supplying the mixture to an internal combustion engine

**car·bu·ret·tor** *also* **car·bu·ret·ter** \ˌkär-byə-ˈre-tər, ˈkär-byə-\ *chiefly Brit var of* CARBURETOR

**car·case** *Brit var of* CARCASS

**car·cass** \ˈkär-kəs\ *n* : a dead body; *esp* : one of an animal dressed for food

**car·cin·o·gen** \kär-ˈsi-nə-jən\ *n* : a substance or agent causing cancer — **car·ci·no·gen·ic** \ˌkärs-ᵊn-ō-ˈje-nik\ *adj* — **car·ci·no·ge·nic·i·ty** \-jə-ˈni-sə-tē\ *n*

**car·ci·no·ma** \ˌkärs-ᵊn-ˈō-mə\ *n, pl* **-mas** *also* **-ma·ta** \-tə\ : a malignant tumor of epithelial origin — **car·ci·no·ma·tous** \-təs\ *adj*

[1]**card** \ˈkärd\ *vb* : to comb with a card : cleanse and untangle before spinning ⟨~*ed* cotton⟩ — **card·er** *n*

[2]**card** *n* : an instrument for combing fibers (as wool or cotton)

[3]**card** *n* **1** : PLAYING CARD **2** *pl* : a game played with playing cards; *also* : card playing **3** : an emotional issue used to one's advantage (as in a political campaign) **4** : a usu. clownishly amusing person : WAG **5** : a flat stiff usu. small piece of paper, cardboard, or plastic often bearing pictures or information **6** : PROGRAM; *esp* : a sports program — **in the cards** : INEVITABLE

[4]**card** *vb* **1** : to list or schedule on a card **2** : SCORE **3** : to ask for identification (as at a bar)

[5]**card** *abbr* cardinal

**car·da·mom** \ˈkär-də-məm\ *n* : the aromatic capsular fruit of an Indian herb related to the ginger whose seeds are used as a spice or condiment and in medicine; *also* : this plant

**card·board** \ˈkärd-ˌbórd\ *n* : a material thicker than paper and made from cellulose fiber

**card–car·ry·ing** \ˈkärd-ˌkar-ē-iŋ\ *adj* : being a regularly enrolled member of an organization (as a political party)

**card catalog** *n* : a catalog (as of books) in which the entries are arranged systematically on cards

**car·di·ac** \ˈkär-dē-ˌak\ *adj* [L *cardiacus*, fr. Gk *kardiakos*, fr. *kardia* heart] **1** : of, relating to, or located near the heart  **2** : of, relating to, or affected with heart disease ⟨~ patients⟩

**car·di·gan** \'kär-di-gən\ *n* : a sweater or jacket usu. without a collar and with a full-length opening in the front

**¹car·di·nal** \'kärd-nəl, 'kär-d⁰n-əl\ *n* **1** : an ecclesiastical official of the Roman Catholic Church ranking next below the pope  **2** : a crested No. American finch that is nearly completely red in the male

**²cardinal** *adj* [ME, fr. LL *cardinalis*, fr. L serving as a hinge, fr. *cardo* hinge] **1** : of basic importance : CHIEF, MAIN, PRIMARY ⟨a ~ principle⟩ **2** : very serious ⟨a ~ sin⟩ — **car·di·nal·ly** *adv*

**car·di·nal·ate** \'kärd nə lət, 'kär-d⁰n-ə-let, -‚lāt\ *n* : the office, rank, or dignity of a cardinal

**cardinal flower** *n* : a No. American plant that bears a spike of brilliant red flowers

**cardinal number** *n* : a number (as 1, 5, 82, 357) that is used in simple counting and answers the question "how many?" — compare ORDINAL NUMBER

**cardinal point** *n* : one of the four principal compass points north, south, east, and west

**car·dio** \'kär-dē-ō\ *adj* : CARDIOVASCULAR **2**

**car·di·ol·o·gy** \‚kär-dē-'ä-lə-jē\ *n* : the study of the heart and its action and diseases — **car·di·ol·o·gist** \-jist\ *n*

**car·dio·pul·mo·nary resuscitation** \‚kär-dē-ō-'pùl-mə-‚ner-ē-\ *n* : a procedure to restore normal breathing after cardiac arrest that includes the clearance of air passages to the lungs, mouth-to-mouth method of artificial respiration, and heart massage by the exertion of pressure on the chest

**car·dio·vas·cu·lar** \-'vas-kyə-lər\ *adj* **1** : of or relating to the heart and blood vessels  **2** : causing a temporary increase in heart rate ⟨a ~ workout⟩

**card-sharp** \-‚shärp\ *or* **card-sharp·er** \'kärd-‚shär-pər\ *n* : a cheater at cards

**¹care** \'ker\ *n* **1** : a disquieted state of uncertainty and responsibility : ANXIETY  **2** : watchful attention : HEED **3** : CHARGE, SUPERVISION ⟨under a doctor's ~⟩ **4** : a person or thing that is an object of anxiety or solicitude

**²care** *vb* **cared; car·ing 1** : to feel anxiety  **2** : to feel interest **3** : to give care **4** : to have a liking, fondness, taste, or inclination  **5** : to be concerned about ⟨~ what happens⟩

**CARE** *abbr* Cooperative for American Relief to Everywhere

**ca·reen** \kə-'rēn\ *vb* **1** : to put (a ship or boat) on a beach esp. in order to clean or repair its hull  **2** : to sway from side to side **3** : CAREER

**¹ca·reer** \kə-'rir\ *n* [MF *carrière*, fr. Old Occitan *carriera* street, fr. ML *carraria* road for vehicles, fr. L *carrus* car] **1** : COURSE, PASSAGE; *also* : speed in a course ⟨ran at full ~⟩ **2** : an occupation or profession followed as a life's work

**²career** *vb* : to go at top speed esp. in a headlong manner

**care-free** \'ker-‚frē\ *adj* : free from care or worry

**care-ful** \-fəl\ *adj* **care·ful·ler; care·ful·lest 1** : using or taking care : VIGILANT  **2** : marked by solicitude, caution, or prudence — **care·ful·ly** *adv* — **care·ful·ness** *n*

**care·giv·er** \-‚gi-vər\ *n* : a person who provides direct care (as for children, elderly people, or the chronically ill)

**care·less** \-ləs\ *adj* **1** : free from care : UNTROUBLED **2** : UNCONCERNED, INDIFFERENT ⟨~ of the consequences⟩ **3** : not taking care **4** : not showing or receiving care — **care·less·ly** *adv* — **care·less·ness** *n*

**care package** *n* : a package of useful or pleasurable items given as a gift to another

**¹ca·ress** \kə-'res\ *vb* : to touch or stroke tenderly or lovingly — **ca·ress·er** *n*

**²caress** *n* : a tender or loving touch or embrace

**car·et** \'ker-ət\ *n* [L, there is lacking, fr. *carēre* to lack, be without] : a mark ^ used to indicate the place where something is to be inserted

**care·tak·er** \'ker-‚tā-kər\ *n* **1** : one in charge usu. as occupant in place of an absent owner  **2** : one temporarily fulfilling the functions of an office

**care·worn** \-‚wórn\ *adj* : showing the effects of grief or anxiety

**car·fare** \'kär-‚fer\ *n* : passenger fare (as on a streetcar or bus)

**car·go** \'kär-gō\ *n, pl* **cargoes** *or* **cargos** : the goods carried in a ship, airplane, or vehicle : FREIGHT

**Ca·rib·be·an** \‚ker-ə-'bē-ən, kə-'ri-bē-ən\ *adj* : of or relating to the eastern and southern West Indies or the Caribbean Sea

**car·i·bou** \'ker-ə-‚bü\ *n, pl* **caribou** *or* **caribous** : a large circumpolar gregarious deer of northern taiga and tundra that usu. has large branched antlers usu. in both sexes — used esp. for one of the New World

**car·i·ca·ture** \'ker-i-kə-‚chùr\ *n* **1** : distorted representation to produce a ridiculous effect  **2** : a representation esp. in literature or art having the qualities of caricature — **caricature** *vb* — **car·i·ca·tur·ist** \-ist\ *n*

**car·ies** \'ker-ēz\ *n, pl* **caries** : tooth decay

**car·il·lon** \'ker-ə-‚län\ *n* : a set of tuned bells sounded by hammers controlled from a keyboard

**car·i·ous** \'ker-ē-əs\ *adj* : affected with caries

**car·jack·ing** \'kär-ja-kiŋ\ *n* : the theft of an automobile by force or intimidation — **car·jack·er** *n*

**car·load** \'kär-‚lōd\ *n* : a load that fills a car

**car·mi·na·tive** \kär-'mi-nə-tiv\ *adj* : expelling gas from the stomach or intestines — **carminative** *n*

**car·mine** \'kär-mən, -‚mīn\ *n* : a vivid red

**car·nage** \'kär-nij\ *n* : great destruction of life : SLAUGHTER

**car·nal** \\\'kär-n\ᵊl\ *adj* [ME, fr. LL *carnalis*, fr. L *carn-, caro* flesh] **1** : of or relating to the body **2** : relating to or given to sensual pleasures and appetites — **car·nal·i·ty** \\kär-'na-lə-tē\ *n* — **car·nal·ly** *adv*

**car·na·tion** \\kär-'nā-shən\ *n* : a cultivated pink of any of numerous usu. double-flowered varieties derived from an Old World species

**car·nau·ba wax** \\kär-'nȯ-bə-, -'naȯ-, ˌkär-nə-'ü-bə-\ *n* : a brittle yellowish wax from a Brazilian palm that is used esp. in polishes

**car·ne·lian** \\kär-'nēl-yən\ *n* : a hard red chalcedony used as a gem

**car·ni·val** \\'kär-nə-vəl\ *n* [It *carnevale,* alter. of *carnelevare,* lit., removal of meat] **1** : a festival of merrymaking just before Lent **2** : a boisterous merrymaking **3** : a traveling enterprise offering amusements **4** : an organized program of entertainment

**car·ni·val·esque** \\ˌkär-nə-və-'lesk\ *adj* : suggestive of a carnival

**car·niv·o·ra** \\kär-'ni-və-rə\ *n pl* : carnivorous mammals

**car·ni·vore** \\'kär-nə-ˌvȯr\ *n* : a flesh-eating animal; *esp* : any of an order of mammals (as dogs, cats, bears, minks, and seals) feeding mostly on animal flesh

**car·niv·o·rous** \\kär-'ni-və-rəs\ *adj* **1** : feeding on animal tissues **2** : of or relating to the carnivores — **car·niv·o·rous·ly** *adv* — **car·niv·o·rous·ness** *n*

**car·ny** *or* **car·ney** *or* **car·nie** \\'kär-nē\ *n, pl* **carnies** *or* **carneys** **1** : CARNIVAL **3 2** : one who works with a carnival

**car·ol** \\'ker-əl\ *n* : a song of joy or devotion — **carol** *vb* — **car·ol·er** *or* **car·ol·ler** *n*

**car·om** \\'ker-əm\ *n* **1** : a shot in billiards in which the cue ball strikes two other balls **2** : a rebounding esp. at an angle — **carom** *vb*

**car·o·tene** \\'ker-ə-ˌtēn\ *n* : any of several orange to red pigments (as beta-carotene) formed esp. in plants and used as a source of vitamin A

**ca·rot·en·oid** \\kə-'rä-tə-ˌnȯid\ *n* : any of various usu. yellow to red pigments (as carotenes) found widely in plants and animals

**ca·rot·id** \\kə-'rä-təd\ *adj* : of, relating to, or being the chief artery or pair of arteries that pass up the neck and supply the head — **carotid** *n*

**ca·rous·al** \\kə-'raȯ-zəl\ *n* : CAROUSE

**ca·rouse** \\kə-'raȯz\ *n* [MF *carrousse,* fr. *carous,* adv., all out (in *boire carous* to empty the cup), fr. G *garaus*] : a drunken revel — **carouse** *vb* — **ca·rous·er** *n*

**car·ou·sel** *also* **car·rou·sel** \\ˌker-ə-'sel, 'kar-ə-ˌsel\ *n* **1** : MERRY-GO-ROUND **2** : a circular conveyor ⟨a baggage ~⟩

**¹carp** \\'kärp\ *vb* : to find fault : CAVIL, COMPLAIN — **carp** *n* — **carp·er** *n*

**²carp** *n, pl* **carp** *or* **carps** : a large variable Asian freshwater fish of sluggish waters often raised for food

**¹car·pal** \\'kär-pəl\ *adj* : of or relating to the wrist or the bones of the wrist

**²carpal** *n* : a carpal element or bone

**carpal tunnel syndrome** *n* : a condition characterized esp. by weakness, pain, and disturbances of sensation (as numbness) in the hand and fingers and caused by compression of a nerve in the wrist

**car·pe di·em** \\'kär-pe-'dē-ˌem, -'dī-\ *n* [L, lit., pluck the day] : enjoyment of the present without concern for the future

**car·pel** \\'kär-pəl\ *n* : one of the highly modified leaves that together form the ovary of a flower of a seed plant

**car·pen·ter** \\'kär-pən-tər\ *n* : one who builds or repairs wooden structures — **carpenter** *vb* — **car·pen·try** \\-trē\ *n*

**car·pet** \\'kär-pət\ *n* : a heavy fabric used as a floor covering — **carpet** *vb*

**car·pet·bag** \\-ˌbag\ *n* : a traveling bag common in the 19th century

**car·pet·bag·ger** \\-ˌba-gər\ *n* : a Northerner in the South after the American Civil War usu. seeking private gain under the reconstruction governments

**car·pet·ing** \\'kär-pə-tiŋ\ *n* : material for carpets; *also* : CARPETS

**car pool** *n* : an arrangement in which a group of people commute together by car; *also* : a group having this arrangement — **car·pool** \\-ˌpül\ *vb*

**car·port** \\'kär-ˌpȯrt\ *n* : an open-sided automobile shelter

**car·pus** \\'kär-pəs\ *n* : the wrist or its bones

**car·ra·geen·an** *or* **car·ra·geen·in** \\ˌker-ə-'gē-nən\ *n* : a colloid extracted esp. from a dark purple branching seaweed and used in foods esp. to stabilize and thicken them

**car·rel** \\'ker-əl\ *n* : a table often partitioned or enclosed for individual study in a library

**car·riage** \\'ker-ij\ *n* **1** : the act of carrying **2** : manner of holding the body **3** : a wheeled vehicle **4** *Brit* : a railway passenger coach **5** : a movable part of a machine for supporting some other moving part ⟨a typewriter ~⟩

**carriage trade** *n* : trade from well-to-do or upper-class people

**car·ri·er** \\'ker-ē-ər\ *n* **1** : one that carries **2** : a person or organization in the transportation business **3** : AIRCRAFT CARRIER **4** : one whose system carries the causative agents of a disease but who is immune to the disease **5** : an individual having a gene for a trait or condition that is not expressed outwardly **6** : an electromagnetic wave whose amplitude or frequency is varied in order to convey a radio or television signal

**carrier pigeon** *n* : a pigeon used esp. to carry messages

**car·ri·on** \\'ker-ē-ən\ *n* : dead and decaying flesh

**car·rot** \\'ker-ət\ *n* : the elongated usu. orange root of a common garden plant that is eaten as a vegetable; *also* : this plant

**carrousel** *var of* CAROUSEL

**¹car·ry** \\'ka-rē, 'ker-ē\ *vb* **car·ried; car·ry·ing** [ME *carien,* fr. AF *carier,* fr. *carre* vehicle, fr. L *carrus*] **1** : to move while supporting : TRANSPORT, CONVEY, TAKE **2** : to influence by mental or emotional appeal **3** : to get possession or control of : CAPTURE, WIN **4** : to transfer from one place (as a column) to another ⟨~ a number in adding⟩ **5** : to have or wear on one's person; *also* : to bear within one **6** : INVOLVE, IMPLY **7** : to hold or bear (oneself) in a specified way **8** : to keep in stock for sale **9** : to sustain the weight or burden of : SUPPORT **10** : to prolong in space, time, or degree **11** : to keep on one's books as a debtor **12** : to succeed in (an election) **13** : to win adoption (as in a legislature) **14** : PUBLISH, PRINT **15** : to reach or penetrate to a distance ⟨voices ~ well over water⟩

²**carry** *n* **1** : the range of a gun or projectile or of a struck or thrown ball **2** : PORTAGE **3** : an act or method of carrying ⟨fireman's ~⟩

**car·ry·all** \⸱ȯl\ *n* : a capacious bag or case

**carry away** *vb* : to arouse to a high and often excessive degree of emotion

**carrying charge** *n* : a charge added to the price of merchandise sold on the installment plan

**car·ry·on** \⸱ȯn, ⸱än\ *n* : a piece of luggage suitable for being carried aboard an airplane by a passenger — **carry-on** *adj*

**carry on** *vb* **1** : CONDUCT, MANAGE **2** : to behave in a foolish, excited, or improper manner **3** : to continue in spite of hindrance or discouragement

**carry out** *vb* **1** : to bring to a successful conclusion **2** : to put into execution

**car·sick** \'kär-ˌsik\ *adj* : affected with motion sickness esp. in an automobile — **car sickness** *n*

¹**cart** \'kärt\ *n* **1** : a heavy 2-wheeled wagon **2** : a small wheeled vehicle

²**cart** *vb* : to convey in or as if in a cart — **cart·er** *n*

**cart·age** \'kär-tij\ *n* : the act of or rate charged for carting

**carte blanche** \'kärt-'blä<sup>n</sup>sh\ *n, pl* **cartes blanches** \*same or* -'blä<sup>n</sup>-shəz\ [F, lit., blank document] : full discretionary power

**car·tel** \kär-'tel\ *n* : a combination of independent business enterprises designed to limit competition ♦ **Synonyms** POOL, SYNDICATE, MONOPOLY, TRUST

**car·ti·lage** \'kär-tə-lij\ *n* : a usu. translucent somewhat elastic tissue that composes most of the skeleton of young vertebrate embryos and later is mostly converted to bone in higher vertebrates — **car·ti·lag·i·nous** \ˌkär-tə-'la-jə-nəs\ *adj*

**cartilaginous fish** *n* : a class of fishes (as a shark or ray) having the skeleton wholly or largely composed of cartilage

**car·tog·ra·phy** \kär-'tä-grə-fē\ *n* : the making of maps — **car·tog·ra·pher** *n* — **car·to·graph·ic** \ˌkär-tə-'gra-fik\ *adj*

**car·ton** \'kär-t<sup>ə</sup>n\ *n* : a cardboard box or container

**car·toon** \kär-'tün\ *n* **1** : a preparatory sketch (as for a painting) **2** : a drawing intended as humor, caricature, or satire **3** : COMIC STRIP — **cartoon** *vb* — **cartoon·ist** *n*

**car·tridge** \'kär-trij\ *n* **1** : a tube containing a complete charge for a firearm **2** : a container of material for insertion into an apparatus **3** : a small case containing a phonograph needle and transducer that is attached to a tonearm **4** : a case containing a magnetic tape or disk **5** : a case for holding integrated circuits containing a computer program

**cart·wheel** \'kärt-ˌhwēl\ *n* **1** : a large coin (as a silver dollar) **2** : a lateral handspring with arms and legs extended

**carve** \'kärv\ *vb* **carved; carv·ing 1** : to cut with care or precision : shape by cutting **2** : to cut into pieces or slices **3** : to slice and serve meat at table — **carv·er** *n*

**cary·at·id** \ˌker-ē-'a-təd\ *n, pl* **-ids** *or* **-i·des** \-'a-tə-ˌdēz\ : a sculptured draped female figure used as an architectural column

**CAS** *abbr* certificate of advanced study

**ca·sa·ba** \kə-'sä-bə\ *n* : any of several muskmelons with a yellow rind and sweet flesh

¹**cas·cade** \kas-'kād\ *n* **1** : a steep usu. small waterfall **2** : something arranged in a series or succession of stages so that each stage derives from or acts upon the product of the preceding

²**cascade** *vb* **cas·cad·ed; cas·cad·ing** : to fall, pass, or connect in or as if in a cascade ⟨water *cascaded* over the rocks⟩

**cas·cara** \ka-'ska-rə\ *n* : the dried bark of a small Pacific coastal tree of the U.S. and southern Canada used as a laxative; *also* : this tree

¹**case** \'kās\ *n* [ME *cas,* fr. AF, fr. L *casus* fall, chance, fr. *cadere* to fall] **1** : a particular instance or situation **2** : an inflectional form of a noun, pronoun, or adjective indicating its grammatical relation to other words; *also* : such a relation whether indicated by inflection or not **3** : what actually exists or happens : FACT **4** : a suit or action in law : CAUSE **5** : a convincing argument **6** : an instance of disease or injury; *also* : PATIENT **7** : INSTANCE, EXAMPLE — **in case** : as a precaution — **in case of** : in the event of

²**case** *n* [ME *cas,* fr. AF *case, chase,* fr. L *capsa*] **1** : a box or container for holding something; *also* : a box with its contents **2** : an outer covering **3** : a divided tray for holding printing type **4** : CASING 2

³**case** *vb* **cased; cas·ing 1** : to enclose in or cover with a case **2** : to inspect esp. with intent to rob

**ca·sein** \'kā-ˌsēn, kā-'\ *n* : any of several phosphorus-containing proteins occurring in or produced from milk

**case·ment** \'kās-mənt\ *n* : a window that opens like a door

**case·work** \-ˌwərk\ *n* : social work that involves the individual person or family — **case·work·er** *n*

¹**cash** \'kash\ *n* [MF or It; MF *casse* money box, fr. It *cassa,* fr. L *capsa* chest, case] **1** : ready money **2** : money or its equivalent paid at the time of purchase or delivery

²**cash** *vb* : to pay or obtain cash for

**ca·shew** \'ka-ˌshü, kə-'shü\ *n* : an edible

kidney-shaped nut of a tropical American tree related to the sumacs; *also* : the tree

¹**ca·shier** \ka-'shir\ *vb* : to dismiss from service; *esp* : to dismiss in disgrace

²**cash·ier** \ka-'shir\ *n* 1 : a bank official responsible for moneys received and paid out 2 : a person who receives and records payments

**cashier's check** *n* : a check drawn by a bank upon its own funds and signed by its cashier

**cash in** *vb* 1 : to convert into cash ⟨*cash in* bonds⟩ 2 : to settle accounts and withdraw from a gambling game or business deal 3 : to obtain financial profit or advantage

**cash·less** \'kash-ləs\ *adj* : relying on monetary transactions that use electronic means rather than cash

**cash·mere** \'kazh-ˌmir, 'kash-\ *n* : fine wool from the undercoat of an Indian goat (**cashmere goat**) or a yarn spun of this; *also* : a soft twilled fabric orig. woven from this yarn

**cash out** *vb* : to convert noncash assets into cash

**cash register** *n* : a business machine that usu. has a money drawer, indicates each sale, and records the money received

**cash-strapped** \'kash-ˌstrapt\ *adj* : lacking sufficient money

**cas·ing** \'kā-siŋ\ *n* 1 : something that encases 2 : the frame of a door or window

**ca·si·no** \kə-'sē-nō\ *n, pl* **-nos** [It, fr. *casa* house] 1 : a building or room for social amusements; *esp* : one used for gambling 2 *also* **cas·si·no** : a card game in which players win cards by matching those on the table

**cask** \'kask\ *n* : a barrel-shaped container usu. for liquids; *also* : the quantity held by such a container

**cas·ket** \'kas-kət\ *n* 1 : a small box (as for jewels) 2 : COFFIN

**casque** \'kask\ *n* : HELMET

**cas·sa·va** \kə-'sä-və\ *n* : any of several tropical spurges with rootstocks yielding a nutritious starch from which tapioca is prepared; *also* : the rootstock or its starch

**cas·se·role** \'ka-sə-ˌrōl\ *n* 1 : a dish in which food may be baked and served 2 : food cooked and served in a casserole

**cas·sette** *also* **ca·sette** \kə-'set\ *n* 1 : a lightproof container for photographic plates or film 2 : a plastic case containing magnetic tape

**cas·sia** \'ka-shə\ *n* 1 : a dried coarse cinnamon bark 2 : any of a genus of leguminous herbs, shrubs, and trees of warm regions including several which yield senna

**cas·sit·er·ite** \kə-'si-tə-ˌrīt\ *n* : a dark mineral that is the chief tin ore

**cas·sock** \'ka-sək\ *n* : an ankle-length garment worn esp. by Roman Catholic and Anglican clergy

**cas·so·wary** \'ka-sə-ˌwer-ē\ *n, pl* **-war·ies** : any of a genus of large flightless birds closely related to the emu

¹**cast** \'kast\ *vb* **cast; cast·ing** 1 : THROW,

FLING 2 : DIRECT ⟨∼ a glance⟩ 3 : to deposit (a ballot) formally 4 : to throw off, out, or away : DISCARD, SHED 5 : COMPUTE; *esp* : to add up 6 : to assign the parts of (a play) to actors; *also* : to assign to a role or part 7 : to shape (a substance) by pouring in liquid or plastic form into a mold and letting harden without pressure 8 : to make (as a knot or stitch) by looping or catching up

²**cast** *n* 1 : THROW, FLING 2 : a throw of dice 3 : the set of actors in a dramatic production 4 : something formed in or as if in a mold; *also* : a rigid surgical casing (as for protecting and supporting a fractured bone) 5 : TINGE, HUE 6 : APPEARANCE, LOOK ⟨features of delicate ∼⟩ 7 : something thrown out or off, shed, or expelled ⟨worm ∼s⟩

**cas·ta·net** \ˌkas-tə-'net\ *n* [Sp *castañeta,* fr. *castaña* chestnut, fr. L *castanea*] : a rhythm instrument consisting of two small wooden, ivory, or plastic shells held in the hand and clicked together

**cast·away** \'kas-tə-ˌwā\ *adj* 1 : thrown away : REJECTED 2 : cast adrift or ashore as a survivor of a shipwreck — **castaway** *n*

**caste** \'kast\ *n* [Pg *casta,* lit., race, lineage, fr. fem. of *casto* pure, chaste, fr. L *castus*] 1 : one of the hereditary social classes in Hinduism 2 : a division of a society based on wealth, inherited rank, or occupation 3 : social position : PRESTIGE 4 : a system of rigid social stratification

**cas·tel·lat·ed** \'kas-tə-ˌlā-təd\ *adj* : having battlements like a castle

**cast·er** \'kas-tər\ *n* 1 *or* **cas·tor** : a small container to hold salt or pepper at the table 2 : a small wheel that turns freely and is used to support and move furniture, trucks, and equipment

**cas·ti·gate** \'kas-tə-ˌgāt\ *vb* **-gat·ed; -gat·ing** : to punish or criticize severely — **cas·ti·ga·tion** \ˌkas-tə-'gā-shən\ *n* — **cas·ti·ga·tor** \'kas-tə-ˌgā-tər\ *n*

**cast·ing** \'kas-tiŋ\ *n* 1 : CAST 7 2 : something cast in a mold

**casting vote** *n* : a deciding vote cast by a presiding officer to break a tie

**cast iron** *n* : a hard brittle alloy of iron, carbon, and silicon cast in a mold

**cas·tle** \'ka-səl\ *n* 1 : a large fortified building or set of buildings 2 : a large or imposing house 3 : ³ROOK

**castle in the air** : an impracticable project

**cast–off** \'kast-ˌôf\ *adj* : thrown away or aside — **cast-off** *n*

**cas·tor oil** \'kas-tər-\ *n* : a thick yellowish oil extracted from the poisonous seeds of an herb (**castor–oil plant**) and used as a lubricant and purgative

**cas·trate** \'kas-ˌtrāt\ *vb* **cas·trat·ed; cas·trat·ing** : to deprive of sex glands and esp. testes — **cas·tra·tion** \kas-'trā-shən\ *n* — **cas·tra·tor** \-ər\ *n*

**ca·su·al** \'ka-zhə-wəl\ *adj* 1 : resulting from or occurring by chance 2 : OCCASIONAL, INCIDENTAL ⟨∼ employment⟩ 3 : OFFHAND, NONCHALANT ⟨a ∼ approach to cooking⟩  **4** : designed for informal use ⟨∼ clothing⟩ — **ca·su·al·ly** *adv* — **ca·su·al·ness** *n*

**ca·su·al·ty** \'ka-zhəl-tē, 'ka-zhə-wəl-\ *n, pl* **-ties  1** : serious or fatal accident  **2** : a military person lost through death, injury, sickness, or capture or through being missing in action  **3** : a person or thing injured, lost, or destroyed

**ca·su·ist·ry** \'ka-zhə-wə-strē\ *n, pl* **-ries** : specious argument : RATIONALIZATION — **ca·su·ist** \-wist\ *n* — **ca·su·is·tic** \ka-zhə-'wis-tik\ *or* **ca·su·is·ti·cal** \-ti-kəl\ *adj*

**ca·sus bel·li** \kä-səs-'be-ͺlē, ͺkä-səs-'beͺlī\ *n, pl* **ca·sus belli** \kä-ͺsüs-, ͺkä-\ [NL, occasion of war] : a cause or pretext for a declaration of war

¹**cat** \'kat\ *n*  **1** : a carnivorous mammal long domesticated as a pet and for catching rats and mice  **2** : any of a family of animals (as the lion, lynx, or leopard) including the domestic cat  **3** : a malicious woman  **4** : GUY

²**cat** *abbr* catalog

**ca·tab·o·lism** \kə-'ta-bə-ͺli-zəm\ *n* : destructive metabolism involving the release of energy and resulting in the breakdown of complex materials — **cat·a·bol·ic** \ͺka-tə-bä-lik\ *adj*

**cat·a·clysm** \'ka-tə-ͺkli-zəm\ *n* : a violent change or upheaval — **cat·a·clys·mal** \ͺka-tə-'kliz-məl\ *or* **cat·a·clys·mic** \-'kliz-mik\ *adj*

**cat·a·comb** \'ka-tə-ͺkōm\ *n* : an underground burial place with galleries and recesses for tombs

**cat·a·falque** \'ka-tə-ͺfalk, -ͺfȯlk, -ͺfȯk\ *n* : an ornamental structure sometimes used in solemn funerals to hold the body

**cat·a·lep·sy** \'ka-tə-ͺlep-sē\ *n, pl* **-sies** : a trancelike state characterized esp. by loss of voluntary motion — **cat·a·lep·tic** \ͺka-tə-'lep-tik\ *adj or n*

¹**cat·a·log** *or* **cat·a·logue** \'ka-tə-ͺlȯg\ *n*  **1** : LIST, REGISTER  **2** : a systematic list of items with descriptive details; *also* : a book containing such a list

²**catalog** *or* **catalogue** *vb* **-loged** *or* **-logued; -log·ing** *or* **-logu·ing  1** : to make a catalog of  **2** : to enter in a catalog — **cat·a·log·er** *or* **cat·a·logu·er** *n*

**ca·tal·pa** \kə-'tal-pə\ *n* : any of a genus of broad-leaved trees with showy flowers and long slim pods

**ca·tal·y·sis** \kə-'ta-lə-səs\ *n, pl* **-y·ses** \-ͺsēz\ : a change and esp. increase in the rate of a chemical reaction brought about by a substance (**cat·a·lyst** \'ka-tə-list\) that is itself unchanged at the end of the reaction — **cat·a·lyt·ic** \ͺka-tə-'li-tik\ *adj* — **cat·a·lyt·i·cal·ly** \-ti-k(ə-)lē\ *adv*

**catalytic converter** *n* : an automobile exhaust-system component in which a catalyst changes harmful gases into mostly harmless products

**cat·a·lyze** \'ka-tə-ͺlīz\ *vb* **-lyzed; -lyz·ing** : to bring about the catalysis of (a chemical reaction)

**cat·a·ma·ran** \ͺka-tə-mə-'ran\ *n* [Tamil, a language of southern India) *kaṭṭumaram,*

fr. *kaṭṭu* to tie + *maram* tree] : a boat with twin hulls

**cat·a·mount** \'ka-tə-ͺmau̇nt\ *n* : COUGAR; *also* : LYNX

**cat·a·pult** \'ka-tə-ͺpəlt, -ͺpu̇lt\ *n*  **1** : an ancient military machine for hurling missiles  **2** : a device for launching an airplane (as from an aircraft carrier) — **catapult** *vb*

**cat·a·ract** \'ka-tə-ͺrakt\ *n*  **1** : a cloudiness of the lens of the eye obstructing vision  **2** : a large waterfall; *also* : steep rapids in a river

**ca·tarrh** \kə-'tär\ *n* : inflammation of a mucous membrane esp. of the nose and throat — **ca·tarrh·al** \-əl\ *adj*

**ca·tas·tro·phe** \kə-'tas-trə-(ͺ)fē\ *n* [Gk *katastrophē,* fr. *katastrephein* to overturn, fr. *kata-* down + *strephein* to turn]  **1** : a great disaster or misfortune  **2** : utter failure — **cat·a·stroph·ic** \ͺka-tə-'strä-fik\ *adj* — **cat·a·stroph·i·cal·ly** \-fi-k(ə-)lē\ *adv*

**cat·a·ton·ic** \ͺka-tə-'tä-nik\ *adj* : of, relating to, or marked by schizophrenia characterized esp. by stupor, negativism, rigidity, purposeless excitement, and bizarre posturing — **catatonic** *n*

**cat·bird** \'kat-ͺbərd\ *n* : an American songbird with a catlike mewing call

**cat·boat** \'kat-ͺbōt\ *n* : a single-masted sailboat with a single large sail extended by a long boom

**cat·call** \-ͺkȯl\ *n* : a loud cry made esp. to express disapproval — **catcall** *vb*

¹**catch** \'kach, 'kech\ *vb* **caught** \'kȯt\; **catch·ing** [ME *cacchen,* fr. AF *cacher, chucher, chacer* to hunt, ultim. fr. L *captare* to chase]  **1** : to capture esp. after pursuit  **2** : TRAP  **3** : to discover unexpectedly ⟨*caught* in the act⟩  **4** : to become suddenly aware of  **5** : to take hold of : SNATCH ⟨∼ at a straw⟩  **6** : INTERCEPT  **7** : to get entangled  **8** : to become affected with or by ⟨∼ fire⟩ ⟨∼ cold⟩  **9** : to seize and hold firmly; *also* : FASTEN  **10** : OVERTAKE  **11** : to be in time for ⟨∼ a train⟩  **12** : to take in and retain  **13** : to look at or listen to ⟨∼ a TV show⟩

²**catch** *n*  **1** : something caught  **2** : the act of catching; *also* : a game consisting of throwing and catching a ball  **3** : something that catches or checks or holds immovable ⟨a door ∼⟩  **4** : one worth catching esp. as a mate  **5** : FRAGMENT, SNATCH  **6** : a concealed difficulty or complication

**catch·all** \'kach-ͺȯl, 'kech-\ *n* : something to hold a variety of odds and ends

**catch–as–catch–can** *adj* : using any means available

**catch·er** \'ka-chər, 'ke-\ *n* : one that catches; *esp* : a player positioned behind home plate in baseball

**catch·ing** *adj*  **1** : INFECTIOUS, CONTAGIOUS  **2** : ALLURING, CATCHY

**catch·ment** \'kach-mənt, 'kech-\ *n*  **1** : something that catches water  **2** : the action of catching water

**catch on** *vb*  **1** : UNDERSTAND  **2** : to become popular

**catch·pen·ny** \'kach-ˌpe-nē, 'kech-\ *adj* : using sensationalism or cheapness for appeal ⟨a ∼ newspaper⟩

**catch·phrase** \-ˌfrāz\ *n* : a word or expression frequently used to represent or characterize a person, group, idea, or point of view

**catch–22** \-ˌtwen-tē-'tü\ *n, pl* **catch–22's** *or* **catch–22s** *often cap C* [fr. *Catch-22*, a paradoxical rule found in the novel *Catch-22* (1961) by Joseph Heller] : a problematic situation for which the only solution is denied by a circumstance inherent in the problem or by a rule; *also* : the circumstance or rule that denies a solution

**catchup** *var of* KETCHUP

**catch up** *vb* : to travel or work fast enough to overtake or complete

**catch·word** \'kach-ˌwərd, 'kech-\ *n* **1** : GUIDE WORD **2** : CATCHPHRASE

**catchy** \'ka-chē, 'ke-\ *adj* **catch·i·er; -est** **1** : likely to catch the interest or attention **2** : TRICKY ⟨a ∼ question⟩

**cat·e·chism** \'ka-tə-ˌki-zəm\ *n* : a summary or test (as of religious doctrine) usu. in the form of questions and answers — **cat·e·chist** \-ˌkist\ *n* — **cat·e·chize** \-ˌkīz\ *vb*

**cat·e·chu·men** \ˌka-tə-'kyü-mən\ *n* : a religious convert receiving training before baptism

**cat·e·gor·i·cal** \ˌka-tə-'gȯr-i-kəl\ *adj* **1** : ABSOLUTE, UNQUALIFIED ⟨a ∼ denial⟩ **2** : of, relating to, or constituting a category — **cat·e·gor·i·cal·ly** \-i-k(ə-)lē\ *adv*

**cat·e·go·rise** *Brit var of* CATEGORIZE

**cat·e·go·rize** \'ka-ti-gə-ˌrīz\ *vb* **-rized; -riz·ing** : to put into a category : CLASSIFY — **cat·e·go·ri·za·tion** \ˌka-ti-gə-rə-'zā-shən\ *n*

**cat·e·go·ry** \'ka-tə-ˌgȯr-ē\ *n, pl* **-ries** : a division used in classification; *also* : CLASS, GROUP, KIND

**ca·ter** \'kā-tər\ *vb* [obs. *cater* buyer of provisions, fr. ME *catour*, short for *acatour*, fr. AF, fr. *acater*, *achater* to buy] **1** : to provide a supply of food **2** : to supply what is wanted — **ca·ter·er** *n*

**catercorner** *or* **cater-cornered** *var of* KITTY-CORNER

**cat·er·pil·lar** \'ka-tər-ˌpi-lər\ *n* [ME *catyrpel*, fr. OF *catepelose*, lit., hairy cat] : a wormlike often hairy insect larva esp. of a butterfly or moth

**cat·er·waul** \'ka-tər-ˌwȯl\ *vb* : to make a harsh cry — **caterwaul** *n*

**cat·fish** \'kat-ˌfish\ *n* : any of an order of chiefly freshwater stout-bodied fishes with slender tactile processes around the mouth

**cat·gut** \-ˌgət\ *n* : a tough cord made usu. from sheep intestines

**ca·thar·sis** \kə-'thär-səs\ *n, pl* **ca·thar·ses** \-ˌsēz\ **1** : an act of purging or purification **2** : elimination of a complex by bringing it to consciousness and affording it expression

**¹ca·thar·tic** \kə-'thär-tik\ *adj* : of, relating to, or producing catharsis

**²cathartic** *n* : PURGATIVE

**ca·the·dral** \kə-'thē-drəl\ *n* : the principal church of a diocese

**cath·e·ter** \'ka-thə-tər\ *n* : a tube for insertion into a bodily passage or cavity usu. for injecting or drawing off material or for keeping a passage open

**cath·e·ter·i·za·tion** \ˌka-thə-tə-rə-'zā-shən\ *n* : the use of or introduction of a catheter — **cath·e·ter·ize** \'ka-thə-tə-ˌrīz\ *vb*

**cath·ode** \'ka-ˌthōd\ *n* **1** : the negative electrode of an electrolytic cell **2** : the positive terminal of a battery **3** : the electron-emitting electrode of an electron tube — **cath·od·al** \'ka-ˌthō-dᵊl\ *adj* — **ca·thod·ic** \ka-'thä-dik\ *adj*

**cathode–ray tube** *n* : a vacuum tube in which a beam of electrons is projected on a phosphor-coated screen to produce a luminous spot

**cath·o·lic** \'kath-lik, 'ka-thə-\ *adj* [ME *catholik* relating to the church universal, ultim. fr. Gk *katholikos* universal, general, fr. *katholou* in general] **1** *cap* : of or relating to Catholics and esp. Roman Catholics **2** : GENERAL, UNIVERSAL

**Cath·o·lic** \'kath-lik, 'ka-thə-\ *n* : a member of a church claiming historical continuity from the ancient undivided Christian church; *esp* : a member of the Roman Catholic Church — **Ca·thol·i·cism** \kə-'thä-lə-ˌsi-zəm\ *n*

**cath·o·lic·i·ty** \ˌka-thə-'li-sə-tē\ *n, pl* **-ties** **1** *cap* : the character of being in conformity with a Catholic church **2** : liberality of sentiments or views **3** : comprehensive range

**cat·ion** \'kat-ˌī-ən\ *n* : the ion in an electrolyte that migrates to the cathode; *also* : a positively charged ion

**cat·kin** \'kat-kən\ *n* : a long flower cluster (as of a willow) bearing crowded flowers and prominent bracts

**cat·like** \-ˌlīk\ *adj* : resembling a cat or its behavior; *esp* : STEALTHY

**cat·nap** \-ˌnap\ *n* : a very short light nap — **catnap** *vb*

**cat·nip** \-ˌnip\ *n* : an aromatic mint that is esp. attractive to cats

**cat-o'-nine-tails** \ˌka-tə-'nīn-ˌtālz\ *n, pl* **cat-o'-nine-tails** : a whip made of usu. nine knotted cords fastened to a handle

**CAT scan** \'kat-\ *n* [computerized *axial tomography*] : an image made by computed tomography

**CAT scanner** *n* : a medical instrument consisting of integrated X-ray and computing equipment that is used to make CAT scans

**cat's cradle** *n* : a game played with a string looped on the fingers in such a way as to resemble a small cradle

**cat's-eye** \'kats-ˌī\ *n, pl* **cat's-eyes** : any of various iridescent gems

**cat's-paw** \-ˌpȯ\ *n, pl* **cat's-paws** : a person used by another as a tool

**cat·suit** \'kat-ˌsüt\ *n* : a close-fitting one-piece garment that covers the torso and the legs

**catsup** *var of* KETCHUP

**cat·tail** \'kat-ˌtāl\ *n* : any of a genus of tall

reedlike marsh plants with furry brown spikes of tiny flowers

**cat·tle** \'ka-t³l\ *n pl* : LIVESTOCK; *esp* : domestic bovines (as cows, bulls, or calves) — **cat·tle·man** \-mən, -ˌman\ *n*

**cat·ty** \'ka-tē\ *adj* **cat·ti·er; -est** : slyly spiteful ⟨∼ comments⟩ — **cat·ti·ly** \'ka-tə-lē\ *adv* — **cat·ti·ness** *n*

**catty–corner** *or* **catty–cornered** *var of* KITTY-CORNER

**CATV** *abbr* community antenna television

**cat·walk** \'kat-ˌwȯk\ *n* : a narrow walk (as along a bridge)

**Cau·ca·sian** \kȯ-'kā-zhən\ *adj* : of or relating to the white race of humankind — **Caucasian** *n* — **Cau·ca·soid** \'kȯ-kə-ˌsȯid\ *adj or n*

**cau·cus** \'kȯ-kəs\ *n* : a meeting of a group of persons belonging to the same political party or faction usu. to decide upon policies and candidates — **caucus** *vb*

**cau·dal** \'kȯ-d³l\ *adj* : of, relating to, or located near the tail or the hind end of the body — **cau·dal·ly** *adv*

**cau·di·llo** \kaü-'thē-(ˌ)yō, -'thēl-\ *n, pl* **-llos** : a Spanish or Latin-American military dictator

**caught** \'kȯt\ *past and past part of* CATCH

**caul** \'kȯl\ *n* : the inner fetal membrane of higher vertebrates esp. when covering the head at birth

**caul·dron** \'kȯl-drən\ *n* : a large kettle

**cau·li·flow·er** \'kȯ-li-ˌflaü(-ə)r\ *n* [It *cavolfiore*, fr. *cavolo* cabbage + *fiore* flower] : a garden plant closely related to cabbage and grown for its compact edible head of undeveloped flowers; *also* : this head used as a vegetable

**cauliflower ear** *n* : an ear deformed from injury and excessive growth of scar tissue

¹**caulk** *or* **calk** \'kȯk\ *vb* [ME, fr. AF *cauker, calcher* to trample, fr. L *calcare*, fr. *calx* heel] : to stop up and make tight against leakage (as a boat or its seams) — **caulk·er** *n*

²**caulk** *or* **calk** *also* **caulk·ing** *or* **calk·ing** *n* : material used to caulk

**caus·al** \'kȯ-zəl\ *adj* 1 : expressing or indicating cause 2 : relating to or acting as a cause — **cau·sal·i·ty** \kȯ-'za-lə-tē\ *n* — **caus·al·ly** *adv*

**cau·sa·tion** \kȯ-'zā-shən\ *n* 1 : the act or process of causing 2 : the means by which an effect is produced

¹**cause** \'kȯz\ *n* 1 : REASON, MOTIVE 2 : something that brings about a result; *esp* : a person or thing that is the agent of bringing something about 3 : a suit or action in court : CASE 4 : a question or matter to be decided 5 : a principle or movement earnestly supported — **cause·less** *adj*

²**cause** *vb* **caused; caus·ing** : to be the cause or occasion of — **caus·a·tive** \'kȯ-zə-tiv\ *adj* — **caus·er** *n*

**cause cé·lè·bre** \ˌkȯz-sā-'lebr³, ˌkȯz-\ *n, pl* **causes célèbres** \*same*\ [F, lit., celebrated case] : a legal case that excites widespread interest 2 : a notorious person, thing, incident, or episode

**cau·se·rie** \ˌkōz-³rē, ˌkō-zə-\ *n* [F] 1 : an

informal conversation : CHAT 2 : a short informal essay

**cause·way** \'kȯz-ˌwā\ *n* : a raised way or road across wet ground or water

¹**caus·tic** \'kȯ-stik\ *adj* 1 : CORROSIVE 2 : SHARP, INCISIVE ⟨∼ wit⟩

²**caustic** *n* 1 : a substance that burns or destroys organic tissue by chemical action 2 : SODIUM HYDROXIDE

**cau·ter·ize** \'kȯ-tə-ˌrīz\ *vb* **-ized; -iz·ing** : to burn or sear usu. to prevent infection or bleeding — **cau·ter·i·za·tion** \ˌkȯ-tə-rə-'zā-shən\ *n*

¹**cau·tion** \'kȯ-shən\ *n* 1 : ADMONITION, WARNING 2 : prudent forethought to minimize risk 3 : one that astonishes — **cau·tion·ary** \-shə-ˌner-ē\ *adj*

²**caution** *vb* : to advise caution to

**cau·tious** \'kȯ-shəs\ *adj* : marked by or given to caution : CAREFUL — **cau·tious·ly** *adv* — **cau·tious·ness** *n*

**cav** *abbr* 1 cavalry 2 cavity

**cav·al·cade** \ˌka-vəl-'kād\ *n* 1 : a procession of riders or carriages; *also* : a procession of vehicles 2 : a dramatic sequence or procession ⟨a ∼ of films⟩

¹**cav·a·lier** \ˌka-və-'lir\ *n* [MF, fr. It *cavaliere*, fr. Old Occitan *cavalier*, fr. LL *caballarius* horseman, fr. L *caballus* horse] 1 : a mounted soldier : KNIGHT 2 *cap* : an adherent of Charles I of England 3 : GALLANT

²**cavalier** *adj* 1 : DEBONAIR 2 : DISDAINFUL, HAUGHTY ⟨a ∼ attitude toward money⟩ — **cav·a·lier·ly** *adv*

**cav·al·ry** \'ka-vəl-rē\ *n, pl* **-ries** : troops mounted on horseback or moving in motor vehicles — **cav·al·ry·man** \-mən, -ˌman\ *n*

¹**cave** \'kāv\ *n* : a natural underground chamber open to the surface

²**cave** *vb* **caved; cav·ing** 1 : to collapse or cause to collapse 2 : to cease to resist : SUBMIT — usu. used with *in*

**ca·ve·at** \'ka-vē-ˌät, -ˌat; 'kä-vē-ˌät\ *n* [L, let him beware] : WARNING

**caveat emp·tor** \-'emp-tȯr, -ˌtȯr\ *n* [NL, let the buyer beware] : a principle in commerce: without a warranty the buyer takes a risk

**cave–in** \'kā-ˌvin\ *n* 1 : the action of caving in 2 : a place where earth has caved in

**cave·man** \'kāv-ˌman\ *n* 1 : a cave dweller esp. of the Stone Age 2 : a man who acts in a rough or crude manner

**cav·ern** \'ka-vərn\ *n* : CAVE; *esp* : one of large or unknown size — **cav·ern·ous** *adj* — **cav·ern·ous·ly** *adv*

**cav·i·ar** *also* **cav·i·are** \'ka-vē-ˌär, 'kä-\ *n* : the salted roe of a large fish (as sturgeon) used as an appetizer

**cav·il** \'ka-vəl\ *vb* **-iled** *or* **-illed; -il·ing** *or* **-il·ling** : to make frivolous objections or raise trivial objections to — **cavil** *n* — **cav·il·er** *or* **cav·il·ler** *n*

**cav·ing** \'kā-viŋ\ *n* : the sport of exploring caves : SPELUNKING

**cav·i·ta·tion** \ˌka-və-'tā-shən\ *n* : the formation of partial vacuums in a liquid by a swiftly moving solid body (as a propeller) or by high-intensity sound waves

**cav·i·ty** \'ka-və-tē\ *n, pl* **-ties** **1** : an un-filled space within a mass : a hollow place **2** : an area of decay in a tooth

**ca·vort** \kə-'vort\ *vb* : PRANCE, CAPER

**ca·vy** \'kā-vē\ *n, pl* **cavies** : GUINEA PIG 1

**caw** \'kö\ *vb* : to utter the harsh call of the crow or a similar cry — **caw** *n*

**cay** \'kē, 'kā\ *n* : [4]KEY

**cay·enne pepper** \,kī-'en-, ,kā-\ *n* : a condiment consisting of ground dried fruits or seeds of a hot pepper

**cayman** *var of* CAIMAN

**Ca·yu·ga** \kā-'ü-gə, kī-\ *n, pl* **Cayuga** or **Cayugas** : a member of an American Indian people of New York

**Cay·use** \'kī-,yüs, kī-'\ *n* **1** *pl* **Cayuse** or **Cayuses** : a member of an American Indian people of Oregon and Washington **2** *pl* **cayuses, not cap, West** : a native range horse

**Cb** *symbol* columbium

**CB** \'sē-'bē\ *n* **1** : CITIZENS BAND; *also* : the radio set used for citizens-band communications

**CBC** *abbr* Canadian Broadcasting Corporation

**CBD** *abbr* cash before delivery

**CBS** *abbr* Columbia Broadcasting System

**CBW** *abbr* chemical and biological warfare

**cc** *abbr* cubic centimeter

**CC** *abbr* **1** carbon copy **2** community college **3** country club

**CCD** \,sē-,sē-'dē\ *n* : CHARGE-COUPLED DEVICE

**CCTV** *abbr* closed-circuit television

**CCU** *abbr* **1** cardiac care unit **2** coronary care unit **3** critical care unit

**ccw** *abbr* counterclockwise

**cd** *abbr* cord

**Cd** *symbol* cadmium

**[1]CD** \,sē-'dē\ *n* : CERTIFICATE OF DEPOSIT

**[2]CD** *n* : a small optical disk usu. containing recorded music or computer data; *also* : the content of a CD

**[3]CD** *abbr* Civil Defense

**CDR** *abbr* commander

**CD-ROM** \,sē-,dē-'räm\ *n* : a CD containing computer data that cannot be altered

**CDT** *abbr* central daylight (saving) time

**Ce** *symbol* cerium

**CE** *abbr* **1** chemical engineer **2** civil engineer **3** Corps of Engineers

**cease** \'sēs\ *vb* **ceased**; **ceas·ing** : to come or bring to an end : STOP

**cease-fire** \'sēs-'fī(-ə)r\ *n* : a suspension of active hostilities

**cease·less** \'sēs-ləs\ *adj* : being without pause or stop : CONTINUOUS — **cease-less·ly** *adv* — **cease·less·ness** *n*

**ce·cum** *also* **cae·cum** \'sē-kəm\ *n, pl* **ce-ca** \-kə\ : the blind pouch at the beginning of the large intestine into which the small intestine opens — **ce·cal** *also* **cae-cal** \-kəl\ *adj*

**ce·dar** \'sē-dər\ *n* : any of numerous coniferous trees (as a juniper) noted for their fragrant durable wood; *also* : this wood

**cede** \'sēd\ *vb* **ced·ed**; **ced·ing** **1** : to yield or give up esp. by treaty **2** : ASSIGN, TRANSFER — **ced·er** *n*

**ce·di** \'sā-dē\ *n* — see MONEY table

**ce·dil·la** \si-'di-lə\ *n* : a mark placed under the letter *c* (as ç) to show that the *c* is to be pronounced like *s*

**ceil·ing** \'sē-liŋ\ *n* **1** : the overhead inside lining of a room **2** : the height above the ground of the base of the lowest layer of clouds when over half of the sky is obscured **3** : the greatest height at which an airplane can operate efficiently **4** : a prescribed upper limit ⟨price ~⟩

**cel·an·dine** \'se-lən-,dīn, -,dēn\ *n* : a yellow-flowered herb related to the poppies

**cel·e·brant** \'se-lə-brənt\ *n* : one who celebrates; *esp* : a priest officiating at the Eucharist

**cel·e·brate** \'se-lə-,brāt\ *vb* **-brat·ed**; **-brat·ing** **1** : to perform (as a sacrament) with appropriate rites **2** : to honor (as a holiday) by solemn ceremonies or by refraining from ordinary business **3** : to observe a notable occasion with festivities **4** : EXTOL — **cel·e·bra·tion** \,se-lə-'brā-shən\ *n* — **cel·e·bra·tor** \'se-lə-'brā-tər\ *n* — **cel·e·bra·to·ry** \-brə-,tör-ē, ,se-lə-'brā-tə-rē\ *adj*

**celebrated** *adj* : widely known and often referred to ⟨a ~ author⟩ ♦ **Synonyms** DISTINGUISHED, RENOWNED, NOTED, FAMOUS, ILLUSTRIOUS, NOTORIOUS

**ce·leb·ri·ty** \sə-'le-brə-tē\ *n, pl* **-ties** **1** : the state of being celebrated : RENOWN **2** : a celebrated person

**ce·ler·i·ty** \sə-'ler-ə-tē\ *n* : SPEED, RAPIDITY

**cel·ery** \'se-lə-rē\ *n, pl* **-er·ies** : a European herb related to the carrot and widely grown for the crisp edible stems of its leaves

**celery cabbage** *n* : CHINESE CABBAGE 2

**ce·les·ta** \sə-'les-tə\ or **ce·leste** \sə-'lest\ *n* : a keyboard instrument with hammers that strike steel plates

**ce·les·tial** \sə-'les-chəl\ *adj* **1** : HEAVENLY, DIVINE **2** : of or relating to the sky ⟨~ bodies⟩ — **ce·les·tial·ly** *adv*

**celestial navigation** *n* : navigation by observation of the positions of stars

**celestial sphere** *n* : an imaginary sphere of infinite radius against which the celestial bodies appear to be projected

**cel·i·ba·cy** \'se-lə-bə-sē\ *n* **1** : the state of being unmarried; *esp* : abstention by vow from marriage **2** : abstention from sexual intercourse

**cel·i·bate** \'se-lə-bət\ *n* : one who lives in celibacy — **celibate** *adj*

**cell** \'sel\ *n* **1** : a small room (as in a convent or prison) usu. for one person; *also* : a small compartment, cavity, or bounded space **2** : a tiny mass of protoplasm that usu. contains a nucleus, is enclosed by a membrane, and forms the smallest structural unit of living matter capable of functioning independently **3** : a container holding an electrolyte either for generating electricity or for use in electrolysis **4** : a single unit in a device for converting radiant energy into electrical energy — **celled** \'seld\ adj

**cel·lar** \'se-lər\ n 1 : BASEMENT 1 2 : the lowest place in the standings (as in an athletic league) 3 : a stock of wines

**cel·lar·ette** or **cel·lar·et** \,se-lə-'ret\ n : a case or cabinet for a few bottles of wine or liquor

**cell body** n : the nucleus-containing central part of a neuron exclusive of its processes

**cel·lo** \'che-lō\ n, pl **cellos** : a bass member of the violin family tuned an octave below the viola — **cel·list** \-list\ n

**cel·lo·phane** \'se-lə-,fān\ n : a thin transparent material made from cellulose and used as a wrapping

**cell phone** n : a portable cordless telephone for use in a cellular system

**cel·lu·lar** \'sel-yə-lər\ adj 1 : of, relating to, or consisting of cells (~ proteins) 2 : of, relating to, or being a radiotelephone system in which a geographical area is divided into small sections each served by a transmitter of limited range

**cel·lu·lite** \'sel-yə-,līt\ n : deposits of lumpy fat within connective tissue (as in the thighs, hips, and buttocks)

**cel·lu·lose** \'sel-yə-,lōs\ n : a complex carbohydrate of the cell walls of plants used esp. in making paper or rayon — **cel·lu·los·ic** \,sel-yə-'lō-sik\ adj or n

**Cel·si·us** \'sel-sē-əs\ adj : relating to or having a scale for measuring temperature on which the interval between the triple point and the boiling point of water is divided into 99.99 degrees with 0.01° being the triple point and 100.00° the boiling point; also : CENTIGRADE

**Celt** \'kelt, 'selt\ n : a member of any of a group of peoples (as the Irish or Welsh) of western Europe — **Celt·ic** adj

**cem·ba·lo** \'chem-bə-,lō\ n, pl **-ba·li** \-,lē\ or **-balos** [It] : HARPSICHORD

¹**ce·ment** \si-'ment\ n 1 : CONCRETE; also : a powder that is produced from a burned mixture chiefly of clay and limestone and that is used in mortar and concrete 2 : a binding element or agency 3 : CEMENTUM; also : a substance for filling cavities in teeth

²**cement** vb 1 : to unite by or as if by cement 2 : to cover with concrete — **ce·ment·er** n

**ce·men·tum** \si-'men-təm\ n : a specialized external bony layer covering the dentin of the part of a tooth normally within the gum

**cem·e·tery** \'se-mə-,ter-ē\ n, pl **-ter·ies** [ME cimitery, fr. AF cimiterie, fr. LL coemeterium, fr. Gk koimētērion sleeping chamber, burial place, fr. koiman to put to sleep] : a burial ground : GRAVEYARD

**cen·o·bite** \'se-nə-,bīt\ n : a member of a religious group living together in a monastic community — **cen·o·bit·ic** \,se-nə-'bi-tik\ adj

**cen·o·taph** \'se-nə-,taf\ n [F cénotaphe, fr. L cenotaphium, fr. Gk kenotaphion, fr. kenos empty + taphos tomb] : a tomb or a monument erected in honor of a person whose body is elsewhere

**Ce·no·zo·ic** \,sē-nə-'zō-ik, ,se-\ adj : of, relating to, or being the era of geologic history that extends from about 65 million years ago to the present — **Cenozoic** n

**cen·ser** \'sen-sər\ n : a vessel for burning incense (as in a religious ritual)

¹**cen·sor** \'sen-sər\ n 1 : a person who inspects printed matter or motion pictures with power to suppress anything objectionable 2 : one of two early Roman magistrates whose duties included taking the census — **cen·so·ri·al** \sen-'sòr-ē-əl\ adj

²**censor** vb : to subject to censorship

**cen·so·ri·ous** \sen-'sòr-ē-əs\ adj : marked by or given to censure : CRITICAL — **cen·so·ri·ous·ly** adv — **cen·so·ri·ous·ness** n

**cen·sor·ship** \'sen-sər-,ship\ n 1 : the action of a censor esp. in stopping the transmission or publication of matter considered objectionable 2 : the office of a Roman censor

¹**cen·sure** \'sen-chər\ n 1 : the act of blaming or condemning sternly 2 : an official reprimand

²**censure** vb **cen·sured; cen·sur·ing** : to find fault with and criticize as blameworthy — **cen·sur·able** adj — **cen·sur·er** n

**cen·sus** \'sen-səs\ n 1 : a periodic governmental count of population 2 : COUNT, TALLY — **cen·sus** vb

¹**cent** \'sent\ n [F, hundred, fr. L centum] 1 — see birr, dollar, euro, leone, lilangeni, nakfa, rand, rupee, shilling at MONEY table 2 : a coin, token, or note representing one cent 3 : a monetary unit formerly used in Suriname (¹/₁₀₀ gulden), Malta (¹/₁₀₀ lira), and Cyprus (¹/₁₀₀ pound)

²**cent** abbr 1 centigrade 2 central 3 century

**cen·tas** \'sen-,täs\ n, pl **cen·tai** \-,tī\ or **cen·tu** \-,tü\ : a monetary unit equal to ¹/₁₀₀ litas formerly used in Lithuania

**cen·taur** \'sen-,tòr\ n : any of a race of creatures in Greek mythology half man and half horse

¹**cen·ta·vo** \sen-'tä-(,)vō\ n, pl **-vos** 1 — see boliviano, cordoba, lempira, peso, quetzal at MONEY table 2 : a monetary unit equal to ¹/₁₀₀ sucre formerly used in Ecuador

²**cen·ta·vo** \-'tä-(,)vü, -(,)vō\ n, pl **-vos** 1 — see escudo, metical, real at MONEY table 2 : a former monetary unit equal to ¹/₁₀₀ Portuguese escudo

**cen·te·nar·i·an** \,sen-tə-'ner-ē-ən\ n : a person who is 100 or more years old

**cen·te·na·ry** \sen-'te-nə-rē, 'sen-tə-,ner-ē\ n, pl **-ries** : CENTENNIAL — **centenary** adj

**cen·ten·ni·al** \sen-'te-nē-əl\ n : a 100th anniversary or its celebration — **centennial** adj

¹**cen·ter** \'sen-tər\ n 1 : the point that is equally distant from all points on the circumference of a circle or surface of a sphere; also : MIDDLE 1 2 : the point about which an activity concentrates or from which something originates 3 : a region of concentrated population 4 : a

middle part  **5** *often cap* : political figures holding moderate views esp. between those of conservatives and liberals  **6** : a player occupying a middle position (as in football or basketball)

²**center** *vb*  **1** : to place or fix at or around a center or central area  **2** : to give a central focus or basis : CONCENTRATE  **3** : to have a center : FOCUS

**cen·ter·board** \'sen-tər-,bórd\ *n* : a retractable keel used esp. in sailboats

**cen·ter·piece** \-,pēs\ *n*  **1** : an object in a central position; *esp* : an adornment in the center of a table  **2** : one that is of central importance or interest in a larger whole ⟨tax reform was the ∼ of his speech⟩

**cen·tes·i·mal** \sen-'te-sə-məl\ *adj* : marked by or relating to division into hundredths

¹**cen·tes·i·mo** \chen-'te-zə-,mō\ *n, pl* **-mi** \-(,)mē\ : a former monetary unit equal to ¹⁄₁₀₀ Italian lira

²**cen·tes·i·mo** \sen-'te-sə-,mō\ *n, pl* **-mos** — see *balboa, peso* at MONEY table

**cen·ti·grade** \'sen-tə-,grād, 'sän-\ *adj* : relating to, conforming to, or having a thermometer scale on which the interval between the freezing and boiling points of water is divided into 100 degrees with 0° representing the freezing point and 100° the boiling point ⟨10° ∼⟩ — compare CELSIUS

**cen·ti·gram** \-,gram\ *n* — see METRIC SYSTEM table

**cen·ti·li·ter** \'sen-ti-,lē-tər\ *n* — see METRIC SYSTEM table

**cen·time** \'sän-,tēm\ *n*  **1** : a former monetary unit of any of several countries (as Belgium, France, and Luxembourg) equal to ¹⁄₁₀₀ franc  **2** — see *dinar, dirham, franc, gourde* at MONEY table

**cen·ti·me·ter** \'sen-tə-,mē-tər, 'sän-\ *n* — see METRIC SYSTEM table

**centimeter–gram–second** *adj* : of, relating to, or being a system of units based on the centimeter as the unit of length, the gram as the unit of mass, and the second as the unit of time

**cen·ti·mo** \'sen-tə-,mō\ *n, pl* **-mos**  **1** — see *bolivar, colón, dobra, guarani, sol* at MONEY table  **2** : a former monetary unit equal to ¹⁄₁₀₀ peseta

**cen·ti·pede** \'sen-tə-,pēd\ *n* [L *centipeda,* fr. *centum* hundred + *pes* foot] : any of a class of long flattened segmented arthropods with one pair of legs on each segment except the first which has a pair of poison fangs

¹**cen·tral** \'sen-trəl\ *adj*  **1** : constituting a center  **2** : ESSENTIAL, PRINCIPAL ⟨the novel's ∼ character⟩  **3** : situated at, in, or near the center  **4** : centrally placed and superseding separate units ⟨∼ heating⟩ — **cen·tral·ly** *adv*

²**central** *n* : a central controlling office

**cen·tral·ise** *Brit var of* CENTRALIZE

**cen·tral·ize** \'sen-trə-,līz\ *vb* **-ized; -izing** : to bring to a central point or under central control — **cen·tral·i·za·tion** \,sen-trə-lə-'zā-shən\ *n* — **cen·tral·iz·er** \'sen-trə-,lī-zər\ *n*

**central nervous system** *n* : the part of the nervous system which integrates nervous function and activity and which in vertebrates consists of the brain and spinal cord

**cen·tre** *chiefly Brit var of* CENTER

**cen·trif·u·gal** \sen-'tri-fyə-gəl, -fi-\ *adj* [NL *centrifugus,* fr. *centr-* center + L *fugere* to flee]  **1** : proceeding or acting in a direction away from a center or axis  **2** : using or acting by centrifugal force

**centrifugal force** *n* : the apparent force felt by an object moving in a curved path and acting outward from a center of rotation

**cen·tri·fuge** \'sen-trə-,fyüj\ *n* : a machine using centrifugal force (as for separating substances of different densities or for removing moisture)

**cen·trip·e·tal** \sen-'tri-pə-t³l\ *adj* [NL *centripetus,* fr. *centr-* center + L *petere* to seek] : proceeding or acting in a direction toward a center or axis

**centripetal force** *n* : the force needed to keep an object revolving about a point moving in a circular path

**cen·trist** \'sen-trist\ *n*  **1** *often cap* : a member of a center party  **2** : one who holds moderate views

**cen·tu·ri·on** \sen-'tür-ē-ən, -'tyür-\ *n* : an officer commanding a Roman century

**cen·tu·ry** \'sen-chə-rē\ *n, pl* **-ries**  **1** : a subdivision of a Roman legion  **2** : a group or sequence of 100 like things  **3** : a period of 100 years

**century plant** *n* : a Mexican agave maturing and flowering only once in many years and then dying

**CEO** \,sē-(,)ē-'ō\ *n* : the executive with the chief decision-making authority in an organization or business

**ce·phal·ic** \sə-'fa-lik\ *adj*  **1** : of or relating to the head  **2** : directed toward or situated on or in or near the head

**ce·ram·ic** \sə-'ra-mik\ *n*  **1** *pl* : the art or process of making articles from a nonmetallic mineral (as clay) by firing  **2** : a product produced by ceramics — **ceramic** *adj*

**ce·ram·ist** \sə-'ra-mist\ *or* **ce·ram·i·cist** \sə-'ra-mə-sist\ *n* : one who engages in ceramics

¹**ce·re·al** \'sir-ē-əl\ *adj* [L *cerealis,* fr. *Ceres,* the Roman goddess of agriculture] : relating to grain or to the plants that produce it; *also* : made of grain

²**cereal** *n*  **1** : a grass (as wheat) yielding grain suitable for food; *also* : its grain  **2** : a food and esp. a breakfast food prepared from the grain of a cereal

**cer·e·bel·lum** \,ser-ə-'be-ləm\ *n, pl* **-bellums** *or* **-bel·la** \-lə\ [ML, fr. L, dim. of *cerebrum* brain] : a part of the brain that projects over the medulla and is concerned esp. with coordination of muscular action and with bodily balance — **cer·e·bel·lar** \-lər\ *adj*

**ce·re·bral** \sə-'rē-brəl, 'ser-ə-\ *adj*  **1** : of or relating to the brain, intellect, or cerebrum  **2** : appealing to or involving the intellect — **ce·re·bral·ly** *adv*

**cerebral cortex** *n* : the surface layer of

gray matter of the cerebrum that functions chiefly in coordination of sensory and motor information

**cerebral palsy** n : a disorder caused by brain damage usu. before, during, or shortly after birth and marked esp. by defective muscle control

**cer·e·brate** \'ser-ə-ˌbrāt\ vb -brat·ed; -brat·ing : THINK — **cer·e·bra·tion** \ˌser-ə-'brā-shən\ n

**ce·re·brum** \sə-'rē-brəm, 'ser-ə-\ n, pl -brums or -bra \-brə\ [L, brain] : the enlarged front and upper part of the brain that contains the higher nervous centers

**cere·ment** \'ser-ə-mənt, 'sir-mənt\ n : a shroud for the dead

**¹cer·e·mo·ni·al** \ˌser-ə-'mō-nē-əl\ adj : of, relating to, or forming a ceremony; also : stressing careful attention to form and detail — **cere·mo·ni·al·ly** adv

**²ceremonial** n : a ceremonial act or system : RITUAL, FORM

**cer·e·mo·ni·ous** \ˌser-ə-'mō-nē-əs\ adj 1 : devoted to forms and ceremony 2 : CEREMONIAL 3 : according to formal usage or procedure 4 : marked by ceremony — **cer·e·mo·ni·ous·ly** adv — **cer·e·mo·ni·ous·ness** n

**cer·e·mo·ny** \'ser-ə-ˌmō-nē\ n, pl -nies 1 : a formal act or series of acts prescribed by law, ritual, or convention 2 : a conventional act of politeness 3 : a mere outward form with no deeper significance 4 : FORMALITY

**ce·re·us** \'sir-ē-əs\ n : any of various cacti of the western U.S. and tropical America

**ce·rise** \sə-'rēs\ n [F, lit., cherry] : a moderate red color

**ce·ri·um** \'sir-ē-əm\ n : a malleable metallic chemical element used esp. in alloys

**cor·met** \'sər-ˌmet\ n : a strong alloy of a heat-resistant compound and a metal used esp. for turbine blades

**cert** abbr certificate; certification; certified; certify

**¹cer·tain** \'sər-t²n\ adj 1 : FIXED, SETTLED 2 : of a specific but unspecified character ⟨~ people in authority⟩ 3 : DEPENDABLE, RELIABLE 4 : INDISPUTABLE, UNDENIABLE ⟨it is ~ that we exist⟩ 5 : assured in mind or action ⟨I am ~ that they are right⟩ — **cer·tain·ly** adv

**²certain** pron : certain ones

**cer·tain·ty** \-tē\ n, pl -ties 1 : something that is certain 2 : the quality or state of being certain

**cer·tif·i·cate** \sər-'ti-fi-kət\ n 1 : a document testifying to the truth of a fact 2 : a document testifying that one has fulfilled certain requirements (as of a course) 3 : a document giving evidence of ownership or debt ⟨a stock ~⟩

**certificate of deposit** : a money-market bond redeemable without penalty only on maturity

**cer·ti·fi·ca·tion** \ˌsər-tə-fə-'kā-shən\'n 1 : the act of certifying : the state of being certified 2 : a certified statement

**certified mail** n : first class mail for which proof of delivery may be secured but no indemnity value is claimed

**certified public accountant** n : an accountant who has met the requirements of a state law and has been granted a certificate

**cer·ti·fy** \'sər-tə-ˌfī\ vb -fied; -fy·ing 1 : VERIFY, CONFIRM 2 : to endorse officially 3 : to guarantee (a bank check) as good by a statement to that effect stamped on its face 4 : to recognize as having met specific qualifications within a field ⟨certified teachers⟩ ♦ **Synonyms** ACCREDIT, APPROVE, SANCTION, ENDORSE — **cer·ti·fi·able** \-ə-bəl\ adj — **cer·ti·fi·ably** \-blē\ adv — **cer·ti·fi·er** n

**cer·ti·tude** \'sər-tə-ˌtüd, -ˌtyüd\ n : the state of being or feeling certain

**ce·ru·le·an** \sə-'rü-lē-ən\ adj : AZURE

**ce·ru·men** \sə-'rü-mən\ n : EARWAX

**cer·vi·cal** \'sər-vi-kəl\ adj : of or relating to a neck or cervix

**cervical cap** n : a contraceptive device in the form of a thimble-shaped molded cap that fits snugly over the uterine cervix and blocks sperm from entering the uterus

**cer·vix** \'sər-viks\ n, pl **cer·vi·ces** \-və-ˌsēz\ or **cer·vix·es** 1 : NECK; esp : the back part of the neck 2 : a constricted portion of an organ or part; esp : the narrow outer end of the uterus

**ce·sar·e·an** or **cae·sar·e·an** also **ce·sar·i·an** or **cae·sar·i·an** \si-'zer-ē-ən\ n, often cap : CESAREAN SECTION — **cesarean** or **caesarean** also **cesarian** or **caesarian** adj

**cesarean section** also **caesarean section** n, often cap C [fr. the legendary association of such a delivery with the Roman cognomen Caesar] : surgical incision of the walls of the abdomen and uterus for delivery of offspring

**ce·si·um** \'sē-zē-əm\ n : a silver-white soft ductile chemical element

**ces·sa·tion** \se-'sā-shən\ n : a temporary or final ceasing (as of action)

**ces·sion** \'se-shən\ n : a yielding (as of rights) to another

**cess·pool** \'ses-ˌpül\ n 1 : an underground pit or tank for receiving household sewage 2 : a filthy or corrupt situation

**ce·ta·cean** \si-'tā-shən\ n : any of an order of aquatic mostly marine mammals that includes whales, porpoises, dolphins, and related forms — **cetacean** adj

**cf** abbr [L. confer] compare

**Cf** symbol californium

**CF** abbr cystic fibrosis

**CFC** abbr chlorofluorocarbon

**CFL** abbr compact fluorescent lamp; compact fluorescent light bulb

**CFO** abbr chief financial officer

**cg** abbr centigram

**CG** abbr 1 coast guard 2 commanding general

**cgs** abbr centimeter-gram-second

**ch** abbr 1 chain 2 champion 3 chapter 4 church

**CH** abbr 1 clearinghouse 2 courthouse 3 customhouse

**Cha·blis** \sha-'blē, shə-, shä-; 'sha-ˌblē\ n, pl **Cha·blis** \-'blēz, -(ˌ)blēz\ 1 : a dry sharp white Burgundy wine **2** : a white California wine

**cha·cha** \'chä-ˌchä\ *n* : a fast rhythmic ballroom dance of Latin American origin

**chafe** \'chāf\ *vb* **chafed; chaf·ing** **1** : IRRITATE, VEX **2** : FRET **3** : to warm by rubbing **4** : to rub so as to wear away; *also* : to make sore by rubbing

**cha·fer** \'chā-fər\ *n* : any of various scarab beetles

**¹chaff** \'chaf\ *n* **1** : debris (as husks) separated from grain in threshing **2** : something comparatively worthless — **chaffy** *adj*

**²chaff** *n* : light jesting talk : BANTER

**³chaff** *vb* : to tease good-naturedly

**chaf·fer** \'cha-fər\ *vb* : BARGAIN, HAGGLE — **chaf·fer·er** *n*

**chaf·finch** \'cha-ˌfinch\ *n* : a common European finch with a cheerful song

**chaf·ing dish** \'chā-fiŋ-\ *n* : a utensil for cooking food at the table

**¹cha·grin** \shə-'grin\ *n* : mental uneasiness or annoyance caused by failure, disappointment, or humiliation

**²chagrin** *vb* **cha·grined** \-'grind\; **cha·grin·ing** : to cause to feel chagrin

**¹chain** \'chān\ *n* [ME *cheyne*, fr. AF *chaene*, fr. L *catena*] **1** : a flexible series of connected links **2** : a chainlike surveying instrument; *also* : a unit of length equal to 66 feet (about 20 meters) **3** *pl* : BONDS, FETTERS **4** : a series of things linked together ⟨mountain ~s⟩; *also* : a group of usu. identical enterprises with a single owner ⟨fast-food ~s⟩ ♦ **Synonyms** TRAIN, STRING, SEQUENCE, SUCCESSION, SERIES

**²chain** *vb* : to fasten, bind, or connect with a chain; *also* : FETTER

**chain gang** *n* : a gang of convicts chained together

**chain letter** *n* : a letter sent to several persons with a request that each send copies to an equal number of persons

**chain mail** *n* : flexible armor of interlocking metal rings

**chain reaction** *n* **1** : a series of events in which each event initiates the succeeding one **2** : a chemical or nuclear reaction yielding products that cause further reactions of the same kind

**chain saw** *n* : a portable power saw that has teeth linked together to form an endless chain — **chain-saw** \'chān-ˌsȯ\ *vb*

**chain–smoke** \'chān-'smōk\ *vb* : to smoke esp. cigarettes continuously

**¹chair** \'cher\ *n* [ME *chaiere*, fr. AF, fr. L *cathedra*, fr. Gk *kathedra*, fr. *kata-* down + *hedra* seat] **1** : a seat with a back for one person **2** : ELECTRIC CHAIR **3** : an official seat; *also* : an office or position of authority or dignity **4** : CHAIRMAN

**²chair** *vb* : to act as chairman of

**chair·lift** \'cher-ˌlift\ *n* : a motor-driven conveyor for skiers consisting of seats hung from a moving cable

**chair·man** \-mən\ *n* : the presiding officer of a meeting, committee, or event — **chair·man·ship** *n*

**chair·per·son** \-ˌpər-sən\ *n* : CHAIRMAN

**chair·wom·an** \-ˌwu̇-mən\ *n* : a woman who serves as chairman

**chaise** \'shāz\ *n* : a 2-wheeled horse-drawn carriage with a folding top

**chaise longue** \'shāz-'lȯŋ\ *n, pl* **chaise longues** \*same or* -'lȯŋz\ [F, lit., long chair] : a long reclining chair

**chaise lounge** \-'lau̇nj\ *n* : CHAISE LONGUE

**chal·ced·o·ny** \kal-'se-d°n-ē\ *n, pl* **-nies** : a translucent quartz of various colors

**chal·co·py·rite** \ˌkal-kə-'pī-ˌrīt\ *n* : a yellow mineral constituting an important copper ore

**cha·let** \sha-'lā\ *n* **1** : a herdsman's cabin in the Swiss mountains **2** : a building in the style of a Swiss cottage with a wide roof overhang

**chal·ice** \'cha-ləs\ *n* : a drinking cup; *esp* : the eucharistic cup

**¹chalk** \'chȯk\ *n* **1** : a soft limestone **2** : chalk or chalky material esp. when used as a crayon — **chalky** *adj*

**²chalk** *vb* **1** : to rub or mark with chalk **2** : to record with or as if with chalk — usu. used with *up*

**chalk·board** \'chȯk-ˌbȯrd\ *n* : BLACKBOARD

**chalk up** *vb* **1** : ASCRIBE, CREDIT **2** : ATTAIN, ACHIEVE ⟨*chalk up* a victory⟩

**¹chal·lenge** \'cha-lənj\ *vb* **chal·lenged; chal·leng·ing** [ME *chalengen* to accuse, fr. AF *chalenger*, fr. L *calumniari* to accuse falsely, fr. *calumnia* calumny] **1** : to order to halt and prove identity **2** : to take exception to : DISPUTE ⟨~ a ruling⟩ **3** : to issue an invitation to compete ⟨*challenged* me to another game⟩ **4** : to stimulate by presenting difficulties ⟨a job that ~s her⟩ — **chal·leng·er** *n*

**²challenge** *n* **1** : a summons to a duel **2** : an invitation to compete in a sport **3** : a calling into question **4** : an exception taken to a juror **5** : a sentry's command to halt and prove identity **6** : a stimulating or interesting task or problem

**challenged** *adj* : presented with difficulties (as by a disability)

**chal·lis** \'sha-lē\ *n, pl* **chal·lises** \-lēz\ : a lightweight clothing fabric of wool, cotton, or synthetic yarns

**cham·ber** \'chām-bər\ *n* **1** : ROOM; *esp* : BEDROOM **2** : an enclosed space or cavity **3** : a hall for meetings of a legislative body **4** : a judge's consultation room — usu. used in pl. **5** : a legislative or judicial body; *also* : a council for a business purpose **6** : the part of a firearm that holds the cartridge or powder charge during firing — **cham·bered** \-bərd\ *adj*

**cham·ber·lain** \'chām-bər-lən\ *n* **1** : a chief officer in the household of a king or nobleman **2** : TREASURER

**cham·ber·maid** \-ˌmād\ *n* : a maid who takes care of bedrooms

**chamber music** *n* : music intended for performance by a few musicians before a small audience

**chamber of commerce** : an association of businesspeople for promoting commercial and industrial interests in the community

**cham·bray** \'sham-ˌbrā\ n : a lightweight clothing fabric of white and colored threads

**cha·me·leon** \kə-'mēl-yən\ n [ME *camelion*, fr. MF, fr. L *chamaeleon*, fr. Gk *chamaileōn*, fr. *chamai* on the ground + *leōn* lion] : a small lizard whose skin changes color esp. according to its surroundings

¹**cham·fer** \'cham-fər\ vb 1 : to cut a furrow in (as a column) : GROOVE 2 : to make a chamfer on : BEVEL

²**chamfer** n : a beveled edge

**cham·ois** \'sha-mē\ n, pl **cham·ois** \*same* or -mēz\ 1 : a small goatlike ruminant mammal of Europe and the Caucasus region of Russia 2 also **cham·my** \'sha-mē\ : a soft leather made esp. from the skin of the sheep or goat 3 : a cotton fabric made in imitation of chamois leather

**cham·o·mile** or **cam·o·mile** \'ka-mə-ˌmī(-ə)l, -ˌmēl\ n : any of a genus of strong-scented herbs related to the daisies and having flower heads that yield a bitter substance used esp. in tonics and teas

¹**champ** \'champ, 'chämp\ vb 1 : to chew noisily 2 : to show impatience of delay or restraint

²**champ** \'champ\ n : CHAMPION

**cham·pagne** \sham-'pān\ n : a white effervescent wine

¹**cham·pi·on** \'cham-pē-ən\ n 1 : a militant advocate or defender 2 : one that wins first prize or place in a contest 3 : one that is acknowledged to be better than all others

²**champion** vb : to protect or fight for as a champion ♦ **Synonyms** BACK, ADVOCATE, UPHOLD, SUPPORT

**cham·pi·on·ship** \-ˌship\ n 1 : the position or title of a champion 2 : the act of championing : DEFENSE 3 : a contest held to determine a champion

¹**chance** \'chans\ n 1 : something that happens without apparent cause 2 : the unpredictable element in existence : LUCK, FORTUNE 3 : OPPORTUNITY 4 : the likelihood of a particular outcome in an uncertain situation : PROBABILITY 5 : RISK 6 : a raffle ticket — **chance** adj — **by chance** : in the haphazard course of events

²**chance** vb **chanced; chanc·ing** 1 : to take place by chance : HAPPEN 2 : to come casually and unexpectedly — used with *upon* 3 : to leave to chance 4 : to accept the risk of

**chan·cel** \'chan-səl\ n : the part of a church including the altar and choir

**chan·cel·lery** or **chan·cel·lory** \'chan-sə-lə-rē\ n, pl **-ler·ies** or **-lor·ies** 1 : the position or office of a chancellor 2 : the building or room where a chancellor works 3 : the office or staff of an embassy or consulate

**chan·cel·lor** \'chan-sə-lər\ n 1 : a high state official in various countries 2 : the head of a university 3 : a judge in the equity court in various states of the U.S. 4 : the chief minister of state in some European countries — **chan·cel·lor·ship** n

**chan·cery** \'chan-sə-rē\ n, pl **-cer·ies** 1 : a record office for public or diplomatic archives 2 : any of various courts of equity in the U.S. and Britain 3 : a chancellor's court or office 4 : the office of an embassy 5 : the business office of a diocese

**chan·cre** \'shaŋ-kər\ n [F, fr. OF, fr. L *cancer*] : a primary sore or ulcer at the site of entry of an infective agent (as of syphilis)

**chan·croid** \'shaŋ-ˌkròid\ n : a sexually transmitted disease caused by a bacterium and characterized by chancres that differ from those of syphilis in lacking hardened margins

**chancy** \'chan-sē\ adj **chanc·i·er; -est** 1 *Scot* : AUSPICIOUS 2 : RISKY

**chan·de·lier** \ˌshan-də-'lir\ n : a branched lighting fixture suspended from a ceiling

**chan·dler** \'chand-lər\ n [ME *chandeler* a maker or seller of candles, fr. AF, fr. *chandele* candle, fr. L *candela*] : a dealer in provisions and supplies of a specified kind ⟨ship's ~⟩ — **chan·dlery** n

¹**change** \'chānj\ vb **changed; chang·ing** 1 : to make or become different : ALTER 2 : to replace with another 3 : to give or receive an equivalent sum in notes or coins of usu. smaller denominations or of another currency 4 : to put fresh clothes or covering on ⟨~ a bed⟩ 5 : to put on different clothes 6 : EXCHANGE — **change·able** adj — **chang·er** n

²**change** n 1 : the act, process, or result of changing 2 : a fresh set of clothes 3 : money given in exchange for other money of higher denomination 4 : money returned when a payment exceeds the sum due 5 : coins esp. of small denominations — **change·ful** adj

**change·ling** \'chānj-liŋ\ n : a child secretly exchanged for another in infancy

**change of life** : MENOPAUSE

**change·over** \'chānj-ˌō-vər\ n : CONVERSION, TRANSITION

**change ringing** n : the art or practice of ringing a set of tuned bells in continually varying order

¹**chan·nel** \'cha-nᵊl\ n 1 : the bed of a stream 2 : the deeper part of a waterway 3 : STRAIT 4 : a means of passage or transmission 5 : a range of frequencies of sufficient width for a single radio or television transmission 6 : a usu. tubular enclosed passage : CONDUIT 7 : a long gutter, groove, or furrow

²**channel** vb **-neled** or **-nelled; -nel·ing** or **-nel·ling** 1 : to make a channel in 2 : to direct into or through a channel

**chan·nel·ize** \'cha-nə-ˌlīz\ vb **-ized; -iz·ing** : CHANNEL — **chan·nel·i·za·tion** \ˌcha-nə-lə-'zā-shən\ n

**chan·son** \shä⁻-'sō⁻\ n, pl **chan·sons** \*same* or -'sō⁻z\ : SONG; *esp* : a cabaret song

¹**chant** \'chant\ vb 1 : SING; *esp* : to sing a chant 2 : to utter or recite in the manner of a chant 3 : to celebrate or praise in song — **chant·er** n

²**chant** n 1 : a repetitive melody in which several words are sung to one tone

: SONG; *esp* : a liturgical melody  **2** : a manner of singing or speaking in musical monotones

**chan·te·relle** \ˌshan-tə-ˈrel\ *n* : a fragrant edible mushroom

**chan·teuse** \shäⁿ-ˈtərz, shan-ˈtüz\ *n, pl* **chan·teuses** \*same or* -ˈtər-zəz, -ˈtü-zəz\ [F] : a woman who is a concert or night-club singer

**chan·tey** *or* **chan·ty** \ˈshan-tē, ˈchan-\ *n, pl* **chanteys** *or* **chanties** : a song sung by sailors in rhythm with their work

**chan·ti·cleer** \ˌchan-tə-ˈklir, ˌshan-\ *n* : ROOSTER

**Chanukah** *var of* HANUKKAH

**cha·os** \ˈkā-ˌäs\ *n* **1** *often cap* : the confused unorganized state existing before the creation of distinct forms  **2** : the inherent unpredictability in the behavior of a complex natural system (as the atmosphere or the beating heart)  **3** : complete disorder  ♦ *Synonyms* CONFUSION, JUMBLE, SNARL, MUDDLE, DISARRAY — **cha·ot·ic** \kā-ˈä-tik\ *adj* — **cha·ot·i·cal·ly** \-ti-k(ə-)lē\ *adv*

**chaos theory** *n* : a branch of mathematical and physical theory concerned with chaotic systems

¹**chap** \ˈchap\ *vb* **chapped; chap·ping** : to dry and crack open usu. from wind and cold ⟨*chapped* lips⟩

²**chap** *n* : a jaw with its fleshy covering — usu. used in pl.

³**chap** *n, chiefly Brit* : FELLOW

⁴**chap** *abbr* chapter

**chap·ar·ral** \ˌsha-pə-ˈral\ *n* **1** : a dense impenetrable thicket of shrubs or dwarf trees  **2** : an ecological community esp. of southern California composed of shrubby plants

**chap·book** \ˈchap-ˌbùk\ *n* : a small book of ballads, tales, or tracts

**cha·peau** \sha-ˈpō\ *n, pl* **cha·peaus** \-ˈpōz\ *or* **cha·peaux** \-ˈpō, -ˈpōz\ [MF] : HAT

**cha·pel** \ˈcha-pəl\ *n* [ME, fr. AF *chapele*, fr. ML *cappella*, fr. LL *cappa* cloak; fr. the cloak of St. Martin of Tours preserved as a sacred relic in a chapel built for that purpose]  **1** : a private or subordinate place of worship  **2** : an assembly at an educational institution usu. including devotional exercises  **3** : a place of worship used by a Christian group other than an established church

¹**chap·er·one** *or* **chap·er·on** \ˈsha-pə-ˌrōn\ *n* [F *chaperon*, lit., hood, fr. MF, head covering, fr. *chape* cape, fr. LL *cappa*]  **1** : a person (as a matron) who accompanies young unmarried women in public for propriety  **2** : an older person who accompanies young people at a social gathering to ensure proper behavior

²**chaperone** *or* **chaperon** *vb* **-oned; -on·ing**  **1** : ESCORT, GUIDE  **2** : to act as a chaperone to or for ⟨∼ a dance⟩ ⟨∼ teenagers⟩ — **chap·er·on·age** \-ˌrō-nij\ *n*

**chap·fall·en** \ˈchap-ˌfò-lən, ˈchäp-\ *adj*  **1** : having the lower jaw hanging loosely  **2** : DEJECTED, DEPRESSED

**chap·lain** \ˈcha-plən\ *n*  **1** : a member of the clergy officially attached to a special group (as the army)  **2** : a person chosen to conduct religious exercises (as for a club) — **chap·lain·cy** \-sē\ *n*

**chap·let** \ˈcha-plət\ *n*  **1** : a wreath for the head  **2** : a string of beads : NECKLACE

**chap·man** \ˈchap-mən\ *n, Brit* : an itinerant dealer : PEDDLER

**chaps** \ˈshaps, ˈchaps\ *n pl* [MexSp *chaparreras*] : leather leggings resembling pants without a seat that are worn esp. by western ranch hands

**chap·ter** \ˈchap-tər\ *n*  **1** : a main division of a book  **2** : a body of canons (as of a cathedral)  **3** : a local branch of a society or fraternity

¹**char** \ˈchär\ *n, pl* **char** *or* **chars** : any of a genus of trouts (as the common brook trout) with small scales

²**char** *vb* **charred; char·ring**  **1** : to burn or become burned to charcoal  **2** : SCORCH

³**char** *vb* **charred; char·ring** : to work as a cleaning woman

**char·ac·ter** \ˈker-ik-tər\ *n* [ME *caracter*, fr. L *character* mark, distinctive quality, fr. Gk *charaktēr*, fr. *charassein* to scratch, engrave]  **1** : a graphic symbol (as a letter) used in writing or printing  **2** : a symbol that represents information; *also* : a representation of such a character that may be accepted by a computer  **3** : a distinguishing feature : ATTRIBUTE  **4** : the complex of mental and ethical traits marking a person or a group  **5** : a person marked by conspicuous often peculiar traits  **6** : one of the persons in a novel or play  **7** : REPUTATION ⟨an attack on his ∼⟩  **8** : moral excellence

¹**char·ac·ter·is·tic** \ˌker-ik-tə-ˈris-tik\ *n* : a distinguishing trait, quality, or property

²**characteristic** *adj* : serving to mark individual character  ♦ *Synonyms* INDIVIDUAL, PECULIAR, DISTINCTIVE — **char·ac·ter·is·ti·cal·ly** \-ti-k(ə-)lē\ *adv*

**char·ac·ter·ize** \ˈker-ik-tə-ˌrīz\ *vb* **-ized; -iz·ing**  **1** : to describe the character of  **2** : to be characteristic of — **char·ac·ter·i·za·tion** \ˌker-ik-tə-rə-ˈzā-shən\ *n*

**cha·rades** \shə-ˈrādz\ *n sing or pl* : a game in which some of the players try to guess a word or phrase from the actions of another player who may not speak

**char·coal** \ˈchär-ˌkōl\ *n*  **1** : a porous carbon prepared from vegetable or animal substances  **2** : a piece of fine charcoal used in drawing; *also* : a drawing made with charcoal

**chard** \ˈchärd\ *n* : SWISS CHARD

**char·don·nay** \ˌshar-dᵊn-ˈā\ *n, often cap* [F] : a dry white wine made from a single variety of white grape

¹**charge** \ˈchärj\ *n*  **1** : a quantity (as of fuel or ammunition) required to fill something to capacity  **2** : a store or accumulation of force  **3** : an excess or deficiency of electrons in a body  **4** : THRILL, KICK  **5** : a task or duty imposed  **6** : CARE, RESPONSIBILITY  **7** : one given into another's care  **8** : instructions from a judge to a jury  **9** : COST, EXPENSE, PRICE; *also*

: a debit to an account **10** : ACCUSATION, INDICTMENT **11** : ATTACK, ASSAULT

²**charge** *vb* **charged; charg·ing 1** : to load or fill to capacity **2** : to give an electric charge to; *also* : to restore the activity of (a storage battery) by means of an electric current **3** : to impose a task or responsibility on **4** : COMMAND, ORDER **5** : ACCUSE **6** : to rush against : rush forward in assault **7** : to make liable for payment; *also* : to record a debt or liability against **8** : to fix as a price — **charge·able** *adj*

**charge–coupled device** *n* : a semiconductor device used esp. as an optical sensor

**char·gé d'af·faires** \shär-ˌzhā-də-ˈfer\ *n, pl* **chargés d'affaires** \-ˌzhā-, -ˌzhāz-\ [F] : a diplomat who substitutes for an ambassador or minister

¹**charg·er** \ˈchär-jər\ *n* : a large platter

²**charg·er** *n* **1** : a device or a worker that charges something **2** : WARHORSE 1

**char·i·ot** \ˈcher-ē-ət\ *n* : a 2-wheeled horse-drawn vehicle of ancient times used esp. in war and in races — **char·i·o·teer** \ˌcher-ē-ə-ˈtir\ *n*

**cha·ris·ma** \kə-ˈriz-mə\ *n* : a personal quality of leadership arousing popular loyalty or enthusiasm — **char·is·mat·ic** \ˌkar-əz-ˈma-tik\ *adj*

**char·i·ta·ble** \ˈcher-ə-tə-bəl\ *adj* **1** : liberal in giving to needy people **2** : merciful or lenient in judging others ♦ **Synonyms** BENEVOLENT, PHILANTHROPIC, ALTRUISTIC, HUMANITARIAN — **char·i·ta·ble·ness** *n* — **char·i·ta·bly** \-blē\ *adv*

**char·i·ty** \ˈcher-ə-tē\ *n, pl* **-ties 1** : goodwill toward or love of humanity **2** : an act or feeling of generosity **3** : the giving of aid to the poor; *also* : ALMS **4** : an institution engaged in relief of the poor **5** : leniency in judging others ♦ **Synonyms** MERCY, CLEMENCY, LENITY

**char·la·tan** \ˈshär-lə-tən\ *n* : a person making usu. showy pretenses to knowledge or ability : FRAUD, FAKER

**Charles·ton** \ˈchärl-stən\ *n* : a lively dance in which the knees are swung in and out and the heels are turned sharply outward on each step

**char·ley horse** \ˈchär-lē-ˌhȯrs\ *n* : a muscular pain, cramping, or stiffness from a strain or bruise

¹**charm** \ˈchärm\ *n* [ME *charme*, fr. AF, fr. L *carmen* song, fr. *canere* to sing] **1** : a practice or expression believed to have magic power **2** : something worn about the person to ward off evil or bring good fortune : AMULET **3** : a trait that fascinates or allures **4** : physical grace or attraction **5** : a small ornament worn on a bracelet or chain **6** : a quark with a charge of +⅔ and a measured energy of approximately 1.5 billion electron volts

²**charm** *vb* **1** : to affect by or as if by a magic spell **2** : to protect by or as if by charms **3** : FASCINATE, ENCHANT ♦ **Synonyms** ALLURE, CAPTIVATE, BEWITCH, ATTRACT — **charm·er** *n*

**charmed** \ˈchärmd\ *adj* : extremely lucky or prosperous ⟨a ∼ life⟩

**charm·ing** \ˈchär-miŋ\ *adj* : PLEASING, DELIGHTFUL — **charm·ing·ly** *adv*

**char·nel house** \ˈchär-nᵊl-\ *n* : a building or chamber in which bodies or bones are deposited

¹**chart** \ˈchärt\ *n* **1** : MAP **2** : a sheet giving information in the form of a table, list, or diagram; *also* : GRAPH

²**chart** *vb* **1** : PLAN ⟨∼ a course⟩ **2** : to make a chart of **3** : CHRONICLE ⟨∼ed his adventures⟩

¹**char·ter** \ˈchär-tər\ *n* **1** : an official document granting rights or privileges (as to a colony, town, or college) from a sovereign or a governing body **2** : CONSTITUTION **3** : a written instrument from a society creating a branch **4** : a mercantile lease of a ship

²**charter** *vb* **1** : to grant a charter to **2** *Brit* : CERTIFY ⟨∼ed engineer⟩ **3** : to hire, rent, or lease for temporary use ⟨∼ a bus⟩ — **char·ter·er** *n*

**charter member** *n* : an original member of an organization

**char·treuse** \shär-ˈtrüz, -ˈtrüs\ *n* : a brilliant yellow green

**char·wom·an** \ˈchär-ˌwu̇-mən\ *n* : a cleaning woman esp. in large buildings

**chary** \ˈcher-ē\ *adj* **char·i·er; -est** [ME, sorrowful, dear, fr. OE *cearig* sorrowful, fr. *caru* sorrow] **1** : CAUTIOUS, CIRCUMSPECT **2** : SPARING — **char·i·ly** \-ə-lē\ *adv*

¹**chase** \ˈchās\ *n* **1** : PURSUIT; *also* : HUNTING **2** : QUARRY **3** : a tract of unenclosed land used as a game preserve

²**chase** *vb* **chased; chas·ing 1** : to follow rapidly : PURSUE **2** : HUNT **3** : to seek out ⟨*chasing* down clues⟩ **4** : to cause to depart or flee : drive away **5** : RUSH, HASTEN

³**chase** *vb* **chased; chas·ing** : to decorate (a metal surface) by embossing or engraving

⁴**chase** *n* : FURROW, GROOVE

**chas·er** \ˈchā-sər\ *n* **1** : one that chases **2** : a mild drink (as beer) taken after hard liquor

**chasm** \ˈka-zəm\ *n* : GORGE 2

**chas·sis** \ˈcha-sē, ˈsha-sē\ *n, pl* **chas·sis** \-sēz\ : the supporting frame of a structure (as an automobile or television set)

**chaste** \ˈchāst\ *adj* **chast·er; chast·est 1** : innocent of unlawful sexual intercourse : VIRTUOUS, PURE **2** : CELIBATE **3** : pure in thought : MODEST **4** : severe or simple in design — **chaste·ly** *adv* — **chaste·ness** *n*

**chas·ten** \ˈchā-sᵊn\ *vb* : to correct through punishment or suffering : DISCIPLINE; *also* : PURIFY — **chas·ten·er** *n*

**chas·tise** \chas-ˈtīz\ *vb* **chas·tised; chas·tis·ing** [ME *chastisen*, alter. of *chasten*] **1** : to punish esp. bodily **2** : to censure severely : CASTIGATE — **chas·tise·ment** \-mənt, ˈchas-təz-\ *n*

**chas·ti·ty** \ˈchas-tə-tē\ *n* : the quality or state of being chaste; *esp* : sexual purity

**cha·su·ble** \ˈcha-zə-bəl, -sə-\ *n* : the outer vestment of the priest at mass

**chat** \ˈchat\ *n* **1** : light familiar informal

talk **2** : online discussion in a chat room — **chat** vb

**châ·teau** \sha-'tō\ n, pl **châ·teaus** \-'tōz\ or **châ·teaux** \-'tō, -'tōz\ [F, fr. OF *chastel*, fr. L *castellum* castle, dim. of *castra* camp] **1** : a feudal castle in France **2** : a large country house **3** : a French vineyard estate

**chat·e·laine** \'shat-ə-ˌlān\ n **1** : the mistress of a chateau **2** : a clasp or hook for a watch, purse, or keys

**chat room** n : a real-time online interactive discussion group

**chat·tel** \'cha-tᵊl\ n **1** : an item of tangible property other than real estate **2** : SLAVE, BONDMAN

**chat·ter** \'cha-tər\ vb **1** : to utter speechlike but meaningless sounds **2** : to talk idly, incessantly, or fast **3** : to click repeatedly or uncontrollably — **chatter** n — **chat·ter·er** n

**chat·ter·box** \'cha-tər-ˌbäks\ n : one who talks incessantly

**chat·ty** \'cha-tē\ adj **chat·ti·er; -est** : TALKATIVE — **chat·ti·ly** \-tᵊl-ē\ adv — **chat·ti·ness** \-tē-nəs\ n

**¹chauf·feur** \'shō-fər, shō-'fər\ n [F, lit., stoker, fr. *chauffer* to heat] : a person employed to drive an automobile

**²chauffeur** vb **1** : to do the work of a chauffeur **2** : to transport in the manner of a chauffeur ⟨~ed the kids to school⟩

**chaunt** var of CHANT

**chau·vin·ism** \'shō-və-ˌni-zəm\ n [F *chauvinisme*, fr. Nicolas *Chauvin*, fictional soldier of excessive patriotism and devotion to Napoleon] **1** : excessive or blind patriotism **2** : an attitude of superiority toward members of the opposite sex — **chau·vin·ist** \-nist\ n or adj — **chau·vin·is·tic** \ˌshō-və-'nis-tik\ adj — **chau·vin·is·ti·cal·ly** \-ti-k(ə-)lē\ adv

**cheap** \'chēp\ adj **1** : INEXPENSIVE **2** : costing little effort to obtain ⟨~ tickets⟩ **3** : worth little : SHODDY, TAWDRY ⟨~ workmanship⟩ **4** : worthy of scorn **5** : STINGY — **cheap** adv — **cheap·ly** adv — **cheap·ness** n

**cheap·en** \'chē-pən\ vb **1** : to make or become cheap or cheaper in price or value **2** : to make tawdry

**cheap·skate** \'chēp-ˌskāt\ n : a miserly or stingy person; esp : one who tries to avoid paying a fair share of costs

**¹cheat** \'chēt\ vb **1** : to deprive of something through fraud or deceit ⟨~ed workers of their pay⟩ **2** : to practice fraud or trickery **3** : to violate rules dishonestly ⟨~ at cards⟩ **4** : to be sexually unfaithful — **cheat·er** n

**²cheat** n **1** : the act of deceiving : FRAUD, DECEPTION **2** : one that cheats : a dishonest person

**¹check** \'chek\ n **1** : exposure of a chess king to an attack **2** : a sudden stoppage of progress **3** : a sudden pause or break **4** : something that stops or restrains **5** : a standard for testing or evaluation **6** : EXAMINATION, INVESTIGATION **7** : the act of testing or verifying **8** : a written order to a bank to pay money **9** : a ticket or token showing ownership or identity **10**

: a slip indicating an amount due **11** : a pattern in squares; also : a fabric in such a pattern **12** : a mark typically ✓ placed beside an item to show that it has been noted **13** : CRACK, SPLIT

**²check** vb **1** : to put (a chess king) in check **2** : to slow down or stop : BRAKE **3** : to restrain the action or force of : CURB **4** : to compare with a source, original, or authority : VERIFY **5** : to inspect or test for satisfactory condition **6** : to mark with a check as examined **7** : to consign for shipment for one holding a passenger ticket **8** : to mark into squares **9** : to leave or accept for safekeeping in a checkroom **10** : to prove to be consistent or truthful **11** : CRACK, SPLIT

**check·book** \'chek-ˌbùk\ n : a book containing blank checks

**¹check·er** \'che-kər\ n : a piece in the game of checkers

**²checker** vb **1** : to variegate with different colors or shades **2** : to vary with contrasting elements ⟨a ~ed career⟩ **3** : to mark into squares

**³checker** n : one that checks; esp : an employee who checks out purchases in a store

**check·er·ber·ry** \'che-kər-ˌber-ē\ n : WINTERGREEN 1; also : the spicy red fruit of this plant

**check·er·board** \-ˌbòrd\ n : a board of 64 squares of alternate colors used in various games

**check·ered** \'che-kərd\ adj : marked by inconsistent fortune or recurring problems ⟨his ~ past⟩

**check·ers** \'che-kərz\ n : a checkerboard game for 2 players each with 12 pieces

**check in** vb : to report one's presence or arrival (as at a hotel)

**check·list** \'chek-ˌlist\ n : a list of things to be checked or done; also : a comprehensive list

**check·mate** \'chek-ˌmāt\ vb [ME *chekmaten*, fr. *chekmate*, interj. used to announce checkmate, fr. AF *eschec mat*, fr. Ar *shāh māt*, fr. Pers, lit., the king is left unable to escape] **1** : to thwart completely : DEFEAT, FRUSTRATE **2** : to attack (an opponent's king) in chess so that escape is impossible — **checkmate** n

**check·off** \'chek-ˌòf\ n : the deduction of union dues from a worker's paycheck by the employer

**check·out** \'chek-ˌaùt\ n **1** : the action or an instance of checking out **2** : a counter at which checking out is done **3** : the process of examining and testing something as to readiness for intended use

**check out** vb **1** : to settle one's account (as at a hotel) and leave **2** : to total or have totaled the cost of purchases in a store and to make or receive payment for them

**check·point** \'chek-ˌpòint\ n : a point at which a check is performed

**check·room** \-ˌrüm, -ˌrùm\ n : a room at which baggage, parcels, or clothing is left for safekeeping

**checks and balances** n pl : a system allowing each branch of a government to restrict the actions of another branch (as by a veto)

**check-up** \'chek-ˌəp\ *n* : EXAMINATION; *esp* : a general physical examination

**ched-dar** \'che-dər\ *n, often cap* : a hard mild to sharp white or yellow cheese of smooth texture

**cheek** \'chēk\ *n* **1** : the fleshy side part of the face **2** : IMPUDENCE, BOLDNESS, AUDACITY **3** : BUTTOCK 1 — **cheeked** \'chēkt\ *adj*

**cheek-bone** \'chēk-ˌbōn\ *n* : the bone or bony ridge below the eye

**cheeky** \'chē-kē\ *adj* **cheek-i-er; -est** : IMPUDENT, SAUCY — **cheek-i-ly** \-kə-lē\ *adv* — **cheek-i-ness** \-kē-nəs\ *n*

**cheep** \'chēp\ *vb* : to utter faint shrill sounds : PEEP — **cheep** *n*

**¹cheer** \'chir\ *n* [ME *chere* face, cheer, fr. AF, face, fr. ML *cara*, prob. fr. Gk *kara* head, face] **1** : state of mind or heart : SPIRIT **2** : ANIMATION, GAIETY **3** : hospitable entertainment : WELCOME **4** : food and drink for a feast **5** : something that gladdens **6** : a shout of applause or encouragement

**²cheer** *vb* **1** : to give hope or courage to : COMFORT **2** : to make glad **3** : to urge on esp. by shouts **4** : to applaud with shouts **5** : to grow or be cheerful — usu. used with *up* — **cheer-er** *n*

**cheer-ful** \'chir-fəl\ *adj* **1** : having or showing good spirits **2** : conducive to good spirits : pleasant and bright — **cheer-ful-ly** *adv* — **cheer-ful-ness** *n*

**cheer-lead-er** \'chir-ˌlē-dər\ *n* : a person who directs organized cheering esp. at a sports event — **cheer-lead-ing** *n*

**cheer-less** \'chir-ləs\ *adj* : BLEAK, DISPIRITING ⟨a ~ office⟩ — **cheer-less-ly** *adv* — **cheer-less-ness** *n*

**cheery** \'chir-ē\ *adj* **cheer-i-er; -est** : CHEERFUL ⟨~ music⟩ — **cheer-i-ly** \-ə-lē\ *adv* — **cheer-i-ness** \-ē-nəs\ *n*

**cheese** \'chēz\ *n* : the curd of milk usu. pressed into cakes and cured for use as food

**cheese-burg-er** \-ˌbər-gər\ *n* : a hamburger topped with cheese

**cheese-cake** \-ˌkāk\ *n* **1** : a dessert consisting of a creamy filling usu. containing cheese baked in a shell **2** : photographs of shapely scantily clad women

**cheese-cloth** \-ˌklȯth\ *n* : a lightweight coarse cotton gauze

**cheese-par-ing** \-ˌper-iŋ\ *n* : miserly economizing — **cheeseparing** *adj*

**cheese-steak** \-ˌstāk\ *n* : a sandwich of thinly sliced beef topped with melted cheese

**cheesy** \'chē-zē\ *adj* **chees-i-er; -est** **1** : resembling, suggesting, or containing cheese **2** : CHEAP **3** ⟨~ motels⟩

**chee-tah** \'chē-tə\ *n* [Hindi *cītā* & Urdu *cītā* leopard, fr. Skt *citraka*, fr. *citra* bright, variegated] : a large long-legged swift-moving spotted cat of Africa and formerly Asia

**chef** \'shef\ *n* : COOK; *esp* : one who manages a kitchen (as of a restaurant)

**chef d'oeu-vre** \shā-'dœvrᵊ\ *n, pl* **chefs d'oeuvre** \*same*\ : MASTERPIECE

**chem** *abbr* chemical; chemist; chemistry

**¹chem-i-cal** \'ke-mi-kəl\ *adj* **1** : of, relating to, used in, or produced by chemistry ⟨~ reactions⟩ **2** : acting or operated or produced by chemicals — **chem-i-cal-ly** \-k(ə-)lē\ *adv*

**²chemical** *n* **1** : a substance obtained by a chemical process or producing a chemical effect **2** : DRUG

**chemical engineering** *n* : engineering dealing with the industrial application of chemistry — **chemical engineer** *n*

**chemical warfare** *n* : warfare using incendiary mixtures, smokes, or irritant, burning, or asphyxiating gases

**chemical weapon** *n* : a weapon used in chemical warfare

**che-mise** \shə-'mēz\ *n* **1** : a woman's one-piece undergarment **2** : a loose straight-hanging dress

**chem-ist** \'ke-mist\ *n* **1** : one trained in chemistry **2** *Brit* : PHARMACIST

**chem-is-try** \'ke-mə-strē\ *n, pl* **-tries** **1** : the science that deals with the composition, structure, and properties of substances and of the changes they undergo **2** : chemical composition or properties ⟨the ~ of gasoline⟩ **3** : a strong mutual attraction; *also* : harmonious interaction among people (as on a team)

**che-mo** \'kē-mo\ *n* : CHEMOTHERAPY

**che-mo-ther-a-py** \ˌkē-mō-'ther-ə-pē\ *n* : the use of chemicals in the treatment or control of disease — **che-mo-ther-a-peu-tic** \-ˌther-ə-'pyü-tik\ *adj*

**che-nille** \shə-'nēl\ *n* [F, lit., caterpillar, fr. OF, fr. L *canicula*, dim. of *canis* dog] : a fabric with a deep fuzzy pile often used for bedspreads and rugs

**cheque** *chiefly Brit var of* ¹CHECK 7

**che-quer** *chiefly Brit var of* CHECKER

**cher-ish** \'cher-ish\ *vb* **1** : to hold dear : treat with care and affection **2** : to keep deeply in mind ⟨~ a memory⟩ — **cher-ish-able** *adj* — **cher-ish-er** *n*

**Cher-o-kee** \'cher-ə-(ˌ)kē\ *n, pl* **Cherokee** *or* **Cherokees** : a member of an American Indian people orig. of Tennessee and No. Carolina; *also* : their language

**che-root** \shə-'rüt\ *n* : a cigar cut square at both ends

**cher-ry** \'cher-ē\ *n, pl* **cherries** [ME *chery*, fr. AF *cherise, cirice* (taken as a plural), fr. LL *ceresia*, fr. L *cerasus* cherry tree, fr. Gk *kerasos*] **1** : the small fleshy pale yellow to deep blackish red fruit of a tree related to the roses; *also* : the tree or its wood **2** : a moderate red

**chert** \'chərt, 'chat\ *n* : a rock resembling flint and consisting essentially of fine crystalline quartz and fibrous chalcedony — **cherty** *adj*

**cher-ub** \'cher-əb\ *n* **1** *pl* **cher-u-bim** \'cher-ə-ˌbim\ : an angel of the 2d highest rank **2** *pl* **cherubs** : a chubby rosy person — **che-ru-bic** \chə-'rü-bik\ *adj*

**chess** \'ches\ *n* : a game for 2 played on a chessboard with each player having 16 pieces — **chess-man** \-ˌman, -mən\ *n*

**chess-board** \'ches-ˌbȯrd\ *n* : a checkerboard used in the game of chess

**chest** \'chest\ *n* **1** : a box, case, or boxlike receptacle for storage or shipping **2** : the part of the body enclosed by the ribs and sternum — **chest·ed** \'ches-təd\ adj — **chest·ful** \'chest-ˌfu̇l\ n

**ches·ter·field** \'ches-tər-ˌfēld\ n : an overcoat with a velvet collar

**chest·nut** \'ches-(ˌ)nət\ n **1** : the edible nut of any of a genus of trees related to the beeches and oaks; also : this tree or its wood **2** : a grayish to reddish brown **3** : an old joke or story

**chet·rum** \'che-trəm\ n, pl **chetrums** or **chetrum** — see *ngultrum* at MONEY table

**che·val glass** \shə-'val-\ n : a full-length mirror that may be tilted in a frame

**che·va·lier** \ˌshe-və-'lir, shə-'val-ˌyā\ n : a member of one of various orders of knighthood or of merit

**chev·i·ot** \'she-vē-ət\ n, often cap **1** : a twilled fabric with a rough nap **2** : a sturdy soft-finished cotton fabric

**chev·ron** \'she-vrən\ n : a sleeve badge of one or more V-shaped or inverted V-shaped stripes worn to indicate rank or service (as in the armed forces)

**¹chew** \'chü\ vb : to crush or grind with the teeth — **chew·able** adj — **chew·er** n — **chewy** \'chü-ē\ adj — **chew on** : to think about : PONDER ⟨*chew on* the proposals⟩ — **chew the fat** : to make conversation : CHAT

**²chew** n **1** : an act of chewing **2** : something for chewing

**Chey·enne** \shī-'an, -'en\ n, pl **Cheyenne** or **Cheyennes** [AmerF, fr. Dakota *šahíyena*] : a member of an American Indian people of the western plains of the U.S.; also : their language

**chg** abbr **1** change **2** charge

**chi** \'kī\ n : the 22d letter of the Greek alphabet — X or χ

**Chi·an·ti** \kē-'än-tē, -'an-\ n : a dry usu. red wine

**chiar·oscu·ro** \kē-ˌär-ə-'sku̇r-ō, -'skyu̇r-\ n, pl **-ros** [It, fr. *chiaro* clear, light + *oscuro* obscure, dark] **1** : pictorial representation in terms of light and shade without regard to color **2** : the arrangement or treatment of light and dark parts in a pictorial work of art

**¹chic** \'shēk\ n : STYLISHNESS

**²chic** adj : cleverly stylish : SMART; also : currently fashionable

**Chi·ca·na** \chi-'kä-nə also shi-\ n : an American woman or girl of Mexican descent — **Chicana** adj

**chi·cane** \shi-'kān\ n : CHICANERY

**chi·ca·nery** \-'kā-nə-rē\ n, pl **-ner·ies** : TRICKERY, DECEPTION

**Chi·ca·no** \chi-'kä-nō\ n, pl **-nos** : a usu. male American of Mexican descent — **Chicano** adj

**chi-chi** \'shē-(ˌ)shē, 'chē-(ˌ)chē\ adj [F] **1** : SHOWY, FRILLY **2** : ARTY, PRECIOUS ⟨~ poetry⟩ **3** : CHIC ⟨~ nightclubs⟩ — **chichi** n

**chick** \'chik\ n **1** : a young chicken; also : a young bird **2** slang : GIRL, WOMAN

**chick·a·dee** \'chi-kə-(ˌ)dē\ n : any of several small grayish American birds with black or brown caps

**Chick·a·saw** \'chi-kə-ˌsȯ\ n, pl **Chicka-** saw or **Chickasaws** : a member of an American Indian people of Mississippi and Alabama

**¹chick·en** \'chi-kən\ n **1** : a common domestic fowl esp. when young; also : its flesh used as food **2** : COWARD

**²chicken** adj **1** : COWARDLY **2** slang : insistent on petty esp. military discipline

**chicken feed** n, slang : an insignificant sum of money

**chick·en-heart·ed** \ˌchi-kən-'här-təd\ adj : TIMID, COWARDLY

**chicken out** vb : to lose one's courage

**chicken pox** n : an acute contagious viral disease esp. of children characterized by a low fever and blisters

**chicken wire** n : a light wire netting of hexagonal mesh

**chick·pea** \'chik-ˌpē\ n : an Asian herb of the legume family cultivated for its short pods with one or two edible seeds; also : its seed

**chick·weed** \'chik-ˌwēd\ n : any of several low-growing small-leaved weeds related to the pinks

**chi·cle** \'chi-kəl\ n : a gum from the latex of a tropical tree used as the chief ingredient of chewing gum

**chic·o·ry** \'chi-kə-rē\ n, pl **-ries** : a usu. blue-flowered herb related to the daisies and grown for its root and for use in salads; also : its dried ground root used to flavor or adulterate coffee

**chide** \'chīd\ vb **chid** \'chid\ or **chid·ed** \'chī-dəd\; **chid** or **chid·den** \'chid-ᵊn\ or **chided**; **chid·ing** : to speak disapprovingly to ♦ **Synonyms** REPROACH, REPROVE, REPRIMAND, ADMONISH, SCOLD, REBUKE

**¹chief** \'chēf\ adj **1** : highest in rank ⟨the ~ executive⟩ **2** : most important ⟨the ~ complaint⟩ ♦ **Synonyms** PRINCIPAL, MAIN, LEADING, MAJOR — **chief·ly** adv

**²chief** n **1** : the leader of a body or organization : HEAD **2** : the principal or most valuable part — **chief·dom** n

**chief master sergeant** n : a noncommissioned officer of the highest rank in the air force

**chief of staff 1** : the ranking officer of a staff in the armed forces **2** : the ranking office of the army or air force

**chief of state** : the formal head of a national state as distinguished from the head of the government

**chief petty officer** n : an enlisted person in the navy ranking next below a senior chief petty officer

**chief·tain** \'chēf-tən\ n : a chief esp. of a band, tribe, or clan — **chief·tain·cy** \-sē\ n — **chief·tain·ship** n

**chief warrant officer** n : a warrant officer of senior rank

**chif·fon** \shi-'fän, 'shi-ˌ\ n [F, lit., rag, fr. *chiffe* old rag] : a sheer fabric esp. of silk

**chif·fo·nier** \ˌshi-fə-'nir\ n : a high narrow chest of drawers

**chig·ger** \'chi-gər\ n : a bloodsucking larval mite that causes intense itching

**chi·gnon** \'shēn-ˌyän\ n [F, fr. MF *chaignon* chain, collar, nape] : a knot of hair worn at the back of the head

**Chi·hua·hua** \chə-'wä-,wä\ *n* : any of a breed of very small large-eared dogs that originated in Mexico

**chil·blain** \'chil-,blān\ *n* : a sore or inflamed swelling (as on the feet or hands) caused by exposure to cold

**child** \'chī-(ə)ld\ *n, pl* **chil·dren** \'chil-drən\ **1** : an unborn or recently born person **2** : a young person between the periods of infancy and youth **3** : a male or female offspring : SON, DAUGHTER **4** : one strongly influenced by another or by a place or state of affairs — **child·ish** *adj* — **child·ish·ly** *adv* — **child·ish·ness** *n* — **child·less** *adj* — **child·less·ness** *n* — **child·like** *adj*

**child·bear·ing** \'chīld-,ber-iŋ\ *n* : CHILDBIRTH — **childbearing** *adj*

**child·birth** \-,bərth\ *n* : the act or process of giving birth to offspring

**child·hood** \-,hůd\ *n* : the state or time of being a child

**¹child·proof** \-,prüf\ *adj* **1** : made to prevent opening or use by children ⟨~ lighters⟩ **2** : made safe for children

**²childproof** *vb* : to make childproof ⟨~ a house⟩

**child's play** *n* : a simple task or act

**chili** *also* **chile** *or* **chil·li** \'chil-lē\ *n, pl* **chil·ies** *also* **chil·es** *or* **chilis** *or* **chil·lies** **1** : any of various pungent peppers related to the tomato **2** : a thick sauce of meat and chilis **3** : CHILI CON CARNE

**chili con car·ne** \,chil-ē-kän-'kär-nē\ *n* [AmerSp *chile con carne* chili with meat] : a spiced stew of ground beef and chilies or chili powder usu. with beans

**chili powder** *n* : a seasoning made of ground chilis and other spices

**chili sauce** *n* : a tomato sauce usu. made with red and green peppers

**¹chill** \'chil\ *n* **1** : a feeling of coldness accompanied by shivering **2** : moderate coldness **3** : a check to enthusiasm or warmth of feeling

**²chill** *adj* **1** : moderately cold **2** : COLD, RAW **3** : DISTANT, FORMAL ⟨a ~ reception⟩ **4** : DEPRESSING, DISPIRITING

**³chill** *vb* **1** : to make or become cold or chilly **2** : to make cool esp. without freezing **3** : RELAX — **chill·er** *n*

**chill·ing** \'chil-liŋ\ *adj* : gravely disturbing or frightening ⟨a ~ scene⟩

**chilly** \'chil-lē\ *adj* **chill·i·er; -est 1** : noticeably cold **2** : unpleasantly affected by cold **3** : lacking warmth of feeling ⟨a ~ reception⟩ — **chill·i·ness** *n*

**chimaera** *chiefly Brit var of* CHIMERA

**¹chime** \'chīm\ *n* **1** : a set of bells musically tuned **2** : the sound of a set of bells — usu. used in pl. **3** : a musical sound suggesting bells

**²chime** *vb* **chimed; chim·ing 1** : to make bell-like sounds **2** : to indicate (as the time of day) by chiming **3** : to be or act in accord : be in harmony

**chime in** *vb* : to break into or join in a conversation

**chi·me·ra** \kī-'mir-ə, kə-\ *n* [L *chimaera*, fr. Gk *chimaira* she-goat, chimera] **1** : an imaginary monster made up of incongru-

ous parts **2** : an illusion or fabrication of the mind; *esp* : an impossible dream

**chi·me·ri·cal** \ki-'mer-i-kəl\ *also* **chi·me·ric** \-ik\ *adj* **1** : FANTASTIC, IMAGINARY **2** : inclined to fantastic schemes

**chim·ney** \'chim-nē\ *n, pl* **chimneys 1** : a vertical structure extending above the roof of a building for carrying off smoke **2** : a glass tube around a lamp flame

**chimp** \'chimp\ *n* : CHIMPANZEE

**chim·pan·zee** \,chim-,pan-'zē, chim-'pan-zē\ *n* : an African ape related to the much larger gorilla

**¹chin** \'chin\ *n* : the part of the face below the lower lip including the prominence of the lower jaw — **chin·less** *adj*

**²chin** *vb* **chinned; chin·ning** : to raise (oneself) while hanging by the hands until the chin is level with the support

**chi·na** \'chī-nə\ *n* : porcelain ware; *also* : domestic pottery in general

**Chi·na·town** \-,taůn\ *n* : the Chinese quarter of a city

**chinch bug** \'chinch \ *n* : a small black and white bug destructive to cereal grasses

**chin·chil·la** \chin-'chi-lə\ *n* **1** : either of two small So. American rodents with soft pearl-gray fur; *also* : this fur **2** : a heavy long-napped woolen cloth

**chine** \'chīn\ *n* : BACKBONE, SPINE; *also* : a cut of meat including all or part of the backbone

**Chi·nese** \chī-'nēz, -'nēs\ *n, pl* **Chinese 1** : a native or inhabitant of China **2** : any of a group of related languages of China — **Chinese** *adj*

**Chinese cabbage** *n* **1** : BOK CHOY **2** : an Asian garden plant related to the cabbage and widely grown in the U.S. for its tight elongate cylindrical heads of pale green to cream-colored leaves

**Chinese checkers** *n* : a game in which each player in turn transfers a set of marbles from a home point to the opposite point of a pitted 6-pointed star

**Chinese gooseberry** *n* : a subtropical vine that bears kiwifruit; *also* : KIWIFRUIT

**Chinese lantern** *n* : a collapsible translucent cover for a light

**¹chink** \'chiŋk\ *n* : a small crack or fissure

**²chink** *vb* : to fill the chinks of : stop up

**³chink** *n* : a slight sharp metallic sound

**⁴chink** *vb* : to make a slight sharp metallic sound

**chi·no** \'chē-nō\ *n, pl* **chinos 1** : a usu. khaki cotton twill **2** *pl* : an article of clothing made of chino

**Chi·nook** \shə-'nůk, chə-, -'nůk\ *n, pl* **Chinook** *or* **Chinooks** : a member of an American Indian people of Oregon

**chintz** \'chints\ *n* : a usu. glazed printed cotton cloth

**chintzy** \'chint-sē\ *adj* **chintz·i·er; -est 1** : decorated with or as if with chintz **2** : GAUDY, CHEAP ⟨a ~ low-budget film⟩ **3** : STINGY — **chintz·i·ness** *n*

**chin-up** \'chin-,əp\ *n* : the act of chinning oneself

**¹chip** \'chip\ *n* **1** : a small usu. thin and flat piece (as of wood) cut or broken off

**2** : a thin crisp morsel of food **3** : a counter used in games (as poker) **4** *pl, slang* : MONEY **5** : a flaw left after a chip is broken off **6** : INTEGRATED CIRCUIT **7** : a very small slice of silicon containing electronic circuits — **chip off the old block** : a child that resembles his or her parent

²**chip** *vb* **chipped; chip·ping 1** : to cut or break chips from **2** : to break off in small pieces at the edges **3** : to play a chip shot

**chip in** *vb* : CONTRIBUTE

**chip·munk** \'chip-ˌməŋk\ *n* [earlier *chitmunk*, prob. fr. Ojibwa *ačitamoˀnˀ* red squirrel] : any of a genus of small striped No. American and Asian rodents closely related to the squirrels and marmots

**chi·pot·le** \chə-'pōt-lā\ *n* : a smoked and usu. dried jalapeño pepper

**chipped beef** \'chipt-\ *n* : smoked dried beef sliced thin

¹**chip·per** \'chi-pər\ *n* : one that chips

²**chipper** *adj* : LIVELY, CHEERFUL

**Chip·pe·wa** \'chi-pə-ˌwȯ, -ˌwä, -ˌwā, -wə\ *n, pl* **Chippewa** *or* **Chippewas** : OJIBWA

**chip shot** *n* : a short usu. low shot to the green in golf

**chi·rog·ra·phy** \kī-'rä-grə-fē\ *n* : HANDWRITING, PENMANSHIP — **chi·ro·graph·ic** \ˌkī-rə-'gra-fik\ *adj*

**chi·rop·o·dy** \kə-'rä-pə-dē, shə-\ *n* : PODIATRY — **chi·rop·o·dist** \-dist\ *n*

**chi·ro·prac·tic** \'kī-rə-ˌprak-tik\ *n* : a system of therapy based esp. on manipulation of body structures — **chi·ro·prac·tor** \-tər\ *n*

**chirp** \'chərp\ *n* : a short sharp sound characteristic of a small bird or cricket — **chirp** *vb* — **chirpy** \'chər-pē\ *adj*

¹**chis·el** \'chi-zəl\ *n* : a metal tool with a sharpened edge at one end used to chip, carve, or cut into a solid material (as wood or stone)

²**chisel** *vb* **-eled** *or* **-elled; -el·ing** *or* **-el·ling 1** : to work with or as if with a chisel **2** : to obtain by shrewd often unfair methods; *also* : CHEAT — **chis·el·er** *n*

¹**chit** \'chit\ *n* [ME *chitte* kitten, cub] **1** : CHILD **2** : a pert young woman

²**chit** *n* [Hindi *ciṭṭhī* letter, note] : a signed voucher for a small debt

**chit·chat** \'chit-ˌchat\ *n* : casual or trifling conversation — **chitchat** *vb*

**chi·tin** \'kī-tⁿn\ *n* : a sugar polymer that forms part of the hard outer integument esp. of insects — **chi·tin·ous** *adj*

**chit·ter·lings** *or* **chit·lins** \'chit-lənz\ *n pl* : the intestines of hogs esp. when prepared as food

**chi·val·ric** \shə-'val-rik\ *adj* : relating to chivalry : CHIVALROUS

**chiv·al·rous** \'shi-vəl-rəs\ *adj* **1** : of or relating to chivalry **2** : marked by honor, courtesy, and generosity **3** : marked by especial courtesy to women — **chiv·al·rous·ly** *adv* — **chiv·al·rous·ness** *n*

**chiv·al·ry** \'shi-vəl-rē\ *n, pl* **-ries 1** : mounted men-at-arms **2** : the system or practices of knighthood **3** : the spirit or character of the ideal knight

**chive** \'chīv\ *n* : an herb related to the onion that has slender leaves used for flavoring; *also* : its leaves

**chla·myd·ia** \klə-'mi-dē-ə\ *n, pl* **-i·ae** \-dē-ˌē\ **1** : any of a genus of bacteria that cause various diseases of the eye and urogenital tract **2** : a disease or infection caused by chlamydiae

**chlo·ral hydrate** \'klȯr-əl-\ *n* : a white crystalline compound used as a hypnotic and sedative

**chlor·dane** \'klȯr-ˌdān\ *n* : a highly chlorinated persistent insecticide

**chlo·ride** \'klȯr-ˌīd\ *n* : a compound of chlorine with another element or group

**chlo·ri·nate** \'klȯr-ə-ˌnāt\ *vb* **-nat·ed; -nat·ing** : to treat or combine with chlorine or a chlorine compound — **chlo·ri·na·tion** \ˌklȯr-ə-'nā-shən\ *n* — **chlo·ri·na·tor** \'klȯr-ə-ˌnā-tər\ *n*

**chlo·rine** \'klȯr-ˌēn\ *n* : a nonmetallic chemical element that is found alone as a strong-smelling greenish-yellow irritating gas and is used as a bleach, oxidizing agent, and disinfectant

**chlorine monoxide** *n* : a reactive radical that plays a major role in stratospheric ozone depletion

**chlo·rite** \'klȯr-ˌīt\ *n* : a usu. green mineral found with and resembling mica

**chlo·ro·flu·o·ro·car·bon** \ˌklȯr-ə-ˈflȯr-ə-ˌkär-bən, -ˈflu̇r-\ *n* : any of several gaseous compounds that contain carbon, chlorine, fluorine, and sometimes hydrogen and are used esp. as solvents, refrigerants, and aerosol propellants

¹**chlo·ro·form** \'klȯr-ə-ˌfȯrm\ *n* : a colorless heavy fluid with etherlike odor used as a solvent

²**chloroform** *vb* : to treat with chloroform to produce anesthesia or death

**chlo·ro·phyll** \-ˌfil\ *n* : the green coloring matter of plants that functions in photosynthesis

**chlo·ro·plast** \'klȯr-ə-ˌplast\ *n* : a cytoplasmic organelle that contains chlorophyll and is the site of photosynthesis

**chm** *abbr* chairman

**chock** \'chäk\ *n* : a wedge for steadying something or for blocking the movement of a wheel — **chock** *vb*

**chock·a·block** \'chä-kə-ˌbläk\ *adj* : very full : CROWDED

**chock-full** \'chək-'fu̇l, 'chäk-\ *adj* : full to the limit : CRAMMED

**choc·o·late** \'chä-k(ə-)lət, 'chȯ-\ *n* [Sp, fr. Nahuatl *chocolātl*] **1** : a food prepared from ground roasted cacao beans; *also* : a drink prepared from this **2** : a candy made of or with a coating of chocolate **3** : a dark brown color — **choc·o·laty** *or* **choc·o·lat·ey** \-k(ə-)lə-tē\ *adj*

**Choc·taw** \'chäk-ˌtȯ\ *n, pl* **Choctaw** *or* **Choctaws** : a member of an American Indian people of Mississippi, Alabama, and Louisiana; *also* : their language

¹**choice** \'chȯis\ *n* **1** : the act of choosing : SELECTION **2** : the power or opportunity of choosing : OPTION **3** : the best part **4** : a person or thing selected **5** : a variety offered for selection

²**choice** *adj* **choic·er; choic·est 1** : wor-

thy of being chosen **2** : selected with care **3** : of high quality

**choir** \'kwī(-ə)r\ *n* **1** : an organized company of singers (as in a church service) **2** : the part of a church occupied by the singers or by the clergy

**choir·boy** \'kwī(-ə)r-ˌbȯi\ *n* : a boy member of a choir

**choir·mas·ter** \-ˌmas-tər\ *n* : the director of a choir (as in a church)

**¹choke** \'chōk\ *vb* **choked; chok·ing 1** : to hinder breathing (as by obstructing the trachea) : STRANGLE **2** : to check the growth or action of **3** : CLOG, OBSTRUCT **4** : to enrich the fuel mixture of (a motor) by restricting the carburetor air intake **5** : to perform badly in a critical situation

**²choke** *n* **1** : the act of choking **2** : a narrowing in size toward the muzzle in the bore of a gun **3** : a valve for choking a gasoline engine

**choke hold** *n* **1** : a hold that involves strong choking pressure **2** : absolute control

**chok·er** \'chō-kər\ *n* : something (as a necklace) worn tightly around the neck

**cho·ler** \'kä-lər, 'kō-\ *n* : a tendency toward anger : IRASCIBILITY

**chol·era** \'kä-lə-rə\ *n* : any of several bacterial diseases usu. marked by severe vomiting and dysentery

**cho·ler·ic** \'kä-lə-rik, kə-'ler-ik\ *adj* **1** : IRASCIBLE **2** : ANGRY, IRATE

**cho·les·ter·ol** \kə-'les-tə-ˌrȯl\ *n* : a physiologically important waxy steroid alcohol found in animal tissues and in high concentrations implicated as a cause of arteriosclerosis

**chomp** \'chämp, 'chȯmp\ *vb* : to chew or bite on something heavily

**chon** \'chän\ *n, pl* **chon** — see **won** at MONEY table

**choose** \'chüz\ *vb* **chose** \'chōz\; **cho·sen** \'chō-zᵊn\, **choos·ing** \'chü-ziŋ\ **1** : to select esp. after consideration **2** : DECIDE **3** : to have a preference for — **choos·er** *n*

**choosy** *or* **choos·ey** \'chü-zē\ *adj* **choos·i·er; -est** : very particular in making choices

**¹chop** \'chäp\ *vb* **chopped; chop·ping 1** : to cut by repeated blows **2** : to cut into small pieces : MINCE **3** : to strike (a ball) with a short quick downward stroke

**²chop** *n* **1** : a sharp downward blow or stroke **2** : a small cut of meat often including part of a rib **3** : a short abrupt motion (as of a wave)

**³chop** *n* **1** : an official seal or stamp **2** : a mark on goods to indicate quality or kind; *also* : QUALITY, GRADE

**chop·house** \'chäp-ˌhaus\ *n* : RESTAURANT

**chop·per** \'chä-pər\ *n* **1** : one that chops **2** *pl, slang* : TEETH **3** : HELICOPTER

**chop·pi·ness** \'chä-pē-nəs\ *n* : the quality or state of being choppy

**¹chop·py** \'chä-pē\ *adj* **chop·pi·er; -est 1** : rough with small waves ⟨a ∼ sea⟩ **2** : JERKY, DISCONNECTED ⟨short ∼ sentences⟩ — **chop·pi·ly** \-pə-lē\ *adv*

**²choppy** *adj* **chop·pi·er; -est** : CHANGEABLE, VARIABLE ⟨a ∼ wind⟩

**chops** \'chäps\ *n pl* **1** : the fleshy covering of the jaws **2** : expertise in a particular field or activity ⟨acting ∼⟩

**chop·stick** \'chäp-ˌstik\ *n* : one of a pair of sticks used chiefly in Asian countries for lifting food to the mouth

**chop su·ey** \chäp-'sü-ē\ *n, pl* **chop su·eys** : a dish made of vegetables (as bean sprouts, bamboo shoots, water chestnuts, onions, mushrooms) and meat or fish and served with rice

**cho·ral** \'kȯr-əl\ *adj* : of, relating to, or sung by a choir or chorus or in chorus — **cho·ral·ly** *adv*

**cho·rale** \kə-'ral, -'räl\ *n* **1** : a hymn or psalm sung in church; *also* : a harmonization of a traditional melody **2** : CHORUS, CHOIR

**¹chord** \'kȯrd\ *n* [alter. of ME *cord*, short for *accord*] : three or more musical tones sounded simultaneously

**²chord** *n* **1** : CORD 2 **2** : a straight line joining two points on a curve

**chore** \'chȯr\ *n* [ME *char* turn, piece of work, fr. OE *chierr*] **1** *pl* : the daily light work of a household or farm **2** : a routine task or job **3** : a difficult or disagreeable task

**cho·rea** \kə-'rē-ə\ *n* : any of various nervous disorders marked by spasmodic uncontrolled movements

**cho·re·og·ra·phy** \ˌkȯr-ē-'ä-grə-fē\ *n, pl* **-phies** : the art of composing and arranging dances and esp. ballets — **cho·re·o·graph** \'kȯr-ē-ə-ˌgraf\ *vb* — **cho·re·og·ra·pher** \ˌkȯr-ē-'ä-grə-fər\ *n* — **cho·re·o·graph·ic** \ˌkȯr-ē-ə-'gra-fik\ *adj* — **cho·re·o·graph·i·cal·ly** \-fi-k(ə-)lē\ *adv*

**cho·ris·ter** \'kȯr-ə-stər\ *n* : a singer in a choir

**chor·tle** \'chȯr-tᵊl\ *vb* **chor·tled; chor·tling** : to laugh or chuckle esp. in satisfaction or exultation — **chortle** *n*

**¹chorus** \'kȯr-əs\ *n* **1** : an organized company of singers : CHOIR **2** : a group of dancers and singers (as in a musical comedy) **3** : a part of a song repeated at intervals **4** : a composition to be sung by a chorus; *also* : group singing **5** : sounds uttered by a number of persons or animals together ⟨a ∼ of boos⟩

**²chorus** *vb* : to sing or utter in chorus

**chose** *past of* CHOOSE

**cho·sen** \'chō-zᵊn\ *adj* : selected or marked for special favor or privilege

**chou·croute** \shü-'krüt\ *n* **1** : SAUERKRAUT **2** *or* **choucroute gar·nie** \-gär-'nē\ : sauerkraut cooked and served with meat

**¹chow** \'chau\ *n* : FOOD

**²chow** *vb* : EAT — often used with *down*

**³chow** *n* : CHOW CHOW

**chow-chow** \'chau-ˌchau\ *n* : chopped mixed pickles in mustard sauce

**chow chow** \'chau-ˌchau\ *n* : any of a breed of thick-coated muscular dogs of Chinese origin with a blue-black tongue and a short tail curled close to the back

**chow·der** \'chau-dər\ *n* : a soup or stew

made from seafood or vegetables and containing milk or tomatoes

**chow mein** \'chaù-'mān\ n : a seasoned stew of shredded or diced meat, mushrooms, and vegetables that is usu. served with fried noodles

**chrism** \'kri-zəm\ n : consecrated oil used esp. in baptism, confirmation, and ordination

**Christ** \'krīst\ n [ME *Crist*, fr. OE, fr. L *Christus*, fr. Gk *Christos*, lit., anointed] : Jesus esp. as the Messiah — **Christ·like** adj — **Christ·ly** adj

**chris·ten** \'kri-s°n\ vb 1 : BAPTIZE 2 : to name at baptism 3 : to name or dedicate (as a ship) by a ceremony suggestive of baptism — **chris·ten·ing** n

**Chris·ten·dom** \'kri-s°n-dəm\ n 1 : CHRISTIANITY 2 : the part of the world in which Christianity prevails

¹**Chris·tian** \'kris-chən\ n : an adherent of Christianity

²**Christian** adj 1 : of or relating to Christianity 2 : based on or conforming with Christianity 3 : of or relating to a Christian 4 : professing Christianity

**Chris·ti·an·i·ty** \ˌkris-chē-'a-nə-tē\ n : the religion derived from Jesus Christ, based on the Bible as sacred scripture, and professed by Christians

**Chris·tian·ize** \'kris-chə-ˌnīz\ vb -ized; -iz·ing : to make Christian

**Christian name** n : GIVEN NAME

**Christian Science** n : a religion and system of healing founded by Mary Baker Eddy and taught by the Church of Christ, Scientist — **Christian Scientist** n

**chris·tie** or **chris·ty** \'kris-tē\ n, pl **chris·ties** : a skiing turn made by shifting body weight forward and skidding into a turn with parallel skis

**Christ·mas** \'kris-məs\ n : December 25 celebrated as a church festival in commemoration of the birth of Christ and observed as a legal holiday

**Christmas club** n : a savings account in which regular deposits are made to provide money for Christmas shopping

**Christ·mas·tide** \'kris-məs-ˌtīd\ n : the season of Christmas

**chro·mat·ic** \krō-'ma-tik\ adj 1 : of or relating to color 2 : proceeding by half steps of the musical scale — **chro·mat·i·cism** \-tə-ˌsi-zəm\ n

**chro·mato·graph** \krō-'ma-tə-ˌgraf\ n : an instrument used in chromatography

**chro·ma·tog·ra·phy** \ˌkrō-mə-'tä-grə-fē\ n : the separation of a complex mixture into its component compounds as a result of the different rates at which the compounds travel through or over a stationary substance due to differing affinities for the substance — **chro·mato·graph·ic** \krō-ˌma-tə-'gra-fik\ adj — **chro·mato·graph·i·cal·ly** \-fi-k(ə-)lē\ adv

**chrome** \'krōm\ n 1 : CHROMIUM 2 : a chromium pigment 3 : something plated with an alloy of chromium

**chro·mi·um** \'krō-mē-əm\ n : a bluish white metallic element used esp. in alloys and chrome plating

**chro·mo·some** \'krō-mə-ˌsōm, -ˌzōm\ n [G *Chromosom*, fr. Gk *chrōma* color, pigment + *sōma* body] : any of the rod= shaped or threadlike DNA-containing structures of cellular organisms that contain most or all of the genes of the organism — **chro·mo·som·al** \ˌkrō-mə-'sō-məl, -'zō-\ adj

**chro·mo·sphere** \'krō-mə-ˌsfir\ n : the lower part of a star's atmosphere

**chron** abbr 1 chronicle 2 chronological; chronology

**Chron** abbr Chronicles

**chron·ic** \'krä-nik\ adj : marked by long duration or frequent recurrence ⟨a ∼ disease⟩; also : HABITUAL ⟨a ∼ grumbler⟩ — **chron·i·cal·ly** \-ni-k(ə-)lē\ adv

**chronic fatigue syndrome** n : a disorder of unknown cause that is characterized by persistent profound fatigue

¹**chron·i·cle** \'krä-ni-kəl\ n : HISTORY, NARRATIVE

²**chronicle** vb **-cled; -cling** : to record in or as if in a chronicle — **chron·i·cler** n

**Chronicles** n — see BIBLE table

**chro·no·graph** \'krä-nə-ˌgraf\ n : an instrument for measuring and recording time intervals with accuracy — **chro·no·graph·ic** \ˌkrä-nə-'gra-fik\ adj — **chro·nog·ra·phy** \krə-'nä-grə-fē\ n

**chro·nol·o·gy** \krə-'nä-lə-jē\ n, pl **-gies** 1 : the science that deals with measuring time and dating events 2 : a chronological list or table 3 : arrangement of events in the order of their occurrence — **chron·o·log·i·cal** \ˌkrän-ᵊl-'ä-ji-kəl\ adj — **chron·o·log·i·cal·ly** \-k(ə-)lē\ adv — **chro·nol·o·gist** \krə-'nä-lə-jist\ n

**chro·nom·e·ter** \krə-'nä-mə-tər\ n : a very accurate timepiece

**chrys·a·lid** \'kri-sə-ləd\ n : CHRYSALIS

**chrys·a·lis** \'kri-sə-ləs\ n, pl **chry·sal·i·des** \kri-'sa-lə-ˌdēz\ or **chrys·a·lis·es** : an insect pupa in a firm case without a cocoon

**chry·san·the·mum** \kri-'san-thə-məm\ n [L, fr. Gk *chrysanthemon*, fr. *chrysos* gold + *anthemon* flower] : any of various plants related to the daisies including some grown for their showy brightly colored flowers or for medicinal products or insecticides; also : a flower of a chrysanthemum

**chub** \'chəb\ n, pl **chub** or **chubs** : any of various small freshwater fishes related to the carp

**chub·by** \'chə-bē\ adj **chub·bi·er; -est** : PLUMP ⟨a ∼ child⟩ — **chub·bi·ness** n

¹**chuck** \'chək\ vb 1 : to give a pat or tap 2 : TOSS 3 : DISCARD; also : EJECT 4 : to have done with ⟨∼ed his job⟩

²**chuck** n 1 : a light pat under the chin 2 : TOSS

³**chuck** n 1 : a cut of beef including most of the neck and the parts around the shoulder blade and the first three ribs 2 : a device for holding work or a tool in a machine (as a lathe)

**chuck·hole** \'chək-ˌhōl\ n : POTHOLE

**chuck·le** \'chə-kəl\ vb **chuck·led; chuck·ling** : to laugh in a quiet hardly audible manner — **chuckle** n

**chuck wagon** *n* : a wagon equipped with a stove and food supplies

[1]**chug** \'chəg\ *n* : a dull explosive sound made by or as if by a laboring engine

[2]**chug** *vb* **chugged; chug·ging** : to move or go with chugs

**chuk·ka** \'chə-kə\ *n* : a usu. ankle-length leather boot

**chuk·ker** \'chə-kər\ *also* **chuk·ka** \'chə-kə\ *n* : a playing period of a polo game

[1]**chum** \'chəm\ *n* : a close friend

[2]**chum** *vb* **chummed; chum·ming 1** : to room together **2** : to be a close friend

**chum·my** \'chə-mē\ *adj* **chum·mi·er; -est** : quite friendly — **chum·mi·ly** \-mə-lē\ *adv* — **chum·mi·ness** \-mē-nəs\ *n*

**chump** \'chəmp\ *n* : FOOL, BLOCKHEAD

**chunk** \'chəŋk\ *n* **1** : a short thick piece ⟨a ~ of meat⟩ **2** : a sizable amount

**chunky** \'chəŋ-kē\ *adj* **chunk·i·er; -est 1** : STOCKY **2** : containing chunks

**church** \'chərch\ *n* [ME *chirche*, fr. OE *cirice*, ultim. fr. LGk *kyriakon*, fr. Gk, neut. of *kyriakos* of the lord, fr. *kyrios* lord, master] **1** : a building esp. for Christian public worship **2** *often cap* : the whole body of Christians **3** : DENOMINATION **4** : CONGREGATION **5** : public divine worship

**church·go·er** \'chərch-ˌgō-ər\ *n* : one who habitually attends church — **church·go·ing** *adj or n*

**church·less** \'chərch-ləs\ *adj* : not affiliated with a church

**church·man** \'chərch-mən\ *n* **1** : CLERGYMAN **2** : a member of a church

**church·war·den** \'chərch-ˌwȯr-d²n\ *n* : WARDEN 5

**church·yard** \-ˌyärd\ *n* : a yard that belongs to a church and is often used as a burial ground

**churl** \'chərl\ *n* **1** : a medieval peasant **2** : RUSTIC **3** : a rude ill-bred person — **churl·ish** *adj* — **churl·ish·ly** *adv* — **churl·ish·ness** *n*

[1]**churn** \'chərn\ *n* : a container in which milk or cream is agitated in making butter

[2]**churn** *vb* **1** : to stir in a churn; *also* : to make (butter) by such stirring **2** : to shake around violently

**churn out** *vb* : to produce mechanically or in large quantity

**chute** \'shüt\ *n* **1** : an inclined surface, trough, or passage down or through which something may pass ⟨a coal ~⟩ ⟨a mail ~⟩ **2** : PARACHUTE

**chut·ney** \'chət-nē\ *n, pl* **chutneys** : a thick sauce containing fruits, vinegar, sugar, and spices

**chutz·pah** \'hu̇t-spə, 'ku̇t-, -(ˌ)spä\ *n* : supreme self-confidence

**CIA** *abbr* Central Intelligence Agency

**cía** *abbr* [Sp *compañia*] company

**cia·bat·ta** \chə-'bä-tə\ *n* [It, lit., slipper] : a flat bread with a moist interior and a crispy crust

**ciao** \'chau̇\ *interj* — used to express greeting or farewell

**ci·ca·da** \sə-'kä-də\ *n* : any of a family of stout-bodied insects related to the aphids and having wide blunt heads and large transparent wings

**ci·ca·trix** \'si-kə-ˌtriks\ *n, pl* **ci·ca·tri·ces** \ˌsi-kə-'trī-ˌsēz\ [L] : a scar resulting from formation and contraction of fibrous tissue in a wound

**ci·ce·ro·ne** \ˌsi-sə-'rō-nē, ˌchē-chə-\ *n, pl* **-ni** \-(ˌ)nē\ : a guide who conducts sightseers

**CID** *abbr* Criminal Investigation Department

**ci·der** \'sī-dər\ *n* : juice pressed from fruit (as apples) and used as a beverage, vinegar, or flavoring

**cie** *abbr* [F *compagnie*] company

**ci·gar** \si-'gär\ *n* [Sp *cigarro*] : a roll of tobacco for smoking

**cig·a·rette** \ˌsi-gə-'ret, 'si-gə-ˌret\ *n* [F, dim. of *cigare* cigar] : a slender roll of cut tobacco enclosed in paper for smoking

**cig·a·ril·lo** \ˌsi-gə-'ri-lō, -'re-ō\ *n, pl* **-los** [Sp] **1** : a very small cigar **2** : a cigarette wrapped in tobacco rather than paper

**ci·lan·tro** \si-'län-trō, -'lan-\ *n* : leaves of coriander used as a flavoring or garnish; *also* : the coriander plant

**cil·i·ate** \'si-lē-ˌət\ *n* : any of a group of protozoans characterized by cilia

**cil·i·um** \'si-lē-əm\ *n, pl* **cil·ia** \-lē-ə\ **1** : a minute short hairlike process; *esp* : one of a cell **2** : EYELASH

**C in C** *abbr* commander in chief

**cinch** \'sinch\ *n* **1** : a girth for a pack or saddle **2** : a sure or an easy thing — **cinch** *vb*

**cin·cho·na** \siŋ-'kō-nə\ *n* : any of a genus of So. American trees related to the madder; *also* : the bitter quinine-containing bark of a cinchona

**cinc·ture** \'siŋk-chər\ *n* : BELT, SASH

**cin·der** \'sin-dər\ *n* **1** : SLAG **2** *pl* : ASHES **3** : a hot piece of partly burned wood or coal **4** : a fragment of lava from an erupting volcano — **cin·dery** *adj*

**cinder block** *n* : a building block made of cement and coal cinders

**cin·e·ma** \'si-nə-mə\ *n* **1** : a motion-picture theater **2** : MOVIES — **cin·e·mat·ic** \ˌsi-nə-'ma-tik\ *adj*

**cin·e·ma·theque** \ˌsi-nə-mə-'tek\ *n* : a small movie house specializing in avant-garde films

**cin·e·ma·tog·ra·phy** \ˌsi-nə-mə-'tä-grə-fē\ *n* : motion-picture photography — **cin·e·ma·tog·ra·pher** *n* — **cin·e·mat·o·graph·ic** \-ˌma-tə-'gra-fik\ *adj*

**cine·phile** \'si-nə-ˌfī(-ə)l\ *n* : a lover of motion pictures

**cin·e·plex** \'si-nə-ˌpleks\ *n* : a complex that houses several movie theaters

**cin·er·ar·i·um** \ˌsi-nə-'rer-ē-əm\ *n, pl* **-ia** \-ē-ə\ : a place to receive the ashes of the cremated dead — **cin·er·ary** \'si-nə-ˌrer-ē\ *adj*

**cin·na·bar** \'si-nə-ˌbär\ *n* **1** : a red mineral that is the only important ore of mercury **2** : a deep vivid red

**cin·na·mon** \'si-nə-mən\ *n* : a spice prepared from the highly aromatic bark of any of several Asian trees related to the true laurel; *also* : a tree that yields cinnamon

**cinque·foil** \'siŋk-ˌfȯi(-ə)l, 'saŋk-\ n : any of a genus of plants related to the roses with leaves having five lobes

**¹ci·pher** \'sī-fər\ n [ME, fr. ML cifra, fr. Ar ṣifr empty, zero] **1** : ZERO, NAUGHT **2** : a method of secret writing

**²cipher** vb : to compute arithmetically

**cir** or **circ** abbr circular

**cir·ca** \'sər-kə\ prep : ABOUT ⟨~ 1600⟩

**cir·ca·di·an** \ˌsər-'kā-dē-ən\ adj : being, having, characterized by, or occurring in approximately 24-hour intervals (as of biological activity)

**¹cir·cle** \'sər-kəl\ n **1** : a closed curve every point of which is equally distant from a fixed point within it **2** : something circular **3** : an area of action or influence **4** : CYCLE **5** : a group bound by a common tie ⟨sewing ~⟩

**²circle** vb **cir·cled; cir·cling 1** : to enclose in a circle **2** : to move or revolve around; also : to move in a circle

**cir·clet** \'sər-klət\ n : a small circle; esp : a circular ornament

**cir·cuit** \'sər-kət\ n **1** : a boundary around an enclosed space **2** : a course around a periphery **3** : a regular tour (as by a judge) around an assigned territory **4** : the complete path of an electric current; also : an assemblage of electronic components **5** : LEAGUE; also : a chain of theaters

**circuit board** n : BOARD 7

**circuit breaker** n : a switch that automatically interrupts the current of an overloaded circuit

**circuit court** n : a court that sits at two or more places within one judicial district

**cir·cu·i·tous** \ˌsər-'kyü-ə-təs\ adj **1** : having a circular or winding course ⟨a ~ route⟩ **2** : not being forthright or direct in language or action ⟨a ~ explanation⟩

**cir·cuit·ry** \'sər-kə-trē\ n, pl **-ries** : the plan or the components of an electric circuit

**cir·cu·ity** \ˌsər-'kyü-ə-tē\ n, pl **-ities** : INDIRECTION

**¹cir·cu·lar** \'sər-kyə-lər\ adj **1** : having the form of a circle : ROUND **2** : moving in or around a circle **3** : CIRCUITOUS **4** : intended for circulation ⟨a ~ letter⟩ — **cir·cu·lar·i·ty** \ˌsər-kyə-'ler-ə-tē\ n

**²circular** n : a paper (as a leaflet) intended for wide distribution

**cir·cu·lar·ise** Brit var of CIRCULARIZE

**cir·cu·lar·ize** \'sər-kyə-lə-ˌrīz\ vb **-ized; -iz·ing 1** : to send circulars to **2** : to poll by questionnaire **3** : to make circular

**circular saw** n : a power saw with a round cutting blade

**cir·cu·late** \'sər-kyə-ˌlāt\ vb **-lat·ed; -lat·ing 1** : to move or cause to move in a circle, circuit, or orbit **2** : to pass from place to place or from person to person — **cir·cu·la·tion** \ˌsər-kyə-'lā-shən\ n

**cir·cu·la·to·ry** \'sər-kyə-lə-ˌtȯr-ē\ adj : of or relating to circulation or the circulatory system

**circulatory system** n : the system of blood, blood vessels, lymphatic vessels, and heart concerned with the circulation of the blood and lymph

**cir·cum·am·bu·late** \ˌsər-kəm-'am-byə-ˌlāt\ vb **-lat·ed; -lat·ing** : to circle on foot esp. as part of a ritual

**cir·cum·cise** \'sər-kəm-ˌsīz\ vb **-cised; -cis·ing** [ME, fr. L circumcisus, pp. of circumcidere, lit., to cut around, fr. circum around + caedere to cut] : to cut off the foreskin of — **cir·cum·ci·sion** \ˌsər-kəm-'si-zhən\ n

**cir·cum·fer·ence** \sər-'kəm-f(ə-)rəns\ n **1** : the perimeter of a circle **2** : the external boundary or surface of a figure or object

**cir·cum·flex** \'sər-kəm-ˌfleks\ n : the mark ^ over a vowel

**cir·cum·lo·cu·tion** \ˌsər-kəm-lō-'kyü-shən\ n : the use of unnecessary words in expressing an idea

**cir·cum·lu·nar** \-'lü-nər\ adj : revolving about or surrounding the moon

**cir·cum·nav·i·gate** \-'na-və-ˌgāt\ vb : to go completely around (as the earth) esp. by water — **cir·cum·nav·i·ga·tion** \-ˌna-və-'gā-shən\ n

**cir·cum·po·lar** \-'pō-lər\ adj **1** : continually visible above the horizon ⟨a ~ star⟩ **2** : surrounding or found near a pole of the earth ⟨a ~ current⟩

**cir·cum·scribe** \'sər-kəm-ˌskrīb\ vb **1** : to constrict the range or activity of **2** : to draw a line around — **cir·cum·scrip·tion** \ˌsər-kəm-'skrip-shən\ n

**cir·cum·spect** \'sər-kəm-ˌspekt\ adj : careful to consider all circumstances and consequences : PRUDENT — **cir·cum·spec·tion** \ˌsər-kəm-'spek-shən\ n

**cir·cum·stance** \'sər-kəm-ˌstans\ n **1** : a fact or event that must be considered along with another fact or event **2** : surrounding conditions **3** : CHANCE, FATE **4** : pl : situation with regard to wealth **5** : CEREMONY ⟨pomp and ~⟩

**cir·cum·stan·tial** \ˌsər-kəm-'stan-chəl\ adj **1** : consisting of or depending on circumstances **2** : INCIDENTAL **3** : containing full details — **cir·cum·stan·tial·ly** adv

**cir·cum·vent** \ˌsər-kəm-'vent\ vb : to check or defeat esp. by stratagem — **cir·cum·ven·tion** \-'vent-shən\ n

**cir·cus** \'sər-kəs\ n **1** : a usu. traveling show that features feats of physical skill, wild animal acts, and performances by clowns **2** : a circus performance; also : the equipment, livestock, and personnel of a circus

**cirque** \'sərk\ n : a deep steep-walled mountain basin usu. forming the blunt end of a valley

**cir·rho·sis** \sə-'rō-səs\ n, pl **-rho·ses** \-ˌsēz\ [NL, fr. Gk kirrhos orange-colored] : fibrosis of the liver — **cir·rhot·ic** \-'rä-tik\ adj or n

**cir·rus** \'sir-əs\ n, pl **cir·ri** \'sir-ˌī\ : a wispy white cloud usu. of minute ice crystals at high altitudes

**cis·lu·nar** \(ˌ)sis-'lü-nər\ adj : lying between the earth and the moon or the moon's orbit

**cis·sy** Brit var of SISSY

**cis·tern** \'sis-tərn\ n : an often underground tank for storing water

**cit** *abbr* **1** citation; cited **2** citizen

**cit·a·del** \'si-tə-dəl, -,del\ *n* **1** : a fortress commanding a city **2** : STRONGHOLD

**ci·ta·tion** \sī-'tā-shən\ *n* **1** : an official summons to appear (as before a court) **2** : QUOTATION **3** : a formal statement of the achievements of a person; *also* : a specific reference in a military dispatch to meritorious performance of duty

**cite** \'sīt\ *vb* **cit·ed**; **cit·ing** **1** : to summon to appear before a court **2** : QUOTE **3** : to refer to esp. in commendation or praise

**cit·i·fied** \'si-ti-,fīd\ *adj* : of, relating to, or characterized by an urban style of living

**cit·i·zen** \'si-tə-zən\ *n* **1** : an inhabitant of a city or town **2** : a person who owes allegiance to a government and is entitled to its protection — **cit·i·zen·ship** *n*

**cit·i·zen·ry** \-rē\ *n, pl* **-ries** : a whole body of citizens

**citizens band** *n* : a range of radio frequencies set aside for private radio communications

**cit·ric acid** \'si-trik-\ *n* : a sour organic acid obtained from lemon and lime juices or by fermentation of sugars and used chiefly as a flavoring

**cit·ron** \'si-trən\ *n* **1** : the oval lemonlike fruit of a citrus tree; *also* : the tree **2** : a small hard-fleshed watermelon used esp. in pickles and preserves

**cit·ro·nel·la** \,si-trə-'ne-lə\ *n* : a lemon-scented oil obtained from a fragrant grass of southern Asia and used in perfumes and as an insect repellent

**cit·rus** \'si-trəs\ *n, pl* **citrus** *or* **cit·rus·es** : any of a genus of often thorny evergreen trees or shrubs grown in warm regions for their fruits (as the orange, lemon, lime, and grapefruit); *also* : the fruit

**city** \'si-tē\ *n, pl* **cit·ies** [ME *citie* large or small town, fr. AF *cité*, fr. ML *civitas*, fr. L, citizenship, state, city of Rome, fr. *civis* citizen] **1** : an inhabited place larger or more important than a town **2** : a municipality in the U.S. governed under a charter granted by the state; *also* : an incorporated municipal unit of the highest class in Canada

**city manager** *n* : an official employed by an elected council to direct the administration of a city government

**city–state** \'si-tē-,stāt\ *n* : an autonomous state consisting of a city and surrounding territory

**civ** *abbr* **1** civil; civilian **2** civilization

**civ·et** \'si-vət\ *n* : a yellowish strong-smelling substance obtained from a cat-like Old World mammal (**civet cat**) and used in making perfumes

**civ·ic** \'si-vik\ *adj* : of or relating to a city, citizenship, or civic affairs

**civ·ics** \-viks\ *n* : a social science dealing with the rights and duties of citizens

**civ·il** \'si-vəl\ *adj* **1** : of or relating to citizens or to the state as a political body **2** : COURTEOUS, POLITE **3** : of or relating to legal proceedings in connection with private rights and obligations 〈the ~ code〉 **4** : of or relating to the general population : not military or ecclesiastical

**civil defense** *n* : protective measures and emergency relief activities conducted by civilians in case of enemy attack or natural disaster

**civil disobedience** *n* : refusal to obey governmental commands esp. as a nonviolent means of protest

**civil engineer** *n* : an engineer whose training or occupation is in the design and construction esp. of public works (as roads or harbors) — **civil engineering** *n*

**ci·vil·ian** \sə-'vil-yən\ *n* : a person not on active duty in a military, police, or firefighting force

**civ·i·li·sa·tion, civ·i·lise** *chiefly Brit var of* CIVILIZATION, CIVILIZE

**civ·il·i·ty** \sə-'vi-lə-tē\ *n, pl* **-ties** **1** : POLITENESS, COURTESY **2** : a polite act or expression

**civ·i·li·za·tion** \,si-və-lə-'zā-shən\ *n* **1** : a relatively high level of cultural and technological development **2** : the culture characteristic of a time or place — **civ·i·li·za·tion·al** \-shə-nᵊl\ *adj*

**civ·i·lize** \'si-və-,līz\ *vb* **-lized**; **-liz·ing** **1** : to raise from a primitive state to an advanced and ordered stage of cultural development **2** : REFINE — **civ·i·lized** *adj*

**civil liberty** *n* : freedom from arbitrary governmental interference specifically by denial of governmental power — usu. used in pl.

**civ·il·ly** \'si-vəl-lē\ *adv* **1** : in terms of civil rights, matters, or law 〈~ dead〉 **2** : in a civil manner : POLITELY

**civil rights** *n pl* : the nonpolitical rights of a citizen; *esp* : those guaranteed by the 13th and 14th amendments to the Constitution and by acts of Congress

**civil servant** *n* : a member of a civil service

**civil service** *n* : the administrative service of a government

**civil war** *n* : a war between opposing groups of citizens of the same country

**civ·vies** \'si-vēz\ *n pl* : civilian clothes as distinguished from a military uniform

**CJ** *abbr* chief justice

**ck** *abbr* **1** cask **2** check

**cl** *abbr* **1** centiliter **2** class

**Cl** *symbol* chlorine

**¹clack** \'klak\ *vb* **1** : CHATTER, PRATTLE **2** : to make or cause to make a clatter

**²clack** *n* **1** : rapid continuous talk : CHATTER **2** : a sound of clacking 〈the ~ of a typewriter〉

**clad** \'klad\ *adj* **1** : CLOTHED, COVERED **2** : being or consisting of coins made of outer layers of one metal bonded to a core of a different metal

**¹claim** \'klām\ *vb* [ME, fr. AF *claimer, clamer*, fr. L *clamare* to cry out, shout] **1** : to ask for as one's own; *also* : to take as the rightful owner **2** : to call for : REQUIRE **3** : to state as a fact : MAINTAIN

**²claim** *n* **1** : a demand for something due 〈an insurance ~〉 **2** : a right to something usu. in another's possession **3** : an assertion open to challenge **4** : something claimed (as a tract of land)

**claim·ant** \'klā-mənt\ *n* : a person making a claim

**clair·voy·ant** \klar-'vȯi-ənt\ *adj* [F, fr. *clair* clear + *voyant* seeing] **1** : able to see beyond the range of ordinary perception **2** : having the power of discerning objects not present to the senses — **clair·voy·ance** \-əns\ *n* — **clairvoyant** *n*

**clam** \'klam\ *n* **1** : any of numerous bivalve mollusks including many that are edible **2** : DOLLAR

**clam·bake** \-ˌbāk\ *n* : a party or gathering (as at the seashore) at which food is cooked usu. on heated rocks covered by seaweed

**clam·ber** \'klam-bər\ *vb* : to climb awkwardly — **clam·ber·er** *n*

**clam·my** \'kla-mē\ *adj* **clam·mi·er; -est** : being damp, soft, sticky, and usu. cool — **clam·mi·ness** *n*

**clam·or** \'kla-mər\ *n* **1** : a noisy shouting **2** : a loud continuous noise **3** : insistent public expression (as of support or protest) — **clamor** *vb* — **clam·or·ous** *adj*

**clam·our** *chiefly Brit var of* CLAMOR

**¹clamp** \'klamp\ *n* : a device that holds or presses parts together firmly

**²clamp** *vb* : to fasten with or as if with a clamp

**clamp down** *vb* : to impose restrictions : become repressive — **clamp·down** \'klamp-ˌdau̇n\ *n*

**clam·shell** \'klam-ˌshel\ *n* **1** : the shell of a clam **2** : a bucket or grapnel (as on a dredge) having two hinged jaws

**clam up** *vb* : to become silent

**clan** \'klan\ *n* [ME, fr. ScGael *clann* offspring, clan, fr. Old Irish *cland* plant, offspring, fr. L *planta* plant] : a group (as in the Scottish Highlands) made up of households whose heads claim descent from a common ancestor — **clan·nish** *adj* — **clan·nish·ness** *n*

**clan·des·tine** \klan-'des-tən\ *adj* : held in or conducted with secrecy

**clang** \'klaŋ\ *n* : a loud metallic ringing sound — **clang** *vb*

**clan·gor** \'klaŋ-ər, -gər\ *n* : a resounding clang or medley of clangs

**clan·gour** *chiefly Brit var of* CLANGOR

**clank** \'klaŋk\ *n* : a sharp brief metallic ringing sound — **clank** *vb*

**¹clap** \'klap\ *vb* **clapped; clap·ping 1** : to strike noisily **2** : APPLAUD

**²clap** *n* **1** : a loud noisy crash **2** : the noise made by clapping the hands

**³clap** *n* : GONORRHEA

**clap·board** \'kla-bərd, -ˌbȯrd; 'klap-ˌbȯrd\ *n* : a narrow board thicker at one edge than the other used for siding — **clap·board** *vb*

**clap·per** \'kla-pər\ *n* : one that claps; *esp* : the tongue of a bell

**clap·trap** \'klap-ˌtrap\ *n* : pretentious nonsense

**claque** \'klak\ *n* [F, fr. *claquer* to clap] **1** : a group hired to applaud at a performance **2** : a group of sycophants

**clar·et** \'kler-ət\ *n* [ME, fr. AF (*vin*) *claret* clear wine] : a dry red wine

**clar·i·fy** \'kler-ə-ˌfī\ *vb* **-fied; -fy·ing 1** : to make or become clear — **clar·i·fi·ca·tion** \ˌkler-ə-fə-'kā-shən\ *n*

**clar·i·net** \ˌkler-ə-'net\ *n* : a single-reed woodwind instrument in the form of a cylindrical tube with a moderately flaring end — **clar·i·net·ist** *or* **clar·i·net·tist** \-'ne-tist\ *n*

**clar·i·on** \'kler-ē-ən\ *adj* : brilliantly clear ⟨a ∼ call⟩

**clar·i·ty** \'kler-ə-tē\ *n* : CLEARNESS

**¹clash** \'klash\ *vb* **1** : to make or cause to make a clash **2** : CONFLICT, COLLIDE

**²clash** *n* **1** : a noisy usu. metallic sound of collision **2** : a hostile encounter **3** : a sharp conflict ⟨a ∼ of opinions⟩

**clasp** \'klasp\ *n* **1** : a device (as a hook) for holding objects or parts together **2** : EMBRACE, GRASP — **clasp** *vb*

**¹class** \'klas\ *n* [F *classe*, fr. L *classis* group called to military service, fleet, class] **1** : a group of students meeting regularly in a course; *also* : a group graduating together **2** : a course of instruction; *also* : the period when such a course is taught **3** : social rank; *also* : high quality **4** : a group of the same general status or nature; *esp* : a major category in biological classification that is above the order and below the phylum **5** : a division or rating based on grade or quality — **class·less** *adj*

**²class** *vb* : CLASSIFY

**class action** *n* : a legal action undertaken in behalf of the plaintiffs and all others having an identical interest in the alleged wrong

**¹clas·sic** \'kla-sik\ *adj* **1** : serving as a standard of excellence ⟨a ∼ novel⟩; *also* : TRADITIONAL **2** : CLASSICAL **2 3** : notable esp. as the best example ⟨his winning goal was ∼⟩ **4** : AUTHENTIC ⟨a ∼ folk dance⟩

**²classic** *n* **1** : a work of enduring excellence and esp. of ancient Greece or Rome; *also* : its author **2** : a traditional event ⟨a football ∼⟩

**clas·si·cal** \'kla-si-kəl\ *adj* **1** : CLASSIC **2** : of or relating to the ancient Greek and Roman classics **3** : of or relating to a form or system of primary significance before modern times ⟨∼ economics⟩ **4** : concerned with a general study of the arts and sciences — **clas·si·cal·ly** \-k(ə-)lē\ *adv*

**clas·si·cism** \'kla-sə-ˌsi-zəm\ *n* **1** : the principles or style of the literature or art of ancient Greece and Rome **2** : adherence to traditional standards believed to be universally valid — **clas·si·cist** \-sist\ *n*

**clas·si·fied** \'kla-sə-ˌfīd\ *adj* : withheld from general circulation for reasons of national security

**clas·si·fieds** \-ˌfīdz\ *n pl* : advertisements grouped by subject

**clas·si·fy** \'kla-sə-ˌfī\ *vb* **-fied; -fy·ing** : to arrange in or assign to classes — **clas·si·fi·able** *adj* — **clas·si·fi·ca·tion** \ˌkla-sə-fə-'kā-shən\ *n* — **clas·si·fi·er** *n*

**class·mate** \'klas-ˌmāt\ *n* : a member of the same class (as in a college)

**class·room** \-ˌrüm-, -ˌru̇m\ *n* : a place where classes meet

**classy** \'kla-sē\ *adj* **class·i·er; -est** : EL-

EGANT, STYLISH ⟨a ~ clientele⟩ — **class·i·ness** *n*

**clat·ter** \'kla-tər\ *n* : a rattling sound ⟨the ~ of dishes⟩ — **clatter** *vb*

**clause** \'klȯz\ *n* **1** : a group of words having its own subject and predicate but forming only part of a compound or complex sentence **2** : a separate part of an article or document

**claus·tro·pho·bia** \ˌklȯ-strə-'fō-bē-ə\ *n* : abnormal dread of being in closed or narrow spaces — **claus·tro·pho·bic** \-bik\ *adj*

**clav·i·chord** \'kla-və-ˌkȯrd\ *n* : an early keyboard instrument in use before the piano

**clav·i·cle** \'kla-vi-kəl\ *n* [F *clavicule*, fr. NL *clavicula*, fr. L, dim. of L *clavis* key] : COLLARBONE

**clavier** \klə-'vir; 'klā-vē-ər\ *n* **1** : the keyboard of a musical instrument **2** : an early keyboard instrument

**¹claw** \'klȯ\ *n* **1** : a sharp usu. curved nail on the toe of an animal **2** : a sharp curved process (as on the foot of an insect); *also* : a pincerlike organ at the end of a limb of some arthropods (as a lobster) — **clawed** \'klȯd\ *adj*

**²claw** *vb* : to rake, seize, or dig with or as if with claws

**clay** \'klā\ *n* **1** : an earthy material that is plastic when moist but hard when fired and is used in making pottery; *also* : finely divided soil consisting largely of such clay **2** : EARTH, MUD **3** : a plastic substance used for modeling **4** : the mortal human body — **clay·ey** \'klā-ē\ *adj*

**clay·more** \'klā-ˌmȯr\ *n* : a large 2-edged sword formerly used by Scottish Highlanders

**clay pigeon** *n* : a saucer-shaped target thrown from a trap in trapshooting

**¹clean** \'klēn\ *adj* **1** : free from dirt, disease, or pollution ⟨~ air⟩ **2** : PURE ⟨the ~ thrill of one's first flight⟩; *also* : HONORABLE **3** : THOROUGH ⟨made a ~ sweep⟩ **4** : TRIM ⟨a ~ edge⟩ ⟨a ship with ~ lines⟩; *also* : EVEN **5** : habitually neat — **clean** *adv* — **clean·ly** \'klēn-lē\ *adv* — **clean·ness** \'klēn-nəs\ *n*

**²clean** *vb* : to make or become clean — **clean·able** \'klē-nə-bəl\ *adj* — **clean·er** *n*

**clean–cut** \'klēn-'kət\ *adj* **1** : cut so that the surface or edge is smooth and even **2** : sharply defined or outlined **3** : giving an effect of wholesomeness

**clean·ly** \'klen-lē\ *adj* **clean·li·er; -est** **1** : careful to keep clean **2** : habitually kept clean — **clean·li·ness** *n*

**clean room** \'klēn-ˌrüm, -ˌrùm\ *n* : an uncontaminated room maintained for the manufacture or assembly of objects (as precision parts)

**cleanse** \'klenz\ *vb* **cleansed; cleans·ing** : to make clean — **cleans·er** *n*

**¹clean–up** \'klēn-ˌəp\ *n* **1** : an act or instance of cleaning **2** : a very large profit

**²cleanup** *adj* : being 4th in the batting order of a baseball team — **cleanup** *adv*

**clean up** *vb* : to make a spectacular business profit

**¹clear** \'klir\ *adj* [ME *clere*, fr. AF *cler*, fr. L. *clarus*] **1** : BRIGHT, LUMINOUS; *also* : UNTROUBLED, SERENE **2** : CLOUDLESS **3** : CLEAN, PURE; *also* : TRANSPARENT **4** : easily heard, seen, or understood **5** : capable of sharp discernment; *also* : free from doubt **6** : INNOCENT ⟨a ~ conscience⟩ **7** : free from restriction, obstruction, or entanglement — **clear** *adv* — **clear·ness** *n*

**²clear** *vb* **1** : to make or become clear **2** : to go away : DISPERSE **3** : to free from accusation or blame; *also* : to certify as trustworthy **4** : EXPLAIN **5** : to get free from obstruction : SETTLE **6** : to free from obstruction : SETTLE **6** : to get rid of : REMOVE ⟨~ed the snow off the driveway⟩ **9** : to jump or go by without touching; *also* : PASS ⟨the bill ~ed the legislature⟩

**³clear** *n* : a clear space or part

**clear·ance** \'klir-əns\ *n* **1** : an act or process of clearing **2** : the distance by which one object clears another **3** : AUTHORIZATION

**clear–cut** \'klir-'kət\ *adj* **1** : sharply outlined **2** : DEFINITE, UNEQUIVOCAL ⟨a ~ victory⟩

**clear–cut·ting** \-ˌkə-tiŋ\ *n* : removal of all the trees in a stand of timber — **clear–cut** \-ˌkət\ *vb*

**clear·head·ed** \-'he-dəd\ *adj* : having a clear understanding : PERCEPTIVE

**clear·ing** \'klir-iŋ\ *n* **1** : a tract of land cleared of wood and brush **2** : the passage of checks and claims through a clearinghouse

**clear·ing·house** \-ˌhaús\ *n* : an institution maintained by banks for making an exchange of checks and claims held by each bank against other banks; *also* : an informal channel for information or assistance

**clear·ly** \'klir-lē\ *adv* **1** : in a clear manner **2** : it is clear

**cleat** \'klēt\ *n* : a piece of wood or metal fastened on or projecting from something to give strength, provide a grip, or prevent slipping

**cleav·age** \'klē-vij\ *n* **1** : a splitting apart : SPLIT **2** : the depression between a woman's breasts esp. when exposed by a low-cut dress

**¹cleave** \'klēv\ *vb* **cleaved** \'klēvd\ *or* **clove** \'klōv\; **cleaved; cleav·ing** : ADHERE, CLING ⟨the child *cleaved* to her mother⟩

**²cleave** *vb* **cleaved** \'klēvd\ *also* **cleft** \'kleft\ *or* **clove** \'klōv\; **cleaved** *also* **cleft** *or* **clo·ven** \'klō-vən\; **cleav·ing** **1** : to divide by force : split asunder ⟨~ logs⟩ **2** : DIVIDE

**cleav·er** \'klē-vər\ *n* : a heavy chopping knife for cutting meat

**clef** \'klef\ *n* : a sign placed on the staff in music to show what pitch is represented by each line and space

**cleft** \'kleft\ *n* : FISSURE, CRACK

**cleft lip** *n* : a birth defect in which the upper lip is vertically split

**cleft palate** *n* : a split in the roof of the mouth that appears as a birth defect

**clem·a·tis** \'kle-mə-təs; kli-'ma-təs\ *n* : any of a genus of vines or herbs related to the buttercups that have showy usu. white or purple flowers

**clem·en·cy** \'kle-mən-sē\ *n, pl* **-cies** 1 : disposition to be merciful 2 : mildness of weather

**clem·ent** \'kle-mənt\ *adj* 1 : MERCIFUL, LENIENT ⟨a ~ judge⟩ 2 : TEMPERATE, MILD ⟨~ weather for this time of year⟩

**clem·en·tine** \'kle-mən-₁tēn\ *n* : a small citrus fruit that is probably a hybrid between a tangerine and an orange

**clench** \'klench\ *vb* 1 : CLINCH 1 2 : to hold fast 3 : to set or close tightly

**clere·sto·ry** \'klir-₁stȯr-ē\ *n* : an outside wall of a room or building that rises above an adjoining roof and contains windows

**cler·gy** \'klər-jē\ *n* : a body of religious officials authorized to conduct services

**cler·gy·man** \-mən\ *n* : a member of the clergy

**cler·gy·per·son** \-₁pər-s°n\ *n* : a member of the clergy

**cler·ic** \'kler-ik\ *n* : a member of the clergy

**cler·i·cal** \'kler-i-kəl\ *adj* 1 : of or relating to the clergy ⟨~ vestments⟩ 2 : of or relating to a clerk

**cler·i·cal·ism** \'kler-i-kə-₁li-zəm\ *n* : a policy of maintaining or increasing the power of a religious hierarchy

**clerk** \'klərk, *Brit* 'klärk\ *n* 1 : CLERIC 2 : an official responsible for correspondence, records, and accounts; *also* : a person employed to perform general office work 3 : a store salesperson — **clerk** *vb* — **clerk·ship** *n*

**clev·er** \'kle-vər\ *adj* 1 : showing skill or resourcefulness 2 : marked by wit or ingenuity — **clev·er·ly** *adv* — **clev·er·ness** *n*

**clev·is** \'kle-vəs\ *n* : a U-shaped shackle used for fastening

¹**clew** \'klü\ *n* 1 : CLUE 2 : a metal loop on a lower corner of a sail

²**clew** *vb* : to haul (a sail) up or down by ropes through the clews

**cli·ché** \kli-'shā\ *n* [F] : a trite phrase or expression — **cli·chéd** \-'shād\ *adj*

¹**click** \'klik\ *vb* 1 : to make or cause to make a click 2 : to fit or work together smoothly 3 : to select or make a selection on a computer by pressing a button on a control device (as a mouse) — **click·able** \'kli-kə-bəl\ *adj*

²**click** *n* 1 : a slight sharp noise 2 : an instance of clicking ⟨a mouse ~⟩

**click·er** \'kli-kər\ *n* : REMOTE CONTROL 2

**cli·ent** \'klī-ənt\ *n* 1 : DEPENDENT 2 : a person who engages the professional services of another; *also* : PATRON, CUSTOMER 3 : a computer in a network that uses the services (access to files) provided by a server

**cli·en·tele** \₁klī-ən-'tel, ₁klē-ä\ *n* : a body of clients and esp. customers

**cliff** \'klif\ *n* : a high steep face of rock, earth, or ice

**cliff-hang·er** \-₁haŋ-ər\ *n* 1 : an adventure serial or melodrama usu. presented in installments each of which ends in suspense 2 : a contest whose outcome is in doubt up to the very end

**cli·mac·ter·ic** \klī-'mak-tə-rik\ *n* 1 : a major turning point or critical stage 2 : MENOPAUSE; *also* : a corresponding period in the male

**cli·mate** \'klī-mət\ *n* [ME *climat*, fr. MF, fr. LL *clima*, fr. Gk *klima* inclination, latitude, climate, fr. *klinein* to lean] 1 : a region having specific climatic conditions 2 : the average weather conditions at a place over a period of years 3 : the prevailing set of conditions (as temperature and humidity) indoors 4 : a prevailing atmosphere or environment ⟨the ~ of opinion⟩ — **cli·mat·ic** \klī-'ma-tik\ *adj* — **cli·mat·i·cal·ly** \-ti-k(ə-)lē\ *adv*

**cli·ma·tol·o·gy** \₁klī-mə-'tä-lə-jē\ *n* : the science that deals with climates — **cli·ma·to·log·i·cal** \-mə-tə-'lä-ji-kəl\ *adj* — **cli·ma·to·log·i·cal·ly** \-k(ə-)lē\ *adv* — **cli·ma·tol·o·gist** \-mə-'tä-lə-jist\ *n*

¹**cli·max** \'klī-₁maks\ *n* [L, fr. Gk *klimax*, lit., ladder, fr. *klinein* to lean] 1 : a series of ideas or statements so arranged that they increase in force and power from the first to the last; *also* : the last member of such a series 2 : the highest point ⟨the ~ of her career⟩ 3 : ORGASM — **cli·mac·tic** \klī-'mak-tik\ *adj*

²**climax** *vb* : to come or bring to a climax

¹**climb** \'klīm\ *vb* 1 : to rise to a higher point 2 : to go up or down esp. by use of hands and feet; *also* : to ascend in growing — **climb·er** *n*

²**climb** *n* 1 : a place where climbing is necessary 2 : the act of climbing : ascent by climbing

**clime** \'klīm\ *n* : CLIMATE ⟨warmer ~s⟩

¹**clinch** \'klinch\ *vb* 1 : to turn over or flatten the end of something sticking out ⟨~ a nail⟩; *also* : to fasten by clinching 2 : to make final : SETTLE ⟨~ a deal⟩ 3 : to hold a boxing opponent 4 : to hold fast or firmly

²**clinch** *n* 1 : a fastening by means of a clinched nail, rivet, or bolt 2 : an act or instance of clinching in boxing

**clinch·er** \'klin-chər\ *n* : one that clinches; *esp* : a decisive fact, argument, act, or remark

**cling** \'kliŋ\ *vb* **clung** \'kləŋ\; **cling·ing** 1 : to adhere as if glued; *also* : to hold or hold on tightly 2 : to have a strong emotional attachment — **clingy** \'kliŋ-ē\ *adj*

**cling·stone** \'kliŋ-₁stōn\ *n* : any of various fruits (as some peaches) whose flesh adheres strongly to the pit

**clin·ic** \'kli-nik\ *n* 1 : a medical class in which patients are examined and discussed 2 : a group meeting for teaching a certain skill and working on individual problems ⟨a reading ~⟩ 3 : a facility (as of a hospital) for diagnosis and treatment of outpatients

**clin·i·cal** \'kli-ni-kəl\ *adj* 1 : of, relating to, or typical of a clinic; *esp* : involving direct observation of the patient ⟨~ studies⟩ 2 : scientifically dispassionate — **clin·i·cal·ly** \-k(ə-)lē\ *adv*

**cli·ni·cian** \kli-'ni-shən\ *n* : a person qualified in the clinical practice of medicine, psychiatry, or psychology as distinguished from one specializing in laboratory or research techniques or in theory

¹**clink** \'kliŋk\ vb : to make or cause to make a sharp short metallic sound

²**clink** n : a clinking sound

**clin·ker** \'kliŋ-kər\ n : stony matter fused together : SLAG

¹**clip** \'klip\ vb **clipped; clip·ping** : to fasten with a clip

²**clip** n **1** : a device that grips, clasps, or hooks **2** : a cartridge holder for a rifle

³**clip** vb **clipped; clip·ping 1** : to cut or cut off with shears ⟨clipped a recipe from the magazine⟩ **2** : CURTAIL, DIMINISH **3** : HIT, PUNCH **4** : to illegally block (an opponent) in football

⁴**clip** n **1** : a 2-bladed instrument for cutting esp. the nails **2** : a sharp blow **3** : a rapid pace ⟨the train moved at a good ∼⟩

**clip art** n : ready-made usu. copyright-free illustrations

**clip·board** \'klip-,bȯrd\ n **1** : a small writing board with a spring clip at the top for holding papers **2** : a section of computer memory that temporarily stores data esp. to facilitate its movement or duplication

**clip joint** n, slang : an establishment (as a nightclub) that makes a practice of defrauding its customers

**clip·per** \'kli-pər\ n **1** : an implement for clipping esp. the hair or nails — usu. used in pl. **2** : a fast sailing ship

**clip·ping** \'kli-piŋ\ n : a piece clipped from something (as a newspaper)

**clique** \'klēk, 'klik\ n [F] : a small exclusive group of people : COTERIE ⟨high school ∼s⟩ — **cliqu·ey** \'klē-kē, 'kli-\ adj — **cliqu·ish** \-kish\ adj

**cli·to·ris** \'kli-tə-rəs\ n, pl **cli·to·ris·es** : a small erectile organ at the anterior or ventral part of the vulva homologous to the penis — **cli·to·ral** \-rəl\ adj

**clk** abbr clerk

**clo** abbr clothing

¹**cloak** \'klōk\ n **1** : a loose outer garment **2** : something that conceals

²**cloak** vb : to cover or hide with a cloak

**cloak-and-dagger** adj : involving or suggestive of espionage

**clob·ber** \'klä-bər\ vb **1** : to pound mercilessly; also : to hit with force : SMASH **2** : to defeat overwhelmingly

**cloche** \'klōsh\ n [F, lit., bell] : a woman's small close-fitting hat

¹**clock** \'kläk\ n : a timepiece not intended to be carried on the person

²**clock** vb **1** : to time (a person or a performance) by a timing device **2** : to register (as speed) on a mechanical recording device — **clock·er** n

³**clock** n : an ornamental figure on a stocking or sock

**clock·wise** \'kläk-,wīz\ adv : in the direction in which the hands of a clock move — **clockwise** adj

**clock·work** \-,wərk\ n **1** : the machinery that runs a mechanical device (as a clock

or toy) **2** : the precision or regularity associated with a clock

**clod** \'kläd\ n **1** : a lump esp. of earth or clay **2** : a dull or insensitive person

**clod·hop·per** \-,hä-pər\ n **1** : an uncouth rustic **2** : a large heavy shoe

¹**clog** \'kläg\ n **1** : a weight attached esp. to an animal to impede motion **2** : a thick-soled shoe

²**clog** vb **clogged; clog·ging 1** : to impede with a clog : HINDER **2** : to obstruct passage through **3** : to become filled with extraneous matter

**cloi·son·né** \,klȯi-zə-'nā\ adj : a colored decoration made of enamels poured into the divided areas in a design outlined with wire or metal strips

¹**clois·ter** \'klȯi-stər\ n [ME cloistre, fr. AF, fr. ML claustrum, fr. L, bar, bolt, fr. claudere to close] **1** : a monastic establishment **2** : a covered usu. colonnaded passage on the side of a court — **clois·tral** \-strəl\ adj

²**cloister** vb : to shut away from the world

**clone** \'klōn\ n [Gk klōn twig, slip] **1** : the collection of genetically identical cells or organisms produced asexually from a single ancestral cell or organism; also : an individual grown from a single cell and genetically identical to it ⟨a sheep ∼⟩ **2** : a group of replicas of a biological molecule (as DNA) **3** : one that appears to be a copy of an original form — **clon·al** \'klō-n²l\ adj — **clone** vb

**clop** \'kläp\ n : a sound made by or as if by a hoof or wooden shoe against pavement — **clop** vb

¹**close** \'klōz\ vb **closed; clos·ing 1** : to bar passage through : SHUT **2** : to suspend the operations (as of a school) **3** : END, TERMINATE **4** : to bring together the parts or edges of; also : to fill up **5** : GRAPPLE ⟨∼ with the enemy⟩ **6** : to enter into an agreement — **clos·able** or **close·able** adj

²**close** \'klōz\ n : CONCLUSION, END

³**close** \'klōs\ adj **clos·er; clos·est 1** : having no openings **2** : narrowly restricting or restricted **3** : limited to a privileged class **4** : SECLUDED; also : SECRETIVE **5** : RIGOROUS ⟨keep ∼ watch⟩ **6** : SULTRY, STUFFY **7** : STINGY **8** : having little space between items or units **9** : fitting tightly; also : SHORT ⟨∼ haircut⟩ **10** : NEAR ⟨at ∼ range⟩ **11** : INTIMATE ⟨∼ friends⟩ **12** : ACCURATE **13** : decided by a narrow margin ⟨a ∼ game⟩ — **closo** adv — **close·ly** adv — **close·ness** n

**closed-circuit** \'klōzd-'sər-kət\ adj : used in, shown on, or being a television installation in which the signal is transmitted by wire to a limited number of receivers

**closed shop** n : an establishment having only members of a labor union on the payroll

**close-fist·ed** \'klōz-'fis-təd, 'klōs-\ adj : STINGY

**close-knit** \'klōs-'nit\ adj : closely bound together by social, cultural, economic, or political ties

**close·mouthed** \'klōz-'maůthd, 'klōs-'maůtht\ *adj* : cautious or reticent in speaking

**close-out** \'klōz-,aůt\ *n* : a sale of a business's entire stock at low prices

**close out** *vb* 1 : to dispose of by a close-out 2 : to dispose of a business : SELL OUT

**clos·er** \'klō-zər\ *n* : one that closes; *esp* : a relief pitcher who specializes in finishing games

**¹clos·et** \'klä-zət, 'klȯ-\ *n* 1 : a small room for privacy 2 : a small compartment for household utensils or clothing 3 : a state or condition of secrecy ⟨came out of the ~⟩

**²closet** *vb* : to take into a private room for an interview

**close–up** \'klōs-,əp\ *n* 1 : a photograph or movie shot taken at close range 2 : an intimate view or examination

**clo·sure** \'klō-zhər\ *n* 1 : an act of closing : the condition of being closed 2 : something that closes 3 : CLOTURE

**clot** \'klät\ *n* : a mass formed by a portion of liquid (as blood) thickening and sticking together — **clot** *vb*

**cloth** \'klȯth\ *n, pl* **cloths** \'klȯthz, 'klȯths\ 1 : a pliable fabric made usu. by weaving or knitting natural or synthetic fibers and filaments 2 : TABLECLOTH 3 : distinctive dress of the clergy; *also* : CLERGY

**clothe** \'klȯth\ *vb* **clothed** *or* **clad** \'klad\; **cloth·ing** 1 : DRESS; *also* : to provide with clothes 2 : to express by suitably significant language ⟨policies *clothed* in rhetoric⟩

**clothes** \'klȯthz, 'klȯz\ *n pl* 1 : CLOTHING 2 : BEDCLOTHES

**clothes·horse** \-,hȯrs\ *n* 1 : a frame on which to hang clothes 2 : a conspicuously dressy person

**¹clothes·line** \-,līn\ *n* : a rope or cord on which clothes are hung to dry

**²clothesline** *vb* : to knock down by catching by the neck with one's outstretched arm

**clothes moth** *n* : any of several small pale moths whose larvae eat wool, fur, and feathers

**clothes·pin** \'klȯthz-,pin, 'klȯz-\ *n* : a device for fastening clothes on a line

**clothes·press** \-,pres\ *n* : a receptacle for clothes

**cloth·ier** \'klȯth-yər, 'klō-thē-ər\ *n* : a maker or seller of clothing

**cloth·ing** \'klō-thiŋ\ *n* : garments in general

**clo·ture** \'klō-chər\ *n* : the closing or limitation (as by calling for a vote) of debate in a legislative body

**¹cloud** \'klaůd\ *n* [ME, rock, cloud, fr. OE *clūd*] 1 : a visible mass of particles of condensed vapor (as water or ice) suspended in the atmosphere 2 : a usu. visible mass of minute airborne particles; *also* : a mass of obscuring matter in interstellar space 3 : CROWD, SWARM ⟨a ~ of mosquitoes⟩ 4 : something having a dark or threatening aspect ⟨a ~ of suspicion⟩ 5 : something that obscures or blemishes

⟨a ~ of ambiguity⟩ — **cloud·i·ness** \'klaů-dē-nəs\ *n* — **cloud·less** *adj* — **cloudy** *adj*

**²cloud** *vb* 1 : to darken or hide with or as if with a cloud 2 : OBSCURE ⟨~ed in mystery⟩ 3 : TAINT, SULLY ⟨a ~ed reputation⟩

**cloud·burst** \-,bərst\ *n* : a sudden heavy rainfall

**cloud·let** \-lət\ *n* : a small cloud

**cloud nine** *n* : a feeling of extreme well-being or elation — usu. used with *on*

**¹clout** \'klaůt\ *n* 1 : a blow esp. with the hand 2 : PULL, INFLUENCE

**²clout** *vb* : to hit forcefully

**¹clove** \'klōv\ *n* : one of the small bulbs that grows at the base of the scales of a large bulb ⟨a ~ of garlic⟩

**²clove** *past of* CLEAVE

**³clove** *n* [ME *clowe*, fr. AF *clou* (*de girofle*), lit., nail of clove, fr. L *clavus* nail] : the dried flower bud of a tropical tree used esp. as a spice

**clo·ven** \'klō-vən\ *past part of* CLEAVE

**cloven foot** *n* : CLOVEN HOOF — **clo·ven–foot·ed** \-'fů-təd\ *adj*

**cloven hoof** *n* : a foot (as of a sheep) with the front part divided into two parts — **cloven–hoofed** \-'hůft, -'hůvd\ *adj*

**clo·ver** \'klō-vər\ *n* : any of a genus of leguminous herbs with usu. 3-parted leaves and dense flower heads

**clo·ver·leaf** \-,lēf\ *n, pl* **cloverleafs** \-,lēfs\ *or* **clo·ver·leaves** \-,lēvz\ : an interchange between two major highways that from above resembles a 4-leaf clover

**¹clown** \'klaůn\ *n* 1 : BOOR 2 : a fool or comedian in an entertainment (as a circus) 3 : a person given to joking and buffoonery — **clown·ish** *adj* — **clown·ish·ly** *adv* — **clown·ish·ness** *n*

**²clown** *vb* : to act like a clown

**cloy** \'klȯi\ *vb* : to disgust or nauseate with excess of something orig. pleasing — **cloy·ing·ly** *adv*

**clr** *abbr* clear

**¹club** \'kləb\ *n* 1 : a heavy wooden stick or staff used as a weapon; *also* : BAT 2 : any of a suit of playing cards marked with a black figure resembling a clover leaf 3 : a group of persons associated for a common purpose; *also* : the meeting place of such a group 4 : CLUB SANDWICH

**²club** *vb* **clubbed; club·bing** 1 : to strike with a club 2 : to unite or combine for a common cause 3 : to patronize nightclubs

**club·foot** \'kləb-'fůt\ *n* : a misshapen foot twisted out of position from birth; *also* : this deformed condition — **club·foot·ed** \-'fů-təd\ *adj*

**club·house** \'kləb-,haůs\ *n* 1 : a house occupied by a club 2 : locker rooms used by an athletic team 3 : a building at a golf course with locker rooms and usu. a pro shop and a restaurant

**club sandwich** *n* : a sandwich of three slices of bread with two layers of meat (as turkey) and lettuce, tomato, and mayonnaise

**club soda** *n* : SODA WATER

**cluck** \'klək\ *n* : the call of a hen esp. to her chicks — **cluck** *vb*

¹**clue** \'klü\ *n* 1 : something that guides through an intricate procedure or maze; *esp* : a piece of evidence leading to the solution of a problem 2 : IDEA, NOTION ⟨has no ∼ what he's doing⟩

²**clue** *vb* **clued; clu·ing** *or* **clu·ing** : to provide with a clue; *also* : to give information to ⟨∼ me in⟩

¹**clump** \'kləmp\ *n* 1 : a group of things clustered together 2 : a heavy tramping sound

²**clump** *vb* : to tread clumsily and noisily

**clum·sy** \'kləm-zē\ *adj* **clum·si·er; -est** 1 : lacking dexterity, nimbleness, or grace 2 : not tactful or subtle ⟨a ∼ attempt at a joke⟩ — **clum·si·ly** \-zə-lē\ *adv* — **clum·si·ness** \-zē-nəs\ *n*

**clung** *past and past part of* CLING

**clunk·er** \'kləŋ-kər\ *n* 1 : a dilapidated automobile 2 : a notable failure

¹**clus·ter** \'kləs-tər\ *n* : GROUP, BUNCH

²**cluster** *vb* : to grow or gather in a cluster

¹**clutch** \'kləch\ *vb* : to grasp with or as if with the hand

²**clutch** *n* 1 : the claws or a hand in the act of grasping; *also* : CONTROL, POWER 2 : a device for gripping an object 3 : a coupling used to connect and disconnect a driving and a driven part of a mechanism; *also* : a lever or pedal operating such a coupling 4 : a crucial situation

³**clutch** *adj* : made, done, or successful in a crucial situation

⁴**clutch** *n* 1 : a nest or batch of eggs; *also* : a brood of chicks 2 : GROUP, BUNCH

¹**clut·ter** \'klə-tər\ *vb* : to fill or cover with a disorderly scattering of things

²**clutter** *n* : a crowded mass

**cm** *abbr* centimeter

**Cm** *symbol* curium

**CM** *abbr* [Commonwealth of the Northern Mariana Islands] Northern Mariana Islands

**cmdr** *abbr* commander

**cml** *abbr* commercial

**CMSgt** *abbr* chief master sergeant

**Cn** *symbol* copernicium

**CNO** *abbr* chief of naval operations

**CNS** *abbr* central nervous system

**co** *abbr* 1 company 2 county

**Co** *symbol* cobalt

**CO** *abbr* 1 Colorado 2 commanding officer 3 conscientious objector

**c/o** *abbr* care of

¹**coach** \'kōch\ *n* [MF *coche*, ultim. fr. Hung *kocsi (szekér)*, lit., (wagon) of Kocs (town in Hungary)] 1 : a large closed 4-wheeled carriage with an elevated outside front seat for the driver 2 : a railroad passenger car esp. for day travel 3 : BUS 4 : a private tutor; *also* : one who instructs or trains ⟨an acting ∼⟩ ⟨a soccer ∼⟩

²**coach** *vb* : to instruct, direct, or prompt as a coach

**coach·man** \-mən\ *n* : a man who drives a coach or carriage

**co·ad·ju·tor** \kō-ə-'jü-tər, kō-'a-jə-tər\ *n* : ASSISTANT; *esp* : an assistant bishop having the right of succession

**co·ag·u·lant** \kō-'a-gyə-lənt\ *n* : something that produces coagulation

**co·ag·u·late** \-,lāt\ *vb* **-lat·ed; -lat·ing** : CLOT — **co·ag·u·la·tion** \kō-,a-gyə-'lā-shən\ *n*

¹**coal** \'kōl\ *n* 1 : EMBER 2 : a black solid combustible mineral used as fuel

²**coal** *vb* 1 : to supply with coal 2 : to take in coal

**co·alesce** \,kō-ə-'les\ *vb* **co·alesced; co·alesc·ing** : to grow together; *also* : FUSE ♦ *Synonyms* MERGE, BLEND, MINGLE, MIX — **co·ales·cence** \-ᵊns\ *n*

**coal·field** \'kōl-,fēld\ *n* : a region rich in coal deposits

**coal gas** *n* : gas from coal; *esp* : gas distilled from bituminous coal and used for heating

**co·a·li·tion** \,kō-ə-'li-shən\ *n* : UNION; *esp* : a temporary union for a common purpose — **co·a·li·tion·ist** *n*

**coal oil** *n* : KEROSENE

**coal tar** *n* : tar distilled from bituminous coal and used in dyes and drugs

**co·an·chor** \'kō-'aŋ-kər\ *n* : a newscaster who shares the duties of head broadcaster

**coarse** \'kȯrs\ *adj* **coars·er; coars·est** 1 : of ordinary or inferior quality 2 : composed of large parts or particles ⟨∼ sand⟩ 3 : CRUDE ⟨∼ manners⟩ 4 : ROUGH, HARSH — **coarse·ly** *adv* — **coarse·ness** *n*

**coars·en** \'kȯr-sᵊn\ *vb* : to make or become coarse

¹**coast** \'kōst\ *n* [ME *cost*, fr. AF *coste*, fr. L *costa* rib, side] 1 : SEASHORE 2 : a slide down a slope 3 : the immediate area of view — used in the phrase *the coast is clear* — **coast·al** *adj*

²**coast** *vb* 1 : to sail along the shore 2 : to move (as downhill on a sled) without effort

**coast·er** *n* 1 : one that coasts 2 : a shallow container or a plate or mat to protect a surface

**coaster brake** *n* : a brake in the hub of the rear wheel of a bicycle

**coast guard** *n* : a military force employed in guarding or patrolling a coast — **coast·guards·man** \'kōst-,gärdz-mən\ *n*

**coast·line** \'kōst-,līn\ *n* : the outline or shape of a coast

¹**coat** \'kōt\ *n* 1 : an outer garment for the upper part of the body 2 : an external growth (as of fur or feathers) on an animal 3 : a covering layer ⟨a ∼ of paint⟩ — **coat·ed** \'kō-təd\ *adj*

²**coat** *vb* : to cover usu. with a finishing or protective coat

**coat·ing** \'kō-tiŋ\ *n* : COAT, COVERING

**coat of arms** : the heraldic bearings (as of a person) usu. depicted on an escutcheon

**coat of mail** : a garment of metal scales or rings worn as armor

**co·au·thor** \'kō-'ȯ-thər\ *n* : a joint or associate author — **coauthor** *vb*

**coax** \'kōks\ *vb* : WHEEDLE; *also* : to gain by gentle urging or flattery

**co·ax·i·al** \'kō-'ak-sē-əl\ *adj* : having co-incident axes — **co·ax·i·al·ly** *adv*

**coaxial cable** *n* : a cable that consists of a tube of electrically conducting material surrounding a central conductor

**cob** \'käb\ *n* **1** : a male swan **2** : CORN-COB **3** : a short-legged stocky horse

**co·balt** \'kō-,bȯlt\ *n* [G *Kobalt,* alter. of *Kobold,* lit., goblin; fr. its occurrence in silver ore, believed to be due to goblins] : a tough shiny silver-white magnetic metallic chemical element found with iron and nickel

**cob·ble** \'kä-bəl\ *vb* **cob·bled; cob·bling** : to make or put together roughly or hastily ⟨— together a solution⟩

**cob·bler** \'kä-blər\ *n* **1** : a mender or maker of shoes **2** : a deep-dish fruit pie with a thick crust

**cob·ble·stone** \'kä-bəl-,stōn\ *n* : a naturally rounded stone larger than a pebble and smaller than a boulder

**co·bra** \'kō-brə\ *n* [Pg *cobra (de capello),* lit., hooded snake] : any of several venomous snakes of Asia and Africa that when excited expand the skin of the neck into a broad hood

**cob·web** \'käb-,web\ *n* [ME *coppeweb,* fr. *coppe* spider, fr. OE ātor*coppe*] **1** : SPIDERWEB; *also* : a thread spun by a spider or insect larva **2** : something flimsy or entangling — **cob·web·by** \-,we-bē\ *adj*

**co·caine** \kō-'kān, 'kō-,kān\ *n* : a drug obtained from the leaves of a So. American shrub (**co·ca** \'kō-kə\) that can result in severe psychological dependence and is sometimes used in medicine as a local anesthetic and illegally as a stimulant of the central nervous system

**coc·cus** \'kä-kəs\ *n, pl* **coc·ci** \'käk-,sī\ : a spherical bacterium

**coc·cyx** \'käk-siks\ *n, pl* **coc·cy·ges** \'käk-sə-,jēz\ *also* **coc·cyx·es** \'käk-sik-səz\ : the end of the spinal column beyond the sacrum esp. in humans

**co·chi·neal** \'kä-chə-,nēl\ *n* : a red dye made from the dried bodies of females of a tropical American insect (**cochineal insect**)

**co·chlea** \'kō-klē-ə, 'kä-\ *n, pl* **co·chle·as** *or* **co·chle·ae** \-klē-,ē, -,ī\ : the usu. spiral part of the inner ear containing nerve endings which carry information about sound to the brain — **co·chle·ar** \-klē-ər\ *adj*

¹**cock** \'käk\ *n* **1** : the adult male of a bird and esp. of the common domestic chicken **2** : VALVE, FAUCET **3** : LEADER **4** : the hammer of a firearm; *also* : the position of the hammer when ready for firing

²**cock** *vb* **1** : to draw back the hammer of a firearm **2** : to set or draw back in readiness for some action ⟨— your arm to throw⟩ **3** : to turn or tilt usu. to one side ⟨— one's head⟩

³**cock** *n* : a small pile (as of hay)

**cock·ade** \kä-'kād\ *n* : an ornament worn on the hat as a badge

**cock·a·tiel** \,kä-kə-'tēl\ *n* : a small crested gray parrot often kept as a cage bird

**cock·a·too** \'kä-kə-,tü\ *n, pl* **-toos** [D *kaketoe,* fr. Malay *kakatua*] : any of various

large noisy crested parrots chiefly of Australia

**cock·a·trice** \'kä-kə-trəs, -,trīs\ *n* : a legendary serpent with a deadly glance

**cock·crow** \'käk-,krō\ *n* : DAWN

**cocked hat** \'käkt-\ *n* : a hat with the brim turned up on two or three sides

**cock·er·el** \'kä-kə-rəl\ *n* : a young male domestic chicken

**cock·er spaniel** \'kä-kər-\ *n* [*cocking* woodcock hunting] : any of a breed of small spaniels with long ears, square muzzle, and silky coat

**cock·eyed** \'kä-'kīd\ *adj* **1** : turned or tilted to one side **2** : slightly crazy : FOOLISH

**cock·fight** \'käk-,fīt\ *n* : a contest of gamecocks usu. fitted with metal spurs

¹**cock·le** \'kä-kəl\ *n* : any of several weedy plants related to the pinks

²**cockle** *n* : a bivalve mollusk with a heart-shaped shell

**cock·le·shell** \-,shel\ *n* **1** : the shell of a cockle **2** : a light flimsy boat

**cock·ney** \'käk-nē\ *n, pl* **cockneys** : a native of London and esp. of the East End of London; *also* : the dialect of a cockney

**cock·pit** \'käk-,pit\ *n* **1** : a pit for cockfights **2** : a space or compartment in a vehicle from which it is steered, piloted, or driven

**cock·roach** \'käk-,rōch\ *n* [Sp *cucaracha*] : any of an order or suborder of active nocturnal insects including some which infest houses and ships

**cock·sure** \'käk-'shùr\ *adj* **1** : perfectly sure : CERTAIN **2** : COCKY

**cock·tail** \'käk-,tāl\ *n* **1** : an iced drink made of liquor and flavoring ingredients **2** : an appetizer (as tomato juice) served as a first course of a meal

**cocky** \'kä-kē\ *adj* **cock·i·er; -est** : marked by overconfidence : PERT, CONCEITED — **cock·i·ly** \-kə-lē\ *adv* — **cock·i·ness** \-kē-nəs\ *n*

**co·coa** \'kō-kō\ *n* **1** : CACAO **2** : chocolate deprived of some of its fat and powdered; *also* : a drink made of this heated with water or milk

**cocoa butter** *n* : a pale vegetable fat obtained from cacao beans

**co·co·nut** \'kō-kə-(,)nət\ *n* : a large edible hard-shelled fruit produced by a tall tropical palm (**coconut palm**)

**co·coon** \kə-'kün\ *n* **1** : a case usu. of silk formed by some insect larvae for protection during the pupal stage **2** : something that offers protection or isolation

**cod** \'käd\ *n, pl* **cod** *also* **cods** : a bottom-dwelling bony fish of the North Atlantic that is an important food fish; *also* : a related fish of the Pacific Ocean

**COD** *abbr* **1** cash on delivery **2** collect on delivery

**co·da** \'kō-də\ *n* : a closing section in a musical composition that is formally distinct from the main structure

**cod·dle** \'kä-dᵊl\ *vb* **cod·dled; cod·dling** **1** : to cook slowly in water below the boiling point **2** : PAMPER

¹**code** \'kōd\ *n* [ME, fr. MF, fr. L *caudex, codex* trunk of a tree, document formed orig. from wooden tablets] **1** : a systematic statement of a body of law **2** : a system of principles or rules ⟨moral ~⟩ **3** : a system of signals **4** : a system of symbols (as in secret communication) with special meanings **5** : GENETIC CODE

²**code** *vb* **cod·ed; cod·ing** : to put into the form or symbols of a code

**co·deine** \'kō-,dēn\ *n* : a narcotic drug obtained from opium and used esp. as an analgesic and cough suppressant

**co·dex** \'kō-,deks\ *n, pl* **co·di·ces** \'kō-də-,sēz, 'kä-\ : a manuscript book (as of the Scriptures or classics)

**cod·fish** \'käd-,fish\ *n* : COD

**cod·ger** \'kä-jər\ *n* : an odd or cranky and usu. elderly fellow

**cod·i·cil** \'kä-də-səl, -,sil\ *n* : a legal instrument modifying an earlier will

**cod·i·fy** \'kä-də-,fī, 'kō-də\ *vb* **-fied; -fy·ing** : to arrange in a systematic form — **cod·i·fi·ca·tion** \,kä-də-fə-'kā-shən, ,kō-\ *n*

**co·ed** \'kō-,ed\ *n* : a female student in a coeducational institution — **coed** *adj*

**co·ed·u·ca·tion** \,kō-,e-jə-'kā-shən\ *n* : the education of male and female students at the same institution — **co·ed·u·ca·tion·al** \-shə-nəl\ *adj* — **co·ed·u·ca·tion·al·ly** *adv*

**co·ef·fi·cient** \,kō-ə-'fi-shənt\ *n* **1** : a constant factor as distinguished from a variable in a mathematical term **2** : a number that serves as a measure of some property (as of a substance, device, or process)

**coe·len·ter·ate** \si-'len-tə-,rāt, -rət\ *n* : any of a phylum of radially symmetrical invertebrate animals including the corals, sea anemones, and jellyfishes

**co·equal** \kō-'ē-kwəl\ *adj* : equal with another — **coequal** *n* — **co·equal·i·ty** \,kō-ē-'kwä-lə-tē\ *n* — **co·equal·ly** *adv*

**co·erce** \kō-'ərs\ *vb* **co·erced; co·erc·ing 1** : RESTRAIN, REPRESS **2** : COMPEL **3** : ENFORCE — **co·er·cion** \-'ər-zhən, -shən\ *n* — **co·er·cive** \-'ər-siv\ *adj*

**co·e·val** \kō-'ē-vəl\ *adj* : of the same age — **coeval** *n*

**co·ex·ist** \,kō-ig-'zist\ *vb* **1** : to exist together or at the same time **2** : to live in peace with each other — **co·ex·is·tence** \-'zis-təns\ *n*

**co·ex·ten·sive** \,kō-ik-'sten-siv\ *adj* : having the same scope or extent in space or time

**C of C** *abbr* Chamber of Commerce

**cof·fee** \'kó-fē\ *n* [It & Turk; It *caffè*, fr. Turk *kahve*, fr. Ar *qahwah*] : a drink made from the roasted and ground seeds of a fruit of a tropical shrub or tree; *also* : these seeds (**coffee beans**) or a plant producing them

**cof·fee·house** \-,haus\ *n* : a place where refreshments (as coffee) are sold

**coffee klatch** \-,klach\ *n* : KAFFEE·KLATSCH

**cof·fee·pot** \-,pät\ *n* : a pot for brewing or serving coffee

**coffee shop** *n* : a small restaurant

**coffee table** *n* : a low table customarily placed in front of a sofa

**cof·fer** \'kó-fər\ *n* : a chest or box used esp. for valuables

**cof·fer·dam** \-,dam\ *n* : a watertight enclosure from which water is pumped to expose the bottom of a body of water and permit construction

**cof·fin** \'kó-fən\ *n* : a box or chest for burying a corpse

**C of S** *abbr* chief of staff

¹**cog** \'käg\ *n* : a tooth on the rim of a wheel or gear — **cogged** \'kägd\ *adj*

²**cog** *abbr* cognate

**co·gen·er·a·tion** \,kō-je-nə-'rā-shən\ *n* : the simultaneous generation of electricity and heat from the same fuel

**co·gent** \'kō-jənt\ *adj* : having power to compel or constrain : CONVINCING ⟨a ~ argument⟩ — **co·gen·cy** \-jən-sē\ *n*

**cog·i·tate** \'kä-jə-,tāt\ *vb* **-tat·ed; -tat·ing** : THINK, PONDER ⟨*cogitated* about his future⟩ — **cog·i·ta·tion** \,kä-jə-'tā-shən\ *n* — **cog·i·ta·tive** \'kä-jə-,tā-tiv\ *adj*

**co·gnac** \'kōn-,yak\ *n* : a French brandy

**cog·nate** \'käg-,nāt\ *adj* **1** : of the same or similar nature **2** : RELATED; *esp* : related by descent from the same ancestral language — **cognate** *n*

**cog·ni·tive** \'käg-nə-tiv\ *adj* : of, relating to, or being conscious intellectual activity (as thinking, remembering, reasoning, or using language) — **cog·ni·tion** \käg-'ni-shən\ *n* — **cog·ni·tive·ly** *adv*

**cog·ni·zance** \'käg-nə-zəns\ *n* **1** : apprehension by the mind : AWARENESS ⟨had no ~ of the crime⟩ **2** : NOTICE, HEED — **cog·ni·zant** \'käg-nə-zənt\ *adj*

**cog·no·men** \käg-'nō-mən, 'käg-nə-\ *n, pl* **cognomens** *or* **cog·no·mi·na** \käg-'nä-mə-nə, -'nō-\ : NAME; *esp* : NICKNAME

**co·gno·scen·te** \,kän-yə-'shen-tē, ,kō-\ *n, pl* **-scen·ti** \-tē\ [obs. It] : CONNOISSEUR

**cog·wheel** \'käg-,hwēl\ *n* : a wheel with cogs or teeth

**co·hab·it** \kō-'ha-bət\ *vb* : to live together as a couple — **co·hab·i·ta·tion** \-,ha-bə-'tā-shən\ *n*

**co·here** \kō-'hir\ *vb* **co·hered; co·her·ing** : to stick together

**co·her·ent** \kō-'hir-ənt\ *adj* **1** : having the quality of cohering **2** : logically consistent ⟨a ~ explanation⟩ — **co·her·ence** \-əns\ *n* — **co·her·ent·ly** *adv*

**co·he·sion** \kō-'hē-zhən\ *n* **1** : a sticking together **2** : molecular attraction by which the particles of a body are united — **co·he·sive** \-siv\ *adj* — **co·he·sive·ly** *adv* — **co·he·sive·ness** *n*

**co·ho** \'kō-,hō\ *n, pl* **cohos** *or* **coho** : a rather small Pacific salmon with light-colored flesh

**co·hort** \'kō-,hórt\ *n* **1** : a group of warriors or followers **2** : COMPANION, ACCOMPLICE

**coif** \'kóif; 2 *usu* 'kwäf\ *n* **1** : a close-fitting hat **2** : COIFFURE

**coif·feur** \kwä-'fər\ *n* [F] : HAIRDRESSER

**coif·feuse** \kwä-'fərz, -'fōz, -'füz, -'fyüz\ *n* : a female hairdresser

**coif·fure** \kwä-'fyür\ *n* : a manner of arranging the hair

¹**coil** \'kȯi(-ə)l\ *vb* : to wind in a spiral shape

²**coil** *n* : a series of rings or loops (as of coiled rope, wire, or pipe) : RING, LOOP

¹**coin** \'kȯin\ *n* [ME, wedge, corner, image on a coin, fr. AF *coing*, fr. L *cuneus* wedge] **1** : a piece of metal issued by government authority as money **2** : metal money

²**coin** *vb* **1** : to make (a coin) esp. by stamping : MINT **2** : CREATE, INVENT ⟨~ a phrase⟩ — **coin·er** *n*

**coin·age** \'kȯi-nij\ *n* **1** : the act or process of coining **2** : COINS

**co·in·cide** \ˌkō-ən-'sīd, 'kō-ən-ˌsīd\ *vb* **-cid·ed; -cid·ing 1** : to occupy the same place in space or time **2** : to correspond or agree exactly

**co·in·ci·dence** \kō-'in-sə-dəns\ *n* **1** : exact agreement **2** : occurrence together apparently without reason; *also* : an event that so occurs

**co·in·ci·dent** \-sə-dənt\ *adj* **1** : of similar nature **2** : occupying the same space or time — **co·in·ci·den·tal** \kō-ˌin-sə-'den-t³l\ *adj*

**co·i·tus** \'kō-ə-təs\ *n* [L, fr. *coire* to come together] : SEXUAL INTERCOURSE **1** — **co·i·tal** \-t³l\ *adj*

¹**coke** \'kōk\ *n* : a hard gray porous fuel made by heating soft coal to drive off most of its volatile material

²**coke** *n* : COCAINE

¹**col** *abbr* **1** colonial; colony **2** column

²**col** *or* **coll** *abbr* **1** collect, collected, collection **2** college, collegiate

**Col** *abbr* **1** colonel **2** Colorado **3** Colossians

**COL** *abbr* **1** colonel **2** cost of living

**co·la** \'kō-lə\ *n* : a carbonated soft drink usu. containing sugar, caffeine, caramel, and special flavoring

**col·an·der** \'kə-lən-dər, 'kä-\ *n* : a perforated utensil for draining food

¹**cold** \'kōld\ *adj* **1** : having a low or decidedly subnormal temperature **2** : lacking warmth of feeling **3** : suffering or uncomfortable from lack of warmth — **cold·ly** *adv* — **cold·ness** *n* — **in cold blood** : with premeditation : DELIBERATELY ⟨murdered her *in cold blood*⟩

²**cold** *n* **1** : a condition marked by low temperature; *also* : cold weather **2** : a chilly feeling **3** : a bodily disorder popularly associated with chilling; *esp* : COMMON COLD

³**cold** *adv* **1** : TOTALLY, FINALLY ⟨stopped them ~⟩ **2** : without notice or preparation ⟨performed the song ~⟩

**cold–blood·ed** \'kōld-'blə-dəd\ *adj* **1** : lacking normal human feelings **2** : having a body temperature not internally regulated but close to that of the environment **3** : sensitive to cold

**cold cuts** *n pl* : sliced assorted cold cooked meats

**cold feet** *n pl* : doubt or fear that prevents action

**cold front** *n* : an advancing edge of a cold air mass

**cold shoulder** *n* : cold or unsympathetic behavior — **cold–shoul·der** *vb*

**cold sore** *n* : a group of fluid-filled blisters appearing in or about the mouth in the oral form of herpes simplex

**cold sweat** *n* : concurrent perspiration and chill usu. associated with fear, pain, or shock

¹**cold turkey** *n* : abrupt complete cessation of the use of an addictive drug

²**cold turkey** *adv* **1** : without a period of adjustment **2** : without preparation

**cold war** *n* : a conflict characterized by the use of means short of sustained overt military action

**cole·slaw** \'kōl-ˌslȯ\ *n* [D *koolsla*, fr. *kool* cabbage + *sla* salad] : a salad made of raw cabbage

**col·ic** \'kä-lik\ *n* **1** : sharp sudden abdominal pain **2** : a condition marked by recurrent episodes of crying and irritability in an otherwise healthy infant — **col·icky** \'kä-li-kē\ *adj*

**col·i·se·um** \ˌkä-lə-'sē-əm\ *n* : a large structure esp. for athletic contests

**co·li·tis** \kō-'lī-təs\ *n* : inflammation of the colon

**col·lab·o·rate** \kə-'la-bə-ˌrāt\ *vb* **-rat·ed; -rat·ing 1** : to work jointly with others (as in writing a book) **2** : to cooperate with an enemy force occupying one's country — **col·lab·o·ra·tion** \-ˌla-bə-'rā-shən\ *n* — **col·lab·o·ra·tive** \-'la-bə-ˌrā-tiv, -b(ə-)rə-\ *adj* — **col·lab·o·ra·tor** \-'la-bə-ˌrā-tər\ *n*

**col·lage** \kə-'läzh\ *n* [F, lit., gluing] : an artistic composition of fragments (as of printed matter) pasted on a surface; *also* : a work that combines various elements into a cohesive whole

**col·la·gen** \'kä-lə-jən\ *n* : any of a group of fibrous proteins widely found in vertebrate connective tissue

¹**col·lapse** \kə-'laps\ *vb* **col·lapsed; col·laps·ing 1** : to shrink together abruptly **2** : DISINTEGRATE; *also* : to fall in : give way **3** : to break down physically or mentally; *esp* : to fall helpless or unconscious **4** : to fold down compactly — **col·laps·ible** *adj*

²**collapse** *n* : BREAKDOWN

¹**col·lar** \'kä-lər\ *n* **1** : a band, strip, or chain worn around the neck or the neckline of a garment **2** : something resembling a collar — **col·lar·less** *adj*

²**collar** *vb* : to seize by the collar; *also* : ARREST, GRAB ⟨~ a fugitive⟩

**col·lar·bone** \-ˌbōn\ *n* : the bone of the shoulder that joins the breastbone and the shoulder blade

**col·lard** \'kä-lərd\ *n* : a stalked smooth-leaved kale — usu. used in pl.

**col·late** \kə-'lāt; 'kä-ˌlāt, 'kō-\ *vb* **col·lat·ed; col·lat·ing 1** : to compare (as two texts) carefully and critically **2** : to assemble in proper order

¹**col·lat·er·al** \kə-'la-tə-rəl\ *adj* **1** : associated but of secondary importance **2** : descended from the same ancestors but not in the same line **3** : PARALLEL **4** : of, relating to, or being collateral used as security; *also* : secured by collateral

²**collateral** *n* : property (as stocks) used as security for the repayment of a loan

**col·la·tion** \kä-ˈlā-shən, kō-\ *n* **1** : a light meal **2** : the act, process, or result of collating

**col·league** \ˈkä-ˌlēg\ *n* : an associate esp. in a profession

**¹col·lect** \ˈkä-likt, -ˌlekt\ *n* : a short prayer comprising an invocation, petition, and conclusion

**²col·lect** \kə-ˈlekt\ *vb* **1** : to bring or come together into one body or place : GATH-ER **2** : to accumulate (as coins) as a hobby **3** : to gain control of ⟨∼ his thoughts⟩ **4** : to receive payment of — **col·lect·ible** *or* **col·lect·able** *adj or n* — **col·lec·tor** \-ˈlek-tər\ *n*

**³col·lect** \kə-ˈlekt\ *adv or adj* : to be paid for by the receiver

**col·lect·ed** \kə-ˈlek-təd\ *adj* **1** : gathered together ⟨his ∼ poems⟩ **2** : SELF-POS-SESSED, CALM

**col·lec·tion** \kə-ˈlek-shən\ *n* **1** : the act or process of collecting ⟨garbage ∼⟩ **2** : something collected ⟨a stamp ∼⟩ **3** : GROUP, AGGREGATE

**¹col·lec·tive** \kə-ˈlek-tiv\ *adj* **1** : of, relating to, or denoting a group of individuals considered as a whole **2** : involving all members of a group as distinct from its individuals ⟨∼ action⟩ **3** : shared or assumed by all members of the group ⟨a ∼ groan⟩ — **col·lec·tive·ly** *adv*

**²collective** *n* **1** : GROUP **2** : a cooperative unit or organization

**collective bargaining** *n* : negotiation between an employer and a labor union

**col·lec·tiv·ise** *chiefly Brit var of* COLLEC-TIVIZE

**col·lec·tiv·ism** \kə-ˈlek-ti-ˌvi-zəm\ *n* : a political or economic theory advocating collective control esp. over production and distribution

**col·lec·tiv·ize** \-ˌvīz\ *vb* **-ized; -iz·ing** : to organize under collective control — **col·lec·tiv·i·za·tion** \-ˌlek-ti-və-ˈzā-shən\ *n*

**col·leen** \kä-ˈlēn, ˈkä-ˌlēn\ *n* : an Irish girl

**col·lege** \ˈkä-lij\ *n* [ME, endowed body of clergy or scholars, fr. AF, fr. L *collegium* society, fr. *collega* colleague, fr. *com-* with + *legare* to depute] **1** : a building used for an educational or religious purpose **2** : an institution of higher learning or division of a university granting a bachelor's degree; *also* : an institution offering instruction esp. in a vocational or technical field ⟨barber ∼⟩ **3** : an organized body of persons having common interests or duties ⟨∼ of cardinals⟩ — **col·le·giate** \kə-ˈlē-jət\ *adj*

**col·le·gi·al·i·ty** \kə-ˌlē-jē-ˈa-lə-tē\ *n* : the relationship of colleagues

**col·le·gian** \kə-ˈlē-jən\ *n* : a college student or recent college graduate

**col·le·gi·um** \kə-ˈlē-gē-əm, -ˈlā-\ *n, pl* **-gia** \-gē-ə\ *or* **-giums** : a group in which each member has approximately equal power

**col·lide** \kə-ˈlīd\ *vb* **col·lid·ed; col·lid·ing 1** : to come together with solid impact **2** : to come into conflict : CLASH

**col·lid·er** \kə-ˈlī-dər\ *n* : a particle accelerator in which two beams of particles are made to collide

**col·lie** \ˈkä-lē\ *n* : any of a breed of large dogs developed in Scotland for herding sheep that occur in rough-coated and smooth-coated varieties

**col·lier** \ˈkäl-yər\ *n* **1** : a coal miner **2** : a ship for carrying coal

**col·liery** \ˈkäl-yə-rē\ *n, pl* **-lier·ies** : a coal mine and its associated buildings

**col·li·mate** \ˈkä-lə-ˌmāt\ *vb* **-mat·ed; -mat·ing** : to make (as light rays) parallel

**col·li·sion** \kə-ˈli-zhən\ *n* : an act or instance of colliding

**col·lo·ca·tion** \ˌkä-lə-ˈkā-shən\ *n* : the act or result of placing or arranging together; *esp* : a noticeable arrangement or conjoining of linguistic elements (as words)

**col·loid** \ˈkä-ˌlȯid\ *n* : a substance in the form of submicroscopic particles that when in solution or suspension do not settle out; *also* : such a substance together with the medium in which it is dispersed — **col·loi·dal** \kə-ˈlȯi-dᵊl\ *adj*

**colloq** *abbr* colloquial

**col·lo·qui·al** \kə-ˈlō-kwē-əl\ *adj* : of, relating to, or characteristic of conversation and esp. of familiar and informal conversation

**col·lo·qui·al·ism** \-ˈlō-kwē-ə-ˌli-zəm\ *n* : a colloquial expression

**col·lo·qui·um** \kə-ˈlō-kwē-əm\ *n, pl* **-quiums** *or* **-quia** \-ə\ : CONFERENCE, SEMI-NAR

**col·lo·quy** \ˈkä-lə-kwē\ *n, pl* **-quies** : a usu. formal conversation or conference

**col·lu·sion** \kə-ˈlü-zhən\ *n* : secret agreement or cooperation for an illegal or deceitful purpose — **col·lu·sive** \-ˈsiv\ *adj*

**Colo** *abbr* Colorado

**co·logne** \kə-ˈlōn\ *n* [*Cologne*, Germany] : a perfumed liquid — **co·logned** \-ˈlōnd\ *adj*

**Co·lom·bi·an** \kə-ˈləm-bē-ən\ *n* : a native or inhabitant of Colombia — **Colombian** *adj*

**¹co·lon** \ˈkō-lən\ *n, pl* **colons** *or* **co·la** \-lə\ : the part of the large intestine extending from the cecum to the rectum — **co·lon·ic** \kō-ˈlä-nik\ *adj*

**²colon** *n, pl* **colons** : a punctuation mark : used esp. to direct attention to following matter (as a list)

**co·lón** *also* **co·lone** \kə-ˈlōn\ *n, pl* **co·lo·nes** \-ˈlō-ˌnās\ — *see* MONEY table

**col·o·nel** \ˈkər-nᵊl\ *n* [alter. of *coronel*, fr. MF, fr. It *colonnello* column of soldiers, colonel, ultim. fr. L *columna* column] : a commissioned officer (as in the army) ranking next below a brigadier general

**¹co·lo·nial** \kə-ˈlō-nē-əl\ *adj* **1** : of, relating to, or characteristic of a colony; *also* : possessing or composed of colonies **2** *often cap* : of or relating to the original 13 colonies forming the U.S.

**²colonial** *n* **1** : a member or inhabitant of a colony **2** : a house built in the style of the American colonial period

**co·lo·nial·ism** \-ə-ˌli-zəm\ *n* : control by one power over a dependent area or people; *also* : a policy advocating or based on such control — **co·lo·nial·ist** \-list\ *n or adj*

**col·o·nise** *Brit var of* COLONIZE

**col·o·nist** \ˈkä-lə-nist\ *n* **1** : COLONIAL **2**

: one that colonizes or settles in a new country

**col·o·nize** \'kä-lə-ˌnīz\ vb **-nized; -niz·ing** 1 : to establish a colony in or on 2 : SETTLE — **col·o·ni·za·tion** \ˌkä-lə-nə-'zā-shən\ n — **col·o·niz·er** n

**col·on·nade** \ˌkä-lə-'nād\ n : an evenly spaced row of columns usu. supporting the base of a roof structure

**co·lo·nos·co·py** \ˌkō-lə-'näs-kə-pē\ n, pl **-pies** : endoscopic examination of the colon — **co·lon·o·scope** \kō-'lä-nə-ˌskōp\ n

**col·o·ny** \'kä-lə-nē\ n, pl **-nies** 1 : a body of people living in a new territory; also : the territory inhabited by these people 2 : a localized population of organisms ⟨a ∼ of bees⟩ 3 : a group with common interests situated in close association ⟨a writers' ∼⟩; also : the area occupied by such a group

**col·o·phon** \'kä-lə-fən, -ˌfän\ n 1 : an inscription placed at the end of a book with facts relative to its production 2 : an identifying mark used by a printer or publisher

¹**col·or** \'kə-lər\ n 1 : a phenomenon of light (as red or blue) or visual perception that enables one to differentiate otherwise identical objects; also : a hue as contrasted with black, white, or gray 2 : APPEARANCE 3 : complexion tint 4 pl : FLAG; also : military service (a call to the ∼s) 5 : VIVIDNESS, INTEREST — **col·or·ful** adj — **col·or·less** adj

²**color** vb 1 : to give color to; also : to change the color of 2 : BLUSH

**Col·o·ra·do potato beetle** \ˌkä-lə-'ra-dō-, -'rä-\ n : a black-and-yellow striped beetle that feeds on the leaves of the potato

**col·or·ation** \ˌkə-lə-'rā-shən\ n : use or arrangement of colors

**col·or·a·tu·ra** \ˌkə-lə-rə-'tùr-ə, -'tyùr-\ n 1 : elaborate ornamentation in vocal music 2 : a soprano specializing in coloratura

**col·or–blind** \'kə-lər-ˌblīnd\ adj 1 : partially or totally unable to distinguish one or more chromatic colors 2 : not influenced by differences of race — **color blindness** n

**co·lo·rec·tal** \ˌkō-lō-'rek-tᵊl\ adj : relating to or affecting the colon and rectum ⟨∼ cancer⟩

**col·ored** \'kə-lərd\ adj 1 : having color 2 : SLANTED, BIASED

**col·or·fast** \'kə-lər-ˌfast\ adj : having color that does not fade or run — **col·or·fast·ness** n

**col·or·ize** \'kə-lə-ˌrīz\ vb **-ized; -iz·ing** : to add color to by means of a computer — **col·or·i·za·tion** \ˌkə-lə-rə-'zā-shən\ n

**co·los·sal** \kə-'lä-səl\ adj : of very great size or degree ⟨a ∼ feat⟩

**Co·los·sians** \kə-'lä-shənz\ n — see BIBLE table

**co·los·sus** \kə-'lä-səs\ n, pl **co·los·si** \-ˌsī\ [L] : a gigantic statue; also : something of immense size or power

**col·our** chiefly Brit var of COLOR

**col·por·teur** \'käl-ˌpòr-tər\ n [F] : a peddler of religious books

**colt** \'kōlt\ n : FOAL; also : a young male horse, ass, or zebra — **colt·ish** adj

**col·um·bine** \'kä-ləm-ˌbīn\ n [ME, fr. AF, fr. ML columbina, fr. L, fem. of columbinus dovelike, fr. columba dove] : any of a genus of plants with showy spurred flowers that are related to the buttercups

**co·lum·bi·um** \kə-'ləm-bē-əm\ n : NIOBIUM

**Columbus Day** \kə-'ləm-bəs-\ n : the 2d Monday in October or formerly October 12 observed as a legal holiday in many states in commemoration of the landing of Columbus in the Bahamas in 1492

**col·umn** \'kä-ləm\ n 1 : one of two or more vertical sections of a printed page; also : one in a usu. regular series of articles (as in a newspaper) 2 : a supporting pillar; esp : one consisting of a usu. round shaft, a capital, and a base 3 : something resembling a column ⟨a ∼ of water⟩ 4 : a long row (as of soldiers) 5 : a statistical category tracked vertically (as on a spreadsheet) — **co·lum·nar** \kə-'ləm-nər\ adj

**col·um·nist** \'kä-ləm-nist\ n : a person who writes a newspaper or magazine column

**com** abbr 1 comedy; comic 2 comma 3 commercial organization

**co·ma** \'kō-mə\ n : a state of deep unconsciousness caused by disease, injury, or poison — **co·ma·tose** \'kō-mə-ˌtōs, 'kä-\ adj

**Co·man·che** \kə-'man-chē\ n, pl **Comanche** or **Comanches** : a member of an American Indian people ranging from Wyoming and Nebraska south into New Mexico and Texas

¹**comb** \'kōm\ n 1 : a toothed instrument for arranging the hair or for separating and cleaning textile fibers 2 : a fleshy crest on the head of a fowl 3 : HONEYCOMB

²**comb** vb 1 : to pass a comb through 2 : to search through systematically

³**comb** abbr combination; combining

**com·bat** \kəm-'bat, 'käm-ˌbat\ vb **-bat·ed** or **-bat·ted; -bat·ing** or **-bat·ting** 1 : FIGHT, CONTEND 2 : to struggle against : OPPOSE — **com·bat** \'käm-ˌbat\ n — **com·bat·ant** \kəm-'ba-tᵊnt, 'käm-bə-tənt\ n — **com·bat·ive** \kəm-'ba-tiv\ adj

**combat fatigue** n : a traumatic psychological reaction occurring under wartime conditions (as combat) that cause intense stress

**comb·er** \'kō-mər\ n 1 : one that combs 2 : a long curling wave of the sea

**com·bi·na·tion** \ˌkäm-bə-'nä-shən\ n 1 : a result or product of combining 2 : a sequence of letters or numbers chosen in setting a lock 3 : the act or process of combining; also : the quality or state of being combined

¹**com·bine** \kəm-'bīn\ vb **com·bined; com·bin·ing** : to become one : UNITE

²**com·bine** \'käm-ˌbīn\ n : a combination esp. of business or political interests

2 : a machine that harvests and threshes grain while moving over a field

**comb·ings** \'kō-miŋz\ n pl : loose hairs or fibers removed by a comb

**combining form** n : a linguistic form that occurs only in compounds or derivatives

**com·bo** \'käm-bō\ n, pl **combos** : a small jazz or dance band

**comb-over** \'kōm-ˌō-vər\ n : a hairstyle in which hair from the side of the head is combed over a bald spot

**com·bus·ti·ble** \kəm-'bəs-tə-bəl\ adj 1 : capable of being burned 2 : easily excited — **com·bus·ti·bil·i·ty** \-ˌbəs-tə-'bi-lə-tē\ n — **combustible** n

**com·bus·tion** \kəm-'bəs-chən\ n 1 : an act or instance of burning 2 : slow oxidation (as in the animal body)

**comdg** abbr commanding

**comdr** abbr commander

**comdt** abbr commandant

**come** \'kəm\ vb **came** \'kām\; **come**; **com·ing** \'kə-miŋ\ 1 : APPROACH 2 : ARRIVE 3 : to reach the point of being or becoming ⟨∼ to a boil⟩ 4 : AMOUNT ⟨the bill came to $10⟩ 5 : to take place 6 : ORIGINATE, ARISE ⟨wine ∼s from grapes⟩ 7 : to be available ⟨∼s in three sizes⟩ 8 : REACH, EXTEND ⟨grass that ∼s to our knees⟩ — **come across** 1 : to make a specified impression ⟨came across as rude⟩ 2 : to find esp. by chance ⟨came across an intriguing story⟩ — **come clean** : CONFESS — **come into** : ACQUIRE, ACHIEVE — **come of age** : MATURE — **come to grips with** : to meet or deal with frankly — **come to pass** : HAPPEN — **come to terms** : to reach an agreement

**come·back** \'kəm-ˌbak\ n 1 : RETORT 2 : a return to a former position or condition — **come back** vb

**co·me·di·an** \kə-'mē-dē-ən\ n 1 : an actor in comedy 2 : a comic person; esp : an entertainer specializing in comedy

**co·me·di·enne** \-ˌmē-dē-'en\ n : a woman who is a comedian

**come·down** \'kəm-ˌdaún\ n : a descent in rank or dignity

**com·e·dy** \'kä-mə-dē\ n, pl **-dies** [ME, narrative that ends happily, fr. ML comoedia, fr. L, play with a happy ending, fr. Gk kōmōidia, fr. kōmos revel + aeidein to sing] 1 : a light amusing play with a happy ending 2 : a literary work treating a comic theme or written in a comic style 3 : humorous entertainment — **co·me·dic** \kə-'mē-dik\ adj

**come·ly** \'kəm-lē\ adj **come·li·er; -est** : ATTRACTIVE, HANDSOME — **come·li·ness** n

**come off** vb 1 : APPEAR, SEEM ⟨comes off as crass⟩ 2 : SUCCEED 3 : to have recently ended ⟨is coming off surgery⟩

**come-on** \'kə-ˌmòn, -ˌmän\ n : INDUCEMENT, LURE

**come out** vb 1 : to come into public view 2 : to declare oneself 6 : TURN OUT 6 ⟨everything came out all right⟩ — **come out with** : SAY 1

**com·er** \'kə-mər\ n 1 : one that comes ⟨all ∼s⟩ 2 : a promising beginner

¹**co·mes·ti·ble** \kə-'mes-tə-bəl\ adj : EDIBLE

²**comestible** n : FOOD — usu. used in pl.

**com·et** \'kä-mət\ n [ME comete, fr. OE cometa, fr. L, fr. Gk komētēs, lit., long-haired, fr. komē hair] : a small bright celestial body that develops a long tail when near the sun

**come to** vb : to regain consciousness

**come·up·pance** \kə-'mə-pəns\ n : a deserved rebuke or penalty

**com·fit** \'kəm-fət\ n : a candied fruit or nut

¹**com·fort** \'kəm-fərt\ vb 1 : to give strength and hope to 2 : CONSOLE

²**comfort** n 1 : CONSOLATION 2 : freedom from pain, trouble, or anxiety; also : something that gives such freedom

**com·fort·able** \'kəm-fər-tə-bəl, 'kəmf-tər-\ adj 1 : providing comfort or security 2 : feeling at ease — **com·fort·ably** \-blē\ adv

**com·fort·er** \'kəm-fər-tər\ n 1 : one that comforts 2 : QUILT

**com·frey** \'kəm-frē\ n, pl **comfreys** : any of a genus of perennial herbs that have coarse hairy leaves and are often used in herbal remedies

**com·fy** \'kəm-fē\ adj : COMFORTABLE

¹**com·ic** \'kä-mik\ adj 1 : relating to comedy or comic strips 2 : provoking laughter or amusement ♦ Synonyms LAUGHABLE, FUNNY, FARCICAL — **com·i·cal** adj

²**comic** n 1 : COMEDIAN 2 pl : the part of a newspaper devoted to comic strips

**comic book** n : a magazine containing sequences of comic strips

**comic strip** n : a group of cartoons in narrative sequence

**coming** adj 1 : APPROACHING, NEXT 2 : gaining importance ⟨the ∼ trend⟩

**co·mi·ty** \'kä-mə-tē, 'kō-\ n, pl **-ties** : friendly civility : COURTESY

**coml** abbr commercial

**comm** abbr 1 command; commander 2 commerce; commercial 3 commission; commissioner 4 committee 5 common 6 commonwealth

**com·ma** \'kä-mə\ n : a punctuation mark , used esp. as a mark of separation within the sentence

¹**com·mand** \kə-'mand\ vb 1 : to direct authoritatively : ORDER 2 : DOMINATE, CONTROL, GOVERN 3 : to overlook from a strategic position

²**command** n 1 : an order given 2 : ability to control : MASTERY 3 : the act of commanding 4 : a signal that actuates a device (as a computer); also : the activation of a device by means of a signal 5 : a body of troops under a commander; also : an area or position that one commands 6 : a position of highest authority

**com·man·dant** \'kä-mən-ˌdant, -ˌdänt\ n : an officer in command

**com·man·deer** \ˌkä-mən-'dir\ vb : to take possession of by force

**com·mand·er** \kə-'man-dər\ n 1 : LEADER, CHIEF; esp : an officer commanding an army or subdivision of an army 2 : a commissioned officer in the navy ranking next below a captain

**commander in chief** : the supreme commander of the armed forces

**com·mand·ment** \kə-ˈmand-mənt\ n : COMMAND, ORDER; esp : any of the Ten Commandments

**command module** n : a space vehicle module designed to carry the crew and reentry equipment

**com·man·do** \kə-ˈman-dō\ n, pl **-dos** or **-does** : a member of a military unit trained for surprise raids

**command sergeant major** n : a noncommissioned officer in the army ranking above a sergeant major

**com·mem·o·rate** \kə-ˈme-mə-ˌrāt\ vb **-rat·ed; -rat·ing** 1 : to call or recall to mind 2 : to serve as a memorial of — **com·mem·o·ra·tion** \-ˌme-mə-ˈrā-shən\ n

**com·mem·o·ra·tive** \kə-ˈmem-rə-tiv, -ˈme-mə-ˌrā-tiv\ adj : intended to commemorate an event ⟨a ~ stamp⟩

**com·mence** \kə-ˈmens\ vb **commenced; comenc·ing** : BEGIN, START ⟨~ the festivities⟩

**com·mence·ment** \-mənt\ n 1 : the act or time of a beginning 2 : the graduation exercises of a school or college

**com·mend** \kə-ˈmend\ vb 1 : to commit to one's care 2 : RECOMMEND 3 : PRAISE — **com·mend·able** \-ˈmen-də-bəl\ adj — **com·mend·ably** \-blē\ adv — **com·men·da·tion** \ˌkä-mən-ˈdā-shən, -ˌmen-\ n — **com·mend·er** n

**com·men·su·ra·ble** \kə-ˈmen-sə-rə-bəl\ adj : having a common measure or a common divisor

**com·men·su·rate** \kə-ˈmen-sə-rət, -ˈmen-chə-\ adj : equal in measure or extent; also : PROPORTIONAL, CORRESPONDING ⟨a job ~ with her abilities⟩

**com·ment** \ˈkä-ˌment\ n 1 : an expression of opinion 2 : an explanatory, illustrative, or critical note or observation : REMARK — **comment** vb

**com·men·tary** \ˈkä-mən-ˌter-ē\ n, pl **-tar·ies** : a systematic series of comments

**com·men·ta·tor** \-ˌtā-tər\ n : one who comments; esp : a person who discusses news events on radio or television

**com·merce** \ˈkä-(ˌ)mərs\ n : the buying and selling of commodities : TRADE

¹**com·mer·cial** \kə-ˈmər-shəl\ adj : having to do with commerce; also : designed for profit or for mass appeal — **com·mer·cial·ly** adv

²**commercial** n : an advertisement broadcast on radio or television

**com·mer·cial·ise** Brit var of COMMERCIALIZE

**com·mer·cial·ism** \kə-ˈmər-shə-ˌli-zəm\ n 1 : a spirit, method, or practice characteristic of business 2 : excessive emphasis on profit

**com·mer·cial·ize** \-ˌlīz\ vb **-ized; -iz·ing** 1 : to manage on a business basis for profit 2 : to exploit for profit

**com·mi·na·tion** \ˌkä-mə-ˈnā-shən\ n : DENUNCIATION — **com·mi·na·to·ry** \ˈkä-mə-nə-ˌtȯr-ē\ adj

**com·min·gle** \kə-ˈmiŋ-gəl\ vb : MINGLE, BLEND

**com·mis·er·ate** \kə-ˈmi-zə-ˌrāt\ vb **-at·ed; -at·ing** : to feel or express pity : SYMPATHIZE — **com·mis·er·a·tion** \-ˌmi-zə-ˈrā-shən\ n

**com·mis·sar** \ˈkä-mə-ˌsär\ n [Russ komissar] : a Communist party official

**com·mis·sar·i·at** \ˌkä-mə-ˈser-ē-ət\ n 1 : a system for supplying troops with food 2 : a department headed by a commissar

**com·mis·sary** \ˈkä-mə-ˌser-ē\ n, pl **-sar·ies** : a store for equipment and provisions esp. for military personnel

¹**com·mis·sion** \kə-ˈmi-shən\ n 1 : a warrant granting certain powers and imposing certain duties 2 : a certificate conferring military rank and authority 3 : authority to act as agent for another; also : something to be done by an agent 4 : a body of persons charged with performing a duty 5 : the doing of some act ⟨~ of a crime⟩; also : the thing done 6 : the allowance made to an agent for transacting business for another

²**commission** vb 1 : to give a commission to 2 : to order to be made ⟨~ a portrait⟩ 3 : to put (a ship) into a state of readiness for service

**commissioned officer** n : an officer of the armed forces holding rank by a commission from the president

**com·mis·sion·er** \kə-ˈmi-shə-nər\ n 1 : a member of a commission 2 : an official in charge of a department of public service ⟨a police ~⟩ 3 : the administrative head of a professional sport — **com·mis·sion·er·ship** n

**com·mit** \kə-ˈmit\ vb **com·mit·ted; com·mit·ting** 1 : to put into charge or trust : ENTRUST 2 : to put in a prison or mental institution : TRANSFER, CONSIGN 3 : to carry into action : PERPETRATE ⟨~ a crime⟩ 4 : to pledge or assign to some particular course or use — **com·mit·ment** n — **com·mit·tal** n

**com·mit·tee** \kə-ˈmi-tē\ n : a body of persons selected to consider and act or report on some matter — **com·mit·tee·man** \-mən\ n — **com·mit·tee·wom·an** \-ˌwu̇-mən\ n

**commo** abbr commodore

**com·mode** \kə-ˈmōd\ n [F, fr. commode, adj., suitable, convenient, fr. L commodus, fr. com- with + modus measure] 1 : a movable washstand with cupboard below 2 : TOILET 3

**com·mo·di·ous** \kə-ˈmō-dē-əs\ adj : comfortably spacious : ROOMY

**com·mod·i·ty** \kə-ˈmä-də-tē\ n, pl **-ties** 1 : a product of agriculture or mining 2 : an article of commerce 3 : something useful or valued ⟨that valuable ~ patience⟩

**com·mo·dore** \ˈkä-mə-ˌdȯr\ n 1 : a commissioned officer in the navy ranking next below a rear admiral 2 : an officer commanding a group of merchant ships 3 : the chief officer of a yacht club

¹**com·mon** \ˈkä-mən\ adj 1 : belonging to or serving the community : PUBLIC 2 : shared by a number in a group 3 : wide-

ly or generally known, found, or observed : FAMILIAR ⟨~ knowledge⟩ 4 : VERNACULAR 3 ⟨~ names of plants⟩ 5 : not above the average esp. in social status ♦ *Synonyms* UNIVERSAL, GENERAL, GENERIC — **com·mon·ly** *adv*

²**common** *n* 1 *pl* : the common people 2 *pl* : a dining hall 3 *pl, cap* : the lower house of the British and Canadian parliaments 4 : a piece of land subject to common use — **in common** : shared together

**com·mon·al·ty** \ˈkä-mə-nᵊl-tē\ *n, pl* **-ties** : the common people

**common cold** *n* : a contagious respiratory disease caused by a virus and characterized by a sore, swollen, and inflamed nose and throat, usu. by much mucus, and by coughing and sneezing

**common denominator** *n* 1 : a common multiple of the denominators of a group of fractions 2 : a common trait or theme

**common divisor** *n* : a number or expression that divides two or more numbers or expressions without remainder

**com·mon·er** \ˈkä-mə-nər\ *n* : one of the common people : a person having no rank of nobility

**common fraction** *n* : a fraction (as ½ or ¾) in which the numerator and denominator are both integers and are separated by a horizontal or slanted line

**common law** *n* : a group of legal practices and traditions based on judges' decisions and social customs and usu. having the same force as laws passed by legislative bodies

**common logarithm** *n* : a logarithm whose base is 10

**common market** *n* : an economic association formed to remove trade barriers among members

**common multiple** *n* : a multiple of each of two or more numbers or expressions

¹**com·mon·place** \ˈkä-mən-ˌplās\ *n* : something that is ordinary or trite

²**commonplace** *adj* : ORDINARY

**common sense** *n* : ordinary good sense and judgment — **com·mon·sen·si·cal** \ˈkä-mən-ˈsen-si-kəl\ *adj*

**com·mon·weal** \ˈkä-mən-ˌwēl\ *n* 1 *archaic* : COMMONWEALTH 2 : the general welfare

**com·mon·wealth** \-ˌwelth\ *n* 1 : the body of people politically organized into a state 2 : STATE; *also* : an association or federation of autonomous states

**com·mo·tion** \kə-ˈmō-shən\ *n* 1 : DISTURBANCE, UPRISING 2 : AGITATION

**com·mu·nal** \kə-ˈmyü-nᵊl, ˈkäm-yə-nᵊl\ *adj* 1 : of or relating to a commune or community 2 : marked by collective ownership and use of property 3 : shared or used in common

¹**com·mune** \kə-ˈmyün\ *vb* **com·muned**; **com·mun·ing** : to communicate intimately ⟨~ with nature⟩

²**com·mune** \ˈkäm-ˌyün; kə-ˈmyün\ *n* 1 : the smallest administrative district in some European countries 2 : a community organized on a communal basis

**com·mu·ni·ca·ble** \kə-ˈmyü-ni-kə-bəl\

*adj* : capable of being communicated ⟨~ diseases⟩ — **com·mu·ni·ca·bil·i·ty** \-ˌmyü-ni-kə-ˈbi-lə-tē\ *n*

**com·mu·ni·cant** \-ˈmyü-ni-kənt\ *n* 1 : a church member entitled to receive Communion 2 : one that communicates; *esp* : INFORMANT

**com·mu·ni·cate** \kə-ˈmyü-nə-ˌkāt\ *vb* **-cat·ed**; **-cat·ing** 1 : to make known 2 : to pass from one to another : TRANSMIT 3 : to receive Communion 4 : to be in communication 5 : JOIN, CONNECT — **com·mu·ni·ca·tor** \-ˌkā-tər\ *n*

**com·mu·ni·ca·tion** \kə-ˌmyü-nə-ˈkā-shən\ *n* 1 : an act of transmitting 2 : MESSAGE 3 : exchange of information or opinions 4 : a means of communicating — **com·mu·ni·ca·tive** \-ˈmyü-nə-ˌkā-tiv, -ni-kə-tiv\ *adj*

**com·mu·nion** \kə-ˈmyün-nyən\ *n* 1 : a sharing of something with others 2 *cap* : a Christian sacrament in which bread and wine are consumed as the substance or symbols of Christ's body and blood in commemoration of the death of Christ 3 : intimate fellowship or rapport 4 : a body of Christians having a common faith and discipline ⟨the Anglican ~⟩

**com·mu·ni·qué** \kə-ˈmyü-nə-ˌkā, -ˌmyü-nə-ˈkā\ *n* : BULLETIN 1

**com·mu·nism** \ˈkäm-yə-ˌni-zəm\ *n* 1 : social organization in which goods are held in common 2 : a theory of social organization advocating common ownership of means of production and a distribution of products of industry based on need 3 *cap* : a political doctrine based on revolutionary Marxist socialism that was the official ideology of the U.S.S.R. and some other countries; *also* : a system of government in which one party controls state-owned means of production — **com·mu·nist** \-nist\ *n or adj, often cap* — **com·mu·nis·tic** \ˌkäm-yə-ˈnis-tik\ *adj, often cap*

**com·mu·ni·ty** \kə-ˈmyü-nə-tē\ *n, pl* **-ties** 1 : a body of people living in the same place under the same laws; *also* : a natural population of plants and animals that interact ecologically and live in one place (as a pond) 2 : society at large 3 : joint ownership ⟨~ of goods⟩ 4 : SIMILARITY, LIKENESS ⟨~ of interests⟩

**community college** *n* : a 2-year government-supported college that offers an associate degree

**community property** *n* : property held jointly by husband and wife

**com·mu·ta·tion** \ˌkäm-yə-ˈtā-shən\ *n* : substitution of one form of payment or penalty for another

**com·mu·ta·tive** \ˈkäm-yə-ˌtā-tiv, kə-ˈmyü-tə-\ *adj* : of, having, or being the property that the result obtained using a mathematical operation on any two elements of a set does not differ with the order in which the elements are used ⟨$a \times b = b \times a$ because multiplication is ~⟩ — **com·mu·ta·tiv·i·ty** \kə-ˌmyü-tə-ˈti-və-tē, ˌkäm-yə-tə-\ *n*

**com·mu·ta·tor** \ˈkäm-yə-ˌtā-tər\ *n* : a device (as on a generator or motor) for changing the direction of electric current

¹**com·mute** \kə-ˈmyüt\ vb **com·mut·ed; com·mut·ing** 1 : EXCHANGE 2 : to revoke (a sentence) and impose a milder penalty 3 : to travel back and forth regularly — **com·mut·er** n

²**commute** n : a trip made in commuting

**comp** abbr 1 comparative; compare 2 compensation 3 compiled; compiler 4 composition; compositor 5 compound 6 comprehensive 7 comptroller

¹**com·pact** \kəm-ˈpakt, ˈkäm-ˌpakt\ adj 1 : SOLID, DENSE 2 : BRIEF, SUCCINCT 3 : occupying a small volume by efficient use of space ⟨~ camera⟩ — **com·pact·ly** adv — **com·pact·ness** n

²**compact** vb : to pack together — COMPRESS — **com·pac·tor** \kəm-ˈpak-tər, ˈkäm-ˌpak-\ n

³**com·pact** \ˈkäm-ˌpakt\ n 1 : a small case for cosmetics 2 : a small automobile

⁴**com·pact** \ˈkäm-ˌpakt\ n : AGREEMENT, COVENANT

**compact disc** \ˈkäm-ˌpakt-\ n : CD

**com·pa·dre** \kəm-ˈpä-drā\ n : a close friend : BUDDY

¹**com·pan·ion** \kəm-ˈpan-yən\ n [ME companoun, fr. AF cumpaing, cumpaignun, fr. LL companion-, companio, fr. L com-together + panis bread] 1 : an intimate friend or associate : COMRADE 2 : one that is closely connected with something similar 3 : a celestial body that appears close to another but that may not be associated with it in space — **com·pan·ion·able** adj — **com·pan·ion·ship** n

²**companion** n : COMPANIONWAY

**com·pan·ion·way** \-ˌwā\ n : a ship's stairway from one deck to another

**com·pa·ny** \ˈkəm-pə-nē\ n, pl **-nies** 1 : association with others : FELLOWSHIP; also : COMPANIONS 2 : GUESTS 3 : a group of persons or things 4 : an infantry unit consisting of two or more platoons and normally commanded by a captain 5 : a group of musical or dramatic performers 6 : the officers and crew of a ship 7 : an association of persons for carrying on a business ◆ Synonyms PARTY, BAND, TROOP, TROUPE, CORPS, OUTFIT

**com·pa·ra·ble** \ˈkäm-pə-rə-bəl, -prə-\ adj : capable of being compared ⟨singers of ~ talent⟩ ◆ Synonyms PARALLEL, SIMILAR, LIKE, ALIKE, CORRESPONDING — **com·pa·ra·bil·i·ty** \ˌkäm-pə-rə-ˈbi-lə-tē\ n

¹**com·par·a·tive** \kəm-ˈper-ə-tiv\ adj 1 : of, relating to, or constituting the degree of grammatical comparison that denotes increase in quality, quantity, or relation 2 : RELATIVE ⟨a ~ stranger⟩ — **com·par·a·tive·ly** adv

²**comparative** n : the comparative degree or form in a language

¹**com·pare** \kəm-ˈper\ vb **com·pared; com·par·ing** 1 : to represent as similar : LIKEN 2 : to examine for likenesses and differences 3 : to inflect or modify (an adjective or adverb) according to the degrees of comparison

²**compare** n : the possibility of comparing ⟨beauty beyond ~⟩

**com·par·i·son** \kəm-ˈper-ə-sən\ n 1 : the act of comparing 2 : change in the form of an adjective or adverb to show different levels of quality, quantity, or relation

**com·part·ment** \kəm-ˈpärt-mənt\ n 1 : a separate division 2 : a section of an enclosed space : ROOM

**com·part·men·tal·ise** Brit var of COMPARTMENTALIZE

**com·part·men·tal·ize** \kəm-ˌpärt-ˈmen-tᵊl-ˌīz\ vb **-ized; -iz·ing** : to separate into compartments

¹**com·pass** \ˈkəm-pəs, ˈkäm-\ vb [ME, fr. AF cumpasser to measure, fr. VL *compassare to pace off, fr. L com- + passus pace] 1 : CONTRIVE, PLOT 2 : ENCIRCLE, ENCOMPASS 3 : BRING ABOUT, ACHIEVE

²**compass** n 1 : BOUNDARY, CIRCUMFERENCE 2 : an enclosed space 3 : RANGE, SCOPE 4 : a device for determining direction by means of a magnetic needle swinging freely and pointing to the magnetic north; also : a nonmagnetic device that indicates direction 5 : an instrument for drawing circles or transferring measurements consisting of two legs joined by a pivot

**com·pas·sion** \kəm-ˈpa-shən\ n : sympathetic feeling : PITY, MERCY — **com·pas·sion·ate** \-shə-nət\ adj — **com·pas·sion·ate·ly** adv

**com·pat·i·ble** \kəm-ˈpa-tə-bəl\ adj : able to exist or act together harmoniously ⟨~ colors⟩ ⟨~ drugs⟩ ◆ Synonyms CONSONANT, CONGENIAL, SYMPATHETIC — **com·pat·i·bil·i·ty** \-ˌpa-tə-ˈbi-lə-tē\ n

**com·pa·tri·ot** \kəm-ˈpā-trē-ət, -ˌät\ n : a fellow countryman

**com·peer** \ˈkäm-ˌpir\ n : EQUAL, PEER

**com·pel** \kəm-ˈpel\ vb **com·pelled; com·pel·ling** : to drive or urge with force

**com·pen·di·ous** \kəm-ˈpen-dē-əs\ adj : concise and comprehensive; also : COMPREHENSIVE ⟨a ~ almanac⟩

**com·pen·di·um** \kəm-ˈpen-dē-əm\ n, pl **-di·ums** or **-dia** \-ə\ 1 : a brief summary of a larger work or of a field of knowledge 2 : COLLECTION

**com·pen·sate** \ˈkäm-pən-ˌsāt\ vb **-sat·ed; -sat·ing** 1 : to be equivalent to : make up for 2 : PAY, REMUNERATE ◆ Synonyms BALANCE, OFFSET, COUNTERBALANCE, COUNTERPOISE — **com·pen·sa·tion** \ˌkäm-pən-ˈsā-shən\ n — **com·pen·sa·to·ry** \kəm-ˈpen-sə-ˌtȯr-ē\ adj

**com·pete** \kəm-ˈpēt\ vb **com·pet·ed; com·pet·ing** : CONTEND, VIE ⟨~ for the title⟩ ⟨~ for customers⟩

**com·pe·tence** \ˈkäm-pə-təns\ n 1 : adequate means for subsistence 2 : FITNESS, ABILITY ⟨trusted his doctor's ~⟩

**com·pe·ten·cy** \-tən-sē\ n, pl **-cies** : COMPETENCE

**com·pe·tent** \-tənt\ adj : CAPABLE, FIT, QUALIFIED ⟨a ~ mechanic⟩ ⟨a ~ juror⟩

**com·pe·ti·tion** \ˌkäm-pə-ˈti-shən\ n 1 : the act of competing : RIVALRY 2 : CONTEST, MATCH; also : one's competitors — **com·pet·i·tive** \kəm-'pe-tə-tiv\ *adj* — **com·pet·i·tive·ly** *adv* — **com·pet·i·tive·ness** *n*

**com·pet·i·tor** \kəm-'pe-tə-tər\ *n* : one that competes : RIVAL

**com·pile** \kəm-'pī(-ə)l\ *vb* **com·piled; com·pil·ing** [ME, fr. AF *compiler*, fr. L *compilare* to plunder] **1** : to compose out of materials from other documents **2** : to collect and edit into a volume **3** : to translate (a computer program) with a compiler **4** : to build up gradually ⟨~ a record of four wins and two losses⟩ — **com·pi·la·tion** \ˌkäm-pə-'lā-shən\ *n*

**com·pil·er** \kəm-'pī-lər\ *n* **1** : one that compiles **2** : a computer program that translates any program correctly written in a specific programming language into machine language

**com·pla·cence** \kəm-'plā-sᵊns\ *n* : COMPLACENCY — **com·pla·cent** \-sᵊnt\ *adj* — **com·pla·cent·ly** *adv*

**com·pla·cen·cy** \-sᵊn-sē\ *n, pl* **-cies** : SATISFACTION; *esp* : SELF-SATISFACTION

**com·plain** \kəm-'plān\ *vb* **1** : to express grief, pain, or discontent **2** : to make a formal accusation — **com·plain·ant** *n* — **com·plain·er** *n*

**com·plaint** \kəm-'plānt\ *n* **1** : expression of grief, pain, or dissatisfaction **2** : a bodily ailment or disease **3** : a formal accusation against a person

**com·plai·sance** \kəm-'plā-sᵊns, ˌkäm-plā-'zans\ *n* [F] : disposition to please — **com·plai·sant** \-sᵊnt, -'zant\ *adj* — **com·plai·sant·ly** *adv*

**com·pleat** \kəm-'plēt\ *adj* : PROFICIENT

**com·plect·ed** \kəm-'plek-təd\ *adj* : having a specified facial complexion ⟨dark-*complected*⟩

**¹com·ple·ment** \'käm-plə-mənt\ *n* **1** : something that fills up or completes; *also* : the full quantity, number, or amount that makes a thing complete **2** : an added word by which a predicate is made complete **3** : a group of proteins in blood that combines with antibodies to destroy antigens — **com·ple·men·ta·ry** \ˌkäm-plə-'men-t(ə-)rē\ *adj*

**²com·ple·ment** \-ˌment\ *vb* : to be complementary to : fill out

**complementary medicine** *n* : ALTERNATIVE MEDICINE

**¹com·plete** \kəm-'plēt\ *adj* **com·plet·er; -est** **1** : having all parts or elements **2** : brought to an end **3** : fully carried out; *also* : ABSOLUTE **2** ⟨~ silence⟩ — **com·plete·ly** *adv* — **com·plete·ness** *n* — **com·ple·tion** \-'plē-shən\ *n*

**²complete** *vb* **com·plet·ed; com·plet·ing** **1** : FINISH, CONCLUDE **2** : to make whole or perfect ⟨the hat ~s the outfit⟩

**com·plet·ist** \kəm-'plē-tist\ *n* : one who wants to make something (as a collection) complete

**¹com·plex** \'käm-ˌpleks\ *n* **1** : a whole made up of or involving intricately interrelated elements **2** : a group of repressed desires and memories that exert a dominating influence on one's personality and behavior ⟨a guilt ~⟩

**²com·plex** \käm-'pleks, 'käm-ˌpleks\ *adj*

**1** : composed of two or more parts **2** : consisting of a main clause and one or more subordinate clauses ⟨~ sentence⟩ **3** : hard to separate, analyze, or solve — **com·plex·i·ty** \käm-'plek-sə-tē\ *n* — **com·plex·ly** *adv*

**complex fraction** *n* : a fraction with a fraction or mixed number in the numerator or denominator or both

**com·plex·ion** \kəm-'plek-shən\ *n* **1** : the hue or appearance of the skin esp. of the face **2** : overall appearance — **com·plex·ioned** \-shənd\ *adj*

**complex number** *n* : a number of the form $a + b \sqrt{-1}$ where $a$ and $b$ are real numbers

**com·pli·ance** \kəm-'plī-əns\ *n* **1** : the act of complying to a demand or proposal **2** : a disposition to yield — **com·pli·ant** \-ənt\ *adj*

**com·pli·cate** \'käm-plə-ˌkāt\ *vb* **-cat·ed; -cat·ing** : to make or become complex or intricate

**com·pli·cat·ed** \'käm-plə-ˌkā-təd\ *adj* **1** : consisting of parts intricately combined **2** : difficult to analyze, understand, or explain ⟨a ~ issue⟩ — **com·pli·cat·ed·ly** *adv*

**com·pli·ca·tion** \ˌkäm-plə-'kā-shən\ *n* **1** : the quality or state of being complicated; *also* : a complex feature **2** : a disease or condition that develops during and affects the course of a primary disease or condition

**com·plic·i·ty** \kəm-'pli-sə-tē\ *n, pl* **-ties** : the state of being an accomplice

**¹com·pli·ment** \'käm-plə-mənt\ *n* **1** : an expression of approval or admiration; *esp* : a flattering remark **2** *pl* : best wishes : REGARDS

**²com·pli·ment** \-ˌment\ *vb* : to pay a compliment to

**com·pli·men·ta·ry** \ˌkäm-plə-'men-t(ə-)rē\ *adj* **1** : containing or expressing a compliment **2** : given free as a courtesy ⟨~ ticket⟩

**com·ply** \kəm-'plī\ *vb* **com·plied; com·ply·ing** : CONFORM, YIELD

**¹com·po·nent** \kəm-'pō-nənt, 'käm-ˌpō-\ *n* : a component part ♦ *Synonyms* INGREDIENT, ELEMENT, FACTOR, CONSTITUENT

**²component** *adj* : serving to form a part of : CONSTITUENT

**com·port** \kəm-'pōrt\ *vb* **1** : AGREE, ACCORD ⟨actions that ~ with policy⟩ **2** : CONDUCT ⟨~ oneself with dignity⟩ ♦ *Synonyms* BEHAVE, ACQUIT, DEPORT — **com·port·ment** *n*

**com·pose** \kəm-'pōz\ *vb* **com·posed; com·pos·ing** **1** : to form by putting together : FASHION **2** : to produce (as pages of type) by composition **3** : ADJUST, ARRANGE **4** : CALM, QUIET ⟨~ yourself before acting⟩ **5** : to practice composition ⟨~ music⟩ — **com·pos·er** *n*

**¹com·pos·ite** \käm-'pä-zət\ *adj* **1** : made up of distinct parts or elements **2** : of, relating to, or being a large family of flowering plants (as a daisy or aster) that bear many small flowers united into compact heads resembling single flowers

²**composite** n 1 : something composite 2 : a plant of the composite family ♦ **Synonyms** BLEND, COMPOUND, MIXTURE, AMALGAMATION

**com·po·si·tion** \ˌkäm-pə-ˈzi-shən\ n 1 : the act or process of composing; esp : arrangement esp. in artistic form 2 : the arrangement or production of type for printing 3 : general makeup 4 : a product of mixing various elements or ingredients 5 : a literary, musical, or artistic product; esp : ESSAY

**com·po·si·tion·ist** \-ˈzi-shə-nist\ n : a teacher of writing

**com·pos·i·tor** \kəm-ˈpä-zə-tər\ n : one who sets type

**com·post** \ˈkäm-ˌpōst\ n : a fertilizing material consisting largely of decayed organic matter — **compost** vb

**com·po·sure** \kəm-ˈpō-zhər\ n : CALMNESS, SELF-POSSESSION

**com·pote** \ˈkäm-ˌpōt\ n 1 : fruits cooked in syrup 2 : a bowl (as of glass) usu. with a base and stem for serving esp. fruit or compote

¹**com·pound** \käm-ˈpaund, ˈkäm-ˌ\ vb [ME compounen, fr. AF *cumpundre, fr. L componere, fr. com- together + ponere to put] 1 : COMBINE 2 : to form by combining parts ⟨~ a medicine⟩ 3 : SETTLE ⟨~ a dispute⟩; also : to refrain from prosecuting (an offense) in return for a consideration 4 : to increase (as interest) by an amount that can itself vary; also : to add to

²**com·pound** \ˈkäm-ˌpaund\ adj 1 : made up of individual parts 2 : composed of united similar parts esp. of a kind usu. independent ⟨a ~ plant ovary⟩ 3 : formed by the combination of two or more otherwise independent elements ⟨~ sentence⟩

³**com·pound** \ˈkäm-ˌpaund\ n 1 : a word consisting of parts that are words 2 : something formed from a union of elements or parts; esp : a distinct substance formed by the union of two or more chemical elements ♦ **Synonyms** MIXTURE, COMPOSITE, BLEND, ADMIXTURE, ALLOY

⁴**com·pound** \ˈkäm-ˌpaund\ n [by folk etymology fr. Malay kampung group of buildings, village] : an enclosure containing buildings

**compound interest** n : interest computed on the sum of an original principal and accrued interest

**com·pre·hend** \ˌkäm-pri-ˈhend\ vb 1 : UNDERSTAND 2 : INCLUDE — **com·pre·hen·si·ble** \-ˈhen-sə-bəl\ adj — **com·pre·hen·sion** \-ˈhen-chən\ n

**com·pre·hen·sive** \ˌkäm-pri-ˈhen-siv\ adj : covering completely or broadly ⟨~ insurance⟩ — **com·pre·hen·sive·ly** adv — **com·pre·hen·sive·ness** n

¹**com·press** \kəm-ˈpres\ vb 1 : to squeeze together 2 : to reduce in size as if by squeezing ♦ **Synonyms** CONSTRICT, CONTRACT, SHRINK — **com·pres·sor** \-ˈpre-sər\ n

²**com·press** \ˈkäm-ˌpres\ n : a folded pad or cloth used to press upon a body part

**compressed air** n : air under pressure greater than that of the atmosphere

**com·pres·sion** \kəm-ˈpre-shən\ n 1 : the act or process of compressing 2 : the process of compressing the fuel mixture in an internal combustion engine 3 : conversion (as of data) in order to reduce the space occupied or the bandwidth required

**com·prise** \kəm-ˈprīz\ vb **com·prised**; **com·pris·ing** 1 : INCLUDE, CONTAIN 2 : to be made up of ⟨the play ~s three acts⟩ 3 : COMPOSE, CONSTITUTE

¹**com·pro·mise** \ˈkäm-prə-ˌmīz\ n : a settlement of differences reached by mutual concessions

²**compromise** vb **-mised**; **-mis·ing** 1 : to settle by compromise 2 : to expose to suspicion or loss of reputation

**comp·trol·ler** \kən-ˈtrō-lər, ˈkämp-ˌtrō-\ n : an official who audits and supervises expenditures and accounts

**com·pul·sion** \kəm-ˈpəl-shən\ n 1 : an act of compelling 2 : a force that compels 3 : an irresistible persistent impulse to perform an act ♦ **Synonyms** CONSTRAINT, FORCE, VIOLENCE, DURESS — **com·pul·sive** \-siv\ adj — **com·pul·sive·ly** adv — **com·pul·so·ry** \-sə-rē\ adj

**com·punc·tion** \kəm-ˈpəŋk-shən\ n : anxiety arising from guilt : REMORSE

**com·pute** \kəm-ˈpyüt\ vb **com·put·ed**; **com·put·ing** : CALCULATE, RECKON — **com·pu·ta·tion** \ˌkäm-pyü-ˈtā-shən\ n — **com·pu·ta·tion·al** adj

**computed tomography** n : radiography in which a three-dimensional image of a body structure is constructed by computer from a series of plane cross-sectional images made along an axis

**com·put·er** \kəm-ˈpyü-tər\ n : a programmable electronic device that can store, retrieve, and process data

**com·put·er·ise** chiefly Brit var of COMPUTERIZE

**com·put·er·ize** \kəm-ˈpyü-tə-ˌrīz\ vb **-ized**; **-iz·ing** 1 : to carry out, control, or produce by means of a computer 2 : to provide with computers 3 : to store in a computer; also : put into a form that a computer can use — **com·put·er·i·za·tion** \-ˌpyü-tə-rə-ˈzā-shən\ n

**computerized axial tomography** n : COMPUTED TOMOGRAPHY

**com·rade** \ˈkäm-ˌrad\ n [MF camarade group sleeping in one room, roommate, companion, fr. Sp camarada, fr. cámara room, fr. LL camera] : COMPANION, ASSOCIATE — **com·rade·ly** adj — **com·rade·ship** n

¹**con** \ˈkän\ vb **conned**; **con·ning** 1 : MEMORIZE 2 : STUDY

²**con** adv : in opposition : AGAINST

³**con** n : an opposing argument, person, or position ⟨pros and ~⟩

⁴**con** vb **conned**; **con·ning** 1 : SWINDLE 2 : PERSUADE, CAJOLE

⁵**con** n : CONVICT

**conc** abbr concentrated

**con·cat·e·nate** \kän-ˈka-tə-ˌnāt\ vb **-nat·ed**; **-nat·ing** : to link together in a series or chain — con·cat·e·na·tion \(ˌ)kän-ˌka-tə-ˈnā-shən\ n

con·cave \kän-ˈkāv, ˈkän-ˌ\ adj : curved or rounded inward like the inside of a bowl — con·cav·i·ty \kän-ˈka-və-tē\ n

con·ceal \kən-ˈsēl\ vb : to place out of sight : HIDE ⟨~ evidence⟩ — con·ceal·er n — con·ceal·ment n

con·cede \kən-ˈsēd\ vb con·ced·ed; con·ced·ing 1 : to admit to be true 2 : GRANT, YIELD ♦ Synonyms ALLOW, ACKNOWLEDGE, AVOW, CONFESS

con·ceit \kən-ˈsēt\ n 1 : excessively high opinion of one's self or ability : VANITY 2 : an elaborate or strained metaphor — con·ceit·ed adj — con·ceit·ed·ly adv — con·ceit·ed·ness n

con·ceive \kən-ˈsēv\ vb con·ceived; con·ceiv·ing 1 : to become pregnant or pregnant with ⟨~ a child⟩ 2 : to form an idea of : THINK, IMAGINE ⟨~ a plan⟩ — con·ceiv·able \-ˈsē-və-bəl\ adj — con·ceiv·ably \-blē\ adv

con·cel·e·brant \kən-ˈse-lə-brənt\ n : one that jointly participates in celebrating the Eucharist

1con·cen·trate \ˈkän-sən-ˌtrāt\ vb -trat·ed; -trat·ing 1 : to gather into one body, mass, or force 2 : to make less dilute 3 : to fix one's powers, efforts, or attentions

2concentrate n : something concentrated

con·cen·tra·tion \ˌkän-sən-ˈtrā-shən\ n 1 : the act or process of concentrating : the state of being concentrated; esp : direction of attention on a single object 2 : the amount of a component in a given area or volume

concentration camp n : a camp where persons (as prisoners of war or political prisoners) are confined

con·cen·tric \kən-ˈsen-trik\ adj 1 : having a common center ⟨~ circles⟩ 2 : COAXIAL

1con·cept \ˈkän-ˌsept\ n : THOUGHT, NOTION, IDEA — con·cep·tu·al \kən-ˈsep-chə-wəl\ adj — con·cep·tu·al·ly adv

2concept adj 1 : organized around a main idea or theme ⟨~ album⟩ 2 : created to illustrate a concept ⟨a ~ car⟩

con·cep·tion \kən-ˈsep-shən\ n 1 : the process of conceiving or being conceived 2 : the power to form or understand ideas or concepts 3 : IDEA, CONCEPT 4 : the originating of something

con·cep·tu·al·ise Brit var of CONCEPTUALIZE

con·cep·tu·al·ize \-ˈsep-chə-wə-ˌlīz\ vb -ized; -iz·ing : to form a conception of

1con·cern \kən-ˈsərn\ vb 1 : to relate to 2 : to be the business of : INVOLVE 3 : ENGAGE, OCCUPY

2concern n 1 : INTEREST, ANXIETY 2 : AFFAIR, MATTER 3 : a business organization ♦ Synonyms CARE, WORRY, DISQUIET, UNEASE

con·cerned \-ˈsərnd\ adj 1 : ANXIOUS, UNEASY ⟨~ for their safety⟩ 2 : INVOLVED ⟨is ~ed with films⟩

con·cern·ing \-ˈsər-niŋ\ prep : relating to : REGARDING ⟨news ~ his business⟩

con·cern·ment \kən-ˈsərn-mənt\ n 1 : something in which one is concerned 2 : IMPORTANCE, CONSEQUENCE

1con·cert \ˈkän-(ˌ)sərt\ n 1 : agreement in a plan or design 2 : a public performance (as of music)

2con·cert \kən-ˈsərt\ vb : to plan together

con·cert·ed \kən-ˈsər-təd\ adj : mutually agreed on; also : performed in unison

con·cer·ti·na \ˌkän-sər-ˈtē-nə\ n : an instrument of the accordion family

concertina wire n : a coiled wire with sharp points for use as an obstacle

con·cert·mas·ter \ˈkän-sərt-ˌmas-tər\ or con·cert·meis·ter \-ˌmī-stər\ n : the leader of the first violins of an orchestra and assistant to the conductor

con·cer·to \kən-ˈcher-tō\ n, pl -ti \-(ˌ)tē\ or -tos [It] : a piece for one or more solo instruments and orchestra in three movements

con·ces·sion \kən-ˈse-shən\ n 1 : an act of conceding or yielding 2 : something yielded 3 : a grant by a government of land or of a right to use it 4 : a grant of a portion of premises for some specific purpose; also : the activities or enterprise carried on — con·ces·sion·ary \-ˈse-shə-ˌner-ē\ adj

con·ces·sion·aire \kən-ˌse-shə-ˈner\ n : one that owns or operates a concession

conch \ˈkäŋk, ˈkänch\ n, pl conchs \ˈkäŋks\ or conch·es \ˈkän-chəz\ : a large spiral-shelled marine gastropod mollusk; also : its shell

con·cierge \kōⁿ-ˈsyerzh\ n, pl con·cierg·es \same or -ˈsyer-zhəz\ [F] 1 : a resident in an apartment building who performs services for the tenants 2 : a usu. multilingual hotel staff member who usu. handles mail and reservations

con·cil·i·ate \kən-ˈsi-lē-ˌāt\ vb -at·ed; -at·ing 1 : to bring into agreement : RECONCILE 2 : to gain the goodwill of — con·cil·i·a·tion \-ˌsi-lē-ˈā-shən\ n — con·cil·i·a·tor \-ˈsi-lē-ˌā-tər\ n — con·cil·i·a·to·ry \-ˈsi-lē-ə-ˌtȯr-ē\ adj

con·cise \kən-ˈsīs\ adj : expressing much in few words : BRIEF ⟨a ~ history⟩ — con·cise·ly adv — con·cise·ness n

con·clave \ˈkän-ˌklāv\ n [ME, fr. ML, fr. L, room that can be locked, fr. com- together + clavis key] : a private gathering; also : CONVENTION

con·clude \kən-ˈklüd\ vb con·clud·ed; con·clud·ing 1 : to bring to a close : END 2 : DECIDE, JUDGE 3 : to bring about as a result ♦ Synonyms CLOSE, FINISH, TERMINATE, COMPLETE, HALT

con·clu·sion \kən-ˈklü-zhən\ n 1 : the logical consequence of a reasoning process 2 : TERMINATION, END 3 : OUTCOME, RESULT — con·clu·sive \-siv\ adj — con·clu·sive·ly adv — con·clu·sive·ness n

con·coct \kən-ˈkäkt, kän-\ vb 1 : to prepare by combining raw materials 2 : DEVISE — con·coc·tion \-ˈkäk-shən\ n

con·com·i·tant \kən-ˈkä-mə-tənt\ adj : ACCOMPANYING, ATTENDING — concomitant n

con·cord \ˈkän-ˌkȯrd, ˈkäŋ-\ n : AGREEMENT, HARMONY

**con·cor·dance** \kən-'kȯr-dᵊns\ n 1 : an alphabetical index of words in a book or in an author's works with the passages in which they occur 2 : AGREEMENT, COVENANT

**con·cor·dant** \-dᵊnt\ adj : HARMONIOUS, AGREEING

**con·cor·dat** \kən-'kȯr-ˌdat\ n : CONCORDANCE 2

**con·course** \'kän-ˌkȯrs\ n 1 : a spontaneous coming together : GATHERING 2 : an open space or hall (as in a bus terminal) where crowds gather

¹**con·crete** \kän-'krēt, 'kän-ˌkrēt\ adj 1 : naming a real thing or class of things : not abstract 2 : not theoretical : ACTUAL 3 : made of or relating to concrete

²**con·crete** \'kän-ˌkrēt, kän-'krēt\ vb **con·cret·ed**; **con·cret·ing** 1 : SOLIDIFY 2 : to cover with concrete

³**con·crete** \'kän-ˌkrēt, kän-'krēt\ n : a hard building material made by mixing cement, sand, and gravel with water

**con·cre·tion** \kän-'krē-shən\ n : a hard mass esp. when formed abnormally in the body

**con·cu·bine** \'käŋ-kyù-ˌbīn\ n [ME, fr. AF, fr. L concubina, fr. com- with + cubare to lie] : a woman who is not legally a wife but lives with a man and sometimes has a recognized position in his household; also : MISTRESS — **con·cu·bi·nage** \kän-'kyü-bə-nij\ n

**con·cu·pis·cence** \kän-'kyü-pə-səns\ : ardent sexual desire : LUST

**con·cur** \kən-'kər\ vb **con·curred**; **con·cur·ring** 1 : to act together 2 : AGREE 3 : COINCIDE ♦ **Synonyms** UNITE, COMBINE, COOPERATE, BAND, JOIN

**con·cur·rence** \-'kər-əns\ n 1 : agreement in action or opinion 2 : occurrence together : CONJUNCTION

**con·cur·rent** \-'kər-ənt\ adj 1 : happening or operating at the same time 2 : joint and equal in authority

**con·cus·sion** \kən-'kə-shən\ n 1 : a hard blow or collision; also : bodily injury (as to the brain) resulting from a sudden jar 2 : AGITATION, SHAKING

**con·demn** \kən-'dem\ vb 1 : to declare to be wrong 2 : to convict of guilt 3 : to sentence judicially 4 : to pronounce unfit for use ⟨∼ a building⟩ 5 : to declare forfeited or taken for public use ♦ **Synonyms** DENOUNCE, CENSURE, BLAME, CRITICIZE, REPREHEND — **con·dem·na·tion** \ˌkän-ˌdem-'nā-shən\ n — **con·dem·na·to·ry** \kən-'dem-nə-ˌtȯr-ē\ adj

**con·den·sate** \'kän-dən-ˌsāt, kən-'den-\ n : a product of condensation

**con·dense** \kən-'dens\ vb **con·densed**; **con·dens·ing** 1 : to make or become more compact or dense : CONCENTRATE 2 : to change from vapor to liquid ♦ **Synonyms** CONTRACT, SHRINK, COMPRESS, CONSTRICT — **con·den·sa·tion** \ˌkän-den-'sā-shən\ n

**con·dens·er** \kən-'den-sər\ n 1 : one that condenses 2 : CAPACITOR

**con·de·scend** \ˌkän-di-'send\ vb : to assume an air of superiority — **con·de·scend·ing·ly** \-'sen-diŋ-lē\ adv — **con·de·scen·sion** \-'sen-chən\ n

**con·dign** \kən-'dīn, 'kän-ˌdīn\ adj : DESERVED, APPROPRIATE ⟨∼ punishment⟩

**con·di·ment** \'kän-də-mənt\ n : something used to make food savory; esp : a pungent seasoning (as pepper)

¹**con·di·tion** \kən-'di-shən\ n 1 : something essential to the occurrence of some other thing 2 : state of being 3 : social status 4 pl : state of affairs : CIRCUMSTANCES 5 : a bodily state in which something is wrong ⟨a heart ∼⟩ 6 : a state of health, fitness, or working order ⟨in good ∼⟩

²**condition** vb 1 : to put into proper condition for action or use 2 : to adapt, modify, or mold to respond in a particular way 3 : to modify so that an act or response previously associated with one stimulus becomes associated with another

**con·di·tion·al** \kən-'di-shə-nəl\ adj : containing, implying, or depending on a condition — **con·di·tion·al·ly** adv

**con·di·tioned** \-'di-shənd\ adj : determined or established by conditioning

**con·di·tion·er** \-'di-shə-nər\ n : a preparation used to improve the condition of hair

**con·do** \'kän-(ˌ)dō\ n : CONDOMINIUM 3

**con·dole** \kən-'dōl\ vb **con·doled**; **con·dol·ing** : to express sympathetic sorrow — **con·do·lence** \kən-'dō-ləns\ n

**con·dom** \'kän-dəm, 'kən-\ n : a usu. rubber sheath worn over the penis (as to prevent pregnancy or venereal infection during sexual intercourse)

**con·do·min·i·um** \ˌkän-də-'mi-nē-əm\ n, pl -ums 1 : joint sovereignty (as by two or more nations) 2 : a politically dependent territory under condominium 3 : individual ownership of a unit (as an apartment) in a multiunit structure; also : a unit so owned

**con·done** \kən-'dōn\ vb **con·doned**; **con·don·ing** : to overlook or forgive esp. by treating (an offense) as harmless or trivial ♦ **Synonyms** EXCUSE, PARDON, FORGIVE, REMIT — **con·do·na·tion** \ˌkän-də-'nā-shən\ n

**con·dor** \'kän-dər, -ˌdȯr\ n [Sp cóndor, fr. Quechua kuntur] : a very large American vulture of the high Andes; also : a related nearly extinct vulture of southern California now resident only in captivity

**con·duce** \kən-'düs, -'dyüs\ vb **con·duced**; **con·duc·ing** : to lead or contribute to a particular result — **con·du·cive** adj

¹**con·duct** \'kän-(ˌ)dəkt\ n 1 : MANAGEMENT, DIRECTION 2 : BEHAVIOR

²**con·duct** \kən-'dəkt\ vb 1 : GUIDE, ESCORT 2 : MANAGE, DIRECT 3 : to act as a medium for conveying or transmitting 4 : BEHAVE — **con·duc·tion** \-'dək-shən\ n

**con·duc·tance** \kən-'dək-təns\ n : the readiness with which a conductor transmits an electric current

**con·duc·tive** \kən-'dək-tiv\ adj : having the power to conduct (as heat or electricity) — **con·duc·tiv·i·ty** \ˌkän-ˌdək-'ti-və-tē\ n

**con·duc·tor** \kən-'dək-tər\ *n* **1** : one that conducts; *esp* : a material that permits an electric current to flow easily **2** : a collector of fares in a public conveyance **3** : the leader of a musical ensemble

**con·duit** \'kän-,dü-ət, ,dyü-, -dwət\ *n* **1** : a channel for conveying fluid **2** : a tube or trough for protecting electric wires or cables **3** : a means of transmitting or distributing

**con·dyle** \'kän-,dīl(-ə)l, -d°l\ *n* : an articular prominence of a bone — **con·dy·lar** \-də-lər\ *adj*

**cone** \'kōn\ *n* **1** : the scaly usu. ovate fruit of trees of most conifers **2** : a solid figure formed by rotating a right triangle about one of its legs **3** : a solid figure that slopes evenly to a point from a usu. circular base **4** : any of the conical light-sensitive receptor cells of the retina that function in color vision **5** : something shaped like a cone

**cone·flow·er** \'kōn-,flau̇(-ə)r\ *n* : any of several composite plants having cone-shaped flower disks

**Con·es·to·ga wagon** \,kä-nə-'stō-gə-\ *n* : a broad-wheeled covered wagon used esp. for transporting freight across the prairies

**co·ney** *or* **co·ny** \'kō-nē\ *n, pl* **coneys** *or* **conies** \-nēz\ **1** : RABBIT; *also* : its fur **2** : PIKA

**conf** *abbr* **1** conference **2** confidential

**con·fab** \'kän-,fab, kən-'fab\ *n* : CONFABULATION 1

**con·fab·u·la·tion** \kən-,fab-yə-'lā-shən\ *n* **1** : CHAT; *also* : CONFERENCE **2** : a filling in of gaps in memory by fabrication — **con·fab·u·late** \-'fa-byə-,lāt\ *vb*

**con·fec·tion** \kən-'fek-shən\ *n* **1** : something put together from varied material **2** : a fancy dish or sweet; *also* : CANDY — **con·fect** \kən-'fekt\ *vb*

**con·fec·tion·er** \-sh(ə-)nər\ *n* : a maker of or dealer in confections

**con·fec·tion·ery** \-sha-,ner-ē\ *n, pl* **-er·ies** **1** : sweet foods **2** : a confectioner's place of business

**Confed** *abbr* Confederate

**con·fed·er·a·cy** \kən-'fe-də-rə-sē\ *n, pl* **-cies** **1** : LEAGUE, ALLIANCE **2** *cap* : the 11 southern states that seceded from the U.S. in 1860 and 1861

**¹con·fed·er·ate** \kən-'fe-də-rət\ *adj* **1** : united in a league : ALLIED **2** *cap* : of or relating to the Confederacy

**²confederate** *n* **1** : ALLY, ACCOMPLICE **2** *cap* : an adherent of the Confederacy

**³con·fed·er·ate** \-'fe-də-,rāt\ *vb* **-at·ed;** **-at·ing** : to unite in a confederacy

**con·fed·er·a·tion** \kən-,fe-də-'rā-shən\ *n* **1** : an act of confederating : ALLIANCE **2** : LEAGUE

**con·fer** \kən-'fər\ *vb* **con·ferred;** **con·fer·ring** **1** : GRANT, BESTOW ⟨~ an award⟩ **2** : to exchange views : CONSULT — **con·fer·ee** \kän-fə-'rē\ *n*

**con·fer·ence** \'kän-f(ə-)rəns\ *n* **1** : an interchange of views; *also* : a meeting for this purpose **2** : an association of athletic teams

**con·fer·enc·ing** \'kän-f(ə-)rən-siŋ\ *n*

: the holding of conferences esp. by means of electronic devices

**con·fess** \kən-'fes\ *vb* **1** : to acknowledge or disclose one's misdeed, fault, or sin **2** : to acknowledge one's sins to God or to a priest **3** : to receive the confession of (a penitent)  ♦ **Synonyms** ADMIT, OWN, AVOW, CONCEDE, GRANT

**con·fessed·ly** \-'fe-səd-lē\ *adv* : by confession : ADMITTEDLY

**con·fes·sion** \-'fe-shən\ *n* **1** : an act of confessing (as in the sacrament of penance) **2** : an acknowledgment of guilt **3** : a formal statement of religious beliefs **4** : a religious body having a common creed — **con·fes·sion·al** *adj*

**con·fes·sion·al** \-'fe-shə-nəl\ *n* : a place where a priest hears confessions

**con·fes·sor** \kən-'fe-sər\ *n* **1** : one that confesses **2** : a priest who hears confessions

**con·fet·ti** \kən-'fe-tē\ *n* [It, pl. of *confetto* sweetmeat, fr. ML *confectum*, fr. L, neut. of *confectus*, pp. of *conficere* to prepare] : bits of colored paper or ribbon for throwing (as at weddings)

**con·fi·dant** \'kän-fə-,dänt, -,dant\ *n* : one to whom secrets are confided

**con·fi·dante** \-,dänt, -,dant\ *n* : CONFIDANT; *esp* : one who is a woman

**con·fide** \kən-'fīd\ *vb* **con·fid·ed;** **con·fid·ing** **1** : to have or show faith : TRUST ⟨~ in a friend⟩ **2** : to tell confidentially ⟨~ a secret⟩ **3** : ENTRUST

**¹con·fi·dence** \'kän-fə-dəns\ *n* **1** : TRUST, RELIANCE **2** : SELF-ASSURANCE, BOLDNESS **3** : a state of trust or intimacy **4** : SECRET **2** — **con·fi·dent** \-dənt\ *adj* — **con·fi·dent·ly** *adv*

**²confidence** *adj* : of or relating to swindling by false promises ⟨a ~ game⟩

**con·fi·den·tial** \,kän-fə-'den-shəl\ *adj* **1** : SECRET, PRIVATE ⟨~ information⟩ **2** : entrusted with confidences ⟨~ clerk⟩ — **con·fi·den·ti·al·i·ty** \-,den-shē-'a-lə-tē\ *n* — **con·fi·den·tial·ly** \-'den-shə-lē\ *adv*

**con·fig·u·ra·tion** \kən-,fi-gyə-'rā-shən\ *n* : structural arrangement of parts : SHAPE

**con·fig·ure** \kən-'fi-gyər\ *vb* **-ured; -ur·ing** : to set up for operation esp. in a particular way

**con·fine** \kən-'fīn\ *vb* **con·fined;** **con·fin·ing** **1** : to hold within a location; *also* : IMPRISON **2** : to keep within limits ⟨will ~ my remarks to one subject⟩ — **con·fine·ment** *n* — **con·fin·er** *n*

**con·fines** \'kän-,fīnz\ *n pl* : BOUNDS, BORDERS

**con·firm** \kən-'fərm\ *vb* **1** : to give approval to : RATIFY **2** : to make firm or firmer **3** : to administer the rite of confirmation to **4** : VERIFY, CORROBORATE — **con·fir·ma·to·ry** \-'fər-mə-,tȯr-ē\ *adj*

**con·fir·ma·tion** \,kän-fər-'mā-shən\ *n* **1** : a religious ceremony admitting a person to full membership in a church or synagogue **2** : an act of ratifying or corroborating; *also* : PROOF

**con·fis·cate** \'kän-fə-,skāt\ *vb* **-cat·ed;** **-cat·ing** [L *confiscare,* fr. *com-* with + *fiscus* treasury] : to take possession of by or as if by public authority — **con·fis·ca·tion** \ˌkän-fə-ˈskā-shən\ n — **con·fis·ca·to·ry** \kən-ˈfis-kə-ˌtōr-ē\ adj

**con·fit** \kōn-ˈfē\ n : a garnish of fruit or vegetables cooked in a seasoned liquid

**con·fla·gra·tion** \ˌkän-flə-ˈgrā-shən\ n : FIRE; esp : a large disastrous fire

**¹con·flict** \ˈkän-ˌflikt\ n 1 : WAR 2 : a clash between hostile or opposing elements, ideas, or forces

**²con·flict** \kən-ˈflikt\ vb : to show opposition or irreconcilability : CLASH

**con·flu·ence** \ˈkän-ˌflü-əns, kən-ˈflü-\ n 1 : a coming together at one point 2 : the meeting or place of meeting of two or more streams — **con·flu·ent** \-ənt\ adj

**con·flux** \ˈkän-ˌfləks\ n : CONFLUENCE

**con·form** \kən-ˈfórm\ vb 1 : to be similar or identical; also : AGREE 2 : to obey customs or standards; also : COMPLY ⟨∼ to regulations⟩ — **con·form·able** adj — **con·form·ist** \-ˈfór-mist\ adj

**con·for·mance** \kən-ˈfór-məns\ n : CONFORMITY

**con·for·ma·tion** \ˌkän-fór-ˈmā-shən\ n : a forming into a whole by arranging parts

**con·for·mi·ty** \kən-ˈfór-mə-tē\ n, pl **-ties** 1 : HARMONY, AGREEMENT 2 : COMPLIANCE, OBEDIENCE

**con·found** \kən-ˈfaůnd, kän-\ vb 1 : to throw into disorder or confusion 2 : CONFUSE 2 ♦ **Synonyms** BEWILDER, PUZZLE, PERPLEX, BEFOG

**con·fra·ter·ni·ty** \ˌkän-frə-ˈtər-nə-tē\ n : a society devoted esp. to a religious or charitable cause

**con·frere** \ˈkän-ˌfrer, ˈkōⁿ-\ n : COLLEAGUE, COMRADE

**con·front** \kən-ˈfrənt\ vb 1 : to face esp. in challenge : OPPOSE; also : to deal unflinchingly with ⟨∼ed the issue⟩ 2 : to cause to face or meet — **con·fron·ta·tion** \ˌkän-frən-ˈtā-shən\ n — **con·fron·ta·tion·al** \-shə-nᵊl\ adj

**Con·fu·cian** \kən-ˈfyü-shən\ adj : of or relating to the Chinese philosopher Confucius or his teachings — **Con·fu·cian·ism** \-shə-ˌni-zəm\ n

**con·fuse** \kən-ˈfyüz\ vb **con·fused; con·fus·ing** 1 : to make mentally unclear or uncertain; also : to disturb the composure of 2 : to mix up : JUMBLE ♦ **Synonyms** MUDDLE, BEFUDDLE, ADDLE, FLUSTER — **con·fus·ed·ly** \-ˈfyü-zəd-lē\ adv — **con·fus·ing·ly** \-ˈfyü-ziŋ-lē\ adv

**con·fu·sion** \-ˈfyü-zhən\ n 1 : an act or instance of confusing 2 : the quality or state of being confused

**con·fute** \kən-ˈfyüt\ vb **con·fut·ed; con·fut·ing** : to overwhelm by argument : REFUTE ⟨∼ a proposition⟩ — **con·fu·ta·tion** \ˌkän-fyü-ˈtā-shən\ n

**cong** abbr congress; congressional

**con·ga** \ˈkäŋ-gə\ n : a Cuban dance of African origin performed by a group usu. in single file

**con·geal** \kən-ˈjēl\ vb 1 : FREEZE 2 : to make or become hard or thick

**con·gee** \ˈkän-jē\ n : porridge made from rice

**con·ge·ner** \ˈkän-jə-nər\ n : one related to another; esp : a plant or animal of the same taxonomic genus as another — **con·ge·ner·ic** \ˌkän-jə-ˈner-ik\ adj

**con·ge·nial** \kən-ˈjē-nyəl\ adj 1 : KINDRED, SYMPATHETIC ⟨∼ companions⟩ 2 : suited to one's taste or nature : AGREEABLE — **con·ge·ni·al·i·ty** \-ˌjē-nē-ˈa-lə-tē\ n — **con·ge·nial·ly** adv

**con·gen·i·tal** \kən-ˈje-nə-tᵊl\ adj : existing at or dating from birth ⟨∼ deafness⟩ ♦ **Synonyms** INBORN, INNATE, NATURAL

**con·ger eel** \ˈkän-gər-\ n : a large edible marine eel of the Atlantic

**con·ge·ries** \ˈkän-jə-(ˌ)rēz\ n, pl **congeries** : AGGREGATION, COLLECTION

**con·gest** \kən-ˈjest\ vb 1 : to cause excessive fullness of the blood vessels of (as a lung) 2 : to obstruct by overcrowding — **con·ges·tion** \-ˈjes-chən\ n — **con·ges·tive** \-ˈjes-tiv\ adj

**congestive heart failure** n : heart failure in which the heart is unable to keep enough blood circulating in the tissues or is unable to pump out the blood returned to it by the veins

**¹con·glom·er·ate** \kən-ˈglä-mə-rət\ adj [L conglomerare to roll together, fr. com- together + glomerare to wind into a ball, fr. glomer-, glomus ball] : made up of parts from various sources

**²con·glom·er·ate** \-ˌrāt\ vb **-at·ed; -at·ing** : to form into a mass — **con·glom·er·a·tion** \-ˌglä-mə-ˈrā-shən\ n

**³con·glom·er·ate** \-rət\ n 1 : a mass formed of fragments from various sources; esp : a rock composed of fragments varying from pebbles to boulders held together by a cementing material 2 : a widely diversified corporation

**con·grat·u·late** \kən-ˈgra-chə-ˌlāt\ vb **-lat·ed; -lat·ing** : to express sympathetic pleasure to on account of success or good fortune : FELICITATE — **con·grat·u·la·tion** \-ˌgra-chə-ˈlā-shən\ n — **con·grat·u·la·to·ry** \-ˈgra-chə-lə-ˌtōr-ē\ adj

**con·gre·gate** \ˈkäŋ-gri-ˌgāt\ vb **-gat·ed; -gat·ing** [ME, fr. L congregatus, pp. of congregare, fr. com- together + greg-, grex flock] : ASSEMBLE

**con·gre·ga·tion** \ˌkäŋ-gri-ˈgā-shən\ n 1 : an assembly of persons met esp. for worship; also : a group that habitually so meets 2 : a religious community or order 3 : the act or an instance of congregating

**con·gre·ga·tion·al** \-shə-nəl\ adj 1 : of or relating to a congregation 2 cap : observing the faith and practice of certain Protestant churches which recognize the independence of each congregation in church matters — **con·gre·ga·tion·al·ism** \-nə-ˌli-zəm\ n, often cap — **con·gre·ga·tion·al·ist** \-list\ n, often cap

**con·gress** \ˈkäŋ-grəs\ n 1 : an assembly esp. of delegates for discussion and usu. action on some question 2 : the body of senators and representatives constituting a nation's legislature — **con·gres·sio·nal** \kən-ˈgre-shə-nəl\ adj

**con·gress·man** \ˈkäŋ-grəs-mən\ n : a member of a congress

**con·gress·wom·an** \-ˌwů-mən\ n : a woman who is a member of a congress

**con·gru·ence** \kən-'grü-əns, 'kän-grü-\ *n* : the quality of agreeing or coinciding : CONGRUITY — **con·gru·ent** \kən-'grü-ənt, 'kän-grü-\ *adj*

**con·gru·en·cy** \-sē\ *n, pl* **-cies** : CONGRUENCE

**con·gru·ity** \kän-'grü-ə-tē\ *n, pl* **-ities** : correspondence between things — **con·gru·ous** \'kän-grü-əs\ *adj*

**con·ic** \'kä-nik\ *adj* 1 : of or relating to a cone 2 : CONICAL

**con·i·cal** \'kä-ni-kəl\ *adj* : resembling a cone esp. in shape

**co·ni·fer** \'kä-nə-fər, 'kō-\ *n* : any of an order of shrubs or trees (as the pines) that usu. are evergreen and bear cones — **co·nif·er·ous** \kō-'ni-fə-rəs\ *adj*

**conj** *abbr* conjunction

**con·jec·ture** \kən-'jek-chər\ *n* : GUESS, SURMISE — **con·jec·tur·al** \-chə-rəl\ *adj* — **conjecture** *vb*

**con·join** \kən-'join\ *vb* : to join together — **con·joint** \-'joint\ *adj*

**con·ju·gal** \'kän-ji-gəl\ *adj* : of or relating to marriage : MATRIMONIAL

¹**con·ju·gate** \'kän-ji-gət, -jə-,gāt\ *adj* 1 : united esp. in pairs : COUPLED 2 : of kindred origin and meaning ⟨*sing* and *song* are ~⟩ — **con·ju·gate·ly** *adv*

²**con·ju·gate** \-jə-,gāt\ *vb* **-gat·ed; -gat·ing** 1 : INFLECT ⟨~ a verb⟩ 2 : to join together : COUPLE

**con·ju·ga·tion** \,kän-jə-'gā-shən\ *n* 1 : an arrangement of the inflectional forms of a verb 2 : the act of conjugating : the state of being conjugated

**con·junct** \kän-'jəŋkt\ *adj* : JOINED, UNITED

**con·junc·tion** \kən-'jəŋk-shən\ *n* 1 : COMBINATION 2 : occurrence at the same time 3 : a word that joins together sentences, clauses, phrases, or words

**con·junc·ti·va** \,kän-jəŋk-'tī-və\ *n, pl* **-vas** *or* **-vae** \-(,)vē\ : the mucous membrane lining the inner surface of the eyelids and continuing over the forepart of the eyeball

**con·junc·tive** \kən-'jəŋk-tiv\ *adj* 1 : CONNECTIVE 2 : CONJUNCT ⟨the ~ operation of different factors⟩ 3 : being or functioning like a conjunction

**con·junc·ti·vi·tis** \kən-,jəŋk-ti-'vī-təs\ *n* : inflammation of the conjunctiva

**con·junc·ture** \kən-'jəŋk-chər\ *n* : CONJUNCTION, UNION : JUNCTURE 3

**con·jun·to** \kōn-'hün-tō\ *n* : Mexican-American music influenced by the music of German immigrants to Texas

**con·jure** \'kän-jər, 'kən- *for 1, 2;* kən-'jùr *for 3*\ *vb* **con·jured; con·jur·ing** 1 : to implore earnestly or solemnly 2 : to practice magic; *esp* : to summon (as a devil) by sorcery 3 : to practice sleight of hand — **con·ju·ra·tion** \,kän-jù-'rā-shən, ,kən-\ *n* — **con·jur·er** *or* **con·ju·ror** \'kän-jər-ər, 'kən-\ *n*

**conk** \'käŋk\ *vb* : BREAK DOWN; *esp* : STALL ⟨the motor ~ed out⟩

**Conn** *abbr* Connecticut

**con·nect** \kə-'nekt\ *vb* 1 : to JOIN, LINK 2 : to associate in one's mind 3 : to establish a communications connection ⟨~ to the Internet⟩ — **con·nect·able** *adj* — **con·nec·tor** *n*

**con·nec·tion** \kə-'nek-shən\ *n* 1 : JUNCTION, UNION 2 : logical relationship : COHERENCE; *esp* : relation of a word to other words in a sentence 3 : family relationship 4 : BOND, LINK 5 : a person related by blood or marriage 6 : relationship in social affairs or in business 7 : an association of persons; *esp* : a religious denomination 8 : a means of communication or transport ⟨a telephone ~⟩

¹**con·nec·tive** \kə-'nek-tiv\ *adj* : serving to connect — **con·nec·tiv·i·ty** \,kä-,nek-'ti-və-tē\ *n*

²**connective** *n* : a word (as a conjunction) that connects words or word groups

**connective tissue** *n* : a tissue (as bone or cartilage) that forms a supporting framework for the body or its parts

**con·nex·ion** *chiefly Brit var of* CONNECTION

**con·ning tower** \'kä-niŋ-\ *n* : a raised structure on the deck of a submarine

**con·nip·tion** \kə-'nip-shən\ *n* : a fit of rage, hysteria, or alarm

**con·nive** \kə-'nīv\ *vb* **con·nived; con·niv·ing** [F or L: F *conniver*, fr. L *conivēre* to close the eyes, connive] 1 : to pretend ignorance of something one ought to oppose as wrong 2 : to cooperate secretly : give secret aid — **con·niv·ance** *n* — **con·niv·er** *n*

**con·nois·seur** \,kä-nə-'sər\ *n* : a critical judge in matters of art or taste

**con·no·ta·tion** \,kä-nə-'tā-shən\ *n* : a meaning in addition to or apart from the thing explicitly named or described by a word

**con·no·ta·tive** \'kä-nə-,ta-tiv, kə-'no-tə-\ *adj* 1 : connoting or tending to connote 2 : relating to connotation

**con·note** \kə-'nōt\ *vb* **con·not·ed; con·not·ing** : to suggest or mean as a connotation

**con·nu·bi·al** \kə-'nü-bē-əl, -'nyü-\ *adj* : of or relating to marriage : CONJUGAL

**con·quer** \'käŋ-kər\ *vb* 1 : to gain by force of arms : WIN 2 : to get the better of : OVERCOME ♦ *Synonyms* DEFEAT, SUBJUGATE, SUBDUE, OVERTHROW, VANQUISH — **con·quer·or** \-ər\ *n*

**con·quest** \'kän-,kwest, 'käŋ-\ *n* 1 : an act of conquering : VICTORY 2 : something conquered

**con·quis·ta·dor** \kōn-'kēs-tə-,dór, kän-'kwis-\ *n, pl* **-do·res** \-,kēs-tə-'dór-ēz, -,kwis-\ *or* **-dors** : CONQUEROR; *esp* : a leader in the Spanish conquest of the Americas in the 16th century

**cons** *abbr* consonant

**con·san·guin·i·ty** \,kän-,san-'gwi-nə-tē, -,saŋ-\ *n, pl* **-ties** : blood relationship — **con·san·guin·e·ous** \-nē-əs\ *adj*

**con·science** \'kän-chəns\ *n* : consciousness of the moral right and wrong of one's own acts or motives — **conscience·less** *adj*

**con·sci·en·tious** \,kän-chē-'en-chəs\ *adj* : guided by one's own sense of right and wrong ♦ *Synonyms* SCRUPULOUS,

HONORABLE, HONEST, UPRIGHT, JUST — **con·sci·en·tious·ly** adv

**conscientious objector** n : a person who refuses to serve in the armed forces or to bear arms on moral or religious grounds

¹**con·scious** \ˈkän-chəs\ adj 1 : AWARE 2 : known or felt by one's inner self 3 : mentally awake or alert : not asleep or unconscious 4 : done with awareness or purpose ⟨a ~ decision⟩ — **con·scious·ly** adv — **con·scious·ness** n

²**conscious** n : the upper level of mental life of which a person is aware : CONSCIOUSNESS

**con·script** \kən-ˈskript\ vb : to enroll by compulsion for military or naval service — **conscript** \ˈkän-ˌskript\ n — **con·scrip·tion** \kən-ˈskrip-shən\ n

**con·se·crate** \ˈkän-sə-ˌkrāt\ vb **-crat·ed; -crat·ing** [ME, fr. L consecratus, pp. of consecrare, fr. com- together + sacrare to set aside as sacred, fr. sacer sacred] 1 : to induct (as a bishop) into an office with a religious rite 2 : to make or declare sacred ⟨~ a church⟩ 3 : to devote solemnly to a purpose — **con·se·cra·tion** \ˌkän-sə-ˈkrā-shən\ n

**con·sec·u·tive** \kən-ˈse-kyə-tiv\ adj : following in regular order : SUCCESSIVE — **con·sec·u·tive·ly** adv

**con·sen·su·al** \kən-ˈsen-chə-wəl\ adj : involving or based on mutual consent

**con·sen·sus** \kən-ˈsen-səs\ n 1 : agreement in opinion, testimony, or belief 2 : collective opinion

¹**con·sent** \kən-ˈsent\ vb : to give assent or approval ⟨~ed to the marriage⟩

²**consent** n : approval or acceptance of something done or proposed by another

²**con·se·quence** \ˈkän-sə-ˌkwens\ n 1 : RESULT 2 : IMPORTANCE ♦ **Synonyms** EFFECT, OUTCOME, AFTERMATH, UPSHOT

**con·se·quent** \-kwənt, -ˌkwent\ adj : following as a result or effect

**con·se·quen·tial** \ˌkän-sə-ˈkwen-chəl\ adj 1 : having significant consequences 2 : showing self-importance

**con·se·quent·ly** \ˈkän-sə-ˌkwent-lē, -kwənt-\ adv : as a result : ACCORDINGLY

**con·ser·van·cy** \kən-ˈsər-vən-sē\ n, pl **-cies** : an organization or area designated to conserve natural resources

**con·ser·va·tion** \ˌkän-sər-ˈvā-shən\ n : PRESERVATION; esp : planned management of natural resources

**con·ser·va·tion·ist** \-shə-nist\ n : a person who advocates conservation esp. of natural resources

**con·ser·va·tism** \kən-ˈsər-və-ˌti-zəm\ n : disposition to keep to established ways : opposition to change

¹**con·ser·va·tive** \kən-ˈsər-və-tiv\ adj 1 : PRESERVATIVE 2 : disposed to maintain existing views, conditions, or institutions 3 : MODERATE, CAUTIOUS ⟨a ~ investment⟩ — **con·ser·va·tive·ly** adv

²**conservative** n : a person who is conservative esp. in politics

**con·ser·va·tor** \kən-ˈsər-və-tər, ˈkän-sər-ˌvā-\ n 1 : PROTECTOR, GUARDIAN 2 : one named by a court to protect the interests of an incompetent (as a child)

**con·ser·va·to·ry** \kən-ˈsər-və-ˌtōr-ē\ n, pl **-ries** 1 : GREENHOUSE 2 : a place of instruction in one of the fine arts (as music)

¹**con·serve** \kən-ˈsərv\ vb **con·served; con·serv·ing** : to keep from losing or wasting : PRESERVE ⟨~ energy⟩

²**con·serve** \ˈkän-ˌsərv\ n 1 : CONFECTION 2; esp : a candied fruit 2 : PRESERVE; esp : one prepared from a mixture of fruits

**con·sid·er** \kən-ˈsi-dər\ vb [ME, fr. AF considerer, fr. L considerare to observe, think about, fr. com- together + sider-, sidus heavenly body] 1 : THINK, PONDER 2 : HEED, REGARD 3 : JUDGE, BELIEVE — **con·sid·ered** adj

**con·sid·er·able** \-ˈsi-dər-ə-bəl, -ˈsi-drə-bəl\ adj 1 : IMPORTANT 2 : large in extent, amount, or degree — **con·sid·er·ably** \-blē\ adv

**con·sid·er·ate** \kən-ˈsi-də-rət\ adj : observant of the rights and feelings of others ♦ **Synonyms** THOUGHTFUL, ATTENTIVE

**con·sid·er·ation** \kən-ˌsi-də-ˈrā-shən\ n 1 : careful thought : DELIBERATION 2 : a matter taken into account 3 : thoughtful attention 4 : JUDGMENT, OPINION 5 : RECOMPENSE

**con·sid·er·ing** \-ˈsi-d(ə-)riŋ\ prep : in view of : taking into account ⟨did well ~ his limitations⟩

**con·sign** \kən-ˈsīn\ vb 1 : ENTRUST, COMMIT 2 : to deliver formally 3 : to send (goods) to an agent for sale — **con·sign·ee** \ˌkän-sə-ˈnē, -ˌsī-; kən-ˌsī-\ n — **con·sign·or** \ˌkän-sə-ˈnȯr, -ˌsī-; kən-ˌsī-\ n

**con·sign·ment** \kən-ˈsīn-mənt\ n : something intended esp. in a single shipment

**con·sil·ience** \kən-ˈsil-yəns\ n : the linking together of principles from different disciplines when forming a comprehensive theory

**con·sist** \kən-ˈsist\ vb 1 : to be inherent : LIE — usu. used with in 2 : to be composed or made up — usu. used with of

**con·sis·tence** \kən-ˈsis-təns\ n : CONSISTENCY

**con·sis·ten·cy** \-tən-sē\ n, pl **-cies** 1 : COHESIVENESS, FIRMNESS 2 : agreement or harmony in parts or of different things 3 : UNIFORMITY ⟨~ of behavior⟩ — **con·sis·tent** \-tənt\ adj — **con·sis·tent·ly** adv

**con·sis·to·ry** \kən-ˈsis-tə-rē\ n, pl **-ries** : a solemn assembly (as of Roman Catholic cardinals)

**consol** abbr consolidated

¹**con·sole** \ˈkän-ˌsōl\ n [F] 1 : the desklike part of an organ at which the organist sits 2 : the combination of displays and controls of a device or system 3 : a cabinet for a radio or television set resting directly on the floor 4 : a small storage cabinet between bucket seats in an automobile

²**con·sole** \kən-ˈsōl\ vb **con·soled; con·sol·ing** : to soothe the grief of : COMFORT, SOLACE — **con·so·la·tion** \ˌkän-

sə-'lā-shən\ *n* — **con·so·la·to·ry** \kən-'sō-lə-ˌtȯr-ē, -'sä-\ *adj*

**con·sol·i·date** \kən-'sä-lə-ˌdāt\ *vb* **-dat·ed; -dat·ing** 1 : to unite or become united into one whole : COMBINE 2 : to make firm or secure 3 : to form into a compact mass — **con·sol·i·da·tion** \-ˌsä-lə-'dā-shən\ *n* — **con·sol·i·da·tor** \-'sä-lə-ˌdā-tər\ *n*

**con·som·mé** \ˌkän-sə-'mā\ *n* [F] : a clear soup made from well-seasoned stock

**con·so·nance** \'kän-sə-nəns\ *n* 1 : AGREEMENT, HARMONY 2 : repetition of consonants esp. as an alternative to rhyme in verse

¹**con·so·nant** \-nənt\ *adj* : having consonance, harmony, or agreement ♦ *Synonyms* CONSISTENT, COMPATIBLE, CONGRUOUS, CONGENIAL, SYMPATHETIC — **con·so·nant·ly** *adv*

²**consonant** *n* 1 : a speech sound (as \p\, \g\, \n\, \l\, \s\, \r\) characterized by constriction or closure at one or more points in the breath channel 2 : a letter other than *a*, *e*, *i*, *o*, and *u* — **con·so·nan·tal** \ˌkän-sə-'nan-t³l\ *adj*

¹**con·sort** \'kän-ˌsȯrt\ *n* 1 : a ship accompanying another 2 : SPOUSE, MATE

²**con·sort** \kən-'sȯrt\ *vb* 1 : to keep company 2 : ACCORD, HARMONIZE

**con·sor·tium** \kən-'sȯr-shəm; -shē-əm, -tē-\ *n, pl* **-sor·tia** \-shə-; -shē-ə, -tē-\ [L, fellowship] : an agreement or combination (as of companies) formed to undertake a large enterprise

**con·spec·tus** \kən-'spek-təs\ *n* 1 : a brief survey or summary 2 : SUMMARY

**con·spic·u·ous** \kən-'spi-kyə-wəs\ *adj* : attracting attention : PROMINENT, STRIKING ♦ *Synonyms* NOTICEABLE, REMARKABLE, OUTSTANDING — **con·spic·u·ous·ly** *adv*

**con·spir·a·cy** \kən-'spir-ə-sē\ *n, pl* **-cies** : an agreement among conspirators : PLOT

**con·spir·a·tor** \kən-'spir-ə-tər\ *n* : one who conspires — **con·spir·a·to·ri·al** \-ˌspir-ə-'tȯr-ē-əl\ *adj*

**con·spire** \kən-'spī(-ə)r\ *vb* **conspired; con·spir·ing** [ME, fr. AF *conspirer*, fr. L *conspirare* to be in harmony, conspire, fr. *com-* together + *spirare* to breathe] : to plan secretly an unlawful act : PLOT

**const** *abbr* 1 constant 2 constitution; constitutional

**con·sta·ble** \'kän-stə-bəl, 'kən-\ *n* [ME *conestable*, fr. AF, fr. LL *comes stabuli*, lit., officer of the stable] : a public officer responsible for keeping the peace

**con·stab·u·lary** \kən-'sta-byə-ˌler-ē\ *n, pl* **-lar·ies** 1 : the police of a particular district or country 2 : a police force organized like the military

**con·stan·cy** \'kän-stən-sē\ *n, pl* **-cies** 1 : firmness of mind 2 : STABILITY

¹**con·stant** \-stənt\ *adj* 1 : STEADFAST, FAITHFUL ⟨∼ friends⟩ 2 : FIXED, UNCHANGING ⟨a ∼ flow⟩ 3 : continually recurring : REGULAR ⟨a ∼ annoyance⟩ — **con·stant·ly** *adv*

²**constant** *n* : something unchanging

**con·stel·la·tion** \ˌkän-stə-'lā-shən\ *n* 1 : any of 88 groups of stars forming patterns 2 : a group of usu. related persons, qualities, or things

**con·ster·na·tion** \ˌkän-stər-'nā-shən\ *n* : amazed dismay and confusion

**con·sti·pa·tion** \ˌkän-stə-'pā-shən\ *n* : abnormally difficult or infrequent bowel movements — **con·sti·pate** \'kän-stə-ˌpāt\ *vb*

**con·stit·u·en·cy** \kən-'sti-chə-wən-sē\ *n, pl* **-cies** : a body of constituents; *also* : an electoral district

¹**con·stit·u·ent** \-wənt\ *n* 1 : a person entitled to vote for a representative for a district 2 : a component part

²**constituent** *adj* 1 : COMPONENT ⟨∼ parts⟩ 2 : having power to create a government or frame or amend a constitution

**con·sti·tute** \'kän-stə-ˌtüt, -ˌtyüt\ *vb* **-tut·ed; -tut·ing** 1 : to appoint to an office or duty 2 : SET UP, ESTABLISH ⟨∼ a law⟩ 3 : MAKE UP, COMPOSE

**con·sti·tu·tion** \ˌkän-stə-'tü-shən, -'tyü-\ *n* 1 : an established law or custom 2 : the physical makeup of the individual 3 : the structure, composition, or makeup of something ⟨∼ of the sun⟩ 4 : the basic law in a politically organized body; *also* : a document containing such law

¹**con·sti·tu·tion·al** \-shə-nəl\ *adj* 1 : of or relating to the constitution of body or mind 2 : being in accord with the constitution of a state or society; *also* : of or relating to such a constitution — **con·sti·tu·tion·al·ly** *adv*

²**constitutional** *n* : an exercise (as a walk) taken for one's health

**con·sti·tu·tion·al·i·ty** \-ˌtü-shə-'na-lə-tē, -ˌtyü-\ *n* : the quality or state of being constitutional

**con·sti·tu·tive** \'kän-stə-ˌtü-tiv, -ˌtyü-; kən-'sti-chə-tiv\ *adj* 1 : CONSTRUCTIVE 2 : CONSTITUENT, ESSENTIAL

**constr** *abbr* construction

**con·strain** \kən-'strān\ *vb* 1 : COMPEL, FORCE 2 : CONFINE 3 : RESTRAIN

**con·straint** \-'strānt\ *n* 1 : COMPULSION; *also* : RESTRAINT 2 : repression of one's natural feelings

**con·strict** \kən-'strikt\ *vb* : to draw together : SQUEEZE — **con·stric·tion** \-'strik-shən\ *n* — **con·stric·tive** \-'strik-tiv\ *adj*

**con·stric·tor** \kən-'strik-tər\ *n* : a snake that coils around and compresses its prey

**con·struct** \kən-'strəkt\ *vb* : BUILD, MAKE — **con·struc·tor** \-'strək-tər\ *n*

**con·struc·tion** \kən-'strək-shən\ *n* 1 : INTERPRETATION 2 : the art, process, or manner of building; *also* : something built, created, or established : STRUCTURE 3 : syntactical arrangement of words in a sentence — **con·struc·tive** \-tiv\ *adj*

**con·struc·tion·ist** \-shə-nist\ *n* : a person who construes a legal document (as the U.S. Constitution) in a specific way ⟨a strict ∼⟩

**con·strue** \kən-'strü\ *vb* **con·strued; con·stru·ing** 1 : to analyze the mutual relations of words in a sentence; *also*

: TRANSLATE **2** : EXPLAIN, INTERPRET ⟨*construed* the act as hostile⟩ — **con-stru-able** *adj* — **con-stru-al** \-'strü-əl\ *n*

**con-sub-stan-ti-a-tion** \ˌkän-səb-ˌstan-chē-'ā-shən\ *n* : the actual substantial presence and combination of the body and blood of Christ with the eucharistic bread and wine

**con-sul** \'kän-səl\ *n* **1** : a chief magistrate of the Roman republic **2** : a government official who resides in a foreign country to care for the commercial interests of the appointing government's citizens — **con-sul-ar** \-sə-lər\ *adj* — **con-sul-ate** \-lət\ *n* — **con-sul-ship** *n*

**con-sult** \kən-'səlt\ *vb* **1** : to ask the advice or opinion of **2** : CONFER — **con-sul-tant** \-'səl-t²nt\ *n* — **con-sul-ta-tion** \ˌkän-səl-'tā-shən\ *n*

**con-sume** \kən-'süm\ *vb* **con-sum-ing; con-sum-ing 1** : DESTROY ⟨*consumed* by fire⟩ **2** : to spend wastefully **3** : to eat up : DEVOUR **4** : to absorb the attention of : ENGROSS ⟨*consumed* with jealousy⟩ **5** : to utilize as a customer — **con-sum-able** *adj* — **con-sum-er** *n*

**con-sum-er-ism** \kən-'sü-mə-ˌri-zəm\ *n* : the promotion of consumers' interests (as against false advertising)

**consumer price index** *n* : an index measuring the change in the cost of widely purchased goods and services from the cost in some base period

¹**con-sum-mate** \'kän-sə-mət, kən-'sə\ *adj* : PERFECT ⟨a ~ team player⟩ ♦ *Synonyms* FINISHED, ACCOMPLISHED

²**con-sum-mate** \'kän-sə-ˌmāt\ *vb* **-mat-ed; -mat-ing** : to make complete : FINISH, ACHIEVE — **con-sum-ma-tion** \ˌkän-sə-'mā-shən\ *n*

**con-sump-tion** \kən-'səmp-shən\ *n* **1** : progressive bodily wasting away; *also* : TUBERCULOSIS **2** : the act of consuming or using up **3** : the use of economic goods

¹**con-sump-tive** \-'səmp-tiv\ *adj* **1** : tending to consume **2** : relating to or affected with consumption

²**consumptive** *n* : a person who has consumption

**cont** *abbr* **1** containing **2** contents **3** continent; continental **4** continued **5** control

¹**con-tact** \'kän-ˌtakt\ *n* **1** : a touching or meeting of bodies **2** : ASSOCIATION, RELATIONSHIP; *also* : CONNECTION, COMMUNICATION **3** : a person serving as a go-between or source of information **4** : CONTACT LENS

²**contact** *vb* **1** : to come or bring into contact : TOUCH **2** : to get in communication with ⟨~*ed* his lawyer⟩

**contact lens** *n* : a thin lens fitting over the cornea usu. to correct vision

**con-ta-gion** \kən-'tā-jən\ *n* [ME, fr. L *contagio*, fr. *contingere* to have contact with, pollute, fr. *com-* together + *tangere* to touch] **1** : a contagious disease **2** : *also* : the transmission of such a disease **2** : a disease-producing agent (as a virus) **3** : transmission of an influence on the mind or emotions

**con-ta-gious** \-jəs\ *adj* **1** : able to be passed by contact between individuals ⟨colds are ~⟩ ⟨~ disease⟩; *also* : capable of passing on a contagious disease **2** : communicated or transmitted like a contagious disease; *esp* : exciting similar emotion or conduct in others

**con-tain** \kən-'tān\ *vb* **1** : RESTRAIN **2** : to have within : HOLD **3** : COMPRISE, INCLUDE — **con-tain-able** \-'tā-nə-bəl\ *adj* — **con-tain-ment** \-'tān-mənt\ *n*

**con-tain-er** \kən-'tā-nər\ *n* : RECEPTACLE

**con-tam-i-nant** \kən-'ta-mə-nənt\ *n* : something that contaminates

**con-tam-i-nate** \kən-'ta-mə-ˌnāt\ *vb* **-nat-ed; -nat-ing** : to soil, stain, or infect by contact or association — **con-tam-i-na-tion** \-ˌta-mə-'nā-shən\ *n*

**contd** *abbr* continued

**con-temn** \kən-'tem\ *vb* : to view or treat with contempt : DESPISE

**con-tem-plate** \'kän-təm-ˌplāt\ *vb* **-plat-ed; -plat-ing** [L *contemplari*, fr. *com-* with + *templum* space marked out for observation of auguries] **1** : to view or consider with continued attention **2** : INTEND — **con-tem-pla-tion** \ˌkän-təm-'plā-shən\ *n* — **con-tem-pla-tive** \kən-'tem-plə-tiv, 'kän-təm-ˌplā-\ *adj*

**con-tem-po-ra-ne-ous** \kən-ˌtem-pə-'rā-nē-əs\ *adj* : CONTEMPORARY 1

**con-tem-po-rary** \kən-'tem-pə-ˌrer-ē\ *adj* **1** : occurring or existing at the same time **2** : marked by characteristics of the present period — **contemporary** *n*

**con-tempt** \kən-'tempt\ *n* **1** : the act of despising : the state of mind of one who despises **2** : the state of being despised **3** : disobedience to or open disrespect of a court or legislature

**con-tempt-ible** \kən-'temp-tə-bəl\ *adj* : deserving contempt : DESPICABLE — **con-tempt-ibly** \-blē\ *adv*

**con-temp-tu-ous** \-'temp-chə-wəs\ *adj* : feeling or expressing contempt — **con-temp-tu-ous-ly** *adv*

**con-tend** \kən-'tend\ *vb* **1** : to strive against rivals or difficulties **2** : ARGUE **3** : MAINTAIN, ASSERT — **con-tend-er** *n*

¹**con-tent** \kən-'tent\ *adj* : SATISFIED

²**content** *vb* : SATISFY; *esp* : to limit (oneself) in requirements or actions

³**content** *n* : CONTENTMENT ⟨ate to his heart's ~⟩

⁴**con-tent** \'kän-ˌtent\ *n* **1** : something contained ⟨~*s* of a room⟩ **2** : subject matter or topics treated (as in a book) **3** : material (as text or music) offered by a website **4** : MEANING, SIGNIFICANCE **5** : the amount of material contained

**con-tent-ed** \kən-'ten-təd\ *adj* : SATISFIED — **con-tent-ed-ly** *adv* — **con-tent-ed-ness** *n*

**con-ten-tion** \kən-'ten-chən\ *n* **1** : CONTEST, STRIFE **2** : an idea or point for which a person argues — **con-ten-tious** \-chəs\ *adj* — **con-ten-tious-ly** *adv*

**con-tent-ment** \kən-'tent-mənt\ *n* : ease of mind : SATISFACTION

**con-ter-mi-nous** \kän-'tər-mə-nəs\ *adj* : having the same or a common boundary — **con-ter-mi-nous-ly** *adv*

¹**con·test** \kən-'test\ vb **1** : to engage in a struggle or competition : COMPETE, VIE **2** : CHALLENGE, DISPUTE ⟨∼ the accusations⟩ — **con·tes·tant** \-'tes-tənt\ n
²**con·test** \'kän-,test\ n : STRUGGLE, COMPETITION

**con·text** \'kän-,tekst\ n [ME, fr. L contextus connection of words, coherence, fr. contexere to weave together] : the parts of a discourse that surround a word or passage and help to explain its meaning; also : the circumstances surrounding an act or event ⟨the ∼ of the war⟩ — **con·tex·tu·al·ly** adv

**con·tig·u·ous** \kən-'ti-gyə-wəs\ adj : being in contact : TOUCHING ⟨the 48 ∼ states⟩; also : NEXT, ADJOINING — **con·ti·gu·i·ty** \,kän-tə-'gyü-ə-tē\ n

**con·ti·nence** \'kän-tə-nəns\ n **1** : SELF-RESTRAINT, esp : a refraining from sexual intercourse **2** : the ability to retain urine or feces voluntarily

¹**con·ti·nent** \'kän-tə-nənt\ adj : exercising continence
²**continent** n **1** : any of the great divisions of land on the globe **2** cap : the continent of Europe

¹**con·ti·nen·tal** \,kän-tə-'nen-t³l\ adj **1** : of or relating to a continent; esp, often cap : of or relating to the continent of Europe **2** often cap : of or relating to the colonies later forming the U.S. **3** : of or relating to cuisine based on classical European cooking
²**continental** n **1** often cap : a soldier in the Continental army **2** : EUROPEAN

**continental drift** n : a slow movement of the continents over a fluid layer deep within the earth

**continental shelf** n : a shallow submarine plain forming a border to a continent

**continental slope** n : a comparatively steep slope from a continental shelf to the ocean floor

**con·tin·gen·cy** \kən-'tin-jən-sē\ n, pl **-cies** : a chance or possible event

¹**con·tin·gent** \-jənt\ adj **1** : liable but not certain to happen : POSSIBLE **2** : happening by chance : not planned **3** : dependent on something that may or may not occur **4** : CONDITIONAL ♦ **Synonyms** ACCIDENTAL, CASUAL, INCIDENTAL, ODD
²**contingent** n : a quota (as of troops) supplied from an area or group

**con·tin·u·al** \kən-'tin-yə-wəl\ adj **1** : CONTINUOUS, UNBROKEN **2** : steadily recurring — **con·tin·u·al·ly** adv

**con·tin·u·ance** \-yə-wəns\ n **1** : unbroken succession **2** : the extent of continuing : DURATION **3** : adjournment of legal proceedings

**con·tin·u·a·tion** \kən-,tin-yə-'wā-shən\ n **1** : extension or prolongation of a state or activity **2** : resumption after an interruption; also : something that carries on after a pause or break

**con·tin·ue** \kən-'tin-yü\ vb **-tin·ued; -tin·u·ing 1** : to maintain without interruption **2** : ENDURE, LAST ⟨the tradition ∼s⟩ **3** : to remain in a place or condition ⟨∼ at this job⟩ **4** : to resume (as a story)

after an intermission **5** : EXTEND ⟨∼ a subscription⟩; also : to persist in ⟨will ∼ to remind you⟩ **6** : to allow to remain **7** : to keep (a legal case) on the calendar or undecided

**con·ti·nu·i·ty** \,kän-tə-'nü-ə-tē, -'nyü-\ n, pl **-ties 1** : the state of being continuous **2** : something (as a film script) that has or provides continuity

**con·tin·u·ous** \kən-'tin-yə-wəs\ adj : continuing without interruption — **con·tin·u·ous·ly** adv

**con·tin·u·um** \-yə-wəm\ n, pl **-ua** \-yə-wə\ also **-u·ums** : something that is the same throughout or consists of a series of variations or of a sequence of things in regular order

**con·tort** \kən-'tort\ vb : to twist out of shape ⟨a ∼ed face⟩ ⟨∼ the truth⟩ — **con·tor·tion** \-'tor-shən\ n

**con·tor·tion·ist** \-'tor-shə-nist\ n : an acrobat able to twist the body into unusual postures

**con·tour** \'kän-,tür\ n [F, fr. It contorno fr. contornare to round off, fr. ML, to turn around, fr. L com- together + tornare to turn on a lathe, fr. tornus lathe] **1** : OUTLINE **2** : SHAPE, FORM — often used in pl. ⟨the ∼s of a statue⟩

**contr** abbr contract; contraction

**con·tra·band** \'kän-trə-,band\ n : goods legally prohibited in trade; also : smuggled goods

**con·tra·cep·tion** \,kän-trə-'sep-shən\ n : intentional prevention of conception and pregnancy — **con·tra·cep·tive** \-'sep-tiv\ adj or n

¹**con·tract** \'kän-,trakt\ n **1** : a binding agreement; also : a document stating its terms **2** : an undertaking to win a specified number of tricks in bridge — **contract** adj — **con·trac·tu·al** \kən-'trak-chə-wəl\ adj — **con·trac·tu·al·ly** adv

²**con·tract** \kən-'trakt, 2 usu 'kän-,trakt\ vb **1** : to become affected with ⟨∼ a disease⟩ **2** : to establish or undertake by contract **3** : SHRINK, LESSEN; esp : to draw together esp. so as to shorten ⟨∼ a muscle⟩ **4** : to shorten (a word) by omitting letters or sounds in the middle — **con·tract·ible** \kən-'trak-tə-bəl, 'kän-,\ adj — **con·trac·tion** \kən-'trak-shən\ n — **con·trac·tor** \'kän-,trak-tər, kən-'trak-\ n

**con·trac·tile** \kən-'trak-t³l\ adj : able to contract — **con·trac·til·i·ty** \,kän-,trak-'ti-lə-tē\ n

**con·tra·dict** \,kän-trə-'dikt\ vb : to assert the contrary of : deny the truth of ⟨∼ a rumor⟩ — **con·tra·dic·tion** \-'dik-shən\ n — **con·tra·dic·to·ry** \-'dik-tə-rē\ adj

**con·tra·dis·tinc·tion** \,kän-trə-dis-'tiŋk-shən\ n : distinction by contrast

**con·trail** \'kän-,trāl\ n : a streak of condensed water vapor created by an airplane or rocket at high altitudes

**con·tra·in·di·cate** \,kän-trə-'in-də-,kāt\ vb : to make (a treatment or procedure) inadvisable — **con·tra·in·di·ca·tion** \-,in-də-'kā-shən\ n

**con·tral·to** \kən-'tral-tō\ n, pl **-tos** : the

lowest female voice; *also* : a singer having such a voice

**con·trap·tion** \kən-'trap-shən\ *n* : CONTRIVANCE, DEVICE

**con·tra·pun·tal** \ˌkän-trə-'pən-tᵊl\ *adj* : of or relating to counterpoint

**con·tra·ri·ety** \ˌkän-trə-'rī-ə-tē\ *n, pl* **-eties** : the state of being contrary : DISAGREEMENT, INCONSISTENCY

**con·trari·wise** \'kän-ˌtrer-ē-ˌwīz, kən-'trer-\ *adv* **1** : on the contrary **2** : VICE VERSA

**con·trary** \'kän-ˌtrer-ē; *4 often* kən-'trer-ē\ *adj* **1** : opposite in nature or position **2** : COUNTER, OPPOSED **3** : UNFAVORABLE — used of wind or weather **4** : unwilling to accept control or advice — **con·trar·i·an** \kən-'trer-ē-ən, kän-\ *n or adj* — **con·trari·ly** \'kän-ˌtrer-ə-lē, kən-'trer-\ *adv* — **con·trary** \*n is* 'kän-ˌtrer-ē, *adv is like adj*\ *n or adv*

¹**con·trast** \kən-'trast\ *vb* [F *contraster*, fr. MF, to oppose, resist, fr. VL *contrastare*, fr. L *contra-* against + *stare* to stand] **1** : to show differences when compared **2** : to compare in such a way as to show differences

²**con·trast** \'kän-ˌtrast\ *n* **1** : diversity of adjacent parts in color, emotion, tone, or brightness ⟨the ∼ of a photograph⟩ **2** : unlikeness as shown when things are compared : DIFFERENCE

**con·tra·vene** \ˌkän-trə-'vēn\ *vb* **-vened; -ven·ing 1** : to go or act contrary to ⟨∼ a law⟩ **2** : CONTRADICT ⟨∼ a claim⟩

**con·tre·temps** \'kän-trə-ˌtäⁿ, kōⁿ-trə-'täⁿ\ *n, pl* **con·tre·temps** \-ˌtäⁿ, -ˌtäⁿz\ [F] : an inopportune or embarrassing occurrence

**contrib** *abbr* contribution; contributor

**con·trib·ute** \kən-'tri-byət\ *vb* **-ut·ed; -ut·ing** : to give along with others (as to a fund); *also* : HELP, ASSIST — **con·tri·bu·tion** \ˌkän-trə-'byü-shən\ *n* — **con·trib·u·tor** \kən-'tri-byə-tər\ *n* — **con·trib·u·to·ry** \-byə-ˌtȯr-ē\ *adj*

**con·trite** \'kän-ˌtrīt, kən-'trīt\ *adj* : PENITENT, REPENTANT — **con·trite·ly** *adv* — **con·tri·tion** \kən-'tri-shən\ *n*

**con·triv·ance** \kən-'trī-vəns\ *n* **1** : a mechanical device **2** : SCHEME, PLAN

**con·trive** \kən-'trīv\ *vb* **con·trived; con·triv·ing 1** : PLAN, DEVISE **2** : FRAME, MAKE **3** : to bring about with difficulty — **con·triv·er** *n*

**con·trived** \-'trīvd\ *adj* : lacking in natural quality ⟨a ∼ plot⟩

¹**con·trol** \kən-'trōl\ *vb* **con·trolled; con·trol·ling** [ME *controllen* to verify, fr. AF *countrerouler*, fr. *countrereule* copy of an account, audit, fr. ML *contrarotulus*, fr. L *contra* against + ML *rotulus* roll] **1** : to exercise restraining or directing influence over : REGULATE **2** : DOMINATE, RULE — **con·trol·la·ble** \-'trō-lə-bəl\ *adj*

²**control** *n* **1** : power to direct or regulate **2** : RESERVE, RESTRAINT **3** : a device for regulating a mechanism

**con·trol·ler** \kən-'trō-lər, 'kän-ˌtrō-lər\ *n* **1** : COMPTROLLER **2** : a person or thing that controls ⟨an air traffic ∼⟩ ⟨a game ∼⟩

**con·tro·ver·sy** \'kän-trə-ˌvər-sē\ *n, pl* **-sies** : a clash of opposing views : DISPUTE — **con·tro·ver·sial** \ˌkän-trə-ˌvər-shəl, -sē-əl\ *adj*

**con·tro·vert** \'kän-trə-ˌvərt, ˌkän-trə-'vərt\ *vb* : DENY, CONTRADICT ⟨∼ an allegation⟩ — **con·tro·vert·ible** *adj*

**con·tu·ma·cious** \ˌkän-tü-'mā-shəs, -tyü-\ *adj* : stubbornly disobedient
♦ *Synonyms* REBELLIOUS, INSUBORDINATE, SEDITIOUS — **con·tu·ma·cy** \kən-'tü-mə-sē, -'tyü-; 'kän-tyə-\ *n* — **con·tu·ma·cious·ly** *adv*

**con·tu·me·ly** \kən-'tü-mə-lē, -'tyü-; 'kän-tə-ˌmē-lē, -tyə-\ *n, pl* **-lies** : contemptuous treatment : INSULT

**con·tu·sion** \kən-'tü-zhən, -'tyü-\ *n* : BRUISE — **con·tuse** \-'tüz, -'tyüz\ *vb*

**co·nun·drum** \kə-'nən-drəm\ *n* : RIDDLE

**conv** *abbr* **1** convention **2** convertible

**con·va·lesce** \ˌkän-və-'les\ *vb* **-lesced; -lesc·ing** : to recover health gradually — **con·va·les·cence** \-'le-sᵊns\ *n* — **con·va·les·cent** \-sᵊnt\ *adj or n*

**con·vec·tion** \kən-'vek-shən\ *n* : circulatory motion in a fluid due to warmer portions rising and cooler denser portions sinking; *also* : the transfer of heat by such motion — **con·vec·tion·al** \-shə-nəl\ *adj* — **con·vec·tive** \-'vek-tiv\ *adj*

**convection oven** *n* : an oven with a fan that circulates hot air uniformly and continuously around the food

**con·vene** \kən-'vēn\ *vb* **con·vened; con·ven·ing** : ASSEMBLE, MEET

**con·ve·nience** \kən-'vē-nyəns\ *n* **1** : SUITABLENESS **2** : a laborsaving device **3** : a suitable time ⟨at your ∼⟩ **4** : personal comfort : EASE

**convenience store** *n* : a small market that is open long hours

**con·ve·nient** \-nyənt\ *adj* **1** : suited to personal comfort or ease **2** : placed near at hand — **con·ve·nient·ly** *adv*

**con·vent** \'kän-vənt, -ˌvent\ *n* [ME *covent*, fr. AF, fr. ML *conventus*, fr. L, assembly, fr. *convenire* to come together] : a local community or house of a religious order esp. of nuns — **con·ven·tu·al** \kän-'ven-chə-wəl\ *adj*

**con·ven·ti·cle** \kən-'ven-ti-kəl\ *n* : MEETING; *esp* : a secret meeting for worship

**con·ven·tion** \kən-'ven-chən\ *n* **1** : an agreement esp. between states on a matter of common concern **2** : MEETING, ASSEMBLY **3** : an assembly of persons convened for some purpose **4** : generally accepted custom, practice, or belief

**con·ven·tion·al** \-chə-nəl\ *adj* **1** : sanctioned by general custom **2** : COMMONPLACE, ORDINARY — **con·ven·tion·al·i·ty** \-ˌven-chə-'na-lə-tē\ *n* — **con·ven·tion·al·ize** \-'ven-chə-nə-ˌlīz\ *vb* — **con·ven·tion·al·ly** *adv*

**con·verge** \kən-'vərj\ *vb* **con·verged; con·verg·ing** : to approach one common center or single point ⟨*converging* paths⟩ — **con·ver·gence** \kən-'vər-jəns\ *n* — **con·ver·gent** \-jənt\ *adj*

**con·ver·sant** \kən-'vər-sᵊnt\ *adj* : having knowledge and experience — used with *with*

**con·ver·sa·tion** \ˌkän-vər-ˈsā-shən\ *n* : an informal talking together — **con·ver·sa·tion·al** \-shə-nᵊl\ *adj* — **con·ver·sa·tion·al·ly** *adv*

**con·ver·sa·tion·al·ist** \-shə-nᵊl-ist\ *n* : a person who converses a great deal or who excels in conversation

¹**con·verse** \ˈkän-ˌvərs\ *n* : CONVERSATION

²**con·verse** \kən-ˈvərs\ *vb* **con·versed; con·vers·ing** : to engage in conversation

³**con·verse** \ˈkän-ˌvərs\ *n* : a statement related to another statement by having its hypothesis and conclusion or its subject and predicate reversed or interchanged

⁴**con·verse** \-ˈvərs, ˈkän-ˌvərs\ *adj* : reversed in order or relation — **con·verse·ly** *adv*

**con·ver·sion** \kən-ˈvər-zhən\ *n*   1 : a change in nature or form   2 : an experience associated with a decisive adoption of religion

¹**con·vert** \kən-ˈvərt\ *vb*   1 : to turn from one belief or party to another   2 : TRANSFORM, CHANGE   3 : MISAPPROPRIATE   4 : EXCHANGE — **con·vert·er** *or* **con·ver·tor** \-ˈvər-tər\ *n*

²**con·vert** \ˈkän-ˌvərt\ *n* : a person who has undergone religious conversion

¹**con·vert·ible** \kən-ˈvər-tə-bəl\ *adj* : capable of being converted

²**convertible** *n* : an automobile with a top that may be lowered or removed

**con·vex** \kän-ˈveks, ˈkän-ˌveks\ *adj* : curved or rounded outward like the exterior of a sphere or circle — **con·vex·i·ty** \ˈvek-sə-tē\ *n*

**con·vey** \kən-ˈvā\ *vb*   1 : CARRY, TRANSPORT ⟨a river ⁓ing logs⟩   2 : TRANSFER, COMMUNICATE ⟨⁓ a message⟩ — **con·vey·or** *also* **con·vey·er** \-ər\ *n*

**con·vey·ance** \-ˈvā-əns\ *n*   1 : the act of conveying   2 : a legal paper transferring ownership of property   3 : VEHICLE

¹**con·vict** \kən-ˈvikt\ *vb* : to prove or find guilty

²**con·vict** \ˈkän-ˌvikt\ *n* : a person serving a prison sentence

**con·vic·tion** \kən-ˈvik-shən\ *n*   1 : the act of convicting esp. in a court   2 : the state of being convinced : BELIEF

**con·vince** \kən-ˈvins\ *vb* **con·vinced; con·vinc·ing** : to bring (as by argument) to belief or action — **con·vinc·ing** *adj* — **con·vinc·ing·ly** *adv*

**con·viv·ial** \kən-ˈviv-yəl, -ˈvi-vē-əl\ *adj* [LL convivialis, fr. L convivium banquet, fr. com- together + vivere to live] : enjoying companionship and the pleasures of feasting and drinking : JOVIAL, FESTIVE ⟨a ⁓ gathering⟩ — **con·viv·i·al·i·ty** \-ˌvi-vē-ˈa-lə-tē\ *n* — **con·viv·ial·ly** *adv*

**con·vo·ca·tion** \ˌkän-və-ˈkā-shən\ *n*   1 : a ceremonial assembly (as of the clergy)   2 : the act of convoking

**con·voke** \kən-ˈvōk\ *vb* **con·voked; con·vok·ing** : to call together to a meeting ⟨convoked a meeting of the delegates⟩

**con·vo·lut·ed** \ˈkän-və-ˌlü-təd\ *adj*   1 : folded in curved or tortuous windings   2 : INVOLVED, INTRICATE ⟨⁓ logic⟩

**con·vo·lu·tion** \ˌkän-və-ˈlü-shən\ *n* : a tortuous or winding structure; *esp* : one of the ridges of the brain

¹**con·voy** \ˈkän-ˌvȯi, kən-ˈvȯi\ *vb* : to accompany for protection

²**con·voy** \ˈkän-ˌvȯi\ *n*   1 : one that convoys; *esp* : a protective escort (as for ships)   2 : the act of convoying   3 : a group of moving vehicles

**con·vulse** \kən-ˈvəls\ *vb* **con·vulsed; con·vuls·ing** : to agitate violently

**con·vul·sion** \kən-ˈvəl-shən\ *n*   1 : an abnormal and violent involuntary contraction or series of contractions of muscle   2 : a violent disturbance — **con·vul·sive** \-siv\ *adj* — **con·vul·sive·ly** *adv*

**cony** *var of* CONEY

**coo** \ˈkü\ *n* : a soft low sound made by doves or pigeons; *also* : a sound like this — **coo** *vb*

**COO** *abbr* chief operating officer

¹**cook** \ˈkuk\ *n* : a person who prepares food for eating

²**cook** *vb*   1 : to prepare food for eating   2 : to subject to heat or fire   3 : CONCOCT, FABRICATE — usu. used with *up* ⟨⁓ up a scheme⟩ — **cook·er** *n* — **cook·ware** \-ˌwer\ *n*

**cook·book** \-ˌbuk\ *n* : a book of cooking directions and recipes

**cook·ery** \ˈku-kə-rē\ *n, pl* **-er·ies** : the art or practice of cooking

**cook·ie** *or* **cooky** \ˈku-kē\ *n, pl* **cook·ies** [D koekje, dim. of koek cake]   1 : a small sweet flat cake   2 cookie : a file containing information about a website user created and read by a website server and stored on the user's computer

**cookie–cutter** *adj* : marked by a lack of originality or distinction ⟨⁓ malls⟩

**cook·out** \ˈkuk-ˌaut\ *n* : an outing at which a meal is cooked and served in the open

¹**cool** \ˈkül\ *adj*   1 : moderately cold   2 : not excited : CALM   3 : not friendly   4 : IMPUDENT   5 : protecting from heat   6 *slang* : very good   7 *slang* : FASHIONABLE

♦ **Synonyms** UNFLAPPABLE, COMPOSED, COLLECTED, UNRUFFLED, NONCHALANT — **cool·ly** *adv* — **cool·ness** *n*

²**cool** *vb* : to make or become cool

³**cool** *n*   1 : a cool time or place   2 : INDIFFERENCE; *also* : SELF-ASSURANCE, COMPOSURE ⟨kept his ⁓⟩

**cool·ant** \ˈkü-lənt\ *n* : a usu. fluid cooling agent

**cool·er** \ˈkü-lər\ *n*   1 : a container for keeping food or drink cool   2 : JAIL, PRISON   3 : a tall iced drink

**coo·lie** \ˈkü-lē\ *n* [Hindi & Urdu qulī] : an unskilled laborer usu. in or from the Far East

**coon** \ˈkün\ *n* : RACCOON

**coon·hound** \-ˌhaund\ *n* : a sporting dog trained to hunt raccoons

**coon·skin** \-ˌskin\ *n* : the pelt of a raccoon; *also* : something (as a cap) made of this

¹**coop** \ˈküp, ˈkup\ *n* : a small enclosure or building usu. for poultry

²**coop** *vb* : to confine in or as if in a coop — usu. used with *up*

**co-op** \ˈkō-ˌäp\ *n* : COOPERATIVE

**coo·per** \'kü-pər, 'kú-\ n : one who makes or repairs barrels or casks — **cooper** vb — **coo·per·age** \-pə-rij\ n

**co·op·er·ate** \kō-'ä-pə-ˌrāt\ vb : to act jointly or in compliance with others — **co·op·er·a·tion** \-ˌä-pə-'rā-shən\ n — **co·op·er·a·tor** \-'ä-pə-ˌrā-tər\ n

¹**co·op·er·a·tive** \kō-'ä-prə-tiv, -'ä-pə-ˌrā-\ adj **1** : willing to work with others **2** : of or relating to an association formed to enable its members to buy or sell to better advantage by eliminating middlemen's profits

²**cooperative** n : a cooperative association

**co–opt** \kō-'äpt\ vb **1** : to choose or elect as a colleague **2** : ABSORB, ASSIMILATE; also : TAKE OVER ⟨a style ∼ed by advertisers⟩

¹**co·or·di·nate** \kō-'òr-də-nət\ adj **1** : equal in rank or order **2** : of equal rank in a compound sentence ⟨∼ clause⟩ **3** : joining words or word groups of the same rank — **co·or·di·nate·ly** adv

²**co·or·di·nate** \-'òr-də-ˌnāt\ vb **-nat·ed; -nat·ing 1** : to make or become coordinate ⟨∼ our schedules⟩ **2** : to work or act together harmoniously ⟨a coordinated wardrobe⟩ — **co·or·di·na·tion** \-ˌòr-də-'nā-shən\ n — **co·or·di·na·tor** \-'òr-də-ˌnā-tər\ n

³**co·or·di·nate** \-'òr-də-nət\ n **1** : one of a set of numbers used in specifying the location of a point on a surface or in space **2** pl : articles (as of clothing) designed to be used together and to attain their effect through pleasing contrast

**coot** \'küt\ n **1** : a dark-colored ducklike bird related to the rails **2** : any of several No. American sea ducks **3** : a harmless simple person

**coo·tie** \'kü-tē\ n : a body louse

¹**cop** \'käp\ n : POLICE OFFICER

²**cop** vb **1** slang : STEAL ⟨∼ a glance⟩ **2** slang : ADMIT — used with to ⟨∼ to the charges⟩ **3** : ADOPT ⟨∼ an attitude⟩

**co–pay** \'kō-ˌpā\ n : CO-PAYMENT

**co–pay·ment** \'kō-ˌpā-mənt, ˌkō-'\ n : a fixed fee required of a patient by a health insurer (as an HMO) at the time of each outpatient service or filling of a prescription

¹**cope** \'kōp\ n : a long cloaklike ecclesiastical vestment

²**cope** vb **coped; cop·ing** : to struggle to overcome problems or difficulties ⟨∼ with tragedy⟩

**co·per·nic·i·um** \ˌkō-pər-'ni-sē-əm\ n [NL, fr. Nikolaus Copernicus] : a short-lived artificially produced radioactive element

**cop·i·er** \'kä-pē-ər\ n : one that copies; esp : a machine for making copies

**co·pi·lot** \'kō-ˌpī-lət\ n : an assistant pilot of an aircraft or spacecraft

**cop·ing** \'kō-piŋ\ n : the top layer of a wall

**co·pi·ous** \'kō-pē-əs\ adj : LAVISH, ABUNDANT ⟨a ∼ harvest⟩ — **co·pi·ous·ly** adv — **co·pi·ous·ness** n

**cop–out** \'käp-ˌaút\ n : an excuse for copping out; also : an act of copping out

**cop out** vb : to back out (as of an unwanted responsibility)

**cop·per** \'kä-pər\ n **1** : a malleable reddish metallic element that is one of the best conductors of heat and electricity **2** : a coin or token made of copper — **cop·pery** adj

**cop·per·head** \'kä-pər-ˌhed\ n : a largely coppery brown pit viper esp. of the eastern and central U.S.

**cop·pice** \'kä-pəs\ n : THICKET

**co·pra** \'kō-prə\ n : dried coconut meat yielding coconut oil

**copse** \'käps\ n : THICKET

**cop·ter** \'käp-tər\ n : HELICOPTER

**cop·u·la** \'kä-pyə-lə\ n : LINKING VERB — **cop·u·la·tive** \-lə-tiv, -ˌlā-\ adj

**cop·u·late** \'kä-pyə-ˌlāt\ vb **-lat·ed; -lat·ing** : to engage in sexual intercourse — **cop·u·la·tion** \ˌkä-pyə-'lā-shən\ n — **cop·u·la·to·ry** \'kä-pyə-lə-ˌtòr-ē\ adj

¹**copy** \'kä-pē\ n, pl **cop·ies 1** : an imitation or reproduction of an original work **2** : material to be set in type **3** : DUPLICATE ♦ Synonyms DUPLICATE, REPRODUCTION, FACSIMILE, REPLICA

²**copy** vb **cop·ied; copy·ing 1** : to make a copy of **2** : IMITATE — **copy·ist** n

**copy·book** \'kä-pē-ˌbùk\ n : a book formerly used to teach handwriting containing examples to be copied

**copy·boy** \-ˌbòi\ n : a person who carries copy and runs errands (as in a newspaper office)

**copy·cat** \-ˌkat\ n : a slavish imitator

**copy·desk** \-ˌdesk\ n : the desk at which newspaper copy is edited

**copy editor** n : one who edits or prepares copy (as headlines) esp. for a newspaper

**copy·read·er** \-ˌrē-dər\ n : COPY EDITOR

¹**copy·right** \-ˌrīt\ n : the sole right to reproduce, publish, sell, or distribute a literary or artistic work

²**copyright** vb : to secure a copyright on

**copy·writ·er** \'kä-pē-ˌrī-tər\ n : a writer of advertising copy

**co·quet** or **co·quette** \kō-'ket\ vb **co·quet·ted; co·quet·ting** : FLIRT — **co·quet·ry** \'kō-kə-trē, kō-'ke-trē\ n

**co·quette** \kō-'ket\ n [F, fem. of coquet, flirtatious man, dim. of coq cock] : FLIRT — **co·quett·ish** adj

**cor** abbr corner

**Cor** abbr Corinthians

**cor·a·cle** \'kòr-ə-kəl\ n [W corwgl] : a boat made of a frame covered usu. with hide or tarpaulin

**cor·al** \'kòr-əl\ n **1** : a stony or horny material that forms the skeleton of colonies of tiny sea polyps and includes a red form used in jewelry; also : a coral-forming polyp or polyp colony **2** : a deep pink color — **coral** adj

**coral snake** n : any of several venomous chiefly tropical New World snakes brilliantly banded in red, black, and yellow or white

**cor·bel** \'kòr-bəl\ n : a bracket-shaped architectural member that projects from a wall and supports a weight

¹**cord** \'kòrd\ n **1** : a usu. heavy string consisting of several strands woven or twisted together **2** : a long slender anatomical structure (as a tendon or nerve) **3** : a

small flexible insulated electrical cable used to connect an appliance with a receptacle **4** : a cubic measure used esp. for firewood and equal to a stack 4×4×8 feet **5** : a rib or ridge on cloth

²**cord** vb **1** : to tie or furnish with a cord **2** : to pile (wood) in cords

**cord·age** \'kȯr-dij\ n : ROPES, CORDS; esp : ropes in the rigging of a ship

¹**cor·dial** \'kȯr-jəl\ adj [ME, fr. ML cordialis, fr. L cord-, cor heart] : warmly receptive or welcoming : HEARTFELT, HEARTY — **cor·di·al·i·ty** \ˌkȯr-jē-'a-lə-tē, kȯr-'ja-\ n — **cor·dial·ly** adv

²**cordial** n **1** : a stimulating medicine or drink **2** : LIQUEUR

**cor·dil·le·ra** \ˌkȯr-dəl-'yer-ə, -də-'ler-\ n [Sp] : a series of parallel mountain ranges

**cord·less** \'kȯrd-ləs\ adj : having no cord; esp : powered by a battery ⟨a ~ phone⟩ — **cordless** n

**cór·do·ba** \'kȯr-də-bə, -və\ n — see MONEY table

**cor·don** \'kȯr-d³n\ n **1** : an ornamental cord or ribbon **2** : an encircling line (as of troops or police) — **cordon** vb

**cor·do·van** \'kȯr-də-vən\ n : a soft fine-grained leather

**cor·du·roy** \'kȯr-də-ˌrȯi\ n, pl **-roys** : a heavy ribbed fabric; also, pl : pants of this material

**cord·wain·er** \'kȯrd-ˌwā-nər\ n : SHOEMAKER

¹**core** \'kȯr\ n **1** : the central usu. inedible part of some fruits (as the apple); also : an inmost part of something **2** : GIST, ESSENCE

²**core** vb **cored; cor·ing** : to take out the core of — **cor·er** n

**CORE** \'kȯr\ abbr Congress of Racial Equality

**co·re·op·sis** \ˌkȯr-ē-'äp-səs\ n, pl **coreopsis** : any of a genus of widely cultivated composite herbs with showy often yellow flower heads

**co·re·spon·dent** \ˌkō-ri-'spän-dənt\ n : a person named as guilty of adultery with the defendant in a divorce suit

**co·ri·an·der** \'kȯr-ē-ˌan-dər\ n : an herb related to the carrot; also : its aromatic dried fruit used as a flavoring

**Cor·in·thi·ans** \kə-'rin-thē-ənz\ n — see BIBLE table

¹**cork** \'kȯrk\ n **1** : the tough elastic bark of a European oak (**cork oak**) used esp. for stoppers and insulation; also : a stopper of this **2** : a tissue of a woody plant making up most of the bark — **corky** adj

²**cork** vb : to furnish with or stop up with cork or a cork ⟨~ a bottle⟩

**cork·screw** \'kȯrk-ˌskrü\ n : a device for drawing corks from bottles

**corm** \'kȯrm\ n : a solid bulblike underground part of a stem (as of the crocus or gladiolus)

**cor·mo·rant** \'kȯr-mə-rənt, -ˌrant\ n [ME cormeraunt, fr. MF cormorant, fr. OF cormareng, fr. corp raven + marenc of the sea, fr. L marinus] : any of various dark-colored water birds with a long neck, hooked bill, and distensible throat pouch

¹**corn** \'kȯrn\ n **1** Brit : the seeds of a cereal grass and esp. of the chief cereal crop of a region (as wheat in Britain); also : a cereal grass **2 a** : a tall widely cultivated cereal grass grown for its large ears of starchy seeds **b** : the typically yellow or whitish seeds of corn used esp. as a food **c** : an ear of corn

²**corn** vb : to salt (as beef) in brine and preservatives

³**corn** n : a local hardening and thickening of skin (as on a toe)

¹**corn·ball** \'kȯrn-ˌbȯl\ n : an unsophisticated person; also : something corny

²**cornball** adj : CORNY ⟨~ humor⟩

**corn bread** n : bread made with cornmeal

**corn·cob** \-ˌkäb\ n : the woody core on which the kernels of corn are arranged

**corn·crib** \-ˌkrib\ n : a crib for storing ears of corn

**cor·nea** \'kȯr-nē-ə\ n : the transparent part of the coat of the eyeball covering the iris and the pupil — **cor·ne·al** adj

**corn ear·worm** \-'ir-ˌwərm\ n : a moth whose larva is destructive esp. to corn

¹**cor·ner** \'kȯr-nər\ n [ME, fr. AF cornere, fr. corne horn, corner, fr. L cornu horn, point] **1** : the point or angle formed by the meeting of lines, edges, or sides **2** : the place where two streets come together **3** : a quiet secluded place **4** : a position from which retreat or escape is impossible **5** : control of enough of the available supply (as of a commodity) to permit manipulation of the price — **cornered** adj — **around the corner** : IMMINENT ⟨has a birthday just around the corner⟩

²**cor·ner** vb **1** : to drive into a corner **2** : to get a corner on ⟨~ the wheat market⟩ **3** : to turn a corner

**cor·ner·stone** \'kȯr-nər-ˌstōn\ n **1** : a stone forming part of a corner in a wall; esp : such a stone laid at a formal ceremony **2** : something of basic importance

**cor·net** \kȯr-'net\ n : a brass band instrument resembling the trumpet

**corn flour** n, Brit : CORNSTARCH

**corn·flow·er** \'kȯrn-ˌflau̇(-ə)r\ n : BACHELOR'S BUTTON

**cor·nice** \'kȯr-nəs\ n : the horizontal projecting part crowning the wall of a building

**corn·meal** \'kȯrn-ˌmēl\ n : meal ground from corn

**corn·row** \-ˌrō\ n : a section of hair braided flat to the scalp in rows — **cornrow** vb

**corn·stalk** \-ˌstȯk\ n : a stalk of corn

**corn·starch** \-ˌstärch\ n : a starch made from corn and used in cookery as a thickening agent

**corn syrup** n : a sweet syrup obtained from cornstarch

**cor·nu·co·pia** \ˌkȯr-nə-'kō-pē-ə, -nyə-\ n [LL, fr. L cornu copiae horn of plenty] **1** : a horn-shaped container filled with fruits and grain emblematic of abundance **2** : ABUNDANCE

**corny** \'kȯr-nē\ adj **corn·i·er; -est** : tiresomely simple or sentimental

**co·rol·la** \kə-'rä-lə, -'rō-\ n : the petals of a flower

**cor·ol·lary** \'kòr-ə-ˌler-ē\ *n, pl* **-lar·ies** **1** : a deduction from a proposition proved true **2** : CONSEQUENCE, RESULT

**co·ro·na** \kə-'rō-nə\ *n* **1** : a colored circle often seen around and close to a luminous body (as the sun or moon) **2** : the outermost part of the atmosphere of a star (as the sun) — **co·ro·nal** \'kòr-ə-nˀl, kə-'rō-\ *adj*

**cor·o·nal** \'kòr-ə-nˀl\ *n* : a circlet for the head

**¹cor·o·nary** \'kòr-ə-ˌner-ē\ *adj* : of or relating to the heart or its blood vessels

**²coronary** *n, pl* **-nar·ies** **1** : a coronary blood vessel **2** : CORONARY THROMBOSIS; *also* : HEART ATTACK

**coronary thrombosis** *n* : the blocking by a thrombus of one of the arteries supplying the heart tissues

**cor·o·na·tion** \ˌkòr-ə-'nā-shən\ *n* : the act or ceremony of crowning a monarch

**cor·o·ner** \'kòr-ə-nər\ *n* [ME, an officer of the crown, fr. AF, fr. *corone* crown, fr. L *corona*] : a public official who investigates causes of deaths possibly not due to natural causes

**cor·o·net** \ˌkòr-ə-'net\ *n* **1** : a small crown **2** : an ornamental band worn around the temples

**corp** *abbr* **1** corporal **2** corporation

**¹cor·po·ral** \'kòr-p(ə-)rəl\ *adj* : of or relating to the body ⟨∼ punishment⟩

**²corporal** *n* : a noncommissioned officer (as in the army) ranking next below a sergeant

**cor·po·rate** \'kòr-p(ə-)rət\ *adj* **1** : INCORPORATED; also : belonging to an incorporated body **2** : of or relating to large-scale business ⟨∼ mergers⟩ **3** : combined into one body

**cor·po·ra·tion** \ˌkòr-pə-'rā-shən\ *n* **1** : the municipal authorities of a town or city **2** : a legal creation authorized to act with the rights and liabilities of a person; *also* : COMPANY

**cor·po·rat·ize** \'kòr-pə-rə-ˌtīz\ *vb* **-ized; -iz·ing** : to subject to corporate control ⟨∼ education⟩

**cor·po·re·al** \kòr-'pòr-ē-əl\ *adj* **1** : PHYSICAL, MATERIAL **2** *archaic* : BODILY — **cor·po·re·al·i·ty** \ˌkòr-ˌpòr-ē-'a-lə-tē\ *n* — **cor·po·re·al·ly** *adv*

**corps** \'kòr\ *n, pl* **corps** \'kòrz\ [F, fr. OF *cors*, fr. L *corpus* body] **1** : an organized subdivision of a country's military forces **2** : a group acting under common direction

**corpse** \'kòrps\ *n* : a dead body

**corps·man** \'kòr-mən, 'kòrz-\ *n* : an enlisted person trained to give first aid

**cor·pu·lence** \'kòr-pyə-ləns\ *n* : excessive fatness : OBESITY

**cor·pu·lent** \-lənt\ *adj* : OBESE

**cor·pus** \'kòr-pəs\ *n, pl* **cor·po·ra** \-pə-rə\ [ME, fr. L] **1** : BODY; *esp* : CORPSE **2** : a body of writings or works

**cor·pus·cle** \'kòr-pə-səl, -ˌpə-\ *n* **1** : a minute particle **2** : a living cell (as in blood or cartilage) not aggregated into continuous tissues — **cor·pus·cu·lar** \kòr-'pəs-kyə-lər\ *adj*

**cor·pus de·lic·ti** \ˌkòr-pəs-di-'lik-ˌtī, -tē\

*n, pl* **cor·po·ra de·lic·ti** [NL, lit., body of the crime] **1** : the substantial fact proving that a crime has been committed **2** : the body of a victim of murder

**corr** *abbr* **1** correct; corrected; correction **2** correspondence; correspondent; corresponding

**cor·ral** \kə-'ral\ *n* [Sp] : an enclosure for confining or capturing animals; *also* : an enclosure of wagons for defending a camp — **corral** *vb*

**¹cor·rect** \kə-'rekt\ *vb* **1** : REPROVE, CHASTISE ⟨∼ an error⟩ **2** : REPROVE, CHASTISE ⟨∼ed the child⟩ — **cor·rect·able** \-'rek-tə-bəl\ *adj* — **cor·rec·tion** \-'rek-shən\ *n* — **cor·rec·tion·al** \-'rek-sh(ə-)nəl\ *adj* — **cor·rec·tive** \-'rek-tiv\ *adj*

**²correct** *adj* **1** : conforming to a conventional standard ⟨∼ behavior⟩ **2** : agreeing with fact or truth ⟨a ∼ answer⟩ **3** : conforming to the standards of a specific ideology ⟨environmentally ∼⟩ — **cor·rect·ly** *adv* — **cor·rect·ness** *n*

**cor·re·late** \'kòr-ə-ˌlāt\ *vb* **-lat·ed; -lat·ing** : to connect in a systematic way : establish the mutual relations of — **cor·re·late** \-lət, -ˌlāt\ *n* — **cor·re·la·tion** \ˌkòr-ə-'lā-shən\ *n*

**cor·rel·a·tive** \kə-'re-lə-tiv\ *adj* **1** : reciprocally related **2** : regularly used together (as *either* and *or*) — **correlative** *n* — **cor·rel·a·tive·ly** *adv*

**cor·re·spond** \ˌkòr-ə-'spänd\ *vb* **1** : to be in agreement : SUIT, MATCH **2** : to communicate by letter — **cor·re·spond·ing·ly** *adv*

**cor·re·spon·dence** \-'spän-dəns\ *n* **1** : agreement between particular things **2** : communication by letters; *also* : the letters exchanged

**¹cor·re·spon·dent** \-dənt\ *adj* **1** : SIMILAR **2** : FITTING, CONFORMING

**²correspondent** *n* **1** : something that corresponds **2** : a person with whom one communicates by letter **3** : a person employed to contribute news regularly from a place ⟨a war ∼⟩

**cor·ri·dor** \'kòr-ə-dər, -ˌdòr\ *n* **1** : a passageway into which compartments or rooms open (as in a hotel or school) **2** : a narrow strip of land esp. through foreign-held territory **3** : a densely populated strip of land including two or more major cities **4** : an area identified by a common characteristic or purpose ⟨a ∼ of liberalism⟩

**cor·ri·gen·dum** \ˌkòr-ə-'jen-dəm\ *n, pl* **-da** \-də\ [L] : an error in a printed work discovered after printing and shown with its correction on a separate sheet

**cor·ri·gi·ble** \'kòr-ə-jə-bəl\ *adj* : CORRECTABLE

**cor·rob·o·rate** \kə-'rä-bə-ˌrāt\ *vb* **-rat·ed; -rat·ing** [L *corroborare*, fr. *robur* strength] : to support with evidence : CONFIRM — **cor·rob·o·ra·tion** \-ˌrä-bə-'rā-shən\ *n* — **cor·rob·o·ra·tive** \-'rä-bə-ˌrā-tiv, -'rä-brə-\ *adj* — **cor·rob·o·ra·to·ry** \-'rä-bə-rə-ˌtòr-ē\ *adj*

**cor·rode** \kə-'rōd\ *vb* **cor·rod·ed; cor·rod·ing** : to wear or be worn away gradually (as by chemical action) — **cor·ro·**

**sion** \-'rō-zhən\ n — **cor·ro·sive** \-'rō-siv\ adj or n

**cor·ru·gate** \'kòr-ə-,gāt\ vb **-gat·ed; -gat·ing** : to form into wrinkles or ridges and grooves — **cor·ru·gat·ed** adj — **cor·ru·ga·tion** \,kòr-ə-'gā-shən\ n

¹**cor·rupt** \kə-'rəpt\ vb **1** : to make evil : DEPRAVE; esp : BRIBE **2** : ROT, SPOIL — **cor·rupt·ible** adj — **cor·rup·tion** \-'rəp-shən\ n

²**corrupt** adj : morally degenerate; also : characterized by improper conduct ⟨~ officials⟩

**cor·sage** \kòr-'säzh, -'säj\ n [F, bust, bodice, fr. OF, bust, fr. cors body, fr. L corpus] **1** : the waist or bodice of a dress **2** : a bouquet to be worn or carried

**cor·sair** \'kòr-,ser\ n : PIRATE

**cor·set** \'kòr-sət\ n : a stiffened undergarment worn for support or to give shape to the waist and hips

**cor·tege** also **cor·tège** \kòr-'tezh, 'kòr-,tezh\ n [F] : PROCESSION; esp : a funeral procession

**cor·tex** \'kòr-,teks\ n, pl **cor·ti·ces** \'kòr-tə-,sēz\ or **cor·tex·es** : an outer or covering layer of an organism or one of its parts ⟨the adrenal ~⟩ ⟨~ of a plant stem⟩; esp : CEREBRAL CORTEX — **cor·ti·cal** \'kòr-ti-kəl\ adj

**cor·ti·co·ste·roid** \,kòr-ti-kō-'stir-,òid, -'ster-\ n : any of various steroids made in the adrenal cortex and used medically as anti-inflammatory agents

**cor·ti·sone** \'kòr-tə-,sōn, -,zōn\ n : a corticosteroid used esp. in treating rheumatoid arthritis

**co·run·dum** \kə-'rən-dəm\ n : a very hard aluminum-containing mineral used as an abrasive or as a gem

**cor·us·cate** \'kòr-ə-,skāt\ vb **-cat·ed; -cat·ing** : FLASH, SPARKLE — **cor·us·ca·tion** \,kòr-ə-'skā-shən\ n

**cor·vette** \kòr-'vet\ n **1** : a naval sailing ship smaller than a frigate **2** : an armed escort ship smaller than a destroyer

**co·ry·za** \kə-'rī-zə\ n : an inflammatory disorder of the upper respiratory tract; esp : COMMON COLD

**cos** abbr cosine

**COS** abbr **1** cash on shipment **2** chief of staff

**co·sig·na·to·ry** \kō-'sig-nə-,tòr-ē\ n : a joint signer

**co·sign·er** \'kō-,sī-nər\ n : COSIGNATORY; esp : a joint signer of a promissory note

**co·sine** \'kō-,sīn\ n : the trigonometric function that is the ratio between the side next to an acute angle in a right triangle and the hypotenuse

¹**cos·met·ic** \käz-'me-tik\ adj [Gk kosmētikos skilled in adornment, fr. kosmein to arrange, adorn, fr. kosmos order, ornament, universe] **1** : intended to beautify the hair or complexion **2** : correcting physical defects esp. to improve appearance ⟨~ dentistry⟩ **3** : SUPERFICIAL ⟨~ changes⟩ — **cos·met·i·cal·ly** \-ti-k(ə-)lē\ adv

²**cosmetic** n : a cosmetic preparation

**cos·me·tol·o·gist** \,käz-mə-'tä-lə-jist\ n : one who gives beauty treatments — **cos·me·tol·o·gy** \-jē\ n

**cos·mic** \'käz-mik\ also **cos·mi·cal** \-mi-kəl\ adj **1** : of or relating to the cosmos **2** : VAST, GRAND **3** : of or relating to spiritual or metaphysical ideas ⟨a ~ thinker⟩ — **cos·mi·cal·ly** adv

**cosmic ray** n : a stream of very penetrating atomic nuclei that enter the earth's atmosphere from outer space

**cos·mog·o·ny** \käz-'mä-gə-nē\ n, pl **-nies** : the origin or creation of the world or universe

**cos·mol·o·gy** \-'mä-lə-jē\ n, pl **-gies** : a branch of astronomy dealing with the origin and structure of the universe — **cos·mo·log·i·cal** \,käz-mə-'lä-ji-kəl\ adj — **cos·mol·o·gist** \käz-'mä-lə-jist\ n

**cos·mo·naut** \'käz-mə-,nòt\ n : a Soviet or Russian astronaut

**cos·mo·pol·i·tan** \,käz-mə-'pä-lə-tən\ adj : belonging to all the world : not local ♦ Synonyms UNIVERSAL, GLOBAL, CATHOLIC — **cosmopolitan** n

**cos·mos** \'käz-məs, 1 also -,mōs, -,mäs\ n **2** : UNIVERSE **2** : a tall garden herb related to the daisies

**co·spon·sor** \'kō-,spän-sər, -'spän-\ n : a joint sponsor — **cosponsor** vb

**Cos·sack** \'kä-,sak, -sək\ n [Pol & Ukrainian kozak, of Turkic origin] : a member of one of several autonomous communities drawn from various ethnic groups in southern Russia; also : a mounted soldier from one of these communities

¹**cost** \'kòst\ n **1** : the amount paid or charged for something : PRICE **2** : the loss or penalty incurred in gaining something **3** pl : expenses incurred in a lawsuit — **at all costs** : regardless of consequences ⟨win at all costs⟩

²**cost** vb **cost; cost·ing 1** : to require a specified amount in payment **2** : to cause to pay, suffer, or lose

**co–star** \'kō-,stär\ n : one of two leading players in a motion picture or play — **co–star** vb

**cos·tive** \'käs-tiv\ adj : affected with or causing constipation

**cost·ly** \'kòst-lē\ adj **cost·li·er; -est 1** : of great cost or value ⟨~ gems⟩ **2** : done at great expense or sacrifice ⟨a ~ error⟩ ♦ Synonyms DEAR, VALUABLE, EXPENSIVE — **cost·li·ness** n

**cos·tume** \'käs-,tüm, -,tyüm\ n [F, fr. It, custom, dress, fr. L consuetudo custom] **1** : the style of attire characteristic of a period or country **2** : a special or fancy dress ⟨Halloween ~s⟩. — **cos·tum·er** \käs-,tü-mər, -,tyü-\ n

**costume jewelry** n : inexpensive jewelry

**cosy** chiefly Brit var of COZY

¹**cot** \'kät\ n : a small house : COTTAGE

²**cot** n : a small often collapsible bed

**cote** \'kōt, 'kät\ n : a small shed or coop (as for sheep or doves)

**co·te·rie** \'kō-tə-,rē, ,kō-tə-'rē\ n [F] : an intimate often exclusive group of persons with a common interest

**co·ter·mi·nous** \,kō-'tər-mə-nəs\ adj : having the same scope or duration

**co·til·lion** \kō-ˈtil-yən, kə-\ n : a formal ball

**cot·tage** \ˈkä-tij\ n : a small house — **cot·tag·er** n

**cottage cheese** n : a soft uncured cheese made from soured skim milk

**cot·tar** or **cot·ter** \ˈkä-tər\ n : a peasant or farm laborer occupying a cottage and often a small holding

**cotter pin** n : a metal strip bent into a pin whose ends can be spread apart after insertion through a hole or slot

**cot·ton** \ˈkä-t³n\ n [ME coton, fr. AF cotun, fr. Ar quṭun] 1 : a soft fibrous usu. white substance composed of hairs attached to the seeds of various tropical plants related to the mallow; also : this plant 2 : thread or cloth made of cotton — **cot·tony** adj

**cotton candy** n : a candy made of spun sugar

**cot·ton·mouth** \ˈkä-t³n-ˌmaúth\ n : WATER MOCCASIN

**cot·ton·seed** \-ˌsēd\ n : the seed of the cotton plant yielding a protein-rich meal and a fatty oil (**cottonseed oil**) used esp. in cooking

**cot·ton·tail** \-ˌtāl\ n : a No. American rabbit with a white-tufted tail

**cot·ton·wood** \-ˌwùd\ n : a poplar having seeds with cottony hairs

**cot·y·le·don** \ˌkä-tə-ˈlē-d³n\ n : the first leaf or one of the first pair or whorl of leaves developed by a seed plant

¹**couch** \ˈkaúch\ vb 1 : to lie or place on a couch 2 : to phrase in a specified manner ⟨proposals ∼ed in jargon⟩

²**couch** n : a piece of furniture (as a bed or sofa) that one can sit or lie on

**couch·ant** \ˈkaù-chənt\ adj : lying down with the head raised ⟨coat of arms with lion ∼⟩

**couch potato** n : one who spends a great deal of time watching television

**cou·gar** \ˈkü-gər\ n, pl **cougars** also **cougar** [F couguar, fr. NL cuguacuarana, modif. of Tupi (a Brazilian Indian language) stwasuarána, fr. stwásu deer + -ran resembling] : a large powerful tawny brown wild American cat

**cough** \ˈkóf\ vb : to force air from the lungs with short sharp noises; also : to expel by coughing — **cough** n

**could** \kəd, ˈkùd\ past of CAN — used as an auxiliary in the past or as a polite or less forceful alternative to can in the present

**cou·lee** \ˈkü-lē\ n 1 : a small stream 2 : a dry streambed 3 : GULLY

**cou·lomb** \ˈkü-ˌläm, -ˌlóm\ n : a unit of electric charge equal to the electricity transferred by a current of one ampere in one second

**coun·cil** \ˈkaún-səl\ n 1 : ASSEMBLY, MEETING 2 : an official body of lawmakers ⟨city ∼⟩ — **coun·cil·lor** or **coun·cil·or** \-s(ə-)lər\ n — **coun·cil·man** \-mən\ n — **coun·cil·wom·an** \-ˌwù-mən\ n

¹**coun·sel** \ˈkaún-səl\ n 1 : ADVICE 2 : a plan of action 3 : deliberation together 4 pl **counsel** : LAWYER

²**counsel** vb -seled or -selled; -sel·ing or -sel·ling 1 : ADVISE 2 : CONSULT

**coun·sel·or** or **coun·sel·lor** \ˈkaún-sə-lər\ n 1 : ADVISER 2 : LAWYER 3 : one who has supervisory duties at a summer camp

¹**count** \ˈkaúnt\ vb [ME, fr. AF cunter, counter, fr. L computare, fr. com- with + putare to consider] 1 : to name or indicate one by one in order to find the total number 2 : to recite numbers in order 3 : CONSIDER, ACCOUNT 4 : RELY ⟨you can ∼ on me⟩ 5 : to be of value or account ⟨∼s toward your grade⟩ — **count·able** adj

²**count** n 1 : the act of counting; also : the total obtained by counting 2 : a particular charge in an indictment or legal declaration ⟨two ∼s of murder⟩

³**count** n [ME, fr. AF cunte, fr. LL comes, fr. L, companion, one of the imperial court, fr. com- with + ire to go] : a European nobleman whose rank corresponds to that of a British earl

**count·down** \ˈkaúnt-ˌdaún\ n : a backward counting in fixed units (as seconds) to indicate the time remaining before an event (as the launching of a rocket) — **count down** vb

¹**coun·te·nance** \ˈkaún-t³n-əns\ n 1 : the human face 2 : FAVOR, APPROVAL

²**countenance** vb -nanced; -nanc·ing : SANCTION, TOLERATE

¹**count·er** \ˈkaún-tər\ n 1 : a piece (as of metal or plastic) used in reckoning or in games 2 : a level surface over which business is transacted, food is served, or work is conducted

²**count·er** n : a device for recording a number or amount

³**coun·ter** vb : to act in opposition to

⁴**coun·ter** adv : in an opposite direction : CONTRARY

⁵**coun·ter** n 1 : OPPOSITE, CONTRARY 2 : an answering or offsetting force or blow

⁶**coun·ter** adj : CONTRARY, OPPOSITE

**coun·ter·act** \ˌkaún-tər-ˈakt\ vb : to lessen the force of : OFFSET — **coun·ter·ac·tive** \-ˈak-tiv\ adj

**coun·ter·at·tack** \ˈkaún-tər-ə-ˌtak\ n : an attack made to oppose an enemy's attack — **counterattack** vb

¹**coun·ter·bal·ance** \ˈkaún-tər-ˌba-ləns\ n : a weight or influence that balances another

²**counterbalance** \ˌkaún-tər-ˈba-ləns\ vb : to oppose with equal weight or influence

**coun·ter·claim** \ˈkaún-tər-ˌklām\ n : an opposing claim esp. in law

**coun·ter·clock·wise** \ˌkaún-tər-ˈkläk-ˌwīz\ adv : in a direction opposite to that in which the hands of a clock rotate — **counterclockwise** adj

**coun·ter·cul·ture** \ˈkaún-tər-ˌkəl-chər\ n : a culture with values and mores that run counter to those of established society

**coun·ter·es·pi·o·nage** \ˌkaún-tər-ˈes-pē-ə-ˌnäzh, -nij\ n : activities intended to discover and defeat enemy espionage

¹**coun·ter·feit** \'kaún-tər-ˌfit\ *adj* : SHAM, SPURIOUS; *also* : FORGED ⟨∼ money⟩

²**counterfeit** *vb* **1** : to copy or imitate in order to deceive **2** : PRETEND, FEIGN — **coun·ter·feit·er** *n*

³**counterfeit** *n* : something counterfeit : FORGERY ♦ *Synonyms* FRAUD, SHAM, FAKE, IMPOSTURE, DECEIT, DECEPTION

**coun·ter·in·sur·gen·cy** \ˌkaún-tər-in-ˈsər-jən-sē\ *n* : military activity designed to deal with insurgents

**coun·ter·in·tel·li·gence** \ in-ˈte-lə-jəns\ *n* : organized activity of an intelligence service designed to counter the activities of an enemy's intelligence service

**coun·ter·in·tu·i·tive** \-in-ˈtü-ə-tiv, -ˈtyü-\ *adj* : contrary to what would intuitively be expected

**count·er·man** \'kaún-tər-ˌman, -mən\ *n* : one who tends a counter

**coun·ter·mand** \'kaún-tər-ˌmand\ *vb* : to withdraw (an order already given) by a contrary order

**coun·ter·mea·sure** \-ˌme-zhər\ *n* : an action or device designed to counter another action or other

**coun·ter·of·fen·sive** \-ə-ˌfen-siv\ *n* : a large-scale counterattack

**coun·ter·pane** \-ˌpān\ *n* : BEDSPREAD

**coun·ter·part** \-ˌpärt\ *n* : a person or thing very closely like or corresponding to another person or thing

**coun·ter·point** \-ˌpóint\ *n* : music in which one melody is accompanied by one or more other melodies all woven into a harmonious whole

**coun·ter·poise** \-ˌpóiz\ *n* : COUNTERBALANCE

**coun·ter·rev·o·lu·tion** \ˌkaún-tər-ˌre-və-ˈlü-shən\ *n* : a revolution opposed to a current or earlier one — **coun·ter·rev·o·lu·tion·ary** \-shə-ˌner-ē\ *adj or n*

**coun·ter·sign** \'kaún-tər-ˌsīn\ *n* **1** : a confirmatory signature added to a writing already signed by another person **2** : a military secret signal that must be given by a person who wishes to pass a guard — **countersign** *vb*

**coun·ter·sink** \-ˌsiŋk\ *vb* **-sunk** \-ˌsəŋk\; **-sink·ing** **1** : to form a funnel-shaped enlargement at the outer end of a drilled hole **2** : to set the head of (as a screw) at or below the surface — **countersink** *n*

**coun·ter·spy** \-ˌspī\ *n* : a spy engaged in counterespionage

**coun·ter·ten·or** \-ˌte-nər\ *n* : a tenor with an unusually high range

**coun·ter·vail** \ˌkaún-tər-ˈvāl\ *vb* : COUNTERACT

**coun·ter·weight** \'kaún-tər-ˌwāt\ *n* : COUNTERBALANCE

**count·ess** \'kaún-təs\ *n* **1** : the wife or widow of a count or an earl **2** : a woman holding the rank of a count or an earl in her own right

**count·ing·house** \'kaún-tiŋ-ˌhaús\ *n* : a building or office for keeping books and conducting business

**count·less** \'kaúnt-ləs\ *adj* : INNUMERABLE

**coun·tri·fied** *also* **coun·try·fied** \'kən-tri-ˌfīd\ *adj* **1** : RURAL, RUSTIC **2** : UNSO-PHISTICATED **3** : played or sung in the manner of country music

¹**coun·try** \'kən-trē\ *n, pl* **countries** [ME *contree,* fr. AF *cuntree, contré,* fr. ML *contrata,* fr. L *contra* against, on the opposite side] **1** : REGION, DISTRICT **2** : FATHERLAND **3** : a nation or its territory **4** : rural regions as opposed to towns and cities **5** : COUNTRY MUSIC

²**country** *adj* **1** : RURAL **2** : of or relating to country music ⟨a ∼ singer⟩

**country and western** *n* : COUNTRY MUSIC

**country club** *n* : a suburban club for social life and recreation; *esp* : one having a golf course — **country-club** *adj*

**coun·try-dance** \'kən-trē-ˌdans\ *n* : an English dance in which partners face each other esp. in rows

**coun·try·man** \'kən-trē-mən, *2 often* -ˌman\ *n* **1** : an inhabitant of a specified country **2** : COMPATRIOT **3** : one raised or living in the country : RUSTIC

**country music** *n* : music derived from or imitating the folk style of the southern U.S. or of the Western cowboy

**coun·try·side** \'kən-trē-ˌsīd\ *n* : a rural area or its people

**coun·ty** \'kaún-tē\ *n, pl* **counties** **1** : the domain of a count **2** : a territorial division of a country or state for purposes of local government

**coup** \'kü\ *n, pl* **coups** \'küz\ [F, blow, stroke] **1** : a brilliant sudden stroke or stratagem **2** : COUP D'ÉTAT

**coup de grace** \ˌkü-də-ˈgräs\ *n, pl* **coups de grace** \*same*\ [F *coup de grâce,* lit., stroke of mercy] : DEATHBLOW; *also* : a final decisive stroke or event

**coup d'état** \ˌkü-dā-ˈtä\ *n, pl* **coups d'état** \*same or* -ˈtäz\ [F, lit., stroke of state] : a sudden violent overthrow of a government by a small group

**cou·pé** *or* **coupe** \kü-ˈpā, *2 often* ˈküp\ *n* [F *coupé,* fr. *couper* to cut] **1** : a closed horse-drawn carriage for two persons inside with an outside seat for the driver **2** *usu* **coupe** : a 2-door automobile with an enclosed body

¹**cou·ple** \'kə-pəl\ *n* **1** : two persons married, engaged, or otherwise romantically paired **2** : PAIR **3** : BOND, TIE **4** : an indefinite small number : FEW ⟨a ∼ of days ago⟩

²**couple** *vb* **cou·pled; cou·pling** : to link together

**cou·plet** \'kə-plət\ *n* : two successive rhyming lines of verse

**cou·pling** \'kə-pliŋ (*usual for* 2), -pə-liŋ\ *n* **1** : CONNECTION **2** : a device for connecting two parts or things

**cou·pon** \'kü-ˌpän, 'kyü-\ *n* **1** : a statement attached to a bond showing interest due and designed to be cut off and presented for payment **2** : a form surrendered in order to obtain an article, service, or accommodation **3** : a printed document or slip used to submit orders or inquiries or to obtain a discount on merchandise or services

**cour·age** \'kər-ij\ *n* : ability to conquer fear or despair : BRAVERY, VALOR —

**cou·ra·geous** \kə-'rā-jəs\ *adj* — **cou·ra·geous·ly** *adv*

**cou·ri·er** \'kúr-ē-ər, 'kər-ē-\ *n* : one who bears messages or information esp. for the diplomatic or military services

¹**course** \'kórs\ *n* **1** : PROGRESS, PASSAGE; *also* : direction of progress **2** : the ground or path over which something moves **3** : method of procedure : CONDUCT, BEHAVIOR **4** : an ordered series of acts or proceedings : sequence of events **5** : a series of instruction periods dealing with a subject **6** : the series of studies leading to graduation from a school or college **7** : the part of a meal served at one time — **of course** : as might be expected

²**course** *vb* **coursed; cours·ing** **1** : to hunt with dogs **2** : to run or go speedily

**cours·er** \'kór-sər\ *n* : a swift or spirited horse

¹**court** \'kórt\ *n* [ME, fr. AF, fr. L *cohort-, cohors* enclosure, group, retinue, cohort] **1** : the residence of a sovereign or similar dignitary **2** : a sovereign's formal assembly of officials and advisers as a governing power **3** : an assembly of the retinue of a sovereign **4** : an open space enclosed by a building or buildings **5** : a space walled or marked off for playing a game (as tennis or basketball) **6** : the place where justice is administered; *also* : a judicial body or a meeting of a judicial body **7** : attention intended to win favor

²**court** *vb* **1** : to try to gain the favor of **2** : WOO **3** : ATTRACT, TEMPT

**cour·te·ous** \'kər-tē-əs\ *adj* : marked by respect for others : CIVIL, POLITE — **cour·te·ous·ly** *adv*

**cour·te·san** \'kór-tə-zən, -,zan\ *n* : PROSTITUTE

**cour·te·sy** \'kər-tə-sē\ *n, pl* **-sies** **1** : courteous behavior : POLITENESS **2** : a favor courteously performed

**court·house** \'kórt-,haús\ *n* : a building in which courts of law are held or county offices are located

**court·ier** \'kórt-ē-ər\ *n* : a person in attendance at a royal court

**court·ly** \'kórt-lē\ *adj* **court·li·er; -est** : REFINED, ELEGANT, POLITE ♦ **Synonyms** GALLANT, GRACIOUS — **court·li·ness** *n*

**court–mar·tial** \'kórt-,mär-shəl\ *n, pl* **courts–martial** : a military or naval court for trial of offenses against military or naval law; *also* : a trial by this court — **court–martial** *vb*

**court·room** \-,rüm, -,rúm\ *n* : a room in which a court of law is held

**court·ship** \-,ship\ *n* : the act of courting : WOOING

**court·yard** \-,yärd\ *n* : an enclosure next to a building

**cous·cous** \'küs-,küs\ *n* : a No. African dish of steamed semolina usu. served with meat or vegetables; *also* : the semolina itself

**cous·in** \'kə-zən\ *n* [ME *cosin,* fr. AF, fr. L *consobrinus,* fr. *com-* with + *sobrinus* second cousin, fr. *soror* sister] : a child of one's uncle or aunt

**cou·ture** \kü-'túr, -'tuer\ *n* [F] : the business of designing fashionable custom-made women's clothing; *also* : the designers and establishments engaged in this business

**cou·tu·ri·er** \kü-'túr-ē-ər, -ē-,ā\ *n* [F, dressmaker] : the owner of an establishment engaged in couture

**cove** \'kōv\ *n* : a small sheltered inlet or bay

**co·ven** \'kə-vən\ *n* : an assembly or band of witches

**cov·e·nant** \'kə-və-nənt\ *n* : a formal binding agreement : COMPACT — **cov·e·nant** \-nənt, -,nant\ *vb*

¹**cov·er** \'kə-vər\ *vb* **1** : to bring or hold within range of a firearm **2** : PROTECT, GUARD ⟨*~ed* by insurance⟩ ⟨*~* third base⟩ **3** : HIDE, CONCEAL ⟨*~* up a crime⟩ **4** : to place something over or upon **5** : INCLUDE, COMPRISE **6** : to have as one's field of activity ⟨one salesman *~s* the state⟩ **7** : to buy (stocks) in order to have them for delivery on a previous short sale

²**cover** *n* **1** : something that protects or shelters **2** : LID, TOP **3** : CASE, BINDING **4** : TABLECLOTH **5** : a cloth used on a bed **6** : SCREEN, DISGUISE **7** : an envelope or wrapper for mail

**cov·er·age** \'kə-və-rij\ *n* **1** : the act or fact of covering **2** : the total group covered : SCOPE

**cov·er·all** \'kə-vər-,ól\ *n* : a one-piece outer garment worn to protect one's clothes — usu. used in pl.

**cover charge** *n* : a charge made by a restaurant or nightclub in addition to the charge for food and drink

**cover crop** *n* : a crop planted to prevent soil erosion and to provide humus

**cov·er·let** \'kə-vər-lət\ *n* : BEDSPREAD

¹**co·vert** \'kō-,vərt, 'kə-vərt\ *adj* **1** : HIDDEN, SECRET ⟨a *~* operation⟩ **2** : SHELTERED — **co·vert·ly** *adv*

²**co·vert** \'kə-vərt, 'kō-\ *n* **1** : a secret or sheltered place; *esp* : a thicket sheltering game **2** : a feather covering the bases of the quills of the wings and tail of a bird

**cov·er–up** \'kə-vər-,əp\ *n* **1** : a device for masking or concealing **2** : a usu. concerted effort to keep an illegal or unethical act or situation from being made public

**cov·et** \'kə-vət\ *vb* : to desire enviously (what belongs to another) — **cov·et·ous** *adj* — **cov·et·ous·ness** *n*

**cov·ey** \'kə-vē\ *n, pl* **coveys** [ME, fr. AF *covee* sitting (of a hen), fr. *cover* to sit on, brood over, fr. L *cubare* to lie] **1** : a bird with her brood of young **2** : a small flock (as of quail) **3** : GROUP 1

¹**cow** \'kaú\ *n* **1** : the mature female of cattle or of an animal (as the moose, elephant, or whale) of which the male is called *bull* **2** : any domestic bovine animal irrespective of sex or age

²**cow** *vb* : INTIMIDATE, DAUNT, OVERAWE

**cow·ard** \'kaú(-ə)rd\ *n* [ME, fr. AF *cuard,* fr. *cue, coe* tail, fr. L *cauda*] : one who lacks courage or shows shameful fear or timidity — **coward** *adj* — **cow·ard·ice** \'kaú-ər-dəs\ *n* — **cow·ard·ly** *adv or adj*

**cow·bird** \'kau̇-ˌbərd\ *n* : a small No. American blackbird that lays its eggs in the nests of other birds

**cow·boy** \-ˌbȯi\ *n* : one (as a mounted ranch hand) who tends cattle or horses

**cow·er** \'kau̇-(ə)r\ *vb* : to shrink or crouch down from fear or cold : QUAIL

**cow·girl** \'kau̇-ˌgərl\ *n* : a girl or woman who tends cattle or horses

**cow·hand** \'kau̇-ˌhand\ *n* : COWBOY

**cow·herd** \-ˌhərd\ *n* : one who tends cows

**cow·hide** \-ˌhīd\ *n* **1** : the hide of a cow; *also* : leather made from it **2** : a coarse whip of braided rawhide

**cowl** \'kau̇(-ə)l\ *n* : a monk's hood

**cow·lick** \'kau̇-ˌlik\ *n* : a turned-up tuft of hair that resists control

**cowl·ing** \'kau̇-liŋ\ *n* : a usu. metal covering for the engine or another part of an airplane

**cow·man** \'kau̇-mən, -ˌman\ *n* : COWBOY; *also* : a cattle owner or rancher

**co·work·er** \'kō-ˌwər-kər\ *n* : a fellow worker

**cow·poke** \'kau̇-ˌpōk\ *n* : COWBOY

**cow pony** *n* : a strong and agile horse trained for herding cattle

**cow·pox** \'kau̇-ˌpäks\ *n* : a mild disease of the cow that when communicated to humans protects against smallpox

**cow·punch·er** \-ˌpən-chər\ *n* : COWBOY

**cow·slip** \'kau̇-ˌslip\ *n* **1** : a yellow-flowered European primrose **2** : MARSH MARIGOLD

**cox·comb** \'käks-ˌkōm\ *n* : a conceited foolish person : FOP

**cox·swain** \'käk-sən, -ˌswän\ *n* : the steersman of a ship's boat or a racing shell

**coy** \'kȯi\ *adj* [ME, quiet, shy, fr. AF *quei, quoi, koi* quiet, fr. L *quietus*] **1** : BASHFUL, SHY **2** : marked by artful playfulness : COQUETTISH — **coy·ly** *adv* — **coy·ness** *n*

**coy·ote** \'kī-ˌōt, kī-'ō-tē\ *n, pl* **coyotes** *or* **coyote** : a mammal of No. America smaller than the related wolves

**coy·pu** \'kȯi-pü\ *n* : NUTRIA 2

**coz·en** \'kə-zᵊn\ *vb* : CHEAT, DEFRAUD — **coz·en·age** \-ij\ *n* — **coz·en·er** *n*

**¹co·zy** \'kō-zē\ *adj* **co·zi·er; -est** : SNUG, COMFORTABLE \a ~ cabin\ — **co·zi·ly** \-zə-lē\ *adv* — **co·zi·ness** \-zē-nəs\ *n*

**²cozy** *n, pl* **co·zies** : a padded covering for a vessel (as a teapot) to keep the contents hot

**cp** *abbr* **1** compare **2** coupon

**CP** *abbr* **1** cerebral palsy **2** chemically pure **3** command post **4** communist party

**CPA** *abbr* certified public accountant

**CPB** *abbr* Corporation for Public Broadcasting

**cpd** *abbr* compound

**CPI** *abbr* consumer price index

**Cpl** *abbr* corporal

**CPO** *abbr* chief petty officer

**CPOM** *abbr* master chief petty officer

**CPOS** *abbr* senior chief petty officer

**CPR** *abbr* cardiopulmonary resuscitation

**CPT** *abbr* captain

**CPU** \ˌsē-ˌpē-'yü\ *n* [central processing unit] : the part of a computer that performs its basic operations, manages its components, and exchanges data with memory or peripherals

**CQ** *abbr* charge of quarters

**cr** *abbr* credit; creditor

**Cr** *symbol* chromium

**¹crab** \'krab\ *n, pl* **crabs** *also* **crab** : any of various crustaceans with a short broad shell and small abdomen

**²crab** *n* : an ill-natured person

**³crab** *vb* **crabbed; crab·bing** : COMPLAIN, GROUSE

**crab apple** *n* : a small often highly colored sour apple; *also* : a tree that produces crab apples

**crab·bed** \'kra-bəd\ *adj* **1** : MOROSE, PEEVISH \a ~ view of human nature\ **2** : CRAMPED, IRREGULAR \~ handwriting\

**crab·by** \'kra-bē\ *adj* **crab·bi·er; -est** : CROSS, ILL-NATURED

**crab·grass** \'krab-ˌgras\ *n* : a weedy grass with creeping or sprawling stems that root freely at the nodes

**crab louse** *n* : a louse infesting the pubic region in humans

**¹crack** \'krak\ *vb* **1** : to break with a sharp sudden sound **2** : to break with or without completely separating into parts **3** : to fail in tone or become harsh \her voice ~ed\ **4** : to subject (as a petroleum oil) to heat for breaking down into lighter products (as gasoline)

**²crack** *n* **1** : a sudden sharp noise **2** : a witty or sharp remark **3** : a narrow break or opening : FISSURE **4** : a sharp blow **5** : ATTEMPT, TRY **6** : a potent form of cocaine in small chips used illicitly for smoking

**³crack** *adj* : extremely proficient

**crack·down** \'krak-ˌdau̇n\ *n* : an act or instance of taking positive disciplinary action \a ~ on gambling\ — **crack down** *vb*

**crack·er** \'kra-kər\ *n* **1** : FIRECRACKER **2** : a dry thin crispy baked bread product made of flour and water

**crack·er·jack** \-ˌjak\ *adj* : EXCELLENT, GREAT \a ~ salesperson\ — **crack·er·jack** *n*

**crack·le** \'kra-kəl\ *vb* **crack·led; crack·ling** **1** : to make small sharp snapping noises **2** : to develop fine cracks in a surface — **crackle** *n* — **crack·ly** \-k(ə-)lē\ *adj*

**crack·pot** \'krak-ˌpät\ *n* : an eccentric person

**crack–up** \'krak-ˌəp\ *n* : CRASH, WRECK; *also* : BREAKDOWN

**crack up** *vb* **1** : PRAISE \isn't all it's *cracked up* to be\ **2** : to laugh or cause to laugh out loud **3** : to crash a vehicle

**¹cra·dle** \'krā-dᵊl\ *n* **1** : a baby's bed or cot **2** : a framework or support (as for a telephone receiver) **3** : INFANCY \from ~ to the grave\ **4** : a place of origin

**²cradle** *vb* **cra·dled; cra·dling** **1** : to place in or as if in a cradle **2** : SHELTER, REAR

**craft** \'kraft\ *n* **1** : ART, SKILL; *also* : an occupation requiring special skill **2**

: CUNNING, GUILE ⟨used ∼ to close the deal⟩ **3** *pl usu* **craft** : a boat esp. of small size; *also* : AIRCRAFT, SPACECRAFT

**crafts·man** \'krafts-mən\ *n* : a skilled artisan — **crafts·man·ship** *n*

**crafty** \'kraf-tē\ *adj* **craft·i·er; -est** : CUNNING, DECEITFUL, SUBTLE — **craft·i·ly** \-tə-lē\ *adv* — **craft·i·ness** \-tē-nəs\ *n*

**crag** \'krag\ *n* : a steep rugged cliff or rock — **crag·gy** *adj*

**cram** \'kram\ *vb* **crammed; cram·ming** **1** : to pack in tight : JAM **2** : to eat greedily **3** : to study rapidly under pressure for an examination

¹**cramp** \'kramp\ *n* **1** : a sudden painful contraction of muscle **2** : sharp abdominal pain — usu. used in pl.

²**cramp** *vb* **1** : to affect with a cramp or cramps **2** : to restrain from free action : HAMPER

**cran·ber·ry** \'kran-,ber-ē, -bə-rē\ *n* : the red acid berry of any of several trailing plants related to the heaths; *also* : one of these plants

¹**crane** \'krān\ *n* **1** : any of a family of tall wading birds related to the rails; *also* : any of several herons **2** : a machine for lifting and carrying heavy objects

²**crane** *vb* **craned; cran·ing** : to stretch one's neck to see better

**crane fly** *n* : any of a family of long-legged slender dipteran flies that resemble large mosquitoes but do not bite

**cranial nerve** *n* : any of the nerves that arise in pairs from the lower surface of the brain and pass through openings in the skull to the periphery of the body

**cra·ni·um** \'krā-nē-əm\ *n, pl* **-ni·ums** or **-nia** \-ə\ : SKULL; *esp* : the part enclosing the brain — **cra·ni·al** \-əl\ *adj*

¹**crank** \'krank\ *n* **1** : a bent part of an axle or shaft or an arm at right angles to the end of a shaft by which circular motion is imparted to or received from it **2** : an eccentric person **3** : a bad-tempered person : GROUCH

²**crank** *vb* : to start or operate by or as if by turning a crank

**crank·case** \'krank-,kās\ *n* : the housing of a crankshaft

**crank out** *vb* : to produce in a mechanical manner

**crank·shaft** \'krank-,shaft\ *n* : a shaft turning or driven by a crank

**cranky** \'kran-kē\ *adj* **crank·i·er; -est 1** : IRRITABLE **2** : operating uncertainly or imperfectly ⟨a ∼ old tractor⟩

**cran·ny** \'kra-nē\ *n, pl* **crannies** : CREVICE, CHINK

**craps** \'kraps\ *n* : a gambling game played with two dice

**crap·shoot·er** \'krap-,shü-tər\ *n* : a person who plays craps

¹**crash** \'krash\ *vb* **1** : to break noisily : SMASH **2** : to damage an airplane in landing **3** : to enter or attend without invitation or without paying ⟨∼ a party⟩ **4** : to suffer a sudden major failure usu. with loss of data ⟨my computer ∼ed⟩

²**crash** *n* **1** : a loud sound (as of things smashing) **2** : an instance of crashing ⟨a plane ∼⟩; *also* : COLLISION **3** : a sudden failure (as of a business)

³**crash** *adj* : marked by concentrated effort over the shortest possible time ⟨a ∼ diet⟩

⁴**crash** *n* : coarse linen fabric used for towels and draperies

**crash–land** \'krash-'land\ *vb* : to land an aircraft or spacecraft under emergency conditions usu. with damage to the craft — **crash landing** *n*

**crass** \'kras\ *adj* : GROSS, INSENSITIVE ⟨∼ ignorance⟩ — **crass·ly** *adv* — **crass·ness** *n*

**crate** \'krāt\ *n* : a container often of wooden slats — **crate** *vb*

**cra·ter** \'krā-tər\ *n* [L, mixing bowl, crater, fr. Gk *kratēr*, fr. *kerannynai* to mix] **1** : the depression around the opening of a volcano **2** : a depression formed by the impact of a meteorite or by the explosion of a bomb or shell

**cra·vat** \krə-'vat\ *n* : NECKTIE

**crave** \'krāv\ *vb* **craved; crav·ing 1** : to ask for earnestly : BEG **2** : to long for : DESIRE

**cra·ven** \'krā-vən\ *adj* : COWARDLY — **craven** *n* — **cra·ven·ly** *adv*

**crav·ing** \'krā-viŋ\ *n* : an urgent or abnormal desire

**craw·fish** \'krȯ-,fish\ *n* **1** : CRAYFISH 1 **2** : SPINY LOBSTER

¹**crawl** \'krȯl\ *vb* **1** : to move slowly by drawing the body along the ground **2** : to advance feebly, cautiously, or slowly **3** : to be swarming with or feel as if swarming with creeping things ⟨a place ∼ing with ants⟩ ⟨her flesh ∼ed⟩

²**crawl** *n* **1** : a very slow pace **2** : a prone speed swimming stroke

**cray·fish** \'krā-,fish\ *n* **1** : any of numerous freshwater crustaceans usu. much smaller than the related lobsters **2** : SPINY LOBSTER

**cray·on** \'krā-,än, -ən\ *n* : a stick of chalk or wax used for writing, drawing, or coloring; *also* : a drawing made with such material — **crayon** *vb*

¹**craze** \'krāz\ *vb* **crazed; craz·ing** [ME *crasen* to crush, craze, of Scand origin] : to make or become insane

²**craze** *n* : FAD, MANIA

**cra·zy** \'krā-zē\ *adj* **cra·zi·er; -est 1** : mentally disordered : INSANE **2** : wildly impractical ⟨a ∼ plan⟩; *also* : ERRATIC ⟨∼ drivers⟩ — **cra·zi·ly** \-zə-lē\ *adv* — **cra·zi·ness** \-zē-nəs\ *n*

**CRC** *abbr* Civil Rights Commission

**creak** \'krēk\ *vb* : to make a prolonged squeaking or grating sound — **creak** *n* — **creaky** *adj*

¹**cream** \'krēm\ *n* **1** : the yellowish fat-rich part of milk **2** : a thick smooth sauce, confection, or cosmetic **3** : the choicest part **4** : a pale yellow color — **creamy** *adj*

²**cream** *vb* **1** : to prepare with a cream sauce **2** : to beat or blend into creamy consistency **3** : to defeat decisively

**cream cheese** *n* : a cheese made from whole milk enriched with cream

**cream·ery** \'krē-mə-rē\ *n, pl* **-er·ies** : an

establishment where butter and cheese are made or milk and cream are prepared for sale

**crease** \'krēs\ *n* : a mark or line made by or as if by folding — **crease** *vb*

**cre·ate** \krē-'āt\ *vb* **cre·at·ed; cre·at·ing** : to bring into being : cause to exist : MAKE, PRODUCE — **cre·a·tive** \-'ā-tiv\ *adj* — **cre·a·tive·ness** *n* — **cre·a·tiv·i·ty** \ˌkrē-(ˌ)ā-'ti-və-tē\ *n*

**cre·a·tion** \krē-'ā-shən\ *n* **1** : the act of creating or producing (~ of the world) **2** : something that is created **3** : all created things : WORLD

**cre·a·tion·ism** \krē-'ā-shə-ˌni-zəm\ *n* : a doctrine or theory holding that matter, the various forms of life, and the world were created by God out of nothing — **cre·a·tion·ist** \-nIst\ *n or adj*

**ore·a·tor** \krē-'ā-tər\ *n* **1** : one that creates : MAKER, AUTHOR **2** *cap* : GOD 1

**crea·ture** \'krē-chər\ *n* : a lower animal; *also* : a human being

**crèche** \'kresh\ *n* [F, manger, crib, fr. OF *creche*, of Gmc origin] : a representation of the Nativity scene

**cre·dence** \'krē-dᵊns\ *n* : mental acceptance as true or real

**cre·den·tial** \kri-'den-chəl\ *n* : something that gives a basis for credit or confidence

**cre·den·za** \kri-'den-zə\ *n* [It, lit., belief, confidence] : a sideboard, buffet, or bookcase usu. without legs

**cred·i·ble** \'kre-də-bəl\ *adj* : TRUSTWORTHY, BELIEVABLE — **cred·i·bil·i·ty** \ˌkre-də-'bi-lə-tē\ *n* — **cred·i·bly** \'kre-də-blē\ *adv*

¹**cred·it** \'kre-dət\ *n* [MF, fr. It *credito*, fr. L *creditum* something entrusted to another, loan, fr. *credere* to believe, entrust] **1** : the balance (as in a bank) in a person's favor **2** : time given for payment for goods sold on trust **3** : an accounting entry of payment received **4** : BELIEF, FAITH **5** : financial trustworthiness **6** : ESTEEM **7** : a source of honor or distinction **8** : a unit of academic work

²**credit** *vb* **1** : BELIEVE **2** : to give credit to ⟨the players all ~ed their coach⟩

**cred·it·able** \'kre-də-tə-bəl\ *adj* : worthy of esteem or praise ⟨did a ~ job⟩ — **cred·it·ably** \-blē\ *adv*

**credit card** *n* : a card authorizing purchases on credit

**cred·i·tor** \'kre-də-tər\ *n* : a person to whom money is owed

**cre·do** \'krē-dō, 'krā-\ *n, pl* **credos** [ME, fr. L, I believe] : CREED

**cred·u·lous** \'kre-jə-ləs\ *adj* : inclined to believe esp. on slight evidence — **cre·du·li·ty** \kri-'dü-lə-tē, -'dyü-\ *n* — **cred·u·lous·ly** *adv*

**Cree** \'krē\ *n, pl* **Cree** or **Crees** : a member of an American Indian people of Canada

**creed** \'krēd\ *n* [ME *crede*, fr. OE *crēda*, fr. L *credo* I believe, first word of the Apostles' and Nicene Creeds] : a statement of the essential beliefs of a religious faith

**creek** \'krēk, 'krik\ *n* **1** *chiefly Brit* : a small inlet **2** : a stream smaller than a river and larger than a brook

**Creek** \'krēk\ *n* : a member of an American Indian people of Alabama, Georgia, and Florida

**creel** \'krēl\ *n* : a wicker basket esp. for carrying fish

**creep** \'krēp\ *vb* **crept** \'krept\; **creep·ing** **1** : CRAWL **2** : to feel as though insects were crawling on the skin **3** : to spread or grow over a surface like ivy — **creep** *n* — **creep·er** *n*

**creep·ing** \'krē-pin\ *adj* : developing or advancing by imperceptible degrees

**creepy** \'krē-pē\ *adj* **creep·i·er; -est** : having or producing a nervous shivery fear

**cre·mate** \'krē-ˌmāt\ *vb* **cre·mat·ed; cre·mat·ing** : to reduce (a dead body) to ashes with fire — **cre·ma·tion** \kri-'mā-shən\ *n*

**cre·ma·to·ry** \'krē-mə-ˌtōr-ē, 'krē-\ *n, pl* **-ries** : a furnace for cremating; *also* : a structure containing such a furnace

**crème** or **creme** \'krem, 'krēm\ *n, pl* **crèmes** or **cremes** \*same or* 'kremz, 'krēmz\ [F, lit., cream] : a sweet liqueur

**cren·el·lat·ed** or **cren·el·at·ed** \'kre-nə-lā-təd\ *adj* : having battlements — **cren·el·la·tion** \ˌkre-nə-'lā-shən\ *n*

**Cre·ole** \'krē-ˌōl\ *n* **1** : a descendant of early French or Spanish settlers of the U.S. Gulf states preserving their speech and culture; *also* : a person of mixed French or Spanish and black descent speaking a dialect of French or Spanish **2** *not cap* : a language that has evolved from a pidgin but serves as the native language of a speech community

**cre·o·sote** \'krē-ə-ˌsōt\ *n* : an oily liquid obtained by distillation of coal tar and used in preserving wood

**crepe** or **crêpe** \'krāp\ *n* : a light crinkled fabric of any of various fibers

**crêpe su·zette** \ˌkrāp-sü-'zet\ *n, pl* **crêpes suzette** \*same or* ˌkrāps-\ or **crêpe suzettes** \-sü-'zets\ *often cap S* : a thin folded or rolled pancake in a hot orange-butter sauce that is sprinkled with a liqueur and set ablaze for serving

**cre·pus·cu·lar** \kri-'pəs-kyə-lər\ *adj* **1** : of, relating to, or resembling twilight **2** : occurring or active during twilight ⟨~ insects⟩

**cre·scen·do** \krə-'shen-dō\ *adv or adj* [It] : increasing in loudness — used as a direction in music — **crescendo** *n*

**cres·cent** \'kre-sᵊnt\ *n* [ME *cressant*, fr. AF fr. prp. of *crestre* to grow, increase, fr. L *crescere*] : the moon at any stage between new moon and first quarter and between last quarter and new moon; *also* : something shaped like the figure of the crescent moon with a convex and a concave edge — **cres·cen·tic** \kre-'sen-tik\ *adj*

**cress** \'kres\ *n* : any of several salad plants related to the mustards

¹**crest** \'krest\ *n* **1** : a tuft or process on the head of an animal (as a bird) **2** : a heraldic device **3** : an upper part, edge,

or limit ⟨the ∼ of a hill⟩ — **crest·ed** \'kres-təd\ *adj* — **crest·less** *adj*

²**crest** *vb* **1** : CROWN **2** : to reach the crest of **3** : to rise to a crest

**crest·fall·en** \'krest-ˌfȯ-lən\ *adj* : DISPIRITED, DEJECTED

**Cre·ta·ceous** \kri-'tā-shəs\ *adj* : of, relating to, or being the latest period of the Mesozoic era marked by great increase in flowering plants, diversification of mammals, and extinction of the dinosaurs — **Cretaceous** *n*

**cre·tin** \'krē-t³n\ *n* [F *crétin*, fr. F dial. *cretin*, lit., wretch, innocent victim, fr. L *christianus* Christian] **1** : one affected with cretinism **2** : a stupid person

**cre·tin·ism** \-ˌi-zəm\ *n* : a usu. congenital abnormal condition characterized by physical stunting and mental retardation

**cre·tonne** \'krē-ˌtän\ *n* : a strong unglazed cotton cloth for curtains and upholstery

**cre·vasse** \kri-'vas\ *n* : a deep fissure esp. in a glacier

**crev·ice** \'kre-vəs\ *n* : a narrow fissure

¹**crew** \'krü\ *chiefly Brit past of* CROW

²**crew** *n* [ME *crue*, fr. MF, a reinforcement, lit., increase, fr. *croistre* to grow, fr. L *crescere*] **1** : a body of people trained to work together for certain purposes **2** : a group of people who operate a ship, train, aircraft, or spacecraft **3** : the rowers and coxswain of a racing shell; *also* : the sport of rowing engaged in by a crew — **crew·man** \-mən\ *n*

**crew cut** *n* : a very short bristly haircut

**crew·el** \'krü-əl\ *n* : slackly twisted worsted yarn used for embroidery — **crewel·work** \-ˌwərk\ *n*

¹**crib** \'krib\ *n* **1** : a manger for feeding animals **2** : a child's bedstead with high sides **3** : a building or bin for storage (as of grain) **4** : something used for cheating in an exam

²**crib** *vb* **cribbed; crib·bing 1** : to put in a crib **2** : STEAL, PLAGIARIZE — **crib·ber** *n*

**crib·bage** \'kri-bij\ *n* : a card game usu. played by two players and scored on a board (**cribbage board**)

**crib death** *n* : SUDDEN INFANT DEATH SYNDROME

**crick** \'krik\ *n* : a painful spasm of muscles (as of the neck)

¹**crick·et** \'kri-kət\ *n* [ME *criket*, fr. AF, of imit. origin] : any of a family of leaping insects related to the grasshoppers and noted for the chirping noises of the male

²**cricket** *n* [MF *criquet* goal stake in a bowling game] : a game played with a bat and ball by two teams on a field centering upon two wickets each defended by a batsman

**cri·er** \'krī-(-ə)r\ *n* : one who calls out proclamations and announcements

**crime** \'krīm\ *n* : a serious offense against the public law

¹**crim·i·nal** \'kri-mə-n³l\ *adj* **1** : involving or being a crime **2** : relating to crime or its punishment — **crim·i·nal·i·ty** \ˌkri-mə-'na-lə-tē\ *n* — **crim·i·nal·ly** *adv*

²**criminal** *n* : one who has committed a crime

**crim·i·nol·o·gy** \ˌkri-mə-'nä-lə-jē\ *n* : the scientific study of crime and criminals — **crim·i·no·log·i·cal** \-mə-nə-'lä-ji-kəl\ *adj* — **crim·i·nol·o·gist** \ˌkri-mə-'nä-lə-jist\ *n*

¹**crimp** \'krimp\ *vb* : to cause to become crinkled, wavy, or bent

²**crimp** *n* : something (as a curl in hair) produced by or as if by crimping

**crim·son** \'krim-zən\ *n* : a deep purplish red color — **crimson** *adj*

**cringe** \'krinj\ *vb* **cringed; cring·ing** : to shrink in fear ; WINCE, COWER

**crin·kle** \'kriŋ-kəl\ *vb* **crin·kled; crinkling** : to form many short bends or curves; *also* : WRINKLE — **crinkle** *n* — **crin·kly** \-kə-lē\ *adj*

**crin·o·line** \'kri-nə-lən\ *n* **1** : an open-weave cloth used for stiffening and lining **2** : a full stiff skirt or underskirt made of crinoline

¹**crip·ple** \'kri-pəl\ *n* : one that is disabled or deficient in a specified manner ⟨a social ∼⟩

²**cripple** *vb* **crip·pled; crip·pling 1** : to make lame **2** : to make useless or imperfect — **crip·pler** \'kri-p(ə-)lər\ *n*

**cri·sis** \'krī-səs\ *n, pl* **cri·ses** \-ˌsēz\ [ME, fr. L, fr. Gk *krisis*, lit., decision, fr. *krinein* to decide] **1** : the turning point for better or worse in an acute disease or fever **2** : a decisive or critical moment

**crisp** \'krisp\ *adj* **1** : CURLY, WAVY **2** : BRITTLE ⟨a ∼ potato chip⟩ **3** : FIRM, FRESH ⟨∼ lettuce⟩ **4** : being sharp and clear ⟨a ∼ photo⟩ **5** : LIVELY, SPARKLING **6** : FROSTY, SNAPPY; *also* : INVIGORATING — **crisp** *vb* — **crisp·ly** *adv* — **crisp·ness** *n* — **crispy** *adj*

¹**criss·cross** \'kris-ˌkrȯs\ *vb* **1** : to mark with crossed lines **2** : to go or pass back and forth

²**crisscross** *adj* : marked or characterized by crisscrossing — **crisscross** *adv*

³**crisscross** *n* : a pattern formed by crossed lines

**crit** *abbr* critical; criticism

**cri·te·ri·on** \krī-'tir-ē-ən\ *n, pl* **-ria** \-ē-ə\ : a standard on which a judgment may be based

**crit·ic** \'kri-tik\ *n* **1** : a person who judges literary or artistic works **2** : one inclined to find fault

**crit·i·cal** \'kri-ti-kəl\ *adj* **1** : being or relating to a condition or disease involving danger of death ⟨∼ care⟩ **2** : being a crisis **3** : inclined to criticize **4** : relating to criticism or critics **5** : requiring careful judgment ⟨∼ thinking⟩ — **crit·i·cal·ly** \-k(ə-)lē\ *adv*

**crit·i·cise** *Brit var of* CRITICIZE

**crit·i·cism** \'kri-tə-ˌsi-zəm\ *n* **1** : the act of criticizing; *esp* : CENSURE **2** : a judgment or review **3** : the art of judging works of literature or art

**crit·i·cize** \'kri-tə-ˌsīz\ *vb* **-cized; -ciz·ing 1** : to judge as a critic : EVALUATE **2** : to find fault : express criticism ♦ *Synonyms* BLAME, CENSURE, CONDEMN

**cri·tique** \krə-'tēk\ *n* : a critical estimate or discussion

**crit·ter** \'kri-tər\ *n* : CREATURE

**croak** \'krōk\ *n* : a hoarse harsh cry (as of a frog) — **croak** *vb*

**croak·er** \'krō-kər\ *n* : an animal that croaks 2 : a fish that produces croaking or grunting noises

**Croat** \'krō-,at\ *n* : CROATIAN

**Cro·atian** \krō-'ā-shən\ *n* 1 : a native or inhabitant of Croatia 2 : a Slavic language spoken by Croatians — **Croatian** *adj*

**cro·chet** \krō-'shā\ *n* : needlework done with a single thread and hooked needle — **crochet** *vb*

**crock** \'kräk\ *n* : a thick earthenware pot or jar

**crock·ery** \'krä-kə-rē\ *n* : EARTHENWARE

**croc·o·dile** \'krä-kə-,dī(-ə)l\ *n* [ME & L; ME *cocodrille*, fr. AF, fr. ML *cocodrillus*, alter. of L *crocodilus*, fr. Gk *krokodilos* lizard, crocodile, fr. *krokē* shingle, pebble + *drillos* worm] : any of several thick-skinned long-bodied carnivorous reptiles of tropical and subtropical waters

**cro·cus** \'krō-kəs\ *n, pl* **cro·cus·es** *also* **crocus** *or* **cro·ci** \-,kī\ : any of a large genus of low herbs related to the irises and having brightly colored flowers borne singly in early spring

**Crohn's disease** \'krōnz\ *n* : a chronic inflammatory disease of the gastrointestinal tract and esp. the ileum

**crois·sant** \krô-'sänt, krwä-'sä"\ *n, pl* **croissants** \*same or* -'sänts, -'sä"z\ : a rich crescent-shaped roll

**Cro-Ma·gnon** \krō-'mag-nən, -'man-yən\ *n* : a hominid of a tall erect race known from skeletal remains found in southern France and usu. classified as the same species as present-day humans — **Cro-Magnon** *adj*

**crone** \'krōn\ *n* : HAG

**cro·ny** \'krō-nē\ *n, pl* **cronies** : a close friend esp. of long standing

**¹crook** \'krúk\ *vb* : to curve or bend sharply

**²crook** *n* 1 : a bent or curved implement 2 : a bent or curved part; *also* : BEND, CURVE 3 : SWINDLER, THIEF

**crook·ed** \'krú-kəd\ *adj* 1 : having a crook : BENT, CURVED 2 : DISHONEST — **crook·ed·ly** *adv* — **crook·ed·ness** *n*

**croon** \'krün\ *vb* : to sing or hum in a gentle murmuring voice — **croon·er** *n*

**¹crop** \'kräp\ *n* 1 : the handle of a whip; *also* : a short riding whip 2 : a pouch in the throat of many birds and insects where food is received 3 : something (as a plant product) that can be harvested; *also* : the yield at harvest

**²crop** *vb* **cropped; crop·ping** 1 : to remove the tips of : cut off short; *also* : TRIM 2 : to feed on by cropping 3 : to devote (land) to crops 4 : to appear unexpectedly ⟨new problems have **cropped** up⟩

**crop duster** *n* : a person who uses an airplane to spray crops with insecticidal dusts; *also* : an airplane so used

**crop·land** \-,land\ *n* : land devoted to the production of plant crops

**crop·per** \'krä-pər\ *n* : a raiser of crops; *esp* : SHARECROPPER

**cro·quet** \krō-'kā\ *n* : a game in which mallets are used to drive wooden balls through a series of wickets set out on a lawn

**cro·quette** \krō-'ket\ *n* [F] : a small often rounded mass of minced meat, fish, or vegetables fried in deep fat

**cro·sier** *or* **cro·zier** \'krō-zhər\ *n* : a staff carried by bishops and abbots

**¹cross** \'krós\ *n* 1 : a structure consisting of an upright beam and a crossbar used esp. by the ancient Romans for execution 2 : a figure of the cross on which Christ was crucified used as a Christian symbol 3 : a hybridizing of unlike individuals or strains; *also* : a product of this 4 : a punch delivered with a circular motion over an opponent's lead

**²cross** *vb* 1 : to lie or place across; *also* : INTERSECT 2 : to cancel by marking a cross on or by lining through 3 : THWART, OBSTRUCT 4 : to go or extend across : TRAVERSE 5 : HYBRIDIZE 6 : to meet and pass on the way ⟨our letters *—ed* in the mail⟩

**³cross** *adj* 1 : lying across 2 : CONTRARY, OPPOSED 3 : marked by bad temper 4 : HYBRID — **cross·ly** *adv*

**cross·bar** \'krós-,bär\ *n* : a transverse bar or piece

**cross·bow** \-,bō\ *n* : a short bow mounted crosswise at the end of a wooden stock that shoots short arrows

**cross·breed** \'krós-,brēd, -'brēd\ *vb* **-bred** \-'bred\; **breed·ing** : HYBRIDIZE

**cross-coun·try** \-'kən-trē\ *adj* 1 : extending or moving across a country 2 : proceeding over the countryside (as fields and woods) and not by roads 3 : of or relating to racing or skiing over the countryside instead of over a track or run — **cross-country** *adv*

**cross-cur·rent** \-'kər-ənt\ *n* 1 : a current running counter to another 2 : a conflicting tendency — usu. used in pl.

**¹cross·cut** \-,kət\ *vb* : to cut or saw crosswise esp. of the grain of wood

**²crosscut** *adj* 1 : made or used for crosscutting ⟨a ~ saw⟩ 2 : cut across the grain

**³crosscut** *n* : something that cuts through transversely

**cross-ex·am·ine** \,kró-sig-'za-mən\ *vb* : to examine with questions to check the answers to previous questions — **cross-ex·am·i·na·tion** \-,za-mə-'nā-shən\ *n* — **cross-ex·am·in·er** *n*

**cross-eyed** \'kró-,sīd\ *adj* : having one or both eyes turned inward toward the nose

**cross-fer·til·i·za·tion** \-,fər-tə-lə-'zā-shən\ *n* 1 : fertilization between sex cells produced by separate individuals or sometimes by individuals of different kinds; *also* : CROSS-POLLINATION 2 : a broadening or productive interchange (as between cultures) — **cross-fer·til·ize** \-'fərt-tə-,līz\ *vb*

**cross fire** n **1** : crossing lines of fire in combat **2** : rapid or angry interchange

**cross·hair** \'kros-ˌher\ n : a fine wire or thread in the eyepiece of an optical instrument used as a reference line

**cross·hatch** \'kros-ˌhach\ vb :' to mark with two series of parallel lines that intersect — **cross–hatch·ing** n

**cross·ing** \'kro-siŋ\ n **1** : a place or structure for crossing something (as a river) **2** : a point of intersection (as of a street and a railroad track)

**cross·over** \'kros-ˌō-vər\ n **1** : CROSSING **2** : a member of a political party who votes in the primary of the other party **3** : a broadening of the popular appeal of an artist (as a musician) by a change in the artist's style, genre, or medium **4** : an instance of breaking into another category

**cross over** vb : to achieve broader popularity by a change of medium or style

**cross·piece** \'kros-ˌpēs\ n : a horizontal member

**cross–pol·li·na·tion** \ˌkros-ˌpä-lə-'nā-shən\ n : transfer of pollen from one flower to the stigma of another — **cross–pol·li·nate** \-'pä-lə-ˌnāt\ vb

**cross–pur·pose** \'kros-'pər-pəs\ n : a purpose contrary to another purpose ⟨working at ∼s⟩

**cross–ques·tion** \-'kwes-chən\ vb : CROSS-EXAMINE — **cross–question** n

**cross–re·fer** \ˌkros-ri-'fər\ vb : to refer by a notation or direction from one place to another (as in a book or list) — **cross–ref·er·ence** \'kros-'re-frəns\ n

**cross·road** \'kros-ˌrōd\ n **1** : a road that crosses a main road or runs between main roads **2** : a place where roads meet — usu. used in pl. **3** : a crucial point where a decision must be made — usu. used in pl.

**cross section** n **1** : a section cut across something; also : a representation made by or as if by such cutting **2** : a number of persons or things selected from a group that show the general nature of the whole group — **cross–sec·tion·al** adj

**cross·walk** \'kros-ˌwok\ n : a marked path for pedestrians crossing a street

**cross·ways** \-ˌwāz\ adv : CROSSWISE

**cross·wind** \-ˌwind\ n : a wind not parallel to a course (as of an airplane)

**cross·wise** \-ˌwīz\ adv : so as to cross something : ACROSS — **crosswise** adj

**cross·word** \'kros-ˌwərd\ n : a puzzle in which words are put into a pattern of numbered squares in answer to clues

**cros·ti·ni** \krȯ-'stē-nē\ n pl : small slices of toasted bread served with a topping

**crotch** \'kräch\ n : an angle or area formed by the parting of two legs, branches, or members

**crotch·et** \'krä-chət\ n : an odd notion : WHIM — **crotch·ety** adj

**crouch** \'krauch\ vb **1** : to stoop or bend low **2** : CRINGE, COWER — **crouch** n

**croup** \'krüp\ n : laryngitis esp. of infants marked by a hoarse ringing cough and difficult breathing — **croupy** adj

**crou·pi·er** \'krü-pē-ər, -pē-ˌā\ n [F, lit.,

rider on the rump of a horse, fr. *croupe* rump] : an employee of a gambling casino who collects and pays bets at a gaming table

**crou·ton** \'krü-ˌtän\ n [F *croûton*, dim. of *croûte* crust] : a small cube of bread toasted or fried crisp

**¹crow** \'krō\ n **1** : any of various large glossy black birds related to the jays **2** cap : a member of an American Indian people of a region in Montana and Wyoming; also : the language of the Crow people

**²crow** vb **1** : to make the loud shrill sound characteristic of the cock **2** : to utter a sound expressive of pleasure **3** : EXULT, GLOAT; also : BRAG, BOAST

**³crow** n : the cry of the cock

**crow·bar** \'krō-ˌbär\ n : a metal bar usu. wedge-shaped at the end for use as a pry or lever

**¹crowd** \'kraud\ vb **1** : to press close **2** : to collect in numbers : THRONG **3** : CRAM, STUFF ⟨a box ∼ed with toys⟩

**²crowd** n : a large number of people gathered together at random : THRONG

**¹crown** \'kraun\ n **1** : a mark of victory or honor; esp : the title of a champion in a sport **2** : a royal headdress **3** : the top of the head; also : the part of a hat that covers the top of the head **4** : the highest part (as of a tree or tooth) **5** often cap : sovereign power; also : MONARCH **6** : a formerly used British silver coin — **crowned** \'kraund\ adj

**²crown** vb **1** : to place a crown on **2** : HONOR **3** : TOP, SURMOUNT **4** : to fit (a tooth) with an artificial crown

**crown vetch** n : a Eurasian leguminous herb with umbels of pink-and-white flowers and sharp-angled pods

**crow's-foot** \'krōz-ˌfut\ n, pl **crow's-feet** \-ˌfēt\ : any of the wrinkles around the outer corners of the eyes — usu. used in pl.

**crow's nest** n : a partly enclosed platform high on a ship's mast for use as a lookout

**crozier** var of CROSIER

**¹CRT** \ˌsē-(ˌ)är-'tē\ n, pl **CRTs** or **CRT's** : CATHODE-RAY TUBE; also : a display device incorporating a cathode-ray tube

**²CRT** abbr carrier route

**cru·cial** \'krü-shəl\ adj : DECISIVE ⟨a ∼ step⟩; also : IMPORTANT, SIGNIFICANT ⟨a ∼ question⟩

**cru·ci·ate** \'krü-shē-ˌāt\ adj : CRUCIFORM

**cru·ci·ble** \'krü-sə-bəl\ n : a heat-resistant container in which material can be subjected to great heat

**cru·ci·fix** \'krü-sə-ˌfiks\ n : a representation of Christ on the cross

**cru·ci·fix·ion** \ˌkrü-sə-'fik-shən\ n **1** cap : the crucifying of Christ **2** : the act of crucifying

**cru·ci·form** \'krü-sə-ˌform\ adj : shaped like a cross

**cru·ci·fy** \'krü-sə-ˌfī\ vb **-fied; -fy·ing 1** : to put to death by nailing or binding the hands and feet to a cross **2** : MORTIFY 1 **3** : TORTURE, PERSECUTE

**¹crude** \'krüd\ adj **crud·er; crud·est 1**

: not refined : RAW ⟨~ oil⟩ ⟨~ statistics⟩ **2** : lacking grace, taste, tact, or polish : RUDE — **crude·ly** *adv* — **crude·ness** *n* — **cru·di·ty** \'krü-də-tē\ *n*

²**crude** *n* : unrefined petroleum

**cru·el** \'krü-əl\ *adj* **cru·el·er** *or* **cru·el·ler**; **cru·el·est** *or* **cru·el·lest** [ME, fr. AF, fr. L *crudelis*, fr. *crudus* crude] : causing pain and suffering to others : MERCILESS — **cru·el·ly** *adv* — **cru·el·ty** \-tē\ *n*

**cru·et** \'krü-ət\ *n* : a small usu. glass bottle for vinegar, oil, or sauce

**cruise** \'krüz\ *vb* **cruised; cruis·ing** [D *kruisen* to make a cross, cruise] **1** : to sail about touching at a series of ports **2** : to travel for enjoyment **3** : to sail about the streets at random **4** : to travel at the most efficient operating speed ⟨the *cruising* speed of an airplane⟩ **5** : SURF 2 — **cruise** *n*

**cruis·er** \'krü-zər\ *n* **1** : SQUAD CAR **2** : a large fast moderately armored and gunned warship **3** : a motorboat equipped for living aboard

**cruis·er·weight** \-ˌwāt\ *n* : a boxer weighing no more than 190 pounds

**crul·ler** \'krə-lər\ *n* **1** : a small sweet cake in the form of a twisted strip fried in deep fat **2** *Northern & Midland* : an unraised doughnut

¹**crumb** \'krəm\ *n* : a small fragment

²**crumb** *vb* **1** : to break into crumbs **2** : to cover with crumbs

**crum·ble** \'krəm-bəl\ *vb* **crum·bled; crum·bling** : to break into small pieces : DISINTEGRATE — **crum·bly** *adj*

**crum·my** *also* **crumby** \'krə-mē\ *adj* **crum·mi·er** *also* **crumb·i·er; -est** : very poor or inferior : LOUSY

**crum·pet** \'krəm-pət\ *n* : a small round unsweetened bread cooked on a griddle

**crum·ple** \'krəm-pəl\ *vb* **crum·pled; crum·pling** **1** : to crush together : RUMPLE **2** : COLLAPSE

¹**crunch** \'krənch\ *vb* : to chew with a grinding noise; *also* : to grind or press with a crushing noise

²**crunch** *n* **1** : an act of or a sound made by crunching **2** : a tight or critical situation — **crunchy** *adj*

**cru·sade** \krü-'sād\ *n* **1** *cap* : any of the expeditions in the 11th, 12th, and 13th centuries undertaken by Christian countries to take the Holy Land from the Muslims **2** : a reforming enterprise undertaken with zeal — **crusade** *vb* — **cru·sad·er** *n*

**cruse** \'krüz, 'krüs\ *n* : a jar for water or oil

¹**crush** \'krəsh\ *vb* **1** : to squeeze out of shape **2** : HUG, EMBRACE **3** : to grind or pound to small bits **4** : OVERWHELM, SUPPRESS

²**crush** *n* **1** : an act of crushing **2** : a violent crowding **3** : INFATUATION

**crust** \'krəst\ *n* **1** : the outside part of bread; *also* : a piece of old dry bread **2** : the cover of a pie **3** : a hard or brittle surface layer — **crust·al** *adj*

**crus·ta·cean** \ˌkrəs-'tā-shən\ *n* : any of a large class of mostly aquatic arthropods

(as lobsters or crabs) having a firm crustlike shell — **crustacean** *adj*

**crusty** \'krəs-tē\ *adj* **crust·i·er; -est** **1** : having or being a crust **2** : CROSS, GRUMPY

**crutch** \'krəch\ *n* : a supporting device; *esp* : a support fitting under the armpit for use by the disabled in walking

**crux** \'krəks, 'krúks\ *n, pl* **crux·es** [L, cross, torture] **1** : a puzzling or difficult problem **2** : a crucial point

¹**cry** \'krī\ *vb* **cried; cry·ing 1** : to call out : SHOUT **2** : to proclaim publicly : ADVERTISE **3** : WEEP

²**cry** *n, pl* **cries 1** : a loud outcry **2** : APPEAL, ENTREATY **3** : a fit of weeping **4** : the characteristic sound uttered by an animal **5** : DISTANCE — usu. used in the phrase *a far cry*

**cry·ba·by** \'krī-ˌbā-bē\ *n* : one who cries easily or often

**cryo·gen·ic** \ˌkrī-ə-'je-nik\ *adj* : of or relating to the production of very low temperatures; *also* : involving the use of a very low temperature — **cryo·gen·i·cal·ly** \-ni-k(ə-)lē\ *adv*

**cryo·gen·ics** \-niks\ *n* : a branch of physics that relates to the production and effects of very low temperatures

**cryo·lite** \'krī-ə-ˌlīt\ *n* : a usu. white mineral formerly used in making aluminum

**crypt** \'kript\ *n* : a chamber wholly or partly underground

**cryp·tic** \'krip-tik\ *adj* : meant to be puzzling or mysterious ⟨~ messages⟩

**cryp·to·gram** \'krip-tə-ˌgram\ *n* : a communication in cipher or code

**cryp·tog·ra·phy** \krip-'tä-grə-fē\ *n* : the coding and decoding of secret messages — **cryp·tog·ra·pher** \-fər\ *n*

**cryp·to·sys·tem** \ˌkrip-tō-'sis-təm\ *n* : a method for coding and decoding messages

**crys·tal** \'kris-t³l\ *n* [ME *cristal*, fr. AF, fr. L *crystallum*, fr. Gk *krystallos* ice, crystal] **1** : transparent quartz **2** : something resembling crystal (as in transparency); *esp* : a clear colorless glass of superior quality **3** : a body that is formed by solidification of a substance and has a regular repeating arrangement of atoms and often of external plane faces ⟨a salt ~⟩ **4** : the transparent cover of a watch dial

**crystal clear** *adj* : perfectly or transparently clear

**crys·tal·line** \'kris-tə-lən\ *adj* **1** : made of or resembling crystal **2** : very clear or sparkling

**crys·tal·lise** *Brit var of* CRYSTALLIZE

**crys·tal·lize** \'kris-tə-ˌlīz\ *vb* **-lized; -liz·ing 1** : to assume or cause to assume a crystalline form **2** : to take or cause to take a definite form ⟨publicity can ~ public opinion⟩ — **crys·tal·li·za·tion** \ˌkris-tə-lə-'zā-shən\ *n*

**crys·tal·log·ra·phy** \ˌkris-tə-'lä-grə-fē\ *n* : the science dealing with the forms and structures of crystals — **crys·tal·log·ra·pher** *n*

**cs** *abbr* case; cases

**Cs** *symbol* cesium

**CS** *abbr* **1** civil service **2** county seat

**CSA** *abbr* Confederate States of America

**C–section** \'sē-,sek-shən\ *n* : CESAREAN SECTION

**CSM** *abbr* command sergeant major

**CST** *abbr* central standard time

**ct** *abbr* **1** carat **2** cent **3** count **4** county **5** court

**CT** *abbr* **1** central time **2** Connecticut

**ctn** *abbr* carton

**ctr** *abbr* **1** center **2** counter

**CT scan** \,sē-'tē-\ *n* : CAT SCAN

**cu** *abbr* cubic

**Cu** *symbol* [L *cuprum*] copper

**cub** \'kəb\ *n* : a young individual of some animals (as a fox, bear, or lion)

**Cu·ban sandwich** \'kyü-bən-\ *n* : a usu. grilled and pressed sandwich served on a long split roll

**cub·by·hole** \'kə-bē-,hōl\ *n* : a snug place (as for storing things)

¹**cube** \'kyüb\ *n* **1** : a solid having 6 equal square sides **2** : the result of raising a number to the third power ⟨the ~ of 3 is 27⟩

²**cube** *vb* **cubed; cub·ing 1** : to raise to the third power **2** : to form into a cube **3** : to cut into cubes

**cube root** *n* : a number whose cube is a given number

**cu·bic** \'kyü-bik\ *also* **cu·bi·cal** *adj* **1** : having the form of a cube **2** : being the volume of a cube whose edge is a specified unit **3** : having length, width, and height

**cu·bi·cle** \'kyü-bi-kəl\ *n* : a small separate space (as for sleeping, studying, or working)

**cubic measure** *n* : a unit (as cubic inch) for measuring volume — see METRIC SYSTEM table, WEIGHT table

**cubic zir·co·nia** \-,zər-'kō-nē-ə\ *also* **cubic zirconium** *n* : a synthetic gemstone resembling a diamond made from an oxide of zirconium

**cub·ism** \'kyü-,bi-zəm\ *n* : a style of art characterized by the abstraction of natural forms into fragmented geometric shapes — **cub·ist** \-bist\ *n or adj*

**cu·bit** \'kyü-bət\ *n* : an ancient unit of length equal to about 18 inches (46 centimeters)

**Cub Scout** *n* : a member of the program of the Boy Scouts for boys in the first through fifth grades in school

**cuck·old** \'kə-kəld, 'kü-\ *n* : a man whose wife is unfaithful — **cuckold** *vb*

¹**cuck·oo** \'kü-kü, 'kù-\ *n, pl* **cuckoos** : a largely grayish brown European bird that lays its eggs in the nests of other birds for them to hatch

²**cuckoo** *adj* : SILLY, FOOLISH

**cu·cum·ber** \'kyü-(,)kəm-bər\ *n* : the long fleshy many-seeded fruit of a vine of the gourd family that is grown as a garden vegetable; *also* : this vine

**cud** \'kəd\ *n* : food brought up into the mouth by some animals (as cows) from the rumen to be chewed again

**cud·dle** \'kə-d²l\ *vb* **cud·dled; cud·dling** : to lie close : SNUGGLE

**cud·gel** \'kə-jəl\ *n* : a short heavy club — **cudgel** *vb*

¹**cue** \'kyü\ *n* **1** : a word, phrase, or action in a play serving as a signal for the next actor to speak or act **2** : HINT — **cue** *vb*

²**cue** *n* : a tapered rod for striking the balls in billiards or pool

**cue ball** *n* : the ball a player strikes with a cue in billiards or pool

¹**cuff** \'kəf\ *n* **1** : a part (as of a sleeve or glove) encircling the wrist **2** : the folded hem of a trouser leg

²**cuff** *vb* : to strike esp. with the open hand : SLAP

³**cuff** *n* : a blow with the hand esp. when open

**cui·sine** \kwi-'zēn\ *n* : style of cooking; *also* : the food prepared

**cuke** \'kyük\ *n* : CUCUMBER

**cul–de–sac** \'kəl-di-'sak, ,kül-\ *n, pl* **culs–de–sac** \*same or* ,kəlz-, ,külz-\ *also* **cul–de–sacs** \,kəl-də-'saks, ,kül-\ [F, lit., bottom of the bag] : a street or passage closed at one end

**cu·li·nary** \'kə-lə-,ner-ē, 'kyü-\ *adj* : of or relating to the kitchen or cookery

¹**cull** \'kəl\ *vb* : to pick out from a group

²**cull** *n* : something rejected from a group or lot as worthless or inferior

**cul·mi·nate** \'kəl-mə-,nāt\ *vb* **-nat·ed; -nat·ing** : to reach the highest point — **cul·mi·na·tion** \,kəl-mə-'nā-shən\ *n*

**cu·lotte** \'kü-,lät, ,kyü-, kü-,lät, kyü-\ *n* [F, breeches, fr. dim. of *cul* backside] : a divided skirt; *also* : a garment having a divided skirt — often used in pl.

**cul·pa·ble** \'kəl-pə-bəl\ *adj* : deserving blame — **cul·pa·bil·i·ty** \,kəl-pə-'bi-lə-tē\ *n*

**cul·prit** \'kəl-prət\ *n* [AF *cul.* (abbr. of *culpable* guilty) + *prest, prit* ready (i.e., to prove it), fr. L *praestus*] : one accused or guilty of a crime

**cult** \'kəlt\ *n* **1** : formal religious veneration **2** : a religious system; *also* : its adherents **3** : faddish devotion; *also* : a group of persons showing such devotion — **cult·ish** \'kəl-tish\ *adj* — **cult·ist** \-tist\ *n*

**cul·ti·va·ble** \'kəl-tə-və-bəl\ *adj* : capable of being cultivated

**cul·ti·var** \'kəl-tə-,vär, -,ver\ *n* : a plant variety originating and persisting under cultivation

**cul·ti·vate** \'kəl-tə-,vāt\ *vb* **-vat·ed; -vat·ing 1** : to prepare for the raising of crops **2** : to foster the growth of by tilling or by labor and care ⟨~ vegetables⟩ **3** : REFINE, IMPROVE ⟨~ the mind⟩ **4** : ENCOURAGE, FURTHER ⟨~ the arts⟩ **5** : to seek the friendship of — **cul·ti·va·tion** \,kəl-tə-'vā-shən\ *n* — **cul·ti·va·tor** \'kəl-tə-,vā-tər\ *n*

**cul·ture** \'kəl-chər\ *n* **1** : TILLAGE, CULTIVATION **2** : the act of developing by education and training **3** : refinement of intellectual and artistic taste **4** : the customary beliefs, social forms, and material traits of a racial, religious, or social group — **cul·tur·al** \'kəl-chə-rəl\ *adj* — **cul·tur·al·ly** *adv* — **cul·tured** \-chərd\ *adj*

**cul·vert** \'kəl-vərt\ *n* : a drain crossing under a road or railroad

**cum** *abbr* cumulative

**cum·ber** \'kəm-bər\ *vb* : to weigh down : BURDEN, HINDER

**cum·ber·some** \'kəm-bər-səm\ *adj* : hard to handle or manage because of size or weight — **cum·ber·some·ly** *adv*

**cum·brous** \'kəm-brəs\ *adj* : CUMBERSOME — **cum·brous·ly** *adv* — **cumbrous·ness** *n*

**cum·in** \'kə-mən, 'kyü-\ *n* : the seedlike fruit of a small annual herb related to the carrot that is used as a spice; *also* : this herb

**cum·mer·bund** \'kə-mər-,bənd, 'kəm-bər-\ *n* [Hindi & Urdu *kamarband*, fr. Pers. fr. *kamar* waist + *band* band] : a broad sash worn as a waistband

**cu·mu·la·tive** \'kyü-myə-lə-tiv, -,lā-\ *adj* : increasing in force or value by successive additions

**cu·mu·lo·nim·bus** \,kyü-myə-lō-'nim-bəs\ *n* : an anvil-shaped cumulus cloud extending to great heights

**cu·mu·lus** \'kyü-myə-ləs\ *n, pl* **-li** \-,lī, -,lē\ : a dense puffy cloud having a flat base and rounded outlines

**cu·ne·i·form** \kyù-'nē-ə-,förm\ *adj* 1 : wedge-shaped 2 : composed of wedge-shaped characters

**cun·ni·lin·gus** \,kə-ni-'liŋ-gəs\ *also* **cun·ni·linc·tus** \-'liŋk-təs\ *n* : oral stimulation of the vulva or clitoris

¹**cun·ning** \'kə-niŋ\ *adj* 1 : SKILLFUL, DEXTEROUS 2 : marked by wiliness and trickery ⟨~ schemes⟩ 3 : CUTE ⟨a ~ kitten⟩ — **cun·ning·ly** *adv*

²**cunning** *n* 1 : SKILL 2 : SLYNESS

¹**cup** \'kəp\ *n* 1 : a small bowl-shaped drinking vessel 2 : the contents of a cup 3 : the consecrated wine of the Communion 4 : something resembling a cup : a small bowl or hollow 5 : a half pint — **cup·ful** *n* — **cup·like** \-,lik\ *adj*

²**cup** *vb* **cupped; cup·ping** : to curve into the shape of a cup

**cup·board** \'kə-bərd\ *n* : a small closet with shelves for food or dishes

**cup·cake** \'kəp-,kāk\ *n* : a small cake baked in a cup-shaped mold

**cu·pid** \'kyü-pəd\ *n* : a winged naked figure of an infant often with a bow and arrow that represents the god Cupid

**cu·pid·i·ty** \kyü-'pi-də-tē\ *n, pl* **-ties** : excessive desire for money

**cu·po·la** \'kyü-pə-lə, -,lō\ *n* : a small structure on top of a roof or building

¹**cur** \'kər\ *n* : a mongrel dog

²**cur** *abbr* 1 currency 2 current

**cu·rate** \'kyür-ət\ *n* 1 : a member of the clergy who is in charge of a parish 2 : a member of the clergy who assists a rector or vicar — **cu·ra·cy** \-ə-sē\ *n*

**cu·ra·tive** \-ə-tiv\ *adj* : relating to or used in the cure of diseases ⟨~ therapy⟩ ⟨~ powers⟩ — **curative** *n*

**cu·ra·tor** \'kyür-'ā-tər, kyù-'rā-\ *n* : CUSTODIAN; *esp* : one in charge of a place of exhibit (as a museum or zoo)

¹**curb** \'kərb\ *n* 1 : a bit that exerts pressure on a horse's jaws 2 : CHECK, RESTRAINT 3 : a raised edging (as of stone or concrete) along a paved street

²**curb** *vb* : to hold in or back : RESTRAIN

**curb·ing** \'kər-biŋ\ *n* 1 : the material for a curb 2 : CURB

**curd** \'kərd\ *n* : the thick protein-rich part of coagulated milk

**cur·dle** \'kər-d³l\ *vb* **cur·dled; cur·dling** : to form curds; *also* : SPOIL, SOUR

¹**cure** \'kyür\ *n* 1 : spiritual care 2 : recovery or relief from disease 3 : a curative agent : REMEDY 4 : a course or period of treatment

²**cure** *vb* **cured; cur·ing** 1 : to restore to health : HEAL, REMEDY; *also* : to become cured 2 : to process for storage or use ⟨~ bacon⟩ — **cur·able** *adj*

**cu·ré** \kyù-'rā\ *n* [F] : a parish priest

**cure–all** \'kyür-,öl\ *n* : a remedy for all ills : PANACEA

**cu·ret·tage** \,kyür-ə-'täzh\ *n* : a surgical scraping or cleaning of a body part (as the uterus)

**cur·few** \'kər-fyü\ *n* [ME, fr. AF *covre-feu*, signal given to bank the hearth fire, curfew, fr. *coverir* to cover + *fu, feu* fire, fr. L *focus* hearth] : a regulation that specified persons (as children) be off the streets at a set hour of the evening; *also* : the sounding of a signal (as a bell) at this hour

**cu·ria** \'kyür-ē-ə, 'kür-\ *n, pl* **cu·ri·ae** \'kyür-ē-,ē, 'kür-ē-,ī\ *often cap* : the body of congregations, tribunals, and offices through which the pope governs the Roman Catholic Church

**cu·rie** \'kyür-ē\ *n* : a unit of radioactivity equal to 37 billion disintegrations per second

**cu·rio** \'kyür-ē-,ō\ *n, pl* **cu·ri·os** : an object or article valued because it is strange or rare

**cu·ri·ous** \'kyur-ē-əs\ *adj* 1 : having a desire to investigate and learn 2 : STRANGE, UNUSUAL, ODD ⟨a ~ coincidence⟩ — **cu·ri·os·i·ty** \,kyür-ē-'ä-sə-tē\ *n* — **cu·ri·ous·ness** *n*

**cu·ri·ous·ly** *adv* 1 : in a curious manner 2 : as is curious

**cu·ri·um** \'kyür-ē-əm\ *n* : a metallic radioactive element produced artificially

¹**curl** \'kərl\ *vb* 1 : to form into ringlets 2 : CURVE, COIL — **curl·er** *n*

²**curl** *n* 1 : a lock of hair that coils : RINGLET 2 : something having a spiral or twisted form — **curly** *adj*

**cur·lew** \'kər-lü, 'kər-,yü\ *n, pl* **curlews** *or* **curlew** : any of various long-legged brownish birds that have a down-curved bill and are related to the sandpipers and snipes

**curli·cue** \'kər-li-,kyü\ *n* : a fancifully curved or spiral figure

**cur·rant** \'kər-ənt\ *n* 1 : a small seedless raisin 2 : the acid berry of various shrubs related to the gooseberry; *also* : this plant

**cur·ren·cy** \'kər-ən-sē\ *n, pl* **-cies** 1 : general use or acceptance 2 : something that is in circulation as a medium of exchange : MONEY

¹**cur·rent** \'kər-ənt\ *adj* 1 : occurring in or belonging to the present ⟨the ~ crisis⟩ 2 : used as a medium of exchange 3 : generally accepted or practiced

²**current** *n* **1** : the part of a body of fluid moving continuously in a certain direction; *also* : the swiftest part of a stream **2** : a flow of electric charge; *also* : the rate of such flow

**cur·ric·u·lum** \kə-'ri-kyə-ləm\ *n, pl* **-la** \-lə\ *also* **-lums** [L, running, course, fr. *currere* to run] : the courses offered by an educational institution

¹**cur·ry** \'kər-ē\ *vb* **cur·ried; cur·ry·ing 1** : to clean the coat of (a horse) with a currycomb **2** : to treat (tanned leather) esp. by incorporating oil or grease — **curry favor** : to seek to gain favor by flattery or attention

²**cur·ry** *n, pl* **cur·ries** : a powder of pungent spices used in cooking; *also* : a food seasoned with curry

**cur·ry·comb** \-,kōm\ *n* : a comb used esp. to curry horses — **currycomb** *vb*

¹**curse** \'kərs\ *n* **1** : a prayer for harm to come upon one **2** : something that is cursed **3** : evil or misfortune coming as if in response to a curse

²**curse** *vb* **cursed; curs·ing 1** : to call on divine power to send injury upon **2** : BLASPHEME **3** : AFFLICT ♦ *Synonyms* EXECRATE, DAMN, ANATHEMATIZE, OBJURGATE

**cur·sive** \'kər-siv\ *adj* : written with the strokes of the letters joined together and the angles rounded

**cur·sor** \'kər-sər\ *n* : a visual cue (as a pointer) on a computer screen that indicates position (as for data entry)

**cur·so·ry** \'kər-sə-rē\ *adj* : rapidly and often superficially done : HASTY ⟨a ~ reading of the report⟩ — **cur·so·ri·ly** \-rə-lē\ *adj*

**curt** \'kərt\ *adj* : rudely short or abrupt — **curt·ly** *adv* — **curt·ness** *n*

**cur·tail** \(,)kər-'tāl\ *vb* : to cut off the end of : SHORTEN — **cur·tail·ment** *n*

**cur·tain** \'kər-t³n\ *n* **1** : a hanging screen that can be drawn back esp. at a window **2** : the screen between the stage and auditorium of a theater — **curtain** *vb*

**curt·sy** *also* **curt·sey** \'kərt-sē\ *n, pl* **curt·sies** *or* **curtseys** : a courteous bow made by women chiefly by bending the knees — **curtsy** *also* **curtsey** *vb*

**cur·va·ceous** *also* **cur·va·cious** \,kər-'vā-shəs\ *adj* : having curves suggestive of a well-proportioned feminine figure

**cur·va·ture** \'kər-və-,chùr\ *n* : a measure or amount of curving : BEND

¹**curve** \'kərv\ *vb* **curved; curv·ing** : to bend from a straight line or course

²**curve** *n* **1** : a line esp. when curved **2** : something that bends or curves without angles ⟨a ~ in the road⟩ **3** : a baseball pitch thrown so that it swerves esp. downward and to one side

**cur·vet** \(,)kər-'vet\ *n* : a prancing leap of a horse — **curvet** *vb*

¹**cush·ion** \'kù-shən\ *n* [ME *cusshin*, fr. AF *cussin, quissin*, fr. VL \*coxinus, fr. L *coxa* hip] **1** : a soft pillow or pad to rest on or against **2** : the springy pad inside the rim of a billiard table **3** : something soft that prevents discomfort or protects against injury

²**cushion** *vb* **1** : to provide (as a seat) with a cushion **2** : to soften or lessen the force or shock of

**cusp** \'kəsp\ *n* : a pointed end or part (as of a tooth)

**cus·pid** \'kəs-pəd\ *n* : a canine tooth

**cus·pi·dor** \'kəs-pə-,dór\ *n* : SPITTOON

**cus·tard** \'kəs-tərd\ *n* : a sweetened cooked mixture of milk and eggs

**cus·to·di·al** \,kəs-'tō-dē-əl\ *adj* : marked by watching and protecting rather than seeking to cure ⟨~ care⟩

**cus·to·di·an** \,kəs-'tō-dē-ən\ *n* : one who has custody (as of a building)

**cus·to·dy** \'kəs-tə-dē\ *n, pl* **-dies** : immediate charge and control

¹**cus·tom** \'kəs-təm\ *n* **1** : habitual course of action : recognized usage **2** *pl* : taxes levied on imports **3** : business patronage

²**custom** *adj* **1** : made to personal order **2** : doing work only on order

**cus·tom·ary** \'kəs-tə-,mer-ē\ *adj* **1** : based on or established by custom **2** : commonly practiced or observed : HABITUAL — **cus·tom·ar·i·ly** *adv*

**cus·tom–built** \'kəs-təm-'bilt\ *adj* : built to individual order

**cus·tom·er** \'kəs-tə-mər\ *n* : BUYER, PURCHASER; *esp* : a regular or frequent buyer

**cus·tom·house** \'kəs-təm-,hàus\ *n* : the building where customs are paid

**cus·tom·ise** *Brit var of* CUSTOMIZE

**cus·tom·ize** \'kəs-tə-,mīz\ *vb* **-ized; -iz·ing** : to build, fit, or alter according to individual specifications

**cus·tom–made** \'kəs-təm-'mād\ *adj* : made to individual order

¹**cut** \'kət\ *vb* **cut; cut·ting 1** : to penetrate or divide with a sharp edge : CLEAVE, GASH; *also* : to experience the growth of (a tooth) through the gum **2** : to hurt the feelings of **3** : to strike sharply **4** : SHORTEN, REDUCE **5** : to remove by severing or paring **6** : INTERSECT, CROSS **7** : to divide into parts **8** : to go quickly or change direction abruptly **9** : to cause to stop

²**cut** *n* **1** : something made by cutting : GASH, CLEFT **2** : SHARE **3** : a segment or section of a meat carcass **4** : an excavated channel or roadway **5** : BAND **4 6** : a sharp stroke or blow **7** : REDUCTION ⟨a ~ in wages⟩ **8** : the shape or manner in which a thing is cut

**cut–and–dried** \,kət-³n-'drīd\ *also* **cut–and–dry** \-'drī\ *adj* : according to a plan, set procedure, or formula

**cu·ta·ne·ous** \kyù-'tā-nē-əs\ *adj* : of, relating to, or affecting the skin

**cut·back** \'kət-,bak\ *n* **1** : something cut back **2** : REDUCTION

**cute** \'kyüt\ *adj* **cut·er; cut·est** [short for *acute*] **1** : CLEVER, SHREWD **2** : daintily attractive : PRETTY

**cu·ti·cle** \'kyü-ti-kəl\ *n* **1** : an outer layer (as of skin or a leaf) **2** : dead or horny epidermis esp. around a fingernail — **cu·tic·u·lar** \kyü-'ti-kyə-lər\ *adj*

**cut in** *vb* **1** : to thrust oneself between others **2** : to interrupt a dancing couple and take one as one's partner

**cut·lass** \'kət-ləs\ *n* : a short heavy curved sword

**cut·ler** \'kət-lər\ *n* [ME, fr. AF *cuteler*, fr. LL *cultellarius*, fr. L *cultellus* knife] : one who makes, deals in, or repairs cutlery

**cut·lery** \'kət-lə-rē\ *n* : edged or cutting tools; *esp* : implements for cutting and eating food

**cut·let** \'kət-lət\ *n* : a slice of meat (as veal) for broiling or frying

**cut·off** \'kət-ˌȯf\ *n* **1** : the channel formed when a stream cuts through the neck of an oxbow; *also* : SHORTCUT **2** : a device for cutting off **3** *pl* : shorts orig. made from jeans with the legs cut off at the knees or higher

**cut·out** \'kət-ˌau̇t\ *n* : something cut out or prepared for cutting out from something else

**cut out** *vb* **1** : to determine or assign through necessity ⟨had her work *cut out* for her⟩ **2** : DISCONNECT **3** : to cease operating ⟨the engine *cut out*⟩ **4** : ELIMINATE ⟨*cut out* unnecessary expense⟩

**cut–rate** \'kət-ˈrāt\ *adj* : relating to or dealing in goods sold at reduced rates

**cut·ter** \'kə-tər\ *n* **1** : a tool or a machine for cutting **2** : a ship's boat for carrying stores and passengers **3** : a small armed vessel in government service **4** : a light sleigh

**¹cut·throat** \'kət-ˌthrōt\ *n* : MURDERER

**²cutthroat** *adj* **1** : MURDEROUS, CRUEL **2** : RUTHLESS ⟨~ competition⟩

**cutthroat trout** *n* : a large American trout with a red mark under the jaw

**¹cut·ting** \'kə-tiŋ\ *n* : a piece of a plant able to grow into a new plant

**²cutting** *adj* **1** : SHARP, EDGED **2** : marked by piercing cold **3** : likely to hurt the feelings : SARCASTIC ⟨a ~ remark⟩

**cut·tle·fish** \'kə-t⁰l-ˌfish\ *n* : any of various marine mollusks having eight arms and two usu. longer tentacles and an internal shell (**cut·tle·bone** \-ˌbōn\) composed of calcium compounds

**cut·up** \'kət-ˌəp\ *n* : a person who clowns or acts boisterously — **cut up** *vb*

**cut·worm** \-ˌwərm\ *n* : any of various smooth-bodied moth larvae that feed on plants at night

**cw** *abbr* clockwise

**CWO** *abbr* **1** cash with order **2** chief warrant officer

**cwt** *abbr* hundredweight

**-cy** \sē\ *n suffix* **1** : action : practice ⟨mendan*cy*⟩ **2** : rank : office ⟨chaplain*cy*⟩ **3** : body : class ⟨constituen*cy*⟩ **4** : state : quality ⟨accura*cy*⟩

**cy·an** \'sī-ˌan, -ən\ *n* : a greenish blue color

**cy·a·nide** \'sī-ə-ˌnīd, -nəd\ *n* : a poisonous compound of carbon and nitrogen with another element (as potassium)

**cy·ber** \'sī-bər\ *adj* : of, relating to, or involving computers or computer networks

**cyber-** *comb form* : computer : computer network

**cy·ber·bul·ly·ing** \'sī-bər-ˌbu̇-lē-iŋ, -ˌbə-\ *n* : the electronic posting of mean-spirited messages about a person

**cy·ber·ca·fe** \'sī-bər-ka-ˌfā\ *n* : a small restaurant offering use of computers with Internet access

**cy·ber·net·ics** \ˌsī-bər-ˈne-tiks\ *n* : the science of communication and control theory that is concerned esp. with the comparative study of automatic control systems — **cy·ber·net·ic** *adj*

**cy·ber·punk** \'sī-bər-ˌpəŋk\ *n* **1** : science fiction dealing with computer-dominated future societies **2** : HACKER 3

**cy·ber·sex** \'sī-bər-ˌseks\ *n* **1** : online sex-oriented conversations **2** : sex-oriented material available on a computer

**cy·ber·space** \'sī-bər-ˌspās\ *n* : the online world of the Internet

**cy·ber·ter·ror·ism** \-ˌter-ər-ˌi-zəm\ *n* : terrorist activities intended to damage or disrupt computer systems

**cy·cla·men** \'sī-klə-mən\ *n* : any of a genus of plants related to the primroses and having showy nodding flowers

**¹cy·cle** \'sī-kəl\ *n* **1** : a period of time occupied by a series of events that repeat themselves regularly and in the same order **2** : a recurring round of operations or events **3** : one complete occurrence of a periodic process (as a vibration or current alternation) **4** : a circular or spiral arrangement **5** : a long period of time : AGE **6** : BICYCLE **7** : MOTORCYCLE — **cy·clic** \'sī-klik, 'si-\ *or* **cy·cli·cal** \'klī-kəl\ *adj* — **cy·cli·cal·ly** \-k(ə-)lē\ *also* **cy·clic·ly** *adv*

**²cy·cle** \'sī-kəl\ *vb* **cy·cled; cy·cling** : to ride a cycle — **cy·clist** \'sī-klist, -kə-list\ *n*

**cy·clone** \'sī-ˌklōn\ *n* **1** : a storm or system of winds that rotates about a center of low atmospheric pressure and advancing at 20 to 30 miles (about 30 to 50 kilometers) an hour **2** : TORNADO — **cy·clon·ic** \sī-ˈklä-nik\ *adj*

**cy·clo·pe·dia** *also* **cy·clo·pae·dia** \ˌsī-klə-ˈpē-dē-ə\ *n* : ENCYCLOPEDIA

**cy·clo·tron** \'sī-klə-ˌträn\ *n* : a device for giving high speed to charged particles by magnetic and electric fields

**cy·der** *Brit var of* CIDER

**cyg·net** \'sig-nət\ *n* : a young swan

**cyl** *abbr* cylinder

**cyl·in·der** \'si-lən-dər\ *n* : the solid figure formed by turning a rectangle about one side as an axis; *also* : a body or space of this form ⟨an engine ~⟩ ⟨a bullet in the ~ of a revolver⟩ — **cy·lin·dri·cal** \sə-ˈlin-dri-kəl\ *adj*

**cym·bal** \'sim-bəl\ *n* : a concave brass plate that produces a brilliant clashing sound

**cyn·ic** \'si-nik\ *n* : one who attributes all actions to selfish motives — **cyn·i·cal** \-ni-kəl\ *adj* — **cyn·i·cal·ly** \-k(ə-)lē\ *adv* — **cyn·i·cism** \-nə-ˌsi-zəm\ *n*

**cy·no·sure** \'sī-nə-ˌshu̇r, 'si-\ *n* [MF & L; MF, Ursa Minor, fr. L *cynosura*, fr. Gk *kynosoura* Ursa Minor, guide, fr. L *Cynosura* Ursa Minor, fr. Gk *kynosoura*, fr. *kynos oura*, lit., dog's tail] : a center of attraction

**CYO** *abbr* Catholic Youth Organization

**cy·pher** *chiefly Brit var of* CIPHER

**cy·press** \'sī-prəs\ *n* **1** : any of a genus of scaly-leaved evergreen trees and shrubs **2** : BALD CYPRESS **3** : the wood of a cypress

**cyst** \'sist\ *n* : an abnormal closed bodily sac usu. containing liquid — **cys·tic** \'sis-tik\ *adj*

**cystic fibrosis** *n* : a common hereditary disease marked esp. by deficiency of pancreatic enzymes, by respiratory symptoms, and by excessive loss of salt in the sweat

**cy·tol·o·gy** \sī-'tä-lə-jē\ *n* : a branch of biology dealing with cells — **cy·to·log·i·cal** \ˌsī-tə-'lä-ji-kəl\ *or* **cy·to·log·ic** \-jik\ *adj* — **cy·tol·o·gist** \sī-'tä-lə-jist\ *n*

**cy·to·plasm** \'sī-tə-ˌpla-zəm\ *n* : the protoplasm of a cell that lies external to the nucleus — **cy·to·plas·mic** \ˌsī-tə-'plaz-mik\ *adj*

**cy·to·sine** \'sī-tə-ˌsēn\ *n* : a chemical base that is a pyrimidine coding genetic information in DNA and RNA

**CZ** *abbr* **1** Canal Zone **2** cubic zirconia

**czar** *also* **tsar** *or* **tzar** \'zär, 'tsär\ *n* [NL, fr. Russ *tsar'*, ultim. fr. L *Caesar* Caesar] : the ruler of Russia until 1917; *also* : one having agreat authority — **czar·ist** *also* **tsar·ist** *or* **tzarist** \-ist\ *n or adj*

**cza·ri·na** \zä-'rē-nə\ *n* : the wife of a czar

**Czech** \'chek\ *n* **1** : a native or inhabitant of Czechoslovakia or the Czech Republic **2** : the language of the Czechs — **Czech** *adj*

**¹d** \'dē\ *n, pl* **d's** *or* **ds** \'dēz\ *often cap* **1** : the 4th letter of the English alphabet **2** : a grade rating a student's work as poor **3** : DEFENSE

**²d** *abbr, often cap* **1** date **2** daughter **3** day **4** dead **5** deceased **6** degree **7** Democrat **8** [L *denarius, denarii*] penny; pence **9** depart; departure **10** diameter

**D** *symbol* deuterium

**DA** *abbr* **1** deposit account **2** district attorney **3** don't answer

**¹dab** \'dab\ *n* **1** : a sudden blow or thrust : POKE; *also* : PECK **2** : a gentle touch or stroke : PAT

**²dab** *vb* **dabbed; dab·bing 1** : to strike or touch gently : PAT **2** : to apply lightly or irregularly : DAUB — **dab·ber** *n*

**³dab** *n* **1** : DAUB **2** : a small amount

**dab·ble** \'da-bəl\ *vb* **dab·bled; dab·bling 1** : to wet by splashing : SPATTER **2** : to paddle or play in or as if in water **3** : to work or involve oneself without serious effort — **dab·bler** *n*

**da ca·po** \dä-'kä-(ˌ)pō\ *adv or adj* [It] : from the beginning — used as a direction in music to repeat

**dace** \'dās\ *n, pl* **dace** : any of various small No. American freshwater fishes related to the carp

**da·cha** \'dä-chə\ *n* [Russ] : a Russian country house

**dachs·hund** \'däks-ˌhùnt\ *n* [G, fr. *Dachs* badger + *Hund* dog] : any of a breed of long-bodied short-legged dogs of German origin

**dac·tyl** \'dak-t³l\ *n* [ME *dactile*, fr. L *dactylus*, fr. Gk *daktylos*, lit., finger; fr. the fact that the three syllables have the first one longest like the joints of the finger] : a metrical foot of one accented syllable followed by two unaccented syllables — **dac·tyl·ic** \dak-'ti-lik\ *adj or n*

**dad** \'dad\ *n* : FATHER 1

**Da·da** \'dä-(ˌ)dä\ *n* : a movement in art and literature based on deliberate irrationality and negation of traditional artistic values — **da·da·ism** \-ˌi-zəm\ *n, often cap* — **da·da·ist** \-ˌist\ *n or adj, often cap*

**dad·dy** \'da-dē\ *n, pl* **daddies** : FATHER 1

**dad·dy long·legs** \ˌda-dē-'lòŋ-ˌlegz\ *n, pl* **daddy longlegs** : any of an order of arachnids resembling the true spiders but having small rounded bodies and long slender legs

**daemon** *var of* DEMON

**daf·fo·dil** \'da-fə-ˌdil\ *n* : any of various bulbous herbs with usu. large flowers having a trumpetlike corolla

**daf·fy** \'da-fē\ *adj* **daf·fi·er; -est** : DAFT

**daft** \'daft\ *adj* : FOOLISH; *also* : INSANE — **daft·ness** *n*

**dag** *abbr* dekagram

**dag·ger** \'da-gər\ *n* **1** : a sharp pointed knife for stabbing **2** : a character † used as a reference mark or to indicate a death date

**da·guerre·o·type** \də-'ger-(ē-)ə-ˌtīp\ *n* : an early photograph produced on a silver or a silver-covered copper plate

**dahl·ia** \'dal-yə, 'däl-\ *n* : any of a genus of tuberous herbs related to the daisies and having showy flowers

**¹dai·ly** \'dā-lē\ *adj* **1** : occurring, done, or used every day or every weekday **2** : of or relating to every day ⟨~ visitors⟩ **3** : computed in terms of one day ⟨~ wages⟩ ♦ *Synonyms* DIURNAL, QUOTIDIAN — **dai·li·ness** \-lē-nəs\ *n* — **daily** *adv*

**²daily** *n, pl* **dailies** : a newspaper published every weekday

**daily double** *n* : a system of betting on races in which the bettor must pick the winners of two stipulated races in order to win

**¹dain·ty** \'dān-tē\ *n, pl* **dainties** [ME *deinte* high esteem, delight, fr. AF *deinté*, fr. L *dignitas* dignity, worth] : something delicious or pleasing to the taste : DELICACY

**²dainty** *adj* **dain·ti·er; -est 1** : pleasing to the taste **2** : delicately pretty **3** : having or showing delicate taste; *also* : FASTIDIOUS ♦ *Synonyms* CHOICE, DELICATE, EXQUISITE, RARE, RECHERCHÉ — **dain·ti·ly** \-ti-lē\ *adv* — **dain·ti·ness** \-tē-nəs\ *n*

**dai·qui·ri** \'dä-kə-rē, 'dī-\ *n* [*Daiquirí*, Cuba] : a cocktail made usu. of rum, lime juice, and sugar

**dairy** \'der-ē\ *n, pl* **dair·ies** [ME *deyerie,* fr. *deye* dairymaid, fr. OE *dæge* kneader of bread] **1** : CREAMERY **2** : a farm specializing in milk production

**dairy·ing** \'der-ē-iŋ\ *n* : the business of operating a dairy

**dairy·maid** \-ˌmād\ *n* : a woman employed in a dairy

**dairy·man** \-mən, -ˌman\ *n* : a person who operates a dairy farm or works in a dairy

**da·is** \'dā-əs\ *n* : a raised platform usu. above the floor of a hall or large room

**dai·sy** \'dā-zē\ *n, pl* **daisies** [ME *dayeseye,* fr. OE *dægesēage,* fr. *dæg* day + *ēage* eye] : any of numerous composite plants having flower heads in which the marginal flowers resemble petals

**dai·sy-chain** \-ˌchān\ *vb* : to link (as computer components) together in series — **daisy chain** *n*

**daisy wheel** *n* : a disk with spokes bearing type that serves as the printing element of an electric typewriter or printer; *also* : a printer that uses such a disk

**Da·ko·ta** \də-'kō-tə\ *n, pl* **Dakotas** *also* **Dakota** : a member of an American Indian people of the northern Mississippi valley; *also* : their language

**dal** *abbr* dekaliter

**da·la·si** \dä-'lä-sē\ *n, pl* **dalasi** *or* **dalasis** — see MONEY table

**dale** \'dāl\ *n* : VALLEY

**dal·ly** \'da-lē\ *vb* **dal·lied; dal·ly·ing 1** : to act playfully; *esp* : to play amorously **2** : to waste time **3** : LINGER, DAWDLE
   ♦ *Synonyms* FLIRT, COQUET, TOY, TRIFLE — **dal·li·ance** \-lē-əns\ *n*

**dal·ma·tian** \dal-'mā-shən\ *n, often cap* : any of a breed of medium-sized dogs having a white short-haired coat with many black or brown spots

**¹dam** \'dam\ *n* : the female parent of an animal and esp. of a domestic animal

**²dam** *n* : a barrier (as across a stream) to stop the flow of water — **dam** *vb*

**³dam** *abbr* dekameter

**¹dam·age** \'da-mij\ *n* **1** : loss or harm due to injury to persons, property, or reputation **2** *pl* : compensation in money imposed by law for loss or injury ⟨bring a suit for ∼*s*⟩

**²damage** *vb* **dam·aged; dam·ag·ing** : to cause damage to ⟨∼ the furniture⟩

**dam·a·scene** \'da-mə-ˌsēn\ *vb* **-scened; -scen·ing** : to ornament (as iron or steel) with wavy patterns or with inlaid work of precious metals

**dam·ask** \'da-məsk\ *n* **1** : a firm lustrous reversible figured fabric used for household linen **2** : a tough steel having decorative wavy lines

**dame** \'dām\ *n* **1** : a woman of rank, station, or authority **2** : an elderly woman **3** : WOMAN

**damn** \'dam\ *vb* [ME *dampnen,* fr. AF *dampner,* fr. L *damnare,* fr. *damnum* damage, loss, fine] **1** : to condemn esp. to hell **2** : CURSE — **damned** *adj*

**dam·na·ble** \'dam-nə-bəl\ *adj* **1** : liable to or deserving punishment **2** : DETEST-

ABLE ⟨∼ weather⟩ — **dam·na·bly** \-blē\ *adv*

**dam·na·tion** \dam-'nā-shən\ *n* **1** : the act of damning **2** : the state of being damned

**¹damp** \'damp\ *n* **1** : a noxious gas **2** : MOISTURE

**²damp** *vb* : DAMPEN

**³damp** *adj* : MOIST — **damp·ness** *n*

**damp·en** \'dam-pən\ *vb* **1** : to check or diminish in activity or vigor ⟨∼ enthusiasm⟩ **2** : to make or become damp ⟨∼ a sponge⟩

**damp·er** \'dam-pər\ *n* **1** : a dulling or deadening influence ⟨put a ∼ on the party⟩ **2** : one that damps; *esp* : a valve or movable plate (as in the flue of a stove, furnace, or fireplace) to regulate the draft

**dam·sel** \'dam-zəl\ *n* : MAIDEN, GIRL

**dam·sel·fly** \-ˌflī\ *n* : any of a group of insects that are closely related to the dragonflies but fold their wings above the body when at rest

**dam·son** \'dam-zən\ *n* : a plum with acid purple fruit; *also* : its fruit

**Dan** *abbr* Daniel

**¹dance** \'dans\ *vb* **danced; danc·ing 1** : to glide, step, or move through a set series of movements usu. to music **2** : to move quickly up and down or about **3** : to perform or take part in as a dancer — **danc·er** *n*

**²dance** *n* **1** : an act or instance of dancing **2** : a social gathering for dancing **3** : a piece of music (as a waltz) by which dancing may be guided **4** : the art of dancing

**D & C** *n* [*dilation and curettage*] : a surgical procedure that involves stretching the cervix and scraping the inside walls of the uterus (as to test for cancer or to perform an abortion)

**dan·de·li·on** \'dan-də-ˌlī-ən, dē-\ *n* [ME *dendelyoun,* fr. AF *dent de lion,* lit., lion's tooth] : any of a genus of common yellow-flowered composite herbs

**dan·der** \'dan-dər\ *n* : ANGER, TEMPER

**dan·di·fy** \'dan-di-ˌfī\ *vb* **-fied; -fy·ing** : to cause to resemble a dandy

**dan·dle** \'dan-dºl\ *vb* **dan·dled; dan·dling** : to move up and down in one's arms or on one's knee in affectionate play ♦ *Synonyms* CARESS, FONDLE, LOVE, PET

**dan·druff** \'dan-drəf\ *n* : scaly white or grayish flakes of dead skin cells that come off the scalp — **dan·druffy** \-drə-fē\ *adj*

**¹dan·dy** \'dan-dē\ *n, pl* **dandies 1** : a man unduly attentive to personal appearance **2** : something excellent in its class ♦ *Synonyms* FOP, COXCOMB, POPINJAY

**²dandy** *adj* **dan·di·er; -est** : very good : FIRST-RATE

**Dane** \'dān\ *n* **1** : a native or inhabitant of Denmark **2** : GREAT DANE

**dan·ger** \'dān-jər\ *n* [ME *daunger* control, resistance, peril, fr. AF *dangier,* fr. VL *\*dominiarium,* fr. L *dominium* ownership] **1** : exposure or liability to injury, harm, or evil **2** : something that may cause injury or harm ♦ *Synonyms* PER-IL, HAZARD, RISK, JEOPARDY

**dan·ger·ous** \'dān-jə-rəs\ *adj* **1** : HAZ-ARDOUS, PERILOUS ⟨a ∼ slope⟩ **2** : able or likely to inflict injury ⟨a ∼ man⟩ — **dan·ger·ous·ly** *adv*

**dan·gle** \'daŋ-gəl\ *vb* **dan·gled; dan·gling** **1** : to hang loosely esp. with a swinging motion : SWING **2** : to be a hanger-on or dependent **3** : to be left without proper grammatical connection in a sentence ⟨a *dangling* participle⟩ **4** : to keep hanging uncertainly **5** : to offer as an inducement

**Dan·iel** \'dan-yəl\ *n* — see BIBLE table

**Dan·ish** \'dā-nish\ *n* : the language of the Danes — **Danish** *adj*

**Danish pastry** *n* : a pastry made of a rich yeast-raised dough

**dank** \'daŋk\ *adj* : disagreeably wet or moist : DAMP — **dank·ness** *n*

**dan·seuse** \dänⁿ-'sərz, -'səz; dän-'süz\ *n* [F] : a female ballet dancer

**dap·per** \'da-pər\ *adj* **1** : SPRUCE, TRIM **2** : being alert and lively in movement and manners : JAUNTY

**dap·ple** \'da-pəl\ *vb* **dap·pled; dap·pling** : to mark with different-colored spots

**DAR** *abbr* Daughters of the American Revolution

**¹dare** \'der\ *vb* **dared; dar·ing** **1** : to have sufficient courage : be bold enough to **2** : CHALLENGE ⟨*dared* him to jump⟩ **3** : to confront boldly

**²dare** *n* : an act or instance of daring : CHALLENGE

**dare·dev·il** \-,de-vəl\ *n* : a recklessly bold person — **daredevil** *adj*

**dar·ing** \'der-iŋ\ *n* : venturesome boldness — **daring** *adj* — **dar·ing·ly** *adv*

**¹dark** \'därk\ *adj* **1** : being without light or without much light **2** : not light in color ⟨a ∼ suit⟩ **3** : GLOOMY ⟨a ∼ outlook⟩ **4** *often cap* : being a period of stagnation or decline ⟨the *Dark* Ages⟩ **5** : SECRETIVE ⟨∼ dealings⟩ ♦ *Synonyms* DIM, DUSKY, MURKY, TENEBROUS — **dark·ly** *adv* — **dark·ness** *n*

**²dark** *n* **1** : absence of light : DARKNESS; *esp* : NIGHT **2** : a dark or deep color — **in the dark** **1** : in secrecy **2** : in ignorance ⟨kept *in the dark* about the plans⟩

**dark·en** \'där-kən\ *vb* **1** : to make or grow dark or darker **2** : DIM **3** : BESMIRCH, TARNISH **4** : to make or become gloomy or forbidding

**dark horse** *n* : a contestant or a political figure whose abilities and chances as a contender are not known

**dark·ling** \'där-kliŋ\ *adj* **1** : DARK ⟨a ∼ plain⟩ **2** : MYSTERIOUS

**dark·room** \'därk-,rüm, -,rum\ *n* : a light-proof room in which photographic materials are processed

**¹dar·ling** \'där-liŋ\ *n* **1** : a dearly loved person **2** : FAVORITE

**²darling** *adj* **1** : dearly loved : FAVORITE **2** : very pleasing : CHARMING

**darm·stadt·i·um** \,därm-'sta-tē-əm\ *n* : a short-lived radioactive chemical element produced artificially

**¹darn** \'därn\ *vb* : to mend with darning stitches — **darn·er** *n*

**²darn** *or* **darned** \'därnd\ *adv* : VERY, EXTREMELY ⟨a ∼ good job⟩

**darning needle** *n* **1** : a needle for darning **2** : DRAGONFLY

**¹dart** \'därt\ *n* **1** : a small missile with a point on one end and feathers on the other; *also, pl* : a game in which darts are thrown at a target **2** : something causing a sudden pain **3** : a stitched tapering fold in a garment **4** : a quick movement

**²dart** *vb* **1** : to throw with a sudden movement **2** : to thrust or move suddenly or rapidly ⟨∼ed across the street⟩ **3** : to shoot with a dart containing a usu. tranquilizing drug

**dart·er** \'där-tər\ *n* : any of numerous small No. American freshwater fishes related to the perches

**Dar·win·ism** \'där-wə-,ni-zəm\ *n* : a theory explaining the origin and continued existence of new species of plants and animals by means of natural selection acting on chance variations — **Dar·win·ist** \-nist\ *n or adj*

**¹dash** \'dash\ *vb* **1** : SMASH **2** : to knock, hurl, or thrust violently **3** : SPLASH, SPATTER **4** : RUIN **5** : DEPRESS, SADDEN **6** : to perform or finish hastily ⟨∼ off a letter⟩ **7** : to move with sudden speed ⟨∼ed down the hall⟩

**²dash** *n* **1** : a sudden burst or splash **2** : a stroke of a pen **3** : a punctuation mark — that is used esp. to indicate a break in the thought or structure of a sentence **4** : a small addition ⟨a ∼ of salt⟩ **5** : flashy showiness **6** : animation in style and action **7** : a sudden rush or attempt ⟨made a ∼ for the door⟩ **8** : a short foot race **9** : DASHBOARD

**dash·board** \-,bórd\ *n* : a panel in an automobile or aircraft below the windshield usu. containing dials and controls

**dash·er** \'da-shər\ *n* : a device (as in a churn) for agitating something

**da·shi·ki** \də-'shē-kē\ *also* **dai·shi·ki** \dī-\ *n* [modif. of Yoruba (an African language) *dànṣíkí*] : a usu. brightly colored loose-fitting pullover garment

**dash·ing** \'da-shiŋ\ *adj* **1** : marked by vigorous action **2** : marked by smartness esp. in dress and manners ♦ *Synonyms* STYLISH, CHIC, FASHIONABLE, MODISH, SMART, SWANK

**das·tard** \'das-tərd\ *n* **1** : COWARD **2** : a person who acts treacherously — **das·tard·ly** *adj*

**dat** *abbr* dative

**da·ta** \'dā-tə, 'da-, 'dä-\ *n sing or pl* [L, pl. of *datum*] : factual information (as measurements or statistics) used as a basis for reasoning, discussion, or calculation

**da·ta·base** \-,bās\ *n* : a usu. large collection of data organized esp. for rapid search and retrieval (as by a computer) — **database** *vb*

**data processing** *n* : the action or process of supplying a computer with information and having the computer use it to produce a desired result

**¹date** \'dāt\ *n* [ME, fr. AF, ultim. fr. L *dac-*

tylus, fr. Gk *daktylos*, lit., finger] : the oblong edible fruit of a tall palm; *also* : this palm

²**date** *n* [ME, fr. AF, fr. LL *data*, fr. *data* (as in *data Romae* given at Rome), fem. of L *datus*, pp. of *dare* to give] **1** : the day, month, or year of an event **2** : a statement giving the time of execution or making (as of a coin or check) **3** : the period to which something belongs **4** : APPOINTMENT; *esp* : a social engagement between two persons that often has a romantic character **5** : a person with whom one has a usu. romantic date — **to date** : up to the present moment

³**date** *vb* **dat·ed; dat·ing** **1** : to record the date of or on **2** : to determine, mark, or reveal the date, age, or period of **3** : go on a date or dates with ⟨~ed her for a year⟩ **4** : ORIGINATE ⟨~s from ancient times⟩ **5** : EXTEND ⟨dating back to childhood⟩ **6** : to show qualities typical of a past period

**dat·ed** \'dā-təd\ *adj* **1** : provided with a date **2** : OLD-FASHIONED ⟨a ~ custom⟩
♦ *Synonyms* ANTIQUATED, ARCHAIC, OLD HAT, OUTDATED, OUTMODED, PASSÉ

**date·less** \'dāt-ləs\ *adj* **1** : ENDLESS **2** : having no date **3** : too ancient to be dated **4** : TIMELESS

**date·line** \'dāt-,līn\ *n* : a line in a publication giving the date and place of composition or issue — **dateline** *vb*

**date rape** *n* : rape committed by the victim's date

**da·tive** \'dā-tiv\ *adj* : of, relating to, or constituting a grammatical case marking typically the indirect object of a verb — **dative** *n*

**da·tum** \'dā-təm, 'da-, 'dä-\ *n, pl* **da·ta** \-tə\ *or* **datums** : a single piece of data : FACT

**dau** *abbr* daughter

¹**daub** \'dòb\ *vb* **1** : to cover with soft adhesive matter **2** : SMEAR, SMUDGE **3** : to paint crudely — **daub·er** *n*

²**daub** *n* **1** : something daubed on : SMEAR **2** : a crude picture

**daugh·ter** \'dò-tər\ *n* **1** : a female offspring esp. of human beings **2** : a female adopted child **3** : a human female descendant — **daughter** *adj* — **daugh·ter·less** \-ləs\ *adj*

**daugh·ter–in–law** \'dò-tə-rən-,lò\ *n, pl* **daugh·ters–in–law** \-tər-zən-\ : the wife of one's son

**daunt** \'dònt\ *vb* [ME, fr. AF *danter*, *daunter*, fr. L *domitare* to tame] : to lessen the courage of : INTIMIDATE, OVERWHELM

**daunt·ing** \'dòn-tiŋ\ *adj* : tending to overwhelm or intimidate ⟨a ~ task⟩

**daunt·less** \-ləs\ *adj* : FEARLESS, UNDAUNTED ♦ *Synonyms* BRAVE, BOLD, COURAGEOUS, LIONHEARTED — **daunt·less·ly** *adv*

**dau·phin** \'dò-fən\ *n, often cap* : the eldest son of a king of France

**DAV** *abbr* Disabled American Veterans

**dav·en·port** \'da-vən-,pòrt\ *n* : a large upholstered sofa

**da·vit** \'dā-vət, 'da-\ *n* : a small crane on a

ship used in pairs esp. to raise or lower boats

**daw·dle** \'dò-d²l\ *vb* **daw·dled; daw·dling** **1** : to spend time wastefully or idly **2** : LOITER — **daw·dler** *n*

¹**dawn** \'dòn\ *vb* **1** : to begin to grow light as the sun rises **2** : to begin to appear or develop **3** : to begin to be understood ⟨the solution ~ed on him⟩

²**dawn** *n* **1** : the first appearance of light in the morning **2** : a first appearance : BEGINNING ⟨the ~ of a new era⟩

**day** \'dā\ *n* **1** : the period of light between one night and the next; *also* : DAYLIGHT, DAYTIME **2** : the period of rotation of a planet (as earth) or a moon on its axis **3** : a period of 24 hours beginning at midnight **4** : a specified day or date ⟨wedding ~⟩ **5** : a specified time or period : AGE ⟨in olden ~s⟩ **6** : the conflict or contention of the day **7** : the time set apart by usage or law for work ⟨the 8-hour ~⟩

**day·bed** \'dā-,bed\ *n* : a couch that can be converted into a bed

**day·book** \-,bùk\ *n* : DIARY, JOURNAL

**day·break** \-,brāk\ *n* : DAWN

**day care** *n* : supervision of and care for children or disabled adults provided during the day; *also* : a program offering day care

**day·dream** \'dā-,drēm\ *n* : a pleasant reverie — **daydream** *vb*

**day·light** \'dā-,līt\ *n* **1** : the light of day **2** : DAYTIME **3** : DAWN **4** : understanding of something that has been obscure **5** *pl* : CONSCIOUSNESS; *also* : WITS **6** : a perceptible space, gap, or difference

**daylight saving time** *n* : time usu. one hour ahead of standard time

**Day of Atonement** : YOM KIPPUR

**day school** *n* : a private school without boarding facilities

**day student** *n* : a student who attends regular classes at a college or preparatory school but does not live there

**day·time** \'dā-,tīm\ *n* : the period of daylight

**daze** \'dāz\ *vb* **dazed; daz·ing** **1** : to stupefy esp. by a blow **2** : DAZZLE — **daze** *n* — **da·zed·ly** \'dā-zəd-lē\ *adv*

**daz·zle** \'da-zəl\ *vb* **daz·zled; daz·zling** **1** : to overpower with light **2** : to impress greatly or confound with brilliance ⟨dazzled by her wit⟩ — **dazzle** *n*

**dB** *abbr* decibel

**Db** *symbol* dubnium

**d/b/a** *abbr* doing business as

**dbl** *or* **dble** *abbr* double

**DC** *abbr* **1** [It *da capo*] from the beginning **2** direct current **3** District of Columbia **4** doctor of chiropractic

**DD** *abbr* **1** days after date **2** demand draft **3** dishonorable discharge **4** doctor of divinity

**D–day** *n* [D, abbr. for *day*] : a day set for launching an operation (as an invasion)

**DDS** *abbr* doctor of dental surgery

**DDT** \,dē-(,)dē-'tē\ *n* : a persistent insecticide poisonous to many higher animals

**DE** *abbr* Delaware

**dea·con** \'dē-kən\ *n* [ME *dekene*, fr. OE *dēacon*, fr. LL *diaconus*, fr. Gk *diakonos*, lit., servant] : a subordinate officer in a Christian church

**dea·con·ess** \'dē-kə-nəs\ *n* : a woman chosen to assist in the church ministry

**de·ac·ti·vate** \dē-'ak-tə-ˌvāt\ *vb* : to make inactive or ineffective

¹**dead** \'ded\ *adj* 1 : LIFELESS 2 : DEATHLIKE, DEADLY ⟨in a ~ faint⟩ 3 : NUMB 4 : very tired 5 : UNRESPONSIVE 6 : EXTINGUISHED ⟨~ coals⟩ 7 : INANIMATE, INERT 8 : no longer active or functioning ⟨a ~ battery⟩ 9 : lacking power, significance, or effect ⟨a ~ custom⟩ 10 : OBSOLETE ⟨a ~ language⟩ 11 : lacking in gaiety or animation ⟨a ~ party⟩ 12 : QUIET, IDLE, UNPRODUCTIVE ⟨~ capital⟩ 13 : lacking elasticity ⟨a ~ tennis ball⟩ 14 : not circulating : STAGNANT ⟨~ air⟩ 15 : lacking warmth, vigor, or taste ⟨~ wine⟩ 16 : absolutely uniform ⟨~ level⟩ 17 : UNERRING, EXACT ⟨a ~ shot⟩ 18 : ABRUPT ⟨a ~ stop⟩ 19 : COMPLETE ⟨a ~ loss⟩

²**dead** *n, pl* **dead** 1 : one that is dead — usu. used collectively ⟨the living and the ~⟩ 2 : the time of greatest quiet ⟨the ~ of the night⟩

³**dead** *adv* 1 : UTTERLY ⟨~ right⟩ 2 : in a sudden and complete manner ⟨stopped ~⟩ 3 : DIRECTLY ⟨~ ahead⟩

**dead·beat** \-ˌbēt\ *n* : a person who persistently fails to pay personal debts or expenses

**dead duck** *n* : GONER

**dead·en** \'de-dᵊn\ *vb* 1 : to impair in vigor or sensation : BLUNT ⟨~ pain⟩ 2 : to lessen the luster or spirit of 3 : to make (as a wall) soundproof

**dead end** *n* 1 : an end (as of a street) without an exit 2 : a position, situation, or course of action that leads to nothing further — **dead–end** \ˌded-ˌend\ *adj*

**dead heat** *n* : a contest in which two or more contestants tie (as by crossing the finish line simultaneously)

**dead horse** *n* : an exhausted topic or issue

**dead letter** *n* 1 : something that has lost its force or authority without being formally abolished 2 : a letter that cannot be delivered or returned

**dead·line** \'ded-ˌlīn\ *n* : a date or time before which something must be done

**dead·lock** \'ded-ˌläk\ *n* 1 : a stoppage of action because neither faction in a struggle will give in 2 : a tie score — **deadlock** *vb*

¹**dead·ly** \'ded-lē\ *adj* **dead·li·er; -est** 1 : likely to cause or capable of causing death 2 : HOSTILE, IMPLACABLE 3 : very accurate : UNERRING 4 : tending to deprive of force or vitality ⟨a ~ habit⟩ 5 : suggestive of death 6 : very great : EXTREME — **dead·li·ness** *n*

²**deadly** *adv* 1 : suggesting death ⟨~ pale⟩ 2 : EXTREMELY ⟨~ dull⟩

**deadly sin** *n* : one of seven sins of pride, covetousness, lust, anger, gluttony, envy, and sloth held to be fatal to spiritual progress

**dead meat** *n* : one that is doomed

¹**dead·pan** \'ded-ˌpan\ *adj* : marked by an impassive manner or expression ⟨~ humor⟩ — **deadpan** *vb* — **deadpan** *adv*

²**deadpan** *n* : a completely expressionless face

**dead reckoning** *n* : the determination of the position of a ship or aircraft solely from the record of the direction and distance of its course

**dead·weight** \'ded-'wāt\ *n* 1 : the unrelieved weight of an inert mass 2 : a ship's load including the weight of cargo, fuel, crew, and passengers

**dead·wood** \-ˌwud\ *n* 1 : wood dead on the tree 2 : useless personnel or material

**deaf** \'def\ *adj* 1 : unable to hear 2 : unwilling to hear or listen ⟨~ to all suggestions⟩ — **deaf·ness** *n*

**deaf·en** \'de-fən\ *vb* : to make deaf

¹**deal** \'dēl\ *n* 1 : a usu. large or indefinite quantity or degree ⟨a great ~ of support⟩ 2 : the act or right of distributing cards to players in a card game; *also* : HAND

²**deal** *vb* **dealt** \'delt\; **deal·ing** 1 : DISTRIBUTE; *esp* : to distribute playing cards to players in a game 2 : ADMINISTER, DELIVER ⟨*dealt* him a blow⟩ 3 : to concern itself : TREAT ⟨the book ~s with crime⟩ 4 : to take action in regard to something ⟨~ with offenders⟩ 5 : TRADE; *also* : to sell or distribute something as a business ⟨~ in used cars⟩ 6 : to reach a state of acceptance ⟨~ with her child's death⟩ — **deal·er** *n*

³**deal** *n* 1 : BARGAINING, NEGOTIATION 2 : TRANSACTION; *esp* : an agreement by contract 3 : treatment received ⟨a raw ~⟩ 4 : an often secret agreement or arrangement for mutual advantage 5 : BARGAIN

⁴**deal** *n* : wood or a board of fir or pine

**deal·er·ship** \'dē-lər-ˌship\ *n* : an authorized sales agency ⟨an auto ~⟩

**deal·ing** \'dē-liŋ\ *n* 1 : a way of acting or of doing business 2 *pl* : friendly or business transactions

**dean** \'dēn\ *n* [ME *deen*, fr. AF *deien*, fr. LL *decanus*, lit., chief of ten, fr. Gk *dekanos*, fr. *deka* ten] 1 : a clergyman who is head of a group of canons or of joint pastors of a church 2 : the head of a division, faculty, college, or school of a university 3 : a college or secondary school administrator in charge of counseling and disciplining students 4 : DOYEN ⟨the ~ of a diplomatic corps⟩ — **dean·ship** *n*

**dean·ery** \'dē-nə-rē\ *n, pl* **-er·ies** : the office, jurisdiction, or official residence of a clerical dean

¹**dear** \'dir\ *adj* 1 : highly valued : PRECIOUS 2 : AFFECTIONATE, FOND 3 : EXPENSIVE 4 : HEARTFELT — **dear·ly** *adv* — **dear·ness** *n*

²**dear** *n* : a loved one : DARLING

**Dear John** \-'jän\ *n* : a letter (as to a soldier) in which a woman breaks off a marital or romantic relationship

**dearth** \'dərth\ *n* 1 : SCARCITY, FAMINE

**2** : an inadequate supply : LACK ⟨a ~ of jobs⟩

**death** \'deth\ *n* **1** : the end of life **2** : the cause of loss of life **3** : a cause of ruin **4** : the state of being dead **5** : DESTRUCTION, EXTINCTION **6** : SLAUGHTER — **death·like** *adj*

**death·bed** \-,bed\ *n* **1** : the bed in which a person dies **2** : the last hours of life

**death·blow** \-,blō\ *n* : a destructive or killing stroke or event

**death grip** *n* : an extremely tight grip or hold

**death·less** \-ləs\ *adj* : IMMORTAL, IMPERISHABLE ⟨~ fame⟩

**death·ly** \-lē\ *adj* **1** : FATAL **2** : of, relating to, or suggestive of death ⟨a ~ pallor⟩ — **deathly** *adv*

**death rattle** *n* : a sound produced by air passing through mucus in the lungs and air passages of a dying person

**death's-head** \'deths-,hed\ *n* : a human skull emblematic of death

**death·watch** \'deth-,wäch\ *n* : a vigil kept over the dead or dying

**deb** \'deb\ *n* : DEBUTANTE

**de·ba·cle** \di-'bä-kəl, -'ba-\ *also* **dé·bâ·cle** \*same or* dā-'bäk\ *n* [F *débâcle*] : DISASTER, FAILURE, ROUT ⟨stock market ~⟩

**de·bar** \di-'bär\ *vb* : to bar from having or doing something : PRECLUDE

**de·bark** \di-'bärk\ *vb* : DISEMBARK — **bar·ka·tion** \dē-,bär-'kā-shən\ *n*

**de·base** \di-'bās\ *vb* : to lower in character, quality, or value ♦ *Synonyms* DEGRADE, CORRUPT, DEPRAVE — **de·base·ment** *n*

**de·bate** \di-'bāt\ *vb* **de·bat·ed; de·bat·ing 1** : to discuss a question by considering opposed arguments **2** : to take part in a debate — **de·bat·able** *adj* — **debate** *n* — **de·bat·er** *n*

**de·bauch** \di-'bȯch\ *vb* : SEDUCE, CORRUPT ♦ *Synonyms* DEBASE, DEMORALIZE, DEPRAVE, PERVERT — **de·bauch·ery** \-'bȯ-chə-rē\ *n*

**de·ben·ture** \di-'ben-chər\ *n* : BOND; *esp* : one secured by the general credit of the issuer rather than a lien on particular assets

**de·bil·i·tate** \di-'bi-lə-,tāt\ *vb* **-tat·ed; -tat·ing** : to impair the health or strength of ♦ *Synonyms* WEAKEN, DISABLE, ENFEEBLE, UNDERMINE

**de·bil·i·ty** \di-'bi-lə-tē\ *n, pl* **-ties** : an infirm or weakened state

¹**deb·it** \'de-bət\ *vb* : to enter as a debit : charge with or as a debit

²**debit** *n* **1** : an entry in an account showing money paid out or owed **2** : DISADVANTAGE, SHORTCOMING

**debit card** *n* : a card by which money may be withdrawn or the cost of purchases paid directly from the holder's bank account

**deb·o·nair** \,de-bə-'ner\ *adj* [ME *debonere*, fr. AF *debonoire*, fr. *de bon aire* of good family or nature] : SUAVE, URBANE; *also* : LIGHTHEARTED

**de·bouch** \di-'baúch, -'büsh\ *vb* [F *dé-*

*boucher*, fr. *dé-* out of + *bouche* mouth] : to come out into an open area : EMERGE

**de·brief** \di-'brēf\ *vb* **1** : to question (as a pilot back from a mission) in order to obtain useful information **2** : to review carefully upon completion

**de·bris** \də-'brē, dā-; 'dā-,brē\ *n, pl* **de·bris** \-'brēz, -,brēz\ **1** : the remains of something broken down or destroyed **2** : an accumulation of rock fragments **3** : RUBBISH

**debt** \'det\ *n* **1** : SIN, TRESPASS **2** : something owed : OBLIGATION **3** : a condition of owing

**debt·or** \'de-tər\ *n* **1** : one guilty of neglect or violation of duty **2** : one that owes a debt

**de·bug** \(,)dē-'bəg\ *vb* : to eliminate errors in ⟨~ a computer program⟩

**de·bunk** \dē-'bəŋk\ *vb* : to expose the sham or falseness of ⟨~ a legend⟩

¹**de·but** \'dā-,byü, dā-'byü\ *n* **1** : a first appearance **2** : a formal entrance into society

²**debut** *vb* : to make a debut; *also* : INTRODUCE

**deb·u·tante** \'de-byü-,tänt\ *n* : a young woman making her formal entrance into society

**dec** *abbr* **1** deceased **2** decrease

**Dec** *abbr* December

**de·cade** \'de-,kād, de-'kād\ *n* : a period of 10 years

**dec·a·dence** \'de-kə-dəns, di-'kā-dⁿs\ *n* : DETERIORATION, DECLINE — **dec·a·dent** \'de-kə-dənt, di-'kā-dⁿt\ *adj or n*

**de·caf** \'dē-,kaf\ *n* : decaffeinated coffee

**de·caf·fein·at·ed** \(,)dē-'ka-fə-,nā-təd\ *adj* : having the caffeine removed ⟨~ coffee⟩

**deca·gon** \'de-kə-,gän\ *n* : a plane polygon of 10 angles and 10 sides

**de·cal** \'dē-,kal\ *n* : a picture, design, or label made to be transferred (as to glass) from specially prepared paper

**de·cal·co·ma·nia** \di-,kal-kə-'mā-nē-ə\ *n* [F *décalcomanie*, fr. *décalquer* to copy by tracing (fr. *calquer* to trace, fr. It *calcare*, lit., to tread, fr. L) + *manie* mania, fr. LL *mania*] : the process of making decals; *also* : DECAL

**Deca·logue** \'de-kə-,lȯg\ *n* : TEN COMMANDMENTS

**de·camp** \di-'kamp\ *vb* **1** : to break up a camp **2** : to depart suddenly ♦ *Synonyms* ESCAPE, ABSCOND, FLEE

**de·cant** \di-'kant\ *vb* : to pour (as wine) from one vessel into another

**de·cant·er** \di-'kan-tər\ *n* : an ornamental glass bottle for serving wine

**de·cap·i·tate** \di-'ka-pə-,tāt\ *vb* **-tat·ed; -tat·ing** : BEHEAD — **de·cap·i·ta·tion** \-,ka-pə-'tā-shən\ *n* — **de·cap·i·ta·tor** \-'ka-pə-,tā-tər\ *n*

**deca·syl·lab·ic** \,de-kə-sə-'la-bik\ *adj* : having or composed of verses having 10 syllables — **decasyllabic** *n*

**de·cath·lon** \di-'kath-lən, -,län\ *n* : a 10-event athletic contest

**de·cay** \di-'kā\ *vb* **1** : to decline from a sound or prosperous condition ⟨a ~ing town⟩ **2** : to cause or undergo decomposition ⟨radium *∼s* slowly⟩; *esp* : to break down while spoiling : ROT ⟨*∼ing* teeth⟩ — **decay** *n*

**decd** *abbr* deceased

**de·cease** \di-'sēs\ *n* : DEATH

¹**de·ceased** \-'sēst\ *adj* : no longer living; *esp* : recently dead

²**deceased** *n, pl* **deceased** : a dead person

**de·ce·dent** \di-'sē-d°nt\ *n* : a deceased person

**de·ceit** \di-'sēt\ *n* **1** : DECEPTION **2** : TRICK **3** : DECEITFULNESS ♦ **Synonyms** DISSIMULATION, DUPLICITY, GUILE

**de·ceit·ful** \-fəl\ *adj* **1** : practicing or tending to practice deceit **2** : MISLEADING, DECEPTIVE ⟨a *∼* answer⟩ — **de·ceit·ful·ly** *adv* — **de·ceit·ful·ness** *n*

**de·ceive** \di-'sēv\ *vb* **de·ceived; de·ceiv·ing 1** : to cause to believe an untruth **2** : to use or practice deceit ♦ **Synonyms** BEGUILE, BETRAY, DELUDE, MISLEAD — **de·ceiv·er** *n*

**de·cel·er·ate** \dē-'se-lə-,rāt\ *vb* **-at·ed; -at·ing** : to slow down

**De·cem·ber** \di-'sem-bər\ *n* [ME *Decembre,* fr. OE or AF, both fr. L *December* (tenth month), fr. *decem* ten] : the 12th month of the year

**de·cen·cy** \'dē-s°n-sē\ *n, pl* **-cies 1** : PROPRIETY **2** : conformity to standards of taste, propriety, or quality **3** : standard of propriety — usu. used in pl.

**de·cen·ni·al** \di-'se-nē-əl\ *adj* **1** : consisting of 10 years **2** : happening every 10 years ⟨*∼* census⟩

**de·cent** \'dē-s°nt\ *adj* **1** : conforming to standards of propriety, good taste, or morality **2** : modestly clothed **3** : free from immodesty or obscenity **4** : ADEQUATE ⟨*∼* housing⟩ — **de·cent·ly** *adv*

**de·cen·tral·i·za·tion** \dē-,sen-trə-lə-'zā-shən\ *n* **1** : the distribution of powers from a central authority to regional and local authorities **2** : the redistribution of population and industry from urban centers to outlying areas — **de·cen·tral·ize** \-'sen-trə-,līz\ *vb*

**de·cep·tion** \di-'sep-shən\ *n* **1** : the act of deceiving **2** : the fact or condition of being deceived **3** : FRAUD, TRICK — **de·cep·tive** \-'sep-tiv\ *adj* — **de·cep·tive·ly** *adv* — **de·cep·tive·ness** *n*

**deci·bel** \'de-sə-,bel, -bəl\ *n* : a unit for measuring the relative loudness of sounds

**de·cide** \di-'sīd\ *vb* **de·cid·ed; de·cid·ing** [ME, fr. L *decidere,* lit., to cut off, fr. *de-* off + *caedere* to cut] **1** : make a final choice or judgment **2** : to bring to a definitive end ⟨one blow *decided* the fight⟩ **3** : to induce to come to a choice

**de·cid·ed** \di-'sī-dəd\ *adj* **1** : UNQUESTIONABLE ⟨a *∼* advantage⟩ **2** : FIRM, DETERMINED — **de·cid·ed·ly** *adv*

**de·cid·u·ous** \di-'si-jə-wəs\ *adj* : falling off or out usu. at the end of a period of growth or function ⟨*∼* leaves⟩ ⟨a *∼* tooth⟩ **2** : having deciduous parts ⟨*∼* trees⟩

**deci·gram** \'de-sə-,gram\ *n* — see METRIC SYSTEM table

**deci·li·ter** \-,lē-tər\ *n* — see METRIC SYSTEM table

¹**dec·i·mal** \'de-sə-məl\ *adj* : based on the number 10 : reckoning by tens

²**decimal** *n* : any number expressed in base 10; *esp* : DECIMAL FRACTION

**decimal fraction** *n* : a fraction or mixed number in which the denominator is a power of 10 and that is usu. expressed with a decimal point ⟨the *decimal fraction* .25 is equivalent to the common fraction $^{25}/_{100}$⟩

**decimal place** *n* : the position of a digit as counted to the right of the decimal point in a decimal fraction

**decimal point** *n* : a period, centered dot, or in some countries a comma at the left of a decimal fraction (as .678) less than one or between a whole number and a decimal fraction in a mixed number (as 3.678)

**dec·i·mate** \'de-sə-,māt\ *vb* **-mat·ed; -mat·ing 1** : to take or destroy the 10th part of **2** : to cause great destruction or harm to ⟨factories *decimated* by fire⟩

**deci·me·ter** \'de-sə-,mē-tər\ *n* — see METRIC SYSTEM table

**de·ci·pher** \di-'sī-fər\ *vb* **1** : DECODE **2** : to make out the meaning of despite indistinctness — **de·ci·pher·able** *adj*

**de·ci·sion** \di-'si-zhən\ *n* **1** : the act or result of deciding **2** : promptness and firmness in deciding : DETERMINATION

**de·ci·sive** \-'sī-siv\ *adj* **1** : having the power to decide ⟨the *∼* vote⟩ **2** : RESOLUTE, DETERMINED **3** : CONCLUSIVE ⟨a *∼* victory⟩ — **de·ci·sive·ly** *adv* — **de·ci·sive·ness** *n*

¹**deck** \'dek\ *n* **1** : a floorlike platform of a ship; *also* : something resembling the deck of a ship **2** : a pack of playing cards

²**deck** *vb* **1** : ARRAY ⟨men *∼ed* out in suits⟩ **2** : DECORATE **3** : to furnish with a deck **4** : KNOCK DOWN, FLOOR

**deck·hand** \'dek-,hand\ *n* : a sailor who performs manual duties

**de·claim** \di-'klām\ *vb* : to speak or deliver in the manner of a formal speech ⟨an actor *∼ing* his lines⟩ — **dec·la·ma·tion** \,de-klə-'mā-shən\ *n* — **de·clam·a·to·ry** \di-'kla-mə-,tòr-ē\ *adj*

**de·clar·a·tive** \di-'kler-ə-tiv\ *adj* : making a declaration ⟨*∼* sentence⟩

**de·clare** \di-'kler\ *vb* **de·clared; de·clar·ing 1** : to make known formally, officially, or explicitly : ANNOUNCE ⟨*∼* war⟩ **2** : to state emphatically : AFFIRM **3** : to make a full statement of ♦ **Synonyms** BLAZON, BROADCAST, PROCLAIM, PUBLISH — **dec·la·ra·tion** \,de-klə-'rā-shən\ *n* — **de·clar·a·to·ry** \di-'kler-ə-,tòr-ē\ *adj* — **de·clar·er** *n*

**de·clas·si·fy** \dē-'kla-sə-,fī\ *vb* : to remove the security classification of ⟨*∼* documents⟩ — **de·clas·si·fi·ca·tion** \-,kla-sə-fə-'kā-shən\ *n*

**de·clen·sion** \di-'klen-chən\ *n* **1** : the inflectional forms of a noun, pronoun, or adjective **2** : DECLINE, DETERIORATION **3** : DESCENT, SLOPE

¹**de·cline** \di-'klīn\ *vb* **de·clined; de·clin·ing 1** : to slope downward : DESCEND **2**

: DROOP **3** : RECEDE ⟨morale *declined*⟩ **4** : WANE **5** : to withhold consent; *also* : REFUSE, REJECT ⟨∼ an invitation⟩ ⟨∼ to answer⟩ **6** : INFLECT 2 ⟨∼ a noun⟩ — **de·clin·able** *adj* — **dec·li·na·tion** \de-klə-'nā-shən\ *n*

**²decline** *n* **1** : a gradual sinking and wasting away **2** : a change to a lower state or level **3** : the time when something is approaching its end ⟨an empire in ∼⟩ **4** : a descending slope

**de·cliv·i·ty** \di-'kli-və-tē\ *n, pl* **-ties** : a steep downward slope

**de·code** \dē-'kōd\ *vb* : to convert (a coded message) into ordinary language — **de·cod·er** *n*

**dé·col·le·tage** \dā-,kä-lə-'tàzh\ *n* : the low-cut neckline of a dress

**dé·col·le·té** \dā-,käl-'tā\ *adj* [F] **1** : wearing a strapless or low-necked gown **2** : having a low-cut neckline

**de·com·mis·sion** \dē-kə-'mi-shən\ *vb* : to remove from service

**de·com·pose** \dē-kəm-'pōz\ *vb* **1** : to separate into constituent parts **2** : to break down in decay : ROT — **de·com·po·si·tion** \dē-,käm-pə-'zi-shən\ *n*

**de·com·press** \dē-kəm-'pres\ *vb* : to release from pressure or compression — **de·com·pres·sion** \-'pre-shən\ *n*

**decompression sickness** *n* : ²BEND 3

**de·con·ges·tant** \dē-kən-'jes-tənt\ *n* : an agent that relieves congestion (as of mucous membranes)

**de·con·struc·tion** \dē-kən-'strək-shən\ *n* : the analysis of something (as language or literature) by the separation and individual examination of its basic elements — **de·con·struct** \-'strəkt\ *vb*

**de·con·tam·i·nate** \dē-kən-'ta-mə-,nāt\ *vb* : to rid of contamination (as radioactive material) — **de·con·tam·i·na·tion** \-,ta-mə-'nā-shən\ *n*

**de·con·trol** \dē-kən-'trōl\ *vb* : to end control of ⟨∼ prices⟩ — **decontrol** *n*

**de·cor** *or* **dé·cor** \dā-'kòr, 'dā-,kòr\ *n* : DECORATION; *esp* : the style and layout of interior furnishings

**dec·o·rate** \'de-kə-,rāt\ *vb* **-rat·ed; -rat·ing** **1** : to furnish with something ornamental ⟨∼ a room⟩ **2** : to award a mark of honor (as a medal) to ⟨*decorated* soldiers⟩ ✦ *Synonyms* ADORN, BEAUTIFY, BEDECK, GARNISH, ORNAMENT

**dec·o·ra·tion** \de-kə-'rā-shən\ *n* **1** : ORNAMENT **2** : a badge of honor

**dec·o·ra·tive** \'de-kə-rə-tiv\ *adj* : ORNAMENTAL

**dec·o·ra·tor** \'de-kə-,rā-tər\ *n* : one that decorates; *esp* : a person who designs or executes interiors and their furnishings

**de·co·rous** \'de-kə-rəs, di-'kòr-əs\ *adj* : PROPER, SEEMLY, CORRECT

**de·co·rum** \di-'kòr-əm\ *n* [L] **1** : conformity to accepted standards of conduct **2** : ORDERLINESS, PROPRIETY

**¹de·coy** \'dē-,kòi, di-'kòi\ *n* [prob. fr. D *de kooi*, lit., the cage] **1** : something that lures or entices; *esp* : an artificial bird used to attract live birds within shot **2**

: something used to draw attention away from another

**²de·coy** \di-'kòi, 'dē-,kòi\ *vb* : to lure by or as if by a decoy : ENTICE

**¹de·crease** \di-'krēs\ *vb* **de·creased; de·creas·ing** : to grow or cause to grow less : DIMINISH

**²de·crease** \'dē-,krēs\ *n* **1** : the process of decreasing **2** : REDUCTION

**¹de·cree** \di-'krē\ *n* **1** : ORDER, EDICT **2** : a judicial decision

**²de·cree** *vb* **de·creed; de·cree·ing** **1** : COMMAND **2** : to determine or order judicially ✦ *Synonyms* DICTATE, ORDAIN, PRESCRIBE

**dec·re·ment** \'de-krə-mənt\ *n* **1** : gradual decrease **2** : the quantity lost by diminution or waste

**de·crep·it** \di-'kre-pət\ *adj* : broken down with age : WORN-OUT — **de·crep·i·tude** \-pə-,tüd, -,tyüd\ *n*

**de·cre·scen·do** \dā-krə-'shen-dō\ *adv or adj* : with a decrease in volume — used as a direction in music

**de·crim·i·nal·ize** \dē-'kri-mə-nə-,līz\ *vb* : to remove or reduce the criminal status of

**de·cry** \di-'krī\ *vb* : to express strong disapproval of ⟨∼ welfare policies⟩

**ded·i·cate** \'de-di-,kāt\ *vb* **-cat·ed; -cat·ing** **1** : to devote to the worship of a divine being esp. with sacred rites **2** : to set apart for a definite purpose **3** : to inscribe or address as a compliment ⟨∼ a novel⟩ — **ded·i·ca·tion** \de-di-'kā-shən\ *n* — **ded·i·ca·tor** \'de-di-,kā-tər\ *n* — **ded·i·ca·to·ry** \-kə-,tòr-ē\ *adj*

**de·duce** \di-'düs, -'dyüs\ *vb* **de·duced; de·duc·ing** **1** : to derive by reasoning : INFER **2** : to trace the course of — **de·duc·ible** *adj*

**de·duct** \di-'dəkt\ *vb* : SUBTRACT — **de·duct·ible** *adj*

**de·duc·tion** \di-'dək-shən\ *n* **1** : SUBTRACTION **2** : something that is or may be subtracted **3** : the deriving of a conclusion by reasoning : the conclusion so reached — **de·duc·tive** \-'dək-tiv\ *adj* — **de·duc·tive·ly** *adv*

**¹deed** \'dēd\ *n* **1** : something done **2** : FEAT, EXPLOIT **3** : a document containing some legal transfer, bargain, or contract

**²deed** *vb* : to convey or transfer by deed

**dee·jay** \'dē-,jā\ *n* : DISC JOCKEY

**deem** \'dēm\ *vb* : THINK, JUDGE ✦ *Synonyms* CONSIDER, ACCOUNT, RECKON, REGARD, VIEW

**de·em·pha·size** \dē-'em-fə-,sīz\ *vb* : to reduce in relative importance; *also* : to attach little importance to — **de·em·pha·sis** \-səs\ *n*

**¹deep** \'dēp\ *adj* **1** : extending far down, back, within, or outward ⟨a ∼ well⟩ **2** : having a specified extension downward or backward ⟨3 feet ∼⟩ **3** : difficult to understand; *also* : MYSTERIOUS, OBSCURE ⟨a ∼ dark secret⟩ **4** : WISE **5** : ENGROSSED, INVOLVED ⟨∼ in thought⟩ **6** : INTENSE, PROFOUND ⟨∼ sleep⟩ **7** : dark and rich in color ⟨a ∼ red⟩ **8** : having a low musical pitch or range ⟨a

~ voice⟩ **9** : situated well within **10** : covered, enclosed, or filled often to a specified degree — **deep·ly** adv

²**deep** adv **1** : DEEPLY **2** : far on : LATE ⟨~ in the night⟩

³**deep** n **1** : an extremely deep place or part; esp : OCEAN **2** : the middle or most intense part ⟨the ~ of winter⟩

**deep·en** \'dē-pən\ vb : to make or become deep or deeper

**deep–freeze** \'dēp-'frēz\ vb **-froze** \-'frōz\; **-fro·zen** \-'frō-z²n\ : QUICK-FREEZE

**deep–fry** vb : to cook in enough oil to cover the food being fried

**deep pocket** n **1** : one having substantial financial resources **2** pl : substantial financial resources

**deep–root·ed** \'dēp-'rü-təd, -'rü-\ adj : deeply implanted or established

**deep–sea** \'dēp-'sē\ adj : of, relating to, or occurring in the deeper parts of the sea ⟨~ fishing⟩

**deep–seat·ed** \'dēp-'sē-təd\ adj **1** : situated far below the surface **2** : firmly established ⟨~ convictions⟩

**deer** \'dir\ n, pl **deer** [ME, deer, animal, fr. OE dēor beast] : any of numerous ruminant mammals with cloven hoofs and usu. antlers esp. in the males

**deer·fly** \-,flī\ n : any of numerous small horseflies

**deer·skin** \-,skin\ n : leather made from the skin of a deer; also : a garment of such leather

**deer tick** n : a tick that transmits the bacterium causing Lyme disease

**de·es·ca·late** \dē-'es-kə-,lāt\ vb : to decrease in extent, volume, or scope : LIMIT — **de·es·ca·la·tion** \-,es-kə-'lā-shən\ n

**deet** \'dēt\ n, often all cap : a colorless oily liquid insect and tick repellent

¹**def** \'def\ adj **def·fer; def·fest** slang : very good : COOL

²**def** abbr **1** defendant **2** definite **3** definition

**de·face** \di-'fās\ vb : to destroy or mar the face or surface of ⟨~ a desk⟩ — **de·face·ment** n — **de·fac·er** n

**de fac·to** \di-'fak-tō, dā-\ adj or adv **1** : existing though not formally recognized ⟨a de facto recession⟩ **2** : actually exercising power ⟨de facto government⟩

**de·fal·ca·tion** \di-,fal-'kā-shən, -,fȯl-; ,de-fȯl-\ n : EMBEZZLEMENT

**de·fame** \di-'fām\ vb **de·famed; de·fam·ing** : to injure or destroy the reputation of by libel or slander ◆ **Synonyms** CALUMNIATE, DENIGRATE, LIBEL, MALIGN, SLANDER, VILIFY — **def·a·ma·tion** \,de-fə-'mā-shən\ n — **de·fam·a·to·ry** \di-'fa-mə-,tȯr-ē\ adj

**de·fault** \di-'fȯlt\ n **1** : failure to do something required by duty or law; also : failure to appear for a legal proceeding **2** : failure to compete in or to finish an appointed contest ⟨lose a race by ~⟩ **3** : a choice made without active consideration due to lack of viable alternatives **4** : a selection made automatically by a computer in the absence of a choice by the user — **default** vb — **de·fault·er** n

¹**de·feat** \di-'fēt\ vb **1** : FRUSTRATE, NULLIFY **2** : to win victory over : BEAT — **de·feat·able** \-'fē-tə-bəl\ adj

²**defeat** n **1** : FRUSTRATION **2** : an overthrow of an army in battle **3** : loss of a contest

**de·feat·ism** \-'fē-,ti-zəm\ n : acceptance of or resignation to defeat — **de·feat·ist** \-tist\ n or adj

**def·e·cate** \'de-fi-,kāt\ vb **-cat·ed; -cat·ing 1** : to free from impurity or corruption **2** : to discharge feces from the bowels — **def·e·ca·tion** \,de-fi-'kā-shən\ n

¹**de·fect** \'dē-,fekt, di-'fekt\ n : BLEMISH, FAULT, IMPERFECTION

²**de·fect** \di-'fekt\ vb : to desert a cause, party, or nation esp. in order to espouse another — **de·fec·tion** \-'fek-shən\ n — **de·fec·tor** \-'fek-tər\ n

**de·fec·tive** \di-'fek-tiv\ adj : FAULTY, DEFICIENT — **defective** n

**de·fence** chiefly Brit var of DEFENSE

**de·fend** \di-'fend\ vb [ME, fr. AF defendre, fr. L defendere, fr. de- from + -fendere to strike] **1** : to repel danger or attack from ⟨~ the fort⟩ **2** : to act as attorney for **3** : to oppose the claim of another in a lawsuit : CONTEST **4** : to maintain against opposition ⟨~ an idea⟩ **5** : to try to retain against a challenge ⟨~ed his title⟩ — **de·fend·er** n

**de·fen·dant** \di-'fen-dənt\ n : a person required to make answer in a legal action or suit

**de·fense** \di-'fens\ n **1** : the act of defending : resistance against attack **2** : means, method, or capability of defending **3** : an argument in support **4** : the answer made by the defendant in a legal action **5** : a defending party, group, or team — **de·fense·less** adj — **de·fen·si·ble** adj

**defense mechanism** n : an often unconscious mental process (as repression) that assists in reaching compromise solutions to personal problems

¹**de·fen·sive** \di-'fen-siv\ adj **1** : serving or intended to defend or protect **2** : of or relating to the attempt to keep an opponent from scoring (as in a game) — **de·fen·sive·ly** adv — **de·fen·sive·ness** n

²**defensive** n : a defensive position

¹**de·fer** \di-'fər\ vb **de·ferred; de·fer·ring** [ME differren, differen, fr. MF differer, fr. L differre to postpone, be different] : POSTPONE, PUT OFF

²**defer** vb **deferred; deferring** [ME deferren, differren, fr. MF deferer, defferer, fr. LL deferre, fr. L, to bring down, bring, fr. de- down + ferre to carry] : to submit or yield to the opinion or wishes of another — **de·fer·ral** \-əl\ n

**def·er·ence** \'de-fər-əns\ n : courteous, respectful, or ingratiating regard for another's wishes ◆ **Synonyms** HONOR, HOMAGE, OBEISANCE, REVERENCE — **def·er·en·tial** \,de-fə-'ren-chəl\ adj

**de·fer·ment** \di-'fər-mənt\ n : the act of delaying; esp : official postponement of military service

**de·fi·ance** \di-'fī-əns\ n **1** : CHALLENGE **2** : disposition to resist or contend

**de·fi·ant** \-ənt\ *adj* : full of defiance : BOLD, IMPUDENT — **de·fi·ant·ly** *adv*

**de·fi·bril·la·tor** \dē-'fi-brə-ˌlā-tər\ *n* : an electronic device that applies an electric shock to restore the rhythm of a fibrillating heart — **de·fi·bril·late** \-ˌlāt\ *vb* — **de·fi·bril·la·tion** \-ˌfi-brə-'lā-shən\ *n*

**deficiency disease** *n* : a disease (as scurvy or beriberi) caused by a lack of essential dietary elements and esp. a vitamin or mineral

**de·fi·cient** \di-'fi-shənt\ *adj* : lacking in something necessary; *also* : not up to a normal standard — **de·fi·cien·cy** \-shən-sē\ *n*

**def·i·cit** \'de-fə-sət\ *n* : a deficiency in amount; *esp* : an excess of expenditures over revenue

¹**de·file** \di-'fī(-ə)l\ *vb* **de·filed; de·fil·ing** 1 : to make filthy 2 : CORRUPT 3 : to violate the chastity of 4 : to violate the sanctity of : DESECRATE 5 : DISHONOR ♦ *Synonyms* CONTAMINATE, POLLUTE, SOIL, TAINT — **de·file·ment** *n*

²**de·file** \di-'fī(-ə)l, 'dē-ˌfī(-ə)l\ *n* : a narrow passage or gorge

**de·fine** \di-'fīn\ *vb* **de·fined; de·fin·ing** 1 : to set forth the meaning of ⟨~ a word⟩ 2 : to fix or mark the limits of 3 : to clarify in outline or character — **de·fin·able** *adj* — **de·fin·er** *n*

**def·i·nite** \'de-fə-nət\ *adj* 1 : having distinct limits : FIXED 2 : clear in meaning 3 : typically designating an identified or immediately identifiable person or thing ⟨a ~ article⟩ — **def·i·nite·ly** *adv* — **def·i·nite·ness** *n*

**def·i·ni·tion** \ˌde-fə-'ni-shən\ *n* 1 : an act of determining or settling 2 : a statement of the meaning of a word or word group; *also* : the action or process of defining 3 : the action or the power of making definite and clear : CLARITY, DISTINCTNESS

**de·fin·i·tive** \di-'fi-nə-tiv\ *adj* 1 : DECISIVE, CONCLUSIVE 2 : authoritative and apparently exhaustive ⟨a ~ edition⟩ 3 : serving to define or specify precisely ⟨~ laws⟩

**de·flate** \di-'flāt\ *vb* **de·flat·ed; de·flat·ing** 1 : to release air or gas from 2 : to reduce in size, importance, or effectiveness; *also* : to reduce from a state of inflation 3 : to become deflated

**de·fla·tion** \-'flā-shən\ *n* 1 : an act or instance of deflating : the state of being deflated 2 : reduction in the volume of available money or credit resulting in a decline of the general price level

**de·flect** \di-'flekt\ *vb* : to turn aside — **de·flec·tion** \-'flek-shən\ *n*

**de·flo·ra·tion** \ˌde-flə-'rā-shən\ *n* : rupture of the hymen

**de·flow·er** \dē-'flaů(-ə)r\ *vb* : to deprive of virginity

**de·fog** \dē-'fȯg, -'fäg\ *vb* : to remove fog or condensed moisture from ⟨~ a windshield⟩ — **de·fog·ger** *n*

**de·fo·li·ant** \dē-'fō-lē-ənt\ *n* : a chemical spray or dust used to defoliate plants

**de·fo·li·ate** \-ˌāt\ *vb* : to deprive of leaves esp. prematurely — **de·fo·li·a·tion** \dē-

ˌfō-lē-'ā-shən\ *n* — **de·fo·li·a·tor** \dē-'fō-lē-ˌā-tər\ *n*

**de·for·es·ta·tion** \dē-ˌfȯr-ə-'stā-shən\ *n* : the action or process of clearing an area of forests; *also* : the state of having been cleared of forests — **de·for·est** \(ˌ)dē-'fȯr-əst, -'fär-\ *vb*

**de·form** \di-'fȯrm\ *vb* 1 : DISFIGURE, DEFACE 2 : to make or become misshapen or changed in shape — **de·for·ma·tion** \ˌdē-ˌfȯr-'mā-shən, ˌde-fər\ *n*

**de·for·mi·ty** \di-'fȯr-mə-tē\ *n, pl* **-ties** 1 : the state of being deformed 2 : a physical blemish or distortion

**de·fraud** \di-'frȯd\ *vb* : CHEAT

**de·fray** \di-'frā\ *vb* : to provide for the payment of : PAY — **de·fray·al** *n*

**de·frock** \(ˌ)dē-'fräk\ *vb* : to deprive (as a priest) of the right to exercise the functions of office

**de·frost** \di-'frȯst\ *vb* 1 : to thaw out 2 : to free from ice — **de·frost·er** *n*

**deft** \'deft\ *adj* : quick and neat in action — **deft·ly** *adv* — **deft·ness** *n*

**de·funct** \di-'fəŋkt\ *adj* : DEAD, EXTINCT ⟨a ~ language⟩

**de·fuse** \dē-'fyüz\ *vb* 1 : to remove the fuse from (as a bomb) 2 : to make less harmful, potent, or tense

**de·fy** \di-'fī\ *vb* **de·fied; de·fy·ing** [ME, to renounce faith in, challenge, fr. AF *desfier*, *defier*, fr. *de-* from + *fier* to entrust, ultim. fr. L *fidere* to trust] 1 : CHALLENGE, DARE 2 : to refuse boldly to obey or to yield to : DISREGARD ⟨~ the law⟩ 3 : WITHSTAND, BAFFLE ⟨a scene that *defies* description⟩

**deg** *abbr* degree

**de·gas** \dē-'gas\ *vb* : to remove gas from

**de·gen·er·a·cy** \di-'je-nə-rə-sē\ *n, pl* **-cies** 1 : the state of being degenerate 2 : the process of becoming degenerate 3 : PERVERSION

¹**de·gen·er·ate** \di-'je-nə-rət\ *adj* : fallen or deteriorated from a former, higher, or normal condition — **de·gen·er·a·tion** \-ˌje-nə-'rā-shən\ *n* — **de·gen·er·a·tive** \-'je-nə-ˌrā-tiv\ *adj*

²**de·gen·er·ate** \di-'je-nə-ˌrāt\ *vb* : to undergo deterioration (as in morality, intelligence, structure, or function)

³**de·gen·er·ate** \-rət\ *n* : a degenerate person; *esp* : a sexual pervert

**de·grad·able** \di-'grā-də-bəl\ *adj* : capable of being chemically degraded

**de·grade** \di-'grād\ *vb* 1 : to reduce from a higher to a lower rank or degree 2 : DEBASE, CORRUPT 3 : DECOMPOSE — **deg·ra·da·tion** \ˌde-grə-'dā-shən\ *n*

**de·gree** \di-'grē\ *n* [ME, fr. AF *degré*, fr. VL *\*degradus*, fr. L *de-* down + *gradus* step, grade] 1 : a step in a series 2 : a rank or grade of official, ecclesiastical, or social position; *also* : the civil condition of a person 3 : the extent, intensity, or scope of something esp. as measured by a graded series 4 : one of the forms or sets of forms used in the comparison of an adjective or adverb 5 : a title conferred upon students by a college, university, or professional school on completion of a program of study 6 : a line or space of the musical staff; *also* : a note or tone of a musical scale **7** : a unit of measure for angles that is equal to an angle with its vertex at the center of a circle and its sides cutting off $\frac{1}{360}$ of the circumference; *also* : a unit of measure for arcs of a circle that is equal to the amount of arc extending $\frac{1}{360}$ of the circumference **8** : any of various units for measuring temperature

**de·horn** \dē-'hòrn\ *vb* : to deprive of horns

**de·hu·man·ize** \dē-'hyü-mə-,nīz\ *vb* : to deprive of human qualities, personality, or spirit — **de·hu·man·i·za·tion** \,dē-,hyü-mə-nə-'zā-shən\ *n*

**de·hu·mid·i·fy** \dē-hyü-'mi-də-,fī\ *vb* : to remove moisture from (as the air) — **de·hu·mid·i·fi·er** *n*

**de·hy·drate** \dē-'hī-,drāt\ *vb* : to remove water from; *also* : to lose liquid — **de·hy·dra·tion** \,dē-hī-'drā-shən\ *n*

**de·hy·dro·ge·na·tion** \dē-(,)hī-,drā-jə-'nā-shən, -drə-\ *n* : the removal of hydrogen from a chemical compound — **de·hy·dro·ge·nate** \dē-(,)hī-'drä-jə-,nāt, dē-'hī-drə-jə-\ *vb*

**de·ice** \dē-'īs\ *vb* : to keep free or rid of ice ⟨~ a plane⟩ — **de·ic·er** *n*

**de·i·fy** \'dē-ə-,fī, 'dā-\ *vb* **-fied; -fy·ing** **1** : to make a god of **2** : WORSHIP, GLORIFY — **de·i·fi·ca·tion** \,dē-ə-fə-'kā-shən, ,dā-\ *n*

**deign** \'dān\ *vb* [ME, fr. AF *deigner*, fr. L *dignare, dignari*, fr. *dignus* worthy] : CONDESCEND

**de·ion·ize** \dē-'ī-ə-,nīz\ *vb* : to remove ions from

**de·ism** \'dē-,i-zəm, 'dā-\ *n, often cap* : a system of thought advocating natural religion based on human morality and reason rather than divine revelation — **de·ist** \-ist\ *n, often cap* — **de·is·tic** \dē-'is-tik, dā-\ *adj*

**de·i·ty** \'dē-ə-tē, 'dā-\ *n, pl* **-ties** **1** : DIVINITY **2** *cap* : GOD **1** **3** : a god or goddess

**dé·jà vu** \,dā-,zhä-'vü\ *n* [F, adj., already seen] : the feeling that one has seen or heard something before

**de·ject·ed** \di-'jek-təd\ *adj* : low in spirits : SAD — **de·ject·ed·ly** *adv*

**de·jec·tion** \di-'jek-shən\ *n* : lowness of spirits

**de ju·re** \dē-'jùr-ē\ *adv or adj* [ML] : by legal right

**deka·gram** \'de-kə-,gram\ *n* — see METRIC SYSTEM table

**deka·li·ter** \-,lē-tər\ *n* — see METRIC SYSTEM table

**deka·me·ter** \-,mē-tər\ *n* — see METRIC SYSTEM table

**del** *abbr* delegate; delegation

**Del** *abbr* Delaware

**Del·a·ware** \'de-lə-,wer\ *n, pl* **Delaware** *or* **Delawares** : a member of an American Indian people orig. of the Delaware valley; *also* : their language

**¹de·lay** \di-'lā\ *n* **1** : the act of delaying : the state of being delayed **2** : the time for which something is delayed

**²delay** *vb* **1** : POSTPONE, PUT OFF **2** : to

stop, detain, or hinder for a time **3** : to move or act slowly

**de·lec·ta·ble** \di-'lek-tə-bəl\ *adj* **1** : highly pleasing : DELIGHTFUL **2** : DELICIOUS

**de·lec·ta·tion** \,dē-,lek-'tā-shən\ *n* : DELIGHT, PLEASURE, DIVERSION

**¹del·e·gate** \'de-li-gət, -,gāt\ *n* **1** : DEPUTY, REPRESENTATIVE **2** : a member of the lower house of the legislature of Maryland, Virginia, or West Virginia

**²del·e·gate** \-,gāt\ *vb* **-gat·ed; -gat·ing** **1** : to entrust to another ⟨~ authority⟩ **2** : to appoint as one's delegate

**del·e·ga·tion** \,de-li-'gā-shən\ *n* **1** : the act of delegating **2** : one or more persons chosen to represent others

**de·le·git·i·mize** \,dē-lə-'ji-tə-,mīz\ *vb* : to diminish or destroy the legitimacy, prestige, or authority of

**de·lete** \di-'lēt\ *vb* **de·let·ed; de·let·ing** [L *deletus*, pp. of *delēre* to wipe out, destroy] : to eliminate esp. by blotting out, cutting out, or erasing ⟨~ a computer file⟩ — **de·le·tion** \-'lē-shən\ *n*

**del·e·te·ri·ous** \,de-lə-'tir-ē-əs\ *adj* : HARMFUL, NOXIOUS

**delft** \'delft\ *n* **1** : a Dutch pottery with an opaque white glaze and predominantly blue decoration **2** : glazed pottery esp. when blue and white

**delft·ware** \-,wer\ *n* : DELFT

**deli** \'de-lē\ *n, pl* **del·is** : DELICATESSEN

**de·lib·er·ate** \di-'li-bə-,rāt\ *vb* **-at·ed; -at·ing** : to consider carefully — **de·lib·er·a·tion** \-,li-bə-'rā-shən\ *n* — **de·lib·er·a·tive** \-'li-bə-,rā-tiv, -brə-tiv\ *adj* — **de·lib·er·a·tive·ly** *adv*

**²de·lib·er·ate** \di-'li-bə-rət, -'li-brət\ *adj* **1** : determined after careful thought **2** : done or said intentionally **3** : UNHURRIED, SLOW — **de·lib·er·ate·ly** *adv* — **de·lib·er·ate·ness** *n*

**del·i·ca·cy** \'de-li-kə-sē\ *n, pl* **-cies** **1** : something pleasing to eat and considered rare or luxurious **2** : FINENESS, DAINTINESS; *also* : FRAILTY **3** : nicety or expressiveness of touch **4** : precise perception and discrimination : SENSITIVITY **5** : sensibility in feeling or conduct; *also* : SQUEAMISHNESS **6** : the quality or state of requiring delicate handling

**del·i·cate** \'de-li-kət\ *adj* **1** : pleasing to the senses of taste or smell esp. in a mild or subtle way **2** : marked by daintiness or charm : EXQUISITE **3** : FASTIDIOUS, SQUEAMISH ⟨a person of ~ tastes⟩ **4** : easily damaged : FRAGILE; *also* : SICKLY **5** : requiring skill or tact **6** : marked by care, skill, or tact **7** : marked by minute precision : very sensitive ⟨a ~ instrument⟩ — **del·i·cate·ly** *adv*

**del·i·ca·tes·sen** \,de-li-kə-'te-s³n\ *n pl* [G, pl. of *Delicatesse* delicacy, fr. F *délicatesse*] **1** : ready-to-eat food products (as cooked meats and prepared salads) **2** *sing, pl* **delicatessens** : a store where delicatessen are sold

**de·li·cious** \di-'li-shəs\ *adj* : affording great pleasure : DELIGHTFUL; *esp* : very pleasing to the taste or smell — **de·li·cious·ly** *adv* — **de·li·cious·ness** *n*

**¹de·light** \di-'līt\ *n* **1** : great pleasure or

satisfaction : JOY  **2** : something that gives great pleasure — **de·light·ful** \-fəl\ *adj* — **de·light·ful·ly** *adv*

²**delight** *vb* **1** : to take great pleasure **2** : to satisfy greatly : PLEASE

**de·light·ed** *adj* : highly pleased : GRATIFIED — **de·light·ed·ly** *adv*

**de·lim·it** \di-'li-mət\ *vb* : to fix the limits of

**de·lin·eate** \di-'li-nē-,āt\ *vb* -**eat·ed; -eat·ing** **1** : SKETCH, PORTRAY **2** : to picture in words : DESCRIBE — **de·lin·ea·tion** \-,li-nē-'ā-shən\ *n*

**de·lin·quen·cy** \di-'liŋ-kwən-sē\ *n, pl* -**cies** : the quality or state of being delinquent

¹**de·lin·quent** \-kwənt\ *n* : a delinquent person

²**delinquent** *adj* **1** : offending by neglect or violation of duty or of law **2** : being overdue in payment

**del·i·quesce** \,de-li-'kwes\ *vb* -**quesced; -quesc·ing** : MELT, DISSOLVE — **del·i·ques·cent** \-'kwe-s³nt\ *adj*

**de·lir·i·um** \di-'lir-ē-əm\ *n* [L, fr. *delirare* to be crazy, lit., to leave the furrow (in plowing), fr. *de-* from + *lira* furrow] : mental disturbance marked by confusion, disordered speech, and hallucinations; *also* : frenzied excitement — **de·lir·i·ous** \-ē-əs\ *adj* — **de·lir·i·ous·ly** *adv*

**delirium tre·mens** \-'trē-mənz, -'tre-\ *n* : a violent delirium with tremors that is induced by excessive and prolonged use of alcoholic liquors

**de·liv·er** \di-'li-vər\ *vb* -**ered; -er·ing** **1** : to set free : SAVE **2** : CONVEY, TRANSFER ⟨~ a letter⟩ **3** : to assist in giving birth or at the birth of; *also* : to give birth to **4** : UTTER, COMMUNICATE **5** : to send to an intended target or destination — **de·liv·er·able** \-'li-v(ə-)rə-bəl\ *adj* — **de·liv·er·ance** \-v(ə-)rəns\ *n* — **de·liv·er·er** *n*

**de·liv·ery** \di-'li-və-rē\ *n, pl* -**er·ies** : the act of delivering something; *also* : something delivered — **de·liv·ery·man** \-,man\ *n*

**dell** \'del\ *n* : a small secluded valley

**de·louse** \dē-'laùs\ *vb* : to remove lice from

**del·phin·i·um** \del-'fi-nē-əm\ *n* : any of a genus of mostly perennial herbs related to the buttercups with tall branching spikes of irregular flowers

**del·ta** \'del-tə\ *n* **1** : the 4th letter of the Greek alphabet — Δ or δ **2** : something shaped like a capital Δ; *esp* : the triangular silt-formed land at the mouth of a river — **del·ta·ic** \del-'tā-ik\ *adj*

**del·toid** \'del-,tȯid\ *n* : a large triangular muscle that covers the shoulder joint and raises the arm laterally

**de·lude** \di-'lüd\ *vb* **de·lud·ed; de·lud·ing** : MISLEAD, DECEIVE, TRICK

¹**del·uge** \'del-,yüj\ *n* **1** : a flooding of land by water **2** : a drenching rain **3** : a great amount or number ⟨a ~ of mail⟩

²**deluge** *vb* **del·uged; del·ug·ing** **1** : INUNDATE, FLOOD **2** : to overwhelm as if with a deluge ⟨*deluged* with e-mails⟩

**de·lu·sion** \di-'lü-zhən\ *n* : a deluding or

being deluded; *esp* : a persistent false psychotic belief — **de·lu·sion·al** \-'lü-zhə-nəl\ *adj* — **de·lu·sive** \-'lü-siv\ *adj*

**de·luxe** \di-'lúks, -'ləks, -'lüks\ *adj* : notably luxurious or elegant

**delve** \'delv\ *vb* **delved; delv·ing** **1** : DIG **2** : to seek laboriously for information

**dely** *abbr* delivery

**Dem** *abbr* Democrat; Democratic

**de·mag·ne·tize** \dē-'mag-nə-,tīz\ *vb* : to cause to lose magnetic properties — **de·mag·ne·ti·za·tion** \dē-,mag-nə-tə-'zā-shən\ *n*

**dem·a·gogue** *also* **dem·a·gog** \'de-mə-,gäg\ *n* [Gk *dēmagōgos,* fr. *dēmos* people + *agōgos* leading, fr. *agein* to lead] : a person who appeals to the emotions and prejudices of people esp. in order to gain political power — **dem·a·gogu·ery** \-,gä-gə-rē\ *n* — **dem·a·gogy** \-,gä-gē, -,gä-jē\ *n*

¹**de·mand** \di-'mand\ *n* **1** : an act of demanding; *also* : something claimed as due or just **2** : the ability and desire to buy goods or services; *also* : the quantity of goods wanted at a stated price **3** : a seeking or being sought after : urgent need **4** : a pressing need or requirement

²**demand** *vb* **1** : to ask for with authority : claim as due or just **2** : to ask earnestly or in the manner of a command **3** : REQUIRE, NEED ⟨a patient who ~s constant care⟩

**de·mar·cate** \di-'mär-,kāt, 'dē-,mär-\ *vb* -**cat·ed; -cat·ing** **1** : DELIMIT **2** : to set apart : DISTINGUISH — **de·mar·ca·tion** \,dē-,mär-'kā-shən\ *n*

**dé·marche** *or* **de·marche** \dā-'märsh\ *n* : a course of action : MANEUVER

¹**de·mean** \di-'mēn\ *vb* **de·meaned; de·mean·ing** : to behave or conduct (oneself) usu. in a proper manner

²**demean** *vb* **de·meaned; de·mean·ing** : DEGRADE, DEBASE

**de·mean·or** \di-'mē-nər\ *n* : CONDUCT, BEARING

**de·mean·our** *Brit var of* DEMEANOR

**de·ment·ed** \di-'men-təd\ *adj* : MAD, INSANE — **de·ment·ed·ly** *adv*

**de·men·tia** \di-'men-chə\ *n* **1** : deterioration of cognitive functioning (as in Alzheimer's disease) **2** : INSANITY

**de·mer·it** \di-'mer-ət\ *n* **1** : FAULT **2** : a mark placed against a person's record for some fault or offense

**de·mesne** \di-'mān, -'mēn\ *n* **1** : REALM **2** : manorial land actually possessed by the lord and not held by free tenants **3** : ESTATE **4** : REGION

**demi·god** \'de-mi-,gäd\ *n* : a mythological being with more power than a mortal but less than a god

**demi·john** \'de-mi-,jän\ *n* [F *dame-jeanne,* lit., Lady Jane] : a large narrow-necked bottle usu. enclosed in wickerwork

**de·mil·i·ta·rize** \dē-'mi-lə-tə-,rīz\ *vb* : to strip of military forces, weapons, or fortifications — **de·mil·i·tar·i·za·tion** \-,mi-lə-tə-rə-'zā-shən\ *n*

**demi·mon·daine** \,de-mi-,män-'dän\ *n* : a woman of the demimonde

**demi·monde** \'de-mi-ˌmänd\ *n* [F *demi= monde*, fr. *demi-* half + *monde* world] **1** : a class of women on the fringes of respectable society supported by wealthy lovers **2** : a distinct isolated group having low reputation or prestige

**de·min·er·al·ize** \dē-ˈmi-nə-rə-ˌlīz\ *vb* : to remove the mineral matter from — **de·min·er·al·i·za·tion** \-ˌmi-nə-rə-lə-ˈzā-shən\ *n*

**de·mise** \di-ˈmīz\ *n* **1** : LEASE **2** : transfer of sovereignty to a successor ⟨~ of the crown⟩ **3** : DEATH **4** : loss of status

**demi·tasse** \'de-mi-ˌtas\ *n* : a small cup of black coffee; *also* : the cup used to serve it

**demo** \'de-mō\ *n, pl* **dem·os** **1** : DEMONSTRATION **2** : a product used to show performance or merits to prospective buyers **3** : a recording used to show off a song or performer

**de·mo·bi·lize** \di-ˈmō-bə-ˌlīz, dē-\ *vb* **1** : DISBAND **2** : to discharge from military service — **de·mo·bi·li·za·tion** \di-ˌmō-bə-lə-ˈzā-shən, dē-\ *n*

**de·moc·ra·cy** \di-ˈmä-krə-sē\ *n, pl* **-cies** [MF *democratie*, fr. LL *democratia*, fr. Gk *dēmokratia*, fr. *dēmos* people + *kratos* strength, power] **1** : government by the people; *esp* : rule of the majority **2** : a government in which the supreme power is held by the people **3** : a political unit that has a democratic government **4** *cap* : the principles and policies of the Democratic party in the U.S. **5** : the common people esp. when constituting the source of political authority **6** : the absence of hereditary or arbitrary class distinctions or privileges

**dem·o·crat** \'de-mə-ˌkrat\ *n* **1** : one who believes in or practices democracy **2** *cap* : a member of the Democratic party of the U.S.

**dem·o·crat·ic** \ˌde-mə-ˈkra-tik\ *adj* **1** : of, relating to, or favoring democracy **2** *often cap* : of or relating to one of the two major political parties in the U.S. associated in modern times with policies of broad social reform and internationalism **3** : relating to or appealing to the common people ⟨~ art⟩ **4** : not snobbish — **dem·o·crat·i·cal·ly** \-ti-k(ə-)lē\ *adv*

**de·moc·ra·tize** \di-ˈmä-krə-ˌtīz\ *vb* **-tized; -tiz·ing** : to make democratic

**dé·mo·dé** \ˌdā-mō-ˈdā\ *adj* [F] : no longer fashionable : OUT-OF-DATE

**de·mo·graph·ics** \ˌde-mə-ˈgra-fiks, ˌdē-\ *n pl* : the statistical characteristics of human populations

**de·mog·ra·phy** \di-ˈmä-grə-fē\ *n* : the statistical study of human populations and esp. their size and distribution and the number of births and deaths — **de·mog·ra·pher** \-fər\ *n* — **de·mo·graph·ic** \ˌde-mə-ˈgra-fik, ˌdē-\ *adj* — **de·mo·graph·i·cal·ly** \-fi-k(ə-)lē\ *adv*

**dem·oi·selle** \ˌdem-wə-ˈzel\ *n* [F] : a young woman

**de·mol·ish** \di-ˈmä-lish\ *vb* **1** : to destroy by breaking apart **2** : RAZE **3** : SMASH **3** : to put an end to ⟨~ a theory⟩

**de·mo·li·tion** \ˌde-mə-ˈli-shən, ˌdē-\ *n* : the act of demolishing; *esp* : destruction by means of explosives

**de·mon** *or* **dae·mon** \'dē-mən\ *n* **1** : an evil spirit : DEVIL **2** *usu daemon* : an attendant power or spirit **3** : one that has unusual drive or effectiveness ⟨a ~ for work⟩

**de·mon·e·tize** \dē-ˈmä-nə-ˌtīz, -ˈmə-\ *vb* : to stop using as money or as a monetary standard ⟨~ silver⟩ — **de·mon·e·ti·za·tion** \dē-ˌmä-nə-tə-ˈzā-shən, -ˌmə-\ *n*

**de·mo·ni·ac** \di-ˈmō-nē-ˌak\ *also* **de·mo·ni·a·cal** \ˌdē-mə-ˈnī-ə-kəl\ *adj* **1** : possessed or influenced by a demon **2** : DEMONIC

**de·mon·ic** \di-ˈmä-nik\ *also* **de·mon·i·cal** \-ni-kəl\ *adj* : DEVILISH, FIENDISH ⟨~ cruelty⟩

**de·mon·ize** \'dē-mə-ˌnīz\ *vb* **-ized; -iz·ing** **1** : to convert into a demon **2** : to characterize or treat as evil or harmful

**de·mon·ol·o·gy** \ˌdē-mə-ˈnä-lə-jē\ *n* **1** : the study of demons **2** : belief in demons

**de·mon·stra·ble** \di-ˈmän-strə-bəl\ *adj* : capable of being demonstrated **2** : APPARENT, EVIDENT — **de·mon·stra·bly** \-blē\ *adv*

**dem·on·strate** \'de-mən-ˌstrāt\ *vb* **-strat·ed; -strat·ing** **1** : to show clearly **2** : to prove or make clear by reasoning or evidence **3** : to explain esp. with many examples **4** : to show publicly ⟨~ a new car⟩ **5** : to make a public display ⟨~ in protest⟩ — **dem·on·stra·tion** \ˌde-mən-ˈstrā-shən\ *n* — **dem·on·stra·tor** \'de-mən-ˌstrā-tər\ *n*

**¹de·mon·stra·tive** \di-ˈmän-strə-tiv\ *adj* **1** : demonstrating as real or true **2** : characterized by demonstration **3** : pointing out the one referred to and distinguishing it from others of the same class ⟨~ pronoun⟩ **4** : marked by display of feeling : EFFUSIVE — **de·mon·stra·tive·ly** *adv* — **de·mon·stra·tive·ness** *n*

**²demonstrative** *n* : a demonstrative word and esp. a pronoun

**de·mor·al·ize** \di-ˈmȯr-ə-ˌlīz\ *vb* **1** : to corrupt in morals **2** : to weaken in discipline or spirit : DISORGANIZE — **de·mor·al·i·za·tion** \-ˌmȯr-ə-lə-ˈzā-shən\ *n*

**de·mote** \di-ˈmōt\ *vb* **de·mot·ed; de·mot·ing** : to reduce to a lower grade or rank — **de·mo·tion** \-ˈmō-shən\ *n*

**de·mot·ic** \di-ˈmä-tik\ *adj* : COMMON, POPULAR ⟨~ idiom⟩

**de·mur** \di-ˈmər\ *vb* **de·murred; de·mur·ring** [ME *demuren, demeren* to linger, fr. AF *demurer, demoerer*, fr. L *demorari, morari* to linger, fr. *mora* delay] : to take exception : OBJECT — **de·mur** *n*

**de·mure** \di-ˈmyu̇r\ *adj* **1** : quietly modest : DECOROUS **2** : affectedly modest, reserved, or serious : PRIM ♦ *Synonyms* SHY, BASHFUL, COY, DIFFICULT, RETIRING, UNASSERTIVE — **de·mure·ly** *adv*

**de·mur·rer** \di-ˈmər-ər\ *n* : a claim by the defendant in a legal action that the plaintiff does not have sufficient grounds to proceed

**den** \'den\ *n* **1** : LAIR **1** **2** : HIDEOUT ⟨a robber's ~⟩; *also* : a place like a hideout or a center of secret activity ⟨opium ∼⟩ ⟨a ∼ of iniquity⟩ **3** : a cozy private little room

**Den** *abbr* Denmark

**de·nar** \'de-ˌnär, 'dä\ — see MONEY table

**de·na·ture** \dē-'nā-chər\ *vb* **de·na·tured; de·na·tur·ing** : to remove or change the natural qualities of; *esp* : to make (alcohol) unfit for drinking

**den·drol·o·gy** \den-'drä-lə-jē\ *n* : the study of trees — **den·drol·o·gist** \-jist\ *n*

**den·gue** \'deŋ-gē, -ˌgā\ *n* [Sp] : an acute infectious disease characterized by headache, severe joint pain, and rash

**de·ni** \'de-ˌnē, 'dā-\ *n pl* — see *denar* at MONEY table

**de·ni·al** \di-'nī(-ə)l\ *n* **1** : rejection of a request **2** : refusal to admit the truth of a statement or charge; *also* : assertion that something alleged is false ⟨ : DISAVOWAL ⟩ **4** : restriction on one's own activity or desires

**de·nier** \'den-yər\ *n* : a unit of fineness for yarn

**den·i·grate** \'de-ni-ˌgrāt\ *vb* **-grat·ed; -grat·ing** [L *denigrare*, fr. *nigrare* to blacken, fr. *niger* black] : to cast aspersions on : DEFAME — **den·i·gra·tion** \ˌde-ni-'grā-shən\ *n*

**den·im** \'de-nəm\ *n* [F (*serge*) *de Nîmes* serge of Nîmes, France] **1** : a firm durable twilled usu. cotton fabric woven with colored warp and white filling threads **2** *pl* : overalls or pants of usu. blue denim

**den·i·zen** \'de-nə-zən\ *n* : INHABITANT

**de·nom·i·nate** \di-'nä-mə-ˌnāt\ *vb* : to give a name to : DESIGNATE

**de·nom·i·na·tion** \di-ˌnä-mə-'nā-shən\ *n* **1** : an act of denominating **2** : a value or size of a series of related values (as of money) **3** : NAME, DESIGNATION; *esp* : a general name for a category **4** : a religious organization uniting local congregations in a single body — **de·nom·i·na·tion·al** \-shə-nəl\ *adj*

**de·nom·i·na·tor** \di-'nä-mə-ˌnā-tər\ *n* : the part of a fraction that is below the line indicating division

**de·no·ta·tive** \'dē-nō-ˌtā-tiv, di-'nō-tə-tiv\ *adj* **1** : denoting or tending to denote **2** : relating to denotation

**de·note** \di-'nōt\ *vb* **1** : to mark out plainly : INDICATE **2** : to make known **3** : MEAN, NAME — **de·no·ta·tion** \ˌdē-nō-'tā-shən\ *n*

**de·noue·ment** \ˌdā-ˌnü-'mäⁿ\ *n* [F *dénouement*, lit., untying] : the final outcome of the dramatic complications in a literary work

**de·nounce** \di-'naúns\ *vb* **de·nounced; de·nounc·ing 1** : to pronounce esp. publicly to be blameworthy or evil **2** : to inform against : ACCUSE **3** : to announce formally the termination of (as a treaty) — **de·nounce·ment** *n*

**de no·vo** \di-'nō-vō\ *adv or adj* [L] : over again : ANEW ⟨a case tried ∼⟩

**dense** \'dens\ *adj* **dens·er; dens·est 1** : marked by compactness or crowding together of parts : THICK ⟨∼ forest⟩ ⟨a ∼ fog⟩ **2** : DULL, STUPID — **dense·ly** *adv* — **dense·ness** *n*

**den·si·ty** \'den-sə-tē\ *n, pl* **-ties 1** : the quality or state of being dense **2** : the quantity of something per unit volume, unit area, or unit length

**dent** \'dent\ *n* **1** : a small depressed place made by a blow or by pressure **2** : an impression or weakening effect made usu. against resistance **3** : initial progress — **dent** *vb*

**den·tal** \'den-tᵊl\ *adj* : of or relating to teeth or dentistry — **den·tal·ly** *adv*

**dental floss** *n* : a thread used to clean between the teeth

**dental hygienist** *n* : a person licensed to clean and examine teeth

**den·tate** \'den-ˌtāt\ *adj* : having pointed projections : NOTCHED

**den·ti·frice** \'den-tə-frəs\ *n* [ME *dentifricie*, fr. L *dentifricium*, fr. *dent-, dens* tooth + *fricare* to rub] : a powder, paste, or liquid for cleaning the teeth

**den·tin** \'den-tᵊn\ *or* **den·tine** \'den-ˌtēn, den-'tēn\ *n* : a calcareous material like bone but harder and denser that composes the principal mass of a tooth

**den·tist** \'den-tist\ *n* : a person licensed in the care, treatment, and replacement of teeth — **den·tist·ry** *n*

**den·ti·tion** \den-'ti-shən\ *n* : the number, kind, and arrangement of teeth (as of a person or animal); *also* : TEETH

**den·ture** \'den-chər\ *n* : a set of teeth; *esp* : a partial or complete set of false teeth

**de·nude** \di-'nüd, -'nyüd\ *vb* **de·nud·ed; de·nud·ing** : to strip the covering from — **de·nu·da·tion** \ˌdē-nü-'dā-shən, -nyü-\ *n*

**de·nun·ci·a·tion** \di-ˌnən-sē-'ā-shən\ *n* : the act of denouncing; *esp* : a public condemnation — **de·nun·ci·a·to·ry** \-'nən-sē-ə-ˌtōr-ē\ *adj*

**de·ny** \di-'nī\ *vb* **de·nied; de·ny·ing 1** : to declare untrue **2** : to refuse to recognize or acknowledge : DISAVOW **3** : to refuse to grant ⟨∼ a request⟩ **4** : to reject as false ⟨∼ a theory⟩

**de·o·dar** \'dē-ə-ˌdär\ *n* [Hindi & Urdu *devadār, deodār*, fr. Skt *devadāru*, fr. *deva* god + *dāru* wood] : a Himalayan cedar

**de·odor·ant** \dē-'ō-də-rənt\ *n* : a preparation that destroys or masks unpleasant odors

**de·odor·ize** \dē-'ō-də-ˌrīz\ *vb* : to eliminate the offensive odor of

**de·ox·i·dize** \dē-'äk-sə-ˌdīz\ *vb* : to remove esp. elemental oxygen from

**de·oxy·ri·bo·nu·cle·ic acid** \dē-ˌäk-si-ˌrī-bō-nü-ˌklē-ik-, -nyü-\ *n* : DNA

**de·oxy·ri·bose** \dē-ˌäk-si-'rī-ˌbōs\ *n* : a sugar with five carbon and four oxygen atoms in each molecule that is part of DNA

**dep** *abbr* **1** depart; departure **2** deposit **3** deputy

**de·part** \di-'pärt\ *vb* **1** : to go away : go away from : LEAVE **2** : DIE **3** : to turn aside : DEVIATE

**de·part·ee** \di-ˌpär-'tē\ *n* : a person who is departing or who has departed

**de·part·ment** \di-'pärt-mənt\ *n* **1** : a distinct sphere or category esp. of an activity or attribute **2** : a functional or territorial division (as of a government, business, or college) — **de·part·men·tal** \di-ˌpärt-ˈmen-t⁰l, ˌdē-\ adj — **de·part·men·tal·ly** adv

**department store** n : a store having separate sections for a wide variety of goods

**de·par·ture** \di-ˈpär-chər\ n **1** : the act of going away **2** : a starting out (as on a journey) **3** : DIVERGENCE ⟨a ∼ from tradition⟩

**de·pend** \di-ˈpend\ vb **1** : to be determined, based, or contingent ⟨life ∼s on food⟩ **2** : TRUST, RELY ⟨you can ∼ on me⟩ **3** : to be dependent esp. for financial support **4** : to hang down ⟨a vine ∼ing from a tree⟩

**de·pend·able** \di-ˈpen-də-bəl\ adj : TRUSTWORTHY, RELIABLE — **de·pend·abil·i·ty** \-ˌpen-də-ˈbi-lə-tē\ n

**de·pen·dence** also **de·pen·dance** \di-ˈpen-dəns\ n **1** : the quality or state of being dependent; esp : the quality or state of being influenced by or subject to another **2** : RELIANCE, TRUST **3** : something on which one relies **4** : drug addiction; also : HABITUATION 2

**de·pen·den·cy** \-dən-sē\ n, pl **-cies 1** : DEPENDENCE **2** : a territory under the jurisdiction of a nation but not formally annexed by it

¹**de·pen·dent** \-dənt\ adj **1** : hanging down **2** : determined or conditioned by another; also : affected with drug dependence **3** : relying on another for support **4** : subject to another's jurisdiction **5** : SUBORDINATE 4 ⟨∼ clauses⟩

²**dependent** also **de·pen·dant** \-dənt\ n : one that is dependent; esp : a person who relies on another for support

**dependent variable** n : a variable whose value is determined by that of one or more other variables in a function

**de·pict** \di-ˈpikt\ vb **1** : to represent by a picture **2** : to describe in words — **de·pic·tion** \-ˈpik-shən\ n

**de·pil·a·to·ry** \di-ˈpi-lə-ˌtȯr-ē\ n, pl **-ries** : a preparation for removing hair, wool, or bristles

**de·plane** \dē-ˈplān\ vb : to get out of an airplane

**de·plete** \di-ˈplēt\ vb **de·plet·ed; de·plet·ing** : to exhaust esp. of strength or resources — **de·ple·tion** \-ˈplē-shən\ n

**de·plor·able** \di-ˈplȯr-ə-bəl\ adj **1** : LAMENTABLE ⟨a ∼ death⟩ **2** : WRETCHED — **de·plor·ably** adv

**de·plore** \-ˈplȯr\ vb **de·plored; de·plor·ing 1** : to feel or express grief for **2** : to regret strongly **3** : to consider unfortunate or deserving of disapproval

**de·ploy** \di-ˈplȯi\ vb : to spread out (as troops or ships) in order for battle — **de·ploy·ment** \-mənt\ n

**de·po·nent** \di-ˈpō-nənt\ n : one who gives evidence

**de·pop·u·late** \dē-ˈpä-pyə-ˌlāt\ vb : to reduce greatly the population of — **de·pop·u·la·tion** \-ˌpä-pyə-ˈlā-shən\ n

**de·port** \di-ˈpȯrt\ vb **1** : CONDUCT, BEHAVE **2** : BANISH, EXILE — **de·por·ta·tion** \ˌdē-ˌpȯr-ˈtā-shən\ n

**de·port·ment** \di-ˈpȯrt-mənt\ n : BEHAVIOR, BEARING

**de·pose** \di-ˈpōz\ vb **de·posed; de·pos·ing 1** : to remove from high office (as of king) **2** : to testify under oath or by affidavit

¹**de·pos·it** \di-ˈpä-zət\ vb **de·pos·it·ed \-zə-təd\; de·pos·it·ing 1** : to place for safekeeping or as a pledge; esp : to put money in a bank **2** : to lay down : PLACE **3** : to let fall or sink ⟨silt ∼ed by a flood⟩ — **de·pos·i·tor** \-ˈpä-zə-tər\ n

²**deposit** n **1** : the state of being deposited ⟨money on ∼⟩ **2** : something placed for safekeeping; esp : money deposited in a bank **3** : money given as a pledge **4** : an act of depositing **5** : something laid down ⟨a ∼ of silt⟩ **6** : a natural accumulation (as of a mineral)

**de·po·si·tion** \ˌde-pə-ˈzi-shən, ˌdē-\ n **1** : an act of removing from a position of authority **2** : TESTIMONY **3** : the process of depositing **4** : DEPOSIT

**de·pos·i·to·ry** \di-ˈpä-zə-ˌtȯr-ē\ n, pl **-ries** : a place where something is deposited esp. for safekeeping

**de·pot** \l, 2 usu ˈde-pō, 3 usu ˈdē-\ n **1** : a place for storing goods or vehicles **2** : a place where military supplies or replacements are kept or assembled **3** : a building for railroad or bus passengers

**depr** abbr depreciation

**de·prave** \di-ˈprāv\ vb **de·praved; de·prav·ing** [ME, fr. AF depraver, fr. L depravare to pervert, fr. pravus crooked, bad] : CORRUPT, PERVERT — **de·praved** adj — **de·prav·i·ty** \-ˈpra-və-tē\ n

**dep·re·cate** \ˈde-pri-ˌkāt\ vb **-cat·ed; -cat·ing** [L deprecari to avert by prayer, fr. precari to pray] **1** : to express disapproval of **2** : BELITTLE — **dep·re·ca·tion** \ˌde-pri-ˈkā-shən\ n

**dep·re·ca·to·ry** \ˈde-pri-kə-ˌtȯr-ē\ adj **1** : APOLOGETIC **2** : serving to deprecate : DISAPPROVING

**de·pre·ci·ate** \di-ˈprē-shē-ˌāt\ vb **-at·ed; -at·ing** [ME, fr. LL depreciatus, pp. of depretiare, fr. L pretium price] **1** : BELITTLE, DISPARAGE **2** : to lessen in price or value — **de·pre·cia·ble** \-shə-bəl\ adj — **de·pre·ci·a·tion** \-ˌprē-shē-ˈā-shən\ n

**dep·re·da·tion** \ˌde-prə-ˈdā-shən\ n : a laying waste or plundering — **dep·re·date** \ˈde-prə-ˌdāt\ vb

**de·press** \di-ˈpres\ vb **1** : to press down : cause to sink to a lower position **2** : to lessen the activity or force of **3** : SADDEN, DISCOURAGE **4** : to lessen in price or value — **de·pres·sor** \-ˈpre-sər\ n

**de·pres·sant** \di-ˈpre-s⁰nt\ n : one that depresses; esp : a chemical substance (as a drug) that reduces bodily functional activity — **depressant** adj

**de·pressed** \-ˈprest\ adj **1** : low in spirits; also : affected with psychological depression **2** : suffering from economic depression

**de·pres·sion** \di-ˈpre-shən\ n **1** : an act of depressing : a state of being depressed **2** : a pressing down : LOWERING **3** : a state of feeling sad **4** : a psychological disorder marked esp. by sadness, inactivity, difficulty in thinking and concentration, and feelings of dejection 5 : a depressed area or part 6 : a period of low general economic activity with widespread unemployment

**¹de·pres·sive** \di-'pre-siv\ *adj* 1 : tending to depress 2 : characterized or affected by psychological depression

**²depressive** *n* : a person affected with or prone to psychological depression

**de·pres·sur·ize** \(ˌ)dē-'pre-shə-ˌrīz\ *vb* : to release pressure from

**dep·ri·va·tion** \ˌde-prə-'vā-shən\ *n* 1 : an act or instance of depriving : LOSS 2 : PRIVATION 2

**de·prive** \di-'prīv\ *vb* **de·prived; de·priv·ing** 1 : to take something away from 2 : to stop from having something

**deprived** *adj* : marked by deprivation esp. of the necessities of life

**de·pro·gram** \(ˌ)dē-'prō-ˌgram, -grəm\ *vb* : to dissuade from convictions usu. of a religious nature often by coercive means

**dept** *abbr* department

**depth** \'depth\ *n, pl* **depths** \'depths\ 1 : something that is deep; *esp* : the deep part of a body of water 2 : a part that is far from the outside or surface; *also* : the middle or innermost part 3 : ABYSS 4 : a profound or intense state ⟨the ~s of reflection⟩; *also* : the worst part ⟨during the ~s of the depression⟩ 5 : a reprehensibly low condition 6 : the distance from top to bottom or from front to back 7 : the quality of being deep 8 : the degree of intensity

**depth charge** *n* : an explosive device for use underwater esp. against submarines

**dep·u·ta·tion** \ˌde-pyə-'tā-shən\ *n* 1 : the act of appointing a deputy 2 : DELEGATION

**de·pute** \di-'pyüt\ *vb* **de·put·ed; de·put·ing** : DELEGATE

**dep·u·tize** \'de-pyə-ˌtīz\ *vb* **-tized; -tiz·ing** : to appoint or act as deputy

**dep·u·ty** \'de-pyə-tē\ *n, pl* **-ties** 1 : a person appointed to act for or in place of another 2 : an assistant empowered to act as a substitute in the absence of a superior 3 : a member of a lower house of a legislative assembly

**der** *or* **deriv** *abbr* derivation; derivative

**de·rail** \di-'rāl\ *vb* : to leave or cause to leave the rails — **de·rail·ment** *n*

**de·rail·leur** \di-'rā-lər\ *n* [F *dérailleur*] : a device for shifting gears on a bicycle by moving the chain from one set of exposed gears to another

**de·range** \di-'rānj\ *vb* **de·ranged; de·rang·ing** 1 : DISARRANGE, UPSET 2 : to make insane — **de·range·ment** *n*

**der·by** \'dər-bē, *Brit* 'där-\ *n, pl* **derbies** 1 : a horse race usu. for three-year-olds held annually 2 : a race or contest open to all 3 : a stiff felt hat with dome-shaped crown and narrow brim

**de·re·cho** \də-'rā-(ˌ)chō\ *n, pl* **-chos** [Sp, straight (contrasted with *tornado*, taken to mean "turned")]: a complex of thunderstorms with powerful winds

**de·reg·u·la·tion** \(ˌ)dē-ˌre-gyü-'lā-shən\ *n*
: the act of removing restrictions or regulations — **de·reg·u·late** \-'re-gyù-ˌlāt\ *vb*

**¹der·e·lict** \'der-ə-ˌlikt\ *adj* 1 : abandoned by the owner or occupant 2 : NEGLIGENT ⟨~ in his duty⟩

**²derelict** *n* 1 : something voluntarily abandoned; *esp* : a ship abandoned on the high seas 2 : a destitute homeless social misfit : VAGRANT, BUM

**der·e·lic·tion** \ˌder-ə-'lik-shən\ *n* 1 : the act of abandoning : the state of being abandoned 2 : intentional neglect ⟨~ of duty⟩

**de·ride** \di-'rīd\ *vb* **de·rid·ed; de·rid·ing** [L *deridēre*, fr. *ridēre* to laugh] : to laugh at scornfully : RIDICULE

**de ri·gueur** \də-rē-'gər\ *adj* [F] : prescribed or required by fashion, etiquette, or custom : PROPER

**de·ri·sion** \də-'ri-zhən\ *n* : RIDICULE

**de·ri·sive** \-'rī-siv\ *adj* — **de·ri·sive·ly** *adv* — **de·ri·sive·ness** *n* — **de·ri·so·ry** \-'rī-sə-rē\ *adj*

**der·i·va·tion** \ˌder-ə-'vā-shən\ *n* 1 : the formation of a word from an earlier word or root; *also* : an act of ascertaining or stating the derivation of a word 2 : ETYMOLOGY 3 : SOURCE, ORIGIN; *also* : DESCENT 4 : an act or process of deriving

**de·riv·a·tive** \di-'ri-və-tiv\ *n* 1 : a word formed by derivation 2 : something derived 3 : the limit of the ratio of the change of a function's value to the change in its independent variable as the latter change approaches zero — **derivative** *adj*

**de·rive** \di-'rīv\ *vb* **de·rived; de·riv·ing** [ME, fr. AF *deriver*, fr. L *derivare*, lit., to draw off (water), fr. *de-* from + *rivus* stream] 1 : to receive or obtain from a source 2 : to obtain from a parent substance 3 : INFER, DEDUCE 4 : to trace the derivation of 5 : to come from a certain source

**der·mal** \'dər-məl\ *adj* : of or relating to the skin : CUTANEOUS

**der·ma·ti·tis** \ˌdər-mə-'tī-təs\ *n, pl* **-tit·i·des** \-'ti-zə-ˌdēz\ *or* **-ti·tis·es** : inflammation of the skin

**der·ma·tol·o·gy** \-'tä-lə-jē\ *n* : a branch of medical science dealing with the structure, functions, and diseases of the skin — **der·ma·tol·o·gist** \-jist\ *n*

**der·mis** \'dər-məs\ *n* : the sensitive vascular inner layer of the skin

**der·o·gate** \'der-ə-ˌgāt\ *vb* **-gat·ed; -gat·ing** 1 : to cause to seem inferior : DISPARAGE 2 : DETRACT — **der·o·ga·tion** \ˌder-ə-'gā-shən\ *n* — **de·rog·a·tive** \di-'rä-gə-tiv\ *adj*

**de·rog·a·to·ry** \di-'rä-gə-ˌtȯr-ē\ *adj* : intended to lower the reputation of a person or thing : DISPARAGING — **de·rog·a·to·ri·ly** \-ˌrä-gə-'tȯr-ə-lē\ *adv*

**der·rick** \'der-ik\ *n* [obs. *derrick* hangman, gallows, fr. *Derick*, name of 17th cent. Eng. hangman] 1 : a hoisting apparatus : CRANE 2 : a framework over a drill hole (as for oil) for supporting machinery

**der·ri·ere** *or* **der·ri·ère** \ˌder-ē-'er\ *n* : BUTTOCKS

**der·ring–do** \ˌder-iŋ-ˈdü\ n : DARING

**der·rin·ger** \ˈder-ən-jər\ n : a short-barreled pocket pistol

**der·vish** \ˈdər-vish\ n [Turk *derviş*, lit., beggar, fr. Pers *darvīsh*] : a member of a Muslim religious order noted for devotional exercises (as bodily movements leading to a trance)

**de·sal·i·nate** \dē-ˈsa-lə-ˌnāt\ vb -nat·ed; -nat·ing : DESALT — **de·sal·i·na·tion** \ˌsa-lə-ˈnā-shən\ n

**de·sal·i·nize** \dē-ˈsa-lə-ˌnīz\ vb -nized; -niz·ing : DESALT — **de·sal·i·ni·za·tion** \ˌsa-lə-nə-ˈzā-shən\ n

**de·salt** \dē-ˈsȯlt\ vb : to remove salt from ⟨∼ seawater⟩ — **de·salt·er** n

**des·cant** \ˈdes-ˌkant\ vb 1 : to sing or play part music : SING 2 : to discourse or write at length

**de·scend** \di-ˈsend\ vb 1 : to pass from a higher to a lower place or level : pass, move, or climb down or down along 2 : DERIVE ⟨∼ed from royalty⟩ 3 : to pass by inheritance or transmission 4 : to incline, lead, or extend downward 5 : to swoop down or appear suddenly (as in an attack)

¹**de·scen·dant** *also* **de·scen·dent** \di-ˈsen-dənt\ adj 1 : DESCENDING 2 : proceeding from an ancestor or source

²**descendant** *also* **descendent** n 1 : one descended from another or from a common stock 2 : one deriving directly from a precursor or prototype

**de·scent** \di-ˈsent\ n 1 : ANCESTRY, BIRTH, LINEAGE 2 : the act or process of descending 3 : SLOPE 4 : a descending way (as a downgrade) 5 : a sudden hostile raid or assault 6 : a downward step (as in station or value) : DECLINE

**de·scram·ble** \dē-ˈskram-bəl\ vb : UNSCRAMBLE 2 ⟨∼ satellite transmissions⟩ — **de·scram·bler** \-b(ə-)ler\ n

**de·scribe** \di-ˈskrīb\ vb **de·scribed**; **de·scrib·ing** 1 : to represent or give an account of in words 2 : to trace the outline of — **de·scrib·able** adj

**de·scrip·tion** \di-ˈskrip-shən\ n 1 : an account of something; *esp* : an account that presents a picture to a person who reads or hears it 2 : KIND, SORT — **de·scrip·tive** \-ˈskrip-tiv\ adj

**de·scry** \di-ˈskrī\ vb **de·scried**; **de·scry·ing** 1 : to catch sight of 2 : to discover by observation or investigation

**des·e·crate** \ˈde-si-ˌkrāt\ vb -crat·ed; -crat·ing : PROFANE — **des·e·cra·tion** \ˌde-si-ˈkrā-shən\ n

**de·seg·re·gate** \dē-ˈse-gri-ˌgāt\ vb : to eliminate segregation in; *esp* : to free of any law or practice requiring isolation on the basis of race — **de·seg·re·ga·tion** \-ˌse-gri-ˈgā-shən\ n

**de·sen·si·tize** \dē-ˈsen-sə-ˌtīz\ vb : to make (a sensitized or hypersensitive individual) insensitive or nonreactive to a sensitizing agent — **de·sen·si·ti·za·tion** \-ˌsen-sə-tə-ˈzā-shən\ n

¹**des·ert** \ˈde-zərt\ n : dry land with few plants and little rainfall

²**des·ert** \ˈde-zərt\ adj : of, relating to, or resembling a desert; *esp* : being barren and without life ⟨a ∼ island⟩

³**de·sert** \di-ˈzərt\ n 1 : the quality or fact of deserving reward or punishment 2 : a just reward or punishment

⁴**de·sert** \di-ˈzərt\ vb 1 : to withdraw from 2 : ABANDON, FORSAKE — **de·sert·er** n — **de·ser·tion** \-ˈzər-shən\ n

**de·serve** \di-ˈzərv\ vb **de·served**; **de·serv·ing** : to be worthy of : MERIT — **de·serv·ing** adj

**de·serv·ed·ly** \-ˈzər-vəd-lē\ adv : according to merit : JUSTLY

**deshabille** *var of* DISHABILLE

**des·ic·cate** \ˈde-si-ˌkāt\ vb -cat·ed; -cat·ing : DRY, DEHYDRATE — **des·ic·ca·tion** \ˌde-si-ˈkā-shən\ n — **des·ic·ca·tor** \ˈde-si-ˌkā-tər\ n

**de·sid·er·a·tum** \di-ˌsi-də-ˈrä-təm, -ˌzi-, -ˈrā-\ n, pl **-ta** \-tə\ [L] : something desired as essential

¹**de·sign** \di-ˈzīn\ vb 1 : to conceive and plan out in the mind : INTEND 2 : to devise for a specific function or end 4 : to make a pattern or sketch of 5 : to conceive and draw the plans for

²**design** n 1 : a particular purpose : deliberate planning 2 : a mental project or scheme : PLAN 3 : a secret project or scheme : PLOT 4 pl : aggressive or evil intent — used with *on* or *against* 5 : a preliminary sketch or plan 6 : an underlying scheme that governs functioning, developing, or unfolding : MOTIF ⟨the general ∼ of the epic⟩ 7 : the arrangement of elements or details in a product or a work of art 8 : a decorative pattern ⟨a floral ∼⟩ 9 : the art of executing designs

¹**des·ig·nate** \ˈde-zig-ˌnāt, -nət\ adj : chosen but not yet installed ⟨ambassador ∼⟩

²**des·ig·nate** \-ˌnāt\ vb -nat·ed; -nat·ing 1 : to appoint and set apart for a special purpose 2 : to mark or point out : INDICATE; *also* : SPECIFY, STIPULATE 3 : to call by a name or title — **des·ig·na·tion** \ˌde-zig-ˈnā-shən\ n

**designated driver** n : a person chosen to abstain from alcohol so as to transport others safely

**designated hitter** n : a baseball player designated at the start of the game to bat in place of the pitcher without causing the pitcher to be removed from the game

**de·sign·er** \di-ˈzī-nər\ n 1 : one who creates plans for a project or structure 2 : one who designs and manufactures high-fashion clothing — **designer** adj

**designer drug** n : a synthetic version of an illicit drug that has been chemically altered to avoid its prohibition

**de·sign·ing** \di-ˈzī-niŋ\ adj : CRAFTY, SCHEMING

**de·sir·able** \di-ˈzī-rə-bəl\ adj 1 : PLEASING, ATTRACTIVE 2 : ADVISABLE ⟨∼ legislation⟩ — **de·sir·abil·i·ty** \-ˌzī-rə-ˈbi-lə-tē\ n — **de·sir·able·ness** n — **de·sir·ably** \-ˈzī-rə-blē\ adv

¹**de·sire** \di-ˈzī(-ə)r\ vb **de·sired**; **de·sir·ing** [ME, fr. AF *desirer*, fr. L *desiderare*, fr. *sider-*, *sidus* heavenly body] 1 : to long

or hope for : exhibit or feel desire for **2** : REQUEST

**²de·sire** n **1** : a strong wish : LONGING, CRAVING **2** : sexual urge or appetite **3** : a usu. formal request for action **4** : something desired

**de·sir·ous** \di-'zī(-ə)r-əs\ adj : eagerly wishing : DESIRING ⟨~ of fame⟩

**de·sist** \di-'zist, -'sist\ vb : to cease to proceed or act

**desk** \'desk\ n [ME deske, fr. ML desca, fr. It desco table, fr. L discus dish, disc] **1** : a table, frame, or case esp. for writing and reading **2** : a counter, stand, or booth at which a person performs duties **3** : a specialized division of an organization (as a newspaper) ⟨city ~⟩

**desk·top publishing** \'desk-ˌtäp-\ n : the production of printed matter by means of a microcomputer

**¹des·o·late** \'de-sə-lət, -zə-\ adj **1** : DESERTED, ABANDONED **2** : FORSAKEN, LONELY **3** : DILAPIDATED **4** : BARREN, LIFELESS ⟨a ~ landscape⟩ **5** : CHEERLESS, GLOOMY ⟨~ memories⟩ — **des·o·late·ly** adv — **des·o·late·ness** n

**²des·o·late** \-ˌlāt\ vb -lat·ed; -lat·ing : to make desolate : lay waste : make wretched

**des·o·la·tion** \ˌde-sə-'lā-shən, -zə-\ n **1** : the action of desolating **2** : GRIEF, SADNESS **3** : LONELINESS **4** : DEVASTATION, RUIN **5** : barren wasteland

**des·oxy·ri·bo·nu·cle·ic acid** \de-ˌzäk-sē-ˈrī-bō-nü-ˌklē-ik-, -nyü-\ n : DNA

**¹de·spair** \di-'sper\ vb : to lose all hope or confidence — **de·spair·ing** \-iŋ\ adj — **de·spair·ing·ly** adv

**²despair** n **1** : utter loss of hope **2** : a cause of hopelessness

**des·patch** chiefly Brit var of DISPATCH

**des·per·a·do** \ˌdes-pə-'rä-dō, -'rä-\ n, pl **-does** or **-dos** : a bold or reckless criminal

**des·per·ate** \'des-pə-rət, -prət\ adj **1** : being beyond or almost beyond hope : causing despair **2** : RASH ⟨a ~ attempt⟩ **3** : extremely intense — **des·per·ate·ly** adv — **des·per·ate·ness** n

**des·per·a·tion** \ˌdes-pə-'rā-shən\ n **1** : a loss of hope and surrender to despair **2** : a state of hopelessness leading to rashness

**de·spi·ca·ble** \di-'spi-kə-bəl, 'des-pi-\ adj : deserving to be despised — **de·spi·ca·bly** \-blē\ adv

**de·spise** \di-'spīz\ vb **de·spised**; **de·spis·ing** **1** : to look down on with contempt or aversion : DISDAIN, DETEST **2** : to regard as negligible, worthless, or distasteful

**de·spite** \di-'spīt\ prep : in spite of

**de·spoil** \di-'spȯi(-ə)l\ vb : to strip of belongings, possessions, or value — **de·spoil·er** n — **de·spoil·ment** n

**de·spo·li·a·tion** \di-ˌspō-lē-'ā-shən\ n : the act of plundering : the state of being despoiled

**¹de·spond** \di-'spänd\ vb : to become discouraged or disheartened

**²despond** n : DESPONDENCY

**de·spon·den·cy** \-'spän-dən-sē\ n : DEJECTION, HOPELESSNESS — **de·spon·dent** \-dənt\ adj — **de·spon·dent·ly** adv

**des·pot** \'des-pət, -ˌpät\ n [MF despote, fr. Gk despotēs master, lord, autocrat] **1** : a ruler with absolute power and authority **2** : a person exercising power tyrannically — **des·pot·ic** \des-'pä-tik\ adj — **des·po·tism** \'des-pə-ˌti-zəm\ n

**des·sert** \di-'zərt\ n : a course of sweet food, fruit, or cheese served at the close of a meal

**de·stig·ma·tize** \dē-'stig-mə-ˌtīz\ vb : to remove associations of shame or disgrace from

**des·ti·na·tion** \ˌdes-tə-'nā-shən\ n **1** : a purpose for which something is destined **2** : an act of appointing, setting aside for a purpose, or predetermining **3** : a place to which one is journeying or to which something is sent

**des·tine** \'des-tən\ vb **des·tined**; **des·tin·ing** **1** : to settle in advance **2** : to designate, assign, or dedicate in advance **3** : to direct or set apart for a specific purpose or place

**des·ti·ny** \'des-tə-nē\ n, pl **-nies** **1** : something to which a person or thing is destined : FATE, FORTUNE **2** : a predetermined course of events

**des·ti·tute** \'des-tə-ˌtüt, -ˌtyüt\ adj **1** : lacking something needed or desirable **2** : suffering extreme poverty — **des·ti·tu·tion** \ˌdes-tə-'tü-shən, -'tyü-\ n

**de·stroy** \di-'strȯi\ vb **1** : to put an end to : RUIN **2** : KILL

**de·stroy·er** \di-'strȯi-ər\ n **1** : one that destroys **2** : a small speedy warship

**de·struc·ti·ble** \di-'strək-tə-bəl\ adj : capable of being destroyed — **de·struc·ti·bil·i·ty** \-ˌstrək-tə-'bi-lə-tē\ n

**de·struc·tion** \di-'strək-shən\ n **1** : RUIN **2** : the action or process of destroying something **3** : a destroying agency

**de·struc·tive** \di-'strək-tiv\ adj **1** : causing destruction : RUINOUS **2** : designed or tending to hurt or destroy — **de·struc·tive·ly** adv — **de·struc·tive·ness** n

**de·sue·tude** \'de-swi-ˌtüd, -ˌtyüd\ n : DISUSE

**des·ul·to·ry** \'de-səl-ˌtȯr-ē\ adj : passing aimlessly from one thing or subject to another : DISCONNECTED

**det** abbr **1** detached; detachment **2** detail

**de·tach** \di-'tach\ vb **1** : to separate esp. from a larger mass **2** : DISENGAGE, WITHDRAW — **de·tach·able** adj

**de·tached** \di-'tacht\ adj **1** : not joined or connected : SEPARATE **2** : ALOOF, IMPARTIAL ⟨a ~ attitude⟩

**de·tach·ment** \di-'tach-mənt\ n **1** : SEPARATION **2** : the dispatching of a body of troops or part of a fleet from the main body for special service; also : the portion so dispatched **3** : a small permanent military unit of special composition **4** : indifference to worldly concerns : ALOOFNESS **5** : IMPARTIALITY

**¹de·tail** \di-'tāl, 'dē-ˌtāl\ n [F détail, fr. OF detail slice, piece, fr. detaillier to cut in pieces, fr. taillier to cut] **1** : a dealing with something item by item ⟨go into

~\>; *also* : ITEM, PARTICULAR ⟨the ~s of a story⟩ **2** : selection (as of soldiers) for special duty; *also* : the persons thus selected

²**de·tail** *vb* **1** : to report in particulars : SPECIFY **2** : to assign to a special duty

**de·tailed** \di-'tāld, 'dē-₁tāld\ *adj* : marked by abundant detail

**de·tail·ing** \'dē-₁tāl-iŋ\ *n* : the meticulous cleaning and refurbishing of an automobile

**de·tain** \di-'tān\ *vb* **1** : to hold in or as if in custody **2** : STOP, DELAY

**de·tect** \di-'tekt\ *vb* : to discover the nature, existence, presence, or fact of — **de·tect·able** *adj* — **de·tec·tion** \-'tek-shən\ *n* — **de·tec·tor** \-'tek-tər\ *n*

¹**de·tec·tive** \di-'tek-tiv\ *adj* **1** : fitted or used for detection **2** : of or relating to detectives

²**detective** *n* : a person employed or engaged in detecting lawbreakers or getting information that is not readily accessible

**dé·tente** *or* **de·tente** \dā-'tänt\ *n* [F] : a relaxation of strained relations or tensions (as between nations)

**de·ten·tion** \di-'ten-chən\ *n* **1** : the act or fact of detaining : CONFINEMENT; *esp* : a period of temporary custody prior to disposition by a court **2** : a forced delay

**de·ter** \di-'tər\ *vb* **de·terred; de·ter·ring** [L *deterrēre*, fr. *terrēre* to frighten] **1** : to turn aside, discourage, or prevent from acting (as by fear) **2** : INHIBIT

**de·ter·gent** \di-'tər-jənt\ *n* : a cleansing agent; *esp* : a chemical product similar to soap in its cleaning ability

**de·te·ri·o·rate** \di-'tir-ē-ə-₁rāt\ *vb* **-rat·ed; -rat·ing** : to make or become worse in quality or condition — **de·te·ri·o·ra·tion** \-₁tir-ē-ə-'rā-shən\ *n*

**de·ter·min·able** \-'tər-mə-nə-bəl\ *adj* : capable of being determined; *esp* : ASCERTAINABLE

**de·ter·mi·nant** \-mə-nənt\ *n* **1** : something that determines or conditions **2** : GENE

**de·ter·mi·nate** \di-'tər-mə-nət\ *adj* **1** : having fixed limits : DEFINITE ⟨a ~ period of time⟩ **2** : definitely settled ⟨in ~ order⟩ — **de·ter·mi·nate·ness** *n*

**de·ter·mi·na·tion** \di-₁tər-mə-'nā-shən\ *n* **1** : the act of coming to a decision; *also* : the decision or conclusion reached **2** : a fixing of the extent, position, or character of something **3** : accurate measurement (as of length or volume) **4** : firm or fixed purpose — **de·ter·mi·na·tive** \-'tər-mə-₁nā-tiv, -'tər-mə-nə-\ *adj*

**de·ter·mine** \di-'tər-mən\ *vb* **-mined; -min·ing 1** : to fix conclusively or authoritatively **2** : to come to a decision : SETTLE, RESOLVE **3** : to fix the form or character of beforehand : ORDAIN; *also* : REGULATE **4** : to find out the limits, nature, dimensions, or scope of ⟨~ a position at sea⟩ **5** : to bring about as a result

**de·ter·mined** \-'tər-mənd\ *adj* **1** : firmly resolved **2** : characterized by or showing determination — **de·ter·mined·ly** \-mənd-lē, -mə-nəd-lē\ *adv* — **de·ter·mined·ness** *n*

**de·ter·min·ism** \di-'tər-mə-₁ni-zəm\ *n* : a doctrine that acts of the will, natural events, or social changes are determined by preceding events or natural causes — **de·ter·min·ist** \-nist\ *n or adj*

**de·ter·rence** \di-'tər-əns\ *n* : the inhibition of criminal behavior by fear esp. of punishment

**de·ter·rent** \-ənt\ *adj* **1** : serving to deter ⟨the law's ~ effect⟩ **2** : relating to deterrence — **deterrent** *n*

**de·test** \di-'test\ *vb* [L *detestari*, lit., to curse while calling a deity to witness, fr. *de-* from + *testari* to call to witness, fr. *testis* witness] : LOATHE, HATE — **de·test·able** *adj* — **de·tes·ta·tion** \₁dē-₁tes-'tā-shən\ *n*

**de·throne** \di-'thrōn\ *vb* : to remove from a throne : DEPOSE — **de·throne·ment** *n*

**det·o·nate** \'de-t³n-₁āt\ *vb* **-nat·ed; -nat·ing** : to explode or cause to explode with violence — **det·o·na·tion** \₁de-t³n-'ā-shən\ *n*

**det·o·na·tor** \'de-t³n-₁ā-tər\ *n* : a device for detonating an explosive

¹**de·tour** \'dē-₁tůr\ *n* : an indirect way replacing part of a route

²**detour** *vb* : to go by detour

**de·tox** \'dē-₁täks, dē-'täks\ *n* : detoxification from an intoxicating or addictive substance — **detox** *vb*

**de·tox·i·fy** \dē-'täk-sə-₁fī\ *vb* **-fied; -fy·ing 1** : to remove a poison or toxin or the effect of such from **2** : to free (as a drug user) from an intoxicating or addictive substance or from dependence on it — **de·tox·i·fi·ca·tion** \-₁täk-sə-fə-'kā-shən\ *n*

**de·tract** \di-'trakt\ *vb* **1** : to take away or diminish the value or effect of something **2** : DIVERT ⟨~s attention from the real issue⟩ — **de·trac·tion** \-'trak-shən\ *n* — **de·trac·tor** \-'trak-tər\ *n*

**de·train** \dē-'trān\ *vb* : to leave or cause to leave a railroad train

**det·ri·ment** \'de-trə-mənt\ *n* : INJURY, DAMAGE; *also* : a cause of injury or damage — **det·ri·men·tal** \₁de-trə-'ment-³l\ *adj* — **det·ri·men·tal·ly** *adv*

**de·tri·tus** \di-'trī-təs\ *n, pl* **de·tri·tus** : fragments resulting from disintegration (as of rocks) : DEBRIS

**deuce** \'düs, 'dyüs\ *n* **1** : a two in cards or dice **2** : a tie in a tennis game with both sides at 40 **3** : DEVIL — used chiefly as a mild oath

**Deut** *abbr* Deuteronomy

**deu·te·ri·um** \dü-'tir-ē-əm, dyü-\ *n* : an isotope of hydrogen that has twice the mass of ordinary hydrogen

**Deu·ter·on·o·my** \₁dü-tə-'rä-nə-mē, ₁dyü-\ *n* — see BIBLE table

**deut·sche mark** \'doi-chə-₁märk\ *n* : a former basic monetary unit of Germany

**dev** *abbr* deviation

**de·val·ue** \dē-'val-yü\ *vb* : to reduce the international exchange value of ⟨~ a currency⟩ — **de·val·u·a·tion** \-₁val-yə-'wā-shən\ *n*

**dev·as·tate** \'de-və-₁stāt\ *vb* **-tat·ed; -tat·**

ing **1** : to bring to ruin **2** : to reduce to chaos or helplessness — **dev·as·tat·ing·ly** *adv* — **dev·as·ta·tion** \‚de-və-'stā-shən\ *n*

**de·vel·op** \di-'ve-ləp\ *vb* **1** : to unfold gradually or in detail **2** : to place (exposed photographic material) in chemicals to produce a visible image **3** : to bring out the possibilities of **4** : to make more available or usable ⟨∼ land⟩ **5** : to acquire gradually ⟨∼ a taste for olives⟩ **6** : to go through a natural process of growth, differentiation, or evolution **7** : to come into being gradually — **de·vel·op·er** *n* — **de·vel·op·ment** *n* — **de·vel·op·men·tal** \‚ve-ləp-'men-t⁰l\ *adj* — **de·vel·op·men·tal·ly** \-t⁰l-ē\ *adv*

**de·vi·ant** \'dē-ve-ənt\ *adj* : deviating esp. from some accepted norm ⟨∼ behavior⟩ — **de·vi·ance** \-əns\ *n* — **de·vi·an·cy** \-ən-sē\ *n* — **deviant** *n*

**de·vi·ate** \'dē-vē-‚āt\ *vb* **-at·ed; -at·ing** [LL *deviare*, fr. L *de-* from + *via* way] : to turn aside from a course, standard, principle, or topic — **de·vi·ate** \-vē-ət, -vē-‚āt\ *n* — **de·vi·a·tion** \‚dē-vē-'ā-shən\ *n*

**de·vice** \di-'vīs\ *n* **1** : SCHEME, STRATAGEM **2** : a piece of equipment or a mechanism for a special purpose **3** : DESIRE, INCLINATION ⟨left to my own ∼s⟩ **4** : an emblematic design

¹**dev·il** \'de-vəl\ *n* [ME *devel*, fr. OE *dēofol*, fr. LL *diabolus*, fr. Gk *diabolos*, lit., slanderer, fr. *diaballein* to throw across, slander, fr. *dia-* across + *ballein* to throw] **1** *often cap* : the personal supreme spirit of evil **2** : DEMON **3** : a wicked person **4** : an energetic, reckless, or dashing person **5** : FELLOW ⟨poor ∼⟩ ⟨lucky ∼⟩

²**devil** *vb* **-iled** *or* **-illed; -il·ing** *or* **-il·ling 1** : to season highly ⟨∼ed eggs⟩ **2** : TEASE, ANNOY

**dev·il·ish** \'de-və-lish\ *adj* **1** : befitting a devil : EVIL; *also* : MISCHIEVOUS **2** : EXTREME ⟨in a ∼ hurry⟩ — **dev·il·ish·ly** *adv* — **dev·il·ish·ness** *n*

**dev·il·ment** \'de-vəl-mənt, -‚ment\ *n* : MISCHIEF

**dev·il·ry** \-rē\ *or* **dev·il·try** \-trē\ *n, pl* **-il·ries** *or* **-il·tries 1** : action performed with the help of the devil **2** : MISCHIEF

**de·vi·ous** \'dē-vē-əs\ *adj* **1** : deviating from a straight line : ROUNDABOUT **2** : ERRANT **3** : TRICKY, CUNNING

¹**de·vise** \di-'vīz\ *vb* **de·vised; de·vis·ing** [ME, fr. AF *deviser* to divide, distinguish, invent, fr. VL *divisare*, fr. L *dividere* to divide] **1** : INVENT **2** : PLOT **3** : to give (real estate) by will

²**devise** *n* **1** : a disposing of real property by will **2** : a will or clause of a will disposing of real property **3** : property given by will

**de·vi·tal·ize** \dē-'vī-tə-‚līz\ *vb* : to deprive of life or vitality

**de·void** \di-'void\ *adj* : being without : VOID ⟨a book ∼ of interest⟩

**de·voir** \də-'vwär\ *n* **1** : DUTY **2** : a formal act of civility or respect

**de·volve** \di-'välv\ *vb* **de·volved; de·volv·ing** : to pass (as rights or responsibility) from one to another usu. by suc-

cession or transmission — **dev·o·lu·tion** \‚de-və-'lü-shən, ‚dē-\ *n*

**De·vo·ni·an** \di-'vō-nē-ən\ *adj* : of, relating to, or being the period of the Paleozoic era between the Silurian and the Mississippian — **Devonian** *n*

**de·vote** \di-'vōt\ *vb* **de·vot·ed; de·vot·ing 1** : to commit to wholly or chiefly ⟨∼s herself to serving the poor⟩ **2** : to set apart for a special purpose : DEDICATE

**de·vot·ed** \-'vō-təd\ *adj* : characterized by loyalty and devotion : FAITHFUL ⟨∼ fans⟩

**dev·o·tee** \‚de-və-'tē, -'tā\ *n* : an ardent follower, supporter, or enthusiast

**de·vo·tion** \di-'vō-shən\ *n* **1** : religious fervor **2** : an act of prayer or private worship — usu. used in pl. **3** : a religious exercise for private use **4** : the fact or state of being dedicated and loyal ⟨∼ to music⟩; *also* : the act of devoting — **de·vo·tion·al** \-shə-nəl\ *adj*

**de·vour** \di-'vau̇(-ə)r\ *vb* **1** : to eat up greedily or ravenously **2** : WASTE, ANNIHILATE ⟨the forest was ∼ed by fire⟩ **3** : to enjoy avidly ⟨∼ a book⟩ — **de·vour·er** *n*

**de·vout** \di-'vau̇t\ *adj* **1** : devoted to religion : PIOUS **2** : expressing devotion or piety **3** : EARNEST, SERIOUS ⟨a ∼ baseball fan⟩ — **de·vout·ly** *adv* — **de·vout·ness** *n*

**dew** \'dü, 'dyü\ *n* : moisture that condenses on the surfaces of cool bodies at night — **dewy** *adj*

**dew·ber·ry** \'dü-‚ber-ē, 'dyü-\ *n* : any of several sweet edible berries related to and resembling blackberries; *also* : a trailing bramble bearing these

**dew·claw** \‚klȯ\ *n* : a digit on the foot of a mammal that does not reach the ground; *also* : its claw or hoof

**dew·lap** \-‚lap\ *n* : loose skin hanging under the neck of an animal

**dew point** *n* : the temperature at which the moisture in the air begins to condense

**dex·ter·i·ty** \dek-'ster-ə-tē\ *n, pl* **-ties 1** : mental skill or quickness **2** : readiness and grace in physical activity; *esp* : skill and ease in using the hands

**dex·ter·ous** \'dek-strəs\ *adj* **1** : CLEVER **2** : done with skillfulness **3** : skillful and competent with the hands — **dex·ter·ous·ly** *adv*

**dex·trose** \'dek-‚strōs\ *n* : the naturally occurring form of glucose found in plants and blood

**DFC** *abbr* Distinguished Flying Cross

**dg** *abbr* decigram

**DG** *abbr* **1** [LL *Dei gratia*] by the grace of God **2** director general

**DH** \‚dē-'āch\ *n* : DESIGNATED HITTER

**dhow** \'dau̇\ *n* : an Arab sailing ship usu. having a long overhang forward and a high poop

**DI** *abbr* drill instructor

**dia** *abbr* diameter

**di·a·be·tes** \‚dī-ə-'bē-tēz, -təs\ *n* : an abnormal state marked by passage of excessive amounts of urine; *esp* : one (**diabetes**

**mel·li·tus** \-'me-lə-təs\) characterized by deficient insulin, by excess sugar in the blood and urine, and by thirst, hunger, and loss of weight — **di·a·bet·ic** \-'be-tik\ *adj or n*

**di·a·bol·i·cal** \dī-ə-'bä-li-kəl\ *or* **di·a·bol·ic** \-lik\ *adj* : DEVILISH ⟨a ~ plot⟩ — **di·a·bol·i·cal·ly** \-k(ə-)lē\ *adv*

**di·a·crit·ic** \dī-ə-'kri-tik\ *n* : a mark accompanying a letter and indicating a sound value different from that of the same letter when unmarked — **di·a·crit·i·cal** \-ti-kəl\ *adj*

**di·a·dem** \'dī-ə-,dem\ *n* : CROWN; *esp* : a royal headband

**di·aer·e·sis** *or* **di·er·e·sis** \dī-'er-ə-səs\, *pl* **-e·ses** \-,sēz\ : a mark " placed over a vowel to show that it is pronounced in a separate syllable (as in *naïve*)

**diag** *abbr* 1 diagonal 2 diagram

**di·ag·no·sis** \dī-ig-'nō-səs\ *n*, *pl* **-no·ses** \-,sēz\ : the art or act of identifying a disease from its signs and symptoms; *also* : the decision reached by diagnosis — **di·ag·nose** \'dī-ig-,nōs\ *vb* — **di·ag·nos·tic** \dī-ig-'näs-tik\ *adj* — **di·ag·nos·ti·cian** \-,näs-'ti-shən\ *n*

**¹di·ag·o·nal** \dī-'a-gə-nəl\ *adj* 1 : extending from one corner to the opposite corner in a 4-sided figure 2 : running in a slanting direction ⟨~ stripes⟩ 3 : having slanting markings or parts ⟨a ~ weave⟩ — **di·ag·o·nal·ly** *adv*

**²diagonal** *n* 1 : a diagonal line 2 : a diagonal row, pattern, or direction 3 : SLASH 3

**¹di·a·gram** \'dī-ə-,gram\ *n* : a design and esp. a drawing that makes something easier to understand — **di·a·gram·ma·ble** \-,gra-mə-bəl\ *adj* — **di·a·gram·mat·ic** \dī-ə-grə-'ma-tik\ *adj* — **di·a·gram·mat·i·cal·ly** \-ti-k(ə-)lē\ *adv*

**²diagram** *vb* **-grammed** *or* **-gramed** \-,gramd\; **-gram·ming** *or* **-gram·ing** : to represent by a diagram

**¹di·al** \'dī(-ə)l\ *n* [ME *dyal*, fr. ML *dialis* clock wheel revolving daily, fr. L *dies* day] 1 : the face of a sundial 2 : the face of a timepiece 3 : a face with a pointer and numbers that indicate something ⟨the ~ of a gauge⟩ 4 : a device used for making electrical connections or for regulating operation (as of a radio)

**²dial** *vb* **di·aled** *or* **di·alled**; **di·al·ing** *or* **di·al·ling** 1 : to manipulate a dial so as to operate or select 2 : to make a telephone call or connection

**³dial** *abbr* dialect

**di·a·lect** \'dī-ə-,lekt\ *n* : a regional variety of a language

**di·a·lec·tic** \,dī-ə-'lek-tik\ *n* : the process or art of reasoning by discussion of conflicting ideas; *also* : the tension between opposing elements — **di·a·lec·ti·cal** \-ti-kəl\ *adj*

**dialog box** *n* : a window on a computer screen for choosing options or inputting information

**di·a·logue** \'dī-ə-,lòg\ *n* 1 : a conversation between two or more parties 2 : the parts of a literary or dramatic work that represent conversation

**di·al·y·sis** \dī-'a-lə-səs\ *n*, *pl* **-y·ses** \-,sēz\ 1 : the separation of substances from solution by means of their unequal diffusion through semipermeable membranes 2 : the medical procedure of removing blood from an artery, purifying it by dialysis, and returning it to a vein

**diam** *abbr* diameter

**di·am·e·ter** \dī-'a-mə-tər\ *n* [ME *diametre*, fr. MF, fr. L *diametros*, fr. Gk, fr. *dia-* through + *metron* measure] 1 : a straight line passing through the center of a figure or body; *esp* : one that divides a circle in half 2 : the length of a diameter

**di·a·met·ric** \,dī-ə-'me-trik\ *or* **di·a·met·ri·cal** \-tri-kəl\ *adj* 1 : of, relating to, or constituting a diameter 2 : completely opposed or opposite — **di·a·met·ri·cal·ly** \-k(ə-)lē\ *adv*

**di·a·mond** \'dī-mənd, 'dī-ə-\ *n* 1 : a hard brilliant mineral that consists of crystalline carbon and is used as a gem 2 : a flat figure having four equal sides, two acute angles, and two obtuse angles 3 : any of a suit of playing cards marked with a red diamond 4 : INFIELD; *also* : the entire playing field in baseball

**di·a·mond·back rattlesnake** \-,bak-\ *n* : either of two large and deadly rattlesnakes of the southern U.S.

**di·an·thus** \dī-'an-thəs\ *n* : ¹PINK 1

**di·a·pa·son** \,dī-ə-'pā-zⁿn, -sⁿn\ *n* 1 : the organ stop governing the flue pipes that form the primary basis of organ tone 2 : the entire range of musical tones

**¹di·a·per** \'dī-pər, 'dī-ə-\ *n* 1 : a cotton or linen fabric woven in a simple geometric pattern 2 : a garment for a baby drawn up between the legs and fastened about the waist

**²diaper** *vb* 1 : to ornament with diaper designs 2 : to put a diaper on

**di·aph·a·nous** \dī-'a-fə-nəs\ *adj* : of so fine a texture as to be transparent

**di·a·pho·ret·ic** \,dī-ə-fə-'re-tik\ *adj* : having the power to increase perspiration — **diaphoretic** *n*

**di·a·phragm** \'dī-ə-,fram\ *n* 1 : a sheet of muscle between the chest and abdominal cavities of a mammal 2 : a vibrating disk (as in a microphone) 3 : a cup-shaped device usu. of thin rubber fitted over the uterine cervix to act as a mechanical contraceptive barrier — **di·a·phrag·mat·ic** \,dī-ə-frəg-'ma-tik, -,frag-\ *adj*

**di·a·rist** \'dī-ə-rist\ *n* : one who keeps a diary

**di·a·ris·tic** \,dī-ə-'ris-tik\ *adj* : of, relating to, or characteristic of a diary

**di·ar·rhea** \,dī-ə-'rē-ə\ *n* [ME *diaria*, fr. LL *diarrhoea*, fr. Gk *diarrhoia*, fr. *diarrhein* to flow through, fr. *dia-* through + *rhein* to flow] : abnormally frequent and watery bowel movements — **di·ar·rhe·al** \-'rē-əl\ *adj*

**di·ar·rhoea** *chiefly Brit var of* DIARRHEA

**di·a·ry** \'dī-ə-rē\ *n*, *pl* **-ries** : a daily record esp. of personal experiences; *also* : a book used as a diary

**di·as·po·ra** \dī-'as-pə-rə\ *n* 1 *cap* : the settling of scattered colonies of Jews outside Palestine after the Babylonian exile

**2** *cap* : the Jews living outside Palestine or modern Israel **3** : the migration or scattering of a people away from an ancestral homeland

**di·as·to·le** \dī-'as-tə-(ˌ)lē\ *n* : the stretching of the chambers of the heart during which they fill with blood — **di·a·stol·ic** \ˌdī-ə-'stä-lik\ *adj*

**dia·ther·my** \'dī-ə-ˌthər-mē\ *n* : the generation of heat in tissue by electric currents for medical purposes

**di·a·tom** \'dī-ə-ˌtäm\ *n* : any of a class of planktonic one-celled or colonial algae with skeletons of silica

**di·atom·ic** \ˌdī-ə-'tä-mik\ *adj* : having two atoms in the molecule

**di·a·tribe** \'dī-ə-ˌtrīb\ *n* : biting or abusive speech or writing

**di·az·e·pam** \dī-'a-zə-ˌpam\ *n* : a tranquilizer used esp. to relieve anxiety, tension, and muscle spasms

**dib·ble** \'di-bəl\ *n* : a pointed hand tool for making holes (as for planting bulbs) in the ground — **dibble** *vb*

**¹dice** \'dīs\ *n, pl* **dice** : DIE 1

**²dice** *vb* **diced; dic·ing** **1** : to cut into small cubes ⟨∼ carrots⟩ **2** : to play games with dice

**di·chot·o·my** \dī-'kä-tə-mē\ *n, pl* **-mies** : a division or the process of dividing into two esp. mutually exclusive or contradictory groups — **di·chot·o·mous** \-məs\ *adj*

**dick·er** \'di-kər\ *vb* : BARGAIN, HAGGLE

**dick·ey** *or* **dicky** \'di-kē\ *n, pl* **dickeys** *or* **dick·ies** : a small fabric insert worn to fill in the neckline

**di·cot·y·le·don** \ˌdī-ˌkä-tə-'lēd-ᵊn\ *n* : any of a group of seed plants having an embryo with two cotyledons — **di·cot·y·le·don·ous** *adj*

**dict** *abbr* dictionary

**¹dic·tate** \'dik-ˌtāt\ *vb* **dic·tat·ed; dic·tat·ing** **1** : to speak or read for a person to transcribe or for a machine to record **2** : COMMAND, ORDER — **dic·ta·tion** \dik-'tā-shən\ *n*

**²dic·tate** \'dik-ˌtāt\ *n* : an authoritative rule, prescription, or injunction : COMMAND ⟨the ∼s of conscience⟩

**dic·ta·tor** \'dik-ˌtā-tər\ *n* **1** : a person ruling absolutely and often brutally and oppressively **2** : one that dictates

**dic·ta·to·ri·al** \ˌdik-tə-'tȯr-ē-əl\ *adj* : of, relating to, or characteristic of a dictator or a dictatorship

**dic·ta·tor·ship** \dik-'tā-tər-ˌship, 'dik-ˌtā-\ *n* **1** : the office of a dictator **2** : autocratic rule, control, or leadership **3** : a government or country in which absolute power is held by a dictator or a small clique

**dic·tion** \'dik-shən\ *n* **1** : choice of words esp. with regard to correctness, clearness, or effectiveness : WORDING **2** : ENUNCIATION

**dic·tio·nary** \'dik-shə-ˌner-ē\ *n, pl* **-nar·ies** : a reference book containing words usu. alphabetically arranged along with information about their forms, pronunciations, functions, etymologies, meanings, and syntactical and idiomatic uses

**dic·tum** \'dik-təm\ *n, pl* **dic·ta** \-tə\ *also* **dic·tums** : a noteworthy, formal, or authoritative statement or observation

**did** *past of* DO

**di·dac·tic** \dī-'dak-tik\ *adj* **1** : intended to instruct, inform, or teach a moral lesson **2** : making moral observations

**di·do** \'dī-dō\ *n, pl* **didoes** *or* **didos** : a mischievous act : PRANK

**¹die** \'dī\ *vb* **died; dy·ing** \'dī-iŋ\ [ME *dien*, fr. or akin to ON *deyja* to die] **1** : to stop living : EXPIRE **2** : to pass out of existence ⟨a *dying* race⟩ **3** : SUBSIDE **4** ⟨the wind *died* down⟩ **4** : to long keenly ⟨*dying* to go⟩ **5** : STOP ⟨the motor *died*⟩

**²die** \'dī\ *n* [ME *dee*, fr. AF *dé*] **1** *pl* **dice** \'dīs\ : a small cube marked on each face with one to six spots and used usu. in pairs in games and gambling **2** *pl* **dies** \'dīz\ : a device used to shape, finish, or impress an object

**die·hard** \'dī-ˌhärd\ *n* : one who is strongly devoted or determined — **die–hard** *adj*

**dieresis** *var of* DIAERESIS

**die·sel** \'dē-zəl, -səl\ *n* **1** : DIESEL ENGINE **2** : a vehicle driven by a diesel engine **3** : DIESEL FUEL

**diesel engine** *n* : an internal combustion engine in whose cylinders air is compressed to a temperature sufficiently high to ignite the fuel

**diesel fuel** *n* : a heavy mineral oil used as fuel in diesel engines

**die·sel·ing** \'dē-zə-liŋ\ *n* : the continued operation of an internal combustion engine after the ignition has been turned off

**¹di·et** \'dī-ət\ *n* [ME *diete*, fr. AF, fr. L *diaeta*, fr. Gk *diaita*, lit., manner of living, fr. *diaitasthai* to lead one's life] **1** : food and drink regularly consumed : FARE **2** : an allowance of food prescribed for a special reason (as to lose weight) — **di·e·tary** \-ə-ˌter-ē\ *adj or n*

**²diet** *vb* : to eat or cause to eat or drink less or according to a prescribed rule — **di·et·er** *n*

**dietary supplement** *n* : a product taken orally that contains ingredients (as vitamins or amino acids) intended to supplement one's diet

**di·e·tet·ics** \ˌdī-ə-'te-tiks\ *n sing or pl* : the science or art of applying the principles of nutrition to diet — **di·e·tet·ic** *adj*

**di·e·ti·tian** *or* **di·e·ti·cian** \ˌdī-ə-'ti-shən\ *n* : a specialist in dietetics

**dif** *or* **diff** *abbr* difference

**dif·fer** \'di-fər\ *vb* **dif·fered; dif·fer·ing** **1** : to be unlike **2** : VARY **3** : DISAGREE

**dif·fer·ence** \'di-frəns, 'di-fə-rəns\ *n* **1** : UNLIKENESS ⟨∼ in their looks⟩ **2** : distinction or discrimination in preference **3** : DISAGREEMENT; *also* : an instance or cause of disagreement ⟨unable to settle their ∼s⟩ **4** : the amount by which one number or quantity differs from another

**dif·fer·ent** \'di-frənt, 'di-fə-rənt\ *adj* **1** : unlike in nature or quality **2** : DISTINCT ⟨∼ age groups⟩; *also* : VARIOUS ⟨∼ members of the club⟩ **3** : ANOTHER ⟨try a ∼ channel⟩ **4** : UNUSUAL, SPECIAL ⟨a quite ∼ style⟩ — **dif·fer·ent·ly** *adv*

¹**dif·fer·en·tial** \ˌdi-fə-ˈren-chəl\ *adj* : showing, creating, or relating to a difference

²**differential** *n* **1** : the amount or degree by which things differ **2** : an arrangement of gears in an automobile that allows one wheel to turn faster than another (as in rounding curves)

**differential gear** *n* : DIFFERENTIAL 2

**dif·fer·en·ti·ate** \ˌdi-fə-ˈren-chē-ˌāt\ *vb* **-at·ed; -at·ing** **1** : to make or become different **2** : to attain a specialized adult form and function during development **3** : to recognize or state the difference ⟨∼ between them⟩ — **dif·fer·en·ti·a·tion** \-ˌren-chē-ˈā-shən\ *n*

**dif·fi·cult** \ˈdi-fi-(ˌ)kəlt\ *adj* **1** : hard to do or make ⟨a ∼ climb⟩ **2** : hard to understand or deal with ⟨∼ reading⟩ ⟨a ∼ child⟩

**dif·fi·cul·ty** \-(ˌ)kəl-tē\ *n, pl* **-ties** [ME *difficulte,* fr. AF *difficulté,* fr. L *difficilis* not easy, fr. *dis-* not + *facilis* easy] **1** : difficult nature ⟨the ∼ of a task⟩ **2** : DISAGREEMENT ⟨settled their *difficulties*⟩ **3** : OBSTACLE ⟨overcome *difficulties*⟩ **4** : TROUBLE ⟨in financial *difficulties*⟩

♦ **Synonyms** HARDSHIP, RIGOR, VICISSITUDE

**dif·fi·dent** \ˈdi-fə-dənt\ *adj* **1** : lacking confidence **2** : RESERVED 1 — **dif·fi·dence** \-dəns\ *n* — **dif·fi·dent·ly** *adv*

**dif·frac·tion** \di-ˈfrak-shən\ *n* : the bending or spreading of waves (as of light) esp. when passing through narrow slits

¹**dif·fuse** \di-ˈfyüs\ *adj* **1** : VERBOSE, WORDY ⟨∼ writing⟩ **2** : not concentrated or localized ⟨∼ light⟩

²**dif·fuse** \di-ˈfyüz\ *vb* **dif·fused; dif·fus·ing** **1** : to pour out or spread widely **2** : to undergo or cause to undergo diffusion **3** : to break up light by diffusion

**dif·fu·sion** \di-ˈfyü-zhən\ *n* **1** : a diffusing or a being diffused **2** : movement of particles (as of a gas) from a region of high to one of lower concentration **3** : the reflection of light from a rough surface or the passage of light through a translucent material

¹**dig** \ˈdig\ *vb* **dug** \ˈdəg\; **dig·ging** **1** : to turn up the soil (as with a spade) **2** : to hollow out or form by removing earth ⟨∼ a hole⟩ **3** : to uncover or seek by turning up earth ⟨∼ potatoes⟩ **4** : DISCOVER ⟨∼ up information⟩ **5** : POKE, THRUST ⟨∼ a person in the ribs⟩ **6** : to work hard **7** : UNDERSTAND, APPRECIATE; *also* : LIKE, ADMIRE

²**dig** *n* **1** : THRUST, POKE; *also* : a cutting remark : GIBE **2** *pl* : living or working accommodations

³**dig** *abbr* digest

¹**di·gest** \ˈdī-ˌjest\ *n* : a summarized or shortened version esp. of a literary work

²**di·gest** \dī-ˈjest, də-\ *vb* **1** : to think over and arrange in the mind **2** : to convert (food) into simpler forms that can be absorbed by the body **3** : to compress into a short summary — **di·gest·ibil·i·ty** \-ˌjes-tə-ˈbi-lə-tē\ *n* — **di·gest·ible** *adj* — **di·ges·tion** \-ˈjes-chən\ *n* — **di·ges·tive** \-ˈjes-tiv\ *adj*

**di·ges·tif** \ˌdē-zhes-ˈtēf\ *n* : an alcoholic drink taken after a meal

**dig in** *vb* **1** : to take a defensive stand esp. by digging trenches **2** : to firmly set to work **3** : to begin eating

**dig·it** \ˈdi-jət\ *n* [ME, fr. L *digitus* finger, toe] **1** : any of the Arabic numerals 1 to 9 and usu. the symbol 0 **2** : FINGER, TOE

**dig·i·tal** \ˈdi-jə-tᵊl\ *adj* **1** : of, relating to, or done with a finger or toe **2** : of, relating to, or using calculation by numerical methods or by discrete units **3** : relating to or employing communications signals in the form of binary digits ⟨a ∼ broadcast⟩ **4** : providing a readout in numerical digits ⟨a ∼ watch⟩ **5** : ELECTRONIC; *also* : characterized by computerized technology ⟨the ∼ age⟩ — **dig·i·tal·ly** *adv*

**digital camera** *n* : a camera that records images as digital data instead of on film

**dig·i·tal·is** \ˌdi-jə-ˈta-ləs\ *n* : a drug from the common foxglove that is a powerful heart stimulant; *also* : FOXGLOVE

**digital versatile disc** *n* : DVD

**digital video disc** *n* : DVD

**dig·ni·fied** \ˈdig-nə-ˌfīd\ *adj* : showing or expressing dignity

**dig·ni·fy** \-ˌfī\ *vb* **-fied; -fy·ing** : to give dignity, distinction, or attention to

**dig·ni·tary** \ˈdig-nə-ˌter-ē\ *n, pl* **-tar·ies** : a person of high position or honor

**dig·ni·ty** \ˈdig-nə-tē\ *n, pl* **-ties** **1** : the quality or state of being worthy, honored, or esteemed **2** : high rank, office, or position **3** : formal reserve of manner, language, or appearance

**di·graph** \ˈdī-ˌgraf\ *n* : a group of two successive letters whose phonetic value is a single sound (as *ea* in *bread*)

**di·gress** \dī-ˈgres, də-\ *vb* : to turn aside esp. from the main subject or argument — **di·gres·sion** \-ˈgre-shən\ *n* — **di·gres·sive** \-ˈgre-siv\ *adj*

**Di·jon mustard** \ˈdē-ˌzhän-, di-ˈzhän-\ *n* : a mustard made from dark mustard seeds, white wine, and spices

**dike** \ˈdīk\ *n* : a bank of earth constructed to control water : LEVEE

**dil** *abbr* dilute

**di·lap·i·dat·ed** \də-ˈla-pə-ˌdā-təd\ *adj* : fallen into partial ruin or decay — **di·lap·i·da·tion** \-ˌla-pə-ˈdā-shən\ *n*

**di·late** \dī-ˈlāt, ˈdī-ˌlāt\ *vb* **di·lat·ed; di·lat·ing** : SWELL, DISTEND, EXPAND ⟨her pupils were *dilated*⟩ — **di·la·ta·tion** \ˌdi-lə-ˈtā-shən\ *n* — **di·la·tion** \dī-ˈlā-shən\ *n*

**dil·a·to·ry** \ˈdi-lə-ˌtȯr-ē\ *adj* **1** : DELAYING **2** : TARDY, SLOW

**di·lem·ma** \də-ˈle-mə\ *n* **1** : a usu. undesirable or unpleasant choice; *also* : a situation involving such a choice **2** : PREDICAMENT

**dil·et·tante** \ˌdi-lə-ˈtänt, -ˈtant\ *n, pl* **-tantes** *or* **-tan·ti** \-ˈtän-tē, -ˈtan-\ [It, fr. prp. of *dilettare* to delight, fr. L *dilectare*] : a person having a superficial interest in an art or a branch of knowledge

**dil·i·gent** \ˈdi-lə-jənt\ *adj* : characterized by steady, earnest, and energetic effort : PAINSTAKING — **dil·i·gence** \-jəns\ *n* — **dil·i·gent·ly** *adv*

**dill** \'dil\ *n* : an herb related to the carrot with aromatic leaves and seeds used as a seasoning and in pickles

**dil·ly** \'di-lē\ *n, pl* **dil·lies** : one that is remarkable or outstanding

**dil·ly·dal·ly** \'di-lē-,da-lē\ *vb* : to waste time by loitering or delaying

¹**di·lute** \dī-'lüt, də-\ *vb* **di·lut·ed; di·lut·ing** : to lessen the consistency or strength of by mixing with something else — **di·lu·tion** \-'lü-shən\ *n*

²**dilute** *adj* : DILUTED, WEAK

¹**dim** \'dim\ *adj* **dim·mer; dim·mest** 1 : LUSTERLESS, DULL \\(\sim\) colors\\) 2 : not bright or distinct : OBSCURE, FAINT 3 : not seeing or understanding clearly — **dim·ly** *adv* **dim·ness** *n*

²**dim** *vb* **dimmed; dim·ming** 1 : to make or become dim or lusterless 2 : to reduce the light from

³**dim** *abbr* 1 dimension 2 diminished 3 diminutive

**dime** \'dīm\ *n* [ME, tenth part, tithe, fr. AF *disme, dime,* fr. L *decima,* fr. fem of *decimus* tenth, fr. *decem* ten] : a U.S. coin worth ¹⁄₁₀ dollar

**di·men·sion** \də-'men-chən, dī-\ *n* 1 : the physical property of length, breadth, or thickness; *also* : a measure of this 2 : EXTENT, SCOPE, PROPORTIONS — usu. used in pl. \\(the \sim s of this problem\\) — **di·men·sion·al** \-'men-chə-nəl\ *adj* — **di·men·sion·al·i·ty** \-,men-chə-'na-lə-tē\ *n*

**di·min·ish** \də-'mi-nish\ *vb* 1 : to make less or cause to appear less 2 : BELITTLE 3 : DWINDLE 4 : TAPER — **dim·i·nu·tion** \,di-mə-'nü-shən, -'nyü-\ *n*

**di·min·u·en·do** \də-,min-yə-'wen-dō\ *adv or adj* : DECRESCENDO

¹**di·min·u·tive** \də-'min-yə-tiv\ *n* 1 : a diminutive word or affix \\(the word "kitchenette" is a \sim\\) 2 : a diminutive individual

²**diminutive** *adj* 1 : indicating small size and sometimes the state or quality of being lovable, pitiable, or contemptible \\(the \sim suffixes *-ette* and *-ling*\\) 2 : extremely small : TINY

**dim·i·ty** \'di-mə-tē\ *n, pl* **-ties** : a thin usu. corded cotton fabric

**dim·mer** \'di-mər\ *n* : a device for controlling the amount of light from an electric lighting unit

**di·mor·phic** \(,)dī-'mȯr-fik\ *adj* : occurring in two distinct forms — **di·mor·phism** \-,fi-zəm\ *n*

¹**dim·ple** \'dim-pəl\ *n* : a small depression esp. in the cheek or chin

²**dimple** *vb* **dim·pled; dim·pling** : to form dimples (as in smiling)

**din** \'din\ *n* : a loud confused mixture of noises

**di·nar** \di-'när\ *n* 1 — see MONEY table 2 — see *rial* at MONEY table

**dine** \'dīn\ *vb* **dined; din·ing** [ME, fr. AF *disner, diner* to eat, have a meal, fr. VL \*disjejunare to break one's fast, ultim. fr. L *jejunus* fasting] 1 : to eat dinner 2 : to give a dinner to

**din·er** \'dī-nər\ *n* 1 : one that dines 2 : a railroad dining car 3 : a restaurant usu. resembling a dining car

**di·nette** \dī-'net\ *n* : an alcove or small room used for dining

**ding** \'diŋ\ *vb* : to cause minor damage to a surface — **ding** *n*

**din·ghy** \'diŋ-ē\ *n, pl* **dinghies** 1 : a small boat 2 : LIFE RAFT

**din·gle** \'diŋ-gəl\ *n* : a small wooded valley

**din·go** \'diŋ-gō\ *n, pl* **dingoes** : a reddish brown wild dog of Australia

**din·gus** \'diŋ-gəs, -əs\ *n* : DOODAD

**din·gy** \'din-jē\ *adj* **din·gi·er; -est** : DIRTY, UNCLEAN; *also* : SHABBY — **din·gi·ness** *n*

**dink** \'diŋk\ *n, often all cap* [double income, no kids] : a couple with two incomes and no children; *also* : a member of such a couple

**din·ky** \'diŋ-kē\ *adj* **din·ki·er; -est** : overly small \\(a \sim apartment\\)

**din·ner** \'di-nər\ *n* : the main meal of the day; *also* : a formal banquet

**din·ner·ware** \'di-nər-,wer\ *n* : tableware other than flatware

**di·no** \'dī-nō\ *n, pl* **dinos** : DINOSAUR

**di·no·fla·gel·late** \,dī-nō-'fla-jə-lət, -,lāt\ *n* : any of an order of planktonic plantlike unicellular flagellates of which some cause red tide

**di·no·saur** \'dī-nə-,sȯr\ *n* [ultim. fr. Gk *deinos* terrifying + *sauros* lizard] : any of a group of extinct long-tailed Mesozoic reptiles often of huge size

**dint** \'dint\ *n* 1 : FORCE \\(by \sim of sheer grit\\) 2 : DENT

**di·o·cese** \'dī-ə-səs, -,sēz, -,ses\ *n, pl* **-ces·es** \-sə-səz, -,sē-zəz, -,sē-səz\ : the territorial jurisdiction of a bishop — **di·oc·e·san** \dī-'ä-sə-sən, ,dī-ə-'sē-z°n\ *adj or n*

**di·ode** \'dī-,ōd\ *n* : an electronic device with two electrodes or terminals used esp. as a rectifier

**di·ox·in** \dī-'äk-sən\ *n* : a persistent toxic hydrocarbon that occurs esp. as a byproduct of industrial processes and waste incineration

¹**dip** \'dip\ *vb* **dipped; dip·ping** 1 : to plunge temporarily or partially under the surface (as of a liquid) 2 : to thrust in a way to suggest immersion 3 : to scoop up or out : LADLE 4 : to lower and then raise quickly \\(\sim a flag in salute\\) 5 : to drop or slope down esp. suddenly \\(the moon *dipped* below the crest\\) 6 : to decrease moderately and usu. temporarily \\(prices *dipped*\\) 7 : to reach inside or as if inside or below a surface \\(*dipped* into their savings\\) 8 : to delve casually into something; *esp* : to read superficially \\(\sim into a book\\)

²**dip** *n* 1 : an act of dipping; *esp* : a short swim 2 : inclination downward : DROP 3 : something obtained by or used in dipping 4 : a sauce or soft mixture into which food may be dipped 5 : a liquid into which something may be dipped (as for cleansing or coloring)

**diph·the·ria** \dif-'thir-ē-ə\ *n* : an acute contagious bacterial disease marked by fever and by coating of the air passages with a membrane that interferes with breathing

**diph·thong** \'dif-ˌthȯŋ, 'dip-\ *n* : two vowel sounds joined in one syllable to form one speech sound (as *ou* in *out*)

**dip·loid** \'di-ˌplȯid\ *adj* : having two haploid sets of chromosomes ⟨~ somatic cells⟩ — **diploid** *n*

**di·plo·ma** \də-'plō-mə\ *n* : an official record of graduation from or of a degree conferred by a school

**di·plo·ma·cy** \də-'plō-mə-sē\ *n* **1** : the art and practice of conducting negotiations between nations **2** : TACT

**dip·lo·mat** \'di-plə-ˌmat\ *n* : one employed or skilled in diplomacy — **dip·lo·mat·ic** \ˌdi-plə-'ma-tik\ *adj*

**di·plo·ma·tist** \də-'plō-mə-tist\ *n* : DIPLOMAT

**dip·per** \'di-pər\ *n* **1** : any of a genus of birds that are related to the thrushes and are skilled in diving **2** : something (as a ladle or scoop) that dips or is used for dipping **3** *cap* : BIG DIPPER **4** *cap* : LITTLE DIPPER

**dip·so·ma·nia** \ˌdip-sə-'mā-nē-ə\ *n* : an uncontrollable craving for alcoholic liquors — **dip·so·ma·ni·ac** \-nē-ˌak\ *n*

**dip·stick** \'dip-ˌstik\ *n* : a graduated rod for indicating depth

**dip·ter·an** \'dip-tə-rən\ *adj* : of, relating to, or having a fly (sense 2) — **dipteran** *n* — **dip·ter·ous** \-rəs\ *adj*

**dir** *abbr* **1** direct **2** director

**di·ram** \dē-'ram\ *n* — see *somoni* at MONEY table

**dire** \'dī(-ə)r\ *adj* **dir·er; dir·est 1** : very horrible : DREADFUL ⟨~ suffering⟩ **2** : warning of disaster **3** : EXTREME ⟨~ poverty⟩

**¹di·rect** \də-'rekt, dī-\ *vb* **1** : ADDRESS ⟨~ a letter⟩; *also* : to impart orally : AIM ⟨~ a remark to the gallery⟩ **2** : to regulate the activities or course of : guide the supervision, organizing, or performance of **3** : to cause to turn, move, or point or to follow a certain course **4** : to point, extend, or project in a specified line or course **5** : to request or instruct with authority **6** : to show or point out the way

**²direct** *adj* **1** : stemming immediately from a source ⟨~ result⟩ **2** : being or passing in a straight line of descent : LINEAL ⟨~ ancestor⟩ **3** : leading from one point to another in time or space without turn or stop : STRAIGHT **4** : NATURAL, STRAIGHTFORWARD ⟨a ~ manner⟩ **5** : operating without an intervening agency or step ⟨~ action⟩ **6** : effected by the action of the people or the electorate and not by representatives ⟨~ democracy⟩ **7** : consisting of or reproducing the exact words of a speaker or writer — **direct** *adv* — **di·rect·ly** *adv* — **di·rect·ness** *n*

**direct broadcast satellite** *n* : a television broadcasting system in which satellite transmissions are received at the viewing location

**direct current** *n* : an electric current flowing in one direction only

**direct deposit** *n* : a method of payment in which money is transferred to the payee's account without the use of checks or cash

**di·rec·tion** \də-'rek-shən, dī-\ *n* **1** : MANAGEMENT, GUIDANCE **2** : COMMAND, ORDER, INSTRUCTION **3** : the course or line along which something moves, lies, or points **4** : TENDENCY, TREND — **di·rec·tion·al** \-shə-nəl\ *adj*

**di·rec·tive** \də-'rek-tiv, dī-\ *n* : something that directs and usu. impels toward an action or goal; *esp* : an order issued by a high-level body or official

**direct mail** *n* : printed matter used for soliciting business or contributions and mailed direct to individuals

**di·rec·tor** \də-'rek-tər, dī-\ *n* **1** : one that directs : MANAGER, SUPERVISOR, CONDUCTOR **2** : one of a group of persons who direct the affairs of an organized institution — **di·rec·to·ri·al** \-ˌrek-'tȯr-ē-əl\ *adj* — **di·rec·tor·ship** *n*

**di·rec·tor·ate** \-tə-rət\ *n* **1** : the office or position of director **2** : a board of directors; *also* : membership on such a board **3** : an executive staff

**director's cut** *n* : a version of a motion picture that is edited according to the director's wishes

**di·rec·to·ry** \-tə-rē\ *n, pl* **-ries 1** : an alphabetical or classified list esp. of names and addresses **2** : FOLDER 4

**dire·ful** \'dī(-ə)r-fəl\ *adj* : DREADFUL ⟨a ~ disease⟩; *also* : OMINOUS

**dirge** \'dərj\ *n* [ME *dirige* church service for the dead, fr. the first word of a LL anthem, fr. L, imper. of *dirigere* to direct] : a song of lamentation; *also* : a slow mournful piece of music

**dir·ham** \'dir-həm\ *n* **1** — see MONEY table **2** — see *dinar, riyal* at MONEY table

**di·ri·gi·ble** \'dir-ə-jə-bəl, də-'ri-jə-\ *n* : AIRSHIP

**dirk** \'dərk\ *n* : DAGGER 1

**dirndl** \'dərn-dᵊl\ *n* [short for G *Dirndlkleid*, fr. G dial. *Dirndl* girl + G *Kleid* dress] : a full skirt with a tight waistband

**dirt** \'dərt\ *n* **1** : a filthy or soiling substance (as mud, dust, or grime) **2** : loose or packed earth : SOIL **3** : moral uncleanness **4** : scandalous gossip **5** : embarrassing or incriminating information

**¹dirty** \'dər-tē\ *adj* **dirt·i·er; -est 1** : SOILED, FILTHY **2** : INDECENT, SMUTTY ⟨~ jokes⟩ **3** : BASE, UNFAIR ⟨a ~ trick⟩ **4** : STORMY, FOGGY ⟨~ weather⟩ **5** : not clear in color : DULL ⟨a ~ red⟩ — **dirt·i·ness** *n* — **dirty** *adv*

**²dirty** *vb* **dirt·ied; dirty·ing** : to make or become dirty

**dis·able** \di-'sā-bəl\ *vb* **dis·abled; dis·abling 1** : to disqualify legally **2** : to make unable to perform by or as if by illness, injury, or malfunction — **dis·abil·i·ty** \ˌdi-sə-'bi-lə-tē\ *n*

**dis·abled** *adj* : incapacitated by illness or injury; *also* : physically or mentally impaired

**dis·abuse** \ˌdi-sə-'byüz\ *vb* : to free from error, fallacy, or misconception

**dis·ad·van·tage** \ˌdi-səd-'van-tij\ *n* **1** : loss or damage esp. to reputation or finances **2** : an unfavorable, inferior, or prejudicial condition, quality, or circumstance — **dis·ad·van·ta·geous** \di-,sad-,van-'tā-jəs, -vən-\ adj

**dis·ad·van·taged** \-tijd\ adj : lacking in basic resources or conditions believed necessary for an equal position in society

**dis·af·fect** \,di-sə-'fekt\ vb : to alienate the affection or loyalty of — **dis·af·fec·tion** \-'fek-shən\ n

**dis·agree** \,di-sə-'grē\ vb 1 : to fail to agree 2 : to differ in opinion 3 : to cause discomfort or distress ⟨fried foods ∼ with her⟩ — **dis·agree·ment** n

**dis·agree·able** \-ə-bəl\ adj 1 : causing discomfort : UNPLEASANT, OFFENSIVE ⟨a ∼ odor⟩ 2 : ILL-TEMPERED, PEEVISH — **dis·agree·able·ness** n — **dis·agree·ably** \-blē\ adv

**dis·al·low** \,di-sə-'laů\ vb : to refuse to admit or recognize : REJECT ⟨∼ a claim⟩ — **dis·al·low·ance** n

**dis·ap·pear** \,di-sə-'pir\ vb 1 : to pass out of sight 2 : to cease to be : become lost — **dis·ap·pear·ance** n

**dis·ap·point** \,di-sə-'pȯint\ vb : to fail to fulfill the expectation or hope of — **dis·ap·point·ment** n

**dis·ap·pro·ba·tion** \dis-,a-prə-'bā-shən\ n : DISAPPROVAL

**dis·ap·prov·al** \,dis-ə-'prü-vəl\ n : adverse judgment : CENSURE

**dis·ap·prove** \-'prüv\ vb 1 : CONDEMN 2 : to feel or express disapproval ⟨∼s of smoking⟩ 3 : REJECT — **dis·ap·prov·ing·ly** \-'prü-viŋ-lē\ adv

**dis·arm** \dis-'ärm\ vb 1 : to take arms or weapons from 2 : to reduce the size and strength of the armed forces of a country 3 : to make harmless, peaceable, or friendly : win over ⟨a ∼ing smile⟩ — **dis·ar·ma·ment** \-'är-mə-mənt\ n

**dis·ar·range** \,dis-ə-'rānj\ vb : to disturb the arrangement or order of — **dis·ar·range·ment** n

**dis·ar·ray** \-'rā\ n 1 : DISORDER, CONFUSION 2 : disorderly or careless dress

**dis·as·sem·ble** \,dis-ə-'sem-bəl\ vb : to take apart

**dis·as·so·ci·ate** \-'sō-shē-,āt, -sē-\ vb : to detach from association

**di·sas·ter** \di-'zas-tər, -'sas-\ n [MF desastre, fr. It disastro, fr. astro star, fr. L astrum] : a sudden or great misfortune — **di·sas·trous** \-'zas-trəs\ adj — **di·sas·trous·ly** adv

**dis·avow** \,dis-ə-'vaů\ vb : to deny responsibility for : REPUDIATE — **dis·avow·al** \-'vaů(-ə)l\ n

**dis·band** \dis-'band\ vb : to break up the organization of : DISPERSE

**dis·bar** \dis-'bär\ vb : to expel from the legal profession — **dis·bar·ment** n

**dis·be·lieve** \,dis-bə-'lēv\ vb 1 : to hold not worthy of belief : not believe 2 : to withhold or reject belief — **dis·be·lief** \-'lēf\ n — **dis·be·liev·er** n

**dis·bur·den** \dis-'bər-d²n\ vb : to rid of a burden

**dis·burse** \dis-'bərs\ vb **dis·bursed; dis·burs·ing** 1 : to pay out : EXPEND 2 : DISTRIBUTE — **dis·burse·ment** n

¹**disc** var of DISK

²**disc** abbr discount

**dis·card** \dis-'kärd, 'dis-,kärd\ vb 1 : to let go a playing card from one's hand; also : to play (a card) from a suit other than a trump but different from the one led 2 : to get rid of as unwanted — **dis·card** \'dis-,kärd\ n

**disc brake** n : a brake that operates by the friction of a pair of plates pressing against the sides of a rotating disc

**dis·cern** \di-'sərn, -'zərn\ vb 1 : to detect with the eyes : DISTINGUISH 2 : DISCRIMINATE 3 : to come to know or recognize mentally ⟨∼ right from wrong⟩ — **dis·cern·ible** adj — **dis·cern·ment** n

**dis·cern·ing** adj : revealing insight and understanding ⟨a ∼ critic⟩

¹**dis·charge** \dis-'chärj, 'dis-,chärj\ vb 1 : to relieve of a charge, load, or burden : UNLOAD; esp : to remove the electrical energy from ⟨∼ a storage battery⟩ 2 : to let or put off ⟨∼ passengers⟩ 3 : SHOOT ⟨∼ an arrow⟩ 4 : to set free ⟨∼ a prisoner⟩ 5 : to dismiss from service or employment ⟨∼ a soldier⟩ 6 : to get rid of by paying or doing ⟨∼ a debt⟩ 7 : to give forth fluid ⟨the river ∼s into the ocean⟩

²**dis·charge** \'dis-,chärj, dis-'chärj\ n 1 : the act of discharging, unloading, or releasing 2 : something that discharges; esp : a certification of release or payment 3 : a firing off (as of a gun) 4 : a flowing out (as of blood from a wound); also : something that is emitted ⟨a purulent ∼⟩ 5 : release or dismissal esp. from an office or employment; also : complete separation from military service 6 : a flow of electricity (as through a gas)

**dis·ci·ple** \di-'sī pəl\ n [ultim. fr. LL discipulus follower of Jesus in his lifetime, fr. L, pupil] 1 : one who accepts and helps to spread the teachings of another; also : a convinced adherent 2 cap : a member of the Disciples of Christ

**dis·ci·pli·nar·i·an** \,di-sə-plə-'ner-e-ən\ n : one who enforces order

**dis·ci·plin·ary** \'di-sə-plə-,ner-ē\ adj : of or relating to discipline; also : CORRECTIVE ⟨take ∼ action⟩

¹**dis·ci·pline** \'di-sə-plən\ n 1 : PUNISHMENT 2 : a field of study : SUBJECT 3 : training that corrects, molds, or perfects 4 : control gained by obedience or training : orderly conduct 5 : a system of rules governing conduct

²**discipline** vb **-plined; -plin·ing** 1 : PUNISH 2 : to train or develop by instruction and exercise esp. in self-control 3 : to bring under control ⟨∼ troops⟩; also : to impose order upon

**disc jockey** or **disk jockey** n : an announcer of a radio show of popular recorded music

**dis·claim** \dis-'klām\ vb : DENY, DISAVOW — **dis·claim·er** n

**dis·close** \dis-'klōz\ vb : to expose to view — **dis·clo·sure** \-'klō-zhər\ n

**dis·co** \'dis-kō\ n, pl **discos** 1 : a nightclub for dancing to live or recorded music 2 : popular dance music characterized by hypnotic rhythm, repetitive lyrics, and electronically produced sounds

**dis·col·or** \dis-'kə-lər\ *vb* : to alter or change in hue or color esp. for the worse — **dis·col·or·ation** \-,kə-lə-'rā-shən\ *n*

**dis·com·bob·u·late** \,dis-kəm-'bä-byə-,lāt\ *vb* **-lat·ed; -lat·ing** : UPSET, CONFUSE

**dis·com·fit** \dis-'kəm-fət, *esp Southern* ,dis-kəm-'fit\ *vb* : UPSET, FRUSTRATE — **dis·com·fi·ture** \dis-'kəm-fə-,chúr\ *n*

¹**dis·com·fort** \dis-'kəm-fərt\ *vb* : to make uncomfortable or uneasy

²**discomfort** *n* : mental or physical uneasiness

**dis·com·mode** \,dis-kə-'mōd\ *vb* **-mod·ed; -mod·ing** : INCONVENIENCE, TROUBLE

**dis·com·pose** \-kəm-'pōz\ *vb* **1** : to destroy the calmness or peace of **2** : DISARRANGE — **dis·com·po·sure** \-'pō-zhər\ *n*

**dis·con·cert** \,dis-kən-'sərt\ *vb* : CONFUSE, UPSET ⟨the bad news ~ed her⟩

**dis·con·nect** \,dis-kə-'nekt\ *vb* : to undo the connection of — **dis·con·nec·tion** \-'nek-shən\ *n*

**dis·con·nect·ed** *adj* : not connected; *also* : INCOHERENT — **dis·con·nect·ed·ly** *adv* — **dis·con·nect·ed·ness** *n*

**dis·con·so·late** \dis-'kän-sə-lət\ *adj* **1** : CHEERLESS **2** : hopelessly sad — **dis·con·so·late·ly** *adv*

**dis·con·tent** \,dis-kən-'tent\ *n* : uneasiness of mind : DISSATISFACTION — **dis·con·tent·ed** *adj*

**dis·con·tin·ue** \,dis-kən-'tin-yü\ *vb* **1** : to break the continuity of : cease to operate, use, or take **2** : END — **dis·con·tin·u·ance** \-yə-wəns\ *n* — **dis·con·ti·nu·i·ty** \dis-,kän-tə-'nü-ə-tē, -'nyü-\ *n* — **dis·con·tin·u·ous** \,dis-kən-'tin-yə-wəs\ *adj*

**dis·cord** \'dis-,kórd\ *n* **1** : lack of agreement or harmony : DISSENSION, CONFLICT **2** : a harsh combination of musical sounds **3** : a harsh or unpleasant sound — **dis·cor·dant** \dis-'kór-dᵊnt\ *adj* — **dis·cor·dant·ly** *adv*

**dis·co·theque** *or* **discothèque** \'dis-kə-,tek\ *n* : DISCO 1

¹**dis·count** \'dis-,kaúnt\ *n* **1** : a reduction made from a regular or list price **2** : a deduction of interest in advance when lending money

²**dis·count** \'dis-,kaúnt, dis-'kaúnt\ *vb* **1** : to deduct from the amount of a bill, debt, or charge usu. for cash or prompt payment; *also* : to sell or offer for sale at a discount **2** : to lend money after deducting the discount ⟨~ a note⟩ **3** : DISREGARD; *also* : MINIMIZE **4** : to make allowance for bias or exaggeration **5** : to take into account (as a future event) in present calculations — **dis·count·able** *adj* — **dis·count·er** *n*

³**dis·count** \'dis-,kaúnt\ *adj* : selling goods or services at a discount; *also* : sold at or reflecting a discount

**dis·coun·te·nance** \dis-'kaún-tə-nənts\ *vb* **1** : EMBARRASS, DISCONCERT **2** : to look with disfavor on

**dis·cour·age** \dis-'kər-ij\ *vb* **-aged; -ag·ing** **1** : to deprive of courage or confidence : DISHEARTEN **2** : to hinder by disfavoring **3** : to attempt to dissuade — **dis·cour·age·ment** *n* — **dis·cour·ag·ing·ly** *adv*

¹**dis·course** \'dis-,kórs\ *n* [ME *discours,* fr. ML & LL *discursus;* ML, argument, fr. LL, conversation, fr. L, act of running about, fr. *discurrere* to run about, fr. *currere* to run] **1** : CONVERSATION **2** : formal and usu. extended expression of thought on a subject

²**dis·course** \dis-'kórs\ *vb* **dis·coursed; dis·cours·ing** **1** : to express oneself in esp. oral discourse **2** : TALK, CONVERSE

**dis·cour·te·ous** \(,)dis-'kər-tē-əs\ *adj* : lacking courtesy : UNCIVIL, RUDE — **dis·cour·te·ous·ly** *adv*

**dis·cour·te·sy** \-'kər-tə-sē\ *n* : RUDENESS; *also* : a rude act

**dis·cov·er** \dis-'kə-vər\ *vb* **1** : to make known or visible **2** : to obtain sight or knowledge of for the first time; *also* : FIND OUT — **dis·cov·er·er** *n*

**dis·cov·ery** \dis-'kə-və-rē\ *n, pl* **-er·ies** **1** : the act or process of discovering **2** : something discovered **3** : the disclosure usu. before a civil trial of pertinent facts or documents

¹**dis·cred·it** \(,)dis-'kre-dət\ *vb* **1** : DISBELIEVE **2** : to cause disbelief in the accuracy or authority of **3** : DISGRACE — **dis·cred·it·able** *adj*

²**discredit** *n* **1** : loss of reputation **2** : lack or loss of belief or confidence

**dis·creet** \dis-'krēt\ *adj* : showing good judgment; *esp* : capable of observing prudent silence — **dis·creet·ly** *adv*

**dis·crep·an·cy** \dis-'kre-pən-sē\ *n, pl* **-cies** **1** : DIFFERENCE, DISAGREEMENT **2** : an instance of being discrepant

**dis·crep·ant** \-pənt\ *adj* [ME *discrepaunt,* fr. L *discrepans,* prp. of *discrepare* to sound discordantly, fr. *discrepare* to rattle, creak] : being at variance : DISAGREEING ⟨~ conclusions⟩

**dis·crete** \dis-'krēt, 'dis-,krēt\ *adj* **1** : individually distinct ⟨several ~ sections⟩ **2** : NONCONTINUOUS

**dis·cre·tion** \dis-'kre-shən\ *n* **1** : the quality of being discreet : PRUDENCE **2** : individual choice or judgment ⟨left the decision to his ~⟩ **3** : power of free decision or latitude of choice — **dis·cre·tion·ary** *adj*

**dis·crim·i·nate** \dis-'kri-mə-,nāt\ *vb* **-nat·ed; -nat·ing** **1** : DISTINGUISH, DIFFERENTIATE **2** : to make a difference in treatment on a basis other than individual merit — **dis·crim·i·na·tion** \-,kri-mə-'nā-shən\ *n*

**dis·crim·i·nat·ing** *adj* : marked by discrimination; *esp* : DISCERNING, JUDICIOUS — **dis·crim·i·nat·ing·ly** *adv*

**dis·crim·i·na·to·ry** \dis-'kri-mə-nə-,tòr-ē\ *adj* : marked by esp. unjust discrimination ⟨~ treatment⟩

**dis·cur·sive** \dis-'kər-siv\ *adj* : passing from one topic to another : RAMBLING ⟨a ~ speech⟩ — **dis·cur·sive·ly** *adv* — **dis·cur·sive·ness** *n*

**dis·cus** \'dis-kəs\ *n, pl* **dis·cus·es** : a heavy disk that is hurled for distance in a track-and-field contest

**dis·cuss** \di-'skəs\ vb [ME, fr. AF discusser, fr. L discussus, pp. of discutere to disperse, fr. dis- apart + quatere to shake] **1** : to argue or consider carefully by presenting the various sides **2** : to talk about — **dis·cus·sion** \-'skə-shən\ n

**dis·cus·sant** \di-'skə-sᵊnt\ n : one who takes part in a formal discussion

¹**dis·dain** \dis-'dān\ n : CONTEMPT, SCORN ⟨a look of ∼⟩ — **dis·dain·ful** \-fəl\ adj — **dis·dain·ful·ly** adv

²**disdain** vb **1** : to look on with scorn **2** : to reject or refrain from because of disdain ⟨∼ed gambling⟩

**dis·ease** \di-'zēz\ n : an abnormal bodily condition that impairs normal functioning and can usu. be recognized by signs and symptoms : SICKNESS — **dis·eased** \-'zēzd\ adj

**dis·em·bark** \,di-səm-'bärk\ vb : to go or put ashore from a ship — **dis·em·bar·ka·tion** \di-,sem-,bär-'kā-shən\ n

**dis·em·body** \,di-səm-'bä-dē\ vb : to deprive of bodily existence

**dis·em·bow·el** \-'baú-(ə)l\ vb : EVISCERATE 1 — **dis·em·bow·el·ment** n

**dis·em·pow·er** \dis-im-'paú(-ə)r\ vb : to deprive of power, authority, or influence

**dis·en·chant** \dis-in-'chant\ vb : DISILLUSION — **dis·en·chant·ment** \-mənt\ n

**dis·en·chant·ed** \-'chan-təd\ adj : DISAPPOINTED, DISSATISFIED

**dis·en·cum·ber** \dis-ᵊn-'kəm-bər\ vb : to free from something that burdens

**dis·en·fran·chise** \dis-in-'fran-,chīz\ vb : to deprive of a franchise, a legal right, or a privilege; esp : to deprive of the right to vote — **dis·en·fran·chise·ment** n

**dis·en·gage** \dis-ᵊn-'gāj\ vb : RELEASE, EXTRICATE, DISENTANGLE ⟨∼ from a harness⟩ — **dis·en·gage·ment** n

**dis·en·gaged** \-'gājd\ adj : IMPARTIAL, DETACHED ⟨a ∼ observer⟩

**dis·en·tan·gle** \,dis-in-'tan-gəl\ vb : to free from entanglement : UNRAVEL

**dis·equi·lib·ri·um** \dis-,ē-kwə-'li-brē-əm\ n : loss or lack of equilibrium

**dis·es·tab·lish** \,dis-ə-'sta-blish\ vb : to end the establishment of; esp : to deprive of the status of an established church — **dis·es·tab·lish·ment** n

**dis·es·teem** \,dis-ə-'stēm\ n : lack of esteem : DISFAVOR, DISREPUTE

**dis·fa·vor** \(,)dis-'fā-vər\ n **1** : DISAPPROVAL, DISLIKE **2** : the state or fact of being no longer favored

**dis·fig·ure** \dis-'fi-gyər\ vb : to spoil the appearance of ⟨disfigured by a scar⟩ — **dis·fig·ure·ment** n

**dis·fran·chise** \dis-'fran-,chīz\ vb : DISENFRANCHISE — **dis·fran·chise·ment** n

**disfunction** var of DYSFUNCTION

**dis·gorge** \-'gòrj\ vb : VOMIT; also : to discharge forcefully or confusedly

¹**dis·grace** \dis-'krās, -'grās\ vb : to bring reproach or shame to

²**disgrace** n **1** : SHAME, DISHONOR; also : a cause of shame **2** : the condition of being out of favor : loss of respect — **dis·grace·ful** \-fəl\ adj — **dis·grace·ful·ly** adv

**dis·grun·tle** \dis-'grən-tᵊl\ vb **dis·grun-**

**tled; dis·grun·tling** : to put in bad humor ⟨disgruntled employees⟩

¹**dis·guise** \dis-'gīz\ vb **dis·guised; dis·guis·ing** **1** : to change the appearance of so as to conceal the identity or to resemble another **2** : HIDE, CONCEAL

²**disguise** n **1** : clothing put on to conceal one's identity or counterfeit another's **2** : an outward appearance that hides what something really is

¹**dis·gust** \dis-'gəst\ n : AVERSION, REPUGNANCE — **dis·gust·ful** \-fəl\ adj

²**disgust** vb : to provoke to loathing, repugnance, or aversion : to be offensive to — **dis·gust·ed·ly** adv — **dis·gust·ing** \-'gəs-tiŋ\ adj — **dis·gust·ing·ly** \-'gəs-tiŋ\ adv

¹**dish** \'dish\ n [ME, fr. OE disc plate, fr. L discus quoit, disk, dish, fr. Gk diskos, fr. dikein to throw] **1** : a vessel used for serving food **2** : the food served in a dish ⟨a ∼ of berries⟩ **3** : food prepared in a particular way **4** : something resembling a dish esp. in being shallow and concave **5** : SATELLITE DISH **6** : GOSSIP 2

²**dish** vb **1** : to put into a dish **2** : to make concave like a dish **3** : GOSSIP

**dis·ha·bille** \,di-sə-'bēl\ or **des·ha·bille** \,de-\ n [F déshabillé] : the state of being dressed in a casual or careless manner

**dis·har·mo·ny** \(,)dis-'här-mə-nē\ n : lack of harmony — **dis·har·mo·ni·ous** \,dis-(,)här-'mō-nē-əs\ adj

**dish·cloth** \'dish-,klòth\ n : a cloth for washing dishes

**dis·heart·en** \dis-'här-tᵊn\ vb : DISCOURAGE, DEJECT

**dished** \'disht\ adj : CONCAVE

**di·shev·el** \di-'she-vəl\ vb **-shev·eled** or **-shev·elled; -shev·el·ing** or **-shev·el·ling** [ME discheveled bareheaded, with disordered hair, fr. AF deschevelé, fr. des- apart + chevoil hair, fr. L capillus] : to throw into disorder or disarray — **di·shev·eled** or **di·shev·elled** adj — **di·shev·el·ment** \-mənt\ n

**dis·hon·est** \di-'sä-nəst\ adj : not honest : UNTRUSTWORTHY, DECEITFUL — **dis·hon·est·ly** adv — **dis·hon·es·ty** \-nə-stē\ n

¹**dis·hon·or** \dis-'ä-nər\ n **1** : lack or loss of honor **2** : SHAME, DISGRACE **3** : a cause of disgrace **4** : the act of dishonoring a negotiable instrument when presented for payment — **dis·hon·or·able** \dis-'ä-nə-rə-bəl\ adj — **dis·hon·or·ably** \-blē\ adv

²**dishonor** vb **1** : DISGRACE **2** : to refuse to accept or pay ⟨∼ a check⟩

**dish out** vb : to give freely

**dish·rag** \'dish-,rag\ n : DISHCLOTH

**dish·wash·er** \-,wò-shər, -,wä-\ n : a person or machine that washes dishes

**dish·wa·ter** \-,wò-tər, -,wä-\ n : water used for washing dishes

**dis·il·lu·sion** \,di-sə-'lü-zhən\ vb : to free from illusion — **dis·il·lu·sion·ment** n

**dis·il·lu·sioned** adj : DISAPPOINTED, DISSATISFIED

**dis·in·cli·na·tion** \dis-,in-klə-'nā-shən\ n : a preference for avoiding something : slight aversion

**dis·in·cline** \ˌdis-in-ˈklīn\ vb : to make unwilling

**dis·in·clined** adj : unwilling because of dislike or disapproval

**dis·in·fect** \ˌdis-in-ˈfekt\ vb : to cleanse of infection-causing germs — **dis·in·fec·tant** \-ˈfek-tənt\ n — **dis·in·fec·tion** \-ˈfek-shən\ n

**dis·in·for·ma·tion** \-ˌin-fər-ˈmā-shən\ n : false information deliberately and often covertly spread

**dis·in·gen·u·ous** \ˌdis-in-ˈjen-yə-wəs\ adj : lacking in candor; also : giving a false appearance of simple frankness

**dis·in·her·it** \ˌdis-in-ˈher-ət\ vb : to deprive of the right to inherit

**dis·in·te·grate** \dis-ˈin-tə-ˌgrāt\ vb 1 : to break or decompose into constituent parts or small particles 2 : to destroy the unity or integrity of — **dis·in·te·gra·tion** \-ˌin-tə-ˈgrā-shən\ n

**dis·in·ter** \ˌdis-in-ˈtər\ vb 1 : to take from the grave or tomb 2 : UNEARTH

**dis·in·ter·est·ed** \(ˌ)dis-ˈin-tə-rəs-təd, -ˌres-\ adj 1 : not interested 2 : free from selfish motive or interest : UNBIASED — **dis·in·ter·est·ed·ness** n

**dis·join** \dis-ˈjoin\ vb : SEPARATE

**dis·joint** \(ˌ)dis-ˈjoint\ vb : to disturb the orderly arrangement of; also : to separate at the joints

**dis·joint·ed** adj 1 : INCOHERENT ⟨~ conversation⟩ 2 : separated at or as if at the joint

**disk** or **disc** \ˈdisk\ n 1 : something round and flat; esp : a flat rounded anatomical structure (as the central part of the flower head of a composite plant or a pad of cartilage between vertebrae) 2 usu disc : a phonograph record 3 : a round flat plate coated with a magnetic substance on which data for a computer is stored 4 usu disc : OPTICAL DISK

**disk drive** n : a device for accessing or storing data on a magnetic disk

**dis·kette** \dis-ˈket\ n : FLOPPY DISK

**disk jockey** var of DISC JOCKEY

¹**dis·like** \(ˌ)dis-ˈlīk\ n : a feeling of aversion or disapproval

²**dislike** vb : to regard with dislike : DISAPPROVE

**dis·lo·cate** \ˈdis-lō-ˌkāt, dis-ˈlō-\ vb 1 : to put out of place; esp : to displace (a bone or joint) from normal connections ⟨~ a shoulder⟩ 2 : DISRUPT — **dis·lo·ca·tion** \ˌdis-(ˌ)lō-ˈkā-shən\ n

**dis·lodge** \(ˌ)dis-ˈläj\ vb : to force out of a place esp. of rest, hiding, or defense

**dis·loy·al** \(ˌ)dis-ˈloi-(ə)l\ adj : lacking in loyalty — **dis·loy·al·ty** n

**dis·mal** \ˈdiz-məl\ adj [ME, fr. dismal, n., days marked as unlucky in medieval calendars, fr. AF, fr. ML dies mali, lit., evil days] 1 : showing or causing gloom or depression 2 : lacking merit ⟨a ~ performance⟩ — **dis·mal·ly** adv

**dis·man·tle** \(ˌ)dis-ˈman-tᵊl\ vb -tled; -tling 1 : to take apart 2 : to strip of furniture and equipment — **dis·man·tle·ment** n

**dis·may** \dis-ˈmā\ vb : to cause to lose courage or resolution from alarm or fear : DAUNT — **dismay** n — **dis·may·ing·ly** adv

**dis·mem·ber** \dis-ˈmem-bər\ vb 1 : to cut off or separate the limbs or parts of 2 : to break up or tear into pieces — **dis·mem·ber·ment** n

**dis·miss** \dis-ˈmis\ vb 1 : to send away 2 : DISCHARGE 5 3 : to put aside or out of mind 4 : to put out of judicial consideration ⟨~ed all charges⟩ — **dis·miss·al** n — **dis·mis·sive** \-ˈmi-siv\ adj — **dis·mis·sive·ly** adv

**dis·mount** \dis-ˈmaunt\ vb 1 : to get down from something (as a horse or bicycle) 2 : UNHORSE 3 : DISASSEMBLE

**dis·obe·di·ence** \ˌdis-ə-ˈbē-dē-əns\ n : neglect or refusal to obey — **dis·obe·di·ent** \-ənt\ adj

**dis·obey** \ˌdis-ə-ˈbā\ vb : to fail to obey : be disobedient

**dis·oblige** \ˌdis-ə-ˈblīj\ vb 1 : to go counter to the wishes of 2 : INCONVENIENCE

¹**dis·or·der** \dis-ˈor-dər\ vb 1 : to disturb the order of 2 : to disturb the regular or normal functions of

²**disorder** n 1 : lack of order : CONFUSION 2 : breach of the peace or public order : TUMULT 3 : an abnormal physical or mental condition : AILMENT

**dis·or·der·ly** \-lē\ adj 1 : offensive to public order 2 : marked by disorder ⟨a ~ desk⟩ — **dis·or·der·li·ness** n

**dis·or·ga·nize** \dis-ˈor-gə-ˌnīz\ vb : to break up the regular system of : throw into disorder — **dis·or·ga·ni·za·tion** \dis-ˌor-gə-nə-ˈzā-shən\ n

**dis·ori·ent** \dis-ˈor-ē-ˌent\ vb : to cause to be confused or lost — **dis·ori·en·ta·tion** \dis-ˌor-ē-ən-ˈtā-shən\ n

**dis·own** \dis-ˈōn\ vb : REPUDIATE, RENOUNCE, DISCLAIM ⟨her parents ~ed her⟩

**dis·par·age** \di-ˈsper-ij\ vb -aged; -aging [ME, to degrade by marriage below one's class, disparage, fr. AF desparager to marry below one's class, fr. parage equality, lineage, fr. per peer] 1 : to lower in rank or reputation : DEGRADE 2 : BELITTLE — **dis·par·age·ment** n — **dis·par·ag·ing·ly** adv

**dis·pa·rate** \ˈdis-pə-rət, di-ˈsper-ət\ adj : distinct in quality or character — **dis·par·i·ty** \di-ˈsper-ə-tē\ n

**dis·pas·sion·ate** \(ˌ)dis-ˈpa-shə-nət\ adj : not influenced by strong feeling : CALM, IMPARTIAL — **dis·pas·sion** \-ˈpa-shən\ n — **dis·pas·sion·ate·ly** adv

¹**dis·patch** \di-ˈspach\ vb 1 : to send off or away with promptness or speed esp. on official business 2 : to put to death 3 : to attend to rapidly or efficiently 4 : DEFEAT — **dis·patch·er** n

²**dis·patch** \di-ˈspach, ˈdis-ˌpach\ n 1 : MESSAGE 2 : a news item sent in by a correspondent to a newspaper 3 : the act of dispatching; esp : SHIPMENT 4 : the act of putting to death 5 : promptness and efficiency in performing a task

**dis·pel** \di-ˈspel\ vb dis·pelled; dis·pel·ling : to drive away by scattering : DISSIPATE ⟨~ a rumor⟩

**dis·pens·able** \di-'spen-sə-bəl\ *adj* : capable of being dispensed with

**dis·pen·sa·ry** \di-'spen-sə-rē\ *n, pl* **-ries** : a place where medicine or medical or dental aid is dispensed

**dis·pen·sa·tion** \ˌdis-pən-'sā-shən\ *n* **1** : a system of rules for ordering affairs **2** : a particular arrangement or provision esp. of nature **3** : an exemption from a rule or from a vow or oath **4** : the act of dispensing **5** : something dispensed or distributed

**dis·pense** \di-'spens\ *vb* **dis·pensed**; **dis·pens·ing 1** : to portion out **2** : ADMINISTER ⟨~ justice⟩ **3** : EXEMPT **4** : to make up and give out (remedies) — **dis·pens·er** *n* — **dispense with 1** : SUSPEND **2** : to do without

**dis·perse** \di-'spərs\ *vb* **dis·persed**; **dis·pers·ing** : to break up and scatter about : SPREAD — **dis·per·sal** \-'spər-səl\ *n* — **dis·per·sion** \-'spər-zhən\ *n*

**dis·pir·it** \dis-'pir-ət\ *vb* : DEPRESS, DISCOURAGE, DISHEARTEN

**dis·place** \dis-'plās\ *vb* **1** : to remove from the usual or proper place; *esp* : to expel or force to flee from home or native land ⟨*displaced* persons⟩ **2** : to move out of position ⟨water *displaced* by a floating object⟩ **3** : to take the place of : REPLACE

**dis·place·ment** \-mənt\ *n* **1** : the act of displacing : the state of being displaced **2** : the volume or weight of a fluid (as water) displaced by a floating body **3** : the difference between the initial position of an object and a later position

**¹dis·play** \di-'splā\ *vb* [ME, fr. AF *desplaier, desploier*, lit., to unfold, fr. *des-* un- + *ploier, plier* to fold, fr. L *plicare*] : to present to view : make evident

**²display** *n* **1** : a displaying of something **2** : an electronic device (as a cathode-ray tube) that gives information in visual form; *also* : the visual information

**dis·please** \ˌdis-'plēz\ *vb* **1** : to arouse the disapproval and dislike of **2** : to be offensive to : give displeasure

**dis·plea·sure** \-'ple-zhər\ *n* : a feeling of dislike and irritation

**dis·port** \di-'spōrt\ *vb* **1** : DIVERT, AMUSE **2** : FROLIC **3** : DISPLAY

**dis·pos·able** \di-'spō-zə-bəl\ *adj* **1** : remaining after deduction of taxes ⟨~ income⟩ **2** : designed to be used once and then thrown away ⟨~ diapers⟩ — **disposable** *n*

**dis·pos·al** \di-'spō-zəl\ *n* **1** : CONTROL, COMMAND **2** : an orderly arrangement **3** : a getting rid of **4** : MANAGEMENT, ADMINISTRATION **5** : presenting or bestowing something ⟨~ of favors⟩ **6** : a device used to reduce waste matter (as by grinding)

**dis·pose** \di-'spōz\ *vb* **dis·posed**; **dis·pos·ing 1** : to give a tendency to : INCLINE ⟨*disposed* to accept⟩ **2** : to put in place : ARRANGE ⟨troops *disposed* for withdrawal⟩ **3** : SETTLE — **dis·pos·er** *n* — **dispose of 1** : to transfer to the control of another **2** : to get rid of **3** : to deal with conclusively

**dis·po·si·tion** \ˌdis-pə-'zi-shən\ *n* **1** : the act or power of disposing : DISPOSAL **2** : RELINQUISHMENT **3** : ARRANGEMENT **4** : TENDENCY, INCLINATION **5** : natural attitude toward things ⟨a cheerful ~⟩

**dis·pos·sess** \ˌdis-pə-'zes\ *vb* : to put out of possession or occupancy — **dis·pos·ses·sion** \-'ze-shən\ *n*

**dis·praise** \dis-'prāz\ *vb* : DISPARAGE — **dispraise** *n* — **dis·prais·er** *n*

**dis·pro·por·tion** \ˌdis-prə-'pȯr-shən\ *n* : lack of proportion, symmetry, or proper relation — **dis·pro·por·tion·ate** \-shə-nət\ *adj*

**dis·prove** \ˌdis-'prüv\ *vb* : to prove to be false — **dis·proof** \-'prüf\ *n*

**dis·pu·tant** \dis-'pyü-t³nt, 'dis-pyə-tənt\ *n* : one that is engaged in a dispute

**dis·pu·ta·tion** \ˌdis-pyü-'tā-shən\ *n* **1** : DEBATE **2** : an oral defense of an academic thesis

**dis·pu·ta·tious** \-shəs\ *adj* : inclined to dispute : ARGUMENTATIVE

**¹dis·pute** \di-'spyüt\ *vb* **dis·put·ed**; **dis·put·ing 1** : ARGUE, DEBATE **2** : WRANGLE **3** : to deny the truth or rightness of **4** : to struggle against or over : OPPOSE **dis·put·able** \di-'spyü-tə-bəl, 'dis-pyə-tə-bəl\ *adj* — **dis·put·er** *n*

**²dispute** *n* **1** : DEBATE **2** : QUARREL

**dis·qual·i·fy** \ˌdis-'kwä-lə-ˌfī\ *vb* : to make or declare unfit or not qualified — **dis·qual·i·fi·ca·tion** \-ˌkwä-lə-fə-'kā-shən\ *n*

**¹dis·qui·et** \ˌdis-'kwī-ət\ *vb* : to make uneasy or restless : DISTURB ⟨was ~ed by the news⟩ — **dis·qui·et·ing** *adj*

**²disquiet** *n* : lack of peace or tranquillity : ANXIETY

**dis·qui·etude** \ˌdis-'kwī-ə-ˌtüd, -ˌtyüd\ *n* : AGITATION, ANXIETY

**dis·qui·si·tion** \ˌdis-kwə-'zi-shən\ *n* : a formal inquiry or discussion

**¹dis·re·gard** \ˌdis-ri-'gärd\ *vb* : to pay no attention to : treat as unworthy of notice or regard

**²disregard** *n* : the act of disregarding : state of being disregarded : NEGLECT — **dis·re·gard·ful** *adj*

**dis·re·pair** \ˌdis-ri-'per\ *n* : the state of being in need of repair

**dis·rep·u·ta·ble** \ˌdis-'re-pyü-tə-bəl\ *adj* : having a bad reputation

**dis·re·pute** \ˌdis-ri-'pyüt\ *n* : lack of decline of reputation : low esteem

**dis·re·spect** \ˌdis-ri-'spekt\ *n* : DISCOURTESY — **dis·re·spect·ful** *adj*

**dis·robe** \dis-'rōb\ *vb* : UNDRESS

**dis·rupt** \dis-'rəpt\ *vb* **1** : to break apart **2** : to throw into disorder **3** : INTERRUPT — **dis·rup·tion** \-'rəp-shən\ *n* — **dis·rup·tive** \-'rəp-tiv\ *adj*

**dis·sat·is·fac·tion** \di-ˌsa-təs-'fak-shən\ *n* : DISCONTENT

**dis·sat·is·fy** \di-'sa-təs-ˌfī\ *vb* : to fail to satisfy : DISPLEASE

**dis·sect** \dī-'sekt, di-\ *vb* **1** : to divide into parts esp. for examination and study **2** : ANALYZE — **dis·sec·tion** \-'sek-shən\ *n* — **dis·sec·tor** \-'sek-tər\ *n*

**dis·sect·ed** adj : cut deeply into narrow lobes ⟨a ～ leaf⟩

**dis·sem·ble** \di-'sem-bəl\ vb -bled; -bling 1 : to hide under or put on a false appearance : conceal facts, intentions, or feelings under some pretense 2 : SIMULATE — **dis·sem·bler** n

**dis·sem·i·nate** \di-'se-mə-ˌnāt\ vb -nat·ed; -nat·ing : to spread abroad as if sowing seed ⟨～ ideas⟩ — **dis·sem·i·na·tion** \-ˌse-mə-'nā-shən\ n

**dis·sen·sion** \di-'sen-chən\ n : disagreement in opinion : DISCORD

¹**dis·sent** \di-'sent\ vb 1 : to withhold assent 2 : to differ in opinion

²**dissent** n 1 : difference of opinion; esp : religious nonconformity 2 : a written statement in which a justice disagrees with the opinion of the majority

**dis·sent·er** \di-'sen-tər\ n 1 : one that dissents 2 cap : an English Nonconformist

**dis·ser·ta·tion** \ˌdi-sər-'tā-shən\ n : an extended usu. written treatment of a subject; esp : one submitted for a doctorate

**dis·ser·vice** \di-'sər-vəs\ n : INJURY, HARM, MISCHIEF

**dis·sev·er** \di-'se-vər\ vb : SEPARATE, DISUNITE

**dis·si·dent** \'di-sə-dənt\ adj [L dissidens, prp. of dissidēre to sit apart, disagree, fr. dis- apart + sedēre to sit] : disagreeing esp. with an established religious or political system, organization, or belief — **dis·si·dence** \-dəns\ n — **dissident** n

**dis·sim·i·lar** \di-'si-mə-lər\ adj : UNLIKE — **dis·sim·i·lar·i·ty** \di-ˌsi-mə-'ler-ə-tē\ n

**dis·sim·u·late** \di-'si-myə-ˌlāt\ vb : to hide under a false appearance : DISSEMBLE — **dis·sim·u·la·tion** \di-ˌsi-myə-'lā-shən\ n

**dis·si·pate** \'di-sə-ˌpāt\ vb -pat·ed; -pat·ing 1 : to break up and drive off : DISPERSE, SCATTER ⟨the breeze dissipated the fog⟩ 2 : SQUANDER 3 : to break up and vanish 4 : to be dissolute; esp : to drink alcoholic beverages to excess — **dis·si·pat·ed** adj — **dis·si·pa·tion** \ˌdi-sə-'pā-shən\ n

**dis·so·ci·ate** \di-'sō-shē-ˌāt\ vb -at·ed; -at·ing : DISCONNECT, DISUNITE — **dis·so·ci·a·tion** \di-ˌsō-shē-'ā-shən\ n — **dis·so·cia·tive** \di-'sō-shē-ˌā-tiv\ adj

**dis·so·lute** \'di-sə-ˌlüt\ adj : loose in morals or conduct — **dis·so·lute·ly** adv — **dis·so·lute·ness** n

**dis·so·lu·tion** \ˌdi-sə-'lü-shən\ n 1 : the action or process of dissolving 2 : separation of a thing into its parts 3 : DECAY; also : DEATH 4 : the termination or breaking up of (as an assembly)

**dis·solve** \di-'zälv\ vb 1 : to separate into component parts 2 : to pass or cause to pass into solution ⟨sugar ～s in water⟩ 3 : TERMINATE, DISPERSE ⟨～ parliament⟩ 4 : to waste or fade away ⟨his courage dissolved⟩ 5 : to be overcome emotionally ⟨～ in tears⟩ 6 : to resolve itself as if by dissolution

**dis·so·nance** \'di-sə-nəns\ n : DISCORD — **dis·so·nant** \-nənt\ adj

**dis·suade** \di-'swād\ vb **dis·suad·ed**; **dis·suad·ing** : to advise against a course of action : persuade or try to persuade not to do something — **dis·sua·sion** \-'swā-zhən\ n — **dis·sua·sive** \-'swā-siv\ adj

**dist** abbr 1 distance 2 district

¹**dis·taff** \'dis-ˌtaf\ n, pl **distaffs** \-ˌtafs, -ˌtavz\ [ME distaf, fr. OE distæf, fr. dis- bunch of flax + stæf stick, staff] 1 : a staff for holding the flax, tow, or wool in spinning 2 : a woman's work or domain 3 : the female branch or side of a family

²**distaff** adj 1 : MATERNAL 2 ⟨the ～ side of the family⟩ 2 : FEMALE 1 ⟨～ executives⟩

**dis·tal** \'dis-tᵊl\ adj 1 : situated away from the point of attachment or origin esp. on the body 2 : of, relating to, or being the surface of a tooth that is farthest from the middle of the front of the jaw — **dis·tal·ly** adv

¹**dis·tance** \'dis-təns\ n 1 : measure of separation in space or time 2 : EXPANSE 3 : the full length ⟨go the ～⟩ 4 : spatial remoteness 5 : COLDNESS, RESERVE 6 : DIFFERENCE, DISPARITY 7 : a distant point

²**distance** vb **dis·tanced**; **dis·tanc·ing** : to leave far behind : OUTSTRIP

³**distance** adj : taking place via electronic media linking instructors and students ⟨～ learning⟩

**dis·tant** \'dis-tənt\ adj 1 : separate in space : AWAY 2 : FAR-OFF ⟨a ～ galaxy⟩ 3 : far apart or behind 4 : not close in relationship ⟨a ～ cousin⟩ 5 : different in kind 6 : RESERVED, ALOOF, COLD ⟨～ politeness⟩ 7 : going a long distance ⟨～ voyages⟩ — **dis·tant·ly** adv — **dis·tant·ness** n

**dis·taste** \(ˌ)dis-'tāst\ n : DISINCLINATION, DISLIKE — **dis·taste·ful** adj

**dis·tem·per** \(ˌ)dis-'tem-pər\ n : a bodily disorder usu. of a domestic animal; esp : a contagious often fatal virus disease of dogs

**dis·tend** \di-'stend\ vb : EXPAND, SWELL — **dis·ten·si·ble** \-'sten-sə-bəl\ adj — **dis·ten·sion** or **dis·ten·tion** \-chən\ n

**dis·tich** \'dis-(ˌ)tik\ n : a unit of two lines of poetry

**dis·till** also **dis·til** \di-'stil\ vb **dis·tilled**; **dis·till·ing** 1 : to fall or let fall in drops 2 : to obtain or purify by distillation — **dis·till·er** n — **dis·till·ery** \-'sti-lə-rē\ n

**dis·til·late** \'dis-tə-ˌlāt, -lət\ n : a liquid product condensed from vapor during distillation

**dis·til·la·tion** \ˌdis-tə-'lā-shən\ n : the process of purifying a liquid by successive evaporation and condensation

**dis·tinct** \di-'stiŋkt\ adj 1 : SEPARATE, INDIVIDUAL ⟨a ～ cultural group⟩ 2 : presenting a clear unmistakable impression — **dis·tinct·ly** adv — **dis·tinct·ness** n

**dis·tinc·tion** \di-'stiŋk-shən\ n 1 : the distinguishing of a difference; also : the difference distinguished 2 : something that distinguishes 3 : special honor or recognition

**dis·tinc·tive** \di-'stiŋk-tiv\ adj 1 : serving

to distinguish ⟨the ~ flight of the crane⟩ **2** : having or giving style or distinction

**dis·tinc·tive·ly** *adv* — **dis·tinc·tive·ness** *n*

**dis·tin·guish** \di-'stin-gwish\ *vb* [alter. of ME *distinguen*, fr. AF *distinguer*, fr. L *distinguere*, lit., to separate by pricking] **1** : to recognize by some mark or characteristic **2** : to hear or see clearly : DISCERN **3** : to make distinctions ⟨~ between right and wrong⟩ **4** : to give prominence or distinction to; *also* : to take special notice of — **dis·tin·guish·able** *adj*

**dis·tin·guished** \-gwisht\ *adj* **1** : marked by eminence or excellence **2** : befitting an eminent person

**dis·tort** \di-'stort\ *vb* **1** : to twist out of the true meaning **2** : to twist out of a natural, normal, or original shape or condition **3** : to cause to be perceived unnaturally — **dis·tor·tion** \-'stor-shən\ *n*

**distr** *abbr* distribution; distribution

**dis·tract** \di-'strakt\ *vb* **1** : to draw (the attention or mind) to a different object : DIVERT **2** : to stir up or confuse with conflicting emotions or motives — **dis·trac·tion** \-'strak-shən\ *n*

**dis·trait** \di-'strā\ *adj* : DISTRAUGHT 1

**dis·traught** \di-'strot\ *adj* **1** : agitated with doubt or mental conflict or pain **2** : INSANE

**¹dis·tress** \di-'stres\ *n* **1** : suffering of body or mind : PAIN, ANGUISH **2** : TROUBLE, MISFORTUNE **3** : a condition of danger or desperate need — **dis·tress·ful** *adj*

**²distress** *vb* **1** : to subject to great strain or difficulties **2** : UPSET

**dis·tressed** \-'strest\ *adj* : experiencing economic decline or difficulty

**dis·trib·ute** \di-'stri-byüt\ *vb* **-ut·ed; -ut·ing 1** : to divide among several or many **2** : to spread out : SCATTER; *also* : DELIVER **3** : CLASSIFY — **dis·tri·bu·tion** \,dis-trə-'byü-shən\ *n*

**dis·trib·u·tive** \di-'stri-byú-tiv\ *adj* **1** : of or relating to distribution **2** : of, having, or being the property of producing the same value when an operation is carried out on a whole expression and when it is carried out on each part of an expression with the results then collected together ⟨*a*(*b* + *c*) = *ab* + *ac* because multiplication is ~⟩ — **dis·trib·u·tive·ly** *adv*

**dis·trib·u·tor** \di-'stri-byü-tər\ *n* **1** : one that distributes **2** : one that markets goods **3** : a device for directing current to the spark plugs of an engine

**dis·trict** \'dis-(,)trikt\ *n* **1** : a fixed territorial division (as for administrative or electoral purposes) **2** : an area, region, or section with a distinguishing character

**district attorney** *n* : the prosecuting attorney of a judicial district

**¹dis·trust** \dis-'trəst\ *n* : a lack or absence of trust — **dis·trust·ful** \-fəl\ *adj* — **dis·trust·ful·ly** *adv*

**²distrust** *vb* : to have no trust or confidence in

**dis·turb** \dis-'stərb\ *vb* **1** : to interfere with : INTERRUPT **2** : to alter the position or arrangement of; *also* : to upset the natural and esp. the ecological balance of **3** : to destroy the tranquillity or composure of : make uneasy **4** : to throw into disorder **5** : INCONVENIENCE — **dis·tur·bance** \-'stər-bəns\ *n* — **dis·turb·er** *n* — **dis·turb·ing·ly** \-'stər-biŋ-lē\ *adv*

**dis·turbed** \-'stərbd\ *adj* : showing symptoms of mental illness

**dis·unite** \,dis-yü-'nīt\ *vb* : DIVIDE, SEPARATE

**dis·uni·ty** \dis-'yü-nə-tē\ *n* : lack of unity; *esp* : DISSENSION

**dis·use** \-'yüs\ *n* : a cessation of use or practice

**dis·used** \-'yüzd\ *adj* : no longer used or occupied

**¹ditch** \'dich\ *n* : a long narrow channel or trench dug in the earth

**²ditch** *vb* **1** : to enclose with a ditch; *also* : to dig a ditch in **2** : to get rid of : DISCARD **3** : to make a forced landing of an airplane on water

**dith·er** \'di-thər\ *n* : a highly nervous, excited, or agitated state

**dit·to** \'di-tō\ *n, pl* **dittos** [It *ditto, detto*, pp. of *dire* to say, fr. L *dicere*] **1** : a thing mentioned previously or above — used to avoid repeating a word **2** : a mark " or " used as a symbol for the word *ditto*

**dit·ty** \'di-tē\ *n, pl* **ditties** : a short simple song

**dit·zy** *or* **dit·sy** \'dit-sē\ *adj* **ditz·i·er** *or* **dits·i·er; -est** : eccentrically silly, giddy, or inane

**di·uret·ic** \,dī-yə-'re-tik\ *adj* : tending to increase urine flow — **diuretic** *n*

**di·ur·nal** \dī-'ər-n²l\ *adj* **1** : DAILY ⟨a ~ chore⟩ **2** : of, relating to, occurring, or active in the daytime ⟨~ animals⟩

**div** *abbr* **1** divided **2** dividend **3** division **4** divorced

**di·va** \'dē-və\ *n, pl* **divas** *or* **di·ve** \-,vā\ [It, lit., goddess, fr. L, fem. of *dīvus* divine, god] **1** : PRIMA DONNA **2** : a usu. glamorous and successful female performer or personality

**di·va·gate** \'dī-və-,gāt\ *vb* **-gat·ed; -gat·ing** : to wander or stray from a course or subject : DIVERGE — **di·va·ga·tion** \,dī-və-'gā-shən\ *n*

**di·van** \'dī-,van, di-'van\ *n* : COUCH, SOFA

**¹dive** \'dīv\ *vb* **dived** \'dīvd\ *or* **dove** \'dōv\; **dived; div·ing 1** : to plunge into water headfirst **2** : SUBMERGE **3** : to come or drop down precipitously **4** : to descend in an airplane at a steep angle **5** : to plunge into some matter or activity **6** : DART, LUNGE — **div·er** *n*

**²dive** *n* **1** : the act or an instance of diving **2** : a sharp decline **3** : a disreputable bar or place of amusement

**di·verge** \də-'vərj, dī-\ *vb* **di·verged; di·verg·ing 1** : to move or extend in different directions from a common point : draw apart **2** : to differ in character, form, or opinion **3** : DEVIATE **4** : DEFLECT — **di·ver·gence** \-'vər-jəns\ *n* — **di·ver·gent** \-jənt\ *adj*

**di·vers** \'dī-vərz\ *adj* : VARIOUS

**di·verse** \dī-'vərs, də-, 'dī-,vərs\ *adj* **1**

: UNLIKE **2** : composed of distinct forms or qualities — **di·verse·ly** *adv*

**di·ver·si·fy** \də-'vər-sə-ˌfī, dī-\ *vb* **-fied**; **-fy·ing** : to make different or various in form or quality — **di·ver·si·fi·ca·tion** \-ˌvər-sə-fə-'kā-shən\ *n*

**di·ver·sion** \də-'vər-zhən, dī-\ *n* **1** : a turning aside from a course, activity, or use : DEVIATION **2** : something that diverts or amuses : PASTIME

**di·ver·si·ty** \də-'vər-sə-tē, dī-\ *n, pl* **-ties 1** : the condition of being diverse : VARIETY **2** : an instance of being diverse

**di·vert** \də-'vərt, dī-\ *vb* **1** : to turn from a course or purpose : DEFLECT **2** : DISTRACT **3** : ENTERTAIN, AMUSE

**di·vert·ing** \-'vər-tiŋ\ *adj* : providing amusement or entertainment

**di·vest** \dī-'vest, də-\ *vb* **1** : to deprive or dispossess esp. of property, authority, or rights **2** : to strip esp. of clothing, ornament, or equipment

**¹di·vide** \də-'vīd\ *vb* **di·vid·ed**; **di·vid·ing 1** : SEPARATE; *also* : CLASSIFY **2** : CLEAVE, PART ⟨a ship *dividing* the waves⟩ **3** : DISTRIBUTE, APPORTION **4** : to possess or make use of in common : share in **5** : to cause to be separate, distinct, or apart from one another **6** : to separate into opposing sides or parties **7** : to mark divisions on **8** : to subject to or use in mathematical division; *also* : to be used as a divisor with respect to **9** : to branch out

**²divide** *n* : WATERSHED 1

**div·i·dend** \'di-və-ˌdend\ *n* **1** : an individual share of something distributed **2** : BONUS **3** : a number to be divided **4** : a sum or fund to be divided or distributed

**di·vid·er** \də-'vī-dər\ *n* **1** : one that divides (as a partition) ⟨room ∼⟩ **2** *pl* : COMPASS 5

**div·i·na·tion** \ˌdi-və-'nā-shən\ *n* **1** : the art or practice of using omens or magic powers to foretell the future **2** : unusual insight or intuitive perception

**¹di·vine** \də-'vīn\ *adj* **di·vin·er**; **-est 1** : of, relating to, or being God or a god **2** : supremely good : SUPERB; *also* : HEAVENLY — **di·vine·ly** *adv*

**²divine** *n* **1** : CLERGYMAN **2** : THEOLOGIAN

**³divine** *vb* **di·vined**; **di·vin·ing 1** : INFER, CONJECTURE **2** : PROPHESY **3** : DOWSE — **di·vin·er** *n*

**divining rod** *n* : a forked rod believed to reveal the presence of water or minerals by dipping downward when held over a vein

**di·vin·i·ty** \də-'vi-nə-tē\ *n, pl* **-ties 1** : THEOLOGY **2** : the quality or state of being divine **3** : a divine being; *esp* : GOD 1

**di·vis·i·ble** \də-'vi-zə-bəl\ *adj* : capable of being divided ⟨9 is ∼ by 3⟩ — **di·vis·i·bil·i·ty** \-ˌvi-zə-'bi-lə-tē\ *n*

**di·vi·sion** \də-'vi-zhən\ *n* **1** : DISTRIBUTION, SEPARATION **2** : one of the parts or groupings into which a whole is divided **3** : DISAGREEMENT, DISUNITY **4** : something that divides or separates **5** : the mathematical operation of finding how many times one number is contained in another **6** : a large self-contained military unit **7** : an administrative or operating unit of a governmental, business, or educational organization — **di·vi·sion·al** \-'vi-zhə-nəl\ *adj*

**di·vi·sive** \də-'vī-siv, -'vi-ziv\ *adj* : creating disunity or dissension — **di·vi·sive·ly** *adv* — **di·vi·sive·ness** *n*

**di·vi·sor** \də-'vī-zər\ *n* : the number by which a dividend is divided

**di·vorce** \də-'vòrs\ *n* **1** : an act or instance of legally dissolving a marriage **2** : SEPARATION, SEVERANCE — **divorce** *vb* — **di·vorce·ment** *n*

**di·vor·cé** \də-ˌvòr-'sā\ *n* [F] : a divorced man

**di·vor·cée** \də-ˌvòr-'sā, -'sē\ *n* : a divorced woman

**div·ot** \'di-vət\ *n* : a piece of turf dug from a golf fairway in making a stroke

**di·vulge** \də-'vəlj, dī-\ *vb* **di·vulged**; **di·vulg·ing** : REVEAL, DISCLOSE

**Dix·ie·land** \'dik-sē-ˌland\ *n* : jazz music in duple time played in a style developed in New Orleans

**diz·zy** \'di-zē\ *adj* **diz·zi·er; -est** [ME *disy*, fr. OE *dysig* stupid] **1** : FOOLISH, SILLY **2** : having a sensation of whirling : GIDDY **3** : causing or caused by giddiness — **diz·zi·ly** \-zə-lē\ *adv* — **diz·zi·ness** \-zē-nəs\ *n*

**DJ** *n, often not cap* : DISC JOCKEY

**dk** *abbr* **1** dark **2** deck **3** dock

**dl** *abbr* deciliter

**DLitt** *or* **DLit** *abbr* [NL *doctor litterarum*] doctor of letters; doctor of literature

**DLO** *abbr* dead letter office

**dm** *abbr* decimeter

**DMD** *abbr* [NL *dentariae medicinae doctor*] doctor of dental medicine

**DMZ** *abbr* demilitarized zone

**dn** *abbr* down

**DNA** \ˌdē-ˌen-'ā\ *n* : any of various nucleic acids that are usu. the molecular basis of heredity and are localized esp. in cell nuclei

**DNR** *abbr* do not resuscitate

**¹do** \'dü\ *vb* **did** \'did\; **done** \'dən\; **do·ing; does** \'dəz\ **1** : to bring to pass : ACCOMPLISH **2** : ACT, BEHAVE ⟨∼ as I say⟩ **3** : to be active or busy ⟨up and ∼*ing*⟩ **4** : HAPPEN ⟨what's ∼*ing*?⟩ **5** : to be engaged in the study or practice of : work at ⟨he *does* tailoring⟩ **6** : COOK ⟨steak *done* rare⟩ **7** : to put in order (as by cleaning or arranging) ⟨∼ the dishes⟩ **8** : DECORATE ⟨*did* the hall in blue⟩ **9** : GET ALONG ⟨∼ well in school⟩ **10** : CARRY ON, MANAGE **11** : RENDER ⟨sleep will ∼ you good⟩ **12** : FINISH ⟨when he had *done*⟩ **13** : EXERT ⟨*did* my best⟩ **14** : PRODUCE ⟨*did* a poem⟩ **15** : to play the part of **16** : CHEAT ⟨*did* him out of his share⟩ **17** : TRAVERSE, TOUR **18** : TRAVEL **19** : to spend or serve out a period of time ⟨*did* ten years in prison⟩ **20** : SUFFICE, SUIT **21** : to be fitting or proper **22** : USE ⟨doesn't ∼ drugs⟩ **23** — used as an auxiliary verb (1) before the subject in an interrogative sentence ⟨*does* he work?⟩ and after some adverbs ⟨never *did* she say so⟩, (2) in a negative statement ⟨I *don't* know⟩, (3) for emphasis ⟨you ~ know⟩, and (4) as a substitute for a preceding predicate ⟨he works harder than I ~⟩ — **do·able** \'dü-ə-bəl\ *adj* — **do away with 1** : to put an end to **2** : DESTROY, KILL — **do by** : to deal with : TREAT ⟨*did* right *by* her⟩ — **do for** *chiefly Brit* : to bring about the death or ruin of — **do the trick** : to produce a desired result

²**do** *n* **1** : AFFAIR, PARTY **2** : a command or entreaty to do something ⟨list of ~s and don'ts⟩ **3** : HAIRSTYLE

³**do** *abbr* ditto

**DOA** *abbr* dead on arrival

**DOB** *abbr* date of birth

**dob·bin** \'dä-bən\ *n* [*Dobbin*, nickname for *Robert*] **1** : a farm horse **2** : a quiet plodding horse

**Do·ber·man pin·scher** \'dō-bər-mən-'pin-chər\ *n* : any of a German breed of short-haired medium-sized dogs

**do·bra** \'dō-brə\ *n* — see MONEY table

¹**doc** \'däk\ *n* : DOCTOR

²**doc** *abbr* document

**do·cent** \'dō-sᵊnt, dōt-'sent\ *n* [obs. G (now *Dozent*), fr. L *docens*, prp. of *docere* to teach] : TEACHER, LECTURER; *also* : a person who leads a guided tour

**doc·ile** \'dä-səl\ *adj* [L *docilis*, fr. *docere* to teach] : easily taught, led, or managed : TRACTABLE — **do·cil·i·ty** \dä-'si-lə-tē\ *n*

¹**dock** \'däk\ *n* : any of a genus of coarse weedy herbs related to buckwheat

²**dock** *vb* **1** : to cut off the end of : cut short **2** : to take away a part of : deduct from ⟨~ a worker's wages⟩

³**dock** *n* **1** : an artificial basin to receive ships **2** : ²SLIP **2** : a wharf or platform for loading or unloading materials or for mooring a boat

⁴**dock** *vb* **1** : to bring or come into dock **2** : to join (as two spacecraft) mechanically in space

⁵**dock** *n* : the place in a court where a prisoner stands or sits during trial

**dock·age** \'dä-kij\ *n* : docking facilities

**dock·et** \'dä-kət\ *n* **1** : a formal abridged record of the proceedings in a legal action; *also* : a register of such records **2** : a list of legal causes to be tried **3** : a calendar of matters to be acted on : AGENDA **4** : a label attached to a document containing identification or directions — **docket** *vb*

**dock·hand** \'däk-ˌhand\ *n* : LONGSHOREMAN

**dock·work·er** \-ˌwər-kər\ *n* : LONGSHOREMAN

**dock·yard** \-ˌyärd\ *n* : SHIPYARD

¹**doc·tor** \'däk-tər\ *n* [ME *doctour* teacher, doctor, fr. AF & ML; AF, fr. ML *doctor*, fr. L, teacher, fr. *docere* to teach] **1** : a person holding one of the highest academic degrees (as a PhD) conferred by a university **2** : a person skilled in healing arts; *esp* : one (as a physician, dentist, or veterinarian) academically and legally qualified to practice **3** : a person who restores or repairs things — **doc·tor·al** \-tə-rəl\ *adj*

²**doctor** *vb* **1** : to give medical treatment to **2** : to practice medicine **3** : REPAIR **4** : to adapt or modify for a desired end **5** : to alter deceptively

**doc·tor·ate** \'däk-tə-rət\ *n* : the degree, title, or rank of a doctor

**doc·tri·naire** \ˌdäk-trə-'ner\ *n* [F] : one who attempts to put an abstract theory into effect without regard to practical difficulties — **doctrinaire** *adj*

**doc·trine** \'däk-trən\ *n* **1** : something that is taught **2** : DOGMA, TENET — **doc·tri·nal** \-trə-nᵊl\ *adj*

**docu·dra·ma** \'dä-kyə-ˌdrä-mə, -ˌdra-\ *n* : a drama made for television, motion pictures, or theater that deals freely with historical events

**doc·u·ment** \'dä-kyə-mənt\ *n* **1** : a paper that furnishes information, proof, or support of something else **2** : a computer file containing information input by a computer user usu. via a word processor — **doc·u·ment** \-ˌment\ *vb* — **doc·u·men·ta·tion** \ˌdä-kyə-mən-'tā-shən\ *n* — **doc·u·ment·er** *n*

**doc·u·men·ta·ry** \ˌdä-kyə-'men-tə-rē\ *adj* **1** : consisting of documents; *also* : being in writing ⟨~ proof⟩ **2** : giving a factual presentation in artistic form ⟨a ~ movie⟩ — **documentary** *n*

**DOD** *abbr* Department of Defense

¹**dod·der** \'dä-dər\ *n* : any of a genus of leafless parasitic twining vines that are highly deficient in chlorophyll

²**dodder** *vb* **dod·dered; dod·der·ing 1** : to tremble or shake usu. from age **2** : to progress feebly and unsteadily

¹**dodge** \'däj\ *n* **1** : an act of evading by sudden bodily movement **2** : an artful device to evade, deceive, or trick **3** : EXPEDIENT

²**dodge** *vb* **dodged; dodg·ing 1** : to evade usu. by trickery **2** : to move suddenly aside; *also* : to avoid or evade by so doing — **dodg·er** *n*

**do·do** \'dō-dō\ *n, pl* **dodoes** *or* **dodos** [Pg *doudo*, fr. *doudo* silly, stupid] **1** : an extinct heavy flightless bird of the island of Mauritius related to the pigeons and larger than a turkey **2** : one hopelessly behind the times; *also* : a stupid person

**doe** \'dō\ *n, pl* **does** *or* **doe** : an adult female of various mammals (as a deer, rabbit, or kangaroo) of which the male is called *buck*

**DOE** *abbr* Department of Energy

**do·er** \'dü-ər\ *n* : one that does

**does** *pres 3d sing of* DO; *pl of* DOE

**doff** \'däf\ *vb* [ME, fr. *don* to do + *of* off] **1** : to take off (the hat) in greeting or as a sign of respect **2** : to rid oneself of

¹**dog** \'dȯg\ *n* **1** : a flesh-eating domestic mammal related to the wolves; *esp* : a male of this animal **2** : a worthless or contemptible person **3** : FELLOW, CHAP ⟨you lucky ~⟩ **4** : a mechanical device for holding something **5** : uncharacteristic or affected stylishness or dignity ⟨put on the ~⟩ **6** *pl* : RUIN ⟨gone to the ~s⟩

²**dog** *vb* **dogged; dog·ging 1** : to hunt or track like a hound **2** : to worry as if by pursuit with dogs : PLAGUE

**dog·bane** \'dȯg-ˌbān\ n : any of a genus of mostly poisonous herbs with milky juice and often showy flowers

**dog·cart** \-ˌkärt\ n : a light one-horse carriage with two seats back to back

**dog·catch·er** \-ˌka-chər, -ˌke-\ n : a community official assigned to catch and dispose of stray dogs

**dog-ear** \'dȯg-ˌir\ n : the turned-down corner of a leaf of a book — **dog-ear** vb — **dog-eared** \-ˌird\ adj

**dog·fight** \'dȯg-ˌfīt\ n : a fight between fighter planes at close range

**dog·fish** \-ˌfish\ n : any of various small usu. bottom-dwelling sharks

**dog·ged** \'dȯ-gəd\ adj : stubbornly determined : TENACIOUS — **dog·ged·ly** adv — **dog·ged·ness** n

**dog·ger·el** \'dȯ-gə-rəl\ n : verse that is loosely styled and irregular in measure esp. for comic effect

**dog·gie bag** or **doggy bag** \'dȯ-gē-\ n : a container for carrying home leftover food from a restaurant meal

¹**dog·gy** or **dog·gie** \'dȯ-gē\ n, pl **doggies** : a small dog

²**dog·gy** adj **dog·gi·er; -est** : of or resembling a dog ⟨a ~ odor⟩

**dog·house** \'dȯg-ˌhau̇s\ n : a shelter for a dog — **in the doghouse** : in a state of disfavor

**do·gie** \'dō-gē\ n, chiefly West : a motherless calf in a range herd

**dog·leg** \'dȯg-ˌleg\ n : a sharp bend or angle (as in a road or golf fairway) — **dogleg** vb

**dog·ma** \'dȯg-mə\ n, pl **dogmas** also **dog·ma·ta** \-mə-tə\ [L, fr. Gk, fr. dokein to think, have an opinion] 1 : a tenet or code of tenets 2 : a doctrine or body of doctrines formally proclaimed by a church

**dog·ma·tism** \'dȯg-mə-ˌti-zəm\ n : positiveness in stating matters of opinion esp. when unwarranted or arrogant — **dog·mat·ic** \dȯg-'ma-tik\ adj — **dog·mat·i·cal·ly** \-ti-k(ə-)lē\ adv

**do–good·er** \'dü-ˌgu̇-dər\ n : an earnest often naive humanitarian or reformer

**dog·tooth violet** \'dȯg-ˌtüth-\ n : any of a genus of small spring-flowering bulbous herbs related to the lilies

**dog·trot** \'dȯg-ˌträt\ n : a gentle trot — **dogtrot** vb

**dog·wood** \'dȯg-ˌwu̇d\ n : any of a genus of trees and shrubs having heads of small flowers often with showy white, pink, or red bracts

**doi·ly** \'dȯi-lē\ n, pl **doilies** : a small often decorative mat

**do in** vb 1 : RUIN 2 : KILL 3 : TIRE, EXHAUST ⟨the climb did him in⟩ 4 : CHEAT

**do·ings** \'dü-iŋz\ n pl : GOINGS-ON

**do–it–yourself** n : the activity of doing or making something without professional training or help — **do–it–your·self·er** n

**dol** abbr dollar

**dol·drums** \'dōl-drəmz, 'däl-\ n pl 1 : a spell of listlessness or despondency 2 often cap : a part of the ocean near the

equator known for calms 3 : a state or period of inactivity, stagnation, or slump

¹**dole** \'dōl\ n 1 : a distribution esp. of food, money, or clothing to the needy; also : something so distributed 2 : a grant of government funds to the unemployed

²**dole** vb **doled; dol·ing** : to give or distribute as a charity — usu. used with out

**dole·ful** \'dōl-fəl\ adj : full of grief : SAD — **dole·ful·ly** adv

**dole out** vb 1 : to give or deliver in small portions 2 : DISH OUT

**doll** \'däl, 'dȯl\ n 1 : a small figure of a human being used esp. as a child's plaything 2 : a pretty woman 3 : an attractive person — **doll·ish** \'dä-lish, 'dȯ-\ adj

**dol·lar** \'dä-lər\ n [Dutch or LG daler, fr. G Taler, short for Joachimstaler, fr. Sankt Joachimsthal, Bohemia, where talers were first made] 1 : any of various basic monetary units (as in the U.S. and Canada) — see MONEY table 2 : a coin, note, or token representing one dollar 3 : RINGGIT

**dol·lop** \'dä-ləp\ n 1 : LUMP, GLOB 2 : PORTION 1 — **dollop** vb

**doll up** vb 1 : to dress elegantly or extravagantly 2 : to make more attractive 3 : to get dolled up

**dol·ly** \'dä-lē\ n, pl **dollies** : a small cart or wheeled platform (as for a television or movie camera)

**dol·men** \'dōl-mən, 'däl-\ n : a prehistoric monument consisting of two or more upright stones supporting a horizontal stone slab

**do·lo·mite** \'dō-lə-ˌmīt, 'dä-\ n : a mineral found in broad layers as a compact limestone

**do·lor** \'dō-lər, 'dä-\ n : mental suffering or anguish : SORROW — **do·lor·ous** adj — **do·lor·ous·ly** adv

**do·lour** chiefly Brit var of DOLOR

**dol·phin** \'däl-fən\ n 1 : any of various small whales with conical teeth and an elongated beaklike snout 2 : either of two active food fishes of tropical and temperate seas

**dolt** \'dōlt\ n : a stupid person — **dolt·ish** \'dōl-tish\ adj — **dolt·ish·ness** n

**dom** abbr 1 domestic 2 dominant 3 dominion

**-dom** n suffix 1 : dignity : office ⟨dukedom⟩ 2 : realm : jurisdiction ⟨kingdom⟩ 3 : state or fact of being ⟨freedom⟩ 4 : those having a (specified) office, occupation, interest, or character ⟨officialdom⟩

**do·main** \dō-'mān\ n 1 : complete and absolute ownership of land 2 : land completely owned 3 : a territory over which dominion is exercised 4 : a sphere of knowledge, influence, or activity ⟨the ~ of science⟩ 5 : a subdivision of the Internet made up of computers whose URLs share a characteristic abbreviation (as com or gov)

**domain name** n : a sequence of characters (as Merriam-Webster.com) that specifies a group of online resources and forms part of its URL

**dome** \'dōm\ n 1 : a large hemispherical

roof or ceiling **2** : a structure or natural formation that resembles the dome of a building **3** : a roofed sports stadium — **dome** vb

¹**do·mes·tic** \də-'mes-tik\ adj **1** : living near or about human habitations **2** : TAME, DOMESTICATED **3** : relating and limited to one's own country or the country under consideration **4** : of or relating to the household or the family **5** : devoted to home duties and pleasures **6** : INDIGENOUS — **do·mes·ti·cal·ly** \-ti-k(ə-)lē\ adv

²**domestic** n : a household servant

**do·mes·ti·cate** \də-'mes-ti-ˌkāt\ vb **-cat·ed; -cat·ing** : to adapt to life in association with and to the use of humans

**do·mes·ti·ca·tion** \-ˌmes-ti-'ka-shən\ n

**do·mes·tic·i·ty** \ˌdō-ˌmes-'ti-sə-tē, də-\ n, pl **-ties** **1** : the quality or state of being domestic or domesticated **2** : domestic activities or life

**domestic violence** n : the inflicting of injury by one family or household member on another

**do·mi·cile** \'dä-mə-ˌsī(-ə)l, 'dō-; 'dä-mə-səl\ n : a dwelling place : HOME — **domicile** vb — **dom·i·cil·i·ary** \ˌdä-mə-'si-lē-ˌer-ē, ˌdō-\ adj

**dom·i·nance** \'dä-mə-nəns\ n **1** : AUTHORITY, CONTROL **2** : the property of one of a pair of alleles or traits that suppresses expression of the other when both are present

¹**dom·i·nant** \-nənt\ adj **1** : controlling or prevailing over all others **2** : overlooking from a high position **3** : exhibiting genetic dominance

²**dominant** n : a dominant gene or trait

**dom·i·nate** \'dä-mə-ˌnāt\ vb **-nat·ed; -nat·ing** **1** : RULE, CONTROL **2** : to have a commanding position or controlling power over **3** : to rise high above in a position suggesting power to dominate — **dom·i·na·tor** \ ˌnā tər\ n

**dom·i·na·tion** \ˌdä-mə-'nā-shən\ n **1** : supremacy or preeminence over another **2** : exercise of mastery, ruling power, or preponderant influence

**do·mi·na·trix** \ˌdä-mə-'nā-triks\ n, pl **-trices** \-'nā-trə-ˌsēz, -nə-'trī-sēz\ : a woman who dominates her sexual partner; also : a dominating woman

**dom·i·neer** \ˌdä-mə-'nir\ vb **1** : to rule in an arrogant manner **2** : to be overbearing

**do·mi·nie** \1 usu 'dä-mə-nē, 2 usu 'dō-\ n **1** chiefly Scot : SCHOOLMASTER **2** : CLERGYMAN

**do·min·ion** \də-'min-yən\ n **1** : DOMAIN **2** : supreme authority : SOVEREIGNTY **3** often cap : a self-governing nation of the Commonwealth

**dom·i·no** \'dä-mə-ˌnō\ n, pl **-noes** or **-nos** **1** : a long loose hooded cloak usu. worn with a half mask as a masquerade costume **2** : a flat rectangular block used as a piece in a game (**dominoes**)

¹**don** \'dän\ vb **donned; don·ning** [ME, fr. don to do + on] : to put on (as clothes)

²**don** n [Sp, fr. L dominus lord, master] **1** : a Spanish nobleman or gentleman —

used as a title prefixed to the Christian name **2** : a head, tutor, or fellow in an English university

**do·ña** \'dō-nyə\ n : a Spanish woman of rank — used as a title prefixed to the Christian name

**do·nate** \'dō-ˌnāt\ vb **do·nat·ed; do·nat·ing** **1** : to make a gift of : CONTRIBUTE **2** : to make a donation

**do·na·tion** \dō-'nā-shən\ n **1** : the making of a gift esp. to a charity **2** : a free contribution : GIFT

¹**done** \'dən\ past part of DO

²**done** adj **1** : doomed to failure, defeat, or death **2** : gone by : OVER ⟨when day is ~⟩ **3** : cooked sufficiently **4** : conformable to social convention

**done deal** n : FAIT ACCOMPLI

**dong** \'dȯŋ, 'däŋ\ n — see MONEY table

**don·key** \'däŋ-kē, 'dȯŋ-\ n, pl **donkeys** **1** : a sturdy and patient domestic mammal classified with the asses **2** : a stupid or obstinate person

**don·ny·brook** \'dä-nē-ˌbrùk\ n, often cap [Donnybrook Fair, annual Irish event known for its brawls] : an uproarious brawl

**do·nor** \'dō-nər\ n : one that gives, donates, or presents

**donut** var of DOUGHNUT

**doo·dad** \'dü-ˌdad\ n : an often small article whose common name is unknown or forgotten

**doo·dle** \'dü-dᵊl\ vb **doo·dled; doo·dling** : to draw or scribble aimlessly while occupied with something else — **doodle** n — **doo·dler** n

**doom** \'düm\ n **1** : JUDGMENT; esp : a judicial condemnation or sentence **2** : DESTINY **3** : RUIN, DEATH — **doom** vb

**dooms·day** \'dümz-ˌdā\ n : JUDGMENT DAY

**door** \'dōr\ n **1** : a barrier by which an entry is closed and opened; also : a similar part of a piece of furniture **2** : DOORWAY **3** : a means of access or participation : OPPORTUNITY

**door·keep·er** \-ˌkē-pər\ n : a person who tends a door

**door·knob** \-ˌnäb\ n : a knob that when turned releases a door latch

**door·man** \-ˌman, -mən\ n : a usu. uniformed attendant at the door of a building (as a hotel)

**door·mat** \-ˌmat\ n : a mat placed before or inside a door for wiping dirt from the shoes

**door·plate** \-ˌplāt\ n : a nameplate on a door

**door·step** \-ˌstep\ n : a step or series of steps before an outer door

**door·way** \-ˌwā\ n **1** : the opening that a door closes **2** : DOOR 3

**do·pa** \'dō-pə\ n : a form of an amino acid that is used esp. in the treatment of Parkinson's disease

**do·pa·mine** \'dō-pə-ˌmēn\ n : an organic compound that occurs esp. as a neurotransmitter in the brain

¹**dope** \'dōp\ n **1** : a preparation for giving a desired quality **2** : an illicit, habit-forming, or narcotic drug; esp : MARI-

JUANA **3** : a stupid person **4** : INFORMATION

²**dope** *vb* **doped; dop·ing 1** : to treat with dope; *esp* : to give a narcotic to **2** : FIGURE OUT — usu. used with *out* **3** : to take dope — **dop·er** *n*

**dop·ey** *also* **dopy** \'dō-pē\ *adj* **dop·i·er; -est 1** : dulled by alcohol or a narcotic **2** : SLUGGISH : STUPID — **dop·i·ness** *n*

**doping** *n* : the use of a substance or technique to illegally improve athletic performance

**Dopp·ler effect** \'dä-plər-\ *n* : a change in the frequency at which waves (as of sound) reach an observer from a source in motion with respect to the observer

**do–rag** \'dü-ˌrag\ *n* : a kerchief worn esp. to cover the hair

**dork** \'dȯrk\ *n, slang* : NERD; *also* : JERK 2

**dorm** \'dȯrm\ *n* : DORMITORY

**dor·mant** \'dȯr-mənt\ *adj* : INACTIVE; *esp* : not actively growing or functioning ⟨~ buds⟩ — **dor·man·cy** \-mən-sē\ *n*

**dor·mer** \'dȯr-mər\ *n* [MF *dormeor* dormitory, fr. L *dormitorium*, fr. *dormire* to sleep] : a window built upright in a sloping roof; *also* : the roofed structure containing such a window

**dor·mi·to·ry** \'dȯr-mə-ˌtōr-ē\ *n, pl* **-ries 1** : a room for sleeping; *esp* : a large room containing a number of beds **2** : a residence hall providing sleeping rooms

**dor·mouse** \'dȯr-ˌmaůs\ *n* : any of numerous Old World rodents that resemble small squirrels

**dor·sal** \'dȯr-səl\ *adj* : of, relating to, or located near or on the surface of the body that in humans is the back but in most other animals is the upper surface — **dor·sal·ly** *adv*

**do·ry** \'dȯr-ē\ *n, pl* **dories** : a flat-bottomed boat with high flaring sides and a sharp bow

**DOS** *abbr* disk operating system

¹**dose** \'dōs\ *n* [ME, fr. MF, fr. LL *dosis*, fr. Gk, lit., act of giving, fr. *didonai* to give] **1** : a measured quantity (as of medicine) to be taken or administered at one time **2** : the quantity of radiation administered or absorbed — **dos·age** \'dō-sij\ *n*

²**dose** *vb* **dosed; dos·ing 1** : to give in doses **2** : to give medicine to

**do·sim·e·ter** \dō-'si-mə-tər\ *n* : a device for measuring doses of radiations (as X-rays) — **do·sim·e·try** \-mə-trē\ *n*

**dos·sier** \'dȯs-ˌyā, 'dȯ-sē-ˌā\ *n* [F, bundle of documents labeled on the back, dossier, fr. *dos* back, fr. OF, fr. L *dorsum*] : a file containing detailed records on a particular person or subject

¹**dot** \'dät\ *n* **1** : a small spot : SPECK **2** : a small round mark **3** : a precise point esp. in time ⟨be here on the ~⟩

²**dot** *vb* **dot·ted; dot·ting 1** : to mark with a dot ⟨~ an *i*⟩ **2** : to cover with or as if with dots — **dot·ter** *n*

**DOT** *abbr* Department of Transportation

**dot·age** \'dō-tij\ *n* : feebleness of mind esp. in old age : SENILITY

**dot·ard** \-tərd\ *n* : a person in dotage

**dot–com** \'dät-ˌkäm\ *n* : a company that

markets its products or services usu. exclusively via a website

**dote** \'dōt\ *vb* **dot·ed; dot·ing 1** : to be feebleminded esp. from old age **2** : to be lavish or excessive in one's attention, affection, or fondness ⟨*doted* on her niece⟩

**dot matrix** *n* : a rectangular arrangement of dots from which alphanumeric characters can be formed (as by a computer printer)

**Dou·ay Version** \dü-'ā-\ *n* : an English translation of the Vulgate used by Roman Catholics

¹**dou·ble** \'də-bəl\ *adj* [ME, fr. AF, fr. L *duplus*, fr. *duo* two + *-plus* multiplied by] **1** : TWOFOLD, DUAL ⟨serving a ~ function⟩ **2** : consisting of two members or parts **3** : being twice as great or as many **4** : folded in two **5** : having more than one whorl of petals ⟨~ roses⟩

²**double** *vb* **dou·bled; dou·bling 1** : to make, be, or become twice as great or as many **2** : to make a call in bridge that increases the trick values and penalties of (an opponent's bid) **3** : FOLD **4** : CLENCH **5** : to be or cause to be bent over **6** : to take the place of another **7** : to hit a double **8** : to turn sharply and suddenly; *esp* : to turn back on one's course

³**double** *adv* **1** : DOUBLY **2** : two together ⟨sleep ~⟩

⁴**double** *n* **1** : something twice another in size, strength, speed, quantity, or value **2** : a base hit that enables the batter to reach second base **3** : COUNTERPART, DUPLICATE; *esp* : a person who closely resembles another **4** : UNDERSTUDY, SUBSTITUTE **5** : a sharp turn : REVERSAL **6** : FOLD **7** : a combined bet placed on two different contests **8** *pl* : a game between two pairs of players **9** : an act of doubling in a card game

**double bond** *n* : a chemical bond in which two atoms in a molecule share two pairs of electrons

**double cross** *n* : an act of betraying or cheating esp. an associate — **dou·ble–cross** \ˌdə-bəl-'krȯs\ *vb* — **dou·ble–cross·er** *n*

**dou·ble–deal·ing** \ˌdə-bəl-'dē-liŋ\ *n* : DUPLICITY — **dou·ble–deal·er** \-'dē-lər\ *n* — **double–dealing** *adj*

**dou·ble–deck·er** \-'de-kər\ *n* : something having two decks, levels, or layers — **dou·ble–deck** \-ˌdek\ *or* **dou·ble–decked** \-ˌdekt\ *adj*

**dou·ble–dig·it** \ˌdə-bəl-'di-jət\ *adj* : amounting to 10 percent or more

**double down** *vb* : to become more tenacious, zealous, or resolute

**dou·ble en·ten·dre** \ˌdüb-əl-ä[n]-ˈtä[n]d, ˌdə-bəl-, -ˈtänd-rᵊ\ *n, pl* **double entendres** \*same or* -ˈtän-drəz\ [obs. F, lit., double meaning] : a word or expression capable of two interpretations with one usu. risqué

**dou·ble·head·er** \ˌdə-bəl-'he-dər\ *n* : two games played consecutively on the same day

**double helix** *n* : a helix or spiral consisting of two strands (as of DNA) in the surface of a cylinder which coil around its axis

**dou·ble–hung** \ˌdə-bəl-'həŋ\ *adj, of a window* : having an upper and a lower sash that can slide past each other

**dou·ble–joint·ed** \-'jȯin-təd\ *adj* : having a joint that permits an exceptional degree of freedom of motion of the parts joined ⟨a ~ finger⟩

**dou·ble–park** \ˌdə-bəl-'pärk\ *vb* : to park a vehicle beside a row of vehicles already parked parallel to the curb

**double play** *n* : a play in baseball by which two players are put out

**double pneumonia** *n* : pneumonia affecting both lungs

**double standard** *n* : a set of principles that applies differently and usu. more rigorously to one group of people or circumstances than to another

**dou·blet** \'də-blət\ *n* **1** : a man's close-fitting jacket worn in Europe esp. in the 16th century **2** : one of two similar or identical things

**dou·ble take** \'də-bəl-ˌtāk\ *n* : a delayed reaction to a surprising or significant situation after an initial failure to notice anything unusual

**dou·ble–talk** \-ˌtȯk\ *n* : language that appears to be meaningful but in fact is a mixture of sense and nonsense

**double up** *vb* : to share accommodations designed for one

**double whammy** *n* : a combination of two usu. adverse forces, circumstances, or effects

**dou·bloon** \ˌdə-'blün\ *n* : a former gold coin of Spain and Spanish America

**dou·bly** \'də-blē\ *adv* **1** : in a twofold manner **2** : to twice the degree ⟨~ glad⟩

¹**doubt** \'daùt\ *vb* **1** : to be uncertain about **2** : to lack confidence in : DISTRUST **3** : to consider unlikely — **doubt·able** *adj* — **doubt·er** *n*

²**doubt** *n* **1** : uncertainty of belief or opinion **2** : a condition causing uncertainty, hesitation, or suspense ⟨the outcome was in ~⟩ **3** : DISTRUST **4** : an inclination not to believe or accept

**doubt·ful** \'daùt-fəl\ *adj* **1** : QUESTIONABLE ⟨~ they knew what happened⟩ **2** : UNDECIDED ⟨the outcome of the election is ~⟩ — **doubt·ful·ly** *adv* — **doubt·ful·ness** *n*

¹**doubt·less** \'daùt-ləs\ *adv* **1** : without doubt **2** : PROBABLY

²**doubtless** *adj* : free from doubt : CERTAIN — **doubt·less·ly** *adv*

**douche** \'düsh\ *n* [F] **1** : a jet of fluid (as water) directed against a part or into a cavity of the body; *also* : a cleansing with a douche **2** : a device for giving douches — **douche** *vb*

**dough** \'dō\ *n* **1** : a mixture that consists of flour or meal and a liquid (as milk or water) and is stiff enough to knead or roll **2** : something resembling dough esp. in consistency **3** : MONEY — **doughy** \'dō-ē\ *adj*

**dough·boy** \-ˌbȯi\ *n* : an American infantryman esp. in World War I

**dough·nut** *also* **do·nut** \-(ˌ)nət\ *n* : a small usu. ring-shaped cake fried in fat

**dough·ty** \'daù-tē\ *adj* **dough·ti·er; -est** : ABLE, VALIANT ⟨a ~ warrior⟩

**Doug·las fir** \'də-gləs-\ *n* : a tall evergreen timber tree of the western U.S.

**dou·la** \'dü-lə\ *n* : a woman who provides assistance to a mother before, during, and just after childbirth

**do up** *vb* **1** : to prepare (as by cleaning) for use **2** : to wrap up **3** : CLOTHE, DECORATE **4** : FASTEN

**dour** \'daù(-ə)r, 'dù(r\ *adj* [ME, fr. L *durus* hard] **1** : STERN, HARSH **2** : OBSTINATE **3** : SULLEN — **dour·ly** *adv*

**douse** \'daùs, 'daùz\ *vb* **doused; dous·ing 1** : to plunge into water **2** : DRENCH **3** : EXTINGUISH ⟨~ a match⟩

¹**dove** \'dəv\ *n* **1** : any of numerous pigeons; *esp* : a small wild pigeon **2** : an advocate of peace or of a peaceful policy — **dov·ish** \'də-vish\ *adj*

²**dove** \'dōv\ *past of* DIVE

¹**dove·tail** \'dəv-ˌtāl\ *n* : something that resembles a dove's tail; *esp* : a flaring tenon and a mortise into which it fits tightly

²**dovetail** *vb* **1** : to join by means of dovetails **2** : to fit skillfully together to form a whole ⟨our plans ~ nicely⟩

**dow·a·ger** \'daù-i-jər\ *n* **1** : a widow owning property or a title from her deceased husband **2** : a dignified elderly woman

**dowdy** \'daù-dē\ *adj* **dowd·i·er; -est** : lacking neatness and charm : SHABBY, UNTIDY; *also* : lacking smartness

**dow·el** \'daù(-ə)l\ *n* **1** : a pin used for fastening together two pieces of wood **2** : a round rod (as of wood) — **dowel** *vb*

¹**dow·er** \'daù(-ə)r\ *n* [ME *dowere*, fr. AF *dower, douaire*, fr. ML *dotarium*, fr. L *dot-, dos* gift, marriage portion] **1** : the part of a deceased husband's real estate which the law gives for life to his widow **2** : DOWRY

²**dower** *vb* : to supply with a dower or dowry : ENDOW

**dow·itch·er** \'daù-i-chər\ *n* : any of several long-billed wading birds related to the sandpipers

¹**down** \'daùn\ *adv* [ME *doun*, fr. OE *dūne*, short for *adūne*, of *dūne*, lit., from (the) hill] **1** : toward or in a lower physical position **2** : to a lying or sitting position **3** : toward or to the ground, floor, or bottom **4** : as a down payment ⟨paid $5 ~⟩ **5** : on paper ⟨put ~ what he says⟩ **6** : in a direction that is the opposite of up **7** : SOUTH **8** : to or in a lower or worse condition or status **9** : from a past time **10** : to or in a state of less activity **11** : into defeat ⟨voted the motion ~⟩

²**down** *prep* : down in, on, along, or through : toward the bottom of ⟨fell ~ a hole⟩ ⟨lives ~ the road⟩

³**down** *vb* **1** : to go or cause to go or come down ⟨~ed a warplane⟩ **2** : DEFEAT **3** : to cause (a football) to be out of play **4** : CONSUME **3** ⟨~ed two beers⟩

⁴**down** *adj* **1** : occupying a low position; *esp* : lying on the ground **2** : directed or going downward **3** : being in a state of

reduced or low activity **4** : DEPRESSED, DEJECTED **5** : SICK ⟨~ with a cold⟩ **6** : FINISHED, DONE **7** : completely mastered ⟨got her lines ~⟩ **8** : being on record ⟨you're ~ for two tickets⟩

⁵**down** *n* **1** : a low or falling period (as in activity, emotional life, or fortunes) **2** : one of a series of attempts to advance a football **3** : a quark with a charge of -⅓ that is one of the constituents of the proton and neutron

⁶**down** *n* : a rolling usu. treeless upland with sparse soil — usu. used in pl.

⁷**down** *n* **1** : a covering of soft fluffy feathers; *also* : such feathers **2** : a downlike covering or material

**down·beat** \'daun-,bēt\ *n* : the downward stroke of a conductor indicating the principally accented note of a measure of music

**down·burst** \-,bərst\ *n* : a powerful downdraft usu. associated with a thunderstorm that is a hazard for low-flying aircraft; *also* : MICROBURST

**down·cast** \-,kast\ *adj* **1** : DEJECTED **2** : directed down ⟨a ~ glance⟩

**down·draft** \-,draft\ *n* : a downward current of gas (as air)

**down·er** \'daù-nər\ *n* **1** : a depressant drug; *esp* : BARBITURATE **2** : someone or something depressing

**down·fall** \'daun-,fol\ *n* **1** : a sudden fall (as from high rank) **2** : something that causes a downfall — **down·fall·en** \-,fo-lən\ *adj*

¹**down·grade** \'daun-,grād\ *n* **1** : a downward slope (as of a road) **2** : a decline toward a worse condition

²**downgrade** *vb* : to lower in quality, value, extent, or status

**down·heart·ed** \-'här-təd\ *adj* : DEJECTED

¹**down·hill** \'daun-'hil\ *adv* : toward the bottom of a hill — **downhill** \-,hil\ *adj*

²**down·hill** \-,hil\ *n* : the sport of skiing downhill usu. in a race against time

¹**down·load** \'daun-,lōd\ *n* : an act or instance of downloading something; *also* : the item downloaded

²**download** *vb* : to transfer (data) from a computer to another device — **download·able** \-,lō-də-bəl\ *adj*

**down payment** *n* : a part of the full price paid at the time of purchase or delivery with the balance to be paid later

**down·play** \'daun-,plā\ *vb* : DE-EMPHA-SIZE ⟨~ed the allegations⟩

**down·pour** \'daun-,pór\ *n* : a heavy rain

**down·range** \-'rānj\ *adv* : away from a launching site

¹**down·right** \-,rīt\ *adv* : THOROUGHLY

²**downright** *adj* **1** : ABSOLUTE, UTTER ⟨a ~ lie⟩ **2** : PLAIN, BLUNT ⟨a ~ man⟩

**down·shift** \-,shift\ *vb* : to shift an automotive vehicle into a lower gear

**down·size** \-,sīz\ *vb* : to reduce or undergo reduction in size or numbers

**down·spout** \-,spaùt\ *n* : a vertical pipe used to drain rainwater from a roof

**Down syndrome** \'daun-\ *or* **Down's syndrome** \'daunz-\ *n* : a birth defect characterized by mental retardation, slanting eyes, a broad short skull, broad hands with short fingers, and the presence of an extra chromosome

**down·stage** \'daun-'stāj\ *adv or adj* : toward or at the front of a theatrical stage — **down·stage** \-,stāj\ *n*

**down·stairs** \-'sterz\ *adv* : on or to a lower floor and esp. the main or ground floor — **down·stairs** \-,sterz\ *adj or n*

**down·stream** \-'strēm\ *adv or adj* : in the direction of flow of a stream

**down·stroke** \-,strōk\ *n* : a downward stroke

**down·swing** \-,swiŋ\ *n* **1** : a swing downward **2** : DOWNTURN

**down–to–earth** *adj* : PRACTICAL, REAL-ISTIC

**down·town** \'daun-,taun\ *n* : the main business district of a town or city — **downtown** \'daun-'taun\ *adj or adv*

**down·trod·den** \'daun-'trä-d²n\ *adj* : suffering oppression

**down·turn** \-,tərn\ *n* : a downward turn esp. in economic activity

¹**down·ward** \'daun-wərd\ *or* **downwards** \-wərdz\ *adv* **1** : from a higher to a lower place or condition **2** : from an earlier time **3** : from an ancestor or predecessor

²**downward** *adj* : directed toward or situated in a lower place or condition

**down·wind** \'daun-'wind\ *adv or adj* : in the direction that the wind is blowing

**downy** \'daú-nē\ *adj* **down·i·er; -est** : resembling or covered with down

**downy mildew** *n* : any of various parasitic fungi producing whitish masses esp. on the underside of plant leaves; *also* : a plant disease caused by downy mildew

**downy woodpecker** *n* : a small black-and-white woodpecker of No. America

**dow·ry** \'daú-(ə)r-ē\ *n, pl* **dowries** [ME *dowarie*, fr. AF, alter. of *dower, douaire* dower] : the property that a woman brings to her husband in marriage

**dowse** \'daúz\ *vb* **dowsed; dows·ing** : to use a divining rod esp. to find water — **dows·er** *n*

**dox·ol·o·gy** \däk-'sä-lə-jē\ *n, pl* **-gies** : a usu. short hymn of praise to God

**doy·en** \'dói-ən, 'dwä-,ya^n\ *n* : the senior or most experienced person in a group

**doy·enne** \dói-'yen, dwä-'yen\ *n* : a woman who is a doyen

**doy·ley** *chiefly Brit var of* DOILY

**doz** *abbr* dozen

**doze** \'dōz\ *vb* **dozed; doz·ing** : to sleep lightly — **doze** *n*

**doz·en** \'də-z²n\ *n, pl* **dozens** *or* **dozen** [ME *dozeine*, fr. AF *duzeine*, fr. *duze* twelve, fr. L *duodecim*, fr. *duo* two + *decem* ten] : a group of twelve — **doz·enth** \-z²nth\ *adj*

¹**DP** \,dē-'pē\ *n, pl* **DP's** *or* **DPs 1** : a displaced person **2** : DOUBLE PLAY

²**DP** *abbr* data processing

**dpt** *abbr* department

**DPT** *abbr* diphtheria-pertussis-tetanus (vaccines)

**dr** *abbr* **1** debtor **2** dram **3** drive **4** drum

**Dr** *abbr* doctor

**DR** *abbr* **1** dead reckoning **2** dining room

**drab** \'drab\ *adj* **drab·ber; drab·best 1** : being of a light olive-brown color **2** : DULL, MONOTONOUS, CHEERLESS — **drab·ly** *adv* — **drab·ness** *n*

**drach·ma** \'drak-mə\ *n, pl* **drach·mas** or **drach·mai** \-ˌmī\ or **drach·mae** \-ˌ(ˌ)mē\ : the former basic monetary unit of Greece

**dra·co·ni·an** \drā-'kō-nē-ən, drə-\ *adj, often cap* : CRUEL; *also* : SEVERE

**¹draft** \'draft, 'draft\ *n* **1** : the act of drawing or hauling **2** : the act or an instance of drinking or inhaling; *also* : the portion drunk or inhaled in one such act **3** : DOSE, POTION **4** : DELINEATION, PLAN, DESIGN; *also* : a preliminary sketch, outline, or version ⟨a rough ~ of a speech⟩ **5** : the act of drawing (as from a cask); *also* : a portion of liquid so drawn **6** : the depth of water a ship draws esp. when loaded **7** : a system for or act of selecting persons (as for sports teams or compulsory military service); *also* : the persons so selected **8** : an order for the payment of money drawn by one person or bank on another **9** : a heavy demand : STRAIN **10** : a current of air; *also* : a device to regulate air supply (as in a stove) — **on draft** : ready to be drawn from a receptacle ⟨beer *on draft*⟩

**²draft** *adj* **1** : used or adapted for drawing loads ⟨~ horses⟩ **2** : being or having been on draft ⟨~ beer⟩

**³draft** *vb* **1** : to select usu. on a compulsory basis; *esp* : to conscript for military service **2** : to draw the preliminary sketch, version, or plan of **3** : COMPOSE, PREPARE **4** : to draw off or away

**draft·ee** \draf-'tē, dräf-\ *n* : a person who is drafted

**drafts·man** \'draft-smən, 'dräft-\ *n* : a person who draws plans (as for buildings or machinery) — **drafts·man·ly** \-lē\ *adj*

**drafty** \'draf-tē, 'dräf-\ *adj* **draft·i·er; -est** : exposed to or abounding in drafts of air ⟨a ~ room⟩

**¹drag** \'drag\ *n* **1** : a device pulled along under water for detecting or gathering **2** : something (as a harrow or sledge) that is dragged along over a surface **3** : the act or an instance of dragging **4** : something that hinders progress; *also* : something boring ⟨thinks school is a ~⟩ **5** : STREET ⟨the main ~⟩ **6** : clothing typical of one sex worn by a member of the opposite sex

**²drag** *vb* **dragged; drag·ging 1** : HAUL **2** : to move or proceed with slowness or difficulty ⟨*dragged* himself out of bed⟩ ⟨the lecture *dragged* on⟩ **3** : to force into or out of some situation, condition, or course of action **4** : PROTRACT ⟨~ a story out⟩ **5** : to hang or lag behind **6** : to explore, search, or fish with a drag **7** : to trail along on the ground **8** : DRAW, PUFF ⟨~ on a cigarette⟩ **9** : to move (items on a computer screen) esp. by using a mouse — **drag·ger** *n* — **drag one's feet** *also* **drag one's heels** : to act slowly or with hesitation

**drag·net** \-ˌnet\ *n* **1** : NET, TRAWL **2** : a network of planned actions for pursuing and catching ⟨a police ~⟩

**drag·o·man** \'dra-gə-mən\ *n, pl* **-mans** or **-men** \-mən\ : an interpreter employed esp. in the Near East

**drag·on** \'dra-gən\ *n* [ME, fr. AF *dragun*, fr. L *dracon-, draco* serpent, dragon, fr. Gk *drakōn* serpent] : a fabulous animal usu. represented as a huge winged scaly serpent with a crested head and large claws

**drag·on·fly** \-ˌflī\ *n* : any of a group of large harmless 4-winged insects that hold the wings horizontal and unfolded in repose

**¹dra·goon** \drə-'gün, dra-\ *n* [F *dragon* dragon, dragoon, fr. MF] **1** : a heavily armed mounted soldier **2** : CAVALRYMAN

**²dragoon** *vb* : to force or attempt to force into submission : COERCE

**drag race** *n* : an acceleration contest between vehicles — **drag racer** *n*

**drag·ster** \'drag-stər\ *n* : a usu. high-powered vehicle used in a drag race

**drag strip** *n* : a site for drag races

**¹drain** \'drān\ *vb* **1** : to draw off or flow off gradually or completely **2** : to exhaust physically or emotionally ⟨~ed by the work⟩ **3** : to make or become gradually dry or empty ⟨~ a swamp⟩ **4** : to carry away the surface water of : discharge surface or surplus water **5** : EMPTY, EXHAUST ⟨~ed our savings⟩ — **drain·er** *n*

**²drain** *n* **1** : a means (as a channel or sewer) of draining **2** : the act of draining **3** : a gradual outflow; *also* : something causing an outflow ⟨a ~ on our savings⟩

**drain·age** \'drā-nij\ *n* **1** : the act or process of draining; *also* : something that is drained off **2** : a means for draining : DRAIN, SEWER **3** : an area drained

**drain·pipe** \'drān-ˌpīp\ *n* : a pipe for drainage

**drake** \'drāk\ *n* : a male duck

**¹dram** \'dram\ *n* **1** — see WEIGHT table **2** : FLUID DRAM **3** : a small drink

**²dram** \'dräm\ *n* — see MONEY table

**dra·ma** \'drä-mə, 'dra-\ *n* [LL, fr. Gk, deed, drama, fr. *dran* to do, act] **1** : a literary composition designed for theatrical presentation; *also* : a production (as a film) with a serious tone or subject **2** : dramatic art, literature, or affairs **3** : a series of events involving conflicting forces — **dra·mat·ic** \drə-'ma-tik\ *adj* — **dra·mat·i·cal·ly** \-ti-k(ə-)lē\ *adv* — **dra·ma·tist** \'dra-mə-tist, 'drä-\ *n*

**dram·a·ti·sa·tion, dra·ma·tise** *Brit var of* DRAMATIZATION, DRAMATIZE

**dra·ma·tize** \'dra-mə-ˌtīz, 'drä-\ *vb* **-tized; -tiz·ing 1** : to adapt for or be suitable for theatrical presentation **2** : to present or represent in a dramatic manner — **dram·a·ti·za·tion** \ˌdra-mə-tə-'zā-shən, ˌdrä-\ *n*

**dra·me·dy** \'drä-mə-ˌdē, 'dra-\ *n* : a comedy having dramatic moments

**drank** *past and past part of* DRINK

**¹drape** \'drāp\ *vb* **draped; drap·ing 1** : to cover or adorn with or as if with folds of cloth ⟨kings *draped* in robes⟩ **2** : to cause to hang or stretch out loosely or carelessly **3** : to arrange or become arranged in flowing lines or folds

²**drape** n **1** : CURTAIN **2** : arrangement in or of folds **3** : the cut or hang of clothing

**drap·er** \'drā-pər\ n, chiefly Brit : a dealer in cloth and sometimes in clothing and dry goods

**drap·ery** \'drā-pə-rē\ n, pl **-er·ies 1** Brit : DRY GOODS **2** : a decorative fabric esp. when hung loosely and in folds; also : hangings of heavy fabric used as a curtain

**dras·tic** \'dras-tik\ adj : HARSH, RIGOROUS, SEVERE ⟨∼ punishment⟩ — **dras·ti·cal·ly** \-ti-k(ə-)lē\ adv

**draught** \'draft\, **draughty** \'draf-tē\ chiefly Brit var of DRAFT, DRAFTY

**draughts** \'drafts\ n, Brit : CHECKERS

**draughts·man** chiefly Brit var of DRAFTS-MAN

**Dra·vid·i·an** \drə-'vi-dē-ən\ n : a language family of south Asia that includes the major literary languages of southern India

¹**draw** \'drò\ vb **drew** \'drü\; **drawn** \'dròn\; **draw·ing 1** : to cause to move toward a force exerted **2** : to cause to go in a certain direction ⟨drew him aside⟩ **3** : to move or go steadily or gradually ⟨night ∼s near⟩ **4** : ATTRACT, ENTICE **5** : PROVOKE, ROUSE ⟨drew enemy fire⟩ **6** : INHALE ⟨∼ a deep breath⟩ **7** : to bring or pull out ⟨drew a gun⟩ **8** : to cause to come out of a container or source ⟨∼ blood⟩ ⟨∼ water for a bath⟩ **9** : EVISCERATE **10** : to require (a specified depth) to float in **11** : ACCUMULATE, GAIN ⟨∼ing interest⟩ **12** : to take money from a place of deposit : WITHDRAW **13** : to receive regularly ⟨∼ a salary⟩ **14** : to take (cards) from a stack or the dealer **15** : to receive or take at random ⟨∼ a winning number⟩ **16** : to bend (a bow) by pulling back the string **17** : WRINKLE, SHRINK **18** : to change shape by or as if by pulling or stretching ⟨a face drawn with sorrow⟩ **19** : to leave (a contest) undecided : TIE **20** : DELINEATE, SKETCH **21** : to write out in due form : DRAFT ⟨∼ up a will⟩ **22** : FORMULATE ⟨∼ comparisons⟩ **23** : INFER ⟨∼ a conclusion⟩ **24** : to spread or elongate (metal) by hammering or by pulling through dies **25** : to produce or allow a draft or current of air ⟨the chimney ∼s well⟩ **26** : to swell out in a wind ⟨all sails ∼ing⟩ — **draw a blank** : to be unable to think of something — **draw the line** or **draw a line** : to fix an arbitrary boundary usu. between two things

²**draw** n **1** : the act, process, or result of drawing **2** : a lot or chance drawn at random **3** : a contest left undecided or deadlocked : TIE **4** : one that draws attention or patronage : ATTRACTION

**draw·back** \'drò-ˌbak\ n : DISADVANTAGE **2** ⟨the ∼s of rural living⟩

**draw·bridge** \-ˌbrij\ n : a bridge made to be raised, lowered, or turned to permit or deny passage

**draw·er** \'dròr, 'dró-ər\ n **1** : one that

draws **2** pl : an undergarment for the lower part of the body **3** : a sliding boxlike compartment (as in a table or desk)

**draw·ing** \'dró-iŋ\ n **1** : an act or instance of drawing; esp : an occasion when something is decided by drawing lots ⟨tonight's lottery ∼⟩ **2** : the act or art of making a figure, plan, or sketch by means of lines **3** : a representation made by drawing : SKETCH

**drawing card** n : DRAW 4

**drawing room** n : a formal reception room

**drawl** \'dròl\ vb : to speak or utter slowly with vowels greatly prolonged — **drawl** n

**draw on** vb : APPROACH ⟨night draws on⟩

**draw out** vb **1** : PROLONG **2** : to cause to speak freely

**draw·string** \'dró-ˌstriŋ\ n : a string, cord, or tape for use in closing a bag or controlling fullness in garments or curtains

**draw up** vb **1** : to prepare a draft or version of **2** : to pull oneself erect **3** : to bring or come to a stop

**dray** \'drā\ n : a strong low cart for carrying heavy loads

¹**dread** \'dred\ vb **1** : to fear greatly **2** : to feel extreme reluctance to meet or face

²**dread** n : great fear esp. of some harm to come

³**dread** adj **1** : causing great fear or anxiety ⟨a ∼ disease⟩ **2** : inspiring awe

**dread·ful** \'dred-fəl\ adj **1** : inspiring dread or awe : FRIGHTENING **2** : extremely distasteful, unpleasant, or shocking ⟨a ∼ accident⟩ — **dread·ful·ly** adv

**dread·locks** \'dred-ˌläks\ n pl : long braids of hair over the entire head

**dread·nought** \'dred-ˌnòt\ n : BATTLESHIP

¹**dream** \'drēm\ n [ME dreem, fr. OE drēam noise, joy, and ON draumr dream] **1** : a series of thoughts, images, or emotions occurring during sleep **2** : a dreamlike vision : DAYDREAM, REVERIE **3** : something notable for its beauty, excellence, or enjoyable quality **4** : IDEAL — **dream·like** \-ˌlīk\ adj — **dreamy** adj

²**dream** \'drēm\ vb **dreamed** \'dremt, 'drēmd\ or **dreamt** \'dremt\; **dream·ing 1** : to have a dream of **2** : to indulge in daydreams or fantasies : pass (time) in reverie or inaction **3** : IMAGINE — **dream·er** n

**dream·boat** \'drēm-ˌbōt\ n, slang : something highly desirable; esp : a very attractive person

**dream·land** \'drēm-ˌland\ n : an unreal delightful country that exists in imagination or in dreams

**dream up** vb : INVENT, CONCOCT

**dream·world** \-ˌwərld\ n : a world of illusion or fantasy

**drear** \'drir\ adj : DREARY

**drea·ry** \'drir-ē\ adj **drea·ri·er; -est** [ME drery, fr. OE drēorig sad, bloody, fr. drēor gore] **1** : DOLEFUL, SAD **2** : DISMAL, GLOOMY — **drea·ri·ly** \-ə-lē\ adv

¹**dredge** \'drej\ vb **dredged; dredg·ing** : to gather or search with or as if with a dredge — **dredg·er** n

**²dredge** n : a machine or barge for removing earth or silt

**³dredge** vb **dredged; dredg·ing** : to coat (food) by sprinkling (as with flour)

**dregs** \\'dregz\\ n pl 1 : SEDIMENT 1 2 : the most undesirable part ⟨the ∼ of humanity⟩

**drench** \\'drench\\ vb : to wet thoroughly

**¹dress** \\'dres\\ vb [ME, fr. AF dresser to direct, put right, fr. VL *directiare, fr. L directus direct] 1 : to make or set straight : ALIGN 2 : to prepare for use; esp : BUTCHER 3 : TRIM, EMBELLISH ⟨∼ a store window⟩ 4 : to put clothes on : CLOTHE; also : to put on or wear formal or fancy clothes 5 : to apply dressings or medicine to ⟨∼ a wound⟩ 6 : to arrange (the hair) by combing, brushing, or curling 7 : to apply fertilizer to ⟨∼ a field⟩ 8 : SMOOTH FINISH ⟨∼ leather⟩

**²dress** n 1 : APPAREL, CLOTHING ⟨casual ∼⟩ 2 : a garment usu. consisting of a one-piece bodice and skirt — **dress·mak·er** \\-ˌmā-kər\\ n — **dress·mak·ing** \\-ˌmā-kiŋ\\ n

**³dress** adj : suitable for a formal occasion; also : requiring formal dress

**dres·sage** \\drə-'säzh\\ n [F] : the execution by a trained horse of complex movements in response to barely perceptible signals from its rider

**dress down** vb : to scold severely

**¹dress·er** \\'dre-sər\\ n : a chest of drawers or bureau with a mirror

**²dresser** n : one that dresses

**dress·ing** \\'dre-siŋ\\ n 1 : the act or process of one who dresses 2 : a sauce for adding to a dish (as a salad) 3 : a seasoned mixture usu. used as stuffing 4 : material used to cover an injury (as a wound)

**dressing gown** n : a loose robe worn esp. while dressing or resting

**dressy** \\'dre-sē\\ adj **dress·i·er; -est** 1 : showy in dress 2 : STYLISH, SMART

**drew** past of DRAW

**¹drib·ble** \\'dri-bəl\\ vb **drib·bled; drib·bling** 1 : to fall or flow in drops : TRICKLE 2 : DROOL 3 : to propel by successive slight taps or bounces

**²dribble** n 1 : a small trickling stream or flow 2 : a drizzling shower 3 : the dribbling of a ball or puck

**drib·let** \\'dri-blət\\ n 1 : a trifling amount 2 : a drop of liquid

**dri·er** or **dry·er** \\'drī-ər\\ n 1 : a substance that speeds drying (as of paint or ink) 2 usu dryer : a device for drying

**¹drift** \\'drift\\ n 1 : the motion or course of something drifting; also : a gradual shift of position 2 : a mass of matter (as snow or sand) piled up esp. by wind 3 : earth, gravel, and rock deposited by a glacier 4 : a general underlying design or tendency : MEANING ⟨catch my ∼⟩

**²drift** vb 1 : to float or be driven along by or as if by a current of water or air ⟨∼ing logs⟩ 2 : to become piled up by wind or water ⟨∼ing snow⟩

**drift·er** \\'drif-tər\\ n : a person who moves about aimlessly

**drift net** n : a fishing net often miles in extent arranged to drift with the tide or current

**drift·wood** \\'drift-ˌwu̇d\\ n : wood drifted or floated by water

**¹drill** \\'dril\\ n 1 : a tool for boring holes 2 : the training of soldiers in marching and the handling of arms 3 : a regularly practiced exercise ⟨a shooting ∼⟩

**²drill** vb 1 : to instruct and exercise by repetition 2 : to train in or practice military drill 3 : to bore with a drill ⟨∼ a hole⟩ — **drill·er** n

**³drill** n 1 : a shallow furrow or trench in which seed is sown 2 : an agricultural implement for making furrows and dropping seed into them

**⁴drill** n : a firm cotton twilled fabric

**drill·mas·ter** \\'dril-ˌmas-tər\\ n : an instructor in military drill

**drill press** n : an upright drilling machine in which the drill is pressed to the work usu. by a hand lever

**drily** var of DRYLY

**¹drink** \\'driŋk\\ vb **drank** \\'draŋk\\; **drunk** \\'drəŋk\\ or **drank; drink·ing** 1 : to swallow liquid : IMBIBE 2 : ABSORB 3 : to take in through the senses ⟨∼ in the beautiful scenery⟩ 4 : to give or join in a toast 5 : to drink alcoholic beverages esp. to excess — **drink·able** adj — **drink·er** n

**²drink** n 1 : BEVERAGE; also : an alcoholic beverage 2 : a draft or portion of liquid 3 : excessive consumption of alcoholic beverages

**¹drip** \\'drip\\ vb **dripped; drip·ping** 1 : to fall or let fall in drops 2 : to let fall drops of moisture or liquid ⟨a dripping faucet⟩ 3 : to overflow with or as if with moisture ⟨clothes dripping with sweat⟩ ⟨stories dripping with irony⟩

**²drip** n 1 : a falling in drops 2 : liquid that falls, overflows, or is extruded in drops 3 : the sound made by or as if by falling drops

**¹drive** \\'drīv\\ vb **drove** \\'drōv\\; **driv·en** \\'dri-vən\\; **driv·ing** 1 : to urge, push, or force onward 2 : to carry through strongly ⟨∼ a bargain⟩ 3 : to set or keep in motion or operation 4 : to direct the movement or course of 5 : to convey in a vehicle ⟨drove her to school⟩ 6 : to bring into a specified condition ⟨the noise ∼s me crazy⟩ 7 : FORCE, COMPEL ⟨driven by hunger to steal⟩ 8 : to project, inject, or impress forcefully ⟨drove the lesson home⟩ 9 : to produce by opening a way ⟨∼ a well⟩ 10 : to progress with strong momentum ⟨a driving rain⟩ 11 : to propel an object of play (as a golf ball) by a hard blow — **driv·er** n

**²drive** n 1 : a trip in a carriage or automobile 2 : a driving or collecting of animals ⟨a cattle ∼⟩ 3 : the guiding of logs downstream to a mill 4 : the act of driving a ball; also : the flight of a ball 5 : DRIVEWAY 6 : a public road for driving (as in a park) 7 : the state of being hurried and under pressure 8 : an intensive campaign ⟨membership ∼⟩ 9 : the apparatus by which motion is imparted to a machine 10 : an offensive or aggressive move : a military attack **11** : NEED, LONGING ⟨the ~ to succeed⟩ **12** : dynamic quality **13** : a device for reading and writing on magnetic media (as magnetic tape or disks)

**drive–in** \'drī-ˌvin\ *adj* : accommodating patrons while they remain in their automobiles — **drive–in** *n*

¹**driv·el** \'dri-vəl\ *vb* -**eled** *or* -**elled**; -**el·ing** *or* -**el·ling 1** : DROOL, SLAVER **2** : to talk or utter stupidly, carelessly, or in an infantile way — **driv·el·er** *n*

²**drivel** *n* : NONSENSE

**drive·shaft** \'drīv-ˌshaft\ *n* : a shaft that transmits mechanical power

**drive–through** *also* **drive–thru** \'drīv-ˌthrü\ *adj* : designed for the service of patrons remaining in their automobiles — **drive–through** *also* **drive–thru** *n*

**drive·way** \-ˌwā\ *n* : a short private road leading from the street to a house, garage, or parking lot

¹**driz·zle** \'dri-zəl\ *n* : a fine misty rain

²**drizzle** *vb* **driz·zled**; **driz·zling** : to rain in very small drops

**drogue** \'drōg\ *n* : a small parachute for slowing down or stabilizing something (as a space capsule)

**droid** \'dróid\ *n* : ANDROID

**droll** \'drōl\ *adj* [F *drôle*, fr. *drôle* scamp, fr. MF *drôle*, fr. MD, imp] : having a humorous, whimsical, or odd quality ⟨a ~ expression⟩ — **droll·ery** \'drō-lə-rē\ *n* — **drol·ly** *adv*

**drom·e·dary** \'drä-mə-ˌder-ē\ *n, pl* -**dar·ies** [ME *dromedarie*, fr. MF *dromedaire*, fr. LL *dromedarius*, fr. L *dromad-, dromas*, fr. Gk, running] : CAMEL; *esp* : a domesticated one-humped camel of western Asia and northern Africa

¹**drone** \'drōn\ *n* **1** : a male honeybee **2** : one that lives on the labors of others : PARASITE **3** : an unmanned aircraft or ship guided by remote control **4** : one whose work is menial or monotonous

²**drone** *vb* **droned**; **dron·ing** : to sound with a low dull monotonous murmuring sound : speak monotonously

³**drone** *n* : a deep monotonous sound ⟨the ~ of engines⟩

**drool** \'drül\ *vb* **1** : to let liquid flow from the mouth **2** : to talk foolishly — **drool** *n*

**droop** \'drüp\ *vb* **1** : to hang or incline downward **2** : to sink gradually **3** : LANGUISH — **droop** *n* — **droopy** *adj*

¹**drop** \'dräp\ *n* **1** : the quantity of fluid that falls in one spherical mass **2** *pl* : a dose of medicine measured by drops **3** : a small quantity of drink **4** : the smallest practical unit of liquid measure **5** : something (as a pendant or a small round candy) that resembles a liquid drop **6** : FALL **7** : a decline in quantity or quality **8** : a descent by parachute **9** : the distance through which something drops **10** : a slot into which something is to be dropped **11** : something that drops or has dropped

²**drop** *vb* **dropped**; **drop·ping 1** : to fall or let fall in drops **2** : to let fall : LOWER ⟨~ a glove⟩ ⟨*dropped* his voice⟩ **3**

: SEND ⟨~ me a note⟩ **4** : to let go : DISMISS ⟨~ the subject⟩ **5** : MENTION ⟨~ a suggestion⟩ **6** : to knock down : cause to fall **7** : to go lower : become less ⟨prices *dropped*⟩ **8** : SPEND, LOSE ⟨~ $20⟩ ⟨*dropped* ten pounds⟩ **9** : to come or go unexpectedly or informally ⟨a friend *dropped* in⟩ **10** : to pass from one state into a less active one ⟨~ off to sleep⟩ **11** : to move downward or with a current **12** : QUIT ⟨*dropped* out of the race⟩ — **drop back** : to move toward the rear — **drop behind** : to fail to keep up

**drop–down** \'dräp-ˌdaun\ *adj* : PULL-DOWN

**drop·kick** \-'kik\ *n* : a kick made by dropping a ball to the ground and kicking it at the moment it starts to rebound — **drop·kick** *vb*

**drop·let** \'dräp-lət\ *n* : a tiny drop

**drop–off** \'dräp-ˌóf\ *n* **1** : a steep or perpendicular descent **2** : a marked decline ⟨a ~ in attendance⟩ **3** : an act or instance of delivering or depositing something ⟨~ points along the route⟩

**drop off** *vb* : to fall asleep

**drop out** *vb* : to withdraw from participation or membership; *esp* : to leave school before graduation — **drop·out** \'dräp-ˌaut\ *n*

**drop·per** \'drä-pər\ *n* **1** : one that drops **2** : a short glass tube with a rubber bulb used to measure out liquids by drops

**drop·pings** *n pl* : MANURE, DUNG

**drop·sy** \'dräp-sē\ *n* [ME *dropesie*, short for *ydropesie*, fr. AF, fr. L *hydropisis*, fr. Gk *hydrōps*, fr. *hydōr* water] : EDEMA — **drop·si·cal** \-si-kəl\ *adj*

**drop–top** \'dräp-ˌtäp\ *n* : CONVERTIBLE

**dross** \'dräs\ *n* **1** : the scum that forms on the surface of a molten metal **2** : waste matter : REFUSE

**drought** \'draut\ *also* **drouth** \'drauth\ *n* : a long spell of dry weather

¹**drove** \'drōv\ *n* **1** : a group of animals driven or moving in a body **2** : a large number : CROWD — usu. used in pl. ⟨tourists arriving in ~s⟩

²**drove** *past of* DRIVE

**drov·er** \'drō-vər\ *n* : one who drives domestic animals usu. to market

**drown** \'draun\ *vb* **drowned** \'draund\; **drown·ing 1** : to suffocate by submersion esp. in water **2** : to become drowned **3** : to cover with water **4** : to cause to be muted (as a sound) by a loud noise **5** : OVERPOWER, OVERWHELM

**drowse** \'drauz\ *vb* **drowsed**; **drows·ing** : DOZE — **drowse** *n*

**drowsy** \'drau-zē\ *adj* **drows·i·er**; -**est 1** : ready to fall asleep **2** : making one sleepy ⟨~ music⟩ — **drows·i·ly** \-zə-lē\ *adv* — **drows·i·ness** \-zē-nəs\ *n*

**drub** \'drəb\ *vb* **drubbed**; **drub·bing 1** : to beat severely **2** : to berate critically **3** : to defeat decisively

**drudge** \'drəj\ *vb* **drudged**; **drudg·ing** : to do hard, menial, or monotonous work — **drudge** *n* — **drudg·ery** \'drə-jə-rē\ *n*

¹**drug** \'drəg\ *n* **1** : a substance used as a medicine or in making medicine **2** : a

substance (as heroin or marijuana) that can cause addiction, habituation, or a marked change in mental status

²**drug** vb **drugged; drug·ging** : to affect with or as if with drugs; esp : to stupefy with a narcotic

**drug·gist** \'drə-gist\ n : a dealer in drugs and medicines; also : PHARMACIST

**drug·store** \'drəg-ˌstȯr\ n : a retail shop where medicines and miscellaneous articles are sold

**dru·id** \'drü-əd\ n, often cap : one of an ancient Celtic priesthood appearing in Irish, Welsh, and Christian legends as magicians and wizards

¹**drum** \'drəm\ n 1 : a percussion instrument usu. consisting of a hollow cylinder with a skin or plastic head stretched over one or both ends that is beaten with the hands or with a stick 2 : the sound of a drum; also : a similar sound 3 : a drum-shaped object (as a structure or container)

²**drum** vb **drummed; drum·ming** 1 : to beat a drum 2 : to sound rhythmically : THROB, BEAT 3 : to summon or enlist by or as if by beating a drum ⟨drummed into service⟩ 4 : EXPEL — usu. used with out 5 : to drive or force by steady effort ⟨~ the facts into memory⟩ 6 : to strike or tap repeatedly so as to produce rhythmic sounds

**drum·beat** \'drəm-ˌbēt\ n : a stroke on a drum or its sound

**drum major** n : the leader of a marching band

**drum ma·jor·ette** \-ˌmā-jə-'ret\ n : a girl or woman who leads a marching band; also : a baton twirler who accompanies a marching band

**drum·mer** \'drə-mər\ n 1 : one that plays a drum 2 : a traveling salesman

**drum·stick** \'drəm-ˌstik\ n 1 : a stick for beating a drum 2 : the lower segment of a fowl's leg

**drum up** vb 1 : to bring about by persistent effort ⟨drum up business⟩ 2 : INVENT, ORIGINATE ⟨drum up a new method⟩

¹**drunk** past part of DRINK

²**drunk** \'drəŋk\ adj 1 : having the faculties impaired by alcohol ⟨~ drivers⟩ 2 : dominated by an intense feeling ⟨~ with power⟩ 3 : of, relating to, caused by, or characterized by intoxication

³**drunk** n 1 : a period of excessive drinking 2 : a drunken person

**drunk·ard** \'drəŋ-kərd\ n : one who is habitually drunk

**drunk·en** \'drəŋ-kən\ adj 1 : DRUNK 2 : given to habitual excessive use of alcohol 3 : of, relating to, or resulting from intoxication ⟨a ~ brawl⟩ 4 : unsteady or lurching as if from intoxication ⟨walked with a ~ shuffle⟩ — **drunk·en·ly** adv — **drunk·en·ness** n

**drupe** \'drüp\ n : a partly fleshy fruit (as a plum or cherry) having one seed enclosed in a hard inner shell

¹**dry** \'drī\ adj **dri·er** \'drī-ər\; **dri·est** \-əst\ 1 : free or freed from water or liquid ⟨~ fruits⟩; also : not being in or under water

2 : characterized by lack of water or moisture ⟨~ climate⟩ 3 : lacking freshness : STALE 4 : devoid of natural moisture; also : THIRSTY 5 : no longer liquid or sticky ⟨the ink is ~⟩ 6 : not giving milk ⟨a ~ cow⟩ 7 : marked by the absence of alcoholic beverages ⟨a ~ dormitory⟩ 8 : prohibiting the making or distributing of alcoholic beverages 9 : not sweet ⟨~ wine⟩ 10 : solid as opposed to liquid ⟨~ groceries⟩ 11 : containing or employing no liquid 12 : SEVERE; also : UNINTERESTING, WEARISOME 13 : not productive ⟨a writer's ~ spell⟩ 14 : marked by a matter-of-fact, ironic, or terse manner of expression ⟨~ humor⟩ — **dri·ly** or **dry·ly** adv — **dry·ness** n

²**dry** vb **dried; dry·ing** : to make or become dry

³**dry** n, pl **drys** : PROHIBITIONIST

**dry·ad** \'drī-əd, -ˌad\ n : WOOD NYMPH

**dry cell** n : a battery whose contents are not spillable

**dry-clean** \'drī-ˌklēn\ vb : to clean (fabrics) chiefly with solvents other than water — **dry cleaning** n

**dry dock** \'drī-ˌdäk\ n : a dock that can be kept dry during ship construction or repair

**dryer** var of DRIER

**dry farm·ing** n : farming without irrigation in areas of limited rainfall — **dry-farm** vb — **dry farmer** n

**dry goods** \'drī-ˌgu̇dz\ n pl : cloth goods (as fabrics, ribbon, and ready-to-wear clothing)

**dry ice** n : solid carbon dioxide

**dry measure** n : a series of units of capacity for dry commodities — see METRIC SYSTEM table, WEIGHT table

**dry rot** n : decay of timber in which fungi consume the wood's cellulose

**dry run** n : REHEARSAL, TRIAL

**dry·wall** \'drī-ˌwȯl\ n : a wallboard consisting of fiberboard, paper, or felt over a plaster core

**Ds** symbol darmstadtium

**DSC** abbr 1 Distinguished Service Cross 2 doctor of surgical chiropody

**DSM** abbr Distinguished Service Medal

**DST** abbr daylight saving time

**DTP** abbr diphtheria, tetanus, pertussis (vaccines)

**d.t.'s** \ˌdē-'tēz\ n pl, often cap D&T : DELIRIUM TREMENS

**du·al** \'dü-əl, 'dyü-\ adj 1 : TWOFOLD, DOUBLE 2 : having a double character or nature — **du·al·ism** \-ə-ˌli-zəm\ n — **du·al·i·ty** \dü-'a-lə-tē, dyü-\ n

**du·ath·lon** \dü-'ath-lən, -ˌlän\ n : a long-distance race involving running and bicycling — **du·ath·lete** n

¹**dub** \'dəb\ vb **dubbed; dub·bing** 1 : to confer knighthood upon 2 : NAME, NICKNAME

²**dub** n : a clumsy person : DUFFER

³**dub** vb **dubbed; dub·bing** : to add (sound effects) to a motion picture or to a radio or television production

**du·bi·e·ty** \dü-'bī-ə-tē, dyü-\ n, pl **-eties** 1 : UNCERTAINTY 2 : a matter of doubt

**du·bi·ous** \'dü-bē-əs, 'dyü-\ adj 1 : UN-

CERTAIN **2** : QUESTIONABLE ⟨a ∼ choice⟩ **3** : feeling doubt : UNDECIDED — **du·bi·ous·ly** adv — **du·bi·ous·ness** n

**dub·ni·um** \'düb-nē-əm, 'dəb-\ n : a short-lived radioactive chemical element produced artificially

**du·cal** \'dü-kəl, 'dyü-\ adj : of or relating to a duke or dukedom

**duc·at** \'də-kət\ n : a gold coin formerly used in various European countries

**duch·ess** \'də-chəs\ n **1** : the wife or widow of a duke **2** : a woman holding the rank of duke in her own right

**duchy** \'də-chē\ n, pl **duch·ies** : the territory of a duke or duchess : DUKEDOM

¹**duck** \'dək\ n, pl **ducks** : any of various swimming birds related to but smaller than geese and swans

²**duck** vb **1** : to thrust or plunge under water **2** : to lower the head or body suddenly : BOW; also : DODGE **3** : to evade a duty, question, or responsibility ⟨∼ the issue⟩

³**duck** n **1** : a durable closely woven usu. cotton fabric **2** pl : light clothes made of duck

**duck·bill** \'dək-,bil\ n : PLATYPUS

**duck·ling** \-liŋ\ n : a young duck

**duck·pin** \-,pin\ n **1** : a small bowling pin shorter and wider in the middle than a tenpin **2** pl but sing in constr : a bowling game using duckpins

**duck sauce** n : a thick sweet sauce made with fruits and seasonings and used in Chinese cuisine

**duct** \'dəkt\ n **1** : a tube or canal for conveying a bodily fluid **2** : a pipe or tube through which a fluid (as air) flows — **duct·less** adj

**duc·tile** \'dək-t⁰l\ adj **1** : capable of being drawn out into wire or thread **2** : easily led : DOCILE — **duc·til·i·ty** \,dək-'ti-lə-tē\ n

**ductless gland** n : an endocrine gland

**duct tape** n : a cloth adhesive tape orig. designed for sealing certain ducts and joints — **duct–tape** vb

**dud** \'dəd\ n **1** pl : CLOTHING **2** : one that fails completely; also : a bomb or missile that fails to explode

**dude** \'düd, 'dyüd\ n **1** : DANDY **1** **2** : a city dweller; esp : an Easterner in the West **3** : FELLOW, GUY — sometimes used as an informal form of address

**dude ranch** n : a vacation resort offering activities (as horseback riding) typical of western ranches

**dud·geon** \'də-jən\ n : a fit or state of indignation ⟨in high ∼⟩

¹**due** \'dü, 'dyü\ adj [ME, fr. AF deu, pp. of dever to owe, fr. L debēre] **1** : owed or owing as a debt **2** : owed or owing as a right ⟨is ∼ a fair trial⟩ **3** : APPROPRIATE, FITTING ⟨with all ∼ respect⟩ **4** : SUFFICIENT, ADEQUATE **5** : REGULAR, LAWFUL ⟨∼ process of law⟩ **6** : ATTRIBUTABLE, ASCRIBABLE ⟨∼ to negligence⟩ **7** : PAYABLE ⟨a bill ∼ today⟩ **8** : SCHEDULED ⟨∼ to arrive soon⟩

²**due** n **1** : something that rightfully belongs to one ⟨give everyone their ∼⟩ **2** : DEBT **3** pl : FEES, CHARGES

³**due** adv : DIRECTLY, EXACTLY ⟨∼ north⟩

**du·el** \'dü-əl, 'dyü-\ n : a combat between two persons; esp : one fought with weapons in front of witnesses — **duel** vb — **du·el·ist** \-ə-list\ n

**du·en·de** \dü-'en-dā\ n [Sp dial., charm, fr. Sp, ghost, goblin, fr. duen de casa, prob. fr. dueño de casa owner of a house] : the power to attract through personal magnetism and charm

**du·en·na** \dü-'e-nə, dyü-\ n **1** : an elderly woman in charge of the younger ladies in a Spanish or Portuguese family **2** : CHAPERONE

**du·et** \dü-'et, dyü-\ n : a musical composition for two performers

**due to** prep : BECAUSE OF

**duf·fel bag** \'də-fəl-\ n : a soft oblong bag for personal belongings

**duf·fer** \'də-fər\ n : an incompetent or clumsy person

**dug** past and past part of DIG

**dug·out** \'dəg-,aùt\ n **1** : a boat made by hollowing out a log **2** : a shelter dug in the ground **3** : a low shelter facing a baseball diamond that contains the players' bench

**DUI** n : the act or crime of driving while under the influence of alcohol

**duke** \'dük, 'dyük\ n **1** : a sovereign ruler of a continental European duchy **2** : a nobleman of the highest rank; esp : a member of the highest grade of the British peerage **3** slang : FIST **1** ⟨put up your ∼s⟩ — **duke·dom** n

**dul·cet** \'dəl-sət\ adj **1** : pleasing to the ear **2** : AGREEABLE, SOOTHING

**dul·ci·mer** \'dəl-sə-mər\ n **1** : a stringed instrument of trapezoidal shape played with light hammers held in the hands **2** or **dul·ci·more** \-,mōr\ : an American folk instrument with three or four strings that is held on the lap and played by plucking or strumming

¹**dull** \'dəl\ adj **1** : mentally slow : STUPID **2** : slow in perception or sensibility **3** : LISTLESS **4** : slow in action : SLUGGISH ⟨a ∼ market⟩ **5** : lacking intensity ⟨a ∼ pain⟩; also : not resonant or ringing **6** : BLUNT **7** : lacking brilliance or luster ⟨a ∼ finish⟩ **8** : low in saturation and lightness ⟨∼ color⟩ **9** : CLOUDY, OVERCAST ⟨∼ weather⟩ **10** : TEDIOUS, UNINTERESTING ⟨a ∼ lecture⟩ — **dull·ness** also **dul·ness** n — **dul·ly** adv

²**dull** vb : to make or become dull

**dul·lard** \'də-lərd\ n : a stupid person

**du·ly** \'dü-lē, 'dyü-\ adv : in a due manner or time

**dumb** \'dəm\ adj **1** often offensive : lacking the power of speech **2** : SILENT **3** : STUPID — **dumb·ly** adv

**dumb·bell** \'dəm-,bel\ n **1** : a bar with weights at the end used for exercise **2** : one who is stupid

**dumb down** vb : to lower the level of intelligence or intellectual content of

**dumb·found** also **dum·found** \,dəm-'faùnd\ vb : ASTONISH, AMAZE — **dumb·found·ing·ly** \-'faùn-diŋ-lē\ adv

**dumb·wait·er** \'dəm-ˌwā-tər\ n : a small elevator for conveying food and dishes from one floor to another

**dum·my** \'də-mē\ n, pl **dummies** 1 : a person who cannot speak, *also* : a stupid person 2 : the exposed hand in bridge played by the declarer in addition to that player's own hand; *also* : a bridge player whose hand is a dummy 3 : an imitative substitute for something; *also* : MANNEQUIN 4 : one seeming to act alone but really acting for another 5 : a mock-up of matter to be reproduced esp. by printing

¹**dump** \'dəmp\ vb : to let fall in a pile ⟨∼ laundry on the floor⟩; *also* : to get rid of carelessly ⟨∼ed her boyfriend⟩

²**dump** n 1 : a place for dumping something (as refuse) 2 : a reserve supply; *also* : a place where such supplies are kept ⟨an ammunition ∼⟩ 3 : a messy or objectionable place

**dump·ing** \'dəm-piŋ\ n : the selling of goods in quantity at below market price

**dump·ling** \'dəm-pliŋ\ n 1 : a small mass of boiled or steamed dough 2 : a dessert of fruit baked in biscuit dough

**dumps** \'dəmps\ n pl : a gloomy state of mind : low spirits ⟨in the ∼⟩

**dump truck** n : a truck for transporting and dumping bulk material

**dumpy** \'dəm-pē\ adj **dump·i·er; -est** 1 : short and thick in build 2 : SHABBY

¹**dun** \'dən\ n : a brownish dark gray

²**dun** vb **dunned; dun·ning** 1 : to make persistent demands for payment 2 : PLAGUE, PESTER — **dun** n

**dunce** \'dəns\ n [John *Duns* Scotus, whose once accepted writings were ridiculed in the 16th cent.] : a slow stupid person

**dun·der·head** \'dən-dər-ˌhed\ n : DUNCE, BLOCKHEAD

**dune** \'dün, 'dyün\ n : a hill or ridge of sand piled up by the wind

**dune buggy** n : a motor vehicle with oversize tires for use on sand

¹**dung** \'dəŋ\ n : MANURE

²**dung** vb : to dress (land) with dung

**dun·ga·ree** \ˌdəŋ-gə-'rē\ n 1 : a heavy coarse cotton twill; *esp* : blue denim 2 pl : clothes made of blue denim

**dun·geon** \'dən-jən\ n [ME *dongeoun* fortress, prison, fr. AF *donjun*, fr. VL *\*dominion-*, *\*domnio* keep, mastery, fr. L *dominus* lord] : a dark prison commonly underground

**dung·hill** \'dəŋ-ˌhil\ n : a manure pile

**dunk** \'dəŋk\ vb 1 : to dip or submerge temporarily in liquid 2 : to submerge oneself in water 3 : to shoot a basketball into the basket from above the rim

**duo** \'dü-(ˌ)ō, 'dyü-\ n, pl **du·os** 1 : DUET 2 : PAIR 3

**duo·dec·i·mal** \ˌdü-ə-'de-sə-məl, ˌdyü-\ adj : of, relating to, or being a system of numbers with a base of 12

**du·o·de·num** \ˌdü-ə-'dē-nəm, ˌdyü-, dü-'ä-də-nəm, dyü-\ n, pl **-de·na** \-'dē-nə, -də-nə\ or **-denums** : the first part of the small intestine extending from the stomach to the jejunum — **du·o·de·nal** \-'dēn-ᵊl, -də-nᵊl\ adj

**dup** abbr 1 duplex 2 duplicate

¹**dupe** \'düp, 'dyüp\ n : one who is easily deceived or cheated : FOOL

²**dupe** vb **duped; dup·ing** : to make a dupe of : DECEIVE, FOOL

**du·ple** \'dü-pəl, 'dyü-\ adj : having two beats or a multiple of two beats to the measure ⟨∼ time⟩

¹**du·plex** \'dü-ˌpleks, 'dyü-\ adj : DOUBLE

²**duplex** n : something duplex; *esp* : a 2-family house

¹**du·pli·cate** \'dü-pli-kət, 'dyü-\ adj 1 : consisting of or existing in two corresponding or identical parts or examples 2 : being the same as another

²**du·pli·cate** \'dü-pli-ˌkāt, 'dyü-\ vb **-cat·ed; -cat·ing** 1 : to make double or twofold 2 : to make a copy of — **du·pli·ca·tion** \ˌdü-pli-'kā-shən, ˌdyü-\ n

³**du·pli·cate** \-kət\ n : a thing that exactly resembles another in appearance, pattern, or content : COPY

**du·pli·ca·tor** \'dü-pli-ˌkā-tər, 'dyü-\ n : COPIER

**du·plic·i·ty** \dü-'pli-sə-tē, dyü-\ n, pl **-ties** : the disguising of true intentions by deceptive words or action — **du·plic·i·tous** \-təs\ adj — **du·plic·i·tous·ly** adv

**du·ra·ble** \'dur-ə-bəl, 'dyur-\ adj : able to exist for a long time without significant deterioration ⟨∼ goods⟩ — **du·ra·bil·i·ty** \ˌdur-ə-'bi-lə-tē, ˌdyur-\ n

**du·rance** \'dur-əns, 'dyur-\ n : restraint 'by or as if by physical force ⟨held in ∼ vile⟩

**du·ra·tion** \du-'rā-shən, dyu-\ n : the time during which something exists or lasts

**du·ress** \du-'res, dyu-\ n : compulsion by threat ⟨confession made under ∼⟩

**dur·ing** \'dur-iŋ, 'dyur-\ prep 1 : THROUGHOUT ⟨swims every day ∼ the summer⟩ 2 : at some point in ⟨broke in ∼ the night⟩

**dusk** \'dəsk\ n 1 : the darker part of twilight esp. at night 2 : partial darkness

**dusky** \'dəs-kē\ adj **dusk·i·er; -est** 1 : somewhat dark in color 2 : SHADOWY — **dusk·i·ly** \-kə-lē\ adv — **dusk·i·ness** n

¹**dust** \'dəst\ n 1 : fine particles of matter 2 : the particles into which something disintegrates 3 : something worthless 4 : the surface of the ground — **dust·less** adj — **dusty** adj

²**dust** vb 1 : to make free of or remove dust ⟨∼ the furniture⟩ 2 : to sprinkle with fine particles ⟨popcorn ∼ed with salt⟩ 3 : to sprinkle in the form of dust 4 : to defeat badly

**dust bowl** n : a region suffering from long droughts and dust storms

**dust devil** n : a small whirlwind containing sand or dust

**dust·er** \'dəs-tər\ n 1 : one that removes dust 2 : a dress-length housecoat 3 : one that scatters fine particles; *esp* : a device for applying insecticides to crops

**dust·pan** \'dəst-ˌpan\ n : a flat-ended pan for sweepings

**dust storm** *n* : a violent wind carrying dust across a dry region

**dutch** \'dəch\ *adv, often cap* : with each person paying his or her own way ⟨go ~⟩

**Dutch** \'dəch\ *n* **1 Dutch** *pl* : the people of the Netherlands **2** : the language of the Netherlands — **Dutch** *adj* — **Dutch-man** \-mən\ *n*

**Dutch elm disease** *n* : a fungus disease of elms characterized by yellowing of the foliage, defoliation, and death

**dutch treat** *n, often cap D* : an entertainment (as a meal) for which each person pays his or her own way — **dutch treat** *adv, often cap D*

**du·te·ous** \'dü-tē-əs, 'dyü-\ *adj* : DUTIFUL, OBEDIENT

**du·ti·able** \'dü-tē-ə-bəl, 'dyü-\ *adj* : subject to a duty ⟨~ imports⟩

**du·ti·ful** \'dü-ti-fəl, 'dyü-\ *adj* **1** : motivated by a sense of duty ⟨a ~ son⟩ **2** : coming from or showing a sense of duty ⟨~ affection⟩ — **du·ti·ful·ly** *adv* — **du·ti·ful·ness** *n*

**du·ty** \'dü-tē, 'dyü-\ *n, pl* **duties 1** : conduct or action required by one's occupation or position **2** : assigned service or business; *esp* : active military service **3** : a moral or legal obligation **4** : TAX **5** : the service required (as of a machine) : USE ⟨a heavy-*duty* tire⟩

**DV** *abbr* **1** [L *Deo volente*] God willing **2** Douay Version

**DVD** \,dē-,vē-'dē\ *n* [*digital video disk*] : a high-capacity optical disk format; *also* : an optical disk using such a format

**DVM** *abbr* doctor of veterinary medicine

**DVR** \,dē-,vē-'är\ *n* [*digital video recorder*] : a device that records and plays back television programs

¹**dwarf** \'dwȯrf\ *n, pl* **dwarfs** \'dwȯrfs\ *also* **dwarves** \'dwȯrvz\ : one that is much below normal size — **dwarf·ish** *adj* — **dwarf·ism** \'dwȯr-,fi-zəm\ *n*

²**dwarf** *vb* **1** : to restrict the growth or development of : STUNT **2** : to cause to appear smaller ⟨*dwarfed* by comparison⟩

**dwarf planet** *n* : a spherical celestial body that orbits the sun but is too small to disturb other objects from its orbit

**dwell** \'dwel\ *vb* **dwelt** \'dwelt\ *or* **dwelled** \'dweld, 'dwelt\; **dwell·ing** [ME, fr. OE *dwellan* to go astray, hinder] **1** : ABIDE, REMAIN **2** : RESIDE, EXIST **3** : to keep the attention directed **4** : to write or speak insistently — used with *on* or *upon* — **dwell·er** *n*

**dwell·ing** \'dwe-liŋ\ *n* : RESIDENCE

**DWI** \,dē-,dəb-əl-(,)yü-'ī\ *n* [*driving while intoxicated*] : DUI

**dwin·dle** \'dwin-d°l\ *vb* **dwin·dled; dwin·dling** : to make or become steadily less : DIMINISH

**dwt** *abbr* pennyweight

**Dy** *symbol* dysprosium

**dyb·buk** \'di-bək\ *n, pl* **dyb·bu·kim** \,di-bu̇-'kēm\ *also* **dybbuks** : a wandering soul believed in Jewish folklore to enter and possess a person

¹**dye** \'dī\ *n* **1** : color produced by dyeing **2** : material used for coloring or staining

²**dye** *vb* **dyed; dye·ing 1** : to impart a new color to esp. by impregnating with a dye **2** : to take up or impart color in dyeing — **dy·er** \'dī-(ə)r\ *n*

**dye·stuff** \'dī-,stəf\ *n* : DYE 2

**dying** *pres part of* DIE

**dyke** *chiefly Brit var of* DIKE

**dy·nam·ic** \dī-'na-mik\ *also* **dy·nam·i·cal** \-mi-kəl\ *adj* : of or relating to physical force producing motion : ENERGETIC, FORCEFUL

¹**dy·na·mite** \'dī-nə-,mīt\ *n* : an explosive made of nitroglycerin absorbed in a porous material; *also* : an explosive made without nitroglycerin

²**dynamite** *vb* **-mit·ed; -mit·ing** : to blow up with dynamite

³**dynamite** *adj* : TERRIFIC, WONDERFUL

**dy·na·mo** \'dī-nə-,mō\ *n, pl* **-mos 1** : an electrical generator **2** : a forceful energetic individual

**dy·na·mom·e·ter** \,dī-nə-'mä-mə-tər\ *n* : an instrument for measuring mechanical power (as of an engine)

**dy·nas·ty** \'dī-nəs-tē, -,nas-\ *n, pl* **-ties 1** : a succession of rulers of the same family **2** : a powerful group or family that maintains its position for a long time — **dy·nas·tic** \dī-'nas-tik\ *adj*

**dys·en·tery** \'di-s°n-,ter-ē\ *n, pl* **-ter·ies** : a disease marked by diarrhea with blood and mucus in the feces; *also* : DIARRHEA

**dys·func·tion** *also* **dis·func·tion** \dis-'fəŋk-shən\ *n* **1** : impaired or abnormal functioning ⟨liver ~⟩ **2** : abnormal or unhealthy behavior within a group ⟨family ~⟩ — **dys·func·tion·al** \-shə-nəl\ *adj*

**dys·lex·ia** \dis-'lek-sē-ə\ *n* : a learning disability marked by difficulty in reading, writing, and spelling — **dys·lex·ic** \-'sik\ *adj or n*

**dys·pep·sia** \dis-'pep-shə, -sē-ə\ *n* : INDIGESTION — **dys·pep·tic** \-'pep-tik\ *adj or n*

**dys·pla·sia** \dis-'plā-zh(ē-)ə\ *n* : abnormal growth or development

**dys·pro·si·um** \dis-'prō-zē-əm\ *n* : a metallic chemical element that forms highly magnetic compounds

**dys·tro·phy** \'dis-trə-fē\ *n, pl* **-phies** : a disorder involving atrophy of muscular tissue; *esp* : MUSCULAR DYSTROPHY

**dz** *abbr* dozen

¹e \'ē\ n, pl e's or es \'ēz\ often cap 1 : the 5th letter of the English alphabet 2 : the base of the system of natural logarithms having the approximate value 2.71828 3 : a grade rating a student's work as poor or failing

²e abbr, often cap 1 east; eastern 2 error 3 excellent

e- comb form : electronic ⟨e-commerce⟩

ea abbr each

¹each \'ēch\ adj : being one of the class named ⟨∼ player⟩

²each pron : every individual one

³each adv : APIECE ⟨cost five cents ∼⟩

each other pron : each of two or more in reciprocal action or relation ⟨looked at each other⟩

ea·ger \'ē-gər\ adj : marked by urgent or enthusiastic desire or interest ⟨∼ to learn⟩ ♦ Synonyms AVID, ANXIOUS, ARDENT, KEEN — ea·ger·ly adv — ea·ger·ness n

¹ea·gle \'ē-gəl\ n 1 : a large bird of prey related to the hawks 2 : a score of two under par on a hole in golf

²eagle vb ea·gled; ea·gling : to score an eagle on a golf hole

ea·glet \'ē-glət\ n : a young eagle

-ean — see -AN

E and OE abbr errors and omissions excepted

¹ear \'ir\ n 1 : the organ of hearing; also : the outer part of this in a vertebrate 2 : something resembling a mammal's ear in shape, position, or function 3 : an ability to understand and appreciate something heard ⟨a good ∼ for music⟩ 4 : sympathetic attention

²ear n : the fruiting spike of a cereal (as wheat or corn)

ear·ache \-,āk\ n : an ache or pain in the ear

ear·drum \-,drəm\ n : a thin membrane that receives and transmits sound waves in the ear

eared \'ird\ adj : having ears esp. of a specified kind or number ⟨a long-eared dog⟩

ear·ful \'ir-,ful\ n : a verbal outpouring (as of news, gossip, or complaint)

earl \'ərl\ n [ME erl, fr. OE eorl warrior, nobleman] : a member of the British peerage ranking below a marquess and above a viscount — earl·dom \-dəm\ n

ear·lobe \'ir-,lōb\ n : the pendent part of the ear

¹ear·ly \'ər-lē\ adv ear·li·er; -est : at an early time (as in a period or series)

²early adj ear·li·er; -est 1 : of, relating to, or occurring near the beginning 2 : ANCIENT, PRIMITIVE ⟨∼ tools⟩ 3 : occurring before the usual time ⟨an ∼ breakfast⟩; also : occurring in the near future

¹ear·mark \'ir-,märk\ n : an identification mark (as on the ear of an animal); also : a distinguishing mark ⟨∼s of poverty⟩

²earmark vb 1 : to mark with an earmark 2 : to designate for a specific purpose ⟨money ∼ed for education⟩

ear·muff \-,məf\ n : one of a pair of ear coverings worn to protect against cold

earn \'ərn\ vb 1 : to receive as a return for service 2 : DESERVE, MERIT ♦ Synonyms GAIN, SECURE, GET, OBTAIN, ACQUIRE, WIN — earn·er n

earned run n : a run in baseball that scores without benefit of an error before the fielding team has had a chance to make the third putout of the inning

earned run average n : the average number of earned runs per game scored against a pitcher in baseball

¹ear·nest \'ər-nəst\ n : an intensely serious state of mind ⟨spoke in ∼⟩

²earnest adj 1 : seriously intent and sober ⟨an ∼ face⟩ ⟨an ∼ attempt⟩ 2 : GRAVE, IMPORTANT ♦ Synonyms SOLEMN, SEDATE, STAID — ear·nest·ly adv — ear·nest·ness n

³earnest n 1 : something of value given by a buyer to a seller to bind a bargain 2 : PLEDGE

earn·ings \'ər-ninz\ n pl 1 : something (as wages) earned 2 : the balance of revenue after deduction of costs and expenses

ear·phone \'ir-,fōn\ n : a device that reproduces sound and is worn over or in the ear

ear·piece \-,pēs\ n : a part of an instrument which is placed against or in the ear; esp : EARPHONE

ear·plug \-,pləg\ n : a protective device for insertion into the opening of the ear

ear·ring \-,rin\ n : an ornament for the earlobe

ear·shot \-,shät\ n : range of hearing

ear·split·ting \-,spli-tin\ adj : intolerably loud or shrill

earth \'ərth\ n 1 : SOIL, DIRT 2 : LAND, GROUND 3 often cap : the planet on which we live that is 3d in order from the sun

earth·en \'ər-thən\ adj : made of earth or baked clay

earth·en·ware \-,wer\ n : slightly porous opaque pottery fired at low heat

earth·ling \'ərth-lin\ n : an inhabitant of the earth

earth·ly \'ərth-lē\ adj : having to do with the earth esp. as distinguished from heaven — earth·li·ness n

earth·quake \-,kwāk\ n : a shaking or trembling of a portion of the earth

earth science n : any of the sciences (as geology or meteorology) that deal with the earth or one of its parts

earth·shak·ing \'ərth-,shā-kin\ adj : of great importance : MOMENTOUS

earth·ward \-wərd\ also earth·wards \-wərdz\ adv : toward the earth

earth·work \'ərth-,wərk\ n : an embankment or fortification of earth

**earth·worm** \-ˌwərm\ n : a long segmented worm found in damp soil

**earthy** \'ər-thē\ adj **earth·i·er; -est 1** : of, relating to, or consisting of earth; *also* : suggesting earth ⟨~ flavors⟩ **2** : PRACTICAL **4 3** : COARSE, GROSS ⟨~ humor⟩ — **earth·i·ness** n

**ear·wax** \'ir-ˌwaks\ n : the yellow waxy secretion from the ear

**ear·wig** \-ˌwig\ n : any of numerous insects with slender antennae and a pair of appendages resembling forceps at the end of the body

¹**ease** \'ēz\ n **1** : comfort of body or mind **2** : naturalness of manner **3** : freedom from difficulty or effort ♦ *Synonyms* RELAXATION, REST, REPOSE, LEISURE

²**ease** vb **eased; eas·ing 1** : to relieve from distress **2** : to lessen the pressure or tension of **3** : to make or become less difficult ⟨~ credit⟩

**ea·sel** \'ē-zəl\ n [Dutch *ezel*, lit., ass] : a frame for supporting something (as an artist's canvas)

¹**east** \'ēst\ adv : to or toward the east

²**east** adj **1** : situated toward or at the east ⟨an ~ window⟩ **2** : coming from the east ⟨an ~ wind⟩

³**east** n **1** : the general direction of sunrise **2** : the compass point directly opposite to west **3** cap : regions or countries east of a specified or implied point — **east·er·ly** \'ē-stər-lē\ adv or adj — **east·ward** adv or adj — **east·wards** adv

**Eas·ter** \'ē-stər\ n : a church feast observed on a Sunday in March or April in commemoration of Christ's resurrection

**east·ern** \'ē-stərn\ adj **1** often cap : of, relating to, or characteristic of a region designated East **2** cap : of, relating to, or being the Christian churches originating in the Church of the Eastern Roman Empire **3** : lying toward or coming from the east — **East·ern·er** n

**easy** \'ē-zē\ adj **eas·i·er; -est 1** : marked by ease ⟨an ~ life⟩; esp : not causing distress or difficulty ⟨~ tasks⟩ **2** : MILD, LENIENT ⟨be ~ on him⟩ **3** : GRADUAL ⟨an ~ slope⟩ **4** : LEISURELY ⟨an ~ pace⟩ **5** : free from pain, trouble, or worry **6** : COMFORTABLE ⟨an ~ chair⟩ **7** : showing ease : NATURAL ⟨an ~ manner⟩ — **eas·i·ly** \'ē-zə-lē\ adv — **eas·i·ness** \-zē-nəs\ n

**easy·go·ing** \ˌē-zē-'gō-iŋ\ adj : relaxed and casual in style or manner

**eat** \'ēt\ vb **ate** \'āt\; **eat·en** \'ēt-ᵊn\; **eat·ing 1** : to take in as food : take food **2** : to use up : DEVOUR **3** : CORRODE — **eat·able** adj or n — **eat·er** n

**eat·ery** \'ē-tə-rē\ n, pl **-er·ies** : LUNCHEONETTE, RESTAURANT

**eaves** \'ēvz\ n pl : the overhanging lower edge of a roof

**eaves·drop** \'ēvz-ˌdräp\ vb : to listen secretly — **eaves·drop·per** n

¹**ebb** \'eb\ n **1** : the flowing back from shore of water brought in by the tide **2** : a point or state of decline

²**ebb** vb **1** : to recede from the flood **2** : DECLINE ⟨his fortunes ~ed⟩

**EBCDIC** \'eb-sə-ˌdik\ n [extended *b*inary *c*oded *d*ecimal *i*nterchange *c*ode] : a computer code for representing alphanumeric information

**Ebo·la** \ē-'bō-lə\ n : an often fatal hemorrhagic fever caused by a virus (**Ebola virus**) of African origin

¹**eb·o·ny** \'e-bə-nē\ n, pl **-nies** : a hard heavy blackish wood of various tropical trees related to the persimmon

²**ebony** adj **1** : made of or resembling ebony **2** : BLACK, DARK

**e-book** \'ē-ˌbu̇k\ n : a book in digital form for display on a computer screen or a handheld device

**ebul·lient** \i-'bu̇l-yənt, -'bəl-\ adj **1** : BOILING, AGITATED **2** : EXUBERANT — **ebul·lience** \-yəns\ n

**EC** abbr European Community

**ec·cen·tric** \ik-'sen-trik\ adj **1** : deviating from a usual or accepted pattern **2** : deviating from a circular path ⟨~ orbits⟩ **3** : set with axis or support off center ⟨an ~ cam⟩; also : being off center ♦ *Synonyms* ERRATIC, QUEER, SINGULAR, CURIOUS, ODD — **eccentric** n — **ec·cen·tri·cal·ly** \-tri-k(ə-)lē\ adv — **ec·cen·tric·i·ty** \ˌek-ˌsen-'tri-sə-tē\ n

**Eccles** abbr Ecclesiastes

**Ec·cle·si·as·tes** \i-ˌklē-zē-'as-tēz\ n — see BIBLE table

**ec·cle·si·as·tic** \i-ˌklē-zē-'as-tik\ n : CLERGYMAN

**ec·cle·si·as·ti·cal** \-ti-kəl\ or **ec·cle·si·as·tic** \-tik\ adj : of or relating to a church esp. as an institution ⟨~ art⟩ — **ec·cle·si·as·ti·cal·ly** \-ti-k(ə-)lē\ adv

**Ec·cle·si·as·ti·cus** \i-ˌklē-zē-'as-ti-kəs\ n — see BIBLE table

**Ecclus** abbr Ecclesiasticus

**ECG** abbr electrocardiogram

**ech·e·lon** \'e-shə-ˌlän\ n [F *échelon*, lit., rung of a ladder] **1** : a steplike arrangement (as of troops or airplanes) **2** : a level (as of authority or responsibility) within an organization

**ech·i·na·cea** \ˌe-ki-'nā-sē-ə, -shə\ n : the dried root of three composite herbs that is used primarily in herbal remedies to boost the immune system; also : any of these herbs

**echi·no·derm** \i-'kī-nə-ˌdərm\ n : any of a phylum of marine animals (as starfishes and sea urchins) having similar body parts (as the arms of a starfish) arranged around a central axis and often having a calcium-containing outer skeleton

**echo** \'e-kō\ n, pl **ech·oes** also **ech·os** : repetition of a sound caused by a reflection of the sound waves; also : the reflection of a radar signal by an object — **echo** vb — **echo·ic** \e-'kō-ik\ adj

**echo·lo·ca·tion** \ˌe-kō-lō-'kā-shən\ n : a process for locating distant or invisible objects by sound waves reflected back to the sender (as a bat) from the objects

**echt** \'ekt\ adj [G] : TRUE, GENUINE ⟨an ~ New Yorker⟩

**éclair** \ā-'kler\ n [F, lit., lightning] : an oblong shell of light pastry with whipped cream or custard filling

**éclat** \ā-ˈklä\ n [F] **1** : a dazzling effect or success **2** : ACCLAIM

**eclec·tic** \e-ˈklek-tik\ adj : selecting or made up of what seems best of varied sources — **eclectic** n — **eclec·ti·cism** \-ˈklek-tə-ˌsi-zəm\ n

**¹eclipse** \i-ˈklips\ n **1** : the total or partial obscuring of one heavenly body by another; also : a passing into the shadow of a heavenly body **2** : a falling into obscurity or decline ⟨the author's fame has been in ~⟩

**²eclipse** vb **eclipsed; eclips·ing** : to cause an eclipse of; also : SURPASS

**eclip·tic** \i-ˈklip-tik\ n : the great circle of the celestial sphere that is the apparent path of the sun

**ec·logue** \ˈek-ˌlog, -ˌläg\ n : a pastoral poem

**ECM** abbr European Common Market

**ecol** abbr ecological; ecology

**E. coli** \ˌē-ˈkō-ˌlī\ n, pl **E. coli** : a rod-shaped bacterium that sometimes causes intestinal illness

**ecol·o·gy** \i-ˈkä-lə-jē, e-\ n, pl **-gies** [G Ökologie, fr. Gk oikos house + logos word] **1** : a branch of science concerned with the relationships between organisms and their environment **2** : the pattern of relations between one or more organisms and the environment — **eco·log·i·cal** \ˌē-kə-ˈlä-ji-kəl, ˌe-\ also **eco·log·ic** \-jik\ adj — **eco·log·i·cal·ly** \-ji-k(ə-)lē\ adv — **ecol·o·gist** \i-ˈkä-lə-jist, e-\ n

**e-com·merce** \ˈē-ˌkä-kə-(ˌ)mərs\ n : commerce conducted via the Internet

**econ** abbr economics; economist; economy

**eco·nom·ic** \ˌe-kə-ˈnä-mik, ˌē-\ adj : of or relating to the production, distribution, and consumption of goods and services

**eco·nom·i·cal** \-ˈnä-mi-kəl\ adj **1** : THRIFTY **2** : operating with little waste or at a saving ♦ **Synonyms** FRUGAL, SPARING, PROVIDENT — **eco·nom·i·cal·ly** \-k(ə-)lē\ adv

**eco·nom·ics** \ˌe-kə-ˈnä-miks, ˌē-\ n sing or pl : a social science dealing with the production, distribution, and consumption of goods and services — **econ·o·mist** \i-ˈkä-nə-mist\ n

**econ·o·mise** Brit var of ECONOMIZE

**econ·o·mize** \i-ˈkä-nə-ˌmīz\ vb **-mized; -miz·ing** : to practice economy : be frugal — **econ·o·miz·er** n

**¹econ·o·my** \i-ˈkä-nə-mē\ n, pl **-mies** [MF yconomie, tr. ML oeconomia, fr. Gk oikonomia, fr. oikonomos household manager, fr. oikos house + nemein to manage] **1** : thrifty and efficient use of resources; also : an instance of this **2** : manner of arrangement or functioning : ORGANIZATION **3** : an economic system ⟨a money ~⟩

**²economy** adj : ECONOMICAL ⟨~ cars⟩

**eco·sys·tem** \ˈē-kō-ˌsis-təm, ˈe-\ n : the complex of an ecological community and its environment functioning as a unit in nature

**eco·tour·ism** \ˌē-kō-ˈtu̇r-ˌi-zəm, ˌe-\ n : the touring of natural habitats in a manner meant to minimize ecological impact — **eco·tour·ist** \-ˈtu̇r-ist\ n

**ecru** \ˈe-krü, ˈā-\ n [F écru, lit., unbleached] : BEIGE — **ecru** adj

**ec·sta·sy** \ˈek-stə-sē\ n, pl **-sies 1** : extreme and usu. rapturous emotional excitement **2** often cap : an illicit drug with hallucinogenic properties that is chemically related to amphetamine — **ec·stat·ic** \ek-ˈsta-tik, ik-\ adj — **ec·stat·i·cal·ly** \-ti-k(ə-)lē\ adv

**Ecua** abbr Ecuador

**ec·u·men·i·cal** \ˌe-kyu̇-ˈme-ni-kəl\ adj **1** : general in extent or influence **2** : promoting or tending toward worldwide Christian unity — **ec·u·men·i·cal·ly** \-k(ə-)lē\ adv

**ec·ze·ma** \ig-ˈzē-mə, ˈeg-zə-mə, ˈek-sə-\ n : an itching skin inflammation with oozing and then crusted lesions — **ec·zem·a·tous** \ig-ˈze-mə-təs\ adj

**ed** abbr **1** edited; edition; editor **2** education

**¹-ed** \d after a vowel or b, g, j, l, m, n, ŋ, r, th, v, z, zh; əd, id after d, t; t after other sounds\ vb suffix or adj suffix **1** — used to form the past participle of regular weak verbs ⟨ended⟩ ⟨faded⟩ ⟨tried⟩ ⟨patted⟩ **2** : having : characterized by ⟨cultured⟩ ⟨2-legged⟩; also : having the characteristics of ⟨bigoted⟩

**²-ed** vb suffix — used to form the past tense of regular weak verbs ⟨judged⟩ ⟨denied⟩ ⟨dropped⟩

**Edam** \ˈē-dəm, -ˌdam\ n : a yellow Dutch pressed cheese made in balls

**ed·a·ma·me** \ˌe-də-ˈmä-mä\ n [Jp, fr. eda branch + mame beans] : immature green soybeans usu. in the pod

**ed·dy** \ˈe-dē\ n, pl **eddies** : WHIRLPOOL — **eddy** vb

**edel·weiss** \ˈā-dᵊl-ˌwīs, -ˌvīs\ n [G, fr. edel noble + weiss white] : a small perennial woolly composite herb that grows high in the Alps

**ede·ma** \i-ˈdē-mə\ n : abnormal accumulation of watery fluid in connective tissue or in a serous cavity — **edem·a·tous** \-ˈde-mə-təs\ adj

**Eden** \ˈē-dᵊn\ n : PARADISE 2

**¹edge** \ˈej\ n **1** : the cutting side of a blade **2** : SHARPNESS; also : FORCE, EFFECTIVENESS **3** : the line where something begins or ends; also : the area adjoining such an edge **4** : ADVANTAGE ⟨has an ~ on the competition⟩ — **edged** \ˈejd\ adj

**²edge** vb **edged; edg·ing 1** : to give or form an edge **2** : to move or force gradually ⟨~ into a crowd⟩ **3** : to defeat by a small margin ⟨edged out her opponent⟩ — **edg·er** n

**edge·wise** \ˈej-ˌwīz\ adv : SIDEWAYS

**edg·ing** \ˈe-jiŋ\ n : something that forms an edge or border ⟨a lace ~⟩

**edgy** \ˈe-jē\ adj **edg·i·er; -est 1** : SHARP ⟨an ~ tone⟩ **2** : TENSE, NERVOUS **3** : having a bold, provocative, or unconventional quality — **edg·i·ness** n

**ed·i·ble** \ˈe-də-bəl\ adj : fit or safe to be eaten — **ed·i·bil·i·ty** \ˌe-də-ˈbi-lə-tē\ n — **edible** n

**edict** \ˈē-ˌdikt\ n : ORDER, DECREE

**ed·i·fi·ca·tion** \ˌe-də-fə-ˈkā-shən\ n : instruction and improvement esp. in morality — **ed·i·fy** \ˈe-də-ˌfī\ vb

**ed·i·fice** \'e-də-fəs\ *n* : a usu. large building

**ed·it** \'e-dət\ *vb* **1** : to revise, assemble, or prepare for publication or release (as a motion picture) **2** : to direct the publication and policies of (as a newspaper) **3** : DELETE — **ed·i·tor** \'e-də-tər\ *n* — **ed·i·tor·ship** *n* — **ed·i·tress** \-trəs\ *n*

**edi·tion** \i-'di-shən\ *n* **1** : the form in which a text is published **2** : the total number of copies (as of a book) published at one time **3** : VERSION

**¹ed·i·to·ri·al** \ˌe-də-'tór-ē-əl\ *adj* **1** : of or relating to an editor or editing **2** : being or resembling an editorial — **ed·i·to·ri·al·ly** *adv*

**²editorial** *n* : an article (as in a newspaper) giving the views of the editors or publishers; *also* : an expression of opinion resembling an editorial ⟨a television ∼⟩

**ed·i·to·ri·al·ize** \ˌe-də-'tór-ē-ə-ˌlīz\ *vb* **-ized; -iz·ing 1** : to express an opinion in an editorial **2** : to introduce opinions into factual reporting **3** : to express an opinion — **ed·i·to·ri·al·iza·tion** \-ˌtór-ē-ə-lə-'zā-shən\ *n* — **ed·i·to·ri·al·iz·er** *n*

**EDP** *abbr* electronic data processing

**EDT** *abbr* Eastern daylight (saving) time

**educ** *abbr* education; educational

**ed·u·ca·ble** \'e-jə-kə-bəl\ *adj* : capable of being educated

**ed·u·cate** \'e-jə-ˌkāt\ *vb* **-cat·ed; -cat·ing** [ME, to rear, fr. L *educatus*, pp. of *educare*, fr. *educere* to lead forth, draw out] **1** : to provide with schooling **2** : to develop mentally and morally; *also* : to provide with information ♦ *Synonyms* TRAIN, DISCIPLINE, SCHOOL, INSTRUCT, TEACH — **ed·u·ca·tor** \-ˌkā-tər\ *n*

**ed·u·ca·tion** \ˌe-jə-'kā-shən\ *n* **1** : the action or process of educating or being educated **2** : a field of study dealing with methods of teaching and learning — **ed·u·ca·tion·al** \-shə-nəl\ *adj* — **ed·u·ca·tion·al·ly** *adv*

**educational television** *n* **1** : television that provides educational programming (as for students) **2** : television (as public television) that receives support from contributions rather than from commercials

**educe** \i-'düs, -'dyüs\ *vb* **educed; educing 1** : ELICIT, EVOKE **2** : DEDUCE ♦ *Synonyms* EXTRACT, EVINCE, EXTORT

**ed·u·tain·ment** \ˌe-jə-'tān-mənt\ *n* : entertainment that is designed to be educational

**¹-ee** \'ē, (ˌ)ē\ *n suffix* **1** : one that receives or benefits from (a specified action or thing) ⟨grant*ee*⟩ ⟨patent*ee*⟩ **2** : a person who does (a specified action) ⟨escap*ee*⟩

**²-ee** *n suffix* **1** : a particular esp. small kind of ⟨boot*ee*⟩ **2** : one resembling or suggestive of ⟨goat*ee*⟩

**EE** *abbr* electrical engineer

**EEC** *abbr* European Economic Community

**EEG** *abbr* **1** electroencephalogram **2** electroencephalograph

**eel** \'ēl\ *n* : any of numerous snakelike bony fishes with a smooth slimy skin

**EEO** *abbr* equal employment opportunity

**ee·rie** *also* **ee·ry** \'ir-ē\ *adj* **ee·ri·er; -est** : WEIRD, UNCANNY — **ee·ri·ly** \'ir-ə-lē\ *adv*

**eff** *abbr* efficiency

**ef·face** \i-'fās, e-\ *vb* **ef·faced; ef·fac·ing** : to obliterate or obscure by or as if by rubbing out ♦ *Synonyms* ERASE, DELETE, ANNUL, CANCEL, EXPUNGE — **ef·face·able** *adj* — **ef·face·ment** *n*

**¹ef·fect** \i-'fekt\ *n* **1** : MEANING, INTENT **2** : RESULT **3** : APPEARANCE **4** : INFLUENCE **5** *pl* : GOODS, POSSESSIONS **6** : the quality or state of being operative : OPERATION ♦ *Synonyms* CONSEQUENCE, OUTCOME, UPSHOT, AFTERMATH, ISSUE

**²effect** *vb* : to cause to happen ⟨∼ repairs⟩ ⟨∼ changes⟩

**ef·fec·tive** \i-'fek-tiv\ *adj* **1** : producing a decisive or desired effect **2** : IMPRESSIVE, STRIKING **3** : ready for service or action ⟨∼ manpower⟩ **4** : being in effect — **ef·fec·tive·ly** *adv* — **ef·fec·tive·ness** *n*

**ef·fec·tu·al** \i-'fek-chə-wəl\ *adj* : producing an intended effect : ADEQUATE — **ef·fec·tu·al·ly** *adv*

**ef·fec·tu·ate** \i-'fek-chə-ˌwāt\ *vb* **-at·ed; -at·ing** : BRING ABOUT, EFFECT

**ef·fem·i·nate** \ə-'fe-mə-nət\ *adj* : marked by qualities more typical of women than men — **ef·fem·i·na·cy** \-nə-sē\ *n*

**ef·fen·di** \e-'fen-dē\ *n* [Turk *efendi* master, fr. ModGk *authentēs*] : a man of property, authority, or education in an eastern Mediterranean country

**ef·fer·ent** \'e-fə-rənt\ *adj* : bearing or conducting outward from a more central part ⟨∼ nerves⟩

**ef·fer·vesce** \ˌe-fər-'ves\ *vb* **-vesced; -vesc·ing 1** : to bubble and hiss as gas escapes **2** : to show liveliness or exhilaration — **ef·fer·ves·cence** \-'ve-s⁰ns\ *n* — **ef·fer·ves·cent** \-s⁰nt\ *adj* — **ef·fer·ves·cent·ly** *adv*

**ef·fete** \e-'fēt\ *adj* **1** : having lost character, vitality, or strength; *also* : DECADENT **2** : EFFEMINATE

**ef·fi·ca·cious** \ˌe-fə-'kā-shəs\ *adj* : producing an intended effect ⟨∼ remedies⟩ ♦ *Synonyms* EFFECTUAL, EFFECTIVE, EFFICIENT — **ef·fi·ca·cy** \'e-fi-kə-sē\ *n*

**ef·fi·cient** \i-'fi-shənt\ *adj* : productive of desired effects esp. without waste — **ef·fi·cien·cy** \-shən-sē\ *n* — **ef·fi·cient·ly** *adv*

**ef·fi·gy** \'e-fə-jē\ *n, pl* **-gies** : IMAGE; *esp* : a crude figure of a hated person

**ef·flo·res·cence** \ˌe-flə-'re-s⁰ns\ *n* **1** : the period or state of flowering **2** : the action or process of developing **3** : fullness of development : FLOWERING

**ef·flu·ence** \'e-ˌflü-əns\ *n* : something that flows out

**ef·flu·ent** \'e-ˌflü-ənt\ *n* : something that flows out; *esp* : a fluid (as sewage) discharged as waste — **effluent** *adj*

**ef·flu·vi·um** \e-'flü-vē-əm\ *n, pl* **-via** \-vē-ə\ *also* **-vi·ums** [L, outflow] **1** : a usu. unpleasant emanation **2** : a by-product usu. in the form of waste

**ef·fort** \'e-fərt\ *n* **1** : EXERTION, ENDEAVOR; *also* : a product of effort **2** : active or applied force — **ef·fort·less** *adj* — **ef·fort·less·ly** *adv*

**ef·fron·tery** \i-'frən-tə-rē\ *n, pl* **-ter·ies** : shameless boldness : IMPUDENCE
♦ *Synonyms* TEMERITY, AUDACITY, BRASS, GALL, NERVE, CHUTZPAH

**ef·ful·gence** \i-'ful-jəns, -'fəl-\ *n* : radiant splendor : BRILLIANCE ⟨the ~ of its golden age⟩ — **ef·ful·gent** \-jənt\ *adj*

**ef·fu·sion** \i-'fyü-zhən, e-\ *n* : a gushing forth; *also* : unrestrained utterance — **ef·fuse** \-'fyüz, e-\ *vb* — **ef·fu·sive** \i-'fyü-siv, e-\ *adj* — **ef·fu·sive·ly** *adv*

**eft** \'eft\ *n* : NEWT

**EFT** *or* **EFTS** *abbr* electronic funds transfer (system)

**e.g.** *abbr* [L *exempli gratia*] for example

**Eg** *abbr* Egypt; Egyptian

**egal·i·tar·i·an·ism** \i-,ga-lə-'ter-ē-ə-,ni-zəm\ *n* : a belief in human equality esp. in social, political, and economic affairs — **egal·i·tar·i·an** *adj or n*

¹**egg** \'eg\ *vb* [ME, fr. ON *eggja*; akin to OE *ecg* edge] : to urge to action — usu. used with *on*

²**egg** *n* [ME *egge*, fr. ON *egg*; akin to OE *æg* egg, L *ovum*] **1** : a rounded usu. hardshelled reproductive body esp. of birds and reptiles from which the young hatches; *also* : the egg of the common domestic chicken as an article of food **2** : a germ cell produced by a female

**egg·beat·er** \'eg-,bē-tər\ *n* : a hand-operated kitchen utensil for beating, stirring, or whipping

**egg cell** *n* : EGG 2

**egg foo yong** *or* **egg foo young** *or* **egg foo yung** \-'fü-'yəŋ\ : a fried egg patty

**egg·head** \-,hed\ *n* : INTELLECTUAL, HIGHBROW

**egg·nog** \-,näg\ *n* : a drink consisting of eggs beaten with sugar, milk or cream, and often alcoholic liquor

**egg·plant** \-,plant\ *n* : the edible usu. large and dark purplish fruit of a plant related to the potato; *also* : the plant

**egg roll** *n* : a thin egg-dough casing filled with minced vegetables and often bits of meat and usu. deep-fried

**egg·shell** \'eg-,shel\ *n* : the hard exterior covering of an egg

**egis** *var of* AEGIS

**eg·lan·tine** \'e-glən-,tīn, -,tēn\ *n* : SWEETBRIAR

**ego** \'ē-gō\ *n, pl* **egos** [L, I] **1** : the self as distinguished from others **2** : the one of the three divisions of the psyche in psychoanalytic theory that is the organized conscious mediator between the person and reality

**ego·cen·tric** \,ē-gō-'sen-trik\ *adj* : concerned or overly concerned with the self; *esp* : SELF-CENTERED

**ego·ism** \'ē-gō-,i-zəm\ *n* **1** : a doctrine holding self-interest to be the motive or the valid end of action **2** : excessive concern for oneself with or without exaggerated feelings of self-importance — **ego·ist** \-ist\ *n* — **ego·is·tic** \,ē-gō-'is-tik\ *adj* — **ego·is·ti·cal·ly** *adv*

**ego·tism** \'ē-gə-,ti-zəm\ *n* **1** : the practice of talking about oneself too much **2** : an

exaggerated sense of self-importance : CONCEIT — **ego·tist** \-tist\ *n* — **ego·tis·tic** \,ē-gə-'tis-tik\ *or* **ego·tis·ti·cal** \-ti-kəl\ *adj* — **ego·tis·ti·cal·ly** *adv*

**ego trip** *n* : an act that enhances and satisfies one's ego

**egre·gious** \i-'grē-jəs\ *adj* [L *egregius*, outstanding, fr. *ex, e* out of + *greg-, grex* flock, herd] : notably bad : FLAGRANT ⟨~ errors⟩ — **egre·gious·ly** *adv* — **egre·gious·ness** *n*

**egress** \'ē-,gres\ *n* : a way out : EXIT

**egret** \'ē-grət, i-'gret\ *n* : any of various herons that bear long plumes during the breeding season

**Egyp·tian** \i-'jip-shən\ *n* **1** : a native or inhabitant of Egypt **2** : the language of the ancient Egyptians from earliest times to about the 3d century A.D. — **Egyptian** *adj*

**ei·der** \'ī-dər\ *n* : any of several northern sea ducks that yield a soft down

**ei·der·down** \-,daun\ *n* **1** : the down of the eider **2** : a comforter filled with eiderdown

**ei·do·lon** \ī-'dō-lən\ *n, pl* **-lons** *or* **-la** \-lə\ **1** : PHANTOM **2** : IDEAL

**eight** \'āt\ *n* **1** : one more than seven **2** : the 8th in a set or series **3** : something having eight units — **eight** *adj or pron* — **eighth** \'ātth\ *adj or adv or n*

**eight ball** *n* : a black pool ball numbered 8 — **behind the eight ball** : in a highly disadvantageous position

**eigh·teen** \'āt-'tēn\ *n* : one more than 17 — **eighteen** *adj or pron* — **eigh·teenth** \-'tēnth\ *adj or n*

**eighty** \'ā-tē\ *n, pl* **eight·ies** : eight times 10 — **eight·i·eth** \'ā-tē-əth\ *adj or n* — **eighty** *adj or pron*

**ein·stei·ni·um** \īn-'stī-nē-əm\ *n* : an artificially produced radioactive element

**ei·re·nic** *chiefly Brit var of* IRENIC

¹**ei·ther** \'ē-thər, 'ī-\ *adj* **1** : being the one and the other of two : EACH ⟨trees on ~ side⟩ **2** : being the one or the other of two ⟨take ~ road⟩

²**either** *pron* : the one or the other

³**either** *conj* — used as a function word before the first of two or more words or word groups of which the last is preceded by *or* to indicate that they represent alternatives ⟨a statement is ~ true or false⟩

**ejac·u·late** \i-'ja-kyə-,lāt\ *vb* **-lat·ed; -lat·ing 1** : to eject a fluid (as semen) **2** : to utter suddenly : EXCLAIM — **ejac·u·la·tion** \-,ja-kyə-'lā-shən\ *n* — **ejac·u·la·to·ry** \-'ja-kyə-lə-,tör-ē\ *adj*

**eject** \i-'jekt\ *vb* : to drive or throw out or off ♦ *Synonyms* EXPEL, OUST, EVICT, DISMISS — **ejec·tion** \-'jek-shən\ *n*

**eke** \'ēk\ *vb* **eked; ek·ing** : to gain, supplement, or extend usu. with effort — usu. used with *out* ⟨~ out a living⟩

**EKG** *abbr* [G *Elektrokardiogramm*] electrocardiogram; electrocardiograph

**el** *abbr* elevation

¹**elab·o·rate** \i-'la-bə-rət, -'la-brət\ *adj* **1** : planned or carried out with great care **2** : being complex and usu. ornate — **elab·o·rate·ly** *adv* — **elab·o·rate·ness** *n*

²**elab·o·rate** \i-'la-bə-,rāt\ *vb* **-rat·ed; -rat-**

ing **1** : to build up from simpler ingredients **2** : to work out in detail : develop fully — **elab·o·ra·tion** \-ˌla-bə-'rā-shən\ n

**élan** \ā-'lä[n]\ n [F] : ARDOR, SPIRIT

**eland** \'ē-lənd, -ˌland\ n, pl **eland** also **elands** [Afrikaans] : either of two large African antelopes with spirally twisted horns in both sexes

**elapse** \i-'laps\ vb **elapsed; elaps·ing** : to slip by : PASS

¹**elas·tic** \i-'las-tik\ adj **1** : SPRINGY **2** : FLEXIBLE, PLIABLE ⟨an ∼ bandage⟩ **3** : ADAPTABLE ⟨an ∼ plan⟩ ♦ *Synonyms* RESILIENT, SUPPLE, STRETCH — **elas·tic·i·ty** \-ˌlas-'ti-sə-tē, ˌē-ˌlas-\ n

²**elastic** n **1** : elastic material **2** : a rubber band

**elate** \i-'lāt\ vb **elat·ed; elat·ing** : to fill with joy — **ela·tion** \-'lā-shən\ n

¹**el·bow** \'el-ˌbō\ n [ME elbowe, fr. OE elboga, fr. el- (akin to eln ell) + boga bow] **1** : the joint of the arm; also : the outer curve of the bent arm **2** : a bend or joint resembling an elbow in shape

²**elbow** vb : to push aside with the elbow; also : to make one's way by elbowing

**el·bow room** \'el-ˌbō-ˌrüm, -ˌrüm\ n : enough space for work or operation

¹**el·der** \'el-dər\ n : ELDERBERRY 2

²**elder** adj **1** : OLDER **2** : EARLIER, FORMER **3** : of higher rank : SENIOR

³**elder** n **1** : an older individual : SENIOR **2** : one having authority by reason of age and experience **3** : a church officer

**el·der·ber·ry** \'el-dər-ˌber-ē\ n **1** : the edible black or red fruit of a shrub or tree related to the honeysuckle and bearing flat clusters of small white or pink flowers **2** : a tree or shrub bearing elderberries

**el·der·ly** \'el-dər-lē\ adj **1** : rather old; esp : past middle age **2** : of, relating to, or characteristic of later life

**el·dest** \'el-dəst\ adj : of the greatest age

**El Do·ra·do** \ˌel-də-'rä-dō, -'rä-\ n [Sp, lit., the gilded one] : a place of vast riches, abundance, or opportunity

**elec** abbr electric; electrical; electricity

¹**elect** \i-'lekt\ adj **1** : CHOSEN, SELECT **2** : elected but not yet installed in office ⟨the president-*elect*⟩

²**elect** n, pl **elect 1** : a selected person **2** pl : a select or exclusive group

³**elect** vb **1** : to select by vote (as for office or membership) **2** : CHOOSE, PICK

**elec·tion** \i-'lek-shən\ n **1** : an act or process of electing **2** : the fact of being elected

**elec·tion·eer** \i-ˌlek-shə-'nir\ vb : to work for the election of a candidate or party

¹**elec·tive** \i-'lek-tiv\ adj **1** : chosen or filled by election **2** : permitting a choice : OPTIONAL

²**elective** n : an elective course or subject of study

**elec·tor** \i-'lek-tər\ n **1** : one qualified to vote in an election **2** : one elected to an electoral college — **elec·tor·al** \i-'lek-tə-rəl\ adj

**electoral college** n : a body of electors who elect the president and vice president of the U.S.

**elec·tor·ate** \i-'lek-tə-rət\ n : a body of persons entitled to vote

**elec·tric** \i-'lek-trik\ adj [NL electricus produced from amber by friction, electric, fr. ML, of amber, fr. L electrum amber, fr. Gk ēlektron] **1** or **elec·tri·cal** \-tri-kəl\ : of, relating to, operated by, or produced by electricity **2** : ELECTRIFYING, THRILLING ⟨an ∼ performance⟩ — **elec·tri·cal·ly** adv

**electrical storm** n : THUNDERSTORM

**electric chair** n : a chair used to carry out the death penalty by electrocution

**electric eye** n : PHOTOELECTRIC CELL

**elec·tri·cian** \i-ˌlek-'tri-shən\ n : a person who installs, operates, or repairs electrical equipment

**elec·tric·i·ty** \i-ˌlek-'tri-sə-tē\ n, pl **-ties 1** : a form of energy that occurs naturally (as in lightning) or is produced (as in a generator) and that is expressed in terms of the movement and interaction of electrons **2** : electric current

**elec·tri·fy** \i-'lek-trə-ˌfī\ vb **-fied; -fy·ing 1** : to charge with electricity **2** : to equip for use of electric power **3** : THRILL — **elec·tri·fi·ca·tion** \i-ˌlek-trə-fə-'kā-shən\ n

**elec·tro·car·dio·gram** \i-ˌlek-trō-'kär-dē-ə-ˌgram\ n : the tracing made by an electrocardiograph

**elec·tro·car·dio·graph** \-ˌgraf\ n : a device for recording the changes of electrical potential occurring during the heartbeat — **elec·tro·car·dio·graph·ic** \-ˌkär-dē-ə-'gra-fik\ adj — **elec·tro·car·di·og·ra·phy** \-dē-'ä-grə-fē\ n

**elec·tro·chem·is·try** \-'ke-mə-strē\ n : a branch of chemistry that deals with the relation of electricity to chemical changes — **elec·tro·chem·i·cal** \-'ke-mi-kəl\ adj

**elec·tro·cute** \i-'lek-trə-ˌkyüt\ vb **-cut·ed; -cut·ing 1** : to kill (a criminal) by electricity **2** : to kill by electric shock — **elec·tro·cu·tion** \-ˌlek-trə-'kyü-shən\ n

**elec·trode** \i-'lek-ˌtrōd\ n : a conductor used to establish electrical contact with a nonmetallic part of a circuit

**elec·tro·en·ceph·a·lo·gram** \i-ˌlek-trō-in-'se-fə-lə-ˌgram\ n : the tracing made by an electroencephalograph

**elec·tro·en·ceph·a·lo·graph** \-ˌgraf\ n : an apparatus for detecting and recording brain waves — **elec·tro·en·ceph·a·lo·graph·ic** \-ˌse-fə-lə-'gra-fik\ adj — **elec·tro·en·ceph·a·log·ra·phy** \-'lä-grə-fē\ n

**elec·trol·o·gist** \i-ˌlek-'trä-lə-jist\ n : one that uses electrical means to remove hair, warts, moles, and birthmarks from the body

**elec·trol·y·sis** \i-ˌlek-'trä-lə-səs\ n **1** : the production of chemical changes by passage of an electric current through an electrolyte **2** : the destruction of hair roots with an electric current — **elec·tro·lyt·ic** \-trə-'li-tik\ adj

**elec·tro·lyte** \i-'lek-trə-ˌlīt\ n : a nonmetallic electric conductor in which current is carried by the movement of ions; *also* : a substance whose solution or molten form is such a conductor

**elec·tro·mag·net** \i-ˌlek-trō-ˈmag-nət\ *n* : a core of magnetic material (as iron) surrounded by a coil of wire through which an electric current is passed to magnetize the core

**elec·tro·mag·net·ic** \-mag-ˈne-tik\ *adj* : of, relating to, or produced by electromagnetism — **elec·tro·mag·net·i·cal·ly** *adv*

**electromagnetic radiation** *n* : energy in the form of electromagnetic waves; *also* : a series of electromagnetic waves

**electromagnetic wave** *n* : a wave (as a radio wave, an X-ray, or a wave of visible light) that consists of associated magnetic and electric effects and that travels at the speed of light

**elec·tro·mag·ne·tism** \i-ˌlek-trō-ˈmag-nə-ˌti-zəm\ *n* 1 : magnetism developed by a current of electricity 2 : a natural force responsible for interactions between charged particles which result from their charge

**elec·tro·mo·tive force** \i-ˌlek-trə-ˈmō-tiv-\ *n* : the potential difference derived from an electrical source per unit quantity of electricity passing through the source

**elec·tron** \i-ˈlek-ˌträn\ *n* : a negatively charged elementary particle

**elec·tron·ic** \i-ˌlek-ˈträ-nik\ *adj* 1 : of or relating to electrons or electronics 2 : involving a computer — **elec·tron·i·cal·ly** \-ni-k(ə-)lē\ *adv*

**electronic mail** *n* : E-MAIL

**elec·tron·ics** \i-ˌlek-ˈträ-niks\ *n* 1 : the physics of electrons and electronic devices 2 : electronic components, devices, or equipment

**electron microscope** *n* : an instrument in which a beam of electrons is used to produce an enlarged image of a minute object

**electron tube** *n* : a device in which electrical conduction by electrons takes place within a sealed container and which is used for the controlled flow of electrons

**electron volt** *n* : a unit of energy equal to $1.60 \times 10^{-19}$ joule

**elec·tro·pho·re·sis** \i-ˌlek-trə-fə-ˈrē-səs\ *n* : the movement of suspended particles through a medium (as paper or gel) by an electromotive force — **elec·tro·pho·ret·ic** \-ˈre-tik\ *adj*

**elec·tro·plate** \i-ˈlek-trə-ˌplāt\ *vb* : to coat (as with metal) by electrolysis

**elec·tro·shock therapy** \i-ˈlek-trō-ˌshäk-\ *n* : the treatment of mental disorder by applying electric current to the head and inducing convulsions

**elec·tro·stat·ics** \i-ˌlek-trə-ˈsta-tiks\ *n* : physics dealing with the interactions of stationary electric charges

**el·ee·mos·y·nary** \ˌe-li-ˈmäs-sə-ˌner-ē\ *adj* : CHARITABLE

**el·e·gance** \ˈe-li-gəns\ *n* 1 : refined gracefulness; *also* : tasteful richness (as of design) 2 : something marked by elegance — **el·e·gant** \-gənt\ *adj* — **el·e·gant·ly** *adv*

**ele·gi·ac** \ˌe-lə-ˈjī-ək, -ˌak\ *adj* : of or relating to an elegy

**el·e·gy** \ˈe-lə-jē\ *n, pl* **-gies** : a song, poem, or speech expressing grief for one who is dead; *also* : a reflective poem usu. melancholy in tone

**elem** *abbr* elementary

**el·e·ment** \ˈe-lə-mənt\ *n* 1 *pl* : weather conditions; *esp* : severe weather (boards exposed to the ~*s*) 2 : natural environment (in her ~) 3 : a constituent part 4 *pl* : the simplest principles (as of an art or science) : RUDIMENTS 5 : a member of a mathematical set 6 : any of the fundamental substances that consist of atoms of only one kind ♦ *Synonyms* COMPONENT, INGREDIENT, CONSTITUENT — **el·e·men·tal** \ˌe-lə-ˈment-ᵊl\ *adj*
☞ the ELEMENT table is on page 232

**el·e·men·ta·ry** \ˌe-lə-ˈmen-trē, -tə-rē\ *adj* 1 : SIMPLE, RUDIMENTARY; *also* : of, relating to, or teaching the basic subjects of education

**elementary particle** *n* : a subatomic particle of matter and energy that does not appear to be made up of other smaller particles

**elementary school** *n* : a school usu. including the first six or the first eight grades

**el·e·phant** \ˈe-lə-fənt\ *n, pl* **elephants** *also* **elephant** : any of a family of huge thickset nearly hairless mammals that have the snout lengthened into a trunk and two long curving pointed ivory tusks

**el·e·phan·ti·a·sis** \ˌe-lə-fən-ˈtī-ə-səs\ *n, pl* **-a·ses** \-ˌsēz\ : enlargement and thickening of tissues in response esp. to infection by minute parasitic worms

**el·e·phan·tine** \ˌe-lə-ˈfan-ˌtēn, -ˌtīn, ˈe-lə-fən-\ *adj* 1 : of great size or strength 2 : CLUMSY, PONDEROUS (~ verse)

**elev** *abbr* elevation

**el·e·vate** \ˈe-lə-ˌvāt\ *vb* **-vat·ed; -vat·ing** 1 : to lift up : RAISE 2 : EXALT, ENNOBLE (great books that ~ their readers) 3 : ELATE

**el·e·va·tion** \ˌe-lə-ˈvā-shən\ *n* 1 : the height to which something is raised (as above sea level) 2 : a lifting up 3 : something (as a hill) that is elevated

**el·e·va·tor** \ˈe-lə-ˌvā-tər\ *n* 1 : a cage or platform for conveying people or things from one level to another 2 : a building for storing and discharging grain 3 : a movable surface on an airplane to produce motion up or down

**elev·en** \i-ˈle-vən\ *n* 1 : one more than 10 2 : the 11th in a set or series 3 : something having 11 units; *esp* : a football team — **eleven** *adj or pron* — **elev·enth** \-vənth\ *adj or n*

**elf** \ˈelf\ *n, pl* **elves** \ˈelvz\ : a mischievous fairy — **elf·ish** \ˈel-fish\ *adj*

**ELF** *abbr* extremely low frequency

**elf·in** \ˈel-fən\ *adj* : of, relating to, or resembling an elf

**elic·it** \i-ˈli-sət\ *vb* : to draw out or forth ♦ *Synonyms* EVOKE, EDUCE, EXTRACT, EXTORT

# CHEMICAL ELEMENTS

| ELEMENT NAME | SYMBOL & ATOMIC NUMBER | ATOMIC WEIGHT[1] | ELEMENT NAME | SYMBOL & ATOMIC NUMBER | ATOMIC WEIGHT[1] |
|---|---|---|---|---|---|
| actinium | (Ac = 89) | 227.0277 | meitnerium | (Mt = 109) | (268) |
| aluminum | (Al = 13) | 26.98154 | mendelevium | (Md = 101) | (258) |
| americium | (Am = 95) | (243) | mercury | (Hg = 80) | 200.59 |
| antimony | (Sb = 51) | 121.760 | molybdenum | (Mo = 42) | 95.94 |
| argon | (Ar = 18) | 39.948 | neodymium | (Nd = 60) | 144.24 |
| arsenic | (As = 33) | 74.92160 | neon | (Ne = 10) | 20.180 |
| astatine | (At = 85) | (210) | neptunium | (Np = 93) | (237) |
| barium | (Ba = 56) | 137.33 | nickel | (Ni = 28) | 58.6934 |
| berkelium | (Bk = 97) | (247) | niobium | (Nb = 41) | 92.90638 |
| beryllium | (Be = 4) | 9.012182 | nitrogen | (N = 7) | 14.0067 |
| bismuth | (Bi = 83) | 208.98038 | nobelium | (No = 102) | (259) |
| bohrium | (Bh = 107) | (264) | osmium | (Os = 76) | 190.23 |
| boron | (B = 5) | 10.81 | oxygen | (O = 8) | 15.9994 |
| bromine | (Br = 35) | 79.904 | palladium | (Pd = 46) | 106.42 |
| cadmium | (Cd = 48) | 112.41 | phosphorus | (P = 15) | 30.973761 |
| calcium | (Ca = 20) | 40.078 | platinum | (Pt = 78) | 195.078 |
| californium | (Cf = 98) | (251) | plutonium | (Pu = 94) | (244) |
| carbon | (C = 6) | 12.011 | polonium | (Po = 84) | (209) |
| cerium | (Ce = 58) | 140.116 | potassium | (K = 19) | 39.0983 |
| cesium | (Cs = 55) | 132.90545 | praseodymium | (Pr = 59) | 140.90765 |
| chlorine | (Cl = 17) | 35.453 | promethium | (Pm = 61) | (145) |
| chromium | (Cr = 24) | 51.996 | protactinium | (Pa = 91) | (231) |
| cobalt | (Co = 27) | 58.93320 | radium | (Ra = 88) | (226) |
| copernicium | (Cn = 112) | (285) | radon | (Rn = 86) | (222) |
| copper | (Cu = 29) | 63.546 | rhenium | (Re = 75) | 186.207 |
| curium | (Cm = 96) | (247) | rhodium | (Rh = 45) | 102.90550 |
| darmstadtium | (Ds = 110) | (269) | roentgenium | (Rg = 111) | (280) |
| dubnium | (Db = 105) | (262) | rubidium | (Rb = 37) | 85.4678 |
| dysprosium | (Dy = 66) | 162.50 | ruthenium | (Ru = 44) | 101.07 |
| einsteinium | (Es = 99) | (252) | rutherfordium | (Rf = 104) | (261) |
| erbium | (Er = 68) | 167.259 | samarium | (Sm = 62) | 150.36 |
| europium | (Eu = 63) | 151.964 | scandium | (Sc = 21) | 44.95591 |
| fermium | (Fm = 100) | (257) | seaborgium | (Sg = 106) | (266) |
| fluorine | (F = 9) | 18.998403 | selenium | (Se = 34) | 78.96 |
| francium | (Fr = 87) | (223) | silicon | (Si = 14) | 28.0855 |
| gadolinium | (Gd = 64) | 157.25 | silver | (Ag = 47) | 107.8682 |
| gallium | (Ga = 31) | 69.723 | sodium | (Na = 11) | 22.989770 |
| germanium | (Ge = 32) | 72.64 | strontium | (Sr = 38) | 87.62 |
| gold | (Au = 79) | 196.96655 | sulfur | (S = 16) | 32.07 |
| hafnium | (Hf = 72) | 178.49 | tantalum | (Ta = 73) | 180.9479 |
| hassium | (Hs = 108) | (277) | technetium | (Tc = 43) | (98) |
| helium | (He = 2) | 4.002602 | tellurium | (Te = 52) | 127.60 |
| holmium | (Ho = 67) | 164.93032 | terbium | (Tb = 65) | 158.92534 |
| hydrogen | (H = 1) | 1.0079 | thallium | (Tl = 81) | 204.3833 |
| indium | (In = 49) | 114.818 | thorium | (Th = 90) | 232.0381 |
| iodine | (I = 53) | 126.90447 | thulium | (Tm = 69) | 168.93421 |
| iridium | (Ir = 77) | 192.217 | tin | (Sn = 50) | 118.71 |
| iron | (Fe = 26) | 55.845 | titanium | (Ti = 22) | 47.867 |
| krypton | (Kr = 36) | 83.80 | tungsten | (W = 74) | 183.84 |
| lanthanum | (La = 57) | 138.9055 | uranium | (U = 92) | (238) |
| lawrencium | (Lr = 103) | (262) | vanadium | (V = 23) | 50.9415 |
| lead | (Pb = 82) | 207.2 | xenon | (Xe = 54) | 131.29 |
| lithium | (Li = 3) | 6.941 | ytterbium | (Yb = 70) | 173.04 |
| lutetium | (Lu = 71) | 174.967 | yttrium | (Y = 39) | 88.90585 |
| magnesium | (Mg = 12) | 24.305 | zinc | (Zn = 30) | 65.39 |
| manganese | (Mn = 25) | 54.93805 | zirconium | (Zr = 40) | 91.224 |

[1]Weights are based on the naturally occurring isotope compositions and scaled to $^{12}C = 12$. For elements lacking stable isotopes, the mass number of the most stable nuclide is shown in parentheses.

**elide** \i-'līd\ vb **elid·ed; elid·ing** : to suppress or alter by elision

**el·i·gi·ble** \'e lə jə bəl\ adj : qualified to participate or to be chosen — **el·i·gi·bil·i·ty** \,e-lə-jə-'bi-lə-tē\ n — **eligible** n

**elim·i·nate** \i-'li-mə-,nāt\ vb **-nat·ed; -nat·ing** [L eliminatus, pp. of eliminare, fr. limen threshold] **1** : REMOVE, ERADICATE **2** : to pass (wastes) from the body **3** : to leave out : IGNORE — **elim·i·na·tion** \-,li-mə-'nā-shən\ n

**eli·sion** \i-'li-zhən\ n : the omission of a final or initial sound or of a word; esp : the omission of an unstressed vowel or syllable in a verse to achieve a uniform rhythm

**elite** \ā-'lēt, ē-\ n [F élite] **1** : the choice part; also : a superior group **2** : a typewriter type providing 12 characters to the inch — **elite** adj

**elit·ism** \-'lē-,ti-zəm\ n : leadership or rule by an elite; also : advocacy of such elitism — **elit·ist** \-'tist\ n or adj

**elix·ir** \i-'lik-sər\ n [ME, fr. ML, fr. Ar al-iksīr the elixir, fr. al the + iksīr elixir] **1** : a substance held capable of prolonging life indefinitely; also : PANACEA **2** : a sweetened alcoholic medicinal solution

**Eliz·a·be·than** \i-,li-zə-'bē-thən\ adj : of, relating to, or characteristic of Elizabeth I of England or her times

**elk** \'elk\ n, pl **elk** or **elks** **1** : MOOSE — used for one of the Old World **2** : a large gregarious deer of No. America, Europe, Asia, and northwestern Africa with curved antlers having many branches

**¹ell** \'el\ n [ME eln, fr. OE; akin to L ulna forearm, Gk ōlenē elbow] : a former English cloth measure of 45 inches

**²ell** n : an extension at right angles to a building

**el·lipse** \i-'lips, e-\ n : a closed curve of oval shape

**el·lip·sis** \i-'lip-səs, e-\ n, pl **el·lip·ses** \-,sēz\ **1** : omission from an expression of a word clearly implied **2** : marks (as . . .) to show omission

**el·lip·soid** \i-'lip-,sȯid, e-\ n : a surface all plane sections of which are circles or ellipses — **el·lip·soi·dal** \-,lip-'sȯi-d²l\ also **ellipsoid** adj

**el·lip·ti·cal** \i-'lip-ti-kəl, e-\ or **el·lip·tic** \-tik\ adj **1** : of, relating to, or shaped like an ellipse **2** : of, relating to, or marked by ellipsis — **el·lip·ti·cal·ly** \-ti-k(ə-)lē\ adv

**elm** \'elm\ n : any of a genus of large trees that have toothed leaves and nearly circular one-seeded winged fruits and are often grown as shade trees; also : the wood of an elm

**El Ni·ño** \el-'nē-nyō\ n : a flow of unusually warm Pacific Ocean water moving toward and along the west coast of So. America

**el·o·cu·tion** \,e-lə-'kyü-shən\ n : the art of effective public speaking — **el·o·cu·tion·ist** \-shə-nist\ n

**elon·gate** \i-'lȯŋ-,gāt\ vb **-gat·ed; -gat·ing** : to make or grow longer ♦ **Synonyms** EXTEND, LENGTHEN, PROLONG,

PROTRACT — **elon·ga·tion** \(,)ē-,lȯŋ-'gā-shən\ n

**elope** \i-'lōp\ vb **eloped; elop·ing** : to run away esp. to be married — **elope·ment** n — **elop·er** n

**el·o·quent** \'e-lə-kwənt\ adj **1** : having or showing clear and forceful expression ⟨an ~ speaker⟩ **2** : clearly showing some feeling or meaning — **el·o·quence** \-kwəns\ n — **el·o·quent·ly** adv

**¹else** \'els\ adv **1** : in a different or additional manner or place or at a different or additional time ⟨where ~ can we meet⟩ **2** : OTHERWISE ⟨obey or ~ you'll be sorry⟩

**²else** adj : OTHER; esp : being in addition ⟨what ~ do you want⟩

**else·where** \-,hwer\ adv : in or to another place ⟨took my business ~⟩

**elu·ci·date** \i-'lü-sə-,dāt\ vb **-dat·ed; -dat·ing** : to make clear usu. by explanation ♦ **Synonyms** CLARIFY, EXPLAIN, ILLUMINATE — **elu·ci·da·tion** \-,lü-sə-'dā-shən\ n

**elude** \ē-'lüd\ vb **elud·ed; elud·ing** **1** : EVADE **2** : to escape the notice of

**elu·sive** \ē-'lü-siv\ adj : tending to elude : EVASIVE ⟨the solution remains ~⟩ — **elu·sive·ly** adv — **elu·sive·ness** n

**el·ver** \'el-vər\ n [alter. of eelfare migration of eels] : a young eel

**elves** pl of ELF

**Ely·si·um** \i-'li-zhē-əm, -zē-\ n, pl **-si·ums** or **-sia** \-zhē-ə, -zē-\ : PARADISE 2 — **Ely·sian** \-'li-zhən\ adj

**em** \'em\ n : a length approximately the width of the letter M

**EM** abbr **1** electromagnetic **2** electron microscope **3** enlisted man

**ema·ci·ate** \i-'mā-shē-,āt\ vb **-at·ed; -at·ing** : to become or cause to become very thin — **ema·ci·a·tion** \-,mā-shē-'ā-shən, -sē-\ n

**e–mail** \'ē-,māl\ n **1** : a system for transmitting messages between computers on a network **2** : a message or messages sent and received through an e-mail system

**emalangeni** pl of LILANGENI

**em·a·nate** \'e-mə-,nāt\ vb **-nat·ed; -nat·ing** : to come out from a source ♦ **Synonyms** PROCEED, SPRING, RISE, ARISE, ORIGINATE — **em·a·na·tion** \,e-mə-'nā-shən\ n

**eman·ci·pate** \i-'man-sə-,pāt\ vb **-pat·ed; -pat·ing** : to set free ♦ **Synonyms** LIBERATE, RELEASE, DELIVER, DISCHARGE — **eman·ci·pa·tion** \-,man-sə-'pā-shən\ n — **eman·ci·pa·tor** \-'man-sə-,pā-tər\ n

**emas·cu·late** \i-'mas-kyù-,lāt\ vb **-lat·ed; -lat·ing** : to deprive of virility : CASTRATE; also : WEAKEN — **emas·cu·la·tion** \-,mas-kyù-'lā-shən\ n

**em·balm** \im-'bäm, -'bälm\ vb : to treat (a corpse) so as to protect from decay — **em·balm·er** n

**em·bank·ment** \im-'baŋk-mənt\ n : a raised structure (as of earth) to hold back water or carry a roadway

**em·bar·go** \im-'bär-gō\ n, pl **-goes** [Sp, fr. embargar to bar] : a prohibition on commerce — **embargo** vb

**em·bark** \im-'bärk\ vb **1** : to put or go on

board a ship or airplane **2** : to make a start — **em·bar·ka·tion** \,em-,bär-'kā-shən\ *n*

**em·bar·rass** \im-'ber-əs\ *vb* **1** : CONFUSE, DISCONCERT **2** : to involve in financial difficulties **3** : to cause to experience self-conscious distress **4** : HINDER, IMPEDE — **em·bar·rass·ing·ly** *adv* — **em·bar·rass·ment** *n*

**em·bas·sy** \'em-bə-sē\ *n, pl* **-sies** **1** : a group of representatives headed by an ambassador **2** : the function, position, or mission of an ambassador **3** : the official residence and offices of an ambassador

**em·bat·tle** \im-'ba-t°l\ *vb* : to arrange in order for battle; *also* : FORTIFY

**em·bat·tled** *adj* **1** : engaged in battle, conflict, or controversy **2** : being a site of battle, conflict, or controversy **3** : characterized by conflict or controversy ⟨an ~ presidency⟩

**em·bed** \im-'bed\ *vb* **em·bed·ded; em·bed·ding 1** : to enclose closely in a surrounding mass **2** : to make something an integral part of

**em·bel·lish** \im-'be-lish\ *vb* **1** : ADORN, DECORATE **2** : to add ornamental details to ♦ *Synonyms* BEAUTIFY, DECK, BEDECK, GARNISH, ORNAMENT, DRESS — **em·bel·lish·er** *n* — **em·bel·lish·ment** *n*

**em·ber** \'em-bər\ *n* **1** : a glowing or smoldering fragment from a fire **2** *pl* : the smoldering remains of a fire

**em·bez·zle** \im-'be-zəl\ *vb* **-zled; -zling** : to steal (as money) by falsifying records — **em·bez·zle·ment** *n* — **em·bez·zler** *n*

**em·bit·ter** \im-'bi-tər\ *vb* **1** : to arouse bitter feelings in **2** : to make bitter

**em·bla·zon** \im-'blā-z°n\ *vb* **1** : to adorn with heraldic devices **2** : to display conspicuously

**em·blem** \'em-bləm\ *n* : something (as an object or picture) suggesting another object or an idea : SYMBOL — **em·blem·at·ic** \,em-blə-'ma-tik\ *also* **em·blem·at·i·cal** \-ti-kəl\ *adj*

**em·body** \im-'bä-dē\ *vb* **em·bod·ied; em·body·ing 1** : INCARNATE **2** : to express in definite form **3** : to incorporate into a system or body **4** : PERSONIFY ♦ *Synonyms* COMBINE, INTEGRATE — **em·bodi·ment** \-di-mənt\ *n*

**em·bold·en** \im-'bōl-dən\ *vb* : to inspire with courage ⟨his speech ~ed the soldiers⟩

**em·bo·lism** \'em-bə-,li-zəm\ *n* : the obstruction of a blood vessel by a foreign or abnormal particle

**em·bon·point** \äⁿ-bōⁿ-'pwaⁿ\ *n* [F] : plumpness of person : STOUTNESS

**em·boss** \im-'bäs, -'bòs\ *vb* : to ornament with raised work

**em·bou·chure** \'äm-bù-,shùr, ,äm-bù-'shùr\ *n* [F, ultim. fr. *bouche* mouth] : the position and use of the lips, tongue, and teeth in playing a wind instrument

**em·bow·er** \im-'baù(-ə)r\ *vb* : to shelter or enclose in a bower

¹**em·brace** \im-'brās\ *vb* **em·braced; em·brac·ing 1** : to clasp in the arms; *also* : CHERISH, LOVE **2** : ENCIRCLE **3** : TAKE UP, ADOPT ⟨*embraced* the cause⟩; *also*

: WELCOME ⟨*embraced* the opportunity⟩ **4** : INCLUDE **5** : to participate in an embrace ♦ *Synonyms* COMPREHEND, INVOLVE, ENCOMPASS, EMBODY

²**embrace** *n* : an encircling with the arms

**em·bra·sure** \im-'brā-zhər\ *n* **1** : an opening in a wall through which a cannon is fired **2** : a recess of a door or window

**em·bro·ca·tion** \,em-brə-'kā-shən\ *n* : LINIMENT

**em·broi·der** \im-'bròi-dər\ *vb* **1** : to ornament with or do needlework **2** : to elaborate with exaggerated detail

**em·broi·dery** \im-'bròi-də-rē\ *n, pl* **-der·ies 1** : the forming of decorative designs with needlework **2** : something embroidered

**em·broil** \im-'bròi(-ə)l\ *vb* **1** : to throw into confusion or disorder **2** : to involve in conflict or difficulties ⟨~ed in a dispute⟩ — **em·broil·ment** *n*

**em·bryo** \'em-brē-,ō\ *n, pl* **embryos** : a living thing in its earliest stages of development — **em·bry·on·ic** \,em-brē-'ä-nik\ *adj*

**em·bry·ol·o·gy** \,em-brē-'ä-lə-jē\ *n* : a branch of biology dealing with embryos and their development — **em·bry·o·log·i·cal** \-brē-ə-'lä-ji-kəl\ *adj* — **em·bry·ol·o·gist** \-brē-'ä-lə-jist\ *n*

**em·cee** \,em-'sē\ *n* : MASTER OF CEREMONIES — **emcee** *vb*

**emend** \ē-'mend\ *vb* : to correct usu. by altering the text of ♦ *Synonyms* RECTIFY, REVISE, AMEND — **emen·da·tion** \,ē-,men-'dā-shən\ *n*

**emer** *abbr* emeritus

¹**em·er·ald** \'em-rəld, 'e-mə-\ *n* : a green beryl prized as a gem

²**emerald** *adj* : brightly or richly green

**emerge** \i-'mərj\ *vb* **emerged; emerging** : to rise, come forth, or come out into view — **emer·gence** \-'mər-jəns\ *n* — **emer·gent** \-jənt\ *adj*

**emer·gen·cy** \i-'mər-jən-sē\ *n, pl* **-cies** : an unforeseen event or condition requiring prompt action ♦ *Synonyms* EXIGENCY, CONTINGENCY, CRISIS, JUNCTURE

**emergency room** *n* : a hospital room for receiving and treating persons needing immediate medical care

**emer·i·ta** \i-'mer-ə-tə\ *adj* : EMERITUS — used of a woman

**emer·i·tus** \i-'mer-ə-təs\ *adj* [L] : retired from active duty ⟨professor ~⟩

**em·ery** \'e-mə-rē\ *n, pl* **em·er·ies** : a dark granular mineral consisting primarily of corundum and used as an abrasive

**emet·ic** \i-'me-tik\ *n* : an agent that induces vomiting — **emetic** *adj*

**emf** *n* [electromotive *force*] : POTENTIAL DIFFERENCE

**em·i·grate** \'e-mə-,grāt\ *vb* **-grat·ed; -grat·ing** : to leave a place (as a country) to settle elsewhere — **em·i·grant** \-mi-grənt\ *n* — **em·i·gra·tion** \,e-mə-'grā-shən\ *n*

**émi·gré** *also* **emi·gré** \'e-mi-,grā, ,e-mi-'grā\ *n* [F] : a person who emigrates esp. because of political conditions

**em·i·nence** \'e-mə-nəns\ *n* **1** : high rank or position; *also* : a person of high rank or attainment **2** : a lofty place

**em·i·nent** \'e-mə-nənt\ *adj* **1** : CONSPICUOUS, EVIDENT **2** : DISTINGUISHED, PROMINENT ⟨an ∼ physician⟩ — **em·i·nent·ly** *adv*

**eminent domain** *n* : a right of a government to take private property for public use

**emir** *or* **amir** \ə-'mir, ā-\ *n* [Ar *amīr* commander] : a ruler, chief, or commander in Islamic countries — **emir·ate** \'e-mər-ət\ *n*

**em·is·sary** \'e-mə-ˌser-ē\ *n, pl* **-sar·ies** : AGENT; *esp* : a secret agent

**emis·sion** \ē-'mi-shən\ *n* : something emitted; *esp* : substances discharged into the air

**emit** \ē-'mit\ *vb* **emit·ted; emit·ting** **1** : to give off or out ⟨∼ light⟩; *also* : EJECT **2** : EXPRESS, UTTER ⟨emitted a groan⟩ — **emit·ter** *n*

**emol·lient** \i-'mäl-yənt\ *adj* : making soft or supple; *also* : soothing esp. to the skin or mucous membrane ⟨an ∼ hand lotion⟩ — **emol·lient** *n*

**emol·u·ment** \i-'mäl-yə-mənt\ *n* [ME, fr. L *emolumentum* advantage, fr. *emolere* to produce by grinding] : the product (as salary or fees) of an employment

**emote** \i-'mōt\ *vb* **emot·ed; emot·ing** : to give expression to emotion in or as if in a play

**emo·ti·con** \i-'mō-ti-ˌkän\ *n* : a group of keyboard characters (as :)) that represents a facial expression esp. in online communications

**emo·tion** \i-'mō-shən\ *n* : a usu. intense feeling (as of love, hate, or despair) — **emo·tion·al** \-shə-nəl\ *adj* — **emo·tion·al·ly** *adv*

**emo·tive** \i-'mō-tiv\ *adj* **1** : of or relating to the emotions **2** : appealing to or expressing emotion

**emp** *abbr* emperor; empress

**empanel** *var of* IMPANEL

**em·pa·thy** \'em-pə-thē\ *n* : the experiencing as one's own of the feelings of another; *also* : the capacity for this — **em·path·ic** \em-'pa-thik\ *adj*

**em·pen·nage** \ˌäm-pə-'näzh, ˌem-\ *n* [F] : the tail assembly of an airplane

**em·per·or** \'em-pər-ər\ *n* : the sovereign male ruler of an empire

**em·pha·sis** \'em-fə-səs\ *n, pl* **-pha·ses** \-ˌsēz\ : particular prominence given (as to a syllable in speaking or to a phase of action)

**em·pha·sise** *Brit var of* EMPHASIZE

**em·pha·size** \-ˌsīz\ *vb* **-sized; -siz·ing** : to place emphasis on : STRESS

**em·phat·ic** \im-'fa-tik, em-\ *adj* : uttered with emphasis : STRESSED ⟨an ∼ refusal⟩ — **em·phat·i·cal·ly** \-ti-k(ə-)lē\ *adv*

**em·phy·se·ma** \ˌem-fə-'zē-mə, -'sē-\ *n* : a condition marked esp. by abnormal expansion of the air spaces of the lungs resulting in severe breathlessness

**em·pire** \'em-ˌpī(-ə)r\ *n* **1** : a large state or a group of states under a single sovereign who is usu. an emperor; *also* : something resembling a political empire **2** : imperial sovereignty or dominion

**em·pir·i·cal** \im-'pir-i-kəl\ *also* **em·pir·ic** \-ik\ *adj* : based on observation; *also* : subject to verification by observation or experiment ⟨∼ laws⟩ — **em·pir·i·cal·ly** \-i-k(ə-)lē\ *adv*

**em·pir·i·cism** \im-'pir-ə-ˌsi-zəm, em-\ *n* : the practice of relying on observation and experiment esp. in the natural sciences — **em·pir·i·cist** \-sist\ *n*

**em·place·ment** \im-'plās-mənt\ *n* **1** : a prepared position for weapons or military equipment **2** : PLACEMENT

**¹em·ploy** \im-'ploi\ *vb* **1** : to make use of **2** : to use the services of **3** : OCCUPY, DEVOTE — **em·ploy·er** *n*

**²em·ploy** \im-'ploi; 'im-ˌploi, 'em-\ *n* : EMPLOYMENT

**em·ploy·ee** *also* **em·ploye** \im-ˌploi-'ē, -ˌem-; im-'ploi-ˌē, em-\ *n* : a person who works for another

**em·ploy·ment** \im-'ploi-mənt\ *n* **1** : OCCUPATION, ACTIVITY **2** : the act of employing : the condition of being employed

**em·po·ri·um** \im-'pōr-ē-əm, em-\ *n, pl* **-ri·ums** *also* **-ria** \-ē-ə\ [L, fr. Gk *emporion*, fr. *emporos* traveler, trader] : a commercial center; *esp* : a store carrying varied articles

**em·pow·er** \im-'pau̇(-ə)r\ *vb* : to give authority or power to; *also* : ENABLE — **em·pow·er·ment** \-mənt\ *n*

**em·press** \'em-prəs\ *n* **1** : the wife or widow of an emperor **2** : a sovereign female ruler of an empire

**¹emp·ty** \'emp-tē\ *adj* **emp·ti·er; -est** [ME, fr. OE *ǣmettig* unoccupied, fr. *ǣmetta* leisure] **1** : containing nothing ⟨∼ shelves⟩ **2** : UNOCCUPIED, UNINHABITED ⟨an ∼ building⟩ **3** : lacking value, force, sense, or purpose ♦ *Synonyms* VACANT, BLANK, VOID, STARK, VACUOUS — **emp·ti·ness** *n*

**²empty** *vb* **emp·tied; emp·ty·ing** **1** : to make or become empty **2** : to discharge contents; *also* : to remove from what holds or encloses

**³empty** *n, pl* **empties** : an empty bottle or can

**emp·ty–hand·ed** \ˌemp-tē-'han-dəd\ *adj* **1** : having or bringing nothing **2** : having acquired or gained nothing

**em·py·re·an** \ˌem-ˌpī-'rē-ən, -pə-\ *n* **1** : the highest heaven; *also* : FIRMAMENT **2** : an ideal place or state

**EMT** \ˌē-(ˌ)em-'tē\ *n* [emergency medical technician] : a specially trained medical technician certified to provide basic medical services before and during transport to a hospital

**¹emu** \'ē-myü, -mü\ *n* : a swift-running flightless Australian bird smaller than the related ostrich

**²emu** *abbr* electromagnetic unit

**em·u·late** \'em-yù-ˌlāt\ *vb* **-lat·ed; -lat·ing** : to strive to equal or excel : IMITATE — **em·u·la·tion** \ˌem-yù-'lā-shən\ *n* — **em·u·lous** \'em-yù-ləs\ *adj*

**emul·si·fi·er** \i-'məl-sə-ˌfī(-ə)r\ *n* : a substance (as a soap) that helps to form and stabilize an emulsion

**emul·si·fy** \-ˌfī\ *vb* **-fied; -fy·ing** : to disperse (as an oil) in an emulsion — **emul·si·fi·ca·tion** \-ˌməl-sə-fə-ˈkā-shən\ *n*

**emul·sion** \i-ˈməl-shən\ *n* **1** : a mixture of mutually insoluble liquids in which one is dispersed in droplets throughout the other ⟨an ~ of oil in water⟩ **2** : a light-sensitive coating on photographic film or paper

**en** \ˈen\ *n* : a length approximately half the width of the letter *M*

**¹-en** *also* **-n** *adj suffix* : made of : consisting of ⟨earth*en*⟩

**²-en** *vb suffix* **1** : become or cause to be ⟨sharp*en*⟩ **2** : cause or come to have ⟨length*en*⟩

**en·able** \i-ˈnā-bəl\ *vb* **en·abled; en·abling** **1** : to make able or feasible ⟨wings that ~ one to fly⟩ **2** : to give legal power, capacity, or sanction to

**en·act** \i-ˈnakt\ *vb* **1** : to make into law **2** : to act out — **en·act·ment** *n*

**enam·el** \i-ˈna-məl\ *n* **1** : a glasslike substance used to coat the surface of metal or pottery **2** : the hard outer layer of a tooth **3** : a usu. glossy paint that forms a hard coat — **enamel** *vb*

**enam·el·ware** \-ˌwer\ *n* : metal utensils coated with enamel

**en·am·or** \i-ˈna-mər\ *vb* : to inflame with love

**en·am·our** *chiefly Brit var of* ENAMOR

**en bloc** \äⁿ-ˈbläk\ *adv or adj* : as a whole : in a mass

**enc** *or* **encl** *abbr* enclosure

**en·camp** \in-ˈkamp\ *vb* : to make camp — **en·camp·ment** *n*

**en·cap·su·late** \in-ˈkap-sə-ˌlāt\ *vb* **-lated; -lating** **1** : to encase or become encased in a capsule **2** : SUMMARIZE — **en·cap·su·la·tion** \-ˌkap-sə-ˈlā-shən\ *n*

**en·case** \in-ˈkās\ *vb* : to enclose in or as if in a case — **en·case·ment** \-ˈkā-smənt\ *n*

**-ence** *n suffix* **1** : action or process ⟨emerg*ence*⟩ : instance of an action or process ⟨refer*ence*⟩ **2** : quality or state ⟨depend*ence*⟩

**en·ceinte** \äⁿ-ˈsant\ *adj* : PREGNANT 1

**ceph·a·li·tis** \in-ˌse-fə-ˈlī-təs\ *n, pl* **-lit·i·des** \-ˈli-tə-ˌdēz\ : inflammation of the brain — **en·ceph·a·lit·ic** \-ˈli-tik\ *adj*

**en·ceph·a·lop·a·thy** \in-ˌse-fə-ˈlä-pə-thē\ *n, pl* **-thies** : a disease of the brain

**en·chain** \in-ˈchān\ *vb* : FETTER, CHAIN

**en·chant** \in-ˈchant\ *vb* **1** : BEWITCH **2** : ENRAPTURE, FASCINATE ⟨was ~*ed* by his poetry⟩ — **en·chant·er** *n* — **en·chant·ing·ly** *adv* — **en·chant·ment** *n* — **en·chant·ress** \-ˈchan-trəs\ *n*

**en·chi·la·da** \ˌen-chə-ˈlä-də\ *n* : a tortilla rolled around a filling, covered with chili sauce, and usu. baked

**en·ci·pher** \in-ˈsī-fər, en-\ *vb* : ENCODE

**en·cir·cle** \in-ˈsər-kəl\ *vb* : to pass completely around : SURROUND — **en·cir·cle·ment** *n*

**en·clave** \ˈen-ˌklāv; ˈän-ˌklāv\ *n* : a distinct territorial, cultural, or social unit

enclosed within or as if within foreign territory

**en·close** \in-ˈklōz\ *vb* **1** : to shut up or in; *esp* : to surround with a fence **2** : to include along with something else in a parcel or envelope ⟨~ a check⟩ — **en·clo·sure** \-ˈklō-zhər\ *n*

**en·code** \in-ˈkōd, en-\ *vb* : to convert (a message) into code

**en·co·mi·um** \en-ˈkō-mē-əm\ *n, pl* **-miums** *also* **-mia** \-mē-ə\ : high or glowing praise

**en·com·pass** \in-ˈkəm-pəs\ *vb* **1** : ENCIRCLE **2** : ENVELOP, INCLUDE

**en·core** \ˈän-ˌkȯr\ *n* **1** : a demand for repetition or reappearance **2** : a further performance or appearance demanded by an audience **3** : a second achievement that usu. surpasses the first — **encore** *vb*

**¹en·coun·ter** \in-ˈkaȯn-tər\ *vb* **1** : to meet as an enemy : FIGHT **2** : to meet usu. unexpectedly ⟨~ problems⟩

**²encounter** *n* **1** : a hostile usu. violent meeting **2** : a chance meeting **3** : an experience shared with another ⟨a romantic ~⟩

**en·cour·age** \in-ˈkər-ij\ *vb* **-aged; -aging** **1** : to inspire with courage and hope **2** : STIMULATE, INCITE ⟨tax cuts to ~ spending⟩ **3** : FOSTER — **en·cour·age·ment** *n* — **en·cour·ag·ing·ly** *adv*

**en·croach** \in-ˈkrōch\ *vb* [ME *encrochen* to seize, fr. AF *encrocher*, fr. *croche* hook] : to enter gradually or stealthily upon another's property or rights — **en·croach·er** *n* — **en·croach·ment** *n*

**en·crust** *also* **in·crust** \in-ˈkrəst\ *vb* : to provide with or form a crust

**en·crus·ta·tion** \ˌ(ˌ)in-ˌkrəs-ˈtā-shən, ˌen-\ *var of* INCRUSTATION

**en·cum·ber** \in-ˈkəm-bər\ *vb* **1** : to weigh down : BURDEN **2** : to hinder the function or activity of ⟨relations ~*ed* by mistrust⟩ — **en·cum·brance** \-brəns\ *n*

**ency** *or* **encyc** *abbr* encyclopedia

**¹en·cyc·li·cal** \in-ˈsi-kli-kəl, en-\ *adj* : addressed to all the individuals of a group

**²encyclical** *n* : an encyclical letter; *esp* : a papal letter to the bishops of the church

**en·cy·clo·pae·dia, en·cy·clo·pae·dic** *chiefly Brit var of* ENCYCLOPEDIA, ENCYCLOPEDIC

**en·cy·clo·pe·dia** \in-ˌsī-klə-ˈpē-dē-ə\ *n* [ML *encyclopaedia* course of general education, fr. Gk *enkyklios paideia* general education] : a work treating the various branches of learning — **en·cy·clo·pe·dic** \-ˈpē-dik\ *adj*

**en·cyst** \in-ˈsist, en-\ *vb* : to form or become enclosed in a cyst — **en·cyst·ment** *n*

**¹end** \ˈend\ *n* **1** : the part of an area that lies at the boundary; *also* : a point which marks the extent or limit of something or at which something ceases to exist **2** : a ceasing of a course (as of action or activity); *also* : DEATH **3** : the ultimate state; *also* : RESULT, ISSUE **4** : REMNANT **5** : PURPOSE, OBJECTIVE **6** : a player stationed at the extremity of a line (as in football) **7** : a share, operation, or aspect of an undertaking

²**end** *vb* **1** : to bring or come to an end **2** : DESTROY; *also* : DIE **3** : to form or be at the end of ♦ **Synonyms** CLOSE, CONCLUDE, TERMINATE, FINISH, COMPLETE

**en·dan·ger** \in-'dān-jər\ *vb* : to bring into danger; *also* : to create danger

**en·dan·gered** *adj* : being or relating to an endangered species

**endangered species** *n* : a species threatened with extinction

**en·dear** \in-'dir\ *vb* : to cause to become beloved or admired

**en·dear·ment** \-mənt\ *n* : a sign of affection : CARESS

**en·deav·or** \in-'de-vər\ *vb* : TRY, ATTEMPT — **endeavor** *n*

**en·deav·our** *chiefly Brit var of* ENDEAVOR

**en·dem·ic** \en-'de-mik, in-\ *adj* : restricted to a particular place ⟨~ plants⟩ ⟨an ~ disease⟩ — **endemic** *n*

**end·ing** \'en-diŋ\ *n* : something that forms an end; *esp* : SUFFIX

**en·dive** \'en-,dīv\ *n* **1** : an herb related to chicory and grown as a salad plant **2** : the blanched shoot of chicory

**end·less** \'end-ləs\ *adj* **1** : having or seeming to have no end : ETERNAL ⟨~ debates⟩ **2** : united at the ends : CONTINUOUS ⟨an ~ belt⟩ ♦ **Synonyms** INTERMINABLE, EVERLASTING, UNCEASING, CEASELESS, UNENDING — **end·less·ly** *adv*

**end·most** \-,mōst\ *adj* : situated at the very end

**end·note** \-,nōt\ *n* : a note placed at the end of a text

**en·do·crine** \'en-də-krən, -,krīn, -,krēn\ *adj* : producing secretions that are distributed by way of the bloodstream ⟨~ glands⟩ — **endocrine** *n* — **en·do·cri·nol·o·gist** \,kri-'nä-lə-jist\ *n*   **en·do·cri·nol·o·gy** \-jē\ *n*

**en·dog·e·nous** \en-'dä-jə-nəs\ *adj* : caused or produced by factors inside the organism or system ⟨~ depression⟩ — **en·dog·e·nous·ly** *adv*

**en·do·me·tri·um** \,en-dō-'mē-trē-əm\ *n, pl* **-tria** \-trē-ə\ : the mucous membrane lining the uterus — **en·do·me·tri·al** \-trē-əl\ *adj*

**en·dor·phin** \en-'dȯr-fən\ *n* : any of a group of endogenous morphinelike proteins found esp. in the brain

**en·dorse** *also* **in·dorse** \in-'dȯrs\ *vb* **en·dorsed; en·dors·ing** [ME *endosen*, fr. AF *endosser* to put on, don, write on the back of, fr. *dos* back, fr. L *dorsum*] **1** : to sign one's name on the back of (as a check) **2** : APPROVE, SANCTION **3** : to recommend (as a product) usu. for financial compensation — **en·dorse·ment** *also* **in·dorse·ment** *n*

**en·do·scope** \'en-də-,skōp\ *n* : an illuminated usu. fiber-optic instrument for visualizing the interior of a hollow organ or part (as the colon or esophagus) — **en·do·scop·ic** \,en-də-'skä-pik\ *adj* — **en·dos·co·py** \en-'däs-kə-pē\ *n*

**en·do·ther·mic** \,en-də-'thər-mik\ *adj*

: characterized by or formed with absorption of heat

**en·dow** \in-'dau̇\ *vb* **1** : to furnish with funds for support ⟨~ a school⟩ **2** : to furnish with something freely or naturally ⟨~ed with intellect⟩ — **en·dow·ment** *n*

**en·due** \in-'dü, -'dyü\ *vb* **en·dued; en·du·ing** : PROVIDE, ENDOW

**en·dur·ance** \in-'dur-əns, -'dyur-\ *n* **1** : DURATION **2** : the ability to withstand hardship or stress : FORTITUDE

**en·dure** \in-'dur, -'dyur\ *vb* **en·dured; en·dur·ing** **1** : LAST, PERSIST **2** : to suffer firmly or patiently : BEAR **3** : TOLERATE — **en·dur·able** *adj*

**end·ways** \'end-,wāz\ *adv or adj* **1** : LENGTHWISE **2** : with the end forward **3** : on end

**end·wise** \-,wīz\ *adv or adj* : ENDWAYS

**ENE** *abbr* east-northeast

**en·e·ma** \'e-nə-mə\ *n, pl* **enemas** *also* **ene·ma·ta** \,e-nə-'mä-tə, 'e-nə-mə-tə\ : injection of liquid into the rectum; *also* : material so injected

**en·e·my** \'e-nə-mē\ *n, pl* **-mies** [ME *enemi*, fr. AF, fr. L *inimicus*, fr. *in-* not + *amicus* friend] : one that attacks or tries to harm another : FOE; *esp* : a military opponent

**en·er·get·ic** \,e-nər-'je-tik\ *adj* : marked by energy : ACTIVE, VIGOROUS ♦ **Synonyms** STRENUOUS, LUSTY, VIGOROUS, VITAL — **en·er·get·i·cal·ly** \-ti-k(ə-)lē\ *adv*

**en·er·gise** *Brit var of* ENERGIZE

**en·er·gize** \'e-nər-,jīz\ *vb* **-gized; -giz·ing** : to give energy to

**en·er·gy** \'e-nər-jē\ *n, pl* **-gies** **1** : vigorous action : EFFORT **2** : capacity for action **3** : a fundamental entity of nature usu. regarded as the capacity for performing work **4** : usable power (as heat or electricity); *also* : the resources for producing such power

**energy level** *n* : one of the stable states of constant energy that may be assumed by a physical system (as the electrons in an atom)

**en·er·vate** \'e-nər-,vāt\ *vb* **-vat·ed; -vat·ing** : to lessen the strength or vigor of : weaken in mind or body ⟨*enervated* by work⟩ — **en·er·vat·ing·ly** \-,vā-tiŋ-lē\ *adv* — **en·er·va·tion** \,e-nər-'vā-shən\ *n*

**en·fee·ble** \in-'fē-bəl\ *vb* **-bled; -bling** : to make feeble ♦ **Synonyms** WEAKEN, DEBILITATE, SAP, UNDERMINE, CRIPPLE — **en·fee·ble·ment** *n*

**en·fi·lade** \'en-fə-,lād, -,läd\ *n* : gunfire directed along the length of an enemy battle line — **enfilade** *vb*

**en·fold** \in-'fōld\ *vb* **1** : ENVELOP ⟨darkness ~ed the city⟩ **2** : EMBRACE

**en·force** \in-'fȯrs\ *vb* **1** : COMPEL ⟨~ obedience by threats⟩ **2** : to execute effectively ⟨~ the law⟩ — **en·force·able** *adj* — **en·force·ment** *n*

**en·forc·er** \in-'fȯr-sər\ *n* : one that enforces; *esp* : a player (as in ice hockey) known for rough play

**en·fran·chise** \in-'fran-,chīz\ *vb* **-chised; -chis·ing** **1** : to set free (as from slavery)

**2** : to admit to citizenship; *also* : to grant the vote to — **en·fran·chise·ment** \-ˌchīz-mənt, -chəz-\ *n*

**eng** *abbr* engine; engineer; engineering

**Eng** *abbr* England; English

**en·gage** \in-'gāj\ *vb* **en·gaged; en·gag·ing 1** : PLEDGE; *esp* : to bind by a pledge to marry **2** : EMPLOY, HIRE **3** : to attract and hold esp. by interesting; *also* : to cause to participate **4** : to commence or take part in a venture ⟨*engaged* in shady deals⟩ **5** : to bring or enter into conflict ⟨~ the enemy⟩ **6** : to connect or interlock with : MESH; *also* : to cause to mesh

**en·gage·ment** \in-'gāj-mənt\ *n* **1** : APPOINTMENT **2** : EMPLOYMENT **3** : a mutual promise to marry : BETROTHAL **4** : a hostile encounter

**en·gag·ing** *adj* : ATTRACTIVE ⟨an ~ smile⟩ — **en·gag·ing·ly** *adv*

**en·gen·der** \in-'jen-dər\ *vb* **1** : BEGET **2** : BRING ABOUT, CREATE ⟨~ controversy⟩ ♦ **Synonyms** GENERATE, BREED, OCCASION, PRODUCE

**en·gine** \'en-jən\ *n* [ME *engin*, fr. AF, fr. L *ingenium* natural disposition, talent] **1** : a mechanical device **2** : a machine for converting energy into mechanical motion **3** : LOCOMOTIVE **4** : software that performs a fundamental function esp. of a larger program — **en·gine·less** *adj*

¹**en·gi·neer** \ˌen-jə-'nir\ *n* **1** : a member of a military unit specializing in engineering work **2** : a designer or builder of engines **3** : one trained in engineering **4** : one that operates an engine

²**engineer** *vb* **1** : to lay out or manage as an engineer **2** : to guide the course of ⟨~ a rally⟩ ♦ **Synonyms** PILOT, LEAD, STEER

**en·gi·neer·ing** *n* : the practical applications of scientific and mathematical principles

**En·glish** \'iŋ-glish\ *n* **1** : the language of England, the U.S., and many areas now or formerly under British rule **2 English** *pl* : the people of England **3** : spin imparted to a ball that is driven or rolled — **English** *adj* — **En·glish·man** \-mən\ *n* — **En·glish·wom·an** \-ˌwu̇-mən\ *n*

**English horn** *n* : a woodwind instrument longer than and having a range lower than the oboe

**English setter** *n* : any of a breed of hunting dogs with a flat silky coat of white or white with color

**English sparrow** *n* : HOUSE SPARROW

**English system** *n* : a system of weights and measures in which the foot is the principal unit of length and the pound is the principal unit of weight

**engr** *abbr* **1** engineer **2** engraved

**en·gram** \'en-ˌgram\ *n* : a hypothetical change in neural tissue postulated in order to account for persistence of memory

**en·grave** \in-'grāv\ *vb* **en·graved; en·grav·ing 1** : to produce (as letters or lines) by incising a surface **2** : to cut figures, letters, or designs on for printing; *also* : to print from an engraved plate ⟨~ an invitation⟩ **3** : PHOTOENGRAVE — **en·grav·er** *n*

**en·grav·ing** \in-'grā-viŋ\ *n* **1** : the art of one who engraves **2** : an engraved plate; *also* : a print made from it

**en·gross** \in-'grōs\ *vb* : to take up the whole interest or attention of ♦ **Synonyms** MONOPOLIZE, ABSORB, CONSUME

**en·gulf** \in-'gəlf\ *vb* : to flow over and enclose : OVERWHELM ⟨~ed in flames⟩

**en·hance** \in-'hans\ *vb* **en·hanced; en·hanc·ing** : to increase or improve (as in value or desirability) ♦ **Synonyms** HEIGHTEN, INTENSIFY, MAGNIFY — **en·hance·ment** *n*

**enig·ma** \i-'nig-mə\ *n* [L *aenigma*, fr. Gk *ainigma*, fr. *ainissesthai* to speak in riddles, fr. *ainos* fable] : something obscure or hard to understand

**enig·mat·ic** \ˌe-nig-'ma-tik\ *adj* : resembling an enigma ♦ **Synonyms** OBSCURE, CRYPTIC, MYSTIFYING — **en·ig·mat·i·cal·ly** \-ti-k(ə-)lē\ *adv*

**en·join** \in-'jȯin\ *vb* **1** : COMMAND, ORDER ⟨~ed us to desist⟩ **2** : FORBID ♦ **Synonyms** DIRECT, BID, CHARGE, COMMAND, INSTRUCT

**en·joy** \in-'jȯi\ *vb* **1** : to have for one's benefit or use ⟨~ good health⟩ **2** : to take pleasure or satisfaction in ⟨~ed the concert⟩ — **en·joy·able** *adj* — **en·joy·ment** *n*

**enl** *abbr* **1** enlarged **2** enlisted

**en·large** \in-'lärj\ *vb* **en·larged; en·larg·ing 1** : to make or grow larger **2** : ELABORATE ♦ **Synonyms** INCREASE, AUGMENT, MULTIPLY, EXPAND — **en·large·ment** *n*

**en·light·en** \in-'lī-tᵊn\ *vb* **1** : INSTRUCT, INFORM **2** : to give spiritual insight to — **en·light·en·ment** *n*

**en·list** \in-'list\ *vb* **1** : to secure the aid or support of **2** : to engage for service in the armed forces — **en·list·ee** \-ˌlis-'tē\ *n* — **en·list·ment** \-'list-mənt\ *n*

**en·list·ed** \in-'lis-təd\ *adj* : of, relating to, or forming the part of a military force below commissioned or warrant officers

**enlisted man** *n* : a man or woman in the armed forces ranking below a commissioned or warrant officer

**en·liv·en** \in-'lī-vən\ *vb* : to give life, action, or spirit to : ANIMATE

**en masse** \äⁿ-'mas\ *adv* [F] : in a body : as a whole

**en·mesh** \in-'mesh\ *vb* : to catch or entangle in or as if in meshes

**en·mi·ty** \'en-mə-tē\ *n, pl* **-ties** : ILL WILL; *esp* : mutual hatred ♦ **Synonyms** HOSTILITY, ANTIPATHY, ANIMOSITY, RANCOR, ANTAGONISM

**en·no·ble** \i-'nō-bəl\ *vb* **-bled; -bling** : EXALT, ELEVATE; *esp* : to raise to noble rank — **en·no·ble·ment** *n*

**en·nui** \ˌän-'wē\ *n* [F] : BOREDOM

**enor·mi·ty** \i-'nȯr-mə-tē\ *n, pl* **-ties 1** : an outrageous, vicious, or immoral act **2** : great wickedness **3** : IMMENSITY

**enor·mous** \i-'nȯr-məs\ *adj* [L *enormis*, fr. *e, ex* out of + *norma* rule] **1** : exceedingly wicked **2** : great in size, number, or degree : HUGE ♦ **Synonyms** IMMENSE,

VAST, GIGANTIC, COLOSSAL, MAMMOTH, ELEPHANTINE — **enor·mous·ly** *adv*

**¹enough** \i-'nəf\ *adj* : SUFFICIENT

**²enough** *adv* **1** : SUFFICIENTLY **2** : FULLY, QUITE **3** : TOLERABLY

**³enough** *pron* : a sufficient number, quantity, or amount

**en·quire** \in-'kwī(-ə)r\, **en·qui·ry** \'in-ˌkwī(-ə)r-ē, in-'; 'in-kwə-rē, 'iŋ-\ *chiefly Brit var of* INQUIRE, INQUIRY

**en·rage** \in-'rāj\ *vb* : to fill with rage

**en·rap·ture** \in-'rap-chər\ *vb* **en·rap·tured; en·rap·tur·ing** : DELIGHT

**en·rich** \in-'rich\ *vb* **1** : to make rich or richer **2** : ORNAMENT, ADORN — **en·rich·ment** *n*

**en·roll** *also* **en·rol** \in-'rōl\ *vb* **en·rolled; en·roll·ing 1** : to enter or register on a roll or list **2** : to offer (oneself) for enrolling — **en·roll·ment** *n*

**en route** \än-'rüt, en-\ *adv or adj* : on or along the way ⟨stalled while *en route* to work⟩

**ENS** *abbr* ensign

**en·sconce** \in-'skäns\ *vb* **en·sconced; en·sconc·ing 1** : SHELTER, CONCEAL **2** : to settle snugly or securely ◆ *Synonyms* SECRETE, HIDE, CACHE, STASH

**en·sem·ble** \än-'säm-bəl\ *n* [F, fr. *ensemble* together, fr. L *insimul* at the same time] : a group (as of singers, dancers, or players) or a set (as of clothes) producing a single effect

**en·sheathe** \in-'shēth\ *vb* : to cover with or as if with a sheath

**en·shrine** \in-'shrīn\ *vb* **1** : to enclose in or as if in a shrine **2** : to cherish as sacred — **en·shrine·ment** \-mənt\ *n*

**en·shroud** \in-'shraud\ *vb* : SHROUD, OBSCURE

**en·sign** \'en-sən, *1 also* 'en-ˌsīn\ *n* **1** : FLAG; *also* : BADGE, EMBLEM **2** : a commissioned officer in the navy ranking next below a lieutenant junior grade

**en·slave** \in-'slāv\ *vb* : to make a slave of — **en·slave·ment** *n*

**en·snare** \in-'sner\ *vb* : SNARE, TRAP ◆ *Synonyms* ENTRAP, BAG, CATCH, CAPTURE

**en·sue** \in-'sü\ *vb* **en·sued; en·su·ing** : to follow in time or as a result ⟨the birds escaped and chaos *ensued*⟩

**en·sure** \in-'shur\ *vb* **en·sured; en·sur·ing** : INSURE, GUARANTEE

**en·tail** \in-'tāl\ *vb* **1** : to limit the inheritance of (property) to the owner's lineal descendants or to a class thereof **2** : to include or involve as a necessary step or result ⟨the sacrifices that parenting ∼s⟩ — **en·tail·ment** *n*

**en·tan·gle** \in-'taŋ-gəl\ *vb* : TANGLE, CONFUSE — **en·tan·gle·ment** *n*

**en·tente** \än-'tänt\ *n* [F] : an understanding providing for joint action; *also* : parties linked by such an entente

**en·ter** \'en-tər\ *vb* **1** : to go or come in or into **2** : to become a member of : JOIN ⟨∼ the ministry⟩ **3** : BEGIN **4** : to take part in : CONTRIBUTE **5** : to go into or upon and take possession **6** : to set down (as in a list) : REGISTER ⟨∼ the data⟩ **7**

: to place (a complaint) before a court; *also* : to put on record ⟨∼ a complaint⟩

**en·ter·i·tis** \ˌen-tə-'rī-təs\ *n* : intestinal inflammation; *also* : a disease marked by this

**en·ter·prise** \'en-tər-ˌprīz\ *n* **1** : UNDERTAKING, PROJECT **2** : readiness for daring action : INITIATIVE **3** : a business organization

**en·ter·pris·ing** \-ˌprī-ziŋ\ *adj* : bold and vigorous in action : ENERGETIC

**en·ter·tain** \ˌen-tər-'tān\ *vb* **1** : to treat or receive as a guest **2** : AMUSE, DIVERT ⟨∼*ed* us with jokes⟩ **3** : to hold in mind ⟨∼*ed* thoughts of retirement⟩ ◆ *Synonyms* HARBOR, SHELTER, LODGE, HOUSE, BILLET — **en·ter·tain·er** *n* — **en·ter·tain·ment** *n*

**en·thrall** *or* **en·thral** \in-'throl\ *vb* **en·thralled; en·thrall·ing 1** : ENSLAVE **2** : to hold spellbound

**en·throne** \in-'thrōn\ *vb* **1** : to seat on or as if on a throne **2** : EXALT

**en·thuse** \in-'thüz, -'thyüz\ *vb* **en·thused; en·thus·ing 1** : to make enthusiastic **2** : to show enthusiasm

**en·thu·si·asm** \in-'thü-zē-ˌa-zəm, -'thyü-\ *n* [Gk *enthousiasmos*, fr. *enthousiazein* to be inspired, irreg. fr. *entheos* inspired, fr. *theos* god] **1** : strong warmth of feeling : keen interest : FERVOR **2** : a cause of fervor — **en·thu·si·ast** \-ˌast, -əst\ *n* — **en·thu·si·as·tic** \in-ˌthü-zē-'as-tik, -ˌthyü-\ *adj* — **en·thu·si·as·ti·cal·ly** \-ti-k(ə-)lē\ *adv*

**en·tice** \in-'tīs\ *vb* **en·ticed; en·tic·ing** : ALLURE, TEMPT — **en·tice·ment** *n*

**en·tire** \in-'tī(-ə)r\ *adj* : COMPLETE, WHOLE ◆ *Synonyms* SOUND, PERFECT, INTACT, UNDAMAGED — **en·tire·ly** *adv*

**en·tire·ty** \in-'tī-rə-tē, -'tī(-ə)r-tē\ *n, pl* **-ties 1** : COMPLETENESS **2** : WHOLE, TOTALITY

**en·ti·tle** \in-'tī-t⁰l\ *vb* **en·ti·tled; en·ti·tling 1** : NAME, DESIGNATE **2** : to give a right or claim to ⟨*entitled* to a fair trial⟩

**en·ti·tle·ment** \in-'tī-t⁰l-mənt\ *n* : a government program providing benefits to members of a specified group

**en·ti·ty** \'en-tə-tē\ *n, pl* **-ties 1** : EXISTENCE, BEING **2** : something with separate and real existence

**en·tomb** \in-'tüm\ *vb* : to place in a tomb : BURY — **en·tomb·ment** *n*

**en·to·mol·o·gy** \ˌen-tə-'mä-lə-jē\ *n* : a branch of zoology that deals with insects — **en·to·mo·log·i·cal** \-mə-'lä-ji-kəl\ *adj* — **en·to·mol·o·gist** \-jist\ *n*

**en·tou·rage** \ˌän-tu̇-'räzh\ *n* [F] : RETINUE

**en·tr'acte** \'än-ˌtrakt\ *n* [F] **1** : something (as a dance) performed between two acts of a play **2** : the interval between two acts of a play

**en·trails** \'en-ˌtrālz\ *n pl* : VISCERA; *esp* : INTESTINES

**¹en·trance** \'en-trəns\ *n* **1** : permission or right to enter **2** : the act of entering **3** : a means or place of entry

**²en·trance** \in-'trans\ *vb* **en·tranced; en·tranc·ing** : CHARM, DELIGHT

**en·trant** \'en-trənt\ n : one that enters esp. as a competitor

**en·trap** \in-'trap\ vb : ENSNARE, TRAP — **en·trap·ment** n

**en·treat** \in-'trēt\ vb : to ask urgently : BESEECH ♦ *Synonyms* BEG, IMPLORE, PLEAD, SUPPLICATE — **en·treaty** \-'trē-tē\ n

**en·trée** or **en·tree** \'än-ˌtrā\ n [F *entrée*] 1 : freedom of entry or access 2 : the main course of a meal in the U.S. ♦ *Synonyms* ADMISSION, ADMITTANCE, ENTRANCE

**en·trench** \in-'trench\ vb 1 : to place within or surround with a trench esp. for defense; *also* : to establish solidly <~ed customs> 2 : ENCROACH, TRESPASS — **en·trench·ment** n

**en·tre·pre·neur** \ˌän-trə-prə-'nər, -'nu̇r, -'nyu̇r\ n [F, fr. OF, fr. *entreprendre* to undertake] : one who organizes and assumes the risk of a business or enterprise — **en·tre·pre·neur·ial** \-'nu̇r-ē-əl, -'nyu̇r-, -'nər-\ adj — **en·tre·pre·neur·ship** \-ˌship\ n

**en·tro·py** \'en-trə-pē\ n, pl **-pies** 1 : the degree of disorder in a system 2 : an ultimate state of inert uniformity

**en·trust** \in-'trəst\ vb 1 : to commit something to as a trust 2 : to commit to another with confidence ♦ *Synonyms* CONFIDE, CONSIGN, RELEGATE, COMMEND

**en·try** \'en-trē\ n, pl **entries** 1 : ENTRANCE 2 : ENTRANCE 3; *also* : VESTIBULE 1 3 : an entering in a record; *also* : an item so entered 4 : a headword with its definition or identification; *also* : VOCABULARY ENTRY 5 : one entered in something (as a contest or market)

**en·twine** \in-'twīn\ vb : to twine together or around

**enu·mer·ate** \i-'nü-mə-ˌrāt, -'nyü-\ vb **-at·ed; -at·ing** 1 : to determine the number of : COUNT 2 : LIST — **enu·mer·a·tion** \-ˌnü-mə-'rā-shən, -ˌnyü-\ n

**enun·ci·ate** \ē-'nən-sē-ˌāt\ vb **-at·ed; -at·ing** 1 : to state definitely; *also* : ANNOUNCE, PROCLAIM 2 : PRONOUNCE, ARTICULATE <~ every syllable> — **enun·ci·a·tion** \-ˌnən-sē-'ā-shən\ n

**en·ure·sis** \ˌen-yu̇-'rē-səs\ n : involuntary discharge of urine : BED-WETTING

**env** abbr envelope

**en·vel·op** \in-'ve-ləp\ vb : to enclose completely with or as if with a covering — **en·vel·op·ment** n

**en·ve·lope** \'en-və-ˌlōp, 'än-\ n 1 : a usu. paper container for a letter 2 : WRAPPER, COVERING 3 : a conventionally accepted limit <fashions that push the ~>

**en·ven·om** \in-'ve-nəm\ vb 1 : to make poisonous 2 : EMBITTER

**en·vi·able** \'en-vē-ə-bəl\ adj : highly desirable — **en·vi·ably** \-blē\ adv

**en·vi·ous** \'en-vē-əs\ adj : feeling or showing envy — **en·vi·ous·ly** adv — **en·vi·ous·ness** n

**en·vi·ron·ment** \in-'vī-rən-mənt, -'vī(-ə)rn-\ n 1 : SURROUNDINGS 2 : the whole complex of factors (as soil, climate, and living things) that influence the form and the ability to survive of a plant or animal or ecological community — **en·vi·ron·men·tal** \-ˌvī-rən-'men-t³l, -ˌvīrn-\ adj — **en·vi·ron·men·tal·ly** \-t³l-ē\ adv

**en·vi·ron·men·tal·ist** \-ˌvī-rən-'men-təl-ist, -ˌvīr(-ə)n-\ n : a person concerned about environmental quality esp. with respect to control of pollution — **en·vi·ron·men·tal·ism** \-ˌvī-rən-'men-tə-ˌli-zəm, -ˌvī(-ə)rn-\

**en·vi·rons** \in-'vī-rənz\ n pl 1 : SUBURBS 2 : SURROUNDINGS; *also* : VICINITY

**en·vis·age** \in-'vi-zij\ vb **-aged; -ag·ing** : to have a mental picture of

**en·vi·sion** \in-'vi-zhən, en-\ vb : to picture to oneself <~s world peace>

**en·voy** \'en-ˌvȯi, 'än-\ n 1 : a diplomatic agent 2 : REPRESENTATIVE, MESSENGER

**¹en·vy** \'en-vē\ n [ME *envie*, fr. AF, fr. L *invidia*, fr. *invidus* envious, fr. *invidēre* to look askance at, envy, fr. *vidēre* to see] : painful or resentful awareness of another's advantages; *also* : an object of envy

**²envy** vb **en·vied; en·vy·ing** : to feel envy toward or on account of

**en·zyme** \'en-ˌzīm\ n : any of various complex proteins produced by living cells that catalyze specific biochemical reactions at body temperatures — **en·zy·mat·ic** \ˌen-zə-'ma-tik\ adj

**Eo·cene** \'ē-ə-ˌsēn\ adj : of, relating to, or being the epoch of the Tertiary between the Paleocene and the Oligocene — **Eo·cene** n

**EOE** abbr equal opportunity employer

**eo·lian** \ē-'ō-lē-ən\ adj : borne, deposited, or produced by the wind

**EOM** abbr end of month

**eon** var of AEON

**EP** abbr European plan

**EPA** abbr Environmental Protection Agency

**ep·au·let** also **ep·au·lette** \ˌe-pə-'let\ n [F *épaulette*, dim. of *épaule* shoulder] : a shoulder ornament esp. on a coat or military uniform

**épée** \'e-ˌpā, ā-'pā\ n [F] : a fencing or dueling sword

**Eph** or **Ephes** abbr Ephesians

**ephed·rine** \i-'fe-drən\ n : a stimulant drug used to treat asthma and nasal congestion

**ephem·era** \i-'fe-mər-ə\ n pl : paper items (as posters or tickets) of little original value collected usu. as a hobby

**ephem·er·al** \i-'fe-mə-rəl\ adj [Gk *ephēmeros* lasting a day, daily, fr. *epi-* on + *hēmera* day] : SHORT-LIVED, TRANSITORY ♦ *Synonyms* PASSING, FLEETING, TRANSIENT, EVANESCENT — **ephem·er·al·i·ty** \i-ˌfe-mə-'ra-lə-tē\ n

**Ephe·sians** \i-'fē-zhənz\ n — see BIBLE table

**ep·ic** \'e-pik\ n : a long poem in elevated style narrating the deeds of a hero — **epic** adj

**epi·cen·ter** \'e-pi-ˌsen-tər\ n : the point on the earth's surface directly above the point of origin of an earthquake

**epi·cure** \'e-pi-ˌkyu̇r\ n : a person with

sensitive and discriminating tastes esp. in food and wine

**ep·i·cu·re·an** \ˌe-pi-kyu̇-ˈrē-ən, -ˈkyu̇r-ē-\ *n* : EPICURE — **epicurean** *adj*

¹**ep·i·dem·ic** \ˌe-pə-ˈde-mik\ *adj* **1** : affecting many persons at one time ⟨∼ disease⟩; *also* : excessively prevalent

²**epidemic** *n* : an epidemic outbreak esp. of disease

**ep·i·de·mi·ol·o·gy** \ˌep-ə-ˌdē-mē-ˈä-lə-jē\ *n* : the study of the incidence, distribution, and control of disease in a population — **ep·i·de·mi·o·log·i·cal** \-ˌdē-mē-ə-ˈlä-ji-kəl\ *also* **ep·i·de·mi·o·log·ic** \-jik\ *adj* — **ep·i·de·mi·ol·o·gist** \-ˈä-lə-jist\ *n*

**epi·der·mis** \ˌe-pə-ˈdər-məs\ *n* : an outer layer esp. of skin — **epi·der·mal** \-məl\ *adj*

**epi·du·ral** \ˌe-pi-ˈd(y)u̇r-əl\ *adj* : administered into the space outside the membrane that envelops the spinal cord ⟨∼ anesthesia⟩ — **epidural** *n*

**epi·glot·tis** \ˌe-pə-ˈglä-təs\ *n* : a thin plate of flexible tissue protecting the tracheal opening during swallowing

**ep·i·gram** \ˈe-pə-ˌgram\ *n* : a short witty poem or saying — **ep·i·gram·mat·ic** \ˌe-pə-grə-ˈma-tik\ *adj*

**ep·i·lep·sy** \ˈe-pə-ˌlep-sē\ *n, pl* **-sies** [ultim. fr. Gk *epilēpsia*, fr. *epilambanein* to seize] : a disorder marked by abnormal electrical discharges in the brain and typically manifested by sudden periods of diminished consciousness or by convulsions — **ep·i·lep·tic** \ˌe-pə-ˈlep-tik\ *adj or n*

**ep·i·logue** *also* **ep·i·log** \ˈe-pə-ˌlȯg, -ˌläg\ *n* **1** : a concluding section of a literary work **2** : a speech addressed to the spectators by an actor at the end of a play

**epi·neph·rine** \ˌe-pə-ˈne-frən\ *n* : an adrenal hormone used medicinally esp. as a heart stimulant, a muscle relaxant, and a vasoconstrictor

**epiph·a·ny** \i-ˈpi-fə-nē\ *n, pl* **-nies 1** *cap* : January 6 observed as a church festival in commemoration of the coming of the Magi to Jesus at Bethlehem **2** : a sudden striking understanding of something

**epis·co·pa·cy** \i-ˈpis-kə-pə-sē\ *n, pl* **-cies 1** : government of a church by bishops **2** : EPISCOPATE

**epis·co·pal** \i-ˈpis-kə-pəl\ *adj* **1** : of or relating to a bishop or episcopacy **2** *cap* : of or relating to the Protestant Episcopal Church

**Epis·co·pa·lian** \i-ˌpis-kə-ˈpāl-yən\ *n* : a member of the Protestant Episcopal Church

**epis·co·pate** \i-ˈpis-kə-pət, -ˌpāt\ *n* **1** : the rank, office, or term of a bishop **2** : a body of bishops

**ep·i·sode** \ˈe-pə-ˌsōd\ *n* [Gk *epeisodion*, fr. *epeisodios* coming in besides, fr. *eisodios* coming in, fr. *eis* into + *hodos* road, journey] **1** : a unit of action in a dramatic or literary work **2** : an incident in a course of events : OCCURRENCE ⟨a feverish ∼⟩ — **ep·i·sod·ic** \ˌe-pə-ˈsä-dik\ *adj*

**epis·tle** \i-ˈpi-səl\ *n* **1** *cap* : one of the

letters of the New Testament **2** : LETTER — **epis·to·lary** \i-ˈpis-tə-ˌler-ē\ *adj*

**ep·i·taph** \ˈe-pə-ˌtaf\ *n* : an inscription in memory of a dead person

**ep·i·tha·la·mi·um** \ˌe-pə-thə-ˈlā-mē-əm\ *or* **ep·i·tha·la·mi·on** \-mē-ən\ *n, pl* **-mi·ums** *or* **-mia** \-mē-ə\ : a song or poem in honor of a bride and bridegroom

**ep·i·the·li·um** \ˌe-pə-ˈthē-lē-əm\ *n, pl* **-lia** \-lē·ə\ : a cellular membrane covering a bodily surface or lining a cavity — **ep·i·the·li·al** \-lē-əl\ *adj*

**ep·i·thet** \ˈe-pə-ˌthet, -thət\ *n* : a characterizing and often abusive word or phrase ⟨a racial ∼⟩

**epit·o·me** \i-ˈpi-tə-mē\ *n* **1** : ABSTRACT, SUMMARY **2** : EMBODIMENT ⟨the ∼ of elegance⟩ — **epit·o·mize** \-ˌmīz\ *vb*

**ep·och** \ˈe-pək, ˈe-ˌpäk\ *n* : a usu. extended period : ERA, AGE — **ep·och·al** \-pə-kəl, -ˌpä-\ *adj*

**ep·onym** \ˈe-pə-ˌnim\ *n* **1** : one for whom something is or is believed to be named **2** : a name (as of a disease) based on or derived from an eponym — **epon·y·mous** \i-ˈpä-nə-məs\ *adj*

**ep·oxy** \i-ˈpäk-sē\ *vb* **ep·ox·ied** *or* **ep·oxyed**; **ep·oxy·ing** : to glue, fill, or coat with epoxy resin

**epoxy resin** *n* : a synthetic resin used in coatings and adhesives

**ep·si·lon** \ˈep-sə-ˌlän, -lən\ *n* : the 5th letter of the Greek alphabet — E or ε

**Ep·som salts** \ˈep-səm-\ *n* : a bitter colorless or white magnesium salt with cathartic properties

**eq** *abbr* **1** equal **2** equation

**equa·ble** \ˈe-kwə-bəl, ˈē-\ *adj* : UNIFORM, EVEN; *esp* : free from unpleasant extremes — **equa·bil·i·ty** \ˌe-kwə-ˈbi-lə-tē, ˌē-\ *n* — **equa·bly** \ˈe-kwə-blē, ˈē-\ *adv*

¹**equal** \ˈē-kwəl\ *adj* **1** : of the same measure, quantity, value, quality, number, degree, or status as another ⟨∼ opportunity⟩ **2** : IMPARTIAL ⟨∼ justice⟩ **3** : free from extremes **4** : able to cope with a situation or task — **equal·i·ty** \i-ˈkwä-lə-tē\ *n* — **equal·ly** *adv*

²**equal** *vb* **equaled** *or* **equalled**; **equal·ing** *or* **equal·ling** : to be or become equal to; *also* : to be identical in value to

³**equal** *n* : one that is equal

**equal·ise, equal·is·er** *Brit var of* EQUAL-IZE, EQUALIZER

**equal·ize** \ˈē-kwə-ˌlīz\ *vb* **-ized; -iz·ing** : to make equal, uniform, or constant — **equal·i·za·tion** \ˌē-kwə-lə-ˈzā-shən\ *n* — **equal·iz·er** *n*

**equals sign** *or* **equal sign** *n* : a sign = indicating equivalence

**equa·nim·i·ty** \ˌē-kwə-ˈni-mə-tē, ˌe-\ *n, pl* **-ties** : COMPOSURE

**equate** \i-ˈkwāt\ *vb* **equat·ed; equat·ing** : to make, treat, or regard as equal or comparable ⟨∼s liars with thieves⟩

**equa·tion** \i-ˈkwā-zhən\ *n* **1** : an act of equating : the state of being equated **2** : a usu. formal statement of equivalence esp. of mathematical expressions

**equa·tor** \i-ˈkwā-tər, ˈē-\ *n* : an imaginary circle around the earth that is everywhere equally distant from the two poles — **equa·to·ri·al** \ˌē-kwə-ˈtȯr-ē-əl, ˌe-\ *adj*

**equer·ry** \ˈe-kwə-rē, i-ˈkwer-ē\ *n, pl* **-ries** **1** : an officer in charge of the horses of a prince or noble **2** : a personal attendant of a member of the British royal family

¹**eques·tri·an** \i-ˈkwes-trē-ən\ *adj* : of or relating to horseback riding ⟨~ competition⟩; *also* : representing a person on horseback ⟨an ~ statue⟩

²**equestrian** *n* : one who rides a horse

**eques·tri·enne** \i-ˌkwes-trē-ˈen\ *n* : a female rider on horseback

**equi·dis·tant** \ˌē-kwə-ˈdis-tənt\ *adj* : equally distant

**equi·lat·er·al** \ˌē-kwə-ˈla-tə-rəl\ *adj* : having all sides or faces equal ⟨~ triangles⟩

**equi·lib·ri·um** \ˌē-kwə-ˈli-brē-əm, ˌe-\ *n, pl* **-ri·ums** *or* **-ria** \-brē-ə\ : a state of intellectual or emotional balance; *also* : a state of balance between opposing forces or actions ♦ *Synonyms* POISE, BALANCE, EQUIPOISE

**equine** \ˈē-ˌkwīn, ˈe-\ *adj* [L *equinus*, fr. *equus* horse] : of or relating to the horse — **equine** *n*

**equi·noc·tial** \ˌē-kwə-ˈnäk-shəl, ˌe-\ *adj* : relating to an equinox

**equi·nox** \ˈē-kwə-ˌnäks, ˈe-\ *n* : either of the two times each year when the sun appears directly overhead at the equator and day and night are everywhere on earth of equal length

**equip** \i-ˈkwip\ *vb* **equipped; equipping** [AF *eskiper* to load on board a ship, outfit, man, of Gmc origin] **1** : to supply with needed resources **2** : to make ready : PREPARE ⟨*equipped* for the challenge⟩

**eq·ui·page** \ˈe-kwə-pij\ *n* : a horse-drawn carriage usu. with its servants

**equip·ment** \i-ˈkwip-mənt\ *n* **1** : things used in equipping : SUPPLIES, OUTFIT **2** : the equipping of a person or thing : the state of being equipped

**equi·poise** \ˈe-kwə-ˌpȯiz, ˈē-\ *n* **1** : BALANCE, EQUILIBRIUM **2** : COUNTERBALANCE

**eq·ui·ta·ble** \ˈe-kwə-tə-bəl\ *adj* : JUST, FAIR — **eq·ui·ta·bly** \-blē\ *adv*

**eq·ui·ta·tion** \ˌe-kwə-ˈtā-shən\ *n* : the act or art of riding on horseback

**eq·ui·ty** \ˈe-kwə-tē\ *n, pl* **-ties** **1** : JUSTNESS, IMPARTIALITY **2** : value of a property or of an interest in it in excess of claims against it

**equiv** *abbr* equivalent

**equiv·a·lent** \i-ˈkwi-və-lənt\ *adj* : EQUAL; *also* : virtually identical — **equiv·a·lence** \-ləns\ *n* — **equivalent** *n*

**equiv·o·cal** \i-ˈkwi-və-kəl\ *adj* **1** : AMBIGUOUS ⟨~ answers⟩ **2** : UNCERTAIN, UNDECIDED **3** : SUSPICIOUS, DUBIOUS ⟨~ behavior⟩ ♦ *Synonyms* OBSCURE, DARK, VAGUE, ENIGMATIC — **equiv·o·cal·ly** *adv*

**equiv·o·cate** \i-ˈkwi-və-ˌkāt\ *vb* **-cat·ed; -cat·ing 1** : to use misleading language **2** : to avoid giving a definite answer — **equiv·o·ca·tion** \-ˌkwi-və-ˈkā-shən\ *n*

¹**-er** \ər\ *adj suffix or adv suffix* — used to form the comparative degree of adjectives and adverbs of one or two syllables ⟨hotter⟩ ⟨drier⟩ ⟨sillier⟩ and sometimes of longer ones

²**-er** \ər\ *also* **-ier** \ē-ər, yər\ *or* **-yer** \yər\ *n suffix* **1** : a person occupationally connected with ⟨furrier⟩ ⟨lawyer⟩ **2** : a person or thing belonging to or associated with ⟨old-timer⟩ **3** : a native of : resident of ⟨New Zealander⟩ **4** : one that has ⟨double-decker⟩ **5** : one that produces or yields ⟨porker⟩ **6** : one that does or performs (a specified action) ⟨batter⟩ **7** : one that is a suitable object of (a specified action) ⟨broiler⟩ **8** : one that is ⟨foreigner⟩

**Er** *symbol* erbium

**ER** *abbr* emergency room

**era** \ˈer-ə, ˈe-rə, ˈir-ə\ *n* [LL *aera*, fr. L, counters, pl. of *aes* copper, money] **1** : a chronological order or system of notation reckoned from a given date as basis **2** : a period identified by some special feature ⟨the ~ of industrialization⟩ **3** : any of the four major divisions of geologic time ♦ *Synonyms* AGE, EPOCH, PERIOD, TIME

**ERA** *abbr* **1** earned run average **2** Equal Rights Amendment

**erad·i·cate** \i-ˈra-də-ˌkāt\ *vb* **-cat·ed; -cat·ing** [L *eradicatus*, pp. of *eradicare*, fr. *e-* out + *radix* root] : UPROOT, ELIMINATE ♦ *Synonyms* EXTERMINATE, ANNIHILATE, ABOLISH, EXTINGUISH — **erad·i·ca·ble** \-di-kə-bəl\ *adj* — **erad·i·ca·tion** \-ˌra-də-ˈkā-shən\ *n*

**erase** \i-ˈrās\ *vb* **erased; eras·ing** : to rub or scratch out (as written words); *also* : OBLITERATE ♦ *Synonyms* CANCEL, EFFACE, DELETE, EXPUNGE — **eras·er** *n* — **era·sure** \i-ˈrā-shər\ *n*

**er·bi·um** \ˈər-bē-əm\ *n* : a rare metallic element found with yttrium

¹**ere** \ˈer\ *prep* : BEFORE

²**ere** *conj* : BEFORE

¹**erect** \i-ˈrekt\ *adj* **1** : not leaning or lying down : UPRIGHT **2** : being in a state of physiological erection

²**erect** *vb* **1** : BUILD **2** : to fix or set in an upright position ⟨~ an antenna⟩ **3** : SET UP; *also* : ESTABLISH, DEVELOP

**erec·tile** \i-ˈrek-tᵊl, -ˈrek-ˌtī(-ə)l\ *adj* : capable of becoming erect ⟨~ tissue⟩ ⟨~ feathers of a bird⟩

**erec·tion** \i-ˈrek-shən\ *n* **1** : the turgid state of a previously flaccid bodily part when it becomes dilated with blood **2** : CONSTRUCTION ⟨the ~ of a building⟩

**ere·long** \er-ˈlȯn\ *adv* : before long

**er·e·mite** \ˈer-ə-ˌmīt\ *n* : HERMIT

**er·go** \ˈer-gō, ˈər-\ *adv* [L] : THEREFORE

**er·go·nom·ics** \ˌər-gə-ˈnä-miks\ *n sing or pl* : an applied science concerned with designing and arranging things people use in order to improve efficiency and safety — **er·go·nom·ic** \-mik\ *adj*

**er·got** \ˈər-gət, -ˌgät\ *n* **1** : a disease of rye and other cereals caused by a fungus; *also* : this fungus **2** : a medicinal compound or preparation derived from an ergot fungus

**er·mine** \ˈər-mən\ *n, pl* **ermines 1** : any of several weasels with winter fur mostly white; *also* : this white fur **2** : a rank or office whose official robe is ornamented with ermine

**erode** \i-'rōd\ *vb* **erod·ed; erod·ing** : to diminish or destroy by degrees; *esp* : to gradually eat into or wear away ⟨soil *eroded* by wind and water⟩ — **erod·ible** *also* **erod·able** \-'rō-də-bəl\ *adj*

**erog·e·nous** \i-'rä-jə-nəs\ *adj* **1** : sexually sensitive ⟨~ zones⟩ **2** : of, relating to, or arousing sexual feelings

**ero·sion** \i-'rō-zhən\ *n* : the process or state of being eroded — **ero·sion·al** \-'rō-zhə-nəl\ *adj* — **ero·sion·al·ly** *adv*

**ero·sive** \i-'rō-siv\ *adj* : tending to erode — **ero·sive·ness** *n*

**erot·ic** \i-'rä-tik\ *adj* : relating to or dealing with sexual love : AMATORY ⟨~ art⟩ — **erot·i·cal·ly** \-ti-k(ə-)lē\ *adv* — **erot·i·cism** \-tə-ˌsi-zəm\ *n*

**err** \'er, 'ər\ *vb* : to be or do wrong

**er·rand** \'er-ənd\ *n* : a short trip taken to do something; *also* : the object or purpose of such a trip

**er·rant** \'er-ənt\ *adj* **1** : WANDERING ⟨an ~ knight⟩ **2** : straying outside proper bounds ⟨an ~ throw⟩ **3** : behaving wrongly ⟨an ~ child⟩

**er·ra·ta** \e-'rä-tə\ *n* : a list of corrigenda

**er·rat·ic** \i-'ra-tik\ *adj* **1** : having no fixed course **2** : INCONSISTENT ⟨~ dieting⟩; *also* : ECCENTRIC ⟨~ behavior⟩ — **er·rat·i·cal·ly** \-ti-k(ə-)lē\ *adv*

**er·ra·tum** \e-'rä-təm\ *n, pl* **-ta** \-tə\ : CORRIGENDUM

**er·ro·ne·ous** \i-'rō-nē-əs, e-'rō-\ *adj* : INCORRECT — **er·ro·ne·ous·ly** *adv*

**er·ror** \'er-ər\ *n* **1** : a usu. ignorant or unintentional deviating from accuracy or truth ⟨made an ~ in adding⟩ **2** : a defensive misplay in baseball **3** : the state of one that errs ⟨to be in ~⟩ **4** : a product of mistake ⟨a typographical ~⟩ — **er·ror·less** *adj*

**er·satz** \'er-ˌzäts\ *adj* [G *ersatz-*, fr. *Ersatz*, n., substitute] : being usu. an artificial and inferior substitute ⟨~ diamonds⟩

**erst** \'ərst\ *adv, archaic* : ERSTWHILE

**¹erst·while** \-ˌhwī(-ə)l\ *adv* : in the past : FORMERLY

**²erstwhile** *adj* : FORMER, PREVIOUS ⟨~ friends⟩

**er·u·di·tion** \ˌer-ə-'di-shən, ˌer-yə-\ *n* : SCHOLARSHIP, LEARNING — **er·u·dite** \'er-ə-ˌdīt, 'er-yə-\ *adj*

**erupt** \i-'rəpt\ *vb* **1** : to burst forth or cause to burst forth : EXPLODE **2** : to break through a surface ⟨teeth ~*ing* through the gum⟩ **3** : to break out with or as if with a skin rash — **erup·tion** \-'rəp-shən\ *n* — **erup·tive** \-tiv\ *adj*

**-ery** *n suffix* **1** : qualities collectively : character : -NESS ⟨snob*bery*⟩ **2** : art : practice ⟨cook*ery*⟩ **3** : place of doing, keeping, producing, or selling (the thing specified) ⟨fish*ery*⟩ ⟨bak*ery*⟩ **4** : collection : aggregate ⟨fin*ery*⟩ **5** : state or condition ⟨slav*ery*⟩

**ery·sip·e·las** \ˌer-ə-'si-pə-ləs, ˌir-\ *n* : an acute bacterial disease marked by fever and severe skin inflammation

**er·y·the·ma** \ˌer-ə-'thē-mə\ *n* : abnormal redness of the skin due to capillary congestion (as in inflammation)

**eryth·ro·cyte** \i-'ri-thrə-ˌsīt\ *n* : RED BLOOD CELL

**Es** *symbol* einsteinium

**¹-es** \əz, iz *after* s, z, sh, ch; z *after* v *or a vowel*\ *n pl suffix* — used to form the plural of most nouns that end in *s* ⟨glass*es*⟩, *z* ⟨fuzz*es*⟩, *sh* ⟨bush*es*⟩, *ch* ⟨peach*es*⟩, or a final *y* that changes to *i* ⟨lad*ies*⟩ and of some nouns ending in *f* that changes to *v* ⟨loa*ves*⟩

**²-es** *vb suffix* — used to form the third person singular present of most verbs that end in *s* ⟨bless*es*⟩, *z* ⟨fizz*es*⟩, *sh* ⟨hush*es*⟩, *ch* ⟨catch*es*⟩, or a final *y* that changes to *i* ⟨def*ies*⟩

**es·ca·late** \'es-kə-ˌlāt\ *vb* **-lat·ed; -lat·ing** : to increase in extent, volume, number, intensity, or scope ⟨the violence *escalated*⟩ — **es·ca·la·tion** \ˌes-kə-'lā-shən\ *n*

**es·ca·la·tor** \'es-kə-ˌlā-tər\ *n* : a moving set of stairs

**escallop** *var of* SCALLOP

**es·ca·pade** \'es-kə-ˌpād\ *n* [F, action of escaping] : a mischievous adventure

**¹es·cape** \is-'kāp\ *vb* **es·caped; es·cap·ing** [ME, fr. AF *escaper, eschaper*, fr. VL *excappare*, fr. L *ex-* out + LL *cappa* head covering, cloak] **1** : to get free or away **2** : to avoid a threatening evil **3** : AVOID ⟨~ injury⟩ **4** : ELUDE ⟨his name ~*s* me⟩ **5** : to be produced or uttered involuntarily by ⟨let a sob ~ him⟩

**²escape** *n* **1** : flight from or avoidance of something unpleasant **2** : LEAKAGE **3** : a means of escape

**³escape** *adj* : providing a means or way of escape

**es·cap·ee** \is-ˌkā-'pē, ˌes-(ˌ)kā-\ *n* : one that has escaped esp. from prison

**escape velocity** *n* : the minimum velocity needed by a body (as a rocket) to escape from the gravitational field of a celestial body (as the earth)

**es·cap·ism** \is-'kā-ˌpi-zəm\ *n* : diversion of the mind to imaginative activity as an escape from routine — **es·cap·ist** \-pist\ *adj or n*

**es·car·got** \ˌes-ˌkär-'gō\ *n, pl* **-gots** \-'gō(z)\ : a snail prepared for use as food

**es·ca·role** \'es-kə-ˌrōl\ *n* : ENDIVE 1

**es·carp·ment** \is-'kärp-mənt\ *n* **1** : a steep slope in front of a fortification **2** : a long cliff

**es·chew** \is-'chü\ *vb* : SHUN, AVOID

**¹es·cort** \'es-ˌkòrt\ *n* : one (as a person or warship) accompanying another esp. as a protection or courtesy

**²es·cort** \is-'kòrt, es-\ *vb* : to accompany as an escort

**es·crow** \'es-ˌkrō\ *n* [AF *escrowe* scroll, strip of parchment] : something (as a deed or a sum of money) delivered by one person to another to be delivered to a third party only upon the fulfillment of a condition; *also* : a fund or deposit serving as an escrow

**es·cu·do** \is-'kü-dō\ *n, pl* **-dos** **1** : the former basic monetary unit of Portugal **2** — see MONEY table

**es·cutch·eon** \is-'kə-chən\ *n* : the usu.

shield-shaped surface on which a coat of arms is shown

**Esd** *abbr* Esdras

**Es·dras** \'ez-drəs\ *n* — see BIBLE table

**ESE** *abbr* east-southeast

**Es·ki·mo** \'es-kə-‚mō\ *n* **1** : a member of a group of peoples of northern Canada, Greenland, Alaska, and eastern Siberia **2** : any of the languages of the Eskimo peoples

**Eskimo dog** *n* : a sled dog of American origin

**ESL** *abbr* English as a second language

**esoph·a·gus** \i-'sä-fə-gəs\ *n, pl* **-gi** \-‚gī, -‚jī\ : a muscular tube that leads from the cavity behind the mouth to the stomach — **esoph·a·ge·al** \-‚sä-fə-'jē-əl\ *adj*

**es·o·ter·ic** \‚e-sə-'ter-ik\ *adj* **1** : designed for or understood only by the specially initiated **2** : PRIVATE, SECRET

**esp** *abbr* especially

**ESP** \‚ē-(‚)es-'pē\ *n* : EXTRASENSORY PERCEPTION

**es·pa·drille** \'es-pə-‚dril\ *n* [F] : a flat sandal usu. having a fabric upper and a flexible sole

**es·pal·ier** \i-'pal-yər, -‚yā\ *n* : a plant (as a fruit tree) trained to grow flat against a support — **espalier** *vb*

**es·pe·cial** \is-'pe-shəl\ *adj* : SPECIAL, PARTICULAR — **es·pe·cial·ly** *adv*

**Es·pe·ran·to** \‚es-pə-'ran-tō, -'rän-\ *n* : an artificial international language based esp. on words common to the chief European languages

**es·pi·o·nage** \'es-pē-ə-‚näzh, -nij\ *n* [F *espionnage*] : the practice of spying

**es·pla·nade** \'es-plə-‚näd\ *n* : a level open stretch or area; *esp* : one for walking or driving along a shore

**es·pous·al** \i-'spau̇-zəl\ *n* **1** : BETROTHAL; *also* : WEDDING **2** : a taking up (as of a cause) as a supporter ⟨~ of human rights⟩ — **es·pouse** \-'spau̇z\ *vb*

**espres·so** \e-'spre-sō\ *n, pl* **-sos** : coffee brewed by forcing steam or hot water through finely ground darkly roasted coffee beans

**es·prit** \i-'sprē\ *n* : sprightly wit

**es·prit de corps** \i-‚sprē-də-'kȯr\ *n* [F] : the common spirit existing in the members of a group

**es·py** \i-'spī\ *vb* **es·pied; es·py·ing** : to catch sight of ♦ *Synonyms* BEHOLD, SEE, VIEW, DESCRY

**Esq** *or* **Esqr** *abbr* esquire

**es·quire** \'es-‚kwī(-ə)r\ *n* [ME, fr. AF *esquier* squire, fr. LL *scutarius*, fr. L *scutum* shield] **1** : a man of the English gentry ranking next below a knight **2** : a candidate for knighthood serving as attendant to a knight **3** — used as a title of courtesy

**-ess** \əs, ‚es\ *n suffix* : female ⟨author*ess*⟩

**¹es·say** \e-'sā, 'e-‚sā\ *vb* : ATTEMPT, TRY

**²es·say** \'e-‚sā, *in sense 1* e-'sā\ *n* **1** : ATTEMPT **2** \'e-‚sā\ : a literary composition usu. dealing with a subject from a limited or personal point of view — **es·say·ist** \'e-‚sā-ist\ *n*

**es·sence** \'e-s³ns\ *n* **1** : fundamental nature or quality **2** : a substance distilled or extracted from another substance (as a plant or drug) and having the special qualities of the original substance **3** : PERFUME **4** : the most significant element or aspect of something ⟨the ~ of the issue⟩

**¹es·sen·tial** \i-'sen-chəl\ *adj* **1** : of, relating to, or constituting an essence ⟨voting is an ~ right of citizenship⟩ ⟨~ oils⟩ **2** : of the utmost importance : INDISPENSABLE ⟨water is ~ for life⟩ **3** : being a substance that must be obtained from the diet because it is not sufficiently produced by the body ⟨~ amino acids⟩ ♦ *Synonyms* IMPERATIVE, NECESSARY, NECESSITOUS — **es·sen·tial·ly** *adv*

**²essential** *n* : something essential

**est** *abbr* **1** established **2** estimate; estimated

**EST** *abbr* eastern standard time

**¹-est** \əst, ist\ *adj suffix or adv suffix* — used to form the superlative degree of adjectives and adverbs of one or two syllables ⟨fatt*est*⟩ ⟨lat*est*⟩ ⟨lucki*est*⟩ ⟨often*est*⟩ and less often of longer ones

**²-est** \əst, ist\ *or* **-st** \st\ *vb suffix* — used to form the archaic second person singular of English verbs ⟨with *thou*⟩ ⟨did*st*⟩

**es·tab·lish** \i-'sta-blish\ *vb* **1** : to institute permanently ⟨~ a law⟩ **2** : FOUND ⟨~ a settlement⟩; *also* : EFFECT **3** : to make firm or stable **4** : to put on a firm basis : SET UP ⟨~ a son in business⟩ **5** : to gain acceptance or recognition of ⟨the movie ~ed her as a star⟩; *also* : PROVE ⟨~ed his innocence⟩

**es·tab·lish·ment** \-mənt\ *n* **1** : something established **2** : a place of residence or business with its furnishings and staff **3** : an established ruling or controlling group ⟨the literary ~⟩ **4** : the act or state of establishing or being established

**es·tate** \i-'stāt\ *n* **1** : STATE, CONDITION; *also* : social standing **2** : a social or political class ⟨the three ~s of nobility, clergy, and commons⟩ **3** : a person's possessions : FORTUNE **4** : a landed property

**¹es·teem** \i-'stēm\ *n* : high regard

**²esteem** *vb* **1** : REGARD ⟨was highly ~ed⟩ **2** : to set a high value on ♦ *Synonyms* RESPECT, ADMIRE, REVERE

**es·ter** \'es-tər\ *n* : an often fragrant organic compound formed by the reaction of an acid and an alcohol

**Esth** *abbr* Esther

**Es·ther** \'es-tər\ *n* — see BIBLE table

**esthete, esthetic, esthetically, esthetics** *var of* AESTHETE, AESTHETIC, AESTHETICALLY, AESTHETICS

**es·ti·ma·ble** \'es-tə-mə-bəl\ *adj* : worthy of esteem ⟨an ~ adversary⟩

**¹es·ti·mate** \'es-tə-‚māt\ *vb* **-mat·ed; -mat·ing** **1** : to give or form an approximation (as of value, size, or cost) **2** : JUDGE, CONCLUDE ♦ *Synonyms* EVALUATE, VALUE, RATE, APPRAISE, ASSAY, ASSESS — **es·ti·ma·tor** \-‚mā-tər\ *n*

**²es·ti·mate** \'es-tə-mət\ *n* **1** : OPINION, JUDGMENT **2** : a rough or approximate calculation **3** : a statement of the cost of work to be done

# 245 — estimation • eucalyptus

es·ti·ma·tion \,es-tə-'mā-shən\ n 1 : JUDGMENT, OPINION 2 : ESTIMATE 3 : ESTEEM, HONOR

es·ti·vate \'es-tə-,vāt\ vb -vat·ed; -vat·ing : to pass the summer in an inactive or resting state ⟨creatures estivating in the cool mud⟩ — es·ti·va·tion \,es-tə-'vā-shən\ n

es·trange \i-'strānj\ vb es·tranged; es·trang·ing : to alienate the affections or confidence of — es·trange·ment n

es·tro·gen \'es-trə-jən\ n : a steroid (as a sex hormone) that tends to cause estrus and the development of female secondary sex characteristics — es·tro·gen·ic \,es-trə-'je-nik\ adj

estrous cycle n : the cycle of changes in the endocrine and reproductive systems of a female mammal from the beginning of one period of estrus to the beginning of the next

es·trus \'es-trəs\ n : a periodic state of sexual excitability during which the female of most mammals is willing to mate with the male and is capable of becoming pregnant : HEAT — es·trous \-trəs\ adj

es·tu·ary \'es-chə-,wer-ē\ n, pl -ar·ies : an arm of the sea at the mouth of a river — es·tu·a·rine \-wə-,rīn, -,rēn, -rin\ adj

ET abbr eastern time

eta \'ā-tə\ n : the 7th letter of the Greek alphabet — H or η

ETA abbr estimated time of arrival

et al \et-'al\ abbr [L et alii (masc.), et aliae (fem.), or et alia (neut.)] and others

etc abbr et cetera

et cet·era \et-'se-tə-rə, -'se-trə\ [L] and others esp. of the same kind

etch \'ech\ vb [D etsen, fr. G ätzen to etch, corrode, fr. OHG azzen to feed] 1 : to produce (as a design) on a hard material by corroding its surface (as by acid) 2 : to delineate clearly — etch·er n

etch·ing n 1 : the action, process, or art of etching 2 : a design produced on or print made from an etched plate

ETD abbr estimated time of departure

eter·nal \i-'tər-nᵊl\ adj : EVERLASTING, PERPETUAL — eter·nal·ly adv

eter·ni·ty \i-'tər-nə-tē\ n, pl -ties 1 : infinite duration 2 : IMMORTALITY

¹-eth \əth, ith\ or -th \th\ vb suffix — used to form the archaic third person singular present of verbs ⟨doth⟩

²-eth — see ²-TH

eth·ane \'e-,thān\ n : a colorless odorless gaseous hydrocarbon found in natural gas and used esp. as a fuel

eth·a·nol \'e-thə-,nȯl\ n : ALCOHOL 1

ether \'ē-thər\ n 1 : the upper regions of space; also : the gaseous element formerly held to fill these regions 2 : a light flammable liquid used as an anesthetic and solvent

ethe·re·al \i-'thir-ē-əl\ adj 1 : CELESTIAL, HEAVENLY 2 : exceptionally delicate : AIRY, DAINTY ⟨~ flaky pastry⟩ — ethe·re·al·ly adv — ethe·re·al·ness n

Ether·net \'ē-thər-,net\ n : a computer network architecture for local area networks

eth·i·cal \'e-thi-kəl\ adj 1 : of or relating to ethics 2 : conforming to accepted and esp. professional standards of conduct ♦ Synonyms VIRTUOUS, MORAL, PRINCIPLED — eth·i·cal·ly adv

eth·ics \'e-thiks\ n sing or pl 1 : a discipline dealing with good and evil and with moral duty 2 : moral principles or practice

¹eth·nic \'eth-nik\ adj [ME, heathen, fr. LL ethnicus, fr. Gk ethnikos national, gentile, fr. ethnos nation, people] : of or relating to races or large groups of people classed according to common traits and customs — eth·ni·cal·ly adv

²ethnic n : a member of a minority ethnic group who retains its customs, language, or social views

eth·nol·o·gy \eth-'nä-lə-jē\ n : a science dealing with the races of human beings, their origin, distribution, characteristics, and relations — eth·no·log·i·cal \,eth-nə-'lä-ji-kəl\ adj — eth·nol·o·gist \eth-'nä-lə-jist\ n

ethol·o·gy \ē-'thä-lə-jē\ n : the scientific and objective study of animal behavior — etho·log·i·cal \,ē-thə-'lä-ji-kəl, ,e-\ adj — ethol·o·gist \ē-'thä-lə-jist\ n

ethos \'ē-,thäs\ n : the distinguishing character, sentiment, moral nature, or guiding beliefs of a person, group, or institution

ethyl alcohol n : ALCOHOL 1

eth·yl·ene \'e-thə-,lēn\ n : a colorless flammable gas found in coal gas or obtained from petroleum

eti·ol·o·gy \,ē-tē-'ä-lə-jē\ n : the causes of a disease or abnormal condition; also : a branch of medicine concerned with the causes and origins of diseases — eti·o·log·ic \,ē-tē-ə-'lä-jik\ or eti·o·log·i·cal \-ji-kəl\ adj

et·i·quette \'e-ti-kət, -,ket\ n [F étiquette, lit., label, list] : the forms prescribed by custom or authority to be observed in social, official, or professional life ♦ Synonyms PROPRIETY, DECORUM, DECENCY, DIGNITY

Etrus·can \i-'trəs-kən\ n 1 : the language of the Etruscans 2 : an inhabitant of ancient Etruria — Etruscan adj

et seq abbr [L et sequens] and the following one; [L et sequentes (masc. & fem. pl.) or et sequentia (neut. pl.)] and the following ones

-ette \'et, ,et, ət, it\ n suffix 1 : little one ⟨dinette⟩ 2 : female ⟨usherette⟩

étude \'ā-,tüd, -,tyüd\ n [F, lit., study] : a musical composition for practice to develop technical skill

et·y·mol·o·gy \,e-tə-'mä-lə-jē\ n, pl -gies 1 : the history of a linguistic form (as a word) shown by tracing its development and relationships 2 : a branch of linguistics dealing with etymologies — et·y·mo·log·i·cal \-mə-'lä-ji-kəl\ adj — et·y·mol·o·gist \-'mä-lə-jist\ n

Eu symbol europium

EU abbr European Union

eu·ca·lyp·tus \,yü-kə-'lip-təs\ n, pl -ti \-,tī\ or -tus·es : any of a genus of mostly Australian evergreen trees widely grown for shade or their wood, oils, resins, and gums

**Eu·cha·rist** \'yü-kə-rəst\ n : COMMUNION 2 — **eu·cha·ris·tic** \,yü-kə-'ris-tik\ adj, often cap

¹**eu·chre** \'yü-kər\ n : a card game in which the side naming the trump must take three of five tricks to win

²**euchre** vb **eu·chred; eu·chring** : CHEAT, TRICK

**eu·clid·e·an** also **eu·clid·i·an** \yü-'kli-dē-ən\ adj, often cap : of or relating to the geometry of Euclid or a geometry based on similar axioms

**eu·gen·ics** \yù-'je-niks\ n : a science dealing with the improvement (as by selective breeding) of hereditary qualities esp. of human beings — **eu·gen·ic** \-nik\ adj

**eu·lo·gy** \'yü-lə-jē\ n, pl **-gies** 1 : a speech in praise of some person or thing esp. in honor of a deceased person 2 : high praise — **eu·lo·gis·tic** \,yü-lə-'jis-tik\ adj — **eu·lo·gize** \'yü-lə-,jīz\ vb

**eu·nuch** \'yü-nək\ n : a castrated man

**eu·phe·mism** \'yü-fə-,mi-zəm\ n [Gk euphēmismos, fr. euphēmos auspicious, sounding good, fr. eu- good + phēmē speech] : the substitution of a mild or pleasant expression for one offensive or unpleasant; also : the expression substituted — **eu·phe·mis·tic** \,yü-fə-'mis-tik\ adj — **eu·phe·mis·ti·cal·ly** \-tī-k(ə)lē\ adv

**eu·pho·ni·ous** \yù-'fō-nē-əs\ adj : pleasing to the ear — **eu·pho·ni·ous·ly** adv

**eu·pho·ny** \'yü-fə-nē\ n, pl **-nies** : the effect produced by words so combined as to please the ear

**eu·pho·ria** \yù-'fór-ē-ə\ n : a marked feeling of well-being or elation — **eu·phor·ic** \-'fór-ik\ adj

**Eur** abbr Europe; European

**Eur·asian** \yù-'rā-zhən, -shən\ adj 1 : of mixed European and Asian origin 2 : of or relating to Europe and Asia — **Eurasian** n

**eu·re·ka** \yù-'rē-kə\ interj [Gk heurēka I have found, fr. heuriskein to find; fr. the exclamation attributed to Archimedes on discovering a method for determining the purity of gold] — used to express triumph on a discovery

**eu·ro** \'yùr-ō\ n, pl **euros** : the common basic monetary unit of most countries of the European Union — see MONEY table

**Eu·ro-Amer·i·can** \,yùr-ō-ə-'mer-ə-kən\ n 1 : a person of mixed European and American ancestry 2 : CAUCASIAN

**Eu·ro·bond** \'yùr-ō-,bänd\ n : a bond of a U.S. corporation that is sold outside the U.S. but that is valued and paid for in dollars and yields interest in dollars

**Eu·ro·cur·ren·cy** \,yùr-ō-'kər-ən-sē\ n : moneys (as of the U.S. and Japan) held outside their countries of origin and used in the money markets of Europe

**Eu·ro·dol·lar** \'yùr-ō-,dä-lər\ n : a U.S. dollar held as Eurocurrency

**Eu·ro·pe·an** \,yùr-ə-'pē-ən\ n 1 : a native or inhabitant of Europe 2 : a person of

European descent — **European** adj — **Eu·ro·pe·an·ize** \-ə-,nīz\ vb

**European–American** n : EURO-AMERICAN

**Eu·ro·pe·an·ism** \,yùr-,ō-'pē-ə-ni-zəm\ n 1 : allegiance to the traditions, interests, or ideals of Europeans 2 : advocacy of political and economic integration of Europe — **eu·ro·pe·an·ist** \-nist\ n

**European plan** n : a hotel plan whereby the daily rates cover only the cost of the room

**eu·ro·pi·um** \yù-'rō-pē-əm\ n : a rare metallic chemical element

**eu·sta·chian tube** \yù-'stā-shən-\ n, often cap E : a tube connecting the inner cavity of the ear with the throat and equalizing air pressure on both sides of the eardrum

**eu·tha·na·sia** \,yü-thə-'nā-zhə\ n [Gk, easy death, fr. eu- good + thanatos death] : the act or practice of killing or permitting the death of hopelessly sick or injured persons or animals with as little pain as possible for reasons of mercy

**EVA** abbr extravehicular activity

**evac·u·ate** \i-'va-kyə-,wāt\ vb **-at·ed; -at·ing** 1 : EMPTY 2 : to discharge wastes from the body 3 : to remove or withdraw from : VACATE — **evac·u·a·tion** \-,va-kyə-'wā-shən\ n

**evac·u·ee** \i-,va-kyə-'wē\ n : a person removed from a dangerous place

**evade** \i-'vād\ vb **evad·ed; evad·ing** : to manage to avoid esp. by dexterity or slyness : ELUDE, EVADE ⟨evaded capture⟩

**eval·u·ate** \i-'val-yü-,wāt\ vb **-at·ed; -at·ing** : APPRAISE, VALUE ⟨~ the candidates⟩ — **eval·u·a·tion** \-,val-yü-'wā-shən\ n

**ev·a·nes·cent** \,e-və-'ne-s³nt\ adj : tending to vanish like vapor ⟨~ pleasures⟩
♦ **Synonyms** PASSING, TRANSIENT, TRANSITORY, MOMENTARY — **ev·a·nes·cence** \-s³ns\ n

**evan·gel·i·cal** \,ē-,van-'je-li-kəl, ,e-vən-\ adj [LL evangelium gospel, fr. Gk evangelion, fr. euangelos bringing good news, fr. eu- good + angelos messenger] 1 : of or relating to the Christian gospel esp. as presented in the four Gospels 2 : of or relating to certain Protestant churches emphasizing the authority of Scripture and the importance of preaching as contrasted with ritual 3 : ZEALOUS ⟨~ fervor⟩ — **Evangelical** n — **Evan·gel·i·cal·ism** \-kə-,li-zəm\ n — **evan·gel·i·cal·ly** adv

**evan·ge·lism** \i-'van-jə-,li-zəm\ n 1 : the winning or revival of personal commitments to Christ 2 : militant or crusading zeal — **evan·ge·lis·tic** \-,van-jə-'lis-tik\ adj — **evan·ge·lis·ti·cal·ly** adv

**evan·ge·list** \i-'van-jə-list\ n 1 often cap : the writer of any of the four Gospels 2 : a person who evangelizes; esp : a Protestant minister or layman who preaches at special services

**evan·ge·lize** \i-'van-jə-,līz\ vb **-lized; -liz·ing** 1 : to preach the gospel 2 : to convert to Christianity

**evap** abbr evaporate

**evap·o·rate** \i-'va-pə-,rāt\ vb **-rat·ed;**

-rat·ing 1 : to pass off or cause to pass off in vapor 2 : to disappear quickly 3 : to drive out the moisture from (as by heat) — **evap·o·ra·tion** \-,va-pə-'rā-shən\ n — **evap·o·ra·tor** \-,rā-tər\ n

**evap·o·rite** \i-'va-pə-,rīt\ n : a sedimentary rock that originates by the evaporation of seawater in an enclosed basin

**eva·sion** \i-'vā-zhən\ n 1 : a means of evading 2 : an act or instance of evading ⟨arrested for tax ~⟩ — **eva·sive** \i-'vā-siv\ adj — **eva·sive·ness** n

**eve** \'ēv\ n 1 : EVENING 2 : the period just before some important event

¹**even** \'ē-vən\ adj 1 : LEVEL, FLAT ⟨~ ground⟩ 2 : REGULAR, SMOOTH 3 : EQUAL, FAIR ⟨an ~ exchange⟩ 4 : BALANCED; also : fully revenged 5 : divisible by two 6 : EXACT ⟨an ~ dollar⟩ — **even·ly** adv — **even·ness** n

²**even** adv 1 : EXACTLY, PRECISELY 2 : FULLY, QUITE 3 : at the very time 4 — used as an intensive to stress identity ⟨~ I know that⟩ 5 — used as an intensive to emphasize something extreme or highly unlikely ⟨so simple ~ a child can do it⟩ 6 — used as an intensive to stress the comparative degree ⟨did ~ better⟩ 7 — used as an intensive to indicate a small or minimum degree ⟨didn't ~ try⟩

³**even** vb : to make or become even

**even·hand·ed** \,ē-vən-'han-dəd\ adj : FAIR, IMPARTIAL ⟨an ~ assessment⟩ — **even·hand·ed·ly** adv

**eve·ning** \'ēv-niŋ\ n 1 : the end of the day and early part of the night 2 chiefly Southern & Midland : AFTERNOON

**evening primrose** n : a coarse biennial herb with yellow flowers that open in the evening

**evening star** n : a bright planet (as Venus) seen esp. in the western sky at or after sunset

**even·song** \'ē-vən-,soŋ\ n, often cap 1 : VESPERS 2 : evening prayer esp. when sung

**event** \i-'vent\ n [MF or L; MF, fr. L eventus, fr. evenire to happen, fr. venire to come] 1 : OCCURRENCE 2 : a noteworthy happening 3 : CONTINGENCY ⟨in the ~ of rain⟩ 4 : a contest in a program of sports — **event·ful** adj

**even·tide** \'ē-vən-,tīd\ n : EVENING

**even·tu·al** \i-'ven-chü-wəl\ adj : coming at some later time : ULTIMATE — **even·tu·al·ly** adv

**even·tu·al·i·ty** \i-,ven-chü-'wa-lə-tē\ n, pl -ties : a possible event or outcome

**even·tu·ate** \i-'ven-chü-,wāt\ vb -at·ed; -at·ing : to result finally

**ev·er** \'e-vər\ adv 1 : ALWAYS ⟨~ faithful⟩ 2 : at any time 3 : in any way : AT ALL ⟨how can I ~ thank you⟩

**ev·er·glade** \'e-vər-,glād\ n : a low-lying tract of swampy or marshy land

**ev·er·green** \-,grēn\ adj : having foliage that remains green ⟨most coniferous trees are ~⟩ — **evergreen** n

¹**ev·er·last·ing** \,e-vər-'las-tiŋ\ adj 1 : enduring forever : ETERNAL 2 : having or being flowers or foliage that retain form

or color for a long time when dried — **ev·er·last·ing·ly** adv

²**everlasting** n 1 : ETERNITY ⟨from ~⟩ 2 : a plant with everlasting flowers; also : its flower

**ev·er·more** \,e-vər-'mór\ adv : FOREVER

**ev·ery** \'ev-rē\ adj [ME everich, every, fr. OE æfre ælc, fr. æfre ever + ælc each] 1 : being each one of a group 2 : all possible ⟨given ~ chance⟩; also : COMPLETE ⟨have ~ confidence⟩

**ev·ery·body** \'ev-ri-,bä-dē, -bə-\ pron : every person

**ev·ery·day** \'ev-rē-,dā\ adj : encountered or used routinely : ORDINARY

**ev·ery·one** \-(,)wən\ pron : EVERYBODY

**ev·ery·thing** \'ev-rē-,thiŋ\ pron 1 : all that exists 2 : all that is relevant

**ev·ery·where** \'ev-rē-,hwer\ adv : in every place or part

**evg** abbr evening

**evict** \i-'vikt\ vb 1 : to put (a person) out from a property by legal process 2 : EXPEL ♦ Synonyms EJECT, OUST, DISMISS — **evic·tion** \-'vik-shən\ n

¹**ev·i·dence** \'e-və-dəns\ n 1 : an outward sign 2 : PROOF, TESTIMONY; esp : matter submitted in court to determine the truth of alleged facts

²**evidence** vb : PROVE, EVINCE

**ev·i·dent** \-dənt\ adj : clear to the vision and understanding ♦ Synonyms MANIFEST, DISTINCT, OBVIOUS, APPARENT, PLAIN

**ev·i·dent·ly** \'e-və-dənt-lē, ,e-və-'dent-\ adv 1 : in an evident manner 2 : on the basis of available evidence

¹**evil** \'ē-vəl\ adj evil·er or evil·ler; evil·est or evil·lest 1 : WICKED 2 : causing or threatening distress or harm : PERNICIOUS — **evil·ly** adv

²**evil** n 1 : the fact of suffering, misfortune, and wrongdoing 2 : a source of sorrow, distress, or calamity

**evil·do·er** \,ē-vəl-'dü-ər\ n : one who does evil

**evil–mind·ed** \-'mīn-dəd\ adj : having an evil disposition or evil thoughts — **evil–mind·ed·ly** adv

**evince** \i-'vins\ vb evinced; evinc·ing : SHOW, REVEAL ⟨evinced an interest in art⟩

**evis·cer·ate** \i-'vi-sə-,rāt\ vb -at·ed; -at·ing 1 : to remove the entrails of 2 : to deprive of vital content or force — **evis·cer·a·tion** \-,vi-sə-'rā-shən\ n

**evoke** \i-'vōk\ vb evoked; evok·ing : to call forth or up — **evo·ca·tion** \,ē-vō-'kā-shən, ,e-və-\ n — **evoc·a·tive** \i-'vä-kə-tiv\ adj

**evo·lu·tion** \,e-və-'lü-shən\ n 1 : one of a set of prescribed movements (as in a dance) 2 : a process of change in a particular direction 3 : a theory that the various kinds of plants and animals are descended from other kinds that lived in earlier times and that the differences are due to inherited changes that occurred over many generations — **evo·lu·tion·ary** \-shə-,ner-ē\ adj — **evo·lu·tion·ist** \-shə-nist\ n

**evolve** \i-'välv\ vb evolved; evolv·ing [L

*evolvere* to unroll] : to develop or change by or as if by evolution

**EW** *abbr* enlisted woman

**e-waste** \'ē-ˌwāst\ *n* : waste consisting of discarded electronic products

**ewe** \'yü\ *n* : a female sheep

**ew·er** \'yü-ər\ *n* : a water pitcher

**¹ex** \'eks\ *prep* [L] : out of : FROM

**²ex** *n* : a former spouse

**³ex** *abbr* **1** example **2** express **3** extra

**Ex** *abbr* Exodus

**ex-** \e *also occurs in this prefix where only* i *is shown below (as in* "express") *and* ks *sometimes occurs where only* gz *is shown (as in* "exact")\ *prefix* **1** : out of : outside **2** : former ⟨*ex*-president⟩

**ex·ac·er·bate** \ig-ˈza-sər-ˌbāt\ *vb* **-bat·ed; -bat·ing** : to make more violent, bitter, or severe ⟨comments that ∼ the dispute⟩ — **ex·ac·er·ba·tion** \-ˌza-sər-ˈbā-shən\ *n*

**¹ex·act** \ig-ˈzakt\ *vb* **1** : to compel to furnish **2** : to call for as suitable or necessary — **ex·ac·tion** \-ˈzak-shən\ *n*

**²exact** *adj* : precisely accurate or correct — **ex·act·ly** *adv* — **ex·act·ness** *n*

**ex·act·ing** \ig-ˈzak-tiŋ\ *adj* **1** : greatly demanding ⟨an ∼ taskmaster⟩ **2** : requiring close attention and precision

**ex·ac·ti·tude** \ig-ˈzak-tə-ˌtüd, -ˌtyüd\ *n* : the quality or state of being exact

**ex·ag·ger·ate** \ig-ˈza-jə-ˌrāt\ *vb* **-at·ed; -at·ing** [L *exaggeratus*, pp. of *exaggerare*, lit., to heap up, fr. *agger* heap] : to enlarge (as a statement) beyond normal : OVERSTATE — **ex·ag·ger·at·ed·ly** *adv* — **ex·ag·ger·a·tion** \-ˌza-jə-ˈrā-shən\ *n* — **ex·ag·ger·a·tor** \-ˈza-jə-ˌrā-tər\ *n*

**ex·alt** \ig-ˈzȯlt\ *vb* **1** : to raise up esp. in rank, power, or dignity **2** : GLORIFY ⟨the poem ∼s her beauty⟩ — **ex·al·ta·tion** \ˌeg-ˌzȯl-ˈtā-shən, ˌek-ˌsȯl-\ *n*

**ex·am** \ig-ˈzam\ *n* : EXAMINATION

**ex·am·ine** \ig-ˈza-mən\ *vb* **ex·am·ined; ex·am·in·ing 1** : to inspect closely **2** : QUESTION; *esp* : to test by questioning ♦ **Synonyms** INTERROGATE, QUERY, QUIZ, CATECHIZE — **ex·am·i·na·tion** \-ˌza-mə-ˈnā-shən\ *n*

**ex·am·ple** \ig-ˈzam-pəl\ *n* **1** : something forming a model to be followed or avoided **2** : a representative sample **3** : a problem to be solved in order to show the application of some rule

**ex·as·per·ate** \ig-ˈzas-pə-ˌrāt\ *vb* **-at·ed; -at·ing** : VEX, IRRITATE — **ex·as·per·a·tion** \ig-ˌzas-pə-ˈrā-shən\ *n*

**exc** *abbr* **1** excellent **2** except

**ex·ca·vate** \'ek-skə-ˌvāt\ *vb* **-vat·ed; -vat·ing 1** : to hollow out; *also* : to form by hollowing out **2** : to dig out and remove (as earth) **3** : to reveal to view by digging away a covering — **ex·ca·va·tion** \ˌek-skə-ˈvā-shən\ *n* — **ex·ca·va·tor** \'ek-skə-ˌvā-tər\ *n*

**ex·ceed** \ik-ˈsēd\ *vb* **1** : to go or be beyond the limit of **2** : SURPASS ⟨∼ed our expectations⟩ — **ex·ceed·ance** \-ˈsē-dᵊns\ *n*

**ex·ceed·ing·ly** \-ˈsē-diŋ-lē\ *also* **ex·ceed·ing** *adv* : EXTREMELY, VERY

**ex·cel** \ik-ˈsel\ *vb* **ex·celled; ex·cel·ling** : SURPASS, OUTDO

**ex·cel·lence** \'ek-sə-ləns\ *n* **1** : the quality of being excellent **2** : an excellent or valuable quality : VIRTUE **3** : EXCELLENCY 2

**ex·cel·len·cy** \-lən-sē\ *n, pl* **-cies 1** : EXCELLENCE **2** — used as a title of honor

**ex·cel·lent** \-lənt\ *adj* : very good of its kind : FIRST-CLASS — **ex·cel·lent·ly** *adv*

**ex·cel·si·or** \ik-ˈsel-sē-ər\ *n* : fine curled wood shavings used esp. for packing fragile items

**¹ex·cept** \ik-ˈsept\ *also* **ex·cept·ing** *prep* : with the exclusion or exception of ⟨daily ∼ Sundays⟩

**²except** *vb* **1** : to take or leave out ⟨children were ∼ed from the study⟩ **2** : OBJECT

**³except** *also* **excepting** *conj* **1** : UNLESS ⟨∼ you repent⟩ **2** : ONLY ⟨I'd go, ∼ it's too far⟩

**ex·cep·tion** \ik-ˈsep-shən\ *n* **1** : the act of excepting **2** : something excepted ⟨an ∼ to the rule⟩ **3** : OBJECTION

**ex·cep·tion·able** \ik-ˈsep-shə-nə-bəl\ *adj* : OBJECTIONABLE

**ex·cep·tion·al** \ik-ˈsep-shə-nəl\ *adj* **1** : UNUSUAL ⟨an ∼ number of rainy days⟩ **2** : SUPERIOR ⟨∼ skill⟩ — **ex·cep·tion·al·ly** *adv*

**ex·cerpt** \'ek-ˌsərpt, 'eg-ˌzərpt\ *n* : a passage selected or copied : EXTRACT — **excerpt** \ek-ˈsərpt, eg-ˈzərpt; 'ek-ˌsərpt, 'eg-ˌzərpt\ *vb*

**ex·cess** \ik-ˈses, 'ek-ˌses\ *n* **1** : SUPERFLUITY, SURPLUS **2** : the amount by which one quantity exceeds another **3** : INTEMPERANCE; *also* : an instance of intemperance ⟨the dictator's ∼es⟩ — **excess** *adj* — **ex·ces·sive** \ik-ˈse-siv\ *adj* — **ex·ces·sive·ly** *adv*

**exch** *abbr* exchange; exchanged

**¹ex·change** \iks-ˈchānj\ *n* **1** : the giving or taking of one thing in return for another : TRADE **2** : a substituting of one thing for another **3** : interchange of valuables and esp. of bills of exchange or money of different countries **4** : a place where things and services are exchanged; *esp* : a marketplace for securities **5** : a central office in which telephone lines are connected for communication

**²exchange** *vb* **ex·changed; ex·chang·ing** : to transfer in return for some equivalent : BARTER, SWAP — **ex·change·able** \iks-ˈchān-jə-bəl\ *adj*

**ex·che·quer** \'eks-ˌche-kər\ *n* [ME *escheker*, fr. AF, chessboard, counting table, office charged with revenue collection, fr. *eschec* check (in chess), chess] : TREASURY; *esp* : a national treasury

**ex·cise** \'ek-ˌsīz\ *n* : a tax on the manufacture, sale, or consumption of a commodity

**ex·ci·sion** \ik-ˈsi-zhən\ *n* : removal by or as if by cutting out esp. by surgical means — **ex·cise** \ik-ˈsīz\ *vb*

**ex·cit·able** \ik-ˈsī-tə-bəl\ *adj* : easily excited — **ex·cit·abil·i·ty** \-ˌsī-tə-ˈbi-lə-tē\ *n*

**ex·cite** \ik-ˈsīt\ *vb* **ex·cit·ed; ex·cit·ing 1** : to stir up the emotions of : ROUSE **2** : to increase the activity of : STIMULATE ♦ **Synonyms** PROVOKE, PIQUE, QUICK-

EN — **ex·ci·ta·tion** \ˌek-ˌsī-ˈtā-shən, ˌek-sə-\ n — **ex·cit·ed·ly** adv — **ex·cit·ing·ly** adv

**ex·cite·ment** \ik-ˈsīt-mənt\ n : AGITATION, STIR

**ex·claim** \iks-ˈklām\ vb : to cry out, speak, or utter sharply or vehemently — **ex·cla·ma·tion** \ˌcks-klə-ˈmā-shən\ n — **ex·clam·a·to·ry** \iks-ˈkla-mə-ˌtōr-ē\ adj

**exclamation point** n : a punctuation mark ! used esp. after an interjection or exclamation

**ex·clude** \iks-ˈklüd\ vb **ex·clud·ed; ex·clud·ing** 1 : to prevent from using or participating : BAR 2 : to put out : EXPEL — **ex·clu·sion** \-ˈklü-zhən\ n — **ex·clu·sion·ary** \-zhə-ˌner-ē\ adj

**ex·clu·sive** \iks-ˈklü-siv\ adj 1 : reserved for particular persons 2 : snobbishly aloof; also : STYLISH 3 : SOLE ⟨~ rights⟩; also : UNDIVIDED ⟨my ~ attention⟩
♦ **Synonyms** CHIC, MODISH, SMART, SWANK, FASHIONABLE — **exclusive** n — **ex·clu·sive·ly** adv — **ex·clu·sive·ness** n — **ex·clu·siv·i·ty** \ˌeks-ˌklü-si-və-tē, iks-, -zl-\ n

**exclusive of** prep : not taking into account

**ex·cog·i·tate** \ek-ˈskä-jə-ˌtāt\ vb : to think out : DEVISE

**ex·com·mu·ni·cate** \ˌek-skə-ˈmyü-nə-ˌkāt\ vb : to cut off officially from the rites of the church — **ex·com·mu·ni·ca·tion** \-ˌmyü-nə-ˈkā-shən\ n

**ex·co·ri·ate** \ek-ˈskōr-ē-ˌāt\ vb **-at·ed; -at·ing** : to criticize severely — **ex·co·ri·a·tion** \(ˌ)ek-ˌskōr-ē-ˈā-shən\ n

**ex·cre·ment** \ˈek-skrə-mənt\ n : waste discharged from the body; esp : FECES — **ex·cre·men·tal** \ˌek-skrə-ˈmen-t³l\ adj

**ex·cres·cence** \ik-ˈskre-s³ns\ n : OUTGROWTH; esp : an abnormal outgrowth (as a wart)

**ex·cre·ta** \ik-ˈskrē-tə\ n pl : waste matter (as feces) separated or eliminated from the body

**ex·crete** \ik-ˈskrēt\ vb **ex·cret·ed; ex·cret·ing** : to separate and eliminate wastes from the body esp. in urine or sweat — **ex·cre·tion** \-ˈskrē-shən\ n — **ex·cre·to·ry** \ˈek-skrə-ˌtōr-ē\ adj

**ex·cru·ci·at·ing** \ik-ˈskrü-shē-ˌā-tiŋ\ adj [L excruciare to torture, fr. cruciare to crucify, fr. crux cross] : intensely painful or distressing ♦ **Synonyms** AGONIZING, HARROWING, TORTUROUS — **ex·cru·ci·at·ing·ly** adv

**ex·cul·pate** \ˈek-(ˌ)skəl-ˌpāt\ vb **-pat·ed; -pat·ing** : to clear from alleged fault or guilt ♦ **Synonyms** ABSOLVE, EXONERATE, ACQUIT, VINDICATE, CLEAR

**ex·cur·sion** \ik-ˈskər-zhən\ n 1 : EXPEDITION; esp : a pleasure trip 2 : DIGRESSION — **ex·cur·sion·ist** \-zhə-nist\ n

**ex·cur·sive** \-ˈskər-siv\ adj : constituting or characterized by digression

¹**ex·cuse** \ik-ˈskyüz\ vb **ex·cused; ex·cus·ing** [ME, fr. AF excuser, fr. L excusare, fr. causa cause, explanation] 1 : to make apology for 2 : PARDON 3 : to release from an obligation 4 : JUSTIFY — **ex·cus·able** adj

²**excuse** \ik-ˈskyüs\ n 1 : an act of excusing 2 : something that excuses or is a reason for excusing : JUSTIFICATION

**exec** n : EXECUTIVE

**ex·e·cra·ble** \ˈek-si-krə-bəl\ adj 1 : DETESTABLE ⟨~ crimes⟩ 2 : very bad ⟨~ spelling⟩

**ex·e·crate** \ˈek-sə-ˌkrāt\ vb **-crat·ed; -crat·ing** [L exsecratus, pp. of exsecrari to put under a curse, fr. ex- out of + sacer sacred] : to denounce as evil or detestable; also : DETEST — **ex·e·cra·tion** \ˌek-sə-ˈkrā-shən\ n

**ex·e·cute** \ˈek-si-ˌkyüt\ vb **-cut·ed; -cut·ing** 1 : to carry out fully : put completely into effect 2 : to do what is called for (as by a law) 3 : to put to death in accordance with a legal sentence 4 : to produce by carrying out a design 5 : to do what is needed to give validity to ⟨~ a deed⟩ — **ex·e·cu·tion** \ˌek-si-ˈkyü-shən\ n — **ex·e·cu·tion·er** n

¹**ex·ec·u·tive** \ig-ˈze-kyə-tiv\ adj 1 : of or relating to the enforcement of laws and the conduct of affairs 2 : designed for or related to carrying out plans or purposes

²**executive** n 1 : the branch of government with executive duties 2 : one having administrative or managerial responsibility

**ex·ec·u·tor** \ig-ˈze-kyə-tər\ n : the person named in a will to execute it

**ex·ec·u·trix** \ig-ˈze-kyə-ˌtriks\ n, pl **ex·ec·u·tri·ces** \-ˌze-kyə-ˈtrī-ˌsēz\ or **ex·ec·u·trix·es** \-ˈze-kyə-ˌtrik-səz\ : a woman who is an executor

**ex·e·ge·sis** \ˌek-sə-ˈjē-səs\ n, pl **-ge·ses** \-ˈjē-ˌsēz\ : explanation or critical interpretation of a text

**ex·e·gete** \ˈek-sə-ˌjēt\ n : one who practices exegesis — **ex·e·get·i·cal** \ˌek-sə-ˈje-ti-kəl\ adj

**ex·em·plar** \ig-ˈzem-ˌplär, -plər\ n 1 : one that serves as a model or example; esp : an ideal model ⟨an ~ of courage⟩ 2 : a typical instance or example

**ex·em·pla·ry** \ig-ˈzem-plə-rē\ adj : serving as a pattern; also : COMMENDABLE ⟨~ courage⟩

**ex·em·pli·fy** \ig-ˈzem-plə-ˌfī\ vb **-fied; -fy·ing** : to illustrate by example : serve as an example of — **ex·em·pli·fi·ca·tion** \-ˌzem-plə-fə-ˈkā-shən\ n

¹**ex·empt** \ig-ˈzempt\ adj : free from some liability to which others are subject ⟨~ from taxation⟩

²**exempt** vb : to make exempt : EXCUSE — **ex·emp·tion** \ig-ˈzemp-shən\ n

¹**ex·er·cise** \ˈek-sər-ˌsīz\ n 1 : EMPLOYMENT, USE ⟨~ of authority⟩ 2 : exertion made for the sake of training or physical fitness 3 : a task or problem done to develop skill 4 pl : a public exhibition or ceremony

²**exercise** vb **-cised; -cis·ing** 1 : EXERT ⟨~ control⟩ 2 : to train by or engage in exercise 3 : WORRY, DISTRESS ⟨issues that ~ voters⟩ — **ex·er·cis·er** n

**ex·ert** \ig-ˈzərt\ vb : to bring or put into action ⟨~ influence⟩ ⟨~ed himself⟩ — **ex·er·tion** \-ˈzər-shən\ n

**ex·fo·li·ate** \eks-ˈfō-lē-ˌāt\ vb **-at·ed; -at-**

ing : to cast off in scales, layers, or splinters — **ex·fo·li·a·tion** \-ˌfō-lē-ˈā-shən\ *n*

**ex·hale** \eks-ˈhāl\ *vb* **ex·haled; ex·hal·ing** **1** : to breathe out **2** : to give or pass off in the form of vapor — **ex·ha·la·tion** \ˌeks-hə-ˈlā-shən\ *n*

**¹ex·haust** \ig-ˈzȯst\ *vb* **1** : to use up wholly **2** : to tire or wear out **3** : to draw off or let out completely; *also* : EMPTY **4** : to develop (a subject) completely

**²exhaust** *n* **1** : the escape of used vapor or gas from an engine; *also* : the gas that escapes **2** : a system of pipes through which exhaust escapes

**ex·haus·tion** \ig-ˈzȯs-chən\ *n* : extreme weariness : FATIGUE

**ex·haus·tive** \ig-ˈzȯ-stiv\ *adj* : covering all possibilities : THOROUGH ⟨an ~ investigation⟩ — **ex·haus·tive·ly** *adv*

**¹ex·hib·it** \ig-ˈzi-bət\ *vb* **1** : to display esp. publicly **2** : to present to a court in legal form ♦ *Synonyms* DISPLAY, SHOW, PARADE, FLAUNT — **ex·hi·bi·tion** \ˌek-sə-ˈbi-shən\ *n* — **ex·hib·i·tor** \ig-ˈzi-bə-tər\ *n*

**²exhibit** *n* **1** : an act or instance of exhibiting; *also* : something exhibited **2** : something produced and identified in court for use as evidence

**ex·hi·bi·tion·ism** \ˌek-sə-ˈbi-shə-ˌni-zəm\ *n* **1** : a perversion marked by a tendency to indecently expose one's genitals **2** : the act or practice of behaving so as to attract attention to oneself — **ex·hi·bi·tion·ist** \-nist\ *n or adj*

**ex·hil·a·rate** \ig-ˈzi-lə-ˌrāt\ *vb* **-rat·ed; -rat·ing** : ENLIVEN, STIMULATE — **ex·hil·a·ra·tion** \-ˌzi-lə-ˈrā-shən\ *n*

**ex·hort** \ig-ˈzȯrt\ *vb* : to urge, advise, or warn earnestly — **ex·hor·ta·tion** \ˌek-ˌsȯr-tā-shən, ˌeg-ˌzȯr-, -zər-\ *n*

**ex·hume** \ig-ˈzyüm, iks-ˈhyüm\ *vb* **ex·humed; ex·hum·ing** [ME fr. ML *exhumare*, fr. L *ex* out of + *humus* earth] : DISINTER — **ex·hu·ma·tion** \ˌeks-hyü-ˈmā-shən, ˌeg-zü-\ *n*

**ex·i·gen·cy** \ˈek-sə-jən-sē, ig-ˈzi-jən-\ *n, pl* **-cies** **1** *pl* : REQUIREMENTS **2** : urgent need — **ex·i·gent** \ˈek-sə-jənt\ *adj*

**ex·ig·u·ous** \ig-ˈzi-gyə-wəs\ *adj* : scanty in amount — **ex·i·gu·i·ty** \ˌeg-zi-ˈgyü-ə-tē\ *n*

**¹ex·ile** \ˈeg-ˌzī(-ə)l, ˈek-ˌsī(-ə)l\ *n* **1** : BANISHMENT; *also* : voluntary absence from one's country or home **2** : a person driven from his or her native place

**²exile** *vb* **ex·iled; ex·il·ing** : BANISH, EXPEL ♦ *Synonyms* EXPATRIATE, DEPORT, OSTRACIZE

**ex·ist** \ig-ˈzist\ *vb* **1** : to have being **2** : to continue to be : LIVE

**ex·is·tence** \ig-ˈzis-təns\ *n* **1** : continuance in living **2** : actual or present occurrence ⟨~ of a state of war⟩ — **ex·is·tent** \-tənt\ *adj*

**ex·is·ten·tial** \ˌeg-zis-ˈten-chəl, ˌek-sis-\ *adj* **1** : of or relating to existence **2** : EMPIRICAL **3** : having being in time and space **4** : of or relating to existentialism or existentialists

**ex·is·ten·tial·ism** \ˌeg-zis-ˈten-chə-ˌli-zəm\ *n* : a philosophy centered on indi-

vidual existence and personal responsibility for acts of free will in the absence of certain knowledge of what is right or wrong — **ex·is·ten·tial·ist** \-list\ *adj or n*

**ex·it** \ˈeg-zət, ˈek-sət\ *n* **1** : a departure from a stage **2** : a going out or away; *also* : DEATH **3** : a way out of an enclosed space **4** : a point of departure from an expressway — **exit** *vb*

**exo·bi·ol·o·gy** \ˌek-sō-bī-ˈä-lə-jē\ *n* : biology concerned with life originating or existing outside the earth or its atmosphere — **exo·bi·ol·o·gist** \-jist\ *n*

**exo·crine gland** \ˈek-sə-krən-, -ˌkrīn-, -ˌkrēn-\ *n* : a gland (as a salivary gland) that releases a secretion externally by means of a canal or duct

**Exod** *abbr* Exodus

**ex·o·dus** \ˈek-sə-dəs\ *n* **1** *cap* — see BIBLE table **2** : a mass departure : EMIGRATION

**ex of·fi·cio** \ˌek-sə-ˈfi-shē-ˌō\ *adv or adj* : by virtue of or because of an office ⟨*ex officio* chairman⟩

**ex·og·e·nous** \ek-ˈsä-jə-nəs\ *adj* : caused or produced by factors outside the organism or system — **ex·og·e·nous·ly** *adv*

**ex·on·er·ate** \ig-ˈzä-nə-ˌrāt\ *vb* **-at·ed; -at·ing** [ME, fr. L *exoneratus*, pp. of *exonerare* to unburden, fr. *ex-* out + *onus* load] : to free from blame ♦ *Synonyms* ACQUIT, ABSOLVE, EXCULPATE, VINDICATE — **ex·on·er·a·tion** \-ˌzä-nə-ˈrā-shən\ *n*

**exo·plan·et** \ˈek-sō-ˌpla-nət\ *n* : a planet orbiting a star that is not our sun

**ex·or·bi·tant** \ig-ˈzȯr-bə-tənt\ *adj* : exceeding what is usual or proper

**ex·or·cise** \ˈek-ˌsȯr-ˌsīz, -sər-\ *vb* **-cised; -cis·ing** **1** : to get rid of by or as if by solemn command **2** : to free of an evil spirit — **ex·or·cism** \-ˌsi-zəm\ *n* — **ex·or·cist** \-ˌsist\ *n*

**exo·sphere** \ˈek-sō-ˌsfir\ *n* : the outermost region of the atmosphere

**exo·ther·mic** \ˌek-sō-ˈthər-mik\ *adj* : characterized by or formed with evolution of heat

**ex·ot·ic** \ig-ˈzä-tik\ *adj* **1** : introduced from another country ⟨~ plants⟩ **2** : strikingly, excitingly, or mysteriously different or unusual ⟨~ flavors⟩ — **exotic** *n* — **ex·ot·i·cal·ly** \-ti-k(ə-)lē\ *adv* — **ex·ot·i·cism** \-tə-ˌsi-zəm\ *n*

**exp** *abbr* **1** expense **2** experiment **3** export **4** express

**ex·pand** \ik-ˈspand\ *vb* **1** : to open up : UNFOLD **2** : ENLARGE **3** : to develop in detail ♦ *Synonyms* AMPLIFY, SWELL, DISTEND, INFLATE, DILATE — **ex·pand·able** \-ˈspan-də-bəl\ *adj* — **ex·pand·er** *n*

**ex·panse** \ik-ˈspans\ *n* : a broad extent (as of land or sea)

**ex·pan·sion** \ik-ˈspan-chən\ *n* **1** : the act or process of expanding **2** : the quality or state of being expanded **3** : an expanded part or thing

**expansion slot** *n* : a socket on a motherboard for a circuit board (**expansion card**) offering additional capabilities

**ex·pan·sive** \ik-ˈspan-siv\ *adj* **1** : tending to expand or to cause expansion **2**

: warmly benevolent, generous, or ready to talk   **3** : of large extent or scope — **ex·pan·sive·ly** adv — **ex·pan·sive·ness** n

**ex parte** \eks-'pär-tē\ adv or adj [ML] : from a one-sided point of view

**ex·pa·ti·ate** \ek-'spā-shē-,āt\ vb **-at·ed; -at·ing** : to talk or write at length — **ex·pa·ti·a·tion** \ek-,spā-shē-'ā-shən\ n

**¹ex·pa·tri·ate** \ek-'spā-trē-,āt\ vb **-at·ed; -at·ing** : EXILE — **ex·pa·tri·a·tion** \ek-,spā-trē-'ā-shən\ n

**²ex·pa·tri·ate** \ek-'spā-trē-,āt, -trē-ət\ adj : living in a foreign country — **expatri·ate** n

**ex·pect** \ik-'spekt\ vb   **1** : SUPPOSE, THINK   **2** : to look forward to : ANTICI-PATE   **3** : to consider reasonable, due, or necessary   **4** : to consider to be obliged

**ex·pec·tan·cy** \-'spek-tan-sē\ n, pl **-cies**   **1** : EXPECTATION   **2** : the expected amount (as of years of life)

**ex·pec·tant** \-tənt\ adj : marked by expectation; esp : expecting the birth of a child ⟨~ parents⟩ — **ex·pec·tant·ly** adv

**ex·pec·ta·tion** \,ek-,spek-'tā-shən\ n   **1** : the act or state of expecting   **2** : prospect of inheritance — usu. used in pl.   **3** : something expected

**ex·pec·to·rant** \ik-'spek-tə-rənt\ n : an agent that promotes the discharge or expulsion of mucus from the respiratory tract — **expectorant** adj

**ex·pec·to·rate** \-,rāt\ vb **-rat·ed; -rat·ing** : SPIT — **ex·pec·to·ra·tion** \-,spek-tə-'rā-shən\ n

**ex·pe·di·ence** \ik-'spē-dē-əns\ n : EXPE-DIENCY

**ex·pe·di·en·cy** \-ən-sē\ n, pl **-cies**   **1** : fitness to some end   **2** : use of expedient means and methods; also : something expedient

**¹ex·pe·di·ent** \-ənt\ adj [ME, fr. AF or L; AF, fr. L expediens, prp. of expedire to extricate, prepare, be useful, fr. ex- out + ped-, pes foot]   **1** : adapted for achieving a particular end   **2** : marked by concern with what is advantageous; esp : governed by self-interest

**²expedient** n : something expedient; esp : a temporary means to an end

**ex·pe·dite** \'ek-spə-,dīt\ vb **-dit·ed; -dit·ing** : to carry out promptly, also : to speed up ⟨~ a lawsuit⟩

**ex·pe·dit·er** \-,dī-tər\ n : one that expedites; esp : one employed to ensure efficient movement of goods or supplies in a business

**ex·pe·di·tion** \,ek-spə-'di-shən\ n   **1** : a journey for a particular purpose; also : the persons making it   **2** : efficient promptness

**ex·pe·di·tion·ary** \-'di-shə-,ner-ē\ adj : of, relating to, or constituting an expedition; also : sent on military service abroad

**ex·pe·di·tious** \-'di-shəs\ adj : marked by or acting with prompt efficiency ♦ **Synonyms** SWIFT, FAST, RAPID, SPEEDY

**ex·pel** \ik-'spel\ vb **ex·pelled; ex·pel·ling** : to drive or force out : EJECT

**ex·pend** \ik-'spend\ vb   **1** : to pay out

: SPEND   **2** : UTILIZE ⟨~ resources⟩; also : USE UP — **ex·pend·able** adj

**ex·pen·di·ture** \ik-'spen-di-chər, -,chür\ n   **1** : the act or process of expending   **2** : something expended

**ex·pense** \ik-'spens\ n   **1** : EXPENDITURE   **2** : COST   **3** : a cause of expenditure   **4** : SACRIFICE ⟨had a laugh at my ~⟩

**ex·pen·sive** \ik-'spen-siv\ adj : COSTLY, DEAR — **ex·pen·sive·ly** adv

**¹ex·pe·ri·ence** \ik-'spir-ē-əns\ n   **1** : observation of or participation in events resulting in or tending toward knowledge   **2** : knowledge, practice, or skill derived from observation or participation in events; also : the length of such participation   **3** : something encountered, undergone, or lived through (as by a person or community)

**²experience** vb **-enced; -enc·ing**   **1** : FIND OUT, DISCOVER   **2** : to have experience of : UNDERGO ⟨~ the loss of a pet⟩

**ex·pe·ri·enced** adj : made capable through experience ⟨an ~ pilot⟩

**¹ex·per·i·ment** \ik-'sper-ə-mənt\ n : a controlled procedure carried out to discover, test, or demonstrate something; also : the process of testing — **ex·per·i·men·tal** \-,sper-ə-'men-t³l\ adj — **ex·per·i·men·tal·ly** \-'men-t³l-ē\ adv

**²ex·per·i·ment** \-,ment\ vb : to make experiments — **ex·per·i·men·ta·tion** \ik-,sper-ə-mən-'tā-shən\ n — **ex·per·i·men·ter** n

**¹ex·pert** \'ek-,spərt\ adj : showing special skill or knowledge — **ex·pert·ly** adv — **ex·pert·ness** n

**²ex·pert** \'ek-,spərt\ n : an expert person : SPECIALIST ⟨a computer ~⟩

**ex·per·tise** \,ek-(,)spər-'tēz\ n : the skill of an expert ⟨~ in legal matters⟩

**expert system** n : computer software that attempts to mimic the reasoning of a human specialist

**ex·pi·ate** \'ek-spē-,āt\ vb **-at·ed; -at·ing** : to give satisfaction for : ATONE ⟨~ sin⟩ — **ex·pi·a·tion** \,ek-spē-'ā-shən\ n

**ex·pi·a·to·ry** \'ek-spē-ə-,tōr-ē\ adj : serving to expiate

**expiration date** n   **1** : the date after which something is no longer in effect   **2** : the date after which a product is expected to decline in quality or effectiveness

**ex·pire** \ik-'spī(-ə)r, ek-\ vb **ex·pired; ex·pir·ing**   **1** : to breathe one's last breath : DIE   **2** : to come to an end   **3** : to breathe out from or as if from the lungs — **ex·pi·ra·tion** \,ek-spə-'rā-shən\ n

**ex·plain** \ik-'splān\ vb [ME explanen, fr. L explanare, lit., to make level, fr. planus level, flat]   **1** : to make clear   **2** : to give the reason for — **ex·pla·na·tion** \,ek-splə-'nā-shən\ n — **ex·plan·a·to·ry** \ik-'spla-nə-,tōr-ē\ adj

**ex·ple·tive** \'ek-splə-tiv\ n : a usu. profane exclamation

**ex·pli·ca·ble** \ek-'spli-kə-bəl, 'ek-(,)spli-\ adj : capable of being explained

**ex·pli·cate** \'ek-splə-,kāt\ vb **-cat·ed; -cat·ing** : to give a detailed explanation of — **ex·pli·ca·tion** \,ek-spli-'kā-shən\ n

**ex·plic·it** \ik-'spli-sət\ *adj* : clearly and precisely expressed ⟨∼ directions⟩ — **ex·plic·it·ly** *adv* — **ex·plic·it·ness** *n*

**ex·plode** \ik-'splōd\ *vb* **ex·plod·ed; ex·plod·ing** [L *explodere* to drive off the stage by clapping, fr. *ex-* out + *plaudere* to clap] **1** : DISCREDIT ⟨∼ a belief⟩ **2** : to burst or cause to burst violently and noisily ⟨∼ a bomb⟩ ⟨the boiler *exploded*⟩ **3** : to undergo a rapid chemical or nuclear reaction with production of heat and violent expansion of gas ⟨dynamite ∼*s*⟩ **4** : to give forth a sudden strong and noisy outburst of emotion **5** : to increase rapidly ⟨the city's population *exploded*⟩

**exploded** *adj* : showing the parts separated but in correct relationship to each other ⟨an ∼ view of a carburetor⟩

**¹ex·ploit** \'ek-,splȯit\ *n* : DEED; *esp* : a notable or heroic act

**²ex·ploit** \ik-'splȯit\ *vb* **1** : to make productive use of : UTILIZE ⟨∼ natural resources⟩ **2** : to use unfairly for one's own advantage ⟨∼ migrant workers⟩ — **ex·ploi·ta·tion** \,ek-,splȯi-'tā-shən\ *n*

**ex·plore** \ik-'splȯr\ *vb* **ex·plored; ex·plor·ing 1** : to look into or travel over thoroughly **2** : to examine carefully ⟨∼ a wound⟩ — **ex·plo·ra·tion** \,ek-splə-'rā-shən\ *n* — **ex·plor·a·to·ry** \ik-'splȯr-ə-,tȯr-ē\ *adj* — **ex·plor·er** *n*

**ex·plo·sion** \ik-'splō-zhən\ *n* : the act or an instance of exploding

**ex·plo·sive** \ik-'splō-siv\ *adj* **1** : relating to or able to cause explosion **2** : tending to explode ⟨an ∼ temper⟩ — **explosive** *n* — **ex·plo·sive·ly** *adv*

**ex·po** \'ek-,spō\ *n, pl* **expos** : EXPOSITION 2

**ex·po·nent** \ik-'spō-nənt, 'ek-,spō-\ *n* **1** : a symbol written above and to the right of a mathematical expression (as $^3$ in $a^3$) to signify how many times it is to be used as a factor **2** : INTERPRETER, EXPOUNDER **3** : ADVOCATE, CHAMPION — **ex·po·nen·tial** \,ek-spə-'nen-chəl\ *adj* — **ex·po·nen·tial·ly** *adv*

**ex·po·nen·ti·a·tion** \,ek-spə-,nen-chē-'ā-shən\ *n* : the mathematical operation of raising a quantity to a power

**¹ex·port** \ek-'spȯrt, 'ek-,spȯrt\ *vb* : to send (as merchandise) to foreign countries — **ex·por·ta·tion** \,ek-spȯr-'tā-shən, -spər-\ *n* — **ex·port·er** *n*

**²ex·port** \'ek-,spȯrt\ *n* **1** : something exported esp. for trade **2** : the act of exporting

**ex·pose** \ik-'spōz\ *vb* **ex·posed; ex·pos·ing 1** : to deprive of shelter or protection **2** : to submit or subject to an action or influence; *esp* : to subject (as photographic film) to radiant energy (as light) **3** : to bring to light : DISCLOSE ⟨∼ a scam⟩ **4** : to cause to be open to view

**ex·po·sé** \,ek-spō-'zā\ *n* : an exposure of something discreditable

**ex·po·si·tion** \,ek-spə-'zi-shən\ *n* **1** : a setting forth of the meaning or purpose (as of a writing); *also* : discourse designed to convey information **2** : a public exhibition

**ex·pos·i·tor** \ik-'spä-zə-tər\ *n* : one who explains — COMMENTATOR

**ex post fac·to** \,eks-'pōst-,fak-tō\ *adv or adj* : after the fact

**ex·pos·tu·late** \ik-'späs-chə-,lāt\ *vb* : to reason earnestly with a person esp. in dissuading : REMONSTRATE — **ex·pos·tu·la·tion** \-,späs-chə-'lā-shən\ *n*

**ex·po·sure** \ik-'spō-zhər\ *n* **1** : the fact or condition of being exposed **2** : the act or an instance of exposing **3** : the length of time for which a film is exposed **4** : a section of a photographic film for one picture

**ex·pound** \ik-'spaúnd\ *vb* **1** : STATE **2** : INTERPRET, EXPLAIN — **ex·pound·er** *n*

**¹ex·press** \ik-'spres\ *adj* **1** : EXPLICIT; *also* : EXACT, PRECISE **2** : SPECIFIC ⟨this ∼ purpose⟩ **3** : traveling at high speed and esp. with few stops ⟨an ∼ train⟩; *also* : adapted to high-speed use ⟨∼ roads⟩ — **ex·press·ly** *adv*

**²express** *adv* : by express ⟨ship it ∼⟩

**³express** *n* **1** : a system for the prompt transportation of goods; *also* : a company operating such a service or the shipments so transported **2** : an express vehicle

**⁴express** *vb* **1** : to make known : SHOW, STATE ⟨∼ regret⟩; *also* : SYMBOLIZE **2** : to squeeze out : extract by pressing **3** : to send by express **4** : to manifest or produce by a genetic process

**ex·pres·sion** \ik-'spre-shən\ *n* **1** : UTTERANCE **2** : something that represents or symbolizes : SIGN; *esp* : a mathematical symbol or combination of signs and symbols representing a quantity or operation **3** : the detectable effect of a gene **4** : a significant word or phrase; *also* : manner of expressing (as in writing or music) **5** : facial aspect or vocal intonation indicative of feeling — **ex·pres·sion·less** *adj*

**ex·pres·sion·ism** \ik-'spre-shə-,ni-zəm\ *n* : a theory or practice in art of seeking to depict the artist's subjective responses to objects and events — **ex·pres·sion·ist** \-nist\ *n or adj* — **ex·pres·sion·is·tic** \-,spre-shə-'nis-tik\ *adj*

**ex·pres·sive** \ik-'spre-siv\ *adj* **1** : of or relating to expression **2** : serving to express ⟨an ∼ gesture⟩ — **ex·pres·sive·ly** *adv* — **ex·pres·sive·ness** *n*

**ex·press·way** \ik-'spres-,wā\ *n* : a divided superhighway with limited access

**ex·pro·pri·ate** \ek-'sprō-prē-,āt\ *vb* **-at·ed; -at·ing** : to deprive of possession or the right to own — **ex·pro·pri·a·tion** \(,)ek-,sprō-prē-'ā-shən\ *n*

**expt** *abbr* experiment

**ex·pul·sion** \ik-'spəl-shən\ *n* : an expelling or being expelled : EJECTION

**ex·punge** \ik-'spənj\ *vb* **ex·punged; ex·pung·ing** [L *expungere* to mark for deletion by dots, fr. *ex-* out + *pungere* to prick] : OBLITERATE, ERASE

**ex·pur·gate** \'ek-spər-,gāt\ *vb* **-gat·ed; -gat·ing** : to clear (as a book) of objectionable passages — **ex·pur·ga·tion** \,ek-spər-'gā-shən\ *n*

**ex·qui·site** \ek-'skwi-zət, 'ek-(,)skwi-\ *adj* [ME *exquisit*, fr. L *exquisitus*, pp. of *ex-*

*quirere* to search out, fr. *ex* out + *quaerere* to seek] **1** : marked by flawless form or workmanship **2** : keenly appreciative or sensitive **3** : pleasingly beautiful or delicate **4** : INTENSE ⟨∼ pain⟩

**ext** *abbr* **1** extension **2** exterior **3** external **4** extra **5** extract

**ex·tant** \'ek-stənt; ek-'stant\ *adj* : EXISTENT; *esp* : not lost or destroyed

**ex·tem·po·ra·ne·ous** \ek-,stem-pə-'rā-nē-əs\ *adj* : not planned beforehand : IMPROMPTU — **ex·tem·po·ra·ne·ous·ly** *adv*

**ex·tem·po·rary** \ik-'stem-pə-,rer-ē\ *adj* : EXTEMPORANEOUS

**ex·tem·po·re** \ik-'stem-pə-(,)rē\ *adv* : EXTEMPORANEOUSLY

**ex·tem·po·rise** *Brit var of* EXTEMPORIZE

**ex·tem·po·rize** \ik-'stem-pə-,rīz\ *vb* **-rized; -riz·ing** : to do something extemporaneously ⟨∼ a speech⟩

**ex·tend** \ik-'stend\ *vb* **1** : to spread or stretch forth or out (as in reaching) **2** : to exert or cause to exert to full capacity **3** : PROFFER ⟨∼ credit⟩ **4** : PROLONG ⟨∼ a note⟩ **5** : to make greater or broader ⟨∼ knowledge⟩ **6** : to stretch out or reach across a distance, space, or time ♦ *Synonyms* LENGTHEN, ELONGATE, PROTRACT — **ex·tend·able** *also* **ex·tend·ible** \-'sten-də-bəl\ *adj*

**ex·ten·sion** \ik-'sten-chən\ *n* **1** : an extending or being extended **2** : a program that geographically extends the educational resources of an institution **3** : an additional part; *also* : an extra telephone connected to a line

**ex·ten·sive** \ik-'sten-siv\ *adj* : of considerable extent : FAR-REACHING, BROAD ⟨∼ training⟩ — **ex·ten·sive·ly** *adv*

**ex·tent** \ik-'stent\ *n* **1** : the range or space over which something extends ⟨a property of large ∼⟩ **2** : the point or degree to which something extends ⟨to the fullest ∼ of the law⟩

**ex·ten·u·ate** \ik-'sten-yù-,wāt\ *vb* **-at·ed; -at·ing** : to lessen the seriousness of — **ex·ten·u·a·tion** \-,sten-yù-'wā-shən\ *n*

**¹ex·te·ri·or** \ik-'stir-ē-ər\ *adj* **1** : EXTERNAL **2** : suitable for use on an outside surface ⟨∼ paint⟩

**²exterior** *n* : an exterior part or surface

**ex·ter·mi·nate** \ik-'stər-mə-,nāt\ *vb* **-nat·ed; -nat·ing** : to get rid of completely usu. by killing off ♦ *Synonyms* EXTIRPATE, ERADICATE, ABOLISH, ANNIHILATE — **ex·ter·mi·na·tion** \-,stər-mə-'nā-shən\ *n* — **ex·ter·mi·na·tor** \-'stər-mə-,nā-tər\ *n*

**¹ex·ter·nal** \ek-'stər-n°l\ *adj* **1** : outwardly perceivable; *also* : SUPERFICIAL **2** : of, relating to, or located on the outside or an outer part **3** : arising or acting from without; *also* : FOREIGN ⟨∼ affairs⟩ — **ex·ter·nal·ly** *adv*

**²external** *n* : an external feature

**ex·tinct** \ik-'stiŋkt\ *adj* **1** : EXTINGUISHED; *also* : no longer active ⟨an ∼ volcano⟩ **2** : no longer existing or in use ⟨dinosaurs are ∼⟩ ⟨∼ languages⟩ — **ex·tinc·tion** \ik-'stiŋk-shən\ *n*

**ex·tin·guish** \ik-'stiŋ-gwish\ *vb* : to cause

to stop burning; *also* : to bring to an end (as by destroying) — **ex·tin·guish·able** *adj* — **ex·tin·guish·er** *n*

**ex·tir·pate** \'ek-stər-,pāt\ *vb* **-pat·ed; -pat·ing** [L *exstirpatus,* pp. of *exstirpare,* fr. *ex-* out + *stirps* trunk, root] **1** : to destroy completely ⟨∼ a heresy⟩ **2** : UPROOT ♦ *Synonyms* EXTERMINATE, ERADICATE, ABOLISH, ANNIHILATE — **ex·tir·pa·tion** \,ek-stər-'pā-shən\ *n*

**ex·tol** *also* **ex·toll** \ik-'stōl\ *vb* **ex·tolled; ex·tol·ling** : to praise highly : GLORIFY

**ex·tort** \ik-'stȯrt\ *vb* [L *extortus,* pp. of *extorquēre* to wrench out, extort, fr. *ex-* out + *torquēre* to twist] : to obtain by force or improper pressure ⟨∼ a bribe⟩ — **ex·tor·tion** \-'stȯr-shən\ *n* — **ex·tor·tion·er** *n* — **ex·tor·tion·ist** *n*

**ex·tor·tion·ate** \ik-'stȯr-shə-nət\ *adj* : EXCESSIVE, EXORBITANT ⟨∼ prices⟩ — **ex·tor·tion·ate·ly** *adv*

**¹ex·tra** \'ek-strə\ *adj* **1** : ADDITIONAL ⟨∼ work⟩ **2** : SUPERIOR ⟨∼ quality⟩

**²extra** *n* **1** : a special edition of a newspaper **2** : an added charge **3** : an additional worker or performer (as in a motion picture)

**³extra** *adv* : beyond what is usual ⟨∼ large⟩

**¹ex·tract** \ik-'strakt, *esp for 3* 'ek-,strakt\ *vb* **1** : to draw out; *esp* : to pull out forcibly ⟨∼ a tooth⟩ **2** : to withdraw (as a juice or a constituent) by a physical or chemical process **3** : to select for citation : QUOTE — **ex·tract·able** *adj* — **ex·trac·tion** \ik-'strak-shən\ *n* — **ex·trac·tor** \-tər\ *n*

**²ex·tract** \'ek-,strakt\ *n* **1** : EXCERPT, CITATION **2** : a product (as a juice or concentrate) obtained by extracting

**ex·tra·cur·ric·u·lar** \,ek-strə-kə-'ri-kyə-lər\ *adj* : lying outside the regular curriculum; *esp* : of or relating to school-connected activities (as sports) usu. carrying no academic credit

**ex·tra·dite** \'ek-strə-,dīt\ *vb* **-dit·ed; -dit·ing** : to obtain by or deliver up to extradition

**ex·tra·di·tion** \,ek-strə-'di-shən\ *n* : the surrender of an alleged criminal to a different jurisdiction for trial

**ex·tra·mar·i·tal** \,ek-strə-'ma-rə-t°l\ *adj* : of or relating to sexual intercourse by a married person with someone other than his or her spouse

**ex·tra·mu·ral** \-'myur-əl\ *adj* : existing or functioning beyond the bounds of an organized unit

**ex·tra·ne·ous** \ek-'strā-nē-əs\ *adj* **1** : coming from without ⟨∼ light⟩ **2** : not forming a vital part; *also* : IRRELEVANT — **ex·tra·ne·ous·ly** *adv*

**ex·tra·net** \'ek-strə-,net\ *n* : a network like an intranet but also allowing access by certain outside parties

**ex·traor·di·nary** \ik-'strȯr-də-,ner-ē, ,ek-strə-'ȯr-\ *adj* **1** : notably unusual or exceptional **2** : employed on special service ⟨an ambassador ∼⟩ — **ex·traor·di·nari·ly** \-,strȯr-də-'ner-ə-lē, ,ek-strə-,ȯr-\ *adv*

**ex·trap·o·late** \ik-'stra-pə-,lāt\ *vb* **-lat·ed; -lat·ing** : to infer (unknown data) from known data — **ex·trap·o·la·tion** \-ₗstra-pə-ˈlā-shən\ *n*

**ex·tra·sen·so·ry** \ˌek-strə-ˈsen-sə-rē\ *adj* : not acting or occurring through the known senses

**extrasensory perception** *n* : perception (as in telepathy) of events external to the self not gained through the senses and not deducible from previous experience

**ex·tra·so·lar** \-ˈsō-lər\ *adj* : originating or existing outside the solar system

**ex·tra·ter·res·tri·al** \-tə-ˈres-trē-əl\ *adj* : originating or existing outside the earth or its atmosphere ⟨∼ life⟩ — **extraterrestrial** *n*

**ex·tra·ter·ri·to·ri·al** \ˌter-ə-ˈtōr-ē-əl\ *adj* : existing or taking place outside the territorial limits of a jurisdiction

**ex·tra·ter·ri·to·ri·al·i·ty** \-ˌtōr-ē-ˌa-lə-tē\ *n* : exemption from the application or jurisdiction of local law or tribunals ⟨diplomats enjoy ∼⟩

**ex·trav·a·gant** \ik-ˈstra-vi-gənt\ *adj* 1 : EXCESSIVE ⟨∼ claims⟩ 2 : unduly lavish : WASTEFUL 3 : too costly ♦ **Synonyms** IMMODERATE, EXORBITANT, EXTREME, INORDINATE, UNDUE — **ex·trav·a·gance** \-gəns\ *n* — **ex·trav·a·gant·ly** *adv*

**ex·trav·a·gan·za** \ik-ˌstra-və-ˈgan-zə\ *n* 1 : a literary or musical work marked by extreme freedom of style and structure 2 : a spectacular show

**ex·tra·ve·hic·u·lar** \ˌek-strə-vē-ˈhi-kyə-lər\ *adj* : taking place outside a vehicle (as a spacecraft) ⟨∼ activity⟩

¹**ex·treme** \ik-ˈstrēm\ *adj* 1 : very great or intense ⟨∼ cold⟩ 2 : very severe or radical ⟨∼ measures⟩ 3 : going to great lengths or beyond normal limits ⟨politically ∼⟩ 4 : most remote ⟨the ∼ end⟩ 5 : UTMOST; *also* : MAXIMUM — **ex·treme·ly** *adv*

²**extreme** *n* 1 : something located at one end or the other of a range or series 2 : EXTREMITY 4

**extremely low frequency** *n* : a radio frequency in the lowest range of the radio spectrum

**ex·trem·ism** \ik-ˈstrē-ˌmi-zəm\ *n* : the quality or state of being extreme; *esp* : advocacy of extreme political measures — **ex·trem·ist** \-mist\ *n or adj*

**ex·trem·i·ty** \ik-ˈstre-mə-tē\ *n, pl* **-ties** 1 : the most remote part or point 2 : a limb of the body; *esp* : a human hand or foot 3 : the greatest need or danger 4 : the utmost degree ⟨the *extremities* of suffering⟩ 5 : a drastic or desperate measure

**ex·tri·cate** \ˈek-strə-ˌkāt\ *vb* **-cat·ed; -cat·ing** [L *extricatus,* pp. of *extricare,* fr. *ex-* out + *tricae* trifles, perplexities] : to free from an entanglement or difficulty ♦ **Synonyms** DISENTANGLE, UNTANGLE, DISENCUMBER — **ex·tri·ca·ble** \ik-ˈstri-kə-bəl, ek-; ˈek-(ₗ)stri-\ *adj* — **ex·tri·ca·tion** \ˌek-strə-ˈkā-shən\ *n*

**ex·trin·sic** \ek-ˈstrin-zik, -sik\ *adj* 1 : not forming part of or belonging to a thing 2 : EXTERNAL — **ex·trin·si·cal·ly** \-zi-k(ə-)lē, -si-\ *adv*

**ex·tro·vert** *also* **ex·tra·vert** \ˈek-strə-ˌvərt\ *n* : a gregarious and unreserved person — **ex·tro·ver·sion** *or* **ex·tra·ver·sion** \ˌek-strə-ˈvər-zhən\ *n* — **ex·tro·vert·ed** *also* **ex·tra·vert·ed** *adj*

**ex·trude** \ik-ˈstrüd\ *vb* **ex·trud·ed; ex·trud·ing** 1 : to force, press, or push out 2 : to shape (as plastic) by forcing through a die — **ex·tru·sion** \-ˈstrü-zhən\ *n* — **ex·trud·er** *n*

**ex·u·ber·ant** \ig-ˈzü-bə-rənt\ *adj* 1 : unrestrained in enthusiasm or style 2 : PROFUSE ⟨∼ vegetation⟩ — **ex·u·ber·ance** \-rəns\ *n* — **ex·u·ber·ant·ly** *adv*

**ex·ude** \ig-ˈzüd\ *vb* **ex·ud·ed; ex·ud·ing** [L *exsudare,* fr. *ex-* out + *sudare* to sweat] 1 : to discharge slowly through pores or cuts : OOZE 2 : to display conspicuously or abundantly ⟨∼s charm⟩ — **ex·u·date** \ˈek-sù-ˌdāt, -syù-\ *n* — **ex·u·da·tion** \ˌek-sù-ˈdā-shən, -syù-\ *n*

**ex·ult** \ig-ˈzəlt\ *vb* : REJOICE, GLORY ⟨∼ed in their victory⟩ — **ex·ul·tant** \-ˈzəl-tᵊnt\ *adj* — **ex·ul·tant·ly** *adv* — **ex·ul·ta·tion** \ˌeg-zəl-ˈtā-shən, ˌeg-(ₗ)zul-\ *n*

**ex·urb** \ˈek-ˌsərb, ˈeg-ˌzərb\ *n* : a region outside a city and its suburbs inhabited chiefly by well-to-do families — **ex·ur·ban** \ek-ˈsər-bən, eg-ˈzər-\ *adj*

**ex·ur·ban·ite** \ek-ˈsər-bə-ˌnīt; eg-ˈzər-\ *n* : one who lives in an exurb

**ex·ur·bia** \ek-ˈsər-bē-ə, eg-ˈzər-\ *n* : the generalized region of exurbs

**-ey** — see -Y

¹**eye** \ˈī\ *n* 1 : an organ of sight typically consisting in vertebrates of a globular structure that is located in a socket of the skull, is lined with a sensitive retina, and is normally paired 2 : VISION, PERCEPTION; *also* : faculty of discrimination ⟨an ∼ for bargains⟩ 3 : POINT OF VIEW, JUDGMENT — often used in pl. ⟨in the ∼s of the law⟩ 4 : something suggesting an eye (as the hole of a needle or the bud of a potato) 5 : the calm center of a cyclone — **eyed** \ˈīd\ *adj*

²**eye** *vb* **eyed; eye·ing** *or* **ey·ing** : to look at : WATCH

¹**eye·ball** \ˈī-ˌbȯl\ *n* : the globular capsule of the vertebrate eye

²**eyeball** *vb* : to look at intently

**eye·brow** \-ˌbrau̇\ *n* : the ridge over the eye or the hair growing on it

**eye·drop·per** \-ˌdrä-pər\ *n* : DROPPER 2

**eye·glass** \-ˌglas\ *n* : a lens worn to aid vision; *also, pl* : GLASSES

**eye·lash** \-ˌlash\ *n* 1 : the fringe of hair edging the eyelid — usu. used in pl. 2 : a single hair of the eyelashes

**eye·let** \-lət\ *n* 1 : a small hole intended for ornament or for passage of a cord or lace 2 : a typically metal ring for reinforcing an eyelet : GROMMET

**eye·lid** \-ˌlid\ *n* : either of the movable folds of skin and muscle that can be closed over the eyeball

**eye·lin·er** \-ˌlī-nər\ *n* : makeup used to emphasize the contour of the eyes

**eye-open·er** \-ˌō-pə-nər\ *n* : something startling or surprising — **eye-open·ing** *adj*

**eye·piece** \-ˌpēs\ *n* : the lens or combination of lenses at the eye end of an optical instrument

**eye shadow** *n* : a colored cosmetic applied to the eyelids to accent the eyes

**eye·sight** \-ˌsīt\ *n* : SIGHT, VISION

**eye·sore** \-ˌsȯr\ *n* : something offensive to view

**eye·strain** \-ˌstrān\ *n* : weariness or a strained state of the eye

**eye·tooth** \-ˈtüth\ *n* : a canine tooth of the upper jaw

**eye·wash** \-ˌwȯsh, -ˌwäsh\ *n* 1 : an eye lotion 2 : misleading or deceptive statements, actions, or procedures

**eye·wit·ness** \-ˈwit-nəs\ *n* : a person who actually sees something happen

**ey·rie** *chiefly Brit var of* AERIE

**ey·rir** \'ā-ˌrir\ *n, pl* **au·rar** \'au̇ ˌrär\ *see* **krona** at MONEY table

**Ez** *or* **Ezr** *abbr* Ezra

**Ezech** *abbr* Ezechiel

**Eze·chiel** \i-ˈzē-kyəl\ *n* — see BIBLE table

**Ezek** *abbr* Ezekiel

**Eze·kiel** \i-ˈzē-kyəl\ *n* — see BIBLE table

**e-zine** \'ē-ˌzēn\ *n* : an online magazine

**Ez·ra** \'ez-rə\ *n* — see BIBLE table

**f** \'ef\ *n, pl* **f's** *or* **fs** \'efs\ *often cap* 1 : the 6th letter of the English alphabet 2 : a grade rating a student's work as failing

²**f** *abbr, often cap* 1 Fahrenheit 2 false 3 family 4 farad 5 female 6 feminine 7 forte 8 French 9 frequency 10 Friday

³**f** *symbol* focal length

**F** *symbol* fluorine

**FAA** *abbr* Federal Aviation Administration

**fab** \'fab\ *adj* : FABULOUS

**Fa·bi·an** \'fā-bē-ən\ *adj* : of, relating to, or being a society of socialists organized in England in 1884 to spread socialist principles gradually — **Fabian** *n* — **Fa·bi·an·ism** *n*

**fa·ble** \'fā-bəl\ *n* 1 : a legendary story of supernatural happenings 2 : a narration intended to teach a lesson; *esp* : one in which animals speak and act like people 3 : FALSEHOOD

**fa·bled** \'fā-bəld\ *adj* 1 : FICTITIOUS 2 : told or celebrated in fable ⟨~ deeds⟩

**fab·ric** \'fa-brik\ *n* [MF *fabrique,* fr. L *fabrica* workshop, structure] 1 : STRUCTURE, FRAMEWORK ⟨the ~ of society⟩ 2 : CLOTH; *also* : a material that resembles cloth

**fab·ri·cate** \'fa-bri-ˌkāt\ *vb* **-cat·ed; -cat·ing** 1 : INVENT, CREATE 2 : to make up for the sake of deception ⟨reporters *fabricating* news stories⟩ 3 : CONSTRUCT, MANUFACTURE ⟨~ tools⟩ — **fab·ri·ca·tion** \ˌfa-bri-ˈkā-shən\ *n*

**fab·u·lous** \'fa-byə-ləs\ *adj* 1 : resembling a fable; *also* : INCREDIBLE, MARVELOUS ⟨had a ~ time⟩ 2 : told in or based on fable — **fab·u·lous·ly** *adv*

**fac** *abbr* 1 facsimile 2 faculty

**fa·cade** *also* **fa·çade** \fə-ˈsäd\ *n* [F *façade,* fr. It *facciata,* fr. *faccia* face] 1 : the principal face or front of a building 2 : a false, superficial, or artificial appearance
  ◆ **Synonyms** MASK, DISGUISE, FRONT, GUISE, PRETENSE, VENEER

¹**face** \'fās\ *n* 1 : the front part of the head 2 : PRESENCE ⟨in the ~ of danger⟩ 3 : facial expression : LOOK ⟨put a sad ~ on⟩ 4 : GRIMACE ⟨made a ~⟩ 5 : outward appearance ⟨looks easy on the ~

of it⟩ 6 : CONFIDENCE; *also* : BOLDNESS 7 : DIGNITY, PRESTIGE ⟨afraid to lose ~⟩ 8 : SURFACE; *esp* : a front, principal, bounding, or contacting surface ⟨~ of a cliff⟩ ⟨the ~s of a cube⟩ ⟨the ~ of a golf club⟩ — **faced** \'fāst, 'fā-səd\ *adj*

²**face** *vb* **faced; fac·ing** 1 : to confront brazenly 2 : to line near the edge esp. with a different material; *also* : to cover the front or surface of ⟨~ a building with marble⟩ 3 : to meet or bring in direct contact or confrontation ⟨*faced* the problem⟩ 4 : to stand or sit with the face toward ⟨~ the sun⟩ 5 : to have the front oriented toward ⟨a house *facing* the park⟩ 6 : to have as or be a prospect ⟨~ a grim future⟩ 7 : to turn the face or body in a specified direction — **face the music** : to meet the unpleasant consequences of one's actions

**face·down** \ˌfās-ˈdau̇n\ *adv* : with the face downward ⟨cards turned ~⟩

**face·less** \-ləs\ *n* 1 : lacking character or individuality 2 : lacking a face

**face-lift** \'fās-ˌlift\ *n* 1 : plastic surgery on the face and neck to remove defects (as wrinkles) typical of aging 2 : MODERNIZATION — **face-lift** *vb*

**face-off** \'fās-ˌȯf\ *n* 1 : a method of beginning play by dropping a puck or ball (as in hockey) between two opposing players each of whom attempts to control it 2 : CONFRONTATION — **face off** *vb*

**fac·et** \'fa-sət\ *n* [F *facette,* dim. of *face*] 1 : a small plane surface of a cut gem 2 : ASPECT, PHASE

**fa·ce·tious** \fə-ˈsē-shəs\ *adj* 1 : joking often inappropriately ⟨~ remarks⟩ 2 : JOCULAR, JOCOSE ◆ **Synonyms** WITTY, HUMOROUS — **fa·ce·tious·ly** *adv* — **fa·ce·tious·ness** *n*

¹**fa·cial** \'fā-shəl\ *adj* 1 : of or relating to the face 2 : used to improve the appearance of the face

²**facial** *n* : a facial treatment

**fac·ile** \'fa-səl\ *adj* 1 : easily accomplished, handled, or attained 2 : SIMPLISTIC 3 : readily manifested and often insincere ⟨~ prose⟩ 4 : READY, FLUENT ⟨a ~ writer⟩

**fa·cil·i·tate** \fə-ˈsi-lə-ˌtāt\ *vb* **-tat·ed; -tat·ing** : to make easier — **fa·cil·i·ta·tion** \-ˌsi-lə-ˈtā-shən\ *n* — **fa·cil·i·ta·tor** \-ˈsi-lə-ˌtā-tər\ *n*

**fa·cil·i·ty** \fə-ˈsi-lə-tē\ *n, pl* **-ties 1** : the quality of being easily performed **2** : ease in performance : APTITUDE **3** : PLIANCY **4** : something that makes easier an action, operation, or course of conduct; *also* : REST ROOM — often used in pl. **5** : something (as a hospital) built or installed for a particular purpose

**fac·ing** \ˈfā-siŋ\ *n* **1** : a lining at the edge esp. of a garment **2** *pl* : the collar, cuffs, and trimmings of a uniform coat **3** : an ornamental or protective layer **4** : material for facing

**fac·sim·i·le** \fak-ˈsi-mə-lē\ *n* [L *fac simile* make similar] **1** : an exact copy **2** : a system of transmitting and reproducing printed matter or pictures by means of signals sent over telephone lines

**fact** \ˈfakt\ *n* **1** : DEED; *esp* : CRIME ⟨accessory after the ∼⟩ **2** : the quality of being actual **3** : something that exists or occurs **4** : a piece of information — **in fact** : in truth

**fac·tion** \ˈfak-shən\ *n* : a group or combination (as in a government) acting together within and usu. against a larger body : CLIQUE — **fac·tion·al·ism** \-shə-nə-ˌli-zəm\ *n*

**fac·tious** \ˈfak-shəs\ *adj* **1** : of, relating to, or caused by faction **2** : inclined to faction or the formation of factions : causing dissension ♦ *Synonyms* INSUBORDINATE, CONTUMACIOUS, INSURGENT, SEDITIOUS, REBELLIOUS

**fac·ti·tious** \fak-ˈti-shəs\ *adj* : ARTIFICIAL, SHAM ⟨a ∼ display of grief⟩

**fac·toid** \ˈfak-ˌtȯid\ *n* **1** : an invented fact believed to be true because of its appearance in print **2** : a brief usu. trivial fact

**¹fac·tor** \ˈfak-tər\ *n* **1** : AGENT **2** : something that actively contributes to a result ⟨a ∼ in her decision⟩ **3** : GENE **4** : any of the numbers or symbols in mathematics that when multiplied together form a product; *esp* : any of the integers that divide a given integer without a remainder

**²factor** *vb* **1** : to work as a factor **2** : to find the mathematical factors of and esp. the prime mathematical factors of

**¹fac·to·ri·al** \fak-ˈtȯr-ē-əl\ *adj* : of, relating to, or being a factor

**²factorial** *n* : the product of all the positive integers from 1 to a given integer *n*

**fac·to·ry** \ˈfak-trē, -tə-rē\ *n, pl* **-ries 1** : a trading post where resident brokers trade **2** : a group or buildings used for manufacturing

**fac·to·tum** \fak-ˈtō-təm\ *n* [NL, lit., do everything, fr. L *fac* do + *totum* everything] : a person (as a servant) having numerous or varied duties

**facts of life** : the physiological processes and behavior involved in sex and reproduction

**fac·tu·al** \ˈfak-chə-wəl\ *adj* : of or relating to facts; *also* : based on fact — **fac·tu·al·ly** *adv*

**fac·ul·ty** \ˈfa-kəl-tē\ *n, pl* **-ties 1** : ability

to act or do : POWER; *also* : natural aptitude **2** : one of the powers of the mind or body ⟨the ∼ of hearing⟩ **3** : the teachers in a school or college or one of its divisions

**fad** \ˈfad\ *n* : a practice or interest followed for a time with exaggerated zeal : CRAZE — **fad·dish** *adj* — **fad·dish·ly** *adv* — **fad·dist** *n*

**¹fade** \ˈfād\ *vb* **fad·ed; fad·ing 1** : WITHER **2** : to lose or cause to lose freshness or brilliance of color **3** : VANISH ⟨a *fading* memory⟩ **4** : to grow dim or faint

**²fade** *n* : a short haircut in which hair on top of the head stands high

**FADM** *abbr* fleet admiral

**fae·cal, fae·ces** *chiefly Brit var of* FECAL, FECES

**fae·er·ie** *also* **fa·ery** \ˈfā-rē, ˈfer-ē\ *n, pl* **fae·er·ies 1** : FAIRYLAND **2** : FAIRY

**¹fag** \ˈfag\ *vb* **fagged; fag·ging 1** : DRUDGE **2** : TIRE, EXHAUST ⟨*fagged* by the work⟩

**²fag** *n* : MENIAL, DRUDGE

**³fag** *n* : an English public-school boy who acts as servant to another

**⁴fag** *vb* : to act as a fag

**⁵fag** *n* : CIGARETTE

**fag end** *n* **1** : REMNANT **2** : the extreme end **3** : the last part or coarser end of a web of cloth **4** : the untwisted end of a rope

**fag·ot** *or* **fag·got** \ˈfa-gət\ *n* : a bundle of sticks or twigs

**fag·ot·ing** *or* **fag·got·ing** *n* : an embroidery produced by tying threads in hourglass-shaped clusters

**Fah** *or* **Fahr** *abbr* Fahrenheit

**Fahr·en·heit** \ˈfer-ən-ˌhīt\ *adj* : relating to, conforming to, or having a thermometer scale with the boiling point of water at 212 degrees and the freezing point at 32 degrees above zero

**fa·ience** *or* **fa·ïence** \fā-ˈäns\ *n* [F] : earthenware decorated with opaque colored glazes

**¹fail** \ˈfāl\ *vb* **1** : to become feeble; *esp* : to decline in health **2** : to die away **3** : to stop functioning **4** : to fall short ⟨∼ed in his duty⟩ **5** : to be or become absent or inadequate **6** : to be unsuccessful esp. in achieving a passing grade **7** : to become bankrupt **8** : DISAPPOINT **9** : NEGLECT ⟨∼ed to lock the door⟩

**²fail** *n* : FAILURE ⟨without ∼⟩

**¹fail·ing** \ˈfā-liŋ\ *n* : WEAKNESS, SHORTCOMING

**²failing** *prep* : in the absence or lack of

**faille** \ˈfī(-ə)l\ *n* : a somewhat shiny closely woven ribbed fabric (as silk)

**fail-safe** \ˈfāl-ˌsāf\ *adj* **1** : incorporating a counteractive feature for a possible source of failure **2** : having no chance of failure — **fail-safe** *n*

**fail·ure** \ˈfāl-yər\ *n* **1** : a failing to do or perform **2** : a state of inability to perform a normal function adequately ⟨heart ∼⟩; *also* : an abrupt cessation of functioning ⟨a power ∼⟩ **3** : a fracturing or giving way under stress **4** : a lack of success **5** : BANKRUPTCY **6** : DEFICIEN-

CY ⟨crop ∼⟩   7 : DETERIORATION, DE-
CAY   8 : one that has failed

¹**fain** \'fān\ adj   1 archaic : GLAD; also : IN-
CLINED   2 : being obliged or compelled

ᵘ**fain** adv   1 : with pleasure   2 : by preference

¹**faint** \'fānt\ adj [ME faint, feint, fr. AF, fr.
faindre, feindre to feign, lose heart]   1
: COWARDLY, SPIRITLESS ⟨∼ of heart⟩   2
: weak, dizzy, and likely to faint   3 : lacking vigor or strength : FEEBLE ⟨∼
praise⟩   4 : hardly perceptible ⟨∼ hand-
writing⟩ — **faint·ly** adv — **faint·ness** n

²**faint** vb : to lose consciousness

³**faint** n : the action of fainting; also : the
resulting condition

**faint-heart·ed** \ˌfānt-'här-təd\ adj : lacking courage : TIMID

¹**fair** \'fer\ adj   1 : pleasing in appearance
: BEAUTIFUL   2 : superficially pleasing
: SPECIOUS   3 : CLEAN, PURE   4 : CLEAR,
LEGIBLE   5 : not stormy or cloudy   6
: JUST   7 : conforming with the rules : AL-
LOWED; also : being within the foul lines
⟨∼ ball⟩   8 : open to legitimate pursuit
or attack ⟨∼ game⟩   9 : PROMISING,
LIKELY ⟨a ∼ chance of winning⟩   10
: favorable to a ship's course ⟨a ∼ wind⟩
  11 : light in complexion : BLOND   12
: ADEQUATE   13 : significant in size ⟨a ∼
amount of traffic⟩ — **fair·ness** n

²**fair** adv   1 : in a fair manner ⟨play ∼⟩   2
chiefly Brit : FAIRLY   4

³**fair** n   1 : a gathering of buyers and sellers
at a stated time and place for trade   2 : a
competitive exhibition (as of farm products)   3 : a sale of assorted articles usu.
for a charitable purpose ⟨a book ∼⟩   4
: an exhibition that promotes available
services ⟨a job ∼⟩

**fair·ground** \-ˌgraund\ n : an area where
outdoor fairs, circuses, or exhibitions are
held

**fair·ing** \'fer-iŋ\ n : a structure for producing a smooth outline and reducing
drag (as on an airplane)

**fair·ly** \'fer-lē\ adv   1 : HANDSOMELY   2
: in a manner of speaking ⟨∼ bursting
with pride⟩   3 : without bias   4 : to a full
degree or extent : PLAINLY, DISTINCTLY
  5 : SOMEWHAT, RATHER ⟨a ∼ easy job⟩

**fair–spo·ken** \'fer-ˌspō-kən\ adj : pleasant and courteous in speech

**fair–trade** \-'trād\ adj : of, relating to, or
being an agreement between a producer
and a seller that branded merchandise
will be sold at or above a specified price
— **fair–trade** vb

**fair·way** \-ˌwā\ n : the mowed part of a
golf course between tee and green

**fairy** \'fer-ē\ n, pl **fair·ies** [ME fairie fairyland, enchantment, fr. AF faerie, fr. fee
fairy, fr. L Fata, goddess of fate, fr. fatum
fate] : an imaginary being of folklore and
romance usu. having diminutive human
form and magic powers — **fairy** adj

**fairy·land** \-ˌland\ n   1 : the land of fairies
  2 : a beautiful or charming place

**fairy tale** n   1 : a children's story usu.
about mythical beings (as fairies)   2 : FIB

**fait ac·com·pli** \ˌfāt-ˌa-ˌkōⁿ-'plē\ n, pl
**faits accomplis** \same or -'plēz\ [F, accomplished fact] : a thing accomplished
and presumably irreversible

**faith** \'fāth\ n, pl **faiths** \'fāths, 'fāthz\
[MF feith, fr. AF feid, fei, fr. L fides]   1
: allegiance to duty or a person : LOYAL-
TY   2 : belief and trust in God   3 : complete trust   4 : a system of religious beliefs — **faith·ful** \-fəl\ adj — **faith·ful·ly**
adv — **faith·ful·ness** n

**faith·less** \'fāth-ləs\ adj   1 : DISLOYAL   2
: not to be relied on — ♦ **Synonyms**
FALSE, TRAITOROUS, TREACHEROUS, UN-
FAITHFUL — **faith·less·ly** adv — **faith-
less·ness** n

**fa·ji·ta** \fə-'hē-tə\ n : a marinated strip
usu. of beef or chicken grilled or broiled
and served usu. with a flour tortilla and
savory fillings

¹**fake** \'fāk\ adj : COUNTERFEIT, SHAM

²**fake** n   1 : IMITATION, FRAUD; also : IM-
POSTOR   2 : a simulated move in sports
(as a pretended pass)

³**fake** vb **faked; fak·ing**   1 : to treat so as
to falsify   2 : COUNTERFEIT   3 : to deceive
(an opponent) in a sports contest by making a fake — **fak·er** n

**fa·kir** \fə-'kir\ n [Ar faqīr, lit., poor man]
  1 : a Muslim mendicant : DERVISH   2 : a
wandering Hindu ascetic

**fal·con** \'fal-kən, 'fȯl-\ n   1 : a hawk
trained for use in falconry   2 : any of
various swift long-winged long-tailed
hawks having a notched beak and usu.
inhabiting open areas

**fal·con·ry** \'fal-kən-rē, 'fȯl-\ n   1 : the art
of training hawks to hunt in cooperation
with a person   2 : the sport of hunting
with hawks — **fal·con·er** n

¹**fall** \'fȯl\ vb **fell** \'fel\; **fall·en** \'fȯ-lən\;
**fall·ing**   1 : to descend freely by the force
of gravity   2 : to hang freely   3 : to come
or go as if by falling ⟨darkness fell⟩   4 : to
become uttered   5 : to lower or become
lowered : DROP ⟨her eyes fell⟩   6 : to
leave an erect position suddenly and involuntarily   7 : STUMBLE, STRAY   8 : to
drop down wounded or dead esp. in battle   9 : to become captured ⟨the city fell
to the enemy⟩   10 : to suffer ruin, defeat,
or failure   11 : to commit an immoral act
  12 : to move or extend in a downward
direction   13 : SUBSIDE, ABATE   14 : to
decline in quality, activity, quantity, or
value   15 : to assume a look of shame or
dejection ⟨her face fell⟩   16 : to occur at
a certain time   17 : to come by chance
  18 : DEVOLVE ⟨the duties fell to him⟩   19
: to have the proper place or station ⟨the
accent ∼s on the first syllable⟩   20 : to
come within the scope of something   21
: to pass from one condition to another
⟨fell ill⟩   22 : to set about heartily or actively ⟨∼ to work⟩ — **fall all over oneself** or **fall over backward** : to display
excessive eagerness — **fall flat** : to produce no response or result — **fall for**   1
: to fall in love with   2 : to become a victim of — **fall from grace** : BACKSLIDE —
**fall into line** : to comply with a certain
course of action — **fall short**   1 : to be
deficient   2 : to fail to attain

²**fall** n   1 : the act of falling   2 : a falling

out, off, or away : DROPPING **3** : AUTUMN **4** : a thing or quantity that falls ⟨a light ∼ of snow⟩ **5** : COLLAPSE, DOWNFALL **6** : the surrender or capture of a besieged place **7** : departure from virtue or goodness **8** : SLOPE **9** : WATERFALL — usu. used in pl. **10** : a decrease in size, quantity, degree, or value ⟨a ∼ in price⟩ **11** : the distance which something falls **12** : an act of forcing a wrestler's shoulders to the mat; *also* : a bout of wrestling

**fal·la·cious** \fə-'lā-shəs\ *adj* **1** : embodying a fallacy ⟨a ∼ argument⟩ **2** : MISLEADING, DECEPTIVE

**fal·la·cy** \'fa-lə-sē\ *n, pl* **-cies** **1** : a false or mistaken idea **2** : an often plausible argument using false or illogical reasoning

**fall back** *vb* : RETREAT, RECEDE

**fall guy** *n* : SCAPEGOAT

**fal·li·ble** \'fa-lə-bəl\ *adj* **1** : liable to be erroneous **2** : capable of making a mistake — **fal·li·bly** \-blē\ *adv*

**fall·ing-out** \ˌfo-liŋ-'aút\ *n, pl* **fallings-out** *or* **falling-outs** : QUARREL

**falling star** *n* : METEOR

**fal·lo·pi·an tube** \fə-'lō-pē-ən-\ *n, often cap F* : either of the pair of anatomical tubes that carry the eggs from the ovary to the uterus

**fall·out** \'fól-ˌaút\ *n* **1** : the often radioactive particles that result from a nuclear explosion and descend through the air **2** : a secondary and often lingering effect or result

**fall out** *vb* : QUARREL

**¹fal·low** \'fa-(ˌ)lō\ *n* : fallow land; *also* : the state or period of being fallow — **fallow** *vb*

**²fallow** *adj* **1** : left without tilling or sowing after plowing **2** : DORMANT, INACTIVE ⟨a writer's ∼ period⟩

**false** \'fóls\ *adj* **fals·er; fals·est** **1** : not genuine : ARTIFICIAL ⟨∼ teeth⟩ **2** : intentionally untrue **3** : adjusted or made so as to deceive ⟨∼ scales⟩ **4** : tending to mislead : DECEPTIVE ⟨∼ promises⟩ **5** : not true ⟨∼ concepts⟩ **6** : not faithful or loyal : TREACHEROUS **7** : not essential or permanent ⟨∼ front⟩ **8** : inaccurate in pitch **9** : based on mistaken ideas — **false·ly** *adv* — **false·ness** *n* — **fal·si·ty** \'fól-sə-tē\ *n*

**false·hood** \'fóls-ˌhúd\ *n* **1** : LIE **2** : absence of truth or accuracy **3** : the practice of lying

**fal·set·to** \fól-'se-tō\ *n, pl* **-tos** [It, fr. dim. of *falso* false] : an artificially high voice; *esp* : an artificial singing voice that overlaps and extends above the range of the full voice esp. of a tenor

**fal·si·fy** \'fól-sə-ˌfī\ *vb* **-fied; -fy·ing** **1** : to prove to be false **2** : to alter so as to deceive **3** : LIE; *also* : MISREPRESENT — **fal·si·fi·able** \ˌfól-sə-'fī-ə-bəl\ *adj* — **fal·si·fi·ca·tion** \ˌfól-sə-fə-'kā-shən\ *n*

**fal·ter** \'fól-tər\ *vb* **1** : to move unsteadily : STUMBLE, TOTTER **2** : to hesitate in speech : STAMMER **3** : to hesitate in purpose or action : WAVER, FLINCH **4** : to lose effectiveness ⟨a ∼*ing* business⟩ — **fal·ter·ing·ly** *adv*

**fam** *abbr* **1** familiar **2** family

**fame** \'fām\ *n* : public reputation : RENOWN — **famed** \'fāmd\ *adj*

**fa·mil·ial** \fə-'mil-yəl\ *adj* **1** : of, relating to, or suggestive of a family **2** : tending to occur in more members of a family than expected by chance alone ⟨a ∼ disorder⟩

**¹fa·mil·iar** \fə-'mil-yər\ *n* **1** : COMPANION **2** : a spirit held to attend and serve or guard a person **3** : one who frequents a place

**²familiar** *adj* **1** : closely acquainted : INTIMATE **2** : of or relating to a family **3** : INFORMAL ⟨a ∼ style⟩ **4** : FORWARD, PRESUMPTUOUS **5** : frequently seen or experienced ⟨a ∼ face⟩ **6** : of everyday occurrence — **fa·mil·iar·ly** *adv*

**fa·mil·iar·ise** *Brit var of* FAMILIARIZE

**fa·mil·iar·i·ty** \fə-ˌmil-'yer-ə-tē, -ˌmi-lē-'er-\ *n, pl* **-ties** **1** : close friendship : INTIMACY **2** : INFORMALITY **3** : an unduly bold or forward act or expression : IMPROPRIETY **4** : close acquaintance with something ⟨∼ with current software⟩

**fa·mil·iar·ize** \fə-'mil-yə-ˌrīz\ *vb* **-ized; -iz·ing** **1** : to make known or familiar **2** : to make thoroughly acquainted

**fam·i·ly** \'fam-lē, 'fa-mə-\ *n, pl* **-lies** [ME *familie*, fr. L *familia* household, fr. *famulus* servant] **1** : a group of individuals living under one roof and under one head : HOUSEHOLD **2** : a group of persons of common ancestry : CLAN **3** : a group of things having common characteristics; *esp* : a group of related plants or animals ranking in biological classification above a genus and below an order **4** : a social unit usu. consisting of one or two parents and their children

**family planning** *n* : planning intended to determine the number and spacing of one's children by using birth control

**family tree** *n* : GENEALOGY; *also* : a genealogical diagram

**fam·ine** \'fa-mən\ *n* **1** : an extreme scarcity of food **2** : a great shortage

**fam·ish** \'fa-mish\ *vb* **1** : STARVE **2** : to suffer for lack of something necessary

**fa·mous** \'fā-məs\ *adj* **1** : widely known **2** : honored for achievement **3** : EXCELLENT, FIRST-RATE ♦ *Synonyms* RENOWNED, CELEBRATED, NOTED, NOTORIOUS, DISTINGUISHED, EMINENT, ILLUSTRIOUS

**fa·mous·ly** *adv* : SPLENDIDLY, EXCELLENTLY ⟨got along ∼⟩

**¹fan** \'fan\ *n* : a device (as a hand-waved triangular piece or a mechanism with blades) for producing a current of air

**²fan** *vb* **fanned; fan·ning** **1** : to drive away the chaff from grain by winnowing **2** : to move (air) with or as if with a fan **3** : to direct a current of air upon ⟨∼ a fire⟩ **4** : to stir up to activity : STIMULATE **5** : to spread like a fan **6** : to strike out in baseball

**³fan** *n* : an enthusiastic follower or admirer

**fa·nat·ic** \fə-'na-tik\ *or* **fa·nat·i·cal** \-ti-kəl\ *adj* [L *fanaticus* inspired by a deity, frenzied, fr. *fanum* temple] : marked by excessive enthusiasm and often intense uncritical devotion — **fanatic** *n* — **fa-nat-i-cism** \-tə-₁si-zəm\ *n*

**fan-ci-er** \'fan-sē-ər\ *n* 1 : one that has a special liking or interest 2 : a person who breeds or grows some kind of animal or plant for points of excellence

**fan-ci-ful** \'fan-si-fəl\ *adj* 1 : marked by, existing in, or given to unrestrained imagination or whim rather than reason 2 : curiously made or shaped ⟨a ∼ design⟩ — **fan-ci-ful-ly** *adv*

¹**fan-cy** \'fan-sē\ *vb* **fan-cied; fan-cy-ing** 1 : LIKE 2 : IMAGINE 3 : to believe without evidence or certainty 4 : to visualize or interpret as

²**fancy** *n, pl* **fancies** [ME *fantasie, fantsy* imagination, image, preference, fr. AF *fantasie* illusion, fr. L *phantasia*, fr. Gk, appearance, imagination] 1 : LIKING, IN-CLINATION; *also* : LOVE 2 : WHIM, NO-TION, IDEA ⟨a passing ∼⟩ 3 : IMAGINA-TION 4 : TASTE, JUDGMENT ♦ **Syn-onyms** CAPRICE, CROTCHET, VAGARY

³**fancy** *adj* **fan-ci-er; -est** 1 : WHIMSICAL 2 : not plain : ORNAMENTAL, POSH 3 : of particular excellence 4 : bred esp. for a showy appearance 5 : EXCESSIVE 6 : ex-ecuted with technical skill and style — **fan-ci-ly** \'fan-sə-lē\ *adv*

**fancy dress** *n* : a costume (as for a mas-querade) chosen to suit a fancy

**fan-cy-free** \₁fan-sē-'frē\ *adj* : free from amorous attachment; *also* : free to imag-ine

**fan-cy-work** \'fan-sē-₁wərk\ *n* : ornamen-tal needlework (as embroidery)

**fan-dan-go** \fan-'dan-gō\ *n, pl* **-gos** 1 : a lively Spanish or Spanish-American dance 2 : TOMFOOLERY

**fane** \'fān\ *n* 1 : TEMPLE 2 : CHURCH

**fan-fare** \'fan-₁fer\ *n* 1 : a flourish of trumpets 2 : a showy display

**fan fiction** *n* : stories involving fictional characters that are written by fans

**fang** \'faŋ\ *n* : a long sharp tooth; *esp* : a grooved or hollow tooth of a venomous snake — **fanged** \'faŋd\ *adj*

**fan-light** \'fan-₁līt\ *n* : a semicircular win-dow with radiating bars like a fan that is set over a door or window

**fan-ny** \'fa-nē\ *n, pl* **fannies** : BUTTOCKS

**fan-tail** \'fan-₁tāl\ *n* 1 : a fan-shaped tail or end 2 : an overhang at the stern of a ship

**fan-ta-sia** \fan-'tā-zhə, -zhē-ə, -zē-ə; ₁fan-tə-'zē-ə\ *n* : a musical composition free and fanciful in form

**fan-ta-sise** *Brit var of* FANTASIZE

**fan-ta-size** \'fan-tə-₁sīz\ *vb* **-sized; -siz-ing** : IMAGINE, DAYDREAM

**fan-tas-tic** \fan-'tas-tik\ *also* **fan-tas-ti-cal** \-ti-kəl\ *adj* 1 : IMAGINARY, UNREAL 2 : conceived by unrestrained fancy 3 : exceedingly or unbelievably great 4 : ECCENTRIC ♦ **Synonyms** CHIMERI-CAL, FANCIFUL, IMAGINARY — **fan-tas-ti-cal-ly** \-ti-k(ə-)lē\ *adv*

**fan-ta-sy** *also* **phan-ta-sy** \'fan-tə-sē\ *n, pl* **-sies** 1 : IMAGINATION, FANCY 2 : a product of the imagination : ILLUSION 3 : FANTASIA — **fantasy** *vb*

**FAQ** *abbr* frequently asked question

¹**far** \'fär\ *adv* **far-ther** \-thər\ *or* **fur-ther** \'fər-\; **far-thest** *or* **fur-thest** \-thəst\ 1 : at or to a considerable distance in space or time ⟨∼ from home⟩ 2 : by a broad interval : WIDELY, MUCH ⟨∼ better⟩ 3 : to or at a definite distance, point, or de-gree ⟨as ∼ as I know⟩ 4 : to an advanced point or extent ⟨go ∼ in his field⟩ — **by far** : by a considerable margin — **far and away** : DECIDEDLY — **so far** : until now

²**far** *adj* **farther** *or* **further; farthest** *or* **furthest** 1 : remote in space or time 2 : DIFFERENT 3 : LONG ⟨a ∼ journey⟩ 4 : being the more distant of two ⟨on the ∼ side of the lake⟩

**far-ad** \'fer-₁ad, -əd\ *n* : a unit of capaci-tance equal to the capacitance of a ca-pacitor having a potential difference of one volt between its plates when it is charged with one coulomb of electricity

**far-away** \'fär-ə-₁wā\ *adj* 1 : DISTANT, RE-MOTE ⟨∼ lands⟩ 2 : DREAMY

**farce** \'färs\ *n* 1 : a broadly satirical com-edy with an improbable plot 2 : the hu-mor characteristic of farce or pretense 3 : a ridiculous or empty display — **far-ci-cal** \'fär-si-kəl\ *adj*

**far cry** *n* 1 : a long distance 2 : some-thing notably different ⟨a *far cry* from what we expected⟩

¹**fare** \'fer\ *vb* **fared; far-ing** 1 : GO, TRAV-EL 2 : GET ALONG, SUCCEED ⟨fared well in math⟩ 3 : EAT, DINE

²**fare** *n* 1 : range of food : DIET; *also* : ma-terial provided for use, consumption, or enjoyment 2 : the price charged to trans-port a person 3 : a person paying a fare : PASSENGER

¹**fare-well** \fer-'wel\ *vb imper* : get along well — used interjectionally to or by one departing

²**farewell** *n* 1 : a wish of well-being at part-ing : GOOD-BYE 2 : LEAVE-TAKING

³**fare-well** \fer-₁wel\ *adj* : PARTING, FINAL ⟨a ∼ concert⟩

**far-fetched** \'fär-'fecht\ *adj* : not easily or naturally deduced or introduced : IM-PROBABLE ⟨a ∼ story⟩

**far-flung** \-'fləŋ\ *adj* : widely spread or distributed ⟨a ∼ empire⟩

**fa-ri-na** \fə-'rē-nə\ *n* [L, meal, flour] : a fine meal (as of wheat) used in puddings or as a breakfast cereal

**far-i-na-ceous** \₁fer-ə-'nā-shəs\ *adj* 1 : having a mealy texture or surface 2 : containing or rich in starch

¹**farm** \'färm\ *n* [ME *ferme* rent, lease, fr. AF, fr. *fermer* to fix, rent, fr. L *firmare* to make firm, fr. *firmus* firm] 1 : a tract of land used for raising crops or livestock 2 : a minor-league subsidiary of a major-league team

²**farm** *vb* : to use (land) as a farm ⟨∼ed 200 acres⟩; *also* : to raise crops or livestock

**farm-er** *n*

**farm-hand** \'färm-₁hand\ *n* : a farm la-borer

**farm-house** \-₁haus\ *n* : a dwelling on a farm

**farm-ing** \'fär-miŋ\ *n* : the occupation or business of a person who farms

**farm·land** \'färm-,land\ n : land used or suitable for farming

**farm out** vb : to turn over (as a task) to another

**farm·stead** \'färm-,sted\ n : a farm with its buildings

**farm·yard** \-,yärd\ n : land around or enclosed by farm buildings

**far–off** \'fär-'óf\ adj : remote in time or space : DISTANT

**fa·rouche** \fə-'rüsh\ adj [F] 1 : WILD 2 : marked by shyness and lack of polish

**far–out** \'fär-'aút\ adj : very unconventional 〈~ clothes〉

**far·ra·go** \fə-'rä-gō, -'rä-\ n, pl **-goes** [L, mixed fodder, mixture] : a confused collection : MIXTURE

**far–reach·ing** \'fär-'rē-chiŋ\ adj : having a wide range or effect

**far·ri·er** \'fer-ē-ər\ n [alter. of ME ferrour, fr. AF, blacksmith, fr. ferrer to shoe (horses)] : a person who shoes horses

¹**far·row** \'fer-ō\ vb : to give birth to a litter of pigs

²**farrow** n : a litter of pigs

**far–see·ing** \'fär-,sē-iŋ\ adj 1 : FAR-SIGHTED 1 2 : FARSIGHTED 2

**far·sight·ed** \'fär-,sī-təd\ adj 1 : seeing or able to see to a great distance 2 : JUDICIOUS, WISE, SHREWD 3 : affected with an eye condition in which vision is better for distant than near objects — **far·sight·ed·ness** n

¹**far·ther** \'fär-thər\ adv 1 : at or to a greater distance or more advanced point 2 : to a greater degree or extent

²**farther** adj 1 : more distant 2 : ADDITIONAL

**far·ther·most** \-,mōst\ adj : FARTHEST

¹**far·thest** \'fär-thəst\ adj : most distant

²**farthest** adv 1 : to or at the greatest distance : REMOTEST 〈hit the ball ~〉 2 : to the most advanced point 3 : by the greatest degree or extent : MOST

**far·thing** \'fär-thiŋ\ n 1 : a former British monetary unit equal to ¹/₄ of a penny; also : a coin representing this unit 2 : something of small value

**fas·cia** \1 is usu 'fā-sh(ē-)ə, 2 is usu 'fa-\ n, pl **-ci·ae** \-shē-,ē\ or **-cias** 1 : a flat usu. horizontal part (as a band or board) of or on a building 2 : a sheet of connective tissue covering body structures (as muscles)

**fas·ci·cle** \'fa-si-kəl\ n 1 : a small or slender bundle (as of pine needles or nerve fibers) 2 : one of the divisions of a book published in parts — **fas·ci·cled** \-kəld\ adj

**fas·ci·nate** \'fa-sə-,nāt\ vb **-nat·ed; -nat·ing** [L fascinare, fr. fascinum evil spell] 1 : to transfix and hold spellbound by an irresistible power 2 : ALLURE 3 : to be irresistibly attractive — **fas·ci·na·tion** \,fa-sə-'nā-shən\ n

**fas·cism** \'fa-,shi-zəm\ n, often cap : a political philosophy, movement, or regime that exalts nation and often race and stands for a centralized autocratic often militaristic government — **fas·cist** \-shist\ n or adj, often cap — **fas·cis·tic** \fa-'shis-tik\ adj, often cap

¹**fash·ion** \'fa-shən\ n 1 : the make or form of something 2 : MANNER, WAY 3 : a prevailing custom, usage, or style 4 : the prevailing style (as in dress) ♦ **Synonyms** MODE, VOGUE, RAGE, TREND

²**fashion** vb 1 : MOLD, CONSTRUCT 〈~ a vase out of clay〉 2 : FIT, ADAPT

**fash·ion·able** \'fa-shə-nə-bəl\ adj 1 : dressing or behaving according to fashion : STYLISH 2 : of or relating to the world of fashion 〈~ resorts〉 ♦ **Synonyms** CHIC, MODISH, SMART, SWANK — **fash·ion·ably** \-blē\ adv

¹**fast** \'fast\ adj 1 : firmly fixed 2 : tightly shut 3 : adhering firmly 4 : STUCK 5 : STAUNCH 〈~ friends〉 6 : characterized by quick motion, operation, or effect 〈a ~ trip〉 〈a ~ track〉 7 : indicating ahead of the correct time 〈the clock is ~〉 8 : not easily disturbed : SOUND 〈a ~ sleep〉 9 : permanently dyed; also : being proof against fading 〈colors ~ to sunlight〉 10 : DISSIPATED, WILD 〈a ~ crowd〉 11 : sexually promiscuous ♦ **Synonyms** RAPID, SWIFT, FLEET, QUICK, SPEEDY, HASTY

²**fast** adv 1 : in a firm or fixed manner 〈stuck ~ in the mud〉 2 : SOUNDLY, DEEPLY 〈~ asleep〉 3 : SWIFTLY 4 : RECKLESSLY

³**fast** vb 1 : to abstain from food 2 : to eat sparingly or abstain from some foods

⁴**fast** n 1 : the act or practice of fasting 2 : a time of fasting

**fast·back** \'fast-,bak\ n : an automobile having a roof with a long slope to the rear

**fast·ball** \-,ból\ n : a baseball pitch thrown at full speed

**fas·ten** \'fa-sᵊn\ vb 1 : to attach or join by or as if by pinning, tying, or nailing 2 : to make fast : fix securely 3 : to become fixed or joined 4 : to focus attention 〈~ed onto the newest trends〉 — **fas·ten·er** n

**fas·ten·ing** n : something that fastens : FASTENER

**fast–food** \,fast-'füd\ adj : specializing in food that is prepared and served quickly 〈a ~ restaurant〉

**fast–for·ward** \-'fór-wərd\ n 1 : a function of an electronic device that advances a recording rapidly 2 : a state of rapid advancement — **fast–forward** vb

**fas·tid·i·ous** \fa-'sti-dē-əs\ adj 1 : overly difficult to please 2 : showing a meticulous or demanding attitude 〈~ workmanship〉 ♦ **Synonyms** NICE, FINICKY, FUSSY, PARTICULAR, PERSNICKETY, SQUEAMISH — **fas·tid·i·ous·ly** adv — **fas·tid·i·ous·ness** n

**fast·ness** \'fast-nəs\ n 1 : the quality or state of being fast 2 : a fortified or secure place : STRONGHOLD

**fast–talk** \'fast-'tók\ vb : to influence by persuasive and usu. deceptive talk

**fast–track** \'fast-,trak\ vb : to speed up the processing or production of

**fast track** n : a course leading to rapid advancement or success

¹**fat** \'fat\ adj **fat·ter; fat·test** 1 : PLUMP, OBESE 2 : OILY, GREASY 3 : well filled

out : BIG  **4** : well stocked : ABUNDANT **5** : richly rewarding — **fat·ness** n

**²fat** n  **1** : animal tissue rich in greasy or oily matter  **2** : any of various energy-rich esters that occur naturally in animal fats and in plants and are soluble in organic solvents (as ether) but not in water  **3** : the best or richest portion ⟨lived on the ~ of the land⟩  **4** : OBESITY  **5** : excess matter ⟨trim the ~ from the budget⟩

**fa·tal** \'fāt-ʾl\ adj  **1** : FATEFUL ⟨that ~ day⟩  **2** : causing death or ruin ⟨a ~ mistake⟩ — **fa·tal·ly** adv

**fa·tal·ism** \-ˌi-zəm\ n : the belief that events are determined by fate — **fa·tal·ist** \-ist\ n — **fa·tal·is·tic** \ˌfāt-ʾl-'is-tik\ adj — **fa·tal·is·ti·cal·ly** \-ti-k(ə-)lē\ adv

**fa·tal·i·ty** \fā-'ta-lə-tē, fə-\ n, pl **-ties**  **1** : DEADLINESS  **2** : FATE  **3** : death resulting from a disaster or accident; also : one who suffers such a death

**fat·back** \'fat-ˌbak\ n : a fatty strip from the back of the hog usu. cured by salting and drying

**fat cat** n  **1** : a wealthy contributor to a political campaign  **2** : a wealthy privileged person

**fate** \'fāt\ n [ME, fr. MF or L; MF, fr. L fatum, lit., what has been spoken, fr. fari to speak]  **1** : the cause or will that is held to determine events : DESTINY  **2** : LOT, FORTUNE  **3** : DISASTER; esp : DEATH **4** : END, OUTCOME  **5** pl, cap : the three goddesses of classical mythology who determine the course of human life

**fat·ed** \'fā-təd\ adj : decreed, controlled, or marked by fate

**fate·ful** \'fāt-fəl\ adj  **1** : OMINOUS, PROPHETIC  **2** : IMPORTANT, DECISIVE **3** : DEADLY, DESTRUCTIVE  **4** : determined by fate — **fate·ful·ly** adv

**fath** abbr fathom

**fat·head** \'fat-ˌhed\ n : a stupid person — **fat·head·ed** \-'he-dəd\ adj

**¹fa·ther** \'fä-thər\ n  **1** : a male parent **2** cap : God esp. as the first person of the Trinity  **3** : FOREFATHER  **4** : one deserving the respect and love given to a father **5** often cap : an early Christian writer accepted by the church as an authoritative witness to its teaching and practice  **6** : ORIGINATOR ⟨the ~ of modern radio⟩; also : SOURCE  **7** : PRIEST — used esp. as a title  **8** : one of the leading men ⟨city ~s⟩ — **fa·ther·hood** \-ˌhu̇d\ n — **fa·ther·less** adj — **fa·ther·ly** adj

**²father** vb  **1** : BEGET  **2** : to be the founder, producer, or author of  **3** : to treat or care for as a father

**father–in–law** \'fä-thə-rən-ˌlȯ\ n, pl **fathers–in–law** \-thər-zən-\ : the father of one's husband or wife

**fa·ther·land** \'fä-thər-ˌland\ n  **1** : the native land of one's ancestors  **2** : one's native land

**fath·om** \'fa-thəm\ n [ME fadme, fr. OE fæthm length of the outstretched arms] : a unit of length equal to 6 feet (about 1.8 meters) used esp. for measuring the depth of water

**²fathom** vb  **1** : to measure by a sounding line  **2** : PROBE  **3** : to penetrate and come

to understand ⟨~ the problem⟩ — **fath·om·able** \'fa-thə-mə-bəl\ adj

**fath·om·less** \'fa-thəm-ləs\ adj : incapable of being fathomed

**¹fa·tigue** \fə-'tēg\ n [F]  **1** : manual or menial work performed by military personnel  **2** pl : the uniform or work clothing worn on fatigue and in the field  **3** : weariness from labor or stress  **4** : the tendency of a material to break under repeated stress

**²fatigue** vb **fa·tigued; fa·tigu·ing** : WEARY, TIRE

**fat·ten** \'fa-tᵊn\ vb : to make or grow fat

**Fat Tuesday** n : MARDI GRAS

**fat·ty** \'fa-tē\ adj **fat·ti·er; -est**  **1** : containing fat esp. in unusual amounts  **2** : GREASY

**²fatty** n, pl **fat·ties** : a fat person

**fatty acid** n : any of numerous acids that contain only carbon, hydrogen, and oxygen and that occur naturally in fats and various oils

**fa·tu·i·ty** \fə-'tü-ə-tē, -'tyü-\ n, pl **-ities** : FOOLISHNESS, STUPIDITY

**fat·u·ous** \'fa-chù-wəs\ adj : FOOLISH, INANE, SILLY — **fat·u·ous·ly** adv

**fau·bourg** \fō-'bu̇r\ n  **1** : a suburb esp. of a French city  **2** : a city quarter

**fau·ces** \'fȯ-ˌsēz\ n pl [L, throat] : the narrow passage located between the soft palate and the base of the tongue that joins the mouth to the pharynx

**fau·cet** \'fȯ-sət, 'fä-\ n : a fixture for drawing off a liquid (as from a pipe)

**¹fault** \'fȯlt\ n  **1** : a weakness in character : FAILING  **2** : IMPERFECTION, IMPAIRMENT, DEFECT  **3** : an error esp. in service in a net or racket game  **4** : MISDEMEANOR; also : MISTAKE  **5** : responsibility for something wrong  **6** : a fracture in the earth's crust accompanied by a displacement of one side relative to the other — **fault·i·ly** \'fȯl-tə-lē\ adv — **fault·less** adj — **fault·less·ly** adv — **faulty** adj

**²fault** vb  **1** : to commit a fault : ERR  **2** : to fracture so as to produce a geologic fault **3** : to find a fault in  **4** : BLAME, CRITICIZE

**fault·find·er** \'fȯlt-ˌfīn-dər\ n : a person who tends to find fault or complain ◆ **Synonyms** CRITIC, CARPER, CAVILER, COMPLAINER — **fault·find·ing** n or adj

**faun** \'fȯn\ n : a Roman god similar to but gentler than a satyr

**fau·na** \'fȯ-nə\ n, pl **faunas** also **fau·nae** \-ˌnē, -ˌnī\ [NL, fr. L Fauna, sister of Faunus (the Roman god of animals)] : animals or animal life esp. of a region, period, or environment — **fau·nal** \-nᵊl\ adj

**fau·vism** \'fō-ˌvi-zəm\ n, often cap : a movement in painting characterized by vivid colors, free treatment of form, and a vibrant and decorative effect — **fauvist** \-vist\ n, often cap

**faux pas** \'fō-ˌpä, fō-'\ n, pl **faux pas** \same or -ˌpäz, -'päz\ [F, lit., false step] : BLUNDER; esp : a social blunder

**fa·va bean** \'fä-və-\ n : the large flat edible seed of an Old World vetch; also : this plant

**¹fa·vor** \'fā-vər\ n  **1** : friendly regard

shown toward another esp. by a superior **2** : APPROVAL **3** : PARTIALITY **4** : POPULARITY **5** : gracious kindness; *also* : an act of such kindness **6** *pl* : effort in one's behalf : ATTENTION **7** : a token of love (as a ribbon) usu. worn conspicuously **8** : a small gift or decorative item given out at a party **9** : a special privilege **10** : sexual privileges — usu. used in pl. **11** *archaic* : LETTER **12** : BEHALF, INTEREST ⟨acted in his own ∼⟩

²**favor** *vb* **1** : to regard or treat with favor **2** : OBLIGE **3** : ENDOW ⟨∼ed by nature⟩ **4** : to treat gently or carefully : SPARE ⟨∼ a lame leg⟩ **5** : PREFER **6** : SUPPORT, SUSTAIN ⟨∼ed the tax reform⟩ **7** : FACILITATE ⟨darkness ∼s attack⟩ **8** : RESEMBLE ⟨he ∼s his father⟩

**fa·vor·able** \'fā-və-rə-bəl\ *adj* **1** : APPROVING ⟨a ∼ response⟩ **2** : HELPFUL, PROMISING, ADVANTAGEOUS ⟨∼ weather⟩ — **fa·vor·ably** \-blē\ *adv*

**fa·vor·ite** \'fā-və-rət, -vrət\ *n* **1** : a person or a thing that is favored above others **2** : a competitor regarded as most likely to win — **favorite** *adj*

**favorite son** *n* : a candidate supported by the delegates of his state at a presidential nominating convention

**fa·vor·it·ism** \'fā-və-rə-,ti-zəm\ *n* : PARTIALITY, BIAS

**fa·vour** *chiefly Brit var of* FAVOR

¹**fawn** \'fȯn, 'fän\ *vb* **1** : to show affection ⟨a dog ∼ing on its master⟩ **2** : to court favor by a cringing or flattering manner ♦ *Synonyms* GROVEL, KOWTOW, TOADY, TRUCKLE

²**fawn** *n* **1** : a young deer **2** : a light grayish brown — **fawny** \'fȯ-nē, 'fä-\ *adj*

**fax** \'faks\ *n* **1** : FACSIMILE 2 **2** : a device used to send or receive facsimile communications; *also* : such a communication — **fax** *vb*

**fay** \'fā\ *n* : FAIRY, ELF — **fay** *adj*

**faze** \'fāz\ *vb* **fazed**; **faz·ing** : to disturb the composure or courage of : DAUNT

**FBI** *abbr* Federal Bureau of Investigation

**FCC** *abbr* Federal Communications Commission

**FD** *abbr* fire department

**FDA** *abbr* Food and Drug Administration

**FDIC** *abbr* Federal Deposit Insurance Corporation

**Fe** *symbol* [L *ferrum*] iron

**fe·al·ty** \'fē-(ə)l-tē\ *n*, *pl* **-ties** : LOYALTY, ALLEGIANCE ♦ *Synonyms* FIDELITY, DEVOTION, FAITHFULNESS, PIETY

¹**fear** \'fir\ *vb* **1** : to have a reverent awe of ⟨∼ God⟩ **2** : to be afraid of ⟨∼s spiders⟩ **3** : to be apprehensive

²**fear** *n* **1** : an unpleasant often strong emotion caused by expectation or awareness of danger; *also* : an instance of or a state marked by this emotion **2** : anxious concern : SOLICITUDE **3** : profound reverence esp. toward God ♦ *Synonyms* DREAD, FRIGHT, ALARM, PANIC, TERROR, TREPIDATION

**fear·ful** \-fəl\ *adj* **1** : causing fear **2** : filled with fear **3** : showing or caused by fear **4** : extremely bad, intense, or large ⟨paid a ∼ price⟩ — **fear·ful·ly** *adv*

**fear·less** \-ləs\ *adj* : free from fear : BRAVE — **fear·less·ly** *adv* — **fear·less·ness** *n*

**fear·some** \-səm\ *adj* **1** : causing fear **2** : TIMID **3** : INTENSE ⟨∼ determination⟩

**fea·si·ble** \'fē-zə-bəl\ *adj* [ME *faisible*, fr. AF *faisable*, fr.-*sip*-, stem of *faire* to make, do] **1** : capable of being done or carried out ⟨a ∼ plan⟩ **2** : SUITABLE **3** : REASONABLE, LIKELY ♦ *Synonyms* POSSIBLE, PRACTICABLE, VIABLE, WORKABLE — **fea·si·bil·i·ty** \,fē-zə-'bi-lə-tē\ *n* — **fea·si·bly** \'fē-zə-blē\ *adv*

¹**feast** \'fēst\ *n* **1** : an elaborate meal : BANQUET **2** : ABUNDANCE ⟨a ∼ of good books⟩ **3** : FESTIVAL 1

²**feast** *vb* **1** : to take part in a feast; *also* : to give a feast for **2** : to enjoy some unusual pleasure or delight **3** : DELIGHT, GRATIFY

**feat** \'fēt\ *n* : DEED, EXPLOIT, ACHIEVEMENT; *esp* : an act notable for courage, skill, endurance, or ingenuity

¹**feath·er** \'fe-thər\ *n* **1** : any of the light horny outgrowths that form the external covering of the body of a bird **2** : the vane of an arrow **3** : PLUMAGE **4** : KIND, NATURE ⟨birds of a ∼⟩ **5** : ATTIRE, DRESS ⟨in full ∼⟩ **6** : CONDITION, MOOD ⟨in fine ∼⟩ — **feath·ered** \-thərd\ *adj* — **feath·er·less** *adj* — **feath·ery** *adj* — **a feather in one's cap** : a mark of distinction : HONOR

²**feather** *vb* **1** : to furnish with a feather ⟨∼ an arrow⟩ **2** : to cover, clothe, line, or adorn with or as if with feathers — **feather one's nest** : to provide for oneself financially esp. while exploiting a position of trust

**feath·er·bed·ding** \'fe-thər-,be-diŋ\ *n* : the requiring of an employer usu. under a union rule or safety statute to employ more workers than are needed

**feath·er·edge** \-,ej\ *n* : a very thin sharp edge

**feath·er·weight** \-,wāt\ *n* : one that is very light in weight; *esp* : a boxer weighing more than 118 but not over 126 pounds

¹**fea·ture** \'fē-chər\ *n* [ME *fetūre*, fr. AF, fr. L *factura* act of making, fr. *facere* to make] **1** : the shape or appearance of the face or its parts **2** : a part of the face ⟨her eyes are her best ∼⟩ **3** : a prominent part or characteristic **4** : a special attraction (as in a newspaper) **5** : something offered to the public or advertised as particularly attractive ⟨a new car's ∼s⟩ — **fea·ture·less** *adj*

²**feature** *vb* **1** : to picture in the mind : IMAGINE **2** : to give special prominence to ⟨the show ∼s new artists⟩ **3** : to play an important part

**Feb** *abbr* February

**fe·brile** \'fe-,brī(-ə)l\ *adj* : FEVERISH

**Feb·ru·ary** \'fe-b(y)ə-,wer-ē, 'fe-brə-\ *n* [ME *Februarie*, fr. L *Februarius*, fr. *Februa*, pl., feast of purification] : the 2d month of the year

**fe·ces** \'fē-,sēz\ *n pl* : bodily waste discharged from the intestine : EXCREMENT — **fe·cal** \-kəl\ *adj*

**feck·less** \'fek-ləs\ *adj* **1** : WEAK, INEFFECTIVE **2** : WORTHLESS, IRRESPONSIBLE 〈~ drifters〉

**fe·cund** \'fe-kənd, 'fē-\ *adj* : FRUITFUL, PROLIFIC 〈~ fields〉 — **fe·cun·di·ty** \fi-'kən-də-tē, fe-\ *n*

**fe·cun·date** \'fe-kən-ˌdāt, 'fē-\ *vb* **-dat·ed; -dat·ing** **1** : to make fecund **2** : IMPREGNATE — **fe·cun·da·tion** \ˌfe-kən-'dā-shən, ˌfē-\ *n*

**fed** *abbr* federal; federation

**fed·er·al** \'fe-də-rəl, -drəl\ *adj* **1** : formed by a compact between political units that surrender individual sovereignty to a central authority but retain certain limited powers **2** : of or constituting a form of government in which power is distributed between a central authority and constituent territorial units **3** : of or relating to the central government of a federation **4** *cap* : FEDERALIST **5** *often cap* : of, relating to, or loyal to the federal government or the Union armies of the U.S. in the American Civil War — **fed·er·al·ly** *adv*

**Federal** *n* : a supporter of the U.S. government in the Civil War; *esp* : a soldier in the federal armies

**federal district** *n* : a district (as the District of Columbia) set apart as the seat of the central government of a federation

**fed·er·al·ism** \'fe-də-rə-li-zəm, -drə-\ *n* *often cap* : the distribution of power in an organization (as a government) between a central authority and the constituent units **2** : support or advocacy of federalism **3** *cap* : the principles of the Federalists

**fed·er·al·ist** \-list\ *n* **1** : an advocate of federalism **2** *often cap* : an advocate of a federal union between the American colonies after the Revolution and of adoption of the U.S. Constitution **3** *cap* : a member of a major political party in the early years of the U.S. favoring a strong centralized national government — **fed·eralist** *adj, often cap*

**fed·er·al·ize** \'fe-də-rə-ˌlīz, -drə-\ *vb* **-ized; -iz·ing** **1** : to unite in or under a federal system **2** : to bring under the jurisdiction of a federal government

**fed·er·ate** \'fe-də-ˌrāt\ *vb* **-at·ed; -at·ing** : to join in a federation

**fed·er·a·tion** \ˌfe-də-'rā-shən\ *n* **1** : a political or societal entity formed by uniting smaller entities **2** : a federal government **3** : a union of organizations **4** : the forming of a federal union

**fedn** *abbr* federation

**fe·do·ra** \fi-'dȯr-ə\ *n* : a low soft felt hat with the crown creased lengthwise

**fed up** *adj* : utterly sated, tired, or disgusted 〈*fed up* with bureaucracy〉

**fee** \'fē\ *n* [ME, fr. AF *fé, fief,* of Gmc origin; akin to OE *feoh* cattle, property] **1** : an estate in land held from a feudal lord **2** : an inherited or heritable estate in land **3** : a fixed charge; *also* : a charge for a service

**fee·ble** \'fē-bəl\ *adj* **fee·bler** \-bə-lər\; **fee·blest** \-bə-ləst\ [ME *feble,* fr. AF, fr. L *flebilis* lamentable, wretched, fr. *flēre* to

weep] **1** : DECREPIT, FRAIL **2** : INEFFECTIVE, INADEQUATE 〈a ~ protest〉 — **fee·ble·ness** *n* — **fee·bly** \-blē\ *adv*

**fee·ble-mind·ed** \ˌfē-bəl-'mīn-dəd\ *adj* : lacking normal intelligence — **fee·ble-mind·ed·ness** *n*

**¹feed** \'fēd\ *vb* **fed** \'fed\; **feed·ing** **1** : to give food to; *also* : to give as food **2** : EAT **1**; *also* : PREY **3** : to furnish what is necessary to the development or function of 〈used wood to ~ the fire〉 **4** : to supply for another to use 〈~ a pass〉 〈*fed* the actor his lines〉 — **feed·er** *n*

**²feed** *n* **1** : a usu. large meal **2** : food for livestock **3** : a mechanism for feeding material to a machine

**feed·back** \'fēd-ˌbak\ *n* **1** : the return to the input of a part of the output of a machine, system, or process **2** : response esp. to one in authority about an activity or policy **3** : sound (as whistling) resulting from the retransmission of an amplified or broadcast signal

**feed·lot** \'fēd-ˌlät\ *n* : land on which cattle are fattened for market

**feed·stuff** \-ˌstəf\ *n* : FEED 2

**¹feel** \'fēl\ *vb* **felt** \'felt\; **feel·ing** **1** : to perceive or examine through physical contact : TOUCH, HANDLE **2** : EXPERIENCE; *also* : to suffer from **3** : to ascertain by cautious trial 〈~ out public senti­ment〉 **4** : to be aware of **5** : to be conscious of an inward impression, state of mind, or physical condition **6** : BELIEVE, THINK 〈say what you ~〉 **7** : to search for something with the fingers : GROPE **8** : SEEM 〈it ~s like spring〉 **9** : to have sympathy or pity

**²feel** *n* **1** : the sense of touch **2** : SENSATION, FEELING **3** : the quality of a thing as imparted through touch

**feel·er** \'fē-lər\ *n* **1** : one that feels; *esp* : a tactile organ (as on the head of an insect) **2** : a proposal or remark made to find out the views of other people

**¹feel·ing** \'fē-liŋ\ *n* **1** : the sense of touch; *also* : a sensation perceived by this **2** : a state of mind 〈a ~ of loneliness〉 **3** *pl* : general emotional condition : SENSIBILITIES 〈hurt their ~s〉 **4** : OPINION, BELIEF **5** : capacity to respond emotionally

**²feeling** *adj* **1** : SENSITIVE; *esp* : easily moved emotionally **2** : expressing emotion or sensitivity — **feel·ing·ly** *adv*

**feet** *pl of* FOOT

**feign** \'fān\ *vb* **1** : to give a false appearance of : SHAM 〈~ illness〉 **2** : to assert as if true : PRETEND

**feint** \'fānt\ *n* : something feigned; *esp* : a mock blow or attack intended to distract attention from the real point of attack — **feint** *vb*

**feisty** \'fī-stē\ *adj* **feist·i·er; -est** : having or showing a lively aggressiveness 〈a ~ heroine〉

**feld·spar** \'feld-ˌspär\ *n* : any of a group of crystalline minerals consisting of silicates of aluminum with another element (as potassium or sodium)

**fe·lic·i·tate** \fi-'li-sə-ˌtāt\ *vb* **-tat·ed; -tat·ing** : CONGRATULATE 〈felicitated the winner⟩ — **fe·lic·i·ta·tion** \-ˌli-sə-ˈtā-shən\ *n*

**fe·lic·i·tous** \fi-ˈli-sə-təs\ *adj* **1** : well chosen : APT **2** : PLEASANT, DELIGHTFUL — **fe·lic·i·tous·ly** *adv*

**fe·lic·i·ty** \fi-ˈli-sə-tē\ *n, pl* **-ties** **1** : the quality or state of being happy; *esp* : great happiness **2** : something that causes happiness **3** : a pleasing manner or quality esp. in art or language ⟨her ∼ with words⟩ **4** : an apt expression

**fe·line** \ˈfē-ˌlīn\ *adj* [L *felinus,* fr. *felis* cat] **1** : of or relating to cats or their kin **2** : sleekly graceful **3** : SLY, TREACHEROUS **4** : STEALTHY — **feline** *n*

**¹fell** \ˈfel\ *n* : SKIN, HIDE, PELT

**²fell** *vb* **1** : to cut, beat, or knock down; *also* : KILL **2** : to sew (a seam) by folding one raw edge under the other

**³fell** *past of* FALL

**⁴fell** *adj* : CRUEL, FIERCE; *also* : DEADLY — **in one fell swoop** *also* **at one fell swoop** : all at once : with a single effort

**fel·lah** \ˈfe-lə, fə-ˈlä\ *n, pl* **fel·la·hin** *or* **fel·la·heen** \ˌfe-lə-ˈhēn\ : a peasant or agricultural laborer in Arab countries (as Egypt or Syria)

**fel·la·tio** \fə-ˈlā-shē-ˌō\ *also* **fel·la·tion** \-shən\ *n* : oral stimulation of the penis

**fel·low** \ˈfe-lō\ *n* [ME *felawe,* fr. OE *fēolaga,* fr. ON *fēlagi,* fr. *fēlag* partnership (fr. *fē* cattle, money) + *lag* act of laying] **1** : COMRADE, ASSOCIATE **2** : EQUAL, PEER **3** : one of a pair : MATE **4** : a member of an incorporated literary or scientific society **5** : MAN, BOY **6** : BOYFRIEND **7** : a person granted a stipend for advanced study

**fellow man** *n* : a kindred human being

**fel·low·ship** \ˈfe-lō-ˌship\ *n* **1** : the condition of friendly relationship existing among persons : COMRADESHIP **2** : a community of interest or feeling **3** : a group with similar interests **4** : the position of a fellow (as of a university) **5** : the stipend granted a fellow

**fellow traveler** *n* : a sympathetic supporter of another's cause; *esp* : a person who sympathizes with and often furthers the ideals and program of an organized group (as the Communist party) without joining it

**fel·on** \ˈfe-lən\ *n* **1** : one who has committed a felony **2** : WHITLOW

**fel·o·ny** \ˈfe-lə-nē\ *n, pl* **-nies** : a serious crime punishable by a heavy sentence — **fe·lo·ni·ous** \fə-ˈlō-nē-əs\ *adj*

**fel·spar** *chiefly Brit var of* FELDSPAR

**¹felt** \ˈfelt\ *n* **1** : a cloth made of wool and fur often mixed with natural or synthetic fibers **2** : a material resembling felt

**²felt** *past and past part of* FEEL

**fem** *abbr* **1** female **2** feminine

**FEMA** *abbr* Federal Emergency Management Agency

**fe·male** \ˈfē-ˌmāl\ *adj* [ME, alter. of *femel,* fr. AF *femele,* fr. ML *femella,* fr. L, girl, dim. of *femina* woman] **1** : of, relating to, or being the sex that bears young; *also* : PISTILLATE **2** : characteristic of girls or women ⟨∼ voices⟩ ♦ *Synonyms* FEMI-

NINE, WOMANLY, WOMANLIKE, WOMAN-ISH, EFFEMINATE — **female** *n*

**¹fem·i·nine** \ˈfe-mə-nən\ *adj* **1** : of the female sex; *also* : characteristic of or appropriate or peculiar to women **2** : of, relating to, or constituting the gender that includes most words or grammatical forms referring to females — **fem·i·nin·i·ty** \ˌfe-mə-ˈni-nə-tē\ *n*

**²feminine** *n* : a noun, pronoun, adjective, or inflectional form or class of the feminine gender; *also* : the feminine gender

**fem·i·nism** \ˈfe-mə-ˌni-zəm\ *n* **1** : the theory of the political, economic, and social equality of the sexes **2** : organized activity on behalf of women's rights and interests — **fem·i·nist** \-nist\ *n or adj*

**femme fa·tale** \ˌfem-fə-ˈtal\ *n, pl* **femmes fa·tales** \*same or* -ˈtalz\ [F, lit., disastrous woman] : a seductive woman

**fe·mur** \ˈfē-mər\ *n, pl* **fe·murs** *or* **fem·o·ra** \ˈfe-mə-rə\ : the long leg bone extending from the hip to the knee — **fem·o·ral** \ˈfe-mə-rəl\ *adj*

**fen** \ˈfen\ *n* : low swampy land

**fen** \ˈfən\ *n, pl* **fen** — see *yuan* at MONEY table

**¹fence** \ˈfens\ *n* [ME *fens,* short for *defens* defense] **1** : a barrier (as of wood or wire) to prevent escape or entry or to mark a boundary **2** : a person who receives stolen goods; *also* : a place where stolen goods are disposed of — **on the fence** : in a position of neutrality or indecision

**²fence** *vb* **fenced; fenc·ing** **1** : to enclose with a fence **2** : to keep in or out with a fence **3** : to practice fencing **4** : to use tactics of attack and defense esp. in debate — **fenc·er** *n*

**fenc·ing** *n* **1** : the art or practice of attack and defense with the foil, épée, or saber **2** : the fences of a property or region **3** : material used for building fences

**fend** \ˈfend\ *vb* **1** : to keep or ward off : REPEL **2** : SHIFT ⟨∼ for yourself⟩

**fend·er** \ˈfen-dər\ *n* : a protective device (as a guard over the wheel of an automobile)

**fen·es·tra·tion** \ˌfe-nə-ˈstrā-shən\ *n* : the arrangement and design of windows and doors in a building

**Fe·ni·an** \ˈfē-nē-ən\ *n* : a member of a secret 19th century Irish and Irish-American organization dedicated to overthrowing British rule in Ireland

**fen·ing** \ˈfe-niŋ\ *n, pl* **fening** *or* **fen·inga** \-niŋ-ə\ — see *marka* at MONEY table

**fen·nel** \ˈfe-nᵊl\ *n* : a garden plant related to the carrot and grown for its aromatic foliage and seeds

**FEPC** *abbr* Fair Employment Practices Commission

**fe·ral** \ˈfir-əl, ˈfer-\ *adj* **1** : SAVAGE **2** : WILD 1 **3** : having escaped from domestication and become wild

**fer–de–lance** \ˈfer-də-ˈlans\ *n, pl* **fer–de–lance** [F, lit., lance iron, spearhead] : a large venomous pit viper of Central and So. America

**¹fer·ment** \fər-ˈment\ *vb* **1** : to cause or undergo fermentation **2** : to be or cause to be in a state of agitation or intense activity

²**fer·ment** \'fər-,ment\ n 1 : a living organism (as a yeast) causing fermentation by its enzymes; also : ENZYME 2 : AGITATION, TUMULT

**fer·men·ta·tion** \,fər-mən-'tā-shən, -,men-\ n 1 : chemical decomposition of an organic substance (as in the souring of milk or the formation of alcohol from sugar) by enzymatic action in the absence of oxygen often with formation of gas 2 : FERMENT 2

**fer·mi·um** \'fer-mē-əm, 'fər-\ n : an artificially produced radioactive metallic chemical element

**fern** \'fərn\ n : any of an order of vascular plants resembling seed plants in having roots, stems, and leaflike fronds but reproducing by spores instead of by flowers and seeds

**fern·ery** \'fər-nə-rē\ n, pl **-er·ies** 1 : a place for growing ferns 2 : a collection of growing ferns

**fe·ro·cious** \fə-'rō-shəs\ adj 1 : FIERCE, SAVAGE 2 : extremely intense — **fe·ro·cious·ly** adv — **fe·ro·cious·ness** n

**fe·roc·i·ty** \fə-'rä-sə-tē\ n : the quality or state of being ferocious

¹**fer·ret** \'fer-ət\ n : a partially domesticated usu. white European mammal related to the weasels

²**ferret** vb 1 : to hunt game with ferrets 2 : to drive out of a hiding place 3 : to find and bring to light by searching ⟨∼ out the truth⟩

**fer·ric** \'fer-ik\ adj : of, relating to, or containing iron

**ferric oxide** n : an oxide of iron found in nature as hematite and as rust and used esp. as a pigment, for polishing, and in magnetic materials

**Fer·ris wheel** \'fer-əs-\ n : an amusement device consisting of a large upright powerdriven wheel with seats that remain horizontal around its rim

**fer·ro·mag·net·ic** \,fer-ō-mag-'ne-tik\ adj : of or relating to substances that are easily magnetized

**fer·rous** \'fer-əs\ adj : of, relating to, or containing iron

**fer·rule** \'fer-əl\ n : a metal ring or cap around a slender wooden shaft to prevent splitting

¹**fer·ry** \'fer-ē\ vb **fer·ried; fer·ry·ing** [ME ferien, fr. OE ferian to carry, convey] 1 : to carry by boat across a body of water 2 : to cross by a ferry 3 : to convey from one place to another

²**ferry** n, pl **ferries** 1 : a place where persons or things are ferried 2 : FERRYBOAT

**fer·ry·boat** \'fer-ē-,bōt\ n : a boat used in ferrying

**fer·tile** \'fər-t³l\ adj 1 : producing plentifully : PRODUCTIVE ⟨∼ soils⟩ ⟨a ∼ mind⟩ 2 : capable of developing or reproducing ⟨∼ seed⟩ ⟨a ∼ bull⟩ ♦ **Synonyms** FRUITFUL, PROLIFIC, FECUND, PRODUCTIVE — **fer·til·i·ty** \(,)fər-'ti-lə-tē\ n

**fer·til·ize** \'fər-tə-,līz\ vb **-ized; -iz·ing** 1 : to unite with in the process of fertiliza-

tion ⟨a sperm ∼s an egg⟩ 2 : to apply fertilizer to — **fer·til·i·za·tion** \,fər-tə-lə-'zā-shən\ n

**fer·til·iz·er** \'fər-tə-,lī-zər\ n : material (as manure or a chemical mixture) for enriching land

**fer·ule** \'fer-əl\ n : a rod or ruler used to punish children

**fer·ven·cy** \'fər-vən-sē\ n, pl **-cies** : FERVOR

**fer·vent** \'fər-vənt\ adj 1 : very hot : GLOWING 2 : marked by great intensity of feeling ♦ **Synonyms** IMPASSIONED, ARDENT, FERVID, FIERY, PASSIONATE — **fer·vent·ly** adv

**fer·vid** \-vəd\ adj 1 : very hot 2 : ARDENT, ZEALOUS — **fer·vid·ly** adv

**fer·vor** \'fər-vər\ n 1 : intense heat 2 : intensity of feeling or expression **fervour** chiefly Brit var of FERVOR

**fes·cue** \'fes-kyü\ n : any of a genus of tufted perennial grasses

**fes·tal** \'fes-t³l\ adj : FESTIVE

**fes·ter** \'fes-tər\ vb 1 : to form pus 2 : PUTREFY, ROT 3 : RANKLE

**fes·ti·val** \'fes-tə-vəl\ n 1 : a time of celebration marked by special observances; esp : an occasion marked with religious ceremonies 2 : a periodic season or program of cultural events or entertainment ⟨a dance ∼⟩

**fes·tive** \'fes-tiv\ adj 1 : of, relating to, or suitable for a feast or festival 2 : JOYFUL, GAY — **fes·tive·ly** adv

**fes·tiv·i·ty** \fes-'ti-və-tē\ n, pl **-ties** 1 : FESTIVAL 1 2 : the quality or state of being festive 3 : festive activity

¹**fes·toon** \fes-'tün\ n [F feston, fr. It festone, fr. festa festival] 1 : a decorative chain or strip hanging between two points 2 : a carved, molded, or painted ornament representing a decorative chain

²**festoon** vb 1 : to hang or form festoons on 2 : to shape into festoons

**fe·ta** \'fe-tə\ n : a white crumbly Greek cheese made from sheep's or goat's milk

**fe·tal** \'fēt-³l\ adj : of, relating to, or being a fetus

**fetch** \'fech\ vb 1 : to go or come after and bring or take back ⟨teach a dog to ∼ a stick⟩ 2 : to bring in (as a price) 3 : to cause to come : bring out ⟨∼ed tears from the eyes⟩ 4 : to give by striking ⟨∼ him a blow⟩

**fetch·ing** adj : ATTRACTIVE, PLEASING ⟨a ∼ smile⟩ — **fetch·ing·ly** adv

¹**fete** or **fête** \'fāt, 'fet\ n [F fête, fr. OF feste] 1 : FESTIVAL 2 : a large elaborate entertainment or party

²**fete** or **fête** vb **fet·ed** or **fêt·ed; fet·ing** or **fêt·ing** 1 : to honor or commemorate with a fete 2 : to pay high honor to

**fet·id** \'fe-təd\ adj : having an offensive smell : STINKING

**fe·tish** also **fe·tich** \'fe-tish\ n [F & Pg; F fétiche, fr. Pg feitiço, fr. feitiço artificial, false, fr. L facticius factitious] 1 : an object (as an idol or image) believed to have magical powers (as in curing disease) 2 : an object of unreasoning devotion or concern 3 : an object whose real or fantasied presence is psychologically necessary for sexual gratification

**fe·tish·ism** \-ti-,shi-zəm\ n 1 : belief in or devotion to fetishes 2 : the pathological transfer of sexual interest and gratification to a fetish — **fe·tish·ist** \-shist\ n — **fe·tish·is·tic** \,fe-ti-'shis-tik\ adj

**fe·tish·ize** \-ti-,shīz\ vb -ized -iz·ing : to make a fetish of

**fet·lock** \'fet-,läk\ n : a projection on the back of a horse's leg above the hoof; also : a tuft of hair on this

**fet·ter** \'fe-tər\ n 1 : a chain or shackle for the feet 2 : something that confines : RESTRAINT — **fetter** vb

**fet·tle** \'fe-t²l\ n : a state of fitness or order : CONDITION ⟨in fine ∼⟩

**fe·tus** \'fē-təs\ n : an unborn or unhatched vertebrate esp. after its basic structure is laid down; esp : a developing human in the uterus from usu. three months after conception to birth

**feud** \'fyüd\ n : a prolonged quarrel; esp : a lasting conflict between families or clans marked by violent attacks made for revenge — **feud** vb

**feu·dal** \'fyü-d²l\ adj 1 : of, relating to, or having the characteristics of a medieval fee 2 : of, relating to, or characteristic of feudalism

**feu·dal·ism** \'fyü-də-,li-zəm\ n : a system of political organization prevailing in medieval Europe in which a vassal renders service to a lord and receives protection and land in return; also : a similar political or social system — **feu·dal·is·tic** \,fyü-d²l-'is-tik\ adj

**¹feu·da·to·ry** \'fyü-də-,tór-ē\ adj : owing feudal allegiance

**²feudatory** n, pl -ries 1 : FIEF 2 : a person who holds lands by feudal law or usage

**fe·ver** \'fē-vər\ n 1 : a rise in body temperature above the normal; also : a disease of which this is a chief symptom 2 : a state of heightened emotion or activity 3 : CRAZE ⟨football ∼⟩ — **fe·ver·ish** adj — **fe·ver·ish·ly** adv

**¹few** \'fyü\ pron : not many : a small number

**²few** adj 1 : consisting of or amounting to a small number 2 : not many but some ⟨caught a ∼ fish⟩ — **few·ness** n — **few and far between** : RARE 3

**³few** n 1 : a small number of units or individuals ⟨a ∼ of them⟩ 2 : a special limited number ⟨among the ∼⟩

**few·er** \'fyü-ər\ pron : a smaller number of persons or things

**fey** \'fā\ adj 1 chiefly Scot : fated to die; also : marked by a foreboding of death or calamity 2 : able to see into the future : VISIONARY 3 : marked by an otherworldly air or attitude 4 : CRAZY, TOUCHED

**fez** \'fez\ n, pl **fez·zes** also **fez·es** : a round red felt hat that has a flat top and a tassel but no brim

**ff** abbr 1 folios 2 [following] and the following ones 3 fortissimo

**FHA** abbr Federal Housing Administration

**fi·an·cé** \,fē-,än-'sā\ n [F, fr. MF, fr. pp. of *fiancer* to promise, betroth, fr. OF *fiancier*, fr. *fiance* promise, trust, fr. *fier* to trust, ultim. fr. L *fidere*] : a man engaged to be married

**fi·an·cée** \,fē-,än-'sā\ n : a woman engaged to be married

**fi·as·co** \fē-'as-kō\ n, pl **-coes** [F] : a complete failure

**fi·at** \'fē-ət, -,at, -,ät; 'fī-ət, -,at\ n [L, let it be done] : an authoritative and often arbitrary order or decree

**¹fib** \'fib\ n : a trivial or childish lie

**²fib** vb **fibbed; fib·bing** : to tell a fib — **fib·ber** n

**fi·ber** \'fī-bər\ n 1 : a threadlike substance or structure (as a muscle cell or fine root); esp : a natural (as wool or flax) or artificial (as rayon) filament capable of being spun or woven 2 : indigestible material in food that stimulates the intestine to move its contents along 3 : an element that gives texture or substance 4 : basic toughness : STRENGTH ⟨moral ∼⟩ — **fi·brous** \-brəs\ adj

**fi·ber·board** \'fī-bər-,bórd\ n : a material made by compressing fibers (as of wood) into stiff sheets

**fi·ber·fill** \-,fil\ n : synthetic fibers used as a filling material (as for cushions)

**fi·ber·glass** \-,glas\ n : glass in fibrous form used in making various products (as insulation)

**fiber optics** n 1 pl : thin transparent fibers of glass or plastic that are enclosed by a less refractive material and that transmit light by internal reflection; also : a bundle of such fibers used in an instrument 2 : the technique of the use of fiber optics — **fiber-optic** adj

**fibre** chiefly Brit var of FIBER

**fi·bril** \'fī-brəl, 'fi-\ n : a small fiber

**fi·bril·la·tion** \,fi-brə-'lā-shən, ,fī-\ n : rapid irregular contractions of the heart muscle fibers resulting in a lack of synchronism between heartbeat and pulse — **fib·ril·late** \'fi-brə-,lāt, 'fī-\ vb

**fi·brin** \'fī-brən\ n : a white insoluble fibrous protein formed in the clotting of blood

**¹fi·broid** \'fī-bróid, 'fi-\ adj : resembling, forming, or consisting of fibrous tissue ⟨∼ tumors⟩

**²fibroid** n : a benign tumor of the uterus

**fi·bro·my·al·gia** \,fī-,brō-,mī-'al-jə\ n : any of a group of rheumatic disorders affecting soft tissues (as muscles or tendons)

**fi·bro·sis** \fī-'brō-səs\ n : a condition marked by abnormal increase of fiber-containing tissue

**fib·u·la** \'fi-byə-lə\ n, pl **-lae** \-lē, -lī\ or **-las** : the outer and usu. the smaller of the two bones between the knee and ankle — **fib·u·lar** \-lər\ adj

**FICA** abbr Federal Insurance Contributions Act

**-fication** n comb form : making : production ⟨simplifi*cation*⟩

**fiche** \'fēsh\ n, pl **fiche** : MICROFICHE

**fi·chu** \'fi-shü\ n [F] : a woman's light triangular scarf draped over the shoulders and fastened in front

**fick·le** \'fi-kəl\ *adj* : not firm or steadfast in disposition or character : INCONSTANT ⟨∼ friends⟩ — **fick·le·ness** *n*

**fic·tion** \'fik-shən\ *n* **1** : something (as a story) invented by the imagination **2** : fictitious literature (as novels) — **fic·tion·al** \-shə-nəl\ *adj* — **fic·tion·al·ly** *adv*

**fic·ti·tious** \fik-'ti-shəs\ *adj* **1** : of, relating to, or characteristic of fiction : IMAGINARY **2** : FALSE, ASSUMED ⟨a ∼ name⟩ **3** : FEIGNED ◆ *Synonyms* CHIMERICAL, FANCIFUL, FANTASTIC, UNREAL

¹**fid·dle** \'fi-d³l\ *n* : VIOLIN

²**fiddle** *vb* **fid·dled**; **fid·dling 1** : to play on a fiddle **2** : to move the hands or fingers restlessly **3** : PUTTER **4** : MEDDLE, TAMPER — **fid·dler** *n*

**fid·dle·head** \'fi-d³l-₁hed\ *n* : one of the young unfurling fronds of some ferns that are often eaten as greens

**fiddler crab** *n* : any of a genus of burrowing crabs with one claw much enlarged in the male

**fid·dle·stick** \'fi-d³l-₁stik\ *n* **1** : a violin bow **2** *pl* : NONSENSE — used as an interjection

**fi·del·i·ty** \fə-'de-lə-tē, fī-\ *n, pl* **-ties 1** : the quality or state of being faithful **2** : ACCURACY ⟨∼ in sound reproduction⟩ ◆ *Synonyms* ALLEGIANCE, LOYALTY, DEVOTION, FEALTY

¹**fidg·et** \'fi-jət\ *n* **1** : uneasiness or restlessness as shown by nervous movements — usu. used in pl. **2** : one that fidgets — **fidg·ety** *adj*

²**fidget** *vb* : to move or cause to move or act restlessly or nervously

**fi·du·cia·ry** \fə-'dü-shē-₁er-ē, -'dyü-, -shə-rē\ *adj* **1** : involving a confidence or trust **2** : held or holding in trust for another ⟨∼ accounts⟩ — **fiduciary** *n*

**fie** \'fī\ *interj* — used to express disgust or disapproval

**fief** \'fēf\ *n* [F, fr. OF] : a feudal estate : FEE

¹**field** \'fēld\ *n* **1** : open country **2** : a piece of cleared land for cultivation or pasture **3** : a piece of land yielding some special product **4** : the place where a battle is fought; *also* : BATTLE **5** : an area, division, or sphere of activity ⟨the ∼ of science⟩ ⟨salesmen in the ∼⟩ **6** : an area for military exercises **7** : an area for sports **8** : a background on which something is drawn or projected ⟨a flag with white stars on a ∼ of blue⟩ **9** : a region or space in which a given effect (as magnetism) exists — **field** *adj*

²**field** *vb* **1** : to handle a batted or thrown baseball while on defense **2** : to put into the field **3** : to answer satisfactorily ⟨∼ a tough question⟩ — **field·er** *n*

**field day** *n* **1** : a day devoted to outdoor sports and athletic competition **2** : a time of extraordinary pleasure or opportunity

**field event** *n* : a track-and-field event (as weight-throwing) other than a race

**field glass** *n* : a hand-held binocular telescope — usu. used in pl.

**field guide** *n* : a manual for identifying natural objects, plants, or animals

**field hockey** *n* : a field game played between two teams of 11 players each whose object is to knock a ball into the opponent's goal with a curved stick

**field marshal** *n* : an officer (as in the British army) of the highest rank

**field–test** \-₁test\ *vb* : to test (as a new product) in actual situations reflecting intended use — **field test** *n*

**fiend** \'fēnd\ *n* **1** : DEVIL **2** : DEMON **3** : an extremely wicked or cruel person **4** : a person excessively devoted to a pursuit ⟨a golf ∼⟩ **5** : ADDICT ⟨a dope ∼⟩ — **fiend·ish** *adj* — **fiend·ish·ly** *adv*

**fierce** \'firs\ *adj* **fierc·er**; **fierc·est 1** : violently hostile or aggressive in temperament **2** : PUGNACIOUS **3** : INTENSE ⟨∼ pain⟩ **4** : furiously active or determined **5** : wild or menacing in appearance ◆ *Synonyms* FEROCIOUS, BARBAROUS, SAVAGE, CRUEL — **fierce·ly** *adv* — **fierce·ness** *n*

**fi·ery** \'fī-ə-rē\ *adj* **fi·er·i·er; -est 1** : consisting of fire **2** : BURNING, BLAZING **3** : FLAMMABLE **4** : hot like a fire : INFLAMED, FEVERISH **5** : RED ⟨a ∼ sunset⟩ **6** : full of emotion or spirit **7** : IRRITABLE — **fi·er·i·ness** \-rē-nəs\ *n*

**fi·es·ta** \fē-'es-tə\ *n* [Sp] : FESTIVAL

**fife** \'fīf\ *n* [G *Pfeife* pipe, fife] : a small flute

**FIFO** *abbr* first in, first out

**fif·teen** \fif-'tēn\ *n* : one more than 14 — **fifteen** *adj or pron* — **fif·teenth** \-'tēnth\ *adj or n*

**fifth** \'fifth\ *n* **1** : one that is number five in a countable series **2** : one of five equal parts of something **3** : a unit of measure for liquor equal to ¹⁄₅ U.S. gallon (0.757 liter) — **fifth** *adj or adv*

**fifth column** *n* : a group of secret supporters of a nation's enemy that engage in espionage or sabotage within the country — **fifth columnist** *n*

**fifth wheel** *n* : one that is unnecessary and often burdensome

**fif·ty** \'fif-tē\ *n, pl* **fifties** : five times 10 — **fif·ti·eth** \-tē-əth\ *adj or n* — **fifty** *adj or pron*

**fif·ty–fif·ty** \₁fif-tē-'fif-tē\ *adj* **1** : shared equally ⟨a ∼ proposition⟩ **2** : half favorable and half unfavorable

¹**fig** \'fig\ *n* : a soft usu. pear-shaped edible fruit of a tree related to the mulberry; *also* : a tree bearing figs

²**fig** *abbr* **1** figurative; figuratively **2** figure

¹**fight** \'fīt\ *vb* **fought** \'fȯt\; **fight·ing 1** : to contend against another in battle or physical combat **2** : BOX **3** : to put forth a determined effort **4** : STRUGGLE, CONTEND **5** : to attempt to prevent the success or effectiveness of **6** : WAGE ⟨∼ a war⟩ **7** : to gain by struggle

²**fight** *n* **1** : a hostile encounter : BATTLE **2** : a boxing match **3** : a verbal disagreement **4** : a struggle for a goal or an objective **5** : strength or disposition for fighting ⟨full of ∼⟩

**fight·er** \'fī-tər\ *n* **1** : one that fights; *esp* : WARRIOR **2** : BOXER **1 3** : a fast maneuverable warplane for destroying enemy aircraft

**fig·ment** \'fig-mənt\ *n* : something imagined or made up

**fig·u·ra·tion** \ˌfig-gyə-'rā-shən, -gə-\ *n* 1 : FORM, OUTLINE 2 : an act or instance of representation in figures and shapes

**fig·u·ra·tive** \'fig-gyə-rə-tiv, -gə-\ *adj* 1 : EMBLEMATIC 2 : SYMBOLIC, METAPHORICAL ⟨∼ language⟩ — **fig·u·ra·tive·ly** *adv*

**¹fig·ure** \'fi-gyər, -gər\ *n* [ME, fr. AF, fr. L *figura*, fr. *fingere* to shape] 1 : NUMERAL 2 *pl* : arithmetical calculations 3 : a written or printed character 4 : PRICE, SUM ⟨sold at a low ∼⟩ 5 : a combination of points, lines, or surfaces in geometry ⟨a circle is a closed plane ∼⟩ 6 : SHAPE, FORM, OUTLINE 7 : the graphic representation of a form esp. of a person 8 : a diagram or pictorial illustration of textual matter 9 : PATTERN, DESIGN 10 : appearance made or impression produced ⟨they cut quite a ∼⟩ 11 : a series of movements (as in a dance) 12 : PERSONAGE ⟨a well-known sports ∼⟩

**²figure** *vb* **fig·ured; fig·ur·ing** 1 : to represent by or as if by a figure or outline 2 : to decorate with a pattern 3 : to indicate or represent by numerals 4 : REGARD, CONSIDER 5 : to be or appear important or conspicuous 6 : COMPUTE, CALCULATE ⟨*figured* the cost⟩

**fig·ure·head** \'fi-gyər-ˌhed, -gər-\ *n* 1 : a figure on the bow of a ship 2 : a head or chief in name only

**figure of speech** : a form of expression (as a simile or metaphor) that often compares or identifies one thing with another to convey meaning or heighten effect

**figure out** *vb* 1 : FIND OUT, DISCOVER 2 : SOLVE ⟨*figure out* a math problem⟩

**figure skating** *n* : skating that includes various jumps, spins, and dance movements

**fig·u·rine** \ˌfig-gyə-'rēn, -gə-\ *n* : a small carved or molded figure

**fil·a·ment** \'fi-lə-mənt\ *n* : a fine thread or threadlike object, part, or process — **fil·a·men·tous** \ˌfi-lə-'men-təs\ *adj*

**fil·bert** \'fil-bərt\ *n* : the sweet thick-shelled nut of either of two European hazels; *also* : a shrub or small tree bearing filberts

**filch** \'filch\ *vb* : to steal furtively

**¹file** \'fī(-ə)l\ *n* : a usu. steel tool with a ridged or toothed surface used esp. for smoothing a hard substance

**²file** *vb* **filed; fil·ing** : to rub, smooth, or cut away with a file

**³file** *vb* **filed; fil·ing** [ME, fr. ML *filare* to string documents on a string or wire, fr. *filum* file of documents, lit., thread, fr. L] 1 : to arrange in order 2 : to enter or record officially or as prescribed by law ⟨∼ a lawsuit⟩ 3 : to send (copy) to a newspaper

**⁴file** *n* 1 : a device (as a folder or cabinet) by means of which papers may be kept in order 2 : a collection of papers or publications usu. arranged or classified 3 : a collection of data (as text) treated by a computer as a unit

**⁵file** *n* : a row of persons, animals, or things arranged one behind the other

**⁶file** *vb* **filed; fil·ing** : to march or proceed in file

**fi·let mi·gnon** \ˌfi-(ˌ)lā-mēn-'yōⁿ, fi-ˌlā-\ *n*, *pl* **filets mignons** \-(ˌ)lā-mēn-'yōⁿz, -ˌlā-\ [F, lit., dainty fillet] : a thick slice of beef cut from the narrow end of a beef tenderloin

**fil·ial** \'fi-lē-əl, 'fil-yəl\ *adj* : of, relating to, or befitting a son or daughter

**fil·i·bus·ter** \'fi-lə-ˌbəs-tər\ *n* [Sp *filibustero*, lit., freebooter] 1 : a military adventurer; *esp* : an American engaged in fomenting 19th century Latin American uprisings 2 : the use of delaying tactics (as extremely long speeches) esp. in a legislative assembly; *also* : an instance of this practice — **filibuster** *vb* — **fil·i·bus·ter·er** *n*

**fil·i·cide** \'fi-lə-ˌsīd\ *n* : the murder of one's own daughter or son

**fil·i·gree** \'fi-lə-ˌgrē\ *n* [F *filigrane*] : ornamental openwork (as of fine wire) — **fil·i·greed** \-ˌgrēd\ *adj*

**fil·ing** \'fī-liŋ\ *n* 1 : the act or instance of using a file 2 : a small piece scraped off by a file ⟨iron ∼s⟩

**Fil·i·pi·no** \ˌfi-lə-'pē-nō\ *n*, *pl* **Filipinos** : a native or inhabitant of the Philippines — **Filipino** *adj*

**¹fill** \'fil\ *vb* 1 : to make or become full 2 : to stop up : PLUG ⟨∼ a cavity⟩ 3 : FEED, SATIATE 4 : SATISFY, FULFILL ⟨∼ all requirements⟩ 5 : to occupy fully 6 : to spread through ⟨laughter ∼ed the room⟩ 7 : OCCUPY ⟨∼ the office of president⟩ 8 : to put a person in ⟨∼ a vacancy⟩ 9 : to supply as directed ⟨∼ a prescription⟩

**²fill** *n* 1 : a full supply; *esp* : a quantity that satisfies or satiates 2 : material used esp. for filling a low place

**¹fill·er** \'fi-lər\ *n* 1 : one that fills 2 : a substance added to another substance (as to increase bulk or weight) 3 : a material used for filling cracks and pores in wood before painting

**²fil·ler** \'fi-ˌler\ *n*, *pl* **fillers** *or* **filler** — see *forint* at MONEY table

**¹fil·let** \'fi-lət, in sense 2 fi-'lā, 'fi-(ˌ)lā\ *also* **fi·let** \fi-'lā, 'fi-(ˌ)lā\ *n* [ME *filet*, fr. AF, dim. of *fil* thread] 1 : a narrow band, strip, or ribbon 2 : a piece or slice of boneless meat or fish; *esp* : the tenderloin of beef

**²fil·let** \'fi-lət, in sense 2 also fi-'lā, 'fi-(ˌ)lā\ *vb* 1 : to bind or adorn with or as if with a fillet 2 : to cut into fillets

**fill in** *vb* 1 : to provide necessary or recent information 2 : to serve as a temporary substitute

**fill·ing** \'fi-liŋ\ *n* 1 : material used to fill something ⟨a ∼ for a tooth⟩ 2 : the yarn interlacing the warp in a fabric 3 : a food mixture used to fill pastry or sandwiches

**filling station** *n* : GAS STATION

**fil·lip** \'fi-ləp\ *n* 1 : a blow or gesture made by a flick or snap of the finger across the thumb 2 : something that serves to arouse or excite — **fillip** *vb*

**fill-up** \'fil-,əp\ *n* : an act or instance of filling something

**fil-ly** \'fi-lē\ *n, pl* **fillies** : a young female horse usu. less than four years old

**¹film** \'film\ *n* **1** : a thin skin or membrane **2** : a thin coating or layer **3** : a flexible strip of chemically treated material used in taking pictures **4** : MOTION PICTURE — **filmy** *adj*

**²film** *vb* **1** : to cover with a film **2** : to make a motion picture of

**film-dom** \'film-dəm\ *n* : the motion-picture industry

**film-og-ra-phy** \fil-'mä-grə-fē\ *n, pl* **-phies** : a list of motion pictures featuring the work of a film figure or a particular topic

**film-strip** \'film-,strip\ *n* : a strip of film bearing a sequence of images for projection as still pictures

**¹fils** \'fēs\ *n* [F] : SON — used after a family name to distinguish a son from his father

**²fils** \'fils\ *n, pl* **fils** — see *dinar, dirham, rial* at MONEY table

**¹fil-ter** \'fil-tər\ *n* **1** : a porous material through which a fluid is passed to separate out matter in suspension; *also* : a device containing such material **2** : a device for suppressing waves of certain frequencies; *esp* : one (as for a camera) that absorbs light of certain colors **3** : software for sorting or blocking certain online material

**²filter** *vb* **1** : to remove by means of a filter **2** : to pass through a filter — **fil-ter-able** *also* **fil-tra-ble** \-tə-rə-bəl, -trə-\ *adj* — **fil-tra-tion** \fil-'trā-shən\ *n*

**filth** \'filth\ *n* [ME, fr. OE *fylth*, fr. *fūl* foul] **1** : foul matter; *esp* : loathsome dirt or refuse **2** : moral corruption **3** : OBSCENITY — **filth-i-ness** *n* — **filthy** \'fil-thē\ *adj*

**filthy** *adv* : VERY, EXTREMELY ⟨~ *dirty*⟩ ⟨~ *rich*⟩

**fil-trate** \'fil-,trāt\ *n* : fluid that has passed through a filter

**¹fin** \'fin\ *n* **1** : a thin external process by which an aquatic animal (as a fish) moves through water **2** : a fin-shaped part (as on an airplane) **3** : FLIPPER **2** — **finned** \'find\ *adj*

**²fin** *abbr* **1** finance; financial **2** finish

**fi-na-gle** \fə-'nā-gəl\ *vb* **-gled; -gling 1** : to obtain by indirect or dishonest means : WANGLE **2** : to use devious dishonest methods to achieve one's ends — **fi-na-gler** *n*

**¹fi-nal** \'fī-nᵊl\ *adj* **1** : not to be altered or undone ⟨all sales are ~⟩ **2** : ULTIMATE **3** : relating to or occurring at the end or conclusion ⟨the ~ results⟩ — **fi-nal-i-ty** \fī-'na-lə-tē, fī-\ *n* — **fi-nal-ly** *adv*

**²final** *n* **1** : a deciding match or game — usu. used in pl. **2** : the last examination in a course — often used in pl.

**fi-na-le** \fə-'na-lē, fi-'nä-\ *n* : the close or end of something; *esp* : the last section of a musical composition

**fi-nal-ise** *Brit var of* FINALIZE

**fi-nal-ist** \'fī-nə-list\ *n* : a contestant in the finals of a competition

**fi-nal-ize** \'fī-nə-,līz\ *vb* **-ized; -iz-ing** : to put in final or finished form

**¹fi-nance** \fə-'nans, 'fī-,nans\ *n* [ME, ending, payment, fr. AF, fr. *finer* to end, pay, fr. *fin* end, fr. L *finis* boundary, end] **1** *pl* : money resources available esp. to a government or business **2** : management of money affairs

**²finance** *vb* **fi-nanced; fi-nanc-ing 1** : to raise or provide funds for **2** : to furnish with necessary funds **3** : to sell or supply on credit

**finance company** *n* : a company that makes usu. small short-term loans usu. to individuals

**fi-nan-cial** \fə-'nan-chəl, fī-\ *adj* : relating to finance or financiers ⟨~ *problems*⟩ — **fi-nan-cial-ly** *adv*

**fi-nan-cials** \-shəlz\ *n pl* : financial statistics

**fi-nan-cier** \,fi-nən-'sir, ,fī-,nan-\ *n* **1** : a person skilled in managing public moneys **2** : a person who deals with large-scale finance and investment

**finch** \'finch\ *n* : any of numerous songbirds with strong conical bills

**¹find** \'fīnd\ *vb* **found** \'faund\; **find-ing 1** : to meet with either by chance or by searching or study : ENCOUNTER, DISCOVER **2** : to obtain by effort or management ⟨~ time to read⟩ **3** : to arrive at : REACH ⟨the bullet *found* its mark⟩ **4** : EXPERIENCE, FEEL ⟨*found* happiness⟩ **5** : to gain or regain the use of ⟨*found* his voice again⟩ **6** : to determine and make a statement about ⟨~ a verdict⟩

**²find** *n* **1** : an act or instance of finding **2** : something found; *esp* : a valuable item of discovery

**find-er** \'fīn-dər\ *n* : one that finds; *esp* : VIEWFINDER

**fin de siè-cle** \,faⁿ-də-sē-'eklᵊ\ *adj* [F, end of century] **1** : of, relating to, or characteristic of the close of the 19th century **2** : of or relating to the end of a century

**find-ing** \'fīn-diŋ\ *n* **1** : the act of finding **2** : FIND **2 3** : the result of a judicial proceeding or inquiry

**find out** *vb* : to learn by study, observation, or search : DISCOVER

**¹fine** \'fīn\ *n* : money exacted as a penalty for an offense

**²fine** *vb* **fined; fin-ing** : to impose a fine on : punish by a fine

**³fine** *adj* **fin-er; fin-est 1** : free from impurity **2** : very thin in gauge or texture **3** : not coarse ⟨~ sand⟩ **4** : SUBTLE, SENSITIVE ⟨a ~ distinction⟩ **5** : superior in quality or appearance **6** : ELEGANT, REFINED ⟨~ manners⟩ — **fine-ly** *adv* — **fine-ness** *n*

**⁴fine** *adv* **1** : very well **2** — used to express agreement

**fine art** *n* : art (as painting, sculpture, or music) concerned primarily with the creation of beautiful objects — usu. used in pl.

**fin-ery** \'fī-nə-rē\ *n, pl* **-er-ies** : ORNAMENT, DECORATION; *esp* : showy clothing and jewels

**fine-spun** \'fīn-'spən\ *adj* : developed

with extremely or excessively fine delicacy or detail

**fi·nesse** \fə-'nes\ n 1 : refinement or delicacy of workmanship, structure, or texture 2 : CUNNING, SUBTLETY ⟨handled the questions with ~⟩ — **finesse** vb

**fine–tune** \'fīn-'tün\ vb : to adjust so as to bring to the highest level of performance or effectiveness

**fin·fish** \'fin-,fish\ n : FISH 2

¹**fin·ger** \'fiŋ-gər\ n 1 : any of the five divisions at the end of the hand; esp : one other than the thumb 2 : something that resembles or does the work of a finger 3 : a part of a glove into which a finger is inserted

²**finger** vb **fin·gered; fin·ger·ing** 1 : to touch or feel with the fingers : HANDLE 2 : to perform with the fingers or with a certain fingering 3 : to mark the notes of a piece of music as a guide in playing 4 : to point out ⟨was ~ed as a suspect⟩

**fin·ger·board** \'fiŋ-gər-,bórd\ n : the part of a stringed instrument against which the fingers press the strings to vary the pitch

**finger bowl** n : a small water bowl for rinsing the fingers at the table

**fin·ger·ing** \'fiŋ-gə-riŋ\ n 1 : handling or touching with the fingers 2 : the act or method of using the fingers in playing an instrument 3 : the marking of the method of fingering

**fin·ger·ling** \'fiŋ-gər-liŋ\ n : a small fish

**fin·ger·nail** \'fiŋ-gər-,nāl\ n : the nail of a finger

**fin·ger·print** \-,print\ n : the pattern of marks made by pressing the tip of a finger or thumb on a surface; esp : an ink impression of such a pattern taken for the purpose of identification — **fingerprint** vb

**fin·ger·tip** \-,tip\ n : the tip of a finger

**fin·i·al** \'fi-nē-əl\ n : an ornamental projection or end (as on a spire)

**fin·ick·ing** \'fi-ni-kiŋ\ adj : FINICKY

**fin·icky** \'fi-ni-kē\ adj : excessively particular in taste or standards ⟨a ~ eater⟩

**fi·nis** \'fi-nəs\ n : END, CONCLUSION

¹**fin·ish** \'fi-nish\ vb 1 : TERMINATE 2 : to use or dispose of entirely 3 : to bring to completion : ACCOMPLISH 4 : to put a final coat or surface on 5 : to come to the end of a course or undertaking ⟨my horse ~ed third⟩ — **fin·ish·er** n

²**finish** n 1 : END, CONCLUSION 2 : something that completes or perfects 3 : the final treatment or coating of a surface

**fi·nite** \'fī-,nīt\ adj 1 : having definite or definable limits; also : having a limited nature or existence 2 : being less than some positive integer in number or measure and greater than its negative 3 : showing distinction of grammatical person and number ⟨a ~ verb⟩

**fink** \'fiŋk\ n 1 : a contemptible person 2 : STRIKEBREAKER 3 : INFORMER

**Finn** \'fin\ n : a native or inhabitant of Finland

**fin·nan had·die** \,fi-nən-'ha-dē\ n : smoked haddock

¹**Finn·ish** \'fi-nish\ adj : of or relating to Finland, the Finns, or Finnish

²**Finnish** n : the language of the Finns

**fin·ny** \'fi-nē\ adj 1 : having or characterized by fins 2 : relating to or being fish

**fiord** var of FJORD

**fir** \'fər\ n : any of a genus of usu. large evergreen trees related to the pines; also : the light soft wood of a fir

¹**fire** \'fī(-ə)r\ n 1 : the light or heat and esp. the flame of something burning 2 : ENTHUSIASM, ZEAL 3 : fuel that is burning (as in a stove or fireplace) 4 : destructive burning (as of a house) 5 : the firing of weapons — **fire·less** adj

²**fire** vb **fired; fir·ing** 1 : KINDLE, IGNITE ⟨~ a house⟩ 2 : STIR, ENLIVEN ⟨~ the imagination⟩ 3 : to dismiss from employment 4 : SHOOT ⟨~ a gun⟩ ⟨~ an arrow⟩ 5 : BAKE ⟨firing pottery in a kiln⟩ 6 : to apply fire or fuel to something ⟨~ a furnace⟩

**fire ant** n : either of two small fiercely stinging So. American ants introduced into the southeastern U.S. where they are agricultural pests

**fire·arm** \'fī(-ə)r-,ärm\ n : a weapon (as a pistol) from which a shot is discharged by gunpowder

**fire·ball** \-,ból\ n 1 : a ball of fire 2 : a very bright meteor 3 : the highly luminous cloud of vapor and dust created by a nuclear explosion 4 : a highly energetic person

**fire·boat** \-,bōt\ n : a boat equipped for fighting fires

**fire·bomb** \-,bäm\ n : an incendiary bomb — **firebomb** vb

**fire·box** \-,bäks\ n 1 : a chamber (as of a furnace) that contains a fire 2 : a box containing a fire alarm

**fire·brand** \-,brand\ n 1 : a piece of burning wood 2 : a person who creates unrest or strife : AGITATOR

**fire·break** \-,brāk\ n : a barrier of cleared or plowed land intended to check a forest or grass fire

**fire·bug** \-,bəg\ n : a person who deliberately sets destructive fires

**fire·crack·er** \-,kra-kər\ n : a usu. paper tube containing an explosive and a fuse and set off to make a noise

**fire department** n : an organization for preventing or extinguishing fires; also : its members

**fire engine** n : a motor vehicle with equipment for extinguishing fires

**fire escape** n : a stairway or ladder for escape from a burning building

**fire·fight·er** \'fī(-ə)r-,fī-tər\ n : a person who fights fires; esp : a member of a fire department

**fire·fly** \-,flī\ n : any of various small night-flying beetles that produce flashes of light for courtship purposes

**fire·house** \-,haús\ n : FIRE STATION

**fire irons** n pl : tools for tending a fire esp. in a fireplace

**fire·man** \'fī(-ə)r-mən\ n 1 : STOKER 2 : FIREFIGHTER

**fire off** vb : to write and send

**fire·place** \-,plās\ n 1 : a framed opening

made in a chimney to hold an open fire **2** : an outdoor structure of brick or stone for an open fire

**fire·plug** \-ˌpləg\ *n* : HYDRANT

**fire·pow·er** \-ˌpau̇(-ə)r\ *n* : the ability to deliver gunfire or warheads on a target

**¹fire·proof** \-ˈprüf\ *adj* : resistant to fire

**²fireproof** *vb* : to make fireproof

**fire–sale** \-ˌsāl\ *adj* : heavily discounted ⟨~ prices⟩

**fire screen** *n* : a protective screen before a fireplace

**¹fire·side** \ˈfī(-ə)r-ˌsīd\ *n* **1** : a place near the fire or hearth **2** : HOME

**²fireside** *adj* : having an informal or intimate quality

**fire station** *n* : a building housing fire engines and usu. firefighters

**fire·storm** \ˈfī(-ə)r-ˌstȯrm\ *n* **1** : a large destructive very hot fire **2** : a sudden or violent outburst ⟨~ of criticism⟩

**fire tower** *n* : a tower (as in a forest) from which a watch for fires is kept

**fire·trap** \ˈfī(-ə)r-ˌtrap\ *n* : a building or place apt to catch on fire or difficult to escape from in case of fire

**fire truck** *n* : FIRE ENGINE

**fire·wall** \-ˌwȯl\ *n* : computer hardware or software for preventing unauthorized access to data

**fire·wa·ter** \ˈfī(-ə)r-ˌwȯ-tər, -ˌwä-\ *n* : intoxicating liquor

**fire·wood** \-ˌwu̇d\ *n* : wood used for fuel

**fire·work** \-ˌwərk\ *n* : a device designed to produce a striking display by the burning of explosive or flammable materials

**firing line** *n* **1** : a line from which fire is delivered against a target **2** : the forefront of an activity

**¹firm** \ˈfərm\ *adj* **1** : securely fixed in place **2** : SOLID, VIGOROUS ⟨a ~ handshake⟩ **3** : having a solid or compact texture **4** : not subject to change or fluctuation : STEADY ⟨~ prices⟩ **5** : STEADFAST **6** : indicating firmness or resolution — **firm·ly** *adv* — **firm·ness** *n*

**²firm** *vb* : to make or become firm

**³firm** *n* [G *Firma*, fr. It, signature, ultim. fr. L *firmare* to make firm, confirm] **1** : the name under which a company transacts business **2** : a business partnership of two or more persons **3** : a business enterprise

**fir·ma·ment** \ˈfər-mə-mənt\ *n* : the arch of the sky : HEAVENS

**firm·ware** \ˈfirm-ˌwer\ *n* : computer programs contained permanently in a hardware device

**¹first** \ˈfərst\ *adj* : preceding all others as in time, order, or importance

**²first** *adv* **1** : before any other **2** : for the first time **3** : in preference to something else

**³first** *n* **1** : number one in a countable series **2** : something that is first **3** : the lowest forward gear in an automotive vehicle **4** : the winning or highest place in a competition or examination

**first aid** *n* : emergency care or treatment given an injured or ill person

**first–born** \ˈfərst-ˈbȯrn\ *adj* : ELDEST — **firstborn** *n*

**first class** *n* : the best or highest group in a classification — **first–class** *adj or adv*

**first·hand** \ˈfərst-ˈhand\ *adj* : coming from direct personal observation or experience — **firsthand** *adv*

**first lady** *n, often cap F&L* : the wife or hostess of the chief executive of a political unit (as a country)

**first lieutenant** *n* : a commissioned officer (as in the army) ranking next below a captain

**first·ling** \ˈfərst-liŋ\ *n* : one that comes or is produced first

**first·ly** \-lē\ *adv* : in the first place : FIRST

**¹first–rate** \-ˈrāt\ *adj* : of the first order of size, importance, or quality

**²first–rate** *adv* : very well

**first sergeant** *n* **1** : a noncommissioned officer serving as the chief assistant to the commander of a military unit **2** : a rank in the army below a sergeant major and in the marine corps below a master gunnery sergeant

**first strike** *n* : a preemptive nuclear attack

**first–string** \ˈfərst-ˈstriŋ\ *adj* : being a regular as distinguished from a substitute — **first–string·er** \-ˌstriŋ-ər\ *n*

**firth** \ˈfərth\ *n* [ME, fr. ON *fjorthr*] : ESTUARY

**fis·cal** \ˈfis-kəl\ *adj* [L *fiscalis*, fr. *fiscus* basket, treasury] **1** : of or relating to taxation, public revenues, or public debt **2** : of or relating to financial matters — **fis·cal·ly** *adv*

**¹fish** \ˈfish\ *n, pl* **fish** *or* **fish·es 1** : a water-dwelling animal — usu. used in combination ⟨star*fish*⟩ ⟨shell*fish*⟩ **2** : any of numerous cold-blooded water-breathing vertebrates with fins, gills, and usu. scales that include the bony fishes and usu. the cartilaginous and jawless fishes **3** : the flesh of fish used as food

**²fish** *vb* **1** : to attempt to catch fish **2** : to seek something by roundabout means ⟨~ for praise⟩ **3** : to search for something underwater **4** : to engage in a search by groping **5** : to draw forth

**fish–and–chips** *n pl* : fried fish and french fried potatoes

**fish·bowl** \ˈfish-ˌbōl\ *n* **1** : a bowl for the keeping of live fish **2** : a place or condition that affords no privacy

**fish·er** \ˈfi-shər\ *n* **1** : one that fishes **2** : a dark brown No. American carnivorous mammal related to the weasels

**fish·er·man** \-mən\ *n* **1** : a person engaged in fishing **2** : a fishing boat

**fish·ery** \ˈfi-shə-rē\ *n, pl* **-er·ies 1** : the business of catching fish **2** : a place for catching fish

**fish·hook** \ˈfish-ˌhu̇k\ *n* : a usu. barbed hook for catching fish

**fish ladder** *n* : an arrangement of pools in steps by which fish can pass over a dam in going upstream

**fish·net** \ˈfish-ˌnet\ *n* **1** : netting for catching fish **2** : a coarse open-mesh fabric

**fish·tail** \-ˌtāl\ *vb* : to have the rear end slide from side to side out of control while moving forward

**fish·wife** \-ˌwīf\ *n* **1** : a woman who sells fish **2** : a vulgar abusive woman

**fishy** \ˈfi-shē\ *adj* **fish·i·er; -est 1** : of or resembling fish **2** : QUESTIONABLE ⟨the story sounds ∼ to me⟩

**fis·sion** \ˈfi-shən, -zhən\ *n* [L *fissio,* fr. *findere* to split] **1** : a cleaving into parts **2** : a method of reproduction in which a living cell or body divides into two or more parts each of which grows into a whole new individual **3** : the splitting of an atomic nucleus resulting in the release of large amounts of energy — **fis·sion·able** \ˈfi-shə-nə-bəl, -zhə-\ *adj*

**fis·sure** \ˈfi-shər\ *n* : a narrow opening or crack

**fist** \ˈfist\ *n* **1** : the hand with fingers folded into the palm **2** : INDEX 6

**fist bump** *n* : a gesture in which two people bump their fists together — **fist-bump** *vb*

**fist·ful** \ˈfist-ˌfůl\ *n* : HANDFUL

**fist·i·cuffs** \ˈfis-ti-ˌkəfs\ *n pl* : a fight with the fists

**fist pump** *n* : a celebratory gesture in which the fist is raised and lowered quickly and vigorously — **fist-pump** *vb*

**fis·tu·la** \ˈfis-chə-lə\ *n, pl* **-las** *or* **-lae** : an abnormal passage leading from an abscess or hollow organ — **fis·tu·lous** \-ləs\ *adj*

**¹fit** \ˈfit\ *adj* **fit·ter; fit·test 1** : adapted to a purpose : APPROPRIATE **2** : PROPER, RIGHT ⟨a movie ∼ for children⟩ **3** : PREPARED, READY **4** : physically and mentally sound — **fit·ly** *adv* — **fit·ness** *n*

**²fit** *n* **1** : a sudden violent attack (as in epilepsy) **2** : a sudden outburst

**³fit** *vb* **fit·ted** *also* **fit; fit·ting 1** : to be suitable for or to **2** : to be correctly adjusted to or shaped for **3** : to insert or adjust until correctly in place **4** : to make a place or room for **5** : to be in agreement or accord with **6** : PREPARE **7** : ADJUST **8** : SUPPLY, EQUIP ⟨*fitted* out with gear⟩ **9** : BELONG — **fit·ter** *n*

**⁴fit** *n* : the fact, condition, or manner of fitting or being fitted

**fit·ful** \ˈfit-fəl\ *adj* : not regular : INTERMITTENT ⟨∼ sleep⟩ — **fit·ful·ly** *adv*

**¹fit·ting** \ˈfi-tiŋ\ *adj* : APPROPRIATE, SUITABLE ⟨a ∼ tribute⟩ — **fit·ting·ly** *adv*

**²fitting** *n* **1** : the action or act of one that fits; *esp* : a trying on of clothes being made or altered **2** : a small often standardized part ⟨a plumbing ∼⟩

**five** \ˈfīv\ *n* **1** : one more than four **2** : the 5th in a set or series **3** : something having five units; *esp* : a basketball team **4** : a 5-dollar bill — **five** *adj or pron*

**¹fix** \ˈfiks\ *vb* **1** : to make firm, stable, or fast **2** : to give a permanent or final form to **3** : AFFIX, ATTACH **4** : to hold or direct steadily ⟨∼es his eyes on the horizon⟩ **5** : ESTABLISH, SET **6** : ASSIGN ⟨∼ the blame⟩ **7** : to set in order : ADJUST **8** : PREPARE. **9** : to make whole or sound again **10** : to get even with **11** : to influence by improper or illegal methods ⟨∼ a race⟩ — **fix·er** *n*

**²fix** *n* **1** : PREDICAMENT **2** : a determination of position (as of a ship) **3** : an accurate determination or understanding **4** : an act of improper influence **5** : a supply or dose of something (as an addictive drug) strongly desired or craved **6** : something that fixes or restores

**fix·a·tion** \fik-ˈsā-shən\ *n* : an obsessive or unhealthy preoccupation or attachment — **fix·ate** \ˈfik-ˌsāt\ *vb*

**fix·a·tive** \ˈfik-sə-tiv\ *n* : something that stabilizes or sets

**fixed** \ˈfikst\ *adj* **1** : securely placed or fastened : STATIONARY **2** : not volatile **3** : SETTLED, FINAL **4** : INTENT, CONCENTRATED ⟨a ∼ stare⟩ **5** : supplied with a definite amount of something needed (as money) — **fixed·ly** \ˈfik-səd-lē\ *adv* — **fixed·ness** \ˈfik-səd-nəs\ *n*

**fix·i·ty** \ˈfik-sə-tē\ *n, pl* **-ties** : the quality or state of being fixed or stable

**fix·ture** \ˈfiks-chər\ *n* **1** : something firmly attached as a permanent part of some other thing **2** : a familiar feature in a particular setting; *esp* : a person associated with a place or activity

**¹fizz** \ˈfiz\ *vb* : to make a hissing or sputtering sound

**²fizz** *n* : an effervescent beverage

**¹fiz·zle** \ˈfi-zəl\ *vb* **fiz·zled; fiz·zling 1** : FIZZ **2** : to fail after a good start — often used with *out*

**²fizzle** *n* : FAILURE

**fjord** \fē-ˈôrd\ *n* [Norw] : a narrow inlet of the sea between cliffs or steep slopes

**fl** *abbr* **1** [L *floruit*] flourished **2** fluid

**FL** *or* **Fla** *abbr* Florida

**flab** \ˈflab\ *n* : soft flabby body tissue

**flab·ber·gast** \ˈfla-bər-ˌgast\ *vb* : ASTOUND

**flab·by** \ˈfla-bē\ *adj* **flab·bi·er; -est** : lacking firmness : FLACCID ⟨∼ muscles⟩ — **flab·bi·ness** \-bē-nəs\ *n*

**flac·cid** \ˈfla-səd\ *adj* : lacking firmness ⟨∼ muscles⟩

**¹flag** \ˈflag\ *n* : any of various irises; *esp* : a wild iris

**²flag** *n* **1** : a usu. rectangular piece of fabric of distinctive design that is used as a symbol (as of a nation) or as a signaling device **2** : something used like a flag to signal or attract attention **3** : one of the cross strokes of a musical note less than a quarter note in value

**³flag** *vb* **flagged; flag·ging 1** : to signal with or as if with a flag; *esp* : to signal to stop ⟨∼ a taxi⟩ **2** : to mark or identify with or as if with a flag **3** : to call a penalty on ⟨∼ a football player⟩

**⁴flag** *vb* **flagged; flag·ging 1** : to hang loose or limp **2** : to become unsteady, feeble, or spiritless **3** : to decline in interest or attraction ⟨the topic *flagged*⟩

**⁵flag** *n* : a hard flat stone suitable for paving

**flag·el·late** \ˈfla-jə-ˌlāt\ *vb* **-lat·ed; -lat·ing** : to punish by whipping — **flag·el·la·tion** \ˌfla-jə-ˈlā-shən\ *n*

**fla·gel·lum** \flə-ˈje-ləm\ *n, pl* **-la** \-lə\ *also* **-lums** : a long whiplike process that is the primary organ of motion of many microorganisms — **fla·gel·lar** \-lər\ *adj*

**fla·geo·let** \ˌfla-jə-ˈlet, -ˈlā\ *n* [F] : a small

woodwind instrument belonging to the flute class

**fla·gi·tious** \flə-'ji-shəs\ adj : grossly wicked : VILLAINOUS

**flag·on** \'fla-gən\ n : a container for liquids usu. with a handle, spout, and lid

**flag·pole** \'flag-,pōl\ n : a pole on which to raise a flag

**fla·grant** \'flā-grənt\ adj [L flagrans, prp. of flagrare to burn] : conspicuously bad <~ abuse of power> — **fla·grant·ly** adv

**fla·gran·te de·lic·to** \flə-,gran-tē-di-'lik-tō\ adv : IN FLAGRANTE DELICTO

**flag·ship** \'flag-,ship\ n 1 : the ship that carries the commander of a fleet or subdivision thereof and flies his flag 2 : the most important one of a group

**flag·staff** \-,staf\ n : FLAGPOLE

**flag·stone** \-,stōn\ n : ¹FLAG

¹**flail** \'flāl\ n : a tool for threshing grain by hand

²**flail** vb : to strike or swing with or as if with a flail

**flair** \'fler\ n [F, lit., sense of smell, fr. OF, odor, fr. flairier to give off an odor, fr. VL *flagrare, alter. of L fragrare] 1 : ability to appreciate or make good use of something : BENT, TALENT 2 : a unique style

**flak** \'flak\ n, pl **flak** [G, fr. Fliegerabwehrkanonen, fr. Flieger flyer + Abwehr defense + Kanonen cannons] 1 : antiaircraft guns or bursting shells fired from them 2 : CRITICISM, OPPOSITION

¹**flake** \'flāk\ n 1 : a small loose mass or bit 2 : a thin flattened piece or layer : CHIP — **flaky** adj

²**flake** vb **flaked; flak·ing** : to form or separate into flakes

³**flake** n : a markedly eccentric person : ODDBALL — **flak·i·ness** \'flā-kē-nəs\ n — **flaky** adj

**flam·beau** \'flam-,bō\ n, pl **flambeaux** \-,bōz\ or **flambeaus** [F, fr. MF, fr. flambe flame] : a flaming torch

**flam·boy·ant** \flam-'bȯi-ənt\ adj : marked by or given to strikingly elaborate or colorful display or behavior — **flam·boy·ance** \-əns\ n — **flam·boy·an·cy** \-ən-sē\ n — **flam·boy·ant·ly** adv

**flame** \'flām\ n 1 : the glowing gaseous part of a fire 2 : a state of blazing combustion 3 : a flamelike condition 4 : burning zeal or passion 5 : BRILLIANCE 6 : SWEETHEART 7 : an angry, hostile, or abusive electronic message — **flame** vb

**fla·men·co** \flə-'meŋ-kō\ n, pl **-cos** [Sp, fr. flamenco of the Gypsies, lit., Flemish, fr. MD Vlaminc Fleming] : a vigorous rhythmic dance style of the Spanish Gypsies

**flame·throw·er** \'flām-,thrō-ər\ n : a device that expels from a nozzle a burning stream of liquid or semiliquid fuel under pressure

**fla·min·go** \flə-'miŋ-gō\ n, pl **-gos** also **-goes** : any of several long-legged long-necked tropical water birds with scarlet wings and a broad bill bent downward

**flam·ma·ble** \'fla-mə-bəl\ adj : easily ignited and quick-burning — **flam·ma·bil·i·ty** \,fla-mə-'bi-lə-tē\ n — **flammable** n

**flan** \'flan, 'flän\ n 1 : an open pie with a sweet or savory filling 2 : custard baked with a caramel glaze

**flange** \'flanj\ n : a rim used for strengthening or guiding something or for attachment to another object

¹**flank** \'flaŋk\ n 1 : the fleshy part of the side between the ribs and the hip; also : the side of a quadruped 2 : SIDE 3 : the right or left of a formation

²**flank** vb 1 : to be situated on the side of : BORDER 2 : to attack or threaten the flank of

**flank·er** \'flaŋ-kər\ n : a football player stationed wide of the formation slightly behind the line of scrimmage as a pass receiver

**flan·nel** \'fla-nᵊl\ n 1 : a soft twilled wool or worsted fabric with a napped surface 2 : a stout cotton fabric napped on one side 3 pl : flannel underwear or pants

¹**flap** \'flap\ n 1 : a stroke with something broad : SLAP 2 : something broad, limber, or flat and usu. thin that hangs loose 3 : the motion or sound of something broad and limber as it swings to and fro 4 : a state of excitement or confusion

²**flap** vb **flapped; flap·ping** 1 : to beat with something broad and flat 2 : FLING 3 : to move (as wings) with a beating motion 4 : to sway loosely usu. with a noise of striking

**flap·jack** \'flap-,jak\ n : PANCAKE

**flap·per** \'fla-pər\ n 1 : one that flaps 2 : a young woman of the 1920s who showed freedom from conventions (as in conduct)

¹**flare** \'fler\ n 1 : a blaze of light used esp. to signal or illuminate; also : a device for producing such a blaze 2 : an unsteady glaring light

²**flare** vb **flared; flar·ing** 1 : to flame with a sudden unsteady light 2 : to become suddenly excited or angry <after his harangue, I flared up> 3 : to spread outward

**flare–up** \-,əp\ n : a sudden outburst or intensification

¹**flash** \'flash\ vb 1 : to break forth in or like a sudden flame 2 : to appear or pass suddenly or with great speed 3 : to send out in or as if in flashes <~ a message> 4 : to make a sudden display (as of brilliance or feeling) 5 : to gleam or glow intermittently 6 : to fill by a sudden rush of water 7 : to expose to view very briefly <~ a badge> ♦ **Synonyms** GLANCE, GLINT, SPARKLE, TWINKLE — **flash·er** n

²**flash** n 1 : a sudden burst of light 2 : a movement of a flag or light in signaling 3 : a sudden and brilliant burst (as of wit) 4 : a brief time : SHOW, DISPLAY; esp : ostentatious display 6 : one that attracts notice; esp : an outstanding athlete 7 : GLIMPSE, LOOK 8 : a first brief news report 9 : FLASHLIGHT 10 : a device for producing a brief and very bright flash of light for taking photographs 11 : a quick-spreading flame or momentary intense outburst of radiant heat

³**flash** adj : of sudden origin and short duration <a ~ fire> <a ~ flood>

⁴**flash** adv : by very brief exposure to an

intense agent (as heat or cold) ⟨∼ fry⟩ ⟨∼ freeze⟩

**flash·back** \'flash-ˌbak\ n  1 : interruption of the chronological sequence (as of a film or literary work) by an event of earlier occurrence  2 : a past event remembered vividly

**flash back** vb  1 : to vividly remember a past incident  2 : to employ a flashback

**flash·bulb** \-ˌbəlb\ n : an electric bulb that can be used only once to produce a brief and very bright flash of light for taking photographs

**flash card** n : a card bearing words, numbers, or pictures briefly displayed usu. as a learning aid

**flash·gun** \ˌgən\ n : a device for producing a bright flash of light for photography

**flash·ing** \'fla-shiŋ\ n : sheet metal used in waterproofing (as at the angle between a chimney and a roof)

**flash·light** \'flash-ˌlīt\ n : a battery-operated portable electric light

**flash memory** n : a computer memory chip not requiring connection to a power source to retain its data

**flashy** \'fla-shē\ adj **flash·i·er; -est**  1 : momentarily dazzling  2 : superficially attractive or impressive : SHOWY ⟨∼ clothes⟩ — **flash·i·ly** \-shə-lē\ adv — **flash·i·ness** \-shē-nəs\ n

**flask** \'flask\ n : a flattened bottle-shaped container ⟨a whiskey ∼⟩

**¹flat** \'flat\ adj **flat·ter; flat·test**  1 : spread out along a surface; also : being or characterized by a horizontal line  2 : having a smooth, level, or even surface  3 : having a broad smooth surface and little thickness  4 : DOWNRIGHT, POSITIVE ⟨a ∼ refusal⟩  5 : FIXED, UNCHANGING ⟨charge a ∼ rate⟩  6 : EXACT, PRECISE ⟨in four minutes ∼⟩  7 : DULL, UNINTERESTING; also : INSIPID  8 : DEFLATED ⟨a ∼ tire⟩  9 : lower than the true pitch; also : lower by a half step  10 : free from gloss ⟨a ∼ paint⟩  11 : lacking depth of characterization — **flat·ly** adv — **flat·ness** n

**²flat** n  1 : a level surface of land : PLAIN  2 : a flat part or surface  3 : a character ♭ that indicates that a specified note is to be lowered by a half step; also : the resulting note  4 : something flat  5 : an apartment on one floor  6 : a deflated tire

**³flat** adv  1 : FLATLY  2 : COMPLETELY ⟨∼ broke⟩  3 : below the true musical pitch

**⁴flat** vb **flat·ted; flat·ting**  1 : FLATTEN  2 : to lower in pitch esp. by a half step

**flat·bed** \'flat-ˌbed\ n : a truck or trailer with a body in the form of a platform or shallow box

**flat·boat** \-ˌbōt\ n : a flat-bottomed boat used esp. for carrying bulky freight

**flat·car** \-ˌkär\ n : a railroad freight car without sides or roof

**flat·fish** \-ˌfish\ n : any of an order of flattened marine bony fishes with both eyes on the upper side

**flat·foot** \-ˌfu̇t, -'fu̇t\ n, pl **flat·feet** \-ˌfēt, -'fēt\ : a condition in which the arch of the foot is flattened so that the entire sole

rests upon the ground — **flat–foot·ed** \-'fu̇-təd\ adj

**Flat·head** \-ˌhed\ n, pl **Flatheads** or **Flathead** : a member of an American Indian people of Montana

**flat·iron** \-ˌī(-ə)rn\ n : IRON 3

**flat·land** \-ˌland\ n : land lacking significant variation in elevation

**flat–out** \'flat-ˌau̇t\ adj  1 : being or going at maximum effort or speed  2 : OUT-AND-OUT, DOWNRIGHT ⟨it was a ∼ lie⟩

**flat out** adv  1 : BLUNTLY, DIRECTLY  2 : at top speed  3 usu **flat–out** : to the greatest degree : COMPLETELY ⟨is just flat-out confusing⟩

**flat–pan·el** \-'pa-nᵊl\ adj : relating to or being a thin flat video display

**flat·ten** \'fla-tᵊn\ vb : to make or become flat

**flat·ter** \'fla-tər\ vb [ME flateren, fr. AF flater to lap, flatter]  1 : to praise too much or without sincerity  2 : to represent too favorably ⟨the portrait ∼s him⟩  3 : to display to advantage  4 : to judge (oneself) favorably or too favorably — **flat·ter·er** n

**flat·tery** \'fla-tə-rē\ n, pl **-ter·ies** : flattering speech or attentions : insincere or excessive praise

**flat·top** \'flat-ˌtäp\ n  1 : AIRCRAFT CARRIER  2 : CREW CUT

**flat·u·lent** \'fla-chə-lənt\ adj  1 : full of gas ⟨a ∼ stomach⟩  2 : INFLATED, POMPOUS — **flat·u·lence** \-ləns\ n

**fla·tus** \'flā-təs\ n : gas formed in the intestine or stomach

**flat·ware** \'flat-ˌwer\ n : eating and serving utensils

**flat·worm** \-ˌwu̇rm\ n : any of a phylum of flattened mostly parasitic segmented worms (as trematodes and tapeworms)

**flaunt** \'flȯnt\ vb  1 : to display oneself to public notice  2 : to wave or flutter showily  3 : to display ostentatiously or impudently : PARADE — **flaunt** n

**flau·ta** \'flau̇-tə\ n : a tortilla rolled around a filling and deep-fried

**flau·tist** \'flȯ-tist, 'flau̇-\ n [It flautista] : FLUTIST

**¹fla·vor** \'flā-vər\ n  1 : the quality of something that affects the sense of taste or of taste and smell  2 : a substance that adds flavor  3 : characteristic or predominant quality — **fla·vored** \-vərd\ adj — **fla·vor·ful** \-fəl\ adj — **fla·vor·less** adj — **fla·vor·some** adj

**²flavor** vb : to give or add flavor to

**fla·vor·ing** n : FLAVOR 2

**fla·vour** chiefly Brit var of FLAVOR

**flaw** \'flȯ\ n : a small often hidden defect — **flaw·less** adj — **flaw·less·ly** adv — **flaw·less·ness** n

**flax** \'flaks\ n : a fiber that is the source of linen; also : a blue-flowered plant grown for this fiber and its oily seeds

**flax·en** \'flak-sən\ adj  1 : made of flax  2 : resembling flax esp. in pale soft straw color

**flay** \'flā\ vb  1 : to strip off the skin or surface of  2 : to criticize harshly

**fl dr** abbr fluid dram

**flea** \'flē\ *n* : any of an order of small wingless leaping bloodsucking insects

**flea-bane** \'flē-,bān\ *n* : any of various plants of the daisy family once believed to drive away fleas

**flea-bit-ten** \-,bi-t³n\ *adj* : bitten by or infested with fleas

**flea market** *n* : a usu. open-air market for secondhand articles and antiques

¹**fleck** \'flek\ *vb* : STREAK, SPOT

²**fleck** *n* **1** : SPOT, MARK **2** : FLAKE, PARTICLE

**fledge** \'flej\ *vb* **fledged; fledg-ing** : to develop the feathers necessary for flying or independent activity

**fledg-ling** \'flej-liŋ\ *n* **1** : a young bird just fledged **2** : an immature or inexperienced person

**flee** \'flē\ *vb* **fled** \'fled\; **flee-ing** **1** : to run away often from danger or evil **2** : VANISH **3** : to run away from : SHUN

¹**fleece** \'flēs\ *n* **1** : the woolly coat of an animal and esp. a sheep **2** : a soft or woolly covering — **fleecy** *adj*

²**fleece** *vb* **fleeced; fleec-ing** **1** : to strip of money or property by fraud or extortion **2** : SHEAR

¹**fleet** \'flēt\ *vb* : to pass rapidly

²**fleet** *n* [ME *flete*, fr. OE *flēot* ship, fr. *flēotan* to float] **1** : a group of warships under one command **2** : a group (as of ships, planes, or trucks) under one management

³**fleet** *adj* **1** : SWIFT, NIMBLE **2** : not enduring : FLEETING — **fleet-ness** *n*

**fleet admiral** *n* : an admiral of the highest rank in the navy

**fleet-ing** \'flē-tiŋ\ *adj* : passing swiftly

**Flem-ing** \'fle-miŋ\ *n* : a member of a Germanic people inhabiting chiefly northern Belgium

**Flem-ish** \-mish\ *n* **1** : the Dutch language as spoken by the Flemings — **Flemish** *pl* — **FLEMINGS** — **Flemish** *adj*

¹**flesh** \'flesh\ *n* **1** : the soft parts of an animal's body; *esp* : muscular tissue **2** : MEAT **3** : the physical nature of humans as distinguished from the soul **4** : human beings; *also* : living beings **5** : STOCK, KINDRED **6** : fleshy plant tissue (as fruit pulp) — **fleshed** \'flesht\ *adj*

²**flesh** *vb* : to make fuller or more nearly complete — usu. used with *out* ⟨*flesh out* a schedule⟩

**flesh fly** *n* : a dipteran fly whose maggots feed on flesh

**flesh-ly** \'flesh-lē\ *adj* **1** : CORPOREAL, BODILY **2** : not spiritual : WORLDLY **3** : CARNAL, SENSUAL ⟨~ appetites⟩

**flesh-pot** \'flesh-,pät\ *n* **1** *pl* : bodily comfort : LUXURY **2** : a place of lascivious entertainment — usu. used in pl.

**fleshy** \'fle-shē\ *adj* **flesh-i-er; -est** **1** : consisting of or resembling animal flesh **2** : PLUMP, FAT

**flew** *past of* ¹FLY

**flex** \'fleks\ *vb* : to bend esp. repeatedly — **flex** *n*

**flex-i-ble** \'flek-sə-bəl\ *adj* **1** : capable of being flexed : PLIANT **2** : yielding to influence : TRACTABLE **3** : readily changed or changing : ADAPTABLE ♦ **Synonyms**

ELASTIC, SUPPLE, RESILIENT, SPRINGY — **flex-i-bil-i-ty** \,flek-sə-'bi-lə-tē\ *n*

**flex-or** \'flek-sər, -,sòr\ *n* : a muscle serving to bend a body part

**flex-ure** \'flek-shər\ *n* : TURN, FOLD

**flib-ber-ti-gib-bet** \,fli-bər-tē-'ji-bət\ *n* : a silly flighty person

¹**flick** \'flik\ *n* **1** : a light sharp jerky stroke or movement **2** : a sound produced by a flick **3** : ²FLICKER

²**flick** *vb* **1** : to strike lightly with a quick sharp motion **2** : FLUTTER, FLIT

³**flick** *n* : MOVIE

¹**flick-er** \'fli-kər\ *vb* **1** : to move irregularly or unsteadily : FLUTTER **2** : to burn fitfully or with a fluctuating light — **flick-er-ing-ly** *adv*

²**flicker** *n* **1** : an act of flickering **2** : a sudden brief movement ⟨a ~ of an eyelid⟩ **3** : a momentary stirring ⟨a ~ of interest⟩ **4** : a slight indication : HINT **5** : a wavering light

³**flicker** *n* : a large barred and spotted No. American woodpecker with a brown back that occurs in an eastern form with yellow on the underside of the wings and tail and a western form with red in these areas

**flied** *past and past part of* ³FLY

**fli-er** \'flī-(ə)r\ *n* **1** : one that flies; *esp* : PILOT **2** : a reckless or speculative undertaking **3** *usu* **fly-er** : an advertising circular

¹**flight** \'flīt\ *n* **1** : an act or instance of flying **2** : the ability to fly **3** : a passing through air or space **4** : the distance covered in a flight **5** : swift movement **6** : a trip made by or in an airplane or spacecraft **7** : a group of similar individuals (as birds or airplanes) flying as a unit **8** : a passing (as of the imagination) beyond ordinary limits **9** : a series of stairs from one landing to another — **flight-less** *adj*

²**flight** *n* : an act or instance of running away

**flight bag** *n* **1** : a lightweight traveling bag with zippered outside pockets **2** : a small canvas satchel

**flight line** *n* : a parking and servicing area for airplanes

**flighty** \'flī-tē\ *adj* **flight-i-er; -est** **1** : easily upset : VOLATILE **2** : easily excited : SKITTISH **3** : CAPRICIOUS, SILLY — **flight-i-ness** \-tē-nəs\ *n*

**flim-flam** \'flim-,flam\ *n* : DECEPTION, FRAUD — **flim-flam-mery** \-,fla-mə-re\ *n*

**flim-sy** \'flim-zē\ *adj* **flim-si-er; -est** **1** : lacking strength or substance **2** : of inferior materials and workmanship **3** : having little worth or plausibility ⟨a ~ excuse⟩ — **flim-si-ly** \-zə-lē\ *adv* — **flim-si-ness** \-zē-nəs\ *n*

**flinch** \'flinch\ *vb* [MF *flenchir* to bend] : to shrink from or as if from pain : WINCE — **flinch** *n*

¹**fling** \'fliŋ\ *vb* **flung** \'fləŋ\; **fling-ing** **1** : to move hastily, brusquely, or violently ⟨flung out of the room⟩ **2** : to kick or plunge vigorously **3** : to throw with force or recklessness; *also* : to cast as if by throwing **4** : to put suddenly into a state or condition

²**fling** n **1** : an act or instance of flinging **2** : a casual try : ATTEMPT **3** : a period of self-indulgence

**flint** \'flint\ n **1** : a hard dark quartz that produces a spark when struck by steel **2** : an alloy used for producing a spark in lighters — **flinty** adj

**flint glass** n : heavy glass containing an oxide of lead and used in lenses and prisms

**flint·lock** \'flint-ˌläk\ n **1** : a lock for a gun using a flint to ignite the charge **2** : a firearm fitted with a flintlock

¹**flip** \'flip\ vb **flipped; flip·ping 1** : to turn by tossing ⟨~ a coin⟩ **2** : to turn over; also : to leaf through **3** : FLICK, JERK ⟨~ a light switch⟩ **4** : to lose self-control — **flip** n

²**flip** adj : FLIPPANT, IMPERTINENT

**flip·pant** \'fli-pənt\ adj : lacking proper respect or seriousness — **flip·pan·cy** \'fli-pən-sē\ n

**flip·per** \'fli-pər\ n **1** : a broad flat limb (as of a seal) adapted for swimming **2** : a paddlelike shoe used in skin diving

**flip side** n : the reverse and usu. less popular side of a phonograph record

¹**flirt** \'flərt\ vb **1** : to move erratically : FLIT **2** : to behave amorously without serious intent **3** : to show casual interest ⟨~ed with the idea⟩; also : to come close to ⟨~ with danger⟩ — **flir·ta·tion** \flər-'tā-shən\ n — **flir·ta·tious** \-shəs\ adj

²**flirt** n **1** : an act or instance of flirting **2** : a person who flirts

**flit** \'flit\ vb **flit·ted; flit·ting** : to pass or move quickly or abruptly from place to place : DART — **flit** n

**flitch** \'flich\ n : a side of cured meat; esp : a side of bacon

**fliv·ver** \'fli-vər\ n : a small cheap usu. old automobile

¹**float** \'flōt\ n **1** : something (as a raft) that floats **2** : a cork buoying up the baited end of a fishing line **3** : a hollow ball that floats at the end of a lever in a cistern or tank and regulates the liquid level **4** : a vehicle with a platform to carry an exhibit **5** : a soft drink with ice cream floating in it

²**float** vb **1** : to rest on the surface of or be suspended in a fluid **2** : to move gently on or through a fluid **3** : to cause to float **4** : WANDER **5** : to offer (securities) in order to finance an enterprise **6** : to finance by floating an issue of stocks or bonds **7** : to arrange for ⟨~ a loan⟩ — **float·er** n

**floaty** \'flō-tē\ adj **float·i·er; -est 1** : tending to float : BUOYANT **2** : light and billowy ⟨a ~ skirt⟩

¹**flock** \'fläk\ n **1** : a group of animals (as birds or sheep) assembled or herded together **2** : a group of people under the guidance of a leader; esp : CONGREGATION **3** : a large number ⟨a ~ of tourists⟩

²**flock** vb : to gather or move in a flock ⟨people ~ed to the beach⟩

**floe** \'flō\ n : a flat mass of floating ice

**flog** \'fläg\ vb **flogged; flog·ging 1** : to beat with or as if with a rod or whip **2** : SELL ⟨~ encyclopedias⟩ — **flog·ger** n

¹**flood** \'fləd\ n **1** : a great flow of water over the land **2** : the flowing in of the tide **3** : an overwhelming volume

²**flood** vb **1** : to cover or become filled with a flood **2** : to fill abundantly or excessively; esp : to supply an excess of fuel to **3** : to pour forth in a flood — **flood·er** n

**flood·gate** \'fləd-ˌgāt\ n : a gate for controlling a body of water : SLUICE

**flood·light** \-ˌlīt\ n : a lamp that throws a broad beam of light; also : the beam itself — **floodlight** vb

**flood·plain** \-ˌplān\ n : a plain along a river or stream subject to periodic flooding

**flood tide** n **1** : a rising tide **2** : an overwhelming quantity **3** : a high point

**flood·wa·ter** \'fləd-ˌwȯ-tər, -ˌwä-\ n : the water of a flood

¹**floor** \'flȯr\ n **1** : the bottom of a room on which one stands **2** : a ground surface **3** : a story of a building **4** : a main level space (as in a legislative chamber) distinguished from a platform or gallery **5** : AUDIENCE **6** : the right to address an assembly **7** : a lower limit ⟨put a ~ under wheat prices⟩ — **floor·ing** n

²**floor** vb **1** : to furnish with a floor **2** : to knock down **3** : AMAZE, DUMBFOUND ⟨was ~ed by the news⟩ **4** : to press (a vehicle's accelerator) to the floorboard esp. rapidly

**floor·board** \-ˌbȯrd\ n **1** : a board in a floor **2** : the floor of an automobile

**floor leader** n : a member of a legislative body who has charge of a party's organization and strategy on the floor

**floor show** n : a series of acts presented in a nightclub

**floor·walk·er** \'flȯr-ˌwȯ-kər\ n : a person employed in a retail store to oversee the sales force and aid customers

**floo·zy** or **floo·zie** \'flü-zē\ n, pl **floozies** : a usu. young woman of loose morals

**flop** \'fläp\ vb **flopped; flop·ping 1** : FLAP **2** : to throw oneself down heavily, clumsily, or in a relaxed manner ⟨flopped into a chair⟩ **3** : FAIL ⟨the show flopped⟩ — **flop** n — **flop** adv — **flop·per** n

**flop·house** \'fläp-ˌhau̇s\ n : a cheap hotel

¹**flop·py** \'flä-pē\ adj **flop·pi·er; -est** : tending to flop; esp : soft and flexible — **flop·pi·ly** \-pə-lē\ adv

²**floppy** n, pl **flop·pies** : FLOPPY DISK

**floppy disk** n : a thin plastic disk with a magnetic coating on which computer data can be stored

**flop sweat** n : sweat caused by the fear of failing

**flo·ra** \'flȯr-ə\ n, pl **floras** also **flo·rae** \-ˌē, -ˌī\ [L Flora, Roman goddess of flowers] : plants or plant life esp. of a region or period

**flo·ral** \'flȯr-əl\ adj : of, relating to, or depicting flowers ⟨a ~ design⟩

**flo·res·cence** \flȯ-'re-sᵊns, flə-\ n : a state or period of being in bloom or flourishing — **flo·res·cent** \-ᵊnt\ adj

**flor·id** \'flȯr-əd\ adj **1** : very flowery in

style : ORNATE ⟨~ prose⟩ **2** : tinged with red : RUDDY **3** : marked by emotional or sexual fervor ⟨~ love letters⟩

**flo·rin** \'flȯr-ən\ *n* **1** : an old gold coin first struck at Florence, Italy, in 1252 **2** : a gold coin of a European country patterned after the florin of Florence **3** : any of several modern silver coins issued in Commonwealth countries **4** : GULDEN

**flo·rist** \'flȯr-ist\ *n* : a person who sells flowers or ornamental plants

**¹floss** \'fläs\ *n* **1** : soft thread of silk or mercerized cotton for embroidery **2** : DENTAL FLOSS **3** : fluffy fibrous material

**²floss** *vb* : to use dental floss on (one's teeth)

**flossy** \'flä-sē\ *adj* **floss·i·er; -est 1** : of, relating to, or having the characteristics of floss **2** : STYLISH, GLAMOROUS ⟨~ hotels⟩ — **floss·i·ly** \-sə-lē\ *adv*

**flo·ta·tion** \flō-'tā-shən\ *n* : the process or an instance of floating

**flo·til·la** \flō-'ti-lə\ *n* [Sp, dim. of *flota* fleet] : a fleet esp. of small ships

**flot·sam** \'flät-səm\ *n* : floating wreckage of a ship or its cargo

**¹flounce** \'flaůns\ *vb* **flounced; flounc·ing 1** : to move with exaggerated jerky or bouncy motions **2** : to go with sudden determination

**²flounce** *n* : an act or instance of flouncing — **flouncy** \'flaůn-sē\ *adj*

**³flounce** *n* : a strip of fabric attached by one edge; *also* : a wide ruffle

**¹floun·der** \'flaůn-dər\ *n, pl* **flounder** or **flounders** : FLATFISH; *esp* : any of various important marine food fishes

**²flounder** *vb* **1** : to struggle to move or obtain footing **2** : to proceed clumsily ⟨~ed through the speech⟩

**¹flour** \'flaů(-ə)r\ *n* [ME, flower, best of anything, flour, fr. AF *flur* flower] : finely ground and sifted meal of a grain (as wheat); *also* : a fine soft powder — **floury** *adj*

**²flour** *vb* : to coat with or as if with flour

**¹flour·ish** \'flər-ish\ *vb* **1** : THRIVE, PROSPER **2** : to be in a state of activity or production ⟨~ed about 1850⟩ **3** : to reach a height of development or influence **4** : to make bold and sweeping gestures **5** : BRANDISH ⟨~ed his sword⟩

**²flourish** *n* **1** : a florid bit of speech or writing; *also* : an ornamental touch or decorative detail **2** : FANFARE ⟨a ~ of trumpets⟩ **3** : WAVE ⟨with a ~ of his cane⟩ **4** : showiness in doing something

**¹flout** \'flaůt\ *vb* : to treat with contemptuous disregard ⟨~ the law⟩ — **flout·er** *n*

**²flout** *n* : TAUNT

**¹flow** \'flō\ *vb* **1** : to issue or move in a stream **2** : RISE ⟨the tide ebbs and ~s⟩ **3** : ABOUND **4** : to proceed smoothly and readily **5** : to have a smooth continuity **6** : to hang loose and billowing **7** : COME, ARISE **8** : MENSTRUATE

**²flow** *n* **1** : an act of flowing **2** : FLOOD 1, 2 **3** : a smooth uninterrupted movement **4** : STREAM; *also* : a mass of material that has flowed when molten **5** : the quantity

that flows in a certain time **6** : MENSTRUATION **7** : a continuous transfer of energy — **flow·age** \'flō-ij\ *n*

**flow·chart** \'flō-,chärt\ *n* : a symbolic diagram showing step-by-step progression through a procedure

**flow diagram** *n* : FLOWCHART

**¹flow·er** \'flaů(-ə)r\ *n* [ME *flour*, fr. AF *flur, flour*, fr. L *flor-, flos*] **1** : a plant shoot modified for reproduction and bearing leaves specialized into floral organs; *esp* : one of a seed plant consisting of a calyx, corolla, stamens, and carpels **2** : a plant cultivated for its blossoms **3** : the best part or example **4** : the finest most vigorous period **5** : a state of blooming or flourishing — **flow·ered** \'flaů(-ə)rd\ *adj* — **flow·er·less** *adj* — **flow·er·like** \-,līk\ *adj*

**²flower** *vb* **1** : DEVELOP; *also* : FLOURISH **2** : to produce flowers : BLOOM

**flower girl** *n* : a little girl who carries flowers at a wedding

**flower head** *n* : a compact cluster of small flowers without stems suggesting a single flower

**flowering plant** *n* : any of a major group of vascular plants (as magnolias, grasses, or roses) that produce flowers and fruit and have the seeds enclosed in an ovary

**flow·er·pot** \'flaů(-ə)r-,pät\ *n* : a pot in which to grow plants

**flow·ery** \'flaů(-ə)r-ē\ *adj* **1** : of, relating to, or resembling flowers **2** : full of fine words or phrases ⟨a ~ speech⟩ — **flow·er·i·ness** \-ē-nəs\ *n*

**flown** \'flōn\ *past part of* ¹FLY

**fl oz** *abbr* fluid ounce

**flu** \'flü\ *n* **1** : INFLUENZA **2** : any of several virus diseases marked esp. by respiratory or intestinal symptoms — **flu·like** \-,līk\ *adj*

**flub** \'fləb\ *vb* **flubbed; flub·bing** : BOTCH, BLUNDER — **flub** *n*

**fluc·tu·ate** \'flək-chə-,wāt\ *vb* **-at·ed; -at·ing 1** : WAVER **2** : to move up and down or back and forth — **fluc·tu·a·tion** \,flək-chə-'wā-shən\ *n*

**flue** \'flü\ *n* : a passage (as in a chimney) for directing a current (as of smoke or gases)

**flu·ent** \'flü-ənt\ *adj* **1** : capable of flowing : FLUID **2** : ready or facile in speech ⟨~ in French⟩; *also* : having or showing mastery in a subject or skill **3** : effortlessly smooth and rapid ⟨~ speech⟩ — **flu·en·cy** \-ən-sē\ *n* — **flu·ent·ly** *adv*

**flue pipe** *n* : an organ pipe whose tone is produced by an air current striking the beveled opening of the pipe

**¹fluff** \'fləf\ *n* **1** : ¹DOWN 1 ⟨~ from a pillow⟩ **2** : something fluffy **3** : something inconsequential **4** : BLUNDER; *esp* : an actor's lapse of memory

**²fluff** *vb* **1** : to make or become fluffy ⟨~ up a pillow⟩ **2** : to make a mistake

**fluffy** \'flə-fē\ *adj* **fluff·i·er; -est 1** : covered with or resembling fluff **2** : being light and soft or airy ⟨a ~ omelet⟩ **3** : lacking in meaning or substance — **fluff·i·ly** \-fə-lē\ *adv*

**¹flu·id** \'flü-əd\ *adj* **1** : capable of flowing

**2** : subject to change or movement **3** : showing a smooth easy style ⟨∼ movements⟩ **4** : available for a different use; *esp* : LIQUID **5** ⟨∼ assets⟩ — **flu·id·i·ty** \flü-'i-də-tē\ *n* — **flu·id·ly** *adv*

²**fluid** *n* : a substance (as a liquid or gas) tending to flow or take the shape of its container

**fluid dram** *or* **flu·i·dram** \,flü-ə-'dram\ *n* — see WEIGHT table

**fluid ounce** *n* — see WEIGHT table

¹**fluke** \'flük\ *n* : any of various trematode flatworms

²**fluke** *n* **1** : the part of an anchor that fastens in the ground **2** : a lobe of a whale's tail

³**fluke** *n* : a stroke of luck — **fluky** *also* **fluk·ey** \'flü-kē\ *adj*

**flume** \'flüm\ *n* **1** : an inclined channel for carrying water **2** : a ravine or gorge with a stream running through it

**flung** *past and past part of* FLING

**flunk** \'fləŋk\ *vb* : to fail esp. in an examination or course — **flunk** *n*

**flun·ky** *also* **flun·key** *or* **flun·kie** \'fləŋ-kē\ *n, pl* **flunkies** *also* **flunkeys** **1** : a liveried servant; *also* : one performing menial or miscellaneous duties **2** : YESMAN

**fluo·res·cence** \flò-'re-sᵊns\ *n* : luminescence caused by radiation absorption that ceases almost immediately after the incident radiation has stopped; *also* : the emitted radiation — **fluo·resce** \-'res\ *vb* — **fluo·res·cent** \-'re-sᵊnt\ *adj*

**fluorescent lamp** *n* : a tubular electric lamp in which light is produced by the action of ultraviolet light on a fluorescent material that coats the inner surface of the lamp

**fluo·ri·date** \'flòr-ə-,dāt\ *vb* **-dat·ed; -dat·ing** : to add a fluoride to (as drinking water) to reduce tooth decay — **fluo·ri·da·tion** \,flòr-ə-'dā-shən\ *n*

**fluo·ride** \'flòr-,īd\ *n* : a compound of fluorine

**fluo·ri·nate** \'flòr-ə-,nāt\ *vb* **-nat·ed; -nat·ing** : to treat or cause to combine with fluorine or a compound of fluorine — **fluo·ri·na·tion** \,flòr-ə-'nā-shən\ *n*

**fluo·rine** \'flòr-,ēn, -ən\ *n* : a pale yellowish flammable irritating toxic gaseous chemical element

**fluo·rite** \'flòr-,īt\ *n* : a mineral that consists of the fluoride of calcium used as a flux and in making glass

**fluo·ro·car·bon** \,flòr-ō-'kär-bən\ *n* : a compound containing fluorine and carbon used chiefly as a lubricant, refrigerant, or nonstick coating; *also* : CHLOROFLUOROCARBON

**fluo·ro·scope** \'flòr-ə-,skōp\ *n* : an instrument for observing the internal structure of an opaque object (as the living body) by means of X-rays — **fluo·ro·scop·ic** \,flòr-ə-'skä-pik\ *adj* — **fluo·ros·co·py** \-'ä-skə-pē\ *n*

**fluo·ro·sis** \flù-'rō-səs, ,flò-\ *n* : an abnormal condition (as spotting of the teeth) caused by fluorine or its compounds

**flu·ox·e·tine** \flü-'äk-sə-,tēn\ *n* : an anti-depressant drug that enhances serotonin activity

**flur·ry** \'flər-ē\ *n, pl* **flurries 1** : a gust of wind **2** : a brief light snowfall **3** : COMMOTION, BUSTLE **4** : a brief outburst of activity ⟨a ∼ of trading⟩ — **flurry** *vb*

¹**flush** \'fləsh\ *vb* : to cause (a bird) to fly away suddenly

²**flush** *n* : a hand of cards all of the same suit

³**flush** *n* **1** : a sudden flow (as of water) **2** : a surge esp. of emotion ⟨a ∼ of triumph⟩ **3** : a tinge of red : BLUSH **4** : a fresh and vigorous state ⟨in the ∼ of youth⟩ **5** : a passing sensation of extreme heat

⁴**flush** *vb* **1** : to flow and spread suddenly and freely **2** : to glow brightly **3** : BLUSH **4** : to wash out with a rush of fluid **5** : INFLAME, EXCITE ⟨was ∼ed with anger⟩ **6** : to cause to blush

⁵**flush** *adj* **1** : of a ruddy healthy color **2** : full of life and vigor **3** : filled to overflowing **4** : AFFLUENT **5** : readily available : ABUNDANT **6** : having an unbroken or even surface **7** : directly abutting : immediately adjacent **8** : set even with an edge of a type page or column — **flush·ness** *n*

⁶**flush** *adv* **1** : in a flush manner **2** : SQUARELY ⟨a blow ∼ on the chin⟩

⁷**flush** *vb* : to make flush

**flus·ter** \'fləs-tər\ *vb* : to put into a state of agitated confusion — **fluster** *n*

**flute** \'flüt\ *n* **1** : a hollow pipelike musical instrument **2** : a grooved pleat **3** : GROOVE — **flute** *vb* — **flut·ed** *adj*

**flut·ing** *n* : fluted decoration

**flut·ist** \'flü-tist\ *n* : a flute player

¹**flut·ter** \'flə-tər\ *vb* [ME *floteren* to float, flutter, fr. OE *floterian*, fr. *flotian* to float] **1** : to flap the wings rapidly **2** : to move with quick wavering or flapping motions **3** : to vibrate in irregular spasms **4** : to move about or behave in an agitated aimless manner — **flut·tery** \-tə-rē\ *adj*

²**flutter** *n* **1** : an act of fluttering **2** : a state of nervous confusion **3** : FLURRY

¹**flux** \'fləks\ *n* **1** : an act of flowing **2** : a state of continuous change **3** : a substance used to aid in fusing metals

²**flux** *vb* : FUSE

¹**fly** \'flī\ *vb* **flew** \'flü\; **flown** \'flōn\; **fly·ing 1** : to move in or pass through the air with wings **2** : to move through the air or before the wind **3** : to float or cause to float, wave, or soar in the air **4** : FLEE **5** : to fade and disappear : VANISH **6** : to move or pass swiftly ⟨time *flies*⟩ **7** : to become expended or dissipated rapidly **8** : to journey or travel in an aircraft or spacecraft **9** : to journey over by flying **10** : AVOID, SHUN **11** : to transport by flying

²**fly** *n, pl* **flies 1** : the action or process of flying : FLIGHT **2** *pl* : the space over a theater stage **3** : a garment closing concealed by a fold of cloth **4** : the length of an extended flag from its staff or support **5** : a baseball hit high into the air **6** : the outer canvas of a tent with a double top — **on the fly** : while still in the air

**³fly** *vb* **flied; fly·ing** : to hit a fly in baseball

**⁴fly** *n, pl* **flies** **1** : a winged insect — usu. used in combination ⟨butter*fly*⟩ **2** : any of a large order of insects mostly with one pair of functional wings and another pair that if present are reduced to balancing organs and often with larvae without a head, eyes, or legs; *esp* : one (as a housefly) that is large and stout-bodied **3** : a fishhook dressed to suggest an insect

**fly·able** \'flī-ə-bəl\ *adj* : suitable for flying or being flown

**fly ball** *n* : ²FLY 5

**fly-blown** \'flī-,blōn\ *adj* : not pure : TAINTED, CORRUPT

**fly·by** \-,bī\ *n, pl* **flybys** **1** : a usu. low-altitude flight by an aircraft over a public gathering **2** : a flight of a spacecraft past a heavenly body (as Jupiter) close enough to obtain scientific data

**fly-by-night** \-bī-,nīt\ *adj* **1** : seeking a quick profit usu. by shady acts **2** : TRANSITORY, PASSING ⟨~ fashions⟩

**fly casting** *n* : the casting of artificial flies in fly-fishing or as a competitive sport

**fly·catch·er** \-,ka-chər, -,ke-\ *n* : any of various passerine birds that feed on insects caught in flight

**flyer** *var of* FLIER

**fly-fish·ing** \'flī-,fi-shin\ *n* : a method of fishing in which an artificial fly is used for bait

**flying boat** *n* : a seaplane with a hull designed for floating

**flying buttress** *n* : a projecting arched structure to support a wall or building

**flying fish** *n* : any of numerous marine bony fishes capable of long gliding flights out of water by spreading their large fins like wings

**flying saucer** *n* : an unidentified flying object reported to be saucer-shaped or disk-shaped

**flying squirrel** *n* : either of two small nocturnal No. American squirrels with folds of skin connecting the forelegs and hind legs that enable them to make long gliding leaps

**fly·leaf** \'flī-,lēf\ *n, pl* **fly·leaves** \-,lēvz\ : a blank leaf at the beginning or end of a book

**fly·pa·per** \-,pā-pər\ *n* : paper poisoned or coated with a sticky substance for killing or catching flies

**fly·speck** \-,spek\ *n* **1** : a speck of fly dung **2** : something small and insignificant

**fly·way** \-,wā\ *n* : an established air route of migratory birds

**fly·wheel** \-,hwēl\ *n* : a heavy wheel for regulating the speed of machinery

**fm** *abbr* fathom

**Fm** *symbol* fermium

**FM** \'ef-,em\ *n* : a broadcasting system using frequency modulation; *also* : a radio receiver of such a system

**fn** *abbr* footnote

**fo** *or* **fol** *abbr* folio

**FO** *abbr* foreign office

**¹foal** \'fōl\ *n* : a young horse or related animal; *esp* : one under one year

**²foal** *vb* : to give birth to a foal

**¹foam** \'fōm\ *n* **1** : a mass of bubbles formed on the surface of a liquid : FROTH, SPUME **2** : material (as rubber) in a lightweight cellular form — **foamy** *adj*

**²foam** *vb* : to form foam : FROTH

**fob** \'fäb\ *n* **1** : a short strap, ribbon, or chain attached esp. to a pocket watch **2** : a small ornament worn on a fob

**FOB** *abbr* free on board

**fob off** *vb* **1** : to put off with a trick, excuse, or inferior substitute **2** : to pass or offer as genuine **3** : to put aside

**FOC** *abbr* free of charge

**focal length** *n* : the distance of a focus from a lens or curved mirror

**fo'c'sle** *var of* FORECASTLE

**fo·cus** \'fō-kəs\ *n, pl* **fo·ci** \-,sī\ *also* **fo·cus·es** [NL, tr. L, hearth] **1** : a point at which rays (as of light, heat, or sound) meet or diverge or appear to diverge; *esp* : the point at which an image is formed by a mirror, lens, or optical system **2** : FOCAL LENGTH **3** : adjustment (as of eyes or eyeglasses) that gives clear vision **4** : central point : CENTER — **fo·cal** \'fō-kəl\ *adj* — **fo·cal·ly** *adv*

**²focus** *vb* **-cused** *also* **-cussed; -cus·ing** *also* **-cus·sing** **1** : to bring or come to a focus ⟨~ rays of light⟩ **2** : CENTER ⟨~ attention on a problem⟩ **3** : to adjust the focus of

**fod·der** \'fä-dər\ *n* **1** : coarse dry food (as cornstalks) for livestock **2** : available material used to supply a heavy demand

**foe** \'fō\ *n* [ME *fo*, fr. OE *fāh*, fr. *fāh* hostile] : ENEMY

**FOE** *abbr* Fraternal Order of Eagles

**foehn** *or* **föhn** \'fərn, 'fœn, 'fān\ *n* [G *Föhn*] : a warm dry wind blowing down a mountainside

**foe·man** \'fō-mən\ *n* : FOE

**foe·tal, foe·tus** *chiefly Brit var of* FETAL, FETUS

**¹fog** \'fóg, 'fäg\ *n* **1** : fine particles of water suspended in the lower atmosphere **2** : mental confusion ⟨was in a ~ as what to do next⟩ — **fog·gy** *adj*

**²fog** *vb* **fogged; fog·ging** : to obscure or be obscured with or as if with fog

**fog·horn** \'fóg-,hórn, 'fäg-\ *n* : a horn sounded in a fog to give warning

**fo·gy** *also* **fo·gey** \'fō-gē\ *n, pl* **fogies** *also* **fogeys** : a person with old-fashioned ideas ⟨an old ~⟩

**foi·ble** \'fói-bəl\ *n* : a minor failing or weakness in character or behavior

**foie gras** \'fwä-'grä\ *n* [F, lit., fat liver] : the fattened liver of an animal and esp. of a goose usu. served as a pâté

**¹foil** \'fói(-ə)l\ *vb* [ME, alter. of *fullen* to full cloth, fr. AF *foller*] **1** : to prevent from attaining an end : DEFEAT **2** : to bring to naught : THWART

**²foil** *n* [ME, leaf, fr. AF *fuille, foille*, fr. L *folia*, pl. of *folium* leaf] **1** : a very thin sheet of metal ⟨aluminum ~⟩ **2** : one that serves as a contrast to another ⟨acted as a ~ for a comedian⟩

**³foil** *n* : a light fencing sword with a flexible blade tapering to a blunt point

**foist** \ˈfȯist\ vb : to pass off (something false or worthless) as genuine

¹**fold** \ˈfōld\ n 1 : an enclosure for sheep 2 : a group of people with a common faith, belief, or interest

²**fold** vb : to house (sheep) in a fold

³**fold** vb 1 : to lay one part over or against another part 2 : to clasp together 3 : EMBRACE 4 : to bend (as a layer of rock) into folds 5 : to incorporate into a mixture by overturning repeatedly without stirring or beating 6 : to become doubled or pleated 7 : FAIL, COLLAPSE ⟨the business ~ed⟩

⁴**fold** n 1 : a doubling or folding over 2 : a part doubled or laid over another part

**fold·a·way** \ˈfōld-ə-ˌwā\ adj : designed to fold out of the way or out of sight

**fold·er** \ˈfōl-dər\ n 1 : one that folds 2 : a folded printed circular 3 : a folded cover or large envelope for loose papers 4 : an object in a computer operating system used to organize files or other folders

**fol·de·rol** \ˈfäl-də-ˌräl\ n 1 : a useless trifle 2 : NONSENSE

**fold·out** \ˈfōld-ˌau̇t\ n : a folded leaf (as in a magazine) larger in some dimension than the page

**fo·li·age** \ˈfō-lē-ij\ n : a mass of leaves (as of a plant or forest)

**fo·li·at·ed** \ˈfō-lē-ˌā-təd\ adj : composed of or separable into layers

**fo·lic acid** \ˈfō-lik-\ n : a vitamin of the vitamin B complex used esp. to treat nutritional anemias

**fo·lio** \ˈfō-lē-ˌō\ n, pl **fo·li·os** 1 : a leaf of a book; also : a page number 2 : the size of a piece of paper cut two from a sheet 3 : a book printed on folio pages

¹**folk** \ˈfōk\ n, pl **folk** or **folks** 1 : the largest number or most characteristic part of a group of people forming a tribe or nation 2 pl : PEOPLE, PERSONS ⟨country ~⟩ ⟨old ~s⟩ 3 **folks** pl : the persons of one's own family

²**folk** adj : of, relating to, or originating among the common people ⟨~ music⟩

**folk art** n : the traditional anonymous art of usu. untrained people

**folk·lore** \ˈfōk-ˌlȯr\ n : customs, beliefs, stories, and sayings of a people handed down from generation to generation — **folk·lor·ic** \-ˌlȯr-ik\ adj — **folk·lor·ist** \-ist\ n

**folk mass** n : a mass in which traditional liturgical music is replaced by folk music

**folk·sing·er** \ˈfōk-ˌsiŋ-ər\ n : a singer of folk songs — **folk·sing·ing** n

**folksy** \ˈfōk-sē\ adj **folks·i·er; -est** 1 : SOCIABLE, FRIENDLY 2 : informal, casual, or familiar in manner or style ⟨~ humor⟩

**folk·way** \ˈfōk-ˌwā\ n : a way of thinking, feeling, or acting common to a given group of people; esp : a traditional social custom

**fol·li·cle** \ˈfä-li-kəl\ n 1 : a small anatomical cavity or gland ⟨a hair ~⟩ 2 : a small fluid-filled cavity in the ovary of a mammal enclosing a developing egg — **fol·lic·u·lar** \fə-ˈli-kyə-lər\ adj

**fol·low** \ˈfä-lō\ vb 1 : to go or come after

2 : to proceed along ⟨~ the path⟩ 3 : to engage in as a way of life ⟨~ the sea⟩ ⟨~ a profession⟩ 4 : OBEY ⟨~ instructions⟩ 5 : PURSUE 6 : to come after in order or rank or natural sequence 7 : to keep one's attention fixed on 8 : to result from ♦ **Synonyms** SUCCEED, ENSUE, SUPERVENE — **fol·low·er** n — **follow suit** 1 : to play a card of the same suit as the card led 2 : to follow an example set

¹**fol·low·ing** \ˈfä-lə-wiŋ\ adj 1 : next after : SUCCEEDING ⟨the ~ day⟩ 2 : that immediately follows ⟨trains will leave at the ~ times⟩

²**following** n : a group of followers, adherents, or partisans

³**following** prep : subsequent to : AFTER ⟨~ the lecture tea was served⟩

**follow-up** \ˈfä-lō-ˌəp\ n : a system or instance of pursuing an initial effort by supplementary action

**fol·ly** \ˈfä-lē\ n, pl **follies** [ME folie, fr. AF, fr. fol fool] 1 : lack of good sense 2 : a foolish act or idea : FOOLISHNESS 3 : an excessively costly or unprofitable undertaking

**fo·ment** \fō-ˈment\ vb : INCITE

**fo·men·ta·tion** \ˌfō-mən-ˈtā-shən, -ˌmen-\ n 1 : a hot moist material (as a damp cloth) applied to the body to ease pain 2 : the act of fomenting : INSTIGATION

**fond** \ˈfänd\ adj [ME, fr. fonne fool] 1 : FOOLISH, SILLY ⟨~ pride⟩ 2 : prizing highly : DESIROUS ⟨~ of praise⟩ 3 : strongly attracted or predisposed ⟨~ of music⟩ 4 : foolishly tender : INDULGENT; also : LOVING, AFFECTIONATE 5 : CHERISHED, DEAR ⟨his ~est hopes⟩ — **fond·ly** adv — **fond·ness** n

**fon·dant** \ˈfän-dənt\ n : a creamy preparation of sugar used as a basis for candies or icings

**fon·dle** \ˈfän-dᵊl\ vb **fon·dled; fon·dling** : to touch or handle lovingly : CARESS

**fon·due** also **fon·du** \fän-ˈdü, -ˈdyü\ n [F] : a preparation of melted cheese often flavored with white wine

¹**font** \ˈfänt\ n 1 : a receptacle for baptismal or holy water 2 : FOUNTAIN, SOURCE ⟨a ~ of information⟩

²**font** n : an assortment of printing type of one style and sometimes one size

**food** \ˈfüd\ n 1 : material taken into an organism and used for growth, repair, and vital processes and as a source of energy; also : organic material produced by green plants and used by them as food 2 : nourishment in solid form 3 : something that nourishes, sustains, or supplies ⟨~ for thought⟩

**food chain** n 1 : a hierarchical arrangement of organisms in an ecological community such that each uses the next usu. lower member as a food source 2 : a hierarchy based on power or importance

**food court** n : an area (as within a shopping mall) set apart for food concessions

**food poisoning** n : a digestive illness caused by bacteria or by chemicals in food

**food·stuff** \ˈfüd-ˌstəf\ n : a substance with

food value; *esp* : a specific nutrient (as fat or protein)

**¹fool** \'fül\ *n* [ME, fr. AF *fol*, fr. LL *follis*, fr. L, bellows, bag] **1** : a person who lacks sense or judgment **2** : JESTER **3** : DUPE **4** : IDIOT

**²fool** *vb* **1** : to spend time idly or aimlessly **2** : to meddle or tamper thoughtlessly or ignorantly **3** : JOKE **4** : DECEIVE **5** : FRITTER ⟨∼ed away his time⟩

**fool·ery** \'fü-lə-rē\ *n, pl* **-er·ies 1** : a foolish act, utterance, or belief **2** : foolish behavior

**fool·har·dy** \'fül-,här-dē\ *adj* : foolishly daring : RASH — **fool·har·di·ness** \-dē-nəs\ *n*

**fool·ish** \'fü-lish\ *adj* **1** : showing or arising from folly or lack of judgment **2** : ABSURD, RIDICULOUS **3** : ABASHED — **fool·ish·ly** *adv* — **fool·ish·ness** *n*

**fool·proof** \'fül-,prüf\ *adj* : so simple or reliable as to leave no opportunity for error, misuse, or failure ⟨a ∼ plan⟩

**fools·cap** \'fül-,skap\ *n* [fr. the watermark of a fool's cap formerly applied to such paper] : a size of paper typically 16×13 inches

**fool's gold** *n* : PYRITE

**¹foot** \'fut\ *n, pl* **feet** \'fēt\ *also* **foot 1** : the end part of a leg below the ankle of a vertebrate animal **2** — see WEIGHT table **3** : a group of syllables forming the basic unit of verse meter **4** : something resembling an animal's foot in position or use **5** : the lowest part : BOTTOM **6** : the part at the opposite end from the head **7** : the part (as of a stocking) that covers the foot

**²foot** *vb* **1** : DANCE **2** : to go on foot **3** : to add up **4** : to pay or provide for paying

**foot·age** \'fu-tij\ *n* **1** : length expressed in feet **2** : the length of film used for a scene; *also* : the material contained on such footage

**foot–and–mouth disease** *n* : an acute contagious viral disease esp. of cattle

**foot·ball** \'fut-,bȯl\ *n* **1** : any of several games played by two teams on a rectangular field with goalposts at each end in which the object is to get the ball over the goal line or between goalposts by running, passing, or kicking **2** : the ball used in football

**foot·board** \-,bȯrd\ *n* **1** : a narrow platform on which to stand or brace the feet **2** : a board forming the foot of a bed

**foot·bridge** \-,brij\ *n* : a bridge for pedestrians

**foot·ed** \'fu-təd\ *adj* : having a foot or feet of a specified kind or number ⟨flat-footed⟩ ⟨four-footed⟩

**-foot·er** \'fu-tər\ *comb form* : one that is a specified number of feet in height, length, or breadth ⟨a six-footer⟩

**foot·fall** \'fut-,fȯl\ *n* : the sound of a footstep

**foot·hill** \-,hil\ *n* : a hill at the foot of higher hills or mountains

**foot·hold** \-,hōld\ *n* **1** : a hold for the feet : FOOTING **2** : a position usable as a base for further advance

**foot·ing** *n* **1** : the placing of one's feet in

a stable position **2** : the act of moving on foot **3** : a place or space for standing : FOOTHOLD **4** : position with respect to one another : STATUS **5** : BASIS

**foot·less** \'fut-ləs\ *adj* **1** : having no feet ⟨∼ tights⟩ **2** : INEPT, INEFFECTUAL

**foot·lights** \-,līts\ *n pl* **1** : a row of lights along the front of a stage floor **2** : the stage as a profession ⟨succeeded in the ∼⟩

**foo·tling** \'füt-liŋ\ *adj* **1** : INEPT ⟨∼ amateurs⟩ **2** : TRIVIAL

**foot·lock·er** \'fut-,lä-kər\ *n* : a small trunk designed to be placed at the foot of a bed (as in a barracks)

**foot·loose** \-,lüs\ *adj* : having no ties : FREE, UNTRAMMELED

**foot·man** \-mən\ *n* : a male servant who attends a carriage or waits on table, admits visitors, and runs errands

**foot·note** \-,nōt\ *n* **1** : a note of reference, explanation, or comment placed usu. at the bottom of a page **2** : COMMENTARY

**foot·pad** \-,pad\ *n* : a round somewhat flat foot on the leg of a spacecraft for distributing weight to minimize sinking into a surface

**foot·path** \-,path, -,päth\ *n* : a narrow path for pedestrians

**foot·print** \-,print\ *n* **1** : an impression of the foot **2** : the area on a surface covered by something ⟨a tire with a wide ∼⟩

**foot·race** \-,rās\ *n* : a race run on foot

**foot·rest** \-,rest\ *n* : a support for the feet

**foot·sore** \-,sȯr\ *adj* : having sore or tender feet (as from much walking)

**foot·step** \-,step\ *n* **1** : the mark of the foot : TRACK **2** : TREAD **3** : distance covered by a step : PACE **4** : a step on which to ascend or descend **5** : a way of life, conduct, or action

**foot·stool** \-,stül\ *n* : a low stool to support the feet

**foot·wear** \-,wer\ *n* : apparel (as shoes or boots) for the feet

**foot·work** \-,wərk\ *n* : the management of the feet (as in boxing)

**fop** \'fäp\ *n* : DANDY **1** — **fop·pery** \'fä-pə-rē\ *n* — **fop·pish** *adj*

**¹for** \fər, 'fȯr\ *prep* **1** : as a preparation toward ⟨dress ∼ dinner⟩ **2** : toward the purpose or goal of ⟨need time ∼ study⟩ ⟨money ∼ a trip⟩ **3** : so as to reach or attain ⟨run ∼ cover⟩ **4** : as being ⟨took him ∼ a fool⟩ **5** : because of ⟨cry ∼ joy⟩ **6** : used to indicate a recipient ⟨a letter ∼ you⟩ **7** : in support of ⟨fought ∼ his country⟩ **8** : directed at : AFFECTING ⟨a cure ∼ what ails you⟩ **9** : used with a noun or pronoun followed by an infinitive to form the equivalent of a noun clause ⟨∼ you to go would be silly⟩ **10** : in exchange as equal to : so as to return the value of ⟨a lot of trouble ∼ nothing⟩ ⟨pay $10 ∼ a hat⟩ **11** : CONCERNING ⟨a stickler ∼ detail⟩ **12** : CONSIDERING ⟨tall ∼ her age⟩ **13** : through the period of ⟨served ∼ three years⟩ **14** : in honor of ⟨named ∼ her grandmother⟩

**²for** *conj* : BECAUSE

³**for** *abbr* **1** foreign **2** forestry

**fora** *pl of* FORUM

¹**for·age** \ˈfȯr-ij\ *n* [ME, fr. AF, fr. *fuerre*, *foer* fodder, straw, of Gmc origin] **1** : food for animals esp. when taken by browsing or grazing **2** : a search for food or supplies

²**forage** *vb* **for·aged; for·ag·ing 1** : to collect forage from **2** : to search for food or supplies **3** : to get by foraging **4** : to make a search : RUMMAGE

**for·ay** \ˈfȯr-ˌā, fȯ-ˈrā\ *vb* : to raid esp. in search of plunder : PILLAGE — **foray** *n*

¹**for·bear** \fȯr-ˈber\ *vb* **-bore** \-ˈbȯr\; **-borne** \-ˈbȯrn\; **-bear·ing 1** : to refrain from : ABSTAIN **2** : to be patient — **for·bear·ance** \-ˈber-əns\ *n*

²**forbear** *var of* FOREBEAR

**for·bid** \fər-ˈbid\ *vb* **-bade** \-ˈbad, -ˈbād\ *also* **-bad** \-ˈbad\; **-bid·den** \-ˈbi-dᵊn\; **-bid·ding 1** : to command against : PROHIBIT **2** : HINDER, PREVENT ♦ *Synonyms* ENJOIN, INTERDICT, INHIBIT, BAN

**forbidding** *adj* : DISAGREEABLE, REPELLENT ⟨a ~ task⟩

¹**force** \ˈfȯrs\ *n* **1** : strength or energy esp. of an exceptional degree : active power **2** : capacity to persuade or convince **3** : military strength; *also, pl* : the whole military strength (as of a nation) **4** : a body (as of persons or ships) available for a particular purpose **5** : VIOLENCE, COMPULSION **6** : an influence (as a push or pull) that causes motion or a change of motion — **force·ful** \-fəl\ *adj* — **force·ful·ly** *adv* — **in force 1** : in great numbers **2** : VALID, OPERATIVE ⟨the ban remains *in force*⟩

²**force** *vb* **forced; forc·ing 1** : COMPEL, COERCE ⟨*forced* to admit defeat⟩ **2** : to cause through necessity **3** : to press, attain to, or effect against resistance or inertia ⟨~ your way through⟩ **4** : to raise or accelerate to the utmost ⟨~ the pace⟩ **5** : to produce with unnatural or unwilling effort ⟨*forced* a smile⟩ **6** : to hasten (as in growth) by artificial means

**for·ceps** \ˈfȯr-səps\ *n, pl* **forceps** [L] : a handheld instrument for grasping, holding, or pulling objects esp. for delicate operations (as by a surgeon)

**forc·ible** \ˈfȯr-sə-bəl\ *adj* **1** : obtained or done by force **2** : showing force or energy : POWERFUL — **forc·i·bly** \-blē\ *adv*

¹**ford** \ˈfȯrd\ *n* : a place where a stream may be crossed by wading

²**ford** *vb* : to cross (a body of water) by wading

¹**fore** \ˈfȯr\ *adv* : in, toward, or adjacent to the front : FORWARD

²**fore** *adj* : being or coming before in time, order, or space

³**fore** *n* : something that occupies a front position

⁴**fore** *interj* — used by a golfer to warn anyone within range of the probable line of flight of the ball

**fore–and–aft** \ˌfȯr-ə-ˈnaft\ *adj* : lying, running, or acting along the length of a structure (as a ship)

¹**fore·arm** \(ˌ)fȯr-ˈärm\ *vb* : to arm in advance : PREPARE

²**fore·arm** \ˈfȯr-ˌärm\ *n* : the part of the arm between the elbow and the wrist

**fore·bear** \-ˌber\ *n* : ANCESTOR, FOREFATHER

**fore·bode** *also* **for·bode** \fȯr-ˈbōd\ *vb* **1** : to have a premonition esp. of misfortune **2** : FORETELL, PREDICT ♦ *Synonyms* AUGUR, BODE, FORESHADOW, PORTEND, PROMISE — **fore·bod·ing** *n or adj* — **fore·bod·ing·ly** *adv*

**fore·cast** \ˈfȯr-ˌkast\ *vb* **-cast** *also* **-cast·ed; -cast·ing 1** : PREDICT, CALCULATE ⟨~ weather conditions⟩ **2** : to indicate as likely to occur — **forecast** *n* — **fore·cast·er** *n*

**fore·cas·tle** *or* **fo'·c'sle** \ˈfōk-səl\ *n* **1** : the forward part of the upper deck of a ship **2** : the crew's quarters usu. in a ship's bow

**fore·close** \fȯr-ˈklōz\ *vb* **1** : to shut out : PRECLUDE **2** : to take legal measures to terminate a mortgage and take possession of the mortgaged property

**fore·clo·sure** \-ˈklō-zhər\ *n* : the act of foreclosing; *esp* : the legal procedure of foreclosing a mortgage

**fore·doom** \fȯr-ˈdüm\ *vb* : to doom beforehand

**fore·fa·ther** \ˈfȯr-ˌfä-thər\ *n* **1** : ANCESTOR **2** : a person of an earlier period and common heritage

**forefend** *var of* FORFEND

**fore·fin·ger** \-ˌfiŋ-gər\ *n* : INDEX FINGER

**fore·foot** \-ˌfut\ *n* : either of the front feet of a quadruped; *also* : the front part of the human foot

**fore·front** \-ˌfrənt\ *n* : the foremost part or place

**foregather** *var of* FORGATHER

¹**fore·go** \fȯr-ˈgō\ *vb* **-went** \-ˈwent\; **-gone** \-ˈgȯn\; **-go·ing** : PRECEDE

²**forego** *var of* FORGO

**foregoing** *adj* : PRECEDING ⟨the ~ statement can be proven⟩

**fore·gone** \ˈfȯr-ˌgȯn\ *adj* : determined in advance ⟨a ~ conclusion⟩

**fore·ground** \-ˌgraund\ *n* **1** : the part of a scene or representation that appears nearest to and in front of the spectator **2** : a position of prominence

**fore·hand** \-ˌhand\ *n* : a stroke (as in tennis) made with the palm of the hand turned in the direction in which the hand is moving; *also* : the side on which such a stroke is made — **forehand** *adj*

**fore·hand·ed** \(ˌ)fȯr-ˈhan-dəd\ *adj* : mindful of the future : PRUDENT

**fore·head** \ˈfȯr-əd, ˈfȯr-ˌhed\ *n* : the part of the face above the eyes

**for·eign** \ˈfȯr-ən\ *adj* [ME *forein*, fr. AF, fr. LL *foranus* on the outside, fr. L *foris* outside] **1** : situated outside a place or country and esp. one's own country **2** : born in, belonging to, or characteristic of some place or country other than the one under consideration ⟨~ language⟩ **3** : not connected, pertinent, or characteristically present **4** : related to or dealing with other nations ⟨~ affairs⟩ **5**

: occurring in an abnormal situation in the living body ⟨a ~ body in the eye⟩

**for·eign·er** \ˈfȯr-ə-nər\ n : a person belonging to or owing allegiance to a foreign country

**foreign minister** n : a governmental minister for foreign affairs

**fore·know** \fȯr-ˈnō\ vb **-knew** \-ˈnü, -ˈnyü\; **-known** \-ˈnōn\; **-know·ing** : to have previous knowledge of — **fore·knowl·edge** \ˈfȯr-ˌnä-lij, fȯr-ˈnä-\ n

**fore·la·dy** \ˈfȯr-ˌlā-dē\ n : FOREWOMAN

**fore·leg** \-ˌleg\ n : a front leg

**fore·limb** \-ˌlim\ n : a front or upper limb (as a wing, arm, fin, or leg)

**fore·lock** \-ˌläk\ n : a lock of hair growing from the front part of the head

**fore·man** \-mən\ n 1 : a spokesperson of a jury 2 : a person in charge of a group of workers

**fore·mast** \-ˌmast\ n : the mast nearest the bow of a ship

**fore·most** \-ˌmōst\ adj : first in time, place, or order : most important : PREEMINENT — **foremost** adv

**fore·name** \-ˌnām\ n : a first name

**fore·named** \-ˌnāmd\ adj : previously named : AFORESAID

**fore·noon** \-ˌnün\ n : MORNING

¹**fo·ren·sic** \fə-ˈren-sik\ adj [L forensis public, forensic, fr. forum forum] 1 : belonging to, used in, or suitable to courts of law or to public speaking or debate 2 : relating to the application of scientific knowledge to legal problems ⟨~ medicine⟩

²**forensic** n 1 : an argumentative exercise 2 pl : the art or study of argumentative discourse 3 pl : scientific analysis of physical evidence ⟨from a crime scene⟩

**fore·or·dain** \ˌfȯr-ȯr-ˈdān\ vb : to ordain or decree beforehand : PREDESTINE

**fore·part** \ˈfȯr-ˌpärt\ n 1 : the anterior part of something 2 : the earlier part of a period of time

**fore·quar·ter** \-ˌkwȯr-tər\ n : the front half of a lateral half of the body or carcass of a quadruped ⟨a ~ of beef⟩

**fore·run·ner** \-ˌrə-nər\ n 1 : one that goes before to give notice of the approach of others : HARBINGER 2 : PREDECESSOR, ANCESTOR ♦ Synonyms PRECURSOR, HERALD

**fore·sail** \-ˌsāl, -səl\ n 1 : the lowest sail on the foremast of a square-rigged ship or schooner 2 : the principal sail forward of the foremast (as of a sloop)

**fore·see** \fȯr-ˈsē\ vb **-saw** \-ˈsȯ\; **-seen** \-ˈsēn\; **-see·ing** : to see or realize beforehand : EXPECT ♦ Synonyms FOREKNOW, DIVINE, APPREHEND, ANTICIPATE — **fore·see·able** adj

**fore·shad·ow** \-ˈsha-dō\ vb : to give a hint or suggestion of beforehand

**fore·short·en** \fȯr-ˈshȯr-tᵊn\ vb : to shorten (a detail) in a drawing or painting so that it appears to have depth

**fore·sight** \ˈfȯr-ˌsīt\ n 1 : the act or power of foreseeing 2 : care or provision for the future : PRUDENCE 3 : an act of looking forward; also : a view forward — **fore·sight·ed** \-ˌsī-təd\ adj — **fore·sight·ed·ly** adv — **fore·sight·ed·ness** n

**fore·skin** \-ˌskin\ n : a fold of skin enclosing the end of the penis

¹**for·est** \ˈfȯr-əst\ n [ME, fr. AF, fr. LL forestis (silva) unenclosed (woodland), fr. L foris outside] : a large thick growth of trees and underbrush — **for·est·ed** \ˈfȯr-ə-stəd\ adj — **for·est·land** \ˈfȯr-əst-ˌland\ n

**fore·stall** \fȯr-ˈstȯl\ vb : to counter, hinder, or prevent by measures taken in advance ⟨his comments ~ed the criticism⟩

**forest ranger** n : a person in charge of the management and protection of a portion of a forest

**for·est·ry** \ˈfȯr-ə-strē\ n : the science of growing and caring for forests — **for·est·er** \ˈfȯr-ə-stər\ n

**fore·swear** var of FORSWEAR

¹**fore·taste** \ˈfȯr-ˌtāst\ n : an advance indication, warning, or notion ⟨a ~ of winter⟩

²**fore·taste** \fȯr-ˈtāst\ vb : to taste beforehand : ANTICIPATE

**fore·tell** \fȯr-ˈtel\ vb **-told** \-ˈtōld\; **-tell·ing** : to tell of beforehand : PREDICT ♦ Synonyms FORECAST, PROPHESY, PROGNOSTICATE

**fore·thought** \ˈfȯr-ˌthȯt\ n 1 : PREMEDITATION 2 : consideration for the future

**fore·to·ken** \fȯr-ˈtō-kən\ vb : to indicate in advance

**fore·top** \ˈfȯr-ˌtäp\ n : a platform near the top of a ship's foremast

**for·ev·er** \fȯr-ˈe-vər\ adv 1 : for a limitless time 2 : at all times : ALWAYS

**for·ev·er·more** \-ˌe-vər-ˈmȯr\ adv : FOREVER

**fore·warn** \fȯr-ˈwȯrn\ vb : to warn beforehand — **fore·warn·ing** \-ˈwȯr-niŋ\ n

**forewent** past of FOREGO

**fore·wing** \ˈfȯr-ˌwiŋ\ n : either of the anterior wings of a 4-winged insect

**fore·wom·an** \ˈfȯr-ˌwù-mən\ n : a woman having the responsibilities of a foreman

**fore·word** \-ˌwərd\ n : PREFACE

¹**for·feit** \ˈfȯr-fət\ n [ME forfait, fr. AF, fr. pp. of forfaire, forsfaire to commit a crime, forfeit, fr. fors outside + faire to do] 1 : something forfeited : PENALTY, FINE 2 : FORFEITURE 3 : something deposited and then redeemed on payment of a fine 4 pl : a game in which forfeits are exacted

²**forfeit** vb : to lose or lose the right to esp. by some error, offense, or crime

**for·fei·ture** \ˈfȯr-fə-ˌchùr\ n 1 : the act of forfeiting 2 : something forfeited : PENALTY

**for·fend** \fȯr-ˈfend\ vb 1 : PREVENT 2 : PROTECT, PRESERVE

**for·gath·er** or **fore·gath·er** \fȯr-ˈga-thər\ vb 1 : to come together : ASSEMBLE 2 : to meet someone usu. by chance

¹**forge** \ˈfȯrj\ n [ME, fr. AF, fr. L fabrica, fr. faber smith] : a furnace or shop with its furnace where metal is heated and worked

²**forge** vb **forged**; **forg·ing** 1 : to form (metal) by heating and hammering 2

: FASHION, SHAPE ⟨~ an agreement⟩ 3 : to make or imitate falsely esp. with intent to defraud ⟨~ a signature⟩ — forg·er n — forg·ery \'for-jə-rē\ n

³forge vb forged; forg·ing : to move ahead steadily but gradually

for·get \fər-'get\ vb -got \-'gät\; -got·ten \-'gät-⁹n\ or -got; -get·ting 1 : to be unable to think of or recall 2 : to fail to become mindful of at the proper time 3 : NEGLECT, DISREGARD ⟨forgot their old friends⟩ 4 : to give up hope for or expectation of — for·get·ful \-'get-fəl\ adj — for·get·ful·ly adv — for·get·ful·ness n

for·get–me–not \fər-'get-mē-,nät\ n : any of a genus of small herbs with bright blue or white flowers

forg·ing n : a piece of forged work

for·give \fər-'giv\ vb -gave \-'gāv\; -giv·en \-'gi-vən\; -giv·ing 1 : to give up resentment of 2 : PARDON, ABSOLVE 3 : to grant relief from payment of ⟨~ a debt⟩ — for·giv·able adj — for·give·ness n — for·giv·er n

forgiving adj 1 : willing or able to forgive 2 : allowing room for error or weakness ⟨a ~ recipe⟩

for·go \for-'gō\ vb -went \-'went\; -gone \-'gon\; -go·ing : to give up the enjoyment or advantage of : do without

fo·rint \'for-int\ n, pl forints also forint — see MONEY table

¹fork \'fork\ n 1 : an implement with two or more prongs for taking up (as in eating), pitching, or digging 2 : a forked part, tool, or piece of equipment 3 : a dividing into branches or a place where something branches; also : a branch of such a fork

²fork vb 1 : to divide into two or more branches 2 : to give the form of a fork to ⟨~ing her fingers⟩ 3 : to raise or pitch with a fork ⟨~ hay⟩ 4 : PAY, CONTRIBUTE — used with over, out, or up

forked \'forkt, 'for-kəd\ adj : having a fork : shaped like a fork ⟨~ lightning⟩

fork·lift \'fork-,lift\ n : a machine for lifting heavy objects by means of steel fingers inserted under the load

for·lorn \fər-'lorn, for-\ adj 1 : sad and lonely because of isolation or desertion 2 : WRETCHED 3 : nearly hopeless — for·lorn·ly adv — for·lorn·ness n

¹form \'form\ n 1 : SHAPE, STRUCTURE 2 : a body esp. of a person : FIGURE 3 : the essential nature of a thing 4 : established manner of doing or saying something 5 : FORMULA 6 : a document with blank spaces for insertion of information ⟨tax ~⟩ 7 : CEREMONY 8 : manner of performing according to recognized standards 9 : a long seat : BENCH 10 : a model of the human figure used for displaying clothes 11 : MOLD ⟨a ~ for concrete⟩ 12 : type or plates in a frame ready for printing 13 : MODE, KIND, VARIETY ⟨coal is a ~ of carbon⟩ 14 : orderly method of arrangement; also : a particular kind or instance of such arrangement ⟨the sonnet ~ in poetry⟩ 15 : the structural element, plan, or design of a work of art 16 : a bounded surface

or volume 17 : a grade in a British school or in some American private schools 18 : RACING FORM 19 : known ability to perform; also : condition (as of an athlete) suitable for performing 20 : one of the ways in which a word is changed to show difference in use ⟨the plural ~ of a noun⟩ — form·less adj

²form vb 1 : to give form or shape to : FASHION, MAKE 2 : TRAIN, INSTRUCT 3 : CONSTITUTE, COMPOSE 4 : DEVELOP, ACQUIRE ⟨~ a habit⟩ 5 : to arrange in order ⟨~ a battle line⟩ 6 : to take form : ARISE ⟨clouds are ~ing⟩ 7 : to take a definite form, shape, or arrangement

¹for·mal \'for-məl\ adj 1 : according to conventional forms and rules ⟨a ~ dinner party⟩ 2 : done in due or lawful form ⟨a ~ contract⟩ 3 : CEREMONIOUS, PRIM ⟨a ~ manner⟩ 4 : NOMINAL — for·mal·ly adv

²formal n : something (as a social event) formal in character

form·al·de·hyde \for-'mal-də-,hīd\ n : a colorless pungent gas used in water solution as a preservative and disinfectant

for·mal·ise Brit var of FORMALIZE

for·mal·ism \'for-mə-,li-zəm\ n : strict adherence to set forms

for·mal·i·ty \for-'ma-lə-tē\ n, pl -ties 1 : compliance with formal or conventional rules 2 : the quality or state of being formal 3 : an established form that is required or conventional

for·mal·ize \'for-mə-,līz\ vb -ized; -iz·ing 1 : to give a certain or definite form to 2 : to make formal; also : to give formal status or approval to

¹for·mat \'for-,mat\ n 1 : the general composition or style of a publication 2 : the general plan or arrangement of something 3 : a method of organizing data ⟨various file ~s⟩

²format vb for·mat·ted; for·mat·ting : to arrange (as material to be printed) in a particular format — for·mat·ter n

for·ma·tion \for-'mā-shən\ n 1 : an act of giving form to something : DEVELOPMENT 2 : something that is formed 3 : STRUCTURE, SHAPE 4 : an arrangement of persons or things in a prescribed manner or for a certain purpose

for·ma·tive \'for-mə-tiv\ adj 1 : giving or capable of giving form : CONSTRUCTIVE 2 : of, relating to, or characterized by important growth or formation ⟨a child's ~ years⟩

for·mer \'for-mər\ adj 1 : PREVIOUS, EARLIER 2 : FOREGOING ⟨the ~ part of the chapter⟩ 3 : being first mentioned or in order of two or more things

for·mer·ly \-lē\ adv : in time past : PREVIOUSLY

form–fit·ting \'form-,fi-tin\ adj : conforming to the outline of the body ⟨a ~ sweater⟩

for·mi·da·ble \'for-mə-də-bəl, for-'mi-\ adj 1 : exciting fear, dread, or awe ⟨a ~ foe⟩ 2 : imposing serious difficulties ⟨a ~ barrier⟩ — for·mi·da·bly \-blē\ adv

form letter n 1 : a letter on a frequently recurring topic that can be sent to different people at different times **2** : a letter for mass circulation sent out in many printed copies

**for·mu·la** \'fȯr myə lə\ *n, pl* **-las** *or* **-lae** \-,lē, -,lī\ **1** : a set form of words for ceremonial use **2** : RECIPE, PRESCRIPTION **3** : a milk mixture or substitute for a baby **4** : a group of symbols or figures joined to express information concisely **5** : a customary or set form or method

**for·mu·late** \-,lāt\ *vb* **-lat·ed; -lat·ing 1** : to express in a formula **2** : DESIGN, DEVISE ⟨∼ a policy⟩ **3** : to prepare according to a formula — **for·mu·la·tion** \,fȯr-myə-'lā-shən\ *n*

**for·ni·ca·tion** \,fȯr-nə-'kā-shən\ *n* : consensual sexual intercourse between two persons not married to each other — **for·ni·cate** \'fȯr-nə-,kāt\ *vb* — **for·ni·ca·tor** \-,kā-tər\ *n*

**for·sake** \fər-'sāk, fȯr-\ *vb* **for·sook** \-'sùk\; **for·sak·en** \-'sā-kən\; **for·sak·ing** [ME, fr. OE *forsacan*, fr. *sacan* to dispute] : to renounce or turn away from entirely ⟨*forsook* teaching for a film career⟩

**for·sooth** \fər-'süth\ *adv* : in truth : INDEED

**for·swear** \fȯr-'swer\ *vb* **-swore** \-'swȯr\; **-sworn** \-'swȯrn\; **-swear·ing 1** : to swear falsely : commit perjury **2** : to renounce earnestly or under oath **3** : to deny under oath

**for·syth·ia** \fər-'si-thē-ə\ *n, pl* **-ias** *also* **-ia** : any of a genus of shrubs related to the olive and having yellow bell-shaped flowers appearing before the leaves in early spring

**fort** \'fȯrt\ *n* [ME *forte*, fr. AF *fort*, fr. *fort* strong, fr. L *fortis*] **1** : a fortified place **2** : a permanent army post

¹**forte** \'fȯrt, 'fȯr-,tā\ *n* [F *fort*, fr. *fort*, adj., strong] : one's strong point

²**for·te** \'fȯr-,tā\ *adv or adj* [It, fr. *forte* strong] : LOUD — used as a direction in music

**forth** \'fȯrth\ *adv* **1** : FORWARD, ONWARD ⟨from this day ∼⟩ **2** : out into view ⟨plants putting ∼ leaves⟩

**forth·com·ing** \'fȯrth-'kə-min\ *adj* **1** : coming or available soon ⟨the ∼ holidays⟩ **2** : marked by openness and candor : OUTGOING

**forth·right** \'fȯrth-,rīt\ *adj* : free from ambiguity or evasiveness : going straight to the point ⟨a ∼ answer⟩ — **forth·right·ly** *adv* — **forth·right·ness** *n*

**forth·with** \,fȯrth-'with\ *adv* : IMMEDIATELY

**for·ti·fy** \'fȯr-tə-,fī\ *vb* **-fied; -fy·ing 1** : to strengthen by military defenses **2** : to give physical strength or endurance to **3** : ENCOURAGE **4** : to strengthen or enrich with a material ⟨∼ bread with vitamins⟩ — **for·ti·fi·ca·tion** \,fȯr-tə-fə-'kā-shən\ *n*

**for·tis·si·mo** \fȯr-'ti-sə-,mō\ *adv or adj* : very loud — used as a direction in music

**for·ti·tude** \'fȯr-tə-,tüd, -,tyüd\ *n* : strength of mind that enables one to meet danger or bear pain or adversity

with courage ♦ *Synonyms* GRIT, BACKBONE, PLUCK, GUTS

**fort·night** \'fȯrt-,nīt\ *n* [ME *fourtenight*, alter. of *fourtene night* fourteen nights] : two weeks — **fort·night·ly** \-lē\ *adj or adv*

**for·tress** \'fȯr-trəs\ *n* : FORT 1

**for·tu·itous** \fȯr-'tü-ə-təs, -'tyü-\ *adj* **1** : happening by chance ⟨a ∼ discovery⟩ **2** : FORTUNATE — **for·tu·itous·ly** *adv*

**for·tu·ity** \-ə-tē\ *n, pl* **-ities 1** : the quality or state of being fortuitous **2** : a chance event or occurrence

**for·tu·nate** \'fȯr-chə-nət\ *adj* **1** : bringing some good thing not foreseen **2** : LUCKY

**for·tu·nate·ly** \-lē\ *adv* **1** : in a fortunate manner **2** : it is fortunate that

**for·tune** \'fȯr-chən\ *n* **1** : prosperity attained partly through luck, *also* : CHANCE, LUCK **2** : what happens to a person : good or bad luck **3** : FATE, DESTINY **4** : RICHES, WEALTH

**fortune hunter** *n* : a person who seeks wealth esp. by marriage

**for·tune–tell·er** \-,te-lər\ *n* : a person who professes to foretell future events — **for·tune–tell·ing** *n or adj*

**for·ty** \'fȯr-tē\ *n, pl* **forties** : four times 10 — **for·ti·eth** \'fȯr-tē-əth\ *adj or n* — **for·ty** *adj or pron*

**for·ty–five** \,fȯr-tē-'fīv\ *n* **1** : a .45 caliber handgun — usu. written .45 **2** : a phonograph record designed to be played at 45 revolutions per minute — usu. written 45

**for·ty–nin·er** \-'nī-nər\ *n* : a person in the rush to California for gold in 1849

**forty winks** *n sing or pl* : a short sleep

**fo·rum** \'fȯr-əm\ *n, pl* **forums** *also* **fo·ra** \-ə\ [L] **1** : the marketplace or central meeting place of an ancient Roman city **2** : a medium (as a publication or online service) of open discussion **3** : COURT **4** : a public assembly, lecture, or program involving audience or panel discussion

¹**for·ward** \'fȯr-wərd\ *adj* **1** : being near or at or belonging to the front **2** : EAGER, READY **3** : BRASH, BOLD **4** : notably advanced or developed : PRECOCIOUS **5** : moving, tending, or leading toward a position in front **6** : EXTREME, RADICAL **7** : of, relating to, or getting ready for the future — **for·ward·ness** *n*

²**forward** *adv* : to or toward what is ahead or in front

³**forward** *vb* **1** : to help onward : ADVANCE **2** : to send forward : TRANSMIT **3** : to send or ship onward

⁴**forward** *n* : a player who plays at the front of a team's offensive formation near the opponent's goal

**for·ward·er** \-wər-dər\ *n* : one that forwards; *esp* : an agent who forwards goods

**for·wards** \'fȯr-wərdz\ *adv* : FORWARD

**forwent** *past of* FORGO

¹**fos·sil** \'fä-səl\ *adj* [L *fossilis* obtained by digging, fr. *fodere* to dig] **1** : preserved from a past geologic age ⟨∼ plants⟩ **2** : of or relating to fossil fuels

²**fossil** *n* **1** : a trace or impression or the remains of a plant or animal of a past geologic age preserved in the earth's

crust **2** : a person whose ideas are out-of-date — **fos·sil·ize** \'fä-sə-ˌlīz\ *vb*

**fossil fuel** *n* : a fuel (as coal or oil) that is formed in the earth from plant or animal remains

¹**fos·ter** \'fȯs-tər\ *adj* [ME, fr. OE *fōstor-*, fr. *fōstor* food, feeding] : affording, receiving, or sharing nourishment or parental care though not related by blood or legal ties ⟨~ parent⟩ ⟨~ child⟩

²**foster** *vb* **1** : to give parental care to : NURTURE **2** : to promote the growth or development of : ENCOURAGE

**foster home** *n* : a household in which an orphaned, neglected, or delinquent child is placed for care

**fos·ter·ling** \-tər-liŋ\ *n* : a foster child

**Fou·cault pendulum** \ˌfü-'kō-\ *n* : a device that consists of a heavy weight hung by a long wire and that swings in a constant direction which appears to change showing that the earth rotates

**fought** *past and past part of* FIGHT

¹**foul** \'fau̇(-ə)l\ *adj* **1** : offensive to the senses : LOATHSOME; *also* : clogged with dirt **2** : ODIOUS, DETESTABLE ⟨a ~ crime⟩ **3** : OBSCENE, ABUSIVE ⟨~ language⟩ **4** : DISAGREEABLE, STORMY ⟨~ weather⟩ **5** : TREACHEROUS, DISHONORABLE, UNFAIR ⟨by fair means or ~⟩ **6** : marking the bounds of a playing field ⟨~ lines⟩; *also* : being outside the foul line ⟨~ ball⟩ ⟨~ territory⟩ **7** : containing marked-up corrections **8** : ENTANGLED — **foul·ly** *adv* — **foul·ness** *n*

²**foul** *n* **1** : an entanglement or collision in fishing or sailing **2** : an infraction of the rules in a game or sport; *also* : a baseball hit outside the foul line

³**foul** *vb* **1** : to make or become foul or filthy **2** : to entangle or become entangled **3** : OBSTRUCT, BLOCK **4** : to collide with **5** : to make or hit a foul

⁴**foul** *adv* : in a foul manner

**fou·lard** \fu̇-'lärd\ *n* : a lightweight silk of plain or twill weave usu. decorated with a printed pattern

**foul·mouthed** \'fau̇(-ə)l-ˈmau̇t͟hd, -ˈmau̇tht\ *adj* : given to the use of obscene, profane, or abusive language

**foul of** *prep* : AFOUL OF

**foul play** *n* : VIOLENCE; *esp* : MURDER

**foul-up** \'fau̇(-ə)l-ˌəp\ *n* : a state of being fouled up **2** : a mechanical difficulty

**foul up** *vb* **1** : to spoil by mistakes or poor judgment **2** : to cause a foul-up : BUNGLE

¹**found** \'fau̇nd\ *past and past part of* FIND

²**found** *vb* [ME, fr. AF *funder, fonder*, fr. L *fundare*, fr. *fundus* bottom] **1** : to take the first steps in building **2** : to set or ground on something solid : BASE **3** : to establish (as an institution) often with provision for future maintenance — **found·er** *n*

**foun·da·tion** \fau̇n-'dā-shən\ *n* **1** : the act of founding **2** : a basis upon which something stands or is supported ⟨suspicions without ~⟩ **3** : funds given for the permanent support of an institution : ENDOWMENT; *also* : an institution so endowed **4** : supporting structure : BASE **5**

: CORSET — **foun·da·tion·al** \-shə-nəl\ *adj*

**foun·der** \'fau̇n-dər\ *vb* **1** : to make or become lame ⟨the horse ~ed⟩ **2** : COLLAPSE **3** : SINK ⟨a ~ing ship⟩ **4** : FAIL

**found·ling** \'fau̇nd-liŋ\ *n* : an infant found after its unknown parents have abandoned it

**found·ry** \'fau̇n-drē\ *n, pl* **foundries** : a building or works where metal is cast

**fount** \'fau̇nt\ *n* : SOURCE, FOUNTAIN

**foun·tain** \'fau̇n-tᵊn\ *n* **1** : a spring of water **2** : SOURCE **3** : an artificial jet of water **4** : a container for liquid that can be drawn off as needed

**foun·tain·head** \-ˌhed\ *n* : SOURCE

**fountain pen** *n* : a pen with a reservoir that feeds the writing point with ink

**four** \'fȯr\ *n* **1** : one more than three **2** : the 4th in a set or series **3** : something having four units — **four** *adj or pron*

**4x4** *also* **four-by-four** \'fȯr-bī-ˌfȯr\ *n* : a four-wheel automobile with four-wheel drive

**four-flush** \-ˌfləsh\ *vb* : to make a false claim : BLUFF — **four-flush·er** *n*

**four·fold** \-ˌfōld, -ˈfōld\ *adj* **1** : being four times as great or as many **2** : having four units or members — **four·fold** \-ˈfōld\ *adv*

**4-H** \'fȯr-'āch\ *adj* [fr. the fourfold aim of improving the head, heart, hands, and health] : of or relating to a program set up by the U.S. Department of Agriculture to help young people become productive citizens — **4-H'·er** *n*

**Four Hundred** *or* **400** *n* : the exclusive social set of a community — used with *the*

**four-in-hand** \'fȯr-ən-ˌhand\ *n* **1** : a team of four horses driven by one person; *also* : a vehicle drawn by such a team **2** : a necktie tied in a slipknot with long ends overlapping vertically in front

**four-o'clock** \'fȯr-ə-ˌkläk\ *n* : a garden plant with fragrant yellow, red, or white flowers without petals that open late in the afternoon

**four-post·er** \ˌfȯr-'pō-stər\ *n* : a bed with tall corner posts orig. designed to support curtains or a canopy

**four·score** \'fȯr-'skȯr\ *adj* : being four times twenty : EIGHTY

**four·some** \'fȯr-səm\ *n* **1** : a group of four persons or things **2** : a golf match between two pairs of partners

**four·square** \-'skwer\ *adj* **1** : SQUARE **2** : marked by boldness and conviction : FORTHRIGHT — **foursquare** *adv*

**four·teen** \fȯr-'tēn\ *n* : one more than 13 — **fourteen** *adj or pron* — **four·teenth** \-'tēnth\ *adj or n*

**fourth** \'fȯrth\ *n* **1** : one that is number four in a countable series **2** : one of four equal parts of something — **fourth** *adj or adv*

**fourth estate** *n, often cap F&E* : the public press

**fourth wall** *n* : an imaginary wall that keeps performers from recognizing or directly addressing their audience

**4WD** *abbr* four-wheel drive

**four–wheel** \\'fȯr-,hwēl\\ *or* **four–wheeled** \\-,hwēld\\ *adj* : acting on or by means of four wheels of a motor vehicle ⟨~ disc brakes⟩

**four-wheel drive** *n* : an automotive drive mechanism that acts on all four wheels of the vehicle; *also* : a vehicle with such a drive

¹**fowl** \\'fau̇(-ə)l\\ *n, pl* **fowl** *or* **fowls**  **1** : BIRD  **2** : a cock or hen of the domestic chicken; *also* : the flesh of these used as food

²**fowl** *vb* : to hunt wildfowl

¹**fox** \\'fäks\\ *n, pl* **fox·es** *also* **fox**  **1** : any of various flesh-eating mammals related to the wolves but smaller and with shorter legs and a more pointed muzzle; *also* : the fur of a fox  **2** : a clever crafty person  **3** *cap* : a member of an American Indian people formerly living in what is now Wisconsin

²**fox** *vb* : TRICK, OUTWIT

**fox·glove** \\'fäks-,gləv\\ *n* : a common plant related to the snapdragons that is grown for its showy spikes of dotted white or purple tubular flowers and as a source of digitalis

**fox·hole** \\-,hōl\\ *n* : a pit dug for protection against enemy fire

**fox·hound** \\-,hau̇nd\\ *n* : any of various large swift powerful hounds used in hunting foxes

**fox·ing** \\'fäk-siŋ\\ *n* : brownish spots on old paper

**fox terrier** *n* : a small lively terrier that occurs in varieties with smooth dense coats or with harsh wiry coats

**fox–trot** \\'fäks-,trät\\ *n*  **1** : a short broken slow trotting gait  **2** : a ballroom dance in duple time

**foxy** \\'fäk-sē\\ *adj* **fox·i·er; -est  1** : resembling or suggestive of a fox  **2** : WILY  **3** : physically attractive

**foy·er** \\'fȯi(-ə)r, 'fȯi-,yā\\ *n* [F, lit., fireplace, fr. OF *foier*, fr. VL *\*focarium*, fr. L *focus* hearth] : LOBBY; *also* : an entrance hallway

**fpm** *abbr* feet per minute

**FPO** *abbr* fleet post office

**fps** *abbr* feet per second

**fr  1** father  **2** franc  **3** friar  **4** from

¹**Fr** *abbr*  **1** France; French  **2** Friday

²**Fr** *symbol* francium

**fra·cas** \\'frā-kəs, 'fra-\\ *n, pl* **fra·cas·es** \\-kə-səz\\ [F, din, row, fr. It *fracasso*, fr. *fracassare* to shatter] : BRAWL

**frack·ing** \\'fra-kiŋ\\ *n* [by shortening & alter. fr. *(hydraulic) fracturing*] : the injection of fluid into shale beds so as to free up petroleum — **frack** \\'frak\\ *vb*

**frac·tal** \\'frak-t³l\\ *n* : an irregular curve or shape that repeats itself at any scale on which it is examined — **fractal** *adj*

**frac·tion** \\'frak-shən\\ *n*  **1** : a numerical representation (as $\frac{1}{2}$, $\frac{3}{4}$, or 3.323) indicating the quotient of two numbers  **2** : FRAGMENT  **3** : PORTION ⟨a small ~ of voters⟩ — **frac·tion·al** \\-shə-nəl\\ *adj* — **frac·tion·al·ly** *adv*

**frac·tious** \\'frak-shəs\\ *adj*  **1** : tending to be troublesome : hard to handle or control  **2** : QUARRELSOME, IRRITABLE

**frac·ture** \\'frak-chər\\ *n*  **1** : a breaking of something or a bone  **2** : CRACK, CLEFT — **fracture** *vb*

**frag·ile** \\'fra-jəl, -,jī(-ə)l\\ *adj* : easily broken : DELICATE — **fra·gil·i·ty** \\frə-'ji-lə-tē\\ *n*

¹**frag·ment** \\'frag-mənt\\ *n* : a part broken off, detached, or incomplete

²**frag·ment** \\-,ment\\ *vb* : to break into fragments — **frag·men·ta·tion** \\,frag-mən-'tā-shən, -,men-\\ *n*

**frag·men·tary** \\'frag-mən-,ter-ē\\ *adj* : made up of fragments : INCOMPLETE ⟨a ~ account⟩

**fra·grant** \\'frā-grənt\\ *adj* : sweet or agreeable in smell — **fra·grance** \\-grəns\\ *n* — **fra·grant·ly** *adv*

**frail** \\'frāl\\ *adj* [ME, fr. AF *fraile*, fr. L *fragilis* fragile, fr. *frangere* to break]  **1** : morally or physically weak  **2** : FRAGILE, DELICATE

**frail·ty** \\'frāl-tē\\ *n, pl* **frailties  1** : the quality or state of being frail  **2** : a fault due to weakness

¹**frame** \\'frām\\ *vb* **framed; fram·ing  1** : PLAN, CONTRIVE  **2** : SHAPE, CONSTRUCT  **3** : FORMULATE  **4** : DRAW UP ⟨~ a constitution⟩  **5** : to make appear guilty  **6** : to fit or adjust for a purpose : ARRANGE  **7** : to provide with or enclose in a frame — **fram·er** *n*

²**frame** *n*  **1** : something made of parts fitted and joined together  **2** : the physical makeup of the body  **3** : an arrangement of structural parts that gives form or support  **4** : a supporting or enclosing border or open case (as for a window or picture)  **5** : one picture of a series (as on a length of film)  **6** : FRAME-UP

³**frame** *adj* : having a wood frame ⟨~ houses⟩

**frame of mind** *n* : mental attitude or outlook : MOOD

**frame–up** \\'frā-,məp\\ *n*  **1** : an act or series of actions in which someone is framed  **2** : an action that is planned, contrived, or formulated

**frame·work** \\'frām-,wərk\\ *n* : a basic supporting part or structure

**franc** \\'fraŋk\\ *n*  **1** : any of various former basic monetary units (as of Belgium, France, and Luxembourg)  **2** — see MONEY table

**fran·chise** \\'fran-,chīz\\ *n* [ME, fr. AF, fr. *franchir* to free, fr. *franc* free]  **1** : a right or license granted to an individual or group ⟨a ~ to operate a ferry⟩  **2** : a constitutional or statutory right or privilege; *esp* : the right to vote  **3** : the right of membership in a professional sports league; *also* : a team having such membership

**fran·chi·see** \\,fran-,chī-'zē, -chə-\\ *n* : one granted a franchise

**fran·chis·er** \\'fran-,chī-zər\\ *n*  **1** : FRANCHISEE  **2** : FRANCHISOR

**fran·chi·sor** \\,fran-,chī-'zȯr, -chə-\\ *n* : one that grants a franchise

**fran·ci·um** \\'fran-sē-əm\\ *n* : a radioactive metallic chemical element

**Fran·co–Amer·i·can** \\,fraŋ-kō-ə-'mer-ə-kən\\ *n* : an American of French or esp.

French-Canadian descent — **Franco–American** adj

**fran·gi·ble** \'fran-jə-bəl\ adj : BREAK-ABLE — **fran·gi·bil·i·ty** \ˌfran-jə-'bi-lə-tē\ n

¹**frank** \'fraŋk\ adj : marked by free, forth-right, and sincere expression — **frank·ness** n

²**frank** vb : to mark (a piece of mail) with an official sign so that it can be mailed free; also : to mail free

³**frank** n 1 : the signature or mark on a piece of mail indicating free or paid post-age 2 : the privilege of sending mail free

⁴**frank** n : FRANKFURTER

**Fran·ken·stein** \'fraŋ-kən-ˌstīn\ n 1 : a monstrous creation that usu. ruins its originator 2 : a monster in the shape of a man

**frank·furt·er** \'fraŋ-fər-tər, -ˌfər-\ or **frank·furt** \-fərt\ n : a seasoned sausage (as of beef or beef and pork)

**frank·in·cense** \'fraŋ-kən-ˌsens\ n : a fra-grant resin burned as incense

**frank·ly** \'fraŋ-klē\ adv 1 : in a frank manner ⟨~ speaking⟩ 2 : in truth : INDEED ⟨~, I don't know⟩

**fran·tic** \'fran-tik\ adj : marked by un-controlled emotion or disordered anx-ious activity — **fran·ti·cal·ly** \-ti-k(ə-)lē\ adv

**frap·pé** \fra-'pā\ or **frappe** \same or 'frap\ n [F frappé, fr. pp. of frapper to strike, chill] 1 : an iced or frozen drink 2 : a thick milk shake — **frap·pé** \fra-'pā\ adj

**fra·ter·nal** \frə-'tər-n⁹l\ adj 1 : of, relat-ing to, or involving brothers 2 : of, relat-ing to, or being a fraternity or society 3 : derived from two ova ⟨~ twins⟩ 4 : FRIENDLY, BROTHERLY — **fra·ter·nal·ly** adv

**fra·ter·ni·ty** \frə-'tər-nə-tē\ n, pl **-ties** 1 : a social, honorary, or professional group; esp : a men's student organization 2 : BROTHERLINESS, BROTHERHOOD 3 : persons of the same class, profession, or tastes

**frat·er·nize** \'fra-tər-ˌnīz\ vb **-nized; -niz·ing** 1 : to mingle as friends 2 : to associ-ate on close terms with members of a hostile group — **frat·er·ni·za·tion** \ˌfra-tər-nə-'zā-shən\ n

**frat·ri·cide** \'fra-trə-ˌsīd\ n 1 : one that kills a sibling or countryman 2 : the act of a fratricide — **frat·ri·cid·al** \ˌfra-trə-'sī-d⁹l\ adj

**fraud** \'frȯd\ n 1 : DECEIT, TRICKERY 2 : TRICK 3 : IMPOSTOR, CHEAT

**fraud·ster** \'frȯd-stər\ n, chiefly Brit : a person who engages in fraud

**fraud·u·lent** \'frȯ-jə-lənt\ adj : character-ized by, based on, or done by fraud : DE-CEITFUL — **fraud·u·lence** \-ləns\ n — **fraud·u·lent·ly** adv

**fraught** \'frȯt\ adj : full of or accompa-nied by something specified ⟨~ with danger⟩

¹**fray** \'frā\ n : FIGHT, STRUGGLE; also : QUARREL, DISPUTE

²**fray** vb 1 : to wear (as an edge of cloth) by rubbing 2 : to separate the threads at the

edge of 3 : STRAIN, IRRITATE ⟨~ed nerves⟩

**fraz·zle** \'fra-zəl\ vb **fraz·zled; fraz·zling** 1 : FRAY 2 : to put in a state of extreme physical or nervous fatigue — **frazzle** n

¹**freak** \'frēk\ n 1 : WHIM, CAPRICE 2 : a strange, abnormal, or unusual person or thing 3 slang : a person who uses an il-licit drug 4 : an ardent enthusiast — **freak·ish** adj — **freaky** \'frē-kē\ adj

²**freak** vb 1 : to experience the effects (as hallucinations) of taking illicit drugs — often used with out 2 : to distress or be-come distressed — often used with out — **freak–out** \'frē-ˌkaút\ n

**freck·le** \'fre-kəl\ n : a small brownish spot on the skin — **freckle** vb

¹**free** \'frē\ adj **fre·er; fre·est** 1 : having liberty 2 : enjoying political or personal independence; also : not subject to or al-lowing slavery 3 : made or done volun-tarily : SPONTANEOUS 4 : relieved from or lacking something unpleasant 5 : not subject to a duty, tax, or charge 6 : not obstructed : CLEAR 7 : not being used or occupied ⟨waved with my ~ hand⟩ 8 : not fastened ⟨the ~ end of the rope⟩ 9 : LAVISH 10 : OPEN, FRANK ⟨a ~ ex-change of ideas⟩ 11 : given without charge 12 : not literal or exact ⟨~ trans-lation⟩ 13 : not restricted by conven-tional forms ⟨~ skating⟩ — **free·ly** adv

²**free** vb **freed; free·ing** 1 : to set free 2 : RELIEVE, RID 3 : DISENTANGLE, CLEAR
♦ **Synonyms** RELEASE, LIBERATE, DIS-CHARGE, EMANCIPATE, LOOSE

³**free** adv 1 : FREELY 2 : without charge

**free·base** \'frē-ˌbās\ n : purified cocaine smoked as crack or heated to produce vapors for inhalation — **freebase** vb

**free·bie** or **free·bee** \'frē-bē\ n : some-thing given without charge

**free·board** \'frē-ˌbȯrd\ n : the vertical distance between the waterline and the upper edge of the side of a boat

**free·boot·er** \-ˌbü-tər\ n [D vrijbuiter, fr. vrijbuit plunder, fr. vrij free + buit booty] : PLUNDERER, PIRATE

**free·born** \-'bȯrn\ adj 1 : not born in vas-salage or slavery 2 : of, relating to, or befitting one that is freeborn

**freed·man** \'frēd-mən, -ˌman\ n : a per-son freed from slavery

**free·dom** \'frē-dəm\ n 1 : the quality or state of being free : INDEPENDENCE 2 : EXEMPTION, RELEASE 3 : EASE, FACIL-ITY ⟨spoke the language with ~⟩ 4 : FRANKNESS 5 : unrestricted use 6 : a political right; also : FRANCHISE, PRIVI-LEGE

**freedom fighter** n : a person who takes part in a resistance movement against an oppressive political or social establish-ment

**free enterprise** n : freedom of private business to operate with little regulation by the government

**free–for–all** \'frē-fə-ˌrȯl\ n : a competi-tion or fight open to all comers and usu. with no rules : BRAWL — **free–for–all** adj

**free·hand** \-ˌhand\ adj : done without mechanical aids or devices ⟨∼ drawing⟩

**free·hold** \ˈfrē-ˌhōld\ n : ownership of an estate for life usu. with the right to bequeath it to one's heirs; also : an estate thus owned — **free·hold·er** n

**free·lance** \-ˌlans\ n : one who pursues a profession (as writing) without a long-term commitment to any one employer — **free·lance** adj or vb

**free–living** \ˈfrē-ˈli-vin\ adj 1 : unrestricted in pursuing personal pleasures 2 : being neither parasitic nor symbiotic ⟨∼ organisms⟩

**free·load** \ˈfrē-ˌlōd\ vb : to impose upon another's hospitality — **free·load·er** n

**free love** n 1 : the practice of living openly with one of the opposite sex without marriage 2 : sexual relations without any commitments by either partner

**free·man** \ˈfrē-mən, -ˌman\ n 1 : one who has civil or political liberty 2 : one having the full rights of a citizen

**Free·ma·son** \-ˌmā-sᵊn\ n : a member of a secret fraternal society called Free and Accepted Masons — **Free·ma·son·ry** \-rē\ n

**free radical** n : an esp. reactive atom or group of atoms with one or more unpaired electrons; esp : one that can cause bodily damage (as by altering the chemical structure of cells)

**free·range** \ˈfrē-ˌrānj\ adj : allowed to range and forage with relative freedom ⟨∼ chickens⟩; also : produced by free-range animals ⟨∼ eggs⟩

**free speech** n : speech that is protected by the First Amendment to the U.S. Constitution

**free spirit** n : NONCONFORMIST

**free·stand·ing** \ˈfrē-ˈstan-diŋ\ adj : standing alone or on its own foundation free of support

**free·stone** \ˈfrē-ˌstōn\ n 1 : a stone that may be cut freely without splitting 2 : a fruit stone to which the flesh does not cling; also : a fruit (as a peach or cherry) having such a stone

**free·think·er** \-ˈthiŋ-kər\ n : one who forms opinions on the basis of reason independently of authority; esp : one who doubts or denies religious dogma — **free·think·ing** n or adj

**free trade** n : trade between nations without restrictions (as high taxes on imports)

**free verse** n : verse whose meter is irregular or whose rhythm is not metrical

**free·ware** \ˈfrē-ˌwer\ n : software that is free or that has a small usu. optional cost

**free·way** \ˈfrē-ˌwā\ n : an expressway without tolls

**free·wheel** \-ˈhwēl\ vb : to move, live, or play freely or irresponsibly

**free·will** \ˈfrē-ˌwil\ adj : VOLUNTARY

**free will** n : voluntary choice or decision

¹**freeze** \ˈfrēz\ vb **froze** \ˈfrōz\; **fro·zen** \ˈfrō-zᵊn\; **freez·ing** 1 : to harden or cause to harden into a solid (as ice) by loss of heat 2 : to withstand freezing 3 : to chill or become chilled with cold 4 : to damage by frost 5 : to adhere solidly by or as if by freezing 6 : to become

fixed, motionless, or incapable of speech 7 : to cause to grip tightly 8 : to become clogged with ice 9 : to fix at a certain stage or level ⟨∼ wages⟩

²**freeze** n 1 : an act or instance of freezing 2 : the state of being frozen 3 : a state of weather marked by low temperature

**freeze–dry** \ˈfrēz-ˈdrī\ vb : to dry in a frozen state under vacuum esp. for preservation — **freeze–dried** adj

**freez·or** \ˈfrō-zər\ n : a compartment, device, or room for freezing food or keeping it frozen

¹**freight** \ˈfrāt\ n 1 : payment for carrying goods 2 : CARGO 3 : BURDEN 4 : the carrying of goods by a common carrier 5 : a train that carries freight

²**freight** vb 1 : to load with goods for transportation 2 : BURDEN CHARGE 3 : to ship or transport by freight

**freight·er** \ˈfrā-tər\ n : a ship or airplane used chiefly to carry freight

**French** \ˈfrench\ n 1 : the language of France 2 **French** pl : the people of France 3 : strong language ⟨pardon my ∼⟩ — **French** adj — **French·man** \-mən\ n — **French·wom·an** \-ˌwu̇-mən\ n

**French door** n : a door with small panes of glass extending the full length

**French dressing** n 1 : a thin salad dressing usu. made of vinegar and oil with spices 2 : a creamy salad dressing flavored with tomatoes

**french fry** n, often cap 1st F : a strip of potato fried in deep fat until brown — **french fry** vb, often cap 1st F

**French horn** n : a curved brass instrument with a funnel-shaped mouthpiece and a flaring bell

**French press** n : a coffeepot in which ground beans are infused and then pressed by a plunger

**French toast** n : bread dipped in a mixture of eggs and milk and fried at a low heat

**French twist** n : a woman's hairstyle in which the hair is coiled at the rear and secured in place

**fren·e·my** \ˈfre-nə-mē\ n, pl -mies : one who pretends to be a friend but is actually an enemy

**fre·net·ic** \fri-ˈne-tik\ adj : FRANTIC — **fre·net·i·cal·ly** \-ti-k(ə-)lē\ adv

**fren·zy** \ˈfren-zē\ n, pl **frenzies** 1 : temporary madness or a violently agitated state 2 : intense often disordered activity — **fren·zied** \-zēd\ adj

**freq** abbr frequency; frequent; frequently

**fre·quen·cy** \ˈfrē-kwən-sē\ n, pl -cies 1 : the fact or condition of occurring frequently 2 : rate of occurrence 3 : the number of cycles per second of an alternating current 4 : the number of waves (as of sound or electromagnetic energy) that pass a fixed point each second

**frequency modulation** n : variation of the frequency of a carrier wave according to another signal; also : FM

¹**fre·quent** \frē-ˈkwent, ˈfrē-kwənt\ vb : to associate with, be in, or resort to habitually — **fre·quent·er** n

²**fre·quent** \'frē-kwənt\ *adj* **1** : happening often or at short intervals ⟨making ∼ stops⟩ **2** : HABITUAL ⟨a ∼ visitor⟩ — **fre·quent·ly** *adv*

**fre·quent–fli·er** \'frē-kwənt-'flī-ər\ *adj* : of, relating to, or being an airline program offering awards for specified numbers of air miles traveled

**fres·co** \'fres-kō\ *n, pl* **frescoes** [It, fr. *fresco* fresh] : the art of painting on fresh plaster; *also* : a painting done by this method

**fresh** \'fresh\ *adj* **1** : VIGOROUS, RE-FRESHED **2** : not stale, sour, or decayed ⟨∼ bread⟩ **3** : not faded **4** : not worn or rumpled **5** : not altered by processing (as freezing or canning) **6** : not containing salt **7** : free from taint : PURE ⟨∼ air⟩ **8** : fairly strong : BRISK ⟨∼ breeze⟩ **9** : experienced, made, or received newly or anew **10** : ADDITIONAL, ANOTHER ⟨made a ∼ start⟩ **11** : ORIGINAL, VIVID ⟨a ∼ portrayal⟩ **12** : INEXPERIENCED **13** : newly come or arrived ⟨∼ from school⟩ **14** : IMPUDENT — **fresh·ly** *adv* — **fresh·ness** *n*

**fresh·en** \'fre-shən\ *vb* : to make, grow, or become fresh

**fresh·et** \'fre-shət\ *n* : an overflowing of a stream (as by heavy rains)

**fresh·man** \'fresh-mən\ *n* **1** : a 1st-year student **2** : BEGINNER, NEWCOMER

**fresh·wa·ter** \-,wȯ-tər, -,wä-\ *n* : water that is not salty — **freshwater** *adj*

¹**fret** \'fret\ *vb* **fret·ted**; **fret·ting** [ME, to devour, fret, fr. OE *fretan* to devour] **1** : WEAR, CORRODE; *also* : FRAY **2** : RUB, CHAFE **3** : to make by wearing away **4** : to become irritated : WORRY, VEX ⟨∼ ted over his taxes⟩ **5** : GRATE; *also* : AGITATE

²**fret** *n* : an irritated or worried state ⟨in a ∼ about the interview⟩

³**fret** *n* : ornamental work esp. of straight lines in symmetrical patterns

⁴**fret** *n* : one of a series of ridges across the fingerboard of a stringed musical instrument — **fret·ted** *adj*

**fret·ful** \'fret-fəl\ *adj* : IRRITABLE — **fret·ful·ly** *adv* — **fret·ful·ness** *n*

**fret·saw** \-,sȯ\ *n* : a narrow-bladed handsaw used for cutting curved outlines

**fret·work** \-,wərk\ *n* **1** : decoration consisting of frets **2** : ornamental openwork or work in relief

**Fri** *abbr* Friday

**fri·a·ble** \'frī-ə-bəl\ *adj* : easily crumbled or pulverized ⟨∼ soil⟩

**fri·ar** \'frī(-ə)r\ *n* [ME *frere, fryer*, fr. AF *frere, friere*, lit., brother, fr. L *frater*] : a member of a religious order that orig. lived by alms

**fri·ary** \'frī(-ə)r-ē\ *n, pl* **-ar·ies** : a monastery of friars

¹**fric·as·see** \'fri-kə-,sē, ,fri-kə-'sē\ *n* : a dish made of meat (as chicken) cut into pieces, stewed in stock, and served in sauce

²**fricassee** *vb* **-seed; -see·ing** : to cook as a fricassee

**fric·tion** \'frik-shən\ *n* **1** : the rubbing of one body against another **2** : the force that resists motion between bodies in contact **3** : clash in opinions between persons or groups : DISAGREEMENT — **fric·tion·al** *adj*

**friction tape** *n* : a usu. cloth adhesive tape impregnated with insulating material and used esp. to protect and insulate electrical conductors

**Fri·day** \'frī-dē, -(,)dā\ *n* : the sixth day of the week

**fridge** \'frij\ *n* : REFRIGERATOR

**fried·cake** \'frīd-,kāk\ *n* : DOUGHNUT, CRULLER

**fried rice** *n* : a dish of boiled or steamed rice that is stir-fried with soy sauce and typically includes egg, meat, and vegetables

**friend** \'frend\ *n* **1** : one attached to another by respect or affection **2** : AC-QUAINTANCE **3** : one who is not hostile **4** : one who supports or favors something ⟨a ∼ of art⟩ **5** *cap* : a member of the Society of Friends : QUAKER — **friend·less** *adj* — **friend·li·ness** \-lē-nəs\ *n* — **friend·ly** *adj* — **friend·ship** \-,ship\ *n*

**frieze** \'frēz\ *n* : an ornamental often sculptured band extending around something (as a building or room)

**frig·ate** \'fri-gət\ *n* **1** : a square-rigged warship **2** : a warship smaller than a destroyer

**fright** \'frīt\ *n* **1** : sudden terror : ALARM **2** : something that is ugly or shocking

**fright·en** \'frī-t⁰n\ *vb* **1** : to make afraid **2** : to drive away or out by frightening **3** : to become frightened — **fright·en·ing·ly** *adv*

**fright·ful** \'frīt-fəl\ *adj* **1** : TERRIFYING **2** : STARTLING **3** : EXTREME ⟨∼ thirst⟩ — **fright·ful·ly** *adv* — **fright·ful·ness** *n*

**frig·id** \'fri-jəd\ *adj* **1** : intensely cold **2** : lacking warmth or ardor : INDIFFERENT **3** : abnormally averse to or unable to achieve orgasm during sexual intercourse — used esp. of women — **fri·gid·i·ty** \fri-'ji-də-tē\ *n*

**frigid zone** *n* : the area or region between the arctic circle and the north pole or between the antarctic circle and the south pole

**frill** \'fril\ *n* **1** : a gathered, pleated, or ruffled edging **2** : something unessential — **frilly** *adj*

**fringe** \'frinj\ *n* [ME *frenge*, fr. AF, fr. VL *\*frimbia*, alter. of L *fimbriae* (pl.)] **1** : an ornamental border consisting of short threads or strips hanging from an edge or band **2** : something that resembles a fringe : EDGE ⟨operated on the ∼s of the law⟩ **3** : something that is additional or secondary to an activity, process, or subject — **fringe** *vb*

**fringe benefit** *n* **1** : an employment benefit paid for by an employer without affecting basic wage rates **2** : any additional benefit

**frip·pery** \'fri-pə-rē\ *n, pl* **-per·ies** [MF *friperie*] **1** : FINERY **2** : pretentious display

**frisk** \'frisk\ *vb* **1** : to leap, skip, or dance in a lively or playful way : GAMBOL **2** : to search (a person) esp. for concealed weapons by running the hand rapidly over the clothing

**frisky** \'fris-kē\ adj **frisk·i·er; -est** : PLAYFUL — **frisk·i·ly** \-kə-lē\ adv — **frisk·i·ness** \-kē-nəs\ n

¹**frit·ter** \'fri-tər\ n : a small lump of fried batter often containing fruit or meat

²**fritter** vb 1 : to reduce or waste piecemeal 2 : to break into small fragments

**fritz** \'frits\ n : a state of disorder or disrepair — used in the phrase *on the fritz*

**friv·o·lous** \'fri-və-ləs\ adj 1 : of little importance : TRIVIAL 2 : lacking in seriousness — **fri·vol·i·ty** \fri-'vä-lə-tē\ n — **friv·o·lous·ly** adv

**frizz** \'friz\ vb : to form into small tight curls — **frizz** n — **frizzy** adj

**friz·zies** \'fri-zēz\ n pl : hair which has become difficult to manage (as due to humidity)

¹**friz·zle** \'fri-zəl\ vb **friz·zled; friz·zling** : FRIZZ, CURL — **frizzle** n

²**frizzle** vb **friz·zled; friz·zling** 1 : to fry until crisp and curled 2 : to cook with a sizzling noise

**fro** \'frō\ adv : BACK, AWAY — used in the phrase *to and fro*

**frock** \'fräk\ n 1 : an outer garment worn by monks and friars 2 : an outer garment worn esp. by men 3 : a woman's or girl's dress

**frock coat** n : a man's knee-length usu. double-breasted coat

**frog** \'frog, 'fräg\ n 1 : any of various largely aquatic smooth-skinned tailless leaping amphibians 2 : an ornamental braiding for fastening the front of a garment by a loop through which a button passes 3 : a condition in the throat causing hoarseness 4 : a small holder (as of metal, glass, or plastic) with perforations or spikes that is placed in a bowl or vase to keep cut flowers in position

**frog·man** \'frog-,man, 'fräg-, -mən\ n : a swimmer equipped to work underwater for long periods of time

¹**frol·ic** \'frä-lik\ vb **frol·icked; frol·ick·ing** 1 : to make merry 2 : to play about happily : ROMP

²**frolic** n : a playful or mischievous action 2 : FUN, MERRIMENT — **frol·ic·some** \-səm\ adj

**from** \'frəm, 'främ\ prep 1 — used to show a starting point ⟨a letter ∼ home⟩ 2 — used to show removal or separation ⟨subtract 3 ∼ 9⟩ 3 — used to show a material, source, or cause ⟨suffering ∼ a cold⟩

**frond** \'fränd\ n : a usu. large divided leaf esp. of a fern or palm tree

¹**front** \'frənt\ n 1 : FOREHEAD; also : the whole face 2 : external and often feigned appearance 3 : a region of active fighting; also : a sphere of activity 4 : a political coalition 5 : the side of a building containing the main entrance 6 : the forward part or surface 7 : FRONTAGE 8 : a boundary between two dissimilar air masses 9 : a position directly before or ahead of something else 10 : a person, group, or thing used to mask the identity of the actual controlling agent

²**front** vb 1 : to have the principal side adjacent to something 2 : to serve as a front 3 : CONFRONT

**front·age** \'frən-tij\ n 1 : a piece of land lying adjacent (as to a street or the ocean) 2 : the length of a frontage 3 : the front side of a building

**front·al** \'frən-t°l\ adj 1 : of, relating to, or next to the forehead 2 : of, relating to, or directed at the front ⟨a ∼ attack⟩ — **fron·tal·ly** adv

**fron·tier** \,frən-'tir\ n 1 : a border between two countries 2 : a region that forms the margin of settled territory 3 : the outer limits of knowledge or achievement ⟨the ∼s of science⟩ — **fron·tiers·man** \-'tirz-mən\ n

**fron·tis·piece** \'frən-tə-,spēs\ n : an illustration preceding and usu. facing the title page of a book

**front man** n : a person serving as a front or figurehead

**front·ward** \'frənt-wərd\ or **front·wards** \-wərdz\ adv or adj : toward the front

¹**frost** \'frost\ n 1 : freezing temperature 2 : a covering of tiny ice crystals on a cold surface — **frosty** adj

²**frost** vb 1 : to cover with frost 2 : to put icing on (as a cake) 3 : to produce a slightly roughened surface on (as glass) 4 : to injure or kill by frost

¹**frost·bite** \'frost-,bīt\ vb **-bit** \-,bit\; **-bit·ten** \-,bi-t°n\; **-bit·ing** : to injure by frost or frostbite

²**frostbite** n : the freezing or the local effect of a partial freezing of some part of the body

**frost heave** n : an upthrust of pavement caused by freezing of moist soil

**frost·ing** \'fros-tiŋ\ n 1 : ICING 2 : dull finish on metal or glass

**froth** \'froth\ n, pl **froths** \'froths, 'frothz\ [ME, fr. ON *frotha*] 1 : bubbles formed in or on a liquid 2 : something light or worthless — **frothy** adj

**frou·frou** \'frü-,frü\ n [F] 1 : a rustling esp. of a woman's skirts 2 : showy or frilly ornamentation

**fro·ward** \'frō-wərd\ adj : DISOBEDIENT, WILLFUL

**frown** \'fraún\ vb 1 : to wrinkle the forehead (as in displeasure or thought) 2 : to look with disapproval 3 : to express with a frown — **frown** n

**frow·sy** or **frow·zy** \'fraú-zē\ adj **frow·si·er** or **frow·zi·er; -est** : having a slovenly or uncared-for appearance

**froze** past of FREEZE

**fro·zen** \'frō-z°n\ adj 1 : treated, affected, or crusted over by freezing 2 : subject to long and severe cold 3 : incapable of being changed, moved, or undone : FIXED ⟨∼ wages⟩ 4 : not available for present use ⟨∼ capital⟩ 5 : expressing or characterized by cold unfriendliness

**FRS** abbr Federal Reserve System

**frt** abbr freight

**fruc·ti·fy** \'frək-tə-,fī, 'frúk-\ vb **-fied; -fy·ing** 1 : to bear fruit 2 : to make fruitful or productive

**fruc·tose** \'frək-,tōs, 'frúk-\ n : a very

sweet soluble sugar that occurs esp. in fruit juices and honey

**fru·gal** \'frü-gəl\ adj : ECONOMICAL, THRIFTY — **fru·gal·i·ty** \frü-'ga-lə-tē\ n — **fru·gal·ly** adv

¹**fruit** \'früt\ n [ME, fr. AF frut, fruit, fr. L fructus fruit, use, fr. frui to enjoy, have the use of] **1** : a product of plant growth; esp : a usu. edible and sweet reproductive body (as a strawberry or apple) of a seed plant **2** : a product of fertilization in a plant; esp : the ripe ovary of a seed plant with its contents and appendages **3** : CONSEQUENCE, RESULT — **fruit·ed** \'frü-təd\ adj

²**fruit** vb : to bear or cause to bear fruit

**fruit·cake** \'früt-ˌkāk\ n : a rich cake containing nuts, dried or candied fruits, and spices

**fruit fly** n : any of various small dipteran flies whose larvae feed on fruit or decaying vegetable matter

**fruit·ful** \'früt-fəl\ adj **1** : yielding or producing fruit **2** : very productive; also : bringing results ⟨a ~ idea⟩ — **fruit·ful·ly** adv — **fruit·ful·ness** n

**fru·ition** \frü-'i-shən\ n **1** : ENJOYMENT **2** : the state of bearing fruit **3** : REALIZATION, ACCOMPLISHMENT ⟨guided the project to ~⟩

**fruit·less** \'früt-ləs\ adj **1** : not bearing fruit **2** : UNSUCCESSFUL ⟨a ~ attempt⟩ — **fruit·less·ly** adv

**fruity** \'frü-tē\ adj **fruit·i·er**; **-est** : resembling a fruit esp. in flavor

**frumpy** \'frəm-pē\ adj **frump·i·er**; **-est** : DOWDY, DRAB ⟨a ~ dress⟩

**frus·trate** \'frəs-ˌtrāt\ vb **frus·trat·ed**; **frus·trat·ing 1** : to balk or defeat in an endeavor **2** : to induce feelings of insecurity, discouragement, or dissatisfaction in **3** : to bring to nothing — **frus·trat·ing·ly** adv — **frus·tra·tion** \ˌfrəs-'trā-shən\ n

**frus·tum** \'frəs-təm\ n, pl **frustums** or **frus·ta** \-tə\ : the part of a cone or pyramid formed by cutting off the top by a plane parallel to the base

**frwy** abbr freeway

¹**fry** \'frī\ vb **fried**; **fry·ing** [ME frien, fr. AF frire, fr. L frigere to roast] **1** : to cook in a pan or on a griddle over heat esp. with the use of fat **2** : to undergo frying **3** : to damage or destroy by overheating esp. by high voltage

²**fry** n, pl **fries 1** : a social gathering where fried food is eaten **2** : a dish of something fried; esp, pl : FRENCH FRIES

³**fry** n, pl **fry** [ME, fr. AF frie, fr. freier, frier to rub, spawn, fr. L fricare to rub] **1** : recently hatched fishes; also : very small adult fishes **2** : members of a group or class ⟨small ~⟩

**fry·er** \'frī-(ə)r\ n **1** : something (as a young chicken) suitable for frying **2** : a deep utensil for frying foods

**FSLIC** abbr Federal Savings and Loan Insurance Corporation

**ft** abbr **1** feet; foot **2** fort

**FTC** abbr Federal Trade Commission

**FTP** \ˌef-ˌtē-'pē\ n [file transfer protocol] : a system for transferring computer files esp. via the Internet — **FTP** vb

**fuch·sia** \'fyü-shə\ n **1** : any of a genus of shrubs related to the evening primrose and grown for their showy nodding often red or purple flowers **2** : a vivid reddish purple color

**fud·dle** \'fə-dᵊl\ vb **fud·dled**; **fud·dling** : MUDDLE, CONFUSE

**fud·dy–dud·dy** \'fə-dē-ˌdə-dē\ n, pl **-dies** : one that is old-fashioned, unimaginative, or conservative

¹**fudge** \'fəj\ vb **fudged**; **fudg·ing 1** : to exceed the proper bounds of something **2** : CHEAT; also : FALSIFY ⟨fudged their data⟩ **3** : to fail to come to grips with

²**fudge** n **1** : NONSENSE **2** : a soft candy of milk, sugar, butter, and flavoring

¹**fu·el** \'fyü-əl, 'fyül\ n : a material used to produce heat or power by burning; also : a material from which nuclear energy can be liberated

²**fuel** vb **-eled** or **-elled**; **-el·ing** or **-el·ling** : to provide with or take in fuel

**fuel cell** n : a device that continuously changes the chemical energy of a fuel directly into electrical energy

**fuel injection** n : a system for injecting a precise amount of atomized fuel into an internal combustion engine — **fuel–in·ject·ed** \'fyül-in-ˌjek-təd\ adj

¹**fu·gi·tive** \'fyü-jə-tiv\ adj **1** : running away or trying to escape **2** : likely to vanish suddenly : not fixed or lasting

²**fugitive** n **1** : one who flees or tries to escape **2** : something elusive or hard to find

**fugue** \'fyüg\ n **1** : a musical composition in which different parts successively repeat the theme **2** : a disturbed state of consciousness characterized by acts that are not recalled upon recovery

**füh·rer** or **fueh·rer** \'fyúr-ər, 'fír-\ n [G] : LEADER; esp : TYRANT

¹**-ful** \fəl\ adj suffix, sometimes **-ful·er**; sometimes **-ful·lest 1** : full of ⟨prideful⟩ **2** : characterized by ⟨peaceful⟩ **3** : having the qualities of ⟨masterful⟩ **4** : tending, given, or liable to ⟨helpful⟩

²**-ful** \ˌfúl\ n suffix : number or quantity that fills or would fill ⟨roomful⟩

**ful·crum** \'fúl-krəm, 'fəl-\ n, pl **ful·crums** or **ful·cra** \-krə\ [LL, fr. L, bedpost] : the support on which a lever turns

**ful·fill** or **ful·fil** \fúl-'fil\ vb **ful·filled**; **ful·fill·ing 1** : to put into effect **2** : to bring to an end **3** : SATISFY ⟨~ed expectations⟩ — **ful·fill·ment** or **ful·fil·ment** n

¹**full** \'fúl\ adj **1** : FILLED **2** : complete esp. in detail, number, or duration **3** : having all the distinguishing characteristics ⟨a ~ member⟩ **4** : MAXIMUM ⟨~ strength⟩ **5** : rounded in outline ⟨a ~ figure⟩ **6** : possessing or containing an abundance ⟨~ of wrinkles⟩ **7** : having an abundance of material ⟨a ~ skirt⟩ **8** : satisfied esp. with food or drink **9** : having volume or depth of sound **10** : completely occupied with a thought or plan — **full·ness** also **ful·ness** n

²**full** adv **1** : VERY, EXTREMELY **2** : ENTIRELY ⟨fill a glass ~⟩ **3** : STRAIGHT, SQUARELY ⟨hit him ~ in the face⟩

³**full** n **1** : the highest or fullest state or

degree **2** : the utmost extent — **in full** : to the requisite or complete amount

**⁴full** vb : to shrink and thicken (woolen cloth) by moistening, heating, and pressing — **full·er** n

**full·back** \'fŭl-,bak\ n : a football back stationed between the halfbacks

**full–blood·ed** \'fŭl-'blə-dəd\ adj : of unmixed ancestry : PUREBRED

**full–blown** \-'blōn\ adj **1** : being at the height of bloom **2** : fully mature or developed

**full–bod·ied** \-'bä-dēd\ adj : marked by richness and fullness

**full dress** n : the style of dress worn for ceremonial or formal occasions

**full–fledged** \'fŭl-'flejd\ adj **1** : fully developed **2** : having attained complete status ⟨a ~ lawyer⟩

**full house** n : a poker hand containing three of a kind and a pair

**full moon** n : the moon with its whole disk illuminated

**full–on** \-,ȯn, -,än\ adj : COMPLETE, FULL-FLEDGED

**full–scale** \'fŭl-'skāl\ adj **1** : identical to an original in proportion and size ⟨~ drawing⟩ **2** : involving full use of available resources ⟨a ~ revolt⟩

**full–term** \-,tərm\ adj : retained in the uterus for the normal period of gestation before birth ⟨a ~ baby⟩

**full tilt** adv : at high speed

**full–time** \'fŭl-'tīm\ adj or adv : involving or working a normal or standard schedule

**ful·ly** \'fŭ-lē\ adv **1** : in a full manner or degree : COMPLETELY **2** : at least ⟨~ nine tenths of us⟩

**ful·mi·nate** \'fŭl-mə-,nat, 'fəl-\ vb **-nat·ed; -nat·ing** [ME, fr. ML *fulminatus*, pp. of *fulminare*, fr. L, to strike (of lightning), fr. *fulmen* lightning] : to utter or send out censure or invective : condemn severely ⟨*fulminated* against the tax increase⟩ — **ful·mi·na·tion** \,fŭl-mə-'nā-shən, ,fəl-\ n

**ful·some** \'fŭl-səm\ adj **1** : COPIOUS, ABUNDANT ⟨~ detail⟩ **2** : generous in amount or extent ⟨a ~ victory⟩ **3** : excessively flattering ⟨~ praise⟩

**fu·ma·role** \'fyü-mə-,rōl\ n : a hole in a volcanic region from which hot gases issue

**fum·ble** \'fəm-bəl\ vb **fum·bled; fum·bling 1** : to grope about clumsily **2** : to fail to hold, catch, or handle properly — **fumble** n

**¹fume** \'fyüm\ n : a usu. irritating smoke, vapor, or gas

**²fume** vb **fumed; fum·ing 1** : to treat with fumes **2** : to give off fumes **3** : to express anger or annoyance

**fu·mi·gant** \'fyü-mi-gənt\ n : a substance used for fumigation

**fu·mi·gate** \'fyü-mə-,gāt\ vb **-gat·ed; -gat·ing** : to treat with fumes to disinfect or destroy pests — **fu·mi·ga·tion** \,fyü-mə-'gā-shən\ n — **fu·mi·ga·tor** \'fyü-mə-,gā-tər\ n

**¹fun** \'fən\ n [E dial. *fun* to hoax] **1** : something that provides amusement or enjoyment **2** : ENJOYMENT

**²fun** adj : full of fun ⟨a ~ person⟩ ⟨had a ~ time⟩

**¹func·tion** \'fəŋk-shən\ n **1** : OCCUPATION **2** : special purpose **3** : the particular purpose for which a person or thing is specially fitted or used or for which a thing exists ⟨the ~ of a hammer⟩; *also* : the natural or proper action of a bodily part in a living thing ⟨the ~ of the heart⟩ **4** : a formal ceremony or social affair **5** : a mathematical relationship that assigns to each element of a set one and only one element of the same or another set **6** : a variable (as a quality, trait, or measurement) that depends on and varies with another ⟨height is a ~ of age in children⟩ **7** : a computer subroutine that performs a calculation with variables provided by a program — **func·tion·al** \-shə-nəl\ adj — **func·tion·al·ly** adv

**²function** vb : to have or carry on a function ⟨the computer ~s well⟩

**func·tion·ary** \'fəŋk-shə-,ner-ē\ n, pl **-ar·ies** : one who performs a certain function; *esp* : OFFICIAL

**function word** n : a word (as a preposition, auxiliary verb, or conjunction) expressing the grammatical relationship between other words

**¹fund** \'fənd\ n [L *fundus* bottom, country estate] **1** : a sum of money or resources intended for a special purpose **2** : STORE, SUPPLY **3** pl : available money **4** : an organization administering a special fund

**²fund** vb **1** : to provide funds for ⟨~ed cancer research⟩ **2** : to convert (a short-term obligation) into a long-term interest-bearing debt — **fund·er** n

**fun·da·men·tal** \,fən-də-'men-t⁽ᵊ⁾l\ adj **1** : serving as an origin : PRIMARY **2** : BASIC, ESSENTIAL **3** : RADICAL ⟨~ change⟩ **4** : of central importance : PRINCIPAL ⟨~ purpose⟩ — **fundamental** n — **fun·da·men·tal·ly** adv

**fun·da·men·tal·ism** \-tə-,li-zəm\ n **1** often cap : a Protestant religious movement emphasizing the literal infallibility of the Bible **2** : a movement or attitude stressing strict adherence to a set of basic principles — **fun·da·men·tal·ist** \-list\ adj or n

**¹fu·ner·al** \'fyü-nə-rəl\ adj **1** : of, relating to, or constituting a funeral **2** : FUNEREAL 2

**²funeral** n : the ceremonies held for a dead person usu. before burial

**fu·ner·ary** \'fyü-nə-,rer-ē\ adj : of, used for, or associated with burial ⟨~ rites⟩

**fu·ne·re·al** \fyü-'nir-ē-əl\ adj **1** : of or relating to a funeral **2** : suggesting a funeral ⟨a ~ mood⟩

**fun·gi·cide** \'fən-jə-,sīd, 'fən-gə-\ n : an agent that kills or checks the growth of fungi — **fun·gi·cid·al** \,fən-jə-'sī-d⁽ᵊ⁾l, ,fən-gə-\ adj

**fun·gus** \'fən-gəs\ n, pl **fun·gi** \'fən-jī, 'fən-,gī\ also **fun·gus·es** \'fən-gə-səz\ : any of a kingdom of parasitic spore-producing organisms (as molds, mildews, and mushrooms) formerly classified as plants — **fun·gal** \-gəl\ adj — **fun·gous** \-gəs\ adj

**fu·nic·u·lar** \fyù-'ni-kyə-lər, fə-\ *n* : a cable railway ascending a mountain

¹**funk** \'fəŋk\ *n* : a strong offensive smell

²**funk** *n* : a depressed state of mind

**funky** \'fəŋ-kē\ *adj* **funk·i·er; -est** 1 : having an earthy unsophisticated style and feeling; *esp* : having the style and feeling of older black American music 2 : odd or quaint in appearance or style ⟨a ~ little restaurant⟩ — **funk·i·ness** *n*

¹**fun·nel** \'fə-n°l\ *n* 1 : a cone-shaped utensil with a tube used for catching and directing a downward flow (as of liquid) 2 : FLUE, SMOKESTACK

²**funnel** *vb* **-neled** *also* **-nelled; -nel·ing** *also* **-nel·ling** 1 : to pass through or as if through a funnel 2 : to move to a central point or into a central channel

**fun·nies** \'fə-nēz\ *n pl* : a comic strip or a comic section (as of a newspaper) — used with *the*

**fun·ny** \'fə-nē\ *adj* **fun·ni·er; -est** 1 : AMUSING 2 : FACETIOUS 3 : PECULIAR 3 4 : UNDERHANDED — **funny** *adv*

**funny bone** *n* : a place at the back of the elbow where a blow easily compresses a nerve and causes a painful tingling sensation

**fun·plex** \'fən-ˌpleks\ *n* : a center containing various entertainment facilities

¹**fur** \'fər\ *n* 1 : an article of clothing made of or with fur 2 : the hairy coat of a mammal esp. when fine, soft, and thick; *also* : this coat dressed for use — **fur** *vb* — **furred** \'fərd\ *adj*

²**fur** *abbr* furlong

**fur·be·low** \'fər-bə-ˌlō\ *n* 1 : FLOUNCE, RUFFLE 2 : showy trimming

**fur·bish** \'fər-bish\ *vb* 1 : to make lustrous : POLISH 2 : to give a new look to : RENOVATE

**fu·ri·ous** \'fyúr-ē-əs\ *adj* 1 : FIERCE, ANGRY, VIOLENT 2 : BOISTEROUS 3 : INTENSE ⟨~ growth⟩ — **fu·ri·ous·ly** *adv*

**furl** \'fərl\ *vb* 1 : to wrap or roll (as a sail or a flag) close to or around something 2 : to curl in furls — **furl** *n*

**fur·long** \'fər-ˌlòŋ\ *n* [ME, fr. OE *furlang*, fr. *furh* furrow + *lang* long] : a unit of distance equal to 220 yards (about 201 meters)

**fur·lough** \'fər-lō\ *n* [D *verlof*, lit., permission] : a leave of absence from duty granted esp. to a soldier — **furlough** *vb*

**fur·nace** \'fər-nəs\ *n* : an enclosed structure in which heat is produced

**fur·nish** \'fər-nish\ *vb* 1 : to provide with what is needed : EQUIP 2 : SUPPLY, GIVE ⟨~ed them with food⟩

**fur·nish·ings** \-ni-shiŋz\ *n pl* 1 : articles or accessories of dress 2 : FURNITURE

**fur·ni·ture** \'fər-ni-chər\ *n* : equipment that is necessary or desirable; *esp* : movable articles (as chairs or beds) for a room

**fu·ror** \'fyúr-ˌòr\ *n* 1 : ANGER, RAGE 2 : a contagious excitement; *esp* : a fashionable craze 3 : UPROAR

**fu·rore** \-ˌòr\ *n* [It] : FUROR 2, 3

**fur·ri·er** \'fər-ē-ər\ *n* : one who prepares or deals in fur

**fur·ring** \'fər-iŋ\ *n* : wood or metal strips applied to a wall or ceiling to form a level surface or an air space

**fur·row** \'fər-ō\ *n* 1 : a trench in the earth made by a plow 2 : a narrow groove or wrinkle — **furrow** *vb*

**fur·ry** \'fər-ē\ *adj* **fur·ri·er; -est** 1 : resembling or consisting of fur 2 : covered with fur

¹**fur·ther** \'fər-thər\ *adv* 1 : FARTHER 1 2 : in addition : MOREOVER 3 : to a greater extent or degree

²**further** *vb* : to help forward — **fur·ther·ance** \'fər-thə-rəns\ *n*

³**further** *adj* 1 : FARTHER 1 2 : ADDITIONAL ⟨~ education⟩

**fur·ther·more** \'fər-thər-ˌmòr\ *adv* : in addition to what precedes : BESIDES

**fur·ther·most** \-ˌmōst\ *adj* : most distant : FARTHEST

**fur·thest** \'fər-thəst\ *adv or adj* : FARTHEST

**fur·tive** \'fər-tiv\ *adj* [F or L; F *furtif*, fr. L *furtivus*, fr. *furtum* theft, fr. *fur* thief] : done by stealth : SLY ⟨a ~ glance⟩ — **fur·tive·ly** *adv* — **fur·tive·ness** *n*

**fu·ry** \'fyúr-ē\ *n, pl* **furies** 1 : intense and often destructive rage 2 : extreme fierceness or violence 3 : FRENZY

**furze** \'fərz\ *n* : GORSE

¹**fuse** \'fyüz\ *vb* **fused; fus·ing** 1 : MELT 2 : to unite by or as if by melting together — **fus·ible** *adj*

²**fuse** *n* : an electrical safety device having a metal wire or strip that melts and interrupts the circuit when the current becomes too strong

³**fuse** *n* 1 : a cord or cable that is set afire to ignite an explosive charge 2 *usu* **fuze** : a mechanical or electrical device for setting off the explosive charge of a projectile, bomb, or torpedo

⁴**fuse** *also* **fuze** \'fyüz\ *vb* **fused** *also* **fuzed; fus·ing** *also* **fuz·ing** : to equip with a fuse

**fu·se·lage** \'fyü-sə-ˌläzh, -zə-\ *n* : the central body portion of an aircraft

**fu·sil·lade** \'fyü-sə-ˌläd, -ˌläd; ˌfyü-sə-ˈläd, -ˈläd\ *n* : a number of shots fired simultaneously or in rapid succession

**fu·sion** \'fyü-zhən\ *n* 1 : the act or process of melting or making plastic by heat 2 : union by or as if by melting 3 : the union of light atomic nuclei to form heavier nuclei with the release of huge quantities of energy

¹**fuss** \'fəs\ *n* 1 : needless bustle or excitement : COMMOTION 2 : effusive praise 3 : a state of agitation 4 : OBJECTION, PROTEST 5 : DISPUTE

²**fuss** *vb* : to make a fuss ⟨~ed over the baby⟩

**fuss·bud·get** \'fəs-ˌbə-jət\ *n* : one who fusses or is fussy about trifles

**fussy** \'fə-sē\ *adj* **fuss·i·er; -est** 1 : IRRITABLE 2 : overly decorative ⟨a ~ wallpaper pattern⟩ 3 : requiring or giving close attention or concern to details or niceties — **fuss·i·ly** \-sə-lē\ *adv* — **fuss·i·ness** \-sē-nəs\ *n*

**fus·tian** \'fəs-chən\ *n* 1 : a strong usu. cotton fabric 2 : pretentious writing or speech — **fustian** *adj*

**fus·ty** \'fəs-tē\ *adj* **fus·ti·er; -est** [prob. alter. of ME *fotsted, fotsi* musty, fr. *fotsi* wine cask, fr. AF *fust, fuist* wood, tree trunk, cask] **1** : MUSTY **2** : OLD-FASHIONED ⟨~ notions⟩

**fut** *abbr* future

**fu·tile** \'fyü-t[ə]l, 'fyü-,tī(-ə)l\ *adj* **1** : USELESS, VAIN **2** : FRIVOLOUS, TRIVIAL — **fu·tile·ly** *adv* — **fu·til·i·ty** \fyü-'ti-lə-tē\ *n*

**fu·ton** \'fü-,tän\ *n* [Jp] : a usu. cotton-filled mattress used on the floor or in a frame as a bed, couch, or chair

¹**fu·ture** \'fyü-chər\ *adj* **1** : of, relating to, or constituting a verb tense that expresses time yet to come **2** : coming after the present

²**future** *n* **1** : time that is to come **2** : what is going to happen **3** : an expectation of advancement or progressive development **4** : the future tense; *also* : a verb form in it

**fu·tur·ism** \'fyü-chə-,ri-zəm\ *n* : a modern movement in art, music, and literature that tries esp. to express the energy and activity of mechanical processes — **fu·tur·ist** \'fyü-chə-rist\ *n*

**fu·tur·is·tic** \,fyü-chə-'ris-tik\ *adj* : of or relating to the future or to futurism; *also* : very modern

**fu·tur·i·ty** \fyü-'tùr-ə-tē, -'tyùr-\ *n, pl* **-ties** **1** : FUTURE **2** : the quality or state of being future **3** *pl* : future events or prospects

**fuze** *var of* FUSE

**fuzz** \'fəz\ *n* : fine light particles or fibers (as of down or fluff)

**fuzzy** \'fə-zē\ *adj* **fuzz·i·er; -est** **1** : having or resembling fuzz **2** : INDISTINCT ⟨~ photos⟩ **3** : being or relating to pleasant usu. sentimental emotions ⟨~ feelings⟩ — **fuzz·i·ness** \-zē-nəs\ *n*

**fuzzy logic** *n* : a system of logic in which a statement can be true, false, or any of a continuum of values in between

**fwd** *abbr* forward

**FWD** *abbr* front-wheel drive

**FY** *abbr* fiscal year

**-fy** *vb suffix* : make : form into ⟨dandi*fy*⟩

**FYI** *abbr* for your information

¹**g** \'jē\ *n, pl* **g's** *or* **gs** \'jēz\ *often cap* **1** : the 7th letter of the English alphabet **2** : a unit of force equal to the force exerted by gravity on a body at rest and used to indicate the force to which a body is subjected when accelerated **3** *slang* : a sum of $1000

²**g** *abbr, often cap* **1** game **2** gauge **3** good **4** gram **5** gravity

**ga** *abbr* gauge

¹**Ga** *abbr* Georgia

²**Ga** *symbol* gallium

**GA** *abbr* **1** general assembly **2** general average **3** general of the army **4** Georgia

**gab** \'gab\ *vb* **gabbed; gab·bing** : to talk in a rapid or thoughtless manner — **gab** *n*

**gab·ar·dine** \'ga-bər-,dēn\ *n* **1** : GABERDINE 1 **2** : a firm durable twilled fabric having diagonal ribs and made of various fibers; *also* : a garment of gabardine

**gab·ble** \'ga-bəl\ *vb* **gab·bled; gab·bling** : JABBER, BABBLE

**gab·by** \'ga-bē\ *adj* **gab·bi·er; -est** : TALKATIVE, GARRULOUS

**gab·er·dine** \'ga-bər-,dēn\ *n* **1** : a long loose outer garment worn in medieval times and associated esp. with Jews **2** : GABARDINE 2

**gab·fest** \'gab-,fest\ *n* **1** : an informal gathering for general talk **2** : an extended conversation

**ga·ble** \'gā-bəl\ *n* : the vertical triangular end of a building formed by the sides of the roof sloping from the ridge down to the eaves — **ga·bled** \-bəld\ *adj*

**gad** \'gad\ *vb* **gad·ded; gad·ding** : to be constantly active without specific purpose — usu. used with *about* ⟨*gadded* about Europe for a year⟩ — **gad·der** *n*

**gad·about** \'ga-də-,baüt\ *n* : a person who flits about in social activity

**gad·fly** \'gad-,flī\ *n* **1** : a fly that bites or harasses livestock **2** : a person who annoys esp. by persistent criticism

**gad·get** \'ga-jət\ *n* : DEVICE, CONTRIVANCE — **gad·get·ry** \'ga-jə-trē\ *n*

**gad·o·lin·i·um** \,ga-də-'li-nē-əm\ *n* : a magnetic metallic chemical element

¹**Gael** \'gāl\ *n* : a Celtic inhabitant of Ireland or Scotland

²**Gael** *abbr* Gaelic

**Gael·ic** \'gā-lik\ *adj* : of or relating to the Gaels or their languages — **Gaelic** *n*

**gaff** \'gaf\ *n* **1** : a spear used in taking fish or turtles; *also* : a metal hook for holding or lifting heavy fish **2** : the spar supporting the top of a fore-and-aft sail **3** : rough treatment : ABUSE — **gaff** *vb*

**gaffe** \'gaf\ *n* : a usu. social blunder

**gaf·fer** \'ga-fər\ *n* **1** : an old man **2** : a lighting electrician on a motion-picture or television set

¹**gag** \'gag\ *vb* **gagged; gag·ging** **1** : to restrict use of the mouth of with a gag **2** : to prevent from speaking freely **3** : to retch or cause to retch **4** : OBSTRUCT, CHOKE **5** : BALK **6** : to make quips — **gag·ger** *n*

²**gag** *n* **1** : something thrust into the mouth esp. to prevent speech or outcry **2** : an official check or restraint on free speech **3** : a laugh-provoking remark or act **4** : PRANK, TRICK

¹**gage** \'gāj\ *n* **1** : a token of defiance; *esp* : a glove or cap cast on the ground as a pledge of combat **2** : SECURITY

²**gage** *var of* GAUGE

**gag·gle** \'ga-gəl\ *n* [ME *gagyll,* fr. *gagelen* to cackle] **1** : a flock of geese **2** : an unorganized group

**gai·ety** *also* **gay·ety** \'gā-ə-tē\ *n, pl* **-eties** **1** : festive activity : MERRYMAKING **2** : MERRIMENT **3** : FINERY ♦ **Synonyms** MIRTH, FESTIVITY, GLEE, HILARITY, JOLLITY

**gai·ly** *also* **gay·ly** \'gā-lē\ *adv* : in a gay manner ⟨chatting ∼⟩

¹**gain** \'gān\ *n* **1** : PROFIT **2** : ACQUISITION, ACCUMULATION **3** : INCREASE

²**gain** *vb* **1** : to get possession of : EARN **2** : WIN ⟨∼ a victory⟩ **3** : to increase in ⟨∼ momentum⟩ **4** : PERSUADE **5** : to arrive at **6** : ACHIEVE ⟨∼ strength⟩ **7** : to run fast ⟨the watch ∼s a minute a day⟩ **8** : PROFIT **9** : INCREASE **10** : to improve in health ♦ **Synonyms** ACCOMPLISH, ATTAIN, REALIZE — **gain·er** *n*

**gain·ful** \'gān-fəl\ *adj* : PROFITABLE ⟨∼ employment⟩ — **gain·ful·ly** *adv*

**gain·say** \gān-'sā\ *vb* **-said** \-'sād, -'sed\; **-say·ing; -says** \-'sāz, -'sez\ [ME *gainsayen,* fr. *gain-* against + *sayen* to say] **1** : DENY, DISPUTE **2** : to speak against ♦ **Synonyms** CONTRADICT, CONTRAVENE, IMPUGN, NEGATE — **gain·say·er** *n*

**gait** \'gāt\ *n* : manner of moving on foot; *also* : a particular pattern or style of such moving — **gait·ed** *adj*

**gai·ter** \'gā-tər\ *n* **1** : a leg covering reaching from the instep to ankle, midcalf, or knee **2** : an overshoe with a fabric upper **3** : an ankle-high shoe with elastic gores in the sides

¹**gal** \'gal\ *n* : GIRL

²**gal** *abbr* gallon

**Gal** *abbr* Galatians

**ga·la** \'gā-lə, 'ga-, 'gä-\ *n* : a festive celebration : FESTIVITY — **gala** *adj*

**ga·lac·tic** \gə-'lak-tik\ *adj* : of or relating to a galaxy

**Ga·la·tians** \gə-'lā-shənz\ *n* — see BIBLE table

**gal·axy** \'ga-lək-sē\ *n, pl* **-ax·ies** [ME *galaxie, galaxias,* fr. LL *galaxias,* fr. Gk, fr. *galakt-, gala* milk] **1** *often cap* : MILKY WAY GALAXY — used with *the* **2** : a very large group of stars **3** : an assemblage of brilliant or famous persons or things

**gale** \'gāl\ *n* **1** : a strong wind **2** : an emotional outburst ⟨∼s of laughter⟩

**ga·le·na** \gə-'lē-nə\ *n* : a lustrous bluish gray mineral that consists of the sulfide of lead and is the chief ore of lead

¹**gall** \'gȯl\ *n* **1** : BILE **2** : something bitter to endure **3** : RANCOR **4** : IMPUDENCE ♦ **Synonyms** EFFRONTERY, BRASS, CHEEK, CHUTZPAH, AUDACITY, PRESUMPTION

²**gall** *n* : a skin sore caused by chafing

³**gall** *vb* **1** : CHAFE; *esp* : to become sore or worn by rubbing **2** : VEX, HARASS

⁴**gall** *n* : an abnormal outgrowth of plant tissue usu. due to parasites

¹**gal·lant** \gə-'lant, -'länt; 'ga-lənt\ *n* **1** : a young man of fashion **2** : a man who

shows a marked fondness for the company of women and who is esp. attentive to them : SUITOR

²**gal·lant** \'ga-lənt *(usual for 2, 3, 4)*; gə-'lant, -'länt *(usual for 5)*\ *adj* **1** : showy in dress or bearing : SMART **2** : SPLENDID, STATELY **3** : SPIRITED, BRAVE **4** : CHIVALROUS, NOBLE **5** : polite and attentive to women — **gal·lant·ly** *adv*

**gal·lant·ry** \'ga-lən-trē\ *n, pl* **-ries** **1** *archaic* : gallant appearance **2** : an act of marked courtesy **3** : courteous attention to a woman **4** : conspicuous bravery ♦ **Synonyms** HEROISM, VALOR, PROWESS

**gall·blad·der** \'gȯl-,bla-dər\ *n* : a membranous muscular sac attached to the liver and serving to store bile

**gal·le·on** \'ga-lē-ən\ *n* : a large square-rigged sailing ship formerly used esp. by the Spanish

**gal·le·ria** \,ga-lə-'rē-ə\ *n* [It] : a roofed and usu. glass-enclosed promenade or court

**gal·lery** \'ga-lə-rē\ *n, pl* **-ler·ies** **1** : an outdoor balcony; *also* : PORCH, VERANDA **2** : a long narrow passage, apartment, or hall **3** : a narrow passage (as one made underground by a miner or through wood by an insect) **4** : a room where works of art are exhibited; *also* : an organization dealing in works of art **5** : a balcony in a theater, auditorium, or church; *esp* : the highest one in a theater **6** : the spectators at a sporting event (as a tennis or golf match) **7** : a photographer's studio — **gal·ler·ied** \-rēd\ *adj*

**gal·ley** \'ga-lē\ *n, pl* **galleys** **1** : a long low ship propelled esp. by oars and formerly used esp. in the Mediterranean Sea **2** : the kitchen esp. of a ship or airplane **3** : a proof of typeset matter esp. in a single column

**Gal·lic** \'ga-lik\ *adj* : of or relating to Gaul or France

**gal·li·mau·fry** \,ga-lə-'mȯ-frē\ *n, pl* **-fries** [MF *galimafree* stew] : HODGEPODGE

**gal·li·nule** \'ga-lə-,nül, -,nyül\ *n* : any of several aquatic birds related to the rails

**gal·li·um** \'ga-lē-əm\ *n* : a bluish-white metallic chemical element used esp. in semiconductors

**gal·li·vant** \'ga-lə-,vant\ *vb* : to travel, roam, or move about for pleasure

**gal·lon** \'ga-lən\ *n* — see WEIGHT table

¹**gal·lop** \'ga-ləp\ *vb* **1** : to go or cause to go at a gallop **2** : to run fast — **gal·lop·er** *n*

²**gallop** *n* **1** : a bounding gait of a quadruped; *esp* : a fast 3-beat gait of a horse **2** : a ride or run at a gallop

**gal·lows** \'ga-lōz\ *n, pl* **gallows** *or* **gallows·es** : a frame usu. of two upright posts and a crosspiece from which criminals are hanged; *also* : the punishment of hanging

**gall·stone** \'gȯl-,stōn\ *n* : an abnormal concretion occurring in the gallbladder or bile passages

**gal·lus·es** \'ga-lə-səz\ *n pl* : SUSPENDERS

**ga·lore** \gə-ˈlȯr\ adj [Ir go leor enough] : ABUNDANT, PLENTIFUL

**ga·losh** \gə-ˈläsh\ n : a high overshoe

**galv** abbr galvanized

**gal·va·nise** Brit var of GALVANIZE

**gal·va·nize** \ˈgal-və-ˌnīz\ vb **-nized; -niz·ing** **1** : to stimulate as if by an electric shock ⟨~ public opinion⟩ **2** : to coat (iron or steel) with zinc — **gal·va·ni·za·tion** \ˌgal-və-nə-ˈzā-shən\ n — **gal·va·niz·er** n

**gal·va·nom·e·ter** \ˌgal-və-ˈnä-mə-tər\ n : an instrument for detecting or measuring a small electric current

**gam·bit** \ˈgam-bət\ n [It gambetto, lit., act of tripping someone, fr. gamba leg] **1** : a chess opening in which a player risks one or more minor pieces to gain an advantage in position **2** : a calculated move : STRATAGEM ♦ Synonyms TRICK, ARTIFICE, GIMMICK, MANEUVER, PLAY, RUSE

**¹gam·ble** \ˈgam-bəl\ vb **gam·bled; gam·bling** **1** : to play a game for money or property **2** : BET, WAGER **3** : VENTURE, HAZARD — **gam·bler** n

**²gamble** n : a risky undertaking

**gam·bol** \ˈgam-bəl\ vb **-boled or -bolled; -bol·ing or -bol·ling** : to skip about in play : FRISK — **gambol** n

**gam·brel roof** \ˈgam-brəl-\ n : a roof with a lower steeper slope and an upper flatter one on each side

**¹game** \ˈgām\ n **1** : AMUSEMENT, DIVERSION **2** : SPORT, FUN ⟨made ~ of the strange boy⟩ **3** : SCHEME, PROJECT **4** : a line of work : PROFESSION **5** : CONTEST **6** : animals hunted for sport or food; also : the flesh of a game animal

**²game** vb **gamed; gam·ing 1** : to play for a stake **2** : to take dishonest advantage of ⟨~ the tax system⟩

**³game** adj : PLUCKY, RESOLUTE — **game·ly** adv — **game·ness** n

**⁴game** adj : LAME ⟨a ~ leg⟩

**game·cock** \ˈgām-ˌkäk\ n : a rooster trained for fighting

**game fish** n : SPORT FISH

**game·keep·er** \ˈgām-ˌkē-pər\ n : a person in charge of the breeding and protection of game animals or birds on a private preserve

**game show** n : a television program on which contestants compete usu. for prizes in a game

**game·some** \ˈgām-səm\ adj : MERRY ♦ Synonyms PLAYFUL, FROLICSOME, SPORTIVE, ANTIC

**game·ster** \ˈgām-stər\ n : GAMBLER

**gam·ete** \ˈga-ˌmēt\ n : a mature germ cell — **ga·met·ic** \gə-ˈme-tik\ adj

**game theory** n : the analysis of a situation involving conflicting interests (as in business) in terms of gains and losses among opposing players

**gam·in** \ˈga-mən\ n [F] **1** : a boy who hangs around on the streets **2** : GAMINE 2

**ga·mine** \ga-ˈmēn\ n **1** : a girl who hangs around on the streets **2** : a small playfully mischievous girl

**gam·ma** \ˈga-mə\ n : the 3d letter of the Greek alphabet — Γ or γ

**gamma globulin** n : a blood protein fraction rich in antibodies; also : a solution of this from human blood donors that is given to provide immunity against some infectious diseases (as measles)

**gamma ray** n : a photon emitted by a radioactive substance; also : a photon of higher energy than that of an X-ray — usu. used in pl.

**gam·mon** \ˈga-mən\ n, chiefly Brit : a cured ham or side of bacon

**gam·ut** \ˈga-mət\ n : an entire range or series ♦ Synonyms SCALE, SPECTRUM

**gamy** or **gam·ey** \ˈgā-mē\ adj **gam·i·er; -est 1** : GAME, PLUCKY **2** : having the flavor of game esp. when near tainting ⟨~ meat⟩ **3** : SCANDALOUS, also : DISREPUTABLE — **gam·i·ness** \-mē-nəs\ n

**¹gan·der** \ˈgan-dər\ n : a male goose

**²gander** n : LOOK, GLANCE

**¹gang** \ˈgaŋ\ n **1** : a set of implements or devices arranged to operate together **2** : a group of persons working or associated together; esp : a group of criminals or young delinquents

**²gang** vb **1** : to attack in a gang — usu. used with up **2** : to form into or move or act as a gang

**gang·land** \ˈgaŋ-ˌland\ n : the world of organized crime

**gan·gling** \ˈgaŋ-gliŋ\ adj : loosely and awkwardly built : LANKY

**gan·gli·on** \ˈgaŋ-glē-ən\ n, pl **-glia** \-ə\ also **-gli·ons** : a mass of nerve tissue containing cell bodies of neurons outside the central nervous system; also : NUCLEUS 3 — **gan·gli·on·ic** \ˌgaŋ-glē-ˈä-nik\ adj

**gan·gly** \ˈgaŋ-glē\ adj : GANGLING

**gang·plank** \ˈgaŋ-ˌplaŋk\ n : a movable bridge from a ship to the shore

**gang·plow** \-ˌplau̇\ n : a plow that turns two or more furrows at one time

**gan·grene** \ˈgaŋ-ˌgrēn, gaŋ-ˈgrēn\ n : the death of soft tissues in a local area of the body due to loss of the blood supply — **gangrene** vb — **gan·gre·nous** \ˈgaŋ-grə-nəs\ adj

**gang·sta** \ˈgaŋ-stə\ n : a member of an urban street gang

**gangsta rap** n : rap music with usu. hostile lyrics portraying urban gang life

**gang·ster** \ˈgaŋ-stər\ n : a member of a gang of criminals : RACKETEER

**gang·way** \ˈgaŋ-ˌwā\ n **1** : PASSAGEWAY; also : GANGPLANK **2** : clear passage through a crowd

**gan·net** \ˈga-nət\ n, pl **gannets** also **gannet** : any of several large fish-eating usu. white and black seabirds that breed chiefly on offshore islands

**gantlet** var of GAUNTLET

**gan·try** \ˈgan-trē\ n, pl **gantries** : a frame structure on side supports over or around something

**GAO** abbr General Accounting Office

**gaol** \ˈjāl\, **gaol·er** \ˈjā-lər\ chiefly Brit var of JAIL, JAILER

**gap** \ˈgap\ n **1** : BREACH, CLEFT **2** : a

mountain pass **3** : a blank space; *also* : an incomplete or deficient area **4** : a wide difference in character or attitude **5** : a problem caused by a disparity ⟨credibility ∼⟩

**gape** \'gāp\ *vb* **gaped; gap·ing 1** : to open the mouth wide **2** : to open or part widely **3** : to stare with mouth open **4** : YAWN — **gape** *n*

¹**gar** \'gär\ *n* : any of several fishes that have a long body resembling that of a pike and long narrow jaws

²**gar** *abbr* garage

**GAR** *abbr* Grand Army of the Republic

¹**ga·rage** \gə-'räzh, -'räj\ *n* [F, act of docking, garage, fr. *garer* to dock, fr. MF *garrer*, prob. ultim. fr. ON *vara* to beware, take care] : a shelter or repair shop for automobiles

²**garage** *vb* **ga·raged; ga·rag·ing** : to keep or put in a garage

**garage sale** *n* : a sale of used household or personal articles held on the seller's own premises

**garb** \'gärb\ *n* **1** : style of dress **2** : outward form : APPEARANCE — **garb** *vb*

**gar·bage** \'gär-bij\ *n* **1** : food waste **2** : unwanted or useless material

**gar·bage·man** \-ˌman\ *n* : a person who collects and removes garbage

**gar·ble** \'gär-bəl\ *vb* **gar·bled; gar·bling** : to distort the meaning of ⟨∼ a story⟩

**gar·çon** \gär-'sōⁿ, *n, pl* **garçons** \*same or* gär-'sōⁿz\ [F, boy, servant] : WAITER

¹**gar·den** \'gär-dᵊn\ *n* **1** : a plot for growing fruits, flowers, or vegetables **2** : a public recreation area; *esp* : one for displaying plants or animals

²**garden** *vb* : to lay out or work in a garden — **gar·den·er** *n*

**gar·de·nia** \gär-'dē-nyə\ *n* [NL, genus name, fr. Alexander *Garden* †1791 Scot. naturalist] : any of a genus of tropical trees or shrubs that are related to the madder and have fragrant white or yellow flowers

**garden–variety** *adj* : COMMONPLACE, ORDINARY ⟨∼ police dramas⟩

**gar·fish** \'gär-ˌfish\ *n* : GAR

**gar·gan·tuan** \gär-'gan-chə-wən\ *adj, often cap* : tremendous in size, volume, or degree ⟨∼ waterfalls⟩ ♦ **Synonyms** HUGE, COLOSSAL, GIGANTIC, MAMMOTH, MONSTROUS, TITANIC

**gar·gle** \'gär-gəl\ *vb* **gar·gled; gar·gling** : to rinse the throat with liquid agitated by air forced through it from the lungs — **gargle** *n*

**gar·goyle** \'gär-ˌgȯi(-ə)l\ *n* **1** : a waterspout in the form of a grotesque human or animal figure projecting from the roof or eaves of a building **2** : a grotesquely carved figure

**gar·ish** \'ger-ish\ *adj* : FLASHY, GLARING, SHOWY, GAUDY ⟨a ∼ wardrobe⟩

¹**gar·land** \'gär-lənd\ *n* : WREATH, CHAPLET

²**garland** *vb* : to form into or deck with a garland

**gar·lic** \'gär-lik\ *n* [ME *garlek*, fr. OE *gārlēac*, fr. *gār* spear + *lēac* leek] : an herb related to the lilies and grown for its pun-

gent bulbs used in cooking; *also* : its bulb — **gar·licky** \-li-kē\ *adj*

**gar·ment** \'gär-mənt\ *n* : an article of clothing

**gar·ner** \'gär-nər\ *vb* **1** : to gather into storage **2** : to acquire by effort ⟨∼ evidence⟩ **3** : ACCUMULATE, COLLECT

**gar·net** \'gär-nət\ *n* [ME *gernet*, fr. AF *gernete*, fr. *gernet* dark red, fr. *pume gernete* pomegranate] : a transparent deep red mineral sometimes used as a gem

**gar·nish** \'gär-nish\ *vb* **1** : DECORATE, EMBELLISH **2** : to add decorative or savory touches to (food) **3** : GARNISHEE — **garnish** *n*

**gar·nish·ee** \ˌgär-nə-'shē\ *vb* **-eed; -ee·ing 1** : to serve with a garnishment **2** : to take (as a debtor's wages) by legal authority

**gar·nish·ment** \'gär-nish-mənt\ *n* **1** : GARNISH **2** : a legal warning concerning the attachment of property to satisfy a debt; *also* : the attachment of such property

**gar·ni·ture** \-ni-chər, -ˌchúr\ *n* : EMBELLISHMENT, TRIMMING

**gar·ret** \'ger-ət\ *n* : the part of a house just under the roof : ATTIC

**gar·ri·son** \'ger-ə-sən\ *n* [ME *garisoun* protection, fr. AF *garisun* healing, protection, fr. *garir* to heal, protect, of Gmc origin] **1** : a military post; *esp* : a permanent military installation **2** : the troops stationed at a garrison — **garrison** *vb*

**garrison state** *n* : a state organized on a primarily military basis

**gar·rote** *or* **ga·rotte** \gə-'rät, -'rōt\ *n* [Sp *garrote*] **1** : a method of execution by strangulation; *also* : the apparatus used **2** : an implement (as a wire with handles) for strangulation — **garrote** *or* **garotte** *vb*

**gar·ru·lous** \'ger-ə-ləs\ *adj* : TALKATIVE, WORDY — **gar·ru·li·ty** \gə-'rü-lə-tē\ *n* — **gar·ru·lous·ly** *adv* — **gar·ru·lous·ness** *n*

**gar·ter** \'gär-tər\ *n* : a band or strap worn to hold up a stocking or sock

**garter snake** *n* : any of a genus of harmless American snakes with longitudinal stripes on the back

¹**gas** \'gas\ *n, pl* **gas·es** *also* **gas·ses** [NL, alter. of L *chaos* space, chaos] **1** : a fluid (as hydrogen or air) that tends to expand indefinitely **2** : a gas or mixture of gases used as a fuel or anesthetic **3** : a substance that can be used to produce a poisonous, asphyxiating, or irritant atmosphere **4** : GASOLINE — **gas·eous** \'ga-sē-əs, -shəs\ *adj*

²**gas** *vb* **gassed; gas·sing 1** : to treat with gas; *also* : to poison with gas **2** : to fill with gasoline ⟨∼ up the car⟩

**gash** \'gash\ *n* : a deep long cut — **gash** *vb*

**gas·ket** \'gas-kət\ *n* : material (as rubber) or a part used to seal a joint

**gas·light** \'gas-ˌlīt\ *n* **1** : light made by burning illuminating gas **2** : a gas flame; *also* : a gas lighting fixture

**gas mask** *n* : a mask with a chemical air

filter used to protect the face and lungs against poison gas

**gas·o·line** \'ga-sə-ˌlēn, ˌga-sə-'lēn\ *n* : a flammable liquid mixture made from petroleum and used esp. as a motor fuel

**gasp** \'gasp\ *vb* **1** : to catch the breath audibly (as with shock) **2** : to breathe laboriously : PANT **3** : to utter in a gasping manner — **gasp** *n*

**gas station** *n* : a retail station for servicing and fueling motor vehicles

**gas·tric** \'gas-trik\ *adj* : of or relating to the stomach

**gastric juice** *n* : the acid digestive secretion of the stomach

**gas·tri·tis** \gas-'trī-təs\ *n* : inflammation of the lining of the stomach

**gas·tro·en·ter·i·tis** \ˌgas-trō-ˌen-tə-'rī-təs\ *n* : inflammation of the lining membrane of the stomach and intestines

**gas·tro·en·ter·ol·o·gy** \ˌgas-trō-ˌen-tə-'rä-lə-jē\ *n* : a branch of medicine concerned with the structure, functions, and diseases of the stomach and intestines — **gas·tro·en·ter·ol·o·gist** \-jist\ *n*

**gas·tro·in·tes·ti·nal** \ˌgas-trō-in-'tes-tə-nᵊl\ *adj* : of, relating to, affecting, or including both the stomach and intestine ⟨~ tract⟩ ⟨~ distress⟩

**gas·tron·o·my** \gas-'trä-nə-mē\ *n* [F *gastronomie*, fr. Gk *Gastronomia*, title of a 4th cent. B.C. poem, fr. *gastēr* belly + *-nomia* system of laws] : the art of good eating — **gas·tro·nom·ic** \ˌgas-trə-'nä-mik\ *also* **gas·tro·nom·i·cal** \-mi-kəl\ *adj* — **gas·tro·nom·i·cal·ly** \-k(ə-)lē\ *adv*

**gas·tro·pod** \'gas-trə-ˌpäd\ *n* : any of a large class of mollusks (as snails and slugs) with a muscular foot and a spiral shell or none — **gastropod** *adi*

**gas·works** \'gas-ˌwərks\ *n sing or pl* : a plant for manufacturing gas

**gate** \'gāt\ *n* **1** : an opening for passage in a wall or fence **2** : a city or castle entrance often with defensive structures **3** : the frame or door that closes a gate **4** : a device (as a valve) for controlling the passage of a fluid or signal **5** : the total admission receipts or the number of people at an event

**-gate** \ˌgāt\ *n comb form* [Water*gate*, scandal that resulted in the resignation of President Richard Nixon in 1974] : usu. political scandal often involving the concealment of wrongdoing

**gate–crash·er** \'gāt-ˌkra-shər\ *n* : a person who enters without paying admission or attends without invitation

**gate·keep·er** \-ˌkē-pər\ *n* : a person who tends or guards a gate

**gate·post** \-ˌpōst\ *n* : the post to which a gate is hung or the one against which it closes

**gate·way** \-ˌwā\ *n* **1** : an opening for a gate **2** : a means of entrance or exit

¹**gath·er** \'ga-thər\ *vb* **1** : to bring together : COLLECT **2** : PICK, HARVEST **3** : to pick up little by little **4** : to scoop up from a resting place ⟨~ed up the child⟩ **5** : to gain or win by gradual increase **6** : AT-TRACT, ACCUMULATE ⟨~ dust⟩ **7** : to summon up ⟨~ courage to dive⟩ **8** : to

gain control of ⟨~ed his wits⟩ **9** : to draw abreast of or close to something **10** : to pull (fabric) along a line of stitching into puckers **11** : GUESS, DEDUCE, INFER **12** : ASSEMBLE **13** : to swell out and fill with pus **14** : GROW, INCREASE ♦ *Synonyms* CONGREGATE, FORGATHER — **gath·er·er** *n*

²**gather** *n* : a puckering in cloth made by gathering

**GATT** \'gat\ *abbr* General Agreement on Tariffs and Trade

**gauche** \'gōsh\ *adj* [F, lit., left] **1** : lacking social experience or grace; *also* : not tactful **2** : crudely made or done ♦ *Synonyms* CLUMSY, HEAVY-HANDED, INEPT, MALADROIT

**gau·che·rie** \ˌgō-shə-'rē\ *n* : a tactless or awkward action

**gau·cho** \'gaú-chō\ *n, pl* **gauchos** : a cowboy of the So. American pampas

**gaud** \'gód\ *n* : ORNAMENT, TRINKET

**gaudy** \'gò-dē\ *adj* **gaud·i·er; -est 1** : ostentatiously or tastelessly ornamented **2** : marked by showiness or extravagance **1** : OUTLANDISH **3** : EXCEPTIONAL ⟨a ~ batting average⟩ ♦ *Synonyms* GARISH, FLASHY, GLARING, TAWDRY — **gaud·i·ly** \-də-lē\ *adv* — **gaud·i·ness** \-dē-nəs\ *n*

¹**gauge** *also* **gage** \'gāj\ *n* **1** : measurement according to some standard or system **2** : DIMENSIONS, SIZE **3** *usu* **gage** : an instrument for measuring, testing, or registering

²**gauge** *also* **gage** *vb* **gauged** *also* **gaged; gaug·ing** *also* **gag·ing 1** : MEASURE **2** : to determine the capacity or contents of **3** : ESTIMATE, JUDGE

**gaunt** \'gónt\ *adj* **1** : excessively thin and angular ⟨a ~ face⟩ **2** : BARREN, DESOLATE ♦ *Synonyms* BONY, LANK, LANKY, LEAN, RAWBONED, SKINNY — **gaunt·ness** *n*

¹**gaunt·let** *also* **gant·let** \'gónt-lət\ *n* **1** : a protective glove **2** : an open challenge (as to combat) **3** : a dress glove extending above the wrist

²**gauntlet** *also* **gantlet** *n* **1** : a double file of men armed with weapons (as clubs) with which to strike at an individual who is made to run between them **2** : ORDEAL **3** : a line or series of something to be greeted or managed

**gauss** \'gaús\ *n* : the centimeter-gram-second unit of magnetic flux density that is equal to $1 \times 10^{-4}$ tesla

**gauze** \'góz\ *n* : a very thin often transparent fabric used esp. for draperies and surgical dressings

**gauzy** \'gò-zē\ *adj* **gauz·i·er; -est 1** : made of or resembling gauze **2** : marked by vagueness or fuzziness ⟨a ~ memory⟩

**gave** *past of* GIVE

**gav·el** \'ga-vəl\ *n* : a mallet used by a presiding officer or auctioneer

**ga·votte** \gə-'vät\ *n* : a dance of French peasant origin marked by the raising rather than sliding of the feet

**gawk** \'gók\ *vb* : to gape or stare stupidly — **gawk·er** *n*

**gawky** \'gȯ-kē\ adj **gawk·i·er; -est**
: AWKWARD, CLUMSY — **gawk·i·ly** \-kə-
lē\ adv — **gawk·i·ness** n

**gay** \'gā\ adj **1** : MERRY **2** : BRIGHT,
LIVELY **3** : brilliant in color **4** : given to
social pleasures; also : LICENTIOUS **5**
: HOMOSEXUAL; also : of, relating to, or
used by homosexuals ⟨a ~ bar⟩

**gayety, gayly** var of GAIETY, GAILY

**gaz** abbr gazette

**gaze** \'gāz\ vb **gazed; gaz·ing** : to fix the
eyes in a steady intent look ♦ **Synonyms** GAPE, GAWK, GLARE, GOGGLE,
PEER, STARE — **gaz·er** n

**ga·ze·bo** \gə-'zē-bō\ n, pl **-bos 1** : BEL-
VEDERE **2** : a freestanding roofed structure usu. open on the sides

**ga·zelle** \gə-'zel\ n, pl **gazelles** also **ga-
zelle** : any of numerous small swift
graceful antelopes

**ga·zette** \gə-'zet\ n **1** : NEWSPAPER **2**
: an official journal

**gaz·et·teer** \,ga-zə-'tir\ n : a geographical
dictionary

**ga·zil·lion** \gə-'zil-yən\ n : ZILLION —
**gazillion** adj — **ga·zil·lionth** \-yənth\
adj

**gaz·pa·cho** \gəz-'pä-(,)chō, gə-'spä-\ n, pl
**-chos** [Sp] : a spicy soup usu. made from
raw vegetables and served cold

**GB** abbr Great Britain

**GCA** abbr ground-controlled approach

**gd** abbr good

**Gd** symbol gadolinium

**GDR** abbr German Democratic Republic

**Ge** symbol germanium

**gear** \'gir\ n **1** : CLOTHING **2** : movable
property : GOODS **3** : EQUIPMENT ⟨fish-
ing ~⟩ **4** : a mechanism that performs a
specific function ⟨steering ~⟩ **5** : a
toothed wheel **6** : working order or adjustment ⟨got her career in ~⟩ **7** : an
adjustment of transmission gears (as of
an automobile or bicycle) that determines speed and direction of travel —
**gear** vb

**gear·box** \'gir-,bäks\ n : TRANSMISSION 3

**gear·shift** \-,shift\ n : a mechanism by
which transmission gears are shifted

**gear·wheel** \-,hwēl\ n : GEAR 5

**gecko** \'ge-kō\ n, pl **geck·os** also **geck-
oes** : any of numerous small chiefly
tropical insect-eating lizards

**GED** abbr general equivalency diploma

**geek** \'gēk\ n : a person of an intellectual
bent who is often disliked — **geek·i-
ness** n — **geeky** adj

**geese** pl of GOOSE

**gee·zer** \'gē-zər\ n : an odd or eccentric
person usu. of old age

**Gei·ger counter** \'gī-gər-\ n : an electronic instrument for detecting the presence
of cosmic rays or radioactive substances

**gei·sha** \'gā-shə, 'gē-\ n, pl **geisha** or **gei-
shas** [Jp, fr. gei art + -sha person] : a
Japanese girl or woman who is trained to
provide entertaining company for men

**gel** \'jel\ n : a solid jellylike colloid (as
gelatin dessert) — **gel** vb

**gel·a·tin** also **gel·a·tine** \'je-lə-tən\ n
: glutinous material and esp. protein obtained from animal tissues by boiling and

used as a food, in dyeing, and in photography; also : an edible jelly formed with
gelatin — **ge·lat·i·nous** \jə-'la-tə-nəs\
adj

**geld** \'geld\ vb : CASTRATE

**geld·ing** n : a castrated male horse

**gel·id** \'je-ləd\ adj : extremely cold

**gem** \'jem\ n **1** : JEWEL **2** : a usu. valuable stone cut and polished for ornament
**3** : something valued for beauty or perfection ⟨a ~ of colonial architecture⟩

**Gem·i·ni** \'je-mə-(,)nē, -,nī; 'ge-mə-,nē\ n
**1** : a zodiacal constellation between Taurus and Cancer usu. pictured as twins sitting together **2** : the 3d sign of the zodiac
in astrology; also : one born under this
sign

**gem·ol·o·gy** or **gem·mol·o·gy** \je-'mä-
lə-jē, jə-\ n : the science of gems — **gem-
olog·i·cal** \,je-mə-'lä-ji-kəl\ adj — **gem-
ol·o·gist** also **gem·mol·o·gist** \-jist\ n

**gem·stone** \'jem-,stōn\ n : a mineral or
petrified material that when cut and polished can be used in jewelry

**gen** abbr **1** general **2** genitive

**Gen** abbr Genesis

**Gen AF** abbr general of the air force

**gen·darme** \'zhän-,därm, 'jän-\ n [F, intended as sing. of gensdarmes, pl. of gent
d'armes, lit., armed people] : a member of
a body of soldiers esp. in France serving
as an armed police force

**gen·der** \'jen-dər\ n [ME gendre, fr. AF
genre, gendre, fr. L gener-, genus birth,
race, kind, gender] **1** : any of two or
more divisions within a grammatical
class that determine agreement with and
selection of other words or grammatical
forms **2** : SEX 1

**gene** \'jēn\ n : a part of DNA or RNA
that contains chemical information needed to make a particular protein (as an
enzyme) controlling or influencing an
inherited bodily trait (as eye color) or activity (as metabolism) or that influences
or controls the activity of another gene
or genes — **gen·ic** \'jē-nik, 'je-\ adj

**ge·ne·al·o·gy** \,jē-nē-'ä-lə-jē, ,je-, -'a-\ n,
pl **-gies** : PEDIGREE, LINEAGE; also : the
study of family pedigrees — **ge·ne·a-
log·i·cal** \,jē-nē-ə-'lä-ji-kəl, ,je-\ adj —
**ge·ne·a·log·i·cal·ly** \-k(ə-)lē\ adv — **ge-
ne·al·o·gist** \,jē-nē-'ä-lə-jist, ,je-; -'a-\ n

**gene pool** n : the total genetic information contained in a population of interbreeding organisms

**genera** pl of GENUS

**¹gen·er·al** \'je-nə-rəl, 'jen-rəl\ adj **1** : of or
relating to the whole **2** : taken as a whole
**3** : relating to or covering all instances **4**
: not special or specialized **5** : common
to many ⟨a ~ custom⟩ **6** : not limited in
meaning : not specific **7** : holding superior rank ⟨inspector ~⟩ ♦ **Synonyms**
GENERIC, UNIVERSAL

**²general** n **1** : something that involves or
is applicable to the whole **2** : a commissioned officer ranking next below a general of the army or a general of the air
force **3** : a commissioned officer of the
highest rank in the marine corps — **in
general** : for the most part

**general assembly** *n* **1** : a legislative assembly; *esp* : a U.S. state legislature **2** *cap G&A* : the supreme deliberative body of the United Nations

**gen·er·al·i·sa·tion, gen·er·al·ise, gen·er·al·ised** *Brit var of* GENERALIZATION, GENERALIZE, GENERALIZED

**gen·er·a·lis·si·mo** \ˌje-nə-rə-ˈli-sə-ˌmō\ *n, pl* -mos [It, fr. *generale* general] : the chief commander of an army

**gen·er·al·i·ty** \ˌje-nə-ˈra-lə-tē\ *n, pl* -ties **1** : the quality or state of being general **2** : GENERALIZATION 2 **3** : a vague or inadequate statement **4** : the greatest part : BULK

**gen·er·al·i·za·tion** \ˌje-nə-rə-lə-ˈzā-shən, ˌjen-rə-\ *n* **1** : the act or process of generalizing **2** : a general statement, law, principle, or proposition

**gen·er·al·ize** \ˈje-nə-rə-ˌlīz, ˈjen-rə-\ *vb* -ized; -iz·ing **1** : to make general **2** : to draw general conclusions from **3** : to reach a general conclusion esp. on the basis of particular instances **4** : to extend throughout the body

**gen·er·al·ly** \ˈjen-rə-lē, ˈje-nə-\ *adv* **1** : in a general manner **2** : as a rule

**general of the air force** : a commissioned officer of the highest rank in the air force

**general of the army** : a commissioned officer of the highest rank in the army

**general practitioner** *n* : a physician or veterinarian whose practice is not limited to a specialty

**gen·er·al·ship** \ˈje-nə-rəl-ˌship, ˈjen-rəl-\ *n* **1** : office or tenure of office of a general **2** : LEADERSHIP **3** : military skill as a high commander

**general store** *n* : a retail store that carries a wide variety of goods but is not divided into departments

**gen·er·ate** \ˈje-nə-ˌrāt\ *vb* -at·ed; -at·ing : to bring into existence : PRODUCE ✦ *Synonyms* CREATE, ORIGINATE, PROCREATE, SPAWN

**gen·er·a·tion** \ˌje-nə-ˈrā-shən\ *n* **1** : a body of living beings constituting a single step in the line of descent from an ancestor; *also* : the average period between generations **2** : PRODUCTION

**Generation X** *n* : the generation of Americans born in the 1960s and 1970s

**gen·er·a·tive** \ˈje-nə-rə-tiv, -ˌrā-tiv\ *adj* : having the power or function of generating, originating, producing, or reproducing ⟨~ organs⟩

**gen·er·a·tor** \ˈje-nə-ˌrā-tər\ *n* : one that generates; *esp* : a machine by which mechanical energy is changed into electrical energy

**ge·ner·ic** \jə-ˈner-ik\ *adj* **1** : not specific : GENERAL **2** : not protected by a trademark ⟨a ~ drug⟩ **3** : of or relating to a biological genus **4** : having no particularly distinctive quality ⟨~ towns⟩ — **generic** *n* — **ge·ner·i·cal·ly** \-i-k(ə-)lē\ *adv*

**gen·er·ous** \ˈje-nə-rəs\ *adj* **1** : free in giving or sharing ⟨~ donors⟩ **2** : HIGH-MINDED, NOBLE **3** : ABUNDANT, AMPLE, COPIOUS ⟨a ~ salary⟩ ✦ *Synonyms*

LIBERAL, BOUNTIFUL, MUNIFICENT, OPENHANDED — **gen·er·os·i·ty** \ˌje-nə-ˈrä-sə-tē\ *n* — **gen·er·ous·ly** \ˈje-nə-rəs-lē\ *adv* — **gen·er·ous·ness** *n*

**gen·e·sis** \ˈje-nə-səs\ *n, pl* -e·ses \-ˌsēz\ : the origin or coming into existence of something

**Genesis** *n* — see BIBLE table

**gene–splic·ing** \-ˌspli-siŋ\ *n* : the process of preparing recombinant DNA

**gene therapy** *n* : the insertion of normal or altered genes into cells esp. to replace defective genes in the treatment of genetic disorders or to provide a specialized disease-fighting function

**ge·net·ic** \jə-ˈne-tik\ *adj* : of or relating to the origin, development, or causes of something; *also* : of, relating to, or caused by genes or genetics ⟨~ research⟩ — **ge·net·i·cal·ly** \-ti-k(ə-)lē\ *adv*

**genetic code** *n* : the chemical code that is the basis of genetic inheritance and consists of units of three linked chemical groups in DNA and RNA which specify particular amino acids used to make proteins or which start or stop the process of making proteins

**genetic engineering** *n* : the alteration of genetic material esp. by cutting up and joining together DNA from one or more species of organism and inserting the result into an organism — **genetically engineered** *adj*

**ge·net·ics** \jə-ˈne-tiks\ *n* : a branch of biology dealing with heredity and variation — **ge·net·i·cist** \-tə-sist\ *n*

**ge·nial** \ˈjēn-yəl, ˈjē-nē-əl\ *adj* **1** : favorable to growth or comfort ⟨~ sunshine⟩ **2** : CHEERFUL, KINDLY ⟨a ~ host⟩ ✦ *Synonyms* AFFABLE, CONGENIAL, CORDIAL, GRACIOUS, SOCIABLE — **ge·nial·i·ty** \ˌjē-nē-ˈa-lə-tē, jēn-ˈya-\ *n* — **ge·nial·ly** *adv*

**-gen·ic** \ˈje-nik\ *adj comb form* **1** : producing : forming **2** : produced by : formed from **3** : suitable for production or reproduction by (such) a medium

**ge·nie** \ˈjē-nē\ *n, pl* **ge·nies** *also* **ge·nii** \-nē-ˌī\ [F *génie*, fr. Ar *jinnī*] : a supernatural spirit that often takes human form usu. serving the person who calls on it

**gen·i·tal** \ˈje-nə-tᵊl\ *adj* **1** : concerned with reproduction ⟨~ organs⟩ **2** : of, relating to, or characterized by the stage of psychosexual development in psychoanalytic theory in which oral and anal impulses are subordinated to adaptive interpersonal mechanisms — **gen·i·tal·ly** *adv*

**gen·i·ta·lia** \ˌje-nə-ˈtāl-yə\ *n pl* : reproductive organs; *esp* : the external genital organs — **gen·i·ta·lic** \-ˈta-lik, -ˈtā-\ *adj*

**gen·i·tals** \ˈje-nə-tᵊlz\ *n pl* : GENITALIA

**gen·i·tive** \ˈje-nə-tiv\ *adj* : of, relating to, or constituting a grammatical case marking typically a relationship of possessor or source — **genitive** *n*

**gen·i·to·uri·nary** \ˌje-nə-tō-ˈyur-ə-ˌner-ē\ *adj* : of or relating to the genital and urinary organs or functions

**ge·nius** \ˈjē-nyəs\ *n, pl* **ge·nius·es** *or* **ge-**

**nii** \-ˈnē-ˌī\ [L, tutelary spirit, natural inclinations, fr. *gignere* to beget] **1** *pl genii* : an attendant spirit of a person or place; *also* : a person who influences another for good or evil **2** : a strong leaning or inclination **3** : a peculiar or distinctive character or spirit (as of a nation or a language) **4** *pl usu genii* : SPIRIT, GENIE **5** *pl usu geniuses* : a single strongly marked capacity or aptitude **6** : extraordinary intellectual power; *also* : a person having such power ♦ **Synonyms** GIFT, FACULTY, FLAIR, KNACK, TALENT

**genl** *abbr* general

**geno·cide** \ˈje-nə-ˌsīd\ *n* : the deliberate and systematic destruction of a racial, political, or cultural group

**ge·nome** \ˈjē-ˌnōm\ *n* **1** : one haploid set of chromosomes **2** : the genetic material of an organism

**ge·no·mics** \jē-ˈnō-miks\ *n* : a branch of biotechnology concerned esp. with investigating and collecting data about the structure and function of all or part of an organism's genome

**-genous** \jə-nəs\ *adj comb form* **1** : producing : yielding ⟨erogenous⟩ **2** : having (such) an origin ⟨endogenous⟩

**genre** \ˈzhän-rə, ˈzhän-, ˈzhäⁿr; ˈjän-rə\ *n* **1** : a distinctive type or category esp. of literary composition **2** : a style of painting in which everyday subjects are treated realistically

**gens** \ˈjenz, ˈgens\ *n, pl* **gen·tes** \ˈjen-ˌtēz, ˈgen-ˌtās\ [L] : a Roman clan embracing the families of the same stock in the male line

**gent** *n* : GENTLEMAN

**gen·teel** \jen-ˈtēl\ *adj* **1** : ARISTOCRATIC **2** : ELEGANT, STYLISH **3** : POLITE, REFINED **4** : maintaining the appearance of superior social status **5** : marked by false delicacy, prudery, or affectation — **genteel·ly** *adv* — **gen·teel·ness** *n*

**gen·tian** \ˈjen-chən\ *n* : any of numerous herbs with opposite leaves and showy usu. blue flowers in the fall

**gen·tile** \ˈjen-ˌtī(-ə)l\ *n* [ME, fr. LL *gentilis* heathen, pagan, fr. L *gent-, gens* clan, nation] *1 often cap* : a person who is not Jewish; *esp* : a Christian as distinguished from a Jew **2** : HEATHEN, PAGAN — **gentile** *adj, often cap*

**gen·til·i·ty** \jen-ˈti-lə-tē\ *n, pl* **-ties** **1** : good birth and family **2** : the qualities characteristic of a well-bred person **3** : good manners **4** : superior social status shown in manners or mode of life

**¹gen·tle** \ˈjen-t³l\ *adj* **gen·tler** \ˈjent-lər, -t³l-ər\; **gen·tlest** \ˈjent-ləst, -t³l-əst\ **1** : belonging to a family of high social station **2** : of, relating to, or characteristic of a gentleman **3** : KIND, AMIABLE ⟨a ~ pastor⟩ **4** : TRACTABLE, DOCILE ⟨a ~ dog⟩ **5** : not harsh, stern, or violent **6** : SOFT, DELICATE **7** : MODERATE — **gentle·ness** *n* — **gent·ly** *adv*

**²gentle** *vb* **gen·tled**; **gen·tling** **1** : to make or become mild, docile, soft, or moderate **2** : MOLLIFY, PLACATE

**gen·tle·folk** \ˈjen-t³l-ˌfōk\ *also* **gen·tle-**

**folks** \-ˌfōks\ *n* : persons of good family and breeding

**gen·tle·man** \-mən\ *n* **1** : a man of good family **2** : a well-bred man **3** : MAN — used in pl. as a form of address — **gentle·man·ly** *adj*

**gen·tle·wom·an** \-ˌwu̇-mən\ *n* **1** : a woman of good family **2** : a woman attending a lady of rank **3** : a woman with very good manners : LADY

**gen·tri·fi·ca·tion** \ˌjen-trə-fə-ˈkā-shən\ *n* : the process of renewal accompanying the influx of middle-class people into deteriorating areas that often displaces earlier usu. poorer residents — **gen·tri·fy** \ˈjen-trə-ˌfī\ *vb*

**gen·try** \ˈjen-trē\ *n, pl* **gentries** **1** : people of good birth, breeding, and education **2** : ARISTOCRACY **3** : the class of English people between the nobility and the yeomanry **4** : persons of a designated class

**gen·u·flect** \ˈjen-yu̇-ˌflekt\ *vb* : to bend the knee esp. in worship — **gen·u·flec·tion** \ˌjen-yu̇-ˈflek-shən\ *n*

**gen·u·ine** \ˈjen-yə-wən\ *adj* **1** : AUTHENTIC, REAL ⟨a ~ signature⟩ **2** : SINCERE, HONEST ⟨their love is ~⟩ ♦ **Synonyms** BONA FIDE, TRUE, VERITABLE — **gen·u·ine·ly** *adv* — **gen·u·ine·ness** *n*

**ge·nus** \ˈjē-nəs\ *n, pl* **gen·era** \ˈje-nə-rə\ [L, birth, race, kind] : a category of biological classification that ranks between the family and the species and contains related species

**geo·cen·tric** \ˌjē-ō-ˈsen-trik\ *adj* **1** : relating to or measured from the earth's center **2** : having or relating to the earth as a center

**geo·chem·is·try** \-ˈke-mə-strē\ *n* : a branch of geology that deals with the chemical composition of and chemical changes in the earth — **geo·chem·i·cal** \-mi-kəl\ *adj* — **geo·chem·ist** \-mist\ *n*

**ge·ode** \ˈjē-ˌōd\ *n* : a nodule of stone having a cavity lined with mineral matter

**¹geo·de·sic** \ˌjē-ə-ˈde-sik\ *adj* : made of light straight structural elements ⟨a ~ dome⟩

**²geodesic** *n* : the shortest line between two points on a surface

**geo·det·ic** \ˌjē-ə-ˈde-tik\ *adj* : of, relating to, or being precise measurement of the earth and its features ⟨a ~ survey⟩

**geog** *abbr* geographic; geographical; geography

**ge·og·ra·phy** \jē-ˈä-grə-fē\ *n, pl* **-phies** **1** : a science that deals with the natural features of the earth and its climate, products, and inhabitants **2** : the natural features of a region — **ge·og·ra·pher** \-fər\ *n* — **geo·graph·ic** \ˌjē-ə-ˈgra-fik\ *or* **geo·graph·i·cal** \-fi-kəl\ *adj* — **geo·graph·i·cal·ly** \-fi-k(ə-)lē\ *adv*

**geol** *abbr* geologic; geological; geology

**ge·ol·o·gy** \jē-ˈä-lə-jē\ *n, pl* **-gies** **1** : a science that deals with the history of the earth and its life esp. as recorded in rocks; *also* : a study of the features of a celestial body (as the moon) **2** : the geologic features of an area — **geo·log·ic** \ˌjē-ə-ˈlä-jik\ *or* **geo·log·i·cal** \-ji-kəl\ *adj*

— **geo·log·i·cal·ly** \-ji-k(ə-)lē\ *adv*

**ge·ol·o·gist** \jē-'ä-lə-jist\ *n*

**geom** *abbr* geometric; geometrical; geometry

**geo·mag·net·ic** \,jē-ō-mag-'ne-tik\ *adj* : of or relating to the magnetism of the earth — **geo·mag·ne·tism** \-'mag-nə-,ti-zəm\ *n*

**geometric mean** *n* : the *n*th root of the product of *n* numbers; *esp* : a number that is the second term of three consecutive terms of a geometric progression ⟨the *geometric mean* of 9 and 4 is 6⟩

**geometric progression** *n* : a progression (as 1, ¹/₂, ¹/₄) in which the ratio of a term to its predecessor is always the same

**ge·om·e·try** \jē-'ä-mə-trē\ *n, pl* **-tries** [ultim. fr. Gk *geōmetria*, fr. *geōmetrein* to measure the earth, fr. gē earth + *metron* measure] : a branch of mathematics dealing with the relations, properties, and measurements of solids, surfaces, lines, points, and angles — **ge·om·e·ter** \-tər\ *n* — **geo·met·ric** \jē-ə-'me-trik\ *or* **geo·met·ri·cal** \-tri-kəl\ *adj*

**geo·phys·ics** \jē-ō-'fi-ziks\ *n* : the physics of the earth — **geo·phys·i·cal** \-zi-kəl\ *adj* — **geo·phys·i·cist** \-zə-sist\ *n*

**geo·pol·i·tics** \-'pä-lə-,tiks\ *n* : a combination of political and geographic factors relating to a state — **geo·po·lit·i·cal** \-pə-'li-ti-kəl\ *adj*

**geo·ther·mal** \,jē-ō-'thər-məl\ *adj* : of, relating to, or using the heat of the earth's interior ⟨∼ energy⟩

**ger** *abbr* gerund

**Ger** *abbr* German; Germany

**ge·ra·ni·um** \jə-'rā-nē-əm\ *n* [L, fr. Gk *geranion*, fr. *geranos* crane] : any of a genus of herbs with usu. deeply cut leaves and typically pink, purple, or white flowers; *also* : any of a related genus of herbs that are native to southern Africa and are widely grown for their clusters of showy usu. red, pink, or white flowers

**ger·bil** *also* **ger·bile** \'jər-bəl\ *n* : any of numerous Old World burrowing desert rodents with long hind legs

**ge·ri·at·ric** \,jer-ē-'a-trik\ *adj* **1** : of or relating to geriatrics or the process of aging **2** : of, relating to, or appropriate for elderly people **3** : OLD

**ge·ri·at·rics** \-triks\ *n* : a branch of medicine dealing with the problems and diseases of old age and aging

**germ** \'jərm\ *n* **1** : a bit of living matter capable of growth and development (as into an organism) **2** : SOURCE, RUDIMENTS **3** : MICROORGANISM; *esp* : one causing disease

**Ger·man** \'jər-mən\ *n* **1** : a native or inhabitant of Germany **2** : the language of Germany, Austria, and parts of Switzerland — **German** *adj* — **Ger·man·ic** \jər-'ma-nik\ *adj*

**ger·mane** \jər-'mān\ *adj* [ME *germain*, lit., having the same parents, fr. AF, fr. L *germanus*, fr. *germen* sprout, bud] : RELEVANT, APPROPRIATE ♦ ***Synonyms*** APPLICABLE, MATERIAL, PERTINENT

**ger·ma·ni·um** \jər-'mā-nē-əm\ *n* : a grayish white hard chemical element used esp. in semiconductor and optical materials and as a catalyst

**German measles** *n sing or pl* : an acute contagious virus disease milder than typical measles but damaging to the fetus when occurring early in pregnancy

**German shepherd** *n* : any of a breed of intelligent responsive working dogs of German origin often used in police work and as guide dogs for the blind

**germ cell** *n* : an egg or sperm or one of their antecedent cells

**ger·mi·cide** \'jər-mə-,sīd\ *n* : an agent that destroys germs — **ger·mi·cid·al** \,jər-mə-'sī-d³l\ *adj*

**ger·mi·nal** \'jər-mə-nəl\ *adj* : of or relating to a germ or germ cell; *also* : EMBRYONIC

**ger·mi·nate** \'jər-mə-,nāt\ *vb* **-nat·ed;** **-nat·ing 1** : to cause to develop : begin to develop : SPROUT **2** : to come into being : EVOLVE — **ger·mi·na·tion** \,jər-mə-'nā-shən\ *n*

**ger·on·tol·o·gy** \,jer-ən-'tä-lə-jē\ *n* : a scientific study of aging and the problems of the aged — **ge·ron·to·log·i·cal** \jə-,rän-tə-'lä-ji-kəl\ *adj* — **ger·on·tol·o·gist** \,jer-ən-'tä-lə-jist\ *n*

**ger·ry·man·der** \'jer-ē-,man-dər\ *vb* : to divide into election districts so as to give one political party an advantage — **gerrymander** *n*

**ger·und** \'jer-ənd\ *n* : a word having the characteristics of both verb and noun

**ge·sta·po** \gə-'stä-pō\ *n, pl* **-pos** [G, fr. *Geheime Staatspolizei*, lit., secret state police] : a usu. terrorist secret-police organization operating against persons suspected of disloyalty

**ges·ta·tion** \je-'stä-shən\ *n* : PREGNANCY, INCUBATION — **ges·tate** \'jes-,tāt\ *vb*

**ges·tic·u·late** \je-'sti-kyə-,lāt\ *vb* **-lat·ed;** **-lat·ing** : to make gestures esp. when speaking — **ges·tic·u·la·tion** \-,sti-kyə-'lā-shən\ *n*

**ges·ture** \'jes-chər\ *n* **1** : a movement usu. of the body or limbs that expresses or emphasizes an idea, sentiment, or attitude **2** : something said or done by way of formality or courtesy, as a symbol or token, or for its effect on the attitudes of others — **ges·tur·al** \-chə-rəl\ *adj* — **gesture** *vb*

**ge·sund·heit** \gə-'zùnt-,hīt\ *interj* [G, lit., health] — used to wish good health esp. to one who has just sneezed

**¹get** \'get\ *vb* **got** \'gät\; **got** *or* **got·ten** \'gä-t³n\; **get·ting 1** : to gain possession of (as by receiving, acquiring, earning, buying, or winning) : PROCURE, OBTAIN, FETCH **2** : to succeed in coming or going ⟨*got* away to the lake⟩ **3** : to cause to come or go ⟨*got* the car to the station⟩ **4** : BEGET **5** : to cause to be in a certain condition or position ⟨don't ∼ wet⟩ **6** : BECOME ⟨∼ sick⟩ **7** : PREPARE **8** : SEIZE **9** : to move emotionally; *also* : IRRITATE **10** : BAFFLE, PUZZLE **11** : KILL **12** : HIT **13** : to be subjected to ⟨∼ the measles⟩ **14** : to receive as punishment **15** : to find out by calculation **16** : HEAR; *also* : UNDERSTAND ⟨*got* the joke⟩ **17**

: PERSUADE, INDUCE **18** : HAVE ⟨he's *got* no money⟩ **19** : to have as an obligation or necessity ⟨you have *got* to come⟩ **20** : to establish communication with **21** : to be able ⟨finally *got* to go to med school⟩ **22** : to come to be ⟨*got* talking about old times⟩ **23** : to leave at once — **get ahead** : to achieve success — **get a move on** : HURRY — **get away with** : to avoid punishment for (as a crime) — **get into** : to become strongly involved or interested in ⟨*got into* music⟩ — **get over** : to reconcile oneself to ⟨*got over* the breakup⟩

²**get** \'get\ *n* : OFFSPRING, PROGENY

**get along** *vb* **1** : GET BY **2** : to be on friendly terms

**get·away** \'ge-tə-,wā\ *n* **1** : ESCAPE **2** : START **3** : a usu. brief vacation

**get by** *vb* : to meet one's needs

**get–to·geth·er** \'get-tə-,ge-thər\ *n* : an informal social gathering

**get·up** \'get-,əp\ *n* **1** : OUTFIT, COSTUME **2** : general composition or structure

**gew·gaw** \'gü-,gȯ, 'gyü-\ *n* : a showy trifle : BAUBLE, TRINKET

**gey·ser** \'gī-zər\ *n* [Icelandic *Geysir*, hot spring in Iceland] : a spring that intermittently shoots up hot water and steam

**g–force** \'jē-,fȯrs\ *n* : the force of gravity or acceleration on a body

**ghast·ly** \'gast-lē\ *adj* **ghast·li·er; -est 1** : HORRIBLE, SHOCKING **2** : resembling a ghost : DEATHLIKE, PALE ♦ **Synonyms** GRUESOME, GRIM, LURID, GRISLY, MACABRE

**ghat** \'gȯt\ *n* [Hindi & Urdu *ghāṭ*] : a broad flight of steps on an Indian riverbank that provides access to the water

**gher·kin** \'gər-kən\ *n* **1** : a small prickly fruit of a vine related to the cucumber used to make pickles **2** : an immature cucumber

**ghet·to** \'ge-tō\ *n, pl* **ghettos** *or* **ghet·toes** : a quarter of a city in which members of a minority group live because of social, legal, or economic pressure

¹**ghost** \'gōst\ *n* **1** : the seat of life : SOUL **2** : a disembodied soul; *esp* : the soul of a dead person believed to be an inhabitant of the unseen world or to appear in bodily form to living people **3** : SPIRIT, DEMON **4** : a faint trace ⟨a ~ of a smile⟩ **5** : a false image in a photographic negative or on a television screen — **ghost·ly** *adv*

²**ghost** *vb* : GHOSTWRITE

**ghost·write** \-,rīt\ *vb* **-wrote** \-,rōt\; **-writ·ten** \-,ri-t°n\ : to write for and in the name of another — **ghost·writ·er** *n*

**ghoul** \'gül\ *n* [Ar *ghūl*] : a legendary evil being that robs graves and feeds on corpses — **ghoul·ish** *adj*

**GHQ** *abbr* general headquarters

**gi** *abbr* gill

¹**GI** \,jē-'ī\ *adj* [galvanized *i*ron; fr. abbr. used in listing such articles as garbage cans, but taken as abbr. for *government issue*] **1** : provided by an official U.S. military supply department ⟨~ shoes⟩ **2** : of, relating to, or characteristic of U.S. military personnel **3** : conforming to

military regulations or customs ⟨a ~ haircut⟩

²**GI** *n, pl* **GIs** *or* **GI's** \-'īz\ : a member or former member of the U.S. armed forces; *esp* : an enlisted person

³**GI** *abbr* **1** galvanized iron **2** gastrointestinal **3** general issue **4** government issue

**gi·ant** \'jī-ənt\ *n* **1** : a legendary humanlike being of great size and strength **2** : a living being or thing of extraordinary size or powers — **giant** *adj*

**gi·ant·ess** \'jī-ən-təs\ *n* : a female giant

**giant panda** *n* : PANDA 2

**gib·ber** \'ji-bər\ *vb* : to speak rapidly, inarticulately, and often foolishly

**gib·ber·ish** \'ji-bə-rish\ *n* : unintelligible or confused speech or language

¹**gib·bet** \'ji-bət\ *n* : GALLOWS

²**gibbet** *vb* **1** : to hang on a gibbet **2** : to expose to public scorn **3** : to execute by hanging

**gib·bon** \'gi-bən\ *n* : any of several tailless apes of southeastern Asia

**gib·bous** \'ji-bəs, 'gi-\ *adj* **1** : rounded like the exterior of a sphere or circle **2** : seen with more than half but not all of the apparent disk illuminated ⟨~ moon⟩ **3** : having a hump : HUMPBACKED

**gibe** *or* **jibe** \'jīb\ *vb* **gibed** *or* **jibed; gib·ing** *or* **jib·ing** : to utter taunting words : SNEER — **gibe** *or* **jibe** *n*

**gib·lets** \'jib-ləts\ *n pl* : the edible viscera of a fowl

**Gib·son girl** \'gib-sən-\ *adj* : of or relating to a style in women's clothing characterized by high necks, full sleeves, and slender waistlines

**gid·dy** \'gi-dē\ *adj* **gid·di·er; -est 1** : DIZZY **2** : causing dizziness ⟨a ~ height⟩ **3** : not serious : FRIVOLOUS, SILLY — **gid·di·ness** \-dē-nəs\ *n*

**gid·dy·ap** \,gi-dē-'ap, -'əp\ *or* **gid·dy·up** \-'əp\ *vb imper* — a command (as to a horse) to go ahead or go faster

**GIF** \'gif, 'jif\ *n* [*g*raphic *i*nterchange *f*ormat] : a computer file format for digital images; *also* : the image itself

**gift** \'gift\ *n* **1** : a special ability : TALENT **2** : something given : PRESENT **3** : the act or power of giving

**gift card** *n* : a card entitling the recipient to goods or services of a specified value from the issuer

**gift·ed** \'gif-təd\ *adj* : TALENTED

¹**gig** \'gig\ *n* **1** : a long light ship's boat **2** : a light 2-wheeled one-horse carriage

²**gig** *n* : a pronged spear for catching fish — **gig** *vb*

³**gig** *n* : a job for a specified time; *esp* : an entertainer's engagement

⁴**gig** *n* : a military demerit — **gig** *vb*

**giga·byte** \'ji-gə-,bīt, 'gi-\ *n* : 1024 megabytes or 1,073,741,824 bytes; *also* : one billion bytes

**gi·gan·tic** \jī-'gan-tik\ *adj* : exceeding the usual (as in size or force)

**gig·gle** \'gi-gəl\ *vb* **gig·gled; gig·gling** : to laugh with repeated short catches of the breath — **giggle** *n* — **gig·gly** \-gə-lē\ *adj*

**GIGO** *abbr* garbage in, garbage out

**gig·o·lo** \'ji-gə-,lō\ *n, pl* **-los 1** : a man

supported by a woman usu. in return for his attentions **2** : a professional dancing partner or male escort

**Gi·la monster** \'hē-lə-\ *n* : a large orange and black venomous lizard of the south western U.S.

**¹gild** \'gild\ *vb* **gild·ed** *or* **gilt** \'gilt\; **gild·ing 1** : to overlay with or as if with a thin covering of gold **2** : to give an attractive but often deceptive appearance to

**²gild** *var of* GUILD

**¹gill** \'jil\ *n* — see WEIGHT table

**²gill** \'gil\ *n* : an organ (as of a fish) for obtaining oxygen from water

**¹gilt** \'gilt\ *adj* : of the color of gold

**²gilt** *n* : gold or a substance resembling gold laid on the surface of an object

**³gilt** *n* : a young female swine

**¹gim·crack** \'jim-,krak\ *n* : a showy object of little use or value

**²gimcrack** *adj* : CHEAP, SHODDY

**gim·let** \'gim-lət\ *n* : a small tool with screw point and cross handle for boring holes

**gim·me cap** \'gi-mē-\ *n* : an adjustable visored cap featuring a corporate logo or slogan

**gim·mick** \'gi-mik\ *n* **1** : CONTRIVANCE, GADGET **2** : an important feature that is not immediately apparent : CATCH **3** : a new and ingenious scheme **4** : a device used to attract business or attention — **gim·micky** \-mi-kē\ *adj*

**gim·mick·ry** \'gi-mi-krē\ *n, pl* **-ries** : an array of or the use of gimmicks

**gimpy** \'gim-pē\ *adj* : LAME 1

**¹gin** \'jin\ *n* [ME *gin*, short for *engin* engine] **1** : TRAP, SNARE **2** : a machine to separate seeds from cotton — **gin** *vb*

**²gin** *n* [by shortening & alter. fr. *geneva*, kind of gin] : a liquor distilled from a grain mash and flavored with juniper berries

**gin·ger** \'jin-jər\ *n* : the pungent aromatic rootstock of a tropical plant used esp. as a spice and in medicine; *also* : the spice or the plant

**ginger ale** *n* : a carbonated soft drink flavored with ginger

**gin·ger·bread** \'jin-jər-,bred\ *n* **1** : a cake made with molasses and flavored with ginger **2** : lavish or superfluous ornament esp. in architecture

**gin·ger·ly** \'jin-jər-lē\ *adj* : very cautious or careful — **gingerly** *adv*

**gin·ger·snap** \-,snap\ *n* : a thin brittle molasses cookie flavored with ginger

**ging·ham** \'gin-əm\ *n* : a cotton cloth that is often marked with a pattern of colored squares

**gin·gi·vi·tis** \,jin-jə-'vī-təs\ *n* : inflammation of the gums

**gink·go** *also* **ging·ko** \'gin-(,)kō\ *n, pl* **ginkgoes** *or* **ginkgos** *also* **ginkgoes** *or* **gingkoes 1** : a tree of eastern China with fan-shaped leaves often grown as a shade tree **2** : GINKGO BILOBA

**ginkgo bi·lo·ba** \-,bī-'lō-bə\ *n* : an extract of the leaves of ginkgo that is held to enhance mental functioning

**gin·seng** \'jin-,sen\ *n* : an aromatic root of a Chinese or No. American herb used

esp. in Chinese medicine; *also* : one of these herbs

**Gip·sy** *chiefly Brit var of* GYPSY

**gi·raffe** \jə-'raf\ *n, pl* **giraffes** [It *giraffa*, fr. Ar *zirafa*] : an African ruminant mammal with a very long neck and a short coat with dark blotches

**gird** \'gərd\ *vb* **gird·ed** *or* **girt** \'gərt\; **gird·ing 1** : to encircle or fasten (as a sword) with or as if with a belt **2** : to invest esp. with power or authority **3** : PREPARE, BRACE

**gird·er** \'gər-dər\ *n* : a horizontal main supporting beam

**gir·dle** \'gər-dᵊl\ *n* **1** : something (as a belt or sash) that encircles or confines **2** : a woman's supporting undergarment that extends from the waist to below the hips — **girdle** *vb*

**girl** \'gərl\ *n* **1** : a female child **2** : a young woman **3** : SWEETHEART — **girl·hood** \-,hu̇d\ *n* — **girl·ish** *adj*

**girl Friday** *n* : a female assistant (as in an office) entrusted with a wide variety of tasks

**girl·friend** \'gərl-,frend\ *n* **1** : a female friend **2** : a regular female companion in a romantic or sexual relationship

**Girl Scout** *n* : a member of any of the scouting programs of the Girl Scouts of the United States of America

**girth** \'gərth\ *n* **1** : a band around an animal by which something (as a saddle) may be fastened on its back **2** : a measure around something

**gist** \'jist\ *n* [AF, it lies, fr. *gesir* to lie, ultim. fr. L *jacēre*] : the main point or part ⟨the ~ of his speech⟩

**git** *dial var of* GET

**¹give** \'giv\ *vb* **gave** \'gāv\; **giv·en** \'gi-vən\; **giv·ing 1** : to make a present of **2** : to bestow by formal action **3** : to accord or yield to another **4** : to yield to force, strain, or pressure **5** : to put into the possession or keeping of another **6** : PROFFER ⟨*gave* her his hand⟩ **7** : DELIVER ⟨*gave* the bride away⟩ **8** : to present in public performance or to view **9** : PROVIDE ⟨~ a party⟩ **10** : ATTRIBUTE **11** : to make, form, or yield as a product or result ⟨cows ~ milk⟩ **12** : PAY **13** : to deliver by some bodily action ⟨*gave* me a push⟩ **14** : to offer as a pledge ⟨I ~ you my word⟩ **15** : DEVOTE **16** : to cause to have or receive ⟨~ me time⟩

**²give** *n* **1** : capacity or tendency to yield to force or strain **2** : the quality or state of being springy

**give–and–take** \,giv-ən-'tāk\ *n* **1** : COMPROMISE **2** : a usu. good-natured exchange (as of remarks or ideas)

**give·away** \'gi-və-,wā\ *n* **1** : an unintentional revelation or betrayal **2** : something given away free; *esp* : PREMIUM

**give in** *vb* : SUBMIT, SURRENDER

**¹giv·en** \'gi-vən\ *adj* **1** : DISPOSED, INCLINED ⟨~ to swearing⟩ **2** : SPECIFIED, PARTICULAR ⟨at a ~ time⟩

**²given** *n* : something taken for granted : a basic condition or assumption

**³given** *prep* : CONSIDERING

**given name** *n* : a name that precedes one's surname

**give out** *vb* 1 : EMIT 2 : BREAK DOWN 3 : to become exhausted : COLLAPSE

**give up** *vb* 1 : SURRENDER 2 : to abandon (oneself) to a feeling, influence, or activity 3 : QUIT ⟨*gave up* his job⟩

**giz·mo** *also* **gis·mo** \ˈgiz-mō\ *n, pl* **giz·mos** *also* **gismos** : GADGET

**giz·zard** \ˈgi-zərd\ *n* : the muscular usu. horny-lined enlargement of the alimentary canal of a bird used for churning and grinding up food

**gla·cial** \ˈglā-shəl\ *adj* 1 : extremely cold 2 : of or relating to glaciers 3 : being or relating to a past period of time when a large part of the earth was covered by glaciers 4 *cap* : PLEISTOCENE 5 : very slow ⟨a ~ pace⟩ — **gla·cial·ly** *adv*

**gla·ci·ate** \ˈglā-shē-ˌāt\ *vb* **-at·ed; -at·ing** 1 : to subject to glacial action 2 : to produce glacial effects in or on — **gla·ci·a·tion** \ˌglā-shē-ˈā-shən, -sē-\ *n*

**gla·cier** \ˈglā-shər\ *n* [F, fr. MF dial. (Savoy), fr. *glace* ice, fr. L *glacies*] : a large body of ice moving slowly down a slope or spreading outward on a land surface

**¹glad** \ˈglad\ *adj* **glad·der; glad·dest** 1 : experiencing pleasure, joy, or delight 2 : PLEASED 3 : very willing ⟨was ~ to help⟩ 4 : PLEASANT, JOYFUL 5 : CHEERFUL ⟨a ~ morning⟩ — **glad·ly** *adv* — **glad·ness** *n*

**²glad** *n* : GLADIOLUS

**glad·den** \ˈgla-dᵊn\ *vb* : to make glad

**glade** \ˈglād\ *n* : a grassy open space surrounded by woods

**glad·i·a·tor** \ˈgla-dē-ˌā-tər\ *n* 1 : a person engaged in a fight to the death for public entertainment in ancient Rome 2 : a person engaging in a public fight or controversy; *also* : PRIZEFIGHTER — **glad·i·a·to·ri·al** \ˌgla-dē-ə-ˈtȯr-ē-əl\ *adj*

**glad·i·o·lus** \ˌgla-dē-ˈō-ləs\ *n, pl* **-oli** \-ˈō-(ˌ)lē, -ˌlī\ *or* **-olus** *also* **-o·lus·es** [L, fr. dim. of *gladius* sword] : any of a genus of chiefly African plants related to the irises and having erect sword-shaped leaves and stalks of bright-colored flowers

**glad·some** \ˈglad-səm\ *adj* : giving or showing joy : CHEERFUL

**glad·stone** \ˈglad-ˌstōn\ *n, often cap* : a suitcase with flexible sides on a rigid frame that opens flat into two compartments

**glam** \ˈglam\ *n* : extravagantly showy glamour — **glam** *adj*

**glam·or·ise** *Brit var of* GLAMORIZE

**glam·or·ize** *also* **glam·our·ize** \ˈgla-mə-ˌrīz\ *vb* **-ized; -iz·ing** : to make or look upon as glamorous

**glam·our** *also* **glam·or** \ˈgla-mər\ *n* [Sc *glamour* magic spell, alter. of E *grammar*; fr. the popular association of erudition with occult practices] : an exciting and often illusory and romantic attractiveness; *esp* : alluring personal attraction — **glam·or·ous** *also* **glam·our·ous** \-mə-rəs\ *adj*

**¹glance** \ˈglans\ *vb* **glanced; glanc·ing** 1 : to strike and fly off to one side 2 : GLEAM 3 : to give a quick look

**²glance** *n* 1 : a quick intermittent flash or gleam 2 : a deflected impact or blow 3 : a quick look

**gland** \ˈgland\ *n* : a cell or group of cells that prepares and secretes a substance (as saliva or sweat) for further use in or discharge from the body

**glan·du·lar** \ˈglan-jə-lər\ *adj* : of, relating to, or involving glands

**glans** \ˈglanz\ *n, pl* **glan·des** \ˈglan-ˌdēz\ [L, lit., acorn] : a conical vascular body forming the extremity of the penis or clitoris

**¹glare** \ˈgler\ *vb* **glared; glar·ing** 1 : to shine with a harsh dazzling light 2 : to stare fiercely or angrily

**²glare** *n* 1 : a harsh dazzling light 2 : an angry or fierce stare

**glaring** *adj* : very conspicuous ⟨a ~ error⟩ — **glar·ing·ly** *adv*

**glass** \ˈglas\ *n* 1 : a hard brittle amorphous usu. transparent or translucent material consisting typically of silica 2 : something made of glass; *esp* : TUMBLER 3 *pl* : a pair of lenses used to correct defects of vision : SPECTACLES 4 : the quantity held by a glass container — **glass** *adj* — **glass·ful** \-ˌfùl\ *n* — **glassy** *adj*

**glass·blow·ing** \-ˌblō-iŋ\ *n* : the art of shaping a mass of glass that has been softened by heat by blowing air into it through a tube — **glass·blow·er** *n*

**glass·ware** \-ˌwer\ *n* : articles made of glass

**glau·co·ma** \glaù-ˈkō-mə, glȯ-\ *n* : a disease of the eye marked by increased pressure within the eyeball resulting in damage to the retina and gradual loss of vision

**¹glaze** \ˈglāz\ *vb* **glazed; glaz·ing** 1 : to furnish (as a window frame) with glass 2 : to apply glaze to

**²glaze** *n* : a glassy coating or surface

**gla·zier** \ˈglā-zhər\ *n* : a person who sets glass in window frames

**¹gleam** \ˈglēm\ *n* 1 : a transient subdued or partly obscured light 2 : GLINT 3 : a faint trace ⟨a ~ of hope⟩

**²gleam** *vb* 1 : to shine with subdued light or moderate brightness 2 : to appear briefly or faintly ♦ **Synonyms** FLASH, GLIMMER, GLISTEN, GLITTER, SHIMMER, SPARKLE

**glean** \ˈglēn\ *vb* 1 : to gather grain left by reapers 2 : to collect little by little or with patient effort ⟨antiques ~ed from flea markets⟩ — **glean·able** *adj* — **glean·er** *n*

**glean·ings** \ˈglē-niŋz\ *n pl* : things acquired by gleaning

**glee** \ˈglē\ *n* [ME, fr. OE *glēo* entertainment, music] 1 : JOY, HILARITY 2 : a part-song for three usu. male voices — **glee·ful** *adj* — **glee·ful·ly** *adv*

**glee club** *n* : a chorus organized for singing usu. short choral pieces

**glen** \ˈglen\ *n* : a narrow hidden valley

**glen·gar·ry** \glen-ˈga-rē\ *n, pl* **-ries** *often cap* : a woolen cap of Scottish origin

**glib** \ˈglib\ *adj* **glib·ber; glib·best**

: speaking or spoken with careless ease — **glide·ly** *adv*

**glide** \'glīd\ *vb* **glid·ed; glid·ing** **1** : to move smoothly and effortlessly **2** : to descend gradually without engine power ⟨∼ in an airplane⟩ — **glide** *n*

**glid·er** \'glī-dər\ *n* **1** : one that glides **2** : an aircraft resembling an airplane but having no engine **3** : a porch seat suspended from an upright frame

**¹glim·mer** \'gli-mər\ *vb* : to shine faintly or unsteadily

**²glimmer** *n* **1** : a faint unsteady light **2** : INKLING **3** : a small amount : HINT

**¹glimpse** \'glimps\ *vb* **glimpsed; glimps·ing** : to take a brief look : see momentarily or incompletely

**²glimpse** *n* **1** : a faint idea : GLIMMER **2** : a short hurried look

**glint** \'glint\ *vb* **1** : to shine by reflection : SPARKLE, GLITTER, GLEAM **2** : to appear briefly or faintly — **glint** *n*

**glis·san·do** \gli-'sän-(ˌ)dō\ *n, pl* **-di** \-(ˌ)dē\ *or* **-dos** : a rapid sliding up or down the musical scale

**glis·ten** \'gli-sᵊn\ *vb* : to shine by reflection with a soft luster or sparkle

**glis·ten** \'gli-sᵊn\ *n* : GLITTER, SPARKLE

**glis·ter** \'gli-stər\ *vb* : GLITTER

**glitch** \'glich\ *n* : MALFUNCTION; *also* : SNAG **2**

**¹glit·ter** \'gli-tər\ *vb* **1** : to shine with brilliant or metallic luster : SPARKLE **2** : to shine with strong emotion : FLASH ⟨eyes ∼ing in anger⟩ **3** : to be brilliantly attractive esp. in a superficial way

**²glitter** *n* **1** : sparkling brilliancy, showiness, or attractiveness **2** : small glittering objects used for ornamentation — **glit·tery** \'gli-tə-rē\ *adj*

**¹glitz** \'glits\ *n* : extravagant showiness — **glitzy** \'glit-sē\ *adj*

**²glitz** *vb* : to make flashy or extravagant in appearance — often used with *up*

**gloam·ing** \'glō-miŋ\ *n* : TWILIGHT, DUSK

**gloat** \'glōt\ *vb* : to think about something with triumphant and often malicious delight ⟨∼ing over their victory⟩

**glob** \'gläb\ *n* **1** : a small drop **2** : a large rounded mass

**glob·al** \'glō-bəl\ *adj* **1** : WORLDWIDE **2** : COMPREHENSIVE, GENERAL — **glob·al·ly** *adv*

**glob·al·i·za·tion** \ˌglō-bə-lə-'zā-shən\ *n* : the development of an increasingly integrated global economy

**Global Positioning System** *n* : GPS

**global warming** *n* : an increase in the earth's atmospheric and oceanic temperatures due to an increase in the greenhouse effect

**globe** \'glōb\ *n* **1** : BALL, SPHERE **2** : EARTH; *also* : a spherical representation of the earth

**globe–trot·ter** \'glōb-ˌträ-tər\ *n* : a person who travels widely — **globe–trot·ting** *n or adj*

**glob·u·lar** \'glä-byə-lər\ *adj* : having the shape of a globe or globule

**glob·ule** \'glä-(ˌ)byül\ *n* : a tiny globe or ball esp. of a liquid

**glob·u·lin** \'glä-byə-lən\ *n* : any of a class

of simple proteins insoluble in pure water but soluble in dilute salt solutions that occur widely in plant and animal tissues

**glock·en·spiel** \'glä-kən-ˌshpēl, -ˌspēl\ *n* [G, fr. *Glocke* bell + *Spiel* play] : a percussion musical instrument consisting of a series of metal bars played with two hammers

**gloom** \'glüm\ *n* **1** : partial or total darkness **2** : lowness of spirits : DEJECTION **3** : an atmosphere of despondency ⟨a ∼ fell over the household⟩ — **gloom·i·ly** \'glü-mə-lē\ *adv* — **gloom·i·ness** \-mē-nəs\ *n* — **gloomy** \'glü-mē\ *adj*

**Gloomy Gus** \-'gəs\ *n, pl* **Gloomy Guses** : a person who is habitually gloomy

**glop** \'gläp\ *n* : a messy mass or mixture

**glo·ri·fy** \'glór-ə-ˌfī\ *vb* **-fied; -fy·ing** **1** : to raise to heavenly glory **2** : to light up brilliantly **3** : EXTOL **4** : to give glory to (as in worship) — **glo·ri·fi·ca·tion** \ˌglór-ə-fə-'kā-shən\ *n*

**glo·ri·ous** \'glór-ē-əs\ *adj* **1** : possessing or deserving glory : PRAISEWORTHY **2** : conferring glory **3** : RESPLENDENT, MAGNIFICENT ⟨a ∼ sunset⟩ **4** : DELIGHTFUL, WONDERFUL ⟨had a ∼ weekend⟩ — **glo·ri·ous·ly** *adv*

**¹glo·ry** \'glór-ē\ *n, pl* **glories** **1** : RENOWN **2** : honor and praise rendered in worship **3** : something that secures praise or renown **4** : a distinguishing quality or asset **5** : RESPLENDENCE, MAGNIFICENCE **6** : heavenly bliss **7** : a height of prosperity or achievement

**²glory** *vb* **glo·ried; glo·ry·ing** : to rejoice proudly : EXULT

**¹gloss** \'gläs, 'glós\ *n* **1** : LUSTER, SHEEN, BRIGHTNESS **2** : outward show

**²gloss** *vb* **1** : to give a false appearance of acceptableness to ⟨∼ over inadequacies⟩ **2** : to deal with too lightly or not at all ⟨∼ed over the problem⟩

**³gloss** *n* [alter. of *gloze*, fr. ME *glose*, fr. AF, fr. ML *glosa, glossa*, fr. Gk *glōssa, glōtta* tongue, language, unusual word] **1** : an explanatory note (as in the margin of a text) **2** : GLOSSARY **3** : an interlinear translation **4** : a continuous commentary accompanying a text

**⁴gloss** *vb* : to furnish glosses for

**glos·sa·ry** \'glä-sə-rē, 'gló-\ *n, pl* **-ries** : a collection of difficult or specialized terms with their meanings — **glos·sar·i·al** \glä-'ser-ē-əl, gló-\ *adj*

**glos·so·la·lia** \ˌglä-sə-'lā-lē-ə, ˌglò-\ *n* [ultim. fr. Gk *glōssa* tongue, language + *lalia* chatter] : TONGUE **6**

**¹glossy** \'glä-sē, 'gló-\ *adj* **gloss·i·er; -est** : having a surface luster or brightness — **gloss·i·ly** \-sə-lē\ *adv* — **gloss·i·ness** \-sē-nəs\ *n*

**²glossy** *n, pl* **gloss·ies** : a photograph printed on smooth shiny paper

**glot·tis** \'glä-təs\ *n, pl* **glot·tis·es** *or* **glot·ti·des** \-tə-ˌdēz\ : the slitlike opening between the vocal cords in the larynx — **glot·tal** \'glä-tᵊl\ *adj*

**glove** \'gləv\ *n* **1** : a covering for the hand having separate sections for each finger **2** : a padded leather covering for the hand for use in a sport

¹**glow** \'glō\ *vb* **1** : to shine with or as if with intense heat **2** : to have a rich warm usu. ruddy color : FLUSH, BLUSH **3** : to feel hot **4** : to show exuberance or elation ⟨∼ with pride⟩

²**glow** *n* **1** : brightness or warmth of color; *esp* : REDNESS **2** : warmth of feeling or emotion **3** : a sensation of warmth **4** : light such as is emitted from a heated substance

**glow·er** \'glaù(-ə)r\ *vb* : to stare angrily : SCOWL — **glower** *n*

**glow·worm** \'glō-ˌwərm\ *n* : any of various insect larvae or adults that give off light

**glox·in·ia** \gläk-'si-nē-ə\ *n* : any of a genus of tropical herbs related to the African violets; *esp* : one with showy bell-shaped or slipper-shaped flowers

**gloze** \'glōz\ *vb* **glozed; gloz·ing** : to make appear right or acceptable : GLOSS

**glu·cose** \'glü-ˌkōs\ *n* **1** : a form of crystalline sugar; *esp* : DEXTROSE **2** : a sweet light-colored syrup made from cornstarch

**glue** \'glü\ *n* : a jellylike protein substance made from animal materials and used for sticking things together; *also* : any of various other strong adhesives — **glue** *vb* — **glu·ey** \'glü-ē\ *adj*

**glum** \'gləm\ *adj* **glum·mer; glum·mest** **1** : broodingly morose : SULLEN **2** : DREARY, GLOOMY ⟨a ∼ countenance⟩
♦ **Synonyms** CRABBED, DOUR, SATURNINE, SULKY

¹**glut** \'glət\ *vb* **glut·ted; glut·ting** **1** : OVERSUPPLY **2** : to fill esp. with food to satiety : SATIATE

²**glut** *n* : an excessive supply

**glu·ten** \'glü-tⁿn\ *n* : a gluey protein substance that causes dough to be sticky

**glu·ti·nous** \'glü-tə-nəs\ *adj* : STICKY

**glut·ton** \'glə-tⁿn\ *n* : one that eats to excess — **glut·ton·ous** \'glə-tə-nəs\ *adj* — **glut·tony** \'glə-tə-nē\ *n*

**glyc·er·in** *or* **glyc·er·ine** \'gli-sə-rən\ *n* : GLYCEROL

**glyc·er·ol** \'gli-sə-ˌròl, -ˌrōl\ *n* : a sweet syrupy alcohol usu. obtained from fats and used esp. as a solvent

**gly·co·gen** \'glī-kə-jən\ *n* : a white tasteless substance that is the chief storage carbohydrate of animals

**gm** *abbr* gram

**GM** *abbr* **1** general manager **2** guided missile

**G–man** \'jē-ˌman\ *n* : a special agent of the Federal Bureau of Investigation

**GMT** *abbr* Greenwich mean time

**gnarled** \'närld\ *adj* **1** : KNOTTY ⟨∼ hands⟩ **2** : GLOOMY, SULLEN

**gnash** \'nash\ *vb* : to grind (as teeth) together

**gnat** \'nat\ *n* : any of various small usu. biting dipteran flies

**gnaw** \'nò\ *vb* **1** : to consume, wear away, or make by persistent biting or nibbling **2** : to affect as if by gnawing — **gnaw·er** *n*

**gneiss** \'nīs\ *n* : a layered rock similar in composition to granite

**gnome** \'nōm\ *n* : a dwarf of folklore who lives inside the earth and guards precious ore or treasure — **gnome-like** \-ˌlīk\ *adj* — **gnom·ish** *adj*

**GNP** *abbr* gross national product

**gnu** \'nü\ *n, pl* **gnu** *or* **gnus** : WILDEBEEST

¹**go** \'gō\ *vb* **went** \'went\; **gone** \'gòn, 'gän\; **go·ing; goes** \'gōz\ **1** : to move on a course : PROCEED ⟨∼ slow⟩ **2** : LEAVE, DEPART **3** : to take a certain course or follow a certain procedure ⟨reports ∼ through department channels⟩ **4** : EXTEND, RUN ⟨his land ∼es to the river⟩; *also* : LEAD ⟨that door ∼es to the cellar⟩ **5** : to be habitually in a certain state ⟨∼es barefoot⟩ **6** : to become lost, consumed, or spent; *also* : DIE **7** : ELAPSE, PASS **8** : to pass by sale ⟨went for a good price⟩ **9** : to become impaired or weakened ⟨his hearing started to ∼⟩ **10** : to give way under force or pressure : BREAK **11** : to move along in a specified manner ⟨it went well⟩ **12** : to be in general or on an average ⟨cheap, as yachts ∼⟩ **13** : to become esp. as the result of a contest ⟨the decision went against him⟩ **14** : to put or subject oneself ⟨∼ to great expense⟩ **15** : RESORT ⟨went to court to recover damages⟩ **16** : to begin or maintain an action or motion **17** : to function properly ⟨the clock doesn't ∼⟩ **18** : to be known ⟨∼es by an alias⟩ **19** : to be or act in accordance ⟨a good rule to ∼ by⟩ **20** : to come to be applied **21** : to pass by award, assignment, or lot **22** : to contribute to a result ⟨qualities that ∼ to make a hero⟩ **23** : to be about, intending, or expecting something ⟨is ∼ing to leave town⟩ **24** : to arrive at a certain state or condition ⟨∼ to sleep⟩ **25** : to come to be ⟨the tire went flat⟩ **26** : to be capable of being sung or played ⟨the tune ∼es like this⟩ **27** : to be suitable or becoming : HARMONIZE **28** : to be capable of passing, extending, or being contained or inserted ⟨this coat will ∼ in the trunk⟩ **29** : to have a usual or proper place or position : BELONG ⟨these books ∼ on the top shelf⟩ **30** : to be capable of being divided ⟨3 ∼es into 6 twice⟩ **31** : to have a tendency ⟨that ∼es to show that he is honest⟩ **32** : to be acceptable, satisfactory, or adequate ⟨any color will ∼ with black⟩ **33** : to empty the bladder or bowels **34** : to proceed along or according to : FOLLOW **35** : TRAVERSE **36** : BET, BID ⟨willing to ∼ $50⟩ **37** : to assume the function or obligation of ⟨∼ bail for a friend⟩ **38** : to participate to the extent of ⟨∼ halves⟩ **39** : WEIGH **40** : ENDURE, TOLERATE **41** : AFFORD ⟨can't ∼ the price⟩ **42** : SAY — used chiefly in oral narration of speech **43** : to engage in ⟨don't ∼ telling everyone⟩ — **go at 1** : ATTACK, ATTEMPT **2** : UNDERTAKE — **go back on 1** : ABANDON **2** : BETRAY **3** : FAIL — **go by the board** : to be discarded — **go for 1** : to pass for or serve as **2** : to try to secure **3** : FAVOR — **go one better** : OUTDO, SURPASS — **go over 1** : EXAMINE **2** : REPEAT **3** : STUDY, REVIEW — **go places** : to be on

the way to success — **go steady** : to date one person exclusively — **go to bat for** : DEFEND, CHAMPION — **go to town** 1 : to work or act efficiently 2 : to be very successful

²**go** n, pl **goes** 1 : the act or manner of going 2 : the height of fashion ⟨boots are all the ∼⟩ 3 : a turn of affairs : OCCURRENCE 4 : ENERGY, VIGOR 5 : ATTEMPT, TRY ⟨give it a ∼⟩ 6 : a spell of activity ⟨finished the job at one ∼⟩ — **no go** : USELESS, HOPELESS — **on the go** : constantly active

³**go** adj : functioning properly ⟨declared all systems ∼⟩

**goad** \'gōd\ n [ME gode, fr. OE gād spear, goad] 1 : a pointed rod used to urge on an animal 2 : something that urges
**♦ Synonyms** STIMULUS, IMPETUS, INCENTIVE, SPUR, STIMULANT — **goad** vb

**go-ahead** \'gō-ə-,hed\ n : authority to proceed ⟨got the ∼ for the project⟩

**goal** \'gōl\ n 1 : the mark set as limit to a race; also : an area to be reached safely in children's games 2 : AIM, PURPOSE 3 : an area or object toward which play is directed to score; also : a successful attempt to score

**goal·ie** \'gō-lē\ n : GOALKEEPER

**goal·keep·er** \'gōl-,kē-pər\ n : a player who defends the goal in various games

**goal·post** \-,pōst\ n : one of the two vertical posts with a crossbar that constitute the goal in various games

**goat** \'gōt\ n, pl **goats** or **goat** : any of various hollow-horned ruminant mammals related to the sheep that have backward-curving horns, a short tail, and usu. straight hair

**goa·tee** \gō-'tē\ n : a small trim pointed or tufted beard on a man's chin

**goat·herd** \'gōt-,hərd\ n : a person who tends goats

**goat·skin** \-,skin\ n : the skin of a goat or a leather made from it

¹**gob** \'gäb\ n : LUMP, MASS

²**gob** n : SAILOR

**gob·bet** \'gä-bət\ n : LUMP, MASS

¹**gob·ble** \'gä-bəl\ vb **gob·bled; gob·bling** 1 : to swallow or eat greedily 2 : to take eagerly : GRAB

²**gobble** vb **gob·bled; gob·bling** : to make the natural guttural noise of a male turkey

**gob·ble·dy·gook** also **gob·ble·de·gook** \'gä-bəl-dē-,gük, -,gük\ n : generally unintelligible jargon

**gob·bler** \'gä-blər\ n : a male turkey

**go-be·tween** \'gō-bə-,twēn\ n : an intermediate agent : BROKER

**gob·let** \'gä-blət\ n : a drinking glass with a foot and stem

**gob·lin** \'gä-blən\ n : an ugly or grotesque sprite that is mischievous and sometimes evil and malicious

**go·by** \'gō-bē\ n, pl **gobies** also **goby** : any of numerous spiny-finned fishes usu. having the pelvic fins united to form a ventral sucking disk

**god** \'gäd, 'gód\ n 1 cap : the supreme reality; esp : the Being worshiped as the creator and ruler of the universe 2 : a

being or object believed to have supernatural attributes and powers and to require worship 3 : a thing of supreme value 4 : an extraordinarily attractive person

**god·child** \'gäd-,chī(-ə)ld, 'gód-\ n : a person for whom another person stands as sponsor at baptism

**god·daugh·ter** \-,do-tər\ n : a female godchild

**god·dess** \'gä-dəs, 'gó-\ n 1 : a female god 2 : a woman whose charm or beauty arouses adoration

**god·fa·ther** \'gäd-,fä-thər, 'gód-\ n 1 : a man who sponsors a person at baptism 2 : the leader of an organized crime syndicate

**god·head** \-,hed\ n 1 : divine nature or essence 2 cap : GOD 1; also : the nature of God esp. as existing in three persons

**god·hood** \-,hud\ n : DIVINITY

**god·less** \-ləs\ adj : not acknowledging a deity or divine law — **god·less·ness** n

**god·like** \-,līk\ adj : resembling or having the qualities of God or a god

**god·ly** \-lē\ adj **god·li·er; -est** 1 : DIVINE 2 : PIOUS, DEVOUT — **god·li·ness** n

**god·moth·er** \-,mə-thər\ n : a woman who sponsors a person at baptism

**god·par·ent** \-,per-ənt\ n : a sponsor at baptism

**god·send** \-,send\ n : a desirable or needed thing or event that comes unexpectedly

**god·son** \-,sən\ n : a male godchild

**God·speed** \-'spēd\ n : a prosperous journey : SUCCESS ⟨bade him ∼⟩

**go·fer** or **go·pher** \'gō-fər\ n [alter. of go for] : an employee whose duties include running errands

**go-get·ter** \'gō-,ge-tər\ n : an aggressively enterprising person — **go-get·ting** adj or n

**gog·gle** \'gä-gəl\ vb **gog·gled; gog·gling** : to stare with wide or protuberant eyes

**gog·gles** \'gä-gəlz\ n pl : protective glasses set in a flexible frame that fits snugly against the face

**go-go** \'gō-,gō\ adj 1 : related to, being, or employed to entertain in a disco ⟨∼ dancers⟩ 2 : aggressively enterprising and energetic ⟨∼ entrepreneurs⟩

**go·ings-on** \,gō-in-'zón, -'zän\ n pl : ACTIONS, EVENTS

**goi·ter** \'gói-tər\ n : an abnormally enlarged thyroid gland visible as a swelling at the base of the neck — **goi·trous** \-trəs, -tə-rəs\ adj

**goi·tre** chiefly Brit var of GOITER

**go-kart** \'gō-,kärt\ n : a small motorized vehicle used esp. for racing

**gold** \'gōld\ n 1 : a malleable yellow metallic chemical element used esp. for coins and jewelry 2 : gold coins; also : MONEY 3 : a yellow color

**gold·brick** \'gōld-,brik\ n : a person who shirks assigned work — **goldbrick** vb

**gold coast** n, often cap G&C : an exclusive residential district

**gold digger** n : a person who uses charm to extract money or gifts from others

**gold·en** \'gōl-dən\ adj 1 : made of or relating to gold  **2** : having the color of gold; *also* : BLOND  **3** : SHINING, LUSTROUS  **4** : SUPERB  **5** : FLOURISHING, PROSPEROUS  **6** : radiantly youthful and vigorous  **7** : FAVORABLE, ADVANTAGEOUS ⟨a ∼ opportunity⟩  **8** : MELLOW, RESONANT ⟨a ∼ tenor⟩

**gold·en·ag·er** \'gōl-dən-ˌā-jər\ *n* : an elderly and often retired person usu. engaging in club activities

**golden eagle** *n* : a large dark brown eagle with gold-colored feathers on the back of the head and neck

**golden hamster** *n* : a small tawny hamster often kept as a pet

**golden handcuffs** *n pl* : special benefits offered to an employee as an inducement to continue service

**golden handshake** *n* : a generous severance agreement given esp. as an inducement to early retirement

**golden retriever** *n* : any of a breed of retrievers with a flat golden coat

**gold·en·rod** \'gōl-dən-ˌräd\ *n* : any of numerous herbs related to the daisies that have tall slender stalks with many tiny usu. yellow flower heads

**golden years** *n pl* : the advanced years in a lifetime

**gold·finch** \-ˌfinch\ *n*  **1** : a small largely red, black, and yellow Old World finch often kept in a cage  **2** : any of three small related American finches of which the males usu. become bright yellow and black in summer

**gold·fish** \-ˌfish\ *n* : a small usu. golden-orange carp often kept as an aquarium or pond fish

**gold·smith** \-ˌsmith\ *n* : a person who makes or deals in articles of gold

**golf** \'gälf, 'gȯlf\ *n* : a game played with a small ball and various clubs on a course having 9 or 18 holes — **golf** *vb* — **golf·er** *n*

**-gon** \ˌgän\ *n comb form* : figure having (so many) angles ⟨hexa*gon*⟩

**go·nad** \'gō-ˌnad\ *n* : a sperm- or egg-producing gland : OVARY, TESTIS — **go·nad·al** \gō-'na-dᵊl\ *adj*

**go·nad·o·trop·ic** \ˌgō-ˌna-də-'trä-pik\ *also* **go·nad·o·tro·phic** \-'trō-fik, -'trä-\ *adj* : acting on or stimulating the gonads

**go·nad·o·tro·pin** \-'trō-pən\ *also* **go·nad·o·tro·phin** \-fən\ *n* : a gonadotropic hormone

**gon·do·la** \'gän-də-lə (*usual for 1*), gän-'dō-\ *n* [It. dial. (Venice), prob. fr. MGk *kontoura* small vessel]  **1** : a long narrow boat used on the canals of Venice  **2** : a railroad car used for hauling loose freight (as coal)  **3** : an enclosure beneath an airship or balloon  **4** : an enclosed car suspended from a cable and used esp. for transporting skiers

**gon·do·lier** \ˌgän-də-'lir\ *n* : a person who propels a gondola

**¹gone** \'gȯn\ *past part of* GO

**²gone** *adj*  **1** : LOST, RUINED  **2** : DEAD  **3** : SINKING, WEAK  **4** : INVOLVED, ABSORBED  **5** : INFATUATED  **6** : PREGNANT  **7** : PAST

**gon·er** \'gȯ-nər\ *n* : one whose case is hopeless

**gong** \'gäŋ, 'gȯŋ\ *n* : a metallic disk that produces a resounding tone when struck

**gono·coc·cus** \ˌgä-nə-'kä-kəs\ *n, pl* **-coc·ci** \-'käk-ˌsī, -(ˌ)sē, -'kä-ˌkī, -(ˌ)kē\ : a pus-producing bacterium causing gonorrhea — **gono·coc·cal** \-'kä-kəl\ *adj*

**gon·or·rhea** \ˌgä-nə-'rē-ə\ *n* : a contagious sexually transmitted inflammation of the genital tract caused by the gonococcus — **gon·or·rhe·al** \-'rē-əl\ *adj*

**goo** \'gü\ *n*  **1** : a viscid or sticky substance  **2** : sentimental tripe — **goo·ey** \-ē\ *adj*

**goo·ber** \'gü-bər, 'gu-\ *n, Southern & Midland* : PEANUT

**¹good** \'gu̇d\ *adj* **bet·ter** \'be-tər\; **best** \'best\  **1** : of a favorable character or tendency  **2** : BOUNTIFUL, FERTILE ⟨∼ land⟩  **3** : COMELY, ATTRACTIVE  **4** : SUITABLE, FIT  **5** : SOUND, WHOLE ⟨only one ∼ arm⟩  **6** : AGREEABLE, PLEASANT ⟨had a ∼ time⟩  **7** : SALUTARY, WHOLESOME  **8** : CONSIDERABLE, AMPLE ⟨a ∼ bit of time⟩  **9** : FULL ⟨waited a ∼ hour⟩  **10** : WELL-FOUNDED  **11** : TRUE ⟨holds ∼ for everybody⟩  **12** : legally valid or effectual  **13** : ADEQUATE, SATISFACTORY  **14** : conforming to a standard ⟨∼ English⟩  **15** : DISCRIMINATING  **16** : COMMENDABLE, VIRTUOUS  **17** : KIND  **18** : UPPER-CLASS  **19** : COMPETENT  **20** : LOYAL, CLOSE ⟨a ∼ friend⟩ — **good·ish** *adj*

**²good** *n*  **1** : something good  **2** : GOODNESS  **3** : BENEFIT, WELFARE ⟨for the ∼ of mankind⟩  **4** : something that has economic utility  **5** *pl* : personal property  **6** *pl* : CLOTH  **7** *pl* : WARES, MERCHANDISE ⟨canned ∼s⟩  **8** : good persons ⟨the ∼ die young⟩  **9** *pl* : proof of wrongdoing — **for good** : FOREVER, PERMANENTLY — **to the good** : in a position of net gain or profit ⟨$10 *to the good*⟩

**³good** *adv* : WELL

**good–bye** *or* **good–by** \gu̇d-'bī, gə-\ *n* : a concluding remark at parting

**good cholesterol** *n* : HDL

**good–for–noth·ing** \'gu̇d-fər-ˌnə-thiŋ\ *adj* : of no use or value — **good–for–nothing** *n*

**Good Friday** *n* : the Friday before Easter observed as the anniversary of the crucifixion of Christ

**good–heart·ed** \'gu̇d-'här-təd\ *adj* : having a kindly generous disposition — **good–heart·ed·ly** *adv* — **good–heart·ed·ness** *n*

**good–look·ing** \'gu̇d-'lu̇-kiŋ\ *adj* : having an attractive appearance

**good·ly** \'gu̇d-lē\ *adj* **good·li·er; -est**  **1** : of pleasing appearance  **2** : LARGE, CONSIDERABLE ⟨a ∼ sum of money⟩

**good·man** \'gu̇d-mən\ *n, archaic* : MR.

**good–na·tured** \'gu̇d-'nā-chərd\ *adj* : of a cheerful disposition — **good–na·tured·ly** \-chərd-lē\ *adv*

**good·ness** \-nəs\ *n* : EXCELLENCE, VIRTUE

**good·wife** \-ˌwīf\ *n, archaic* : MRS.

**good·will** \-'wil\ *n*  **1** : BENEVOLENCE  **2**

: the value of the trade a business has built up over time **3** : cheerful consent **4** : willing effort

**goody** *or* **good·ie** \'gù-dē\ *n, pl* **good·ies** : something that is good esp. to eat

**goody–goody** \,gù-dē-'gù-dē\ *adj* : affectedly good — **goody–goody** *n*

**goof** \'güf\ *vb* **1** : to spend time idly or foolishly — usu. used with *off* **2** : BLUNDER — usu. used with *up* — **goof** *n*

**goof·ball** \'güf-,bȯl\ *n* **1** *slang* : a barbiturate sleeping pill **2** : a goofy person

**go off** *vb* **1** : EXPLODE **2** : to follow a course ⟨the party *went off* well⟩

**goof–off** \'güf-,ȯf\ *n* : one who evades work or responsibility

**goofy** \'gù-fē\ *adj* **goof·i·er; -est** : CRAZY, SILLY — **goof·i·ness** \-fē-nəs\ *n*

**goo·gle** \'gü-gəl\ *vb* **goo·gled; goo·gling** [*Google*, trademark for a search engine] : to use the Google search engine to obtain information on the World Wide Web

**goon** \'gün\ *n* : a man hired to terrorize or kill opponents

**go on** *vb* **1** : to continue in a course of action **2** : to take place : HAPPEN

**goose** \'güs\ *n, pl* **geese** \'gēs\ **1** : any of numerous long-necked web-footed birds related to the swans and ducks; *also* : a female goose as distinguished from a gander **2** : a foolish person **3** *pl* **goos·es** : a tailor's smoothing iron

**goose·ber·ry** \'güs-,ber-ē, 'güz-, -bə-rē\ *n* : the acid berry of any of several shrubs related to the currant and used esp. in jams and pies

**goose bumps** *n pl* : roughening of the skin caused usu. by cold, fear, or a sudden feeling of excitement

**goose·flesh** \-,flesh\ *n* : GOOSE BUMPS

**goose pimples** *n pl* : GOOSE BUMPS

**go out** *vb* **1** : to become extinguished **2** : to become a candidate ⟨*went out* for the football team⟩

**go over** *vb* : SUCCEED

**GOP** *abbr* Grand Old Party (Republican)

**¹go·pher** \'gō-fər\ *n* **1** : a burrowing American land tortoise **2** : any of a family of No. American burrowing rodents with large cheek pouches opening beside the mouth **3** : any of several small ground squirrels of the prairie region of No. America

**²gopher** *var of* GOFER

**go·pik** \gō-'pēk, -'pik\ *n, pl* **gopik** — see *manat* at MONEY table

**¹gore** \'gȯr\ *n* : a tapering or triangular piece (as of cloth in a skirt)

**²gore** *vb* **gored; gor·ing** : to pierce or wound with something pointed

**³gore** *n* **1** : BLOOD **2** : gruesomeness depicted in vivid detail

**¹gorge** \'gȯrj\ *n* **1** : THROAT **2** : a narrow ravine **3** : a mass of matter that chokes up a passage

**²gorge** *vb* **gorged; gorg·ing** : to eat greedily : stuff to capacity : GLUT

**gor·geous** \'gȯr-jəs\ *adj* : resplendently beautiful

**Gor·gon·zo·la** \,gȯr-gən-'zō-lə\ *n* : a pungent blue cheese of Italian origin

**go·ril·la** \gə-'ri-lə\ *n* [NL, fr. Gk *Gorillai*, a tribe of hairy women in an account of a voyage around Africa] : an African anthropoid ape related to but much larger than the chimpanzee

**gor·man·dise** *chiefly Brit var of* GORMANDIZE

**gor·man·dize** \'gȯr-mən-,dīz\ *vb* **-dized; -diz·ing** : to eat ravenously — **gor·man·diz·er** *n*

**gorp** \'gȯrp\ *n* : a snack consisting of high-calorie food (as raisins and nuts)

**gorse** \'gȯrs\ *n* : a spiny yellow-flowered European evergreen shrub of the legume family

**gory** \'gȯr-ē\ *adj* **gor·i·er; -est** **1** : BLOODSTAINED **2** : HORRIBLE, SENSATIONAL ⟨the ~ details⟩

**gos·hawk** \'gäs-,hȯk\ *n* : any of several long-tailed hawks with short rounded wings

**gos·ling** \'gäz-liŋ, 'gȯz-\ *n* : a young goose

**¹gos·pel** \'gäs-pəl\ *n* [ME, fr. OE *gōdspel*, fr. *gōd* good + *spell* message, news] **1** : the teachings of Christ and the apostles **2** *cap* : any of the first four books of the New Testament **3** : something accepted or promoted as infallible truth

**²gospel** *adj* **1** : of, relating to, or emphasizing the gospel **2** : relating to or being American religious songs associated with evangelism

**gos·sa·mer** \'gä-sə-mər\ *n* [ME *gossomer*, fr. *gos* goose + *somer* summer] **1** : a film of cobwebs floating in the air **2** : something light, delicate, or tenuous

**¹gos·sip** \'gä-səp\ *n* **1** : a person who habitually reveals personal or sensational facts **2** : rumor or report of an intimate nature **3** : an informal conversation — **gos·sip·y** *adj*

**²gossip** *vb* : to spread gossip

**got** *past and past part of* GET

**Goth** \'gäth\ *n* : a member of a Germanic people that early in the Christian era overran the Roman Empire

**¹Goth·ic** \'gä-thik\ *adj* **1** : of or relating to the Goths **2** : of or relating to a style of architecture prevalent in western Europe from the middle 12th to the early 16th century

**²Gothic** *n* **1** : the Germanic language of the Goths **2** : the Gothic architectural style or decoration

**gotten** *past part of* GET

**Gou·da** \'gü-də\ *n* : a mild Dutch milk cheese shaped in balls

**¹gouge** \'gaúj\ *n* **1** : a rounded troughlike chisel **2** : a hole or groove made with or as if with a gouge

**²gouge** *vb* **gouged; goug·ing** **1** : to cut holes or grooves in with or as if with a gouge **2** : DEFRAUD, CHEAT

**gou·lash** \'gü-,läsh, -,lash\ *n* [Hungarian *gulyás*] : a stew made with meat, assorted vegetables, and paprika

**go under** *vb* : to be overwhelmed, defeated, or destroyed : FAIL

**gourd** \'gȯrd, 'gùrd\ *n* **1** : any of a family of tendril-bearing vines including the cucumber, squash, and melon **2** : the fruit of a gourd; *esp* : any of various inedible hard-shelled fruits used esp. for ornament or implements

**gourde** \'gurd\ *n* — see MONEY table

**gour·mand** \'gur-,mänd\ *n* 1 : one who is excessively fond of eating and drinking 2 : GOURMET

**gour·met** \'gur-,mā, gur-'mā\ *n* [F, fr. MF, alter. of *gromet* boy servant, vintner's assistant] : a connoisseur of food and drink

**gout** \'gaut\ *n* : a metabolic disease marked by painful inflammation and swelling of the joints — **gouty** *adj*

**gov** *abbr* 1 government 2 governor 3 governmental institution — used in World Wide Web addresses

**gov·ern** \'gə-vərn\ *vb* [ME, fr. AF *governer*, fr. L *gubernare* to steer, govern, fr. Gk *kybernan*] 1 : to control and direct the making and administration of policy in : RULE 2 : CONTROL, DIRECT, INFLUENCE 3 : DETERMINE, REGULATE 4 : RESTRAIN — **gov·ern·able** \-vər-nə-bəl\ *adj* — **gov·er·nance** \-vər-nəns\ *n*

**gov·ern·ess** \'gə-vər-nəs\ *n* : a woman who teaches and trains a child esp. in a private home

**gov·ern·ment** \'gə-vərn-mənt\ *n* 1 : authoritative direction or control : RULE 2 : the making of policy 3 : the organization or agency through which a political unit exercises authority 4 : the complex of institutions, laws, and customs through which a political unit is governed 5 : the governing body — **gov·ern·men·tal** \,gə-vərn-'men-t³l\ *adj* — **gov·ern·men·tal·ly** \-t³l-ē\ *adv*

**gov·er·nor** \'gə-vər-nər\ *n* 1 : one that governs; *esp* : a ruler, chief executive, or head of a political unit (as a state) 2 : an attachment to a machine for automatic control of speed — **gov·er·nor·ship** *n*

**govt** *abbr* government

**gown** \'gaun\ *n* 1 : a loose flowing outer garment 2 : an official robe worn esp. by a judge, clergyman, or teacher 3 : a woman's dress ⟨evening ~s⟩ 4 : a loose robe 5 : an academic community within a town or city — **gown** *vb*

**gp** *abbr* group

**GP** *abbr* general practitioner

**GPO** *abbr* 1 general post office 2 Government Printing Office

**GPS** \,jē-,pē-'es\ *n* [Global Positioning System] : a navigation system that uses satellite signals to fix location; *also* : the signal receiver itself

**GQ** *abbr* general quarters

**gr** *abbr* 1 grade 2 grain 3 gram 4 gravity 5 gross

**grab** \'grab\ *vb* **grabbed; grab·bing** : to take hastily : SNATCH — **grab** *n*

¹**grace** \'grās\ *n* 1 : unmerited help given to people by God (as in overcoming temptation) 2 : freedom from sin through divine grace 3 : a virtue coming from God 4 — used as a title for a duke, a duchess, or an archbishop 5 : a short prayer at a meal 6 : a temporary respite (as from the payment of a debt) 7 : APPROVAL, ACCEPTANCE ⟨in his good ~s⟩

8 : CHARM 9 : ATTRACTIVENESS, BEAUTY 10 : fitness or proportion of line or expression 11 : ease of movement 12 : a musical trill or ornament — **grace·ful** \-fəl\ *adj* — **grace·ful·ly** *adv* — **grace·ful·ness** *n* — **grace·less** *adj*

²**grace** *vb* **graced; grac·ing** 1 : HONOR 2 : ADORN, EMBELLISH

**gra·cious** \'grā-shəs\ *adj* 1 : marked by kindness and courtesy ⟨a ~ host⟩ 2 : GRACEFUL 3 : characterized by charm and good taste 4 : MERCIFUL — **gra·cious·ly** *adv* — **gra·cious·ness** *n*

**grack·le** \'gra-kəl\ *n* : any of several large American blackbirds with glossy iridescent plumage

**grad** *abbr* graduate; graduated

**gra·da·tion** \grā-'dā-shən, grə-\ *n* 1 : a series forming successive stages 2 : a step, degree, or stage in a series 3 : an advance by regular degrees 4 : the act or process of grading

¹**grade** \'grād\ *n* [L *gradus* step, degree, fr. *gradi* to step, go] 1 : a position in a scale of rank, quality, or order 2 : a stage in a process or ranking 3 : a division of the school course representing one year's work; *also* : the pupils in such a division 4 : a class of persons or things of the same rank or quality 5 : a mark or rating esp. of accomplishment in school 6 : the degree of slope (as of a road); *also* : SLOPE 7 *pl* : the elementary school system

²**grade** *vb* **grad·ed; grad·ing** 1 : to arrange in grades : SORT 2 : to make level or evenly sloping ⟨~ a highway⟩ 3 : to give a grade to ⟨~ a pupil in history⟩ 4 : to assign to a grade

**grade inflation** *n* : the assigning of grades higher than previously assigned for given levels of achievement

**grad·er** \'grā-dər\ *n* 1 : a machine for leveling earth 2 : a pupil in a school grade

**grade school** *n* : ELEMENTARY SCHOOL

**gra·di·ent** \'grā-dē-ənt\ *n* : SLOPE, GRADE

**grad·u·al** \'gra-jə-wəl\ *adj* : proceeding or changing by steps or degrees ⟨~ improvements⟩ — **grad·u·al·ly** *adv*

**grad·u·al·ism** \-wə-,li-zəm\ *n* : the policy of approaching a desired end gradually

¹**grad·u·ate** \'gra-jə-wət\ *n* 1 : a holder of an academic degree or diploma 2 : a graduated container for measuring contents

²**graduate** *adj* 1 : holding an academic degree or diploma 2 : of or relating to studies beyond the first or bachelor's degree ⟨~ school⟩

³**grad·u·ate** \'gra-jə-,wāt\ *vb* **-at·ed; -at·ing** 1 : to grant or receive an academic degree or diploma 2 : to divide into grades, classes, or intervals 3 : to admit to a particular standing or grade

**grad·u·a·tion** \,gra-jə-'wā-shən\ *n* 1 : a mark that graduates something 2 : an act or process of graduating 3 : COMMENCEMENT 2

**graf·fi·ti** \grə-'fē-(,)tē\ *n* : unauthorized writing or drawing on a public surface

**graf·fi·to** \gra-'fē-tō, grə-\ *n, pl* **-ti** \-(,)tē\

: an inscription or drawing made on a public surface (as a wall)

¹**graft** \'graft\ *n* **1** : a grafted plant; *also* : the point of union in this **2** : material (as skin) used in grafting **3** : the getting of money or advantage dishonestly; *also* : the money or advantage so gained

²**graft** *vb* **1** : to insert a shoot from one plant into another so that they join and grow; *also* : to join one thing to another as in plant grafting ⟨∼ skin over a burn⟩ **2** : to get (as money) dishonestly — **graft·er** *n*

**gra·ham cracker** \'grā-əm-, 'gram-\ *n* : a slightly sweet cracker made chiefly of whole wheat flour

**Grail** \'grāl\ *n* **1** : the cup or platter used according to medieval legend by Christ at the Last Supper and thereafter the object of knightly quests **2** *not cap* : the object of an extended or difficult quest

**grain** \'grān\ *n* **1** : a seed or fruit of a cereal grass **2** : seeds or fruits of various food plants and esp. cereal grasses, *also* : a plant (as wheat) producing grain **3** : a small hard particle **4** : a unit of weight based on the weight of a grain of wheat — see WEIGHT table **5** : TEXTURE; *also* : the arrangement of fibers in wood **6** : natural disposition ⟨lying goes against my ∼⟩ — **grained** \'grānd\ *adj*

**grain alcohol** *n* : ALCOHOL 1

**grainy** \'grā-nē\ *adj* **grain·i·er; -est 1** : resembling or having some characteristic of grain : not smooth or fine **2** *of a photograph* : appearing to be composed of grain-like particles

¹**gram** \'gram\ *n* [F *gramme*, fr. LL *gramma*, a small weight, fr. Gk *gramma* letter, writing, a small weight, fr *graphein* to write] : a metric unit of mass and weight equal to $^1/_{1000}$ kilogram — see METRIC SYSTEM table

²**gram** *abbr* grammar; grammatical

**-gram** \,gram\ *n comb form* : drawing : writing : record ⟨telegram⟩

**gram·mar** \'gra-mər\ *n* **1** : the study of the classes of words, their inflections, and their functions and relations in the sentence **2** : a study of what is to be preferred and what avoided in inflection and syntax **3** : speech or writing evaluated according to its conformity to grammatical rules — **gram·mar·i·an** \grə-'mer-ē-ən, -'mar-\ *n* — **gram·mat·i·cal** \-'ma-ti-kəl\ *adj* — **gram·mat·i·cal·ly** \-k(ə-)lē\ *adv*

**grammar school** *n* **1** : a secondary school emphasizing Latin and Greek in preparation for college; *also* : a British college preparatory school **2** : a school intermediate between the primary grades and high school **3** : ELEMENTARY SCHOOL

**gramme** \'gram\ *chiefly Brit var of* GRAM

**gram·o·phone** \'gra-mə-ˌfōn\ *n* : PHONOGRAPH

**gra·na·ry** \'grā-nə-rē, 'gra-\ *n, pl* **-ries 1** : a storehouse for grain **2** : a region producing grain in abundance

¹**grand** \'grand\ *adj* **1** : higher in rank or importance : FOREMOST, CHIEF **2** : great

in size **3** : INCLUSIVE, COMPLETE ⟨a ∼ total⟩ **4** : MAGNIFICENT, SPLENDID **5** : showing wealth or high social standing **6** : IMPRESSIVE, STATELY **7** : very good : FINE ⟨had a ∼ time⟩ — **grand·ly** *adv* — **grand·ness** *n*

²**grand** *n, pl* **grand** *slang* : a thousand dollars

**grand·dam** \'gran-ˌdam, -dəm\ *or* **gran·dame** \-ˌdām, -dəm\ *n* : an old woman

**grand·child** \'grand-ˌchī(-ə)ld\ *n* : a child of one's son or daughter

**grand·daugh·ter** \'gran-ˌdȯ-tər\ *n* : a daughter of one's son or daughter

**grande dame** \'grän-'däm\ *n, pl* **grandes dames** : a usu. elderly woman of great prestige or ability

**gran·dee** \gran-'dē\ *n* : a high-ranking Spanish or Portuguese nobleman

**gran·deur** \'gran-jər\ *n* **1** : the quality or state of being grand : MAGNIFICENCE **2** : something that is grand

**grand·fa·ther** \'grand-ˌfä-thər\ *n* : the father of one's father or mother; *also* : ANCESTOR

**grandfather clock** *n* : a tall clock that stands on the floor

**gran·dil·o·quence** \gran-'di-lə-kwəns\ *n* : pompous eloquence — **gran·dil·o·quent** \-kwənt\ *adj*

**gran·di·ose** \'gran-dē-ˌōs, ˌgran-dē-'ōs\ *adj* : IMPRESSIVE, IMPOSING; *also* : affectedly splendid — **gran·di·ose·ly** *adv* — **gran·di·os·i·ty** \ˌgran-dē-'ä-sə-tē\ *n*

**grand jury** *n* : a jury that examines accusations of crime against persons and makes formal charges on which the persons are later tried

**grand mal** \'grän-ˌmäl; 'grand-ˌmal\ *n* [F, lit., great illness] : severe epilepsy

**grand·moth·er** \'grand-ˌmə-thər\ *n* : the mother of one's father or mother; *also* : a female ancestor

**grand·par·ent** \-ˌper-ənt\ *n* : a parent of one's father or mother

**grand piano** *n* : a piano with horizontal frame and strings

**grand prix** \'grän-'prē\ *n, pl* **grand prix** \*same or* -'prēz\ *often cap G&P* : a long-distance auto race over a road course; *also* : a high-level competition in another sport (as sailing)

**grand slam** *n* **1** : a total victory or success **2** : a home run hit with three runners on base

**grand·son** \'grand-ˌsən\ *n* : a son of one's son or daughter

**grand·stand** \-ˌstand\ *n* : a usu. roofed stand for spectators at a racecourse or stadium

**grange** \'grānj\ *n* **1** : a farm or farmhouse with its various buildings **2** *cap* : one of the lodges of a national association originally made up of farmers; *also* : the association itself — **Grang·er** \'grān-jər\ *n*

**gran·ite** \'gra-nət\ *n* : a hard granular igneous rock used esp. for building — **gra·nit·ic** \gra-'ni-tik\ *adj*

**gran·ite·ware** \'gra-nət-ˌwer\ *n* : ironware with mottled enamel

**gra·no·la** \grə-ˈnō-lə\ n : a cereal made of rolled oats and usu. raisins and nuts

¹**grant** \ˈgrant\ vb 1 : to consent to : ALLOW, PERMIT 2 : GIVE, BESTOW ⟨~ed land to settlers⟩ 3 : to admit as true — **grant·er** n — **grant·or** \ˈgran-tər, -ˌtȯr\ n

²**grant** n 1 : the act of granting 2 : something granted; esp : a gift for a particular purpose ⟨a ~ for study abroad⟩ 3 : a transfer of property by deed or writing; also : the instrument by which such a transfer is made 4 : the property transferred by grant — **grant·ee** \gran-ˈtē\ n

**gran·u·lar** \ˈgra-nyə-lər\ adj : consisting of or appearing to consist of granules — **gran·u·lar·i·ty** \ˌgra-nyə-ˈlar-ə-tē\ n

**gran·u·late** \ˈgra-nyə-ˌlāt\ vb -lat·ed; -lat·ing : to form into grains or crystals — **gran·u·la·tion** \ˌgra-nyə-ˈlā-shən\ n

**gran·ule** \ˈgra-nyül\ n : a small grain or particle

**grape** \ˈgrāp\ n [ME, fr. AF, grape stalk, bunch of grapes, grape, of Gmc origin] 1 : a smooth-skinned juicy edible greenish white, deep red, or purple berry that is the chief source of wine 2 : any of numerous woody vines widely grown for their bunches of grapes

**grape·fruit** \ˈgrāp-ˌfrüt\ n 1 pl grapefruit or grapefruits : a large edible yellow-skinned citrus fruit 2 : a tree bearing grapefruit

**grape hyacinth** n : any of several small bulbous herbs related to the lilies that produce clusters of usu. blue flowers in the spring

**grape·shot** \ˈgrāp-ˌshät\ n : a cluster of small iron balls formerly fired at people from short range by a cannon

**grape·vine** \-ˌvīn\ n 1 : GRAPE 2 2 : RUMOR; also : an informal means of circulating information or gossip

**graph** \ˈgraf\ n : a diagram that usu. by means of dots and lines shows change in one variable factor in comparison with one or more other factors — **graph** vb

**-graph** \ˌgraf\ n comb form 1 : something written ⟨autograph⟩ 2 : instrument for making or transmitting records ⟨seismograph⟩

¹**graph·ic** \ˈgra-fik\ also **graph·i·cal** \-fi-kəl\ adj 1 : of or relating to the arts **(graphic arts)** of representation, decoration, and printing on flat surfaces 2 : being written, drawn, or engraved 3 : vividly described ⟨~ details⟩ — **graph·i·cal·ly** \-fi-k(ə-)lē\ adv

²**graphic** n 1 : a picture, map, or graph used for illustration 2 : a pictorial image displayed on a computer screen

**graphical user interface** n : a computer program designed to allow easy user interaction esp. by having graphic menus or icons

**graph·ics tablet** \-fiks-\ n : a computer input device for entering pictorial information by drawing or tracing

**graph·ite** \ˈgra-ˌfīt\ n [G Graphit, fr. Gk graphein to write] : a soft black form of carbon used esp. for lead pencils and lubricants

**grap·nel** \ˈgrap-nəl\ n : a small anchor used esp. to recover a sunken object or to anchor a small boat

¹**grap·ple** \ˈgra-pəl\ n : the act of grappling

²**grapple** vb grap·pled; grap·pling 1 : to seize or hold with or as if with a hooked implement 2 : to come to grips with : WRESTLE

¹**grasp** \ˈgrasp\ vb 1 : to make the motion of seizing 2 : to take or seize firmly 3 : to enclose and hold with the fingers or arms 4 : COMPREHEND

²**grasp** n 1 : HANDLE 2 : EMBRACE 3 : HOLD, CONTROL 4 : the reach of the arms 5 : the power of seizing and holding or attaining 6 : COMPREHENSION

**grasp·ing** adj : GREEDY, AVARICIOUS

**grass** \ˈgras\ n 1 : herbage for grazing animals 2 : any of a large family of plants (as wheat, bamboo, or sugarcane) with jointed stems and narrow leaves 3 : grass-covered land 4 : MARIJUANA — **grass·like** \-ˌlīk\ adj — **grassy** adj

**grass·hop·per** \-ˌhä-pər\ n : any of numerous leaping plant-eating insects

**grass·land** \-ˌland\ n : land covered naturally or under cultivation with grasses and low-growing herbs

**grass roots** n pl : society at the local level as distinguished from the centers of political leadership

¹**grate** \ˈgrāt\ vb grat·ed; grat·ing 1 : to pulverize by rubbing against something rough 2 : to grind or rub against with a rasping noise 3 : IRRITATE — **grat·er** n — **grat·ing·ly** adv

²**grate** n 1 : GRATING 2 : a frame of iron bars for holding fuel while it burns

**grate·ful** \ˈgrāt-fəl\ adj 1 : THANKFUL, APPRECIATIVE; also : expressing gratitude 2 : PLEASING — **grate·ful·ly** adv — **grate·ful·ness** n

**grat·i·fy** \ˈgra-tə-ˌfī\ vb -fied; -fy·ing : to afford pleasure to — **grat·i·fi·ca·tion** \ˌgra-tə-fə-ˈkā-shən\ n

**grat·ing** \ˈgrā-tiŋ\ n : a framework with parallel bars or crossbars

**gra·tis** \ˈgra-təs, ˈgrā-\ adv or adj : without charge or recompense : FREE

**grat·i·tude** \ˈgra-tə-ˌtüd, -ˌtyüd\ n : THANKFULNESS

**gra·tu·itous** \grə-ˈtü-ə-təs, -ˈtyü-\ adj 1 : done or provided without recompense : FREE 2 : UNWARRANTED ⟨a ~ assumption⟩ ⟨~ violence in movies⟩

**gra·tu·ity** \-ə-tē\ n, pl -ities : ¹⁰TIP

**gra·va·men** \grə-ˈvä-mən\ n, pl -va·mens or -vam·i·na \-ˈva-mə-nə\ [LL, burden] : the basic or significant part of a grievance or complaint

¹**grave** \ˈgrāv\ vb graved; grav·en \ˈgrā-vən\ or graved; grav·ing : SCULPTURE, ENGRAVE

²**grave** n : an excavation in the earth as a place of burial; also : TOMB

³**grave** \ˈgrāv; 5 also ˈgräv\ adj 1 : IMPORTANT 2 : threatening great harm or danger 3 : DIGNIFIED, SOLEMN 4 : drab in color : SOMBER 5 : of, marked by, or being an accent mark having the form ` — **grave·ly** adv — **grave·ness** n

**grav·el** \ˈgra-vəl\ n : pebbles and small

pieces of rock larger than grains of sand
— **grav·el·ly** adj

**Graves' disease** \'grāvz-\ n : hyperthyroidism characterized by goiter and often protrusion of the eyeballs

**grave·stone** \'grāv-ˌstōn\ n : a burial monument

**grave·yard** \-ˌyärd\ n : CEMETERY

**grav·id** \'gra-vəd\ adj [L gravidus, fr. gravis heavy] : PREGNANT

**gra·vi·me·ter** \gra-'vi-mə-tər, 'gra-və-ˌmē-\ n : a device for measuring variations in a gravitational field

**grav·i·tate** \'gra-və-ˌtāt\ vb -tat·ed; -tat·ing : to move or tend to move toward something

**grav·i·ta·tion** \ˌgra-və-'tā-shən\ n 1 : a natural force of attraction that tends to draw bodies together and that occurs because of the mass of the bodies 2 : the action or process of gravitating — **grav·i·ta·tion·al** \-shə-nəl\ adj — **grav·i·ta·tion·al·ly** adv

**grav·i·ty** \'gra-və-tē\ n, pl -ties 1 : IMPORTANCE; esp : SERIOUSNESS 2 : ²MASS 5 3 : the gravitational attraction of the mass of a celestial object (as earth) for bodies close to it; also : GRAVITATION 1

**gra·vure** \grə-'vyu̇r\ n [F] : PHOTOGRAVURE

**gra·vy** \'grā-vē\ n, pl **gravies** 1 : a sauce made from the thickened and seasoned juices of cooked meat 2 : unearned or illicit gain : GRAFT

¹**gray** also **grey** \'grā\ adj 1 : of the color gray; also : dull in color 2 : having gray hair 3 : CHEERLESS, DISMAL ⟨a ∼ day⟩ 4 : intermediate in position or character ⟨an ethically ∼ area⟩ — **gray·ish** adj — **gray·ness** n

²**gray** also **grey** n 1 : something of a gray color 2 : a neutral color ranging between black and white

³**gray** also **grey** vb : to make or become gray

**gray·beard** \'grā-ˌbird\ n : an old man

**gray·ling** \'grā-liŋ\ n, pl **grayling** also **graylings** : any of several slender freshwater food and sport fishes related to the trouts

**gray matter** n 1 : the grayish part of nervous tissue consisting mostly of the cell bodies of neurons 2 : INTELLIGENCE

**gray wolf** n : a large wolf of northern No. America and Asia that is usu. gray

¹**graze** \'grāz\ vb **grazed**; **graz·ing** [ME grasen, fr. OE grasian, fr. græs grass] 1 : to feed on herbage or pasture 2 : to feed (livestock) on grass or pasture — **graz·er** n

²**graze** vb **grazed**; **graz·ing** 1 : to touch lightly in passing 2 : SCRATCH, ABRADE

¹**grease** \'grēs\ n 1 : rendered animal fat 2 : oily material 3 : a thick lubricant — **greasy** \'grē-sē, -zē\ adj

²**grease** \'grēs, 'grēz\ vb **greased**; **greas·ing** : to smear or lubricate with grease

**grease·paint** \'grēs-ˌpānt\ n : theater makeup

¹**great** \'grāt\ adj 1 : large in size : BIG 2 : ELABORATE, AMPLE ⟨in ∼ detail⟩ 3 : large in number : NUMEROUS 4 : being

beyond the average : MIGHTY, INTENSE ⟨a ∼ weight⟩ ⟨in ∼ pain⟩ 5 : EMINENT, GRAND 6 : long continued ⟨a ∼ while⟩ 7 : MAIN, PRINCIPAL ⟨a reception in the ∼ hall⟩ 8 : more distant in a family relationship by one generation ⟨a great-grandfather⟩ 9 : markedly superior in character, quality, or skill ⟨∼ at bridge⟩ 10 : EXCELLENT, FINE ⟨had a ∼ time⟩ — **great·ly** adv — **great·ness** n

**great ape** n : any of a family of primates including the gorilla, orangutan, and chimpanzees

**great blue heron** n : a large crested grayish-blue American heron

**great circle** n : a circle on the surface of a sphere that has the same center as the sphere; esp : one on the surface of the earth an arc of which is the shortest travel distance between two points

**great·coat** \'grāt-ˌkōt\ n : a heavy overcoat

**Great Dane** n : any of a breed of very tall powerful smooth-coated dogs

**great·er** adj, often cap : consisting of a central city together with adjacent areas ⟨∼ London⟩

**great·heart·ed** \'grāt-'här-təd\ adj 1 : COURAGEOUS 2 : MAGNANIMOUS

**great power** n, often cap G&P : one of the nations that figure most decisively in international affairs

**great white shark** n : a large and dangerous shark of warm seas that has large saw-edged teeth and is whitish below and bluish or brownish above

**grebe** \'grēb\ n : any of a family of lobe-toed diving birds related to the loons

**Gre·cian** \'grē-shən\ adj : GREEK

**greed** \'grēd\ n : acquisitive or selfish desire beyond reason — **greed·i·ly** \'grē-də-lē\ adv — **greed·i·ness** \-dē-nəs\ n — **greedy** \'grē-dē\ adj

¹**Greek** \'grēk\ n 1 : a native or inhabitant of Greece 2 : the ancient or modern language of Greece

²**Greek** adj 1 : of, relating to, or characteristic of Greece, the Greeks, or Greek 2 : ORTHODOX 3

¹**green** \'grēn\ adj 1 : of the color green 2 : covered with verdure; also : consisting of green plants or of the leafy parts of plants ⟨a ∼ salad⟩ 3 : UNRIPE; also : IMMATURE 4 : having a sickly appearance 5 : not fully processed or treated ⟨∼ liquor⟩ ⟨∼ hides⟩ 6 : INEXPERIENCED; also : NAIVE 7 : concerned with or supporting environmentalism ⟨∼ companies⟩ — **green·ish** adj — **green·ness** n

²**green** vb : to make or become green

³**green** n 1 : a color between blue and yellow in the spectrum : the color of growing fresh grass or of the emerald 2 : something of a green color 3 : green vegetation; esp, pl : leafy herbs or leafy parts of a vegetable ⟨collard ∼s⟩ ⟨beet ∼s⟩ 4 : a grassy plot; esp : a smooth grassy area around the hole into which the ball must be played in golf

**green·back** \'grēn-ˌbak\ n : a U.S. legal-tender note

**green bean** n : a kidney bean that is used

as a snap bean when the pods are colored green

**green·belt** \'grēn-ˌbelt\ n : a belt of parks or farmlands around a community

**green card** n : an identity card attesting the permanent resident status of an alien in the U.S.

**green·ery** \'grē-nə-rē\ n, pl **-er·ies** : green foliage or plants

**green–eyed** \'grē-ˈnīd\ adj : JEALOUS

**green·gro·cer** \'grēn-ˌgrō-sər\ n, chiefly Brit : a retailer of fresh vegetables and fruit

**green·horn** \-ˌhȯrn\ n : an inexperienced person; also : NEWCOMER

**green·house** \-ˌhaůs\ n : a glass structure for the growing of tender plants

**greenhouse effect** n : warming of a planet's atmosphere that occurs when the sun's radiation passes through the atmosphere, is absorbed by the planet, and is reradiated as radiation of longer wavelength that can be absorbed by atmospheric gases

**green manure** n : an herbaceous crop (as clover) plowed under when green to enrich the soil

**green onion** n : a young onion pulled before the bulb has enlarged and used esp. in salads : SCALLION

**green pepper** n : a sweet pepper before it turns red at maturity

**green·room** \'grēn-ˌrüm, -ˌrům\ n : a room (as in a theater or studio) where performers can relax before, between, or after appearances

**green·sward** \-ˌswȯrd\ n : turf that is green with growing grass

**green thumb** n : an unusual ability to make plants grow

**green·wash·ing** \'grēn-ˌwȯ-shiŋ, -ˌwä-\ n : expressions of environmentalist concerns as a cover for products, policies, or activities deleterious to the environment

**Green·wich mean time** \'gri-nij-, 'gre-, -nich-\ n [Greenwich, England] : the time of the meridian of Greenwich used historically as the basis of worldwide standard time

**Greenwich time** n : GREENWICH MEAN TIME

**green·wood** \'grēn-ˌwůd\ n : a forest that is green with foliage

**greet** \'grēt\ vb 1 : to address with expressions of kind wishes 2 : to meet or react to in a specified manner 3 : to be perceived by — **greet·er** n

**greet·ing** n 1 : a salutation on meeting 2 pl : best wishes : REGARDS

**greeting card** n : a card that bears a message usu. sent on a special occasion

**gre·gar·i·ous** \gri-ˈger-ē-əs\ adj [L gregarius of a flock or herd, fr. greg-, grex flock, herd] 1 : SOCIAL, COMPANIONABLE 2 : tending to flock together — **gre·gar·i·ous·ly** adv — **gre·gar·i·ous·ness** n

**grem·lin** \'grem-lən\ n : a cause of error or equipment malfunction conceived of as a small gnome

**gre·nade** \grə-ˈnād\ n [MF, lit., pomegranate, fr. LL granata, fr. L, fem. of granatus seedy, fr. granum grain] : a small bomb that is thrown by hand or launched (as by a rifle)

**gren·a·dier** \ˌgre-nə-ˈdir\ n : a member of a European regiment formerly armed with grenades

**gren·a·dine** \ˌgre-nə-ˈdēn, 'gre-nə-ˌdēn\ n : a syrup flavored with pomegranates and used in mixed drinks

**grew** past of GROW

**grey** var of GRAY

**grey·hound** \'grā-ˌhaůnd\ n : any of a breed of tall slender dogs noted for speed and keen sight

**grid** \'grid\ n 1 : GRATING 2 : a network of conductors for distributing electric power 3 : a network of horizontal and perpendicular lines (as for locating points on a map) 4 : GRIDIRON 2; also : FOOTBALL

**grid·dle** \'gri-dᵊl\ n : a flat usu. metal surface for cooking food

**griddle cake** n : PANCAKE

**grid·iron** \'grid-ˌī(-ə)rn\ n 1 : a grate for broiling food 2 : a football field

**grid·lock** \-ˌläk\ n : a traffic jam in which an intersection is so blocked that vehicles cannot move

**grief** \'grēf\ n 1 : emotional distress caused by or as if by bereavement; also : a cause of such distress 2 : DISASTER ⟨the expedition came to ~⟩; also : MISHAP

**griev·ance** \'grē-vəns\ n 1 : a cause of distress affording reason for complaint or resistance 2 : COMPLAINT

**grieve** \'grēv\ vb **grieved; griev·ing** [ME greven, fr. AF grever, fr. L gravare to burden, fr. gravis heavy, grave] 1 : to cause grief or sorrow to : DISTRESS 2 : to feel grief : SORROW

**griev·ous** \'grē-vəs\ adj 1 : causing suffering, grief, or sorrow : SEVERE ⟨a ~ wound⟩ 2 : OPPRESSIVE, ONEROUS ⟨~ costs of war⟩ 3 : SERIOUS, GRAVE ⟨a ~ fault⟩ — **griev·ous·ly** adv

¹**grill** \'gril\ vb 1 : to broil on a grill; also : to fry or toast on a griddle 2 : to question intensely ⟨~ a suspect⟩

²**grill** n 1 : a cooking utensil of parallel bars on which food is grilled 2 : a usu. informal restaurant

**grille** or **grill** \'gril\ n : a grating that forms a barrier or screen

**grill·work** \'gril-ˌwərk\ n : work constituting or resembling a grille

**grim** \'grim\ adj **grim·mer; grim·mest** 1 : CRUEL, FIERCE 2 : harsh and forbidding in appearance 3 : ghastly or repellent in character 4 : RELENTLESS — **grim·ly** adv — **grim·ness** n

**gri·mace** \'gri-məs, gri-ˈmās\ n : a facial expression usu. of disgust or disapproval — **grimace** vb

**grime** \'grīm\ n : soot, smut, or dirt adhering to or embedded in a surface; also : accumulated dirtiness and disorder — **grimy** adj

**grin** \'grin\ vb **grinned; grin·ning** : to draw back the lips so as to show the teeth esp. in amusement — **grin** n

¹**grind** \'grīnd\ vb **ground** \'graůnd\; **grind·ing** 1 : to reduce to small particles

2 : to wear down, polish, or sharpen by friction 3 : OPPRESS 4 : to press with a grating noise : GRIT ⟨~ the teeth⟩ 5 : to operate or produce by turning a crank 6 : DRUDGE; *esp* : to study hard 7 : to move with difficulty or friction ⟨gears ~*ing*⟩

²**grind** *n* 1 : dreary monotonous labor, routine, or study 2 : one who works or studies excessively

**grind·er** \ˈgrīn-dər\ *n* 1 : MOLAR 2 *pl* : TEETH 3 : one that grinds 4 : SUBMARINE 2 5 : an athlete who succeeds through hard work and determination

**grind·stone** \ˈgrīnd-ˌstōn\ *n* : a flat circular stone of natural sandstone that revolves on an axle and is used for grinding, shaping, or smoothing

¹**grip** \ˈgrip\ *vb* **gripped; grip·ping** 1 : to seize or hold firmly 2 : to hold the interest of strongly ⟨*gripped* by the story⟩

²**grip** *n* 1 : GRASP; *also* : strength in gripping 2 : a firm tenacious hold 3 : UNDERSTANDING 4 : a device for gripping 5 : TRAVELING BAG

**gripe** \ˈgrīp\ *vb* **griped; grip·ing** 1 : IRRITATE, VEX 2 : to cause or experience spasmodic pains in the bowels 3 : COMPLAIN — **gripe** *n*

**grippe** \ˈgrip\ *n* : INFLUENZA

**gris–gris** \ˈgrē-ˌgrē\ *n, pl* **gris–gris** \-ˌgrēz\ [F] : an amulet or incantation used chiefly by people of black African ancestry

**gris·ly** \ˈgriz-lē\ *adj* **gris·li·er; -est** : HORRIBLE, GRUESOME

**grist** \ˈgrist\ *n* : grain to be ground or already ground

**gris·tle** \ˈgri-səl\ *n* : CARTILAGE — **gris·tly** \ˈgris-lē\ *adj*

**grist·mill** \ˈgrist-ˌmil\ *n* : a mill for grinding grain

¹**grit** \ˈgrit\ *n* 1 : a hard sharp granule (as of sand); *also* : material composed of such granules 2 : unyielding courage ⟨the pioneers' ~⟩ — **grit·ty** *adj*

²**grit** *vb* **grit·ted; grit·ting** : GRIND, GRATE

**grits** \ˈgrits\ *n pl* : coarsely ground hulled grain ⟨hominy ~⟩

**griz·zled** \ˈgri-zəld\ *adj* : streaked or mixed with gray; *also* : having gray hair

**griz·zly** \ˈgriz-lē\ *adj* **griz·zli·er; -est** : GRIZZLED

**grizzly bear** *n* : a large powerful brownish bear of western No. America

**gro** *abbr* gross

**groan** \ˈgrōn\ *vb* 1 : MOAN 2 : to make a harsh sound under sudden or prolonged strain ⟨the chair ~ed under his weight⟩ — **groan** *n*

**groat** \ˈgrōt\ *n* : an old British coin worth four pennies

**gro·cer** \ˈgrō-sər\ *n* [ME, fr. AF *groser* wholesaler, fr. *gros* coarse, wholesale, fr. L *grossus* coarse] : a dealer esp. in staple foodstuffs — **gro·cery** \ˈgrōs-rē, ˈgrōsh-, ˈgrō-sə-\ *n*

**grog** \ˈgräg\ *n* [*Old Grog*, nickname of Edward Vernon †1757 Eng. admiral responsible for diluting the sailors' rum] : alcoholic liquor; *esp* : liquor (as rum) mixed with water

**grog·gy** \ˈgrä-gē\ *adj* **grog·gi·er; -est** :

weak and unsteady on the feet or in action — **grog·gi·ly** \-gə-lē\ *adv* — **grog·gi·ness** \-gē-nəs\ *n*

**groin** \ˈgröin\ *n* 1 : the juncture of the lower abdomen and inner part of the thigh; *also* : the region of this juncture 2 : the curved line or rib on a ceiling along which two vaults meet

**grok** \ˈgräk\ *vb* **grokked; grok·king** : to understand profoundly and intuitively

**grom·met** \ˈgrä-mət, ˈgrə-\ *n* 1 : a ring of rope 2 : an eyelet of firm material to strengthen or protect an opening

¹**groom** \ˈgrüm, ˈgrùm\ *n* 1 : a person responsible for the care of horses 2 : BRIDEGROOM

²**groom** *vb* 1 : to clean and care for (an animal) 2 : to make neat or attractive 3 : PREPARE

**grooms·man** \ˈgrümz-mən, ˈgrùmz-\ *n* : a male friend who attends a bridegroom at his wedding

**groove** \ˈgrüv\ *n* 1 : a long narrow channel 2 : a fixed routine — **groove** *vb*

**groovy** \ˈgrü-vē\ *adj* **groov·i·er; -est** 1 : EXCELLENT 2 : HIP

**grope** \ˈgrōp\ *vb* **groped; grop·ing** 1 : to feel about or search for blindly or uncertainly ⟨~ for the right word⟩ 2 : to feel one's way by groping

**gros·beak** \ˈgrōs-ˌbēk\ *n* : any of several finches of Europe or America with large stout conical bills

**gro·schen** \ˈgrō-shən\ *n, pl* **groschen** : a former Austrian monetary unit equal to ¹⁄₁₀₀ schilling

**gros·grain** \ˈgrō-ˌgrān\ *n* [F *gros grain* coarse texture] : a silk or rayon fabric with crosswise cotton ribs

¹**gross** \ˈgrōs\ *adj* 1 : glaringly noticeable 2 : OUT-AND-OUT, UTTER 3 : BIG, BULKY; *esp* : excessively fat 4 : GENERAL, BROAD 5 : consisting of an overall total exclusive of deductions ⟨~ earnings⟩ 6 : CARNAL, EARTHY ⟨~ pleasures⟩ 7 : UNREFINED; *also* : crudely vulgar 8 : lacking knowledge — **gross·ly** *adv* — **gross·ness** *n*

²**gross** *n* : an overall total exclusive of deductions — **gross** *vb*

³**gross** *n, pl* **gross** : a total of 12 dozen things ⟨a ~ of pencils⟩

**gross domestic product** *n* : the gross national product excluding the value of net income earned abroad

**gross national product** *n* : the total value of the goods and services produced in a nation during a year

**gro·szy** \ˈgrō-shē\ *n, pl* **groszy** — see *zloty* at MONEY table

**grot** \ˈgrät\ *n* : GROTTO

**gro·tesque** \grō-ˈtesk\ *adj* 1 : FANCIFUL, BIZARRE 2 : absurdly incongruous 3 : ECCENTRIC — **gro·tesque·ly** *adv*

**grot·to** \ˈgrä-tō\ *n, pl* **grottoes** *also* **grottos** 1 : CAVE 2 : an artificial cavelike structure

**grouch** \ˈgraùch\ *n* 1 : a fit of bad temper 2 : a habitually irritable or complaining person — **grouch** *vb* — **grouchy** *adj*

¹**ground** \ˈgraùnd\ *n* 1 : the bottom of a body of water 2 *pl* : sediment at the bottom of a liquid 3 : a basis for belief, ac-

tion, or argument **4** : BACKGROUND **5** : the surface of the earth; *also* : SOIL **6** : an area with a particular use ⟨fishing ~*s*⟩ **7** *pl* : the area about and belonging to a building **8** : a conductor that makes electrical connection with the earth — **ground·less** *adj*

²**ground** *vb* **1** : to bring to or place on the ground **2** : to run or cause to run aground **3** : to provide a reason or justification for **4** : to furnish with a foundation of knowledge **5** : to connect electrically with a ground **6** : to restrict to the ground; *also* : prohibit from some activity ⟨~*ed* the boy for a week⟩

³**ground** *past and past part of* GRIND

**ground ball** *n* : a batted baseball that rolls or bounces along the ground

**ground cover** *n* : low plants that grow over and cover the soil; *also* : a plant suitable for use as ground cover

**ground·ed** \'graún-dəd\ *adj* : mentally and emotionally stable

**ground·er** \'graún-dər\ *n* : GROUND BALL

**ground·hog** \'graúnd-ˌhóg, -ˌhäg\ *n* : WOODCHUCK

**ground·ling** \'graúnd-liŋ\ *n* : a spectator in the pit of an Elizabethan theater

**ground rule** *n* **1** : a sports rule adopted to modify play on a particular field, court, or course **2** : a rule of procedure

**ground squirrel** *n* : any of various burrowing squirrels of No. America and Eurasia that often live in colonies in open areas

**ground swell** *n* **1** : a broad deep ocean swell caused by an often distant gale or earthquake **2** *usu* **ground-swell** : a rapid spontaneous growth (as of political opinion)

**ground·wa·ter** \'graúnd-ˌwó-tər, -ˌwä-\ *n* : water within the earth that supplies wells and springs

**ground·work** \-ˌwərk\ *n* : FOUNDATION, BASIS

**ground zero** *n* **1** : the point above, below, or at which a nuclear explosion occurs **2** : the center or origin of rapid, intense, or violent activity

¹**group** \'grüp\ *n* **1** : a number of individuals related by a common factor (as physical association, community of interests, or blood) **2** : a combination of atoms commonly found together in a molecule ⟨a methyl ~⟩

²**group** *vb* : to associate in groups : CLUSTER, AGGREGATE

**grou·per** \'grü-pər\ *n, pl* **groupers** *also* **grouper** : any of numerous large solitary bottom fishes of warm seas

**group home** *n* : a residence for persons requiring care or supervision

**group·ie** \'grü-pē\ *n* : a fan of a rock group who usu. follows the group around on concert tours; *also* : ENTHUSIAST, FAN

**group therapy** *n* : therapy in the presence of a therapist in which several patients discuss their personal problems

**group·ware** \'grüp-ˌwer\ *n* : software that enables users to work jointly via a network on projects or files

¹**grouse** \'graús\ *n, pl* **grouse** *or* **grouses**

: any of various chiefly ground-dwelling game birds that have feathered legs and are usu. of reddish brown or other protective color

²**grouse** *vb* **groused; grous·ing** : COMPLAIN, GRUMBLE

**grout** \'graút\ *n* : material (as mortar) used for filling spaces — **grout** *vb*

**grove** \'grōv\ *n* : a small wood usu. without underbrush

**grov·el** \'grä-vəl, 'grə-\ *vb* **-eled** *or* **-elled; -el·ing** *or* **-el·ling** **1** : to creep or lie with the body prostrate in fear or humility **2** : to abase oneself

**grow** \'grō\ *vb* **grew** \'grü\; **grown** \'grōn\; **grow·ing** **1** : to spring up and develop to maturity **2** : to be able to grow : THRIVE **3** : to take on some relation through or as if through growth ⟨tree limbs *grown* together⟩ **4** : INCREASE, EXPAND **5** : to develop from a parent source **6** : BECOME **7** : to have an increasing influence **8** : to cause to grow ⟨~ a business⟩ — **grow·er** *n*

**growing pains** *n pl* **1** : pains in the legs of growing children having no known relation to growth **2** : the stresses and strains attending a new project or development

**growl** \'graú(-ə)l\ *vb* **1** : RUMBLE **2** : to utter a deep throaty sound **3** : GRUMBLE — **growl** *n*

**grown-up** \'grō-ˌnəp\ *adj* : not childish : ADULT — **grown-up** *n*

**growth** \'grōth\ *n* **1** : stage or condition attained in growing **2** : a process of growing esp. through progressive development or increase **3** : a result or product of growing ⟨a fine ~ of hair⟩; *also* : an abnormal mass of tissue (as a tumor)

**growth hormone** *n* : a vertebrate hormone that is secreted by the pituitary gland and regulates growth

**growth industry** *n* : a business, interest, or activity that is increasingly popular, profitable, or trendy

¹**grub** \'grəb\ *vb* **grubbed; grub·bing** **1** : to clear or root out by digging **2** : to dig in the ground usu. for a hidden object **3** : to search about

²**grub** *n* **1** : a soft thick wormlike insect larva ⟨beetle ~*s*⟩ **2** : DRUDGE; *also* : a slovenly person **3** : FOOD

**grub·by** \'grə-bē\ *adj* **grub·bi·er; -est** : DIRTY, SLOVENLY ⟨~ clothes⟩ — **grub·bi·ness** \-bē-nəs\ *n*

**grub·stake** \'grəb-ˌstāk\ *n* : supplies or funds furnished a mining prospector in return for a share in his finds

¹**grudge** \'grəj\ *vb* **grudged; grudg·ing** : to be reluctant to give : BEGRUDGE

²**grudge** *n* : a feeling of deep-seated resentment or ill will

**gru·el** \'grü-əl\ *n* : a thin porridge

**gru·el·ing** *or* **gru·el·ling** \'grü-liŋ, 'grü-ə-\ *adj* : requiring extreme effort : EXHAUSTING ⟨a ~ race⟩

**grue·some** \'grü-səm\ *adj* [fr. earlier *growsome*, fr. E dial. *grow, grue* to shiver] : inspiring horror or repulsion — **grue·some·ly** *adv* — **grue·some·ness** *n*

**gruff** \'grəf\ *adj* **1** : rough in speech or

manner **2** : being deep and harsh : HOARSE — **gruff·ly** *adv*

**grum·ble** \'grəm-bəl\ *vb* **grum·bled; grum·bling** **1** : to mutter in discontent **2** : GROWL, RUMBLE — **grum·bler** *n*

**grumpy** \'grəm-pē\ *adj* **grump·i·er; -est** : moodily cross : SURLY — **grump·i·ly** \-pə-lē\ *adv* — **grump·i·ness** \-pē-nəs\ *n*

**grunge** \'grənj\ *n* **1** : one that is grungy **2** : heavy metal rock music expressing alienation and discontent **3** : untidy or tattered clothing typically worn by grunge fans

**grun·gy** \'grən-jē\ *adj* **grun·gi·er; -est** : shabby or dirty in character or condition

**grun·ion** \'grən-yən\ *n* : a fish of the California coast which comes inshore to spawn at nearly full moon

**grunt** \'grənt\ *n* : a deep throaty sound (as that of a hog) — **grunt** *vb*

**GSA** *abbr* **1** General Services Administration **2** Girl Scouts of America

**G suit** *n* [gravity] : a suit for a pilot or astronaut designed to counteract the physiological effects of acceleration

**GSUSA** *abbr* Girl Scouts of the United States of America

**gt** *abbr* great

**Gt Brit** *abbr* Great Britain

**gtd** *abbr* guaranteed

**GU** *abbr* Guam

**gua·ca·mo·le** \ˌgwä-kə-'mō-lē\ *n* [MexSp, fr. Nahuatl *ahuacamolli*, fr. *ahuacatl* avocado + *mōlli* sauce] : mashed and seasoned avocado

**gua·nine** \'gwä-ˌnēn\ *n* : a purine base that codes genetic information in the molecular chain of DNA and RNA

**gua·no** \'gwä-nō\ *n* [Sp, fr. Quechua *wanu* fertilizer, dung] : excrement esp. of seabirds or bats; *also* : a fertilizer composed chiefly of this excrement

**gua·ra·ni** \ˌgwär-ə-'nē\ *n, pl* **guaranies** *also* **guaranis** — see MONEY table

¹**guar·an·tee** \ˌger-ən-'tē\ *n* **1** : GUARANTOR **2** : GUARANTY 1 **3** : an agreement by which one person undertakes to secure another in the possession or enjoyment of something **4** : an assurance of the quality of or of the length of use to be expected from a product offered for sale **5** : GUARANTY 4

²**guarantee** *vb* **-teed; -tee·ing** **1** : to undertake to answer for the debt, failure to perform, or faulty performance of (another) **2** : to undertake an obligation to establish, perform, or continue **3** : to give security to

**guar·an·tor** \ˌger-ən-'tȯr\ *n* : one who gives a guarantee

¹**guar·an·ty** \'ger-ən-tē\ *n, pl* **-ties** **1** : an undertaking to answer for another's failure to pay a debt or perform a duty **2** : GUARANTEE **3** : GUARANTOR **4** : PLEDGE, SECURITY

²**guaranty** *vb* **-tied; -ty·ing** : GUARANTEE

¹**guard** \'gärd\ *n* **1** : a person or a body of persons on sentinel duty **2** *pl* : troops assigned to protect a sovereign **3** : a defensive position (as in boxing) **4** : the act or duty of protecting or defending **5** : PRO-

TECTION **6** : a protective or safety device **7** : a football lineman playing between center and tackle; *also* : a basketball player stationed farthest from the goal — **on guard** : WATCHFUL, ALERT

²**guard** *vb* **1** : PROTECT, DEFEND **2** : to watch over **3** : to be on guard

**guard·house** \'gärd-ˌhaus\ *n* **1** : a building occupied by a guard or used as a headquarters by soldiers on guard duty **2** : a military jail

**guard·ian** \'gär-dē-ən\ *n* **1** : CUSTODIAN **2** : one who has the care of the person or property of another — **guard·ian·ship** *n*

**guard·room** \'gärd-ˌrüm\ *n* **1** : a room used by a military guard while on duty **2** : a room where military prisoners are confined

**guards·man** \'gärdz-mən\ *n* : a member of a military body called *guard* or *guards*

**gua·va** \'gwä-və\ *n* : the sweet yellow or pink acid fruit of a shrubby tropical American tree used esp. for making jam and jelly; *also* : the tree

**gu·ber·na·to·ri·al** \ˌgü-bər-nə-'tȯr-ē-əl\ *adj* : of or relating to a governor

**guer·don** \'gər-dᵊn\ *n* : REWARD, RECOMPENSE

**Guern·sey** \'gərn-zē\ *n, pl* **Guernseys** : any of a breed of usu. reddish-brown and white dairy cattle that produce rich yellowish milk

**guer·ril·la** *or* **gue·ril·la** \gə-'ri-lə\ *n* [Sp *guerrilla*, fr. dim. of *guerra* war, of Gmc origin] : one who engages in irregular warfare esp. as a member of an independent unit

**guess** \'ges\ *vb* **1** : to form an opinion from little or no evidence **2** : BELIEVE, SUPPOSE **3** : to conjecture correctly about : DISCOVER — **guess** *n*

**guest** \'gest\ *n* **1** : a person to whom hospitality (as of a house or a club) is extended **2** : a patron of a commercial establishment (as a hotel) **3** : a person not a regular member of a cast who appears on a program

**guest·house** \'gest-ˌhaus\ *n* : a house run as a boarding house or bed-and-breakfast

**guf·faw** \(ˌ)gə-'fȯ\ *n* : a loud burst of laughter — **guf·faw** *vb*

**guid·ance** \'gī-dᵊns\ *n* **1** : the act or process of guiding **2** : ADVICE, DIRECTION

¹**guide** \'gīd\ *n* **1** : one who leads or directs another's course **2** : one who shows and explains points of interest **3** : something that provides guiding information; *also* : SIGNPOST **4** : a device to direct the motion of something

²**guide** *vb* **guid·ed; guid·ing** **1** : to act as a guide to **2** : MANAGE, DIRECT **3** : to superintend the training of — **guid·able** \'gī-də-bəl\ *adj*

**guide·book** \'gīd-ˌbuk\ *n* : a book of information for travelers

**guided missile** *n* : a missile whose course may be altered during flight

**guide dog** *n* : a dog trained to lead the blind

**guide·line** \'gīd-ˌlīn\ *n* : an indication or outline of policy or conduct

**guide word** *n* : a term at the head of a

page of an alphabetical reference work that indicates the alphabetically first or last word on that page

**gui·don** \'gī-ˌdän, 'gī-dᵊn\ n : a small flag (as of a military unit)

**guild** \'gild\ n : an association of people with common aims and interests; esp : a medieval association of merchants or craftsmen — **guild·hall** \-ˌhȯl\ n

**guil·der** \'gil-dər\ n : GULDEN

**guile** \'gī(-ə)l\ n : deceitful cunning : DU-PLICITY — **guile·ful** adj — **guile·less** adj — **guile·less·ness** n

**guil·lo·tine** \'gi-lə-ˌtēn, ˌgē-ə-'tēn\ n [F, fr. Joseph Guillotin †1814 Fr. physician] : a machine for beheading persons — **guil·lotine** vb

**guilt** \'gilt\ n 1 : the fact of having committed an offense esp. against the law 2 : BLAMEWORTHINESS 3 : a feeling of responsibility for wrongdoing — **guilt·less** adj

**guilt–trip** \'gilt-ˌtrip\ vb : to cause feelings of guilt in

**guilty** \'gil-tē\ adj **guilt·i·er; -est** 1 : having committed a breach of conduct or a crime 2 : suggesting or involving guilt 3 : aware of or suffering from guilt — **guilt·i·ly** \-tə-lē\ adv — **guilt·i·ness** \-tē-nəs\ n

**guin·ea** \'gi-nē\ n 1 : a British gold coin no longer issued worth 21 shillings 2 : a unit of value equal to 21 shillings

**guinea fowl** n : a gray and white spotted West African bird related to the pheasants and widely raised for food; also : any of several related birds

**guinea hen** n : a female guinea fowl; also : GUINEA FOWL

**guinea pig** n 1 : a small stocky short-eared and nearly tailless So. American rodent often kept as a pet or used in lab research 2 : a subject of research or testing

**guise** \'gīz\ n 1 : a form or style of dress : COSTUME 2 : external appearance : SEMBLANCE

**gui·tar** \gi-'tär\ n : a musical instrument with usu. six strings plucked with a pick or with the fingers

**gulch** \'gəlch\ n : RAVINE

**gul·den** \'gül-dən, 'gu̇l-\ n, pl **guldens** or **gulden** : the basic monetary unit of the Netherlands until 2002 2 : the basic monetary unit of Suriname until 2004

**gulf** \'gəlf\ n [ME goulf, fr. MF golfe, fr. It golfo, fr. LL colpus, fr. Gk kolpos bosom, gulf] 1 : a part of an ocean or sea partly or mostly surrounded by land 2 : ABYSS, CHASM 3 : a wide separation ⟨the ~ between generations⟩

¹**gull** \'gəl\ n : any of numerous mostly white or gray long-winged web-footed seabirds

²**gull** vb : to make a dupe of : DECEIVE

³**gull** n : DUPE

**gul·let** \'gə-lət\ n : ESOPHAGUS; also : THROAT

**gull·ible** \'gə-lə-bəl\ adj : easily duped or cheated

**gul·ly** \'gə-lē\ n, pl **gullies** : a trench worn

in the earth by and often filled with running water after rains

**gulp** \'gəlp\ vb 1 : to swallow hurriedly or greedily 2 : SUPPRESS ⟨~ down a sob⟩ 3 : to catch the breath as if in taking a long drink — **gulp** n

¹**gum** \'gəm\ n : the oral tissue that surrounds the necks of the teeth

²**gum** n [ME gomme, fr. MF, fr. L cummi, gummi, fr. Gk kommi, fr. Egyptian qmy.t] 1 : a sticky plant exudate; esp : one that hardens on drying 2 : a sticky substance 3 : a preparation usu. of a plant gum sweetened and flavored and used for chewing — **gum·my** adj

**gum arabic** n : a water-soluble gum obtained from several acacias and used esp. in making inks, adhesives, confections, and pharmaceuticals

**gum·bo** \'gəm-bō\ n [AmerF gombo, of Bantu origin] : a rich thick soup usu. thickened with okra

**gum·drop** \'gəm-ˌdräp\ n : a candy made usu. from corn syrup with gelatin and coated with sugar crystals

**gump·tion** \'gəmp-shən\ n 1 chiefly dial : shrewd common sense 2 : ENTERPRISE, INITIATIVE ⟨lacked the ~ to try⟩

**gum·shoe** \'gəm-ˌshü\ n : DETECTIVE — **gumshoe** vb

¹**gun** \'gən\ n 1 : CANNON 2 : a portable firearm 3 : a discharge of a gun 4 : something suggesting a gun in shape or function 5 : THROTTLE — **gunned** \'gənd\ adj

²**gun** vb **gunned; gun·ning** 1 : to hunt with a gun 2 : SHOOT 3 : to open up the throttle of so as to increase speed

**gun·boat** \'gən-ˌbōt\ n : a small lightly armed ship for use in shallow waters

**gun·fight** \-ˌfīt\ n : a duel with guns — **gun·fight·er** n

**gun·fire** \-ˌfī(-ə)r\ n : the firing of guns

**gung ho** \'gəŋ-'hō\ adj : extremely zealous or enthusiastic

**gun·man** \-mən\ n : a man armed with a gun; esp : a professional killer

**gun·ner** \'gə-nər\ n 1 : a soldier or airman who operates or aims a gun 2 : one who hunts with a gun

**gun·nery** \'gə-nə-rē\ n : the use of guns; esp : the science of the flight of projectiles and effective use of guns

**gunnery sergeant** n : a noncommissioned officer in the marine corps ranking next below a master sergeant

**gun·ny·sack** \'gə-nē-ˌsak\ n : a sack made of a coarse heavy fabric (as burlap)

**gun·point** \'gən-ˌpȯint\ n : the muzzle of a gun — **at gunpoint** : under a threat of death by being shot

**gun·pow·der** \-ˌpau̇-dər\ n : an explosive powder used in guns and blasting

**gun·shot** \-ˌshät\ n 1 : shot fired from a gun 2 : the range of a gun ⟨within ~⟩

**gun–shy** \-ˌshī\ adj 1 : afraid of a loud noise 2 : markedly distrustful

**gun·sling·er** \-ˌsliŋ-ər\ n : a skilled gunman esp. in the American West

**gun·smith** \-ˌsmith\ n : one who designs, makes, or repairs firearms

**gun·wale** *also* **gun·nel** \ˈgə-nᵊl\ *n* : the upper edge of a ship's or boat's side

**gup·py** \ˈgə-pē\ *n, pl* **guppies** [R.J.L. *Guppy* †1916 Trinidadian naturalist] : a small brightly colored tropical fish

**gur·gle** \ˈgər-gəl\ *vb* **gur·gled; gur·gling** : to make a sound like that of an irregularly flowing or gently splashing liquid — **gurgle** *n*

**Gur·kha** \ˈgùr-kə, ˈgər-\ *n* : a soldier from Nepal in the British or Indian army

**gur·ney** \ˈgər-nē\ *n, pl* **gurneys** : a wheeled cot or stretcher

**gu·ru** \ˈgùr-ü\ *n, pl* **gurus** [ultim. fr. Sanskrit *guru*, fr. *guru*, adj., heavy, venerable] **1** : a personal religious and spiritual teacher in Hinduism **2** : a teacher in matters of fundamental concern **3** : EXPERT ⟨a fitness ∼⟩

**gush** \ˈgəsh\ *vb* **1** : to issue or pour forth copiously or violently : SPOUT **2** : to make an effusive display of affection or enthusiasm

**gush·er** \ˈgə-shər\ *n* : one that gushes; *esp* : an oil well with a large natural flow

**gushy** \ˈgə-shē\ *adj* **gush·i·er; -est** : marked by effusive sentimentality

**gus·set** \ˈgə-sət\ *n* : a triangular insert (as in a seam of a sleeve) to give width or strength — **gusset** *vb*

**gus·sy up** \ˈgə-sē-\ *vb* **gus·sied up; gus·sy·ing up 1** : to dress in best or formal clothes **2** : to make more attractive, glamorous, or fancy

**¹gust** \ˈgəst\ *n* **1** : a sudden brief rush of wind **2** : a sudden outburst : SURGE ⟨a ∼ of emotion⟩ — **gusty** *adj*

**²gust** *vb* : to blow in gusts

**gus·ta·to·ry** \ˈgəs-tə-ˌtór-ē\ *adj* : relating to or associated with the sense of taste

**gus·to** \ˈgəs-tō\ *n, pl* **gustoes** : enthusiastic enjoyment; *also* : VITALITY 4

**¹gut** \ˈgət\ *n* **1** *pl* : BOWELS, ENTRAILS **2** : the alimentary canal or a part of it (as the intestine); *also* : BELLY, ABDOMEN **3** *pl* : the inner essential parts ⟨a car's ∼s⟩ **4** *pl* : COURAGE, PLUCK

**²gut** *vb* **gut·ted; gut·ting 1** : EVISCERATE **2** : to destroy the inside of ⟨fire *gutted* the building⟩

**gut check** *n* : a test of courage, character, or determination

**gutsy** \ˈgət-sē\ *adj* **guts·i·er; -est** : marked by courage and determination

**gut·ter** \ˈgə-tər\ *n* : a groove or channel for carrying off esp. rainwater

**gut·ter·snipe** \-ˌsnīp\ *n* : a street urchin

**gut·tur·al** \ˈgə-tə-rəl\ *adj* **1** : sounded in the throat **2** : being or marked by an utterance that is strange, unpleasant, or disagreeable — **guttural** *n*

**gut·ty** \ˈgə-tē\ *adj* **gut·ti·er; -est 1** : GUTSY **2** : having a vigorous challenging quality ⟨a ∼ role in a play⟩

**gut-wrench·ing** \ˈgət-ˌren-chiŋ\ *adj* : causing emotional anguish

**¹guy** \ˈgī\ *n* : a rope, chain, or rod attached to something as a brace or guide

**²guy** *vb* : to steady or reinforce with a guy

**³guy** *n* : MAN, FELLOW; *also, pl* : PERSONS

**⁴guy** *vb* : to make fun of : RIDICULE

**guz·zle** \ˈgə-zəl\ *vb* **guz·zled; guz·zling** : to drink greedily

**gym** \ˈjim\ *n* : GYMNASIUM

**gym·kha·na** \jim-ˈka-nə\ *n* : a meet featuring sports contests; *esp* : a contest of automobile-driving skill

**gym·na·si·um** \*for 1* jim-ˈnā-zē-əm, -zhəm, *for 2* gim-ˈnä-zē-əm\ *n, pl* **-si·ums** *or* **-na·sia** \-ˈnā-zē-ə, -ˈnä-zhə; -ˈnä-zē-ə\ [L, exercise ground, school, fr. Gk *gymnasion*, fr. *gymnazein* to exercise naked, fr. *gymnos* naked] **1** : a room or building for indoor sports **2** : a European secondary school that prepares students for the university

**gym·nas·tics** \jim-ˈnas-tiks\ *n* : a competitive sport developed from physical exercises designed to demonstrate strength, balance, and body control — **gym·nast** \ˈjim-ˌnast\ *n* — **gym·nas·tic** *adj*

**gym·no·sperm** \ˈjim-nə-ˌspərm\ *n* : any of a group of woody vascular seed plants (as conifers) that produce naked seeds not enclosed in an ovary

**gyn** *or* **gynecol** *abbr* gynecology

**gy·nae·col·o·gy** *chiefly Brit var of* GYNECOLOGY

**gy·ne·col·o·gy** \ˌgī-nə-ˈkä-lə-jē\ *n* : a branch of medicine that deals with the diseases and routine care of the reproductive system of women — **gy·ne·co·log·ic** \-ni-kə-ˈlä-jik\ *or* **gy·ne·co·log·i·cal** \-ji-kəl\ *adj* — **gy·ne·col·o·gist** \-nə-ˈkä-lə-jist\ *n*

**gy·no·cen·tric** \ˌgī-nə-ˈsen-trik\ *adj* : emphasizing feminine interests or a feminine point of view

**gyp** \ˈjip\ *n* **1** : CHEAT, SWINDLER **2** : FRAUD, SWINDLE — **gyp** *vb*

**gyp·sum** \ˈjip-səm\ *n* : a calcium-containing mineral used in making plaster of paris

**Gyp·sy** \ˈjip-sē\ *n, pl* **Gypsies** [by shortening & alter. fr. *Egyptian*] : a member of a traditionally traveling people coming orig. from India and living chiefly in Europe, Asia, and No. America; *also* : the language of the Gypsies

**gypsy moth** *n* : an Old World moth that was introduced into the U.S. where its caterpillar is a destructive defoliator of many trees

**gy·rate** \ˈjī-ˌrāt\ *vb* **gy·rat·ed; gy·rat·ing 1** : to revolve around a point or axis **2** : to oscillate with or as if with a circular or spiral motion — **gy·ra·tion** \jī-ˈrā-shən\ *n*

**gyr·fal·con** \ˈjər-ˌfal-kən, -ˌfòl-\ *n* : an arctic falcon with several color forms that is the largest of all falcons

**¹gy·ro** \ˈjī-rō\ *n, pl* **gyros** : GYROSCOPE

**²gy·ro** \ˈyē-ˌrō, ˈzhir-ō\ *n, pl* **gyros** : a sandwich esp. of lamb and beef, tomato, onion, and yogurt sauce on pita bread

**gy·ro·scope** \ˈjī-rō-ˌskōp\ *n* : a wheel or disk mounted to spin rapidly about an axis that is free to turn in various directions

**Gy Sgt** *abbr* gunnery sergeant

**gyve** \ˈjīv, ˈgīv\ *n* : FETTER — **gyve** *vb*

¹**h** \'āch\ *n, pl* **h's** *or* **hs** \'ā-chəz\ *often cap* : the 8th letter of the English alphabet

²**h** *abbr, often cap* **1** hard; hardness **2** heroin **3** hit **4** husband

**H** *symbol* hydrogen

¹**ha** \'hä\ *interj* — used esp. to express surprise or joy

²**ha** *abbr* hectare

**Hab** *abbr* Habacuc; Habakkuk

**Ha·ba·cuc** \'ha-bə-,kək, hə-'ba-kək\ *n* : HABAKKUK

**Ha·bak·kuk** \'ha-bə-,kək, hə-'ba-kək\ *n* — see BIBLE table

**ha·ba·ne·ra** \,hä-bə-'ner-ə\ *n* [Sp *(danza) habanera,* lit., dance of Havana] : a Cuban dance in slow time; *also* : the music for this dance

**ha·ba·ne·ro** *also* **ha·ba·ñe·ro** \,(h)ä-bə-'n(y)er-ō\ *n* : a very hot chili pepper that is usu. orange when mature

**ha·be·as cor·pus** \'hā-bē-əs-'kòr-pəs\ *n* [ME, fr. ML, lit., you should have the body (the opening words of the writ)] : a writ issued to bring a party before a court

**hab·er·dash·er** \'ha-bər-,da-shər\ *n* : a dealer in men's clothing and accessories

**hab·er·dash·ery** \-,da-shə-rē\ *n, pl* **-er·ies** **1** : goods sold by a haberdasher **2** : a haberdasher's shop

**ha·bil·i·ment** \hə-'bi-lə-mənt\ *n* **1** *pl* : TRAPPINGS, EQUIPMENT **2** : DRESS; *esp* : the dress characteristic of an occupation or occasion — usu. used in pl.

**hab·it** \'ha-bət\ *n* **1** : DRESS, GARB **2** : BEARING, CONDUCT **3** : PHYSIQUE **4** : mental makeup **5** : a usual manner of behavior : CUSTOM **6** : a behavior pattern acquired by frequent repetition ⟨has a ∼ of swearing⟩ **7** : ADDICTION ⟨a drug ∼⟩ **8** : mode of growth or occurrence ⟨trees with a spreading ∼⟩

**hab·it·able** \'ha-bə-tə-bəl\ *adj* : capable of being lived in — **hab·it·abil·i·ty** \,ha-bə-tə-'bi-lə-tē\ *n*

**hab·i·tat** \'ha-bə-,tat\ *n* [L, it inhabits] : the place or environment where a plant or animal naturally occurs

**hab·i·ta·tion** \,ha-bə-'tā-shən\ *n* **1** : OCCUPANCY **2** : a dwelling place : RESIDENCE **3** : SETTLEMENT

**hab·it-form·ing** \'ha-bət-,fòr-miŋ\ *adj* : causing addiction : ADDICTIVE

**ha·bit·u·al** \hə-'bi-chə-wəl\ *adj* **1** : CUSTOMARY **2** : doing, practicing, or acting by force of habit **3** : inherent in an individual ⟨∼ grace⟩ — **ha·bit·u·al·ly** *adv* — **ha·bit·u·al·ness** *n*

**ha·bit·u·ate** \hə-'bi-chə-,wāt\ *vb* **-at·ed;** **-at·ing** **1** : ACCUSTOM **2** : to cause or undergo habituation

**ha·bit·u·a·tion** \hə-,bi-chə-'wā-shən\ *n* **1** : the process of making habitual **2** : psychological dependence on a drug after a period of use

**ha·bi·tué** *also* **ha·bi·tue** \hə-'bi-chə-,wā\

*n* [F] **1** : one who may be regularly found in or at (as a place of entertainment) **2** : DEVOTEE

**ha·ci·en·da** \,hä-sē-'en-də\ *n* **1** : a large estate in a Spanish-speaking country **2** : the main building of a farm or ranch

¹**hack** \'hak\ *vb* **1** : to cut or sever with repeated irregular blows **2** : to cough in a short dry manner **3** : to manage successfully; *also* : TOLERATE ⟨can't ∼ the pressure⟩ **4** : to gain access to a computer illegally

²**hack** *n* **1** : an implement for hacking **2** : a short dry cough **3** : a hacking blow

³**hack** *n* **1** : a horse hired or used for varied work **2** : a horse worn out in service **3** : a light easy often 3-gaited saddle horse **4** : HACKNEY, TAXICAB **5** : a person who works solely for mercenary reasons; *esp* : a writer working solely for commercial success — **hack** *adj*

⁴**hack** *vb* : to operate a taxicab

**hack·er** \'ha-kər\ *n* **1** : one that hacks; *also* : a person unskilled at something **2** : an expert at using a computer **3** : a person who illegally gains access to and sometimes tampers with information in a computer system

**hack·ie** \'ha-kē\ *n* : a taxicab driver

**hack·le** \'ha-kəl\ *n* **1** : one of the long feathers on the neck or back of a bird **2** *pl* : hairs (as on a dog's neck) that can be erected **3** *pl* : TEMPER, DANDER

**hack·man** \'hak-mən\ *n* : HACKIE

¹**hack·ney** \'hak-nē\ *n, pl* **hackneys** **1** : a horse for riding or driving **2** : a carriage or automobile kept for hire

²**hackney** *vb* : to make trite

**hack·neyed** \'hak-nēd\ *adj* : lacking in freshness or originality ⟨∼ slogans⟩

**hack·saw** \'hak-,sò\ *n* : a fine-tooth saw in a frame for cutting metal

**hack·work** \-,wərk\ *n* : work done on order usu. according to a formula

**had** *past and past part of* HAVE

**had·dock** \'ha-dək\ *n, pl* **haddock** *also* **haddocks** : an Atlantic food fish usu. smaller than the related cod

**Ha·des** \'hā-(,)dēz\ *n* **1** : the abode of the dead in Greek mythology **2** *often not cap* : HELL

**haem** *chiefly Brit var of* HEME

**hae·ma·tite** *Brit var of* HEMATITE

**haf·ni·um** \'haf-nē-əm\ *n* : a gray metallic chemical element

**haft** \'haft\ *n* : the handle of a weapon or tool

**hag** \'hag\ *n* **1** : an ugly or evil-looking old woman **2** : WITCH 1

**Hag** *abbr* Haggai

**Hag·gai** \'ha-gē-,ī, 'ha-,gī\ *n* — see BIBLE table

**hag·gard** \'ha-gərd\ *adj* : having a worn or emaciated appearance ⟨∼ faces⟩
◆ **Synonyms** CAREWORN, WASTED,

DRAWN — **hag·gard·ly** adv — **hag·gard·ness** n

**hag·gis** \'ha-gəs\ n : a traditionally Scottish dish made of the heart, liver, and lungs of a sheep or a calf minced with suet, onions, oatmeal, and seasonings

**hag·gle** \'ha-gəl\ vb **hag·gled; hag·gling** : to argue in bargaining — **hag·gler** n

**Ha·gi·og·ra·pha** \,ha-gē-'ä-grə-fə, ,hä-jē-\ n pl — see WRITINGS

**ha·gi·o·graph·ic** \,ha-gē-ə-'gra-fik, ,hä-,-jē-\ adj : of or relating to hagiography; esp : excessively flattering

**ha·gi·og·ra·phy** \,ha-gē-'ä-grə-fē, ,hä-jē-\ n 1 : biography of saints or venerated persons 2 : idealizing or idolizing biography — **ha·gi·og·ra·pher** \-fər\ n

**hai·ku** \'hī-(,)kü\ n, pl haiku [Jp] : an unrhymed Japanese verse form of three lines containing usu. five, seven, and five syllables respectively; also : a poem in this form

¹**hail** \'hāl\ n 1 : precipitation in the form of small lumps of ice 2 : something that gives the effect of falling hail

²**hail** vb 1 : to precipitate hail 2 : to pour down and strike like hail

³**hail** interj [ME, fr. ON heill, fr. heill healthy] — used to express acclamation

⁴**hail** vb 1 : SALUTE, GREET 2 : SUMMON

⁵**hail** n 1 : an expression of greeting, approval, or praise 2 : hearing distance

**Hail Mary** n 1 : a salutation and prayer to the Virgin Mary 2 : a long forward pass in football thrown as a final attempt to score

**hail·stone** \'hāl-,stōn\ n : a pellet of hail

**hail·storm** \-,storm\ n : a storm accompanied by hail

**hair** \'her\ n : a threadlike outgrowth esp. from the skin of a mammal; also : a covering or growth of hairs of an animal or a body part — **haired** \'herd\ adj — **hairless** adj

**hair·breadth** \'her-,bredth\ or **hairs·breadth** \'herz-\ n : a very small distance or margin

**hair·brush** \-,brəsh\ n : a brush for the hair

**hair·cloth** \-,klòth\ n : a stiff wiry fabric used esp. for upholstery

**hair·cut** \-,kət\ n : the act, process, or style of cutting and shaping the hair

**hair·do** \-,dü\ n, pl hairdos : HAIRSTYLE

**hair·dress·er** \-,dre-sər\ n : a person who dresses or cuts hair — **hair·dress·ing** n

**hair·line** \-,līn\ n 1 : a very thin line 2 : the outline of the hair on the head

**hair·piece** \-,pēs\ n 1 : supplementary hair (as a switch) used in some women's hairdos 2 : TOUPEE

**hair·pin** \-,pin\ n 1 : a U-shaped pin to hold the hair in place 2 : a sharp U-shaped turn in a road — **hairpin** adj

**hair–rais·ing** \'her-,rā-ziŋ\ adj : causing terror or astonishment

**hair·split·ter** \-,spli-tər\ n : a person who makes excessively fine distinctions in reasoning — **hair·split·ting** \-,spli-tiŋ\ adj or n

**hair·spray** \'her-,sprā\ n : a liquid sprayed onto the hair to hold it in place

**hair·style** \-,stī(-ə)l\ n : a way of wearing the hair — **hair·styl·ing** n

**hair·styl·ist** \-,stī-list\ n : HAIRDRESSER

**hair–trigger** adj : immediately responsive to the slightest stimulus

**hairy** \'her-ē\ adj **hair·i·er; -est** 1 : covered with or as if with hair 2 : tending to cause nervous tension ⟨a few ∼ moments⟩ 3 : difficult to deal with — **hair·i·ness** \-ē-nəs\ n

**hairy woodpecker** n : a common No. American woodpecker with a white back that is larger than the similarly marked downy woodpecker

**hajj** \'haj\ n : a pilgrimage to Mecca prescribed as a religious duty for Muslims

**hajji** \'ha-jē\ n : one who has made a pilgrimage to Mecca — often used as a title

**hake** \'hāk\ n : any of several marine food fishes related to the cod

**ha·la·la** \hə-'lä-lə\ n, pl halala or halalas — see riyal at MONEY table

**hal·berd** \'hal-bərd, 'hòl-\ also **hal·bert** \-bərt\ n : a weapon esp. of the 15th and 16th centuries consisting of a battle-ax and pike on a long handle

**hal·cy·on** \'hal-sē-ən\ adj [Gk halkyōn, alkyōn, a mythical bird believed to nest at sea and to calm the waves] 1 : CALM, PEACEFUL ⟨a ∼ lake⟩ 2 : being a time of happiness, success, or prosperity

¹**hale** \'hāl\ adj : free from defect, disease, or infirmity ♦ **Synonyms** HEALTHY, SOUND, ROBUST, WELL

²**hale** vb haled; hal·ing 1 : HAUL, PULL 2 : to compel to go

**ha·ler** \'hä-lər\ n, pl ha·le·ru \'hä-lə-,rü\ — see koruna at MONEY table

¹**half** \'haf, 'häf\ n, pl halves \'havz, 'hävz\ 1 : either of two equal parts into which something is divisible 2 : one of a pair

²**half** adj 1 : being one of two equal parts 2 : amounting to nearly half 3 : PARTIAL, INCOMPLETE — **half** adv

**half–and–half** \,haf-ʲn-'haf, ,häf-ʲn-'häf\ n : something that is half one thing and half another

**half·back** \'haf-,bak, 'häf-\ n 1 : a football back stationed on or near the flank 2 : a player stationed immediately behind the forward line

**half–baked** \-'bākt\ adj 1 : poorly planned 2 : lacking common sense 3 : not thoroughly baked

**half–breed** \-,brēd\ n, often disparaging : one of mixed racial descent — **half·breed** adj, often disparaging

**half brother** n : a brother related through one parent only

**half–caste** \'haf-,kast, 'häf-\ n : HALF-BREED — **half–caste** adj

**half–cocked** \'haf-'käkt, 'häf-\ adj : lacking adequate preparation

**half–dol·lar** \-'dä-lər\ n 1 : a coin representing one half of a dollar 2 : the sum of fifty cents

**half–heart·ed** \-'här-təd\ adj : lacking spirit or interest — **half·heart·ed·ly** adv — **half·heart·ed·ness** n

**half–life** \-,līf\ n : the time required for

half of something (as atoms or a drug) to undergo a process

**half–mast** \-'mast\ *n* : a point about halfway down from the top of a mast or staff

**half note** *n* : a musical note equal in time to one half that of a whole note

**half·pen·ny** \'hāp-nē\ *n, pl* **half·pence** \'hā-pəns\ *or* **halfpennies** : a former British coin representing one half of a penny

**half–pint** \'haf-ˌpīnt, 'häf-\ *adj* : of less than average size — **half–pint** *n*

**half sister** *n* : a sister related through one parent only

**half sole** *n* : a shoe sole extending from the shank forward — **half–sole** *vb*

**half–staff** \'haf-'staf, 'häf-\ *n* : HALF-MAST

**half step** *n* : a musical interval equivalent to one twelfth of an octave

**half·time** \'haf-ˌtīm, 'häf-\ *n* : an intermission between halves of a game

**half–track** \-ˌtrak\ *n* : a motor vehicle propelled by an endless chain-track drive system; *esp* : such a vehicle lightly armored for military use

**half–truth** \-ˌtrüth\ *n* : a statement that is only partially true; *esp* : one that deliberately mixes truth and falsehood

**half·way** \-'wā\ *adj* 1 : midway between two points 2 : PARTIAL 1 — **halfway** *adv*

**half–wit** \-ˌwit\ *n* : a foolish or imbecilic person — **half–wit·ted** \-'wi-təd\ *adj* — **half–wit·ted·ness** *n*

**hal·i·but** \'ha-lə-bət\ *n, pl* **halibut** *also* **halibuts** [ME *halybutte*, fr. *haly, holy* holy + *butte* flatfish; fr. its being eaten on holy days] : any of several large edible marine flatfishes

**ha·lite** \'ha-ˌlīt, 'hā-\ *n* : ROCK SALT

**hal·i·to·sis** \ˌha-lə-'tō-səs\ *n* : the condition of having fetid breath

**hall** \'hól\ *n* 1 : the residence of a medieval king or noble; *also* : the house of a landed proprietor 2 : a large public building 3 : a college or university building; *also* : DORMITORY 4 : LOBBY; *also* : CORRIDOR 5 : AUDITORIUM

**hal·le·lu·jah** \ˌha-lə-'lü-yə\ *interj* [Heb *hallēlūyāh* praise (ye) the Lord] — used to express praise, joy, or thanks

**hall·mark** \'hól-ˌmärk\ *n* 1 : a mark put on an article to indicate origin, purity, or genuineness 2 : a distinguishing characteristic

**hal·low** \'ha-lō\ *vb* 1 : CONSECRATE 2 : REVERE, VENERATE ⟨our ~ed leader⟩ — **hal·lowed** \-lōd, -lə-wəd\ *adj*

**Hal·low·een** *also* **Hal·low·e'en** \ˌha-lə-'wēn, ˌhä-\ *n* : the evening of October 31 observed esp. by children in merrymaking and masquerading

**hal·lu·ci·nate** \hə-'lü-sə-ˌnāt\ *vb* **-nat·ed; -nat·ing** : to have hallucinations or experience as a hallucination

**hal·lu·ci·na·tion** \hə-ˌlü-sə-'nā-shən\ *n* : perception of objects with no reality due usu. to use of drugs (as LSD) or to disorder of the nervous system; *also* : something so perceived ♦ **Synonyms** DELUSION, ILLUSION, MIRAGE — **hal·lu·ci·na·to·ry** \-'lü-sə-nə-ˌtór-ē\ *adj*

**hal·lu·ci·no·gen** \hə-'lü-sə-nə-jən\ *n* : a substance that induces hallucinations — **hal·lu·ci·no·gen·ic** \-ˌlü-sə-nə-'je-nik\ *adj or n*

**hall·way** \'hól-ˌwā\ *n* 1 : an entrance hall 2 : CORRIDOR

**ha·lo** \'hā-lō\ *n, pl* **halos** *or* **haloes** [L *halos,* fr. Gk *halōs* threshing floor, disk, halo] 1 : a circle of light appearing to surround a shining body (as the sun) 2 : the aura of glory surrounding an idealized person or thing

**¹hal·o·gen** \'ha-lə-jən\ *n* : any of the five elements fluorine, chlorine, bromine, iodine, and astatine

**²hal·o·gen** *adj* : containing, using, or being a halogen ⟨a ~ lamp⟩

**¹halt** \'hólt\ *adj* : LAME 1

**²halt** *n* : STOP

**³halt** *vb* 1 : to stop marching or traveling 2 : DISCONTINUE, END ⟨~ protests⟩

**¹hal·ter** \'hól-tər\ *n* 1 : a rope or strap for leading or tying an animal; *also* : HEADSTALL 2 : NOOSE 3 : a brief blouse held in place by straps around the neck and across the back

**²halter** *vb* **hal·tered; hal·ter·ing** 1 : to catch with or as if with a halter; *also* : to put a halter on (as a horse) 2 : HANG 3 : IMPEDE, RESTRAIN

**halt·ing** \'hól-tiŋ\ *adj* : UNCERTAIN, FALTERING — **halt·ing·ly** *adv*

**halve** \'hav, 'häv\ *vb* **halved; halv·ing** 1 : to divide into two equal parts 2 : to reduce to one half

**halv·ers** \'ha-vərz, 'hä-\ *n pl* : half shares : HALVES

**halves** *pl of* HALF

**hal·yard** \'hal-yərd\ *n* : a rope or tackle for hoisting and lowering (as sails)

**¹ham** \'ham\ *n* 1 : a buttock with its associated thigh — usu. used in pl. 2 : a cut of meat and esp. pork from the thigh 3 : a showy performer 4 : an operator of an amateur radio station — **ham** *adj*

**²ham** *vb* **hammed; ham·ming** : to overplay a part : OVERACT

**ham·burg·er** \'ham-ˌbər-gər\ *or* **hamburg** \-ˌbərg\ *n* [G *Hamburger* of Hamburg, Germany] 1 : ground beef 2 : a sandwich consisting of a ground-beef patty in a round roll

**ham·let** \'ham-lət\ *n* : a small village

**¹ham·mer** \'ha-mər\ *n* 1 : a hand tool used for pounding; *also* : something resembling a hammer in form or function 2 : the part of a gun whose striking action causes explosion of the charge 3 : a metal sphere hurled by a flexible handle for distance in a track-and-field event (**hammer throw**) 4 : ACCELERATOR 2

**²hammer** *vb* 1 : to beat, drive, or shape with repeated blows of a hammer : POUND 2 : to produce or bring about as if by repeated blows — usu. used with *out* 3 : to criticize severely

**ham·mer·head** \'ha-mər-ˌhed\ *n* 1 : the striking part of a hammer 2 : any of a family of medium-sized sharks with eyes at the ends of lateral extensions of the flattened head

**ham·mer·lock** \-ˌläk\ *n* : a wrestling hold

in which an opponent's arm is held bent behind the back

**ham·mer·toe** \-ˌtō\ *n* : a toe deformed by having one or more joints permanently flexed

¹**hammock** \'ha-mək\ *n* [Sp *hamaca*, of AmerInd origin] : a swinging couch hung by cords at each end

²**hammock** *n* : a fertile elevated area of the southern U.S. and esp. Florida with hardwood vegetation and soil rich in humus

¹**ham·per** \'ham-pər\ *vb* : IMPEDE; *also* : RESTRAIN ◆ **Synonyms** TRAMMEL, CLOG, FETTER, SHACKLE

²**hamper** *n* : a large usu. lidded basket

**ham·ster** \'ham-stər\ *n* [G, fr. OHG *hamustro*, of Slavic origin] : any of a subfamily of small Old World rodents with large cheek pouches

¹**ham·string** \'ham-ˌstriŋ\ *n* : any of several muscles at the back of the thigh or tendons at the back of the knee

²**hamstring** *vb* **-strung** \-ˌstrəŋ\; **-string·ing** 1 : to make ineffective or powerless ⟨*hamstrung* by guilt⟩ 2 : to cripple by cutting the leg tendons

**hand** \'hand\ *n* 1 : the end of a front limb when modified (as in humans) for grasping 2 : an indicator or pointer on a dial 3 : personal possession — usu. used in pl.; *also* : CONTROL 4 : SIDE 5 5 : a pledge esp. of betrothal 6 : HANDWRITING 7 : SKILL, ABILITY; *also* : a significant part ⟨had a ~ in the victory⟩ 8 : ASSISTANCE; *also* : PARTICIPATION ⟨had no ~ in the affair⟩ 9 : an outburst of applause 10 : a single round in a card game; *also* : the cards held by a player after a deal 11 : WORKER, EMPLOYEE; *also* : a member of a ship's crew — **hand·less** *adj* — **at hand** : near in time or place — **on hand** : in present possession or readily available — **out of hand** : out of control

²**hand** *vb* 1 : to lead, guide, or assist with the hand 2 : to give, pass, or transmit with the hand ⟨~ed her the letter⟩

**hand·bag** \'hand-ˌbag\ *n* : a bag for carrying small personal articles and money

**hand·ball** \-ˌbȯl\ *n* : a game played by striking a small rubber ball against a wall with the hand

**hand·bill** \-ˌbil\ *n* : a small printed sheet for distribution by hand

**hand·book** \-ˌbu̇k\ *n* : a concise reference book : MANUAL

**hand·car** \-ˌkär\ *n* : a small 4-wheeled railroad car propelled by hand or by a small motor

**hand·clasp** \-ˌklasp\ *n* : HANDSHAKE

**hand·craft** \-ˌkraft\ *vb* : to fashion by manual skill

¹**hand·cuff** \-ˌkəf\ *n* : a metal fastening that can be locked around a wrist and is usu. connected with another such fastening — usu. used in pl.

²**handcuff** *vb* : MANACLE

**hand·ed** \'han-dəd\ *adj* : having or using such or so many hands ⟨a left-*handed* person⟩ — **hand·ed·ness** *n*

**hand·ful** \'hand-ˌfu̇l\ *n*, *pl* **hand·fuls** \-ˌfu̇lz\ *also* **hands·ful** \'handz-ˌfu̇l\ 1

: as much or as many as the hand will grasp 2 : a small number 3 : as much as one can manage

**hand·gun** \-ˌgən\ *n* : a firearm held and fired with one hand

¹**hand-held** \-ˌheld\ *adj* : designed for use while being held in the hand — **hand-held** *n*

¹**hand·i·cap** \'han-di-ˌkap\ *n* [obs. E *handicap*, a game in which forfeit money was held in a cap, fr. *hand in cap*] 1 : a contest in which an artificial advantage is given or disadvantage imposed on a contestant to equalize chances of winning; *also* : the advantage given or disadvantage imposed 2 : a disadvantage that makes achievement difficult

²**handicap** *vb* **-capped; -cap·ping** 1 : to give a handicap to 2 : to put at a disadvantage

**hand·i·capped** *adj, sometimes offensive* : having a physical or mental disability

**hand·i·cap·per** \-ˌka-pər\ *n* : a person who predicts the winners in a contest

**hand·i·craft** \'han-di-ˌkraft\ *n* 1 : manual skill 2 : an occupation requiring manual skill 3 : the articles fashioned by those engaged in handicraft — **hand·i·craft·er** \-ˌkraf-tər\ *n* — **hand·i·crafts·man** \-ˌkrafts-mən\ *n*

**hand in glove** *or* **hand and glove** *adv* : in an extremely close relationship

**hand·i·work** \'han-di-ˌwərk\ *n* : work done personally or by the hands

**hand·ker·chief** \'haŋ-kər-chəf, -ˌchef\ *n*, *pl* **-chiefs** \-chəfs, -ˌchefs\ *also* **-chieves** \-ˌchēvz\ : a small piece of cloth used for various personal purposes (as the wiping of the face)

¹**han·dle** \'han-dᵊl\ *n* 1 : a part (as of a tool) designed to be grasped by the hand 2 : NAME; *also* : NICKNAME — **han·dled** \-dᵊld\ *adj* — **off the handle** : into a state of sudden and violent anger — usu. used with *fly*

²**handle** *vb* **han·dled; han·dling** 1 : to touch, hold, or manage with the hands 2 : to have responsibility for 3 : to deal or trade in 4 : to behave in a certain way when managed or directed ⟨a car that ~s well⟩ — **han·dler** *n*

**han·dle·bar** \'han-dᵊl-ˌbär\ *n* : a usu. bent bar with a grip at each end (as for steering a bicycle) — usu. used in pl.

**hand·made** \'hand-ˌmad\ *adj* : made by hand or by a hand process

**hand·maid·en** \-ˌma-dᵊn\ *also* **hand·maid** \-ˌmad\ *n* : a female attendant

**hand-me-down** \-me-ˌdau̇n\ *adj* : used by one person after having been used by another — **hand-me-down** *n*

**hand·out** \'hand-ˌau̇t\ *n* 1 : a portion (as of food) given to a beggar 2 : a piece of printed information for free distribution; *also* : a prepared statement released to the press

**hand over** *vb* : to yield control of

**hand·pick** \'hand-'pik\ *vb* : to select personally ⟨a ~ed candidate⟩

**hand·rail** \-ˌrāl\ *n* : a narrow rail for grasping as a support

**hand·saw** \-₁sȯ\ *n* : a saw designed to be used with one hand

**hands down** *adv* **1** : with little effort **2** : without question

**hand·sel** \'han-səl\ *n* **1** : a gift made as a token of good luck **2** : a first installment : earnest money

**hand·set** \'hand-₁set\ *n* : a combined telephone transmitter and receiver mounted on a handheld device

**hand·shake** \-₁shāk\ *n* : a clasping usu. of right hands by two people

**hands–off** \'handz-'ȯf\ *adj* : characterized by noninterference

**hand·some** \'han-səm\ *adj* **hand·som·er; -est** [ME *handsom* easy to manipulate] **1** : SIZABLE, AMPLE ⟨a ~ profit⟩ **2** : GENEROUS, LIBERAL **3** : pleasing and usu. impressive in appearance ♦ *Synonyms* BEAUTIFUL, LOVELY, PRETTY, COMELY, FAIR — **hand·some·ly** *adv* — **hand·some·ness** *n*

**hands–on** \'handz-'ȯn, -'än\ *adj* **1** : being or providing direct practical experience in the operation of something **2** : characterized by active personal involvement ⟨~ management⟩

**hand·spring** \'hand-₁spriŋ\ *n* : an acrobatic feat in which the body turns in a full circle from a standing position and lands first on the hands and then on the feet

**hand·stand** \-₁stand\ *n* : an act of supporting the body on the hands with the trunk and legs balanced in the air

**hand–to–hand** *adj* : involving physical contact or very close range ⟨~ fighting⟩ — **hand to hand** *adv*

**hand–to–mouth** *adj* : having or providing nothing to spare ⟨lived a ~ existence⟩ — **hand to mouth** *adv*

**hand·wo·ven** \'hand-₁wō-vən\ *adj* : produced on a hand-operated loom

**hand·writ·ing** \-₁rī-tiŋ\ *n* : writing done by hand; *also* : the form of writing peculiar to a person — **hand·writ·ten** \-₁rit-ᵊn\ *adj*

**handy** \'han-dē\ *adj* **hand·i·er; -est** **1** : conveniently near **2** : easily used ⟨a ~ tool⟩ **3** : DEXTEROUS — **hand·i·ly** \-də-lē\ *adv* — **hand·i·ness** \-dē-nəs\ *n*

**handy·man** \-₁man\ *n* **1** : one who does odd jobs **2** : one competent in a variety of small skills or repair work

¹**hang** \'haŋ\ *vb* **hung** \'həŋ\ *also* **hanged; hang·ing** **1** : to fasten or remain fastened to an elevated point without support from below; *also* : to fasten or be fastened so as to allow free motion on the point of suspension ⟨~ a door⟩ **2** : to suspend by the neck until dead; *also* : to die by hanging **3** : DROOP ⟨*hung* his head in shame⟩ **4** : to fasten to a wall ⟨~ wallpaper⟩ **5** : to prevent (a jury) from coming to a decision **6** : to display (pictures) in a gallery **7** : to remain stationary in the air **8** : to be imminent **9** : DEPEND **10** : to take hold for support **11** : to be burdensome **12** : to undergo delay **13** : to incline downward; *also* : to fit or fall from the figure in easy lines **14** : to be raptly attentive **15** : to pass time idly by

relaxing or socializing ⟨~*ing* at the mall⟩ — often used with *around* or *out* —

**hang out to dry** : to subject to ruin by abandonment

²**hang** *n* **1** : the manner in which a thing hangs **2** : an understanding of something ⟨got the ~ of skiing⟩

**han·gar** \'haŋ-ər\ *n* [F] : a covered and usu. enclosed area for housing and repairing aircraft

**hang·dog** \'haŋ-₁dȯg\ *adj* **1** : SAD, DEJECTED ⟨a ~ look on his face⟩ **2** : SHEEPISH

**hang·er** \'haŋ-ər\ *n* **1** : one that hangs **2** : a device that fits inside or around a garment for hanging from a hook or rod

**hang·er–on** \'haŋ-ər-'ȯn, -'än\ *n, pl* **hangers–on** : one who hangs around a person or place esp. for personal gain

**hang in** *vb* : to persist tenaciously

**hang·ing** *n* **1** : an execution by strangling or snapping the neck by a suspended noose **2** : something hung

**hang·man** \'haŋ-mən\ *n* **1** : a public executioner **2** : a game in which players must identify an unknown word by guessing the letters that comprise it within a designated number of chances

**hang·nail** \-₁nāl\ *n* : a bit of skin hanging loose at the edge of a fingernail

**hang on** *vb* **1** : to keep hold onto something **2** : HANG IN **3** : to await something desired

**hang·out** \'haŋ-₁au̇t\ *n* : a favorite place for spending time

**hang·over** \-₁ō-vər\ *n* **1** : something that remains from what is past **2** : disagreeable physical effects following heavy drinking or the use of drugs

**hang–up** \'haŋ-₁əp\ *n* : a source of mental or emotional difficulty

**hang up** *vb* **1** : to place on a hook or hanger **2** : to end a telephone conversation by breaking the connection **3** : to keep delayed or suspended

**hank** \'haŋk\ *n* : COIL, LOOP ⟨a ~ of rope⟩

**han·ker** \'haŋ-kər\ *vb* : to desire strongly or persistently — **han·ker·ing** *n*

**han·kie** *or* **han·ky** \'haŋ-kē\ *n, pl* **han·kies** : HANDKERCHIEF

**han·ky–pan·ky** \₁haŋ-kē-'paŋ-kē\ *n* **1** : questionable or underhanded activity **2** : sexual dalliance

**hansel** *var of* HANDSEL

**han·som** \'han-səm\ *n* : a 2-wheeled covered carriage with the driver's seat elevated at the rear

**han·ta·virus** \'hän-tə-₁vī-rəs, 'hən-, 'han-\ *n* : any of a genus of viruses including some transmitted by rodents that cause pneumonia or hemorrhagic fevers

**Ha·nuk·kah** *also* **Cha·nu·kah** \'ḵä-nə-kə, 'hä-\ *n* [Heb *ḥănukkāh* dedication] : an 8-day Jewish holiday commemorating the rededication of the Temple of Jerusalem after its defilement by Antiochus of Syria

**hap** \'hap\ *n* **1** : HAPPENING **2** : CHANCE, FORTUNE

¹**hap·haz·ard** \hap-'ha-zərd\ *n* : CHANCE

²**haphazard** *adj* : marked by lack of plan

or order — **hap·haz·ard·ly** *adv* — **hap·haz·ard·ness** *n*

**hap·less** \'hap-ləs\ *adj* : UNFORTUNATE — **hap·less·ly** *adv* — **hap·less·ness** *n*

**hap·loid** \'hap-ˌlȯid\ *adj* : having the number of chromosomes characteristic of gametic cells — **haploid** *n*

**hap·ly** \'hap-lē\ *adv* : by chance

**hap·pen** \'ha-pən\ *vb* 1 : to occur by chance 2 : to take place 3 : CHANCE 2

[1]**hap·pen·ing** *n* 1 : OCCURRENCE 2 : an event that is especially interesting, entertaining, or important

[2]**happening** *adj* 1 : very fashionable 2 : offering much stimulating activity ⟨a ~ nightclub⟩

**hap·pi·ly** \'ha-pə-lē\ *adv* 1 : LUCKILY 2 : in a happy manner or state ⟨lived ~ ever after⟩ 3 : APTLY, SUCCESSFULLY

**hap·pi·ness** \'ha-pē-nəs\ *n* 1 : a state of well-being and contentment; *also* : a pleasurable satisfaction 2 : APTNESS

**hap·py** \'ha-pē\ *adj* **hap·pi·er; -est** 1 : FORTUNATE 2 : APT, FELICITOUS 3 : enjoying well-being and contentment ⟨a ~ childhood⟩ 4 : PLEASANT ⟨a ~ ending⟩; *also* : PLEASED, GRATIFIED ⟨~ to meet you⟩ 5 : quick or enthusiastic to use or do something ⟨trigger-*happy*⟩ ⟨a cliché-*happy* writer⟩ ♦ **Synonyms** GLAD, CHEERFUL, LIGHTHEARTED, JOYFUL, JOYOUS

**hap·py-go-lucky** \ˌha-pē-gō-'lə-kē\ *adj* : CAREFREE

**happy hour** *n* : a period of time when the price of drinks at a bar is reduced

**hara-kiri** \ˌha-ri-'kir-ē, -'ka-rē\ *n* [Jp *harakiri*, fr. *hara* belly + *kiri* cutting] : ritual suicide by disembowelment

**ha·rangue** \hə-'raŋ\ *n* 1 : a ranting speech or writing 2 : LECTURE — **harangue** *vb* — **ha·rangu·er** *n*

**ha·rass** \hə-'ras, 'ha-rəs\ *vb* [F *harasser*, fr. MF, fr. *harer* to set a dog on, fr. OF *hare*, interj. used to incite dogs, of Gmc origin] 1 : EXHAUST, FATIGUE 2 : to worry and impede by repeated raids 3 : to annoy continually 4 : to create an unpleasant or hostile situation for esp. by one's verbal or physical conduct ♦ **Synonyms** HARRY, PLAGUE, PESTER, TEASE, BEDEVIL — **ha·rass·ment** *n*

**har·bin·ger** \'här-bən-jər\ *n* : one that announces or foreshadows what is coming : PRECURSOR; *also* : PORTENT

[1]**har·bor** \'här-bər\ *n* 1 : a place of security and comfort 2 : a part of a body of water protected and deep enough to furnish anchorage : PORT

[2]**harbor** *vb* 1 : to give or take refuge : SHELTER ⟨~ a fugitive⟩ ⟨~ed in the barn⟩ 2 : to be the home or habitat of; *also* : LIVE 3 : to hold a thought or feeling ⟨~ a grudge⟩

**har·bor·age** \'här-bə-rij\ *n* : HARBOR

**har·bour** *chiefly Brit var of* HARBOR

**hard** \'härd\ *adj* 1 : not easily penetrated : not easily yielding to pressure 2 : high in alcoholic content 3 : containing salts that prevent lathering with soap ⟨~ water⟩ 4 : stable in value ⟨~ currency⟩ 5 : physically fit 6 : FIRM, DEFINITE ⟨~

agreement⟩; *also* : based on clear fact ⟨~ evidence⟩ 7 : CLOSE, SEARCHING ⟨a ~ look⟩ 8 : REALISTIC ⟨good ~ sense⟩ 9 : OBDURATE, UNFEELING ⟨a ~ heart⟩ 10 : difficult to bear ⟨~ times⟩; *also* : HARSH, SEVERE 11 : RESENTFUL ⟨~ feelings⟩ 12 : STRICT, UNRELENTING ⟨a ~ bargain⟩ 13 : INCLEMENT ⟨a ~ winter⟩ 14 : intense in force or manner ⟨a ~ gust of wind⟩ 15 : ARDUOUS, STRENUOUS ⟨~ work⟩ 16 : sounding as in *arc*ing and *geese* respectively — used of *c* and *g* 17 : TROUBLESOME ⟨a ~ problem⟩ 18 : having difficulty in doing something ⟨~ of hearing⟩ 19 : addictive and gravely detrimental to health ⟨~ drugs⟩ 20 : of or relating to the natural sciences and esp. the physical sciences — **hard** *adv* — **hard·ness** *n*

**hard-and-fast** *adj* : rigidly binding : STRICT ⟨a ~ rule⟩

**hard·back** \'härd-ˌbak\ *n* : a hardcover book

**hard·ball** \-ˌbȯl\ *n* 1 : BASEBALL 2 : forceful uncompromising methods

**hard-bit·ten** \-'bi-tᵊn\ *adj* : SEASONED, TOUGH ⟨~ campaigners⟩

**hard·board** \-ˌbȯrd\ *n* : a very dense fiberboard

**hard-boiled** \-'bȯi(-ə)ld\ *adj* 1 *of an egg* : boiled until both white and yolk have solidified 2 : lacking sentiment : TOUGH; *also* : HARDHEADED 2

**hard·bound** \-ˌbau̇nd\ *adj* : HARDCOVER

**hard copy** *n* : a copy of textual or graphic information (as from computer storage) produced on paper

**hard-core** \'härd-'kȯr\ *adj* 1 : extremely resistant to solution or improvement 2 : being the most determined or dedicated members of a specified group 3 : containing explicit depictions of sex acts — **hard core** *n*

**hard·cov·er** \-'kə-vər\ *adj* : having rigid boards on the sides covered in cloth or paper ⟨~ books⟩

**hard disk** *n* : a sealed rigid metal disk used as a computer storage device; *also* : HARD DRIVE

**hard drive** *n* : a data-storage device consisting of a drive and one or more hard disks

**hard·en** \'här-dᵊn\ *vb* 1 : to make or become hard or harder 2 : to confirm or become confirmed in disposition or action — **hard·en·er** *n*

**hard·hack** \'härd-ˌhak\ *n* : an American spirea with dense clusters of pink or white flowers and leaves having a hairy rusty yellow underside

**hard hat** *n* 1 : a protective hat worn esp. by construction workers 2 : a construction worker

**hard-head·ed** \'härd-'he-dəd\ *adj* 1 : STUBBORN, WILLFUL 2 : SOBER, REALISTIC ⟨some ~ advice⟩ — **hard-head·ed·ly** *adv* — **hard·head·ed·ness** *n*

**hard-heart·ed** \-'härt-əd\ *adj* : PITILESS, CRUEL — **hard-heart·ed·ly** *adv* — **hard-heart·ed·ness** *n*

**har·di·hood** \'här-dē-ˌhu̇d\ *n* 1 : resolute

courage and fortitude 2 : VIGOR, RO-BUSTNESS

**hard–line** \\'härd-'lin\\ *adj* : advocating or involving a rigidly uncompromising course of action ⟨a ~ conservative⟩ — **hard–lin·er** \\'-'li-nər\\ *n*

**hard·luck** \\-,lək\\ *adj* : marked by or relating to bad luck ⟨~ losing teams⟩

**hard·ly** \\'härd-lē\\ *adv* 1 : with force 2 : SEVERELY 3 : with difficulty 4 : only just : BARELY ⟨can ~ tell the difference⟩ 5 : certainly not ⟨is ~ a friend of mine⟩

**hard–nosed** \\'härd-'nōzd\\ *adj* : TOUGH, UNCOMPROMISING; *also* : HARDHEADED 2

**hard palate** *n* : the bony anterior part of the palate forming the roof of the mouth

**hard·pan** \\'härd-,pan\\ *n* : a compact layer in soil that is impenetrable by roots

**hard–pressed** \\-'prest\\ *adj* : HARD PUT; *esp* : being under financial strain

**hard put** *adj* 1 : barely able 2 : faced with difficulty or perplexity

**hard rock** *n* : rock music marked by a heavy beat, high amplification, and usu. frenzied performances

**hard–shell** \\'härd-,shel\\ *or* **hard–shelled** \\-,sheld\\ *adj* 1 : having a hard shell 2 : HIDEBOUND, UNCOMPROMISING ⟨a ~ conservative⟩

**hard·ship** \\-,ship\\ *n* 1 : SUFFERING, PRIVATION 2 : something that causes suffering or privation

**hard·tack** \\-,tak\\ *n* : a saltless hard biscuit, bread, or cracker

**hard·top** \\-,täp\\ *n* : an automobile having a permanent rigid top

**hard·ware** \\-,wer\\ *n* 1 : ware (as cutlery or tools) made of metal 2 : the physical components (as electronic devices) of a vehicle (as a spacecraft) or an apparatus (as a computer)

**hard·wired** \\-,wi(-ə)rd\\ *adj* 1 : connected or incorporated by or as if by permanent electrical connections 2 : genetically or innately determined or predisposed ⟨~ reactions⟩ ⟨is ~ to avoid change⟩

**hard·wood** \\-,wud\\ *n* : the wood of a broad-leaved usu. deciduous tree as distinguished from that of a conifer; *also* : such a tree — **hardwood** *adj*

**hard·work·ing** \\-'wər-kin\\ *adj* : INDUSTRIOUS, DILIGENT

**har·dy** \\'här-dē\\ *adj* **har·di·er; -est** 1 : BOLD, BRAVE ⟨~ pioneers⟩ 2 : AUDACIOUS, BRAZEN 3 : ROBUST; *also* : able to withstand adverse conditions (as of weather) ⟨~ shrubs⟩ — **har·di·ly** \\-də-lē\\ *adv* — **har·di·ness** \\-dē-nəs\\ *n*

**hare** \\'her\\ *n, pl* **hare** *or* **hares** : any of various swift timid long-eared mammals like the related rabbits but born with open eyes and fur

**hare·bell** \\'her-,bel\\ *n* : a slender herb with bright blue bell-shaped flowers

**hare·brained** \\-'brānd\\ *adj* : FOOLISH, ABSURD ⟨~ notions⟩

**hare·lip** \\-'lip\\ *n, sometimes offensive* : CLEFT LIP

**ha·rem** \\'her-əm\\ *n* [Ar *ḥarīm*, lit., something forbidden & *ḥaram*, lit., sanctuary] 1 : a house or part of a house allotted to women in a Muslim household 2 : the women and servants occupying a harem 3 : a group of females associated with one male

**hark** \\'härk\\ *vb* : LISTEN

**harken** *var of* HEARKEN

**har·le·quin** \\'här-li-kən, -kwən\\ *n* 1 *cap* : a character (as in comedy) with a shaved head, masked face, variegated tights, and wooden sword 2 : CLOWN 2

**har·lot** \\'här-lət\\ *n* : PROSTITUTE

¹**harm** \\'härm\\ *n* 1 : physical or mental damage : INJURY 2 : MISCHIEF, HURT — **harm·ful** \\-fəl\\ *adj* — **harm·ful·ly** *adv* — **harm·ful·ness** *n* — **harm·less** *adj* — **harm·less·ly** *adv* — **harm·less·ness** *n*

²**harm** *vb* : to cause harm to : INJURE

¹**har·mon·ic** \\här-'mä-nik\\ *adj* 1 : of or relating to musical harmony or harmonics 2 : pleasing to the ear — **har·mon·i·cal·ly** \\-ni-k(ə-)lē\\ *adv*

²**harmonic** *n* : a musical overtone

**har·mon·i·ca** \\här-'mä-ni-kə\\ *n* : a small wind instrument in which the sound is produced by metal reeds

**har·mo·ni·ous** \\här-'mō-nē-əs\\ *adj* 1 : musically concordant 2 : CONGRUOUS 3 : marked by accord in sentiment or action ⟨a ~ relationship⟩ — **har·mo·ni·ous·ly** *adv* — **har·mo·ni·ous·ness** *n*

**har·mo·nise** *Brit var of* HARMONIZE

**har·mo·ni·um** \\här-'mō-nē-əm\\ *n* : a keyboard wind instrument in which the wind acts on a set of metal reeds

**har·mo·nize** \\'här-mə-,nīz\\ *vb* **-nized; -niz·ing** 1 : to play or sing in harmony 2 : to be in harmony 3 : to bring into consonance or accord — **har·mo·ni·za·tion** \\,här-mə-nə-'zā-shən\\ *n*

**har·mo·ny** \\'här-mə-nē\\ *n, pl* **-nies** [ME *armony*, fr. AF *armonie*, fr. L *harmonia*, fr. Gk, joint, harmony, fr. *harmos* joint] 1 : musical agreement of sounds; *esp* : the combination of tones into chords and progressions of chords 2 : a pleasing arrangement of parts; *also* : ACCORD 3 : internal calm

¹**har·ness** \\'här-nəs\\ *n* 1 : the gear other than a yoke of a draft animal 2 : something that resembles a harness

²**harness** *vb* 1 : to put a harness on; *also* : YOKE 2 : UTILIZE ⟨~ one's potential⟩

¹**harp** \\'härp\\ *n* : a musical instrument consisting of a triangular frame set with strings plucked by the fingers — **harp·ist** \\'här-pist\\ *n*

²**harp** *vb* 1 : to play on a harp 2 : to dwell on a subject tiresomely — **harp·er** *n*

**har·poon** \\här-'pün\\ *n* : a barbed spear used esp. in hunting whales — **harpoon** *vb* — **har·poon·er** *n*

**harp·si·chord** \\'härp-si-,kord\\ *n* : a keyboard instrument producing tones by the plucking of its strings with quills or with leather or plastic points

**har·py** \\'här-pē\\ *n, pl* **harpies** [L *Harpyia*, a malign creature of myth having a woman's head and a bird's body, fr. Gk] 1 : a predatory person : LEECH 2 : a shrewish woman

**har·ri·dan** \\'her-ə-dən\\ *n* : SHREW

¹**har·ri·er** \\'her-ē-ər\\ *n* 1 : any of a breed

of medium-sized foxhounds **2** : a runner on a cross-country team

²**harrier** *n* : a slender long-legged hawk

¹**har·row** \'her-ō\ *n* : a cultivating tool that has spikes, spring teeth, or disks and is used esp. to pulverize and smooth the soil

²**harrow** *vb* **1** : to cultivate with a harrow **2** : TORMENT, VEX

**har·rumph** \hə-'rəmf\ *vb* : to comment disapprovingly as though clearing the throat

**har·ry** \'her-ē\ *vb* **har·ried; har·ry·ing 1** : RAID, PILLAGE **2** : to torment by or as if by constant attack ♦ **Synonyms** WORRY, ANNOY, PLAGUE, PESTER

**harsh** \'härsh\ *adj* **1** : disagreeably rough **2** : causing discomfort or pain **3** : unduly exacting : SEVERE — **harsh·ly** *adv* — **harsh·ness** *n*

**harsh·en** \'här-shən\ *vb* : to make or become harsh ⟨~ed his voice⟩

**hart** \'härt\ *n, chiefly Brit* : STAG

**har·um—scar·um** \,har-əm-'skar-əm\ *adj* : RECKLESS, IRRESPONSIBLE

¹**har·vest** \'här-vəst\ *n* **1** : the season for gathering in crops; *also* : the act of gathering in a crop **2** : a mature crop **3** : the product or reward of effort

²**harvest** *vb* **1** : to gather in a crop : REAP **2** : to gather, hunt, or kill (as deer) for human use or population control **3** : to remove cells, tissues, or organs from a living or recently deceased body esp. for transplanting — **har·vest·er** *n*

**has** *pres 3d sing of* HAVE

**has—been** \'haz-,bin\ *n* : one that has passed the peak of ability, power, effectiveness, or popularity

¹**hash** \'hash\ *vb* [F *hacher*, fr. OF *hachier*, fr. *hache* battle-ax, fr. of Gmc origin] **1** : to chop into small pieces **2** : to talk about — often used with *over* or *out*

²**hash** *n* **1** : chopped meat mixed with potatoes and browned **2** : HODGEPODGE, JUMBLE

³**hash** *n* : HASHISH

**hash browns** *n pl* : boiled potatoes that have been diced, mixed with chopped onions and shortening, and fried

**hash·ish** \'ha-,shēsh, ha-'shēsh\ *n* [Ar *ḥashīsh*] : the intoxicating concentrated resin from the flowering tops of the female hemp plant

**hash·tag** \'hash-,tag\ *n* : a word or phrase preceded by the symbol # that classifies the accompanying text

**hasp** \'hasp\ *n* : a fastener (as for a door) consisting of a hinged metal strap that fits over a staple and is secured by a pin or padlock

**has·si·um** \'ha-sē-əm\ *n* : an artificially produced radioactive metallic chemical element

**has·sle** \'ha-səl\ *n* **1** : WRANGLE; *also* : FIGHT **2** : an annoying or troublesome concern — **hassle** *vb*

**has·sock** \'ha-sək\ *n* : a cushion that serves as a seat or leg rest; *also* : a cushion to kneel on in prayer

**haste** \'hāst\ *n* **1** : rapidity of motion or action : SPEED **2** : rash or headlong action **3** : excessive eagerness — **hast·i·ly** \'hā-stə-lē\ *adv* — **hast·i·ness** \-stē-nəs\ *n* — **hasty** \'hā-stē\ *adj*

**has·ten** \'hā-sᵊn\ *vb* **1** : to urge on **2** : to move or act quickly : HURRY ♦ **Synonyms** SPEED, ACCELERATE, QUICKEN

**hat** \'hat\ *n* : a covering for the head usu. having a shaped crown and brim — **under one's hat** : SECRET ⟨kept the plans *under his hat*⟩

**hat·box** \'hat-,bäks\ *n* : a round piece of luggage often for carrying hats

¹**hatch** \'hach\ *n* **1** : a small door or opening **2** : a door or cover for access down into a compartment of a ship

²**hatch** *vb* **1** : to produce by incubation; *also* : INCUBATE **2** : to emerge from an egg or pupa; *also* : to give forth young **3** : ORIGINATE ⟨~ a scheme⟩ — **hatch·ery** \'ha-chə-rē\ *n*

**hatch·back** \'hach-,bak\ *n* : an automobile with a rear hatch that opens upward

**hatch·et** \'ha-chət\ *n* **1** : a short-handled ax with a hammerlike part opposite the blade **2** : TOMAHAWK

**hatchet man** *n* : a person hired for murder, coercion, or unscrupulous attack

**hatch·ing** \'ha-chiŋ\ *n* : the engraving or drawing of closely spaced fine lines chiefly to give an effect of shading; *also* : the pattern so created

**hatch·way** \'hach-,wā\ *n* : a hatch giving access usu. by a ladder or stairs

¹**hate** \'hāt\ *n* **1** : intense hostility and aversion **2** : an object of hatred — **hate·ful** \-fəl\ *adj* — **hate·ful·ly** *adv* — **hate·ful·ness** *n*

²**hate** *vb* **hat·ed; hat·ing 1** : to express or feel extreme enmity **2** : to find distasteful ♦ **Synonyms** DETEST, ABHOR, ABOMINATE, LOATHE — **hat·er** *n*

**ha·tred** \'hā-trəd\ *n* : HATE; *also* : prejudiced hostility or animosity

**hat·ter** \'ha-tər\ *n* : one that makes, sells, or cleans and repairs hats

**hau·berk** \'hȯ-bərk\ *n* : a coat of mail

**haugh·ty** \'hȯ-tē\ *adj* **haugh·ti·er; -est** [obs. *haught*, fr. ME *haute*, fr. AF *halt, haut*, lit., high, fr. L *altus*] : disdainfully proud ♦ **Synonyms** INSOLENT, LORDLY, OVERBEARING, ARROGANT — **haugh·ti·ly** \-tə-lē\ *adv* — **haugh·ti·ness** \-tē-nəs\ *n*

¹**haul** \'hȯl\ *vb* **1** : to exert traction on : DRAW, PULL **2** : to furnish transportation : CART — **haul·er** *n*

²**haul** *n* **1** : PULL, TUG **2** : the result of an effort to obtain, collect, or win **3** : the length or course of a transportation route; *also* : LOAD

**haul·age** \'hȯ-lij\ *n* **1** : the act or process of hauling **2** : a charge for hauling

**haunch** \'hȯnch\ *n* **1** : ²HIP 1 **2** : HINDQUARTER 2 — usu. used in pl. **3** : HINDQUARTER 1

¹**haunt** \'hȯnt\ *vb* **1** : to visit often : FREQUENT **2** : to have a disquieting effect on ⟨was ~ed by his past⟩; *also* : to reappear continually in **3** : to visit or inhabit as a ghost — **haunt·er** *n* — **haunt·ing·ly** *adv*

²**haunt** \'hȯnt, 2 *is usu* 'hant\ *n* **1** : a place habitually frequented **2** *chiefly dial* : GHOST

**haute cou·ture** \ˌōt-kú-'túr\ *n* [F] : the establishments or designers that create exclusive and often trend-setting fashions for women; *also* : the fashions created

**haute cui·sine** \-kwi-'zēn\ *n* : artful or elaborate cuisine

**hau·teur** \hō-'tər, ō-, hō-\ *n* : ARROGANCE, HAUGHTINESS

¹**have** \'hav, həv, v; *in sense 2 before "to" usu* 'haf\ *vb* **had** \'had, həd\; **hav·ing**; **has** \'haz, həz, v; *in sense 2 before "to" usu* 'has\ **1** : to hold in possession; *also* : to hold in one's use, service, or regard ⟨*has* a good job⟩ **2** : to be compelled or forced ⟨~ to go now⟩ **3** : to stand in relationship to ⟨*has* many enemies⟩ **4** : OBTAIN; *also* : RECEIVE, ACCEPT **5** : to be marked by ⟨*has* red hair⟩ **6** : SHOW; *also* : USE, EXERCISE ⟨~ mercy⟩ **7** : EXPERIENCE; *also* : TAKE ⟨~ a look⟩ **8** : to entertain in the mind ⟨~ an idea⟩ **9** : to cause to **10** : ALLOW **11** : to be competent in **12** : to hold in a disadvantageous position; *also* : TRICK **13** : BEGET **14** : to partake of **15** — used as an auxiliary with the past participle to form the present perfect, past perfect, or future perfect — **have at** : ATTACK — **have coming** : DESERVE — **have done with** : to be finished with — **have had it** : to have endured all one will permit or can stand — **have to do with** : to have in the way of relation with or effect on

²**have** \'hav\ *n* : one that has material wealth

**ha·ven** \'hā-vən\ *n* **1** : HARBOR, PORT **2** : a place of safety **3** : a place offering favorable conditions ⟨an artist's ~⟩

**have–not** \'hav-ˌnät, -'nät\ *n* : one that is poor in material wealth

**hav·er·sack** \'ha-vər-ˌsak\ *n* [F *havresac*, fr. G *Habersack* bag for oats] : a bag similar to a knapsack but worn over one shoulder

**hav·oc** \'ha-vək\ *n* **1** : wide and general destruction **2** : great confusion and disorder

**haw** \'hȯ\ *n* : a hawthorn berry; *also* : HAWTHORN

**Ha·wai·ian** \hə-'wä-yən\ *n* **1** : a native or resident of Hawaii; *esp* : one of Polynesian ancestry **2** : the Polynesian language of Hawaii

¹**hawk** \'hȯk\ *n* **1** : any of numerous mostly small or medium-sized day-flying birds of prey (as a falcon or kite) **2** : a supporter of a war or a warlike policy — **hawk·ish** *adj*

²**hawk** *vb* : to make a harsh coughing sound in or as if in clearing the throat; *also* : to raise by hawking

³**hawk** *vb* : to offer goods for sale by calling out in the street — **hawk·er** *n*

**hawk·weed** \'hȯk-ˌwēd\ *n* : any of several plants related to the daisies usu. having yellow flowers

**haw·ser** \'hȯ-zər\ *n* : a large rope for towing, mooring, or securing a ship

**haw·thorn** \'hȯ-ˌthȯrn\ *n* : any of a genus of spiny spring-flowering shrubs or small trees related to the apple

¹**hay** \'hā\ *n* **1** : herbage (as grass) mowed and cured for fodder **2** : REWARD **3** *slang* : BED ⟨hit the ~⟩ **4** : a small amount of money

²**hay** *vb* : to cut, cure, and store for hay

**hay·cock** \'hā-ˌkäk\ *n* : a small conical pile of hay

**hay fever** *n* : an acute allergic reaction esp. to plant pollen that resembles a cold

**hay·loft** \'hā-ˌlȯft\ *n* : a loft for hay

**hay·mow** \-ˌmaú\ *n* : a mow of or for hay

**hay·rick** \-ˌrik\ *n* : a large sometimes thatched outdoor stack of hay

**hay·seed** \-ˌsēd\ *n, pl* **hayseed** *or* **hayseeds** **1** : clinging bits of straw or chaff from hay **2** : BUMPKIN, YOKEL

**hay·stack** \-ˌstak\ *n* : a stack of hay

**hay·wire** \-ˌwī(-ə)r\ *adj* : being out of order or control ⟨things went ~⟩; *also* : CRAZY

¹**haz·ard** \'ha-zərd\ *n* [ME, a dice game, fr. AF *hasard*, fr. Sp *azar*, Ar *al-zahr* the die] **1** : a source of danger **2** : CHANCE; *also* : ACCIDENT **3** : an obstacle on a golf course — **haz·ard·ous** *adj*

²**hazard** *vb* : VENTURE, RISK ⟨~ a guess⟩

¹**haze** \'hāz\ *n* **1** : fine dust, smoke, or light vapor causing lack of transparency in the air **2** : vagueness of mind or perception

²**haze** *vb* **hazed; haz·ing** : to harass by abusive and humiliating tricks usu. by way of initiation

**ha·zel** \'hā-zəl\ *n* **1** : any of a genus of shrubs or small trees related to the birches and bearing edible brown nuts (**ha·zel·nuts** \-ˌnəts\) **2** : a light brown color

**hazy** \'hā-zē\ *adj* **haz·i·er; -est 1** : obscured or darkened by haze **2** : VAGUE, INDEFINITE ⟨a ~ memory⟩; *also* : UNCERTAIN — **haz·i·ly** \-zə-lē\ *adv* — **haz·i·ness** \-zē-nəs\ *n*

**Hb** *abbr* hemoglobin

**HBM** *abbr* Her Britannic Majesty; His Britannic Majesty

**H–bomb** \'āch-ˌbäm\ *n* : HYDROGEN BOMB

**HC** *abbr* **1** Holy Communion **2** House of Commons

**hd** *abbr* head

**HD** *abbr* **1** heavy-duty **2** high definition

**hdbk** *abbr* handbook

**hdkf** *abbr* handkerchief

**HDL** \ˌāch-(ˌ)dē-'el\ *n* [*high-density lipoprotein*] : a cholesterol-poor protein-rich lipoprotein of blood plasma correlated with reduced risk of atherosclerosis

**hdwe** *abbr* hardware

**he** \'hē\ *pron* **1** : that male one **2** : a person : the person ⟨~ who hesitates is lost⟩

**He** *symbol* helium

**HE** *abbr* **1** Her Excellency **2** His Eminence **3** His Excellency

¹**head** \'hed\ *n* **1** : the front or upper part of the body containing the brain, the chief sense organs, and the mouth **2** : MIND; *also* : natural aptitude ⟨has a ~ for math⟩ **3** : POISE ⟨a level ~⟩ **4** : the obverse of a coin **5** : INDIVIDUAL; *also, pl* **head** : one of a number (as of cattle) **6** : the end that is upper or higher or opposite the foot; *also* : either end of something (as a drum) whose two ends need not be distinguished **7** : a compact mass

of plant parts (as leaves or flowers) **8** : the source of a stream **9** : DIRECTOR, LEADER; *also* : a leading element (as of a procession) **10** : a projecting part; *also* : the striking part of a weapon **11** : the place of leadership or honor **12** : a separate part or topic **13** : the foam on a fermenting or effervescing liquid **14** : a critical point ⟨events came to a ∼⟩ — **head·ed** \'he-dəd\ *adj* — **head·less** *adj* — **over one's head** : beyond one's comprehension or competence

²**head** *adj* : PRINCIPAL, CHIEF

³**head** *vb* **1** : to provide with or form a head; *also* : to form the head of **2** : LEAD, CONDUCT ⟨∼ed the search⟩ **3** : to get in front of esp. so as to stop; *also* : SURPASS **4** : to put or stand at the head **5** : to point or proceed in a certain direction ⟨∼ed west⟩

**head·ache** \'he-ˌdāk\ *n* **1** : pain in the head **2** : a baffling situation or problem — **head·achy** *also* **head·achey** \-ˌā-ke\ *adj*

**head·band** \'hed-ˌband\ *n* : a band worn on or around the head

**head·bang·er** \-ˌbaŋ-ər\ *n* : one who performs or enjoys hard rock

**head·board** \-ˌbȯrd\ *n* : a board forming the head (as of a bed)

**head cold** *n* : a common cold centered in the nasal passages and adjacent mucous tissues

**head·dress** \'hed-ˌdres\ *n* : an often elaborate covering for the head

**head·first** \-'fərst\ *adv* : HEADLONG 1 ⟨dove ∼ into the water⟩ — **headfirst** *adj*

**head·gear** \-ˌgir\ *n* : a covering or protective device for the head

**head·hunt·er** \-ˌhən-tər\ *n* **1** : one that engages in head-hunting **2** : a recruiter of esp. executive personnel

**head·hunt·ing** \-ˌhən-tiŋ\ *n* : the practice of seeking out and decapitating enemies and preserving their heads as trophies

**head·ing** \'he-diŋ\ *n* **1** : the compass direction in which the longitudinal axis of a ship or airplane points **2** : something that appears at the top or beginning of something else (as a document)

**head·land** \'hed-lənd, -ˌland\ *n* : PROMONTORY

**head·light** \-ˌlīt\ *n* : a light mounted on the front of a vehicle to illuminate the road ahead

¹**head·line** \-ˌlīn\ *n* : a head of a newspaper story or article usu. printed in large type

²**headline** *vb* **1** : to provide with a headline **2** : to publicize highly **3** : to be a leading performer in

**head·lock** \-ˌläk\ *n* : a wrestling hold in which one encircles the opponent's head with one arm

¹**head·long** \-'lȯŋ\ *adv* **1** : with the head foremost **2** : RECKLESSLY **3** : without delay

²**head·long** \-ˌlȯŋ\ *adj* **1** : PRECIPITATE, RASH ⟨∼ flight⟩ **2** : plunging with the head foremost

**head·man** \'hed-'man, -ˌman\ *n* : one who is a leader : CHIEF

**head·mas·ter** \-ˌmas-tər\ *n* : a man who is head of a private school

**head·mis·tress** \-ˌmis-trəs\ *n* : a woman who is head of a private school

**head of steam** : strong driving force : MOMENTUM

**head–on** \'hed-'ȯn, -'än\ *adj* : having the front facing in the direction of initial contact or line of sight ⟨∼ collision⟩ — **head–on** *adv*

**head·phone** \-ˌfōn\ *n* : an earphone held on by a band over the head

**head·piece** \-ˌpēs\ *n* : a covering for the head

**head·pin** \-ˌpin\ *n* : a bowling pin that stands foremost in the arrangement of pins

**head·quar·ters** \-ˌkwȯr-tərz\ *n sing or pl* **1** : a place from which a commander exercises command **2** : the administrative center of an enterprise

**head·rest** \-ˌrest\ *n* **1** : a support for the head **2** : a pad at the top of the back of an automobile seat

**head·room** \-ˌrüm, -ˌrùm\ *n* : vertical space in which to stand, sit, or move

**head–scratcher** \-ˌskra-chər\ *n* : PUZZLE, MYSTERY

**head·set** \-ˌset\ *n* : a pair of headphones

**head·ship** \-ˌship\ *n* : the position, office, or dignity of a head

**heads·man** \'hedz-mən\ *n* : EXECUTIONER

**head·stall** \'hed-ˌstȯl\ *n* : a part of a bridle or halter that encircles the head

**head·stone** \-ˌstōn\ *n* : a memorial stone at the head of a grave

**head·strong** \'hed-ˌstrȯŋ\ *adj* **1** : not easily restrained **2** : directed by ungovernable will ♦ **Synonyms** UNRULY, INTRACTABLE, WILLFUL, PERTINACIOUS, REFRACTORY, STUBBORN

**heads–up** \'hedz-'əp\ *n* : WARNING

**head·wait·er** \-'wā-tər\ *n* : the head of the dining-room staff of a restaurant or hotel

**head·wa·ter** \-ˌwȯ-tər, -ˌwä-\ *n* : the source of a stream — usu. used in pl.

**head·way** \-ˌwā\ *n* : forward motion; *also* : PROGRESS

**head·wind** \-ˌwind\ *n* : a wind blowing in a direction opposite to a course esp. of a ship or aircraft

**head·word** \'hed-ˌwərd\ *n* **1** : a word or term placed at the beginning of a chapter qualified by a modifier **2** : a word

**head·work** \-ˌwərk\ *n* : mental work or effort : THINKING

**heady** \'he-dē\ *adj* **head·i·er; -est 1** : WILLFUL, RASH; *also* : IMPETUOUS **2** : INTOXICATING ⟨a ∼ wine⟩ **3** : SHREWD

**heal** \'hēl\ *vb* **1** : to make or become healthy, sound, or whole **2** : CURE, REMEDY — **heal·er** *n*

**health** \'helth\ *n* **1** : sound physical or mental condition; *also* : overall condition of the body ⟨in poor ∼⟩ **2** : WELL-BEING **3** : a toast to someone's health or prosperity

**health care** *n* : efforts made to maintain

or restore health — usu. hyphenated when used attributively

**health club** n : a commercial establishment providing health and fitness facilities and equipment for members

**health·ful** \'helth-fəl\ adj 1 : beneficial to health 2 : HEALTHY — **health·ful·ly** adv — **health·ful·ness** n

**health maintenance organization** n : HMO

**healthy** \'hel-thē\ adj **health·i·er; -est** 1 : enjoying or typical of good health : WELL 2 : evincing or conducive to health 3 : PROSPEROUS ⟨a ~ economy⟩; also : CONSIDERABLE 2 ⟨a ~ savings⟩ — **health·i·ly** \-thə-lē\ adv — **health·i·ness** \-thē-nəs\ n

¹**heap** \'hēp\ n : PILE ⟨rubbish ~⟩; also : LOT 5 ⟨a ~ of fun⟩

²**heap** vb 1 : to throw or lay in a heap 2 : to give in large quantities; also : to load heavily

**hear** \'hir\ vb **heard** \'hərd\; **hear·ing** 1 : to perceive by the ear 2 : to gain knowledge of by hearing : LEARN 3 : HEED; also : ATTEND 4 : to give a legal hearing to or take testimony from — **hear·er** n

**hear·ing** n 1 : the process, function, or power of perceiving sound; esp : the special sense by which noises and tones are received as stimuli 2 : EARSHOT 3 : opportunity to be heard 4 : a listening to arguments (as in a court); also : a session (as of a legislative committee) in which testimony is taken from witnesses

**hear·ken** \'här-kən\ vb : to give attention : LISTEN ♦ Synonyms HEAR, HARK, HEED

**hear·say** \'hir-ˌsā\ n : RUMOR

**hearse** \'hərs\ n : a vehicle for carrying the dead to the grave

**heart** \'härt\ n 1 : a hollow muscular organ that by rhythmic contraction keeps up the circulation of the blood in the body; also : something resembling a heart in shape 2 : any of a suit of playing cards marked with a red figure of a heart; also, pl : a card game in which the object is to avoid taking tricks containing hearts 3 : the whole personality; also : the emotional or moral as distinguished from the intellectual nature 4 : COURAGE 5 : one's innermost being ⟨knew it in his ~⟩ 6 : CENTER; also : the essential part 7 : the younger central part of a compact leafy cluster (as of lettuce) — **heart·ed** \'här-təd\ adj — **by heart** : by rote or from memory

**heart·ache** \-ˌāk\ n : anguish of mind

**heart attack** n : an acute episode of heart disease due to insufficient blood supply to the heart muscle

**heart·beat** \'härt-ˌbēt\ n : one complete pulsation of the heart

**heart·break** \-ˌbrāk\ n : crushing grief

**heart·break·ing** \-ˌbrā-kiŋ\ adj : causing extreme sorrow or distress — **heart·break·er** \-ˌbrā-kər\ n — **heart·break·ing·ly** adv

**heart·bro·ken** \-ˌbrō-kən\ adj : overcome by sorrow

**heart·burn** \-ˌbərn\ n : a burning distress behind the sternum due esp. to the backward flow of acid from the stomach to the esophagus

**heart disease** n : an abnormal organic condition of the heart or of the heart and circulation

**heart·en** \'här-t³n\ vb : ENCOURAGE, CHEER ⟨were ~ed by the victory⟩

**heart·felt** \'härt-ˌfelt\ adj : deeply felt : SINCERE ⟨~ thanks⟩

**hearth** \'härth\ n 1 : an area (as of brick) in front of a fireplace; also : the floor of a fireplace 2 : HOME

**hearth·stone** \'härth-ˌstōn\ n 1 : stone forming a hearth 2 : HOME

**heart·less** \'härt-ləs\ adj : CRUEL

**heart·rend·ing** \-ˌren-diŋ\ adj : HEARTBREAKING

**heart·sick** \-ˌsik\ adj : very despondent — **heart·sick·ness** n

**heart–stop·ping** \-ˌstä-piŋ\ adj : extremely shocking or exciting

**heart·strings** \-ˌstriŋz\ n pl : the deepest emotions or affections

**heart·throb** \-ˌthräb\ n 1 : the throb of a heart 2 : sentimental emotion 3 : SWEETHEART 4 : an entertainer noted for his sex appeal

**heart–to–heart** adj : SINCERE, FRANK

**heart·warm·ing** \'härt-ˌwȯr-miŋ\ adj : inspiring sympathetic feeling

**heart·wood** \-ˌwu̇d\ n : the older harder nonliving and usu. darker wood of the central part of a tree trunk

¹**hearty** \'här-tē\ adj **heart·i·er; -est** 1 : giving full support; also : JOVIAL 2 : vigorously healthy 3 : ABUNDANT; also : NOURISHING ⟨~ soups⟩ ♦ Synonyms SINCERE, WHOLEHEARTED, UNFEIGNED, HEARTFELT — **heart·i·ly** \-tə-lē\ adv — **heart·i·ness** \-tē-nəs\ n

²**hearty** n, pl **heart·ies** : an enthusiastic jovial fellow; also : SAILOR

¹**heat** \'hēt\ vb 1 : to make or become warm or hot 2 : EXCITE ⟨a ~ed discussion⟩ — **heat·ed·ly** adv — **heat·er** n

²**heat** n 1 : a condition of being hot : WARMTH 2 : a form of energy that when added to a body causes the body to rise in temperature, to fuse, to evaporate, or to expand 3 : high temperature 4 : intensity of feeling; also : sexual excitement esp. in a female mammal 5 : a preliminary race for narrowing the competition 6 : pungency of flavor 7 slang : POLICE 8 : PRESSURE, COERCION; also : ABUSE, CRITICISM ⟨took ~ for my mistakes⟩

**heat exchanger** n : a device (as an automobile radiator) for transferring heat from one fluid to another without allowing them to mix

**heat exhaustion** n : a condition marked by weakness, nausea, dizziness, and profuse sweating resulting from physical exertion in a hot environment

**heath** \'hēth\ n 1 : a tract of wasteland 2 : any of a family of often evergreen shrubby plants (as a blueberry or heather) of wet acid soils — **heathy** adj

**hea·then** \'hē-thən\ n, pl **heathens** or **heathen** 1 : an unconverted member of a people or nation that does not acknowledge the God of the Bible **2** : an uncivilized or irreligious person — **heathen** *adj* — **hea·then·dom** *n* — **hea·then·ish** *adj* — **hea·then·ism** *n*

**heath·er** \'he-thər\ *n* : a northern and alpine evergreen heath with usu. lavender flowers — **heath·ery** *adj*

**heat lightning** *n* : flashes of light without thunder ascribed to distant lightning reflected by high clouds

**heat·stroke** \'hēt-,strōk\ *n* : a disorder marked esp. by high body temperature without sweating and by collapse that follows prolonged exposure to excessive heat

¹**heave** \'hēv\ *vb* **heaved** *or* **hove** \'hōv\; **heav·ing 1** : to rise or lift upward **2** : THROW **3** : to rise and fall rhythmically; *also* : PANT **4** : RETCH **5** : PULL, PUSH — **heav·er** *n*

²**heave** *n* **1** : an effort to lift or raise **2** : THROW, CAST **3** : an upward motion **4** *pl* : a chronic lung disease of horses marked by difficult breathing and persistent cough

**heav·en** \'he-vən\ *n* **1** : FIRMAMENT — usu. used in pl. **2** *often cap* : the abode of the Deity and of the blessed dead; *also* : a spiritual state of everlasting communion with God **3** *cap* : GOD 1 **4** : a place of supreme happiness — **heav·en·ly** *adj* — **heav·en·ward** *adv or adj*

¹**heavy** \'he-vē\ *adj* **heavi·er; -est 1** : having great weight **2** : hard to bear **3** : SERIOUS **4** : DEEP, PROFOUND ⟨a ∼ silence⟩ **5** : burdened with something oppressive; *also* : PREGNANT **6** : SLUGGISH **7** : DRAB; *also* : DOLEFUL **8** : DROWSY **9** : greater than the average of its kind or class **10** : very rich and hard to digest; *also* : not properly raised or leavened **11** : producing goods (as steel) used in the production of other goods — **heavi·ly** \-və lē\ *adv* — **heavi·ness** \-vē-nəs\ *n*

²**heavy** *n, pl* **heav·ies** : a theatrical role representing a dignified or imposing person; *also* : a villain esp. in a story

**heavy–du·ty** \,he-vē-'dü-tē, -'dyü-\ *adj* : able to withstand unusual strain

**heavy–hand·ed** \-'han-dəd\ *adj* **1** : CLUMSY **2** : OPPRESSIVE, HARSH

**heavy–heart·ed** \-'här-təd\ *adj* : SADDENED, DESPONDENT

**heavy lifting** *n* : a burdensome or laborious duty

**heavy metal** *n* : energetic and highly amplified electronic rock music

**heavy–set** \,he-vē-'set\ *adj* : stocky and compact in build

**heavy water** *n* : water enriched in deuterium

**heavy·weight** \'he-vē-,wāt\ *n* : one above average in weight; *esp* : a boxer in an unlimited weight division

**Heb** *abbr* Hebrews

**He·bra·ism** \'hē-brā-,i-zəm\ *n* : the thought, spirit, or practice characteristic of the Hebrews — **He·bra·ic** \hi-'brā-ik\ *adj*

**He·bra·ist** \'hē-,brā-ist\ *n* : a specialist in Hebrew and Hebraic studies

**He·brew** \'hē-brü\ *n* **1** : the language of the Hebrews **2** : a member of or descendant from a group of Semitic peoples; *esp* : ISRAELITE — **Hebrew** *adj*

**He·brews** \'hē-(,)brüz\ *n* — see BIBLE table

**hec·a·tomb** \'he-kə-,tōm\ *n* : an ancient Greek and Roman sacrifice of 100 oxen or cattle

**heck·le** \'he-kəl\ *vb* **heck·led; heck·ling** : to harass with questions or gibes : BADGER — **heck·ler** *n*

**hect·are** \'hek-,ter\ *n* — see METRIC SYSTEM table

**hec·tic** \'hek-tik\ *adj* **1** : being hot and flushed **2** : filled with excitement, activity, or confusion — **hec·ti·cal·ly** \-ti-k(ə-)lē\ *adv*

**hecto·gram** \'hek-tə-,gram\ *n* — see METRIC SYSTEM table

**hec·to·li·ter** \'hek-tə-,lē-tər\ *n* — see METRIC SYSTEM table

**hec·to·me·ter** \'hek-tə-,mē-tər, hek-'tä-mə-tər\ *n* — see METRIC SYSTEM table

**hec·tor** \'hek-tər\ *vb* [*hector* bully, fr. *Hector*, champion of Troy in Greek legend] **1** : SWAGGER **2** : to intimidate by bluster or personal pressure

¹**hedge** \'hej\ *n* **1** : a fence or boundary formed of shrubs or small trees **2** : BARRIER **3** : a means of protection (as against financial loss)

²**hedge** *vb* **hedged; hedg·ing 1** : ENCIRCLE **2** : HINDER **3** : to protect oneself financially by a counterbalancing action **4** : to evade the risk of commitment — **hedg·er** *n*

**hedge·hog** \'hej-,hóg, -,häg\ *n* : a small Old World insect-eating mammal covered with spines; *also* : PORCUPINE

**hedge·hop** \-,häp\ *vb* : to fly an airplane very close to the ground

**hedge·row** \-,rō\ *n* : a row of shrubs or trees bounding or separating fields

**he·do·nism** \'hē-də-,ni-zəm\ *n* [Gk *hēdonē* pleasure] : the doctrine that pleasure is the chief good in life; *also* : a way of life based on this — **he·do·nist** \ nist\ *n* — **he·do·nis·tic** \,hēdə-'ni-stik\ *adj*

¹**heed** \'hēd\ *vb* : to pay attention

²**heed** *n* : ATTENTION, NOTICE — **heed·ful** \-fəl\ *adj* — **heed·ful·ly** *adv* — **heed·ful·ness** *n* — **heed·less** *adj* — **heed·less·ly** *adv* — **heed·less·ness** *n*

¹**heel** \'hēl\ *n* **1** : the hind part of the foot **2** : one of the crusty ends of a loaf of bread **3** : a solid attachment forming the back of the sole of a shoe **4** : a rear, low, or bottom part **5** : a contemptible person

²**heel** *vb* : to tilt to one side : LIST

¹**heft** \'heft\ *n* : WEIGHT, HEAVINESS

²**heft** *vb* : to test the weight of by lifting

**hefty** \'hef-tē\ *adj* **heft·i·er; -est 1** : marked by bigness, bulk, and usu. strength **2** : impressively large ⟨got a ∼ raise⟩

**he·ge·mo·ny** \hi-'je-mə-nē\ *n* : preponderant influence or authority over others : DOMINATION

**he·gi·ra** \hi-'jī-rə\ *n* [the *Hegira*, flight of Muhammad from Mecca in A.D. 622, fr. ML, fr. Ar *hijra*, lit., departure] : a journey esp. when undertaken to escape a dangerous or undesirable environment

**heif·er** \'he-fər\ *n* : a young cow; *esp* : one that has not had a calf

**height** \'hīt\ *n* **1** : the highest part or point **2** : the distance from the bottom to the top of something standing upright **3** : ALTITUDE

**height·en** \'hī-t³n\ *vb* **1** : to increase in amount or degree **2** : to make or become high or higher ♦ *Synonyms* ENHANCE, INTENSIFY, AGGRAVATE, MAGNIFY

**Heim·lich maneuver** \'hīm-lik-\ *n* [Henry J. *Heimlich b*1920 Am. surgeon] : the manual application of sudden upward pressure on the upper abdomen of a choking victim to force a foreign object from the trachea

**hei·nous** \'hā-nəs\ *adj* [ME, fr. AF *hainus, heinous,* fr. *haine* hate, fr. *hair* to hate] : hatefully or shockingly evil — **hei·nous·ly** *adv* — **hei·nous·ness** *n*

**heir** \'er\ *n* : one who inherits or is entitled to inherit property, rank, title, or office — **heir·ship** *n*

**heir apparent** *n, pl* **heirs apparent** : an heir whose right to succeed (as to a title) cannot be taken away if he or she survives the present holder

**heir·ess** \'er-əs\ *n* : a female heir esp. to great wealth

**heir·loom** \'er-,lüm\ *n* **1** : a piece of personal property that descends by inheritance **2** : something handed on from one generation to another

**heir presumptive** *n, pl* **heirs presumptive** : an heir whose present right to inherit could be lost through the birth of a nearer relative

**heist** \'hīst\ *vb* : to commit armed robbery on; *also* : STEAL — **heist** *n*

**held** *past and past part of* HOLD

**he·li·cal** \'he-li-kəl, 'hē-\ *adj* : SPIRAL

**he·li·cop·ter** \'he-lə-,käp-tər, 'hē-\ *n* [F *hélicoptère,* fr. Gk *helik-, helix* spiral + *pteron* wing] : an aircraft that is supported in the air by one or more rotors revolving on substantially vertical axes

**he·lio·cen·tric** \,hē-lē-ō-'sen-trik\ *adj* : having or relating to the sun as center

**he·li·o·sphere** \'hē-lē-ə-,sfir, -ō-\ *n* : the region in space influenced by the sun or solar wind

**he·lio·trope** \'hē-lē-ə-,trōp\ *n* [L *heliotropium,* fr. Gk *hēliotropion,* fr. *hēlios* sun + *tropos* turn; fr. its flowers' turning toward the sun] : any of a genus of herbs or shrubs related to the forget-me-nots that have small white or purple flowers

**he·li·port** \'he-lə-,pōrt\ *n* : a landing and takeoff place for a helicopter

**he·li·um** \'hē-lē-əm\ *n* [NL, fr. Gk *hēlios* sun] : a very light inert gaseous chemical element occurring in various natural gases

**he·lix** \'hē-liks\ *n, pl* **he·li·ces** \'he-lə-,sēz, 'hē-\ *also* **he·lix·es** \'hē-lik-səz\ : something spiral in form

**hell** \'hel\ *n* **1** : a nether world in which the dead continue to exist **2** : the realm of the devil in which the damned suffer everlasting punishment **3** : a place or

state of torment or destruction — **hell·ish** *adj*

**hel·la·cious** \,he-'lā-shəs\ *adj* **1** : exceptionally powerful or violent ⟨~ winds⟩ **2** : remarkably good **3** : extremely difficult ⟨a ~ schedule⟩ **4** : extraordinarily large

**hell–bent** \'hel-,bent\ *adj* : stubbornly determined ⟨~ on revenge⟩

**hell·cat** \-,kat\ *n* **1** : WITCH 2 **2** : a violently temperamental person; *esp* : an ill-tempered woman

**hel·le·bore** \'he-lə-,bōr\ *n* **1** : any of a genus of poisonous herbs related to the buttercups; *also* : the dried root of a hellebore **2** : a poisonous plant related to the lilies; *also* : its dried roots used in medicine and insecticides

**Hel·lene** \'he-,lēn\ *n* : GREEK

**Hel·le·nism** \'he-lə-,ni-zəm\ *n* : a body of humanistic and classical ideals associated with ancient Greece — **Hel·len·ic** \he-'le-nik\ *adj* — **Hel·le·nist** \'he-lə-nist\ *n*

**Hel·le·nis·tic** \,he-lə-'nis-tik\ *adj* : of or relating to Greek history, culture, or art after Alexander the Great

**hell–for–leather** *adv* : at full speed

**hell·gram·mite** \'hel-grə-,mīt\ *n* : an aquatic insect larva that is used as bait in fishing

**hell·hole** \'hel-,hōl\ *n* : a place of extreme misery or squalor

**hel·lion** \'hel-yən\ *n* : a troublesome or mischievous person

**hel·lo** \hə-'lō, he-\ *n, pl* **hellos** : an expression of greeting — used interjectionally

**helm** \'helm\ *n* **1** : a lever or wheel for steering a ship **2** : a position of control

**hel·met** \'hel-mət\ *n* : a protective covering for the head

**helms·man** \'helmz-mən\ *n* : the person at the helm : STEERSMAN

**helms·per·son** \-,pər-s³n\ *n* : HELMSMAN

**hel·ot** \'he-lət\ *n* : SLAVE, SERF

**¹help** \'help\ *vb* **1** : AID, ASSIST **2** : IMPROVE, RELIEVE **3** : to be of use; *also* : PROMOTE **4** : to change for the better **5** : to refrain from; *also* : PREVENT **6** : to serve with food or drink ⟨~ yourself⟩ — **help·er** *n*

**²help** *n* **1** : AID, ASSISTANCE; *also* : a source of aid **2** : REMEDY, RELIEF **3** : one who assists another **4** : EMPLOYEE — **help·ful** \-fəl\ *adj* — **help·ful·ly** *adv* — **help·ful·ness** *n* — **help·less** *adj* — **help·less·ly** *adv* — **help·less·ness** *n*

**helper T cell** *n* : a T cell that participates in the immune response by recognizing foreign antigens and has a protein on its surface to which HIV attaches

**help·ing** *n* : a portion of food

**help·mate** \'help-,māt\ *n* **1** : HELPER **2** : WIFE

**help·meet** \-,mēt\ *n* : HELPMATE

**hel·ter–skel·ter** \,hel-tər-'skel-tər\ *adv* **1** : in undue haste or disorder **2** : HAPHAZARDLY

**helve** \'helv\ *n* : a handle of a tool or weapon

**Hel·ve·tian** \hel-'vē-shən\ *adj* : SWISS — **Helvetian** *n*

**¹hem** \'hem\ n 1 : a border of an article (as of cloth) doubled back and stitched down 2 : RIM, MARGIN

**²hem** vb **hemmed; hem·ming** 1 : to make a hem in sewing; also : BORDER, EDGE 2 : to surround restrictively

**he–man** \'hē-,man\ n : a strong virile man

**he·ma·tite** \'hē-mə-,tīt\ n : a mineral that consists of an oxide of iron and that constitutes an important iron ore

**he·ma·tol·o·gy** \,hē mə 'tä lə jē\ n : a branch of biology that deals with the blood and blood-forming organs — **he·ma·to·log·ic** \-tə-'läj-ik\ also **he·ma·to·log·i·cal** \-ji-kəl\ adj — **he·ma·tol·o·gist** \-'lä-lə-jist\ n

**he·ma·to·ma** \-'tō-mə\ n, pl **-mas** also **-ma·ta** \-mə-tə\ : a usu. clotted mass of blood forming as a result of a broken blood vessel

**heme** \'hēm\ n : the deep red iron-containing part of hemoglobin

**hemi·sphere** \'he-mə-,sfir\ n 1 : one of the halves of the earth as divided by the equator into northern and southern parts or by a meridian into eastern and western parts 2 : either of two half spheres formed by a plane through the sphere's center — **hemi·spher·ic** \,he-mə-'sfir-ik, -'sfer-\ or **hemi·spher·i·cal** \-'sfir-i-kəl, -'sfer-\ adj

**hem·line** \'hem-,līn\ n : the line formed by the lower edge of a garment

**hem·lock** \'hem-,läk\ n 1 : any of several poisonous herbs related to the carrot 2 : an evergreen tree related to the pines; also : its soft light wood

**he·mo·glo·bin** \'hē-mə-,glō-bən\ n : an iron-containing compound found in red blood cells that carries oxygen from the lungs to the body tissues

**he·mo·phil·ia** \,hē-mə-'fi-lē-ə\ n : a hereditary blood defect usu. of males that slows blood clotting with resulting difficulty in stopping bleeding — **he·mo·phil·i·ac** \-lē-,ak\ adj or n

**hem·or·rhage** \'hem-rij, 'he-mə-\ n : a large discharge of blood from the blood vessels — **hemorrhage** vb — **hem·or·rhag·ic** \,he-mə-'ra-jik\ adj

**hemorrhagic fever** n : any of a group of virus diseases characterized chiefly by sudden onset, fever, aching, and bleeding in the internal organs

**hem·or·rhoid** \'hem-,roid, 'he-mə-\ n : a swollen mass of dilated veins at or just within the anus — usu. used in pl.

**hemp** \'hemp\ n : a tall widely grown Asian herb that is the source of a tough fiber used in rope and of marijuana and hashish from its flowers and leaves; also : the fiber — **hemp·en** \'hem-pən\ adj

**hem·stitch** \'hem-,stich\ vb : to embroider (fabric) by drawing out parallel threads and stitching the exposed threads in groups to form designs

**hen** \'hen\ n : a female chicken esp. over a year old; also : a female bird

**hence** \'hens\ adv 1 : AWAY 2 : from this time ⟨four years ∼⟩ 3 : CONSEQUENTLY 4 : from this source or origin

**hence·forth** \hens ,fórth\ adv : from this point on

**hence·for·ward** \-'fór-wərd\ adv : HENCEFORTH

**hench·man** \'hench-mən\ n [ME hengestman groom, fr. hengest stallion] : a trusted follower or supporter

**hen·na** \'he-nə\ n 1 : an Old World tropical shrub with fragrant white flowers; also : a reddish brown dye obtained from its leaves and used esp. on hair 2 : the color of henna dye

**hen·peck** \'hen-,pek\ vb : to nag and boss one's husband

**hep** \'hep\ adj : HIP

**hep·a·rin** \'he-pə-rən\ n : a compound found esp. in liver that slows the clotting of blood and is used medically

**he·pat·ic** \hi-'pa-tik\ adj : of, relating to, or associated with the liver

**he·pat·i·ca** \hi-'pa-ti-kə\ n : any of a genus of herbs related to the buttercups that have lobed leaves and delicate white, pink, or bluish flowers

**hep·a·ti·tis** \,he-pə-'tī-təs\ n, pl **-tit·i·des** \-'ti-tə-,dēz\ : inflammation of the liver; also : a virus disease of which this is a feature

**hep·tam·e·ter** \hep-'ta-mə-tər\ n : a line of verse containing seven metrical feet

**hep·tath·lon** \hep-'tath-lən, -,län\ n : a 7-event athletic contest for women

**¹her** \'hər\ adj : of or relating to her or herself

**²her** pron, objective case of SHE

**¹her·ald** \'her-əld\ n 1 : an official crier or messenger 2 : HARBINGER 3 : ANNOUNCER 4 : ADVOCATE

**²herald** vb 1 : to give notice of 2 : HAIL, GREET; also : PUBLICIZE

**he·ral·dic** \he-'ral-dik, hə-\ adj : of or relating to heralds or heraldry

**her·ald·ry** \'her-əl-drē\ n, pl **-ries** 1 : the practice of devising and granting armorial insignia and of tracing genealogies 2 : INSIGNIA 3 : PAGEANTRY

**herb** \'ərb, 'hərb\ n 1 : a seed plant that lacks woody tissue and dies to the ground at the end of a growing season 2 : a plant or plant part valued for medicinal or savory qualities — **her·ba·ceous** \,ər-'bā-shəs, ,hər-\ adj

**herb·age** \'ər-bij, 'hər-\ n : green plants esp. when used or fit for grazing

**her·bal** \'ər-bəl, 'hər-\ adj : of, relating to, utilizing, or made of herbs

**herb·al·ist** \'ər-bə-list, 'hər-\ n 1 : a person who practices healing by the use of herbs 2 : a person who collects or grows herbs

**her·bar·i·um** \,ər-'ber-ē-əm, ,hər-\ n, pl **-ia** \-ē-ə\ 1 : a collection of dried plant specimens 2 : a place that houses an herbarium

**her·bi·cide** \'ər-bə-,sīd, 'hər-\ n : an agent used to destroy or inhibit plant growth — **her·bi·cid·al** \,ər-bə-'sī-dᵊl, ,hər-\ adj

**her·biv·o·rous** \,ər-'bi-və-rəs, ,hər-\ adj : feeding on plants — **her·bi·vore** \'ər-bə-,vór, 'hər-\ n

**her·cu·le·an** \,hər-kyə-'lē-ən, ,hər-'kyü-lē-\ adj, often cap [Hercules, hero of

Greek myth renowned for his strength] : of extraordinary power, size, or difficulty ⟨a ∼ task⟩

¹**herd** \'hərd\ n 1 : a group of animals of one kind kept or living together 2 : a group of people with a common bond ⟨a ∼ of tourists⟩ 3 : MOB

²**herd** vb : to assemble or move in a herd — **herd·er** n

**herds·man** \'hərdz-mən\ n : one who manages, breeds, or tends livestock

¹**here** \'hir\ adv 1 : in or at this place; also : NOW 2 : at or in this point, particular, or case 3 : in the present life or state 4 : to this place ⟨come ∼⟩

²**here** n : this place ⟨get away from ∼⟩

**here·abouts** \'hir-ə-,bauts\ or **here·about** \-,baut\ adv : in this vicinity

¹**here·af·ter** \hir-'af-tər\ adv 1 : after this in sequence or in time 2 : in some future time or state

²**hereafter** n, often cap 1 : FUTURE 2 : an existence beyond earthly life

**here·by** \hir-'bī\ adv : by means of this

**he·red·i·tary** \hə-'re-də-,ter-ē\ adj 1 : genetically passed or passable from parent to offspring 2 : passing by inheritance; also : having title or possession through inheritance 3 : of a kind established by tradition

**he·red·i·ty** \-də-tē\ n : the characteristics and potentialities genetically derived from one's ancestors; also : the passing of these from ancestor to descendant

**Her·e·ford** \'hər-fərd\ n : any of a breed of red-coated beef cattle with white faces and markings

**here·in** \hir-'in\ adv : in this

**here·of** \-'əv, -'äv\ adv : of this

**here·on** \-'ȯn, -'än\ adv : on this

**her·e·sy** \'her-ə-sē\ n, pl **-sies** [ME heresie, fr. AF, fr. LL haeresis, fr. LGk hairesis, fr. Gk, action of taking, choice, sect, fr. hairein to take] 1 : adherence to a religious opinion contrary to church dogma 2 : an opinion or doctrine contrary to church dogma 3 : dissent from a dominant theory, opinion, or practice — **her·e·tic** \-,tik\ n — **he·ret·i·cal** \hə-'re-ti-kəl\ adj

**here·to** \hir-'tü\ adv : to this document

**here·to·fore** \'hir-tə-,fȯr\ adv : up to this time

**here·un·der** \hir-'ən-dər\ adv : under this or according to this writing

**here·un·to** \hir-'ən-tü\ adv : to this

**here·upon** \'hir-ə-,pȯn, -,pän\ adv : on this or immediately after this

**here·with** \'hir-'with, -'with\ adv 1 : with this 2 : HEREBY

**her·i·ta·ble** \'her-ə-tə-bəl\ adj : capable of being inherited

**her·i·tage** \'her-ə-tij\ n 1 : property that descends to an heir 2 : LEGACY 3 : BIRTHRIGHT

**her·maph·ro·dite** \(,)hər-'ma-frə-,dīt\ n : an animal or plant having both male and female reproductive organs — **her·maphrodite** adj — **her·maph·ro·dit·ic** \(,)hər-,ma-frə-'di-tik\ adj

**her·met·ic** \hər-'me-tik\ also **her·met·i-**

cal \-ti-kəl\ adj : AIRTIGHT — **her·met·i·cal·ly** \-ti-k(ə-)lē\ adv

**her·mit** \'hər-mət\ n [ME heremite, eremite, fr. AF, fr. LL eremita, fr. LGk erēmitēs, fr. Gk, adj., living in the desert, fr. erēmia desert, fr. erēmos desolate] : one who lives in solitude esp. for religious reasons

**her·mit·age** \-mə-tij\ n 1 : the dwelling of a hermit 2 : a secluded dwelling

**hermit crab** n : any of numerous crabs that occupy empty mollusk shells

**her·nia** \'hər-nē-ə\ n, pl **-ni·as** or **-ni·ae** \-nē-,ē, -nē-,ī\ : a protrusion of a bodily part (as a loop of intestine) into a pouch of the weakened wall of a cavity in which it is normally enclosed — **her·ni·ate** \-nē-,āt\ vb — **her·ni·a·tion** \,hər-nē-'ā-shən\ n

**he·ro** \'hē-rō\ n, pl **heroes** 1 : a mythological or legendary figure of great strength or ability 2 : a man admired for his achievements and qualities 3 : the chief male character in a literary or dramatic work 4 pl usu **heros** : SUBMARINE 2 — **he·ro·ic** \hi-'rō-ik\ adj — **he·ro·i·cal·ly** \-i-k(ə-)lē\ adv

**heroic couplet** n : a rhyming couplet in iambic pentameter

**he·ro·ics** \hi-'rō-iks\ n pl : heroic or showy behavior

**her·o·in** \'her-ə-wən\ n : an illicit addictive narcotic drug made from morphine

**her·o·ine** \'her-ə-wən\ n 1 : a woman admired for her achievements and qualities 2 : the chief female character in a literary or dramatic work

**her·o·ism** \'her-ə-,wi-zəm\ n 1 : heroic conduct 2 : the qualities of a hero
♦ **Synonyms** VALOR, PROWESS, GALLANTRY

**her·on** \'her-ən\ n, pl **herons** also **heron** : any of various long-legged long-billed wading birds with soft plumage

**her·pes** \'hər-pēz\ n : any of several virus diseases characterized by the formation of blisters on the skin or mucous membranes

**herpes sim·plex** \-'sim-,pleks\ n : either of two virus diseases marked in one by watery blisters above the waist (as on the mouth and lips) and in the other on the sex organs

**herpes zos·ter** \-'zäs-tər\ n : SHINGLES

**her·pe·tol·o·gy** \,hər-pə-'tä-lə-jē\ n : a branch of zoology dealing with reptiles and amphibians — **her·pe·tol·o·gist** \,hər-pə-'tä-lə-jist\ n

**her·ring** \'her-iŋ\ n, pl **herring** or **herrings** : a valuable narrow-bodied food fish of the No. Atlantic; also : a related fish of the No. Pacific harvested esp. for its roe

**her·ring·bone** \'her-iŋ-,bōn\ n : a pattern made up of rows of parallel lines with adjacent rows slanting in reverse directions; also : a twilled fabric with this pattern

**hers** \'hərz\ pron : one or the ones belonging to her

**her·self** \hər-'self\ pron : SHE, HER — used reflexively, for emphasis, or in absolute constructions

**hertz** \'hərts, 'herts\ *n, pl* **hertz** : a unit of frequency equal to one cycle per second

**hes·i·tant** \'he-zə-tənt\ *adj* : tending to hesitate — **hes·i·tance** \-təns\ *n* — **hes·i·tan·cy** \-tən-sē\ *n* — **hes·i·tant·ly** *adv*

**hes·i·tate** \'he-zə-ˌtāt\ *vb* **-tat·ed; -tat·ing** **1** : to hold back (as in doubt) **2** : PAUSE
♦ **Synonyms** WAVER, VACILLATE, FALTER, SHILLY-SHALLY — **hes·i·ta·tion** \ˌhe-zə-'tā-shən\ *n*

**het·er·o·dox** \'he-tə-rə-ˌdäks\ *adj* **1** : differing from an acknowledged standard **2** : holding unorthodox opinions — **het·er·o·doxy** \-ˌdäk-sē\ *n*

**het·er·o·ge·neous** \ˌhe-tə-rə-'jē-nē-əs, -nyəs\ *adj* : consisting of dissimilar ingredients or constituents : MIXED — **het·er·o·ge·ne·ity** \-jə-'nē-ə-tē\ *n* — **het·er·o·ge·neous·ly** *adv*

**het·ero·glos·sia** \ˌhe-tə-rō-'glä-sē-ə, -'glȯ-\ *n* : a diversity of voices, styles of discourse, or points of view in a literary work

**het·ero·sex·ism** \ˌhe-tə-rō-'sek-si-zəm\ *n* : discrimination or prejudice by heterosexuals against homosexuals

**het·ero·sex·u·al** \ˌhe-tə-rō-ˌsek-shə-wəl\ *adj* **1** : of, relating to, or marked by sexual interest in the opposite sex; *also* : of, relating to, or involving sexual intercourse between members of opposite sex **2** : of or relating to different sexes — **heterosexual** *n* — **het·ero·sex·u·al·i·ty** \-ˌsek-shə-'wa-lə-tē\ *n*

**hew** \'hyü\ *vb* **hewed;** **hewed** *or* **hewn** \'hyün\; **hew·ing** **1** : to cut or fell with blows (as of an ax) **2** : to give shape to with or as if with an ax **3** : to conform strictly ⟨∼ed to the rules⟩ — **hew·er** *n*

**HEW** *abbr* Department of Health, Education, and Welfare

**¹hex** \'heks\ *vb* **1** : to practice witchcraft **2** : JINX

**²hex** *n* : SPELL, JINX

**³hex** *adj* : HEXAGONAL

**⁴hex** *abbr* hexagon

**hexa·gon** \'hek-sə-ˌgän\ *n* [ultim. fr. Gk *hex* six + *gōnia* angle] : a polygon having six angles and six sides — **hex·ag·o·nal** \hek-'sa-gən-ᵊl\ *adj*

**hex·am·e·ter** \hek-'sa-mə-tər\ *n* : a line of verse containing six metrical feet

**hey** \'hā\ *interj* — used esp. to call attention or to express doubt, surprise, or joy

**hey·day** \'hā-ˌdā\ *n* : a period of greatest strength, vigor, or prosperity

**hf** *abbr* half

**Hf** *symbol* hafnium

**HF** *abbr* high frequency

**hg** *abbr* hectogram

**Hg** *symbol* [NL *hydrargyrum,* lit., water silver] mercury

**hgt** *abbr* height

**hgwy** *abbr* highway

**HH** *abbr* **1** Her Highness **2** His Highness **3** His Holiness

**HHS** *abbr* Department of Health and Human Services

**HI** *abbr* **1** Hawaii **2** humidity index

**hi·a·tus** \hī-'ā-təs\ *n* [L, fr. *hiare* to yawn] **1** : a break in an object : GAP **2** : a period

when something is suspended or interrupted

**hi·ba·chi** \hi-'bä-chē\ *n* [Jp] : a charcoal brazier

**hi·ber·nate** \'hī-bər-ˌnāt\ *vb* **-nat·ed; -nat·ing** : to pass the winter in a torpid or resting state — **hi·ber·na·tion** \ˌhī-bər-'nā-shən\ *n* — **hi·ber·na·tor** \'hī-bər-ˌnā-tər\ *n*

**hi·bis·cus** \hī-'bis-kəs, hə-\ *n* : any of a genus of herbs, shrubs, and trees related to the mallows and noted for large showy flowers

**hic·cup** *also* **hic·cough** \'hi-(ˌ)kəp\ *n* **1** : a spasmodic breathing movement checked by sudden closing of the glottis accompanied by a peculiar sound; *also, pl* : an attack of hiccuping **2** : a slight irregularity, error, or malfunction **3** : a brief minor interruption or change — **hiccup** *vb*

**hick** \'hik\ *n* [*Hick,* nickname for *Richard*] : an unsophisticated provincial person — **hick** *adj*

**hick·o·ry** \'hi-kə-rē\ *n, pl* **-ries** : any of a genus of No. American hardwood trees related to the walnuts; *also* : the wood of a hickory — **hickory** *adj*

**hi·dal·go** \hi-'dal-gō\ *n, pl* **-gos** *often cap* [Sp, fr. earlier *fijo dalgo,* lit., son of something] : a member of the lower nobility of Spain

**hidden tax** *n* **1** : a tax ultimately paid by someone other than the person on whom it is formally levied **2** : an economic injustice that reduces one's income or buying power

**¹hide** \'hīd\ *vb* **hid** \'hid\; **hid·den** \'hid-ᵊn\ *or* **hid; hid·ing** **1** : to put or remain out of sight **2** : to conceal for shelter or protection; *also* : to seek protection **3** : to keep secret **4** : to turn away in shame or anger — **hid·er** *n*

**²hide** *n* : the skin of an animal

**hide-and-seek** \ˌhīd-ᵊn-'sēk\ *n* : a children's game in which everyone hides from one player who tries to find them

**hide·away** \'hī-də-ˌwā\ *n* : HIDEOUT

**hide·bound** \'hīd-ˌbau̇nd\ *adj* : being inflexible or conservative

**hid·eous** \'hi-dē-əs\ *adj* [ME *hidous,* fr. AF *hidus, hisdos,* fr. *hisde,* fride terror] **1** : offensive to one of the senses : UGLY **2** : morally offensive : SHOCKING ♦ **Synonyms** GHASTLY, GRISLY, GRUESOME, HORRIBLE, LURID, MACABRE — **hideous·ly** *adv* — **hide·ous·ness** *n*

**hide·out** \'hīd-ˌau̇t\ *n* : a place of refuge or concealment

**hie** \'hī\ *vb* **hied; hy·ing** *or* **hie·ing** : HASTEN

**hi·er·ar·chy** \'hī-ə-ˌrär-kē\ *n, pl* **-chies** **1** : a ruling body of clergy organized into ranks **2** : persons or things arranged in a graded series — **hi·er·ar·chi·cal** \ˌhī-ə-'rär-ki-kəl\ *adj* — **hi·er·ar·chi·cal·ly** \-k(ə-)lē\ *adv*

**hi·ero·glyph·ic** \ˌhī-ə-rə-'gli-fik\ *n* [MF *hieroglyphique,* adj., ultim. fr. Gk *hieroglyphikos,* fr. *hieros* sacred + *glyphein* to carve] **1** : a character in a system of picture writing (as of the ancient Egyptians) **2** : a symbol or sign difficult to decipher

**hi-fi** \'hī-'fī\ *n* **1** : HIGH FIDELITY **2** : equipment for reproduction of sound with high fidelity

**hig-gle-dy-pig-gle-dy** \,hi-gəl-dē-'pi-gəl-dē\ *adv* : in confusion

**¹high** \'hī\ *adj* **1** : ELEVATED; *also* : TALL **2** : advanced toward fullness or culmination; *also* : slightly tainted **3** : advanced esp. in complexity ⟨∼*er* mathematics⟩ **4** : long past **5** : SHRILL, SHARP **6** : far from the equator ⟨∼ latitudes⟩ **7** : exalted in character **8** : of greater degree, size, or amount than average ⟨∼ in cholesterol⟩ **9** : of relatively great importance **10** : FORCIBLE, STRONG ⟨∼ winds⟩ **11** : showing elation or excitement **12** : INTOXICATED; *also* : excited or stupefied by or as if by a drug — **high·ly** *adv*

**²high** *adv* **1** : at or to a high place or degree **2** : LUXURIOUSLY ⟨living ∼⟩

**³high.** *n* **1** : an elevated place **2** : a region of high barometric pressure **3** : a high point or level **4** : the gear of a vehicle giving the highest speed **5** : an excited or stupefied state produced by or as if by a drug

**high·ball** \'hī-,bȯl\ *n* : a usu. tall drink of liquor mixed with water or a carbonated beverage

**high beam** *n* : a vehicle headlight with a long-range focus

**high·born** \'hī-'bȯrn\ *adj* : of noble birth

**high·boy** \-,bȯi\ *n* : a high chest of drawers mounted on a base with legs

**high·bred** \-'bred\ *adj* : coming from superior stock

**high·brow** \-,braủ\ *n* : a person of superior learning or culture — **highbrow** *adj* — **high·brow·ism** \-,braủ-,i-zəm\ *n*

**high–definition** *adj* : being or relating to a television system with twice as many scan lines per frame as a conventional system

**high–density li·po·pro·tein** \-,lī-pō-'prō-tēn, -,li-\ *n* : HDL

**high·er–up** \,hī-ər-'əp\ *n* : a superior officer or official

**high·fa·lu·tin** \,hī-fə-'lü-t²n\ *adj* : PRETENTIOUS, POMPOUS

**high fashion** *n* **1** : HIGH STYLE **2** : HAUTE COUTURE

**high fidelity** *n* : the reproduction of sound or image with a high degree of faithfulness to the original

**high five** *n* : a slapping of upraised right hands by two people (as in celebration) — **high–five** *vb*

**high–flown** \'hī-'flōn\ *adj* **1** : EXALTED **2** : BOMBASTIC

**high frequency** *n* : a radio frequency between 3 and 30 megahertz

**high gear** *n* **1** : HIGH 4 **2** : a state of intense or maximum activity

**high–hand·ed** \'hī-'han-dəd\ *adj* : OVERBEARING — **high–hand·ed·ly** *adv* — **high–hand·ed·ness** *n*

**high–hat** \-'hat\ *adj* : SUPERCILIOUS, SNOBBISH — **high–hat** *vb*

**high·land** \'hī-lənd\ *n* : elevated or mountainous land

**high·land·er** \-lən-dər\ *n* **1** : an inhabitant of a highland **2** *cap* : an inhabitant of the Scottish Highlands

**high–lev·el** \'hī-'le-vəl\ *adj* **1** : being of high importance or rank **2** : being or relating to highly concentrated and environmentally hazardous nuclear waste

**¹high·light** \-,līt\ *n* : an event or detail of major importance

**²highlight** *vb* **1** : EMPHASIZE **2** : to constitute a highlight of **3** : to mark (text) with a highlighter **4** : to cause to be displayed in a way that stands out on a computer screen

**high·light·er** \-,līt-ər\ *n* : a pen with transparent ink used for marking text passages

**high–mind·ed** \-'mīn-dəd\ *adj* : marked by elevated principles and feelings — **high–mind·ed·ness** *n*

**high·ness** \'hī-nəs\ *n* **1** : the quality or state of being high **2** — used as a title (as for kings)

**high–pres·sure** \-'pre-shər\ *adj* : using or involving aggressive and insistent sales techniques

**high–rise** \-'rīz\ *adj* **1** : having several stories and being equipped with elevators ⟨∼ apartments⟩ **2** : of or relating to high-rise buildings

**high road** *n* : HIGHWAY

**high school** *n* : a school usu. including grades 9 to 12 or 10 to 12

**high sea** *n* : the open sea outside territorial waters — usu. used in pl.

**high–sound·ing** \'hī-'saủn-diŋ\ *adj* : POMPOUS, IMPOSING ⟨∼ rhetoric⟩

**high–spir·it·ed** \-'spir-ə-təd\ *adj* : characterized by a bold or energetic spirit

**high–strung** \-'strəŋ\ *adj* : having an extremely nervous or sensitive temperament

**high style** *n* : the newest in fashion or design

**high·tail** \'hī-,tāl\ *vb* : to retreat at full speed

**high tech** \-'tek\ *n* : HIGH TECHNOLOGY

**high technology** *n* : technology involving the use of advanced devices

**high–ten·sion** \'hī-'ten-chən\ *adj* : having or using a high voltage

**high–test** \-'test\ *adj* : having a high octane number

**high–tick·et** \-'ti-kət\ *adj* : EXPENSIVE

**high–toned** \-'tōnd\ *adj* **1** : high in social, moral, or intellectual quality **2** : PRETENTIOUS, POMPOUS

**high·way** \'hī-,wā\ *n* : a main direct road

**high·way·man** \'hī-,wā-mən\ *n* : a thief who robs travelers on a road

**hi·jab** \hē-'jäb, -'jab\ *n* [Ar *ḥijāb* cover, screen, veil] : the covering for the hair and neck that is worn by Muslim women

**hi·jack** *also* **high·jack** \'hī-,jak\ *vb* : to steal esp. by stopping a vehicle on the highway; *also* : to commandeer a flying airplane — **hijack** *n* — **hi·jack·er** *n*

**¹hike** \'hīk\ *vb* **hiked; hik·ing 1** : to move or raise with a sudden motion **2** : to take a long walk — **hik·er** *n*

²**hike** n **1** : a long walk **2** : RISE, INCREASE ⟨price ~⟩

**hi·lar·i·ous** \hi-'ler-ē-əs, hī-\ adj : marked by or providing boisterous merriment — **hi·lar·i·ous·ly** adv — **hi·lar·i·ty** \-ə-tē\ n

**hill** \'hil\ n **1** : a usu. rounded elevation of land **2** : a little heap or mound (as of earth) — **hilly** adj

**hill·bil·ly** \'hil-,bi-lē\ n, pl **-lies** : a person from a backwoods area

**hill·ock** \'hil-lək\ n : a small hill

**hill·side** \'hil-,sīd\ n : the part of a hill between the summit and the foot

**hill·top** \-,täp\ n : the top of a hill

**hilt** \'hilt\ n : a handle esp. of a sword or dagger

**him** \'him\ pron, objective case of HE

**him·self** \him-'self\ pron : HE, HIM — used reflexively, for emphasis, or in absolute constructions

¹**hind** \'hīnd\ n, pl **hinds** also **hind** : a female of a common Eurasian deer

²**hind** adj : REAR ⟨the dog's ~ legs⟩

¹**hin·der** \'hin-dər\ vb **1** : to impede the progress of **2** : to hold back ♦ **Synonyms** OBSTRUCT, BLOCK, BAR, IMPEDE

²**hind·er** \'hīn-dər\ adj : HIND

**Hin·di** \'hin-dē\ n : a literary and official language of northern India

**hind·most** \'hīnd-,mōst\ adj : farthest to the rear

**hind·quar·ter** \-,kwȯr-tər\ n **1** : one side of the back half of the carcass of a quadruped **2** pl : the part of the body of a quadruped behind the junction of hind limbs and trunk

**hin·drance** \'hin-drəns\ n **1** : the state of being hindered **2** : IMPEDIMENT 1 **3** : the action of hindering

**hind·sight** \'hīnd-,sīt\ n : understanding of an event after it has happened

**Hindu–Arabic** adj : relating to, being, or composed of Arabic numerals

**Hin·du·ism** \'hin-dü-,i-zəm\ n : a body of religious beliefs and practices native to India — **Hin·du** n or adj

**hind wing** n : either of the posterior wings of a 4-winged insect

¹**hinge** \'hinj\ n : a jointed device on which a swinging part (as a door, gate, or lid) turns

²**hinge** vb **hinged; hing·ing 1** : to attach by or furnish with hinges **2** : to be contingent on a single consideration

**hint** \'hint\ n **1** : an indirect or summary suggestion **2** : CLUE **3** : a very small amount ♦ **Synonyms** DASH, SOUPÇON, SUSPICION, TINCTURE, TOUCH — **hint** vb

**hin·ter·land** \'hin-tər-,land\ n **1** : a region behind a coast **2** : a region remote from cities

¹**hip** \'hip\ n : the fruit of a rose

²**hip** n **1** : the part of the body on either side below the waist consisting of the side of the pelvis and the upper thigh **2** : HIP JOINT

³**hip** adj **hip·per; hip·pest** : keenly aware of or interested in the newest developments or styles — **hip·ness** n

⁴**hip** vb **hipped; hip·ping** : TELL, INFORM

**hip·bone** \'hip-'bōn, -,bōn\ n : the large flaring bone that makes a lateral half of the pelvis in mammals

**hip–hop** \'hip-,häp\ n **1** : a subculture esp. of inner-city youths who are devotees of rap music **2** : the stylized rhythmic music that accompanies rap — **hip–hop** adj

**hip–hug·gers** \'hip-,hə-gərz\ n pl : low-slung close-fitting pants that rest on the hips

**hip joint** n : the articulation between the femur and the hipbone

**hipped** \'hipt\ adj : having hips esp. of a specified kind ⟨broad-hipped⟩

**hip·pie** or **hip·py** \'hi-pē\ n, pl **hippies** : a usu. young person who rejects established mores and advocates nonviolence; also : a long-haired unconventionally dressed young person

**hip·po** \'hi-pō\ n, pl **hippos** : HIPPOPOTAMUS

**hip·po·drome** \'hi-pə-,drōm\ n : an arena for equestrian performances

**hip·po·pot·a·mus** \,hi-pə-'pä-tə-məs\ n, pl **-mus·es** or **-mi** \-,mī\ [L, fr. Gk hippopotamos, alter. of hippos potamios, lit., river horse] : a large thick-skinned aquatic mammal of sub-Saharan Africa that is related to the swine

¹**hire** \'hī(-ə)r\ n **1** : payment for labor or personal services : WAGES **2** : EMPLOYMENT **3** : one who is hired

²**hire** vb **hired; hir·ing 1** : to employ for pay **2** : to engage the temporary use of for pay **3** : to take employment

**hire·ling** \'hī(-ə)r-liŋ\ n : a hired person; esp : one with mercenary motives

**hir·sute** \'hər-,süt, 'hir-\ adj : HAIRY

¹**his** \'hiz\ adj : of or relating to him or himself

²**his** pron : one or the ones belonging to him

**His·pan·ic** \hi-'spa-nik\ adj : of, relating to, or being a person of Latin-American descent living in the U.S. — **Hispanic** n

**hiss** \'his\ vb : to make a sharp sibilant sound; also : to express disapproval of by hissing — **hiss** n

**hissy fit** \'hi-sē-\ n : TANTRUM

**hist** abbr historian; historical; history

**his·ta·mine** \'his-tə-,mēn, -mən\ n : a compound widespread in animal tissues that plays a major role in allergic reactions (as hay fever)

**his·to·gram** \'his-tə-,gram\ n : a representation of statistical data by rectangles whose widths represent class intervals and whose heights usu. represent corresponding frequencies

**his·tol·o·gy** \his-'tä-lə-jē\ n, pl **-gies** : a branch of anatomy dealing with tissue structure **2** : tissue structure or organization — **his·to·log·i·cal** \,his-tə-'lä-ji-kəl\ or **his·to·log·ic** \-'lä-jik\ adj — **his·tol·o·gist** \-'tä-lə-jist\ n

**his·to·ri·an** \hi-'stȯr-ē-ən\ n : a student or writer of history

**his·to·ric·i·ty** \,his-tə-'ri-sə-tē\ n : historical actuality

**his·to·ri·og·ra·pher** \hi-,stȯr-ē-'ä-grə-fər\ n : HISTORIAN

**his·to·ry** \'his-tə-rē\ n, pl **-ries** [ultim. fr.

L *historia,* fr. Gk, inquiry, history, fr. *histōr, istōr* knowing, learned] **1** : a chronological record of significant events often with an explanation of their causes **2** : a branch of knowledge that records and explains past events **3** : events that form the subject matter of history **4** : an established record ⟨a convict's ∼ of violence⟩ — **his·tor·ic** \hi-'stòr-ik\ *adj* — **his·tor·i·cal** \-i-kəl\ *adj* — **his·tor·i·cal·ly** \-k(ə-)lē\ *adv*

**his·tri·on·ic** \,his-trē-'ä-nik\ *adj* [LL *histrionicus,* fr. L *histrio* actor] **1** : deliberately affected **2** : of or relating to actors, acting, or the theater — **his·tri·on·i·cal·ly** \-ni-k(ə-)lē\ *adv*

**his·tri·on·ics** \-niks\ *n pl* **1** : theatrical performances **2** : deliberate display of emotion for effect

¹**hit** \'hit\ *vb* **hit; hit·ting** **1** : to reach with a blow : STRIKE; *also* : to arrive with a force like a blow ⟨the storm ∼⟩ **2** : to make or bring into contact : COLLIDE **3** : to affect detrimentally ⟨was ∼ by the flu⟩ **4** : to make a request of **5** : to come upon **6** : to accord with : SUIT **7** : REACH, ATTAIN **8** : to indulge in often to excess — **hit·ter** *n*

²**hit** *n* **1** : an act or instance of hitting or being hit **2** : a great success **3** : BASE HIT **4** : a dose of a drug **5** : a murder committed by a gangster **6** : an instance of connecting to a particular website **7** : a successful match in a search (as of the Internet)

¹**hitch** \'hich\ *vb* **1** : to move by jerks **2** : to catch or fasten esp. by a hook or knot **3** : HITCHHIKE

²**hitch** *n* **1** : JERK, PULL **2** : a sudden halt **3** : a connection between something towed and its mover **4** : KNOT

**hitch·hike** \'hich-,hīk\ *vb* : to travel by securing free rides from passing vehicles — **hitch·hik·er** *n*

¹**hith·er** \'hi-thər\ *adv* : to this place

²**hither** *adj* : being on the near or adjacent side

**hith·er·to** \-,tü\ *adv* : up to this time

**HIV** \,āch-(,)ī-'vē\ *n* [*human immunodeficiency virus*] : any of several retroviruses that infect and destroy helper T cells causing the great reduction in their numbers that is diagnostic of AIDS

**hive** \'hīv\ *n* **1** : a container for housing honeybees **2** : a colony of bees **3** : a place swarming with busy occupants — **hive** *vb*

**hives** \'hīvz\ *n sing or pl* : an allergic disorder marked by raised itching patches on the skin or mucous membranes

**hl** *abbr* hectoliter

**HL** *abbr* House of Lords

**hm** *abbr* hectometer

**HM** *abbr* **1** Her Majesty; Her Majesty's **2** His Majesty; His Majesty's

**HMO** \,āch-(,)em-'ō\ *n* [*health maintenance organization*] : a comprehensive health-care organization financed by periodic fixed payments by voluntarily enrolled individuals and families

**HMS** *abbr* **1** Her Majesty's ship **2** His Majesty's ship

**Ho** *symbol* holmium

**hoa·gie** *also* **hoa·gy** \'hō-gē\ *n, pl* **hoagies** : SUBMARINE 2

**hoard** \'hòrd\ *n* : a hidden accumulation — **hoard** *vb* — **hoard·er** *n*

**hoar·frost** \'hòr-,fròst\ *n* : FROST 2

**hoarse** \'hòrs\ *adj* **hoars·er; hoars·est** **1** : rough and harsh in sound **2** : having a grating voice — **hoarse·ly** *adv* — **hoarse·ness** *n*

**hoary** \'hòr-ē\ *adj* **hoar·i·er; -est** **1** : gray or white with or as if with age **2** : ANCIENT — **hoar·i·ness** \'hòr-ē-nəs\ *n*

**hoax** \'hōks\ *n* : an act intended to trick or dupe; *also* : something accepted or established by fraud — **hoax** *vb* — **hoax·er** *n*

**hob** \'häb\ *n* : MISCHIEF, TROUBLE ⟨raising ∼⟩

¹**hob·ble** \'hä-bəl\ *vb* **hob·bled, hob·bling** **1** : to limp along; *also* : to make lame **2** : FETTER

²**hobble** *n* **1** : a hobbling movement **2** : something used to hobble an animal

**hob·by** \'hä-bē\ *n, pl* **hobbies** : a pursuit or interest engaged in for relaxation — **hob·by·ist** \-ist\ *n*

**hob·by·horse** \'hä-bē-,hòrs\ *n* **1** : a stick with a horse's head on which children pretend to ride **2** : a toy horse mounted on rockers **3** : a topic to which one constantly reverts

**hob·gob·lin** \'häb-,gäb-lən\ *n* **1** : a mischievous goblin **2** : BOGEY 1

**hob·nail** \-,nāl\ *n* : a short large-headed nail for studding shoe soles — **hob·nailed** \-,nāld\ *adj*

**hob·nob** \-,näb\ *vb* **hob·nobbed; hob·nob·bing** : to associate familiarly

**ho·bo** \'hō-bō\ *n, pl* **hoboes** *also* **hobos** : TRAMP 2

¹**hock** \'häk\ *n* : a joint or region in the hind limb of a quadruped just above the foot and corresponding to the human ankle

²**hock** *n* [D *hok* pen, prison] : ²PAWN 2 ⟨got his watch out of ∼⟩; *also* : DEBT 3 ⟨trying to get out of ∼⟩ — **hock** *vb*

**hock·ey** \'hä-kē\ *n* **1** : FIELD HOCKEY **2** : ICE HOCKEY

**ho·cus–po·cus** \,hō-kəs-'pō-kəs\ *n* **1** : SLEIGHT OF HAND **2** : nonsense or sham used to conceal deception

**hod** \'häd\ *n* : a long-handled carrier for mortar or bricks

**hodge·podge** \'häj-,päj\ *n* : a heterogeneous mixture : JUMBLE

**Hodgkin's disease** \'häj-kinz-\ *n* : a neoplastic disease of lymphoid tissue characterized esp. by enlargement of lymph nodes, spleen, and liver

**hoe** \'hō\ *n* : a long-handled implement with a thin flat blade used esp. for cultivating, weeding, or loosening the earth around plants — **hoe** *vb*

**hoe·cake** \'hō-,kāk\ *n* : a small cornmeal cake

**hoe·down** \-,daùn\ *n* **1** : SQUARE DANCE **2** : a gathering featuring hoedowns

¹**hog** \'hòg, 'häg\ *n, pl* **hogs** *also* **hog** **1** : a domestic swine esp. when grown **2** : a

selfish, gluttonous, or filthy person —
**hog·gish** adj

²**hog** vb **hogged; hog·ging** : to take or
hold selfishly ⟨*hogged* the limelight⟩

**no·gan** \'hō-,gän\ n : a Navajo Indian
dwelling usu. made of logs and mud

**hog·back** \'hòg-,bak, 'häg-\ n : a ridge
with a sharp summit and steep sides

**hog·nose snake** \'hòg-,nōz-, 'häg-\ or
**hog·nosed snake** \-,nōzd-\ n : any of a
genus of rather small harmless stout-
bodied No. American snakes that seldom
bite but hiss wildly and often play dead
when disturbed

**hogs·head** \'hògz-,hed, 'hägz-\ n 1 : a
large cask or barrel 2 : a liquid measure
equal to 63 U.S. gallons

**hog·tie** \'hòg-,tī, 'häg-\ vb 1 : to tie together the feet of ⟨~ a calf⟩ 2 : to make
helpless

**hog·wash** \-,wòsh, -,wäsh\ n 1 : SWILL,
SLOP 2 : NONSENSE, BALONEY

**hog wild** adj : lacking in restraint

**hoi pol·loi** \,hòi-pə-'lòi\ n pl [Gk, the
many] : the general populace

**hoi·sin sauce** \'hòi-,sin-\ n : a thick reddish sauce of soybeans, spices, and garlic
used in Asian cookery

¹**hoist** \'hòist\ vb : RAISE, LIFT

²**hoist** n 1 : LIFT 2 : an apparatus for
hoisting

**hoke** \'hōk\ vb **hoked; hok·ing** : FAKE
— usu. used with *up*

**hok·ey** \'hō-kē\ adj **hok·i·er; -est** 1
: CORNY ⟨~ songs⟩ 2 : PHONY ⟨a ~
excuse⟩

**ho·kum** \'hō-kəm\ n : NONSENSE

¹**hold** \'hōld\ vb **held** \'held\; **hold·ing** 1
: POSSESS; also : KEEP 2 : RESTRAIN
3 : to have a grasp on 4 : to support, remain, or keep in a particular situation or
position 5 : SUSTAIN; also : RESERVE 6
: BEAR, COMPORT 7 : to maintain in being or action : PERSIST 8 : CONTAIN, AC-
COMMODATE 9 : HARBOR, ENTERTAIN;
also : CONSIDER, REGARD 10 : to carry
on by concerted action; also : CONVOKE
11 : to occupy esp. by appointment or
election 12 : to be valid 13 : HALT,
PAUSE — **hold·er** n — **hold forth** : to
speak at length — **hold to** : to adhere to
: MAINTAIN — **hold with** : to agree with
or approve of

²**hold** n 1 : STRONGHOLD 2 : CONFINE-
MENT; also : PRISON 3 : the act or manner of holding : GRIP 4 : a restraining,
dominating, or controlling influence 5
: something that may be grasped as a support 6 : an order or indication that something is to be reserved or delayed — **on
hold** : in a temporary state of waiting (as
during a phone call); also : in a state of
postponement ⟨plans *on hold*⟩

³**hold** n 1 : the interior of a ship below
decks; esp : a ship's cargo deck 2 : an
airplane's cargo compartment

**hold·ing** n 1 : land or other property
owned 2 : a ruling of a court esp. on an
issue of law

**holding pattern** n : a course flown by an
aircraft waiting to land

**hold out** vb 1 : to continue to fight or

work 2 : to refuse to come to an agreement — **hold·out** \'hōl-,daut\ n

**hold·over** \'hōl-,dō-vər\ n : one that is
held over

**hold·up** \'hōl-,dəp\ n 1 . DELAY 2 . robbery at the point of a gun

**hole** \'hōl\ n 1 : an opening into or
through something 2 : a hollow place (as
a pit or cave) 3 : DEN, BURROW 4 : a
wretched or dingy place 5 : a unit of play
from tee to cup in golf 6 : an awkward
position — **hole** vb

**hol·i·day** \'hä-lə-,dā\ n [ME, fr. OE *hälig-
dæg*, fr. *hälig* holy + *dæg* day] 1 : a day
set aside for special religious observance
2 : a day of freedom from work; esp : one
in commemoration of an event 3 : VACA-
TION — **holiday** vb

**ho·li·ness** \'hō-lē-nəs\ n : the quality or
state of being holy — used as a title for
various high religious officials

**ho·lis·tic** \hō-'lis-tik\ adj : relating to or
concerned with integrated wholes or
complete systems rather than with the
analysis or treatment of separate parts
⟨~ medicine⟩ ⟨~ ecology⟩

**hol·lan·daise** \,hä-lən-'dāz\ n : a rich
sauce made basically of butter, egg yolks,
and lemon juice or vinegar

**hol·ler** \'hä-lər\ vb : to cry out : SHOUT —
**holler** n

¹**hol·low** \'hä-lō\ n 1 : CAVITY, HOLE 2 : a
surface depression

²**hollow** adj **hol·low·er** \'hä-lə-wər\; **hol-
low·est** \-lə-wəst\ 1 : CONCAVE, SUNKEN
2 : having a cavity within 3 : lacking in
real value, sincerity, or substance; also
: FALSE 4 : MUFFLED ⟨a ~ sound⟩
**hol·low·ness** n

³**hollow** vb : to make or become hollow

**hol·low·ware** or **hol·lo·ware** \'hä-lə-
,war\ n : vessels (as bowls or cups) with a
significant depth and volume

**hol·ly** \'hä-lē\ n, pl **hollies** : either of two
trees or shrubs with branches of usu. evergreen glossy spiny-margined leaves and
red berries

**hol·ly·hock** \'hä-lē-,häk, -,hòk\ n [ME *ho-
lihoc*, fr. *holi* holy + *hoc* mallow] : a biennial or perennial herb related to the mallows that is widely grown for its tall
stalks of showy flowers

**hol·mi·um** \'hōl-mē-əm\ n : a metallic
chemical element

**ho·lo·caust** \'hä-lə-,kòst, 'hō-\ n 1 : a
thorough destruction esp. by fire 2 often
cap : the killing of European Jews by the
Nazis during World War II; also : GENO-
CIDE

**Ho·lo·cene** \'hō-lə-,sēn\ adj : of, relating
to, or being the present geologic epoch
— **Holocene** n

**ho·lo·gram** \'hō-lə-,gram, 'hä-\ n : a
three-dimensional image produced by an
interference pattern of light (as laser
light)

**ho·lo·graph** \'hō-lə-,graf, 'hä-\ n : a document wholly in the handwriting of its author

**ho·log·ra·phy** \hō-'lä-grə-fē\ n : the process of making a hologram — **ho·lo-
graph·ic** \,hō-lə-'gra-fik, ,hä-\ adj

**Hol·stein** \'hōl-,stēn, -,stīn\ n : any of a breed of large black-and-white dairy cattle that produce large quantities of comparatively low-fat milk

**Hol·stein–Frie·sian** \-'frē-zhən\ n : HOLSTEIN

**hol·ster** \'hōl-stər\ n [D] : a usu. leather case for a firearm

**ho·ly** \'hō-lē\ adj **ho·li·er; -est 1** : worthy of absolute devotion **2** : SACRED **3** : having a divine quality ◆ Synonyms HALLOWED, BLESSED, SANCTIFIED, CONSECRATED — **ho·li·ly** \-lə-lē\ adv

**Holy Spirit** n : the third person of the Christian Trinity

**ho·ly·stone** \'hō-lē-,stōn\ n : a soft sandstone used to scrub a ship's wooden decks — **holystone** vb

**hom·age** \'ä-mij, 'hä-\ n [ME, fr. AF homage, omage, fr. home man, vassal, fr. L homo human being] : expression of high regard; also : TRIBUTE 3

**hom·bre** \'äm-,brā, 'əm-, -brē\ n : GUY, FELLOW

**hom·burg** \'häm-,bərg\ n [Homburg, Germany] : a man's felt hat with a stiff curled brim and a high crown creased lengthwise

**¹home** \'hōm\ n **1** : one's residence; also : HOUSE **2** : the social unit formed by a family living together **3** : a congenial environment; also : HABITAT **4** : a place of origin **5** : the objective in various games

**²home** vb **homed; hom·ing 1** : to go or return home **2** : to proceed to or toward a source of radiated energy used as a guide

**home·body** \'hōm-,bä-dē\ n : one whose life centers on home

**home·boy** \-,bói\ n **1** : a boy or man from one's neighborhood, hometown, or region **2** : a fellow member of a youth gang **3** : an inner-city youth

**home·bred** \-'bred\ adj : produced at home : INDIGENOUS

**home·com·ing** \-,kə-miŋ\ n **1** : a return home **2** : an annual celebration for alumni at a college or university

**home computer** n : a small inexpensive microcomputer

**home economics** n : the theory and practice of homemaking

**home·girl** \'hōm-,gərl\ n **1** : a girl or woman from one's neighborhood, hometown, or region **2** : a girl or woman who is a member of one's peer group **3** : an inner-city girl or woman

**home·grown** \'hōm-'grōn\ adj **1** : grown domestically ⟨∼ peaches⟩ **2** : LOCAL, INDIGENOUS ⟨a ∼ artist⟩

**home·land** \-,land\ n **1** : native land **2** : an area set aside to be a state for a people of a particular national, cultural, or racial origin

**home·less** \-ləs\ adj : having no home or permanent residence — **home·less·ness** n

**home·ly** \'hōm-lē\ adj **home·li·er; -est 1** : FAMILIAR **2** : unaffectedly natural **3** : lacking beauty or proportion — **home·li·ness** \-lē-nəs\ n

**home·made** \'hōm-,mād\ adj : made in

the home, on the premises, or by one's own efforts

**home·mak·er** \-,mā-kər\ n : one who manages a household esp. as a wife and mother — **home·mak·ing** \-kiŋ\ n

**ho·me·op·a·thy** \,hō-mē-'ä-pə-thē\ n : a system of medical practice that treats disease esp. with minute doses of a remedy that would in larger amounts produce symptoms in healthy persons similar to those of the disease — **ho·meo·path** \'hō-mē-ə-,path\ n — **ho·meo·path·ic** \,hō-mē-ə-'pa-thik\ adj

**ho·meo·sta·sis** \,hō-mē-ō-'stā-səs\ n : the maintenance of a relatively stable state of equilibrium between interrelated physiological, psychological, or social factors characteristic of an individual or group — **ho·meo·stat·ic** \-'sta-tik\ adj

**home page** n : the page usu. encountered first at a website that usu. contains hyperlinks to the other pages of the site

**home plate** n : a slab at the apex of a baseball diamond that a base runner must touch in order to score

**hom·er** \'hō-mər\ n : HOME RUN — **homer** vb

**home·room** \'hōm-,rüm, -,rùm\ n : a classroom where pupils report at the beginning of each school day

**home run** n : a hit in baseball that enables the batter to go around all the bases and score a run

**home·school** \'hōm-,skül\ vb : to teach school subjects to one's children at home — **home·school·er** \-,skü-lər\ n

**home·sick** \'hōm-,sik\ adj : longing for home and family while absent from them — **home·sick·ness** n

**home·spun** \-,spən\ adj **1** : spun or made at home; also : made of a loosely woven usu. woolen or linen fabric **2** : SIMPLE, HOMELY

**¹home·stead** \-,sted\ n : the home and land occupied by a family

**²homestead** vb : to acquire or settle on public land — **home·stead·er** n

**home·stretch** \-'strech\ n **1** : the part of a racecourse between the last curve and the winning post **2** : a final stage (as of a project)

**home theater** n : an entertainment system (as a television with surround sound and a DVD player) for the home

**home video** n : prerecorded videocassettes or videodiscs for home viewing

**¹home·ward** \-wərd\ or **home·wards** \-wərdz\ adv : toward home

**²homeward** adj : being or going toward home

**home·work** \-,wərk\ n **1** : an assignment given a student to be completed outside the classroom **2** : preparatory reading or research

**¹hom·ey** \'hō-mē\ adj **hom·i·er; -est** : characteristic of home

**²homey** or **hom·ie** \'hō-mē\ n, pl **homeys** or **homies** : HOMEBOY

**ho·mi·cide** \'hä-mə-,sīd, 'hō-\ n [L homicida murderer & homicidium manslaughter; both fr. homo human being + caedere to cut, kill] **1** : a person who kills another **2** : a killing of one human being by another — **hom·i·cid·al** \ˌhä-mə-'sī-d³l\ *adj*

**hom·i·ly** \'hä-mə-lē\ *n, pl* **-lies** : SERMON — **hom·i·let·ic** \ˌhä-mə-'le-tik\ *adj*

**homing pigeon** *n* : a racing pigeon trained to return home

**hom·i·nid** \'hä-mə-nəd, -ˌnid\ *n* : any of a family of primate mammals that comprise all living humans and extinct ancestral and related forms — **hominid** *adj*

**hom·i·ny** \'hä-mə-nē\ *n* : hulled corn with the germ removed

**ho·mo·cys·te·ine** \ˌhō-mō-'sis-tə-ˌēn\ *n* : an amino acid associated with an increased risk of heart disease when occurring at high levels in the blood

**ho·mo·erot·ic** \ˌhō-mō-i-'rä-tik\ *adj* : marked by or portraying homosexual desire — **ho·mo·erot·i·cism** \-'rä-tə-ˌsi-zəm\ *n*

**ho·mo·ge·neous** \ˌhō-mə-'jē-nē-əs, -nyəs\ *adj* : of the same or a similar kind; *also* : of uniform structure — **ho·mo·ge·ne·i·ty** \-jə-'nē-ə-tē\ *n* — **ho·mo·ge·neous·ly** *adv*

**ho·mo·e·ni·sa·tion**,     **ho·mog·e·nise** *Brit var of* HOMOGENIZATION, HOMOGENIZE

**ho·mog·e·nize** \hō-'mä-jə-ˌnīz, hə-\ *vb* **-nized; -niz·ing 1** : to make homogeneous **2** : to reduce the particles in (as milk) to uniform size and distribute them evenly throughout the liquid — **ho·mog·e·ni·za·tion** \-ˌmä-jə-nə-'zā-shən\ *n* — **ho·mog·e·niz·er** *n*

**ho·mo·graph** \'hä-mə-ˌgraf, 'hō-\ *n* : one of two or more words spelled alike but different in origin, meaning, or pronunciation (as the *bow* of a ship, a *bow* and arrow)

**ho·mol·o·gy** \hō-'mä-lə-jē, hə-\ *n, pl* **-gies 1** : structural likeness between corresponding parts of different plants or animals due to evolution from a common ancestor **2** : structural likeness between different parts of the same individual — **ho·mol·o·gous** \-'mä-lə-gəs\ *adj*

**hom·onym** \'hä-mə-ˌnim, 'hō-\ *n* **1** : HOMOPHONE, HOMOGRAPH **2** : one of two or more words spelled and pronounced alike but different in meaning (as *pool* of water and *pool* the game)

**ho·mo·pho·bia** \ˌhō-mə-'fō-bē-ə\ *n* : irrational fear, aversion to, or discrimination against homosexuality or homosexuals — **ho·mo·phobe** \'hō-mə-ˌfōb\ *n* — **ho·mo·pho·bic** \-'fō-bik\ *adj*

**ho·mo·phone** \'hä-mə-ˌfōn, 'hō-\ *n* : one of two or more words (as *to, too, two*) pronounced alike but different in meaning or derivation or spelling

**Ho·mo sa·pi·ens** \ˌhō-mō-'sä-pē-ənz, -'sa-\ *n* : HUMANKIND

**ho·mo·sex·u·al** \ˌhō-mō-'sek-shə-wəl\ *adj* : of, relating to, or marked by sexual interest in the same sex as oneself; *also* : of, relating to, or involving sexual intercourse between members of the same sex — **homosexual** *n* — **ho·mo·sex·u·al·i·ty** \-ˌsek-shə-'wa-lə-tē\ *n*

**hon** *abbr* honor; honorable; honorary

**hone** \'hōn\ *n* : WHETSTONE — **hone** *vb* — **hon·er** *n*

**hone in** *vb* : to move toward or direct attention to an objective

**¹hon·est** \'ä-nəst\ *adj* [ME, fr. AF, fr. L *honestus* honorable, fr. *honos, honor* honor] **1** : free from deception : TRUTHFUL; *also* : GENUINE, REAL **2** : REPUTABLE **3** : CREDITABLE ⟨an ~ day's work⟩ **4** : marked by integrity **5** : FRANK ♦ *Synonyms* UPRIGHT, JUST, CONSCIENTIOUS, HONORABLE — **hon·est·ly** *adv* — **hon·es·ty** \-ə-stē\ *n*

**²honest** *adv* : HONESTLY; *also* : with all sincerity ⟨I didn't do it, ~⟩

**hon·ey** \'hə-nē\ *n, pl* **honeys** : a sweet sticky substance made by honeybees from the nectar of flowers — **hon·eyed** \-nēd\ *adj*

**hon·ey·bee** \'hə-nē-ˌbē\ *n* : a honey-producing bee often kept in hives

**¹hon·ey·comb** \-ˌkōm\ *n* : a mass of 6-sided wax cells built by honeybees; *also* : something of similar structure or appearance

**²honeycomb** *vb* : to make or become full of cavities like a honeycomb

**hon·ey·dew** \-ˌdü, -ˌdyü\ *n* : a sweetish deposit secreted on plants by aphids, scale insects, or fungi

**honeydew melon** *n* : a smooth-skinned muskmelon with sweet green flesh

**honey locust** *n* : a tall usu. spiny No. American leguminous tree with hard durable wood and long twisted pods

**hon·ey·moon** \'hə-nē-ˌmün\ *n* **1** : a period of harmony esp. just after marriage **2** : a holiday taken by a newly married couple — **honeymoon** *vb* — **hon·ey·moon·er** *n*

**hon·ey·suck·le** \'hə-nē-ˌsə-kəl\ *n* : any of a genus of shrubs with fragrant tube-shaped flowers rich in nectar

**honk** \'häŋk, 'hȯŋk\ *n* : the cry of a goose, *also* : a similar sound (as of a horn) — **honk** *vb* — **honk·er** *n*

**hon·ky–tonk** \'häŋ-kē-ˌtäŋk, 'hȯŋ-kē-ˌtȯŋk\ *n* : a tawdry nightclub or dance hall — **honky–tonk** *adj*

**¹hon·or** \'ä-nər\ *n* **1** : good name : REPUTATION; *also* : outward respect **2** : PRIVILEGE **3** : a person of superior standing — used esp. as a title **4** : one who brings respect or fame ⟨an ~ to the class⟩ **5** : an evidence or symbol of distinction **6** : CHASTITY, PURITY **7** : INTEGRITY ♦ *Synonyms* HOMAGE, REVERENCE, DEFERENCE, OBEISANCE

**²honor** *vb* **1** : to regard or treat with honor **2** : to confer honor on **3** : to fulfill the terms of; *also* : to accept as payment — **hon·or·ee** \ˌä-nə-'rē\ *n* — **hon·or·er** *n*

**hon·or·able** \'ä-nə-rə-bəl\ *adj* **1** : deserving of honor **2** : of great renown **3** : accompanied by marks of honor **4** : doing credit to the possessor **5** : characterized by integrity — **hon·or·able·ness** *n* — **hon·or·ably** \-blē\ *adv*

**hon·o·rar·i·um** \ˌä-nə-'rer-ē-əm\ *n, pl* **-ia** \-ē-ə\ *also* **-i·ums** : a reward usu. for services on which custom or propriety forbids a price to be set

**hon·or·ary** \'ä-nə-ˌrer-ē\ adj **1** : having or conferring distinction **2** : conferred in recognition of achievement without the usual prerequisites ⟨∼ degree⟩ **3** : UNPAID, VOLUNTARY ⟨an ∼ chairman⟩ — **hon·or·ari·ly** \ˌä-nə-'rer-ə-lē\ adv

**hon·or·if·ic** \ˌä-nə-'ri-fik\ adj : conferring or conveying honor ⟨∼ titles⟩

**hon·our, hon·our·able** chiefly Brit var of HONOR, HONORABLE

**¹hood** \'hủd\ n **1** : a covering for the head and neck and sometimes the face **2** : an ornamental fold (as at the back of an ecclesiastical vestment) **3** : a cover for parts of mechanisms; esp : the covering over an automobile engine — **hood·ed** \'hủ-dəd\ adj

**²hood** \'hủd, 'hủd\ n : HOODLUM

**³hood** \'hủd\ n : an inner-city neighborhood; also : INNER CITY

**-hood** \ˌhủd\ n suffix **1** : state : condition : quality : character ⟨boyhood⟩ ⟨hardihood⟩ **2** : instance of a (specified) state or quality ⟨falsehood⟩ **3** : individuals sharing a (specified) state or character ⟨brotherhood⟩

**hood·ie** \'hủ-dē\ n : a hooded sweatshirt

**hood·lum** \'hủd-ləm, 'hủd-\ n **1** : THUG **2** : a young ruffian

**hoo·doo** \'hủ-dü\ n, pl **hoodoos 1** : a body of magical practices traditional esp. among blacks in the southern U.S. **2** : something that brings bad luck — **hoodoo** vb

**hood·wink** \'hủd-ˌwiŋk\ vb : to deceive by false appearance

**hoo·ey** \'hủ-ē\ n : NONSENSE

**hoof** \'hủf, 'hủf\ n, pl **hooves** \'hủvz, 'hủvz\ also **hoofs** : a horny covering that protects the ends of the toes of ungulate mammals (as horses or cattle); also : a hoofed foot — **hoofed** \'hủft, 'hủft\ adj

**¹hook** \'hủk\ n **1** : a curved or bent device for catching, holding, or pulling **2** : something curved or bent like a hook **3** : a flight of a ball (as in golf) that curves in a direction opposite to the dominant hand of the player propelling it **4** : a short punch delivered with a circular motion and with the elbow bent and rigid

**²hook** vb **1** : CURVE, CROOK **2** : to seize or make fast with a hook **3** : STEAL **4** : to work as a prostitute

**hoo·kah** \'hủ-kə, 'hủ-\ n [Ar huqqa bottle of a water pipe] : WATER PIPE

**hook·er** \'hủ-kər\ n **1** : one that hooks **2** : PROSTITUTE

**hook·up** \'hủ-ˌkəp\ n : an assemblage (as of apparatus or circuits) used for a specific purpose (as in radio)

**hook up** vb : to become involved in a working, social, or sexual relationship

**hook·worm** \'hủk-ˌwərm\ n : any of several parasitic intestinal nematode worms having hooks or plates around the mouth; also : infestation with or disease caused by hookworms

**hoo·li·gan** \'hủ-li-gən\ n : RUFFIAN, HOODLUM — **hoo·li·gan·ism** \-gə-ˌni-zəm\ n

**hoop** \'hủp, 'hủp\ n **1** : a circular strip used esp. for holding together the staves

of a barrel **2** : a circular figure or object : RING **3** : a circle of flexible material for expanding a woman's skirt **4** : BASKETBALL — usu. used in pl.

**hoop·la** \'hủp-ˌlä, 'hủp-\ n [F houp-là, interj.] : TO-DO; also : BALLYHOO

**hoop·ster** \'hủp-stər\ n : a basketball player

**hoo·ray** \hủ-'rā\ interj — used to express joy, approval, or encouragement

**hoose·gow** \'hủs-ˌgaủ\ n [Sp juzgado panel of judges, courtroom] : JAIL

**¹hoot** \'hủt\ vb **1** : to shout or laugh usu. in contempt **2** : to make the natural throat noise of an owl — **hoot·er** n

**²hoot** n **1** : a sound of hooting **2** : the least bit ⟨don't give a ∼⟩ **3** : something or someone amusing ⟨the play is a real ∼⟩

**hoo·te·nan·ny** \'hủ-tə-ˌna-nē\ n, pl **-nies** : a gathering at which folksingers entertain often with the audience joining in

**¹hop** \'häp\ vb **hopped; hop·ping 1** : to move by quick springy leaps **2** : to make a quick trip **3** : to ride on esp. surreptitiously and without authorization

**²hop** n **1** : a short brisk leap esp. on one leg **2** : DANCE **3** : a short trip by air

**³hop** n : a vine related to the hemp plant whose ripe dried pistillate catkins are used esp. in flavoring malt liquors; also, pl : its pistillate catkins

**¹hope** \'hōp\ vb **hoped; hop·ing** : to desire with expectation of fulfillment

**²hope** n **1** : TRUST, RELIANCE **2** : desire accompanied by expectation of fulfillment; also : something hoped for **3** : one that gives promise for the future — **hope·ful** \-fəl\ adj — **hope·ful·ness** n — **hope·less** adj — **hope·less·ly** adv — **hope·less·ness** n

**HOPE** abbr Health Opportunity for People Everywhere

**hope·ful·ly** \'hōp-fə-lē\ adv **1** : in a hopeful manner **2** : it is hoped

**Ho·pi** \'hō-pē\ n, pl **Hopi** or **Hopis** : a member of an American Indian people of Arizona; also : the language of the Hopi people

**hopped–up** \'häpt-'əp\ adj **1** : being under the influence of a narcotic; also : full of enthusiasm or excitement **2** : having more than usual power ⟨a ∼ engine⟩

**hop·per** \'hä-pər\ n **1** : a usu. immature hopping insect (as a grasshopper) **2** : a usu. funnel-shaped container for delivering material (as grain) **3** : a freight car with hinged doors in a sloping bottom **4** : a box into which a bill is to be considered by a legislative body is dropped **5** : a tank holding a liquid and having a device for releasing its contents through a pipe

**hop·scotch** \'häp-ˌskäch\ n : a child's game in which a player tosses an object (as a stone) into areas of a figure drawn on the ground and hops through the figure to pick up the object

**hor** abbr horizontal

**horde** \'hȯrd\ n : THRONG, SWARM

**ho·ri·zon** \hə-'rī-zᵊn\ n [ME, fr. LL, fr. Gk horizont-, horizōn, fr. prp. of horizein to bound, fr. horos limit, boundary] **1**

: the apparent junction of earth and sky **2** : range of outlook or experience

**hor·i·zon·tal** \ˌhȯr-ə-ˈzän-tᵊl\ *adj* : parallel to the horizon : LEVEL — **horizontal** *n* — **hor·i·zon·tal·ly** *adv*

**hor·mon·al** \hȯr-ˈmō-nᵊl\ *adj* : of, relating to, or effected by hormones — **hor·mon·al·ly** \-nᵊl-ē\ *adv*

**hor·mone** \ˈhȯr-ˌmōn\ *n* [Gk *hormōn*, prp. of *horman* to stir up, fr. *hormē* impulse, assault] : a product of living cells that circulates in body fluids and has a specific effect on the activity of cells remote from its point of origin

**horn** \ˈhȯrn\ *n* **1** : one of the hard projections of bone or keratin on the head of many hoofed mammals **2** : something resembling or suggesting a horn **3** : a brass wind instrument **4** : a usu. electrical device that makes a noise (an auto mobile ∼) — **horned** \ˈhȯrnd\ *adj* — **horn·less** *adj*

**horn·book** \ˈhȯrn-ˌbůk\ *n* **1** : a child's primer consisting of a sheet of parchment or paper protected by a sheet of transparent horn **2** : a rudimentary treatise

**horned toad** *n* : any of several small harmless insect-eating lizards with spines on the head resembling horns and spiny scales on the body

**hor·net** \ˈhȯr-nət\ *n* : any of the larger social wasps

**horn in** *vb* : to participate without invitation : INTRUDE

**horn·pipe** \ˈhȯrn-ˌpīp\ *n* : a lively folk dance of the British Isles

**horny** \ˈhȯr-nē\ *adj* **horn·i·er; -est 1** : of or made of horn; *also* : HARD, CALLOUS **2** : having horns **3** : desiring sexual gratification; *also* : excited sexually

**ho·rol·o·gy** \hə-ˈrä-lə-jē\ *n* : the science of measuring time or constructing time-indicating instruments — **hor·o·log·i·cal** \ˌhȯr-ə-ˈlä-ji-kəl\ *adj* — **ho·rol·o·gist** \hə-ˈrä-lə-jist\ *n*

**horo·scope** \ˈhȯr-ə-ˌskōp\ *n* [ME *horoscopum*, fr. L *horoscopus*, fr. Gk *hōroskopos*, fr. *hōra* hour + *skopos* watcher] **1** : a diagram of the relative positions of planets and signs of the zodiac at a particular time for use by astrologers to foretell events of a person's life **2** : an astrological forecast

**hor·ren·dous** \hȯ-ˈren-dəs\ *adj* : DREADFUL, HORRIBLE

**hor·ri·ble** \ˈhȯr-ə-bəl\ *adj* **1** : marked by or conducive to horror **2** : highly disagreeable ⟨a ∼ mistake⟩ — **hor·ri·ble·ness** *n* — **hor·ri·bly** \-blē\ *adv*

**hor·rid** \ˈhȯr-əd\ *adj* **1** : HIDEOUS **2** : REPULSIVE — **hor·rid·ly** *adv*

**hor·rif·ic** \hȯ-ˈri-fik\ *adj* : having the power to horrify ⟨a ∼ crime⟩ — **hor·rif·i·cal·ly** \-fi-k(ə-)lē\ *adv*

**hor·ri·fy** \ˈhȯr-ə-ˌfī\ *vb* **-fied; -fy·ing** : to cause to feel horror ♦ **Synonyms** APPALL, DAUNT, DISMAY

**hor·ror** \ˈhȯr-ər\ *n* **1** : painful and intense fear, dread, or dismay **2** : intense repugnance **3** : something that horrifies

**horror story** *n* : an account of an unsettling or unfortunate occurrence

**hors de com·bat** \ˌȯr-də-kōⁿ-ˈbä\ *adv or adj* : in a disabled condition

**hors d'oeuvre** \ȯr-ˈdərv\ *n, pl* **hors d'oeuvres** \*same or* -ˈdərvz\ *also* **hors d'oeuvre** [F *hors-d'oeuvre*, lit., outside of the work] : any of various savory foods usu. served as appetizers

**horse** \ˈhȯrs\ *n, pl* **hors·es** *also* **horse 1** : a large solid-hoofed herbivorous mammal domesticated as a draft and saddle animal **2** : a supporting framework usu. with legs — **horse·less** *adj*

**¹horse·back** \ˈhȯrs-ˌbak\ *n* : the back of a horse

**²horseback** *adv* : on horseback

**horse chestnut** *n* : a large tree with palmate leaves, erect conical clusters of showy flowers, and large glossy brown seeds enclosed in a prickly bur; *also* : its seed

**horse·flesh** \ˈhȯrs-ˌflesh\ *n* : horses for riding, driving, or racing

**horse·fly** \-ˌflī\ *n* : any of a family of large dipteran flies with bloodsucking females

**horse·hair** \-ˌher\ *n* **1** : the hair of a horse esp. from the mane or tail **2** : cloth made from horsehair

**horse·hide** \-ˌhīd\ *n* **1** : the dressed or raw hide of a horse **2** : the ball used in baseball

**horse latitudes** *n pl* : either of two calm regions near 30°N and 30°S latitude

**horse·laugh** \ˈhȯrs-ˌlaf, -ˌläf\ *n* : a loud boisterous laugh

**horse·man** \-mən\ *n* **1** : one who rides horseback; *also* : one skilled in managing horses **2** : a breeder or raiser of horses — **horse·man·ship** *n*

**horse·play** \-ˌplā\ *n* : rough boisterous play

**horse·play·er** \-ər\ *n* : a bettor on horse races

**horse·pow·er** \ˈhȯrs-ˌpaů(-ə)r\ *n* : a unit of power equal in the U.S. to 746 watts

**horse·rad·ish** \-ˌra-dish\ *n* : a tall white-flowered herb related to the mustards whose pungent root is used as a condiment; *also* : the pungent condiment

**horse·shoe** \ˈhȯrs-ˌshü\ *n* **1** : a usu. U-shaped protective metal plate fitted to the rim of a horse's hoof **2** *pl* : a game in which horseshoes are pitched at a fixed object — **horse·shoe** *vb* — **horse·sho·er** *n*

**horseshoe crab** *n* : any of several marine arthropods with a broad crescent-shaped combined head and thorax

**horse·tail** \ˈhȯrs-ˌtāl\ *n* : any of a genus of primitive spore-producing plants with hollow jointed stems and leaves reduced to sheaths about the joints

**horse·whip** \-ˌhwip\ *vb* : to flog with a whip made to be used on a horse

**horse·wom·an** \-ˌwů-mən\ *n* **1** : a woman skilled in riding horseback or in caring for or managing horses **2** : a woman who breeds or raises horses

**hors·ey** *also* **horsy** \ˈhȯr-sē\ *adj* **hors·i·er; -est 1** : of, relating to, or suggesting a horse **2** : having to do with horses or horse racing

**hort** *abbr* horticultural; horticulture

**hor·ta·tive** \'hòr-tə-tiv\ *adj* : giving exhortation ⟨a ∼ appeal⟩

**hor·ta·to·ry** \'hòr-tə-ˌtòr-ē\ *adj* : HORTATIVE

**hor·ti·cul·ture** \'hòr-tə-ˌkəl-chər\ *n* : the science and art of growing fruits, vegetables, flowers, and ornamental plants — **hor·ti·cul·tur·al** \ˌhòr-tə-'kəl-chə-rəl\ *adj* — **hor·ti·cul·tur·ist** \-rist\ *n*

**Hos** *abbr* Hosea

**ho·san·na** \hō-'za-nə, -'zä-\ *interj* [Gk *hōsanna*, fr. Heb *hōshī'āh-nnā* pray, save (us)!] — used as a cry of acclamation and adoration — **hosanna** *n*

¹**hose** \'hōz\ *n, pl* **hose** *or* **hos·es** 1 *pl* **hose** : STOCKING, SOCK; *also* : a close-fitting garment covering the legs and waist 2 : a flexible tube for conveying fluids (as from a faucet)

²**hose** *vb* **hosed; hos·ing** : to spray, water, or wash with a hose

**Ho·sea** \hō-'zā-ə, -'zē-\ *n* — see BIBLE table

**ho·siery** \'hō-zhə-rē, -zə-\ *n* : STOCKINGS, SOCKS

**hosp** *abbr* hospital

**hos·pice** \'häs-pəs\ *n* 1 : a lodging for travelers or for young persons or the underprivileged 2 : a facility or program for caring for dying persons

**hos·pi·ta·ble** \hä-'spi-tə-bəl, 'häs-(ˌ)pi-\ *adj* 1 : given to generous and cordial reception of guests 2 : readily receptive — **hos·pi·ta·bly** \-blē\ *adv*

**hos·pi·tal** \'häs-ˌpi-t°l\ *n* [ME, fr. AF, fr. ML *hospitale* hospice, guest house, fr. neut. of L *hospitalis* of a guest, fr. *hospit-, hospes* guest, host] : an institution where the sick or injured receive medical or surgical care

**hos·pi·tal·ise** *Brit var of* HOSPITALIZE

**hos·pi·tal·i·ty** \ˌhäs-pə-'ta-lə-tē\ *n, pl* **-ties** : hospitable treatment, reception, or disposition

**hos·pi·tal·ize** \'häs-ˌpi-tə-ˌlīz\ *vb* **-ized; -iz·ing** : to place in a hospital as a patient — **hos·pi·tal·i·za·tion** \ˌhäs-ˌpi-t°l-ə-'zā-shən\ *n*

¹**host** \'hōst\ *n* [ME, fr. AF *ost*, fr. LL *hostis*, fr. L, stranger, enemy] 1 : ARMY 2 : MULTITUDE ⟨a ∼ of options⟩

²**host** *n* [ME *hoste* host, guest, fr. AF, fr. L *hospit-, hospes*] 1 : one who receives or entertains guests 2 : an animal or plant on or in which a parasite lives 3 : one into which something (as an organ) is transplanted 4 : SERVER 2 — **host** *vb*

³**host** *n, often cap* [ultim. fr. L *hostia* sacrifice] : the eucharistic bread

**hos·tage** \'häs-tij\ *n* 1 : a person kept as a pledge pending the fulfillment of an agreement 2 : a person taken by force to secure the taker's demands

**hos·tel** \'häs-t°l\ *n* [ME, fr. AF, fr. ML *hospitale* hospice] 1 : INN 2 : a supervised lodging for youth — **hos·tel·er** *or* **hos·tel·ler** *n*

**hos·tel·ry** \-rē\ *n, pl* **-ries** : INN, HOTEL

**host·ess** \'hō-stəs\ *n* : a woman who acts as host

**hos·tile** \'häs-t°l, -ˌtī(-ə)l\ *adj* : marked by

usu. overt antagonism : UNFRIENDLY — **hostile** *n* — **hos·tile·ly** *adv*

**hos·til·i·ty** \hä-'sti-lə-tē\ *n, pl* **-ties** 1 : an unfriendly state or action 2 *pl* : overt acts of war

**hos·tler** \'häs-lər, 'äs-\ *n* : one who takes care of horses or mules

**hot** \'hät\ *adj* **hot·ter; hot·test** 1 : marked by a high temperature or an uncomfortable degree of body heat 2 : giving a sensation of heat or of burning 3 : ARDENT, FIERY 4 : sexually excited 5 : EAGER 6 : newly made or received 7 : PUNGENT 8 : unusually lucky or favorable ⟨∼ dice⟩ 9 : recently and illegally obtained ⟨∼ jewels⟩ — **hot** *adv* — **hot·ly** *adv* — **hot·ness** *n*

**hot·bed** \-ˌbed\ *n* 1 : a glass-covered bed of soil heated (as by fermenting manure) and used esp. for raising seedlings 2 : an environment that favors rapid growth or development

**hot–blood·ed** \-'blə-dəd\ *adj* : easily roused or excited ⟨∼ rebels⟩

**hot·box** \-ˌbäks\ *n* : a bearing (as of a railroad car) overheated by friction

**hot button** *n* : an emotional issue or concern that triggers immediate intense reaction

**hot·cake** \-ˌkāk\ *n* : PANCAKE

**hot dog** *n* : a cooked frankfurter usu. served in a long split roll

**ho·tel** \hō-'tel\ *n* [F *hôtel*, fr. OF *hostel*, fr. ML *hospitale* hospice] : a building where lodging and usu. meals, entertainment, and various personal services are provided for the public

**hot flash** *n* : a sudden brief flushing and sensation of heat usu. associated with menopausal endocrine imbalance

**hot·head·ed** \-'he-dəd\ *adj* : FIERY, IMPETUOUS ⟨a ∼ troublemaker⟩ — **hot·head** \-ˌhed\ *n* — **hot·head·ed·ly** *adv* — **hot·head·ed·ness** *n*

**hot·house** \-ˌhaùs\ *n* : a heated greenhouse esp. for raising tropical plants

**hotline** *n* : a telephone line for emergency use (as between governments or to a counseling service)

**hot pants** *n pl* : very short shorts

**hot pepper** *n* : a small usu. thin-walled pepper with a pungent taste; *also* : a plant bearing hot peppers

**hot plate** *n* : a simple portable appliance for heating or for cooking

**hot potato** *n* : an embarrassing or controversial issue

**hot rod** *n* : an automobile modified for high speed and fast acceleration — **hot–rod·der** \-'rä-dər\ *n*

**hots** \'häts\ *n pl* : strong sexual desire — usu. used with *the*

**hot seat** *n* : a position of anxiety or embarrassment

**hot·shot** \'hät-ˌshät\ *n* : a showily skillful person ⟨a ∼ lawyer⟩

**hot tub** *n* : a large tub of hot water for one or more bathers

**hot water** *n* : TROUBLE, DIFFICULTY

**hot–wire** \'hät-ˌwī(-ə)r\ *vb* : to start (an automobile) by short-circuiting the ignition system

¹**hound** \'haůnd\ *n* **1** : any of various hunting dogs that track prey by scent or sight **2** : FAN, ADDICT ⟨autograph ∼*s*⟩

²**hound** *vb* : to pursue relentlessly

**hour** \'au̇(-ə)r\ *n* **1** : the 24th part of a day : 60 minutes **2** : the time of day **3** : a particular or customary time **4** : a class session — **hour·ly** *adv or adj*

**hour·glass** \'au̇(-ə)r-ˌglas\ *n* : a glass vessel for measuring time in which sand runs from an upper compartment to a lower compartment in an hour

**hou·ri** \'hu̇r-ē\ *n* [F, fr. Pers *hūrī*, fr. Ar *hūrīya*] : one of the beautiful maidens of the Muslim paradise

¹**house** \'haůs\ *n, pl* **hous·es** \'hau̇-zəz\ **1** : a building for human habitation **2** : an animal shelter (as a den or nest) **3** : a building in which something is stored **4** : HOUSEHOLD; *also* : FAMILY **5** : a residence for a religious community or for students; *also* : those in residence **6** : a legislative body **7** : a place of business or entertainment **8** : a business organization **9** : the audience in a theater or concert hall — **house·ful** *n*

²**house** \'hau̇z\ *vb* **housed; hous·ing** **1** : to provide with or have shelter : LODGE **2** : STORE ⟨paintings *housed* in a gallery⟩

**house·boat** \'hau̇s-ˌbōt\ *n* : a pleasure boat fitted for use as a dwelling or for leisurely cruising

**house·boy** \-ˌbȯi\ *n* : a boy or man hired to act as a household servant

**house·break** \-ˌbrāk\ *vb* **-broke; -broken; -break·ing** : to train (a pet) in excretory habits acceptable in indoor living

**house·break·ing** \-ˌbrā-kiŋ\ *n* : the act of breaking into a dwelling with the intent of committing a felony

**house·clean** \-ˌklēn\ *vb* : to clean a house and its furniture — **house·clean·ing** *n*

**house·coat** \-ˌkōt\ *n* : a woman's often long-skirted informal garment for wear around the house

**house·fly** \-ˌflī\ *n* : a dipteran fly that is common about human habitations

¹**house·hold** \-ˌhōld\ *n* : those who dwell as a family under the same roof — **house·hold·er** *n*

²**household** *adj* **1** : DOMESTIC **2** : FAMILIAR, COMMON ⟨a ∼ name⟩

**house·keep·er** \-ˌkē-pər\ *n* : a woman employed to take care of a house

**house·keep·ing** \-ˌkē-piŋ\ *n* : the care and management of a house or institutional property

**house·lights** \-ˌlīts\ *n pl* : the lights that illuminate the auditorium of a theater

**house·maid** \-ˌmād\ *n* : a girl or woman who is a servant employed to do housework

**house·moth·er** \-ˌmə-thər\ *n* : a woman acting as hostess, chaperone, and often housekeeper in a group residence

**house·plant** \-ˌplant\ *n* : a plant grown or kept indoors

**house sparrow** *n* : a Eurasian sparrow widely introduced in urban and agricultural areas

**house·top** \'hau̇s-ˌtäp\ *n* : ROOF

**house·wares** \-ˌwerz\ *n pl* : small articles of household equipment

**house·warm·ing** \-ˌwȯr-miŋ\ *n* : a party to celebrate the taking possession of a house or premises

**house·wife** \-ˌwīf\ *n* : a married woman in charge of a household — **house·wife·ly** *adj* — **house·wif·ery** \-ˌwī-fə-rē\ *n*

**house·work** \-ˌwərk\ *n* : the work of housekeeping

¹**hous·ing** \'hau̇-ziŋ\ *n* **1** : SHELTER; *also* : dwellings provided for people **2** : something that covers or protects

²**housing** *n* : CAPARISON 1

**HOV** *abbr* high-occupancy vehicle

**hove** *past and past part of* HEAVE

**hov·el** \'hə-vəl, 'hä-\ *n* : a small, wretched, and often dirty house : HUT

**hov·er** \'hə-vər, 'hä-\ *vb* **hov·ered; hov·er·ing** **1** : FLUTTER; *also* : to move to and fro **2** : to be in an uncertain state

**hov·er·craft** \-ˌkraft\ *n* : a vehicle that rides on a cushion of air over a surface

¹**how** \'hau̇\ *adv* **1** : in what way or manner ⟨∼ was it done⟩ **2** : with what meaning ⟨∼ do we interpret such behavior⟩ **3** : for what reason ⟨∼ could you have done such a thing⟩ **4** : to what extent or degree ⟨∼ deep is it⟩ **5** : in what state or condition ⟨∼ are you⟩ — **how about** : what do you say to or think of ⟨*how about* coming with me⟩ — **how come** : why is it that

²**how** *conj* **1** : the way or manner in which ⟨remember ∼ they fought⟩ **2** : HOWEVER ⟨do it ∼ you like⟩

¹**how·be·it** \hau̇-'bē-ət\ *conj* : ALTHOUGH

²**howbeit** *adv* : NEVERTHELESS

**how·dah** \'hau̇-də\ *n* [Hindi & Urdu *haudā*, fr. Ar *haudaj*] : a seat or covered pavilion on the back of an elephant or camel

¹**how·ev·er** \hau̇-'e-vər\ *conj* : in whatever manner that

²**however** *adv* **1** : in whatever manner; *also* : to whatever degree **2** : in spite of that

**how·it·zer** \'hau̇-ət-sər\ *n* : a short cannon that shoots shells at a high angle

**howl** \'hau̇(-ə)l\ *vb* **1** : to emit a loud long doleful sound characteristic of dogs **2** : to cry loudly — **howl** *n*

**howl·er** \'hau̇-lər\ *n* **1** : one that howls **2** : a humorous and ridiculous blunder

**howl·ing** *adj* **1** : DESOLATE, WILD **2** : very great ⟨a ∼ success⟩

**how·so·ev·er** \ˌhau̇-sə-'we-vər\ *adv* : HOWEVER 1

**hoy·den** \'hȯi-dᵊn\ *n* : a girl or woman of saucy, boisterous, or carefree behavior — **hoy·den·ish** *adj*

**hp** *abbr* horsepower

**HP** *abbr* high pressure

**HPF** *abbr* highest possible frequency

**HQ** *abbr* headquarters

**hr** *abbr* **1** here **2** hour

**HR** *abbr* House of Representatives

**HRH** *abbr* **1** Her Royal Highness **2** His Royal Highness

**hryv·nia** \(h)riv-nē-ə\ *n, pl* **hryvnia** *or* **hryvnias** — see MONEY table

**hrzn** *abbr* horizon

**Hs** *symbol* hassium

**HS** *abbr* high school

**HST** *abbr* Hawaiian standard time

**ht** *abbr* height

**HT** *abbr* **1** Hawaii time **2** high-tension

**HTML** \ā̱ch-¸tē-¸em-ᵗel\ *n* [*hypertext markup language*] : a computer language used to create World Wide Web documents

**http** *abbr* hypertext transfer protocol

**hua·ra·che** \wə-ʳrä-chē\ *n* [MexSp] : a sandal with an upper made of interwoven leather strips

**hub** \ʰhəb\ *n* **1** : the central part of a circular object (as a wheel) **2** : a center of activity; *esp* : an airport or city through which an airline routes most of its traffic

**hub-bub** \ʰhə-bəb\ *n* : UPROAR ⟨the ∼ in the stadium⟩; *also* : TURMOIL ⟨the ∼ following the war⟩

**hub·cap** \ʰhəb-¸kap\ *n* : a removable metal cap over the end of an axle

**hu·bris** \ʰhyü-brəs\ *n* : exaggerated pride or self-confidence

**huck·le·ber·ry** \ʰhə-kəl-¸ber-ē\ *n* **1** : any of a genus of American shrubs of the heath family; *also* : its edible dark blue berry **2** : BLUEBERRY

**huck·ster** \ʰhək-stər\ *n* : PEDDLER, HAWKER — **huck·ster·ism** \-stə-¸ri-zəm\ *n*

**HUD** *abbr* Department of Housing and Urban Development

¹**hud·dle** \ʰhə-dᵉl\ *vb* **hud·dled; hud·dling** **1** : to crowd together **2** : CONFER

²**huddle** *n* **1** : a closely packed group **2** : MEETING, CONFERENCE

**hue** \ʰhyü\ *n* **1** : COLOR; *also* : gradation of color **2** : the attribute of colors that permits them to be classed as red, yellow, green, blue, or an intermediate color — **hued** \ʰhyüd\ *adj*

**hue and cry** *n* : a clamor of pursuit or protest

**huff** \ʰhəf\ *n* : a fit of anger or pique — **huff** *vb* — **huff·i·ly** \ʰhə-fə-lē\ *adv* — **huffy** \ʰhə-fē\ *adj*

**hug** \ʰhəg\ *vb* **hugged; hug·ging** **1** : EMBRACE **2** : to stay close to — **hug** *n*

**huge** \ʰhyüj\ *adj* **hug·er; hug·est** : very large or extensive — **huge·ly** *adv* — **huge·ness** *n*

**hug·ger–mug·ger** \ʰhə-gər-¸mə-gər\ *n* **1** : SECRECY **2** : CONFUSION, MUDDLE

**Hu·gue·not** \ʰhyü-gə-¸nät\ *n* : a French Protestant of the 16th and 17th centuries

**hu·la** \ʰhü-lə\ *n* : a sinuous Polynesian dance usu. accompanied by chants

**hulk** \ʰhəlk\ *n* **1** : a heavy clumsy ship **2** : an old ship unfit for service **3** : a bulky or unwieldy person or thing

**hulk·ing** \ʰhəl-kiŋ\ *adj* : BURLY, MASSIVE

¹**hull** \ʰhəl\ *n* **1** : the outer covering of a fruit or seed **2** : the frame or body esp. of a ship or boat

²**hull** *vb* : to remove the hulls of — **hull·er** *n*

**hul·la·ba·loo** \ʰhə-lə-bə-¸lü\ *n, pl* **-loos** : a confused noise : UPROAR

**hul·lo** \¸hə-ʰlō\ *chiefly Brit var of* HELLO

**hum** \ʰhəm\ *vb* **hummed; hum·ming** **1** : to utter a sound like that of the speech sound \m\ prolonged **2** : DRONE **3** : to be busily active **4** : to run smoothly **5** : to sing with closed lips — **hum** *n* — **hum·mer** *n*

¹**hu·man** \ʰhyü-mən, ᵗyü-\ *adj* **1** : of, relating to, being, or characteristic of humans **2** : having human form or attributes — **hu·man·ly** *adv* — **hu·man·ness** *n*

²**human** *n* : any of a species of bipedal primate mammals comprising all living persons and their recent ancestors; *also* : HOMINID — **hu·man·like** \-¸līk\ *adj*

**hu·mane** \hyü-ʰmān, yü-\ *adj* **1** : marked by compassion, sympathy, or consideration for others **2** : HUMANISTIC — **hu·mane·ly** *adv* — **hu·mane·ness** *n*

**human immunodeficiency virus** *n* : HIV

**hu·man·ism** \ʰhyü-mə-¸ni-zəm, ᵗyü-\ *n* **1** : devotion to the humanities; *also* : the revival of classical letters characteristic of the Renaissance **2** : a doctrine or way of life centered on human interests or values — **hu·man·ist** \-nist\ *n or adj* — **hu·man·is·tic** \¸hyü-mə-ʰnis-tik, ¸yü-\ *adj*

**hu·man·i·tar·i·an** \hyü-¸ma-nə-ʰter-ē-ən, yü-\ *n* : one who practices philanthropy — **humanitarian** *adj* — **hu·man·i·tar·i·an·ism** *n*

**hu·man·i·ty** \hyü-ʰma-nə-tē, yü-\ *n, pl* **-ties** **1** : the quality or state of being human or humane **2** *pl* : the branches of learning dealing with human concerns (as philosophy) as opposed to natural processes (as physics) **3** : the human race

**hu·man·ize** \ʰhyü-mə-¸nīz, ᵗyü-\ *vb* **-ized; -iz·ing** : to make human or humane — **hu·man·i·za·tion** \¸hyü-mə-nə-ʰzā-shən, ¸yü-\ *n* — **hu·man·iz·er** *n*

**hu·man·kind** \ʰhyü-mən-¸kīnd, ᵗyü-\ *n* : the human race

**hu·man·oid** \ʰhyü-mə-¸nȯid, ᵗyü-\ *adj* : having human form or characteristics — **humanoid** *n*

**human pap·il·lo·ma·virus** \-¸pa-pə-ʰlō-mə-¸vī-rəs\ *n* : any of numerous DNA-containing viruses that cause various human warts

¹**hum·ble** \ʰhəm-bəl\ *adj* **hum·bler** \-bə-lər\; **hum·blest** \-bə-ləst\ [ME, fr. AF, fr. L *humilis* low, humble, fr. *humus* earth] **1** : not proud or haughty **2** : not pretentious : UNASSUMING **3** : INSIGNIFICANT

♦ *Synonyms* MEEK, MODEST, LOWLY — **hum·ble·ness** *n* — **hum·bly** *adv*

²**humble** *vb* **hum·bled; hum·bling** **1** : to make humble **2** : to destroy the power or prestige of — **hum·bler** *n*

¹**hum·bug** \ʰhəm-¸bəg\ *n* **1** : HOAX, FRAUD **2** : NONSENSE

²**humbug** *vb* **hum·bugged; hum·bug·ging** : DECEIVE

**hum·ding·er** \ʰhəm-ʰdiŋ-ər\ *n* : a person or thing of striking excellence

**hum·drum** \ʰhəm-¸drəm\ *adj* : MONOTONOUS, DULL — **humdrum** *n*

**hu·mer·us** \ʰhyü-mə-rəs\ *n, pl* **hu·meri** \ʰhyü-mə-¸rī, -¸rē\ : the long bone extending from shoulder to elbow

**hu·mid** \ʰhyü-məd, ᵗyü-\ *adj* : containing or characterized by perceptible moisture : DAMP — **hu·mid·ly** *adv*

**hu·mid·i·fy** \hyü-ʰmi-də-¸fī\ *vb* **-fied; -fy-**

ing : to make humid — **hu·mid·i·fi·ca·tion** \-,mi-də-fə-'ka-shən\ n — **hu·mid·i·fi·er** \-'mi-də-,fī-ər\ n

**hu·mid·i·ty** \hyü-'mi-də-tē, yü-\ n, pl **-ties** : the amount of atmospheric moisture

**hu·mi·dor** \'hyü-mə-,dòr, 'yü-\ n : a case (as for storing cigars) in which the air is kept properly humidified

**hu·mil·i·ate** \hyü-'mi-lē-,āt, yü-\ vb **-at·ed; -at·ing** : to injure the self-respect of : MORTIFY — **hu·mil·i·at·ing·ly** adv — **hu·mil·i·a·tion** \-,mi-lē-'ā-shən\ n

**hu·mil·i·ty** \hyü-'mi-lə-tē, yü-\ n : the quality or state of being humble

**hum·ming·bird** \'hə-miŋ-,bərd\ n : any of a family of tiny brightly colored American birds related to the swifts

**hum·mock** \'hə-mək\ n : a rounded mound : KNOLL — **hum·mocky** \-mə-kē\ adj

**hum·mus** \'hə-məs, 'hu-\ n [Ar ḥummuṣ chickpeas] : a paste of pureed chickpeas usu. mixed with sesame oil or paste

**hu·mon·gous** \hyü-'məŋ-gəs, -'mäŋ-\ adj [perh. alter. of huge + monstrous] : extremely large \a ~ stadium\

¹**hu·mor** \'hyü-mər, 'yü-\ n **1** : TEMPERAMENT **2** : MOOD **3** : WHIM **4** : a quality that appeals to a sense of the ludicrous or incongruous; also : a keen perception of the ludicrous or incongruous **5** : comical or amusing entertainment — **hu·mor·ist** \'hyü-mə-rist, 'yü-\ n — **hu·mor·less** \'hyü-mər-ləs, 'yü-\ adj — **hu·mor·less·ly** adv — **hu·mor·less·ness** n — **hu·mor·ous** \'hyü-mə-rəs, 'yü-\ adj — **hu·mor·ous·ly** adv — **hu·mor·ous·ness** n

²**humor** vb : to comply with the wishes or mood of \~ed his boss\

**hu·mour** chiefly Brit var of HUMOR

**hump** \'həmp\ n **1** : a rounded protuberance (as on the back of a camel) **2** : a difficult phase or obstacle \over the ~\ — **humped** adj

**hump·back** \'həmp-,bak; 1 also -'bak\ n **1** : HUNCHBACK **2** : HUMPBACK WHALE — **hump·backed** adj

**humpback whale** n : a large baleen whale having very long flippers

**hu·mus** \'hyü-məs, 'yü-\ n : the dark organic part of soil formed from decaying matter

**Hun** \'hən\ n : a member of an Asian people that invaded Europe about A.D. 450

¹**hunch** \'hənch\ vb **1** : to thrust oneself forward **2** : to assume or cause to assume a bent or crooked posture

²**hunch** n **1** : PUSH **2** : a strong intuitive feeling about what will happen

**hunch·back** \'hənch-,bak\ n : a person with a crooked back; also : a back with a hump — **hunch·backed** adj

**hun·dred** \'hən-drəd\ n, pl **hundreds** or **hundred** : 10 times 10 — **hundred** adj — **hun·dredth** \-drədth\ adj or n

**hun·dred·weight** \-,wāt\ n, pl **hundredweight** or **hundredweights** — see WEIGHT table

¹**hung** past and past part of HANG

²**hung** adj : unable to reach a decision or verdict \a ~ jury\

**Hung** abbr Hungarian; Hungary

**Hun·gar·i·an** \həŋ-'ger-ē-ən\ n **1** : a native or inhabitant of Hungary **2** : the language of the Hungarians — **Hungarian** adj

**hun·ger** \'həŋ-gər\ n **1** : a craving or urgent need for food **2** : a strong desire — **hunger** vb — **hun·gri·ly** adv — **hun·gry** adj

**hung·over** \'həŋ-'ō-vər\ adj : having a hangover

**hung up** adj **1** : DELAYED **2** : ENTHUSIASTIC; also : PREOCCUPIED — usu. used with on \hung up on winning\

**hunk** \'həŋk\ n **1** : a large piece **2** : an attractive well-built man — **hunky** adj

**hun·ker** \'həŋ-kər\ vb **1** : CROUCH, SQUAT usu. used with down **2** : to settle in for a sustained period — used with down

**hun·ky-do·ry** \,həŋ-kē-'dòr-ē\ adj : quite satisfactory : FINE

¹**hunt** \'hənt\ vb **1** : to pursue for food or in sport; also : to take part in a hunt **2** : to try to find : SEEK **3** : to drive or chase esp. by harrying **4** : to traverse in search of prey — **hunt·er** n

²**hunt** n : an act, practice, or instance of hunting

**Hun·ting·ton's disease** \'hən-tiŋ-tənz-\ n : a chorea that usu. begins in middle age and leads to dementia

**hunt·ress** \'hən-trəs\ n : a woman who hunts game

**hunts·man** \'hənts-mən\ n **1** : HUNTER **2** : a person who manages a hunt and looks after the hounds

**hur·dle** \'hər-dᵊl\ n **1** : a barrier to leap over in a race **2** : OBSTACLE — **hurdle** vb — **hur·dler** n

**hur·dy-gur·dy** \,hər-dē-'gər-dē, 'hər-dē-,gər-dē\ n, pl **-gur·dies** : a musical instrument in which the sound is produced by turning a crank

**hurl** \'hərl\ vb **1** : to move or cause to move vigorously **2** : to throw down with violence **3** : FLING; also : PITCH — **hurl** n — **hurl·er** n

**hur·ly-bur·ly** \,hər-lē-'bər-lē\ n : UPROAR, TUMULT

**Hu·ron** \'hyür-ən, 'hyür-,än\ n, pl **Hurons** or **Huron** : a member of a confederacy of American Indian peoples formerly living between Georgian Bay and Lake Ontario

**hur·rah** \hù-'rò, -'rä\ also **hur·ray** \hù-'rä\ interj — used to express joy, approval, or encouragement

**hur·ri·cane** \'hər-ə-,kān\ n [Sp huracán, of AmerInd origin] : a tropical cyclone with winds of 74 miles (118 kilometers) per hour or greater that is usu. accompanied by rain, thunder, and lightning

¹**hur·ry** \'hər-ē\ vb **hur·ried; hur·ry·ing** **1** : to carry or cause to go with haste **2** : to impel to a greater speed **3** : to move or act with haste — **hurried** adj — **hur·ried·ly** adv

²**hurry** n : extreme haste or eagerness

¹**hurt** \'hərt\ vb **hurt; hurt·ing** **1** : to feel or cause to feel physical or emotional pain **2** : to do harm to : DAMAGE **3** : OF-

FEND  4 : HAMPER  5 : to be in need — usu. used with *for* — **hurt** *adj*

²**hurt** *n*  1 : a bodily injury or wound  2 : SUFFERING  3 : HARM, WRONG — **hurt·ful** *adj* — **hurt·ful·ness** *n*

**hur·tle** \'hǝr-t³l\ *vb* **hur·tled; hur·tling**  1 : to move rapidly or forcefully  2 : HURL, FLING

¹**hus·band** \'hǝz-bǝnd\ *n* [ME *husbonde*, fr. OE *hūsbonda* master of a house, fr. ON *hūsbōndi*, fr. *hūs* house + *bōndi* householder] : a male partner in a marriage

²**husband** *vb* : to manage prudently

**hus·band·man** \'hǝz-bǝnd-mǝn\ *n* : FARMER

**hus·band·ry** \'hǝz-bǝn-drē\ *n*  1 : the control or judicious use of resources  2 : AGRICULTURE  3 : the production and care of domestic animals

¹**hush** \'hǝsh\ *vb*  1 : to make or become quiet or calm  2 : SUPPRESS

²**hush** *n* : SILENCE, QUIET

**hush–hush** \'hǝsh-,hǝsh\ *adj* : SECRET, CONFIDENTIAL

¹**husk** \'hǝsk\ *n*  1 : a usu. thin dry outer covering of a seed or fruit  2 : an outer layer : SHELL

²**husk** *vb* : to strip the husk from — **husk·er** *n*

¹**hus·ky** \'hǝs-kē\ *adj* **hus·ki·er; -est** : HOARSE — **hus·ki·ly** \-kǝ-lē\ *adv* — **hus·ki·ness** \-kē-nǝs\ *n*

²**husky** *n, pl* **huskies**  1 : a heavy-coated working dog of the New World Arctic  2 : SIBERIAN HUSKY

³**husky** *adj*  1 : BURLY, ROBUST  2 : LARGE

**hus·sar** \(,)hǝ-'zär\ *n* [Hung *huszár*] : a member of any of various European cavalry units

**hus·sy** \'hǝ-zē, -sē\ *n, pl* **hussies** [alter. of *housewife*]  1 : a lewd or brazen woman  2 : a pert or mischievous girl

**hus·tings** \'hǝs-tiŋz\ *n pl* : a place where political campaign speeches are made; *also* : the proceedings in an election campaign

**hus·tle** \'hǝ-sǝl\ *vb* **hus·tled; hus·tling**  1 : JOSTLE, SHOVE  2 : HASTEN, HURRY  3 : to work energetically — **hustle** *n* — **hus·tler** \'hǝs-lǝr\ *n*

**hut** \'hǝt\ *n* : a small and often temporary dwelling : SHACK

**hutch** \'hǝch\ *n*  1 : a chest or compartment for storage  2 : a cupboard usu. surmounted with open shelves  3 : a pen or coop for an animal  4 : HUT

**huz·zah** *or* **huz·za** \(,)hǝ-'zä\ *n* : a shout of acclaim — often used interjectionally to express joy or approbation

**HV** *abbr*  1 high velocity  2 high voltage

**HVAC** *abbr* heating, ventilating and air-conditioning

**hvy** *abbr* heavy

**HW** *abbr* hot water

**hwy** *abbr* highway

**hy·a·cinth** \'hī-ǝ-(,)sinth\ *n* : a bulbous Mediterranean herb related to the lilies that is widely grown for its spikes of fragrant bell-shaped flowers

**hy·brid** \'hī-brǝd\ *n*  1 : an offspring of genetically differing parents (as members

of different breeds or species)  2 : one of mixed origin or composition — **hybrid** *adj* — **hy·brid·i·za·tion** \,hī-brǝ-dǝ-'zā-shǝn\ *n* — **hy·brid·ize** \'hī-brǝ-,dīz\ *vb* — **hy·brid·iz·er** *n*

**hy·dra** \'hī-drǝ\ *n* : any of numerous small tubular freshwater coelenterates that are polyps having at one end a mouth surrounded by tentacles

**hy·dran·gea** \hī-'drān-jǝ\ *n* : any of a genus of shrubs related to the currants and grown for their showy clusters of white, pink, or bluish flowers

**hy·drant** \'hī-drǝnt\ *n* : a pipe with a valve and spout at which water may be drawn from a main pipe

**hy·drate** \'hī-,drāt\ *n* : a compound formed by union of water with some other substance — **hydrate** *vb*

**hy·drau·lic** \hī-'dró-lik\ *adj* [ultim. fr. Gk *hydraulis* pipe organ using water pressure, fr. *hydōr* water + *aulos* reed instrument]  1 : operated, moved, or effected by means of water  2 : of or relating to hydraulics  3 : operated by the resistance offered or the pressure transmitted when a quantity of liquid is forced through a small orifice or through a tube  4 : hardening or setting under water

**hy·drau·lics** \-liks\ *n* : a science that deals with practical applications of liquid (as water) in motion

**hydro** \'hī-drō\ *n* : HYDROPOWER

**hy·dro·car·bon** \'hī-drō-,kär-bǝn\ *n* : an organic compound containing only carbon and hydrogen

**hy·dro·ceph·a·lus** \,hī-drō-'se-fǝ-lǝs\ *n* : abnormal increase in the amount of fluid in the cranial cavity accompanied by enlargement of the skull and atrophy of the brain

**hy·dro·chlo·ric acid** \,hī-drǝ-'klór-ik-\ *n* : a sharp-smelling corrosive acid used in the laboratory and in industry and present in dilute form in gastric juice

**hy·dro·dy·nam·ics** \,hī-drō-dī-'na-miks\ *n* : a science that deals with the motion of fluids and the forces acting on moving bodies immersed in fluids — **hy·dro·dy·nam·ic** *adj*

**hy·dro·elec·tric** \,hī-drō-i-'lek-trik\ *adj* : of or relating to production of electricity by waterpower — **hy·dro·elec·tric·i·ty** \-,lek-'tri-sǝ-tē\ *n*

**hy·dro·foil** \'hī-drǝ-,fói(-ǝ)l\ *n* : a boat that has fins attached to the bottom by struts for lifting the hull clear of the water to allow faster speeds

**hy·dro·gen** \'hī-drǝ-jǝn\ *n* [F *hydrogène*, fr. Gk *hydōr* water + *-genēs* born; fr. the fact that water is generated by its combustion] : a gaseous colorless odorless highly flammable chemical element that is the lightest of the elements — **hy·drog·e·nous** \hī-'drä-jǝ-nǝs\ *adj*

**hy·dro·ge·nate** \hī-'drä-jǝ-,nāt, 'hī-drǝ-\ *vb* **-nat·ed; -nat·ing** : to combine or treat with hydrogen; *esp* : to add hydrogen to the molecule of — **hy·dro·ge·na·tion** \hī-,drä-jǝ-'nā-shǝn, ,hī-drǝ-\ *n*

**hydrogen bomb** *n* : a bomb whose violent explosive power is due to the sudden release of atomic energy resulting from the fusion of light nuclei (as of hydrogen atoms)

**hydrogen peroxide** *n* : an unstable compound of hydrogen and oxygen used esp. as an oxidizing and bleaching agent, an antiseptic, and a propellant

**hy·dro·graph·ic** \ˌhī-drə-ˈgra-fik\ *adj* : of or relating to the description and study of bodies of water — **hy·drog·ra·pher** *n* — **hy·drog·ra·phy** \hī-ˈdrä-grə-fē\ *n*

**hy·drol·o·gy** \hī-ˈdrä-lə-jē\ *n* : a science dealing with the properties, distribution, and circulation of water — **hy·dro·log·ic** \ˌhī-drə-ˈlä-jik\ *or* **hy·dro·log·i·cal** \-ji-kəl\ *adj* — **hy·drol·o·gist** \hī-ˈdrä-lə-jist\ *n*

**hy·dro·ly·sis** \hī-ˈdrä-lə-səs\ *n* : a chemical decomposition involving the addition of the elements of water

**hy·drom·e·ter** \hī-ˈdrä-mə-tər\ *n* : a floating instrument for determining specific gravities of liquids and hence the strength (as of alcoholic liquors)

**hy·dro·pho·bia** \ˌhī-drə-ˈfō-bē-ə\ *n* [LL, fr. Gk, fr. *hydōr* water + *phobos* fear] : RABIES

**hy·dro·phone** \ˈhī-drə-ˌfōn\ *n* : an underwater listening device

**¹hy·dro·plane** \ˈhī-drə-ˌplān\ *n* **1** : a powerboat designed for racing that skims the surface of the water **2** : SEAPLANE

**²hydroplane** *vb* : to skid on a wet road due to loss of contact between the tires and road

**hy·dro·pon·ics** \ˌhī-drə-ˈpä-niks\ *n* : the growing of plants in nutrient solutions — **hy·dro·pon·ic** *adj*

**hy·dro·pow·er** \ˈhī-drə-ˌpau̇(-ə)r\ *n* : hydroelectric power

**hy·dro·sphere** \ˈhī-drə-ˌsfir\ *n* : the water (as vapor or lakes) of the earth

**hy·dro·stat·ic** \ˌhī-drə-ˈsta-tik\ *adj* : of or relating to fluids at rest or to the pressures they exert or transmit

**hy·dro·ther·a·py** \ˌhī-drə-ˈther-ə-pē\ *n* : the use of water esp. externally in the treatment of disease or disability

**hy·dro·ther·mal** \ˌhī-drə-ˈthər-məl\ *adj* : of or relating to hot water

**hy·drous** \ˈhī-drəs\ *adj* : containing water

**hy·drox·ide** \hī-ˈdräk-ˌsīd\ *n* **1** : a negatively charged ion consisting of one atom of oxygen and one atom of hydrogen **2** : a compound of hydroxide with an element or group

**hy·e·na** \hī-ˈē-nə\ *n* [ME *hyene*, fr. L *hyaena*, fr. Gk *hyaina*, fr. *hys* hog] : any of several large doglike carnivorous mammals of Asia and Africa

**hy·giene** \ˈhī-ˌjēn\ *n* **1** : a science concerned with establishing and maintaining good health **2** : conditions or practices conducive to health — **hy·gien·ic** \hī-ˈje-nik, -ˈjē-\ *adj* — **hy·gien·i·cal·ly** \-ni-k(ə-)lē\ *adv* — **hy·gien·ist** \hī-ˈjē-nist, ˈhī-ˌjē-, hī-ˈje-\ *n*

**hy·grom·e·ter** \hī-ˈgrä-mə-tər\ *n* : any of several instruments for measuring the humidity of the atmosphere

**hy·gro·scop·ic** \ˌhī-grə-ˈskä-pik\ *adj* : readily taking up and retaining moisture

**hying** *pres part of* HIE

**hy·men** \ˈhī-mən\ *n* : a fold of mucous membrane partly closing the opening of the vagina

**hy·me·ne·al** \ˌhī-mə-ˈnē-əl\ *adj* : NUPTIAL

**hymn** \ˈhim\ *n* : a song of praise esp. to God — **hymn** *vb*

**hym·nal** \ˈhim-nəl\ *n* : a book of hymns

**hyp** *abbr* hypothesis; hypothetical

**¹hype** \ˈhīp\ *vb* **hyped**; **hyp·ing 1** : STIMULATE usu. used with *up* **2** : INCREASE — **hyped–up** *adj*

**²hype** *vb* **hyped**; **hyping 1** : DECEIVE **2** : PUBLICIZE

**³hype** *n* **1** : DECEPTION, PUT-ON **2** : PUBLICITY

**hy·per** \ˈhī-pər\ *adj* **1** : HIGH-STRUNG, EXCITABLE **2** : extremely active

**hy·per·acid·i·ty** \ˌhī-pər-ə-ˈsi-də-tē\ *n* : the condition of containing excessive acid esp. in the stomach — **hy·per·ac·id** \-ˈa-səd\ *adj*

**hy·per·ac·tive** \-ˈak-tiv\ *adj* : excessively or pathologically active — **hy·per·ac·tiv·i·ty** \-ˌak-ˈti-və-tē\ *n*

**hy·per·bar·ic** \ˌhī-pər-ˈber-ik\ *adj* : of, relating to, or utilizing greater than normal pressure

**hy·per·bo·la** \hī-ˈpər-bə-lə\ *n, pl* **-las** *or* **-lae** \-(ˌ)lē\ : a curve formed by the intersection of a double right circular cone with a plane that cuts both halves of the cone — **hy·per·bol·ic** \ˌhī-pər-ˈbä-lik\ *adj*

**hy·per·bo·le** \hī-ˈpər-bə-(ˌ)lē\ *n* : extravagant exaggeration used as a figure of speech

**hy·per·crit·i·cal** \ˌhī-pər-ˈkri-ti-kəl\ *adj* : excessively critical — **hy·per·crit·i·cal·ly** \-k(ə-)lē\ *adv*

**hy·per·drive** \ˈhī-pər-ˌdrīv\ *n* : a state of extremely heightened activity

**hy·per·ex·tend** \ˌhī-pər-ik-ˈstend\ *vb* : to extend beyond the normal range of motion — **hy·per·ex·ten·sion** \-ˈsten-shən\ *n*

**hy·per·gly·ce·mia** \ˌhī-pər-glī-ˈsē-mē-ə\ *n* : excess of sugar in the blood — **hy·per·gly·ce·mic** \-mik\ *adj*

**hy·per·ki·net·ic** \-kə-ˈne-tik\ *adj* : characterized by fast-paced or frenetic activity

**hy·per·link** \ˈhī-pər-ˌliŋk\ *n* : a connecting element (as highlighted text) between one place in a hypertext or hypermedia document and another

**hy·per·me·dia** \ˌhī-pər-ˈmē-dē-ə\ *n* : a database format offering direct access to text, sound, or images related to that on display

**hy·per·opia** \ˌhī-pə-ˈrō-pē-ə\ *n* : a condition in which visual images come to focus behind the retina resulting esp. in defective vision for near objects — **hy·per·opic** \-ˈrō-pik, -ˈrä-\ *adj*

**hy·per·sen·si·tive** \-ˈsen-sə-tiv\ *adj* **1** : excessively or abnormally sensitive **2** : abnormally susceptible physiologically to a specific agent (as a drug) — **hy·per·sen·si·tive·ness** *n* — **hy·per·sen·si·tiv·i·ty** \-ˌsen-sə-ˈti-və-tē\ *n*

**hy·per·ten·sion** \'hī-pər-‚ten-chən\ *n* : high blood pressure — **hy·per·ten·sive** \‚hī-pər-'ten-siv\ *adj or n*

**hy·per·text** \'hī-pər-‚tekst\ *n* : a database format in which information related to that on display can be accessed directly from the display

**hy·per·thy·roid·ism** \‚hī-pər-'thī-‚rȯi-‚di-zəm\ *n* : excessive activity of the thyroid gland; *also* : the resulting bodily condition — **hy·per·thy·roid** \-'thī-‚rȯid\ *adj*

**hy·per·tro·phy** \hī-'pər-trə-fē\ *n, pl* **-phies** : excessive development of a body part — **hy·per·tro·phic** \‚hī-pər-'trō-fik\ *adj* — **hypertrophy** *vb*

**hy·per·ven·ti·late** \‚hī-pər-'ven-tə-‚lāt\ *vb* : to breathe rapidly and deeply esp. to the point of losing an abnormal amount of carbon dioxide from the blood — **hy·per·ven·ti·la·tion** \-‚ven-tə-'lā-shən\ *n*

**hy·phen** \'hī-fən\ *n* : a punctuation mark - used esp. to divide or to compound words or word parts — **hyphen** *vb*

**hy·phen·ate** \'hī-fə-‚nāt\ *vb* **-at·ed; -at·ing** : to connect or divide with a hyphen — **hy·phen·ation** \‚hī-fə-'nā-shən\ *n*

**hyp·no·sis** \hip-'nō-səs\ *n, pl* **-no·ses** \-‚sēz\ : an induced state that resembles sleep and in which the subject is responsive to suggestions of the inducer (**hyp·no·tist** \'hip-nə-tist\) — **hyp·no·tism** \'hip-nə-‚ti-zəm\ *n* — **hyp·no·tiz·able** \'hip-nə-‚tī-zə-bəl\ *adj* — **hyp·no·tize** \-‚tīz\ *vb*

¹**hyp·not·ic** \hip-'nä-tik\ *adj* **1** : inducing sleep : SOPORIFIC  **2** : of or relating to hypnosis or hypnotism  **3** : readily holding the attention — **hyp·not·i·cal·ly** \-ti-k(ə-)lē\ *adv*

²**hypnotic** *n* : a sleep-inducing drug

**hy·po** \'hī-pō\ *n, pl* **hypos** : SODIUM THIOSULFATE; *also* : a solution of sodium thiosulfate

**hy·po·al·ler·gen·ic** \‚hī-pō-‚a-lər-'je-nik\ *adj* : having little likelihood of causing an allergic response

**hy·po·cen·ter** \'hī-pə-‚sen-tər\ *n* : the point of origin of an earthquake

**hy·po·chon·dria** \‚hī-pə-'kän-drē-ə\ *n* [NL, fr. LL, pl., upper abdomen (formerly regarded as the seat of hypochondria), fr. Gk, lit., the parts under the cartilage (of the breastbone), fr. *hypo-* under + *chondros* cartilage] : depression of mind often centered on imaginary physical ailments — **hy·po·chon·dri·ac** \-drē-‚ak\ *adj or n*

**hy·poc·ri·sy** \hi-'pä-krə-sē\ *n, pl* **-sies** : a

feigning to be what one is not or to believe what one does not; *esp* : the false assumption of an appearance of virtue or religion — **hyp·o·crite** \'hi-pə-‚krit\ *n* — **hyp·o·crit·i·cal** \‚hi-pə-'kri-ti-kəl\ *adj* — **hyp·o·crit·i·cal·ly** \-k(ə-)lē\ *adv*

¹**hy·po·der·mic** \‚hī-pə-'dər-mik\ *adj* : administered by or used in making an injection beneath the skin

²**hypodermic** *n* : HYPODERMIC SYRINGE; *also* : an injection made with this

**hypodermic needle** *n* : NEEDLE 3; *also* : HYPODERMIC SYRINGE

**hypodermic syringe** *n* : a small syringe with a hollow needle for injecting material into or through the skin

**hy·po·gly·ce·mia** \‚hī-pō-glī-'sē-mē-ə\ *n* : abnormal decrease of sugar in the blood — **hy·po·gly·ce·mic** \-mik\ *adj*

**hy·pot·e·nuse** \hī-'pä-tə-‚nüs, -‚nyüs, -‚nüz, -‚nyüz\ *n* : the side of a right triangle that is opposite the right angle; *also* : its length

**hy·po·thal·a·mus** \‚hī-pō-'tha-lə-məs\ *n* : a part of the brain that lies beneath the thalamus and is a control center for the autonomic nervous system

**hy·poth·e·sis** \hī-'pä-thə-səs\ *n, pl* **-e·ses** \-‚sēz\ : an assumption made esp. in order to test its logical or empirical consequences — **hy·po·thet·i·cal** \‚hī-pə-'the-ti-kəl\ *adj* — **hy·po·thet·i·cal·ly** \-k(ə-)lē\ *adv*

**hy·poth·e·size** \-‚sīz\ *vb* **-sized; -siz·ing** : to adopt as a hypothesis

**hy·po·thy·roid·ism** \‚hī-pō-'thī-‚rȯi-‚di-zəm\ *n* : deficient activity of the thyroid gland; *also* : a resultant lowered metabolic rate and general loss of vigor — **hy·po·thy·roid** *adj*

**hys·sop** \'hi-səp\ *n* : a European mint sometimes used as a potherb

**hys·ter·ec·to·my** \‚his-tə-'rek-tə-mē\ *n, pl* **-mies** : surgical removal of the uterus

**hys·te·ria** \hi-'ster-ē-ə, -'stir-\ *n* [NL, fr. E *hysteric*, adj., fr. L *hystericus*, fr. Gk *hysterikos*, fr. *hystera* womb; fr. the Greek notion that hysteria was peculiar to women and caused by disturbances in the uterus]  **1** : a nervous disorder marked esp. by defective emotional control  **2** : unmanageable fear or outburst of emotion — **hys·ter·ic** \-'ster-ik\ *n* — **hys·ter·i·cal** \-'ster-i-kəl\ *also* **hysteric** *adj* — **hys·ter·i·cal·ly** \-k(ə-)lē\ *adv*

**hys·ter·ics** \-'ster-iks\ *n pl* : a fit of uncontrollable laughter or crying

**Hz** *abbr* hertz

**¹i** \'ī\ *n, pl* **i's** *or* **is** \'īz\ *often cap* : the 9th letter of the English alphabet
**²i** *abbr, often cap* island; isle
**³i** *symbol* imaginary unit
**¹I** \'ī, ə\ *pron* : the one speaking or writing
**²I** *abbr* interstate
**³I** *symbol* iodine
**Ia** *or* **IA** *abbr* Iowa
**-ial** *adj suffix* : -AL ⟨manor*ial*⟩
**iamb** \'ī-,am *or* **iam·bus** \ī-'am-bəs\ *n, pl* **iambs** \'ī-,amz\ *or* **iam·bus·es** : a metrical foot of one unaccented syllable followed by one accented syllable — **iam·bic** \ī-'am-bik\ *adj or n*
**-ian** — see -AN
**-iatric** *also* **-iatrical** *adj comb form* : of or relating to (such) medical treatment or healing ⟨pedi*atric*⟩
**-iatrics** *n pl comb form* : medical treatment ⟨pedi*atrics*⟩
**ib** *or* **ibid** *abbr* ibidem
**ibex** \'ī-,beks\ *n, pl* **ibex** *or* **ibex·es** [L] : any of several Old World wild goats with large curved horns
**ibi·dem** \'i-bə-,dem, i-'bī-dəm\ *adv* [L] : in the same place
**-ibility** — see -ABLE
**ibis** \'ī-bəs\ *n, pl* **ibis** *or* **ibis·es** [L, fr. Gk, fr. Egypt *hbw*] : any of various wading birds related to the herons but having a downwardly curved bill
**-ible** — see -ABLE
**ibu·pro·fen** \ī-byü-'prō-fən\ *n* : a nonsteroidal anti-inflammatory drug used to relieve pain and fever
**IC** \ī-'sē\ *n* : INTEGRATED CIRCUIT
**¹-ic** *adj suffix* **1** : of, relating to, or having the form of : being ⟨panoram*ic*⟩ **2** : related to, derived from, or containing ⟨alcohol*ic*⟩ **3** : in the manner of : like that of : characteristic of **4** : associated or dealing with : utilizing ⟨electron*ic*⟩ **5** : characterized by : exhibiting ⟨nostalg*ic*⟩ **6** : affected with ⟨allerg*ic*⟩ **7** : caused by ⟨analges*ic*⟩ : tending to produce ⟨analges*ic*⟩
**²-ic** *n suffix* : one having the character or nature of : one belonging to or associated with : one exhibiting or affected by : one that produces
**-ical** *adj suffix* : -IC ⟨symmetr*ical*⟩ ⟨geolog*ical*⟩ — **-ically** *adv suffix*
**ICBM** \ī-,sē-(,)bē-'em\ *n, pl* **ICBM's** *or* **ICBMs** \-'emz\ : an intercontinental ballistic missile
**ICC** *abbr* Interstate Commerce Commission
**¹ice** \'īs\ *n* **1** : frozen water **2** : a substance resembling ice **3** : a state of coldness (as from formality or reserve) **4** : a flavored frozen dessert; *esp* : one containing no milk or cream
**²ice** *vb* **iced; ic·ing 1** : FREEZE **2** : CHILL **3** : to cover with or as if with icing
**ice age** *n* : a time of widespread glaciation

**ice bag** *n* : a waterproof bag to hold ice for local application of cold to the body
**ice·berg** \'īs-,bərg\ *n* : a large floating mass of ice broken off from a glacier
**iceberg lettuce** *n* : any of various crisp light green lettuces that form a compact head like a cabbage
**ice·boat** \'īs-,bōt\ *n* : a boatlike frame on runners propelled on ice by sails
**ice·bound** \-,baùnd\ *adj* : surrounded, obstructed, or covered by ice
**ice·box** \-,bäks\ *n* : REFRIGERATOR
**ice·break·er** \-,brā kər\ *n* : a ship equipped (as with a reinforced bow) to make a channel through ice
**ice cap** *n* : a glacier forming on relatively level land and flowing outward from its center
**ice cream** *n* : a frozen food containing sweetened or flavored cream or butterfat
**ice hockey** *n* : a game in which two teams of ice-skating players try to shoot a puck into the opponent's goal
**ice·house** \'īs-,haùs\ *n* : a building in which ice is made or stored
**¹Ice·lan·dic** \īs-'lan-dik\ *adj* : of, relating to, or characteristic of Iceland, the Icelanders, or their language
**²Icelandic** *n* : the language of Iceland
**ice·man** \'īs-,man\ *n* : one who sells or delivers ice
**ice milk** *n* : a sweetened frozen food made of skim milk
**ice pick** *n* : a hand tool ending in a spike for chipping ice
**ice·skate** \'īs-,skāt\ *vb* : to skate on ice — **ice–skater** *n*
**ice storm** *n* : a storm in which falling rain freezes on contact
**ice water** *n* : chilled or iced water esp. for drinking
**ich·thy·ol·o·gy** \ik-thē-'ä-lə-jē\ *n* : a branch of zoology dealing with fishes — **ich·thy·ol·o·gist** \-jist\ *n*
**ici·cle** \'ī-,sī-kəl\ *n* [ME *isikel*, fr. *is* ice + *ikel* icicle, fr. OE *gicel*] : a hanging mass of ice formed by the freezing of dripping water
**ic·ing** \'ī-siŋ\ *n* : a sweet usu. creamy mixture used to coat baked goods
**ICJ** *abbr* International Court of Justice
**icky** \'i-kē\ *adj* **ick·i·er; -est** : OFFENSIVE, DISTASTEFUL — **ick·i·ness** *n*
**icon** *also* **ikon** \'ī-,kän\ *n* **1** : IMAGE; *esp* : a religious image painted on a wood panel **2** : a small picture on a computer display that suggests the purpose of an available function — **icon·ic** \ī-'kä-nik\ *adj*
**icon·o·clasm** \ī-'kä-nə-,kla-zəm\ *n* : the doctrine, practice, or attitude of an iconoclast
**icon·o·clast** \-,klast\ *n* [ML *iconoclastes*, fr. MGk *eikonoklastēs*, lit., image destroyer, fr. Gk *eikōn* image + *klan* to

break] **1** : one who destroys religious images or opposes their veneration **2** : one who attacks cherished beliefs or institutions

**-ics** \iks\ *n sing or pl suffix* **1** : study : knowledge : skill : practice ⟨linguist*ics*⟩ ⟨electron*ics*⟩ **2** : characteristic actions or activities ⟨acrobat*ics*⟩ **3** : characteristic qualities, operations, or phenomena ⟨mechan*ics*⟩

**ic·tus** \'ik-təs\ *n* : the recurring stress or beat in a rhythmic or metrical series of sounds

**ICU** *abbr* intensive care unit

**icy** \'ī-sē\ *adj* **ic·i·er; -est** **1** : covered with, abounding in, or consisting of ice **2** : intensely cold **3** : being cold and unfriendly — **ic·i·ly** \'ī-sə-lē\ *adv* — **ic·i·ness** \-sē-nəs\ *n*

¹**id** \'id\ *n* [L, it] : the part of the psyche in psychoanalytic theory that is completely unconscious and concerned with instinctual needs and drives

²**id** *abbr* idem

¹**ID** \'ī-'dē\ *n* : a document with identifying information about an individual whose name appears on it

²**ID** *vb* **ID'd** *or* **IDed; ID'ing** *or* **IDing** : IDENTIFY

³**ID** *abbr* **1** Idaho **2** identification

**idea** \ī-'dē-ə\ *n* **1** : a plan for action : DESIGN **2** : something imagined or pictured in the mind **3** : a central meaning or purpose ♦ **Synonyms** CONCEPT, CONCEPTION, NOTION, IMPRESSION

¹**ide·al** \ī-'dēl\ *adj* **1** : existing only in the mind : IMAGINARY; *also* : lacking practicality **2** : of or relating to an ideal or to perfection : PERFECT

²**ideal** *n* **1** : a standard of excellence **2** : one regarded as a model worthy of imitation **3** : GOAL ♦ **Synonyms** ARCHETYPE, EXAMPLE, EXEMPLAR, PARADIGM, PATTERN

**ide·al·ise** *Brit var of* IDEALIZE

**ide·al·ism** \ī-'dē-ə-ˌli-zəm\ *n* : the practice of forming ideals or living under their influence; *also* : an idealized representation — **ide·al·ist** \-list\ *n* — **ide·al·is·tic** \ī-ˌdē-ə-'lis-tik\ *adj* — **ide·al·is·ti·cal·ly** \-ti-k(ə-)lē\ *adv*

**ide·al·ize** \ī-'dē-ə-ˌlīz\ *vb* **-ized; -iz·ing** : to think of or represent as ideal — **ide·al·i·za·tion** \-ˌdē-ə-lə-'zā-shən\ *n*

**ide·al·ly** \ī-'dē-lē, -'dē-ə-lē\ *adv* **1** : in idea or imagination : MENTALLY **2** : in agreement with an ideal : PERFECTLY

**ide·a·tion** \ˌī-dē-'ā-shən\ *n* : the forming or entertaining of ideas — **ide·ate** \'ī-dē-ˌāt\ *vb* — **ide·a·tion·al** \ˌī-dē-'ā-shə-nəl\ *adj*

**idem** \'ī-ˌdem, 'ē-, 'i-\ *pron* [L, same] : the same as something previously mentioned

**iden·ti·cal** \ī-'den-ti-kəl\ *adj* **1** : being the same **2** : essentially alike ♦ **Synonyms** EQUIVALENT, EQUAL, TANTAMOUNT

**iden·ti·fi·ca·tion** \ī-ˌden-tə-fə-'kā-shən\ *n* **1** : an act of identifying : the state of being identified **2** : evidence of identity **3** : an unconscious psychological process by which an individual models thoughts,

feelings, and actions after another person or an object

**iden·ti·fy** \ī-'den-tə-ˌfī\ *vb* **-fied; -fy·ing 1** : to regard as identical **2** : ASSOCIATE : to establish the identity of **4** : to practice psychological identification — **iden·ti·fi·able** \-ˌden-tə-'fī-ə-bəl\ *adj* — **iden·ti·fi·ably** \-blē\ *adv* — **iden·ti·fi·er** \-ˌfī(-ə)r\ *n*

**iden·ti·ty** \ī-'den-tə-tē\ *n, pl* **-ties 1** : sameness of essential character **2** : INDIVIDUALITY **3** : the fact of being the same person or thing as claimed

**identity crisis** *n* : psychological conflict esp. in adolescence involving confusion about one's social role and one's personality

**identity theft** *n* : the illegal use of someone else's personal information to obtain money or credit

**ideo·gram** \'ī-dē-ə-ˌgram, 'i-\ *n* **1** : a picture or symbol used in a system of writing to represent a thing or an idea **2** : a character or symbol used in a system of writing to represent an entire word

**ideo·logue** *also* **idea·logue** \'ī-dē-ə-ˌlȯg\ *n* : a partisan advocate or adherent of a particular ideology

**ide·ol·o·gy** \ˌī-dē-'ä-lə-jē, ˌi-\ *also* **ide·al·o·gy** \-'ä-lə-jē, -'a-\ *n, pl* **-gies 1** : the body of ideas characteristic of a particular individual, group, or culture **2** : the assertions, theories, and aims that constitute a political, social, and economic program — **ide·o·log·i·cal** \ˌī-dē-ə-'lä-ji-kəl, ˌi-\ *adj* — **ideo·log·i·cal·ly** \-'lä-ji-k(ə-)lē\ *adv* — **ide·ol·o·gist** \-dē-'ä-lə-jist\ *n*

**ides** \'īdz\ *n sing or pl* : the 15th day of March, May, July, or October or the 13th day of any other month in the ancient Roman calendar

**id·i·o·cy** \'i-dē-ə-sē\ *n, pl* **-cies 1** *usu offensive* : extreme mental retardation **2** : something notably stupid or foolish

**id·i·om** \'i-dē-əm\ *n* **1** : the language peculiar to a person or group **2** : the characteristic form or structure of a language **3** : an expression that cannot be understood from the meanings of its separate words (as *give way*) — **id·i·o·mat·ic** \ˌi-dē-ə-'ma-tik\ *adj* — **id·i·o·mat·i·cal·ly** \-ti-k(ə-)lē\ *adv*

**id·i·o·path·ic** \ˌi-dē-ə-'pa-thik\ *adj* : arising spontaneously or from an obscure or unknown cause ⟨an ~ disease⟩

**id·i·o·syn·cra·sy** \ˌi-dē-ə-'siŋ-krə-sē\ *n, pl* **-sies** : personal peculiarity — **id·i·o·syn·crat·ic** \ˌi-dē-ō-sin-'kra-tik\ *adj* — **id·i·o·syn·crat·i·cal·ly** \-'kra-ti-k(ə-)lē\ *adv*

**id·i·ot** \'i-dē-ət\ *n* [ME, fr. AF *ydiote*, fr. L *idiota* ignorant person, fr. Gk *idiōtēs* one in a private station, layman, ignorant person, fr. *idios* one's own, private] **1** *usu offensive* : a person affected with idiocy **2** : a foolish or stupid person — **id·i·ot·ic** \ˌi-dē-'ä-tik\ *adj* — **id·i·ot·i·cal·ly** \-ti-k(ə-)lē\ *adv*

**id·i·ot-proof** \'i-dē-ət-ˌprüf\ *adj* : extremely easy to operate or maintain

¹**idle** \'ī-dᵊl\ *adj* **idler** \'ī-də-lər\; **idlest** \'ī-də-ləst\ **1** : GROUNDLESS, WORTHLESS, USELESS ⟨~ talk⟩ **2** : not occupied or

employed : INACTIVE **3** : LAZY — **idle-ness** n — **idly** \'īd-lē\ adv

²**idle** vb **idled; idling 1** : to spend time doing nothing **2** : to make idle **3** : to run without being connected so that power is not used for useful work — **idler** n

**idol** \'ī-dᵊl\ n **1** : an image worshipped as a god; also : a false god **2** : an object of passionate devotion ⟨a sports ∼⟩

**idol·a·ter** or **idol·a·tor** \ī-'dä-lə-tər\ n : a worshiper of idols

**idol·a·try** \-trē\ n, pl **-tries 1** : the worship of a physical object as a god **2** : excessive devotion — **idol·a·trous** \-trəs\ adj

**idol·ize** \'ī-də-ˌlīz\ vb **-ized; -iz·ing** : to make an idol of ⟨idolized his father⟩ — **idol·i·za·tion** \ˌī-də-lə-'zā-shən\ n

**idyll** \'ī-dᵊl\ n **1** : a simple work of writing or poetry that describes country life or suggests a peaceful setting **2** : a fit subject for an idyll — **idyl·lic** \ī-'di-lik\ adj

**i.e.** \'ī-'ē\ abbr [L id est] that is

**IE** abbr industrial engineer

**IED** abbr improvised explosive device

**-ier** — see -ER

**if** \'if\ conj **1** : in the event that ⟨∼ he stays, I leave⟩ **2** : WHETHER ⟨ask ∼ he left⟩ **3** — used as a function word to introduce an exclamation expressing a wish ⟨∼ it would only rain⟩ **4** : even though ⟨an interesting ∼ untenable argument⟩ **5** : and perhaps not even ⟨few ∼ any changes are expected⟩

**IF** abbr intermediate frequency

**if·fy** \'i-fē\ adj : full of contingencies or unknown conditions

**-i·fy** \ə-ˌfī\ vb suffix : -FY

**IG** abbr inspector general

**ig·loo** \'i-glü\ n, pl **igloos** [Inuit (an Eskimo language) iglu house] : an Eskimo house or hut often made of snow blocks and in the shape of a dome

**ig·ne·ous** \'ig-nē-əs\ adj **1** : FIERY **2** : formed by solidification of molten rock

**ig·nite** \ig-'nīt\ vb **ig·nit·ed; ig·nit·ing** : to set afire or catch fire — **ig·nit·able** \-'nī-tə-bəl\ adj

**ig·ni·tion** \ig-'ni-shən\ n **1** : a setting on fire **2** : the process or means (as an electric spark) of igniting the fuel mixture in an engine **3** : a device that activates an ignition system

**ig·no·ble** \ig-'nō-bəl\ adj **1** : of common birth **2** : not honorable : BASE, MEAN ♦ **Synonyms** DESPICABLE, SCURVY, SORDID, VILE, WRETCHED — **ig·no·bly** adv

**ig·no·min·i·ous** \ˌig-nə-'mi-nē-əs\ adj **1** : DISHONORABLE **2** : DESPICABLE **3** : HUMILIATING, DEGRADING ♦ **Synonyms** DISREPUTABLE, DISCREDITABLE, DISGRACEFUL, INGLORIOUS — **ig·no·min·i·ous·ly** adv — **ig·no·mi·ny** \'ig-nə-ˌmi-nē, ig-'nä-mə-nē\ n

**ig·no·ra·mus** \ˌig-nə-'rā-məs\ n, pl **-mus·es** also **-mi** \-mē\ [Ignoramus, ignorant lawyer in Ignoramus (1615), play by George Ruggle] : an utterly ignorant person

**ig·no·rance** \'ig-nə-rəns\ n : the state of being ignorant

**ig·no·rant** \'ig-nə-rənt\ adj **1** : lacking knowledge **2** : resulting from or showing lack of knowledge or intelligence **3** : UNAWARE, UNINFORMED ♦ **Synonyms** BENIGHTED, ILLITERATE, UNEDUCATED, UNLETTERED, UNTUTORED — **ig·no·rant·ly** adv

**ig·nore** \ig-'nȯr\ vb **ig·nored; ig·nor·ing** : to refuse to take notice of ♦ **Synonyms** OVERLOOK, SLIGHT, NEGLECT

**igua·na** \i-'gwä-nə\ n : any of various large tropical American lizards

**ihp** abbr indicated horsepower

**IHS** \ˌī-ˌāch-'es\ [LL, part transliteration of Gk IHΣ, abbr. for IHΣΟΥΣ Iēsous Jesus] — used as a Christian symbol and monogram for Jesus

**ikon** var of ICON

**IL** abbr Illinois

**il·e·itis** \ˌi-lē-'ī-təs\ n : inflammation of the ileum

**il·e·um** \'i-lē-əm\ n, pl **il·ea** \-lē-ə\ : the part of the small intestine between the jejunum and the large intestine

**il·i·ac** \'i-lē-ˌak\ adj : of, relating to, or located near the ilium

**il·i·um** \'i-lē-əm\ n, pl **il·ia** \-lē-ə\ : the uppermost and largest of the three bones making up either side of the pelvis

**ilk** \'ilk\ n : SORT, KIND

¹**ill** \'il\ adj **worse** \'wərs\; **worst** \'wərst\ **1** : attended or caused by an evil intent ⟨∼ deeds⟩ **2** : not normal or sound ⟨∼ health⟩; also : not in good health : SICK **3** : BAD, UNLUCKY ⟨an ∼ omen⟩ **4** : not right or proper ⟨∼ manners⟩ **5** : UNFRIENDLY, HOSTILE ⟨∼ feeling⟩

²**ill** adv **worse; worst 1** : with displeasure **2** : in a harsh manner **3** : HARDLY, SCARCELY ⟨can ∼ afford it⟩ **4** : BADLY, UNLUCKILY **5** : in a faulty way

³**ill** n **1** : EVIL **2** : MISFORTUNE, DISTRESS **3** : AILMENT, SICKNESS; also : TROUBLE

⁴**ill** abbr illustrated; illustration; illustrator

**Ill** abbr Illinois

**ill-ad·vised** \ˌil-əd-'vīzd\ adj : not well counseled ⟨∼ efforts⟩ — **ill-ad·vis·ed·ly** \-'vī-zəd-lē\ adv

**ill-bred** \-'bred\ adj : badly brought up : IMPOLITE ⟨an ∼ child⟩

**il·le·gal** \il-'lē-gəl\ adj : not lawful; also : not sanctioned by official rules ♦ **Synonyms** UNLAWFUL, CRIMINAL, ILLEGITIMATE, ILLICIT, WRONGFUL — **il·le·gal·i·ty** \ˌil-li-'ga-lə-tē\ n — **il·le·gal·ly** adv

**il·leg·i·ble** \il-'le-jə-bəl\ adj : not legible — **il·leg·i·bil·i·ty** \il-ˌle-jə-'bi-lə-tē\ n — **il·leg·i·bly** \il-'le-jə-blē\ adv

**il·le·git·i·mate** \ˌi-li-'ji-tə-mət\ adj **1** : born of unmarried parents **2** : ILLOGICAL **3** : ILLEGAL — **il·le·git·i·ma·cy** \-'ji-tə-mə-sē\ n — **il·le·git·i·mate·ly** adv

**ill-fat·ed** \'il-'fā-təd\ adj : UNFORTUNATE ⟨an ∼ expedition⟩

**ill-fa·vored** \-'fā-vərd\ adj : UGLY, UNATTRACTIVE

**ill-got·ten** \-'gä-tᵊn\ adj : acquired by improper means ⟨∼ gains⟩

**ill-hu·mored** \-'hyü-mərd, -'yü-\ adj : SURLY, IRRITABLE

**il·lib·er·al** \il-'li-bə-rəl\ adj : not liberal : NARROW, BIGOTED il·lic·it \il-'li-sət\ adj : not permitted : UNLAWFUL — il·lic·it·ly adv

il·lim·it·able \il-'li-mə-tə-bəl\ adj : BOUNDLESS, MEASURELESS — il·lim·it·ably \-blē\ adv

Il·li·nois \ˌi-lə-'nȯi also -'nȯiz\ n, pl Illinois : a member of an American Indian people of Illinois, Iowa, and Wisconsin

il·lit·er·ate \il-'li-tə-rət\ adj 1 : having little or no education; esp : unable to read or write 2 : showing a lack of familiarity with the fundamentals of a particular field of knowledge — il·lit·er·a·cy \-'li-tə-rə-sē\ n — illiterate n

ill–man·nered \ˈil-'ma-nərd\ adj : marked by bad manners : RUDE

ill–na·tured \-'nā-chərd\ adj : CROSS, SURLY — ill–na·tured·ly adv

ill·ness \'il-nəs\ n : SICKNESS

il·log·i·cal \il-'lä-ji-kəl\ adj : lacking sound reasoning; also : SENSELESS — il·log·i·cal·ly \-k(ə)-lē\ adv

ill–starred \'il-'stärd\ adj : UNLUCKY 1 ⟨an ~ venture⟩

ill–tem·pered \-'tem-pərd\ adj : CROSS

ill–treat \-'trēt\ vb : to treat cruelly or improperly : MALTREAT — ill–treat·ment n

il·lu·mi·nate \i-'lü-mə-ˌnāt\ vb -nat·ed; -nat·ing 1 : to supply or brighten with light : light up 2 : to make clear : ELUCIDATE; also : to bring to the fore 3 : to decorate (as a manuscript) with designs or pictures in gold or colors — il·lu·mi·nat·ing·ly adv — il·lu·mi·na·tion \-ˌlü-mə-'nā-shən\ n — il·lu·mi·na·tor \-'lü-mə-ˌnā-tər\ n

il·lu·mine \i-'lü-mən\ vb -mined; -mining : ILLUMINATE

ill–us·age \'il-'yü-sij\ n : harsh, unkind, or abusive treatment

ill–use \-'yüz\ vb : MALTREAT, ABUSE

il·lu·sion \i-'lü-zhən\ n [ME, fr. AF, fr. LL illusio, fr. L, action of mocking, fr. illudere to mock at, fr. ludere to play, mock] 1 : a mistaken idea : MISCONCEPTION 2 : a misleading visual image; also : HALLUCINATION

il·lu·sion·ist \i-'lü-zhə-nist\ n : one that produces illusions; esp : a sleight-of-hand performer

il·lu·sive \i-'lü-siv\ adj : DECEPTIVE

il·lu·so·ry \i-'lü-sə-rē, -zə-\ adj : DECEPTIVE ⟨~ hopes⟩

illust or illus abbr illustrated; illustration

il·lus·trate \'i-ləs-ˌtrāt\ vb -trat·ed; -trating [L illustrare, fr. lustrare to purify, make bright] 1 : to explain by use of examples; also : DEMONSTRATE 2 : to provide with pictures or figures that explain or decorate 3 : to serve to explain or decorate — il·lus·tra·tor \'i-ləs-ˌtrā-tər\ n

il·lus·tra·tion \ˌi-ləs-'trā-shən\ n 1 : the act of illustrating : the condition of being illustrated 2 : an example or instance that helps make something clear 3 : a picture or diagram that explains or decorates

il·lus·tra·tive \i-'ləs-trə-tiv, 'i-lə-ˌstrā-\ adj : serving, tending, or designed to illustrate — il·lus·tra·tive·ly adv

il·lus·tri·ous \i-'ləs-trē-əs\ adj : notably outstanding because of rank or achievement ♦ Synonyms DISTINGUISHED, EMINENT, FAMOUS, GREAT, NOTABLE, PROMINENT — il·lus·tri·ous·ness n

ill will n : unfriendly feeling

ILS abbr instrument landing system

¹im·age \'i-mij\ n 1 : a likeness or imitation of a person or thing; esp : STATUE 2 : a picture of an object formed by a device (as a mirror or lens) 3 : a visual representation of something ⟨a computer ~⟩ 4 : a person strikingly like another person ⟨he is the ~ of his father⟩ 5 : a mental picture or conception : IMPRESSION, IDEA, CONCEPT 6 : a vivid representation or description

²image vb im·aged; im·ag·ing 1 : to call up a mental picture of 2 : to describe or portray in words 3 : to create a representation of 4 : REFLECT, MIRROR 5 : to make appear : PROJECT

im·ag·ery \'i-mij-rē\ n, pl -er·ies 1 : IMAGES; also : the art of making images 2 : figurative language 3 : mental images; esp : the products of imagination

imag·in·able \i-'ma-jə-nə-bəl\ adj : capable of being imagined : CONCEIVABLE — imag·in·ably adv

imag·i·nary \i-'ma-jə-ˌner-ē\ adj 1 : existing only in the imagination 2 : containing or relating to a quantity (imaginary unit) that is the positive square root of minus 1 (√-1)

imaginary number n : a complex number (as 2 + 3i) with a nonzero term (imaginary part) containing the imaginary unit as a factor

imag·i·na·tion \i-ˌma-jə-'nā-shən\ n 1 : the act or power of forming a mental image of something not present to the senses or not previously known or experienced 2 : creative ability 3 : RESOURCEFULNESS 4 : a mental image : a creation of the mind — imag·i·na·tive \i-'ma-jə-nə-tiv, -ˌnā-\ adj — imag·i·na·tive·ly adv

imag·ine \i-'ma-jən\ vb imag·ined; imag·in·ing 1 : to form a mental picture of something not present 2 : THINK, GUESS ⟨I ~ it will rain⟩

imag·in·ings \-'maj-niŋz, -'ma-jə-\ n pl : products of the imagination

im·ag·ism \'i-mi-ji-zəm\ n, often cap : a movement in poetry advocating free verse and the expression of ideas and emotions through clear precise images — im·ag·ist \-jist\ n

ima·go \i-'mā-gō, -'mä-\ n, pl imagoes or ima·gi·nes \-'mä-gə-ˌnēz, -'mä-\ [NL, fr. L, image] : an insect in its final adult stage — ima·gi·nal \i-'mā-gə-nᵊl, -'mä-\ adj

im·bal·ance \'im-'ba-ləns\ n : lack of balance : the state of being out of equilibrium or out of proportion

im·be·cile \'im-bə-səl, -ˌsil\ n 1 usu offensive : a person affected with moderate mental retardation 2 : FOOL, IDIOT — imbecile or im·be·cil·ic \ˌim-bə-'si-lik\ adj — im·be·cil·i·ty \ˌim-bə-'si-lə-tē\ n

imbed var of EMBED

im·bibe \im-'bīb\ vb im·bibed; im·bib-

**ing 1** : to receive and retain in the mind **2** : to drink alcoholic beverages **3** : to take in or up : ABSORB — **im·bib·er** n

**im·bri·ca·tion** \,im-brə-'kā-shən\ n **1** : an overlapping of edges (as of tiles) **2** : a pattern showing imbrication — **im·bri·cate** \'im-bri-kət\ adj

**im·bro·glio** \im-'brōl-yō\ n, pl **-glios** [It, fr. imbrogliare to entangle] **1** : a confused mass **2** : a complicated situation; also : a serious or embarrassing misunderstanding

**im·brue** \im-'brü\ vb **im·brued; im·bru·ing** : STAIN ⟨hands imbrued with blood⟩

**im·bue** \-'byü\ vb **im·bued; im·bu·ing 1** : to permeate or influence as if by dyeing **2** : to tinge or dye deeply

**IMF** abbr International Monetary Fund

**imit** abbr imitative

**im·i·ta·ble** \'i-mə-tə-bəl\ adj : capable or worthy of being imitated or copied

**im·i·tate** \'i-mə-,tāt\ vb **-tat·ed; -tat·ing 1** : to follow as a model : COPY **2** : RESEMBLE **3** : REPRODUCE **4** : MIMIC, COUNTERFEIT — **im·i·ta·tor** \-,tā-tər\ n

**im·i·ta·tion** \,i-mə-'tā-shən\ n **1** : an act of imitating **2** : COPY, COUNTERFEIT **3** : a literary work that reproduces the style of another author — **imitation** adj

**im·i·ta·tive** \'i-mə-,tā-tiv\ adj **1** : marked by imitation **2** : inclined to imitate **3** : COUNTERFEIT

**im·mac·u·late** \i-'ma-kyə-lət\ adj **1** : being without stain or blemish : PURE **2** : spotlessly clean ⟨~ linen⟩ — **im·mac·u·late·ly** adv

**im·ma·nent** \'i-mə-nənt\ adj **1** INHERENT **2** : being within the limits of experience or knowledge — **im·ma·nence** \-nəns\ n — **im·ma·nen·cy** \-nən-sē\ n

**im·ma·te·ri·al** \,i-mə-'tir-ē-əl\ adj **1** : not consisting of matter : SPIRITUAL **2** : UNIMPORTANT, TRIFLING   ♦ **Synonyms** BODILESS, DISEMBODIED, INCORPOREAL, INSUBSTANTIAL, NONPHYSICAL — **im·ma·te·ri·al·i·ty** \-,tir-ē-'a-lə-tē\ n

**im·ma·ture** \,i-mə-'tůr, -'tyůr\ adj : lacking complete development : not yet mature ⟨~ behavior⟩ — **im·ma·tu·ri·ty** \-'tůr-ə-tē, -'tyůr-\ n

**im·mea·sur·able** \(,)i-'me-zhə-rə-bəl\ adj : not capable of being measured : indefinitely extensive : ILLIMITABLE — **im·mea·sur·ably** \-blē\ adv

**im·me·di·a·cy** \i-'mē-dē-ə-sē\ n, pl **-cies 1** : the quality or state of being immediate **2** : something that is of immediate importance

**im·me·di·ate** \i-'mē-dē-ət\ adj **1** : acting directly and alone : DIRECT ⟨the ~ cause of death⟩ **2** : being next in line or relation ⟨members of the ~ family⟩ **3** : not distant : CLOSE **4** : made or done at once ⟨an ~ response⟩ **5** : near to or related to the present time ⟨the ~ future⟩ — **im·me·di·ate·ly** adv

**im·me·mo·ri·al** \,i-mə-'mȯr-ē-əl\ adj : extending beyond the reach of memory, record, or tradition ⟨from time ~⟩

**im·mense** \i-'mens\ adj [ME, fr. MF, fr. L immensus immeasurable, fr. mensus, pp. of metiri to measure] **1** : very great in

size or degree : VAST, HUGE **2** : EXCELLENT — **im·mense·ly** adv — **im·men·si·ty** \-'men-sə-tē\ n

**im·merse** \i-'mərs\ vb **im·mersed; im·mers·ing 1** : to plunge or dip esp. into a fluid **2** : ENGROSS, ABSORB **3** : to baptize by immersing — **im·mer·sion** \-'mər-zhən\ n

**im·mi·grant** \'i-mi-grənt\ n **1** : a person who immigrates **2** : a plant or animal that becomes established where it did not previously occur

**im·mi·grate** \'i-mə-,grāt\ vb **-grat·ed; -grat·ing** : to come into a foreign country and take up residence — **im·mi·gra·tion** \,i-mə-'grā-shən\ n

**im·mi·nent** \'i-mə-nənt\ adj : ready to take place; esp : hanging threateningly over one's head ⟨in ~ danger⟩ — **im·mi·nence** \-nəns\ n — **im·mi·nent·ly** adv

**im·mis·ci·ble** \(,)i-'mi-sə-bəl\ adj : incapable of mixing — **im·mis·ci·bil·i·ty** \-,mi-sə-'bi-lə-tē\ n

**im·mis·er·a·tion** \(,)i-,mi-zə-'rā-shən\ n : IMPOVERISHMENT

**im·mo·bile** \(,)i-'mō-bəl\ adj : incapable of being moved : FIXED — **im·mo·bil·i·ty** \,i-mō-'bi-lə-tē\ n

**im·mo·bi·lize** \i-'mō-bə-,līz\ vb : to make immobile — **im·mo·bi·li·za·tion** \i-,mō-bə-lə-'zā-shən\ n

**im·mod·er·ate** \(,)i-'mä-də-rət\ adj : lacking in moderation : EXCESSIVE ⟨~ drinking⟩ — **im·mod·er·a·cy** \-rə-sē\ n — **im·mod·er·ate·ly** adv

**im·mod·est** \(,)i-'mä-dəst\ adj : not modest : BRAZEN, INDECENT ⟨an ~ dress⟩ ⟨~ conduct⟩ — **im·mod·est·ly** adv — **im·mod·es·ty** \-də-stē\ n

**im·mo·late** \'i-mə-,lāt\ vb **-lat·ed; -lat·ing** [L immolare, to sprinkle with meal before sacrificing, sacrifice, fr. mola sacrificial barley cake, lit., millstone] : to offer in sacrifice; esp : to kill as a sacrificial victim — **im·mo·la·tion** \,i-mə-'lā-shən\ n

**im·mor·al** \(,)i-'mȯr-əl\ adj : not moral — **im·mor·al·ly** adv

**im·mo·ral·i·ty** \,i-mȯ-'ra-lə-tē, ,i-mə-\ n **1** : WICKEDNESS; esp : UNCHASTITY **2** : an immoral act or practice

¹**im·mor·tal** \(,)i-'mȯr-t⁷l\ adj **1** : not mortal : exempt from death ⟨~ gods⟩ **2** : destined to be remembered forever ⟨those ~ words⟩ — **im·mor·tal·ly** adv

²**immortal** n **1** : one exempt from death **2** pl, often cap : the gods in Greek and Roman mythology **3** : a person whose fame is lasting ⟨an ~ of baseball⟩

**im·mor·tal·ise** Brit var of IMMORTALIZE

**im·mor·tal·i·ty** \,i-mȯr-'ta-lə-tē\ n : the quality or state of being immortal; esp : unending existence

**im·mor·tal·ize** \i-'mȯr-tə-,līz\ vb **-ized; -iz·ing** : to make immortal

**im·mov·able** \(,)i-'mü-və-bəl\ adj **1** : firmly fixed, settled, or fastened : FAST, STATIONARY ⟨~ mountains⟩ **2** : STEADFAST, UNYIELDING **3** : IMPASSIVE — **im·mov·abil·i·ty** \i-,mü-və-'bi-lə-tē\ n — **im·mov·ably** \-blē\ adv

**im·mune** \i-'myün\ adj **1** : EXEMPT **2** : having a special capacity for resistance (as to a disease) **3** : containing or producing antibodies — **im·mu·ni·ty** \-'myü-nə-tē\ n

**immune response** n : a response of the body to an antigen resulting in the formation of antibodies and cells designed to react with the antigen and render it harmless

**immune system** n : the bodily system that protects the body from foreign substances, cells, and tissues by producing the immune response and that includes esp. the thymus, spleen, lymph nodes, and lymphocytes

**im·mu·nize** \'i-myə-ˌnīz\ vb **-nized; -niz·ing** : to make immune — **im·mu·ni·za·tion** \ˌi-myə-nə-'zā-shən\ n

**im·mu·no·de·fi·cien·cy** \ˌi-myə-nō-di-'fi-shən-sē\ n : inability to produce the normal number of antibodies or immunologically sensitized cells esp. in response to specific antigens — **im·mu·no·de·fi·cient** \-'fi-shənt\ adj

**im·mu·no·glob·u·lin** \ˌi-myə-nō-'glä-byə-lən\ n : ANTIBODY

**im·mu·nol·o·gy** \ˌi-myə-'nä-lə-jē\ n : a science that deals with the immune system, immunity, and the immune response — **im·mu·no·log·ic** \-nə-'lä-jik\ or **im·mu·no·log·i·cal** \-ji-kəl\ adj — **im·mu·no·log·i·cal·ly** \-ji-k(ə-)lē\ adv — **im·mu·nol·o·gist** \-'nä-lə-jist\ n

**im·mu·no·sup·pres·sion** \ˌi-myə-nō-sə-'pre-shən\ n : suppression (as by drugs) of natural immune responses — **im·mu·no·sup·press** \-'pres\ vb — **im·mu·no·sup·pres·sant** \-'pre-sⁿnt\ n or adj — **im·mu·no·sup·pres·sive** \-'pre-siv\ adj

**im·mu·no·ther·a·py** \-'ther-ə-pē\ n : the treatment or prevention of disease by attempting to induce immunity

**im·mure** \i-'myùr\ vb **im·mured; im·mur·ing 1** : to enclose within or as if within walls **2** : to build into a wall; esp : to entomb in a wall

**im·mu·ta·ble** \(ˌ)i-'myü-tə-bəl\ adj : UNCHANGEABLE, UNCHANGING — **im·mu·ta·bil·i·ty** \-ˌmyü-tə-'bi-lə-tē\ n — **im·mu·ta·bly** \-'myü-tə-blē\ adv

**¹imp** \'imp\ n **1** : a small demon : FIEND **2** : a mischievous child

**²imp** abbr **1** imperative **2** imperfect **3** imperial **4** import; imported

**¹im·pact** \im-'pakt\ vb **1** : to press together **2** : to have an impact on

**²im·pact** \'im-ˌpakt\ n **1** : a forceful contact, collision, or onset; also : the impetus communicated in or as if in a collision **2** : EFFECT

**im·pact·ed** \im-'pak-təd\ adj **1** : packed or wedged in **2** : wedged between the jawbone and another tooth

**im·pair** \im-'per\ vb : to diminish in quantity, value, excellence, or strength : DAMAGE, LESSEN — **im·pair·ment** n

**im·paired** \-'perd\ adj : being in a less than perfect or whole condition; esp : disabled or functionally defective — often used in combination ⟨hearing-impaired⟩

**im·pa·la** \im-'pa-lə\ n, pl impalas or impala : a large brownish African antelope

that in the male has slender curved horns with ridges

**im·pale** \im-'pāl\ vb **im·paled; im·pal·ing** : to pierce with or as if with something pointed — **im·pale·ment** n

**im·pal·pa·ble** \(ˌ)im-'pal-pə-bəl\ adj **1** : unable to be felt by touch : INTANGIBLE **2** : not easily seen or understood — **im·pal·pa·bly** \-blē\ adv

**im·pan·el** or **em·pan·el** \im-'pan-ᵊl\ vb : to enter in or on a panel : ENROLL ⟨~ a jury⟩

**im·part** \im-'pärt\ vb **1** : to give from one's store or abundance ⟨the sun ~s warmth⟩ **2** : to make known

**im·par·tial** \(ˌ)im-'pär-shəl\ adj : not partial : UNBIASED, JUST — **im·par·tial·i·ty** \-ˌpär-shē-'a-lə-tē\ n — **im·par·tial·ly** adv

**im·pass·able** \(ˌ)im-'pa-sə-bəl\ adj : incapable of being passed, traversed, or crossed ⟨~ roads⟩ — **im·pass·ably** \-blē\ adv

**im·passe** \'im-ˌpas\ n **1** : a predicament from which there is no obvious escape **2** : an impassable road or way

**im·pas·si·ble** \(ˌ)im-'pa-sə-bəl\ adj : incapable of feeling : IMPASSIVE

**im·pas·sioned** \im-'pa-shənd\ adj : filled with passion or zeal : showing great warmth or intensity of feeling ♦ **Synonyms** PASSIONATE, ARDENT, FERVENT, FERVID

**im·pas·sive** \(ˌ)im-'pa-siv\ adj : showing no signs of feeling, emotion, or interest : EXPRESSIONLESS, INDIFFERENT ♦ **Synonyms** STOIC, PHLEGMATIC, APATHETIC, STOLID — **im·pas·sive·ly** adv — **im·pas·siv·i·ty** \ˌim-ˌpa-'si-və-tē\ n

**im·pas·to** \im-'pas-tō, -'päs-\ n : the thick application of a pigment to a canvas or panel in painting; also : the body of pigment so applied

**im·pa·tiens** \im-'pā-shənz, -shəns\ n : any of a genus of herbs with usu. spurred flowers and seed capsules that readily split open

**im·pa·tient** \(ˌ)im-'pā-shənt\ adj **1** : not patient : restless or short of temper esp. under irritation, delay, or opposition **2** : INTOLERANT ⟨~ of poverty⟩ **3** : prompted or marked by impatience ⟨an ~ reply⟩ **4** : ANXIOUS — **im·pa·tience** \-shəns\ n — **im·pa·tient·ly** adv

**im·peach** \im-'pēch\ vb [ME empechen to accuse, fr. AF empecher, enpechier to ensnare, impede, prosecute, fr. LL impedicare to fetter, fr. L pedica fetter, fr. ped-, pes foot] **1** : to charge (a public official) before an authorized tribunal with misconduct in office **2** : to challenge the credibility or validity of **3** : to remove from public office for misconduct — **im·peach·ment** n

**im·pec·ca·ble** \(ˌ)im-'pe-kə-bəl\ adj **1** : not capable of sinning or wrongdoing **2** : FAULTLESS, IRREPROACHABLE ⟨a man of ~ character⟩ — **im·pec·ca·bil·i·ty** \-ˌpe-kə-'bi-lə-tē\ n — **im·pec·ca·bly** \-'pe-kə-blē\ adv

**im·pe·cu·nious** \ˌim-pi-'kyü-nyəs, -nē-əs\ adj : having little or no money — **im·pe·cu·nious·ness** n

**im·ped·ance** \im-'pē-dᵊns\ n : the opposition in an electrical circuit to the flow of an alternating current

**im·pede** \im-'pēd\ vb **im·ped·ed; im·ped·ing** [L *impedīre*, fr. *ped-, pes* foot] : to interfere with the progress of

**im·ped·i·ment** \im-'pe-də-mənt\ n **1** : something that impedes, hinders, or obstructs **2** : a speech defect

**im·ped·i·men·ta** \im-,pe-də-'men-tə\ n pl : things that impede

**im·pel** \im-'pel\ vb **im·pelled; im·pel·ling** : to urge or drive forward or on : FORCE; *also* : PROPEL

**im·pel·ler** *also* **im·pel·lor** \im-'pe-lər\ n : a rotor esp. in a pump

**im·pend** \im-'pend\ vb **1** : to hover or hang over threateningly : MENACE **2** : to be about to occur

**im·pen·e·tra·ble** \(,)im-'pe-nə-trə-bəl\ adj **1** : incapable of being penetrated or pierced ⟨an ∼ jungle⟩ **2** : incapable of being comprehended : INSCRUTABLE ⟨an ∼ mystery⟩ — **im·pen·e·tra·bil·i·ty** \-,pe-nə-trə-'bi-lə-tē\ n — **im·pen·e·tra·bly** \-'pe-nə-trə-blē\ adv

**im·pen·i·tent** \(,)im-'pe-nə-tənt\ adj : not penitent : not repenting of sin — **im·pen·i·tence** \-təns\ n

**im·per·a·tive** \im-'per-ə-tiv\ adj **1** : expressing a command, request, or encouragement ⟨∼ sentence⟩ **2** : having power to restrain, control, or direct **3** : NECESSARY ⟨an ∼ duty⟩ — **imperative** n — **im·per·a·tive·ly** adv

**im·per·cep·ti·ble** \,im-pər-'sep-tə-bəl\ adj : not perceptible; *esp* : too slight to be perceived ⟨∼ changes⟩ — **im·per·cep·ti·bly** \-blē\ adv

**im·per·cep·tive** \,im-pər-'sep-tiv\ adj : not perceptive ⟨an ∼ reader⟩

**imperf** *abbr* imperfect

**¹im·per·fect** \(,)im-'pər-fikt\ adj **1** : not perfect : DEFECTIVE, INCOMPLETE **2** : of, relating to, or being a verb tense used to designate a continuing state or an incomplete action esp. in the past — **im·per·fect·ly** adv

**²imperfect** n : the imperfect tense; *also* : a verb form in it

**im·per·fec·tion** \,im-pər-'fek-shən\ n : the quality or state of being imperfect; *also* : FAULT, BLEMISH

**im·pe·ri·al** \im-'pir-ē-əl\ adj **1** : of, relating to, or befitting an empire or an emperor; *also* : of or relating to the United Kingdom or to the Commonwealth or British Empire **2** : ROYAL, SOVEREIGN; *also* : REGAL, IMPERIOUS **3** : of unusual size or excellence

**im·pe·ri·al·ism** \im-'pir-ē-ə-,li-zəm\ n : the policy of seeking to extend the power, dominion, or territories of a nation — **im·pe·ri·al·ist** \-list\ n or adj — **im·pe·ri·al·is·tic** \-,pir-ē-ə-'lis-tik\ adj — **im·pe·ri·al·is·ti·cal·ly** \-ti-k(ə-)lē\ adv

**im·per·il** \im-'per-əl\ vb **-iled** *or* **-illed; -il·ing** *or* **-il·ling** : ENDANGER

**im·pe·ri·ous** \im-'pir-ē-əs\ adj **1** : COMMANDING, LORDLY **2** : ARROGANT, DOMINEERING **3** : IMPERATIVE, URGENT ⟨∼ problems⟩ — **im·pe·ri·ous·ly** adv

**im·per·ish·able** \(,)im-'per-i-shə-bəl\ adj : not perishable or subject to decay

**im·per·ma·nent** \(,)im-'pər-mə-nənt\ adj : not permanent : TRANSIENT — **im·per·ma·nent·ly** adv

**im·per·me·able** \(,)im-'pər-mē-ə-bəl\ adj : not permitting passage (as of a fluid) through its substance

**im·per·mis·si·ble** \,im-pər-'mi-sə-bəl\ adj : not permissible ⟨∼ by law⟩

**im·per·son·al** \(,)im-'pər-sə-nəl\ adj **1** : not referring to any particular person or thing **2** : not involving human emotions — **im·per·son·al·i·ty** \-,pər-sə-'na-lə-tē\ n — **im·per·son·al·ly** adv

**im·per·son·ate** \im-'pər-sə-,nāt\ vb **-at·ed; -at·ing** : to assume or act the character of — **im·per·son·a·tion** \-,pər-sə-'nā-shən\ n — **im·per·son·a·tor** \-'pər-sə-,nā-tər\ n

**im·per·ti·nent** \(,)im-'pər-tə-nənt\ adj **1** : IRRELEVANT **2** : not restrained within due or proper bounds : RUDE, INSOLENT, SAUCY ⟨an ∼ reply⟩ — **im·per·ti·nence** \-nəns\ n — **im·per·ti·nent·ly** adv

**im·per·turb·able** \,im-pər-'tər-bə-bəl\ adj : marked by extreme calm, impassivity, and steadiness : SERENE

**im·per·vi·ous** \(,)im-'pər-vē-əs\ adj **1** : incapable of being penetrated (as by moisture) **2** : not capable of being affected or disturbed ⟨∼ to criticism⟩

**im·pe·ti·go** \,im-pə-'tē-gō, -'tī-\ n : a contagious skin disease characterized by vesicles, pustules, and yellowish crusts

**im·pet·u·ous** \im-'pe-chə-wəs\ adj **1** : marked by impulsive vehemence ⟨∼ temper⟩ **2** : marked by force and violence ⟨with ∼ speed⟩ — **im·pet·u·os·i·ty** \(,)im-,pe-chə-'wä-sə-tē\ n — **im·pet·u·ous·ly** adv

**im·pe·tus** \'im-pə-təs\ n [L, assault, impetus, fr. *impetere* to attack, fr. *petere* to go to, seek] **1** : a driving force : IMPULSE; *also* : INCENTIVE **2** : MOMENTUM

**im·pi·e·ty** \(,)im-'pī-ə-tē\ n, pl **-ties** **1** : the quality or state of being impious **2** : an impious act

**im·pinge** \im-'pinj\ vb **im·pinged; im·ping·ing** **1** : to strike or dash esp. with a sharp collision **2** : ENCROACH, INFRINGE — **im·pinge·ment** n

**im·pi·ous** \'im-pē-əs, (,)im-'pī-\ adj : not pious : IRREVERENT, PROFANE

**imp·ish** \'im-pish\ adj : of, relating to, or befitting an imp; *esp* : MISCHIEVOUS — **imp·ish·ly** adv — **imp·ish·ness** n

**im·pla·ca·ble** \(,)im-'pla-kə-bəl, -'plā-\ adj : not capable of being appeased, pacified, mitigated, or changed ⟨an ∼ enemy⟩ — **im·pla·ca·bil·i·ty** \-,pla-kə-'bi-lə-tē, -,plā-\ n — **im·pla·ca·bly** \-'pla-kə-blē\ adv

**im·plant** \im-'plant\ vb **1** : to set firmly or deeply **2** : to fix in the mind or spirit **3** : to insert in living tissue (as for growth or absorption) — **im·plant** \'im-,plant\ n — **im·plan·ta·tion** \,im-,plan-'tā-shən\ n

**im·plau·si·ble** \(,)im-'plȯ-zə-bəl\ adj : not plausible — **im·plau·si·bil·i·ty** \-,plȯ-zə-bi-lə-tē\ n — **im·plau·si·bly** \-'plȯ-zə-blē\ adv

**im·ple·ment** \'im-plə-mənt\ n [ME, fr. AF, fr. ML *implementum* item making a full complement, appurtenance, tool, fr. LL, act of filling up, fr. L *implēre* to fill up] : TOOL, UTENSIL, INSTRUMENT

²**im·ple·ment** \-ˌment\ vb 1 : CARRY OUT; *esp* : to put into practice ⟨~ a plan⟩ 2 : to provide implements for — **im·ple·men·ta·tion** \ˌim-plə-mən-'tā-shən\ n

**im·pli·cate** \'im-plə-ˌkāt\ vb -cat·ed; -cat·ing 1 : IMPLY 2 : INVOLVE — **im·pli·ca·tion** \ˌim-plə-'kā-shən\ n

**im·plic·it** \im-'pli-sət\ adj 1 : understood though not directly stated or expressed : IMPLIED; *also* : POTENTIAL 2 : COMPLETE, UNQUESTIONING, ABSOLUTE ⟨~ faith⟩ — **im·plic·it·ly** adv

**im·plode** \im-'plōd\ vb im·plod·ed; im·plod·ing 1 : to burst or collapse inward 2 : SELF-DESTRUCT — **im·plo·sion** \-'plō-zhən\ n — **im·plo·sive** \-siv\ adj

**im·plore** \im-'plȯr\ vb im·plored; im·plor·ing : BESEECH, ENTREAT ⟨*implored* him not to go⟩ ♦ *Synonyms* SUPPLICATE, BEG, IMPORTUNE, PLEAD

**im·ply** \im-'plī\ vb im·plied; im·ply·ing 1 : to involve or indicate by inference, association, or necessary consequence rather than by direct statement ⟨war *implies* fighting⟩ 2 : to express indirectly : hint at : SUGGEST

**im·po·lite** \ˌim-pə-'līt\ adj : not polite : RUDE, DISCOURTEOUS

**im·pol·i·tic** \(ˌ)im-'pä-lə-ˌtik\ adj : not politic : UNWISE

**im·pon·der·a·ble** \(ˌ)im-'pän-də-rə-bəl\ adj : incapable of being weighed or evaluated with exactness — **imponderable** n

¹**im·port** \im-'pȯrt\ vb 1 : MEAN, SIGNIFY 2 : to bring (as merchandise) into a place or country from a foreign or external source — **im·port·er** n

²**im·port** \'im-ˌpȯrt\ n 1 : IMPORTANCE, SIGNIFICANCE 2 : MEANING, SIGNIFICATION 3 : something (as merchandise) brought in from another country

**im·por·tance** \im-'pȯr-t°ns\ n : the quality or state of being important : MOMENT, SIGNIFICANCE ♦ *Synonyms* CONSEQUENCE, IMPORT, WEIGHT

**im·por·tant** \im-'pȯr-t°nt\ adj 1 : marked by importance : SIGNIFICANT 2 : giving an impression of importance — **im·por·tant·ly** adv

**im·por·ta·tion** \ˌim-ˌpȯr-'tā-shən, -pər-\ n 1 : the act or practice of importing 2 : something imported

**im·por·tu·nate** \im-'pȯr-chə-nət\ adj 1 : troublesomely urgent or persistent 2 : BURDENSOME, TROUBLESOME

**im·por·tune** \ˌim-pər-'tün, -'tyün; im-'pȯr-chən\ vb -tuned; -tun·ing : to urge or beg with troublesome persistence — **im·por·tu·ni·ty** \-pər-'tü-nə-tē, -'tyü-\ n

**im·pose** \im-'pōz\ vb im·posed; im·pos·ing 1 : to establish or apply by authority ⟨~ a tax⟩; *also* : to establish by force ⟨*imposed* a government⟩ 2 : OBTRUDE ⟨*imposed* herself on others⟩ 3 : to take unwarranted advantage of something ⟨~ on her good nature⟩ — **im·po·si·tion** \ˌim-pə-'zi-shən\ n

**im·pos·ing** adj : impressive because of size, bearing, dignity, or grandeur — **im·pos·ing·ly** adv

**im·pos·si·ble** \(ˌ)im-'pä-sə-bəl\ adj 1 : incapable of being or of occurring 2 : enormously difficult 3 : extremely undesirable : UNACCEPTABLE — **im·pos·si·bil·i·ty** \-ˌpä-sə-'bi-lə-tē\ n — **im·pos·si·bly** \-'pä-sə-blē\ adv

¹**im·post** \'im-ˌpōst\ n : TAX, DUTY

²**impost** n : a block, capital, or molding from which an arch springs

**im·pos·tor** or **im·pos·ter** \im-'päs-tər\ n : one that assumes an identity or title not one's own in order to deceive

**im·pos·ture** \im-'päs-chər\ n : DECEPTION; *esp* : fraudulent impersonation

**im·po·tent** \'im-pə-tənt\ adj 1 : lacking in power or strength : HELPLESS 2 : unable to copulate; *also* : STERILE — **im·po·tence** \-təns\ n — **im·po·ten·cy** \-tən-sē\ n — **im·po·tent·ly** adv

**im·pound** \im-'paûnd\ vb 1 : CONFINE, ENCLOSE ⟨~ stray dogs⟩ 2 : to seize and hold in legal custody 3 : to collect in a reservoir ⟨~ water⟩ — **im·pound·ment** n

**im·pov·er·ish** \im-'pä-və-rish\ vb : to make poor; *also* : to deprive of strength, richness, or fertility — **im·pov·er·ish·ment** n

**im·prac·ti·ca·ble** \(ˌ)im-'prak-ti-kə-bəl\ adj : not practicable : incapable of being put into practice or use ⟨an ~ plan⟩

**im·prac·ti·cal** \(ˌ)im-'prak-ti-kəl\ adj 1 : not practical 2 : IMPRACTICABLE

**im·pre·cate** \'im-pri-ˌkāt\ vb -cat·ed; -cat·ing : CURSE — **im·pre·ca·tion** \ˌim-pri-'kā-shən\ n

**im·pre·cise** \ˌim-pri-'sīs\ adj : not precise — **im·pre·cise·ly** adv — **im·pre·cise·ness** n — **im·pre·ci·sion** \-'si-zhən\ n

**im·preg·na·ble** \im-'preg-nə-bəl\ adj : incapable of being taken by assault : UNCONQUERABLE, UNASSAILABLE — **im·preg·na·bil·i·ty** \(ˌ)im-ˌpreg-nə-'bi-lə-tē\ n

**im·preg·nate** \im-'preg-ˌnāt\ vb -nat·ed; -nat·ing 1 : to fertilize or make pregnant 2 : to cause to be filled, permeated, or saturated — **im·preg·na·tion** \ˌim-ˌpreg-'nā-shən\ n

**im·pre·sa·rio** \ˌim-prə-'sär-ē-ˌō\ n, pl -ri·os [it, fr. *impresa* undertaking, fr. *imprendere* to undertake] 1 : the manager or conductor of an opera or concert company 2 : one who puts on an entertainment 3 : MANAGER, PRODUCER

¹**im·press** \im-'pres\ vb 1 : to apply with or produce (as a mark) by pressure : IMPRINT 2 : to press, stamp, or print in or upon 3 : to produce a vivid impression of 4 : to affect esp. forcibly or deeply — **im·press·ible** adj

²**im·press** \'im-ˌpres\ n 1 : a characteristic or distinctive mark 2 : IMPRESSION, EFFECT 3 : an impression or image of something formed by or as if by pressure; *also* : a product of pressure or influence

³**im·press** \im-'pres\ vb 1 : to force into naval service 2 : to get the aid or services

of by forcible argument or persuasion —
**im·press·ment** *n*

**im·pres·sion** \im-ˈpre-shən\ *n* 1 : a characteristic trait or feature resulting from influence : IMPRESS 2 : a stamp, form, or figure made by impressing : IMPRINT 3 : an esp. marked influence or effect on feeling, sense, or mind 4 : a single print or copy (as from type or from an engraved plate or book) 5 : all the copies of a publication (as a book) printed for one issue : PRINTING 6 : a usu. vague notion or remembrance 7 : an imitation in caricature of a noted personality as a form of entertainment

**im·pres·sion·able** \im-ˈpre-shə-nə-bəl\ *adj* : capable of being easily impressed : easily molded or influenced

**im·pres·sion·ism** \im-ˈpre-shə-ˌni-zəm\ *n, often cap* : a theory or practice in modern art of depicting the natural appearances of objects by dabs or strokes of primary unmixed colors in order to simulate actual reflected light — **im·pres·sion·is·tic** \-ˌpre-shə-ˈnis-tik\ *adj*

**im·pres·sion·ist** \im-ˈpre-shə-nist\ *n* 1 *often cap* : a painter who practices impressionism 2 : an entertainer who does impressions

**im·pres·sive** \im-ˈpre-siv\ *adj* : making or tending to make a marked impression ⟨an ~ speech⟩ — **im·pres·sive·ly** *adv* — **im·pres·sive·ness** *n*

**im·pri·ma·tur** \ˌim-prə-ˈmä-ˌtùr\ *n* [NL, let it be printed] 1 : a license to print or publish; *also* : official approval of a publication by a censor 2 : SANCTION, APPROVAL

¹**im·print** \im-ˈprint, ˈim-ˌprint\ *vb* 1 : to stamp or mark by or as if by pressure : IMPRESS 2 : to fix firmly (as on the memory)

²**im·print** \ˈim-ˌprint\ *n* 1 : something imprinted or printed 2 : a publisher's name printed at the foot of a title page 3 : an indelible distinguishing effect or influence ⟨put her ~ on the company⟩

**im·pris·on** \im-ˈpri-zᵊn\ *vb* : to put in or as if in prison : CONFINE — **im·pris·on·ment** *n*

**im·prob·a·ble** \(ˌ)im-ˈprä-bə-bəl\ *adj* : unlikely to be true or to occur — **im·prob·a·bil·i·ty** \-ˌprä-bə-ˈbi-lə-tē\ *n* — **im·prob·a·bly** \-ˈprä-bə-blē\ *adv*

**im·promp·tu** \im-ˈprämp-tü, -ˌtyü\ *adj* [F, fr. *impromptu* extemporaneously, fr. L *in promptu* in readiness] 1 : made or done on or as if on the spur of the moment 2 : EXTEMPORANEOUS, UNREHEARSED ⟨an ~ speech⟩ — **impromptu** *adv or n*

**im·prop·er** \(ˌ)im-ˈprä-pər\ *adj* 1 : not proper, fit, or suitable 2 : INCORRECT, INACCURATE 3 : not in accord with propriety, modesty, or good manners — **im·prop·er·ly** *adv*

**improper fraction** *n* : a fraction whose numerator is equal to or larger than the denominator

**im·pro·pri·e·ty** \ˌim-prə-ˈprī-ə-tē\ *n, pl* **-ties** 1 : an improper act or remark; *esp* : an unacceptable use of a word or of language 2 : the quality or state of being improper

**im·prov** \ˈim-ˌpräv\ *adj* : of, relating to, or being an improvised comedy routine — **improv** *n*

**im·prove** \im-ˈprüv\ *vb* **im·proved; im·prov·ing** 1 : to enhance or increase in value or quality 2 : to grow or become better ⟨your work is *improving*⟩ 3 : to make good use of ⟨~ the time by reading⟩ — **im·prov·able** \-ˈprü-və-bəl\ *adj*

**im·prove·ment** \im-ˈprüv-mənt\ *n* 1 : the act or process of improving 2 : increased value or excellence of something 3 : something that adds to the value or appearance of a thing

**im·prov·i·dent** \(ˌ)im-ˈprä-və-dənt\ *adj* : not providing for the future — **im·prov·i·dence** \-dəns\ *n*

**im·pro·vise** \ˈim-prə-ˌvīz\ *vb* **-vised; -vis·ing** [F *improviser*, fr. It *improvvisare*, fr. *improvviso* sudden, fr. L *improvisus*, lit., unforeseen] 1 : to compose, recite, play, or sing on the spur of the moment : EXTEMPORIZE ⟨~ on the piano⟩ 2 : to make, invent, or arrange offhand ⟨~ a sail out of shirts⟩ — **im·pro·vi·sa·tion** \im-ˌprä-və-ˈzā-shən, ˌim-prə-və-\ *n* — **im·pro·vis·er** *or* **im·pro·vi·sor** \ˌim-prə-ˈvī-zər, ˈim-prə-ˌvī-\ *n*

**im·pru·dent** \(ˌ)im-ˈprü-dᵊnt\ *adj* : not prudent : lacking discretion, wisdom, or good judgement — **im·pru·dence** \-dᵊns\ *n* — **im·pru·dent·ly** *adv*

**im·pu·dent** \ˈim-pyü-dənt\ *adj* : marked by contemptuous boldness or disregard of others — **im·pu·dence** \-dəns\ *n* — **im·pu·dent·ly** *adv*

**im·pugn** \im-ˈpyün\ *vb* [ME, to assail, fr. AF *empugner*, fr. L *inpugnare*, fr. *pugnare* to fight] : to attack by words or arguments : oppose or attack as false or as lacking integrity ⟨~ed his rival's character⟩

**im·puis·sance** \im-ˈpwi-sᵊns, -ˈpyü-ə-sᵊns\ *n* [ME, fr. MF] : the quality or state of being powerless : WEAKNESS

**im·pulse** \ˈim-ˌpəls\ *n* 1 : a force that starts a body into motion; *also* : the motion produced by such a force 2 : an arousing of the mind and spirit to some usu. unpremeditated action 3 : NERVE IMPULSE

**im·pul·sion** \im-ˈpəl-shən\ *n* 1 : the act of impelling : the state of being impelled 2 : a force that impels 3 : IMPULSE 2; *also* : COMPULSION 3

**im·pul·sive** \im-ˈpəl-siv\ *adj* 1 : having the power of or actually impelling or impelling 2 : arising from or prone to act on impulse — **im·pul·sive·ly** *adv* — **im·pul·sive·ness** *n*

**im·pu·ni·ty** \im-ˈpyü-nə-tē\ *n* [MF or L; MF *impunité*, fr. L *impunitas*, fr. *impune* without punishment, fr. *poena* penalty, punishment] : exemption from punishment, harm, or loss

**im·pure** \(ˌ)im-ˈpyùr\ *adj* 1 : not pure : UNCHASTE, OBSCENE 2 : DIRTY, FOUL ⟨~ water⟩ 3 : ADULTERATED, MIXED — **im·pu·ri·ty** \-ˈpyùr-ə-tē\ *n*

**im·pute** \im-'pyüt\ *vb* **im·put·ed; im·put·ing** **1** : to lay the responsibility or blame for often falsely or unjustly **2** : to credit to a person or a cause : ATTRIBUTE — **im·put·able** \-'pyü-tə-bəl\ *adj* — **im·pu·ta·tion** \im-pyü-'tā-shən\ *n*

**¹in** \'in\ *prep* **1** — used to indicate physical surroundings ⟨swim ∼ the lake⟩ **2** : INTO 1 ⟨ran ∼ the house⟩ **3** : DURING ⟨∼ the summer⟩ **4** : WITH ⟨written ∼ pencil⟩ **5** — used to indicate one's situation or state of being ⟨∼ luck⟩ ⟨∼ love⟩ **6** — used to indicate manner or purpose ⟨∼ a hurry⟩ ⟨said ∼ reply⟩ **7** : INTO 2 ⟨broke ∼ pieces⟩

**²in** *adv* **1** : to or toward the inside ⟨come ∼⟩; *also* : to or toward some destination or place ⟨flew ∼ from the South⟩ **2** : at close quarters : NEAR ⟨the enemy closed ∼⟩ **3** : into the midst of something ⟨mix ∼ the flour⟩ **4** : to or at its proper place ⟨fit a piece ∼⟩ **5** : WITHIN ⟨locked ∼⟩ **6** : in vogue or season **7** : in one's presence, possession, or control ⟨the results are ∼⟩

**³in** *adj* **1** : located inside or within **2** : that is in position, operation, or power ⟨the ∼ party⟩ **3** : directed inward : INCOMING ⟨the ∼ train⟩ **4** : keenly aware of and responsive to what is new and fashionable ⟨the ∼ crowd⟩; *also* : extremely fashionable ⟨the ∼ thing to do⟩

**⁴in** *n* **1** : one who is in office or power or on the inside **2** : INFLUENCE, PULL ⟨he has an ∼ with the owner⟩

**⁵in** *abbr* **1** inch **2** inlet

**In** *symbol* indium

**IN** *abbr* Indiana

**in-** \(ˌ)in\ *prefix* : not : absence of : NON-, UN-

**in·abil·i·ty** \ˌi-nə-'bi-lə-tē\ *n* : the quality or state of being unable

**in ab·sen·tia** \ˌin-ab-'sen-chə, -chē-ə\ *adv* : in one's absence

**in·ac·ti·vate** \(ˌ)i-'nak-tə-ˌvāt\ *vb* : to make inactive — **in·ac·ti·va·tion** \(ˌ)i-ˌnak-tə-'vā-shən\ *n*

**in·ad·e·quate** \(ˌ)i-'na-di-kwət\ *adj* : not adequate : INSUFFICIENT — **in·ad·e·qua·cy** \-kwə-sē\ *n* — **in·ad·e·quate·ly** *adv* — **in·ad·e·quate·ness** *n*

**in·ad·ver·tent** \ˌi-nəd-'vər-t³nt\ *adj* **1** : HEEDLESS, INATTENTIVE **2** : UNINTENTIONAL ⟨an ∼ omission⟩ — **in·ad·ver·tence** \-'t³ns\ *n* — **in·ad·ver·ten·cy** \-'t³n-sē\ *n* — **in·ad·ver·tent·ly** *adv*

**in·alien·able** \(ˌ)i-'nāl-yə-nə-bəl, -'nā-lē-ə-\ *adj* : incapable of being alienated, surrendered, or transferred ⟨∼ rights⟩ — **in·alien·abil·i·ty** \(ˌ)i-ˌnāl-yə-nə-'bi-lə-tē, -ˌnā-lē-ə-\ *n* — **in·alien·ably** *adv*

**in·amo·ra·ta** \i-ˌnä-mə-'rä-tə\ *n* : a woman with whom one is in love

**inane** \i-'nān\ *adj* **inan·er; -est** : EMPTY, INSUBSTANTIAL; *also* : SHALLOW, SILLY ⟨∼ comments⟩ — **inane·ly** *adv* — **inan·i·ty** \i-'na-nə-tē\ *n*

**in·an·i·mate** \(ˌ)i-'na-nə-mət\ *adj* : not animate or animated : lacking the qualities of living things — **in·an·i·mate·ly** *adv* — **in·an·i·mate·ness** *n*

**in·ap·pre·cia·ble** \ˌi-nə-'prē-shə-bəl\ *adj* : too small to be perceived — **in·ap·pre·cia·bly** \-blē\ *adv*

**in·apt** \(ˌ)i-'napt\ *adj* **1** : not suitable ⟨an ∼ analogy⟩ **2** : INEPT — **in·apt·ly** *adv* — **in·apt·ness** *n*

**in·ar·tic·u·late** \ˌi-när-'ti-kyə-lət\ *adj* **1** : not understandable as spoken words **2** : MUTE **3** : incapable of being expressed by speech ⟨∼ fear⟩; *also* : UNSPOKEN **4** : not having the power of distinct utterance or effective expression — **in·ar·tic·u·late·ly** *adv*

**in·as·much as** \ˌi-nəz-'məch-\ *conj* : seeing that : SINCE

**in·at·ten·tion** \ˌi-nə-'ten-chən\ *n* : failure to pay attention : DISREGARD — **in·at·ten·tive** \-'ten-tiv\ *adj*

**¹in·au·gu·ral** \i-'nȯ-gyə-rəl, -gə-\ *adj* **1** : of or relating to an inauguration **2** : marking a beginning

**²inaugural** *n* **1** : an inaugural address **2** : INAUGURATION

**in·au·gu·rate** \i-'nȯ-gyə-ˌrāt, -gə-\ *vb* **-rat·ed; -rat·ing** **1** : to introduce into an office with suitable ceremonies : INSTALL **2** : to dedicate ceremoniously **3** : BEGIN, INITIATE — **in·au·gu·ra·tion** \-ˌnȯ-gyə-'rā-shən, -gə-\ *n*

**in·board** \'in-ˌbȯrd\ *adv* **1** : inside the hull of a ship **2** : close or closest to the center line of a vehicle or craft — **in·board** *adj*

**in·born** \'in-'bȯrn\ *adj* **1** : present from or as if from birth **2** : HEREDITARY, INHERITED ♦ **Synonyms** INNATE, CONGENITAL, NATIVE

**in·bound** \'in-ˌbaůnd\ *adj* : inward bound ⟨∼ traffic⟩

**in-box** \'in-ˌbäks\ *n* : a receptacle for incoming interoffice letters; *also* : a computer folder for incoming e-mail

**in·bred** \'in-'bred\ *adj* **1** : ingrained in one's nature as deeply as if by heredity **2** : subjected to or produced by inbreeding

**in·breed·ing** \'in-ˌbrē-diŋ\ *n* **1** : the interbreeding of closely related individuals esp. to preserve and fix desirable characters of and to eliminate unfavorable characters from a stock **2** : confinement to a narrow range or a local or limited field of choice — **in·breed** \'in-'brēd\ *vb*

**inc** *abbr* **1** incomplete **2** incorporated **3** increase

**In·ca** \'iŋ-kə\ *n* [Sp, fr. Quechua *inka* ruler of the Inca empire] **1** : a noble or a member of the ruling family of an Indian empire of Peru, Bolivia, and Ecuador until the Spanish conquest **2** : a member of any people under Inca influence

---

| | | | | |
|---|---|---|---|---|
| inaccessibility | inactive | inadvisable | inappropriate | inaudible |
| inaccessible | inactivity | inadmissibility | inaptitude | inaudibly |
| inaccuracy | inadmissible | inapparent | inarguable | inauspicious |
| inaccurate | inadmissible | inapplicable | inartistic | inauthentic |
| inaction | inadvisability | inapposite | inattentive | incautious |
| | | inapproachable | | |

**in·cal·cu·la·ble** \(ˌ)in-ˈkal-kyə-lə-bəl\ *adj* **1** : not capable of being calculated; *esp* : very great **2** : not predictable ⟨∼ consequences⟩ — **in·cal·cu·la·bly** \-blē\ *adv*

**in·can·des·cent** \ˌin-kən-ˈde-sᵊnt\ *adj* **1** : glowing with heat **2** : SHINING, BRILLIANT — **in·can·des·cence** \-ˈsᵊns\ *n*

**incandescent lamp** *n* : LIGHT BULB 1

**in·can·ta·tion** \ˌin-ˌkan-ˈtā-shən\ *n* : a use of spells or verbal charms spoken or sung as a part of a ritual of magic; *also* : a formula of words used in or as if in such a ritual

**in·ca·pa·ble** \(ˌ)in-ˈkā-pə-bəl\ *adj* : lacking ability or qualification for a particular purpose; *also* : UNQUALIFIED — **in·ca·pa·bil·i·ty** \-ˌkā-pə-ˈbi-lə-tē\ *n*

**in·ca·pac·i·tate** \ˌin-kə-ˈpa-sə-ˌtāt\ *vb* **-tat·ed; -tat·ing** : to make incapable or unfit

**in·ca·pac·i·ty** \ˌin-kə-ˈpa-sə-tē\ *n, pl* **-ties** : the quality or state of being incapable

**in·car·cer·ate** \in-ˈkär-sə-ˌrāt\ *vb* **-at·ed; -at·ing** : IMPRISON, CONFINE — **in·car·cer·a·tion** \(ˌ)in-ˌkär-sə-ˈrā-shən\ *n*

**in·car·na·dine** \in-ˈkär-nə-ˌdīn, -ˌdēn\ *vb* **-dined; -din·ing** : REDDEN

**in·car·nate** \in-ˈkär-nət, -ˌnāt\ *adj* **1** : having bodily and esp. human form and substance **2** : PERSONIFIED — **in·car·nate** \-ˌnāt\ *vb*

**in·car·na·tion** \ˌin-ˌkär-ˈnā-shən\ *n* **1** : the embodiment of a deity or spirit in an earthly form **2** *cap* : the union of divine and human natures in Jesus Christ **3** : a person showing a trait or typical character to a marked degree **4** : the act of incarnating : the state of being incarnate

**in·cen·di·ary** \in-ˈsen-dē-ˌer-ē\ *adj* **1** : of or relating to a deliberate burning of property **2** : tending to excite or inflame **3** : designed to start fires ⟨an ∼ bomb⟩ — **incendiary** *n*

**¹in·cense** \ˈin-ˌsens\ *n* **1** : material used to produce a fragrant odor when burned **2** : the perfume or smoke from some spices and gums when burned

**²in·cense** \in-ˈsens\ *vb* **in·censed; in·cens·ing** : to make extremely angry

**in·cen·tive** \in-ˈsen-tiv\ *n* [ME, fr. LL *incentivum*, fr. *incentivus* stimulating, fr. L, setting the tune, fr. *incinere* to play (a tune), fr. *canere* to sing] : something that incites or is likely to incite to determination or action

**in·cep·tion** \in-ˈsep-shən\ *n* : BEGINNING, COMMENCEMENT

**in·cer·ti·tude** \(ˌ)in-ˈsər-tə-ˌtüd, -ˌtyüd\ *n* **1** : UNCERTAINTY, DOUBT, INDECISION **2** : INSECURITY, INSTABILITY

**in·ces·sant** \(ˌ)in-ˈse-sᵊnt\ *adj* : continuing or flowing without interruption ⟨∼ rains⟩ — **in·ces·sant·ly** *adv*

**in·cest** \ˈin-ˌsest\ *n* [ME, fr. L *incestus* sexual impurity, fr. *incestus* impure, fr. *castus* pure] : sexual intercourse between persons so closely related that marriage is illegal — **in·ces·tu·ous** \in-ˈses-chü-wəs\ *adj*

**¹inch** \ˈinch\ *n* [ME, fr. OE *ynce*, fr. L *un-*

*cia* twelfth part, inch, ounce] — see WEIGHT table

**²inch** *vb* : to move by small degrees

**in·cho·ate** \in-ˈkō-ət, ˈin-kə-ˌwāt\ *adj* : being only partly in existence or operation : INCOMPLETE ⟨∼ yearnings⟩

**inch·worm** \ˈinch-ˌwərm\ *n* : LOOPER

**in·ci·dence** \ˈin-sə-dəns\ *n* : rate of occurrence or effect

**¹in·ci·dent** \-dənt\ *n* **1** : OCCURRENCE, HAPPENING **2** : an action likely to lead to grave consequences esp. in diplomatic matters

**²incident** *adj* **1** : occurring or likely to occur esp. in connection with some other happening **2** : falling or striking on something ⟨∼ light rays⟩

**¹in·ci·den·tal** \ˌin-sə-ˈden-tᵊl\ *adj* **1** : subordinate, nonessential, or attendant in position or significance ⟨∼ expenses⟩ **2** : CASUAL, CHANCE

**²incidental** *n* **1** *pl* : minor items (as of expense) that are not individually accounted for **2** : something incidental

**in·ci·den·tal·ly** \ˌin-sə-ˈden-tᵊl-ē, -ˈdent-lē\ *adv* **1** : in an incidental manner **2** : by the way

**in·cin·er·ate** \in-ˈsi-nə-ˌrāt\ *vb* **-at·ed; -at·ing** : to burn to ashes — **in·cin·er·a·tion** \-ˌsi-nə-ˈrā-shən\ *n*

**in·cin·er·a·tor** \in-ˈsi-nə-ˌrā-tər\ *n* : a furnace for burning waste

**in·cip·i·ent** \in-ˈsi-pē-ənt\ *adj* : beginning to be or become apparent

**in·cise** \in-ˈsīz\ *vb* **in·cised; in·cis·ing** **1** : to cut into **2** : CARVE, ENGRAVE

**in·ci·sion** \in-ˈsi-zhən\ *n* : CUT, GASH; *esp* : a surgical cut

**in·ci·sive** \in-ˈsī-siv\ *adj* : impressively direct and decisive — **in·ci·sive·ly** *adv*

**in·ci·sor** \in-ˈsī-zər\ *n* : a front tooth typically adapted for cutting

**in·cite** \in-ˈsīt\ *vb* **in·cit·ed; in·cit·ing** : to arouse to action : stir up — **in·cite·ment** *n* — **in·cit·er** *n*

**in·ci·vil·i·ty** \ˌin-sə-ˈvi-lə-tē\ *n* **1** : RUDENESS, DISCOURTESY **2** : a rude or discourteous act

**incl** *abbr* include; included; including; inclusive

**in·clem·ent** \(ˌ)in-ˈkle-mənt\ *adj* : SEVERE, STORMY ⟨∼ weather⟩ — **in·clem·en·cy** \-mən-sē\ *n*

**in·cli·na·tion** \ˌin-klə-ˈnā-shən\ *n* **1** : PROPENSITY, BENT; *esp* : LIKING **2** : BOW, NOD ⟨an ∼ of the head⟩ **3** : a tilting of something **4** : SLANT, SLOPE

**¹in·cline** \in-ˈklīn\ *vb* **in·clined; in·clin·ing** **1** : BOW, BEND **2** : to be drawn toward an opinion or course of action **3** : to deviate from the vertical or horizontal : SLOPE **4** : INFLUENCE, PERSUADE — **in·clin·er** *n*

**²in·cline** \ˈin-ˌklīn\ *n* : SLOPE

**inclose, inclosure** *var of* ENCLOSE, ENCLOSURE

**in·clude** \in-ˈklüd\ *vb* **in·clud·ed; in·clud·ing** : to take in or comprise as a part of a whole ⟨the price ∼s tax⟩ — **in·clu·sion** \in-ˈklü-zhən\ *n*

**in·clu·sive** \in-ˈklü-siv\ *adj* **1** : including stated limits or extremes ⟨from Monday to Friday ~⟩ 2 : broad in scope; *esp* : covering all items, costs, or services — **in·clu·sive·ly** *adv* — **in·clu·sive·ness** *n*

**incog** *abbr* incognito

¹**in·cog·ni·to** \,in-ˈkäg-ˈnē-to, in-ˈkäg-nə-,tō\ *adv or adj* [It, fr. L *incognitus* unknown, fr. *cognoscere* to know] : with one's identity concealed

²**incognito** *n, pl* **-tos** 1 : one appearing or living incognito 2 : the state or disguise of an incognito

**in·co·her·ent** \,in-kō-ˈhir-ənt, -ˈher-\ *adj* 1 : not sticking closely or compactly together : LOOSE 2 : lacking normal clarity or intelligibility in speech or thought ⟨an ~ patient⟩ — **in·co·her·ence** \-əns\ *n* — **in·co·her·ent·ly** *adv*

**in·come** \ˈin-,kəm\ *n* : a gain usu. measured in money that derives from labor, business, or property

**income tax** *n* : a tax on the net income of an individual or business concern

**in·com·ing** \ˈin-,kə-miŋ\ *adj* : coming in ⟨the ~ tide⟩ ⟨~ freshmen⟩

**in·com·men·su·rate** \,in-kə-ˈmen-sə-rət, -ˈmen-chə-\ *adj* : not commensurate; *esp* : INADEQUATE

**in·com·mode** \,in-kə-ˈmōd\ *vb* **-mod·ed; -mod·ing** : INCONVENIENCE, DISTURB

**in·com·mu·ni·ca·ble** \,in-kə-ˈmyü-ni-kə-bəl\ *adj* : not communicable : not capable of being communicated or imparted; *also* : UNCOMMUNICATIVE

**in·com·mu·ni·ca·do** \,in-kə-,myü-nə-ˈkä-dō\ *adv or adj* : without means of communication; *also* : in solitary confinement ⟨a prisoner held ~⟩

**in·com·pa·ra·ble** \(,)in-ˈkäm-pə-rə-bəl, -prə-\ *adj* 1 : eminent beyond comparison : MATCHLESS 2 : not suitable for comparison — **in·com·pa·ra·bly** \-blē\ *adv*

**in·com·pat·i·ble** \,in-kəm-ˈpa-tə-bəl\ *adj* : incapable of or unsuitable for association or use together ⟨~ colors⟩ ⟨temperamentally ~⟩ — **in·com·pat·i·bil·i·ty** \,in-kəm-,pa-tə-ˈbi-lə-tē\ *n*

**in·com·pe·tent** \(,)in-ˈkäm-pə-tənt\ *adj* 1 : not legally qualified 2 : not competent : lacking sufficient knowledge, skill, or ability — **in·com·pe·tence** \-təns\ *n* — **in·com·pe·ten·cy** \-tən-sē\ *n* — **incompetent** *n*

**in·com·plete** \,in-kəm-ˈplēt\ *adj* : lacking a part or parts : UNFINISHED, IMPERFECT — **in·com·plete·ly** *adv* — **in·com·plete·ness** *n*

**in·com·pre·hen·si·ble** \,in-,käm-pri-ˈhen-sə-bəl\ *adj* : impossible to comprehend : UNINTELLIGIBLE ⟨~ muttering⟩

**in·con·ceiv·able** \,in-kən-ˈsē-və-bəl\ *adj* 1 : impossible to comprehend 2 : UNBELIEVABLE

**in·con·gru·ous** \(,)in-ˈkäŋ-grü-wəs\ *adj* : not consistent with or suitable to the surroundings or associations — **in·con·gru·i·ty** \,in-kən-ˈgrü-ə-tē, -,kän-\ *n* — **in·con·gru·ous·ly** *adv*

**in·con·se·quen·tial** \,in-,kän-sə-ˈkwen-**

chəl\ *adj* 1 : ILLOGICAL; *also* : IRRELEVANT 2 : of no significance : UNIMPORTANT — **in·con·se·quence** \(,)in-ˈkän-sə-,kwens\ *n* — **in·con·se·quen·tial·ly** *adv*

**in·con·sid·er·able** \,in-kən-ˈsi-də-rə-bəl\ *adj* : SLIGHT, TRIVIAL ⟨the cost was not ~⟩

**in·con·sid·er·ate** \,in-kən-ˈsi-də-rət\ *adj* : HEEDLESS, THOUGHTLESS; *esp* : not respecting the rights or feelings of others — **in·con·sid·er·ate·ly** *adv* — **in·con·sid·er·ate·ness** *n*

**in·con·sol·able** \,in-kən-ˈsō-lə-bəl\ *adj* : incapable of being consoled — **in·con·sol·ably** \-blē\ *adv*

**in·con·spic·u·ous** \,in-kən-ˈspi-kyə-wəs\ *adj* : not readily noticeable — **in·con·spic·u·ous·ly** *adv*

**in·con·stant** \(,)in-ˈkän-stənt\ *adj* : not constant : CHANGEABLE ♦ *Synonyms* FICKLE, CAPRICIOUS, MERCURIAL, UNSTABLE, VOLATILE — **in·con·stan·cy** \-stən-sē\ *n* — **in·con·stant·ly** *adv*

**in·con·test·able** \,in-kən-ˈtes-tə-bəl\ *adj* : not contestable : INDISPUTABLE — **in·con·test·ably** \-ˈtes-tə-blē\ *adv*

**in·con·ti·nent** \(,)in-ˈkänt-ᵊn-ənt\ *adj* 1 : lacking self-restraint 2 : unable to retain urine or feces voluntarily — **in·con·ti·nence** \-əns\ *n*

**in·con·tro·vert·ible** \,in-,kän-trə-ˈvər-tə-bəl\ *adj* : not open to question : INDISPUTABLE ⟨~ evidence⟩ — **in·con·tro·vert·ibly** \-blē\ *adv*

¹**in·con·ve·nience** \,in-kən-ˈvē-nyəns\ *n* 1 : something that is inconvenient 2 : the quality or state of being inconvenient

²**inconvenience** *vb* **-nienced; -nienc·ing** : to subject to inconvenience

**in·con·ve·nient** \,in-kən-ˈvē-nyənt\ *adj* : not convenient : causing trouble or annoyance : INOPPORTUNE — **in·con·ve·nient·ly** *adv*

**in·cor·po·rate** \in-ˈkȯr-pə-,rāt\ *vb* **-rat·ed; -rat·ing** 1 : to unite closely or so as to form one body : BLEND 2 : to form, form into, or become a corporation 3 : to give material form to : EMBODY — **in·cor·po·ra·tion** \-,kȯr-pə-ˈrä-shən\ *n*

**in·cor·po·re·al** \,in-kȯr-ˈpȯr-ē-əl\ *adj* : having no material body or form

**in·cor·rect** \,in-kə-ˈrekt\ *adj* 1 : INACCURATE, FAULTY ⟨an ~ transcription⟩ 2 : not true : WRONG 3 : UNBECOMING, IMPROPER — **in·cor·rect·ly** *adv* — **in·cor·rect·ness** *n*

**in·cor·ri·gi·ble** \(,)in-ˈkȯr-ə-jə-bəl\ *adj* : incapable of being corrected, amended, or reformed — **in·cor·ri·gi·bil·i·ty** \(,)in-,kȯr-ə-jə-ˈbi-lə-tē\ *n* — **in·cor·ri·gi·bly** \-ˈkȯr-ə-jə-blē\ *adv*

**in·cor·rupt·ible** \,in-kə-ˈrəp-tə-bəl\ *adj* 1 : not subject to decay or dissolution 2 : incapable of being bribed or morally corrupted — **in·cor·rupt·ibil·i·ty** \-,rəp-tə-ˈbi-lə-tē\ *n* — **in·cor·rupt·ibly** \-ˈrəp-tə-blē\ *adv*

**incr** *abbr* increase; increased

¹**in·crease** \in-ˈkrēs, ˈin-,krēs\ *vb* **in-**

---

| | |
|---|---|
| incombustible | inconclusive |
| incomprehension | incongruent |

| | |
|---|---|
| inconsistency | incoordination |
| inconsistent | |

**creased; in·creas·ing** [ME *encresen*, fr. AF *encreistre*, fr. L *increscere*, fr. *crescere* to grow] **1** : to become greater : GROW **2** : to multiply by the production of young ⟨rabbits ~ rapidly⟩ **3** : to make greater — **increased** *adj* — **in·creas·ing·ly** \-ˈkrē-siŋ-lē\ *adv*

²**in·crease** \ˈin-ˌkrēs, in-ˈkrēs\ *n* **1** : addition or enlargement in size, extent, or quantity : GROWTH **2** : something that is added to an original stock or amount (as by growth)

**in·cred·i·ble** \(ˌ)in-ˈkre-də-bəl\ *adj* : too extraordinary and improbable to be believed; *also* : hard to believe — **in·cred·i·bil·i·ty** \(ˌ)in-ˌkre-də-ˈbi-lə-tē\ *n* — **in·cred·i·bly** \-ˈkre-də-blē\ *adv*

**in·cred·u·lous** \-ˈkre-jə-ləs\ *adj* **1** : SKEPTICAL **2** : expressing disbelief — **in·cre·du·li·ty** \ˌin-kri-ˈdü-lə-tē, -ˈdyü-\ *n* — **in·cred·u·lous·ly** *adv*

**in·cre·ment** \ˈiŋ-krə-mənt, ˈin-\ *n* **1** : the action or process of increasing esp. in quantity or value : ENLARGEMENT **2** : something gained or added; *esp* : one of a series of regular consecutive additions — **in·cre·men·tal** \ˌiŋ-krə-ˈmen-tᵊl, ˌin-\ *adj* — **in·cre·men·tal·ly** *adv*

**In·crim·i·nate** \in-ˈkri-mə-ˌnāt\ *vb* **-nat·ed; -nat·ing** : to charge with or prove involvement in a crime or fault : ACCUSE — **in·crim·i·na·tion** \-ˌkri-mə-ˈnā-shən\ *n* — **in·crim·i·na·to·ry** \-ˈkri-mə-nə-ˌtȯr-ē\ *adj*

**incrust** *var of* ENCRUST

**in·crus·ta·tion** *also* **en·crus·ta·tion** \ˌin-ˌkrəs-ˈtā-shən\ *n* **1** : CRUST; *also* : an accumulation (as of habits, opinions, or customs) resembling a crust **2** : the act of encrusting : the state of being encrusted

**in·cu·bate** \ˈiŋ-kyü-ˌbāt, ˈin-\ *vb* **-bat·ed; -bat·ing** : to sit on (eggs) to hatch by the warmth of the body; *also* : to keep (as an embryo) under conditions favorable for development — **in·cu·ba·tion** \ˌiŋ-kyü-ˈbā-shən, ˌin-\ *n*

**in·cu·ba·tor** \ˈiŋ-kyù-ˌbāt-ər, ˈin-\ *n* : one that incubates; *esp* : an apparatus providing suitable conditions (as of warmth and moisture) for incubating something (as a premature baby)

**in·cu·bus** \ˈiŋ-kyə-bəs, ˈin-\ *n, pl* **-bi** \-ˌbī, -ˌbē\ *also* **-bus·es** [ME, fr. LL, fr. L *incubare* to lie on] **1** : a spirit supposed to work evil on persons in their sleep **2** : NIGHTMARE **3** : one that oppresses like a nightmare

**in·cul·cate** \in-ˈkəl-ˌkāt, ˈin-(ˌ)kəl-\ *vb* **-cat·ed; -cat·ing** [L *inculcare*, lit., to tread on, fr. *calcare* to trample, fr. *calx* heel] : to teach and impress by frequent repetitions or admonitions — **in·cul·ca·tion** \(ˌ)in-(ˌ)kəl-ˈkā-shən\ *n*

**in·cul·pa·ble** \(ˌ)in-ˈkəl-pə-bəl\ *adj* : free from guilt : INNOCENT

**in·cul·pate** \in-ˈkəl-ˌpāt, ˈin-(ˌ)kəl-\ *vb* **-pat·ed; -pat·ing** : INCRIMINATE

**in·cum·ben·cy** \in-ˈkəm-bən-sē\ *n, pl* **-cies** **1** : something that is incumbent **2** : the quality or state of being incumbent

**3** : the office or period of office of an incumbent

¹**in·cum·bent** \in-ˈkəm-bənt\ *n* : the holder of an office or position

²**incumbent** *adj* **1** : imposed as a duty **2** : occupying a specified office **3** : lying or resting on something else

**in·cu·nab·u·lum** \ˌin-kyə-ˈna-byə-ləm, iŋ-\ *n, pl* **-la** \-lə\ [NL, fr. L *incunabula*, pl., bands holding the baby in a cradle, fr. *cunae* cradle] : a book printed before 1501

**in·cur** \in-ˈkər\ *vb* **in·curred; in·cur·ring** : to become liable or subject to : bring down upon oneself

**in·cur·able** \(ˌ)in-ˈkyür-ə-bəl\ *adj* **1** : not curable **2** : not likely to be changed — **incurable** *n* — **in·cur·ably** \(ˌ)in-ˈkyür-ə-blē\ *adv*

**in·cur·sion** \in-ˈkər-zhən\ *n* **1** : a sudden hostile invasion : RAID **2** : an entering in or into (as an activity)

**in·cus** \ˈiŋ-kəs\ *n, pl* **in·cu·des** \iŋ-ˈkyü-(ˌ)dēz\ [NL, fr. L, anvil] : the middle bone of a chain of three small bones in the middle ear of a mammal

**ind** *abbr* **1** independent **2** index **3** industrial; industry

**Ind** *abbr* **1** Indian **2** Indiana

**in·debt·ed** \in-ˈde-təd\ *adj* **1** : owing gratitude or recognition to another **2** : owing money — **in·debt·ed·ness** *n*

**in·de·cent** \(ˌ)in-ˈdē-sᵊnt\ *adj* : not decent; *esp* : grossly improper or offensive — **in·de·cen·cy** \-sᵊn-sē\ *n* — **in·de·cent·ly** *adv*

**in·de·ci·sion** \ˌin-di-ˈsi-zhən\ *n* : a wavering between two or more possible courses of action : IRRESOLUTION

**in·de·ci·sive** \ˌin-di-ˈsī-siv\ *adj* **1** : INCONCLUSIVE ⟨an ~ battle⟩ **2** : marked by or prone to indecision **3** : INDEFINITE — **in·de·ci·sive·ly** *adv* — **in·de·ci·sive·ness** *n*

**in·de·co·rous** \(ˌ)in-ˈde-kə-rəs; ˌin-di-ˈkȯr-əs\ *adj* : conflicting with accepted standards of good conduct or good taste

♦ **Synonyms** IMPROPER, UNSEEMLY, INDECENT, UNBECOMING, INDELICATE — **in·de·co·rous·ly** *adv* — **in·de·co·rous·ness** *n*

**in·deed** \in-ˈdēd\ *adv* **1** : without any question : TRULY — often used interjectionally to express irony, disbelief, or surprise **2** : in reality **3** : all things considered

**in·de·fat·i·ga·ble** \ˌin-di-ˈfa-ti-gə-bəl\ *adj* : UNTIRING ⟨an ~ worker⟩ — **in·de·fat·i·ga·bly** \-blē\ *adv*

**in·de·fea·si·ble** \-ˈfē-zə-bəl\ *adj* : not capable of being annulled or voided — **in·de·fea·si·bly** \-blē\ *adv*

**in·de·fen·si·ble** \-ˈfen-sə-bəl\ *adj* **1** : incapable of being maintained as right or valid **2** : INEXCUSABLE ⟨~ comments⟩ **3** : incapable of being protected against physical attack

**in·de·fin·able** \-ˈfī-nə-bəl\ *adj* : incapable of being precisely described or analyzed — **in·de·fin·ably** \-blē\ *adv*

**in·def·i·nite** \(ˌ)in-'de-fə-nət\ *adj* **1** : not defining or identifying ⟨*an* is an ∼ article⟩ **2** : not precise : VAGUE **3** : having no fixed limits — **in·def·i·nite·ly** *adv* — **in·def·i·nite·ness** *n*

**in·del·i·ble** \in-'de-lə-bəl\ *adj* [ME, fr. ML *indelibilis*, alter. of L *indelebilis*, fr. *delēre* to delete, destroy] **1** : not capable of being removed or erased **2** : making marks that cannot be erased **3** : LASTING, UNFORGETTABLE ⟨an ∼ performance⟩ — **in·del·i·bly** \in-'de-lə-blē\ *adv*

**in·del·i·cate** \(ˌ)in-'de-li-kət\ *adj* : not delicate; *esp* : IMPROPER, COARSE, TACTLESS ♦ *Synonyms* INDECENT, UNSEEMLY, INDECOROUS, UNBECOMING — **in·del·i·ca·cy** \in-'de-lə-kə-sē\ *n*

**in·dem·ni·fy** \in-'dem-nə-ˌfī\ *vb* **-fied; -fying** [L *indemnis* unharmed, fr. *in-* not + *damnum* damage] **1** : to secure against hurt, loss, or damage **2** : to make compensation to for hurt, loss, or damage — **in·dem·ni·fi·ca·tion** \-ˌdem-nə-fə-'kā-shən\ *n*

**in·dem·ni·ty** \in-'dem-nə-tē\ *n, pl* **-ties** **1** : security against hurt, loss, or damage; *also* : exemption from incurred penalties or liabilities **2** : something that indemnifies

¹**in·dent** \in-'dent\ *vb* [ME, fr. AF *endenter*, fr. *dent* tooth, fr. L *dent-, dens*] **1** : to notch the edge of **2** : INDENTURE **3** : to set (as a line of a paragraph) in from the margin

²**indent** *vb* **1** : to force inward so as to form a depression **2** : to form a dent in

**in·den·ta·tion** \ˌin-ˌden-'tā-shən\ *n* **1** : NOTCH; *also* : a recess in a surface **2** : the action of indenting : the condition of being indented **3** : DENT **4** : INDENTION 2

**in·den·tion** \in-'den-chən\ *n* **1** : INDENTATION 2 **2** : the blank space produced by indenting

¹**in·den·ture** \in-'den-chər\ *n* **1** : a written certificate or agreement; *esp* : a contract binding one person (as an apprentice) to work for another for a given period of time — often used in pl. **2** : INDENTATION 1 **3** : DENT

²**indenture** *vb* **in·den·tured; in·den·turing** : to bind (as an apprentice) by indentures

**in·de·pen·dence** \ˌin-də-'pen-dəns\ *n* : the quality or state of being independent : FREEDOM

**Independence Day** *n* : July 4 observed as a legal holiday in the U.S. in commemoration of the adoption of the Declaration of Independence in 1776

**in·de·pen·dent** \ˌin-də-'pen-dənt\ *adj* **1** : SELF-GOVERNING; *also* : not affiliated with a larger controlling unit **2** : not requiring or relying on something else or somebody else ⟨an ∼ conclusion⟩ ⟨∼ of her parents⟩ **3** : not easily influenced : showing self-reliance and personal freedom ⟨an ∼ mind⟩ **4** : not committed to a political party ⟨an ∼ voter⟩ **5** : MAIN

⟨an ∼ clause⟩ — **independent** *n* — **in·de·pen·dent·ly** *adv*

**independent variable** *n* : a variable whose value is not determined by that of any other variable in a function

**in·de·scrib·able** \ˌin-di-'skrī-bə-bəl\ *adj* **1** : that cannot be described **2** : being too intense or great for description — **in·de·scrib·ably** \-blē\ *adv*

**in·de·ter·mi·nate** \ˌin-di-'tər-mə-nət\ *adj* **1** : VAGUE; *also* : not known in advance **2** : not limited in advance; *also* : not leading to a definite end or result — **in·de·ter·mi·na·cy** \-nə-sē\ *n* — **in·de·ter·mi·nate·ly** *adv*

¹**in·dex** \'in-ˌdeks\ *n, pl* **in·dex·es** *or* **in·di·ces** \-də-ˌsēz\ **1** : POINTER **2** : SIGN, INDICATION ⟨an ∼ of character⟩ **3** : a guide for facilitating references; *esp* : an alphabetical list of items treated in a printed work with the page number where each item may be found **4** : a list of restricted or prohibited material **5** *pl usu* **indices** : a number or symbol or expression (as an exponent) associated with another to indicate a mathematical operation or use or position in an arrangement or expansion **6** : a character ☞ used to direct attention (as to a note) **7** : INDEX NUMBER

²**index** *vb* **1** : to provide with or put into an index **2** : to serve as an index of **3** : to regulate by indexation

**in·dex·ation** \ˌin-ˌdek-'sā-shən\ *n* : a system of economic control in which a body of variables (as wages and interest) rise or fall at the same rate as an index of the cost of living

**index finger** *n* : the finger next to the thumb

**in·dex·ing** *n* : INDEXATION

**index number** *n* : a number used to indicate change in magnitude (as of cost) as compared with the magnitude at some specified time

**index of refraction** : REFRACTIVE INDEX

**in·dia ink** \'in-dē-ə-\ *n, often cap 1st I* **1** : a solid black pigment used in drawing **2** : a fluid made from india ink

**In·di·an** \'in-dē-ən\ *n* **1** : a native or inhabitant of India or of the East Indies; *also* : a person of Indian descent **2** : AMERICAN INDIAN — **Indian** *adj*

**Indian corn** *n* **1** : CORN 2 **2** : corn having hard kernels of various colors (as reddish-brown or purple) used esp. for ornament

**Indian meal** *n* : CORNMEAL

**Indian paintbrush** *n* : any of a genus of herbaceous plants related to the snapdragons that have brightly colored bracts

**Indian pipe** *n* : a waxy white leafless saprophytic herb of Asia and the U.S.

**Indian summer** *n* : a period of mild weather in late autumn or early winter

**In·dia paper** \'in-dē-ə-\ *n* **1** : a thin absorbent paper used esp. for taking impressions (as of steel engravings) **2** : a thin tough opaque printing paper

**in·di·cate** \'in-də-ˌkāt\ *vb* **-cat·ed; -cat·ing** **1** : to point out or to **2** : to show

---

**indemonstrable**     **indestructible**     **indeterminable**

indirectly **3** : to state briefly — **in·di·ca·tion** \ˌin-də-ˈkā-shən\ n — **in·di·ca·tor** \ˈin-də-ˌkā-tər\ n

¹**in·dic·a·tive** \in-ˈdi-kə-tiv\ adj **1** : of, relating to, or being a verb form that represents an act or state as a fact ⟨∼ mood⟩ **2** : serving to indicate ⟨actions ∼ of fear⟩

²**indicative** n **1** : the indicative mood of a language **2** : a form in the indicative mood

**in·di·cia** \in-ˈdi-shə, -shē-ə\ n pl **1** : distinctive marks **2** : postal markings often imprinted on mail or mailing labels

**in·dict** \in-ˈdīt\ vb [alter. of earlier *indite*, fr. ME, fr. AF *enditter* to write, point out, indict, ultim. fr. L *indicere* to make known formally, fr. *dicere* to say] **1** : to charge with a fault or offense **2** : to charge with a crime by the finding of a jury — **in·dict·able** adj — **in·dict·ment** n

**in·die** \ˈin-dē\ n **1** : one that is independent; esp : an unaffiliated record or motion-picture production company **2** : something produced by an indie — **indie** adj

**in·dif·fer·ent** \in-ˈdi-frənt, -fə-rənt\ adj **1** : UNBIASED, UNPREJUDICED **2** : of no importance one way or the other **3** : marked by no special liking for or dislike of something **4** : being neither excessive nor inadequate **5** : PASSABLE, MEDIOCRE **6** : being neither right nor wrong — **in·dif·fer·ence** \-frəns, -fə-rəns\ n — **in·dif·fer·ent·ly** adv

**in·dig·e·nous** \in-ˈdi-jə-nəs\ adj : produced, growing, or living naturally in a particular region

**in·di·gent** \ˈin-di-jənt\ adj : IMPOVERISHED, NEEDY — **in·di·gence** \-jəns\ n

**in·di·gest·ible** \ˌin-dī-ˈjes-tə-bəl, -də-\ adj : not readily digested

**in·di·ges·tion** \-ˈjes-chən\ n : inadequate or difficult digestion : DYSPEPSIA

**in·dig·nant** \in-ˈdig-nənt\ adj : filled with or marked by indignation — **in·dig·nant·ly** adv

**in·dig·na·tion** \ˌin-dig-ˈnā-shən\ n : anger aroused by something unjust, unworthy, or mean

**in·dig·ni·ty** \in-ˈdig-nə-tē\ n, pl **-ties** : an offense against personal dignity or self-respect; also : humiliating treatment

**in·di·go** \ˈin-di-ˌgō\ n, pl **-gos** or **-goes** [It dial., fr. L *indicum*, fr. Gk *indikon*, fr. *indikos* Indic, fr. *Indos* India] **1** : a blue dye obtained from plants or synthesized **2** : a deep reddish blue color

**in·di·rect** \ˌin-də-ˈrekt, -dī-\ adj **1** : not straight ⟨an ∼ route⟩ **2** : not straightforward and open ⟨∼ methods⟩ **3** : not having a plainly seen connection ⟨an ∼ cause⟩ **4** : not directly to the point ⟨an ∼ answer⟩ — **in·di·rec·tion** \-ˈrek-shən\ n — **in·di·rect·ly** adv — **in·di·rect·ness** n

**in·dis·creet** \ˌin-di-ˈskrēt\ adj : not discreet : IMPRUDENT — **in·dis·creet·ly** adv

**in·dis·cre·tion** \ˌin-di-ˈskre-shən\ n **1** : IMPRUDENCE ⟨dietary ∼⟩ **2** : something marked by lack of discretion; esp : an act deviating from accepted morality

**in·dis·crim·i·nate** \ˌin-di-ˈskri-mə-nət\ adj **1** : not careful in making choices **2** : HAPHAZARD, RANDOM ⟨an application of a law⟩ **3** : UNRESTRAINED **4** : MOTLEY — **in·dis·crim·i·nate·ly** adv

**in·dis·pens·able** \ˌin-di-ˈspen-sə-bəl\ adj : absolutely essential : REQUISITE — **in·dis·pens·abil·i·ty** \-ˌspen-sə-ˈbi-lə-tē\ n — **indispensable** n — **in·dis·pens·ably** \-ˈspen-sə-blē\ adv

**in·dis·posed** \-ˈspōzd\ adj **1** : slightly ill **2** : AVERSE — **in·dis·po·si·tion** \ˌ(ˌ)in-ˌdis-pə-ˈzi-shən\ n

**in·dis·put·able** \ˌin-di-ˈspyü-tə-bəl, (ˌ)in-ˈdis-pyə-\ adj : not disputable : UNQUESTIONABLE ⟨∼ proof⟩ — **in·dis·put·ably** \-blē\ adv

**in·dis·sol·u·ble** \ˌin-di-ˈsäl-yə-bəl\ adj : not capable of being dissolved, undone, or broken : PERMANENT ⟨an ∼ contract⟩

**in·dis·tinct** \ˌin-di-ˈstiŋkt\ adj **1** : not sharply outlined or separable : BLURRED, FAINT, DIM **2** : not readily distinguishable : UNCERTAIN — **in·dis·tinct·ly** adv — **in·dis·tinct·ness** n

**in·dite** \in-ˈdīt\ vb **in·dit·ed**; **in·dit·ing** : COMPOSE ⟨∼ a poem⟩; also : to put in writing ⟨∼ a letter⟩

**in·di·um** \ˈin-dē-əm\ n : a malleable silvery metallic chemical element

**indiv** abbr individual

¹**in·di·vid·u·al** \ˌin-də-ˈvi-jə-wəl\ adj **1** : of, relating to, or associated with an individual ⟨∼ traits⟩ **2** : being an individual : existing as an indivisible whole **3** : intended for one person **4** : SEPARATE ⟨∼ copies⟩ **5** : having marked individuality ⟨an ∼ style⟩ — **in·di·vid·u·al·ly** adv

²**individual** n **1** : a single member of a category : a particular person, animal, or thing **2** : PERSON ⟨a disagreeable ∼⟩

**in·di·vid·u·al·ise** Brit var of INDIVIDUALIZE

**in·di·vid·u·al·ism** \ˌin-də-ˈvi-jə-wə-ˌli-zəm\ n **1** : a doctrine that the interests of the individual are primary **2** : a doctrine holding that the individual has political or economic rights with which the state must not interfere **3** : INDIVIDUALITY

**in·di·vid·u·al·ist** \-list\ n **1** : one that pursues a markedly independent course in thought or action **2** : one that advocates or practices individualism — **individualist** or **in·di·vid·u·al·is·tic** \ˌvi-jə-wə-ˈlis-tik\ adj

**in·di·vid·u·al·i·ty** \-ˌvi-jə-ˈwa-lə-tē\ n, pl **-ties 1** : the sum of qualities that characterize and distinguish an individual from all others; also : PERSONALITY **2** : separate or distinct existence **3** : INDIVIDUAL, PERSON

**in·di·vid·u·al·ize** \-ˈvi-jə-wə-ˌlīz\ vb **-ized**;

**-iz·ing 1** : to make individual in character **2** : to treat or notice individually : PARTICULARIZE **3** : to adapt to the needs of an individual

**individual retirement account** *n* : IRA

**in·di·vid·u·ate** \ˌin-də-ˈvi-jə-ˌwāt\ *vb* **-at·ed; -at·ing** : to give individuality to : form into an individual — **in·di·vid·u·a·tion** \-ˌvi-jə-ˈwā-shən\ *n*

**in·di·vis·i·ble** \ˌin-də-ˈvi-zə-bəl\ *adj* : impossible to divide or separate — **in·di·vis·i·bil·i·ty** \-ˌvi-zə-ˈbi-lə-tē\ *n* — **in·di·vis·i·bly** *adv*

**In·do-Ar·y·an** \ˌin-dō-ˈer-ē-ən\ *n* : a branch of the Indo-European language family that includes Hindi and other languages of south Asia

**in·doc·tri·nate** \in-ˈdäk-trə-ˌnāt\ *vb* **-nat·ed; -nat·ing** : to instruct esp. in fundamentals or rudiments : TEACH **2** : to teach the beliefs and doctrines of a particular group — **in·doc·tri·na·tion** \(ˌ)ˌdäk-trə-ˈnā-shən\ *n* — **in·doc·tri·na·tor** *n*

**In·do-Eu·ro·pe·an** \ˌin-dō-ˌyùr-ə-ˈpē-ən\ *adj* : of, relating to, or constituting a family of languages comprising those spoken in most of Europe and in the parts of the world colonized by Europeans since 1500 and also in Persia, the subcontinent of India, and some other parts of Asia

**in·do·lent** \ˈin-də-lənt\ *adj* [LL *indolens* insensitive to pain, fr. L *dolēre* to feel pain] **1** : slow to develop or heal ⟨∼ ulcers⟩ **2** : LAZY — **in·do·lence** \-ləns\ *n* — **in·do·lent·ly** *adv*

**in·dom·i·ta·ble** \in-ˈdä-mə-tə-bəl\ *adj* : UNCONQUERABLE ⟨∼ courage⟩ — **in·dom·i·ta·bly** \-blē\ *adv*

**in·door** \ˈin-ˌdòr\ *adj* **1** : of or relating to the inside of a building **2** : living, located, or carried on within a building

**in·doors** \in-ˈdòrz\ *adv* : in or into a building

**indorse, indorsement** *var of* ENDORSE, ENDORSEMENT

**in·du·bi·ta·ble** \(ˌ)in-ˈdü-bə-tə-bəl, -ˈdyü-\ *adj* : UNQUESTIONABLE ⟨∼ truths⟩ — **in·du·bi·ta·bly** \-blē\ *adv*

**in·duce** \in-ˈdüs, -ˈdyüs\ *vb* **in·duced; in·duc·ing 1** : PERSUADE, INFLUENCE **2** : BRING ABOUT **3** : to produce (as an electric current) by induction **4** : to determine by induction; *esp* : to infer from particulars — **in·duc·er** *n*

**in·duce·ment** \-mənt\ *n* **1** : something that induces : MOTIVE **2** : the act or process of inducing

**in·duct** \in-ˈdəkt\ *vb* **1** : to place in office **2** : to admit as a member **3** : to enroll for military training or service — **in·duct·ee** \-ˌdək-ˈtē\ *n*

**in·duc·tance** \in-ˈdək-təns\ *n* : a property of an electric circuit by which a varying current produces an electromotive force in that circuit or in a nearby circuit; *also* : the measure of this property

**in·duc·tion** \in-ˈdək-shən\ *n* **1** : the act or process of inducting; *also* : INITIATION **2** : the formality by which a civilian is in-

ducted into military service **3** : inference of a generalized conclusion from particular instances; *also* : a conclusion so reached **4** : the act of causing or bringing on or about **5** : the process by which an electric current, an electric charge, or magnetism is produced in a body by the proximity of an electric or magnetic field

**in·duc·tive** \in-ˈdək-tiv\ *adj* : of, relating to, or employing induction

**in·duc·tor** \in-ˈdək-tər\ *n* : an electrical component that acts upon another or is itself acted upon by induction

**in·dulge** \in-ˈdəlj\ *vb* **in·dulged; in·dulg·ing 1** : to give free rein to : GRATIFY **2** : HUMOR **3** : to gratify one's taste or desire for ⟨∼ in alcohol⟩

**in·dul·gence** \in-ˈdəl-jəns\ *n* **1** : remission of temporal punishment due in Roman Catholic doctrine for sins whose eternal punishment has been remitted by reception of the sacrifice of penance **2** : the act of indulging : the state of being indulgent **3** : an indulgent act **4** : the thing indulged in **5** : SELF-INDULGENCE — **in·dul·gent** \-jənt\ *adj* — **in·dul·gent·ly** *adv*

**in·du·rat·ed** \ˈin-dyù-ˌrā-təd, -dù-\ *adj* : physically or emotionally hardened — **in·du·ra·tion** \in-dyù-ˈrā-shən, -dù-\ *n*

**in·dus·tri·al** \in-ˈdəs-trē-əl\ *adj* **1** : of or relating to industry **2** : HEAVY-DUTY ⟨an ∼ zipper⟩ **3** : characterized by highly developed industries — **in·dus·tri·al·ly** *adv*

**in·dus·tri·al·ise** *Brit var of* INDUSTRIALIZE

**in·dus·tri·al·ist** \-ə-list\ *n* : a person owning or engaged in the management of an industry

**in·dus·tri·al·ize** \in-ˈdəs-trē-ə-ˌlīz\ *vb* **-ized; -iz·ing** : to make or become industrial — **in·dus·tri·al·i·za·tion** \-ˌdəs-trē-ə-lə-ˈzā-shən\ *n*

**in·dus·tri·ous** \in-ˈdəs-trē-əs\ *adj* : DILIGENT, BUSY — **in·dus·tri·ous·ly** *adv* — **in·dus·tri·ous·ness** *n*

**in·dus·try** \ˈin-(ˌ)dəs-trē\ *n, pl* **-tries 1** : DILIGENCE **2** : a department or branch of a craft, art, business, or manufacture; *esp* : one that employs a large personnel and capital **3** : a distinct group of productive enterprises **4** : manufacturing activity as a whole

**in·dwell** \(ˌ)in-ˈdwel\ *vb* : to exist within as an activating spirit or force

**In·dy car** \ˈin-dē-\ *n* : a single-seat, open-cockpit racing car with the engine in the rear

¹**in·ebri·ate** \i-ˈnē-brē-ˌāt\ *vb* **-at·ed; -at·ing** : to make drunk : INTOXICATE — **in·ebri·a·tion** \-ˌnē-brē-ˈā-shən\ *n*

²**in·ebri·ate** \-ət\ *n* : one that is drunk; *esp* : DRUNKARD

**in·ef·fa·ble** \(ˌ)in-ˈe-fə-bəl\ *adj* **1** : incapable of being expressed in words : INDESCRIBABLE ⟨∼ joy⟩ **2** : UNSPEAKABLE ⟨∼ disgust⟩ **3** : not to be uttered : TABOO — **in·ef·fa·bly** \-blē\ *adv*

**in·ef·fec·tive** \ˌi-nə-ˈfek-tiv\ *adj* **1** : INEF-

FECTUAL **2** : not able to perform efficiently or as expected : INCAPABLE — **in·ef·fec·tive·ly** adv — **in·ef·fec·tive·ness** n

**in·ef·fec·tu·al** \ˌi-ˈfek-chə-wəl\ adj **1** : not producing the proper or usual effect **2** : INEFFECTIVE 2 — **in·ef·fec·tu·al·ly** adv

**in·ef·fi·cient** \ˌi-nə-ˈfi-shənt\ adj **1** : not producing the desired effect **2** : wasteful of time or energy **3** : INCAPABLE, INCOMPETENT — **in·ef·fi·cien·cy** \ˈfi-shən-sē\ n — **in·ef·fi·cient·ly** adv

**in·el·e·gant** \(ˌ)i-ˈne-li-gənt\ adj : lacking in refinement, grace, or good taste — **in·el·e·gance** \-gəns\ n — **in·el·e·gant·ly** adv

**in·el·i·gi·ble** \(ˌ)i-ˈne-lə-jə-bəl\ adj : not qualified for an office or position — **in·el·i·gi·bil·i·ty** \(ˌ)i-ˌne-lə-jə-ˈbi-lə-tē\ n

**in·eluc·ta·ble** \ˌi-ni-ˈlək-tə-bəl\ adj : not to be avoided, changed, or resisted ⟨an ∼ conclusion⟩ — **in·eluc·ta·bly** \-blē\ adv

**in·ept** \i-ˈnept\ adj **1** : lacking in fitness or aptitude : UNFIT **2** : FOOLISH **3** : being out of place : INAPPROPRIATE **4** : generally incompetent : BUNGLING — **in·ept·ly** adv — **in·ept·ness** n

**in·ep·ti·tude** \(ˌ)i-ˈnep-tɪ-ˌtud, -ˌtyüd\ n : the quality or state of being inept; esp : INCOMPETENCE

**in·equal·i·ty** \ˌi-ni-ˈkwä-lə-tē\ n **1** : the quality of being unequal or uneven; esp : UNEVENNESS, DISPARITY **2** : an instance of being unequal

**in·ert** \i-ˈnərt\ adj [L inert-, iners unskilled, idle, fr. art-, ars skill] **1** : powerless to move **2** : SLUGGISH **3** : lacking in active properties ⟨chemically ∼⟩ — **in·ert·ly** adv — **in·ert·ness** n

**in·er·tia** \i-ˈnər-shə, -shē-ə\ n **1** : a property of matter whereby it remains at rest or continues in uniform motion unless acted upon by some outside force **2** : INERTNESS, SLUGGISHNESS — **in·er·tial** \-shəl\ adj

**in·es·cap·able** \ˌi-nə-ˈskä-pə-bəl\ adj : incapable of being escaped : INEVITABLE — **in·es·cap·ably** \-blē\ adv

**in·es·ti·ma·ble** \(ˌ)i-ˈnes-tə-mə-bəl\ adj **1** : incapable of being estimated or computed ⟨∼ errors⟩ **2** : too valuable or excellent to be fully appreciated — **in·es·ti·ma·bly** \-blē\ adv

**in·ev·i·ta·ble** \i-ˈne-və-tə-bəl\ adj : incapable of being avoided or evaded : bound to happen ⟨the ∼ result⟩ — **in·ev·i·ta·bil·i·ty** \(ˌ)i-ˌne-və-tə-ˈbi-lə-tē\ n

**in·ev·i·ta·bly** \-blē\ adv **1** : in an inevitable way **2** : as is to be expected

**in·ex·act** \ˌi-nig-ˈzakt\ adj **1** : not precisely correct or true : INACCURATE **2** : not rigorous and careful — **in·ex·act·ly** adv — **in·ex·act·ness** n

**in·ex·cus·able** \ˌi-nik-ˈskyü-zə-bəl\ . adj : impossible to excuse or justify ⟨∼ rudeness⟩ — **in·ex·cus·ably** \-blē\ adv

**in·ex·haust·ible** \ˌi-nig-ˈzȯ-stə-bəl\ adj **1** : incapable of being used up ⟨an ∼ supply⟩ **2** : UNTIRING ⟨an ∼ hiker⟩ — **in·ex·haust·ibly** \-blē\ adv

**in·ex·o·ra·ble** \(ˌ)i-ˈnek-sə-rə-bəl\ adj : not to be persuaded, moved, or stopped : RELENTLESS — **in·ex·o·ra·bly** adv

**in·ex·pe·ri·ence** \ˌi-nik-ˈspir-ē-əns\ n : lack of experience or of knowledge gained by experience — **in·ex·pe·ri·enced** \-ənst\ adj

**in·ex·pert** \(ˌ)i-ˈnek-ˌspərt\ adj : not expert : UNSKILLED — **in·ex·pert·ly** adv

**in·ex·pi·a·ble** \(ˌ)i-ˈnek-spē-ə-bəl\ adj : not capable of being atoned for

**in·ex·pli·ca·ble** \ˌi-nik-ˈspli-kə-bəl, (ˌ)i-ˈnek-(ˌ)spli-\ adj : incapable of being explained or accounted for ⟨an ∼ mistake⟩ — **in·ex·pli·ca·bly** \-blē\ adv

**in·ex·press·ible** \-ˈspre-sə-bəl\ adj : not capable of being expressed ⟨∼ joy⟩ — **in·ex·press·ibly** \-blē\ adv

**in ex·tre·mis** \ˌin-ik-ˈstrā-məs, -ˈstrē-\ adv : in extreme circumstances; esp : at the point of death

**in·ex·tri·ca·ble** \ˌi-nik-ˈstri-kə-bəl, (ˌ)i-ˈnek-(ˌ)stri-\ adj **1** : forming a maze or tangle from which it is impossible to get free **2** : incapable of being disentangled or untied — **in·ex·tri·ca·bly** \-blē\ adv

**inf** abbr **1** infantry **2** infinitive

**in·fal·li·ble** \(ˌ)in-ˈfa-lə-bəl\ adj **1** : incapable of error : UNERRING ⟨an ∼ marksman⟩ **2** : SURE, CERTAIN ⟨an ∼ remedy⟩ — **in·fal·li·bil·i·ty** \(ˌ)in-ˌfa-lə-ˈbi-lə-tē\ n — **in·fal·li·bly** \(ˌ)in-ˈfa-lə-blē\ adv

**in·fa·mous** \ˈin-fə-məs\ adj **1** : having a reputation of the worst kind **2** : DISGRACEFUL — **in·fa·mous·ly** adv

**in·fa·my** \-mē\ n, pl **-mies 1** : evil reputation brought about by something grossly criminal, shocking, or brutal **2** : an extreme and publicly known criminal or evil act **3** : the state of being infamous

**in·fan·cy** \ˈin-fən-sē\ n, pl **-cies 1** : early childhood **2** : a beginning or early period of existence

**in·fant** \ˈin-fənt\ n [ME enfaunt, fr. AF enfant, fr. L infant-, infans, adj., incapable of speech, young, fr. fant-, fans, prp. of fari to speak] : BABY; also : a person who is a legal minor

**in·fan·ti·cide** \in-ˈfan-tə-ˌsīd\ n : the killing of an infant

**in·fan·tile** \ˈin-fən-ˌtī(-ə)l, -tᵊl, -ˌtēl\ adj : of or relating to infants; also : CHILDISH

**infantile paralysis** n : POLIOMYELITIS

**in·fan·try** \ˈin-fən-trē\ n, pl **-tries** [MF & It; MF infanterie, fr. It infanteria, fr. infante boy, foot soldier] : soldiers trained, armed, and equipped to fight on foot — **in·fan·try·man** \-mən\ n

**in·farct** \ˈin-ˌfärkt\ n [L infarctus, pp. of infarcire to stuff] : an area of dead tissue (as of the heart wall) caused by blocking of local blood circulation — **in·farc·tion** \in-ˈfärk-shən\ n

**in·fat·u·ate** \in-ˈfa-chə-ˌwāt\ vb **-at·ed; -at·ing** : to inspire with a foolish or ex-

---

| | | | |
|---|---|---|---|
| inefficacious | inelasticity | ineradicable | inexpensive |
| inefficacy | inequitable | inerrant | inexpressive |
| inelastic | inequity | inexpedient | inextinguishable |

travagant love or admiration — **in·fat·u·a·tion** \-ˌfa-chə-ˈwā-shən\ *n*

**in·fect** \in-ˈfekt\ *vb* **1** : to contaminate with disease-producing matter **2** : to communicate a pathogen or disease to **3** : to cause to share one's feelings ⟨~ed us with his enthusiasm⟩

**in·fec·tion** \in-ˈfek-shən\ *n* **1** : a disease or condition caused by a germ or parasite; *also* : such a germ or parasite **2** : an act or process of infecting — **in·fec·tious** \-shəs\ *adj* — **in·fec·tive** \-ˈfek-tiv\ *adj*

**infectious mononucleosis** *n* : an acute infectious disease characterized by fever, swelling of lymph glands, and increased numbers of lymph cells in the blood

**in·fe·lic·i·tous** \ˌin-fi-ˈli-sə-təs\ *adj* : not appropriate in application or expression ⟨~ comments⟩ — **in·fe·lic·i·ty** \-sə-tē\ *n*

**in·fer** \in-ˈfər\ *vb* **in·ferred; in·fer·ring** **1** : to derive as a conclusion from facts or premises **2** : GUESS, SURMISE **3** : to lead to as a conclusion or consequence **4** : HINT, SUGGEST ♦ **Synonyms** DEDUCE, CONCLUDE, JUDGE, GATHER — **in·fer·ence** \ˈin-frəns, -fə-rəns\ *n* — **in·fer·en·tial** \ˌin-fə-ˈren-chəl\ *adj*

**in·fe·ri·or** \in-ˈfir-ē-ər\ *adj* **1** : situated lower down **2** : of low or lower degree or rank **3** : of lesser quality **4** : of little or less importance, value, or merit ⟨an ~ opponent⟩ — **inferior** *n* — **in·fe·ri·or·i·ty** \-ˌfir-ē-ˈor-ə-tē\ *n*

**in·fer·nal** \in-ˈfər-nᵊl\ *adj* **1** : of or relating to hell **2** : HELLISH, FIENDISH ⟨~ schemes⟩ **3** : DAMNABLE ⟨an ~ pest⟩ — **in·fer·nal·ly** *adv*

**in·fer·no** \in-ˈfər-nō\ *n, pl* **-nos** [It, hell, fr. LL *infernus*, fr. L, lower] : a place or a state that resembles or suggests hell; *also* : intense heat

**in·fer·tile** \(ˌ)in-ˈfər-tᵊl\ *adj* : not fertile or productive : BARREN — **in·fer·til·i·ty** \ˌin-fər-ˈti-lə-tē\ *n*

**in·fest** \in-ˈfest\ *vb* : to trouble by spreading or swarming in or over; *also* : to live in or on as a parasite — **in·fes·ta·tion** \ˌin-ˌfes-ˈtā-shən\ *n*

**in·fi·del** \ˈin-fə-dᵊl, -fə-ˌdel\ *n* **1** : one who is not a Christian or opposes Christianity **2** : an unbeliever esp. with respect to a particular religion

**in·fi·del·i·ty** \ˌin-fə-ˈde-lə-tē, -fī-\ *n, pl* **-ties** **1** : lack of belief in a religion **2** : unfaithfulness or an instance of it esp. in marriage

**in·field** \ˈin-ˌfēld\ *n* : the part of a baseball field inside the baselines — **in·field·er** *n*

**in·fight·ing** \ˈin-ˌfī-tiŋ\ *n* **1** : fighting at close quarters **2** : dissension or rivalry among members of a group

**in·fil·trate** \in-ˈfil-ˌtrāt, ˈin-(ˌ)fil-\ *vb* **-trat·ed; -trat·ing** **1** : to enter or filter into or through something **2** : to pass into or through by or as if by filtering or permeating — **in·fil·tra·tion** \ˌin-(ˌ)fil-ˈtrā-shən\ *n* — **in·fil·tra·tor** *n*

**in·fi·nite** \ˈin-fə-nət\ *adj* **1** : LIMITLESS, BOUNDLESS, ENDLESS ⟨~ space⟩ ⟨~ pa-

tience⟩ **2** : VAST, IMMENSE; *also* : INEXHAUSTIBLE ⟨~ wealth⟩ **3** : greater than any preassigned finite value however large ⟨~ number of positive integers⟩; *also* : extending to infinity ⟨~ plane surface⟩ — **infinite** *n* — **in·fi·nite·ly** *adv*

**in·fin·i·tes·i·mal** \(ˌ)in-ˌfi-nə-ˈte-sə-məl\ *adj* : immeasurably or incalculably small — **in·fin·i·tes·i·mal·ly** *adv*

**in·fin·i·tive** \in-ˈfi-nə-tiv\ *n* : a verb form having the characteristics of both verb and noun and in English usu. being used with *to*

**in·fin·i·tude** \in-ˈfi-nə-ˌtüd, -ˌtyüd\ *n* **1** : the quality or state of being infinite **2** : something that is infinite esp. in extent

**in·fin·i·ty** \in-ˈfi-nə-tē\ *n, pl* **-ties** **1** : the quality of being infinite **2** : unlimited extent of time, space, or quantity **3** : an indefinitely great number or amount

**in·firm** \in-ˈfərm\ *adj* **1** : deficient in vitality; *esp* : feeble from age **2** : weak of mind, will, or character : IRRESOLUTE **3** : not solid or stable : INSECURE

**in·fir·ma·ry** \in-ˈfər-mə-rē\ *n, pl* **-ries** : a place for the care of the infirm or sick

**in·fir·mi·ty** \in-ˈfər-mə-tē\ *n, pl* **-ties** **1** : FEEBLENESS **2** : DISEASE, AILMENT **3** : a personal failing : FOIBLE

**infl** *abbr* influenced

**in fla·gran·te de·lic·to** \ˌin-flə-ˈgrän-tē-di-ˈlik-tō, -ˈgran-\ *adv* **1** : in the very act of committing a misdeed **2** : in the midst of sexual activity

**in·flame** \in-ˈflām\ *vb* **in·flamed; in·flam·ing** **1** : KINDLE **2** : to excite to excessive or uncontrollable action or feeling; *also* : INTENSIFY **3** : to affect or become affected with inflammation

**in·flam·ma·ble** \in-ˈfla-mə-bəl\ *adj* **1** : FLAMMABLE **2** : easily inflamed, excited, or angered : IRASCIBLE

**in·flam·ma·tion** \ˌin-flə-ˈmā-shən\ *n* : a bodily response to injury in which an affected area becomes red, hot, and painful and congested with blood

**in·flam·ma·to·ry** \in-ˈfla-mə-ˌtor-ē\ *adj* **1** : tending to excite the senses or to arouse anger, disorder, or tumult : SEDITIOUS **2** : causing or accompanied by inflammation ⟨an ~ disease⟩

**in·flate** \in-ˈflāt\ *vb* **in·flat·ed; in·flat·ing** **1** : to swell with air or gas ⟨~ a balloon⟩ **2** : to puff up : ELATE ⟨~ one's ego⟩ **3** : to expand or increase abnormally ⟨~ prices⟩ — **in·flat·able** *adj*

**in·fla·tion** \in-ˈflā-shən\ *n* **1** : an act of inflating : the state of being inflated **2** : empty pretentiousness : POMPOSITY **3** : a continuing rise in the general price level usu. attributed to an increase in the volume of money and credit

**in·fla·tion·ary** \-shə-ˌner-ē\ *adj* : of, characterized by, or productive of inflation

**in·flect** \in-ˈflekt\ *vb* **1** : to turn from a direct line or course : CURVE **2** : to vary a word by inflection **3** : to change or vary the pitch of the voice

**in·flec·tion** \in-ˈflek-shən\ *n* **1** : the act or result of curving or bending **2** : a change

infeasible

in pitch or loudness of the voice **3** : the change of form that words undergo to mark case, gender, number, tense, person, mood, or voice — **in·flec·tion·al** \-shə-nəl\ *adj*

**in·flex·i·ble** \(,)in-'flek-sə-bəl\ *adj* **1** : UNYIELDING **2** : RIGID **3** : incapable of change ⟨an ∼ deadline⟩ — **in·flex·i·bil·i·ty** \-,flek-sə-'bi-lə-tē\ *n* — **in·flex·i·bly** \-'flek-sə-blē\ *adv*

**in·flex·ion** \in-'flek-shən\ *chiefly Brit var of* INFLECTION

**in·flict** \in-'flikt\ *vb* : AFFLICT; *also* : to give by or as if by striking ⟨∼ pain⟩ — **in·flic·tion** \-'flik-shən\ *n*

**in·flo·res·cence** \,in-flə-'re-sᵊn(t)s\ *n* : the manner of development and arrangement of flowers on a stem; *also* : a flowering stem with its appendages : a flower cluster

**in·flow** \'in-,flō\ *n* : a flowing in

**¹in·flu·ence** \'in-,flü-əns\ *n* **1** : the act or power of producing an effect without any apparent force or direct authority **2** : the power or capacity of causing an effect in indirect or intangible ways **3** : one that exerts influence — **in·flu·en·tial** \,in-flü-'en-chəl\ *adj* — **under the influence** : affected by alcohol

**²influence** *vb* **-enced; -enc·ing 1** : to affect or alter by influence : SWAY **2** : to have an effect on the condition or development of : MODIFY

**in·flu·en·za** \,in-flü-'en-zə\ *n* [It, lit., influence, fr. ML *influentia;* fr. the belief that epidemics were due to the influence of the stars] : an acute and highly contagious virus disease marked by fever, prostration, aches and pains, and respiratory inflammation; *also* : any of various feverish usu. virus diseases typically with respiratory symptoms

**in·flux** \'in-,fləks\ *n* : a coming in

**in·fo** \'in-(,)fō\ *n* : INFORMATION

**in·fold** \in-'fōld\ *vb* **1** : ENFOLD **2** : to fold inward or toward one another

**in·fo·mer·cial** \'in-fō-,mər-shəl\ *n* : a television program that is an extended advertisement often including a discussion or demonstration

**in·form** \in-'fȯrm\ *vb* **1** : to communicate knowledge to : TELL **2** : to give information or knowledge **3** : to act as an informer ♦ *Synonyms* ACQUAINT, APPRISE, ADVISE, NOTIFY

**in·for·mal** \in-'fȯr-məl\ *adj* **1** : conducted or carried out without formality or ceremony ⟨an ∼ party⟩ **2** : characteristic of or appropriate to ordinary, casual, or familiar use ⟨∼ clothes⟩ — **in·for·mal·i·ty** \,in-fȯr-'ma-lə-tē, -fər-\ *n* — **in·for·mal·ly** \(,)in-'fȯr-mə-lē\ *adv*

**in·for·mant** \in-'fȯr-mənt\ *n* : a person who gives information : INFORMER

**in·for·ma·tion** \,in-fər-'mā-shən\ *n* **1** : the communication or reception of knowledge or intelligence **2** : knowledge obtained from investigation, study, or instruction : FACTS, DATA **3** : the attribute communicated by one of two or more alternative sequences of something (as nucleotides in DNA or binary digits in a computer program) — **in·for·ma·tion·al** \-shə-nəl\ *adj*

**information superhighway** *n* : INTERNET

**information technology** *n* : technology involving computer systems and networks for the processing and distribution of data

**in·for·ma·tive** \in-'fȯr-mə-tiv\ *adj* : imparting knowledge : INSTRUCTIVE

**in·formed** \in-'fȯrmd\ *adj* **1** : having or based on information ⟨an ∼ decision⟩ **2** : EDUCATED, KNOWLEDGEABLE

**informed consent** *n* : consent to a medical procedure by someone who understands what is involved

**in·form·er** \-'fȯr-mər\ *n* : one that informs; *esp* : a person who informs against others for illegalities esp for financial gain

**in·fo·tain·ment** \,in-fō-'tān-mənt\ *n* : a television program that presents information (as news) in a manner intended to be entertaining

**in·frac·tion** \in-'frak-shən\ *n* [ME, fr. ML *infractio,* fr. L, subduing, fr. *infringere* to break, crush] : the act of infringing : VIOLATION

**in·fra dig** \,in-frə-'dig\ *adj* [short for L *infra dignitatem*] : being beneath one's dignity

**in·fra·red** \,in-frə-'red\ *adj* : being, relating to, or using radiation having wavelengths longer than those of red light — **infrared** *n*

**in·fra·struc·ture** \'in-frə-,strək-chər\ *n* **1** : the underlying foundation or basic framework (as of a system or organization) **2** : the system of public works of a country, state, or region; *also* : the resources (as buildings or equipment) required for an activity

**in·fre·quent** \(,)in-'frē-kwənt\ *adj* **1** : seldom happening : RARE **2** : placed or occurring at wide intervals in space or time ♦ *Synonyms* UNCOMMON, SCARCE, SPORADIC — **in·fre·quent·ly** *adv*

**in·fringe** \in-'frinj\ *vb* **in·fringed; in·fring·ing 1** : VIOLATE, TRANSGRESS ⟨∼ a patent⟩ **2** : ENCROACH, TRESPASS ⟨∼ on our rights⟩ — **in·fringe·ment** *n*

**in·fu·ri·ate** \in-'fyùr-ē-,āt\ *vb* **-at·ed; -at·ing** : to make furious : ENRAGE — **in·fu·ri·at·ing·ly** *adv*

**in·fuse** \in-'fyüz\ *vb* **in·fused; in·fus·ing 1** : to instill a principle or quality in ⟨*infused* the team with confidence⟩ **2** : INSPIRE, ANIMATE **3** : to steep (as tea) without boiling — **in·fu·sion** \-'fyü-zhən\ *n*

**¹-ing** \iŋ\ *n suffix* **1** : action or process ⟨sleep*ing*⟩ : instance of an action or process ⟨a meet*ing*⟩ **2** : product or result of an action or process ⟨an engrav*ing*⟩ ⟨earn*ings*⟩ **3** : something used in an action or process ⟨a bed cover*ing*⟩ **4** : something connected with, consisting of, or used in making (a specified thing) ⟨scaffold*ing*⟩ **5** : something related to (a specified concept) ⟨off*ing*⟩

**²-ing** *n suffix* : one of a (specified) kind

**³-ing** *vb suffix or adj suffix* — used to form the present participle ⟨sail*ing*⟩ and sometimes to form an adjective resembling a present participle but not derived from a verb <swashbuckl*ing*>

**in·gath·er** \'in-,ga-thər\ *vb* : to gather in : ASSEMBLE

**in·ge·nious** \in-'jēn-yəs\ *adj* 1 : marked by special aptitude at discovering, inventing, or contriving 2 : marked by originality, resourcefulness, and cleverness in conception or execution — **in·ge·nious·ly** *adv* — **in·ge·nious·ness** *n*

**in·ge·nue** *or* **in·gé·nue** \'an-jə-,nü, 'än-; 'aⁿ-zhə-, 'äⁿ-\ *n* : a naive girl or young woman; *esp* : an actress portraying such a person

**in·ge·nu·i·ty** \,in-jə-'nü-ə-tē, -'nyü-\ *n, pl* **-ties** : skill or cleverness in planning or inventing : INVENTIVENESS

**in·gen·u·ous** \in-'jen-yə-wəs\ *adj* [L *ingenuus* native, freeborn, fr. *gignere* to beget] 1 : innocently straightforward <*her* ~ *curiosity*> 2 : lacking craft or subtlety <~ *comments*> — **in·gen·u·ous·ly** *adv* — **in·gen·u·ous·ness** *n*

**in·gest** \in-'jest\ *vb* : to take in for or as if for digestion — **in·ges·tion** \-'jes-chən\ *n*

**in·gle·nook** \'iŋ-gəl-,nük\ *n* : a nook by a large open fireplace; *also* : a bench occupying this nook

**in·glo·ri·ous** \(,)in-'glór-ē-əs\ *adj* 1 : SHAMEFUL 2 : not glorious : lacking fame or honor — **in·glo·ri·ous·ly** *adv*

**in·got** \'iŋ-gət\ *n* : a mass of metal cast in a form convenient for storage or transportation

¹**in·grain** \(,)in-'grān\ *vb* : to work indelibly into the natural texture or mental or moral constitution — **in·grained** *adj*

²**in·grain** \'in-,grān\ *adj* 1 : made of fiber that is dyed before being spun into yarn 2 : made of yarn that is dyed before being woven or knitted 3 : INNATE — **in·grain** *n*

**in·grate** \'in-,grāt\ *n* : an ungrateful person

**in·gra·ti·ate** \in-'grā-shē-,āt\ *vb* **-at·ed; -at·ing** : to gain favor by deliberate effort

**in·gra·ti·at·ing** *adj* 1 : capable of winning favor : PLEASING <an ~ *smile*> 2 : FLATTERING <an ~ *manner*>

**in·grat·i·tude** \(,)in-'gra-tə-,tüd, -,tyüd\ *n* : lack of gratitude : UNGRATEFULNESS

**in·gre·di·ent** \in-'grē-dē-ənt\ *n* : one of the substances that make up a mixture or compound : CONSTITUENT

**in·gress** \'in-,gres\ *n* : ENTRANCE, ACCESS — **in·gres·sion** \in-'gre-shən\ *n*

**in·grow·ing** \'in-,grō-iŋ\ *adj* : growing or tending inward

**in·grown** \-,grōn\ *adj* : grown in; *esp* : having the free tip or edge embedded in the flesh <an ~ *toenail*>

**in·gui·nal** \'in-gwə-nºl\ *adj* : of, relating to, or situated in or near the region of the groin <an ~ *hernia*>

**in·hab·it** \in-'ha-bət\ *vb* : to live or dwell in <spiders that ~ *caves*> — **in·hab·it·able** *adj* — **in·hab·i·ta·tion** \in-,ha-bə-'tā-shən\ *n*

**in·hab·i·tant** \in-'ha-bə-tənt\ *n* : a permanent resident in a place

**in·hal·ant** \in-'hā-lənt\ *n* : something (as a medicine) that is inhaled

**in·ha·la·tor** \'in-hə-,lā-tər\ *n* : a device that provides a mixture of carbon dioxide and oxygen for breathing

**in·hale** \in-'hāl\ *vb* **in·haled; in·hal·ing** : to breathe in — **in·ha·la·tion** \,in-hə-'lā-shən\ *n*

**in·hal·er** \in-'hā-lər\ *n* : a device by means of which medicinal material is inhaled

**in·here** \in-'hir\ *vb* **in·hered; in·her·ing** : to be inherent

**in·her·ent** \in-'hir-ənt, -'her-\ *adj* : established as an essential part of something : INTRINSIC <risks ~ in the venture> — **in·her·ent·ly** *adv*

**in·her·it** \in-'her-ət\ *vb* 1 : to receive esp. from one's ancestors 2 : to receive by genetic transmission — **in·her·it·able** \-ə-tə-bəl\ *adj* — **in·her·i·tance** \-ə-təns\ *n* — **in·her·i·tor** \-ə-tər\ *n*

**in·hib·it** \in-'hi-bət\ *vb* 1 : PROHIBIT, FORBID 2 : to hold in check : RESTRAIN <~ed by fear> — **in·hib·i·tor** \-bə-tər\ *n* — **in·hib·i·to·ry** \-bə-,tór-ē\ *adj*

**in·hi·bi·tion** \,in-hə-'bi-shən\ *n* 1 : PROHIBITION, RESTRAINT 2 : a usu. inner check on free activity, expression, or functioning

**in–house** \'in-,haùs, -'haùs\ *adj* : existing, originating, or carried on within a group or organization

**in·hu·man** \(,)in-'hyü-mən, -'yü-\ *adj* 1 : lacking pity, kindness, or mercy : SAVAGE <an ~ *tyrant*> 2 : COLD, IMPERSONAL 3 : not worthy of or conforming to the needs of human beings <~ *living conditions*> 4 : of or suggesting a nonhuman class of beings — **in·hu·man·ly** *adv* — **in·hu·man·ness** *n*

**in·hu·mane** \,in-hyü-'mān, -yü-\ *adj* : not humane : INHUMAN 1

**in·hu·man·i·ty** \-'ma-nə-tē\ *n, pl* **-ties** 1 : the quality or state of being cruel or barbarous 2 : a cruel or barbarous act

**in·im·i·cal** \i-'ni-mi-kəl\ *adj* 1 : being adverse often by reason of hostility <forces ~ to change> 2 : HOSTILE, UNFRIENDLY <~ *factions*> — **in·im·i·cal·ly** *adv*

**in·im·i·ta·ble** \(,)i-'ni-mə-tə-bəl\ *adj* : not capable of being imitated

**in·iq·ui·ty** \i-'ni-kwə-tē\ *n, pl* **-ties** [ME *iniquite*, fr. AF *iniquité*, fr. L *iniquitas*, fr. *iniquus* uneven, fr. *aequus* equal] 1 :· WICKEDNESS 2 : a wicked act — **in·iq·ui·tous** \-təs\ *adj*

¹**ini·tial** \i-'ni-shəl\ *adj* 1 : of or relating to the beginning : INCIPIENT <my ~ *reaction*> 2 : being at the beginning — **ini·tial·ly** *adv*

²**initial** *n* : the first letter of a word or name

³**initial** *vb* **-tialed** *or* **-tialled; -tial·ing** *or* **-tial·ling** : to affix an initial to

¹**ini·ti·ate** \i-'ni-shē-,āt\ *vb* **-at·ed; -at·ing** 1 : START, BEGIN 2 : to induct into membership by or as if by special ceremonies 3 : to instruct in the rudiments or princi-

---

inharmonious          inhospitable          injudicious

ples of something — **ini·ti·a·tion** \-,ni-shē-'ā-shən\ n

²**ini·tiate** \i-'ni-shē-ət\ n  1 : a person who is undergoing or has passed an initiation  2 : a person who is instructed or adept in some special field

**ini·tia·tive** \i-'ni-shə-tiv\ n  1 : an introductory step  2 : self-reliant enterprise ⟨showed great ~⟩  3 : a process by which laws may be introduced or enacted directly by vote of the people

**ini·tia·to·ry** \i-'ni-shē-ə-,tōr-ē\ adj  1 : INTRODUCTORY  2 : tending or serving to initiate ⟨~ rites⟩

**in·ject** \in-'jekt\ vb  1 : to force into something ⟨~ serum with a needle⟩  2 : to introduce as an element into some situation or subject ⟨~ a note of suspicion⟩ — **in·jec·tion** \-'jek-shən\ n

**in·junc·tion** \in-'jəŋk-shən\ n  1 : ORDER, ADMONITION  2 : a court writ whereby one is required to do or to refrain from doing a specified act

**in·jure** \'in-jər\ vb **in·jured**; **in·jur·ing**  1 : WRONG  2 : to damage or hurt esp. physically  ♦ **Synonyms** HARM, IMPAIR, MAR, SPOIL

**in·ju·ry** \'in-jə-rē\ n, pl **-ries**  1 : an act that damages or hurts : WRONG  2 : hurt, damage, or loss sustained — **in·ju·ri·ous** \in-'jür-ē-əs\ adj

**in·jus·tice** \(,)in-'jəs-təs\ n  1 : violation of a person's rights : UNFAIRNESS  2 : an unjust act or deed : WRONG

¹**ink** \'iŋk\ n [ME enke, fr. AF encre, enke, fr. LL encaustum, fr. L encaustus burned in, fr. Gk enkaustos, fr. enkaiein to burn in] : a usu. liquid and colored material for writing and printing — **inky** adj

²**ink** vb : to put ink on; esp : SIGN

**ink·blot test** \'iŋk-,blät-\ n : any of several psychological tests based on the interpretation of irregular figures

**ink·horn** \-,hörn\ n : a small bottle (as of horn) for holding ink

**in–kind** \'in-'kīnd\ adj : consisting of something (as goods) other than money

**ink–jet** n : a computer printer that sprays electrically charged droplets of ink onto paper — **ink–jet** adj

**ink·ling** \'iŋ-kliŋ\ n  1 : HINT, INTIMATION  2 : a vague idea

**ink·stand** \'iŋk-,stand\ n : INKWELL; also : a pen and ink stand

**ink·well** \-,wel\ n : a container for ink

**in·laid** \'in-'lād\ adj : decorated with material set into a surface

¹**in·land** \'in-,land, -lənd\ adj  1 chiefly Brit : not foreign : DOMESTIC ⟨~ revenue⟩  2 : of or relating to the interior of a country ⟨the ~ states⟩

²**inland** n : the interior of a country

³**inland** adv : into or toward the interior

**in–law** \'in-,lö\ n : a relative by marriage

¹**in·lay** \(,)in-'lā, 'in-,lā\ vb **in·laid** \-'lād\; **in·lay·ing** : to set (a material) into a surface or ground material esp. for decoration

²**in·lay** \'in-,lā\ n  1 : inlaid work  2 : a shaped filling cemented into a tooth

**in·let** \'in-,let, -lət\ n  1 : a small or narrow

bay  2 : an opening for intake esp. of a fluid

**in–line skate** n : a roller skate whose four wheels are set in a straight line — **in–line skater** n — **in–line skating** n

**in·mate** \'in-,māt\ n : any of a group occupying a single place of residence; esp : a person confined (as in a hospital or prison)

**in me·di·as res** \in-,mā-dē-əs-'rās\ adv [L, lit., into the midst of things] : in or into the middle of a narrative or plot

**in me·mo·ri·am** \,in-mə-'mör-ē-əm\ prep [L.] : in memory of

**in·most** \'in-,mōst\ adj : deepest within : INNERMOST

**inn** \'in\ n : HOTEL, TAVERN

**in·nards** \'i-nərdz\ n pl [alter. of inwards]  1 : the internal organs of a human being or animal; esp : VISCERA  2 : the internal parts of a structure or mechanism

**in·nate** \i-'nāt\ adj  1 : existing in, belonging to, or determined by factors present in an individual from birth : NATIVE  2 : INHERENT, INTRINSIC ⟨the ~ defects of a plan⟩ — **in·nate·ly** adv

**in·ner** \'i-nər\ adj  1 : situated farther in ⟨the ~ bark⟩  2 : near a center esp. of influence ⟨the ~ circle⟩  3 : of or relating to the mind or spirit ⟨an ~ voice⟩  4 : being a usu. repressed part of one's psychological makeup ⟨the ~ child⟩

**inner city** n : the usu. older, poorer, and more densely populated section of a city — **inner–city** adj

**in·ner–di·rect·ed** \,i-nər-də-'rek-təd, -(,)di-\ adj : directed in thought and action by one's own scale of values as opposed to external norms

**inner ear** n : the part of the ear that is most important for hearing, is located in a cavity in the temporal bone, and contains sense organs of hearing and of awareness of position in space

**in·ner·most** \'i-nər-,mōst\ adj : farthest inward : INMOST

**in·ner·sole** \'i-nər-'sōl\ n : INSOLE

**in·ner·spring** \'i-nər-'spriŋ\ adj : having coil springs inside a padded casing ⟨an ~ mattress⟩

**inner tube** n : an airtight rubber tube inside a tire to hold air under pressure

**in·ning** \'i-niŋ\ n  1 sing or pl : a division of a cricket match  2 : a baseball team's turn at bat; also : a division of a baseball game consisting of a turn at bat for each team

**inn·keep·er** \'in-'kē-pər\ n  1 : a proprietor of an inn  2 : a hotel manager

**in·no·cence** \'i-nə-səns\ n  1 : BLAMELESSNESS; also : freedom from legal guilt  2 : GUILELESSNESS, SIMPLICITY; also : IGNORANCE

**in·no·cent** \-sənt\ adj [ME, fr. AF, fr. L innocens, fr. nocens wicked, fr. nocēre to harm]  1 : free from guilt or sin : BLAMELESS  2 : harmless in effect or intention; also : CANDID ⟨an ~ remark⟩  3 : free from legal guilt or fault : LAWFUL  4 : INGENUOUS ⟨an ~ question⟩  5 : UNAWARE — **innocent** n — **in·no·cent·ly** adv

**in·noc·u·ous** \i-'nä-kyə-wəs\ *adj* **1** : HARMLESS **2** : not offensive; *also* : INSIPID ⟨∼ jokes⟩

**in·nom·i·nate** \i-'nä-mə-nət\ *adj* : having no name; *also* : ANONYMOUS

**in·no·vate** \'i-nə-ˌvāt\ *vb* **-vat·ed; -vat·ing** : to introduce as or as if new : make changes — **in·no·va·tive** \-ˌvā-tiv\ *adj* — **in·no·va·tor** \-ˌvā-tər\ *n*

**in·no·va·tion** \ˌi-nə-'vā-shən\ *n* **1** : the introduction of something new **2** : a new idea, method, or device

**in·nu·en·do** \ˌin-yə-'wen-dō\ *n, pl* **-dos** or **-does** [L, by nodding, fr. *innuere* to nod to, make a sign to, fr. *nuere* to nod] : HINT, INSINUATION; *esp* : a veiled reflection on character or reputation

**in·nu·mer·a·ble** \i-'nü-mə-rə-bəl, -'nyü-\ *adj* : too many to be numbered

**in·oc·u·late** \i-'nä-kyə-lāt\ *vb* **-lat·ed; -lat·ing** [ME, to insert a bud in a plant, fr. L *inoculare*, fr. *oculus* eye, bud] : to introduce something into; *esp* : to introduce a serum or antibody into (an organism) to treat or prevent a disease — **in·oc·u·la·tion** \-ˌnä-kyə-'lā-shən\ *n*

**in·op·er·a·ble** \(ˌ)in-'ä-pə-rə-bəl\ *adj* **1** : not suitable for surgery ⟨an ∼ tumor⟩ **2** : not operable ⟨∼ vehicles⟩

**in·op·er·a·tive** \-'ä-pə-rə-tiv, -'ä-pə-ˌrā-\ *adj* : not functioning

**in·op·por·tune** \(ˌ)in-ˌä-pər-'tün, -'tyün\ *adj* : INCONVENIENT, INAPPROPRIATE — **in·op·por·tune·ly** *adv*

**in·or·di·nate** \in-'ȯr-dᵊn-ət\ *adj* : exceeding reasonable limits : IMMODERATE ⟨drank an ∼ amount of water⟩ — **in·or·di·nate·ly** *adv*

**in·or·gan·ic** \ˌin-ȯr-'ga-nik\ *adj* : being or composed of matter of other than plant or animal origin : MINERAL

**in·pa·tient** \'in-ˌpā-shənt\ *n* : a hospital patient who receives lodging and food as well as treatment

**in·put** \'in-ˌpu̇t\ *n* **1** : something put in **2** : power or energy put into a machine or system **3** : information fed into a computer or data processing system **4** : ADVICE, OPINION — **input** *vb*

**in·quest** \'in-ˌkwest\ *n* **1** : an official inquiry or examination esp. before a jury **2** : INQUIRY, INVESTIGATION

**in·qui·etude** \(ˌ)in-'kwī-ə-ˌtüd, -ˌtyüd\ *n* : UNEASINESS, RESTLESSNESS

**in·quire** \in-'kwī(-ə)r\ *vb* **in·quired; in·quir·ing** **1** : to ask about : ASK **2** : INVESTIGATE, EXAMINE — **in·quir·er** *n* — **in·quir·ing·ly** *adv*

**in·qui·ry** \'in-ˌkwī(-ə)r-ē, in-'kwī(-ə)r-ē; 'in-kwə-rē, 'iṇ-\ *n, pl* **-ries** **1** : a request for information; *also* : RESEARCH **2** : a systematic investigation of a matter of public interest

**in·qui·si·tion** \ˌin-kwə-'zi-shən, ˌiṇ-\ *n* **1** : a judicial or official inquiry usu. before a jury **2** *cap* : a former Roman Catholic tribunal for the discovery and punishment of heresy **3** : a severe questioning — **in·quis·i·tor** \in-'kwi-zə-tər\ *n* — **in·quis·i·to·ri·al** \-ˌkwi-zə-'tȯr-ē-əl\ *adj*

**in·quis·i·tive** \in-'kwi-zə-tiv\ *adj* **1** : given to examination or investigation ⟨an ∼ mind⟩ **2** : unduly curious — **in·quis·i·tive·ly** *adv* — **in·quis·i·tive·ness** *n*

**in re** \in-'rā, -'rē\ *prep* : in the matter of

**INRI** *abbr* [L *Iesus Nazarenus Rex Iudaeorum*] Jesus of Nazareth, King of the Jews

**in·road** \'in-ˌrōd\ *n* **1** : INVASION, RAID **2** : an advance made usu. at the expense of another ⟨made ∼s toward getting the job⟩

**in·rush** \'in-ˌrəsh\ *n* : a crowding or flooding in

**ins** *abbr* **1** inches **2** insurance

**INS** *abbr* Immigration and Naturalization Service

**in·sa·lu·bri·ous** \ˌin-sə-'lü-brē-əs\ *adj* : UNWHOLESOME, NOXIOUS ⟨∼ air⟩

**ins and outs** *n pl* **1** : characteristic peculiarities **2** : RAMIFICATIONS

**in·sane** \(ˌ)in-'sān\ *adj* **1** : exhibiting serious and debilitating mental disorder; *also* : used by or for the insane **2** : ABSURD **3** : greatly exceeding the ordinary, usual, or expected — **in·sane·ly** *adv* — **in·san·i·ty** \in-'sa-nə-tē\ *n*

**in·sa·tia·ble** \(ˌ)in-'sā-shə-bəl\ *adj* : incapable of being satisfied ⟨an ∼ thirst⟩ — **in·sa·tia·bil·i·ty** \(ˌ)in-ˌsā-shə-'bi-lə-tē\ *n* — **in·sa·tia·bly** *adv*

**in·sa·tiate** \(ˌ)in-'sā-shē-ət, -ˌshət\ *adj* : INSATIABLE — **in·sa·tiate·ly** *adv*

**in·scribe** \in-'skrīb\ *vb* **1** : to write, engrave, or print as a lasting record **2** : ENROLL **3** : to write, engrave, or print characters upon **4** : to dedicate to someone **5** : to draw within a figure so as to touch in as many places as possible — **in·scrip·tion** \-'skrip-shən\ *n*

**in·scru·ta·ble** \in-'skrü-tə-bəl\ *adj* : not readily comprehensible : MYSTERIOUS ⟨an ∼ smile⟩ — **in·scru·ta·bly** \-blē\ *adv*

**in·seam** \'in-ˌsēm\ *n* : the seam on the inside of the leg of a pair of pants; *also* : the length of this seam

**in·sect** \'in-ˌsekt\ *n* [L *insectum*, fr. *insectus*, pp. of *insecare* to cut into, fr. *secare* to cut] : any of a class of small usu. winged arthropod animals (as flies, bees, beetles, and moths) with usu. three pairs of legs as adults

**in·sec·ti·cide** \in-'sek-tə-ˌsīd\ *n* : an agent for destroying insects — **in·sec·ti·cid·al** \(ˌ)in-ˌsek-tə-'sī-dᵊl\ *adj*

**in·sec·tiv·o·rous** \ˌin-ˌsek-'ti-və-rəs\ *adj* : feeding on insects

**in·se·cure** \ˌin-si-'kyu̇r\ *adj* **1** : UNCERTAIN **2** : not protected : UNSAFE ⟨an ∼ investment⟩ **3** : LOOSE, SHAKY ⟨an ∼ hinge⟩ **4** : not highly stable ⟨an ∼ marriage⟩; *also* : lacking assurance : ANXIOUS, FEARFUL — **in·se·cure·ly** *adv* — **in·se·cu·ri·ty** \-'kyu̇r-ə-tē\ *n*

**in·sem·i·nate** \in-'se-mə-ˌnāt\ *vb* **-nat·ed; -nat·ing** : to introduce semen into the genital tract of (a female) — **in·sem·i·na·tion** \-ˌse-mə-'nā-shən\ *n*

**in·sen·sate** \(ˌ)in-'sen-ˌsāt, -sət\ *adj* **1** : lacking sense or understanding; *also*

: FOOLISH  **2** : INANIMATE  **3** : BRUTAL, INHUMAN 〈~ rage〉

**in·sen·si·ble** \(,)in-'sen-sə-bəl\ *adj*  **1** : IMPERCEPTIBLE; *also* : SLIGHT, GRADUAL  **2** : INANIMATE  **3** : UNCONSCIOUS  **4** : lacking sensory perception or ability to react 〈~ to pain〉  **5** : APATHETIC, INDIFFERENT; *also* : UNAWARE 〈~ of their danger〉  **6** : MEANINGLESS  **7** : lacking delicacy or refinement — **in·sen·si·bil·i·ty** \-,sen-sə-'bi-lə-tē\ *n* — **in·sen·si·bly** \-'sen-sə-blē\ *adv*

**in·sen·tient** \(,)in-'sen-chē-ənt\ *adj* : lacking perception, consciousness, or animation — **in·sen·tience** \-chē-əns\ *n*

**in·sep·a·ra·ble** \(,)in-'se-prə-bəl, -pə-rə-\ *adj*  **1** : incapable of being separated or disjoined  **2** : very close or intimate 〈~ friends〉 — **in·sep·a·ra·bil·i·ty** \-,se-prə-'bi-lə-tē, -pə-rə-\ *n* — **inseparable** *n* — **in·sep·a·ra·bly** \-'se-prə-blē, -pə-rə-\ *adv*

¹**in·sert** \in-'sərt\ *vb*  **1** : to put or thrust in 〈~ a key in a lock〉 〈~ a comma〉  **2** : INTERPOLATE  **3** : to set in (as a piece of fabric) and make fast

²**in·sert** \'in-,sərt\ *n* : something that is inserted or is for insertion; *esp* : written or printed material inserted (as between the leaves of a book)

**in·ser·tion** \in-'sər-shən\ *n*  **1** : something that is inserted  **2** : the act or process of inserting

**in·set** \'in-,set\ *vb* **inset** *or* **in·set·ted**; **set·ting** : to set in : INSERT — **inset** *n*

¹**in·shore** \'in-'shòr\ *adj*  **1** : situated, living, or carried on near shore  **2** : moving toward shore 〈an ~ current〉

²**inshore** *adv* : to or toward shore

¹**in·side** \in-'sīd, 'in-,sīd\ *n*  **1** : an inner side or surface : INTERIOR  **2** : inward nature, thoughts, or feeling  **3** *pl* : VISCERA, ENTRAILS  **4** : a position of power, trust, or familiarity — **inside** *adj*

²**inside** *adv*  **1** : on the inner side  **2** : in or into the interior

³**inside** *prep*  **1** : in or into the inside of 〈~ the house〉  **2** : WITHIN 〈~ an hour〉

**inside of** *prep* : INSIDE

**inside out** *adv*  **1** : in such a manner that the inner surface becomes the outer 〈turned the shirt *inside out*〉  **2** : in a state of disarray or reorganization 〈turned her life *inside out*〉

**in·sid·er** \in-'sī-dər\ *n* : a person who is in a position of power or has access to confidential information

**in·sid·i·ous** \in-'si-dē-əs\ *adj* [L *insidiosus*, fr. *insidiae* ambush, fr. *insidēre* to sit in, sit on, fr. *sedēre* to sit]  **1** : SLY, TREACHEROUS  **2** : SEDUCTIVE  **3** : having a gradual and cumulative effect : SUBTLE — **in·sid·i·ous·ly** *adv* — **in·sid·i·ous·ness** *n*

**in·sight** \'in-,sīt\ *n* : the power, act, or result of seeing into a situation : UNDERSTANDING 〈a leader of great ~〉 — **in·sight·ful** \'in-,sīt-fəl, in-'sīt-\ *adj*

**in·sig·nia** \in-'sig-nē-ə\ *also* **in·sig·ne** \-(,)nē\ *n, pl* **-nia** *or* **-ni·as** : a distinguish-

ing mark esp. of authority or honor : BADGE

**in·sin·cere** \,in-sin-'sir\ *adj* : not sincere : HYPOCRITICAL — **in·sin·cere·ly** *adv* — **in·sin·cer·i·ty** \-'ser-ə-tē\ *n*

**in·sin·u·ate** \in-'sin-yə-,wāt\ *vb* **-at·ed; -at·ing** [L *insinuare*, fr. *sinuare* to bend, curve, fr. *sinus* curve]  **1** : to introduce gradually or in a subtle, indirect, or artful way  **2** : to imply in a subtle or devious way — **in·sin·u·a·tion** \(,)in-,sin-yə-'wā-shən\ *n*

**in·sin·u·at·ing** *adj*  **1** : winning favor and confidence by imperceptible degrees  **2** : tending gradually to cause doubt, distrust, or change of outlook

**in·sip·id** \in-'si-pəd\ *adj*  **1** : lacking taste or savor  **2** : DULL, FLAT 〈an ~ movie〉 — **in·si·pid·i·ty** \,in-sə-'pi-də-tē\ *n*

**in·sist** \in-'sist\ *vb* [MF or L; MF *insister*, fr. L *insistere* to stand upon, persist, fr. *sistere* to take a stand] : to take a resolute stand 〈~ed on paying〉

**in·sis·tence** \in-'sis-təns\ *n* : the act of insisting; *also* : an insistent attitude or quality : URGENCY

**in·sis·tent** \in-'sis-tənt\ *adj* : disposed to insist — **in·sis·tent·ly** *adv*

**in si·tu** \in-'sī-tü, -'sē-\ *adv or adj* [L, in position] : in the natural or original position 〈an *in situ* cancer〉

**in·so·far as** \,in-sə-'fär-\ *conj* : to the extent or degree that

**insol** *abbr* insoluble

**in·so·la·tion** \,in-(,)sō-'lā-shən\ *n* : solar radiation that has been received

**in·sole** \'in-,sōl\ *n*  **1** : an inside sole of a shoe  **2** : a loose thin strip placed inside a shoe for warmth or comfort

**in·so·lent** \'in-sə-lənt\ *adj* : contemptuous, rude, disrespectful, or bold in behavior or language — **in·so·lence** \-ləns\ *n*

**in·sol·u·ble** \(,)in-'säl-yə-bəl\ *adj*  **1** : having or admitting of no solution or explanation  **2** : difficult or impossible to dissolve — **in·sol·u·bil·i·ty** \-,säl-yə-'bi-lə-tē\ *n*

**in·sol·vent** \(,)in-'säl-vənt\ *adj*  **1** : unable or insufficient to pay all debts 〈an ~ estate〉  **2** : IMPOVERISHED, DEFICIENT — **in·sol·ven·cy** \-vən-sē\ *n*

**in·som·nia** \in-'säm-nē-ə\ *n* : prolonged and usu. abnormal sleeplessness — **in·som·ni·ac** \-nē-,ak\ *n*

**in·so·much as** \,in-sə-'məch-\ *conj* : INASMUCH AS

**insomuch that** *conj* : to such a degree that : SO

**in·sou·ci·ance** \in-'sü-sē-əns, aⁿ-süs-'yäⁿs\ *n* [F] : lighthearted unconcern 〈youthful ~〉 — **in·sou·ci·ant** \in-'sü-sē-ənt, aⁿ-süs-'yäⁿ\ *adj*

**insp** *abbr* inspector

**in·spect** \in-'spekt\ *vb* : to view closely and critically : EXAMINE 〈~ the gem for flaws〉 — **in·spec·tion** \-'spek-shən\ *n* — **in·spec·tor** \-tər\ *n*

**inspector general** *n* : the head of a system of inspection (as of an army)

**in·spi·ra·tion** \,in-spə-'rā-shən\ *n*  **1** : the act or power of moving the intellect or emotions 2 : INHALATION 3 : the quality or state of being inspired; *also* : something that is inspired 4 : an inspiring agent or influence — **in·spi·ra·tion·al** \-shə-nəl\ *adj*

**in·spire** \in-ˈspīr\ *vb* **in·spired; in·spir·ing** 1 : to influence, move, or guide by divine or supernatural inspiration 2 : to exert an animating, enlivening, or exalting influence upon ⟨a painter *inspired* by cubism⟩; *also* : AFFECT 3 : to communicate to an agent supernaturally; *also* : bring out or about 4 : INHALE 5 : INCITE 6 : to spread by indirect means — **in·spir·er** *n*

**in·spir·it** \in-ˈspir-ət\ *vb* : ENCOURAGE, HEARTEN ⟨~ed the team⟩

**inst** *abbr* 1 instant 2 institute; institution; institutional

**in·sta·bil·i·ty** \in-stə-ˈbi-lə-tē\ *n* : lack of steadiness; *esp* : lack of emotional or mental stability

**in·stal** *chiefly Brit var of* INSTALL

**in·stall** \in-ˈstȯl\ *vb* 1 : to place formally in office : induct into an office, rank, or order 2 : to establish in an indicated place, condition, or status 3 : to set up for use or service — **in·stal·la·tion** \in-stə-ˈlā-shən\ *n*

¹**in·stall·ment** *also* **in·stal·ment** \in-ˈstȯl-mənt\ *n* : INSTALLATION

²**installment** *also* **instalment** *n* 1 : one of the parts into which a debt or sum is divided for payment 2 : one of several parts presented at intervals

¹**in·stance** \ˈin-stəns\ *n* 1 : INSTIGATION, REQUEST 2 : EXAMPLE ⟨for ~⟩ 3 : an event or step that is part of a process or series ♦ ***Synonyms*** CASE, ILLUSTRATION, SAMPLE, SPECIMEN

²**instance** *vb* **in·stanced; in·stanc·ing** : to mention as a case or example

¹**in·stant** \ˈin-stənt\ *n* 1 : MOMENT ⟨the ~ we met⟩ 2 : the present or current month

²**instant** *adj* 1 : URGENT 2 : PRESENT, CURRENT 3 : IMMEDIATE ⟨~ relief⟩ 4 : premixed or precooked for easy final preparation ⟨~ cake mix⟩; *also* : immediately soluble in water ⟨~ coffee⟩

**in·stan·ta·neous** \in-stən-ˈtā-nē-əs\ *adj* : done or occurring in an instant or without delay ⟨an ~ chemical reaction⟩ — **in·stan·ta·neous·ly** *adv*

**in·stan·ter** \in-ˈstan-tər\ *adv* : at once

**in·stan·ti·ate** \in-ˈstan-chē-ˌāt\ *vb* **-at·ed; -at·ing** : to represent (an abstraction) by a concrete example — **in·stan·ti·a·tion** \-ˌstan-chē-ˈā-shən\ *n*

**in·stant·ly** \ˈin-stənt-lē\ *adv* : at once : IMMEDIATELY

**in·state** \in-ˈstāt\ *vb* : to establish in a rank or office : INSTALL

**in·stead** \in-ˈsted\ *adv* 1 : as a substitute or equivalent 2 : as an alternative

**instead of** *prep* : as a substitute for or alternative to ⟨use glue *instead of* paste⟩

**in·step** \ˈin-ˌstep\ *n* : the arched part of the human foot in front of the ankle joint; *esp* : its upper surface

**in·sti·gate** \ˈin-stə-ˌgāt\ *vb* **-gat·ed; -gat·ing** : to goad or urge forward : PROVOKE, INCITE ⟨~ a revolt⟩ — **in·sti·ga·tion** \ˌin-stə-ˈgā-shən\ *n* — **in·sti·ga·tor** \ˈin-stə-ˌgā-tər\ *n*

**in·stil** *chiefly Brit var of* INSTILL

**in·still** \in-ˈstil\ *vb* 1 : to cause to enter drop by drop 2 : to impart gradually

¹**in·stinct** \ˈin-ˌstiŋkt\ *n* 1 : a natural aptitude 2 : a largely inheritable and unalterable tendency of an organism to make a complex and specific response to environmental stimuli without involving reason; *also* : behavior originating below the conscious level — **in·stinc·tive** \in-ˈstiŋk-tiv\ *adj* — **in·stinc·tive·ly** *adv*

²**in·stinct** \in-ˈstiŋkt, ˈin-ˌstiŋkt\ *adj* : IMBUED, INFUSED

**in·stinc·tu·al** \in-ˈstiŋk-chə-wəl\ *adj* : of, relating to, or based on instinct

¹**in·sti·tute** \ˈin-stə-ˌtüt, -ˌtyüt\ *vb* **-tut·ed; -tut·ing** 1 : to establish in a position or office 2 : ORGANIZE 3 : INAUGURATE, INITIATE ⟨~ a new policy⟩

²**institute** *n* 1 : an elementary principle recognized as authoritative; *also, pl* : a collection of such principles and precepts 2 : an organization for the promotion of a cause : ASSOCIATION 3 : an educational institution 4 : a brief course of instruction on a particular field

**in·sti·tu·tion** \in-stə-ˈtü-shən, -ˈtyü-\ *n* 1 : an act of originating, setting up, or founding 2 : an established practice, law, or custom 3 : a society or corporation esp. of a public character ⟨a charitable ~⟩; *also* : ASYLUM 3 — **in·sti·tu·tion·al** \-ˈtü-shə-nəl, -ˈtyü-\ *adj* — **in·sti·tu·tion·al·ize** \-nə-ˌlīz\ *vb* — **in·sti·tu·tion·al·ly** *adv*

**instr** *abbr* 1 instructor 2 instrument; instrumental

**in·struct** \in-ˈstrəkt\ *vb* [ME, fr. L *instructus,* pp. of *instruere,* fr. *struere* to build] 1 : TEACH 2 : INFORM 3 : to give an order or a command to

**in·struc·tion** \in-ˈstrək-shən\ *n* 1 : LESSON, PRECEPT 2 : COMMAND, ORDER 3 *pl* : DIRECTIONS 4 : the action, practice, or profession of a teacher — **in·struc·tion·al** \-shə-nəl\ *adj*

**in·struc·tive** \in-ˈstrək-tiv\ *adj* : carrying a lesson : ENLIGHTENING ⟨an ~ book⟩

**in·struc·tor** \in-ˈstrək-tər\ *n* : one that instructs; *esp* : a college teacher below professorial rank — **in·struc·tor·ship** *n*

**in·stru·ment** \ˈin-strə-mənt\ *n* 1 : a device used to produce music 2 : a means by which something is done 3 : a device for doing work and esp. precision work ⟨a drafting ~⟩ 4 : a legal document (as a deed) 5 : a device used in navigating an airplane — **in·stru·ment** \-ˌment\ *vb*

**in·stru·men·tal** \in-strə-ˈmen-t⁹l\ *adj* 1 : acting as a crucial agent or means ⟨was ~ in arranging the deal⟩ 2 : of, relating to, or done with an instrument 3 : relating to, composed for, or performed on a musical instrument

**in·stru·men·tal·ist** \-ˈmen-tə-list\ *n* : a player on a musical instrument

**in·stru·men·tal·i·ty** \in-strə-mən-ˈta-lə-tē, -ˌmen-\ *n, pl* **-ties** 1 : the quality or state of being instrumental 2 : MEANS, AGENCY

**in·stru·men·ta·tion** \in-strə-mən-'tā-shən, -men-\ n  1 : ORCHESTRATION 2 : instruments for a particular purpose

**instrument panel** n : DASHBOARD

**in·sub·or·di·nate** \in-sə-'bȯr-də-nət\ adj : disobedient to authority — **in·sub·or·di·na·tion** \-,bȯr-də-'nā-shən\ n

**in·sub·stan·tial** \in-səb-'stan-chəl\ adj 1 : lacking substance or reality 2 : lacking firmness or solidity

**in·suf·fer·able** \(,)in-'sə-fə-rə-bəl\ adj : not to be endured : INTOLERABLE ⟨an ~ bore⟩ — **in·suf·fer·ably** \-blē\ adv

**in·suf·fi·cient** \in-sə-'fi-shənt\ adj : not sufficient ⟨~ funds⟩; also : lacking capacity — **in·suf·fi·cien·cy** \-'fi-shən-sē\ n — **in·suf·fi·cient·ly** adv

**in·su·lar** \'in-sə-lər, -syə-\ adj 1 : of, relating to, or forming an island 2 : dwelling or situated on an island 3 : NARROW-MINDED ⟨an ~ perspective⟩ — **in·su·lar·i·ty** \in-sə-'lar-ə-tē, -syə-\ n

**in·su·late** \'in-sə-,lāt\ vb -lat·ed; -lat·ing [L insula island] : ISOLATE; esp : to separate a conductor of electricity, heat, or sound from other conducting bodies by means of a nonconductor — **in·su·la·tion** \in-sə-'lā-shən\ n — **in·su·la·tor** \'in-sə-,lā-tər\ n

**in·su·lin** \'in-sə-lən\ n : a pancreatic hormone essential esp. for the metabolism of carbohydrates and the regulation of glucose levels in the blood

**¹in·sult** \in-'səlt\ vb [MF or L; MF insulter, fr. L insultare, lit., to spring upon, fr. saltare to leap] : to treat with insolence or contempt : AFFRONT ⟨were ~ed by his rudeness⟩ — **in·sult·ing·ly** adv

**²in·sult** \'in-,səlt\ n : a gross indignity

**in·su·per·a·ble** \(,)in-'sü-p(ə-)rə-bəl\ adj : incapable of being surmounted, overcome, passed over, or solved — **in·su·per·a·bly** \-blē\ adv

**in·sup·port·able** \in-sə-'pȯr-tə-bəl\ adj 1 : UNENDURABLE 2 : UNJUSTIFIABLE

**in·sur·able** \in-'shu̇r-ə-bəl\ adj : capable of being or proper to be insured

**in·sur·ance** \in-'shu̇r-əns\ n 1 : the business of insuring persons or property 2 : coverage by contract whereby one party agrees to guarantee another against a specified loss 3 : the sum for which something is insured 4 : a means of guaranteeing protection or safety

**in·sure** \in-'shu̇r\ vb **in·sured; in·sur·ing** 1 : to provide or obtain insurance on or for : UNDERWRITE 2 : to make certain : ENSURE

**in·sured** \in-'shu̇rd\ n : a person whose life or property is insured

**in·sur·er** \in-'shu̇r-ər\ n : one that insures; esp : an insurance company

**in·sur·gent** \in-'sər-jənt\ n 1 : a person who revolts against civil authority or an established government : REBEL 2 : a member of a political party who rebels against it — **in·sur·gence** \-jəns\ n — **in·sur·gen·cy** \-jən-sē\ n — **in·sur·gent** adj

**in·sur·mount·able** \in-sər-maun-tə-bəl\ adj : INSUPERABLE ⟨~ problems⟩ — **in·sur·mount·ably** \-blē\ adv

**in·sur·rec·tion** \in-sə-'rek-shən\ n : an act or instance of revolting against civil authority or an established government — **in·sur·rec·tion·ist** \-shə-nist\ n

**int** abbr 1 interest 2 interior 3 internal 4 internal 5 international 6 intransitive

**in·tact** \in-'takt\ adj : untouched esp. by anything that harms or diminishes

**in·ta·glio** \in-'tal-yō\ n, pl **-glios** [It] : an engraving cut deeply into the surface of a hard material (as stone)

**in·take** \'in-,tāk\ n 1 : an opening through which fluid enters 2 : the act of taking in 3 : something taken in

**in·tan·gi·ble** \(,)in-'tan-jə-bəl\ adj : incapable of being touched : IMPALPABLE ⟨~ benefits⟩ — **in·tan·gi·bly** \-blē\ adv

**²intangible** n 1 : an incorporeal asset 2 : an abstract quality or attribute

**in·te·ger** \'in-ti-jər\ n [L, adj., whole, entire] : a number (as 1, 2, 3, 12, 432) that is not a fraction and does not include a fraction, is the negative of such a number, or is 0

**¹in·te·gral** \'in-ti-grəl\ adj 1 : essential to completeness ⟨~ to the company⟩ 2 : formed as a unit with another part 3 : composed of parts that make up a whole 4 : ENTIRE

**²integral** n : the result of a mathematical integration

**in·te·grate** \'in-tə-,grāt\ vb **-grat·ed; -grat·ing** 1 : to find a function that has a given derivative 2 : to form, coordinate, or blend into a functioning whole : UNITE 3 : to incorporate into a larger unit 4 : to end the segregation of and bring into equal membership in society or an organization; also : DESEGREGATE — **in·te·gra·tion** \in-tə-'grā-shən\ n

**integrated circuit** n : a group of tiny electronic components and their connections that is produced in or on a small slice of material (as silicon)

**in·teg·ri·ty** \in-'te-grə-tē\ n 1 : adherence to a code of values : INCORRUPTIBILITY 2 : SOUNDNESS 3 : COMPLETENESS

**in·teg·u·ment** \in-'te-gyə-mənt\ n : a covering layer (as a skin or cuticle) of an organism or one of its parts

**in·tel·lect** \'in-tə-,lekt\ n 1 : the power of knowing : the capacity for knowledge 2 : the capacity for rational or intelligent thought esp. when highly developed 3 : a person with great intellectual powers

**in·tel·lec·tu·al** \in-tə-'lek-chə-wəl\ adj 1 : of, relating to, or performed by the intellect : RATIONAL 2 : given to study, reflection, and speculation ⟨~ games⟩ 3 : engaged in activity requiring the creative use of the intellect — **intellectual** n — **in·tel·lec·tu·al·ly** adv

**in·tel·lec·tu·al·ism** \-chə-wə-,li-zəm\ n : devotion to the exercise of intellect or to intellectual pursuits

**in·tel·li·gence** \in-'te-lə-jəns\ n 1 : ability to learn and understand or to deal with new or trying situations **2** : mental acuteness **3** : INFORMATION, NEWS **4** : an agency engaged in obtaining information esp. concerning an enemy or possible enemy; *also* : the information so gained

**intelligence quotient** *n* : IQ

**in·tel·li·gent** \in-ˈte-lə-jənt\ *adj* [L *intelligens*, fr. *intelligere* to understand, fr. *inter* between + *legere* to select] : having or showing intelligence or intellect ⟨an ~ decision⟩ — **in·tel·li·gent·ly** *adv*

**in·tel·li·gen·tsia** \in-ˌte-lə-ˈjent-sē-ə, -ˈgent-\ *n* [Russ *intelligentsiya*, fr. L *intelligentia* intelligence] : intellectuals forming a vanguard or elite

**in·tel·li·gi·ble** \in-ˈte-lə-jə-bəl\ *adj* : capable of being understood or comprehended ⟨a very ~ plan⟩ — **in·tel·li·gi·bil·i·ty** \-ˌte-lə-jə-ˈbi-lə-tē\ *n* — **in·tel·li·gi·bly** \-ˈte-lə-jə-blē\ *adv*

**in·tem·per·ance** \(ˌ)in-ˈtem-pə-rəns\ *n* : lack of moderation; *esp* : habitual or excessive drinking of intoxicants — **in·tem·per·ate** \-pə-rət\ *adj* — **in·tem·per·ate·ness** *n*

**in·tend** \in-ˈtend\ *vb* [ME *entenden, intenden*, fr. AF *entendre*, fr. L *intendere* to stretch out, direct, aim at, fr. *tendere* to stretch] **1** : to have in mind as a purpose or aim ⟨~s to retire⟩ **2** : to design for a specified use or future ⟨programs ~ed to help students⟩

**in·ten·dant** \in-ˈten-dənt\ *n* : an official (as a governor) esp. under the French, Spanish, or Portuguese monarchies

**¹in·tend·ed** *adj* **1** : expected to be such in the future; *esp* : BETROTHED **2** : INTENTIONAL ⟨an ~ pun⟩

**²intended** *n* : an engaged person

**in·tense** \in-ˈtens\ *adj* **1** : existing in an extreme degree ⟨~ pain⟩ **2** : marked by great zeal, energy, or eagerness ⟨~ effort⟩ **3** : showing strong feeling; *also* : deeply felt — **in·tense·ly** *adv*

**in·ten·si·fy** \in-ˈten-sə-ˌfī\ *vb* **-fied; -fying 1** : to make or become intense or more intensive **2** : to make more acute : SHARPEN ♦ *Synonyms* AGGRAVATE, HEIGHTEN, ENHANCE, MAGNIFY — **in·ten·si·fi·ca·tion** \-ˌten-sə-fə-ˈkā-shən\ *n*

**in·ten·si·ty** \in-ˈten-sə-tē\ *n, pl* **-ties 1** : the quality or state of being intense; *esp* : degree of strength, energy, or force

**¹in·ten·sive** \in-ˈten-siv\ *adj* **1** : highly concentrated **2** : serving to give emphasis — **in·ten·sive·ly** *adv*

**²intensive** *n* : an intensive word, particle, or prefix ⟨the word "very" is an ~⟩

**intensive care** *n* : continuous monitoring and treatment of seriously ill patients; *also* : an area of a hospital providing this treatment

**¹in·tent** \in-ˈtent\ *n* **1** : the state of mind with which an act is done : VOLITION **2** : PURPOSE, AIM ⟨the artist's ~⟩ **3** : MEANING, SIGNIFICANCE

**²intent** *adj* **1** : directed with keen attention ⟨an ~ gaze⟩ **2** : ENGROSSED; *also* : DETERMINED ⟨~ on winning⟩ — **in·tent·ly** *adv* — **in·tent·ness** *n*

**in·ten·tion** \in-ˈten-chən\ *n* **1** : a determination to act in a certain way **2** : PURPOSE, AIM, END ♦ *Synonyms* INTENT, DESIGN, OBJECT, OBJECTIVE, GOAL

**in·ten·tion·al** \in-ˈten-chə-nəl\ *adj* : done by intention or design : INTENDED — **in·ten·tion·al·ly** *adv*

**in·ter** \in-ˈtər\ *vb* **in·terred; in·ter·ring** : BURY

**in·ter·ac·tion** \ˌin-tər-ˈak-shən\ *n* : mutual or reciprocal action or influence — **in·ter·act** \-ˈakt\ *vb*

**in·ter·ac·tive** \-ˈak-tiv\ *adj* **1** : mutually or reciprocally active **2** : involving the actions or input of a user ⟨~ exhibits⟩ **3** : allowing two-way electronic communication (as between a person and a computer) — **in·ter·ac·tive·ly** *adv* — **in·ter·ac·tiv·i·ty** \-ak-ˈti-və-tē\ *n*

**in·ter alia** \ˌin-tər-ˈā-lē-ə, -ˈä-\ *adv* : among other things

**in·ter·atom·ic** \ˌin-tər-ə-ˈtä-mik\ *adj* : existing or acting between atoms

**in·ter·breed** \-ˈbrēd\ *vb* **-bred** \-ˈbred\; **-breed·ing** : to breed together

**in·ter·ca·la·ry** \in-ˈtər-kə-ˌler-ē\ *adj* **1** : INTERCALATED ⟨February 29 is an ~ day⟩ **2** : INTERPOLATED

**in·ter·ca·late** \-ˌlāt\ *vb* **-lat·ed; -lat·ing 1** : to insert (as a day) in a calendar **2** : to insert between or among existing elements or layers — **in·ter·ca·la·tion** \-ˌtər-kə-ˈlā-shən\ *n*

**in·ter·cede** \ˌin-tər-ˈsēd\ *vb* **-ced·ed; -ced·ing** : to act between parties with a view to reconciling differences

**¹in·ter·cept** \ˌin-tər-ˈsept\ *vb* **1** : to stop or interrupt the progress or course of **2** : to include (as part of a curve or solid) between two points, curves, or surfaces **3** : to gain possession of (an opponent's pass) — **in·ter·cep·tion** \-ˈsep-shən\ *n*

**²in·ter·cept** \ˈin-tər-ˌsept\ *n* : INTERCEPTION; *esp* : the interception of a target by an interceptor or missile

**in·ter·cep·tor** \ˌin-tər-ˈsep-tər\ *n* : a fighter plane designed for defense against attacking bombers

**in·ter·ces·sion** \ˌin-tər-ˈse-shən\ *n* **1** : MEDIATION **2** : prayer or petition in favor of another — **in·ter·ces·sor** \-ˈse-sər\ *n* — **in·ter·ces·so·ry** \-ˈse-sə-rē\ *adj*

**¹in·ter·change** \ˌin-tər-ˈchānj\ *vb* **1** : to put each in the place of the other **2** : EXCHANGE **3** : to change places mutually — **in·ter·change·able** \-ˈchān-jə-bəl\ *adj* — **in·ter·change·ably** \-blē\ *adv*

**²in·ter·change** \ˈin-tər-ˌchānj\ *n* **1** : EXCHANGE **2** : a highway junction that by separated levels permits passage between highways without crossing traffic streams

**in·ter·col·le·giate** \ˌin-tər-kə-ˈlē-jət\ *adj* : existing or carried on between colleges ⟨~ sports⟩

**in·ter·com** \ˈin-tər-ˌkäm\ *n* : a two-way system for localized communication

**in·ter·con·nect** \ˌin-tər-kə-ˈnekt\ *vb* : to connect with one another — **in·ter·con·nec·tion** \-ˈnek-shən\ *n*

**in·ter·con·ti·nen·tal** \ˌin-tər-ˌkän-tə-ˈnen-tᵊl\ *adj* **1** : extending among or carried on between continents ⟨~ trade⟩ **2** : capable of traveling between continents ⟨~ ballistic missiles⟩

**in·ter·course** \'in-tər-ˌkŏrs\ *n* **1** : connection or dealings between persons or nations **2** : physical sexual contact between individuals that involves the genitalia of at least one person ⟨anal ∼⟩; *esp* : SEXUAL INTERCOURSE

**in·ter·de·nom·i·na·tion·al** \ˌin-tər-di-ˌnā-mə-'nā-shə-nəl\ *adj* : involving different denominations

**in·ter·de·part·men·tal** \ˌin-tər-di-ˌpärt-'men-tᵊl, -ˌdē-\ *adj* : carried on between or involving different departments (as of a college)

**in·ter·de·pen·dent** \ˌin-tər-di-'pen-dənt\ *adj* : dependent upon one another — **in·ter·de·pen·dence** \-dəns\ *n*

**in·ter·dict** \ˌin-tər-'dikt\ *vb* **1** : to prohibit by decree **2** : to destroy, cut off, or damage (as an enemy line of supply) : INTERCEPT ⟨∼ed drug shipments⟩ — **in·ter·dic·tion** \-'dik-shən\ *n*

**in·ter·dis·ci·plin·ary** \-'di-sə-plə-ˌner-ē\ *adj* : involving two or more academic, scientific, or artistic disciplines

**¹in·ter·est** \'in-trəst; 'in-tə-rəst, -ˌrest\ *n* **1** : right, title, or legal share in something **2** : a charge for borrowed money that is generally a percentage of the amount borrowed; *also* : the return received by capital on its investment **3** : WELFARE, BENEFIT; *also* : SELF-INTEREST **4** : CURIOSITY, CONCERN **5** : readiness to be concerned with or moved by an object or class of objects **6** : a quality in a thing that arouses interest

**²interest** *vb* **1** : to persuade to participate or engage **2** : to engage the attention of

**in·ter·est·ing** *adj* : holding the attention — **in·ter·est·ing·ly** *adv*

**¹in·ter·face** \'in-tər-ˌfās\ *n* **1** : a surface forming a common boundary of two bodies, spaces, or phases ⟨an oil-water ∼⟩ **2** : the place at which two independent systems meet and act on or communicate with each other ⟨the man-machine ∼⟩ **3** : the means by which interaction or communication is achieved at an interface — **in·ter·fa·cial** \ˌin-tər-'fā-shəl\ *adj*

**²interface** *vb* **-faced; -fac·ing 1** : to connect by means of an interface **2** : to serve as an interface

**in·ter·faith** \ˌin-tər-'fāth\ *adj* : involving persons of different religious faiths

**in·ter·fere** \ˌin-tər-'fir\ *vb* **-fered; -fer·ing** [ME *enterferen*, fr. AF *(s)entreferir* to strike one another, fr. *entre* between, among + *ferir* to strike, fr. L *ferire*] **1** : to come in collision or be in opposition : CLASH **2** : to enter into the affairs of others **3** : to affect one another

**in·ter·fer·ence** \-'fir-əns\ *n* **1** : the act or process of interfering : OBSTRUCTION **2** : something that interferes **3** : the mutual effect on meeting of two waves resulting in areas of increased and decreased amplitude **4** : the blocking of an opponent in football to make way for the ballcarrier **5** : the illegal hindering of an opponent in sports

**in·ter·fer·om·e·ter** \ˌin-tər-fə-'rä-mə-tər\ *n* : an apparatus that uses the interference of waves (as of light) for making precise measurements — **in·ter·fer·om·e·try** \-fə-'rä-mə-trē\ *n*

**in·ter·fer·on** \ˌin-tər-'fir-ˌän\ *n* : any of a group of antiviral proteins of low molecular weight produced usu. by animal cells in response to a virus, a parasite in the cell, or a chemical

**in·ter·ga·lac·tic** \ˌin-tər-gə-'lak-tik\ *adj* : relating to or situated in the spaces between galaxies

**in·ter·gen·er·a·tion·al** \-je-nə-'rā-shə-nəl\ *adj* : existing or occurring between generations ⟨∼ conflicts⟩

**in·ter·gla·cial** \-'glā-shəl\ *n* : a warm period between successive glaciations

**in·ter·gov·ern·men·tal** \-ˌgə-vərn-'men-tᵊl\ *adj* : existing or occurring between two governments or levels of government

**in·ter·im** \'in-tə-rəm\ *n* [L, adv., meaning while, fr. *inter* between] : a time intervening : INTERVAL — **interim** *adj*

**in·te·ri·or** \in-'tir-ē-ər\ *adj* **1** : lying, occurring, or functioning within the limiting boundaries : INSIDE, INNER **2** : remote from the surface, border, or shore : INLAND

**²interior** *n* **1** : the inland part (as of a country) **2** : INSIDE **3** : the internal affairs of a state or nation **4** : a scene or view of the interior of a building

**interior decoration** *n* : INTERIOR DESIGN — **interior decorator** *n*

**interior design** *n* : the art or practice of planning and supervising the design and execution of architectural interiors and their furnishings — **interior designer** *n*

**interj** *abbr* interjection

**in·ter·ject** \ˌin-tər-'jekt\ *vb* : to throw in between or among other things

**in·ter·jec·tion** \ˌin-tər-'jek-shən\ *n* : an exclamatory word (as *ouch*) — **in·ter·jec·tion·al·ly** \-shə-nə-lē\ *adv*

**in·ter·lace** \ˌin-tər-'lās\ *vb* **1** : to unite by or as if by lacing together : INTERWEAVE **2** : INTERSPERSE

**in·ter·lard** \ˌin-tər-'lärd\ *vb* : to vary by inserting or interjecting something ⟨a speech ∼ed with anecdotes⟩

**in·ter·leave** \ˌin-tər-'lēv\ *vb* **-leaved; -leav·ing** : to arrange in alternate layers

**in·ter·leu·kin** \ˌin-tər-'lü-kən\ *n* : any of several proteins of low molecular weight that are produced by cells of the body and regulate the immune system and immune responses

**¹in·ter·line** \ˌin-tər-'līn\ *vb* : to insert between lines already written or printed

**²interline** *vb* : to provide (as a coat) with an interlining

**in·ter·lin·ear** \ˌin-tər-'li-nē-ər\ *adj* : inserted between lines already written or printed ⟨an ∼ translation of a text⟩

**in·ter·lin·gual** \ˌin-tər-'liŋ-gwəl\ *adj* : of, relating to, or existing between two or more languages

**in·ter·lin·ing** \'in-tər-ˌlī-niŋ\ *n* : a lining (as of a coat) between the ordinary lining and the outside fabric

**in·ter·link** \ˌin-tər-'liŋk\ *vb* : to link together

**in·ter·lock** \ˌin-tər-'läk\ *vb* **1** : to engage or interlace together : lock together

: UNITE **2** : to connect so that action of one part affects action of another part — **in·ter·lock** \'in-tər-ˌläk\

**in·ter·loc·u·tor** \ˌin-tər-'lä-kyə-tər\ *n* : one who takes part in dialogue or conversation

**in·ter·loc·u·to·ry** \-ˌtȯr-ē\ *adj* : made during the progress of a legal action and not final or definite ⟨an ~ decree⟩

**in·ter·lope** \ˌin-tər-'lōp\ *vb* **-loped; -loping 1** : to encroach on the rights (as in trade) of others **2** : INTRUDE, INTERFERE — **in·ter·lop·er** *n*

**in·ter·lude** \'in-tər-ˌlüd\ *n* **1** : a usu. short simple play or dramatic entertainment **2** : an intervening period, space, or event **3** : a piece of music inserted between the parts of a longer composition or a religious service

**in·ter·mar·riage** \ˌin-tər-'mer-ij\ *n* **1** : marriage within one's own group as required by custom **2** : marriage between members of different groups

**in·ter·mar·ry** \-'mer-ē\ *vb* **1** : to marry each other **2** : to marry within a group **3** : to become connected by intermarriage

¹**in·ter·me·di·ary** \ˌin-tər-'mē-dē-ˌer-ē\ *adj* **1** : INTERMEDIATE **2** : acting as a mediator

²**intermediary** *n, pl* **-ar·ies** : MEDIATOR, GO-BETWEEN

¹**in·ter·me·di·ate** \ˌin-tər-'mē-dē-ət\ *adj* : being or occurring at the middle place or degree or between extremes

²**intermediate** *n* **1** : one that is intermediate **2** : INTERMEDIARY

**intermediate school** *n* **1** : JUNIOR HIGH SCHOOL **2** : a school usu. comprising grades 4–6

**in·ter·ment** \in-'tər-mənt\ *n* : BURIAL

**in·ter·mez·zo** \ˌin-tər-'met-sō, -'med-zō\ *n, pl* **-zi** \-sē, -zē\ *or* **-zos** [It, ultim. fr. L *intermedius* intermediate] : a short movement connecting major sections of an extended musical work (as a symphony); *also* : a short independent instrumental composition

**in·ter·mi·na·ble** \in-'tər-mə-nə-bəl\ *adj* : ENDLESS; *esp* : wearisomely protracted — **in·ter·mi·na·bly** \-blē\ *adv*

**in·ter·min·gle** \ˌin-tər-'miŋ-gəl\ *vb* : to mingle or mix together

**in·ter·mis·sion** \ˌin-tər-'mi-shən\ *n* **1** : INTERRUPTION, BREAK **2** : a temporary halt esp. in a public performance

**in·ter·mit** \-'mit\ *vb* **-mit·ted; -mit·ting** : DISCONTINUE; *also* : to be intermittent

**in·ter·mit·tent** \-'mi-tᵊnt\ *adj* : coming and going at intervals ⟨~ rain⟩ ♦ *Synonyms* RECURRENT, PERIODIC, ALTERNATE — **in·ter·mit·tent·ly** *adv*

**in·ter·mix** \ˌin-tər-'miks\ *vb* : to mix together : INTERMINGLE — **in·ter·mix·ture** \-'miks-chər\ *n*

**in·ter·mo·lec·u·lar** \-mə-'le-kyə-lər\ *adj* : existing or acting between molecules

**in·ter·mon·tane** \ˌin-tər-'män-ˌtān\ *adj* : situated between mountains

¹**in·tern** \'in-ˌtərn, in-'tərn\ *vb* : to confine or impound esp. during a war — **in·tern·ee** \ˌ(ˌ)in-ˌtər-'nē\ *n* — **in·tern·ment** \in-'tərn-mənt\ *n*

²**in·tern** *also* **in·terne** \'in-ˌtərn\ *n* : an advanced student or recent graduate (as in medicine) gaining supervised practical experience — **in·tern·ship** *n*

³**in·tern** \'in-ˌtərn\ *vb* : to work as an intern

**in·ter·nal** \in-'tər-nᵊl\ *adj* **1** : INWARD, INTERIOR **2** : relating to or located in the inside of the body ⟨~ pain⟩ **3** : of, relating to, or occurring within the confines of an organized structure ⟨~ affairs⟩ **4** : of, relating to, or existing within the mind **5** : INTRINSIC, INHERENT ⟨~ evidence⟩ — **in·ter·nal·ly** *adv*

**internal combustion engine** *n* : an engine in which the fuel is ignited within the engine cylinder

**in·ter·nal·ise** *Brit var of* INTERNALIZE

**in·ter·nal·ize** \in-'tər-nə-ˌlīz\ *vb* **-ized; -izing** : to incorporate (as values) within the self through learning or socialization ⟨*internalized* their parents' values⟩ — **in·ter·nal·i·za·tion** \-ˌtər-nə-lə-'zā-shən\ *n*

**internal medicine** *n* : a branch of medicine that deals with the diagnosis and treatment of diseases not requiring surgery

¹**in·ter·na·tion·al** \ˌin-tər-'na-shə-nəl\ *adj* **1** : common to or affecting two or more nations ⟨~ trade⟩ **2** : of, relating to, or constituting a group having members in two or more nations — **in·ter·na·tion·al·ly** *adv*

²**international** *n* : one that is international; *esp* : an organization of international scope

**in·ter·na·tion·al·ise** *Brit var of* INTERNATIONALIZE

**in·ter·na·tion·al·ism** \-'na-shə-nə-ˌli-zəm\ *n* : a policy of cooperation among nations; *also* : an attitude favoring such a policy — **in·ter·na·tion·al·ist** \-ˌlist\ *n or adj*

**in·ter·na·tion·al·ize** \-'na-shə-nə-ˌlīz\ *vb* : to make international; *esp* : to place under international control

**International System of Units** *n* : a system of units based on the metric system and used by international convention esp. for scientific work

**in·ter·ne·cine** \ˌin-tər-'ne-ˌsēn, -'nē-ˌsīn\ *adj* [L *internecinus*, fr. *internecare* to destroy, kill, fr. *necare* to kill, fr. *nec-, nex* violent death] **1** : DEADLY; *esp* : mutually destructive **2** : of, relating to, or involving conflict within a group ⟨~ feuds⟩

**In·ter·net** \'in-tər-ˌnet\ *n* : an electronic communications network that connects computer networks worldwide

**in·tern·ist** \'in-ˌtər-nist\ *n* : a physician who specializes in internal medicine

**in·ter·nun·cio** \ˌin-tər-'nən-sē-ˌō, -'nún-\ *n* [It *internunzio*] : a papal legate of lower rank than a nuncio

**in·ter·of·fice** \-'ȯ-fəs\ *adj* : functioning or communicating between the offices of an organization

**in·ter·per·son·al** \-'pər-sə-nəl\ *adj* : being, relating to, or involving relations between persons ⟨~ communication⟩ — **in·ter·per·son·al·ly** *adv*

**in·ter·plan·e·tary** \ˌin-tər-'pla-nə-ˌter-ē\

*adj* : existing, carried on, or operating between planets ⟨~ space⟩

**in·ter·play** \'in-tər-ˌplā\ *n* : INTERACTION

**in·ter·po·late** \in-'tər-pə-ˌlāt\ *vb* **-lat·ed; -lat·ing 1** : to change (as a text) by inserting new or foreign matter **2** : to insert (as words) into a text or into a conversation **3** : to estimate values of (data or a function) between two known values — **in·ter·po·la·tion** \-ˌtər-pə-'lā-shən\ *n*

**in·ter·pose** \ˌin-tər-'pōz\ *vb* **-posed; -pos·ing 1** : to place between **2** : to thrust in : INTRUDE, INTERRUPT **3** : to inject between parts of a conversation or argument **4** : to come or be between
♦ *Synonyms* INTERFERE, INTERCEDE, INTERMEDIATE, INTERVENE — **in·ter·po·si·tion** \-pə-'zi-shən\ *n*

**in·ter·pret** \in-'tər-prət\ *vb* **1** : to explain the meaning of; *also* : to act as an interpreter : TRANSLATE **2** : to understand according to individual belief, judgment, or interest **3** : to represent artistically — **in·ter·pret·er** *n* — **in·ter·pre·tive** \-'tər-prə-tiv\ *adj*

**in·ter·pre·ta·tion** \in-ˌtər-prə-'tā-shən\ *n* **1** : EXPLANATION ⟨~ of the law⟩ **2** : an instance of artistic interpretation in performance or adaptation — **in·ter·pre·ta·tive** \-'tər-prə-ˌtā-tiv\ *adj*

**in·ter·ra·cial** \-'rā-shəl\ *adj* : of, involving, or designed for members of different races

**in·ter·reg·num** \ˌin-tə-'reg-nəm\ *n, pl* **-nums** *or* **-na** \-nə\ **1** : the time during which a throne is vacant between two successive reigns or regimes **2** : a pause in a continuous series

**in·ter·re·late** \ˌin-tər-ri-'lāt\ *vb* : to bring into or have a mutual relationship — **in·ter·re·lat·ed·ness** \-lā-təd-nəs\ *n* — **in·ter·re·la·tion** \-'lā-shən\ *n* — **in·ter·re·la·tion·ship** *n*

**interrog** *abbr* interrogative

**in·ter·ro·gate** \in-'ter-ə-ˌgāt\ *vb* **-gat·ed; -gat·ing** : to question esp. formally and systematically ⟨~ a suspect⟩ — **in·ter·ro·ga·tion** \-ˌter-ə-'gā-shən\ *n* — **in·ter·ro·ga·tor** \-'ter-ə-ˌgā-tər\ *n*

**in·ter·rog·a·tive** \ˌin-tə-'rä-gə-tiv\ *adj* : asking a question ⟨~ sentence⟩ — **interrogative** *n* — **in·ter·rog·a·tive·ly** *adv*

**in·ter·rog·a·to·ry** \ˌin-tə-'rä-gə-ˌtȯr-ē\ *adj* : INTERROGATIVE

**in·ter·rupt** \ˌin-tə-'rəpt\ *vb* **1** : to stop or hinder by breaking in **2** : to break the uniformity or continuity of **3** : to break in by speaking while another is speaking — **in·ter·rupt·er** *n* — **in·ter·rup·tion** \-'rəp-shən\ *n* — **in·ter·rup·tive** \-'rəp-tiv\ *adv*

**in·ter·scho·las·tic** \ˌin-tər-skə-'las-tik\ *adj* : existing or carried on between schools ⟨~ sports⟩

**in·ter·sect** \ˌin-tər-'sekt\ *vb* **1** : to divide by passing through or across **2** : to meet and cross (as at a point); *also* : OVERLAP — **in·ter·sec·tion** \-'sek-shən\ *n*

**in·ter·sperse** \ˌin-tər-'spərs\ *vb* **-spersed; -spers·ing 1** : to place something at intervals in or among **2** : to insert at intervals among other things — **in·ter·sper·sion** \-'spər-zhən\ *n*

**¹in·ter·state** \ˌin-tər-'stāt\ *adj* : relating to, including, or connecting two or more states esp. of the U.S. ⟨~ commerce⟩

**²in·ter·state** \'in-tər-ˌstāt\ *n* : an interstate highway

**in·ter·stel·lar** \ˌin-tər-'ste-lər\ *adj* : located or taking place among the stars

**in·ter·stice** \in-'tər-stəs\ *n, pl* **-stic·es** \-stə-ˌsēz, -stə-səz\ : a space that intervenes between things : CHINK — **in·ter·sti·tial** \ˌin-tər-'sti-shəl\ *adj*

**in·ter·tid·al** \ˌin-tər-'tī-dᵊl\ *adj* : of, relating to, or being the area that is above low tide mark but exposed to tidal flooding ⟨life in the ~ mud⟩

**in·ter·twine** \-'twīn\ *vb* : to twine or cause to twine about one another : INTERLACE — **in·ter·twine·ment** *n*

**in·ter·twist** \-'twist\ *vb* : INTERTWINE

**in·ter·ur·ban** \-'ər-bən\ *adj* : connecting cities or towns

**in·ter·val** \'in-tər-vəl\ *n* [ME *intervalle,* fr. AF & L; AF *entreval,* fr. L *intervallum* space between ramparts, interval, fr. *inter-* between + *vallum* rampart] **1** : a space of time between events or states : PAUSE **2** : a space between objects, units, or states **3** : the difference in pitch between two tones

**in·ter·vene** \ˌin-tər-'vēn\ *vb* **-vened; -ven·ing 1** : to occur, fall, or come between points of time or between events **2** : to enter or appear as an unrelated feature or circumstance ⟨rain *intervened* and we postponed the trip⟩ **3** : to come in or between in order to stop, settle, or modify ⟨~ in a quarrel⟩ **4** : to occur or lie between two things — **in·ter·ven·tion** \-'ven-chən\ *n*

**in·ter·ven·tion·ism** \-'ven-chə-ˌni-zəm\ *n* : interference by one country in the political affairs of another — **in·ter·ven·tion·ist** \-'ven-chə-nist\ *n or adj*

**in·ter·view** \'in-tər-ˌvyü\ *n* **1** : a formal consultation usu. to evaluate qualifications **2** : a meeting at which a writer or reporter obtains information from a person; *also* : the recorded or written account of such a meeting — **interview** *vb* — **in·ter·view·ee** \ˌin-tər-(ˌ)vyü-'ē\ *n* — **in·ter·view·er** *n*

**in·ter·vo·cal·ic** \ˌin-tər-vō-'ka-lik\ *adj* : immediately preceded and immediately followed by a vowel ⟨an ~ consonant⟩

**in·ter·weave** \ˌin-tər-'wēv\ *vb* **-wove** \-'wōv\ *also* **-weaved; -wo·ven** \-'wō-vən\ *also* **-weaved; -weav·ing** : to weave or blend together : INTERTWINE, INTERMINGLE — **interwoven** *adj*

**in·tes·tate** \in-'tes-ˌtāt, -tət\ *adj* **1** : having made no valid will ⟨died ~⟩ **2** : not disposed of by will ⟨~ estate⟩

**in·tes·tine** \in-'tes-tən\ *n* : the tubular part of the alimentary canal that extends from stomach to anus and consists of a long narrow upper part (**small intestine**) followed by a broader shorter lower part (**large intestine**) — **in·tes·ti·nal** \-tə-nᵊl\ *adj*

**in·ti·fa·da** \ˌin-tə-'fä-də\ *n* : an armed uprising of Palestinians against Israeli occupation of the West Bank and Gaza Strip

¹in·ti·mate \'in-tə-ˌmāt\ *vb* **-mat·ed; -mat·ing** [LL *intimare* to put in, announce, fr. L *intimus* innermost] **1** : ANNOUNCE, NOTIFY **2** : to communicate indirectly : HINT — **in·ti·ma·tion** \ˌin-tə-ˈmā-shən\ *n*

²in·ti·mate \'in-ti-mət\ *adj* **1** : INTRINSIC; *also* : INNERMOST **2** : marked by very close association, contact, or familiarity **3** : marked by a warm friendship ⟨~ friends⟩ **4** : suggesting informal warmth or privacy **5** : of a very personal or private nature ⟨~ feelings⟩ — **in·ti·ma·cy** \'in-tə-mə-sē\ *n* — **in·ti·mate·ly** *adv*

³in·ti·mate \'in-tə-mət\ *n* : an intimate friend, associate, or confidant

in·tim·i·date \in-'ti-mə-ˌdāt\ *vb* **-dat·ed; -dat·ing** : to make timid or fearful : FRIGHTEN; *esp* : to compel or deter by or as if by threats ♦ *Synonyms* COW, BULLDOZE, BULLY, BROWBEAT — **in·tim·i·dat·ing·ly** *adv* — **in·tim·i·da·tion** \-ˌti-mə-'dā-shən\ *n*

**intl** *or* **intnl** *abbr* international

in·to \'in-tü\ *prep* **1** : to the inside of ⟨ran ~ the house⟩ **2** : to the state, condition, or form of ⟨got ~ trouble⟩ **3** : AGAINST ⟨ran ~ a wall⟩

in·tol·er·a·ble \(ˌ)in-'tä-lə-rə-bəl\ *adj* **1** : UNBEARABLE ⟨~ pain⟩ **2** : EXCESSIVE — **in·tol·er·a·bly** \-blē\ *adv*

in·tol·er·ant \(ˌ)in-'tä-lə-rənt\ *adj* **1** : unable or unwilling to endure ⟨is lactose ~⟩ **2** : unwilling to grant equality, freedom, or other social rights : BIGOTED — **in·tol·er·ance** \-rəns\ *n*

in·to·na·tion \ˌin-tō-'nā-shən\ *n* **1** : something that is intoned **2** : the act of intoning and esp. of chanting **3** : the manner of singing, playing, or uttering tones; *esp* : the rise and fall in pitch of the voice in speech

in·tone \in-'tōn\ *vb* **in·toned; in·ton·ing** : to utter in musical or prolonged tones : CHANT ⟨~ a prayer⟩

in to·to \in-'tō-tō\ *adv* [L, on the whole] : TOTALLY, ENTIRELY

in·tox·i·cant \in-'täk-si-kənt\ *n* : something that intoxicates; *esp* : an alcoholic drink — **intoxicant** *adj*

in·tox·i·cate \-sə-ˌkāt\ *vb* **-cat·ed; -cat·ing 1** : to affect by a drug (as alcohol or cocaine) esp. to the point of physical or mental impairment **2** : to excite to enthusiasm or frenzy ⟨*intoxicated* by his power⟩ — **in·tox·i·ca·tion** \-ˌtäk-sə-'kā-shən\ *n*

in·trac·ta·ble \(ˌ)in-'trak-tə-bəl\ *adj* : not easily controlled

in·tra·mu·ral \-'myùr-əl\ *adj* : being or occurring within the walls or limits (as of a city or college) ⟨~ sports⟩

in·tra·mus·cu·lar \-'məs-kyə-lər\ *adj* : situated within, occurring in, or administered by entering a muscle — **in·tra·mus·cu·lar·ly** *adv*

in·tra·net \'in-trə-ˌnet\ *n* a network similar to the World Wide Web but having access limited to certain authorized users

**intrans** *abbr* intransitive

in·tran·si·gent \-jənt\ *adj* : UNCOMPRO-

MISING ⟨an ~ attitude⟩ — **in·tran·si·gence** \-jəns\ *n* — **intransigent** *n*

in·tran·si·tive \(ˌ)in-'tran-sə-tiv, -zə-\ *adj* : not transitive; *esp* : not having or containing an object ⟨an ~ verb⟩ — **in·tran·si·tive·ly** *adv* — **in·tran·si·tive·ness** *n*

in·tra·state \ˌin-trə-'stāt\ *adj* : existing or occurring within a state ⟨~ rivals⟩

in·tra·uter·ine device \-'yü-tə-rən-, -ˌrīn-\ *n* : a device inserted into and left in the uterus to prevent pregnancy

in·tra·ve·nous \ˌin-trə-'vē-nəs\ *adj* : being within or entering by way of the veins ⟨~ feeding⟩; *also* : used in or using intravenous procedures ⟨~ needles⟩ — **in·tra·ve·nous·ly** *adv*

**intrench** *var of* ENTRENCH

in·trep·id \in-'tre-pəd\ *adj* : characterized by resolute fearlessness, fortitude, and endurance ⟨an ~ explorer⟩ — **in·tre·pid·i·ty** \ˌin-trə-'pi-də-tē\ *n*

in·tri·cate \'in-tri-kət\ *adj* [ME, fr. L *intricatus*, pp. of *intricare* to entangle, fr. *tri·cae* trifles, complications] **1** : having many complexly interrelated parts : COMPLICATED **2** : difficult to follow, understand, or solve — **in·tri·ca·cy** \-tri-kə-sē\ *n* — **in·tri·cate·ly** *adv*

¹in·trigue \'in-ˌtrēg, in-'trēg\ *n* **1** : a secret scheme : PLOT **2** : a clandestine love affair

²in·trigue \in-'trēg\ *vb* **in·trigued; in·trigu·ing 1** to accomplish by intrigue **2** : to carry on an intrigue; *esp* : PLOT, SCHEME **3** : to arouse the interest, desire, or curiosity of — **in·trigu·ing·ly** *adv*

in·trin·sic \in-'trin-zik, -sik\ *adj* : belonging to the essential nature or constitution of a thing — **in·trin·si·cal·ly** \-zi-k(ə-)lē, -si-\ *adv*

**introd** *abbr* introduction

in·tro·duce \ˌin-trə-'düs, -'dyüs\ *vb* **-duced; -duc·ing 1** : to lead or bring in esp. for the first time **2** : to bring into practice or use **3** : to cause to be acquainted **4** : to present for discussion **5** : PLACE, INSERT ♦ *Synonyms* INSINUATE, INTERPOLATE, INTERPOSE, INTERJECT — **in·tro·duc·tion** \-'dək-shən\ *n* — **in·tro·duc·to·ry** \-'dək-tə-rē\ *adj*

in·troit \'in-ˌtròit, -ˌtrō-ət\ *n* **1** *often cap* : the first part of the traditional proper of the Mass **2** : a piece of music sung or played at the beginning of a worship service

in·tro·spec·tion \-'spek-shən\ *n* : a reflective looking inward : an examination of one's own thoughts or feelings — **in·tro·spect** \ˌin-trə-'spekt\ *vb* — **in·tro·spec·tive** \-'spek-tiv\ *adj* — **in·tro·spec·tive·ly** *adv*

in·tro·vert \'in-trə-ˌvərt\ *n* : a reserved or shy person — **in·tro·ver·sion** \ˌin-trə-'vər-zhən\ *n* — **introvert** *adj* — **in·tro·vert·ed** \'in-trə-ˌvər-təd\ *adj*

in·trude \in-'trüd\ *vb* **in·trud·ed; in·trud·ing 1** : to thrust, enter, or force in or upon **2** : ENCROACH, TRESPASS — **in·trud·er** *n* — **in·tru·sion** \-'trü-zhən\ *n* — **in·tru·sive** \-'trü-siv\ *adj* — **in·tru·sive·ness** *n*

**intrust** *var of* ENTRUST

**in·tu·it** \in-'tü-ət, -'tyü-\ *vb* : to know, sense, or understand by intuition

**in·tu·ition** \,in-tü-'wi-shən, -tyü-\ *n* **1** : quick and ready insight **2** : the power or faculty of knowing things without conscious reasoning — **in·tu·i·tive** \in-'tü-ə-tiv, -'tyü-\ *adj* — **in·tu·i·tive·ly** *adv*

**In·u·it** \'i-nü-wət, 'in-yü-\ *n* [Inuit *inuit*, pl. of *inuk* person] **1** *pl* **Inuit** or **Inuits** : a member of the indigenous people of No. America and Greenland **2** : the language of the Inuit people

**in·un·date** \'i-nən-,dāt\ *vb* **-dat·ed; -dat·ing** : to cover with or as if with a flood : OVERFLOW — **in·un·da·tion** \,i-nən-'dā-shən\ *n*

**in·ure** \i-'nür, -'nyür\ *vb* **in·ured; in·ur·ing** [ME *enuren*, fr. *in ure* customary, fr. *putten in ure* to use, put into practice, part trans. of AF *mettre en ovre, en uevre*] **1** : to accustom to accept something undesirable ⟨*inured* to violence⟩ **2** : to become of advantage

**in utero** \in-'yü-tə-,rō\ *adv or adj* [L] : in the uterus : before birth

**inv** *abbr* **1** inventor **2** invoice

**in vac·uo** \in-'va-kyü-,wō\ *adv* [L] : in a vacuum

**in·vade** \in-'vād\ *vb* **in·vad·ed; in·vad·ing** **1** : to enter for conquest or plunder **2** : to encroach upon **3** : to spread through and usu. harm ⟨germs ~ the tissues⟩ — **in·vad·er** *n*

**¹in·val·id** \(,)in-'va-ləd\ *adj* : being without foundation or force in fact, reason, or law — **in·va·lid·i·ty** \,in-və-'li-də-tē\ *n* — **in·val·id·ly** *adv*

**²in·va·lid** \'in-və-ləd\ *adj* : being in ill health : SICKLY

**³invalid** \'in-və-ləd\ *n* : a person in usu. chronic ill health — **in·va·lid·ism** \-lə-,di-zəm\ *n*

**⁴in·va·lid** \'in-və-ləd, -,lid\ *vb* **1** : to remove from active duty by reason of sickness or disability **2** : to make sickly or disabled

**in·val·i·date** \(,)in-'va-lə-,dāt\ *vb* : to make invalid ⟨*invalidate* a contract⟩; *esp* : to weaken or make valueless — **in·val·i·da·tion** \in-,va-lə-'dā-shən\ *n*

**in·valu·able** \-'val-yə-bəl, -yə-wə-bəl\ *adj* : valuable beyond estimation

**in·vari·able** \-'ver-ē-ə-bəl\ *adj* : not changing or capable of change : CONSTANT — **in·vari·ably** \-blē\ *adv*

**in·va·sion** \in-'vā-zhən\ *n* : an act or instance of invading; *esp* : entry of an army into a country for conquest

**in·va·sive** \in-'vā-siv, -ziv\ *adj* **1** : tending to spread ⟨~ cancer cells⟩ **2** : involving entry into the living body (as by surgery) ⟨~ therapy⟩

**in·vec·tive** \in-'vek-tiv\ *n* **1** : an abusive expression or speech **2** : abusive language — **invective** *adj*

**in·veigh** \in-'vā\ *vb* : to protest or complain bitterly or vehemently : RAIL

**in·vei·gle** \in-'vā-gəl, -'vē-\ *vb* **in·vei·gled; in·vei·gling** [AF *enveegler, aveogler* to blind, hoodwink, fr. *avogle, enveugle* blind, fr. ML *ab oculis*, lit., lacking eyes] **1** : to win over by flattery : ENTICE **2** : to

acquire by ingenuity or flattery ⟨*inveigled* his way into her confidence⟩

**in·vent** \in-'vent\ *vb* **1** : to think up **2** : to create or produce for the first time — **in·ven·tor** \-'ven-tər\ *n*

**in·ven·tion** \in-'ven-chən\ *n* **1** : INVENTIVENESS **2** : a creation of the imagination; *esp* : a false conception **3** : a device, contrivance, or process originated after study and experiment **4** : the act or process of inventing

**in·ven·tive** \in-'ven-tiv\ *adj* **1** : CREATIVE, INGENIOUS ⟨an ~ composer⟩ **2** : characterized by invention ⟨an ~ turn of mind⟩ — **in·ven·tive·ness** *n*

**in·ven·to·ry** \'in-vən-,tōr-ē\ *n, pl* **-ries** **1** : an itemized list of current goods or assets **2** : SURVEY, SUMMARY **3** : STOCK, SUPPLY **4** : the act or process of taking an inventory — **inventory** *vb*

**¹in·verse** \(,)in-'vərs, 'in-,vərs\ *adj* : opposite in order, nature, or effect : REVERSED — **in·verse·ly** *adv*

**²inverse** *n* : something inverse or resulting in or from inversion : OPPOSITE

**in·ver·sion** \in-'vər-zhən\ *n* **1** : a reversal of position, order, or relationship; *esp* : an increase of temperature with altitude through a layer of air **2** : the act or process of inverting

**in·vert** \in-'vərt\ *vb* **1** : to reverse in position, order, or relationship **2** : to turn upside down or inside out **3** : to turn inward

**in·ver·te·brate** \(,)in-'vər-tə-brət, -,brāt\ *adj* : lacking a backbone; *also* : of or relating to invertebrate animals — **invertebrate** *n*

**¹in·vest** \in-'vest\ *vb* **1** : to install formally in an office or honor **2** : to furnish with power or authority : VEST **3** : to cover completely : ENVELOP **4** : CLOTHE, ADORN **5** : BESIEGE **6** : to endow with a quality or characteristic

**²invest** *vb* **1** : to commit (money) in order to earn a financial return ⟨~ed in real estate⟩ **2** : to expend for future benefits or advantages **3** : to make an investment — **in·ves·tor** \-'ves-tər\ *n*

**in·ves·ti·gate** \in-'ves-tə-,gāt\ *vb* **-gat·ed; -gat·ing** [L *investigare* to track, investigate, fr. *vestigium* footprint, track] : to study by close examination and systematic inquiry — **in·ves·ti·ga·tion** \-,ves-tə-'gā-shən\ *n* — **in·ves·ti·ga·tive** \-'ves-tə-,gā-tiv\ *adj* — **in·ves·ti·ga·tor** \-,gā-tər\ *n*

**in·ves·ti·ture** \in-'ves-tə-,chùr, -chər\ *n* **1** : the act of ratifying or establishing in office **2** : something that covers or adorns

**¹in·vest·ment** \in-'vest-mənt\ *n* **1** : an outer layer : ENVELOPE **2** : INVESTITURE **1** **3** : BLOCKADE, SIEGE

**²investment** *n* : the outlay of money for income or profit; *also* : the sum invested or the property purchased

**in·vet·er·ate** \in-'ve-tə-rət\ *adj* **1** : firmly established by age or long persistence **2** : confirmed in a habit ⟨an ~ liar⟩

**in·vi·a·ble** \(,)in-'vī-ə-bəl\ *adj* : incapable of surviving

**in·vid·i·ous** \in-'vi-dē-əs\ *adj* **1** : tending

to cause discontent, animosity, or envy ⟨an ∼ comparison⟩ **2** : ENVIOUS **3** : OBNOXIOUS ⟨∼ remarks⟩ — **in·vid·i·ous·ly** *adv*

**in·vig·o·rate** \in-'vi-gə-ˌrāt\ *vb* **-rat·ed; -rat·ing** : to give life and energy to : ANIMATE ⟨∼ the economy⟩ — **in·vig·o·ra·tion** \-ˌvi-gə-'rā-shən\ *n*

**in·vin·ci·ble** \(ˌ)in-'vin-sə-bəl\ *adj* : incapable of being conquered, overcome, or subdued — **in·vin·ci·bil·i·ty** \-ˌvin-sə-'bi-lə-tē\ *n* — **in·vin·ci·bly** \-'vin-sə-blē\ *adv*

**in·vi·o·la·ble** \-'vī-ə-lə-bəl\ *adj* **1** : safe from violation or profanation **2** : UNASSAILABLE ⟨∼ borders⟩ — **in·vi·o·la·bil·i·ty** \-ˌvī-ə-lə-'bi-lə-tē\ *n*

**in·vi·o·late** \-'vī-ə-lət\ *adj* : not violated or profaned : PURE ⟨an ∼ principle⟩

**in·vis·i·ble** \-'vi-zə-bəl\ *adj* **1** : incapable of being seen ⟨∼ to the naked eye⟩ **2** : HIDDEN **3** : IMPERCEPTIBLE, INCONSPICUOUS — **in·vis·i·bil·i·ty** \-ˌvi-zə-'bi-lə-tē\ *n* — **in·vis·i·bly** \-'vi-zə-blē\ *adv*

**invisible hand** *n* : a hypothetical economic force that works for the benefit of all

**in·vi·ta·tion·al** \ˌin-və-'tā-shə-nəl\ *adj* : limited to invited participants ⟨an ∼ tournament⟩ — **invitational** *n*

**in·vite** \in-'vīt\ *vb* **in·vit·ed; in·vit·ing 1** : ENTICE, TEMPT **2** : to increase the likelihood of ⟨∼ trouble⟩ **3** : to request the presence or participation of : ASK **4** : to request formally **5** : ENCOURAGE ⟨∼ suggestions⟩ — **in·vi·ta·tion** \ˌin-və-'tā-shən\ *n*

**in·vit·ing** *adj* : ATTRACTIVE, TEMPTING

**in vi·tro** \in-'vē-trō, -'vī-, -'vi-\ *adv or adj* [NL, lit., in glass] : outside the living body and in an artificial environment ⟨*in vitro* fertilization⟩

**in·vo·ca·tion** \ˌin-və-'kā-shən\ *n* **1** : SUPPLICATION; *esp* : a prayer at the beginning of a service **2** : a formula for conjuring : INCANTATION

¹**in·voice** \'in-ˌvȯis\ *n* [modif. of MF *envois,* pl. of *envoi* message] : an itemized list of goods shipped usu. specifying the price and the terms of sale : BILL

²**invoice** *vb* **in·voiced; in·voic·ing** : to send an invoice to or for : BILL

**in·voke** \in-'vōk\ *vb* **in·voked; in·vok·ing 1** : to petition for help or support **2** : to appeal to or cite as authority ⟨∼ a law⟩ **3** : to call forth by incantation : CONJURE ⟨∼ spirits⟩ **4** : to make an earnest request for : SOLICIT ⟨*invoked* mercy⟩ **5** : to put into effect or operation **6** : to bring about : CAUSE

**in·vol·un·tary** \(ˌ)in-'vä-lən-ˌter-ē\ *adj* **1** : done contrary to or without choice **2** : COMPULSORY ⟨∼ servitude⟩ **3** : not controlled by the will : REFLEX ⟨∼ contractions⟩ — **in·vol·un·tari·ly** \-ˌvä-lən-'ter-ə-lē\ *adv*

**in·vo·lute** \'in-və-ˌlüt\ *adj* : INVOLVED, INTRICATE ⟨an ∼ maneuver⟩

**in·vo·lu·tion** \ˌin-və-'lü-shən\ *n* **1** : the act or an instance of enfolding or entangling **2** : COMPLEXITY, INTRICACY

**in·volve** \in-'välv\ *vb* **in·volved; in·volv·ing 1** : to draw in as a participant **2**

to occupy (as oneself) absorbingly; *esp* : to commit oneself emotionally **4** : to relate closely : CONNECT **5** : to have as part of itself : INCLUDE **6** : ENTAIL, IMPLY ⟨the job ∼s traveling⟩ **7** : ²AFFECT — **in·volve·ment** *n*

**in·volved** \-'välvd\ *adj* : INTRICATE, COMPLEX ⟨an ∼ plot⟩

**in·vul·ner·a·ble** \(ˌ)in-'vəl-nə-rə-bəl\ *adj* **1** : incapable of being wounded, injured, or damaged **2** : immune to or proof against attack — **in·vul·ner·a·bil·i·ty** \-ˌvəl-nə-rə-'bi-lə-tē\ *n* — **in·vul·ner·a·bly** \-'vəl-nə-rə-blē\ *adv*

¹**in·ward** \'in-wərd\ *adj* **1** : situated on the inside **2** : MENTAL; *also* : SPIRITUAL **3** : directed toward the interior

²**inward** *or* **in·wards** \-wərdz\ *adv* **1** : toward the inside, center, or interior **2** : toward the inner being ⟨turned his thoughts ∼⟩

**in·ward·ly** \'in-wərd-lē\ *adv* **1** : MENTALLY, SPIRITUALLY **2** : INTERNALLY ⟨bled ∼⟩ **3** : to oneself ⟨cursed ∼⟩

**IOC** *abbr* International Olympic Committee

**io·dide** \'ī-ə-ˌdīd\ *n* : a compound of iodine with another element or group

**io·dine** \'ī-ə-ˌdīn, -dᵊn\ *n* **1** : a nonmetallic chemical element used esp. in medicine and photography **2** : a solution of iodine used as a local antiseptic

**io·dise** *Brit var of* IODIZE

**io·dize** \'ī-ə-ˌdīz\ *vb* **io·dized; io·diz·ing** : to treat with iodine or an iodide

**ion** \'ī-ən, 'ī-ˌän\ *n* [Gk, neut. of *iōn,* prp. of *ienai* to go; so called because in electrolysis it goes to one of the two poles] : an electrically charged particle, atom, or group of atoms — **ion·ic** \ī-'ä-nik\ *adj*

**-ion** *n suffix* : act, process, state, or condition ⟨validation⟩

**ion·ise** *Brit var of* IONIZE

**ion·ize** \'ī-ə-ˌnīz\ *vb* **ion·ized; ion·iz·ing 1** : to convert wholly or partly into ions **2** : to become ionized — **ion·iz·able** \ˌī-ə-'nī-zə-bəl\ *adj* — **ion·i·za·tion** \ˌī-ə-nə-'zā-shən\ *n* — **ion·iz·er** \'ī-ə-ˌnī-zər\ *n*

**ion·o·sphere** \ī-'ä-nə-ˌsfir\ *n* : the part of the earth's atmosphere extending from about 30 miles (50 kilometers) to the exosphere that contains ionized atmospheric gases — **ion·o·spher·ic** \ī-ˌä-nə-'sfir-ik, -'sfer-\ *adj*

**IOOF** *abbr* Independent Order of Odd Fellows

**io·ta** \ī-'ō-tə\ *n* [L, fr. Gk *iōta*] **1** : the 9th letter of the Greek alphabet — I or ι **2** : a very small quantity : JOT

**IOU** \ˌī-(ˌ)ō-'yü\ *n* : an acknowledgement of a debt

**IP** *abbr* innings pitched

**IP address** \'ī-'pē-\ *n* [*Internet protocol*] : the numeric address of a computer on the Internet

**ip·e·cac** \'i-pi-ˌkak\ *n* [Pg *ipecacuanha*] : an emetic and expectorant drug used esp. as a syrup in treating accidental poisoning; *also* : either of two tropical American plants or their rhizomes and roots used to make ipecac

**IPO** \ˌī-ˌpē-ˈō\ *n, pl* **IPOs** : an initial public offering of a company's stock

**ip·so fac·to** \ˌip-sō-ˈfak-tō\ *adv* [NL, lit., by the fact itself] : by the very nature of the case

**iq** *abbr* [L *idem quod*] the same as

**IQ** \ˈī-ˈkyü\ *n* : a number used to express a person's relative intelligence as determined by a standardized test

**¹Ir** *abbr* Irish

**²Ir** *symbol* iridium

**IR** *abbr* infrared

**¹IRA** \ˌī-(ˌ)är-ˈā; ˈī-rə\ *n* [*individual retirement account*] : a retirement savings account in which income taxes are deferred until withdrawals are made

**²IRA** *abbr* Irish Republican Army

**irai·mbi·lan·ja** \ē-ˌrīm-bē-ˈlän(d)-zə\ *n, pl* **iraimbilanja** — see *ariary* at MONEY table

**iras·ci·ble** \i-ˈra-sə-bəl\ *adj* : marked by hot temper and easily provoked anger
  ♦ *Synonyms* CHOLERIC, TESTY, TOUCHY, CRANKY, CROSS — **iras·ci·bil·i·ty** \-ˌra-sə-ˈbi-lə-tē\ *n*

**irate** \ī-ˈrāt\ *adj* **1** : roused to ire ⟨an ~ customer⟩ **2** : arising from anger — **irate·ly** *adv*

**ire** \ˈī(-ə)r\ *n* : ANGER, WRATH — **ire·ful** *adj*

**ire** *abbr* Ireland

**ire·nic** \ī-ˈre-nik\ *adj* : favoring, conducive to, or operating toward peace or conciliation ⟨~ measures⟩

**ir·i·des·cence** \ˌir-ə-ˈde-sᵊns\ *n* : a rainbowlike play of colors — **ir·i·des·cent** \-sᵊnt\ *adj*

**irid·i·um** \ir-ˈi-dē-əm\ *n* : a hard brittle heavy metallic chemical element

**iris** \ˈī-rəs\ *n, pl* **iris·es** *also* **iri·des** \ˈī-rə-ˌdēz, ˈir-ə-\ [ME, fr. L *iris* rainbow, iris plant, fr. Gk, rainbow, iris plant, iris of the eye] **1** : the colored part around the pupil of the eye **2** : any of a large genus of plants with linear basal leaves and large showy flowers

**Irish** \ˈī-rish\ *n* **1 Irish** *pl* : the people of Ireland **2** : the Celtic language of Ireland — **Irish** *adj* — **Irish·man** \-mən\ *n* — **Irish·wom·an** \-ˌwü-mən\ *n*

**Irish bull** *n* : an incongruous statement (as "it was hereditary in his family to have no children")

**Irish coffee** *n* : hot sugared coffee with Irish whiskey and whipped cream

**Irish moss** *n* : the dried and bleached plants of a red alga that is a source of carrageenan; *also* : this red alga

**Irish setter** *n* : any of a breed of hunting dogs with a mahogany-red coat

**irk** \ˈərk\ *vb* : to make weary, irritated, or bored : ANNOY

**irk·some** \ˈərk-səm\ *adj* : tending to irk : ANNOYING — **irk·some·ly** *adv*

**¹iron** \ˈī(-ə)rn\ *n* [ME, fr. OE *īsern, īren*] **1** : a heavy malleable magnetic metallic chemical element that rusts easily and is vital to biological processes **2** : something made of metal and esp. iron; *also* : something (as handcuffs) used to bind or restrain ⟨put them in ~s⟩ **3** : a household device with a flat base that is heated and used for pressing cloth **4** : STRENGTH, HARDNESS

**²iron** *vb* **1** : to press or smooth with or as if with a heated iron **2** : to remove (as wrinkles) by ironing — **iron·er** *n*

**¹iron·clad** \-ˈklad\ *adj* **1** : sheathed in iron armor **2** : so firm or secure as to be unbreakable

**²iron·clad** \-ˌklad\ *n* : an armored naval vessel esp. of the 19th century

**iron curtain** *n* : a political, military, and ideological barrier that isolates an area; *esp, often cap* : one formerly isolating an area under Soviet control

**iron·ic** \ī-ˈrä-nik\ *also* **iron·i·cal** \-ni-kəl\ *adj* **1** : of, relating to, or marked by irony **2** : given to irony

**iron·i·cal·ly** \-ni-k(ə-)lē\ *adv* **1** : in an ironic manner **2** : it is ironic

**iron·ing** *n* : clothes ironed or to be ironed

**iron lung** *n* : a device for artificial respiration that encloses the chest in a chamber in which changes of pressure force air into and out of the lungs

**iron out** *vb* : to remove or lessen difficulties in or extremes of

**iron oxide** *n* : FERRIC OXIDE

**iron·stone** \ˈī(-ə)rn-ˌstōn\ *n* **1** : a hard iron rich sedimentary rock **2** : a hard heavy durable pottery developed in England in the 19th century

**iron·ware** \-ˌwer\ *n* : articles made of iron

**iron·weed** \-ˌwēd\ *n* : any of a genus of mostly weedy plants related to the asters that have terminal heads of red, purple, or white flowers

**iron·wood** \-ˌwud\ *n* : any of numerous trees or shrubs with exceptionally hard wood; *also* : the wood

**iron·work** \-ˌwərk\ *n* **1** : work in iron **2** *pl* : a mill or building where iron or steel is smelted or heavy iron or steel products are made — **iron·work·er** *n*

**iro·ny** \ˈī-rə-nē\ *n, pl* **-nies** [L *ironia*, fr. Gk *eirōnia*, fr. *eirōn* dissembler] **1** : the use of words to express the opposite of what one really means **2** : incongruity between the actual result of a sequence of events and the expected result

**Ir·o·quois** \ˈir-ə-ˌkwȯi\ *n, pl* **Iroquois** \*same or* -ˌkwȯiz\ **1** *pl* : an American Indian confederacy orig. of New York that consisted of the Cayuga, Mohawk, Oneida, Onondaga, and Seneca and later included the Tuscarora **2** : a member of any of the Iroquois peoples

**ir·ra·di·ate** \i-ˈrā-dē-ˌāt\ *vb* **-at·ed; -at·ing** **1** : ILLUMINATE **2** : ENLIGHTEN **3** : to treat by exposure to radiation **4** : RADIATE — **ir·ra·di·a·tion** \-ˌrā-dē-ˈā-shən\ *n*

**¹ir·ra·tio·nal** \(ˌ)i-ˈra-shə-nəl\ *adj* **1** : incapable of reasoning ⟨~ beasts⟩; *also* : defective in mental power ⟨~ with fever⟩ **2** : not based on reason ⟨~ fears⟩ **3** : being or numerically equal to an irrational number — **ir·ra·tio·nal·i·ty** \(ˌ)i-ˌra-shə-ˈna-lə-tē\ *n* — **ir·ra·tio·nal·ly** *adv*

**²irrational** *n* : IRRATIONAL NUMBER

**irrational number** *n* : a real number that cannot be expressed as the quotient of two integers

**ir·rec·on·cil·able** \(ˌ)i-ˌre-kən-ˈsī-lə-bəl,

-'re-kən-ˌsī-\ *adj* : impossible to reconcile, adjust, or harmonize — **ir·rec·on·cil·abil·i·ty** \(ˌ)i-ˌre-kən-ˌsī-lə-'bi-lə-tē\ *n*

**ir·re·cov·er·able** \ˌir-i-'kə-və-rə-bəl\ *adj* : not capable of being recovered or rectified : IRREPARABLE ⟨an ∼ loss⟩ — **ir·re·cov·er·ably** \-blē\ *adv*

**ir·re·deem·able** \ˌir-i-'dē-mə-bəl\ *adj* 1 : not redeemable; *esp* : not terminable by payment of the principal ⟨an ∼ bond⟩ 2 : not convertible into gold or silver at the will of the holder 3 : being beyond remedy : HOPELESS ⟨∼ villains⟩

**ir·re·den·tism** \-'den-ˌti-zəm\ *n* : a principle or policy directed toward the incorporation of a territory historically or ethnically part of another into that other — **ir·re·den·tist** \-tist\ *n or adj*

**ir·re·duc·ible** \ˌir-i-'dü-sə-bəl, -'dyü-\ *adj* : not reducible ⟨an ∼ fraction⟩ — **ir·re·duc·ibly** \-blē\ *adv*

**ir·re·fut·able** \ˌir-i-'fyü-tə-bəl, (ˌ)i-'re-fyət-\ *adj* : impossible to refute

**irreg** *abbr* irregular

**ir·reg·u·lar** \(ˌ)i-'re-gyə-lər\ *adj* 1 : not regular : not natural or uniform 2 : not conforming to the normal or usual manner of inflection ⟨∼ verbs⟩ 3 : not belonging to a regular or organized army ⟨∼ troops⟩ — **irregular** *n* — **ir·reg·u·lar·ly** *adv*

**ir·reg·u·lar·i·ty** \i-ˌre-gyə-'la-rə-tē\ *n, pl* **-ties** 1 : something that is irregular 2 : the quality or state of being irregular 3 : occasional constipation

**ir·rel·e·vant** \i-'re-lə-vənt\ *adj* : not relevant — **ir·rel·e·vance** \-vəns\ *n*

**ir·re·li·gious** \ˌir-i-'li-jəs\ *adj* : lacking religious emotions, doctrines, or practices

**ir·re·me·di·a·ble** \ˌir-i-'mē-dē-ə-bəl\ *adj* : impossible to remedy or correct

**ir·re·mov·able** \-'mü-və-bəl\ *adj* : not removable

**ir·rep·a·ra·ble** \(ˌ)i-'re-pə-rə-bəl\ *adj* : impossible to make good, undo, repair, or remedy ⟨∼ damage⟩

**ir·re·place·able** \ˌir-i-'plā-sə-bəl\ *adj* : not replaceable ⟨∼ antiques⟩

**ir·re·press·ible** \-'pre-sə-bəl\ *adj* : impossible to repress or control ⟨∼ curiosity⟩

**ir·re·proach·able** \-'prō-chə-bəl\ *adj* : not reproachable : BLAMELESS

**ir·re·sist·ible** \ˌir-i-'zis-tə-bəl\ *adj* : impossible to successfully resist ⟨an ∼ craving⟩ — **ir·re·sist·ibly** \-blē\ *adv*

**ir·res·o·lute** \(ˌ)i-'re-zə-ˌlüt\ *adj* : uncertain how to act or proceed : VACILLATING — **ir·res·o·lute·ly** \-ˌlüt-lē; (ˌ)i-ˌre-zə-'lüt-\ *adv* — **ir·res·o·lu·tion** \(ˌ)i-ˌre-zə-'lü-shən\ *n*

**ir·re·spec·tive of** \ˌir-i-'spek-tiv-\ *prep* : without regard to

**ir·re·spon·si·ble** \-'spän-sə-bəl\ *adj* : not responsible ⟨∼ wastrels⟩ — **ir·re·spon·si·bil·i·ty** \-ˌspän-sə-'bi-lə-tē; (ˌ)i-ˌre-\ *n* — **ir·re·spon·si·bly** \-'spän-sə-blē\ *adv*

**ir·re·triev·able** \ˌir-i-'trē-və-bəl\ *adj* : not retrievable : IRRECOVERABLE

**ir·rev·er·ence** \(ˌ)i-'re-və-rəns\ *n* 1 : lack of reverence 2 : an irreverent act or utterance — **ir·rev·er·ent** \-rənt\ *adj* — **ir·rev·er·ent·ly** *adv*

**ir·re·vers·ible** \ˌir-i-'vər-sə-bəl\ *adj* : incapable of being reversed ⟨an ∼ loss⟩

**ir·rev·o·ca·ble** \(ˌ)i-'re-və-kə-bəl\ *adj* : incapable of being revoked or recalled ⟨∼ change⟩ — **ir·rev·o·ca·bly** \-blē\ *adv*

**ir·ri·gate** \'ir-ə-ˌgāt\ *vb* **-gat·ed; -gat·ing** : to supply (as land) with water by artificial means; *also* : to flush with liquid — **ir·ri·ga·tion** \ˌir-ə-'gā-shən\ *n*

**ir·ri·ta·bil·i·ty** \ˌir-ə-tə-'bi-lə-tē\ *n* 1 : the property of living things and of protoplasm that enables reaction to stimuli 2 : the quality or state of being irritable; *esp* : readiness to become annoyed or angry

**ir·ri·ta·ble** \'ir-ə-tə-bəl\ *adj* : capable of being irritated; *esp* : readily or easily irritated — **ir·ri·ta·bly** \-blē\ *adv*

**ir·ri·tate** \'ir-ə-ˌtāt\ *vb* **-tat·ed; -tat·ing** 1 : to excite to anger : EXASPERATE 2 : to make sore or inflamed — **ir·ri·tant** \'ir-ə-tənt\ *adj or n* — **ir·ri·tat·ing·ly** \-ˌtā-tiŋ-lē\ *adv* — **ir·ri·ta·tion** \ˌir-ə-'tā-shən\ *n*

**ir·rupt** \(ˌ)i-'rəpt\ *vb* 1 : to rush in forcibly or violently 2 : to increase suddenly in numbers ⟨rabbits ∼ in cycles⟩ — **ir·rup·tion** \-'rəp-shən\ *n*

**IRS** *abbr* Internal Revenue Service

**is** *pres 3d sing of* BE

**Isa** or **Is** *abbr* Isaiah

**Isa·iah** \ī-'zā-ə\ *n* — see BIBLE table

**Isa·ias** \ī-'zā-əs\ *n* : ISAIAH

**ISBN** *abbr* International Standard Book Number

**is·che·mia** \is-'kē-mē-ə\ *n* : deficient supply of blood to a body part (as the brain) — **is·che·mic** \-mik\ *adj*

**isl** *abbr* island

**Is·lam** \is-'läm, iz-, -'lam, 'is-ˌ, 'iz-ˌ\ *n* [Ar *islām* submission (to the will of God)] : the religious faith of Muslims including belief in Allah as the sole deity and in Muhammad as his prophet; *also* : the civilization built on this faith — **Is·lam·ic** \is-'lä-mik, iz-, -'la-\ *adj*

**is·land** \'ī-lənd\ *n* [ME *iland*, fr. OE *īgland*, fr. *īg* island + *land* land] 1 : a body of land smaller than a continent surrounded by water 2 : something resembling an island in its isolation

**is·land·er** \'ī-lən-dər\ *n* : a native or inhabitant of an island

**isle** \'ī(-ə)l\ *n* : ISLAND; *esp* : a small island

**is·let** \'ī-lət\ *n* : a small island

**ism** \ˌi-zəm\ *n* : a distinctive doctrine, cause, or theory

**-ism** *n suffix* 1 : act : practice : process ⟨criticism⟩ 2 : manner of action or behavior characteristic of a (specified) person or thing ⟨fanaticism⟩ 3 : state : condition : property ⟨dualism⟩ 4 : abnormal state or condition ⟨alcoholism⟩ 5 : doctrine : theory : cult ⟨Buddhism⟩ 6 : adherence to a set of principles ⟨stoicism⟩

**7** : prejudice or discrimination on the basis of a (specified) attribute ⟨*racism*⟩ ⟨*sexism*⟩ **8** : characteristic or peculiar feature or trait ⟨colloquial*ism*⟩

**iso·bar** \ˈī-sə-ˌbär\ *n* : a line on a map connecting places of equal barometric pressure — **iso·bar·ic** \ˌī-sə-ˈbär-ik, -ˈber-\ *adj*

**iso·late** \ˈī-sə-ˌlāt\ *vb* **-lat·ed; -lat·ing** [fr. *isolated* set apart, fr. F *isolé*, fr. It *isolato*, fr. *isola* land, fr. L *insula*] : to place or keep by itself : separate from others — **iso·la·tion** \ˌī-sə-ˈlā-shən\ *n*

**isolated** *adj* **1** : occurring alone or once : UNIQUE **2** : SPORADIC ⟨∼ outbreaks⟩

**iso·la·tion·ism** \ˌī-sə-ˈlā-shə-ˌni-zəm\ *n* : a policy of national isolation by abstention from international political and economic relations — **iso·la·tion·ist** \-shə-nist\ *n or adj*

**iso·mer** \ˈī-sə-mər\ *n* : any of two or more chemical compounds that contain the same numbers of atoms of the same elements but differ in structural arrangement and properties — **iso·mer·ic** \ˌī-sə-ˈmer-ik\ *adj* — **isom·er·ism** \ī-ˈsä-mə-ˌri-zəm\ *n*

**iso·met·rics** \ˌī-sə-ˈme-triks\ *n sing or pl* : exercise involving a series of brief and intense contractions of muscles against each other or against an immovable resistance — **iso·met·ric** *adj*

**iso·prene** \ˈī-sə-ˌprēn\ *n* : a hydrocarbon used esp. in making synthetic rubber

**isos·ce·les** \ī-ˈsä-sə-ˌlēz\ *adj* : having two equal sides ⟨an ∼ triangle⟩

**iso·therm** \ˈī-sə-ˌthərm\ *n* : a line on a map connecting points having the same temperature

**iso·ther·mal** \ˌī-sə-ˈthər-məl\ *adj* : of, relating to, or marked by equality of temperature

**iso·tope** \ˈī-sə-ˌtōp\ *n* [Gk *isos* equal + *topos* place] : any of the forms of a chemical element that differ chiefly in the number of neutrons in an atom — **iso·to·pic** \ˌī-sə-ˈtä-pik, -ˈtō-\ *adj* — **iso·to·pi·cal·ly** \-ˈtä-pi-k(ə-)lē, -ˈtō-\ *adv*

**Isr** *abbr* Israel; Israeli

**Is·ra·el·ite** \ˈiz-rē-ə-ˌlīt\ *n* : a member of the Hebrew people descended from Jacob

**is·su·ance** \ˈi-shü-wəns\ *n* : the act of issuing or giving out esp. officially

**¹is·sue** \ˈi-shü\ *n* [ME, exit, proceeds, fr. AF, fr. *issir* to come out, go out, fr. L. *exire*, fr. *ire* to go] **1** : the action of going, coming, or flowing out : EGRESS, EMERGENCE **2** : EXIT, OUTLET, VENT **3** : OFFSPRING, PROGENY **4** : OUTCOME, RESULT **5** : a point of debate or controversy; *also* : the point at which an unsettled matter is ready for a decision **6** : a discharge (as of blood) from the body **7** : something coming forth from a specified source **8** : the act of officially giving out or printing : PUBLICATION; *also* : the quantity of things given out at one time

**²issue** *vb* **is·sued; is·su·ing 1** : to go, come, or flow out **2** : to come forth or cause to come forth : EMERGE, DISCHARGE, EMIT **3** : ACCRUE **4** : to descend from a specified parent or ancestor **5** : to result in **6** : to put forth or distribute officially **7** : PUBLISH **8** : EMANATE, RESULT — **is·su·er** *n*

**¹-ist** *n suffix* **1** : one that performs a (specified) action ⟨cycl*ist*⟩ **2** : one that makes or produces ⟨novel*ist*⟩ **2** : one that plays a (specified) musical instrument ⟨harp*ist*⟩ **3** : one that operates a (specified) mechanical instrument or contrivance ⟨machin*ist*⟩ **4** : one that specializes in a (specified) art or science or skill ⟨geolog*ist*⟩ **5** : one that adheres to or advocates a (specified) doctrine or system or code of behavior ⟨social*ist*⟩ or that of a (specified) individual ⟨Darwin*ist*⟩

**²-ist** *adj suffix* : -ISTIC

**isth·mi·an** \ˈis-mē-ən\ *adj* : of, relating to, or situated in or near an isthmus

**isth·mus** \ˈis-məs\ *n* : a narrow strip of land connecting two larger portions of land

**¹it** \ˈit, ət\ *pron* **1** : that one — used of a lifeless thing, a plant, a person or animal, or an abstract entity ⟨∼'s a big building⟩ ⟨∼'s a shade tree⟩ ⟨who is ∼⟩ ⟨beauty is everywhere and ∼ is a source of joy⟩ **2** — used as subject of an impersonal verb that expresses a condition or action without reference to an agent ⟨∼ is raining⟩ **3** — used as an anticipatory subject or object ⟨∼'s good to see you⟩

**²it** \ˈit\ *n* : the player in a game who performs the principal action of the game (as trying to find others in hide-and-seek)

**It** *abbr* Italian; Italy

**ital** *abbr* italic; italicized

**Ital** *abbr* Italian

**Ital·ian** \i-ˈtal-yən\ *n* **1** : a native or inhabitant of Italy **2** : the language of Italy — **Italian** *adj*

**ital·ic** \i-ˈta-lik, ī-\ *adj* : relating to type in which the letters slope up toward the right (as in "italic") — **italic** *n*

**ital·i·cise** *Brit var of* ITALICIZE

**ital·i·cize** \i-ˈta-lə-ˌsīz, ī-\ *vb* **-cized; -ciz·ing** : to print in italics — **ital·i·ci·za·tion** \-ˌta-lə-sə-ˈzā-shən\ *n*

**itch** \ˈich\ *n* **1** : an uneasy irritating skin sensation that evokes a desire to scratch the affected area **2** : a skin disorder accompanied by an itch **3** : a persistent desire — **itch** *vb* — **itchy** *adj*

**-ite** *n suffix* **1** : native : resident ⟨suburban*ite*⟩ **2** : adherent : follower ⟨Lenin*ite*⟩ **3** : product ⟨metabol*ite*⟩ **4** : mineral : rock ⟨quartz*ite*⟩

**item** \ˈī-təm\ *n* [L, likewise, also] **1** : a separate particular in a list, account, or series : ARTICLE **2** : a separate piece of news (as in a newspaper)

**item·ise** *Brit var of* ITEMIZE

**item·ize** \ˈī-tə-ˌmīz\ *vb* **-ized; -iz·ing** : to set down in detail : LIST — **item·i·za·tion** \ˌī-tə-mə-ˈzā-shən\ *n*

**it·er·ate** \ˈi-tə-ˌrāt\ *vb* **-at·ed; -at·ing** : REITERATE, REPEAT ⟨*iterated* his innocence⟩

**it·er·a·tion** \ˌi-tə-ˈrā-shən\ *n* **1** : REPETITION; *esp* : a computational process in which a series of operations is repeated until a condition is met **2** : one repetition of the series of operations in iteration **3** : VERSION

**itin·er·ant** \ī-'ti-nə-rənt, ə-\ *adj* : traveling from place to place; *esp* : covering a circuit ⟨an ~ preacher⟩

**itin·er·ary** \ī-'ti-nə-,rer-ē, ə-\ *n, pl* **-ar·ies** **1** : the route of a journey or the proposed outline of one **2** : a travel diary **3** : GUIDEBOOK

**its** \'its\ *adj* : of or relating to it or itself

**it·self** \it-'self\ *pron* : that identical one — used reflexively, for emphasis, or in absolute constructions

**-ity** *n suffix* : quality : state : degree ⟨alkalin*ity*⟩

**IUD** \,ī-(,)yü-'dē\ *n* : INTRAUTERINE DEVICE

**IV** \,ī-'vē\ *n, pl* **IVs** [*intravenous*] : an apparatus used to administer a fluid (as of nutrients) intravenously; *also* : a fluid administered by IV

**-ive** *adj suffix* : that performs or tends toward an (indicated) action ⟨correct*ive*⟩

**ivo·ry** \'ī-vrē, -və-rē\ *n, pl* **-ries** [ME *ivo*-rie, fr. AF *ivoire, ivurie,* fr. L *eboreus* of ivory, fr. *ebur* ivory] **1** : the hard creamy-white material composing the tusks of an elephant or walrus **2** : a pale yellow color **3** : something made of ivory or of a similar substance

**ivory tower** *n* **1** : an impractical lack of concern with urgent problems **2** : a place of learning

**ivy** \'ī-vē\ *n, pl* **ivies** : a trailing woody evergreen vine with small black berries that is related to ginseng

**IWW** *abbr* Industrial Workers of the World

**-ize** *vb suffix* **1** : cause to be or conform to or resemble ⟨American*ize*⟩ : cause to be formed into ⟨union*ize*⟩ **2** : subject to a (specified) action ⟨satir*ize*⟩ **3** : saturate, treat, or combine with ⟨macadam*ize*⟩ **4** : treat like ⟨idol*ize*⟩ **5** : become : become like ⟨crystall*ize*⟩ **6** : be productive in or of : engage in a (specified) activity ⟨philosoph*ize*⟩ **7** : adopt or spread the manner of activity or the teaching of ⟨Christian*ize*⟩

**J**

**¹j** \'jā\ *n, pl* **j's** *or* **js** \'jāz\ *often cap* : the 10th letter of the English alphabet

**²j** *abbr, often cap* **1** jack **2** journal **3** judge **4** justice

**¹jab** \'jab\ *vb* **jabbed; jab·bing** : to thrust quickly or abruptly : POKE

**²jab** *n* : a usu. short straight punch

**jab·ber** \'ja-bər\ *vb* : to talk rapidly, indistinctly, or unintelligibly : CHATTER — **jabber** *n* — **jab·ber·er** *n*

**jab·ber·wocky** \'ja-bər-,wä-kē\ *n* : meaningless speech or writing

**ja·bot** \zha-'bō, 'ja-,bō\ *n* : a ruffle worn down the front of a dress or shirt

**jac·a·ran·da** \,ja-kə-'ran-də\ *n* : any of a genus of pinnate-leaved tropical American trees with clusters of showy blue flowers

**¹jack** \'jak\ *n* **1** : a mechanical device; *esp* : one used to raise a heavy body a short distance **2** : a male donkey **3** : a small target ball in lawn bowling **4** : a small national flag flown by a ship **5** : a small 6-pointed metal object used in a game (**jacks**) **6** : a playing card bearing the figure of a soldier or servant **7** : a socket into which a plug is inserted for connecting electric circuits

**²jack** *vb* **1** : to raise by means of a jack **2** : INCREASE ⟨~ up prices⟩

**jack·al** \'ja-kəl\ *n* [Turk *çakal,* fr. Pers *shaqāl*] : any of several mammals of Asia and Africa related to the wolves

**jack·a·napes** \'ja-kə-,nāps\ *n* **1** : MONKEY, APE **2** : an impudent or conceited person

**jack·ass** \'jak-,as\ *n* **1** : DONKEY; *esp* : a male donkey **2** : a stupid person : FOOL

**jack·boot** \-,büt\ *n* **1** : a heavy military boot of glossy black leather extending above the knee **2** : a laceless military boot reaching to the knee

**jack·daw** \'jak-,dȯ\ *n* : a black and gray Old World crowlike bird

**jack·et** \'ja-kət\ *n* [ME *jaket,* fr. AF *jackés,* pl., dim. of MF *jaque* short jacket, fr. *jacques* peasant, fr. the name *Jacques* James] **1** : a garment for the upper body usu. having a front opening, collar, and sleeves **2** : an outer covering or casing ⟨a book ~⟩

**Jack Frost** *n* : frost or frosty weather personified

**jack·ham·mer** \'jak-,ha-mər\ *n* : a pneumatic percussion tool for drilling rock or breaking pavement

**jack–in–the–box** *n, pl* **jack–in–the–boxes** *or* **jacks–in–the–box** : a toy consisting of a small box out of which a figure springs when the lid is raised

**jack–in–the–pulpit** *n, pl* **jack–in–the–pulpits** *also* **jacks–in–the–pulpit** : a No. American spring-flowering woodland herb having an upright club-shaped spadix arched over by a green and purple spathe

**¹jack·knife** \'jak-,nīf\ *n* **1** : a large pocketknife **2** : a dive in which the diver bends from the waist and touches the ankles before straightening out

**²jackknife** *vb* : to fold like a jackknife ⟨the trailer truck *jackknifed*⟩

**jack·leg** \'jak-,leg\ *adj* **1** : lacking skill or training **2** : MAKESHIFT

**jack–of–all–trades** *n, pl* **jacks–of–all–trades** : one who is able to do passable work at various tasks

**jack–o'–lan·tern** \'ja-kə-,lan-tərn\ *n* : a lantern made of a pumpkin cut to look like a human face

**jack·pot** \'jak-,pät\ *n* **1** : a large sum of money formed by the accumulation of stakes from previous play (as in poker) **2** : an impressive and often unexpected success or reward

**jack·rab·bit** \-,ra-bət\ *n* : any of several large hares of western No. America with very long ears and hind legs

**Jack Russell terrier** \'jak-'rə-səl-\ *n* : any of a breed of small terriers having a white coat with dark markings

**jack·straw** \-,strȯ\ *n* **1** *pl* : a game in which straws or thin sticks are let fall in a heap and each player in turn tries to remove them one at a time without disturbing the rest **2** : one of the pieces used in jackstraws

**jack–tar** \-'tär\ *n, often cap* : SAILOR

**Ja·cob's ladder** \'jā-kəbz-\ *n* : any of several perennial herbs related to phlox that have pinnate leaves and blue or white bell-shaped flowers

**jac·quard** \'ja-,kärd\ *n, often cap* : a fabric of intricate variegated weave or pattern

**¹jade** \'jād\ *n* **1** : a broken-down, vicious, or worthless horse **2** : a disreputable woman

**²jade** *vb* **jad·ed; jad·ing 1** : to wear out by overwork or abuse **2** : to become weary
 ♦ **Synonyms** EXHAUST, FATIGUE, TIRE

**³jade** *n* [F, fr. obs. Sp (*piedra de la*) *ijada*, lit., loin stone; fr. the belief that jade cures renal colic] : a usu. green gemstone that takes a high polish

**jad·ed** *adj* : made dull, apathetic, or cynical by experience or by surfeit

**¹jag** \'jag\ *n* : a sharp projecting part

**²jag** *n* : SPREE ⟨a crying ∼⟩

**jag·ged** \'ja-gəd\ *adj* : sharply notched

**jag·uar** \'ja-,gwär\ *n* : a black-spotted tropical American cat that is larger and stockier than the Old World leopard

**jai alai** \'hī-,lī\ *n* [Sp, fr. Basque, fr. *jai* festival + *alai* merry] : a court game played by usu. two or four players with a ball and a curved wicker basket strapped to the wrist

**jail** \'jāl\ *n* [ME *jaiole*, fr. AF *gaiole, jaiole*, fr. LL *caveola*, dim. of L *cavea* cage] : PRISON; *esp* : one for persons held in lawful custody — **jail** *vb*

**jail·bird** \-,bərd\ *n* : a habitual criminal

**jail·break** \-,brāk\ *n* : a forcible escape from jail

**jail·er** *also* **jail·or** \'jā-lər\ *n* : a keeper of a jail

**jal·ap** \'ja-ləp, 'jä-\ *n* : a powdered purgative drug from the root of a Mexican plant related to the morning glory; *also* : this root or plant

**ja·la·pe·ño** \,hä-lə-'pān-(,)yō\ *n* : a small plump dark green chili pepper

**ja·lo·py** \jə-'lä-pē\ *n, pl* **ja·lop·ies** : a dilapidated vehicle (as an automobile)

**jal·ou·sie** \'ja-lə-sē\ *n* [F, lit., jealousy] : a blind, window, or door with adjustable horizontal slats or louvers

**¹jam** \'jam\ *vb* **jammed; jam·ming 1** : to press into a close or tight position **2** : to cause to become wedged so as to be unworkable; *also* : to make or become un-

workable through the jamming of a movable part **3** : to push forcibly ⟨∼ on the brakes⟩ **4** : CRUSH, BRUISE ⟨*jammed* a finger in the door⟩ **5** : to make unintelligible by sending out interfering signals or messages **6** : to take part in a jam session — **jam·mer** *n*

**²jam** *n* **1** : a crowded mass that impedes or blocks ⟨traffic ∼⟩ **2** : a difficult state of affairs

**³jam** *n* : a food made by boiling fruit and sugar to a thick consistency

**Jam** *abbr* Jamaica

**jamb** \'jam\ *n* [ME *jambe*, fr. AF *jambe, gambe*, lit., leg] : an upright piece forming the side of an opening (as of a door)

**jam·ba·laya** \,jəm-bə-'lī-ə\ *n* [LaF] : rice cooked with ham, sausage, chicken, shrimp, or oysters and seasoned with herbs

**jam·bo·ree** \,jam-bə-'rē\ *n* : a large festive gathering

**James** \'jāmz\ *n* — see BIBLE table

**jam–pack** \'jam-'pak\ *vb* : to pack tightly or to excess

**jam session** *n* : an impromptu performance esp. by jazz musicians

**Jan** *abbr* January

**jan·gle** \'jaŋ-gəl\ *vb* **jan·gled; jan·gling** : to make a harsh or discordant sound — **jangle** *n*

**jan·i·tor** \'ja-nə-tər\ *n* [L, doorkeeper, fr. *janus* arch, gate] : a person who has the care of a building — **jan·i·to·ri·al** \,ja-nə-'tȯr-ē-əl\ *adj*

**Jan·u·ary** \'ja-nyə-,wer-ē\ *n* [ME *Januarie*, fr. L *Januarius*, first month of the ancient Roman year, fr. *Janus*, two-faced god of gates and beginnings] : the 1st month of the year

**¹ja·pan** \jə-'pan\ *n* : a varnish giving a hard brilliant finish

**²japan** *vb* **ja·panned; ja·pan·ning** : to cover with a coat of japan

**Jap·a·nese** \,ja-pə-'nēz, -'nēs\ *n, pl* **Japanese 1** : a native or inhabitant of Japan **2** : the language of Japan — **Japanese** *adj*

**Japanese beetle** *n* : a small metallic green and brown scarab beetle introduced from Japan that is a pest on the roots of grasses as a grub and on foliage and fruits as an adult

**¹jape** \'jāp\ *vb* **japed; jap·ing 1** : JOKE **2** : MOCK

**²jape** *n* : JEST, GIBE

**¹jar** \'jär\ *vb* **jarred; jar·ring 1** : to make a harsh or discordant sound **2** : to have a harsh or disagreeable effect **3** : VIBRATE, SHAKE ⟨tremors *jarred* the house⟩

**²jar** *n* **1** : a state of conflict **2** : a harsh discordant sound **3** : JOLT **4** : a painful effect : SHOCK

**³jar** *n* : a widemouthed container usu. of glass or earthenware

**jar·di·niere** \,jär-də-'nir\ *n* : an ornamental stand for plants or flowers

**jar·gon** \'jär-gən\ *n* **1** : confused unintelligible language **2** : the special vocabulary of a particular group or activity **3** : obscure and often pretentious language

**Jas** *abbr* James

**jas·mine** \'jaz-mən\ *also* **jes·sa·mine** \'jes-mən, 'je-sə-\ *n* [MF *jasmin*, fr. Ar *yāsamīn*, fr. Pers] : any of various climbing shrubs with fragrant flowers

**jas·per** \'jas-pər\ *n* : a usu. red, yellow, or brown opaque quartz

**jaun·dice** \'jȯn-dəs\ *n* : yellowish discoloration of skin, tissues, and body fluids by bile pigments; *also* : an abnormal condition marked by jaundice

**jaun·diced** \-dəst\ *adj* **1** : affected with or as if with jaundice **2** : exhibiting envy, distaste, or hostility ⟨a ~ critic⟩

**jaunt** \'jȯnt\ *n* : a short trip usu. for pleasure

**jaun·ty** \'jȯn-tē\ *adj* **jaun·ti·er; -est** : sprightly in manner or appearance : LIVELY ⟨~ tunes⟩ — **jaun·ti·ly** \-tə-lē\ *adv* — **jaun·ti·ness** \-tē-nəs\ *n*

**jav·e·lin** \'ja-və-lən\ *n* **1** : a light spear **2** : a slender shaft thrown for distance in a track-and-field contest

**¹jaw** \'jȯ\ *n* **1** : either of the bony or cartilaginous structures that support the soft tissues enclosing the mouth and that usu. bear teeth **2** : the parts forming the walls of the mouth and serving to open and close it — usu. used in pl. **3** : one of a pair of movable parts for holding or crushing something — **jawed** \'jȯd\ *adj*

**²jaw** *vb* : to talk abusively, indignantly, or at length ⟨~ing with her sister⟩

**¹jaw·bone** \-,bōn,-\ *n* : JAW 1

**²jawbone** *vb* : to talk forcefully and persuasively

**jaw·break·er** \-,brā-kər\ *n* **1** : a word difficult to pronounce **2** : a round hard candy

**jaw–drop·ping** \'jȯ-,dra-piŋ\ *adj* : causing great surprise or astonishment

**jaw·less fish** \'jȯ-ləs-\ *n* : any of a group of primitive vertebrates (as lampreys) without jaws

**jay** \'jā\ *n* : any of various noisy brightly colored often largely blue birds smaller than the related crows

**jay·bird** \'jā-,bərd\ *n* : JAY

**jay·vee** \jā-'vē\ *n* **1** : JUNIOR VARSITY **2** : a member of a junior varsity team

**jay·walk** \'jā-,wȯk\ *vb* : to cross a street carelessly without regard for traffic regulations — **jay·walk·er** *n*

**¹jazz** \'jaz\ *n* **1** : American music characterized by improvisation, syncopated rhythms, and contrapuntal ensemble playing **2** : empty talk **3** : similar but unspecified things : STUFF

**²jazz** *vb* : ENLIVEN ⟨~ things up⟩

**jazzy** \'ja-zē\ *adj* **jazz·i·er; -est 1** : having the characteristics of jazz **2** : marked by unrestraint, animation, or flashiness

**JCS** *abbr* joint chiefs of staff

**jct** *abbr* junction

**JD** *abbr* **1** [L *juris doctor*] doctor of jurisprudence; doctor of law **2** [L *jurum doctor*] doctor of laws **3** justice department **4** juvenile delinquent

**jeal·ous** \'je-ləs\ *adj* **1** : demanding complete devotion **2** : suspicious of a rival or of one believed to enjoy an advantage ⟨~ of his rich friends⟩ **3** : VIGILANT — **jeal·ous·ly** *adv* — **jeal·ou·sy** \-lə-sē\ *n*

**jeans** \'jēnz\ *n pl* [pl. of *jean* twilled cloth, short for *jean fustian*, fr. ME *Gene* Genoa, Italy] : pants made of durable twilled cotton cloth

**jeep** \'jēp\ *n* : a small four-wheel drive general-purpose motor vehicle used in World War II

**¹jeer** \'jir\ *vb* : to speak or cry out in derision : MOCK ⟨~ed the umpire⟩

**²jeer** *n* : TAUNT ⟨~ed by the bully⟩

**Je·ho·vah** \ji-'hō-və\ *n* : GOD 1

**je·hu** \'jē-hü, -hyü\ *n* : a driver of a coach or cab

**je·june** \ji-'jün\ *adj* [L *jejunus* empty of food, hungry, meager] : lacking interest or significance : DULL

**je·ju·num** \ji-'jü-nəm\ *n* [L] : the section of the small intestine between the duodenum and the ileum — **je·ju·nal** \-'jü-nᵊl\ *adj*

**jell** \'jel\ *vb* **1** : to come to the consistency of jelly **2** : to take shape ⟨my idea began to ~⟩

**jel·ly** \'je-lē\ *n, pl* **jellies 1** : a food with a soft elastic consistency due usu. to the presence of gelatin or pectin; *esp* : a fruit product made by boiling sugar and the juice of a fruit **2** : a substance resembling jelly — **jelly** *vb* — **jel·ly·like** *adj*

**jelly bean** *n* : a bean-shaped candy

**jel·ly·fish** \'je-lē-,fish\ *n* : a marine coelenterate with a nearly transparent jellylike body and stinging tentacles

**jen·net** \'je-nət\ *n* **1** : a small Spanish horse **2** : a female donkey

**jen·ny** \'je-nē\ *n, pl* **jennies** : a female bird or donkey

**jeop·ar·dy** \'je-pər-dē\ *n* [ME *jeopardie*, fr. AF *juparti, jeuparti* alternative, lit., divided game] : exposure to death, loss, or injury ♦ **Synonyms** PERIL, HAZARD, RISK, DANGER — **jeop·ar·dize** \-,dīz\ *vb*

**Jer** *abbr* Jeremiah; Jeremias

**jer·e·mi·ad** \,jer-ə-'mī-əd, -,ad\ *n* : a prolonged lamentation or complaint; *also* : a cautionary or angry harangue

**Jer·e·mi·ah** \,jer-ə-'mī-ə\ *n* — see BIBLE table

**Jer·e·mi·as** \,jer-ə-'mī-əs\ *n* : JEREMIAH

**¹jerk** \'jərk\ *n* **1** : a short quick pull or twist : TWITCH **2** : an annoyingly stupid or foolish person — **jerk·i·ly** \'jər-kə-lē\ *adv* — **jerky** \'jər-kē\ *adj*

**²jerk** *vb* **1** : to give a sharp quick push, pull, or twist **2** : to move in short abrupt motions

**jer·kin** \'jər-kən\ *n* : a close-fitting usu. sleeveless jacket

**jerk·wa·ter** \'jərk-,wȯ-tər, -,wä-\ *adj* [fr. *jerkwater* rural train] : of minor importance : INSIGNIFICANT ⟨~ towns⟩

**jer·ry–built** \'jer-ē-,bilt\ *adj* : built cheaply and flimsily

**jer·ry–rigged** \-,rigd\ *adj* : organized or constructed in a crude or improvised manner

**jer·sey** \'jər-zē\ *n, pl* **jerseys** [*Jersey*, one of the Channel islands] **1** : a plain weftknitted fabric **2** : a close-fitting knitted shirt **3** *often cap* : any of a breed of small usu. fawn-colored dairy cattle

**Jersey barrier** *n* : a concrete slab that is

used with others to block or reroute traffic or to divide a highway

**Je·ru·sa·lem artichoke** \jə-ˈrü-sə-ləm-\ n : a No. American sunflower widely grown for its edible tubers that are used as a vegetable; *also* : its tubers

**jess** \ˈjes\ n : a leg strap by which a captive bird of prey may be controlled

**jessamine** *var of* JASMINE

**jest** \ˈjest\ n **1** : an act intended to provoke laughter **2** : a witty remark **3** : a frivolous mood ⟨said in ∼⟩ — **jest** vb

**jest·er** \ˈjes-tər\ n : a retainer formerly kept to provide casual entertainment

**¹jet** \ˈjet\ n : a velvet-black coal that takes a good polish and is often used for jewelry

**²jet** vb **jet·ted; jet·ting** : to spout or emit in a stream

**³jet** n **1** : a forceful rush (as of liquid or gas) through a narrow opening; *also* : a nozzle for a jet of fluid **2** : a jet-propelled airplane

**⁴jet** vb **jet·ted; jet·ting** : to travel by jet

**jet lag** n : a condition that is marked esp. by fatigue and irritability and occurs following a long flight through several time zones — **jet lagged** adj

**jet·lin·er** \ˈjet-ˌlī-nər\ n : a jet-propelled airliner

**jet·port** \-ˌpȯrt\ n : an airport designed to handle jets

**jet–pro·pelled** \ˌjet-prə-ˈpeld\ adj : driven by an engine (**jet engine**) that produces propulsion (**jet propulsion**) by the rearward discharge of a jet of fluid (as heated air and exhaust gases)

**jet·sam** \ˈjet-səm\ n : jettisoned goods; *esp* : such goods washed ashore

**jet set** n : an international group of wealthy people who frequent fashionable resorts

**jet stream** n : a long narrow high-altitude current of high-speed winds blowing generally from the west

**jet·ti·son** \ˈje-tə-sən\ vb **1** : to throw (goods) overboard to lighten a ship or aircraft in distress **2** : DISCARD ⟨∼ed their old computers⟩ — **jettison** n

**jet·ty** \ˈje-tē\ n, pl **jetties 1** : a pier built to influence the current or to protect a harbor **2** : a landing wharf

**jeu d'es·prit** \zhœ-des-ˈprē\ n, pl **jeux d'esprit** \*same*\ [F, lit., play of the mind] : a witty comment or composition

**Jew** \ˈjü\ n **1** : ISRAELITE **2** : one whose religion is Judaism — **Jew·ish** adj

**¹jew·el** \ˈjü-əl\ n [ME *juel*, fr. AF, dim. of *ju, jeu* game, play, fr. L *jocus* game, joke] **1** : an ornament of precious metal **2** : GEMSTONE, GEM

**²jewel** vb **-eled** or **-elled; -el·ing** or **-el·ling** : to adorn or equip with jewels

**jewel box** n : a thin plastic case for a CD or DVD

**jew·el·er** or **jew·el·ler** \ˈjü-ə-lər\ n : a person who makes or deals in jewelry and related articles

**jew·el·lery** *chiefly Brit var of* JEWELRY

**jew·el·ry** \ˈjü-əl-rē\ n : JEWELS; *esp* : objects of precious metal set with gems and worn for personal adornment

**Jew·ry** \ˈju̇r-ē, ˈjü-ər-ē, ˈjü-rē\ n : the Jewish people

**jg** *abbr* junior grade

**¹jib** \ˈjib\ n : a triangular sail set on a line running forward from the bow to the mast

**²jib** vb **jibbed; jib·bing** : to refuse to proceed further

**¹jibe** *var of* GIBE

**²jibe** \ˈjīb\ vb **jibed; jib·ing** : to be in accord : AGREE ⟨his conclusion does not ∼ with theirs⟩

**ji·ca·ma** \ˈhē-kə-mə\ n : an edible starchy tuber of a tropical American vine of the legume family

**jif·fy** \ˈji-fē\ n, pl **jiffies** : MOMENT, INSTANT ⟨I'll be ready in a ∼⟩

**¹jig** \ˈjig\ n **1** : a lively dance in triple rhythm **2** : TRICK, GAME ⟨the ∼ is up⟩ **3** : a device used to hold work during manufacture or assembly

**²jig** vb **jigged; jig·ging** : to dance a jig

**jig·ger** \ˈji-gər\ n : a measure usu. holding 1 to 2 ounces (30 to 60 milliliters) used in mixing drinks

**jig·gle** \ˈji-gəl\ vb **jig·gled; jig·gling** : to move with quick little jerks — **jiggle** n

**jig·saw** \ˈjig-ˌsȯ\ n : SCROLL SAW 2

**jigsaw puzzle** n : a puzzle consisting of small irregularly cut pieces to be fitted together to form a picture

**ji·had** \ji-ˈhäd, -ˈhad\ n **1** : a Muslim holy war **2** : CRUSADE 2

**ji·had·ist** \ji-ˈhä-dist, -ˈha-\ n : a Muslim who advocates or participates in a jihad

**¹jilt** \ˈjilt\ vb : to drop (as a lover) capriciously or unfeelingly

**²jilt** n : one who jilts a lover

**jim crow** \ˈjim-ˈkrō\ n, often cap J&C : discrimination against blacks esp. by legal enforcement or traditional sanctions — **jim crow** adj, often cap J&C — **jim crow·ism** \-ˈkrō-ˌi-zəm\ n, often cap J&C

**jim–dan·dy** \ˈjim-ˈdan-dē\ n : something excellent of its kind — **jim–dandy** adj

**jim·mies** \ˈji-mēz\ n pl : tiny rod-shaped bits of usu. chocolate-flavored candy often sprinkled on ice cream

**¹jim·my** \ˈji-mē\ n, pl **jimmies** : a small crowbar

**²jimmy** vb **jim·mied; jim·my·ing** : to force open with a jimmy

**jim·son·weed** \ˈjim-sən-ˌwēd\ n, often cap : a coarse poisonous weed related to the tomato that has large trumpet-shaped white or violet flowers

**¹jin·gle** \ˈjin-gəl\ vb **jin·gled; jin·gling** : to make a light clinking or tinkling sound

**²jingle** n **1** : a light clinking or tinkling sound **2** : a short verse or song with catchy repetition

**jin·go·ism** \ˈjin-gō-ˌi-zəm\ n : extreme chauvinism or nationalism marked esp. by a belligerent foreign policy — **jin·go·ist** \-ist\ n — **jin·go·is·tic** \ˌjin-gō-ˈis-tik\ adj

**jin·rik·sha** \jin-ˈrik-ˌshȯ\ n : RICKSHAW

**¹jinx** \ˈjiŋks\ n : one that brings bad luck

**²jinx** vb : to foredoom to failure or misfortune

**jit·ney** \ˈjit-nē\ n, pl **jitneys** : a small bus

that serves a regular route on a flexible schedule

**jit·ter·bug** \'ji-tər-ˌbəg\ n : a dance in which couples two-step, balance, and twirl vigorously in standardized patterns — **jitterbug** vb

**jit·ters** \'ji-tərz\ n pl : extreme nervousness — **jit·tery** \-tə-rē\ adj

¹**jive** \'jīv\ n 1 : swing music or dancing performed to it 2 : glib, deceptive, or foolish talk 3 : the jargon of jazz enthusiasts

²**jive** vb **jived; jiv·ing** 1 : KID, TEASE 2 : to dance to or play jive

**Jn** or **Jno** abbr John

**Jo** abbr Joel

¹**job** \'jäb\ n 1 : a piece of work 2 : something that has to be done : TASK 3 : a regular remunerative position — **job·less** adj

²**job** vb **jobbed; job·bing** 1 : to do occasional pieces of work for hire 2 : to hire or let by the job

**Job** \'jōb\ n — see BIBLE table

**job action** n : a protest action by workers to force compliance with demands

**job·ber** \'jä-bər\ n 1 : a person who buys goods and then sells them to other dealers : MIDDLEMAN 2 : a person who does work by the job

**job·hold·er** \'jäb-ˌhōl-dər\ n : one having a regular job

**jock** \'jäk\ n [jockstrap] : ATHLETE; esp : a school or college athlete

¹**jock·ey** \'jä-kē\ n, pl **jockeys** : one who rides a horse esp. as a professional in a race

²**jockey** vb **jock·eyed; jock·ey·ing** : to maneuver or manipulate by adroit or devious means ⟨rivals ~ed for power⟩

**jock·strap** \'jäk-ˌstrap\ n [E slang jock penis] : ATHLETIC SUPPORTER

**jo·cose** \jō-'kōs\ adj 1 : MERRY ⟨~ partygoers⟩ 2 : HUMOROUS ♦ *Synonyms* JOCULAR, FACETIOUS, WITTY

**joc·u·lar** \'jä-kyə-lər\ adj : marked by jesting : PLAYFUL — **joc·u·lar·i·ty** \ˌjäk-yə-'lar-ə-tē\ n — **joc·u·lar·ly** adv

**jo·cund** \'jä-kənd\ adj : marked by mirth or cheerfulness ⟨a ~ celebration⟩

**jodh·pur** \'jäd-pər\ n 1 pl : riding breeches loose above the knee and tight-fitting below 2 : an ankle-high boot fastened with a strap

**Joe Blow** \'jō-\ n : an average or ordinary man

**Jo·el** \'jō-əl\ n — see BIBLE table

**Joe Six–Pack** \'jō-\ n : a blue-collar worker

¹**jog** \'jäg\ vb **jogged; jog·ging** 1 : to give a slight shake or push to 2 : to go at a slow monotonous pace 3 : to run or ride at a slow trot — **jog·ger** n

²**jog** n 1 : a slight shake 2 : a jogging movement or pace

³**jog** n 1 : a projecting or retreating part of a line or surface 2 : a brief abrupt change in direction

**jog·gle** \'jä-gəl\ vb **jog·gled; jog·gling** : to shake slightly — **joggle** n

**john** \'jän\ n 1 : TOILET 2 : a prostitute's client

**John** \'jän\ n — see BIBLE table

**john·ny** \'jä-nē\ n, pl **johnnies** : a short-sleeved gown opening in the back that is worn by hospital patients

**John·ny–jump–up** \ˌjä-nē-'jəmp-ˌəp\ n : any of various small-flowered cultivated pansies

**joie de vi·vre** \ˌzhwä-də-'vēvrᵃ\ n [F] : keen enjoyment of life

**join** \'jȯin\ vb 1 : to come or bring together so as to form a unit 2 : to come or bring into close association 3 : to become a member of 4 : ADJOIN 5 : to take part in a collective activity

**join·er** \'jȯi-nər\ n 1 : a worker who constructs articles by joining pieces of wood 2 : a gregarious person who joins many organizations

¹**joint** \'jȯint\ n 1 : the point of contact between bones of an animal skeleton with the parts that surround and support it 2 : a cut of meat suitable for roasting 3 : a place where two things or parts are connected 4 : ESTABLISHMENT; esp : a shabby or disreputable establishment 5 : a marijuana cigarette — **joint·ed** adj

²**joint** adj 1 : UNITED 2 : common to two or more — **joint·ly** adv

³**joint** vb 1 : to unite by or provide with a joint 2 : to separate the joints of

**joist** \'jȯist\ n : any of the small beams ranged parallel from wall to wall in a building to support a floor or ceiling

¹**joke** \'jōk\ n : something said or done to provoke laughter; esp : a brief narrative with a humorous climax

²**joke** vb **joked; jok·ing** : to make jokes — **jok·ing·ly** adv

**jok·er** \'jō-kər\ n 1 : a person who jokes 2 : an extra card used in some card games 3 : a misleading part of an agreement that works to one party's disadvantage

**jol·li·fi·ca·tion** \ˌjä-li-fə-'kā-shən\ n : a festive celebration

**jol·li·ty** \'jä-lə-tē\ n, pl **-ties** : GAIETY, MERRIMENT

**jol·ly** \'jä-lē\ adj **jol·li·er; -est** : full of high spirits : MERRY

¹**jolt** \'jōlt\ vb 1 : to give a quick hard knock or blow to 2 : to move with a sudden jerky motion — **jolt·er** n

²**jolt** n 1 : an abrupt jerky blow or movement 2 : a sudden shock

**Jon** abbr Jonah; Jonas

**Jo·nah** \'jō-nə\ n — see BIBLE table

**Jo·nas** \'jō-nəs\ n : JONAH

¹**jones** \'jōnz\ n 1 slang : addiction to heroin 2 slang : HEROIN 3 slang : a craving for something

²**jones** vb, slang : to have a craving for something

**jon·gleur** \zhōⁿ-'glər\ n : an itinerant medieval minstrel

**jon·quil** \'jän-kwəl\ n [F jonquille, fr. Sp junquillo, dim. of junco reed, fr. L juncus] : a narcissus with fragrant clustered white or yellow flowers

**josh** \'jäsh\ vb : TEASE, JOKE

**Josh** abbr Joshua

**Josh·ua** \'jä-shə-wə\ n — see BIBLE table

**Joshua tree** n : a tall branched yucca of the southwestern U.S.

**jos·tle** \'jä-səl\ *vb* **jos·tled; jos·tling 1** : to come in contact or into collision **2** : to make one's way by pushing and shoving ⟨*jostled* his way onto the bus⟩

**Jos·ue** \'jä-shü-ē\ *n* : JOSHUA

**¹jot** \'jät\ *n* : the least bit : IOTA

**²jot** *vb* **jot·ted; jot·ting** : to write briefly and hurriedly

**jot·ting** *n* : a brief note

**joule** \'jül\ *n* : a unit of work or energy equal to the work done by a force of one newton acting through a distance of one meter

**jounce** \'jaůns\ *vb* **jounced; jounc·ing** : JOLT — **jounce** *n*

**jour** *abbr* **1** Journal **2** Journeyman

**jour·nal** \'jər-nᵊl\ *n* [ME, service book containing the day hours, fr. AF *jurnal*, fr. *jurnal* daily, fr. L *diurnalis* fr. *dies* day] **1** : a brief account of daily events **2** : a record of proceedings (as of a legislative body) **3** : a periodical (as a newspaper) dealing esp. with current events **4** : the part of a rotating axle or spindle that turns in a bearing

**jour·nal·ese** \ˌjər-nə-ᵊlez, -ᵊles\ *n* : a style of writing held to be characteristic of newspapers

**jour·nal·ism** \'jər-nə-ˌli-zəm\ *n* **1** : the business of writing for, editing, or publishing periodicals (as newspapers) **2** : writing designed for or characteristic of newspapers — **jour·nal·ist** \-list\ *n* — **jour·nal·is·tic** \ˌjər-nə-ᵊlis-tik\ *adj*

**¹jour·ney** \'jər-nē\ *n, pl* **journeys** [ME, fr. OF *journee* day's journey, fr. *jour* day] : a traveling from one place to another

**²journey** *vb* **jour·neyed; jour·ney·ing** : to go on a journey : TRAVEL

**jour·ney·man** \-mən\ *n* **1** : a worker who has learned a trade and works for another person **2** : an experienced reliable worker

**¹joust** \'jaůst\ *vb* : to engage in a joust

**²joust** *n* : a combat on horseback between two knights with lances esp. as part of a tournament

**jo·vial** \'jō-vē-əl\ *adj* : marked by good humor ⟨in a ~ mood⟩ — **jo·vi·al·i·ty** \ˌjō-vē-ᵊa-lə-tē\ *n* — **jo·vi·al·ly** *adv*

**¹jowl** \'jaů(-ə)l\ *n* : loose flesh about the lower jaw or throat

**²jowl** *n* **1** : the lower jaw **2** : CHEEK

**¹joy** \'joi\ *n* [ME, fr. AF *joie*, fr. L *gaudia*] **1** : a feeling of happiness that comes from success, good fortune, or a sense of well-being **2** : a source of happiness ♦ **Synonyms** BLISS, DELIGHT, ENJOYMENT, PLEASURE — **joy·less** *adj*

**²joy** *vb* : REJOICE

**joy·ful** \-fəl\ *adj* : experiencing, causing, or showing joy ⟨~ news⟩ — **joy·ful·ly** *adv*

**joy·ous** \'joi-əs\ *adj* : JOYFUL — **joy·ous·ly** *adv* — **joy·ous·ness** *n*

**joy·ride** \'joi-ˌrīd\ *n* : a ride for pleasure often marked by reckless driving — **joy·ride** *vb* — **joy·rid·er** *n* — **joy·rid·ing** *n*

**joy·stick** \-ˌstik\ *n* : a control device (as for a computer) consisting of a lever capable of motion in two or more directions

**JP** *abbr* **1** jet propulsion **2** justice of the peace

**JPEG** \'jā-ˌpeg\ *n* [Joint Photographic Experts Group] : a computer file format for usu. high-quality digital images

**Jr** *abbr* junior

**jt** *or* **jnt** *abbr* joint

**ju·bi·lant** \'jü-bə-lənt\ *adj* [L *jubilans*, prp. of *jubilare* to rejoice] : EXULTANT ⟨~ winners⟩ — **ju·bi·lant·ly** *adv*

**ju·bi·la·tion** \ˌjü-bə-ᵊlā-shən\ *n* : EXULTATION

**ju·bi·lee** \'jü-bə-ˌlē, ˌjü-bə-ᵊlē\ *n* [ME, fr. AF & LL; AF *jubilé*, fr. LL *jubilaeus*, fr. LGk *iōbēlaios*, fr. Heb *yōbhēl* ram's horn, trumpet, jubilee] **1** : a 50th anniversary **2** : a season or occasion of celebration

**ju·co** \'jü-ˌkō\ *n, pl* **jucos** : JUNIOR COLLEGE; *also* : an athlete at a junior college

**Jud** *abbr* Judith

**Ju·da·ic** \jü-ᵊdā-ik\ *also* **Ju·da·i·cal** \-ᵊdā-ə-kəl\ *adj* : of, relating to, or characteristic of Jews or Judaism

**Ju·da·ism** \'jü-də-ˌi-zəm, -dā-, -dē-\ *n* : a religion developed among the ancient Hebrews and marked by belief in one God and by the moral and ceremonial laws of the Old Testament and the rabbinic tradition

**Jude** \'jüd\ *n* — see BIBLE table

**Judg** *abbr* Judges

**¹judge** \'jəj\ *vb* **judged; judg·ing 1** : to form an authoritative opinion **2** : to decide as a judge : TRY **3** : to form an estimate or evaluation about something : THINK ♦ **Synonyms** CONCLUDE, DEDUCE, GATHER, INFER

**²judge** *n* **1** : a public official authorized to decide questions brought before a court **2** : UMPIRE **3** : one who gives an authoritative opinion : CRITIC — **judge·ship** *n*

**Judges** *n* — see BIBLE table

**judg·ment** *or* **judge·ment** \'jəj-mənt\ *n* **1** : a decision or opinion given after judging; *esp* : a formal decision given by a court **2** *cap* : the final judging of mankind by God **3** : the process of forming an opinion by discerning and comparing **4** : the capacity for judging : DISCERNMENT

**judg·men·tal** \ˌjəj-ᵊmen-tᵊl\ *adj* **1** : of, relating to, or involving judgment **2** : characterized by a tendency to judge harshly — **judg·men·tal·ly** *adv*

**judgment call** *n* : a subjective decision, ruling, or opinion

**Judgment Day** *n* : the day of the final judging of all human beings by God

**ju·di·ca·ture** \'jü-di-kə-ˌchůr\ *n* **1** : the administration of justice **2** : JUDICIARY 1

**ju·di·cial** \jů-ᵊdi-shəl\ *adj* **1** : of or relating to the administration of justice or the judiciary **2** : ordered or enforced by a court **3** : CRITICAL — **ju·di·cial·ly** *adv*

**ju·di·cia·ry** \jů-ᵊdi-shē-ˌer-ē, -shə-rē\ *n* **1** : a system of courts of law; *also* : the judges of these courts **2** : a branch of government in which judicial power is vested — **judiciary** *adj*

**ju·di·cious** \jü-ᵊdi-shəs\ *adj* : having, exercising, or characterized by sound judgment ⟨a ~ decision⟩ ♦ **Synonyms**

PRUDENT, SAGE, SANE, SENSIBLE, WISE — **ju·di·cious·ly** adv

**Ju·dith** \'jü-dəth\ n — see BIBLE table

**ju·do** \'jü-dō\ n [Jp, fr. jū weakness, gentleness + dō art] : a sport derived from jujitsu that emphasizes the use of quick movement and leverage to throw an opponent — **ju·do·ist** \-ist\ n

**ju·do·ka** \'jü-dō-,kä\ n, pl judoka or ju·dokas : one who participates in judo

¹**jug** \'jəg\ n 1 : a large deep container with a narrow mouth and a handle 2 : JAIL, PRISON

²**jug** vb jugged; jug·ging : JAIL, IMPRISON

**jug-eared** \'jəg-,ird\ adj : having protuberant ears

**jug·ger·naut** \'jə-gər-,nȯt\ n [Hindi Jagannāth, title of Vishnu (a Hindu god), lit., lord of the world] : a massive inexorable force or object that crushes everything in its path

**jug·gle** \'jə-gəl\ vb jug·gled; jug·gling 1 : to keep several objects in motion in the air at the same time 2 : to manipulate esp. in order to achieve a desired end often fraudulent end — **jug·gler** \'jə-glər\ n

**jug·u·lar** \'jə-gyə-lər\ adj : of, relating to, or situated in or on the throat or neck ⟨the ~ veins⟩

**juice** \'jüs\ n 1 : the extractable fluid contents of cells or tissues 2 pl : the natural fluids of an animal body 3 : something that supplies power; esp : ELECTRICITY 2

**juic·er** \'jü-sər\ n : an appliance for extracting juice (as from fruit)

**juice up** vb : to give life, energy, or spirit to ⟨juice up the music⟩

**juicy** \'jü-sē\ adj juic·i·er; -est 1 : SUCCULENT 2 : rich in interest; also : RACY ⟨~ gossip⟩ — **juic·i·ly** \-sə-lē\ adv — **juic·i·ness** \-sē-nəs\ n

**ju·jit·su** also **ju·jut·su** or **jiu·jit·su** \jü-'jit-sü\ n : an art of fighting employing holds, throws, and paralyzing blows

**ju·ju** \'jü-jü\ n : a style of African music characterized by a rapid beat, use of percussion instruments, and vocal harmonies

**ju·jube** \'jü-,jüb, 'jü-jü-,bē\ n : a fruit-flavored gumdrop or lozenge

**juke·box** \'jük-,bäks\ n : a coin-operated machine that automatically plays selected recordings

**Jul** abbr July

**ju·lep** \'jü-ləp\ n [ME, sweetened water, fr. MF, fr. Ar julāb, fr. Pers gulāb, fr. gul rose + āb water] : a drink made of bourbon, sugar, and mint served over crushed ice

**Ju·ly** \ju̇-'lī\ n [ME Julie, fr. OE Julius, fr. L, fr. Gaius Julius Caesar] : the 7th month of the year

¹**jum·ble** \'jəm-bəl\ vb jum·bled; jum·bling : to mix in a confused mass

²**jumble** n : a disorderly mass or pile

**jum·bo** \'jəm-bō\ n, pl jumbos [Jumbo, a huge elephant exhibited by P.T. Barnum] : a very large specimen of its kind ⟨a ~ TV screen⟩ — **jumbo** adj

¹**jump** \'jəmp\ vb 1 : to spring into the air : leap over 2 : to give a start 3 : to rise or

increase suddenly or sharply 4 : to make a sudden attack 5 : to leave hurriedly and often furtively ⟨~ town⟩ 6 : to act or move before (as a signal) — **jump bail** : to abscond after being released from custody on bail — **jump ship** 1 : to leave the company of a ship without authority 2 : to desert a cause — **jump the gun** : to begin something before the proper time

²**jump** n 1 : a spring into the air; esp : one made for height or distance in a track meet 2 : a sharp sudden increase 3 : an initial advantage ⟨got the ~ on his rival⟩

¹**jump·er** \'jəm-pər\ n : one that jumps

²**jumper** n 1 : a loose blouse 2 : a sleeveless one-piece dress worn usu. with a blouse 3 pl : a child's sleeveless coverall

**jumping bean** n : a seed of any of several Mexican shrubs that tumbles about because of the movements of a small moth larva inside it

**jumping-off place** n 1 : a remote or isolated place 2 : a place from which an enterprise is launched

**jump·mas·ter** \'jəmp-,mas-tər\ n : a person who supervises parachutists

**jump-start** \'jəmp-,stärt\ vb : to start (an engine or vehicle) by connection to an external power source

**jump·suit** \'jəmp-,süt\ n 1 : a coverall worn by parachutists in jumping 2 : a one-piece garment consisting of a blouse or shirt with attached pants or shorts

**jumpy** \'jəm-pē\ adj jump·i·er; -est : NERVOUS, JITTERY

**jun** abbr junior

**Jun** abbr June

**junc** abbr junction

**jun·co** \'jəŋ-kō\ n, pl juncos or juncoes : any of a genus of small common pink-billed No. American finches that are largely gray with conspicuous white tail feathers

**junc·tion** \'jəŋk-shən\ n 1 : an act of joining 2 : a place or point of meeting

**junc·ture** \'jəŋk-chər\ n 1 : JOINT, CONNECTION 2 : UNION 3 : a critical time or state of affairs

**June** \'jün\ n [ME, fr. L Junius] : the 6th month of the year

**jun·gle** \'jəŋ-gəl\ n [Hindi & Urdu jangal forest] 1 : a thick tangled mass of tropical vegetation; also : a tract overgrown with vegetation 2 : a place of ruthless struggle for survival

¹**ju·nior** \'jü-nyər\ adj 1 : YOUNGER 2 : lower in rank ⟨a ~ partner⟩ 3 : of or relating to juniors

²**junior** n 1 : a person who is younger or of lower rank than another 2 : a student in the next-to-last year before graduating

**junior college** n : a school that offers studies corresponding to those of the 1st two years of college

**junior high school** n : a school usu. including grades 7–9

**junior varsity** n : a team whose members lack the experience or qualifications required for the varsity

**ju·ni·per** \'jü-nə-pər\ n : any of numerous coniferous shrubs or trees with leaves like needles or scales and female cones like berries

**¹junk** \'jəŋk\ n **1** : old iron, glass, paper, or waste; *also* : discarded articles **2** : a shoddy product **3** : something of little meaning, worth, or significance **4** *slang* : NARCOTICS; *esp* : HEROIN — **junky** *adj*

**²junk** *vb* : DISCARD, SCRAP

**³junk** *n* : a ship of eastern Asia with a high stern and 4-cornered sails

**junk·er** \'jəŋ-kər\ n : something (as an old automobile) ready for scrapping

**Jun·ker** \'yún-kər\ n [G] : a member of the Prussian landed aristocracy

**jun·ket** \'jəŋ-kət\ n **1** : a pudding of sweetened flavored milk set by rennet **2** : a trip made by an official at public expense

**junk food** *n* : food that is high in calories but low in nutritional content

**junk·ie** *also* **junky** \'jəŋ-kē\ n, pl **junkies 1** : a narcotics peddler or addict **2** : one that derives inordinate pleasure from or is dependent on something ⟨a sugar ∼⟩

**jun·ta** \'hùn-tə, 'jən-, 'hən-\ n [Sp, fr. *junto* joined, fr. L *junctus*, pp. of *jungere* to join] : a group of persons controlling a government esp. after a revolutionary seizure of power

**Ju·pi·ter** \'jü-pə-tər\ n : the largest of the planets and the one 5th in order of distance from the sun

**Ju·ras·sic** \jù-'ra-sik\ adj : of, relating to, or being the period of the Mesozoic era between the Triassic and the Cretaceous that is marked esp. by the presence of dinosaurs — **Jurassic** n

**ju·rid·i·cal** \jù-'ri-di-kəl\ *also* **ju·rid·ic** \-dik\ adj **1** : of or relating to the administration of justice **2** : LEGAL — **ju·rid·i·cal·ly** \-di-k(ə-)lē\ adv

**ju·ris·dic·tion** \,jùr-əs-'dik-shən\ n **1** : the power, right, or authority to interpret and apply the law **2** : the authority of a sovereign power **3** : the limits or territory within which authority may be exercised — **ju·ris·dic·tion·al** \-shə-nəl\ adj

**ju·ris·pru·dence** \-'prü-dⁿns\ n **1** : the science or philosophy of law **2** : a system of laws

**ju·rist** \'jùr-ist\ n : one having a thorough knowledge of law; *esp* : JUDGE

**ju·ris·tic** \jù-'ris-tik\ adj **1** : of or relating to a jurist or jurisprudence **2** : of, relating to, or recognized in law

**ju·ror** \'jùr-ər, -,ór\ n : a member of a jury

**¹ju·ry** \'jùr-ē\ n, pl **juries 1** : a body of persons sworn to inquire into a matter submitted to them and to give their verdict **2** : a committee for judging and awarding prizes

**²jury** *adj* : improvised for temporary use esp. in an emergency ⟨a ∼ mast⟩

**jury nullification** *n* : the acquitting of a defendant by a jury in disregard of the judge's instructions and contrary to the jury's findings of fact

**jury-rig** \'jùr-ē-,rig\ vb : to construct or arrange in a makeshift fashion

**¹just** \'jəst\ adj **1** : having a basis in or conforming to fact or reason : REASONABLE ⟨∼ comment⟩ **2** : CORRECT, PROPER ⟨∼ proportions⟩ **3** : morally or legally right ⟨a ∼ title⟩ **4** : DESERVED, MERITED ⟨∼ punishment⟩ ♦ *Synonyms* UPRIGHT, HONORABLE, CONSCIENTIOUS, HONEST — **just·ly** adv — **just·ness** n

**²just** \'jəst, 'jist\ adv **1** : EXACTLY ⟨∼ right⟩ **2** : very recently ⟨has ∼ left⟩ **3** : BARELY ⟨∼ too late⟩ **4** : DIRECTLY ⟨∼ west of here⟩ **5** : ONLY ⟨∼ last year⟩ **6** : QUITE ⟨∼ wonderful⟩ **7** : POSSIBLY ⟨it ∼ might work⟩

**jus·tice** \'jəs-təs\ n **1** : the administration of what is just (as by assigning merited rewards or punishments) **2** : JUDGE **3** : the administration of law **4** : FAIRNESS; *also* : RIGHTEOUSNESS

**justice of the peace** : a local magistrate empowered chiefly to try minor cases, to administer oaths, and to perform marriages

**jus·ti·fy** \'jəs-tə-,fī\ vb **-fied; -fy·ing 1** : to prove to be just, right, or reasonable **2** : to pronounce free from guilt or blame **3** : to adjust spaces in a line of printed text so the margins are even — **jus·ti·fi·able** adj — **jus·ti·fi·ca·tion** \,jəs-tə-fə-'kā-shən\ n

**jut** \'jət\ vb **jut·ted; jut·ting** : PROJECT, PROTRUDE

**jute** \'jüt\ n : a strong glossy fiber from either of two tropical plants used esp. for making sacks and twine

**juv** *abbr* juvenile

**¹ju·ve·nile** \'jü-və-,nī(-ə)l, -nəl\ adj **1** : showing incomplete development **2** : of, relating to, or characteristic of children or young people

**²juvenile** n **1** : a young person; *esp* : one below the legally established age of adulthood **2** : a young animal (as a fish or a bird) or plant **3** : an actor or actress who plays youthful parts

**juvenile delinquency** *n* : violation of the law or antisocial behavior by a juvenile — **juvenile delinquent** *n*

**jux·ta·pose** \'jək-stə-,pōz\ vb **-posed; -pos·ing** : to place side by side — **jux·ta·po·si·tion** \,jək-stə-pə-'zi-shən\ n

**JV** *abbr* junior varsity

¹**k** \'kā\ *n, pl* **k's** *or* **ks** \'kāz\ **1** *often cap* : the 11th letter of the English alphabet **2** *cap* : STRIKEOUT

²**k** *abbr* **1** karat **2** kitchen **3** knit **4** kosher — often enclosed in a circle

¹**K** *abbr* **1** Kelvin **2** kindergarten

²**K** *symbol* [NL *kalium*] potassium

**kab·ba·lah** *also* **kab·ba·la** *or* **ka·ba·la** *or* **ca·ba·la** \kə-ˈbä-lə, ˈka-bə-lə\ *n, often cap* **1** : a medieval Jewish mysticism marked by belief in creation through emanation and a cipher method of interpreting Scripture **2** : esoteric or mysterious doctrine

**kabob** *var of* KEBAB

**Ka·bu·ki** \kə-ˈbü-kē\ *n* : traditional Japanese popular drama with highly stylized singing and dancing

**kad·dish** \'kä-dish\ *n, often cap* : a Jewish prayer recited in the daily synagogue ritual and by mourners at public services after the death of a close relative

**kaf·fee·klatsch** \'kò-fē-,klach, 'kä-\ *n, often cap* [G] : an informal social gathering for coffee and conversation

**kai·ser** \'kī-zər\ *n* : EMPEROR; *esp* : the ruler of Germany from 1871 to 1918

**Ka·lash·ni·kov** \kə-ˈlash-nə-,kòf\ *n* [M. T. *Kalashnikov* b1919 Soviet weapons designer] : a Soviet-designed assault rifle

**kale** \'kāl\ *n* : a hardy cabbage with curled leaves that do not form a head

**ka·lei·do·scope** \kə-ˈlī-də-,skōp\ *n* : a tube containing loose bits of colored material (as glass) and two mirrors at one end that shows many different patterns as it is turned — **ka·lei·do·scop·ic** \-,lī-də-ˈskä-pik\ *adj* — **ka·lei·do·scop·i·cal·ly** \-pi-k(ə-)lē\ *adv*

**ka·ma·ai·na** \,kä-mə-ˈī-nə\ *n* [Hawaiian *kama'āina*, fr. *kama* child + *'āina* land] : one who has lived in Hawaii for a long time

**kame** \'kām\ *n* [Sc. lit., comb] : a short ridge or mound of material deposited by water from a melting glacier

**ka·mi·ka·ze** \,kä-mi-ˈkä-zē\ *n* [Jp, lit., divine wind] : a member of a corps of Japanese pilots assigned to make a suicidal crash on a target; *also* : an airplane flown in such an attack

**Kan** *or* **Kans** *abbr* Kansas

**kan·ga·roo** \,kaŋ-gə-ˈrü\ *n, pl* **-roos** : any of various large leaping marsupial mammals of Australia and adjacent islands with powerful hind legs and a long thick tail used as a support

**kangaroo court** *n* : a court or an illegal self-appointed tribunal characterized by irresponsible, perverted, or irregular procedures

**ka·o·lin** \'kā-ə-lən\ *n* : a fine usu. white clay used in ceramics and refractories and for the treatment of diarrhea

**ka·pey·ka** \kä-ˈpā-kä\ *n, pl* **ka·pe·ek** \kä-ˈpā-ək\ — see *rubel* at MONEY table

**ka·pok** \'kā-,päk\ *n* : silky fiber from the seeds of a tropical tree used esp. as a filling (as for life preservers)

**Kap·o·si's sar·co·ma** \'ka-pə-sēz-sär-ˈkō-mə\ *n* : a neoplastic disease associated esp. with AIDS that affects esp. the skin and mucous membranes and is characterized usu. by the formation of pink to reddish-brown or bluish plaques

**kap·pa** \'ka-pə\ *n* : the 10th letter of the Greek alphabet — K or κ

**ka·put** *also* **ka·putt** \kä-ˈpùt, kə-, -ˈpüt\ *adj* [G, fr. F *capot* not having made a trick at piquet] **1** : utterly defeated or destroyed **2** : unable to function : USELESS

**kar·a·kul** \'ker-ə-kəl\ *n* : the usu. curly glossy black coat of a very young lamb of a hardy Asian breed of sheep

**kar·a·o·ke** \,ker-ē-ˈō-kē\ *n* [Jp] : a device that plays instrumental accompaniments for songs to which the user sings along

**kar·at** \'ker-ət\ *n* : a unit for expressing proportion of gold in an alloy equal to $\frac{1}{24}$ part of pure gold

**ka·ra·te** \kə-ˈrä-tē\ *n* [Jp, lit., empty hand] : an art of self-defense in which an attacker is disabled by crippling kicks and punches

**kar·ma** \'kär-mə\ *n, often cap* [Skt] : the force generated by a person's actions held in Hinduism and Buddhism to perpetuate reincarnation and to determine the nature of the person's next existence — **kar·mic** \-mik\ *adj*

**karst** \'kärst\ *n* [G] : an irregular limestone region with sinks, underground streams, and caverns

**ka·ty·did** \'kā-tē-,did\ *n* : any of several large green tree-dwelling American grasshoppers with long antennae

**kay·ak** \'kī-,ak\ *n* : an Eskimo canoe made of a skin-covered frame with a small opening and propelled by a double-bladed paddle; *also* : a similar portable boat — **kay·ak·er** *n*

**kayo** \(,)kā-ˈō, ˈkā-ō\ *n* : KNOCKOUT — **kayo** *vb*

**ka·zoo** \kə-ˈzü\ *n, pl* **kazoos** : a toy musical instrument consisting of a tube with a membrane sealing one end and a side hole to sing or hum into

**KB** *abbr* kilobyte

**kc** *abbr* kilocycle

**KC** *abbr* **1** Kansas City **2** King's Counsel **3** Knights of Columbus

**kc/s** *abbr* kilocycles per second

**KD** *abbr* knocked down

**ke·bab** *or* **ke·bob** *also* **ka·bob** \kə-ˈbäb\ *n* : cubes of meat cooked with vegetables usu. on a skewer

**kedge** \'kej\ *n* : a small anchor

¹**keel** \'kēl\ *n* **1** : the chief structural mem-

ber of a ship running lengthwise along the center of its bottom **2** : something (as a bird's breastbone) like a ship's keel in form or use — **keeled** \'kēld\ *adj*

**²keel** *vb* : FAINT, SWOON — usu. used with *over* ⟨~*ed* over from the heat⟩

**keel·boat** \'kēl-ˌbōt\ *n* : a shallow covered keeled riverboat for freight that is usu. rowed, poled, or towed

**keel·haul** \-ˌhȯl\ *vb* : to haul under the keel of a ship as punishment

**¹keen** \'kēn\ *adj* **1** : SHARP ⟨a ~ knife⟩ **2** : SEVERE ⟨a ~ wind⟩ **3** : ENTHUSIASTIC ⟨~ about swimming⟩ **4** : mentally alert ⟨a ~ mind⟩ **5** : STRONG, ACUTE ⟨~ eyesight⟩ **6** : WONDERFUL, EXCELLENT — **keen·ly** *adv* — **keen·ness** *n*

**²keen** *n* : a lamentation for the dead uttered in a loud wailing voice or in a wordless cry — **keen** *vb*

**¹keep** \'kēp\ *vb* **kept** \'kept\; **keep·ing 1** : FULFILL, OBSERVE ⟨~ a promise⟩ ⟨~ a holiday⟩ **2** : GUARD ⟨~ us from harm⟩; *also* : to take care of ⟨~ a neighbor's children⟩ **3** : MAINTAIN ⟨~ silence⟩ **4** : to have in one's service or at one's disposal ⟨~ a horse⟩ **5** : to preserve a record in ⟨~ a diary⟩ **6** : to have in stock for sale **7** : to retain in one's possession ⟨~ what you find⟩ **8** : to carry on (as a business) : CONDUCT **9** : HOLD, DETAIN ⟨~ him in jail⟩ **10** : to refrain from revealing ⟨~ a secret⟩ **11** : to continue in good condition ⟨meat will ~ in a freezer⟩ **12** : ABSTAIN, REFRAIN — **keep·er** *n*

**²keep** *n* **1** : FORTRESS **2** : the means or provisions by which one is kept — **for keeps 1** : with the provision that one keep what one has won ⟨play marbles *for keeps*⟩ **2** : PERMANENTLY ⟨came home *for keeps*⟩

**keep–away** \'kēp-ə-ˌwā\ *n* : a game in which players try to keep an object from one or more other players

**keeping** *n* : CONFORMITY ⟨in ~ with good taste⟩

**keeping room** *n* : a common room used for multiple purposes

**keep·sake** \'kēp-ˌsāk\ *n* : MEMENTO

**keep up** *vb* **1** : to persevere in **2** : MAINTAIN, SUSTAIN **3** : to keep informed **4** : to continue without interruption

**keg** \'keg\ *n* : a small cask or barrel

**keg·ger** \'ke-gər\ *n* : a party featuring one or more kegs of beer

**keg·ler** \'ke-glər\ *n* : ¹BOWLER

**kelp** \'kelp\ *n* : any of various coarse brown seaweeds; *also* : a mass of these or their ashes often used as fertilizer

**kel·vin** \'kel-vən\ *n* : a unit of temperature equal to ¹/₂₇₃.₁₆ of the Kelvin scale temperature of the triple point of water and equal to the Celsius degree

**Kelvin** *adj* : relating to, conforming to, or being a temperature scale according to which absolute zero is 0 K, the equivalent of −273.15°C

**ken** \'ken\ *n* **1** : range of vision : SIGHT **2** : range of understanding

**ken·nel** \'ke-nᵊl\ *n* : a shelter for a dog or cat; *also* : an establishment for the breeding or boarding of dogs or cats — **kennel** *vb*

**ke·no** \'kē-nō\ *n* : a game resembling bingo

**ke·no·sis** \kə-'nō-səs\ *n* : the relinquishment of divine attributes by Jesus Christ in becoming human — **ke·not·ic** \-'nä-tik\ *adj*

**ken·te cloth** \'ken-ˌtā-\ *n* : colorfully patterned cloth traditionally woven by hand in Ghana

**Ken·tucky bluegrass** \kən-'tə-kē-\ *n* : a valuable pasture and meadow grass of both Europe and America

**Ke·ogh plan** \'kē-ˌ(ˌ)ō-\ *n* [Eugene James *Keogh* †1989 Am. politician] : an individual retirement account for the self-employed

**ko·pi** \'kü-ˌpē, 'ke-\ *n* [F] : a military cap with a round flat top and a visor

**ker·a·tin** \'ker-ə-tən\ *n* : any of various sulfur-containing proteins that make up hair and horny tissues

**kerb** \'kərb\ *n, Brit* : CURB 3

**ker·chief** \'kər-chəf, -ˌchef\ *n, pl* **kerchiefs** \-chəfs, -ˌchēfs\ *also* **kerchieves** \-ˌchēvz\ [ME *courchef*, fr. AF *coverchef, cuerchief*, fr. *coverir* to cover + *chef* head] **1** : a square of cloth worn esp. as a head covering **2** : HANDKERCHIEF

**kerf** \'kərf\ *n* : a slit or notch made by a saw or cutting torch

**ker·nel** \'kər-nᵊl\ *n* **1** : the inner softer part of a seed, fruit stone, or nut **2** : a whole seed of a cereal ⟨a ~ of corn⟩ **3** : a central or essential part : CORE

**ker·o·sene** *also* **ker·o·sine** \'ker-ə-ˌsēn, ˌker-ə-'sēn\ *n* : a flammable oil produced from petroleum and used for a fuel and as a solvent

**kes·trel** \'kes-trəl\ *n* : any of various small falcons that usu. hover in the air while searching for prey

**ketch** \'kech\ *n* : a large fore-and-aft rigged boat with two masts

**ketch·up** *also* **catch·up** \'ke-chəp, 'ka-\ *or* **cat·sup** \'ke-chəp, 'ka-; 'kat-səp\ *n* : a seasoned tomato puree

**ket·tle** \'ke-tᵊl\ *n* : a metallic vessel for boiling liquids

**ket·tle·drum** \-ˌdrəm\ *n* : a brass, copper, or fiberglass drum with calfskin or plastic stretched across the top

**¹key** \'kē\ *n* **1** : a usu. metal instrument by which the bolt of a lock is turned; *also* : a device having the form or function of a key **2** : a means of gaining or preventing entrance, possession, or control **3** : EXPLANATION, SOLUTION **4** : one of the levers pressed by a finger in operating or playing an instrument **5** : a leading individual or principle **6** : a system of seven tones based on their relationship to a tonic; *also* : the tone or pitch of a voice **7** : a small switch for opening or closing an electric circuit ⟨a telegraph ~⟩

**²key** *vb* **1** : SECURE, FASTEN **2** : to regulate the musical pitch of **3** : to bring into harmony or conformity **4** : to make nervous — usu. used with *up*

**³key** *adj* : BASIC, CENTRAL ⟨~ issues⟩

⁴**key** *n* : a low island or reef (as off the southern coast of Florida)

⁵**key** *n, slang* : a kilogram esp. of marijuana or heroin

**key·board** \-ˌbȯrd\ *n* **1** : a row of keys (as on a piano) **2** : an assemblage of keys for operating a machine

**key club** *n* : a private club serving liquor and providing entertainment

**key·hole** \ˈkē-ˌhōl\ *n* : a hole for receiving a key

¹**key·note** \-ˌnōt\ *n* **1** : the first and harmonically fundamental tone of a scale **2** : the central fact, idea, or mood

²**keynote** *vb* **1** : to set the keynote of **2** : to deliver the major address (as at a convention) — **key·not·er** *n*

**key·punch** \ˈkē-ˌpənch\ *n* : a machine with a keyboard used to cut holes or notches in punch cards — **keypunch** *vb* — **key·punch·er** *n*

**key·stone** \-ˌstōn\ *n* : the wedge-shaped piece at the crown of an arch that locks the other pieces in place

**key·stroke** \-ˌstrōk\ *n* : an act or instance of depressing a key on a keyboard

**key word** *n* : a word that is a key; *esp, usu* **key·word** : a significant word from a title or document used esp. as an indication of the content

**kg** *abbr* kilogram

**KGB** *abbr* [Russ *Komitet gosudarstvennoĭ bezopasnosti*] (Soviet) State Security Committee

**kha·ki** \ˈka-kē, ˈkä-\ *n* [Hindi & Urdu *khākī* dust-colored, fr. *khāk* dust, fr. Pers] **1** : a light yellowish brown color **2** : a khaki-colored cloth; *also* : a military uniform of this cloth

**khan** \ˈkän, ˈkan\ *n* : a Mongol leader; *esp* : a successor of Genghis Khan

**khe·dive** \kə-ˈdēv\ *n* : a ruler of Egypt from 1867 to 1914 governing as a viceroy of the sultan of Turkey

**khoum** \ˈküm\ *n* — see *ouguiya* at MONEY table

**kHz** *abbr* kilohertz

**KIA** *abbr* killed in action

**kib·ble** \ˈki-bəl\ *vb* **kib·bled; kib·bling** : to grind coarsely — **kibble** *n*

**kib·butz** \ki-ˈbu̇ts, -ˈbüts\ *n, pl* **kib·but·zim** \-ˌbu̇t-ˈsēm, -ˌbüt-\ [ModHeb *qibbūṣ*] : a communal farm or settlement in Israel

**ki·bitz·er** \ˈki-bət-sər, kə-ˈbit-\ *n* : one who looks on and usu. offers unwanted advice — **kib·itz** \ˈki-bəts\ *vb*

**ki·bosh** \ˈki-ˌbäsh\ *n* : something that serves as a check or stop ⟨put the ∼ on his plan⟩

¹**kick** \ˈkik\ *vb* **1** : to strike out or hit with the foot; *also* : to score by kicking a ball **2** : to object strongly **3** : to recoil when fired — **kick·er** *n*

²**kick** *n* **1** : a blow or thrust with the foot; *esp* : a propelling of a ball with the foot **2** : the recoil of a gun **3** : a feeling or expression of objection **4** : stimulating effect esp. of pleasure

**kick·back** \ˈkik-ˌbak\ *n* **1** : a sharp violent reaction **2** : a secret return of a part of a sum received

**kick back** *vb* : to assume a relaxed position or attitude

**kick·box·ing** \ˈkik-ˌbäk-siŋ\ *n* : boxing in which boxers are permitted to kick with bare feet — **kick·box·er** \-sər\ *n*

**kick in** *vb* **1** : CONTRIBUTE **2** *slang* : DIE **3** : to begin operating or having an effect ⟨the caffeine started to *kick in*⟩

**kick·off** \ˈkik-ˌȯf\ *n* **1** : a kick that puts the ball in play (as in football) **2** : COMMENCEMENT ⟨campaign ∼⟩

**kick off** *vb* **1** : to start or resume play with a placekick **2** : to begin proceedings ⟨*kick off* a campaign⟩ **3** *slang* : DIE

**kick over** *vb* : to begin or cause to begin to fire — used of an internal combustion engine

**kick·shaw** \ˈkik-ˌshȯ\ *n* [modif. of F *quelque chose* something] **1** : DELICACY **2** : TRINKET

**kick·stand** \ˈkik-ˌstand\ *n* : a swiveling metal bar attached to a 2-wheeled vehicle for holding it up when not in use

**kick–start** \ˈkik-ˌstärt\ *vb* : JUMP-START

**kicky** \ˈki-kē\ *adj* : providing a kick or thrill : EXCITING; *also* : excitingly fashionable

¹**kid** \ˈkid\ *n* **1** : a young goat **2** : the flesh, fur, or skin of a young goat; *also* : something made of kid **3** : CHILD, YOUNGSTER — **kid·dish** *adj*

²**kid** *vb* **kid·ded; kid·ding 1** : FOOL **2** : TEASE — **kid·der** *n* — **kid·ding·ly** *adv*

**kid·do** \ˈki-dō\ *n, pl* **kiddos 1** — used as a familiar form of address ⟨you're okay, ∼⟩ **2** : CHILD, KID

**kid·nap** \ˈkid-ˌnap\ *vb* **kid·napped** *also* **kid·naped** \-ˌnapt\; **kid·nap·ping** *also* **kid·nap·ing** \-ˌna-piŋ\ : to hold or carry a person away by unlawful force or by fraud and against one's will — **kid·nap·per** *also* **kid·nap·er** \-ˌna-pər\ *n*

**kid·ney** \ˈkid-nē\ *n, pl* **kidneys** : either of a pair of organs lying near the backbone that excrete waste products of the body in the form of urine

**kidney bean** *n* **1** : an edible seed of the common cultivated bean; *esp* : one that is large and dark red **2** : a plant bearing kidney beans

**kid·skin** \ˈkid-ˌskin\ *n* : the skin of a young goat used for leather

**kiel·ba·sa** \kēl-ˈbä-sə, kil-\ *n, pl* **-basas** *also* **-ba·sy** \-ˈbä-sē\ [Pol *kiełbasa*] : a smoked sausage of Polish origin

¹**kill** \ˈkil\ *vb* **1** : to deprive of life **2** : to put an end to ⟨∼ competition⟩; *also* : DEFEAT ⟨∼ a proposed amendment⟩ **3** : USE UP ⟨∼ time⟩ **4** : to mark for omission **♦ Synonyms** SLAY, MURDER, ASSASSINATE, EXECUTE — **kill·er** *n*

²**kill** *n* **1** : an act of killing **2** : an animal or animals killed (as in a hunt); *also* : an aircraft, ship, or vehicle destroyed by military action

**kill·deer** \ˈkil-ˌdir\ *n, pl* **killdeers** *or* **killdeer** [imit.] : an American plover with a plaintive penetrating cry

**killer app** \-ˈap\ *n* : a component (as a computer application) that in itself makes something worth having or using

**killer bee** *n* : AFRICANIZED BEE

**killer whale** *n* : a small gregarious black and white flesh-eating whale with a white oval patch behind each eye

**kill·ing** *n* : a sudden notable gain or profit

**killing field** *n* : a scene of mass killing

**kill·joy** \'kil-,jȯi\ *n* : one who spoils the pleasures of others

**kiln** \'kil, 'kiln\ *n* [ME *kilne,* fr. OE *cyln,* fr. L *culina* kitchen] : a heated enclosure (as an oven) for processing a substance by burning, firing, or drying — **kiln** *vb*

**ki·lo** \'kē-lō\ *n, pl* **kilos** : KILOGRAM

**ki·lo·byte** \'kē-lə-,bīt, 'kil-ə\ *n* : 1024 bytes

**kilo·cy·cle** \'kil-ə-,sī-kəl\ *n* : KILOHERTZ

**ki·lo·gram** \'kē-lə-,gram, 'ki-\ *n* 1 : the basic metric unit of mass that is nearly equal to the mass of 1000 cubic centimeters of water at its maximum density — see METRIC SYSTEM table 2 : the weight of a kilogram mass under earth's gravity

**kilo·hertz** \'ki-lə-,hərts, 'kē-, ,herts\ *n* : 1000 hertz

**kilo·li·ter** \'ki-lə-,lē-tər\ *n* — see METRIC SYSTEM table

**ki·lo·me·ter** \ki-'lä-mə-tər, 'ki-lə-,mē-\ *n* : a metric unit of length equal to 1000 meters — see METRIC SYSTEM table

**ki·lo·ton** \'ki-lə-,tən, 'kē-lō-\ *n* 1 : 1000 tons 2 : an explosive force equivalent to that of 1000 tons of TNT

**ki·lo·volt** \-,vōlt\ *n* : 1000 volts

**kilo·watt** \'ki-lə-,wät\ *n* : 1000 watts

**kilowatt–hour** *n* : a unit of energy equal to that expended by one kilowatt in one hour

**kilt** \'kilt\ *n* : a knee-length pleated skirt usu. of tartan worn by men in Scotland

**kil·ter** \'kil-tər\ *n* : proper condition ⟨out of ~⟩

**ki·mo·no** \kə-'mō-nə\ *n, pl* **-nos** 1 : a loose robe with wide sleeves traditionally worn with a wide sash as an outer garment by the Japanese 2 : a loose dressing gown or jacket

**kin** \'kin\ *n* 1 : an individual's relatives 2 : KINSMAN

**ki·na** \'kē-nə\ *n, pl* **kina** — see MONEY table

**ki·na·ra** \kē-'nä-rə\ *n* : a candelabra with seven candlesticks used during Kwanzaa

**¹kind** \'kīnd\ *n* 1 : essential quality or character 2 : a group united by common traits or interests : CATEGORY; *also* : VARIETY 3 : goods or commodities as distinguished from money

**²kind** *adj* 1 : of a sympathetic, forbearing, or pleasant nature 2 : arising from sympathy or forbearance ⟨~ deeds⟩ ♦ **Synonyms** BENEVOLENT, BENIGN, BENIGNANT, KINDLY — **kind·ness** *n*

**kin·der·gar·ten** \'kin-dər-,gär-t³n\ *n* [G, lit., children's garden] : a school or class for children usu. from four to six years old

**kin·der·gart·ner** \-,gärt-nər\ *n* 1 : a kindergarten teacher 2 : a kindergarten pupil

**kind·heart·ed** \,kīnd-'här-təd\ *adj* : marked by a sympathetic nature

**kin·dle** \'kin-d³l\ *vb* **kin·dled; kin·dling** 1 : to set on fire : start burning 2 : to stir up : AROUSE 3 : ILLUMINATE, GLOW

**kin·dling** \'kind-lin, 'kin-lən\ *n* : easily combustible material for starting a fire

**¹kind·ly** \'kīnd-lē\ *adj* **kind·li·er; -est** 1 : of an agreeable or beneficial nature 2 : of a sympathetic or generous nature — **kind·li·ness** *n*

**²kindly** *adv* 1 : READILY ⟨does not take ~ to criticism⟩ 2 : SYMPATHETICALLY 3 : COURTEOUSLY, OBLIGINGLY

**kind of** *adv* : to a moderate degree ⟨it's *kind of* late to begin⟩

**¹kin·dred** \'kin-drəd\ *n* 1 : a group of related individuals 2 : one's relatives

**²kindred** *adj* : of a like nature or character

**kine** \'kīn\ *archaic pl of* COW

**kin·e·ma** \'ki-nə-mə\ *Brit var of* CINEMA

**ki·ne·mat·ics** \,ki-nə-'ma-tiks\ *n* : a science that deals with motion apart from considerations of mass and force — **ki·ne·mat·ic** \-tik\ *or* **ki·ne·mat·i·cal** \-ti-kəl\ *adj*

**kin·es·the·sia** \,ki-nəs-'thē-zhə, -zhē-ə\ *or* **kin·es·the·sis** \-'thē-səs\ *n, pl* **-the·sias** *or* **-the·ses** \-,sēz\ : a sense that perceives bodily movement, position, and weight and is mediated by nervous receptors in tendons, muscles, and joints; *also* : sensory experience derived from this sense — **kin·es·thet·ic** \-'the-tik\ *adj*

**ki·net·ic** \kə-'ne-tik\ *adj* : of or relating to the motion of material bodies and the forces and energy (**kinetic energy**) associated with them

**ki·net·ics** \-'tiks\ *n sing or pl* : a science that deals with the effects of forces upon the motions of material bodies or with changes in a physical or chemical system

**kin·folk** \'kin-,fōk\ *or* **kinfolks** *n pl* : RELATIVES

**king** \'kiŋ\ *n* 1 : a male sovereign 2 : a chief among competitors ⟨home-run ~⟩ 3 : the principal piece in the game of chess 4 : a playing card bearing the figure of a king 5 : a checker that has been crowned — **king·less** *adj* — **king·ly** *adj* — **king·ship** *n*

**king crab** *n* 1 : HORSESHOE CRAB 2 : a large crab of the No. Pacific caught commercially for food

**king·dom** \'kiŋ-dəm\ *n* 1 : a country whose head is a king or queen 2 : a realm or region in which something or someone is dominant ⟨a cattle ~⟩ 3 : one of the three primary divisions of lifeless material, plants, and animals into which natural objects are grouped; *also* : a biological category that ranks above the phylum

**king·fish·er** \-,fi-shər\ *n* : any of numerous usu. bright-colored crested birds that feed chiefly on fish

**king·pin** \'kiŋ-,pin\ *n* 1 : HEADPIN 2 : the leader in a group or undertaking

**Kings** *n* — see BIBLE table

**king–size** \'kiŋ-,sīz\ *or* **king–sized** \-,sīzd\ *adj* 1 : longer than the regular or standard size 2 : unusually large 3 : having dimensions of about 76 by 80 inches (1.9 by 2.0 meters) ⟨a ~ bed⟩; *also* : of a size that fits a king-size bed

**kink** \'kiŋk\ *n* 1 : a short tight twist or curl 2 : a mental peculiarity : QUIRK 3 : CRAMP ⟨a ~ in the back⟩ 4 : an imperfection likely to cause difficulties in operation — **kinky** *adj*

**kin·ship** \'kin-,ship\ *n* : RELATIONSHIP

**kins·man** \'kinz-mən\ *n* : RELATIVE; *esp* : a male relative

**kins·wom·an** \-,wu̇-mən\ *n* : a female relative

**ki·osk** \'kē-,äsk\ *n* 1 : a small structure with one or more open sides 2 : a standalone device providing information and services on a computer screen ⟨interactive ~s at the museum⟩

**Ki·o·wa** \'kī-ə-,wȯ, -,wä, -,wä\ *n*, *pl* **Kiowa** *or* **Kiowas** : a member of an American Indian people of Colorado, Kansas, New Mexico, Oklahoma, and Texas

**kip** \'kip, 'gip\ *n*, *pl* **kip** *or* **kips** — see MONEY table

**kip·per** \'ki-pər\ *n* : a fish (as a herring) preserved by salting and drying or smoking — **kipper** *vb*

**kirk** \'kərk, 'kirk\ *n*, *chiefly Scot* : CHURCH

**kir·tle** \'kər-t°l\ *n* : a long gown or dress worn by women

**kis·met** \'kiz-,met, -mət\ *n*, *often cap* [Turk., fr. Ar *qisma* portion, lot] : FATE

¹**kiss** \'kis\ *vb* 1 : to touch or caress with the lips as a mark of affection or greeting 2 : to touch gently or lightly

²**kiss** *n* 1 : a caress with the lips 2 : a gentle touch or contact 3 : a bite-size candy

**kiss·er** \'ki-sər\ *n* 1 : one that kisses 2 *slang* : MOUTH 3 *slang* : FACE

**kit** \'kit\ *n* 1 : a set of articles for personal use; *also* : a set of tools or implements or of parts to be assembled 2 : a container (as a case) for a kit

**kitch·en** \'ki-chən\ *n* 1 : a room with cooking facilities 2 : the personnel that prepares, cooks, and serves food

**kitch·en·ette** \,ki-chə-'net\ *n* : a small kitchen or an alcove containing cooking facilities

**kitchen police** *n* 1 : KP 2 : the work of KPs

**kitch·en·ware** \'ki-chən-,wer\ *n* : utensils and appliances for kitchen use

**kite** \'kīt\ *n* 1 : any of various longwinged hawks often with deeply forked tails 2 : a light frame covered with paper or cloth and designed to be flown in the air at the end of a long string

**kith** \'kith\ *n* [ME, fr. OE *cȳthth*, fr. *cūth* known] : familiar friends, neighbors, or relatives ⟨~ and kin⟩

**kitsch** \'kich\ *n* [G] : something often of poor quality that appeals to popular or lowbrow taste — **kitschy** \'ki-chē\ *adj*

**kit·ten** \'ki-t°n\ *n* : a young cat — **kit·ten·ish** *adj*

¹**kit·ty** \'ki-tē\ *n*, *pl* **kitties** : CAT; *esp* : KITTEN

²**kitty** *n*, *pl* **kitties** : a fund in a poker game made up of contributions from each pot; *also* : POOL

**kit·ty-cor·ner** *also* **cat·ty-cor·ner** *or* **cat·er-cor·ner** \'ki-tē-,kȯr-nər, 'ka-; 'ka-tə-\ *or* **kit·ty-cor·nered** *or* **cat·ty-cor·nered** *or* **cat·er-cornered** \-nərd\ *adv or adj* : in a diagonal or oblique position

**ki·wi** \'kē-(,)wē\ *n* 1 : any of a small ge-

nus of flightless New Zealand birds 2 : KIWIFRUIT

**ki·wi·fruit** \-,früt\ *n* : a brownish hairy egg-shaped fruit of a subtropical vine that has sweet bright green flesh and small edible black seeds

**KJV** *abbr* King James Version

**KKK** *abbr* Ku Klux Klan

**kl** *abbr* kiloliter

**klatch** *also* **klatsch** \'klach\ *n* [G *Klatsch* gossip] : a gathering marked by informal conversation

**klep·toc·ra·cy** \klep-'tä-krə-sē\ *n*, *pl* **-cies** : government by those who seek chiefly status and personal gain at the expense of the governed

**klep·to·ma·nia** \,klep-tə-'mā-nē-ə\ *n* : a persistent neurotic impulse to steal esp. without economic motive — **klep·to·ma·ni·ac** \-nē-,ak\ *n*

**klieg light** *or* **kleig light** \'klēg-\ *n* : a very bright lamp used in making motion pictures

**klutz** \'klǝts\ *n* [Yiddish *klots*, lit., wooden beam] : a clumsy person — **klutzy** *adj*

**km** *abbr* kilometer

**kn** *abbr* knot

**knack** \'nak\ *n* 1 : a clever way of doing something 2 : natural aptitude

**knap·sack** \'nap-,sak\ *n* : a bag (as of canvas) strapped on the back and used esp. for carrying supplies

**knave** \'nāv\ *n* 1 : ROGUE 2 : JACK 6 — **knav·ery** \'nā-və-rē\ *n* — **knav·ish** \'nā-vish\ *adj*

**knead** \'nēd\ *vb* : to work and press into a mass with the hands; *also* : MASSAGE — **knead·er** *n*

**knee** \'nē\ *n* : the joint in the middle part of the leg — **kneed** \'nēd\ *adj*

**knee·cap** \'nē-,kap\ *n* : a thick flat triangular movable bone forming the front of the knee

**knee·hole** \-,hōl\ *n* : a space (as under a desk) for the knees

**knee-jerk** \'nē-,jərk\ *adj* : readily predictable ⟨a ~ reaction⟩

**kneel** \'nēl\ *vb* **knelt** \'nelt\ *or* **kneeled**; **kneel·ing** : to bend the knee : fall or rest on the knees

¹**knell** \'nel\ *vb* 1 : to ring esp. for a death or disaster 2 : to summon, announce, or proclaim by a knell

²**knell** *n* 1 : a stroke of a bell esp. when tolled (as for a funeral) 2 : an indication of the end or failure of something

**knew** *past of* KNOW

**knick·ers** \'ni-kərz\ *n pl* : loose-fitting short pants gathered at the knee

**knick·knack** \'nik-,nak\ *n* : a small trivial article intended for ornament

¹**knife** \'nīf\ *n*, *pl* **knives** \'nīvz\ 1 : a cutting instrument consisting of a sharp blade fastened to a handle 2 : a sharp cutting tool in a machine

²**knife** *vb* **knifed**; **knif·ing** : to stab, slash, or wound with a knife

¹**knight** \'nīt\ *n* 1 : a mounted warrior of feudal times serving a king 2 : a man honored by a sovereign for merit and in Great Britain ranking below a baronet 3 : a man devoted to the service of a lady 4

: a member of an order or society **5** : a chess piece having an L-shaped move — **knight·ly** adj

²**knight** vb : to make a knight of

**knight·hood** \'nīt-ˌhu̇d\ n **1** : the rank, dignity, or profession of a knight **2** : CHIVALRY **3** : knights as a class or body

**knish** \kə-'nish\ n [Yiddish] : a small round or square of dough stuffed with a filling (as of meat or fruit) and baked or fried

¹**knit** \'nit\ vb **knit** or **knit·ted; knit·ting 1** : to link firmly or closely **2** : WRINKLE ⟨~ her brows⟩ **3** : to form a fabric by interlacing yarn or thread in connected loops with needles **4** : to grow together ⟨the fractured bone *knitted* slowly⟩ — **knit·ter** n

²**knit** n **1** : a basic knitting stitch **2** : a knitted garment or fabric

**knit·wear** \-ˌwer\ n : knitted clothing

**knob** \'näb\ n **1** : a rounded protuberance; *also* : a small rounded ornament or handle **2** : a rounded usu. isolated hill — **knobbed** \'näbd\ adj — **knob·by** \'nä-bē\ adj

¹**knock** \'näk\ vb **1** : to strike with a sharp blow **2** : BUMP, COLLIDE **3** : to make a pounding noise; *esp* : to have engine knock **4** : to find fault with

²**knock** n **1** : a sharp blow **2** : a pounding noise; *esp* : one caused by abnormal ignition in an automobile engine

**knock·down** \'näk-ˌdau̇n\ n **1** : the action of knocking down **2** : something (as a blow) that knocks down **3** : something that can be easily assembled or disassembled

**knock down** vb **1** : to strike to the ground with or as if with a sharp blow **2** : to take apart : DISASSEMBLE **3** : to receive as income or salary : EARN **4** : to make a reduction in

**knock·er** \'nä-kər\ n : one that knocks; *esp* : a device hinged to a door for use in knocking

**knock–knee** \'näk-ˌnē\ n : a condition in which the legs curve inward at the knees — **knock–kneed** \-ˌnēd\ adj

**knock·off** \'näk-ˌȯf\ n : a copy or imitation of someone or something popular

**knock off** vb **1** : to stop doing something **2** : to do quickly, carelessly, or routinely **3** : to deduct from a price **4** : KILL : ROB **6** : COPY, IMITATE

**knock·out** \'näk-ˌau̇t\ n **1** : a blow that fells and immobilizes an opponent (as in boxing) **2** : something sensationally striking or attractive

**knock out** vb **1** : to defeat by a knockout **2** : to make unconscious or inoperative **3** : to tire out : EXHAUST

**knock·wurst** *also* **knack·wurst** \'näk-ˌwərst, -ˌvu̇rst\ n : a short thick heavily seasoned sausage

**knoll** \'nōl\ n : a small round hill

¹**knot** \'nät\ n **1** : an interlacing (as of string) forming a lump or knob and often used for fastening or tying together **2** : PROBLEM **3** : a bond of union; *esp* : the marriage bond **4** : a protuberant lump or swelling in tissue **5** : a rounded cross-grained area in lumber that is a section through the junction of a tree branch with the trunk; *also* : the woody tissue forming this junction in a tree **6** : GROUP, CLUSTER **7** : an ornamental bow of ribbon **8** : one nautical mile per hour; *also* : one nautical mile — **knot·ty** adj

²**knot** vb **knot·ted; knot·ting 1** : to tie in or with a knot **2** : ENTANGLE

**knot·hole** \-ˌhōl\ n : a hole in a board or tree trunk where a knot has come out

**knout** \'nau̇t, 'nüt\ n : a whip used for flogging

**know** \'nō\ vb **knew** \'nü, 'nyü\; **known** \'nōn\; **know·ing 1** : to perceive directly : have understanding or direct cognition of; *also* : to recognize the nature of **2** : to be acquainted or familiar with **3** : to be aware of the truth of **4** : to have a practical understanding of — **know·able** adj — **know·er** n — **in the know** : possessing confidential information

**know–how** \'nō-ˌhau̇\ n : knowledge of how to do something smoothly and efficiently

**knowing** adj **1** : having or reflecting knowledge, intelligence, or information **2** : shrewdly and keenly alert **3** : DELIBERATE ⟨~ interference⟩ ♦ *Synonyms* CLEVER, BRIGHT, SMART — **know·ing·ly** adv

**knowl·edge** \'nä-lij\ n **1** : understanding gained by actual experience ⟨a ~ of carpentry⟩ **2** : range of information ⟨to the best of my ~⟩ **3** : clear perception of truth **4** : something learned and kept in the mind

**knowl·edge·able** \'nä-li-jə-bəl\ adj : having or showing knowledge or intelligence

**knuck·le** \'nə-kəl\ n **1** : the rounded knob at a joint and esp. at a finger joint

**knuckle down** vb : to apply oneself earnestly ⟨*knuckled down* to the task⟩

**knuckle under** vb : SUBMIT, SURRENDER

**knurl** \'nərl\ n **1** : KNOB **2** : one of a series of small ridges on a metal surface to aid in gripping — **knurled** \'nərld\ adj — **knurly** adj

¹**KO** \(ˌ)kā-'ō, 'kā-ˌō\ n : KNOCKOUT

²**KO** vb **KO'd; KO'·ing** : to knock out in boxing

**ko·ala** \kō-'ä-lə\ n : a gray furry Australian marsupial that has large hairy ears and feeds on eucalyptus leaves

**ko·bo** \'kō-(ˌ)bō\ n, pl **kobo** — see *naira* at MONEY table

**K of C** abbr Knights of Columbus

**kohl·ra·bi** \kōl-'rä-bē\ n, pl **-bies** [G, fr. It *cavolo rapa*, lit., cabbage turnip] : a cabbage that forms no head but has a swollen fleshy edible stem

**koi** \'kȯi\ n, pl **koi** [Jp] : a carp bred for large size and a variety of colors and often stocked in ornamental ponds

**ko·lin·sky** \kə-'lin-skē\ n, pl **-skies** : the fur of various Asian minks

**Ko·mo·do dragon** \kə-ˈmō-dō-\ n [*Komodo* Island, Indonesia] : a carnivorous lizard of Indonesia that is the largest of all known lizards

**kook** \'kük\ n : SCREWBALL 2

**kooky** *also* **kook·ie** \'kü-kē\ adj **kook·i-**

**er; -est** : having the characteristics of a kook : CRAZY, ECCENTRIC ⟨a ∼ radical⟩ — **kook·i·ness** n

**Koo·te·nai** or **Ku·te·nai** \'kü-tə-ˌnä\ n, pl **-nai** or **-nais** : a member of an American Indian people of the Rocky Mountains in both the U.S. and Canada; also : their language

**ko·peck** or **ko·pek** \'kō-ˌpek\ n [Russ kopeĭka] — see ruble at MONEY table

**ko·piy·ka** \kō-'pē-kə\ n — see hryvnia at MONEY table

**ko·ra** \'kôr-ə\ n : a 21-stringed African musical instrument

**Ko·ran** or **Qur·an** also **Qur·'an** \kə-'ran, -'rän\ n [Ar qur'ān] : a sacred book of Islam that contains revelations made to Muhammad by Allah

**ko·ru·na** \'kôr-ə-ˌnä\ n, pl **ko·ru·ny** \-ə-nē\ or **korunas** or **ko·run** \-ən\ 1 — see MONEY table 2 : the basic monetary unit of Slovakia from 1992 to 2009

**ko·sher** \'kō-shər\ adj [Yiddish, fr. Heb kāshēr fit, proper] 1 : ritually fit for use according to Jewish law 2 : selling or serving kosher food

**kow·tow** \kaú-'taú, 'kaú-ˌtaú\ vb [Chin kòutóu, fr. kòu to knock + tóu head] 1 : to show obsequious deference 2 : to kneel and touch the forehead to the ground as a sign of homage or deep respect

**KP** \ˌkā-'pē\ n 1 : an enlisted person detailed to help the cooks in a military mess 2 : the work of KPs

**kph** abbr kilometers per hour

**Kr** symbol krypton

**kraal** \'kräl, 'krôl\ n 1 : a native village in southern Africa 2 : an enclosure for domestic animals in southern Africa

**kraut** \'kraút\ n : SAUERKRAUT

**Krem·lin** \'krem-lən\ n : the Russian government

**Krem·lin·ol·o·gist** \ˌkrem-lə-'nä-lə-jist\ n : a specialist in the policies and practices of the government of the Soviet Union

**¹kro·na** \'krō-nə\ n, pl **kro·nor** \-ˌnôr\ [Sw] — see MONEY table

**²kro·na** \'krō-nə\ n, pl **kro·nur** \-nər\ [Icel] — see MONEY table

**kro·ne** \'krō-nə\ n, pl **kro·ner** \-nər\ — see MONEY table

**kroon** \'krōn\ n, pl **kroo·ni** \'krō-nē\ or **kroons** : the basic monetary unit of Estonia from 1928 to 1940 and from 1991 to 2011

**Kru·ger·rand** \'krü-gər-ˌrand, -ˌränd\ n : a 1-ounce gold coin of the Republic of South Africa

**kryp·ton** \'krip-ˌtän\ n : a gaseous chemical element used esp. in electric lamps

**KS** abbr Kansas

**kt** abbr 1 karat 2 knight

**ku·do** \'kü-dō, 'kyü-\ n, pl **kudos** [fr. kudos (taken as pl.)] 1 : AWARD, HONOR 2 : COMPLIMENT, PRAISE

**ku·dos** \'kü-ˌdäs, 'kyü-\ n : fame and renown resulting from achievement

**kud·zu** \'kúd-zü, 'kad-\ n [Jp kuzu] : a fast-growing weedy leguminous vine used for forage and erosion control

**ku·lak** \kü-'lak, kyü-, 'läk\ n [Russ, lit., fist] 1 : a wealthy peasant farmer in 19th century Russia 2 : a farmer characterized by Communists as too wealthy

**kum·quat** \'kəm-ˌkwät\ n : any of several small citrus fruits with sweet spongy rind and acid pulp

**ku·na** \'kü-ˌnä\ n, pl **kuna** or **ku·ne** \-nä\ — see MONEY table

**kung fu** \kəŋ-'fü, kúŋ-\ n : a Chinese art of self-defense resembling karate

**kung pao** \kəŋ-'paú, 'küŋ-, 'kúŋ-\ adj : being stir-fried or deep-fried and served in a spicy hot sauce usu. with peanuts

**kur·ta** \'kər-tə\ n : a long loose-fitting collarless shirt

**ku·rus** \kə-'rüsh\ n, pl **kurus** — see lira at MONEY table

**kV** abbr kilovolt

**kvell** \'kvel\ vb : to be extraordinarily proud

**kvetch** \'kvech, 'kfech\ vb : to complain habitually — **kvetch** n

**kW** abbr kilowatt

**kwa·cha** \'kwä-chə\ n, pl **kwacha** — see MONEY table

**kwan·za** \'kwän-zə\ n, pl **kwanzas** or **kwanza** — see MONEY table

**Kwan·zaa** also **Kwan·za** \'kwän-zə\ n [Swahili kwanza first] : an African-American cultural festival held from December 26 to January 1

**kwash·i·or·kor** \ˌkwä-shē-'ôr-kôr, -ôr-'kôr\ n : a disease of young children caused by deficient intake of protein

**kWh** abbr kilowatt-hour

**Ky** or **KY** abbr Kentucky

**kyat** \'chät\ n, pl **kyats** or **kyat** — see MONEY table

**ky·bosh** chiefly Brit var of KIBOSH

**¹l** \'el\ n, pl **l's** or **ls** \'elz\ often cap : the 12th letter of the English alphabet

**²l** abbr, often cap 1 lake 2 large 3 left 4 [L libra] pound 5 line 6 liter

**¹La** abbr Louisiana

**²La** symbol lanthanum

**LA** abbr 1 law agent 2 Los Angeles 3 Louisiana

**laa·ri** \'lä-rē\ n, pl **laari** — see rufiyaa at MONEY table

**lab** \'lab\ n : LABORATORY

**Lab** n : LABRADOR RETRIEVER

**¹la·bel** \'lä-bəl\ n 1 : a slip attached to something for identification or description 2 : a descriptive or identifying word or phrase 3 : BRAND 3

**label** *vb* **-beled** *or* **-belled; -bel·ing** *or* **-bel·ling 1 :** to affix a label to **2 :** to describe or name with a label

**la·bi·al** \'lā-bē-əl\ *adj* **:** of, relating to, or situated near the lips or labia

**la·bia ma·jo·ra** \'lā-bē-ə-mə-'jȯr-ə\ *n pl* **:** the outer fatty folds of the vulva

**labia mi·no·ra** \-mə-'nȯr-ə\ *n pl* **:** the inner highly vascular folds of the vulva

**la·bile** \'lā-,bī(-ə)l, -bəl\ *adj* **1 :** UNSTABLE ⟨a ~ mineral⟩ **2 :** ADAPTABLE

**la·bi·um** \'lā-bē-əm\ *n, pl* **la·bia** \-ə\ [NL, fr. L, lip] **:** any of the folds at the margin of the vulva

¹**la·bor** \'lā-bər\ *n* **1 :** physical or mental effort; *also* **:** human activity that provides the goods or services in an economy **2 :** the physical efforts of giving birth; *also* **:** the period of such labor **3 :** TASK **4 :** those who do manual labor or work for wages; *also* **:** labor unions or their officials

²**labor** *vb* **1 :** WORK **2 :** to move with great effort **3 :** to be in the labor of giving birth **4 :** to suffer from some disadvantage or distress ⟨~ under a delusion⟩ **5 :** to treat or work out laboriously — **la·bor·er** *n*

**lab·o·ra·to·ry** \'la-brə-,tȯr-ē, -bə-rə-\ *n, pl* **-ries :** a place equipped for making scientific experiments or tests

**Labor Day** *n* **:** the 1st Monday in September observed as a legal holiday in recognition of the working people

**la·bored** \'lā-bərd\ *adj* **:** not freely or easily done ⟨~ breathing⟩

**la·bo·ri·ous** \lə-'bȯr-ē-əs\ *adj* **1 :** INDUSTRIOUS **2 :** requiring great effort — **la·bo·ri·ous·ly** *adv*

**la·bor·sav·ing** \'lā-bər-,sā-viŋ\ *adj* **:** designed to replace or decrease labor

**labor union** *n* **:** an organization of workers formed to advance its members' interest in respect to wages and working conditions

**la·bour** *chiefly Brit var of* LABOR

**lab·ra·dor·ite** \'la-brə-,dȯr-,īt\ *n* **:** an iridescent feldspar used in jewelry

**Lab·ra·dor retriever** \'la-brə-,dȯr-\ *n* **:** any of a breed of strongly built retrievers having a short dense black, yellow, or chocolate coat

**la·bur·num** \lə-'bər-nəm\ *n* **:** any of a genus of leguminous shrubs or trees with hanging clusters of yellow flowers

**lab·y·rinth** \'la-bə-,rinth\ *n* **:** a place constructed of or filled with confusing intricate passageways **:** MAZE

**lab·y·rin·thine** \,la-bə-'rin-thən, -,thīn, -,thēn\ *adj* **:** INTRICATE, INVOLVED ⟨a ~ plot⟩ ⟨~ hallways⟩

**lac** \'lak\ *n* **:** a resinous substance secreted by a scale insect and used chiefly in the form of shellac

¹**lace** \'lās\ *vb* **laced; lac·ing 1 :** TIE **2 :** to adorn with lace **3 :** INTERTWINE **4 :** BEAT, LASH **5 :** to add something that taints (as a drug) or enhances flavor (as a spice) **6 :** to criticize sharply — used with *into* ⟨laced into his opponent⟩

²**lace** *n* [ME, fr. AF *lace, laz,* fr. L *laqueus* snare] **1 :** a cord or string used for drawing together two edges **2 :** an ornamental braid **3 :** a fine openwork usu. figured fabric made of thread — **lacy** \'lā-sē\ *adj*

**lac·er·ate** \'la-sə-,rāt\ *vb* **-at·ed; -at·ing :** to tear roughly — **lac·er·a·tion** \,la-sə-'rā-shən\ *n*

**lace·wing** \'lās-,wiŋ\ *n* **:** any of various insects with delicate wing veins, long antennae, and often brilliant eyes

**lach·ry·mal** *or* **lac·ri·mal** \'la-krə-məl\ *adj* **1** *usu* lacrimal **:** of, relating to, or being glands that produce tears **2 :** of, relating to, or marked by tears

**lach·ry·mose** \'la-krə-,mōs\ *adj* **1 :** TEARFUL **2 :** MOURNFUL ⟨~ songs⟩

¹**lack** \'lak\ *vb* **1 :** to be wanting or missing **2 :** to be deficient in ⟨~s experience⟩

²**lack** *n* **:** the fact or state of being wanting or deficient **:** NEED

**lack·a·dai·si·cal** \,la-kə-'dā-zi-kəl\ *adj* **:** lacking life, spirit, or zest — **lack·a·dai·si·cal·ly** \-k(ə-)lē\ *adv*

**lack·ey** \'la-kē\ *n, pl* **lackeys 1 :** FOOTMAN, SERVANT **2 :** TOADY

**lack·lus·ter** \'lak-,ləs-tər\ *adj* **:** DULL

**la·con·ic** \lə-'kä-nik\ *adj* [L *laconicus* Spartan, fr. Gk *lakōnikos,* fr. the Spartan reputation for terseness of speech] **:** sparing of words **:** TERSE ♦ *Synonyms* CONCISE, CURT, SHORT, SUCCINCT, BRUSQUE — **la·con·i·cal·ly** \-ni-k(ə-)lē\ *adv*

**lac·quer** \'la-kər\ *n* **:** a clear or colored usu. glossy and quick-drying surface coating — **lacquer** *vb*

**lac·ri·ma·tion** \,la-krə-'mā-shən\ *n* **:** secretion of tears

**la·crosse** \lə-'krȯs\ *n* [CanF *la crosse,* lit., the crooked stick] **:** a goal game in which players use a long-handled triangular-headed stick having a mesh pouch for catching, carrying, and throwing the ball

**lac·tate** \'lak-,tāt\ *vb* **lac·tat·ed; lac·tat·ing :** to secrete milk — **lac·ta·tion** \lak-'tā-shən\ *n*

**lac·tic** \'lak-tik\ *adj* **1 :** of or relating to milk **2 :** obtained from sour milk or whey

**lactic acid** *n* **:** a syrupy acid present in blood and muscle tissue and used esp. in food and medicine

**lac·tose** \'lak-,tōs\ *n* **:** a sugar present in milk

**la·cu·na** \lə-'kü-nə, -'kyü-\ *n, pl* **la·cu·nae** \-nē\ *also* **la·cu·nas** [L, pool, pit, gap, fr. *lacus* lake] **:** a blank space or missing part **:** GAP, DEFICIENCY

**lad** \'lad\ *n* **:** YOUTH; *also* **:** FELLOW

**lad·der** \'la-dər\ *n* **1 :** a structure for climbing that consists of two parallel sidepieces joined at intervals by crosspieces **2 :** something resembling a ladder in having ascending steps or stages ⟨a tournament ~⟩

**lad·die** \'la-dē\ *n* **:** a young lad

**lad·en** \'la-d³n\ *adj* **:** LOADED, BURDENED

**lad·ing** \'lā-diŋ\ *n* **:** CARGO, FREIGHT

**la·dle** \'lā-d³l\ *n* **:** a deep-bowled long-handled spoon used in taking up and conveying liquids — **ladle** *vb*

**la·dy** \'lā-dē\ *n, pl* **ladies** [ME, fr. OE *hlǣfdīge,* fr. *hlāf* bread + *-dige* (akin to *dǣge* kneader of bread)] **1 :** a woman of property, rank, or authority; *also* : a woman of superior social position or of refinement **2** : WOMAN **3** : WIFE

**lady beetle** *n* : LADYBUG

**la·dy·bird** \'lā-dē-ˌbərd\ *n* : LADYBUG

**la·dy·bug** \-ˌbəg\ *n* : any of various small nearly hemispherical and usu. brightly colored beetles that feed mostly on other insects

**la·dy·fin·ger** \-ˌfiŋ-gər\ *n* : a small finger-shaped sponge cake

**lady–in–waiting** *n, pl* **ladies–in–waiting** : a lady appointed to attend or wait on a queen or princess

**la·dy·like** \'lā-dē-ˌlīk\ *adj* : WELL-BRED

**la·dy·ship** \-ˌship\ *n* : the condition of being a lady : rank of lady

**lady's slipper** *also* **lady slipper** *n* : any of several No. American orchids with slipper-shaped flowers

**¹lag** \'lag\ *n* **1** : a slowing up or falling behind; *also* : the amount by which one lags **2** : INTERVAL

**²lag** *vb* **lagged**; **lag·ging** **1** : to fail to keep up : stay behind **2** : to slacken gradually ♦ **Synonyms** DAWDLE, DALLY, TARRY, LOITER

**la·ger** \'lä-gər\ *n* : a usu. dry beer slowly brewed and matured under refrigeration

**lag·gard** \'la-gərd\ *adj* : tending to lag ⟨~ workers⟩ — **laggard** *n* — **lag·gard·ly** *adv or adj* — **lag·gard·ness** *n*

**la·gniappe** \'lan-ˌyap\ *n* : something given free esp. with a purchase

**la·goon** \lə-'gün\ *n* : a shallow sound, channel, or pond near or connected to a larger body of water

**laid** *past and past part of* LAY

**laid–back** \'lād-'bak\ *adj* : having a relaxed style or character ⟨~ music⟩

**lain** *past part of* ¹LIE

**lair** \'ler\ *n* **1** : the resting or living place of a wild animal : DEN **2** : a usu. hidden refuge

**laird** \'lerd\ *n, chiefly Scot* : a landed proprietor

**lais·ser–faire** *chiefly Brit var of* LAISSEZ-FAIRE

**lais·sez–faire** \ˌle-ˌsā-'fer, ˌlā-, -ˌzā-\ *n* [F *laissez faire* let do] : a doctrine opposing governmental control of economic affairs beyond that necessary to maintain peace and property rights

**la·ity** \'lā-ə-tē\ *n* **1** : the people of a religious faith as distinct from its clergy **2** : the mass of people as distinct from those of a particular field

**lake** \'lāk\ *n* : an inland body of standing water of considerable size; *also* : a pool of liquid (as lava or pitch)

**La·ko·ta** \lə-'kō-tə\ *n, pl* **Lakota** *also* **Lakotas** : a member of a western division of the Dakota peoples; *also* : their language

**¹lam** \'lam\ *vb* **lammed**; **lam·ming** : to flee hastily — **lam** *n*

**²lam** *abbr* laminated

**Lam** *abbr* Lamentations

**la·ma** \'lä-mə\ *n* : a Buddhist monk of Tibet or Mongolia

**la·ma·sery** \'lä-mə-ˌser-ē\ *n, pl* **-ser·ies** : a monastery for lamas

**¹lamb** \'lam\ *n* **1** : a young sheep; *also* : its

flesh used as food **2** : an innocent or gentle person

**lamb** *vb* : to bring forth a lamb

**lam·baste** *or* **lam·bast** \lam-'bāst, -'bast\ *vb* **1** : BEAT **2** : EXCORIATE ♦ **Synonyms** CASTIGATE, FLAY, LASH

**lamb·da** \'lam-də\ *n* : the 11th letter of the Greek alphabet — Λ or λ

**lam·bent** \'lam-bənt\ *adj* [L *lambens*, prp. of *lambere* to lick] **1** : FLICKERING ⟨a ~ flame⟩ **2** : softly radiant ⟨~ eyes⟩ **3** : marked by lightness or brilliance ⟨~ humor⟩ ♦ **Synonyms** EFFULGENT, INCANDESCENT, LUCENT, LUMINOUS — **lam·ben·cy** \-bən-sē\ *n* — **lam·bent·ly** *adv*

**lamb·skin** \'lam-ˌskin\ *n* : a lamb's skin or a small fine-grade sheepskin or the leather made from either

**¹lame** \'lām\ *adj* **lam·er**; **lam·est** **1** : having a body part and esp. a limb so disabled as to impair freedom of movement; *also* : marked by stiffness and soreness **2** : lacking substance : WEAK ⟨~ excuses⟩ **3** : INFERIOR, PITIFUL ⟨a ~ school⟩ — **lame·ly** *adv* — **lame·ness** *n*

**²lame** *vb* **lamed**; **lam·ing** : to make lame ⟨was *lamed* by a broken leg⟩

**la·mé** \lä-'mā, la-\ *n* [F] : a brocaded clothing fabric with tinsel filling threads (as of gold or silver)

**lame·brain** \'lām-ˌbrān\ *n* : DOLT

**lame duck** *n* : an elected official continuing to hold office between an election and the inauguration of a successor — **lame–duck** *adj*

**¹la·ment** \lə-'ment\ *vb* **1** : to mourn aloud : WAIL **2** : to express sorrow or regret for : BEWAIL — **lam·en·ta·ble** \'la-mən-tə-bəl, lə-'men-tə-\ *adj* — **lam·en·ta·bly** \-blē\ *adv* — **lam·en·ta·tion** \ˌla-mən-'tā-shən\ *n*

**²lament** *n* **1** : a crying out in grief : WAIL **2** : DIRGE, ELEGY **3** : COMPLAINT

**Lamentations** *n* — see BIBLE table

**la·mia** \'lā-mē-ə\ *n* : a female demon

**lam·i·na** \'la-mə-nə\ *n, pl* **-nae** \-ˌnē\ *or* **-nas** : a thin plate or scale

**¹lam·i·nate** \'la-mə-ˌnāt\ *vb* **-nat·ed**; **-nat·ing** : to make by uniting layers of one or more materials — **lam·i·na·tion** \ˌla-mə-'nā-shən\ *n*

**²lam·i·nate** \-nət\ *n* : a product manufactured by laminating

**lamp** \'lamp\ *n* **1** : a vessel with a wick for burning a flammable liquid (as oil) to produce light **2** : a device for producing light or heat

**lamp·black** \-ˌblak\ *n* : black soot used esp. as a pigment

**lamp·light·er** \-ˌlī-tər\ *n* : one that lights a lamp

**lam·poon** \lam-'pün\ *n* : SATIRE; *esp* : a harsh satire directed against an individual — **lampoon** *vb*

**lam·prey** \'lam-prē\ *n, pl* **lampreys** : any of a family of eel-shaped jawless fishes that have well-developed eyes and a large disk-shaped sucking mouth armed with horny teeth

**LAN** \'lan, ˌel-ˌā-'en\ *n* : LOCAL AREA NETWORK

**la·nai** \lə-ˈnī\ n [Hawaiian *lānai*] : PORCH, VERANDA

**¹lance** \ˈlans\ n **1** : a spear carried by mounted soldiers **2** : any of various sharp-pointed implements; *esp* : LANCET

**²lance** *vb* **lanced; lanc·ing** : to pierce or open with a lance ⟨∼ a boil⟩

**lance corporal** n : an enlisted person in the marine corps ranking above a private first class and below a corporal

**lanc·er** \ˈlan-sər\ n : a cavalryman of a unit formerly armed with lances

**lan·cet** \ˈlan-sət\ n : a sharp-pointed and usu. 2-edged surgical instrument

**¹land** \ˈland\ n **1** : the solid part of the surface of the earth; *also* : a part of the earth's surface ⟨fenced ∼⟩ ⟨marshy ∼⟩ **2** : NATION **3** : REALM, DOMAIN ⟨the ∼ of the living⟩ — **land·less** *adj*

**²land** *vb* **1** : DISEMBARK; *also* : to touch at a place on shore **2** : to alight or cause to alight on a surface ⟨∼ a punch⟩ **3** : to bring to or arrive at a destination **4** : to catch and bring in ⟨∼ a fish⟩; *also* : GAIN, SECURE ⟨∼ a job⟩

**lan·dau** \ˈlan-ˌdau\ n : a 4-wheeled carriage with a top divided into two sections that can be lowered, thrown back, or removed

**land·ed** *adj* : having an estate in land ⟨∼ gentry⟩

**land·er** \ˈlan-dər\ n : a space vehicle designed to land on a celestial body

**land·fall** \ˈland-ˌfol\ n : a sighting or making of land (as after a voyage); *also* : the land first sighted

**land·fill** \-ˌfil\ n : a low-lying area on which refuse is buried between layers of earth — **landfill** *vb*

**land·form** \-ˌform\ n : a natural feature of a land surface

**land·hold·er** \-ˌhōl-dər\ n : a holder or owner of land — **land·hold·ing** \-diŋ\ *adj or n*

**land·ing** \ˈlan-diŋ\ n **1** : the action of one that lands **2** : a place for discharging or taking on passengers and cargo **3** : a level part of a staircase

**landing gear** n : the part that supports the weight of an aircraft when it is on the ground

**land·la·dy** \ˈland-ˌlā-dē\ n : a woman who is a landlord

**land·locked** \-ˌläkt\ *adj* **1** : enclosed or nearly enclosed by land ⟨a ∼ country⟩ **2** : confined to fresh water by some barrier ⟨∼ salmon⟩

**land·lord** \-ˌlord\ n **1** : the owner of property leased or rented to another **2** : a person who rents lodgings : INNKEEPER

**land·lub·ber** \-ˌlə-bər\ n : one who knows little of the sea or seamanship

**land·mark** \-ˌmärk\ n **1** : an object that marks a course or boundary or serves as a guide **2** : an event that marks a turning point **3** : a structure of unusual historical and usu. aesthetic interest

**land·mass** \-ˌmas\ n : a large area of land

**land mine** n **1** : a mine placed on or just below the surface of the ground and designed to be exploded by the weight of

someone or something passing over it **2** : a trap for the unwary

**land·own·er** \-ˌō-nər\ n : an owner of land

**¹land·scape** \-ˌskāp\ n **1** : a picture of natural inland scenery **2** : a portion of land that can be seen in one glance

**²landscape** *vb* **land·scaped; land·scap·ing** : to modify (a natural landscape) by grading, clearing, or decorative planting

**land·slide** \-ˌslīd\ n **1** : the slipping down of a mass of rocks or earth on a steep slope; *also* : the mass of material that slides **2** : an overwhelming victory esp. in a political contest

**lands·man** \ˈlandz-mən\ n : a person who lives on land; *esp* : LANDLUBBER

**land·ward** \ˈland-wərd\ *adv or adj* : to or toward the land

**lane** \ˈlān\ n **1** : a narrow passageway (as between fences) **2** : a relatively narrow way or track ⟨traffic ∼⟩

**lang** *abbr* language

**lan·guage** \ˈlaŋ-gwij\ n [ME, fr. AF *langage*, fr. *langue* tongue, language, fr. L *lingua*] **1** : the words, their pronunciation, and the methods of combining them used and understood by a community **2** : form or style of verbal expression ⟨legal ∼⟩ **3** : a system of signs and symbols and rules for using them that is used to carry information

**lan·guid** \ˈlaŋ-gwəd\ *adj* **1** : WEAK **2** : sluggish in character or disposition : LISTLESS ⟨a ∼ summer day⟩ **3** : SLOW — **lan·guid·ly** *adv* — **lan·guid·ness** n

**lan·guish** \ˈlaŋ-gwish\ *vb* **1** : to become languid **2** : to become dispirited : PINE **3** : to appeal for sympathy by assuming an expression of grief

**lan·guor** \ˈlaŋ-gər\ n **1** : a languid feeling **2** : listless indolence or inertia ♦ *Synonyms* LETHARGY, LASSITUDE, TORPIDITY, TORPOR — **lan·guor·ous** *adj* — **lan·guor·ous·ly** *adv*

**La Ni·ña** \lä-ˈnē-nyə\ n : an upwelling of unusually cold ocean water along the west coast of So. America that often follows an El Niño

**lank** \ˈlaŋk\ *adj* **1** : not well filled out **2** : hanging straight and limp ⟨∼ hair⟩

**lanky** \ˈlaŋ-kē\ *adj* **lank·i·er; -est** : ungracefully tall and thin

**lan·o·lin** \ˈlan-ᵊl-ən\ n : the fatty coating of sheep's wool esp. when refined for use in ointments and cosmetics

**lan·ta·na** \lan-ˈta-nə\ n : any of a genus of tropical shrubs related to the vervains with showy heads of small bright flowers

**lan·tern** \ˈlan-tərn\ n [ME *lanterne*, fr. AF, fr. L *lanterna*, fr. Gk *lamptēr*, fr. *lampein* to shine] **1** : a usu. portable light with a protective covering **2** : the chamber in a lighthouse containing the light **3** : a projector for slides

**lan·tha·num** \ˈlan-thə-nəm\ n : a soft malleable metallic chemical element

**lan·yard** \ˈlan-yərd\ n : a piece of rope for fastening something in ships; *also* : any of various cords

**¹lap** \ˈlap\ n **1** : a loose panel of a garment **2** : the clothing that lies on the knees, thighs, and lower part of the trunk when one sits; *also* : the front part of the lower trunk and thighs of a seated person **3** : an environment of nurture ⟨the ∼ of luxury⟩ **4** : CHARGE, CONTROL ⟨in the ∼ of the gods⟩

**²lap** *vb* **lapped; lap·ping 1** : FOLD **2** : WRAP **3** : to lay over or near so as to partly cover

**³lap** *n* **1** : the amount by which an object overlaps another; *also* : the part of an object that overlaps another **2** : an act or instance of going over a course (as a track or swimming pool)

**⁴lap** *vb* **lapped; lap·ping 1** : to scoop up food or drink with the tip of the tongue; *also* : DEVOUR — usu. used with *up* **2** : to splash gently ⟨*lapping* waves⟩

**⁵lap** *n* **1** : an act or instance of lapping **2** : a gentle splashing sound

**lap·a·ros·co·py** \ˌla-pə-ˈräs-kə-pē\ *n, pl* **-pies 1** : visual examination of the abdomen by means of an endoscope; *also* : surgery using laparoscopy — **lap·a·ro·scope** \ˈla-pə-rə-ˌskōp\ *n* — **lap·a·ro·scop·ic** \ˌla-pə-rə-ˈskä-pik\ *adj*

**lap·dog** \ˈlap-ˌdȯg\ *n* : a small dog that may be held in the lap

**la·pel** \lə-ˈpel\ *n* : the fold of the front of a coat that is usu. a continuation of the collar

**¹lap·i·dary** \ˈla-pə-ˌder-ē\ *n, pl* **-dar·ies** : a person who cuts, polishes, or engraves precious stones

**²lapidary** *adj* **1** : of, relating to, or suitable for engraved inscriptions **2** : of, relating to, or suggestive of precious stones or the art of cutting them

**lap·in** \ˈla-pən\ *n* : rabbit fur usu. sheared and dyed

**la·pis la·zu·li** \ˌla-pəs-ˈla-zə-lē, -zhə-\ *n* : a usu. blue semiprecious stone often having sparkling bits of pyrite

**lap·pet** \ˈla-pət\ *n* : a fold or flap on a garment

**¹lapse** \ˈlaps\ *n* [L *lapsus*, fr. *labi* to slip] **1** : a slight error ⟨a mental ∼⟩ **2** : a fall from a higher to a lower state **3** : the termination of a right or privilege through failure to meet requirements **4** : INTERRUPTION **5** : APOSTASY **6** : a passage of time; *also* : INTERVAL ♦ *Synonyms* BLOOPER, BLUNDER, BONER, GOOF, MISTAKE, SLIP

**²lapse** *vb* **lapsed; laps·ing 1** : to commit apostasy **2** : SINK, SLIP ⟨*lapsed* into a coma⟩ **3** : CEASE

**lap·top** \ˈlap-ˌtäp\ *adj* : of a size that can be used conveniently on one's lap ⟨a ∼ computer⟩ — **laptop** *n*

**lap·wing** \ˈlap-ˌwiŋ\ *n* : an Old World crested plover

**lar·board** \ˈlär-bərd\ *n* : ⁵PORT

**lar·ce·ny** \ˈlär-sə-nē\ *n, pl* **-nies** [ME, fr. AF *larecin* theft, fr. L *latrocinium* robbery, fr. *latro* mercenary soldier] : THEFT — **lar·ce·nous** \-nəs\ *adj*

**larch** \ˈlärch\ *n* : any of a genus of trees related to the pines that shed their needles in the fall

**¹lard** \ˈlärd\ *vb* **1** : to insert strips of usu.

pork fat into (meat) before cooking; *also* : GREASE **2** *obs* : ENRICH

**²lard** *n* : a soft white fat obtained by rendering fatty tissue of the hog

**lar·der** \ˈlär-dər\ *n* : a place where foods (as meat) are kept

**large** \ˈlärj\ *adj* **larg·er; larg·est 1** : having more than usual power, capacity, or scope **2** : exceeding most other things of like kind in quantity or size ♦ *Synonyms* BIG, GREAT, OVERSIZE — **large** *adv* — **large·ness** *n* — **at large 1** : UNCONFINED **2** : as a whole

**large·ly** \ˈlärj-lē\ *adv* : to a large extent

**lar·gesse** *or* **lar·gess** \lär-ˈzhes, -ˈjes\ *n* **1** : liberal giving **2** : a generous gift

**¹lar·go** \ˈlär-gō\ *adv or adj* [It, slow, broad, fr. L *largus* abundant] : at a very slow tempo — used as a direction in music

**²largo** *n, pl* **largos** : a largo movement

**lari** \ˈlä-rē\ *n, pl* **lari** — see MONEY table

**lar·i·at** \ˈlar-ē-ət\ *n* [AmerSp *la reata* the lasso, fr. Sp *la* the + AmerSp *reata* lasso, fr. Sp *reatar* to tie again] : a long rope used to catch or tether livestock : LASSO

**¹lark** \ˈlärk\ *n* : any of a family of small songbirds; *esp* : SKYLARK

**²lark** *n* : a source of or quest for fun or adventure

**³lark** *vb* : to engage in harmless fun or mischief — often used with *about*

**lark·spur** \ˈlärk-ˌspər\ *n* : DELPHINIUM; *esp* : any of the widely cultivated annual delphiniums

**lar·va** \ˈlär-və\ *n, pl* **lar·vae** \-(ˌ)vē\ *also* **larvas** [NL, fr. L, specter, mask] : the wingless often wormlike form in which insects hatch from the egg; *also* : any young animal (as a tadpole) that is fundamentally unlike its parent — **lar·val** \-vəl\ *adj*

**lar·yn·gi·tis** \ˌlar-ən-ˈjī-təs\ *n* : inflammation of the larynx

**lar·ynx** \ˈlar-iŋks\ *n, pl* **la·ryn·ges** \lə-ˈrin-ˌjēz\ *or* **lar·ynx·es** : the upper part of the trachea containing the vocal cords — **la·ryn·ge·al** \lə-ˈrin-jəl\ *adj*

**la·sa·gna** \lə-ˈzän-yə\ *n* [It] : boiled broad flat noodles baked with a sauce usu. of tomatoes, cheese, and meat

**las·car** \ˈlas-kər\ *n* : an Indian sailor

**las·civ·i·ous** \lə-ˈsi-vē-əs\ *adj* : LUSTFUL, LEWD ♦ *Synonyms* LICENTIOUS, LECHEROUS, LIBIDINOUS, SALACIOUS — **las·civ·i·ous·ness** *n*

**la·ser** \ˈlā-zər\ *n* [*l*ight *a*mplification by *s*timulated *e*mission of *r*adiation] **1** : a device that produces an intense monochromatic beam of light **2** : something thrown or directed straight with high speed or intensity ⟨threw a ∼ into the end zone⟩

**laser disc** *n* : OPTICAL DISK; *esp* : one containing a video recording

**¹lash** \ˈlash\ *vb* **1** : to move violently or suddenly **2** : WHIP **3** : to attack verbally

**²lash** *n* **1** : a stroke esp. with a whip; *also* : WHIP **2** : a stinging rebuke **3** : EYELASH

**³lash** *vb* : to bind with or as if with a line

**lass** \ˈlas\ *n* : GIRL

**lass·ie** \ˈla-sē\ *n* : LASS

**las·si·tude** \'la-sə-ˌtüd, -ˌtyüd\ *n* **1** : WEARINESS, FATIGUE **2** : LANGUOR

**las·so** \'la-sō, la-'sü\ *n, pl* **lassos** *or* **lassoes** [Sp *lazo*] : a rope or long leather thong with a noose used for catching livestock — **lasso** *vb*

**¹last** \'last\ *vb* **1** : to continue in existence or operation **2** : to remain fresh or unimpaired : ENDURE **3** : to manage to continue **4** : to be enough for the needs of

**²last** *n* : a foot-shaped form on which a shoe is shaped or repaired

**³last** *vb* : to shape with a last

**⁴last** *adv* **1** : at the end **2** : most recently **3** : in conclusion

**⁵last** *adj* **1** : following all the rest : FINAL **2** : next before the present ⟨∼ week⟩ **3** : most up to date **4** : farthest from a specified quality, attitude, or likelihood ⟨the ∼ thing we want⟩ **5** : CONCLUSIVE; *also* : SUPREME — **last·ly** *adv*

**⁶last** *n* : something that is last ⟨the ∼ of them⟩ — **at last** : FINALLY

**last–ditch** \'last-'dich\ *adj* : made as a final effort esp. to avert disaster

**last laugh** *n* : an ultimate satisfaction or triumph despite previous doubt or criticism

**Last Supper** *n* : the supper eaten by Jesus and his disciples on the night of his betrayal

**lat** *abbr* latitude

**Lat** *abbr* Latin

**¹latch** \'lach\ *vb* : to catch or get hold

**²latch** *n* : a catch that holds a door or gate closed

**³latch** *vb* : to make fast with a latch

**latch·et** \'la-chət\ *n* : a strap, thong, or lace for fastening a shoe or sandal

**latch·key** \'lach-ˌkē\ *n* : a key for opening a door latch esp. from the outside

**latch·string** \-ˌstriŋ\ *n* : a string on a latch that may be left hanging outside the door for raising the latch

**¹late** \'lāt\ *adj* **lat·er; lat·est 1** : coming or remaining after the due, usual, or proper time **2** : far advanced toward the close or end **3** : recently deceased **4** : made, appearing, or happening just previous to the present : RECENT ⟨∼ news⟩ — **late·ly** *adv* — **late·ness** *n*

**²late** *adv* **lat·er; lat·est 1** : after the usual or proper time; *also* : at or to an advanced point in time **2** : RECENTLY

**late·com·er** \'lāt-ˌkə-mər\ *n* : one who arrives late

**la·teen** \lə-'tēn\ *adj* : relating to or being a triangular sail extended by a long spar slung to a low mast

**la·tent** \'lāt-ᵊnt\ *adj* : present but not visible or active ♦ *Synonyms* DORMANT, QUIESCENT, POTENTIAL — **la·ten·cy** \-ᵊn-sē\ *n*

**¹lat·er·al** \'la-tə-rəl\ *adj* : situated on, directed toward, or coming from the side ⟨a ∼ view⟩ — **lat·er·al·ly** *adv*

**²lateral** *n* **1** : a branch from the main part **2** : a football pass thrown parallel to the line of scrimmage or away from the opponent's goal

**la·tex** \'lā-ˌteks\ *n, pl* **la·ti·ces** \'lā-tə-ˌsēz, 'la-\ *or* **la·tex·es** **1** : a milky juice pro-

duced by various plant cells (as of milkweeds, poppies, and the rubber tree) **2** : a water emulsion of a synthetic rubber or plastic used esp. in paint

**lath** \'lath, 'lath\ *n, pl* **laths** *or* **lath** : a thin narrow strip of wood used esp. as a base for plaster; *also* : a building material in sheets used for the same purpose — **lath** *vb*

**lathe** \'lāth\ *n* : a machine in which a piece of material is held and turned while being shaped by a tool

**¹lath·er** \'la-thər\ *n* **1** : a foam or froth formed when a detergent is agitated in water; *also* : foam from profuse sweating (as by a horse) **2** : DITHER

**²lather** *vb* : to spread lather over ⟨∼ed his face before shaving⟩; *also* : to form a lather

**Lat·in** \'lat-ᵊn\ *n* **1** : the language of ancient Rome **2** : a member of any of the peoples whose languages derive from Latin — **Latin** *adj*

**La·ti·na** \lə-'tē-nə\ *n* : a woman or girl who is a native or inhabitant of Latin America; *also* : a woman or girl of Latin-American origin living in the U.S.

**Latin American** *n* : a native or inhabitant of any of the countries of No., Central, or So. America whose official language is Spanish or Portuguese — **Latin-American** *adj*

**La·ti·no** \lə-'tē-nō\ *n, pl* **-nos** : a native or inhabitant of Latin America; *also* : a person of Latin-American origin living in the U.S. — **Latino** *adj*

**lat·i·tude** \'la-tə-ˌtüd, -ˌtyüd\ *n* **1** : angular distance north or south from the earth's equator measured in degrees **2** : a region marked by its latitude **3** : freedom of action or choice

**lat·i·tu·di·nar·i·an** \ˌla-tə-ˌtü-də-'ner-ē-ən, -ˌtyü-\ *n* : a person who is liberal in religious belief and conduct

**la·trine** \lə-'trēn\ *n* : TOILET

**lats** \'läts\ *n, pl* **la·ti** \'lä-tē\ *or* **la·tu** \'lä-tü\ : the basic monetary unit of Latvia from 1922 to 1940 and from 1991 through 2013

**lat·ter** \'la-tər\ *adj* **1** : more recent; *also* : FINAL **2** : of, relating to, or being the second of two things referred to

**lat·ter–day** *adj* **1** : of present or recent times **2** : of a later or subsequent time

**Latter–day Saint** *n* : a member of a religious body founded by Joseph Smith in 1830 and accepting the Book of Mormon as divine revelation : MORMON

**lat·ter·ly** \'la-tər-lē\ *adv* **1** : LATER **2** : of late : RECENTLY ⟨the business has grown ∼⟩

**lat·tice** \'la-təs\ *n* **1** : a framework of crossed wood or metal strips; *also* : a window, door, or gate having a lattice **2** : a regular geometrical arrangement

**lat·tice·work** \-ˌwərk\ *n* : LATTICE; *also* : work made of lattices

**Lat·vi·an** \'lat-vē-ən\ *n* **1** : a native or inhabitant of Latvia **2** : the language of the Latvians — **Latvian** *adj*

**¹laud** \'lȯd\ *vb* : PRAISE, ACCLAIM

**²laud** *vb* : PRAISE, EXTOL ♦ *Synonyms*

CELEBRATE, EULOGIZE, GLORIFY, MAGNIFY — **laud·a·ble** *adj* — **laud·a·bly** *adv*

**lau·da·num** \'lȯd-ᵊn-əm\ *n* : a tincture of opium

**lau·da·to·ry** \'lȯ-də-ˌtōr-ē\ *adj* : of, relating to, or expressive of praise

¹**laugh** \'laf, 'làf\ *vb* [ME, fr. OE *hliehhan*] : to show mirth, joy, or scorn with a chuckle or explosive vocal sound; *also* : to become amused or derisive — **laugh·able** *adj* — **laugh·ing·ly** *adv*

²**laugh** *n* **1** : the act of laughing **2** : JOKE; *also* : JEER **3** *pl* : SPORT

**laughing gas** *n* : NITROUS OXIDE

**laugh·ing·stock** \'la-fiŋ-ˌstäk, 'là-\ *n* : an object of ridicule

**laugh·ter** \'laf-tər, 'làf-\ *n* : the action or sound of laughing

¹**launch** \'lȯnch\ *vb* **1** : THROW, HURL; *also* : to send off ⟨~ a rocket⟩ **2** : to set afloat **3** : to set in operation : START ⟨~ a business⟩ — **launch·er** *n*

²**launch** *n* : an act or instance of launching

³**launch** *n* : a small open or half-decked motorboat

**launch·pad** \'lȯnch-ˌpad\ *n* : a platform from which a rocket is launched

**laun·der** \'lȯn-dər\ *vb* **1** : to wash or wash and iron clothing and household linens **2** : to transfer (as money of an illegal origin) through an outside party to conceal the true source — **laun·der·er** *n*

**laun·dress** \'lȯn-drəs\ *n* : a woman who is a laundry worker

**laun·dry** \'lȯn-drē\ *n, pl* **laundries** [fr. obs. *launder* launderer, fr. AF *lavandere*, fr. ML *lavandarius*, fr. L *lavandus* needing to be washed, fr. *lavare* to wash] **1** : a place where laundering is done **2** : clothes or linens that have been or are to be laundered — **laun·dry·man** \-mən\ *n*

**lau·re·ate** \'lȯr-ē-ət\ *n* : the recipient of honor for achievement in an art or science — **lau·re·ate·ship** *n*

**lau·rel** \'lȯ-rəl\ *n* **1** : an evergreen tree or shrub of southern Europe that is related to the sassafras and cinnamon and has glossy aromatic leaves **2** : MOUNTAIN LAUREL **3** : a crown of laurel awarded as an honor — usu. used in pl.

**lav** *abbr* lavatory

**la·va** \'lä-və, 'la-\ *n* [It] : melted rock coming from a volcano; *also* : such rock that has cooled and hardened

**la·vage** \lə-'väzh\ *n* [F] : WASHING; *esp* : the washing out (as of an organ) esp. for medicinal reasons

**lav·a·to·ry** \'la-və-ˌtōr-ē\ *n, pl* **-ries** **1** : a fixed washbowl with running water and drainpipe **2** : BATHROOM

**lave** \'lāv\ *vb* **laved; lav·ing** : WASH

**lav·en·der** \'la-vən-dər\ *n* **1** : a Mediterranean mint or its dried leaves and flowers used to perfume clothing and bed linen **2** : a pale purple color

¹**lav·ish** \'la-vish\ *adj* [ME *laves, lavage*, prob. fr. MF *lavasse, lavache* downpour, fr. *laver* to wash] **1** : expending or bestowing profusely **2** : expended or produced in abundance ⟨~ gifts⟩ **3**

: marked by excess ⟨~ decor⟩ — **lav·ish·ly** *adv* — **lav·ish·ness** *n*

²**lavish** *vb* : to expend or give freely

**law** \'lȯ\ *n* **1** : a rule of conduct or action established by custom or laid down and enforced by a governing authority; *also* : the whole body of such rules **2** : the control brought about by enforcing rules **3** *cap* : the revelation of the divine will set forth in the Old Testament; *also* : the first part of the Jewish scriptures — see BIBLE table **4** : a rule or principle of construction or procedure **5** : the science that deals with laws and their interpretation and application **6** : the profession of a lawyer **7** : a rule or principle stating something that always works in the same way under the same conditions

**law·break·er** \'lȯ-ˌbrā-kər\ *n* : a person who violates the law

**law·ful** \'lȯ-fəl\ *adj* **1** : permitted by law **2** : RIGHTFUL — **law·ful·ly** *adv*

**law·giv·er** \-ˌgi-vər\ *n* : LEGISLATOR

**law·less** \'lȯ-ləs\ *adj* **1** : having no laws **2** : UNRULY, DISORDERLY ⟨a ~ mob⟩ — **law·less·ly** *adv* — **law·less·ness** *n*

**law·mak·er** \-ˌmā-kər\ *n* : LEGISLATOR

**law·man** \'lȯ-mən\ *n* : a law enforcement official (as a sheriff or marshal)

¹**lawn** \'lȯn\ *n* : ground (as around a house) covered with mowed grass

²**lawn** *n* : a fine sheer linen or cotton fabric

**lawn bowling** *n* : a bowling game played on a green with wooden balls which are rolled at a jack

**law·ren·ci·um** \lȯ-'ren-sē-əm\ *n* : a short-lived radioactive element

**law·suit** \'lȯ-ˌsüt\ *n* : a suit in law

**law·yer** \'lȯ-yər\ *n* : one who conducts lawsuits for clients or advises as to legal rights and obligations in other matters — **law·yer·ly** *adv*

¹**lax** \'laks\ *adj* **1** : not strict ⟨~ discipline⟩ **2** : not tense or rigid ♦ *Synonyms* REMISS, NEGLIGENT, NEGLECTFUL, DELINQUENT, DERELICT — **lax·i·ty** \'lak-sə-tē\ *n* — **lax·ly** *adv* — **lax·ness** *n*

¹**lax·a·tive** \'lak-sə-tiv\ *adj* : relieving constipation

²**laxative** *n* : a usu. mild laxative drug

¹**lay** \'lā\ *vb* **laid** \'lād\; **lay·ing** **1** : to beat or strike down **2** : to put on or set down : PLACE **3** : to produce and deposit eggs **4** : SETTLE; *also* : ALLAY **5** : SPREAD **6** : PREPARE, CONTRIVE **7** : WAGER **8** : to impose esp. as a duty or burden **9** : to set in order or position **10** : to bring to a specified condition ⟨*laid* waste the land⟩ **11** : to put forward : SUBMIT

²**lay** *n* : the way in which something lies or is laid in relation to something else

³**lay** *past of* ¹LIE

⁴**lay** *n* **1** : a simple narrative poem **2** : SONG

⁵**lay** *adj* **1** : of or relating to the laity **2** : not of a particular profession; *also* : lacking extensive knowledge of a particular subject

**lay·away** \'lā-ə-ˌwā\ *n* : a purchasing agreement by which a retailer agrees to hold merchandise secured by a deposit until the price is paid in full

**lay·er** \'lā-ər\ n **1** : one that lays **2** : one thickness, course, or fold laid or lying over or under another

**lay·ette** \lā-'et\ n [F, fr. MF, dim. of *laye* box] : an outfit of clothing and equipment for a newborn infant

**lay·man** \'lā-mən\ n : a person who is a member of the laity

**lay·off** \'lā-,ȯf\ n **1** : a period of inactivity **2** : the act of laying off an employee

**lay off** vb **1** : to cease to employ (a worker) often temporarily **2** : to leave undisturbed **3** : to stop doing something

**lay·out** \'lā-,aút\ n : the final arrangement, plan, or design of something

**lay·over** \-,ō-vər\ n : STOPOVER

**lay·per·son** \-,pər-sən\ n : a member of the laity

**lay·wom·an** \'lā-,wu̇-mən\ n : a woman who is a member of the laity

**la·zar** \'la-zər, 'lā-\ n : LEPER

**laze** \'lāz\ vb lazed; laz·ing : to pass time in idleness and relaxation

**la·zy** \'lā-zē\ adj la·zi·er; -est **1** : disliking activity or exertion **2** : encouraging idleness ⟨a ~ day⟩ **3** : SLUGGISH **4** : DROOPY, LAX **5** : not rigorous or strict ⟨~ work habits⟩ — **la·zi·ly** \-zə-lē\ adv — **la·zi·ness** \-zē-nəs\ n

**la·zy·bones** \-,bōnz\ n sing or pl : a lazy person

**lazy Su·san** \,lā-zē-'süz-ʰn\ n : a revolving tray used for serving food

**lb** abbr [L *libra*] pound

**lc** abbr lowercase

**LC** abbr Library of Congress

**¹LCD** \,el-(,)sē-'dē\ n [liquid crystal display] : a display (as of the time in a digital watch) that consists of segments of a liquid crystal whose reflectivity varies with the voltage applied to them

**²LCD** abbr least common denominator; lowest common denominator

**LCDR** abbr lieutenant commander

**LCM** abbr least common multiple; lowest common multiple

**LCpl** abbr lance corporal

**LCS** abbr League Championship Series

**ld** abbr **1** load **2** lord

**LD** abbr learning disabled; learning disability

**LDC** abbr less developed country

**ldg** abbr **1** landing **2** loading

**LDL** \,el-(,)dē-'el\ n [low-density lipoprotein] : a cholesterol-rich protein-poor lipoprotein of blood plasma correlated with increased probability of developing atherosclerosis

**L-do·pa** \'el-'dō-pə\ n : an isomer of dopa used esp. in the treatment of Parkinson's disease

**LDS** abbr Latter-day Saints

**lea** \'lē, 'lā\ n : PASTURE, MEADOW

**leach** \'lēch\ vb : to pass a liquid (as water) through to carry off the soluble components; also : to dissolve out by such means ⟨~ alkali from ashes⟩

**¹lead** \'lēd\ vb led \'led\; lead·ing **1** : to guide on a way **2** : LIVE ⟨~ a quiet life⟩ **3** : to direct the operations, activity, or performance of ⟨~ an orchestra⟩ **4** : to go at the head of : be first ⟨~ a parade⟩

**5** : to begin play with; also : BEGIN, OPEN **6** : to tend toward a definite result ⟨study ~ing to a degree⟩ — **lead·er** n — **lead·er·less** adj — **lead·er·ship** n

**²lead** \'lēd\ n **1** : a position at the front; also : a margin by which one leads **2** : the privilege of leading in cards; also : the card or suit led **3** : EXAMPLE **4** : one that leads **5** : a principal role (as in a play); also : one who plays such a role **6** : INDICATION, CLUE **7** : an insulated electrical conductor

**³lead** \'led\ n **1** : a heavy malleable bluish white chemical element **2** : an article made of lead; esp : a weight for sounding at sea **3** : a thin strip of metal used to separate lines of type in printing **4** : a thin stick of marking substance in or for a pencil

**⁴lead** \'led\ vb **1** : to cover, line, or weight with lead **2** : to fix (glass) in position with lead **3** : to treat or mix with lead or a lead compound

**lead·en** \'led-ʰn\ adj **1** : made of lead; also : of the color of lead **2** : SLUGGISH, DULL ⟨a ~ lecture⟩

**lead off** vb : OPEN, BEGIN; esp : to bat first in an inning — **lead-off** \'lēd-,ȯf\ n or adj

**¹leaf** \'lēf\ n, pl **leaves** \'lēvz\ **1** : a usu. flat and green outgrowth of a plant stem that is a unit of foliage and functions esp. in photosynthesis; also : FOLIAGE **2** : something (as a page or a flat moving part) that is suggestive of a leaf — **leaf·less** adj — **leafy** adj

**²leaf** vb **1** : to produce leaves **2** : to turn the pages of a book

**leaf·age** \'lē-fij\ n : FOLIAGE

**leafed** \'lēft\ adj : LEAVED

**leaf·hop·per** \'lēf-,hä-pər\ n : any of a family of small leaping insects related to the cicadas that suck the juices of plants

**leaf·let** \'lē-flət\ n **1** : a division of a compound leaf **2** : PAMPHLET, FOLDER

**leaf mold** n : a compost or layer composed chiefly of decayed leaves

**leaf·stalk** \'lēf-,stȯk\ n : PETIOLE

**¹league** \'lēg\ n : a unit of distance equal to about three miles (five kilometers)

**²league** n **1** : an association or alliance (as of nations or sports teams) for a common purpose **2** : CLASS, CATEGORY — **league** vb — **leagu·er** \'lē-gər\ n

**¹leak** \'lēk\ vb **1** : to enter or escape through a leak **2** : to let a substance in or out through an opening **3** : to become or make known ⟨~ed the news⟩

**²leak** n **1** : a crack or hole that accidentally admits a fluid or light or lets it escape; also : something that secretly or accidentally permits the admission or escape of something else **2** : LEAKAGE — **leaky** adj

**leak·age** \'lē-kij\ n **1** : the act of leaking **2** : the thing or amount that leaks

**¹lean** \'lēn\ vb **1** : to bend from a vertical position : INCLINE **2** : to cast one's weight to one side for support **3** : to rely on for support **4** : to incline in opinion, taste, or desire — **lean** n

**²lean** adj **1** : lacking or deficient in flesh and esp. in fat ⟨~ meat⟩ **2** : lacking

richness or productiveness ⟨~ profits⟩ 3
: low in fuel content — **lean·ness** n

**leant** \\'lent\ *chiefly Brit past of* LEAN

**lean–to** \\'lēn-,tü\ n, pl **lean–tos** \-,tüz\
: a wing or extension of a building having
a roof of only one slope; *also* : a rough
shed or shelter with a similar roof

¹**leap** \\'lēp\ vb **leapt** \\'lēpt, 'lept\ *or*
**leaped**; **leap·ing** : to spring free from a
surface or over an obstacle : JUMP

²**leap** n : JUMP

**leap·frog** \\'lēp-,frȯg, -,fräg\ n : a game in
which a player bends down and is vaulted
over by another — **leapfrog** vb

**leap year** n : a year containing 366 days
with February 29 as the extra day

**learn** \\'lərn\ vb **learned** \\'lərnd, 'lərnt\;
**learn·ing** 1 : to gain knowledge, understanding, or skill by study or experience;
*also* : MEMORIZE ⟨~ the poem⟩ 2 : to
find out : ASCERTAIN ⟨~ the truth⟩ —
**learn·er** n

**learn·ed** \\'lər-nəd\ adj : SCHOLARLY, ER-
UDITE — **learn·ed·ly** adv — **learn·ed-
ness** n

**learn·ing** \\'lər-niŋ\ n : KNOWLEDGE, ER-
UDITION

**learning disability** n : any of various
conditions (as dyslexia) that interfere
with a person's ability to learn and so result in impaired functioning (as in language) — **learning disabled** adj

**learnt** \\'lərnt\ *chiefly Brit past and past
part of* LEARN

¹**lease** \\'lēs\ n : a contract transferring real
estate for a term of years or at will usu.
for a specified rent

²**lease** vb **leased**; **leas·ing** [AF *lesser,
lescher* to leave, hand over, lease, fr. L
*laxare* to loosen, fr. *laxus* slack] 1 : to
grant by lease 2 : to hold under a lease
♦ **Synonyms** LET, CHARTER, HIRE, RENT

**lease·hold** \\'lēs-,hōld\ n 1 : a tenure by
lease 2 : land held by lease — **lease-
hold·er** n

**leash** \\'lēsh\ n [ME *lees, leshe,* fr. AF
\*lesche, lesse* prob. fr. *lesser* to leave, let
go] 1 : a line for leading or restraining an
animal 2 : a state of restraint ⟨kept
spending on a tight ~⟩ — **leash** vb

¹**least** \\'lēst\ adj 1 : lowest in importance
or position 2 : smallest in size or degree
3 : SLIGHTEST ⟨the ~ sign of trouble⟩

²**least** n : one that is least

³**least** adv : in the smallest or lowest degree

**least common denominator** n : the least
common multiple of two or more denominators

**least common multiple** n : the smallest
common multiple of two or more numbers

**least·wise** \\'lēst-,wīz\ adv : at least

**leath·er** \\'le-thər\ n : animal skin dressed
for use — **leath·ern** \-thərn\ adj —
**leath·ery** adj

**leath·er·back** \-,bak\ n : the largest existing sea turtle with a flexible leathery
carapace

**leath·er·neck** \-,nek\ n : MARINE

¹**leave** \\'lēv\ vb **left** \\'left\; **leav·ing** 1 : to
allow or cause to remain behind 2 : to
have as a remainder 3 : BEQUEATH 4 : to

let stay without interference 5 : to go
away : depart from 6 : GIVE UP, ABAN-
DON ⟨*left* his wife for another woman⟩

²**leave** n 1 : PERMISSION; *also* : authorized
absence from duty 2 : DEPARTURE

³**leave** vb **leaved**; **leav·ing** : LEAF

**leaved** \\'lēvd\ adj : having leaves

**leav·en** \\'le-vən\ n 1 : a substance (as
yeast) used to produce fermentation (as
in dough) 2 : something that modifies or
lightens

²**leaven** vb : to raise (dough) with a leaven;
*also* : to permeate with a modifying or
vivifying element ⟨lectures ~ed with hu-
mor⟩

**leav·en·ing** \\'le-və-niŋ\ n : LEAVEN

**leaves** pl of LEAF

**leave–tak·ing** \\'lēv-,tā-kiŋ\ n : DEPAR-
TURE, FAREWELL

**leav·ings** \\'lē-viŋz\ n pl : REMNANT, RESI-
DUE ⟨the ~ of a meal⟩

**lech·ery** \\'le-chə-rē\ n : inordinate indulgence in sexual activity — **lech·er** \\'le-
chər\ n — **lech·er·ous** \\'le-chə-rəs\ adj
— **lech·er·ous·ly** adv — **lech·er·ous-
ness** n

**lec·i·thin** \\'le-sə-thən\ n : any of several
waxy phosphorus-containing substances
that are common in animals and plants,
form colloidal solutions in water, and
have emulsifying and wetting properties

**lect** abbr lecture; lecturer

**lec·tern** \\'lek-tərn\ n : a stand to support
a book for a standing reader

**lec·tor** \-tər\ n : one whose chief duty is
to read the lessons in a church service

**lec·ture** \\'lek-chər\ n 1 : a discourse giv-
en before an audience esp. for instruction 2 : REPRIMAND — **lec·ture** vb —
**lec·tur·er** n — **lec·ture·ship** n

**led** past and past part of LEAD

**LED** \el-(,)ē-'dē\ n [*l*ight-*e*mitting *d*iode]
: a semiconductor diode that emits light
when a voltage is applied to it and is used
esp. for electronic displays

**le·der·ho·sen** \\'lā-dər-,hōz-ᵊn\ n pl
: leather shorts often with suspenders
worn esp. in Bavaria

**ledge** \\'lej\ n [ME *legge* bar of a gate] 1
: a shelflike projection from a top or an
edge 2 : REEF

**led·ger** \\'le-jər\ n : a book containing accounts to which debits and credits are
transferred in final form

**lee** \\'lē\ n 1 : a protecting shelter 2 : the
side (as of a ship) that is sheltered from
the wind — **lee** adj

**leech** \\'lēch\ n 1 : any of various bloodsucking segmented usu. freshwater
worms that are related to the earthworms
and have a sucker at each end 2 : a hanger-
on who seeks gain

**leek** \\'lēk\ n : an onionlike herb grown
for its mildly pungent leaves and stalk

**leer** \\'lir\ n : a suggestive, knowing, or
malicious look — **leer** vb

**leery** \\'lir-ē\ adj : SUSPICIOUS, WARY

**lees** \\'lēz\ n pl : DREGS ⟨~ in the bottle⟩

¹**lee·ward** \\'lē-wərd, 'lü-ərd\ n : the lee side

²**leeward** adj : situated away from the
wind

**lee·way** \\'lē-,wā\ n 1 : lateral movement

of a ship when under way **2** : an allowable margin of freedom or variation

**¹left** \'left\ *adj* [ME, fr. OE, weak; fr. the left hand's being the weaker in most individuals] **1** : of, relating to, or being the side of the body in which the heart is mostly located; *also* : located nearer to this side than to the right **2** *often cap* : of, adhering to, or constituted by the political left — **left** *adv*

**²left** *n* **1** : the left hand; *also* : the side or part that is on or toward the left side **2** *often cap* : those professing political views marked by desire to reform the established order and usu. to give greater freedom to the common people — **left·ward** \-wərd\ *adv or adj*

**³left** *past and past part of* LEAVE

**left-hand** *adj* **1** : situated on the left **2** : LEFT-HANDED

**left-hand·ed** \'left-'han-dəd\ *adj* **1** : using the left hand habitually or more easily than the right **2** : designed for or done with the left hand **3** : INSINCERE, BACK-HANDED ⟨a ∼ compliment⟩ **4** : COUNTERCLOCKWISE — **left-handed** *adv* **left-hand·ed·ness** *n* — **left-hand·er** \-dər\ *n*

**left·ism** \'lef-,ti-zəm\ *n* **1** : the principles and views of the left **2** : advocacy of the doctrines of the left — **left·ist** \-tist\ *n or adj*

**left·over** \'left-,ō-vər\ *n* : something that remains unused or unconsumed

**lefty** \'lef-tē\ *n, pl* **left·ies** **1** : a left-handed person **2** : an advocate of leftism

**¹leg** \'leg\ *n* **1** : a limb of an animal used esp. for supporting the body and in walking; *also* : the part of the vertebrate leg between knee and foot **2** : something resembling or analogous to an animal leg ⟨table ∼⟩ **3** : the part of an article of clothing that covers the leg **4** : a portion of a trip **5** *pl* : long-term appeal or interest ⟨a musical that has ∼s⟩ — **leg·ged** \'le-gəd\ *adj* — **leg·less** *adj*

**²leg** *vb* **legged**; **leg·ging** : to use the legs in walking or esp. in running

**³leg** *abbr* **1** legal **2** legislative; legislature

**leg·a·cy** \'le-gə-sē\ *n, pl* **-cies** : INHERITANCE; *also* : something that has come from a predecessor or the past

**le·gal** \'lē-gəl\ *adj* **1** : of or relating to law or lawyers **2** : LAWFUL; *also* : STATUTORY **3** : enforced in courts of law — **le·gal·i·ty** \li-'ga-lə-tē\ *n* — **le·gal·ize** \'lē-gə-,līz\ *vb* — **le·gal·ly** *adv*

**le·gal·ese** \,lē-gə-'lēz\ *n* : the specialized language of the legal profession

**le·gal·ism** \'lē-gə-,li-zəm\ *n* **1** : strict, literal, or excessive conformity to the law or to a religious or moral code **2** : a legal term — **le·gal·is·tic** \,lē-gə-'lis-tik\ *adj*

**leg·ate** \'le-gət\ *n* : an official representative

**leg·a·tee** \,le-gə-'tē\ *n* : a person to whom a legacy is bequeathed

**le·ga·tion** \li-'gā-shən\ *n* **1** : a diplomatic mission headed by a minister **2** : the official residence and office of a minister in a foreign country

**le·ga·to** \li-'gä-tō\ *adv or adj* [It, lit., tied]

: in a smooth and connected manner (as of music)

**leg·end** \'le-jənd\ *n* [ME *legende*, fr. AF & ML; AF *legende*, fr. ML *legenda*, fr. L *legere* to read] **1** : a story coming down from the past; *esp* : one popularly accepted as historical though not verifiable **2** : an inscription on an object; *also* : CAPTION **3** : an explanatory list of the symbols on a map or chart

**leg·end·ary** \'le-jən-,der-ē\ *adj* **1** : of, relating to, or characteristic of a legend **2** : FAMOUS ⟨∼ actors⟩ — **leg·en·dari·ly** \,le-jən-'der-ə-lē\ *adv*

**leg·er·de·main** \,le-jər-də-'mān\ *n* [ME, fr. MF *leger de main* light of hand] : SLEIGHT OF HAND

**leg·ging** *or* **leg·gin** \'le-gən, gin\ *n* : a covering for the leg; *also* : TIGHTS

**leg·gy** \'le-gē\ *adj* **leg·gi·er; -est** **1** : having unusually long legs **2** : having long and attractive legs **3** : SPINDLY — used of a plant

**leg·horn** \'leg-,hȯrn, 'le-gərn\ *n* **1** : a fine plaited straw; *also* : a hat made of this straw **2** : any of a Mediterranean breed of small hardy chickens

**leg·i·ble** \'le-jə-bəl\ *adj* : capable of being read : CLEAR — **leg·i·bil·i·ty** \,le-jə-'bi-lə-tē\ *n* — **leg·i·bly** \'le-jə-blē\ *adv*

**¹le·gion** \'lē-jən\ *n* **1** : a unit of the Roman army comprising 3000 to 6000 soldiers **2** : MULTITUDE ⟨∼s of fans⟩ **3** : an association of ex-servicemen — **le·gion·ary** \-jə-,ner-ē\ *n* — **le·gion·naire** \,lē-jə-'nar\ *n*

**²legion** *adj* : MANY, NUMEROUS

**Legionnaires' disease** *also* **Legionnaire's disease** \-'nerz-\ *n* : a lobar pneumonia caused by a bacterium

**legis** *abbr* legislation; legislative; legislature

**leg·is·late** \'le-jəs-,lāt\ *vb* **-lat·ed; -lat·ing** : to make or enact laws; *also* : to bring about by legislation — **leg·is·la·tor** \-,lā-tər\ *n*

**leg·is·la·tion** \,le-jəs-'lā-shən\ *n* **1** : the action of legislating **2** : laws made by a legislative body

**leg·is·la·tive** \'le-jəs-,lā-tiv\ *adj* **1** : having the power of legislating **2** : of or relating to a legislature or legislation

**leg·is·la·ture** \'le-jəs-,lā-chər\ *n* : an organized body of persons having the authority to make laws

**le·git** \li-'jit\ *adj, slang* : LEGITIMATE

**le·git·i·mate** \li-'ji-tə-mət\ *adj* **1** : lawfully begotten **2** : GENUINE **3** : LAWFUL **4** : conforming to recognized principles or accepted rules or standards — **le·git·i·ma·cy** \-mə-sē\ *n* — **le·git·i·mate·ly** *adv*

**²le·git·i·mate** \-,māt\ *vb* : to make legitimate

**le·git·i·mise** *Brit var of* LEGITIMIZE

**le·git·i·mize** \li-'ji-tə-,mīz\ *vb* **-mized; -miz·ing** : LEGITIMATE

**leg·man** \'leg-,man\ *n* **1** : a reporter assigned usu. to gather information **2** : an assistant who gathers information and runs errands

**le·gume** \'le-,gyüm, li-'gyüm\ *n* [F] **1** : any of a large family of plants having fruits that are dry pods and split when ripe and including important food and forage plants (as beans and clover); *also* : the part (as seeds or pods) of a legume used as food **2** : the pod of a legume — **le·gu·mi·nous** \li-ˈgyü-mə-nəs\ *adj*

**¹lei** \ˈlā, ˈlā-ˌē\ *n* : a wreath or necklace usu. of flowers

**²lei** \ˈlā\ *pl of* LEU

**lei·sure** \ˈlē-zhər, ˈle-, ˈlā-\ *n* **1** : time free from work or duties **2** : EASE; *also* : CONVENIENCE ⟨read it at your ∼⟩ ♦ *Synonyms* RELAXATION, REST, REPOSE — **lei·sure·ly** *adj or adv*

**leit·mo·tif** *also* **leit·mo·tiv** \ˈlīt-mō-ˌtēf\ *n* [G *Leitmotiv*, fr. *leiten* to lead + *Motiv* motive] : a dominant recurring theme

**lek** \ˈlek\ *n, pl* **leks** *or* **le·ke** *or* **lekë** \ˈle-kə\ — see MONEY table

**lem·ming** \ˈle-miŋ\ *n* [Norw] : any of various short-tailed rodents found mostly in northern regions and noted for recurrent mass migrations

**lem·on** \ˈle-mən\ *n* **1** : an acid yellow usu. nearly oblong citrus fruit; *also* : a citrus tree that bears lemons **2** : something (as an automobile) unsatisfactory or defective — **lem·ony** *adj*

**lem·on·ade** \ˌle-mə-ˈnād\ *n* : a beverage of lemon juice, sugar, and water

**lemon curd** *n* : a custard made with lemon juice, butter, sugar, and eggs

**lem·on·grass** \ˈle-mən-ˌgras\ *n* : a tropical Asian grass grown for its lemon-scented foliage used as a seasoning

**lem·pi·ra** \lem-ˈpir-ə\ *n* — see MONEY table

**le·mur** \ˈlē-mər\ *n* : any of various arboreal primates largely of Madagascar that have large eyes, very soft woolly fur, and a long furry tail

**Len·a·pe** \ˈle-nə-pē, lə-ˈnä-pē\ *n, pl* **Lenape** *or* **Lenapes** : DELAWARE

**lend** \ˈlend\ *vb* **lent** \ˈlent\; **lend·ing 1** : to give for temporary use on condition that the same or its equivalent be returned **2** : AFFORD, FURNISH **3** : ACCOMMODATE — **lend·er** *n*

**lend–lease** \-ˈlēs\ *n* : the transfer of goods and services to an ally to aid in a common cause with payment made by a return of the items or their use in the cause or by a similar transfer of other goods and services

**length** \ˈleŋth\ *n* **1** : the longer or longest dimension of an object; *also* : a measured distance **2** : duration or extent in time or space **3** : the length of something taken as a unit of measure **4** : a single piece of a series of pieces that may be joined together ⟨a ∼ of pipe⟩ — **at length 1** : in full **2** : FINALLY

**length·en** \ˈleŋ-thən\ *vb* : to make or become longer ♦ *Synonyms* EXTEND, ELONGATE, PROLONG, PROTRACT

**length·wise** \ˈleŋth-ˌwīz\ *adv* : in the direction of the length — **lengthwise** *adj*

**lengthy** \ˈleŋ-thē\ *adj* **length·i·er; -est 1** : protracted excessively **2** : EXTENDED, LONG ⟨a ∼ journey⟩

**le·nient** \ˈlē-nē-ənt, -nyənt\ *adj* : of mild and tolerant disposition or effect ♦ *Syn-*

*onyms* INDULGENT, FORBEARING, MERCIFUL, TOLERANT — **le·ni·en·cy** \ˈlē-nē-ən-sē, -nyən-sē\ *n* — **le·ni·ent·ly** *adv*

**len·i·tive** \ˈle-nə-tiv\ *adj* : alleviating pain or harshness

**len·i·ty** \ˈle-nə-tē\ *n* : LENIENCY

**lens** \ˈlenz\ *n* [L *lent-, lens* lentil; so called fr. the shape of a convex lens] **1** : a curved piece of glass or plastic used singly or combined in an optical instrument for forming an image; *also* : a device for focusing radiation other than light **2** : a transparent body in the eye that focuses light rays on receptors at the back of the eye

**Lent** \ˈlent\ *n* : a 40-day period of penitence and fasting observed from Ash Wednesday to Easter by many churches — **Lent·en** \ˈlen-t³n\ *adj*

**len·til** \ˈlen-t³l\ *n* : a Eurasian annual legume grown for its flat edible seeds and for fodder; *also* : its seed

**Leo** \ˈlē-ō\ *n* [L, lit., lion] **1** : a zodiacal constellation between Cancer and Virgo usu. pictured as a lion **2** : the 5th sign of the zodiac in astrology; *also* : one born under this sign

**le·one** \lē-ˈōn\ *n, pl* **leones** *or* **leone** — see MONEY table

**le·o·nine** \ˈlē-ə-ˌnīn\ *adj* : of, relating to, or resembling a lion

**leop·ard** \ˈle-pərd\ *n* : a large usu. tawny and black-spotted cat of southern Asia and Africa

**le·o·tard** \ˈlē-ə-ˌtärd\ *n* : a close-fitting garment worn esp. by dancers and for exercise

**lep·er** \ˈle-pər\ *n* **1** : a person affected with leprosy **2** : OUTCAST

**lep·re·chaun** \ˈle-prə-ˌkän\ *n* : a mischievous elf of Irish folklore

**lep·ro·sy** \ˈle-prə-sē\ *n* : a chronic bacterial disease marked esp. if not treated by slow-growing swellings with deformity and loss of sensation of affected parts — **lep·rous** \-prəs\ *adj*

**lep·tin** \ˈlep-tən\ *n* : a hormone that is produced by fat-containing cells and plays a role in body weight regulation

**lep·ton** \lep-ˈtän\ *n, pl* **lep·ta** \-ˈtä\ : a former monetary unit equal to ¹/₁₀₀ drachma

**les·bi·an** \ˈlez-bē-ən\ *n* [fr. the reputed homosexual group associated with the poet Sappho of Lesbos] : a woman who is a homosexual — **lesbian** *adj* — **les·bi·an·ism** \-ə-ˌni-zəm\ *n*

**lèse ma·jes·té** *or* **lese maj·es·ty** \ˈläz-ˈma-jə-stē, ˈlez-, ˈlēz-\ *n* [MF *lese majesté*, fr. L *laesa majestas*, lit., injured majesty] : an offense violating the dignity of a sovereign

**le·sion** \ˈlē-zhən\ *n* : an abnormal structural change in the body due to injury or disease; *esp* : one clearly marked off from healthy tissue around it

**¹less** \ˈles\ *adj, comparative of* ¹LITTLE **1** : FEWER ⟨∼ than six⟩ **2** : of lower rank, degree, or importance **3** : SMALLER; *also* : more limited in quantity ⟨∼ than a year⟩

**²less** *adv, comparative of* ²LITTLE : to a lesser extent or degree

³**less** *n, pl* **less 1** : a smaller portion **2** : something of less importance

⁴**less** *prep* : diminished by : MINUS ⟨list price ~ the discount⟩

-**less** \ləs\ *adj suffix* **1** . destitute of : not having ⟨child*less*⟩ **2** : unable to be acted on or to act (in a specified way) ⟨daunt*less*⟩

**les·see** \le-'sē\ *n* : a tenant under a lease

**less·en** \'le-s³n\ *vb* : to make or become less ♦ **Synonyms** DECREASE, DIMINISH, DWINDLE, ABATE

**less·er** \'le-sər\ *adj, comparative of* ¹LITTLE : of less size, quality, or significance

**les·son** \'le-s³n\ *n* **1** : a passage from sacred writings read in a service of worship **2** : a reading or exercise to be studied by a pupil; *also* : something to be learned **3** : a period of instruction **4** : an instructive example

**les·sor** \'le-,sȯr, le-'sȯr\ *n* : one who conveys property by a lease

**lest** \'lest\ *conj* : for fear that

¹**let** \'let\ *n* [ME *lette*, fr. *letten* to delay, hinder, fr. OE *lettan*] **1** : HINDRANCE, OBSTACLE **2** : a shot or point in racket games that does not count

²**let** *vb* **let; let·ting** [ME *leten*, fr. OE *lǣtan*] **1** : to cause to : MAKE ⟨~ it be known⟩ **2** : RENT, LEASE; *also* : to assign esp. after bids **3** : ALLOW, PERMIT ⟨~ me go⟩

-**let** *n suffix* **1** : small one ⟨book*let*⟩ **2** : article worn on ⟨wrist*let*⟩

**let·down** \'let-,daủn\ *n* **1** : DISAPPOINTMENT **2** : a slackening of effort

**le·thal** \'lē-thəl\ *adj* : DEADLY, FATAL ⟨~ weapons⟩ — **le·thal·ly** *adv*

**leth·ar·gy** \'le-thər-jē\ *n* **1** : abnormal drowsiness **2** : the quality or state of being lazy or indifferent ♦ **Synonyms** LANGUOR, LASSITUDE, TORPOR — **le·thar·gic** \li-'thär-jik\ *adj*

**let on** *vb* **1** : REVEAL **1** ⟨knows a lot more than he *lets on*⟩ **2** : PRETEND

¹**let·ter** \'le-tər\ *n* **1** : a symbol that stands for a speech sound and constitutes a unit of an alphabet **2** : a written or printed communication **3** *pl* : LITERATURE; *also* : LEARNING **4** : the literal meaning ⟨the ~ of the law⟩ **5** : a single piece of type

²**letter** *vb* : to mark with letters : INSCRIBE — **let·ter·er** *n*

**letter bomb** *n* : an explosive device concealed in an envelope and mailed to the intended victim

**let·ter·boxed** \'le-tər-,bäkst\ *adj* : being a video recording formatted to display a frame size proportional to a standard theater screen

**letter carrier** *n* : a person who delivers mail

**let·ter·head** \'le-tər-,hed\ *n* : stationery with a printed or engraved heading; *also* : the heading itself

**let·ter-per·fect** \,le-tər-'pər-fikt\ *adj* : correct to the smallest detail

**let·ter·press** \'le-tər-,pres\ *n* : printing done directly by impressing the paper on an inked raised surface

**letters of marque** \-'märk\ : a license granted to a private person by a govern-

ment to fit out an armed ship to capture enemy shipping

**letters patent** *n pl* : a written grant from a government to a person in a form readily open for inspection by all

**let·tuce** \'le-təs\ *n* [ME *letuse*, fr. AF, prob. fr. pl. of *letue* lettuce plant, fr. L *lactuca*, fr. *lac* milk; fr. its milky juice] : a garden composite plant with crisp leaves used esp. in salads

**let-up** \'let-,əp\ *n* : a lessening of effort

**leu** \'leủ\ *n, pl* **lei** \'lā\ — see MONEY table

**leu·kae·mia** *chiefly Brit var of* LEUKEMIA

**leu·ke·mia** \lü-'kē-mē-ə\ *n* : a malignant disease characterized by an abnormal increase in the number of white blood cells in the blood-forming tissues — **leu·ke·mic** \-mik\ *adj or n*

**leu·ko·cyte** \'lü-kə-,sīt\ *n* : WHITE BLOOD CELL

**lev** \'lef\ *n, pl* **le·va** \'le-və\ — see MONEY table

**Lev** *or* **Levit** *abbr* Leviticus

¹**le·vee** \'le-vē\ *n* [F *lever* act of arising] : a reception held by or for a person of distinction

²**lev·ee** \'le-vē\ *n* : an embankment to prevent or confine flooding; *also* : a river landing place

¹**lev·el** \'le-vəl\ *n* **1** : a device for establishing a horizontal line or plane **2** : horizontal condition **3** : a horizontal position, line, or surface often taken as an index of altitude; *also* : a flat area of ground **4** : height, position, rank, or size in a scale

²**level** *vb* **-eled** *or* **-elled; -el·ing** *or* **-el·ling 1** : to make flat or level; *also* : to come to a level **2** : AIM, DIRECT **3** : EQUALIZE **4** : RAZE — **lev·el·er** *n*

³**level** *adj* **1** : having a flat even surface **2** : HORIZONTAL **3** : of the same height or rank; *also* : UNIFORM **4** : steady and cool in judgment ⟨keep a ~ head when in danger⟩ — **lev·el·ly** *adv* — **lev·el·ness** *n*

**lev·el·head·ed** \,le-vəl-'he-dəd\ *adj* : having or showing sound judgment : SENSIBLE ⟨a ~ decision⟩

**le·ver** \'le-vər, 'lē-\ *n* **1** : a bar used for prying or dislodging something; *also* : a means for achieving one's purpose **2** : a rigid piece turning about an axis and used for transmitting and changing force and motion

**le·ver·age** \'le-vrij, 'lē-, -və-rij\ *n* : the action or mechanical effect of a lever

**le·vi·a·than** \li-'vī-ə-thən\ *n* **1** : a large sea animal **2** : something large or formidable ⟨the ocean liner is a ~⟩

**lev·i·tate** \'le-və-,tāt\ *vb* **-tat·ed; -tat·ing** : to rise or cause to rise in the air in seeming defiance of gravitation — **lev·i·ta·tion** \,le-və-'tā-shən\ *n*

**Le·vit·i·cus** \li-'vi-tə-kəs\ *n* — see BIBLE table

**lev·i·ty** \'le-və-tē\ *n* : lack of seriousness ♦ **Synonyms** LIGHTNESS, FLIPPANCY, FRIVOLITY

**le·vo·do·pa** \,le-və-'dō-pə\ *n* : L-DOPA

¹**levy** \'le-vē\ *n, pl* **lev·ies 1** : the imposition or collection of an assessment; *also* : an amount levied **2** : the enlistment or

conscription of men for military service; *also* : troops raised by levy

²**levy** *vb* **lev·ied; levy·ing** **1** : to impose or collect by legal authority ⟨~ taxes⟩ **2** : to enlist for military service **3** : WAGE ⟨~ war⟩ **4** : to seize property

**lewd** \'lüd\ *adj* [ME *lewed* vulgar, fr. OE *lǣwede* lay, ignorant] : sexually unchaste; *also* : OBSCENE, VULGAR — **lewd·ly** *adv* — **lewd·ness** *n*

**lex·i·cog·ra·phy** \ˌlek-sə-'kä-grə-fē\ *n* **1** : the editing or making of a dictionary **2** : the principles and practices of dictionary making — **lex·i·cog·ra·pher** \-fər\ *n* — **lex·i·co·graph·i·cal** \-kō-'gra-fi-kəl\ *or* **lex·i·co·graph·ic** \-fik\ *adj*

**lex·i·con** \'lek-sə-ˌkän\ *n, pl* **lex·i·ca** \-si-kə\ *or* **lexicons** **1** : DICTIONARY **2** : the vocabulary of a language, speaker, or subject

**lg** *abbr* **1** large **2** long

**LH** *abbr* **1** left hand **2** lower half

**li** *abbr* link

**Li** *symbol* lithium

**LI** *abbr* Long Island

**li·a·bil·i·ty** \ˌlī-ə-'bi-lə-tē\ *n, pl* **-ties** **1** : the quality or state of being liable **2** *pl* : DEBTS **3** : DISADVANTAGE

**li·a·ble** \'lī-ə-bəl\ *adj* **1** : legally obligated : RESPONSIBLE **2** : LIKELY, APT ⟨~ to fall⟩ **3** : SUSCEPTIBLE ⟨~ to disease⟩

**li·ai·son** \'lē-ə-ˌzän, lē-'ā-\ *n* [F] **1** : a close bond : INTERRELATIONSHIP **2** : an illicit sexual relationship **3** : communication for mutual understanding (as between parts of an armed force); *also* : one that carries on a liaison

**li·ar** \'lī(-ə)r\ *n* : a person who lies

¹**lib** \'lib\ *n* : LIBERATION

²**lib** *abbr* **1** liberal **2** librarian; library

**li·ba·tion** \lī-'bā-shən\ *n* **1** : an act of pouring a liquid as a sacrifice (as to a god); *also* : the liquid poured **2** : DRINK

¹**li·bel** \'lī-bəl\ *n* [ME, written declaration, fr. AF, fr. L *libellus*, dim. of *liber* book] **1** : a spoken or written statement or a representation that gives an unjustly unfavorable impression of a person or thing **2** : the action or crime of publishing a libel — **li·bel·ous** *or* **li·bel·lous** \-bə-ləs\ *adj*

²**libel** *vb* **-beled** *or* **-belled; -bel·ing** *or* **-bel·ling** : to make or publish a libel — **li·bel·er** *n* — **li·bel·ist** *n*

¹**lib·er·al** \'li-brəl, -bə-rəl\ *adj* [ME, fr. AF, fr. L *liberalis* suitable for a freeman, generous, fr. *liber* free] **1** : of, relating to, or based on the liberal arts **2** : GENEROUS, BOUNTIFUL ⟨a ~ serving⟩ **3** : not literal **4** : not narrow in opinion or judgment : TOLERANT; *also* : not orthodox **5** : not conservative — **lib·er·al·i·ty** \ˌli-bə-'ra-lə-tē\ *n* — **lib·er·al·i·za·tion** \ˌli-brə-lə-'zā-shən, -bə-rə-\ *n* — **lib·er·al·ize** \'li-brə-ˌlīz, -bə-rə-\ *vb* — **lib·er·al·ly** *adv*

²**liberal** *n* : a person who holds liberal views

**liberal arts** *n pl* : the studies (as language, philosophy, history, literature, or abstract science) in a college or university intended to provide chiefly general knowledge and to develop the general intellectual capacities

**lib·er·al·ism** \'li-brə-ˌli-zəm, -bə-rə-\ *n* : liberal principles and theories

**lib·er·ate** \'li-bə-ˌrāt\ *vb* **-at·ed; -at·ing** **1** : to free from bondage or restraint; *also* : to raise to equal rights and status **2** : to free (as a gas) from combination — **lib·er·a·tion** \ˌli-bə-'rā-shən\ *n* — **lib·er·a·tor** \'li-bə-ˌrā-tər\ *n*

**liberated** *adj* : freed from or opposed to traditional social and sexual attitudes or roles ⟨a ~ marriage⟩

**lib·er·tar·i·an** \ˌli-bər-'ter-ē-ən\ *n* **1** : an advocate of the doctrine of free will **2** : one who upholds the principles of unrestricted liberty

**lib·er·tine** \'li-bər-ˌtēn\ *n* : a person who leads a dissolute life

**lib·er·ty** \'li-bər-tē\ *n, pl* **-ties** **1** : FREEDOM **2** : an action going beyond normal limits; *esp* : FAMILIARITY **3** : a short leave from naval duty

**li·bid·i·nous** \lə-'bi-də-nəs\ *adj* **1** : LASCIVIOUS **2** : LIBIDINAL

**li·bi·do** \lə-'bē-dō\ *n, pl* **-dos** [NL, fr. L, desire, lust] **1** : psychic energy derived from basic biological urges **2** : sexual drive — **li·bid·i·nal** \lə-'bi-də-nəl\ *adj*

**Li·bra** \'lē-brə\ *n* [L, lit., scales] **1** : a zodiacal constellation between Virgo and Scorpio usu. pictured as a balance scale **2** : the 7th sign of the zodiac in astrology; *also* : one born under this sign

**li·brar·i·an** \lī-'brer-ē-ən\ *n* : a specialist in the management of a library

**li·brary** \'lī-ˌbrer-ē\ *n, pl* **-brar·ies** **1** : a place in which books and related materials are kept for use but not for sale **2** : a collection of books

**li·bret·to** \lə-'bre-tō\ *n, pl* **-tos** *or* **-ti** \-tē\ [It, dim. of *libro* book, fr. L *liber*] : the text esp. of an opera — **li·bret·tist** \-tist\ *n*

**lice** *pl of* LOUSE

**li·cense** *or* **li·cence** \'lī-s°ns\ *n* **1** : permission to act **2** : a permission granted by authority to engage in an activity **3** : a document, plate, or tag providing proof of a license **4** : freedom used irresponsibly — **license** *vb*

**licensed practical nurse** *n* : a specially trained person who is licensed (as by a state) to provide routine care for the sick

**li·cens·ee** \ˌlī-s°n-'sē\ *n* : a licensed person

**licente** *pl of* SENTE

**li·cen·ti·ate** \lī-'sen-chē-ət\ *n* : one licensed to practice a profession

**li·cen·tious** \lī-'sen-chəs\ *adj* : LEWD, LASCIVIOUS — **li·cen·tious·ly** *adv* — **li·cen·tious·ness** *n*

**lichee** *var of* LITCHI

**li·chen** \'lī-kən\ *n* : any of various complex plantlike organisms made up of an alga and a fungus growing as a unit on a solid surface — **li·chen·ous** *adj*

**lic·it** \'li-sət\ *adj* : LAWFUL

¹**lick** \'lik\ *vb* **1** : to draw the tongue over; *also* : to flicker over like a tongue **2** : THRASH; *also* : DEFEAT

²**lick** *n* **1** : a stroke of the tongue **2** : a small amount **3** : a hasty careless effort

4 : BLOW 5 : a natural deposit of salt that animals lick

**lick·e·ty–split** \ˌli-kə-tē-ˈsplit\ adv : at great speed

**lick·spit·tle** \ˈlik-ˌspi-t⁹l\ n : a fawning subordinate : TOADY

**lic·o·rice** \ˈli-kə-rish, -rəs\ n [ME, tr. AF licoris, fr. LL liquiritia, alter. of L glycyrrhiza, fr. Gk glykyrrhiza, fr. glykys sweet + rhiza root] 1 : the dried root of a European leguminous plant; also : an extract from it used esp. as a flavoring and in medicine 2 : a candy flavored with licorice 3 : a plant yielding licorice

**lid** \ˈlid\ n 1 : a movable cover 2 : EYELID 3 : something that confines or suppresses — **lid·ded** \ˈli-dəd\ adj

**li·do** \ˈlē-dō\ n, pl **lidos** : a fashionable beach resort

**¹lie** \ˈlī\ vb **lay** \ˈlā\; **lain** \ˈlān\; **ly·ing** \ˈlī-iŋ\ 1 : to be in, stay at rest in, or assume a horizontal position; also : to be in a helpless or defenseless state 2 : EXTEND ⟨our route lay to the west⟩ 3 : to occupy a certain relative position 4 : to have an effect esp. through mere presence

**²lie** n : the position in which something lies

**³lie** vb **lied**; **ly·ing** \ˈlī-iŋ\ : to tell a lie

**⁴lie** n : an untrue statement made with intent to deceive

**lied** \ˈlēt\ n, pl **lie·der** \ˈlē-dər\ [G] : a German song esp. of the 19th century

**lie detector** n : a polygraph for detecting physiological evidence of the tension that accompanies lying

**lief** \ˈlēv, ˈlēf\ adv : GLADLY, WILLINGLY

**¹liege** \ˈlēj\ adj : LOYAL, FAITHFUL

**²liege** n 1 : VASSAL 2 : a feudal superior

**lien** \ˈlēn, ˈlē-ən\ n : a legal claim on the property of another for the satisfaction of a debt or duty

**lieu** \ˈlü\ n, archaic : PLACE, STEAD — **in lieu of** : in the place of

**lieut** abbr lieutenant

**lieu·ten·ant** \lü-ˈte-nənt\ n [ME, fr. AF lieu tenant, fr. liu, lieu place + tenant holding, fr. tenir to hold, fr. L tenēre] 1 : a representative of another in the performance of duty 2 : FIRST LIEUTENANT; also : SECOND LIEUTENANT 3 : a commissioned officer in the navy ranking next below a lieutenant commander — **lieu·ten·an·cy** \-nən-sē\ n

**lieutenant colonel** n : a commissioned officer (as in the army) ranking next below a colonel

**lieutenant commander** n : a commissioned officer in the navy ranking next below a commander

**lieutenant general** n : a commissioned officer (as in the army) ranking next below a general

**lieutenant governor** n : a deputy or subordinate governor

**lieutenant junior grade** n, pl **lieutenants junior grade** : a commissioned officer in the navy ranking next below a lieutenant

**life** \ˈlīf\ n, pl **lives** \ˈlīvz\ 1 : the quality that distinguishes a vital and functional being from a dead body or inanimate matter; also : a state of an organism characterized esp. by capacity for metabolism, growth, reaction to stimuli, and reproduction 2 : the physical and mental experiences of an individual 3 : BIOGRAPHY 4 : a specific phase or period ⟨adult ∼⟩ 5 : the period from birth to death; also : a sentence of imprisonment for the remainder of a person's life 6 : a way of living 7 : PERSON ⟨many lives were lost in the fire⟩ 8 : ANIMATION, SPIRIT ⟨danced without ∼⟩ 9 : living beings ⟨forest ∼⟩ 10 : animate activity ⟨signs of ∼⟩ 11 : one providing interest and vigor ⟨∼ of the party⟩ — **life·less** adj — **life·like** adj

**life·blood** \ˈlīf-ˌbləd\ n : a basic source of strength and vitality

**life·boat** \-ˌbōt\ n : a sturdy boat designed for use in saving lives at sea

**life·guard** \-ˌgärd\ n : a usu. expert swimmer employed to safeguard bathers

**life·line** \-ˌlīn\ n 1 : a line to which persons may cling for safety 2 : something considered vital for survival

**life·long** \-ˌlȯŋ\ adj : continuing through life

**life preserver** n : a buoyant device designed to save a person from drowning

**lif·er** \ˈlī-fər\ n 1 : a person sentenced to life imprisonment 2 : a person who makes a career in the armed forces

**life raft** n : a raft for use by people forced into the water

**life·sav·ing** \ˈlīf-ˌsā-viŋ\ n : the skill or practice of saving or protecting lives esp. of drowning persons — **life·sav·er** \-ˌsā-vər\ n

**life science** n : a branch of science (as biology, medicine, and sometimes anthropology or sociology) that deals with living organisms and life processes — usu. used in pl. — **life scientist** n

**¹life·style** \ˈlīf-ˌstī(-ə)l\ n : a way of living

**²lifestyle** adj : associated with, reflecting, or promoting an enhanced or more desirable lifestyle

**life·time** \-ˌtīm\ n : the duration of an individual's existence

**life·work** \-ˈwərk\ n : the entire or principal work of one's lifetime; also : a work extending over a lifetime

**life·world** \-ˌwər(-ə)ld\ n : the total of an individual's physical surroundings and everyday experiences

**LIFO** abbr last in, first out

**¹lift** \ˈlift\ vb 1 : RAISE, ELEVATE; also : RISE, ASCEND 2 : to put an end to : STOP ⟨∼ a ban⟩ 3 : to pay off ⟨∼ a mortgage⟩ — **lift·er** n

**²lift** n 1 : LOAD 2 : the action or an instance of lifting 3 : HELP; also : a ride along one's way 4 : RISE, ADVANCE 5 chiefly Brit : ELEVATOR 6 : an elevation of the spirits 7 : the upward force that is developed by a moving airfoil and that opposes the pull of gravity

**lift·off** \-ˌȯf\ n : a vertical takeoff (as by a rocket)

**lift truck** n : a small truck for lifting and transporting loads

**lig·a·ment** \ˈli-gə-mənt\ n : a band of

tough fibrous tissue that holds bones together or supports an organ in place

**li·gate** \'lī-ˌgāt\ vb **li·gat·ed; li·gat·ing** : to tie with a ligature — **li·ga·tion** \lī-'gā-shən\ n

**lig·a·ture** \'li-gə-ˌchùr, -chər\ n 1 : something that binds or ties; also : a thread used in surgery esp. for tying blood vessels 2 : a printed or written character consisting of two or more letters or characters (as æ) united

**¹light** \'līt\ n 1 : something that makes vision possible : electromagnetic radiation visible to the human eye; also : the sensation aroused by stimulation of the visual sense organs 2 : DAYLIGHT 3 : a source of light (as a candle) 4 : ENLIGHTENMENT; also : TRUTH 5 : public knowledge ⟨facts brought to ∼⟩ 6 : a particular aspect presented to view ⟨saw the matter in a different ∼⟩ 7 : WINDOW 8 pl : STANDARDS ⟨according to his ∼s⟩ 9 : CELEBRITY 10 : LIGHTHOUSE, BEACON; also : TRAFFIC LIGHT 11 : a flame for lighting something

**²light** adj 1 : having light : BRIGHT 2 : PALE 2 ⟨∼ blue⟩ — **light·ness** n

**³light** vb lit \'lit\ or **light·ed; light·ing** 1 : to make or become light 2 : to cause to burn : BURN 3 : to conduct with a light 4 : ILLUMINATE

**⁴light** adj 1 : not heavy 2 : not serious ⟨∼ reading⟩ 3 : SCANTY ⟨∼ rain⟩ 4 : easily disturbed ⟨a ∼ sleeper⟩ 5 : GENTLE ⟨a ∼ blow⟩ 6 : easily endurable ⟨a ∼ cold⟩; also : requiring little effort ⟨∼ exercise⟩ 7 : SWIFT, NIMBLE 8 : FRIVOLOUS 9 : DIZZY 10 : made with lower calorie content or less of some ingredient than usual ⟨∼ salad dressing⟩ 11 : producing goods for direct consumption by the consumer ⟨∼ industry⟩ — **light·ly** adv — **light·ness** n

**⁵light** adv 1 : LIGHTLY 2 : with little baggage ⟨travel ∼⟩

**⁶light** vb lit \'lit\ or **light·ed; light·ing** 1 : SETTLE, ALIGHT 2 : to fall unexpectedly 3 : HAPPEN ⟨∼ed on a solution⟩

**light bulb** n 1 : a lamp in which an electrically heated filament emits light 2 : FLUORESCENT LAMP

**light–emitting diode** n : LED

**¹light·en** \'lī-tᵊn\ vb 1 : ILLUMINATE, BRIGHTEN 2 : to give out flashes of lightning

**²lighten** vb 1 : to relieve of a burden 2 : GLADDEN 3 : to become lighter

**lighten up** vb : to take things less seriously ⟨lighten up and relax⟩

**¹ligh·ter** \'lī-tər\ n : a barge used esp. in loading or unloading ships

**²light·er** \'lī-tər\ n : one that lights; esp : a device for lighting (as a fire or cigarette)

**light·face** \'līt-ˌfās\ n : a type having light thin lines — **light·faced** \-ˌfāst\ adj

**light–head·ed** \'līt-ˌhe-dəd\ adj 1 : feeling confused or dizzy 2 : lacking maturity or seriousness

**light·heart·ed** \-ˌhär-təd\ adj : free from worry — **light·heart·ed·ly** adv — **light·heart·ed·ness** n

**light·house** \-ˌhaùs\ n : a structure with a powerful light for guiding sailors

**light meter** n : a usu. handheld device for indicating correct photographic exposure

**¹light·ning** \'līt-niŋ\ n : the flashing of light produced by a discharge of atmospheric electricity; also : the discharge itself

**²lightning** adj : extremely fast

**lightning bug** n : FIREFLY

**lightning rod** n : a grounded metallic rod set up on a structure to protect it from lightning

**light out** vb : to leave in a hurry

**light·proof** \'līt-ˌprüf\ adj : impenetrable by light

**lights** \'līts\ n pl : the lungs esp. of a slaughtered animal

**light·ship** \'līt-ˌship\ n : a ship with a powerful light moored at a place dangerous to navigation

**light show** n : a kaleidoscopic display (as of colored lights)

**light·some** \'līt-səm\ adj 1 : free from care 2 : NIMBLE

**¹light·weight** \'līt-ˌwāt\ n : one of less than average weight; esp : a boxer weighing not over 135 pounds

**²lightweight** adj 1 : INCONSEQUENTIAL 2 : of less than average weight

**light–year** \'līt-ˌyir\ n 1 : an astronomical unit of distance equal to the distance that light travels in one year in a vacuum or about 5.88 trillion miles (9.46 trillion kilometers) 2 : an extremely large measure of comparison ⟨saw it ∼s ago⟩

**lig·nin** \'lig-nən\ n : a substance related to cellulose that occurs in the woody cell walls of plants and in the cementing material between them

**lig·nite** \'lig-ˌnīt\ n : brownish black soft coal

**¹like** \'līk\ vb **liked; lik·ing** 1 : ENJOY ⟨∼s baseball⟩ 2 : WANT ⟨would ∼ a drink⟩ 3 : CHOOSE ⟨does as she ∼s⟩ — **lik·able** or **like·able** \'lī-kə-bəl\ adj

**²like** n : PREFERENCE

**³like** adj : SIMILAR ♦ **Synonyms** ALIKE, ANALOGOUS, COMPARABLE, PARALLEL, UNIFORM

**⁴like** prep 1 : similar or similarly to ⟨seems ∼ a dream⟩ 2 : typical of 3 : comparable to 4 : as though there would be ⟨looks ∼ rain⟩ 5 : such as ⟨a subject ∼ physics⟩

**⁵like** n 1 : COUNTERPART 2 : one that is similar to another ⟨we may never see his ∼ again⟩ — **and the like** : ET CETERA

**⁶like** conj 1 : AS IF ⟨acted ∼ they were scared⟩ 2 : in the same way that ⟨do it ∼ mom said⟩

**-like** adj comb form : resembling or characteristic of ⟨ladylike⟩ ⟨lifelike⟩

**like·li·hood** \'lī-klē-ˌhùd\ n : PROBABILITY

**¹like·ly** \'lī-klē\ adj **like·li·er; -est** 1 : very probable 2 : BELIEVABLE 3 : PROMISING ⟨a ∼ place to fish⟩

**²likely** adv : in all probability

**lik·en** \'lī-kən\ vb : COMPARE

**like·ness** \'līk-nəs\ n 1 : COPY, PORTRAIT 2 : SEMBLANCE 3 : RESEMBLANCE

**like·wise** \-,wīz\ *adv* **1** : in like manner **2** : in addition : ALSO

**lik·ing** \'lī-kiŋ\ *n* : favorable regard ⟨took a ∼ to the newcomer⟩; *also* : TASTE

**li·lac** \'lī-lək, -,lak, -,läk\ *n* [obs. F (now *lilas*), fr. Ar *līlak*, fr. Pers *nīlak* bluish, fr. *nīl* blue, fr. Skt *nīla* dark blue] **1** : a shrub related to the olive that produces large clusters of fragrant grayish pink, purple, or white flowers **2** : a moderate purple color

**lil·an·ge·ni** \,lil-lən-'ge-ne\ *n*, *pl* **em·a·lan·ge·ni** \,e-mə-lən-'ge-nē\ — see MONEY table

**lil·li·pu·tian** \,li-lə-'pyü-shən\ *adj*, *often cap* **1** : SMALL, MINIATURE **2** : PETTY

**lilt** \'lilt\ *n* **1** : a cheerful lively song or tune **2** : a rhythmical swing or flow

**lily** \'li-lē\ *n*, *pl* **lil·ies** : any of a genus of tall bulbous herbs with leafy stems and usu. funnel-shaped flowers; *also* : any of various related plants

**lily of the valley** : a low perennial herb related to the lilies that produces a raceme of fragrant nodding bell-shaped white flowers

**li·ma bean** \'lī-mə-\ *n* : a bushy or tall-growing bean widely cultivated for its flat edible usu. pale green or whitish seeds; *also* : the seed

**limb** \'lim\ *n* **1** : one of the projecting paired appendages (as legs, arms, or wings) used by an animal esp. in moving or grasping **2** : a large branch of a tree : BOUGH — **limb·less** *adj*

¹**lim·ber** \'lim-bər\ *adj* **1** : FLEXIBLE, SUPPLE **2** : LITHE, NIMBLE

²**limber** *vb* : to make or become limber

**lim·bic** \'lim-bik\ *adj* : of, relating to, or being a group of structures of the brain (**limbic system**) concerned esp. with emotion and motivation

¹**lim·bo** \'lim-bō\ *n*, *pl* **limbos** [ME, fr. ML, abl. of *limbus* limbo, fr. L, border] **1** *often cap* : an abode of souls barred from heaven through no fault of their own **2** : a place or state of confinement, oblivion, or uncertainty ⟨a ∼ of forgotten things⟩

²**limbo** *n*, *pl* **limbos** : an acrobatic dance or contest that involves passing under a horizontal pole

**Lim·burg·er** \'lim-,bər-gər\ *n* : a pungent semisoft surface-ripened cheese

¹**lime** \'līm\ *n* : a caustic powdery white solid that consists of calcium and oxygen, is obtained from limestone or shells, and is used in making cement and in fertilizer — **lime** *vb* — **limy** \'lī-mē\ *adj*

²**lime** *n* : a small yellowish green citrus fruit with juicy acid pulp

**lime·ade** \,līm-'ād, 'lī-,mād\ *n* : a beverage of lime juice, sugar, and water

**lime·light** \'līm-,līt\ *n* **1** : a device in which flame is directed against a cylinder of lime formerly used in the theater to cast a strong white light on the stage **2** : the center of public attention

**lim·er·ick** \'li-mə-rik\ *n* : a light or humorous poem of 5 lines

**lime·stone** \'līm-,stōn\ *n* : a rock that is formed by accumulation of organic remains (as shells), is used in building, and yields lime when burned

¹**lim·it** \'li-mət\ *n* **1** : something that restrains or confines; *also* : the utmost extent **2** : BOUNDARY; *also*, *pl* : BOUNDS **3** : a prescribed maximum or minimum **4** : a number whose value becomes arbitrarily close to that of a function as its independent variable approaches a given value — **lim·it·less** *adj* — **lim·it·less·ness** *n*

²**limit** *vb* **1** : to set limits to **2** : to reduce in quantity or extent — **lim·i·ta·tion** \,li-mə-'tā-shən\ *n*

**lim·it·ed** *adj* **1** : confined within limits **2** : offering faster service esp. by making fewer stops ⟨a ∼ train⟩

**limn** \'lim\ *vb* **limned**; **limn·ing** \'li-miŋ, 'lim-niŋ\ **1** : DRAW; *also* : PAINT **2** : DELINEATE **3** : DESCRIBE

**limo** \'li-(,)mō\ *n*, *pl* **limos** : LIMOUSINE

**li·mo·nite** \'lī-mə-,nīt\ *n* : a ferric oxide that is a major ore of iron — **li·mo·nit·ic** \,lī-mə-'ni-tik\ *adj*

**lim·ou·sine** \'li-mə-,zēn, ,li-mə-'zēn\ *n* [F] **1** : a large luxurious often chauffeur-driven sedan **2** : a large vehicle for transporting passengers to and from an airport

¹**limp** \'limp\ *vb* : to walk lamely; *also* : to proceed with difficulty

²**limp** *n* : a limping movement or gait

³**limp** *adj* **1** : having no defined shape; *also* : not stiff or rigid **2** : lacking in strength or firmness ⟨went ∼ from fatigue⟩ — **limp·ly** *adv* — **limp·ness** *n*

**lim·pet** \'lim-pət\ *n* : any of numerous gastropod sea mollusks with a conical shell that clings to rocks or timbers

**lim·pid** \'lim-pəd\ *adj* : CLEAR, TRANSPARENT ⟨∼ water⟩

**lin** *abbr* **1** lineal **2** linear

**lin·age** \'lī-nij\ *n* : the number of lines of written or printed matter

**linch·pin** \'linch-,pin\ *n* : a locking pin inserted crosswise (as through the end of an axle)

**lin·den** \'lin-dən\ *n* : any of a genus of trees with large heart-shaped leaves and clustered yellowish flowers; *also* : the light white wood of a linden

¹**line** \'līn\ *n* **1** : CORD, ROPE, WIRE; *also* : a length of material used in measuring and leveling **2** : pipes for conveying a fluid ⟨a gas ∼⟩ **3** : a horizontal row of written or printed characters; *also* : VERSE **4** : NOTE **5** : the words making up a part in a drama — usu. used in pl. **6** : something distinct, long, and narrow; *also* : ROUTE **7** : a state of agreement **8** : a course of conduct, action, or thought; *also* : OCCUPATION **9** : LIMIT **10** : an arrangement of persons or objects of one kind in an orderly series ⟨waiting in ∼⟩ **11** : a transportation system **12 a** : the football players who are stationed on the line of scrimmage **b** : a group of three players who play together as a unit in hockey **13** : a long narrow mark; *also* : EQUATOR **14** : a geometric element that is the path of a moving point **15** : CONTOUR **16** : a general plan ⟨thinking along

these ~*s*⟩ **17** : an indication based on insight or investigation

²**line** *vb* **lined; lin·ing 1** : to mark with a line **2** : to place or form a line along **3** : ALIGN ⟨~ up the sheets of paper⟩

³**line** *vb* **lined; lin·ing** : to cover the inner surface of ⟨~ the box with paper⟩

**lin·eage** \'li-nē-ij\ *n* : lineal descent from a common progenitor; *also* : FAMILY

**lin·eal** \'li-nē-əl\ *adj* **1** : LINEAR **2** : consisting of or being in a direct line of ancestry; *also* : HEREDITARY

**lin·ea·ment** \'li-nē-ə-mənt\ *n* : an outline, feature, or contour of a body and esp. of a face — usu. used in pl.

**lin·ear** \'li-nē-ər\ *adj* **1** : of, relating to, resembling, or having a graph that is a line and esp. a straight line : STRAIGHT **2** : composed of simply drawn lines with little attempt at pictorial representation ⟨~ script⟩ **3** : being long and uniformly narrow

**line·back·er** \'līn-,ba-kər\ *n* : a defensive football player who lines up just behind the line of scrimmage

**line drive** *n* : a batted baseball hit in a flatter path than a fly ball

**line–item veto** *n* : the power of a government executive to veto specific items in an appropriations bill

**line·man** \'līn-mən\ *n* **1** : a person who sets up or repairs communication or power lines **2** : a player in the line in football

**lin·en** \'li-nən\ *n* **1** : cloth made of flax; *also* : thread or yarn spun from flax **2** : clothing or household articles made of linen cloth or similar fabric

**line of scrimmage** : an imaginary line in football parallel to the goal lines and tangent to the nose of the ball laid on the ground before a play

¹**lin·er** \'lī-nər\ *n* : a ship or airplane of a regular transportation line

²**liner** *n* : one that lines or is used as a lining — **lin·er·less** *adj*

**line score** *n* : a score of a baseball game giving the runs, hits, and errors made by each team

**lines·man** \'līnz-mən\ *n* **1** : LINEMAN 1 **2** : an official who assists a referee

**line·up** \'lī-,nəp\ *n* **1** : a list of players taking part in a game (as of baseball) **2** : a line of persons arranged esp. for identification by police

**ling** \'liŋ\ *n* : any of various fishes related to the cod

**-ling** *n suffix* **1** : one associated with ⟨nest*ling*⟩ **2** : young, small, or minor one ⟨duck*ling*⟩

**lin·ger** \'liŋ-gər\ *vb* : TARRY; *also* : PROCRASTINATE — **lin·ger·er** *n*

**lin·ge·rie** \,län-jə-'rā, ,la<sup>n</sup>-zhə-, -'rē\ *n* [F, fr. MF, fr. *linge* linen, fr. L *lineus* made of linen, fr. *linum* flax, linen] : women's intimate apparel

**lin·go** \'liŋ-gō\ *n, pl* **lingoes** : a usu. strange or incomprehensible language

**lin·gua fran·ca** \,liŋ-gwə-'fraŋ-kə\ *n, pl* **lingua francas** *or* **lin·guae fran·cae** \-gwē-'fraŋ-,kē\ [It] **1** *often cap* : a common language consisting of Italian mixed

with French, Spanish, Greek, and Arabic that was formerly spoken in Mediterranean ports **2** : a common or commercial tongue among speakers of different languages

**lin·gual** \'liŋ-gwəl\ *adj* : of, relating to, or produced by the tongue

**lin·gui·ca** \liŋ-'gwē-sə\ *n* : a spicy Portuguese sausage

**lin·guist** \'liŋ-gwist\ *n* **1** : a person skilled in languages **2** : a person who specializes in linguistics

**lin·guis·tics** \liŋ-'gwis-tiks\ *n* : the study of human speech including the units, nature, structure, and modification of language — **lin·guis·tic** \-tik\ *adj*

**lin·i·ment** \'li-nə-mənt\ *n* : a liquid preparation rubbed on the skin esp. to relieve pain

**lin·ing** \'lī-niŋ\ *n* : material used to line esp. an inner surface

**link** \'liŋk\ *n* **1** : a connecting structure; *esp* : a single ring of a chain **2** : BOND, TIE **3** : HYPERLINK — **link** *vb* — **link·er** *n*

**link·age** \'liŋ-kij\ *n* **1** : the manner or style of being united **2** : the quality or state of being linked **3** : a system of links

**linking verb** *n* : a word or expression (as a form of *be, become, feel,* or *seem*) that links a subject with its predicate

**links** \'liŋks\ *n pl* : a golf course

**link·up** \'liŋ-,kəp\ *n* **1** : MEETING **2** : something that serves as a linking device or factor

**lin·net** \'li-nət\ *n* : an Old World finch

**li·no·leum** \lə-'nō-lē-əm\ *n* [L *linum* flax + *oleum* oil] : a floor covering with a canvas back and a surface of hardened linseed oil and a filler

**lin·seed** \'lin-,sēd\ *n* : the seeds of flax yielding a yellowish oil (**linseed oil**) used esp. in paints and linoleum

**lin·sey–wool·sey** \,lin-zē-'wúl-zē\ *n* : a coarse sturdy fabric of wool and linen or cotton

**lint** \'lint\ *n* **1** : linen made into a soft fleecy substance **2** : fine ravels and short fibers of yarn or fabric **3** : the fibers that surround cotton seeds and form the cotton lint

**lin·tel** \'lin-t°l\ *n* : a horizontal piece across the top of an opening (as of a door) that carries the weight of the structure above it

**linz·er torte** \'lin-sər-, -zər-\ *n, often cap L* : a baked buttery torte made with chopped almonds, sugar, and spices and filled with jam or preserves

**li·on** \'lī-ən\ *n, pl* **lions** : a large heavily built cat of Africa and southern Asia with a shaggy mane in the male

**li·on·ess** \'lī-ə-nəs\ *n* : a female lion

**li·on·heart·ed** \,lī-ən-'här-təd\ *adj* : COURAGEOUS, BRAVE

**li·on·ise** *Brit var of* LIONIZE

**li·on·ize** \'lī-ə-,nīz\ *vb* **-ized; -iz·ing** : to treat as an object of great interest or importance — **li·on·i·za·tion** \,lī-ə-nə-'zā-shən\ *n*

**lion's den** *n* : a place or state of extreme disadvantage, antagonism, or hostility

**lip** \'lip\ *n* **1** : either of the two fleshy folds that surround the mouth; *also* : the margin of the human lip **2** : a part or projection suggesting a lip **3** : the edge of a hollow vessel or cavity — **lipped** \'lipt\ *adj*

**li·pa** \'lē-,pä, -pə\ *n, pl* **lipa** — see *kuna* at MONEY table

**lip·id** \'li-pəd\ *n* : any of various substances (as fats and waxes) that with proteins and carbohydrates make up the principal structural parts of living cells

**lip–lock** \'lip-,läk\ *n* : a long amorous kiss

**li·po·pro·tein** \,lī-pō-'prō-,tēn, ,li-\ *n* : a protein that is a complex of protein and lipid

**li·po·suc·tion** \'li-pə-,sək-shən, 'lī-\ *n* : surgical removal of local fat deposits (as in the thighs) esp. for cosmetic purposes

**lip·read·ing** \'lip-,rē-diŋ\ *n* : the interpreting of a speaker's words by watching lip and facial movements without hearing the voice

**lip service** *n* : an avowal of allegiance that is not matched by action

**lip·stick** \'lip-,stik\ *n* : a waxy solid colored cosmetic in stick form for the lips — **lip·sticked** \-,stikt\ *adj*

**liq** *abbr* **1** liquid **2** liquor

**liq·ue·fy** *also* **liq·ui·fy** \'li-kwə-,fī\ *vb* **-fied; -fy·ing** : to make or become liquid — **liq·ue·fi·er** \-,fī-(ə)r\ *n*

**li·queur** \li-'kər\ *n* [F] : a distilled alcoholic liquor flavored with aromatic substances and usu. sweetened

**¹liq·uid** \'li-kwəd\ *adj* **1** : flowing freely like water **2** : neither solid nor gaseous **3** : shining and clear ⟨large ∼ eyes⟩ **4** : smooth and musical in tone; *also* : smooth and unconstrained in movement **5** : consisting of or capable of ready conversion into cash ⟨∼ assets⟩ — **li·quid·i·ty** \li-'kwi-də-tē\ *n*

**²liquid** *n* : a liquid substance

**liq·ui·date** \'li-kwə-,dāt\ *vb* **-dat·ed; -dat·ing** : to settle the accounts and distribute the assets of (as a business) **2** : to pay off ⟨∼ a debt⟩ **3** : to get rid of; *esp* : KILL — **liq·ui·da·tion** \,li-kwə-'dā-shən\ *n*

**liquid crystal** *n* : an organic liquid that resembles a crystal in having ordered molecular arrays

**liquid crystal display** *n* : LCD

**liquid measure** *n* : a unit or series of units for measuring liquid capacity — see METRIC SYSTEM table, WEIGHT table

**li·quor** \'li-kər\ *n* [ME *licour*, fr. AF, fr. L *liquor*, fr. *liquēre* to be fluid] : a liquid substance; *esp* : a distilled alcoholic beverage

**li·quo·rice** *chiefly Brit var of* LICORICE

**li·ra** \'lir-ə, 'lē-rə\ *n* **1** *pl* **li·re** \'lē-(,)rā\ : the former basic monetary unit of Italy **2** : the basic monetary unit of Turkey — see MONEY table **3** *pl* **li·ri** \'lē-rē\ : the basic monetary unit of Malta until 2008

**lisente** *pl of* SENTE

**lisle** \'līl\ *n* : a smooth tightly twisted thread usu. made of long-staple cotton

**lisp** \'lisp\ *vb* : to pronounce \s\ and \z\ imperfectly esp. by turning them into \ th\ and \th\; *also* : to speak childishly — **lisp** *n* — **lisp·er** *n*

**lis·some** *also* **lis·som** \'li-səm\ *adj* **1** : easily flexed **2** : LITHE **2** ⟨a ∼ dancer⟩ **3** : NIMBLE — **lis·some·ly** *adv*

**¹list** \'list\ *vb, archaic* : PLEASE; *also* : WISH

**²list** *vb, archaic* : LISTEN

**³list** *n* : a leaning to one side : TILT

**⁴list** *vb* : TILT

**⁵list** *n* **1** : a simple series of words or numerals; *also* : an official roster **2** : CATALOG, CHECKLIST

**⁶list** *vb* : to make a list of; *also* : to include on a list — **list·ee** \lis-'tē\ *n*

**lis·ten** \'li-s³n\ *vb* **1** : to pay attention in order to hear **2** : HEED — **lis·ten·er** *n*

**lis·ten·er·ship** \'li-s³n-ər-,ship\ *n* : the audience for a radio program or recording

**list·ing** \'lis-tiŋ\ *n* **1** : an act or instance of making or including in a list **2** : something that is listed

**list·less** \'list-ləs\ *adj* : SPIRITLESS, LANGUID ⟨a ∼ performance⟩ — **list·less·ly** *adv* — **list·less·ness** *n*

**list price** *n* : the price of an item as published in a catalog, price list, or advertisement before being discounted

**lists** \'lists\ *n pl* : an arena for combat (as jousting)

**¹lit** \'lit\ *past and past part of* LIGHT

**²lit** *abbr* **1** liter **2** literal; literally **3** literary **4** literature

**lit·a·ny** \'li-tə-nē\ *n, pl* **-nies** [ME *letanie*, fr. AF & LL; AF, fr. LL *litania*, fr. LGk *litaneia*, fr. Gk, entreaty, fr. *litanos* suppliant] **1** : a prayer consisting of a series of supplications and responses said alternately by a leader and a group **2** : a lengthy recitation ⟨a ∼ of complaints⟩

**li·tas** \'lē-,täs\ *n, pl* **li·tai** \-,tī\ *or* **li·tu** \-,tü\ : the basic monetary unit of Lithuania from 1923 to 1940 and from 1991 through 2014

**litchi** *var of* LYCHEE

**lite** \'līt\ *adj* **1** : ⁴LIGHT 10 ⟨∼ beer⟩ **2** : lacking in substance or seriousness ⟨∼ news⟩

**li·ter** \'lē-tər\ *n* — see METRIC SYSTEM table

**lit·er·al** \'li-tə-rəl\ *adj* **1** : adhering to fact or to the ordinary or usual meaning (as of a word) **2** : UNADORNED; *also* : PROSAIC **3** : VERBATIM

**lit·er·al·ism** \-rə-,li-zəm\ *n* **1** : adherence to the explicit substance (as of an idea) **2** : fidelity to observable fact — **lit·er·al·ist** \-list\ *n* — **lit·er·al·is·tic** \,li-tə-rə-'lis-tik\ *adj*

**lit·er·al·ly** \'li-tə-rə-lē, 'li-trə-\ *adv* **1** : ACTUALLY ⟨was ∼ insane⟩ **2** : VIRTUALLY ⟨∼ poured out new ideas⟩

**lit·er·ary** \'li-tə-,rer-ē\ *adj* **1** : of or relating to literature **2** : WELL-READ

**lit·er·ate** \'li-trət, -tə-rət\ *adj* **1** : EDUCATED; *also* : able to read and write **2** : LITERARY; *also* : POLISHED, LUCID — **lit·er·a·cy** \'li-trə-sē, -tə-rə-\ *n* — **literate** *n*

**li·te·ra·ti** \,li-tə-'rä-tē\ *n pl* **1** : the educated class **2** : persons interested in literature or the arts

**lit·er·a·ture** \'li-trə-,chùr, -tə-rə-, -,chər\ *n*

**1** : the production of written works having excellence of form or expression and dealing with ideas of permanent interest **2** : the written works produced in a particular language, country, or age

**lithe** \'līth, 'līth\ *adj* **1** : SUPPLE **2** : characterized by effortless grace; *also* : athletically slim ⟨a ~ body⟩

**lithe·some** \'līth-səm, 'līth-\ *adj* : LISSOME

**lith·i·um** \'li-thē-əm\ *n* : a light silver-white metallic chemical element

**li·thog·ra·phy** \li-'thä-grə-fē\ *n* : the process of printing from a plane surface (as a smooth stone or metal plate) on which the image to be printed is ink-receptive and the blank area ink-repellent — **lith·o·graph** \'li-thə-ˌgraf\ *vb* — **lithograph** *n* — **li·thog·ra·pher** \li-'thä-grə-fər, 'li-thə-ˌgra-fər\ *n* — **lith·o·graph·ic** \ˌli-thə-'gra-fik\ *adj* — **lith·o·graph·i·cal·ly** \-fi-k(ə-)lē\ *adv*

**li·thol·o·gy** \li-'thä-lə-jē\ *n, pl* **-gies** : the study of rocks — **lith·o·log·ic** \ˌli-thə-'lä-jik\ *or* **lith·o·log·i·cal** \-ji-kəl\ *adj*

**lith·o·sphere** \'li-thə-ˌsfir\ *n* : the outer part of the solid earth

**Lith·u·a·nian** \ˌli-thə-'wā-nē-ən, -thyü-\ *n* **1** : a native or inhabitant of Lithuania **2** : the language of the Lithuanians — **Lithuanian** *adj*

**lit·i·gant** \'li-ti-gənt\ *n* : a party to a lawsuit — **litigant** *adj*

**lit·i·gate** \-ˌgāt\ *vb* **-gat·ed; -gat·ing** : to carry on a legal contest by judicial process; *also* : to contest at law — **lit·i·ga·tion** \ˌli-tə-'gā-shən\ *n*

**li·ti·gious** \lə-'ti-jəs\ *adj* **1** : CONTENTIOUS **2** : prone to engage in lawsuits **3** : of or relating to litigation — **li·ti·gious·ly** *adv* — **li·ti·gious·ness** *n*

**lit·mus** \'lit-məs\ *n* : a coloring matter from lichens that turns red in acid solutions and blue in alkaline

**litmus test** *n* : a test in which a single factor (as an attitude) is decisive

**Litt D** *or* **Lit D** *abbr* [ML *litterarum doctor*] : doctor of letters; doctor of literature

**¹lit·ter** \'li-tər\ *n* [ME, fr. AF *litere*, fr. *lit* bed, fr. L *lectus*] **1** : a covered and curtained couch with shafts that is used to carry a single passenger; *also* : a device (as a stretcher) for carrying a sick or injured person **2** : material used as bedding for animals; *also* : material used to absorb the urine and feces of animals **3** : the offspring of an animal at one birth **4** : RUBBISH

**²litter** *vb* **1** : to give birth to young **2** : to strew or mark with scattered objects

**lit·ter·bug** \'li-tər-ˌbəg\ *n* : one who litters a public area

**¹lit·tle** \'li-tᵊl\ *adj* **lit·tler** \'li-tᵊl-ər\ *or* **less** \'les\ *or* **less·er** \'le-sər\; **lit·tlest** \'li-tᵊl-əst\ *or* **least** \'lēst\ **1** : not big; *also* : YOUNG **2** : not important **3** : PETTY **3** **4** : not much — **lit·tle·ness** *n*

**²little** *adv* **less** \'les\; **least** \'lēst\ **1** : SLIGHTLY; *also* : not at all **2** : INFREQUENTLY

**³little** *n* **1** : a small amount or quantity **2** : a short time or distance

**Little Dipper** *n* : the seven bright stars of Ursa Minor arranged in a form resembling a dipper

**little finger** *n* : PINKIE

**little theater** *n* : a small theater for low-cost dramatic productions designed for a limited audience

**lit·to·ral** \'li-tə-rəl; ˌli-tə-'ral\ *adj* : of, relating to, or growing on or near a shore esp. of the sea — **littoral** *n*

**lit·ur·gy** \'li-tər-jē\ *n, pl* **-gies** : a rite or body of rites prescribed for public worship — **li·tur·gi·cal** \lə-'tər-ji-kəl\ *adj* — **li·tur·gi·cal·ly** \-k(ə-)lē\ *adv* — **lit·ur·gist** \'li-tər-jist\ *n*

**liv·able** *also* **live·able** \'li-və-bəl\ *adj* **1** : suitable for living in or with ⟨a ~ house⟩ ⟨~ wages⟩ **2** : ENDURABLE — **liv·a·bil·i·ty** \ˌli-və-'bi-lə-tē\ *n*

**¹live** \'liv\ *vb* **lived; liv·ing 1** : to be or continue alive ⟨*lived* 90 years⟩ **2** : SUBSIST **3** : RESIDE ⟨~s next door⟩ **4** : to conduct one's life **5** : to remain in human memory or record ⟨his legacy ~s⟩

**²live** \'līv\ *adj* **1** : having life ⟨~ worms⟩ **2** : ACTUAL ⟨a real ~ celebrity⟩ **3** : BURNING, GLOWING ⟨a ~ cigar⟩ **4** : connected to electric power ⟨a ~ wire⟩ **5** : UNEXPLODED ⟨a ~ bomb⟩ **6** : of continuing interest ⟨a ~ issue⟩ **7** : of or involving the actual presence of real people ⟨~ audience⟩; *also* : broadcast directly at the time of production **8** : being in play ⟨a ~ ball⟩

**lived–in** \'livd-ˌin\ *adj* : of or suggesting long-term human habitation or use

**live down** *vb* : to live so as to wipe out the memory or effects of

**live in** *vb* : to live in one's place of employment — used of a servant — **live–in** \'liv-ˌin\ *adj*

**live·li·hood** \'līv-lē-ˌhùd\ *n* : means of support or subsistence

**live·long** \'liv-ˌlòŋ\ *adj* [ME *lef long*, fr. *lef* dear + *long* long] : WHOLE, ENTIRE ⟨the ~ day⟩

**live·ly** \'līv-lē\ *adj* **live·li·er; -est 1** : ANIMATED ⟨~ debate⟩ **2** : KEEN, VIVID ⟨~ interest⟩ **3** : showing activity or vigor ⟨a ~ manner⟩ **4** : quick to rebound ⟨a ~ ball⟩ **5** : full of life ♦ **Synonyms** VIVACIOUS, SPRIGHTLY, GAY, SPIRITED — **live·li·ness** *n* — **live·ly** *adv*

**liv·en** \'lī-vən\ *vb* : ENLIVEN

**live oak** *n* : any of several American evergreen oaks; *esp* : one of the southeastern U.S. that is often planted as a shade tree

**¹liv·er** \'li-vər\ *n* **1** : a large glandular organ of vertebrates that secretes bile and is a center of metabolic activity **2** : the liver of an animal (as a calf or chicken) eaten as food

**²liver** *n* : one that lives esp. in a specified way ⟨a fast ~⟩

**liv·er·ish** \'li-və-rish\ *adj* **1** : resembling liver esp. in color **2** : BILIOUS **3** : PEEVISH — **liv·er·ish·ness** *adj*

**liver spots** *n pl* : AGE SPOTS

**liv·er·wort** \'li-vər-ˌwərt\ *n* : any of a class of flowerless plants resembling the related mosses

**liv·er·wurst** \-ˌwərst, -ˌwùrst\ *n* [part

trans. of G *Leberwurst*, fr. *Leber* liver + *Wurst* sausage] : a sausage consisting chiefly of liver

**liv·ery** \'li-və-rē\ *n, pl* **-er·ies 1** : a servant's uniform; *also* : distinctive dress **2** : the feeding, care, and stabling of horses for pay; *also* : an establishment (as a stable or business) keeping horses or vehicles for hire — **liv·er·ied** \-rēd\ *adj* — **liv·ery·man** \'li-və-rē-mən\ *n*

**lives** *pl of* LIFE

**live·stock** \'līv-,stäk\ *n* : farm animals kept for use and profit

**live wire** *n* : an alert, active, or aggressive person — **live–wire** *adj*

**liv·id** \'li-vəd\ *adj* [F *livide*, fr. L *lividus*, fr. *livēre* to be blue] **1** : discolored by bruising **2** : ASHEN, PALLID **3** : REDDISH **4** : ENRAGED — **lividity** \li-'vi-də-tē\, *n*

**¹liv·ing** \'li-viŋ\ *adj* **1** : having life **2** : NATURAL **3** : full of life and vigor; *also* : VIVID ⟨in ~ color⟩

**²living** *n* **1** : the condition of being alive **2** : LIVELIHOOD **3** : manner of life

**living room** *n* : a room in a residence used for the common social activities of the occupants

**living wage** *n* : a wage sufficient to provide an acceptable standard of living

**living will** *n* : a document requesting that the signer not be kept alive by artificial means unless there is a reasonable expectation of recovery

**livre** \'lēvrᵊ\ *n* : the pound of Lebanon

**liz·ard** \'li-zərd\ *n* : any of a group of 4-legged reptiles with long tapering tails

**Lk** *abbr* Luke

**ll** *abbr* lines

**lla·ma** \'lä-mə\ *n* [Sp, fr. Quechua] : any of a genus of wild or domesticated So. American mammals related to the camels but smaller and without a hump

**lla·no** \'lä-nō\ *n, pl* **llanos** : an open grassy plain esp. of Latin America

**LLD** *abbr* [NL *legum doctor*] doctor of laws

**LNG** *abbr* liquefied natural gas

**¹load** \'lōd\ *n* **1** : PACK; *also* : CARGO **2** : a mass of weight supported by something **3** : something that burdens the mind or spirits **4** : a large quantity — usu. used in pl. **5** : a standard, expected, or authorized burden

**²load** *vb* **1** : to put a load in or on; *also* : to receive a load **2** : to encumber with an obligation or something heavy or disheartening **3** : to increase the weight of by adding something **4** : to supply abundantly **5** : to put a charge in (as a firearm) **6** : to copy or transfer into a computer's memory esp. from an external source

**load·ed** *adj* **1** *slang* : HIGH **12 2** : having a large amount of money **3** : equipped with an abundance of options ⟨a ~ car⟩

**load·stone** *var of* LODESTONE

**¹loaf** \'lōf\ *n, pl* **loaves** \'lōvz\ : a shaped or molded mass esp. of bread

**²loaf** *vb* : to spend time in idleness : LOUNGE

**loaf·er** \'lō-fər\ *n* **1** : one that loafs : IDLER **2** : a low step-in shoe

**loam** \'lōm, 'lüm\ *n* : SOIL; *esp* : a loose soil of mixed clay, sand, and silt — **loamy** *adj*

**¹loan** \'lōn\ *n* **1** : money lent at interest; *also* : something lent for the borrower's temporary use **2** : the grant of temporary use

**²loan** *vb* : LEND

**loan shark** *n* : a person who lends money at excessive rates of interest — **loan·shark·ing** \'lōn-,shär-kiŋ\ *n*

**loan·word** \'lōn-,wərd\ *n* : a word taken from another language and at least partly naturalized

**loath** *also* **loth** \'lōth, 'lōth\ *or* **loathe** \'lōth, 'lōth\ *adj* : RELUCTANT

**loathe** \'lōth\ *vb* **loathed; loath·ing** : to dislike greatly ♦ *Synonyms* ABOMINATE, ABHOR, DETEST, HATE

**loath·ing** \'lō-thiŋ\ *n* : extreme disgust

**loath·some** \'lōth-səm, 'lōth-\ *adj* : exciting loathing : REPULSIVE

**lob** \'läb\ *vb* **lobbed; lob·bing 1** : to throw, hit, or propel something in a high arc **2** : to direct (as a question) so as to elicit a response — **lob** *n*

**¹lob·by** \'lä-bē\ *n, pl* **lobbies 1** : a corridor used esp. as a passageway or waiting room **2** : a group of persons engaged in lobbying

**²lobby** *vb* **lob·bied; lob·by·ing** : to try to influence public officials and esp. legislators — **lob·by·ist** *n*

**lobe** \'lōb\ *n* : a curved or rounded part esp. of a bodily organ — **lo·bar** \'lō-bər\ *adj* — **lobed** \'lōbd\ *adj*

**lo·be·lia** \lō-'bēl-yə\ *n* : any of a genus of plants grown for their clusters of showy flowers

**lo·bot·o·my** \lō-'bä-tə-mē\ *n, pl* **-mies** : surgical severance of certain nerve fibers in the brain used esp. formerly to relieve some mental disorders

**lob·ster** \'läb-stər\ *n* [ME, fr. OE *loppestre*, fr. *loppe* spider] : any of a family of edible marine crustaceans with two large pincerlike claws and four other pairs of legs; *also* : SPINY LOBSTER

**¹lo·cal** \'lō-kəl\ *adj* **1** : of, relating to, or occupying a particular place **2** : serving a particular limited district; *also* : making all stops ⟨a ~ train⟩ **3** : affecting a small part of the body ⟨a ~ infection⟩ — **lo·cal·ly** *adv*

**²local** *n* : one that is local

**local area network** *n* : a network of personal computers in a small area (as an office)

**lo·cale** \lō-'kal\ *n* : a place that is the setting for a particular event

**lo·cal·ise** *Brit var of* LOCALIZE

**lo·cal·i·ty** \lō-'ka-lə-tē\ *n, pl* **-ties** : a particular spot, situation, or location

**lo·cal·ize** \'lō-kə-,līz\ *vb* **-ized; -iz·ing** : to fix in or confine to a definite place or locality — **lo·cal·i·za·tion** \,lō-kə-lə-'zā-shən\ *n*

**lo·cate** \'lō-,kāt, lō-'kāt\ *vb* **lo·cat·ed; lo·cat·ing 1** : STATION, SETTLE **2** : to determine the site of **3** : to find or fix the place of in a sequence

**lo·ca·tion** \lō-'kā-shən\ *n* **1** : SITUATION,

PLACE **2** : the process of locating **3** : a place outside a studio where a motion picture is filmed

**lo·ca·vore** \'lō-kə-ˌvȯr\ *n* [*local* + *-vore* (as in *carnivore*)] : one who eats foods grown locally whenever possible

**loc cit** *abbr* [L *loco citato*] in the place cited

**loch** \'läk, 'läk\ *n*, *Scot* : LAKE; *also* : a bay or arm of the sea esp. when nearly land-locked

**¹lock** \'läk\ *n* : a tuft, strand, or ringlet of hair; *also* : a cohering bunch (as of wool or flax)

**²lock** *n* **1** : a fastening in which a bolt is operated **2** : the mechanism of a firearm by which the charge is exploded **3** : an enclosure (as in a canal) used in raising or lowering boats from level to level **4** : AIR LOCK **5** : a wrestling hold

**³lock** *vb* **1** : to fasten the lock of; *also* : to make fast with a lock **2** : to confine or exclude by means of a lock **3** : INTER-LOCK **4** : to make or become motionless by the interlocking of parts

**lock·er** \'lä-kər\ *n* **1** : a drawer, cup-board, or compartment for individual storage use **2** : an insulated compart-ment for storing frozen food

**lock·et** \'lä-kət\ *n* : a small usu. metal case for a memento worn suspended from a chain or necklace

**lock·jaw** \'läk-ˌjȯ\ *n* : a symptom of teta-nus marked by spasms of the jaw muscles and inability to open the jaws; *also* : TET-ANUS

**lock·nut** \-ˌnət\ *n* **1** : a nut screwed tight on another to prevent it from slacking back **2** : a nut designed to lock itself when screwed tight

**lock·out** \-ˌau̇t\ *n* : the suspension of work by an employer during a labor dis-pute in order to make employees accept the terms being offered

**lock·smith** \-ˌsmith\ *n* : one who makes or repairs locks

**lock·step** \-ˌstep\ *n* : a mode of marching in step by a body of men moving in a very close single file

**lock·up** \-ˌəp\ *n* : JAIL

**lo·co** \'lō-kō\ *adj* [Sp] *slang* : CRAZY, FRENZIED

**lo·co·mo·tion** \ˌlō-kə-'mō-shən\ *n* **1** : the act or power of moving from place to place **2** : TRAVEL

**¹lo·co·mo·tive** \ˌlō-kə-'mō-tiv\ *adj* : of or relating to locomotion or a locomotive

**²locomotive** *n* : a self-propelled vehicle used to move railroad cars

**lo·co·mo·tor** \ˌlō-kə-'mō-tər\ *adj* : of or relating to locomotion or organs used in locomotion

**lo·co·weed** \'lō-kō-ˌwēd\ *n* : any of sev-eral leguminous plants of western No. America that are poisonous to livestock

**lo·cus** \'lō-kəs\ *n*, *pl* **lo·ci** \'lō-ˌsī\ [L] **1** : PLACE, LOCALITY **2** : the set of all points whose location is determined by stated conditions

**lo·cust** \'lō-kəst\ *n* **1** : a usu. destructive migratory grasshopper **2** : CICADA **3** : any of various leguminous trees; *also* : the wood of a locust

**lo·cu·tion** \lō-'kyü-shən\ *n* : a particular form of expression; *also* : PHRASEOLOGY

**lode** \'lōd\ *n* : an ore deposit

**lode·stone** \-ˌstōn\ *n* : an iron-containing rock with magnetic properties

**¹lodge** \'läj\ *vb* **lodged; lodg·ing 1** : to provide quarters for; *also* : to settle in a place **2** : CONTAIN **3** : to come to a rest and remain ⟨*lodged* in his throat⟩ **4** : to deposit for safekeeping **5** : to vest (as au-thority) in an agent **6** : FILE ⟨~ a com-plaint⟩

**²lodge** *n* **1** : a house set apart for resi-dence in a special season or by an em-ployee on an estate; *also* : INN **2** : a den or lair esp. of gregarious animals **3** : the meeting place of a branch of a fraternal organization; *also* : the members of such a branch

**lodg·er** \'lä-jər\ *n* : a person who occupies a rented room in another's house

**lodg·ing** \'lä-jiŋ\ *n* **1** : DWELLING **2** : a room or suite of rooms in another's house rented as a dwelling place — usu. used in pl.

**lodg·ment** *or* **lodge·ment** \'läj-mənt\ *n* **1** : a lodging place **2** : the act or manner of lodging **3** : DEPOSIT

**loess** \'les, 'ləs\ *n* : a usu. yellowish brown loamy deposit believed to be chiefly deposited by the wind

**lo–fi** \'lō-ˌfī\ *n* : audio production of rough or unpolished sound quality — **lo–fi** *adj*

**¹loft** \'lȯft\ *n* [ME, fr. OE, air, sky, fr. ON *lopt*] **1** : ATTIC **2** : GALLERY ⟨organ ~⟩ **3** : an upper floor (as in a warehouse or barn) esp. when not partitioned **4** : the thickness of a fabric or insulated material (as of a sleeping bag)

**²loft** *vb* : to strike or throw a ball so that it rises high in the air

**lofty** \'lȯf-tē\ *adj* **loft·i·er; -est 1** : NO-BLE; *also* : SUPERIOR ⟨~ ideals⟩ **2** : ex-tremely proud **3** : HIGH, TALL — **loft·i·ly** \'lȯf-tə-lē\ *adv* — **loft·i·ness** \-tē-nəs\ *n*

**¹log** \'lȯg, 'läg\ *n* **1** : a bulky piece of a cut or fallen tree **2** : an apparatus for mea-suring a ship's speed **3** : the daily record of a ship's progress; *also* : a regularly kept record of performance or events ⟨a pi-lot's ~⟩ ⟨a runner's ~⟩

**²log** *vb* **logged; log·ging 1** : to cut (trees) for lumber; *also* : to clear (land) of trees in lumbering **2** : to enter in a log **3** : to sail a ship or fly an airplane for (an indi-cated distance or period of time) **4** : to have (an indicated record) to one's credit : ACHIEVE — **log·ger** \'lȯ-gər, 'lä-\ *n*

**³log** *n* : LOGARITHM

**lo·gan·ber·ry** \'lō-gən-ˌber-ē\ *n* : a red-fruited upright-growing dewberry; *also* : its berry

**log·a·rithm** \'lȯ-gə-ˌri-thəm, 'lä-\ *n* : the exponent that indicates the power to which a base is raised to produce a given number ⟨the ~ of 100 to base 10 is 2 since $10^2 = 100$⟩ — **log·a·rith·mic** \ˌlȯ-gə-'rith-mik, ˌlä-\ *adj*

**loge** \'lōzh\ *n* **1** : a small compartment;

*also* : a box in a theater  **2** : a small partitioned area; *also* : the forward section of a theater mezzanine  **3** : a raised level of seats in a stadium

**log·ger·head** \'lȯ-gər-ˌhed, 'lä-\ *n* : a large sea turtle of subtropical and temperate waters — **at loggerheads** : in a state of quarrelsome disagreement

**log·gia** \'lō-jē-ə, 'lȯ-jä\ *n, pl* **loggias** \'lō-jē-əz, 'lȯ-jäz\ : a roofed open gallery

**log·ic** \'lä-jik\ *n*  **1** : a science that deals with the rules and tests of sound thinking and proof by reasoning  **2** : sound reasoning  **3** : the arrangement of circuit elements for arithmetical computation in a computer — **log·i·cal** \-ji-kəl\ *adj* — **log·i·cal·ly** \-jik(ə-)lē\ *adv* — **lo·gi·cian** \lō-'ji-shən\ *n*

**lo·gis·tics** \lō-'jis-tiks\ *n sing or pl* : the procurement, maintenance, and transportation of matériel, facilities, and personnel — **lo·gis·tic** \-tik\ *or* **lo·gis·ti·cal** \-ti-kəl\ *adj*

**log·jam** \'lȯg-ˌjam, 'läg-\ *n*  **1** : a deadlocked jumble of logs in a watercourse  **2** : DEADLOCK — **logjam** *vt*

**logo** \'lō-gō\ *n, pl* **log·os** \-gōz\ : an identifying symbol (as for advertising)

**log off** *vb* : to end the connection of a computer to a network or system

**log on** *vb* : to start the connection of a computer to a network or system

**logo·type** \'lä-gə-ˌtīp, 'lȯ-\ *n* : LOGO

**log·roll·ing** \-ˌrō-liŋ\ *n* : the trading of votes by legislators to secure favorable action on projects of individual interest

**lo·gy** \'lō-gē\ *also* **log·gy** \'lȯ-gē, 'lä-\ *adj* **lo·gi·er; -est** : deficient in vitality : SLUGGISH

**loin** \'lȯin\ *n* [ME *loyne*, fr. AF *loigne*, fr. VL *lumbea*, fr. L *lumbus*]  **1** : the part of the body on each side of the spinal column and between the hip and the lower ribs; *also* : a cut of meat from this part of an animal  **2** *pl* : the pubic region; *also* : the organs of reproduction

**loin·cloth** \-ˌklȯth\ *n* : a cloth worn about the loins often as the sole article of clothing in warm climates

**loi·ter** \'lȯi-tər\ *vb*  **1** : LINGER  **2** : to hang around idly ♦ **Synonyms** DAWDLE, DALLY, PROCRASTINATE, LAG, TARRY — **loi·ter·er** *n*

**loll** \'läl\ *vb*  **1** : DROOP, DANGLE  **2** : LOUNGE ⟨~ing by the pool⟩

**lol·la·pa·loo·za** \ˌlä-lə-pə-'lü-zə\ *n* : something extraordinarily impressive or outstanding

**lol·li·pop** *or* **lol·ly·pop** \'lä-li-ˌpäp\ *n* : a lump of hard candy on a stick

**lol·ly·gag** \'lä-lē-ˌgag\ *vb* **-gagged; -gagging** : DAWDLE

**Lond** *abbr* London

**lone** \'lōn\ *adj*  **1** : SOLITARY ⟨a ~ sentinel⟩  **2** : SOLE, ONLY ⟨the ~ theater in town⟩  **3** : ISOLATED ⟨a ~ tree⟩

**lone·ly** \'lōn-lē\ *adj* **lone·li·er; -est**  **1** : being without company  **2** : UNFREQUENTED ⟨a ~ spot⟩  **3** : LONESOME — **lone·li·ness** *n*

**lon·er** \'lō-nər\ *n* : one that avoids others

**lone·some** \'lōn-səm\ *adj*  **1** : sad from lack of companionship  **2** : REMOTE; *also* : SOLITARY ⟨a ~ road⟩ — **lone·some·ly** *adv* — **lone·some·ness** *n*

**¹long** \'lȯŋ\ *adj* **lon·ger** \'lȯŋ-gər\; **lon·gest** \'lȯŋ-gəst\  **1** : extending for a considerable distance ⟨a ~ corridor⟩; *also* : TALL, ELONGATED ⟨~ legs⟩  **2** : having a specified length  **3** : extending over a considerable time; *also* : TEDIOUS ⟨~ lectures⟩  **4** : containing many items in a series ⟨a ~ list⟩  **5** : being a syllable or speech sound of relatively great duration  **6** : extending far into the future  **7** : well furnished with something — used with *on* ⟨~ on talent⟩

**²long** *adv* : for or during a long time

**³long** *n* : a long period of time

**⁴long** *vb* **longed; long·ing** \'lȯŋ-iŋ\ : to feel a strong desire or wish ♦ **Synonyms** YEARN, HANKER, PINE, HUNGER, THIRST

**⁵long** *abbr* longitude

**long·boat** \'lȯŋ-ˌbōt\ *n* : a large boat usu. carried by a merchant sailing ship

**long·bow** \-ˌbō\ *n* : a wooden bow drawn by hand and used esp. by medieval English archers

**lon·gev·i·ty** \län-'je-və-tē\ *n* [LL *longaevitas*, fr. L *longaevus* long-lived, fr. *longus* long + *aevum* age] : a long duration of individual life; *also* : length of life

**long·hair** \'lȯŋ-ˌher\ *n*  **1** : a lover of classical music  **2** : HIPPIE  **3** : a domestic cat having long outer fur — **long—haired** \-ˌherd\ *or* **long·hair** *adj*

**long·hand** \-ˌhand\ *n* : HANDWRITING

**long·horn** \-ˌhȯrn\ *n* : any of the cattle with long horns formerly common in the southwestern U.S.

**long hundredweight** *n, Brit* — see WEIGHT table

**long·ing** \'lȯŋ-iŋ\ *n* : a strong desire esp. for something unattainable — **long·ing·ly** *adv*

**lon·gi·tude** \'län-jə-ˌtüd, -ˌtyüd\ *n* : angular distance expressed usu. in degrees east or west from the prime meridian through Greenwich, England

**lon·gi·tu·di·nal** \ˌlän-jə-'tüd-ᵊn-əl, -'tyüd-\ *adj*  **1** : extending lengthwise  **2** : of or relating to length — **lon·gi·tu·di·nal·ly** *adv*

**long—range** \'lȯŋ-'rānj\ *adj*  **1** : relating to or fit for long distances  **2** : involving a long period of time

**long·shore·man** \'lȯŋ-'shȯr-mən\ *n* : a laborer at a wharf who loads and unloads cargo

**long—suf·fer·ing** \-'sə-friŋ, -fə-riŋ\ *adj* : patiently enduring lasting offense or hardship

**long—term** \'lȯŋ-'tərm\ *adj*  **1** : extending over or involving a long period of time  **2** : constituting a financial obligation based on a term usu. of more than 10 years ⟨~ bonds⟩

**long·time** \'lȯŋ-'tīm\ *adj* : of long duration ⟨~ friends⟩

**long ton** *n* — see WEIGHT table

**lon·gueur** \lōⁿ-'gər\ *n, pl* **longueurs** \*same or* -'gərz\ [F, lit., length] : a dull tedious portion (as of a book)

**long–wind·ed** \ˌlȯŋ-ˈwin-dəd\ *adj* : tediously long in speaking or writing

**loo·fah** \ˈlü-fə\ *n* : a sponge consisting of the fibrous skeleton of a gourd

¹**look** \ˈlu̇k\ *vb* 1 : to exercise the power of vision : SEE ⟨∼ what I won⟩ 2 : EXPECT 3 : to have an appearance that befits ⟨∼s the part⟩ 4 : SEEM ⟨∼s thin⟩ 5 : to direct one's attention : HEED ⟨∼ at the sign⟩ 6 : POINT, FACE ⟨∼s east⟩ 7 : to show a tendency — **look after** : to take care of — **look at** 1 : CONSIDER ⟨*looking at* all possibilities⟩ 2 : CONFRONT, FACE ⟨*looking at* stiff fines⟩ — **look for** 1 : EXPECT — **look forward** : to anticipate with pleasure ⟨*look forward* to summer⟩

²**look** *n* 1 : the action of looking : GLANCE 2 : EXPRESSION; *also* : physical appearance 3 : ASPECT

**look down** *vb* : to regard with contempt — used with *on* or *upon*

**looking glass** *n* : MIRROR

**look·out** \ˈlu̇k-ˌau̇t\ *n* 1 : a person assigned to watch (as on a ship) 2 : a careful watch 3 : VIEW 4 : a matter of concern

**look up** *vb* 1 : IMPROVE ⟨business is *looking up*⟩ 2 : to search for in or as if in a reference work 3 : to seek out esp. for a brief visit

¹**loom** \ˈlüm\ *n* : a frame or machine for weaving together threads or yarns into cloth

²**loom** *vb* 1 : to come into sight in an unnaturally large, indistinct, or distorted form 2 : to appear in an impressively exaggerated form

**loon** \ˈlün\ *n* : any of several web-footed black-and-white fish-eating diving birds

**loo·ny** *or* **loo·ney** \ˈlü-nē\ *adj* **loo·ni·er; -est** : CRAZY, FOOLISH

**loony bin** *n* : a psychiatric hospital

**loop** \ˈlüp\ *n* 1 : a fold or doubling of a line through which another line or hook can be passed; *also* : a loop-shaped figure or course ⟨a ∼ in a river⟩ 2 : a circular airplane maneuver executed in the vertical plane 3 : a continuously repeated segment of film, music, or sound — **loop** *vb*

**loop·er** \ˈlü-pər\ *n* : any of numerous rather small hairless moth caterpillars that move with a looping motion

**loop·hole** \ˈlüp-ˌhōl\ *n* 1 : a small opening in a wall through which firearms may be discharged 2 : a means of escape; *esp* : an ambiguity or omission that allows one to evade the intent of a law or contract

**loopy** \ˈlü-pē\ *adj* **loop·i·er; -est** 1 : having loops 2 : CRAZY, BIZARRE — **loop·i·ly** \-pə-lē\ *adv* — **loop·i·ness** \-pē-nəs\ *n*

¹**loose** \ˈlüs\ *adj* **loos·er; loos·est** 1 : not rigidly fastened 2 : free from restraint or obligation 3 : not dense or compact in structure 4 : not chaste : LEWD 5 : SLACK 6 : not precise or exact — **loose·ly** *adv* — **loose·ness** *n*

²**loose** *vb* **loosed; loos·ing** 1 : RELEASE 2 : UNTIE 3 : DETACH 4 : DISCHARGE 5 : RELAX, SLACKEN

³**loose** *adv* : LOOSELY

**loos·en** \ˈlü-sᵊn\ *vb* 1 : FREE 2 : to make

or become loose 3 : to relax the severity of ⟨∼ rules⟩

**loot** \ˈlüt\ *n* [Hindi & Urdu *lūṭ*; akin to Skt *luṇṭati* he plunders] : goods taken in war or by robbery : PLUNDER — **loot** *vb* — **loot·er** *n*

¹**lop** \ˈläp\ *vb* **lopped; lop·ping** : to cut branches or twigs from : TRIM; *also* : to cut off

²**lop** *vb* **lopped; lop·ping** : to hang downward; *also* : to flop or sway loosely

**lope** \ˈlōp\ *n* : an easy bounding gait — **lope** *vb*

**lop·sid·ed** \ˈläp-ˈsī-dəd\ *adj* 1 : leaning to one side 2 : UNSYMMETRICAL — **lop·sid·ed·ly** *adv* — **lop·sid·ed·ness** *n*

**lo·qua·cious** \lō-ˈkwā-shəs\ *adj* : excessively talkative — **lo·quac·i·ty** \-ˈkwa-sə-tē\ *n*

¹**lord** \ˈlȯrd\ *n* [ME *loverd, lord,* fr. OE *hlāford,* fr. *hlāf* loaf + *weard* keeper] 1 : one having power and authority over others; *esp* : a person from whom a feudal fee or estate is held 2 *cap* : GOD 1 3 : a man of rank or high position; *esp* : a British nobleman 4 *pl, cap* : the upper house of the British parliament 5 : a person of great power in some field

²**lord** *vb* : to act like a lord; *esp* : to put on airs — usu. used with *it*

**lord chancellor** *n, pl* **lords chancellor** : a British officer of state who presides over the House of Lords, serves as head of the British judiciary, and is usu. a leading member of the cabinet

**lord·ly** \-lē\ *adj* **lord·li·er; -est** 1 : DIGNIFIED; *also* : NOBLE 2 : HAUGHTY

**lord·ship** \-ˌship\ *n* 1 : the rank or dignity of a lord — used as a title 2 : the authority or territory of a lord

**Lord's Supper** *n* : COMMUNION

**lore** \ˈlȯr\ *n* : KNOWLEDGE; *esp* : traditional knowledge or belief

**lor·gnette** \lȯrn-ˈyet\ *n* [F, fr. *lorgner* to take a sidelong look at, fr. MF, fr. *lorgne* squinting] : a pair of eyeglasses or opera glasses with a handle

**lorn** \ˈlȯrn\ *adj* : FORSAKEN, DESOLATE

**lor·ry** \ˈlȯr-ē\ *n, pl* **lorries** *chiefly Brit* : MOTORTRUCK

**lose** \ˈlüz\ *vb* **lost** \ˈlȯst\; **los·ing** \ˈlü-ziŋ\ 1 : DESTROY 2 : to miss from a customary place : MISLAY 3 : to suffer deprivation of 4 : to fail to use : WASTE ⟨no time to ∼⟩ 5 : to fail to win or obtain ⟨∼ the game⟩ 6 : to fail to keep or maintain ⟨∼ his balance⟩ 7 : to wander from ⟨∼ her way⟩ 8 : to get rid of ⟨should ∼ the beard⟩ — **los·er** *n* — **lose it** 1 : to go crazy 2 : to fail to keep one's composure

**loss** \ˈlȯs\ *n* 1 : RUIN 2 : the harm resulting from losing 3 : something that is lost 4 *pl* : killed, wounded, or captured soldiers 5 : failure to win 6 : an amount by which the cost exceeds the selling price 7 : decrease in amount or degree

**loss leader** *n* : an article sold at a loss in order to draw customers

**lost** \ˈlȯst\ *adj* 1 : not used, won, or claimed 2 : no longer possessed or known 3 : ruined or destroyed physically or morally 4 : DENIED; *also* : HARDENED

**5** : unable to find the way; *also* : HELP-LESS **6** : ABSORBED, RAPT **7** : not appreciated or understood ⟨his jokes were ~ on me⟩ **8** : made obscure : OVERLOOKED ⟨~ in translation⟩ **9** : FUTILE ⟨a ~ cause⟩

**lot** \ˈlät\ *n* **1** : an object used in deciding something by chance; *also* : the use of lots to decide something **2** : SHARE, POR-TION; *also* : FORTUNE, FATE **3** : a plot of land **4** : a group of individuals : SET **5** : a considerable quantity ⟨a ~ of trouble⟩

**loth** *var of* LOATH

**lo·ti** \ˈlō-tē\ *n, pl* **ma·lo·ti** \mə-ˈlō-tē\ — see MONEY table

**lo·tion** \ˈlō-shən\ *n* : a liquid preparation for cosmetic and external medicinal use

**lot·tery** \ˈlä-tə-rē\ *n, pl* **-ter·ies** **1** : a drawing of lots in which prizes are given to the winning names or numbers **2** : a matter determined by chance

**lo·tus** \ˈlō-təs\ *n* **1** : a fruit held in Greek legend to cause dreamy contentment and forgetfulness **2** : any of various water lilies represented esp. in ancient Egyptian and Hindu art **3** : any of several leguminous forage plants

**loud** \ˈlaud\ *adj* **1** : marked by intensity or volume of sound **2** : CLAMOROUS, NOISY **3** : obtrusive or offensive in color or pattern ⟨a ~ tie⟩ — **loud** *adv* — **loud·ly** *adv* — **loud·ness** *n*

**loud-mouthed** \-ˌmautht, -ˌmauthd\ *adj* : given to loud offensive talk

**loud·speak·er** \-ˌspē-kər\ *n* : a device that changes electrical signals into sound

**¹lounge** \ˈlaunj\ *vb* **lounged**; **loung·ing** : to act or move lazily or listlessly

**²lounge** *n* **1** : a room with comfortable furniture; *also* : a room (as in a theater) with lounging, smoking, and toilet facilities **2** : a long couch

**lour, loury** *var of* LOWER, LOWERY

**louse** \ˈlaus\ *n, pl* **lice** \ˈlīs\ **1** : any of various small wingless usu. flattened insects parasitic on warm-blooded animals **2** : a plant pest (as an aphid) **3** *pl* **lous·es** \ˈlau-səz\ : a contemptible person

**lousy** \ˈlau-zē\ *adj* **lous·i·er**; **-est** **1** : infested with lice **2** : POOR, INFERIOR **3** : somewhat ill **4** : amply supplied ⟨~ with money⟩ — **lous·i·ly** \-zə-lē\ *adv* — **lous·i·ness** \-zē-nəs\ *n*

**lout** \ˈlaut\ *n* : a stupid awkward fellow — **lout·ish** *adj* — **lout·ish·ly** *adv*

**lou·ver** *or* **lou·vre** \ˈlü-vər\ *n* **1** : an opening having parallel slanted slats to allow flow of air but to exclude rain or sun or to provide privacy; *also* : a slat in such an opening **2** : a device with movable slats for controlling the flow of air or light

**¹love** \ˈləv\ *n* **1** : strong affection **2** : warm attachment ⟨~ of the sea⟩ **3** : attraction based on sexual desire **4** : a beloved person **5** : unselfish loyal and benevolent concern for others **6** : a score of zero in tennis — **love·less** *adj*

**²love** *vb* **loved**; **lov·ing** **1** : CHERISH **2** : to feel a passion, devotion, or tenderness for **3** : CARESS **4** : to take pleasure in ⟨~s to play bridge⟩ — **lov·able** *also* **love·able** \ˈlə-və-bəl\ *adj* — **lov·er** *n*

**love·bird** \ˈləv-ˌbərd\ *n* : any of various small usu. gray or green parrots that seem to show caring behavior for their mates

**love·lorn** \-ˌlorn\ *adj* : deprived of love or of a lover

**love·ly** \ˈləv-lē\ *adj* **love·li·er**; **-est** : BEAUTIFUL — **love·li·ly** \ˈləv-lə-lē\ *adv* — **love·li·ness** *n* — **lovely** *adv*

**love·mak·ing** \-ˌmā-kiŋ\ *n* **1** : COURT-SHIP **2** : sexual activity; *esp* : COPULA-TION

**love·sick** \-ˌsik\ *adj* **1** : YEARNING ⟨a ~ suitor⟩ **2** : expressing a lover's longing — **love·sick·ness** *n*

**lov·ing** \ˈlə-viŋ\ *adj* **1** : AFFECTIONATE **2** : PAINSTAKING — **lov·ing·ly** *adv*

**¹low** \ˈlō\ *vb* : MOO

**²low** *n* : MOO

**³low** *adj* **low·er** \ˈlō-ər\; **low·est** \ˈlō-əst\ **1** : not high or tall ⟨~ wall⟩; *also* : DÉCOLLETÉ **2** : situated or passing below the normal level or surface ⟨~ ground⟩; *also* : marking a nadir **3** : not loud ⟨~ voice⟩ **4** : being near the equator **5** : humble in status **6** : WEAK; *also* : DEPRESSED **7** : STRICKEN, PROSTRATE **8** : less than usual in number, amount, or value; *also* : of lesser degree than average **9** : falling short of a standard **10** : UNFAVORABLE — **low** *adv* — **low·ness** *n*

**⁴low** *n* **1** : something that is low **2** : a region of low barometric pressure **3** : the arrangement of gears in an automobile transmission that gives the slowest speed and greatest power

**low·ball** \ˈlō-ˌbol\ *vb* : to give a deceptively low price, cost estimate, or offer to

**low beam** *n* : a vehicle headlight beam with short-range focus

**low blow** *n* : an unprincipled attack

**low·brow** \ˈlō-ˌbrau\ *adj* : having little taste or intellectual interest ⟨~ humor⟩ — **lowbrow** *n*

**low–density lipoprotein** *n* : LDL

**low·down** \-ˌdaun\ *n* : pertinent and esp. guarded information

**low–down** \-ˌdaun\ *adj* **1** : MEAN, CON-TEMPTIBLE **2** : deeply emotional

**low–end** \-ˌend\ *adj* : of, relating to, or being the lowest-priced merchandise in a manufacturer's line

**¹low·er** *also* **lour** \ˈlau(-ə)r\ *vb* **1** : FROWN **2** : to become dark, gloomy, and threatening — **lower** *also* **lour** *n*

**²low·er** \ˈlō-ər\ *adj* **1** : relatively low (as in rank) **2** : SOUTHERN ⟨the ~ states⟩ **3** : less advanced in the scale of evolutionary development ⟨~ animals⟩ **4** : situated beneath the earth's surface **5** : constituting the popular and more representative branch of a bicameral legislative body

**³low·er** \ˈlō-ər\ *vb* **1** : DROP; *also* : DIMIN-ISH **2** : to let descend by its own weight; *also* : to reduce the height of **3** : to reduce in value, number, or amount **4** : DEGRADE; *also* : HUMBLE

**low·er·case** \ˌlō-ər-ˈkās\ *adj* : being a letter that belongs to or conforms to the series a, b, c, etc., rather than A, B, C, etc. — **lowercase** *n*

**lower class** *n* : a social class occupying a position below the middle class and having the lowest status in a society — **lower–class** \-'klas\ *adj*

**low·er·most** \'lō-ər-,mōst\ *adj* : LOWEST

**low·ery** *also* **loury** \'laù-(ə-)rē\ *adj* : GLOOMY, LOWERING ⟨a ∼ sky⟩

**lowest common denominator** *n* **1** : LEAST COMMON DENOMINATOR **2** : something designed to appeal to a lowbrow audience; *also* : such an audience

**lowest common multiple** *n* : LEAST COMMON MULTIPLE

**low–key** \'lō-'kē\ *also* **low–keyed** \-'kēd\ *adj* : of low intensity : RESTRAINED

**low·land** \'lō-lənd, -,land\ *n* : low and usu. level country

**low–lev·el** \'lō-'le-vəl\ *adj* **1** : being of low importance or rank **2** : being or relating to nuclear waste of low concentration

**low–life** \'lō-,līf\ *n, pl* **low–lifes** \-,līfs\ *also* **low–lives** \-,līvz\ : a person of low social status or moral character

**low·ly** \'lō-lē\ *adj* **low·li·er; -est** **1** : HUMBLE, MEEK **2** : ranking low in some hierarchy — **low·li·ness** *n*

**low–rise** \'lō-'rīz\ *adj* **1** : having few stories and not equipped with elevators ⟨a ∼ building⟩ **2** : of, relating to, or characterized by low-rise buildings

**low–slung** \'lō-,sləŋ\ *adj* : relatively low to the ground or floor ⟨a ∼ building⟩ ⟨∼ pants⟩

**low–tech** \'lō-'tek\ *adj* : technologically simple or unsophisticated

¹**lox** \'läks\ *n* : liquid oxygen

²**lox** *n, pl* **lox** *or* **lox·es** : salmon cured in brine and sometimes smoked

**loy·al** \'lòi-(ə)l\ *adj* [MF, fr. OF *leial, leel,* fr. L *legalis* legal] **1** : faithful in allegiance to one's government **2** : faithful esp. to a cause or ideal : CONSTANT — **loy·al·ly** \'lòi-ə-lē\ *adv* — **loy·al·ty** \'lòi-(ə)l-tē\ *n*

**loy·al·ist** \'lòi-ə-list\ *n* : one who is or remains loyal to a political party, government, or sovereign

**loz·enge** \'lä-zənj\ *n* **1** : a diamond-shaped figure **2** : a small flat often medicated candy

**LP** *abbr* low pressure

**LPG** *abbr* liquefied petroleum gas

**LPGA** *abbr* Ladies Professional Golf Association

**LPN** \'el-'pē-'en\ *n* : LICENSED PRACTICAL NURSE

**Lr** *symbol* Lawrencium

**LSD** \,el-(,)es-'dē\ *n* [G *Lysergsäure-Diäthylamid* lysergic acid diethylamide] : an illicit and highly potent hallucinogenic drug derived from ergot or produced synthetically

**lt** *abbr* light

**Lt** *abbr* lieutenant

**LT** *abbr* long ton

**LTC** *or* **Lt Col** *abbr* lieutenant colonel

**Lt Comdr** *abbr* lieutenant commander

**ltd** *abbr* limited

**LTG** *or* **Lt Gen** *abbr* lieutenant general

**LTJG** *abbr* lieutenant, junior grade

**ltr** *abbr* letter

**Lu** *symbol* lutetium

**lu·au** \'lü-,aù\ *n* : a Hawaiian feast

**lub** *abbr* lubricant; lubricating

**lub·ber** \'lə-bər\ *n* **1** : LOUT **2** : an unskilled seaman — **lub·ber·ly** *adj*

**lube** \'lüb\ *n* : LUBRICANT; *also* : an application of a lubricant

**lu·bri·cant** \'lü-bri-kənt\ *n* : a material capable of reducing friction when applied between moving parts

**lu·bri·cate** \'lü-brə-,kāt\ *vb* **-cat·ed; -cat·ing** : to apply a lubricant to — **lu·bri·ca·tion** \,lü-brə-'kā-shən\ *n* — **lu·bri·ca·tor** \'lü-brə-,kā-tər\ *n*

**lu·bri·cious** \lü-'bri-shəs\ *or* **lu·bri·cous** \'lü-bri-kəs, -kəs\ *adj* **1** : SMOOTH, SLIPPERY **2** : LECHEROUS; *also* : SALACIOUS — **lu·bric·i·ty** \lü-'bri-sə-tē\ *n*

**lu·cent** \'lü-sᵊnt\ *adj* **1** : LUMINOUS **2** : CLEAR, LUCID — **lu·cent·ly** *adv*

**lu·cerne** \lü-'sərn\ *n, chiefly Brit* : ALFALFA

**lu·cid** \'lü-səd\ *adj* **1** : SHINING **2** : mentally sound **3** : easily understood ⟨a ∼ explanation⟩ — **lu·cid·i·ty** \lü-'si-də-tē\ *n* — **lu·cid·ly** *adv* — **lu·cid·ness** *n*

**Lu·ci·fer** \'lü-sə-fər\ *n* [ME, the morning star, a fallen rebel archangel, the Devil, fr. OE, fr. L, the morning star, fr. *lucifer* light-bearing] : DEVIL, SATAN

¹**luck** \'lək\ *n* **1** : CHANCE, FORTUNE **2** : good fortune — **luck·less** *adj*

²**luck** *vb* **1** : to prosper or succeed esp. through chance or good fortune — usu. used with *out* **2** : to come upon something desirable by chance — usu. used with *out, on, onto,* or *into*

**luck·i·ly** \'lə-kə-lē\ *adv* **1** : in a lucky manner **2** : FORTUNATELY

**lucky** \'lə-kē\ *adj* **luck·i·er; -est** **1** : favored by luck : FORTUNATE **2** : FORTUITOUS **3** : seeming to bring good luck ⟨a ∼ penny⟩ — **luck·i·ness** *n*

**lu·cra·tive** \'lü-krə-tiv\ *adj* : PROFITABLE ⟨∼ business deals⟩ — **lu·cra·tive·ly** *adv* — **lu·cra·tive·ness** *n*

**lu·cre** \'lü-kər\ *n* [ME, fr. AF, fr. L *lucrum*] : PROFIT; *also* : MONEY

**lu·cu·bra·tion** \,lü-kyə-'brā-shən, -kə-\ *n* : laborious study : MEDITATION

**Lud·dite** \'lə-,dīt\ *n* [perh. fr. Ned *Ludd,* 18th cent. Eng. workman who destroyed a knitting frame] : one who is opposed to technological change

**lu·di·crous** \'lü-də-krəs\ *adj* : LAUGHABLE, RIDICULOUS ⟨a ∼ idea⟩ — **lu·di·crous·ly** *adv* — **lu·di·crous·ness** *n*

**luff** \'ləf\ *vb* : to turn the head of a ship toward the wind

¹**lug** \'ləg\ *vb* **lugged; lug·ging** **1** : DRAG, PULL **2** : to carry laboriously

²**lug** *n* **1** : a projecting piece (as for fastening, support, or traction) **2** : a nut securing a wheel on an automobile

**lug·gage** \'lə-gij\ *n* : containers (as suitcases) for carrying personal belongings : BAGGAGE

**lu·gu·bri·ous** \lù-'gü-brē-əs\ *adj* : mournful often to an exaggerated degree ⟨∼ music⟩ — **lu·gu·bri·ous·ly** *adv* — **lu·gu·bri·ous·ness** *n*

**Luke** \'lük\ *n* — see BIBLE table

**luke·warm** \'lük-'wȯrm\ adj 1 : moderately warm : TEPID 2 : not enthusiastic ⟨~ praise⟩ — **luke·warm·ly** adv

¹**lull** \'ləl\ vb 1 : SOOTHE, CALM 2 : to cause to relax vigilance

²**lull** n 1 : a temporary calm (as during a storm) 2 : a temporary drop in activity ⟨a ~ in sales⟩

**lul·la·by** \'lə-lə-,bī\ n, pl **-bies** : a song to lull children to sleep

**lu·ma** \,lü-'mä\ n — see dram at MONEY table

**lum·ba·go** \,ləm-'bā-gō\ n : acute or chronic pain in the lower back

**lum·bar** \'ləm-bər, -,bär\ adj : of, relating to, or constituting the loins or the vertebrae between the thoracic vertebrae and sacrum ⟨~ region⟩

¹**lum·ber** \'ləm-bər\ vb : to move heavily or clumsily ⟨an elephant ~ed along the road⟩

²**lumber** n 1 : surplus or disused articles that are stored away 2 : timber or logs esp. when dressed for use

³**lumber** vb : to cut logs; also : to saw logs into lumber — **lum·ber·man** \-mən\ n

**lum·ber·jack** \-,jak\ n : LOGGER

**lum·ber·yard** \-,yärd\ n : a place where lumber is kept for sale

**lu·mi·nary** \'lü-mə-,ner-ē\ n, pl **-nar·ies** 1 : a very famous person 2 : a source of light; esp : a celestial body

**lu·mi·nes·cence** \,lü-mə-'ne-sᵊns\ n : the low-temperature emission of light (as by a chemical or physiological process); also : such light — **lu·mi·nes·cent** \-sᵊnt\ adj

**lu·mi·nous** \'lü-mə-nəs\ adj 1 : emitting light; also : LIGHTED 2 : CLEAR, INTELLIGIBLE 3 : ILLUSTRIOUS — **lu·mi·nance** \-nəns\ n — **lu·mi·nos·i·ty** \,lü-mə-'nä-sə-tē\ n — **lu·mi·nous·ly** adv

**lum·mox** \'lə-məks\ n : a clumsy person

¹**lump** \'ləmp\ n 1 : a piece or mass of indefinite size and shape 2 : AGGREGATE, TOTALITY 3 : a usu. abnormal swelling — **lump·ish** adj — **lumpy** adj

²**lump** vb 1 : to heap together in a lump 2 : to form into lumps

³**lump** adj : not divided into parts ⟨a ~ sum⟩

**lump·ec·to·my** \,ləm-'pek-tə-mē\ n, pl **-mies** : excision of a breast tumor

**lu·na·cy** \'lü-nə-sē\ n, pl **-cies** 1 : INSANITY 2 : extreme folly

**lu·nar** \'lü-nər\ adj : of or relating to the moon ⟨a ~ eclipse⟩

**lu·nate** \'lü-,nāt\ adj : shaped like a crescent

**lu·na·tic** \'lü-nə-,tik\ adj [ME lunatik, fr. AF & LL; AF lunatike, fr. LL lunaticus, fr. L luna moon; fr. the belief that lunacy fluctuated with the phases of the moon] 1 : INSANE; also : used for insane persons 2 : extremely foolish — **lunatic** n

¹**lunch** \'lənch\ n 1 : a light meal usu. eaten in the middle of the day 2 : the food prepared for a lunch

²**lunch** vb : to eat lunch

**lun·cheon** \'lən-chən\ n : a usu. formal lunch

**lun·cheon·ette** \,lən-chə-'net\ n : a small restaurant serving light lunches

**lunch·room** \'lənch-,rüm, -,rüm\ n 1 : LUNCHEONETTE 2 : a room (as in a school) where lunches are sold and eaten or lunches brought from home may be eaten

**lu·nette** \lü-'net\ n : something shaped like a crescent

**lung** \'ləŋ\ n 1 : one of the usu. paired baglike breathing organs in the chest of an air-breathing vertebrate 2 : a mechanical device to promote breathing and make it easier — **lunged** \'ləŋd\ adj

**lunge** \'lənj\ n 1 : a sudden thrust or pass (as with a sword) 2 : a sudden forward stride or leap — **lunge** vb

**lu·pine** \'lü-pən\ n : any of a genus of leguminous plants with long upright clusters of pealike flowers

**lu·pus** \'lü-pəs\ n [ML, fr. L, wolf] : any of several diseases characterized by skin lesions; esp : SYSTEMIC LUPUS ERYTHEMATOSUS

**lurch** \'lərch\ n : a sudden swaying or tipping movement — **lurch** vb

¹**lure** \'lu̇r\ n 1 : ENTICEMENT; also : APPEAL ⟨the ~ of easy money⟩ 2 : an artificial bait for catching fish

²**lure** vb lured; lur·ing : to draw on with a promise of pleasure or gain

**lu·rid** \'lu̇r-əd\ adj 1 : GRUESOME; also : SENSATIONAL 2 : wan and ghostly pale in appearance 3 : shining with the red glow of fire seen through smoke or cloud
♦ **Synonyms** GHASTLY, GRISLY, GRIM, HORRIBLE, MACABRE — **lu·rid·ly** adv

**lurk** \'lərk\ vb 1 : to move furtively : SNEAK 2 : to lie concealed

**lus·cious** \'lə-shəs\ adj 1 : having a pleasingly sweet taste or smell 2 : sensually appealing ⟨a ~ voice⟩ — **lus·cious·ly** adv — **lus·cious·ness** n

¹**lush** \'ləsh\ adj : having or covered with abundant growth ⟨~ pastures⟩

²**lush** n : a habitual heavy drinker

**lust** \'ləst\ n 1 : usu. intense or unbridled sexual desire : LASCIVIOUSNESS 2 : an intense longing ⟨a ~ to succeed⟩ — **lust** vb — **lust·ful** adj

**lus·ter** or **lus·tre** \'ləs-tər\ n 1 : a shine or sheen esp. from reflected light 2 : BRIGHTNESS, GLITTER 3 : GLORY, SPLENDOR — **lus·ter·less** adj — **lustrous** \-trəs\ adj

**lus·tral** \'ləs-trəl\ adj : serving or intended to purify ⟨~ water⟩

**lusty** \'ləs-tē\ adj **lust·i·er; -est** : full of vitality : ROBUST — **lust·i·ly** \'ləs-tə-lē\ adv — **lust·i·ness** \-tē-nəs\ n

**lute** \'lüt\ n : a stringed musical instrument with a large pear-shaped body and a fretted fingerboard — **lu·te·nist** or **lu·ta·nist** \'lü-tə-nist\ n

**lu·te·tium** also **lu·te·cium** \lü-'tē-shē-əm, -shəm\ n : a metallic chemical element

**Lu·ther·an** \'lü-thə-rən\ n : a member of a Protestant denomination adhering to the doctrines of Martin Luther — **Lu·ther·an·ism** \-rə-,ni-zəm\ n

**lux·u·ri·ant** \,ləg-'zhu̇r-ē-ənt, ,lək-'shu̇r-\ adj 1 : yielding or growing abundantly : LUSH, PRODUCTIVE ⟨~ vegetation⟩ 2 : abundantly rich and varied; also : FLOR-

ID ⟨a ~ fabric⟩ ◆ **Synonyms** EXUBERANT, LAVISH, OPULENT, PRODIGAL, PROFUSE, RIOTOUS — **lux·u·ri·ance** \-ē-əns\ *n* — **lux·u·ri·ant·ly** *adv*

**lux·u·ri·ate** \-ē-ˌāt\ *vb* **-at·ed; -at·ing** 1 : to grow profusely 2 : REVEL

**lux·u·ry** \ˈlək-shə-rē, ˈləg-zhə-\ *n, pl* **-ries** 1 : great ease and comfort 2 : something adding to pleasure or comfort but not absolutely necessary — **lux·u·ri·ous** \ˌləg-ˈzhùr-ē-əs, ˌlək-ˈshùr-\ *adj* — **lux·u·ri·ous·ly** *adv*

**lv** *abbr* leave

**lwei** \lə-ˈwā\ *n, pl* **lwei** — see *kwanza* at MONEY table

**LWV** *abbr* League of Women Voters

**¹-ly** \lē\ *adj suffix* 1 : like in appearance, manner, or nature ⟨queenly⟩ 2 : characterized by regular recurrence in (specified) units of time : every ⟨hourly⟩ ⟨weekly⟩

**²-ly** *adv suffix* 1 : in a (specified) manner ⟨slowly⟩ 2 : from a (specified) point of view ⟨grammatically⟩

**ly·ce·um** \lī-ˈsē-əm, ˈlī-sē-\ *n* 1 : a hall for public lectures 2 : an association providing public lectures, concerts, and entertainments

**ly·chee** *or* **li·tchi** \ˈlē-chē, ˈlī-\ *n* [Ch(Beijing) *lìzhī*] 1 : an oval fruit with a hard scaly outer covering, a small hard seed, and edible flesh 2 : an Asian tree bearing lychees

**lye** \ˈlī\ *n* : a corrosive alkaline substance used esp. in making soap

**ly·ing** \ˈlī-iŋ\ *adj* : UNTRUTHFUL, FALSE

**ly·ing-in** \ˌlī-iŋ-ˈin\ *n, pl* **lyings-in** *or* **ly·ing-ins** : the state during and consequent to childbirth : CONFINEMENT

**Lyme disease** \ˈlīm-\ *n* [*Lyme*, Connecticut, where it was first reported] : an acute inflammatory disease that is caused by a spirochete transmitted by ticks, is characterized usu. by chills and fever, and if left untreated may result in joint pain, arthritis, and cardiac and neurological disorders

**lymph** \ˈlimf\ *n* : a usu. clear fluid consisting chiefly of blood plasma and white blood cells, circulating in thin-walled tubes (**lymphatic vessels**), and bathing the body tissues — **lym·phat·ic** \lim-ˈfa-tik\ *adj*

**lymph·ade·nop·a·thy** \ˌlim-ˌfa-də-ˈnä-pə-thē\ *n, pl* **-thies** : abnormal enlargement of the lymph nodes

**lymph node** *n* : any of the rounded masses of lymphoid tissue surrounded by a capsule of connective tissue

**lym·pho·cyte** \ˈlim-fə-ˌsīt\ *n* : any of the white blood cells arising from lymphoid tissue that are typically found in lymph and blood and that include the cellular mediators (as a B cell or a T cell) of immunity — **lym·pho·cyt·ic** \ˌlim-fə-ˈsi-tik\ *adj*

**lym·phoid** \ˈlim-ˌfòid\ *adj* 1 : of, relating to, or being tissue (as of the lymph nodes) containing lymphocytes 2 : of, relating to, or resembling lymph

**lym·pho·ma** \lim-ˈfō-mə\ *n, pl* **-mas** *also* **-ma·ta** \-mə-tə\ : a usu. malignant tumor of lymphoid tissue

**lynch** \ˈlinch\ *vb* : to put to death by mob action without legal sanction or due process of law — **lynch·er** *n*

**lynx** \ˈliŋks\ *n, pl* **lynx** *or* **lynx·es** : any of several wildcats with a short tail, long legs, and usu. tufted ears

**lyre** \ˈlī(-ə)r\ *n* : a stringed musical instrument of the harp class having a U-shaped frame and used by the ancient Greeks

**¹lyr·ic** \ˈlir-ik\ *n* 1 : a lyric poem 2 *pl* : the words of a popular song — **lyr·i·cal** \-i-kəl\ *adj*

**²lyric** *adj* 1 : suitable for singing : MELODIC 2 : expressing direct and usu. intense personal emotion ⟨~ poetry⟩

**ly·ser·gic acid di·eth·yl·am·ide** \lə-ˈsər-jik . . . ˌdī-ˌe-thə-ˈla-ˌmīd, lī-, -ˈla-məd\ *n* : LSD

**LZ** *abbr* landing zone

**¹m** \ˈem\ *n, pl* **m's** *or* **ms** \ˈemz\ *often cap* : the 13th letter of the English alphabet

**²m** *abbr, often cap* 1 Mach 2 male 3 married 4 masculine 5 medium 6 [L *meridies*] noon 7 meter 8 mile 9 [L *mille*] thousand 10 minute 11 month 12 moon

**ma** \ˈmä, ˈmò\ *n* : MOTHER

**MA** *abbr* [ML *magister artium*] master of arts 1 Massachusetts 3 mental age

**ma'am** \ˈmam, *after "yes" often* əm\ *n* : MADAM

**Mac** *abbr* Machabees

**Mac** *or* **Macc** *abbr* Maccabees

**ma·ca·bre** \mə-ˈkäb; ˈkä-brə, -bər\ *adj* [F] 1 : having death as a subject 2 : GRUESOME 3 : HORRIBLE

**mac·ad·am** \mə-ˈka-dəm\ *n* [John L. McAdam †1836 Brit. engineer] : a roadway or pavement of small closely packed broken stone — **mac·ad·am·ize** \-də-ˌmīz\ *vb*

**mac·a·da·mia nut** \ˌma-kə-ˈdä-mē-ə-\ : a hard-shelled richly flavored nut of any of several Australian trees

**ma·caque** \mə-ˈkak, -ˈkäk\ *n* : any of a genus of short-tailed chiefly Asian monkeys; *esp* : RHESUS MONKEY

**mac·a·ro·ni** \ˌma-kə-ˈrō-nē\ *n* 1 : pasta made chiefly of wheat flour and shaped in the form of slender tubes 2 *pl* **-nis** *or* **-nies** : FOP, DANDY

**mac·a·roon** \ˌma-kə-ˈrün\ *n* : a small cookie made chiefly of egg whites, sugar, and ground almonds or coconut

**ma·caw** \mə-ˈkò\ *n* : any of numerous parrots of Central and So. America

**Mac·ca·bees** \'ma-kə-ˌbēz\ *n* — see BI-BLE table

¹**mace** \'mās\ *n* : a spice made from the fibrous coating of the nutmeg

²**mace** *n* **1** : a heavy often spiked club used as a weapon esp. in the Middle Ages **2** : an ornamental staff carried as a symbol of authority

**mac·er·ate** \'ma-sə-ˌrāt\ *vb* **-at·ed; -at·ing** **1** : to cause to waste away **2** : to soften by steeping or soaking so as to separate the parts — **mac·er·a·tion** \ˌma-sə-'rā-shən\ *n*

**Mac·Guf·fin** *or* **Mc·Guf·fin** \mə-'gə-fən\ *n* : an object, event, or character whose main purpose is to advance the plot of a motion picture

**mach** *abbr* machine; machinery; machinist

**Mach** \'mäk\ *n* : a speed expressed by a Mach number

**Mach·a·bees** \'ma-kə-ˌbēz\ *n* : MACCABEES

**ma·chete** \mə-'she-te\ *n* : a large heavy knife used for cutting sugarcane and underbrush and as a weapon

**Ma·chi·a·vel·lian** \ˌma-kē-ə-'ve-lē-ən\ *adj* [Niccolò *Machiavelli*, †1527 Ital. political philosopher] : characterized by cunning, duplicity, and bad faith — **Ma·chi·a·vel·lian·ism** *n*

**mach·i·na·tion** \ˌma-kə-'nā-shən, ˌma-shə-\ *n* : an act of planning esp. to do harm; *esp* : PLOT — **mach·i·nate** \'ma-kə-ˌnāt, 'ma-shə-\ *vb*

¹**ma·chine** \mə-'shēn\ *n* **1** : CONVEYANCE, VEHICLE; *esp* : AUTOMOBILE **2** : a combination of mechanical parts that transmit forces, motion, and energy one to another **3** : an instrument (as a lever) for transmitting or modifying force or motion **4** : an electrical, electronic, or mechanical device for performing a task ⟨a sewing ∼⟩ **5** : a highly organized political group under the leadership of a boss or small clique

²**machine** *vb* **ma·chined; ma·chin·ing** : to shape or finish by machine-operated tools — **ma·chin·able** \-'shē-nə-bəl\ *adj*

**machine gun** *n* : an automatic gun capable of rapid continuous firing — **ma·chine–gun** *vb* — **machine gunner** *n*

**machine language** *n* : the set of symbolic instruction codes used to represent operations and data in a machine (as a computer)

**machine–readable** *adj* : directly usable by a computer

**ma·chin·ery** \mə-'shē-nə-rē\ *n, pl* **-er·ies** **1** : MACHINES; *also* : the working parts of a machine **2** : the means by which something is done

**ma·chin·ist** \mə-'shē-nist\ *n* : a person who makes or works on machines

**ma·chis·mo** \mä-'chēz-(ˌ)mō, -'chiz-\ *n* : a strong or exaggerated pride in one's masculinity

**Mach number** \'mäk-\ *n* : a number representing the ratio of the speed of a body (as an aircraft) to the speed of sound in the surrounding atmosphere

**ma·cho** \'mä-chō\ *adj* [Sp, lit., male, fr. L *masculus*] : characterized by machismo

**mack·er·el** \'ma-kə-rəl\ *n, pl* **mackerel** *or* **mackerels** : a No. Atlantic food fish greenish above and silvery below

**mack·i·naw** \'ma-kə-ˌnȯ\ *n* : a short heavy plaid coat

**mack·in·tosh** *also* **mac·in·tosh** \'ma-kən-ˌtäsh\ *n* **1** *chiefly Brit* : RAINCOAT **2** : a lightweight waterproof fabric

**mac·ra·mé** *also* **mac·ra·me** \'ma-krə-ˌmā\ *n* [ultim. fr. Ar *miqrama* coverlet] : a coarse lace or fringe made by knotting threads or cords in a geometrical pattern

¹**mac·ro** \'ma-(ˌ)krō\ *adj* : very large; *also* : involving large quantities or being on a large scale ⟨∼ economic policies⟩

²**macro** *n, pl* **macros** : a single computer instruction that stands for a sequence of operations

**mac·ro·bi·ot·ic** \ˌma-krō-bī-'ä-tik, -bē-\ *adj* : relating to or being a very restricted diet (as one containing chiefly whole cereals or grains)

**mac·ro·cosm** \'ma-krə-ˌkä-zəm\ *n* : the great world : UNIVERSE

**ma·cron** \'mā-ˌkrän, 'ma-\ *n* : a mark placed over a vowel (as in \mäk\) to show that the vowel is long

**mac·ro·scop·ic** \ˌma-krə-'skä-pik\ *adj* : visible to the naked eye — **mac·ro·scop·i·cal·ly** \-pi-k(ə-)lē\ *adv*

**mac·u·la** \'ma-kyə-lə\ *n, pl* **-lae** \-ˌlē, -ˌlī\ *also* **-las** : an anatomical spot distinguishable from surrounding tissues — **mac·u·lar** \-lər\ *adj*

¹**mad** \'mad\ *adj* **mad·der; mad·dest 1** : disordered in mind : INSANE **2** : being rash and foolish **3** : FURIOUS, ENRAGED **4** : carried away by enthusiasm ⟨∼ about football⟩ **5** : RABID **6** : marked by wild gaiety and merriment **7** : FRANTIC ⟨a ∼ rush⟩ — **mad·ly** *adv* — **mad·ness** *n*

**mad·am** \'ma-dəm\ *n* **1** *pl* **mes·dames** \mā-'däm\ — used as a form of polite address to a woman **2** *pl* **madams** : the female head of a house of prostitution

**ma·dame** \mə-'dam, *before a surname also* 'ma-dəm\ *n, pl* **mes·dames** \mā-'däm\ : MISTRESS — used as a title equivalent to *Mrs.* for a married woman not of English-speaking nationality

**mad·cap** \'mad-ˌkap\ *adj* : WILD, RECKLESS ⟨a ∼ scheme⟩ — **madcap** *n*

**mad cow disease** *n* : a fatal encephalopathy of cattle that affects the nervous system causing the brain tissue to resemble a porous sponge

**mad·den** \'ma-dᵊn\ *vb* : to make mad — **mad·den·ing·ly** *adv*

**mad·der** \'ma-dər\ *n* : a Eurasian herb with yellow flowers and fleshy red roots; *also* : its root or a dye prepared from it

**made** *past and past part of* MAKE

**Ma·dei·ra** \mə-'dir-ə\ *n* : an amber-colored dessert wine

**ma·de·moi·selle** \ˌma-də-mə-'zel, -mwə-, mam-'zel\ *n, pl* **ma·de·moi·selles** \-'zelz\ *or* **mes·de·moi·selles** \ˌmā-də-me-'zel, -mwə-\ : an unmarried girl or woman — used as a title for an unmarried woman not of English-speaking nationality

**made–to–measure** adj : CUSTOM-MADE

**made–up** \'mād-'əp\ adj 1 : fancifully conceived or falsely devised 2 : marked by the use of makeup

**mad·house** \'mad-,haùs\ n 1 : a place for the detention and care of the insane 2 : a place of great uproar

**mad·man** \'mad-,man, -mən\ n : LUNATIC

**Ma·don·na** \mə-'dä-nə\ n : a representation (as a picture or statue) of the Virgin Mary

**ma·dras** \'ma-drəs; ,mə-'dras, -'dräs\ n [Madras, India] : a fine usu. cotton fabric with various designs (as plaid)

**ma·dras·sa** or **ma·dra·sa** \mə-'dra-sə, -'drä-\ n : a Muslim school, college, or university that is often part of a mosque

**mad·ri·gal** \'ma-dri-gəl\ n [It madrigale] 1 : a short lyrical poem in a strict poetic form 2 : an elaborate part-song esp. of the 16th and 17th centuries

**mad·wom·an** \'mad-,wù-mən\ n : a woman who is insane

**mael·strom** \'māl-strəm\ n 1 : a violent whirlpool 2 : TUMULT

**mae·stro** \'mī-strō\ n, pl **maestros** or **mae·stri** \-,strē\ [It] : a master in an art; esp : an eminent composer, conductor, or teacher of music

**Ma·fia** \'mä-fē-ə\ n [It] : a secret criminal society of Sicily or Italy; also : a similar organization elsewhere

**ma·fi·o·so** \,mä-fē-'ō-(,)sō\ n, pl **-si** \-(,)sē\ : a member of the Mafia

**¹mag** \'mag\ n : MAGAZINE

**²mag** abbr 1 magnetism 2 magneto 3 magnitude

**mag·a·zine** \'ma-gə-,zēn\ n [MF, fr. Old Occitan, fr. Ar makhāzin, pl. of makhzan storehouse] 1 : a storehouse esp. for military supplies 2 : a place for keeping gunpowder in a fort or ship 3 : a publication usu. containing stories, articles, or poems and issued periodically 4 : a container in a gun for holding cartridges; also : a chamber (as on a camera) for film

**ma·gen·ta** \mə-'jen-tə\ n : a deep purplish red color

**mag·got** \'ma-gət\ n : the legless wormlike larva of a dipteran fly — **mag·goty** adj

**ma·gi** \'mā-jì\ n pl, often cap : the three wise men from the East who paid homage to the infant Jesus

**mag·ic** \'ma-jik\ n 1 : the use of means (as charms or spells) believed to have supernatural power over natural forces 2 : an extraordinary power or influence seemingly from a supernatural force 3 : SLEIGHT OF HAND — **magic** adj — **mag·i·cal** \-ji-kəl\ adj — **mag·i·cal·ly** \-ji-k(ə-)lē\ adv

**ma·gi·cian** \mə-'ji-shən\ n : a person skilled in magic

**mag·is·te·ri·al** \,ma-jə-'stir-ē-əl\ adj 1 : AUTHORITATIVE ⟨a ∼ attitude⟩ 2 : of or relating to a magistrate or a magistrate's office or duties

**mag·is·tral** \'ma-jə-strəl\ adj : AUTHORITATIVE

**mag·is·trate** \'ma-jə-,strāt\ n : an official entrusted with administration of the laws — **mag·is·tra·cy** \-strə-sē\ n

**mag·lev** \'mag-lev\ n 1 : the use of magnetic fields to float an object above a solid surface 2 : a train using maglev technology

**mag·ma** \'mag-mə\ n : molten rock material within the earth — **mag·mat·ic** \mag-'ma-tik\ adj

**mag·nan·i·mous** \mag-'na-nə-məs\ adj : showing or suggesting a lofty and courageous spirit 2 : NOBLE, GENEROUS — **mag·na·nim·i·ty** \,mag-nə-'ni-mə-tē\ n — **mag·nan·i·mous·ly** adv — **mag·nan·i·mous·ness** n

**mag·nate** \'mag-,nāt\ n : a person of rank, influence, or distinction

**mag·ne·sia** \mag-'nē-shə, -zhə\ n [NL, fr. magnes carneus, a white earth, lit., flesh magnet] : a light white oxide of magnesium used as a laxative

**mag·ne·sium** \mag-'nē-zē-əm, -zhəm\ n : a silver-white light malleable metallic chemical element

**mag·net** \'mag-nət\ n 1 : LODESTONE 2 : a body that is able to attract iron 3 : something that attracts

**mag·net·ic** \mag-'ne-tik\ adj 1 : having an unusual ability to attract ⟨a ∼ leader⟩ 2 : of or relating to a magnet or magnetism 3 : magnetized or capable of being magnetized — **mag·net·i·cal·ly** \-ti-k(ə-)lē\ adv

**magnetic disk** n : DISK 3

**magnetic levitation** n : MAGLEV 1

**magnetic north** n : the northerly direction in the earth's magnetic field indicated by the north-seeking pole of a compass needle

**magnetic resonance imaging** n : a noninvasive diagnostic technique that produces computerized images of internal body tissues based on electromagnetically induced activity of atoms within the body

**magnetic tape** n : a ribbon coated with a magnetic material on which information (as sound) may be stored

**mag·ne·tise** Brit var of MAGNETIZE

**mag·ne·tism** \'mag-nə-,ti-zəm\ n 1 : the power (as of a magnet) to attract iron 2 : the science that deals with magnetic phenomena 3 : an ability to attract or charm

**mag·ne·tite** \'mag-nə-,tīt\ n : a black mineral that is an important iron ore

**mag·ne·tize** \'mag-nə-,tīz\ vb **-tized; -tiz·ing** 1 : to induce magnetic properties in 2 : to attract like a magnet : CHARM — **mag·ne·tiz·able** adj — **mag·ne·ti·za·tion** \,mag-nə-tə-'zā-shən\ n — **mag·ne·tiz·er** n

**mag·ne·to** \mag-'nē-tō\ n, pl **-tos** : a generator used to produce sparks in an internal combustion engine

**mag·ne·tom·e·ter** \,mag-nə-'tä-mə-tər\ n : an instrument for measuring the strength of a magnetic field

**mag·ne·to·sphere** \mag-'nē-tə-,sfir,

-'ne-\ n : a region around a celestial object (as the earth) in which charged particles are trapped by its magnetic field —
**mag·ne·to·spher·ic** \-,nē-tə-'sfir-ik, -'sfer-\ adj

**mag·ni·fi·ca·tion** \,mag-nə-fə-'kā-shən\ n
**1** : the act of magnifying **2** : the amount by which an optical lens or instrument magnifies

**mag·nif·i·cent** \mag-'ni-fə-sənt\ adj **1** : characterized by grandeur or beauty : SPLENDID **2** : EXALTED, NOBLE ♦ **Synonyms** IMPOSING, STATELY, GRAND, MAJESTIC — **mag·nif·i·cence** \-səns\ n — **mag·nif·i·cent·ly** adv

**mag·ni·fi·co** \mag-'ni-fi-,kō\ n, pl **-coes** or **-cos** **1** : a nobleman of Venice **2** : a person of high position

**mag·ni·fy** \'mag-nə-,fī\ vb **-fied; -fy·ing 1** : EXTOL, LAUD; also : to cause to be held in greater esteem **2** : INTENSIFY; also : EXAGGERATE **3** : to enlarge in fact or in appearance ⟨a microscope magnifies an object⟩ — **mag·ni·fi·er** \'mag-nə-,fī(-ə)r\ n

**mag·nil·o·quent** \mag-'ni-lə-kwənt\ adj : characterized by an exalted and often bombastic style or manner — **mag·nil·o·quence** \-kwəns\ n

**mag·ni·tude** \'mag-nə-,tüd, -,tyüd\ n **1** : greatness of size or extent **2** : SIZE **3** : QUANTITY **4** : a number representing the brightness of a celestial body **5** : a number representing the intensity of an earthquake

**mag·no·lia** \mag-'nōl-yə\ n : any of a genus of usu. spring-flowering shrubs and trees with large often fragrant flowers

**mag·num opus** \'mag-nəm-'ō-pəs\ n [L] : the greatest achievement of an artist or writer

**mag·pie** \'mag-,pī\ n : any of various long-tailed often black-and-white birds related to the jays

**Mag·yar** \'mag-,yär, 'mäg-; 'mä-,jär\ n : a member of the dominant people of Hungary — **Magyar** adj

**ma·ha·ra·ja** or **ma·ha·ra·jah** \,mä-hə-'rä-jə\ n : a Hindu prince ranking above a raja

**ma·ha·ra·ni** or **ma·ha·ra·nee** \-'rä-nē\ n **1** : the wife of a maharaja **2** : a Hindu princess ranking above a rani

**ma·ha·ri·shi** \,mä-hə-'rē-shē\ n : a Hindu teacher of mystical knowledge

**ma·hat·ma** \mə-'hät-mə, -'hat-\ n [Skt mahātman, fr. mahātman great-souled, fr. mahat great + ātman soul] : a person revered for high-mindedness, wisdom, and selflessness

**Ma·hi·can** \mə-'hē-kən\ or **Mo·hi·can** \mō-, mə-\ n, pl **-can** or **-cans** : a member of an American Indian people of the upper Hudson River valley

**ma·hog·a·ny** \mə-'hä-gə-nē\ n, pl **-nies** : the reddish wood of any of various chiefly tropical trees that is used in furniture; also : a tree yielding this wood

**ma·hout** \mə-'haùt\ n [Hindi & Urdu mahāwat, mahāut] : a keeper and driver of an elephant

**maid** \'mād\ n **1** : an unmarried girl or

young woman **2** : MAIDSERVANT; also : a woman or girl employed to do domestic work

**¹maid·en** \'mā-d²n\ n : MAID 1 — **maid·en·ly** adj

**²maiden** adj **1** : UNMARRIED; also : VIRGIN **2** : of, relating to, or befitting a maiden **3** : FIRST ⟨a ship's ∼ voyage⟩

**maid·en·hair fern** \-,her-\ n : any of a genus of ferns with delicate feathery fronds

**maid·en·head** \'mā-d²n-,hed\ n **1** : VIRGINITY **2** : HYMEN

**maid·en·hood** \-,hùd\ n : the condition or time of being a maiden

**maid–in–waiting** n, pl **maids–in–waiting** : a young woman appointed to attend a queen or princess

**maid of honor** : a bride's principal unmarried wedding attendant

**maid·ser·vant** \'mād-,sər-vant\ n : a girl or woman who is a servant

**¹mail** \'māl\ n [ME male bag, fr. AF, of Gmc origin] **1** : material sent or carried in the postal system **2** : a nation's postal system — often used in pl. **3** : E-MAIL

**²mail** vb : to send by mail

**³mail** n [ME maille metal link, mail, fr. AF, fr. L macula spot, mesh] : armor made of metal links or plates

**mail·box** \'māl-,bäks\ n **1** : a public box for the collection of mail **2** : a private box for the delivery of mail

**mail·man** \-,man\ n : a man who delivers mail

**maim** \'mām\ vb : to mutilate, disfigure, or wound seriously

**¹main** \'mān\ n **1** : FORCE ⟨with might and ∼⟩ **2** : MAINLAND; also : HIGH SEA **3** : the chief part **4** : a principal pipe, duct, or circuit of a utility system

**²main** adj **1** : CHIEF, PRINCIPAL ⟨the ∼ idea⟩ **2** : fully exerted ⟨∼ force⟩ **3** : expressing the chief predication in a complex sentence ⟨the ∼ clause⟩ — **main·ly** adv

**main·frame** \'mān-,frām\ n : a large fast computer

**main·land** \-,land, -lənd\ n : a continuous body of land constituting the chief part of a country or continent

**main·line** \-,līn\ vb, slang : to inject a narcotic drug into a vein

**main line** n : a principal highway or railroad line

**main·mast** \'mān-,mast, -məst\ n : the principal mast on a sailing ship

**main·sail** \-,sāl, -səl\ n : the largest sail on the mainmast

**main·spring** \-,sprin\ n **1** : the chief spring in a mechanism (as of a watch) **2** : the chief motive, agent, or cause

**main·stay** \-,stā\ n **1** : a stay running from the head of the mainmast to the foot of the foremast **2** : a chief support

**main·stream** \-,strēm\ n : a prevailing current or direction of activity or influence — **mainstream** adj

**main·tain** \mān-'tān\ vb [ME mainteinen, fr. AF maintenir, maynteiner, fr. ML manutenēre, fr. L manu tenēre to hold in the hand] **1** : to keep in an existing state (as of repair) **2** : to sustain against opposition or danger **3** : to continue in : CARRY ON **4** : to provide for : SUPPORT **5** : AS-SERT ⟨*~ed* his innocence⟩ — **main·tain·abil·i·ty** \-ˌtā-nə-ˈbi-lə-tē\ *n* — **main·tain·able** \-ˈtā-nə-bəl\ *adj* — **main·te·nance** \ˈmān-tə-nəns\ *n*

**main·top** \ˈmān-ˌtäp\ *n* : a platform at the head of the mainmast of a square-rigged ship

**mai·son·ette** \ˌmā-zə-ˈnet\ *n* **1** : a small house **2** : an apartment often on two floors

**mai tai** \ˈmī-ˌtī\ *n* : a cocktail made with liquors and fruit juices

**maî·tre d'** *or* **mai·tre d'** \ˌmā-trə-ˈdē, ˌme-\ *n*, *pl* **maître d's** *or* **maitre d's** \-ˈdēz\ : MAÎTRE D'HÔTEL

**maî·tre d'hô·tel** \ˌmā-trə-dō-ˈtel, ˌme-\ *n*, *pl* **maîtres d'hôtel** \*same*\ [F, lit., master of house] **1** : MAJORDOMO **2** : HEAD-WAITER

**maize** \ˈmāz\ *n* : CORN 2

**Maj** *abbr* major

**maj·es·ty** \ˈma-jə-stē\ *n*, *pl* **-ties 1** : sovereign power, authority, or dignity; *also* : the person of a sovereign — used as a title **2** : GRANDEUR, SPLENDOR — **ma·jes·tic** \mə-ˈjes-tik\ *adj* — **ma·jes·ti·cal·ly** \-ti-k(ə-)lē\ *adv*

**Maj Gen** *abbr* Major General

**ma·jol·i·ca** \mə-ˈjä-li-kə\ *also* **ma·iol·i·ca** \-ˈyä-\ *n* : any of several faiences; *esp* : an Italian tin-glazed pottery

**¹ma·jor** \ˈmā-jər\ *adj* **1** : greater in number, extent, or importance ⟨a ~ poet⟩ **2** : notable or conspicuous in effect or scope ⟨a ~ improvement⟩ **3** : SERIOUS ⟨a ~ illness⟩ **4** : having half steps between the 3d and 4th and the 7th and 8th degrees ⟨~ scale⟩; *also* : based on a major scale ⟨~ key⟩ ⟨~ chord⟩

**²major** *n* **1** : a commissioned officer (as in the army) ranking next below a lieutenant colonel **2** : an academic subject chosen as a field of specialization; *also* : a student specializing in such a field ⟨a history ~⟩

**³major** *vb* : to pursue an academic major

**ma·jor·do·mo** \ˌmā-jər-ˈdō-mō\ *n*, *pl* **-mos** [Sp *mayordomo* or obs. It *maiordomo*, fr. ML *major domus*, lit., chief of the house] **1** : a head steward **2** : BUTLER

**ma·jor·ette** \ˌmā-jə-ˈret\ *n* : DRUM MAJORETTE

**major general** *n* : a commissioned officer (as in the army) ranking next below a lieutenant general

**ma·jor·i·ty** \mə-ˈjȯr-ə-tē\ *n*, *pl* **-ties 1** : the age at which full civil rights are accorded; *also* : the status of one who has attained this age **2** : a number greater than half of a total; *also* : the excess of this greater number over the remainder **3** : the rank of a major

**ma·jus·cule** \ˈma-jəs-ˌkyül, mə-ˈjəs-\ *n* : a large letter (as a capital)

**Ma·kah** \ˈmä-kä\ *n*, *pl* **Makah** *or* **Makahs** : a member of an American Indian people of the northwest coast of No. America

**¹make** \ˈmāk\ *vb* **made** \ˈmād\; **mak·ing 1** : to cause to exist, occur, or appear; *also* : DESTINE ⟨was *made* to be an actor⟩

**2** : FASHION ⟨~ a dress⟩; *also* : COMPOSE **3** : to formulate in the mind ⟨~ plans⟩ **4** : CONSTITUTE ⟨house *made* of stone⟩ **5** : to compute to be **6** : to set in order : PREPARE ⟨~ a bed⟩ **7** : to cause to be or become; *also* : APPOINT **8** : ENACT; *also* : EXECUTE ⟨~ a will⟩ **9** : CONCLUDE ⟨didn't know what to ~ of it⟩ **10** : CARRY OUT, PERFORM ⟨~ a gesture⟩ **11** : COMPEL **12** : to assure the success of ⟨will ~ us or break us⟩ **13** : to amount to in significance ⟨~s no difference⟩ **14** : to be capable of developing or being fashioned into **15** : REACH, ATTAIN; *also* : GAIN **16** : to start out : GO **17** : to have weight or effect ⟨courtesy ~s for safer driving⟩ ♦ **Synonyms** FORM, SHAPE, FABRICATE, MANUFACTURE — **mak·er** *n* — **make believe** : PRETEND — **make do** : to manage with the means at hand — **make fun of** : RIDICULE, MOCK — **make good 1** : INDEMNIFY ⟨*make good* the loss⟩; *also* : to carry out successfully ⟨*make good* his promise⟩ **2** : SUCCEED — **make way 1** : to give room for passing, entering, or occupying **2** : to make progress

**²make** *n* **1** : the manner or style of construction; *also* : BRAND **3 2** : MAKEUP **3** : the action of manufacturing — **on the make** : in search of wealth, social status, or sexual adventure

**make–be·lieve** \ˈmāk-bə-ˌlēv\ *n* : a pretending that what is not real is real

**²make–believe** *adj* : IMAGINED, PRETENDED

**make–do** \-ˌdü\ *adj* : MAKESHIFT

**make out** *vb* **1** : to draw up in writing ⟨*make out* a list⟩ **2** : to find or grasp the meaning of ⟨can you *make* that *out*⟩ **3** : to represent as being **4** : to pretend to be true **5** : DISCERN ⟨*make out* a ship in the fog⟩ **6** : GET ALONG, FARE ⟨*make out* well in life⟩ **7** : to engage in amorous kissing and caressing

**make over** *vb* **1** : REMAKE, REMODEL — **make·over** \ˈmā-ˌkō-vər\ *n*

**make·shift** \ˈmāk-ˌshift\ *n* : a temporary expedient — **makeshift** *adj*

**make·up** \ˈmā-ˌkəp\ *n* **1** : the way in which something is put together; *also* : physical, mental, and moral constitution **2** : cosmetics esp. for the face; *also* : materials (as wigs and cosmetics) used in making up

**make up** *vb* **1** : FORM, COMPOSE **2** : to compensate for a deficiency **3** : SETTLE ⟨*made up* my mind⟩ **4** : INVENT, IMPROVISE **5** : to become reconciled **6** : to put on makeup (as for a play)

**make–work** \ˈmāk-ˌwərk\ *n* : BUSYWORK

**mak·ings** \ˈmā-kiŋz\ *n pl* : the material from which something is made

**Mal** *abbr* Malachi

**Mal·a·chi** \ˈma-lə-ˌkī\ *n* — see BIBLE table

**Mal·a·chi·as** \ˌma-lə-ˈkī-əs\ *n* : MALACHI

**mal·a·chite** \ˈma-lə-ˌkīt\ *n* : a green mineral that is a carbonate of copper used for making ornamental objects

**mal·adapt·ed** \ˌma-lə-ˈdap-təd\ *adj* : poorly suited to a particular use, purpose, or situation

**mal·ad·just·ed** \ˌma-lə-ˈjəs-təd\ adj : poorly or inadequately adjusted (as to one's environment) — **mal·ad·just·ment** \-ˈjəst-mənt\ n

**mal·adroit** \ˌma-lə-ˈdrȯit\ adj : not adroit : INEPT ⟨the ~ handling of the crisis⟩

**mal·a·dy** \ˈma-lə-dē\ n, pl **-dies** : a disease or disorder of body or mind

**mal·aise** \ma-ˈlāz, ma-\ n [F] : a hazy feeling of not being well

**mal·a·mute** \ˈma-lə-ˌmyüt\ n : a dog often used to draw sleds esp. in northern No. America

**mal·a·prop·ism** \ˈma-lə-ˌprä-ˌpi-zəm\ n ; a usu. humorous misuse of a word

**mal·ap·ro·pos** \ˌma-ˌla-prə-ˈpō, ma-ˈla-prə-ˌpō\ adv : in an inappropriate or inopportune way — **malapropos** adj

**ma·lar·ia** \mə-ˈler-e-ə\ n [It, fr. mala aria bad air] : a disease marked by recurring chills and fever and caused by a protozoan parasite of the blood that is transmitted by anopheles mosquitoes — **ma·lar·i·al** \-əl\ adj

**ma·lar·key** \mə-ˈlär-kē\ n : insincere or foolish talk

**mal·a·thi·on** \ˌma-lə-ˈthī-ən, -ˌän\ n : an insecticide with a relatively low toxicity for mammals

**Ma·lay** \mə-ˈlā, ˈmā-ˌlā\ n 1 : a member of a people of the Malay Peninsula and Archipelago 2 : the language of the Malays — **Malay** adj — **Ma·lay·an** \mə-ˈlā-ən, ˈmā-ˌlā-\ n or adj

**mal·con·tent** \ˌmal-kən-ˈtent\ adj : marked by a dissatisfaction with the existing state of affairs : DISCONTENTED — **malcontent** n

**mal de mer** \ˌmal-də-ˈmer\ n [F] : SEASICKNESS

¹**male** \ˈmāl\ n : a male individual

²**male** adj 1 : of, relating to, or being the sex that produces germ cells which fertilize the eggs of a female; also : STAMINATE 2 : MASCULINE — **male·ness** n

**male·dic·tion** \ˌma-lə-ˈdik-shən\ n : CURSE, EXECRATION

**male·fac·tor** \ˈma-lə-ˌfak-tər\ n : EVILDOER; esp : one who commits an offense against the law — **male·fac·tion** \ˌma-lə-ˈfak-shən\ n

**ma·lef·ic** \mə-ˈle-fik\ adj 1 : BALEFUL ⟨~ influences⟩ 2 : MALICIOUS

**ma·lef·i·cent** \-fə-sənt\ adj : working or productive of harm or evil

**ma·lev·o·lent** \mə-ˈle-və-lənt\ adj : having, showing, or arising from ill will, spite, or hatred ♦ **Synonyms** MALIGNANT, MALIGN, MALICIOUS, SPITEFUL — **ma·lev·o·lence** \-ləns\ n

**mal·fea·sance** \mal-ˈfē-zᵊns\ n : wrongful conduct esp. by a public official

**mal·for·ma·tion** \ˌmal-fȯr-ˈmā-shən\ n : irregular or faulty formation or structure; also : an instance of this — **malformed** \mal-ˈfȯrmd\ adj

**mal·func·tion** \mal-ˈfəŋk-shən\ vb : to fail to operate normally — **malfunction** n

**mal·ice** \ˈma-ləs\ n : desire to cause injury or distress to another — **ma·li·cious** \mə-ˈli-shəs\ adj — **ma·li·cious·ly** adv

¹**ma·lign** \mə-ˈlīn\ adj 1 : evil in nature, influence, or effect; also : MALIGNANT 2 2 : moved by ill will

²**malign** vb : to speak evil of : DEFAME

**ma·lig·nant** \mə-ˈlig-nənt\ adj 1 : INJURIOUS, MALIGN 2 : tending to produce death or deterioration ⟨a ~ tumor⟩ — **ma·lig·nan·cy** \-nən-sē\ n — **ma·lig·nant·ly** adv — **ma·lig·ni·ty** \-nə-tē\ n

**ma·lin·ger** \mə-ˈliŋ-gər\ vb [F malingre sickly] : to pretend illness so as to avoid duty — **ma·lin·ger·er** n

**mal·i·son** \ˈma-lə-sən, -zən\ n : CURSE

**mall** \ˈmȯl, ˈmal\ n 1 : a shaded walk : PROMENADE 2 : an urban shopping area featuring a variety of shops surrounding a concourse 3 : a usu. large enclosed suburban shopping area containing various shops

**mal·lard** \ˈma-lərd\ n, pl **mallard** or **mallards** : a common wild duck that is the source of domestic ducks

**mal·lea·ble** \ˈma-lē-ə-bəl\ adj 1 : capable of being extended or shaped by beating with a hammer or by the pressure of rollers 2 : ADAPTABLE, PLIABLE ⟨~ young minds⟩ ♦ **Synonyms** PLASTIC, PLIANT, DUCTILE, SUPPLE — **mal·lea·bil·i·ty** \ˌma-lē-ə-ˈbi-lə-tē\ n

**mal·let** \ˈma-lət\ n 1 : a tool with a large head for driving another tool or for striking a surface without marring it 2 : a long-handled hammerlike implement for striking a ball (as in croquet)

**mal·le·us** \ˈma-lē-əs\ n, pl **mal·lei** \-lē-ˌī, -lē-ˌē\ [NL, fr. L, hammer] : the outermost of the three small bones of the mammalian middle ear

**mal·low** \ˈma-lō\ n : any of a genus of herbs with lobed leaves, usu. showy flowers, and a disk-shaped fruit

**malm·sey** \ˈmälm-zē\ n, often cap : the sweetest variety of Madeira

**mal·nour·ished** \mal-ˈnər-isht\ adj : UNDERNOURISHED

**mal·nu·tri·tion** \ˌmal-nü-ˈtri-shən, -nyü-\ n : faulty and esp. inadequate nutrition

**mal·oc·clu·sion** \ˌma-lə-ˈklü-zhən\ n : faulty coming together of teeth in biting

**mal·odor·ous** \ma-ˈlō-də-rəs\ adj : ill-smelling — **mal·odor·ous·ly** adv — **mal·odor·ous·ness** n

**maloti** pl of LOTI

**mal·prac·tice** \mal-ˈprak-təs\ n : a dereliction of professional duty or a failure of professional skill that results in injury, loss, or damage

**malt** \ˈmȯlt\ n 1 : grain and esp. barley steeped in water until it has sprouted and used in brewing and distilling 2 : liquor made with malt — **malty** adj

**malted milk** \ˈmȯl-təd-\ n : a powder prepared from dried milk and an extract from malt; also : a beverage of this powder in milk or other liquid

**Mal·thu·sian** \mal-ˈthü-zhən, -ˈthyü-\ adj : of or relating to a theory that population unless checked (as by war) tends to increase faster than its means of subsistence — **Malthusian** n — **Mal·thu·sian·ism** \-zhə-ˌni-zəm\ n

**malt·ose** \'mȯl-ˌtōs\ n : a sugar formed esp. from starch by the action of enzymes

**mal·treat** \mal-'trēt\ vb : to treat cruelly or roughly : ABUSE — **mal·treat·ment** n

**mal·ware** \'mal-ˌwer\ n : software designed to interfere with a computer's normal functioning

**ma·ma** or **mam·ma** \'mä-mə\ n : MOTHER

**mam·bo** \'mäm-bō\ n, pl **mambos** : a dance of Cuban origin related to the rumba — **mambo** vb

**mam·mal** \'ma-məl\ n [NL Mammalia, fr. LL, neut. pl. of mammalis of the breast, fr. L mamma breast] : any of a class of warm-blooded vertebrates that includes humans and all other animals which nourish their young with milk and have the skin more or less covered with hair — **mam·ma·li·an** \mə-'mä-lē-ən, ma-\ adj or n

**mam·ma·ry** \'ma-mə-rē\ adj : of, relating to, or being the glands (**mammary glands**) that in female mammals secrete milk

**mam·mo·gram** \'ma-mə-ˌgram\ n : an X-ray photograph of the breasts

**mam·mog·ra·phy** \ma-'mä-grə-fē\ n : X-ray examination of the breasts (as for early detection of cancer)

**mam·mon** \'ma-mən\ n, often cap : material wealth having a debasing influence

**¹mam·moth** \'ma-məth\ n : any of a genus of large hairy extinct elephants

**²mammoth** adj : of very great size : GIGANTIC ♦ **Synonyms** COLOSSAL, ENORMOUS, IMMENSE, VAST, ELEPHANTINE

**¹man** \'man\ n, pl **men** \'men\ 1 : a human being; esp : an adult male 2 : the human race : MANKIND 3 : one possessing in high degree the qualities considered distinctive of manhood 4 : an adult male servant or employee 5 : the individual who can fulfill one's requirements ⟨he's your ~⟩ 6 a : one of the pieces with which various games (as chess) are played b : one of the players on a team 7 often cap : white society or people

**²man** vb **manned; man·ning** 1 : to supply with men ⟨~ a fleet⟩ 2 : FORTIFY, BRACE

**³man** abbr manual

**Man** abbr Manitoba

**man–about–town** n, pl **men–about–town** : a worldly and socially active man

**man·a·cle** \'ma-ni-kəl\ n 1 : a shackle for the hand or wrist 2 : something used as a restraint

**man·age** \'ma-nij\ vb **man·aged; man·ag·ing** 1 : HANDLE, CONTROL ⟨~s her skis well⟩; also : to direct or carry on business or affairs 2 : to make and keep compliant 3 : to treat with care : HUSBAND 4 : to achieve one's purpose : CONTRIVE — **man·age·abil·i·ty** \ˌma-ni-jə-'bi-lə-tē\ n — **man·age·able** \'ma-ni-jə-bəl\ adj — **man·age·able·ness** n — **man·age·ably** \-blē\ adv

**managed care** n : a health-care system that controls costs by limiting doctor's fees and by restricting the patient's choice of doctors

**man·age·ment** \'ma-nij-mənt\ n 1 : the act or art of managing : CONTROL 2 : judicious use of means to accomplish an end 3 : the group of those who manage or direct an enterprise

**man·ag·er** \'ma-ni-jər\ n : one that manages — **man·a·ge·ri·al** \ˌma-nə-'jir-ē-əl\ adj

**ma·ña·na** \mən-'yä-nə\ n [Sp, lit., tomorrow] : an indefinite time in the future

**ma·nat** \mä-'nät\ n, pl **manat** or **manats** — see MONEY table

**man–at–arms** n, pl **men–at–arms** : SOLDIER; esp : one who is heavily armed and mounted

**man·a·tee** \'ma-nə-ˌtē\ n : any of a genus of chiefly tropical plant-eating aquatic mammals having a broad rounded tail

**man·ci·ple** \'man-sə-pəl\ n : a steward or purveyor esp. for a college or monastery

**man·da·mus** \man-'dā-məs\ n [L, we enjoin] : a writ issued by a superior court commanding that an official act or duty be performed

**man·da·rin** \'man-də-rən\ n 1 : a public official of high rank under the Chinese Empire 2 cap : the chief dialect group of China 3 : a yellow to reddish orange loose-skinned citrus fruit; also : a tree that bears mandarins

**man·date** \'man-ˌdāt\ n 1 : an authoritative command 2 : an authorization to act given to a representative 3 : a commission granted by the League of Nations to a member nation for governing conquered territory; also : a territory so governed

**man·da·to·ry** \'man-də-ˌtȯr-ē\ adj 1 : containing or constituting a command : OBLIGATORY 2 : of or relating to a League of Nations mandate

**man·di·ble** \'man-də-bəl\ n 1 : JAW; esp : a lower jaw 2 : either segment of a bird's bill — **man·dib·u·lar** \man-'dib-yə-lər\ adj

**man·do·lin** \ˌman-də-'lin, 'man-də-lən\ n : a stringed musical instrument with a pear-shaped body and a fretted neck

**man·drake** \'man-ˌdrāk\ n 1 : an Old World herb related to the nightshades or its large forked root formerly credited with magical properties 2 : MAYAPPLE

**man·drel** also **man·dril** \'man-drəl\ n 1 : an axle or spindle inserted into a hole in a piece of work to support it during machining 2 : a metal bar used as a core around which material may be cast, shaped, or molded

**man·drill** \'man-drəl\ n : a large baboon of western central Africa

**mane** \'mān\ n : long heavy hair growing about the neck of some mammals (as horses) — **maned** \'mānd\ adj

**man–eat·er** \'man-ˌē-tər\ n : one (as a shark or cannibal) that has or is thought to have an appetite for human flesh — **man–eat·ing** adj

**ma·nège** \ma-'nezh, mə-\ n : the art of horsemanship or of training horses

**ma·nes** \'mä-ˌnās, 'mā-ˌnēz\ n pl, often cap : the spirits of the dead and gods of the lower world in ancient Roman belief

**ma·neu·ver** \mə-'nü-vər, -'nyü-\ *n* [F *manœuvre*, fr. OF *maneuvre* work done by hand, fr. ML *manuopera*, fr. *manu operare* to work by hand] **1** : a military or naval movement; *also* : an armed forces training exercise — often used in pl. **2** : a procedure involving expert physical movement **3** : an evasive movement or shift of tactics; *also* : an action taken to gain a tactical end — **maneuver** *vb* — **ma·neu·ver·abil·i·ty** \-,nü-və-rə-'bi-lə-tē, -,nyü-\ *n* — **ma·neu·ver·able** \-'nü-və-rə-bəl, -'nyü-\ *adj*

**man Friday** *n* : an efficient and devoted aide or employee

**man·ful** \'man-fəl\ *adj* : having or showing courage and resolution ⟨a ~ struggle⟩ — **man·ful·ly** *adv*

**man·ga** \'mäŋ-gə\ *n* [Jp, comic, cartoon, fr. *man-* involuntary, aimless + *-ga* picture] : a Japanese comic book or graphic novel

**man·ga·nese** \'maŋ-gə-,nēz, -,nēs\ *n* : a metallic chemical element resembling iron but not magnetic

**mange** \'mānj\ *n* : any of several contagious itchy skin diseases esp. of domestic animals — **mangy** \'mān-jē\ *adj*

**man·ger** \'mān-jər\ *n* : a trough or open box for livestock feed or fodder

**¹man·gle** \'maŋ-gəl\ *vb* **man·gled; man·gling 1** : to cut, bruise, or hack with repeated blows **2** : to spoil or injure esp. through ineptitude — **man·gler** *n*

**²mangle** *n* : a machine with heated rollers for ironing laundry

**man·go** \'maŋ-gō\ *n, pl* **mangoes** *also* **mangos** [Pg *manga*, prob. fr. Malayalam (Dravidian language of India) *māṇṇa*] : an edible juicy yellowish-red fruit borne by a tropical evergreen tree related to the sumacs; *also* : this tree

**man·grove** \'maŋ-,grōv\ *n* : any of a genus of tropical maritime trees that send out many prop roots and form dense thickets important in coastal land building

**man·han·dle** \'man-,han-d'l\ *vb* : to handle roughly

**man·hat·tan** \man-'ha-t³n\ *n, often cap* : a cocktail made of whiskey and vermouth

**man·hole** \'man-,hōl\ *n* : a hole through which a person may pass esp. to gain access to an underground or enclosed structure

**man·hood** \-,hùd\ *n* **1** : the condition of being an adult male **2** : qualities associated with men : MANLINESS **3** : MEN ⟨the nation's ~⟩

**man-hour** \-'aù(-ə)r\ *n* : a unit of one hour's work by one person

**man·hunt** \-,hənt\ *n* : an organized hunt for a person and esp. for one charged with a crime

**ma·nia** \'mā-nē-ə, -nyə\ *n* **1** : excitement manifested by mental and physical hyperactivity, disorganized behavior, and elevated mood **2** : excessive enthusiasm

**ma·ni·ac** \'mā-nē-,ak\ *n* : LUNATIC, MADMAN

**ma·ni·a·cal** \mə-'nī-ə-kəl\ *also* **ma·ni·ac** \'mā-nē-ak\ *adj* **1** : affected with or sug-

gestive of madness **2** : FRANTIC ⟨a ~ mob⟩

**man·ic** \'ma-nik\ *adj* : affected with, relating to, characterized by, or resulting from mania — **manic** *n* — **man·i·cal·ly** \-ni-k(ə-)lē\ *adv*

**manic depression** *n* : BIPOLAR DISORDER

**man·ic-de·pres·sive** \,ma-nik-di-'pre-siv\ *adj* : characterized by or affected with either mania or depression or alternating episodes of mania and depression — **manic-depressive** *n*

**¹man·i·cure** \'ma-nə-,kyùr\ *n* **1** : MANICURIST **2** : a treatment for the care of the hands and nails

**²manicure** *vb* **-cured; -cur·ing 1** : to do manicure work on **2** : to trim closely and evenly

**man·i·cur·ist** \-,kyùr-ist\ *n* : a person who gives manicure treatments

**¹man·i·fest** \'ma-nə-,fest\ *adj* [ME, fr. AF or L; AF *manifeste*, fr. L *manifestus*, caught in the act, flagrant, obvious, perh. fr. *manus* hand + *-festus* (akin to L *infestus* hostile)] **1** : readily perceived by the senses and esp. by the sight **2** : easily understood : OBVIOUS — **man·i·fest·ly** *adv*

**²manifest** *vb* : to make evident or certain by showing or displaying ♦ *Synonyms* EVINCE, DEMONSTRATE, EXHIBIT

**³manifest** *n* : a list of passengers or an invoice of cargo for a ship or plane

**man·i·fes·ta·tion** \,ma-nə-fə-'stā-shən\ *n* : DISPLAY, DEMONSTRATION

**man·i·fes·to** \,ma-nə-'fes-tō\ *n, pl* **-tos** *or* **-toes** : a public declaration of intentions, motives, or views

**¹man·i·fold** \'ma-nə-,fōld\ *adj* **1** : marked by diversity or variety **2** : consisting of or operating many of one kind combined

**²manifold** *n* : a pipe fitting with several lateral outlets for connecting it with other pipes

**³manifold** *vb* **1** : MULTIPLY **2** : to make a number of copies of (as a letter)

**man·i·kin** *also* **man·ni·kin** \'ma-ni-kən\ *n* **1** : MANNEQUIN **2** : a little man : DWARF

**Ma·nila hemp** \mə-'ni-lə-\ *n* : a tough fiber from a Philippine plant related to the banana that is used for cordage

**manila paper** *n, often cap M* : a tough brownish paper made orig. from Manila hemp

**man·i·oc** \'ma-nē-,äk\ *n* : CASSAVA

**ma·nip·u·late** \mə-'ni-pyə-,lāt\ *vb* **-lat·ed; -lat·ing 1** : to treat or operate manually or mechanically esp. with skill **2** : to manage or use skillfully **3** : to influence esp. with intent to deceive — **ma·nip·u·la·tion** \mə-,ni-pyə-'lā-shən\ *n* — **ma·nip·u·la·tive** \-'ni-pyə-,la-tiv\ *adj* — **ma·nip·u·la·tor** \-,lā-tər\ *n*

**ma·nip·u·la·tives** \mə-'ni-pyə-,lā-tivz\ *n pl* : objects that a student is instructed to use in a way that teaches or reinforces a lesson

**man·kind** *n* **1** \'man-'kīnd\ : the human race **2** \-,kīnd\ : men as distinguished from women

**¹man·ly** \'man-lē\ *adv* : in a manly manner

**²manly** *adj* **man·li·er; -est** : having qualities appropriate to or generally associated with a man : BOLD, RESOLUTE ⟨a ~ competitor⟩ — **man·li·ness** n

**man–made** \'man-'mād\ adj : made by humans rather than nature ⟨~ systems⟩; esp : SYNTHETIC ⟨~ fibers⟩

**man·na** \'ma-nə\ n 1 : food miraculously supplied to the Israelites in the wilderness 2 : something of value that comes unexpectedly : WINDFALL

**manned** \'mand\ adj : carrying or performed by a person ⟨~ spaceflight⟩

**man·ne·quin** \'ma-ni-kən\ n 1 : a form representing the human figure used esp. for displaying clothes 2 : a person employed to model clothing

**man·ner** \'ma-nər\ n 1 : KIND, SORT ⟨what ~ of man is he⟩ 2 : a way of acting or proceeding ⟨worked in a brisk ~⟩; also : normal behavior ⟨spoke bluntly as was his ~⟩ 3 : a method of artistic execution 4 pl : social conduct; also : BEARING 5 pl : BEHAVIOR ⟨taught the child good ~s⟩

**man·nered** \'ma-nərd\ adj 1 : having manners of a specified kind ⟨well-*man-nered*⟩ 2 : having an artificial character ⟨a highly ~ style⟩

**man·ner·ism** \'ma-nə-ˌri-zəm\ n 1 : ARTIFICIALITY, PRECIOSITY 2 : a peculiarity of action, bearing, or treatment ♦ *Synonyms* POSE, AIR, AFFECTATION

**man·ner·ly** \'ma-nər-lē\ adj : showing good manners : POLITE — **man·ner·li·ness** n — **mannerly** adv

**man·nish** \'ma-nish\ adj 1 : resembling or suggesting a man rather than a woman 2 : generally associated with or characteristic of a man ⟨a ~ voice⟩ — **man·nish·ly** adv — **man·nish·ness** n

**ma·no a ma·no** \ˌmä-nō-ä-'mä-nō\ adv or adj : in direct competition or conflict

**ma·noeu·vre** \mə-'nü-vər, -'nyü-\ chiefly Brit var of MANEUVER

**man–of–war** \ˌman-əv-'wȯr\ n, pl **men–of–war** \ˌmen-\ : WARSHIP

**ma·nom·e·ter** \mə-'nä-mə-tər\ n : an instrument for measuring the pressure of gases and vapors — **mano·met·ric** \ˌma-nə-'me-trik\ adj

**man·or** \'ma-nər\ n 1 : the house or hall of an estate; also : a landed estate 2 : an English estate of a feudal lord — **ma·no·ri·al** \mə-'nȯr-ē-əl\ adj — **ma·no·ri·al·ism** \-ə-ˌli-zəm\ n

**man power** n 1 : power available from or supplied by the physical effort of human beings 2 usu **man·pow·er** : the total supply of persons available and fitted for service

**man·qué** \mäⁿ-'kā\ adj [F, fr. pp. of *manquer* to lack, fail] : short of or frustrated in the fulfillment of one's aspirations or talents ⟨a poet ~⟩

**man·sard** \'man-ˌsärd, -sərd\ n : a roof having two slopes on all sides with the lower slope steeper than the upper one

**manse** \'mans\ n : the residence esp. of a Presbyterian minister

**man·ser·vant** \'man-ˌsər-vənt\ n, pl **men·ser·vants** \'men-ˌsər-vənts\ : a male servant

**man·sion** \'man-chən\ n : a large imposing residence; also : a separate apartment in a large structure

**man–size** \'man-ˌsīz\ or **man–sized** \-ˌsīzd\ adj : suitable for or requiring a man ⟨a ~ job⟩

**man·slaugh·ter** \-ˌslȯ-tər\ n : the unlawful killing of a human being without express or implied malice

**man·ta** \'man-tə\ n : a square piece of cloth or blanket used in southwestern U.S. and Latin America as a cloak or shawl

**man·teau** \man-'tō\ n : a loose cloak, coat, or robe

**man·tel** \'man-tᵊl\ n : a beam, stone, or arch serving as a lintel to support the masonry above a fireplace; also : a shelf above a fireplace

**man·tel·piece** \'man-tᵊl-ˌpēs\ n : the shelf of a mantel

**man·til·la** \man-'tē-yə, -'ti-lə\ n : a light scarf worn over the head and shoulders esp. by Spanish and Latin-American women

**man·tis** \'man-təs\ n, pl **man·tis·es** also **man·tes** \-ˌtēz\ [NL, fr. Gk, lit., diviner, prophet] : any of a group of large usu. green insect-eating insects that hold their prey in forelimbs folded as if in prayer

**man·tis·sa** \man-'ti-sə\ n : the part of a logarithm to the right of the decimal point

¹**man·tle** \'man-tᵊl\ n 1 : a loose sleeveless garment worn over other clothes 2 : something that covers, enfolds, or envelops 3 : a lacy sheath that gives light by incandescence when placed over a flame 4 : the portion of the earth lying between the crust and the core 5 : MANTEL

²**mantle** vb **man·tled; man·tling** 1 : to cover with a mantle 2 : BLUSH

**man·tra** \'man-trə\ n : a mystical formula of invocation or incantation (as in Hinduism)

¹**man·u·al** \'man-yə-wəl\ adj 1 : of, relating to, or involving the hands; also : worked by hand ⟨a ~ pump⟩ 2 : requiring or using physical skill and energy ⟨~ labor⟩ — **man·u·al·ly** adv

²**manual** n 1 : a small book; esp : HANDBOOK 2 : the prescribed movements in the handling of a military item and esp. a weapon during a drill or ceremony ⟨the ~ of arms⟩ 3 : a keyboard esp. of an organ

**man·u·fac·to·ry** \ˌman-yə-'fak-tə-rē\ n : FACTORY

¹**man·u·fac·ture** \ˌman-yə-'fak-chər\ n [MF, fr. ML *manufactura*, L *manu factus* made by hand] 1 : something made from raw materials 2 : the process of making wares by hand or by machinery; also : a productive industry using machinery

²**manufacture** vb **-tured; -tur·ing** 1 : to make from raw materials by hand or by machinery; also : to engage in manufacture 2 : INVENT, FABRICATE; also : CREATE — **man·u·fac·tur·er** n

**man·u·mit** \ˌman-yə-'mit\ vb **-mit·ted; -mit·ting** : to free from slavery — **man·u·mis·sion** \-'mi-shən\ n

¹**ma·nure** \mə-'nu̇r, -'nyu̇r\ *vb* **ma·nured;** **ma·nur·ing** : to fertilize land with manure

²**manure** *n* : FERTILIZER; *esp* : refuse from stables and barnyards — **ma·nu·ri·al** \-'nu̇r-ē-əl, -'nyu̇r-\ *adj*

**man·u·script** \'man-yə-ˌskript\ *n* [L *manu scriptus* written by hand] **1** : a written or typewritten composition or document; *also* : a document submitted for publication **2** : writing as opposed to print

**Manx** \'maŋks\ *n pl* : the people of the Isle of Man — **Manx** *adj*

¹**many** \'me-nē\ *adj* **more** \'mȯr\; **most** \'mōst\ : consisting of or amounting to a large but indefinite number ⟨~ years ago⟩

²**many** *pron* : a large number ⟨~ are called⟩

³**many** *n* : a large but indefinite number ⟨a good ~ of them⟩

**many·fold** \ˌme-nē-'fōld\ *adv* : by many times

**many–sid·ed** \-'sī-dəd\ *adj* **1** : having many sides or aspects **2** : VERSATILE

**Mao·ism** \'mau̇-ˌi-zəm\ *n* : the theory and practice of Communism developed in China chiefly by Mao Zedong — **Mao·ist** \'mau̇-ist\ *n or adj*

**Mao·ri** \'mau̇(-ə)r-ē\ *n, pl* **Maori** *or* **Mao·ris** : a member of a Polynesian people native to New Zealand

¹**map** \'map\ *n* [L *mappa*, fr. L *mappa*, napkin, towel] **1** : a representation usu. on a flat surface of the whole or part of an area **2** : a representation of the celestial sphere or part of it

²**map** *vb* **mapped; map·ping 1** : to make a map of **2** : to plan in detail ⟨~ out a program⟩ — **map·pa·ble** \'ma-pə-bəl\ *adj* — **map·per** *n*

**MAP** *abbr* modified American plan

**ma·ple** \'mā-pəl\ *n* : any of a genus of trees or shrubs with 2-winged dry fruit and opposite leaves; *also* : the hard light-colored wood of a maple used esp. for floors and furniture

**maple sugar** *n* : sugar made by boiling maple syrup

**maple syrup** *n* : syrup made by concentrating the sap of maple trees and esp. the sugar maple

**mar** \'mär\ *vb* **marred; mar·ring** : to detract from the wholeness or perfection of : SPOIL ◆ **Synonyms** INJURE, HURT, HARM, DAMAGE, IMPAIR, BLEMISH

**Mar** *abbr* March

**ma·ra·ca** \mə-'rä-kə, -'ra-\ *n* [Pg *maracá*] : a rattle usu. made from a gourd and used as a percussion instrument

**mar·a·schi·no** \ˌmer-ə-'skē-nō-, -'shē-\ *n, often cap* : a cherry preserved in a sweet liqueur made from the juice of a bitter wild cherry

**mar·a·thon** \'mer-ə-ˌthän\ *n* [*Marathon*, Greece, site of a victory of Greeks over Persians in 490 B.C. the news of which was carried to Athens by a long-distance runner] **1** : a long-distance race esp. on foot **2** : an endurance contest

**mar·a·thon·er** \'mer-ə-ˌthä-nər\ *n* : a person who takes part in a marathon — **mar·a·thon·ing** *n*

**ma·raud** \mə-'rȯd\ *vb* : to roam about and raid in search of plunder : PILLAGE — **ma·raud·er** *n*

**mar·ble** \'mär-bəl\ *n* **1** : a limestone that can be polished and used in fine building work **2** : something resembling marble (as in coldness) **3** : a small ball (as of glass) used in various games; *also, pl* : a children's game played with these small balls — **marble** *adj*

**mar·bling** \-bə-liŋ, -bliŋ\ *n* : an intermixture of fat through the lean of a cut of meat

**mar·cel** \mär-'sel\ *n* : a deep soft wave made in the hair by the use of a heated curling iron — **marcel** *vb*

¹**march** \'märch\ *n* : a border region : FRONTIER

²**march** *vb* **1** : to move along in or as if in military formation **2** : to walk in a direct purposeful manner; *also* : PROGRESS, ADVANCE **3** : TRAVERSE ⟨~ed 10 miles⟩ — **march·er** *n*

³**march** *n* **1** : the action of marching; *also* : the distance covered (as by a military unit) in a march **2** : a regular measured stride or rhythmic step used in marching **3** : forward movement **4** : a piece of music with marked rhythm suitable for marching to

**March** *n* [ME, fr. AF, fr. L *martius*, fr. *martius* of Mars, fr. *Mart-, Mars,* Roman god of war] : the 3d month of the year

**mar·chio·ness** \'mär-shə-nəs\ *n* **1** : the wife or widow of a marquess **2** : a woman holding the rank of a marquess in her own right

**Mar·di Gras** \'mär-dē-ˌgrä\ *n* [F, lit., fat Tuesday] : the Tuesday before Ash Wednesday often observed with parades and merrymaking

¹**mare** \'mer\ *n* : an adult female of the horse or a related mammal

²**ma·re** \'mär-(ˌ)ā\ *n, pl* **ma·ria** \'mär-ē-ə\ : any of several large dark areas on the surface of the moon or Mars

**mar·ga·rine** \'mär-jə-rən\ *n* : a food product made usu. from vegetable oils churned with skimmed milk and used as a substitute for butter

**mar·ga·ri·ta** \ˌmär-gə-'rē-tə\ *n* : a cocktail consisting of tequila, lime or lemon juice, and an orange-flavored liqueur

**mar·gin** \'mär-jən\ *n* **1** : the part of a page outside the main body of printed or written matter **2** : EDGE ⟨continental ~⟩ **3** : a spare amount, measure, or degree allowed for use if needed ⟨a safety ~⟩ **4** : measure or degree of difference ⟨a one-vote ~⟩

**mar·gin·al** \-jə-nəl\ *adj* **1** : written or printed in the margin **2** : of, relating to, or situated at a margin or border **3** : close to the lower limit of quality or acceptability **4** : excluded from or existing outside the mainstream of society or a group — **mar·gin·al·ly** *adv*

**mar·gi·na·lia** \ˌmär-jə-'nā-lē-ə\ *n pl* : marginal notes or embellishments

**mar·gin·al·ize** \'mär-jə-nᵊl-ˌīz\ *vb* **-ized;**

**-iz·ing** : to relegate to an unimportant position within a society or group

**mar·grave** \'mär-₁grāv\ *n* : the military governor esp. of a medieval German border province

**ma·ri·a·chi** \₁mär-ē-'ä-chē, ₁mer-\ *n* : a Mexican street band; *also* : a member of or the music of such a band

**mari·gold** \'mer-ə-₁gōld\ *n* : any of a genus of tropical American herbs related to the daisies that are grown for their showy usu. yellow, orange, or maroon flower heads

**mar·i·jua·na** *also* **mar·i·hua·na** \₁mer-ə-'wä-nə, -'hwä-\ *n* [MexSp *marihuana*] : the dried leaves and flowering tops of the female hemp plant smoked usu. illegally for their intoxicating effect; *also* : HEMP

**ma·rim·ba** \mə-'rim-bə\ *n* : a xylophone of southern Africa and Central America; *also* : a modern version of it

**ma·ri·na** \mə-'rē-nə\ *n* : a dock or basin providing secure moorings for pleasure boats

**mar·i·nade** \₁mer-ə-'nād\ *n* : a savory usu. acidic sauce in which meat, fish, or a vegetable is soaked to enrich its flavor or to tenderize it

**mar·i·na·ra** \₁mer-ə-'ner-ə\ *adj* [It *(alla) marinara*, lit., in sailor style] : made with tomatoes, onions, garlic, and spices; *also* : served with marinara sauce

**mar·i·nate** \'mer-ə-₁nāt\ *vb* **-nat·ed; -nat·ing** : to steep (as meat or fish) in a marinade

¹**ma·rine** \mə-'rēn\ *adj* **1** : of or relating to the sea or its navigation or commerce **2** : of or relating to marines

²**marine** *n* **1** : the mercantile and naval shipping of a country **2** : any of a class of soldiers serving on shipboard or with a naval force

**mar·i·ner** \'mer-ə-nər\ *n* : SAILOR

**mar·i·o·nette** \₁mer-ē-ə-'net\ *n* : a puppet moved by strings or by hand

**mar·i·tal** \'mer-ə-t°l\ *adj* : of or relating to marriage : CONJUGAL ♦ *Synonyms* MATRIMONIAL, CONNUBIAL, NUPTIAL

**mar·i·time** \'mer-ə-₁tīm\ *adj* **1** : of, relating to, or bordering on the sea **2** : of or relating to navigation or commerce of the sea

**mar·jo·ram** \'mär-jə-rəm\ *n* : any of various fragrant mints often used as seasoning

¹**mark** \'märk\ *n* **1** : something (as a line or fixed object) designed to record position; *also* : the starting line or position in a track event **2** : TARGET; *also* : GOAL, OBJECT **3** : an object of abuse or ridicule **4** : the question under discussion **5** : NORM ⟨not up to the ∼⟩ **6** : a visible sign : INDICATION; *also* : CHARACTERISTIC **7** : a written or printed symbol **8** : GRADE **5** ⟨a ∼ of B+⟩ **9** : IMPORTANCE, DISTINCTION **10** : a lasting impression ⟨made his ∼ in the world⟩; *also* : a damaging impression left on a surface

²**mark** *vb* **1** : to set apart by a line or boundary **2** : to designate by a mark or make a mark on **3** : CHARACTERIZE ⟨the

vehemence that ∼s his speeches⟩; *also* : SIGNALIZE ⟨this year ∼s our 50th anniversary⟩ **4** : to take notice of : OBSERVE ⟨∼ my words⟩ — **mark·er** *n*

³**mark** *n* : DEUTSCHE MARK

**Mark** \'märk\ *n* — see BIBLE table

**mar·ka** \'mär-kə\ *n*, *pl* **mar·a·ka** \'mär-ə-kə\ *or* **marka** *or* **mar·kas** — see MONEY table

**mark·down** \'märk-₁daůn\ *n* **1** : a lowering of price **2** : the amount by which an original price is reduced

**mark down** *vb* : to put a lower price on

**marked** \'märkt\ *adj* : NOTICEABLE — **mark·ed·ly** \'mär-kəd-lē\ *adv*

¹**mar·ket** \'mär-kət\ *n* **1** : a meeting together of people for trade by purchase and sale; *also* : a public place where such a meeting is held **2** : the rate or price offered for a commodity or security **3** : the course of commercial activity by which the exchange of commodities is effected **4** : a geographical area of demand for commodities; *also* : extent of demand **5** : a retail establishment usu. of a specific kind

²**market** *vb* : to go to a market to buy or sell; *also* : SELL — **mar·ket·able** *adj*

**mar·ket·place** \'mär-kət-₁plās\ *n* **1** : an open square in a town where markets are held **2** : the world of trade or economic activity

**mark·ka** \'mär-₁kä\ *n*, *pl* **mark·kaa** \'mär-₁kä\ *or* **markkas** \-₁käz\ : the basic monetary unit of Finland from 1917 to 2001

**marks·man** \'märks-mən\ *n* : a person skillful at hitting a target — **marks·man·ship** *n*

**mark·up** \'mär-₁kəp\ *n* **1** : a raising of price **2** : an amount added to the cost price of an article to determine the selling price

**mark up** *vb* : to put a higher price on

**markup language** *n* : a system for marking the components and layout of a computer document

**marl** \'märl\ *n* : an earthy deposit rich in lime used esp. as fertilizer — **marly** \'mär-lē\ *adj*

**mar·lin** \'mär-lən\ *n* : any of several large oceanic sport fishes related to sailfishes

**mar·line·spike** *also* **mar·lin·spike** \'mär-lən-₁spīk\ *n* : a pointed iron tool used to separate strands of rope or wire (as in splicing)

**mar·ma·lade** \'mär-mə-₁lād\ *n* : a clear jelly holding in suspension pieces of fruit and fruit rind

**mar·mo·re·al** \mär-'mȯr-ē-əl\ *adj* : of, relating to, or suggestive of marble

**mar·mo·set** \'mär-mə-₁set\ *n* : any of numerous small bushy-tailed monkeys of Central and So. America

**mar·mot** \'mär-mət\ *n* : any of a genus of stout short-legged burrowing No. American rodents

¹**ma·roon** \mə-'rün\ *vb* **1** : to put ashore (as on a desolate island) and leave to one's fate **2** : to leave in isolation and without hope of escape

²**maroon** *n* : a dark red color

¹**mar·quee** \mär-'kē\ *n* [modif. of F *mar-*

*quise,* lit., marchioness] **1 :** a large tent set up (as for an outdoor party) **2 :** a usu. metal and glass canopy over an entrance (as of a theater) **3 :** a sign over the entrance of a theater or arena advertising a performance

**²marquee** *adj* **:** having or being a great attraction **:** PREEMINENT ⟨~ athletes⟩

**mar·quess** \'mär-kwəs\ *or* **mar·quis** \'mär-kwəs, mär-'kē\ *n* **1 :** a nobleman of hereditary rank in Europe and Japan **2 :** a member of the British peerage ranking below a duke and above an earl

**mar·que·try** \'mär-kə-trē\ *n* **:** inlaid work of wood, shell, or ivory (as on a table or cabinet)

**mar·quise** \mär-'kēz\ *n, pl* **mar·quises** \*same or* -'kē-zəz\ **:** MARCHIONESS

**mar·riage** \'mer-ij\ *n* **1 :** the state of being united to another person as a spouse **:** contractual relationship according to law or custom **2 :** a wedding ceremony and attendant festivities **3 :** a close union ⟨a ~ of light and shadow⟩ — **mar·riage·able** *adj*

**married name** *n* **:** a woman's surname acquired through marriage

**mar·row** \'mer-ō\ *n* **:** a soft vascular tissue that fills the cavities of most bones

**mar·row·bone** \'mer-ə-,bōn, 'mer-ō-\ *n* **:** a bone (as a shinbone) rich in marrow

**mar·ry** \'mer-ē\ *vb* **mar·ried; mar·ry·ing 1 :** to join in marriage **2 :** to take as a spouse **:** WED **3 :** to enter into a close union **4 :** COMBINE, UNITE — **mar·ried** *adj or n*

**Mars** \'märz\ *n* **:** the planet 4th from the sun and conspicuous for its red color

**marsh** \'märsh\ *n* **:** a tract of soft wet land — **marshy** *adj*

**¹mar·shal** \'mär-shəl\ *n* [ME, fr. AF *mareschal,* of Gmc origin; akin to OHG *marahscalc* marshal, fr. *marah* horse + *scalc* servant] **1 :** a high official in a medieval household; *also* **:** a person in charge of the ceremonial aspects of a gathering **2 :** a general officer of the highest military rank **3 :** an administrative officer (as of a U.S. judicial district) having duties similar to a sheriff's **4 :** the administrative head of a city police or fire department

**²marshal** *vb* **mar·shaled** *or* **mar·shalled; mar·shal·ing** *or* **mar·shal·ling 1 :** to arrange in order, rank, or position ⟨~ troops⟩ **2 :** to bring together ⟨~ arguments⟩ **3 :** to lead with ceremony **:** USHER

**marsh gas** *n* **:** METHANE

**marsh·mal·low** \'märsh-,me-lō, -,ma-\ *n* **:** a light spongy confection made from corn syrup, sugar, albumen, and gelatin

**marsh marigold** *n* **:** a swamp herb related to the buttercups that has bright yellow flowers

**mar·su·pi·al** \mär-'sü-pē-əl\ *n* **:** any of an order of primitive mammals (as opossums, kangaroos, or wombats) that bear very immature young which are nourished in a pouch on the abdomen of the female — **marsupial** *adj*

**mart** \'märt\ *n* **:** MARKET

**mar·ten** \'mär-t²n\ *n, pl* **marten** *or* **martens :** a slender mammal that is larger than the related weasels and has soft gray or brown fur; *also* **:** this fur

**mar·tial** \'mär-shəl\ *adj* [L *martialis* of Mars, fr. *Mart-, Mars* Mars, Roman god of war] **1 :** of, relating to, or suited for war or a warrior ⟨~ music⟩ **2 :** of or relating to an army or military life **3 :** WARLIKE

**martial art** *n* **:** any of several arts of combat (as karate and judo) practiced as sport

**martial law** *n* **1 :** the law applied in occupied territory by the occupying military forces **2 :** the established law of a country administered by military forces in an emergency when civilian law enforcement agencies are unable to maintain public order and safety

**mar·tian** \'mär-shən\ *adj, often cap* **:** of or relating to the planet Mars or its hypothetical inhabitants — **martian** *n, often cap*

**mar·tin** \'mär-t²n\ *n* **:** any of several swallows and esp. one of No. America with purplish blue plumage

**mar·ti·net** \,mär-tə-'net\ *n* **:** a strict disciplinarian

**mar·tin·gale** \'mär-t²n-,gāl\ *n* **:** a strap connecting a horse's girth to the bit or reins so as to hold down its head

**mar·ti·ni** \mär-'tē-nē\ *n* **:** a cocktail made of gin or vodka and dry vermouth

**¹mar·tyr** \'mär-tər\ *n* [ME, fr. OE, fr. LL, fr. Gk *martyr-, martys* witness] **1 :** a person who dies rather than renounce a religion; *also* **:** a person who makes a great sacrifice for the sake of principle **2 :** a great or constant sufferer

**²martyr** *vb* **1 :** to put to death for adhering to a belief **2 :** TORTURE

**mar·tyr·dom** \'mär-tər-dəm\ *n* **1 :** the suffering and death of a martyr **2 :** TORTURE

**¹mar·vel** \'mär-vəl\ *n* **1 :** one that causes wonder or astonishment **2 :** intense surprise or interest

**²marvel** *vb* **mar·veled** *or* **mar·velled; mar·vel·ing** *or* **mar·vel·ling :** to feel surprise, wonder, or amazed curiosity ⟨~ed at the circus act⟩

**mar·vel·ous** *or* **mar·vel·lous** \'mär-və-ləs\ *adj* **1 :** causing wonder **2 :** of the highest kind or quality — **mar·vel·ous·ly** *adv* — **mar·vel·ous·ness** *n*

**Marx·ism** \'märk-,si-zəm\ *n* **:** the political, economic, and social principles and policies advocated by Karl Marx — **Marx·ist** \-sist\ *n or adj*

**mar·zi·pan** \'märt-sə-,pän, -,pan; 'mär-zə-,pan\ *n* [G, fr. It *marzapane*] **:** a confection of almond paste, sugar, and egg whites

**masc** *abbr* masculine

**mas·cara** \ma-'sker-ə\ *n* **:** a cosmetic esp. for darkening the eyelashes

**mas·car·po·ne** \,mas-kär-'pō-nā\ *n* **:** an Italian cream cheese

**mas·cot** \'mas-,kät, -kət\ *n* [F *mascotte,* fr. Occitan *mascoto,* fr. *masco* witch, fr. ML *masca*] **:** a person, animal, or object adopted usu. by a group to bring good luck

¹**mas·cu·line** \'mas-kyə-lən\ *adj* **1** : MALE; *also* : MANLY **2** : of, relating to, or constituting the gender that includes most words or grammatical forms referring to males — **mas·cu·lin·i·ty** \,mas-kyə-'li-nə-tē\ *n*

²**masculine** *n* : a noun, pronoun, adjective, or inflectional form or class of the masculine gender; *also* : the masculine gender

¹**mash** \'mash\ *n* **1** : a mixture of ground feeds for livestock **2** : crushed malt or grain steeped in hot water to make wort **3** : a soft pulpy mass

²**mash** *vb* **1** : to reduce to a soft pulpy state **2** : CRUSH, SMASH ⟨~ a finger⟩ — **mash·er** *n*

**MASH** *abbr* mobile army surgical hospital

**mash–up** \'mash-,əp\ *n* : something created by combining elements from two or more sources

¹**mask** \'mask\ *n* **1** : a cover for the face usu. for disguise or protection **2** : MASQUE **3** : a figure of a head worn on the stage in antiquity **4** : a copy of a face made by means of a mold ⟨death ~⟩ **5** : something that conceals or disguises **6** : the face of an animal

²**mask** *vb* **1** : to conceal from view : DISGUISE **2** : to cover for protection

**mask·er** \'mas-kər\ *n* : a participant in a masquerade

**mas·och·ism** \'ma-sə-,ki-zəm, 'ma-zə-\ *n* **1** : a sexual perversion characterized by pleasure in being subjected to pain or humiliation **2** : pleasure in being abused or dominated — **mas·och·ist** \-kist\ *n* — **mas·och·is·tic** \,ma-sə-'kis-tik, ,ma-zə-\ *adj*

**ma·son** \'mā-s³n\ *n* **1** : a skilled worker who builds with stone, brick, or concrete **2** *cap* : FREEMASON

**Ma·son·ic** \mə-'sä-nik\ *adj* : of or relating to Freemasons or Freemasonry

**ma·son·ry** \'mā-s³n-rē\ *n, pl* **-ries** **1** : something constructed of materials used by masons **2** : the art, trade, or work of a mason **3** *cap* : FREEMASONRY

**masque** \'mask\ *n* **1** : MASQUERADE **2** : a short allegorical dramatic performance (as of the 17th century)

¹**mas·quer·ade** \,mas-kə-'rād\ *n* **1** : a social gathering of persons wearing masks; *also* : a costume for wear at such a gathering **2** : DISGUISE

²**masquerade** *vb* **-ad·ed; -ad·ing** **1** : to disguise oneself : POSE **2** : to take part in a masquerade — **mas·quer·ad·er** *n*

¹**mass** \'mas\ *n* **1** *cap* : a sequence of prayers and ceremonies forming the eucharistic service of the Roman Catholic Church **2** *often cap* : a celebration of the Eucharist **3** : a musical setting for parts of the Mass

²**mass** *n* **1** : a quantity or aggregate of matter usu. of considerable size **2** : EXPANSE, BULK; *also* : MASSIVENESS **3** : the principal part **4** : AGGREGATE, WHOLE **5** : the quantity of matter that a body possesses as measured by its inertia **6** : a

large quantity, amount, or number **7** : the great body of people — usu. used in pl. — **massy** *adj*

³**mass** *vb* : to form or collect into a mass

**Mass** *abbr* Massachusetts

**mas·sa·cre** \'ma-si-kər\ *n* **1** : the killing of many persons under cruel or atrocious circumstances **2** : a wholesale slaughter — **massacre** *vb*

¹**mas·sage** \mə-'säzh, -'säj\ *n* : manipulation of tissues (as by rubbing and kneading) for therapeutic purposes

²**massage** *vb* **mas·saged; mas·sag·ing** **1** : to subject to massage **2** : to treat flatteringly; *also* : MANIPULATE, DOCTOR ⟨~ data⟩

**mas·seur** \ma-'sər\ *n* : a man who practices massage

**mas·seuse** \-'sərz, -'süz\ *n* : a woman who practices massage

**mas·sif** \ma-'sēf\ *n* : a principal mountain mass

**mas·sive** \'ma-siv\ *adj* **1** : forming or consisting of a large mass **2** : large in structure, scope, or degree — **mas·sive·ly** *adv* — **mas·sive·ness** *n*

**mass·less** \'mas-ləs\ *adj* : having no mass ⟨~ particles⟩

**mass medium** *n, pl* **mass media** : a medium of communication (as the newspapers or television) that is designed to reach the mass of the people

**mass–pro·duce** \,mas-prə-'düs, -'dyüs\ *vb* : to produce in quantity usu. by machinery — **mass production** *n*

¹**mast** \'mast\ *n* **1** : a long pole or spar rising from the keel or deck of a ship and supporting the yards, booms, and rigging **2** : a slender vertical structure — **mast·ed** \'mas-təd\ *adj*

²**mast** *n* : nuts (as acorns) accumulated on the forest floor and often serving as food for animals (as hogs)

**mas·tec·to·my** \ma-'stek-tə-mē\ *n, pl* **-mies** : surgical removal of the breast

¹**mas·ter** \'mas-tər\ *n* **1** : a male teacher; *also* : a person holding an academic degree higher than a bachelor's but lower than a doctor's **2** : one highly skilled (as in an art or profession) **3** : one having authority or control **4** : VICTOR, SUPERIOR **5** : the commander of a merchant ship **6** : a youth or boy too young to be called *mister* — used as a title **7** : an original from which copies are made

²**master** *vb* **1** : to become master of : OVERCOME **2** : to become skilled or proficient in **3** : to produce a master recording of (as a musical performance)

**master chief petty officer** *n* : a petty officer of the highest rank in the navy

**mas·ter·ful** \'mas-tər-fəl\ *adj* **1** : inclined and usu. competent to act as master **2** : having or reflecting the skill of a master ⟨~ verse⟩ — **mas·ter·ful·ly** *adv* — **mas·ter·ful·ness** *n*

**master gunnery sergeant** *n* : a noncommissioned officer in the marine corps ranking above a master sergeant

**master key** *n* : a key designed to open several different locks

**mas·ter·ly** \'mas-tər-lē\ *adj* **1** : indicating

thorough knowledge or superior skill ⟨~ performance⟩ **2** : having the skill of a master ⟨~ a writer⟩ — **mas·ter·ly** adv

**mas·ter·mind** \·,mīnd\ n : a person who directs or provides creative intelligence for a project — **mastermind** vb

**master of ceremonies** : a person who acts as host at a formal event or a program of entertainment

**mas·ter·piece** \'mas-tər-,pēs\ n : a work done with extraordinary skill

**master plan** n : an overall plan

**mas·ter's** \'mas-tərz\ n : a master's degree

**master sergeant** n **1** : a noncommissioned officer in the army ranking next below a sergeant major **2** : a noncommissioned officer in the air force ranking next below a senior master sergeant **3** : a noncommissioned officer in the marine corps ranking next below a master gunnery sergeant

**mas·ter·stroke** \'mas-tər-,strōk\ n : a masterly performance or move

**mas·ter·work** \·,wərk\ n : MASTERPIECE

**mas·tery** \'mas-tə-rē\ n **1** : DOMINION; also : SUPERIORITY **2** : possession or display of great skill or knowledge

**mast·head** \'mast-,hed\ n **1** : the top of a mast **2** : the printed matter in a newspaper or periodical giving the title and details of ownership and rates of subscription or advertising

**mas·tic** \'mas-tik\ n : a pasty material used as a coating or cement

**mas·ti·cate** \'mas-tə-,kāt\ vb **-cat·ed; -cat·ing** : CHEW — **mas·ti·ca·tion** \,mas-tə-'kā-shən\ n

**mas·tiff** \'mas-təf\ n : any of a breed of large smooth-coated dogs used esp. as guard dogs

**mast·odon** \'mas-tə-,dän\ n [NL, fr. Gk mastos breast + odōn, odous tooth] : any of numerous huge extinct mammals related to the mammoths

**mas·toid** \'mas-,tȯid\ n : a bony prominence behind the ear — **mastoid** adj

**mas·tur·ba·tion** \,mas-tər-'bā-shən\ n : stimulation of the genital organs apart from sexual intercourse, usu. to orgasm, and esp. by use of one's own hand — **mas·tur·bate** \'mas-tər-,bāt\ vb — **mas·tur·ba·to·ry** \'mas-tər-bə-,tȯr-ē\ adj

**¹mat** \'mat\ n **1** : a piece of coarse woven or plaited fabric **2** : something made up of many intertwined strands **3** : a large thick pad used as a surface for wrestling and gymnastics

**²mat** vb **mat·ted; mat·ting 1** : to provide with a mat **2** : to form into a tangled mass ⟨dirt matted her hair⟩

**³mat** vb **mat·ted; mat·ting 1** also **matte** or **matt** : to make (as a color) matte **2** : to provide (a picture) with a mat

**⁴mat** var of ²MATTE

**⁵mat** or **matt** or **matte** n : a border going around a picture between picture and frame or serving as the frame

**mat·a·dor** \'mat-ə-,dȯr\ n [Sp, fr. matar to kill] : a bullfighter whose role is to kill the bull in a bullfight

**¹match** \'mach\ n **1** : a person or thing equal or similar to another; also : one able to cope with another : RIVAL **2** : a suitable pairing of persons or objects **3** : a contest or game between two or more individuals **4** : a marriage union; also : a prospective marriage partner — **match·less** adj

**²match** vb **1** : to meet as an antagonist; also : PIT ⟨~ wits⟩ **2** : to provide with a worthy competitor; also : to set in comparison with **3** : MARRY **4** : to combine suitably or congenially ⟨~ed the drapes with the rug⟩; also : ADAPT, SUIT **5** : to act in harmony ⟨his shoes and belt ~⟩ **6** : to provide with a counterpart

**³match** n : a short slender piece of flammable material (as wood) tipped with a combustible mixture that ignites through friction

**match·book** \'mach-,buk\ n : a small folder containing rows of paper matches

**match·lock** \·,läk\ n : a musket with a slow-burning cord lowered over a hole in the breech to ignite the charge

**match·mak·er** \·,mā-kər\ n : one who arranges a match and esp. a marriage

**match·wood** \·,wud\ n : small pieces of wood

**¹mate** \'māt\ vb **mat·ed; mat·ing** : CHECKMATE — **mate** n

**²mate** n **1** : ASSOCIATE, COMPANION; also : HELPER **2** : a deck officer on a merchant ship ranking below the captain **3** : one of a pair; esp : either member of a married couple or a breeding pair of animals

**³mate** vb **mat·ed; mat·ing 1** : to join or fit together **2** : to come or bring together as mates **3** : COPULATE

**¹ma·te·ri·al** \mə-'tir-ē-əl\ adj **1** : PHYSICAL ⟨~ world⟩; also : BODILY ⟨~ needs⟩ **2** : of or relating to matter rather than form ⟨~ cause⟩; also : EMPIRICAL ⟨~ knowledge⟩ **3** : highly important : SIGNIFICANT **4** : of a physical or worldly nature ⟨~ progress⟩ — **ma·te·ri·al·ly** adv

**²material** n **1** : the elements or substance of which something is composed or made **2** : apparatus necessary for doing or making something

**ma·te·ri·al·ise** Brit var of MATERIALIZE

**ma·te·ri·al·ism** \mə-'tir-ē-ə-,li-zəm\ n **1** : a theory that everything can be explained as being or coming from matter **2** : a preoccupation with material rather than intellectual or spiritual things — **ma·te·ri·al·ist** \-ist\ n or adj — **ma·te·ri·al·is·tic** \-,tir-ē-ə-'lis-tik\ adj — **ma·te·ri·al·is·ti·cal·ly** \-ti-k(ə-)lē\ adv

**ma·te·ri·al·ize** \mə-'tir-ē-ə-,līz\ vb **-ized; -iz·ing 1** : to give material form to; also : to assume bodily form **2** : to make an often unexpected appearance — **ma·te·ri·al·i·za·tion** \mə-,tir-ē-ə-lə-'zā-shən\ n

**ma·té·ri·el** or **ma·te·ri·el** \mə-,tir-ē-'el\ n [F matériel] : equipment, apparatus, and supplies used by an organization

**ma·ter·nal** \mə-'tər-n²l\ adj **1** : MOTHERLY **2** : related through or inherited or derived from a female parent ⟨his ~ grandparents⟩ — **ma·ter·nal·ly** adv

**¹ma·ter·ni·ty** \mə-'tər-nə-tē\ n, pl **-ties 1**

: the quality or state of being a mother; *also* : MOTHERLINESS **2** : a hospital facility for the care of women before and during childbirth and for newborn babies

²**maternity** *adj* **1** : designed for wear during pregnancy ⟨a ∼ dress⟩ **2** : effective for the period close to and including childbirth ⟨∼ leave⟩

¹**math** \'math\ *n* : MATHEMATICS

²**math** *abbr* mathematical; mathematician

**math·e·mat·ics** \ˌma-thə-'ma-tiks\ *n* : the science of numbers and their properties, operations, and relations and with shapes in space and their structure and measurement — **math·e·mat·i·cal** \-'ma-ti-kəl\ *adj* — **math·e·mat·i·cal·ly** \-ti-k(ə-)lē\ *adv* — **math·e·ma·ti·cian** \ˌma-thə-mə-'ti-shən\ *n*

**mat·i·nee** *or* **mat·i·née** \ˌma-tə-'nā\ *n* [F *matinée*, lit., morning, fr. OF, fr. *matin* morning, fr. L *matutinum*, fr. neut. of *matutinus* of the morning, fr. *Matuta*, goddess of morning] : a musical or dramatic performance in the daytime and esp. the afternoon

**mat·ins** \'ma-tᵊnz\ *n pl, often cap* **1** : special prayers said between midnight and 4 a.m. **2** : a morning service of liturgical prayer in Anglican churches

**ma·tri·arch** \'mā-trē-ˌärk\ *n* : a woman who rules or dominates a family, group, or state — **ma·tri·ar·chal** \ˌmā-trē-'är-kəl\ *adj* — **ma·tri·ar·chy** \'mā-trē-ˌär-kē\ *n*

**ma·tri·cide** \'ma-trə-ˌsīd, 'mā-\ *n* : the murder of a mother by her child — **ma·tri·cid·al** \ˌma-trə-'sī-dᵊl, ˌmā-\ *adj*

**ma·tric·u·late** \mə-'tri-kyə-ˌlāt\ *vb* **-lat·ed; -lat·ing** : to enroll as a member of a body and esp. of a college or university — **ma·tric·u·la·tion** \-ˌtri-kyə-'lā-shən\ *n*

**mat·ri·mo·ny** \'ma-trə-ˌmō-nē\ *n* [ME, fr. AF *matrimoignie*, fr. L *matrimonium*, fr. *mater* mother, matron] : MARRIAGE — **mat·ri·mo·nial** \ˌma-trə-'mō-nē-əl\ *adj* — **mat·ri·mo·nial·ly** *adv*

**ma·trix** \'mā-triks\ *n, pl* **ma·tri·ces** \'mā-trə-ˌsēz, 'ma-\ *or* **ma·trix·es** \'mā-trik-səz\ **1** : something within or from which something else originates, develops, or takes form **2** : a mold from which a relief surface (as a piece of type) is made

**ma·tron** \'mā-trən\ *n* **1** : a married woman usu. of dignified maturity or social distinction **2** : a woman supervisor (as in a school or police station) — **ma·tron·ly** *adj*

**Matt** *abbr* Matthew

¹**matte** *or* **matt** *var of* ³MAT

²**matte** *also* **matt** \'mat\ *adj* : not shiny : DULL

¹**mat·ter** \'ma-tər\ *n* **1** : a subject of interest or concern **2** *pl* : events or circumstances of a particular situation **3** : the subject of a discourse or writing **4** : TROUBLE, DIFFICULTY ⟨what's the ∼⟩ **5** : the substance of which a physical object is composed **6** : PUS **7** : an indefinite amount or quantity ⟨a ∼ of a few days⟩ **8** : something written or printed **9** : MAIL — **as a matter of fact** : ACTUALLY — **no matter** : without regard to ⟨will follow

*no matter* where you go⟩ — **no matter what** : regardless of the consequences ⟨must win, *no matter what*⟩

²**matter** *vb* : to be of importance

**mat·ter-of-fact** \ˌma-tə-rəv-'fakt\ *adj* : adhering to fact; *also* : being plain, straightforward, or unemotional — **mat·ter-of-fact·ly** *adv* — **mat·ter-of-fact·ness** *n*

**Mat·thew** \'ma-thyü\ *n* — see BIBLE table

**mat·tins** *often cap, chiefly Brit var of* MATINS

**mat·tock** \'ma-tək\ *n* : a digging and grubbing tool with features of an adze and an ax or pick

**mat·tress** \'ma-trəs\ *n* **1** : a fabric case filled with resilient material used as or for a bed **2** : an inflatable airtight sack for use as a mattress

**mat·u·rate** \'ma-chə-ˌrāt\ *vb* **-rat·ed; -rat·ing** : MATURE

**mat·u·ra·tion** \ˌma-chə-'rā-shən\ *n* **1** : the process of becoming mature **2** : the emergence of personal and behavioral characteristics through growth processes — **mat·u·ra·tion·al** \-shə-nəl\ *adj*

¹**ma·ture** \mə-'tūr, -'tyūr\ *adj* **ma·tur·er; -est** **1** : based on slow careful consideration **2** : having attained a final or desired state **3** : of or relating to a condition of full development **4** : suitable only for adults ⟨∼ content⟩ **5** : due for payment — **ma·ture·ly** *adv*

²**mature** *vb* **ma·tured; ma·tur·ing** : to reach or bring to maturity or completion

**ma·tu·ri·ty** \mə-'tūr-ə-tē, -'tyūr-\ *n* **1** : the quality or state of being mature; *esp* : full development **2** : the date when a note becomes due for payment

**ma·tu·ti·nal** \ˌma-chü-'tī-nᵊl; mə-'tü-tə-nᵊl, -'tyü-\ *adj* : of, relating to, or occurring in the morning : EARLY

**mat·zo** *or* **mat·zoh** \'mät-sə\ *n, pl* **mat·zoth** \-ˌsōt, -ˌsōth, -sōs\ *or* **mat·zos** *or* **mat·zohs** [Yiddish *matse*, fr. Heb *maṣé ṣāh*] : unleavened bread eaten esp. at the Passover

**maud·lin** \'mȯd-lən\ *adj* [alter. of Mary *Magdalene;* fr. her depiction as a weeping, penitent sinner] **1** : drunk enough to be silly **2** : weakly and effusively sentimental ⟨a ∼ love story⟩

¹**maul** \'mȯl\ *n* : a heavy hammer often with a wooden head used esp. for driving wedges

²**maul** *vb* **1** : BEAT, BRUISE; *also* : MANGLE **2** : to handle roughly

**maun·der** \'mȯn-dər\ *vb* **1** : to wander slowly and idly **2** : to speak indistinctly or disconnectedly

**mau·so·le·um** \ˌmȯ-sə-'lē-əm, ˌmȯ-zə-\ *n, pl* **-leums** *or* **-lea** \-'lē-ə\ [L, fr. Gk *mausōleion*, fr. *Mausōlos* Mausolus † *ab* 353 B.C. ruler of Caria whose tomb was one of the seven wonders of the ancient world] : a large tomb; *esp* : a usu. stone building for entombment of the dead above ground

**mauve** \'mōv, 'mȯv\ *n* : a moderate purple, violet, or lilac color

**ma·ven** *also* **ma·vin** \'mā-vən\ *n* [Yiddish *meyvn*, fr. LHeb *mēbhīn*] : EXPERT

**mav·er·ick** \'ma-vrik, -və-rik\ *n* [Samuel A. *Maverick* † 1870 Am. pioneer who did not brand his calves] **1** : an unbranded range animal **2** : NONCONFORMIST

**maw** \'mo\ *n* **1** : STOMACH; *also* : the crop of a bird **2** : the throat, gullet, or jaws esp. of a voracious animal

**mawk·ish** \'mo-kish\ *adj* : sickly sentimental ⟨∼ poetry⟩ — **mawk·ish·ly** *adv* — **mawk·ish·ness** *n*

**max** *abbr* maximum

**maxi** \'mak-sē\ *n, pl* **max·is** : a long skirt, dress, or coat

**maxi-** *comb form* **1** : extra long ⟨*maxi*kilt⟩ **2** : extra large ⟨*maxi*-problems⟩

**max·il·la** \mak-'si-lə\ *n, pl* **max·il·lae** \-'si-(ͺ)lē\ *or* **maxillas** : JAW 1; *esp* : an upper jaw — **max·il·lary** \'mak-sə-ͺler-ē\ *adj*

**max·im** \'mak-səm\ *n* : a proverbial saying

**max·i·mal** \'mak-sə-məl\ *adj* : MAXIMUM — **max·i·mal·ly** *adv*

**max·i·mise** *Brit var of* MAXIMIZE

**max·i·mize** \'mak-sə-ͺmīz\ *vb* **-mized; -miz·ing** **1** : to increase to a maximum **2** : to make the most of — **max·i·mi·za·tion** \ͺmak-sə-mə-'zā-shən\ *n*

**max·i·mum** \'mak-sə-məm\ *n, pl* **-ma** \-mə\ *or* **-mums** **1** : the greatest quantity, value, or degree **2** : an upper limit allowed by authority **3** : the largest of a set of numbers — **maximum** *adj*

**max out** *vb* **1** : to push to or reach a limit or an extreme **2** : to use up all available credit on (a credit card)

**may** \'mā\ *verbal auxiliary, past* **might** \'mīt\ *pres sing & pl* **may** **1** : have permission or liberty to ⟨you ∼ go now⟩ **2** : be in some degree likely to ⟨you ∼ be right⟩ **3** — used as an auxiliary to express a wish, purpose, contingency, or concession ⟨∼ the best man win⟩

**May** \'mā\ *n* [ME, fr. OF *mai*, fr. L *Maius*, fr. *Maia*, Roman goddess] : the 5th month of the year

**Ma·ya** \'mī-ə\ *n, pl* **Maya** *or* **Mayas** : a member of a group of American Indian peoples of Yucatán, Guatemala, and adjacent areas — **Ma·yan** \'mī-ən\ *n or adj*

**may·ap·ple** \'mā-ͺa-pəl\ *n* : a No. American woodland herb related to the barberry that has a poisonous root, one or two large leaves, and an edible egg-shaped yellow fruit

**may·be** \'mā-bē, 'me-\ *adv* : PERHAPS

**May Day** \'mā-ͺdā\ *n* : May 1 celebrated as a springtime festival and in some countries as Labor Day

**may·flow·er** \'mā-ͺflaů(-ə)r\ *n* : any of several spring blooming herbs (as the trailing arbutus or an anemone)

**may·fly** \'mā-ͺflī\ *n* : any of an order of insects with an aquatic nymph and a short-lived fragile adult having membranous wings

**may·hem** \'mā-ͺhem, 'mā-əm\ *n* **1** : willful and permanent crippling, mutilation, or disfigurement of a person **2** : needless or willful damage

**may·on·naise** \'mā-ə-ͺnāz\ *n* [F] : a dressing made of egg yolks, vegetable oil, and vinegar or lemon juice

**may·or** \'mā-ər\ *n* : an official elected to act as chief executive or nominal head of a city or borough — **may·or·al** \-əl\ *adj* — **may·or·al·ty** \-əl-tē\ *n*

**may·pole** \'mā-ͺpōl\ *n, often cap* : a tall flower-wreathed pole forming a center for May Day sports and dances

**maze** \'māz\ *n* : a confusing intricate network of passages — **mazy** *adj*

**ma·zur·ka** \mə-'zər-kə\ *n* : a Polish dance in moderate triple measure

**MB** *abbr* Manitoba

**MBA** *abbr* master of business administration

**mc** *abbr* megacycle

¹**MC** *n* : MASTER OF CEREMONIES

²**MC** *abbr* member of Congress

**Mc-** \mək; mə *before forms beginning with* k *or* g\ *prefix* : used to indicate a convenient, low-quality version of a specified thing ⟨*Mc*Book⟩

**Mc·Coy** \mə-'kȯi\ *n* : something that is neither imitation nor substitute ⟨the real ∼⟩

**McGuffin** *var of* MACGUFFIN

**MCPO** *abbr* master chief petty officer

¹**Md** *abbr* Maryland

²**Md** *symbol* mendelevium

**MD** *abbr* **1** [NL *medicinae doctor*] doctor of medicine **2** Maryland **3** muscular dystrophy

**MDMA** \ͺem-dē-ͺem-'ā\ *n* : ECSTASY 2

**mdnt** *abbr* midnight

**mdse** *abbr* merchandise

**MDT** *abbr* mountain daylight (saving) time

**me** \'mē\ *pron, objective case of* I

**Me** *abbr* Maine

**ME** *abbr* **1** Maine **2** mechanical engineer **3** medical examiner

¹**mead** \'mēd\ *n* : an alcoholic beverage brewed from water and honey, malt, and yeast

²**mead** *n, archaic* : MEADOW

**mead·ow** \'me-dō\ *n* : land in or mainly in grass; *esp* : a tract of moist low-lying usu. level grassland — **mead·ow·land** \-ͺland\ *n* — **mead·owy** \'me-də-wē\ *adj*

**mead·ow·lark** \'me-dō-ͺlärk\ *n* : any of several American songbirds related to the orioles that are streaked brown above and in northernmost forms have a yellow breast marked with a black crescent

**mead·ow·sweet** \-ͺswēt\ *n* : a No. American native or naturalized spirea

**mea·ger** *or* **mea·gre** \'mē-gər\ *adj* **1** : THIN **2** : lacking richness, fertility, or strength; *also* : POOR ⟨a ∼ income⟩
♦ *Synonyms* SCANTY, SCANT, SPARE, SPARSE — **mea·ger·ly** *adv* — **mea·ger·ness** *n*

¹**meal** \'mēl\ *n* **1** : an act or the time of eating a portion of food **2** : the portion of food eaten at a meal

²**meal** *n* **1** : usu. coarsely ground seeds of a cereal **2** : a product resembling seed meal — **mealy** *adj*

**meal·time** \'mēl-ͺtīm\ *n* : the usual time at which a meal is served

**mealy·bug** \'mē-lē-ͺbəg\ *n* : any of a family of scale insects with a white cottony or waxy covering that are destructive pests esp. of fruit trees

**mealy·mouthed** \\,mē-lē-,mau̇thd, -,mau̇tht\\ *adj* : not plain and straightforward : DEVIOUS ⟨a ~ politician⟩

**¹mean** \\'mēn\\ *vb* **meant** \\'ment\\; **meaning 1** : to have in the mind as a purpose **2** : to serve to convey, show, or indicate : SIGNIFY ⟨red ~s stop⟩ **3** : to have importance to the degree of ⟨~s the world to me⟩ **4** : to direct to a particular individual ⟨a gift *meant* for me⟩

**²mean** *adj* **1** : HUMBLE **2** : lacking acumen : DULL **3** : SHABBY, CONTEMPTIBLE ⟨no ~ feat⟩ **4** : IGNOBLE, BASE ⟨a ~ trick⟩ **5** : STINGY **6** : pettily selfish or malicious : VEXATIOUS ⟨a ~ dog⟩ **8** : EXCELLENT ⟨throws a ~ slider⟩ — **mean·ly** *adv* — **mean·ness** *n*

**³mean** *adj* **1** : occupying a middle position (as in space, order, or time) **2** : being a mean : AVERAGE ⟨a ~ value⟩

**⁴mean** *n* **1** : a middle point between extremes **2** *pl* : something helpful in achieving a desired end **3** *pl* : material resources affording a secure life : ARITHMETIC MEAN

**¹me·an·der** \\mē-'an-dər\\ *n* [L *maeander*, fr. Gk *maiandros*, fr. *Maiandros* (now *Menderes*), river in Asia Minor] **1** : a winding course **2** : a winding of a stream — **me·an·drous** \\-drəs\\ *adj*

**²meander** *vb* **1** : to follow a winding course **2** : to wander aimlessly or casually

**mean·ing** *n* **1** : the thing one intends to convey esp. by language; *also* : the thing that is thus conveyed **2** : AIM **3** : SIGNIFICANCE; *esp* : implication of a hidden significance **4** : CONNOTATION; *also* : DENOTATION — **mean·ing·ful** \\-fəl\\ *adj* — **mean·ing·ful·ly** *adv* — **mean·ing·less** *adj*

**¹mean·time** \\'mēn-,tīm\\ *n* : the intervening time

**²meantime** *adv* : MEANWHILE

**¹mean·while** \\,-hwī(-ə)l\\ *n* : MEANTIME

**²meanwhile** *adv* **1** : during the intervening time **2** : at the same time

**meas** *abbr* measure

**mea·sles** \\'mē-zəlz\\ *n sing or pl* : an acute virus disease marked by fever and an eruption of distinct circular red spots

**mea·sly** \\'mēz-lē, -zə-lē\\ *adj* **mea·sli·er; -est** : contemptibly small or insignificant

**¹mea·sure** \\'me-zhər, 'mā-\\ *n* **1** : an adequate or moderate portion; *also* : a suitable limit **2** : the dimensions, capacity, or amount of something ascertained by measuring; *also* : an instrument for measuring **3** : a unit of measurement; *also* : a system of such units **4** : the act or process of measuring **5** : rhythmic structure or movement **6** : the part of a musical staff between two bars **7** : CRITERION **8** : a means to an end **9** : a legislative bill — **mea·sure·less** *adj*

**²measure** *vb* **mea·sured; mea·sur·ing 1** : to mark or fix in multiples of a specific unit ⟨~ off five centimeters⟩ **2** : to find out the size, extent, or amount of **3** : to

bring into comparison or competition **4** : to serve as a means of measuring **5** : to have a specified measurement — **mea·sur·able** \\'me-zhə-rə-bəl, 'mā-\\ *adj* — **mea·sur·ably** \\-blē\\ *adv* — **mea·sur·er** *n*

**mea·sure·ment** \\'me-zhər-mənt, 'mā-\\ *n* **1** : the act or process of measuring **2** : a figure, extent, or amount obtained by measuring

**measure up** *vb* **1** : to have necessary or fitting qualifications **2** : to equal esp. in ability

**meat** \\'mēt\\ *n* **1** : FOOD; *esp* : solid food as distinguished from drink **2** : animal and esp. mammal flesh considered as food **3** : the edible part inside a covering (as a shell or rind) — **meaty** *adj*

**meat·ball** \\-,bȯl\\ *n* : a small ball of chopped or ground meat

**meat loaf** *n* : a dish of ground meat seasoned and baked in the form of a loaf

**mec·ca** \\'me-kə\\ *n, often cap* [*Mecca*, Saudi Arabia, a destination of pilgrims in the Islamic world] : a center of a specified activity or interest ⟨a shopping ~⟩

**mech** *abbr* mechanical; mechanics

**¹me·chan·ic** \\mi-'ka-nik\\ *adj* : of or relating to manual work or skill

**²mechanic** *n* **1** : a manual worker **2** : MACHINIST; *esp* : one who repairs cars

**me·chan·i·cal** \\mi-'ka-ni-kəl\\ *adj* **1** : of or relating to machinery, to manual operations, or to mechanics **2** : done as if by a machine : AUTOMATIC ⟨a ~ response⟩ **♦ Synonyms** INSTINCTIVE, IMPULSIVE, SPONTANEOUS — **me·chan·i·cal·ly** \\-k(ə-)lē\\ *adv*

**mechanical drawing** *n* : drawing done with the aid of instruments

**me·chan·ics** \\mi-'ka-niks\\ *n sing or pl* **1** : a branch of physics that deals with energy and forces and their effect on bodies **2** : the practical application of mechanics (as to the operation of machines) **3** : mechanical or functional details ⟨the ~ of the brain⟩

**mech·a·nism** \\'me-kə-,ni-zəm\\ *n* **1** : a piece of machinery; *also* : a process or technique for achieving a result **2** : mechanical operation or action **3** : the fundamental processes involved in or responsible for a natural phenomenon ⟨the visual ~⟩

**mech·a·nis·tic** \\,me-kə-'nis-tik\\ *adj* **1** : mechanically determined ⟨~ universe⟩ **2** : MECHANICAL — **mech·a·nis·ti·cal·ly** \\-ti-k(ə-)lē\\ *adv*

**mech·a·nize** \\'me-kə-,nīz\\ *vb* **-nized; -niz·ing 1** : to make mechanical **2** : to equip with machinery esp. in order to replace human or animal labor **3** : to equip with armed and armored motor vehicles — **mech·a·ni·za·tion** \\,me-kə-nə-'zā-shən\\ *n* — **mech·a·niz·er** *n*

**¹med** \\'med\\ *adj* : MEDICAL ⟨~ school⟩

**²med** *n* : MEDICINE **1** — usu. used in pl.

**³med** *abbr* **1** medical; medicine **2** medieval **3** medium

**MEd** *abbr* master of education

**med·al** \\'me-dºl\\ *n* [MF *medaille*, fr. OIt *medaglia* coin worth half a denarius,

**medal**, fr. VL *medalis* half, altcr. of LL *medialis* middle, fr. L *medius*] **1** : a small usu. metal object bearing a religious emblem or picture **2** : a piece of metal issued to commemorate a person or event or to award excellence or achievement

**med·al·ist** or **med·al·list** \'me-d<sup>ə</sup>l-ist\ n **1** : a designer or maker of medals **2** : a recipient of a medal as an award

**me·dal·lion** \mə-'dal-yən\ n **1** : a large medal **2** : a tablet or panel bearing a portrait or an ornament

**med·dle** \'me-d<sup>ə</sup>l\ vb **med·dled**; **med·dling** : to interfere without right or propriety — **med·dler** \'me-d<sup>ə</sup>l-ər\ n

**med·dle·some** \'me-d<sup>ə</sup>l-səm\ adj : inclined to meddle ⟨a ~ neighbor⟩

**med·e·vac** also **med·i·vac** \'me-də-,vak\ n **1** : emergency evacuation of the sick or wounded **2** : a helicopter used for medevac

**me·dia** \'mē-dē-ə\ n, pl **me·di·as 1** : MEDIUM 4 **2** sing or pl in constr : MASS MEDIA

**me·di·al** \'mē-dē-əl\ adj : occurring in or extending toward the middle

¹**me·di·an** \'mē-dē-ən\ n **1** : a value in an ordered set of values below and above which there are an equal number of values **2** : MEDIAN STRIP

²**median** adj **1** : being in the middle or in an intermediate position **2** : relating to or constituting a statistical median

**median strip** n : a strip dividing a highway into lanes according to the direction of travel

**me·di·ate** \'mē-dē-,āt\ vb **-at·ed**; **-at·ing 1** : to act as an intermediary; esp : to work with opposing sides in order to resolve (as a dispute) or bring about (as a settlement) **2** : to bring about, influence, or transmit (as a physical process or effect) by acting as an intermediate or controlling agent or mechanism ♦ **Synonyms** INTERCEDE, INTERVENE, INTERPOSE, INTERFERE — **me·di·a·tion** \,mē-dē-'ā-shən\ n — **me·di·a·tor** \'mē-dē-,ā-tər\ n

**med·ic** \'me-dik\ n : one engaged in medical work; esp : CORPSMAN

**med·i·ca·ble** \'me-di-kə-bəl\ adj : CURABLE

**Med·ic·aid** \'me-di-,kād\ n : a program of financial assistance for medical care designed for those unable to afford regular medical service and financed jointly by the state and federal governments

**med·i·cal** \'me-di-kəl\ adj : of or relating to the science or practice of medicine or the treatment of disease — **med·i·cal·ly** \-k(ə-)lē\ adv

**medical examiner** n : a public officer who performs autopsies on bodies to find the cause of death

**me·dic·a·ment** \mi-'di-kə-mənt, 'me-di-kə-\ n : a substance used in therapy

**Medi·care** \'me-di-,ker\ n : a government program of financial assistance for medical care esp. for the aged

**med·i·cate** \'me-di-,kāt\ vb **-cat·ed**; **-cat·ing** : to treat with medicine

**med·i·ca·tion** \,me-də-'kā-shən\ n **1** : the act or process of medicating **2** : MEDICINE 1

**me·dic·i·nal** \mə-'di-s<sup>ə</sup>n-əl\ adj : tending or used to cure disease or relieve pain — **me·dic·i·nal·ly** adv

**med·i·cine** \'me-də-sən\ n **1** : a substance or preparation used in treating disease **2** : a science and art dealing with the prevention, alleviation, and cure of disease

**medicine ball** n : a heavy stuffed leather ball used for conditioning exercises

**medicine man** n : a priestly healer or sorcerer esp. among the American Indians : SHAMAN

**med·i·co** \'me-di-,kō\ n, pl **-cos** : a medical practitioner or student

**me·di·e·val** also **me·di·ae·val** \,mē-dē-'ē-vəl, ,mē-, mē-'dē-vəl\ adj **1** : of, relating to, or characteristic of the Middle Ages **2** : having a quality (as cruelty) associated with the Middle Ages **3** : extremely outmoded or antiquated — **me·di·e·val·ism** \-və-,li-zəm\ n — **me·di·e·val·ist** \-list\ n

**me·di·o·cre** \,mē-dē-'ō-kər\ adj [MF, fr. L *mediocris*, fr. *medius* middle + *ocris* stony mountain] : of moderate or low quality : ORDINARY ⟨did a ~ job⟩ — **me·di·oc·ri·ty** \-'ä-krə-tē\ n

**med·i·tate** \'me-də-,tāt\ vb **-tat·ed**; **-tat·ing 1** : to muse over : CONTEMPLATE, PONDER **2** : to engage in deep mental exercise directed toward a heightened level of spiritual awareness **3** : INTEND, PLAN — **med·i·ta·tion** \,me-də-'tā-shən\ n — **med·i·ta·tive** \'me-də-,tā-tiv\ adj — **med·i·ta·tive·ly** adv

**Med·i·ter·ra·nean** \,me-də-tə-'rā-nē-ən, -'rā-nyən\ adj : of or relating to the Mediterranean Sea or to the lands or people around it

¹**me·di·um** \'mē-dē-əm\ n, pl **mediums** or **me·dia** \-dē-ə\ [L] **1** : something in a middle position; also : a middle position or degree **2** : a means of effecting or conveying something **3** : a surrounding or enveloping substance **4** : a channel or system of communication, information, or entertainment **5** : a mode of artistic expression **6** : an individual held to be a channel of communication between the earthly world and a world of spirits **7** : a condition or environment in which something may function or flourish

²**medium** adj : intermediate in amount, quality, position, or degree

**me·di·um·is·tic** \,mē-dē-ə-'mis-tik\ adj : of, relating to, or being a spiritualistic medium

**medivac** var of MEDEVAC

**med·ley** \'med-lē\ n, pl **medleys 1** : HODGEPODGE **2** : a musical composition made up esp. of a series of songs

**me·dul·la** \mə-'də-lə\ n, pl **-las** or **-lae** \-(,)lē, -,lī\ : an inner or deep anatomical part; also : the posterior part (**medulla ob·lon·ga·ta** \-,ä-,blȯŋ-'gä-tə\) of the vertebrate brain that is continuous with the spinal cord

**meed** \'mēd\ n : a fitting return

**meek** \'mēk\ adj **1** : enduring injury with patience and without resentment **2** : de-

ficient in spirit and courage **3** : MODER-
ATE — **meek·ly** adv — **meek·ness** n

**meer·schaum** \'mir-shəm, -ˌshȯm\ n [G,
fr. Meer sea + Schaum foam] : a tobacco
pipe made of a light white clayey mineral

¹**meet** \'mēt\ vb **met** \'met\; **meet·ing 1**
: to come upon : FIND **2** : JOIN, INTER-
SECT **3** : to appear to the perception of **4**
: OPPOSE, FIGHT **5** : to join in conversation or discussion; also : ASSEMBLE **6** : to
conform to ⟨~s requirements⟩ **7** : to
pay fully **8** : to cope with **9** : to provide
for **10** : to be introduced to

²**meet** n : an assembling esp. for a hunt or
for competitive sports

³**meet** adj : SUITABLE, PROPER

**meet·ing** \'mē-tiŋ\ n **1** : an act of coming
together : ASSEMBLY **2** : JUNCTION, IN-
TERSECTION

**meet·ing·house** \-ˌhau̇s\ n : a building
for public assembly and esp. for Protestant worship

**meg** \'meg\ n : MEGABYTE

**mega-** or **meg-** comb form **1** : great
: large ⟨megahit⟩ **2** : million ⟨mega-
hertz⟩

**mega·byte** \'me-gə-ˌbīt\ n : 1024 kilo-
bytes or 1,048,576 bytes; also : one million bytes

**mega·cy·cle** \-ˌsī-kəl\ n : MEGAHERTZ

**mega·death** \-ˌdeth\ n : one million
deaths — used as a unit in reference to
nuclear warfare

**mega·hertz** \'me-gə-ˌhərts, -ˌherts\ n : a
unit of frequency equal to one million
hertz

**mega·lith** \'me-gə-ˌlith\ n : a large stone
used in prehistoric monuments — **mega-
lith·ic** \ˌme-gə-ˈli-thik\ adj

**meg·a·lo·ma·nia** \ˌme-gə-lō-ˈmā-nē-ə,
-nyə\ n : a mental disorder marked by
feelings of personal omnipotence and
grandeur — **meg·a·lo·ma·ni·ac**
\-nē-ˌak\ adj or n — **meg·a·lo·ma·ni·a·cal**
\-mə-ˈnī-ə-kəl\ adj

**meg·a·lop·o·lis** \ˌme-gə-ˈlä-pə-ləs\ n : a
very large urban unit

**mega·phone** \'me-gə-ˌfōn\ n : a cone-
shaped device used to intensify or direct
the voice — **megaphone** vb

**mega·pix·el** \'me-gə-ˌpik-səl\ n : one million pixels

**mega·plex** \-ˌpleks\ n : a cineplex having
usu. at least 16 movie theaters

**mega·ton** \-ˌtän\ n : an explosive force
equivalent to that of one million tons of
TNT

**mega·vi·ta·min** \-ˌvī-tə-mən\ adj : relating to or consisting of very large doses of
vitamins — **mega·vi·ta·mins** n pl

**meh** \'me\ interj — used to express indifference or mild disappointment

**mei·o·sis** \mī-ˈō-səs\ n : a process of cell
division in gamete-producing cells in
which the number of chromosomes is reduced to one half — **mei·ot·ic** \mī-ˈä-tik\
adj

**meit·ner·i·um** \mīt-ˈnir-ē-əm, -ˈner-\ n
: an artificially produced radioactive
chemical element

**mel·an·cho·lia** \ˌme-lən-ˈkō-lē-ə\ n : a

mental condition marked by extreme depression often with delusions

**mel·an·chol·ic** \ˌme-lən-ˈkä-lik\ adj **1**
: DEPRESSED **2** : of or relating to melan-
cholia

**mel·an·choly** \'me-lən-ˌkä-lē\ n, pl **-chol·
ies** [ME malencolie, fr. AF, fr. LL melan-
cholia, fr. Gk, fr. melan-, melas black +
cholē bile; so called fr. the former belief
that it was caused by an excess of black
bile] : depression of spirits : DEJECTION
— **melancholy** adj

**Mel·a·ne·sian** \ˌme-lə-ˈnē-zhən\ n : a
member of the dominant native group of
the Pacific island grouping of Melanesia
— **Melanesian** adj

**mé·lange** \mā-ˈläⁿzh, -ˈlänj\ n : a mixture
esp. of incongruous elements

**mel·a·nin** \'me-lə-nən\ n : any of various
dark brown pigments of animal or plant
structures (as skin or hair)

**mel·a·nism** \'me-lə-ˌni-zəm\ n : an increased amount of black or nearly black
pigmentation

**mel·a·no·ma** \ˌme-lə-ˈnō-mə\ n, pl **-mas**
also **-ma·ta** \-mə-tə\ : a usu. malignant
tumor containing dark pigment

¹**meld** \'meld\ vb : to show or announce
for a score in a card game

²**meld** n : a card or combination of cards
that is or can be melded

**me·lee** \'mā-ˌlā, mā-ˈlā\ n [F mêlée] : a
confused struggle ♦ Synonyms FRA-
CAS, ROW, BRAWL, DONNYBROOK

**me·lio·rate** \'mēl-yə-ˌrāt, ˈmē-lē-ə-\ vb
**-rat·ed; -rat·ing** : AMELIORATE — **me-
lio·ra·tion** \ˌmēl-yə-ˈrā-shən, ˌmē-lē-ə-\ n
— **me·lio·ra·tive** \'mēl-yə-ˌrā-tiv, ˈmē-lē-
ə-\ adj

**mel·lif·lu·ous** \me-ˈli-flə-wəs, mə-\ adj
[ME mellyfluous, fr. LL mellifluus, fr. L
mel honey + fluere to flow] : sweetly flowing ⟨a ~ voice⟩ — **mel·lif·lu·ous·ly** adv
— **mel·lif·lu·ous·ness** n

¹**mel·low** \'me-lō\ adj **1** : soft and sweet
because of ripeness; also : well aged and
pleasingly mild ⟨~ wine⟩ **2** : made gentle by age or experience **3** : being rich
and full but not garish or strident ⟨~
colors⟩ **4** : of soft loamy consistency ⟨~
soil⟩ — **mel·low·ness** n

²**mellow** vb : to make or become mellow
— often used with out

**me·lo·di·ous** \mə-ˈlō-dē-əs\ adj : pleasing
to the ear ⟨~ chimes⟩ — **me·lo·di·ous·
ly** adv — **me·lo·di·ous·ness** n

**melo·dra·ma** \'me-lə-ˌdrä-mə, -ˌdra-\ n **1**
: an extravagantly theatrical play in
which action and plot predominate over
characterization **2** : something having a
sensational or theatrical quality — **melo-
dra·mat·ic** \ˌme-lə-drə-ˈma-tik\ adj —
**melo·dra·mat·i·cal·ly** \-ti-k(ə-)lē\ adv —
**melo·dra·ma·tist** \ˌme-lə-ˈdrä-mə-tist,
-ˈdrä-\ n

**mel·o·dy** \'me-lə-dē\ n, pl **-dies 1** : sweet
or agreeable sound **2** : a particular succession of notes : TUNE, AIR — **me·lod·ic**
\mə-ˈlä-dik\ adj — **me·lod·i·cal·ly** \-di-
k(ə-)lē\ adv

**mel·on** \'me-lən\ n : any of various typically sweet fruits (as a muskmelon or

watermelon) of the gourd family usu. eaten raw

¹**melt** \'melt\ *vb* **1** : to change from a solid to a liquid state usu. by heat **2** : DISSOLVE, DISINTEGRATE; *also* : to cause to disperse or disappear ⟨her anger *~ed* away⟩ **3** : to make or become tender or gentle

²**melt** *n* : a melted substance

**melt-down** \'melt-ˌdau̇n\ *n* **1** : the melting of the core of a nuclear reactor **2** : a collapse of something (as one's self-control)

**melting pot** *n* : a place where different races, cultures, or individuals assimilate into a cohesive whole

**melt-wa-ter** \-ˌwȯ-tər, -ˌwä-\ *n* : water derived from the melting of ice and snow

**mem** *abbr* **1** member **2** memoir **3** memorial

**mem-ber** \'mem-bər\ *n* **1** : a part (as an arm, leg, leaf, or branch) of an animal or plant **2** : one of the individuals composing a group **3** : a part of a whole ⟨*~s* of a set⟩

**mem-ber-ship** \-ˌship\ *n* **1** : the state or status of being a member **2** : the body of members

**mem-brane** \'mem-ˌbrān\ *n* : a thin pliable layer esp. of animal or plant origin — **mem-bra-nous** \-brə-nəs\ *adj*

**me-men-to** \mə-'men-tō\ *n, pl* **-tos** or **-toes** [ME, fr. L, remember, imper. of *meminisse* to remember] : something that serves to warn or remind; *also* : SOUVENIR

**memo** \'me-mō\ *n, pl* **mem-os** : MEMORANDUM

**mem-oir** \'mem-ˌwär\ *n* **1** : MEMORANDUM **2** : AUTOBIOGRAPHY — usu. used in pl. **3** : an account of something noteworthy; *also, pl* : the record of the proceedings of a learned society

**mem-o-ra-bil-ia** \ˌme-mə-rə-'bi-lē-ə, -'bil-yə\ *n pl* [L] **1** : things worthy of remembrance **2** : things associated with a particular interest and that are usu. collectied : MEMENTOS

**mem-o-ra-ble** \'me-mə-rə-bəl\ *adj* : worth remembering : NOTABLE ⟨a *~* quotation⟩ — **mem-o-ra-bil-i-ty** \ˌme-mə-rə-'bi-lə-tē\ *n* — **mem-o-ra-ble-ness** *n* — **mem-o-ra-bly** \-blē\ *adv*

**mem-o-ran-dum** \ˌme-mə-'ran-dəm\ *n, pl* **-dums** or **-da** \-də\ **1** : an informal record; *also* : a written reminder **2** : an informal written note

¹**me-mo-ri-al** \mə-'mȯr-ē-əl\ *adj* : serving to preserve remembrance

²**memorial** *n* **1** : something designed to keep remembrance alive; *esp* : MONUMENT **2** : a statement of facts often accompanied with a petition — **me-mo-ri-al-ize** *vb*

**Memorial Day** *n* : the last Monday in May or formerly May 30 observed as a legal holiday in honor of those who died in war

**mem-o-rise** *Brit var of* MEMORIZE

**mem-o-rize** \'me-mə-ˌrīz\ *vb* **-rized; -riz-ing** : to learn by heart — **mem-o-ri-za-**

**tion** \ˌme-mə-rə-'zā-shən\ *n* — **mem-o-riz-er** *n*

**mem-o-ry** \'me-mə-rē\ *n, pl* **-ries** **1** : the power or process of remembering **2** : the store of things remembered **3** : COMMEMORATION **4** : something remembered **5** : the time within which past events are remembered **6** : a device (as in a computer) in which information can be stored; *esp* : RAM **7** : capacity for storing information ⟨512 megabytes of *~*⟩

♦ **Synonyms** REMEMBRANCE, RECOLLECTION, REMINISCENCE

**men** *pl of* MAN

¹**men-ace** \'me-nəs\ *n* **1** : THREAT **2** : DANGER ⟨those dogs are a *~*⟩; *also* : NUISANCE

²**menace** *vb* **men-aced; men-ac-ing** **1** : THREATEN **2** : ENDANGER — **men-ac-ing-ly** *adv*

**mé-nage** \mā-'näzh\ *n* [F] : HOUSEHOLD

**ménage à trois** \-ˌä-'trwä\ *n* : an arrangement in which three persons share sexual relations esp. while living together

**me-nag-er-ie** \mə-'na-jə-rē\ *n* : a collection of wild animals esp. for exhibition

¹**mend** \'mend\ *vb* **1** : to improve in manners or morals **2** : to put into good shape : REPAIR **3** : to improve in or restore to health : HEAL — **mend-er** *n*

²**mend** *n* **1** : an act of mending **2** : a mended place

**men-da-cious** \men-'dā-shəs\ *adj* : given to deception or falsehood : UNTRUTHFUL

♦ **Synonyms** DISHONEST, DECEITFUL — **men-da-cious-ly** *adv* — **men-dac-i-ty** \-'da-sə-tē\ *n*

**men-de-le-vi-um** \ˌmen-də-'lē-vē-əm, -'lā-\ *n* : a radioactive metallic chemical element artificially produced

**men-di-cant** \'men-di-kənt\ *n* **1** : BEGGAR **2** *often cap* : FRIAR — **men-di-can-cy** \-kən-sē\ *n* — **mendicant** *adj*

**men-folk** \'men-ˌfōk\ or **men-folks** \-ˌfōks\ *n pl* **1** : men in general **2** : the men of a family or community

**men-ha-den** \men-'hā-dᵊn, mən-\ *n, pl* **-den** *also* **-dens** : a marine fish related to the herring that is abundant along the Atlantic coast of the U.S.

¹**me-nial** \'mē-nē-əl, -nyəl\ *n* : a domestic servant

²**menial** *adj* **1** : of or relating to servants **2** : HUMBLE, SERVILE ⟨answered in *~* tones⟩ — **me-ni-al-ly** *adv*

**men-in-gi-tis** \ˌme-nən-'jī-təs\ *n, pl* **-git-i-des** \-'ji-tə-ˌdēz\ : inflammation of the membranes enclosing the brain and spinal cord; *also* : a usu. bacterial disease marked by this

**me-ninx** \'mē-niŋks, 'me-\ *n, pl* **me-nin-ges** \mə-'nin-(ˌ)jēz\ : any of the three membranes that envelop the brain and spinal cord — **men-in-ge-al** \ˌme-nən-'jē-əl\ *adj*

**me-nis-cus** \mə-'nis-kəs\ *n, pl* **me-nis-ci** \-'nis-ˌkī, -ˌkē\ *also* **me-nis-cus-es** **1** : CRESCENT **2** : the curved upper surface of a column of liquid

**men-o-pause** \'me-nə-ˌpȯz\ *n* : the period of life when menstruation stops naturally — **men·o·paus·al** \ˌme-nə-ˈpȯ-zəl\ adj

**me·no·rah** \mə-ˈnȯr-ə\ n [Heb měnōrāh candlestick] : a candelabrum that is used in Jewish worship

**men·ses** \ˈmen-ˌsēz\ n sing or pl : the menstrual flow

**menstrual cycle** n : the complete cycle of physiological changes from the beginning of one menstrual period to the beginning of the next

**men·stru·a·tion** \ˌmen-strə-ˈwā-shən, men-ˈstrā-\ n : a discharging of bloody matter at approximately monthly intervals from the uterus of breeding-age nonpregnant primate females; also : PERIOD 6 — **men·stru·al** \ˈmen-strə-wəl\ adj — **men·stru·ate** \ˈmen-strə-ˌwāt, -ˌstrāt\ vb

**men·su·ra·ble** \ˈmen-sə-rə-bəl, ˈ-chə-\ adj : MEASURABLE

**men·su·ra·tion** \ˌmen-sə-ˈrā-shən, ˌmen-chə-\ n : MEASUREMENT

**-ment** n suffix 1 : concrete result, object, or agent of a (specified) action ⟨embankment⟩ ⟨entanglement⟩ 2 : concrete means or instrument of a (specified) action ⟨entertainment⟩ 3 : action : process ⟨encirclement⟩ ⟨development⟩ 4 : place of a (specified) action ⟨encampment⟩ 5 : state : condition ⟨amazement⟩

**men·tal** \ˈmen-tᵊl\ adj 1 : of or relating to the mind 2 : of, relating to, or affected with a disorder of the mind ⟨∼ illness⟩ — **men·tal·ly** adv

**mental age** n : a measure of a child's mental development in terms of the number of years it takes an average child to reach the same level

**mental deficiency** n : MENTAL RETARDATION

**men·tal·i·ty** \men-ˈta-lə-tē\ n, pl **-ties** 1 : mental power or capacity 2 : mode or way of thought

**mental retardation** n : subaverage intellectual ability present from infancy that is characterized by an IQ of 70 or less and problems in development, learning, and social adjustment — **mentally retarded** adj

**men·tee** \men-ˈtē\ n : PROTÉGÉ

**men·thol** \ˈmen-ˌthȯl, -ˌthōl\ n : an alcohol occurring esp. in mint oils that has the odor and cooling properties of peppermint — **men·tho·lat·ed** \-thə-ˌlā-təd\ adj

**¹men·tion** \ˈmen-chən\ n 1 : a brief or casual reference 2 : a formal citation for outstanding achievement

**²mention** vb 1 : to refer to : CITE 2 : to cite for superior achievement — **not to mention** : not even yet counting or considering

**men·tor** \ˈmen-ˌtȯr, -tər\ n : a trusted counselor or guide; also : TUTOR, COACH — **mentor** vb

**menu** \ˈmen-yü, ˈmān-\ n, pl **menus** [F, fr. menu small, detailed, fr. OF, fr. L minutus minute (adj.)] 1 : a list of the dishes available (as in a restaurant) for a meal; also : the dishes served 2 : a list of offerings or options

**me·ow** \mē-ˈaù\ vb : to make the characteristic cry of a cat — **meow** n

**mer** abbr meridian

**mer·can·tile** \ˈmər-kən-ˌtēl, -ˌtī(-ə)l\ adj : of or relating to merchants or trading

**¹mer·ce·nary** \ˈmər-sə-ˌner-ē\ n, pl **-nar·ies** : a person who serves merely for wages; esp : a soldier hired into foreign service

**²mercenary** adj 1 : serving merely for pay or gain 2 : hired for service in a foreign army

**mer·cer** \ˈmər-sər\ n, Brit : a dealer in usu. expensive fabrics

**mer·cer·ise** Brit var of MERCERIZE

**mer·cer·ize** \ˈmər-sə-ˌrīz\ vb **-ized; -iz·ing** : to treat cotton yarn or cloth with alkali so that it looks silky or takes a better dye

**¹mer·chan·dise** \ˈmər-chən-ˌdīz, -ˌdīs\ n : the commodities or goods that are bought and sold in business

**²mer·chan·dise** \-ˌdīz\ vb **-dised; -dis·ing** : to buy and sell in business : TRADE — **mer·chan·dis·er** n

**mer·chant** \ˈmər-chənt\ n 1 : a buyer and seller of commodities for profit 2 : STOREKEEPER

**mer·chant·able** \ˈmər-chən-tə-bəl\ adj : acceptable to buyers : MARKETABLE

**mer·chant·man** \ˈmər-chənt-mən\ n : a ship used in commerce

**merchant marine** n : the commercial ships of a nation

**merchant ship** n : MERCHANTMAN

**mer·ci·ful·ly** \ˈmər-si-fə-lē\ adv 1 : in a merciful manner 2 : FORTUNATELY 2 ⟨∼ we didn't have to attend⟩

**mer·cu·ri·al** \ˌmər-ˈkyùr-ē-əl\ adj 1 : unpredictably changeable ⟨a ∼ personality⟩ 2 : MERCURIC — **mer·cu·ri·al·ly** adv — **mer·cu·ri·al·ness** n

**mer·cu·ric** \ˌmər-ˈkyùr-ik\ adj : of, relating to, or containing mercury

**mercuric chloride** n : a poisonous compound of mercury and chlorine used as an antiseptic and fungicide

**mer·cu·ry** \ˈmər-kyə-rē\ n, pl **-ries** 1 : a heavy silver-white liquid metallic chemical element used esp. in scientific instruments 2 cap : the planet nearest the sun

**mer·cy** \ˈmər-sē\ n, pl **mercies** [ME, fr. AF merci, fr. ML merced-, merces, fr. L, price paid, wages, fr. merc-, merx merchandise] 1 : compassion shown to an offender; also : imprisonment rather than death for first-degree murder 2 : a blessing resulting from divine favor or compassion; also : a fortunate circumstance 3 : compassion shown to victims of misfortune — **mer·ci·ful** \-si-fəl\ adj — **mer·ci·less** \-si-ləs\ adj — **mer·ci·less·ly** adv — **mercy** adj

**mercy killing** n : EUTHANASIA

**¹mere** \ˈmir\ n : LAKE, POOL

**²mere** adj, superlative **mer·est** 1 : not diluted : PURE 2 : being nothing more than ⟨a ∼ child⟩ — **mere·ly** adv

**mer·e·tri·cious** \ˌmer-ə-ˈtri-shəs\ adj [L meretricius, fr. meretrix prostitute, fr. merēre to earn] : tawdrily attractive ⟨∼

trinkets); *also* : SPECIOUS — **mer·e·tri·cious·ly** *adv* — **mer·e·tri·cious·ness** *n*

**mer·gan·ser** \(ˌ)mər-'gan-sər\ *n* : any of various fish-eating wild ducks with a usu. crested head and a slender bill hooked at the end and serrated along the margins

**merge** \'mərj\ *vb* **merged; merg·ing** 1 : to blend gradually 2 : to combine, unite, or coalesce into one ♦ *Synonyms* MINGLE, AMALGAMATE, FUSE, INTER-FUSE, INTERMINGLE

**merg·er** \'mər-jər\ *n* 1 : the act or process of merging 2 : absorption by a corporation of one or more others

**me·rid·i·an** \mə-'ri-dē-ən\ *n* [ME, fr. AF *meridien*, fr. *meridien* of noon, fr. L *meridianus*, fr. *meridies* noon, south, irreg. fr. *medius* mid + *dies* day] 1 : the highest point : CULMINATION 2 : any of the imaginary circles on the earth's surface passing through the north and south poles 3 : any of the pathways along which the body's vital energy flows according to the theory behind acupuncture — **meridian** *adj*

**me·ringue** \mə-'raŋ\ *n* [F] : a baked dessert topping of stiffly beaten egg whites and powdered sugar

**me·ri·no** \mə-'rē-nō\ *n, pl* **-nos** [Sp] 1 : any of a breed of sheep noted for fine soft wool 2 : a fine soft fabric or yarn of wool or wool and cotton

¹**mer·it** \'mer-ət\ *n* 1 : laudable or blameworthy traits or actions 2 : a praiseworthy quality; *also* : character or conduct deserving reward or honor 3 *pl* : the intrinsic nature of a legal case; *also* : legal significance

²**merit** *vb* : EARN, DESERVE

**mer·i·toc·ra·cy** \ˌmer-ə-'tä-krə-sē\ *n, pl* **-cies** : a system in which the talented are chosen and moved ahead based on their achievement; *also* : leadership by the talented

**mer·i·to·ri·ous** \ˌmer-ə-'tȯr-ē-əs\ *adj* : deserving honor or esteem — **mer·i·to·ri·ous·ly** *adv* — **mer·i·to·ri·ous·ness** *n*

**mer·lin** \'mər-lən\ *n* : a small compact falcon of the northern hemisphere

**mer·lot** \mer-'lō, mar-\ *n* : a dry red wine made from a widely grown grape; *also* : the grape itself

**mer·maid** \'mər-ˌmād\ *n* : a legendary sea creature with a woman's upper body and a fish's tail

**mer·man** \-ˌman, -mən\ *n* : a legendary sea creature with a man's upper body and a fish's tail

**mer·ri·ment** \'mer-i-mənt\ *n* 1 : HILARITY 2 : FESTIVITY

**mer·ry** \'mer-ē\ *adj* **mer·ri·er; -est** 1 : full of gaiety or high spirits 2 : marked by festivity 3 : BRISK ⟨a ∼pace⟩ ♦ *Synonyms* BLITHE, JOCUND, JOVIAL, JOLLY, MIRTHFUL — **mer·ri·ly** \'mer-ə-lē\ *adv*

**merry–go–round** \'mer-ē-gō-ˌraund\ *n* 1 : a circular revolving platform with benches and figures of animals on which people sit for a ride 2 : a busy round of activities

**mer·ry·mak·ing** \'mer-ē-ˌmā-kiŋ\ *n*

: jovial or festive activity 2 : a festive occasion — **mer·ry·mak·er** \-ˌmā-kər\ *n*

**me·sa** \'mā-sə\ *n* [Sp, lit., table, fr. L *mensa*] : a flat-topped hill with steep sides

**mes·cal** \me-'skal, mā-\ *n* 1 : PEYOTE 2 2 : a usu. colorless liquor distilled from the leaves of an agave; *also* : this agave

**mes·ca·line** \'mes-kə-lən, -ˌlēn\ *n* : a hallucinatory alkaloid from the peyote cactus

**mes·clun** \'mes-klən\ *n* : a mixture of young tender greens; *also* : a salad made with mesclun

**mesdames** *pl of* MADAM *or of* MADAME *or of* MRS.

**mesdemoiselles** *pl of* MADEMOISELLE

¹**mesh** \'mesh\ *n* 1 : one of the openings between the threads or cords of a net; *also* : one of the similar spaces in a network 2 : the fabric of a net 3 : NETWORK 4 : working contact (as of the teeth of gears) ⟨in ∼⟩ — **meshed** \'mesht\ *adj*

²**mesh** *vb* 1 : to catch in or as if in a mesh 2 : to be in or come into mesh : ENGAGE 3 : to fit together properly

**mesh·work** \'mesh-ˌwərk\ *n* : NETWORK

**me·si·al** \'mē-zē-əl, -sē-\ *adj* : of, relating to, or being the surface of a tooth that is closest to the middle of the front of the jaw

**mes·mer·ise** *Brit var of* MESMERIZE

**mes·mer·ize** \'mez-mə-ˌrīz\ *vb* **-ized; -iz·ing** : HYPNOTIZE — **mes·mer·ic** \mez-'mer-ik\ *adj* — **mes·mer·ism** \'mez-mə-ˌri-zəm\ *n*

**Me·so·lith·ic** \ˌme-zə-'li-thik\ *adj* : of, relating to, or being a transitional period of the Stone Age between the Paleolithic and the Neolithic periods

**me·so·sphere** \'me-zə-ˌsfir\ *n* : a layer of the atmosphere between the stratosphere and the thermosphere

**Me·so·zo·ic** \ˌme-zə-'zō-ik, ˌmē-\ *adj* : of, relating to, or being the era of geologic history between the Paleozoic and the Cenozoic and extending from about 245 million years ago to about 65 million years ago — **Mesozoic** *n*

**mes·quite** \mə-'skēt, me-\ *n* : any of several spiny leguminous trees and shrubs chiefly of the southwestern U.S. with sugar-rich pods important as fodder; *also* : mesquite wood used esp. in grilling food

¹**mess** \'mes\ *n* [ME *mes*, fr. AF, fr. LL *missus* course at a meal, fr. *missus*, pp. of *mittere* to put, fr. L, to send] 1 : a quantity of food; *also* : enough food of a specified kind for a dish or meal ⟨a ∼ of beans⟩ 2 : a group of persons who regularly eat together; *also* : a meal eaten by such a group 3 : a place where meals are regularly served to a group 4 : a confused, dirty, or offensive state — **messy** *adj*

²**mess** *vb* 1 : to supply with meals; *also* : to take meals with a mess 2 : to make dirty or untidy; *also* : BUNGLE 3 : INTERFERE, MEDDLE ⟨don't ∼ with me⟩ 4 : PUTTER, TRIFLE

**mes·sage** \'me-sij\ *n* : a communication sent by one person to another

**message board** *n* : BULLETIN BOARD 2

**messeigneurs** *pl of* MONSEIGNEUR

**mes·sen·ger** \'me-s³n-jər\ *n* : one who carries a message or does an errand

**messenger RNA** *n* : an RNA that carries the code for a particular protein from DNA in the nucleus to a ribosome in the cytoplasm and acts as a template for the formation of that protein

**Mes·si·ah** \mə-'sī-ə\ *n* **1** : the expected king and deliverer of the Jews **2** : Jesus **3** *not cap* : a professed or accepted leader of a cause — **mes·si·an·ic** \,me-sē-'a-nik\ *adj*

**messieurs** *pl of* MONSIEUR

**mess·mate** \'mes-,māt\ *n* : a member of a group who eat regularly together

**Messrs.** \'me-sərz\ *pl of* MR.

**mes·ti·zo** \me-'stē-zō\ *n, pl* **-zos** [Sp] : a person of mixed blood

**¹met** *past and past part of* MEET

**²met** *abbr* metropolitan

**me·tab·o·lism** \mə-'ta-bə-,li-zəm\ *n* : the processes by which the substance of plants and animals incidental to life is built up and broken down; *also* : the processes by which a substance is handled in the living body ⟨the ~ of sugar⟩ — **met·a·bol·ic** \,me-tə-'bä-lik\ *adj* — **me·tab·o·lize** \mə-'ta-bə-,līz\ *vb*

**me·tab·o·lite** \-,līt\ *n* **1** : a product of metabolism **2** : a substance essential to the metabolism of a particular organism or to a metabolic process

**meta·car·pal** \,me-tə-'kär-pəl\ *n* : any of usu. five more or less elongated bones of the part of the hand or forefoot between the wrist and the bones of the digits — **metacarpal** *adj*

**meta·car·pus** \-'kär-pəs\ *n* : the part of the hand or forefoot that contains the metacarpals

**met·al** \'me-t³l\ *n* **1** : any of various opaque, fusible, ductile, and typically lustrous substances that are good conductors of electricity and heat **2** : METTLE; *also* : the material out of which a person or thing is made — **me·tal·lic** \mə-'ta-lik\ *adj*

**met·al·lur·gy** \'me-t³l-,ər-jē\ *n* : the science and technology of metals — **met·al·lur·gi·cal** \,me-t³l-'ər-ji-kəl\ *adj* — **met·al·lur·gist** \'me-t³l-,ər-jist\ *n*

**met·al·ware** \'me-t³l-,wer\ *n* : metal utensils for household use

**met·al·work** \-,wərk\ *n* : work and esp. artistic work made of metal — **met·al·work·er** \-,wər-kər\ *n* — **met·al·work·ing** *n*

**meta·mor·phism** \,me-tə-'mȯr-,fi-zəm\ *n* : a change in the structure of rock; *esp* : a change to a more compact and more highly crystalline form produced by pressure, heat, and water — **meta·mor·phic** \-'mȯr-fik\ *adj*

**meta·mor·pho·sis** \,me-tə-'mȯr-fə-səs\ *n, pl* **-pho·ses** \-,sēz\ **1** : a change of physical form, structure, or substance esp. by supernatural means; *also* : a striking alteration (as in appearance or character) **2** : a fundamental change in form and often habits of an animal accompa-

nying the transformation of a larva into an adult — **meta·mor·phose** \-,fōz, -,fōs\ *vb*

**met·a·phor** \'me-tə-,fȯr\ *n* : a figure of speech in which a word for one idea or thing is used in place of another to suggest a likeness between them (as in "the ship plows the sea") — **met·a·phor·ic** \,me-tə-'fȯr-ik\ *or* **met·a·phor·i·cal** \-tə-'fȯr-i-kəl\ *adj* — **met·a·phor·i·cal·ly** \-i-k(ə-)lē\ *adv*

**meta·phys·ics** \,me-tə-'fi-ziks\ *n* [ML *Metaphysica*, title of Aristotle's treatise on the subject, fr. Gk (*ta*) *meta* (*ta*) *physika*, lit., the (works) after the physical (works); fr. its position in his collected works] : the philosophical study of the ultimate causes and underlying nature of things — **meta·phys·i·cal** \-'fi-zi-kəl\ *adj* — **meta·phy·si·cian** \-fə-'zi-shən\ *n*

**me·tas·ta·sis** \mə-'tas-tə-səs\ *n, pl* **-ta·ses** \-,sēz\ : the spread of a health-impairing agency (as cancer cells) from the initial or primary site of disease to another part of the body; *also* : a secondary growth of a malignant tumor — **me·tas·ta·size** \-tə-,sīz\ *vb* — **met·a·stat·ic** \,me-tə-'sta-tik\ *adj*

**meta·tar·sal** \,me-tə-'tär-səl\ *n* : any of the bones of the foot between the tarsus and the bones of the digits that in humans include five elongated bones — **metatarsal** *adj*

**meta·tar·sus** \-'tär-səs\ *n* : the part of the human foot or the hind foot in quadrupeds that contains the metatarsals

**¹mete** \'mēt\ *vb* **met·ed; met·ing** **1** *archaic* : MEASURE : ALLOT — usu. used with *out* ⟨~ out punishment⟩

**²mete** *n* : BOUNDARY ⟨~s and bounds⟩

**me·te·or** \'mē-tē-ər, -,ȯr\ *n* **1** : a small particle of matter in the solar system directly observable only by its glow from frictional heating on falling into the earth's atmosphere **2** : the streak of light produced by a meteor

**me·te·or·ic** \,mē-tē-'ȯr-ik\ *adj* **1** : of, relating to, or resembling a meteor **2** : transiently brilliant ⟨a ~ career⟩ — **me·te·or·i·cal·ly** \-i-k(ə-)lē\ *adv*

**me·te·or·ite** \'mē-tē-ə-,rīt\ *n* : a meteor that reaches the surface of the earth

**me·te·or·oid** \'mē-tē-ə-,rȯid\ *n* : a small particle of matter in the solar system

**me·te·o·rol·o·gy** \,mē-tē-ə-'rä-lə-jē\ *n* : a science that deals with the atmosphere and its phenomena and esp. with weather forecasting — **me·te·o·ro·log·ic** \,mē-tē-,ȯr-ə-'lä-jik\ *or* **me·te·o·ro·log·i·cal** \-ji-kəl\ *adj* — **me·te·o·rol·o·gist** \,mē-tē-ə-'rä-lə-jist\ *n*

**¹me·ter** \'mē-tər\ *n* : rhythm in verse or music

**²meter** *n* : the basic metric unit of length — see METRIC SYSTEM table

**³meter** *n* : a measuring and sometimes recording instrument

**⁴meter** *vb* **1** : to measure by means of a meter **2** : to print postal indicia on by means of a postage meter ⟨~ed mail⟩

**meter–kilogram–second** *adj* : of, relating to, or being a system of units based on the meter, the kilogram, and the second

**meter maid** *n* : a woman assigned to write tickets for parking violations

**meth·a·done** \'me-thə-ˌdōn\ *also* **meth·a·don** \-ˌdän\ *n* : a synthetic addictive narcotic drug used esp. as a substitute narcotic in the treatment of heroin addiction

**meth·am·phet·amine** \ˌme-tham-'fe-tə-ˌmēn, -thəm-, -mən\ *n* : a drug used medically in the form of its hydrochloride in the treatment of obesity and often illicitly as a stimulant

**meth·ane** \'me-ˌthān\ *n* : a colorless odorless flammable gas produced by decomposition of organic matter or from coal and used esp. as a fuel

**meth·a·nol** \'me-thə-ˌnȯl, -ˌnōl\ *n* : a volatile flammable poisonous liquid alcohol used esp. as a solvent and as an antifreeze

**meth·aqua·lone** \me-'tha-kwə-ˌlōn\ *n* : a sedative and hypnotic habit-forming drug that is not a barbiturate

**meth·od** \'me-thəd\ *n* [ME, prescribed treatment, fr. L *methodus*, fr. Gk *methodos*, fr. *meta* with + *hodos* way] **1** : a procedure or process for achieving an end **2** : orderly arrangement : PLAN ♦ *Synonyms* MODE, MANNER, WAY, FASHION, SYSTEM — **me·thod·i·cal** \mə-'thä-di-kəl\ *adj* — **me·thod·i·cal·ly** \-k(ə-)lē\ *adv* — **me·thod·i·cal·ness** *n*

**meth·od·ise** *Brit var of* METHODIZE

**Meth·od·ist** \'me-thə-dist\ *n* : a member of a Protestant denomination adhering to the doctrines of John Wesley — **Meth·od·ism** \-ˌdi-zəm\ *n*

**meth·od·ize** \'me-thə-ˌdīz\ *vb* **ized; -iz·ing** : SYSTEMATIZE

**meth·od·ol·o·gy** \ˌme-thə-'dä-lə-jē\ *n, pl* **-gies 1** : a body of methods and rules followed in a science or discipline **2** : the study of the principles or procedures of inquiry in a particular field

**meth·yl** \'me-thəl\ *n* : a chemical radical consisting of carbon and hydrogen

**methyl alcohol** *n* : METHANOL

**meth·yl·mer·cury** \ˌme-thəl-'mər-kyə-rē\ *n* : any of various toxic compounds of mercury that often occur as pollutants which accumulate in animals esp. at the top of a food chain

**met·i·cal** \'me-ti-kəl\ *n, pl* **met·i·cais** \-ˌkī\ *also* **meticals** — see MONEY table

**me·tic·u·lous** \mə-'ti-kyə-ləs\ *adj* [L *meticulosus* fearful, fr. *metus* fear] : extremely careful in attending to details — **me·tic·u·lous·ly** *adv* — **me·tic·u·lous·ness** *n*

**mé·tier** \'me-ˌtyā, me-'tyā\ *n* : an area of activity in which one is expert or successful

**me·tre** \'mē-tər\ *chiefly Brit var of* METER

**met·ric** \'me-trik\ *adj* **1** : of or relating to measurement; *esp* : of or relating to the metric system **2** : METRICAL 1

**met·ri·cal** \'me-tri-kəl\ *adj* **1** : of, relating to, or composed in meter **2** : METRIC 1 — **met·ri·cal·ly** \-k(ə-)lē\ *adv*

**met·ri·ca·tion** \ˌme-tri-'kā-shən\ *n* : the act or process of converting into or expressing in the metric system

**met·ri·cize** \'me-trə-ˌsīz\ *vb* **-cized; -ciz·ing** : to change into or express in the metric system

**metric system** *n* : a decimal system of weights and measures based on the meter and on the kilogram

☞ the METRIC SYSTEM table is on page 452

**metric ton** *n* — see METRIC SYSTEM table

**¹me·tro** \'me-trō\ *n, pl* **metros** : SUBWAY

**²metro** *adj* : of, relating to, or characteristic of a metropolis and sometimes including its suburbs

**met·ro·nome** \'me-trə-ˌnōm\ *n* : an instrument for marking exact time by a regularly repeated tick

**me·trop·o·lis** \mə-'trä-pə-ləs\ *n* [ME, fr. LL, fr. Gk *mētropolis*, fr. *mētēr* mother + *polis* city] : the chief or capital city of a country, state, or region — **met·ro·pol·i·tan** \ˌme-trə-'pä-lə-tən\ *adj*

**met·tle** \'me-tᵊl\ *n* **1** : SPIRIT, COURAGE **2** : quality of temperament

**met·tle·some** \'me-tᵊl-səm\ *adj* : full of mettle : COURAGEOUS ⟨a ~ opponent⟩

**MeV** *abbr* million electron volts

**¹mew** \'myü\ *vb* : MEOW — **mew** *n*

**²mew** *vb* : CONFINE

**mews** \'myüz\ *n sing or pl, chiefly Brit* : stables usu. with living quarters built around a court; *also* : a narrow street with dwellings converted from stables

**Mex** *abbr* Mexican; Mexico

**mez·za·nine** \'me-zə-ˌnēn, ˌme-zə-'\ *n* **1** : a low-ceilinged story between two main stories of a building **2** : the lowest balcony in a theater; *also* : the first few rows of such a balcony

**mez·zo for·te** \ˌmet-(ˌ)sō-'fȯr-ˌtā, ˌmed-(ˌ)zō-, -tē\ *adj or adv* [It] : moderately loud — used as a direction in music

**mez·zo pia·no** \-pē-'ä-(ˌ)nō\ *adj or adv* [It] : moderately soft — used as a direction in music

**mez·zo-so·pra·no** \-sə-'pra-nō, -'prä-\ *n* : a woman's voice having a range between that of the soprano and contralto; *also* : a singer having such a voice

**MFA** *abbr* master of fine arts

**mfr** *abbr* manufacture; manufacturer

**mg** *abbr* milligram

**Mg** *symbol* magnesium

**MG** *abbr* **1** machine gun **2** major general **3** military government

**mgr** *abbr* **1** manager **2** monseigneur **3** monsignor

**mgt** *or* **mgmt** *abbr* management

**MGy Sgt** *abbr* master gunnery sergeant

**MHz** *abbr* megahertz

**mi** *abbr* **1** mile; mileage **2** mill

**MI** *abbr* **1** Michigan **2** military intelligence

**MIA** \ˌem-(ˌ)ī-'ā\ *n* [*missing in action*] : a member of the armed forces whose whereabouts following a combat mission are unknown

**Mi·ami** \mī-'a-mē, -mə\ *n, pl* **Mi·ami** *or* **Mi·am·is** : a member of an American Indian people orig. of Wisconsin and Indiana

**mi·as·ma** \mī-'az-mə, mē-\ *n, pl* **-mas** *also* **-ma·ta** \-mə-tə\ *adj* **1** : a vapor from a

# METRIC SYSTEM

## LENGTH

| UNIT | SYMBOL | METRIC EQUIVALENT | U.S. EQUIVALENT |
|------|--------|-------------------|-----------------|
| kilometer | km | 1,000 meters | 0.62 mile |
| hectometer | hm | 100 meters | 328.08 feet |
| dekameter | dam | 10 meters | 32.81 feet |
| meter | m | | 39.37 inches |
| decimeter | dm | 0.1 meter | 3.94 inches |
| centimeter | cm | 0.01 meter | 0.39 inch |
| millimeter | mm | 0.001 meter | 0.039 inch |
| micrometer | $\mu$m | 0.000001 meter | 0.000039 inch |

## AREA

| UNIT | SYMBOL | METRIC EQUIVALENT | U.S. EQUIVALENT |
|------|--------|-------------------|-----------------|
| square kilometer | sq km or km$^2$ | 1,000,000 square meters | 0.39 square miles |
| hectare | ha | 10,000 square meters | 2.47 acres |
| are | a | 100 square meters | 119.60 square yards |
| square centimeter | sq cm or cm$^2$ | 0.0001 square meter | 0.16 square inch |

## VOLUME

| UNIT | SYMBOL | METRIC EQUIVALENT | U.S. EQUIVALENT |
|------|--------|-------------------|-----------------|
| cubic meter | m$^3$ | | 1.31 cubic yards |
| cubic decimeter | dm$^3$ | 0.001 cubic meter | 61.02 cubic inches |
| cubic centimeter | cu cm or cm$^3$ also cc | 0.000001 cubic meter | 0.061 cubic inch |

## MASS AND WEIGHT

| UNIT | SYMBOL | METRIC EQUIVALENT | U.S. EQUIVALENT |
|------|--------|-------------------|-----------------|
| metric ton | t | 1,000,000 grams | 1.10 short tons |
| kilogram | kg | 1,000 grams | 2.20 pounds |
| hectogram | hg | 100 grams | 3.53 ounces |
| dekagram | dag | 10 grams | 0.35 ounce |
| gram | g | | 0.035 ounce |
| decigram | dg | 0.1 gram | 1.54 grains |
| centigram | cg | 0.01 gram | 0.15 grain |
| milligram | mg | 0.001 gram | 0.015 grain |
| microgram | $\mu$g or mcg | 0.000001 gram | 0.000015 grain |

## CAPACITY

| UNIT | METRIC EQUIVALENT | U.S. EQUIVALENT UNITS | | |
|------|-------------------|-------|-------|-------|
| | | CUBIC | DRY | LIQUID |
| kiloliter (kl) | 1,000 liters | 1.31 cubic yards | 28.38 bushels | 264.17 gallons |
| hectoliter (hl) | 100 liters | 3.53 cubic feet | 2.84 bushels | 26.42 gallons |
| dekaliter (dal) | 10 liters | 0.35 cubic foot | 1.14 pecks | 2.64 gallons |
| liter (l) | | 61.02 cubic inches | 0.91 quart | 1.06 quarts |
| deciliter (dl) | 0.1 liter | 6.10 cubic inches | 0.18 pint | 0.21 pint |
| centiliter (cl) | 0.01 liter | 0.61 cubic inch | | 0.34 fluid ounce |
| milliliter (ml) | 0.001 liter | 0.061 cubic inch | | 0.27 fluid dram |
| microliter ($\mu$l) | 0.000001 liter | 0.000061 cubic inch | | 0.00027 fluid dram |

For metric system equivalents of U.S. system units, see WEIGHTS AND MEASURES table.

swamp formerly believed to cause disease
**2** : a harmful influence or atmosphere ⟨a ~ of smog⟩ — **mi·as·mal** \-məl\ *adj* — **mi·as·mic** \-mik\ *adj*

**mic** \'mīk\ *n* : MICROPHONE

**Mic** *abbr* Micah

**mi·ca** \'mī-kə\ *n* [NL, fr. L, grain, crumb] : any of various mineral silicates readily separable into thin transparent sheets

**Mi·cah** \'mī-kə\ *n* — see BIBLE table

**mice** *pl of* MOUSE

**Mich** *abbr* Michigan

**Mi·che·as** \'mī-kē-əs, mī-'kē-əs\ *n* : MICAH

**Mic·mac** \'mik-ˌmak\ *n, pl* **Micmac** *or* **Micmacs** : a member of an American Indian people of eastern Canada

**micr-** *or* **micro-** *comb form* **1** : small : minute ⟨*micro*capsule⟩ **2** : one millionth part of a specified unit ⟨*micro*second⟩

¹**mi·cro** \'mī-krō\ *adj* **1** : very small; *esp* : MICROSCOPIC **2** : involving minute quantities or variations

²**micro** *n, pl* **micros** : MICROCOMPUTER

**mi·crobe** \'mī-ˌkrōb\ *n* : MICROORGANISM; *esp* : one causing disease — **mi·cro·bi·al** \mī-'krō-bē-əl\ *adj*

**mi·cro·bi·ol·o·gy** \ˌmī-krō-bī-'ä-lə-jē\ *n* : a branch of biology dealing esp. with microscopic forms of life — **mi·cro·bio·log·i·cal** \-ˌbī-ə-'lä-ji-kəl\ *adj* — **mi·cro·bi·ol·o·gist** \-bī-'ä-lə-jist\ *n*

**mi·cro·brew·ery** \'mī-krō-ˌbrü-ə-rē\ *n* : a small brewery making specialty beer in limited quantities

**mi·cro·burst** \-ˌbərst\ *n* : a violent short-lived localized downdraft that creates extreme wind shears at low altitudes

**mi·cro·cap·sule** \'mī-krō-ˌkap-səl, -ˌsül\ *n* : a tiny capsule containing material (as a medicine) released when the capsule is broken, melted, or dissolved

**mi·cro·chip** \-ˌchip\ *n* : INTEGRATED CIRCUIT

**mi·cro·cir·cuit** \-ˌsər-kət\ *n* : a compact electronic circuit

**mi·cro·com·put·er** \-kəm-ˌpyü-tər\ *n* : a small computer that uses a microprocessor; *esp* : PERSONAL COMPUTER

**mi·cro·cosm** \'mī-krə-ˌkä-zəm\ *n* : an individual or community thought of as a miniature world or universe

**mi·cro·elec·tron·ics** \'mī-krō-i-ˌlek-'trä-niks\ *n* : a branch of electronics that deals with the miniaturization of electronic circuits and components — **mi·cro·elec·tron·ic** \-nik\ *adj*

**mi·cro·en·cap·su·late** \ˌmī-krō-in-'kap-sə-ˌlāt\ *vb* : to enclose (as a drug) in a microcapsule — **mi·cro·en·cap·su·la·tion** \-in-ˌkap-sə-'lā-shən\ *n*

**mi·cro·fi·ber** \'mī-krō-ˌfī-bər\ *n* : a fine usu. soft polyester fiber; *also* : fabric made from such fibers

**mi·cro·fiche** \'mī-krō-ˌfēsh, -ˌfish\ *n, pl* **-fiche** *or* **-fiches** \*same or* ˌfē-shəz, ˌfi-\ : a sheet of microfilm containing rows of images of pages of printed matter

**mi·cro·film** \-ˌfilm\ *n* : a film bearing a photographic record (as of print) on a reduced scale — **microfilm** *vb*

**mi·cro·graph** \'mī-krə-ˌgraf\ *n* : a graphic reproduction of the image of an object formed by a microscope

**mi·cro·man·age** \ˌmī-krō-'ma-nij\ *vb* : to manage esp. with excessive control or attention to details — **mi·cro·man·age·ment** \-mənt\ *n* — **mi·cro·man·ag·er** \-ni-jər\ *n*

**mi·cro·me·te·or·ite** \ˌmī-krō-'mē-tē-ə-ˌrīt\ *n* : a very small particle in interplanetary space

**mi·crom·e·ter** \mī-'krä-mə-tər\ *n* : an instrument used with a telescope or microscope for measuring minute distances

**mi·cro·min·ia·tur·iza·tion** \ˌmī-krō-ˌmi-nē-ə-ˌchùr-ə-'zā-shən, -ˌmi-ni-ˌchùr-, -ˌchər-\ *n* : the process of producing things in a very small size and esp. in a size smaller than one considered miniature — **mi·cro·min·ia·tur·ized** \-'mi-nē-ə-chə-ˌrīzd, -'mi-ni-chə-\ *adj*

**mi·cron** \'mī-ˌkrän\ *n* : one millionth of a meter

**mi·cro·or·gan·ism** \ˌmī-krō-'ȯr-gə-ˌni-zəm\ *n* : an organism (as a bacterium) too tiny to be seen by the unaided eye

**mi·cro·phone** \'mī-krə-ˌfōn\ *n* : an instrument for converting sound waves into variations of an electric current for transmitting or recording sound

**mi·cro·pho·to·graph** \ˌmī-krə-'fō-tə-ˌgraf\ *n* : PHOTOMICROGRAPH

**mi·cro·pro·ces·sor** \ˌmī-krō-'prä-ˌse-sər\ *n* : a computer processor contained in a microchip

**mi·cro·scope** \'mī-krə-ˌskōp\ *n* : an instrument for making magnified images of minute objects usu. using light — **mi·cros·co·py** \mī-'kräs-kə-pē\ *n*

**mi·cro·scop·ic** \ˌmī-krə-'skä-pik\ *also* **mi·cro·scop·i·cal** \-pi-kəl\ *adj* **1** : of, relating to, or involving the use of the microscope **2** : too tiny to be seen without the use of a microscope : very small — **mi·cro·scop·i·cal·ly** \-pi-k(ə-)lē\ *adv*

**mi·cro·sec·ond** \'mī-krō-ˌse-kənd\ *n* : one millionth of a second

**mi·cro·sur·gery** \ˌmī-krō-'sər-jə-rē\ *n* : minute dissection or manipulation (as by a laser beam) of living structures or tissue — **mi·cro·sur·gi·cal** \-'sər-ji-kəl\ *adj*

**mi·cro·tech·nol·o·gy** \-tek-'nä-lə-jē\ *n* : technology on a small or microscopic scale

¹**mi·cro·wave** \'mī-krə-ˌwāv\ *n* **1** : a radio wave between one millimeter and one meter in wavelength **2** : MICROWAVE OVEN

²**microwave** *vb* : to heat or cook in a microwave oven — **mi·cro·wav·able** *or* **mi·cro·wave·able** \ˌmī-krə-'wā-və-bəl\ *adj*

**microwave oven** *n* : an oven in which food is cooked by the absorption of microwave energy by water molecules in the food

¹**mid** \'mid\ *adj* : MIDDLE

²**mid** *abbr* middle

**mid-air** \'mid-'er\ *n* : a point or region in the air well above the ground

**mid·day** \'mid-ˌdā, -'dā\ *n* : NOON

**mid·den** \'mi-dᵊn\ *n* : a refuse heap

¹**mid·dle** \'mi-dᵊl\ *adj* **1** : equally distant from the extremes : MEDIAL, CENTRAL **2** : being at neither extreme : INTERMEDIATE **3** *cap* : constituting an intermediate period

²**middle** *n* **1** : a middle part, point, or position **2** : WAIST

**middle age** *n* : the period of life from about 45 to about 64 — **mid·dle-aged** \ˌmi-dᵊl-ᵊājd\ *adj*

**Middle Ages** *n pl* : the period of European history from about A.D. 500 to about 1500

**mid·dle·brow** \'mi-dᵊl-ˌbraú\ *n* : a person who is moderately but not highly cultivated — **middlebrow** *adj*

**middle class** *n* : a social class holding a position between the upper class and the lower class — **middle-class** *adj*

**middle ear** *n* : a small membrane-lined cavity of the ear through which sound waves are transmitted by a chain of tiny bones

**middle finger** *n* : the midmost of the five digits of the hand

**mid·dle·man** \'mi-dᵊl-ˌman\ *n* : INTERMEDIARY; *esp* : one intermediate between the producer of goods and the retailer or consumer

**middle-of-the-road** *adj* : standing for or following a course of action midway between extremes; *esp* : being neither liberal nor conservative in politics — **middle-of-the-road·er** \-ˈrō-dər\ *n* — **middle-of-the-road·ism** \-ˈrō-ˌdi-zəm\ *n*

**middle school** *n* : a school usu. including grades 5 to 8 or 6 to 8

**mid·dle·weight** \'mi-dᵊl-ˌwāt\ *n* : one of average weight; *esp* : a boxer weighing not over 160 pounds

**mid·dling** \'mid-liŋ, -lən\ *adj* **1** : of middle, medium, or moderate size, degree, or quality **2** : MEDIOCRE

**mid·dy** \'mi-dē\ *n, pl* **middies** : MIDSHIPMAN

**midge** \'mij\ *n* : a very small fly : GNAT

**midg·et** \'mi-jət\ *n* **1** : something (as an animal) very small for its kind *sometimes offensive* : a very small person

**midi** \'mi-dē\ *n* : a calf-length dress, coat, or skirt

**MIDI** \'mi-dē\ *n* [*musical instrument digital interface*] : a protocol for the transmission of digitally encoded music

**mid·land** \'mid-lənd, -ˌland\ *n* : the interior or central region of a country

**mid·life** \'mid-ˈlīf\ *n* : MIDDLE AGE

**midlife crisis** *n* : a period of emotional turmoil in middle age characterized esp. by a strong desire for change

**mid·most** \-ˌmōst\ *adj* : being in or near the exact middle — **midmost** *adv*

**mid·night** \-ˌnīt\ *n* : 12 o'clock at night

**mid–ocean ridge** \'mid-ˈō-shən-\ *n* : an elevation on an ocean floor at the boundary of diverging tectonic plates

**mid·point** \'mid-ˌpóint, -ˈpóint\ *n* : a point at or near the center or middle

**mid·riff** \'mi-ˌdrif\ *n* [ME *midrif*, fr. OE *midhrif*, fr. *midde* mid + *hrif* belly] **1** : DIAPHRAGM 1 **2** : the mid-region of the human torso

**mid·sec·tion** \-ˌsek-shən\ *n* : a section midway between the extremes; *esp* : MIDRIFF 2

**mid·ship·man** \'mid-ˌship-mən, (ˌ)mid-ˈship-\ *n* : a student in a naval academy

**mid·ships** \-ˌships\ *adv* : AMIDSHIPS

**midst** \'midst\ *n* **1** : the interior or central part or point **2** : a position of proximity to the members of a group ⟨in our ∼⟩ **3** : the condition of being surrounded or beset — **midst** *prep*

**mid·stream** \'mid-ˈstrēm, -ˌstrēm\ *n* : the middle of a stream

**mid·sum·mer** \-ˈsə-mər, -ˌsə-\ *n* **1** : the middle of summer **2** : the summer solstice

**mid·town** \'mid-ˌtaún, -ˈtaún\ *n* : a central section of a city; *esp* : one situated between sections called *downtown* and *uptown* — **midtown** *adj*

¹**mid·way** \'mid-ˌwā, -ˈwā\ *adv* : in the middle of the way or distance

²**mid·way** \-ˌwā\ *n* : an avenue (as at a carnival) for concessions and amusements

**mid·week** \-ˌwēk\ *n* : the middle of the week — **mid·week·ly** \-ˌwē-klē, -ˈwē-\ *adj or adv*

**mid·wife** \'mid-ˌwīf\ *n* : a person who helps women in childbirth — **mid·wife·ry** \-ˌwi-fə-rē\ *n*

**mid·win·ter** \'mid-ˈwin-tər, -ˌwin-\ *n* **1** : the winter solstice **2** : the middle of winter

**mid·year** \-ˌyir\ *n* **1** : the middle of a year **2** : a midyear examination — **midyear** *adj*

**mien** \'mēn\ *n* **1** : air or bearing esp. as expressive of mood or personality : DEMEANOR **2** : APPEARANCE, ASPECT ⟨dresses of formal ∼⟩

**miff** \'mif\ *vb* : to put into an ill humor

¹**might** \'mīt\ *verbal auxiliary, past of* MAY — used as an auxiliary to express permission or possibility in the past, a present condition contrary to fact, less probability or possibility than *may*, or as a polite alternative to *may, ought,* or *should*

²**might** *n* : the power, authority, or resources of an individual or a group

**mighty** \'mī-tē\ *adj* **might·i·er; -est** **1** : very strong : POWERFUL **2** : GREAT, NOTABLE — **might·i·ly** \'mī-tə-lē\ *adv* — **might·i·ness** \-tē-nəs\ *n* — **mighty** *adv*

**mi·gnon·ette** \ˌmin-yə-ˈnet\ *n* : an annual garden herb with spikes of tiny fragrant flowers

**mi·graine** \'mī-ˌgrān\ *n* [ME *mygreyn*, fr. MF *migraine*, fr. LL *hemicrania* pain in one side of the head, fr. Gk *hēmikrania*, fr. *hēmi-* half + *kranion* cranium] : a condition marked by recurrent severe headache and often nausea; *also* : an attack of migraine

**mi·grant** \'mī-grənt\ *n* : one that migrates; *esp* : a person who moves in order to find work (as picking crops) — **migrant** *adj*

**mi·grate** \'mī-ˌgrāt\ *vb* **mi·grat·ed; mi·grat·ing 1** : to move from one country or place to another **2** : to pass usu. periodically from one region or climate to another for feeding or breeding — **mi-**

**gra·tion** \mi-'grā-shon\ n — **mi·gra·to·ry** \'mī-grə-,tȯr-ē\ adj

**mi·ka·do** \mə-'kä-dō\ n, pl **-dos** : an emperor of Japan

**mike** \'mīk\ n : MICROPHONE

¹**mil** \'mil\ n : a unit of length equal to ¹/₁₀₀₀ inch

²**mil** abbr military

**milch** \'milk, 'milch\ adj : giving milk ⟨~ cow⟩

**mild** \'mī(-ə)ld\ adj 1 : gentle in nature or behavior 2 : moderate in action or effect 3 : TEMPERATE ⟨~ weather⟩ ♦ **Synonyms** EASY, COMPLAISANT, AMIABLE, LENIENT — **mild·ly** adv — **mild·ness** n

**mil·dew** \'mil-,dü, -,dyü\ n : a superficial usu. whitish growth produced on organic matter and on plants by a fungus; also : a fungus producing this growth — **mildew** vb

**mile** \'mī(-ə)l\ n [ME, fr. OE mīl, fr. L milia miles, fr. milia passuum, lit., thousands of paces] — see WEIGHT table 2 : NAUTICAL MILE

**mile·age** \'mī-lij\ n 1 : an allowance for traveling expenses at a certain rate per mile 2 : distance in miles traveled (as in a day) 3 : the amount of service yielded (as by a tire) expressed in terms of miles of travel 4 : the average number of miles a motor vehicle will travel on a gallon of gasoline

**mile·post** \'mī(-ə)l-,pōst\ n : a post indicating the distance in miles from a given point

**mile·stone** \-,stōn\ n 1 : a stone serving as a milepost 2 : a significant point in development

**mi·lieu** \mēl-'yər, -'yü, -'yœ\ n, pl **milieus** or **mi·lieux** \same or -'yərz, -'yüz, -'yœz\ [F] : ENVIRONMENT, SETTING

**mil·i·tant** \'mi-lə-tənt\ adj 1 : engaged in warfare 2 : aggressively active esp. in a cause — **mil·i·tance** \-təns\ n — **mil·i·tan·cy** \-tən-sē\ n — **militant** n — **mil·i·tant·ly** adv

**mil·i·ta·rise** Brit var of MILITARIZE

**mil·i·ta·rism** \'mi-lə-tə-,ri-zəm\ n 1 : predominance of the military class or its ideals 2 : a policy of aggressive military preparedness — **mil·i·ta·rist** \-rist\ n — **mil·i·ta·ris·tic** \,mi-lə-tə-'ris-tik\ adj

**mil·i·ta·rize** \'mi-lə-tə-,rīz\ vb **-rized; -riz·ing** 1 : to equip with military forces and defenses ⟨~ a region⟩ 2 : to give a military character to

¹**mil·i·tary** \'mi-lə-,ter-ē\ adj 1 : of or relating to soldiers, arms, war, or the army 2 : performed by armed forces; also : supported by armed force ♦ **Synonyms** MARTIAL, WARLIKE — **mil·i·tar·i·ly** \,mi-lə-'ter-ə-lē\ adv

²**military** n, pl **military** also **mil·i·tar·ies** 1 : the military, naval, and air forces of a nation 2 : military persons

**military police** n : a branch of an army that exercises guard and police functions

**mil·i·tate** \'mi-lə-,tāt\ vb **-tat·ed; -tat·ing** : to have weight or effect ⟨disagreements ~ against an alliance⟩

**mi·li·tia** \mə-'li-shə\ n : a part of the organized armed forces of a country liable to call only in emergency — **mi·li·tia·man** \-mən\ n

¹**milk** \'milk\ n 1 : a nutritive usu. whitish fluid secreted by female mammals for feeding their young 2 : a milklike liquid (as a plant juice) — **milk·i·ness** \'mil-kē-nəs\ n — **milky** adj

²**milk** vb 1 : to draw off the milk of ⟨~ a cow⟩ 2 : to draw something from as if by milking

**milk·maid** \'milk-,mād\ n : DAIRYMAID

**milk·man** \-,man, -mən\ n : a person who sells or delivers milk

**milk of magnesia** : a milk-white mixture of hydroxide of magnesium and water used as an antacid and laxative

**milk shake** n : a thoroughly blended drink made of milk, a flavoring syrup, and often ice cream

**milk·sop** \'milk-,säp\ n : an unmanly man

**milk·weed** \-,wēd\ n : any of a genus of herbs with milky juice and clustered flowers

**Milky Way** n 1 : a broad irregular band of light that stretches across the sky and is caused by the light of a very great number of faint stars 2 : MILKY WAY GALAXY

**Milky Way galaxy** n : the galaxy of which the sun is a member and which includes the stars that create the light of the Milky Way

¹**mill** \'mil\ n 1 : a building with machinery for grinding grain into flour 2 : a machine used in processing (as by grinding, stamping, cutting, or finishing) raw material 3 : FACTORY

²**mill** vb 1 : to process in a mill 2 : to move in a circle or in an eddying mass

³**mill** n : one tenth of a cent

**mill·age** \'mi-lij\ n : a rate (as of taxation) expressed in mills

¹**mil·len·ni·al** \mə-'le-nē-əl\ adj : of or relating to a millennium

²**millennial** n : a person born in the 1980s or 1990s — usually pl.

**mil·len·ni·um** \mə-'le-nē-əm\ n, pl **-nia** \-nē-ə\ or **-niums** 1 : a period of 1000 years; also : a 1000th anniversary or its celebration 2 : the 1000 years mentioned in Revelation 20 when holiness is to prevail and Christ is to reign on earth 3 : a period of great happiness or human perfection

**mill·er** \'mi-lər\ n 1 : one that operates a mill and esp. a flour mill 2 : any of various moths having powdery wings

**mil·let** \'mi-lət\ n : any of several smallseeded cereal and forage grasses cultivated for grain or hay; also : the grain of a millet

**milli-** comb form : one thousandth part of

**mil·li·am·pere** \,mi-lē-'am-,pir\ n : one thousandth of an ampere

**mil·liard** \'mil-,yärd, 'mi-lē-,ärd\ n, Brit : a thousand millions

**mil·li·bar** \'mi-lə-,bär\ n : a unit of atmospheric pressure

**mil·li·gram** \-,gram\ n — see METRIC SYSTEM table

**mil·li·li·ter** \-,lē-tər\ n — see METRIC SYSTEM table

**mil·lime** \mə-ˈlēm\ n — see *dinar* at MONEY table

**mil·li·me·ter** \ˈmi-lə-ˌmē-tər\ n — see METRIC SYSTEM table

**mil·li·ner** \ˈmi-lə-nər\ n [irreg. fr. *Milan*, Italy; fr. the importation of women's finery from Italy in the 16th century] : a person who designs, makes, trims, or sells women's hats

**mil·li·nery** \ˈmi-lə-ˌner-ē\ n 1 : women's apparel for the head 2 : the business or work of a milliner

**mill·ing** \ˈmil-liŋ\ n : a corrugated edge on a coin

**mil·lion** \ˈmil-yən\ n, pl **millions** or **million** : a thousand thousands — **million** adj — **mil·lionth** \-yənth\ adj or n

**mil·lion·aire** \ˌmil-yə-ˈner, ˈmil-yə-ˌner\ n : one whose wealth is estimated at a million or more (as of dollars or pounds)

**mil·li·pede** \ˈmi-lə-ˌpēd\ n : any of a class of arthropods related to the centipedes and having a long segmented body with a hard covering, two pairs of legs on most segments, and no poison fangs

**mil·li·sec·ond** \-ˌse-kənd\ n : one thousandth of a second

**mil·li·volt** \-ˌvōlt\ n : one thousandth of a volt

**mill·pond** \ˈmil-ˌpänd\ n : a pond made by damming a stream to produce a fall of water for operating a mill

**mill·race** \-ˌrās\ n : a canal in which water flows to and from a mill wheel

**mill·stone** \-ˌstōn\ n : either of two round flat stones used for grinding grain

**mill·stream** \-ˌstrēm\ n : a stream whose flow is used to run a mill; *also* : the stream in a millrace

**mill wheel** n : a waterwheel that drives a mill

**mill·wright** \ˈmil-ˌrīt\ n : a person who builds mills or sets up or maintains their machinery

**milt** \ˈmilt\ n : the sperm-containing fluid of a male fish

**mime** \ˈmīm\ n 1 : MIMIC 2 : PANTOMIME — **mime** vb

**mim·eo·graph** \ˈmi-mē-ə-ˌgraf\ n : a machine for making many copies by means of a stencil through which ink is pressed — **mimeograph** vb

**mi·me·sis** \mə-ˈmē-səs, mī-\ n : IMITATION, MIMICRY

**mi·met·ic** \-ˈme-tik\ adj 1 : IMITATIVE 2 : relating to, characterized by, or exhibiting mimicry

**¹mim·ic** \ˈmi-mik\ n : one that mimics

**²mimic** vb **mim·icked** \-mikt\; **mim·ick·ing** 1 : to imitate closely 2 : to ridicule by imitation 3 : to resemble by biological mimicry

**mim·ic·ry** \ˈmi-mi-krē\ n, pl **-ries** 1 : an instance of mimicking 2 : a superficial resemblance of one organism to another or to natural objects among which it lives that gives it an advantage (as protection from predation)

**mi·mo·sa** \mə-ˈmō-sə, mī-, -zə\ n : any of a genus of trees, shrubs, and herbs of the legume family that occur in warm re-gions and have ball-shaped heads of small white or pink flowers

**min** abbr 1 minim 2 minimum 3 mining 4 minister 5 minor 6 minute

**min·a·ret** \ˌmi-nə-ˈret\ n [F, fr. Turk *minare*, fr. Ar *manāra* lighthouse] : a tall slender tower of a mosque from which a muezzin calls the faithful to prayer

**mi·na·to·ry** \ˈmi-nə-ˌtȯr-ē, ˈmī-\ adj : THREATENING, MENACING

**mince** \ˈmins\ vb **minced; minc·ing** [ME, fr. AF *mincer*, fr. VL *minutiare*, fr. L *minutia* smallness, fr. *minutus* small, fr. pp. of *minuere* to lessen] 1 : to cut into very small pieces 2 : to restrain (words) within the bounds of decorum 3 : to walk in a prim affected manner

**mince·meat** \ˈmins-ˌmēt\ n : a finely chopped mixture esp. of raisins, apples, spices, and often meat used as a filling for a pie

**¹mind** \ˈmīnd\ n 1 : MEMORY 2 : the part of an individual that feels, perceives, thinks, wills, and esp. reasons 3 : INTENTION, DESIRE 4 : normal mental condition 5 : OPINION, VIEW ⟨changed her ∼⟩ 6 : MOOD 7 : mental qualities of a person or group 8 : intellectual ability 9 : ATTENTION ⟨pay him no ∼⟩

**²mind** vb 1 *chiefly dial* : REMEMBER 2 : to attend to closely 3 : HEED, OBEY 4 : to be concerned about; *also* : DISLIKE 5 : to be careful or cautious ⟨∼ the broken stair⟩ 6 : to take charge of 7 : to regard with attention

**mind–bend·ing** \ˈmīnd-ˌben-diŋ\ adj : MIND-BLOWING — **mind–bend·ing·ly** adv

**mind–blow·ing** \-ˌblō-iŋ\ adj : PSYCHEDELIC 1; *also* : MIND-BOGGLING — **mind–blow·er** \-ˌblō-ər\ n — **mind–blow·ing·ly** adv

**mind–bog·gling** \-ˌbä-gə-liŋ\ adj : mentally or emotionally exciting or overwhelming ⟨∼ special effects⟩

**mind·ed** \ˈmīn-dəd\ adj 1 : INCLINED, DISPOSED 2 : having a mind of a specified kind or concerned with a specific thing — usu. used in combination ⟨narrow-**minded**⟩ ⟨health-**minded**⟩

**mind·ful** \ˈmīnd-fəl\ adj : bearing in mind : AWARE ⟨∼ of their needs⟩ — **mind·ful·ly** adv — **mind·ful·ness** n

**mind·less** \-ləs\ adj 1 : marked by a lack of mind or consciousness; *esp* : marked by no use of the intellect 2 : not mindful : HEEDLESS — **mind·less·ly** adv — **mind·less·ness** n

**¹mine** \ˈmīn\ pron : that which belongs to me

**²mine** n 1 : an excavation in the earth from which minerals are taken; *also* : an ore deposit 2 : an underground passage beneath an enemy position 3 : an explosive device for destroying enemy personnel, vehicles, or ships 4 : a rich source of supply

**³mine** vb **mined; min·ing** 1 : to dig a mine 2 : UNDERMINE 3 : to get ore from the earth 4 : to place military mines in — **min·er** n

**mine·field** \ˈmīn-ˌfēld\ n 1 : an area set

with mines **2** : something resembling a minefield esp. in having many dangers ⟨a political ∼⟩

**mine·lay·er** \-ˌlā-ər\ *n* : a naval vessel for laying underwater mines

**min·er·al** \ˈmi-nə-rəl\ *n* **1** : a crystalline substance (as diamond or quartz) of inorganic origin **2** : a naturally occurring substance (as coal, salt, or water) obtained usu. from the ground — **mineral** *adj*

**min·er·al·ise** *Brit var of* MINERALIZE

**min·er·al·ize** \ˈmi-nə-rə-ˌlīz\ *vb* **-ized; -iz·ing 1** : to impregnate or supply with minerals **2** : to change into mineral form — **min·er·al·i·za·tion** \-rə-lə-ˈzā-shən\ *n*

**min·er·al·o·gy** \ˌmi-nə-ˈrä-lə-jē, -ˈra-\ *n* : a science dealing with minerals — **min·er·al·og·i·cal** \ˌmi-nə-rə-ˈlä-ji-kəl\ *adj* — **min·er·al·o·gist** \ˌmi-nə-ˈrä-lə-jist, -ˈra-\ *n*

**mineral oil** *n* : an oil of mineral origin; *esp* : a refined petroleum oil used as a laxative

**mineral water** *n* : water infused with mineral salts or gases

**min·e·stro·ne** \ˌmi-nə-ˈstrō-nē, -ˈströn\ *n* [It, fr. *minestra*, fr. *minestrare* to serve, dish up, fr. L *ministrare*, fr. *minister* servant] : a rich thick vegetable soup

**mine·sweep·er** \ˈmīn-ˌswē-pər\ *n* : a warship for removing or neutralizing underwater mines

**min·gle** \ˈmiŋ-gəl\ *vb* **min·gled; min·gling 1** : to bring or combine together : MIX ⟨*mingling* odors⟩ **2** : ASSOCIATE; *also* : to move about socially ⟨*mingled* with the guests⟩

**ming tree** \ˈmiŋ-\ *n* : a dwarfed usu. evergreen tree grown as bonsai; *also* : an artificial plant resembling this

**mini** \ˈmi-nē\ *n, pl* **min·is** : something small of its kind — **mini** *adj*

**mini-** *comb form* : smaller or briefer than usual, normal, or standard

**min·ia·ture** \ˈmi-nē-ə-ˌchu̇r, ˈmi-ni-ˌchu̇r, -chər\ *n* [It *miniatura* art of illuminating a manuscript, fr. ML, fr. L *miniare* to color with red lead, fr. *minium* red lead] **1** : a copy on a much reduced scale; *also* : something small of its kind **2** : a small painting (as on ivory or metal) — **miniature** *adj* — **min·ia·tur·ist** \-ˌchu̇r-ist, -chər-\ *n*

**min·ia·tur·ize** \ˈmi-nē-ə-ə-ˌchə-ˌrīz, ˈmi-ni-\ *vb* **-ized; -iz·ing** : to design or construct in small size — **min·ia·tur·i·za·tion** \ˌmi-nē-ə-ˌchu̇r-ə-ˈzā-shən, ˌmi-ni-, -chər-\ *n*

**mini·bar** \ˈmi-nē-ˌbär\ *n* : a small refrigerator in a hotel room that is stocked with beverages and snacks

**mini·bike** \ˈmi-nē-ˌbīk\ *n* : a small one-passenger motorcycle

**mini·bus** \-ˌbəs\ *n* : a small bus or van

**mini·com·put·er** \-kəm-ˌpyü-tər\ *n* : a computer between a mainframe and a microcomputer in size and speed

**mini·disc** \ˈmi-nē-ˌdisk\ *n* : a miniature optical disc

**min·im** \ˈmi-nəm\ *n* — see WEIGHT table

**min·i·mal** \ˈmi-nə-məl\ *adj* **1** : relating to or being a minimum : LEAST **2** : of or relating to minimalism or minimal art — **min·i·mal·ly** *adv*

**minimal art** *n* : abstract art consisting primarily of simple geometric forms executed in an impersonal style — **minimal artist** *n*

**min·i·mal·ism** \ˈmi-nə-mə-ˌli-zəm\ *n* : MINIMAL ART; *also* : a style (as in music or literature) marked by extreme spareness or simplicity — **min·i·mal·ist** \-list\ *n*

**mini·mart** \ˈmi-nē-ˌmärt\ *n* : CONVENIENCE STORE

**min·i·mise** *Brit var of* MINIMIZE

**min·i·mize** \ˈmi-nə-ˌmīz\ *vb* **-mized; -miz·ing 1** : to reduce or keep to a minimum **2** : to underestimate intentionally ⟨∼ the defects⟩ ♦ **Synonyms** DEPRECIATE, DECRY, DISPARAGE

**min·i·mum** \ˈmi-nə-məm\ *n, pl* **-ma** \-mə\ *or* **-mums 1** : the least quantity assignable, admissible, or possible **2** : the least of a set of numbers **3** : the lowest degree or amount of variation (as of temperature) reached or recorded — **minimum** *adj*

**min·ion** \ˈmin-yən\ *n* [MF *mignon* darling] **1** : a servile dependent, follower, or underling **2** : one highly favored **3** : a subordinate official

**mini·se·ries** \ˈmi-nē-ˌsir-ēz\ *n* : a television story presented in sequential episodes

**mini·skirt** \-ˌskərt\ *n* : a skirt with the hemline several inches above the knee

**¹min·is·ter** \ˈmi-nə-stər\ *n* **1** : AGENT **2** : a member of the clergy esp. of a Protestant communion **3** : a high officer of state who heads a division of governmental activities **4** : a diplomatic representative to a foreign state — **min·is·te·ri·al** \ˌmi-nə-ˈstir-ē-əl\ *adj*

**²minister** *vb* **1** : to perform the functions of a minister of religion **2** : to give aid or service — **min·is·tra·tion** \ˌmi-nə-ˈstrā-shən\ *n*

**¹min·is·trant** \ˈmi-nə-strənt\ *adj, archaic* : performing service as a minister

**²ministrant** *n* : one that ministers

**min·is·try** \ˈmi-nə-strē\ *n, pl* **-tries 1** : MINISTRATION **2** : the office, duties, or functions of a minister; *also* : the period of service or office **3** : CLERGY **4** : AGENCY **5** *often cap* : the body of ministers governing a nation or state; *also* : a government department headed by a minister

**mini·tow·er** \ˈmi-nē-ˌtau̇-(ə)r\ *n* : a computer tower of intermediate size

**mini·van** \ˈmi-nē-ˌvan\ *n* : a small van

**mink** \ˈmiŋk\ *n, pl* **mink** *or* **minks** : either of two slender flesh-eating mammals resembling the related weasels; *also* : the soft lustrous typically dark brown fur of a mink

**min·ke whale** \ˈmiŋ-kə-\ *n* : a small grayish baleen whale with a whitish underside

**Minn** *abbr* Minnesota

**min·ne·sing·er** \ˈmi-ni-ˌsiŋ-ər, -ˌziŋ-\ *n* [G, fr. Middle High German, fr. *minne* love + *singer* singer] : any of a class of German lyric poets and musicians of the 12th to the 14th centuries

**min·now** \'mi-nō\ *n, pl* **minnows** *also* **minnow** : any of numerous small freshwater fishes

¹**mi·nor** \'mī-nər\ *adj* **1** : inferior in importance, size, or degree **2** : not having reached majority **3** : having the third, sixth, and sometimes the seventh degrees lowered by a half step ⟨~ scale⟩; *also* : based on a minor scale ⟨~ key⟩ **4** : not serious ⟨~ illness⟩

²**minor** *n* **1** : a person who has not attained majority **2** : a subject of academic study chosen as a secondary field of specialization

³**minor** *vb* : to pursue an academic minor ⟨~ed in philosophy⟩

**mi·nor·i·ty** \mə-'nȯr-ə-tē, mī-\ *n, pl* **-ties 1** : the period or state of being a minor **2** : the smaller in number of two groups; *esp* : a group having less than the number of votes necessary for control **3** : a part of a population differing from others (as in race); *also* : a member of a minority

**mi·nox·i·dil** \mə-'näk-sə-ˌdil\ *n* : a drug used orally to treat hypertension and topically in solution to promote hair regrowth in some forms of baldness

**min·ster** \'min-stər\ *n* : a large or important church

**min·strel** \'min-strəl\ *n* **1** : a medieval singer of verses; *also* : MUSICIAN, POET **2** : any of a group of performers usu. with blackened faces in a program of black American songs, jokes, and impersonations ⟨a ~ show⟩

**min·strel·sy** \-sē\ *n* : the singing and playing of a minstrel; *also* : a body of minstrels

¹**mint** \'mint\ *n* **1** : any of a large family of aromatic square-stemmed herbs and shrubs; *esp* : one (as spearmint) that is fragrant and is the source of a flavoring oil **2** : a mint-flavored piece of candy — **minty** *adj*

²**mint** *n* **1** : a place where coins are made **2** : a vast sum ⟨worth a ~⟩

³**mint** *vb* **1** : to make (as coins) out of metal **2** : CREATE; *also* : to give a certain status to ⟨newly ~ed lawyers⟩ — **mint·age** \-ij\ *n* — **mint·er** *n*

⁴**mint** *adj* : unmarred as if fresh from a mint ⟨in ~ condition⟩

**min·u·end** \'min-yə-ˌwend\ *n* : a number from which another is to be subtracted

**min·u·et** \ˌmin-yə-'wet\ *n* : a slow graceful dance

¹**mi·nus** \'mī-nəs\ *prep* **1** : diminished by : LESS ⟨seven ~ three equals four⟩ **2** : LACKING, WITHOUT ⟨~ his hat⟩

²**minus** *n* : a negative quantity or quality

³**minus** *adj* **1** : algebraically negative ⟨~ quantity⟩ **2** : having a negative quality

¹**mi·nus·cule** \'mi-nəs-ˌkyül\ *n* : a lowercase letter

²**minuscule** *also* **min·is·cule** *adj* : very small

**minus sign** *n* : a sign – used in mathematics to indicate subtraction or a negative quantity

¹**min·ute** \'mi-nət\ *n* **1** : the 60th part of an hour or of a degree : 60 seconds **2** : a short space of time **3** *pl* : the official record of the proceedings of a meeting

²**mi·nute** \mī-'nüt, mə-, -'nyüt\ *adj* **mi·nut·er; -est 1** : very small **2** : of little importance : TRIFLING **3** : marked by close attention to details ♦ **Synonyms** DIMINUTIVE, TINY, MINIATURE, WEE — **mi·nute·ly** *adv* — **mi·nute·ness** *n*

**min·ute·man** \'mi-nət-ˌman\ *n* : a member of a group of armed men pledged to take the field at a minute's notice during and immediately before the American Revolution

**mi·nu·tia** \mə-'nü-shə, -'nyü-, -shē-ə\ *n, pl* **-ti·ae** \-shē-ˌē\ [L] : a minute or minor detail — usu. used in pl.

**minx** \'minks\ *n* : a pert girl

**Mio·cene** \'mī-ə-ˌsēn\ *adj* : of, relating to, or being the epoch of the Tertiary between the Oligocene and the Pliocene — **Miocene** *n*

**mir·a·cle** \'mir-i-kəl\ *n* **1** : an extraordinary event manifesting divine intervention in human affairs **2** : an unusual event, thing, or accomplishment : WONDER, MARVEL — **mi·rac·u·lous** \mə-'ra-kyə-ləs\ *adj* — **mi·rac·u·lous·ly** *adv*

**miracle drug** *n* : a usu. newly discovered drug that elicits a dramatic response in a patient's condition

**mi·rage** \mə-'räzh\ *n* **1** : an illusion that often appears as a pool of water or a mirror in which distant objects are seen inverted, is sometimes seen at sea, in the desert, or over a hot pavement, and results from atmospheric conditions **2** : something illusory and unattainable

¹**mire** \'mī(-ə)r\ *n* : heavy and often deep mud or slush — **miry** *adj*

²**mire** *vb* **mired; mir·ing** : to stick or sink in or as if in mire

**mire·poix** \mir-'pwä\ *n, pl* **mirepoix** : a mixture of diced vegetables and sometimes meats used in soups, stews, and sauces

¹**mir·ror** \'mir-ər\ *n* **1** : a polished or smooth surface (as of glass) that forms images by reflection **2** : a true representation

²**mirror** *vb* **1** : to reflect in or as if in a mirror **2** : RESEMBLE ⟨her mood ~s the gloomy weather⟩

**mirth** \'mərth\ *n* : gladness or gaiety accompanied with laughter ♦ **Synonyms** GLEE, JOLLITY, HILARITY, MERRIMENT — **mirth·ful** \-fəl\ *adj* — **mirth·ful·ly** *adv* — **mirth·ful·ness** *n* — **mirth·less** *adj*

**MIRV** \'mərv\ *n* [*multiple independently targeted reentry vehicle*] : an ICBM with multiple warheads that have different targets — **MIRV** *vb*

**mis·ad·ven·ture** \ˌmi-səd-'ven-chər\ *n* : MISFORTUNE, MISHAP

**mis·aligned** \ˌmi-sə-'līnd\ *adj* : not properly aligned — **mis·align·ment** \-'līn-mənt\ *n*

**mis·al·li·ance** \ˌmi-sə-'lī-əns\ *n* : an improper or unsuitable marriage

**mis·al·lo·ca·tion** \ˌmi-ˌsa-lə-'kā-shən\ *n* : faulty or improper allocation

**mis·an·dry** \'mi-ˌsan-drē\ n : a hatred of men — **mis·an·drist** \-drist\ n or adj

**mis·an·thrope** \'mi-sᵊn-ˌthrōp\ n : one who hates humankind — **mis·an·throp·ic** \ˌmi-sᵊn-'thrä-pik\ adj — **mis·an·throp·i·cal·ly** \-pi-k(ə-)lē\ adv — **mis·an·thro·py** \mi-'san-thrə-pē\ n

**mis·ap·ply** \ˌmi-sə-'plī\ vb : to apply wrongly — **mis·ap·pli·ca·tion** \ˌmi-ˌsa-plə-'kā-shən\ n

**mis·ap·pre·hend** \ˌmi-ˌsa-pri-'hend\ vb : MISUNDERSTAND — **mis·ap·pre·hen·sion** \-'hen-chən\ n

**mis·ap·pro·pri·ate** \ˌmi-sə-'prō-prē-ˌāt\ vb : to appropriate wrongly (as by embezzlement) — **mis·ap·pro·pri·a·tion** \-ˌprō-prē-'ā-shən\ n

**mis·be·got·ten** \-bi-'gä-tᵊn\ adj : ILLEGITIMATE; also : ill-conceived

**mis·be·have** \ˌmis-bi-'hāv\ vb : to behave improperly — **mis·be·hav·er** n — **mis·be·hav·ior** \-'hā-vyər\ n

**mis·be·liev·er** \-bə-'lē-vər\ n : one who holds a false or unorthodox belief

**mis·brand** \mis-'brand\ vb : to brand falsely or in a misleading manner

**misc** abbr miscellaneous

**mis·cal·cu·late** \mis-'kal-kyə-ˌlāt\ vb : to calculate wrongly — **mis·cal·cu·la·tion** \ˌmis-ˌkal-kyə-'lā-shən\ n

**mis·call** \mis-'kȯl\ vb : MISNAME

**mis·car·riage** \-'ker-ij\ n 1 : failure in the administration of justice 2 : spontaneous expulsion of a fetus before it is capable of independent life

**mis·car·ry** \-'ker-ē\ vb 1 : to have a miscarriage of a fetus 2 : to go wrong; also : to be unsuccessful

**mis·ce·ge·na·tion** \ˌmi-se-jə-'nā-shən, ˌmi-si-jə-'nā-\ n [L miscere to mix + genus race] : marriage, cohabitation, or sexual intercourse between persons of different races

**mis·cel·la·neous** \ˌmi-sə-'lā-nē-əs\ adj 1 : consisting of diverse things or members 2 : having various traits; also : dealing with or interested in diverse subjects — **mis·cel·la·neous·ly** adv — **mis·cel·la·neous·ness** n

**mis·cel·la·ny** \'mi-sə-ˌlā-nē\ n, pl -nies : a collection of writings on various subjects 2 : HODGEPODGE

**mis·chance** \mis-'chans\ n : bad luck; also : MISHAP

**mis·chief** \'mis-chəf\ n [ME meschief, fr. AF, misfortune, hardship, fr. OF meschever to come out badly, fr. mes- badly + chief head, end] 1 : injury caused by a particular agent 2 : a source of harm or irritation 3 : action that annoys; also : MISCHIEVOUSNESS

**mis·chie·vous** \'mis-chə-vəs\ adj 1 : HARMFUL, INJURIOUS 2 : causing annoyance or minor injury 3 : irresponsibly playful ⟨~ children⟩ — **mis·chie·vous·ly** adv — **mis·chie·vous·ness** n

**mis·ci·ble** \'mi-sə-bəl\ adj : capable of being mixed

**mis·com·mu·ni·ca·tion** \ˌmis-kə-ˌmyü-nə-'kā-shən\ n : failure to communicate clearly

**mis·con·ceive** \ˌmis-kən-'sēv\ vb : to interpret incorrectly — **mis·con·cep·tion** \-'sep-shən\ n

**mis·con·duct** \mis-'kän-(ˌ)dəkt\ n 1 : MISMANAGEMENT 2 : intentional wrongdoing 3 : improper behavior; also : a penalty in a sport for improper behavior

**mis·con·strue** \ˌmis-kən-'strü\ vb : MISINTERPRET — **mis·con·struc·tion** \-'strək-shən\ n

**mis·count** \mis-'kaunt\ vb : to count incorrectly : MISCALCULATE

**mis·cre·ant** \'mis-krē-ənt\ n : one who behaves criminally or viciously — **miscreant** adj

**mis·cue** \mis-'kyü\ n : MISTAKE, ERROR — **miscue** vb

**mis·deed** \mis-'dēd\ n : a wrong deed

**mis·de·mean·or** \ˌmis-di-'mē-nər\ n 1 : a crime less serious than a felony 2 : MISDEED

**mis·di·rect** \ˌmis-də-'rekt, -dī-\ vb : to give a wrong direction to — **mis·di·rec·tion** \-'rek-shən\ n

**mis·do·ing** \mis-'dü-iŋ\ n : WRONGDOING — **mis·do** \-'dü\ vb — **mis·do·er** \-'dü-ər\ n

**mise-en-scène** \ˌmē-ˌzäⁿ-'sen, -ˌsäⁿ\ n, pl **mise-en-scènes** \same or -'senz, -'sänz\ [F] 1 : the arrangement of the scenery, property, and actors on a stage 2 : SETTING; also : ENVIRONMENT

**mi·ser** \'mī-zər\ n [L miser miserable] : a person who hoards and is stingy with money — **mi·ser·li·ness** \-lē-nəs\ n — **mi·ser·ly** adj

**mis·er·a·ble** \'mi-zə-rə-bəl, 'miz-rə-\ adj 1 : wretchedly deficient; also : causing extreme discomfort 2 : being in a state of distress 3 : SHAMEFUL — **mis·er·a·ble·ness** n — **mis·er·a·bly** \-blē\ adv

**mis·ery** \'mi-zə-rē\ n, pl -er·ies 1 : suffering and want caused by poverty or affliction 2 : a cause of suffering or discomfort 3 : emotional distress

**mis·fea·sance** \mis-'fē-zᵊns\ n : the performance of a lawful action in an illegal or improper manner

**mis·file** \-'fī(-ə)l\ vb : to file in the wrong place

**mis·fire** \-'fī(-ə)r\ vb 1 : to fail to fire 2 : to miss an intended effect — **misfire** n

**mis·fit** \'mis-ˌfit, sense 1 also mis-'fit\ n 1 : something that fits badly 2 : a person who is poorly adjusted to a situation or environment

**mis·for·tune** \mis-'fȯr-chən\ n 1 : bad luck 2 : an unfortunate condition or event

**mis·giv·ing** \-'gi-viŋ\ n : a feeling of doubt or suspicion esp. concerning a future event

**mis·gov·ern** \-'gə-vərn\ vb : to govern badly — **mis·gov·ern·ment** n

**mis·guid·ance** \-'gī-dᵊns\ n : faulty guidance — **mis·guide** \-'gīd\ vb

**mis·guid·ed** \-'gī-dəd\ adj : led or prompted by wrong or inappropriate motives or ideals — **mis·guid·ed·ly** adv

**mis·han·dle** \-'han-dᵊl\ vb 1 : MALTREAT 2 : to manage wrongly

**mis·hap** \\'mis-ˌhap\\ n : an unfortunate accident

**mish·mash** \\'mish-ˌmash, -ˌmäsh\\ n : HODGEPODGE, JUMBLE

**mis·in·form** \\ˌmi-sⁿn-'fȯrm\\ vb : to give false or misleading information to — **mis·in·for·ma·tion** \\ˌmi-sin-fər-'mā-shən\\ n

**mis·in·ter·pret** \\ˌmi-sⁿn-'tər-prət\\ vb : to understand or explain wrongly — **mis·in·ter·pre·ta·tion** \\-ˌtər-prə-'tā-shən\\ n

**mis·judge** \\mis-'jəj\\ vb 1 : to estimate wrongly 2 : to have an unjust opinion of — **mis·judg·ment** \\mis-'jəj-mənt\\ n

**mis·la·bel** \\-'lā-bəl\\ vb : to label incorrectly or falsely ⟨was ~ed a liar⟩

**mis·lay** \\mis-'lā\\ vb -**laid** \\-'lād\\; -**lay·ing** : MISPLACE, LOSE ⟨mislaid his keys⟩

**mis·lead** \\mis-'lēd\\ vb -**led** \\-'led\\; -**lead·ing** : to lead in a wrong direction or into a mistaken action or belief — **mis·lead·ing·ly** adv

**mis·like** \\-'līk\\ vb : DISLIKE — **mis·like** n

**mis·man·age** \\-'ma-nij\\ vb : to manage badly — **mis·man·age·ment** n

**mis·match** \\-'mach\\ vb : to match unsuitably or badly — **mis·match** \\mis-'mach, 'mis-ˌmach\\ n

**mis·name** \\-'nām\\ vb : to name incorrectly : MISCALL

**mis·no·mer** \\mis-'nō-mər\\ n : a wrong or inappropriate name or designation

**mi·so** \\'mē-sō\\ n : a high-protein fermented food paste consisting chiefly of soybeans, salt, and usu. grain

**mi·sog·y·ny** \\mə-'sä-jə-nē\\ n [Gk misogynia, fr. misein to hate + gynē woman] : a hatred of women — **mi·sog·y·nist** \\-nist\\ n or adj — **mi·sog·y·nis·tic** \\mə-ˌsä-jə-'nis-tik\\ adj

**mis·ori·ent** \\mi-'sȯr-ē-ˌent\\ vb : to orient improperly or incorrectly — **mis·ori·en·ta·tion** \\mi-ˌsȯr-ē-ən-'tā-shən\\ n

**mis·place** \\mis-'plās\\ vb 1 : to put in a wrong or unremembered place 2 : to set on a wrong object ⟨~ trust⟩

**mis·play** \\-'plā\\ n : a wrong or unskillful play — **mis·play** \\mis-'plā, 'mis-ˌplā\\ vb

**mis·print** \\'mis-ˌprint\\ n : a mistake in printed matter — **mis·print** \\mis-'print\\ vb

**mis·pro·nounce** \\ˌmis-prə-'naúns\\ vb : to pronounce incorrectly — **mis·pro·nun·ci·a·tion** \\-prə-ˌnən-sē-'ā-shən\\ n

**mis·quote** \\mis-'kwōt\\ vb : to quote incorrectly — **mis·quo·ta·tion** \\ˌmis-kwō-'tā-shən\\ n

**mis·read** \\-'rēd\\ vb -**read** \\-'red\\; -**read·ing** \\-'rē-diŋ\\ : to read or interpret incorrectly ⟨~ her expression⟩

**mis·rep·re·sent** \\ˌmis-ˌre-pri-'zent\\ vb : to represent falsely or unfairly ⟨~ the facts⟩ — **mis·rep·re·sen·ta·tion** \\-ˌzen-'tā-shən\\ n

**¹mis·rule** \\mis-'rül\\ vb : MISGOVERN

**²misrule** n 1 : MISGOVERNMENT 2 : DISORDER

**¹miss** \\'mis\\ vb 1 : to fail to hit, reach, or contact 2 : to feel the absence of 3 : to fail to obtain 4 : AVOID ⟨just ~ed hitting the other car⟩ 5 : OMIT 6 : to fail to understand ⟨~ the point⟩ 7 : to fail to perform or attend; also : MISFIRE

**²miss** n 1 : a failure to hit or to attain a result 2 : MISFIRE

**³miss** n 1 cap — used as a title prefixed to the name of an unmarried woman or girl 2 : a young unmarried woman or girl

**Miss** abbr Mississippi

**mis·sal** \\'mi-səl\\ n : a book containing all that is said or sung at mass during the entire year

**mis·send** \\mis-'send\\ vb : to send incorrectly (as to a wrong destination)

**mis·shap·en** \\-'shā-pən\\ adj : badly shaped : having an ugly shape

**mis·sile** \\'mi-səl\\ n [L, fr. neut. of missilis capable of being thrown, fr. mittere to let go, send] : an object (as a stone, bullet, or rocket) thrown or projected usu. so as to strike a target

**miss·ing** \\'mi-siŋ\\ adj : ABSENT; also : LOST ⟨~ in action⟩

**mis·sion** \\'mi-shən\\ n 1 : a group of missionaries; also : a place where missionaries work 2 : a group of envoys to a foreign country; also : a team of specialists or cultural leaders sent to a foreign country 3 : TASK, OBJECTIVE

**¹mis·sion·ary** \\'mi-shə-ˌner-ē\\ adj : of, relating to, or engaged in missions

**²missionary** n, pl -**ar·ies** : a person commissioned by a church to spread its faith or carry on humanitarian work

**mis·sion·er** \\'mi-shə-nər\\ n : MISSIONARY

**Mis·sis·sip·pi·an** \\ˌmi-sə-'si-pē-ən\\ adj 1 : of or relating to Mississippi, its people, or the Mississippi River 2 : of, relating to, or being the period of the Paleozoic era between the Devonian and the Pennsylvanian — **Mississippian** n

**mis·sive** \\'mi-siv\\ n : LETTER

**mis·speak** \\mis-'spēk\\ vb : to say imperfectly or incorrectly

**mis·spell** \\-'spel\\ vb : to spell incorrectly — **mis·spell·ing** n

**mis·spend** \\-'spend\\ vb -**spent** \\-'spent\\; -**spend·ing** : WASTE, SQUANDER ⟨my misspent youth⟩

**mis·state** \\mis-'stāt\\ vb : to state incorrectly — **mis·state·ment** n

**mis·step** \\-'step\\ n 1 : a wrong step 2 : MISTAKE, BLUNDER

**mist** \\'mist\\ n 1 : water in the form of particles suspended or falling in the air 2 : something that obscures understanding — **mist** vb

**mis·tak·able** \\mə-'stā-kə-bəl\\ adj : capable of being misunderstood or mistaken

**¹mis·take** \\mi-'stāk\\ vb -**took** \\-'stúk\\; -**tak·en** \\-'stā-kən\\; -**tak·ing** 1 : to blunder in the choice of 2 : MISINTERPRET 3 : to make a wrong judgment of the character or ability of 4 : to confuse with another — **mis·tak·en·ly** adv — **mis·tak·er** n

**²mistake** n 1 : a wrong judgment : MISUNDERSTANDING 2 : a wrong action or statement : ERROR

**¹mis·ter** \\'mis-tər\\ n 1 cap — used sometimes instead of Mr. 2 : SIR — used without a name in addressing a man

²**mist·er** \'mis-tər\ n : a device for spraying mist

**mis·tle·toe** \'mi-səl-ˌtō\ n : a European parasitic green shrub that grows on trees and has yellowish flowers and waxy white berries

**mis·tral** \'mis-trəl, mi-'sträl\ n [F, fr. Occitan, fr. mistral masterful, fr. LL magistralis of a teacher, fr. L magister master] : a strong cold dry northerly wind of southern France

**mis·treat** \mis-'trēt\ vb : to treat badly : ABUSE — **mis·treat·ment** n

**mis·tress** \'mis-trəs\ n 1 : a woman who has power, authority, or ownership ⟨~ of the house⟩ 2 : something personified as female that rules or dominates ⟨when Rome was ~ of the world⟩ 3 : a woman other than his wife with whom a married man has sexual relations; also, archaic : SWEETHEART 4 — used archaically as a title prefixed to the name of a married or unmarried woman

**mis·tri·al** \'mis-ˌtrī(-ə)l\ n : a trial that has no legal effect

¹**mis·trust** \mis-'trəst\ n : a lack of confidence : DISTRUST — **mis·trust·ful** \-fəl\ adj — **mis·trust·ful·ly** adv — **mis·trust·ful·ness** n

²**mistrust** vb : to have no trust or confidence in : SUSPECT

**misty** \'mis-tē\ adj **mist·i·er; -est** 1 : obscured by or as if by mist : INDISTINCT ⟨a ~ memory⟩ 2 : TEARFUL — **mist·i·ly** \-tə-lē\ adv — **mist·i·ness** \-tē-nəs\ n

**mis·un·der·stand** \ˌmi-ˌsən-dər-'stand\ vb **-stood** \-'stu̇d\; **-stand·ing** 1 : to fail to understand 2 : to interpret incorrectly

**mis·un·der·stand·ing** \-'stan-diŋ\ n 1 : MISINTERPRETATION 2 : DISAGREEMENT, QUARREL

**mis·us·age** \mis-'yü-sij\ n 1 : bad treatment : ABUSE 2 : wrong or improper use

**mis·use** \mis-'yüz\ vb 1 : to use incorrectly : ABUSE, MISTREAT — **mis·use** \-'yüs\ n

¹**mite** \'mīt\ n : any of numerous tiny arthropod animals related to the spiders that often live and feed on animals or plants

²**mite** n 1 : a small coin or sum of money 2 : a small amount : BIT

¹**mi·ter** or **mi·tre** \'mī-tər\ n [ME mitre, fr. AF, fr. L mitra headband, turban, fr. Gk] 1 : a headdress worn by bishops and abbots 2 : MITER JOINT

²**miter** or **mitre** vb **mi·tered** or **mi·tred; mi·ter·ing** or **mi·tring** \'mī-tə-riŋ\ 1 : to match or fit together in a miter joint 2 : to bevel the ends of for making a miter joint

**miter joint** n : a usu. perpendicular joint made by fitting together two parts with the ends cut at an angle

**mit·i·gate** \'mi-tə-ˌgāt\ vb **-gat·ed; -gat·ing** 1 : to make less harsh or hostile 2 : to make less severe or painful — **mit·i·ga·tion** \ˌmi-tə-'gā-shən\ n — **mit·i·ga·tive** \'mi-tə-ˌgā-tiv\ adj

**mi·to·chon·dri·on** \ˌmī-tə-'kän-drē-ən\ n, pl **-dria** \-drē-ə\ : any of various round or long cellular organelles that produce energy for the cell — **mi·to·chon·dri·al** \-drē-əl\ adj

**mi·to·sis** \mī-'tō-səs\ n, pl **-to·ses** \-ˌsēz\ : a process that takes place in the nucleus of a dividing cell and results in the formation of two new nuclei each of which has the same number of chromosomes as the parent nucleus; also : cell division in which mitosis occurs — **mi·tot·ic** \-'tä-tik\ adj

**mitt** \'mit\ n 1 : a baseball catcher's or first baseman's glove 2 slang : HAND

**mit·ten** \'mi-tᵊn\ n : a covering for the hand having a separate section for the thumb only — **mit·tened** \-tᵊnd\ adj

¹**mix** \'miks\ vb 1 : to combine into one mass 2 : ASSOCIATE 3 : to form by mingling components 4 : to produce (a recording) by electronically combining sounds from different sources 5 : HYBRIDIZE 6 : CONFUSE ⟨~es up the facts⟩ 7 : to become involved ♦ **Synonyms** BLEND, MERGE, COALESCE, AMALGAMATE, FUSE — **mix·able** adj — **mix it up** : to engage in a fight, contest, or dispute

²**mix** n : a product of mixing; esp : a commercially prepared mixture of food ingredients

**mixed** \'mikst\ adj 1 : combining features of more than one kind 2 : made up of or involving individuals or items of more than one kind 3 : including or accompanied by different or opposing elements ⟨a ~ blessing⟩ 4 : resulting from the crossing or breeding of individuals of different races or breeds ⟨a stallion of ~ blood⟩

**mixed number** n : a number (as $5^2/_3$) composed of an integer and a fraction

**mixed–up** \'mikst-'əp\ adj : CONFUSED

**mix·er** \'mik-sər\ n 1 : one that mixes; esp : a machine or device for mixing 2 : an event (as a dance) that encourages meeting and socializing 3 : a nonalcoholic beverage used in a cocktail

**mixt** abbr mixture

**mix·ture** \'miks-chər\ n 1 : the act or process of mixing; also : the state of being mixed 2 : a product of mixing

**mix–up** \'miks-ˌəp\ n 1 : an instance of confusion 2 : CONFLICT, FIGHT

**miz·zen** also **miz·en** \'mi-zᵊn\ n 1 : a fore-and-aft sail set on the mizzenmast 2 : MIZZENMAST — **mizzen** also **mizen** adj

**miz·zen·mast** \-ˌmast, -məst\ n : the mast aft or next aft of the mainmast

**mk** abbr 1 mark 2 markka

**Mk** abbr Mark

**mks** abbr meter-kilogram-second

**mkt** abbr market

**mktg** abbr marketing

**ml** abbr milliliter

**Mlle** abbr [F] mademoiselle

**Mlles** abbr [F] mesdemoiselles

**mm** abbr millimeter

**MM** abbr [F] messieurs

**Mme** abbr [F] madame

**Mmes** abbr [F] mesdames

**Mn** symbol manganese

**MN** abbr Minnesota

**mne·mon·ic** \ni-'mä-nik\ adj : assisting

or designed to assist memory; *also* : of or relating to memory

**mo** *abbr* month

**¹Mo** *abbr* **1** Missouri **2** Monday

**²Mo** *symbol* molybdenum

**MO** *abbr* **1** mail order **2** medical officer **3** Missouri **4** modus operandi **5** money order

**moan** \'mōn\ *n* : a low prolonged sound indicative of pain or grief — **moan** *vb*

**moat** \'mōt\ *n* : a deep wide usu. water-filled trench around a castle

**¹mob** \'mäb\ *n* [L *mobile vulgus* vacillating crowd] **1** : MASSES, RABBLE **2** : a disorderly crowd **3** : a criminal gang

**²mob** *vb* **mobbed; mob·bing 1** : to crowd about and attack or annoy ⟨*mobbed* by fans⟩ **2** : to crowd into or around ⟨shoppers *mobbed* the stores⟩

**¹mo·bile** \'mō-bəl, -ˌbī(-ə)l, -ˌbēl\ *adj* **1** : capable of moving or being moved **2** : changeable in appearance, mood, or purpose; *also* : ADAPTABLE **3** : having the opportunity for or undergoing a shift in social status **4** : using vehicles for transportation ⟨~ warfare⟩ **5** : CELLULAR 2 — **mo·bil·i·ty** \mō-'bi-lə-tē\ *n*

**²mo·bile** \'mō-ˌbēl\ *n* : a construction or sculpture (as of wire and sheet metal) with parts that can be set in motion by air currents; *also* : a similar structure suspended so that it is moved by a current of air

**mobile home** *n* : a trailer used as a permanent dwelling

**mo·bi·lise** *chiefly Brit var of* MOBILIZE

**mo·bi·lize** \'mō-bə-ˌlīz\ *vb* **-lized; -liz·ing 1** : to put into movement or circulation **2** : to assemble and make ready for action ⟨~ army reserves⟩ — **mo·bi·li·za·tion** \ˌmō-bə-lə-'zā-shən\ *n* — **mo·bi·liz·er** \'mō-bə-ˌlī-zər\ *n*

**mob·ster** \'mäb-stər\ *n* : a member of a criminal gang

**moc·ca·sin** \'mä-kə-sən\ *n* **1** : a soft leather heelless shoe **2** : WATER MOCCASIN

**mo·cha** \'mō-kə\ *n* [*Mocha*, port in Yemen] **1** : choice coffee grown in Arabia **2** : a mixture of coffee and chocolate or cocoa **3** : a dark chocolate-brown color

**¹mock** \'mäk, 'mȯk\ *vb* **1** : to treat with contempt or ridicule **2** : DELUDE **3** : DEFY **4** : to mimic in sport or derision — **mock·er** *n* — **mock·ery** \'mä-kə-rē, 'mȯ-\ *n* — **mock·ing·ly** *adv*

**²mock** *adj* : SIMULATED ⟨a ~ trial⟩

**mock–he·ro·ic** \ˌmäk-hi-'rō-ik, ˌmȯk-\ *adj* : ridiculing or burlesquing heroic style, character, or action ⟨a ~ poem⟩

**mock·ing·bird** \'mä-kiŋ-ˌbərd, 'mȯ-\ *n* : a grayish No. American songbird related to the catbirds and thrashers that mimics the calls of other birds

**mock–up** \'mä-ˌkəp, 'mȯ-\ *n* **1** : a full-sized structural model built for study, testing, or display ⟨a ~ of a car⟩ **2** : a working sample (as of a magazine) for review

**¹mod** \'mäd\ *adj* **1** : of, relating to, or being the style of the 1960s British youth culture **2** : HIP, TRENDY

**²mod** *abbr* **1** moderate **2** modern **3** modification; modified

**mode** \'mōd\ *n* **1** : a particular form or variety of something; *also* : STYLE **2** : a manner of doing something **3** : the most frequent value of a set of data — **mod·al** \'mō-dᵊl\ *adj*

**¹mod·el** \'mä-dᵊl\ *n* **1** : structural design **2** : a miniature representation; *also* : a pattern of something to be made **3** : an example for imitation or emulation **4** : one who poses (as for an artist or to display clothes) **5** : TYPE, DESIGN ⟨a new car ~⟩

**²model** *vb* **mod·eled** *or* **mod·elled; mod·el·ing** *or* **mod·el·ling 1** : SHAPE, FASHION, CONSTRUCT ⟨~ed in clay⟩ **2** : to work as a fashion model

**³model** *adj* **1** : serving as or worthy of being in a pattern ⟨a ~ student⟩ **2** : being a miniature representation of something ⟨a ~ airplane⟩

**mo·dem** \'mō-dəm, -ˌdem\ *n* : a device that converts signals from one device (as a computer) to a form compatible with another (as a telephone)

**¹mod·er·ate** \'mä-də-rət\ *adj* **1** : avoiding extremes; *also* : TEMPERATE **2** : AVERAGE; *also* : MEDIOCRE **3** : limited in scope or effect **4** : not expensive — **moderate** *n* — **mod·er·ate·ly** *adv* — **mod·er·ate·ness** *n*

**²mod·er·ate** \'mä-də-ˌrāt\ *vb* **-at·ed; -at·ing 1** : to lessen the intensity of : TEMPER **2** : to act as a moderator — **mod·er·a·tion** \ˌmä-də-'rā-shən\ *n*

**mod·er·a·tor** \'mä-də-ˌrā-tər\ *n* **1** : MEDIATOR **2** : one who presides over an assembly, meeting, or discussion

**mod·ern** \'mä-dərn\ *adj* [LL *modernus*, fr. L *modo* just now, fr. *modus* measure] : of, relating to, or characteristic of the present or the immediate past : CONTEMPORARY ⟨~ art⟩ — **modern** *n* — **mo·der·ni·ty** \mə-'dər-nə-tē\ *n* — **mod·ern·ly** *adv* — **mod·ern·ness** *n*

**mod·ern·ise, mod·ern·i·sa·tion** *Brit var of* MODERNIZE, MODERNIZATION

**mod·ern·ism** \'mä-dər-ˌni-zəm\ *n* : a practice, movement, or belief peculiar to modern times

**mod·ern·ize** \'mä-dər-ˌnīz\ *vb* **-ized; -iz·ing** : to make or become modern — **mod·ern·i·za·tion** \ˌmä-dər-nə-'zā-shən\ *n* — **mod·ern·iz·er** *n*

**mod·est** \'mä-dəst\ *adj* **1** : having a moderate estimate of oneself; *also* : DIFFIDENT **2** : observing the proprieties of dress and behavior **3** : limited in size, amount, or scope ⟨a ~ income⟩ — **mod·est·ly** *adv* — **mod·es·ty** \-də-stē\ *n*

**mod·i·cum** \'mä-di-kəm\ *n* : a small amount ⟨a ~ of privacy⟩

**modif** *abbr* modification

**mod·i·fy** \'mä-də-ˌfī\ *vb* **-fied; -fy·ing 1** : MODERATE **2** : to limit the meaning of esp. in a grammatical construction **3** : CHANGE, ALTER — **mod·i·fi·ca·tion** \ˌmä-də-fə-'kā-shən\ *n* — **mod·i·fi·er** \'mä-də-ˌfī-ər\ *n*

**mod·ish** \'mō-dish\ *adj* : FASHIONABLE,

STYLISH ⟨∼ decor⟩ — **mod·ish·ly** *adv* — **mod·ish·ness** *n*

**mo·diste** \mō-ˈdēst\ *n* : a maker of fashionable dresses and hats

**mod·u·lar** \ˈmä-jə-lər\ *adj* : constructed with standardized units ⟨∼ homes⟩

**mod·u·lar·ized** \ˈmä-jə-lə-ˌrīzd\ *adj* : containing or consisting of modules

**mod·u·late** \ˈmä-jə-ˌlāt\ *vb* **-lat·ed; -lat·ing** **1** : to tune to a key or pitch **2** : to keep in proper measure or proportion : TEMPER **3** : to vary the amplitude or frequency of a carrier wave for the transmission of information (as in radio or television) — **mod·u·la·tion** \ˌmä-jə-ˈlā-shən\ *n* — **mod·u·la·tor** \ˈmä-jə-ˌlā-tər\ *n* — **mod·u·la·to·ry** \-lə-ˌtōr-ē\ *adj*

**mod·ule** \ˈmä-jül\ *n* **1** : any in a series of standardized units for use together **2** : an assembly of wired electronic parts for use with other such assemblies **3** : an independent unit that constitutes a part of the total structure of a space vehicle ⟨a propulsion ∼⟩

**mo·dus ope·ran·di** \ˌmō-dəs-ˌä-pə-ˈran-dē, -ˌdī\ *n, pl* **mo·di operandi** \ˌmō-ˌdē-, ˌmō-ˌdī-\ [NL] : a method of procedure

¹**mo·gul** \ˈmō-gəl, mō-ˈgəl\ *n* [fr. *Mogul*, member of a Muslim dynasty ruling northern India] : an important person : MAGNATE ⟨a media ∼⟩

²**mogul** \ˈmō-gəl\ *n* : a bump in a ski run

**mo·hair** \ˈmō-ˌher\ *n* [modif. of obs. It *mocaiarro*, fr. Ar *mukhayyar*, lit., choice] : a fabric or yarn made wholly or in part from the long silky hair of the Angora goat; *also* : this goat hair

**Mo·ham·med·an** *also* **Mu·ham·mad·an** \mō-ˈha-mə-dən, -ˈhä-, mü-\ *n* : MUSLIM — **Mo·ham·med·an·ism** *also* **Mu·ham·mad·an·ism** \-də-ˌni-zəm\ *n*

**Mo·hawk** \ˈmō-ˌhȯk\ *n, pl* **Mohawk** *or* **Mohawks** **1** : a member of an American Indian people of the Mohawk River valley, New York; *also* : the language of the Mohawk people **2** : a hairstyle with a narrow strip of upright hair down the center and the sides shaved

**Mo·he·gan** \mō-ˈhē-gən, mə-\ *or* **Mo·hi·can** \-ˈhē-kən\ *n, pl* **Mohegan** *or* **Mohegans** *or* **Mohican** *or* **Mohicans** : a member of an American Indian people of southeastern Connecticut

**mo·hel** \mō-(h)el, ˈmȯi(-ə)l\ *n, pl* **mo·hels** *also* **mo·hal·im** \mō-hä-ˈlēm\ *also* **mo·hel·im** \-(h)e-ˈlēm\ : a person who performs Jewish circumcisions

**Mohican** *var of* MAHICAN

**moi·e·ty** \ˈmȯi-ə-tē\ *n, pl* **-ties** : one of two equal or approximately equal parts

**moil** \ˈmȯi(-ə)l\ *vb* : to work hard : DRUDGE — **moil** *n* — **moil·er** *n*

**moi·ré** \mȯ-ˈrā, mwä-\ *or* **moire** \*same or* ˈmȯir, ˈmwär\ *n* : a fabric (as silk) having a watered appearance

**moist** \ˈmȯist\ *adj* : slightly or moderately wet — **moist·ly** *adv* — **moist·ness** *n*

**moist·en** \ˈmȯi-sᵊn\ *vb* : to make or become moist — **moist·en·er** *n*

**mois·ture** \ˈmȯis-chər\ *n* : the small amount of liquid that causes dampness

**mois·tur·ise** *Brit var of* MOISTURIZE

**mois·tur·ize** \ˈmȯis-chə-ˌrīz\ *vb* **-ized; -iz·ing** : to add moisture to ⟨∼ the skin⟩ — **mois·tur·iz·er** *n*

**mo·ji·to** \mō-ˈhē-tō\ *n, pl* **-tos** [AmerSp, dim. of *mojo*, *mojo* citrus marinade, fr. Sp *mojar* to moisten] : a cocktail made of rum, sugar, mint, lime juice and soda water

**mol** *abbr* molecular; molecule

**mo·lar** \ˈmō-lər\ *n* [ME *molares*, pl., fr. L *molaris*, fr. *moluris* of a mill, fr. *mola* millstone] : any of the broad teeth adapted to grinding food and located in the back of the jaw — **molar** *adj*

**mo·las·ses** \mə-ˈla-səz\ *n* : the thick brown syrup that is separated from raw sugar in sugar manufacture

¹**mold** \ˈmōld\ *n* : crumbly soil rich in organic matter

²**mold** *n* **1** : distinctive nature or character **2** : the frame on or around which something is constructed **3** : a cavity in which something is shaped; *also* : an object so shaped **4** : MOLDING

³**mold** *vb* **1** : to shape in or as if in a mold **2** : to ornament with molding — **mold·er** *n*

⁴**mold** *n* : a surface growth of fungus esp. on damp or decaying matter; *also* : a fungus that produces mold — **mold·i·ness** \ˈmōl-dē-nəs\ *n* — **moldy** *adj*

⁵**mold** *vb* : to become moldy

**mold·board** \ˈmōld-ˌbȯrd\ *n* : a curved iron plate attached above the plowshare to lift and turn the soil

**mold·er** \ˈmōl-dər\ *vb* : to crumble into small pieces

**mold·ing** \ˈmōl-diŋ\ *n* **1** : an act or process of shaping in a mold; *also* : an object so shaped **2** : a decorative surface, plane, or curved strip

¹**mole** \ˈmōl\ *n* : a small often pigmented spot or protuberance on the skin

²**mole** *n* **1** : any of numerous small burrowing insect-eating mammals related to the shrews and hedgehogs **2** : a spy embedded within an organization

³**mole** *n* : a massive breakwater or jetty

**molecular biology** *n* : a branch of biology dealing with the ultimate physical and chemical organization of living matter and esp. with the molecular basis of inheritance and protein synthesis — **molecular biologist** *n*

**molecular weight** *n* : the mass of a molecule that is equal to the sum of the masses of all atoms contained in the molecule's formula

**mol·e·cule** \ˈmä-li-ˌkyül\ *n* : the smallest particle of matter that is the same chemically as the whole mass — **mo·lec·u·lar** \mə-ˈle-kyə-lər\ *adj*

**mole·hill** \ˈmōl-ˌhil\ *n* : a little ridge of earth thrown up by a mole

**mole·skin** \-ˌskin\ *n* **1** : the skin of the mole used as fur **2** : a heavy durable cotton fabric

**mo·lest** \mə-ˈlest\ *vb* **1** : ANNOY, DISTURB **2** : to make annoying sexual advances to; *esp* : to force physical and usu. sexual contact on — **mo·les·ta·tion** \ˌmō-ˌles-ˈtā-shən\ *n* — **mo·lest·er** *n*

**moll** \\'mäl\ *n* : a gangster's girlfriend

**mol·li·fy** \\'mä-lə-ˌfī\ *vb* **-fied; -fy·ing 1** : to soothe in temper : APPEASE **2** : SOFTEN **3** : to reduce in intensity : ASSUAGE ⟨~ ill feelings⟩ — **mol·li·fi·ca·tion** \ˌmä-lə-fə-'kā-shən\ *n*

**mol·lusk** *or* **mol·lusc** \\'mä-ləsk\ *n* : any of a large phylum of usu. shelled and aquatic invertebrate animals (as snails, clams, and squids) — **mol·lus·can** *also* **mol·lus·kan** \mə-'ləs-kən\ *adj*

[1]**mol·ly·cod·dle** \\'mä-lē-ˌkä-dᵊl\ *n* : a pampered man or boy

[2]**mollycoddle** *vb* **mol·ly·cod·dled; mol·ly·cod·dling** : PAMPER

**Mo·lo·tov cocktail** \\'mä-lə-ˌtöf-, 'mö-\ *n* [Vyacheslav M. *Molotov* †1986 Soviet foreign minister] : a crude bomb made of a bottle filled usu. with gasoline and fitted with a wick (as a saturated rag) that is ignited just prior to hurling

[1]**molt** \\'mōlt\ *vb* : to shed hair, feathers, outer skin, or horns periodically with the cast-off parts being replaced by new growth — **molt·er** *n*

[2]**molt** *n* : the act or process of molting

**mol·ten** \\'mōlt-ᵊn\ *adj* **1** : fused or liquefied by heat **2** : GLOWING

**mo·ly** \\'mō-lē\ *n* : a mythical herb with black root, white flowers, and magic powers

**mo·lyb·de·num** \mə-'lib-də-nəm\ *n* : a metallic chemical element used in strengthening and hardening steel

**mom** \\'mäm, 'məm\ *n* : MOTHER

**mom–and–pop** *adj* : being a small owner-operated business

**mo·ment** \\'mō-mənt\ *n* **1** : a minute portion of time : INSTANT **2** : a time of excellence ⟨he has his ~s⟩ **3** : IMPORTANCE ⟨an event of great ~⟩ ♦ *Synonyms* CONSEQUENCE, SIGNIFICANCE, WEIGHT, IMPORT

**mo·men·tar·i·ly** \ˌmō-mən-'ter-ə-lē\ *adv* **1** : for a moment **2** *archaic* : INSTANTLY **3** : at any moment : SOON

**mo·men·tary** \\'mō-mən-ˌter-ē\ *adj* **1** : continuing only a moment ⟨a ~ pause⟩; *also* : EPHEMERAL **2** : recurring at every moment — **mo·men·tar·i·ness** \-ˌter-ē-nəs\ *n*

**mo·men·tous** \mō-'men-təs\ *adj* : very important ⟨a ~ decision⟩ — **mo·men·tous·ly** *adv* — **mo·men·tous·ness** *n*

**mo·men·tum** \mō-'men-təm\ *n*, *pl* **mo·men·ta** \-'men-tə\ *or* **momentums** : a property that a moving body has due to its mass and motion; *also* : IMPETUS

**mom·my** \\'mä-mē, 'mə-\ *n*, *pl* **mom·mies** : MOTHER

**Mon** *abbr* Monday

**mon·arch** \\'mä-nərk, -ˌnärk\ *n* **1** : a person who reigns over a kingdom or an empire **2** : one holding preeminent position or power **3** : MONARCH BUTTERFLY — **mo·nar·chi·cal** \mə-'när-ki-kəl\ *also* **mo·nar·chic** \-'när-kik\ *adj*

**monarch butterfly** *n* : a large orange and black migratory American butterfly whose larva feeds on milkweed

**mon·ar·chist** \\'mä-nər-kist\ *n* : a believer

in monarchical government — **mon·ar·chism** \-ˌki-zəm\ *n*

**mon·ar·chy** \\'mä-nər-kē\ *n*, *pl* **-chies** : a nation or state governed by a monarch

**mon·as·tery** \\'mä-nə-ˌster-ē\ *n*, *pl* **-ter·ies** : a house for persons under religious vows (as monks)

**mo·nas·tic** \mə-'nas-tik\ *adj* : of or relating to monasteries or to monks or nuns — **monastic** *n* — **mo·nas·ti·cal·ly** \-ti-k(ə-)lē\ *adv* — **mo·nas·ti·cism** \-tə-ˌsi-zəm\ *n*

**mon·au·ral** \mä-'nȯr-əl\ *adj* : MONOPHONIC — **mon·au·ral·ly** *adv*

**Mon·day** \\'mən-dē, -ˌdā\ *n* : the second day of the week

**mon·e·tary** \\'mä-nə-ˌter-ē, 'mə-\ *adj* : of or relating to money or to the mechanisms by which it is supplied and circulated in the economy

**mon·ey** \\'mə-nē\ *n*, *pl* **moneys** *or* **mon·ies** \\'mə-nēz\ **1** : something (as metal currency) accepted as a medium of exchange **2** : wealth reckoned in monetary terms **3** : the 1st, 2d, and 3d places in a horse or dog race

☞ the MONEY TABLE is on pages 465–466

**mon·eyed** \\'mə-nēd\ *adj* **1** : having money : WEALTHY **2** : consisting in or derived from money

**mon·ey·lend·er** \\'mə-nē-ˌlen-dər\ *n* : one (as a bank or pawnbroker) whose business is lending money

**money market** *n* : the trade in short-term negotiable financial instruments

**money of account** : a denominator of value or basis of exchange used in keeping accounts

**money order** *n* : an order purchased at a post office, bank, or telegraph office directing another office to pay a sum of money to a party named on it

**mon·ger** \\'məŋ-gər, 'mäŋ-\ *n* **1** : DEALER **2** : one who tries to stir up or spread something — usu. used in combination ⟨warmonger⟩

**mon·go** \\'mäŋ-(ˌ)gō\ *n*, *pl* **mongo** — see *tugrik* at MONEY table

**Mon·gol** \\'mäŋ-gəl, 'mäŋ-ˌgōl\ *n* : a member of any of several traditionally pastoral peoples of Mongolia — **Mongol** *adj*

**Mon·go·lian** \mäŋ-'gōl-yən, mäŋ-, -'gō-lē-ən\ *n* **1** : a native or inhabitant of Mongolia **2** : a member of the Mongoloid racial stock — **Mongolian** *adj*

**Mon·gol·oid** \\'mäŋ-gə-ˌlȯid\ *adj* : of or relating to a major racial stock native to Asia that includes peoples of northern and eastern Asia, Malaysians, Eskimos, and often American Indians — **Mongoloid** *n*

**mon·goose** \\'män-ˌgüs, 'mäŋ-\ *n*, *pl* **mon·goos·es** *also* **mon·gees·e** \-ˌgēs\ : any of a group of small agile Old World mammals that are related to the civet cats and feed chiefly on small animals and fruits

**mon·grel** \\'mäŋ-grəl, 'məŋ-\ *n* : an offspring of parents of different breeds; *esp* : one of uncertain ancestry

**mon·i·ker** \\'mä-ni-kər\ *n* : NAME, NICKNAME

**mo·nism** \\'mō-ˌni-zəm, 'mä-\ *n* : a view

# MONEY — WORLD CURRENCIES

| NAME | SUBDIVISION | COUNTRY | NAME | SUBDIVISION | COUNTRY |
|---|---|---|---|---|---|
| afghani | 100 puls | Afghanistan | dram | 100 luma | Armenia |
| ariary | 5 iraimbilanja | Madagascar | escudo | 100 centavos | Cape Verde |
| baht | 100 satang | Thailand | euro[5] | 100 cents | Austria, |
| *or* tical | | | | | Belgium, Cyprus, Estonia, Finland, |
| balboa[1] | 100 centesimos | Panama | | | France, Germany, Greece, Ireland, |
| birr | 100 cents | Ethiopia | | | Italy, Latvia, Lithuania, |
| bolivar | 100 centimos | Venezuela | | | Luxembourg, Malta, Netherlands, |
| boliviano | 100 centavos | Bolivia | | | Portugal, Slovakia, Slovenia, Spain |
| cedi | 100 pesewas | Ghana | forint | 100 fillers[2] | Hungary |
| colón | 100 centimos | Costa Rica | franc[6] | 100 centimes | Cameroon, |
| córdoba | 100 centavos | Nicaragua | | | Central African Republic, Chad, |
| dalasi | 100 bututs | Gambia | | | Republic of the Congo, Equatorial |
| denar | 100 deni[2] | Macedonia | | | Guinea[7], Gabon |
| dinar | 100 centimes | Algeria | franc[8] | 100 centimes | Benin, |
| dinar | 1000 fils | Bahrain | | | Burkina Faso, Guinea-Bissau, |
| dinar | 1000 fils | Iraq | | | Ivory Coast, Mali, Niger, Senegal, |
| dinar | 1000 fils | Jordan | | | Togo |
| dinar | 1000 fils | Kuwait | franc | 100 centimes | Burundi |
| dinar | 1000 dirhams | Libya | franc | 100 centimes | Comoros |
| dinar | 1000 millimes | Tunisia | franc | 100 centimes | Democratic |
| dirham | 100 centimes | Morocco | | | Republic of |
| dirham | 100 fils | United Arab | | | the Congo |
| | | Emirates | franc | 100 centimes | Djibouti |
| dobra | 100 centimos | São Tomé | franc | 100 centimes | Guinea |
| | | and Príncipe | franc | 100 centimes[2] | Rwanda |
| dollar[3] | 100 cents | Antigua and | franc | 100 centimes | Switzerland |
| | Barbuda, Dominica, Grenada, St. | | *or* rappen | | |
| | Kitts-Nevis, St. Lucia, St. Vincent | | gourde | 100 centimes | Haiti |
| | and the Grenadines | | guarani | 100 centimos | Paraguay |
| dollar | 100 cents | Australia | hryvnia | 100 kopiykas | Ukraine |
| dollar | 100 cents | Bahamas | kina | 100 toea | Papua New |
| dollar | 100 cents | Barbados | | | Guinea |
| dollar | 100 cents | Belize | kip | 100 at | Laos |
| dollar | 100 cents | Bermuda | koruna | 100 haleru | Czech |
| dollar | 100 sen | Brunei | | | Republic |
| *or* cents | | | krona | 100 aurar | Iceland |
| dollar | 100 cents | Canada | | (*sing* eyrir) | |
| dollar | 100 cents | Fiji | krona | 100 ore | Sweden |
| dollar | 100 cents | Guyana | krone | 100 ore | Denmark |
| dollar | 100 cents | Hong Kong | krone | 100 ore | Norway |
| dollar | 100 cents | Jamaica | kuna | 100 lipa | Croatia |
| dollar | 100 cents | Liberia | kwacha | 100 tambala | Malawi |
| dollar | 100 cents | Namibia | kwacha | 100 ngwee | Zambia |
| dollar | 100 cents | New Zealand | kwanza | 100 lwei | Angola |
| dollar | 100 cents | Singapore | kyat | 100 pyas | Myanmar |
| dollar | 100 cents | Solomon | lari | 100 tetri | Republic of |
| | | Islands | | | Georgia |
| dollar | 100 cents | Suriname | lek | 100 qindarka | Albania |
| dollar | 100 cents | Taiwan | | (*sing* qintar) | |
| *or* yuan | | | lempira | 100 centavos | Honduras |
| dollar | 100 cents | Trinidad and | leone | 100 cents | Sierra Leone |
| | | Tobago | leu | 100 bani | Moldova |
| dollar | 100 cents | United States | | (*sing* ban) | |
| dollar[4] | 100 cents | Zimbabwe | leu | 100 bani | Romania |
| dollar — see RINGGIT, below | | | | (*sing* ban) | |
| dong | 100 xu | Vietnam | lev | 100 stotinki | Bulgaria |

See footnotes at end of table, p. 466.

# MONEY — WORLD CURRENCIES

| NAME | SUBDIVISION | COUNTRY | NAME | SUBDIVISION | COUNTRY |
|------|-------------|---------|------|-------------|---------|
| lilangeni (*pl* emalangeni) | 100 cents | Swaziland | rial *also* riyal | 100 fils | Yemen |
| lira *or* pound | 100 kurus | Turkey | rial — see RIYAL, below | | |
| livre — see POUND, below | | | riel | 100 sen | Cambodia |
| loti | 100 licente (*sing* sente) | Lesotho | ringgit *or* dollar | 100 sen | Malaysia |
| manat | 100 gopik | Azerbaijan | riyal | 100 dirhams | Qatar |
| manat | 100 tenesi (*sing* tenne) | Turkmenistan | riyal *also* rial | 100 halala | Saudi Arabia |
| marka | 100 fening | Bosnia and Herzegovina | riyal — see RIAL, above | | |
| | | | rubel *or* ruble (*sing* kapeyka) | 100 kapeek | Belarus |
| metical | 100 centavos | Mozambique | ruble | 100 kopecks | Russia |
| naira | 100 kobo | Nigeria | rufiyaa | 100 laari | Maldives |
| nakfa | 100 cents | Eritrea | rupee | 100 paisa | India |
| ngultrum | 100 chetrums | Bhutan | rupee | 100 cents | Mauritius |
| ouguiya | 5 khoums | Mauritania | rupee | 100 paisa | Nepal |
| pa'anga | 100 seniti | Tonga | rupee | 100 paisa | Pakistan |
| pataca | 100 avos | Macao | rupee | 100 cents | Seychelles |
| peso | 100 centavos | Argentina | rupee | 100 cents | Sri Lanka |
| peso | 100 centavos | Chile | rupiah | 100 sen | Indonesia |
| peso | 100 centavos | Colombia | shekel | 100 agorot | Israel |
| peso | 100 centavos | Cuba | shilling | 100 cents | Kenya |
| peso | 100 centavos | Dominican Republic | shilling | 100 cents | Somalia |
| | | | shilling | 100 cents | Tanzania |
| peso | 100 centavos | Mexico | shilling | 100 cents | Uganda |
| peso *or* piso | 100 sentimos *or* centavos | Philippines | sol | 100 centimos | Peru |
| | | | som | 100 tyiyn | Kyrgyzstan |
| peso | 100 centesimos | Uruguay | som *or* sum | 100 tiyin | Uzbekistan |
| pound | 100 piastres | Egypt | | | |
| pound *or* livre | 100 piastres | Lebanon | somoni | 100 dirams | Tajikistan |
| | | | taka | 100 paisa *or* poisha | Bangladesh |
| pound | 100 piastres | South Sudan | | | |
| pound | 100 piastres | Sudan | tala | 100 sene | Samoa |
| pound | 100 piastres | Syria | tenge | 100 tiyins | Kazakhstan |
| pound | 100 pence (*sing* penny) | United Kingdom | tical — see BAHT, above | | |
| | | | tugrik | 100 mongo | Mongolia |
| pound — see LIRA, above | | | vatu | | Vanuatu |
| pula | 100 thebe | Botswana | won | 100 chon | North Korea |
| quetzal | 100 centavós | Guatemala | won | 100 chon | South Korea |
| rand | 100 cents | South Africa | yen | 100 sen[2] | Japan |
| real | 100 centavos | Brazil | yuan | 100 fen | China |
| rial | 100 dinars | Iran | yuan — see DOLLAR, above | | |
| rial | 1000 baiza | Oman | zloty | 100 groszy | Poland |

[1] A monetary unit in name only; replaced by the U.S. dollar.
[2] Now a subdivision in name only.
[3] Issued by the Eastern Caribbean Central Bank.
[4] A monetary unit in name only; replaced by multiple foreign currencies.
[5] Replaced the individual monetary units of participating European Union countries.
[6] Issued by the Bank of Central African States.
[7] The franc of Equatorial Guinea is also called the *franco*.
[8] Issued by the West African Economic and Monetary Union.

that reality is basically one unitary organic whole — **mo·nist** \'mō-nist, 'mä-\ n

**mo·ni·tion** \mō-'ni-shən, mə-\ n : WARNING, CAUTION

¹**mon·i·tor** \'mä-nə-tər\ n 1 : a student appointed to assist a teacher 2 : one that monitors; *esp* : a video display screen (as for a computer)

²**monitor** vb : to watch, check, or observe for a special purpose

**mon·i·to·ry** \'mä-nə-ˌtȯr-ē\ adj : giving admonition : WARNING

¹**monk** \'məŋk\ n [ME, fr. OE munuc, fr. LL monachus, fr. LGk monachos, fr. Gk, adj., single, fr. monos alone] : a man belonging to a religious order and living in a monastery — **monk·ish** adj

²**monk** n : MONKEY

¹**mon·key** \'məŋ-kē\ n, pl **monkeys** : a nonhuman primate mammal; esp : one of the smaller, longer-tailed, and usu. more arboreal primates as contrasted with the apes

²**monkey** vb **mon·keyed; mon·key·ing** 1 : FOOL, TRIFLE — often used with around 2 : TAMPER — usu. used with with ⟨don't ~ and with the engines⟩

**monkey bars** n pl : a framework of bars on which children can play

**mon·key·shine** \'məŋ-kē-ˌshīn\ n : PRANK — usu. used in pl.

**monkey wrench** n : a wrench with one fixed and one adjustable jaw at right angles to a handle

**monk·fish** \'məŋk-ˌfish\ n : either of two marine bony fishes that have a large flattened head and are used for food

**monks·hood** \'məŋks-ˌhud\ n : any of a genus of poisonous plants related to the buttercups; esp : a tall Eurasian herb with white or purplish flowers

¹**mono** \'mä-nō\ adj : MONOPHONIC

²**mono** n : INFECTIOUS MONONUCLEOSIS

**mono·chro·mat·ic** \ˌmä-nə-krō-'ma-tik\ adj 1 : having or consisting of one color 2 : consisting of radiation (as light) of a single wavelength

**mono·chrome** \'mä-nə-ˌkrōm\ adj : involving or producing visual images in a single color or in varying tones of a single color ⟨~ television⟩

**mon·o·cle** \'mä-ni-kəl\ n : an eyeglass for one eye

**mono·clo·nal** \ˌmä-nə-'klō-nəl\ adj : produced by, being, or composed of cells derived from a single cell ⟨~ antibodies⟩

**mono·cot·y·le·don** \ˌmä-nə-ˌkat-ə-'lēd²n\ n : any of a class or subclass of chiefly herbaceous seed plants having an embryo with a single cotyledon and usu. parallel-veined leaves

**mon·o·dy** \'mä-nə-dē\ n, pl **-dies** : ELEGY, DIRGE — **mo·nod·ic** \mə-'nä-dik\ or **mo·nod·i·cal** \-di-kəl\ adj — **mon·o·dist** \'mä-nə-dist\ n

**mo·nog·a·my** \mə-'nä-gə-mē\ n 1 : marriage with but one person at a time 2 : the practice of having a single mate during a period of time — **mo·nog·a·mist** \-mist\ n — **mo·nog·a·mous** \-məs\ adj

**mono·gram** \'mä-nə-ˌgram\ n : a sign of

identity composed of the combined initials of a name — **monogram** vb

**mono·graph** \'mä-nə-ˌgraf\ n : a learned treatise on a small area of learning

**mono·lin·gual** \ˌmä-nə-'liŋ-gwəl\ adj : knowing or using only one language

**mono·lith** \'mä-nə-ˌlith\ n 1 : a single great stone often in the form of a monument or column 2 : something large and powerful that acts as a single unified force ⟨a bureaucratic ~⟩ — **mono·lith·ic** \ˌmä-nə-'li-thik\ adj

**mono·logue** also **mono·log** \'mä-nə-ˌlȯg\ n 1 : a dramatic soliloquy; also : a long speech monopolizing conversation 2 : the routine of a stand-up comic — **mono·logu·ist** \-ˌlȯg-ist\ or **mo·nol·o·gist** \mə-'nä-lə-jist; 'mä-nə-ˌlȯ-gist\ n

**mono·ma·nia** \ˌmä-nə-'mā-nē-ə, -nyə\ n 1 : mental disorder limited in expression to one area of thought 2 : excessive concentration on a single object or idea — **mono·ma·ni·ac** \-nē-ˌak\ n or adj

**mono·mer** \'mä-nə-mər\ n : a simple chemical compound that can be polymerized

**mono·nu·cle·o·sis** \ˌmä-nō-ˌnü-klē-'ō-səs, -ˌnyü-\ n : INFECTIOUS MONONUCLEOSIS

**mono·phon·ic** \ˌmä-nə-'fä-nik\ adj : of or relating to sound recording or reproduction involving a single transmission path

**mono·plane** \'mä-nə-ˌplān\ n : an airplane with only one set of wings

**mo·nop·o·ly** \mə-'nä-pə-lē\ n, pl **-lies** [L monopolium, fr. Gk monopōlion, fr. monos alone, single + pōlein to sell] 1 : exclusive ownership (as through command of supply) 2 : a commodity controlled by one party 3 : one that has a monopoly — **mo·nop·o·list** \-list\ n — **mo·nop·o·lis·tic** \mə-ˌnä-pə-'lis-tik\ adj — **mo·nop·o·li·za·tion** \-lə-'zā-shən\ n — **mo·nop·o·lize** \mə-'nä-pə-ˌlīz\ vb

**mono·rail** \'mä-nə-ˌrāl\ n : a single rail serving as a track for a vehicle; also : a vehicle traveling on such a track

**mono·so·di·um glu·ta·mate** \ˌmä-nə-ˌsō-dē-əm-'glü-tə-ˌmāt\ n : a crystalline salt used to enhance the flavor of food

**mono·syl·la·ble** \'mä-nə-ˌsi-lə-bəl\ n : a word of one syllable — **mono·syl·lab·ic** \ˌmä-nə-sə-'la-bik\ adj — **mono·syl·lab·i·cal·ly** \-bi-k(ə-)lē\ adv

**mono·the·ism** \'mä-nə-(ˌ)thē-ˌi-zəm\ n : a doctrine or belief that there is only one deity — **mono·the·ist** \-ˌthē-ist\ n — **mono·the·is·tic** \-ˌthē-'is-tik\ adj

**mono·tone** \'mä-nə-ˌtōn\ n : a succession of syllables, words, or sentences in one unvaried key or pitch

**mo·not·o·nous** \mə-'nä-tə-nəs\ adj 1 : uttered or sounded in one unvarying tone 2 : tediously uniform — **mo·not·o·nous·ly** adv — **mo·not·o·nous·ness** n

**mo·not·o·ny** \mə-'nä-tə-nē\ n : tedious sameness or uniformity

**mono·un·sat·u·rat·ed** \ˌmä-nō-ˌən-'sa-chə-ˌrā-təd\ adj : containing one double or triple bond per molecule — used esp. of an oil, fat, or fatty acid

**mon·ox·ide** \mə-'näk-ˌsīd\ n : an oxide

containing one atom of oxygen in a molecule

**mon·sei·gneur** \ˌmōⁿ-ˌsān-ˈyər\ *n, pl* **mes·sei·gneurs** \ˌmā-ˌsān-ˈyər, -ˈyərz\ : a French dignitary — used as a title

**mon·sieur** \məs-ˈyər\ *n, pl* **mes·sieurs** \*same or* -ˈyərz\ : a Frenchman of high rank or station — used as a title equivalent to *Mister*

**mon·si·gnor** \män-ˈsē-nyər\ *n, pl* **monsignors** *or* **mon·si·gno·ri** \ˌmän-ˌsēn-ˈyȯr-ē\ [It *monsignore*] : a Roman Catholic prelate — used as a title

**mon·soon** \män-ˈsün\ *n* [obs. Dutch *monssoen*, fr. Pg *monção*, fr. Ar *mawsim* time, season] **1** : a periodic wind esp. in the Indian Ocean and southern Asia **2** : the season of the southwest monsoon esp. in India **3** : rainfall associated with the monsoon

**¹mon·ster** \ˈmän-stər\ *n* **1** : an abnormally developed plant or animal **2** : an animal of strange or terrifying shape; *also* : one unusually large of its kind **3** : an extremely ugly, wicked, or cruel person — **mon·stros·i·ty** \ˌmän-ˈsträ-sə-tē\ *n* — **mon·strous** \ˈmän-strəs\ *adj* — **mon·strous·ly** *adv*

**²monster** *adj* : very large : ENORMOUS

**mon·strance** \ˈmän-strəns\ *n* : a vessel in which the consecrated Host is exposed for the adoration of the faithful

**Mont** *abbr* Montana

**mon·tage** \män-ˈtäzh\ *n* [F] **1** : a composite photograph made by combining several separate pictures **2** : an artistic composition made up of several different kinds of elements **3** : a varied mixture : JUMBLE

**month** \ˈmənth\ *n, pl* **months** \ˈməns, ˈmənths\ : one of the 12 parts into which the year is divided — **month·ly** *adv or adj or n*

**month·long** \ˈmənth-ˈlȯṅ\ *adj* : lasting a month

**mon·u·ment** \ˈmän-yə-mənt\ *n* **1** : a lasting reminder; *esp* : a structure erected in remembrance of a person or event **2** : NATIONAL MONUMENT

**mon·u·men·tal** \ˌmän-yə-ˈmen-tᵊl\ *adj* **1** : of or relating to a monument **2** : MASSIVE; *also* : OUTSTANDING ⟨a ~ achievement⟩ **3** : very great ⟨a ~ task⟩ — **mon·u·men·tal·ly** *adv*

**moo** \ˈmü\ *vb* : to make the natural throat noise of a cow — **moo** *n*

**¹mood** \ˈmüd\ *n* **1** : a conscious state of mind or predominant emotion : FEELING **2** : a prevailing attitude : DISPOSITION **3** : a distinctive atmosphere

**²mood** *n* : distinction of form of a verb to express whether its action or state is conceived as fact or in some other manner (as wish)

**moody** \ˈmü-dē\ *adj* **mood·i·er; -est** **1** : GLOOMY **2** : subject to moods : TEMPERAMENTAL — **mood·i·ly** \-də-lē\ *adv* — **mood·i·ness** \-dē-nəs\ *n*

**¹moon** \ˈmün\ *n* **1** : the earth's natural satellite **2** : SATELLITE 2

**²moon** *vb* : to engage in idle reverie

**moon·beam** \ˈmün-ˌbēm\ *n* : a ray of light from the moon

**¹moon·light** \-ˌlīt\ *n* : the light of the moon — **moon·lit** \-ˌlit\ *adj*

**²moonlight** *vb* **moon·light·ed; moon·light·ing** : to hold a second job in addition to a regular one — **moon·light·er** *n*

**moon·roof** \-ˌrüf, -ˌru̇f\ *n* : a glass sunroof

**moon·scape** \-ˌskāp\ *n* : the surface of the moon as seen or as pictured

**moon·shine** \-ˌshīn\ *n* **1** : MOONLIGHT 2 **2** : empty talk **3** : intoxicating liquor usu. illegally distilled

**moon·stone** \-ˌstōn\ *n* : a transparent or translucent feldspar of pearly luster used as a gem

**moon·struck** \-ˌstrək\ *adj* **1** : mentally unbalanced **2** : romantically sentimental **3** : lost in fantasy

**¹moor** \ˈmu̇r\ *n* **1** *chiefly Brit* : an expanse of open rolling infertile land **2** : a boggy area; *esp* : one that is peaty and dominated by grasses and sedges

**²moor** *vb* : to make fast with or as if with cables, lines, or anchors

**Moor** \ˈmu̇r\ *n* : one of the Arab and Berber conquerors of Spain — **Moor·ish** *adj*

**moor·ing** \ˈmu̇r-iṅ\ *n* **1** : a place where or an object to which a craft can be made fast **2** : an established practice or stabilizing influence — usu. used in pl.

**moor·land** \-lənd, -ˌland\ *n* : land consisting of moors

**moose** \ˈmüs\ *n, pl* **moose** : a large heavy-antlered ruminant mammal related to the deer that has humped shoulders and long legs and inhabits northern forested areas

**¹moot** \ˈmüt\ *vb* : to bring up for discussion; *also* : DEBATE

**²moot** *adj* **1** : open to question; *also* : DISPUTED ⟨a ~ assertion⟩ **2** : having no practical significance ⟨the discussion became ~⟩

**¹mop** \ˈmäp\ *n* : an implement made of absorbent material fastened to a handle and used esp. for cleaning floors

**²mop** *vb* **mopped; mop·ping** : to use a mop on : clean with a mop

**mope** \ˈmōp\ *vb* **moped; mop·ing** **1** : to become dull, dejected, or listless **2** : DAWDLE

**mo·ped** \ˈmō-ˌped\ *n* : a light low-powered motorbike that can be pedaled

**mop·pet** \ˈmä-pət\ *n* [obs. E *mop* fool, child] : CHILD

**mo·raine** \mə-ˈrān\ *n* : an accumulation of earth and stones left by a glacier

**¹mor·al** \ˈmȯr-əl\ *adj* **1** : of or relating to principles of right and wrong **2** : conforming to a standard of right behavior; *also* : capable of right and wrong action **3** : probable but not proved ⟨a ~ certainty⟩ **4** : perceptual or psychological rather than tangible or practical in nature or effect ⟨a ~ victory⟩ ♦ *Synonyms* VIRTUOUS, RIGHTEOUS, NOBLE, ETHICAL, PRINCIPLED — **mor·al·ly** *adv*

**²moral** *n* **1** : the practical meaning (as of a story) **2** *pl* : moral practices or teachings ⟨protecting the public ~s⟩

**mo·rale** \mə-ˈral\ *n* **1** : MORALITY **2** : the mental and emotional attitudes of an individual to the tasks at hand; *also* : ESPRIT DE CORPS

**mor·al·ise** *Brit var of* MORALIZE

**mor·al·ist** \ˈmȯr-ə-list\ *n* **1** : one who leads a moral life **2** : a thinker or writer concerned with morals **3** : one concerned with regulating the morals of others — **mor·al·is·tic** \ˌmȯr-ə-ˈlis-tik\ *adj* — **mor·al·is·ti·cal·ly** \-ti-k(ə-)lē\ *adv*

**mo·ral·i·ty** \mə-ˈra-lə-tē\ *n, pl* **-ties** : moral conduct : VIRTUE

**mor·al·ize** \ˈmȯr-ə-ˌlīz\ *vb* **-ized; -iz·ing** : to make moral reflections — **mor·al·i·za·tion** \ˌmȯr-ə-lə-ˈzā-shən\ *n* — **mor·al·iz·er** \ˈmȯr-ə-ˌlī-zər\ *n*

**mo·rass** \mə-ˈras\ *n* [D *moeras*, fr. OF *maresc*, of Gmc origin; akin to OE *mersc* marsh] : SWAMP; *also* : something that entangles, impedes, or confuses

**mor·a·to·ri·um** \ˌmȯr-ə-ˈtȯr-ē-əm\ *n, pl* **-ri·ums** *or* **-ria** \-ē-ə\ [ultim. fr. L *mora* delay] : a suspension of activity

**mo·ray eel** \mə-ˈrā-, ˈmȯr-ˌā-\ *n* : any of numerous often brightly colored biting eels of warm seas

**mor·bid** \ˈmȯr-bəd\ *adj* **1** : of, relating to, or typical of disease; *also* : DISEASED, SICKLY **2** : characterized by gloomy or unwholesome ideas or feelings **3** : GRISLY, GRUESOME ⟨~ details⟩ — **mor·bid·i·ty** \mȯr-ˈbi-də-tē\ *n* — **mor·bid·ly** *adv* — **mor·bid·ness** *n*

**mor·dant** \ˈmȯr-dᵊnt\ *adj* **1** : biting or caustic in manner or style **2** : BURNING, PUNGENT — **mor·dant·ly** *adv*

**¹more** \ˈmȯr\ *adj* **1** : GREATER ⟨something ~ than I expected⟩ **2** : ADDITIONAL ⟨wanted ~ coffee⟩

**²more** *adv* **1** : in addition **2** : to a greater or higher degree ⟨~ evenly matched⟩

**³more** *n* **1** : a greater quantity, number, or amount ⟨the ~ the merrier⟩ **2** : an additional amount ⟨costs a little ~⟩

**⁴more** *pron* : additional persons or things or a greater amount

**mo·rel** \mə-ˈrel\ *n* : any of several pitted edible fungi

**more·over** \mȯr-ˈō-vər\ *adv* : in addition : FURTHER

**mo·res** \ˈmȯr-ˌāz\ *n pl* [L, pl. of *mor-, mos* custom] **1** : the fixed morally binding customs of a group **2** : HABITS, MANNERS ⟨cultural ~⟩

**Mor·gan** \ˈmȯr-gən\ *n* : any of an American breed of lightly built horses

**morgue** \ˈmȯrg\ *n* : a place where the bodies of dead persons are kept until released for burial or autopsy

**mor·i·bund** \ˈmȯr-ə-(ˌ)bənd\ *adj* : being in a dying condition

**Mor·mon** \ˈmȯr-mən\ *n* : a member of the Church of Jesus Christ of Latter-day Saints — **Mor·mon·ism** \-mə-ˌni-zəm\ *n*

**morn** \ˈmȯrn\ *n* : MORNING

**morn·ing** \ˈmȯr-niŋ\ *n* **1** : the early part of the day; *esp* : the time from the sunrise to noon **2** : BEGINNING

**morn·ing-after pill** \ˌmȯr-niŋ-ˈaf-tər-\ *n* : a contraceptive drug taken up to usu. three days after sexual intercourse

**morning glory** *n* : any of various twining plants related to the sweet potato that have often showy bell-shaped or funnel-shaped flowers

**morning sickness** *n* : nausea and vomiting that typically occur in the morning esp. during early pregnancy

**morning star** *n* : a bright planet (as Venus) seen in the eastern sky before or at sunrise

**mo·roc·co** \mə-ˈrä-kō\ *n* : a fine leather made of goatskins tanned with sumac

**mo·ron** \ˈmȯr-ˌän\ *n* **1** *usu. offensive* : a mildly mentally retarded person **2** : a very stupid person — **mo·ron·ic** \mə-ˈrä-nik\ *adj* — **mo·ron·i·cal·ly** \-ni-k(ə-)lē\ *adv*

**mo·rose** \mə-ˈrōs\ *adj* [L *morosus* hard to please, exacting, fr. *mor-, mos* custom, disposition] : having a sullen disposition; *also* : GLOOMY — **mo·rose·ly** *adv* — **mo·rose·ness** *n*

**morph** \ˈmȯrf\ *vb* : to change the form or character of : TRANSFORM

**mor·pheme** \ˈmȯr-ˌfēm\ *n* : a meaningful linguistic unit that contains no smaller meaningful parts — **mor·phe·mic** \mȯr-ˈfē-mik\ *adj*

**mor·phia** \ˈmȯr-fē-ə\ *n* : MORPHINE

**mor·phine** \ˈmȯr-ˌfēn\ *n* [F, fr. Gk *Morpheus*, Greek god of dreams] : an addictive drug obtained from opium and used to ease pain or induce sleep

**mor·phol·o·gy** \mȯr-ˈfä-lə-jē\ *n* **1** : a branch of biology dealing with the form and structure of organisms **2** : a study and description of word formation in a language — **mor·pho·log·i·cal** \ˌmȯr-fə-ˈlä-ji-kəl\ *adj* — **mor·phol·o·gist** \mȯr-ˈfä-lə-jist\ *n*

**mor·ris** \ˈmȯr-əs\ *n* : a vigorous English dance traditionally performed by men wearing costumes and bells

**mor·row** \ˈmär-ō\ *n* : the next day

**Morse code** \ˈmȯrs-\ *n* : either of two codes consisting of dots and dashes or long and short sounds used for transmitting messages

**mor·sel** \ˈmȯr-səl\ *n* [ME, fr. AF, dim. of *mors* bite, fr. L *morsus*, fr. *mordēre* to bite] **1** : a small piece or quantity ⟨chocolate ~s⟩ **2** : a tasty dish

**mor·tal** \ˈmȯr-tᵊl\ *adj* **1** : causing death : FATAL; *also* : leading to eternal punishment ⟨~ sin⟩ **2** : subject to death ⟨~ man⟩ **3** : implacably hostile ⟨~ foe⟩ **4** : very great : EXTREME ⟨~ fear⟩ **5** : HUMAN ⟨~ limitations⟩ — **mortal** *n* — **mor·tal·i·ty** \mȯr-ˈta-lə-tē\ *n* — **mor·tal·ly** \ˈmȯr-tᵊl-ē\ *adv*

**¹mor·tar** \ˈmȯr-tər\ *n* **1** : a strong bowl in which substances are pounded or crushed with a pestle **2** : a short-barreled cannon used to fire shells at high angles

**²mortar** *n* : a building material (as a mixture of lime and cement with sand and water) that is spread between bricks or stones to bind them together as it hardens — **mortar** *vb*

**mor·tar·board** \ˈmȯr-tər-ˌbȯrd\ *n* **1** : a square board for holding mortar **2** : an academic cap with a flat square top

**mort·gage** \'mȯr-gij\ n [ME *morgage*, fr. AF *mortgage*, fr. *mort* dead + *gage* pledge] : a transfer of rights to a piece of property usu. as security for the payment of a loan or debt that becomes void when the debt is paid — **mortgage** vb — **mort·gag·ee** \ˌmȯr-gi-ʹjē\ n — **mort·gag·or** \ˌmȯr-gi-ʹjȯr\ n

**mor·ti·cian** \mȯr-ʹti-shən\ n [L *mort-, mors* death + E *-ician* (as in *physician*)] : UNDERTAKER

**mor·ti·fy** \'mȯr-tə-ˌfī\ vb **-fied; -fy·ing 1** : to subdue (as the body) esp. by abstinence or self-inflicted pain **2** : HUMILIATE ⟨her behavior *mortified* her parents⟩ **3** : to become necrotic or gangrenous — **mor·ti·fi·ca·tion** \ˌmȯr-tə-fə-ʹkā-shən\ n

**mor·tise** also **mor·tice** \'mȯr-təs\ n : a hole cut in a piece of wood into which another piece fits to form a joint

**mor·tu·ary** \'mȯr-chə-ˌwer-ē\ n, pl **-ar·ies** : a place in which dead bodies are kept until burial

**mos** abbr months

**mo·sa·ic** \mō-ʹzā-ik\ n : a surface decoration made by inlaying small pieces (as of colored glass or stone) to form figures or patterns; also : a design made in mosaic — **mosaic** adj

**mo·sey** \'mō-zē\ vb **mo·seyed; mo·sey·ing** : SAUNTER ⟨*moseyed* through the park⟩

**mosh** \'mäsh\ vb : to engage in rough uninhibited dancing near the stage at a rock concert

**mosh pit** n : an area in front of a stage where rough dancing takes place at a rock concert

**Mos·lem** \'mäz-ləm\ var of MUSLIM

**mosque** \'mäsk\ n : a building used for public worship by Muslims

**mos·qui·to** \mə-ʹskē-tō\ n, pl **-toes** also **-tos** : any of a family of dipteran flies the female of which sucks the blood of animals

**mosquito net** n : a net or screen for keeping out mosquitoes

**moss** \'mȯs\ n : any of a class of green plants that lack flowers but have small leafy stems and often grow in clumps — **mossy** adj

**moss·back** \'mȯs-ˌbak\ n : an extremely conservative person : FOGY

**¹most** \'mōst\ adj **1** : GREATEST ⟨the ~ ability⟩ **2** : the majority of ⟨~ people⟩

**²most** adv **1** : to the greatest or highest degree ⟨~ beautiful⟩ **2** : to a very great degree ⟨a ~ careful driver⟩

**³most** n : the greatest amount ⟨the ~ I can do⟩

**⁴most** pron : the greatest number or part ⟨~ became discouraged⟩

**-most** adj suffix : most ⟨inner*most*⟩ : most toward ⟨end*most*⟩

**most·ly** \'mōst-lē\ adv : MAINLY

**mot** \'mō\ n, pl **mots** \same or 'mōz\ [F, word, saying, fr. LL *muttum* grunt] : a witty saying

**mote** \'mōt\ n : a small particle

**mo·tel** \mō-ʹtel\ n [blend of *motor* and *hotel*] : a hotel in which the rooms are accessible from the parking area

**mo·tet** \mō-ʹtet\ n : a choral work on a sacred text for several voices usu. without instrumental accompaniment

**moth** \'mȯth\ n, pl **moths** \'mȯthz, 'mȯths\ : any of various insects belonging to the same order as the butterflies but usu. night-flying and with a stouter body and smaller wings

**moth·ball** \'mȯth-ˌbȯl\ n **1** : a ball (as of naphthalene) used to keep moths out of clothing **2** pl : protective storage ⟨many ships were put in ~s⟩

**¹moth·er** \'mə-thər\ n **1** : a female parent **2** : the superior of a religious community of women **3** : SOURCE, ORIGIN ⟨necessity is the ~ of invention⟩ — **moth·er·hood** \-ˌhůd\ n — **moth·er·less** adj — **moth·er·li·ness** \-lē-nəs\ n — **moth·er·ly** adj

**²mother** vb **1** : to give birth to; also : PRODUCE **2** : to care for or protect like a mother

**moth·er·board** \'mə-thər-ˌbȯrd\ n : the main circuit board esp. of a microcomputer

**moth·er–in–law** \'mə-thər-ən-ˌlȯ\ n, pl **mothers–in–law** \'mə-thərz-\ : the mother of one's spouse

**moth·er·land** \'mə-thər-ˌland\ n **1** : the land of origin of something **2** : the native land of one's ancestors

**moth·er–of–pearl** \ˌmə-thər-əv-ʹpərl\ n : the hard pearly matter forming the inner layer of a mollusk shell

**mother ship** n : a ship serving smaller craft

**mo·tif** \mō-ʹtēf\ n [F, motive, motif] : a dominant idea or central theme (as in a work of art)

**mo·tile** \'mōt-ᵊl, 'mō-ˌtī(-ə)l\ adj : capable of spontaneous movement ⟨~ cells⟩ — **mo·til·i·ty** \mō-ʹti-lə-tē\ n

**¹mo·tion** \'mō-shən\ n **1** : an act, process, or instance of moving **2** : a proposal for action (as by a deliberative body) **3** pl : ACTIVITIES, MOVEMENTS — **mo·tion·less** adj — **mo·tion·less·ly** adv — **mo·tion·less·ness** n

**²motion** vb : to direct or signal by a movement

**motion picture** n : a series of pictures projected on a screen so rapidly that they produce a continuous picture in which persons and objects seem to move

**motion sickness** n : sickness induced by motion and characterized by nausea

**mo·ti·vate** \'mō-tə-ˌvāt\ vb **-vat·ed; -vat·ing** : to provide with a motive : IMPEL — **mo·ti·va·tion** \ˌmō-tə-ʹvā-shən\ n — **mo·ti·va·tion·al** \-shə-nəl\ adj — **mo·ti·va·tor** \'mō-tə-ˌvā-tər\ n

**¹mo·tive** \'mō-tiv, 2 also mō-ʹtēv\ n **1** : something (as a need or desire) that causes a person to act **2** : a recurrent theme in a musical composition **3** : MOTIF — **mo·tive·less** adj

**²mo·tive** \'mō-tiv\ adj **1** : moving to action **2** : of or relating to motion

**mot·ley** \'mät-lē\ adj **1** : variegated in color **2** : made up of diverse often incongruous elements ♦ **Synonyms** HETEROGENEOUS, MISCELLANEOUS, ASSORTED, MIXED, VARIED

¹**mo·tor** \'mō-tər\ *n* [L, fr. *movēre* to move] **1** : one that imparts motion **2** : a machine that produces motion or power for doing work **3** : AUTOMOBILE

²**motor** *vb* : to travel or transport by automobile : DRIVE — **mo·tor·ist** *n*

**mo·tor·bike** \'mō-tər-ˌbīk\ *n* : a small lightweight motorcycle

**mo·tor·boat** \-ˌbōt\ *n* : a boat propelled by a motor

**mo·tor·cade** \-ˌkād\ *n* : a procession of motor vehicles

**mo·tor·car** \-ˌkär\ *n* : AUTOMOBILE

**mo·tor·cy·cle** \'mō-tər-ˌsī-kəl\ *n* : a 2-wheeled automotive vehicle — **mo·tor·cy·clist** \-k(ə-)list\ *n*

**motor home** *n* : a large motor vehicle equipped as living quarters

**motor inn** *n* : MOTEL

**mo·tor·ise** *Brit var of* MOTORIZE

**mo·tor·ize** \'mō-tə-ˌrīz\ *vb* **-ized; -iz·ing 1** : to equip with a motor **2** : to equip with automobiles

**mo·tor·man** \'mō-tər-mən\ *n* : an operator of a motor-driven vehicle (as a streetcar or subway train)

**motor scooter** *n* : a low 2- or 3-wheeled automotive vehicle resembling a child's scooter but having a seat

**mo·tor·truck** \'mō-tər-ˌtrək\ *n* : an automotive truck

**motor vehicle** *n* : an automotive vehicle (as an automobile) not operated on rails

**mot·tle** \'mä-tᵊl\ *vb* **mot·tled; mot·tling** : to mark with spots of different color : BLOTCH

**mot·to** \'mä-tō\ *n, pl* **mottoes** *also* **mottos** [It, fr. LL *muttum* grunt, fr. L *muttire* to mutter] **1** : a sentence, phrase, or word inscribed on something to indicate its character or use **2** : a short expression of a guiding rule of conduct

**moue** \'mü\ *n* : a little grimace

**mould** *chiefly Brit var of* MOLD

**moult** *chiefly Brit var of* MOLT

**mound** \'maund\ *n* **1** : an artificial bank or hill of earth or stones **2** : KNOLL **3** : HEAP, PILE ⟨a ~ of work⟩

¹**mount** \'maunt\ *n* : a high hill

²**mount** *vb* **1** : to increase in amount or extent; *also* : RISE, ASCEND **2** : to get up on something; *esp* : to seat oneself on (as a horse) for riding **3** : to put in position ⟨~ artillery⟩ **4** : to set on something that elevates **5** : to attach to a support **6** : to prepare esp. for examination or display — **mount·able** *adj* — **mount·er** *n*

³**mount** *n* **1** : FRAME, SUPPORT **2** : a means of conveyance; *esp* : SADDLE HORSE

**moun·tain** \'maun-tᵊn\ *n* : a landmass higher than a hill — **moun·tain·ous** \-tə-nəs\ *adj* — **moun·tainy** \-tᵊn-ē\ *adj*

**mountain ash** *n* : any of various trees related to the roses that have pinnate leaves and red or orange-red fruits

**mountain bike** *n* : a bicycle with wide knobby tires, straight handlebars, and 18 or 21 gears that is designed to operate esp. over unpaved terrain

**moun·tain·eer** \ˌmaun-tə-ˈnir\ *n* **1** : a native or inhabitant of a mountainous region **2** : one who climbs mountains for sport

**mountain goat** *n* : a ruminant mammal of mountainous northwestern No. America that resembles a goat

**mountain laurel** *n* : a No. American evergreen shrub or small tree of the heath family with glossy leaves and clusters of rose-colored or white flowers

**mountain lion** *n* : COUGAR

**moun·tain·side** \'maun-tᵊn-ˌsīd\ *n* : the side of a mountain

**moun·tain·top** \-ˌtäp\ *n* : the summit of a mountain

**moun·te·bank** \'maun-ti-ˌbank\ *n* [It *montimbanco*, fr. *montare* to mount + *in* in, on + *banco, banca* bench] : QUACK, CHARLATAN

**Mount·ie** \'maun-tē\ *n* : a member of the Royal Canadian Mounted Police

**mount·ing** \'maun-tiŋ\ *n* : something that serves as a frame or support

**mourn** \'mōrn\ *vb* : to feel or express grief or sorrow — **mourn·er** *n*

**mourn·ful** \-fəl\ *adj* : expressing, feeling, or causing sorrow ⟨a ~ song⟩ — **mourn·ful·ly** *adv* — **mourn·ful·ness** *n*

**mourn·ing** \'mōr-niŋ\ *n* **1** : an outward sign (as black clothes) of grief for a person's death **2** : a period of time during which signs of grief are shown

**mouse** \'maus\ *n, pl* **mice** \'mīs\ **1** : any of numerous small rodents with pointed snout, long body, and slender tail **2** : a small manual device that controls cursor movement on a computer display

**mouse pad** *n* : a thin flat pad on which a computer mouse is used

**mous·er** \'mau-sər\ *n* : a cat proficient at catching mice

**mouse·trap** \'maus-ˌtrap\ *n* **1** : a trap for catching mice **2** : a stratagem that lures one to defeat or destruction — **mousetrap** *vb*

**mousse** \'müs\ *n* [F, lit., froth, moss] **1** : a molded chilled dessert made with sweetened and flavored whipped cream or egg whites and gelatin **2** : a foamy preparation used in styling hair — **mousse** *vb*

**moustache** *var of* MUSTACHE

**mousy** *or* **mous·ey** \'mau-sē, -zē\ *adj* **mous·i·er; -est 1** : QUIET, STEALTHY **2** : TIMID **3** : grayish brown — **mous·i·ness** \'mau-sē-nəs, -zē-\ *n*

¹**mouth** \'mauth\ *n, pl* **mouths** \'mauthz, 'mauths\ **1** : the opening through which an animal takes in food; *also* : the cavity that encloses the tongue, lips, and teeth in the typical vertebrate **2** : something resembling a mouth (as in affording entrance) — **mouthed** \'mauthd, 'mautht\ *adj* — **mouth·ful** *n*

²**mouth** \'mauth\ *vb* **1** : SPEAK; *also* : DECLAIM **2** : to repeat without comprehension or sincerity ⟨~ed platitudes⟩ **3** : to form soundlessly with the lips

**mouth harp** *n* : HARMONICA

**mouth·part** \'mauth-ˌpärt\ *n* : a structure or appendage near the mouth (as of an insect) esp. when adapted for eating

**mouth·piece** \-ˌpēs\ *n* **1** : a part (as of a

musical instrument) that goes in the mouth or to which the mouth is applied **2** : SPOKESMAN

**mouth-to-mouth** *adj* : of, relating to, or being a method of artificial respiration in which air from a rescuer's mouth is forced into a victim's lungs

**mouth-wash** \-ˌwȯsh, -ˌwäsh\ *n* : a usu. antiseptic liquid preparation for cleaning the mouth and teeth

**mou-ton** \ˈmü-ˌtän\ *n* : processed sheepskin that has been sheared or dyed to resemble beaver or seal

**¹move** \ˈmüv\ *vb* **moved; mov-ing** **1** : to change or cause to change position or posture **2** : to go or cause to go from one point to another; *also* : DEPART **3** : to take or cause to take action **4** : to show marked activity **5** : to stir the emotions **6** : to make a formal request, application, or appeal **7** : to change one's residence **8** : EVACUATE **2** — **mov-able** *or* **move-able** \ˈmü-və-bəl\ *adj*

**²move** *n* **1** : an act of moving **2** : a calculated step taken to gain an objective **3** : a change of location **4** : an agile action esp. in sports

**move-ment** \ˈmüv-mənt\ *n* **1** : the act or process of moving : MOVE **2** : a series of organized activities working toward an objective **3** : the moving parts of a mechanism (as of a watch) **4** : RHYTHM **5** : a section of an extended musical composition **6** : an act of voiding the bowels; *also* : STOOL

**mov-er** \ˈmü-vər\ *n* : one that moves; *esp* : one that moves the belongings of others from one location to another

**mov-ie** \ˈmü-vē\ *n* **1** : MOTION PICTURE **2** *pl* : a showing of a motion picture **3** *pl* : the motion-picture industry

**¹mow** \ˈmau̇\ *n* : the part of a barn where hay or straw is stored

**²mow** \ˈmō\ *vb* **mowed; mowed** *or* **mown** \ˈmōn\; **mow-ing 1** : to cut (as grass) with a scythe or machine **2** : to cut the standing herbage of ⟨~ the lawn⟩ — **mow-er** *n*

**mox-ie** \ˈmäk-sē\ *n* **1** : ENERGY, PEP **2** : COURAGE, DETERMINATION

**moz-za-rel-la** \ˌmät-sə-ˈre-lə\ *n* [It] : a moist white unsalted unripened mild cheese of a smooth rubbery texture

**¹MP** \ˈem-ˈpē\ *n* **1** : a member of the military police **2** : an elected member of a parliament

**²MP** *abbr* **1** melting point **2** metropolitan police

**mpg** *abbr* miles per gallon

**mph** *abbr* miles per hour

**Mr.** \ˈmis-tər\ *n, pl* **Messrs.** \ˈme-sərz\ — used as a conventional title of courtesy before a man's surname or his title of office

**MRI** *n* : MAGNETIC RESONANCE IMAGING; *also* : the procedure in which magnetic resonance imaging is used

**Mr. Right** *n* : a man who would make the perfect husband

**Mrs.** \ˈmi-səz, -səs, *esp Southern* ˈmiz-əz, -zəs\ *n, pl* **Mes-dames** \mā-ˈdäm, -ˈdam\

— used as a conventional title of courtesy before a married woman's surname

**Ms.** \ˈmiz\ *n, pl* **Mss.** *or* **Mses.** \ˈmi-zez\ — used instead of *Miss* or *Mrs.*

**MS** *abbr* **1** manuscript **2** master of science **3** military science **4** Mississippi **5** motor ship **6** multiple sclerosis

**msec** *abbr* millisecond

**msg** *abbr* message

**MSG** *abbr* **1** master sergeant **2** monosodium glutamate

**msgr** *abbr* **1** monseigneur **2** monsignor

**MSgt** *abbr* master sergeant

**MSS** *abbr* manuscripts

**MST** *abbr* mountain standard time

**mt** *abbr* mount; mountain

**¹Mt** *abbr* Matthew

**²Mt** *symbol* meitnerium

**MT** *abbr* **1** metric ton **2** Montana **3** mountain time

**mtg** *abbr* **1** meeting **2** mortgage

**mtge** *abbr* mortgage

**mu** \ˈmyü, ˈmü\ *n* : the 12th letter of the Greek alphabet — M or μ

**¹much** \ˈməch\ *adj* **more** \ˈmȯr\; **most** \ˈmōst\ : great in quantity, amount, extent, or degree ⟨~ money⟩

**²much** *adv* **more; most 1** : to a great degree or extent ⟨~ happier⟩ **2** : ALMOST, NEARLY ⟨looks ~ as he did before⟩

**³much** *n* **1** : a great quantity, amount, extent, or degree **2** : something considerable or impressive

**mu-ci-lage** \ˈmyü-sə-lij\ *n* : a watery sticky solution (as of a gum) used esp. as an adhesive — **mu-ci-lag-i-nous** \ˌmyü-sə-ˈla-jə-nəs\ *adj*

**muck** \ˈmək\ *n* **1** : soft moist barnyard manure **2** : FILTH, DIRT **3** : a dark richly organic soil; *also* : MUD, MIRE — **mucky** *adj*

**muck-rake** \-ˌrāk\ *vb* : to expose publicly real or apparent misconduct of a prominent individual or business — **muck-rak-er** *n*

**mu-cus** \ˈmyü-kəs\ *n* : a slimy slippery protective secretion of membranes (**mucous membranes**) lining some body cavities — **mu-cous** \-kəs\ *adj*

**mud** \ˈməd\ *n* : soft wet earth : MIRE

**mud-dle** \ˈmə-dᵊl\ *vb* **mud-dled; muddling 1** : to make muddy **2** : to confuse esp. with liquor **3** : to mix up or make a mess of ⟨*muddled* the household accounts⟩ **4** : to think or act in a confused way

**mud-dle-head-ed** \ˌmə-dᵊl-ˈhe-dəd\ *adj* **1** : mentally confused **2** : INEPT

**¹mud-dy** \ˈmə-dē\ *adj* **mud-di-er; -est 1** : full of or covered with mud **2** : suggestive of mud **3** : CLOUDY, OBSCURE — **mud-di-ness** *n*

**²muddy** *vb* **mud-died; mud-dy-ing 1** : to soil or stain with or as if with mud **2** : to make cloudy or obscure **3** : CONFUSE

**mud-flat** \ˈməd-ˌflat\ *n* : a level tract alternately covered and left bare by the tide

**mud-guard** \ˈməd-ˌgärd\ *n* : a guard over or a flap behind a wheel of a vehicle to catch or deflect mud

**mud-room** \-ˌrüm, -ˌru̇m\ *n* : a room in a

house for removing dirty or wet footwear and clothing

**mud·sling·er** \-ˌsliŋ-ər\ *n* : one who uses invective esp. against a political opponent — **mud·sling·ing** \-ˌsliŋ-iŋ\ *n*

**Muen·ster** \'mən-stər, 'mün-, 'mùn-\ *n* : a semisoft bland cheese

**mu·ez·zin** \mü-'e-z°n, myü-\ *n* : a Muslim crier who calls the hour of daily prayer

**¹muff** \'məf\ *n* : a warm tubular covering for the hands

**²muff** *n* : a bungling performance; *esp* : a failure to hold a ball in attempting a catch — **muff** *vb*

**muf·fin** \'mə-fən\ *n* : a small soft cake baked in a cup-shaped container

**muf·fle** \'mə-fəl\ *vb* **muf·fled; muf·fling** **1** : to wrap up so as to conceal or protect **2** : to wrap or pad with something to dull the sound of **3** : to keep down : SUPPRESS ⟨*muffled* his feelings⟩

**muf·fler** \'mə-flər\ *n* **1** : a scarf worn around the neck **2** : a device (as on a car's exhaust) to deaden noise

**muf·ti** \'məf-tē\ *n* : civilian clothes

**¹mug** \'məg\ *n* : a usu. metal or earthenware cylindrical drinking cup

**²mug** *vb* **mugged; mug·ging 1** : to pose or make faces esp. to attract attention or for a camera **2** : PHOTOGRAPH

**³mug** *vb* **mugged; mug·ging** : to assault usu. with intent to rob — **mug·ger** *n*

**mug·gy** \'mə-gē\ *adj* **mug·gi·er; -est** : being warm and humid — **mug·gi·ness** \-gē-nəs\ *n*

**mug·wump** \'məg-ˌwəmp\ *n* [obs. slang *mugwump* kingpin, fr. Massachusett (Algonquian language of New England) *mugquomp* war leader] : an independent in politics

**Muhammadan, Muhammadanism** *var of* MOHAMMEDAN, MOHAMMEDANISM

**mu·ja·hid·een** *or* **mu·ja·hed·in** \mü-jə-hi-'dēn, -jä-\ *n pl* [Ar *mujāhidīn*, pl. of *mujāhid*, lit., person who wages jihad] : Islamic guerrilla fighters esp. in the Middle East

**muk·luk** \'mək-ˌlək\ *n* **1** : an Eskimo boot of sealskin or reindeer skin **2** : a boot with a soft leather sole worn over several pairs of socks

**mu·lat·to** \mu-'la-tō, myü-, -'lä-\ *n, pl* **-toes** *or* **-tos** [Sp *mulato*, fr. *mulo* mule, fr. L *mulus*] : a first-generation offspring of a black person and a white person; *also* : a person of mixed white and black ancestry

**mul·ber·ry** \'məl-ˌber-ē\ *n* : any of a genus of trees with edible berrylike fruit and leaves used as food for silkworms; *also* : the fruit

**mulch** \'məlch\ *n* : a protective covering (as of straw or leaves) spread on the ground esp. to reduce evaporation or control weeds — **mulch** *vb*

**¹mulct** \'məlkt\ *n* : FINE, PENALTY

**²mulct** *vb* **1** : FINE **2** : CHEAT, DEFRAUD

**¹mule** \'myül\ *n* **1** : a hybrid offspring of a male donkey and a female horse **2** : a very stubborn person — **mul·ish** \'myü-lish\ *adj* — **mul·ish·ly** *adv* — **mu·lish·ness** *n*

**²mule** *n* : a slipper whose upper does not extend around the heel of the foot

**mule deer** *n* : a long-eared deer of western No. America

**mu·le·teer** \ˌmyü-lə-'tir\ *n* : one who drives mules

**¹mull** \'məl\ *vb* : PONDER, MEDITATE

**²mull** *vb* : to heat, sweeten, and flavor (as wine) with spices

**mul·lein** \'mə-lən\ *n* : a tall herb related to the snapdragons that has coarse woolly leaves and flowers in spikes

**mul·let** \'mə-lət\ *n, pl* **mullet** *or* **mullets** : any of a family of largely gray chiefly marine bony fishes including valuable food fishes

**mul·li·gan stew** \'mə-li-gən\ *n* : a stew made from whatever ingredients are available

**mul·li·ga·taw·ny** \ˌmə-li-gə-'tò-nē\ *n* : a soup usu. of chicken stock seasoned with curry

**mul·lion** \'məl-yən\ *n* : a vertical strip separating windowpanes

**multi-** *comb form* **1** : many : multiple ⟨*multi*unit⟩ **2** : many times over ⟨*multi*millionaire⟩

**mul·ti·col·ored** \ˌməl-ti-'kə-lərd\ *adj* : having many colors

**mul·ti·cul·tur·al** \ˌməl-tē-'kəl-chə-rəl, -ˌtī-\ *adj* : of, relating to, reflecting, or adapted to diverse cultures ⟨a ∼ society⟩ — **mul·ti·cul·tur·al·ism** \-rə-ˌli-zəm\ *n* — **mul·ti·cul·tur·al·ist** \-rə-list\ *n or adj*

**mul·ti·di·men·sion·al** \ˌməl-ti-də-'men-chə-nəl, -ˌtī-, -dī-\ *adj* : of, relating to, or having many facets or dimensions ⟨a ∼ problem⟩ ⟨∼ space⟩

**mul·ti·eth·nic** \-'eth-nik\ *adj* : including, involving, or made up of people of various ethnic groups

**mul·ti·fac·et·ed** \-'fa-sə-təd\ *adj* : having many facets or aspects ⟨a ∼ concept⟩

**mul·ti·fam·i·ly** \-'fam-lē, -'fa-mə-\ *adj* : designed for use by several families

**mul·ti·far·i·ous** \ˌməl-tə-'fer-ē-əs\ *adj* : having great variety : DIVERSE ⟨∼ activities⟩ — **mul·ti·far·i·ous·ness** *n*

**mul·ti·form** \'məl-ti-ˌfòrm\ *adj* : having many forms or appearances — **mul·ti·for·mi·ty** \ˌməl-ti-'fòr-mə-tē\ *n*

**mul·ti·lat·er·al** \ˌməl-ti-'la-tə-rəl, -ˌtī-, -'la-trəl\ *adj* : having many sides or participants ⟨∼ treaty⟩ — **mul·ti·lat·er·al·ism** \-'la-tə-rə-ˌli-zəm\ *n* — **mul·ti·lat·er·al·ly** *adv*

**mul·ti·lay·ered** \-'lā-ərd, -'lerd\ *or* **mul·ti·lay·er** \-'lā-ər, -'ler\ *adj* : having or involving several distinct layers or levels

**mul·ti·lev·el** \-'le-vəl\ *adj* : having several levels

**mul·ti·lin·gual** \-'liŋ-gwəl\ *adj* : knowing or using several languages — **mul·ti·lin·gual·ism** \-gwə-ˌli-zəm\ *n*

**¹mul·ti·me·dia** \-'mē-dē-ə\ *adj* : using, involving, or encompassing several media ⟨a ∼ advertising campaign⟩

**²multimedia** *n sing or pl* : the technique of using several media (as in art); *also* : something (as software) that uses or facilitates it

**mul·ti·mil·lion·aire** \ˌməl-ti-ˌmil-yə-'nar,

-,tī-, -'mil-yə-,nar\ *n* : a person worth several million dollars

**mul·ti·na·tion·al** \-'na-shə-nəl\ *adj* 1 : of or relating to several nationalities 2 : relating to or involving several nations 3 : having divisions in several countries ⟨a ~ corporation⟩ — **multinational** *n*

**mul·ti·pack** \'məl-tē-,pak\ *n* : a package of several individually packed items sold as a unit

¹**mul·ti·ple** \'məl-tə-pəl\ *adj* 1 : more than one; *also* : MANY ⟨~ achievements⟩ 2 : VARIOUS

²**multiple** *n* : the product of a quantity by an integer ⟨35 is a ~ of 7⟩

**multiple-choice** *adj* : having several answers given from which the correct one is to be chosen ⟨a ~ question⟩

**multiple personality disorder** *n* : a neurosis in which the personality becomes separated into two or more parts each of which controls behavior part of the time

**multiple sclerosis** *n* : a disease marked by patches of hardened tissue in the brain or spinal cord and associated esp. with partial or complete paralysis and muscular tremor

**mul·ti·plex** \'məl-tə-,pleks\ *n* : CINEPLEX

**mul·ti·pli·cand** \,məl-tə-pli-'kand\ *n* : the number that is to be multiplied by another

**mul·ti·pli·ca·tion** \,məl-tə-plə-'kā-shən\ *n* 1 : INCREASE 2 : a short method of finding the result of adding a figure the number of times indicated by another figure

**multiplication sign** *n* 1 : TIMES SIGN 2 : a centered dot indicating multiplication

**mul·ti·plic·i·ty** \,məl-tə-'pli-sə-tē\ *n, pl* **-ties** : a great number or variety

**mul·ti·pli·er** \'məl-tə-,plī-(ə)r\ *n* : one that multiplies; *esp* : a number by which another number is multiplied

**mul·ti·ply** \'məl-tə-,plī\ *vb* **-plied; -ply·ing** 1 : to increase in number (as by breeding) 2 : to find the product of (by multiplication); *also* : to perform multiplication

**mul·ti·pur·pose** \,məl-ti-'pər-pəs, -,tī-\ *adj* : having or serving several purposes

**mul·ti·ra·cial** \-'rā-shəl\ *adj* : composed of, involving, or representing various races

**mul·ti·sense** \-,sens\ *adj* : having several meanings ⟨~ words⟩

**mul·ti·sto·ry** \-,stòr-ē\ *adj* : having several stories ⟨~ buildings⟩

**mul·ti·task·ing** \'məl-tē-,tas-kiŋ, -,tī-\ *n* 1 : the concurrent performance of several jobs by a computer 2 : the performance of multiple tasks at one time — **mul·ti·task** \-,task\ *vb* — **mul·ti·task·er** \-,taskər\ *n*

**mul·ti·tude** \'məl-tə-,tüd, -,tyüd\ *n* : a great number — **mul·ti·tu·di·nous** \,məl-tə-'tü-d³n-əs, -,tyüd-\ *adj*

**mul·ti·unit** \,məl-ti-'yü-nət, -,tī-\ *adj* : having several units

**mul·ti·vi·ta·min** \-'vī-tə-mən\ *adj* : containing several vitamins and esp. all known to be essential to health — **multivitamin** *n*

¹**mum** \'məm\ *adj* : SILENT

²**mum** *chiefly Brit var of* MOM

³**mum** *n* : CHRYSANTHEMUM

**mum·ble** \'məm-bəl\ *vb* **mum·bled; mum·bling** : to speak in a low indistinct manner — **mumble** *n* — **mum·bler** *n* — **mum·bly** *adj*

**mum·ble·ty-peg** \'məm-bəl-tē-,peg\ *also* **mum·ble-the-peg** \'məm-bəl-thə-\ *n* : a game in which the players try to flip a knife from various positions so that the blade will stick into the ground

**mum·bo jum·bo** \,məm-bō-'jam-bō\ *n* 1 : a complicated ritual with elaborate trappings 2 : GIBBERISH, NONSENSE

**mum·mer** \'mə-mər\ *n* 1 : an actor esp. in a pantomime 2 : a person who goes merrymaking in disguise during festivals — **mum·mery** *n*

**mum·my** \'mə-mē\ *n, pl* **mummies** [ME *mummie* powdered parts of a mummified body used as a drug, fr. AF *mumie*, fr. ML *mumia*, fr. Ar *mūmiya* bitumen, mummy, fr. Per *mūm* wax] : a body embalmed for burial in the manner of the ancient Egyptians — **mum·mi·fi·ca·tion** \,mə-mi-fə-'kā-shən\ *n* — **mum·mi·fy** \'mə-mi-,fī\ *vb*

**mumps** \'məmps\ *n sing or pl* [fr. pl. of obs. *mump* grimace] : a virus disease marked by fever and swelling esp. of the salivary glands

**mun** *or* **munic** *abbr* municipal

**munch** \'mənch\ *vb* : to eat with a chewing action; *also* : to snack on

**munch·ies** \'mən-chēz\ *n pl* 1 : hunger pangs 2 : light snack foods

**mun·dane** \,mən-'dān, 'mən-,dān\ *adj* 1 : of or relating to the world 2 : concerned with the practical details of everyday life — **mun·dane·ly** *adv*

**mung bean** \'məŋ-\ *n* : an erect bushy bean widely grown in warm regions for its edible seeds and as the chief source of bean sprouts; *also* : its seed

**mu·nic·i·pal** \myủ-'ni-sə-pəl\ *adj* 1 : of, relating to, or characteristic of a municipality 2 : restricted to one locality — **mu·nic·i·pal·ly** *adv*

**mu·nic·i·pal·i·ty** \myủ-,ni-sə-'pa-lə-tē\ *n, pl* **-ties** : an urban political unit with corporate status and usu. powers of self-government

**mu·nif·i·cent** \myủ-'ni-fə-sənt\ *adj* : liberal in giving : GENEROUS — **mu·nif·i·cence** \-səns\ *n*

**mu·ni·tion** \myủ-'ni-shən\ *n* : ARMAMENT, AMMUNITION

¹**mu·ral** \'myủr-əl\ *adj* 1 : of or relating to a wall 2 : applied to and made part of a wall or ceiling surface

²**mural** *n* : a mural painting — **mu·ral·ist** *n*

¹**mur·der** \'mər-dər\ *n* 1 : the crime of unlawfully killing a person esp. with malice aforethought 2 : something unusually difficult or dangerous

²**murder** *vb* 1 : to commit a murder; *also* : to kill brutally 2 : to put an end to 3 : to spoil by performing poorly ⟨~ a song⟩ — **mur·der·er** *n*

**mur·der·ess** \'mər-də-rəs\ *n* : a woman who murders

**mur·der·ous** \'mər-də-rəs\ *adj* **1** : having or appearing to have the purpose of murder ⟨~ impulses⟩ **2** : marked by or causing murder or bloodshed ⟨~ gunfire⟩ — **mur·der·ous·ly** *adv*

**murk** \'mərk\ *n* : DARKNESS, GLOOM — **murk·i·ly** \'mər-kə-lē\ *adv* — **murk·i·ness** \-kē-nəs\ *n* — **murky** *adj*

**mur·mur** \'mər-mər\ *n* **1** : a muttered complaint **2** : a low indistinct often continuous sound — **murmur** *vb* — **mur·mur·er** *n* — **mur·mur·ous** *adj*

**mus** *abbr* **1** museum **2** music; musical; musician

**mus·ca·tel** \ˌməs-kə-'tel\ *n* : a sweet fortified wine

**¹mus·cle** \'mə-səl\ *n* [ME, fr. L *musculus,* fr. dim. of *mus* mouse] **1** : a body tissue consisting of long cells that contract when stimulated and produce motion; *also* : an organ consisting of this tissue and functioning in moving a body part **2** : STRENGTH, BRAWN ⟨needs ~ for lifting weights⟩ — **mus·cled** \'mə-səld\ *adj* — **mus·cu·lar** \'məs-kyə-lər\ *adj* — **mus·cu·lar·i·ty** \ˌməs-kyə-'lar-ə-tē\ *n*

**²muscle** *vb* **mus·cled; mus·cling** : to force one's way

**mus·cle-bound** \'mə-səl-ˌbaùnd\ *adj* : having some of the muscles abnormally enlarged and lacking in elasticity (as from excessive exercise)

**mus·cle·man** \-ˌman\ *n* : a man with a muscular physique

**muscular dystrophy** *n* : any of a group of diseases characterized by progressive wasting of muscles

**mus·cu·la·ture** \'məs-kyə-lə-ˌchùr\ *n* : the muscles of the body or its parts

**mus·cu·lo·skel·e·tal** \ˌməs-kyə-lō-'ske-lə-t⁹l\ *adj* : of, relating to, or involving both musculature and skeleton

**¹muse** \'myüz\ *vb* **mused; mus·ing** [ME, fr. AF *muser* to gape, idle, muse, fr. OF \**mus* mouth of an animal, fr. ML *musus*] : to become absorbed in thought ⟨mused about what might have been⟩ — **mus·ing·ly** *adv*

**²muse** *n* [fr. *Muse* any of the nine sister goddesses of learning and the arts in Greek myth, fr. ME, fr. MF, fr. L *Musa,* fr. Gk *Mousa*] : a source of inspiration

**mu·se·um** \myù-'zē-əm\ *n* : an institution devoted to the procurement, care, and display of objects of lasting interest or value

**¹mush** \'məsh\ *n* **1** : cornmeal boiled in water **2** : sentimental drivel

**²mush** *vb* : to travel esp. over snow with a sled drawn by dogs

**¹mush·room** \'məsh-ˌrüm, -ˌrùm\ *n* : the fleshy usu. caplike spore-bearing organ of various fungi esp. when edible; *also* : such a fungus

**²mushroom** *vb* **1** : to spread out : EXPAND **2** : to collect with mushrooms **3** : to grow rapidly ⟨the population ~ed⟩

**mushy** \'mə-shē\ *adj* **mush·i·er; -est** **1** : soft like mush **2** : excessively sentimental ⟨a ~ movie⟩

**mu·sic** \'myü-zik\ *n* **1** : the science or art of combining tones into a composition having structure and continuity; *also* : vocal or instrumental sounds having rhythm, melody, or harmony **2** : an agreeable sound

**¹mu·si·cal** \'myü-zi-kəl\ *adj* **1** : of or relating to music or musicians **2** : having the pleasing tonal qualities of music **3** : fond of or gifted in music ⟨a ~ family⟩ — **mu·si·cal·ly** \-k(ə-)lē\ *adv*

**²musical** *n* : a film or theatrical production consisting of musical numbers and dialogue based on a unifying plot

**mu·si·cale** \ˌmyü-zi-'kal\ *n* : a usu. private social gathering featuring music

**mu·si·cian** \myù-'zi-shən\ *n* : a composer, conductor, or performer of music — **mu·si·cian·ly** *adj* — **mu·si·cian·ship** *n*

**mu·si·col·o·gy** \ˌmyü-zi-'kä-lə-jē\ *n* : the study of music as a field of knowledge or research — **mu·si·co·log·i·cal** \-kə-'lä-ji-kəl\ *adj* — **mu·si·col·o·gist** \-'kä-lə-jist\ *n*

**musk** \'məsk\ *n* : a substance obtained esp. from a small Asian deer (**musk deer**) and used as a perfume fixative — **musk·i·ness** \'məs-kē-nəs\ *n* — **musky** *adj*

**musk·eg** \'məs-ˌkeg\ *n* : BOG; *esp* : a mossy bog in northern No. America

**mus·kel·lunge** \'məs-kə-ˌlənj\ *n, pl* **muskellunge** : a large No. American pike that is a valuable sport fish

**mus·ket** \'məs-kət\ *n* [MF *mousquet,* fr. It *moschetto* small artillery piece, kind of small hawk, fr. dim. of *mosca* fly, fr. L *musca*] : a heavy large-caliber muzzle-loading shoulder firearm — **mus·ke·teer** \ˌməs-kə-'tir\ *n*

**mus·ket·ry** \'məs-kə-trē\ *n* **1** : MUSKETS **2** : MUSKETEERS **3** : musket fire

**musk·mel·on** \'məsk-ˌme-lən\ *n* : a small round to oval melon that has usu. a sweet edible green or orange flesh and a musky odor

**musk ox** *n* : a heavyset shaggy-coated wild ox of Greenland and the arctic tundra of northern No. America

**musk·rat** \'məs-ˌkrat\ *n, pl* **muskrat** or **muskrats** : a large No. American aquatic rodent with webbed feet and dark brown fur; *also* : its fur

**Mus·lim** \'məz-ləm\ *n* : an adherent of Islam — **Muslim** *adj*

**mus·lin** \'məz-lən\ *n* : a plain-woven sheer to coarse cotton fabric

**¹muss** \'məs\ *n* : a state of disorder — **muss·i·ly** \'mə-sə-lē\ *adv* — **muss·i·ness** \-sē-nəs\ *n* — **mussy** *adj*

**²muss** *vb* : to make untidy : DISARRANGE

**mus·sel** \'mə-səl\ *n* **1** : a dark edible saltwater bivalve mollusk **2** : any of various freshwater bivalve mollusks of the central U.S. having shells with a pearly lining

**¹must** \'məst\ *vb* — used as an auxiliary esp. to express a command, requirement, obligation, or necessity

**²must** *n* **1** : an imperative duty **2** : an indispensable item

**mus·tache** *also* **mous·tache** \'məs-ˌtash, (ˌ)məs-'tash\ *n* : the hair growing on the human upper lip — **mus·tached** *also* **mous·tached** \-ˌtasht, -'tasht\ *adj*

**mus·tang** \'məs-ˌtaŋ\ n [MexSp *mestengo*, fr. Sp, stray, fr. *mesteño* strayed, fr. *mesta* annual roundup of cattle that disposed of strays, fr. ML (*animalia*) *mixta* mixed animals] : a small hardy naturalized horse of the western plains of America; *also* : BRONC

**mus·tard** \'məs-tərd\ n 1 : a pungent yellow powder of the seeds of an herb related to the cabbage and used as a condiment or in medicine 2 : a plant that yields mustard; *also* : a closely related plant — **mustardy** *adj*

**mustard gas** n : a poison gas used in warfare that has violent irritating and blistering effects

**¹mus·ter** \'məs-tər\ n 1 : an act of assembling (as for military inspection); *also* : critical examination 2 : an assembled group

**²muster** vb [ME *mustren* to show, muster, fr. AF *mustrer, monstrer*, fr. L *monstrare* to show, fr. *monstrum* evil omen, monster] 1 : CONVENE, ASSEMBLE ⟨~ an army⟩; *also* : to call the roll of 2 : ACCUMULATE ⟨~ed support⟩ 4 : to amount to : COMPRISE

**muster out** vb : to discharge from military service

**musty** \'məs-tē\ adj **mus·ti·er; -est** : MOLDY, STALE; *also* : tasting or smelling of damp or decay — **must·i·ly** \-tə-lē\ adv — **must·i·ness** \-tē-nəs\ n

**mu·ta·ble** \'myü-tə-bəl\ adj 1 : prone to change : FICKLE 2 : capable of or liable to mutation : VARIABLE — **mu·ta·bil·i·ty** \ˌmyü-tə-'bi-lə-tē\ n

**mu·tant** \'myü-tᵊnt\ adj : of, relating to, or produced by mutation — **mutant** n

**mu·tate** \'myü-ˌtāt\ vb **mu·tat·ed; mu·tat·ing** : to undergo or cause to undergo mutation — **mu·ta·tive** \'myü-ˌtā-tiv, -tə-tiv\ adj

**mu·ta·tion** \myü-'tā-shən\ n 1 : CHANGE 2 : an inherited physical or biochemical change in genetic material; *also* : the process of producing a mutation 3 : an individual, strain, or trait resulting from mutation — **mu·ta·tion·al** adj

**¹mute** \'myüt\ adj **mut·er; mut·est** 1 : unable to speak 2 : SILENT — **mute·ly** adv — **mute·ness** n

**²mute** n 1 : a person who cannot or does not speak 2 : a device on a musical instrument that reduces, softens, or muffles the tone

**³mute** vb **mut·ed; mut·ing** : to muffle, reduce, or eliminate the sound of

**mu·ti·late** \'myü-tə-ˌlāt\ vb **-lat·ed; -lat·ing** 1 : to cut up or alter radically so as to make imperfect 2 : MAIM, CRIPPLE — **mu·ti·la·tion** \ˌmyü-tə-'lā-shən\ n — **mu·ti·la·tor** \'myü-tə-ˌlā-tər\ n

**mu·ti·ny** \'myü-tə-nē\ n, pl **-nies** : willful refusal to obey constituted authority; *esp* : revolt against a superior officer — **mu·ti·neer** \ˌmyü-tə-'nir\ n — **mu·ti·nous** \'myü-tə-nəs\ adj — **mu·ti·nous·ly** adv — **mutiny** vb

**mutt** \'mət\ n : MONGREL, CUR

**mut·ter** \'mə-tər\ vb 1 : to speak indistinctly or with a low voice and lips partly closed 2 : GRUMBLE — **mutter** n

**mut·ton** \'mə-tᵊn\ n [ME *motoun* mutton, sheep, fr. AF *mutun* ram, sheep, mutton] : the flesh of a mature sheep used for food — **mut·tony** adj

**mut·ton-chops** \'mə-tᵊn-ˌchäps\ n pl : whiskers on the side of the face that are narrow at the temple and broad and round by the lower jaws

**mu·tu·al** \'myü-chə-wəl\ adj 1 : given and received in equal amount ⟨~ trust⟩ 2 : having the same feelings one for the other ⟨~ enemies⟩ 3 : COMMON, JOINT ⟨a ~ friend⟩ — **mu·tu·al·ly** adv

**mutual fund** n : an investment company that invests money of its shareholders in a usu. diversified group of securities of other corporations

**muu·muu** \'mü-ˌmü\ n : a loose dress of Hawaiian origin

**¹muz·zle** \'mə-zəl\ n 1 : the nose and jaws of an animal; *also* : a covering for the muzzle to prevent biting or eating 2 : the mouth of a gun

**²muzzle** vb **muz·zled; muz·zling** 1 : to put a muzzle on 2 : to restrain from expression : GAG ⟨tried to ~ the press⟩

**mV** abbr millivolt

**MV** abbr motor vessel

**MVP** abbr most valuable player

**MW** abbr megawatt

**my** \'mī\ adj 1 : of or relating to me or myself 2 — used interjectionally esp. to express surprise

**my·col·o·gy** \mī-'kä-lə-jē\ n : a branch of biology dealing with fungi — **my·co·log·i·cal** \ˌmī-kə-'lä-ji-kəl\ adj — **my·col·o·gist** \mī-'kä-lə-jist\ n

**my·elo·ma** \ˌmī-ə-'lō-mə\ n, pl **-mas** or **-ma·ta** \-mə-tə\ : a primary tumor of the bone marrow

**my·nah** or **my·na** \'mī-nə\ n : any of several Asian starlings; *esp* : a dark brown slightly crested bird sometimes taught to mimic speech

**my·o·pia** \mī-'ō-pē-ə\ n : a condition in which visual images come to a focus in front of the retina resulting esp. in defective vision of distant objects — **my·o·pic** \-'ō-pik, -'ä-\ adj — **my·o·pi·cal·ly** \-pi-k(ə-)lē\ adv

**¹myr·i·ad** \'mir-ē-əd\ n [Gk *myriad-, myrias*, fr. *myrioi* countless, ten thousand] : an indefinitely large number

**²myriad** adj : consisting of a very great but indefinite number

**myr·mi·don** \'mər-mə-ˌdän\ n : a loyal follower; *esp* : one who executes orders without protest or pity

**myrrh** \'mər\ n : a fragrant aromatic plant gum used in perfumes and formerly for incense

**myr·tle** \'mər-tᵊl\ n : an evergreen shrub of southern Europe with shiny leaves, fragrant flowers, and black berries; *also* : PERIWINKLE

**my·self** \mī-'self, mə-\ pron : I, ME — used reflexively, for emphasis, or in absolute constructions ⟨I hurt ~⟩ ⟨I ~ did it⟩ ⟨~ busy, I sent him instead⟩

**mys·tery** \'mis-tə-rē\ n, pl **-ter·ies** 1 : a

religious truth known by revelation alone **2** : something not understood or beyond understanding **3** : enigmatic quality or character **4** : a work of fiction dealing with the solution of a mysterious crime — **mys·te·ri·ous** \mis-'tir-ē-əs\ *adj* — **mys·te·ri·ous·ly** *adv* — **mys·te·ri·ous·ness** *n*

**¹mys·tic** \'mis-tik\ *adj* **1** : of or relating to mystics or mysticism **2** : MYSTERIOUS; *also* : MYSTIFYING

**²mystic** *n* : a person who follows, advocates, or experiences mysticism

**mys·ti·cal** \'mis-ti-kəl\ *adj* **1** : SPIRITUAL, SYMBOLIC **2** : of or relating to an intimate knowledge of or direct communion with God (as through contemplation or visions)

**mys·ti·cism** \'mis-tə-ˌsi-zəm\ *n* : the belief that direct knowledge of God or ultimate reality is attainable through immediate intuition or insight

**mys·ti·fy** \'mis-tə-ˌfī\ *vb* **-fied; -fy·ing 1** : to perplex the mind of **2** : to make mysterious — **mys·ti·fi·ca·tion** \ˌmis-tə-fə-'kā-shən\ *n*

**mys·tique** \mi-'stēk\ *n* [F] **1** : an air or attitude of mystery and reverence developing around something or someone **2** : the special esoteric skill essential in a calling or activity

**myth** \'mith\ *n* **1** : a usu. legendary narrative that presents part of the beliefs of a people or explains a practice or natural phenomenon **2** : an imaginary or unverifiable person or thing — **myth·i·cal** \'mi-thi-kəl\ *or* **myth·ic** \-thik\ *adj*

**my·thol·o·gy** \mi-'thä-lə-jē\ *n, pl* **-gies** : a body of myths and esp. of those dealing with the gods and heroes of a people — **myth·o·log·i·cal** \ˌmi-thə-'lä-ji-kəl\ *adj* — **my·thol·o·gist** \mi-'thä-lə-jist\ *n* — **my·thol·o·gize** \-ˌjīz\ *vb*

**n** \'en\ *n, pl* **n's** *or* **ns** \'enz\ *often cap* **1** : the 14th letter of the English alphabet **2** : an unspecified quantity

**²n** *abbr, often cap* **1** net **2** neuter **3** noon **4** normal **5** north; northern **6** note **7** noun **8** number

**N** *symbol* nitrogen

**-n** — see -EN

**Na** *symbol* [NL *natrium*] sodium

**NA** *abbr* **1** no account **2** North America **3** not applicable **4** not available

**NAACP** \ˌen-ˌdə-bəl-ˌā-ˌsē-'pē, ˌen-ˌā-ˌā-ˌsē-\ *abbr* National Association for the Advancement of Colored People

**nab** \'nab\ *vb* **nabbed; nab·bing** : SEIZE; *esp* : ARREST

**NAB** *abbr* New American Bible

**na·bob** \'nā-ˌbäb\ *n* [Hindi *navāb* & Urdu *nawāb*, provincial governor (in the Mogul empire), fr. Ar *nuwwāb*, pl. of *nā'ib* governor] : a person of great wealth or prominence

**na·celle** \nə-'sel\ *n* : an enclosure (as for an engine) on an aircraft

**na·cho** \'nä-chō\ *n, pl* **nachos** [AmerSp] : a tortilla chip topped with melted cheese and often additional savory toppings

**na·cre** \'nā-kər\ *n* : MOTHER-OF-PEARL — **na·cre·ous** \'nā-krē-əs\ *adj*

**na·dir** \'nā-ˌdir, -dər\ *n* [ME, fr. MF, fr. Ar *naḏhīr* opposite] **1** : the point of the celestial sphere that is directly opposite the zenith and directly beneath the observer **2** : the lowest point

**¹nag** \'nag\ *n* : HORSE; *esp* : an old or decrepit horse

**²nag** *vb* **nagged; nag·ging 1** : to find fault incessantly : COMPLAIN **2** : to irritate by constant scolding or urging **3** : to be a continuing source of annoyance ⟨a *nagging* backache⟩

**³nag** *n* : one who nags habitually

**Nah** *abbr* Nahum

**Na·huatl** \'nä-ˌwä-tᵊl\ *n* : a group of American Indian languages of central and southern Mexico

**Na·hum** \'nä-həm, -əm\ *n* — see BIBLE table

**NAIA** *abbr* National Association of Intercollegiate Athletes

**na·iad** \'nā-əd, 'nī-, -ˌad\ *n, pl* **naiads** *or* **na·ia·des** \-ə-ˌdēz\ **1** : one of the nymphs in ancient mythology living in lakes, rivers, springs, and fountains **2** : an aquatic young of some insects (as a dragonfly)

**¹na·if** *or* **na·if** \nä-'ēf\ *adj* : NAIVE

**²naif** *or* **naif** *n* : a naive person

**nail** \'nāl\ *n* **1** : a horny sheath protecting the end of each finger and toe in humans and related primates **2** : a slender pointed fastener with a head designed to be pounded in

**²nail** *vb* : to fasten with or as if with a nail — **nail·er** *n*

**nail down** *vb* : to settle or establish clearly and unmistakably ⟨*nailed down* the victory⟩

**nain·sook** \'nān-ˌsuk\ *n* : a soft lightweight muslin

**nai·ra** \'nī-rə\ *n* — see MONEY table

**na·ive** *or* **na·ïve** \nä-'ēv\ *adj* **na·iv·er; -est** [F *naïve*, fem. of *naïf*, fr. OF, inborn, natural, fr. L *nativus* native] **1** : marked by unaffected simplicity : ARTLESS, INGENUOUS **2** : CREDULOUS ♦ *Synonyms* NATURAL, INNOCENT, SIMPLE, UNAFFECTED, UNSOPHISTICATED, UNSTUDIED — **na·ive·ly** *adv* — **na·ive·ness** *n*

**na·ive·té** *also* **na·ive·te** *or* **na·ïve·té** \ˌnä-ˌē-və-'tā, nä-'ē-və-ˌtā\ *n* **1** : a naive remark or action **2** : the quality or state of being naive

**na·ive·ty** *also* **na·ïve·ty** \nä-'ē-və-tē\ *n, pl* **-ties** : NAÏVETÉ

**na·ked** \'nā-kəd\ *adj* **1** : having no clothes on : NUDE **2** : UNSHEATHED ⟨a ~ sword⟩ **3** : lacking a usual or natural covering (as of foliage or feathers) **4** : PLAIN, UNADORNED ⟨the ~ truth⟩ **5** : not aided by artificial means ⟨seen by the ~ eye⟩ — **na·ked·ly** *adv* — **na·ked·ness** *n*

**¹nak·fa** \'näk-ˌfä\ *n, pl* **nakfa** — see MONEY table

**nam·by–pam·by** \ˌnam-bē-'pam-bē\ *adj* **1** : INSIPID **2** : WEAK, INDECISIVE
♦ **Synonyms** BLAND, FLAT, INANE, JEJUNE, VAPID, WISHY-WASHY

**¹name** \'nām\ *n* **1** : a word or words by which a person or thing is known **2** : a disparaging epithet ⟨call him ~*s*⟩ **3** : REPUTATION; *esp* : distinguished reputation ⟨made a ~ for herself⟩ **4** : FAMILY, CLAN ⟨was a disgrace to their ~⟩ **5** : appearance as opposed to reality ⟨a friend in ~ only⟩

**²name** *vb* **named; nam·ing** **1** : to give a name to : CALL **2** : to mention or identify by name **3** : NOMINATE, APPOINT **4** : to decide on : CHOOSE ⟨*named* the wedding date⟩ **5** : to mention explicitly : SPECIFY ⟨~ a price⟩ — **name·able** *adj*

**³name** *adj* **1** : of, relating to, or bearing a name ⟨~ tag⟩ **2** : having an established reputation ⟨~ brands⟩

**name day** *n* : the church feast day of the saint after whom one is named

**name·less** \'nām-ləs\ *adj* **1** : having no name **2** : not marked with a name ⟨a ~ grave⟩ **3** : not known by name ⟨a ~ hero⟩ **4** : too distressing to be described ⟨~ fears⟩ — **name·less·ly** *adv*

**name·ly** \-lē\ *adv* : that is to say : AS ⟨the cat family, ~, lions, tigers, and similar animals⟩

**name·plate** \-ˌplāt\ *n* : a plate or plaque bearing a name (as of a resident)

**name·sake** \-ˌsāk\ *n* : one that has the same name as another; *esp* : one named after another

**nan·keen** \nan-'kēn\ *n* : a durable brownish yellow cotton fabric orig. woven by hand in China

**nan·ny goat** \'na-nē-\ *n* : a female domestic goat

**nano·me·ter** \'na-nə-ˌmē-tər\ *n* : one billionth of a meter

**nano·scale** \-ˌskāl\ *adj* : having dimensions measured in nanometers

**nano·sec·ond** \-ˌse-kənd\ *n* : one billionth of a second

**nano·tech·nol·o·gy** \ˌna-nō-tek-'nä-lə-jē\ *n* : the manipulation of materials on an atomic or molecular scale

**nano·tube** \'na-nō-ˌtüb\ *n* : a microscopic tube (as of carbon) whose diameter is measured in nanometers

**¹nap** \'nap\ *vb* **napped; nap·ping** **1** : to sleep briefly esp. during the day : DOZE **2** : to be off guard ⟨was caught *napping*⟩

**²nap** *n* : a short sleep esp. during the day

**³nap** *n* : a soft downy fibrous surface (as on yarn and cloth) — **nap·less** *adj* — **napped** \'napt\ *adj*

**na·palm** \'nā-ˌpälm, -ˌpäm\ *n* [*naphthalene + palm*itate, salt of a fatty acid] **1** : a thickener used in jelling gasoline (as for incendiary bombs) **2** : fuel jelled with napalm

**nape** \'nāp, 'nap\ *n* : the back of the neck

**na·pery** \'nā-pə-rē\ *n* : household linen esp. for the table

**naph·tha** \'naf-thə, 'nap-\ *n* : any of various liquid hydrocarbon mixtures used chiefly as solvents

**naph·tha·lene** \-lēn\ *n* : a crystalline substance used esp. in organic synthesis and as a moth repellent

**nap·kin** \'nap-kən\ *n* **1** : a piece of material (as cloth) used at table to wipe the lips or fingers and protect the clothes **2** : a small cloth or towel

**na·po·leon** \nə-'pōl-yən, -'pō-lē-ən\ *n* : an oblong pastry with a filling of cream, custard, or jelly

**Na·po·le·on·ic** \nə-ˌpō-lē-'ä-nik\ *adj* : of, relating to, or characteristic of Napoleon I or his family

**narc** *also* **nark** \'närk\ *n, slang* : a person (as a government agent) who investigates narcotics violations

**nar·cis·sism** \'när-sə-ˌsi-zəm\ *n* [G *Narzissmus*, fr. *Narziss* Narcissus, beautiful youth of Greek mythology who fell in love with his own image] **1** : undue dwelling on one's own self or attainments **2** : love of or sexual desire for one's own body — **nar·cis·sist** \-sist\ *n or adj* — **nar·cis·sis·tic** \ˌnär-sə-'sis-tik\ *adj*

**nar·cis·sus** \när-'si-səs\ *n, pl* **nar·cis·si** \-ˌsī, -ˌsē\ *or* **nar·cis·sus·es** *or* **narcissus** : DAFFODIL; *esp* : one with short-tubed flowers usu. borne separately

**nar·co·lep·sy** \'när-kə-ˌlep-sē\ *n, pl* **-sies** : a condition characterized by brief attacks of deep sleep — **nar·co·lep·tic** \ˌnär-kə-'lep-tik\ *adj or n*

**nar·co·sis** \när-'kō-səs\ *n, pl* **-co·ses** \-ˌsēz\ : a state of stupor, unconsciousness, or arrested activity produced by the influence of chemicals (as narcotics)

**nar·co·ter·ror·ism** \ˌnär-kō-'ter-ər-ˌi-zəm\ *n* : terrorism financed by profits from illegal drug trafficking

**nar·cot·ic** \när-'kä-tik\ *n* [ME *narkotik*, fr. MF *narcotique*, fr. *narcotique*, adj., fr. ML *narcoticus*, fr. Gk *narkōtikos*, fr. *narkoun* to benumb, fr. *narkē* numbness] **1** : a drug (as opium) that dulls the senses, relieves pain, and induces sleep **2** : an illegal drug (as marijuana or LSD) — **narcotic** *adj*

**nar·co·tize** \'när-kə-ˌtīz\ *vb* **-tized; -tiz·ing** **1** : to treat with or subject to a narcotic; *also* : to put into a state of narcosis **2** : to soothe to unconsciousness or unawareness

**nard** \'närd\ *n* : a fragrant ointment of the ancients

**na·res** \'ner-(ˌ)ēz\ *n pl* [L] : the pair of openings of the nose

**Nar·ra·gan·sett** \ˌna-rə-'gan-sət\ *n, pl* **-sett** *or* **-setts** **1** : a member of an American Indian people of Rhode Island **2** : the Algonquian language of the Narragansett people

**nar·rate** \'ner-ˌāt\ *vb* **nar·rat·ed; nar·rat·ing** : to recite the details of (as a story)

: RELATE, TELL — **nar·ra·tion** \na-'rā-shən\ n — **nar·ra·tor** \'ner-ˌā-tər\ n

**nar·ra·tive** \'ner-ə-tiv\ n **1** : something that is narrated : STORY **2** : the art or practice of narrating

**¹nar·row** \'ner-ō\ adj **1** : of slender or less than standard width **2** : limited in size or scope : RESTRICTED **3** : not liberal in views : PREJUDICED **4** : interpreted or interpreting strictly : CLOSE ⟨won by a ~ margin⟩; also : barely successful ⟨a ~ escape⟩ — **nar·row·ly** adv — **nar·row·ness** n

**²narrow** vb : to lessen in width or extent

**³narrow** n : a narrow passage : STRAIT — usu. used in pl.

**nar·row-mind·ed** \ˌner-ō-'mīn-dəd\ adj : not liberal or broad-minded ♦ **Synonyms** ILLIBERAL, BIGOTED, HIDE-BOUND, INTOLERANT

**nar·whal** \'när-ˌhwäl, 'när-wəl\ n : an arctic sea mammal about 20 feet (6 meters) long that is related to the dolphins and in the male has a long twisted ivory tusk

**NAS** abbr naval air station

**NASA** \'na-sə\ abbr National Aeronautics and Space Administration

**¹na·sal** \'nā-zəl\ n **1** : a nasal part **2** : a nasal consonant or vowel

**²nasal** adj **1** : of or relating to the nose **2** : uttered through the nose — **na·sal·ly** adv

**na·sal·ize** \'nā-zə-ˌlīz\ vb **-ized; -iz·ing** : to make nasal or pronounce as a nasal sound — **na·sal·i·za·tion** \ˌnā-zə-lə-'zā-shən\ n

**na·scent** \'na-sᵊnt, 'nā-\ adj : coming into existence : beginning to grow or develop — **na·scence** \-sᵊns\ n

**nas·tur·tium** \nə-'stər-shəm, na-\ n : either of two widely cultivated watery-stemmed herbs with showy spurred flowers and pungent edible seeds

**nas·ty** \'nas-tē\ adj **nas·ti·er; -est 1** : FILTHY **2** : INDECENT, OBSCENE **3** : HARMFUL, DANGEROUS ⟨took a ~ fall⟩ **4** : DISAGREEABLE ⟨~ weather⟩ **5** : MEAN, ILL-NATURED ⟨a ~ temper⟩ **6** : DIFFICULT, VEXATIOUS ⟨a ~ problem⟩ **7** : UNFAIR, DIRTY ⟨a ~ trick⟩ — **nas·ti·ly** \'nas-tə-lē\ adv — **nas·ti·ness** \-tē-nəs\ n

**nat** abbr **1** national **2** native **3** natural

**na·tal** \'nā-tᵊl\ adj **1** : NATIVE **2** : of, relating to, or present at birth

**na·ta·to·ri·um** \ˌnā-tə-'tȯr-ē-əm, ˌna-\ n : a swimming pool esp. indoors

**na·tion** \'nā-shən\ n [ME nacioun, fr. AF nacïun fr. L nation-, natio birth, race, nation, fr. nasci to be born] **1** : NATIONALITY 5; also : a politically organized nationality **2** : a community of people composed of one or more nationalities with its own territory and government **3** : the territory of a nation **4** : a federation of tribes (as of American Indians) — **na·tion·hood** n

**¹na·tion·al** \'na-shə-nəl\ adj **1** : of or relating to a nation **2** : comprising or characteristic of a nationality **3** : FEDERAL 3 — **na·tion·al·ly** adv

**²national** n : one who owes allegiance to

a nation **2** : a competition that is national in scope — usu. used in pl.

**national guard** n **1** : a military force serving as a national constabulary and defense force **2** cap N & G : a militia force recruited by each state of the U.S., equipped by the federal government, and jointly maintained subject to the call of either — **national guardsman** n, often cap

**na·tion·al·ise** chiefly Brit var of NATIONALIZE

**na·tion·al·ism** \'na-shə-nə-ˌli-zəm\ n : devotion to national interests, unity, and independence

**na·tion·al·ist** \-list\ n **1** : an advocate of or believer in nationalism **2** : a member of a political party or group advocating national independence or strong national government — **nationalist** adj — **na·tion·al·is·tic** \ˌna-shə-nə-'lis-tik\ adj

**na·tion·al·i·ty** \ˌna-shə-'na-lə-tē\ n, pl **-ties 1** : national character **2** : a legal relationship involving allegiance of an individual and protection on the part of the state **3** : membership in a particular nation **4** : political independence or existence as a separate nation **5** : a people having a common origin, tradition, and language and capable of forming a state **6** : an ethnic group within a larger unit (as a nation)

**na·tion·al·ize** \'na-shə-nə-ˌlīz\ vb **-ized; -iz·ing 1** : to make national : make a nation of **2** : to remove from private ownership and place under government control — **na·tion·al·i·za·tion** \ˌna-shə-nə-lə-'zā-shən\ n

**national monument** n : a place of historic, scenic, or scientific interest set aside for preservation usu. by presidential proclamation

**national park** n : an area of special scenic, historical, or scientific importance set aside and maintained by a national government esp. for recreation or study

**national seashore** n : a recreational area adjacent to a seacoast and maintained by the federal government

**na·tion·wide** \ˌnā-shən-'wīd\ adj : extending throughout a nation

**¹na·tive** \'nā-tiv\ adj **1** : INBORN, NATURAL ⟨~ talents⟩ **2** : born in a particular place or country **3** : belonging to a person because of the place or circumstances of birth ⟨her ~ language⟩ **4** : grown, produced, or originating in a particular place : INDIGENOUS **5** cap : NATIVE AMERICAN ♦ **Synonyms** ABORIGINAL, AUTOCHTHONOUS, ENDEMIC

**²native** n : one that is native; esp : a person who belongs to a particular country by birth

**Native American** n : a member of any of the aboriginal peoples of No. America and esp. the U.S.

**na·tiv·ism** \'nā-ti-ˌvi-zəm\ n **1** : a policy of favoring native inhabitants over immigrants **2** : the revival or perpetuation of a native culture esp. in opposition to acculturation

**na·tiv·i·ty** \nə-'ti-və-tē, nā-\ n, pl **-ties 1**

: the process or circumstances of being born : BIRTH  **2** *cap* : the birth of Christ

**natl** *abbr* national

**NATO** \'nā-(,)tō\ *abbr* North Atlantic Treaty Organization

**nat·ty** \'na-tē\ *adj* **nat·ti·er; -est** : trimly neat and tidy : SMART — **nat·ti·ly** \-tə-lē\ *adv* — **nat·ti·ness** \-tē-nəs\ *n*

**¹nat·u·ral** \'na-chə-rəl\ *adj* **1** : determined by nature : INBORN, INNATE ⟨∼ ability⟩ **2** : BORN ⟨a ∼ fool⟩ **3** : ILLEGITIMATE ⟨a ∼ child⟩ **4** : HUMAN **5** : of or relating to nature **6** : not artificial **7** : being simple and sincere : not affected **8** : LIFELIKE **9** : being neither sharp nor flat ♦ *Synonyms* INGENUOUS, NAIVE, UNSOPHISTICATED, ARTLESS, GUILELESS — **nat·u·ral·ness** *n*

**²natural** *n* **1** : IDIOT **2** : a character ♮ placed on a line or space of the musical staff to nullify the effect of a preceding sharp or flat **3** : one obviously suitable for a purpose **4** : AFRO

**natural childbirth** *n* : a system of managing childbirth in which the mother prepares to remain conscious and assist in delivery with little or no use of drugs

**natural gas** *n* : a combustible gaseous mixture of hydrocarbons coming from the earth's crust and used chiefly as a fuel and raw material

**natural history** *n* **1** : a treatise on some aspect of nature **2** : the study of natural objects esp. from an amateur or popular point of view

**nat·u·ral·ise** *Brit var of* NATURALIZE

**nat·u·ral·ism** \'na-chə-rə-ˌli-zəm\ *n* **1** : action or thought based only on natural desires and instincts **2** : a doctrine that denies a supernatural explanation of the origin or development of the universe and holds that scientific laws account for all of nature **3** : realism in art and literature — **nat·u·ral·is·tic** \ˌna-chə-rə-'lis-tik\ *adj*

**nat·u·ral·ist** \-list\ *n* **1** : one that advocates or practices naturalism **2** : a student of animals or plants esp. in the field

**nat·u·ral·ize** \-ˌlīz\ *vb* **-ized; -iz·ing 1** : to confer the rights of a citizen on **2** : to become or cause to become established as if native ⟨∼ new forage crops⟩ — **nat·u·ral·i·za·tion** \ˌna-chə-rə-lə-'zā-shən\ *n*

**nat·u·ral·ly** \'na-chə-rə-lē, 'nach-rə-\ *adv* **1** : by nature **2** : as might be expected by ability : by natural character or ability **3** : without artificial aid; *also* : without affectation **4** : REALISTICALLY

**natural science** *n* : a science (as physics, chemistry, or biology) that deals with matter, energy, and their interrelations and transformations or with objectively measurable phenomena — **natural scientist** *n*

**natural selection** *n* : the natural process that results in the survival of individuals or groups best adjusted to their environment

**na·ture** \'nā-chər\ *n* [ME, fr. MF, fr. L *natura*, fr. *natus*, pp. of *nasci* to be born] **1** : the inherent quality or basic constitution of a person or thing; *also* : DISPOSI-

TION, TEMPERAMENT  **2** : KIND, SORT ⟨letters of a personal ∼⟩ **3** : the physical universe **4** : one's natural instincts or way of life ⟨quirks of human ∼⟩; *also* : primitive state ⟨a return to ∼⟩ **5** : natural scenery or environment ⟨beauties of ∼⟩

**¹naught** *also* **nought** \'nȯt, 'nät\ *pron* : NOTHING ⟨efforts came to ∼⟩

**²naught** *also* **nought** *n* **1** : NOTHINGNESS, NONEXISTENCE **2** : the arithmetical symbol 0 : ZERO

**naugh·ty** \'nȯ-tē, 'nä-\ *adj* **naugh·ti·er; -est 1** : guilty of disobedience or misbehavior **2** : lacking in taste or propriety ⟨∼ jokes⟩ — **naugh·ti·ly** \-tə-lē\ *adv* — **naugh·ti·ness** \-tē-nəs\ *n*

**nau·sea** \'nȯ-zē-ə, -sē-; 'nȯ-zhə, -shə\ *n* [L, seasickness, nausea, fr. Gk *nautia, nausia,* fr. *nautēs* sailor] **1** : sickness of the stomach with a desire to vomit **2** : extreme disgust

**nau·se·ate** \'nȯ-zē-ˌāt, -sē-, -zhē-, -shē-\ *vb* **-at·ed; -at·ing** : to affect or become affected with nausea — **nau·se·at·ing·ly** *adv*

**nau·seous** \'nȯ-shəs, -zē-əs\ *adj* **1** : causing nausea or disgust **2** : affected with nausea or disgust

**naut** *abbr* nautical

**nau·ti·cal** \'nȯ-ti-kəl\ *adj* : of or relating to sailors, navigation, or ships ⟨∼ terms⟩ — **nau·ti·cal·ly** \-k(ə-)lē\ *adv*

**nautical mile** *n* : a unit of distance equal to about 6080 feet (1852 meters)

**nau·ti·lus** \'nȯ-tə-ləs\ *n, pl* **-lus·es** *or* **-li** \ˌlī, -ˌlē\ : any of a genus of sea mollusks related to the octopuses but having a spiral chambered shell

**nav** *abbr* **1** naval **2** navigable; navigation

**Na·va·jo** *also* **Na·va·ho** \'na-və-ˌhō, 'nä-\ *n, pl* **-jo** *or* **-jos** *also* **-ho** *or* **-hos** : a member of an American Indian people of northern New Mexico and Arizona; *also* : their language

**na·val** \'nā-vəl\ *adj* : of, relating to, or possessing a navy ⟨a ∼ power⟩

**naval stores** *n pl* : products (as pitch, turpentine, or rosin) obtained from resinous conifers (as pines)

**nave** \'nāv\ *n* [ML *navis,* fr. L, ship] : the central part of a church running lengthwise

**na·vel** \'nā-vəl\ *n* : a depression in the middle of the abdomen that marks the point of attachment of fetus and mother

**navel–gaz·ing** \'nā-vəl-'gā-ziŋ\ *n* : useless or excessive self-contemplation

**navel orange** *n* : a seedless orange having a pit at the blossom end where the fruit encloses a small secondary fruit

**nav·i·ga·ble** \'na-vi-gə-bəl\ *adj* **1** : capable of being navigated ⟨a ∼ river⟩ **2** : capable of being steered — **nav·i·ga·bil·i·ty** \ˌna-vi-gə-'bi-lə-tē\ *n*

**nav·i·gate** \'na-və-ˌgāt\ *vb* **-gat·ed; -gat·ing 1** : to sail on or through ⟨∼ the Atlantic Ocean⟩ **2** : to steer or direct the course of a ship or aircraft **3** : MOVE; *esp* : WALK ⟨could hardly ∼⟩ — **nav·i·ga·tion** \ˌna-və-'gā-shən\ *n* — **nav·i·ga·tor** \'na-və-ˌgā-tər\ *n*

**na·vy** \\'nā-vē\ *n, pl* **navies** **1** : FLEET; *also* : the warships belonging to a nation **2** *often cap* : a nation's organization for naval warfare

**navy yard** *n* : a yard where naval vessels are built or repaired

**¹nay** \\'nā\ *adv* : NO

**²nay** *n* : a negative vote; *also* : a person casting such a vote

**³nay** *conj* : not merely this but also : not only so but ⟨he was happy, ∼, ecstatic⟩

**nay·say·er** \\'nā-,sā-ər\ *n* : one who denies, refuses, or opposes something

**Na·zi** \\'nät-sē, 'nat-\ *n* [G, fr. *Nationalsozialist*, lit., national socialist] : a member of a German fascist party controlling Germany from 1933 to 1945 under Adolf Hitler — **Nazi** *adj* — **Na·zism** \\'nät-,si-zəm, 'nat-\ *also* **Na·zi·ism** \-sē-,i-zəm\ *n*

**Nb** *symbol* niobium

**NB** *abbr* **1** New Brunswick **2** nota bene

**NBA** *abbr* **1** National Basketball Association **2** National Boxing Association

**NBC** *abbr* National Broadcasting Company

**NBS** *abbr* National Bureau of Standards

**NC** *abbr* **1** no charge **2** North Carolina

**NCAA** *abbr* National Collegiate Athletic Association

**NCO** \\,en-,sē-'ō\ *n* : NONCOMMISSIONED OFFICER

**nd** *abbr* no date

**Nd** *symbol* neodymium

**ND** *abbr* North Dakota

**N Dak** *abbr* North Dakota

**Ne** *symbol* neon

**NE** *abbr* **1** Nebraska **2** New England **3** northeast

**Ne·an·der·thal** \nē-'an-dər-,thôl, nā-'än-dər-,täl\ *n* **1** *or* **Ne·an·der·tal** \-,täl\ : an extinct Old World hominid that lived from about 30,000 to 200,000 years ago **2** : a person who resembles or suggests a caveman — **Neanderthal** *or* **Neandertal** *adj*

**neap tide** \\'nep-\ *n* : a tide of minimum range occurring at the first and third quarters of the moon

**¹near** \\'nir\ *adv* **1** : at, within, or to a short distance or time **2** : ALMOST ⟨was ∼ dead⟩

**²near** *prep* : close to

**³near** *adj* **1** : closely related or associated; *also* : INTIMATE **2** : not far away; *also* : being the closer or left-hand member of a pair ⟨the ∼ side of the lake⟩ **3** : barely avoided ⟨a ∼ accident⟩ **4** : DIRECT, SHORT ⟨by the ∼*est* route⟩ **5** : STINGY **6** : not real but very like ⟨∼ silk⟩ — **near·ly** *adv* — **near·ness** *n*

**⁴near** *vb* : APPROACH

**near beer** *n* : any of various malt liquors low in alcohol

**near·by** \nir-'bī, 'nir-,bī\ *adv or adj* : close at hand

**near·sight·ed** \\'nir-'sī-təd\ *adj* : able to see near things more clearly than distant ones : MYOPIC — **near·sight·ed·ly** *adv* — **near·sight·ed·ness** *n*

**neat** \\'nēt\ *adj* [MF *net*, fr. L *nitidus* bright, neat, fr. *nitēre* to shine] **1** : being orderly and clean **2** : not mixed or di-

luted ⟨∼ brandy⟩ **3** : marked by tasteful simplicity **4** : PRECISE, SYSTEMATIC **5** : SKILLFUL, ADROIT **6** : FINE, ADMIRABLE ♦ *Synonyms* SHIPSHAPE, TIDY, TRIG, TRIM — **neat** *adv* — **neat·ly** *adv* — **neat·ness** *n*

**neath** \\'nēth\ *prep, dial* : BENEATH

**neat·nik** \\'nēt-nik\ *n* : a person who is compulsively neat

**neb** \\'neb\ *n* **1** : the beak of a bird or tortoise; *also* : NOSE, SNOUT **2** : NIB

**Neb** *or* **Nebr** *abbr* Nebraska

**NEB** *abbr* New English Bible

**neb·u·la** \\'ne-byə-lə\ *n, pl* **-lae** \-,lē, -,lī\ *also* **-las** [NL, fr. L, mist, cloud] **1** : any of numerous clouds of gas or dust in interstellar space **2** : GALAXY — **neb·u·lar** \-lər\ *adj*

**neb·u·liz·er** \\'ne-byə-,lī-zər\ *n* : ATOMIZER

**neb·u·lous** \\'ne-byə-ləs\ *adj* **1** : of or relating to a nebula **2** : HAZY, INDISTINCT

**¹nec·es·sary** \\'ne-sə-,ser-ē\ *adj* **1** : INEVITABLE, INESCAPABLE; *also* : CERTAIN **2** : PREDETERMINED **3** : COMPULSORY **4** : positively needed : INDISPENSABLE ⟨∼ supplies⟩ ♦ *Synonyms* IMPERATIVE, NECESSITOUS, ESSENTIAL — **nec·es·sar·i·ly** \,ne-sə-'ser-ə-lē\ *adv*

**²necessary** *n, pl* **-sar·ies** : an indispensable item

**ne·ces·si·tate** \ni-'se-sə-,tāt\ *vb* **-tat·ed; -tat·ing** : to make necessary

**ne·ces·si·tous** \ni-'se-sə-təs\ *adj* **1** : NEEDY, IMPOVERISHED **2** : URGENT **3** : NECESSARY ⟨∼ bargaining⟩

**ne·ces·si·ty** \ni-'se-sə-tē\ *n, pl* **-ties** **1** : conditions that cannot be changed **2** : WANT, POVERTY **3** : something that is necessary ⟨water is a ∼⟩ **4** : very great need

**¹neck** \\'nek\ *n* **1** : the part of the body connecting the head and the trunk **2** : the part of a garment covering or near to the neck **3** : a relatively narrow part suggestive of a neck ⟨∼ of a bottle⟩ ⟨∼ of land⟩ **4** : a narrow margin esp. of victory ⟨won by a ∼⟩ — **necked** \\'nekt\ *adj*

**²neck** *vb* : to kiss and caress amorously

**neck and neck** *adv or adj* : very close (as in a race)

**neck·er·chief** \\'ne-kər-chəf, -,chēf\ *n, pl* **-chiefs** \-chəfs, -,chēfs\ *also* **-chieves** \-,chēvz\ : a square of cloth worn folded about the neck like a scarf

**neck·lace** \\'ne-kləs\ *n* : an ornament worn around the neck

**neck·line** \\'nek-,līn\ *n* : the outline of the neck opening of a garment

**neck·tie** \-,tī\ *n* : a strip of cloth worn around the neck and tied in front

**ne·crol·o·gy** \nə-'krä-lə-jē\ *n, pl* **-gies** **1** : OBITUARY **2** : a list of the recently dead

**nec·ro·man·cy** \\'ne-krə-,man-sē\ *n* **1** : the art or practice of conjuring up the spirits of the dead for purposes of magically revealing the future **2** : MAGIC, SORCERY — **nec·ro·man·cer** \-sər\ *n*

**ne·crop·o·lis** \nə-'krä-pə-ləs, ne-\ *n, pl* **-lis·es** *or* **-les** \-,lēz\ *or* **-leis** \-,lās\ *or* **-li** \-,lī, -,lē\ [LL, fr. Gk *nekropolis*, fr. *nekros* dead body + *polis* city] : CEMETERY; *esp* : a large elaborate cemetery of an ancient city

**nec·rop·sy** \'ne-ˌkräp-sē\ *n, pl* **-sies** : AUTOPSY; *esp* : an autopsy performed on an animal

**ne·cro·sis** \nə-'krō-səs, ne-\ *n, pl* **ne·cro·ses** \-ˌsēz\ : usu. local death of body tissue — **ne·crot·ic** \-'krä-tik\ *adj*

**nec·tar** \'nek-tər\ *n* **1** : the drink of the Greek and Roman gods; *also* : any delicious drink **2** : a sweet plant secretion that is the raw material of honey

**nec·tar·ine** \ˌnek-tə-'rēn\ *n* : a smooth-skinned peach

**née** *or* **nee** \'nā\ *adj* [F, lit., born] — used to identify a woman by her maiden family name

**¹need** \'nēd\ *n* **1** : OBLIGATION ⟨no ~ to hurry⟩ **2** : a lack of something requisite, desirable, or useful **3** : a condition requiring supply or relief ⟨when the ~ arises⟩ **4** : POVERTY ♦ **Synonyms** NECESSITY, EXIGENCY

**²need** *vb* **1** : to be in want **2** : to have cause or occasion for : REQUIRE ⟨he ~s advice⟩ **3** : to be under obligation or necessity ⟨we ~ to know the truth⟩

**need·ful** \'nēd-fəl\ *adj* : NECESSARY, REQUISITE ⟨bought only what was ~⟩

**¹nee·dle** \'nē-dᵊl\ *n* **1** : a slender pointed usu. steel implement used in sewing **2** : a slender rod (as for knitting, controlling a small opening, or transmitting vibrations to or from a recording) ⟨a phonograph ~⟩ **3** : a slender hollow instrument by which material is introduced into or withdrawn from the body **4** : a needle indicator on a dial **5** : a needle-shaped leaf (as of a pine)

**²needle** *vb* **nee·dled; nee·dling** : PROD, GOAD; *esp* : to incite to action by repeated gibes ⟨*needled* him into a fight⟩

**nee·dle–nose pliers** \'nē-dᵊl-ˌnōz-\ *n pl* : pliers with long slender jaws for grasping small or thin objects

**nee·dle·point** \'nē-dᵊl-ˌpoint\ *n* **1** : lace worked with a needle over a paper pattern **2** : embroidery done on canvas across counted threads — **needlepoint** *adj*

**need·less** \'nēd-ləs\ *adj* : UNNECESSARY ⟨~ waste⟩ — **need·less·ly** *adv* — **need·less·ness** *n*

**nee·dle·wom·an** \'nē-dᵊl-ˌwu̇-mən\ *n* : a woman who does needlework; *esp* : SEAMSTRESS

**nee·dle·work** \-ˌwərk\ *n* : work done with a needle; *esp* : work (as embroidery) other than plain sewing

**needs** \'nēdz\ *adv* : of necessity : NECESSARILY ⟨must ~ be recognized⟩

**needy** \'nē-dē\ *adj* **need·i·er; -est** : being in want : POVERTY-STRICKEN

**ne'er** \'ner\ *adv* : NEVER

**ne'er–do–well** \'ner-dü-ˌwel\ *n* : an idle worthless person — **ne'er–do–well** *adj*

**ne·far·i·ous** \ni-'fer-ē-əs\ *adj* [L *nefarius*, fr. *nefas* crime, fr. *ne-* not + *fas* right, divine law] : very wicked : EVIL ♦ **Synonyms** BAD, IMMORAL, INIQUITOUS, SINFUL, VICIOUS — **ne·far·i·ous·ly** *adv*

**neg** *abbr* negative

**ne·gate** \ni-'gāt\ *vb* **ne·gat·ed; ne·gat·ing** **1** : to deny the existence or truth of **2** : to cause to be ineffective or invalid : NULLIFY ⟨~ a contract⟩

**ne·ga·tion** \ni-'gā-shən\ *n* **1** : the action or operation of negating or making negative **2** : a negative doctrine or statement

**¹neg·a·tive** \'ne-gə-tiv\ *adj* **1** : marked by denial, prohibition, or refusal ⟨a ~ reply⟩ **2** : not positive or constructive; *esp* : not affirming the presence of what is sought or suspected to be present ⟨test results were ~⟩ **3** : less than zero ⟨a ~ number⟩ **4** : being, relating to, or charged with electricity of which the electron is the elementary unit **5** : having the light and dark parts opposite to what they were in the original photographic subject — **neg·a·tive·ly** *adv* — **neg·a·tive·ness** *n* — **neg·a·tiv·i·ty** \ˌne-gə-'ti-və-tē\ *n*

**²negative** *n* **1** : a negative word or statement **2** : a negative vote or reply; *also* : REFUSAL **3** : something that is the opposite or negation of something else **4** : a negative number **5** : the side that votes or argues for the opposition (as in a debate) **6** : a negative photographic image on transparent material

**³negative** *vb* **-tived; -tiv·ing** **1** : to refuse to accept or approve **2** : to vote against **3** : DISPROVE

**negative income tax** *n* : a system of federal subsidy payments to families with incomes below a stipulated level

**neg·a·tiv·ism** \'ne-gə-ti-ˌvi-zəm\ *n* : an attitude of skepticism and denial of nearly everything affirmed or suggested by others

**¹ne·glect** \ni-'glekt\ *vb* [L *neglectus*, pp. of *neglegere, neclegere*, fr. *nec-* not + *legere* to gather] **1** : DISREGARD **2** : to leave undone or unattended to esp. through carelessness ♦ **Synonyms** OMIT, IGNORE, OVERLOOK, SLIGHT, FORGET, MISS

**²neglect** *n* **1** : an act or instance of neglecting something **2** : the condition of being neglected — **ne·glect·ful** *adj*

**neg·li·gee** *also* **neg·li·gé** \ˌne-glə-'zhā\ *n* : a woman's long flowing dressing gown

**neg·li·gent** \'ne-gli-jənt\ *adj* : marked by neglect ♦ **Synonyms** NEGLECTFUL, REMISS, DELINQUENT, DERELICT — **neg·li·gence** \-jəns\ *n* — **neg·li·gent·ly** *adv*

**neg·li·gi·ble** \'ne-gli-jə-bəl\ *adj* : so small as to be neglected or disregarded

**ne·go·tiant** \ni-'gō-shē-ənt\ *n* : NEGOTIATOR

**ne·go·ti·ate** \ni-'gō-shē-ˌāt\ *vb* **-at·ed; -at·ing** [L *negotiari* to carry on business, fr. *negotium* business, fr. *neg-* not + *otium* leisure] **1** : to confer with another so as to arrive at the settlement of some matter; *also* : to arrange for or bring about by such conferences ⟨~ a treaty⟩ **2** : to transfer to another by delivery or endorsement in return for equivalent value ⟨~ a check⟩ **3** : to get through, around, or over successfully ⟨~ a turn⟩ — **ne·go·tia·ble** \-shə-bəl, -shē-ə-\ *adj* — **ne·**

**go·ti·a·tion** \ni-ˌgō-sē-ˈā-shən, -shē-\ n — **ne·go·ti·a·tor** \-ˈgō-shē-ˌā-tər\ n

**ne·gri·tude** \ˈne-grə-ˌtüd, -ˌtyüd, ˈnē-\ n : a consciousness of and pride in one's African heritage

**No·gro** \ˈnē-grō\ n, pl **Negroes** [Sp or Pg, fr. negro black] sometimes offensive : a member of the human race native to Africa and classified according to physical features (as dark skin pigmentation) — **Negro** adj, sometimes offensive — **Negroid** \ˈnē-ˌgròid\ n or adj, often not cap, sometimes offensive

**Neh** abbr Nehemiah

**Ne·he·mi·ah** \ˌnē-ə-ˈmī-ə\ n — see BIBLE table

**neigh** \ˈnā\ n : a loud prolonged cry of a horse — **neigh** vb

¹**neigh·bor** \ˈnā-bər\ n 1 : one living or located near another 2 : FELLOW MAN

²**neighbor** vb : to be next to or near to : border on

**neigh·bor·hood** \ˈnā-bər-ˌhùd\ n 1 : NEARNESS 2 : a place or region near : VICINITY; also : a number or amount near ⟨costs in the ~ of $10⟩ 3 : the people living near one another 4 : a section lived in by neighbors and usu. having distinguishing characteristics

**neigh·bor·ly** \-lē\ adj : befitting congenial neighbors; esp : FRIENDLY ⟨a ~ welcome⟩ — **neigh·bor·li·ness** n

**neigh·bour** chiefly Brit var of NEIGHBOR

¹**nei·ther** \ˈnē-thər, ˈnī-\ conj 1 : not either ⟨~ good nor bad⟩ 2 : NOR ⟨~ did I⟩

²**neither** pron : neither one : not the one and not the other ⟨~ of the two⟩

³**neither** adj : not either ⟨~ hand⟩

**nel·son** \ˈnel-sən\ n : a wrestling hold in which one applies leverage against an opponent's arm, neck, and head

**nem·a·todo** \ˈne-mə-ˌtōd\ n : any of a phylum of elongated cylindrical worms parasitic in animals or plants or free-living in soil or water

**nem·e·sis** \ˈne-mə-səs\ n, pl **-e·ses** \-ˌsēz\ [L Nemesis, goddess of divine retribution, fr. Gk] 1 : one that inflicts retribution or vengeance 2 : a formidable and usu. victorious rival 3 : an act or effect of retribution; also : CURSE

**neo·clas·sic** \ˌnē-ō-ˈkla-sik\ or **neo·clas·si·cal** \-si-kəl\ adj : of or relating to a revival or adaptation of the classical style esp. in literature, art, or music

**neo·co·lo·nial·ism** \ˌnē-ō-kə-ˈlō-nē-ə-ˌli-zəm\ n : the economic and political policies by which a nation indirectly maintains or extends its influence over other areas or peoples — **neo·co·lo·nial** adj — **neo·co·lo·nial·ist** \-list\ n or adj

**neo·con** \ˈnē-ō-ˌkän\ n : NEOCONSERVATIVE

**neo·con·ser·va·tive** \-kən-ˈsər-və-tiv\ n : a former liberal espousing political conservatism — **neo·con·ser·va·tism** \-və-ˌti-zəm\ n — **neoconservative** adj

**neo·dym·i·um** \ˌnē-ō-ˈdi-mē-əm\ n : a silver-white to yellow metallic chemical element

**neo·im·pres·sion·ism** \ˌnē-ō-im-ˈpre-shə-ˌni-zəm\ n, often cap N&I : a late 19th century French art movement that attempted to make impressionism more precise and to use a pointillist painting technique

**Neo·lith·ic** \ˌnē-ə-ˈli-thik\ adj : of or relating to the latest period of the Stone Age characterized by polished stone implements

**ne·ol·o·gism** \nē-ˈä-lə-ˌji-zəm\ n : a new word or expression

**ne·on** \ˈnē-ˌän\ n [Gk, neut. of neos new] 1 : a gaseous colorless chemical element used in electric lamps 2 : a lamp in which a discharge through neon gives a reddish glow — **neon** adj

**neo·na·tal** \ˌnē-ō-ˈnā-t²l\ adj : of, relating to, or affecting the newborn ⟨a ~ infection⟩ — **neo·na·tal·ly** adv

**ne·o·nate** \ˈnē-ə-ˌnāt\ n : a newborn child

**neo·pa·gan** \ˌnē-ō-ˈpā-gən\ n : a person who practices a contemporary form of paganism

**neo·phyte** \ˈnē-ə-ˌfīt\ n 1 : a new convert : PROSELYTE 2 : NOVICE 3 : BEGINNER
♦ **Synonyms** APPRENTICE, FRESHMAN, NEWCOMER, ROOKIE, TENDERFOOT, TYRO

**neo·plasm** \ˈnē-ə-ˌpla-zəm\ n : a new growth of tissue serving no useful purpose in the body : TUMOR — **neo·plas·tic** \ˌnē-ə-ˈplas-tik\ adj

**neo·prene** \ˈnē-ə-ˌprēn\ n : a synthetic rubber used esp. for special-purpose clothing (as wet suits)

**neo·trop·i·cal** \ˌnē-ō-ˈträ-pi-kəl\ adj, often cap : of or relating to a zoogeographic region of America that extends south from the central plateau of Mexico

**ne·pen·the** \nə-ˈpen-thē\ n 1 : a potion used by the ancients to dull pain and sorrow 2 : something capable of making one forget grief or suffering

**neph·ew** \ˈne-fyü, chiefly Brit -vyü\ n [ME nevew, fr. AF neveu, fr. LL nepot-, nepos, fr. L, grandson, descendant] : a son of one's brother, sister, brother-in-law, or sister-in-law

**ne·phrit·ic** \ni-ˈfri-tik\ adj 1 : RENAL 2 : of, relating to, or affected with nephritis

**ne·phri·tis** \ni-ˈfrī-təs\ n, pl **ne·phrit·i·des** \-ˈfri-tə-ˌdēz\ : kidney inflammation

**ne plus ul·tra** \ˌnē-ˌpləs-ˈəl-trə\ n [NL, (go) no more beyond] : the highest point capable of being attained

**nep·o·tism** \ˈne-pə-ˌti-zəm\ n [F népotisme, fr. It nepotismo, fr. nepote nephew, fr. LL nepot-, nepos] : favoritism shown to a relative (as in the granting of jobs)

**Nep·tune** \ˈnep-ˌtün, -ˌtyün\ n : the planet 8th in order from the sun — **Nep·tu·ni·an** \nep-ˈtü-nē-ən, -ˈtyü-\ adj

**nep·tu·ni·um** \nep-ˈtü-nē-əm, -ˈtyü-\ n : a short-lived radioactive element

**nerd** \ˈnərd\ n : an unstylish or socially inept person; esp : one slavishly devoted to intellectual pursuits — **nerdy** adj

**Ne·re·id** \ˈnir-ē-əd\ n : a sea nymph in Greek mythology

¹**nerve** \ˈnərv\ n 1 : SINEW, TENDON ⟨strain every ~⟩ 2 : any of the strands of nervous tissue that carry nerve impulses between the brain and spinal cord and

every part of the body **3** : power of endurance or control : FORTITUDE; *also* : BOLDNESS, DARING **4** *pl* : NERVOUSNESS **5** : a vein of a leaf or insect wing — **nerved** \'nərvd\ *adj* — **nerve-less** *adj*

**²nerve** *vb* **nerved; nerv·ing** : to give strength or courage to

**nerve cell** *n* : NEURON; *also* : CELL BODY

**nerve gas** *n* : a chemical weapon damaging esp. to the nervous and respiratory systems

**nerve impulse** *n* : a physical and chemical change that moves along a process of a neuron after stimulation and carries a record of sensation or an instruction to act

**nerve–rack·ing** *or* **nerve–wrack·ing** \'nərv-ˌra-kiŋ\ *adj* : extremely trying on the nerves ⟨a ~ noise⟩

**ner·vous** \'nər-vəs\ *adj* **1** : FORCIBLE, SPIRITED **2** : of, relating to, or made up of neurons or nerves **3** : easily excited or annoyed : JUMPY ⟨a ~ horse⟩ **4** : TIMID, APPREHENSIVE ⟨a ~ smile⟩ **5** : UNEASY, UNSTEADY — **ner·vous·ly** *adv* — **ner·vous·ness** *n*

**nervous breakdown** *n* : an attack of mental or emotional disorder of sufficient severity to be incapacitating esp. when requiring hospitalization

**nervous system** *n* : a bodily system that in vertebrates is made up of the brain and spinal cord, nerves, ganglia, and parts of the sense organs and that receives and interprets stimuli and transmits nerve impulses

**nervy** \'nər-vē\ *adj* **nerv·i·er; -est** **1** : showing calm courage ⟨a ~ performer⟩ **2** : marked by impudence or presumption ⟨a ~ salesperson⟩ **3** : EXCITABLE, NERVOUS ◆ *Synonyms* BOLD, CHEEKY, FORWARD, FRESH, IMPUDENT, SAUCY

**-ness** \nəs\ *n suffix* : state : condition : quality : degree ⟨good*ness*⟩

**¹nest** \'nest\ *n* **1** : the shelter prepared by a bird for its eggs and young **2** : a place where eggs (as of insects or fish) are laid and hatched **3** : a place of rest, retreat, or lodging **4** : DEN, HANGOUT ⟨a ~ of thieves⟩ **5** : the occupants of a nest **6** : a series of objects (as bowls or tables) fitting inside or under one another

**²nest** *vb* **1** : to build or occupy a nest **2** : to fit compactly together or within one another

**nest egg** *n* : a fund of money accumulated as a reserve

**nes·tle** \'ne-səl\ *vb* **nes·tled; nes·tling** **1** : to settle snugly or comfortably **2** : to press closely and affectionately : CUDDLE **3** : to settle, shelter, or house as if in a nest

**nest·ling** \'nest-liŋ\ *n* : a bird too young to leave its nest

**¹net** \'net\ *n* **1** : a meshed fabric twisted, knotted, or woven together at regular intervals **2** : a device made all or partly of net and used esp. to catch birds, fish, or insects **3** : something made of net used esp. for protecting, confining, carrying, or dividing ⟨a tennis ~⟩ **4** : SNARE, TRAP **5** *often cap* : INTERNET

**²net** *vb* **net·ted; net·ting** **1** : to cover or enclose with or as if with a net **2** : to catch in or as if in a net

**³net** *adj* : free from all charges or deductions ⟨~ profit⟩ ⟨~ weight⟩

**⁴net** *vb* **net·ted; net·ting** : to gain or produce as profit : CLEAR, YIELD ⟨his business *netted* $50,000 a year⟩

**⁵net** *n* : a net amount, profit, weight, or price

**Neth** *abbr* Netherlands

**neth·er** \'ne-thər\ *adj* : situated down or below ⟨the ~ regions of the earth⟩

**neth·er·most** \-ˌmōst\ *adj* : LOWEST

**neth·er·world** \-ˌwərld\ *n* **1** : the world of the dead **2** : UNDERWORLD

**net·i·quette** \'ne-ti-kət, -ˌket\ *n* : etiquette governing communication on the Internet

**net·roots** \'net-ˌrüts, -ˌrüts\ *n pl* : the grass-roots political activists who communicate via the Internet

**nett** *Brit var of* NET

**net·ting** *n* **1** : NETWORK **2** : the act or process of making a net or network

**¹net·tle** \'ne-t³l\ *n* : any of a genus of coarse herbs with stinging hairs

**²nettle** *vb* **net·tled; net·tling** : PROVOKE, VEX, IRRITATE

**net·tle·some** \'ne-t³l-səm\ *adj* : causing vexation : IRRITATING

**net·work** \'net-ˌwərk\ *n* **1** : NET **2** : a system of elements (as lines or channels) that cross in the manner of the threads in a net **3** : a group or system of related or connected parts; *esp* : a chain of radio or television stations **4** : a system of computers that are connected (as by telephone wires)

**net·work·ing** \'net-ˌwər-kiŋ\ *n* **1** : the exchange of information or services among individuals, groups, or institutions **2** : the cultivation of productive business relationships

**neu·ral** \'nu̇r-əl, 'nyu̇r-\ *adj* : of, relating to, or involving a nerve or the nervous system ⟨~ pathways⟩

**neu·ral·gia** \nu̇-'ral-jə, nyu̇-\ *n* : acute pain that follows the course of a nerve — **neu·ral·gic** \-jik\ *adj*

**neur·as·the·nia** \ˌnu̇r-əs-'thē-nē-ə, ˌnyu̇r-\ *n* [NL, fr. Gk *neuron* nerve + *asthenia* weakness, fr. *asthenēs* weak, fr. *a-* not + *sthenos* strength] : a psychological disorder marked esp. by fatiguing easily, lack of motivation, feelings of inadequacy, and psychosomatic symptoms — **neur·as·then·ic** \-the-nik, -'thē-\ *adj or n*

**neu·ri·tis** \nu̇-'rī-təs, nyu̇-\ *n, pl* **-rit·i·des** \-'ri-tə-ˌdēz\ *or* **-ri·tis·es** : inflammation of a nerve — **neu·rit·ic** \-'ri-tik\ *adj or n*

**neu·ro·bi·ol·o·gy** \ˌnu̇r-ō-bī-'ä-lə-jē\ *n* : a branch of biology that deals with the nervous system — **neu·ro·bi·o·log·i·cal** \-ˌbī-ə-'lä-ji-kəl\ *adj* — **neu·ro·bi·ol·o·gist** \-bī-'ä-lə-jist\ *n*

**neu·rol·o·gy** \nu̇-'rä-lə-jē, nyu̇-\ *n* : the scientific study of the nervous system — **neu·ro·log·i·cal** \ˌnu̇r-ə-'lä-ji-kəl, ˌnyu̇r-\ *or* **neu·ro·log·ic** \-jik\ *adj* — **neu·ro·log·i·cal·ly** \-ji-k(ə-)lē\ *adv* — **neu·rol·o·gist** \nu̇-'rä-lə-jist, nyu̇-\ *n*

**neu·ro·mus·cu·lar** \,nür-ō-'məs-kyə-lər, ,nyùr-\ *adj* : of, relating to, or affecting nerves and muscles ⟨a ~ disease⟩

**neu·ron** \'nü-,rän, 'nyü-\ *n* : a cell with specialized processes that is the fundamental functional unit of nervous tissue — **neu·ro·nal** \'nür-ə-n°l, 'nyùr-\ *adj*

**neu·rone** \-,rōn\ *chiefly Brit var of* NEURON

**neu·ro·sci·ence** \,nür-ō-'sī-əns, ,nyùr-\ *n* : a branch of the life sciences that deals with the anatomy, physiology, biochemistry, or molecular biology of nerves and nervous tissue and esp. with their relation to behavior and learning — **neu·ro·sci·en·tist** \-ən-tist\ *n*

**neu·ro·sis** \nù-'rō-səs, nyù-\ *n, pl* **-ro·ses** \-,sēz\ : a mental and emotional disorder that is less serious than a psychosis, is not characterized by disturbance of the use of language, and is accompanied by various bodily and mental disturbances (as visceral symptoms, anxieties, or phobias)

**neu·ro·sur·gery** \,nür-ō-'sər-jə-rē, ,nyùr-\ *n* : surgery of nervous structures (as nerves, the brain, or the spinal cord) — **neu·ro·sur·geon** \-'sər-jən\ *n*

¹**neu·rot·ic** \nù-'rä-tik, nyù-\ *adj* : of, relating to, being, or affected with a neurosis — **neu·rot·i·cal·ly** \-ti-k(ə-)lē\ *adv*

²**neurotic** *n* : an emotionally unstable or neurotic person

**neu·ro·trans·mit·ter** \,nür-ō-trans-'mi-tər, ,nyùr-, -tranz-\ *n* : a substance (as acetylcholine) that transmits nerve impulses across a synapse

**neut** *abbr* neuter

¹**neu·ter** \'nü-tər, 'nyü-\ *adj* [ME *neutre*, fr. MF & L; MF *neutre*, fr. L *neuter*, lit., neither, fr. *ne-* not + *uter* which of two] 1 : of, relating to, or constituting the gender that includes most words or grammatical forms referring to things classed as neither masculine nor feminine 2 : lacking or having imperfectly developed sex organs

²**neuter** *n* 1 : a noun, pronoun, adjective, or inflectional form or class of the neuter gender; *also* : the neuter gender 2 : WORKER 2; *also* : a spayed or castrated animal

³**neuter** *vb* 1 : CASTRATE, SPAY 2 : to remove the force or effectiveness of

¹**neu·tral** \'nü-trəl, 'nyü-\ *n* 1 : one that is neutral 2 : a neutral color 3 : a position of disengagement (as of gears)

²**neutral** *adj* 1 : not favoring either side in a quarrel, contest, or war 2 : of or relating to a neutral state or power 3 : MIDDLING, INDIFFERENT 4 : having no hue : GRAY; *also* : not decided in color 5 : neither acid nor basic ⟨a ~ solution⟩ 6 : not electrically charged

**neu·tral·ise** *Brit var of* NEUTRALIZE

**neu·tral·ism** \'nü-trə-,li-zəm, 'nyü-\ *n* : a policy or the advocacy of neutrality esp. in international affairs

**neu·tral·i·ty** \nü-'tra-lə-tē, nyü-\ *n* : the quality or state of being neutral; *esp* : refusal to take part in a war between other powers

**neu·tral·ize** \'nü-trə-,līz, 'nyü-\ *vb* **-ized;**

**-iz·ing** : to make neutral; *esp* : COUNTERACT — **neu·tral·i·za·tion** \,nü-trə-lə-'zā-shən, ,nyü-\ *n*

**neu·tri·no** \nü-'trē-nō, nyü-\ *n, pl* **-nos** : an uncharged elementary particle held to be massless or very light

**neu·tron** \'nü-,trän, 'nyü-\ *n* : an uncharged atomic particle that is nearly equal in mass to the proton

**neutron bomb** *n* : a nuclear bomb designed to produce lethal neutrons but less blast and fire damage than other nuclear bombs

**neutron star** *n* : a dense celestial object that results from the collapse of a large star

**Nev** *abbr* Nevada

**nev·er** \'ne-vər\ *adv* 1 : not ever 2 : not in any degree, way, or condition

**nev·er·more** \,ne-vər-'mòr\ *adv* : never again

**nev·er–nev·er land** \,ne-vər-'ne-vər-\ *n* : an ideal or imaginary place

**nev·er·the·less** \,ne-vər-thə-'les\ *adv* : in spite of that : HOWEVER

**ne·vus** \'nē-vəs\ *n, pl* **ne·vi** \-,vī\ : a usu. pigmented area on the skin : MOLE

¹**new** \'nü, 'nyü\ *adj* 1 : not old : RECENT, MODERN 2 : recently discovered, recognized, or learned about ⟨~ drugs⟩ 3 : UNFAMILIAR ⟨visit ~ places⟩ 4 : different from the former 5 : not accustomed ⟨~ to the work⟩ 6 : beginning as a repetition of a previous act or thing ⟨a ~ year⟩ 7 : REFRESHED, REGENERATED ⟨rest made a ~ man of him⟩ 8 : being in a position or place for the first time ⟨a ~ member⟩ 9 *cap* : having been in use after medieval times : MODERN ⟨New Latin⟩ ♦ *Synonyms* NOVEL, NEWFANGLED, FRESH — **new·ish** *adj* — **new·ness** *n*

²**new** *adv* : NEWLY ⟨new-mown hay⟩

¹**new age** *adj, often cap N&A* 1 : of, relating to, or being New Age 2 : CONTEMPORARY, MODERN

²**new age** *n* 1 *cap* : a group of late 20th century social attitudes adapted from a variety of ancient and modern beliefs relating to spirituality, right living, and health 2 : a soft soothing form of instrumental music

**new·bie** \'nü-bē, 'nyü-\ *n* : a newcomer esp. to cyberspace

**new blood** *n* : persons accepted into a group or organization and expected to provide fresh ideas and vitality

¹**new·born** \-,bòrn\ *adj* 1 : recently born 2 : born anew ⟨~ hope⟩

²**newborn** *n, pl* **newborn** *or* **newborns** : a newborn individual

**new·com·er** \-,kə-mər\ *n* 1 : one recently arrived 2 : BEGINNER

**New Deal** *n* : the legislative and administrative program of President F. D. Roosevelt to promote economic recovery and social reform during the 1930s — **New Dealer** *n*

**new·el** \'nü-əl, 'nyü-\ *n* : a post about which the steps of a circular staircase wind; *also* : a post at the foot of a stairway or one at a landing

**new·fan·gled** \'nü-'faŋ-gəld, 'nyü-\ *adj* 1

: attracted to novelty **2** : of the newest style ⟨~ gadgets⟩

**new–fash·ioned** \-'fa-shənd\ *adj* **1** : made in a new fashion or form ⟨~ automobiles⟩ **2** : UP-TO-DATE

**new·found** \-'faünd\ *adj* : newly found

**New Left** *n* : a radical political movement originating in the 1960s

**new·ly** \'nü-lē, 'nyü-\ *adv* **1** : LATELY, RECENTLY ⟨a ~ married couple⟩ **2** : ANEW, AFRESH ⟨~ painted⟩

**new·ly·wed** \-,wed\ *n* : a person recently married

**new moon** *n* : the phase of the moon with its dark side toward the earth; *also* : the thin crescent seen for a few days after the new moon phase

**news** \'nüz, 'nyüz\ *n* **1** : a report of recent events : TIDINGS **2** : material reported in a newspaper or news periodical or on a newscast

**news·boy** \'nüz-,bói, 'nyüz-\ *n* : one who delivers or sells newspapers

**news·cast** \-,kast\ *n* : a radio or television broadcast of news — **news·cast·er** \-,kas-tər\ *n*

**news·group** \-,grüp\ *n* : an Internet bulletin devoted to a certain topic

**news·let·ter** \'nüz-,le-tər, 'nyüz-\ *n* : a small newspaper containing news or information of interest chiefly to a special group

**news·mag·a·zine** \-,ma-gə-,zēn\ *n* : a usu. weekly magazine devoted chiefly to summarizing and analyzing news

**news·man** \-mən, -,man\ *n* : a person who gathers, reports, or comments on the news : REPORTER

**news·pa·per** \-,pā-pər\ *n* : a paper that is published at regular intervals and contains news, articles of opinion, features, and advertising

**news·pa·per·man** \-,pā-pər-,man\ *n* : a person who owns or is employed by a newspaper

**news·print** \-,print\ *n* : paper made chiefly from wood pulp and used mostly for newspapers

**news·reel** \-,rēl\ *n* : a short motion picture portraying current events

**news·stand** \-,stand\ *n* : a place where newspapers and periodicals are sold

**news·week·ly** \-,wēk-lē\ *n* : a weekly newspaper or newsmagazine

**news·wire** \-,wī(-ə)r\ *n* : WIRE SERVICE

**news·wom·an** \-,wu̇-mən\ *n* : a woman who is a reporter

**news·wor·thy** \-,wər-thē\ *adj* : sufficiently interesting to the general public to warrant reporting

**newsy** \'nü-zē, 'nyü-\ *adj* **news·i·er; -est** : filled with news; *esp* : TALKATIVE

**newt** \'nüt, 'nyüt\ *n* [ME, alter. (from misdivision of *an ewte*) of *ewt, evete*, fr. OE *efete*] : any of various small chiefly aquatic salamanders

**New Testament** *n* : the second of the two chief divisions of the Christian Bible — see BIBLE table

**new·ton** \'nü-t²n, 'nyü-\ *n* : the unit of force in the metric system equal to the force required to impart an acceleration

of one meter per second per second to a mass of one kilogram

**new wave** *n, often cap N&W* : the latest and esp. the most outrageous style — **new–wave** *adj*

**New Year** *n* **1** : NEW YEAR'S DAY; *also* : the first days of the year **2** : ROSH HASHANAH

**New Year's Day** *n* : January 1 observed as a legal holiday

¹**next** \'nekst\ *adj* : immediately preceding or following : NEAREST

²**next** *prep* : nearest or adjacent to

³**next** *adv* **1** : in the time, place, or order nearest or immediately succeeding **2** : on the first occasion to come

⁴**next** *n* : one that is next

**nex·us** \'nek-səs\ *n, pl* **nex·us·es** \-sə-səz\ *or* **nex·us** \-səs, -,süs\ : CONNECTION, LINK

**Nez Percé** \'nez-'pərs\ *n* : a member of an American Indian people of Idaho, Washington, and Oregon; *also* : the language of the Nez Percé

**NF** *abbr* Newfoundland

**NFC** *abbr* National Football Conference

**NFL** *abbr* National Football League

**Nfld** *abbr* Newfoundland

**NG** *abbr* **1** National Guard **2** no good

**ngul·trum** \eŋ-'gül-trəm\ *n* — see MONEY table

**ngwee** \eŋ-'gwē\ *n, pl* **ngwee** — see *kwacha* at MONEY table

**NH** *abbr* New Hampshire

**NHL** *abbr* National Hockey League

**Ni** *symbol* nickel

**ni·a·cin** \'nī-ə-sən\ *n* : an organic acid of the vitamin B complex found widely in plants and animals and used esp. against pellagra

**nib** \'nib\ *n* : POINT; *esp* : a pen point

¹**nib·ble** \'ni-bəl\ *vb* **nib·bled; nib·bling** : to bite gently or bit by bit

²**nibble** *n* : a small or cautious bite

**ni·cad** \'nī-,kad\ *n* : a rechargeable dry cell that has a nickel cathode and a cadmium anode

**nice** \'nīs\ *adj* **nic·er; nic·est** [ME, foolish, wanton, fr. AF, silly, simple, fr. L *nescius* ignorant, fr. *nescire* to not know] **1** : FASTIDIOUS, DISCRIMINATING **2** : marked by delicate discrimination or treatment ⟨a ~ distinction between those two words⟩ **3** : PLEASING, AGREEABLE ⟨had a ~ time⟩; *also* : well-executed ⟨a ~ shot⟩ **4** : WELL-BRED ⟨~ people⟩ **5** : VIRTUOUS, RESPECTABLE ◆ **Synonyms** CHOOSY, FINICKY, PARTICULAR, PERSNICKETY, PICKY — **nice·ly** *adv* — **nice·ness** *n*

**nice–nel·ly** \'nīs-'ne-lē\ *adj, often cap 2d N* **1** : marked by euphemism **2** : PRUDISH ⟨his ~ sweetheart⟩ — **nice nelly** *n, often cap 2d N* — **nice–nel·ly·ism** \-,i-zəm\ *n, often cap 2d N*

**nice·ty** \'nī-sə-tē\ *n, pl* **-ties** **1** : a dainty, delicate, or elegant thing ⟨enjoy the *niceties* of life⟩ **2** : a fine point or distinction ⟨*niceties* of workmanship⟩ **3** : EXACTNESS, PRECISION, ACCURACY

**niche** \'nich\ *n* [F] **1** : a recess in a wall esp. for a statue **2** : a place, employment, or activity for which a person or thing is best fitted **3** : the living space or role of an organism in an ecological community esp. with regard to food consumption

**¹nick** \'nik\ *n* **1** : a small notch, groove, or chip **2** : the final critical moment ⟨in the ~ of time⟩

**²nick** *vb* : NOTCH, CHIP

**nick·el** \'ni-kəl\ *n* **1** : a hard silver-white metallic chemical element capable of a high polish and used in alloys **2** : the U.S. 5-cent piece made of copper and nickel; *also* : the Canadian 5-cent piece

**nick·el·ode·on** \,ni-kə-'lō-dē-ən\ *n* **1** : an early movie theater to which admission cost five cents **2** : JUKEBOX

**nick·er** \'ni-kər\ *vb* : NEIGH, WHINNY — **nicker** *n*

**nick·name** \'nik-,nām\ *n* [ME *nekename* additional name, alter. (from misdivision of *an ekename*) of *ekename*, fr. *eke* also + *name*] **1** : a usu. descriptive name given instead of or in addition to the one belonging to a person, place, or thing **2** : a familiar form of a proper name — **nickname** *vb*

**nic·o·tine** \'ni-kə-,tēn\ *n* : a poisonous and addictive substance in tobacco that is used as an insecticide

**nic·o·tin·ic acid** \,ni-kə-'tē-nik-, -'ti-\ *n* : NIACIN

**niece** \'nēs\ *n* : a daughter of one's brother, sister, brother-in-law, or sister-in-law

**nif·ty** \'nif-tē\ *adj* **nif·ti·er; -est** : very good : very attractive

**nig·gard** \'ni-gərd\ *n* : a stingy person : MISER — **nig·gard·li·ness** \-lē-nəs\ *n* — **nig·gard·ly** *adj or adv*

**nig·gling** \'ni-gə-liŋ\ *adj* **1** : PETTY ⟨~ details⟩ **2** : bothersome in a petty way ⟨~ pain⟩ **♦ Synonyms** INCONSEQUENTIAL, MEASLY, PICAYUNE, PIDDLING, TRIFLING, TRIVIAL

**¹nigh** \'nī\ *adv* **1** : near in place, time, or relationship **2** : NEARLY, ALMOST

**²nigh** *adj* : CLOSE, NEAR

**³nigh** *prep* : NEAR

**night** \'nīt\ *n* **1** : the period between dusk and dawn **2** : the darkness of night **3** : a period of misery or unhappiness **4** : NIGHTFALL — **night** *adj*

**night blindness** *n* : reduced visual capacity in faint light (as at night)

**night·cap** \'nīt-,kap\ *n* **1** : a cloth cap worn with nightclothes **2** : a usu. alcoholic drink taken at bedtime

**night·clothes** \-,klōthz, -,klōz\ *n pl* : garments worn in bed

**night·club** \-,kləb\ *n* : a place of entertainment open at night usu. serving food and liquor and providing music for dancing

**night crawl·er** \-,krȯ-lər\ *n* : EARTHWORM; *esp* : a large earthworm found on the soil surface at night

**night·dress** \'nīt-,dres\ *n* : NIGHTGOWN

**night·fall** \-,fȯl\ *n* : the coming of night

**night·gown** \-,gaùn\ *n* : a loose garment for wear in bed

**night·hawk** \-,hȯk\ *n* : any of a genus of American birds related to and resembling the whip-poor-will

**night·in·gale** \'nī-t°n-,gāl, 'nī-tiŋ-\ *n* [ME, fr. OE *nihtegale*, fr. *niht* night + *galan* to sing] : any of several Old World thrushes noted for the sweet usu. nocturnal song of the male

**night·life** \'nīt-,līf\ *n* : the activity of pleasure-seekers at night

**night·ly** \'nīt-lē\ *adj* **1** : happening, done, or produced by night or every night **2** : of or relating to the night or every night — **nightly** *adv*

**night·mare** \'nīt-,mer\ *n* **1** : a frightening dream **2** : a frightening or horrible experience — **nightmare** *adj* — **night·mar·ish** *adj*

**night rider** *n* : a member of a secret band who ride masked at night during violence to punish or terrorize

**night·shade** \'nīt-,shād\ *n* : any of a large genus of herbs, shrubs, and trees that includes poisonous forms (as the belladonna), ornamentals (as the petunias), and important food plants (as the potato and eggplant)

**night·shirt** \-,shərt\ *n* : a nightgown resembling a shirt

**night soil** *n* : human feces used esp. for fertilizing the soil

**night·stick** \'nīt-,stik\ *n* : a police officer's club

**night·time** \-,tīm\ *n* : the time from dusk to dawn

**night·walk·er** \-,wȯ-kər\ *n* : a person who roves about at night esp. with criminal or immoral intent

**ni·hil·ism** \'nī-ə-,li-zəm, 'nē-hə-\ *n* **1** : a viewpoint that traditional values and beliefs are unfounded and that existence is senseless and useless **2** : ANARCHISM — **ni·hil·ist** \-list\ *n or adj* — **ni·hil·is·tic** \,nī-ə-'lis-tik, ,nē-hə-\ *adj*

**nil** \'nil\ *n* : ZERO, NOTHING

**nim·ble** \'nim-bəl\ *adj* **nim·bler; nim·blest** [ME *nimel*, fr. OE *numol* holding much, fr. *niman* to take] **1** : quick and light in motion : AGILE ⟨a ~ dancer⟩ **2** : quick in understanding and learning : CLEVER ⟨a ~ mind⟩ **♦ Synonyms** ACTIVE, BRISK, SPRIGHTLY, SPRY, ZIPPY — **nim·ble·ness** *n* — **nim·bly** \-blē\ *adv*

**nim·bus** \'nim-bəs\ *n, pl* **nim·bi** \-,bī, -bē\ *or* **nim·bus·es** **1** : a figure (as a disk) in an art work suggesting radiant light about the head of a divinity, saint, or sovereign **2** : a rain cloud; *also* : THUNDERHEAD

**NIMBY** \'nim-bē\ *n* [*not in my backyard*] : opposition to the placement of something undesirable (as a prison) in one's neighborhood

**nim·rod** \'nim-,räd\ *n* **1** : HUNTER **2** : IDIOT, JERK

**nin·com·poop** \'nin-kəm-,püp\ *n* : FOOL, SIMPLETON

**nine** \'nīn\ *n* **1** : one more than eight **2** : the 9th in a set or series **3** : something having nine units; *esp* : a baseball team — **nine** *adj or pron* — **ninth** \'nīnth\ *adj or adv or n* — **to the nines** **1** : to perfection **2** : in an elaborate manner ⟨dressed *to the nines*⟩

**nine days' wonder** *n* : something that creates a short-lived sensation

**nine·pins** \'nīn-ˌpinz\ *n* : a bowling game using nine pins arranged usu. in a diamond-shaped configuration

**nine·teen** \nīn-'tēn\ *n* : one more than 18 — **nineteen** *adj or pron* — **nine·teenth** \-'tēnth\ *adj or n*

**nine·ty** \'nīn-tē\ *n, pl* **nineties** : nine times 10 — **nine·ti·eth** \-tē-əth\ *adj or n* — **ninety** *adj or pron*

**nin·ja** \'nin-jə, -ˌ(ˌ)jä\ *n, pl* **ninja** or **ninjas** [Jp] : a person trained in ancient Japanese martial arts and employed esp. for espionage and assassinations

**nin·ny** \'ni-nē\ *n, pl* **ninnies** : FOOL

**ni·o·bi·um** \nī-'ō-bē-əm\ *n* : a gray metallic chemical element used in alloys

¹**nip** \'nip\ *vb* **nipped; nip·ping** 1 : to catch hold of and squeeze tightly between two surfaces, edges, or points 2 : ³CLIP 3 : to destroy the growth, progress, or fulfillment of ⟨*nipped* in the bud⟩ 4 : to injure or make numb with cold : CHILL 5 : SNATCH, STEAL

²**nip** *n* 1 : a sharp stinging cold 2 : a biting or pungent flavor 3 : PINCH, BITE 4 : a small portion : BIT

³**nip** *n* : a small quantity of liquor : SIP

⁴**nip** *vb* **nipped; nip·ping** : to take liquor in nips : TIPPLE

**nip and tuck** *adj or adv* : so close that the lead shifts rapidly from one contestant to another

**nip·per** \'ni-pər\ *n* 1 : one that nips 2 *pl* : PINCERS 3 : CHILD; *esp* : a small boy

**nip·ple** \'ni-pəl\ *n* : the protuberance of a mammary gland through which milk is drawn off : TEAT; *also* : something resembling a nipple

**nip·py** \'ni-pē\ *adj* **nip·pi·er; -est** 1 : PUNGENT, SHARP 2 : CHILLY

**nir·va·na** \nər-'vä-nə\ *n, often cap* [Skt *nirvāṇa*, lit., act of extinguishing, fr. *nis*- out + *vāti* it blows] 1 : the final freeing of a soul from all that enslaves it; *esp* : the supreme happiness that according to Buddhism comes when all passion, hatred, and delusion die out and the soul is released from the necessity of further purification 2 : OBLIVION; *also* : PARADISE

**ni·sei** \nē-'sā, 'nē-ˌsā\ *n, pl* **nisei** *often cap* : a son or daughter of immigrant Japanese parents who is born and educated in America

**ni·si** \'nī-ˌsī\ *adj* [L, unless, fr. *ne*- not + *si* if] : taking effect at a specified time unless previously modified or voided ⟨a divorce decree ∼⟩

**nit** \'nit\ *n* 1 : the egg of a parasitic insect (as a louse); *also* : the young insect 2 : a minor shortcoming

**nite** *var of* NIGHT

**ni·ter** \'nī-tər\ *n* : POTASSIUM NITRATE

**nit–pick·ing** \'nit-ˌpi-kiŋ\ *n* : minute and usu. unjustified criticism — **nit·pick·er** *n*

¹**ni·trate** \'nī-ˌtrāt, -trət\ *n* 1 : a salt or ester of nitric acid 2 : sodium nitrate or potassium nitrate used as a fertilizer

²**ni·trate** \-ˌtrāt\ *vb* **ni·trat·ed; ni·trat·ing**

: to treat or combine with nitric acid or a nitrate — **ni·tra·tion** \nī-'trā-shən\ *n*

**ni·tre** *chiefly Brit var of* NITER

**ni·tric acid** \'nī-trik-\ *n* : a corrosive liquid used esp. in making dyes, explosives, and fertilizers

**ni·tri·fi·ca·tion** \ˌnī-trə-fə-'kā-shən\ *n* : the oxidation (as by bacteria) of ammonium salts to nitrites and then to nitrates — **ni·tri·fy·ing** \'nī-trə-fī-iŋ\ *adj*

**ni·trite** \'nī-ˌtrīt\ *n* : a salt of nitrous acid

**ni·tro** \'nī-trō\ *n, pl* **nitros** : any of various nitrated products; *esp* : NITROGLYCERIN

**ni·tro·gen** \'nī-trə-jən\ *n* : a tasteless odorless gaseous chemical element constituting 78 percent of the atmosphere by volume — **ni·trog·e·nous** \nī-'trä-jə-nəs\ *adj*

**nitrogen narcosis** *n* : a state of euphoria and confusion caused by nitrogen forced into a diver's bloodstream from atmospheric air under pressure

**ni·tro·glyc·er·in** or **ni·tro·glyc·er·ine** \ˌnī-trə-'gli-sə-rən\ *n* : an oily explosive liquid used to make dynamite and in medicine to dilate blood vessels

**ni·trous acid** \'nī-trəs-\ *n* : an unstable nitrogen-containing acid known only in solution or in the form of its salts

**nitrous oxide** *n* : a colorless gas used esp. as an anesthetic in dentistry

**nit·ty–grit·ty** \ni-tē-'gri-tē, ˈni-tē-ˈgri-tē\ *n* : what is essential and basic : specific practical details

**nit·wit** \'nit-ˌwit\ *n* : a scatterbrained or stupid person

¹**nix** \'niks\ *n* : NOTHING

²**nix** *vb* : VETO, REJECT

³**nix** *adv* : NO

**NJ** *abbr* New Jersey

**NL** *abbr* National League

**NLRB** *abbr* National Labor Relations Board

**NM** *abbr* 1 nautical mile 2 New Mexico

**N Mex** *abbr* New Mexico

**NMI** *abbr* no middle initial

**NNE** *abbr* north-northeast

**NNW** *abbr* north-northwest

¹**no** \'nō\ *adv* 1 — used to express the negative of an alternative ⟨shall we continue or ∼⟩ 2 : in no respect or degree ⟨he is ∼ better than the others⟩ 3 : not so ⟨∼, I'm not ready⟩ 4 — used with an adjective to imply a meaning opposite to the positive statement ⟨in ∼ uncertain terms⟩ 5 — used to introduce a more emphatic or explicit statement ⟨has the right, ∼, the duty to continue⟩ 6 — used as an interjection to express surprise or doubt ⟨∼—you don't say⟩ 7 — used in combination with a verb to form a compound adjective ⟨*no*-bake pie⟩ 8 : in negation ⟨shook his head ∼⟩

²**no** *adj* 1 : not any; *also* : hardly any 2 : not a ⟨she's ∼ expert⟩

³**no** \'nō\ *n, pl* **noes** or **nos** \'nōz\ 1 : REFUSAL, DENIAL ⟨got a ∼ in reply⟩ 2 : a negative vote or decision; *also, pl* : persons voting in the negative

⁴**no** *abbr* 1 north; northern 2 [L *numero*, abl. of *numerus*] number

¹**No** *var of* NOH

²**No** *symbol* nobelium

**No·bel·ist** \nō-'be-list\ *n* : a winner of a Nobel prize

**no·bel·i·um** \nō-'be-lē-əm\ *n* : a radioactive metallic chemical element produced artificially

**No·bel prize** \nō-'bel-, 'nō-ˌbel-\ *n* : any of various annual prizes (as in peace, literature, or medicine) established by the will of Alfred Nobel for the encouragement of persons who work for the interests of humanity

**no·bil·i·ty** \nō-'bi-lə-tē\ *n* 1 : the quality or state of being noble 2 : nobles considered as forming a class

¹**no·ble** \'nō-bəl\ *adj* **no·bler; no·blest** [ME, fr. AF, fr. L *nobilis* well known, noble, fr. *noscere* to come to know] 1 : ILLUSTRIOUS; *also* : FAMOUS, NOTABLE 2 : of high birth, rank, or station : ARISTOCRATIC 3 : EXCELLENT 4 : STATELY, IMPOSING ⟨a ~ edifice⟩ 5 : of a superior nature ◆ **Synonyms** AUGUST, BARONIAL, GRAND, GRANDIOSE, MAGNIFICENT, MAJESTIC — **no·ble·ness** *n* — **no·bly** \-blē\ *adv*

²**no·ble** *n* : a person of noble rank or birth

**no·ble·man** \'nō-bəl-mən\ *n* : a member of the nobility : PEER

**no·blesse oblige** \nō-ˌbles-ə-'blēzh\ *n* [F, lit., nobility obligates] : the obligation of honorable, generous, and responsible behavior associated with high rank or birth

**no·ble·wom·an** \'nō-bəl-ˌwu̇-mən\ *n* : a woman of noble rank : PEERESS

¹**no·body** \'nō-ˌbä-dē, -bə-\ *pron* : no person

²**nobody** *n, pl* **no·bod·ies** : a person of no influence or importance

**no–brain·er** \'nō-'brā-nər\ *n* : something that requires a minimum of thought

**noc·tur·nal** \näk-'tər-n²l\ *adj* 1 : of, relating to, or occurring in the night 2 : active at night ⟨a ~ bird⟩

**noc·turne** \'näk-ˌtərn\ *n* : a work of art dealing with night; *esp* : a dreamy pensive composition for the piano

**noc·u·ous** \'nä-kyə-wəs\ *adj* : HARMFUL — **noc·u·ous·ly** *adv*

**nod** \'näd\ *vb* **nod·ded; nod·ding** 1 : to bend the head downward or forward (as in bowing, going to sleep, or giving assent) 2 : to move up and down ⟨tulips *nodding* in the breeze⟩ 3 : to show by a nod of the head ⟨~ agreement⟩ 4 : to make a slip or error in a moment of abstraction ⟨did many good things, but sometimes he *nodded*⟩ — **nod** *n*

**nod·dle** \'nä-d²l\ *n* : HEAD

**nod·dy** \'nä-dē\ *n, pl* **noddies** 1 : FOOL 2 : a stout-bodied tropical tern

**node** \'nōd\ *n* : a thickened, swollen, or differentiated area (as of tissue); *esp* : the part of a stem from which a leaf arises — **nod·al** \-²l\ *adj*

**nod·ule** \'nä-jül\ *n* : a small lump or swelling — **nod·u·lar** \'nä-jə-lər\ *adj*

**no·el** \nō-'el\ *n* [F *noël* Christmas, carol, fr. OF *Nael* (*Deu*), *Noel* Christmas, fr. L *natalis* birthday] 1 : a Christmas carol 2 *cap* : the Christmas season

**noes** *pl of* NO

**no–fault** \'nō-ˌfȯlt\ *adj* 1 : of, relating to, or being a motor vehicle insurance plan under which someone involved in an accident is compensated usu. up to a stipulated limit for actual losses by that person's own insurance company regardless of who is responsible 2 : of, relating to, or being a divorce law under which neither party is held responsible for the breakup of the marriage

**nog·gin** \'nä-gən\ *n* 1 : a small mug or cup; *also* : a small quantity of drink 2 : a person's head

**no–good** \'nō-'gu̇d\ *adj* : having no worth, virtue, use, or chance of success — **no–good** \'nō-ˌgu̇d\ *n*

**Noh** *also* **No** \'nō\ *n, pl* **Noh** *also* **No** : classic Japanese dance-drama having a heroic theme, a chorus, and highly stylized action, costuming, and scenery

**no hit·ter** \(ˌ)nō-'hi-tər\ *n* : a baseball game or part of a game in which a pitcher allows no base hits

**no·how** \'nō-ˌhau̇\ *adv* : in no manner

¹**noise** \'nȯiz\ *n* [ME, fr. AF, disturbance, noise, fr. L *nausea* nausea] 1 : loud, confused, or senseless shouting or outcry 2 : SOUND; *esp* : one that lacks agreeable musical quality or is noticeably unpleasant 3 : unwanted electronic signal or disturbance — **noise·less** *adj* — **noise·less·ly** *adv*

²**noise** *vb* **noised; nois·ing** : to spread by rumor or report ⟨the story was *noised* abroad⟩

**noise·mak·er** \'nȯiz-ˌmā-kər\ *n* : one that makes noise; *esp* : a device used to make noise at parties

**noise pollution** *n* : annoying or harmful noise in an environment

**noi·some** \'nȯi-səm\ *adj* 1 : HARMFUL, UNWHOLESOME 2 : offensive to the senses (as smell) : DISGUSTING ⟨~ habits⟩ ◆ **Synonyms** INSALUBRIOUS, NOXIOUS, SICKLY, UNHEALTHFUL, UNHEALTHY

**noisy** \'nȯi-zē\ *adj* **nois·i·er; -est** 1 : making loud noises 2 : full of noises : LOUD — **nois·i·ly** \-zə-lē\ *adv* — **nois·i·ness** \-zē-nəs\ *n*

**nol·le pro·se·qui** \ˌnä-lē-'prä-sə-ˌkwī\ *n* [L, to be unwilling to pursue] : an entry on the record of a legal action that the prosecutor or plaintiff will proceed no further in an action or suit or in some aspect of it

**no·lo con·ten·de·re** \ˌnō-lō-kən-'ten-də-rē\ *n* [L, I do not wish to contend] : a plea in a criminal prosecution that subjects the defendant to conviction but does not admit guilt or preclude denying the charges in another proceeding

**nol–pros** \ˌnäl-'präs\ *vb* **nol–prossed; nol–pros·sing** : to discontinue by entering a nolle prosequi

**nom** *abbr* nominative

**no·mad** \'nō-ˌmad\ *n* 1 : a member of a people who have no fixed residence but move from place to place 2 : an individual who roams about aimlessly — **no·mad** *adj* — **no·mad·ic** \nō-'ma-dik\ *adj*

**no–man's–land** \'nō-ˌmanz-ˌland\ *n* 1 : an area of unowned, unclaimed, or uninhabited land 2 : an unoccupied area between opposing troops

**nom de guerre** \näm-di-'ger\ *n, pl* **noms de guerre** \*same or* ,nämz-\ [F, lit., war name] : PSEUDONYM

**nom de plume** \-'plüm\ *n, pl* **noms de plume** \*same or* ,nämz-\ [F, pen name; prob. coined in E] : PEN NAME

**no·men·cla·ture** \'nō-mən-,klā-chər\ *n* 1 : NAME, DESIGNATION 2 : a system of terms used in a science or art

**nom·i·nal** \'nä-mə-nᵊl\ *adj* 1 : being something in name or form only ⟨~ head of a party⟩ 2 : TRIFLING ⟨a ~ price⟩ — **nom·i·nal·ly** *adv*

**nom·i·nate** \'nä-mə-,nāt\ *vb* **-nat·ed; -nat·ing** : to choose as a candidate for election, appointment, or honor ♦ *Synonyms* APPOINT, DESIGNATE, NAME, TAP — **nom·i·na·tion** \,nä-mə-'nā-shən\ *n*

**nom·i·na·tive** \'nä-mə-nə-tiv\ *adj* : of, relating to, or constituting a grammatical case marking typically the subject of a verb — **nominative** *n*

**nom·i·nee** \,nä-mə-'nē\ *n* : a person nominated for an office, duty, or position

**non-** \(')nän *or* ,nän *before stressed syllables;* ,nän *elsewhere*\ *prefix* 1 : not : reverse of : absence of 2 : having no importance

**non·age** \'nä-nij, 'nō-\ *n* 1 : legal minority 2 : a period of youth 3 : IMMATURITY

**no·na·ge·nar·i·an** \,nō-nə-jə-'ner-ē-ən, ,nä-\ *n* : a person whose age is in the nineties

**non·aligned** \,nän-ə-'līnd\ *adj* : not allied with other nations

**no–name** \'nō-,näm\ *adj* : not having a readily recognizable name ⟨~ brands⟩

**non·book** \'nän-,bùk\ *n* : a book of little literary merit that is often a compilation (as of pictures or speeches)

¹**nonce** \'näns\ *n* : the one, particular, or present occasion or purpose ⟨for the ~⟩

²**nonce** *adj* : occurring, used, or made only once or for a special occasion ⟨a ~ word⟩

**non·cha·lant** \,nän-shə-'länt\ *adj* [F, fr. OF, fr. prp. of *nonchaloir* to disregard, fr. *non-* not + *chaloir* to concern, fr. L *calēre* to be warm] : giving an effect of unconcern or indifference ♦ *Synonyms* COLLECTED, COMPOSED, COOL, IMPERTURBABLE, UNFLAPPABLE, UNRUFFLED —

**non·cha·lance** \-'läns\ *n* — **non·cha·lant·ly** *adv*

**non–com** \'nän-,käm\ *n* : NONCOMMISSIONED OFFICER

**non·com·ba·tant** \,nän-kəm-'ba-tᵊnt, nän-'käm-bə-tənt\ *n* : a member (as a chaplain) of the armed forces whose duties do not include fighting; *also* : CIVILIAN — **noncombatant** *adj*

**non·com·mis·sioned officer** \,nän-kə-'mi-shənd-\ *n* : a subordinate officer in the armed forces appointed from enlisted personnel

**non·com·mit·tal** \,nän-kə-'mi-tᵊl\ *adj* : indicating neither consent nor dissent ⟨a ~ reply⟩

**non com·pos men·tis** \,nän-,käm-pəs-'men-təs\ *adj* : not of sound mind

**non·con·duc·tor** \,nän-kən-'dək-tər\ *n* : a substance that is a very poor conductor of heat, electricity, or sound

**non·con·form·ist** \-kən-'fòr-mist\ *n* 1 *often cap* : a person who does not conform to an established church and esp. the Church of England 2 : a person who does not conform to a generally accepted pattern of thought or action ♦ *Synonyms* DISSENTER, DISSIDENT, HERETIC, SCHISMATIC, SECTARY, SEPARATIST — **non·con·for·mi·ty** \-'fòr-mə-tē\ *n*

**non·co·op·er·a·tion** \,nän-kō-,ä-pə-'rā-shən\ *n* : failure or refusal to cooperate; *esp* : refusal through civil disobedience of a people to cooperate with the government of a country

**non·cred·it** \(,)nän-'kre-dət\ *adj* : not offering credit toward a degree

**non·cus·to·di·al** \,nän-kə-'stō-dē-əl\ *adj* : of or being a parent who does not have legal custody of a child

**non·dairy** \'nän-'der-ē\ *adj* : containing no milk or milk products ⟨~ margarine⟩

**non·de·script** \,nän-di-'skript\ *adj* 1 : not belonging to any particular class or kind 2 : lacking distinctive qualities ⟨a ~ building⟩

**non·drink·er** \-'driŋ-kər\ *n* : a person who abstains from alcohol

¹**none** \'nən\ *pron* 1 : not any ⟨~ of them went⟩ 2 : not one ⟨~ of the family⟩ 3 : not any such thing or person ⟨half a loaf is better than ~⟩

²**none** *adj, archaic* : not any : NO

---

| | | | |
|---|---|---|---|
| nonabrasive | nonbeliever | noncompliance | nondemocratic |
| nonabsorbent | nonbelligerent | noncomplying | nondenominational |
| nonacademic | nonbiodegradable | nonconducting | |
| nonacceptance | nonbreakable | nonconfidence | nondepartmental |
| nonaccredited | noncaloric | nonconflicting | nondestructive |
| nonacid | noncancerous | nonconformance | nondevelopment |
| nonactivated | noncandidate | nonconforming | nondiscrimination |
| nonadaptive | noncellular | nonconsensual | nondiscriminatory |
| nonaddictive | noncitizen | nonconstructive | nondistinctive |
| nonadhesive | nonclerical | noncontagious | nondurable |
| nonadjacent | noncoital | noncontinuous | noneconomic |
| nonadjustable | noncombat | noncorroding | noneducational |
| nonaggression | noncombative | noncorrosive | nonelastic |
| nonalcoholic | noncombustible | noncriminal | nonelection |
| nonappearance | noncommercial | noncritical | nonelective |
| nonaromatic | noncommunist | noncrystalline | nonelectric |
| nonathletic | noncompeting | nondeductible | nonelectrical |
| nonattendance | noncompetitive | nondelivery | nonemotional |

**³none** *adv* : by no means : not at all ⟨he got there ~ too soon⟩

**non·en·ti·ty** \nän-'en-tə-tē\ *n* **1** : something that does not exist or exists only in the imagination **2** : one of no consequence or significance ♦ *Synonyms* NOBODY, NOTHING, WHIPPERSNAPPER

**nones** \'nōnz\ *n sing or pl* : the 7th day of March, May, July, or October or the 5th day of any other month in the ancient Roman calendar

**non·es·sen·tial** \nän-i-'sen-shəl\ *adj* **1** : not essential **2** : being a substance synthesized by the body in sufficient quantity to satisfy dietary needs

**none·such** \'nən-,səch\ *n* : one without an equal — **nonesuch** *adj*

**none·the·less** \nən-thə-'les\ *adv* : NEVERTHELESS

**non·event** \'nän-i-,vent\ *n* **1** : an event that fails to take place or to satisfy expectations **2** : a highly promoted event of little intrinsic interest

**non·fat** \-'fat\ *adj* : lacking fat solids : having fat solids removed ⟨~ milk⟩

**non·gono·coc·cal** \,nän-,gä-nə-'kä-kəl\ *adj* : not caused by a gonococcus

**non·he·ro** \'nän-'hē-rō\ *n* : ANTIHERO

**non-Hodg·kin's lymphoma** \'nän-'häj-kənz-\ *n* : any of numerous malignant lymphomas not classified as Hodgkin's disease

**non·in·ter·ven·tion** \,nän-,in-tər-'ven-chən\ *n* : refusal or failure to intervene (as in the affairs of other countries)

**non·is·sue** \'nän-'i-shü\ *n* : an issue of little importance or concern

**non·met·al** \'nän-'me-t²l\ *n* : a chemical element (as carbon) that lacks the characteristics of a metal — **non·me·tal·lic** \,nän-mə-'ta-lik\ *adj*

**non·neg·a·tive** \-'ne-gə-tiv\ *adj* : not negative : being either positive or zero

**non·nu·cle·ar** \'nän-'nü-klē-ər\ *adj* **1** : not nuclear **2** : not having, using, or involving nuclear weapons

**non·ob·jec·tive** \nän-əb-'jek-tiv\ *adj* **1** : not objective **2** : representing no natural or actual object, figure, or scene ⟨~ art⟩

**¹non·pa·reil** \-pə-'rel\ *adj* : having no equal : PEERLESS ⟨a ~ performer⟩

**²nonpareil** *n* **1** : an individual of unequaled excellence : PARAGON **2** : a small flat disk of chocolate covered with white sugar pellets

**non·par·ti·san** \'nän-'pär-tə-zən\ *adj* : not partisan; *esp* : not influenced by political party spirit or interests

**non·per·son** \-'pər-s²n\ *n* **1** : UNPERSON **2** : a person having no social or legal status

**non·plus** \'nän-'pləs\ *vb* **-plussed** *also* **-plused** \-'pləst\; **-plus·sing** *also* **-plus·ing** : PUZZLE, PERPLEX

**non·pre·scrip·tion** \,nän-pri-'skrip-shən\ *adj* : available for sale legally without a doctor's prescription

**non·prof·it** \'nän-'prä-fət\ *adj* : not conducted or maintained for the purpose of making a profit ⟨a ~ organization⟩

**non·pro·lif·er·a·tion** \,nän-prə-,li-fə-'rā-shən\ *adj* : providing for the stoppage of proliferation (as of nuclear arms) ⟨a ~ treaty⟩

**non·read·er** \'nän-'rē-dər\ *n* : one who does not read or has difficulty reading

**non·rep·re·sen·ta·tion·al** \,nän-,re-pri-,zen-'tä-shə-nəl\ *adj* : NONOBJECTIVE 2

**non·res·i·dent** \'nän-'re-zə-dənt\ *adj* : not living in a particular place — **non·res·i·dence** \-dəns\ *n* — **nonresident** *n*

**non·re·sis·tance** \,nän-ri-'zis-təns\ *n* : the principles or practice of passive submission to authority even when unjust or oppressive

**non·re·stric·tive** \-ri-'strik-tiv\ *adj* **1** : not serving or tending to restrict **2** : not limiting the reference of the word or phrase modified ⟨a ~ clause⟩

**non·sched·uled** \'nän-'ske-jüld\ *adj* : li-

nonenforcement, nonethical, non-euclidean, nonexclusive, nonexempt, nonexistence, nonexistent, nonexplosive, nonfarm, nonfatal, nonfattening, nonfederated, nonferrous, nonfiction, nonfictional, nonfilamentous, nonfilterable, nonflammable, nonflowering, nonfood, nonfreezing, nonfulfillment, nonfunctional, nonglare, nongraded, nonhazardous, nonhereditary, nonhomogeneous, nonhomologous, nonhuman, nonidentical, nonimportation, nonindustrial, noninfectious, noninflammable, nonintellectual, nonintercourse, noninterference, nonintoxicant, nonintoxicating, noninvasive, nonionizing, nonirritating, nonlegal, nonlethal, nonlife, nonlinear, nonliterary, nonliving, nonlogical, nonmagnetic, nonmalignant, nonmaterial, nonmember, nonmembership, nonmigratory, nonmilitary, nonmoral, nonmotile, nonmoving, nonnegotiable, nonobservance, nonoccurrence, nonofficial, nonoily, nonorthodox, nonparallel, nonparasitic, nonparticipant, nonparticipating, nonpathogenic, nonpaying, nonpayment, nonperformance, nonperishable, nonphysical, nonpoisonous, nonpolar, nonpolitical, nonporous, nonpregnant, nonproductive, nonprofessional, nonprotein, nonradioactive, nonrandom, nonrated, nonreactive, nonreciprocal, nonrecognition, nonrecurrent, nonrecurring, nonrefillable, nonreligious, nonrenewable, nonresidential, nonrestricted, nonreturnable, nonreusable, nonreversible, nonrigid, nonruminant, nonsalable censed to carry passengers or freight by air without a regular schedule

**non·sense** \\'nän-ˌsens, -səns\ *n* **1** : foolish or meaningless words or actions **2** : things of no importance or value — **non·sen·si·cal** \nän-'sen-si-kəl\ *adj* — **non·sen·si·cal·ly** \-k(ə-)lē\ *adv*

**non se·qui·tur** \\'nän-'se-kwə-tər\ *n* [L, it does not follow] : an inference that does not follow from the premises

**non·skid** \\'nän-'skid\ *adj* : designed to prevent skidding ⟨a ~ surface⟩

**non·slip** \-'slip\ *adj* : designed to prevent slipping ⟨a ~ handle⟩

**non·stan·dard** \ˌnän-'stan-dərd\ *adj* **1** : not standard **2** : not conforming to the usage characteristic of educated native speakers of a language

**non·start·er** \\'nän-'stär-tər\ *n* **1** : one that does not start **2** : one that is not productive or effective

**non·stick** \-'stik\ *adj* : allowing easy removal of cooked food particles

**¹non·stop** \\'stäp\ *adj* : done or made without a stop ⟨~ action⟩ — **nonstop** *adv*

**²nonstop** *n* : a nonstop airplane flight

**non·sup·port** \ˌnän-sə-'pórt\ *n* : failure to support; *esp* : failure on the part of one under obligation to provide maintenance

**non·threat·en·ing** \-'thret-niŋ, -'thre-t°n-iŋ\ *adj* : not likely to cause danger or anxiety ⟨a ~ illness⟩ ⟨a ~ environment⟩

**non–U** \\'nän-'yü\ *adj* : not characteristic of the upper classes ⟨~ speech⟩

**non·union** \-'yü-nyən\ *adj* **1** : not belonging to a trade union ⟨~ carpenters⟩ **2** : not recognizing or favoring trade unions or their members ⟨~ employers⟩

**non·us·er** \-'yü-zər\ *n* : one who does not make use of something (as drugs)

**non·vi·o·lence** \ˌnän-'vī-ə-ləns\ *n* **1** : abstention from violence as a matter of principle **2** : avoidance of violence **3** : nonviolent political demonstrations — **non·vi·o·lent** \-lənt\ *adj*

**non·white** \ˌnän-'hwīt, -'wīt\ *n* : a person whose features and esp. skin color are different from those of peoples of northwestern Europe — **nonwhite** *adj*

**non·wo·ven** \ˌnän-'wō-vən\ *adj* : made of fibers held together by interlocking or bonding (as by chemical or thermal means) — **nonwoven** *n*

**noo·dle** \\'nü-d°l\ *n* [G *Nudel*] : a food paste made usu. with egg and shaped typically in ribbon form

**nook** \\'núk\ *n* **1** : an interior angle or corner formed usu. by two walls ⟨a chimney ~⟩ **2** : a sheltered or hidden place ⟨searched every ~ and cranny⟩ **3** : a usu. recessed section of a larger room ⟨a breakfast ~⟩

**noon** \\'nün\ *n* : the middle of the day : 12 o'clock in the daytime — **noon** *adj*

**noon·day** \\'nün-ˌdā\ *n* : NOON, MIDDAY

**no one** *pron* : NOBODY

**noon·tide** \\'nün-ˌtīd\ *n* : NOON

**noon·time** \-ˌtīm\ *n* : NOON

**noose** \\'nüs\ *n* : a loop with a slipknot that binds closer the more it is drawn

**nope** \\'nōp\ *adv* : NO

**nor** \\'nór\ *conj* : and not ⟨not for you ~ for me⟩ — used esp. to introduce and negate the second member and each later member of a series of items preceded by *neither* ⟨neither here ~ there⟩

**Nor·dic** \\'nór-dik\ *adj* **1** : of or relating to the Germanic peoples of northern Europe and esp. of Scandinavia **2** : of or relating to competitive ski events involving cross-country racing, ski jumping, or biathlon — **Nordic** *n*

**nor·epi·neph·rine** \ˌnór-ˌe-pə-'ne-frən\ *n* : a nitrogen-containing neurotransmitter in parts of the sympathetic and central nervous systems

**norm** \\'nórm\ *n* [L *norma*, lit., carpenter's square] **1** : an authoritative standard or model; *esp* : a set standard of development or achievement usu. derived from the average or median achievement of a large group **2** : a typical or widespread practice, procedure, or custom ♦ *Synonyms* AVERAGE, MEAN, MEDIAN, PAR

**¹nor·mal** \\'nór-məl\ *adj* **1** : REGULAR, STANDARD, NATURAL **2** : of average intelligence; *also* : sound in mind and body — **nor·mal·cy** \-sē\ *n* — **nor·mal·i·ty** \nór-'ma-lə-tē\ *n* — **nor·mal·ly** *adv*

**²normal** *n* **1** : one that is normal **2** : the usual condition, level, or quantity

**nor·mal·ise** *Brit var of* NORMALIZE

**nor·mal·ize** \\'nór-mə-ˌlīz\ *vb* **-ized; -iz·ing** : to make or restore to normal ⟨*normalizing* relations⟩ — **nor·mal·i·za·tion** \ˌnór-mə-lə-'zā-shən\ *n*

**Nor·man** \\'nór-mən\ *n* **1** : a native or inhabitant of Normandy **2** : one of the 10th century Scandinavian conquerors of Normandy **3** : one of the Norman-French conquerors of England in 1066 — **Norman** *adj*

**nor·ma·tive** \\'nór-mə-tiv\ *adj* : of, relating to, or determining norms — **nor·ma·tive·ly** *adv* — **nor·ma·tive·ness** *n*

**Norse** \\'nórs\ *n, pl* **Norse 1** : NORWE-

---

| | | | |
|---|---|---|---|
| nonscientific | nonsmoking | nontemporal | nonveteran |
| nonscientist | nonsocial | nontenured | nonviable |
| nonseasonal | nonspeaking | nontheistic | nonvisual |
| nonsectarian | nonspecialist | nonthreatening | nonvocal |
| nonsegregated | nonspecific | nontoxic | nonvolatile |
| nonselective | nonsteroidal | nontraditional | nonvoter |
| non-self-governing | nonstudent | nontransferable | nonvoting |
| nonsexist | nonsuccess | nontypical | nonworker |
| nonsexual | nonsurgical | nonuniform | nonworking |
| nonshrinkable | nontaxable | nonvascular | nonzero |
| nonsinkable | nonteaching | nonvenomous | |
| nonsmoker | nontechnical | nonverbal | |

GIAN; *also* : any of the western Scandinavian dialects or languages **2** *pl* : SCANDINAVIANS; *also* : NORWEGIANS

**Norse-man** \-mən\ *n* : any of the ancient Scandinavians

¹**north** \'nȯrth\ *adv* : to, toward, or in the north

²**north** *adj* **1** : situated toward or at the north **2** : coming from the north

³**north** *n* **1** : the direction to the left of one facing east **2** : the compass point directly opposite to south **3** *cap* : regions or countries north of a specified or implied point — **north-er-ly** \'nȯr-thər-lē\ *adv or adj* — **north-ern** \-thərn\ *adj* — **North-ern-er** \-thər-nər\ *n* — **north-ern-most** \-thərn-ˌmōst\ *adj* — **north-ward** \'nȯrth-wərd\ *adv or adj* — **north-wards** \-wərdz\ *adv*

**north-east** \nȯrth-'ēst\ *n* **1** : the general direction between north and east **2** : the compass point midway between north and east **3** *cap* : regions or countries northeast of a specified or implied point — **northeast** *adj or adv* — **north-east-er-ly** \-'ē-stər-lē\ *adv or adj* — **north-east-ern** \-stərn\ *adj*

**north-east-er** \-'ē-stər\ *n* **1** : a strong northeast wind **2** : a storm with northeast winds

**north-er** \'nȯr-thər\ *n* **1** : a strong north wind **2** : a storm with north winds

**northern lights** *n pl* : AURORA BOREALIS

**north pole** *n, often cap N&P* : the northernmost point of the earth

**North Star** *n* : the star toward which the northern end of the earth's axis points

**north-west** \nȯrth-'west\ *n* **1** : the general direction between north and west **2** : the compass point midway between north and west **3** *cap* : regions or countries northwest of a specified or implied point — **northwest** *adj or adv* — **north-west-er-ly** \-'we-stər-lē\ *adv or adj* — **north-west-ern** \-'we-stərn\ *adj*

**Norw** *abbr* Norway; Norwegian

**Nor-we-gian** \nȯr-'wē-jən\ *n* **1** : a native or inhabitant of Norway **2** : the language of Norway — **Norwegian** *adj*

**nos** *abbr* numbers

¹**nose** \'nōz\ *n* **1** : the part of the face or head containing the nostrils and covering the front of the nasal cavity **2** : the sense of smell **3** : something (as a point, edge, or projecting front part) that resembles a nose ⟨the ~ of a plane⟩ — **nosed** \'nōzd\ *adj* — **on the nose** : on target : ACCURATE — **under one's nose** : extremely near : in one's presence

²**nose** *vb* **nosed; nos-ing 1** : to detect by or as if by smell : SCENT **2** : to push or move with the nose **3** : to touch or rub with the nose : NUZZLE **4** : PRY **5** : to move ahead slowly ⟨the ship *nosed* into her berth⟩

**nose-bleed** \'nōz-ˌblēd\ *n* : a bleeding from the nose

**nose cone** *n* : a protective cone constituting the forward end of an aerospace vehicle

**nose-dive** \'nōz-ˌdīv\ *n* **1** : a downward nose-first plunge (as of an airplane) **2** : a sudden extreme drop (as in prices)

**nose-gay** \'nōz-ˌgā\ *n* : a small bunch of flowers : POSY

**nose out** *vb* **1** : to discover often by prying **2** : to defeat by a narrow margin

**nose-piece** \-ˌpēs\ *n* **1** : a fitting at the lower end of a microscope tube to which the objectives are attached **2** : the bridge of a pair of eyeglasses

**no-show** \'nō-'shō\ *n* : a person who does not show up for an event as expected

**nos-tal-gia** \nä-'stal-jə\ *n* [NL, fr. Gk *nostos* return home + *algos* pain, grief] **1** : HOMESICKNESS **2** : a wistful yearning for something past or irrecoverable — **nos-tal-gic** \-jik\ *adj* — **nos-tal-gist** \-jist\ *n*

**nos-tril** \'näs-trəl\ *n* [ME *nosethirl*, fr. OE *nosthyrl*, fr. *nosu* nose + *thyrel* hole] **1** : either of the nares usu. with the adjoining nasal wall and passage **2** : either fleshy lateral wall of the nose

**nos-trum** \'näs-trəm\ *n* [L, neut. of *noster* our, ours, fr. *nos* we] : a questionable medicine or remedy

**nosy** *or* **nos-ey** \'nō-zē\ *adj* **nos-i-er; -est** : INQUISITIVE, PRYING ⟨~ neighbors⟩

**not** \'nät\ *adv* **1** — used to make negative a group of words or a word ⟨the boys are ~ here⟩ **2** — used to stand for the negative of a preceding group of words ⟨sometimes hard to see and sometimes ~⟩

**no-ta be-ne** \ˌnō-tə-'bē-nē, -'be-\ [L, mark well] — used to call attention to something important

**no-ta-bil-i-ty** \ˌnō-tə-'bi-lə-tē\ *n, pl* **-ties 1** : the quality or state of being notable **2** : NOTABLE

¹**no-ta-ble** \'nō-tə-bəl\ *adj* **1** : NOTEWORTHY, REMARKABLE ⟨a ~ achievement⟩ **2** : DISTINGUISHED, PROMINENT ⟨two ~ politicians made speeches⟩

²**notable** *n* : a person of note ♦ **Synonyms** BIGWIG, EMINENCE, NABOB, PERSONAGE, SOMEBODY, VIP

**no-ta-bly** \'nō-tə-blē\ *adv* **1** : in a notable manner **2** : ESPECIALLY, PARTICULARLY

**no-tar-i-al** \nō-'ter-ē-əl\ *adj* : of, relating to, or done by a notary public

**no-ta-rize** \'nō-tə-ˌrīz\ *vb* **-rized; -riz-ing** : to acknowledge or make legally authentic as a notary public

**no-ta-ry public** \'nō-tə-rē-\ *n, pl* **notaries public** *or* **notary publics** : a public official who attests or certifies writings (as deeds) to make them legally authentic

**no-ta-tion** \nō-'tā-shən\ *n* **1** : ANNOTATION, NOTE **2** : the act, process, or method of representing data by marks, signs, figures, or characters; *also* : a system of symbols (as letters, numerals, or musical notes) used in such notation

¹**notch** \'näch\ *n* **1** : a V-shaped hollow in an edge or surface **2** : a narrow pass between two mountains

²**notch** *vb* **1** : to cut or make notches in **2** : to score or record by or as if by cutting

a series of notches ⟨~ed 20 points for the team⟩

**notch·back** \'näch-ˌbak\ n : an automobile with a trunk whose lid forms a distinct deck

¹**note** \'nōt\ vb **not·ed; not·ing** 1 : to notice or observe with care ⟨noted her reaction⟩; also : to record or preserve in writing 2 : to make special mention of : REMARK

²**note** n 1 : a musical sound 2 : a cry, call, or sound esp. of a bird 3 : a special tone in a person's words or voice ⟨a ~ of fear⟩ 4 : a character in music used to indicate duration of a tone by its shape and pitch by its position on the staff 5 : a characteristic feature : MOOD, QUALITY ⟨a ~ of optimism⟩ 6 : MEMORANDUM 7 : a brief and informal record; also : a written or printed comment or explanation 8 : a written promise to pay a debt 9 : a piece of paper money 10 : a short informal letter 11 : a formal diplomatic or official communication 12 : DISTINCTION, REPUTATION ⟨an artist of ~⟩ 13 : OBSERVATION, NOTICE, HEED ⟨take ~ of the time⟩

**note·book** \'nōt-ˌbuk\ n 1 : a book for notes or memoranda 2 : a portable microcomputer smaller than a laptop computer

**not·ed** \'nō-təd\ adj : well known by reputation : EMINENT ⟨a ~ violinist⟩

**note·wor·thy** \'nōt-ˌwər-thē\ adj : worthy of note : REMARKABLE

¹**noth·ing** \'nə-thiŋ\ pron 1 : no thing ⟨leaves ~ to the imagination⟩ 2 : no part 3 : one of no interest, value, or importance ⟨she's ~ to me⟩ 4 : a light playful remark ⟨sweet ~s⟩

²**nothing** adv : not at all : in no degree

³**nothing** n 1 : something that does not exist 2 : ZERO 3 : a person or thing of little or no value or importance

⁴**nothing** adj : of no account : WORTHLESS

**noth·ing·ness** \'nə-thiŋ-nəs\ n 1 : the quality or state of being nothing 2 : NONEXISTENCE; also : utter insignificance 3 : something insignificant or valueless

¹**no·tice** \'nō-təs\ n 1 : WARNING, ANNOUNCEMENT 2 : notification of the termination of an agreement or contract at a specified time 3 : ATTENTION, HEED ⟨bring the matter to my ~⟩ 4 : a written or printed announcement 5 : a short critical account or examination (as of a play) : REVIEW

²**notice** vb **no·ticed; no·tic·ing** 1 : to make mention of : remark on : NOTE 2 : to take notice of : OBSERVE, MARK

**no·tice·able** \'nō-tə-sə-bəl\ adj 1 : worthy of notice 2 : likely to be noticed ⟨a ~ scar⟩ — **no·tice·ably** \-blē\ adv

**no·ti·fy** \'nō-tə-ˌfī\ vb **-fied; -fy·ing** 1 : to give notice of : report the occurrence of 2 : to give notice to — **no·ti·fi·ca·tion** \ˌnō-tə-fə-'kā-shən\ n

**no·tion** \'nō-shən\ n 1 : IDEA, CONCEPTION ⟨have a ~ of what he means⟩ 2 : a belief held : OPINION, VIEW 3 : WHIM, FANCY ⟨a sudden ~ to go⟩ 4 pl : small

useful articles (as pins, needles, or thread)

**no·tion·al** \'nō-shə-nəl\ adj 1 : existing in the mind only : IMAGINARY, UNREAL 2 : given to foolish or fanciful moods or ideas : WHIMSICAL

**no·to·ri·ous** \nō-'tòr-ē-əs\ adj : generally known and talked of; esp : widely and unfavorably known — **no·to·ri·ety** \ˌnō-tə-'rī-ə-tē\ n — **no·to·ri·ous·ly** \nō-'tòr-ē-əs-lē\ adv

¹**not·with·stand·ing** \ˌnät-with-'stan-diŋ, -with-\ prep : in spite of

²**notwithstanding** adv : NEVERTHELESS

³**notwithstanding** conj : ALTHOUGH

**nou·gat** \'nü-gət\ n [F, fr. Occitan, fr. Old Occitan, nogat, fr. noga nut, ultim. fr. L nuc-, nux] : a confection of nuts or fruit pieces in a sugar paste

**nought** var of NAUGHT

**noun** \'naun\ n : a word that is the name of a subject of discourse (as a person or place)

**nour·ish** \'nər-ish\ vb : to promote the growth or development of

**nour·ish·ing** adj : giving nourishment

**nour·ish·ment** \'nər-ish-mənt\ n 1 : FOOD, NUTRIENT 2 : the action or process of nourishing

**nou·veau riche** \ˌnü-ˌvō-'rēsh\ n, pl **nou·veaux riches** \same\ [F] : a person newly rich : PARVENU

**Nov** abbr November

**no·va** \'nō-və\ n, pl **novas** or **no·vae** \-(ˌ)vē, -ˌvī\ [NL, fem. of L novus new] : a star that suddenly increases greatly in brightness and then within a few months or years grows dim again

¹**nov·el** \'nä-vəl\ adj 1 : having no precedent : NEW 2 : STRANGE, UNUSUAL

²**novel** n : a long invented prose narrative dealing with human experience through a connected sequence of events — **nov·el·ist** \-və-list\ n

**nov·el·ette** \ˌnä-və-'let\ n : a brief novel or long short story

**nov·el·ize** \'nä-və-ˌlīz\ vb **-ized; -iz·ing** : to convert into the form of a novel — **nov·el·iza·tion** \ˌnä-və-lə-'zā-shən\ n

**no·vel·la** \nō-'ve-lə\ n, pl **novellas** or **no·vel·le** \-'ve-lē\ : NOVELETTE

**nov·el·ty** \'nä-vəl-tē\ n, pl **-ties** 1 : something new or unusual : NEWNESS 3 : a small manufactured article intended mainly for personal or household adornment — usu. used in pl.

**No·vem·ber** \nō-'vem-bər\ n [ME Novembre, fr. AF, fr. L November ninth month of the early Roman calendar, fr. novem nine] : the 11th month of the year

**no·ve·na** \nō-'vē-nə\ n : a Roman Catholic nine-day period of prayer

**nov·ice** \'nä-vəs\ n 1 : a new member of a religious order who is preparing to take the vows of religion 2 : one who is inexperienced or untrained

**no·vi·tiate** \nō-'vi-shət\ n 1 : the period or state of being a novice 2 : a house where novices are trained 3 : NOVICE

¹**now** \'nau\ adv 1 : at the present time or moment 2 : in the time immediately before the present 3 : IMMEDIATELY,

FORTHWITH **4** — used with the sense of present time weakened or lost (as to express command, introduce an important point, or indicate a transition) ⟨~ hear this⟩ **5** : SOMETIMES ⟨~ one and ~ another⟩ **6** : under the present circumstances **7** : at the time referred to **8** : by this time

²**now** *conj* : in view of the fact ⟨~ that you're here, we'll start⟩

³**now** *n* : the present time or moment : PRESENT

⁴**now** *adj* **1** : of or relating to the present time ⟨the ~ president⟩ **2** : excitingly new ⟨~ clothes⟩; *also* : constantly aware of what is new ⟨~ people⟩

**NOW** *abbr* **1** National Organization for Women **2** negotiable order of withdrawal

**now·a·days** \'naú-ə-ˌdāz\ *adv* : at the present time

**no·way** \'nō-ˌwā\ *or* **no·ways** \-ˌwāz\ *adv* : NOWISE

**no·where** \-ˌhwer\ *adv* **1** : not anywhere **2** : not at all — usu. used with *near* ⟨~ near enough⟩ — **nowhere** *n*

**no·wise** \'nō-ˌwīz\ *adv* : in no way

**nox·ious** \'näk-shəs\ *adj* : harmful esp. to health or morals

**noz·zle** \'nä-zəl\ *n* : a short tube constricted in the middle or at one end and used (as on a hose) to speed up or direct a flow of fluid

**np** *abbr* **1** no pagination **2** no place (of publication)

**Np** *symbol* neptunium

**NP** *abbr* notary public

**NR** *abbr* not rated

**NRA** *abbr* National Rifle Association

**NS** *abbr* **1** not specified **2** Nova Scotia

**NSA** *abbr* National Security Agency

**NSC** *abbr* National Security Council

**NSF** *abbr* **1** National Science Foundation **2** not sufficient funds

**NSW** *abbr* New South Wales

**NT** *abbr* **1** New Testament **2** Northern Territory **3** Northwest Territories

**nth** \'enth\ *adj* **1** : numbered with an unspecified or indefinitely large ordinal number ⟨for the ~ time⟩ **2** : EXTREME, UTMOST ⟨to the ~ degree⟩

**NTP** *abbr* normal temperature and pressure

**nt wt** *or* **n wt** *abbr* net weight

**nu** \'nü, 'nyü\ *n* : the 13th letter of the Greek alphabet — N or ν

**NU** *abbr* name unknown

**nu·ance** \'nü-ˌäns, 'nyü-, nü-'äns, nyü-\ *n* [F] : a shade of difference : a delicate variation (as in tone or meaning)

**nub** \'nəb\ *n* **1** : KNOB, LUMP **2** : GIST, POINT ⟨the ~ of the story⟩

**nub·bin** \'nə-bən\ *n* **1** : something (as an ear of corn) that is small for its kind, stunted, undeveloped, or imperfect **2** : a small projecting bit

**nu·bile** \'nü-ˌbī(-ə)l, 'nyü-, -bəl\ *adj* **1** : of marriageable condition or age **2** : sexually attractive ⟨~ young women⟩

**nu·cle·ar** \'nü-klē-ər, 'nyü-\ *adj* **1** : of, relating to, or constituting a nucleus **2** : of, relating to, or using the atomic nu-

cleus or energy derived from it **3** : of, relating to, or being a weapon whose destructive power results from an uncontrolled nuclear reaction

**nu·cle·ate** \'nü-klē-ˌāt, 'nyü-\ *vb* -**at·ed**; -**at·ing** : to form, act as, or have a nucleus — **nu·cle·ation** \ˌnü-klē-'ā-shən, ˌnyü-\ *n*

**nu·cle·ic acid** \nü-'klē-ik-, nyü-, -'klā-\ *n* : any of various complex organic acids (as DNA or RNA) found esp. in cell nuclei

**nu·cle·o·tide** \'nü-klē-ə-ˌtīd, 'nyü-\ *n* : any of several compounds that are the basic structural units of nucleic acids

**nu·cle·us** \'nü-klē-əs, 'nyü-\ *n, pl* **nu·clei** \-klē-ˌī\ *also* **nu·cle·us·es** [NL, fr. L, kernel, dim. of *nuc-, nux* nut] **1** : a central mass or part about which matter gathers or is collected : CORE **2** : a cell part that is characteristic of all living things except viruses, bacteria, and certain algae, that is necessary for heredity and for making proteins, that contains the chromosomes with their genes, and that is enclosed in a membrane **3** : a mass of gray matter or group of cell bodies of neurons in the central nervous system **4** : the central part of an atom that comprises nearly all of the atomic mass **5** : a basic or essential part

¹**nude** \'nüd, 'nyüd\ *adj* **nud·er**; **nud·est** **1** : BARE, NAKED, UNCLOTHED **2** : featuring or catering to naked people ⟨a ~ beach⟩ — **nu·di·ty** \'nü-də-tē, 'nyü-\ *n*

²**nude** *n* **1** : a nude human figure esp. as depicted in art **2** : the condition of being nude ⟨in the ~⟩

**nudge** \'nəj\ *vb* **nudged**; **nudg·ing** : to touch or push gently (as with the elbow) usu. in order to seek attention — **nudge** *n*

**nud·ism** \'nü-ˌdi-zəm, 'nyü-\ *n* : the practice of going nude esp. in mixed groups at specially secluded places — **nud·ist** \-dist\ *n*

**nu·ga·to·ry** \'nü-gə-ˌtȯr-ē\ *adj* **1** : INCONSEQUENTIAL, WORTHLESS ⟨his efforts were rendered ~⟩ **2** : having no force : INEFFECTUAL

**nug·get** \'nə-gət\ *n* **1** : a lump of precious metal (as gold) **2** : TIDBIT

**nui·sance** \'nü-s⁰ns, 'nyü-\ *n* : an annoying or troublesome person or thing

**nuisance tax** *n* : an excise tax collected in small amounts directly from the consumer

¹**nuke** \'nük, 'nyük\ *n* **1** : a nuclear weapon **2** : a nuclear power plant

²**nuke** *vb* **nuked**; **nuk·ing** **1** : to attack with nuclear weapons **2** : MICROWAVE

**null** \'nəl\ *adj* **1** : having no legal or binding force : INVALID, VOID **2** : amounting to nothing **3** : INSIGNIFICANT — **nul·li·ty** \'nə-lə-tē\ *n*

**null and void** *adj* : having no force, binding power, or validity

**nul·li·fy** \'nə-lə-ˌfī\ *vb* -**fied**; -**fy·ing** : to make null or valueless; *also* : ANNUL — **nul·li·fi·ca·tion** \ˌnə-lə-fə-'kā-shən\ *n*

**num** *abbr* numeral

**Num** *or* **Numb** *abbr* Numbers

**numb** \ˈnəm\ adj : lacking sensation or emotion : BENUMBED — **numb** vb — **numb·ly** adv — **numb·ness** n

¹**num·ber** \ˈnəm-bər\ n 1 : the total of individuals or units taken together 2 : an indefinite total ⟨a small ~ of tickets remain unsold⟩ 3 : an ascertainable total ⟨the sands of the desert are without ~⟩ 4 : a distinction of word form to denote reference to one or more than one 5 : a unit belonging to a mathematical system and subject to its laws; also, pl : ARITHMETIC 6 : a symbol used to represent a mathematical number; also : such a number used to identify or designate ⟨a phone ~⟩ 7 : one in a series of musical or theatrical performances 8 : an act of transforming or impairing ⟨tripped and did a ~ on her knee⟩

²**number** vb 1 : COUNT, ENUMERATE 2 : to include with or be one of a group 3 : to restrict to a small or definite number 4 : to assign a number to 5 : to comprise in number : TOTAL

**num·ber·less** \-ləs\ adj : INNUMERABLE, COUNTLESS ⟨~ stars in the sky⟩

**Numbers** n — see BIBLE table

**numb·ing** \ˈnə-miŋ\ adj : tending to make numb ⟨a ~ lecture⟩ ⟨a ~ realization⟩

**numbskull** var of NUMSKULL

**nu·mer·a·cy** \ˈnü-mə-rə-sē, ˈnyü-\ n : the capacity for quantitative thought or expression

**nu·mer·al** \ˈnü-mə-rəl, ˈnyü-\ n : a conventional symbol representing a number — **numeral** adj

**nu·mer·ate** \ˈnü-mə-ˌrāt, ˈnyü-\ vb **-at·ed; -at·ing** : ENUMERATE

**nu·mer·a·tor** \-ˌrā-tər\ n : the part of a fraction above the line

**nu·mer·ic** \nü-ˈmer-ik, nyü-\ adj : NUMERICAL; esp : denoting a number or a system of numbers

**nu·mer·i·cal** \-ˈmer-i-kəl\ adj 1 : of or relating to numbers ⟨in ~ order⟩ 2 : expressed in or involving numbers — **nu·mer·i·cal·ly** \-k(ə-)lē\ adv

**nu·mer·ol·o·gy** \ˌnü-mə-ˈrä-lə-jē, ˌnyü-\ n : the study of the occult significance of numbers — **nu·mer·ol·o·gist** \-jist\ n

**nu·mer·ous** \ˈnü-mə-rəs, ˈnyü-\ adj : consisting of, including, or relating to a great number : MANY

**nu·mis·mat·ics** \ˌnü-məz-ˈma-tiks, ˌnyü-\ n : the study or collection of monetary objects — **nu·mis·mat·ic** \-tik\ adj — **nu·mis·ma·tist** \nü-ˈmiz-mə-tist, nyü-\ n

**num·skull** also **numb·skull** \ˈnəm-ˌskəl\ n : a stupid person : DUNCE

**nun** \ˈnən\ n : a woman belonging to a religious order; esp : one under solemn vows of poverty, chastity, and obedience

**nun·cio** \ˈnən-sē-ˌō, ˈnün-\ n, pl **-ci·os** [It, fr. L nuntius messenger] : a permanent high-ranking papal representative to a civil government

**nun·nery** \ˈnə-nə-rē\ n, pl **-ner·ies** : a convent of nuns

¹**nup·tial** \ˈnəp-shəl\ adj : of or relating to marriage or a wedding ⟨~ vows⟩

²**nuptial** n : MARRIAGE, WEDDING — usu. used in pl.

¹**nurse** \ˈnərs\ n [ME norice, nurse, fr. AF nurice, fr. LL nutricia, fr. L, fem. of nutricius nourishing] 1 : a girl or woman employed to take care of children 2 : a person trained to care for sick people

²**nurse** vb **nursed; nurs·ing** 1 : SUCKLE 2 : to take charge of and watch over 3 : TEND ⟨~ an invalid⟩ 4 : to treat with special care ⟨~ a headache⟩ 5 : to hold in one's mind or consideration ⟨~ a grudge⟩ 6 : to act or serve as a nurse

**nurse·maid** \ˈnərs-ˌmād\ n : NURSE 1

**nurse–prac·ti·tion·er** \-prak-ˈti-shə-nər\ n : a registered nurse who is qualified to assume some of the duties formerly assumed only by a physician

**nurs·ery** \ˈnər-sə-rē\ n, pl **-er·ies** 1 : a room for children 2 : a place where children are temporarily cared for in their parents' absence 3 : a place where young plants are grown usu. for transplanting

**nurs·ery·man** \-mən\ n : a man who keeps or works in a plant nursery

**nursery school** n : a school for children under kindergarten age

**nursing home** n : a private establishment providing care for persons (as the aged or the chronically ill) who are unable to care for themselves

**nurs·ling** \ˈnərs-liŋ\ n 1 : one that is solicitously cared for 2 : a nursing child

¹**nur·ture** \ˈnər-chər\ n 1 : TRAINING, UPBRINGING; also : the influences that modify the expression of an individual's heredity 2 : FOOD, NOURISHMENT

²**nurture** vb **nur·tured; nur·tur·ing** 1 : to care for : FEED, NOURISH 2 : EDUCATE, TRAIN ⟨~ students⟩ 3 : FOSTER ⟨~ creativity⟩

**nut** \ˈnət\ n 1 : a dry fruit or seed with a hard shell and a firm inner kernel; also : its kernel 2 : a metal block with a hole through it that is fastened to a bolt or screw by means of a screw thread within the hole 3 : the ridge on the upper end of the fingerboard in a stringed musical instrument over which the strings pass 4 : a foolish, eccentric, or crazy person 5 : ENTHUSIAST

**nut·crack·er** \ˈnət-ˌkra-kər\ n : an instrument for cracking nuts

**nut·hatch** \-ˌhach\ n : any of various small tree-climbing chiefly insect-eating birds

**nut·meg** \-ˌmeg, -ˌmāg\ n [ME notemuge, ultim. fr. Old Occitan noz muscada, lit., musky nut] : a spice made by grinding the nutlike aromatic seed of a tropical tree; also : the seed or tree

**nu·tria** \ˈnü-trē-ə, ˈnyü-\ n [Sp] 1 : the durable usu. light brown fur of a nutria 2 : a large So. American aquatic rodent with webbed hind feet

¹**nu·tri·ent** \ˈnü-trē-ənt, ˈnyü-\ adj : NOURISHING ⟨~ deficiencies⟩

²**nutrient** n : a nutritive substance or ingredient ⟨fruits and vegetables are important ~s⟩

**nu·tri·ment** \-trə-mənt\ n : NUTRIENT

**nu·tri·tion** \nü-ˈtri-shən, nyü-\ n : the act or process of nourishing; esp : the processes by which an individual takes in and utilizes food material — **nu·tri·tion·al** \-shə-nəl\ *adj* — **nu·tri·tion·al·ly** *adv* — **nu·tri·tion·ist** \-shə-nist\ *n* — **nu·tri·tive** \'nü-trə-tiv, 'nyü-\ *adj*

**nu·tri·tious** \-shəs\ *adj* : NOURISHING — **nu·tri·tious·ly** *adv*

**nuts** \'nəts\ *adj* **1** : ENTHUSIASTIC, KEEN **2** : CRAZY, DEMENTED

**nut·shell** \'nət-,shel\ *n* : the shell of a nut — **in a nutshell** : in a few words ⟨that's the story *in a nutshell*⟩

**nut·ty** \'nə-tē\ *adj* **nut·ti·er; -est 1** : containing or suggesting nuts ⟨a ~ flavor⟩ **2** : mentally unbalanced

**nuz·zle** \'nə-zəl\ *vb* **nuz·zled; nuz·zling 1** : to root around, push, or touch with or as if with the nose **2** : NESTLE, SNUGGLE

**NV** *abbr* Nevada

**NW** *abbr* northwest

**NWT** *abbr* Northwest Territories

**NY** *abbr* New York

**NYC** *abbr* New York City

**ny·lon** \'nī-,län\ *n* **1** : any of numerous strong tough elastic synthetic materials used esp. in textiles and plastics **2** *pl* : stockings made of nylon

**nymph** \'nimf\ *n* **1** : any of the lesser goddesses in ancient mythology represented as maidens living in the mountains, forests, meadows, and waters **2** : GIRL **3** : an immature insect resembling the adult but smaller, less differentiated, and usu. lacking developed wings

**nym·pho·ma·nia** \,nim-fə-'mā-nē-ə, -nyə\ *n* : excessive sexual desire by a female — **nym·pho·ma·ni·ac** \-nē-,ak\ *n or adj*

**NZ** *abbr* New Zealand

**¹o** \'ō\ *n, pl* **o's** *or* **os** \'ōz\ *often cap* **1** : the 15th letter of the English alphabet **2** : ZERO

**²o** *abbr, often cap* **1** ocean **2** Ohio **3** ohm

**¹O** *var of* OH

**²O** *symbol* oxygen

**o/a** *abbr* on or about

**oaf** \'ōf\ *n* : a stupid or awkward person — **oaf·ish** *adj*

**oak** \'ōk\ *n, pl* **oaks** *or* **oak** : any of a genus of trees or shrubs related to the beech and chestnut and bearing a rounded thin-shelled nut surrounded at the base by a hardened cup; *also* : the usu. tough hard durable wood of an oak — **oak·en** \'ō-kən\ *adj*

**oa·kum** \'ō-kəm\ *n* [ME *okum,* fr. OE *ācumba* flax fiber, from *ā*- out + *-cumba* (akin to OE *camb* comb)] : loosely twisted hemp or jute fiber impregnated with tar and used esp. in caulking ships

**oar** \'ȯr\ *n* : a long pole with a broad blade at one end used for propelling or steering a boat

**oar·lock** \'ȯr-,läk\ *n* : a U-shaped device for holding an oar in place

**oars·man** \'ȯrz-mən\ *n* : one who rows esp. in a racing crew

**OAS** *abbr* Organization of American States

**oa·sis** \ō-'ā-səs\ *n, pl* **oa·ses** \-,sēz\ : a fertile or green area in an arid region

**oat** \'ōt\ *n* : a cereal grass widely grown for its edible seed; *also* : this seed — **oat·en** \'ō-tᵊn\ *adj*

**oat·cake** \'ōt-,kāk\ *n* : a thin flat oatmeal cake

**oath** \'ōth\ *n, pl* **oaths** \'ōthz, 'ōths\ **1** : a solemn appeal to God to witness to the truth of a statement or the sacredness of a promise **2** : an irreverent or careless use of a sacred name

**oat·meal** \'ōt-,mēl\ *n* **1** : ground or rolled oats **2** : porridge made from ground or rolled oats

**Ob** *or* **Obad** *abbr* Obadiah

**Oba·di·ah** \,ō-bə-'dī-ə\ *n* — see BIBLE table

**ob·bli·ga·to** \,ä-blə-'gä-tō\ *n, pl* **-tos** *also* **-ti** \-'gä-tē\ [It] : an accompanying part usu. played by a solo instrument

**ob·du·rate** \'äb-də-rət, -dyə-\ *adj* : stubbornly resistant : UNYIELDING ⟨an ~ denial⟩ ♦ *Synonyms* INFLEXIBLE, ADAMANT, RIGID, UNCOMPROMISING — **ob·du·ra·cy** \-rə-sē\ *n*

**obe·di·ent** \ō-'bē-dē-ənt\ *adj* : submissive to the restraint or command of authority ♦ *Synonyms* DOCILE, TRACTABLE, AMENABLE, BIDDABLE — **obe·di·ence** \-əns\ *n* — **obe·di·ent·ly** *adv*

**obei·sance** \ō-'bē-səns, -'bā-\ *n* **1** : a bow made to show respect or submission **2** : DEFERENCE, HOMAGE ⟨makes ~ to her mentors⟩

**obe·lisk** \'ä-bə-,lisk\ *n* [MF *obelisque,* fr. L *obeliscus,* fr. Gk *obeliskos,* fr. dim. of *obelos* spit, pointed pillar] : a 4-sided pillar that tapers toward the top and ends in a pyramid

**obese** \ō-'bēs\ *adj* [L *obesus,* fr. *ob*against + *esus,* pp. of *edere* to eat] : having excessive body fat ♦ *Synonyms* CORPULENT, FLESHY, GROSS, OVERWEIGHT, PORTLY, STOUT — **obe·si·ty** \-'bē-sə-tē\ *n*

**obey** \ō-'bā\ *vb* **obeyed; obey·ing 1** : to follow the commands or guidance of : behave obediently **2** : to comply with ⟨~ orders⟩ ♦ *Synonyms* CONFORM, KEEP, MIND, OBSERVE

**ob·fus·cate** \'äb-fə-,skāt\ *vb* **-cat·ed; -cat·ing 1** : to make dark or obscure **2** : to make difficult to understand — **ob·fus·ca·tion** \,äb-fəs-'kā-shən\ *n*

**OB–GYN** *abbr* obstetrician gynecologist; obstetrics gynecology

**obi** \'ō-bē\ *n* [Jp] : a broad sash worn esp. with a Japanese kimono

**obit** \ō-'bit, 'ō-bət\ *n* : OBITUARY

**obi·ter dic·tum** \,ō-bə-tər-'dik-təm\ *n, pl* **obiter dic·ta** \-tə\ [LL, lit., something said in passing] : an incidental remark or observation

**obit·u·ary** \ə-'bi-chə-,wer-ē\ *n, pl* **-ar·ies** : a notice of a person's death usu. with a short biographical account

**obj** *abbr* object; objective

**¹ob·ject** \'äb-jikt\ *n* **1** : something that may be seen or felt; *also* : something that may be perceived or examined mentally **2** : something that arouses an emotional response (as of affection or pity) **3** : AIM, PURPOSE ⟨the ∼ is to raise money⟩ **4** : a word or word group denoting that on or toward which the action of a verb is directed; *also* : a noun or noun equivalent in a prepositional phrase

**²ob·ject** \əb-'jekt\ *vb* **1** : to offer in opposition **2** : to oppose something; *also* : DISAPPROVE ♦ *Synonyms* PROTEST, REMONSTRATE, EXPOSTULATE — **ob·jec·tor** \-'jek-tər\ *n*

**object code** *n* : a computer program after translation from source code

**ob·jec·ti·fy** \əb-'jek-tə-,fī\ *vb* **-fied; -fy·ing** : to make objective

**ob·jec·tion** \əb-'jek-shən\ *n* **1** : the act of objecting **2** : a reason for or a feeling of disapproval

**ob·jec·tion·able** \əb-'jek-shə-nə-bəl\ *adj* : UNDESIRABLE, OFFENSIVE — **ob·jec·tion·ably** \-blē\ *adv*

**¹ob·jec·tive** \əb-'jek-tiv\ *adj* **1** : of or relating to an object or end **2** : existing outside and independent of the mind **3** : of, relating to, or constituting a grammatical case marking typically the object of a verb or preposition **4** : treating or dealing with facts without distortion by personal feelings or prejudices — **ob·jec·tive·ly** *adv* — **ob·jec·tive·ness** *n* — **ob·jec·tiv·i·ty** \,äb-jek-'ti-və-tē\ *n*

**²objective** *n* **1** : the lens (as in a microscope) nearest the object and forming an image of it **2** : an aim, goal, or end of action

**ob·jet d'art** \,ôb-,zhä-'där\ *n, pl* **ob·jets d'art** \*same*\ [F] **1** : an article of artistic worth **2** : CURIO ♦ *Synonyms* KNICKKNACK, BAUBLE, BIBELOT, GEWGAW, NOVELTY, TRINKET

**ob·jet trou·vé** \'ôb-,zhä-trü-'vä\ *n, pl* **objets trouvés** \*same*\ [F, lit., found object] : a found natural or discarded object (as a piece of driftwood or an old bathtub) held to have aesthetic value

**ob·jur·ga·tion** \,äb-jər-'gā-shən\ *n* : a harsh rebuke — **ob·jur·gate** \'äb-jər-,gāt\ *vb*

**obl** *abbr* **1** oblique **2** oblong

**ob·late** \ä-'blāt\ *adj* : flattened or depressed at the poles ⟨an ∼ spheroid⟩

**ob·la·tion** \ə-'blā-shən\ *n* : a religious offering

**ob·li·gate** \'ä-blə-,gāt\ *vb* **-gat·ed; -gat·ing** : to bind legally or morally

**ob·li·ga·tion** \,ä-blə-'gā-shən\ *n* **1** : an act of obligating oneself to a course of action **2** : something (as a promise or a contract) that binds one to a course of action **3** : INDEBTEDNESS; *also* : LIABILITY **4**

: DUTY — **oblig·a·to·ry** \ə-'bli-gə-,tôr-ē\ *adj*

**oblige** \ə-'blīj\ *vb* **obliged; oblig·ing** [ME, fr. AF *obliger*, fr. L *obligare*, lit., to bind to, fr. *ob-* toward + *ligare* to bind] **1** : FORCE, COMPEL ⟨the soldiers were *obliged* to retreat⟩ **2** : to bind by a favor; *also* : to do a favor for or do something as a favor

**oblig·ing** *adj* : willing to do favors — **oblig·ing·ly** *adv*

**oblique** \ō-'blēk\ *adj* **1** : neither perpendicular nor parallel : SLANTING **2** : not straightforward : INDIRECT — **oblique·ly** *adv* — **oblique·ness** *n* — **obliq·ui·ty** \-'bli-kwə-tē\ *n*

**oblique case** *n* : a grammatical case other than the nominative or vocative

**oblit·er·ate** \ə-'bli-tə-,rāt\ *vb* **-at·ed; -at·ing** [L *oblitterare*, fr. *ob* in the way of + *littera* letter] **1** : to remove from recognition or memory **2** : to make undecipherable by wiping out or covering over **3** : CANCEL — **oblit·er·a·tion** \-,bli-tə-'rā-shən\ *n*

**obliv·i·on** \ə-'bli-vē-ən\ *n* **1** : the condition of being oblivious **2** : the condition or state of being forgotten

**obliv·i·ous** \ə-'bli-vē-əs\ *adj* **1** : lacking memory or mindful attention **2** : UNAWARE ⟨∼ of the risks⟩ — **obliv·i·ous·ly** *adv* — **obliv·i·ous·ness** *n*

**ob·long** \'ä-,blôŋ\ *adj* : deviating from a square, circular, or spherical form by elongation in one dimension — **oblong** *n*

**ob·lo·quy** \'ä-blə-kwē\ *n, pl* **-quies** **1** : strongly condemnatory utterance or language **2** : bad repute : DISGRACE ♦ *Synonyms* DISHONOR, SHAME, INFAMY, DISREPUTE, IGNOMINY

**ob·nox·ious** \äb-'näk-shəs\ *adj* : REPUGNANT, OFFENSIVE ⟨∼ behavior⟩ — **ob·nox·ious·ly** *adv* — **ob·nox·ious·ness** *n*

**oboe** \'ō-bō\ *n* [It, fr. F *hautbois*, fr. *haut* high + *bois* wood] : a woodwind instrument with a slender conical tube and a double reed mouthpiece — **obo·ist** \'ō-,bō-ist\ *n*

**ob·scene** \äb-'sēn\ *adj* **1** : REPULSIVE **2** : deeply offensive to morality or decency; *esp* : designed to incite to lust or depravity ♦ *Synonyms* GROSS, VULGAR, COARSE, CRUDE, INDECENT — **ob·scene·ly** *adv* — **ob·scen·i·ty** \-'se-nə-tē\ *n*

**ob·scu·ran·tism** \äb-'skyúr-ən-,ti-zəm, ,äb-skyü-'ran-\ *n* **1** : opposition to the spread of knowledge **2** : deliberate vagueness or abstruseness — **ob·scu·ran·tist** \-tist\ *n or adj*

**¹ob·scure** \äb-'skyúr\ *adj* **1** : DIM, GLOOMY **2** : not readily understood : VAGUE **3** : REMOTE; *also* : HUMBLE ♦ *Synonyms* DARK, DUSKY, MURKY, TENEBROUS — **ob·scure·ly** *adv* — **ob·scu·ri·ty** \-'skyúr-ə-tē\ *n*

**²obscure** *vb* **ob·scured; ob·scur·ing** **1** : to make dark, dim, or indistinct **2** : to conceal or hide by or as if by covering

**ob·se·qui·ous** \əb-'sē-kwē-əs\ *adj* : humbly or excessively attentive (as to a person in authority) : FAWNING, SYCOPHAN-

TIC ♦ *Synonyms* MENIAL, SERVILE, SLAVISH, SUBSERVIENT — **ob·se·qui·ous·ly** *adv* — **ob·se·qui·ous·ness** *n*

**ob·se·quy** \'äb-sə-kwē\ *n, pl* **-quies** : a funeral or burial rite — usu. used in pl.

**ob·serv·able** \əb-'zər-və-bəl\ *adj* 1 : NOTEWORTHY 2 : capable of being observed — **ob·serv·abil·i·ty** \-'bi-lə-tē\ *n*

**ob·ser·vance** \əb-'zər-vəns\ *n* 1 : a customary practice or ceremony 2 : an act or instance of following a custom, rule, or law 3 : OBSERVATION

**ob·ser·vant** \-vənt\ *adj* 1 : WATCHFUL ⟨~ spectators⟩ 2 : KEEN, PERCEPTIVE 3 : MINDFUL ⟨~ of the amenities⟩

¹**ob·ser·va·tion** \ˌäb-sər-'vā-shən, -zər-\ *n* 1 : an act or instance of observing 2 : the gathering of information (as for scientific studies) by noting facts or occurrences 3 : a conclusion drawn from observing; *also* : REMARK, STATEMENT 4 : the fact of being observed — **ob·ser·va·tion·al** \-shə-nəl\ *adj*

²**observation** *adj* : designed for use in viewing or in making observations

**ob·ser·va·to·ry** \əb-'zər-və-ˌtōr-ē\ *n, pl* **-ries** : a place or institution equipped for observation of natural phenomena (as in astronomy)

**ob·serve** \əb-'zərv\ *vb* **ob·served; ob·serv·ing** 1 : to conform one's action or practice to 2 : CELEBRATE 3 : to make a scientific observation of 4 : to see or sense esp. through careful attention 5 : to come to realize esp. through consideration of noted facts 6 : REMARK — **ob·serv·er** *n*

**ob·sess** \əb-'ses\ *vb* : to preoccupy intensely or abnormally

**ob·ses·sion** \äb-'se-shən\ *n* : a persistent disturbing preoccupation with an idea or feeling; *also* : an emotion or idea causing such a preoccupation — **ob·ses·sive** \-'se-siv\ *adj or n* — **ob·ses·sive·ly** *adv*

**obsessive–compulsive** *adj* : relating to, characterized by, or affected with recurring obsessions and compulsions esp. as symptoms of a neurotic state

**ob·sid·i·an** \əb-'si-dē-ən\ *n* : a dark natural glass formed by the cooling of molten lava

**ob·so·les·cent** \ˌäb-sə-'le-s²nt\ *adj* : going out of use : becoming obsolete ⟨~ computers⟩ — **ob·so·les·cence** \-s²ns\ *n*

**ob·so·lete** \ˌäb-sə-'lēt, 'äb-sə-ˌlēt\ *adj* : no longer in use; *also* : OLD-FASHIONED ⟨an ~ technology⟩ ♦ *Synonyms* EXTINCT, OUTWORN, PASSÉ, SUPERSEDED

**ob·sta·cle** \'äb-sti-kəl\ *n* : something that stands in the way or opposes

**ob·stet·rics** \əb-'ste-triks\ *n sing or pl* : a branch of medicine that deals with birth and with its antecedents and sequels — **ob·stet·ric** \-trik\ *or* **ob·stet·ri·cal** \-tri-kəl\ *adj* — **ob·ste·tri·cian** \ˌäb-stə-'tri-shən\ *n*

**ob·sti·nate** \'äb-stə-nət\ *adj* : fixed and unyielding (as in an opinion or course) despite reason or persuasion : STUBBORN ⟨~ opposition⟩ — **ob·sti·na·cy** \-nə-sē\ *n* — **ob·sti·nate·ly** *adv*

**ob·strep·er·ous** \əb-'stre-pə-rəs\ *adj* 1 : uncontrollably noisy 2 : stubbornly resistant to control : UNRULY — **ob·strep·er·ous·ness** *n*

**ob·struct** \əb-'strəkt\ *vb* 1 : to block by an obstacle 2 : to impede the passage, action, or operation of 3 : to cut off from sight — **ob·struc·tive** \-'strək-tiv\ *adj* — **ob·struc·tor** \-tər\ *n*

**ob·struc·tion** \əb-'strək-shən\ *n* 1 : an act of obstructing : the state of being obstructed 2 : something that obstructs : HINDRANCE

**ob·struc·tion·ist** \-'shə-nist\ *n* : a person who hinders progress or business esp. in a legislative body — **ob·struc·tion·ism** \-'shə-ˌni-zəm\ *n*

**ob·tain** \əb-'tān\ *vb* 1 : to gain or attain usu. by planning or effort 2 : to be generally recognized or established ♦ *Synonyms* PROCURE, SECURE, WIN, EARN, ACQUIRE — **ob·tain·able** *adj*

**ob·trude** \əb-'trüd\ *vb* **ob·trud·ed; ob·trud·ing** 1 : to thrust out 2 : to thrust forward without warrant or request 3 : INTRUDE — **ob·tru·sion** \-'trü-zhən\ *n* — **ob·tru·sive** \-'trü-siv\ *adj* — **ob·tru·sive·ly** *adv* — **ob·tru·sive·ness** *n*

**ob·tuse** \äb-'tüs, -'tyüs\ *adj* **ob·tus·er; -est** 1 : exceeding 90 degrees but less than 180 degrees ⟨~ angle⟩ 2 : not pointed or acute : BLUNT 3 : not sharp or quick of wit (is too ~ to take a hint) — **ob·tuse·ly** *adv* — **ob·tuse·ness** *n*

**obv** *abbr* obverse

¹**ob·verse** \äb-'vərs, 'äb-ˌvərs\ *adj* 1 : facing the observer or opponent 2 : being a counterpart or complement — **ob·verse·ly** *adv*

²**ob·verse** \'äb-ˌvərs, äb-'vərs\ *n* 1 : the side (as of a coin) bearing the principal design and lettering 2 : a front or principal surface 3 : a counterpart having the opposite orientation or force

**ob·vi·ate** \'äb-vē-ˌāt\ *vb* **-at·ed; -at·ing** : to anticipate and prevent (as a situation) or make unnecessary (as an action) ♦ *Synonyms* PREVENT, AVERT, FORESTALL, FORFEND, PRECLUDE — **ob·vi·a·tion** \ˌäb-vē-'ā-shən\ *n*

**ob·vi·ous** \'äb-vē-əs\ *adj* [L *obvius,* fr. *obviam* in the way, fr. *ob* in the way of + *viam,* acc. of *via* way] : easily found, seen, or understood : PLAIN ♦ *Synonyms* EVIDENT, MANIFEST, PATENT, CLEAR — **ob·vi·ous·ly** *adv* — **ob·vi·ous·ness** *n*

**OC** *abbr* officer candidate

**oc·a·ri·na** \ˌä-kə-'rē-nə\ *n* [It] : a wind instrument typically having an oval body with finger holes and a projecting mouthpiece

**occas** *abbr* occasionally

¹**oc·ca·sion** \ə-'kā-zhən\ *n* 1 : a favorable opportunity 2 : a direct or indirect cause 3 : the time of an event 4 : EXIGENCY 5 *pl* : AFFAIRS, BUSINESS 6 : a special event : CELEBRATION

²**occasion** *vb* : BRING ABOUT, CAUSE

**oc·ca·sion·al** \ə-'kā-zhə-nəl\ *adj* 1 : happening or met with now and then ⟨~ visits⟩ 2 : used or designed for a special occasion ⟨~ verse⟩ ♦ *Synonyms* IN-

FREQUENT, RARE, SPORADIC — **oc·ca·sion·al·ly** *adv*

**oc·ci·den·tal** \ˌäk-sə-'den-tᵊl\ *adj, often cap* [fr. *Occident* West, fr. ME, fr. AF, fr. L *occident-, occidens*, fr. prp. of *occidere* to fall, set (of the sun)] : WESTERN — **Oc·cidental** *n*

**Oc·ci·tan** \'äk-sə-ˌtan\ *n* [F, fr. ML *occitanus*, fr. Old Occitan *oc* yes (contrasted with OF *oïl* yes)] : a Romance language spoken in southern France

**oc·clude** \ə-'klüd\ *vb* **oc·clud·ed; oc·clud·ing 1** : OBSTRUCT ⟨an *occluded* artery⟩ **2** : to come together with opposing surfaces in contact — used of teeth — **oc·clu·sion** \-'klü-zhən\ *n* — **oc·clu·sive** \-'klü-siv\ *adj*

¹**oc·cult** \ə-'kəlt\ *adj* **1** : not revealed : SECRET **2** : ABSTRUSE, MYSTERIOUS **3** : of or relating to supernatural agencies, their effects, or knowledge of them ⟨the ∼ arts⟩ — **oc·cult·ism** \-'kəl-ˌti-zəm\ *n* — **oc·cult·ist** \-tist\ *n*

²**occult** *n* : occult matters — used with *the*

**oc·cu·pan·cy** \'ä-kyə-pən-sē\ *n, pl* **-cies 1** : the act of occupying : the state of being occupied **2** : an occupied building or part of a building

**oc·cu·pant** \-pənt\ *n* : one who occupies something; *esp* : RESIDENT

**oc·cu·pa·tion** \ˌä-kyə-'pā-shən\ *n* **1** : an activity in which one engages; *esp* : VOCATION **2** : the taking possession of property; *also* : the taking possession of an area by a foreign military force — **oc·cu·pa·tion·al** \-shə-nəl\ *adj* — **oc·cu·pa·tion·al·ly** *adv*

**occupational therapy** *n* : therapy by means of activity; *esp* : creative activity prescribed for its effect in promoting recovery or rehabilitation — **occupational therapist** *n*

**oc·cu·py** \'ä-kyə-ˌpī\ *vb* **-pied; -py·ing 1** : to engage the attention or energies of **2** : to fill up (an extent in space or time) **3** : to take or hold possession of **4** : to reside in as owner or tenant — **oc·cu·pi·er** *n*

**oc·cur** \ə-'kər\ *vb* **oc·curred; oc·cur·ring** [L *occurrere*, fr. *ob-* in the way + *currere* to run] **1** : to be found or met with : APPEAR **2** : HAPPEN ⟨the event will ∼ at noon⟩ **3** : to come to mind

**oc·cur·rence** \ə-'kər-əns\ *n* **1** : something that takes place **2** : the action or process of occurring

**ocean** \'ō-shən\ *n* **1** : the whole body of salt water that covers nearly three fourths of the surface of the earth **2** : any of the large bodies of water into which the great ocean is divided — **ocean·ic** \ˌō-shē-'a-nik\ *adj*

**ocean·ar·i·um** \ˌō-shə-'nar-ē-əm\ *n, pl* **-iums** or **-ia** \-ē-ə\ : a large marine aquarium

**ocean·front** \'ō-shən-ˌfrənt\ *n* : a shore area on the ocean

**ocean·go·ing** \-ˌgō-iŋ\ *adj* : of, relating to, or suitable for travel on the ocean

**ocean·og·ra·phy** \ˌō-shə-'nä-grə-fē\ *n* : a science dealing with the ocean and its phenomena — **ocean·og·ra·pher** \-fər\ *n* — **ocean·o·graph·ic** \-nə-'gra-fik\ *adj*

**oce·lot** \'ä-sə-ˌlät, 'ō-\ *n* : a medium-sized American wildcat ranging southward from Texas to northern Argentina and having a tawny yellow or gray coat with black markings

**ocher** or **ochre** \'ō-kər\ *n* : an earthy usu. red or yellow iron ore used as a pigment; *also* : the color esp. of yellow ocher

**o'·clock** \ə-'kläk\ *adv* : according to the clock

**OCR** *abbr* optical character reader; optical character recognition

**OCS** *abbr* officer candidate school

**oct** *abbr* octavo

**Oct** *abbr* October

**oc·ta·gon** \'äk-tə-ˌgän\ *n* : a polygon of eight angles and eight sides — **oc·tag·o·nal** \äk-'ta-gə-nᵊl\ *adj*

**oc·tane** \'äk-ˌtān\ *n* : OCTANE NUMBER

**octane number** *n* : a number used to measure the antiknock properties of gasoline that increases as the likelihood of knocking decreases

**oc·tave** \'äk-tiv\ *n* **1** : a musical interval embracing eight degrees; *also* : a tone or note at this interval or the whole series of notes, tones, or keys within this interval **2** : a group of eight

**oc·ta·vo** \äk-'tā-vō, -'tä-\ *n, pl* **-vos 1** : the size of a piece of paper cut eight from a sheet **2** : a book printed on octavo pages

**oc·tet** \äk-'tet\ *n* **1** : a musical composition for eight voices or eight instruments; *also* : the performers of such a composition **2** : a group or set of eight

**Oc·to·ber** \äk-'tō-bər\ *n* [ME *Octobre*, fr. OE *October*, fr. L, eighth month of the early Roman calendar, fr. *octo* eight] : the 10th month of the year

**oc·to·ge·nar·i·an** \ˌäk-tə-jə-'ner-ē-ən\ *n* : a person whose age is in the eighties

**oc·to·pus** \'äk-tə-pəs\ *n, pl* **-pus·es** or **-pi** \-ˌpī\ : any of various sea mollusks with eight long muscular arms furnished with suckers

**oc·to·syl·lab·ic** \ˌäk-tə-sə-'la-bik\ *adj* : composed of verses having eight syllables — **octosyllabic** *n*

¹**oc·u·lar** \'ä-kyə-lər\ *adj* **1** : VISUAL **2** : of or relating to the eye or the eyesight

²**ocular** *n* : EYEPIECE

**oc·u·list** \'ä-kyə-list\ *n* **1** : OPHTHALMOLOGIST **2** : OPTOMETRIST

¹**OD** \ˌō-'dē\ *n* : an overdose of a drug and esp. a narcotic

²**OD** *vb* **OD'd** or **ODed; OD'ing; OD's** : to become ill or die from an OD

³**OD** *abbr* **1** doctor of optometry **2** [L *oculus dexter*] right eye **3** officer of the day **4** olive drab **5** overdraft **6** overdrawn

**odd** \'äd\ *adj* [ME *odde*, fr. ON *oddi* point of land, triangle, odd number] **1** : being only one of a pair or set ⟨an ∼ shoe⟩ **2** : somewhat more than the number mentioned ⟨forty ∼ years ago⟩ **3** : being an integer (as 1, 3, or 5) not divisible by two without leaving a remainder **4** : additional to what is usual ⟨∼ jobs⟩ **5**

: STRANGE ⟨an ~ way of behaving⟩ —
**odd·ness** n
**odd·ball** \'äd-,bòl\ n : one that is eccentric — **oddball** adj
**odd·i·ty** \'ä-də-tē\ n, pl **-ties** 1 : one that
is odd 2 : the quality or state of being
odd
**odd·ly** \'äd-lē\ adv 1 : in an odd manner
⟨an ~ shaped roof⟩ 2 : as is odd
**odd·ment** \'äd-mənt\ n : something left
over : REMNANT
**odds** \'ädz\ n pl 1 : a difference by which
one thing is favored over another 2 : DIS-
AGREEMENT — usu. used with at 3 : the
ratio between the amount to be paid for
a winning bet and the amount of the bet
⟨the horse went off at ~ of 6–1⟩
**odds and ends** n pl : miscellaneous
things or matters
**odds–on** \'ädz-'òn, -'än\ adj : having a
better than even chance to win
**ode** \'ōd\ n : a lyric poem that expresses a
noble feeling with dignity
**odi·ous** \'ō-dē-əs\ adj : arousing or deserving hatred or repugnance — **odi-
ous·ly** adv — **odi·ous·ness** n
**odi·um** \'ō-dē-əm\ n 1 : merited loathing
: HATRED 2 : DISGRACE ⟨the ~ of de-
feat⟩
**odom·e·ter** \ō-'dä-mə-tər\ n [F odomètre,
fr. Gk hodometron, fr. hodos way, road +
metron measure] : an instrument for measuring distance traveled (as by a vehicle)
**odor** \'ō-dər\ n 1 : the quality of something that stimulates the sense of smell;
also : a sensation resulting from such
stimulation 2 : REPUTE, ESTIMATION —
**odored** \'ō-dərd\ adj — **odor·less** adj
— **odor·ous** adj
**odor·if·er·ous** \,ō-də-'ri-fə-rəs\ adj : having or yielding an odor
**odour** chiefly Brit var of ODOR
**od·ys·sey** \'ä-də-sē\ n, pl **-seys** [the Od-
yssey, epic poem attributed to Homer re-
counting the long wanderings of Odys-
seus] : a long wandering marked usu. by
many changes of fortune
**oe·cu·men·i·cal** \esp Brit ,ē-\ chiefly Brit
var of ECUMENICAL
**OED** abbr Oxford English Dictionary
**oe·de·ma** chiefly Brit var of EDEMA
**oe·di·pal** \'e-də-pəl, 'ē-\ adj, often cap
: of, relating to, or resulting from the Oedipus complex
**Oe·di·pus complex** \-pəs-\ n : the positive sexual feelings of a child toward the
parent of the opposite sex and hostile or
jealous feelings toward the parent of the
same sex that may be a source of adult
personality disorder when unresolved
**OEO** abbr Office of Economic Opportunity
**o'er** \'òr\ adv or prep : OVER
**OES** abbr Order of the Eastern Star
**oe·soph·a·gus** chiefly Brit var of ESOPH-
AGUS
**oeu·vre** \'ər-vrə, 'œvr³\ n, pl **oeuvres**
\same\ : a substantial body of work constituting the lifework of a writer, an artist, or a composer
**of** \'əv, 'äv\ prep 1 : FROM ⟨a man ~ the
West⟩ 2 : having as a significant back-

ground or character element ⟨a man ~
noble birth⟩ ⟨a woman ~ ability⟩ 3
: owing to ⟨died ~ flu⟩ 4 : BY ⟨the plays
~ Shakespeare⟩ 5 : having as component parts or material, contents, or members ⟨a house ~ brick⟩ ⟨a glass ~ wa-
ter⟩ ⟨a pack ~ fools⟩ 6 : belonging to or
included by ⟨the front ~ the house⟩ ⟨a
time ~ life⟩ ⟨one ~ you⟩ ⟨the best ~
its kind⟩ ⟨the son ~ a doctor⟩ 7 : ABOUT
⟨tales ~ the West⟩ 8 : connected with
: OVER ⟨the queen ~ England⟩ 9 : that
is : signified as ⟨the city ~ Rome⟩ 10 —
used to indicate apposition of the words
it joins ⟨that fool ~ a husband⟩ 11 : as
concerns : FOR ⟨love ~ nature⟩ 12 —
used to indicate the application of an adjective ⟨fond ~ candy⟩ 13 : BEFORE
⟨quarter ~ ten⟩
**OF** abbr outfield
**¹off** \'òf\ adv 1 : from a place or position
⟨drove ~ in a new car⟩; also : ASIDE
⟨turned ~ into a side road⟩ 2 : at a distance in time or space ⟨stood ~ a few
yards⟩ ⟨several years ~⟩ 3 : so as to be
unattached or removed ⟨the lid blew ~⟩
4 : to a state of discontinuance, exhaustion, or completion ⟨shut the radio ~⟩ 5
: away from regular work ⟨took time ~
for lunch⟩
**²off** prep 1 : away from ⟨just ~ the high-
way⟩ ⟨take it ~ the table⟩ 2 : to seaward
of ⟨two miles ~ the coast⟩ 3 : FROM
⟨borrowed a dollar ~ me⟩ 4 : at the expense of ⟨lives ~ his parents⟩ 5 : not
now engaged in ⟨~ duty⟩ 6 : abstaining
from ⟨~ liquor⟩ 7 : below the usual
level of ⟨~ his game⟩
**³off** adj 1 : more removed or distant 2
: started on the way 3 : not operating 4
: not correct 5 : REMOTE, SLIGHT ⟨an ~
chance⟩ 6 : INFERIOR ⟨~ grade of oil⟩
7 : provided for ⟨well ~⟩
**⁴off** abbr office; officer; official
**of·fal** \'ò-fəl\ n [ME, fr. of off + fall fall]
: the waste or by-product of a process;
esp : the viscera and trimmings of a
butchered animal removed in dressing
**off and on** adv : INTERMITTENTLY
⟨rained off and on⟩
**¹off·beat** \'òf-,bēt\ n : the unaccented part
of a musical measure
**²offbeat** adj : ECCENTRIC, UNCONVEN-
TIONAL ⟨an ~ style⟩
**off–col·or** \'òf-'kə-lər\ or **off–col·ored**
\-lərd\ adj 1 : not having the right or
standard color 2 : of doubtful propriety
: verging on indecency ⟨~ stories⟩
**of·fend** \ə-'fend\ vb 1 : SIN, TRANSGRESS
2 : to cause discomfort or pain : HURT 3
: to cause dislike or vexation : ANNOY
♦ **Synonyms** AFFRONT, INSULT, OUT-
RAGE — **of·fend·er** n
**of·fense** or **of·fence** \ə-'fens, esp for 2 &
3 'ä-,fens\ n 1 : something that outrages
the senses 2 : ATTACK, ASSAULT 3 : DIS-
PLEASURE 4 : DISPLEA-
SURE 5 : SIN, MISDEED 6 : an infraction
of law : CRIME
**¹of·fen·sive** \ə-'fen-siv, esp for 1 & 2 'ä-
,fen-\ adj 1 : AGGRESSIVE 2 : of or relat-

ing to an attempt to score in a game; *also* : of or relating to a team in possession of the ball or puck **3** : OBNOXIOUS ⟨an ∼ odor⟩ **4** : INSULTING ⟨∼ remarks⟩ — **of·fen·sive·ly** *adv* — **of·fen·sive·ness** *n*

²**offensive** *n* : ATTACK

¹**of·fer** \'ȯ-fər\ *vb* **of·fered; of·fer·ing 1** : SACRIFICE **2** : to present for acceptance : TENDER; *also* : to propose as payment **3** : PROPOSE, SUGGEST; *also* : to declare one's readiness **4** : to try or begin to exert ⟨∼ resistance⟩ **5** : to place on sale — **of·fer·ing** *n*

²**offer** *n* **1** : PROPOSAL **2** : BID **3** : TRY

**of·fer·to·ry** \'ȯ-fər-ˌtȯr-ē\ *n, pl* **-ries** : the presentation of offerings at a church service; *also* : the musical accompaniment during it

**off–gas·sing** \'ȯf-ˌga-siŋ\ *n* : the emission of esp. noxious gases (as from a building material)

**off·hand** \'ȯf-'hand\ *adv or adj* : without previous thought or preparation

**off–hour** \-ˌau̇(-ə)r\ *n* : a period of time other than a rush hour; *also* : a period of time other than business hours

**of·fice** \'ȯ-fəs\ *n* **1** : a special duty or position; *esp* : a position of authority in government ⟨run for ∼⟩ **2** : a prescribed form or service of worship; *also* : RITE **3** : an assigned or assumed duty or role **4** : a place where a business is transacted or a service is supplied

**of·fice·hold·er** \'ȯ-fəs-ˌhōl-dər\ *n* : one holding a public office

**of·fi·cer** \'ȯ-fə-sər\ *n* **1** : one charged with the enforcement of law **2** : one who holds an office of trust or authority **3** : a person who holds a position of authority or command in the armed forces; *esp* : COMMISSIONED OFFICER

¹**of·fi·cial** \ə-'fi-shəl\ *n* : OFFICER 2

²**official** *adj* **1** : of or relating to an office or to officers **2** : AUTHORIZED, AUTHORITATIVE ⟨∼ statement⟩ **3** : befitting or characteristic of a person in office — **of·fi·cial·ly** *adv*

**of·fi·cial·dom** \ə-'fi-shəl-dəm\ *n* : officials as a class

**of·fi·cial·ism** \ə-'fi-shə-ˌli-zəm\ *n* : lack of flexibility and initiative combined with excessive adherence to regulations

**of·fi·ci·ant** \ə-'fi-shē-ənt\ *n* : one (as a priest) who officiates at a religious rite

**of·fi·ci·ate** \ə-'fi-shē-ˌāt\ *vb* **-at·ed; -at·ing 1** : to perform a ceremony, function, or duty **2** : to act in an official capacity

**of·fi·cious** \ə-'fi-shəs\ *adj* : volunteering one's services where they are neither asked for nor needed ⟨an ∼ busybody⟩ — **of·fi·cious·ly** *adv* — **of·fi·cious·ness** *n*

**off·ing** \'ȯ-fiŋ\ *n* : the near or foreseeable future

**off–line** \'ȯf-'līn\ *adj or adv* : not connected to or controlled directly by a computer

**off of** *prep* : OFF

**off·print** \'ȯf-ˌprint\ *n* : a separately printed ed except (as from a magazine)

**off–road** \-'rōd\ *adj* : of, relating to, or being a vehicle designed for use away

from public roads — **off–road·er** \-'rō-dər\ *n*

**off–sea·son** \-ˌsē-zⁿn\ *n* : a time of suspended or reduced activity

¹**off·set** \-ˌset\ *n* **1** : a sharp bend (as in a pipe) by which one part is turned aside out of line **2** : a printing process in which an inked impression is first made on a rubber-blanketed cylinder and then transferred to the paper

²**off·set** *vb* **off·set; off·set·ting 1** : to place over against : BALANCE **2** : to compensate for **3** : to form an offset in ⟨∼ a wall⟩

**off·shoot** \'ȯf-ˌshüt\ *n* **1** : a collateral or derived branch, descendant, or member **2** : a branch of a main stem (as of a plant)

¹**off·shore** \'ȯf-'shȯr\ *adv* **1** : at a distance from the shore **2** : outside the country : ABROAD

²**off·shore** \'ȯf-ˌshȯr\ *adj* **1** : moving away from the shore **2** : situated off the shore but within waters under a country's control

**off·side** \-'sīd\ *adv or adj* : illegally in advance of the ball or puck

**off·spring** \-ˌspriŋ\ *n, pl* **offspring** *also* **offsprings** : PROGENY, YOUNG

**off·stage** \'ȯf-'stāj, -ˌstāj\ *adv or adj* **1** : off or away from the stage **2** : out of the public view ⟨deals made ∼⟩

**off–the–record** *adj* : given or made in confidence and not for publication

**off–the–shelf** *adj* : available as a stock item : not specially designed or made

**off–the–wall** *adj* : highly unusual : BIZARRE ⟨an ∼ sense of humor⟩

**off·track** \'ȯf-'trak\ *adv or adj* : away from a racetrack

**off–white** \'ȯf-'hwīt\ *n* : a yellowish or grayish white color

**off year** *n* **1** : a year in which no major election is held **2** : a year of diminished activity or production

**oft** \'ȯft\ *adv* : OFTEN

**of·ten** \'ȯ-fən\ *adv* : many times : FREQUENTLY

**of·ten·times** \-ˌtīmz\ *or* **oft·times** \'ȯf-ˌtīmz, 'ȯft-\ *adv* : OFTEN

**ogle** \'ō-gəl\ *vb* **ogled; ogling** : to look at in a flirtatious way — **ogle** *n* — **ogler** *n*

**ogre** \'ō-gər\ *n* **1** : a monster of fairy tales and folklore that eats people **2** : a dreaded person or object

**ogress** \'ō-grəs\ *n* : a female ogre

**oh** \'ō\ *interj* **1** — used to express an emotion or in response to physical stimuli **2** — used in direct address

**OH** *abbr* Ohio

**ohm** \'ōm\ *n* : a unit of electrical resistance equal to the resistance of a circuit in which a potential difference of one volt produces a current of one ampere — **ohm·ic** \'ō-mik\ *adj*

**ohm·me·ter** \'ōm-ˌmē-tər\ *n* : an instrument for indicating resistance in ohms directly

¹**oil** \'ȯi(-ə)l\ *n* [ME *oile*, fr. AF, fr. L *oleum* olive oil, fr. Gk *elaion*, fr. *elaia* olive] **1** : any of numerous fatty or greasy liquid substances obtained from plants, animals, or minerals and used for fuel, food,

medicines, and manufacturing 2 : PE-
TROLEUM 3 : artists' colors made with
oil; *also* : a painting in those colors — **oil·i·ness** \'oi-lē-nəs\ *n* — **oily** \'oi-lē\ *adj*

**²oil** *vb* : to put oil in or on — **oil·er** *n*

**oil·cloth** \'oi-(ə)l-,klȯth\ *n* : cloth treated
with oil or paint and used for table and
shelf coverings

**oil pan** *n* : the lower section of a crank-
case used as an oil reservoir

**oil shale** *n* : a rock (as shale) from which
oil can be recovered

**oil·skin** \'oi(ə)l-,skin\ *n* 1 : an oiled waterproof cloth 2 : an oilskin raincoat 3
*pl* : an oilskin coat and pants

**oink** \'oȯiŋk\ *n* : the natural noise of a hog
— **oink** *vb*

**oint·ment** \'oint-mənt\ *n* : a salve for use
on the skin

**OJ** *abbr* orange juice

**Ojib·wa** *or* **Ojib·way** *or* **Ojibwe** \ō-'jib-,wā\ *n, pl* **Ojibwa** *or* **Ojibwas** *or* **Ojib·way** *or* **Ojibways** *or* **Ojibwe** *or* **Ojibwes**
1 : a member of an American Indian
people of the region around Lake Superior and westward 2 : the Algonquian
language of the Ojibwa people

**OJT** *abbr* on-the-job training

**¹OK** *or* **okay** \ō-'kā\ *adv or adj* : all right

**²OK** *or* **okay** *vb* **OK'd** *or* **okayed; OK'·ing**
*or* **okay·ing** : APPROVE, AUTHORIZE —
**OK** *or* **okay** *n*

**³OK** *abbr* Oklahoma

**Okla** *abbr* Oklahoma

**okra** \'ō-krə\ *n* : a tall annual plant related to the mallows that has edible finger-
like pods; *also* : these pods

**¹old** \'ōld\ *adj* 1 : ANCIENT; *also* : of long
standing 2 *cap* : belonging to an early
period ⟨*Old* Irish⟩ 3 : having existed for
a specified period of time 4 : of or relating to a past era 5 : advanced in years 6
: showing the effects of age or use 7 : no
longer in use — **old·ish** \'ōl-dish\ *adj*

**²old** *n* : old or earlier time ⟨days of ~⟩

**old·en** \'ōl-dən\ *adj* : of or relating to a
bygone era

**¹old–fash·ioned** \'ōld-'fa-shənd\ *adj*
1 : OUT-OF-DATE, ANTIQUATED 2 : CON-
SERVATIVE

**²old–fashioned** *n* : a cocktail usu. made
with whiskey, bitters, sugar, a twist of
lemon peel, and water or soda water

**old–growth** \'ōld-'grōth\ *adj* : of, relating
to, or being a forest with large old trees,
numerous snags and woody debris, and a
multilayered canopy

**old guard** *n, often cap O&G* : the conservative members of an organization

**old hat** *adj* 1 : OLD-FASHIONED ⟨equip-
ment that is now *old hat*⟩ 2 : STALE,
TRITE

**old·ie** \'ōl-dē\ *n* : something old; *esp* : a
popular song from the past

**old–line** \'ōld-'līn\ *adj* 1 : ORIGINAL, ES-
TABLISHED ⟨an ~ business⟩ 2 : adher-
ing to old policies or practices

**old maid** *n* 1 : SPINSTER 2 : a prim fussy
person — **old–maid·ish** \'ōld-'mā-dish\
*adj*

**old man** *n* 1 : HUSBAND 2 : FATHER

**old–school** *adj* : adhering to traditional
policies or practices ⟨an ~ politician⟩

**old·ster** \'ōld-stər\ *n* : an old or elderly
person

**Old Testament** *n* : the first of the two
chief divisions of the Christian Bible —
see BIBLE table

**old–time** \'ōld-'tīm\ *adj* 1 : of, relating
to, or characteristic of an earlier period
2 : of long standing

**old–tim·er** \-'tī-mər\ *n* : VETERAN; *also*
: OLDSTER

**old–world** \-'wərld\ *adj* : having old-fashioned charm ⟨an ~ hotel⟩

**ole·ag·i·nous** \ō-lē-'a-jə-nəs\ *adj* : OILY

**ole·an·der** \'ō-lē-,an-dər\ *n* : a poisonous
evergreen shrub often grown for its fragrant white to red flowers

**oleo** \'ō-lē-,ō\ *n, pl* **ole·os** : MARGARINE

**oleo·mar·ga·rine** \,ō-lē-ō-'mär-jə-rən\ *n*
: MARGARINE

**ol·fac·to·ry** \äl-'fak-tə-rē, ōl-\ *adj* : of or
relating to the sense of smell

**oli·gar·chy** \'ä-lə-,gär-kē, 'ō-\ *n, pl* **-chies**
1 : a government in which power is in the
hands of a few 2 : a state having an oli-
garchy; *also* : the group holding power in
such a state — **oli·garch** \-,gärk\ *n* —
**oli·gar·chic** \,ä-lə-'gär-kik, ,ō-\ *or* **oli·gar·chi·cal** \-ki-kəl\ *adj*

**Oli·go·cene** \'ä-li-gō-,sēn, ə-'li-gə-,sēn\
*adj* : of, relating to, or being the epoch of
the Tertiary between the Eocene and the
Miocene — **Oligocene** *n*

**olio** \'ō-lē-,ō\ *n, pl* **oli·os** : HODGEPODGE,
MEDLEY

**ol·ive** \'ä-liv\ *n* 1 : an Old World evergreen tree grown in warm regions for its
fruit that is a food and the source of an
edible oil (**olive oil**); *also* : the fruit 2 : a
dull yellowish green color

**olive drab** *n* 1 : a grayish olive color 2
: an olive drab wool or cotton fabric; *also*
: a uniform of this fabric

**ol·iv·ine** \'ä-lə-,vēn\ *n* : a usu. greenish
mineral that is a complex silicate of magnesium and iron

**Olym·pic Games** \ō-'lim-pik-\ *n pl* : a
modified revival of an ancient Greek festival consisting of international athletic
contests that are held at separate winter
and summer gatherings at four-year intervals

**om** \'ōm\ *n* : a mantra consisting of the
sound "om" used in contemplating ultimate reality

**Oma·ha** \'ō-mə-,hä, -,hȯ\ *n, pl* **Omaha** *or*
**Omahas** : a member of an American Indian people of northeastern Nebraska

**om·buds·man** \'äm-,bu̇dz-mən, äm-'bu̇dz-\ *n, pl* **-men** \-mən\ 1 : a government official appointed to investigate
complaints made by individuals against
abuses or capricious acts of public officials 2 : one that investigates reported
complaints (as from students or consumers)

**ome·ga** \ō-'mā-gə\ *n* : the 24th and last
letter of the Greek alphabet — Ω *or* ω

**om·e·let** *or* **om·e·lette** \'äm-lət, 'ä-mə-\ *n*
[F *omelette*, alter. of MF *amelette*,
*alemette*, alter. of *alemelle* thin plate, ul-

tim. fr. L *lamella*, dim. of *lamina*] : eggs beaten with milk or water, cooked without stirring until set, and folded over

**omen** \'ō-mən\ *n* : an event or phenomenon believed to be a sign or warning of a future occurrence

**om·i·cron** \'ä-mə-ˌkrän, 'ō-\ *n* : the 15th letter of the Greek alphabet — O or o

**om·i·nous** \'ä-mə-nəs\ *adj* : foretelling evil : THREATENING — **om·i·nous·ly** *adv* — **om·i·nous·ness** *n*

**omis·si·ble** \ō-'mi-sə-bəl\ *adj* : that may be omitted ⟨~ details⟩

**omis·sion** \ō-'mi-shən\ *n* **1** : something neglected or left undone **2** : the act of omitting : the state of being omitted

**omit** \ō-'mit\ *vb* **omit·ted; omit·ting 1** : to leave out or leave unmentioned **2** : to leave undone: FAIL

¹**om·ni·bus** \'äm-ni-(ˌ)bəs\ *n* : BUS

²**omnibus** *adj* : of, relating to, or providing for many things at once ⟨an ~ bill⟩

**om·nip·o·tent** \äm-'ni-pə-tənt\ *adj* **1** *often cap* : ALMIGHTY 1 **2** : having unlimited authority or influence ⟨an ~ ruler⟩ — **om·nip·o·tence** \-təns\ *n* — **om·nip·o·tent·ly** *adv*

**om·ni·pres·ent** \ˌäm-ni-'pre-z°nt\ *adj* : present in all places at all times ⟨an ~ problem⟩ — **om·ni·pres·ence** \-z°ns\ *n*

**om·ni·scient** \äm-'ni-shənt\ *adj* : having infinite awareness, understanding, and insight — **om·ni·science** \-shəns\ *n* — **om·ni·scient·ly** *adv*

**om·ni·um-gath·er·um** \ˌäm-nē-əm-'ga-thə-rəm\ *n, pl* **omnium-gatherums** : a miscellaneous collection

**om·niv·o·rous** \äm-'ni-və-rəs\ *adj* **1** : feeding on both animal and vegetable substances **2** : AVID ⟨an ~ reader⟩ — **om·ni·vore** \'äm-ni-ˌvȯr\ *n* — **om·niv·o·rous·ly** *adv*

¹**on** \'ȯn, 'än\ *prep* **1** : in or to a position over and in contact with ⟨jumped ~ his horse⟩ **2** : touching the surface of ⟨shadows ~ the wall⟩ **3** : AT, TO ⟨~ the right were the mountains⟩ **4** : IN, ABOARD ⟨went ~ the train⟩ **5** : during or at the time of ⟨came ~ Monday⟩ ⟨every hour ~ the hour⟩ **6** : through the agency of ⟨was cut ~ a tin can⟩ **7** : in a state or process of ⟨~ fire⟩ ⟨the ~ the wane⟩ **8** : connected with as a member or participant ⟨~ a committee⟩ ⟨~ tour⟩ **9** — used to indicate a basis, source, or standard of computation ⟨has it ~ good authority⟩ ⟨10 cents ~ the dollar⟩ **10** : with regard to ⟨a monopoly ~ wheat⟩ **11** : at or toward as an object ⟨crept up ~ her⟩ **12** : ABOUT, CONCERNING ⟨a book ~ minerals⟩

²**on** *adv* **1** : in or into a position of contact with or attachment to a surface **2** : FORWARD **3** : into operation

³**on** *adj* : being in operation or in progress

**ON** *abbr* Ontario

¹**once** \'wəns\ *adv* [ME *ones,* fr. genitive of *on* one] **1** : one time only **2** : at any one time ⟨didn't ~ thank me⟩ **3** : FORMERLY ⟨was ~ young⟩ **4** : by one degree of relationship ⟨first cousin ~ removed⟩

²**once** *n* : one single time — **at once 1** : at the same time **2** : IMMEDIATELY

³**once** *adj* : FORMER ⟨a ~ successful actor⟩

⁴**once** *conj* : AS SOON AS ⟨~ we're finished, we can leave⟩

**once-over** \'wəns-ˌō-vər\ *n* : a swift examination or survey

**on·co·gene** \'äŋ-kō-ˌjēn\ *n* : a gene having the potential to cause a normal cell to become cancerous

**on·col·o·gy** \än-'kä-lə-jē\ *n* : the study of tumors — **on·co·log·i·cal** \ˌäŋ-kə-'lä-ji-kəl\ *also* **on·co·log·ic** \-jik\ *adj* — **on·col·o·gist** \än-'kä-lə-jist\ *n*

**on·com·ing** \'ȯn-ˌkə-miŋ, 'än-\ *adj* : APPROACHING ⟨~ traffic⟩

¹**one** \'wən\ *adj* **1** : being a single unit or thing ⟨~ person went⟩ **2** : being one in particular ⟨early ~ morning⟩ **3** : being the same in kind or quality ⟨members of ~ race⟩; *also* : UNITED **4** : being not specified or fixed ⟨~ day soon⟩

²**one** *n* **1** : the number denoting unity **2** : the 1st in a set or series **3** : a single person or thing — **one·ness** \'wən-nəs\ *n*

³**one** *pron* **1** : a certain indefinitely indicated person or thing ⟨saw ~ of his friends⟩ **2** : a person in general ⟨~ never knows⟩ **3** — used in place of a first-person pronoun

**Onei·da** \ō-'nī-də\ *n, pl* **Oneida** *or* **Onei·das** : a member of an American Indian people orig. of New York

**one-man band 1** : a musician who plays several instruments during a solo performance **2** : a person who alone undertakes or is responsible for several tasks

**oner·ous** \'ä-nə-rəs, 'ō-\ *adj* : imposing or constituting a burden : TROUBLESOME ⟨an ~ task⟩ ♦ **Synonyms** OPPRESSIVE, EXACTING, BURDENSOME, WEIGHTY

**one·self** \(ˌ)wən-'self\ *also* **one's self** *pron* : one's own self — usu. used reflexively or for emphasis

**one-sid·ed** \'wən-'sī-dəd\ *adj* **1** : having or occurring on one side only; *also* : having one side prominent or more developed **2** : PARTIAL ⟨a ~ interpretation⟩

**one-time** \-ˌtīm\ *adj* : FORMER ⟨a ~ actor⟩

**one-to-one** \ˌwən-tə-'wən\ *adj* : pairing each element of a set uniquely with an element of another set

**one up** *adj* : being in a position of advantage ⟨was *one up* on the others⟩

**one-way** *adj* : moving, allowing movement, or functioning in only one direction ⟨~ streets⟩

**on·go·ing** \'ȯn-ˌgō-iŋ, 'än-\ *adj* : continuously moving forward

**on·ion** \'ən-yən\ *n* : the pungent edible bulb of a widely cultivated plant related to the lilies; *also* : this plant

**on·ion·skin** \-ˌskin\ *n* : a thin strong translucent paper of very light weight

**on-line** \'ȯn-'līn, 'än-\ *adj or adv* : connected to, served by, or available through a computer network (as the Internet);

*ulso* ; done while online ⟨~ shopping⟩ — **online** *adv*

**on·look·er** \'ȯn-ˌlu̇-kər, 'än-\ *n* : SPECTATOR

**¹on·ly** \'ōn-lē\ *adj* **1** : unquestionably the best **2** : SOLE ⟨the ~ one left⟩

**²only** *adv* **1** : MERELY, JUST ⟨~ $2⟩ **2** : SOLELY ⟨known ~ to me⟩ **3** : at the very least ⟨was ~ too true⟩ **4** : as a final result ⟨will ~ make you sick⟩

**³only** *conj* : except that

**on·o·mato·poe·ia** \ˌä-nə-ˌmä-tə-'pē-ə\ *n* [LL, fr. Gk *onomatopoiia,* fr. *onoma* name + *poiein* to make] **1** : formation of words in imitation of natural sounds (as *buzz* or *hiss*) **2** : the use of words whose sound suggests the sense — **on·o·mato·poe·ic** \-'pē-ik\ *or* **on·o·mato·po·et·ic** \-ˌpō-'e-tik\ *adj* — **on·o·mato·poe·i·cal·ly** \-'pē-ə-k(ə-)lē\ *or* **on·o·mato·po·et·i·cal·ly** \-ˌpō-'e-ti-k(ə-)lē\ *adv*

**On·on·da·ga** \ˌä-nən-'dȯ-gə, -'dä-, -'dä-\ *n, pl* **-ga** *or* **-gas** : a member of an American Indian people of New York and Canada

**on·rush** \'ȯn-ˌrəsh, 'än-\ *n* : a rushing onward — **on·rush·ing** *adj*

**on screen** \'ȯn-ˌskrēn, 'än-\ *adv or adj* : on a computer or television screen

**on·set** \-ˌset\ *n* **1** : ATTACK **2** : BEGINNING ⟨the ~ of winter⟩

**on·shore** \-ˌshȯr\ *adj* **1** : moving toward the shore **2** : situated on or near the shore — **on·shore** \-'shȯr\ *adv*

**on·slaught** \'ȯn-ˌslȯt, 'än-\ *n* : a fierce attack; *also* : something resembling such an attack ⟨an ~ of questions⟩

**Ont** *abbr* Ontario

**on·to** \'ȯn-tü, 'än-\ *prep* : to a position or point on

**onus** \'ō-nəs\ *n* **1** : BURDEN **2** : OBLIGATION **3** : BLAME

**¹on·ward** \'ȯn-wərd, 'än-\ *also* **on·wards** \-wərdz\ *adv* : FORWARD ⟨kept moving ~⟩

**²onward** *adj* : directed or moving onward : FORWARD

**on·yx** \'ä-niks\ *n* [ME *oniche, onyx,* fr. AF & L; AF, fr. L *onyx,* fr. Gk, lit., claw, nail] : a translucent chalcedony in parallel layers of different colors

**oo·dles** \'ü-d⁹lz\ *n pl* : a great quantity

**oo·lite** \'ō-ə-ˌlīt\ *n* : a rock consisting of small round grains cemented together — **oo·lit·ic** \ˌō-ə-'li-tik\ *adj*

**¹ooze** \'üz\ *n* [ME *wose,* fr. OE *wāse* mire] **1** : a soft deposit (as of mud) on the bottom of a body of water **2** : soft wet ground : MUD — **oozy** \'ü-zē\ *adj*

**²ooze** *vb* **oozed; ooz·ing 1** : to flow or leak out slowly or imperceptibly **2** : EXUDE ⟨~ confidence⟩

**³ooze** *n* : something that oozes

**op** *abbr* **1** operation; operative; operator **2** opportunity **3** opus

**OP** *abbr* **1** observation post **2** out of print

**opac·i·ty** \ō-'pa-sə-tē\ *n, pl* **-ties 1** : obscurity of meaning **2** : mental dullness **3** : the quality or state of being opaque **4** : an opaque spot in a normally transparent structure

**opal** \'ō-pəl\ *n* : a mineral with iridescent colors that is used as a gem

**opal·es·cent** \ˌō-pə-'le-s⁹nt\ *adj* : IRIDESCENT — **opal·es·cence** \-s⁹ns\ *n*

**opaque** \ō-'pāk\ *adj* **1** : blocking the passage of radiant energy and esp. light **2** : not easily understood; *also* : OBTUSE — **opaque·ly** *adv* — **opaque·ness** *n*

**op art** \'äp-\ *n* : OPTICAL ART — **op artist** *n*

**op cit** *abbr* [L *opere citato*] in the work cited

**ope** \'ōp\ *vb* **oped; op·ing** *archaic* : OPEN

**OPEC** *abbr* Organization of Petroleum Exporting Countries

**op-ed** \'äp-'ed\ *n, often cap O&E* : a page of special features usu. opposite the editorial page of a newspaper

**¹open** \'ō-pən\ *adj* **open·er; open·est 1** : not shut or shut up ⟨an ~ door⟩ **2** : not secret or hidden; *also* : FRANK **3** : not enclosed or covered ⟨an ~ fire⟩; *also* : not protected **4** : free to be entered or used ⟨an ~ tournament⟩ **5** : easy to get through or see ⟨~ country⟩ **6** : spread out : EXTENDED **7** : not decided ⟨an ~ question⟩ **8** : readily accessible and cooperative; *also* : GENEROUS **9** : having openings, interruptions, or spaces ⟨an ~ mesh⟩; *also* : having components separated by a space in writing and printing ⟨the name *Spanish moss* is an ~ compound⟩ **10** : ready to operate ⟨stores are ~⟩ **11** : free from restraints or controls ⟨~ season⟩ — **open·ly** *adv* — **open·ness** *n*

**²open** \'ō-pən\ *vb* **opened; open·ing 1** : to change or move from a shut position; *also* : to make open by clearing away obstacles **2** : to make accessible **3** : to make openings in **4** : to make or become functional ⟨~ a store⟩ **5** : REVEAL; *also* : ENLIGHTEN **6** : BEGIN ⟨~ talks⟩ — **open·er** *n*

**³open** *n* **1** : OUTDOORS **2** : a contest or tournament open to all

**open–air** *adj* : OUTDOOR ⟨~ theaters⟩

**open arms** *n pl* : an eager or warm welcome

**open–faced** \-'fāst\ *also* **open–face** \-'fās\ *adj* : served without a covering layer of bread ⟨an ~ sandwich⟩

**open·hand·ed** \ˌō-pən-'han-dəd\ *adj* : GENEROUS — **open·hand·ed·ly** *adv*

**open–heart** *adj* : of, relating to, or performed on a heart temporarily relieved of circulatory function and laid open for repair of defects or damage

**open–hearth** *adj* : of, relating to, or being a process of making steel in a furnace that reflects the heat from the roof onto the material

**opening** *n* **1** : an act or instance of making or becoming open **2** : BEGINNING **3** : something that is open **4** : OCCASION; *also* : an opportunity for employment

**open mike** *n* : an event in which amateurs may perform

**open–mind·ed** \ˌō-pən-'mīn-dəd\ *adj* : free from rigidly fixed preconceptions — **open–mind·ed·ness** *n*

**open sentence** *n* : a statement (as in

mathematics) containing at least one blank or unknown so that when the blank is filled or a quantity substituted for the unknown the statement becomes a complete statement that is either true or false

**open shop** *n* : an establishment having members and nonmembers of a labor union on the payroll

**open·work** \\'ō-pən-ˌwərk\\ *n* : work so made as to show openings through its substance ⟨a railing of wrought-iron ∼⟩ — **open–worked** \\-ˌwərkt\\ *adj*

**¹opera** *pl of* OPUS

**²op·era** \\'ä-prə, -pə-rə\\ *n* : a drama set to music — **op·er·at·ic** \\ˌä-pə-'ra-tik\\ *adj*

**op·er·a·ble** \\'ä-pə-rə-bəl\\ *adj* **1** : fit, possible, or desirable to use **2** : likely to result in a favorable outcome upon surgical treatment

**opera glasses** *n pl* : small binoculars for use in a theater

**op·er·ate** \\'ä-pə-ˌrāt\\ *vb* **-at·ed; -at·ing 1** : to perform work : FUNCTION **2** : to produce an effect **3** : to put or keep in operation **4** : to perform or subject to an operation — **op·er·a·tor** \\-ˌrā-tər\\ *n*

**operating system** *n* : software that controls the operation of a computer

**op·er·a·tion** \\ˌä-pə-'rā-shən\\ *n* **1** : a doing or performing of a practical work **2** : an exertion of power or influence; *also* : method or manner of functioning **3** : a surgical procedure **4** : a process of deriving one mathematical expression from others according to a rule **5** : a military action or mission **6** : a usu. small business — **op·er·a·tion·al** \\-shə-nəl\\ *adj*

**¹op·er·a·tive** \\'ä-pə-rə-tiv, -ˌrā-\\ *adj* **1** : producing an appropriate effect; *also* : most significant or essential **2** : OPERATING ⟨an ∼ force⟩ **3** : having to do with physical operations; *also* : WORKING ⟨an ∼ craftsman⟩ **4** : based on or consisting of an operation ⟨∼ dentistry⟩

**²operative** *n* **1** : OPERATOR; *esp* : a secret agent **2** : a person who works toward achieving the objectives of a larger interest

**op·er·et·ta** \\ˌä-pə-'re-tə\\ *n* [It, dim. of *opera* opera] : a light musical-dramatic work with a romantic plot, spoken dialogue, and dancing scenes

**oph·thal·mic** \\äf-'thal-mik, äp-\\ *adj* [Gk *ophthalmikos,* fr. *ophthalmos* eye] : of, relating to, or located near the eye

**oph·thal·mol·o·gy** \\ˌäf-ˌthal-'mä-lə-jē, ˌäp-\\ *n* : a branch of medicine dealing with the structure, functions, and diseases of the eye — **oph·thal·mol·o·gist** \\-jist\\ *n*

**oph·thal·mo·scope** \\äf-'thal-mə-ˌskōp, äp-\\ *n* : an instrument for use in viewing the interior of the eye and esp. the retina

**opi·ate** \\'ō-pē-ət, -pē-ˌāt\\ *n* : a preparation or derivative of opium; *also* : a narcotic or a substance with similar activity — **opiate** *adj*

**opine** \\ō-'pīn\\ *vb* **opined; opin·ing** : to express an opinion : STATE

**opin·ion** \\ə-'pin-yən\\ *n* **1** : JUDGMENT **2** : a belief stronger than impression and less strong than positive knowledge **3** : a formal statement by an expert after careful study

**opin·ion·at·ed** \\ə-'pin-yə-ˌnā-təd\\ *adj* : obstinately adhering to personal opinions

**opi·um** \\'ō-pē-əm\\ *n* [ME, fr. L, fr. Gk *opion,* fr. dim. of *opos* sap] : an addictive narcotic drug that is the dried latex of a Eurasian poppy

**opos·sum** \\ə-'pä-səm\\ *n, pl* **opossums** *also* **opossum** : an omnivorous tree-dwelling No. American marsupial that is active chiefly at night and has a pointed snout and a prehensile tail

**opp** *abbr* opposite

**op·po·nent** \\ə-'pō-nənt\\ *n* : one that opposes : ADVERSARY

**op·por·tune** \\ˌä-pər-'tün, -'tyün\\ *adj* [ME, fr. MF *opportun,* fr. L *opportunus,* fr. *ob-* toward + *portus* port, harbor] : SUITABLE ⟨an ∼ moment⟩ — **op·por·tune·ly** *adv*

**op·por·tun·ism** \\ˌä-pər-'tü-ˌni-zəm, -'tyü-\\ *n* : a taking advantage of opportunities or circumstances esp. with little regard for principles or ultimate consequences — **op·por·tun·ist** \\-nist\\ *n* — **op·por·tu·nis·tic** \\-tü-'nis-tik, -tyü-\\ *adj*

**op·por·tu·ni·ty** \\ˌä-pər-'tü-nə-tē, -'tyü-\\ *n, pl* **-ties 1** : a favorable combination of circumstances, time, and place **2** : a chance for advancement

**op·pose** \\ə-'pōz\\ *vb* **op·posed; op·pos·ing 1** : to place opposite or against something (as to provide resistance or contrast) **2** : to strive against : RESIST — **op·po·si·tion** \\ˌä-pə-'zi-shən\\ *n*

**¹op·po·site** \\'ä-pə-zət\\ *adj* **1** : set over against something that is at the other end or side **2** : OPPOSED, HOSTILE; *also* : CONTRARY **3** : contrarily turned or moving **4** : being the other of a matching or contrasting pair ⟨the ∼ sex⟩ — **op·po·site·ly** *adv* — **op·po·site·ness** *n*

**²opposite** *n* : one that is opposed or contrary

**³opposite** *adv* : on or to an opposite side

**⁴opposite** *prep* : across from and usu. facing ⟨the house ∼ ours⟩

**op·press** \\ə-'pres\\ *vb* **1** : to crush by abuse of power or authority ⟨∼ed minorities⟩ **2** : to weigh down : BURDEN ♦ **Synonyms** AGGRIEVE, WRONG, PERSECUTE — **op·pres·sive** \\-'pre-siv\\ *adj* — **op·pres·sive·ly** *adv* — **op·pres·sor** \\-'pre-sər\\ *n*

**op·pres·sion** \\ə-'pre-shən\\ *n* **1** : unjust or cruel exercise of power or authority **2** : DEPRESSION

**op·pro·bri·ous** \\ə-'prō-brē-əs\\ *adj* : expressing or deserving opprobrium — **op·pro·bri·ous·ly** *adv*

**op·pro·bri·um** \\-brē-əm\\ *n* **1** : something that brings disgrace **2** : public disgrace or ill fame

**¹opt** \\'äpt\\ *vb* : to make a choice; *esp* : to decide in favor of something

**²opt** *abbr* **1** optical; optician; optics **2** option; optional

**op·tic** \\'äp-tik\\ *adj* : of or relating to vision or the eye

**op·ti·cal** \\'äp-ti-kəl\\ *adj* **1** : relating to

optics **2** : OPTIC **3** : of, relating to, or using light

**optical art** *n* : nonobjective art characterized by the use of geometric patterns often for an illusory effect

**optical disk** *n* : a disk on which information has been recorded digitally and which is read using a laser

**optical fiber** *n* : a single fiber-optic strand

**op·ti·cian** \äp-'ti-shən\ *n* **1** : a maker of or dealer in optical items and instruments **2** : a person who makes or orders eyeglasses and contact lenses to prescription and sells them

**op·tics** \'äp-tiks\ *n* : a science that deals with the nature and properties of light

**op·ti·mal** \'äp-tə-məl\ *adj* : most desirable or satisfactory — **op·ti·mal·ly** *adv*

**op·ti·mism** \'äp-tə-ˌmi-zəm\ *n* [F *optimisme*, fr. L *optimum*, n., best, fr. neut. of *optimus* best] **1** : a doctrine that this world is the best possible world **2** : an inclination to anticipate the best possible outcome of actions or events — **op·ti·mist** \-mist\ *n* — **op·ti·mis·tic** \ˌäp-tə-'mis-tik\ *adj* — **op·ti·mis·ti·cal·ly** \-ti-k(ə-)lē\ *adv*

**op·ti·mize** \'äp-tə-ˌmīz\ *vb* **-mized; -miz-ing** : to make as perfect, effective, or functional as possible — **op·ti·mi·za·tion** \ˌäp-tə-mə-'zā-shən\ *n*

**op·ti·mum** \'äp-tə-məm\ *n, pl* **-ma** \-mə\ *also* **-mums** [L] : the amount or degree of something most favorable to an end; *also* : greatest degree attained under implied or specified conditions

**op·tion** \'äp-shən\ *n* **1** : the power or right to choose **2** : a right to buy or sell something at a specified price during a specified period **3** : something offered for choice — **op·tion·al** \-shə-nəl\ *adj*

**op·tom·e·try** \äp-'tä-mə-trē\ *n* : the health-care profession concerned esp. with examining the eyes for defects of vision and with prescribing corrective lenses or eye exercises — **op·to·met·ric** \ˌäp-tə-'me-trik\ *adj* — **op·tom·e·trist** \äp-'tä-mə-trist\ *n*

**opt out** *vb* : to choose not to participate

**op·u·lence** \'ä-pyə-ləns\ *n* **1** : WEALTH **2** : ABUNDANCE

**op·u·lent** \'ä-pyə-lənt\ *adj* **1** : WEALTHY **2** : richly abundant — **op·u·lent·ly** *adv*

**opus** \'ō-pəs\ *n, pl* **opera** \'ō-pə-rə, 'ä-\ *also* **opus·es** \'ō-pə-səz\ : WORK; *esp* : a musical composition

**or** \'ȯr\ *conj* — used as a function word to indicate an alternative ⟨sink ∼ swim⟩

**OR** *abbr* **1** operating room **2** Oregon

**-or** *n suffix* : one that does a (specified) thing ⟨calculator⟩

**or·a·cle** \'ȯr-ə-kəl\ *n* **1** : one held to give divinely inspired answers or revelations **2** : an authoritative or wise utterance; *also* : a person of great authority or wisdom — **or·ac·u·lar** \ȯ-'ra-kyə-lər\ *adj*

¹**oral** \'ȯr-əl\ *adj* **1** : SPOKEN ⟨an ∼ report⟩ **2** : of, given through, or involving the mouth ⟨an ∼ vaccine⟩ **3** : of, relating to, or characterized by the first stage of psychosexual development in psychoanalytic theory in which libidinal gratifi-

cation is derived from intake (as of food), by sucking, and later by biting **4** : relating to or characterized by personality traits of passive dependency and aggressiveness — **oral·ly** *adv*

²**oral** *n* : an oral examination — usu. used in pl.

**oral sex** *n* : oral stimulation of the genitals : CUNNILINGUS, FELLATIO

**orang** \ə-'raŋ\ *n* : ORANGUTAN

**or·ange** \'är-inj, 'ȯr-\ *n* **1** : a juicy citrus fruit with reddish yellow rind; *also* : an evergreen tree with fragrant white flowers that bears this fruit **2** : a color between red and yellow — **or·ange·y** *or* **or·angy** \'är-in-je, 'ȯr-\ *adj*

**or·ange·ade** \ˌär-in-'jād, ˌȯr-\ *n* : a beverage of orange juice, sugar, and water

**orange hawkweed** *n* : a weedy herb related to the daisies with bright orange-red flower heads

**or·ang·ery** \'är-inj-rē, 'ȯr-\ *n, pl* **-ries** : a protected place (as a greenhouse) for raising oranges in cool climates

**orang·utan** \ə-'raŋ-ə-ˌtaŋ, -ˌtan\ *n* [Bazaar Malay (Malay-based pidgin), fr. Malay *orang* man + *hutan* forest] : a large reddish brown tree-living anthropoid ape of Borneo and Sumatra

**orate** \ȯ-'rāt\ *vb* **orat·ed; orat·ing** : to speak in a declamatory manner

**ora·tion** \ə-'rā-shən\ *n* : an elaborate discourse delivered in a formal and dignified manner

**or·a·tor** \'ȯr-ə-tər\ *n* : one noted for skill and power as a public speaker

**or·a·tor·i·cal** \ˌȯr-ə-'tȯr-i-kəl\ *adj* : of, relating to, or characteristic of an orator or oratory — **or·a·tor·i·cal·ly** \-'tȯr-i-k(ə-)lē\ *adv*

**or·a·to·rio** \ˌȯr-ə-'tȯr-ē-ˌō\ *n, pl* **-rios** : a lengthy choral work usu. on a scriptural subject

¹**or·a·to·ry** \'ȯr-ə-ˌtȯr-ē\ *n, pl* **-ries** : a private or institutional chapel

²**oratory** *n* : the art of speaking eloquently and effectively in public ♦ **Synonyms** RHETORIC, ELOCUTION

**orb** \'ȯrb\ *n* : a spherical body; *also* : EYE

¹**or·bit** \'ȯr-bət\ *n* [L *orbita*, lit., path, rut] **1** : a path described by one body in its revolution about another **2** : range or sphere of activity — **or·bit·al** \-hə-tᵊl\ *adj*

²**orbit** *vb* **1** : CIRCLE **2** : to send up and make revolve in an orbit ⟨∼ a satellite⟩ — **or·bit·er** *n*

**or·ca** \'ȯr-kə\ *n* : KILLER WHALE

**orch** *abbr* orchestra

**or·chard** \'ȯr-chərd\ *n* [ME, fr. OE *ortgeard*, fr. *ort-* (fr. L *hortus* garden) + *geard* yard] : a place where fruit trees, sugar maples, or nut trees are grown; *also* : the trees of such a place — **or·chard·ist** \-chär-dist\ *n*

**or·ches·tra** \'ȯr-kə-strə\ *n* **1** : the front section of seats on the main floor of a theater **2** : a group of instrumentalists organized to perform ensemble music — **or·ches·tral** \ȯr-'kes-trəl\ *adj* — **or·ches·tral·ly** *adv*

**or·ches·trate** \'ȯr-kə-ˌstrāt\ *vb* **-trat·ed; -trat·ing** **1** : to compose or arrange for an orchestra **2** : to arrange so as to achieve a desired effect ⟨∼ a campaign⟩ — **or·ches·tra·tion** \ˌȯr-kə-ˈstrā-shən\ *n*

**or·chid** \ˈȯr-kəd\ *n* : any of a large family of plants having often showy flowers with three petals of which the middle one is enlarged into a lip; *also* : a flower of an orchid

**ord** *abbr* **1** order **2** ordnance

**or·dain** \ȯr-ˈdān\ *vb* **1** : to admit to the ministry or priesthood by the ritual of a church **2** : DECREE, ENACT; *also* : DESTINE — **or·dain·ment** *n*

**or·deal** \ȯr-ˈdēl, ˈȯr-ˌdēl\ *n* : a severe trial or experience

**¹or·der** \ˈȯr-dər\ *vb* **1** : ARRANGE, REGULATE **2** : COMMAND **3** : to place an order

**²order** *n* **1** : a group of people formally united; *also* : a badge or medal of such a group **2** : any of the several grades of the Christian ministry; *also, pl* : ORDINATION **3** : a rank, class, or special group of persons or things **4** : a category of biological classification ranking above the family and below the class **5** : ARRANGEMENT, SEQUENCE; *also* : the prevailing state of things **6** : a customary mode of procedure; *also* : the rule of law or proper authority **7** : a specific rule, regulation, or authoritative direction **8** : a style of building; *also* : an architectural column forming the unit of a style **9** : condition esp. with regard to repair **10** : a direction to pay money or to buy or sell goods; *also* : goods bought or sold — **in order** : APPROPRIATE, DESIRABLE ⟨apologies are *in order*⟩ — **in order to** : for the purpose of

**¹or·der·ly** \ˈȯr-dər-lē\ *adj* **1** : arranged according to some order; *also* : NEAT, TIDY **2** : well behaved ⟨an ∼ crowd⟩ ♦ *Synonyms* METHODICAL, SYSTEMATIC, REGULAR — **or·der·li·ness** *n*

**²orderly** *n, pl* **-lies 1** : a soldier who attends a superior officer **2** : a hospital attendant who does general work

**or·di·nal** \ˈȯr-də-nəl\ *adj* : indicating order or rank (as sixth) in a series

**ordinal number** *n* : a number (as first, second, or third) that designates the place of an item in an ordered sequence — compare CARDINAL NUMBER

**or·di·nance** \ˈȯr-də-nəns\ *n* : an authoritative decree or law; *esp* : a municipal regulation

**or·di·nary** \ˈȯr-də-ˌner-ē\ *adj* **1** : to be expected : USUAL **2** : of common quality, rank, or ability ⟨∼ kids⟩; *also* : POOR, INFERIOR ⟨∼ wine⟩ ♦ *Synonyms* CUSTOMARY, ROUTINE, NORMAL, EVERYDAY — **or·di·nar·i·ly** \ˌȯr-də-ˈner-ə-lē\ *adv* — **or·di·nar·i·ness** \ˈȯr-də-ˌner-ē-nəs\ *n*

**or·di·nate** \ˈȯr-də-nət, -ˌnāt\ *n* : the vertical coordinate of a point in a plane coordinate system obtained by measuring parallel to the y-axis

**or·di·na·tion** \ˌȯr-də-ˈnā-shən\ *n* : the act or ceremony by which a person is ordained

**ord·nance** \ˈȯrd-nəns\ *n* **1** : military supplies **2** : CANNON, ARTILLERY

**Or·do·vi·cian** \ˌȯr-də-ˈvi-shən\ *adj* : of, relating to, or being the period of the Paleozoic era between the Cambrian and the Silurian — **Ordovician** *n*

**or·dure** \ˈȯr-jər\ *n* : EXCREMENT

**¹ore** \ˈȯr\ *n* : a naturally occurring mineral mined to obtain a substance that it contains

**²ore** \ˈər-ə\ *n, pl* **ore** — see *krona, krone* at MONEY table

**Ore** or **Oreg** *abbr* Oregon

**oreg·a·no** \ə-ˈre-gə-ˌnō\ *n* : a bushy perennial mint used as a seasoning and a source of oil

**org** *abbr* organization; organized

**or·gan** \ˈȯr-gən\ *n* **1** : a musical instrument having sets of pipes sounded by compressed air and controlled by keyboards; *also* : an electronic keyboard instrument that approximates the sounds of the pipe organ **2** : a differentiated animal or plant structure (as a heart or a leaf) made up of cells and tissues and performing some bodily function **3** : a group that performs a specialized function ⟨the various ∼*s* of government⟩ **4** : PERIODICAL ⟨the official ∼ of the party⟩

**or·gan·dy** also **or·gan·die** \ˈȯr-gən-dē\ *n, pl* **-dies** [F *organdi*] : a fine transparent muslin with a stiff finish

**or·gan·elle** \ˌȯr-gə-ˈnel\ *n* : a specialized cell part that resembles an organ in having a special function

**or·gan·ic** \ȯr-ˈga-nik\ *adj* **1** : of, relating to, or arising in a bodily organ **2** : of, relating to, or derived from living things **3** : of, relating to, or containing carbon compounds **4** : of or relating to a branch of chemistry dealing with carbon compounds **5** : involving, producing, or dealing in foods produced without the use of laboratory-made fertilizers, growth substances, antibiotics, or pesticides ⟨∼ farming⟩ **6** : ORGANIZED ⟨an ∼ whole⟩ — **or·gan·i·cal·ly** \-ni-k(ə-)lē\ *adv*

**or·ga·ni·sa·tion, or·ga·nise** *Brit var of* ORGANIZATION, ORGANIZE

**or·gan·ism** \ˈȯr-gə-ˌni-zəm\ *n* : an individual living thing (as a person, animal, or plant) — **or·gan·is·mic** \ˌȯr-gə-ˈniz-mik\ *adj*

**or·gan·ist** \ˈȯr-gə-nist\ *n* : a person who plays an organ

**or·ga·ni·za·tion** \ˌȯr-gə-nə-ˈzā-shən\ *n* **1** : the act or process of organizing or of being organized; *also* : the condition or manner of being organized **2** : ASSOCIATION, SOCIETY **3** : an administrative structure (as a business or a political party) — **or·ga·ni·za·tion·al** \-shə-nəl\ *adj*

**or·ga·nize** \ˈȯr-gə-ˌnīz\ *vb* **-nized; -niz·ing 1** : to develop an organic structure **2** : to form into a complete and functioning whole **3** : to set up an administrative structure for **4** : to arrange by systematic planning and united effort **5** : to join in a union; *also* : UNIONIZE ♦ *Synonyms* INSTITUTE, FOUND, ESTABLISH, CONSTITUTE — **or·ga·niz·er** *n*

**or·gano·chlo·rine** \ȯr-ˌga-nə-ˈklȯr-ˌēn\ *adj* : of, relating to, or being a chlorinated hydrocarbon pesticide (as DDT) — **organochlorine** n

**or·gano·phos·phate** \-'fäs-ˌfāt\ n : an organophosphorus pesticide — **organo phosphate** adj

**or·gano·phos·pho·rus** \-'fäs-fə-rəs\ also **or·gano·phos·pho·rous** \-'fäs-'fôr-əs\ adj : of, relating to, or being a phosphorus-containing organic pesticide (as malathion)

**or·gan·za** \ôr-'gan-zə\ n : a sheer dress fabric resembling organdy and usu. made of silk, rayon, or nylon

**or·gasm** \'ôr-ˌga-zəm\ n : the climax of sexual excitement — **or·gas·mic** \ôr-'gaz-mik\ adj

**or·gi·as·tic** \ˌôr-jē-'as-tik\ adj : of, relating to, or marked by orgies

**or·gu·lous** \'ôr-gyə-ləs, -gə-\ adj : PROUD

**or·gy** \'ôr-jē\ n, pl **orgies** : a gathering marked by unrestrained indulgence (as in sexual activity, alcohol, or drugs)

**ori·el** \'ôr-ē-əl\ n : a window built out from a wall and usu. supported by a bracket

**ori·ent** \'ôr-ē-ˌent\ vb 1 : to set in a definite position esp. in relation to the points of the compass 2 : to acquaint with an existing situation or environment 3 : to direct toward the interests of a particular group

**Orient** n : EAST 3; esp : the countries of eastern Asia

**ori·en·tal** \ˌôr-ē-'en-t°l\ adj, often cap [fr. Orient East, fr. ME, fr. AF, fr. L orient-, oriens, fr. prp. of oriri to rise] : of or situated in Asia

**ori·en·tate** \'ôr-ē-ən-ˌtāt\ vb **-tat·ed; -tat·ing** 1 : ORIENT 2 : to face east

**ori·en·ta·tion** \ˌôr-ē-ən-tā-shən\ n 1 : the act or state of being oriented 2 : a person's identity based on sexual tendencies

**ori·fice** \'ôr-ə-fəs\ n : OPENING, MOUTH

**ori·flamme** \'ôr-ə-ˌflam\ n : a brightly colored banner used as a standard or ensign in battle

**orig** abbr original; originally

**ori·ga·mi** \ˌôr-ə-'gä-mē\ n : the Japanese art or process of paper folding

**or·i·gin** \'ôr-ə-jən\ n 1 : ANCESTRY 2 : rise, beginning, or derivation from a source; also : CAUSE 3 : the intersection of coordinate axes

¹**orig·i·nal** \ə-'ri-jə-nəl\ n : something from which a copy, reproduction, or translation is made : PROTOTYPE

²**original** adj 1 : FIRST, INITIAL 2 : not copied from something else : FRESH 3 : INVENTIVE — **orig·i·nal·i·ty** \ˌri-jə-'na-lə-tē\ n — **orig·i·nal·ly** \-'ri-jə-n°l-ē\ adv

**orig·i·nate** \ə-'ri-jə-ˌnāt\ vb **-nat·ed; -nat·ing** 1 : to give rise to : INITIATE 2 : to come into existence : BEGIN — **orig·i·na·tor** \-ˌnā-tər\ n

**ori·ole** \'ôr-ē-ˌōl\ n : any of various New World birds of which the males are usu. black and yellow or black and orange

**or·i·son** \'ôr-ə-sən\ n : PRAYER

**or·mo·lu** \'ôr-mə-ˌlü\ n : a golden or gilded brass used for decorative purposes

¹**or·na·ment** \'ôr-nə-mənt\ n : something

that lends grace or beauty — **or·na·men·tal** \ˌôr-nə-'men-t°l\ adj

²**or·na·ment** \-ˌment\ vb : to provide with ornament : ADORN — **or·na·men·la·tion** \ˌôr-nə-mən-'tā-shən\ n

**or·nate** \ôr-'nāt\ adj : elaborately decorated ⟨an ~ mantel⟩ — **or·nate·ly** adv — **or·nate·ness** n

**or·nery** \'ôr-nə-rē, 'ä-nə-\ adj : having an irritable disposition

**or·ni·thol·o·gy** \ˌôr-nə-'thä-lə-jē\ n, pl **-gies** : a branch of zoology dealing with birds — **or·ni·tho·log·i·cal** \-thə-'lä-ji-kəl\ adj — **or·ni·thol·o·gist** \-'thä-lə-jist\ n

**oro·tund** \'ôr-ə-ˌtənd\ adj 1 : SONOROUS ⟨an ~ voice⟩ 2 : POMPOUS ⟨an ~ speech⟩ — **oro·tun·di·ty** \ˌôr-ə-'tən-di-tē\ n

**or·phan** \'ôr-fən\ n : a child deprived by death of one or usu. both parents — **orphan** vb

**or·phan·age** \'ôr-fə-nij\ n : an institution for the care of orphans

**or·tho·don·tia** \ˌôr-thə-'dän-chə, -chē-ə\ n : ORTHODONTICS

**or·tho·don·tics** \ˌôr-thə-'dän-tiks\ n : a branch of dentistry concerned with the correction of faults in the arrangement and placing of the teeth — **or·tho·don·tic** \-tik\ adj — **or·tho·don·tist** \-tist\ n

**or·tho·dox** \'ôr-thə-ˌdäks\ adj [ME orthodoxe, fr. MF or LL; MF orthodoxe, fr. LL orthodoxus, fr. LGk orthodoxos, fr. Gk orthos right + doxa opinion] 1 : conforming to established doctrine esp. in religion 2 : CONVENTIONAL 3 cap : of or relating to a Christian church originating in the church of the Eastern Roman Empire — **or·tho·doxy** \-ˌdäk-sē\ n

**or·thog·ra·phy** \ôr-'thä-grə-fē\ n : SPELLING — **or·tho·graph·ic** \ˌôr-thə-'gra-fik\ adj

**or·tho·pe·dics** also **or·tho·pae·dics** \ˌôr-thə-'pē-diks\ n sing or pl : a branch of medicine concerned with the correction or prevention of skeletal injuries or disorders — **or·tho·pe·dic** also **or·tho·pae·dic** \-dik\ adj — **or·tho·pe·dist** also **or·tho·pae·dist** \-dist\ n

**-ory** adj suffix 1 : of, relating to, or characterized by ⟨anticipatory⟩ 2 : serving for, producing, or maintaining ⟨illusory⟩

**Os** symbol osmium

**OS** abbr 1 [L oculus sinister] left eye 2 ordinary seaman 3 out of stock

**Osage** \ō-'saj\ n, pl **Osag·es** or **Osage** : a member of an American Indian people orig. of Missouri

**os·cil·late** \'ä-sə-ˌlāt\ vb **-lat·ed; -lat·ing** 1 : to swing backward and forward like a pendulum 2 : to move or travel back and forth between two points 3 : VARY, FLUCTUATE — **os·cil·la·tion** \ˌä-sə-'lā-shən\ n — **os·cil·la·tor** \'ä-sə-ˌlā-tər\ n — **os·cil·la·to·ry** \'ä-sə-lə-ˌtôr-ē\ adj

**os·cil·lo·scope** \ä-'si-lə-ˌskōp\ n : an instrument in which variations in current or voltage appear as a visible wave form on a fluorescent screen

**os·cu·late** \'äs-kyə-ˌlāt\ vb **-lat·ed; -lat·ing** : KISS — **os·cu·la·tion** \ˌäs-kyə-'lā-shən\ *n* — **os·cu·la·to·ry** \'äs-kyə-lə-,tōr-ē\ *adj*

**Osee** \'ō-,zē, ō-'zā-ə\ *n* : HOSEA

**OSHA** \'ō-shə\ *abbr* Occupational Safety and Health Administration

**osier** \'ō-zhər\ *n* : any of various willows with pliable twigs used esp. in making baskets and furniture; *also* : a twig from an osier

**os·mi·um** \'äz-mē-əm\ *n* : a very heavy hard brittle metallic chemical element used esp. as a catalyst and in alloys

**os·mo·sis** \äz-'mō-səs, äs-\ *n* : movement of a solvent through a semipermeable membrane into a solution of higher concentration that tends to equalize the concentrations of the solutions on either side of the membrane — **os·mot·ic** \-'mä-tik\ *adj*

**os·prey** \'äs-prē, -,prā\ *n, pl* **ospreys** : a large dark brown and white fish-eating hawk

**os·si·fy** \'ä-sə-,fī\ *vb* **-fied; -fy·ing** : to make or become hardened or set in one's ways ⟨an *ossified* regime⟩ — **os·si·fi·ca·tion** \,ä-sə-fə-'kā-shən\ *n*

**os·su·ary** \'ä-shə-,wer-ē, -syə-\ *n, pl* **-ar·ies** : a depository for the bones of the dead

**os·ten·si·ble** \ä-'sten-sə-bəl\ *adj* : shown outwardly : PROFESSED, APPARENT — **os·ten·si·bly** \-blē\ *adv*

**os·ten·ta·tion** \,äs-tən-'tā-shən\ *n* : pretentious or excessive display — **os·ten·ta·tious** \-shəs\ *adj* — **os·ten·ta·tious·ly** *adv*

**os·te·o·ar·thri·tis** \,äs-tē-ō-är-'thrī-təs\ *n* : arthritis marked by degeneration of the cartilage and bone of joints

**os·teo·path** \'äs-tē-ə-,path\ *n* : a practitioner of osteopathy

**os·te·op·a·thy** \,äs-tē-'ä-pə-thē\ *n* : a system of treating diseases emphasizing manipulation (as of joints) but not excluding other agencies (as the use of medicine and surgery) — **os·teo·path·ic** \,äs-tē-ə-'pa-thik\ *adj*

**os·te·o·po·ro·sis** \,äs-tē-ō-pə-'rō-səs\ *n, pl* **-ro·ses** \-,sēz\ : a condition affecting esp. older women and characterized by fragile and porous bones

**os·tra·cise** *Brit var of* OSTRACIZE

**os·tra·cize** \'äs-trə-,sīz\ *vb* **-cized; -ciz·ing** [Gk *ostrakizein* to banish by voting with potsherds, fr. *ostrakon* shell, potsherd] : to exclude from a group by common consent — **os·tra·cism** \-,si-zəm\ *n*

**os·trich** \'äs-trich, 'ȯs-\ *n* : a very large swift-footed flightless bird of Africa

**Os·we·go tea** \ä-'swē-gō-\ *n* : a No. American mint with showy scarlet flowers

**OT** *abbr* 1 occupational therapy 2 Old Testament 3 overtime

¹**oth·er** \'ə-thər\ *adj* 1 : being the one left; *also* : being the ones distinct from those first mentioned 2 : ALTERNATE ⟨every ~ day⟩ 3 : DIFFERENT 4 : ADDITIONAL 5 : recently past ⟨the ~ night⟩

²**other** *pron* 1 : remaining one or ones 2 : a different or additional one ⟨something or ~⟩

**oth·er·wise** \'ə-thər-,wīz\ *adv* 1 : in a different way 2 : in different circumstances 3 : in other respects 4 : if not 5 : NOT — **otherwise** *adj*

**oth·er·world** \-,wərld\ *n* : a world beyond death or beyond present reality

**oth·er·world·ly** \ə-thər-'wərld-lē\ *adj* : not worldly : concerned with spiritual, intellectual, or imaginative matters

**oti·ose** \'ō-shē-,ōs, 'ō-tē-\ *adj* 1 : FUTILE 2 : IDLE 3 : USELESS ⟨~ details⟩

**oto·lar·yn·gol·o·gy** \,ō-tō-,la-rən-'gä-lə-jē\ *n* : a medical specialty concerned esp. with the ear, nose, and throat — **oto·lar·yn·gol·o·gist** \-jist\ *n*

**oto·rhi·no·lar·yn·gol·o·gy** \,ō-tō-,rī-nō-,la-rən-'gä-lə-jē\ *n* : OTOLARYNGOLOGY — **oto·rhi·no·lar·yn·gol·o·gist** \-jist\ *n*

**OTS** *abbr* officers' training school

**Ot·ta·wa** \'ä-tə-wə, -,wä, -,wȯ\ *n, pl* **Ottawas** *or* **Ottawa** : a member of an American Indian people of Michigan and southern Ontario

**ot·ter** \'ä-tər\ *n, pl* **otters** *also* **otter** : any of various web-footed fish-eating mammals with dark brown fur that are related to the weasels; *also* : the fur

**ot·to·man** \'ä-tə-mən\ *n* : an upholstered seat or couch usu. without a back; *also* : an overstuffed footstool

**ou·bli·ette** \,ü-blē-'et\ *n* [F, fr. MF, fr. *oublier* to forget, ultim. fr. L *oblivisci*] : a dungeon with an opening at the top

**ought** \'ȯt\ *verbal auxiliary* — used to express moral obligation, advisability, natural expectation, or logical consequence ⟨you ~ to apologize⟩

**ou·gui·ya** \ü-'gwē-ə, -'gē-\ *n, pl* **ouguiya** — see MONEY table

**ounce** \'aůns\ *n* [ME, fr. AF *unce*, fr. L *uncia* twelfth part, ounce, fr. *unus* one] 1 : a unit of avoirdupois, troy, and apothecaries' weight — see WEIGHT table 2 : FLUID OUNCE

**our** \är, 'aů(-ə)r\ *adj* : of or relating to us or ourselves

**ours** \'aů(-ə)z, 'ärz\ *pron* : that which belongs to us

**our·selves** \är-'selvz, aů(-ə)r-\ *pron* : our own selves — used reflexively, for emphasis, or in absolute constructions ⟨we pleased ~⟩ ⟨we'll do it ~⟩ ⟨we were tourists ~⟩

**-ous** *adj suffix* : full of : abounding in : having : possessing the qualities of ⟨clamor*ous*⟩ ⟨poison*ous*⟩

**oust** \'aůst\ *vb* : to eject from or deprive of property or position : EXPEL ♦ *Synonyms* EVICT, DISMISS, BANISH, DEPORT

**oust·er** \'aůs-tər\ *n* : EXPULSION

¹**out** \'aůt\ *adv* 1 : in a direction away from the inside or center 2 : beyond control 3 : to extinction, exhaustion, or completion 4 : in or into the open 5 : so as to retire a batter or base runner; *also* : so as to be retired

²**out** *vb* : to become known ⟨the truth will ~⟩

³**out** *prep* 1 : out through ⟨looked ~ the window⟩ 2 : outward on or along ⟨drive ~ the river road⟩

⁴**out** *adj* 1 : situated outside or at a dis-

tance **2** : not in : ABSENT; *also* : not being in power **3** : removed from play as a batter or base runner **4** : not being in vogue or fashion : not up-to-date **5** : attempting a particular activity ⟨won his first time ∼⟩

⁵**out** *n* **1** : one who is out of office **2** : the retiring of a batter or base runner

**out·age** \'aù-tij\ *n* : a period or instance of interruption esp. of electricity

**out-and-out** *adj* : COMPLETE, THOROUGHGOING ⟨an ∼ fraud⟩

**out·bid** \,aùt-'bid\ *vb* : to make a higher bid than

¹**out·board** \'aùt-,bòrd\ *adj* **1** : situated outboard **2** : having or using an outboard motor

²**outboard** *adv* **1** : outside a ship's hull : away from the long axis of a ship **2** : in a position closer to the wing tip of an airplane

**outboard motor** *n* : a small internal combustion engine with propeller attached for mounting at the stern of a small boat

**out·bound** \'aùt-,baùnd\ *adj* : outward bound ⟨∼ traffic⟩

**out·break** \-,brāk\ *n* **1** : a sudden increase in activity, incidence, or numbers **2** : INSURRECTION, REVOLT

**out·build·ing** \-,bil-diŋ\ *n* : a building separate from but accessory to a main house

**out·burst** \-,bərst\ *n* : ERUPTION; *esp* : a violent expression of feeling

**out·cast** \-,kast\ *n* : one that is cast out by society

**out·class** \aùt-'klas\ *vb* : SURPASS

**out·come** \'aùt-,kəm\ *n* : a final consequence : RESULT

**out·crop** \-,kräp\ *n* : a coming out of bedrock to the surface of the ground; *also* : the part of a rock formation that thus appears — outcrop *vb*

**out·cry** \-,krī\ *n* : a loud cry : CLAMOR

**out·dat·ed** \aùt-'dā-təd\ *adj* : OUTMODED

**out·dis·tance** \-'dis-təns\ *vb* : to go far ahead of (as in a race) : OUTSTRIP

**out·do** \-'dü\ *vb* -did \-'did\; -done \-'dən\; -do·ing; -does \-'dəz\ : to go beyond in action or performance

**out·door** \'aùt-,dòr, -'dòr\ *also* **out·doors** \-,dòrz, -'dòrz\ *adj* **1** : of or relating to the outdoors **2** : performed outdoors **3** : not enclosed (as by a roof)

¹**out·doors** \'aùt-,dòrz, -'dòrz\ *adv* : in or into the open air

²**outdoors** *n* **1** : the open air **2** : the world away from human habitation — **out·doorsy** \aùt-'dòr-zē\ *adj*

**out·draw** \aùt-'dro\ *vb* -drew \-'drü\; -drawn \-'dron\; -draw·ing **1** : to attract a larger audience than **2** : to draw a handgun more quickly than

**out·er** \'aù-tər\ *adj* **1** : EXTERNAL **2** : situated farther out; *also* : being away from a center

**outer ear** *n* : the outer visible portion of the ear that collects and directs sound waves toward the eardrum

**out·er·most** \-,mōst\ *adj* : farthest out

**outer space** *n* : SPACE 5

**out·er·wear** \'aù-tər-,wer\ *n* **1** : clothing

for outdoor wear **2** : outer clothing as opposed to underwear

**out·face** \aùt-'fās\ *vb* **1** : to cause to waver or submit **2** : DEFY

**out·field** \'aùt-,fēld\ *n* : the part of a baseball field beyond the infield and within the foul lines; *also* : players in the outfield — **out·field·er** \-,fēl-dər\ *n*

**out·fight** \aùt-'fīt\ *vb* : to surpass in fighting : DEFEAT

¹**out·fit** \'aùt-,fit\ *n* **1** : the equipment or apparel for a special purpose or occasion **2** : GROUP ⟨an insurance ∼⟩

²**outfit** *vb* **out·fit·ted; out·fit·ting** : EQUIP — **out·fit·ter** *n*

**out·flank** \aùt-'flaŋk\ *vb* : to get around the flank of (an opposing force)

**out·flow** \'aùt-,flō\ *n* **1** : a flowing out **2** : something that flows out

**out·fox** \aùt-'fäks\ *vb* : OUTWIT

**out·go** \'aùt-,gō\ *n, pl* **outgoes** : EXPENDITURES, OUTLAY

**out·go·ing** \-,gō-iŋ\ *adj* **1** : going out ⟨∼ tide⟩ **2** : retiring from a place or position **3** : FRIENDLY

**out·grow** \aùt-'grō\ *vb* -grew \-'grü\; -grown \-'grōn\; -grow·ing **1** : to grow faster than **2** : to grow too large for

**out·growth** \'aùt-,grōth\ *n* : a product of growing out : OFFSHOOT; *also* : CONSEQUENCE, RESULT

**out·guess** \aùt-'ges\ *vb* : OUTWIT

**out·gun** \-'gən\ *vb* : to surpass in firepower

**out·house** \'aùt-,haùs\ *n* : OUTBUILDING; *esp* : an outdoor toilet

**out·ing** \'aù-tiŋ\ *n* : a brief stay or trip in the open ⟨a family ∼⟩

**out·land·ish** \aùt-'lan-dish\ *adj* **1** : of foreign appearance or manner; *also* : BIZARRE **2** : remote from civilization — **out·land·ish·ly** *adv*

**out·last** \-'last\ *vb* : to last longer than

¹**out·law** \'aùt-,lò\ *n* **1** : a person excluded from the protection of the law **2** : a lawless person

²**outlaw** *vb* **1** : to deprive of the protection of the law **2** : to make illegal — **out·law·ry** \'aùt-,lòr-ē\ *n*

**out·lay** \'aùt-,lā\ *n* **1** : the act of spending **2** : EXPENDITURE

**out·let** \'aùt-,let, -lət\ *n* **1** : EXIT, VENT **2** : a means of release (as for an emotion) **3** : a medium for usu. public expression : a media organization **4** : a market for a commodity **5** : a receptacle for the plug of an electrical device

¹**out·line** \'aùt-,līn\ *n* **1** : a line marking the outer limits of an object or figure **2** : a drawing in which only contours are marked **3** : SUMMARY, SYNOPSIS ⟨an ∼ of the novel⟩ **4** : PLAN

²**outline** *vb* **1** : to draw the outline of **2** : to indicate the chief features or parts of

**out·live** \aùt-'liv\ *vb* : to live longer than
♦ *Synonyms* OUTLAST, SURVIVE

**out·look** \'aùt-,lùk\ *n* **1** : a place offering a view; *also* : VIEW **2** : STANDPOINT **3** : the prospect for the future

**out·ly·ing** \-,lī-iŋ\ *adj* : distant from a center or main body

**out·ma·neu·ver** \,aùt-mə-'nü-vər, -'nyü-\

*vb* : to defeat by more skillful maneuvering

**out·mod·ed** \aut-'mō-dəd\ *adj* 1 : no longer in style 2 : no longer acceptable or current ⟨∼ technology⟩

**out·num·ber** \-'nəm-bər\ *vb* : to exceed in number

**out of** *prep* 1 : out from within or behind ⟨walk *out of* the room⟩ ⟨look *out of* the window⟩ 2 : from a state of ⟨wake up *out of* a deep sleep⟩ 3 : beyond the limits of ⟨*out of* sight⟩ 4 : BECAUSE OF ⟨asked *out of* curiosity⟩ 5 : FROM, WITH ⟨built it *out of* scrap⟩ 6 : in or into a state of loss or not having ⟨cheated him *out of* $5000⟩ ⟨we're *out of* matches⟩ 7 : from among ⟨one *out of* four⟩ — **out of it** : SQUARE, OLD-FASHIONED

**out–of–bounds** *adv or adj* : outside the prescribed boundaries or limits

**out–of–date** *adj* : no longer in fashion or in use

**out–of–door** *or* **out–of–doors** *adj* : OUTDOOR

**out–of–the–way** *adj* 1 : UNUSUAL 2 : being off the beaten track

**out·pa·tient** \'aut-ˌpā-shənt\ *n* : a patient who visits a hospital or clinic for diagnosis or treatment without staying overnight

**out·per·form** \ˌaut-pər-'fȯrm\ *vb* : to perform better than

**out·play** \aut-'plā\ *vb* : to play more skillfully than

**out·point** \-'pȯint\ *vb* : to win more points than

**out·post** \'aut-ˌpōst\ *n* 1 : a security detachment dispatched by a main body of troops to protect it from enemy surprise; *also* : a military base established (as by treaty) in a foreign country 2 : an outlying or frontier settlement

**out·pour·ing** \-ˌpȯr-iŋ\ *n* : something that pours out or is poured out

**out·pull** \aut-'pul\ *vb* : OUTDRAW 1

¹**out·put** \'aut-ˌput\ *n* 1 : the amount produced (as by a machine or factory) : PRODUCTION 2 : the information produced by a computer

²**output** *vb* **out·put·ted** *or* **output; out·put·ting** : to produce as output

¹**out·rage** \'aut-ˌrāj\ *n* [ME, fr. AF *utrage, outrage* insult, excess, fr. *utre, outre* beyond, fr. L *ultra*] 1 : a violent or shameful act 2 : INJURY, INSULT 3 : the anger or resentment aroused by injury or insult

²**outrage** *vb* **out·raged; out·rag·ing** 1 : RAPE 2 : to subject to violent injury or gross insult 3 : to arouse to intense resentment

**out·ra·geous** \aut-'rā-jəs\ *adj* : extremely offensive, insulting, or shameful : SHOCKING — **out·ra·geous·ly** *adv*

**out·rank** \-'raŋk\ *vb* : to rank higher than

**ou·tré** \ü-'trā\ *adj* [F] : violating convention or propriety : BIZARRE ⟨∼ creations⟩

¹**out·reach** \aut-'rēch\ *vb* 1 : to surpass in reach 2 : to get the better of by trickery

²**out·reach** \'aut-ˌrēch\ *n* 1 : the act of reaching out 2 : the extent of reach 3

: the extending of services beyond usual limits

**out·rid·er** \-ˌrī-dər\ *n* : a mounted attendant

**out·rig·ger** \-ˌri-gər\ *n* 1 : a frame attached to the side of a boat to prevent capsizing 2 : a craft equipped with an outrigger

¹**out·right** \aut-'rīt\ *adv* 1 : COMPLETELY 2 : INSTANTANEOUSLY

²**out·right** \'aut-ˌrīt\ *adj* 1 : being exactly what is stated ⟨an ∼ lie⟩ 2 : given or made without reservation or encumbrance ⟨an ∼ sale⟩

**out·run** \aut-'rən\ *vb* **-ran** \-'ran\; **-run; -run·ning** : to run faster than; *also* : EXCEED

**out·sell** \-'sel\ *vb* **-sold** \-'sōld\; **-sell·ing** : to exceed in sales

**out·set** \'aut-ˌset\ *n* : BEGINNING, START

**out·shine** \aut-'shīn\ *vb* **-shone** \-'shōn\ *or* **-shined; -shin·ing** 1 : to shine brighter than 2 : SURPASS

¹**out·side** \aut-'sīd, 'aut-ˌsīd\ *n* 1 : a place or region beyond an enclosure or boundary 2 : EXTERIOR 3 : the utmost limit or extent

²**outside** *adj* 1 : OUTER 2 : coming from without ⟨∼ influences⟩ 3 : being apart from one's regular duties ⟨∼ activities⟩ 4 : REMOTE ⟨an ∼ chance⟩

³**outside** *adv* : on or to the outside

⁴**outside** *prep* 1 : on or to the outside of 2 : beyond the limits of 3 : EXCEPT

**outside of** *prep* 1 : OUTSIDE 2 : BESIDES

**out·sid·er** \aut-'sī-dər\ *n* : a person who does not belong to a group

**out·size** \'aut-ˌsīz\ *also* **out·sized** \-ˌsīzd\ *adj* : unusually large : extravagant in size or degree

**out·skirts** \-ˌskərts\ *n pl* : the outlying parts (as of a city) : BORDERS

**out·smart** \aut-'smärt\ *vb* : OUTWIT

**out·source** \'aut-ˌsȯrs\ *vb* **-sourced; -sourc·ing** : to obtain (goods or services) from an outside supplier

**out·spend** \-'spend\ *vb* 1 : to exceed the limits of in spending ⟨∼s his income⟩ 2 : to spend more than

**out·spo·ken** \aut-'spō-kən\ *adj* : direct and open in speech or expression — **out·spo·ken·ly** *adv* — **out·spo·ken·ness** *n*

**out·spread** \-'spred\ *vb* **-spread; -spread·ing** : to spread out

**out·stand·ing** \-'stan-diŋ\ *adj* 1 : PROJECTING 2 : UNPAID; *also* : UNRESOLVED ⟨∼ warrants⟩ 3 : publicly issued and sold 4 : CONSPICUOUS; *also* : DISTINGUISHED — **out·stand·ing·ly** *adv*

**out·stay** \-'stā\ *vb* 1 : OVERSTAY 2 : to surpass in endurance

**out·stretch** \ˌaut-'strech\ *vb* : to stretch out : EXTEND

**out·strip** \-'strip\ *vb* 1 : to go faster than 2 : EXCEL, SURPASS

**out·take** \'aut-ˌtāk\ *n* : something taken out; *esp* : a take that is not used in an edited version of a film or videotape

**out·vote** \-'vōt\ *vb* : to defeat by a majority of votes

¹**out·ward** \'aut-wərd\ *adj* 1 : moving or

directed toward the outside **2** : showing outwardly

**²out·ward** *or* **out·wards** \-wərdz\ *adv* : toward the outside

**out·ward·ly** \-wərd-lē\ *adv* : on the outside : EXTERNALLY

**out·wear** \aút-'wer\ *vb* **-wore** \-'wōr\; **-worn** \-'wórn\; **-wear·ing** : to wear longer than : OUTLAST

**out·weigh** \-'wā\ *vb* : to exceed in weight, value, or importance

**out·wit** \-'wit\ *vb* : to get the better of by superior cleverness

**¹out·work** \-'wərk\ *vb* : to outdo in working

**²out·work** \'aút-,wərk\ *n* : a minor defensive position outside a fortified area

**out·worn** \aút-'wórn\ *adj* : OUTMODED

**ou·zo** \'ü-(,)zō\ *n* : a colorless anise-flavored unsweetened Greek liqueur

**ova** *pl of* OVUM

**oval** \'ō-vəl\ *adj* [ML *ovalis*, fr. LL, of an egg, fr. L *ovum* egg] : egg-shaped; *also* : broadly elliptical — **oval** *n*

**ova·ry** \'ō-və-rē\ *n, pl* **-ries** **1** : one of the usu. paired female reproductive organs producing eggs and in vertebrates sex hormones **2** : the part of a flower in which seeds are produced — **ovar·i·an** \ō-'ver-ē-ən\ *adj*

**ovate** \'ō-,vāt\ *adj* : egg-shaped

**ova·tion** \ō-'vā-shən\ *n* [L *ovation-, ovatio*, fr. *ovare* to exult] : an enthusiastic popular tribute

**ov·en** \'ə-vən\ *n* : a chamber (as in a stove) for baking, heating, or drying

**oven·bird** \-,bərd\ *n* : a large olive-green American warbler that builds its dome-shaped nest on the ground

**¹over** \'ō-vər\ *adv* **1** : across a barrier or intervening space **2** : across the brim ⟨boil ∼⟩ **3** : so as to bring the underside up **4** : out of a vertical position **5** : beyond some quantity, limit, or norm **6** : ABOVE **7** : at an end **8** : THROUGH ⟨read it ∼⟩; *also* : THOROUGHLY ⟨still thinking it ∼⟩ **9** : AGAIN ⟨do it ∼⟩

**²over** *prep* **1** : above in position, authority, or scope ⟨towered ∼ her⟩ ⟨obeyed those ∼ him⟩ **2** : more than ⟨cost ∼ $100⟩ **3** : ON, UPON ⟨a cape ∼ her shoulders⟩ **4** : along the length of ⟨∼ the road⟩ **5** : through the medium of : ON ⟨spoke ∼ TV⟩ **6** : all through ⟨showed me ∼ the house⟩ **7** : on or to the other side or beyond ⟨jump ∼ a ditch⟩ **8** : DURING ⟨∼ the past 25 years⟩ **9** : on account of ⟨trouble ∼ money⟩

**³over** *adj* **1** : UPPER, HIGHER **2** : REMAINING **3** : ENDED ⟨those days are ∼⟩

**over-** *prefix* **1** : so as to exceed or surpass **2** : excessive, excessively

**over·act** \,ō-vər-'akt\ *vb* : to exaggerate in acting

**¹over·age** \,ō-vər-'āj\ *adj* **1** : too old to be useful **2** : older than is normal for one's position, function, or grade

**²over·age** \'ō-və-rij\ *n* : SURPLUS

**over·all** \,ō-vər-'ól\ *adj* : including everything ⟨∼ expenses⟩

**over·alls** \'ō-vər-,ólz\ *n pl* : pants of strong material usu. with a piece extending up to cover the chest

**over·arm** \-,ärm\ *adj* : done with the arm raised above the shoulder

**over·awe** \,ō-vər-'ó\ *vb* : to restrain or subdue by awe

**over·bal·ance** \-'ba-ləns\ *vb* **1** : OUTWEIGH **2** : to cause to lose balance

**over·bear·ing** \-'ber-iŋ\ *adj* : ARROGANT, DOMINEERING

**over·bite** \'ō-vər-,bīt\ *n* : the projection of the upper front teeth over the lower

**over·blown** \-'blōn\ *adj* **1** : PORTLY **2** : INFLATED, PRETENTIOUS

**over·board** \'ō-vər-,bórd\ *adv* **1** : over the side of a ship into the water **2** : to extremes of enthusiasm

**¹over·cast** \'ō-vər-,kast\ *adj* : clouded over : GLOOMY

**²overcast** *n* : COVERING; *esp* : a covering of clouds

**over·charge** \,ō-vər-'chärj\ *vb* **1** : to charge too much **2** : to fill or load too full — **over·charge** \'ō-vər-,chärj\ *n*

**over·coat** \'ō-vər-,kōt\ *n* : a warm coat worn over indoor clothing

**over·come** \,ō-vər-'kəm\ *vb* **-came** \-'kām\; **-come**; **-com·ing** **1** : CONQUER **2** : to make helpless or exhausted

**over·do** \,ō-vər-'dü\ *vb* **-did** \-'did\; **-done** \-'dən\; **-do·ing**; **-does** \-'dəz\ **1** : to do too much; *also* : to tire oneself **2** : EXAGGERATE **3** : to cook too long

**over·dose** \'ō-vər-,dōs\ *n* : too great a dose (as of medicine); *also* : a lethal or toxic amount (as of a drug) — **over·dose** \,ō-vər-'dōs\ *vb*

**over·draft** \'ō-vər-,draft\ *n* : an overdrawing of a bank account; *also* : the sum overdrawn

**over·draw** \,ō-vər-'dró\ *vb* **-drew** \-'drü\; **-drawn** \-'drón\; **-draw·ing** **1** : to draw checks on a bank account for more than the balance **2** : EXAGGERATE

**over·drive** \'ō-vər-,drīv\ *n* : an automotive transmission gear that transmits to the driveshaft a speed greater than the engine speed

**over·dub** \,ō-vər-'dəb\ *vb* : to transfer (recorded sound) onto an earlier recording for a combined effect — **over·dub** \'ō-vər-,dəb\ *n*

**over·due** \-'dü, -'dyü\ *adj* **1** : unpaid when due ⟨an ∼ bill⟩; *also* : not appearing or presented on time ⟨an ∼ train⟩ **2** : more than ready

---

| | | | |
|---|---|---|---|
| overabundance | overbid | overcareful | overcritical |
| overabundant | overbold | overcautious | overcrowd |
| overachiever | overbuild | overcompensation | overdecorated |
| overactive | overburden | overconfidence | overdependence |
| overaggressive | overbuy | overconfident | overdetermined |
| overambitious | overcapacity | overconscientious | overdevelop |
| overanxious | overcapitalize | overcook | overdress |

**over·ex·pose** \ˌō-vər-ik-ˈspōz\ *vb* : to expose (as film) for more time than is needed — **over·ex·po·sure** \-ˈspō-zhər\ *n*

¹**over·flow** \-ˈflō\ *vb* 1 : INUNDATE; *also* : to pour forth in a flood 2 : to flow over the brim or top of

²**over·flow** \ˈō-vər-ˌflō\ *n* 1 : FLOOD; *also* : SURPLUS 2 : an outlet for surplus liquid

**over·fly** \ˌō-vər-ˈflī\ *vb* **-flew** \-ˈflü\; **-flown** \-ˈflōn\; **-fly·ing** 1 : to fly over in an aircraft or spacecraft — **over·flight** \ˈō-vər-ˌflīt\ *n*

**over·grow** \ˌō-vər-ˈgrō\ *vb* **-grew** \-ˈgrü\; **-grown** \-ˈgrōn\; **-grow·ing** 1 : to grow over so as to cover 2 : OUTGROW 3 : to grow excessively — **over·growth** \ˈō-vər-ˌgrōth\ *n*

**over·hand** \ˈō-vər-ˌhand\ *adj* : made with the hand brought down from above — **overhand** *adv* — **over·hand·ed** \-ˌhan-dəd\ *adv or adj*

¹**over·hang** \ˈō-vər-ˌhaŋ, ˌō-vər-ˈhaŋ\ *vb* **-hung** \-ˌhəŋ, -ˈhəŋ\; **-hang·ing** 1 : to project over : jut out 2 : to hang over threateningly

²**over·hang** \ˈō-vər-ˌhaŋ\ *n* : a part (as of a roof) that overhangs

**over·haul** \ˌō-vər-ˈhȯl\ *vb* 1 : to examine thoroughly and make necessary repairs and adjustments 2 : OVERTAKE

¹**over·head** \ˌō-vər-ˈhed\ *adv* : ALOFT

²**over·head** \ˈō-vər-ˌhed\ *adj* : operating or lying above ⟨~ storage bins⟩

³**over·head** \ˈō-vər-ˌhed\ *n* : business expenses not chargeable to a particular part of the work

**over·hear** \ˌō-vər-ˈhir\ *vb* **-heard** \-ˈhərd\; **-hear·ing** : to hear without the speaker's knowledge or intention

**over·joyed** \ˌō-vər-ˈjȯid\ *adj* : filled with great joy

**over·kill** \ˈō-vər-ˌkil\ *n* 1 : destructive capacity greatly exceeding that required for a target 2 : a large excess

**over·land** \ˈō-vər-ˌland, -lənd\ *adv or adj* : by, on, or across land

**over·lap** \ˌō-vər-ˈlap\ *vb* 1 : to lap over 2 : to have something in common — **over·lap** \ˈō-vər-ˌlap\ *n*

**over·lay** \ˌō-vər-ˈlā\ *vb* **-laid** \-ˈlād\; **-lay·ing** : to lay or spread over or across — **over·lay** \ˈō-vər-ˌlā\ *n*

**over·leap** \ˌō-vər-ˈlēp\ *vb* **-leaped** *or* **-leapt** \-ˈlēpt, -ˈlept\; **-leap·ing** 1 : to leap over or across 2 : to defeat (oneself) by going too far

**over·lie** \ˌō-vər-ˈlī\ *vb* **-lay** \-ˈlā\; **-lain** \-ˈlān\; **-ly·ing** : to lie over or upon

¹**over·look** \ˌō-vər-ˈlük\ *vb* 1 : INSPECT 2 : to look down on from above 3 : to fail

to see 4 : IGNORE ⟨~ed his faults⟩; *also* : EXCUSE 5 : SUPERINTEND

²**over·look** \ˈō-vər-ˌlük\ *n* : a place from which to look upon a scene below

**over·lord** \ˈō-vər-ˌlȯrd\ *n* : a lord who has supremacy over other lords

**over·ly** \ˈō-vər-lē\ *adv* : EXCESSIVELY

**over·match** \ˌō-vər-ˈmach\ *vb* : to be more than a match for : DEFEAT

**over·much** \-ˈməch\ *adj or adv* : too much

¹**over·night** \-ˈnīt\ *adv* 1 : on or during the night 2 : SUDDENLY ⟨became famous ~⟩

²**overnight** *adj* : of, lasting, or staying the night ⟨~ guests⟩

**over·pass** \ˈō-vər-ˌpas\ *n* 1 : a crossing (as of two highways) at different levels by means of a bridge 2 : the upper level of an overpass

**over·play** \ˌō-vər-ˈplā\ *vb* 1 : EXAGGERATE; *also* : OVEREMPHASIZE 2 : to rely too much on the strength of

**over·pop·u·la·tion** \ˌō-vər-ˌpä-pyə-ˈlā-shən\ *n* : the condition of having a population so dense as to cause a decline in population or in living conditions — **over·pop·u·lat·ed** \-ˈpä-pyə-ˌlā-təd\ *adj*

**over·pow·er** \-ˈpau̇(-ə)r\ *vb* : to overcome by superior force

**over·price** \ˌō-vər-ˈprīs\ *vb* : to price too high

**over·print** \-ˈprint\ *vb* : to print over with something additional — **over·print** \ˈō-vər-ˌprint\ *n*

**over·qual·i·fied** \-ˈkwä-lə-ˌfīd\ *adj* : having more education, training, or experience than a job calls for

**over·reach** \ˌō-vər-ˈrēch\ *vb* : to defeat (oneself) by too great an effort

**over·ride** \-ˈrīd\ *vb* **-rode** \-ˈrōd\; **-rid·den** \-ˈri-dᵊn\; **-rid·ing** 1 : to ride over or across 2 : to prevail over; *also* : to set aside ⟨~ a veto⟩

**over·rule** \-ˈrül\ *vb* 1 : to prevail over 2 : to rule against 3 : to set aside

¹**over·run** \-ˈrən\ *vb* **-ran** \-ˈran\; **-run; -run·ning** 1 : to defeat and occupy the positions of 2 : OVERSPREAD; *also* : INFEST 3 : to go beyond 4 : to flow over

²**over·run** \ˈō-vər-ˌrən\ *n* 1 : an act or instance of overrunning; *esp* : an exceeding of estimated costs 2 : the amount by which something overruns

**over·sea** \ˌō-vər-ˈsē, ˈō-vər-ˌsē\ *adj or adv* : OVERSEAS

**over·seas** \ˌō-vər-ˈsēz, -ˌsēz\ *adv or adj* : beyond or across the sea : ABROAD

**over·see** \ˌō-vər-ˈsē\ *vb* **-saw** \-ˈsȯ\; **-seen** \-ˈsēn\; **-see·ing** 1 : OVERLOOK 2

---

| | | | |
|---|---|---|---|
| overeager | overfatigued | overindulgent | overproduce |
| overeat | overfeed | overinflate | overproduction |
| overeducated | overfill | overlarge | overprotect |
| overemphasis | overgeneralization | overlearn | overprotective |
| overemphasize | overgeneralize | overload | overrate |
| overenthusiastic | overgenerous | overlong | overreact |
| overestimate | overgraze | overmodest | overreaction |
| overexcite | overhasty | overnice | overrefinement |
| overexcited | overheat | overoptimism | overregulate |
| overexert | overhype | overoptimistic | overreliance |
| overexertion | overindulge | overpay | overrepresented |
| overextend | overindulgence | overpraise | overripe |

: INSPECT; *also* : SUPERVISE ⟨∼ the project⟩ — **over-seer** \'ō-vər-ˌsir\ *n*

**over-sell** \ˌō-vər-'sel\ *vb* **-sold; -sell-ing** : to sell too much to or too much of

**over-sexed** \ˌō-vər-'sekst\ *adj* : exhibiting excessive sexual drive or interest

**over-shad-ow** \-'sha-dō\ *vb* **1** : to cast a shadow over **2** : to exceed in importance

**over-shoe** \'ō-vər-ˌshü\ *n* : a protective outer shoe; *esp* : GALOSH

**over-shoot** \ˌō-vər-'shüt\ *vb* **-shot** \-'shät\ **-shoot-ing 1** : to pass swiftly beyond **2** : to shoot over or beyond

**over-sight** \'ō-vər-ˌsīt\ *n* **1** : SUPERVISION **2** : an inadvertent omission or error

**over-size** \ˌō-vər-'sīz\ *or* **over-sized** \-'sīzd\ *adj* : of more than ordinary size

**over-sleep** \ˌō-vər-'slēp\ *vb* **-slept** \-'slept\ **-sleep-ing** : to sleep beyond the time for waking

**over-spread** \-'spred\ *vb* **-spread; -spread-ing** : to spread over or above

**over-state** \-'stāt\ *vb* : EXAGGERATE — **over-state-ment** *n*

**over-stay** \-'stā\ *vb* : to stay beyond the time or limits of ⟨∼ed her welcome⟩

**over-step** \-'step\ *vb* : EXCEED

**over-sub-scribe** \ˌō-vər-səb-'skrīb\ *vb* : to subscribe for more of than is available, asked for, or offered for sale

**overt** \ō-'vərt, 'ō-ˌvərt\ *adj* [ME, fr. AF, fr. pp. of *ovrir* to open] : not secret ⟨∼ hostility⟩ — **overt-ly** *adv*

**over-take** \ˌō-vər-'tāk\ *vb* **-took** \-'tùk\ **-tak-en** \-'tā-kən\, **-tak-ing** : to catch up with; *also* : to catch up with and pass by ⟨∼ the lead runner⟩

**over–the–counter** *adj* : sold lawfully without a prescription ⟨∼ drugs⟩

**over–the–hill** *adj* **1** : past one's prime **2** : advanced in age

**over–the–top** *adj* : extremely flamboyant or outrageous ⟨an ∼ performance⟩

**over-throw** \ˌō-vər-'thrō\ *vb* **-threw** \-'thrü\, **-thrown** \-'thrōn\, **-throw-ing 1** : UPSET **2** : to bring down : DEFEAT ⟨∼ a government⟩ **3** : to throw over or past — **over-throw** \'ō-vər-ˌthrō\ *n*

**over-time** \'ō-vər-ˌtīm\ *n* : time beyond a set limit; *esp* : working time in excess of a standard day or week — **overtime** *adv*

**over-tone** \-ˌtōn\ *n* **1** : one of the higher tones in a complex musical tone **2** : IMPLICATION, SUGGESTION ⟨political ∼s⟩

**over-trick** \'ō-vər-ˌtrik\ *n* : a card trick won in excess of the number bid

**over-ture** \'ō-vər-ˌchùr, -chər\ *n* [ME, lit., opening, fr. AF, fr. VL *opertura*, alter. of L *apertura*] **1** : an opening offer **2** : an orchestral introduction to a musical dramatic work

**over-turn** \ˌō-vər-'tərn\ *vb* **1** : to turn over : UPSET ⟨∼ a vase⟩ **2** : INVALIDATE ⟨∼ a court ruling⟩

**over-view** \'ō-vər-ˌvyü\ *n* : a general survey : SUMMARY

**over-ween-ing** \ˌō-vər-'wē-nin\ *adj* **1** : ARROGANT ⟨∼ pride⟩ **2** : IMMODERATE

**over-weight** \'ō-vər-ˌwāt\ *n* **1** : weight above what is required or allowed **2** : bodily weight greater than normal — **overweight** *adj*

**over-whelm** \-'hwelm\ *vb* **1** : OVERTHROW **2** : SUBMERGE **3** : to overcome completely

**over-whelm-ing** *adj* : EXTREME, GREAT ⟨∼ joy⟩ — **over-whelm-ing-ly** *adv*

**over-win-ter** \-'win-tər\ *vb* : to survive or pass the winter

**over-work** \-'wərk\ *vb* **1** : to work or cause to work too hard or long **2** : to use too much — **overwork** *n*

**over-wrought** \ˌō-vər-'rót\ *adj* **1** : extremely excited **2** : elaborated to excess

**ovi-duct** \'ō-və-ˌdəkt\ *n* : a tube that serves for the passage of eggs from an ovary

**ovip-a-rous** \ō-'vi-pə-rəs\ *adj* : reproducing by eggs that hatch outside the parent's body

**ovoid** \'ō-ˌvóid\ *or* **ovoi-dal** \ō-'vói-dᵊl\ *adj* : egg-shaped : OVAL

**ovu-la-tion** \ˌäv-yə-'lā-shən, ˌōv-\ *n* : the discharge of a mature egg from the ovary — **ovu-late** \'äv-yə-ˌlāt, 'ōv-\ *vb*

**ovule** \'äv-yül, 'ōv-\ *n* : any of the bodies in a plant ovary that after fertilization become seeds

**ovum** \'ō-vəm\ *n, pl* **ova** \-və\ : EGG 2

**ow** \'aú\ *interj* — used esp. to express sudden pain

**owe** \'ō\ *vb* **owed; ow-ing 1** : to be under obligation to pay or render **2** : to be indebted to or for; *also* : to be in debt

**owing to** *prep* : BECAUSE OF

**owl** \'aú(-ə)l\ *n* : any of an order of chiefly nocturnal birds of prey with a large head and eyes and strong talons — **owl-ish** *adj* — **owl-ish-ly** *adv*

**owl-et** \'aú-lət\ *n* : a young or small owl

**¹own** \'ōn\ *adj* : belonging to oneself — used as an intensive after a possessive adjective ⟨her ∼ car⟩

**²own** *vb* **1** : to have or hold as property **2** : to have power or mastery over **3** : ACKNOWLEDGE ⟨would not ∼ up to his mistake⟩; *also* : CONFESS — **own-er** *n* — **own-er-ship** *n*

**³own** *pron* : one or ones belonging to oneself — **on one's own** : for or by oneself : left to one's own resources

**ox** \'äks\ *n, pl* **ox-en** \'äk-sən\ *also* **ox** : any of the large domestic bovine mammals kept for milk, draft, and meat; *esp* : an adult castrated male ox

**ox-blood** \'äks-ˌbləd\ *n* : a moderate reddish brown

**ox-bow** \-ˌbō\ *n* **1** : a U-shaped collar worn by a draft ox **2** : a U-shaped bend in a river — **oxbow** *adj*

**ox-ford** \'äks-fərd\ *n* : a low shoe laced or tied over the instep

---

| | | | |
|---|---|---|---|
| oversensitive | overspecialization | oversubtle | overuse |
| oversensitiveness | overspecialize | oversupply | overvalue |
| oversimple | overspend | overtax | overzealous |
| oversimplification | overstimulation | overtired | |
| oversimplify | overstock | overtrain | |

**ox·i·dant** \'äk-sə-dənt\ *n* : OXIDIZING AGENT — **oxidant** *adj*

**ox·i·da·tion** \,äk-sə-'dā-shən\ *n* : the act or process of oxidizing; *also* : the condition of being oxidized — **ox·i·da·tive** \'äk-sə-,dā-tiv\ *adj*

**ox·ide** \'äk-,sīd\ *n* : a compound of oxygen with another element or group

**ox·i·dize** \'äk-sə-,dīz\ *vb* **-dized; -diz·ing** : to combine with oxygen ⟨iron rusts because it is *oxidized* by exposure to the air⟩ — **ox·i·diz·er** *n*

**oxidizing agent** *n* : a substance (as oxygen or nitric acid) that oxidizes by taking up electrons

**ox·y·gen** \'äk-si-jən\ *n* [F *oxygène*, fr. Gk *oxys* acidic, lit., sharp + *-genēs* giving rise to; so called because it was once thought to be an essential element of all acids] : a colorless odorless gaseous chemical element that is found in the air, is essential to life, and is involved in combustion

**ox·y·gen·ate** \'äk-si-jə-,nāt\ *vb* **-at·ed; -at·ing** : to impregnate, combine, or supply with oxygen — **ox·y·gen·a·tion** \,äk-si-jə-'nā-shən\ *n*

**oxygen mask** *n* : a device worn over the nose and mouth through which oxygen is supplied

**oxygen tent** *n* : a canopy which can be placed over a bedridden person and within which a flow of oxygen can be maintained

**ox·y·mo·ron** \,äk-sē-'môr-,än\ *n* : a combination of contradictory words (as *cruel kindness*) — **ox·y·mo·ron·ic** \-mə-'rä-nik\ *adj*

**oys·ter** \'ȯis-tər\ *n* : any of various marine mollusks with an irregular 2-valved shell that include commercially important edible shellfish and pearl producers — **oys·ter·ing** *n* — **oys·ter·man** \-mən\ *n*

**oz** *abbr* [obs. It *onza* (now *oncia*)] ounce; ounces

**ozone** \'ō-,zōn\ *n* **1** : a bluish gaseous reactive form of oxygen that is formed naturally in the atmosphere and is used for disinfecting, deodorizing, and bleaching **2** : pure and refreshing air

**ozone layer** *n* : an atmospheric layer at heights of about 25 miles (40 kilometers) with high ozone content which blocks most solar ultraviolet radiation

**¹p** \'pē\ *n, pl* **p's** *or* **ps** \'pēz\ *often cap* : the 16th letter of the English alphabet

**²p** *abbr, often cap* **1** page **2** participle **3** past **4** pawn **5** pence; penny **6** per **7** petite **8** pint **9** pressure **10** purl

**P** *symbol* phosphorus

**pa** \'pä, 'pȯ\ *n* **1** : FATHER

**¹Pa** *abbr* **1** pascal **2** Pennsylvania

**²Pa** *symbol* protactinium

**¹PA** \(,)pē-'ā\ *n* **1** : PHYSICIAN'S ASSISTANT

**²PA** *abbr* **1** Pennsylvania **2** per annum **3** power of attorney **4** press agent **5** private account **6** professional association **7** public address **8** purchasing agent

**pa·'an·ga** \pä-'äŋ-gə\ *n* — see MONEY table

**pab·u·lum** \'pa-byə-ləm\ *n* [L, food, fodder] : usu. soft digestible food

**Pac** *abbr* Pacific

**PAC** *abbr* political action committee

**¹pace** \'pās\ *n* **1** : rate of movement or progress (as in walking or working) **2** : a step in walking; *also* : a measure of length based on such a step **3** : GAIT; *esp* : a horse's gait in which the legs on the same side move together

**²pace** *vb* **paced; pac·ing** **1** : to go or cover at a pace or with slow steps **2** : to measure off by paces ⟨∼ off a 15-yard penalty⟩ **3** : to set or regulate the pace of

**³pa·ce** \'pā-sē; 'pä-,kā, -,chä\ *prep* : contrary to the opinion of

**pace·mak·er** \'pās-,mā-kər\ *n* **1** : one that sets the pace for another **2** : a body part (as of the heart) that serves to establish and maintain a rhythmic activity **3** : an electrical device for stimulating or steadying the heartbeat

**pac·er** \'pā-sər\ *n* **1** : a horse that paces **2** : PACEMAKER

**pachy·derm** \'pa-ki-,dərm\ *n* [F *pachyderme*, fr. Gk *pachydermos* thick=skinned, fr. *pachys* thick + *derma* skin] : any of various thick-skinned hoofed mammals (as an elephant)

**pach·ys·an·dra** \,pa-ki-'san-drə\ *n* : any of a genus of low perennial evergreen plants used as a ground cover

**pa·cif·ic** \pə-'si-fik\ *adj* **1** : tending to lessen conflict **2** : CALM, PEACEFUL

**pac·i·fi·er** \'pa-sə-,fī(-ə)r\ *n* : one that pacifies; *esp* : a device for a baby to chew or suck on

**pac·i·fism** \'pa-sə-,fi-zəm\ *n* : opposition to war or violence as a means of settling disputes — **pac·i·fist** \-fist\ *n or adj* — **pac·i·fis·tic** \,pa-sə-'fis-tik\ *adj*

**pac·i·fy** \'pa-sə-,fī\ *vb* **-fied; -fy·ing** **1** : to allay anger or agitation in **: SOOTHE 2** : SETTLE; *also* : SUBDUE — **pac·i·fi·ca·tion** \,pa-sə-fə-'kā-shən\ *n*

**¹pack** \'pak\ *n* **1** : a compact bundle; *also* : a flexible container for carrying a bundle esp. on the back **2** : a large amount : HEAP **3** : a set of playing cards **4** : a group or band of people or animals **5** : wet absorbent material for application to the body

**²pack** *vb* **1** : to stow goods in for transportation **2** : to fill in or surround so as to prevent passage of air, steam, or water **3** : to put into a protective container **4** : to load with a pack ⟨∼ a mule⟩ **5** : to crowd in **6** : to make into a pack **7** : to cause to go without ceremony ⟨∼ them off to school⟩ **8** : WEAR, CARRY ⟨~ a gun⟩

**³pack** *vb* : to make up fraudulently so as to secure a desired result ⟨~ a jury⟩

**¹pack·age** \'pa-kij\ *n* **1** : BUNDLE, PARCEL **2** : a group of related things offered as a whole

**²package** *vb* **pack·aged; pack·ag·ing** : to make into or enclose in a package

**package deal** *n* : an offer containing several items all or none of which must be accepted

**package store** *n* : a store that sells alcoholic beverages in sealed containers for consumption off the premises

**pack·er** \'pa-kər\ *n* : one that packs; *esp* : a wholesale food dealer

**pack·et** \'pa-kət\ *n* **1** : a small bundle or package **2** : a passenger boat carrying mail and cargo on a regular schedule

**pack·horse** \'pak-,hórs\ *n* : a horse used to carry goods or supplies

**pack·ing** \'pa-kiŋ\ *n* : material used to pack something

**pack·ing·house** \-,haús\ *n* : an establishment for processing and packing food and esp. meat and its by-products

**pack rat** *n* **1** : a bushy-tailed rodent of western No. America that hoards food and miscellaneous objects; *also* : any of several rodents of similar habit **2** : a person who collects or saves many esp. unneeded items

**pack·sad·dle** \'pak-,sa-dᵊl\ *n* : a saddle for supporting loads on the back of an animal

**pack·thread** \-,thred\ *n* : strong thread for tying

**pact** \'pakt\ *n* : AGREEMENT, TREATY

**¹pad** \'pad\ *n* **1** : a cushioning part or thing : CUSHION **2** : the cushioned underside of the foot or toes of some mammals **3** : the floating leaf of a water plant **4** : a writing tablet **5** : LAUNCHPAD **6** : living quarters; *also* : BED

**²pad** *vb* **pad·ded; pad·ding 1** : to furnish with a pad or padding **2** : to expand with needless or fraudulent matter

**pad·ding** *n* : the material with which something is padded

**¹pad·dle** \'pa-dᵊl\ *vb* **pad·dled; pad·dling** : to move the hands and feet about in shallow water

**²paddle** *n* **1** : an implement with a flat blade used in propelling and steering a small craft (as a canoe) **2** : an implement used for stirring, mixing, or beating **3** : a broad board on the outer rim of a waterwheel or a paddle wheel

**³paddle** *vb* **pad·dled; pad·dling 1** : to move on or through water by or as if by using a paddle **2** : to beat or stir with a paddle

**paddle wheel** *n* : a wheel with paddles around its outer edge used to move a boat

**paddle wheeler** *n* : a steam-driven vessel propelled by a paddle wheel

**pad·dock** \'pa-dək\ *n* **1** : a usu. enclosed area for pasturing or exercising animals; *esp* : one where racehorses are saddled and paraded before a race **2** : an area at a racecourse where racing cars are parked

**pad·dy** \'pa-dē\ *n, pl* **paddies** : wet land where rice is grown

**paddy wagon** *n* : an enclosed motortruck for carrying prisoners

**pad·lock** \'pad-,läk\ *n* : a removable lock with a curved piece that snaps into a catch — **padlock** *vb*

**pa·dre** \'pä-drā\ *n* [Sp or It or Pg, lit., father, fr. L *pater*] **1** : PRIEST **2** : a military chaplain

**pad thai** \'päd-'tī\ *n, often cap T* : a Thai dish of rice noodles stir-fried with additional ingredients

**pae·an** \'pē-ən\ *n* : an exultant song of praise or thanksgiving

**pae·di·at·ric, pae·di·a·tri·cian, pae·di·at·rics** *chiefly Brit var of* PEDIATRIC, PEDIATRICIAN, PEDIATRICS

**pa·el·la** \pä-'e-lə; -'āl-yə, -'ā-yə\ *n* : a saffron-flavored dish of rice, meat, seafood, and vegetables

**pa·gan** \'pā-gən\ *n* [ME, fr. LL *paganus*, fr. L, civilian, country dweller, fr. *pagus* country district] : HEATHEN — **pagan** *adj* — **pa·gan·ism** \-gə-,ni-zəm\ *n*

**¹page** \'pāj\ *n* : ATTENDANT; *esp* : one employed to deliver messages

**²page** *vb* **paged; pag·ing 1** : to summon by repeatedly calling out the name of **2** : to send a message to via a pager

**³page** *n* **1** : a single leaf (as of a book); *also* : a single side of such a leaf **2** : the information at a single World Wide Web address

**⁴page** *vb* **paged; pag·ing** : to mark or number the pages of

**pag·eant** \'pa-jənt\ *n* [ME *pagyn*, *padgeant*, lit., scene of a play, fr. AF *pagine, pagent*, fr. ML *pagina*, perh. fr. L, page] : an elaborate spectacle, show, or procession esp. with tableaux or floats — **pag·eant·ry** \-jən-trē\ *n*

**page·boy** \'pāj-,bói\ *n* [¹*page*] : an often shoulder-length hairdo with the ends of the hair turned smoothly under

**pag·er** \'pā-jər\ *n* : one that pages; *esp* : a small radio receiver that alerts its user to incoming messages

**pag·i·nate** \'pa-jə-,nāt\ *vb* **-nat·ed; -nat·ing** : ⁴PAGE

**pag·i·na·tion** \,pa-jə-'nā-shən\ *n* **1** : the paging of written or printed matter **2** : the number and arrangement of pages (as of a book)

**pa·go·da** \pə-'gō-də\ *n* : a tower with roofs curving upward at the division of each of several stories

**paid** *past and past part of* PAY

**pail** \'pāl\ *n* : a usu. cylindrical vessel with a handle — **pail·ful** \-,fúl\ *n*

**¹pain** \'pān\ *n* **1** : PUNISHMENT, PENALTY **2** : suffering or distress of body or mind; *also* : a basic bodily sensation marked by discomfort (as throbbing or aching) **3** *pl* : great care **4** : one that irks or annoys — **pain·ful** \-fəl\ *adj* — **pain·ful·ly** *adv* — **pain·less** *adj* — **pain·less·ly** *adv*

**²pain** *vb* : to cause or experience pain

**pain·kill·er** \'pān-,ki-lər\ *n* : something

(as a drug) that relieves pain — **pain·kill·ing** adj

**pains·tak·ing** \-ˌstā-kiŋ\ adj : taking pains : showing care — **pains·taking** n — **pains·tak·ing·ly** adv

¹**paint** \ˈpānt\ vb 1 : to apply color, pigment, or paint to 2 : to produce or portray in lines or colors on a surface; also : to practice the art of painting 3 : to decorate with colors 4 : to use cosmetics 5 : to describe vividly 6 : SWAB — **paint·er** n

²**paint** n 1 : something produced by painting 2 : MAKEUP 3 : a mixture of a pigment and a liquid that forms a thin adherent coating when spread on a surface; also : the dry pigment used in making this mixture 4 : an applied coating of paint

**paint·ball** \ˈpānt-ˌbȯl\ n : a game in which two teams try to capture each other's flag using guns that shoot paint-filled pellets

**paint·brush** \ˈpānt-ˌbrəsh\ n : a brush for applying paint

**painted lady** n : a migratory butterfly with wings mottled in brown, orange, black, and white

**painting** n 1 : a work (as a picture) produced by painting 2 : the art or occupation of painting

¹**pair** \ˈper\ n, pl **pairs** also **pair** [ME paire, fr. AF, fr. L paria equal things, fr. neut. pl. of par equal] 1 : two things of a kind designed for use together 2 : something made up of two corresponding pieces ⟨a ∼ of pants⟩ 3 : a set of two people or animals

²**pair** vb 1 : to arrange in pairs 2 : to form a pair : MATCH 3 : to become associated with another

**pai·sa** \pī-ˈsä\ n, pl **paisa** or **pai·se** \-ˈsā\ — see rupee, taka at MONEY table

**pais·ley** \ˈpāz-lē\ adj, often cap : decorated with colorful curved abstract figures ⟨a ∼ shawl⟩

**Pai·ute** \ˈpī-ˌüt, -ˌyüt\ n : a member of an American Indian people orig. of Utah, Arizona, Nevada, and California

**pa·ja·mas** \pə-ˈjä-məz, -ˈja-\ n pl : a loose suit for sleeping or lounging

**pal** \ˈpal\ n : a close friend

**pal·ace** \ˈpa-ləs\ n [ME palais, fr. AF, fr. L palatium, fr. Palatium, the Palatine Hill in Rome where the emperors' residences were built] 1 : the official residence of a chief of state 2 : MANSION

**pal·a·din** \ˈpa-lə-dən\ n 1 : a trusted military leader (as for a medieval prince) 2 : a leading champion of a cause

**pa·laes·tra** \pə-ˈles-trə\ n, pl **-trae** \-ˌ(ˌ)trē\ : a school in ancient Greece or Rome for sports (as wrestling)

**pa·lan·quin** \ˌpa-lən-ˈkēn\ n : an enclosed couch for one person borne on the shoulders of men by means of poles

**pal·at·able** \ˈpa-lə-tə-bəl\ adj : agreeable to the taste ♦ **Synonyms** APPETIZING, SAVORY, TASTY, TOOTHSOME

**pal·a·tal** \ˈpa-lə-tᵊl\ adj 1 : of or relating to the palate 2 : pronounced with some part of the tongue near or touching the hard palate ⟨the \y\ in yeast or the \sh\ in she are ∼ sounds⟩

**pal·a·tal·ize** \ˈpa-lə-tə-ˌlīz\ vb **-ized; -iz·ing** : to pronounce as or change into a palatal sound — **pal·a·tal·i·za·tion** \ˌpa-lə-tə-lə-ˈzā-shən\ n

**pal·ate** \ˈpa-lət\ n 1 : the roof of the mouth separating the mouth from the nasal cavity 2 : TASTE

**pa·la·tial** \pə-ˈlā-shəl\ adj 1 : of, relating to, or being a palace 2 : MAGNIFICENT

**pa·lat·i·nate** \pə-ˈla-tə-nət\ n : the territory of a palatine

¹**pal·a·tine** \ˈpa-lə-ˌtīn\ adj 1 : possessing royal privileges; also : of or relating to a palatine or a palatinate 2 : of or relating to a palace : PALATIAL

²**palatine** n 1 : a feudal lord having sovereign power within his domains 2 : a high officer of an imperial palace

**pa·la·ver** \pə-ˈla-vər, -ˈlä-\ n [Pg palavra word, speech, fr. LL parabola parable, speech] 1 : a long parley 2 : idle talk — **palaver** vb

¹**pale** \ˈpāl\ n 1 : a stake or picket of a fence 2 : an enclosed place; also : a district or territory within certain bounds or under a particular jurisdiction 3 : LIMITS, BOUNDS ⟨conduct beyond the ∼⟩

²**pale** vb **paled; pal·ing** : to enclose with or as if with pales : FENCE

³**pale** adj **pal·er; pal·est** 1 : deficient in color or intensity : WAN ⟨a ∼ face⟩ 2 : lacking in brightness : DIM ⟨a ∼ star⟩ 3 : not dark or intense in hue ⟨a ∼ blue⟩ — **pale·ness** n

⁴**pale** vb **paled; pal·ing** : to make or become pale

**pale ale** n : a medium-colored very dry ale

**pale·face** \ˈpāl-ˌfās\ n : a white person

**Pa·leo·cene** \ˈpā-lē-ə-ˌsēn\ adj : of, relating to, or being the earliest epoch of the Tertiary — **Paleocene** n

**pa·leo·con·ser·va·tive** \ˌpā-lē-ō-kən-ˈsər-və-tiv\ n : a conservative espousing traditional principles and policies

**pa·le·og·ra·phy** \ˌpā-lē-ˈä-grə-fē\ n [NL palaeographia, fr. Gk palaios ancient + graphein to write] : the study of ancient writings and inscriptions — **pa·le·og·ra·pher** n

**Pa·leo·lith·ic** \ˌpā-lē-ə-ˈli-thik\ adj : of or relating to the earliest period of the Stone Age characterized by rough or chipped stone implements

**pa·le·on·tol·o·gy** \ˌpā-lē-ˌän-ˈtä-lə-jē\ n : a science dealing with the life of past geologic periods as known from fossil remains — **pa·le·on·to·log·i·cal** \-ˌän-tə-ˈlä-ji-kəl\ adj — **pa·le·on·tol·o·gist** \-ˌän-ˈtä-lə-jist, -ən-\ n

**Pa·leo·zo·ic** \ˌpā-lē-ə-ˈzō-ik\ adj : of, relating to, or being the era of geologic history extending from about 570 million years ago to about 245 million years ago — **Paleozoic** n

**pal·ette** \ˈpa-lət\ n : a thin often oval board that a painter holds and mixes colors on; also : the colors on a palette

**pal·frey** \ˈpȯl-frē\ n, pl **palfreys** archaic : a saddle horse that is not a warhorse; esp : one suitable for a woman

**pa·limp·sest** \ˈpa-ləmp-ˌsest\ n [L pa-

*limpsestus,* fr. Gk *palimpsēstos* scraped again] : writing material (as a parchment) used after the erasure of earlier writing

**pal·in·drome** \'pa-lən-ˌdrōm\ *n* : a word, verse, or sentence (as "Able was I ere I saw Elba") or a number (as 1881) that reads the same backward or forward

**pal·ing** \'pā-liŋ\ *n* 1 : a fence of pales 2 : material for pales 3 : PALE, PICKET

**pal·i·sade** \ˌpa-lə-'sād\ *n* 1 : a high fence of stakes esp. for defense 2 : a line of steep cliffs

¹**pall** \'pȯl\ *vb* 1 : to lose in interest or attraction 2 : SATIATE, CLOY

²**pall** *n* 1 : a heavy cloth draped over a coffin 2 : something that produces a gloomy atmosphere

**pal·la·di·um** \pə-'lā-dē-əm\ *n* : a silver-white metallic chemical element used esp. as a catalyst and in alloys

**pall·bear·er** \'pȯl-ˌber-ər\ *n* : a person who attends the coffin at a funeral

¹**pal·let** \'pa-lət\ *n* : a small, hard, or make-shift bed

²**pallet** *n* : a portable platform for transporting and storing materials

**pal·li·ate** \'pa-lē-ˌāt\ *vb* **-at·ed; -at·ing** 1 : to ease (as a disease) without curing 2 : to cover by excuses and apologies ⟨~ faults⟩ — **pal·li·a·tion** \ˌpa-lē-'ā-shən\ *n* — **pal·li·a·tive** \'pa-lē-ˌā-tiv\ *adj or n*

**pal·lid** \'pa-ləd\ *adj* : PALE, WAN

**pal·lor** \'pa-lər\ *n* : PALENESS

¹**palm** \'pä(l)m, 'pȧlm\ *n* [ME, fr. OE, fr. L *palma* palm of the hand, palm tree; fr. the resemblance of the tree's leaves to the outstretched hand] 1 : any of a family of mostly tropical trees, shrubs, or vines usu. with a tall unbranched stem topped by a crown of large leaves 2 : a symbol of victory; *also* : VICTORY

²**palm** *n* : the underpart of the hand between the fingers and the wrist

³**palm** *vb* 1 : to conceal in or with the hand ⟨~ a card⟩ 2 : to impose by fraud

**pal·mate** \'pal-ˌmāt, 'päl-\ *also* **pal·mat·ed** \-ˌmā-təd\ *adj* : resembling a hand with the fingers spread

**pal·met·to** \pal-'me-tō\ *n, pl* **-tos** *or* **-toes** : any of several usu. small palms with fan-shaped leaves

**palm·ist·ry** \'pä-mə-strē, 'päl-\ *n* : the practice of reading a person's character or future from the markings on the palms — **palm·ist** \'pä-mist, 'päl-\ *n*

**Palm Sunday** *n* : the Sunday preceding Easter and commemorating Christ's triumphal entry into Jerusalem

**palm·top** \'päm-ˌtäp, 'pälm-\ *n* : a portable computer small enough to hold in the hand

**palmy** \'pä-mē, 'päl-\ *adj* **palm·i·er; -est** 1 : abounding in or bearing palms 2 : FLOURISHING, PROSPEROUS

**pal·o·mi·no** \ˌpa-lə-'mē-nō\ *n, pl* **-nos** [AmerSp, fr. Sp, like a dove, fr. L *palumbinus,* fr. *palumbes,* a species of dove] : a horse with a pale cream to golden coat and cream or white mane and tail

**pal·pa·ble** \'pal-pə-bəl\ *adj* 1 : capable of being touched or felt : TANGIBLE 2 : OBVIOUS, PLAIN ⟨the resentment was ~⟩

♦ *Synonyms* PERCEPTIBLE, SENSIBLE, APPRECIABLE, TANGIBLE, DETECTABLE — **pal·pa·bly** \-blē\ *adv*

**pal·pate** \'pal-ˌpāt\ *vb* **pal·pat·ed; pal·pat·ing** : to examine by touch esp. medically — **pal·pa·tion** \pal-'pā-shən\ *n*

**pal·pi·tate** \'pal-pə-ˌtāt\ *vb* **-tat·ed; -tat·ing** : to beat rapidly and strongly : THROB — **pal·pi·ta·tion** \ˌpal-pə-'tā-shən\ *n*

**pal·sy** \'pȯl-zē\ *n, pl* **palsies** 1 : PARALYSIS 2 : a condition marked by tremor — **pal·sied** \-zēd\ *adj*

**pal·ter** \'pȯl-tər\ *vb* **pal·tered; pal·ter·ing** 1 : to act insincerely : EQUIVOCATE 2 : HAGGLE

**pal·try** \'pȯl-trē\ *adj* **pal·tri·er; -est** 1 : TRASHY ⟨a ~ pamphlet⟩ 2 : MEAN, DESPICABLE ⟨a ~ trick⟩ 3 : TRIVIAL ⟨~ excuses⟩ 4 : MEAGER, MEASLY ⟨a ~ sum⟩

**pam** *abbr* pamphlet

**pam·pas** \'pam-pəz, 'päm-, -pəs\ *n pl* : wide grassy So. American plains

**pam·per** \'pam-pər\ *vb* : to treat with excessive attention : INDULGE ♦ *Synonyms* CODDLE, HUMOR, BABY, SPOIL

**pam·phlet** \'pam-flət\ *n* [ME *pamflet* unbound booklet, fr. *Pamphilus seu De Amore Pamphilus* or On Love, popular Latin love poem of the 12th cent.] : an unbound printed publication

**pam·phle·teer** \ˌpam-flə-'tir\ *n* : a writer of pamphlets attacking something or urging a cause

¹**pan** \'pan\ *n* 1 : a usu. broad, shallow, and open container for domestic use; *also* : something resembling such a container 2 : a basin or depression in land 3 : HARDPAN

²**pan** *vb* **panned; pan·ning** 1 : to wash earth or gravel in a pan in searching for gold 2 : to criticize severely

**Pan** *abbr* Panama

**pan·a·cea** \ˌpa-nə-'sē-ə\ *n* : a remedy for all ills or difficulties : CURE-ALL

**pa·nache** \pə-'nash, -'näsh\ *n* [MF *pennache,* ultim. fr. LL *pinnaculum* small wing] 1 : an ornamental tuft (as of feathers) esp. on a helmet 2 : dash or flamboyance in style and action

**pan·a·ma** \'pa-nə-ˌmä, -ˌmȯ\ *n, often cap* : a handmade hat braided from strips of the leaves from a tropical American tree

**pan·a·tela** \ˌpa-nə-'te-lə\ *n* : a long slender cigar with straight sides

**pan·cake** \'pan-ˌkāk\ *n* : a flat cake made of thin batter and fried on both sides

**pan·chro·mat·ic** \ˌpan-krō-'ma-tik\ *adj* : sensitive to all colors of visible light ⟨~ film⟩

**pan·cre·as** \'paŋ-krē-əs, 'pan-\ *n* : a large compound gland of vertebrates that produces insulin and discharges enzymes into the intestine — **pan·cre·at·ic** \ˌpaŋ-krē-'a-tik, ˌpan-\ *adj*

**pan·da** \'pan-də\ *n* 1 : a long-tailed reddish brown Himalayan mammal related to and resembling the raccoon 2 : a large black-and-white mammal of China usu. classified with the bears

**pan·dem·ic** \pan-'de-mik\ *n* : a widespread outbreak of disease — **pandemic** *adj*

**pan·de·mo·ni·um** \ˌpan-də-ˈmō-nē-əm\ *n* : a wild uproar : TUMULT

¹**pan·der** \ˈpan-dər\ *vb* : to act as a pander ⟨~s to the public's taste for violence⟩

²**pander** *n* **1** : a go-between in love intrigues; *also* : PIMP **2** : a person who caters to or exploits others' desires or weaknesses

**P & I** *abbr* principal and interest

**P & L** *abbr* profit and loss

**Pan·do·ra's box** \pan-ˈdȯr-əz-\ *n* : a prolific source of troubles

**pan·dow·dy** \pan-ˈdau̇-dē\ *n, pl* **-dies** : a deep-dish apple dessert spiced, sweetened, and covered with a crust

**pane** \ˈpān\ *n* : a sheet of glass (as in a door or window)

**pan·e·gyr·ic** \ˌpa-nə-ˈjir-ik\ *n* : a eulogistic oration or writing ⟨a ~ on war heroes⟩ — **pan·e·gyr·ist** \-ˈjir-ist\ *n*

¹**pan·el** \ˈpa-nᵊl\ *n* [ME, piece of cloth, jury list on a piece of parchment, fr. AF, fr. VL *pannellus*, dim. of L *pannus* cloth, rag] **1** : a list of persons appointed for special duty ⟨a jury ~⟩; *also* : a group of people taking part in a discussion or quiz program **2** : a section of something (as a wall or door) often sunk below the level of the frame; *also* : a flat piece of construction material **3** : a flat piece of wood on which a picture is painted **4** : a mount for controls or dials

²**panel** *vb* **-eled** *or* **-elled**; **-el·ing** *or* **-el·ling** : to decorate with panels

**paneling** *n* : decorative panels

**pan·el·ist** \ˈpa-nᵊl-ist\ *n* : a member of a discussion or quiz panel

**panel truck** *n* : a small motortruck with a fully enclosed body

**pang** \ˈpaŋ\ *n* : a sudden sharp spasm (as of pain) or attack (as of remorse)

¹**pan·han·dle** \ˈpan-ˌhan-dᵊl\ *n* : a narrow projection of a larger territory (as a state) ⟨the Texas ~⟩

²**panhandle** *vb* **-dled**; **-dling** : to ask for money on the street — **pan·han·dler** *n*

¹**pan·ic** \ˈpa-nik\ *n* : a sudden overpowering fright; *also* : extreme anxiety ⟨a ~ disorder⟩ ⟨~ attacks⟩ ◆ *Synonyms* TERROR, CONSTERNATION, DISMAY, ALARM, DREAD, FEAR — **pan·icky** \-ni-kē\ *adj*

²**panic** *vb* **pan·icked** \-nikt\; **pan·ick·ing** : to affect or be affected with panic

**pan·i·cle** \ˈpa-ni-kəl\ *n* : a branched flower cluster (as of a lilac) in which each branch from the main stem has one or more flowers

**pan·jan·drum** \pan-ˈjan-drəm\ *n, pl* **-drums** *also* **-dra** \-drə\ : a powerful personage or pretentious official

**pan·nier** *also* **pan·ier** \ˈpan-yər\ *n* : a large basket esp. for bearing on the back

**pan·o·ply** \ˈpa-nə-plē\ *n, pl* **-plies** **1** : a full suit of armor **2** : a protective covering **3** : an impressive array

**pan·ora·ma** \ˌpa-nə-ˈra-mə, -ˈrä-\ *n* **1** : a picture unrolled before one's eyes **2** : a complete view in every direction — **pan·oram·ic** \-ˈra-mik\ *adj*

**pan out** *vb* : TURN OUT; *esp* : SUCCEED

**pan·sy** \ˈpan-zē\ *n, pl* **pansies** [ME *pancy, pensee*, fr. MF *pensée*, fr. *pensée* thought, fr. *penser* to think, fr. L *pensare* to ponder] **1** : a low-growing garden herb related to the violet; *also* : its showy flower

¹**pant** \ˈpant\ *vb* [ME, fr. AF *panteiser*, fr. VL *phantasiare* to have hallucinations, fr. Gk *phantasioun*, fr. *phantasia* appearance, imagination] **1** : to breathe in a labored manner **2** : YEARN **3** : THROB

²**pant** *n* : a panting breath or sound

³**pant** *n* **1** : an outer garment covering each leg separately and usu. extending from the waist to the ankle — usu. used in pl. **2** *pl* : PANTIE

**pan·ta·loons** \ˌpan-tə-ˈlünz\ *n pl* **1** : close-fitting pants of the 19th century usu. having straps passing under the instep **2** : loose-fitting usu. shorter than ankle-length trousers

**pan·the·ism** \ˈpan-thē-ˌi-zəm\ *n* : a doctrine that equates God with the forces and laws of the universe — **pan·the·ist** \-ist\ *n* — **pan·the·is·tic** \ˌpan-thē-ˈis-tik\ *adj*

**pan·the·on** \ˈpan-thē-ˌän, -ən\ *n* **1** : a temple dedicated to all the gods; *also* : the gods of a people **2** : a group of illustrious people ⟨a ~ of great writers⟩

**pan·ther** \ˈpan-thər\ *n, pl* **panthers** *also* **panther** **1** : LEOPARD; *esp* : a black one **2** : COUGAR **3** : JAGUAR

**pant·ie** *or* **panty** \ˈpan-tē\ *n, pl* **pant·ies** : a woman's or child's short underpants — usu. used in pl.

**pan·to·mime** \ˈpan-tə-ˌmīm\ *n* **1** : a play in which the actors use no words **2** : expression of something by bodily or facial movements only — **pantomime** *vb* — **pan·to·mim·ic** \ˌpan-tə-ˈmi-mik\ *adj*

**pan·try** \ˈpan-trē\ *n, pl* **pantries** : a storage room for food or dishes

**pant·suit** \ˈpant-ˌsüt\ *n* : a woman's outfit consisting usu. of a long jacket and pants of the same material

**panty hose** *n pl* : a one-piece undergarment for women consisting of hosiery combined with a pantie

**panty·waist** \ˈpan-tē-ˌwāst\ *n* : SISSY

**pap** \ˈpap\ *n* : soft food for infants or invalids

**pa·pa** \ˈpä-pə\ *n* : FATHER

**pa·pa·cy** \ˈpā-pə-sē\ *n, pl* **-cies** **1** : the office of pope **2** : a succession of popes **3** : the term of a pope's reign **4** *cap* : the system of government of the Roman Catholic Church

**pa·pa·in** \pə-ˈpā-ən, -ˈpī-ən\ *n* : an enzyme in papaya juice used esp. as a meat tenderizer and in medicine

**pa·pal** \ˈpā-pəl\ *adj* : of or relating to the pope or to the Roman Catholic Church

**papaw** *var of* PAWPAW

**pa·pa·ya** \pə-ˈpī-ə\ *n* : a tropical American tree with large yellow black-seeded edible fruit; *also* : its fruit

**pa·per** \ˈpā-pər\ *n* [ME *papir*, fr. AF, fr. L *papyrus* papyrus, paper, fr. Gk *papyros* papyrus] **1** : a pliable substance made usu. of vegetable matter and used to write or print on, to wrap things in, or to cover walls; *also* : a single sheet of this substance **2** : a printed or written document **3** : NEWSPAPER **4** : WALLPAPER — **paper** *adj or vb* — **pa·pery** \'pā-pə-rē\ *adj*

**pa·per·back** \-,bak\ *n* : a paper-covered book

**pa·per·board** \-,bórd\ *n* : CARDBOARD

**pa·per·hang·er** \'pā-pər-,haŋ-ər\ *n* : one that applies wallpaper — **pa·per·hang·ing** *n*

**pa·per·weight** \-,wāt\ *n* : an object used to hold down loose papers by its weight

**pa·pier–mâ·ché** \,pā-pər-mə-'shā, ,pā-,pyä-mə-, -ma-\ *n* [F, lit., chewed paper] : a molding material of wastepaper and additives (as gluc) — **papier–mâché** *adj*

**pa·pil·la** \pə-'pil-ə\ *n, pl* **-lae** \-(,)lē, -,lī\ [L, nipple] : a small projecting bodily part (as one of the nubs on the surface of the tongue) that resembles a tiny nipple in form — **pap·il·lary** \'pa-pə-,ler-ē, pə-'pil-ə-rē\ *adj*

**pa·poose** \pa-'püs, pə-\ *n* [Narragansett *papoòs*] : a young child of No. American Indian parents

**pa·pri·ka** \pə-'prē-kə, pa-\ *n* [Hung] : a mild red spice made from the fruit of various cultivated sweet peppers

**Pap smear** \'pap-\ *n* : a method for the early detection of cancer esp. of the uterine cervix

**Pap test** *n* : PAP SMEAR

**pap·ule** \'pa-pyül\ *n* : a small solid usu. conical elevation of the skin — **pap·u·lar** \-pyə-lər\ *adj*

**pa·py·rus** \pə-'pī-rəs\ *n, pl* **-ri** \-(,)rē, -,rī\ *or* **-rus·es** **1** : a tall grassy sedge of the Nile valley **2** : paper made from papyrus pith

**¹par** \'pär\ *n* **1** : a stated value (as of a security) **2** : a common level ; EQUALITY **3** : an accepted standard or normal condition **4** : the score standard set for each hole of a golf course — **par** *adj*

**²par** *abbr* **1** paragraph **2** parallel **3** parish

**par·a·ble** \'pa-rə-bəl\ *n* : a simple story told to illustrate a moral truth

**pa·rab·o·la** \pə-'ra-bə-lə\ *n* : a plane curve formed by a point moving so that its distance from a fixed point is equal to its distance from a fixed line — **par·a·bol·ic** \,par-ə-'bä-lik\ *adj*

**para·chute** \'pa-rə-,shüt\ *n* [F, fr. *para-* (as in *parasol*) + *chute* fall] : a device for slowing the descent of a person or object through the air that consists of a usu. hemispherical canopy beneath which the person or object is suspended — **parachute** *vb* — **para·chut·ist** \-'shü-tist\ *n*

**parachute pants** *n pl* : baggy casual pants of lightweight fabric

**¹pa·rade** \pə-'rād\ *n* **1** : a pompous display : EXHIBITION **2** : MARCH, PROCESSION; *esp* : a ceremonial formation and march **3** : a place for strolling

**²parade** *vb* **pa·rad·ed; pa·rad·ing 1** : to march in a parade ; PROMENADE **2** : SHOW OFF ⟨*paraded* her knowledge⟩ **4** : MASQUERADE

**par·a·digm** \'pa-rə-,dīm, -,dim\ **1** : MODEL, PATTERN **2** : a systematic inflection of a verb or noun showing a complete conjugation or declension — **par·a·dig·mat·ic** \,pa-rə-dig-'ma-tik\ *adj*

**par·a·dise** \'pa-rə-,dīs, -,dīz\ *n* [ME *paradis*, fr. AF, fr. LL *paradisus*, fr. Gk *paradeisos*, lit., enclosed park, of Iranian origin] **1** : HEAVEN **2** : a place or state of bliss

**par·a·di·si·a·cal** \,pa-rə-də-'si-ə-kəl\ *or* **par·a·dis·i·ac** \-'di-zē-,ak, -sē-\ *adj* : of, relating to, or resembling paradise

**par·a·dox** \'pa-rə-,däks\ *n* : a statement that seems contrary to common sense and yet is perhaps true — **par·a·dox·i·cal** \,pa-rə-'däk-si-kəl\ *adj* — **par·a·dox·i·cal·ly** \-k(ə-)lē\ *adv*

**par·af·fin** \'pa-rə-fən\ *n* : a waxy substance used esp. for making candles and sealing foods

**para·glid·ing** \'pa-rə-,glī-diŋ\ *n* : the sport of soaring from a slope or cliff using a modified parachute

**par·a·gon** \'pa-rə-,gän, -gən\ *n* : a model of perfection : PATTERN ⟨a ~ of virtue⟩

**¹para·graph** \'pa-rə-,graf\ *n* : a subdivision of a written composition that deals with one point or gives the words of one speaker; *also* : a character (as ¶) marking the beginning of a paragraph

**²paragraph** *vb* : to divide into paragraphs

**par·a·keet** \'pa-rə-,kēt\ *n* : any of numerous usu. small slender parrots with a long graduated tail

**para·le·gal** \,pa-rə-'lē-gəl\ *adj* : of, relating to, or being a paraprofessional who assists a lawyer — **paralegal** *n*

**Par·a·li·pom·e·non** \,pa-rə-lə-'pä-mə-,nän\ *n* : CHRONICLES

**par·al·lax** \'pa-rə-,laks\ *n* : the difference in apparent direction of an object as seen from two different points

**¹par·al·lel** \'pa-rə-,lel\ *adj* [L *parallelus*, fr. Gk *parallēlos*, fr. *para* beside + *allēlōn* of one another, fr. *allos* . . . *allos* one . . . another, fr. *allos* other] **1** : lying or moving in the same direction but always the same distance apart **2** : similar in essential parts — **par·al·lel·ism** \-,le-,li-zəm\ *n*

**²parallel** *n* **1** : a parallel line, curve, or surface **2** : one of the imaginary circles on the earth's surface that parallel the equator and mark the latitude **3** : something essentially similar to another **4** : SIMILARITY, LIKENESS

**³parallel** *vb* **1** : COMPARE **2** : to correspond to **3** : to extend in a parallel direction with

**par·al·lel·o·gram** \,pa-rə-'le-lə-,gram\ *n* : a 4-sided geometric figure with opposite sides equal and parallel

**par·a·lyse** *Brit var of* PARALYZE

**pa·ral·y·sis** \pə-'ra-lə-səs\ *n, pl* **-y·ses** \-,sēz\ : complete or partial loss of function esp. when involving the motion or sensation in a part of the body — **par·a·lyt·ic** \,pa-rə-'li-tik\ *adj or n*

**par·a·lyze** \'pa-rə-,līz\ *vb* **-lyzed; -lyz·ing 1** : to affect with paralysis **2** : to make powerless or inactive ⟨*paralyzed* by fear⟩ — **par·a·lyz·ing·ly** *adv*

**par·a·me·cium** \,pa-rə-'mē-shəm, -shē-əm, -sē-əm\ *n, pl* **-cia** \-shə, -shē-ə, -sē-ə\ *also* **-ci·ums** : any of a genus of slipper-shaped protozoans that move by cilia

**para·med·ic** \ˌpa-rə-ˈme-dik\ *also* **para·med·i·cal** \-di-kəl\ *n* **1** : a person who assists a physician in a paramedical capacity **2** : a specially trained medical technician licensed to provide a wide range of emergency services before or during transportation to a hospital

**para·med·i·cal** \ˌpa-rə-ˈme-di-kəl\ *also* **para·med·ic** \-ˈme-dik\ *adj* : concerned with supplementing the work of trained medical professionals

**pa·ram·e·ter** \pə-ˈra-mə-tər\ *n* **1** : a quantity whose value characterizes a statistical population or a member of a system (as a family of curves) **2** : a physical property whose value determines the characteristics or behavior of a system **3** : a characteristic element : FACTOR — **para·met·ric** \ˌpa-rə-ˈme-trik\ *adj*

**para·mil·i·tary** \ˌpa-rə-ˈmi-lə-ˌter-ē\ *adj* : formed on a military pattern esp. as an auxiliary military force

**par·a·mount** \ˈpa-rə-ˌmaunt\ *adj* : superior to all others : SUPREME ♦ **Synonyms** PREPONDERANT, PREDOMINANT, DOMINANT, CHIEF, SOVEREIGN

**par·amour** \ˈpa-rə-ˌmur\ *n* : an illicit lover

**para·noia** \ˌpa-rə-ˈnoi-ə\ *n* : a psychosis marked by delusions and irrational suspicion usu. without hallucinations — **par·a·noid** \ˈpa-rə-ˌnoid\ *adj or n*

**para·nor·mal** \ˌpa-rə-ˈnor-məl\ *adj* : not scientifically explainable : SUPERNATURAL ⟨~ phenomena⟩

**par·a·pet** \ˈpa-rə-pət, -ˌpet\ *n* **1** : a protecting rampart **2** : a low wall or railing (as at the edge of a bridge)

**par·a·pher·na·lia** \ˌpa-rə-fə-ˈnāl-yə, -fər-\ *n sing or pl* **1** : personal belongings **2** : EQUIPMENT, APPARATUS

**para·phrase** \ˈpa-rə-ˌfrāz\ *n* : a restatement of a text giving the meaning in different words — **paraphrase** *vb*

**para·ple·gia** \ˌpa-rə-ˈplē-jə, -jē-ə\ *n* : paralysis of the lower trunk and legs — **para·ple·gic** \-jik\ *adj or n*

**para·pro·fes·sion·al** \-prə-ˈfe-shə-nəl\ *n* : a trained aide who assists a professional — **paraprofessional** *adj*

**para·psy·chol·o·gy** \ˌpa-rə-sī-ˈkä-lə-jē\ *n* : a field of study concerned with investigating paranormal psychological phenomena (as extrasensory perception) — **para·psy·chol·o·gist** \-jist\ *n*

**par·a·site** \ˈpa-rə-ˌsīt\ *n* [MF, fr. L *parasitus,* fr. Gk *parasitos,* fr. *para-* beside + *sitos* grain, food] **1** : a plant or animal living in, with, or on another organism usu. to its harm **2** : one depending on another and not making adequate return — **par·a·sit·ic** \ˌpa-rə-ˈsi-tik\ *adj* — **par·a·sit·ism** \ˈpa-rə-sə-ˌti-zəm, -ˌsī-ˌti-\ *n* — **par·a·sit·ize** \-sə-ˌtīz\ *vb*

**par·a·si·tol·o·gy** \ˌpa-rə-sə-ˈtä-lə-jē\ *n* : a branch of biology dealing with parasites and parasitism esp. among animals — **par·a·si·tol·o·gist** \-jist\ *n*

**para·sol** \ˈpa-rə-ˌsol\ *n* [F, fr. It *parasole,*

fr. *parare* to shield + *sole* sun, fr. L *sol*] : a lightweight umbrella used as a shield against the sun

**para·sym·pa·thet·ic nervous system** \ˌpa-rə-ˌsim-pə-ˈthe-tik-\ *n* : the part of the autonomic nervous system that tends to induce secretion, to increase the tone and contractility of smooth muscle, and to slow heart rate

**para·thi·on** \ˌpa-rə-ˈthī-ən, -ˌän\ *n* : an extremely toxic insecticide

**para·thy·roid** \-ˈthī-ˌroid\ *n* : PARATHYROID GLAND — **parathyroid** *adj*

**parathyroid gland** *n* : any of usu. four small endocrine glands adjacent to or embedded in the thyroid gland that produce a hormone (**parathyroid hormone**) concerned with calcium and phosphorus metabolism

**para·tran·sit** \ˌpa-rə-ˈtran-sət, -zət\ *n* : transportation service that provides individualized rules without fixed routes or timetables

**para·troop·er** \ˈpa-rə-ˌtrü-pər\ *n* : a member of the paratroops

**para·troops** \-ˌtrüps\ *n pl* : troops trained to parachute from an airplane

**para·ty·phoid** \ˌpa-rə-ˈtī-ˌfoid\ *n* : a bacterial food poisoning resembling typhoid fever

**par·boil** \ˈpär-ˌboi(-ə)l\ *vb* : to boil briefly

¹**par·cel** \ˈpär-səl\ *n* **1** : a tract or plot of land **2** : COLLECTION, LOT ⟨the story was a ~ of lies⟩ **3** : a wrapped bundle : PACKAGE

²**parcel** *vb* **-celed** *or* **-celled; -cel·ing** *or* **-cel·ling** : to divide into portions

**parcel post** *n* **1** : a mail service handling parcels **2** : packages handled by parcel post

**parch** \ˈpärch\ *vb* **1** : to toast under dry heat **2** : to shrivel with heat

**parch·ment** \ˈpärch-mənt\ *n* : the skin of an animal prepared for writing on; *also* : a writing on such material

**pard** \ˈpärd\ *n* : LEOPARD

¹**par·don** \ˈpär-dᵊn\ *n* : excuse of an offense without penalty; *esp* : an official release from legal punishment

²**pardon** *vb* : to free from penalty : EXCUSE, FORGIVE ⟨~ a criminal⟩ ⟨~ a debt⟩ — **par·don·able** \ˈpär-dᵊn-ə-bəl\ *adj*

**par·don·er** \ˈpär-dᵊn-ər\ *n* **1** : a medieval preacher delegated to raise money for religious works by soliciting offerings and granting indulgences **2** : one that pardons

**pare** \ˈper\ *vb* **pared; par·ing** **1** : to trim off an outside part (as the skin or rind) of **2** : to reduce as if by paring ⟨~ expenses⟩ — **par·er** *n*

**par·e·gor·ic** \ˌper-ə-ˈgor-ik\ *n* : an alcoholic preparation of opium and camphor used esp. to relieve pain

**par·ent** \ˈper-ənt\ *n* **1** : one that begets or brings forth offspring : FATHER, MOTHER **2** : one who brings up and cares for another **3** : SOURCE, ORIGIN — **par·ent·age** \-ən-tij\ *n* — **pa·ren·tal** \pə-ˈren-tᵊl\ *adj* — **par·ent·hood** *n*

**pa·ren·the·sis** \pə-ˈren-thə-səs\ *n, pl*

**-the·ses** \-,sēz\ **1** : a word, phrase, or sentence inserted in a passage to explain or modify the thought **2** : one of a pair of punctuation marks ( ) used esp. to enclose parenthetic matter — **par·en·thet·ic** \,per-ən-'the-tik\ *or* **par·en·thet·i·cal** \-ti-kəl\ *adj* — **par·en·thet·i·cal·ly** \-k(ə-)lē\ *adv*

**pa·ren·the·size** \pə-'ren-thə-,sīz\ *vb* **-sized; -siz·ing** : to make a parenthesis of

**par·ent·ing** \'per-ən-tiŋ\ *n* : the raising of a child by its parents

**pa·re·sis** \pə-'rē-səs, 'pa-rə-\ *n, pl* **pa·re·ses** \-,sēz\ : a usu. incomplete paralysis; *also* : insanity caused by syphilitic alteration of the brain that leads to dementia and paralysis

**par ex·cel·lence** \,pär-,ek-sə-'läⁿs\ *adj* [F, lit., by excellence] : being the best of a kind : PREEMINENT

**par·fait** \pär-'fā\ *n* [F, lit., something perfect] : a cold dessert made of layers of fruit, syrup, ice cream, and whipped cream

**pa·ri·ah** \pə-'rī-ə\ *n* : OUTCAST

**pa·ri·etal** \pə-'rī-ə-tᵊl\ *adj* **1** : of, relating to, or forming the walls of an anatomical structure **2** : of or relating to college living or its regulation

**pari-mu·tu·el** \,per-i-'myü-chə-wəl\ *n* : a betting system in which winners share the total stakes minus a percentage for the management

**paring** *n* : a pared-off piece

**pa·ri pas·su** \'pa-ri-'pa-sü\ *adv or adj* [L, with equal step] : at an equal rate or pace

**par·ish** \'per-ish\ *n* **1** : a church district in the care of one pastor; *also* : the residents of such an area **2** : a local church community **3** : a civil division of the state of Louisiana : COUNTY

**pa·rish·io·ner** \pə-'ri-shə-nər\ *n* : a member or resident of a parish

**par·i·ty** \'per-ə-tē\ *n, pl* **-ties** : EQUALITY, EQUIVALENCE

**¹park** \'pärk\ *n* **1** : a tract of ground kept as a game preserve or recreation area **2** : a place where vehicles (as automobiles) are parked **3** : an enclosed stadium used esp. for ball games

**²park** *vb* **1** : to leave a vehicle temporarily (as in a parking lot or garage) **2** : to set and leave temporarily

**par·ka** \'pär-kə\ *n* : a very warm jacket with a hood

**Par·kin·son's disease** \'pär-kən-sənz-\ *n* : a chronic progressive neurological disease chiefly of later life marked esp. by tremor and weakness of resting muscles and by a shuffling gait

**Parkinson's Law** *n* : an observation in office organization: work expands so as to fill the time available for its completion

**par·kour** \pär-'kùr, 'pär-,kúr\ *n* [F, alter. of *parcours* course, route, fr. ML *percursus*, fr. L *percurrere* to run through] : the sport of traversing environmental obstacles by running, climbing, or leaping rapidly

**park·way** \'pärk-,wā\ *n* : a broad landscaped thoroughfare

**par·lance** \'pär-ləns\ *n* **1** : SPEECH **2** : manner of speaking ⟨military ∼⟩

**¹par·lay** \'pär-,lā, -lē\ *vb* : to increase or change into something of much greater value ⟨∼ed a $1000 loan into a multimillion-dollar company⟩

**²parlay** *n* : a series of bets in which the original stake plus its winnings are risked on successive wagers

**par·ley** \'pär-lē\ *n, pl* **parleys** : a conference usu. over matters in dispute : DISCUSSION — **parley** *vb*

**par·lia·ment** \'pär-lə-mənt\ *n* [ME, fr. AF *parlement*, fr. *parler* to speak, fr. ML *parabolare*, fr. LL *parabola* speech, parable] **1** : a formal governmental conference **2** *cap* : an assembly that constitutes the supreme legislative body of a country (as the United Kingdom) — **par·lia·men·ta·ry** \,pär-lə-'men-tə-rē\ *adj*

**par·lia·men·tar·i·an** \,pär-lə-,men-'ter-ē-ən\ *n* *often cap* : an adherent of the parliament during the English Civil War **2** : an expert in parliamentary procedure

**par·lor** \'pär-lər\ *n* **1** : a room for conversation or the reception of guests **2** : a place of business ⟨beauty ∼⟩

**par·lour** \'pär-lər\ *chiefly Brit var of* PARLOR

**par·lous** \'pär-ləs\ *adj* : full of danger or risk : PRECARIOUS — **par·lous·ly** *adv*

**Par·me·san** \'pär-mə-,zän, -,zhän, -,zan\ *n* : a hard dry cheese with a sharp flavor

**par·mi·gia·na** \,pär-mi-'jä-nə, ,pär-mi-'zhän\ *or* **par·mi·gia·no** \-'jä-(,)nō\ *adj* : made or covered with Parmesan cheese ⟨veal ∼⟩

**pa·ro·chi·al** \pə-'rō-kē-əl\ *adj* **1** : of or relating to a church parish **2** : limited in scope : NARROW, PROVINCIAL — **pa·ro·chi·al·ism** \-ə-,li-zəm\ *n*

**parochial school** *n* : a school maintained by a religious body

**par·o·dy** \'per-ə-dē\ *n, pl* **-dies** [L *parodia*, fr. Gk *parōidia*, fr. *para-* beside + *aidein* to sing] : a humorous or satirical imitation — **parody** *vb*

**pa·role** \pə-'rōl\ *n* : a conditional release of a prisoner whose sentence has not expired — **parole** *vb* — **pa·rol·ee** \-,rō-'lē, -'rō-,lē\ *n*

**par·ox·ysm** \'pa-rək-,si-zəm, pə-'räk-\ *n* : a sudden sharp attack (as of pain or coughing) : CONVULSION — **par·ox·ys·mal** \,pa-rək-'siz-məl, pə-,räk-\ *adj*

**par·quet** \'pär-,kā, pär-'kā\ *n* [F] **1** : a flooring of parquetry **2** : the lower floor of a theater; *esp* : the forward part of the orchestra

**par·que·try** \'pär-kə-trē\ *n, pl* **-tries** : fine woodwork inlaid in patterns

**par·ri·cide** \'pa-rə-,sīd\ *n* **1** : one that murders a parent or a close relative **2** : the act of a parricide

**par·rot** \'per-ət\ *n* : any of numerous bright-colored tropical birds that have a stout hooked bill

**parrot fever** *n* : PSITTACOSIS

**par·ry** \'per-ē\ *vb* **par·ried; par·ry·ing 1** : to ward off a weapon or blow **2** : to evade esp. by an adroit answer — **parry** *n*

**parse** \'pärs *also* 'pärz\ *vb* **parsed; parsing** : to give a grammatical description of a word or a group of words

**par·sec** \'pär-ˌsek\ *n* : a unit of measure for interstellar space equal to 3.26 light-years

**par·si·mo·ny** \'pär-sə-ˌmō-nē\ *n* : extreme or excessive frugality — **par·si·mo·ni·ous** \ˌpär-sə-'mō-nē-əs\ *adj* — **par·si·mo·ni·ous·ly** *adv*

**pars·ley** \'pär-slē\ *n* : a garden plant related to the carrot that has finely divided leaves used as a seasoning or garnish; *also* : the leaves

**pars·nip** \'pär-snəp\ *n* : a garden plant related to the carrot that has a long edible usu. whitish root which is cooked as a vegetable; *also* : the root

**par·son** \'pär-sᵊn\ *n* [ME *persone*, fr. AF, fr. ML *persona*, lit., person, fr. L] : MINISTER 2, PASTOR

**par·son·age** \'pär-sə-nij\ *n* : a house provided by a church for its pastor

¹**part** \'pärt\ *n* **1** : a division or portion of a whole **2** : the melody or score for a particular voice or instrument **3** : a spare piece for a machine **4** : DUTY, FUNCTION **5** : one of the sides in a dispute **6** : ROLE; *also* : an actor's lines in a play **7** *pl* : TALENTS, ABILITY ⟨a man of many ∼*s*⟩ **8** : the line where one's hair divides (as in combing)

²**part** *vb* **1** : to take leave of someone **2** : to divide or break into parts : SEPARATE **3** : to go away : DEPART; *also* : DIE **4** : to give up possession ⟨∼*ed* with her jewels⟩ **5** : APPORTION, SHARE

³**part** *abbr* **1** participial; participle **2** particular

**par·take** \pär-'tāk\ *vb* **-took** \-'túk\; **-taken** \-'tā-kən\; **-tak·ing 1** : to have a share or part **2** : to take a portion (as of food) — **par·tak·er** *n*

**par·terre** \pär-'ter\ *n* [F, fr. MF, fr. *par terre* on the ground] **1** : an ornamental garden with paths between the flower beds **2** : the part of a theater floor behind the orchestra

**par·the·no·gen·e·sis** \ˌpär-thə-nō-'je-nə-səs\ *n* [NL, fr. Gk *parthenos* virgin + L *genesis* genesis] : development of a new individual from an unfertilized usu. female sex cell — **par·the·no·ge·net·ic** \-jə-'ne-tik\ *adj*

**par·tial** \'pär-shəl\ *adj* **1** : not total or general : affecting a part only **2** : favoring one party over the other : BIASED **3** : markedly fond — used with *to* — **par·tial·i·ty** \ˌpär-shē-'a-lə-tē\ *n* — **par·tial·ly** *adv*

**par·tic·i·pate** \pär-'ti-sə-ˌpāt\ *vb* **-pat·ed; -pat·ing 1** : to take part in something ⟨∼ in a game⟩ **2** : SHARE — **par·tic·i·pant** \-pənt\ *adj or n* — **par·tic·i·pa·tion** \-ˌti-sə-'pā-shən\ *n* — **par·tic·i·pa·tor** \-'ti-sə-ˌpā-tər\ *n* — **par·tic·i·pa·to·ry** \-ˌti-sə-pə-ˌtór-ē\ *adj*

**par·ti·ci·ple** \'pär-tə-ˌsi-pəl\ *n* : a word having the characteristics of both verb and adjective — **par·ti·cip·i·al** \ˌpär-tə-'si-pē-əl\ *adj*

**par·ti·cle** \'pär-ti-kəl\ *n* **1** : a very small bit of matter **2** : a unit of speech (as an article, preposition, or conjunction) expressing some general aspect of meaning or some connective or limiting relation

**par·ti·cle·board** \-ˌbórd\ *n* : a board made of very small pieces of wood bonded together

**par·ti–col·or** \'pär-tē-ˌkə-lər\ *or* **par·ti–col·ored** \-ˌlord\ *adj* : showing different colors or tints; *esp* : having one main color broken by patches of one or more other colors

¹**par·tic·u·lar** \pər-'ti-kyə-lər\ *adj* **1** : of or relating to a specific person or thing ⟨the laws of a ∼ state⟩ **2** : DISTINCTIVE, SPECIAL ⟨the ∼ point of his talk⟩ **3** : SEPARATE, INDIVIDUAL ⟨each ∼ hair⟩ **4** : attentive to details : PRECISE **5** : hard to please : EXACTING ⟨is ∼ about her clothes⟩ — **par·tic·u·lar·i·ty** \-ˌti-kyə-'lar-ə-tē\ *n* — **par·tic·u·lar·ly** *adv*

²**particular** *n* : an individual fact or detail

**par·tic·u·lar·ise** *Brit var of* PARTICULARIZE

**par·tic·u·lar·ize** \pər-'ti-kyə-lə-ˌrīz\ *vb* **-ized; -iz·ing 1** : to state in detail : SPECIFY **2** : to go into details

**par·tic·u·late** \pər-'ti-kyə-lət, pär-, -ˌlāt\ *adj* : relating to or existing as minute separate particles — **particulate** *n*

¹**part·ing** *n* : a place or point of separation or divergence

²**parting** *adj* : given, taken, or done at parting ⟨a ∼ kiss⟩

**par·ti·san** *also* **par·ti·zan** \'pär-tə-zən, -sən\ *n* **1** : one that takes the part of another : ADHERENT **2** : GUERRILLA — **partisan** *adj* — **par·ti·san·ship** *n*

**par·tite** \'pär-ˌtīt\ *adj* : divided into a usu. specified number of parts

**par·ti·tion** \pär-'ti-shən\ *n* **1** : DIVISION **2** : something that divides or separates; *esp* : an interior dividing wall — **partition** *vb*

**par·ti·tive** \'pär-tə-tiv\ *adj* : of, relating to, or denoting a part

**part·ly** \'pärt-lē\ *adv* : in part : in some measure or degree

**part·ner** \'pärt-nər\ *n* **1** : ASSOCIATE, COLLEAGUE **2** : either of two persons who dance together **3** : one who plays on the same team with another **4** : SPOUSE **5** : one of two or more persons contractually associated as joint principals in a business — **part·ner·ship** *n*

**part of speech** : a class of words (as nouns or verbs) distinguished according to the kind of idea denoted and the function performed in a sentence

**par·tridge** \'pär-trij\ *n, pl* **partridge** *or* **par·tridg·es** : any of various stout-bodied Old World game birds

**part–song** \'pärt-ˌsón\ *n* : a song with two or more voice parts

**part–time** \-'tīm\ *adj or adv* : involving or working less than a full or regular schedule — **part–tim·er** \-ˌtī-mər\ *n*

**par·tu·ri·tion** \ˌpär-tə-'ri-shən, ˌpär-chə-, ˌpär-tyú-\ *n* : CHILDBIRTH

**part·way** \'pärt-ˌwā\ adv : to some extent : PARTLY

**par·ty** \'pär-tē\ n, pl **parties** 1 : a person or group taking one side of a question; esp : a group of persons organized for the purpose of directing the policies of a government 2 : a person or group concerned in an action or affair : PARTICIPANT 3 : a group of persons detailed for a common task 4 : a social gathering

**party animal** n : a person known for frequent attendance at parties

**par·ty·go·er** \'pär-tē-ˌgō-ər\ n : a person who attends a party or who attends parties frequently

**par·ve·nu** \'pär-və-ˌnü, -ˌnyü\ n [F, fr. pp. of parvenir to arrive, fr. L pervenire, fr. per through + venire to come] : one who has recently or suddenly risen to wealth or power but has not yet secured the social position associated with it

**¹pas** \'pä\ n, pl **pas** \same or 'päz\ : a dance step or combination of steps

**pas·cal** \pas-'kal\ n : a unit of pressure in the metric system equal to one newton per square meter

**pas·chal** \'pas-kəl\ adj : of, relating to, appropriate for, or used during Passover or Easter ceremonies

**pa·sha** \'pä-shə, 'pa-, pə-'shä\ n : a man (as formerly a governor in Turkey) of high rank

**pash·mi·na** \ˌpəsh-'mē-nə\ n : a fine wool from the undercoat of domestic Himalayan goats; also : a shawl made from this wool

**¹pass** \'pas\ vb 1 : MOVE, PROCEED 2 : to go away; also : DIE 3 : to move past, beyond, or over 4 : to allow to elapse : SPEND 5 : to go or make way through 6 : to go or allow to go unchallenged 7 : to undergo transfer 8 : to render a legal judgment 9 : OCCUR 10 : to secure the approval of (as a legislature) 11 : to go or cause to go through an inspection, test, or course of study successfully 12 : to be regarded 13 : CIRCULATE ⟨∼ a note⟩ 14 : VOID 2 15 : to transfer the ball or puck to another player 16 : to decline to bid or bet on one's hand in a card game 17 : to give a base on balls to 18 : to let something go by without accepting ⟨∼ed on his offer⟩ — **pass·er** n

**²pass** n : a gap in a mountain range

**³pass** n 1 : the act or an instance of passing 2 : REALIZATION, ACCOMPLISHMENT 3 : a state of affairs 4 : a written authorization to leave, enter, or move about freely 5 : a transfer of a ball or puck from one player to another 6 : BASE ON BALLS 7 : EFFORT, TRY 8 : a sexually inviting gesture or approach

**⁴pass** abbr 1 passenger 2 passive

**pass·able** \'pa-sə-bəl\ adj 1 : capable of being passed or traveled on 2 : just good enough : TOLERABLE ⟨did a ∼ job⟩ — **pass·ably** \-blē\ adv

**pas·sage** \'pa-sij\ n 1 : a means (as a road or corridor) of passing 2 : the action or process of passing 3 : a voyage esp. by sea or air 4 : a right or permission

to pass 5 : ENACTMENT 6 : a usu. brief portion or section (as of a book)

**pas·sage·way** \-ˌwā\ n : a way that allows passage

**pass·book** \'pas-ˌbùk\ n : BANKBOOK

**pas·sé** \pa-'sā\ adj 1 : past one's prime 2 : not up-to-date : OUTMODED

**pas·sel** \'pa-səl\ n : a large number ⟨a ∼ of children⟩

**pas·sen·ger** \'pa-sᵊn-jər\ n : a traveler in a public or private conveyance

**pass·er·by** \'pa-sər-ˌbī\ n, pl **pass·ers·by** : one who passes by

**pas·ser·ine** \'pa-sə-ˌrīn\ adj : of or relating to the large order of birds comprising singing birds that perch

**pas·sim** \'pa-səm\ adv [L, fr. passus scattered, fr. pp. of pandere to spread] : here and there : THROUGHOUT

**pass·ing** n : the act of one that passes or causes to pass; esp : DEATH

**pas·sion** \'pa-shən\ n 1 often cap : the sufferings of Christ between the night of the Last Supper and his death 2 : strong feeling; also, pl : the emotions as distinguished from reason 3 : RAGE, ANGER 4 : LOVE; also : an object of affection or enthusiasm 5 : sexual desire — **pas·sion·ate** \'pa-shə-nət\ adj — **pas·sion·ate·ly** adv — **pas·sion·less** adj

**pas·sion·flow·er** \'pa-shən-ˌflaù-(ə)r\ n [fr. the fancied resemblance of parts of the flower to the instruments of Christ's crucifixion] : any of a genus of chiefly tropical woody climbing vines or erect herbs with showy flowers and pulpy often edible berries (**passion fruit**)

**pas·sive** \'pa-siv\ adj 1 : not active : acted upon 2 : asserting that the grammatical subject is subjected to or affected by the action represented by the verb ⟨∼ voice⟩ 3 : making use of the sun's heat usu. without the aid of mechanical devices 4 : SUBMISSIVE, PATIENT — **passive** n — **pas·sive·ly** adv — **pas·siv·i·ty** \pa-'si-və-tē\ n

**pas·sive–ma·trix** \-'mā-triks\ adj : of, relating to, or being on LCD in which pixels are controlled in groups

**pass·key** \'pas-ˌkē\ n : a key for opening two or more locks

**pass out** vb : to lose consciousness

**Pass·over** \'pas-ˌō-vər\ n [fr. the exemption of the Israelites from the slaughter of the firstborn in Egypt (Exod 12:23–27)] : a Jewish holiday celebrated in March or April in commemoration of the Hebrews' liberation from slavery in Egypt

**pass·port** \'pas-ˌpòrt\ n : an official document issued by a country upon request to a citizen requesting protection during travel abroad

**pass up** vb : DECLINE, REJECT

**pass·word** \'pas-ˌwərd\ n 1 : a word or phrase that must be spoken by a person before being allowed to pass a guard 2 : a sequence of characters required for access to a computer system

**¹past** \'past\ adj 1 : AGO ⟨10 years ∼⟩ 2 : just gone or elapsed ⟨the ∼ month⟩ 3 : having existed or taken place in a period before the present : BYGONE **4** : of, relating to, or constituting a verb tense that expresses time gone by

²**past** *prep or adv* : BEYOND

³**past** *n* **1** : time gone by **2** : something that happened or was done in a former time **3** : the past tense; *also* : a verb form in it **4** : a secret past life

**pas·ta** \ˈpäs-tə\ *n* [It] **1** : a paste in processed form (as macaroni) or in the form of fresh dough (as ravioli) **2** : a dish of cooked pasta

¹**paste** \ˈpāst\ *n* [ME, fr. AF, fr. LL *pasta* dough, paste] **1** : DOUGH **2** : a smooth food product made by evaporation or grinding ⟨tomato ∼⟩ **3** : a shaped dough (as spaghetti or ravioli) **4** : a preparation (as of flour and water) for sticking things together **5** : a brilliant glass used for artificial gems

²**paste** *vb* **past·ed; past·ing** : to cause to adhere by paste : STICK

**paste·board** \ˈpāst-ˌbȯrd\ *n* : CARDBOARD

¹**pas·tel** \pas-ˈtel\ *n* **1** : a paste made of powdered pigment; *also* : a crayon of such paste **2** : a drawing in pastel **3** : a pale or light color

²**pastel** *adj* **1** : of or relating to a pastel **2** : pale in color

**pas·tern** \ˈpas-tərn\ *n* : the part of a horse's foot extending from the fetlock to the top of the hoof

**pas·teur·i·za·tion** \ˌpas-chə-rə-ˈzā-shən, ˌpas-tə-\ *n* : partial sterilization of a substance (as milk) by heat or radiation — **pas·teur·ize** \ˈpas-chə-ˌrīz, ˈpas-tə-\ *vb* — **pas·teur·iz·er** *n*

**pas·tiche** \pas-ˈtēsh\ *n* : a composition (as in literature or music) made up of selections from different works

**pas·tille** \pas-ˈtēl\ *n* : LOZENGE 2

**pas·time** \ˈpas-ˌtīm\ *n* : DIVERSION; *esp* : something that serves to make time pass agreeably

**pas·tor** \ˈpas-tər\ *n* [ME *pastour*, fr. AF, fr. L *pastor*, herdsman, fr. *pascere* to feed, pasture, nurture] : a minister or priest serving a local church or parish — **pas·tor·ate** \-tə-rət\ *n*

¹**pas·to·ral** \ˈpas-tə-rəl\ *adj* **1** : of or relating to shepherds or to rural life **2** : of or relating to spiritual guidance esp. of a congregation **3** : of or relating to the pastor of a church

²**pastoral** *n* : a literary work dealing with shepherds or rural life

**pas·to·rale** \ˌpas-tə-ˈräl, -ˈral\ *n* [It] : a musical composition having a pastoral theme

**past participle** *n* : a participle that typically expresses completed action, that is one of the principal parts of the verb, and that is used in the formation of perfect tenses in the active voice and of all tenses in the passive voice

**pas·tra·mi** \pə-ˈsträ-mē\ *n* [Yiddish *pastrame*] : a highly seasoned smoked beef prepared esp. from shoulder cuts

**pas·try** \ˈpā-strē\ *n, pl* **pastries** : sweet baked goods made of dough or with a crust made of enriched dough

**pas·tur·age** \ˈpas-chə-rij\ *n* : PASTURE

¹**pas·ture** \ˈpas-chər\ *n* **1** : plants (as grass) for the feeding esp. of grazing livestock **2** : land or a plot of land used for grazing

²**pasture** *vb* **pas·tured; pas·tur·ing 1** : GRAZE **2** : to use as pasture

**pasty** \ˈpā-stē\ *adj* **past·i·er; -est** : resembling paste; *esp* : pallid and unhealthy in appearance

¹**pat** \ˈpat\ *n* **1** : a light tap esp. with the hand or a flat instrument; *also* : the sound made by it **2** : something (as butter) shaped into a small flat usu. square individual portion

²**pat** *adv* : in a pat manner : PERFECTLY

³**pat** *vb* **pat·ted; pat·ting 1** : to strike lightly with a flat instrument **2** : to flatten, smooth, or put into place or shape with a pat **3** : to tap gently or lovingly with the hand

⁴**pat** *adj* **1** : exactly suited to the occasion : APT **2** : memorized exactly **3** : UNYIELDING ⟨stood ∼ on the issue⟩

**PAT** *abbr* point after touchdown

**pa·ta·ca** \pə-ˈtä-kə\ *n* — see MONEY table

¹**patch** \ˈpach\ *n* **1** : a piece used to cover a torn or worn place; *also* : one worn on a garment as an ornament or insignia **2** : a small area distinct from that about it **3** : a shield worn over the socket of an injured or missing eye

²**patch** *vb* **1** : to mend or cover with a patch **2** : to make of fragments **3** : to repair usu. in hasty fashion

**patch·ou·li** \ˈpa-chə-lē, pə-ˈchü-lē\ *n* : a heavy perfume made from the fragrant essential oil of an Asian mint; *also* : the plant itself

**patch test** *n* : a test for allergic sensitivity made by applying to the unbroken skin small pads soaked with the allergen to be tested

**patch·work** \ˈpach-ˌwərk\ *n* : something made of pieces of different materials, shapes, or colors

**patchy** \ˈpa-chē\ *adj* **patch·i·er; -est** : marked by or consisting of patches; *also* : irregular in appearance or quality — **patch·i·ness** \-chē-nəs\ *n*

**pate** \ˈpāt\ *n* : HEAD; *esp* : the crown of the head

**pâ·té** *also* **pate** \pä-ˈtā\ *n* [F] **1** : a meat or fish pie or patty **2** : a spread of finely chopped or pureed seasoned meat

**pa·tel·la** \pə-ˈte-lə\ *n, pl* **-lae** \-ˈte-(ˌ)lē, -ˌlī\ *or* **-las** [L] : KNEECAP — **pa·tel·lar** \-ˈte-lər\ *adj*

**pat·en** \ˈpa-tᵊn\ *n* **1** : PLATE; *esp* : one of precious metal for the eucharistic bread **2** : a thin disk

¹**pa·tent** \/1 & 4 are ˈpa-tᵊnt, Brit also ˈpā-, 2 & 3 are ˈpa-tᵊnt, ˈpā-\ *adj* **1** : open to public inspection — used chiefly in the phrase *letters patent* **2** : free from obstruction **3** : EVIDENT, OBVIOUS **4** : protected by a patent ♦ *Synonyms* MANIFEST, DISTINCT, APPARENT, PALPABLE, PLAIN, CLEAR — **pat·ent·ly** *adv*

²**pat·ent** \ˈpa-tᵊnt, *Brit also* ˈpā-\ *n* **1** : an official document conferring a right or privilege **2** : a document securing to an

inventor for a term of years exclusive right to his or her invention **3** : something patented

³**pat·ent** *vb* : to secure by patent

**pat·en·tee** \pa-tᵊn-'tē, *Brit also* ˌpā-\ *n* : one to whom a grant is made or a privilege secured by patent

**patent medicine** \'pa-tᵊnt-\ *n* : a packaged nonprescription drug protected by a trademark; *also* : any proprietary drug

**pa·ter·fa·mil·i·as** \ˌpā-tər-fə-'mi-lē-əs\ *n*, *pl* **pa·tres·fa·mil·i·as** \ˌpā-ˌtrēz-\ [L] : the father of a family : the male head of a household

**pa·ter·nal** \pə-'tər-nᵊl\ *adj* **1** : FATHERLY **2** : related through or inherited or derived from a father — **pa·ter·nal·ly** *adv*

**pa·ter·nal·ism** \-nə-ˌli-zəm\ *n* : a system under which an authority treats those under its control paternally (as by regulating their conduct and supplying their needs)

¹**pa·ter·ni·ty** \pə-'tər-nə-tē\ *n* **1** : FATHERHOOD **2** : descent from a father

²**paternity** *adj* **1** : granted to a father ⟨∼ leave⟩ **2** : of or relating to the determination of paternity ⟨a ∼ suit⟩

¹**path** \'path, 'páth\ *n*, *pl* **paths** \'pathz, 'paths, 'páthz, 'páths\ **1** : a trodden way **2** : ROUTE, COURSE — **path·less** *adj*

²**path** *or* **patho** *abbr* pathology

**path·break·ing** \'path-ˌbrā-kiŋ\ *adj* : TRAILBLAZING

**pa·thet·ic** \pə-'the-tik\ *adj* **1** : evoking tenderness, pity, or sorrow **2** : pitifully inadequate ⟨a ∼ performance⟩ **♦ Synonyms** PITIFUL, PITEOUS, PITIABLE, POOR — **pa·thet·i·cal·ly** \-ti-k(ə-)lē\ *adv*

**path·find·er** \'path-ˌfīn-dər, 'páth-\ *n* : one that discovers a way; *esp* : one that explores untraveled regions to mark out a new route

**patho·gen** \'pa-thə-jən\ *n* : a specific agent (as a bacterium) causing disease — **patho·gen·ic** \ˌpa-thə-'je-nik\ *adj* — **patho·ge·nic·i·ty** \-jə-'ni-sə-tē\ *n*

**pa·thog·ra·phy** \pə-'thä-grə-fē\ *n* : biography focusing on a person's flaws and misfortunes

**pa·thol·o·gy** \pə-'thä-lə-jē\ *n*, *pl* **-gies** **1** : the study of the essential nature of disease **2** : the abnormality of structure and function characteristic of a disease **3** : deviation giving rise to social ills — **path·o·log·i·cal** \ˌpa-thə-'lä-ji-kəl\ *adj* — **pa·thol·o·gist** \pə-'thä-lə-jist\ *n*

**pa·thos** \'pā-ˌthäs, -ˌthōs\ *n* : an element in experience or artistic representation evoking pity or compassion

**path·way** \'path-ˌwā, 'páth-\ *n* : PATH

**pa·tience** \'pā-shəns\ *n* **1** : the capacity, habit, or fact of being patient **2** *chiefly Brit* : SOLITAIRE 2

¹**pa·tient** \'pā-shənt\ *adj* **1** : bearing pain or trials without complaint **2** : showing self-control : CALM **3** : STEADFAST, PERSEVERING — **pa·tient·ly** *adv*

²**patient** *n* : one under medical care

**pa·ti·na** \'pa-tə-nə, pə-'tē-\ *n*, *pl* **pa·ti·nas** \-nəz\ *or* **pa·ti·nae** \pa-tə-ˌnē, -ˌnī\ **1** : a green film formed on copper and bronze

by exposure to moist air **2** : a superficial covering or exterior

**pa·tio** \'pa-tē-ˌō, 'pä-\ *n*, *pl* **pa·ti·os** **1** : COURTYARD **2** : an often paved area near a dwelling used esp. for outdoor dining

**pa·tois** \'pa-ˌtwä\ *n*, *pl* **pa·tois** \-ˌtwäz\ [F] **1** : a dialect other than the standard dialect; *esp* : uneducated or provincial speech **2** : JARGON 2

**pa·tri·arch** \'pā-trē-ˌärk\ *n* **1** : a man revered as father or founder (as of a tribe) **2** : a venerable old man **3** : an ecclesiastical dignitary (as the bishop of an Eastern Orthodox see) — **pa·tri·ar·chal** \ˌpā-trē-'är-kəl\ *adj* — **pa·tri·arch·ate** \'pā-trē-ˌär-kət, -ˌkät\ *n* — **pa·tri·ar·chy** \-ˌär-kē\ *n*

**pa·tri·cian** \pə-'tri-shən\ *n* : a person of high birth : ARISTOCRAT — **patrician** *adj*

**pat·ri·cide** \'pa-trə-ˌsīd\ *n* **1** : one who murders his or her own father **2** : the murder of one's own father

**pat·ri·mo·ny** \'pa-trə-ˌmō-nē\ *n* : something (as an estate) inherited or derived esp. from one's father : HERITAGE — **pat·ri·mo·ni·al** \ˌpa-trə-'mō-nē-əl\ *adj*

**pa·tri·ot** \'pā-trē-ət, -ˌät\ *n* [MF *patriote* compatriot, fr. LL *patriota*, fr. Gk *patriōtēs*, fr. *patria* lineage, fr. *patr-*, *patēr* father] : one who loves his or her country — **pa·tri·ot·ic** \ˌpā-trē-'ä-tik\ *adj* — **pa·tri·ot·i·cal·ly** \-ti-k(ə-)lē\ *adv* — **pa·tri·o·tism** \'pā-trē-ə-ˌti-zəm\ *n*

**pa·tris·tic** \pə-'tris-tik\ *adj* : of or relating to the church fathers or their writings

¹**pa·trol** \pə-'trōl\ *n* : the action of going the rounds (as of an area) for observation or the maintenance of security; *also* : a person or group performing such an action

²**patrol** *vb* **pa·trolled; pa·trol·ling** : to carry out a patrol

**pa·trol·man** \pə-'trōl-mən\ *n* : a police officer assigned to a beat

**patrol wagon** *n* : PADDY WAGON

**pa·tron** \'pā-trən\ *n* [ME, fr. AF, fr. ML & L; ML *patronus* patron saint, patron of a benefice, pattern, fr. L, defender, fr. *patr-*, *pater* father] **1** : a person chosen or named as special protector **2** : a wealthy or influential supporter ⟨∼ of poets⟩; *also* : BENEFACTOR **3** : a regular client or customer ⟨diner ∼s⟩

**pa·tron·age** \'pa-trə-nij, 'pā-\ *n* **1** : the support or influence of a patron **2** : the trade of customers **3** : control of appointment to government jobs

**pa·tron·ess** \'pā-trə-nəs\ *n* : a woman who is a patron

**pa·tron·ise** *Brit var of* PATRONIZE

**pa·tron·ize** \'pā-trə-ˌnīz, 'pa-\ *vb* **-ized; -iz·ing** **1** : to be a customer of **2** : to treat condescendingly, haughtily, or coolly ⟨rich people who ∼ the poor⟩

**pat·ro·nym·ic** \ˌpa-trə-'ni-mik\ *n* : a name derived from the name of one's father or a paternal ancestor usu. by the addition of an affix

**pa·troon** \pə-'trün\ *n* : the proprietor of a manorial estate esp. in New York under Dutch rule

**pat·sy** \'pat-sē\ *n, pl* **pat·sies** : a person who is easily duped or victimized

¹**pat·ter** \'pa-tər\ *vb* : to talk glibly or mechanically ♦ *Synonyms* CHATTER, PRATE, CHAT, PRATTLE, BABBLE

²**patter** *n* **1** : a specialized lingo **2** : extremely rapid talk ⟨a comedian's ∼⟩

³**patter** *vb* : to strike, pat, or tap rapidly

⁴**patter** *n* : a quick succession of taps or pats ⟨the ∼ of rain⟩

¹**pat·tern** \'pa-tərn\ *n* [ME *patron*, fr. AF, fr. ML *patronus*, fr. L, defender, fr. *patr-, pater* father] **1** : an ideal model **2** : something used as a model for making things ⟨a dressmaker's ∼⟩ **3** : SAMPLE **4** : an artistic design **5** : CONFIGURATION **6** : a sample of a person's behaviors or characteristics ⟨a ∼ of violence⟩

²**pattern** *vb* : to form according to a pattern

**pat·ty** *also* **pat·tie** \'pa-tē\ *n, pl* **patties** **1** : a little pie **2** : a small flat cake esp. of chopped food ⟨hamburger *patties*⟩

**pau·ci·ty** \'pò-sə-tē\ *n* : smallness of number or quantity

**paunch** \'pònch\ *n* : a usu. large belly : POTBELLY — **paunchy** *adj*

**pau·per** \'pò-pər\ *n* : a person without means of support except from charity — **pau·per·ism** \-pə-ˌri-zəm\ *n* — **pau·per·ize** \-pə-ˌrīz\ *vb*

¹**pause** \'pòz\ *n* **1** : a temporary stop; *also* : a period of inaction **2** : a brief suspension of the voice **3** : a sign ⌒ or ∾ above or below a musical note or rest to show it is to be prolonged **4** : a reason for pausing **5** : a function of an electronic device that pauses a recording

²**pause** *vb* **paused; paus·ing** : to stop, rest, or linger for a time

**pave** \'pāv\ *vb* **paved; pav·ing** : to cover (as a road) with hard material in order to smooth or firm the surface

**pave·ment** \'pāv-mənt\ *n* **1** : a paved surface **2** : the material with which something is paved

**pa·vil·ion** \pə-'vil-yən\ *n* [ME *pavilloun, pavillioun*, fr. AF, fr. L *papilion-, papilio* butterfly] **1** : a large tent **2** : a usu. open structure (as in a park) used for entertainment or shelter

**pav·ing** \'pā-viŋ\ *n* : PAVEMENT

¹**paw** \'pò\ *n* : the foot of a quadruped (as a dog or lion) having claws

²**paw** *vb* **1** : to touch or strike with a paw; *also* : to scrape with a hoof **2** : to feel or handle clumsily or rudely **3** : to flail about or grab for with the hands

**pawl** \'pòl\ *n* : a pivoted tongue or sliding bolt designed to fall into notches on another machine part to permit motion in one direction only

¹**pawn** \'pòn\ *n* [ME *pown*, fr. AF *peoun, paun*, fr. ML *pedon-, pedo* foot soldier, fr. LL, one with broad feet, fr. L *ped-, pes* foot] **1** : a chess piece of the least value **2** : one used for the purposes of another

²**pawn** *n* **1** : something deposited as security for a loan; *also* : HOSTAGE **2** : the state of being pledged

³**pawn** *vb* : to deposit as a pledge

**pawn·bro·ker** \'pòn-ˌbrō-kər\ *n* : one who lends money on goods pledged

**Paw·nee** \pò-'nē\ *n, pl* **Pawnee** *or* **Pawnees** : a member of an American Indian people orig. of Kansas and Nebraska

**pawn·shop** \'pòn-ˌshäp\ *n* : a pawnbroker's place of business

**paw·paw** *also* **pa·paw** **1** \pə-'pò\ : PAPAYA **2** \'pä-ˌpò, 'pò-\ : a No. American tree with green-skinned edible fruit; *also* : its fruit

¹**pay** \'pā\ *vb* **paid** \'pād\ *also in sense 7* **payed; pay·ing** [ME, fr. AF *paier*, fr. L *pacare* to pacify, fr. *pac-, pax* peace] **1** : to make due return to for goods or services **2** : to discharge indebtedness for : SETTLE ⟨∼ a bill⟩ **3** : to give in forfeit ⟨∼ the penalty⟩ **4** : REQUITE **5** : to give, offer, or make freely or as fitting ⟨∼ attention⟩ **6** : to be profitable to : RETURN **7** : to make slack and allow to run out ⟨∼ out a rope⟩ — **pay·able** *adj* — **pay·ee** \pā-'ē\ *n* — **pay·er** *n*

²**pay** *n* **1** : something paid; *esp* : WAGES **2** : the status of being paid by an employer : EMPLOY

³**pay** *adj* **1** : containing something valuable (as gold) ⟨∼ dirt⟩ **2** : equipped to receive a fee for use ⟨∼ telephone⟩ **3** : requiring payment

**pay·back** \'pā-ˌbak\ *n* **1** : a return on an investment equal to the original capital outlay **2** : something given in return, compensation, or retaliation

**pay·check** \'pā-ˌchek\ *n* **1** : a check in payment of wages or salary **2** : WAGES, SALARY

**pay·load** \-ˌlōd\ *n* : the load carried by a vehicle in addition to what is necessary for its operation; *also* : the weight of such a load

**pay·mas·ter** \-ˌmas-tər\ *n* : one who distributes the payroll

**pay·ment** \'pā-mənt\ *n* **1** : the act of paying **2** : something paid

**pay·off** \-ˌòf\ *n* **1** : PROFIT, REWARD; *also* : RETRIBUTION **2** : the climax of an incident or enterprise ⟨the ∼ of a story⟩

**pay–per–view** *n* : a cable television service by which customers can order access to a single airing of a TV feature

**pay·roll** \-ˌrōl\ *n* : a list of persons entitled to receive pay; *also* : the money to pay those on such a list

**payt** *abbr* payment

**pay up** *vb* : to pay what is due; *also* : to pay in full

**Pb** *symbol* [L *plumbum*] lead

**PBS** *abbr* Public Broadcasting Service

**PBX** \ˌpē-(ˌ)bē-'eks\ *n* [*private branch exchange*] : a private telephone switchboard

¹**PC** \ˌpē-'sē\ *n, pl* **PCs** *or* **PC's** [*personal computer*] : MICROCOMPUTER

²**PC** *abbr* **1** Peace Corps **2** percent; percentage **3** politically correct **4** postcard **5** [L *post cibum*] after meals **6** professional corporation

**PCB** \ˌpē-ˌsē-'bē\ *n* : POLYCHLORINATED BIPHENYL

**PCP** \ˌpē-ˌsē-'pē\ *n* : PHENCYCLIDINE

**pct** *abbr* percent; percentage

**pd** *abbr* paid

**Pd** *symbol* palladium

**PD** *abbr* **1** per diem **2** police department **3** potential difference

**PDA** \ˌpē-ˌdē-ˈā\ *n* [personal digital assistant] : a small microprocessor device for storing and organizing personal information

**PDQ** \ˌpē-ˌdē-ˈkyü\ *adv, often not cap* [abbr. of *pretty damned quick*] : IMMEDIATELY

**PDT** *abbr* Pacific daylight (saving) time

**PE** *abbr* **1** physical education **2** printer's error **3** professional engineer

**pea** \ˈpē\ *n, pl* **peas** *also* **pease** \ˈpēz\ *n* **1** : the round edible protein-rich seed borne in the pod of a widely grown leguminous vine; *also* : this vine **2** : any of various plants resembling or related to the pea

**peace** \ˈpēs\ *n* **1** : a state of calm and quiet; *esp* : public security under law **2** : freedom from disturbing thoughts or emotions **3** : a state of concord (as between persons or governments); *also* : an agreement to end hostilities — **peaceable** \ˈpē-sə-bəl\ *adj* — **peaceably** \-blē\ *adv* — **peaceful** *adj* — **peacefully** *adv*

**peacekeeping** \ˈpēs-ˌkē-piŋ\ *n* : the preserving of peace; *esp* : international enforcement and supervision of a truce — **peacekeeper** *n*

**peacemaker** \-ˌmā-kər\ *n* : one who settles an argument or stops a fight

**peacetime** \-ˌtīm\ *n* : a time when a nation is not at war

**peach** \ˈpēch\ *n* [ME *peche*, fr. AF *pesche, peche,*, fr. LL *persica,* fr. L (*malum*) *Persicum,* lit., Persian fruit] : a sweet juicy fuzzy-skinned fruit of a small usu. pink-flowered tree related to the cherry and plums; *also* : this tree — **peachy** *adj*

**peacock** \ˈpē-ˌkäk\ *n* [ME *pecok,* fr. *pe-* (fr. OE *pēa* peafowl, fr. L *pavo* peacock) + *cok* cock] : the male peafowl that can spread its long tail feathers to make a colorful display

**peafowl** \-ˌfau̇(-ə)l\ *n* : either of two large domesticated Asian pheasants

**peahen** \-ˌhen\ *n* : the female peafowl

¹**peak** \ˈpēk\ *n* **1** : a pointed or projecting part **2** : the top of a hill or mountain; *also* : MOUNTAIN **3** : the front projecting part of a cap **4** : the narrow part of a ship's bow or stern **5** : the highest level or greatest degree — **peak** *adj*

²**peak** *vb* : to bring to or reach a maximum

**peaked** \ˈpē-kəd\ *adj* : THIN, SICKLY

¹**peal** \ˈpēl\ *n* **1** : the loud ringing of bells **2** : a set of tuned bells **3** : a loud sound or succession of sounds

²**peal** *vb* : to give out peals : RESOUND

**peanut** \ˈpē-ˌnət\ *n* **1** : an annual herb related to the pea but having pods that ripen underground; *also* : this pod or one of the edible seeds it bears **2** *pl* : a very small amount **3** : a pellet of polystyrene foam

**pear** \ˈper\ *n* : the fleshy fruit of a tree related to the apple; *also* : this tree

**pearl** \ˈpərl\ *n* **1** : a small hard often lustrous body formed within the shell of some mollusks and used as a gem **2** : one that is choice or precious ⟨~s of wisdom⟩ **3** : a slightly bluish medium gray color — **pearly** \ˈpər-lē\ *adj*

**peasant** \ˈpe-zᵊnt\ *n* **1** : any of a class of small landowners or laborers tilling the soil **2** : a usu. uneducated person of low social status — **peasantry** \-zᵊn-trē\ *n*

**peashooter** \ˈpē-ˌshü-tər\ *n* : a toy blowgun for shooting peas

**peat** \ˈpēt\ *n* : a dark substance formed by partial decay of plants (as mosses) in water — **peaty** *adj*

**peat moss** *n* : SPHAGNUM

¹**pebble** \ˈpe-bəl\ *n* : a small usu. round stone — **pebbly** \-b(ə-)lē\ *adj*

²**pebble** *vb* **pebbled; pebbling** : to produce a rough surface texture in ⟨~ leather⟩

**pec** \ˈpek\ *n* : PECTORAL MUSCLE

**pecan** \pi-ˈkän, -ˈkan; ˈpē-ˌkan\ *n* : the smooth thin-shelled edible nut of a large American hickory; *also* : this tree

**peccadillo** \ˌpe-kə-ˈdi-lō\ *n, pl* **-loes** *or* **-los** : a slight offense

**peccary** \ˈpe-kə-rē\ *n, pl* **-ries** : any of several American chiefly tropical mammals resembling but smaller than the related pigs

**peccavi** \pe-ˈkä-ˌvē\ *n* [L, I have sinned, fr. *peccare* to sin] : an acknowledgment of sin

¹**peck** \ˈpek\ *n* — see WEIGHT table

²**peck** *vb* **1** : to strike or pierce with or as if with the bill **2** : to make (as a hole) by pecking **3** : to pick up with or as if with the bill

³**peck** *n* **1** : an impression made by pecking **2** : a quick sharp stroke

**pecking order** *also* **peck order** *n* : a basic pattern of social organization within a flock of poultry in which each bird pecks another lower in the scale without being pecked in return and submits to pecking by one of higher rank; *also* : a social hierarchy

**pectin** \ˈpek-tən\ *n* : any of various water-soluble plant substances that cause fruit jellies to set — **pectic** \-tik\ *adj*

**pectoral** \ˈpek-tə-rəl\ *adj* : of or relating to the breast or chest

**pectoral muscle** *n* : either of two muscles on each side of the body which connect the front walls of the chest with the bones of the upper arm and shoulder

**peculiar** \pi-ˈkyül-yər\ *adj* [ME *peculier,* fr. L *peculiaris* of private property, special, fr. *peculium* private property, fr. *pecus* cattle] **1** : belonging exclusively to one person or group **2** : CHARACTERISTIC, DISTINCTIVE **3** : QUEER, ODD ⟨her ~ behavior⟩ ♦ *Synonyms* IDIOSYNCRATIC, ECCENTRIC, SINGULAR, STRANGE, WEIRD — **peculiarity** \-ˌkyü-lē-ˈya-rə-tē, -ˌkyül-ˈya-\ *n* — **peculiarly** *adv*

**pecuniary** \pi-ˈkyü-nē-ˌer-ē\ *adj* : of or relating to money : MONETARY

**pedagogue** *also* **pedagog** \ˈpe-də-ˌgäg\ *n* : TEACHER, SCHOOLMASTER

**pedagogy** \ˈpe-də-ˌgō-jē, -ˌgä-\ *n* : the

art or profession of teaching; *esp* : EDU-CATION 2 — **ped·a·gog·ic** \ˌpe-də-ˈgä-jik, -ˈgō-\ *or* **ped·a·gog·i·cal** \-ji-kəl\ *adj*

¹**ped·al** \ˈpe-dᵊl\ *n* : a lever worked by the foot

²**pedal** *adj* : of or relating to the foot

³**pedal** *vb* **ped·aled** *also* **ped·alled; ped·al·ing** *also* **ped·al·ling 1** : to use or work a pedal (as of a piano or bicycle) **2** : to ride a bicycle

**ped·ant** \ˈpe-dᵊnt\ *n* **1** : a person who makes a show of knowledge **2** : a formal uninspired teacher ⟨his piano teacher was a ∼⟩ — **pe·dan·tic** \pi-ˈdan-tik\ *adj* — **ped·ant·ry** \ˈpe-dᵊn-trē\ *n*

**ped·dle** \ˈpe-dᵊl\ *vb* **ped·dled; ped·dling** : to sell or offer for sale from place to place — **ped·dler** *also* **ped·lar** \ˈped-lər\ *n*

**ped·er·ast** \ˈpe-də-ˌrast\ *n* [Gk *paiderastēs*, lit., lover of boys] : one who practices anal intercourse esp. with a boy — **ped·er·as·ty** \ˈpe-də-ˌras-tē\ *n*

**ped·es·tal** \ˈpe-dəs-tᵊl\ *n* **1** : the support or foot of something (as a column, statue, or vase) that is upright **2** : a position of high regard

¹**pe·des·tri·an** \pə-ˈdes-trē-ən\ *adj* **1** : OR-DINARY **2** : going on foot

²**pedestrian** *n* : WALKER

**pe·di·at·rics** \ˌpē-dē-ˈa-triks\ *n* : a branch of medicine dealing with the develop-ment, care, and diseases of children — **pe·di·at·ric** \-trik\ *adj* — **pe·di·a·tri·cian** \ˌpē-dē-ə-ˈtri-shən\ *n*

**pedi·cab** \ˈpe-di-ˌkab\ *n* : a pedal-driven tricycle with seats for a driver and two passengers

**ped·i·cure** \ˈpe-di-ˌkyùr\ *n* : care of the feet, toes, and nails; *also* : a single treat-ment of these parts — **ped·i·cur·ist** \-ˌkyùr-ist\ *n*

**ped·i·gree** \ˈpe-də-ˌgrē\ *n* [ME *pedegru*, fr. AF *pé de grue*, lit., crane's foot; fr. the shape made by the lines of a genealogical chart] **1** : a record of a line of ancestors **2** : an ancestral line — **ped·i·greed** \-ˌgrēd\ *adj*

**ped·i·ment** \ˈpe-də-mənt\ *n* : a low trian-gular gablelike decoration (as over a door or window) on a building

**pe·dom·e·ter** \pi-ˈdä-mə-tər\ *n* : an in-strument that measures the distance one walks

**pe·do·phile** \ˈpe-də-ˌfī(-ə)l, ˈpē-\ *n* : one affected with pedophilia

**pe·do·phil·ia** \ˌpe-də-ˈfi-lē-ə, ˌpē-\ *n* : sex-ual perversion in which children are the preferred sexual object

**pe·dun·cle** \ˈpē-ˌdəŋ-kəl\ *n* : a narrow supporting stalk

**peek** \ˈpēk\ *vb* **1** : to look furtively **2** : to peer from a place of concealment **3** : GLANCE — **peek** *n*

¹**peel** \ˈpēl\ *vb* [ME *pelen*, fr. AF *peler*, fr. L *pilare* to remove the hair from, fr. *pilus* hair] **1** : to strip the skin, bark, or rind from **2** : to strip off (as a coat); *also* : to come off **3** : to lose the skin, bark, or rind

²**peel** *n* : a skin or rind esp. of a fruit

**peel·ing** \ˈpē-liŋ\ *n* : a peeled-off piece or strip (as of skin or rind)

**peen** \ˈpēn\ *n* : the usu. hemispherical or wedge-shaped end of the head of a ham-mer opposite the face

¹**peep** \ˈpēp\ *vb* : to utter a feeble shrill sound or the slightest sound

²**peep** *n* : a feeble shrill sound

³**peep** *vb* **1** : to look slyly esp. through an aperture : PEEK **2** : to begin to emerge **3** : to look at : WATCH — **peep·er** *n*

⁴**peep** *n* **1** : a first faint appearance **2** : a brief or furtive look

**peep·hole** \ˈpēp-ˌhōl\ *n* : a hole to peep through

¹**peer** \ˈpir\ *n* **1** : one of equal standing with another : EQUAL **2** : NOBLE — **peer·age** \-ij\ *n*

²**peer** *vb* **1** : to look intently or curiously **2** : to come slightly into view

**peer·ess** \ˈpir-əs\ *n* : a woman who is a peer

**peer·less** \ˈpir-ləs\ *adj* : having no equal : MATCHLESS ⟨a ∼ cellist⟩ ♦ **Syn-onyms** SUPREME, UNEQUALED, UNPAR-ALLELED, INCOMPARABLE

¹**peeve** \ˈpēv\ *vb* **peeved; peev·ing** : to make resentful : ANNOY

²**peeve** *n* **1** : a feeling or mood of resent-ment **2** : a particular grievance

**pee·vish** \ˈpē-vish\ *adj* : querulous in temperament : FRETFUL ♦ **Synonyms** IRRITABLE, PETULANT, HUFFY — **pee·vish·ly** *adv* — **pee·vish·ness** *n*

**pee·wee** \ˈpē-(ˌ)wē\ *n* **1** : one that is di-minutive or tiny **2** : a level of sports usu. for young children — **peewee** *adj*

¹**peg** \ˈpeg\ *n* **1** : a small pointed piece (as of wood) used to pin down or fasten things or to fit into holes **2** : a projecting piece used as a support or boundary marker **3** : SUPPORT, PRETEXT **4** : STEP, DEGREE **5** : THROW

²**peg** *vb* **pegged; peg·ging 1** : to put a peg into : fasten, pin down, or attach with or as if with pegs **2** : to work hard and steadily : PLUG **3** : HUSTLE **4** : to mark by pegs **5** : to hold (as prices) at a set level or rate **6** : IDENTIFY ⟨was *pegged* as an intellectual⟩ **7** : THROW

**PEI** *abbr* Prince Edward Island

**pei·gnoir** \pān-ˈwär, pen-\ *n* [F, lit., gar-ment worn while combing the hair, fr. MF, fr. *peigner* to comb the hair, fr. L *pectinare*, fr. *pectin-*, *pecten* comb] : NEG-LIGEE

¹**pe·jo·ra·tive** \pi-ˈjòr-ə-tiv\ *n* : a pejorative word or phrase

²**pejorative** *adj* : having negative connota-tions : DISPARAGING — **pe·jo·ra·tive·ly** *adv*

**peke** \ˈpēk\ *n, often cap* : PEKINGESE

**Pe·king·ese** *or* **Pe·kin·ese** \ˌpē-kə-ˈnēz, -ˈnēs; -kiŋ-ˈēz, -ˈēs\ *n, pl* **Pekingese** *or* **Pekinese** : any of a breed of Chinese origin of small short-legged long-haired dogs

**pe·koe** \ˈpē-(ˌ)kō\ *n* : a black tea made from young tea leaves

**pel·age** \ˈpe-lij\ *n* : the hairy covering of a mammal

**pe·lag·ic** \pə-ˈla-jik\ *adj* : OCEANIC

**pelf** \'pelf\ *n* : MONEY, RICHES

**pel·i·can** \'pe-li-kən\ *n* : any of a genus of large web-footed birds having a pouched lower bill used to scoop in fish

**pel·la·gra** \pə-'la-grə, -'lä-\ *n* : a disease caused by a diet with too little niacin and protein and marked by a skin rash, disease of the digestive system, and mental disturbances

**pel·let** \'pe-lot\ *n* **1** : a little ball (as of medicine) **2** : BULLET — **pel·let·al** \-lə-təl\ *adj* — **pel·let·ize** \-ˌtīz\ *vb*

**pell-mell** \'pel-'mel\ *adv* **1** : in mingled confusion ⟨papers strewn ~ on the desk⟩ **2** : HEADLONG ⟨ran ~ for the door⟩

**pel·lu·cid** \pə-'lü-səd\ *adj* : extremely clear : LIMPID, TRANSPARENT ⟨a ~ stream⟩ ♦ *Synonyms* TRANSLUCENT, LUCID, LUCENT

**pe·lo·ton** \ˌpe-lə-'tän\ *n* : the main body of riders in a bicycle race

**¹pelt** \'pelt\ *n* : a skin esp. of a fur-bearing animal

**²pelt** *vb* : to strike with a succession of blows or missiles

**pel·vis** \'pel-vəs\ *n*, *pl* **pel·vis·es** \-və-səz\ *or* **pel·ves** \-ˌvēz\ : a basin-shaped part of the vertebrate skeleton consisting of the large bone of each hip and the nearby bones of the spine — **pel·vic** \-vik\ *adj*

**pem·mi·can** *also* **pem·i·can** \'pe-mi-kən\ *n* : dried meat pounded fine and mixed with melted fat

**¹pen** \'pen\ *vb* **penned; pen·ning** : to shut in or as if in a pen

**²pen** *n* **1** : a small enclosure for animals **2** : a small place of confinement or storage

**³pen** *n* **1** : an implement for writing or drawing with ink or a similar fluid **2** : a writing instrument regarded as a means of expression **3** : STYLUS 3

**⁴pen** *vb* **penned; pen·ning** : WRITE

**⁵pen** *n* : PENITENTIARY

**⁶pen** *abbr* peninsula

**PEN** *abbr* International Association of Poets, Playwrights, Editors, Essayists and Novelists

**pe·nal** \'pē-nᵊl\ *adj* : of or relating to punishment

**pe·nal·ise** *Brit var of* PENALIZE

**pe·nal·ize** \'pē-nə-ˌlīz, 'pe-\ *vb* **-ized; -iz·ing** : to put a penalty on

**pen·al·ty** \'pe-nᵊl-tē\ *n*, *pl* **-ties** **1** : punishment for crime or offense **2** : something forfeited when a person fails to do something agreed to **3** : disadvantage, loss, or hardship (as to a competitor) due to some action

**pen·ance** \'pe-nəns\ *n* **1** : an act performed to show sorrow or repentance for sin **2** : a sacrament (as in the Roman Catholic Church) consisting of confession, absolution, and a penance directed by the confessor

**pence** \'pens\ *pl of* PENNY

**pen·chant** \'pen-chənt\ *n* [F, fr. prp. of *pencher* to incline, fr. VL *\*pendicare*, fr. L *pendere* to weigh] : a strong inclination : LIKING ⟨a ~ for taking risks⟩ ♦ *Synonyms* LEANING, PROPENSITY, PREDILECTION, PREDISPOSITION

**¹pen·cil** \'pen-səl\ *n* : a writing or drawing tool consisting of or containing a slender cylinder of a solid marking substance

**²pencil** *vb* **-ciled** *or* **-cilled; -cil·ing** *or* **-cil·ling** **1** : to draw or write with a pencil **2** : to plan or designate tentatively ⟨~ed in the appointment⟩

**pen·dant** *also* **pen·dent** \'pen-dənt\ *n* : a hanging ornament (as on a necklace)

**pen·dent** *or* **pen·dant** \'pen-dənt\ *adj* : SUSPENDED, OVERHANGING

**¹pend·ing** \'pen-diŋ\ *prep* **1** : DURING **2** : while awaiting ⟨~ approval⟩

**²pending** *adj* **1** : not yet decided ⟨a ~ application⟩ **2** : IMMINENT

**pen·du·lous** \'pen-jə-ləs, -də-\ *adj* : hanging loosely : DROOPING ⟨~ earrings⟩

**pen·du·lum** \-ləm\ *n* : a body that swings freely from a fixed point

**pe·ne·plain** *also* **pe·ne·plane** \'pē-ni-ˌplān\ *n* : a large almost flat land surface shaped by erosion

**pen·e·trate** \'pe-nə-ˌtrāt\ *vb* **-trat·ed; -trat·ing** **1** : to enter into : PIERCE **2** : PERMEATE **3** : to see into : UNDERSTAND **4** : to affect deeply — **pen·e·tra·ble** \-trə-bəl\ *adj* — **pen·e·tra·tion** \ˌpe-nə-'trā-shən\ *n* — **pen·e·tra·tive** \'pe-nə-ˌtrā-tiv\ *adj*

**penetrating** *adj* **1** : having the power of entering, piercing, or pervading ⟨a ~ shriek⟩ ⟨a ~ odor⟩ **2** : ACUTE, DISCERNING ⟨a ~ look⟩

**pen·guin** \'peŋ-gwən, 'pen-\ *n* : any of various erect short-legged flightless seabirds of the southern hemisphere

**pen·i·cil·lin** \ˌpe-nə-'si-lən\ *n* : any of several antibiotics produced by molds or synthetically and used against various bacteria

**pen·in·su·la** \pə-'nin-sə-lə\ *n* [L *paeninsula*, fr. *paene* almost + *insula* island] : a long narrow portion of land extending out into the water — **pen·in·su·lar** \-lər\ *adj*

**pe·nis** \'pē-nəs\ *n*, *pl* **pe·nis·es** *also* **pe·nes** \-ˌnez\ : a male organ of copulation that in the human male also functions as the channel by which urine leaves the body

**¹pen·i·tent** \'pe-nə-tənt\ *adj* : feeling sorrow for sins or offenses : REPENTANT — **pen·i·tence** \-təns\ *n* — **pen·i·ten·tial** \ˌpe-nə-'ten-chəl\ *adj*

**²penitent** *n* : a penitent person

**¹pen·i·ten·tia·ry** \ˌpe-nə-'ten-chə-rē\ *n*, *pl* **-ries** : a state or federal prison

**²penitentiary** *adj* : of, relating to, or incurring confinement in a penitentiary

**pen·knife** \'pen-ˌnīf\ *n* : a small pocketknife

**pen·light** *also* **pen·lite** \-ˌlīt\ *n* : a small flashlight resembling a fountain pen in size or shape

**pen·man** \'pen-mən\ *n* **1** : COPYIST **2** : one skilled in penmanship **3** : AUTHOR

**pen·man·ship** \-ˌship\ *n* : the art or practice of writing with the pen

**Penn** *or* **Penna** *abbr* Pennsylvania

**pen name** *n* : an author's pseudonym

**pen·nant** \'pe-nənt\ *n* **1** : a tapering flag

used esp. for signaling **2** : a flag symbolic of championship

**pen·ne** \'pe-nā\ *n* : short diagonally cut tubular pasta

**pen·ni** \'pe-nē\ *n, pl* **pen·nia** \-nē-ə\ *or* **pen·nis** \-nēz\ : a former monetary unit equal to ¹/₁₀₀ markka

**pen·non** \'pe-nən\ *n* **1** : a long narrow ribbonlike flag borne on a lance **2** : WING

**Penn·syl·va·nian** \,pen-səl-'vā-nyən\ *adj* **1** : of or relating to Pennsylvania or its people **2** : of, relating to, or being the period of the Paleozoic era between the Mississippian and the Permian — **Pennsylvanian** *n*

**pen·ny** \'pe-nē\ *n, pl* **pennies** \-nēz\ *or* **pence** \'pens\ **1** *pl usu* **pence** : a British monetary unit formerly equal to ¹/₁₂ shilling but now equal to ¹/₁₀₀ pound; *also* : a coin of this value — see *pound* at MONEY table **2** *pl* **pennies** : a cent of the U.S. or Canada **3** : a former monetary unit equal to ¹/₁₀₀ Irish pound — **pen·ni·less** \'pe-ni-ləs\ *adj*

**pen·ny–pinch·ing** \'pe-nē-,pin-chiŋ\ *n* : PARSIMONY — **pen·ny–pinch·er** *n* — **penny–pinching** *adj*

**pen·ny·weight** \-,wāt\ *n* — see WEIGHT table

**pen·ny–wise** \-,wīz\ *adj* : wise or prudent only in small matters

**pe·nol·o·gy** \pi-'nä-lə-jē\ *n* : a branch of criminology dealing with prisons and the treatment of offenders

**¹pen·sion** \'pen-chən\ *n* : a fixed sum paid regularly esp. to a person retired from service

**²pension** *vb* : to pay a pension to — **pen·sion·er** *n*

**pen·sive** \'pen-siv\ *adj* : musingly, dreamily, or sadly thoughtful ♦ *Synonyms* REFLECTIVE, SPECULATIVE, CONTEMPLATIVE, MEDITATIVE — **pen·sive·ly** *adv*

**pen·stock** \'pen-,stäk\ *n* **1** : a sluice or gate for regulating a flow **2** : a pipe for carrying water

**pent** \'pent\ *adj* : shut up : CONFINED

**pen·ta·gon** \'pen-tə-,gän\ *n* : a polygon of five angles and five sides — **pen·tag·o·nal** \pen-'ta-gə-nᵊl\ *adj*

**pen·tam·e·ter** \pen-'ta-mə-tər\ *n* : a line of verse containing five metrical feet

**pen·tath·lon** \pen-'tath-lən\ *n* : a composite athletic contest consisting of five events

**Pen·te·cost** \'pen-ti-,kȯst\ *n* : the 7th Sunday after Easter observed as a church festival commemorating the descent of the Holy Spirit on the apostles — **Pen·te·cos·tal** \,pen-ti-'käs-tᵊl\ *adj*

**Pentecostal** *n* : a member of a Christian religious body that stresses expressive worship, evangelism, and spiritual gifts — **Pen·te·cos·tal·ism** \,pen-ti-'käs-tə-,li-zəm\

**pent·house** \'pent-,haus\ *n* [alter. of ME *pentis*, fr. AF *apentiz*, fr. *apent*, pp. of *apendre* to attach, hang against] **1** : a shed or sloping roof attached to a wall or

building **2** : an apartment built on the top floor or roof of a building

**pen·ul·ti·mate** \pi-'nəl-tə-mət\ *adj* : next to the last ⟨~ syllable⟩

**pen·um·bra** \pə-'nəm-brə\ *n, pl* **-brae** \-(,)brē\ *or* **-bras** **1** : the partial shadow surrounding a complete shadow (as in an eclipse) **2** : something that covers or obscures ⟨a ~ of secrecy⟩

**pe·nu·ri·ous** \pə-'nùr-ē-əs, -'nyùr-\ *adj* **1** : marked by penury **2** : MISERLY ♦ *Synonyms* STINGY, CLOSE, TIGHTFISTED, PARSIMONIOUS

**pen·u·ry** \'pe-nyə-rē\ *n* **1** : extreme poverty **2** : extreme frugality

**pe·on** \'pē-,än, -ən\ *n, pl* **peons** *or* **pe·o·nes** \pā-'ō-nēz\ **1** : a member of the landless laboring class in Spanish America **2** : one bound to service for payment of a debt — **pe·on·age** \-ə-nij\ *n*

**pe·o·ny** \'pē-ə-nē\ *n, pl* **-nies** : any of a genus of chiefly Eurasian plants with large often double red, pink, or white flowers; *also* : the flower

**¹peo·ple** \'pē-pəl\ *n, pl* **people** [ME *peple*, fr. AF *peple, peuple,* fr. L *populus*] **1** *pl* : human beings making up a group or linked by a common characteristic or interest **2** *pl* : human beings — often used in compounds instead of *persons* ⟨sales-*people*⟩ or attributively ⟨~ skills⟩ **3** *pl* : the mass of persons in a community : POPULACE; *also* : ELECTORATE ⟨the ~'s choice⟩ **4** *pl* **peoples** : a body of persons (as a tribe, nation, or race) united by a common culture, sense of kinship, or political organization

**²people** *vb* **peo·pled; peo·pling** : to supply or fill with or as if with people

**¹pep** \'pep\ *n* : brisk energy or initiative — **pep·py** *adj*

**²pep** *vb* **pepped; pep·ping** : to put pep into : STIMULATE ⟨~ the team up⟩

**¹pep·per** \'pe-pər\ *n* **1** : either of two pungent condiments from the berry (**pep·per·corn** \-,kȯrn\) of an Indian climbing plant : BLACK PEPPER, WHITE PEPPER; *also* : this plant **2** : a plant related to the tomato and widely grown for its hot or mild sweet fruit; *also* : this fruit

**²pepper** *vb* **pep·pered; pep·per·ing** **1** : to shower with missiles or rapid blows **2** : to sprinkle or season with or as if with pepper **3** : to deliver something in rapid succession ⟨~ed him with questions⟩

**pep·per·mint** \-,mint, -mənt\ *n* : a pungent aromatic mint; *also* : candy flavored with its oil

**pep·per·o·ni** \,pe-pə-'rō-nē\ *n* : a highly seasoned beef and pork sausage

**pepper spray** *n* : a temporarily disabling aerosol that causes irritation and blinding of the eyes and inflammation of the nose, throat, and skin

**pep·pery** \'pe-pə-rē\ *adj* **1** : having the qualities of pepper : PUNGENT, HOT **2** : having a hot temper **3** : FIERY

**pep·sin** \'pep-sən\ *n* : an enzyme of the stomach that promotes digestion by breaking down proteins; *also* : a preparation of this used medicinally

**pep·tic** \'pep-tik\ *adj* [L *pepticus*, fr. Gk

*peptikos,* fr *peptos* cooked, *peptein* to cook, digest] **1** : relating to or promoting digestion **2** : caused by digestive juices ⟨a ~ ulcer⟩

**pep·tide** \'pep-,tīd\ *n* : any of various organic compounds composed of two or more amino acids bonded together

**Pe·quot** \'pē-,kwät\ *n* : a member of an American Indian people of eastern Connecticut

**¹per** \'pər\ *prep* **1** : by means of **2** : to or for each **3** : ACCORDING TO

**²per** *adv* : for each : APIECE

**³per** *abbr* **1** period **2** person

**¹per·ad·ven·ture** \'pər-əd-ə,ven-chər\ *adv, archaic* : PERHAPS

**²peradventure** *n* **1** : DOUBT **2** : CHANCE 4

**per·am·bu·late** \pə-'ram-byə-,lāt\ *vb* -lat·ed; -lat·ing : to travel over esp. on foot — **per·am·bu·la·tion** \-,ram-byə-'lā-shən\ *n*

**per·am·bu·la·tor** \pə-'ram-byə-,lā-tər\ *n, chiefly Brit* : a baby carriage

**per an·num** \(,)pər-'a-nəm\ *adv* [ML] : in or for each year : ANNUALLY

**per·cale** \(,)pər-'kāl, 'pər-,; (,)pər-'kal\ *n* : a fine woven cotton cloth

**per cap·i·ta** \(,)pər-'ka-pə-tə\ *adv or adj* [ML, by heads] : by or for each person

**per·ceive** \pər-'sēv\ *vb* **per·ceived; per·ceiv·ing 1** : to attain awareness : REALIZE **2** : to become aware of through the senses — **per·ceiv·able** *adj*

**¹per·cent** \pər-'sent\ *adv* [*per* + L *centum* hundred] : in each hundred

**²percent** *n, pl* **percent** *or* **percents 1** : one part in a hundred : HUNDREDTH **2** : PERCENTAGE

**per·cent·age** \pər-'sen-tij\ *n* **1** : a part of a whole expressed in hundredths **2** : the result obtained by multiplying a number by a percent **3** : ADVANTAGE, PROFIT **4** : PROBABILITY; *also* : favorable odds

**percentage point** *n* : one hundredth of a whole ⟨rates rose one *percentage point* from 6.5 to 7.5 percent⟩

**per·cen·tile** \pər-'sen-,tī(-ə)l\ *n* : a value on a scale of one hundred indicating the standing of a score or grade in terms of the percentage of scores or grades falling with or below it

**per·cept** \'pər-,sept\ *n* : an impression of an object obtained by use of the senses

**per·cep·ti·ble** \pər-'sep-tə-bəl\ *adj* : capable of being perceived ⟨a barely ~ light⟩ — **per·cep·ti·bly** \-blē\ *adv*

**per·cep·tion** \pər-'sep-shən\ *n* **1** : an act or result of perceiving **2** : awareness of one's environment through physical sensation **3** : ability to understand : INSIGHT, COMPREHENSION ♦ *Synonyms* PENETRATION, DISCERNMENT, DISCRIMINATION

**per·cep·tive** \pər-'sep-tiv\ *adj* : capable of or exhibiting keen perception : OBSERVANT — **per·cep·tive·ly** *adv*

**per·cep·tu·al** \pər-'sep-chə-wəl\ *adj* : of, relating to, or involving sensory response as opposed to abstract concept ⟨~ stimulation⟩ — **per·cep·tu·al·ly** *adv*

**¹perch** \'pərch\ *n* **1** : a roost for a bird **2** : a high station or vantage point

**²perch** *vb* : ROOST

**³porch** *n, pl* **perch** *or* **perch·es** : either of two small freshwater bony fishes used for food; *also* : any of various fishes resembling or related to these

**per·chance** \pər-'chans\ *adv* : PERHAPS

**per·cip·i·ent** \pər-'si-pē-ənt\ *adj* : capable of or characterized by perception — **per·cip·i·ence** \-əns\ *n*

**per·co·late** \'pər-kə-,lāt\ *vb* -lat·ed; -lat·ing **1** : to trickle or filter through a permeable substance **2** : to filter hot water through to extract the essence ⟨~ coffee⟩ — **per·co·la·tor** \-,lā-tər\ *n*

**per con·tra** \(,)pər-'kän-trə\ *adv* [It, by the opposite side (of the ledger)] **1** : on the contrary **2** : by way of contrast

**per·cus·sion** \pər-'kə-shən\ *n* **1** : a sharp blow : IMPACT; *esp* : a blow upon a cap (**percussion cap**) designed to explode the charge in a firearm **2** : the beating or striking of a musical instrument; *also* : instruments sounded by striking, shaking, or scraping

**per di·em** \pər-'dē-əm, -'dī-\ *adv* [ML] : by the day — **per diem** *adj or n*

**per·di·tion** \pər-'di-shən\ *n* **1** : eternal damnation **2** : HELL

**per·du·ra·ble** \(,)pər-'dur-ə-bəl, -'dyur-\ *adj* : very durable — **per·du·ra·bil·i·ty** \-,dur-ə-'bi-lə-tē, -,dyur-\ *n*

**père** \'per\ *n* [F, fr. OF *paire, perre,* fr. L *pater*] FATHER — used after a name to distinguish a father from a son

**per·e·gri·na·tion** \,per-ə-grə-'nā-shən\ *n* : a traveling about esp. on foot

**per·e·grine falcon** \'per-ə-grən, -,grēn\ *n* : a swift nearly cosmopolitan falcon that often nests in cities and is often used in falconry

**pe·remp·to·ry** \pə-'remp-tə-rē\ *adj* **1** : barring a right of action or delay **2** : expressive of urgency or command : IMPERATIVE **3** : marked by arrogant self-assurance ♦ *Synonyms* IMPERIOUS, MASTERFUL, DOMINEERING, MAGISTERIAL — **pe·remp·to·ri·ly** \-tə-rə-lē\ *adv*

**¹pe·ren·ni·al** \pə-'re-nē-əl\ *adj* **1** : present at all seasons of the year ⟨~ streams⟩ **2** : continuing to live from year to year ⟨~ plants⟩ **3** : recurring regularly : PERMANENT ⟨~ problems⟩ ♦ *Synonyms* LASTING, PERPETUAL, ENDURING, EVERLASTING — **pe·ren·ni·al·ly** *adv*

**²perennial** *n* : a perennial plant

**perf** *abbr* **1** perfect **2** perforated

**¹per·fect** \'pər-fikt\ *adj* **1** : being without fault or defect **2** : EXACT, PRECISE **3** : COMPLETE **4** : relating to or being a verb tense that expresses an action or state completed at the time of speaking or at a time spoken of — **per·fect·ly** *adv* — **per·fect·ness** *n*

**²per·fect** \pər-'fekt\ *vb* : to make perfect

**³per·fect** \'pər-fikt\ *n* : the perfect tense; *also* : a verb form in it

**per·fect·ible** \pər-'fek-tə-bəl, 'pər-fik-\ *adj* : capable of improvement or perfection — **per·fect·ibil·i·ty** \pər-,fek-tə-'bi-lə-tē, ,pər-fik-\ *n*

**per·fec·tion** \pər-'fek-shən\ n  1 : the quality or state of being perfect  2 : the highest degree of excellence  3 : the act or process of perfecting

**per·fec·tion·ist** \-shə-nist\ n : a person who will not accept or be content with anything less than perfection

**per·fec·to** \pər-'fek-tō\ n, pl -tos : a cigar that is thick in the middle and tapers almost to a point at each end

**per·fi·dy** \'pər-fə-dē\ n, pl -dies [L perfidia, fr. perfidus faithless, fr. per- detrimental to + fides faith] : violation of faith or loyalty : TREACHERY — **per·fid·i·ous** \pər-'fi-dē-əs\ adj — **per·fid·i·ous·ly** adv

**per·fo·rate** \'pər-fə-ˌrāt\ vb -rat·ed; -rat·ing : to bore through : PIERCE; esp : to make a line of holes in to facilitate separation — **per·fo·ra·tion** \ˌpər-fə-'rā-shən\ n

**per·force** \pər-'fȯrs\ adv : of necessity ⟨we attended ∼⟩

**per·form** \pər-'fȯrm\ vb  1 : FULFILL  2 : CARRY OUT, DO  3 : FUNCTION  4 : to do in a set manner  5 : to give a performance — **per·form·er** n

**per·for·mance** \pər-'fȯr-məns\ n  1 : the act or process of performing  2 : DEED, FEAT  3 : a public presentation

¹**per·fume** \pər-'fyüm, 'pər-ˌfyüm\ n  1 : a usu. pleasant odor : FRAGRANCE  2 : a preparation used for scenting

²**per·fume** \pər-'fyüm, 'pər-ˌfyüm\ vb per·fumed; per·fum·ing : SCENT

**per·fum·ery** \pər-'fyü-mə-rē\ n, pl -er·ies  1 : the art or process of making perfume  2 : PERFUMES  3 : an establishment where perfumes are made

**per·func·to·ry** \pər-'fəŋk-tə-rē\ adj : done merely as a duty — **per·func·to·ri·ly** adv

**per·go·la** \'pər-gə-lə\ n [It] : a structure consisting of posts supporting an open roof in the form of a trellis

**perh** abbr perhaps

**per·haps** \pər-'haps\ adv : possibly but not certainly

**per·i·gee** \'per-ə-ˌjē\ n [MF, fr. NL perigeum, fr. Gk perigeion, fr. peri around, near + gē earth] : the point at which an orbiting object is nearest the body (as the earth) being orbited

**peri·he·lion** \ˌper-ə-'hēl-yən\ n, pl -he·lia \-'hēl-yə\ : the point in the path of a celestial body (as a planet) that is nearest the sun

**per·il** \'per-əl\ n : DANGER; also : a source of danger : RISK — **per·il·ous** adj — **per·il·ous·ly** adv

**pe·rim·e·ter** \pə-'ri-mə-tər\ n  1 : the boundary of a closed plane figure; also : its length  2 : a line bounding or protecting an area

**peri·na·tal** \ˌper-ə-'nā-tᵊl\ adj : occurring in, concerned with, or being in the period around the time of birth ⟨∼ care⟩

¹**pe·ri·od** \'pir-ē-əd\ n [ultim. fr. Gk periodos circuit, period of time, rhetorical period, fr. peri around + hodos way]  1 : SENTENCE; also : the full pause closing the utterance of a sentence : END, STOP  3 : a punctuation mark . used esp. to mark the end of a declarative sentence or an abbreviation  4 : an extent of time; esp : one regarded as a stage or division in a process or development  5 : a portion of time in which a recurring phenomenon completes one cycle and is ready to begin again  6 : a single cyclic occurrence of menstruation

²**period** adj : of or relating to a particular historical period ⟨∼ furniture⟩

**pe·ri·od·ic** \ˌpir-ē-'ä-dik\ adj  1 : occurring at regular intervals of time  2 : happening repeatedly  3 : of or relating to a sentence that has no trailing elements following full grammatical statement of the essential idea

¹**pe·ri·od·i·cal** \ˌpir-ē-'ä-di-kəl\ adj  1 : PERIODIC  2 : published at regular intervals  3 : of or relating to a periodical — **pe·ri·od·i·cal·ly** \-k(ə-)lē\ adv

²**periodical** n : a periodical publication

**periodic table** n : an arrangement of chemical elements based on their atomic structure and on their properties

**peri·odon·tal** \ˌper-ē-ō-'dän-tᵊl\ adj  1 : surrounding a tooth  2 : of or affecting periodontal tissues or regions

**per·i·pa·tet·ic** \ˌper-ə-pə-'te-tik\ adj : performed or performing while moving about : ITINERANT ⟨∼ salesmen⟩

**pe·riph·er·al** \pə-'ri-fər-əl\ n : a device connected to a computer to provide communication or auxiliary functions

**peripheral nervous system** n : the part of the nervous system that is outside the central nervous system and comprises the spinal nerves, the cranial nerves except the one supplying the retina, and the autonomic nervous system

**pe·riph·ery** \pə-'ri-fə-rē\ n, pl -er·ies  1 : the boundary of a rounded figure  2 : outward bounds : border area — **pe·riph·er·al** \-fə-rəl\ adj

**pe·riph·ra·sis** \pə-'ri-frə-səs\ n, pl -ra·ses \-ˌsēz\ : CIRCUMLOCUTION

**peri·scope** \'per-ə-ˌskōp\ n : a tubular optical instrument enabling an observer to see an otherwise blocked field of view

**per·ish** \'per-ish\ vb : to become destroyed or ruined : cease to exist

**per·ish·able** \'per-i-shə-bəl\ adj : easily spoiled ⟨∼ foods⟩ — **perishable** n

**peri·stal·sis** \ˌper-ə-'stȯl-səs, -'stal-\ n, pl -stal·ses : waves of contraction passing along the walls of a hollow muscular organ (as the intestine) and forcing its contents onward — **per·i·stal·tic** \-'stȯl-tik, -'stal-\ adj

**peri·style** \'per-ə-ˌstīl\ n : a row of columns surrounding a building or court

**peri·to·ne·um** \ˌper-ə-tə-'nē-əm\ n, pl -ne·ums or -nea : the smooth transparent serous membrane that lines the cavity of the abdomen — **peri·to·ne·al** \-'nē-əl\ adj

**peri·to·ni·tis** \ˌper-ə-tə-'nī-təs\ n : inflammation of the peritoneum

**peri·wig** \'per-i-ˌwig\ n : WIG

¹**per·i·win·kle** \'per-i-ˌwiŋ-kəl\ n : a usu. blue-flowered creeping plant cultivated as a ground cover

# PERIODIC TABLE

This is the common long form of the table, with atomic numbers given along with the symbols. Roman numerals and letters heading the vertical columns indicate the groups. (There are differences of opinion regarding the letter designations, but those given here are probably the most generally used. International standards favor numbering the groups 1-18 from left to right using Arabic numerals, but the designations shown below remain quite common.) Horizontal rows represent the periods, with two very long periods removed from the two very long periods and represented below the main table.

| IA[1] | IIA[2] | | | | | | | | | | | IIIA | IVA | VA | VIA | VIIA[3] | VIIIA[4] |
|---|---|---|---|---|---|---|---|---|---|---|---|---|---|---|---|---|---|
| 1 H | | | | | | | | | | | | | | | | 1 H | 2 He |
| 3 Li | 4 Be | | | | | | | | | | | 5 B | 6 C | 7 N | 8 O | 9 F | 10 Ne |
| 11 Na | 12 Mg | IIIB | IVB | VB | VIB | VIIB | | VIII | | IB | IIB | 13 Al | 14 Si | 15 P | 16 S | 17 Cl | 18 Ar |
| 19 K | 20 Ca | 21 Sc | 22 Ti | 23 V | 24 Cr | 25 Mn | 26 Fe | 27 Co | 28 Ni | 29 Cu | 30 Zn | 31 Ga | 32 Ge | 33 As | 34 Se | 35 Br | 36 Kr |
| 37 Rb | 38 Sr | 39 Y | 40 Zr | 41 Nb | 42 Mo | 43 Tc | 44 Ru | 45 Rh | 46 Pd | 47 Ag | 48 Cd | 49 In | 50 Sn | 51 Sb | 52 Te | 53 I | 54 Xe |
| 55 Cs | 56 Ba | 57 *La | 72 Hf | 73 Ta | 74 W | 75 Re | 76 Os | 77 Ir | 78 Pt | 79 Au | 80 Hg | 81 Tl | 82 Pb | 83 Bi | 84 Po | 85 At | 86 Rn |
| 87 Fr | 88 Ra | 89 #Ac | 104 Rf | 105 Db | 106 Sg | 107 Bh | 108 Hs | 109 Mt | 110 Ds | 111 Rg | 112 Cn | | | | | | |

| *LANTHANIDE SERIES | 58 Ce | 59 Pr | 60 Nd | 61 Pm | 62 Sm | 63 Eu | 64 Gd | 65 Tb | 66 Dy | 67 Ho | 68 Er | 69 Tm | 70 Yb | 71 Lu |
|---|---|---|---|---|---|---|---|---|---|---|---|---|---|---|
| #ACTINIDE SERIES | 90 Th | 91 Pa | 92 U | 93 Np | 94 Pu | 95 Am | 96 Cm | 97 Bk | 98 Cf | 99 Es | 100 Fm | 101 Md | 102 No | 103 Lr |

[1] Group IA (excluding hydrogen) comprises the alkali metals.
[2] Group IIA comprises the alkaline earth metals.
[3] Group VIIA (excluding hydrogen) comprises the halogens.
[4] Group VIIIA (also called group Zero) comprises the noble gases.

²**periwinkle** *n* : any of various small edible seashore snails

**per·ju·ry** \'pər-jə-rē\ *n* : the voluntary violation of an oath to tell the truth : lying under oath — **per·jure** \'pər-jər\ *vb* — **per·jur·er** *n*

¹**perk** \'pərk\ *vb* **1** : to thrust (as the head) up impudently or jauntily **2** : to regain vigor or spirit **3** : to make trim or brisk : FRESHEN — **perky** *adj*

²**perk** *vb* : PERCOLATE

³**perk** *n* : PERQUISITE — usu. used in pl.

**per·lite** \'pər-ˌlīt\ *n* : volcanic glass that when expanded by heat forms a lightweight material used esp. in concrete and plaster and for potting plants

¹**perm** \'pərm\ *n* : PERMANENT

²**perm** *vb* : to give (hair) a permanent

³**perm** *abbr* permanent

**per·ma·frost** \'pər-mə-ˌfròst\ *n* : a permanently frozen layer below the surface in frigid regions of a planet

¹**per·ma·nent** \'pər-mə-nənt\ *adj* : LASTING, STABLE — **per·ma·nence** \-nəns\ *n* — **per·ma·nen·cy** \-nən-sē\ *n* — **per·ma·nent·ly** *adv*

²**permanent** *n* : a long-lasting hair wave or straightening

**permanent press** *n* : the process of treating fabrics with chemicals (as resin) and heat for setting the shape and for aiding wrinkle resistance

**per·me·able** \'pər-mē-ə-bəl\ *adj* : having small openings that permit liquids or gases to seep through — **per·me·abil·i·ty** \ˌpər-mē-ə-'bi-lə-tē\ *n*

**per·me·ate** \'pər-mē-ˌāt\ *vb* **-at·ed; -at·ing 1** : PERVADE **2** : to seep through the pores of : PENETRATE — **per·me·ation** \ˌpər-mē-'ā-shən\ *n*

**Perm·ian** \'pər-mē-ən\ *adj* : of, relating to, or being the latest period of the Paleozoic era — **Permian** *n*

**per·mis·si·ble** \pər-'mi-sə-bəl\ *adj* : that may be permitted : ALLOWABLE

**per·mis·sion** \pər-'mi-shən\ *n* : formal consent : AUTHORIZATION

**per·mis·sive** \pər-'mi-siv\ *adj* : granting permission; *esp* : INDULGENT — **per·mis·sive·ly** *adv* — **per·mis·sive·ness** *n*

¹**per·mit** \pər-'mit\ *vb* **per·mit·ted; per·mit·ting 1** : to consent to : ALLOW **2** : to make possible

²**per·mit** \'pər-ˌmit, pər-'mit\ *n* : a written permission : LICENSE ⟨a fishing ∼⟩

**per·mu·ta·tion** \ˌpər-myü-'tā-shən\ *n* **1** : a major or fundamental change **2** : the act or process of changing the order of an ordered set of objects ♦ *Synonyms* INNOVATION, MUTATION, VICISSITUDE

**per·ni·cious** \pər-'ni-shəs\ *adj* [ME, fr. AF, fr. L *perniciosus,* fr. *pernicies* destruction, fr. *per-* through + *nec-, nex* violent death] : very destructive or injurious ⟨a ∼ influence⟩ — **per·ni·cious·ly** *adv*

**per·ora·tion** \'per-ə-ˌrā-shən, 'pər-\ *n* : the concluding part of a speech

¹**per·ox·ide** \pə-'räk-ˌsīd\ *n* : an oxide containing a large proportion of oxygen; *esp* : HYDROGEN PEROXIDE

²**peroxide** *vb* **-id·ed; -id·ing** : to bleach with hydrogen peroxide

**perp** *abbr* **1** perpendicular **2** perpetrator

**per·pen·dic·u·lar** \ˌpər-pən-'di-kyə-lər\ *adj* **1** : standing at right angles to the plane of the horizon **2** : forming a right angle with each other or with a given line or plane — **perpendicular** *n* — **per·pen·dic·u·lar·i·ty** \-ˌdi-kyə-'la-rə-tē\ *n* — **per·pen·dic·u·lar·ly** *adv*

**per·pe·trate** \'pər-pə-ˌtrāt\ *vb* **-trat·ed; -trat·ing** : to carry out (as a crime) : COMMIT — **per·pe·tra·tion** \ˌpər-pə-'trā-shən\ *n* — **per·pe·tra·tor** \'pər-pə-ˌtrā-tər\ *n*

**per·pet·u·al** \pər-'pe-chə-wəl\ *adj* **1** : continuing forever : EVERLASTING **2** : occurring continually : CONSTANT ⟨∼ annoyance⟩ ♦ *Synonyms* CEASELESS, UNCEASING, CONTINUAL, CONTINUOUS, INCESSANT, UNREMITTING — **per·pet·u·al·ly** *adv*

**per·pet·u·ate** \pər-'pe-chə-ˌwāt\ *vb* **-at·ed; -at·ing** : to make perpetual : cause to last indefinitely ⟨∼ a belief⟩ — **per·pet·u·a·tion** \-ˌpe-chə-'wā-shən\ *n*

**per·pe·tu·i·ty** \ˌpər-pə-'tü-ə-tē, -'tyü-\ *n, pl* **-ties 1** : ETERNITY 1 **2** : the quality or state of being perpetual

**per·plex** \pər-'pleks\ *vb* : to disturb mentally; *esp* : CONFUSE — **per·plex·i·ty** \-'plek-sə-tē\ *n*

**per·plexed** \-'plekst\ *adj* **1** : filled with uncertainty : PUZZLED ⟨a ∼ look⟩ **2** : full of difficulty : COMPLICATED — **per·plexed·ly** \-'plek-səd-lē\ *adv*

**per·qui·site** \'pər-kwə-zət\ *n* : a privilege or profit beyond regular pay

**pers** *abbr* person; personal

¹**per se** \(ˌ)pər-'sā\ *adv* [L] : by, of, or in itself : as such

²**per se** *adj* : being such inherently, clearly, or as a matter of law

**per·se·cute** \'pər-si-ˌkyüt\ *vb* **-cut·ed; -cut·ing** : to pursue in such a way as to injure or afflict : HARASS; *esp* : to cause to suffer because of belief — **per·se·cu·tion** \ˌpər-si-'kyü-shən\ *n* — **per·se·cu·tor** \'pər-si-ˌkyü-tər\ *n*

**per·se·vere** \ˌpər-sə-'vir\ *vb* **-vered; -ver·ing** : to persist (as in an undertaking) in spite of difficulties — **per·se·ver·ance** \-'vir-əns\ *n*

**Per·sian** \'pər-zhən\ *n* **1** : a native or inhabitant of ancient Persia **2** : a member of one of the peoples of modern Iran **3** : the language of the Persians

**Persian cat** *n* : any of a breed of stocky round-headed domestic cats that have a long silky coat

**Persian lamb** *n* : a pelt with very silky tightly curled fur that is obtained from newborn lambs which are older than those yielding broadtail

**per·si·flage** \'pər-si-ˌfläzh, 'per-\ *n* [F, fr. *persifler* to banter, fr. *per-* thoroughly + *siffler* to whistle, hiss, boo, ultim. fr. L *sibilare*] : lightly jesting or mocking talk

**per·sim·mon** \pər-'si-mən\ *n* : either of two trees related to the ebony; *also* : the edible usu. orange or red plumlike fruit of a persimmon

**per·sist** \pər-'sist, -'zist\ *vb* **1** : to go on resolutely or stubbornly in spite of difficutlies **2** : to continue to exist — **per·sis·tence** \-'sis-təns, -'zis-\ *n* — **per·sis·ten·cy** \-tən-sē\ *n* — **per·sis·tent** \-tənt\ *adj* — **per·sis·tent·ly** *adv*

**per·snick·e·ty** \pər-'sni-kə-tē\ *adj* : fussy about small details

**per·son** \'pər-sən\ *n* [ME, fr. AF *persone*, fr. L *persona* actor's mask, character in a play, person, prob. fr. Etruscan *phersu* mask, fr. Gk *prosōpa*, pl. of *prosōpon* face, mask] **1** : a human being : INDI-VIDUAL — used in combination esp. by those who prefer to avoid *man* in compounds applicable to both sexes ⟨chair-*person*⟩ **2** : one of the three modes of being in the Godhead as understood by Trinitarians **3** : the body of a human being **4** : the individual personality of a human being : SELF **5** : reference of a segment of discourse to the speaker, to one spoken to, or to one spoken of esp. as indicated by certain pronouns

**per·so·na** \pər-'sō-nə\ *n, pl* **-nae** \-nē\ *or* **-nas** : the personality that a person projects in public

**per·son·able** \'pər-sə-nə-bəl\ *adj* : pleasant in person : ATTRACTIVE

**per·son·age** \'pər-sə-nij\ *n* : a person of rank, note, or distinction

**¹per·son·al** \'pər-sə-nəl\ *adj* **1** : of, relating to, or affecting a person : PRIVATE ⟨~ correspondence⟩ **2** : done in person ⟨a ~ inquiry⟩ **3** : relating to the person or body ⟨~ injuries⟩ **4** : relating to an individual esp. in an offensive way ⟨resented such ~ remarks⟩ **5** : of or relating to temporary or movable property as distinguished from real estate **6** : denoting grammatical person **7** : intended for use by one person ⟨a ~ stereo⟩

**²personal** *n* **1** : a short newspaper paragraph relating to a person or group or to personal matters **2** : a short personal or private communication in the classified ads section of a newspaper

**personal computer** *n* : a computer with a microprocessor designed for an individual user to run esp. commercial software

**personal digital assistant** *n* : PDA

**per·son·al·ise** *Brit var of* PERSONALIZE

**per·son·al·i·ty** \,pər-sə-'na-lə-tē\ *n, pl* **-ties 1** : an offensively personal remark ⟨indulges in *personalities*⟩ **2** : the collection of emotional and behavioral traits that characterize a person **3** : distinction of personal and social traits **4** : a well-known person ⟨a TV ~⟩ ◆ *Synonyms* INDIVIDUALITY, TEMPERAMENT, DISPO-SITION, MAKEUP

**per·son·al·ize** \'pər-sə-nə-,līz\ *vb* **-ized; -iz·ing** : to make personal or individual; *esp* : to mark as belonging to a particular person ⟨*personalized* stationery⟩

**per·son·al·ly** \-nə-lē\ *adv* **1** : in person **2** : as a person **3** : as far as oneself is concerned ⟨~, I don't want to go⟩

**per·son·al·ty** \'pər-sə-nəl-tē\ *n, pl* **-ties** : personal property

**per·so·na non gra·ta** \pər-,sō-nə-,nän-'grä-tə, -'grä-\ *adj* [L] : being personally unacceptable or unwelcome

**per·son·ate** \'pər-sə-,nāt\ *vb* **-at·ed; -at·ing** : IMPERSONATE, REPRESENT

**per·son·i·fy** \pər-'sä-nə-,fī\ *vb* **-fied; -fy·ing 1** : to think of or represent as a person **2** : to be the embodiment of : INCAR-NATE ⟨~ the law⟩ — **per·son·i·fi·ca·tion** \-,sä-nə-fə-'kā-shən\ *n*

**per·son·nel** \,pər-sə-'nel\ *n* : a body of persons employed

**per·spec·tive** \pər-'spek-tiv\ *n* **1** : the science of painting and drawing so that objects represented have apparent depth and distance **2** : the aspect in which a subject or its parts are mentally viewed; *esp* : a view of things (as objects or events) in their true relationship or relative importance

**per·spi·ca·cious** \,pər-spə-'kā-shəs\ *adj* : having or showing keen understanding or discernment ⟨a ~ observation⟩ — **per·spi·cac·i·ty** \-'ka-sə-tē\ *n*

**per·spic·u·ous** \pər-'spi-kyə-wəs\ *adj* : plain to the understanding ⟨a ~ argument⟩ — **per·spi·cu·i·ty** \,pər-spə-'kyü-ə-tē\ *n*

**per·spire** \pər-'spī(-ə)r\ *vb* **per·spired; per·spir·ing** : SWEAT — **per·spi·ra·tion** \,pər-spə-'rā-shən\ *n*

**per·suade** \pər-'swād\ *vb* **per·suad·ed; per·suad·ing** : to win over to a belief or course of action by argument or entreaty — **per·sua·sive** \-'swā-siv, -ziv\ *adj* — **per·sua·sive·ly** *adv* — **per·sua·sive·ness** *n*

**per·sua·sion** \pər-'swā-zhən\ *n* **1** : the act or process of persuading **2** : a system of religious beliefs; *also* : a group holding such beliefs

**pert** \'pərt\ *adj* [ME, evident, attractive, saucy, short for *apert* evident, fr. AF, fr. L *apertus* open, fr. pp. of *aperire* to open] **1** : saucily free and forward : IMPUDENT **2** : stylishly trim : JAUNTY **3** : LIVELY

**per·tain** \pər-'tān\ *vb* **1** : to belong to as a part, quality, or function ⟨duties ~ing to the office⟩ **2** : to have reference : RE-LATE ⟨books ~ing to birds⟩

**per·ti·na·cious** \,pər-tə-'nā-shəs\ *adj* **1** : holding resolutely to an opinion or purpose **2** : obstinately persistent ⟨a ~ bill collector⟩ ◆ *Synonyms* DOGGED, MUL-ISH, HEADSTRONG, PERVERSE — **per·ti·nac·i·ty** \-'na-sə-tē\ *n*

**per·ti·nent** \'pər-tə-nənt\ *adj* : relating to the matter under consideration ◆ *Syn-onyms* RELEVANT, GERMANE, APPLICA-BLE, APROPOS — **per·ti·nence** \-əns\ *n*

**per·turb** \pər-'tərb\ *vb* : to disturb greatly esp. in mind : UPSET — **per·tur·ba·tion** \,pər-tər-'bā-shən\ *n*

**per·tus·sis** \pər-'tə-səs\ *n* : WHOOPING COUGH

**pe·ruke** \pə-'rük\ *n* : WIG

**pe·ruse** \pə-'rüz\ *vb* **pe·rused; pe·rus·ing** : READ; *esp* : to read over attentively or leisurely — **pe·rus·al** \-'rü-zəl\ *n*

**per·vade** \pər-'vād\ *vb* **per·vad·ed; per·vad·ing** : to spread through every part of : PERMEATE ⟨excitement *pervaded* the room⟩ — **per·va·sive** \-'vā-siv, -ziv\ *adj*

**per·verse** \pər-'vərs\ *adj* **1** : turned away from what is right or good : CORRUPT **2**

: obstinate in opposing what is reasonable or accepted 3 : marked by perversion — **per·verse·ly** adv — **per·verse·ness** n — **per·ver·si·ty** \-'vər-sə-tē\ n

**per·ver·sion** \pər-'vər-zhən\ n 1 : the action of perverting : the condition of being perverted 2 : a perverted form of something; esp : aberrant sexual behavior

¹**per·vert** \pər-'vərt\ vb 1 : to lead astray : CORRUPT ⟨∼ the young⟩ 2 : to divert to a wrong purpose : MISAPPLY ⟨∼ evidence⟩ ♦ **Synonyms** DEPRAVE, DEBASE, DEBAUCH, DEMORALIZE — **per·vert·er** n

²**per·vert** \'pər-,vərt\ n : one that is perverted; esp : one given to sexual perversion

**pe·se·ta** \pə-'sā-tə\ n : the former basic monetary unit of Spain

**pe·se·wa** \pə-'sā-wə\ n — see cedi at MONEY table

**pes·ky** \'pes-kē\ adj **pes·ki·er; -est** : causing annoyance : TROUBLESOME

**pe·so** \'pā-sō\ n, pl pesos — see MONEY table

**pes·si·mism** \'pe-sə-,mi-zəm\ n [F pessimisme, fr. L pessimus worst] : an inclination to take the least favorable view (as of events) or to expect the worst — **pes·si·mist** \-mist\ n — **pes·si·mis·tic** \,pe-sə-'mis-tik\ adj

**pest** \'pest\ n 1 : a destructive epidemic disease : PLAGUE 2 : a plant or animal detrimental to humans 3 : one that pesters : NUISANCE — **pesty** adj

**pes·ter** \'pes-tər\ vb : to harass with petty irritations : ANNOY

**pes·ti·cide** \'pes-tə-,sīd\ n : an agent used to destroy pests

**pes·tif·er·ous** \pes-'ti-fə-rəs\ adj 1 : PESTILENT ⟨∼ vermin⟩ 2 : ANNOYING

**pes·ti·lence** \'pes-tə-ləns\ n : a destructive infectious swiftly spreading disease; esp : BUBONIC PLAGUE

**pes·ti·lent** \-lənt\ adj 1 : dangerous to life : DEADLY 2 : PERNICIOUS, HARMFUL 3 : TROUBLESOME 4 : INFECTIOUS, CONTAGIOUS ⟨a ∼ disease⟩

**pes·ti·len·tial** \,pes-tə-'len-chəl\ adj 1 : causing or tending to cause pestilence : DEADLY 2 : morally harmful

**pes·tle** \'pes-əl, 'pes-t³l\ n : an implement for grinding substances in a mortar — **pestle** vb

¹**pet** \'pet\ n 1 : FAVORITE, DARLING 2 : a domesticated animal kept for pleasure rather than utility

²**pet** adj 1 : kept or treated as a pet ⟨∼ dog⟩ 2 : expressing fondness ⟨∼ name⟩ 3 : particularly liked or favored

³**pet** vb **pet·ted; pet·ting** 1 : to stroke gently or lovingly 2 : to make a pet of : PAMPER 3 : to engage in amorous kissing and caressing

⁴**pet** n : a fit of peevishness, sulkiness, or anger — **pet·tish** adj

**Pet** abbr Peter

**pet·al** \'pe-t³l\ n : one of the modified leaves of a flower's corolla

**pe·tard** \pə-'tärd, -'tär\ n : a case containing an explosive to break down a door or gate or breach a wall

**pe·ter** \'pē-tər\ vb : to diminish gradually and come to an end ⟨his energy ∼ed out⟩

**Pe·ter** \'pē-tər\ n — see BIBLE table

**pet·i·ole** \'pe-tē-,ōl\ n : a slender stem that supports a leaf

**pe·tite** \pə-'tēt\ adj [F] : small and trim of figure ⟨a ∼ woman⟩ — **petite** n

**pe·tit four** \,pe-tē-'fōr\ n, pl petits fours or petit fours \-'fōrz\ [F, lit., small oven] : a small cake cut from pound or sponge cake and frosted

¹**pe·ti·tion** \pə-'ti-shən\ n : an earnest request : ENTREATY; esp : a formal written request made to an authority

²**petition** vb : to make a request to or for — **pe·ti·tion·er** n

**pe·trel** \'pe-trəl\ n : any of numerous seabirds that fly far from land

**pe·tri dish** \'pē-trē-\ n 1 : a small shallow dish used esp. for growing bacteria 2 : something fostering development or innovation

**pet·ri·fy** \'pe-trə-,fī\ vb **-fied; -fy·ing** 1 : to convert (organic matter) into stone or stony material 2 : to make rigid or inactive (as from fear or awe) — **pet·ri·fac·tion** \,pe-trə-'fak-shən\ n

**pet·ro·chem·i·cal** \,pe-trō-'ke-mi-kəl\ n : a chemical isolated or derived from petroleum or natural gas — **pet·ro·chem·is·try** \-'ke-mə-strē\ n

**pet·rol** \'pe-trəl\ n, chiefly Brit : GASOLINE

**pet·ro·la·tum** \,pe-trə-'lā-təm\ n : PETROLEUM JELLY

**pe·tro·leum** \pə-'trō-lē-əm\ n [ML, fr. Gk petra rock + L oleum oil] : an oily flammable liquid obtained from wells drilled in the ground and refined into gasoline, fuel oils, and other products

**petroleum jelly** n : a tasteless, odorless, and oily or greasy substance from petroleum that is used esp. in ointments and dressings

¹**pet·ti·coat** \'pe-tē-,kōt\ n 1 : a skirt worn under a dress 2 : an outer skirt

²**petticoat** adj : of, relating to, or exercised by women : FEMALE

**pet·ti·fog·ger** \'pe-tē-,fò-gər, -,fä-\ n 1 : a lawyer whose methods are petty, underhanded, or disreputable 2 : one given to quibbling over trifles — **pet·ti·fog·ging** \-gin\ adj or n

**pet·ty** \'pe-tē\ adj **pet·ti·er; -est** [ME pety small, minor, alter. of petit, fr. AF, small] 1 : having secondary rank : MINOR ⟨∼ prince⟩ 2 : of little importance : TRIFLING ⟨∼ faults⟩ 3 : marked by narrowness or meanness — **pet·ti·ly** \'pe-tə-lē\ adv — **pet·ti·ness** \-tē-nəs\ n

**petty officer** n : a subordinate officer in the navy or coast guard appointed from among the enlisted personnel

**petty officer first class** n : a petty officer ranking below a chief petty officer

**petty officer second class** n : a petty officer ranking below a petty officer first class

**petty officer third class** n : a petty officer ranking below a petty officer second class

**pet·u·lant** \'pe-chə-lənt\ adj : marked by capricious ill humor ♦ **Synonyms** IRRITABLE, PEEVISH, FRETFUL, FRACTIOUS, QUERULOUS — **pet·u·lance** \-ləns\ n — **pet·u·lant·ly** adv

**pe·tu·nia** \pi-'tün-yə, -'tyün-\ n : any of a genus of tropical So. American herbs related to the potato and having bright funnel-shaped flowers

**pew** \'pyü\ n [ME pewe, fr. MF puie balustrade, fr. L podia, pl. of podium parapet, podium, fr. Gk podion base, dim. of pod-, pous foot] : any of the benches with backs fixed in rows in a church

**pe·wee** \'pē-(,)wē\ n : any of various small American flycatchers

**pew·ter** \'pyü-tər\ n 1 : an alloy of tin used esp. for household utensils 2 : a bluish gray color — **pewter** adj — **pew·ter·er** n

**pey·o·te** \pā-'ō-tē\ also **pey·otl** \-'ō-t'l\ n 1 : a hallucinogenic drug derived from the peyote cactus and containing mescaline 2 : a small cactus of the southwestern U.S. and Mexico

**pf** abbr 1 pfennig 2 preferred

**PFC** or **Pfc** abbr private first class

**pfd** abbr preferred

**pfen·nig** \'fe-nig\ n, pl **pfennig** also **pfennigs** or **pfen·ni·ge** \'fe-ni-gə\ : a former monetary unit equal to 1/100 deutsche mark

**PFLAG** abbr parents, families, and friends of lesbians and gays

**pg** abbr page

**PG** abbr postgraduate

**PGA** abbr Professional Golfers' Association

**pH** \(,)pē-'āch\ n : a value used to express acidity and alkalinity; also : the condition represented by such a value

**PH** abbr 1 pinch hit 2 public health

**pha·eton** \'fā-ə-t'n\ n [F phaéton, fr. Gk Phaethōn, son of the sun god who persuaded his father to let him drive the chariot of the sun but who lost control of the horses with disastrous consequences] 1 : a light 4-wheeled horse-drawn vehicle 2 : an open automobile with two cross seats

**phage** \'fāj\ n : BACTERIOPHAGE

**pha·lanx** \'fā-,laŋks\ n, pl **pha·lanx·es** or **pha·lan·ges** \fə-'lan-,jēz\ 1 : a group or body (as of troops) in compact formation 2 pl **phalanges** : one of the digital bones of the hand or foot of a vertebrate

**phal·a·rope** \'fa-lə-,rōp\ n, pl **-ropes** : any of a genus of small shorebirds related to sandpipers

**phal·lic** \'fa-lik\ adj 1 : of, relating to, or resembling a phallus 2 : relating to or being the stage of psychosexual development in psychoanalytic theory during which children become interested in their own sexual organs

**phal·lus** \'fa-ləs\ n, pl **phal·li** \'fa-,lī\ or **phal·lus·es** : PENIS; also : a symbolic representation of the penis

**Phan·er·o·zo·ic** \,fa-nə-rə-'zō-ik\ adj : of, relating to, or being an eon of geologic history comprising the Paleozoic, Mesozoic, and Cenozoic

**phan·tasm** \'fan-,ta-zəm\ n : a product of the imagination : ILLUSION — **phan·tas·mal** \fan-'taz-məl\ adj

**phan·tas·ma·go·ria** \fan-,taz-mə-'gór-ē-ə\ n : a constantly shifting complex succession of things seen or imagined; also : a scene that constantly changes or fluctuates

**phantasy** var of FANTASY

**phan·tom** \'fan-təm\ n 1 : something (as a specter) that is apparent to sense but has no substantial existence 2 : a mere show : SHADOW — **phantom** adj

**pha·raoh** \'fer-ō, 'fā-rō\ n, often cap : a ruler of ancient Egypt

**phar·i·sa·ical** \,fa-rə-'sā-ə-kəl\ adj : hypocritically self-righteous

**phar·i·see** \'fa-rə-,sē\ n 1 cap : a member of an ancient Jewish sect noted for strict observance of rites and ceremonies of the traditional law 2 : a self-righteous or hypocritical person — **phar·i·sa·ic** \,fa-rə-'sā-ik\ adj

**pharm** abbr pharmaceutical; pharmacist; pharmacy

**phar·ma·ceu·ti·cal** \,fär-mə-'sü-ti-kəl\ adj : of, relating to, or engaged in pharmacy or the manufacture and sale of medicinal drugs — **pharmaceutical** n

**phar·ma·col·o·gy** \,fär-mə-'kä-lə-jē\ n 1 : the science of drugs esp. as related to medicinal uses 2 : the reactions and properties of one or more drugs — **phar·ma·co·log·i·cal** \-kə-'lä-ji-kəl\ also **phar·ma·co·log·ic** \-kə-'lä-jik\ adj — **phar·ma·col·o·gist** \-'kä-lə-jist\ n

**phar·ma·co·poe·ia** also **phar·ma·co·pe·ia** \-kə-'pē-ə\ n 1 : a book describing drugs and medicinal preparations 2 : a stock of drugs

**phar·ma·cy** \'fär-mə-sē\ n, pl **-cies** : the art, practice, or profession of preparing and dispensing medical drugs 2 : DRUGSTORE — **phar·ma·cist** \-sist\ n

**phar·ynx** \'fa-riŋks\ n, pl **pha·ryn·ges** \fə-'rin-,jēz\ also **phar·ynx·es** : the muscular tubular passage extending from the back of the nasal cavity and mouth to the esophagus — **pha·ryn·ge·al** \fə-'rin-jəl, ,fa-rən-'jē-əl\ adj

**phase** \'fāz\ n 1 : a particular appearance in a recurring series of changes ⟨~s of the moon⟩ 2 : a stage or interval in a process or cycle ⟨first ~ of an experiment⟩ 3 : an aspect or part under consideration — **pha·sic** \'fā-zik\ adj

**phase down** vb : to reduce the size or amount of by phases

**phase in** vb : to introduce in stages

**phase·out** \'fāz-,aút\ n : a gradual stopping of operations or production

**phase out** vb : to stop production or use of in stages ⟨phase out old equipment⟩

**PhD** abbr [L philosophiae doctor] doctor of philosophy

**pheas·ant** \'fe-z'nt\ n, pl **pheasant** or **pheasants** : any of numerous long-tailed brilliantly colored game birds related to the domestic chicken

**phen·cy·cli·dine** \,fen-'sī-klə-,dēn\ n : a drug used esp. as a veterinary anesthetic and sometimes illicitly as a hallucinogenic drug

**phe·no·bar·bi·tal** \,fē-nō-'bär-bə-,tȯl\ *n* : a crystalline drug used as a hypnotic and sedative

**phe·nol** \'fē-,nȯl\ *n* : a corrosive poisonous acidic compound present in coal and wood tars and used in solution as a disinfectant

**phe·nom·e·non** \fi-'nä-mə-,nän, -nən\ *n, pl* **-na** \-nə\ *or* **-nons** [LL *phaenomenon*, fr. Gk *phainomenon*, fr. neut. of *phainomenos*, prp. of *phainesthai* to appear] **1** *pl* **-na** : an observable fact or event **2** : an outward sign of the working of a law of nature **3** *pl* **-nons** : an extraordinary person or thing : PRODIGY — **phe·nom·e·nal** \-'nä-mə-n°l\ *adj* — **phe·nom·e·nal·ly** *adv*

**pher·o·mone** \'fer-ə-,mōn\ *n* : a chemical substance that is usu. produced by an animal and serves to stimulate a behavioral response in other individuals of the same species — **pher·o·mon·al** \,fer-ə-'mō-n°l\ *adj*

**phi** \'fī\ *n* : the 21st letter of the Greek alphabet — Φ or φ

**phi·al** \'fī(-ə)l\ *n* : VIAL

**Phil** *abbr* Philippians

**phi·lan·der** \fə-'lan-dər\ *vb* : to have casual or illicit sexual relations with many women — **phi·lan·der·er** *n*

**phi·lan·thro·py** \fə-'lan-thrə-pē\ *n, pl* **-pies 1** : goodwill toward all people; *esp* : effort to promote human welfare **2** : a charitable act or gift; *also* : an organization that distributes or is supported by donated funds — **phil·an·throp·ic** \,fi-lən-'thrä-pik\ *adj* — **phil·an·throp·i·cal·ly** \-pi-k(ə-)lē\ *adv* — **phi·lan·thro·pist** \fə-'lan-thrə-pist\ *n*

**phi·lat·e·ly** \fə-'la-tə-lē\ *n* : the collection and study of postage and imprinted stamps — **phil·a·tel·ic** \,fi-lə-'te-lik\ *adj* — **phi·lat·e·list** \fə-'la-tə-list\ *n*

**Phi·le·mon** \fə-'lē-mən, fī-\ *n* — see BIBLE table

**Phi·lip·pi·ans** \fə-'li-pē-ənz\ *n* — see BIBLE table

**phi·lip·pic** \fə-'li-pik\ *n* : TIRADE

**phi·lis·tine** \'fi-lə-,stēn; fə-'lis-tən\ *n, often cap* [*Philistine*, inhabitant of ancient Philistia (Palestine)] : a person who is smugly insensitive or indifferent to intellectual or artistic values — **philistine** *adj, often cap*

**Phil·lips** \'fi-ləps\ *adj* : of, relating to, or being a screw having a head with a cross slot or its corresponding screwdriver

**phi·lo·den·dron** \,fi-lə-'den-drən\ *n, pl* **-drons** *also* **-dra** \-drə\ [NL, fr. Gk, neut. of *philodendros* loving trees, fr. *philos* dear, friendly + *dendron* tree] : any of various plants of the arum family grown for their showy foliage

**phi·lol·o·gy** \fə-'lä-lə-jē\ *n* **1** : the study of literature and relevant fields **2** : LINGUISTICS; *esp* : historical and comparative linguistics — **phil·o·log·i·cal** \,fi-lə-'lä-ji-kəl\ *adj* — **phi·lol·o·gist** \fə-'lä-lə-jist\ *n*

**philos** *abbr* philosopher; philosophy

**phi·los·o·pher** \fə-'lä-sə-fər\ *n* **1** : a reflective thinker : SCHOLAR **2** : a student of or specialist in philosophy **3** : a person whose philosophical perspective makes it possible to meet trouble calmly

**phi·los·o·phise** *Brit var of* PHILOSOPHIZE

**phi·los·o·phize** \fə-'lä-sə-,fīz\ *vb* **-phized; -phiz·ing 1** : to reason like a philosopher : THEORIZE **2** : to expound a philosophy esp. superficially

**phi·los·o·phy** \fə-'lä-sə-fē\ *n, pl* **-phies 1** : sciences and liberal arts exclusive of medicine, law, and theology ⟨doctor of ∼⟩ **2** : a critical study of fundamental beliefs and the grounds for them **3** : a system of philosophical concepts ⟨Aristotelian ∼⟩ **4** : a basic theory concerning a particular subject or sphere of activity **5** : the sum of the ideas and convictions of an individual or group ⟨her ∼ of life⟩ **6** : calmness of temper and judgment — **phil·o·soph·i·cal** \-fi-kəl\ *also* **phil·o·soph·ic** \,fi-lə-'sä-fik\ *adj* — **phil·o·soph·i·cal·ly** \-k(ə-)lē\ *adv*

**phil·ter** \'fil-tər\ *n* **1** : a magic potion **2** : a potion, drug, or charm held to arouse sexual passion

**phil·tre** *chiefly Brit var of* PHILTER

**phle·bi·tis** \fli-'bī-təs\ *n* : inflammation of a vein

**phle·bot·o·my** \fli-'bä-tə-mē\ *n, pl* **-mies** : the opening of a vein esp. for removing or releasing blood

**phlegm** \'flem\ *n* [ME *fleume*, fr. AF, fr. LL *phlegma*, fr. Gk, flame, inflammation, phlegm, fr. *phlegein* to burn] : thick mucus secreted in abnormal quantity esp. in the nose and throat

**phleg·mat·ic** \fleg-'ma-tik\ *adj* : having or showing a slow and stolid temperament ⟨was ∼ during the crisis⟩ ♦ *Synonyms* IMPASSIVE, APATHETIC, STOIC

**phlo·em** \'flō-,em\ *n* : a vascular plant tissue external to the xylem that carries dissolved food material and functions in support and storage

**phlox** \'fläks\ *n, pl* **phlox** *or* **phlox·es** : any of a genus of American herbs that have tall stalks with showy spreading terminal clusters of flowers

**pho·bia** \'fō-bē-ə\ *n* : an irrational persistent fear or dread — **pho·bic** \'fō-bik\ *adj*

**phoe·be** \'fē-(,)bē\ *n* : a flycatcher of the eastern U.S. that has a slight crest and is grayish brown above and yellowish white below

**phoe·nix** \'fē-niks\ *n* : a legendary bird held to live for centuries and then to burn itself to death and rise fresh and young from its ashes

**¹phone** \'fōn\ *n* **1** : TELEPHONE **2** : EARPHONE

**²phone** *vb* **phoned; phon·ing** : TELEPHONE

**phone card** *n* : a prepaid card used in paying for telephone calls

**pho·neme** \'fō-,nēm\ *n* : one of the elementary units of speech that distinguish one utterance from another — **pho·ne·mic** \fō-'nē-mik\ *adj*

**pho·net·ics** \fə-'ne-tiks\ *n* : the study and systematic classification of the sounds made in spoken utterance — **pho·net·ic** \-tik\ *adj* — **pho·ne·ti·cian** \ˌfō-nə-'ti-shən\ *n*

**phon·ic** \'fä-nik\ *adj* **1** : of, relating to, or producing sound **2** : of or relating to the sounds of speech or to phonics — **phon·i·cal·ly** \-ni-k(ə-)lē\ *adv*

**phon·ics** \'fä-niks\ *n* : a method of teaching people to read and pronounce words by learning the phonetic value of letters, letter groups, and esp. syllables

**pho·no·graph** \'fō-nə-ˌgraf\ *n* : an instrument for reproducing sounds by means of the vibration of a needle following a spiral groove on a revolving disc

**pho·nol·o·gy** \fə-'nä-lə-jē\ *n* : a study and description of sound changes in a language — **pho·no·log·i·cal** \ˌfō-nə-'lä-ji-kəl\ *adj* — **pho·nol·o·gist** \fə-'nä-lə-jist\ *n*

**pho·ny** *also* **pho·ney** \'fō-nē\ *adj* **pho·ni·er; -est** : not genuine or real : FAKE ⟨a ~ name⟩ — **phony** *n*

**phos·phate** \'fäs-ˌfāt\ *n* : a salt of a phosphoric acid — **phos·phat·ic** \fäs-'fa-tik\ *adj*

**phos·phor** \'fäs-fər\ *n* : a phosphorescent substance

**phos·pho·res·cence** \ˌfäs-fə-'re-s°ns\ *n* **1** : luminescence caused by the absorption of radiations (as light or electrons) and continuing after these radiations stop **2** : an enduring luminescence without sensible heat — **phos·pho·res·cent** \-s°nt\ *adj* — **phos·pho·res·cent·ly** *adv*

**phosphoric acid** \ˌfäs-'for-ik-, -'fär-\ *n* : any of several oxygen-containing acids of phosphorus

**phos·pho·rus** *also* **phos·pho·rous** \'fäs-fə-rəs\ *n* [NL, fr. Gk *phōsphoros* light-bearing, fr. *phōs* light + *pherein* to carry, bring] : a nonmetallic chemical element that has characteristics similar to nitrogen and occurs widely esp. as phosphates — **phos·pho·ric** \fäs-'for-ik, -'fär-\ *adj* — **phos·pho·rous** \'fäs-fə-rəs; fäs-'for-əs\ *adj*

**phot-** *or* **photo-** *comb form* **1** : light ⟨*photo*graphy⟩ **2** : photograph : photographic ⟨*photo*engraving⟩ **3** : photoelectric ⟨*photo*cell⟩

**pho·to** \'fō-tō\ *n, pl* **photos** : PHOTOGRAPH — **photo** *vb or adj*

**pho·to·cell** \'fō-tə-ˌsel\ *n* : PHOTOELECTRIC CELL

**pho·to·chem·i·cal** \ˌfō-tō-'ke-mi-kəl\ *adj* : of, relating to, or resulting from the chemical action of radiant energy

**pho·to·com·pose** \-kəm-'pōz\ *vb* : to compose reading matter for reproduction by means of characters photographed on film — **pho·to·com·po·si·tion** \-ˌkäm-pə-'zi-shən\ *n*

**pho·to·copy** \'fō-tə-ˌkä-pē\ *n* : a photographic reproduction of graphic matter — **photocopy** *vb*

**pho·to·elec·tric** \ˌfō-tō-i-'lek-trik\ *adj* : relating to an electrical effect due to the interaction of light with matter — **pho·to·elec·tri·cal·ly** \-tri-k(ə-)lē\ *adv*

**photoelectric cell** *n* : a device whose electrical properties are modified by the action of light

**pho·to·en·grave** \ˌfō-tō-in-'grav\ *vb* : to make a photoengraving of

**pho·to·en·grav·ing** *n* : a process by which an etched printing plate is made from a photograph or drawing; *also* : a print made from such a plate

**photo finish** *n* : a race finish so close that a photograph of the finish is used to determine the winner

**pho·tog** \fə-'täg\ *n* : PHOTOGRAPHER

**pho·to·gen·ic** \ˌfō-tə-'je-nik\ *adj* : eminently suitable esp. aesthetically for being photographed

**pho·to·graph** \'fō-tə-ˌgraf\ *n* : a picture taken by photography — **photograph** *vb* — **pho·tog·ra·pher** \fə-'tä-grə-fər\ *n*

**pho·tog·ra·phy** \fə-'tä-grə-fē\ *n* : the art or process of producing images on a sensitive surface (as film or a CCD chip) by the action of light — **pho·to·graph·ic** \ˌfō-tə-'gra-fik\ *adj* — **pho·to·graph·i·cal·ly** \-fi-k(ə-)lē\ *adv*

**pho·to·gra·vure** \ˌfō-tə-grə-'vyu̇r\ *n* : a process for making prints from an intaglio plate prepared by photographic methods

**pho·to·li·thog·ra·phy** \ˌfō-tō-li-'thä-grə-fē\ *n* : the process of photographically transferring a pattern to a surface for etching (as in making an integrated circuit)

**pho·tom·e·ter** \fō-'tä-mə-tər\ *n* : an instrument for measuring the intensity of light — **pho·to·met·ric** \ˌfō-tə-'me-trik\ *adj* — **pho·tom·e·try** \fō-'tä-mə-trē\ *n*

**pho·to·mi·cro·graph** \ˌfō-tō-'mī-krə-ˌgraf\ *n* : a photograph of a microscope image — **pho·to·mi·crog·ra·phy** \-mī-'krä-grə-fē\ *n*

**pho·ton** \'fō-ˌtän\ *n* : a quantum of electromagnetic radiation

**photo op** *n* : a situation or event that lends itself to the taking of pictures which favor the individuals photographed

**pho·to·play** \'fō-tō-ˌplā\ *n* : MOTION PICTURE

**pho·to·sen·si·tive** \ˌfō-tə-'sen-sə-tiv\ *adj* : sensitive or sensitized to the action of radiant energy

**pho·to·shop** \'fō-(ˌ)tō-ˌshäp\ *vb, often cap* : to alter a digital image with image-editing software

**pho·to·sphere** \'fō-tə-ˌsfir\ *n* : the luminous surface of a star — **pho·to·spher·ic** \ˌfō-tə-'sfir-ik, -'sfer-\ *adj*

**pho·to·syn·the·sis** \ˌfō-tō-'sin-thə-səs\ *n* : the process by which chlorophyll-containing plants make carbohydrates from water and from carbon dioxide in the air in the presence of light — **pho·to·syn·the·size** \-ˌsīz\ *vb* — **pho·to·syn·thet·ic** \-sin-'the-tik\ *adj*

**phr** *abbr* phrase

**¹phrase** \'frāz\ *n* **1** : a brief expression **2** : a group of two or more grammatically related words that form a sense unit expressing a thought

²**phrase** *vb* **phrased; phras·ing** : to express in words

**phrase·ol·o·gy** \,frā-zē-'ä-lə-jē\ *n, pl* **-gies** : a manner of phrasing : STYLE

**phras·ing** *n* : style of expression

**phre·net·ic** *archaic var of* FRENETIC

**phren·ic** \'fre-nik\ *adj* : of or relating to the diaphragm ⟨~ nerves⟩

**phre·nol·o·gy** \fri-'nä-lə-jē\ *n* : the study of the conformation of the skull based on the belief that it indicates mental faculties and character traits

**phy·lac·tery** \fə-'lak-tə-rē\ *n, pl* **-ter·ies** 1 : one of two small square leather boxes containing slips inscribed with scripture passages and traditionally worn on the left arm and forehead by Jewish men during morning weekday prayers 2 : AMULET

**phy·lum** \'fī-ləm\ *n, pl* **phy·la** \-lə\ [NL, fr. Gk *phylon* tribe, race] : a major category in biological classification esp. of animals that ranks above the class and below the kingdom; *also* : a group (as of people) apparently of common origin

**phys** *abbr* 1 physical 2 physics

¹**phys·ic** \'fi-zik\ *n* 1 : the profession of medicine 2 : MEDICINE; *esp* : PURGATIVE

²**physic** *vb* **phys·icked; phys·ick·ing** : PURGE 2

¹**phys·i·cal** \'fi-zi-kəl\ *adj* 1 : of or relating to nature or the laws of nature 2 : material as opposed to mental or spiritual 3 : of, relating to, or produced by the forces and operations of physics 4 : of or relating to the body — **phys·i·cal·ly** \-k(ə-)lē\ *adv*

²**physical** *n* : PHYSICAL EXAMINATION

**physical education** *n* : instruction in the development and care of the body ranging from simple calisthenics to training in hygiene, gymnastics, and the performance and management of athletic games

**physical examination** *n* : an examination of the bodily functions and condition of an individual

**phys·i·cal·ize** \'fi-zi-kə-,līz\ *vb* **-ized; -iz·ing** : to give physical form or expression to

**physical science** *n* : any of the sciences (as physics and astronomy) that deal primarily with nonliving materials — **physical scientist** *n*

**physical therapy** *n* : the treatment of disease by physical and mechanical means (as massage, exercise, water, or heat) — **physical therapist** *n*

**phy·si·cian** \fə-'zi-shən\ *n* : a doctor of medicine

**physician's assistant** *n* : a person certified to provide basic medical care usu. under a licensed physician's supervision

**phys·i·cist** \'fi-zə-sist\ *n* : a scientist who specializes in physics

**phys·ics** \'fi-ziks\ *n* [L *physica*, pl., natural sciences, fr. Gk *physika*, fr. *physis* growth, nature, fr. *phyein* to bring forth] 1 : the science of matter and energy and their interactions 2 : the physical properties and composition of something

**phys·i·og·no·my** \,fi-zē-'äg-nə-mē\ *n, pl* **-mies** : facial appearance esp. as a reflection of inner character

**phys·i·og·ra·phy** \,fi-zē-'ä-grə-fē\ *n* : geography dealing with physical features of the earth — **phys·io·graph·ic** \,fi-zē-ō-'gra-fik\ *adj*

**phys·i·ol·o·gy** \,fi-zē-'ä-lə-jē\ *n* 1 : a branch of biology dealing with the functions and functioning of living matter and organisms 2 : functional processes in an organism or any of its parts — **phys·i·o·log·i·cal** \-zē-ə-'lä-ji-kəl\ *or* **phys·i·o·log·ic** \-jik\ *adj* — **phys·i·o·log·i·cal·ly** \-ji-k(ə-)lē\ *adv* — **phys·i·ol·o·gist** \-zē-'ä-lə-jist\ *n*

**phys·io·ther·a·py** \,fi-zē-ō-'ther-ə-pē\ *n* : PHYSICAL THERAPY — **phys·io·ther·a·pist** \-pist\ *n*

**phy·sique** \fə-'zēk\ *n* : the build of a person's body : bodily constitution

**phy·to·chem·i·cal** \,fī-tō-'ke-mi-kəl\ *n* : a chemical compound occurring naturally in plants

**phy·to·plank·ton** \'fī-tō-,plaŋk-tən\ *n* : plant life of the plankton

**pi** \'pī\ *n, pl* **pis** \'pīz\ 1 : the 16th letter of the Greek alphabet — Π or π 2 : the symbol π denoting the ratio of the circumference of a circle to its diameter; *also* : the ratio itself equal to approximately 3.1416

**PI** *abbr* private investigator

**pi·a·nis·si·mo** \,pē-ə-'ni-sə-,mō\ *adv or adj* : very softly — used as a direction in music

**pi·a·nist** \pē-'a-nist, 'pē-ə-\ *n* : a person who plays the piano

¹**pi·a·no** \pē-'ä-nō\ *adv or adj* : SOFTLY — used as a direction in music

²**piano** \pē-'a-nō\ *n, pl* **pianos** [It, short for *pianoforte*, fr. *gravicembalo col piano e forte*, lit., harpsichord with soft and loud; fr. the fact that its tones could be varied in loudness] : a musical instrument having steel strings sounded by felt-covered hammers operated from a keyboard

**pi·ano·forte** \pē-,a-nō-'fôr-,tā, -tē; pē-'a-nə-,fôrt\ *n* : PIANO

**pi·as·tre** *also* **pi·as·ter** \pē-'as-tər\ *n* — see *pound* at MONEY table

**pi·az·za** \pē-'a-zə, *esp for 1* -'at-sə\ *n, pl* **piazzas** *or* **pi·az·ze** \-'at-(,)sā, -'ät-\ [It, fr. L *platea* broad street] 1 : an open square esp. in an Italian town 2 : a long hall with an arched roof 3 *dial* : VERANDA, PORCH

**pi·broch** \'pē-,bräk\ *n* : a set of variations for the bagpipe

**pic** \'pik\ *n, pl* **pics** *or* **pix** \'piks\ 1 : PHOTOGRAPH 2 : MOTION PICTURE

**pi·ca** \'pī-kə\ *n* : a typewriter type with 10 characters to the inch

**pi·ca·resque** \,pi-kə-'resk, ,pē-\ *adj* : of or relating to rogues ⟨~ fiction⟩

**pic·a·yune** \,pi-kē-'yün\ *adj* : of little value : TRIVIAL; *also* : PETTY

**pic·ca·lil·li** \,pi-kə-'li-lē\ *n* : a relish of chopped vegetables and spices

**pic·co·lo** \'pi-kə-,lō\ *n, pl* **-los** [It, short for *piccolo flauto* small flute] : a small shrill flute pitched an octave higher than the ordinary flute

**pice** \'pīs\ *n, pl* **pice** : PAISA

**¹pick** \'pik\ *vb* **1** : to pierce or break up with a pointed instrument **2** : to remove bit by bit; *also* : to remove covering matter from **3** : to gather by plucking ⟨~ apples⟩ **4** : CULL, SELECT **5** : ROB ⟨~ a pocket⟩ **6** : PROVOKE ⟨~ a quarrel⟩ **7** : to dig into or pull lightly at **8** : to pluck with fingers or a pick ⟨~ a guitar⟩ **9** : to loosen or pull apart with a sharp point ⟨~ wool⟩ **10** : to unlock with a wire **11** : to eat sparingly ⟨~ at a salad⟩ — **pick·er** *n* — **pick on** : to single out for criticism, teasing, or bullying

**²pick** *n* **1** : the act or privilege of choosing **2** : the best or choicest one **3** : the part of a crop gathered at one time

**³pick** *n* **1** : a heavy wooden-handled tool pointed at one or both ends **2** : a pointed implement used for picking **3** : a small thin piece (as of plastic) used to pluck the strings of a stringed instrument

**pick·a·back** \'pi-gē-ˌbak, 'pi-kə-\ *var of* PIGGYBACK

**pick·ax** \'pik-ˌaks\ *n* : ³PICK 1

**pick·er·el** \'pi-kə-rəl\ *n, pl* **pickerel** *or* **pickerels** : either of two bony fishes related to the pikes; *also* : WALLEYE 2

**pick·er·el·weed** \-ˌwēd\ *n* : a No. American shallow-water herb that bears spikes of purplish blue flowers

**¹pick·et** \'pi-kət\ *n* **1** : a pointed stake (as for a fence) **2** : a detached body of soldiers on outpost duty; *also* : SENTINEL **3** : a person posted by a labor union where workers are on strike; *also* : a person posted for a protest

**²picket** *vb* **1** : to guard with pickets **2** : TETHER ⟨~ a horse⟩ **3** : to post pickets at ⟨~ a factory⟩ **4** : to serve as a picket

**pick·ings** \'pi-kinz, -kənz\ *n pl* **1** : gleanable or eatable fragments : SCRAPS **2** : yield for effort expended : RETURN

**pick·le** \'pi-kəl\ *n* **1** : a brine or vinegar solution for preserving foods; *also* : a food (as a cucumber) preserved in a pickle **2** : a difficult situation : PLIGHT — **pickle** *vb*

**pick·lock** \'pik-ˌläk\ *n* **1** : BURGLAR, THIEF **2** : a tool for picking locks

**pick·pock·et** \'pik-ˌpä-kət\ *n* : one who steals from pockets

**¹pick·up** \'pik-ˌəp\ *n* **1** : a hitchhiker who is given a ride **2** : a temporary chance acquaintance **3** : a picking up **4** : revival of business activity **5** : ACCELERATION **6** : the conversion of mechanical movements into electrical impulses in the reproduction of sound; *also* : a device for making such conversion **7** : a light truck having an enclosed cab and an open body with low sides and a tailgate **8** : a pickup game **9** : a player acquired from another team

**²pickup** *adj* : using or comprising local or available personnel ⟨a ~ game⟩

**pick up** *vb* **1** : to take hold of and lift **2** : IMPROVE **3** : to put in order

**picky** \'pi-kē\ *adj* **pick·i·er; -est** : FUSSY, FINICKY ⟨a ~ eater⟩

**¹pic·nic** \'pik-ˌnik\ *n* : an outing with food usu. provided by members of the group and eaten in the open

**²picnic** *vb* **pic·nicked; pic·nick·ing** : to go on a picnic : eat in picnic fashion

**pi·cot** \'pē-ˌkō\ *n* : one of a series of small loops forming an edging on ribbon or lace

**pic·to·ri·al** \pik-'tōr-ē-əl\ *adj* : of, relating to, or consisting of pictures

**¹pic·ture** \'pik-chər\ *n* **1** : a representation made by painting, drawing, or photography **2** : a vivid description in words **3** : IMAGE, COPY ⟨was the ~ of his father⟩ **4** : a transitory visual image (as on a TV screen) **5** : MOTION PICTURE **6** : SITUATION ⟨a bleak economic ~⟩

**²picture** *vb* **pic·tured; pic·tur·ing** **1** : to paint or draw a picture of **2** : to describe vividly in words **3** : to form a mental image of

**pic·tur·esque** \ˌpik-chə-'resk\ *adj* **1** : resembling a picture ⟨a ~ landscape⟩ **2** : CHARMING, QUAINT ⟨a ~ character⟩ **3** : GRAPHIC 3, VIVID ⟨a ~ account⟩ — **pic·tur·esque·ness** *n*

**picture tube** *n* : a cathode-ray tube on which the picture appears in a television

**pid·dle** \'pi-dᵊl\ *vb* **pid·dled; pid·dling** : to act or work idly : DAWDLE

**pid·dling** \'pi-dᵊl-on, -in\ *adj* : TRIVIAL, PALTRY ⟨spent a ~ sum⟩

**pid·dly** \'pid-lē\ *adj* : TRIVIAL, PIDDLING

**pid·gin** \'pi-jən\ *n* [fr. *pidgin English,* fr. Chinese Pidgin English *pidgin* business] : a simplified speech used for communication between people with different languages

**pie** \'pī\ *n* : a dish consisting of a pastry crust and a filling (as of fruit or meat)

**¹pie·bald** \'pī-ˌbȯld\ *adj* : of different colors; *esp* : blotched with white and black ⟨a ~ horse⟩

**²piebald** *n* : a piebald animal

**¹piece** \'pēs\ *n* **1** : a part of a whole : FRAGMENT, PORTION **2** : one of a group, set, or mass ⟨~s of flatware⟩; *also* : a single item or instance ⟨a ~ of nonsense⟩ ⟨a ~ of news⟩ **3** : a movable object used in a board game **4** : a length, weight, or size in which something is made or sold **5** : a product (as an essay) of creative work **6** : FIREARM **7** : COIN

**²piece** *vb* **pieced; piec·ing** **1** : to repair or complete by adding pieces : PATCH **2** : to join into a whole

**pièce de ré·sis·tance** \pē-ˌes-də-rā-ˌzē-ˈstäns\ *n, pl* **pièces de ré·sis·tance** \*same*\ [F] **1** : the chief dish of a meal **2** : an outstanding item

**piece·meal** \'pēs-ˌmēl\ *adv or adj* : one piece at a time : GRADUALLY

**piece·work** \-ˌwərk\ *n* : work done and paid for by the piece — **piece·work·er** *n*

**pie chart** *n* : a circular chart that shows quantities or frequencies by parts of a circle shaped like pieces of pie

**pied** \'pīd\ *adj* : of two or more colors in blotches : VARIEGATED

**pied–à–terre** \pē-ˌā-də-'ter\ *n, pl* **pieds–à–terre** \*same*\ [F, lit., foot to the ground] : a temporary or second lodging

**pier** \'pir\ *n* **1** : a support for a bridge

span **2** : a structure built out into the water for use as a landing place or a promenade or to protect or form a harbor **3** : an upright supporting part (as a pillar) of a building or structure

**pierce** \'pirs\ *vb* **pierced; pierc·ing 1** : to enter or thrust into sharply or painfully : STAB **2** : to make a hole in or through : PERFORATE 〈*pierced* ears〉 **3** : to force or make a way into or through : PENETRATE **4** : to see through : DISCERN — **pierc·er** *n*

**piercing** *n* : a piece of jewelry attached to pierced flesh

**pies** *pl of* PI *or of* PIE

**pi·ety** \'pī-ə-tē\ *n, pl* **pi·et·ies 1** : fidelity to natural obligations (as to parents) **2** : dutifulness in religion : DEVOUTNESS **3** : a pious act

**pif·fle** \'pi-fəl\ *n* : trifling talk or action

**pig** \'pig\ *n* **1** : SWINE; *esp* : a young domesticated swine **2** : PORK **3** : a dirty, gluttonous, or repulsive person **4** : a crude casting of metal (as iron)

**pi·geon** \'pi-jən\ *n* : any of numerous stout-bodied short-legged birds with smooth thick plumage

**¹pi·geon·hole** \'pi-jən-ˌhōl\ *n* : a small open compartment (as in a desk) for keeping letters or documents

**²pigeonhole** *vb* **1** : to place in or as if in a pigeonhole : FILE **2** : to lay aside **3** : to assign to a usu. restrictive category

**pi·geon–toed** \-ˌtōd\ *adj* : having the toes and forefoot turned inward

**pig·gish** \'pi-gish\ *adj* **1** : GREEDY **2** : STUBBORN

**pig·gy·back** \'pi-gē-ˌbak\ *also* **pick·a·back** \'pi-gē-, 'pi-kə-\ *adv or adj* **1** : up on the back and shoulders **2** : on a railroad flatcar

**pig·head·ed** \'pig-'he-dəd\ *adj* : OBSTINATE, STUBBORN

**pig latin** *n, often cap L* : a jargon that is made by systematic alteration of English

**pig·let** \'pi-glət\ *n* : a small usu. young swine

**pig·ment** \'pig-mənt\ *n* **1** : coloring matter **2** : a powder mixed with a liquid to give color (as in paints) — **pig·ment·ed** \-mən-təd\ *adj*

**pig·men·ta·tion** \ˌpig-mən-'tā-shən\ *n* : coloration with or deposition of pigment; *esp* : an excessive deposition of bodily pigment

**pigmy** *var of* PYGMY

**pig·nut** \'pig-ˌnət\ *n* : the bitter nut of any of several hickory trees; *also* : any of these trees

**pig·pen** \-ˌpen\ *n* **1** : a pen for pigs **2** : a dirty place

**pig·skin** \-ˌskin\ *n* **1** : the skin of a swine or leather made of it **2** : FOOTBALL 2

**pig·sty** \-ˌstī\ *n* : PIGPEN

**pig·tail** \-ˌtāl\ *n* : a tight braid of hair

**pi·ka** \'pē-kə, 'pī-\ *n* : any of various small short-eared mammals related to the rabbits and occurring in rocky uplands of Asia and western No. America

**¹pike** \'pīk\ *n* : a sharp point or spike

**²pike** *n, pl* **pike** *or* **pikes** : a large slender long-snouted freshwater bony fish valued

for food; *also* : any of various related fishes

**³pike** *n* : a long wooden shaft with a pointed steel head formerly used as a foot soldier's weapon

**⁴pike** *n* : TURNPIKE

**pik·er** \'pī-kər\ *n* **1** : one who does things in a small way or on a small scale **2** : TIGHTWAD, CHEAPSKATE

**pike·staff** \'pīk-ˌstaf\ *n* : the staff of a foot soldier's pike

**pi·laf** *also* **pi·laff** \pi-'läf, 'pē-ˌläf\ *or* **pi·lau** \pi-'lȯ, -'lō, 'pē-ˌlō, -ˌlȯ\ *n* : a dish made of seasoned rice often with meat

**pi·las·ter** \pi-'las-tər, 'pī-ˌlas-tər\ *n* : an architectural support that looks like a rectangular column and projects slightly from a wall

**pil·chard** \'pil-chərd\ *n* : a small European marine fish related to the herrings and often packed as a sardine

**¹pile** \'pī(-ə)l\ *n* : a long slender column (as of wood or steel) driven into the ground to support a vertical load

**²pile** *n* **1** : a quantity of things heaped together **2** : PYRE **3** : a great number or quantity : LOT 〈~s of money〉

**³pile** *vb* **piled; pil·ing 1** : to lay in a pile : STACK **2** : to heap up : ACCUMULATE **3** : to press forward in a mass : CROWD

**⁴pile** *n* : a velvety surface of fine short hairs or threads (as on cloth) — **piled** \'pī(-ə)ld\ *adj* — **pile·less** *adj*

**piles** \'pī(-ə)lz\ *n pl* : HEMORRHOIDS

**pil·fer** \'pil-fər\ *vb* : to steal in small quantities 〈~ pens from work〉

**pil·grim** \'pil-grəm\ *n* [ME, fr. AF *pelerin, pilegrin,* fr. LL *pelegrinus,* alter. of L *peregrinus* foreigner, fr. *peregrinus* foreign, fr. *peregri* abroad, fr. *per* through + *ager* land] **1** : one who journeys in foreign lands : WAYFARER **2** : one who travels to a shrine or holy place as an act of devotion **3** *cap* : one of the English settlers founding Plymouth colony in 1620

**pil·grim·age** \-grə-mij\ *n* : a journey of a pilgrim esp. to a shrine or holy place

**pil·ing** \'pī-liŋ\ *n* : a structure of piles

**pill** \'pil\ *n* **1** : a small rounded mass usu. of medicine that is swallowed whole **2** : a disagreeable or tiresome person **3** *often cap* : an oral contraceptive — usu. used with *the*

**pil·lage** \'pi-lij\ *vb* **pil·laged; pil·lag·ing** : to take booty : LOOT, PLUNDER — **pillage** *n* — **pil·lag·er** *n*

**pil·lar** \'pi-lər\ *n* **1** : a strong upright support (as for a roof) **2** : a column or shaft standing alone esp. as a monument **3** : an integral or upstanding member or part **4** : a fundamental tenet 〈the five ~s of Islam〉 — **pil·lared** \-lərd\ *adj*

**pill·box** \'pil-ˌbäks\ *n* **1** : a shallow round box for pills **2** : a low concrete emplacement esp. for machine guns

**pil·lion** \'pil-yən\ *n* **1** : a pad or cushion placed behind a saddle for an extra rider **2** *chiefly Brit* : a motorcycle or bicycle saddle for a passenger

**¹pil·lo·ry** \'pi-lə-rē\ *n, pl* **-ries** : a wooden frame for public punishment having holes in which the head and hands can be locked

**²pillory** *vb* **-ried; -ry·ing 1** : to set in a pillory **2** : to expose to public scorn

**¹pil·low** \'pi-lō\ *n* : a case filled with springy material (as feathers) and used to support the head of a resting person

**²pillow** *vb* : to rest or place on or as if on a pillow; *also* : to serve as a pillow for

**pil·low·case** \-ˌkās\ *n* : a removable covering for a pillow

**¹pi·lot** \'pī-lət\ *n* **1** : HELMSMAN, STEERSMAN **2** : a person qualified and licensed to take ships into and out of a port **3** : GUIDE, LEADER **4** : one that flies an aircraft or spacecraft **5** : a television show filmed or taped as a sample of a proposed series — **pi·lot·less** *adj*

**²pilot** *vb* : CONDUCT, GUIDE; *esp* : to act as pilot of ⟨~ a ship⟩

**³pilot** *adj* : serving as a guiding or activating device or as a testing or trial unit ⟨a ~ light⟩ ⟨a ~ factory⟩

**pi·lot·house** \'pī-lət-ˌhaús\ *n* : a shelter on the upper deck of a ship for the steering gear and the helmsman

**pilot whale** *n* : either of two mostly black medium-sized whales

**pil·sner** *also* **pil·sen·er** \'pilz-nər, 'pilzə-\ *n* [G, lit., of Pilsen (Plzeň), city in the Czech Republic] **1** : a light beer with a strong flavor of hops **2** : a tall slender footed glass for beer

**pi·men·to** \pə-'men-tō\ *n, pl* **pimentos** *or* **plmento** [Sp *ptmienta* allspice, pepper, fr. LL *pigmenta*, pl. of *pigmentum* plant juice, fr. L, pigment] **1** : ALLSPICE **2** : PIMIENTO

**pi·mien·to** \pə-'men-tō\ *n, pl* **-tos** : any of various mild red sweet pepper fruits used esp. to stuff olives and to make paprika

**pimp** \'pimp\ *n* : a man who solicits clients for a prostitute — **pimp** *vb*

**pim·per·nel** \'pim-pər-ˌnel, -nəl\ *n* : any of a genus of herbs related to the primroses

**pim·ple** \'pim-pəl\ *n* : a small inflamed swelling on the skin often containing pus — **pim·ply** \-p(ə-)lē\ *adj*

**¹pin** \'pin\ *n* **1** : a piece of wood or metal used esp. for fastening things together or as a support by which one thing may be suspended from another; *esp* : a small pointed piece of wire with a head used for fastening clothes or attaching papers **2** : an ornament or emblem fastened to clothing with a pin **3** : one of the pieces constituting the target (as in bowling); *also* : the staff of the flag marking a hole on a golf course **4** : LEG

**²pin** *vb* **pinned; pin·ning 1** : to fasten, join, or secure with a pin **2** : to hold fast or immobile **3** : ATTACH, HANG ⟨*pinned* their hopes on one man⟩ **4** : to assign the blame for ⟨~ a crime on someone⟩ **5** : to define clearly : ESTABLISH ⟨~ down an idea⟩

**PIN** *abbr* personal identification number

**pi·ña co·la·da** \ˌpēn-yə-kō-'lä-də, ˌpē-nə-\ *n* [Sp, lit., strained pineapple] : a tall drink made of rum, cream of coconut, and pineapple juice mixed with ice

**pin·afore** \'pi-nə-ˌfōr\ *n* : a sleeveless dress or apron fastened at the back

**pin·ball machine** \'pin-ˌbȯl-\ *n* : an amusement device in which a ball is maneuvered along a slanted surface among a series of targets for points

**pince–nez** \paⁿs-'nā\ *n, pl* **pince–nez** \same *or* -'nāz\ [F, fr. *pincer* to pinch + *nez* nose] : eyeglasses clipped to the nose by a spring

**pin·cer** \'pin-sər\ *n* **1** *pl* : a gripping instrument with two handles and two grasping jaws **2** : a claw (as of a lobster) resembling pincers

**¹pinch** \'pinch\ *vb* [ME, fr. AF *pincher, pincer*, fr. VL *pinctiare, punctiare*, fr. L *punctum* puncture] **1** : to squeeze between the finger and thumb or between the jaws of an instrument **2** : to compress painfully **3** : CONTRACT, SHRIVEL **4** : to be miserly **5** : to subject to strict economy **6** : to confine or limit narrowly **6** : STEAL **7** : ARREST

**²pinch** *n* **1** : a critical point : EMERGENCY **2** : painful effect **3** : an act of pinching **4** : a very small quantity **5** : ARREST

**³pinch** *adj* : SUBSTITUTE ⟨a ~ runner⟩

**pinch–hit** \'pinch-'hit\ *vb* **1** : to bat in the place of another player esp. when a hit is particularly needed **2** : to act or serve in place of another — **pinch hit** *n* — **pinch hitter** *n*

**pin curl** *n* : a curl made usu. by dampening a strand of hair, coiling it, and securing it by a hairpin or clip

**pin·cush·ion** \'pin-ˌkú-shən\ *n* : a cushion for pins not in use

**¹pine** \'pīn\ *n* : any of a genus of evergreen cone-bearing trees; *also* : the light durable resinous wood of a pine

**²pine** *vb* **pined; pin·ing 1** : to lose vigor or health through distress **2** : to long for something intensely ⟨*pined* for home⟩

**pi·ne·al** \'pī-nē-əl, pī-'nē-əl\ *n* : PINEAL GLAND — **pineal** *adj*

**pineal gland** *n* : a small usu. conical appendage of the brain of all vertebrates with a cranium that functions primarily as an endocrine organ

**pine·ap·ple** \'pīn-ˌa-pəl\ *n* : a tropical plant bearing a large edible juicy fruit; *also* : its fruit

**pin·feath·er** \'pin-ˌfe-thər\ *n* : a new feather just coming through the skin

**ping** \'piŋ\ *n* **1** : a sharp sound like that of a bullet striking **2** : engine knock

**pin·hole** \'pin-ˌhōl\ *n* : a small hole made by, for, or as if by a pin

**¹pin·ion** \'pin-yən\ *n* : the end section of a bird's wing; *also* : WING

**²pinion** *vb* : to restrain by binding the arms; *also* : SHACKLE

**³pinion** *n* : a gear with a small number of teeth designed to mesh with a larger wheel or rack

**¹pink** \'piŋk\ *n* **1** : any of a genus of plants with narrow leaves often grown for their showy flowers **2** : the highest degree : HEIGHT ⟨the ~ of condition⟩

**²pink** *n* : a light tint of red

**³pink** *adj* **1** : of the color pink **2** : holding socialistic views — **pink·ish** *adj*

**⁴pink** vb **1** : to perforate in an ornamental pattern **2** : PIERCE, STAB **3** : to cut a saw-toothed edge on

**pink·eye** \'piŋk-ˌī\ n : an acute contagious eye inflammation

**pin·kie** or **pin·ky** \'piŋ-kē\ n, pl **pinkies** : the smallest finger of the hand

**pin·nace** \'pi-nəs\ n **1** : a light sailing ship **2** : a ship's boat

**pin·na·cle** \'pi-ni-kəl\ n [ME pinacle, fr. AF, fr. LL pinnaculum small wing, gable, fr. L pinna wing, battlement] **1** : a turret ending in a small spire **2** : a lofty peak **3** : ACME

**pin·nate** \'pi-ˌnāt\ adj : resembling a feather esp. in having similar parts arranged on each side of an axis ⟨a ~ leaf⟩ — **pin·nate·ly** adv

**pi·noch·le** \'pē-ˌnə-kəl\ n : a card game played with a 48-card deck

**pi·ñon** or **pin·yon** \'pin-ˌyōn, -ˌyän\ n, pl **pi·ñons** or **pin·yons** or **pi·ño·nes** \pin-'yō-nēz\ [AmerSp piñón] : any of various small pines of western No. America with edible seeds; also : the edible seed of a piñon

**pin·point** \'pin-ˌpȯint\ vb : to locate, hit, or aim with great precision

**pin·prick** \-ˌprik\ n **1** : a small puncture made by or as if by a pin **2** : a petty irritation or annoyance

**pins and needles** n pl : a pricking tingling sensation in a limb growing numb or recovering from numbness — **on pins and needles** : in a nervous or jumpy state of anticipation

**pin·stripe** \'pin-ˌstrīp\ n : a narrow stripe on a fabric; also : a suit with such stripes — **pin–striped** \-ˌstrīpt\ adj

**pint** \'pīnt\ n — see WEIGHT table

**pin·to** \'pin-ˌtō\ n, pl **pintos** also **pintoes** : a spotted horse or pony

**pinto bean** n : a spotted seed produced by a kind of kidney bean and used for food

**pin·up** \'pin-ˌəp\ adj : suitable or designed for hanging on a wall; also : suited (as by beauty) to be the subject of a pin-up photograph

**pin·wheel** \-ˌhwēl, -ˌwēl\ n **1** : a fireworks device in the form of a revolving wheel of colored fire **2** : a toy consisting of lightweight vanes that revolve at the end of a stick

**pin·worm** \-ˌwərm\ n : a nematode worm parasitic in the human intestine

**pin·yin** \'pin-'yin\ n, often cap : a system for writing Chinese ideograms by using Roman letters to represent the sounds

**¹pi·o·neer** \ˌpī-ə-'nir\ n **1** : one that originates or helps open up a new line of thought or activity **2** : an early settler in a territory

**²pioneer** vb **1** : to act as a pioneer **2** : to open or prepare for others to follow ⟨~ed a new cancer treatment⟩; also : SETTLE

**pi·ous** \'pī-əs\ adj **1** : marked by reverence for deity : DEVOUT **2** : excessively or affectedly religious **3** : SACRED, DEVOTIONAL **4** : showing loyal reverence for a person or thing : DUTIFUL **5**

: marked by sham or hypocrisy ⟨~ hypocrites⟩ — **pi·ous·ly** adv

**¹pip** \'pip\ n : one of the dots used on dice and dominoes to indicate numerical value

**²pip** n : a small fruit seed (as of an apple)

**¹pipe** \'pīp\ n **1** : a tubular musical instrument played by forcing air through it **2** : BAGPIPE **3** : a tube designed to conduct something (as water, steam, or oil) **4** : a device for smoking having a tube with a bowl at one end and a mouthpiece at the other **5** : a means of transmission (as of computer data)

**pipe** vb **piped; pip·ing 1** : to play on a pipe **2** : to speak in a high or shrill voice **3** : to convey by or as if by pipes — **pip·er** n

**pipe down** vb : to stop talking or making noise

**pipe dream** n : an illusory or fantastic hope

**pipe·line** \'pīp-ˌlīn\ n **1** : a line of pipe with pumps, valves, and control devices for conveying fluids **2** : a channel for information **3** : PIPE 5

**pi·pette** or **pi·pet** \pī-'pet\ n : a device for measuring and transferring small volumes of liquid

**pipe up** vb : to speak loudly and distinctly; also : to express an opinion freely

**pip·ing** \'pī-piŋ\ n **1** : the music of pipes **2** : a narrow fold of material used to decorate edges or seams

**piping hot** adj : very hot

**pip·pin** \'pi-pən\ n : a crisp tart usu. yellowish apple

**pip–squeak** \'pip-ˌskwēk\ n : one that is small or insignificant

**pi·quant** \'pē-kənt\ adj **1** : pleasantly savory : PUNGENT ⟨a ~ sauce⟩ **2** : engagingly provocative; also : having a lively charm — **pi·quan·cy** \-kən-sē\ n

**¹pique** \'pēk\ n [F] : a passing feeling of wounded vanity : RESENTMENT

**²pique** vb **piqued; piqu·ing 1** : IRRITATE **1 2** : to arouse by a provocation or challenge : GOAD

**pi·qué** or **pi·que** \pi-'kā\ n : a durable ribbed clothing fabric

**pi·quet** \pi-'kā\ n : a 2-handed card game played with 32 cards

**pi·ra·cy** \'pī-rə-sē\ n, pl **-cies 1** : robbery on the high seas; also : an act resembling such robbery **2** : the unauthorized use of another's production or invention

**pi·ra·nha** \pə-'rä-nə, -'rän-yə\ n [Pg, fr. Tupi (So. American Indian language) piráña, fr. pirá fish + áña tooth] : any of various usu. small So. American fishes with sharp teeth that include some known to attack humans and large animals

**pi·rate** \'pī-rət\ n [ME, fr. MF or L; MF, fr. L pirata, fr. Gk peiratēs, fr. peiran to attempt, test] : one who commits piracy — **pirate** vb — **pi·rat·i·cal** \pə-'ra-ti-kəl, pī-\ adj

**pir·ou·ette** \ˌpir-ə-'wet\ n [F] : a rapid whirling about of the body; esp : a full turn on the toe or ball of one foot in ballet — **pirouette** vb

**pis** *pl of* PI

**pis·ca·to·ri·al** \ˌpis-kə-ˈtōr-ē-əl\ *adj* : of or relating to fishing

**Pi·sces** \ˈpī-ˌsēz\ *n* [ME, fr. L, lit., fishes] **1** : a zodiacal constellation between Aquarius and Aries usu. pictured as a fish **2** : the 12th sign of the zodiac in astrology; *also* : one born under this sign

**pis·mire** \ˈpis-ˌmī(-ə)r\ *n* : ANT

**pi·so** \ˈpē-(ˌ)sō\ *n* : the peso of the Philippines

**pis·ta·chio** \pə-ˈsta-shē-ˌō, -ˈstä-\ *n, pl* **-chios** : the greenish edible seed of a small Asian tree related to the sumacs; *also* : the tree

**pis·til** \ˈpis-tᵊl\ *n* : the female reproductive organ in a flower — **pis·til·late** \ˈpis-tə-ˌlāt\ *adj*

**pis·tol** \ˈpis-tᵊl\ *n* : a handgun whose chamber is integral with the barrel

**pis·tol–whip** \-ˌhwip\ *vb* : to beat with a pistol

**pis·ton** \ˈpis-tən\ *n* : a sliding piece that receives and transmits motion and that usu. consists of a short cylinder inside a large cylinder

**¹pit** \ˈpit\ *n* **1** : a hole, shaft, or cavity in the ground **2** : an often sunken area designed for a particular use; *also* : an enclosed place (as for cockfights) **3** : HELL; *also, pl* : WORST ⟨it's the ~s⟩ **4** : a natural hollow or indentation in a surface **5** : a small indented mark or scar (as from disease or corrosion) **6** : an area beside a racecourse where cars are fueled and repaired during a race

**²pit** *vb* **pit·ted; pit·ting** **1** : to form pits in or become marred with pits **2** : to match for fighting

**³pit** *n* : the stony seed of some fruits (as the cherry, peach, and date)

**⁴pit** *vb* **pit·ted; pit·ting** : to remove the pit from

**pi·ta** \ˈpē-tə\ *n* [ModGk] : a thin flat bread

**pit–a–pat** \ˈpit-i-ˈpat\ *n* : PITTER-PATTER — **pit–a–pat** *adv or adj*

**pit bull** *n* : a powerful compact shorthaired dog developed for fighting

**¹pitch** \ˈpich\ *n* **1** : a dark sticky substance left over esp. from distilling tar or petroleum **2** : resin from various conifers — **pitchy** *adj*

**²pitch** *vb* **1** : to erect and fix firmly in place ⟨~ a tent⟩ **2** : THROW, FLING **3** : to deliver a baseball to a batter **4** : to toss (as coins) toward a mark **5** : to set at a particular level ⟨~ the voice low⟩ **6** : to fall headlong **7** : to have the front end (as of a ship) alternately plunge and rise **8** : to incline downward : SLOPE

**³pitch** *n* **1** : the action or a manner of pitching **2** : degree of slope ⟨~ of a roof⟩ **3** : the relative level of some quality or state ⟨a high ~ of excitement⟩ **4** : highness or lowness of sound; *also* : a standard frequency for tuning instruments **5** : a presentation delivered to sell or promote something **6** : the delivery of a baseball to a batter; *also* : the baseball delivered

**pitch·blende** \ˈpich-ˌblend\ *n* : a dark mineral that is the chief source of uranium

**¹pitch·er** \ˈpi-chər\ *n* : a container for liquids that usu. has a lip and a handle

**²pitcher** *n* : one that pitches esp. in a baseball game

**pitcher plant** *n* : any of various plants with leaves modified to resemble pitchers in which insects are trapped and digested

**pitch·fork** \ˈpich-ˌfȯrk\ *n* : a long-handled fork used esp. in pitching hay

**pitch in** *vb* **1** : to begin to work **2** : to contribute to a common effort

**pitch·man** \ˈpich-mən\ *n* : SALESMAN; *esp* : one who sells merchandise on the streets or from a concession

**pitch–per·fect** \ˈpich-ˈpər-fikt\ *adj* : having just the right tone or style ⟨a ~ translation⟩

**pit·e·ous** \ˈpi-tē-əs\ *adj* : arousing pity : PITIFUL — **pit·e·ous·ly** *adv*

**pit·fall** \ˈpit-ˌfȯl\ *n* **1** : TRAP, SNARE; *esp* : a covered pit used for capturing animals **2** : a hidden danger or difficulty

**pith** \ˈpith\ *n* **1** : loose spongy tissue esp. in the center of the stem of vascular plants **2** : the essential part : CORE

**pithy** \ˈpi-thē\ *adj* **pith·i·er; -est** **1** : consisting of or filled with pith **2** : having substance and point : CONCISE

**piti·a·ble** \ˈpi-tē-ə-bəl\ *adj* : PITIFUL

**piti·ful** \ˈpi-ti-fəl\ *adj* **1** : arousing or deserving pity ⟨a ~ sight⟩ **2** : lamentably inadequate : MEAGER — **piti·ful·ly** *adv*

**piti·less** \ˈpi-ti-ləs\ *adj* : devoid of pity : HARSH, CRUEL — **pit·i·less·ly** *adv*

**pi·ton** \ˈpē-ˌtän\ *n* [F] : a spike, wedge, or peg that can be driven into a rock or ice surface as a support

**pit·tance** \ˈpi-tᵊns\ *n* : a small portion, amount, or allowance

**pit·ted** \ˈpi-təd\ *adj* : marked with pits

**pit·ter–pat·ter** \ˈpi-tər-ˌpa-tər, ˈpi-tē-\ *n* : a rapid succession of light taps or sounds ⟨the ~ of rain⟩ — **pitter–patter** \ˌpi-tər-ˈpa-tər, ˌpi-tē-\ *adv or adj* — **pitter–patter** ⟨*same as adv*⟩ *vb*

**pi·tu·i·tary** \pə-ˈtü-ə-ˌter-ē, -ˈtyü-\ *n, pl* **-itar·ies** : PITUITARY GLAND — **pituitary** *adj*

**pituitary gland** *n* : a small oval endocrine gland located at the base of the brain that produces various hormones that affect most basic bodily functions (as growth and reproduction)

**pit viper** *n* : any of various mostly New World venomous snakes with a sensory pit on each side of the head and hollow perforated fangs

**¹pity** \ˈpi-tē\ *n, pl* **pit·ies** [ME *pite*, fr. AF *pité*, fr. L *pietas* piety, pity, fr. *pius* pious] **1** : sympathetic sorrow : COMPASSION **2** : something to be regretted

**²pity** *vb* **pit·ied; pity·ing** : to feel pity for

**¹piv·ot** \ˈpi-vət\ *n* : a fixed pin on which something turns — **pivot** *adj*

**²pivot** *vb* : to turn on or as if on a pivot

**piv·ot·al** \ˈpi-və-tᵊl\ *adj* **1** : of or relating to a pivot **2** : vitally important : CRITICAL ⟨a ~ decision⟩

**pix** *pl of* PIC

**pix·el** \ˈpik-səl, -ˌsel\ *n* **1** : any of the

small elements that together make up an image (as on a television screen) **2** : any of the detecting elements of a charge-coupled device used as an optical sensor

**pix·ie** *also* **pixy** \'pik-sē\ *n, pl* **pix·ies** : FAIRY; *esp* : a mischievous sprite

**piz·za** \'pēt-sə\ *n* [It] : an open pie made of rolled bread dough spread with a spiced mixture (as of tomatoes, cheese, and ground meat) and baked

**piz·zazz** *or* **pi·zazz** \pə-'zaz\ *n* **1** : GLAMOUR **2** : VITALITY

**piz·ze·ria** \ˌpēt-sə-'rē-ə\ *n* : an establishment where pizzas are made and sold

**piz·zi·ca·to** \ˌpit-si-'kä-tō\ *adv or adj* [It] : by means of plucking instead of bowing — used as a direction in music

**pj's** \'pē-ˌjāz\ *n pl* : PAJAMAS

**pk** *abbr* **1** park **2** peak **3** peck **4** pike

**pkg** *abbr* package

**pkt** *abbr* **1** packet **2** pocket

**pkwy** *abbr* parkway

**pl** *abbr* **1** place **2** plate **3** plural

**¹plac·ard** \'pla-kərd, -ˌkärd\ *n* : a notice posted in a public place : POSTER

**²plac·ard** \-ˌkärd, -kərd\ *vb* **1** : to cover with or as if with placards **2** : to announce by or as if by posting

**pla·cate** \'plā-ˌkāt, 'pla-\ *vb* **pla·cat·ed; pla·cat·ing** : to soothe esp. by concessions : APPEASE — **pla·ca·ble** \'pla-kə-bəl, 'plā-\ *adj*

**¹place** \'plās\ *n* [ME, fr. AF, open space, fr. L *platea* broad street, fr. Gk *plateia* (*hodos*), fr. fem. of *platys* broad, flat] **1** : SPACE, ROOM **2** : an indefinite region : AREA **3** : a building or locality used for a special purpose **4** : a center of population **5** : a particular part of a surface : SPOT **6** : relative position in a scale or sequence; *also* : position at the end of a competition ⟨last ∼⟩ **7** : ACCOMMODATION; *esp* : SEAT **8** : the position of a figure within a numeral ⟨12 is a two ∼ number⟩ **9** : JOB; *esp* : public office **10** : a public square **11** : 2d place at the finish (as of a horse race) — **in place of** : INSTEAD OF — **out of place** : not in the proper location : INAPPROPRIATE

**²place** *vb* **placed; plac·ing 1** : to put in a particular place : SET **2** : to distribute in an orderly manner : ARRANGE **3** : IDENTIFY **4** : to give an order for ⟨∼ a bet⟩ **5** : to earn a given spot in a competition; *esp* : to come in 2d

**pla·ce·bo** \plə-'sē-bō\ *n, pl* **-bos** [L, I shall please] : an inert medication used for its psychological effect or for purposes of comparison in an experiment

**place·hold·er** \'plās-ˌhōl-dər\ *n* : a symbol in a mathematical or logical expression that may be replaced by the name of any element of a set

**place–kick** \-ˌkik\ *n* : the kicking of a ball placed or held on the ground — **place–kick** *vb* — **place·kick·er** *n*

**place·ment** \'plās-mənt\ *n* : an act or instance of placing

**place–name** \-ˌnām\ *n* : the name of a geographical locality

**pla·cen·ta** \plə-'sen-tə\ *n, pl* **-tas** *or* **-tae** \-ˌtē\ [NL, fr. L, flat cake] : the organ in most mammals by which the fetus is joined to the maternal uterus and is nourished — **pla·cen·tal** \-'sen-t°l\ *adj or n*

**plac·er** \'pla-sər\ *n* : a deposit of sand or gravel containing particles of valuable mineral (as gold)

**plac·id** \'pla-səd\ *adj* : UNDISTURBED, PEACEFUL ♦ *Synonyms* TRANQUIL, SERENE, CALM — **pla·cid·i·ty** \pla-'si-də-tē\ *n* — **plac·id·ly** *adv*

**pla·gia·rise** *Brit var of* PLAGIARIZE

**pla·gia·rize** \'plā-jə-ˌrīz\ *vb* **-rized; -rizing** : to present the ideas or words of another as one's own — **pla·gia·rism** \-ˌri-zəm\ *n* — **pla·gia·rist** \-rist\ *n*

**¹plague** \'plāg\ *n* **1** : a disastrous evil or influx; *also* : NUISANCE **2** : PESTILENCE; *esp* : a destructive contagious bacterial disease (as bubonic plague)

**²plague** *vb* **plagued; plagu·ing 1** : to afflict with or as if with disease or disaster **2** : TEASE, TORMENT ⟨*plagued* by guilt⟩

**plaid** \'plad\ *n* [ScGael *plaide*] **1** : a rectangular length of tartan worn esp. over the left shoulder as part of the Scottish national costume **2** : a twilled woolen fabric with a tartan pattern **3** : a pattern of unevenly spaced repeated stripes crossing at right angles — **plaid** *adj*

**¹plain** \'plān\ *n* : an extensive area of level or rolling treeless country

**²plain** *adj* **1** : lacking ornament ⟨a ∼ dress⟩ **2** : free of extraneous matter **3** : OPEN, UNOBSTRUCTED ⟨∼ view⟩ **4** : EVIDENT, OBVIOUS **5** : easily understood : CLEAR **6** : CANDID, BLUNT **7** : SIMPLE, UNCOMPLICATED ⟨∼ cooking⟩ **8** : lacking beauty or ugliness — **plain·ly** *adv* — **plain·ness** *n*

**plain·clothes·man** \'plān-'klōthz-mən, -'klōz-, -ˌman\ *n* : a police officer who wears civilian clothes instead of a uniform while on duty : DETECTIVE

**plain·spo·ken** \-'spō-kən\ *adj* : FRANK

**plaint** \'plānt\ *n* **1** : LAMENTATION, WAIL **2** : PROTEST, COMPLAINT

**plain·tiff** \'plān-təf\ *n* : the complaining party in a lawsuit

**plain·tive** \'plān-tiv\ *adj* : expressive of suffering or woe : MELANCHOLY ⟨a ∼ sigh⟩ — **plain·tive·ly** *adv*

**plait** \'plāt, 'plat\ *n* **1** : PLEAT **2** : a braid esp. of hair or straw — **plait** *vb*

**¹plan** \'plan\ *n* **1** : a drawing or diagram showing the parts or details of something **2** : a method for accomplishing an objective; *also* : GOAL, AIM

**²plan** *vb* **planned; plan·ning 1** : to form a plan of ⟨∼ a new city⟩ **2** : INTEND ⟨*planned* to go⟩ — **plan·ner** *n*

**¹plane** \'plān\ *vb* **planed; plan·ing** : to smooth or level off with or as if with a plane — **plan·er** *n*

**²plane** *n* : PLANE TREE

**³plane** *n* : a tool for smoothing or shaping a wood surface

**⁴plane** *n* **1** : a level or flat surface **2** : a level of existence, consciousness, or development **3** : AIRPLANE

**⁵plane** *adj* **1** : FLAT, LEVEL **2** : dealing

with flat surfaces or figures ⟨~ geometry⟩

**plane·load** \'plān-ˌlōd\ n : a load that fills an airplane

**plan·et** \'pla-nət\ n [ME *planete*, fr. AF, fr. LL *planeta*, fr. Gk *planēt-*, *planēs*, lit., wanderer, fr. *planasthai* to wander] : any of the large bodies in the solar system that revolve around the sun — **plan·e·tary** \-nə-ˌter-ē\ *adj*

**plan·e·tar·i·um** \ˌpla-nə-'ter-ē-əm\ n, pl **-i·ums** or **-ia** \-ē-ə\ : a building or room housing a device to project images of celestial bodies

**plan·e·tes·i·mal** \ˌpla-nə-'tes-ə-məl\ n : any of numerous small solid celestial bodies which may have existed during the formation of the solar system

**plan·e·toid** \'pla-nə-ˌtȯid\ n : a body resembling a planet; *esp* : ASTEROID

**plane tree** n : any of a genus of trees (as a sycamore) with large lobed leaves and globe-shaped fruit

**plan·gent** \'plan-jənt\ *adj* **1** : having a loud reverberating sound ⟨a ~ roar⟩ **2** : having an expressive esp. plaintive quality ⟨~ lyrics⟩ — **plan·gen·cy** \-jən-sē\ n

**¹plank** \'plaŋk\ n **1** : a heavy thick board **2** : an article in the platform of a political party

**²plank** vb **1** : to cover with planks **2** : to set or lay down forcibly **3** : to cook and serve on a board

**plank·ing** \'plaŋ-kiŋ\ n : a quantity or covering of planks

**plank·ton** \'plaŋk-tən\ n [G, fr. Gk, neut. of *planktos* drifting] : the passively floating or weakly swimming animal and plant life of a body of water — **plank·ton·ic** \plaŋk-'tä-nik\ *adj*

**¹plant** \'plant\ vb **1** : to set in the ground to grow **2** : ESTABLISH, SETTLE **3** : to stock or provide with something **4** : to place firmly or forcibly **5** : to hide or arrange with intent to deceive

**²plant** n **1** : any of a kingdom of living things that usu. have no locomotor ability or obvious sense organs and have cellulose cell walls and usu. capacity for indefinite growth **2** : the land, buildings, and machinery used in carrying on a trade or business

**¹plan·tain** \'plan-tᵊn\ n [ME, fr. AF, fr. L *plantagin-*, *plantago*, fr. *planta* sole of the foot; fr. its broad leaves] : any of a genus of weedy herbs with spikes of tiny greenish flowers

**²plantain** n [Sp *plántano*, *plátano* plane tree, banana tree, fr. ML *plantanus* plane tree, alter. of L *platanus*] : a banana plant with starchy greenish fruit that is eaten cooked; *also* : its fruit

**plan·tar** \'plan-tər, -ˌtär\ *adj* : of or relating to the sole of the foot

**plan·ta·tion** \plan-'tā-shən\ n **1** : a large group of plants and esp. trees under cultivation **2** : an agricultural estate usu. worked by resident laborers

**plant·er** \'plan-tər\ n **1** : one that plants or sows; *esp* : an owner or operator of a plantation **2** : a container for plants

**plant louse** n : APHID

**plaque** \'plak\ n [F] **1** : an ornamental brooch **2** : a flat thin piece (as of metal) used for decoration; *also* : a commemorative tablet **3** : a bacteria-containing film on a tooth

**plash** \'plash\ n : SPLASH — **plash** vb

**plas·ma** \'plaz-mə\ n **1** : the fluid part of blood, lymph, or milk **2** : a gas composed of ionized particles **3** : a display (as a television screen) in which cells of plasma emit light upon receiving an electric current — **plas·mat·ic** \plaz-'ma-tik\ *adj*

**¹plas·ter** \'plas-tər\ n **1** : a dressing consisting of a backing spread with an often medicated substance that clings to the skin ⟨adhesive ~⟩ **2** : a paste that hardens as it dries and is used for coating walls and ceilings

**²plaster** vb : to cover with or as if with plaster — **plas·ter·er** n

**plas·ter·board** \'plas-tər-ˌbȯrd\ n : DRYWALL

**plaster of par·is** \-'pa-rəs\ *often cap 2d P* : a white powder made from gypsum and used as a quick-setting paste with water for casts and molds

**¹plas·tic** \'plas-tik\ *adj* [L *plasticus* of molding, fr. Gk *plastikos*, fr. *plassein* to mold, form] **1** : capable of being molded ⟨~ clay⟩ **2** : characterized by or using modeling ⟨~ arts⟩ **3** : made or consisting of a plastic ♦ **Synonyms** PLIABLE, PLIANT, DUCTILE, MALLEABLE, ADAPTABLE — **plas·tic·i·ty** \plas-'ti-sə-tē\ n

**²plastic** n : a plastic substance; *esp* : a synthetic or processed material that can be formed into rigid objects or into films or filaments

**plastic surgery** n : surgery to repair, restore, or improve lost, injured, defective, or misshapen body parts — **plastic surgeon** n

**¹plat** \'plat\ n **1** : a small plot of ground **2** : a plan of a piece of land with actual or proposed features (as lots)

**²plat** vb **plat·ted**; **plat·ting** : to make a plat of

**¹plate** \'plāt\ n **1** : a flat thin piece of material **2** : domestic hollowware made of or plated with gold, silver, or base metals **3** : DISH **4** : HOME PLATE **5** : the molded metal or plastic cast of a page of type to be printed from **6** : a sheet of glass or plastic coated with a chemical sensitive to light and used in photography **7** : the part of a denture that fits to the mouth; *also* : DENTURE **8** : something printed from an engraving **9** : a huge mobile segment of the earth's crust

**²plate** vb **plat·ed**; **plat·ing** **1** : to overlay with metal (as gold or silver) **2** : to make a printing plate of

**pla·teau** \pla-'tō\ n, pl **plateaus** or **pla·teaux** \-'tōz\ [F] : a large level area of high land

**plate glass** n : rolled, ground, and polished sheet glass

**plate·let** \'plāt-lət\ n : a minute flattened body; *esp* : a minute colorless disklike body of mammalian blood that assists in blood clotting

**plat·en** \'pla-tᵊn\ n **1** : a flat plate; *esp*

: one that exerts or receives pressure (as in a printing press)  **2** : the roller of a typewriter or printer

**plate tectonics** *n*  **1** : a theory in geology that the lithosphere is divided into plates at the boundaries of which much of earth's seismic activity occurs  **2** : the process and dynamics of tectonic plate movement — **plate–tectonic** *adj*

**plat·form** \'plat-,fȯrm\ *n*  **1** : a raised flooring or stage for speakers, performers, or workers  **2** : a declaration of the principles on which a group of persons (as a political party) stands  **3** : OPERATING SYSTEM

**plat·ing** \'plā-tiṇ\ *n* : a coating of metal plates or plate ⟨the ~ of a ship⟩

**plat·i·num** \'pla-tə-nəm\ *n* : a heavy grayish white metallic chemical element

**plat·i·tude** \'pla-tə-,tüd, -,tyüd\ *n* : a flat or trite remark — **plat·i·tu·di·nous** \-'tü-də-nəs, -'tyü-\ *adj*

**pla·ton·ic love** \plə-'tä-nik-, plā-\ *n, often cap P* : a close relationship between two persons without sexual desire

**pla·toon** \plə-'tün\ *n* [F *peloton* small detachment, lit., ball, fr. *pelote* little ball]  **1** : a subdivision of a company-size military unit usu. consisting of two or more squads or sections  **2** : a group of football players trained either for offense or for defense and sent into the game as a body

**platoon sergeant** *n* : a noncommissioned officer in the army ranking below a first sergeant

**plat·ter** \'pla-tər\ *n*  **1** : a large serving plate  **2** : a phonograph record

**platy** \'pla-tē\ *n, pl* **platy** *or* **plat·ys** *or* **plat·ies** : either of two small stocky usu. brilliantly colored bony fishes often kept in tropical aquariums

**platy·pus** \'pla-ti-pəs\ *n, pl* **platy·pus·es** *also* **platy·pi** \-,pī\ [NL, fr. Gk *platypous* flat-footed, fr. *platys* broad, flat + *pous* foot] : a small aquatic egg-laying marsupial mammal of Australia with webbed feet and a fleshy bill like a duck's

**plau·dit** \'plȯ-dət\ *n* : an act of applause

**plau·si·ble** \'plȯ-zə-bəl\ *adj* [L *plausibilis* worthy of applause, fr. *plausus*, pp. of *plaudere* to applaud] : seemingly worthy of belief — **plau·si·bil·i·ty** \,plȯ-zə-'bi-lə-tē\ *n* — **plau·si·bly** \'plȯ-zə-blē\ *adv*

**¹play** \'plā\ *n*  **1** : brisk handling of something (as a weapon)  **2** : the course of a game; *also* : a particular act or maneuver in a game  **3** : recreational activity; *esp* : the spontaneous activity of children  **4** : JEST ⟨said in ~⟩  **5** : the act or an instance of punning  **6** : GAMBLING  **7** : OPERATION ⟨bring extra force into ~⟩  **8** : a brisk or light movement  **9** : free motion (as of part of a machine)  **10** : scope for action  **11** : PUBLICITY  **12** : an effort to arouse liking ⟨made a ~ for her⟩  **13** : a stage representation of a drama; *also* : a dramatic composition  **14** : a function of an electronic device that causes a recording to play — **play·ful** \-fəl\ *adj* — **play·ful·ly** *adv* — **play·ful·ness** *n* — **in play** : in condition or position to be played

**²play** *vb*  **1** : to engage in recreation : FROLIC  **2** : to handle or behave lightly or absentmindedly  **3** : to make a pun ⟨~ on words⟩  **4** : to take advantage ⟨~ on fears⟩  **5** : to move or operate in a brisk or irregular manner ⟨a flashlight ~ed over the wall⟩  **6** : to perform music on a violin⟩; *also* : to perform (music) on an instrument ⟨~ a waltz⟩  **7** : to perform music upon ⟨~ the piano⟩; *also* : to sound in performance ⟨the organ is ~ing⟩  **8** : to cause to emit sounds ⟨~ a radio⟩; *also* : to cause to reproduce recorded material ⟨~ a DVD⟩  **9** : to act in a dramatic medium; *also* : to act in the character of ⟨~ the hero⟩  **10** : GAMBLE  **11** : to produce a specified impression in performance ⟨~s like a comedy⟩  **12** : to behave in a specified way ⟨~ safe⟩; *also* : COOPERATE ⟨~ along with him⟩  **13** : to deal with; *also* : EMPHASIZE ⟨~ up her good qualities⟩  **14** : to perform for amusement ⟨~ a trick⟩  **15** : WREAK  **16** : to use as an esp. political strategy  **17** : to contend with in a game; *also* : to fill (a certain position) on a team  **18** : to make wagers on ⟨~ the races⟩  **19** : WIELD, PLY  **20** : to keep in action — **play·er** *n*

**play·act·ing** \'plā-,ak-tiṇ\ *n*  **1** : performance in theatrical productions  **2** : insincere or artificial behavior

**play·back** \-,bak\ *n* : an act of reproducing recorded sound or pictures — **play back** *vb*

**play·bill** \-,bil\ *n* : a poster advertising the performance of a play

**play·book** \-,bùk\ *n*  **1** : a notebook containing diagrammed football plays  **2** : a stock of usual tactics or methods

**play·boy** \-,bȯi\ *n* : a man whose chief interest is the pursuit of pleasure

**play·date** \-,dāt\ *n* : a usu. prearranged play session for small children

**play·go·er** \-,gō-ər\ *n* : a person who frequently attends plays

**play·ground** \-,graùnd\ *n* : an area used for games and play esp. by children

**play·house** \-,haùs\ *n*  **1** : THEATER  **2** : a small house for children to play in

**playing card** *n* : any of a set of 24 to 78 cards marked to show its rank and suit and used to play a game of cards

**play·let** \'plā-lət\ *n* : a short play

**play·mate** \-,māt\ *n* : a companion in play

**play·off** \-,ȯf\ *n* : a contest or series of contests to break a tie or determine a championship

**play out** *vb* : DEVELOP, UNFOLD ⟨see how things *play out*⟩

**play·pen** \-,pen\ *n* : a portable enclosure in which a young child may play

**play·suit** \-,süt\ *n* : a sports and play outfit for women and children

**play·thing** \-,thiṇ\ *n* : TOY

**play·wright** \-,rīt\ *n* : a writer of plays

**pla·za** \'pla-zə, 'plä-\ *n* [Sp, fr. L *platea* broad street]  **1** : a public square in a city or town  **2** : a shopping center

**PLC** *abbr, Brit* public limited company

**plea** \'plē\ *n*  **1** : a defendant's answer in law to a charge or indictment  **2** : something alleged as an excuse **3** : ENTREATY, APPEAL

**plead** \ˈplēd\ vb **plead·ed** or **pled** \ˈpled\, **plead·ing** **1** : to argue before a court or authority ⟨~ a case⟩ **2** : to answer to a charge or indictment ⟨~ guilty⟩ **3** : to argue for or against something ⟨~ for acquittal⟩ **4** : to appeal earnestly ⟨~s for help⟩ **5** : to offer as a plea (as in defense) ⟨~ed illness⟩ — **plead·er** n

**pleas·ant** \ˈple-zᵊnt\ adj **1** : giving pleasure : AGREEABLE ⟨a ~ experience⟩ **2** : marked by pleasing behavior or appearance ⟨a ~ person⟩ — **pleas·ant·ly** adv — **pleas·ant·ness** n

**pleas·ant·ry** \-zᵊn-trē\ n, pl **-ries** : a pleasant and casual act or speech

**¹please** \ˈplēz\ vb **pleased; pleas·ing** **1** : to give pleasure or satisfaction to **2** : LIKE ⟨do as you ~⟩ **3** : to be the will or pleasure of ⟨may it ~ his Majesty⟩

**²please** adv — used as a function word to express politeness or emphasis in a request ⟨~ come in⟩

**pleasing** adj. : giving pleasure ⟨a ~ fragrance⟩ — **pleas·ing·ly** adv

**plea·sur·able** \ˈple-zhə-rə-bəl\ adj : PLEASANT, GRATIFYING ⟨a ~ cruise⟩ — **plea·sur·ably** \-blē\ adv

**plea·sure** \ˈple-zhər\ n **1** : DESIRE, INCLINATION ⟨await your ~⟩ **2** : a state of gratification : ENJOYMENT **3** : a source of delight or joy ⟨a ~ to see you dance⟩

**¹pleat** \ˈplēt\ vb **1** : FOLD; esp : to arrange in pleats **2** : BRAID

**²pleat** n : a fold (as in cloth) made by doubling material over on itself

**plebe** \ˈplēb\ n : a freshman at a military or naval academy

**¹ple·be·ian** \pli-ˈbē-ən\ n **1** : a member of the Roman plebs **2** : one of the common people

**²plebeian** adj **1** : of or relating to plebeians **2** : COMMON, VULGAR ⟨~ tastes⟩

**pleb·i·scite** \ˈple-bə-ˌsīt, -sət\ n : a vote of the people (as of a country) on a proposal submitted to them

**plebs** \ˈplebz\ n, pl **ple·bes** \ˈplē-bēz\ **1** : the general populace **2** : the common people of ancient Rome

**plec·trum** \ˈplek-trəm\ n, pl **plec·tra** \-trə\ or **plec·trums** [L] : ³PICK 3

**¹pledge** \ˈplej\ n [ME plegge security, fr. AF plege, fr. LL plebium, fr. *plebere to pledge, prob. of Gmc origin] **1** : something given as security for the performance of an act **2** : the state of being held as a security or guaranty **3** : TOAST 3 **4** : PROMISE, VOW

**²pledge** vb **pledged; pledg·ing** **1** : to deposit as a pledge **2** : TOAST 3 **3** : to bind by a pledge : PLIGHT **4** : PROMISE

**Pleis·to·cene** \ˈplī-stə-ˌsēn\ adj : of, relating to, or being the earlier epoch of the Quaternary — **Pleistocene** n

**ple·na·ry** \ˈplē-nə-rē, ˈple-\ adj **1** : FULL ⟨~ power⟩ **2** : including all entitled to attend ⟨~ session⟩

**pleni·po·ten·tia·ry** \ˌple-nə-pə-ˈten-chə-rē, -ˈten-chē-ˌer-ē\ n, pl **-ries** : a diplomatic agent having full authority — **plenipotentiary** adj

**plen·i·tude** \ˈple-nə-ˌtüd, -ˌtyüd\ n **1** : COMPLETENESS **2** : ABUNDANCE

**plen·te·ous** \ˈplen-tē-əs\ adj **1** : FRUITFUL **2** : existing in plenty

**plen·ti·ful** \ˈplen-ti-fəl\ adj **1** : containing or yielding plenty ⟨a ~ harvest⟩ **2** : ABUNDANT — **plen·ti·ful·ly** adv

**plen·ty** \ˈplen-tē\ n : a more than adequate number or amount

**ple·num** \ˈple-nəm, ˈplē-\ n, pl **-nums** or **-na** \-nə\ : a general assembly of all members esp. of a legislative body

**pleth·o·ra** \ˈple-thə-rə\ n : an excessive quantity or fullness; also : PROFUSION

**pleu·ri·sy** \ˈplu̇r-ə-sē\ n : inflammation of the membrane that lines the chest and covers the lungs

**plexi·glass** \ˈplek-si-ˌglas\ n [alter. of Plexiglas, a trademark] : a transparent acrylic plastic often used in place of glass

**plex·us** \ˈplek-səs\ n, pl **plex·us·es** \-sə-səz\ : an interlacing network esp. of blood vessels or nerves

**pli·able** \ˈplī-ə-bəl\ adj **1** : FLEXIBLE **2** : yielding easily to others ⟨a ~ child⟩ ♦ **Synonyms** PLASTIC, PLIANT, DUCTILE, MALLEABLE, ADAPTABLE — **pli·abil·i·ty** \ˌplī-ə-ˈbi-lə-tē\ n

**pli·ant** \ˈplī-ənt\ adj **1** : FLEXIBLE **2** : easily influenced : PLIABLE ⟨a ~ senator⟩ — **pli·an·cy** \-ən-sē\ n

**pli·ers** \ˈplī-ərz\ n pl : small pincers for bending or cutting wire or handling small objects

**¹plight** \ˈplīt\ vb : to put or give in pledge : ENGAGE

**²plight** n : an unfortunate, difficult, or precarious situation

**plinth** \ˈplinth\ n : the lowest part of the base of an architectural column

**Plio·cene** \ˈplī-ə-ˌsēn\ adj : of, relating to, or being the latest epoch of the Tertiary — **Pliocene** n

**PLO** abbr Palestine Liberation Organization

**plod** \ˈpläd\ vb **plod·ded; plod·ding** **1** : to walk heavily or slowly : TRUDGE **2** : to work laboriously and monotonously : DRUDGE — **plod·der** n — **plod·ding·ly** adv

**plonk** var of PLUNK

**plop** \ˈpläp\ vb **plopped; plop·ping** **1** : to fall or move with a sound like that of something dropping into water **2** : to set, drop, or throw heavily or hastily ⟨plopped down on the couch⟩ ⟨~ down 320⟩ — **plop** n

**¹plot** \ˈplät\ n **1** : a small area of ground **2** : a ground plan (as of an area) **3** : the main story (as of a book or movie) **4** : a secret scheme : INTRIGUE

**²plot** vb **plot·ted; plot·ting** **1** : to make a plot or plan of **2** : to mark on or as if on a chart **3** : to plan or contrive esp. secretly — **plot·ter** n

**plo·ver** \ˈplə-vər, ˈplō-\ n, pl **plover** or **plovers** [ME, fr. AF, fr. VL *pluviarius, fr. L pluvia rain] : any of a family of shorebirds that differ from the sandpipers in having shorter stouter bills

**¹plow** or **plough** \ˈplau̇\ n **1** : an implement used to cut, lift, turn over, and partly break up soil **2** : a device (as a snowplow) operating like a plow

**²plow** *or* **plough** *vb* **1** : to open, break up, or work with a plow **2** : to move through like a plow ⟨a ship ~*ing* the waves⟩ **3** : to proceed laboriously ⟨~*ed* through his work⟩ — **plow·able** *adj* — **plow·er** *n*

**plow·boy** \'plaú-ˌbói\ *n* : a boy who leads the horse drawing a plow

**plow·man** \-mən, -ˌman\ *n* **1** : a man who guides a plow **2** : a farm laborer

**plow·share** \-ˌsher\ *n* : a part of a plow that cuts the earth

**ploy** \'plói\ *n* : a tactic intended to embarrass or frustrate an opponent

**¹pluck** \'plək\ *vb* **1** : to pull off or out : PICK; *also* : to pull something from **2** : to play (an instrument) by pulling at the strings **3** : TUG, TWITCH

**²pluck** *n* **1** : an act or instance of plucking **2** : SPIRIT, COURAGE

**plucky** \'plə-kē\ *adj* **pluck·i·er; -est** : COURAGEOUS, SPIRITED ⟨~ recruits⟩

**¹plug** \'pləg\ *n* **1** : STOPPER; *also* : an obstructing mass **2** : a cake of tobacco **3** : a poor or worn-out horse **4** : SPARK PLUG **5** : a lure with several hooks used in fishing **6** : a device on the end of a cord for making an electrical connection **7** : a piece of favorable publicity

**²plug** *vb* **plugged; plug·ging 1** : to stop, make tight, or secure by inserting a plug **2** : HIT, SHOOT **3** : to publicize insistently **4** : PLOD, DRUDGE

**plug and play** *n* : a computer feature enabling the operating system to automatically detect and configure peripherals — **plug-and-play** *adj*

**plugged–in** \'pləgd-'in\ *adj* : technologically or socially informed and connected

**plug–in** \'pləg-ˌin\ *n* : a small piece of software that supplements a larger program

**plum** \'pləm\ *n* [ME, fr. OE *plūme*, modif. of L *prunum* plum, fr. Gk *proumnon*] **1** : a smooth-skinned juicy fruit borne by trees related to the peach and cherry; *also* : a tree bearing plums **2** : a raisin when used in desserts (as puddings) **3** : something excellent; *esp* : something desirable given in return for a favor

**plum·age** \'plü-mij\ *n* : the feathers of a bird — **plum·aged** \-mijd\ *adj*

**¹plumb** \'pləm\ *n* : a weight on the end of a line (**plumb line**) used esp. by builders to show vertical direction

**²plumb** *adv* **1** : VERTICALLY **2** : COMPLETELY ⟨~ tired out⟩ **3** : EXACTLY; *also* : IMMEDIATELY

**³plumb** *vb* : to sound, adjust, or test with a plumb ⟨~ the depth of a well⟩

**⁴plumb** *adj* **1** : VERTICAL **2** : COMPLETE

**plumb·er** \'plə-mər\ *n* : a worker who fits or repairs pipes and fixtures

**plumb·ing** \'plə-miŋ\ *n* : a system of pipes in a building for supplying and carrying off water

**¹plume** \'plüm\ *n* : FEATHER; *esp* : a large, conspicuous, or showy feather — **plumed** \'plümd\ *adj* — **plumy** \'plü-mē\ *adj*

**²plume** *vb* **plumed; plum·ing 1** : to provide or deck with feathers **2** : to indulge (oneself) in pride

**¹plum·met** \'plə-mət\ *n* : PLUMB; *also* : PLUMB LINE

**²plummet** *vb* : to drop or plunge straight down

**¹plump** \'pləmp\ *vb* **1** : to drop or fall suddenly or heavily **2** : to favor something strongly ⟨~*ing* for change⟩

**²plump** *n* : a sudden heavy fall or blow; *also* : the sound made by it

**³plump** *adv* **1** : straight down; *also* : straight ahead **2** : UNQUALIFIEDLY ⟨came out ~ for free trade⟩

**⁴plump** *adj* : having a full rounded usu. pleasing form ♦ **Synonyms** FLESHY, STOUT, ROLY-POLY, ROTUND — **plump·ness** *n*

**¹plun·der** \'plən-dər\ *vb* : to take the goods of by force or wrongfully : PILLAGE — **plun·der·er** *n*

**²plunder** *n* : something taken by force or theft : LOOT

**¹plunge** \'plənj\ *vb* **plunged; plung·ing 1** : IMMERSE, SUBMERGE **2** : to enter or cause to enter a state or course of action suddenly or violently ⟨~ into war⟩ **3** : to cast oneself into or as if into water **4** : to gamble heavily and recklessly **5** : to descend suddenly

**²plunge** *n* : a sudden dive, leap, or rush

**plung·er** \'plən-jər\ *n* **1** : one that plunges **2** : a sliding piece driven by or against fluid pressure : PISTON **3** : a rubber cup on a handle pushed against an opening to free a waste outlet of an obstruction

**plunk** \'pləŋk\ *or* **plonk** \'pläŋk, 'plȯŋk\ *vb* **1** : to make or cause to make a hollow metallic sound **2** : to drop heavily or suddenly — **plunk** *n*

**plu·per·fect** \ˌplü-'pər-fikt\ *adj* [ME *pluperfyth*, modif. of LL *plusquamperfectus*, lit., more than perfect] : of, relating to, or constituting a verb tense that denotes an action or state as completed at or before a past time spoken of — **pluperfect** *n*

**plu·ral** \'plúr-əl\ *adj* [ME, fr. AF & L; AF *plurel*, fr. L *pluralis*, fr. *plur-*, *plus* more] : of, relating to, or constituting a word form used to denote more than one — **plural** *n*

**plu·ral·i·ty** \plú-'ra-lə-tē\ *n, pl* **-ties 1** : the state of being plural **2** : an excess of votes over those cast for an opposing candidate **3** : the greatest number of votes cast when not a majority

**plu·ral·ize** \'plúr-ə-ˌlīz\ *vb* **-ized; -iz·ing** : to make plural or express in the plural form — **plu·ral·i·za·tion** \ˌplúr-ə-lə-'zā-shən\ *n*

**¹plus** \'pləs\ *adj* [L, more] **1** : mathematically positive **2** : having or being in addition to what is anticipated **3** : falling high in a specified range ⟨a grade of B ~⟩

**²plus** *n, pl* **plus·es** \'plə-səz\ *also* **plus·ses 1** : a sign + (**plus sign**) used in mathematics to indicate addition or a positive quantity **2** : an added quantity; *also* : a positive quality : SURPLUS

**³plus** *prep* **1** : increased by : with the addition of ⟨3 ~ 4⟩ **2** : BESIDES

**⁴plus** *conj* : AND ⟨soup ~ salad and bread⟩

**¹plush** \'pləsh\ *n* : a fabric with a pile longer and less dense than velvet pile — **plushy** *adj*

**²plush** *adj* : notably luxurious ⟨a ~ suite⟩ — **plush·ly** *adv* — **plush·ness** *n*

**plus/minus sign** *n* : the sign ± used to indicate a quantity taking on both a positive value and its negative or to indicate a plus or minus quantity

**plus or minus** *adj* : indicating a quantity whose positive and negative values bracket a range of values ⟨plus or minus 3 inches⟩

**plus–size** \'pləs-ˌsīz\ *also* **plus–sized** \-ˌsīzd\ *adj* : extra large ⟨~ clothing⟩ ⟨~ shoppers⟩

**Plu·to** \'plü-tō\ *n* : a dwarf planet whose orbit crosses the orbit of Neptune — see PLANET table

**plu·toc·ra·cy** \plü-'tä-krə-sē\ *n, pl* **-cies** **1** : government by the wealthy **2** : a controlling class of the wealthy — **plu·to·crat** \'plü-tə-ˌkrat\ *n* — **plu·to·crat·ic** \ˌplü-tə-'kra-tik\ *adj*

**plu·to·ni·um** \plü-'tō-nē-əm\ *n* : a radioactive chemical element formed by the decay of neptunium

**plu·vi·al** \'plü-vē-əl\ *adj* **1** : of or relating to rain **2** : characterized by abundant rain

**¹ply** \'plī\ *vb* **plied; ply·ing 1** : to use, practice, or work diligently ⟨~ a trade⟩ **2** : to keep supplying something to ⟨plied them with liquor⟩ **3** : to go or travel regularly esp. by sea

**²ply** *n, pl* **plies** : one of the folds, thicknesses, or strands of which something (as plywood or yarn) is made

**³ply** *vb* **plied; ply·ing** : to twist together ⟨~ yarns⟩

**ply·wood** \'plī-ˌwud\ *n* : material made of thin sheets of wood glued and pressed together

**pm** *abbr* premium

**Pm** *symbol* promethium

**PM** *abbr* **1** paymaster **2** police magistrate **3** postmaster **4** post meridiem — often not cap. and often punctuated **5** postmortem **6** prime minister **7** provost marshal

**pmk** *abbr* postmark

**PMS** \'pē-ˌem-'es\ *n* : PREMENSTRUAL SYNDROME

**pmt** *abbr* payment

**pneu·mat·ic** \nu-'ma-tik, nyu-\ *adj* **1** : of, relating to, or using air or wind **2** : moved by air pressure **3** : filled with compressed air ⟨~ tires⟩ — **pneu·mat·i·cal·ly** \-ti-k(ə-)lē\ *adv*

**pneu·mo·coc·cus** \ˌnü-mə-'kä-kəs, ˌnyü-\ *n, pl* **-coc·ci** \-'käk-ˌsī, -ˌsē; -'kä-ˌkī, -ˌkē\ : a bacterium that causes pneumonia — **pneu·mo·coc·cal** \-'kä-kəl\ *adj*

**pneu·mo·co·ni·o·sis** \ˌnü-mō-ˌkō-nē-'ō-səs, ˌnyü-\ *n* : a disease of the lungs caused by habitual inhalation of irritant mineral or metallic particles

**pneu·mo·nia** \nu-'mō-nyə, nyu-\ *n* : an inflammatory disease of the lungs

**Po** *symbol* polonium

**PO** *abbr* **1** petty officer **2** post office

**¹poach** \'pōch\ *vb* [ME *pocchen*, fr. MF *pocher*, fr. OF *poché* poached, lit., bagged, tr. *poche* bag, pouch, of Gmc origin] : to cook (as an egg or fish) in simmering liquid

**²poach** *vb* : to hunt or fish unlawfully — **poach·er** *n*

**POB** *abbr* post office box

**po·bla·no** \pō-'blä-nō\ *n, pl* **-nos** : a heart-shaped usu. mild chili pepper esp. when fresh and dark green

**po'·boy** \'pō-ˌboi\ *also* **poor boy** *n* : SUBMARINE 2

**pock** \'päk\ *n* : a small swelling on the skin (as in smallpox); *also* : a spot suggesting this

**¹pock·et** \'pä-kət\ *n* **1** : a small bag open at the top or side inserted in a garment **2** : supply of money : MEANS **3** : RECEPTACLE, CONTAINER **4** : a small isolated area or group ⟨~s of fog⟩ **5** : a small body of ore — **pock·et·ful** *n*

**²pocket** *vb* **1** : to put in or as if in a pocket **2** : STEAL ⟨~ed the profits⟩

**³pocket** *adj* **1** : small enough to fit in a pocket; *also* : SMALL, MINIATURE ⟨a ~ park⟩ **2** : carried in or paid from one's own pocket

**¹pock·et·book** \-ˌbuk\ *n* **1** : PURSE; *also* : HANDBAG **2** : financial resources

**²pocketbook** *adj* : relating to money

**pocket gopher** *n* : GOPHER 2

**pock·et·knife** \'pä-kət-ˌnīf\ *n* : a knife with a folding blade to be carried in the pocket

**pocket veto** *n* : an indirect veto of a legislative bill by an executive through retention of the bill unsigned until after adjournment of the legislature

**pock·mark** \'päk-ˌmärk\ *n* : a pit or scar caused by smallpox or acne — **pock·marked** \-ˌmärkt\ *adj*

**po·co** \'pō-kō, 'pò-\ *adv* [It, little, fr. L *paucus*] : SOMEWHAT — used to qualify a direction in music ⟨~ allegro⟩

**po·co a po·co** \ˌpō-kō-ä-'pō-kō, ˌpò-kō-ä-'pò-\ *adv* : little by little : GRADUALLY — used as a direction in music

**pod** \'päd\ *n* **1** : a dry fruit (as of a pea) that splits open when ripe **2** : an external streamlined compartment (as for a jet engine) on an airplane **3** : a compartment (as for personnel, a power unit, or an instrument) on a ship or craft

**POD** *abbr* pay on delivery

**pod·cast** \'päd-ˌkast\ *n* [*iPod*, trademark for a portable media player + broad*cast*] : a program made available in digital format for download over the Internet — **podcast** *vb* — **pod·cast·er** *n*

**po·di·a·try** \pə-'dī-ə-trē, pō-\ *n* : the medical care and treatment of the human foot — **po·di·at·ric** \ˌpō-dē-'a-trik\ *adj* — **po·di·a·trist** \pə-'dī-ə-trist, pō-\ *n*

**po·di·um** \'pō-dē-əm\ *n, pl* **podiums** *or* **po·dia** \-dē-ə\ **1** : a dais esp. for an orchestral conductor **2** : LECTERN

**POE** *abbr* port of entry

**po·em** \'pō-əm\ *n* : a composition in verse

**po·esy** \'pō-ə-zē\ *n* : POETRY

**po·et** \'pō-ət\ n [ME, fr. AF poete, fr. L poeta, fr. Gk poiētēs maker, poet, fr. poiein to make] : a writer of poetry; also : a creative artist of great sensitivity

**po·et·as·ter** \'pō-ə-ˌtas-tər\ n : an inferior poet

**po·et·ess** \'pō-ə-təs\ n : a girl or woman who is a poet

**poetic justice** n : an outcome in which vice is punished and virtue rewarded usu. in a manner peculiarly or ironically appropriate

**po·et·ry** \'pō-ə-trē\ n 1 : metrical writing 2 : POEMS — **po·et·ic** \pō-'e-tik\ or **po·et·i·cal** \-ti-kəl\ adj

**po·grom** \'pō-grəm, pō-'gräm\ n [Yiddish, fr. Russ, lit., devastation] : an organized massacre of helpless people and esp. of Jews

**poi** \'pói\ n, pl poi or pois : a food prepared from the cooked corms of taro that are mashed with water to the consistency of a paste or thick liquid

**poi·gnant** \'pói-nyənt\ adj 1 : painfully affecting the feelings ⟨~ grief⟩ 2 : deeply moving ⟨~ scene⟩ — **poi·gnan·cy** \-nyən-sē\ n

**poin·ci·ana** \ˌpóin-sē-'a-nə\ n : any of several ornamental tropical leguminous trees or shrubs with bright orange or red flowers

**poin·set·tia** \póin-'se-tē-ə\ n : a showy tropical American spurge with usu. scarlet bracts that suggest petals and surround small yellow flowers

**¹point** \'póint\ n 1 : an individual detail; also : the most important essential 2 : PURPOSE ⟨no ~ in continuing⟩ 3 : a geometric element that has position but no size 4 : a particular place : LOCALITY 5 : a particular stage or degree 6 : a sharp end : TIP 7 : a projecting piece of land 8 : a punctuation mark; esp : PERIOD 9 : DECIMAL POINT 10 : one of the divisions of the compass 11 : a unit of counting (as in a game score) — **point·less** adj — **pointy** \'póin-tē\ adj — **beside the point** : IRRELEVANT — **to the point** : RELEVANT, PERTINENT ⟨her remark was to the point⟩

**²point** vb 1 : to furnish with a point : SHARPEN 2 : PUNCTUATE 3 : to separate (a decimal fraction) from an integer by a decimal point — usu. used with off 4 : to indicate the position of esp. by extending a finger 5 : to direct attention to ⟨~ out an error⟩ 6 : AIM, DIRECT 7 : to lie extended, aimed, or turned in a particular direction : FACE, LOOK

**point–and–click** adj : relating to or being a computer interface that allows the activation of a file by selection with a pointing device (as a mouse)

**point–and–shoot** adj : having or using preset or automatically adjusted controls ⟨a ~ camera⟩

**point–blank** \'póint-'blaŋk\ adj 1 : so close to the target that a missile fired will travel in a straight line to the mark 2 : DIRECT, BLUNT ⟨a ~ refusal⟩ — **point–blank** adv

**point·ed** \'póin-təd\ adj 1 : having a

**point** 2 : being to the point : DIRECT 3 : aimed at a particular person or group; also : CONSPICUOUS, MARKED ⟨~ indifference⟩ — **point·ed·ly** adv

**point·er** \'póin-tər\ n 1 : one that points out : INDICATOR 2 : a large short-haired hunting dog 3 : HINT, TIP ⟨gave me some ~s on how to play⟩

**poin·til·lism** \'pwan-tē-ˌyi-zəm, 'póin-tə-ˌli-zəm\ n [F pointillisme, fr. pointiller to stipple, fr. point spot, point] : the theory or practice in painting of applying small strokes or dots of color to a surface so that from a distance they blend together — **poin·til·list** \ˌpwan-tē-'yēst, 'póin-tə-list\ n or adj

**point man** n : a principal spokesman or advocate

**point of no return** : a critical point at which turning back or reversal is not possible

**point of view** : a position from which something is considered or evaluated

**point spread** n : the number of points by which a favorite is expected to defeat an underdog

**¹poise** \'póiz\ vb poised; pois·ing : BALANCE

**²poise** n 1 : BALANCE 2 : self-possessed calmness ⟨kept his ~ even under attack⟩; also : a particular way of carrying oneself

**poi·sha** \'pói-shə\ n, pl poisha : the paisa of Bangladesh

**¹poi·son** \'pói-zᵊn\ n [ME, fr. AF poisun drink, potion, poison, fr. L potion-, potio drink] : a substance that through its chemical action can injure or kill — **poi·son·ous** \-zᵊn-əs\ adj

**²poison** vb 1 : to injure or kill with poison 2 : to treat or taint with poison 3 : to affect destructively : CORRUPT ⟨~ed her mind⟩ — **poi·son·er** n

**poison hemlock** n : a large branching poisonous herb with finely divided leaves and white flowers that is related to the carrot

**poison ivy** n 1 : a usu. climbing plant related to the sumacs that bears leaves composed of three shiny leaflets and produces an irritating oil causing a usu. intensely itching skin rash; also : any of several related plants 2 : a skin rash caused by poison ivy

**poison oak** n : any of several shrubby plants closely related to poison ivy and having similar properties

**poison sumac** n : a No. American swamp shrub with pinnate leaves, greenish flowers, greenish white berries, and irritating properties

**¹poke** \'pōk\ n, chiefly Southern & Midland : BAG, SACK

**²poke** vb poked; pok·ing 1 : PROD; also : to stir up by prodding 2 : to make a prodding or jabbing movement esp. repeatedly 3 : HIT, PUNCH 4 : to thrust forward obtrusively 5 : RUMMAGE ⟨poking around the attic⟩ 6 : MEDDLE, PRY 7 : DAWDLE ⟨poking along toward home⟩ — **poke fun at** : RIDICULE, MOCK

**³poke** n : a quick thrust; also : PUNCH

¹**pok·er** \'pō-kər\ *n* : a metal rod for stirring a fire

²**po·ker** \'pō-kər\ *n* : any of several card games in which the player with the highest hand at the end of the betting wins

**poke·weed** \'pōk-,wēd\ *n* : a coarse American perennial herb with clusters of white flowers and dark purple juicy berries

**poky** *or* **pok·ey** \'pō-kē\ *adj* **pok·i·er; -est** 1 : small and cramped 2 : SHABBY, DULL 3 : annoyingly slow

**pol** \'päl\ *n* : POLITICIAN

**po·lar** \'pō-lər\ *adj* 1 : of or relating to a geographical pole 2 : of or relating to a pole (as of a magnet)

**polar bear** *n* : a large creamy-white bear that inhabits arctic regions

**Po·lar·is** \pō-'lar-əs\ *n* : NORTH STAR

**po·lar·ise** *Brit var of* POLARIZE

**po·lar·i·ty** \pō-'ler-ə-tē\ *n, pl* **-ties** : the condition of having poles and esp. magnetic or electrical poles

**po·lar·i·za·tion** \,pō-lə-rə-'zā-shən\ *n* 1 : the action of polarizing : the state of being polarized 2 : concentration about opposing extremes

**po·lar·ize** \'pō-lə-,rīz\ *vb* **-ized; -iz·ing** 1 : to cause (light waves) to vibrate in a definite way 2 : to give physical polarity to 3 : to break up into opposing groups

**pol·der** \'pōl-dər, 'päl-\ *n* [D] : a tract of low land reclaimed from the sea

¹**pole** \'pōl\ *n* : a long slender piece of wood or metal ⟨telephone ∼⟩

²**pole** *vb* **poled; pol·ing** : to impel or push with a pole ⟨∼ a boat⟩

³**pole** *n* 1 : either end of an axis esp. of the earth 2 : either of the terminals of an electric device (as a battery or generator) 3 : one of two or more regions in a magnetized body at which the magnetism is concentrated — **pole·ward** \'pōl-wərd\ *adj or adv*

¹**pole·ax** \'pōl-,aks\ *n* : a battle-ax with a short handle

²**poleax** *vb* : to attack or fell with or as if with a poleax

**pole·cat** \'pōl-,kat\ *n, pl* **polecats** *or* **polecat** 1 : a European carnivorous mammal of which the ferret is considered a domesticated variety 2 : SKUNK

**po·lem·ic** \pə-'le-mik\ *n* : the art or practice of disputation — usu. used in pl. — **po·lem·i·cal** \-mi-kəl\ *also* **po·lem·ic** \-mik\ *adj* — **po·lem·i·cist** \-sist\ *n*

**pole·star** \'pōl-,stär\ *n* 1 : NORTH STAR 2 : a directing principle : GUIDE

**pole vault** *n* : a field contest in which each contestant uses a pole to vault for height over a crossbar — **pole–vault** *vb* — **pole–vault·er** *n*

¹**po·lice** \pə-'lēs\ *vb* **po·liced; po·lic·ing** 1 : to control, regulate, or keep in order esp. by use of police ⟨∼ a highway⟩ 2 : to make clean and put in order ⟨policed up the concert site⟩

²**police** *n, pl* **police** [F, government, fr. OF, fr. LL *politia*, fr. Gk *politeia*, fr. *politēs* citizen, fr. *polis* city, state] 1 : the department of government that keeps public order and safety and enforces the laws; *also* : the members of this department 2 : a private organization resembling a police force; *also* : its members 3 : military personnel detailed to clean and put in order

**po·lice·man** \-mən\ *n* : POLICE OFFICER

**police officer** *n* : a member of a police force

**police state** *n* : a state characterized by repressive, arbitrary, totalitarian rule by means of secret police

**po·lice·wom·an** \pə-'lēs-,wu̇-mən\ *n* : a woman who is a police officer

¹**pol·i·cy** \'pä-lə-sē\ *n, pl* **-cies** : a definite course or method of action selected to guide and determine present and future decisions

²**policy** *n, pl* **-cies** : a writing whereby a contract of insurance is made

**pol·i·cy·hold·er** \'pä-lə-sē-,hōl-dər\ *n* : one granted an insurance policy

**po·lio** \'pō-lē-,ō\ *n* : POLIOMYELITIS — **polio** *adj*

**po·lio·my·eli·tis** \-,mī-ə-'lī-təs\ *n* : an acute virus disease marked by inflammation of the gray matter of the spinal cord leading usu. to paralysis

¹**pol·ish** \'pä-lish\ *vb* 1 : to make smooth and glossy usu. by rubbing 2 : to refine or improve in manners, condition, or style

²**polish** *n* 1 : a smooth glossy surface : LUSTER 2 : REFINEMENT, CULTURE 3 : the action or process of polishing 4 : a preparation used to produce a gloss

**Pol·ish** \'pō-lish\ *n* : the Slavic language of the Poles — **Polish** *adj*

**polit** *abbr* political; politician

**po·lit·bu·ro** \'pä-lət-,byu̇r-ō, 'pō-, pə-'lit-\ *n* [Russ *politbyuro*] : the principal policy-making committee of a Communist party

**po·lite** \pə-'līt\ *adj* **po·lit·er; -est** 1 : REFINED, CULTIVATED ⟨∼ society⟩ 2 : marked by correct social conduct : COURTEOUS; *also* : CONSIDERATE, TACTFUL — **po·lite·ly** *adv* — **po·lite·ness** *n*

**po·li·tesse** \,pä-li-'tes\ *n* [F] : formal politeness

**pol·i·tic** \'pä-lə-,tik\ *adj* 1 : wise in promoting a policy ⟨a ∼ statesman⟩ 2 : shrewdly tactful ⟨a ∼ move⟩

**po·lit·i·cal** \pə-'li-ti-kəl\ *adj* 1 : of or relating to government or politics 2 : involving or charged or concerned with acts against a government or a political system ⟨∼ prisoners⟩ — **po·lit·i·cal·ly** \-k(ə-)lē\ *adv*

**politically correct** *adj* : conforming to a belief that language and practices which could offend sensibilities (as in matters of sex or race) should be eliminated — **political correctness** *n*

**pol·i·ti·cian** \,pä-lə-'ti-shən\ *n* : a person actively engaged in government or politics

**pol·i·tick** \'pä-lə-,tik\ *vb* : to engage in political discussion or activity

**po·lit·i·co** \pə-'li-ti-,kō\ *n, pl* **-cos** *also* **-coes** : POLITICIAN

**pol·i·tics** \'pä-lə-,tiks\ *n sing or pl* 1 : the art or science of government, of guiding or influencing governmental policy, or of winning and holding control over a government **2** : political affairs or business; *esp* : competition between groups or individuals for power and leadership **3** : political opinions

**pol·i·ty** \'pä-lə-tē\ *n, pl* **-ties** : a politically organized unit; *also* : the form or constitution of such a unit

**pol·ka** \'pōl-kə, 'pō-kə\ *n* [Czech, fr. *Polka* Polish woman, fem. of *Polák* Pole] : a lively couple dance of Bohemian origin; *also* : music for this dance — **polka** *vb*

**pol·ka dot** \'pō-kə-,dät\ *n* : a dot in a pattern of regularly distributed dots — **polka–dot** *or* **polka–dot·ted** \-,dä-təd\ *adj*

**¹poll** \'pōl\ *n* **1** : HEAD **2** : the casting and recording of votes; *also* : the total vote cast **3** : the place where votes are cast — usu. used in pl. **4** : a questioning of persons to obtain information or opinions to be analyzed

**²poll** *vb* **1** : to cut off or shorten a growth or part of : CLIP, SHEAR **2** : to receive and record the votes of **3** : to receive (as votes) in an election **4** : to question in a poll

**pol·lack** *or* **pol·lock** \'pä-lək\ *n, pl* **pollack** *or* **pollock** : an important No. Atlantic food fish that is related to the cods; *also* : a related food fish of the No. Pacific

**pol·len** \'pä-lən\ *n* [NL, fr. L, fine flour] : a mass of male spores of a seed plant usu. appearing as a yellow dust

**pol·li·na·tion** \,pä-lə-'nā-shən\ *n* : the carrying of pollen to the female part of a plant to fertilize the seed — **pol·li·nate** \'pä-lə-,nāt\ *vb* — **pol·li·na·tor** \-,nā-tər\ *n*

**poll·ster** \'pōl-stər\ *n* : one that conducts a poll or compiles data obtained by a poll

**poll tax** *n* : a tax of a fixed amount per person levied on adults and often linked to the right to vote

**pol·lute** \pə-'lüt\ *vb* **pol·lut·ed; pol·lut·ing** : to make impure; *esp* : to contaminate (an environment) esp. with manmade waste — **pol·lut·ant** \-'lü-ᵊnt\ *n* — **pol·lut·er** *n* — **pol·lu·tion** \-'lü-shən\ *n*

**pol·ly·wog** *or* **pol·li·wog** \'pä-lē-,wäg\ *n* : TADPOLE

**po·lo** \'pō-lō\ *n* [Balti (Tibetan language of northern Kashmir), ball] : a game played by two teams on horseback using long-handled mallets to drive a wooden ball

**po·lo·ni·um** \pə-'lō-nē-əm\ *n* : a radioactive metallic chemical element

**pol·ter·geist** \'pōl-tər-,gīst\ *n* [G, fr. *poltern* to knock + *Geist* spirit] : a noisy usu. mischievous ghost held to be responsible for unexplained noises

**pol·troon** \päl-'trün\ *n* : COWARD

**poly-** *comb form* [Gk, fr. *polys* many] **1** : many : several ⟨*poly*syllabic⟩ **2** : polymeric ⟨*poly*ester⟩

**poly·chlo·ri·nat·ed bi·phe·nyl** \,pä-li-'klōr-ə-,nā-təd-,bī-'fen-ᵊl, -'fēn-\ *n* : any of several industrial compounds that are toxic environmental pollutants

**poly·clin·ic** \,pä-li-'kli-nik\ *n* : a clinic or hospital treating diseases of many sorts

**poly·es·ter** \'pä-lē-,es-tər\ *n* : a polymer composed of ester groups used esp. in making fibers or plastics; *also* : a product (as fabric) composed of polyester

**poly·eth·yl·ene** \,pä-lē-'e-thə-,lēn\ *n* : a lightweight plastic resistant to chemicals and moisture and used chiefly in packaging

**po·lyg·a·my** \pə-'li-gə-mē\ *n* : the practice of having more than one wife or husband at one time — **po·lyg·a·mist** \-mist\ *n* — **po·lyg·a·mous** \-məs\ *adj*

**poly·glot** \'pä-li-,glät\ *adj* **1** : speaking or writing several languages **2** : containing or made up of several languages — **polyglot** *n*

**poly·gon** \'pä-li-,gän\ *n* : a closed plane figure bounded by straight lines — **po·lyg·o·nal** \pə-'li-gə-nᵊl\ *adj*

**poly·graph** \'pä-li-,graf\ *n* : an instrument (as a lie detector) for recording variations of several bodily functions (as blood pressure) simultaneously — **po·lyg·ra·pher** \pə-'li-grə-fər, 'pä-li-,gra-fər\ *n*

**poly·he·dron** \,pä-li-'hē-drən\ *n* : a solid formed by plane faces that are polygons — **poly·he·dral** \-drəl\ *adj*

**poly·math** \'pä-li-,math\ *n* : a person of encyclopedic learning

**poly·mer** \'pä-lə-mər\ *n* : a chemical compound formed by union of small molecules and usu. consisting of repeating structural units — **poly·mer·ic** \,pä-lə-'mer-ik\ *adj*

**po·lym·er·i·za·tion** \pə-,li-mə-rə-'zā-shən\ *n* : a chemical reaction in which two or more small molecules combine to form polymers — **po·lym·er·ize** \pə-'li-mə-,rīz\ *vb*

**Poly·ne·sian** \,pä-lə-'nē-zhən\ *n* **1** : a member of any of the indigenous peoples of Polynesia **2** : a group of Austronesian languages spoken in Polynesia — **Polynesian** *adj*

**poly·no·mi·al** \,pä-lə-'nō-mē-əl\ *n* : an algebraic expression having one or more terms each of which consists of a constant multiplied by one or more variables raised to a nonnegative integral power — **polynomial** *adj*

**pol·yp** \'pä-ləp\ *n* **1** : an invertebrate animal (as a coral) that is a coelenterate having a hollow cylindrical body closed at one end **2** : a growth projecting from a mucous membrane (as of the colon or vocal cords)

**po·lyph·o·ny** \pə-'li-fə-nē\ *n* : music consisting of two or more melodically independent but harmonizing voice parts — **poly·phon·ic** \,pä-li-'fä-nik\ *adj*

**poly·pro·pyl·ene** \,pä-li-'prō-pə-,lēn\ *n* : any of various polymer plastics or fibers

**poly·sty·rene** \,pä-li-'stī-,rēn\ *n* : a rigid transparent nonconducting thermoplastic used esp. in molded products and foams

**poly·syl·lab·ic** \-sə-'la-bik\ *adj* **1** : having more than three syllables **2** : characterized by polysyllabic words

**poly·syl·la·ble** \'pä-li-ˌsi-lə-bəl\ *n* : a polysyllabic word

**poly·tech·nic** \ˌpä-li-'tek-nik\ *adj* : of, relating to, or instructing in many technical arts or applied sciences

**poly·the·ism** \'pä-li-thē-ˌi-zəm\ *n* : belief in or worship of many gods — **poly·the·ist** \-ˌthē-ist\ *adj or n* — **poly·the·is·tic** \ˌpä-li-(ˌ)thē-'is-tik\ *adj*

**poly·un·sat·u·rat·ed** \ˌpä-lē-ˌən-'sa-chə-ˌrā-təd\ *adj* : having many double or triple bonds in a molecule — used esp. of an oil or fatty acid

**poly·ure·thane** \ˌpä-lē-'yur-ə-ˌthān\ *n* : any of various polymers used esp. in foams and resins (as for coatings)

**poly·vi·nyl** \ˌpä-li-'vī-nəl\ *adj* : of, relating to, or being a polymerized vinyl compound, resin, or plastic — often used in combination

**pome·gran·ate** \'pä-mə-ˌgra-nət\ *n* [ME *poumgrenet*, fr. AF *pome garnette*, lit., seedy fruit] : a many-seeded reddish fruit that has an edible crimson pulp and is borne by a tropical Asian tree; *also* : the tree

**¹pom·mel** \'pə-məl, 'pä-\ *n* 1 : the knob on the hilt of a sword 2 : the knoblike bulge at the front and top of a saddlebow

**²pom·mel** \'pə-məl\ *vb* **-meled** *or* **-melled**; **-mel·ing** *or* **-mel·ling** : PUMMEL

**pomp** \'pämp\ *n* 1 : brilliant display : SPLENDOR 2 : OSTENTATION

**pom·pa·dour** \'päm-pə-ˌdȯr\ *n* : a style of dressing the hair high over the forehead

**pom·pa·no** \'päm-pə-ˌnō, 'pəm-\ *n, pl* **-no** *or* **-nos** : a narrow silvery fish of coastal waters of the western Atlantic

**pom–pom** \'päm-ˌpäm\ *n* 1 : an ornamental ball or tuft used on a cap or costume 2 : a fluffy ball flourished by cheerleaders

**pom·pon** \'päm-ˌpän\ *n* 1 : POM-POM 2 : a chrysanthemum or dahlia with small rounded flower heads

**pomp·ous** \'päm-pəs\ *adj* 1 : suggestive of pomp; *esp* : OSTENTATIOUS 2 : pretentiously dignified (~ politicians) 3 : excessively elevated or ornate ◆ **Synonyms** ARROGANT, MAGISTERIAL, SELF-IMPORTANT — **pom·pos·i·ty** \päm-'pä-sə-tē\ *n* — **pomp·ous·ly** *adv*

**pon·cho** \'pän-chō\ *n, pl* **ponchos** [AmerSp, fr. Mapuche (American Indian language of Chile)] 1 : a blanket with a slit in the middle for the head so that it can be worn as a garment 2 : a waterproof garment resembling a poncho

**pond** \'pänd\ *n* : a small body of water

**pon·der** \'pän-dər\ *vb* **pon·dered**; **pon·der·ing** 1 : to weigh in the mind 2 : to consider carefully

**pon·der·o·sa pine** \'pän-də-ˌrō-sə-, -zə-\ *n* : a tall pine of western No. America with long needles; *also* : its strong reddish wood

**pon·der·ous** \'pän-də-rəs\ *adj* 1 : of very great weight 2 : UNWIELDY, CLUMSY (a ~ weapon) 3 : oppressively dull (a ~ speech) ◆ **Synonyms** CUMBROUS, CUMBERSOME, WEIGHTY

**pone** \'pōn\ *n, Southern & Midland* : an

oval-shaped cornmeal cake; *also* : corn bread in the form of pones

**pon·iard** \'pän-yərd\ *n* : DAGGER

**pon·tiff** \'pän-təf\ *n* : POPE — **pon·tif·i·cal** \pän-'ti-fi-kəl\ *adj*

**¹pon·tif·i·cate** \pän-'ti-fi-kət, -fə-ˌkāt\ *n* : the state, office, or term of office of a pontiff

**²pon·tif·i·cate** \pän-'ti-fə-ˌkāt\ *vb* **-cat·ed**; **-cat·ing** : to deliver dogmatic opinions

**pon·toon** \pän-'tün\ *n* 1 : a flat-bottomed boat 2 : a boat or float used in building a floating temporary bridge 3 : a float of a seaplane

**po·ny** \'pō-nē\ *n, pl* **ponies** : a small horse

**po·ny·tail** \-ˌtāl\ *n* : a style of arranging hair to resemble the tail of a pony

**pooch** \'püch\ *n* : DOG

**poo·dle** \'pü-dəl\ *n* [G *Pudel*, short for *Pudelhund*, fr. *pudeln* to splash + *Hund* dog] : any of a breed of active intelligent dogs with a dense curly solid-colored coat

**pooh–pooh** \'pü-'pü\ *also* **pooh** \'pü\ *vb* 1 : to express contempt or impatience 2 : DERIDE, SCORN (~ed my idea)

**¹pool** \'pül\ *n* 1 : a small deep body of usu. fresh water 2 : a small body of standing liquid 3 : SWIMMING POOL

**²pool** *vb* : to form a pool

**³pool** *n* 1 : all the money bet on the result of a particular event 2 : any of several games of billiards played on a table having six pockets 3 : the amount contributed by the participants in a joint venture 4 : a combination between competing firms for mutual profit 5 : a readily available supply

**⁴pool** *vb* : to combine (as resources) in a common fund or effort

**¹poop** \'püp\ *n* : an enclosed superstructure at the stern of a ship

**²poop** *n, slang* : INFORMATION

**poop deck** *n* : a partial deck above a ship's main afterdeck

**poor** \'pur\ *adj* 1 : lacking material possessions (~ people) 2 : less than adequate : MEAGER (a ~ crop) 3 : arousing pity (you ~ thing) 4 : inferior in quality or value 5 : UNPRODUCTIVE, BARREN (~ soil) 6 : fairly unsatisfactory (~ prospects); *also* : UNFAVORABLE (~ opinion) — **poor·ly** *adv*

**poor boy** *var of* PO'BOY

**poor·house** \'pur-ˌhaüs\ *n* : a publicly supported home for needy or dependent persons

**poor–mouth** \-ˌmaùth, -ˌmaùth\ *vb* : to plead poverty as a defense or excuse

**¹pop** \'päp\ *vb* **popped**; **pop·ping** 1 : to go, come, enter, or issue forth suddenly or quickly (~ into bed) 2 : to put or thrust suddenly (~ questions) 3 : to burst or cause to burst with a sharp sound; *also* : to make a sharp sound 4 : to protrude from the sockets 5 : SHOOT 6 : to hit a pop-up

**²pop** *n* 1 : a sharp explosive sound 2 : SHOT 3 : SODA POP

**³pop** *n* : FATHER

**⁴pop** *adj* 1 : POPULAR (~ music) 2 : of

or relating to pop music ⟨~ singer⟩ **.3** : of or relating to the popular culture disseminated through the mass media ⟨~ psychology⟩ **4** : of, relating to, or imitating pop art ⟨~ painter⟩

⁵**pop** *n* : pop music or culture; *also* : POP ART

⁶**pop** *abbr* population

**pop art** *n, often cap P&A* : art in which commonplace objects (as comic strips or soup cans) are used as subject matter — **pop artist** *n*

¹**pop·corn** \'päp-ˌkȯrn\ *n* : a corn whose kernels burst open into a white starchy mass when heated; *also* : the burst kernels

²**popcorn** *adj* : having widespread appeal but little artistic merit ⟨~ movies⟩

**pope** \'pōp\ *n, often cap* : the head of the Roman Catholic Church

**pop-eyed** \'päp-ˌīd\ *adj* : having eyes that bulge (as from disease)

**pop fly** *n* : POP-UP

**pop·gun** \'päp-ˌgən\ *n* : a toy gun for shooting pellets with compressed air

**pop·in·jay** \'päp-ən-ˌjā\ *n* [ME *papejay* parrot, fr. MF *papegai, papejai*, fr. Ar *babghā'*] : a strutting supercilious person

**pop·lar** \'pä-plər\ *n* **1** : any of a genus of slender quick-growing trees (as a cottonwood) related to the willows **2** : the wood of a poplar

**pop·lin** \'pä-plən\ *n* : a strong plain-woven fabric with crosswise ribs

**pop·over** \'päp-ˌō-vər\ *n* : a hollow muffin made from a thin batter rich in egg

**pop·per** \'pä-pər\ *n* : a utensil for popping corn

**pop·py** \'pä-pē\ *n, pl* **poppies** : any of a genus of herbs with showy flowers including one that yields opium

**pop·py·cock** \-ˌkäk\ *n* : empty talk or writing : NONSENSE

**pop·u·lace** \'pä-pyə-ləs\ *n* **1** : the common people **2** : POPULATION

**pop·u·lar** \'pä-pyə-lər\ *adj* **1** : of or relating to the general public ⟨~ government⟩ **2** : suited to the tastes of the general public ⟨~ style⟩ **3** : INEXPENSIVE ⟨~ rates⟩ **4** : frequently encountered or widely accepted ⟨~ notion⟩ **5** : commonly liked or approved ⟨a ~ teacher⟩ — **pop·u·lar·i·ty** \ˌpä-pyə-'la-rə-tē\ *n* — **pop·u·lar·ize** \'pä-pyə-lə-ˌrīz\ *vb* — **pop·u·lar·ly** *adv*

**pop·u·late** \'pä-pyə-ˌlāt\ *vb* **-lat·ed; -lat·ing 1** : to have a place in : INHABIT **2** : PEOPLE

**pop·u·la·tion** \ˌpä-pyə-'lā-shən\ *n* **1** : the people or number of people in an area **2** : the organisms inhabiting a particular locality **3** : a group of individuals or items from which samples are taken for statistical measurement

**population explosion** *n* : a pyramiding of numbers of a biological population; *esp* : the recent great increase in human numbers resulting from increased survival and exponential population growth

**pop·u·list** \'pä-pyə-list\ *n* : a believer in or advocate of the rights, wisdom, or virtues of the common people — **pop·u·lism** \-ˌli-zəm\ *n*

**pop·u·lous** \'pä-pyə-ləs\ *adj* **1** : densely populated; *also* : having a large population **2** : CROWDED — **pop·u·lous·ness** *n*

¹**pop-up** \'päp-ˌəp\ *n* : a short high fly in baseball

²**pop-up** *adj* : of, relating to, or having a component or device that pops up

**por·ce·lain** \'pȯr-sə-lən\ *n* : a fine-grained translucent ceramic ware

**porch** \'pȯrch\ *n* : a covered entrance usu. with a separate roof

**por·cine** \'pȯr-ˌsīn\ *adj* : of, relating to, or suggesting swine

**por·ci·ni** \pȯr-'chē-nē\ *n, pl* **porcini** [It] : a large edible brownish mushroom

**por·ci·no** \pȯr-'chē-nō\ *n, pl* **-ni** : PORCINI

**por·cu·pine** \'pȯr-kyə-ˌpīn\ *n* [ME *porke despyne*, fr. MF *porc espin*, fr. It *porcospino*, fr. L *porcus* pig + *spina* spine, prickle] : any of various mammals having stiff sharp spines mingled with their hair

¹**pore** \'pȯr\ *vb* **pored; por·ing 1** : to read studiously or attentively ⟨~ over a book⟩ **2** : PONDER, REFLECT

²**pore** *n* : a tiny hole or space (as in the skin or soil) — **pored** \'pȯrd\ *adj*

**pork** \'pȯrk\ *n* : the flesh of swine dressed for use as food

**pork barrel** *n* : government projects or appropriations yielding rich patronage benefits

**pork·er** \'pȯr-kər\ *n* : HOG; *esp* : a young pig suitable for use as fresh pork

**por·nog·ra·phy** \pȯr-'nä-grə-fē\ *n* : the depiction of erotic behavior intended to cause sexual excitement — **por·no·graph·ic** \ˌpȯr-nə-'gra-fik\ *adj*

**po·rous** \'pȯr-əs\ *adj* **1** : full of pores **2** : permeable to fluids : ABSORPTIVE — **po·ros·i·ty** \pȯ-'rä-sə-tē\ *n*

**por·phy·ry** \'pȯr-fə-rē\ *n, pl* **-ries** : a rock consisting of feldspar crystals embedded in a compact fine-grained base material — **por·phy·rit·ic** \ˌpȯr-fə-'ri-tik\ *adj*

**por·poise** \'pȯr-pəs\ *n* [ME *porpoys*, fr. AF *porpeis*, fr. ML *porcopiscis*, fr. L *porcus* pig + *piscis* fish] : any of a family of small gregarious blunt-snouted whales with spadelike teeth; *also* : DOLPHIN 1

**por·ridge** \'pȯr-ij\ *n* : a soft food made by boiling meal of grains or legumes in milk or water

**por·rin·ger** \'pȯr-ən-jər\ *n* : a low one-handled metal bowl or cup

¹**port** \'pȯrt\ *n* **1** : HARBOR **2** : a city with a harbor **3** : AIRPORT

²**port** *n* **1** : an inlet or outlet (as in an engine) for a fluid **2** : PORTHOLE **3** : JACK 7

³**port** *vb* : to turn or put a helm to the left

⁴**port** *n* : the left side of a ship or airplane looking forward — **port** *adj*

⁵**port** *n* : a sweet fortified wine

**portabella** *or* **portabello** *var of* PORTOBELLO

**por·ta·bil·i·ty** \ˌpȯr-tə-'bil-ə-tē\ *n, pl* **-ties 1** : the quality or state of being portable **2** : the ability to transfer benefits from one pension fund to another when a worker changes jobs

**por·ta·ble** \'pȯr-tə-bəl\ *adj* : capable of being carried — **portable** *n*

¹**por·tage** \'pȯr-tij, pȯr-'täzh\ *n* [ME, fr. AF, fr. *porter* to carry] : the carrying of boats and goods overland between navigable bodies of water; *also* : a route for such carrying

²**portage** *vb* **por·taged; por·tag·ing** : to carry gear over a portage

**por·tal** \'pȯr-t⁹l\ *n* : DOOR, ENTRANCE; *esp* : a grand or imposing one

**portal–to–portal** *adj* : of or relating to the time spent by a worker in traveling from the entrance to an employer's property to the worker's actual job site (as in a mine)

**port·cul·lis** \pȯrt-'kə-ləs\ *n* : a grating at the gateway of a castle or fortress that can be let down to stop entrance

**porte co·chere** \ˌpȯrt-kō-'sher\ *n* [F *porte cochère*, lit., coach door] : a roofed structure extending from the entrance of a building over an adjacent driveway and sheltering those getting in or out of vehicles

**por·tend** \pȯr-'tend\ *vb* **1** : to give a sign or warning of beforehand **2** : INDICATE, SIGNIFY ♦ *Synonyms* AUGUR, PROGNOSTICATE, FORETELL, PREDICT, FORECAST, PROPHESY

**por·tent** \-ˌtent\ *n* **1** : something that foreshadows a coming event : OMEN **2** : MARVEL, PRODIGY

**por·ten·tous** \pȯr-'ten-təs\ *adj* **1** : of, relating to, or constituting a portent **2** : PRODIGIOUS **3** : self-consciously solemn : POMPOUS

¹**por·ter** \'pȯr-tər\ *n, chiefly Brit* : DOORKEEPER

²**porter** *n* **1** : a person who carries burdens; *esp* : one employed (as at a terminal) to carry baggage **2** : an attendant in a railroad car **3** : a dark heavy ale

**por·ter·house** \'pȯr-tər-ˌhau̇s\ *n* : a choice beefsteak with a large tenderloin

**port·fo·lio** \pȯrt-'fō-lē-ˌō\ *n, pl* **-li·os 1** : a portable case for papers or drawings **2** : the office and functions of a minister of state **3** : the securities held by an investor

**port·hole** \'pȯrt-ˌhōl\ *n* : an opening (as a window) in the side of a ship or aircraft

**por·ti·co** \'pȯr-ti-ˌkō\ *n, pl* **-coes** *or* **-cos** [It] : a row of columns supporting a roof around or at the entrance of a building

¹**por·tion** \'pȯr-shən\ *n* **1** : one's part or share ⟨a ~ of food⟩ **2** : DOWRY **3** : an individual's lot **4** : a part of a whole ⟨a ~ of the sky⟩

²**portion** *vb* **1** : to divide into portions **2** : to allot to as a portion

**port·land cement** \ˌpȯrt-lənd-\ *n* : a cement made by calcining and grinding a mixture of clay and limestone

**port·ly** \'pȯrt-lē\ *adj* **port·li·er; -est** : somewhat stout

**port·man·teau** \pȯrt-'man-ˌtō\ *n, pl* **-teaus** *or* **-teaux** \-ˌtōz\ [MF *portemanteau*, fr. *porter* to carry + *manteau* mantle, fr. L *mantellum*] : a large traveling bag

**por·to·bel·lo** \ˌpȯr-tə-'be-lō\ *also* **por·ta·bel·la** \-lə\ *or* **por·ta·bel·lo** \-lō\ *n, pl* **-los** *also* **-las** : a large dark mature mushroom noted for its meaty texture

**port of call** : an intermediate port where ships customarily stop for supplies, repairs, or transshipment of cargo

**port of entry 1** : a place where foreign goods may be cleared through a customhouse **2** : a place where an alien may enter a country

**por·trait** \'pȯr-trət, -ˌträt\ *n* : a picture (as a painting or photograph) of a person usu. showing the face — **por·trait·ist** \-trə-tist\ *n*

**por·trai·ture** \'pȯr-trə-ˌchu̇r\ *n* : the practice or art of making portraits

**por·tray** \pȯr-'trā\ *vb* **1** : to make a picture of : DEPICT **2** : to describe in words **3** : to play the role of — **por·tray·al** *n*

**Por·tu·guese** \ˌpȯr-chə-ˌgēz, -ˌgēs; ˌpȯr-chə-'gēz, -'gēs\ *n, pl* **Portuguese 1** : a native or inhabitant of Portugal **2** : the language of Portugal and Brazil — **Portuguese** *adj*

**Portuguese man–of–war** *n* : any of several large colonial marine invertebrate animals related to the jellyfishes and having a large sac by which the colony floats at the surface

**por·tu·la·ca** \ˌpȯr-chə-'la-kə\ *n* : any of a genus of succulent herbs cultivated for their showy flowers

**pos** *abbr* **1** position **2** positive

¹**pose** \'pōz\ *vb* **posed; pos·ing 1** : to assume or cause to assume a posture usu. for artistic purposes **2** : to set forth : PROPOSE ⟨~ a question⟩ **3** : to affect an attitude or character

²**pose** *n* **1** : a sustained posture; *esp* : one assumed by a model **2** : an attitude assumed for effect : PRETENSE

**pos·er** \'pō-zər\ *n* : a puzzling question

**poser** *n* : a person who poses

**po·seur** \pō-'zər\ *n* [F, lit., poser] : an affected or insincere person

**posh** \'päsh\ *adj* : FASHIONABLE ⟨a ~ restaurant⟩

**pos·it** \'pä-zət\ *vb* : to assume the existence of : POSTULATE

**po·si·tion** \pə-'zi-shən\ *n* **1** : an arranging in order **2** : the stand taken on a question **3** : the point or area occupied by something : SITUATION **4** : a certain arrangement of bodily parts ⟨exercise in a sitting ~⟩ **5** : RANK, STATUS **6** : EMPLOYMENT, JOB — **position** *vb* — **po·si·tion·al** \-shə-nəl\ *adj*

¹**pos·i·tive** \'pä-zə-tiv\ *adj* **1** : expressed definitely ⟨her answer was a ~ no⟩ **2** : CONFIDENT, CERTAIN ⟨~ it was my book⟩ **3** : of, relating to, or constituting the degree of grammatical comparison that denotes no increase in quality, quantity, or relation **4** : not fictitious : REAL **5** : active and effective in function ⟨~ leadership⟩ **6** : having the light and shade as existing in the original subject ⟨a ~ photograph⟩ **7** : numerically greater than zero ⟨a ~ number⟩ **8** : being, relating to, or charged with electricity of which the proton is the elementary unit

**9** : AFFIRMATIVE ⟨a ~ response⟩ **10** : FAVORABLE; *also* : marked by optimism ⟨a ~ attitude⟩ — **pos·i·tive·ly** *adv* — **pos·i·tive·ness** *n*

²**positive** *n* **1** : the positive degree or a positive form in a language **2** : a positive photograph

**pos·i·tron** \'pä-zə-ˌträn\ *n* : a positively charged particle having the same mass and magnitude of charge as the electron

**po·so·le** *or* **po·zo·le** \pō-'sō-lā\ *n* : a thick Mexican soup made with pork, hominy, garlic, and chili

**poss** *abbr* possessive

**pos·se** \'pä-sē\ *n* [ML *posse comitatus*, lit., power or authority of the county] **1** : a body of persons organized to assist a sheriff in an emergency **2** : a body of attendants or followers

**pos·sess** \pə-'zes\ *vb* **1** : to have as property : OWN **2** : to have as an attribute, knowledge, or skill **3** : to enter into and control firmly ⟨~ed by a devil⟩ — **pos·ses·sor** \-'ze-sər\ *n*

**pos·ses·sion** \-'ze-shən\ *n* **1** : control or occupancy of property **2** : OWNERSHIP **3** : something owned : PROPERTY **4** : domination by something (as an evil spirit, a passion, or an idea) **5** : SELF-CONTROL

**pos·ses·sive** \pə-'ze-siv\ *adj* **1** : of, relating to, or constituting a grammatical case denoting ownership **2** : showing the desire to possess ⟨a ~ nature⟩ — **possessive** *n* — **pos·ses·sive·ness** *n*

**pos·si·ble** \'pä-sə-bəl\ *adj* **1** : being within the limits of ability, capacity, or realization **2** : being something that may or may not occur ⟨~ dangers⟩ **3** : able or fitted to become ⟨a ~ site for a bridge⟩ — **pos·si·bil·i·ty** \ˌpä-sə-'bi-lə-tē\ *n* — **pos·si·bly** \'pä-sə-blē\ *adv*

**pos·sum** \'pä-səm\ *n* : OPOSSUM

¹**post** \'pōst\ *n* **1** : an upright piece of timber or metal serving esp. as a support : PILLAR **2** : a pole or stake set up as a mark or indicator

²**post** *vb* **1** : to affix to a usual place (as a wall) for public notices **2** : to publish or announce by or as if by a public notice ⟨~ grades⟩ **3** : to forbid (property) to trespassers by putting up a notice **4** : SCORE ⟨~ed a 70 in the final round⟩ **5** : to publish in an online forum

³**post** *n* **1** *obs* : COURIER **2** *chiefly Brit* : ¹MAIL; *also* : POST OFFICE **3** : something that is published online

⁴**post** *vb* **1** : to ride or travel with haste : HURRY **2** : MAIL ⟨~ a letter⟩ **3** : to enter in a ledger **4** : INFORM ⟨kept him ~ed on new developments⟩

⁵**post** *n* **1** : the place at which a soldier is stationed; *esp* : a sentry's beat or station **2** : a station or task to which a person is assigned **3** : the place at which a body of troops is stationed : CAMP **4** : OFFICE, POSITION **5** : a trading settlement or station

⁶**post** *vb* **1** : to station in a given place **2** : to put up (as bond)

**post·age** \'pō-stij\ *n* : the fee for postal service; *also* : stamps representing this fee

**post·al** \'pōs-t²l\ *adj* : of or relating to the mails or the post office

**postal card** *n* : POSTCARD

**postal service** *n* : a government agency or department handling the transmission of mail

¹**post·card** \'pōst-ˌkärd\ *n* : a card on which a message may be written for mailing without an envelope

²**postcard** *adj* : PICTURESQUE

**post chaise** *n* : a 4-wheeled closed carriage for two to four persons

**post·con·sum·er** \ˌpōst-kən-'sü-mər\ *adj* **1** : discarded by a consumer **2** : having been used and recycled for reuse in another product

**post·date** \ˌpōst-'dāt\ *vb* : to date with a date later than that of execution ⟨~ a check⟩

**post·doc·tor·al** \-'däk-tə-rəl\ *also* **post·doc·tor·ate** \-tə-rət\ *adj* : of, relating to, or engaged in advanced academic or professional work beyond a doctor's degree

**post·er** \'pō-stər\ *n* : a bill or placard for posting often in a public place

¹**pos·te·ri·or** \pō-'stir-ē-ər, pä-\ *adj* **1** : later in time **2** : situated behind

²**pos·te·ri·or** \pä-'stir-ē-ər, pō-\ *n* : the hinder bodily parts; *esp* : BUTTOCKS

**pos·ter·i·ty** \pä-'ster-ə-tē\ *n* **1** : the descendants from one ancestor **2** : all future generations

**pos·tern** \'pōs-tərn, 'päs-\ *n* **1** : a back door or gate **2** : a private or side entrance

**post exchange** *n* : a store at a military post that sells to military personnel and authorized civilians

**post·grad** \'pōst-ˌgrad\ *adj* : POSTGRADUATE

**post·grad·u·ate** \(ˌ)pōst-'gra-jə-wət\ *adj* : of or relating to studies beyond the bachelor's degree — **postgraduate** *n*

**post·haste** \'pōst-'hāst\ *adv* : with all possible speed

**post·hole** \-ˌhōl\ *n* : a hole for a post and esp. a fence post

**post·hu·mous** \'päs-chə-məs\ *adj* [L *posthumus*, alter. of *postumus* last-born, posthumous, fr. superl. of *posterus* coming after] **1** : born after the death of the father **2** : published after the death of the author — **post·hu·mous·ly** *adv*

**post·hyp·not·ic** \ˌpōst-hip-'nä-tik\ *adj* : of, relating to, or characteristic of the period following a hypnotic trance

**pos·til·ion** *or* **pos·til·lion** \pō-'stil-yən\ *n* : a rider on the left-hand horse of a pair drawing a coach

**Post·im·pres·sion·ism** \ˌpōst-im-'pre-shə-ˌni-zəm\ *n* : a late 19th century French theory or practice of art that stresses variously volume, picture structure, or expressionism

**post·lude** \'pōst-ˌlüd\ *n* : an organ solo played at the end of a church service

**post·man** \-mən, -ˌman\ *n* : MAILMAN

**post·mark** \-ˌmärk\ *n* : an official postal marking on a piece of mail; *esp* : the mark canceling the postage stamp — **postmark** *vb*

**post·mas·ter** \-ˌmas-tər\ *n* : a person who has charge of a post office

**postmaster general** *n, pl* **postmasters general** : an official in charge of a national postal service

**post·men·o·paus·al** \ˌpōst-ˌme-nə-ˈpȯ-zəl\ *adj* 1 : having undergone menopause 2 : occurring or administered after menopause

**post me·ri·di·em** \ˌpōst mə-ˈri-dē-əm\ *adj* [L] : being after noon

**post·mis·tress** \ˈpōst-ˌmis-trəs\ *n* : a woman in charge of a post office

**post·mod·ern** \ˌpōst-ˈmä-dərn\ *adj* : of, relating to, or being any of various movements in reaction to modernism

¹**post·mor·tem** \ˌpōst-ˈmȯr-təm\ *adj* [L *post mortem* after death] 1 : done, occurring, or collected after death ⟨a ~ examination⟩ 2 : following the event

²**postmortem** *n* 1 : AUTOPSY 2 : an analysis or discussion of an event after it is over ⟨a ~ of the election⟩

**post·na·sal drip** \ˈpōst-ˌnā-zəl-\ *n* : flow of mucous secretion from the posterior part of the nasal cavity onto the wall of the pharynx

**post·na·tal** \(ˌ)pōst-ˈnā-tᵊl\ *adj* : occurring or being after birth; *esp* : of or relating to a newborn infant

**post office** *n* 1 : POSTAL SERVICE 2 : a local branch of a post office department

**post·op·er·a·tive** \(ˌ)pōst-ˈä-prə-tiv, -pə-ˌrā-\ *adj* : following or having undergone a surgical operation ⟨~ care⟩

**post·paid** \ˈpōst-ˈpād\ *adj* : having the postage paid by the sender and not chargeable to the receiver

**post·par·tum** \(ˌ)pōst-ˈpär təm\ *adj* [NL *post partum* after birth] : following parturition — **postpartum** *adv*

**post·pone** \pōst-ˈpōn\ *vb* **post·poned; post·pon·ing** : to put off to a later time — **post·pone·ment** *n*

**post road** *n* : a road over which mail is carried

**post·script** \ˈpōst-ˌskript\ *n* : a note added esp. to a completed letter

**post time** *n* : the designated time for the start of a horse race

**post–trau·matic** *adj* : occurring after or as a result of trauma ⟨~ stress⟩

**pos·tu·lant** \ˈpäs-chə-lənt\ *n* : a probationary candidate for membership in a religious order

¹**pos·tu·late** \ˈpäs-chə-ˌlāt\ *vb* **-lat·ed; -lat·ing** : to assume as true

²**pos·tu·late** \ˈpäs-chə-lət, -ˌlāt\ *n* : a proposition taken for granted as true esp. as a basis for a chain of reasoning

¹**pos·ture** \ˈpäs-chər\ *n* 1 : the position or bearing of the body or one of its parts 2 : STATE, CONDITION 3 : ATTITUDE ⟨a ~ of arrogance⟩

²**posture** *vb* **pos·tured; pos·tur·ing** : to strike a pose esp. for effect

**post·war** \ˈpōst-ˈwȯr\ *adj* : occurring or existing after a war

**po·sy** \ˈpō-zē\ *n, pl* **posies** 1 : a brief sentiment : MOTTO 2 : a bunch of flowers; *also* : FLOWER

¹**pot** \ˈpät\ *n* : a rounded container used

chiefly for domestic purposes 2 : the total of the bets at stake at one time 3 : RUIN ⟨go to ~⟩ — **pot·ful** *n*

²**pot** *vb* **pot·ted; pot·ting** 1 : to preserve or place in a pot 2 : SHOOT

³**pot** *n* : MARIJUANA

**po·ta·ble** \ˈpō-tə-bəl\ *adj* : suitable for drinking — **po·ta·bil·i·ty** \ˌpō-tə-ˈbi-lə-tē\ *n*

**po·tage** \pȯ-ˈtäzh\ *n* : a thick soup

**pot·ash** \ˈpät-ˌash\ *n* [sing. of *pot ashes*] : potassium or any of its various compounds esp. as used in agriculture

**po·tas·si·um** \pə-ˈta-sē-əm\ *n* : a silver-white soft metallic chemical element that occurs abundantly in nature

**potassium bromide** *n* : a crystalline salt used as a sedative and in photography

**potassium carbonate** *n* : a white salt used in making glass and soap

**potassium nitrate** *n* : a soluble salt used in making gunpowder, as a fertilizer, and in medicine

**po·ta·tion** \pō-ˈtā-shən\ *n* : a usu. alcoholic drink; *also* : the act of drinking

**po·ta·to** \pə-ˈtā-tō\ *n, pl* **-toes** : the edible starchy tuber of a plant related to the tomato; *also* : this plant

**potato beetle** *n* : COLORADO POTATO BEETLE

**potato bug** *n* : COLORADO POTATO BEETLE

**potbellied pig** *n* : any of an Asian breed of small pigs having a straight tail, potbelly, and black, white, or black and white coat

**pot·bel·ly** \ˈpät-ˌbe-lē\ *n* : a protruding abdomen — **pot·bel·lied** \-lēd\ *adj*

**pot·boil·er** \-ˌbȯi-lər\ *n* : a usu. inferior work of art or literature produced chiefly for profit

**po·tent** \ˈpō-tᵊnt\ *adj* 1 : having authority or influence : POWERFUL 2 : chemically or medicinally effective 3 : able to copulate — used esp. of the male ♦ *Synonyms* FORCEFUL, FORCIBLE, MIGHTY, PUISSANT — **po·ten·cy** \-tᵊn-sē\ *n*

**po·ten·tate** \ˈpō-tᵊn-ˌtāt\ *n* : one who wields controlling power : RULER

¹**po·ten·tial** \pə-ˈten-chəl\ *adj* : existing in possibility : capable of becoming actual ⟨a ~ champion⟩ ♦ *Synonyms* DORMANT, LATENT, QUIESCENT — **po·ten·tial·i·ty** \pə-ˌten-chē-ˈa-lə-tē\ *n* — **po·ten·tial·ly** \-ˈten-chə-lē\ *adv*

²**potential** *n* 1 : something that can develop or become actual ⟨a ~ for violence⟩ 2 : the work required to move a unit positive charge from infinity to a point in question; *also* : POTENTIAL DIFFERENCE

**potential difference** *n* : the difference in potential between two points that represents the work involved in the transfer of a unit quantity of electricity from one point to the other

**potential energy** *n* : the energy an object has because of its position or nature or the arrangement of its parts

**po·ten·ti·ate** \pə-ˈten-chē-ˌāt\ *vb* **-at·ed; -at·ing** : to make potent; *esp* : to augment the activity of (as a drug) synergistically — **po·ten·ti·a·tion** \-,ten-chē-'ā-shən\ n

**pot·head** \'pät-,hed\ n : a person who frequently smokes marijuana

**poth·er** \'pä-thər\ n : a noisy disturbance; *also* : FUSS

**pot·herb** \'pät-,ərb, -,hərb\ n : an herb whose leaves or stems are boiled for greens or used to season food

**pot·hole** \'pät-,hōl\ n : a large pit or hole (as in a road surface)

**pot·hook** \-,hu̇k\ n : an S-shaped hook for hanging pots and kettles over an open fire

**po·tion** \'pō-shən\ n : a mixture of liquids (as liquor or medicine)

**pot·luck** \'pät-'lək\ n : the regular meal available to a guest for whom no special preparations have been made

**pot·pie** \-'pī\ n : pastry-covered meat and vegetables cooked in a deep dish

**pot·pour·ri** \,pō-pu̇-'rē\ n [F *pot pourri*, lit., rotten pot] 1 : a mixture of flowers, herbs, and spices used for scent 2 : a miscellaneous collection

**pot·sherd** \'pät-,shərd\ n : a pottery fragment

**pot·shot** \-,shät\ n 1 : a shot taken from ambush or at a random or easy target 2 : a critical remark made in a random or sporadic manner

**pot sticker** n : a crescent-shaped dumpling that is steamed and fried

**pot·tage** \'pä-tij\ n : a thick soup of vegetables and often meat

¹**pot·ter** \'pä-tər\ n : one that makes pottery

²**potter** vb : PUTTER

**pot·tery** \'pä-tə-rē\ n, pl **-ter·ies** 1 : a place where earthen pots and dishes are made 2 : the art of the potter 3 : dishes, pots, and vases made from clay

**pot·ty-mouthed** \'pä-tē-,mau̇thd, -,mau̇tht\ adj : given to the use of vulgar language

¹**pouch** \'pau̇ch\ n [ME *pouche*, fr. AF, of Gmc origin; akin to OE *pocca* bag] 1 : a small bag (as for tobacco) carried on the person 2 : a bag for storing or transporting goods ⟨mail ∼⟩ ⟨diplomatic ∼⟩ 3 : an anatomical sac; *esp* : one for carrying the young on the abdomen of a female marsupial (as a kangaroo)

²**pouch** vb : to put or form into or as if into a pouch

**poult** \'pōlt\ n : a young fowl; *esp* : a young turkey

**poul·ter·er** \'pōl-tər-ər\ n : one that deals in poultry

**poul·tice** \'pōl-təs\ n : a soft usu. heated and medicated mass spread on cloth and applied to a sore or injury — **poultice** vb

**poul·try** \'pōl-trē\ n : domesticated birds kept for eggs or meat — **poul·try·man** \-mən\ n

**pounce** \'pau̇ns\ vb **pounced; pounc·ing** : to spring or swoop upon and seize something

¹**pound** \'pau̇nd\ n, pl **pounds** also **pound** 1 : a unit of avoirdupois, troy, and apothecaries' weight — see WEIGHT table 2 — see MONEY table 3 : the for-

mer basic monetary unit of Ireland 4 : LIRA 3

²**pound** n : a public enclosure where stray animals are kept

³**pound** vb 1 : to crush to a powder or pulp by beating 2 : to strike or beat heavily or repeatedly 3 : DRILL 1 4 : to move or move along heavily

**pound·age** \'pau̇n-dij\ n : POUNDS; *also* : weight in pounds

**pound cake** n : a rich cake made with a large proportion of eggs and shortening

**pound–fool·ish** \'pau̇nd-'fü-lish\ adj : imprudent in dealing with large sums or large matters

**pour** \'pȯr\ vb 1 : to flow or cause to flow in a stream or flood 2 : to rain hard 3 : to supply freely and copiously

**pour·boire** \pu̇r-'bwär\ n [F, fr. *pour boire* for drinking] : TIP, GRATUITY

**pout** \'pau̇t\ vb : to show displeasure by thrusting out the lips; *also* : to look sullen — **pout** n

**pov·er·ty** \'pä-vər-tē\ n [ME *poverte*, fr. AF *poverté*, fr. L *paupertat-, paupertas*, fr. *pauper* poor] 1 : lack of money or material possessions : WANT 2 : poor quality (as of soil)

**poverty line** n : a level of personal or family income below which one is classified as poor according to government standards

**pov·er·ty–strick·en** \'pä-vər-tē-,stri-kən\ adj : very poor : DESTITUTE

**POW** \,pē-(,)ō-'də-bəl-(,)yü\ n : PRISONER OF WAR

¹**pow·der** \'pau̇-dər\ vb 1 : to sprinkle or cover with or as if with powder 2 : to reduce to powder

²**powder** n [ME *poudre*, fr. AF *pudre, podre*, fr. L *pulver-, pulvis* dust] 1 : dry material made up of fine particles; *also* : a usu. medicinal or cosmetic preparation in this form 2 : a solid explosive (as gunpowder) — **pow·dery** adj

**powder room** n : a rest room for women

¹**pow·er** \'pau̇(-ə)r\ n 1 : the ability to act or produce an effect 2 : a position of ascendancy over others : AUTHORITY 3 : one that has control or authority; *esp* : a sovereign state 4 : physical might; *also* : mental or moral vigor 5 : the number of times as indicated by an exponent that a number occurs as a factor in a product ⟨5 to the third ∼ is 125⟩; *also* : the product itself ⟨8 is a ∼ of 2⟩ 6 : force or energy used to do work; *also* : the time rate at which work is done or energy transferred 7 : MAGNIFICATION 2 — **pow·er·ful** \-fəl\ adj — **pow·er·ful·ly** adv — **pow·er·less** adj

²**power** vb : to supply with power and esp. motive power

³**power** adj 1 : operated mechanically or electrically rather than manually 2 : of, relating to, or utilizing strength

**pow·er·boat** \-,bōt\ n : MOTORBOAT

**pow·er·house** \'pau̇(-ə)r-,hau̇s\ n 1 : POWER PLANT 1 2 : one having great drive, energy, or ability

**power plant** n 1 : a building in which electric power is generated 2 : an engine and related parts supplying the motive power of a self-propelled vehicle

**pow·wow** \'pau̇-ˌwau̇\ n **1** : a No American Indian ceremony (as for victory in war) **2** : a meeting for discussion : CONFERENCE

**pox** \'päks\ n, pl **pox** or **pox·es** : any of various diseases (as smallpox or syphilis) marked by a rash on the skin

**pozole** var of POSOLE

**pp** abbr **1** pages **2** pianissimo

**PP** abbr **1** parcel post **2** past participle **3** postpaid **4** prepaid

**ppd** abbr **1** postpaid **2** prepaid

**PPO** \ˌpē-ˌpē-'ō\ n, pl **PPOs** [preferred provider organization] : a health-care organization that gives economic incentives to enrolled individuals who use certain health-care providers

**PPS** abbr [L post postscriptum] an additional postscript

**ppt** abbr precipitate

**PQ** abbr Province of Quebec

**pr** abbr **1** pair **2** price

**Pr** symbol praseodymium

**¹PR** or **p.r.** \'pē-'är\ n : PUBLIC RELATIONS

**²PR** abbr **1** payroll **2** public relations **3** Puerto Rico

**prac·ti·ca·ble** \'prak-ti-kə-bəl\ adj : capable of being put into practice, done, or accomplished ⟨a ~ method⟩ — **prac·ti·ca·bil·i·ty** \ˌprak-ti-kə-'bi-lə-tē\ n

**prac·ti·cal** \'prak-ti-kəl\ adj **1** : of, relating to, or shown in practice ⟨~ questions⟩ **2** : VIRTUAL ⟨~ control⟩ **3** : capable of being put to use ⟨a ~ knowledge of French⟩ **4** : inclined to action as opposed to speculation ⟨a ~ person⟩ **5** : qualified by practice ⟨a good ~ mechanic⟩ — **prac·ti·cal·i·ty** \ˌprak-ti-'ka-lə-tē\ n — **prac·ti·cal·ly** \-k(ə-)lē\ adv

**practical joke** n : a prank intended to trick or embarrass someone or cause physical discomfort

**practical nurse** n : a professional nurse without all of the qualifications of a registered nurse; esp : LICENSED PRACTICAL NURSE

**¹prac·tice** also **prac·tise** \'prak-təs\ vb **prac·ticed** also **prac·tised; prac·tic·ing** also **prac·tis·ing 1** : CARRY OUT, APPLY ⟨~ what you preach⟩ **2** : to perform or work at repeatedly so as to become proficient ⟨~ tennis strokes⟩ **3** : to do or perform customarily ⟨~ politeness⟩ **4** : to be professionally engaged in ⟨~ law⟩

**²practice** also **practise** n **1** : actual performance or application **2** : customary action : HABIT **3** : systematic exercise for proficiency **4** : the exercise of a profession; also : a professional business

**prac·ti·tion·er** \prak-'ti-shə-nər\ n : one who practices a profession

**prae·tor** \'prē-tər\ n : an ancient Roman magistrate ranking below a consul — **prae·to·ri·an** \prē-'tȯr-ē-ən\ adj

**prag·mat·ic** \prag-'ma-tik\ also **prag·mat·i·cal** \-ti-kəl\ adj **1** : of or relating to practical affairs **2** : concerned with the practical consequences of actions or beliefs ⟨a ~ leader⟩ — **pragmatic** n — **prag·mat·i·cal·ly** \-ti-k(ə-)lē\ adv

**prag·ma·tism** \'prag-mə-ˌti-zəm\ n : a practical approach to problems and affairs

**prai·rie** \'prer-ē\ n [F, fr. OF praierie, fr. VL *prataria, fr. L pratum meadow] : a broad tract of level or rolling grassland

**prairie dog** n : an American burrowing black-tailed rodent related to the squirrels and living in colonies

**prairie schooner** n : a covered wagon used by pioneers in cross-country travel

**praise** \'prāz\ vb **praised; prais·ing 1** : to express approval of : COMMEND **2** : to glorify (a divinity or a saint) esp. in song — **praise** n

**praise·wor·thy** \-ˌwər-thē\ adj : LAUDABLE ⟨a ~ effort⟩

**pra·line** \'prä-ˌlēn, 'prā-\ n [F] : a confection of nuts and sugar

**pram** \'pram\ n, chiefly Brit : PERAMBULATOR

**prance** \'prans\ vb **pranced; pranc·ing 1** : to spring from the hind legs ⟨a prancing horse⟩ **2** : SWAGGER; also : CAPER — **prance** n — **pranc·er** n

**prank** \'praŋk\ n : a playful or mildly mischievous act : TRICK

**prank·ster** \'praŋk-stər\ n : a person who plays pranks

**pra·seo·dym·i·um** \ˌprā-zē-ō-'di-mē-əm\ n : a yellowish white metallic chemical element

**prate** \'prāt\ vb **prat·ed; prat·ing** : to talk long and idly : chatter foolishly

**prat·fall** \'prat-ˌfȯl\ n **1** : a fall on the buttocks **2** : a humiliating blunder

**prat·tle** \'pra-tᵊl\ vb **prat·tled; prat·tling** : PRATE, BABBLE

**prattle** n : trifling or childish talk

**prawn** \'prȯn\ n : any of various edible shrimplike crustaceans; also : SHRIMP **1**

**pray** \'prā\ vb **1** : ENTREAT, IMPLORE **2** : to ask earnestly for something **3** : to address God or a god esp. with supplication

**prayer** \'prer\ n **1** : a supplication or expression addressed to God or a god; also : a set order of words used in praying **2** : an earnest request or wish **3** : the act or practice of praying to God or a god **4** : a religious service consisting chiefly of prayers — often used in pl. **5** : something prayed for **6** : a slight chance

**prayer book** n : a book containing prayers and often directions for worship

**prayer·ful** \'prer-fəl\ adj **1** : DEVOUT **2** : EARNEST — **prayer·ful·ly** adv

**praying mantis** n : MANTIS

**PRC** abbr People's Republic of China

**preach** \'prēch\ vb **1** : to deliver a sermon **2** : to set forth in a sermon **3** : to advocate earnestly ⟨~ed tolerance⟩ — **preach·er** n — **preach·ment** n

**pre·ad·o·les·cence** \ˌprē-ˌa-də-'le-sᵊns\ n : the period of human development just preceding adolescence — **pre·ad·o·les·cent** \-sᵊnt\ adj or n

**pre·am·ble** \'prē-ˌam-bəl\ n [ME, fr. MF preambule, fr. ML preambulum, fr. LL, neut. of praeambulus walking in front of, fr. L prae in front of + ambulare to walk]

: an introductory part ⟨the ~ to a constitution⟩

**pre·ar·range** \ˌprē-ə-ˈrānj\ *vb* : to arrange beforehand — **pre·ar·range·ment** *n*

**pre·as·sign** \ˌprē-ə-ˈsīn\ *vb* : to assign beforehand

**Pre·cam·bri·an** \ˈprē-ˈkam-brē-ən, -ˈkam-\ *adj* : of, relating to, or being the era that is earliest in geologic history and is characterized esp. by the appearance of single-celled organisms — **Precambrian** *n*

**pre·can·cel** \ˌ(ˌ)prē-ˈkan-səl\ *vb* : to cancel (a postage stamp) in advance of use — **precancel** *n* — **pre·can·cel·la·tion** \ˌprē-ˌkan-sə-ˈlā-shən\ *n*

**pre·can·cer·ous** \ˌ(ˌ)prē-ˈkan-sə-rəs\ *adj* : likely to become cancerous

**pre·car·i·ous** \pri-ˈker-ē-əs\ *adj* : dependent on uncertain conditions : dangerously insecure : UNSTABLE ⟨a ~ foothold⟩ ⟨~ prosperity⟩ ♦ *Synonyms* DELICATE, SENSITIVE, TICKLISH, TOUCHY, TRICKY — **pre·car·i·ous·ly** *adv* — **pre·car·i·ous·ness** *n*

**pre·cau·tion** \pri-ˈkȯ-shən\ *n* : a measure taken beforehand to prevent harm or secure good — **pre·cau·tion·ary** \-shə-ˌner-ē\ *adj*

**pre·cede** \pri-ˈsēd\ *vb* **pre·ced·ed; pre·ced·ing** : to be, go, or come ahead or in front of (as in rank or time)

**pre·ce·dence** \ˈpre-sə-dəns, pri-ˈsēd-ᵊns\ *n* 1 : the act or fact of preceding 2 : consideration based on order of importance : PRIORITY

¹**pre·ce·dent** \pri-ˈsē-dᵊnt, ˈpre-sə-dənt\ *adj* : prior in time, order, or significance

²**prec·e·dent** \ˈpre-sə-dənt\ *n* : something said or done that may serve to authorize or justify further words or acts of the same or a similar kind

**pre·ced·ing** \pri-ˈsē-diŋ\ *adj* : that precedes ♦ *Synonyms* ANTECEDENT, FOREGOING, PRIOR, FORMER, ANTERIOR

**pre·cen·tor** \pri-ˈsen-tər\ *n* : a leader of the singing of a choir or congregation

**pre·cept** \ˈprē-ˌsept\ *n* : a command or principle intended as a general rule of action or conduct

**pre·cep·tor** \pri-ˈsep-tər, ˈprē-ˌsep-\ *n* : TUTOR

**pre·ces·sion** \prē-ˈse-shən\ *n* : a slow gyration of the rotation axis of a spinning body (as the earth) — **pre·cess** \prē-ˈses\ *vb* — **pre·ces·sion·al** \-ˈse-shə-nəl\ *adj*

**pre·cinct** \ˈprē-ˌsiŋkt\ *n* 1 : an administrative subdivision (as of a city) : DISTRICT ⟨police ~⟩ ⟨electoral ~⟩ 2 : an enclosure bounded by the limits of a building or place — often used in pl. 3 *pl* : ENVIRONS

**pre·ci·os·i·ty** \ˌpre-shē-ˈä-sə-tē\ *n, pl* **-ties** : fastidious refinement

**pre·cious** \ˈpre-shəs\ *adj* 1 : of great value ⟨~ jewels⟩ 2 : greatly cherished : DEAR ⟨~ memories⟩ 3 : AFFECTED ⟨~ language⟩

**prec·i·pice** \ˈpre-sə-pəs\ *n* : a steep cliff

**pre·cip·i·tan·cy** \pri-ˈsi-pə-tən-sē\ *n* : undue hastiness or suddenness

¹**pre·cip·i·tate** \pri-ˈsi-pə-ˌtāt\ *vb* **-tat·ed; -tat·ing** [L *praecipitare*, fr. *praecipit-, praeceps* headlong, fr. *prae* in front of + *caput* head] 1 : to throw violently 2 : to throw down 3 : to cause to happen quickly or abruptly ⟨~ a quarrel⟩ 4 : to cause to separate from solution or suspension 5 : to fall as rain, snow, or hail ♦ *Synonyms* SPEED, ACCELERATE, QUICKEN, HASTEN, HURRY

²**pre·cip·i·tate** \pri-ˈsi-pə-tət, -ˌtāt\ *n* : the solid matter that separates from a solution or suspension

³**pre·cip·i·tate** \pri-ˈsi-pə-tət\ *adj* 1 : showing extreme or unwise haste : RASH 2 : falling with steep descent; *also* : PRECIPITOUS — **pre·cip·i·tate·ly** *adv* — **pre·cip·i·tate·ness** *n*

**pre·cip·i·ta·tion** \pri-ˌsi-pə-ˈtā-shən\ *n* 1 : rash haste 2 : the process of precipitating or forming a precipitate 3 : water that falls to earth esp. as rain or snow; *also* : the quantity of this water

**pre·cip·i·tous** \pri-ˈsi-pə-təs\ *adj* 1 : PRECIPITATE 2 : having the character of a precipice : very steep ⟨a ~ slope⟩; *also* : containing precipices ⟨~ trails⟩ — **pre·cip·i·tous·ly** *adv*

**pré·cis** \prā-ˈsē\ *n, pl* **pré·cis** \-ˈsēz\ [F] : a concise summary of essentials

**pre·cise** \pri-ˈsīs\ *adj* 1 : exactly defined or stated : DEFINITE 2 : highly accurate : EXACT 3 : conforming strictly to a standard : SCRUPULOUS ⟨a ~ teacher⟩ — **pre·cise·ly** *adv* — **pre·cise·ness** *n*

**pre·ci·sion** \pri-ˈsi-zhən\ *n* : the quality or state of being precise

**pre·clude** \pri-ˈklüd\ *vb* **pre·clud·ed; pre·clud·ing** : to make impossible : BAR, PREVENT

**pre·co·cious** \pri-ˈkō-shəs\ *adj* [L *praecoc-, praecox*, lit., ripening early, fr. *prae*-ahead + *coquere* to cook] : early in development and esp. in mental development — **pre·co·cious·ly** *adv* — **pre·coc·i·ty** \pri-ˈkä-sə-tē\ *n*

**pre·con·ceive** \ˌprē-kən-ˈsēv\ *vb* : to form an opinion of beforehand — **pre·con·cep·tion** \-ˈsep-shən\ *n*

**pre·con·di·tion** \-ˈdi-shən\ *vb* : to put in proper or desired condition or frame of mind in advance

**pre·cook** \ˌprē-ˈkuk\ *vb* : to cook partially or entirely before final cooking or reheating

**pre·cur·sor** \pri-ˈkər-sər\ *n* : one that precedes and indicates the approach of another : FORERUNNER

**pred** *abbr* predicate

**pre·da·ceous** *or* **pre·da·cious** \pri-ˈdā-shəs\ *adj* : living by preying on others : PREDATORY

**pre·date** \ˈprē-ˈdāt\ *vb* : ANTEDATE

**pre·da·tion** \pri-ˈdā-shən\ *n* 1 : the act of preying or plundering 2 : a mode of life in which food is primarily obtained by killing and consuming animals

**pred·a·tor** \ˈpre-də-tər\ *n* : an animal that lives by predation

**pred·a·to·ry** \ˈpre-də-ˌtȯr-ē\ *adj* 1 : of or relating to plunder ⟨~ warfare⟩ 2 : disposed to exploit others **3** : preying upon other animals

**pre·dawn** \\(')prē-'dȯn\ adj : of or relating to the time just before dawn

**pre·de·cease** \ˌprē-di-'sēs\ vb -ceased; -ceas·ing : to die before another person

**pre·de·ces·sor** \'pre-də-ˌse-sər, 'prē-\ n : a previous holder of a position to which another has succeeded

**pre·des·ig·nate** \(ˌ)prē-'de-zig-ˌnāt\ vb : to designate beforehand

**pre·des·ti·na·tion** \ˌprē-ˌdes-tə-'na-shən\ n : the act of foreordaining to an earthly lot or eternal destiny by divine decree; also : the state of being so foreordained — **pre·des·ti·nate** \prē-'des-tə-ˌnāt\ vb

**pre·des·tine** \prē-'des-tən\ vb : to settle beforehand : FOREORDAIN

**pre·de·ter·mine** \ˌprē-di-'tər-mən\ vb : to determine beforehand

**pred·i·ca·ble** \'pre-di-kə-bəl\ adj : capable of being predicated or affirmed

**pre·dic·a·ment** \pri-'di-kə-mənt\ n : a difficult or trying situation ◆ *Synonyms* DILEMMA, PICKLE, QUAGMIRE, JAM

¹**pred·i·cate** \'pre-di-kət\ n : the part of a sentence or clause that expresses what is said of the subject

²**pred·i·cate** \'pre-də-ˌkāt\ vb -cat·ed; -cat·ing **1** : AFFIRM **2** : to assert to be a quality or attribute **3** : FOUND, BASE — usu. used with on — **pred·i·ca·tion** \ˌpre-də-'kā-shən\ n

**pre·dict** \pri-'dikt\ vb : to declare in advance — **pre·dict·abil·i·ty** \-ˌdik-tə-'bi-lə-tē\ n — **pre·dict·able** \-'dik-tə-bəl\ adj — **pre·dict·ably** \-blē\ adv — **pre·dic·tion** \-'dik-shən\ n

**pre·di·gest** \ˌprē-dī-'jest\ vb : to simplify for easy use; also : to subject to artificial or natural partial digestion

**pre·di·lec·tion** \ˌpre-də-'lek-shən, ˌprē-\ n : an established preference for something

**pre·dis·pose** \ˌprē-di-'spōz\ vb : to incline in advance : make susceptible \was *predisposed* to infection\ — **pre·dis·po·si·tion** \ˌprē-ˌdis-pə-'zi-shən\ n

**pre·dom·i·nant** \pri-'dä-mə-nənt\ adj : greater in importance, strength, influence, or authority — **pre·dom·i·nance** \-nəns\ n

**pre·dom·i·nant·ly** \-nənt-lē\ adv : for the most part : MAINLY

**pre·dom·i·nate** \pri-'dä-mə-ˌnāt\ vb : to be superior esp. in power or numbers : PREVAIL

**pre·dom·i·nate·ly** \pri-'dä-mə-nət-lē\ adv : PREDOMINANTLY

**pree·mie** \'prē-mē\ n : a premature baby

**pre·em·i·nent** \prē-'e-mə-nənt\ adj : having highest rank : OUTSTANDING — **pre·em·i·nence** \-nəns\ n — **pre·em·i·nent·ly** adv

**pre·empt** \prē-'empt\ vb **1** : to settle upon (public land) with the right to purchase before others; also : to take by such right **2** : to seize upon before someone else can **3** : to take the place of ◆ *Synonyms* USURP, CONFISCATE, APPROPRIATE, EXPROPRIATE — **pre·emp·tion** \-'emp-shən\ n

**pre·emp·tive** \prē-'emp-tiv\ adj : marked by the seizing of the initiative : initiated by oneself \\~ attack\

**preen** \'prēn\ vb [ME *prenen*, alter. of *proynen*, *prunen*, fr. AF *puroindre*, *proindre*, fr. *pur-* thoroughly + *oindre* to anoint, rub, fr. L *unguere*] **1** : to groom with the bill — used of a bird **2** : to dress or smooth up : PRIMP **3** : to pride (oneself) for achievement

**pre·ex·ist** \ˌprē-ig-'zist\ vb : to exist before — **pre·ex·is·tence** \-'zis-təns\ n — **pre·ex·is·tent** \-tənt\ adj

**pref** abbr **1** preface **2** preference **3** preferred **4** prefix

¹**pre·fab** \(ˌ)prē-'fab, 'prē-ˌfab\ adj : produced by prefabrication \a ~ house\

²**prefab** n : a prefabricated structure

**pre·fab·ri·cate** \(ˌ)prē-'fa-brə-ˌkāt\ vb : to manufacture the parts of (a structure) beforehand for later assembly — **pre·fab·ri·ca·tion** \ˌprē-ˌfa-bri-'kā-shən\ n

¹**pref·ace** \'pre-fəs\ n : the introductory remarks of a speaker or writer — **pref·a·to·ry** \'pre-fə-ˌtȯr-ē\ adj

²**preface** vb pref·aced; pref·ac·ing : to introduce with a preface

**pre·fect** \'prē-ˌfekt\ n **1** : a high official; esp : a chief officer or magistrate **2** : a student monitor

**pre·fec·ture** \'prē-ˌfek-chər\ n : the office, term, or residence of a prefect

**pre·fer** \pri-'fər\ vb pre·ferred; pre·fer·ring **1** : PROMOTE **2** : to like better **3** : to bring (as a charge) against a person — **pref·er·a·ble** \'pre-fə-rə-bəl\ adj — **pref·er·a·bly** \-blē\ adv

**pref·er·ence** \'pre-frəns, -fə-rəns\ n **1** : a special liking for one thing over another **2** : CHOICE, SELECTION — **pref·er·en·tial** \ˌpre-fə-'ren-chəl\ adj

**pre·fer·ment** \pri-'fər-mənt\ n : PROMOTION, ADVANCEMENT

**preferred provider organization** n : PPO

**pre·fig·ure** \prē-'fi-gyər\ vb **1** : FORESHADOW **2** : to imagine beforehand

¹**pre·fix** \'prē-ˌfiks, prē-'fiks\ vb : to place before \~ a title to a name\

²**pre·fix** \'prē-ˌfiks\ n : an affix occurring at the beginning of a word

**pre·flight** \ˌprē-'flīt\ adj : preparing for or preliminary to flight

**pre·form** \(ˌ)prē-'fȯrm, 'prē-ˌfȯrm\ vb : to form or shape beforehand

**preg·na·ble** \'preg-nə-bəl\ adj : vulnerable to capture \a ~ fort\

**preg·nant** \'preg-nənt\ adj **1** : containing unborn offspring within the body **2** : rich in significance : MEANINGFUL — **preg·nan·cy** \-nən-sē\ n

**pre·heat** \prē-'hēt\ vb : to heat beforehand; esp : to heat (an oven) to a designated temperature before using

**pre·hen·sile** \prē-'hen-səl, -ˌsī(-ə)l\ adj : adapted for grasping esp. by wrapping around \a monkey with a ~ tail\

**pre·his·tor·ic** \ˌprē-his-'tȯr-ik\ also **pre·his·tor·i·cal** \-i-kəl\ adj : of, relating to, or existing in the period before written history began

**pre·judge** \(ˌ)prē-'jəj\ vb : to judge before full hearing or examination

¹**prej·u·dice** \'pre-jə-dəs\ n **1** : DAMAGE;

*esp* : detriment to one's rights or claims **2** : an opinion made without adequate basis ⟨racial ∼⟩ — **prej·u·di·cial** \ˌpre-jə-ˈdi-shəl\ *adj*

²**prejudice** *vb* **-diced; -dic·ing 1** : to damage by a judgment or action esp. at law **2** : to cause to have prejudice

**pre·kin·der·gar·ten** \(ˈ)prē-ˈkin-dər-ˌgärt²n\ *n* **1** : NURSERY SCHOOL **2** : a class or program preceding kindergarten

**prel·ate** \ˈpre-lət\ *n* : an ecclesiastic (as a bishop) of high rank — **prel·a·cy** \-lə-sē\ *n*

**pre·launch** \ˈprē-ˈlȯnch\ *adj* : preparing for or preliminary to launch

**pre·lim** \ˈprē-ˌlim, pri-ˈlim\ *n or adj* : PRELIMINARY

¹**pre·lim·i·nary** \pri-ˈli-mə-ˌner-ē\ *n, pl* **-nar·ies** : something that precedes or introduces the main business or event

²**preliminary** *adj* : preceding the main discourse or business

**pre·lude** \ˈprel-ˌyüd; ˈprē-ˌlüd, ˈprā-\ *n* **1** : an introductory performance or event **2** : a musical section or movement introducing the main theme; *also* : an organ solo played at the beginning of a church service

**pre·mar·i·tal** \(ˌ)prē-ˈmer-ə-t²l\ *adj* : existing or occurring before marriage

**pre·ma·ture** \ˌprē-mə-ˈtu̇r, -ˈtyu̇r, -ˈchu̇r\ *adj* : happening, coming, born, or done before the usual or proper time ⟨a ∼ birth⟩ — **pre·ma·ture·ly** *adv*

¹**pre·med** \ˈprē-ˈmed\ *n* : a premedical student or course of study

²**premed** *adj* : PREMEDICAL

**pre·med·i·cal** \(ˌ)prē-ˈme-di-kəl\ *adj* : preceding and preparing for the professional study of medicine

**pre·med·i·tate** \pri-ˈme-də-ˌtāt\ *vb* : to consider and plan beforehand — **pre·med·i·ta·tion** \-ˌme-də-ˈtā-shən\ *n*

**pre·men·o·paus·al** \(ˌ)prē-ˌme-nə-ˈpȯ-zəl\ *adj* : of, relating to, or being in the period preceding menopause

**pre·men·stru·al** \(ˌ)prē-ˈmen-strə-wəl\ *adj* : of, relating to, or occurring in the period just before menstruation

**premenstrual syndrome** *n* : a varying group of symptoms manifested by some women prior to menstruation

**premie** *var of* PREEMIE

¹**pre·mier** \pri-ˈmir, -ˈmyir, ˈprē-mē-ər\ *adj* [ME *primer, primier*, fr. AF, first, chief, fr. L *primarius* of the first rank] : first in rank or importance : CHIEF; *also* : first in time : EARLIEST

²**premier** *n* : PRIME MINISTER — **pre·mier·ship** *n*

¹**pre·miere** \pri-ˈmyer, -ˈmir\ *n* : a first performance

²**premiere** *also* **pre·mier** \*same as* ¹PREMIERE\ *vb* pre·miered; pre·mier·ing : to give or receive a first public performance

¹**prem·ise** \ˈpre-məs\ *n* **1** : a statement of fact or a supposition made or implied as a basis of argument **2** *pl* : a piece of land with the structures on it; *also* : the place of business of an enterprise

²**premise** *vb* prem·ised; prem·is·ing : to base on certain assumptions

**pre·mi·um** \ˈprē-mē-əm\ *n* [L *praemium* booty, profit, reward, fr. *prae* before + *emere* to take, buy] **1** : REWARD, PRIZE **2** : a sum over and above the stated value **3** : something paid over and above a fixed wage or price **4** : something given with a purchase **5** : the sum paid for a contract of insurance **6** : an unusually high value

**pre·mix** \ˌprē-ˈmiks\ *vb* : to mix before use

**pre·mo·lar** \(ˌ)prē-ˈmō-lər\ *adj* : situated in front of or preceding the molar teeth; *esp* : being or relating to those teeth of a mammal in front of the true molars and behind the canines — **premolar** *n*

**pre·mo·ni·tion** \ˌprē-mə-ˈni-shən, ˌpre-\ *n* **1** : previous warning **2** : PRESENTIMENT ⟨had a ∼ of disaster⟩ — **pre·mon·i·to·ry** \pri-ˈmä-nə-ˌtȯr-ē\ *adj*

**pre·na·tal** \ˈprē-ˈnā-t²l\ *adj* : occurring, existing, or taking place before birth

**pre·nup·tial** \prē-ˈnəp-shəl\ *adj* : made or occurring before marriage

**prenuptial agreement** *n* : an agreement between a man and woman before marrying in which they give up future rights to each other's property in the event of divorce or death

**pre·oc·cu·pa·tion** \prē-ˌä-kyə-ˈpā-shən\ *n* : complete absorption of the mind or interests; *also* : something that causes such absorption

**pre·oc·cu·pied** \prē-ˈä-kyə-ˌpīd\ *adj* **1** : lost in thought; *also* : absorbed in some preoccupation **2** : already occupied
  ♦ *Synonyms* ABSTRACTED, ABSENT, ABSENTMINDED

**pre·oc·cu·py** \-ˌpī\ *vb* **1** : to occupy the attention of beforehand **2** : to take possession of before another

**pre·op·er·a·tive** \(ˌ)prē-ˈä-prə-tiv, -pə-ˌrā-\ *adj* : occurring before a surgical operation

**pre·or·dain** \ˌprē-ȯr-ˈdān\ *vb* : FOREORDAIN

**pre·owned** \(ˌ)prē-ˈōnd\ *adj* : SECONDHAND ⟨∼ vehicles⟩

**prep** *abbr* **1** preparatory **2** preposition

**pre·pack·age** \(ˌ)prē-ˈpa-kij\ *vb* : to package (as food) before offering for sale to the customer

**preparatory school** *n* **1** : a usu. private school preparing students primarily for college **2** *Brit* : a private elementary school preparing students primarily for British public schools

**pre·pare** \pri-ˈper\ *vb* pre·pared; pre·par·ing **1** : to make or get ready ⟨∼ dinner⟩ ⟨∼ a student for college⟩ **2** : to get ready beforehand **3** : to put together : COMPOUND ⟨∼ a prescription⟩ — **prep·a·ra·tion** \ˌpre-pə-ˈrā-shən\ *n* — **pre·pa·ra·to·ry** \pri-ˈper-ə-ˌtȯr-ē\ *adj*

**pre·pared·ness** \pri-ˈper-əd-nəs\ *n* : a state of adequate preparation

**pre·pay** \(ˌ)prē-ˈpā\ *vb* **-paid** \-ˈpād\; **-pay·ing** : to pay or pay the charge on in advance

**pre·pon·der·ant** \pri-ˈpän-də-rənt\ *adj* : having greater weight, force, influence, or frequency — **pre·pon·der·ance** \-rəns\ *n* — **pre·pon·der·ant·ly** *adv*

**pre·pon·der·ate** \pri-'pän-də-ˌrāt\ vb **-at·ed; -at·ing** [L *praeponderare,* fr. *prae-* ahead + *ponder-, pondus* weight] : to exceed in weight, force, influence, or frequency : PREDOMINATE

**prep·o·si·tion** \ˌpre-pə-'zi-shən\ n : a word that combines with a noun or pronoun to form a phrase — **prep·o·si·tion·al** \-'zish-nəl\ adj

**pre·pos·sess** \ˌprē-pə-'zes\ vb **1** : to cause to be preoccupied **2** : to influence beforehand esp. favorably

**pre·pos·sess·ing** adj : tending to create a favorable impression ⟨a ~ manner⟩

**pre·pos·ses·sion** \-'ze-shən\ n **1** : PREJUDICE **2** : an exclusive concern with one idea or object

**pre·pos·ter·ous** \pri-'päs-tə-rəs\ adj : contrary to nature or reason : ABSURD

**prep·py** *or* **prep·pie** \'pre-pē\ n, pl **preppies 1** : a student at or a graduate of a preparatory school **2** : a person deemed to dress or behave like a preppy

**pre·puce** \'prē-ˌpyüs\ n : FORESKIN

**pre·quel** \'prē-kwəl\ n : a literary or dramatic work whose story precedes that of an earlier work

**pre·re·cord·ed** \ˌ(ˌ)prē-ri-'kȯr-dəd\ adj : recorded for later broadcast or play

**pre·req·ui·site** \prē-'re-kwə-zət\ n : something required beforehand or for the end in view — **prerequisite** adj

**pre·rog·a·tive** \pri-'rä-gə-tiv\ n : an exclusive or special right, power, or privilege ⟨presidential ~s⟩

**pres** abbr **1** present **2** president

¹**pres·age** \'pre-sij\ n [ME, fr. L *praesagium,* fr. *praesagus* having a foreboding, fr. *prae* before + *sagus* prophetic] **1** : something that foreshadows a future event : OMEN **2** : FOREBODING

²**pre·sage** \'pre-sij, pri-'sāj\ vb **pre·saged; pre·sag·ing 1** : to give an omen or warning of : FORESHADOW **2** : FORETELL, PREDICT

**pres·by·o·pia** \ˌprez-bē-'ō-pē-ə\ n : a visual condition in which loss of elasticity of the lens of the eye causes defective accommodation and inability to focus sharply for near vision — **pres·by·o·pic** \-'ō-pik, -'ä-\ adj or n

**pres·by·ter** \'prez-bə-tər\ n [LL, elder, priest, fr. Gk *presbyteros,* compar. of *presbys* elder, old man] **1** : PRIEST, MINISTER **2** : an elder in a Presbyterian church

¹**Pres·by·te·ri·an** \ˌprez-bə-'tir-ē-ən\ n : a member of a Presbyterian church

²**Presbyterian** adj **1** often not cap : characterized by a graded system of representative ecclesiastical bodies (as presbyteries) exercising legislative and judicial powers **2** : of or relating to a group of Protestant Christian bodies that are presbyterian in government — **Pres·by·te·ri·an·ism** \-ə-ˌni-zəm\ n

**pres·by·tery** \'prez-bə-ˌter-ē\ n, pl **-teries 1** : the part of a church reserved for the officiating clergy **2** : a ruling body in Presbyterian churches consisting of the ministers and representative elders of a district

¹**pre·school** \'prē-ˌskül\ adj : of or relating to the period in a child's life from infancy to the age of five or six — **pre·school·er** \-ˌskü-lər\ n

²**preschool** n : NURSERY SCHOOL

**pre·science** \'pre-shəns, 'prē-\ n : foreknowledge of events; also : FORESIGHT — **pre·scient** \-shənt, -shē-ənt\ adj

**pre·scribe** \pri-'skrīb\ vb **pre·scribed; pre·scrib·ing 1** : to lay down as a guide or rule of action **2** : to direct the use of (as a medicine) as a remedy

**pre·scrip·tion** \pri-'skrip-shən\ n **1** : the action of prescribing rules or directions **2** : a written direction for the preparation and use of a medicine; also : a medicine prescribed

**pre·scrip·tive** \pri-'skrip-tiv\ adj **1** : serving to prescribe ⟨~ rules⟩ **2** : acquired by, based on, or determined by prescription or by custom

**pres·ence** \'pre-zⁿns\ n **1** : the fact or condition of being present **2** : the space immediately around a person **3** : one that is present **4** : the bearing of a person; esp : stately bearing

¹**pres·ent** \'pre-zⁿnt\ n : something presented : GIFT

²**pre·sent** \pri-'zent\ vb **1** : to bring into the presence or acquaintance of : INTRODUCE **2** : to bring before the public ⟨~ a play⟩ **3** : to make a gift to **4** : to give formally **5** : to lay (as a charge) before a court for inquiry **6** : to aim or direct (as a weapon) so as to face in a particular direction — **pre·sent·able** adj — **pre·sen·ta·tion** \ˌprē-ˌzen-'tā-shən, ˌpre-zⁿn-\ n — **pre·sent·ment** \pri-'zent-mənt\ n

³**pres·ent** \'pre-zⁿnt\ adj **1** : now existing or in progress ⟨~ conditions⟩ **2** : being in view or at hand ⟨~ at the meeting⟩ **3** : under consideration ⟨the ~ problem⟩ **4** : of, relating to, or constituting a verb tense that expresses present time or the time of speaking

⁴**pres·ent** \'pre-zⁿnt\ n **1** pl : the present legal document **2** : the present tense; also : a verb form in it **3** : the present time

**pres·ent–day** \'pre-zⁿnt-ˈdā\ adj : now existing or occurring : CURRENT

**pre·sen·ti·ment** \pri-'zen-tə-mənt\ n : a feeling that something is about to happen : PREMONITION ⟨a ~ of danger⟩

**pres·ent·ly** \'pre-zⁿnt-lē\ adv **1** : SOON ⟨~ they arrived⟩ **2** : NOW ⟨~ busy⟩

**present participle** n : a participle that typically expresses present action and that in English is formed with the suffix *-ing* and is used in the formation of the progressive tenses

¹**pre·serve** \pri-'zərv\ vb **pre·served; pre·serv·ing 1** : to keep safe : GUARD, PROTECT **2** : to keep from decaying; esp : to process food (as by canning or pickling) to prevent spoilage **3** : MAINTAIN ⟨~ silence⟩ — **pres·er·va·tion** \ˌpre-zər-'vā-shən\ n — **pre·ser·va·tive** \pri-'zər-və-tiv\ adj or n — **pre·serv·er** n

²**preserve** n **1** : preserved fruit — often used in pl. **2** : an area for the protection of natural resources (as animals)

**pre·set** \'prē-,set\ *vb* **-set; -set·ting** : to set beforehand — **preset** *n*

**pre·shrink** \prē-'shriŋk\ *vb* **-shrank** \-'shraŋk\; **-shrunk** \-'shrəŋk\ : to shrink (as a fabric) before making into a garment

**pre·side** \pri-'zīd\ *vb* **pre·sid·ed; pre·sid·ing** [L *praesidēre* to guard, preside over, fr. *prae* in front of + *sedēre* to sit] **1** : to exercise guidance or control **2** : to occupy the place of authority; *esp* : to act as chairman

**pres·i·dent** \'pre-zə-dənt\ *n* **1** : one chosen to preside ⟨~ of the assembly⟩ **2** : the chief officer of an organization (as a corporation or society) **3** : an elected official serving as both chief of state and chief political executive; *also* : a chief of state often with only minimal political powers — **pres·i·den·cy** \-dən-sē\ *n* — **pres·i·den·tial** \,pre-zə-'den-chəl\ *adj*

**pre·si·dio** \pri-'sē-dē-,ō, -'si-\ *n, pl* **-di·os** [Sp] : a military post or fortified settlement in an area currently or orig. under Spanish control

**pre·sid·i·um** \pri-'si-dē-əm\ *n, pl* **-ia** \-dē-ə\ *or* **-iums** [Russ *prezidium*, fr. L *praesidium* garrison] : a permanent executive committee that acts for a larger body in a Communist country

**¹pre·soak** \(,)prē-'sōk\ *vb* : to soak beforehand

**²pre·soak** \'prē-,sōk\ *n* **1** : an instance of presoaking **2** : a preparation used in presoaking clothes

**pre·sort** \(,)prē-'sort\ *vb* : to sort (mail) by zip code usu. before delivery to a post office

**¹press** \'pres\ *n* **1** : a crowded condition : THRONG **2** : a machine for exerting pressure **3** : CLOSET, CUPBOARD **4** : PRESSURE **5** : the properly creased condition of a freshly pressed garment **6** : PRINTING PRESS; *also* : the act or the process of printing **7** : a printing or publishing establishment **8** : the media (as newspapers and magazines) of public news and comment; *also* : persons (as reporters) employed in these media **9** : comment in newspapers and periodicals

**²press** *vb* **1** : to bear down upon : push steadily against **2** : ASSAIL, COMPEL **3** : to squeeze out the juice or contents of ⟨~ grapes⟩ **4** : to squeeze to a desired density, shape, or smoothness; *esp* : IRON **5** : to try hard to persuade : URGE **6** : to follow through : PROSECUTE **7** : CROWD ⟨reporters ~ed around the players⟩ **8** : to force one's way **9** : to require haste or speed in action — **press·er** *n*

**press agent** *n* : an agent employed to establish and maintain good public relations through publicity

**press·ing** *adj* : URGENT ⟨a ~ need⟩

**press·man** \'pres-mən, -,man\ *n* : the operator of a press and esp. a printing press

**press·room** \-,rüm, -,rum\ *n* **1** : a room in a printing plant containing the printing presses **2** : a room for the use of reporters

**¹pres·sure** \'pre-shər\ *n* **1** : the burden of physical or mental distress **2** : the action

of pressing; *esp* : the application of force to something by something else in direct contact with it **3** : the force exerted over a surface divided by its area **4** : the stress or urgency of matters demanding attention

**²pressure** *vb* **pres·sured; pres·sur·ing** : to apply pressure to

**pressure group** *n* : a group that seeks to influence governmental policy but not to elect candidates to office

**pressure suit** *n* : an inflatable suit for high-altitude flight or spaceflight to protect the body from low pressure

**pres·sur·ise** *Brit var of* PRESSURIZE

**pres·sur·ize** \'pre-shə-,rīz\ *vb* **-ized; -iz·ing 1** : to maintain higher pressure within than without; *esp* : to maintain normal atmospheric pressure within (as an airplane cabin) during high-altitude flight or spaceflight **2** : to apply pressure to **3** : to design to withstand pressure — **pres·sur·i·za·tion** \,pre-shə-rə-'zā-shən\ *n*

**pres·ti·dig·i·ta·tion** \,pres-tə-,di-jə-'tā-shən\ *n* : SLEIGHT OF HAND

**pres·tige** \pres-'tēzh, -'tēj\ *n* [F, fr. MF, conjuror's trick, illusion, fr. LL *praestigium*, fr. L *praestigiae*, pl., conjuror's tricks, fr. *praestringere* to graze, blunt, constrict, fr. *prae-* in front of + *stringere* to bind tight] : standing or estimation in the eyes of people : REPUTATION ♦ *Synonyms* INFLUENCE, AUTHORITY, WEIGHT, CACHET — **pres·ti·gious** \-'ti-jəs, -'tē-\ *adj*

**pres·to** \'pres-tō\ *interj* [It, quick, quickly] — used to indicate the sudden appearance or occurrence of something

**²presto** *adv or adj* **1** : suddenly as if by magic : IMMEDIATELY **2** : at a rapid tempo — used as a direction in music

**pre·stress** \(,)prē-'stres\ *vb* : to introduce internal stresses into (as a structural beam) to counteract later load stresses

**pre·sum·ably** \pri-'zü-mə-blē\ *adv* : by reasonable assumption

**pre·sume** \pri-'züm\ *vb* **pre·sumed; pre·sum·ing 1** : to take upon oneself without leave or warrant : DARE **2** : to take for granted : ASSUME **3** : to act or behave with undue boldness — **pre·sum·able** \-'zü-mə-bəl\ *adj*

**pre·sump·tion** \pri-'zəmp-shən\ *n* **1** : presumptuous attitude or conduct : AUDACITY **2** : an attitude or belief dictated by probability; *also* : the grounds lending probability to a belief — **pre·sump·tive** \-tiv\ *adj*

**pre·sump·tu·ous** \pri-'zəmp-chə-wəs\ *adj* : overstepping due bounds : taking liberties — **pre·sump·tu·ous·ly** *adv*

**pre·sup·pose** \,prē-sə-'pōz\ *vb* **1** : to suppose beforehand **2** : to require beforehand as a necessary condition — **pre·sup·po·si·tion** \(,)prē-,sə-pə-'zi-shən\ *n*

**pre·teen** \'prē-'tēn\ *n* : a boy or girl not yet 13 years old — **preteen** *adj*

**pre·tend** \pri-'tend\ *vb* **1** : PROFESS ⟨doesn't ~ to be scientific⟩ **2** : FEIGN ⟨~ to be angry⟩ **3** : to lay claim ⟨~ to a throne⟩ — **pre·tend·er** *n*

**pre·tense** *or* **pre·tence** \'prē-₁tens, pri-'tens\ *n* **1** : CLAIM; *esp* : one not supported by fact : mere display : SHOW **3** : an attempt to attain a certain condition ⟨made a ~ at discipline⟩ **4** : false show : PRETEXT ⟨a ~ of objectivity⟩ — **pre·ten·sion** \pri-'ten-chən\ *n*

**pre·ten·tious** \pri-'ten-chəs\ *adj* **1** : making or possessing usu. unjustified claims (as to excellence) ⟨a ~ literary style⟩ **2** : making demands on one's ability or means : AMBITIOUS ⟨too ~ an undertaking⟩ — **pre·ten·tious·ly** *adv* — **pre·ten·tious·ness** *n*

**pret·er·it** *or* **pret·er·ite** \'pre-tə-rət\ *n* : a verb form expressing action in the past

**pre·term** \(,)prē-'tərm, 'prē-,\ *adj* : of, relating to, being, or brought forth by premature birth ⟨a ~ infant⟩

**pre·ter·nat·u·ral** \,prē-tər-'na-chə-rəl\ *adj* **1** : exceeding what is natural ⟨his ~ stamina⟩ **2** : inexplicable by ordinary means — **pre·ter·nat·u·ral·ly** *adv*

**pre·text** \'prē-,tekst\ *n* : a purpose stated or assumed to cloak the real intention or state of affairs

**pret·ti·fy** \'pri-ti-,fī\ *vb* **-fied; -fy·ing** : to make pretty — **pret·ti·fi·ca·tion** \,pri-ti-fə-'kā-shən\ *n*

¹**pret·ty** \'pri-tē\ *adj* **pret·ti·er; -est** [ME *praty, prety*, fr. OE *prættig* tricky, fr. *prætt* trick] **1** : pleasing by delicacy or grace : having conventionally accepted elements of beauty ⟨~ flowers⟩ **2** : MISERABLE, TERRIBLE ⟨a ~ state of affairs⟩ **3** : moderately large ⟨a ~ profit⟩ **4** : PLEASANT — usu. used in negative constructions ⟨the truth was not so ~⟩ ♦ *Synonyms* COMELY, FAIR, BEAUTIFUL, ATTRACTIVE, LOVELY — **pret·ti·ly** \-tə-lē\ *adv* — **pret·ti·ness** \-tē-nəs\ *n*

²**pretty** *adv* : in some degree : MODERATELY; *also* : QUITE, MAINLY

³**pretty** *vb* **pret·tied; pret·ty·ing** : to make pretty — usu. used with *up*

**pretty boy** *n* : a man who is notably good-looking

**pret·zel** \'pret-səl\ *n* [G *Brezel*, ultim. fr. L *brachiatus* having branches like arms, fr. *brachium* arm] : a brittle or chewy glazed usu. salted slender bread often shaped like a loose knot

**prev** *abbr* previous; previously

**pre·vail** \pri-'vāl\ *vb* **1** : to win mastery : TRIUMPH **2** : to be or become effective : SUCCEED **3** : to urge successfully ⟨~ed upon her to sing⟩ **4** : to be frequent : PREDOMINATE — **pre·vail·ing·ly** *adv*

**prev·a·lent** \'pre-və-lənt\ *adj* : generally or widely existent : WIDESPREAD — **prev·a·lence** \-ləns\ *n*

**pre·var·i·cate** \pri-'ver-ə-,kāt\ *vb* **-cat·ed; -cat·ing** [L *praevaricari* to act in collusion, lit., to straddle, fr. *prae* in front of + *varicare* to straddle, fr. *varus* bow-legged] : to deviate from the truth : EQUIVOCATE — **pre·var·i·ca·tion** \-,ver-ə-'kā-shən\ *n* — **pre·var·i·ca·tor** \-'ver-ə-,kā-tər\ *n*

**pre·vent** \pri-'vent\ *vb* **1** : to keep from happening or existing ⟨steps to ~ war⟩ **2** : to hold back : HINDER, STOP ⟨~ us

from going⟩ — **pre·vent·able** *also* **pre·vent·ible** \-'ven-tə-bəl\ *adj* — **pre·ven·ta·tive** \-'ven-tə-tiv\ *adj or n* — **pre·ven·tion** \-'ven-chən\ *n* — **pre·ven·tive** \-'ven-tiv\ *adj or n*

**pre·ver·bal** \,prē-'vər-bəl\ *adj* : having not yet acquired the faculty of speech

¹**pre·view** \'prē-,vyü\ *vb* : to see or discuss beforehand; *esp* : to view or show in advance of public presentation

²**preview** *n* **1** : FORETASTE **2** : an advance showing or viewing **3** *also* **pre·vue** \-,vyü\ : a showing of snatches from a motion picture advertised for future appearance

**pre·vi·ous** \'prē-vē-əs\ *adj* : going before : EARLIER, FORMER ♦ *Synonyms* FOREGOING, PRIOR, PRECEDING, ANTECEDENT — **pre·vi·ous·ly** *adv*

**pre·vi·sion** \prē-'vi-zhən\ *n* **1** : FORESIGHT, PRESCIENCE **2** : FORECAST, PREDICTION ⟨a ~ of success⟩

**pre·war** \'prē-'wȯr\ *adj* : occurring or existing before a war

¹**prey** \'prā\ *n, pl* **prey** *also* **preys** **1** : an animal taken for food by a predator; *also* : VICTIM **2** : the act or habit of preying

²**prey** *vb* **1** : to raid for booty **2** : to seize and devour prey **3** : to have a harmful or wearing effect

**prf** *abbr* proof

¹**price** \'prīs\ *n* **1** *archaic* : VALUE **2** : the amount of money paid or asked for the sale of a specified thing; *also* : the cost at which something is obtained

²**price** *vb* **priced; pric·ing** **1** : to set a price on **2** : to ask the price of **3** : to drive by raising prices ⟨priced themselves out of the market⟩

**price–fix·ing** \'prīs-,fik-sin\ *n* : the setting of prices artificially (as by producers or government)

**price·less** \-ləs\ *adj* : having a value beyond any price : INVALUABLE ♦ *Synonyms* PRECIOUS, COSTLY, EXPENSIVE

**price support** *n* : artificial maintenance of prices of a commodity at a level usu. fixed through government action

**price war** *n* : a period of commercial competition in which prices are repeatedly cut by the competitors

**pric·ey** *also* **pricy** \'prī-sē\ *adj* **pric·i·er; -est** : EXPENSIVE ⟨a ~ restaurant⟩

¹**prick** \'prik\ *n* **1** : a mark or small wound made by a pointed instrument **2** : something sharp or pointed **3** : an instance of pricking; *also* : a sensation of being pricked

²**prick** *vb* **1** : to pierce slightly with a sharp point; *also* : to have or cause a pricking sensation **2** : to affect with anguish or remorse ⟨~s his conscience⟩ **3** : to outline with punctures ⟨~ out a pattern⟩ **4** : to stand or cause to stand erect ⟨the dog's ears ~ed up at the sound⟩ ♦ *Synonyms* PUNCH, PUNCTURE, PERFORATE, BORE, DRILL

**prick·er** \'pri-kər\ *n* : BRIAR; *also* : THORN

¹**prick·le** \'pri-kəl\ *n* **1** : a small sharp process (as on a plant) **2** : a slight stinging pain — **prick·ly** \'pri-klē\ *adj*

²**prickle** *vb* **prick·led; prick·ling 1** : to prick lightly **2** : TINGLE

**prickly heat** *n* : a red cutaneous eruption with intense itching and tingling caused by inflammation around the ducts of the sweat glands

**prickly pear** *n* : any of numerous cacti with usu. yellow flowers and prickly flat or rounded joints; *also* : the sweet pulpy pear-shaped edible fruit of various prickly pears

¹**pride** \'prīd\ *n* **1** : CONCEIT **2** : justifiable self-respect **3** : elation over an act or possession ⟨took ∼ in her work⟩ **4** : haughty behavior : DISDAIN **5** : ostentatious display — **pride·ful** *adj*

²**pride** *vb* **prid·ed; prid·ing** : to indulge (as oneself) in pride

**priest** \'prēst\ *n* [ME *preist*, fr. OE *prēost*, ultim. fr. LL *presbyter* elder, priest, fr. Gk *presbyteros*, fr. compar. of *presbys* old man, elder] : a person having authority to perform the sacred rites of a religion; *esp* : a member of the Anglican, Eastern, or Roman Catholic clergy ranking below a bishop and above a deacon — **priest·hood** *n* — **priest·li·ness** *n* — **priest·ly** *adj*

**priest·ess** \'prēs-təs\ *n* : a woman authorized to perform the sacred rites of a religion

**prig** \'prig\ *n* : one who irritates by rigid or pointed observance of proprieties — **prig·gish** \'pri-gish\ *adj* — **prig·gish·ly** *adv*

¹**prim** \'prim\ *adj* **prim·mer; prim·mest** : stiffly formal and precise — **prim·ly** *adv* — **prim·ness** *n*

²**prim** *abbr* **1** primary **2** primitive

**pri·ma·cy** \'prī-mə-sē\ *n* **1** : the state of being first (as in rank) **2** : the office, rank, or character of an ecclesiastical primate

**pri·ma don·na** \ˌpri-mə-'dä-nə\ *n, pl* **prima donnas** [It, lit., first lady] **1** : a principal female singer (as in an opera company) **2** : a vain undisciplined usu. uncooperative person

**pri·ma fa·cie** \ˌprī-mə-'fā-shə, -sē, -shē\ *adj or adv* [L, at first view] **1** : based on immediate impression : APPARENT **2** : SELF-EVIDENT

**pri·mal** \'prī-məl\ *adj* **1** : ORIGINAL, PRIMITIVE **2** : first in importance

**pri·mar·i·ly** \prī-'mer-ə-lē\ *adv* **1** : FUNDAMENTALLY **2** : ORIGINALLY

¹**pri·ma·ry** \'prī-ˌmer-ē, -mə-rē\ *adj* **1** : first in order of time or development; *also* : PREPARATORY **2** : of first rank or importance; *also* : FUNDAMENTAL **3** : not derived from or dependent on something else ⟨∼ sources⟩

²**primary** *n, pl* **-ries** : a preliminary election in which voters nominate or express a preference among candidates usu. of their own party

**primary care** *n* : health care provided by a medical professional with whom a patient has initial contact

**primary color** *n* : any of a set of colors from which all other colors may be derived

**primary school** *n* **1** : a school usu. including grades 1-3 and sometimes kindergarten **2** : ELEMENTARY SCHOOL

**pri·mate** \'prī-ˌmāt *or esp for 1* -mət\ *n* **1** *often cap* : the highest-ranking bishop of a province or nation **2** : any of an order of mammals including humans, apes, and monkeys

¹**prime** \'prīm\ *n* **1** : the earliest stage of something; *esp* : SPRINGTIME **2** : the most active, thriving, or successful stage or period (as of one's life) **3** : the best individual; *also* : the best part of something **4** : any integer other than 0, +1, or –1 that is not divisible without remainder by any integer except +1, –1, and plus or minus itself; *esp* : any such integer that is positive

²**prime** *adj* **1** : standing first (as in time, rank, significance, or quality) ⟨∼ requisite⟩ **2** : of, relating to, or being a number that is prime

³**prime** *vb* **primed; prim·ing 1** : FILL, LOAD **2** : to lay a preparatory coating upon (as in painting) **3** : to put in working condition **4** : to instruct beforehand : COACH ⟨primed the witness⟩

**prime meridian** *n* : the meridian of 0° longitude which runs through Greenwich, England, and from which other longitudes are reckoned east and west

**prime minister** *n* **1** : the chief minister of a ruler or state **2** : the chief executive of a parliamentary government

¹**prim·er** \'pri-mər\ *n* [ME, layperson's prayer book, fr. AF, fr. ML *primarium*, fr. LL, neut. of *primarius* primary] **1** : a small book for teaching children to read **2** : a small introductory book on a subject ⟨a ∼ of modern art⟩ **3** : a short informative piece of writing

²**prim·er** \'prī-mər\ *n* **1** : one that primes **2** : a device for igniting an explosive **3** : material for priming a surface

**prime rate** *n* : an interest rate announced by a bank to be the lowest available to its most credit-worthy customers

**prime time** *n* **1** : the time period when the television or radio audience is largest; *also* : television shows aired in prime time **2** : the choicest or busiest time

**pri·me·val** \prī-'mē-vəl\ *adj* : of or relating to the earliest ages : PRIMITIVE

¹**prim·i·tive** \'pri-mə-tiv\ *adj* **1** : ORIGINAL, PRIMARY **2** : of, relating to, or characteristic of an early stage of development or evolution **3** : ELEMENTAL, NATURAL **4** : of, relating to, or produced by a tribal people or culture **5** : SELF-TAUGHT; *also* : produced by a self-taught artist — **prim·i·tive·ly** *adv* — **prim·i·tive·ness** *n* — **prim·i·tiv·i·ty** \ˌpri-mə-'ti-və-tē\ *n*

²**primitive** *n* **1** : something primitive **2** : a primitive artist **3** : a member of a primitive people

**prim·i·tiv·ism** \'pri-mə-ti-ˌvi-zəm\ *n* **1** : primitive practices or procedures; *also* : a primitive quality or state **2** : belief in the superiority of a simple way of life close to nature **3** : the style of art of primitive peoples or primitive artists

**pri·mo·gen·i·tor** \ˌprī-mō-ˈje-nə-tər\ *n* : ANCESTOR, FOREFATHER

**pri·mo·gen·i·ture** \-ˈje-nə-ˌchùr\ *n* 1 : the state of being the firstborn of a family 2 : an exclusive right of inheritance belonging to the eldest son

**pri·mor·di·al** \prī-ˈmȯr-dē-əl\ *adj* : first created or developed : existing in its original state : PRIMEVAL

**primp** \ˈprimp\ *vb* : to dress in a careful or finicky manner

**prim·rose** \ˈprim-ˌrōz\ *n* : any of a genus of perennial herbs with large leaves arranged at the base of the stem and clusters of showy flowers

**prin** *abbr* 1 principal 2 principle

**prince** \ˈprins\ *n* [ME, fr. AF, fr. L *princeps* leader, initiator, fr. *primus* first + *capere* to take] 1 : MONARCH, KING 2 : a male member of a royal family; *esp* : a son of the monarch 3 : a person of high standing (as in a class) ⟨a ~ of poets⟩ — **prince·dom** \-dəm\ *n* — **prince·ly** *adj*

**prince·ling** \-liŋ\ *n* : a petty prince

**prin·cess** \ˈprin-səs, -ˌses\ *n* 1 : a female member of a royal family 2 : the consort of a prince

¹**prin·ci·pal** \ˈprin-sə-pəl\ *adj* : most important — **prin·ci·pal·ly** *adv*

²**principal** *n* 1 : a leading person (as in a play) 2 : the chief officer of an educational institution 3 : the person from whom an agent's authority derives 4 : a capital sum earning interest or used as a fund

**prin·ci·pal·i·ty** \ˌprin-sə-ˈpa-lə-tē\ *n, pl* **-ties** : the position, territory, or jurisdiction of a prince

**principal parts** *n pl* : the inflected forms of a verb

**prin·ci·ple** \ˈprin-sə-pəl\ *n* 1 : a general or fundamental law, doctrine, or assumption 2 : a rule or code of conduct; *also* : devotion to such a code 3 : the laws or facts of nature underlying the working of an artificial device 4 : a primary source : ORIGIN; *also* : an underlying faculty or endowment 5 : the active part (as of a drug)

**prin·ci·pled** \-pəld\ *adj* : exhibiting, based on, or characterized by principle ⟨high-*principled*⟩

**prink** \ˈpriŋk\ *vb* : PRIMP

¹**print** \ˈprint\ *n* [ME *prente*, fr. AF, fr. *preint, prient*, pp. of *priendre* to press, fr. L, *premere*] 1 : a mark made by pressure 2 : something stamped with an impression 3 : printed state or form 4 : printed matter 5 : a copy made by printing 6 : cloth with a pattern applied by printing

²**print** *vb* 1 : to stamp (as a mark) in or on something 2 : to produce impressions of (as from type) 3 : to write in letters like those of printer's type 4 : to make (a positive picture) from a photographic negative

**print·able** \ˈprin-tə-bəl\ *adj* 1 : capable of being printed or of being printed from 2 : worthy or fit to be published

**print·er** \ˈprin-tər\ *n* : one that prints; *esp* : a device that produces printout

**print·ing** *n* 1 : reproduction in printed form 2 : the art, practice, or business of a printer 3 : IMPRESSION 5

**printing press** *n* : a machine that produces printed copies

**print·out** \ˈprint-ˌaùt\ *n* : a printed output produced by a computer — **print out** *vb*

¹**pri·or** \ˈprī(-ə)r\ *n* : the superior ranking next to the abbot or abbess of a religious house

²**prior** *adj* 1 : earlier in time or order 2 : taking precedence logically or in importance — **pri·or·i·ty** \prī-ˈȯr-ə-tē\ *n*

**pri·or·ess** \ˈprī-ə-rəs\ *n* : a nun corresponding in rank to a prior

**pri·or·i·tize** \prī-ˈȯr-ə-ˌtīz, ˈprī-ə-rə-ˌtīz\ *vb* **-tized; -tiz·ing** : to list or rate in order of priority

**prior to** *prep* : in advance of : BEFORE

**pri·o·ry** \ˈprī-ə-rē\ *n, pl* **-ries** : a religious house under a prior or prioress

**prise** *chiefly Brit var of* ²PRIZE

**prism** \ˈpri-zəm\ *n* [LL *prisma*, fr. Gk, lit., something sawed, fr. *priein* to saw] 1 : a solid whose two sides are parallelograms and whose ends are parallel and alike in shape and size 2 : a usu. 3-sided transparent object that refracts light so that it breaks up into rainbow colors — **pris·mat·ic** \priz-ˈma-tik\ *adj*

**pris·on** \ˈpri-zᵊn\ *n* : a place or state of confinement esp. for criminals

**pris·on·er** \ˈpri-zᵊn-ər\ *n* : a person deprived of liberty; *esp* : one on trial or in prison

**prisoner of war** *n* : a person captured in war

**pris·sy** \ˈpri-sē\ *adj* **pris·si·er; -est** : being overly prim and precise : PRIGGISH — **pris·si·ness** \-sē-nəs\ *n*

**pris·tine** \ˈpris-ˌtēn, pri-ˈstēn\ *adj* 1 : PRIMITIVE 2 : having the purity of its original state : UNSPOILED

**prith·ee** \ˈpri-thē\ *interj, archaic* — used to express a wish or request

**pri·va·cy** \ˈprī-və-sē\ *n, pl* **-cies** 1 : the quality or state of being apart from others 2 : SECRECY

¹**pri·vate** \ˈprī-vət\ *adj* 1 : belonging to or intended for a particular individual or group ⟨~ property⟩ 2 : restricted to the individual : PERSONAL ⟨~ opinion⟩ 3 : carried on by the individual independently ⟨~ study⟩ 4 : not holding public office ⟨a ~ citizen⟩ 5 : withdrawn from company or observation ⟨a ~ place⟩ 6 : not known publicly ⟨~ dealings⟩ — **pri·vate·ly** *adv*

²**private** *n* : an enlisted person of the lowest rank in the marine corps or of one of the two lowest ranks in the army — **in private** : not openly or in public

**pri·va·teer** \ˌprī-və-ˈtir\ *n* : an armed private ship licensed to attack enemy shipping; *also* : a sailor on such a ship

**private first class** *n* : an enlisted person ranking next below a corporal in the army and next below a lance corporal in the marine corps

**pri·va·tion** \prī-ˈvā-shən\ *n* 1 : DEPRIVATION 1 2 : the state of being deprived; *esp* : lack of what is needed for existence

**priv·et** \ˈpri-vət\ *n* : a nearly evergreen

shrub related to the olive and widely used for hedges

**¹priv·i·lege** \'priv-lij, 'priv-ə-\ n [ME, fr. AF, fr. L *privilegium* law for or against a private person, fr. *privus* private + *leg-, lex* law] : a right or immunity granted as an advantage or favor esp. to some and not others

**²privilege** vb **-leged; -leg·ing 1 :** to grant a privilege to **2 :** to accord a higher value to : FAVOR

**privileged** adj **1 :** having or enjoying one or more privileges ⟨~ classes⟩ **2 :** not subject to disclosure in a court of law ⟨a ~ communication⟩

**¹privy** \'pri-vē\ adj **1 :** PERSONAL, PRI-VATE **2 :** SECRET **3 :** admitted as one sharing in a secret ⟨~ to the conspiracy⟩ — **priv·i·ly** \'pri-və-lē\ adv

**²privy** n, pl **priv·ies :** TOILET; esp : OUT-HOUSE

**¹prize** \'prīz\ n **1 :** something offered or striven for in competition or in contests of chance **2 :** something exceptionally desirable

**²prize** adj **1 :** awarded or worthy of a prize ⟨a ~ essay⟩; also : awarded as a prize ⟨a ~ medal⟩ **2 :** OUTSTANDING

**³prize** vb **prized; priz·ing :** to value highly : ESTEEM ⟨a *prized* possession⟩

**⁴prize** n : property (as a ship) lawfully captured in time of war

**⁵prize** vb **prized; priz·ing :** PRY

**prize·fight** \'prīz-ˌfīt\ n : a professional boxing match — **prize·fight·er** n — **prize·fight·ing** n

**prize·win·ner** \-ˌwi-nər\ n : a winner of a prize — **prize·win·ning** adj

**¹pro** \'prō\ n, pl **pros :** a favorable argument, person, or position

**²pro** adv : in favor of : FOR

**³pro** n or adj : PROFESSIONAL

**PRO** abbr public relations officer

**pro·ac·tive** \prō-'ak-tiv\ adj : acting in anticipation of future problems or needs — **pro·ac·tive·ly** adv

**pro–am** \'prō-'am\ adj : involving professionals competing alongside or against amateurs ⟨a ~ tournament⟩ — **pro–am** n

**prob** abbr **1** probable; probably **2** problem

**prob·a·bil·i·ty** \ˌprä-bə-'bi-lə-tē\ n, pl **-ties 1 :** the quality or state of being probable **2 :** something probable **3 :** a measure of how often a particular event will occur if something (as tossing a coin) is done repeatedly which results in any of a number of possible events

**prob·a·ble** \'prä-bə-bəl\ adj **1 :** apparently or presumably true ⟨a ~ hypothesis⟩ **2 :** likely to be or become true or real ⟨a ~ result⟩ — **prob·a·bly** \-bə-blē\ adv

**¹pro·bate** \'prō-ˌbāt\ n : the judicial determination of the validity of a will

**²pro·bate** vb **pro·bat·ed; pro·bat·ing :** to establish (a will) by probate as genuine and valid

**pro·ba·tion** \prō-'bā-shən\ n **1 :** subjection of an individual to a period of testing and trial to ascertain fitness (as for a job)

**2 :** the action of giving a convicted offender freedom during good behavior under the supervision of a probation officer — **pro·ba·tion·ary** \-shə-ˌner-ē\ adj

**pro·ba·tion·er** \-shə-nər\ n **1 :** a person (as a newly admitted student nurse) whose fitness is being tested during a trial period **2 :** a convicted offender on probation

**pro·ba·tive** \'prō-bə-tiv\ adj **1 :** serving to test or try **2 :** serving to prove

**¹probe** \'prōb\ n **1 :** a slender instrument for examining a cavity (as a wound) **2 :** an information-gathering device sent into outer space **3 :** a penetrating investigation ◆ **Synonyms** INQUIRY, IN-QUEST, RESEARCH, INQUISITION

**²probe** vb **probed; prob·ing 1 :** to examine with a probe **2 :** to investigate thoroughly

**pro·bi·ty** \'prō-bə-tē\ n : UPRIGHTNESS, HONESTY

**prob·lem** \'prä-bləm\ n **1 :** a question raised for consideration or solution **2 :** an intricate unsettled question **3 :** a source of perplexity or vexation — **problem** adj

**prob·lem·at·ic** \ˌprä-blə-'ma-tik\ also **prob·lem·at·i·cal** \-ti-kəl\ adj **1 :** difficult to solve or decide : PUZZLING **2 :** DUBIOUS, QUESTIONABLE

**pro·bos·cis** \prə-'bä-səs, -'bäs-kəs\ n, pl **-bos·cis·es** also **-bos·ci·des** \-ˈbä-sə-ˌdēz\ [L, fr. Gk *proboskis*, fr. *pro-* before + *boskein* to feed] : a long flexible snout (as the trunk of an elephant)

**proc** abbr proceedings

**pro·caine** \'prō-ˌkān\ n : a drug used esp. as a local anesthetic

**pro·ce·dure** \prə-'sē-jər\ n **1 :** a particular way of doing something ⟨democratic ~⟩ **2 :** a series of steps followed in a regular order ⟨a surgical ~⟩ — **pro·ce·dur·al** \-ˈsē-jə-rəl\ adj

**pro·ceed** \prō-'sēd\ vb **1 :** to come forth : ISSUE **2 :** to go on in an orderly way; also : CONTINUE **3 :** to begin and carry on an action **4 :** to take legal action **5 :** to go forward : ADVANCE

**pro·ceed·ing** n **1 :** PROCEDURE **2** pl : DOINGS **3** pl : legal action **4 :** TRANSAC-TION **5** pl : an official record of things said or done

**pro·ceeds** \'prō-ˌsēdz\ n pl : the total amount or the profit arising from a business deal : RETURN

**¹pro·cess** \'prä-ˌses, 'prō-\ n, pl **pro·cess·es** \-ˌse-səz, -sə-səz, -ˌsēz\ **1 :** PROG-RESS, ADVANCE **2 :** something going on : PROCEEDING **3 :** a natural phenomenon marked by gradual changes that lead toward a particular result ⟨the ~ of growth⟩ **4 :** a series of actions or operations directed toward a particular result ⟨a manufacturing ~⟩ **5 :** legal action **6 :** a mandate issued by a court; esp : SUM-MONS **7 :** a projecting part of an organism or organic structure

**²process** vb : to subject to a special process

**pro·ces·sion** \prə-'se-shən\ n : a group of

individuals moving along in an orderly often ceremonial way

**pro·ces·sion·al** \-'se-shə-nəl\ *n* 1 : music for a procession 2 : a ceremonial procession

**pro·ces·sor** \'prä-ˌse-sər, 'prō-\ *n* 1 : one that processes 2 : CPU

**pro–choice** \(ˌ)prō-'chȯis\ *adj* : favoring the legalization of abortion

**pro·claim** \prō-'klām\ *vb* : to make known publicly : DECLARE

**proc·la·ma·tion** \ˌprä-klə-'mā-shən\ *n* : an official public announcement

**pro·cliv·i·ty** \prō-'kli-və-tē\ *n, pl* **-ties** : an inherent inclination esp. toward something objectionable

**pro·con·sul** \-'kän-səl\ *n* 1 : a governor or military commander of an ancient Roman province 2 : an administrator in a modern colony or occupied area — **pro·con·su·lar** \-sə-lər\ *adj*

**pro·cras·ti·nate** \prə-'kras-tə-ˌnāt, prō-\ *vb* **-nat·ed; -nat·ing** [L *procrastinare*, fr. *pro-* forward + *crastinus* of tomorrow, fr. *cras* tomorrow] : to put off usu. habitually doing something that should be done ♦ **Synonyms** DAWDLE, DELAY — **pro·cras·ti·na·tion** \-ˌkras-tə-'nā-shən\ *n* — **pro·cras·ti·na·tor** \-'kras-tə-ˌnā-tər\ *n*

**pro·cre·ate** \'prō-krē-ˌāt\ *vb* **-at·ed; -at·ing** : to beget or bring forth offspring ♦ **Synonyms** REPRODUCE, BREED, GENERATE, PROPAGATE — **pro·cre·ation** \ˌprō-krē-'ā-shən\ *n* — **pro·cre·ative** \'prō-krē-ˌā-tiv\ *adj* — **pro·cre·ator** \-ˌā-tər\ *n*

**pro·crus·te·an** \prə-'krəs-tē-ən\ *adj, often cap* [fr. *Procrustes*, villain of Greek mythology who made victims fit his bed by stretching them or cutting off their legs] : marked by arbitrary often ruthless disregard of individual differences or special circumstances

**proc·tor** \'präk-tər\ *n* : one appointed to supervise students (as at an examination) — **proctor** *vb* — **proc·to·ri·al** \präk-'tȯr-ē-əl\ *adj*

**proc·u·ra·tor** \'prä-kyə-ˌrā-tər\ *n* : a Roman provincial administrator

**pro·cure** \prə-'kyür\ *vb* **pro·cured; pro·cur·ing** 1 : to get possession of : OBTAIN 2 : to make women available for promiscuous sexual intercourse 3 : ACHIEVE ♦ **Synonyms** SECURE, ACQUIRE, GAIN, WIN, EARN — **pro·cur·able** \-'kyür-ə-bəl\ *adj* — **pro·cure·ment** *n* — **pro·cur·er** *n*

¹**prod** \'präd\ *vb* **prod·ded; prod·ding** 1 : to thrust a pointed instrument into : GOAD 2 : INCITE, STIR — **prod** *n*

²**prod** *abbr* product, production

**prod·i·gal** \'prä-di-gəl\ *adj* 1 : recklessly extravagant; *also* : LUXURIANT 2 : WASTEFUL, LAVISH ♦ **Synonyms** PROFUSE, LUSH, OPULENT — **prodigal** *n* — **prod·i·gal·i·ty** \ˌprä-də-'ga-lə-tē\ *n*

**pro·di·gious** \prə-'di-jəs\ *adj* 1 : exciting wonder 2 : extraordinary in size or degree : ENORMOUS ♦ **Synonyms** MONSTROUS, TREMENDOUS, STUPENDOUS, MONUMENTAL — **pro·di·gious·ly** *adv*

**prod·i·gy** \'prä-də-jē\ *n, pl* **-gies** 1

: something extraordinary : WONDER 2 : a highly talented child

¹**pro·duce** \prə-'düs, -'dyüs\ *vb* **pro·duced; pro·duc·ing** 1 : to present to view : EXHIBIT 2 : to give birth or rise to : YIELD 3 : EXTEND, PROLONG 4 : to give being or form to : BRING ABOUT, MAKE; *esp* : MANUFACTURE 5 : to sponsor or oversee the making of 6 : to cause to accrue ⟨~ a profit⟩ — **pro·duc·er** *n*

²**pro·duce** \'prä-(ˌ)düs, 'prō- *also* -(ˌ)dyüs\ *n* : PRODUCT 2; *also* : agricultural products and esp. fresh fruits and vegetables

**prod·uct** \'prä-(ˌ)dəkt\ *n* 1 : the number resulting from multiplication 2 : something produced

**pro·duc·tion** \prə-'dək-shən\ *n* 1 : something produced : PRODUCT 2 : the act or process of producing — **pro·duc·tive** \-'dək-tiv\ *adj* — **pro·duc·tive·ness** *n* — **pro·duc·tiv·i·ty** \(ˌ)prō-ˌdək-'ti-və-tē, ˌprä-(ˌ)dək-\ *n*

**product placement** *n* : the inclusion of a product in a television program or film as a means of advertising

**pro·em** \'prō-ˌem\ *n* 1 : preliminary comment : PREFACE 2 : PRELUDE

¹**prof** \'präf\ *n* : PROFESSOR

²**prof** *abbr* professional

¹**pro·fane** \prō-'fān\ *vb* **pro·faned; pro·fan·ing** 1 : to treat (something sacred) with irreverence or contempt 2 : to debase by an unworthy use — **prof·a·na·tion** \ˌprä-fə-'nā-shən\ *n*

²**profane** *adj* [ME *prophane*, fr. MF, fr. L *profanus*, fr. *pro-* before + *fanum* temple] 1 : not concerned with religion : SECULAR 2 : not holy because unconsecrated, impure, or defiled 3 : serving to debase what is holy : IRREVERENT 4 : OBSCENE, VULGAR — **pro·fane·ly** *adv* — **pro·fane·ness** *n*

**pro·fan·i·ty** \prō-'fa-nə-tē\ *n, pl* **-ties** 1 : the quality or state of being profane 2 : the use of profane language : profane language

**pro·fess** \prə-'fes\ *vb* 1 : to declare or admit openly : AFFIRM 2 : to declare in words only : PRETEND 3 : to confess one's faith in 4 : to practice or claim to be versed in (a calling or occupation) — **pro·fess·ed·ly** \-'fe-səd-lē\ *adv*

**pro·fes·sion** \prə-'fe-shən\ *n* 1 : an open declaration or avowal of a belief or opinion 2 : a calling requiring specialized knowledge and often long academic preparation 3 : the whole body of persons engaged in a calling

¹**pro·fes·sion·al** \prə-'fe-shə-nəl\ *adj* 1 : of, relating to, or characteristic of a profession 2 : engaged in one of the professions 3 : participating for gain in an activity often engaged in by amateurs — **pro·fes·sion·al·ly** *adv*

²**professional** *n* : one that engages in an activity professionally

**pro·fes·sion·al·ism** \-nə-ˌli-zəm\ *n* 1 : the conduct, aims, or qualities that characterize or mark a profession or a professional person 2 : the following of a profession (as athletics) for gain or livelihood pro·fes·sion·al·ize \-nə-,līz\ vb -ized; -iz·ing : to give a professional nature to

pro·fes·sor \prə-'fe-sər\ n : a teacher at a university or college; esp : a faculty member of the highest academic rank — pro·fes·so·ri·al \,prō-fə-'sòr-ē-əl, ,prä-\ adj — pro·fes·sor·ship n

prof·fer \'prä-fər\ vb prof·fered; prof·fer·ing : to present for acceptance : OF-FER — proffer n

pro·fi·cient \prə-'fi-shənt\ adj : well advanced in an art, occupation, or branch of knowledge ♦ Synonyms ADEPT, SKILLFUL, EXPERT, MASTERFUL, MAS-TERLY — pro·fi·cien·cy \-shən-sē\ n — proficient n — pro·fi·cient·ly adv

¹pro·file \'prō-,fī(-ə)l\ n [It profilo, fr. profilare to draw in outline, fr. pro- forward (fr. L) + filare to spin, fr. LL, fr. L filum thread] 1 : a representation of something in outline; esp : a human head seen in side view 2 : a concise biographical sketch 3 : degree or level of public exposure ⟨keep a low ∼⟩

²profile vb pro·filed; pro·fil·ing : to write or draw a profile of

profiling n : the act of suspecting or targeting a person solely on the basis of observed characteristics or behavior ⟨racial ∼⟩

¹prof·it \'prä-fət\ n 1 : a valuable return : GAIN 2 : the excess of the selling price of goods over their cost — prof·it·less adj

²profit vb 1 : to be of use : BENEFIT 2 : to derive benefit : GAIN ⟨∼ed from his mistakes⟩ — prof·it·able \'prä-fə-tə-bəl\ adj — prof·it·ably \-blē\ adv

prof·i·teer \,prä-fə-'tir\ n : one who makes what is considered an unreasonable profit — profiteer vb

prof·li·gate \'prä-fli-gət, -flə-,gāt\ adj 1 : completely given up to dissipation and licentiousness 2 : wildly extravagant — prof·li·ga·cy \-gə-sē\ n — profligate n — prof·li·gate·ly adv

pro for·ma \(,)prō-'fòr-mə\ adj : done or existing as a matter of form

pro·found \prə-'faùnd, prō-\ adj 1 : marked by intellectual depth or insight ⟨a ∼ thought⟩ 2 : coming from or reaching to a depth ⟨a ∼ sigh⟩ 3 : deeply felt : INTENSE ⟨∼ sympathy⟩ — pro·found·ly adv — pro·fun·di·ty \-'fən-də-tē\ n

pro·fuse \prə-'fyüs, prō-\ adj : pouring forth liberally : ABUNDANT ⟨∼ bleeding⟩ ♦ Synonyms LAVISH, PRODIGAL, LUXU-RIANT, EXUBERANT — pro·fuse·ly adv — pro·fu·sion \-'fyü-zhən\ n

prog abbr program

pro·gen·i·tor \prō-'je-nə-tər\ n 1 : a direct ancestor : FOREFATHER 2 : ORIGI-NATOR, PRECURSOR

prog·e·ny \'prä-jə-nē\ n, pl -nies : OFF-SPRING, CHILDREN, DESCENDANTS

pro·ges·ter·one \prō-'jes-tə-,rōn\ n : a female hormone that causes the uterus to undergo changes so as to provide a suitable environment for a fertilized egg

prog·na·thous \'präg-nə-thəs\ adj : having the lower jaw projecting beyond the upper part of the face

prog·no·sis \präg-'nō-səs\ n, pl -no·ses \-,sēz\ 1 : the prospect of recovery from disease 2 : FORECAST

¹prog·nos·tic \präg-'näs-tik\ n 1 : POR-TENT 2 : PROPHECY

²prognostic adj : of, relating to, or serving as ground for prognostication or a prognosis

prog·nos·ti·cate \präg-'näs-tə-,kāt\ vb -cat·ed; -cat·ing : to foretell from signs or symptoms — prog·nos·ti·ca·tion \-,näs-tə-'kā-shən\ n — prog·nos·ti·ca·tor \-'näs-tə-,kā-tər\ n

¹pro·gram \'prō-,gram, -grəm\ n [F programme agenda, public notice, fr. Gk programma, fr. prographein to write in advance, fr. pro- before + graphein to write] 1 : a brief outline of the order to be pursued or the subjects included (as in a public entertainment); also : PERFOR-MANCE 2 : a plan of procedure esp. toward a goal 3 : coded instructions for a computer — pro·gram·mat·ic \,prō-grə-'ma-tik\ adj

²program also programme vb -grammed or -gramed; -gram·ming or -gram·ing 1 : to arrange or furnish a program of or for 2 : to enter in a program 3 : to provide (as a computer) with a program — pro·gram·ma·bil·i·ty \(,)grə-ma-bə-'bi-lə-tē\ n — pro·gram·ma·ble \'prō-,grə-mə-bəl\ adj — pro·gram·mer also pro·gram·er \'prō-,gra-mər, -grə-\ n

programme chiefly Brit var of PROGRAM

programmed instruction n : instruction through information given in small steps with each requiring a correct response by the learner before going on to the next step

pro·gram·ming also pro·gram·ing n 1 : the planning, scheduling, or performing of a program 2 : the process of instructing or learning by means of an instruction program 3 : the process of preparing an instruction program

¹prog·ress \'prä-grəs, -,gres\ n 1 : a forward movement : ADVANCE 2 : a gradual betterment ⟨the ∼ of science⟩

²pro·gress \prə-'gres\ vb 1 : to move forward : PROCEED 2 : to develop to a more advanced stage : IMPROVE

pro·gres·sion \prə-'gre-shən\ n 1 : an act of progressing : ADVANCE 2 : a continuous and connected series

¹pro·gres·sive \prə-'gre-siv\ adj 1 : of, relating to, or characterized by progress ⟨a ∼ city⟩ 2 : moving forward or onward : ADVANCING 3 : increasing in extent or severity ⟨a ∼ disease⟩ 4 often cap : of or relating to political Progressives 5 : of, relating to, or constituting a verb form that expresses action in progress at the time of speaking or a time spoken of — pro·gres·sive·ly adv

²progressive n 1 : one that is progressive 2 : a person believing in moderate political change and social improvement by government action; esp, cap : a member of a Progressive Party in the U.S.

pro·hib·it \prō-'hi-bət\ vb 1 : to forbid by

authority   2 : to prevent from doing something

**pro·hi·bi·tion** \‚prō-ə-'bi-shən\ *n*  1 : the act of prohibiting  2 : the forbidding by law of the sale or manufacture of alcoholic beverages — **pro·hi·bi·tion·ist** \-'bi-shə-nist\ *n* — **pro·hib·i·tive** \prō-'hi-bə-tiv\ *adj* — **pro·hib·i·tive·ly** *adv* — **pro·hib·i·to·ry** \-'hi-bə-‚tȯr-ē\ *adj*

¹**proj·ect** \'prä-‚jekt, -jikt\ *n*  1 : a specific plan or design : SCHEME  2 : a planned undertaking ⟨a research ∼⟩

²**pro·ject** \prə-'jekt\ *vb*  1 : to devise in the mind : DESIGN  2 : to throw forward  3 : PROTRUDE  4 : to cause (light or shadow) to fall into space or (an image) to fall on a surface ⟨∼ a beam of light⟩  5 : to attribute (a thought, feeling, or personal characteristic) to a person, group, or object  6 : to display outwardly — **pro·jec·tion** \-'jek-shən\ *n*

**pro·jec·tile** \prə-'jek-t³l, -'jek-tī(-ə)l\ *n* : a body hurled or projected by external force; *esp* : a missile for a firearm  2 : a self-propelling weapon

**pro·jec·tion·ist** \prə-'jek-shə-nist\ *n* : one that operates a motion-picture projector or television equipment

**pro·jec·tor** \-'jek-tər\ *n* : one that projects; *esp* : a device for projecting pictures on a screen

**pro·lapse** \prō-'laps, 'prō-‚\ *n* : the falling down or slipping of a body part from its usual position

**pro·le·gom·e·non** \‚prō-li-'gä-mə-‚nän, -nən\ *n, pl* **-e·na** \-nə\ : prefatory remarks

**pro·le·tar·i·an** \‚prō-lə-'ter-ē-ən\ *n* [L *proletarius* belonging to the lowest class of citizens, fr. *proles* progeny, fr. *pro-* forth + *-oles* (akin to *alere* to nourish)] : a member of the proletariat — **proletarian** *adj*

**pro·le·tar·i·at** \-ē-ət\ *n* : the laboring class; *esp* : industrial workers who sell their labor to live

**pro-life** \(‚)prō-'līf\ *n* : ANTIABORTION

**pro·lif·er·ate** \prə-'li-fə-‚rāt\ *vb* **-at·ed; -at·ing** : to grow or increase by rapid production of new units (as cells, offspring, or nuclear weapons) — **pro·lif·er·a·tion** \-‚li-fə-'rā-shən\ *n*

**pro·lif·ic** \prə-'li-fik\ *adj*  1 : producing young or fruit abundantly  2 : marked by abundant inventiveness or productivity ⟨a ∼ writer⟩ — **pro·lif·i·cal·ly** \-fi-k(ə-)lē\ *adv*

**pro·lix** \prō-'liks, 'prō-‚liks\ *adj* : VERBOSE ♦ *Synonyms* WORDY, DIFFUSE, REDUNDANT — **pro·lix·i·ty** \prō-'lik-sə-tē\ *n*

**pro·logue** *also* **pro·log** \'prō-‚lȯg, -‚läg\ *n* : PREFACE ⟨∼ of a play⟩

**pro·long** \prə-'lȯŋ\ *vb* : to lengthen in time : CONTINUE ⟨∼ a meeting⟩  2 : to lengthen in extent or range ⟨∼ an airport runway⟩ ♦ *Synonyms* PROTRACT, EXTEND, ELONGATE, STRETCH — **pro·lon·ga·tion** \‚prō-‚lȯŋ-'gā-shən\ *n*

**prom** \'präm\ *n* : a formal dance given by a high school or college class

¹**prom·e·nade** \‚prä-mə-'näd, -'näd\ *vb*

**-nad·ed; -nad·ing**  1 : to take a promenade  2 : to walk about in or on

²**promenade** *n* [F, fr. *promener* to take for a walk, fr. MF, alter. of OF *pourmener*, fr. *pour-* completely (fr. L *pro-*) + *mener* to lead, fr. LL *minare* to drive, fr. L *minari* to threaten]  1 : a place for strolling  2 : a leisurely walk for pleasure or display  3 : an opening grand march at a formal ball

**pro·me·thi·um** \prə-'mē-thē-əm\ *n* : a metallic chemical element obtained from uranium or neodymium

**prom·i·nence** \'prä-mə-nəns\ *n*  1 : something prominent  2 : the quality, state, or fact of being prominent or conspicuous  3 : a mass of cloudlike gas that arises from the sun's chromosphere

**prom·i·nent** \-nənt\ *adj*  1 : jutting out : PROJECTING  2 : readily noticeable : CONSPICUOUS  3 : DISTINGUISHED, EMINENT ⟨a ∼ lawyer⟩ ♦ *Synonyms* REMARKABLE, OUTSTANDING, STRIKING, SALIENT — **prom·i·nent·ly** *adv*

**pro·mis·cu·ous** \prə-'mis-kyə-wəs\ *adj*  1 : consisting of various sorts and kinds : MIXED  2 : not restricted to one class or person  3 : having a number of sexual partners ♦ *Synonyms* MISCELLANEOUS, ASSORTED, HETEROGENEOUS, MOTLEY, VARIED — **pro·mis·cu·i·ty** \‚prä-mis-'kyü-ə-tē, ‚prō-‚mis-\ *n* — **pro·mis·cu·ous·ly** *adv* — **pro·mis·cu·ous·ness** *n*

¹**prom·ise** \'prä-məs\ *n*  1 : a pledge to do or not to do something specified  2 : ground for expectation of success or improvement  3 : something promised

²**promise** *vb* **prom·ised; prom·is·ing**  1 : to engage to do, bring about, or provide ⟨∼ help⟩  2 : to suggest beforehand ⟨dark clouds ∼ rain⟩  3 : to give ground for expectation ⟨it ∼s to be a good game⟩

**promising** *adj* : likely to succeed or yield good results ⟨a ∼ new medicine⟩ — **prom·is·ing·ly** *adv*

**prom·is·so·ry** \'prä-mə-‚sȯr-ē\ *adj* : containing a promise

**prom·on·to·ry** \'prä-mən-‚tȯr-ē\ *n, pl* **-ries** : a point of land jutting into the sea : HEADLAND

**pro·mote** \prə-'mōt\ *vb* **pro·mot·ed; pro·mot·ing**  1 : to advance in station, rank, or honor  2 : to contribute to the growth or prosperity of : FURTHER  3 : LAUNCH — **pro·mo·tion** \-'mō-shən\ *n* — **pro·mo·tion·al** \-shə-nəl\ *adj*

**pro·mot·er** \-'mō-tər\ *n* : one that promotes; *esp* : one that assumes the financial responsibilities of a sports event ⟨a boxing ∼⟩

¹**prompt** \'prämpt\ *vb*  1 : INCITE  2 : to assist (one acting or reciting) by suggesting the next words  3 : INSPIRE, URGE — **prompt·er** *n*

²**prompt** *adj*  1 : being ready and quick to act; *also* : PUNCTUAL  2 : performed readily or immediately ⟨∼ service⟩ — **prompt·ly** *adv* — **prompt·ness** *n*

**prompt·book** \-‚bu̇k\ *n* : a copy of a play

with directions for performance used by a theater prompter

**promp·ti·tude** \'prämp-tə-ˌtüd, -ˌtyüd\ *n* : the quality or habit of being prompt : PROMPTNESS

**pro·mul·gate** \'prä-məl-ˌgāt; prō-'məl-\ *vb* **-gat·ed; -gat·ing** : to make known or put into force by open declaration — **prom·ul·ga·tion** \ˌprä-məl-'gā-shən, ˌprō-(ˌ)məl-\ *n*

**pron** *abbr* 1 pronoun 2 pronounced 3 pronunciation

**prone** \'prōn\ *adj* 1 : having a tendency or inclination : DISPOSED 2 : lying face downward; *also* : lying flat or prostrate
♦ *Synonyms* SUBJECT, EXPOSED, OPEN, LIABLE, SUSCEPTIBLE — **prone·ness** *n*

**prong** \'prȯŋ\ *n* : one of the sharp points of a fork : TINE; *also* : a slender projecting part (as of an antler) — **pronged** \'prȯŋd\ *adj*

**prong·horn** \'prȯŋ-ˌhȯrn\ *n, pl* **pronghorn** *or* **pronghorns** : a swift horned ruminant mammal chiefly of grasslands of western No. America that resembles an antelope

**pro·noun** \'prō-ˌnau̇n\ *n* : a word used as a substitute for a noun

**pro·nounce** \prə-'nau̇ns\ *vb* **pro·nounced; pro·nounc·ing** 1 : to utter officially or as an opinion (~ sentence) 2 : to employ the organs of speech in order to produce (~ a word); *esp* : to say or speak correctly (she can't ~ his name) — **pro·nounce·able** *adj* — **pro·nun·ci·a·tion** \-ˌnən-sē-'ā-shən\ *n*

**pro·nounced** *adj* : strongly marked : DECIDED (a ~ dislike)

**pro·nounce·ment** \prə-'nau̇ns-mənt\ *n* : a formal declaration of opinion; *also* : ANNOUNCEMENT

**pron·to** \'prän-ˌtō\ *adv* [Sp, fr. L *promptus* prompt] : QUICKLY

**pro·nu·clear** \'prō-'nü-klē-ər, -'nyü-\ *adj* : supporting the use of nuclear-powered electric generating stations

**pro·nun·ci·a·men·to** \prō-ˌnən-sē-ə-'men-ˌtō\ *n, pl* **-tos** *or* **-toes** : PROCLAMATION, MANIFESTO

¹**proof** \'prüf\ *n* [ME *prof*, *prove*, alter. of *preve*, fr. AF *preove*, fr. LL *proba*, fr. L *probare* to test, prove, fr. *probus* good, honest] 1 : the evidence that compels acceptance by the mind of a truth or fact 2 : a process or operation that establishes validity or truth : TEST 3 : a trial impression (as from type) 4 : a trial print from a photographic negative 5 : alcoholic content (as of a beverage) indicated by a number that is twice the percent by volume of alcohol present (whiskey of 90 ~ is 45% alcohol)

²**proof** *adj* 1 : successful in resisting or repelling (~ against tampering) (waterproof) 2 : of standard strength or quality or alcoholic content

**proof·read** \-ˌrēd\ *vb* : to read and mark corrections in — **proof·read·er** *n*

¹**prop** \'präp\ *n* : something that props

²**prop** *vb* **propped; prop·ping** 1 : to support by placing something under or against 2 : SUSTAIN, STRENGTHEN

³**prop** *n* : PROPERTY 4

⁴**prop** *n* : PROPELLER

⁵**prop** *abbr* 1 property 2 proposition 3 proprietor

**pro·pa·gan·da** \ˌprä-pə-'gan-də, ˌprō-\ *n* [NL, fr. *Congregatio de propaganda fide* Congregation for propagating the faith, organization established by Pope Gregory XVI] : the spreading of ideas or information to further or damage a cause; *also* : ideas or allegations spread for such a purpose — **pro·pa·gan·dist** \-dist\ *n*

**pro·pa·gan·dize** \-ˌdīz\ *vb* **-dized; -diz·ing** : to subject to or carry on propaganda

**prop·a·gate** \'prä-pə-ˌgāt\ *vb* **-gat·ed; -gat·ing** 1 : to reproduce or cause to reproduce biologically : MULTIPLY 2 : to cause to spread (*propagating* the faith) — **prop·a·ga·tion** \ˌprä-pə-'gā-shən\ *n*

**pro·pane** \'prō-ˌpān\ *n* : a heavy flammable gas found in petroleum and natural gas and used esp. as a fuel

**pro·pel** \prə-'pel\ *vb* **pro·pelled; pro·pel·ling** : to drive forward or onward ♦ *Synonyms* PUSH, SHOVE, THRUST

**pro·pel·lant** *also* **pro·pel·lent** \-'pe-lənt\ *n* : something (as a fuel) that propels — **propellant** *also* **propellent** *adj*

**pro·pel·ler** \prə-'pe-lər\ *n* : a device consisting of a hub fitted with blades that is used to propel a vehicle (as a motorboat or an airplane)

**pro·pen·si·ty** \prə-'pen-sə-tē\ *n, pl* **-ties** : an often intense natural inclination or preference

¹**prop·er** \'prä-pər\ *adj* 1 : referring to one individual only (~ noun) 2 : belonging characteristically to a species or individual : PECULIAR 3 : very satisfactory : EXCELLENT 4 : strictly limited to a specified thing (the city ~) 5 : CORRECT (the ~ way to proceed) 6 : strictly decorous : GENTEEL 7 : marked by suitability or rightness (~ punishment) ♦ *Synonyms* MEET, APPROPRIATE, FITTING, SEEMLY — **prop·er·ly** *adv*

²**proper** *n* : the parts of the Mass that vary according to the liturgical calendar

**prop·er·tied** \'prä-pər-tēd\ *adj* : owning property and esp. much property

**prop·er·ty** \'prä-pər-tē\ *n, pl* **-ties** 1 : a quality peculiar to an individual or thing 2 : something owned; *esp* : a piece of real estate 3 : OWNERSHIP 4 : an article or object used in a play or motion picture other than painted scenery and actor's costumes

**proph·e·cy** *also* **proph·e·sy** \'prä-fə-sē\ *n, pl* **-cies** *also* **-sies** 1 : an inspired utterance of a prophet 2 : PREDICTION

**proph·e·sy** \-ˌsī\ *vb* **-sied; -sy·ing** 1 : to speak or utter by divine inspiration 2 : PREDICT — **proph·e·si·er** *n*

**proph·et** \'prä-fət\ *n* [ME *prophete*, fr. AF, fr. L *propheta*, fr. Gk *prophētēs*, fr. *pro* for + *phanai* to speak] 1 : one who utters divinely inspired revelations 2 : one who foretells future events

**proph·et·ess** \'prä-fə-təs\ *n* : a woman who is a prophet

**pro·phet·ic** \prə-'fe-tik\ *or* **pro·phet·i·cal**

\-ti-kəl\ *adj* : of, relating to, or characteristic of a prophet or prophecy — **prophet·i·cal·ly** \-ti-k(ə-)lē\ *adv*

**Proph·ets** \'prä-fəts\ *n pl* — see BIBLE table

¹**pro·phy·lac·tic** \,prō-fə-'lak-tik, ,prä-\ *adj* 1 : preventing or guarding from the spread or occurrence of disease or infection 2 : PREVENTIVE

²**prophylactic** *n* : something prophylactic; *esp* : a device (as a condom) for preventing venereal infection or conception

**pro·phy·lax·is** \-'lak-səs\ *n, pl* **-lax·es** \-'lak-,sēz\ : measures designed to preserve health and prevent the spread of disease

**pro·pin·qui·ty** \prə-'piŋ-kwə-tē\ *n* 1 : KINSHIP 2 : nearness in place or time : PROXIMITY

**pro·pi·ti·ate** \prō-'pi-shē-,āt\ *vb* **-at·ed; -at·ing** : to gain or regain the favor of : APPEASE 〈~ the angry gods〉 — **pro·pi·ti·a·tion** \-,pi-shē-'ā-shən\ *n* — **pro·pi·tia·to·ry** \'pi-shē-ə-,tōr-ē\ *adj*

**pro·pi·tious** \prə-'pi-shəs\ *adj* 1 : favorably disposed 〈~ deities〉 2 : being of good omen 〈~ circumstances〉

**prop·man** \'präp-,man\ *n* : one who is in charge of stage properties

**pro·po·nent** \prə-'pō-nənt\ *n* : one who argues in favor of something

¹**pro·por·tion** \prə-'pȯr-shən\ *n* 1 : BALANCE, SYMMETRY 2 : SHARE, QUOTA 3 : the relation of one part to another or to the whole with respect to magnitude, quantity, or degree : RATIO 4 : SIZE, DEGREE — **in proportion** : PROPORTIONAL

²**proportion** *vb* **-tioned; -tion·ing** 1 : to adjust (a part or thing) in size relative to other parts or things 2 : to make the parts of harmonious

**pro·por·tion·al** \prə-'pȯr-shə-nəl\ *adj* : corresponding in size, degree, or intensity; *also* : having the same or a constant ratio — **pro·por·tion·al·ly** *adv*

**pro·por·tion·ate** \prə-'pȯr-shə-nət\ *adj* : PROPORTIONAL — **pro·por·tion·ate·ly** *adv*

**pro·pose** \prə-'pōz\ *vb* **pro·posed; pro·pos·ing** 1 : PLAN, INTEND 〈~s to buy a house〉 2 : to make an offer of marriage 3 : to offer for consideration : SUGGEST 〈~ a policy〉 — **pro·pos·al** \-'pō-zəl\ *n* — **pro·pos·er** *n*

¹**prop·o·si·tion** \,prä-pə-'zi-shən\ *n* 1 : something proposed for consideration : PROPOSAL 2 : a request for sexual intercourse 3 : a statement of something to be discussed, proved, or explained 4 : SITUATION, AFFAIR 〈a tough ~〉 — **prop·o·si·tion·al** \-'zi-shə-nəl\ *adj*

²**proposition** *vb* **-tioned; -tion·ing** : to make a proposal to; *esp* : to suggest sexual intercourse to

**pro·pound** \prə-'pau̇nd\ *vb* : to set forth for consideration 〈~ a doctrine〉

**pro·pri·e·tary** \prə-'prī-ə-,ter-ē\ *adj* 1 : of, relating to, or characteristic of a proprietor 〈~ rights〉 2 : made and sold by one with the sole right to do so 〈~ med­icines〉 〈~ software〉

**pro·pri·e·tor** \prə-'prī-ə-tər\ *n* : OWNER — **pro·pri·e·tor·ship** *n*

**pro·pri·e·tress** \-'prī-ə-trəs\ *n* : a woman who is a proprietor

**pro·pri·e·ty** \prə-'prī-ə-tē\ *n, pl* **-ties** 1 : the standard of what is socially acceptable in conduct or speech 2 *pl* : the customs of polite society

**props** \'präps\ *n sing or pl* 1 *slang* : DUE 1 〈gave him his ~〉 2 *slang* : RESPECT 2 〈earned the ~ of his peers〉 3 *slang* : ACKNOWLEDGMENT 〈deserves ~ for the effort〉

**pro·pul·sion** \prə-'pəl-shən\ *n* 1 : the action or process of propelling 2 : something that propels — **pro·pul·sive** \-siv\ *adj*

**pro ra·ta** \(,)prō-'rä-tə, -'rä-\ *adv* : in proportion to the share of each : PROPORTIONATELY

**pro·rate** \(,)prō-'rāt\ *vb* **pro·rat·ed; pro·rat·ing** : to divide, distribute, or assess proportionately

**pro·rogue** \prə-'rōg\ *vb* **pro·rogued; pro·rogu·ing** : to suspend or end a session of (a legislative body) — **pro·ro·ga·tion** \,prō-rō-'gā-shən\ *n*

**pros** *pl of* PRO

**pro·sa·ic** \prō-'zā-ik\ *adj* : lacking imagination or excitement : DULL

**pro·sce·ni·um** \prō-'sē-nē-əm\ *n* 1 : the part of a stage in front of the curtain 2 : the wall containing the arch that frames the stage

**pro·scribe** \prō-'skrīb\ *vb* **pro·scribed; pro·scrib·ing** 1 : OUTLAW 2 : to condemn or forbid as harmful — **pro·scrip·tion** \-'skrip-shən\ *n*

**prose** \'prōz\ *n* [ME, fr. AF, fr. L *prosa*, fr. fem. of *prorsus, prosus*, straightforward, being in prose, alter. of *proversus*, pp. of *provertere* to turn forward] : the ordinary language people use in speaking or writing

**pros·e·cute** \'prä-si-,kyüt\ *vb* **-cut·ed; -cut·ing** 1 : to follow to the end 〈~ an investigation〉 2 : to seek legal punishment of 〈~ a forger〉 — **pros·e·cu·tion** \,prä-si-'kyü-shən\ *n* — **pros·e·cu·tor** \'prä-si-,kyü-tər\ *n* — **pros·e·cu·to·ri·al** \,prä-si-kyü-'tȯr-ē-əl\ *adj*

¹**pros·e·lyte** \'prä-sə-,līt\ *n* : a new convert to a religion, belief, or party — **pros·e·ly·tism** \-,lī-,ti-zəm\ *n*

²**proselyte** *vb* **-lyt·ed; -lyt·ing** : PROSELYTIZE

**pros·e·ly·tise** *Brit var of* PROSELYTIZE

**pros·e·ly·tize** \'prä-sə-lə-,tīz\ *vb* **-tized; -tiz·ing** 1 : to induce someone to convert to one's faith 2 : to recruit someone to join one's party, institution, or cause

**pros·o·dy** \'prä-sə-dē, -zə-\ *n, pl* **-dies** : the study of versification and esp. of metrical structure — **pro·sod·ic** \prə-'sä-dik\ *adj*

¹**pros·pect** \'prä-,spekt\ *n* 1 : an extensive view; *also* : OUTLOOK 2 : the act of looking forward 3 : a mental vision of something to come 4 : something that is awaited or expected : POSSIBILITY 5 : a potential buyer or customer; *also* : a likely candidate (as for a job) — **pro·spec·**

**tive** \prə-'spek-tiv, 'prä-ˌspek-\ *adj* — **pro·spec·tive·ly** *adv*

²**pros·pect** \'prä-ˌspekt\ *vb* : to explore esp. for mineral deposits — **pros·pec·tor** \-ˌspek-tər, prä-'spek-\ *n*

**pro·spec·tus** \prə-'spek-təs\ *n* : a preliminary statement that describes an enterprise and is distributed to prospective buyers or participants

**pros·per** \'präs-pər\ *vb* **pros·pered; pros·per·ing** : SUCCEED; *esp* : to achieve economic success

**pros·per·i·ty** \präs-'per-ə-tē\ *n* : thriving condition : SUCCESS; *esp* : economic well=being

**pros·per·ous** \'präs-pə-rəs\ *adj* **1** : FAVORABLE ⟨~ winds⟩ **2** : marked by success or economic well-being ⟨a ~ business⟩

**pros·ta·glan·din** \ˌpräs-tə-'glan-dən\ *n* : any of various oxygenated unsaturated fatty acids of animals that perform a variety of hormonelike actions

**pros·tate** \'präs-ˌtāt\ *n* [NL *prostata*, fr. Gk *prostatēs*, fr. *proïstanai* to put in front] : PROSTATE GLAND — **pros·tat·ic** \prä-'sta-tik\ *adj*

**prostate gland** *n* : a glandular body about the base of the male urethra that produces a secretion which is a major part of the fluid ejaculated during an orgasm

**pros·ta·ti·tis** \ˌpräs-tə-'tī-təs\ *n* : inflammation of the prostate gland

**pros·the·sis** \präs-'thē-səs, 'präs-thə-\ *n, pl* **-the·ses** \-ˌsēz\ : an artificial replacement for a missing body part — **pros·thet·ic** \präs-'the-tik\ *adj*

**pros·thet·ics** \-'the-tiks\ *n pl* : the surgical or dental specialty concerned with the design, construction, and fitting of prostheses

¹**pros·ti·tute** \'präs-tə-ˌtüt, -ˌtyüt\ *vb* **-tut·ed; -tut·ing** **1** : to offer indiscriminately for sexual activity esp. for money **2** : to devote to corrupt or unworthy purposes — **pros·ti·tu·tion** \ˌpräs-tə-'tü-shən, -'tyü-\ *n*

²**prostitute** *n* : one who engages in sexual activities for money

¹**pros·trate** \'prä-ˌstrāt\ *adj* **1** : stretched out with face on the ground in adoration or submission **2** : lying flat **3** : completely overcome ⟨~ with a cold⟩

²**prostrate** *vb* **pros·trat·ed; pros·trat·ing** **1** : to throw or put into a prostrate position **2** : to reduce to a weak or powerless condition — **pros·tra·tion** \prä-'strā-shən\ *n*

**prosy** \'prō-zē\ *adj* **pros·i·er; -est** **1** : PROSAIC, ORDINARY **2** : TEDIOUS

**Prot** *abbr* Protestant

**prot·ac·tin·i·um** \ˌprō-ˌtak-'ti-nē-əm\ *n* : a metallic radioactive chemical element of relatively short life

**pro·tag·o·nist** \prō-'ta-gə-nist\ *n* **1** : the principal character in a drama or story **2** : a leader or supporter of a cause

**pro·te·an** \'prō-tē-ən\ *adj* : able to assume different shapes or roles

**pro·tect** \prə-'tekt\ *vb* : to shield from injury : GUARD

**pro·tec·tion** \prə-'tek-shən\ *n* **1** : the act of protecting : the state of being protected **2** : one that protects ⟨wear a helmet as a ~⟩ **3** : the supervision or support of one that is smaller and weaker **4** : the freeing of producers from foreign competition in their home market by high duties on foreign competitive goods — **pro·tec·tive** \-'tek-tiv\ *adj*

**pro·tec·tion·ist** \-shə-nist\ *n* : an advocate of government economic protection for domestic producers through restrictions on foreign competitors — **pro·tec·tion·ism** \-shə-ˌni-zəm\ *n*

**pro·tec·tor** \prə-'tek-tər\ *n* **1** : one that protects : GUARDIAN **2** : a device used to prevent injury : GUARD **3** : REGENT 1

**pro·tec·tor·ate** \-tə-rət\ *n* **1** : government by a protector **2** : the relationship of superior authority assumed by one state over a dependent one; *also* : the dependent political unit in such a relationship

**pro·té·gé** \'prō-tə-ˌzhā\ *n* [F] : one who is protected, trained, or guided by an influential person

**pro·tein** \'prō-ˌtēn\ *n* [F *protéine*, fr. LGk *prōteios* primary, fr. Gk *prōtos* first] : any of various complex nitrogen-containing substances that consist of chains of amino acids, are present in all living cells, and are an essential part of the human diet

**pro tem** \prō-'tem\ *adv* : PRO TEMPORE

**pro tem·po·re** \prō-'tem-pə-rē\ *adv* [L] : for the time being

**Pro·te·ro·zo·ic** \ˌprä-tə-rə-'zō-ik, ˌprō-\ *adj* : of, relating to, or being the eon of geologic history between the Archean and the Phanerozoic — **Proterozoic** *n*

¹**pro·test** \'prō-ˌtest\ *n* **1** : the act of protesting; *esp* : an organized public demonstration of disapproval **2** : a complaint or objection against an idea, an act, or a course of action

²**pro·test** \prō-'test\ *vb* **1** : to assert positively : make solemn declaration of ⟨~s his innocence⟩ **2** : to object strongly : make a protest against ⟨~ a ruling⟩ — **pro·tes·ta·tion** \ˌprä-təs-'tā-shən\ *n* — **pro·test·er** *or* **pro·tes·tor** \-tər\ *n*

**Prot·es·tant** \'prä-təs-tənt, *3 also* prə-'tes-\ *n* **1** : a member or adherent of one of the Christian churches deriving from the Reformation **2** : a Christian not of a Catholic or Orthodox church **3** *not cap* : one who makes a protest — **Prot·es·tant·ism** \'prä-təs-tən-ˌti-zəm\ *n*

**pro·tha·la·mi·on** \ˌprō-thə-'lā-mē-ən\ *or* **pro·tha·la·mi·um** \-mē-əm\ *n, pl* **-mia** \-mē-ə\ : a song in celebration of a marriage

**pro·to·col** \'prō-tə-ˌkȯl\ *n* [MF *protocole*, fr. ML *protocollum*, fr. LGk *prōtokollon* first sheet of a papyrus roll bearing data of manufacture, fr. Gk *prōtos* first + *kollan* to glue together, fr. *kolla* glue] **1** : an original draft or record **2** : a preliminary memorandum of diplomatic negotiation **3** : a code of diplomatic or military etiquette **4** : a set of conventions for formatting data in an electronic communications system

**pro·ton** \'prō-ˌtän\ *n* [Gk *prōton*, neut. of *protos* first] : a positively charged atomic particle present in all atomic nuclei — **pro·ton·ic** \-'tä-nik\ *adj*

**pro·to·plasm** \'prō-tə-ˌpla-zəm\ *n* : the complex colloidal largely protein substance of living plant and animal cells — **pro·to·plas·mic** \ˌprō-tə-'plaz-mik\ *adj*

**pro·to·type** \'prō-tə-ˌtīp\ *n* : an original model : ARCHETYPE

**pro·to·zo·an** \ˌprō-tə-'zō-ən\ *n* : any of a phylum or subkingdom of unicellular lower invertebrate animals that include some pathogenic parasites of humans and domestic animals — **protozoan** *adj*

**pro·tract** \prō-'trakt\ *vb* : to prolong in time or space ♦ *Synonyms* EXTEND, LENGTHEN, ELONGATE, STRETCH

**pro·trac·tor** \-'trak-tər\ *n* : an instrument for drawing and measuring angles

**pro·trude** \prō-'trüd\ *vb* **pro·trud·ed; pro·trud·ing** : to stick out or cause to stick out : jut out — **pro·tru·sion** \-'trü-zhən\ *n*

**pro·tu·ber·ance** \prō-'tü-bə-rəns, -'tyü-\ *n* : something that protrudes

**pro·tu·ber·ant** \-rənt\ *adj* : extending beyond the surrounding surface in a bulge

**proud** \'praud\ *adj* 1 : having or showing excessive self-esteem : HAUGHTY 2 : highly pleased : EXULTANT 3 : having proper self-respect *⟨too ~ to beg⟩* 4 : GLORIOUS *⟨a ~ occasion⟩* 5 : SPIRITED *⟨a ~ steed⟩* ♦ *Synonyms* ARROGANT, INSOLENT, OVERBEARING, DISDAINFUL — **proud·ly** *adv*

**prov** *abbr* 1 province; provincial 2 provisional

**Prov** *abbr* Proverbs

**prove** \'prüv\ *vb* **proved; proved** or **prov·en** \'prü-vən\; **prov·ing** 1 : to test by experiment or by a standard 2 : to establish the truth of by argument or evidence 3 : to show to be correct, valid, or genuine 4 : to turn out esp. after trial or test *⟨the car proved to be a good choice⟩* — **prov·able** \'prü-və-bəl\ *adj*

**prov·e·nance** \'prä-və-nəns\ *n* : ORIGIN, SOURCE

**Pro·ven·çal** \ˌprō-vän-'säl, ˌprä-vən-\ *n* 1 : a native or inhabitant of Provence 2 : OCCITAN — **Provençal** *adj*

**prov·en·der** \'prä-vən-dər\ *n* 1 : dry food for domestic animals : FEED 2 : FOOD, VICTUALS

**pro·ve·nience** \prə-'vē-nyəns\ *n* : ORIGIN, SOURCE

**prov·erb** \'prä-ˌvərb\ *n* : a pithy popular saying : ADAGE

**pro·ver·bi·al** \prə-'vər-bē-əl\ *adj* 1 : of, relating to, or resembling a proverb 2 : commonly spoken of

**Proverbs** *n* — see BIBLE table

**pro·vide** \prə-'vīd\ *vb* **pro·vid·ed; pro·vid·ing** [ME, fr. L *providēre*, lit., to see ahead, fr. *pro-* forward + *vidēre* to see] 1 : to take measures beforehand *⟨~ against inflation⟩* 2 : to make a proviso or stipulation 3 : to supply what is need-

ed *⟨~ for a family⟩* 4 : EQUIP 5 : to supply for use : YIELD — **pro·vid·er** *n*

**pro·vid·ed** *conj* : on condition that : IF

**prov·i·dence** \'prä-və-dəns\ *n* 1 *often cap* : divine guidance or care 2 *cap* : GOD 1 3 : the quality or state of being provident

**prov·i·dent** \-dənt\ *adj* : making provision for the future : PRUDENT 2 : FRUGAL — **prov·i·dent·ly** *adv*

**prov·i·den·tial** \ˌprä-və-'den-chəl\ *adj* 1 : of, relating to, or determined by Providence 2 : OPPORTUNE, LUCKY

**providing** *conj* : PROVIDED

**prov·ince** \'prä-vəns\ *n* 1 : an administrative district or division of a country 2 *pl* : all of a country except the metropolises 3 : proper business or scope : SPHERE *⟨the ~ of the jury⟩*

**pro·vin·cial** \prə-'vin-chəl\ *adj* 1 : of or relating to a province 2 : limited in outlook : NARROW *⟨~ ideas⟩* — **pro·vin·cial·ism** \-chə-ˌli-zəm\ *n*

**proving ground** *n* : a place for scientific experimentation or testing

¹**pro·vi·sion** \prə-'vi-zhən\ *n* 1 : the act or process of providing; *also* : a measure taken beforehand 2 : a stock of needed supplies; *esp* : a stock of food — usu. used in pl. 3 : PROVISO

²**provision** *vb* : to supply with provisions

**pro·vi·sion·al** \-'vi-zhə-nəl\ *adj* : provided for a temporary need : CONDITIONAL — **pro·vi·sion·al·ly** *adv*

**pro·vi·so** \prə-'vī-zō\ *n*, *pl* **-sos** *also* **-soes** [ME, fr. ML *proviso quod* provided that] : an article or clause that introduces a condition : STIPULATION

**pro·vo·ca·teur** \prō-ˌvä-kə-'tər\ *n* : one who provokes

**prov·o·ca·tion** \ˌprä-və-'kā-shən\ *n* 1 : the act of provoking 2 : something that provokes

**pro·voc·a·tive** \prə-'vä-kə-tiv\ *adj* : serving to provoke or excite

**pro·voke** \prə-'vōk\ *vb* **pro·voked; pro·vok·ing** 1 : to incite to anger : INCENSE 2 : to call forth : EVOKE *⟨a remark that provoked laughter⟩* 3 : to stir up on purpose *⟨~ an argument⟩* ♦ *Synonyms* IRRITATE, EXASPERATE, AGGRAVATE, INFLAME, RILE, PIQUE — **pro·vok·er** *n*

**pro·vo·lo·ne** \ˌprō-və-'lō-nē\ *n* : a usu. firm pliant often smoked Italian cheese

**pro·vost** \'prō-ˌvōst, 'prä-vəst\ *n* : a high official : DIGNITARY; *esp* : a high-ranking university administrative officer

**pro·vost mar·shal** \ˌprō-ˌvō-'mär-shəl\ *n* : an officer who supervises the military police of a command

**prow** \'prau\ *n* : the bow of a ship

**prow·ess** \'prau-əs\ *n* 1 : military valor and skill 2 : extraordinary ability

**prowl** \'praul\ *vb* : to roam about stealthily — **prowl** *n* — **prowl·er** *n*

**prox·i·mal** \'präk-sə-məl\ *adj* 1 : next to or nearest the point of attachment or origin; *esp* : located toward the center of the body 2 : of, relating to, or being the mesial and distal surfaces of a tooth — **prox·i·mal·ly** *adv*

**prox·i·mate** \'präk-sə-mət\ *adj* 1 : DIRECT *⟨the ~ cause⟩* 2 : very near

**prox·im·i·ty** \präk-'si-mə-tē\ *n* : NEAR-NESS ⟨lives in ~ to a bus stop⟩

**prox·i·mo** \'präk-sə-,mō\ *adj* [L *proximo mense* in the next month] : of or occurring in the next month after the present

**proxy** \'präk-sē\ *n, pl* **prox·ies** [ME *proxi, procurie,* alter. of *procuracie,* fr. AF, fr. ML *procuratia,* alter. of L *procuratio* appointment of another as an agent, fr. *procurare* to take care of] : the authority or power to act for another; *also* : a document giving such authorization — **proxy** *adj*

**prude** \'prüd\ *n* : a person who shows or affects extreme modesty — **prud·ery** \'prü-də-rē\ *n* — **prud·ish** *adj* — **prud·ish·ly** *adv*

**pru·dent** \'prü-dᵊnt\ *adj* **1** : shrewd in the management of practical affairs **2** : CAUTIOUS, DISCREET **3** : PROVIDENT, FRUGAL ♦ **Synonyms** JUDICIOUS, FORESIGHTED, SENSIBLE, SANE — **pru·dence** \-dᵊns\ *n* — **pru·den·tial** \prü-'den-chəl\ *adj* — **pru·dent·ly** *adv*

**¹prune** \'prün\ *n* : a dried plum

**²prune** *vb* **pruned; prun·ing** : to cut off unwanted parts (as of a tree)

**pru·ri·ent** \'prur-ē-ənt\ *adj* : LASCIVIOUS; *also* : exciting to lasciviousness — **pru·ri·ence** \-ē-əns\ *n*

**¹pry** \'prī\ *vb* **pried; pry·ing** : to look closely or inquisitively; *esp* : SNOOP

**²pry** *vb* **pried; pry·ing 1** : to raise, move, or pull apart with a pry or lever **2** : to detach or open with difficulty

**³pry** *n* : a tool for prying

**Ps** *or* **Psa** *abbr* Psalms

**PS** *abbr* **1** [L *postscriptum*] postscript **2** public school

**PSA** *abbr* public service announcement

**psalm** \'säm, 'sälm\ *n, often cap* [ME, fr. OE *psealm,* fr. LL *psalmus,* fr. Gk *psalmos,* lit., twanging of a harp, fr. *psallein* to pluck, play a stringed instrument] : a sacred song or poem; *esp* : one of the hymns collected in the Book of Psalms — **psalm·ist** *n*

**psalm·o·dy** \'sä-mə-dē, 'säl-\ *n* : the singing of psalms in worship

**Psalms** *n* — see BIBLE table

**Psal·ter** \'sȯl-tər\ *n* : the Book of Psalms; *also* : a collection of the Psalms arranged for devotional use

**pseud** *abbr* pseudonym; pseudonymous

**pseu·do** \'sü-dō\ *adj* : SPURIOUS, SHAM

**pseu·do·nym** \'sü-də-,nim\ *n* : a fictitious name — **pseu·don·y·mous** \sü-'dä-nə-məs\ *adj*

**pseu·do·sci·ence** \,sü-dō-'sī-əns\ *n* : a system of theories, assumptions, and methods erroneously regarded as scientific — **pseu·do·sci·en·tif·ic** \-,sī-ən-'ti-fik\ *adj*

**PSG** *abbr* platoon sergeant

**¹psi** \'sī, 'psī\ *n* : the 23d letter of the Greek alphabet — Ψ *or* ψ

**²psi** *abbr* pounds per square inch

**psit·ta·co·sis** \,si-tə-'kō-səs\ *n* : an infectious disease of birds marked by diarrhea and wasting and transmissible to humans

**pso·ri·a·sis** \sə-'rī-ə-səs\ *n* : a chronic skin disease characterized by red patches covered with white scales

**PST** *abbr* Pacific standard time

**¹psych** *or* **psyche** \'sīk\ *vb* **psyched; psych·ing 1** : OUTWIT, OUTGUESS; *also* : to analyze beforehand **2** : INTIMIDATE; *also* : to prepare oneself psychologically ⟨get *psyched* up for the game⟩

**²psych** *abbr* psychology

**psy·che** \'sī-kē\ *n* : SOUL, PERSONALITY; *also* : MIND

**psy·che·del·ic** \,sī-kə-'de-lik\ *adj* **1** : of, relating to, or causing abnormal psychic effects ⟨~ drugs⟩ **2** : relating to the taking of psychedelic drugs ⟨~ experience⟩ **3** : imitating, suggestive of, or reproducing the effects of psychedelic drugs ⟨~ art⟩ ⟨~ colors⟩ — **psychedelic** *n* — **psy·che·del·i·cal·ly** \-li-k(ə-)lē\ *adv*

**psy·chi·a·try** \sə-'kī-ə-trē, sī-\ *n* [prob. fr. F *psychiatrie,* fr. *psychiatre* psychiatrist, fr. Gk *psychē* breath, soul + *iatros* physician] : a branch of medicine dealing with mental, emotional, and behavioral disorders — **psy·chi·at·ric** \,sī-kē-'a-trik\ *adj* — **psy·chi·a·trist** \sə-'kī-ə-trist, sī-\ *n*

**¹psy·chic** \'sī-kik\ *also* **psy·chi·cal** \-ki-kəl\ *adj* **1** : of or relating to the psyche **2** : lying outside the sphere of physical science **3** : sensitive to nonphysical or supernatural forces — **psy·chi·cal·ly** \-k(ə-)lē\ *adv*

**²psychic** *n* : a person apparently sensitive to nonphysical forces; *also* : MEDIUM **6**

**psy·cho** \'sī-kō\ *n, pl* **psychos** : a mentally disturbed person — **psycho** *adj*

**psy·cho·ac·tive** \,sī-kō-'ak-tiv\ *adj* : affecting the mind or behavior

**psy·cho·anal·y·sis** \,sī-kō-ə-'na-lə-səs\ *n* : a method of dealing with psychic disorders by having the patient talk freely about personal experiences and esp. about early childhood and dreams — **psy·cho·an·a·lyst** \-'a-nə-list\ *n* — **psy·cho·an·a·lyt·ic** \-,a-nə-'li-tik\ *adj* — **psy·cho·an·a·lyze** \-'a-nə-,līz\ *vb*

**psy·cho·bab·ble** \'sī-kō-,ba-bəl\ *n* : psychological jargon esp. when used in a trite or simplistic manner

**psy·cho·dra·ma** \,sī-kə-'drä-mə, -'dra-\ *n* **1** : an extemporized dramatization designed to afford catharsis for one or more of the participants from whose life the plot is taken **2** : a dramatic event or story with psychological overtones

**psy·cho·gen·ic** \-'je-nik\ *adj* : originating in the mind or in mental or emotional conflict

**psy·cho·graph·ics** \,sī-kə-'gra-fiks\ *n sing or pl* : market research or statistics classifying population groups according to psychological variables

**psychol** *abbr* psychologist; psychology

**psy·chol·o·gy** \sī-'kä-lə-jē\ *n, pl* **-gies 1** : the science of mind and behavior **2** : the mental and behavioral characteristics of an individual or group — **psy·cho·log·i·cal** \,sī-kə-'lä-ji-kəl\ *adj* — **psy·cho·log·i·cal·ly** \-ji-k(ə-)lē\ *adv* — **psy·chol·o·gist** \sī-'kä-lə-jist\ *n*

**psy·cho·path** \'sī-kō-,path\ *n* : a mentally ill or unstable person; *esp* : a person who engages in antisocial behavior and exhibits a pervasive disregard for the rights, feelings, and safety of others — **psy·cho·path·ic** \ˌsī-kə-ˈpa-thik\ *adj*

**psy·cho·sex·u·al** \ˌsī-kō-ˈsek-shə-wəl\ *adj* **1** : of or relating to the mental, emotional, and behavioral aspects of sexual development **2** : of or relating to the physiological psychology of sex

**psy·cho·sis** \sī-ˈkō-səs\ *n, pl* **-cho·ses** \-ˌsēz\ : a serious mental illness (as schizophrenia) marked by loss of or greatly lessened ability to test whether what one is thinking and feeling about the real world is really true

**psy·cho·so·cial** \ˌsī-kō-ˈso-shəl\ *adj* : involving both psychological and social aspects **2** : relating social conditions to mental health

**psy·cho·so·mat·ic** \ˌsī-kō-sə-ˈma-tik\ *adj* : of, relating to, involving, or concerned with bodily symptoms caused by mental or emotional disturbance

**psy·cho·ther·a·py** \ˌsī-kō-ˈther-ə-pē\ *n* : treatment of mental or emotional disorder or of related bodily ills by psychological means — **psy·cho·ther·a·pist** \-pist\ *n*

**psy·chot·ic** \sī-ˈkä-tik\ *adj* : of or relating to psychosis ⟨∼ behavior⟩ ⟨a ∼ patient⟩ — **psychotic** *n*

**psy·cho·tro·pic** \ˌsī-kə-ˈtrō-pik\ *adj* : acting on the mind ⟨∼ drugs⟩

**pt** *abbr* **1** part **2** payment **3** pint **4** point **5** port

**Pt** *symbol* platinum

**PT** *abbr* **1** Pacific time **2** part-time **3** physical therapy **4** physical training

**PTA** *abbr* Parent-Teacher Association

**ptar·mi·gan** \ˈtär-mi-gən\ *n, pl* **-gan** *or* **-gans** : any of various grouses of northern regions with completely feathered feet

**PT boat** \ˌ(ˌ)pē-ˈtē-\ *n* [*patrol torpedo*] : a small fast patrol craft usu. armed with torpedos

**pte** *abbr, Brit* private

**ptg** *abbr* printing

**PTO** *abbr* **1** Parent-Teacher Organization **2** please turn over

**pto·maine** \ˈtō-ˌmān\ *n* : any of various chemical substances formed by bacteria in decaying matter (as meat) and including a few poisonous ones

**Pu** *symbol* plutonium

¹**pub** \ˈpəb\ *n* **1** *chiefly Brit* : PUBLIC HOUSE **2** : TAVERN

²**pub** *abbr* **1** public **2** publication **3** published; publisher; publishing

**pu·ber·ty** \ˈpyü-bər-tē\ *n* : the condition of being or period of becoming first capable of reproducing sexually — **pu·ber·tal** \-bər-tᵊl\ *adj*

**pu·bes** \ˈpyü-bēz\ *n, pl* **pubes** [NL, fr. L, manhood, body hair, pubic region] **1** : the hair that appears upon the lower middle region of the abdomen at puberty **2** : the pubic region

**pu·bes·cence** \pyü-ˈbe-sᵊns\ *n* **1** : the quality or state of being pubescent **2** : a pubescent covering or surface

**pu·bes·cent** \-sᵊnt\ *adj* **1** : arriving at or having reached puberty **2** : covered with fine soft short hairs

**pu·bic** \ˈpyü-bik\ *adj* : of, relating to, or situated near the pubes or the pubis

**pu·bis** \ˈpyü-bəs\ *n, pl* **pu·bes** \-bēz\ : the ventral and anterior of the three principal bones composing either half of the pelvis

**publ** *abbr* **1** publication **2** published; publisher

¹**pub·lic** \ˈpə-blik\ *adj* **1** : exposed to general view ⟨the story became ∼⟩ **2** : of, relating to, or affecting the people as a whole ⟨∼ opinion⟩ **3** : CIVIC, GOVERNMENTAL ⟨∼ expenditures⟩ **4** : of, relating to, or serving the community ⟨∼ officials⟩ **5** : not private : SOCIAL ⟨∼ morality⟩ **6** : open to all ⟨∼ library⟩ **7** : well known : PROMINENT ⟨∼ figures⟩ **8** : supported by public funds and private contributions rather than by income from commercials — **pub·lic·ly** *adv*

²**public** *n* **1** : the people as a whole : POPULACE **2** : a group of people having common interests ⟨the movie-going ∼⟩

**pub·li·can** \ˈpə-bli-kən\ *n* **1** : a Jewish tax collector for the ancient Romans **2** *chiefly Brit* : the licensee of a pub

**pub·li·ca·tion** \ˌpə-blə-ˈkā-shən\ *n* **1** : the act or process of publishing **2** : a published work

**public house** *n* **1** : INN **2** *chiefly Brit* : a licensed saloon or bar

**pub·li·cise** *Brit var of* PUBLICIZE

**pub·li·cist** \ˈpə-blə-sist\ *n* : one that publicizes; *esp* : PRESS AGENT

**pub·lic·i·ty** \(ˌ)pə-ˈbli-sə-tē\ *n* **1** : information with news value issued to gain public attention or support **2** : public attention or acclaim

**pub·li·cize** \ˈpə-blə-ˌsīz\ *vb* **-cized; -ciz·ing** : to bring to public attention : ADVERTISE ⟨*publicizing* his book⟩

**pub·lic–key** \ˈpə-blik-ˈkē\ *n* : the publicly shared element of a code usable only to encode messages

**public relations** *n sing or pl* : the business of fostering public goodwill toward a person, firm, or institution; *also* : the degree of goodwill and understanding achieved

**public school** *n* **1** : an endowed secondary boarding school in Great Britain offering a classical curriculum and preparation for the universities or public service **2** : a free tax-supported school controlled by a local governmental authority

**pub·lic–spir·it·ed** *adj* : motivated by devotion to the general or national welfare

**public works** *n pl* : works (as schools or highways) constructed with public funds for public use

**pub·lish** \ˈpə-blish\ *vb* **1** : to make generally known : announce publicly **2** : to produce or release literature, information, musical scores or sometimes recordings, or art for sale to the public — **pub·lish·er** *n*

¹**puck** \ˈpək\ *n* : a mischievous sprite — **puck·ish** *adj* — **puck·ish·ly** *adv*

²**puck** *n* : a disk used in ice hockey

¹**puck·er** \ˈpə-kər\ *vb* : to contract into folds or wrinkles

²**pucker** *n* : FOLD, WRINKLE

**pud·ding** \ˈpu̇-diŋ\ *n* : a soft, spongy, or thick creamy dessert

**pud·dle** \ˈpə-d³l\ *n* : a very small pool of usu. dirty or muddy water

**pu·den·dum** \pyu̇-ˈden-dəm\ *n, pl* -**da** \-də\ [NL, fr. L *pudēre* to be ashamed] : the human external genital organs esp. of a woman

**pudgy** \ˈpə-jē\ *adj* **pudg·i·er; -est** : being short and plump : CHUBBY

**pueb·lo** \ˈpwe-blō, pü-ˈe-\ *n, pl* -**los** [Sp, village, lit., people, fr. L *populus*] **1** : an American Indian village of Arizona or New Mexico that consists of flat-roofed stone or adobe houses joined in groups sometimes several stories high **2** *cap* : a member of a group of American Indian peoples of the southwestern U.S.

**pu·er·ile** \ˈpyu̇-ə-rəl\ *adj* : CHILDISH, SILLY ⟨~ remarks⟩ — **pu·er·il·i·ty** \ˌpyu̇-ə-ˈri-lə-tē\ *n*

**pu·er·per·al** \pyu̇-ˈər-pə-rəl\ *adj* : of, relating to, or occurring during childbirth or the period immediately following ⟨~ infection⟩ ⟨~ depression⟩

**puerperal fever** *n* : an abnormal condition that results from infection of the placental site following childbirth or abortion

¹**puff** \ˈpəf\ *vb* **1** : to blow in short gusts **2** : PANT **3** : to emit small whiffs or clouds **4** : BLUSTER, BRAG **5** : INFLATE, SWELL **6** : to make proud or conceited **7** : to praise extravagantly

²**puff** *n* **1** : a short discharge (as of air or smoke); *also* : a slight explosive sound accompanying it **2** : a light fluffy pastry **3** : a slight swelling **4** : a fluffy mass; *also* : a small pad for applying cosmetic powder **5** : a laudatory notice or review — **puffy** *adj*

³**puff** *adj* : of, relating to, or designed for promotion or flattery ⟨~ articles on the new TV series⟩

**puff·ball** \ˈpəf-ˌbȯl\ *n* : any of various globe-shaped and often edible fungi

**puf·fin** \ˈpə-fən\ *n* : any of several seabirds having a short neck and a deep grooved parti-colored bill

¹**pug** \ˈpəg\ *n* **1** : any of a breed of small stocky short-haired dogs with a wrinkled face **2** : a close coil of hair

²**pug** *n* : ¹BOXER

**pu·gi·lism** \ˈpyü-jə-ˌli-zəm\ *n* : BOXING — **pu·gi·list** \-list\ *n* — **pu·gi·lis·tic** \ˌpyü-jə-ˈlis-tik\ *adj*

**pug·na·cious** \ˌpəg-ˈnā-shəs\ *adj* : having a quarrelsome or combative nature

♦ **Synonyms** BELLIGERENT, BELLICOSE, CONTENTIOUS, TRUCULENT — **pug·nac·i·ty** \-ˈna-sə-tē\ *n*

**puis·sance** \ˈpwi-səns, ˈpyü-ə-\ *n* : POWER, STRENGTH ⟨the ~ of the king⟩ — **puis·sant** \-sənt\ *adj*

**puke** \ˈpyük\ *vb* **puked; puk·ing** : VOMIT — **puke** *n*

**puk·ka** \ˈpə-kə\ *adj* [Hindi *pakkā* cooked, ripe, solid, fr. Skt *pakva*] : GENUINE, AUTHENTIC; *also* : FIRST-CLASS, COMPLETE

**pul** \ˈpül\ *n, pl* **puls** \ˈpülz\ *or* **pul** — see *afghani* at MONEY table

**pu·la** \ˈpü-lə, ˈpyü-\ *n, pl* **pula** — see MONEY table

**pul·chri·tude** \ˈpəl-krə-ˌtüd, -ˌtyüd\ *n* : BEAUTY — **pul·chri·tu·di·nous** \ˌpəl-krə-ˈtü-d³n-əs, -ˈtyü-\ *adj*

**pule** \ˈpyül\ *vb* **puled; pul·ing** : WHINE, WHIMPER

¹**pull** \ˈpu̇l\ *vb* **1** : to exert force so as to draw (something) toward the force; *also* : MOVE ⟨~ out of a driveway⟩ **2** : PLUCK; *also* : EXTRACT ⟨~ a tooth⟩ **3** : STRETCH, STRAIN ⟨~ a tendon⟩ **4** : to draw apart : TEAR **5** : to make (as a proof) by printing **6** : REMOVE ⟨~ed the pitcher in the third inning⟩ **7** : DRAW ⟨~ a gun⟩ **8** : to carry out esp. with daring ⟨~ a robbery⟩ **9** : PERPETRATE, COMMIT **10** : ATTRACT **11** : to express strong sympathy — **pull·er** *n*

²**pull** *n* **1** : the act or an instance of pulling **2** : the effort expended in moving **3** : ADVANTAGE ⟨had the ~ of a respected family name⟩; *esp* : special influence **4** : a device for pulling something or for operating by pulling **5** : a force that attracts or compels **6** : an injury from abnormal straining or stretching ⟨a muscle ~⟩

**pull·back** \ˈpu̇l-ˌbak\ *n* : an orderly withdrawal of troops

**pull–down** *adj* : appearing below a selected item (as a menu title) on a computer display ⟨a ~ menu⟩

**pul·let** \ˈpu̇-lət\ *n* : a young hen esp. of the domestic chicken when less than a year old

**pul·ley** \ˈpu̇-lē\ *n, pl* **pulleys** : a wheel used to transmit power by means of a belt, rope, or chain; *esp* : one with a grooved rim that forms part of a tackle for hoisting or for changing the direction of a force

**Pull·man** \ˈpu̇l-mən\ *n* : a railroad passenger car with comfortable furnishings esp. for night travel

**pull off** *vb* : to accomplish successfully

**pull·out** \ˈpu̇l-ˌau̇t\ *n* : PULLBACK

**pull·over** \ˈpu̇l-ˌō-vər\ *adj* : put on by being pulled over the head ⟨~ sweater⟩ — **pull·over** *n*

**pull–up** \ˈpu̇l-ˌəp\ *n* : CHIN-UP

**pull up** *vb* : to bring or come to an often abrupt halt : STOP

**pul·mo·nary** \ˈpu̇l-mə-ˌner-ē, ˈpəl-\ *adj* : of, relating to, or carried on by the lungs ⟨the ~ circulation⟩

**pulp** \ˈpəlp\ *n* **1** : the soft juicy or fleshy part of a fruit or vegetable **2** : a soft moist mass **3** : the soft sensitive tissue that fills the central cavity of a tooth **4** : a material (as from wood) used in making paper **5** : a magazine using cheap paper and often dealing with sensational material — **pulpy** *adj*

**pul·pit** \ˈpu̇l-ˌpit\ *n* : a raised platform or high reading desk used in preaching or conducting a worship service

**pulp·wood** \ˈpəlp-ˌwu̇d\ *n* : wood used in making pulp for paper

**pul·sar** \ˈpəl-ˌsär\ *n* : a celestial source of pulsating electromagnetic radiation (as radio waves)

**pul·sate** \ˈpəl-ˌsāt\ *vb* **pul·sat·ed; pul·**

**sat·ing** : to expand and contract rhythmically : BEAT ⟨an artery ∼s⟩ — **pul·sa·tion** \ˌpəl-'sā-shən\ n

**pulse** \'pəls\ n 1 : the regular throbbing in the arteries caused by the contractions of the heart 2 : rhythmical beating, vibrating, or sounding 3 : a brief change in electrical current or voltage — **pulse** vb

**pul·ver·ise** Brit var of PULVERIZE

**pul·ver·ize** \'pəl-və-ˌrīz\ vb **-ized; -iz·ing** 1 : to reduce (as by crushing or grinding) or be reduced to very small particles 2 : DEMOLISH

**pu·ma** \'pü-mə, 'pyü-\ n, pl **pumas** also **puma** [Sp, fr. Quechua] : COUGAR

**pum·ice** \'pə-məs\ n : a light porous volcanic glass used esp. for smoothing and polishing

**pum·mel** \'pə-məl\ vb **-meled** also **-melled; -mel·ing** also **-mel·ling** : POUND, BEAT ⟨∼ed the intruder⟩

¹**pump** \'pəmp\ n : a device for raising, transferring, or compressing fluids esp. by suction or pressure

²**pump** vb 1 : to raise (as water) with a pump 2 : to draw fluid from with a pump; also : to fill by means of a pump ⟨∼ up a tire⟩ 3 : to force or propel in the manner of a pump — **pump·er** n

³**pump** n : a low shoe that grips the foot chiefly at the toe and heel

**pumped** \'pəmpt\ adj : filled with energetic excitement and enthusiasm

**pum·per·nick·el** \'pəm-pər-ˌni-kəl\ n : a dark rye bread

**pump·kin** \'pəmp-kən, 'pəŋ-kən\ n : the large usu. orange fruit of a vine of the gourd family that is widely used as food; also : this vine

**pun** \'pən\ n : the humorous use of a word in a way that suggests two or more interpretations — **pun** vb

¹**punch** \'pənch\ n : a tool for piercing, stamping, cutting, or forming

²**punch** vb 1 : PROD, POKE; also : DRIVE, HERD ⟨∼ing cattle⟩ 2 : to strike with the fist 3 : to emboss, perforate, or make with a punch 4 : to operate, produce, or enter (as data) by or as if by punching — **punch·er** n

³**punch** n 1 : a quick blow with or as if with the fist 2 : effective energy or forcefulness

⁴**punch** n [perh. fr. Hindi pāc five, fr. Skt pañca; fr. the number of ingredients] : a drink usu. composed of wine or alcoholic liquor and nonalcoholic beverages; also : a drink composed of nonalcoholic beverages

**punch card** n : a card with holes punched in particular positions to represent data

**punch–drunk** \'pənch-ˌdrəŋk\ adj 1 : suffering from brain injury resulting from repeated head blows received in boxing 2 : DAZED, CONFUSED

**pun·cheon** \'pən-chən\ n : a large cask

**punch line** n : the sentence or phrase in a joke that makes the point

**punch list** n : a list of tasks to be completed at the end of a project

**punchy** \'pən-chē\ adj **punch·i·er; -est** 1 : having punch : FORCEFUL 2 : DAZED,

CONFUSED ⟨a ∼ boxer⟩ 3 : VIVID, VIBRANT ⟨∼ graphics⟩

**punc·til·io** \ˌpəŋk-'ti-lē-ˌō\ n, pl **-i·os** 1 : a nice detail of conduct in a ceremony or in observance of a code 2 : careful observance of forms (as in social conduct)

**punc·til·i·ous** \ˌpəŋk-'ti-lē-əs\ adj : marked by precise accordance with codes or conventions ♦ **Synonyms** METICULOUS, SCRUPULOUS, CAREFUL, PUNCTUAL

**punc·tu·al** \'pəŋk-chə-wəl\ adj : being on time : PROMPT — **punc·tu·al·i·ty** \ˌpəŋk-chə-'wa-lə-tē\ n — **punc·tu·al·ly** adv

**punc·tu·ate** \'pəŋk-chə-ˌwāt\ vb **-at·ed; -at·ing** 1 : to mark or divide (written matter) with punctuation marks 2 : to break into at intervals 3 : EMPHASIZE

**punc·tu·a·tion** \ˌpəŋk-chə-'wā-shən\ n : the act, practice, or system of inserting standardized marks in written matter to clarify the meaning and separate structural units

¹**punc·ture** \'pəŋk-chər\ n 1 : an act of puncturing 2 : a small hole or wound made by puncturing

²**puncture** vb **punc·tured; punc·tur·ing** 1 : to make a hole in : PIERCE 2 : to make useless as if by a puncture

**pun·dit** \'pən-dət\ n [Hindi paṇḍit, fr. Skt paṇḍita, fr. paṇḍita learned] 1 : a learned person : TEACHER 2 : AUTHORITY, CRITIC

**pun·dit·oc·ra·cy** \ˌpən-dət-'ä-krə-sē\ n, pl **-cies** : a group of powerful and influential political commentators

**pun·gent** \'pən-jənt\ adj 1 : having a sharp incisive quality : CAUSTIC ⟨a ∼ editorial⟩ 2 : causing a sharp, intense, or irritating sensation (as of taste or smell); esp : ACRID ⟨a ∼ odor⟩ — **pun·gen·cy** \-jən-sē\ n — **pun·gent·ly** adv

**pun·ish** \'pə-nish\ vb 1 : to impose a penalty on for a fault or crime ⟨∼ an offender⟩ 2 : to inflict a penalty for ⟨∼ treason with death⟩ 3 : to inflict injury on : HURT ♦ **Synonyms** CHASTISE, CASTIGATE, CHASTEN, DISCIPLINE, CORRECT — **pun·ish·able** adj

**pun·ish·ment** n 1 : retributive suffering, pain, or loss : PENALTY 2 : rough treatment

**pu·ni·tive** \'pyü-nə-tiv\ adj : inflicting, involving, or aiming at punishment

¹**punk** \'pəŋk\ n 1 : a young inexperienced person 2 : a petty hoodlum

²**punk** adj : very poor : INFERIOR

³**punk** n : dry crumbly wood useful for tinder; also : a substance made from fungi for use as tinder

**pun·ster** \'pən-stər\ n : one who is given to punning

¹**punt** \'pənt\ n : a long narrow flat-bottomed boat with square ends

²**punt** vb : to propel (as a punt) with a pole

³**punt** vb : to kick a football or soccer ball dropped from the hands before it touches the ground

⁴**punt** n : the act or an instance of punting a ball

**pu·ny** \'pyü-nē\ adj **pu·ni·er; -est** [AF

*puisné* younger, weakly, lit., born afterward, fr. *puis* afterward (fr. L *post*) + *né* born, fr. L *natus*] : slight in power, size, or importance : WEAK ⟨a ~ body⟩ ⟨~ sales⟩

**pup** \ˈpəp\ *n* : a young dog; *also* : one of the young of some other animals

**pu·pa** \ˈpyü-pə\ *n, pl* **pu·pae** \-(ˌ)pē\ *or* **pupas** [NL, fr. L *pupa* doll] : a form of some insects (as a bee, moth, or beetle) between the larva and the adult that usu. has a protective covering (as a cocoon) — **pu·pal** \-pəl\ *adj*

¹**pu·pil** \ˈpyü-pəl\ *n* 1 : a child or young person in school or in the charge of a tutor 2 : DISCIPLE

²**pupil** *n* : the dark central opening of the iris of the eye

**pup·pet** \ˈpə-pət\ *n* [ME *popet* youth, doll, fr. MF *poupette*, ultim. fr. L *pupa* doll] 1 : a small figure of a person or animal moved by hand or by strings or wires 2 : DOLL 3 : one whose acts are controlled by an outside force or influence

**pup·pe·teer** \ˌpə-pə-ˈtir\ *n* : one who manipulates puppets

**pup·py** \ˈpə-pē\ *n, pl* **puppies** : a young domestic dog

**pu·pu** \ˈpü-ˌpü\ *n* : an Asian dish consisting of a variety of foods

**pur·blind** \ˈpər-ˌblīnd\ *adj* 1 : partly blind 2 : lacking in insight : OBTUSE

¹**pur·chase** \ˈpər-chəs\ *vb* **pur·chased; pur·chas·ing** : to obtain by paying money or its equivalent : BUY — **pur·chas·able** \-chə-sə-bəl\ *adj* — **pur·chas·er** *n*

²**purchase** *n* 1 : an act or instance of purchasing 2 : something purchased 3 : a secure hold or grasp; *also* : advantageous leverage

**pur·dah** \ˈpər-də\ *n* : seclusion of women from public observation among Muslims and some Hindus esp. in India; *also* : a state of seclusion

**pure** \ˈpyu̇r\ *adj* **pur·er; pur·est** 1 : unmixed with any other matter : free from taint ⟨~ gold⟩ ⟨~ water⟩ 2 : SHEER, ABSOLUTE ⟨~ nonsense⟩ 3 : ABSTRACT, THEORETICAL ⟨~ mathematics⟩ 4 : free from what vitiates, weakens, or pollutes ⟨speaks a ~ French⟩ 5 : free from moral fault : INNOCENT 6 : CHASTE, CONTINENT — **pure·ly** *adv*

**pure-blood·ed** \-ˌblə-dəd\ *or* **pure-blood** \-ˌbləd\ *adj* : FULL-BLOODED — **pure-blood** *n*

**pure·bred** \-ˈbred\ *adj* : bred from members of a recognized breed, strain, or kind without crossbreeding over many generations — **pure·bred** \-ˌbred\ *n*

¹**pu·ree** \pyu̇-ˈrā, -ˈrē\ *n* [F *purée*, fr. MF, fr. fem. of *puré*, pp. of *purer* to purify, strain, fr. L *purare* to purify] : a paste or thick liquid suspension usu. made from finely ground cooked food; *also* : a thick soup made of pureed vegetables

²**puree** *vb* **pu·reed; pu·ree·ing** : to make a puree of

**pur·ga·tion** \ˌpər-ˈgā-shən\ *n* : the act or result of purging

¹**pur·ga·tive** \ˈpər-gə-tiv\ *adj* : purging or tending to purge

²**purgative** *n* : a strong laxative : CATHARTIC

**pur·ga·to·ry** \ˈpər-gə-ˌtȯr-ē\ *n, pl* **-ries** 1 : an intermediate state after death for expiatory purification 2 : a place or state of temporary punishment — **pur·ga·to·ri·al** \ˌpər-gə-ˈtȯr-ē-əl\ *adj*

¹**purge** \ˈpərj\ *vb* **purged; purg·ing** 1 : to cleanse or purify esp. from sin 2 : to have or cause strong and usu. repeated emptying of the bowels 3 : to get rid of ⟨the leaders had been *purged*⟩

²**purge** *n* 1 : something that purges; *esp* : PURGATIVE 2 : an act or result of purging; *esp* : a ridding of persons regarded as treacherous or disloyal

**pu·ri·fy** \ˈpyu̇r-ə-ˌfī\ *vb* **-fied; -fy·ing** : to make or become pure ⟨~ water⟩ ⟨~ the mind⟩ — **pu·ri·fi·ca·tion** \ˌpyu̇r-ə-fə-ˈkā-shən\ *n* — **pu·ri·fi·ca·to·ry** \pyu̇-ˈri-fi-kə-ˌtȯr-ē\ *adj* — **pu·ri·fi·er** *n*

**Pu·rim** \ˈpu̇r-(ˌ)im\ *n* : a Jewish holiday celebrated in February or March in commemoration of the deliverance of the Jews from the massacre plotted by Haman

**pu·rine** \ˈpyu̇r-ˌēn\ *n* : any of a group of bases including several (as adenine or guanine) that are constituents of DNA or RNA

**pur·ism** \ˈpyu̇r-ˌi-zəm\ *n* : rigid adherence to or insistence on purity or nicety esp. in use of words — **pur·ist** \-ist\ *n* — **pu·ris·tic** \pyu̇-ˈris-tik\ *adj*

**pu·ri·tan** \ˈpyu̇r-ə-tən\ *n* 1 *cap* : a member of a 16th and 17th century Protestant group in England and New England opposing the ceremonies and government of the Church of England 2 : one who practices or preaches a stricter or professedly purer moral code than that which prevails — **pu·ri·tan·i·cal** \ˌpyu̇r-ə-ˈta-ni-kəl\ *adj* — **pu·ri·tan·i·cal·ly** *adv*

**pu·ri·ty** \ˈpyu̇r-ə-tē\ *n* : the quality or state of being pure

¹**purl** \ˈpərl\ *n* : a stitch in knitting

²**purl** *vb* : to knit in purl stitch

³**purl** *n* : a gentle murmur or movement (as of purling water)

⁴**purl** *vb* 1 : EDDY, SWIRL 2 : to make a soft murmuring sound

**pur·lieu** \ˈpər-lü, ˈpər-lyü\ *n* 1 : an outlying district : SUBURB 2 *pl* : ENVIRONS

**pur·loin** \(ˌ)pər-ˈlȯin, ˈpər-ˌlȯin\ *vb* : STEAL, FILCH

¹**pur·ple** \ˈpər-pəl\ *adj* **pur·pler; pur·plest** 1 : of the color purple 2 : highly rhetorical ⟨a ~ passage⟩ 3 : PROFANE ⟨~ language⟩ — **pur·plish** *adj*

²**purple** *n* 1 : a bluish red color 2 : a purple robe emblematic esp. of regal rank or authority

¹**pur·port** \ˈpər-ˌpȯrt\ *n* [ME, fr. AF, content, tenor, fr. *purporter* to carry, mean, purport, fr. *pur-* thoroughly + *porter* to carry] : meaning conveyed or implied; *also* : GIST ⟨the ~ of her letter⟩

²**pur·port** \(ˌ)pər-ˈpȯrt\ *vb* : to convey or profess outwardly as the meaning or in-

tention : CLAIM ⟨∼s to be objective⟩ —
**pur·port·ed·ly** \-'pȯr-tad-lē\ adv

¹**pur·pose** \'pər-pəs\ n   1 : an object or
result aimed at : INTENTION   2 : RESOLU-
TION, DETERMINATION — **pur·pose·ful**
\-fəl\ adj — **pur·pose·ful·ly** adv — **pur·
pose·less** adj — **pur·pose·ly** adv

²**purpose** vb **pur·posed; pur·pos·ing** : to
propose as an aim to oneself

**purr** \'pər\ n : a low murmur typical of a
contented cat — **purr** vb

¹**purse** \'pərs\ n   1 : a receptacle (as a
pouch) to carry money and often other
small objects in   2 : RESOURCES   3 : a sum
of money offered as a prize or present

²**purse** vb **pursed; purs·ing** : PUCKER

**purs·er** \'pər-sər\ n : an official on a ship
who keeps accounts and attends to the
comfort of passengers

**purs·lane** \'pər-slən, -ˌslān\ n : a fleshy-
leaved weedy trailing plant with tiny yellow flowers that is sometimes used in
salads

**pur·su·ance** \pər-'sü-əns\ n : the act of
carrying out or into effect

**pur·su·ant to** \-'sü-ənt-\ prep : in carrying
out : ACCORDING TO

**pur·sue** \pər-'sü\ vb **pur·sued; pur·su·
ing**   1 : to follow in order to overtake or
overcome : CHASE   2 : to seek to accomplish ⟨∼ a goal⟩   3 : to proceed along
⟨∼ a course⟩   4 : to engage in ⟨∼ a ca-
reer⟩ — **pur·su·er** n

**pur·suit** \pər-'süt\ n   1 : the act of pursuing   2 : OCCUPATION, BUSINESS

**pu·ru·lent** \'pyur-ə-lənt, -yə-\ adj : containing or accompanied by pus ⟨a ∼ dis-
charge⟩ — **pu·ru·lence** \-ləns\ n

**pur·vey** \(ˌ)pər-'vā\ vb **pur·veyed; pur·
vey·ing** : to supply (as provisions) usu. as
a business — **pur·vey·ance** \-əns\ n —
**pur·vey·or** \-ər\ n

**pur·view** \'pər-ˌvyü\ n   1 : the range or
limit esp. of authority, responsibility, or
intention   2 : range of vision, understanding, or cognizance

**pus** \'pəs\ n : thick yellowish white fluid
matter (as in a boil) formed at a place of
inflammation and infection (as an abscess) and containing germs, white blood
cells, and tissue debris

¹**push** \'pu̇sh\ vb [ME possen, pusshen,
prob. fr. OF pousser to exert pressure, fr.
L pulsare, fr. pellere to drive, strike]   1
: to press against with force in order to
drive or impel   2 : to thrust forward,
downward, or outward   3 : to urge on
: press forward   4 : to cause to increase
⟨∼ prices to record levels⟩   5 : to urge or
press the advancement, adoption, or
practice of; esp : to make aggressive efforts to sell   6 : to engage in the illicit sale
of narcotics

²**push** n   1 : a vigorous effort : DRIVE ⟨a ∼
for higher wages⟩   2 : an act of pushing   3
: vigorous enterprise : ENERGY

**push–button** adj   1 : operated or done by
means of push buttons   2 : using or dependent on complex and more or less
automatic mechanisms ⟨∼ warfare⟩

**push button** n : a small button or knob

that when pushed operates something
esp. by closing an electric circuit

**push·cart** \'pu̇sh-ˌkärt\ n : a cart or barrow pushed by hand

**push·er** \'pu̇-shər\ n : one that pushes;
esp : one that pushes illegal drugs

**push·over** \-ˌō-vər\ n   1 : something easily accomplished   2 : an opponent easy to
defeat   3 : SUCKER ⟨she's nobody's ∼⟩

**push–up** \-ˌəp\ n : a conditioning exercise performed in a prone position by
raising and lowering the body with the
straightening and bending of the arms
while keeping the back straight and supporting the body on the hands and toes

**pushy** \'pu̇-shē\ adj **push·i·er; -est** : aggressive often to an objectionable degree

**pu·sil·lan·i·mous** \ˌpyü-sə-'la-nə-məs\
adj [LL pusillanimis, fr. L pusillus very
small (dim. of pusus boy) + animus spirit]
: contemptibly timid : COWARDLY — **pu·
sil·la·nim·i·ty** \ˌpyü-sə-lə-'ni-mə-tē\ n

¹**puss** \'pu̇s\ n : CAT

²**puss** n, slang : FACE

**pussy** \'pu̇-sē\ n, pl **puss·ies** : CAT

**pus·sy** \'pə-sē\ adj **pus·si·er; -est** : full
of or resembling pus

**pussy·cat** \'pu̇-sē-ˌkat\ n : CAT

**pussy·foot** \-ˌfu̇t\ vb   1 : to tread or move
warily or stealthily   2 : to refrain from
committing oneself

**pussy willow** \'pu̇-sē-\ n : a willow having large silky catkins

**pus·tule** \'pəs-chül\ n : a pus-filled pimple

**put** \'pu̇t\ vb **put; put·ting**   1 : to bring
into a specified position : PLACE ⟨∼ the
book on the table⟩   2 : SEND, THRUST   3
: to throw with an upward pushing motion ⟨∼ the shot⟩   4 : to bring into a
specified state ⟨∼ the plan into effect⟩   5
: SUBJECT ⟨∼ traitors to death⟩   6 : IM-
POSE   7 : to set before one for decision
⟨∼ the question⟩   8 : EXPRESS, STATE
⟨∼ my feelings into words⟩   9 : TRANS-
LATE, ADAPT   10 : APPLY, ASSIGN ⟨∼
them to work⟩   11 : ESTIMATE ⟨∼ the
number at 20⟩   12 : ATTACH, ATTRIBUTE
⟨∼ a high value on it⟩   13 : to take a
specified course ⟨the ship ∼ out to sea⟩

**pu·ta·tive** \'pyü-tə-tiv\ adj   1 : commonly
accepted ⟨∼ expert⟩   2 : assumed to exist or to have existed

**put–down** \'pu̇t-ˌdau̇n\ n : a belittling remark

**put in** vb   1 : to come in with : INTERPOSE
⟨put in a good word for me⟩   2 : to spend
time at some occupation or job ⟨put in
eight hours at the office⟩

**put off** vb : POSTPONE, DELAY ⟨put off my
visit⟩

¹**put–on** \'pu̇t-ˌȯn, -ˌän\ adj : PRETENDED,
ASSUMED ⟨a ∼ accent⟩

²**put–on** n   1 : a deliberate act of misleading someone   2 : PARODY, SPOOF

**put·out** \'pu̇t-ˌau̇t\ n : the retiring of a
base runner or batter in baseball

**put out** vb   1 : EXTINGUISH   2 : ANNOY;
also : INCONVENIENCE   3 : to cause to be
out (as in baseball)

**pu·tre·fy** \'pyü-trə-ˌfī\ vb **-fied; -fy·ing**
: to make or become putrid : ROT ⟨putre-

*fied* meat⟩ — **pu·tre·fac·tion** \ˌpyü-trə-ˈfak-shən\ *n* — **pu·tre·fac·tive** \-tiv\ *adj*

**pu·tres·cent** \pyü-ˈtres-sᵊnt\ *adj* : becoming putrid : ROTTING ⟨∼ carcasses⟩ — **pu·tres·cence** \-sᵊns\ *n*

**pu·trid** \ˈpyü-trəd\ *adj* 1 : ROTTEN, DECAYED ⟨∼ meat⟩ 2 : VILE, CORRUPT — **pu·trid·i·ty** \pyü-ˈtri-də-tē\ *n*

**putsch** \ˈpu̇ch\ *n* [G] : a secretly plotted and suddenly executed attempt to overthrow a government

**putt** \ˈpət\ *n* : a golf stroke made on the green to cause the ball to roll into the hole — **putt** *vb*

**put·ta·nes·ca** \ˌpü-tä-ˈnes-kä\ *adj* : served with or being a pungent tomato sauce

**put·tee** \ˌpə-ˈtē, ˈpə-tē\ *n* [Hindi *paṭṭī* strip of cloth] 1 : a cloth strip wrapped around the lower leg 2 : a leather legging

**¹put·ter** \ˈpu̇-tər\ *n* : one that puts

**²putt·er** \ˈpə-tər\ *n* 1 : a golf club used in putting 2 : one that putts

**³put·ter** \ˈpə-tər\ *vb* 1 : to move or act aimlessly or idly 2 : TINKER

**put·ty** \ˈpə-tē\ *n, pl* **putties** [F *potée* potter's glaze, lit., potful, fr. OF, fr. *pot* pot] 1 : a doughlike cement used esp. to fasten glass in sashes 2 : one who is easily manipulated — **putty** *vb*

**put up** *vb* 1 : SHEATHE 2 : to prepare so as to preserve for later use 3 : to offer for public sale ⟨*put* the house *up* for auction⟩ 4 : ACCOMMODATE, LODGE ⟨*put* us *up* for the night⟩ 5 : BUILD 6 : to engage in ⟨*put up* a struggle⟩ 7 : CONTRIBUTE, PAY — **put up with** : TOLERATE 2

**¹puz·zle** \ˈpə-zəl\ *vb* **puz·zled; puz·zling** 1 : to bewilder mentally : PERPLEX 2 : to solve with difficulty or ingenuity ⟨∼ out a riddle⟩ 3 : to be in a quandary ⟨∼ over what to do⟩ 4 : to attempt a solution of a puzzle ⟨∼ over a person's words⟩ ♦ *Synonyms* MYSTIFY, BEWILDER, NONPLUS, CONFOUND — **puz·zle·ment** *n* — **puz·zler** *n*

**²puzzle** *n* 1 : something that puzzles 2 : a question, problem, or contrivance designed for testing ingenuity

**PVC** *abbr* polyvinyl chloride

**pvt** *abbr* private

**PW** *abbr* prisoner of war

**pwt** *abbr* pennyweight

**PX** *abbr* post exchange

**pya** \pē-ˈä\ *n* — see *kyat* at MONEY table

**pyg·my** *also* **pig·my** \ˈpig-mē\ *n, pl* **pyg·mies** *also* **pigmies** [ME *pigmei*, fr. L *pygmaeus* of a pygmy, dwarfish, fr. Gk *pygmaios*, fr. *pygmē* fist, measure of length] 1 *cap* : any of a small people of equatorial Africa 2 : an unusually small person; *also* : an insignificant or unimpressive person — **pygmy** *adj*

**py·ja·mas** \pə-ˈjä-məz\ *chiefly Brit var of* PAJAMAS

**py·lon** \ˈpī-ˌlän, -lən\ *n* 1 : a usu. massive gateway; *esp* : an Egyptian one flanked by flat-topped pyramids 2 : a tower that supports wires over a long span 3 : a post or tower marking the course in an airplane race

**py·or·rhea** \ˌpī-ə-ˈrē-ə\ *n* : an inflammation with pus of the sockets of the teeth

**¹pyr·a·mid** \ˈpir-ə-ˌmid\ *n* 1 : a massive structure with a square base and four triangular faces meeting at a point 2 : a geometrical solid having a polygon for its base and three or more triangles for its sides that meet at a point to form the top — **py·ra·mi·dal** \pə-ˈra-mə-dᵊl, ˌpir-ə-ˈmid-\ *adj*

**²pyramid** *vb* 1 : to build up in the form of a pyramid : heap up 2 : to increase rapidly on a broadening base

**pyramid scheme** *n* : a usu. illegal operation in which participants pay to join and profit from payments made by subsequent participants

**pyre** \ˈpī(-ə)r\ *n* : a combustible heap for burning a dead body as a funeral rite

**py·re·thrum** \pī-ˈrē-thrəm\ *n* : an insecticide made from the dried heads of any of several Old World chrysanthemums

**py·rim·i·dine** \pī-ˈri-mə-ˌdēn\ *n* : any of a group of bases including several (as cytosine, thymine, or uracil) that are constituents of DNA or RNA

**py·rite** \ˈpī-ˌrīt\ *n* : a mineral containing sulfur and iron that is brass-yellow in color

**py·rol·y·sis** \pī-ˈrä-lə-səs\ *n* : chemical change caused by the action of heat

**py·ro·ma·nia** \ˌpī-rō-ˈmā-nē-ə\ *n* : an irresistible impulse to start fires — **py·ro·ma·ni·ac** \-nē-ˌak\ *n*

**py·ro·tech·nics** \ˌpī-rə-ˈtek-niks\ *n pl* 1 : a display of fireworks 2 : a spectacular display (as of extreme virtuosity) ⟨musical ∼⟩ — **py·ro·tech·nic** \-nik\ *also* **py·ro·tech·ni·cal** \-ni-kəl\ *adj*

**Pyr·rhic** \ˈpir-ik\ *adj* : achieved at excessive cost ⟨a ∼ victory⟩; *also* : costly to the point of outweighing expected benefits

**Py·thag·o·re·an theorem** \pī-ˌtha-gə-ˈrē-ən-\ *n* : a theorem in geometry: the square of the length of the hypotenuse of a right triangle equals the sum of the squares of the lengths of the other two sides

**py·thon** \ˈpī-ˌthän, -thən\ *n* [L, monstrous serpent killed by the god Apollo, fr. Gk *Pythōn*] : a large snake (as a boa) that squeezes and suffocates its prey; *esp* : any of the large Old World snakes that include the largest snakes living at the present time

**pyx** \ˈpiks\ *n* : a small case used to carry the Eucharist to the sick

¹**q** \'kyü\ *n, pl* **q's** *or* **qs** \'kyüz\ *often cap*
: the 17th letter of the English alphabet

²**q** *abbr, often cap* **1** quart **2** quarto **3**
queen **4** query **5** question

**QB** *abbr* quarterback

**QED** *abbr* [L *quod erat demonstrandum*]
which was to be demonstrated

**qin·tar** \kin-'tär\ *n, pl* **qin·dar·ka** \kin-
'där-kə\ — see *lek* at MONEY table

**qi·vi·ut** \'kē-vē-,üt\ *n* [Inuit] : the wool of
the undercoat of the musk ox

**Qld** *abbr* Queensland

**QM** *abbr* quartermaster

**QMC** *abbr* quartermaster corps

**QMG** *abbr* quartermaster general

**qq v** *abbr* [L *quae vide*] which (*pl*) see

**qr** *abbr* quarter

**Q rating** *n* [quotient] : a scale measuring
popularity based on dividing an assessment of familiarity or recognition by an
assessment of favorable opinion; *also*
: position on such a scale

**qt** *abbr* quart

**q.t.** \,kyü-'tē\ *n, often cap Q&T* : QUIET —
usu. used in the phrase *on the q.t.*

**qto** *abbr* quarto

**qty** *abbr* quantity

**qu** *or* **ques** *abbr* question

¹**quack** \'kwak\ *vb* : to make the characteristic cry of a duck

²**quack** *n* : a sound made by quacking

³**quack** *n* **1** : CHARLATAN **2** : a pretender
to medical skill ♦ *Synonyms* FAKER,
IMPOSTOR, MOUNTEBANK — **quack** *adj*
— **quack·ery** \'kwa-kə-rē\ *n* — **quack-
ish** *adj*

¹**quad** \'kwäd\ *n* : QUADRANGLE

²**quad** *n* **1** : QUADRUPLET **2** : a ski lift that
accommodates four people

³**quad** *abbr* quadrant

**quad·ran·gle** \'kwä-,draŋ-gəl\ *n* **1**
: QUADRILATERAL **2** : a 4-sided courtyard or enclosure — **quad·ran·gu·lar**
\kwä-'draŋ-gyə-lər\ *adj*

**quad·rant** \'kwä-drənt\ *n* **1** : one quarter
of a circle : an arc of 90° **2** : any of the
four quarters into which something is divided by two lines intersecting each other
at right angles

**qua·drat·ic** \kwä-'dra-tik\ *adj* : having or
being a term in which the variable (as *x*)
is squared but containing no term in
which the variable is raised to a higher
power than a square ⟨a ∼ equation⟩ —
**quadratic** *n*

**qua·dren·ni·al** \kwä-'dre-nē-əl\ *adj* **1**
: consisting of or lasting for four years **2**
: occurring every four years

**qua·dren·ni·um** \-nē-əm\ *n, pl* **-ni·ums**
*or* **-nia** \-nē-ə\ : a period of four years

**quad·ri·ceps** \'kwä-drə-,seps\ *n* : a muscle of the front of the thigh that is divided
into four parts

¹**quad·ri·lat·er·al** \,kwä-drə-'la-tə-rəl\ *n* : a
polygon of four sides

²**quadrilateral** *adj* : having four sides

**qua·drille** \kwä-'dril, kə-\ *n* : a square
dance made up of five or six figures in
various rhythms

**quad·ri·par·tite** \,kwä-drə-'pär-,tīt\ *adj* **1**
: consisting of four parts **2** : shared by
four parties or persons

**quad·ri·ple·gia** \,kwä-drə-'plē-jə, -jē-ə\ *n*
: paralysis of both arms and both legs —
**quad·ri·ple·gic** \-jik\ *adj or n*

**qua·driv·i·um** \kwä-'dri-vē-əm\ *n* : the
four liberal arts of arithmetic, music, geometry, and astronomy in a medieval
university

**quad·ru·ped** \'kwä-drə-,ped\ *n* : an animal having four feet — **qua·dru·pe·dal**
\kwä-'drü-pə-dəl, ,kwä-drə-'pe-\ *adj*

¹**qua·dru·ple** \kwä-'drü-pəl, -'drə-; 'kwä-
drə-\ *vb* **qua·dru·pled; qua·dru·pling**
: to make or become four times as great
or as many

²**quadruple** *adj* : FOURFOLD

**qua·dru·plet** \kwä-'drə-plət, -'drü-; 'kwä-
drə-\ *n* **1** : a combination of four of a
kind **2** : one of four offspring born at
one birth

¹**qua·dru·pli·cate** \kwä-'drü-pli-kət\ *adj* **1**
: repeated four times **2** : FOURTH

²**qua·dru·pli·cate** \-plə-,kāt\ *vb* **-cat·ed;
-cat·ing 1** : QUADRUPLE **2** : to prepare
in quadruplicate — **qua·dru·pli·ca·tion**
\-,drü-plə-'kā-shən\ *n*

³**qua·dru·pli·cate** \-'drü pli-kət\ *n* **1**
: four copies all alike ⟨typed in ∼⟩ **2**
: one of four like things

**quaff** \'kwäf, 'kwaf\ *vb* : to drink deeply
or repeatedly — **quaff** *n*

**quag·mire** \'kwag-,mī(-ə)r, 'kwäg-\ *n* **1**
: soft miry land that yields under the foot
**2** : PREDICAMENT

**qua·hog** \'kō-,hòg, 'kwò-, 'kwō-, -,häg\ *n*
[modif. of Narragansett *poquaûhock*] : a
round thick-shelled edible clam of the
U.S.

**quai** \'kā\ *n* : QUAY

¹**quail** \'kwāl\ *n, pl* **quail** *or* **quails** [ME
*quaile*, fr. AF, fr. ML *quaccula*, of imit.
origin] : any of numerous small short-
winged plump game birds (as a bobwhite)
related to the domestic chicken

²**quail** *vb* [ME, to grow feeble, fr. MD *quel-
en*] : to lose heart : COWER ⟨∼ed at the
daunting task⟩ ♦ *Synonyms* RECOIL,
SHRINK, FLINCH, WINCE, BLANCH

**quaint** \'kwānt\ *adj* : unusual or different in character or appearance; *esp*
: pleasingly old-fashioned or unfamiliar
♦ *Synonyms* ODD, QUEER, CURIOUS,
STRANGE — **quaint·ly** *adv* — **quaint-
ness** *n*

¹**quake** \'kwāk\ *vb* **quaked; quak·ing 1**
: to shake usu. from shock or instability
**2** : to tremble usu. from cold or fear

²**quake** *n* : a shaking or trembling; *esp*
: EARTHQUAKE

**Quak·er** \'kwā-kər\ *n* : FRIEND 5

**qual** *abbr* quality

**qual·i·fi·ca·tion** \,kwä-lə-fə-'kā-shən\ *n* 1 : LIMITATION, MODIFICATION ⟨her statement stands without ∼⟩ 2 : a special skill that fits a person for some work or position 3 : REQUIREMENT ⟨a ∼ for membership⟩

**qual·i·fied** \'kwä-lə-,fīd\ *adj* 1 : fitted for a given purpose or job 2 : limited in some way ⟨∼ approval⟩

**qual·i·fi·er** \'kwä-lə-,fī(-ə)r\ *n* 1 : one that satisfies requirements 2 : a word or word group that limits the meaning of another word or word group

**qual·i·fy** \'kwä-lə-,fī\ *vb* **-fied; -fy·ing** 1 : to reduce from a general to a particular form : MODIFY 2 : to make less harsh 3 : to limit the meaning of (as a noun) 4 : to fit by skill or training for some purpose 5 : to give or have a legal right to do something 6 : to demonstrate the necessary ability ⟨∼ for the finals⟩ ♦ *Synonyms* MODERATE, TEMPER

**qual·i·ta·tive** \'kwä-lə-,tā-tiv\ *adj* : of, relating to, or involving quality — **qual·i·ta·tive·ly** *adv*

¹**qual·i·ty** \'kwä-lə-tē\ *n, pl* **-ties** 1 : peculiar and essential character : NATURE 2 : degree of excellence 3 : high social status 4 : a distinguishing attribute

²**quality** *adj* : being of high quality

**qualm** \'kwäm, 'kwälm\ *n* 1 : a sudden attack (as of nausea) 2 : a sudden feeling of doubt, fear, or uneasiness esp. in not following one's conscience or better judgment

**qualm·ish** \'kwä-mish, 'kwäl-\ *adj* 1 : feeling qualms : NAUSEATED 2 : overly scrupulous : SQUEAMISH 3 : of, relating to, or producing qualms

**quan·da·ry** \'kwän-drē\ *n, pl* **-ries** : a state of perplexity or doubt

**quan·ti·fy** \'kwän-tə-,fī\ *vb* **-fied; -fy·ing** : to determine, express, or measure the quantity of — **quan·ti·fi·able** \,kwän-tə-'fī-ə-bəl\ *adj*

**quan·ti·ta·tive** \'kwän-tə-,tā-tiv\ *adj* : of, relating to, or involving quantity — **quan·ti·ta·tive·ly** *adv*

**quan·ti·ty** \'kwän-tə-tē\ *n, pl* **-ties** 1 : AMOUNT, NUMBER 2 : a considerable amount ⟨buys food in ∼⟩

**quan·tize** \'kwän-,tīz\ *vb* **quan·tized; quan·tiz·ing** : to subdivide (as energy) into small units

¹**quan·tum** \'kwän-təm\ *n, pl* **quan·ta** \-tə\ [L, neut. of *quantus* how much] 1 : QUANTITY, AMOUNT 2 : an elemental unit of energy

²**quantum** *adj* 1 : LARGE, SIGNIFICANT 2 : relating to or employing the principles of quantum mechanics

**quantum mechanics** *n sing or pl* : a theory of matter based on the concept of possession of wave properties by elementary particles — **quantum mechanical** *adj* — **quantum mechanically** *adv*

**quantum theory** *n* 1 : a theory in physics based on the idea that radiant energy (as light) is composed of small separate packets of energy 2 : QUANTUM MECHANICS

**quar** *abbr* quarterly

**quar·an·tine** \'kwȯr-ən-,tēn\ *n* [modif. of It *quarantena*, lit., period of forty days, fr. *quaranta* forty, fr. L *quadraginta*] 1 : a period during which a ship suspected of carrying contagious disease is forbidden contact with the shore 2 : a restraint on the movements of persons or goods to prevent the spread of pests or disease 3 : a place or period of quarantine 4 : a state of enforced isolation — **quarantine** *vb*

**quark** \'kwȯrk, 'kwärk\ *n* : a hypothetical elementary particle that carries a fractional charge and is held to be a constituent of heavier particles (as protons and neutrons)

¹**quar·rel** \'kwȯr-əl\ *n* 1 : a ground of dispute 2 : a verbal clash : CONFLICT — **quar·rel·some** \-səm\ *adj*

²**quarrel** *vb* **-reled** *or* **-relled; -rel·ing** *or* **-rel·ling** 1 : to find fault 2 : to dispute angrily : WRANGLE

¹**quar·ry** \'kwȯr-ē\ *n, pl* **quarries** [ME *querre* entrails of game given to the hounds, fr. AF *curée, quereie*, fr. *quir, cuir* skin, hide (on which the entrails were placed), fr. L *corium*] 1 : game hunted with hawks 2 : PREY

²**quarry** *n, pl* **quarries** [ME *quarey*, alter. of *quarrere*, fr. AF, fr. VL *\*quadraria*, fr. LL *quadrus* hewn (lit., squared) stone, fr. L *quadrum* square] : an open excavation usu. for obtaining building stone or limestone — **quarry** *vb*

³**quart** \'kwȯrt\ *n* — see WEIGHT table

¹**quar·ter** \'kwȯr-tər\ *n* 1 : one of four equal parts 2 : a fourth of a dollar; *also* : a coin of this value 3 : a district of a city 4 *pl* : LODGINGS ⟨moved into new ∼s⟩ 5 : MERCY, CLEMENCY ⟨gave no ∼⟩ 6 : a fourth part of the moon's period

²**quarter** *vb* 1 : to divide into four equal parts 2 : to provide with shelter

¹**quar·ter·back** \-,bak\ *n* : a football player who calls the signals and directs the offensive play for the team

²**quarterback** *vb* 1 : to direct the offensive play of a football team 2 : LEAD, BOSS

**quar·ter·deck** \-,dek\ *n* : the stern area of a ship's upper deck

**quarter horse** *n* : any of a breed of compact muscular saddle horses characterized by great endurance and by high speed for short distances

¹**quar·ter·ly** \'kwȯr-tər-lē\ *adv* : at 3-month intervals

²**quarterly** *adj* : occurring, issued, or payable at 3-month intervals

³**quarterly** *n, pl* **-lies** : a periodical published four times a year

**quar·ter·mas·ter** \-,mas-tər\ *n* 1 : a petty officer who attends to a ship's helm, binnacle, and signals 2 : an army officer who provides clothing and subsistence for troops

**quar·ter·staff** \-,staf\ *n, pl* **-staves** \-,stavz, -,stävz\ : a long stout staff formerly used as a weapon

**quar·tet** *also* **quar·tette** \kwȯr-'tet\ *n* 1

: a musical composition for four instruments or voices **2** : a group of four and esp. of four musicians

**quar·to** \'kwȯr-tō\ *n, pl* **quartos 1** : the size of a piece of paper cut four from a sheet **2** : a book printed on quarto pages

**quartz** \'kwȯrts\ *n* : a common often transparent crystalline mineral that is a form of silica

**quartz·ite** \'kwȯrt-ˌsīt\ *n* : a compact granular rock composed of quartz and derived from sandstone

**qua·sar** \'kwā-ˌzär, -ˌsär\ *n* : any of a class of extremely distant starlike celestial objects

¹**quash** \'kwäsh, 'kwȯsh\ *vb* : to suppress or extinguish summarily and completely : QUELL

²**quash** *vb* : to nullify by judicial action

**qua·si** \'kwā-ˌzī, -ˌsī; 'kwä-zē, -sē\ *adj* : being in some sense or degree ⟨a ~ corporation⟩

**quasi-** *comb form* [L, as if, as it were, approximately, fr. *quam* as + *si* if] : in some sense or degree ⟨*quasi*-historical⟩

**qua·si–gov·ern·men·tal** \ˌga-vərn-'men-t²l\ *adj* : supported by the government but managed privately

**Qua·ter·na·ry** \'kwä-tər-ˌner-ē, kwə-'tər-nə-rē\ *adj* : of, relating to, or being the geologic period from the end of the Tertiary to the present — **Quaternary** *n*

**qua·train** \'kwä-ˌtrān\ *n* : a unit of four lines of verse

**qua·tre·foil** \'ka-tər-ˌfȯi(-ə)l, 'ka-trə-\ *n* : a stylized figure often of a flower with four petals

**qua·ver** \'kwā-vər\ *vb* **1** : TREMBLE, SHAKE ⟨~ed with nervousness⟩ **2** : TRILL **3** : to speak in tremulous tones ◆ **Synonyms** SHUDDER, QUAKE, TWITTER, QUIVER, SHIVER — **quaver** *n*

**quay** \'kē, 'kwā, 'kā\ *n* : WHARF

**Que** *abbr* Quebec

**quean** \'kwēn\ *n* : PROSTITUTE

**quea·sy** \'kwē-zē\ *adj* **quea·si·er; -est** : NAUSEATED — **quea·si·ly** \-zə-lē\ *adv* — **quea·si·ness** \-zē-nəs\ *n*

**Que·chua** \'ke-chə-wə, 'kech-wə\ *n* : a family of languages spoken in Peru and adjacent countries of the So. American Andes

**queen** \'kwēn\ *n* [ME *quene*, fr. OE *cwēn* woman, wife, queen] **1** : the wife or widow of a king **2** : a female monarch **3** : a woman notable for rank, power, or attractiveness **4** : the most powerful piece in the game of chess **5** : a playing card bearing the figure of a queen **6** : a fertile female of a social insect (as a bee or termite) — **queen·ly** *adj*

**Queen Anne's lace** \-'anz-\ *n* : a widely naturalized Eurasian herb from which the cultivated carrot originated

**queen consort** *n, pl* **queens consort** : the wife of a reigning king

**queen mother** *n* : a dowager queen who is mother of the reigning sovereign

**queen–size** *adj* : having dimensions of approximately 60 inches by 80 inches ⟨a ~ bed⟩; *also* : of a size that fits a queen-size bed

¹**queer** \'kwir\ *adj* **1** : COUNTERFEIT ⟨~ money⟩ **2** : differing from the usual or normal : PECULIAR, STRANGE **3** *often disparaging* : HOMOSEXUAL; *also, sometimes offensive* : of, relating to, or used by homosexuals ◆ **Synonyms** WEIRD, BIZARRE, ECCENTRIC, CURIOUS — **queer** *n* — **queer·ly** *adv* — **queer·ness** *n*

²**queer** *vb* : to spoil the effect of : DISRUPT ⟨~ed our plans⟩

**queer theory** *n* : an approach to literary and cultural study that rejects traditional categories of gender and sexuality

**quell** \'kwel\ *vb* **1** : to put an end to by force ⟨~ a riot⟩ **2** : CALM, PACIFY ⟨~ fears⟩

**quench** \'kwench\ *vb* **1** : PUT OUT, EXTINGUISH **2** : SUBDUE **3** : SLAKE, SATISFY ⟨~ed his thirst⟩ — **quench·able** *adj* — **quench·er** *n* — **quench·less** *adj*

**quer·u·lous** \'kwer-ə-ləs, -yə-\ *adj* **1** : constantly complaining **2** : FRETFUL, WHINING ⟨a ~ voice⟩ ◆ **Synonyms** PETULANT, PETTISH, IRRITABLE, PEEVISH, HUFFY — **quer·u·lous·ly** *adv* — **quer·u·lous·ness** *n*

**que·ry** \'kwir-ē, 'kwer-\ *n, pl* **queries** : QUESTION — **query** *vb*

**que·sa·dil·la** \ˌkā-sə-'dē-ə\ *n* : a tortilla filled with a savory mixture, folded, and usu. fried

**quest** \'kwest\ *n* : SEARCH ⟨in ~ of game⟩ — **quest** *vb*

¹**ques·tion** \'kwes-chən\ *n* **1** : an interrogative expression **2** : a subject for debate; *also* : a proposition to be voted on **3** : INQUIRY **4** : DISPUTE ⟨true beyond ~⟩

²**question** *vb* **1** : to ask questions **2** : DOUBT, DISPUTE ⟨~ed the verdict⟩ **3** : to subject to analysis : EXAMINE ◆ **Synonyms** INTERROGATE, QUIZ, QUERY — **ques·tion·er** *n*

**ques·tion·able** \'kwes-chə-nə-bəl\ *adj* **1** : not certain or exact : DOUBTFUL **2** : not believed to be true, sound, or moral ◆ **Synonyms** DUBIOUS, PROBLEMATICAL, MOOT, DEBATABLE — **ques·tion·ably** \-blē\ *adv*

**question mark** *n* : a punctuation mark ? used esp. at the end of a sentence to indicate a direct question

**ques·tion·naire** \ˌkwes-chə-'ner\ *n* : a set of questions for obtaining information

**quet·zal** \ket-'säl, -'sal\ *n, pl* **quetzals** *or* **quet·za·les** \-'sä-läs, -'sa-\ **1** : a Central American bird with brilliant plumage **2** *pl* **quetzales** — see MONEY table

¹**queue** \'kyü\ *n* [F, lit., tail, fr. OF *cue, coe*, fr. L *cauda, coda*] **1** : a braid of hair usu. worn hanging at the back of the head **2** : a waiting line (as of persons)

²**queue** *vb* **queued; queu·ing** *or* **queue·ing** : to line up in a queue

**quib·ble** \'kwi-bəl\ *n* **1** : an evasion of or shifting from the point at issue **2** : a minor objection or criticism — **quibble** *vb* — **quib·bler** *n*

¹**quick** \'kwik\ *adj* **1** : LIVING **2** : RAPID, SPEEDY ⟨~ steps⟩ **3** : prompt to understand, think, or perceive : ALERT **4** : easily aroused ⟨a ~ temper⟩ **5** : turning or

bending sharply ⟨a ~ turn in the road⟩
♦ **Synonyms** FLEET, FAST, HASTY, EXPEDITIOUS — **quick** adv — **quick·ly** adv — **quick·ness** n

²**quick** n **1** : a sensitive area of living flesh **2** : a vital part : HEART

**quick bread** n : a bread made with a leavening agent that permits immediate baking of the dough or batter

**quick·en** \'kwi-kən\ vb **1** : to come to life : REVIVE **2** : AROUSE, STIMULATE ⟨curiosity ~ed my interest⟩ **3** : to increase in speed : HASTEN **4** : to show vitality (as by growing or moving) ♦ **Synonyms** ANIMATE, ENLIVEN, LIVEN, VIVIFY

**quick–freeze** \'kwik-'frēz\ vb **-froze** \-'frōz\; **-fro·zen** \-'frō-z°n\; **-freez·ing** : to freeze (food) for preservation so rapidly that the natural juices and flavor are not lost

**quick·ie** \'kwi-kē\ n : something hurriedly done or made

**quick·lime** \'kwik-,līm\ n : ¹LIME

**quick·sand** \-,sand\ n : a deep mass of loose sand mixed with water

**quick·sil·ver** \-,sil-vər\ n : MERCURY 1

**quick·step** \-,step\ n : a spirited march tune or dance

**quick–wit·ted** \'kwik-'wi-təd\ adj : mentally alert ♦ **Synonyms** CLEVER, BRIGHT, SMART, INTELLIGENT

**quid** \'kwid\ n : a lump of something chewable ⟨a ~ of tobacco⟩

**quid pro quo** \,kwid-,prō-'kwō\ n [NL, something for something] : something given or received for something else

**qui·es·cent** \kwī-'e-s°nt\ adj : being at rest : QUIET ⟨a ~ state⟩ ♦ **Synonyms** LATENT, DORMANT, POTENTIAL — **qui·es·cence** \-s°ns\ n

¹**qui·et** \'kwī-ət\ n : REPOSE

²**quiet** adj **1** : marked by little motion or activity : CALM **2** : GENTLE, MILD ⟨a ~ disposition⟩ **3** : enjoyed in peace and relaxation ⟨a ~ cup of tea⟩ **4** : free from noise or uproar **5** : not showy : MODEST ⟨~ clothes⟩ **6** : SECLUDED ⟨a ~ nook⟩ — **quiet** adv — **qui·et·ly** adv — **qui·et·ness** n

³**quiet** vb **1** : CALM, PACIFY **2** : to become quiet — usu. used with down

**qui·etude** \'kwī-ə-,tüd, -,tyüd\ n : QUIETNESS, REPOSE

**qui·etus** \kwī-'ē-təs\ n [ME quietus est, fr. ML, he is quit, formula of discharge from obligation] **1** : final settlement (as of a debt) **2** : DEATH

**quill** \'kwil\ n **1** : a large stiff feather; also : the hollow tubular part of a feather **2** : one of the hollow sharp spines of a hedgehog or porcupine **3** : a pen made from a feather

¹**quilt** \'kwilt\ n : a padded bed coverlet

²**quilt** vb **1** : to fill, pad, or line like a quilt **2** : to stitch or sew in layers with padding in between **3** : to make quilts

**quince** \'kwins\ n : a hard yellow applelike fruit; also : a tree related to the roses that bears this fruit

**qui·nine** \'kwī-,nīn\ n : a bitter white drug obtained from cinchona bark and used esp. in treating malaria

**qui·noa** \'kēn-,wä, kē-'nō-ə\ n [Sp, fr. Quechua kinua] : the starchy seeds of an annual herb related to spinach which are used as food and ground into flour; also : this herb

**quint** \'kwint\ n : QUINTUPLET

**quin·tal** \'kwin-t°l, 'kan-\ n : HUNDREDWEIGHT

**quin·tes·sence** \kwin-'te-s°ns\ n **1** : the purest essence of something **2** : the most typical example ⟨the ~ of self-control⟩ — **quin·tes·sen·tial** \,kwin-tə-'sen-chəl\ adj — **quin·tes·sen·tial·ly** adv

**quin·tet** \kwin-'tet\ n **1** : a musical composition for five instruments or voices **2** : a group of five and esp. of five musicians

¹**quin·tu·ple** \kwin-'tü-pəl, -'tyü-, -'tə-\ adj **1** : having five units or members **2** : being five times as great or as many — **quintuple** n

²**quintuple** vb **quin·tu·pled**; **quin·tu·pling** : to make or become five times as great or as many

**quin·tu·plet** \kwin-'tə-plət, -'tü-, -'tyü-\ n **1** : a group of five of a kind **2** : one of five offspring born at one birth

¹**quin·tu·pli·cate** \kwin-'tü-pli-kət, -'tyü-\ adj **1** : repeated five times **2** : FIFTH ⟨file the ~ copy⟩

²**quintuplicate** n **1** : one of five like things **2** : five copies all alike ⟨typed in ~⟩

³**quin·tu·pli·cate** \-plə-,kāt\ vb **-cat·ed**; **-cat·ing** **1** : QUINTUPLE **2** : to provide in quintuplicate

¹**quip** \'kwip\ n : a clever remark : GIBE

²**quip** vb **quipped**; **quip·ping** **1** : to make quips : GIBE **2** : to jest or gibe at

**quire** \'kwī(-ə)r\ n : a set of 24 or sometimes 25 sheets of paper of the same size and quality

**quirk** \'kwərk\ n : a peculiarity of action or behavior — **quirky** adj

**quirt** \'kwərt\ n : a riding whip with a short handle and a rawhide lash

**quis·ling** \'kwiz-liŋ\ n [Vidkun Quisling †1945 Norw. politician who collaborated with the Nazis] : one who helps the invaders of one's own country

**quit** \'kwit\ vb **quit** also **quit·ted**; **quit·ting** **1** : CONDUCT, BEHAVE ⟨~ themselves well⟩ **2** : to depart from : LEAVE; also : to bring to an end **3** : to give up for good ⟨~ smoking⟩ ⟨~ my job⟩ ♦ **Synonyms** ACQUIT, COMPORT, DEPORT, DEMEAN — **quit·ter** n

**quite** \'kwīt\ adv **1** : COMPLETELY, WHOLLY ⟨not ~ finished⟩ **2** : to an extreme : POSITIVELY **3** : to a considerable extent : RATHER ⟨~ rich⟩

**quits** \'kwits\ adj : even or equal with another

**quit·tance** \'kwi-t°ns\ n : REQUITAL

¹**quiv·er** \'kwi-vər\ n : a case for carrying arrows

²**quiver** vb **quiv·ered**; **quiv·er·ing** : to shake with a slight trembling motion ⟨~ed with rage⟩ ♦ **Synonyms** SHIVER, SHUDDER, QUAVER, QUAKE, TREMBLE — **quiv·er·ing·ly** adv

³**quiver** n : the act or action of quivering : TREMOR

**qui vive** \kē-'vēv\ *n* [F *qui-vive,* fr. *qui vive?* long live who?, challenge of a French sentry] : ALERT ⟨on the *qui vive* for prowlers⟩

**quix·ot·ic** \kwik-'sä-tik\ *adj* [fr. Don Quixote, hero of the novel *Don Quixote de la Mancha* by Cervantes] : foolishly impractical esp. in the pursuit of ideals — **quix·ot·i·cal·ly** \-ti-kə-lē\ *adv*

¹**quiz** \'kwiz\ *n, pl* **quiz·zes** 1 : an eccentric person 2 : PRACTICAL JOKE 3 : a short oral or written test

²**quiz** *vb* **quizzed; quiz·zing** 1 : MOCK 2 : to look at inquisitively 3 : to question closely ♦ *Synonyms* ASK, INTERROGATE, QUERY

**quiz·zi·cal** \'kwi-zi-kəl\ *adj* 1 : comically quaint 2 : mildly teasing or mocking 3 : expressive of puzzlement, curiosity, or disbelief ⟨gave me a ~ look⟩

**quoit** \'kwät, 'kwóit, 'kóit\ *n* 1 : a flattened ring of iron or circle of rope used in a throwing game 2 *pl* : a game in which quoits are thrown at an upright pin in an attempt to ring the pin

**quon·dam** \'kwän-dəm, -ˌdam\ *adj* [L, at one time, formerly, fr. *quom, cum* when] : FORMER ⟨a ~ friend⟩

**quo·rum** \'kwór-əm\ *n* : the number of members required to be present for business to be legally transacted

**quot** *abbr* quotation

**quo·ta** \'kwō-tə\ *n* : a proportional part esp. when assigned : SHARE

**quot·able** \'kwō-tə-bəl\ *adj* : fit for or worth quoting ⟨a ~ comment⟩ — **quot·abil·i·ty** \ˌkwō-tə-'bi-lə-tē\ *n*

**quo·ta·tion** \kwō-'tā-shən\ *n* 1 : the act or process of quoting 2 : the price currently bid or offered for something 3 : something that is quoted

**quotation mark** *n* : one of a pair of punctuation marks " " or ' ' used esp. to indicate the beginning and end of a quotation in which exact phraseology is directly cited

**quote** \'kwōt\ *vb* **quot·ed; quot·ing** [ML *quotare* to mark the number of, number references, fr. L *quotus* of what number or quantity, fr. *quot* how many, (as) many as] 1 : to speak or write a passage from another usu. with acknowledgment; *also* : to repeat a passage in substantiation or illustration 2 : to state the market price of a commodity, stock, or bond 3 : to inform a hearer or reader that matter following is quoted — **quote** *n*

**quoth** \'kwōth\ *vb past* [ME, past of *quethen* to say, fr. OE *cwethan*] *archaic* : SAID — usu. used in the 1st and 3d persons with the subject following

**quo·tid·i·an** \kwō-'ti-dē-ən\ *adj* 1 : DAILY 2 : COMMONPLACE, ORDINARY ⟨~ concerns⟩

**quo·tient** \'kwō-shənt\ *n* : the number obtained by dividing one number by another

**Quran** *also* **Qur'an** *var of* KORAN

**qv** *abbr* [L *quod vide*] which see

**qy** *abbr* query

¹**r** \'är\ *n, pl* **r's** *or* **rs** \'ärz\ *often cap* : the 18th letter of the English alphabet

²**r** *abbr, often cap* 1 rabbi 2 radius 3 rare 4 Republican 5 rerun 6 resistance 7 right 8 river 9 roentgen 10 rook 11 run

**Ra** *symbol* radium

**RA** *abbr* 1 regular army 2 Royal Academy 3 research assistant

¹**rab·bet** \'ra-bət\ *n* : a groove in the edge or face of a surface (as a board) esp. to receive another piece

²**rabbet** *vb* : to cut a rabbet in; *also* : to join by means of a rabbet

**rab·bi** \'ra-ˌbī\ *n* [ME, fr. OE, fr. LL, fr. Gk *rhabbi,* fr. Heb *rabbī* my master, fr. *rabh* master + -*ī* my] 1 : MASTER, TEACHER — used by Jews as a term of address 2 : a Jew trained and ordained for professional religious leadership — **rab·bin·ic** \rə-'bi-nik\ *or* **rab·bin·i·cal** \-ni-kəl\ *adj*

**rab·bin·ate** \'ra-bə-nət, -ˌnāt\ *n* 1 : the office of a rabbi 2 : the whole body of rabbis

**rab·bit** \'ra-bət\ *n, pl* **rabbit** *or* **rabbits** : any of various long-eared short-tailed burrowing mammals distinguished from the related hares by being blind, furless, and helpless at birth; *also* : the pelt of a rabbit

**rabbit ears** *n pl* : an indoor V-shaped television antenna

**rab·ble** \'ra-bəl\ *n* 1 : MOB 2 2 : the lowest class of people

**rab·ble–rous·er** \'ra-bəl-ˌraú-zər\ *n* : one that stirs up (as to hatred or violence) the masses of the people

**ra·bid** \'ra-bəd\ *adj* 1 : VIOLENT, FURIOUS 2 : being fanatical or extreme ⟨~ supporters⟩ 3 : affected with rabies — **ra·bid·ly** *adv*

**ra·bies** \'rā-bēz\ *n, pl* **rabies** [NL, fr. L, madness] : an acute deadly virus disease of the nervous system transmitted by the bite of an affected animal

**rac·coon** \ra-'kün\ *n, pl* **raccoon** *or* **raccoons** : a gray No. American chiefly tree-dwelling mammal with a black mask, a bushy ringed tail, and nocturnal habits; *also* : its pelt

¹**race** \'rās\ *n* 1 : a strong current of running water; *also* : its channel 2 : an onward course (as of time or life) 3 : a contest of speed 4 : a contest for a desired end (as election to office)

²**race** *vb* **raced; rac·ing** 1 : to run in a race 2 : to run swiftly : RUSH 3 : to engage in a race with 4 : to drive or ride at high speed — **rac·er** *n*

³**race** n 1 : a family, tribe, people, or nation of the same stock 2 : a group of individuals within a biological species able to breed together 3 : a category of humankind that shares certain distinctive physical traits — **ra·cial** \'rā-shəl\ adj — **ra·cial·ly** adv

**race·course** \'rās-,kōrs\ n : a course for racing

**race·horse** \-,hòrs\ n : a horse bred or kept for racing

**ra·ceme** \rā-'sēm\ n [L racemus bunch of grapes] : a flower cluster with flowers borne along a stem and blooming from the base toward the tip — **rac·e·mose** \'ra-sə-,mōs\ adj

**race·track** \'rās-,trak\ n : a usu. oval course on which races are run

**race·way** \-,wā\ n 1 : a channel for a current of water 2 : RACECOURSE

**ra·cial·ism** \'rā-shə-,li-zəm\ n : a theory that race determines human traits and capacities; also : RACISM — **ra·cial·ist** \-list\ n — **ra·cial·is·tic** \,rā-shə-'lis-tik\ adj

**ra·cial·ize** \'rā-shə-,līz\ vb **-ized**; **-iz·ing** : to give a racial character to

**racing form** n : a paper giving data about racehorses for use by bettors

**rac·ism** \'rā-,si-zəm\ n : a belief that some races are by nature superior to others; also : discrimination based on such belief — **rac·ist** \-sist\ n

¹**rack** \'rak\ n 1 : an instrument of torture on which a body is stretched 2 : a framework on or in which something may be placed (as for display or storage) 3 : a bar with teeth on one side to mesh with a pinion or worm gear

²**rack** vb 1 : to torture on or as if on a rack 2 : to stretch or strain by force 3 : TORMENT 4 : to place on or in a rack

¹**rack·et** or **rac·quet** \'ra-kət\ n [MF raquette, ultim. fr. ML rasceta wrist, carpus, fr. Ar rusgh wrist] : a light bat made of netting stretched in an oval open frame having a handle and used for striking a ball or shuttlecock

²**racket** n 1 : confused noise : DIN 2 : a fraudulent or dishonest scheme or activity ⟨a criminal ∼⟩

³**racket** vb : to make a racket

**rack·e·teer** \,ra-kə-'tir\ n : a person who obtains money by an illegal enterprise usu. involving intimidation — **rack·e·teer·ing** n

**rack up** vb : ACHIEVE, GAIN ⟨racked up their 10th victory⟩

**ra·con·teur** \,ra-,kän-'tər\ n : one good at telling anecdotes

**rac·quet·ball** \'ra-kət-,bòl\ n : a game similar to handball that is played on a 4-walled court with a short-handled racket

**racy** \'rā-sē\ adj **rac·i·er**; **-est** 1 : full of zest 2 : PUNGENT, SPICY 3 : RISQUÉ, SUGGESTIVE ⟨∼ jokes⟩ — **rac·i·ly** \'rā-sə-lē\ adv — **rac·i·ness** \-sē-nəs\ n

**rad** abbr 1 radical 2 radius

**ra·dar** \'rā-,där\ n [radio detecting and ranging] : a device that emits radio waves for detecting and locating an object by the reflection of the radio waves and that may use this reflection to determine the object's direction and speed

**radar gun** n : a handheld device that uses radar to measure the speed of a moving object

**ra·dar·scope** \'rā-,där-,skōp\ n : a visual display for a radar receiver

¹**ra·di·al** \'rā-dē-əl\ adj : arranged or having parts arranged like rays around a common center ⟨the ∼ form of a starfish⟩ — **ra·di·al·ly** adv

²**radial** n : a pneumatic tire with cords laid perpendicular to the center line

**radial engine** n : an internal combustion engine with cylinders arranged radially like the spokes of a wheel

**ra·di·an** \'rā-dē-ən\ n : a unit of measure for angles that is equal to approximately 57.3 degrees

**ra·di·ant** \'rā-dē-ənt\ adj 1 : SHINING, GLOWING 2 : beaming with happiness ⟨a ∼ smile⟩ 3 : transmitted by radiation
♦ **Synonyms** BRILLIANT, BRIGHT, LUMINOUS, LUSTROUS — **ra·di·ance** \-əns\ n — **ra·di·ant·ly** adv

**radiant energy** n : energy traveling as electromagnetic waves

**ra·di·ate** \'rā-dē-,āt\ vb **-at·ed**; **-at·ing** 1 : to send out rays : SHINE, GLOW 2 : to issue in or as if in rays ⟨light ∼s⟩ 3 : to spread around as from a center

**ra·di·a·tion** \,rā-dē-'ā-shən\ n 1 : the action or process of radiating 2 : the process of emitting radiant energy in the form of waves or particles; also : something (as an X-ray beam) that is radiated

**radiation sickness** n : sickness that results from exposure to radiation and is commonly marked by fatigue, nausea, vomiting, loss of teeth and hair, and in more severe cases by damage to blood-forming tissue

**radiation therapy** n : RADIOTHERAPY

**ra·di·a·tor** \'rā-dē-,ā-tər\ n : any of various devices (as a set of pipes or tubes) for transferring heat from a fluid within to an area or object outside

¹**rad·i·cal** \'ra-di-kəl\ adj [ME, fr. LL radicalis, fr. L radic-, radix root] 1 : FUNDAMENTAL, EXTREME, THOROUGHGOING 2 : of or relating to radicals in politics — **rad·i·cal·ism** \-kə-,li-zəm\ n — **rad·i·cal·ly** adv

²**radical** n 1 : a person who favors rapid and sweeping changes in laws and methods of government 2 : FREE RADICAL; also : a group of atoms considered as a unit in certain reactions or as a subunit of a larger molecule 3 : a mathematical expression indicating a root by means of a radical sign; also : RADICAL SIGN

**rad·i·cal·ise** Brit var of RADICALIZE

**rad·i·cal·ize** \-kə-,līz\ vb **-ized**; **-iz·ing** : to make radical esp. in politics — **rad·i·cal·i·za·tion** \,ra-di-kə-lə-'zā-shən\ n

**radical sign** n : the sign √ placed before a mathematical expression to indicate that its root is to be taken

**ra·dic·chio** \ra-'di-kē-ō\ n, pl **–chios** : a chicory with reddish variegated leaves

**radii** pl of RADIUS

**¹ra·dio** \'rā-dē-‚ō\ *n, pl* **ra·di·os 1** : the wireless transmission or reception of signals using electromagnetic waves **2** : a radio receiving set **3** : the radio broadcasting industry — **radio** *adj*

**²radio** *vb* : to communicate or send a message to by radio

**ra·dio·ac·tiv·i·ty** \‚rā-dē-ō-‚ak-'ti-və-tē\ *n* : the property that some elements or isotopes have of spontaneously emitting energetic particles by the disintegration of their atomic nuclei — **ra·dio·ac·tive** \-'ak-tiv\ *adj*

**radio astronomy** *n* : astronomy dealing with radio waves received from outside the earth's atmosphere

**ra·dio·car·bon** \‚rā-dē-ō-'kär-bən\ *n* : CARBON 14

**radio frequency** *n* : an electromagnetic wave frequency intermediate between audio frequencies and infrared frequencies used esp. for communication and radar signals

**ra·dio·gram** \'rā-dē-ō-‚gram\ *n* : a message transmitted by radio

**ra·dio·graph** \-‚graf\ *n* : a photograph made by some form of radiation other than light; *esp* : an X-ray photograph — **radiograph** *vb* — **ra·dio·graph·ic** \‚rā-dē-ō-'gra-fik\ *adj* — **ra·dio·graph·i·cal·ly** \-fi-k(ə-)lē\ *adv* — **ra·di·og·ra·phy** \‚rā-dē-'ä-grə-fē\ *n*

**ra·dio·iso·tope** \‚rā-dē-ō-'ī-sə-‚tōp\ *n* : a radioactive isotope

**ra·di·ol·o·gy** \‚rā-dē-'ä-lə-jē\ *n* : the use of radiant energy (as X-rays and radium radiations) in medicine — **ra·di·ol·o·gist** \-jist\ *n*

**ra·dio·man** \'rā-dē-ō-‚man\ *n* : a radio operator or technician

**ra·di·om·e·ter** \‚rā-dē-'ä-mə-tər\ *n* : an instrument for measuring the intensity of radiant energy — **ra·dio·met·ric** \‚rā-dē-ō-'me-trik\ *adj* — **ra·di·om·e·try** \-mə-trē\ *n*

**ra·dio·phone** \'rā-dē-ə-‚fōn\ *n* : RADIOTELEPHONE

**ra·dio·sonde** \'rā-dē-ō-‚sänd\ *n* : a small radio transmitter carried aloft (as by balloon) and used to transmit meteorological data

**ra·dio·tele·phone** \‚ra-dē-ō-'te-lə-‚fōn\ *n* : a telephone that uses radio waves wholly or partly instead of connecting wires — **ra·dio·te·le·pho·ny** \-tə-'le-fə-nē, -'te-lə-‚fō-nē\ *n*

**radio telescope** *n* : a radio receiver-antenna combination used for observation in radio astronomy

**ra·dio·ther·a·py** \‚rā-dē-ō-'ther-ə-pē\ *n* : the treatment of disease by means of radiation (as X-rays) — **ra·dio·ther·a·pist** \-pist\ *n*

**rad·ish** \'ra-dish\ *n* [ME, alter. of OE *rǣdic*, fr. L *radic-, radix* root, radish] : a pungent fleshy root usu. eaten raw; *also* : a plant related to the mustards that produces this root

**ra·di·um** \'rā-dē-əm\ *n* [NL, fr. L *radius* ray] : a very radioactive metallic chemical element that is used in the treatment of cancer

**ra·di·us** \'rā-dē-əs\ *n, pl* **ra·dii** \-ē-‚ī\ *also* **ra·di·us·es 1** : a straight line extending from the center of a circle or a sphere to the circumference or surface; *also* : the length of a radius **2** : the bone on the thumb side of the human forearm **3** : a circular area defined by the length of its radius ◆ *Synonyms* RANGE, REACH, SCOPE, COMPASS

**RADM** *abbr* rear admiral

**ra·don** \'rā-‚dän\ *n* : a heavy radioactive gaseous chemical element

**RAF** *abbr* Royal Air Force

**raf·fia** \'ra-fē-ə\ *n* : fiber used esp. for making baskets and hats that is obtained from the stalks of the leaves of a tropical African palm (**raffia palm**)

**raff·ish** \'ra-fish\ *adj* : jaunty or sporty esp. in a flashy or vulgar manner — **raff·ish·ly** *adv* — **raff·ish·ness** *n*

**¹raf·fle** \'ra-fəl\ *vb* **raf·fled; raf·fling** : to dispose of by a raffle

**²raffle** *n* : a lottery in which the prize is won by one of a number of persons buying chances

**¹raft** \'raft\ *n* **1** : a number of logs or timbers fastened together to form a float **2** : a flat structure for support or transportation on water

**²raft** *vb* **1** : to travel or transport by raft **2** : to make into a raft

**³raft** *n* : a large amount or number

**raf·ter** \'raf-tər\ *n* : any of the parallel beams that support a roof

**¹rag** \'rag\ *n* **1** : a waste piece of cloth **2** : a sleazy newspaper

**²rag** *n* : a composition in ragtime

**ra·ga** \'rä-gə\ *n* **1** : a traditional melodic pattern or mode in Indian music **2** : an improvisation based on a raga

**rag·a·muf·fin** \'ra-gə-‚mə-fən\ *n* [ME *Ragamuffyn*, name for a ragged, oafish person] : a ragged dirty person; *esp* : a poorly clothed often dirty child

**¹rage** \'rāj\ *n* **1** : violent and uncontrolled anger **2** : VOGUE, FASHION

**²rage** *vb* **raged; rag·ing 1** : to be furiously angry : RAVE **2** : to continue out of control ⟨the fire *raged*⟩

**rag·ged** \'ra-gəd\ *adj* **1** : TORN, TATTERED ⟨a ~ dress⟩; *also* : wearing tattered clothes **2** : done in an uneven way ⟨a ~ performance⟩ — **rag·ged·ly** *adv* — **rag·ged·ness** *n*

**rag·lan** \'ra-glən\ *n* : an overcoat with sleeves (**raglan sleeves**) sewn in with seams slanting from neck to underarm

**ra·gout** \ra-'gü\ *n* [F *ragoût*, fr. *ragoûter* to revive the taste, fr. MF *ragouster*, fr. *re-* + *a-* to (fr. L *ad-*) + *goust* taste, fr. L *gustus*] : a highly seasoned meat stew with vegetables

**rag·pick·er** \'rag-‚pi-kər\ *n* : one who collects rags and refuse for a living

**rag·time** \-‚tīm\ *n* : music in which there is more or less continuous syncopation in the melody

**rag·top** \'rag-‚täp\ *n* : CONVERTIBLE

**rag·weed** \-‚wēd\ *n* : any of several chiefly No. American weedy composite herbs with allergenic pollen

¹**raid** \'rād\ *n* : a sudden usu. surprise attack or invasion : FORAY

²**raid** *vb* : to make a raid on — **raid·er** *n*

¹**rail** \'rāl\ *n* [ME *raile*, fr. AF *raille, reille* bar, rule, fr. L *regula* straightedge, rule, fr. *regere* to keep straight, direct] **1** : a bar extending from one support to another as a guard or barrier **2** : a bar of steel forming a track for wheeled vehicles **3** : RAILROAD

²**rail** *vb* : to provide with a railing

³**rail** *n, pl* **rail** *or* **rails** : any of numerous small wading birds often hunted as game birds

⁴**rail** *vb* [ME, fr. MF *railler* to mock, prob. fr. OF *reillier* to growl, mutter, fr. VL *\*ragulare* to bray, fr. LL *ragere* to neigh] : to complain angrily : SCOLD, REVILE — **rail·er** *n*

**rail·ing** \'rā-liŋ\ *n* : a barrier of rails

**rail·lery** \'rā-lə-rē\ *n, pl* **-ler·ies** : good-natured ridicule : BANTER

¹**rail·road** \'-,rōd\ *n* : a permanent road with rails fixed to ties providing a track for cars; *also* : such a road and its assets constituting a property

²**railroad** *vb* **1** : to put through (as a law) too hastily **2** : to convict hastily or with insufficient or improper evidence **3** : to send by rail **4** : to work on a railroad — **rail·road·er** *n* — **rail·road·ing** *n*

**rail·way** \'-,wā\ *n* : RAILROAD

**rai·ment** \'rā-mənt\ *n* : CLOTHING

¹**rain** \'rān\ *n* **1** : water falling in drops from the clouds **2** : a shower of objects ⟨a ∼ of bullets⟩ — **rainy** *adj*

²**rain** *vb* **1** : to send down rain **2** : to fall as or like rain **3** : to pour down

¹**rain·bow** \'-,bō\ *n* : an arc or circle of colors formed by the refraction and reflection of the sun's rays in rain, spray, or mist

²**rainbow** *adj* **1** : having many colors **2** : of, relating to, or made up of people of different races or cultural backgrounds

**rainbow trout** *n* : a large stout-bodied fish of western No. America closely related to the salmons of the Pacific and usu. marked red or pink stripes with black dots along its side

**rain check** *n* **1** : a ticket stub good for a later performance when the scheduled one is rained out **2** : an assurance of a deferred extension of an offer

**rain·coat** \'rān-,kōt\ *n* : a waterproof or water-repellent coat

**rain date** *n* : an alternative date for an event postponed due to rain

**rain·drop** \'-,dräp\ *n* : a drop of rain

**rain·fall** \'-,fol\ *n* **1** : amount of precipitation measured by depth **2** : a fall of rain

**rain forest** *n* : a tropical woodland having an annual rainfall of at least 100 inches (254 centimeters) and marked by lofty broad-leaved evergreen trees forming a continuous canopy

**rain·mak·ing** \'rān-,mā-kiŋ\ *n* : the action or process of producing or attempting to produce rain by artificial means — **rain·mak·er** *n*

**rain out** *vb* : to interrupt or prevent by rain

**rain·storm** \'rān-,stȯrm\ *n* : a storm of or with rain

**rain·wa·ter** \-,wȯ-tər, -,wä-\ *n* : water fallen as rain

¹**raise** \'rāz\ *vb* **raised; rais·ing 1** : to cause or help to rise : LIFT ⟨∼ a window⟩ **2** : AWAKEN, AROUSE ⟨enough to ∼ the dead⟩ **3** : BUILD, ERECT ⟨∼ a monument⟩ **4** : PROMOTE ⟨was *raised* to captain⟩ **5** : END ⟨∼ a siege⟩ **6** : COLLECT ⟨∼ money⟩ **7** : BREED, GROW ⟨∼ cattle⟩ ⟨∼ corn⟩; *also* : BRING UP ⟨∼ a family⟩ **8** : PROVOKE ⟨∼ a laugh⟩ **9** : to bring to notice ⟨∼ an objection⟩ **10** : INCREASE ⟨∼ prices⟩; *also* : to bet more than **11** : to make light and spongy ⟨∼ dough⟩ **12** : to multiply a quantity by itself a specified number of times ⟨∼ 2 to the third power⟩ **13** : to cause to form ⟨∼ a blister⟩ ♦ *Synonyms* LIFT, HOIST, BOOST, ELEVATE — **rais·er** *n*

**raise the bar** : to set a higher standard

²**raise** *n* : an increase in amount (as of a bid or bet); *also* : an increase in pay

**rai·sin** \'rā-zⁿn\ *n* [ME, fr. AF, grape, raisin, fr. L *racemus* cluster of grapes or berries] : a grape dried for food

**rai·son d'être** \,rā-,zōⁿ-'detrᵊ\ *n, pl* **rai·sons d'être** \-,zōⁿz-\ : reason or justification for existence

**ra·ja** *or* **ra·jah** \'rä-jə\ *n* [Hindi *rājā*, fr. Skt *rājan* king] : an Indian prince

¹**rake** \'rāk\ *n* : a long-handled garden tool having a crossbar with prongs

²**rake** *vb* **raked; rak·ing 1** : to gather, loosen, or smooth with or as if with a rake **2** : to sweep the length of (as a trench or ship) with gunfire

³**rake** *n* : inclination from either perpendicular or horizontal : SLANT

⁴**rake** *n* : a dissolute man : LIBERTINE

**rake–off** \'rāk-,ȯf\ *n* : a percentage or cut taken

¹**rak·ish** \'rā-kish\ *adj* : DISSOLUTE — **rak·ish·ly** *adv* — **rak·ish·ness** *n*

²**rakish** *adj* **1** : having a trim appearance indicative of speed ⟨a ∼ sloop⟩ **2** : JAUNTY, SPORTY ⟨∼ clothes⟩ — **rak·ish·ly** *adv* — **rak·ish·ness** *n*

¹**ral·ly** \'ra-lē\ *vb* **ral·lied; ral·ly·ing 1** : to bring together for a common purpose; *also* : to bring back to order ⟨a leader ∼ing his forces⟩ **2** : to arouse to activity or from depression or weakness **3** : to make a comeback ♦ *Synonyms* STIR, ROUSE, AWAKEN, WAKEN, KINDLE

²**rally** *n, pl* **rallies 1** : an act of rallying **2** : a mass meeting to arouse enthusiasm **3** : a competitive automobile event run over public roads

³**rally** *vb* **ral·lied; ral·ly·ing** : BANTER

**rallying cry** *n* : WAR CRY 2

¹**ram** \'ram\ *n* **1** : a male sheep **2** : BATTERING RAM

²**ram** *vb* **rammed; ram·ming 1** : to force or drive in or through **2** : CRAM, CROWD **3** : to strike against violently

**RAM** \'ram\ *n* : a computer memory that provides the main internal storage for programs and data

¹**ram·ble** \'ram-bəl\ *vb* **ram·bled; ram-**

**bling** : to go about aimlessly : ROAM, WANDER

²**ramble** *n* : a leisurely excursion; *esp* : an aimless walk

**ram·bler** \'ram-blər\ *n* **1** : a person who rambles **2** : any of various climbing roses with large clusters of small often double flowers

**ram·bunc·tious** \ram-'bəŋk-shəs\ *adj* : UNRULY

**ra·mie** \'rā-mē, 'ra-\ *n* : a strong lustrous bast fiber from an Asian nettle

**ram·i·fi·ca·tion** \ra-mə-fə-'kā-shən\ *n* **1** : the act or process of branching **2** : CONSEQUENCE, OUTGROWTH ⟨the ∼s of the decision⟩

**ram·i·fy** \'ra-mə-ˌfī\ *vb* **-fied; -fy·ing** : to branch out

**ramp** \'ramp\ *n* : a sloping passage or roadway connecting different levels

¹**ram·page** \'ram-ˌpāj, (ˌ)ram-'pāj\ *vb* **rampaged; ram·pag·ing** : to rush about wildly ⟨*rampaging* soccer fans⟩

²**ram·page** \'ram-ˌpāj\ *n* : a course of violent or riotous action or behavior — **ram·pa·geous** \ram-'pā-jəs\ *adj*

**ram·pant** \'ram-pənt\ *adj* : unchecked in growth or spread : RIFE ⟨fear was ∼ in the town⟩ — **ram·pan·cy** \-pən-sē\ *n* — **ram·pant·ly** *adv*

**ram·part** \'ram-ˌpärt\ *n* **1** : a protective barrier **2** : a broad embankment raised as a fortification

¹**ram·rod** \'ram-ˌräd\ *n* **1** : a rod used to ram a charge into a muzzle-loading gun **2** : a cleaning rod for small arms **3** : BOSS, OVERSEER

²**ramrod** *adj* : marked by rigidity or severity ⟨his ∼ posture⟩

³**ramrod** *vb* : to direct, supervise, and control ⟨*ramrodded* the project forward⟩

**ram·shack·le** \'ram-ˌsha-kəl\ *adj* : RICKETY, TUMBLEDOWN

**ran** *past of* RUN

¹**ranch** \'ranch\ *n* [MexSp *rancho* small ranch, fr. Sp. camp, hut & Sp dial., small farm, fr. Old Spanish *ranchear* (*se*) to take up quarters, fr. MF (*se*) *ranger* to take up a position, fr. *ranger* to set in a row] **1** : an establishment for the raising and grazing of livestock (as cattle, sheep, or horses) **2** : a large farm devoted to a specialty **3** : RANCH HOUSE 2

²**ranch** *vb* : to live or work on a ranch — **ranch·er** *n*

**ranch house** *n* **1** : the main house on a ranch **2** : a one-story house typically with a low-pitched roof

**ran·cho** \'ran-chō, 'rän-\ *n, pl* **ranchos** : RANCH 1

**ran·cid** \'ran-səd\ *adj* **1** : having a rank smell or taste **2** : OFFENSIVE **3** — **ran·cid·i·ty** \ran-'si-də-tē\ *n*

**ran·cor** \'ran-kər\ *n* : bitter deep-seated ill will ◆ *Synonyms* ANTAGONISM, ANIMOSITY, ANTIPATHY, ENMITY, HOSTILITY — **ran·cor·ous** *adj*

**ran·cour** *Brit var of* RANCOR

**rand** \'rand, 'ränd, 'ränt\ *n, pl* **rand** — see MONEY table

**R & B** *abbr* rhythm and blues

**R & D** *abbr* research and development

**ran·dom** \'ran-dəm\ *adj* : CHANCE, HAPHAZARD — **ran·dom·ly** *adv* — **ran·dom·ness** *n*

**random–access** *adj* : allowing access to stored data in any order the user desires

**random–access memory** *n* : RAM

**ran·dom·ize** \'ran-də-ˌmīz\ *vb* **-ized; -iz·ing** : to select, assign, or arrange in a random way — **ran·dom·i·za·tion** \ˌran-də-mə-'zā-shən\ *n*

**R & R** *abbr* rest and recreation; rest and recuperation

**rang** *past of* RING

¹**range** \'rānj\ *n* **1** : a series of things in a row **2** : a cooking stove having an oven and a flat top with burners **3** : open land where animals (as livestock) may roam and graze **4** : the region throughout which an organism occurs **5** : the act of ranging about **6** : the distance a weapon will shoot or is to be shot **7** : a place where shooting is practiced **8** : the space or extent included, covered, or used : SCOPE **9** : a variation within limits ◆ *Synonyms* REACH, COMPASS, RADIUS, CIRCLE

²**range** *vb* **ranged; rang·ing** [ME, fr. AF *renger*, fr. *renc, reng* line, place, row, of Gmc origin] **1** : to set in a row or in a proper order **2** : to set in place among others of the same kind **3** : to roam over or through : EXPLORE **4** : to roam at large or freely **5** : to correspond in direction or line **6** : to vary within limits **7** : to find the range of an object by instrument (as radar)

**rang·er** \'rān-jər\ *n* **1** : FOREST RANGER **2** : a member of a body of troops who range over a region **3** : an expert in close-range fighting and raiding tactics

**rangy** \'rān-jē\ *adj* **rang·i·er; -est** : being long-limbed and slender ⟨a ∼ teenager⟩ — **rang·i·ness** \-jē-nəs\ *n*

**ra·ni** *or* **ra·nee** \rä-'nē, 'rä-ˌnē\ *n* : a raja's wife

¹**rank** \'rank\ *adj* **1** : strong and vigorous and usu. coarse in growth **2** : unpleasantly strong-smelling — **rank·ly** *adv* — **rank·ness** *n*

²**rank** *n* **1** : ROW ⟨∼s of houses⟩ **2** : a line of soldiers ranged side by side **3** *pl* : the body of enlisted personnel ⟨rose from the ∼s⟩ **4** : position in a group **5** : superior position **6** : a grade of official standing (as in an army) **7** : an orderly arrangement **8** : CLASS, DIVISION — usu. used in pl.

³**rank** *vb* **1** : to arrange in lines or in regular formation **2** : RATE **3** : to rate above (as in official standing) **4** : to take or have a relative position

**rank and file** *n* : the general membership of a body as contrasted with its leaders

**rank·ing** \'ran-kin\ *adj* **1** : having a high position : of the highest rank **2** : being next to the chairman in seniority

**ran·kle** \'ran-kəl\ *vb* **ran·kled; ran·kling** [ME *ranclen* to fester, fr. AF *rancler*, fr. OF *draoncler, raoncler*, fr. *draoncle, raoncle* festering sore, fr. ML *dracunculus*, fr. L, dim. of *draco* serpent] : to cause anger, irritation, or bitterness

**ran·sack** \'ran-ˌsak\ *vb* : to search thoroughly; *esp* : to search through and rob

**¹ran·som** \'ran-səm\ *n* [ME *ransoun*, fr. OF *rançun*, fr. L *redemption-, redemptio* act of buying back, fr. *redimere* to buy back, redeem] **1** : something paid or demanded for the freedom of a captive **2** : the act of ransoming

**²ransom** *vb* : to free from captivity or punishment by paying a price — **ran·som·er** *n*

**rant** \'rant\ *vb* **1** : to talk loudly and wildly **2** : to scold violently ⟨~*ed* against his opponent⟩ — **rant·er** *n* — **rant·ing·ly** *adv*

**¹rap** \'rap\ *n* **1** : a sharp blow **2** : a sharp rebuke **3** : a negative often undeserved reputation ⟨a bum ~⟩ **4** : responsibility for or consequences of an action ⟨take the ~⟩

**²rap** *vb* **rapped; rap·ping 1** : to strike sharply : KNOCK **2** : to utter sharply **3** : to criticize sharply

**³rap** *vb* **rapped; rap·ping 1** : to talk freely and frankly **2** : to perform rap music — **rap·per** *n*

**⁴rap** *n* **1** : TALK, CONVERSATION **2** : a rhythmic chanting of usu. rhymed couplets to a musical accompaniment; *also* : a piece so performed

**ra·pa·cious** \rə-'pā-shəs\ *adj* **1** : excessively greedy or covetous **2** : living on prey **3** : RAVENOUS 2 ⟨a ~ appetite⟩ — **ra·pa·cious·ly** *adv* — **ra·pa·cious·ness** *n* — **ra·pac·i·ty** \-'pa-sə-tē\ *n*

**¹rape** \'rāp\ *n* : an Old World herb related to the mustards that is grown as a forage crop and for its seeds (**rapeseed** \-ˌsēd\)

**²rape** *vb* **raped; rap·ing** : to commit rape on — **rap·er** *n* — **rap·ist** \'rā-pist\ *n*

**³rape** *n* **1** : a carrying away by force **2** : unlawful sexual activity and usu. sexual intercourse carried out forcibly or under threat of injury

**¹rap·id** \'ra-pəd\ *adj* [L *rapidus* strongflowing, rapid, fr. *rapere* to seize, carry away] : very fast : SWIFT ◆ **Synonyms** FLEET, QUICK, SPEEDY — **ra·pid·i·ty** \rə-'pi-də-tē\ *n* — **rap·id·ly** *adv*

**²rapid** *n* : a place in a stream where the current flows very fast usu. over obstructions — usu. used in pl.

**rapid eye movement** *n* : rapid conjugate movement of the eyes associated with REM sleep

**rapid transit** *n* : fast passenger transportation (as by subway) in cities

**¹ra·pi·er** \'rā-pē-ər\ *n* : a straight 2-edged sword with a narrow pointed blade

**²rapier** *adj* : extremely sharp or keen ⟨~ wit⟩

**rap·ine** \'ra-pən, -ˌpīn\ *n* : PILLAGE, PLUNDER

**rap·pel** \ra-'pel, ra-\ *vb* **-pelled; -pel·ling** : to descend (as from a cliff) by sliding down a rope

**rap·pen** \'rä-pən\ *n, pl* **rappen** : the centime of Switzerland

**rap·port** \ra-'pȯr\ *n* : RELATION; *esp* : relation characterized by harmony

**rap·proche·ment** \ˌra-ˌprōsh-'mäⁿ, ra-**

'prōsh-ˌmäⁿ\ *n* : the establishment of or a state of having cordial relations

**rap·scal·lion** \rap-'skal-yən\ *n* : RASCAL, SCAMP

**rapt** \'rapt\ *adj* **1** : carried away with emotion **2** : ABSORBED, ENGROSSED ⟨listened with ~ attention⟩ — **rapt·ly** \'rapt-lē\ *adv* — **rapt·ness** *n*

**rap·tor** \'rap-tər, -ˌtȯr\ *n* **1** : BIRD OF PREY **2** : a usu. small-to-medium-sized predatory dinosaur

**rap·ture** \'rap-chər\ *n* : spiritual or emotional ecstasy — **rap·tur·ous** \-chə-rəs\ *adj* — **rap·tur·ous·ly** *adv*

**rapture of the deep** : NITROGEN NARCOSIS

**ra·ra avis** \ˌrer-ə-'ā-vəs, ˌrär-ə-'ä-wəs\ *n, pl* **ra·ra avis·es** \-'ā-və-səz\ *or* **ra·rae aves** \ˌrär-ˌī-'ä-ˌwās\ [L, rare bird] : a rare person or thing : RARITY

**¹rare** \'rer\ *adj* **rar·er; rar·est 1** : not thick or dense : THIN ⟨~ air⟩ **2** : unusually fine : EXCELLENT, SPLENDID **3** : seldom met with — **rare·ly** *adv* — **rare·ness** *n* — **rar·i·ty** \'rar-ə-tē\ *n*

**²rare** *adj* **rar·er; rar·est** : cooked so that the inside is still red ⟨~ beef⟩

**rare·bit** \'rer-bət\ *n* : WELSH RABBIT

**rar·efac·tion** \ˌrer-ə-'fak-shən\ *n* **1** : the action or process of rarefying **2** : the state of being rarefied

**rar·e·fy** *also* **rar·i·fy** \'rer-ə-ˌfī\ *vb* **-fied; -fy·ing** : to make or become rare, thin, or less dense

**rar·ing** \'rer-ən, -iŋ\ *adj* : full of enthusiasm or eagerness ⟨~ to go⟩

**ras·cal** \'ras-kəl\ *n* [ME *rascaile* foot soldiers, commoners, worthless person, fr. AF *rascaille*, fr. OF dial. \**rasquer* to scrape, clean off, ultim. fr. L *radere* to scrape, shave] **1** : a mean or dishonest person **2** : a mischievous person — **ras·cal·i·ty** \ra-'ska-lə-tē\ *n* — **ras·cal·ly** \'ras-kə-lē\ *adv*

**¹rash** \'rash\ *adj* : having or showing little regard for consequences : too hasty in decision, action, or speech : RECKLESS ◆ **Synonyms** DARING, FOOLHARDY, ADVENTUROUS, VENTURESOME — **rash·ly** *adv* — **rash·ness** *n*

**²rash** *n* : an eruption on the body

**rash·er** \'ra-shər\ *n* : a thin slice of bacon or ham broiled or fried; *also* : a portion consisting of several such slices

**¹rasp** \'rasp\ *vb* **1** : to rub with or as if with a rough file **2** : to grate harshly on (as one's nerves) **3** : to speak in a grating tone ⟨"Don't touch me," she ~*ed*⟩

**²rasp** *n* : a coarse file with cutting points instead of ridges

**rasp·ber·ry** \'raz-ˌber-ē, -bə-rē\ *n* **1** : any of various edible usu. black or red berries produced by some brambles; *also* : such a bramble **2** : a sound of contempt made by protruding the tongue through the lips and expelling air forcibly

**¹rat** \'rat\ *n* **1** : any of numerous rodents larger than the related mice **2** : a contemptible person; *esp* : one that betrays friends or associates

**²rat** *vb* **rat·ted; rat·ting 1** : to betray or

inform on one's associates **2** : to hunt or catch rats

**rat cheese** *n* : CHEDDAR

**ratch·et** \'ra-chət\ *n* : a device that consists of a bar or wheel having slanted teeth into which a pawl drops so as to allow motion in only one direction

¹**rate** \'rāt\ *vb* **rat·ed; rat·ing** : to scold violently

²**rate** *n* **1** : quantity, amount, or degree measured by some standard **2** : an amount (as of payment) measured by its relation to some other amount (as of time) **3** : a charge, payment, or price fixed according to a ratio, scale, or standard ⟨tax ∼⟩ **4** : RANK, CLASS

³**rate** *vb* **rat·ed; rat·ing 1** : ESTIMATE **2** : CONSIDER, REGARD ⟨*rated* as a good pianist⟩ **3** : to settle the relative rank or class of **4** : to be classed : RANK **5** : to have a right to : DESERVE ⟨the new museum ∼s a visit⟩ **6** : to be of consequence — **rat·er** *n*

**rath·er** \'ra-thər, 'rä-, 'rə-\ *adv* [ME, fr. OE *hrathor*, compar. of *hrathe* quickly] **1** : more properly **2** : PREFERABLY ⟨I'd ∼ not go⟩ **3** : more correctly speaking **4** : to the contrary : INSTEAD **5** : SOMEWHAT ⟨∼ warm⟩

**rather than** *prep* : INSTEAD OF

**raths·kel·ler** \'rät-ˌske-lər, 'rat-\ *n* [obs. G (now *Ratskeller*), city-hall basement restaurant, fr. *Rat* council + *Keller* cellar] : a usu. basement tavern or restaurant

**rat·i·fy** \'ra-tə-ˌfī\ *vb* **-fied; -fy·ing** : to approve and accept formally — **rat·i·fi·ca·tion** \ˌra-tə-fə-'kā-shən\ *n*

**rat·ing** \'rā-tiŋ\ *n* **1** : a classification according to grade : RANK **2** *Brit* : an enlisted person in the navy **3** : an estimate of the credit standing and business responsibility of a person or firm

**ra·tio** \'rā-shō, -shē-ō\ *n, pl* **ra·tios 1** : the indicated quotient of two numbers or mathematical expressions **2** : the relationship in number, quantity, or degree between two or more things

**ra·ti·o·ci·na·tion** \ˌra-tē-ˌō-sə-'nā-shən, -ˌä-\ *n* : exact thinking : REASONING — **ra·ti·o·ci·nate** \-'ō-sə-ˌnāt, -'ä-\ *vb* — **ra·ti·o·ci·na·tive** \-'ō-sə-ˌnā-tiv, -'ä-\ *adj* — **ra·ti·o·ci·na·tor** \-'ō-sə-ˌnā-tər, -'ä-sə-\ *n*

¹**ra·tion** \'ra-shən, 'rā-\ *n* **1** : a food allowance for one day **2** : FOOD, PROVISIONS, DIET — usu. used in pl. **3** : SHARE, ALLOTMENT

²**ration** *vb* **1** : to supply with or allot as rations **2** : to use or allot sparingly

♦ *Synonyms* APPORTION, PORTION, PRORATE, PARCEL

¹**ra·tio·nal** \'ra-shə-nəl\ *adj* **1** : having reason or understanding **2** : of or relating to reason **3** : relating to, consisting of, or being one or more rational numbers — **ra·tio·nal·ly** *adv*

²**rational** *n* : RATIONAL NUMBER

**ra·tio·nale** \ˌra-shə-'nal\ *n* **1** : an explanation of principles controlling belief or practice **2** : an underlying reason

**ra·tio·nal·ise** *Brit var of* RATIONALIZE

**ra·tio·nal·ism** \'ra-shə-nə-ˌli-zəm\ *n* : the practice of guiding one's actions and opinions solely by what seems reasonable — **ra·tio·nal·ist** \-list\ *n* — **rationalist** *or* **ra·tio·nal·is·tic** \ˌra-shə-nə-'lis-tik\ *adj* — **ra·tio·nal·is·ti·cal·ly** \-ti-k(ə-)lē\ *adv*

**ra·tio·nal·i·ty** \ˌra-shə-'na-lə-tē\ *n, pl* **-ties** : the quality or state of being rational

**ra·tio·nal·ize** \'ra-shə-nə-ˌlīz\ *vb* **-ized; -iz·ing 1** : to make (something irrational) appear rational or reasonable **2** : to provide a natural explanation of (as a myth) **3** : to justify (as one's behavior or weaknesses) esp. to oneself **4** : to find plausible but untrue reasons for conduct — **ra·tio·nal·i·za·tion** \ˌra-shə-nə-lə-'zā-shən\ *n*

**rational number** *n* : a number that can be expressed as an integer or the quotient of an integer divided by a nonzero integer

**rat race** *n* : strenuous, tiresome, and usu. competitive activity or rush

**rat·tan** \ra-'tan, rə-\ *n* : a cane or switch made from one of the long stems of an Asian climbing palm; *also* : this palm

**rat·ter** \'ra-tər\ *n* : a rat-catching dog or cat

¹**rat·tle** \'ra-tᵊl\ *vb* **rat·tled; rat·tling 1** : to make or cause to make a series of clattering sounds **2** : to move with a clattering sound **3** : to say or do in a brisk lively fashion ⟨∼ off the answers⟩ **4** : CONFUSE, UPSET ⟨∼ a witness⟩

²**rattle** *n* **1** : a toy that produces a rattle when shaken **2** : a series of clattering and knocking sounds **3** : a rattling organ at the end of a rattlesnake's tail

**rat·tler** \'rat-lər\ *n* : RATTLESNAKE

**rat·tle·snake** \'ra-tᵊl-ˌsnāk\ *n* : any of various American pit vipers with a rattle at the end of the tail

**rat·tle·trap** \'ra-tᵊl-ˌtrap\ *n* : something (as an old car) rickety and full of rattles

**rat·tling** \'rat-liŋ\ *adj* **1** : LIVELY, BRISK ⟨moved at a ∼ pace⟩ **2** : FIRST-RATE, SPLENDID

**rat·trap** \'rat-ˌtrap\ *n* **1** : a trap for rats **2** : a dilapidated building

**rat·ty** \'ra-tē\ *adj* **rat·ti·er; -est 1** : infested with rats **2** : of, relating to, or suggestive of rats **3** : SHABBY ⟨a ∼ old coat⟩

**rau·cous** \'ro-kəs\ *adj* **1** : HARSH, HOARSE, STRIDENT ⟨∼ voices⟩ **2** : boisterously disorderly — **rau·cous·ly** *adv* — **rau·cous·ness** *n*

**raun·chy** \'ron-chē, 'rän-\ *adj* **raun·chi·er; -est 1** : SLOVENLY, DIRTY **2** : OBSCENE, SMUTTY ⟨∼ jokes⟩ — **raun·chi·ness** \-chē-nəs\ *n*

¹**rav·age** \'ra-vij\ *n* [F] : an act or result of ravaging : DEVASTATION

²**ravage** *vb* **rav·aged; rav·ag·ing** : to lay waste : DEVASTATE — **rav·ag·er** *n*

¹**rave** \'rāv\ *vb* **raved; rav·ing 1** : to talk wildly in or as if in delirium : STORM, RAGE **2** : to talk with extreme enthusiasm ⟨*raved* about the show⟩ — **rav·er** *n*

²**rave** *n* **1** : an act or instance of raving **2** : an extravagantly favorable criticism

¹**rav·el** \'ra-vəl\ *vb* **-eled** *or* **-elled; -el·ing** *or* **-el·ling 1** : UNRAVEL, UNTWIST **2** : TANGLE, CONFUSE

²**ravel** *n* **1** : something tangled **2** : something raveled out; *esp* : a loose thread

¹**ra·ven** \'rā-vən\ *n* : a large black bird related to the crow

²**raven** *adj* : black and glossy like a raven's feathers

³**rav·en** \'ra-vən\ *vb* **1** : to devour greedily **2** : DESPOIL, PLUNDER **3** : PREY

**rav·en·ous** \'ra-və-nəs\ *adj* **1** : RAPACIOUS, VORACIOUS ⟨~ wolves⟩ **2** : eager for food : very hungry — **rav·en·ous·ly** *adv* — **rav·en·ous·ness** *n*

**ra·vine** \rə-'vēn\ *n* : a small narrow steep-sided valley larger than a gully

**rav·i·o·li** \ˌra-vē-'ō-lē\ *n, pl* **ravioli** *also* **raviolis** [It, fr. It dial., pl. of *raviolo*, lit., little turnip, dim. of *rava* turnip, fr. L *rapa*] : small cases of dough with a savory filling (as of meat or cheese)

**rav·ish** \'ra-vish\ *vb* **1** : to seize and take away by violence **2** : to overcome with emotion and esp. with joy or delight ⟨~ed by her beauty⟩ **3** : RAPE — **rav·ish·er** *n* — **rav·ish·ment** *n*

¹**raw** \'rȯ\ *adj* **raw·er** \'rȯ-ər\; **raw·est** \'rȯ-əst\ **1** : not cooked **2** : changed little from the original form : not processed ⟨~ materials⟩ **3** : having the surface abraded or irritated ⟨a ~ sore⟩ **4** : not trained or experienced ⟨~ recruits⟩ **5** : VULGAR, COARSE ⟨~ language⟩ **6** : disagreeably cold and damp ⟨a ~ day⟩ **7** : UNFAIR ⟨~ deal⟩ — **raw·ness** *n*

²**raw** *n* : a raw place or state — **in the raw** : NAKED

**raw-boned** \'rȯ-ˌbōnd\ *adj* : LEAN, GAUNT; *also* : having a heavy frame that seems to have little flesh

**raw·hide** \'rȯ-ˌhīd\ *n* : the untanned skin of cattle; *also* : a whip made of this

¹**ray** \'rā\ *n* : any of an order of large flat cartilaginous fishes that have the eyes on the upper surface and the hind end of the body slender and taillike

²**ray** *n* [ME, fr. AF *rai*, fr. L *radius* rod, ray] **1** : any of the lines of light that appear to radiate from a bright object **2** : a thin beam of radiant energy (as light) **3** : light from a beam **4** : a thin line like a beam of light **5** : an animal or plant structure resembling a ray **6** : a tiny bit : PARTICLE ⟨a ~ of hope⟩

**ray·on** \'rā-ˌän\ *n* : a fiber made from cellulose; *also* : a yarn, thread, or fabric made from such fibers

**raze** \'rāz\ *vb* **razed**; **raz·ing** **1** : to scrape, cut, or shave off **2** : to destroy to the ground : DEMOLISH

**ra·zor** \'rā-zər\ *n* : a sharp cutting instrument used to shave off hair

**ra·zor–backed** \'rā-zər-ˌbakt\ *or* **ra·zor·back** \-ˌbak\ *adj* : having a sharp narrow back ⟨a ~ horse⟩

**razor clam** *n* : any of a family of marine bivalve mollusks having a long narrow curved thin shell

**razor wire** *n* : coiled wire fitted with sharp edges and used as an obstacle or barrier

¹**razz** \'raz\ *n* : RASPBERRY 2

²**razz** *vb* : RIDICULE, TEASE ⟨fans ~ed visiting players⟩

**Rb** *symbol* rubidium

**RBC** *abbr* red blood cells

**RBI** \ˌär-(ˌ)bē-'ī, 'ri-bē\ *n, pl* **RBIs** *or* **RBI** [*run batted in*] : a run in baseball that is driven in by a batter

**RC** *abbr* **1** Red Cross **2** Roman Catholic

**RCAF** *abbr* Royal Canadian Air Force

**RCMP** *abbr* Royal Canadian Mounted Police

**RCN** *abbr* Royal Canadian Navy

**rct** *abbr* recruit

**rd** *abbr* **1** road **2** round

**RD** *abbr* rural delivery

**RDA** *abbr* recommended daily allowance; recommended dietary allowance

**re** \'rā, 'rē\ *prep* : with regard to

**Re** *symbol* rhenium

**re-** \rē, ˌrē, 'rē\ *prefix* **1** : again : for a second time **2** : anew : in a new or different form **3** : back : backward

¹**reach** \'rēch\ *vb* **1** : to stretch out **2** : to touch or attempt to touch or seize **3** : to extend to **4** : to communicate with **5** : to arrive at ♦ *Synonyms* GAIN, REALIZE, ACHIEVE, ATTAIN — **reach·able** *adj* — **reach·er** *n*

²**reach** *n* **1** : an unbroken stretch of a river **2** : the act of reaching **3** : a reachable distance; *also* : ability to reach **4** : a range of knowledge or comprehension

**re·act** \rē-'akt\ *vb* **1** : to exert a return or counteracting influence **2** : to have or show a reaction **3** : to act in opposition to a force or influence **4** : to move or tend in a reverse direction **5** : to undergo chemical reaction

**re·ac·tant** \rē-'ak-tənt\ *n* : a chemically reacting substance

**re·ac·tion** \rē-'ak-shən\ *n* **1** : the act or process of reacting **2** : a counter tendency; *esp* : a tendency toward a former esp. outmoded political or social order or policy **3** : bodily, mental, or emotional response to a stimulus **4** : chemical change **5** : a process involving change in atomic nuclei

**re·ac·tion·ary** \rē-'ak-shə-ˌner-ē\ *adj* : relating to, marked by, or favoring esp. political reaction — **reactionary** *n*

**re·ac·tive** \rē-'ak-tiv\ *adj* : reacting or tending to react ⟨a ~ chemical⟩

**re·ac·tor** \rē-'ak-tər\ *n* **1** : one that reacts **2** : a device for the controlled release of nuclear energy

¹**read** \'rēd\ *vb* **read** \'red\; **read·ing** [ME *reden* to advise, interpret, read, fr. OE *rǣdan*] **1** : to understand language by interpreting written symbols for speech sounds **2** : to utter aloud written or printed words **3** : to learn by observing ⟨~ nature's signs⟩ **4** : to study by a course of reading ⟨~s law⟩ **5** : to discover the meaning of ⟨~ the clues⟩ **6** : to recognize or interpret as if by reading **7** : to attribute (a meaning) to something ⟨~ guilt in his manner⟩ **8** : INDICATE ⟨thermometer ~s 10°⟩ **9** : to consist in phrasing or meaning ⟨the two versions

---

reabsorb　　　reacquire　　　reactivate　　　reactivation

~ differently⟩ — **read·abil·i·ty** \ˌrē-də-'bi-lə-tē\ n — **read·able** \'rē-də-bəl\ adj — **read·ably** \-blē\ adv — **read·er** n

²**read** \'red\ adj : informed by reading ⟨widely ~⟩

**read·er·ship** \'rē-dər-ˌship\ n : the mass or a particular group of readers

**read·ing** n 1 : something read or for reading 2 : a particular version 3 : data indicated by an instrument ⟨thermometer ~⟩ 4 : a particular interpretation (as of a law) 5 : a particular performance (as of a musical work) 6 : an indication of a certain state of affairs

**read–only memory** n : ROM

**read·out** \'rēd-ˌaut\ n 1 : the process of removing information from an automatic device (as a computer) and displaying it in an understandable form; also : the information removed from such a device 2 : an electronic device that presents information in visual form

**read out** vb 1 : to read aloud 2 : to expel from an organization

¹**ready** \'re-dē\ adj **read·i·er; -est** 1 : prepared for use or action 2 : likely to do something indicated; also : willingly disposed : INCLINED 3 : spontaneously prompt ⟨her ~ wit⟩ 4 : immediately available ⟨~ cash⟩ — **read·i·ly** \'re-də-lē\ adv — **read·i·ness** \-dē-nəs\ n — **at the ready** : ready for immediate use

²**ready** vb **read·ied; ready·ing** : to make ready : PREPARE

**ready–made** \ˌre-dē-'mād\ adj : already made up for general sale : not specially made — **ready–made** n

**ready room** n : a room in which pilots are briefed and await orders

**re·agent** \rē-'ā-jənt\ n : a substance that takes part in or brings about a particular chemical reaction

¹**re·al** \'rēl\ adj [ME, real, relating to things (in law), fr. AF, fr. ML & LL; ML *realis* relating to things (in law), fr. LL, real, fr. L *res* thing, fact] 1 : of or relating to fixed or immovable things (as land) ⟨~ property⟩ 2 : not artificial : GENUINE; also : not imaginary — **re·al·ness** n — **for real** 1 : in earnest 2 : GENUINE ⟨the threat was *for real*⟩

²**real** adv : VERY ⟨had a ~ good time⟩

³**re·al** \rā-'äl\ n — see MONEY table

**real estate** n : property in buildings and land

**re·al·ism** \'rē-ə-ˌli-zəm\ n 1 : the disposition to face facts and to deal with them practically 2 : true and faithful portrayal of nature and of people in art or literature — **re·al·ist** \-list\ adj or n — **re·al·is·tic** \ˌrē-ə-'lis-tik\ adj — **re·al·is·ti·cal·ly** \-ti-k(ə-)lē\ adv

**re·al·i·ty** \rē-'a-lə-tē\ n, pl **-ties** 1 : the quality or state of being real 2 : something real 3 : the totality of real things and events

**re·al·ize** \'rē-ə-ˌlīz\ vb **-ized; -iz·ing** 1 : to make actual : ACCOMPLISH 2 : to convert into money ⟨~ assets⟩ 3 : OBTAIN, GAIN ⟨~ a profit⟩ 4 : to be aware of : UNDERSTAND — **re·al·iz·able** adj — **re·al·i·za·tion** \ˌrē-ə-lə-'zā-shən\ n

**re·al·ly** \'rē-lē, 'ri-\ adv : in truth : in fact : ACTUALLY

**realm** \'relm\ n 1 : KINGDOM 2 : SPHERE, DOMAIN ⟨within the ~ of possibility⟩

**real number** n : a number that has no imaginary part ⟨the set of all *real numbers* comprises the rationals and the irrationals⟩

**re·al·po·li·tik** \rā-'äl-ˌpō-li-ˌtēk\ n, often cap [G] : politics based on practical and material factors rather than on theoretical or ethical objectives

**real time** n : the actual time during which something takes place — **real–time** adj

¹**ream** \'rēm\ n [ME *reme*, fr. AF, ultim. fr. Ar *rizma*, lit., bundle] : a quantity of paper that is variously 480, 500, or 516 sheets

²**ream** vb : to enlarge, shape, or clear with a reamer

**ream·er** \'rē-mər\ n : a tool with cutting edges that is used to enlarge or shape a hole

**reap** \'rēp\ vb 1 : to cut or clear with a scythe, sickle, or machine 2 : to gather by or as if by cutting : HARVEST ⟨~ a reward⟩ — **reap·er** n

¹**rear** \'rir\ vb 1 : to erect by building 2 : to set or raise upright 3 : to breed and raise for use or market ⟨~ livestock⟩ 4 : BRING UP, FOSTER 5 : to lift or rise up; esp : to rise on the hind legs

²**rear** n 1 : the unit (as of an army) or area farthest from the enemy 2 : BACK; also : the position at the back of something

³**rear** adj : being at the back

**rear admiral** n : a commissioned officer in the navy or coast guard ranking next below a vice admiral

¹**rear·ward** \'rir-wərd\ adj 1 : being at or toward the rear 2 : directed toward the rear ⟨a ~ glance⟩

²**rear·ward** also **rear·wards** \-wərdz\ adv : at or toward the rear ⟨looking ~⟩

**reas** abbr : reasonable

¹**rea·son** \'rē-zᵊn\ n [ME *resoun*, fr. AF *raisun*, fr. L *ration-, ratio* reason, computation] 1 : a statement offered in explanation or justification 2 : GROUND, CAUSE 3 : the power to think : INTELLECT 4 : a sane or sound mind 5 : due exercise of the faculty of logical thought

²**reason** vb 1 : to talk with another to

| | | | |
|---|---|---|---|
| readdress | reallocate | reappearance | rearm |
| readjust | reallocation | reapplication | rearmament |
| readjustment | reanalysis | reapply | rearouse |
| readmission | reanalyze | reappoint | rearrange |
| readmit | reanimate | reappointment | rearrangement |
| reaffirm | reanimation | reapportion | rearrest |
| reaffirmation | reannex | reapportionment | reascend |
| realign | reannexation | reappraisal | |
| realignment | reappear | reappraise | |

cause a change of mind **2** : to use the faculty of reason : THINK **3** : to discover or formulate by the use of reason — **rea·son·er** *n* — **rea·son·ing** *n*

**rea·son·able** \'rē-z°n-ə-bəl\ *adj* **1** : being within the bounds of reason : not extreme **2** : INEXPENSIVE **3** : able to reason : RATIONAL — **rea·son·able·ness** *n* — **rea·son·ably** \-blē\ *adv*

**re·as·sure** \ˌrē-ə-'shu̇r\ *vb* **1** : to assure again **2** : to restore confidence to : free from fear — **re·as·sur·ance** \-'shu̇r-əns\ *n* — **re·as·sur·ing·ly** *adv*

¹**re·bate** \'rē-ˌbāt\ *vb* **re·bat·ed; re·bat·ing** : to make or give a rebate

²**rebate** *n* : a return of part of a payment
♦ ***Synonyms*** DEDUCTION, ABATEMENT, DISCOUNT

¹**reb·el** \'re-bəl\ *adj* [ME, fr. AF, fr. L *re-bellis*, fr. *re-* + *bellum* war] : of or relating to rebels

²**rebel** *n* : one that rebels against authority

³**re·bel** \ri-'bel\ *vb* **re·belled; re·bel·ling 1** : to resist the authority of one's government **2** : to act in or show disobedience **3** : to feel or exhibit anger or revulsion

**re·bel·lion** \ri-'bel-yən\ *n* : resistance to authority; *esp* : defiance against a government through uprising or revolt

**re·bel·lious** \-yəs\ *adj* **1** : given to or engaged in rebellion **2** : inclined to resist authority — **re·bel·lious·ly** *adv* — **re·bel·lious·ness** *n*

**re·birth** \ˌrē-'bərth\ *n* **1** : a new or second birth **2** : RENAISSANCE, REVIVAL

**re·born** \-'bȯrn\ *adj* : born again : RE-GENERATED, REVIVED

¹**re·bound** \ˌrē-'bau̇nd, 'rē-ˌbau̇nd\ *vb* **1** : to spring back on or as if on striking another body **2** : to recover from a setback or frustration ⟨*~ed* quickly from the loss⟩

²**re·bound** \'rē-ˌbau̇nd\ *n* **1** : the action of rebounding **2** : a rebounding ball **3** : a reaction to setback or frustration

**re·buff** \ri-'bəf\ *vb* : to reject or criticize sharply : SNUB — **rebuff** *n*

**re·build** \ˌˌ)rē-'bild\ *vb* **-built** \-'bilt\; **-build·ing 1** : REPAIR, RECONSTRUCT; *also* : REMODEL **2** : to build again

¹**re·buke** \ri-'byük\ *vb* **re·buked; re·buk·ing** : to reprimand sharply : REPROVE

²**rebuke** *n* : a sharp reprimand

**re·bus** \'rē-bəs\ *n* [L, by things, abl. pl. of *res* thing] : a representation of syllables or words by means of pictures; *also* : a riddle composed of such pictures

**re·but** \ri-'bət\ *vb* **re·but·ted; re·but·ting** : to refute esp. formally (as in debate) by evidence and arguments ♦ ***Synonyms*** DISPROVE, CONTROVERT, CONFUTE — **re·but·ter** *n*

**re·but·tal** \ri-'bə-t°l\ *n* : the act of rebutting

**rec** *abbr* **1** receipt **2** record; recording **3** recreation

**re·cal·ci·trant** \ri-'kal-sə-trənt\ *adj* [LL *recalcitrant-, recalcitrans,* prp. of *recalcitrare* to be stubbornly disobedient, fr. L, to kick back, fr. *re-* back, again + *calcitrare* to kick, fr. *calc-, calx* heel] **1** : stubbornly resisting authority ⟨a *~* prisoner⟩ **2** : resistant to handling or treatment
♦ ***Synonyms*** REFRACTORY, HEAD-STRONG, WILLFUL, UNRULY, UNGOV-ERNABLE — **re·cal·ci·trance** \-trəns\ *n*

¹**re·call** \ri-'kȯl\ *vb* **1** : REVOKE, CANCEL **2** : to call back **3** : REMEMBER, RECOL-LECT ⟨*~ed* their last meeting⟩

²**re·call** \ri-'kȯl, 'rē-ˌkȯl\ *n* **1** : a summons to return **2** : the procedure of removing an official by popular vote **3** : remembrance of things learned or experienced **4** : the act of revoking **5** : a call by a manufacturer for the return of a product that may be defective or contaminated

**re·cant** \ri-'kant\ *vb* : to take back (something one has said) publicly : make an open confession of error — **re·can·ta·tion** \ˌrē-ˌkan-'tā-shən\ *n*

¹**re·cap** \'rē-ˌkap, rē-'kap\ *vb* **re·capped; re·cap·ping** : RECAPITULATE — **re·cap** \'rē-ˌkap\ *n*

²**recap** *vb* **re·capped; re·cap·ping** : RE-TREAD — **re·cap** \'rē-ˌkap\ *n*

**re·ca·pit·u·late** \ˌrē-kə-'pi-chə-ˌlāt\ *vb* **-lat·ed; -lat·ing** : to restate briefly : SUM-MARIZE ⟨*~* recent news stories⟩ — **re·ca·pit·u·la·tion** \-ˌpi-chə-'lā-shən\ *n*

**re·cap·ture** \ˌˌ)rē-'kap-chər\ *vb* **1** : to capture again **2** : to experience again ⟨*~* happy times⟩

**re·cast** \ˌ)rē-'kast\ *vb* **1** : to cast again **2** : REVISE, REMODEL ⟨*~* a sentence⟩

**recd** *abbr* received

**re·cede** \ri-'sēd\ *vb* **re·ced·ed; re·ced·ing 1** : to move back or away ⟨a *receding* hairline⟩ **2** : to slant backward **3** : DI-MINISH, CONTRACT ⟨a *receding* deficit⟩

¹**re·ceipt** \ri-'sēt\ *n* **1** : RECIPE **2** : the act of receiving **3** : something received — usu. used in pl. **4** : a written acknowledg-ment of something received

²**receipt** *vb* **1** : to give a receipt for **2** : to mark as paid

**re·ceiv·able** \ri-'sē-və-bəl\ *adj* **1** : capa-ble of being received; *esp* : acceptable as legal ⟨*~* certificates⟩ **2** : subject to call for payment ⟨notes *~*⟩

**re·ceive** \ri-'sēv\ *vb* **re·ceived; re·ceiv·ing 1** : to take in or accept (as something sent or paid) : come into possession of : GET **2** : CONTAIN, HOLD **3** : to permit to enter : GREET, WELCOME **4** : to be at home to visitors **5** : to accept as true or authoritative **6** : to be the subject of : UNDERGO, EXPERIENCE ⟨*~* a shock⟩ **7**

---

| | | | |
|---|---|---|---|
| reassemble | reassume | reawaken | reburial |
| reassembly | reattach | rebaptism | rebury |
| reassert | reattachment | rebaptize | recalculate |
| reassess | reattain | rebid | recalculation |
| reassessment | reattempt | rebind | |
| reassign | reauthorization | reboil | |
| reassignment | reauthorize | rebroadcast | |

: to change incoming radio waves into sounds or pictures ⟨∼ a broadcast⟩

**re·ceiv·er** \ri-'sē-vər\ *n* **1** : one that receives **2** : a person legally appointed to receive and have charge of property or money involved in a lawsuit **3** : a device for converting electromagnetic waves or signals into audio or visual form ⟨telephone ∼⟩

**re·ceiv·er·ship** \-,ship\ *n* **1** : the office or function of a receiver **2** : the condition of being in the hands of a receiver

**re·cen·cy** \'rē-s⁾n-sē\ *n* : RECENTNESS

**re·cent** \'rē-s⁾nt\ *adj* **1** : of the present time or time just past ⟨∼ history⟩ **2** : having lately come into existence : NEW, FRESH ⟨∼ buds⟩ **3** *cap* : HOLOCENE — **re·cent·ly** *adv* — **re·cent·ness** *n*

**re·cep·ta·cle** \ri-'sep-ti-kəl\ *n* **1** : something used to receive and hold something else : CONTAINER **2** : the enlarged end of a flower stalk upon which the parts of the flower grow **3** : an electrical fitting containing the live parts of a circuit

**re·cep·tion** \ri-'sep-shən\ *n* **1** : the act of receiving **2** : a social gathering at which guests are formally welcomed

**re·cep·tion·ist** \ri-'sep-shə-nist\ *n* : a person employed to greet callers

**re·cep·tive** \ri-'sep-tiv\ *adj* : able or inclined to receive; *esp* : open and responsive to ideas, impressions, or suggestions ⟨a ∼ audience⟩ — **re·cep·tive·ly** *adv* — **re·cep·tive·ness** *n* — **re·cep·tiv·i·ty** \,rē-,sep-'ti-və-tē\ *n*

**re·cep·tor** \ri-'sep-tər\ *n* **1** : one that receives stimuli : SENSE ORGAN **2** : a chemical group or molecule in the outer cell membrane or in the cell interior that has an affinity for a specific chemical group, molecule, or virus

**¹re·cess** \'rē-,ses, ri-'ses\ *n* **1** : a secret or secluded place **2** : an indentation in a line or surface (as an alcove in a room) **3** : a suspension of business or procedure for rest or relaxation

**²recess** *vb* **1** : to put into a recess **2** : to make a recess in **3** : to interrupt for a recess **4** : to take a recess

**re·ces·sion** \ri-'se-shən\ *n* **1** : the act of receding : WITHDRAWAL **2** : a departing procession (as at the end of a church service) **3** : a period of reduced economic activity

**re·ces·sion·al** \ri-'se-shə-nəl\ *n* **1** : a hymn or musical piece at the conclusion of a service or program **2** : RECESSION 2

**¹re·ces·sive** \ri-'se-siv\ *adj* **1** : tending to recede **2** : producing or being a bodily characteristic that is masked or not expressed when a contrasting dominant gene or trait is present ⟨∼ genes⟩ ⟨∼ traits⟩

**²recessive** *n* : a recessive characteristic or gene; *also* : an individual that has one or more recessive characteristics

**re·cher·ché** \rə-,sher-'shā, -'sher-,shā\ *adj* [F] **1** : CHOICE, RARE **2** : excessively refined ⟨∼ poetry⟩

**re·cid·i·vism** \ri-'si-də-,vi-zəm\ *n* : a ten-

dency to relapse into a previous condition; *esp* : relapse into criminal behavior — **re·cid·i·vist** \-vist\ *n*

**rec·i·pe** \'re-sə-(,)pē\ *n* [L, take, imperative of *recipere* to take, receive, fr. *re-* back + *capere* to take] **1** : a set of instructions for making something from various ingredients **2** : a method of procedure : FORMULA

**re·cip·i·ent** \ri-'si-pē-ənt\ *n* : one that receives

**¹re·cip·ro·cal** \ri-'si-prə-kəl\ *adj* **1** : inversely related **2** : MUTUAL, SHARED **3** : serving to reciprocate **4** : mutually corresponding — **re·cip·ro·cal·ly** *adv*

**²reciprocal** *n* **1** : something in a reciprocal relationship to another **2** : one of a pair of numbers (as ²⁄₃ and ³⁄₂) whose product is one

**re·cip·ro·cate** \ri-'si-prə-,kāt\ *vb* **-cat·ed; -cat·ing 1** : to move backward and forward alternately **2** : to give and take mutually **3** : to make a return for something done or given — **re·cip·ro·ca·tion** \-,si-prə-'kā-shən\ *n*

**rec·i·proc·i·ty** \,re-sə-'prä-sə-tē\ *n, pl* **-ties 1** : the quality or state of being reciprocal **2** : mutual exchange of privileges (as trade advantages between countries)

**re·cit·al** \ri-'sī-t⁾l\ *n* **1** : an act or instance of reciting : ACCOUNT **2** : a public reading or recitation ⟨a poetry ∼⟩ **3** : a concert given by a musician, dancer, or dance troupe **4** : a public exhibition of skill given by music or dance pupils — **re·cit·al·ist** \-t⁾l-ist\ *n*

**rec·i·ta·tion** \,re-sə-'tā-shən\ *n* **1** : RECITING, RECITAL **2** : delivery before an audience usu. of something memorized ⟨∼ of a poem⟩ **3** : a classroom exercise in which pupils answer questions on a lesson they have studied

**re·cite** \ri-'sīt\ *vb* **re·cit·ed; re·cit·ing 1** : to repeat verbatim (as something memorized) **2** : to recount in some detail : RELATE **3** : to reply to a teacher's questions on a lesson — **re·cit·er** *n*

**reck·less** \'re-kləs\ *adj* : lacking caution ⟨a ∼ driver⟩ ♦ *Synonyms* HASTY, BRASH, HOTHEADED, THOUGHTLESS — **reck·less·ly** *adv* — **reck·less·ness** *n*

**reck·on** \'re-kən\ *vb* **1** : COUNT, CALCULATE, COMPUTE **2** : CONSIDER, REGARD ⟨was ∼ed as the leader⟩ **3** *chiefly dial* : THINK, SUPPOSE, GUESS

**reck·on·ing** *n* **1** : an act or instance of reckoning **2** : a settling of accounts ⟨day of ∼⟩

**re·claim** \ri-'klām\ *vb* **1** : to recall from wrong conduct : REFORM **2** : to change from an undesirable to a desired condition ⟨∼ marshy land⟩ **3** : to obtain from a waste product or by-product ⟨∼ed plastic⟩ **4** : to demand or obtain the return of — **re·claim·able** *adj* — **rec·la·ma·tion** \,re-klə-'mā-shən\ *n*

**re·cline** \ri-'klīn\ *vb* **re·clined; re·clin-**

| | | | |
|---|---|---|---|
| rechannel | rechargeable | recheck | reclassification |
| recharge | recharter | rechristen | reclassify |

**ing 1** : to lean or incline backward **2** : to lie down : REST

**re·clin·er** \ri-ˈklī-nər\ *n* : a chair with an adjustable back and footrest

**re·cluse** \ˈre-ˌklüs, ri-ˈklüs\ *n* : a person who leads a secluded or solitary life : HERMIT — **re·clu·sive** \ri-ˈklü-siv\ *adj*

**rec·og·nise** *chiefly Brit var of* RECOGNIZE

**rec·og·ni·tion** \ˌre-kəg-ˈni-shən\ *n* **1** : the act of recognizing : the state of being recognized : ACKNOWLEDGMENT ⟨in ∼ of their achievements⟩ **2** : special notice or attention

**re·cog·ni·zance** \ri-ˈkäg-nə-zəns\ *n* : a promise recorded before a court or magistrate to do something (as to appear in court or to keep the peace) usu. under penalty of a money forfeiture

**rec·og·nize** \ˈre-kəg-ˌnīz\ *vb* **-nized; -niz·ing 1** : to acknowledge (as a speaker in a meeting) as one entitled to be heard at the time **2** : to acknowledge the existence or the independence of (a country or government) **3** : to take notice of **4** : to acknowledge with appreciation **5** : to acknowledge acquaintance with **6** : to identify as previously known **7** : to perceive clearly : REALIZE — **rec·og·niz·able** \ˈre-kəg-ˌnī-zə-bəl\ *adj* — **rec·og·niz·ably** \-blē\ *adv*

¹**re·coil** \ri-ˈkȯi(-ə)l\ *vb* [ME *reculen, recoilen,* fr. AF *reculer, reculier,* fr. *re-* back + *cul* backside, fr. L *culus*] **1** : to draw back : RETREAT **2** : to spring back to or as if to a starting point ♦ *Synonyms* SHRINK, FLINCH, WINCE, QUAIL, BLENCH

²**re·coil** \ˈrē-ˌkȯi(-ə)l, ri-ˈkȯil\ *n* : the action of recoiling (as of a gun or spring)

**re·coil·less** \-ˌkȯi(-ə)l-ləs, -ˈkȯi(-ə)l-\ *adj* : venting expanding propellant gas before recoil is produced ⟨∼ gun⟩

**rec·ol·lect** \ˌre-kə-ˈlekt\ *vb* : to recall to mind : REMEMBER ♦ *Synonyms* RECALL, REMIND, REMINISCE, BETHINK

**rec·ol·lec·tion** \ˌre-kə-ˈlek-shən\ *n* **1** : the act or power of recollecting **2** : something recollected

**re·com·bi·nant** \(ˌ)rē-ˈkäm-bə-nənt\ *adj* **1** : relating to genetic recombination **2** : containing or produced by recombinant DNA ⟨∼ vaccines⟩

**recombinant DNA** *n* : genetically engineered DNA prepared in vitro by joining together DNA usu. from more than one species of organism

**re·com·bi·na·tion** \ˌrē-ˌkäm-bə-ˈnā-shən\ *n* : the formation of new combinations of genes

**rec·om·mend** \ˌre-kə-ˈmend\ *vb* **1** : to present as deserving of acceptance or trial **2** : to give in charge : COMMIT **3** : to make acceptable **4** : ADVISE, COUNSEL

— **rec·om·mend·able** \-ˈmen-də-bəl\ *adj*

**rec·om·men·da·tion** \ˌre-kə-mən-ˈdā-shən\ *n* **1** : the act of recommending **2** : something recommended **3** : something that recommends

¹**rec·om·pense** \ˈre-kəm-ˌpens\ *vb* **-pensed; -pens·ing 1** : to give compensation to : pay for ⟨was *recompensed* for their losses⟩ **2** : to return in kind : REQUITE ♦ *Synonyms* REIMBURSE, INDEMNIFY, REPAY, COMPENSATE

²**recompense** *n* : COMPENSATION

**rec·on·cile** \ˈre-kən-ˌsī(-ə)l\ *vb* **-ciled; -cil·ing 1** : to cause to be friendly or harmonious again **2** : ADJUST, SETTLE ⟨∼ differences⟩ **3** : to bring to submission or acceptance ♦ *Synonyms* CONFORM, ACCOMMODATE, HARMONIZE, COORDINATE — **rec·on·cil·able** *adj* — **rec·on·cile·ment** *n* — **rec·on·cil·er** *n*

**rec·on·cil·i·a·tion** \ˌre-kən-ˌsi-lē-ˈā-shən\ *n* **1** : the action of reconciling **2** : the Roman Catholic sacrament of penance

**re·con·dite** \ˈre-kən-ˌdīt\ *adj* **1** : hard to understand : ABSTRUSE ⟨∼ terminology⟩ **2** : little known : OBSCURE

**re·con·di·tion** \ˌre-kən-ˈdi-shən\ *vb* **1** : to restore to good condition (as by replacing parts) **2** : to condition anew

**re·con·nais·sance** \ri-ˈkä-nə-zəns, -səns\ *n* [F, lit., recognition] : a preliminary survey of an area; *esp* : an exploratory military survey of enemy territory

**re·con·noi·ter** *or* **re·con·noi·tre** \ˌrē-kə-ˈnȯi-tər, ˌre-\ *vb* **-noi·tered** *or* **-noi·tred; -noi·ter·ing** *or* **-noi·tring** : to make a reconnaissance of : engage in reconnaissance ⟨∼ed to locate enemy positions⟩

**re·con·sid·er** \ˌrē-kən-ˈsi-dər\ *vb* : to consider again with a view to changing or reversing ⟨∼ed his decision⟩ — **re·con·sid·er·a·tion** \-ˌsi-də-ˈrā-shən\ *n*

**re·con·sti·tute** \ˌrē-ˈkän-stə-ˌtüt, -ˌtyüt\ *vb* : to restore to a former condition by adding water ⟨∼ powdered milk⟩

**re·con·struct** \ˌrē-kən-ˈstrəkt\ *vb* : to construct again : REBUILD

**re·con·struc·tion** \ˌrē-kən-ˈstrək-shən\ *n* **1** : the action of reconstructing : the state of being reconstructed **2** *often cap* : the reorganization and reestablishment of the seceded states in the Union after the American Civil War **3** : something reconstructed

¹**re·cord** \ri-ˈkȯrd\ *vb* [ME, lit., to recall, fr. AF *recorder,* fr. L *recordari,* fr. *re-* back, again + *cord-, cors* heart] **1** : to set down in writing ⟨∼ed her observations⟩ **2** : to register permanently **3** : INDICATE, READ **4** : to give evidence of **5** : to cause (as sound or visual images) to be registered

| | | | |
|---|---|---|---|
| recoin | recompile | recondense | recontact |
| recolonization | recompose | reconfirm | recontaminate |
| recolonize | recomputation | reconfirmation | recontamination |
| recolor | recompute | reconnect | reconvene |
| recombine | reconceive | reconquer | reconvert |
| recommence | reconcentrate | reconquest | recook |
| recommission | reconception | reconsecrate | recopy |
| recommit | recondensation | reconsecration | |

(as on a disc or a magnetic tape) in a form that permits reproduction

²**rec·ord** \'re-kərd\ *n* **1** : the act of being recorded **2** : a written account of proceedings **3** : known facts about a person; *also* : a collection of items of information (as in a database) treated as a unit **4** : an attested top performance **5** : something on which sound or visual images have been recorded

³**re·cord** \ri-'kȯrd\ *n* : a function of an electronic device that causes it to record

**re·cord·er** \ri-'kȯr-dər\ *n* **1** : a judge in some city courts **2** : one who records transactions officially **3** : a recording device **4** : a wind instrument with a whistle mouthpiece and eight fingerholes

**ro·cord·ing** *n* : RECORD.5

**re·cord·ist** \ri-'kȯr-dist\ *n* : one who records sound esp. on film

¹**re·count** \ri-'kaunt\ *vb* : to relate in detail : TELL   ♦ **Synonyms** RECITE, REHEARSE, NARRATE, DESCRIBE, STATE, REPORT

²**re·count** \'rē-,kaunt, (,)rē-'kaunt\ *vb* : to count again

³**re·count** \'rē-,kaunt, (,)rē-'kaunt\ *n* : a second or fresh count

**re·coup** \ri-'küp\ *vb* : to get an equivalent or compensation for : make up for something lost ⟨*~ed* their costs⟩

**re·course** \'rē-,kȯrs, ri-'kȯrs\ *n* **1** : a turning to someone or something for assistance or protection : a source of aid : RESORT

**re·cov·er** \ri-'kə-vər\ *vb* **1** : to get back again : REGAIN, RETRIEVE **2** : to regain normal health, poise, or status **3** : to make up for : RECOUP ⟨*~ed* all his losses⟩ **4** : RECLAIM ⟨*~* land from the sea⟩ **5** : to obtain a legal judgment in one's favor — **re·cov·er·able** *adj*

**re–cov·er** \,rē-'kə-vər\ *vb* : to cover again

**recovering** *adj* : being in the process of overcoming a shortcoming or problem ⟨a *~* alcoholic⟩

**re·cov·ery** \ri-'kə-və-rē\ *n* **1** : an act or instance of recovering; *esp* : an economic upturn **2** : the process of combating a disorder or problem

¹**rec·re·ant** \'re-krē-ənt\ *adj* [ME, fr. AF, fr. prp. of (se) *recreire* to give up, yield, fr. ML (se) *recredere* to resign oneself (to a judgment), fr. L *re-* back + *credere* to believe] **1** : COWARDLY **2** : UNFAITHFUL ⟨were *~* to their duties⟩

²**recreant** *n* **1** : COWARD **2** : DESERTER

**rec·re·ate** \'re-krē-,āt\ *vb* **-at·ed; -at·ing** **1** : to give new life or freshness to **2** : to take recreation ⟨*recreated* at the beach⟩ — **rec·re·ative** \-,ā-tiv\ *adj*

**re–cre·ate** \,rē-krē-'āt\ *vb* : to create again ⟨*re-created* the battle scene⟩ — **re–cre·ation** \-'ā-shən\ *n* — **re–cre·ative** \-'ā-tiv\ *adj*

**rec·re·ation** \,re-krē-'ā-shən\ *n* : a refreshing of strength or spirits after work; *also* : a means of refreshment  ♦ **Synonyms** DIVERSION, ENTERTAINMENT, AMUSEMENT — **rec·re·ation·al** \-shə-nəl\ *adj*

**recreational vehicle** *n* : a vehicle designed for recreational use (as camping)

**re·crim·i·na·tion** \ri-,kri-mə-'nā-shən\ *n* : a retaliatory accusation — **re·crim·i·nate** \-'kri-mə-,nāt\ *vb* — **re·crim·i·na·tory** \-'kri-mə-nə-,tȯr-ē\ *adj*

**re·cru·des·cence** \,rē-krü-'de-sᵊns\ *n* : a renewal or breaking out again esp. of something unhealthful or dangerous

¹**re·cruit** \ri-'krüt\ *vb* **1** : to form or strengthen with new members ⟨*~* an army⟩ **2** : to enlist as a member of an armed service **3** : to secure the services of **4** : to seek to enroll **5** : to restore or increase in health or vigor ⟨resting to *~* his strength⟩ — **re·cruit·er** *n* — **re·cruit·ment** *n*

²**recruit** *n* [F *recrute, recrue* fresh growth, new levy of soldiers, fr. MF, fr. *recroistre* to grow up again, fr. L *recrescere*] : a newcomer to an activity or field; *esp* : a newly enlisted member of the armed forces

**rec·tal** \'rek-tᵊl\ *adj* : of or relating to the rectum — **rec·tal·ly** *adv*

**rect·an·gle** \'rek-,taŋ-gəl\ *n* : a 4-sided figure with four right angles; *esp* : one with adjacent sides of unequal length — **rect·an·gu·lar** \rek-'taŋ-gyə-lər\ *adj*

**rec·ti·fi·er** \'rek-tə-,fī-(ə)r\ *n* : one that rectifies; *esp* : a device for converting alternating current into direct current

**rec·ti·fy** \'rek-tə-,fī\ *vb* **-fied; -fy·ing** : to make or set right : CORRECT  ♦ **Synonyms** EMEND, AMEND, MEND, RIGHT — **rec·ti·fi·ca·tion** \,rek-tə-fə-'kā-shən\ *n*

**rec·ti·lin·ear** \,rek-tə-'li-nē-ər\ *adj* **1** : moving in a straight line ⟨*~* motion⟩ **2** : characterized by straight lines

**rec·ti·tude** \'rek-tə-,tüd, -,tyüd\ *n* **1** : moral integrity **2** : correctness of procedure  ♦ **Synonyms** VIRTUE, GOODNESS, MORALITY, PROBITY

**rec·to** \'rek-tō\ *n, pl* **rectos** : a right-hand page

**rec·tor** \'rek-tər\ *n* **1** : a priest or minister in charge of a parish **2** : the head of a university or school — **rec·to·ri·al** \rek-'tȯr-ē-əl\ *adj*

**rec·to·ry** \'rek-tə-rē\ *n, pl* **-ries** : the residence of a rector or a parish priest

**rec·tum** \'rek-təm\ *n, pl* **rectums** or **rec·ta** \-tə\ [ME, fr. ML, fr. *rectum intestinum*, lit., straight intestine] : the last part of the intestine joining the colon and anus

**re·cum·bent** \ri-'kəm-bənt\ *adj* : lying down : RECLINING

**re·cu·per·ate** \ri-'kü-pə-,rāt-, -'kyü-\ *vb* **-at·ed; -at·ing** : to get back (as health or strength) : RECOVER — **re·cu·per·a·tion** \-,kü-pə-'rā-shən, -,kyü-\ *n* — **re·cu·per·a·tive** \-'kü-pə-,rā-tiv, -'kyü-\ *adj*

**re·cur** \ri-'kər\ *vb* **re·curred; re·cur·ring** **1** : to go or come back in thought or discussion **2** : to occur or appear again esp. after an interval : occur time after time ⟨*recurring* headaches⟩ — **re·cur·rence** \-'kər-əns\ *n* — **re·cur·rent** \-ənt\ *adj*

---

**recross**       **recrystallize**       **recut**

**re·cy·cle** \rē-'sī-kəl\ vb **1** : to pass again through a cycle of changes or treatment **2** : to process (as liquid body waste, glass, or cans) in order to regain materials for human use — **re·cy·cla·bil·i·ty** \-,sī-klə-'bil-ə-tē\ n — **re·cy·cla·ble** \-k(ə)lə-bəl\ adj — **recycle** n

¹**red** \'red\ adj **red·der; red·dest** **1** : of the color red **2** : endorsing radical social or political change esp. by force **3** often cap : of or relating to the former U.S.S.R. or its allies **4** : tending to support Republican candidates ⟨∼ states⟩ — **red·ly** adv — **red·ness** n

²**red** n **1** : the color of blood or of the ruby **2** : a revolutionary in politics **3** cap : COMMUNIST **4** : the condition of showing a loss ⟨in the ∼⟩

**re·dact** \ri-'dakt\ vb **1** : to put in writing : FRAME ⟨∼ed the proclamation⟩ **2** : EDIT — **re·dac·tor** \-'dak-tər\ n

**re·dac·tion** \-'dak-shən\ n **1** : an act or instance of redacting **2** : EDITION

**red alga** n : any of a group of reddish usu. marine algae

**red blood cell** n : any of the hemoglobin-containing cells that carry oxygen from the lungs to the tissues and are responsible for the red color of vertebrate blood

**red·breast** \'red-,brest\ n : ROBIN

**red–carpet** adj : marked by ceremonial courtesy ⟨was given the ∼ treatment⟩

**red cedar** n : an American juniper with scalelike leaves and fragrant close-grained red wood; also : its wood

**red clover** n : a European clover that has globe-shaped heads of reddish flowers and is widely cultivated for hay and forage

**red·coat** \'red-,kōt\ n : a British soldier esp. during the Revolutionary War

**red·den** \'re-d²n\ vb : to make or become red or reddish : FLUSH, BLUSH

**red·dish** \'re-dish\ adj : tinged with red — **red·dish·ness** n

**red dwarf** n : a star with lower temperature and less mass than the sun

**re·deem** \ri-'dēm\ vb [ME redemen, fr. AF redemer, modif. of L redimere, fr. re-, red- back, again + emere to take, buy] **1** : to recover (property) by discharging an obligation **2** : to ransom, free, or rescue by paying a price **3** : to free from the consequences of sin **4** : to remove the obligation of by payment ⟨the government ∼s savings bonds⟩; also : to convert into something of value **5** : to make good (a promise) by performing : FULFILL **6** : to atone for — **re·deem·able** adj — **re·deem·er** n

**re·demp·tion** \ri-'demp-shən\ n : the act of redeeming : the state of being redeemed — **re·demp·tive** \-tiv\ adj — **re·demp·to·ry** \-tə-rē\ adj

**re·de·ploy** \,rē-di-'ploi\ vb **1** : to transfer from one area or activity to another **2** : to relocate men or equipment — **re·de·ploy·ment** n

**red–eye** \'red-,ī\ n **1** : cheap whiskey **2** : a late night or overnight flight

**red·fish** \'red-,fish\ n : any of various reddish marine fishes of the Atlantic including some used for food

**red fox** n : a fox with orange-red to reddish brown fur

**red giant** n : a very large star with a relatively low surface temperature

**red–hand·ed** \'red-'han-dəd\ adv or adj : in the act of committing a misdeed

**red·head** \-,hed\ n : a person having red hair — **red·head·ed** \-,he-dəd\ adj

**red herring** n : a diversion intended to distract attention from the real issue

**red–hot** \'red-'hät\ adj **1** : extremely hot; esp : glowing with heat **2** : EXCITED, FURIOUS **3** : very new ⟨∼ news⟩

**re·dial** \'rē-,dī(-ə)l\ n : a telephone function that automatically repeats the dialing of the last number called — **redial** vb

**re·dis·trib·ute** \,rē-də-'stri-byüt\ vb **1** : to alter the distribution of **2** : to spread to other areas — **re·dis·tri·bu·tion** \(,)rē-,dis-trə-'byü-shən\ n

**re·dis·trict** \,rē-'dis-(,)trikt\ vb : to organize into new territorial and esp. political divisions

**red–let·ter** \'red-,le-tər\ adj : of special significance : MEMORABLE ⟨a ∼ day⟩

**red–light** adj : having many houses of prostitution ⟨a ∼district⟩

**re·do** \(,)rē-'dü\ vb : to do over or again; esp : REDECORATE

**red oak** n : any of various No. American oaks with leaves usu. having spiny-tipped lobes and acorns that take two years to mature; also : the wood of a red oak

**re·do·lent** \'re-də-lənt\ adj **1** : FRAGRANT, AROMATIC **2** : having a specified fragrance ⟨a room ∼ of cooked cabbage⟩ **3** : REMINISCENT, SUGGESTIVE ⟨a tavern ∼ of colonial times⟩ — **red·o·lence** \-ləns\ n — **red·o·lent·ly** adv

**re·dou·ble** \(,)rē-'də-bəl\ vb : to make twice as great in size or amount; also : INTENSIFY

**re·doubt** \ri-'daut\ n [F redoute, fr. It ridotto, fr. ML reductus secret place, fr. L, withdrawn, fr. reducere to lead back, fr. re- back + ducere to lead] : a small usu. temporary fortification

**re·doubt·able** \ri-'daù-tə-bəl\ adj [ME redoutable, fr. AF, fr. reduter to dread, fr. re- back, again + duter to doubt] : arousing dread or fear : FORMIDABLE

**re·dound** \ri-'daund\ vb **1** : to have an effect ⟨the change may ∼ to her benefit⟩ **2** : to become added or transferred : ACCRUE

**red pepper** n **1** : CAYENNE PEPPER **2** : a mature red hot pepper or sweet pepper

---

¹**re·dress** \ri-'dres\ vb **1** : to set right : REMEDY ⟨~ injustice⟩ **2** : COMPENSATE **3** : to remove the cause of (a grievance) **4** : AVENGE

²**re·dress** n **1** : relief from distress **2** : means or possibility of seeking a remedy **3** : compensation for loss or injury **4** : an act or instance of redressing

**red·shift** \'red-'shift\ n : displacement of the spectrum of a heavenly body toward longer wavelengths; also : a measure of this displacement

**red snapper** n : any of various reddish fishes including several food fishes

**red spider** n : SPIDER MITE

**red squirrel** n : a common No. American squirrel with the upper parts chiefly red

**red–tailed hawk** \'red-,tāld-\ n : a rodent-eating No. American hawk with a rather short typically reddish tail

**red tape** n [fr. the red tape formerly used to bind legal documents in England] : official routine or procedure marked by excessive complexity which results in delay or inaction

**red tide** n : seawater discolored by the presence of large numbers of dinoflagellates which produce a toxin that renders infected shellfish poisonous

**re·duce** \ri-'düs, -'dyüs\ vb **re·duced; re·duc·ing** **1** : LESSEN **2** : to bring to a specified state or condition ⟨reduced them to tears⟩ **3** : to put in a lower rank or grade **4** : CONQUER ⟨~ a fort⟩ **5** : to bring into a certain order or classification **6** : to correct (as a fracture) by restoration of displaced parts **7** : to lessen one's weight ◆ *Synonyms* DECREASE, DIMINISH, ABATE, DWINDLE, RECEDE — **re·duc·er** n — **re·duc·ible** \-'dü-sə-bəl, -'dyü-\ adj

**re·duc·tion** \ri-'dək-shən\ n **1** : the act of reducing : the state of being reduced **2** : something made by reducing **3** : the amount taken off in reducing something

**re·dun·dan·cy** \ri-'dən-dən-sē\ n, pl **-cies** **1** : the quality or state of being redundant : SUPERFLUITY **2** : something redundant or in excess **3** : the use of surplus words

**re·dun·dant** \-dənt\ adj **1** : exceeding what is needed or normal : SUPERFLUOUS; esp : using more words than necessary **2** : marked by repetition — **re·dun·dant·ly** adv

**red–winged blackbird** \'red-,wiŋd-\ n : a No. American blackbird of which the adult male is black with a patch of bright scarlet on the wings

**red·wood** \'red-,wud\ n : a tall coniferous timber tree esp. of coastal California; also : its durable wood

**reed** \'rēd\ n **1** : any of various tall slender grasses of wet areas; also : a stem or growth of reed **2** : a musical instrument made from the hollow stem of a reed **3** : an elastic tongue of cane, wood, or metal by which tones are produced in organ pipes and certain other wind instruments — **reedy** adj

**re·ed·u·cate** \(,)rē-'e-jə-,kāt\ vb : to train again; esp : to rehabilitate through education — **re·ed·u·ca·tion** n

¹**reef** \'rēf\ n **1** : a part of a sail taken in or let out in regulating the sail's size **2** : reduction in sail area by reefing

²**reef** vb : to reduce the area of a sail by rolling or folding part of it

³**reef** n : a ridge of rocks, sand or coral at or near the surface of the water

**reef·er** \'rē-fər\ n : a marijuana cigarette

¹**reek** \'rēk\ n : a strong or disagreeable fume or odor

²**reek** vb **1** : to give off or become permeated with a strong or offensive odor **2** : to give a strong impression of some constituent quality ⟨an excuse that ~ed of falsehood⟩ — **reek·er** n — **reeky** \'rē-kē\ adj

¹**reel** \'rēl\ n : a revolvable device on which something flexible (as film or tape) is wound; also : a quantity of something wound on such a device

²**reel** vb **1** : to wind on or as if on a reel **2** : to pull or draw (as a fish) by reeling a line — **reel·able** adj — **reel·er** n

³**reel** vb **1** : WHIRL; also : to be giddy **2** : to waver or fall back (as from a blow) **3** : to walk or move unsteadily

⁴**reel** n : a reeling motion

⁵**reel** n : a lively Scottish dance or its music

**reel off** vb **1** : to tell or recite rapidly and easily ⟨reeled off the right answers⟩ **2** : to achieve usu. consecutively ⟨reeled off six straight wins⟩

**re·en·try** \rē-'en-trē\ n **1** : a second or new entry **2** : the action of reentering the earth's atmosphere from space

**reeve** \'rēv\ vb **rove** \'rōv\ or **reeved; reev·ing** : to pass (as a rope) through a hole in a block or cleat

¹**ref** \'ref\ n : REFEREE 2

²**ref** abbr **1** reference **2** referred **3** reformed **4** refunding

**re·fec·tion** \ri-'fek-shən\ n **1** : refreshment esp. after hunger or fatigue **2** : food and drink together : REPAST

**re·fec·to·ry** \ri-'fek-tə-rē\ n, pl **-ries** : a dining hall (as in a monastery or college)

**re·fer** \ri-'fər\ vb **re·ferred; re·fer·ring** [ME referren, fr. AF referer, referir, fr. L referre to bring back, report, refer, fr. re-back + ferre to carry] **1** : to assign to a certain source, cause, or relationship **2** : to direct or send to some person or place (as for information or help) **3** : to submit to someone else for consideration or action **4** : to have recourse (as for information or aid) **5** : to have connection

| | | | |
|---|---|---|---|
| reecho | reemphasize | reenlist | reevaluate |
| reedit | reemploy | reenlistment | reevaluation |
| reelect | reemployment | reenter | reexamination |
| reelection | reenact | reequip | reexamine |
| reemerge | reenactment | reestablish | reexport |
| reemergence | reenergize | reestablishment | refashion |
| reemphasis | | | |

: RELATE **6** : to direct attention : speak of : MENTION, ALLUDE ♦ **Synonyms** RECUR, REPAIR, RESORT, APPLY, GO, TURN — **re·fer·able** \'re-fə-rə-bəl, ri-'fər-ə-\ *adj*

**¹ref·er·ee** \ˌre-fə-'rē\ *n* **1** : a person to whom an issue esp. in law is referred for investigation or settlement **2** : an umpire in certain games

**²referee** *vb* **-eed; -ee·ing** : to act as referee

**ref·er·ence** \'re-frəns, -fə-rəns\ *n* **1** : the act of referring **2** : RELATION, RESPECT **3** : ALLUSION, MENTION **4** : something that refers a reader to another passage or book **5** : consultation esp. for obtaining information ⟨books for ∼⟩ **6** : a person of whom inquiries as to character or ability can be made **7** : a written recommendation of a person for employment

**ref·er·en·dum** \ˌre-fə-'ren-dəm\ *n, pl* **-da** \-də\ *or* **-dums** : the submitting of legislative measures to the voters for approval or rejection; *also* : a vote on a measure so submitted

**ref·er·ent** \'re-frənt, -fə-rənt\ *n* : one that refers or is referred to; *esp* : the thing a word stands for — **referent** *adj*

**re·fer·ral** \ri-'fər-əl\ *n* **1** : the act or an instance of referring **2** : one that is referred

**¹re·fill** \ˌrē-'fil\ *vb* : to fill again : REPLENISH — **re·fill·able** *adj*

**²re·fill** \'rē-ˌfil\ *n* : a new or fresh supply of something

**re·fi·nance** \ˌrē-fə-'nans, (ˌ)rē-'fī-nans\ *vb* : to renew or reorganize the financing of

**re·fine** \ri-'fīn\ *vb* **re·fined; re·fin·ing** **1** : to free from impurities or waste matter **2** : IMPROVE, PERFECT **3** : to free or become free of what is coarse or uncouth **4** : to make improvements by introducing subtle changes — **re·fin·er** *n*

**re·fined** \ri-'fīnd\ *adj* **1** : freed from impurities **2** : CULTURED, CULTIVATED **3** : PRECISE, EXACT

**re·fine·ment** \ri-'fīn-mənt\ *n* **1** : the action of refining **2** : the quality or state of being refined **3** : a refined feature or method; *also* : something intended to improve or perfect

**re·fin·ery** \ri-'fī-nə-rē\ *n, pl* **-er·ies** : a building and equipment for refining metals, oil, or sugar

**re·flect** \ri-'flekt\ *vb* [ME, fr. L *reflectere* to bend back, fr. *re-* back + *flectere* to bend] **1** : to bend or cast back (as light, heat, or sound) **2** : to give back a likeness or image of as a mirror does **3** : to bring as a result ⟨∼*ed* credit on him⟩ **4** : to make apparent : SHOW ⟨figures that ∼ economic growth⟩ **5** : to cast reproach or blame ⟨their bad conduct ∼*ed* on their training⟩ **6** : PONDER, MEDITATE — **re·flec·tion** \-'flek-shən\ *n* — **re·flec·tive** \-tiv\ *adj* — **re·flec·tiv·i·ty** \(ˌ)rē-ˌflek-'ti-və-tē\ *n*

**re·flec·tor** \ri-'flek-tər\ *n* : one that re-

flects; *esp* : a polished surface for reflecting radiation (as light)

**¹re·flex** \'rē-ˌfleks\ *n* **1** : an automatic and usu. inborn response to a stimulus not involving higher mental centers **2** *pl* : the power of acting or responding with enough speed ⟨an athlete with great ∼*es*⟩

**²reflex** *adj* **1** : bent or directed back **2** : of, relating to, or produced by a reflex ⟨a ∼ action⟩ — **re·flex·ly** *adv*

**¹re·flex·ive** \ri-'flek-siv\ *adj* : of or relating to an action directed back upon the doer or the grammatical subject ⟨a ∼ verb⟩ ⟨the ∼ pronoun *himself*⟩ — **re·flex·ive·ly** *adv* — **re·flex·ive·ness** *n*

**²reflexive** *n* : a reflexive verb or pronoun

**re·flex·ol·o·gy** \ˌrē-ˌflek-'sä-lə-jē\ *n* : massage in which pressure is applied to specific points on the hands or feet

**re·flux** \'rē-ˌfləks\ *n* : a flowing back

**re·fo·cus** \(ˌ)rē-'fō-kəs\ *vb* **1** : to focus again **2** : to change the emphasis or direction of ⟨∼*ed* her life⟩

**re·for·es·ta·tion** \ˌrē-ˌfȯr-ə-'stā-shən\ *n* : the action of renewing forest cover by planting seeds or young trees — **re·for·est** \rē-'fȯr-əst\ *vb*

**¹re·form** \ri-'fȯrm\ *vb* **1** : to make better or improve by removal of faults **2** : to correct or improve one's own character or habits ♦ **Synonyms** CORRECT, RECTIFY, EMEND, REMEDY, REDRESS, REVISE — **re·form·able** *adj* — **re·for·ma·tive** \-'fȯr-mə-tiv\ *adj*

**²reform** *n* : improvement or correction of what is corrupt or defective

**re–form** \ˌrē-'fȯrm\ *vb* : to form again

**ref·or·ma·tion** \ˌre-fər-'mā-shən\ *n* **1** : the act of reforming : the state of being reformed **2** *cap* : a 16th century religious movement marked by the establishment of the Protestant churches

**¹re·for·ma·to·ry** \ri-'fȯr-mə-ˌtȯr-ē\ *adj* : aiming at or tending toward reformation : REFORMATIVE

**²reformatory** *n, pl* **-ries** : a penal institution for reforming esp. young or first offenders

**re·form·er** \ri-'fȯr-mər\ *n* **1** : one that works for or urges reform **2** *cap* : a leader of the Protestant Reformation

**refr** *abbr* refraction

**re·fract** \ri-'frakt\ *vb* [L *refractus,* pp. of *refringere* to break open, break up, fr. *re-* back + *frangere* to break] : to subject to refraction

**re·frac·tion** \ri-'frak-shən\ *n* : the bending of a ray (as of light) when it passes obliquely from one medium into another in which its speed is different — **re·frac·tive** \-tiv\ *adj*

**refractive index** *n* : the ratio of the speed of radiation in one medium to that in another medium

**re·frac·to·ry** \ri-'frak-tə-rē\ *adj* **1** : OBSTINATE, STUBBORN, UNMANAGEABLE **2** : capable of enduring high temperature

⟨~ bricks⟩ ♦ *Synonyms* RECALCI-TRANT, INTRACTABLE, UNGOVERNABLE, UNRULY, HEADSTRONG, WILLFUL — **re·frac·to·ri·ness** \ri-'frak-tə-rē-nəs\ *n* — **refractory** *n*

¹**re·frain** \ri-'frān\ *vb* : to hold oneself back : FORBEAR ⟨~ from interfering⟩ — **re·frain·ment** *n*

²**refrain** *n* : a phrase or verse recurring regularly in a poem or song

**re·fresh** \ri-'fresh\ *vb* **1** : to make or become fresh or fresher **2** : to revive by or as if by renewal of supplies ⟨~ one's memory⟩ **3** : to freshen up **4** : to supply or take refreshment **5** : to update or renew esp. by sending a new signal ⟨~ the Web page⟩ ♦ *Synonyms* RESTORE, REJUVENATE, RENOVATE, REFURBISH — **re·fresh·er** *n* — **re·fresh·ing·ly** *adv*

**re·fresh·ment** \-mənt\ *n* **1** : the act of refreshing : the state of being refreshed **2** : something that refreshes **3** *pl* : a light meal; *also* : assorted light foods

**re·fried beans** \'rē-,frīd-\ *n pl* : beans cooked with seasonings, fried, then mashed and fried again

**refrig** *abbr* refrigerating; refrigeration

**re·frig·er·ate** \ri-'fri-jə-,rāt\ *vb* **-at·ed; -at·ing** : to make cool; *esp* : to chill or freeze (food) for preservation — **re·frig·er·ant** \-jə-rənt\ *adj or n* — **re·frig·er·a·tion** \-,fri-jə-'rā-shən\ *n* — **re·frig·er·a·tor** \-'fri-jə-,rā-tər\ *n*

**ref·uge** \'re-,fyüj\ *n* **1** : shelter or protection from danger or distress **2** : a place that provides protection

**ref·u·gee** \,re-fyü-'jē\ *n* : one who flees for safety esp. to a foreign country

**re·ful·gence** \ri-'ful-jəns, -'fəl-\ *n* : a radiant or resplendent quality or state — **re·ful·gent** \-jənt\ *adj*

¹**re·fund** \ri-'fənd, 'rē-,fənd\ *vb* : to give or put back (money) : REPAY — **re·fund·able** *adj*

²**re·fund** \'rē-,fənd\ *n* **1** : the act of refunding **2** : a sum refunded

**re·fur·bish** \ri-'fər-bish\ *vb* : to brighten or freshen up : RENOVATE

¹**re·fuse** \ri-'fyüz\ *vb* **re·fused; re·fus·ing** **1** : to decline to accept : REJECT **2** : to decline to do, give, or grant : DENY — **re·fus·al** \-'fyü-zəl\ *n*

²**ref·use** \'re-,fyüs, -,fyüz\ *n* : rejected or worthless matter : RUBBISH, TRASH

**re·fute** \ri-'fyüt\ *vb* **re·fut·ed; re·fut·ing** [L *refutare* to check, suppress, refute] : to prove to be false by argument or evidence — **ref·u·ta·tion** \,re-fyü-'tā-shən\ *n* — **re·fut·er** *n*

¹**reg** \'reg\ *n* : REGULATION

²**reg** *abbr* **1** region **2** register; registered; registration **3** regular

**re·gal** \'rē-gəl\ *adj* **1** : of, relating to, or befitting a king : ROYAL **2** : STATELY, SPLENDID — **re·gal·ly** *adv*

**re·gale** \ri-'gāl\ *vb* **re·galed; re·gal·ing** **1** : to entertain richly or agreeably **2** : to give pleasure or amusement to ⟨*regaled*

us with stories⟩ ♦ *Synonyms* GRATIFY, DELIGHT, PLEASE, REJOICE, GLADDEN

**re·ga·lia** \ri-'gāl-yə\ *n pl* **1** : the emblems, symbols, or paraphernalia of royalty (as the crown and scepter) **2** : the insignia of an office or order **3** : special costume : FINERY

¹**re·gard** \ri-'gärd\ *n* **1** : CONSIDERATION, HEED; *also* : CARE, CONCERN **2** : GAZE, GLANCE, LOOK **3** : RESPECT, ESTEEM ⟨held in high ~⟩ **4** *pl* : friendly greetings implying respect and esteem **5** : an aspect to be considered : PARTICULAR — **re·gard·ful** *adj* — **re·gard·less** *adj*

²**regard** *vb* **1** : to think of : CONSIDER **2** : to pay attention to **3** : to show respect for : HEED ⟨~s his elders⟩ **4** : to hold in high esteem : care for **5** : to look at : gaze upon ⟨~ed the landscape⟩ **6** *archaic* : to relate to

**re·gard·ing** *prep* : CONCERNING

**regardless of** \ri-'gärd-ləs-\ *prep* : in spite of

**re·gat·ta** \ri-'gä-tə, -'ga-\ *n* : a boat race or a series of boat races

**re·gen·cy** \'rē-jən-sē\ *n, pl* **-cies** **1** : the office or government of a regent or body of regents **2** : a body of regents **3** : the period during which a regent governs

**re·gen·er·a·cy** \ri-'je-nə-rə-sē\ *n* : the state of being regenerated

¹**re·gen·er·ate** \ri-'je-nə-rət\ *adj* **1** : formed or created again **2** : spiritually reborn or converted

²**re·gen·er·ate** \ri-'je-nə-,rāt\ *vb* **1** : to subject to spiritual renewal **2** : to reform completely **3** : to replace (a body part) by a new growth of tissue **4** : to give new life to : REVIVE — **re·gen·er·a·tion** \-,je-nə-'rā-shən\ *n* — **re·gen·er·a·tive** \-'je-nə-,rā-tiv\ *adj* — **re·gen·er·a·tor** \-,rā-tər\ *n*

**re·gent** \'rē-jənt\ *n* **1** : a person who rules during the childhood, absence, or incapacity of the sovereign **2** : a member of a governing board (as of a state university) — **regent** *adj*

**reg·gae** \'re-,gā\ *n* : popular music of Jamaican origin that combines native styles with elements of rock and soul music

**reg·i·cide** \'re-jə-,sīd\ *n* **1** : one who murders a king **2** : murder of a king

**re·gift** \(,)rē-'gift\ *vb* : to give a previously received gift to someone else

**re·gime** *also* **ré·gime** \rā-'zhēm, ri-\ *n* **1** : REGIMEN **2** : a form or system of government **3** : a government in power; *also* : a period of rule

**reg·i·men** \'re-jə-mən\ *n* [ME, fr. ML, position of authority, direction, set of rules, fr. L, steering, control, fr. *regere* to direct] **1** : a systematic course of treatment or training ⟨a strict dietary ~⟩ **2** : GOVERNMENT

¹**reg·i·ment** \'re-jə-mənt\ *n* : a military unit consisting usu. of a number of battalions — **reg·i·men·tal** \,re-jə-'ment-təl\ *adj*

---

refreeze              refurnish              regain              regather
refuel

²**reg·i·ment** \'re-jə-,ment\ *vb* : to organize rigidly esp. for regulation or central control; *also* : to subject to order or uniformity — **reg·i·men·ta·tion** \,re-jə-mən-'tā-shən\ *n*

**reg·i·men·tals** \,re-jə-'men-təlz\ *n pl* 1 : a regimental uniform 2 : military dress

**re·gion** \'rē-jən\ *n* [ME, fr. AF *regiun*, fr. L *region-, regio*, line, direction, area, fr. *regere* to rule] : an often indefinitely defined part or area

**re·gion·al** \'rē-jə-nəl\ *adj* 1 : affecting a particular region : LOCALIZED 2 : of, relating to, characteristic of, or serving a region — **re·gion·al·ly** *adv*

¹**reg·is·ter** \'re-jə-stər\ *n* 1 : a record of items or details; *also* : a book or system for keeping such a record 2 : the range of a voice or instrument 3 : a device to regulate ventilation or heating 4 : an automatic device recording a number or quantity 5 : CASH REGISTER

²**register** *vb* **-tered; -ter·ing** 1 : to enter in a register (as in a list of guests) 2 : to record automatically 3 : to secure special care for (mail matter) by paying additional postage 4 : to convey an impression of : EXPRESS 5 : to make or adjust so as to correspond exactly

**registered nurse** *n* : a graduate trained nurse who has been licensed to practice by a state authority after passing qualifying examinations

**reg·is·trant** \'re-jə-strənt\ *n* : one that registers or is registered

**reg·is·trar** \-,strär\ *n* : an official recorder or keeper of records (as at an educational institution)

**reg·is·tra·tion** \,re-jə-'strā-shən\ *n* 1 : the act of registering 2 : an entry in a register 3 : the number of persons registered : ENROLLMENT 4 : a document certifying an act of registering

**reg·is·try** \'re-jə-strē\ *n, pl* **-tries** 1 : ENROLLMENT, REGISTRATION 2 : a place of registration 3 : an official record book or an entry in one

**reg·nant** \'reg-nənt\ *adj* 1 : REIGNING 2 : DOMINANT 3 : of common or widespread occurrence

¹**re·gress** \'rē-,gres\ *n* 1 : an act or the privilege of going or coming back 2 : RETROGRESSION

²**re·gress** \ri-'gres\ *vb* : to go or cause to go back or to a lower level — **re·gres·sive** *adj* — **re·gres·sor** \-'gre-sər\ *n*

**re·gres·sion** \ri-'gre-shən\ *n* : the act or an instance of regressing; *esp* : reversion to an earlier mental or behavioral level

¹**re·gret** \ri-'gret\ *vb* **re·gret·ted; re·gret·ting** 1 : to mourn the loss or death of 2 : to be very sorry for 3 : to experience regret — **re·gret·ta·ble** \-'gre-tə-bəl\ *adj* — **re·gret·ter** *n*

²**regret** *n* 1 : sorrow caused by something beyond one's power to remedy 2 : an expression of sorrow 3 *pl* : a note politely declining an invitation — **re·gret·ful** \-fəl\ *adj* — **re·gret·ful·ly** *adv*

**re·gret·ta·bly** \-'gre-tə-blē\ *adv* 1 : to a regrettable extent 2 : it is to be regretted

**re·group** \(,)rē-'grüp\ *vb* : to form into a new grouping

**regt** *abbr* regiment

¹**reg·u·lar** \'re-gyə-lər\ *adj* [ME *reguler*, fr. AF, fr. LL *regularis* regular, fr. L, of a bar, fr. *regula* rule, straightedge, fr. *regere* to keep straight, direct] 1 : belonging to a religious order 2 : made, built, or arranged according to a rule, standard, or type; *also* : even or symmetrical in form or structure 3 : ORDERLY, METHODICAL ⟨~ habits⟩; *also* : not varying : STEADY ⟨a ~ pace⟩ 4 : made, selected, or conducted according to rule or custom 5 : properly qualified ⟨not a ~ lawyer⟩ 6 : conforming to the normal or usual manner or inflection 7 : of, relating to, or constituting the permanent standing military force of a state — **reg·u·lar·i·ty** \,re-gyə-'la-rə-tē\ *n* — **reg·u·lar·ize** \'re-gyə-lə-,rīz\ *vb* — **reg·u·lar·ly** *adv*

²**regular** *n* 1 : one that is regular (as in attendance) 2 : a member of the regular clergy 3 : a soldier in a regular army 4 : a player on an athletic team who is usu. in the starting lineup

**reg·u·late** \'re-gyə-,lāt\ *vb* **-lat·ed; -lat·ing** 1 : to govern or direct according to rule : CONTROL 2 : to bring under the control of law or authority 3 : to put in good order 4 : to fix or adjust the time, amount, degree, or rate of — **reg·u·la·tive** \-,lā-tiv\ *adj* — **reg·u·la·tor** \-,lā-tər\ *n* — **reg·u·la·to·ry** \-lə-,tȯr-ē\ *adj*

**reg·u·la·tion** \,re-gyə-'lā-shən\ *n* 1 : the act of regulating : the state of being regulated 2 : a rule dealing with details of procedure 3 : an order issued by an executive authority of a government and having the force of law

**re·gur·gi·tate** \rē-'gər-jə-,tāt\ *vb* **-tat·ed; -tat·ing** [ML *regurgitare*, fr. L re- re- + LL *gurgitare* to engulf, fr. L *gurgit-, gurges* whirlpool] : to throw or be thrown back, up, or out ⟨~ food⟩ — **re·gur·gi·ta·tion** \-,gər-jə-'tā-shən\ *n*

**re·hab** \'rē-,hab\ *n* 1 : REHABILITATION 2 : a rehabilitated building — **rehab** *vb*

**re·ha·bil·i·tate** \,rē-hə-'bi-lə-,tāt, ,rē-ə-\ *vb* **-tat·ed; -tat·ing** 1 : to restore to a former capacity, rank, or right : REINSTATE 2 : to restore to good condition or health — **re·ha·bil·i·ta·tion** \-,bi-lə-'tā-shən\ *n* — **re·ha·bil·i·ta·tive** \-,tā-tiv\ *adj*

**re·hash** \,rē-'hash\ *vb* : to present again in another form without real change or improvement — **rehash** *n*

**re·hear·ing** \,rē-'hir-iŋ\ *n* : a second or new hearing by the same tribunal

**re·hears·al** \ri-'hər-səl\ *n* 1 : something told again : RECITAL 2 : a private performance or practice session preparatory to a public appearance

**re·hearse** \ri-'hərs\ *vb* **re·hearsed; re·hears·ing** 1 : to say again : REPEAT 2 : to recount in order : ENUMERATE; *also* : RELATE 1 3 : to give a rehearsal of 4

---

| regild | regrade | regrow | rehandle |
| regive | regrind | regrowth | rehear |

: to train by rehearsal  **5** : to engage in a rehearsal — **re·hears·er** n

¹**reign** \'rān\ n  **1** : the authority or rule of a sovereign  **2** : the time during which a sovereign rules

²**reign** vb  **1** : to rule as a sovereign  **2** : to be predominant or prevalent

**re·im·burse** \ˌrē-əm-'bərs\ vb **-bursed;** **-burs·ing** [re- re- + obs. E imburse to put in the pocket, pay, fr. ML imbursare to put into a purse, fr. L in in : ML bursa purse, fr. LL. hide of an ox, fr. Gk byrsa] : to pay back : make restitution : REPAY ⟨was reimbursed for her travel expenses⟩ ♦ **Synonyms** INDEMNIFY, RECOMPENSE, REQUITE, COMPENSATE — **re·im·burs·able** adj — **re·im·burse·ment** n

¹**rein** \'rān\ n  **1** : a strap fastened to a bit by which a rider or driver controls an animal  **2** : a restraining influence : CHECK  **3** : controlling or guiding power  **4** : complete freedom — usu. used in the phrase give rein to

²**rein** vb : to check or direct by reins

**re·in·car·na·tion** \ˌrē-(ˌ)in-(ˌ)kär-'nā-shən\ n : rebirth of the soul in a new body — **re·in·car·nate** \ˌrē-in-'kär-ˌnāt\ vb

**rein·deer** \'rān-ˌdir\ n [ME reindere, fr. ON hreinn reindeer + ME deer animal, deer] : CARIBOU — used esp. for one of the Old World

**reindeer moss** n : a gray, erect, tufted, and much-branched edible lichen of northern regions that is an important food of reindeer

**re·in·fec·tion** \ˌrē-in-'fek-shən\ n : infection following another infection of the same type

**re·in·force** \ˌrē-ən-'fȯrs\ vb  **1** : to strengthen with additional forces ⟨~ our troops⟩  **2** : to strengthen with new force, aid, material, or support — **re·in·force·ment** n — **re·in·forc·er** n

**re·in·scribe** \ˌrē-ən-'skrīb\ vb : to reestablish or rename in a new and esp. stronger form or context

**re·in·state** \ˌrē-in-'stāt\ vb **-stat·ed;** **-stat·ing** : to restore to a former position, condition, or capacity — **re·in·state·ment** n

**re·in·vent** \ˌrē-in-'vent\ vb  **1** : to make as if for the first time something already invented ⟨~ the wheel⟩  **2** : to remake completely

**re·it·er·ate** \rē-'i-tə-ˌrāt\ vb **-at·ed; -at·ing** : to state or do over again or repeatedly — **re·it·er·a·tion** \-ˌi-tə-'rā-shən\ n

¹**re·ject** \ri-'jekt\ vb  **1** : to refuse to accept, consider, use, or submit to  **2** : to refuse to hear, receive, or admit : REPEL  **3** : to rebuff or withhold love from  **4** : to throw out esp. as useless or unsatisfactory  **5** : to subject (a transplanted tissue) to an attack by immune system components of the recipient organism — **re·jec·tion** \-'jek-shən\ n

²**re·ject** \'rē-ˌjekt\ n : a rejected person or thing

**re·joice** \ri-'jȯis\ vb **re·joiced; re·joic·ing**  **1** : to give joy to : GLADDEN  **2** : to feel joy or great delight — **re·joic·er** n

**re·join** \(ˌ)rē-'jȯin for 1, ri- for 2\ vb  **1** : to join again  **2** : to say in answer (as to a plaintiff's plea in court) : REPLY

**re·join·der** \ri-'jȯin-dər\ n : REPLY; esp : an answer to a reply

**re·ju·ve·nate** \ri-'jü-və-ˌnāt\ vb **-nat·ed; -nat·ing** : to make young or youthful again : give new vigor to ♦ **Synonyms** RENEW, REFRESH, RENOVATE, RESTORE — **re·ju·ve·na·tion** \-ˌjü-və-'nā-shən\ n

**rel** abbr  **1** relating; relative  **2** religion; religious

¹**re·lapse** \ri-'laps, 'rē-ˌlaps\ n [ME, fr. ML relapsus, fr. L relabi to slide back]  **1** : the act or process of backsliding or worsening  **2** : a recurrence of illness after a period of improvement

²**re·lapse** \ri-'laps\ vb **re·lapsed; re·laps·ing** : to slip or fall back into a former worse state (as of illness)

**re·late** \ri-'lāt\ vb **re·lat·ed; re·lat·ing**  **1** : to give an account of : TELL, NARRATE  **2** : to show or establish logical or causal connection between  **3** : to have relationship or connection  **4** : to have or establish relationship ⟨the way a child ~s to a teacher⟩  **5** : to respond favorably ⟨can't ~ to that kind of music⟩ — **re·lat·able** adj — **re·lat·er** or **re·la·tor** \-'lā-tər\ n

**re·lat·ed** adj  **1** : connected by some understood relationship  **2** : connected through membership in the same family — **re·lat·ed·ness** n

**re·la·tion** \ri-'lā-shən\ n  **1** : NARRATION, ACCOUNT  **2** : CONNECTION, RELATIONSHIP  **3** : connection by blood or marriage : KINSHIP; also : RELATIVE  **4** : REFERENCE, RESPECT ⟨in ~ to⟩  **5** : the state of being mutually interested or involved (as in social or commercial matters)  **6** pl : DEALINGS, AFFAIRS ⟨foreign ~s⟩  **7** pl : SEXUAL INTERCOURSE — **re·la·tion·al** \-shə-nəl\ adj

**re·la·tion·ship** \-ˌship\ n : the state of being related or interrelated

¹**rel·a·tive** \'re-lə-tiv\ n  **1** : a word referring grammatically to an antecedent  **2** : a thing having a relation to or a dependence upon another thing  **3** : a person connected with another by blood or marriage

²**relative** adj  **1** : introducing a subordinate clause qualifying an expressed or implied antecedent ⟨~ pronoun⟩; also : introduced by such a connective ⟨~ clause⟩  **2** : PERTINENT, RELEVANT ⟨matters ~ to world peace⟩  **3** : not absolute or independent : COMPARATIVE  **4** : expressed as the ratio of the specified quantity to the total magnitude or to the mean of all quantities involved ♦ **Synonyms** DE-

| | | | |
|---|---|---|---|
| reheat | reinsertion | reinvention | reissue |
| rehouse | reintegrate | reinvest | rejudge |
| reimpose | reinterpret | reinvestment | rekindle |
| reimposition | reinterpretation | reinvigorate | reknit |
| reincorporate | reintroduce | reinvigoration | |
| reinsert | reintroduction | | |

PENDENT, CONTINGENT, CONDITIONAL — **rel·a·tive·ly** adv — **rel·a·tive·ness** n

**relative humidity** n : the ratio of the amount of water vapor actually present in the air to the greatest amount possible at the same temperature

**rel·a·tiv·is·tic** \,re-lə-ti-'vis-tik\ adj **1** : of, relating to, or characterized by relativity **2** : moving at a velocity that is a significant fraction of the speed of light so that effects predicted by the theory of relativity become evident ⟨a ~ electron⟩ — **rel·a·tiv·is·ti·cal·ly** \-ti-k(ə-)lē\ adv

**rel·a·tiv·i·ty** \,re-lə-'ti-və-tē\ n, pl **-ties** **1** : the quality or state of being relative **2** : a theory in physics that considers mass and energy to be equivalent and that predicts changes in mass, dimension, and time which are related to speed but are noticeable esp. at speeds approaching that of light; also : an extension of the theory to include gravitation and related acceleration phenomena

**re·lax** \ri-'laks\ vb **1** : to make or become less firm, tense, or rigid **2** : to make less severe or strict **3** : to seek rest or recreation — **re·lax·er** n

**¹re·lax·ant** \ri-'lak-sənt\ adj : of, relating to, or producing relaxation

**²relaxant** n : a relaxing agent; esp : a drug that induces muscular relaxation

**re·lax·ation** \,rē-,lak-'sā-shən\ n **1** : the act of relaxing or state of being relaxed : a lessening of tension **2** : DIVERSION, RECREATION

**¹re·lay** \'rē-,lā\ n [ME, set of fresh hounds, fr. relayen to release fresh hounds, take a fresh horse, fr. MF relaier, fr. re- again + laier to let go, leave] **1** : a fresh supply (as of horses or men) arranged beforehand to relieve others **2** : a race between teams in which each team member covers a specified part of a course **3** : an electromagnetic device in which the opening or closing of one circuit activates another device (as a switch in another circuit) **4** : the act of passing along by stages

**²re·lay** \'rē-,lā, ri-'lā\ vb **re·layed; re·lay·ing 1** : to place in or provide with relays **2** : to pass along by relays **3** : to control or operate by a relay

**³re·lay** \(,)rē-'lā\ vb **-laid** \-'lād\; **-lay·ing** : to lay again

**¹re·lease** \ri-'lēs\ vb **re·leased; re·leas·ing 1** : to set free from confinement or restraint; also : DISMISS ⟨released from her job⟩ **2** : to relieve from something that oppresses, confines, or burdens **3** : RELINQUISH ⟨~ a claim⟩ **4** : to permit publication, performance, exhibition, or sale of; also : to make available to the public ✦ **Synonyms** EMANCIPATE, DISCHARGE, FREE, LIBERATE

**²release** n **1** : relief or deliverance from sorrow, suffering, or trouble **2** : discharge from an obligation or responsibility **3** : an act of setting free : the state of being freed **4** : a document effecting a legal release **5** : a releasing for performance or publication; also : the matter

released (as to the press) **6** : a device for holding or releasing a mechanism as required

**rel·e·gate** \'re-lə-,gāt\ vb **-gat·ed; -gat·ing 1** : to send into exile : BANISH **2** : to remove or dismiss to some less prominent position **3** : to assign to a particular class or sphere **4** : to submit to someone or something for appropriate action : DELEGATE ✦ **Synonyms** COMMIT, ENTRUST, CONSIGN, COMMEND — **rel·e·ga·tion** \,re-lə-'gā-shən\ n

**re·lent** \ri-'lent\ vb **1** : to become less stern, severe, or harsh **2** : SLACKEN

**re·lent·less** \-ləs\ adj : showing or promising no abatement of severity, intensity, or pace ⟨~ pressure⟩ — **re·lent·less·ly** adv — **re·lent·less·ness** n

**rel·e·vance** \'re-lə-vəns\ n : relation to the matter at hand; also : practical and esp. social applicability

**rel·e·van·cy** \-vən-sē\ n : RELEVANCE

**rel·e·vant** \'re-lə-vənt\ adj : bearing on the matter at hand : PERTINENT ✦ **Synonyms** GERMANE, MATERIAL, APPLICABLE, APROPOS — **rel·e·vant·ly** adv

**re·li·able** \ri-'lī-ə-bəl\ adj : fit to be trusted or relied on : DEPENDABLE, TRUSTWORTHY — **re·li·abil·i·ty** \-,lī-ə-'bi-lə-tē\ n — **re·li·able·ness** n — **re·li·ably** \-'lī-ə-blē\ adv

**re·li·ance** \ri-'lī-əns\ n **1** : the act of relying **2** : the state of being reliant **3** : one relied on

**re·li·ant** \ri-'lī-ənt\ adj : having reliance on someone or something : DEPENDENT

**rel·ic** \'re-lik\ n **1** : an object venerated because of its association with a saint or martyr **2** : SOUVENIR, MEMENTO **3** pl : REMAINS, RUINS **4** : a remaining trace : VESTIGE

**rel·ict** \'re-likt\ n : WIDOW

**re·lief** \ri-'lēf\ n **1** : removal or lightening of something oppressive, painful, or distressing **2** : WELFARE **2 3** : military assistance to an endangered post or force **4** : release from a post or from performance of a duty; also : one that takes the place of another on duty **5** : legal remedy or redress **6** : projection of figures or ornaments from the background (as in sculpture) **7** : the state of being distinguished by contrast **8** : the elevations of a land surface

**relief pitcher** n : a baseball pitcher who takes over for another during a game

**re·lieve** \ri-'lēv\ vb **re·lieved; re·liev·ing 1** : to free partly or wholly from a burden or from distress **2** : to bring about the removal or alleviation of : MITIGATE **3** : to release from a post or duty; also : to take the place of **4** : to break the monotony of **5** : to discharge the bladder or bowels of (oneself) ✦ **Synonyms** ALLEVIATE, LIGHTEN, ASSUAGE, ALLAY — **re·liev·er** n

**relig** abbr religion

**re·li·gion** \ri-'li-jən\ n **1** : the service and worship of God or the supernatural **2** : devotion to a religious faith **3** : a per-

---

relaunch          relearn                    relight

sonal set or institutionalized system of religious beliefs, attitudes, and practices **4** : a cause, principle, or belief held to with faith and ardor — **re·li·gion·ist** *n*

¹**re·li·gious** \ri-'li-jəs\ *adj* **1** : relating or devoted to an acknowledged ultimate reality or deity **2** : of or relating to religious beliefs or observances **3** : scrupulously and conscientiously faithful **4** : FERVENT, ZEALOUS ⟨∼ about football⟩ — **re·li·gious·ly** *adv*

²**religious** *n, pl* **religious** : a member of a religious order under monastic vows

**re·lin·quish** \ri-'liŋ-kwish, -'lin-\ *vb* **1** : to withdraw or retreat from : ABANDON, QUIT **2** : GIVE UP ⟨∼ a title⟩ **3** : to let go of : RELEASE ♦ **Synonyms** YIELD, LEAVE, RESIGN, SURRENDER, CEDE, WAIVE — **re·lin·quish·ment** *n*

**rel·i·quary** \'re-lə-ˌkwer-ē\ *n, pl* **-quar·ies** : a container for religious relics

¹**rel·ish** \'re-lish\ *n* [ME *reles* taste, fr. OF, something left behind, release, fr. *relessier* to relax, release, fr. L *relaxare*] **1** : characteristic flavor : SAVOR **2** : keen enjoyment or delight in something : GUSTO **3** : APPETITE, INCLINATION ⟨has no ∼ for sports⟩ **4** : a highly seasoned sauce (as of pickles) eaten with other food to add flavor

²**relish** *vb* **1** : to add relish to **2** : to take pleasure in : ENJOY **3** : to eat with pleasure — **rel·ish·able** *adj*

**re·live** \(ˌ)rē-'liv\ *vb* : to live again or over again; *esp* : to experience again in the imagination

**re·lo·cate** \(ˌ)rē-'lō-ˌkāt, ˌrē-lō-'kāt\ *vb* **1** : to locate again **2** : to move to a new location — **re·lo·ca·tion** \ˌrē-lō-'kā-shən\ *n*

**re·luc·tant** \ri-'lək-tənt\ *adj* : feeling or showing aversion, hesitation, or unwillingness ⟨∼ to get involved⟩ ♦ **Synonyms** DISINCLINED, INDISPOSED, HESITANT, LOATH, AVERSE — **re·luc·tance** \-təns\ *n* — **re·luc·tant·ly** *adv*

**re·ly** \ri-'lī\ *vb* **re·lied; re·ly·ing** [ME *relien* to rally, fr. AF *relier* to retie, gather, rally, fr. L *religare* to tie out of the way, fr. *re-* back + *ligare* to tie] : to place faith or confidence : DEPEND

**REM** \'rem\ *n* : RAPID EYE MOVEMENT

**re·main** \ri-'mān\ *vb* **1** : to be left after others have been removed, subtracted, or destroyed **2** : to be something yet to be shown, done, or treated ⟨it ∼s to be seen⟩ **3** : to stay after others have gone **4** : to continue unchanged

**re·main·der** \ri-'mān-dər\ *n* **1** : that which is left over : a remaining group, part, or trace **2** : the number left after a subtraction **3** : the number that is left over from the dividend after division and that is less than the divisor **4** : a book sold at a reduced price by the publisher after sales have slowed ♦ **Synonyms** LEAVINGS, REST, BALANCE, REMNANT, RESIDUE

**re·mains** \ri-'mānz\ *n pl* **1** : a remaining part or trace ⟨the ∼ of a meal⟩ **2** : a dead body

¹**re·make** \(ˌ)rē-'māk\ *vb* **-made** \-'mād\; **-mak·ing** : to make anew or in a different form

²**re·make** \'rē-ˌmāk\ *n* : one that is remade; *esp* : a new version of a motion picture

**re·mand** \ri-'mand\ *vb* : to order back; *esp* : to return to custody pending trial or for further detention

¹**re·mark** \ri-'märk\ *n* **1** : the act of remarking : OBSERVATION, NOTICE **2** : a passing observation or comment

²**remark** *vb* **1** : to take notice of : OBSERVE **2** : to express as an observation or comment : SAY

**re·mark·able** \ri-'mär-kə-bəl\ *adj* : worthy of being or likely to be noticed : UNUSUAL, EXTRAORDINARY, NOTEWORTHY — **re·mark·able·ness** *n*

**re·mark·ably** \ri-'mär-kə-blē\ *adv* **1** : in a remarkable manner **2** : as is remarkable ⟨∼, no one was hurt⟩

**re·me·di·a·ble** \ri-'mē-dē-ə-bəl\ *adj* : capable of being remedied

**re·me·di·al** \ri-'mē-dē-əl\ *adj* : intended to remedy or improve ⟨a class in ∼ math⟩

¹**rem·e·dy** \'re-mə-dē\ *n, pl* **-dies** [ME *remedie*, fr. AF, fr. L *remedium*, fr. *re-* back, again + *mederi* to heal] **1** : a medicine or treatment that cures or relieves a disease or condition **2** : something that corrects or counteracts an evil or compensates for a loss

²**remedy** *vb* **-died; -dy·ing** : to provide or serve as a remedy for

**re·mem·ber** \ri-'mem-bər\ *vb* **-bered; -ber·ing** **1** : to bring to mind or think of again : RECOLLECT **2** : to keep from forgetting : keep in mind **3** : to convey greetings from **4** : COMMEMORATE

**re·mem·brance** \-brəns\ *n* **1** : an act of remembering : RECOLLECTION **2** : the ability to remember : MEMORY **3** : the period over which one's memory extends **4** : a memory of a person, thing, or event **5** : something that serves to bring to mind : REMINDER **6** : a greeting or gift recalling or expressing friendship or affection

**re·mind** \ri-'mīnd\ *vb* : to put in mind of something : cause to remember — **re·mind·er** *n*

**rem·i·nisce** \ˌre-mə-'nis\ *vb* **-nisced; -nisc·ing** : to indulge in reminiscence

**rem·i·nis·cence** \-'ni-s⁰ns\ *n* **1** : a recalling or telling of a past experience **2** : an account of a memorable experience

**rem·i·nis·cent** \-s⁰nt\ *adj* **1** : of or relating to reminiscence **2** : marked by or given to reminiscence **3** : serving to remind : SUGGESTIVE — **rem·i·nis·cent·ly** *adv*

**re·miss** \ri-'mis\ *adj* **1** : negligent or careless in the performance of work or duty **2** : showing neglect or inattention

♦ *Synonyms* LAX, NEGLECTFUL, DELINQUENT, DERELICT — **re·miss·ness** *n*

**re·mis·sion** \ri-'mi-shən\ *n* 1 : the act or process of remitting 2 : a state or period during which something is remitted

**re·mit** \ri-'mit\ *vb* **re·mit·ted; re·mit·ting** 1 : FORGIVE, PARDON ⟨~ sins⟩ 2 : to give or gain relief from (as pain) 3 : to refer for consideration, report, or decision 4 : to refrain from exacting or enforcing (as a penalty) 5 : to send (money) in payment of a bill

**re·mit·tal** \ri-'mi-t²l\ *n* : REMISSION

**re·mit·tance** \ri-'mi-t²ns\ *n* 1 : a sum of money remitted 2 : transmittal of money (as to a distant place)

**rem·nant** \'rem-nənt\ *n* 1 : a usu. small part or trace remaining 2 : an unsold or unused end of a fabric that is sold by the yard

**re·mod·el** \ˌrē-'mä-d²l\ *vb* : to alter the structure of : MAKE OVER

**re·mon·strance** \ri-'män-strəns\ *n* : an act or instance of remonstrating

**re·mon·strant** \-strənt\ *adj* : vigorously objecting or opposing — **remonstrant** *n* — **re·mon·strant·ly** *adv*

**re·mon·strate** \ri-'män-ˌstrāt\ *vb* **-strat·ed; -strat·ing** : to plead in opposition to something : speak in protest or reproof ♦ *Synonyms* EXPOSTULATE, OBJECT, PROTEST — **re·mon·stra·tion** \ri-ˌmän-'strā-shən, ˌre-mən-\ *n* — **re·mon·stra·tor** \ri-'män-ˌstrā-tər\ *n*

**rem·o·ra** \'re-mə-rə\ *n* : any of a family of marine bony fishes with sucking organs on the head by which they cling esp. to other fishes

**re·morse** \ri-'mórs\ *n* [ME, fr. AF *remors*, fr. ML *remorsus*, fr. LL, act of biting again, fr. L *remordēre* to bite again, fr. *re-* again + *mordēre* to bite] : a gnawing distress arising from a sense of guilt for past wrongs ♦ *Synonyms* PENITENCE, REPENTANCE, CONTRITION — **re·morse·ful** *adj*

**re·morse·less** \-ləs\ *adj* 1 : MERCILESS 2 : PERSISTENT, RELENTLESS

¹**re·mote** \ri-'mōt\ *adj* **re·mot·er; -est** 1 : far off in place or time : not near 2 : not closely related : DISTANT 3 : located out of the way : SECLUDED 4 : acting, acted on, or controlled indirectly or from a distance 5 : small in degree : SLIGHT ⟨a ~ chance⟩ 6 : distant in manner ⟨became ~ in her old age⟩ — **re·mote·ly** *adv* — **re·mote·ness** *n*

²**remote** *n* 1 : a radio or television program or a portion of a program originating outside the studio 2 : REMOTE CONTROL 2

**remote control** *n* 1 : control (as by radio signal) of operation from a point at some distance removed 2 : a device or mechanism for controlling something from a distance

¹**re·mount** \ˌ(ˌ)rē-'maúnt\ *vb* 1 : to mount again 2 : to furnish remounts to

²**re·mount** \'rē-ˌmaúnt\ *n* : a fresh horse to replace one no longer available

¹**re·move** \ri-'müv\ *vb* **re·moved; re·mov·ing** 1 : to move from one place to another : TRANSFER 2 : to move by lifting or taking off or away 3 : DISMISS, DISCHARGE 4 : to get rid of : ELIMINATE ⟨~ a fire hazard⟩ 5 : to change one's residence or location 6 : to go away : DEPART 7 : to be capable of being removed — **re·mov·able** *adj* — **re·mov·al** \-'mü-vəl\ *n* — **re·mov·er** *n*

²**remove** *n* 1 : a transfer from one location to another : MOVE 2 : a degree or stage of separation

**REM sleep** *n* : a state of sleep that recurs cyclically several times during normal sleep and is associated with rapid eye movements and dreaming

**re·mu·ner·ate** \ri-'myü-nə-ˌrāt\ *vb* **-at·ed; -at·ing** : to pay an equivalent for or to : RECOMPENSE ⟨their services were *remunerated*⟩ — **re·mu·ner·a·tor** \-ˌrā-tər\ *n*

**re·mu·ner·a·tion** \ri-ˌmyü-nə-'rā-shən\ *n* : COMPENSATION, PAYMENT

**re·mu·ner·a·tive** \ri-'myü-nə-rə-tiv, -ˌrā-\ *adj* : serving to remunerate : GAINFUL

**re·nais·sance** \ˌre-nə-'säns, -'zäns\ *n* 1 *cap* : the cultural revival and beginnings of modern science in Europe in the 14th–17th centuries; *also* : the period of the Renaissance 2 *often cap* : a movement or period of vigorous artistic and intellectual activity 3 : REBIRTH, REVIVAL

**re·nal** \'rē-n²l\ *adj* : of, relating to, or located in or near the kidneys

**re·na·scence** \ri-'na-s²ns, -'nä-\ *n, often cap* : RENAISSANCE

**rend** \'rend\ *vb* **rent** \'rent\; **rend·ing** 1 : to remove by violence : WREST 2 : to tear forcibly apart : SPLIT

**ren·der** \'ren-dər\ *vb* 1 : to extract (as lard) by heating 2 : to give to another; *also* : YIELD 3 : to give in return 4 : to do (a service) for another ⟨~ aid⟩ 5 : to cause to be or become : MAKE 6 : to reproduce or represent by artistic or verbal means 7 : TRANSLATE ⟨~ into English⟩

¹**ren·dez·vous** \'rän-di-ˌvü, -dā-\ *n, pl* **rendez·vous** \-ˌvüz\ [MF, fr. *rendez vous* present yourselves] 1 : a place appointed for a meeting; *also* : a meeting at an appointed place 2 : a place of popular resort 3 : the process of bringing two spacecraft together

²**rendezvous** *vb* **-voused** \-ˌvüd\; **-vous·ing** \-ˌvü-iŋ\; **-vouses** \-ˌvüz\ : to come or bring together at a rendezvous

**ren·di·tion** \ren-'di-shən\ *n* : an act or a result of rendering ⟨first ~ of the work into English⟩

**ren·e·gade** \'re-ni-ˌgād\ *n* [Sp *renegado*, fr. ML *renegatus*, fr. pp. of *renegare* to deny, fr. L *re-* re- + *negare* to deny] : a deserter from one faith, cause, principle, or party for another

**re·nege** \ri-'neg\ *vb* **re·neged; re·neg·ing** 1 : to go back on a promise or commitment 2 : to fail to follow suit when able in a card game in violation of the rules — **re·neg·er** *n*

---

remold     rename     renegotiate     renegotiation

**re·new** \ri-'nü-, -'nyü-\ *vb* **1** : to make or become new, fresh, or strong again **2** : to restore to existence : RECREATE, REVIVE **3** : to make or do again : REPEAT ⟨∼ a complaint⟩ **4** : to begin again : RESUME ⟨∼ed his efforts⟩ **5** : REPLACE ⟨∼ the lining of a coat⟩ **6** : to grant or obtain an extension of or on ⟨∼ a lease⟩ ⟨∼ a subscription⟩ — **re·new·er** *n*

**re·new·able** \ri-'nü-ə-bəl, -'nyü-\ *adj* **1** : capable of being renewed **2** : capable of being replaced by natural ecological cycles or sound management procedures ⟨∼ resources⟩

**re·new·al** \ri-'nü-əl, -'nyü-\ *n* **1** : the act of renewing : the state of being renewed **2** : something renewed

**ren·net** \'re-nət\ *n* **1** : the contents of the stomach of an unweaned animal (as a calf) or the lining membrane of the stomach used for curdling milk **2** : rennin or a substitute used to curdle milk

**ren·nin** \'re-nən\ *n* : a stomach enzyme that coagulates casein and is used commercially to curdle milk in the making of cheese

**re·nounce** \ri-'naúns\ *vb* **re·nounced; re·nounc·ing 1** : to give up, refuse, or resign usu. by formal declaration **2** : to refuse further to follow, obey, or recognize : REPUDIATE — **re·nounce·ment** *n*

**ren·o·vate** \'re-nə-ˌvāt\ *vb* **-vat·ed; -vat·ing 1** : to make like new again : put in good condition : REPAIR ⟨renovated the kitchen⟩ **2** : to restore to vigor or activity — **ren·o·va·tion** \ˌre-nə-'vā-shən\ *n* — **ren·o·va·tor** \'re-nə-ˌvā-tər\ *n*

**re·nown** \ri-'naún\ *n* : a state of being widely acclaimed and honored : FAME, CELEBRITY ⟨writers of ∼⟩ ◆ **Synonyms** HONOR, GLORY, REPUTATION, REPUTE — **re·nowned** \-'naúnd\ *adj*

**¹rent** \'rent\ *n* **1** : money or the amount of money paid or due at intervals for the use of another's property **2** : property rented or for rent

**²rent** *vb* **1** : to give possession and use of in return for rent **2** : to take and hold under an agreement to pay rent **3** : to be for rent ⟨∼s for $100 a month⟩ — **rent·er** *n*

**³rent** *n* **1** : a tear made by or as if by rending **2** : a split in a party or organized group : SCHISM

**¹rent·al** \'ren-təl\ *n* **1** : an amount paid or collected as rent **2** : something that is rented **3** : an act of renting

**²rental** *adj* : of or relating to rent

**re·nun·ci·a·tion** \ri-ˌnən-sē-'ā-shən\ *n* : the act of renouncing : REPUDIATION

**¹rep** \'rep\ *n* : REPRESENTATIVE ⟨sales ∼s⟩

**²rep** *abbr* **1** repair **2** repeat **3** report; reporter **4** republic

**Rep** *abbr* Republican

**re·pack·age** \(ˌ)rē-'pa-kij\ *vb* : to package again or anew; *esp* : to put into a more attractive form

**¹re·pair** \ri-'per\ *vb* [ME, fr. AF *repairer* to go back, return, fr. LL *repatriare* to go home again, fr. L *re-* back + *patria* native country] : to make one's way : GO ⟨∼ed to the drawing room⟩

**²repair** *vb* [ME, fr. AF *reparer*, fr. L *reparare*, fr. *re-* back + *parare* to prepare] **1** : to restore to good condition : FIX **2** : to restore to a healthy state **3** : REMEDY ⟨∼ a wrong⟩ — **re·pair·er** *n* — **re·pair·man** \-ˌman\ *n*

**³repair** *n* **1** : a result of repairing **2** : an act of repairing **3** : condition with respect to need of repairing ⟨in bad ∼⟩

**rep·a·ra·tion** \ˌre-pə-'rā-shən\ *n* **1** : the act of making amends for a wrong **2** : amends made for a wrong; *esp* : money paid by a defeated nation in compensation for damages caused during hostilities — usu. used in pl. ◆ **Synonyms** REDRESS, RESTITUTION, INDEMNITY

**re·par·a·tive** \ri-'pa-rə-tiv\ *adj* **1** : of, relating to, or effecting repairs **2** : serving to make amends

**rep·ar·tee** \ˌre-pər-'tē\ *n* **1** : a witty reply **2** : a succession of clever replies; *also* : skill in making such replies

**re·past** \ri-'past, 'rē-ˌpast\ *n* : a supply of food and drink served as a meal

**re·pa·tri·ate** \rē-'pā-trē-ˌāt\ *vb* **-at·ed; -at·ing** : to send or bring back to the country of origin or citizenship ⟨∼ prisoners of war⟩ — **re·pa·tri·ate** \-trē-ət, -trē-ˌāt\ *n* — **re·pa·tri·a·tion** \-ˌpā-trē-'ā-shən\ *n*

**re·pay** \rē-'pā\ *vb* **-paid** \-'pād\; **-pay·ing 1** : to pay back : REFUND **2** : to give or do in return or requital **3** : to make a return payment to : RECOMPENSE, REQUITE ◆ **Synonyms** REMUNERATE, COMPENSATE, REIMBURSE, INDEMNIFY — **re·pay·able** *adj* — **re·pay·ment** *n*

**re·peal** \ri-'pēl\ *vb* [ME *repelen*, fr. AF *repeler*, lit., to call back, fr. *re-* back + *upeler* to appeal, call] : to annul by authoritative and esp. legislative action ⟨∼ a law⟩ — **repeal** *n* — **re·peal·er** *n*

**¹re·peat** \ri-'pēt\ *vb* **1** : to say again **2** : to do again **3** : to say over from memory — **re·peat·able** *adj* — **re·peat·er** *n*

**²re·peat** \ri-'pēt, 'rē-ˌpēt\ *n* **1** : the act of repeating **2** : something repeated or to be repeated (as a radio or television program)

**³re·peat** \ri-'pēt\ *adj* : of, relating to, or being one that repeats an offense, achievement, or action

**re·peat·ed** \ri-'pē-təd\ *adj* : done or recurring again and again : FREQUENT ⟨∼ requests⟩ — **re·peat·ed·ly** *adv*

**re·pel** \ri-'pel\ *vb* **re·pelled; re·pel·ling 1** : to drive away : REPULSE **2** : to fight against : RESIST **3** : to turn away : REJECT **4** : to cause aversion in : DISGUST

**¹re·pel·lent** *also* **re·pel·lant** \ri-'pe-lənt\ *adj* **1** : tending to drive away ⟨a mosquito-*repellent* spray⟩ **2** : causing disgust

**²repellent** *also* **repellant** *n* : something

---

renominate reoccur reorganize repack
renomination reopen reorient repaint
renumber reorder reorientation repass
reoccupy reorganization

that repels; *esp* : a substance that repels insects

**re·pent** \ri-ˈpent\ *vb* **1** : to turn from sin and resolve to reform one's life **2** : to feel sorry for (something done) : REGRET ⟨~ed his decision⟩ — **re·pen·tance** \ri-ˈpen-t³ns\ *n* — **re·pen·tant** \-t³nt\ *adj*

**re·per·cus·sion** \ˌrē-pər-ˈkə-shən, ˌre-\ *n* **1** : REVERBERATION **2** : a reciprocal action or effect **3** : a widespread, indirect, or unforeseen effect of something done or said

**rep·er·toire** \ˈre-pər-ˌtwär\ *n* [F] **1** : a list of plays, operas, pieces, or parts which a company or performer is prepared to present **2** : a list of the skills or devices possessed by a person or needed in a person's occupation

**rep·er·to·ry** \ˈre-pər-ˌtȯr-ē\ *n, pl* **-ries** **1** : REPOSITORY **2** : REPERTOIRE **3** : a company that presents its repertoire in the course of one season at one theater

**rep·e·ti·tion** \ˌre-pə-ˈti-shən\ *n* **1** : the act or an instance of repeating **2** : the fact of being repeated

**rep·e·ti·tious** \-ˈti-shəs\ *adj* : marked by repetition; *esp* : tediously repeating ⟨~ work⟩ — **rep·e·ti·tious·ly** *adv* — **rep·e·ti·tious·ness** *n*

**re·pet·i·tive** \ri-ˈpe-ti-tiv\ *adj* : REPETITIOUS — **re·pet·i·tive·ly** *adv* — **re·pet·i·tive·ness** *n*

**re·pine** \ri-ˈpīn\ *vb* **re·pined; re·pin·ing** **1** : to feel or express discontent or dejection **2** : to long for something

**repl** *abbr* replace; replacement

**re·place** \ri-ˈplās\ *vb* **1** : to restore to a former place or position **2** : to take the place of : SUPPLANT **3** : to put something new in the place of — **re·place·able** *adj* — **re·plac·er** *n*

**re·place·ment** \ri-ˈplās-mənt\ *n* **1** : the act of replacing : the state of being replaced **2** : one that replaces another esp. in a job or function

**¹re·play** \(ˌ)rē-ˈplā\ *vb* : to play again or over

**²re·play** \ˈrē-ˌplā\ *n* **1** : an act or instance of replaying **2** : the playing of a tape (as a videotape)

**re·plen·ish** \ri-ˈple-nish\ *vb* : to fill or build up again : stock or supply anew — **re·plen·ish·ment** *n*

**re·plete** \ri-ˈplēt\ *adj* **1** : fully provided ⟨a kit ~ with instructions⟩ **2** : FULL; *esp* : full of food — **re·plete·ness** *n* — **re·ple·tion** \ri-ˈplē-shən\ *n*

**rep·li·ca** \ˈre-pli-kə\ *n* [It, repetition, fr. *replicare* to repeat, fr. LL, fr. L, to fold back, fr. *re-* back + *plicare* to fold] **1** : an exact reproduction (as of a painting) executed by the original artist **2** : a copy exact in all details : DUPLICATE

**¹rep·li·cate** \ˈre-plə-ˌkāt\ *vb* **-cat·ed; -cat·ing** : DUPLICATE, REPEAT

**²rep·li·cate** \-pli-kət\ *n* : one of several identical experiments or procedures

**rep·li·ca·tion** \ˌre-plə-ˈkā-shən\ *n* **1** : ANSWER, REPLY **2** : precise copying or re-

production; *also* : an act or process of this ⟨~ of DNA⟩

**re·ply** \ri-ˈplī\ *vb* **re·plied; re·ply·ing** : to say or do in answer : RESPOND

**reply** *n, pl* **replies** : ANSWER, RESPONSE

**repo** \ˈrē-ˌpō\ *adj* : of, relating to, or being in the business of repossessing property (as a car)

**¹re·port** \ri-ˈpȯrt\ *n* [ME, fr. AF, fr. *reporter* to bring back, report, fr. L *reportare*, fr. *re-* back + *portare* to carry] **1** : common talk : RUMOR **2** : FAME, REPUTATION ⟨a person of good ~⟩ **3** : a usu. detailed account or statement **4** : an explosive noise

**²report** *vb* **1** : to give an account of : RELATE, TELL **2** : to serve as carrier of (a message) **3** : to prepare or present (as an account of an event) for a newspaper or a broadcast **4** : to make a charge of misconduct against **5** : to present oneself (as for work) **6** : to make known to the authorities ⟨~ a fire⟩ **7** : to return or present (as a matter referred to a committee) with conclusions and recommendations **8** : to work as a subordinate ⟨~s to the vice president⟩ — **re·port·able** *adj*

**re·port·age** \ri-ˈpȯr-tij, *esp for* 2 ˌre-pər-ˈtäzh, ˌre-ˌpȯr-ˈ\ *n* [F] **1** : the act or process of reporting news **2** : writing intended to give an account of observed or documented events

**report card** *n* : a periodic report on a student's grades

**re·port·ed·ly** \ri-ˈpȯr-təd-lē\ *adv* : according to report ⟨is ~ about to be fired⟩

**re·port·er** \ri-ˈpȯr-tər\ *n* : one that reports; *esp* : a person who gathers and reports news for a news medium — **re·por·to·ri·al** \ˌre-pər-ˈtȯr-ē-əl\ *adj*

**¹re·pose** \ri-ˈpōz\ *vb* **re·posed; re·pos·ing** **1** : to lay at rest **2** : to lie at rest **3** : to lie dead **4** : to take a rest **5** : to rest for support : LIE

**²repose** *n* **1** : a state of resting (as after exertion); *esp* : SLEEP **2** : eternal or heavenly rest **3** : CALM, PEACE ⟨the ~ of the bayous⟩ **4** : cessation or absence of activity, movement, or animation **5** : composure of manner : POISE — **re·pose·ful** *adj*

**³repose** *vb* **re·posed; re·pos·ing** **1** : to place (as trust) in someone or something **2** : to place for control, management, or use

**re·pos·i·to·ry** \ri-ˈpä-zə-ˌtȯr-ē\ *n, pl* **-ries** **1** : a place where something is deposited or stored **2** : a person to whom something is entrusted

**re·pos·sess** \ˌrē-pə-ˈzes\ *vb* **1** : to regain possession of **2** : to take possession of in default of the payment of installments due — **re·pos·ses·sion** \-ˈze-shən\ *n*

**rep·re·hend** \ˌre-pri-ˈhend\ *vb* : to express disapproval of : CENSURE ♦ **Synonyms** CRITICIZE, CONDEMN, DENOUNCE, BLAME, PAN — **rep·re·hen·sion** \-ˈhen-chən\ *n*

**rep·re·hen·si·ble** \-ˈhen-sə-bəl\ *adj* : deserving blame or censure : CULPABLE — **rep·re·hen·si·bly** \-blē\ *adv*

**rep·re·sent** \re-pri-'zent\ *vb* **1** : to present a picture or a likeness of : PORTRAY, DEPICT **2** : to serve as a sign or symbol of **3** : to act the role of **4** : to stand in the place of : act or speak for; *also* : to manage the legal and business affairs of **5** : to be a member or example of : TYPIFY **6** : to serve as an elected representative of **7** : to describe as having a specified quality or character **8** : to state with the purpose of affecting judgment or action

**rep·re·sen·ta·tion** \re-pri-,zen-'tā-shən\ *n* **1** : the act of representing **2** : one (as a picture or image) that represents something else **3** : the state of being represented in a legislative body; *also* : the body of persons representing a constituency **4** : a usu. formal statement made to effect a change

**¹rep·re·sen·ta·tive** \re-pri-'zen-tə-tiv\ *adj* **1** : serving to represent **2** : standing or acting for another **3** : founded on the principle of representation : carried on by elected representatives ⟨~ government⟩ — **rep·re·sen·ta·tive·ly** *adv* — **rep·re·sen·ta·tive·ness** *n*

**²representative** *n* **1** : one that represents another; *esp* : one representing a district in a legislative body usu. as a member of a lower house **2** : a typical example of a group, class, or quality

**re·press** \ri-'pres\ *vb* **1** : CURB, SUBDUE **2** : RESTRAIN, SUPPRESS **3** : to exclude from consciousness ⟨~ a painful memory⟩ — **re·pres·sion** \-'pre-shən\ *n* — **re·pres·sive** \-'pre-siv\ *adj*

**¹re·prieve** \ri-'prēv\ *vb* **re·prieved; re·priev·ing 1** : to delay the punishment or execution of **2** : to give temporary relief to

**²reprieve** *n* **1** : the act of reprieving : the state of being reprieved **2** : a formal temporary suspension of a sentence esp. of death **3** : a temporary respite

**¹rep·ri·mand** \'re-prə-,mand\ *n* : a severe or formal reproof

**²reprimand** *vb* : to reprove severely or formally ⟨~ed the sergeant⟩

**¹re·print** \(,)rē-'print\ *vb* : to print again

**²re·print** \'rē-,print\ *n* : a reproduction of printed matter

**re·pri·sal** \ri-'prī-zəl\ *n* : an act in retaliation for something done by another

**re·prise** \ri-'prēz\ *n* : a recurrence, renewal, or resumption of an action; *also* : a musical repetition

**¹re·proach** \ri-'prōch\ *n* **1** : an expression of disapproval : DISGRACE, DISCREDIT **3** : the act of reproaching : REBUKE **4** : a cause or occasion of blame or disgrace — **re·proach·ful** \-fəl\ *adj* — **re·proach·ful·ly** *adv* — **re·proach·ful·ness** *n*

**²reproach** *vb* **1** : CENSURE, REBUKE **2** : to cast discredit on ♦ *Synonyms* CHIDE, ADMONISH, REPROVE, REPRIMAND — **re·proach·able** *adj*

**rep·ro·bate** \'re-prə-,bāt\ *n* **1** : a person

foreordained to damnation **2** : a thoroughly bad person : SCOUNDREL — **rep·robate** *adj*

**rep·ro·ba·tion** \,re-prə-'bā-shən\ *n* : strong disapproval : CONDEMNATION

**re·pro·duce** \,rē-prə-'düs, -'dyüs\ *vb* **1** : to produce again or anew **2** : to produce offspring — **re·pro·duc·ible** \-'dü-sə-bəl, -'dyü-\ *adj* — **re·pro·duc·tion** \-'dək-shən\ *n* — **re·pro·duc·tive** \-'dək-tiv\ *adj*

**re·proof** \ri-'prüf\ *n* : blame or censure for a fault

**re·prove** \ri-'prüv\ *vb* **re·proved; re·prov·ing 1** : to administer a rebuke to **2** : to express disapproval of ♦ *Synonyms* REPRIMAND, ADMONISH, REPROACH, CHIDE — **re·prov·er** *n*

**rept** *abbr* report

**rep·tile** \'rep-tī(-ə)l, -t⁰l\ *n* [ME *reptil*, fr. MF or LL; MF *reptile*, fr. LL *reptile*, fr. L *repere* to crawl] : any of a large class of air-breathing scaly vertebrates including snakes, lizards, alligators, turtles, and extinct related forms (as dinosaurs) — **rep·til·i·an** \rep-'ti-lē-ən\ *adj or n*

**re·pub·lic** \ri-'pə-blik\ *n* [F *république*, fr. MF *republique*, fr. L *respublica*, fr. *res* thing, wealth + *publica*, fem. of *publicus* public] **1** : a government having a chief of state who is not a monarch and is usu. a president; *also* : a nation or other political unit having such a government **2** : a government in which supreme power is held by the citizens entitled to vote and is exercised by elected officers and representatives governing according to law; *also* : a nation or other political unit having such a form of government **3** : a constituent political and territorial unit of the former nations of Czechoslovakia, the U.S.S.R., or Yugoslavia

**¹re·pub·li·can** \-bli-kən\ *n* **1** : one that favors or supports a republican form of government **2** *cap* : a member of a republican party and esp. of the Republican party of the U.S.

**²republican** *adj* **1** : of, relating to, or resembling a republic **2** : favoring or supporting a republic **3** *cap* : of, relating to, or constituting one of the two major political parties in the U.S. evolving in the mid-19th century — **re·pub·li·can·ism** *n, often cap*

**re·pu·di·ate** \ri-'pyü-dē-,āt\ *vb* **-at·ed; -at·ing** [L *repudiare* to cast off, divorce, fr. *repudium* rejection of a prospective spouse, divorce] **1** : to cast off : DISOWN **2** : to refuse to have anything to do with : refuse to acknowledge, accept, or pay ⟨~ a charge⟩ ⟨~ a debt⟩ ♦ *Synonyms* SPURN, REJECT, DECLINE — **re·pu·di·a·tion** \-,pyü-dē-'ā-shən\ *n* — **re·pu·di·a·tor** \-'pyü-dē-,ā-tər\ *n*

**re·pug·nance** \ri-'pəg-nəns\ *n* **1** : the quality or fact of being contradictory or inconsistent **2** : strong dislike, distaste, or antagonism

**re·pug·nant** \-nənt\ *adj* **1** : marked by

reprice                 reprogram                 republication             republish
reprocess

repugnance 2 : contrary to a person's tastes or principles : exciting distaste or aversion ♦ **Synonyms** REPELLENT, ABHORRENT, DISTASTEFUL, OBNOXIOUS, REVOLTING, LOATHSOME — **re·pug·nant·ly** adv

¹**re·pulse** \ri-'pəls\ vb **re·pulsed; re·puls·ing** 1 : to drive or beat back : REPEL 2 : to repel by discourtesy or denial : REBUFF 3 : to cause a feeling of repulsion in : DISGUST ⟨repulsed by the violence⟩

²**repulse** n 1 : REBUFF, REJECTION 2 : the action of repelling an attacker : the fact of being repelled

**re·pul·sion** \ri-'pəl-shən\ n 1 : the action of repulsing : the state of being repulsed 2 : the force with which bodies, particles, or like forces repel one another 3 : a feeling of aversion

**re·pul·sive** \-siv\ adj 1 : serving or tending to repel or reject 2 : arousing aversion or disgust ♦ **Synonyms** REPUGNANT, REVOLTING, LOATHSOME, NOISOME — **re·pul·sive·ly** adv — **re·pul·sive·ness** n

**re·pur·pose** \(ˌ)rē-'pər-pəs\ vb : to give a new purpose or use to

**rep·u·ta·ble** \'re-pyə-tə-bəl\ adj : having a good reputation : ESTIMABLE ⟨a ~ lawyer⟩ — **rep·u·ta·bly** \-blē\ adv

**rep·u·ta·tion** \ˌre-pyù-'tā-shən\ n 1 : overall quality or character as seen or judged by people in general 2 : place in public esteem or regard

¹**re·pute** \ri-'pyüt\ vb **re·put·ed; re·put·ing** : BELIEVE, CONSIDER ⟨reputed to be a millionaire⟩

²**repute** n 1 : REPUTATION ⟨knew her by ~⟩ 2 : the state of being favorably known or spoken of

**re·put·ed** \ri-'pyü-təd\ adj 1 : REPUTABLE 2 : according to reputation : SUPPOSED — **re·put·ed·ly** adv

**req** abbr 1 request 2 require; required 3 requisition

¹**re·quest** \ri-'kwest\ n 1 : an act or instance of asking for something 2 : a thing asked for 3 : the condition of being asked for ⟨available on ~⟩

²**request** vb 1 : to make a request to or of 2 : to ask for — **re·quest·er** or **re·quest·or** n

**re·qui·em** \'re-kwē-əm, 'rā-\ n [ME, fr. L (first word of the requiem mass), acc. of requies rest, fr. quies quiet, rest] 1 : a mass for a dead person; also : a musical setting for this 2 : a musical service or hymn in honor of the dead

**re·quire** \ri-'kwī(-ə)r\ vb **re·quired; re·quir·ing** 1 : to demand as necessary or essential 2 : COMMAND, ORDER ⟨the law ~s that everyone pay the tax⟩

**re·quire·ment** \-mənt\ n 1 : something (as a condition or quality) required ⟨entrance ~s⟩ 2 : NECESSITY ⟨production was sufficient to satisfy military ~s⟩

**req·ui·site** \'re-kwə-zət\ adj : REQUIRED, NECESSARY — **requisite** n

**req·ui·si·tion** \ˌre-kwə-'zi-shən\ n 1 : formal application or demand (as for supplies) 2 : the state of being in demand or use — **requisition** vb

**re·quite** \ri-'kwīt\ vb **re·quit·ed; re·quit·ing** 1 : to make return for : REPAY 2 : to make retaliation for : AVENGE 3 : to make return to — **re·quit·al** \-'kwī-t°l\ n

**rere·dos** \'rer-ə-ˌdäs\ n : a usu. ornamental wood or stone screen or partition wall behind an altar

**re·run** \'rē-ˌrən, (ˌ)rē-'rən\ n : the act or an instance of running again or anew; esp : a showing of a motion picture or television program after its first run — **re·run** \(ˌ)rē-'rən\ vb

**res** abbr 1 research 2 reservation; reserve 3 reservoir 4 residence; resident 5 resolution

**re·sale** \'rē-ˌsāl, (ˌ)rē-'sāl\ n : the act of selling again usu. to a new party — **re·sal·able** \(ˌ)rē-'sā-lə-bəl\ adj

**re·scind** \ri-'sind\ vb : REPEAL, CANCEL, ANNUL — **re·scis·sion** \-'si-zhən\ n

**re·script** \'rē-ˌskript\ n : an official or authoritative order or decree

**res·cue** \'res-kyü\ vb **res·cued; res·cu·ing** [ME rescouen, rescuen, fr. AF rescure, fr. re- back, again + escure to shake off, fr. L excutere] : to free from danger, harm, or confinement — **rescue** n — **res·cu·er** n

**re·search** \ri-'sərch, 'rē-ˌsərch\ n 1 : careful or diligent search 2 : studious inquiry or examination aimed at the discovery and interpretation of new knowledge 3 : the collecting of information about a particular subject — **research** vb — **re·search·er** n

**re·sec·tion** \ri-'sek-shən\ n : the surgical removal of part of an organ or structure

**re·sem·blance** \ri-'zem-bləns\ n : the quality or state of resembling

**re·sem·ble** \ri-'zem-bəl\ vb **-bled; -bling** : to be like or similar to

**re·sent** \ri-'zent\ vb : to feel or exhibit annoyance or indignation at ⟨~ed his interference⟩ — **re·sent·ful** \-fəl\ adj — **re·sent·ful·ly** adv — **re·sent·ment** n

**re·ser·pine** \ri-'sər-ˌpēn, -pən\ n : a drug used in treating high blood pressure and nervous tension

**res·er·va·tion** \ˌre-zər-'vā-shən\ n 1 : an act of reserving 2 : something (as a room in a hotel) arranged for in advance 3 : something reserved; esp : a tract of public land set aside for special use 4 : a limiting condition

¹**re·serve** \ri-'zərv\ vb **re·served; re·serv·ing** 1 : to store for future or special use 2 : to hold back for oneself 3 : to set aside or arrange to have set aside or held for special use

²**reserve** n 1 : something reserved : STOCK, STORE 2 : a military force with-

repurchase     rerecord     rescore     reseed
reradiate     reroute     rescreen     resell
reread     reschedule     reseal
rereading

held from action for later use — usu. used in pl. **3** : the military forces of a country not part of the regular services; *also* : RESERVIST **4** : a tract set apart **I RESERVATION 5** : an act of reserving **6** : restraint or caution in one's words or bearing **7** : money or its equivalent kept in hand or set apart to meet liabilities

**re·served** \ri-'zərvd\ *adj* **1** : restrained in words and actions **2** : set aside for future or special use — **re·serv·ed·ly** \-'zər-vəd-lē\ *adv* — **re·serv·ed·ness** \-vəd-nas\ *n*

**re·serv·ist** \ri-'zər-vist\ *n* : a member of a military reserve

**res·er·voir** \'re-zə-,vwär, -zər-, -,vwȯr\ *n* [F] : a place where something is kept in store; *esp* : an artificial lake where water is collected and kept for use

**re·shuf·fle** \rē-'shə-fəl\ *vb* **1** : to shuffle again **2** : to reorganize usu. by redistribution of existing elements ⟨*reshuffled* our schedule⟩ — **reshuffle** *n*

**re·side** \ri-'zīd\ *vb* **re·sid·ed; re·sid·ing** **1** : to make one's home : DWELL **2** : to be present as a quality or vested as a right

**res·i·dence** \'re-zə-dəns\ *n* **1** : the act or fact of residing in a place as a dweller or in discharge of a duty or an obligation **2** : the place where one actually lives **3** : a building used as a home : DWELLING **4** : the period of living in a place

**res·i·den·cy** \'re-zə-dən-sē\ *n, pl* **-cies** **1** : the residence of or the territory under a diplomatic resident **2** : a period of advanced training in a medical specialty

¹**res·i·dent** \-dənt\ *adj* **1** : RESIDING **2** : being in residence **3** : not migratory

²**resident** *n* **1** : one who resides in a place **2** : a diplomatic representative with governing powers (as in a protectorate) **3** : a physician serving a residency

**res·i·den·tial** \,re-zə-'den-chəl\ *adj* **1** : used as a residence or by residents **2** : occupied by or restricted to residences — **res·i·den·tial·ly** *adv*

¹**res·id·u·al** \ri-'zi-jə-wəl\ *n* **1** : a residual product or substance **2** : a payment (as to an actor or writer) for each rerun after an initial showing (as of a taped TV show)

²**residual** *adj* : being a residue or remainder

**re·sid·u·ary** \ri-'zi-jə-,wer-ē\ *adj* : of, relating to, or constituting a residue esp. of an estate

**res·i·due** \'re-zə-,dü, -,dyü\ *n* : a part remaining after another part has been taken away : REMAINDER

**re·sid·u·um** \ri-'zi-jə-wəm\ *n, pl* **re·sid·ua** \-jə-wə\ [L] **1** : something remaining or residual after certain deductions are made **2** : a residual product

¹**re·sign** \ri-'zīn\ *vb* [ME, fr. AF *resigner*, fr. L *resignare*, lit., to unseal, cancel, fr. *signare* to sign, seal] **1** : to give up deliberately (as one's position) esp. by a formal act **2** : to give (oneself) over (as to grief or despair) without resistance — **re·sign·ed·ly** \-'zī-nəd-lē\ *adv*

²**re·sign** \(,)rē-'sīn\ *vb* : to sign again

**res·ig·na·tion** \,re-zig-'nā-shən\ *n* **1** : an act or instance of resigning; *also* : a formal notification of such an act **2** : the quality or state of being resigned

**re·sil·ience** \ri-'zil-yəns\ *n* **1** : the ability of a body to regain its original size and shape after being compressed, bent, or stretched **2** : an ability to recover from or adjust easily to change or misfortune

**re·sil·ien·cy** \-yən-sē\ *n* : RESILIENCE

**re·sil·ient** \-yənt\ *adj* : marked by resilience ⟨∼ players⟩

**res·in** \'re-z³n\ *n* : any of various substances obtained from the gum or sap of some trees and used esp. in varnishes, plastics, and medicine; *also* : a comparable synthetic product — **res·in·ous** *adj*

¹**re·sist** \ri-'zist\ *vb* **1** : to fight against ; OPPOSE ⟨∼ aggression⟩ **2** : to withstand the force or effect of ⟨*∼ed* temptation⟩ ⟨∼ disease⟩ ♦ *Synonyms* COMBAT, REPEL — **re·sist·ible** \-'zis-tə-bəl\ *adj* — **re·sist·less** *adj*

²**resist** *n* : something (as a coating) that resists or prevents a particular action

**re·sis·tance** \ri-'zis-təns\ *n* **1** : the act or an instance of resisting : OPPOSITION **2** : the power or capacity to resist; *esp* : the inherent ability of an organism to resist harmful influences (as disease or infection) **3** : the opposition offered by a body to the passage through it of a steady electric current

**re·sis·tant** \-tənt\ *adj* : giving, capable of, or exhibiting resistance

**re·sis·tor** \ri-'zis-tər\ *n* : a device used to provide resistance to the flow of an electric current in a circuit

**res·o·lute** \'re-zə-,lüt\ *adj* : firmly determined in purpose : RESOLVED ⟨a ∼ leader⟩ ♦ *Synonyms* STEADFAST, STAUNCH, FAITHFUL, TRUE, LOYAL — **res·o·lute·ly** *adv* — **res·o·lute·ness** *n*

**res·o·lu·tion** \,re-zə-'lü-shən\ *n* **1** : the act or process of resolving; *also* : SOLUTION **3** : the quality of being resolute : FIRMNESS, DETERMINATION **4** : a formal statement expressing the opinion, will, or intent of a body of persons **5** : a measure of the sharpness of an image or of the fineness with which a device can produce or record such an image

¹**re·solve** \ri-'zälv\ *vb* **re·solved; re·solv·ing** **1** : to break up into constituent parts : ANALYZE **2** : to distinguish between or make visible adjacent parts of **3** : to find an answer to : SOLVE ⟨∼ a dispute⟩ **4** : DETERMINE, DECIDE **5** : to make or pass a formal resolution — **re·solv·able** *adj*

²**resolve** *n* **1** : fixity of purpose **2** : something resolved

**res·o·nance** \'re-zə-nəns\ *n* **1** : the quality or state of being resonant **2** : a reinforcement of sound in a vibrating body caused by waves from another body vibrating at nearly the same rate

---

reset                      resettlement             reshow                   resocialization
resettle                   resew

**res·o·nant** \-nənt\ *adj* **1** : continuing to sound : RESOUNDING **2** : relating to or exhibiting resonance **3** : intensified and enriched by or as if by resonance — **res·o·nant·ly** *adv*

**res·o·nate** \-,nāt\ *vb* **-nat·ed; -nat·ing 1** : to produce or exhibit resonance **2** : REVERBERATE, RESOUND **3** : to relate harmoniously ⟨∼ with voters⟩

**res·o·na·tor** \-,nā-tər\ *n* : something that resounds or exhibits resonance

**re·sorp·tion** \rē-'sȯrp-shən, -'zȯrp-\ *n* : the action or process of breaking down and assimilating something (as a tooth or an embryo)

**¹re·sort** \ri-'zȯrt\ *n* [ME, return, source of aid, fr. AF, fr. *resortir* to rebound, resort, fr. *sortir* to go out, leave] **1** : one looked to for help : REFUGE **2** : RECOURSE **3** : frequent or general visiting ⟨place of ∼⟩ **4** : a frequently visited place : HAUNT **5** : a place providing recreation esp. to vacationers

**²resort** *vb* **1** : to go often or habitually **2** : to have recourse ⟨∼ed to violence⟩

**re·sound** \ri-'zaůnd\ *vb* **1** : to become filled with sound : REVERBERATE, RING **2** : to sound loudly

**re·sound·ing** *adj* **1** : RESONATING, RESONANT **2** : impressively sonorous ⟨∼ name⟩ **3** : EMPHATIC, UNEQUIVOCAL ⟨a ∼ success⟩ — **re·sound·ing·ly** *adv*

**re·source** \'rē-,sȯrs, ri-'sȯrs\ *n* [F *ressource*, fr. OF *ressourse* relief, resource, fr. *resourdre* to relieve, lit., to rise again, fr. L *resurgere*, fr. *re-* again + *surgere* to rise] **1** : a source of supply or support — usu. used in pl. **2** : a natural feature or phenomenon that enhances the quality of human life **3** *pl* : available funds **4** : a possibility of relief or recovery **5** : a means of spending leisure time **6** : ability to meet and handle situations — **re·source·ful** \-'sȯrs-fəl\ *adj* — **re·source·ful·ness** *n*

**¹re·spect** \ri-'spekt\ *n* **1** : relation to something usu. specified : REGARD ⟨in ∼ to⟩ **2** : high or special regard : ESTEEM **3** *pl* : an expression of respect or deference **4** : DETAIL, PARTICULAR — **re·spect·ful** \-fəl\ *adj* — **re·spect·ful·ly** *adv* — **re·spect·ful·ness** *n*

**²respect** *vb* **1** : to consider deserving of high regard : ESTEEM **2** : to refrain from interfering with ⟨∼ another's privacy⟩ **3** : to have reference to : CONCERN — **re·spect·er** *n*

**re·spect·able** \ri-'spek-tə-bəl\ *adj* **1** : worthy of respect : ESTIMABLE **2** : decent or correct in conduct : PROPER **3** : fair in size, quantity, or quality ⟨a ∼ score⟩ : MODERATE, TOLERABLE **4** : fit to be seen : PRESENTABLE — **re·spect·a·bil·i·ty** \-,spek-tə-'bi-lə-tē\ *n* — **re·spect·ably** \-'spek-tə-blē\ *adv*

**re·spect·ing** *prep* : with regard to

**re·spec·tive** \-tiv\ *adj* : PARTICULAR, SEPARATE ⟨returned to their ∼ homes⟩

**re·spec·tive·ly** \-lē\ *adv* **1** : as relating to each **2** : each in the order given

**res·pi·ra·tion** \,res-pə-'rā-shən\ *n* **1** : an act or the process of breathing **2** : the physical and chemical processes (as breathing and oxidation) by which a living thing obtains oxygen and eliminates waste gases (as carbon dioxide) — **res·pi·ra·to·ry** \'res-pə-rə-,tȯr-ē, ri-'spī-rə-\ *adj* — **re·spire** \ri-'spī-(ə)r\ *vb*

**res·pi·ra·tor** \'res-pə-,rā-tər\ *n* **1** : a device covering the mouth and nose esp. to prevent inhaling harmful vapors **2** : a device for artificial respiration

**re·spite** \'res-pət\ *n* [ME *respit*, fr. AF, fr. ML *respectus*, fr. L, act of looking back] **1** : a temporary delay **2** : an interval of rest or relief

**re·splen·dent** \ri-'splen-dənt\ *adj* : shining brilliantly : gloriously bright : SPLENDID ⟨∼ uniforms⟩ — **re·splen·dence** \-dəns\ *n* — **re·splen·dent·ly** *adv*

**re·spond** \ri-'spänd\ *vb* **1** : ANSWER, REPLY **2** : REACT ⟨∼ed to a call for help⟩ **3** : to show favorable reaction ⟨∼ to medication⟩ — **re·spond·er** *n*

**re·spon·dent** \ri-'spän-dənt\ *n* : one who responds; *esp* : one who answers in various legal proceedings — **respondent** *adj*

**re·sponse** \ri-'späns\ *n* **1** : an act of responding **2** : something constituting a reply or a reaction

**re·spon·si·bil·i·ty** \ri-,spän-sə-'bi-lə-tē\ *n, pl* **-ties 1** : the quality or state of being responsible **2** : something for which one is responsible

**re·spon·si·ble** \ri-'spän-sə-bəl\ *adj* **1** : liable to be called upon to answer for one's acts or decisions : ANSWERABLE **2** : able to fulfill one's obligations : RELIABLE, TRUSTWORTHY **3** : able to choose for oneself between right and wrong **4** : involving accountability or important duties ⟨∼ position⟩ — **re·spon·si·ble·ness** *n* — **re·spon·si·bly** \-blē\ *adv*

**re·spon·sive** \-siv\ *adj* **1** : RESPONDING **2** : quick to respond : SENSITIVE **3** : using responses ⟨∼ readings⟩ — **re·spon·sive·ly** *adv* — **re·spon·sive·ness** *n*

**¹rest** \'rest\ *n* **1** : REPOSE, SLEEP **2** : freedom from work or activity **3** : a state of motionlessness or inactivity **4** : a place of shelter or lodging **5** : a silence in music equivalent in duration to a note of the same value; *also* : a character indicating this **6** : something used as a support — **rest·ful** \-fəl\ *adj* — **rest·ful·ly** *adv*

**²rest** *vb* **1** : to get rest by lying down; *esp* : SLEEP **2** : to cease from action or motion **3** : to give rest to : set at rest **4** : to sit or lie fixed or supported **5** : to place on or against a support **6** : to remain based or founded **7** : to cause to be firmly fixed : GROUND **8** : to remain for action : DEPEND

**³rest** *n* : something left over

**res·tau·rant** \'res-trənt, -tə-,ränt\ *n* [F, fr. prp. of *restaurer* to restore, fr. L *restaurare*] : a public eating place

**res·tau·ra·teur** \,res-tə-rə-'tər\ *also* **res·tau·ran·teur** \-,rän-\ *n* : the operator or proprietor of a restaurant

---

**rest home** *n* : an establishment that gives care for the aged or convalescent

**res·ti·tu·tion** \ˌres-tə-ˈtü-shən, -ˈtyü-\ *n* : the act of restoring : the state of being restored; *esp* : restoration of something to its rightful owner ♦ **Synonyms** AMENDS, REDRESS, REPARATION, INDEMNITY, COMPENSATION

**res·tive** \ˈres-tiv\ *adj* [ME *restyf*, fr. AF *restif*, fr. *rester* to stop, resist, remain, fr. L *restare*, fr. re- back + *stare* to stand] 1 : BALKY 2 : UNEASY, FIDGETY ♦ **Synonyms** RESTLESS, IMPATIENT, NERVOUS — **res·tive·ly** *adv* — **res·tive·ness** *n*

**rest·less** \ˈrest-ləs\ *adj* 1 : lacking or denying rest ⟨a ∼ night⟩ 2 : never resting or settled : always moving ⟨the ∼ sea⟩ 3 : marked by or showing unrest esp. of mind ⟨∼ pacing back and forth⟩ ♦ **Synonyms** RESTIVE, IMPATIENT, NERVOUS, FIDGETY — **rest·less·ly** *adv* — **rest·less·ness** *n*

**re·stor·able** \ri-ˈstȯr-ə-bəl\ *adj* : fit for restoring or reclaiming

**res·to·ra·tion** \ˌres-tə-ˈrā-shən\ *n* 1 : an act of restoring : the state of being restored 2 : something (as a building) that has been restored

**re·stor·ative** \ri-ˈstȯr-ə-tiv\ *n* : something that restores esp. to consciousness or health — **restorative** *adj*

**re·store** \ri-ˈstȯr\ *vb* **re·stored; re·stor·ing** 1 : to give back : RETURN 2 : to put back into use or service 3 : to put or bring back into a former or original state 4 : to put again in possession of something — **re·stor·er** *n*

**re·strain** \ri-ˈstrān\ *vb* 1 : to prevent from doing something 2 : to limit, restrict, or keep under control : CURB 3 : to place under restraint or arrest — **re·strain·able** *adj* — **re·strain·er** *n*

**re·strained** \ri-ˈstrānd\ *adj* : marked by restraint : DISCIPLINED — **re·strain·ed·ly** \-ˈstrā-nəd-lē\ *adv*

**restraining order** *n* : a legal order directing one person to stay away from another

**re·straint** \ri-ˈstrānt\ *n* 1 : an act of restraining : the state of being restrained 2 : a restraining force, agency, or device 3 : deprivation or limitation of liberty : CONFINEMENT 4 : control over one's feelings : RESERVE

**re·strict** \ri-ˈstrikt\ *vb* 1 : to confine within bounds : LIMIT 2 : to place under restriction as to use — **re·stric·tive** *adj* — **re·stric·tive·ly** *adv*

**re·stric·tion** \ri-ˈstrik-shən\ *n* 1 : something (as a law or rule) that restricts 2 : an act of restricting : the state of being restricted

**rest room** *n* : a room or suite of rooms that includes sinks and toilets

¹**re·sult** \ri-ˈzəlt\ *vb* [ME, fr. ML *resultare*, fr. L, to rebound, fr. re- re- + *saltare* to leap] : to come about as an effect or con-

sequence ⟨an injury ∼ing from a fall⟩ — **re·sul·tant** \-ˈzəl-tᵊnt\ *adj or n*

²**result** *n* 1 : something that results : EFFECT, CONSEQUENCE 2 : beneficial or discernible effect 3 : something obtained by calculation or investigation

**re·sume** \ri-ˈzüm\ *vb* **re·sumed; re·sum·ing** 1 : to take or assume again 2 : to return to or begin again after interruption 3 : to take back to oneself — **re·sump·tion** \-ˈzəmp-shən\ *n*

**ré·su·mé** *or* **re·su·me** *or* **re·su·mé** \ˈre-zə-ˌmā, ˌre-zə-ˈmā\ *n* [F *résumé*] 1 : SUMMARY; *esp* : a short account of one's career and qualifications usu. prepared by a job applicant 2 : a set of accomplishments ⟨a musical ∼⟩

**re·sur·gence** \ri-ˈsər-jəns\ *n* : a rising again into life, activity, or prominence — **re·sur·gent** \-jənt\ *adj*

**res·ur·rect** \ˌre-zə-ˈrekt\ *vb* 1 : to raise from the dead 2 : to bring to attention or use again

**res·ur·rec·tion** \ˌre-zə-ˈrek-shən\ *n* 1 *cap* : the rising of Christ from the dead 2 *often cap* : the rising to life of all human dead before the final judgment 3 : REVIVAL ⟨the ∼ of her career⟩

**re·sus·ci·tate** \ri-ˈsə-sə-ˌtāt\ *vb* **-tat·ed; -tat·ing** : to revive from apparent death or unconsciousness; *also* : REVITALIZE — **re·sus·ci·ta·tion** \ri-ˌsə-sə-ˈtā-shən, ˌrē-\ *n* — **re·sus·ci·ta·tor** \ri-ˈsə-sə-ˌtā-tər\ *n*

**ret** *abbr* retired

¹**re·tail** \ˈrē-ˌtāl, *esp for 2 also* ri-ˈtāl\ *vb* 1 : to sell in small quantities directly to the ultimate consumer 2 : to tell in detail or to one person after another — **re·tail·er** *n*

²**re·tail** \ˈrē-ˌtāl\ *n* : the sale of goods in small amounts to ultimate consumers — **retail** *adj or adv*

**re·tain** \ri-ˈtān\ *vb* 1 : to hold in possession or use 2 : to engage (as a lawyer) by paying a fee in advance 3 : to keep in a fixed place or position ♦ **Synonyms** DETAIN, WITHHOLD, RESERVE

¹**re·tain·er** \ri-ˈtā-nər\ *n* 1 : one that retains 2 : a servant in a wealthy household; *also* : EMPLOYEE 3 : a device that holds something (as teeth) in place

²**retainer** *n* : a fee paid to secure services (as of a lawyer)

¹**re·take** \(ˌ)rē-ˈtāk\ *vb* **-took** \-ˈtůk\; **-tak·en** \-ˈtā-kən\; **-tak·ing** 1 : to take or seize again 2 : to photograph again

²**re·take** \ˈrē-ˌtāk\ *n* : a second photographing of a motion-picture scene

**re·tal·i·ate** \ri-ˈta-lē-ˌāt\ *vb* **-at·ed; -at·ing** : to return like for like; *esp* : to get revenge — **re·tal·i·a·tion** \-ˌta-lē-ˈā-shən\ *n* — **re·tal·ia·to·ry** \-ˈtal-yə-ˌtōr-ē\ *adj*

**re·tard** \ri-ˈtärd\ *vb* : to hold back : delay the progress of ♦ **Synonyms** SLOW, SLACKEN, DETAIN — **re·tar·da·tion** \ˌrē-ˌtär-ˈdā-shən, ri-\ *n* — **re·tard·er** *n*

---

| | |
|---|---|
| restock | restuff |
| restrengthen | restyle |
| restructure | resubmit |
| restudy | |

| | |
|---|---|
| resummon | resurvey |
| resupply | resynthesis |
| resurface | resynthesize |

re·tar·dant \ri-'tär-d°nt\ adj : serving or tending to retard — **retardant** n

re·tard·ed adj, sometimes offensive : slow or limited in intellectual, emotional, or academic progress

retch \'rech\ vb : to try to vomit; also : VOMIT

re·ten·tion \ri-'ten-chən\ n 1 : the act of retaining : the state of being retained 2 : the power of retaining esp. in the mind : RETENTIVENESS

re·ten·tive \-'ten-tiv\ adj : having the power of retaining; esp : retaining knowledge easily — **re·ten·tive·ness** n

re·think \(ˌ)rē-'think\ vb -thought \-'thȯt\; -think·ing : to think about again : RECONSIDER

ret·i·cent \'re-tə-sənt\ adj 1 : tending not to talk or give out information 2 : RELUCTANT ♦ **Synonyms** RESERVED, TACITURN, CLOSEMOUTHED — **ret·i·cence** \-səns\ n — **ret·i·cent·ly** adv

ret·i·na \'re-tə-nə\ n, pl retinas or ret·i·nae \-ˌnē\ : the sensory membrane lining the eye that receives the image formed by the lens — **ret·i·nal** \'re-tə-nəl\ adj

ret·i·nue \'re-tə-ˌnü, -ˌnyü\ n : the body of attendants or followers of a distinguished person

re·tire \ri-'tī(-ə)r\ vb re·tired; re·tir·ing 1 : RETREAT 2 : to withdraw esp. for privacy 3 : to withdraw from one's occupation or position : conclude one's career 4 : to withdraw from use or service 5 : to go to bed 6 : to cause to be out in baseball — **re·tire·ment** n

re·tired \ri-'tī(-ə)rd\ adj 1 : SECLUDED, QUIET 2 : withdrawn from active duty or from one's career

re·tir·ee \ri-ˌtī-'rē\ n : a person who has retired from a career

re·tir·ing adj : SHY, RESERVED

re·tool \(ˌ)rē-'tül\ vb 1 : to reequip with tools 2 : to modify with usu. minor improvements <~ed the team for next year>

¹re·tort \ri-'tȯrt\ vb [L retortus, pp. of retorquēre, lit., to twist back, hurl back, fr. re- back + torquēre to twist] 1 : to say in reply : answer back usu. sharply 2 : to answer (an argument) by a counter argument 3 : RETALIATE

²retort n : a quick, witty, or cutting reply

³re·tort \ri-'tȯrt, 'rē-ˌtȯrt\ n [MF retorte, fr. ML retorta, fr. L, fem. of retortus, pp. of retorquēre to twist back; fr. its shape] 1 : a vessel in which substances are distilled or broken up by heat

re·touch \(ˌ)rē-'təch\ vb : TOUCH UP; esp : to change (as a photographic negative) in order to produce a more desirable appearance

re·trace \(ˌ)rē-'trās\ vb : to go over again or in a reverse direction <retraced his steps>

re·tract \ri-'trakt\ vb 1 : to draw back or in 2 : to withdraw (as a charge or promise) : DISAVOW — **re·tract·able** adj — **re·trac·tion** \-'trak-shən\ n

re·trac·tile \ri-'trak-t°l, -'trak-ˌtī(-ə)l\ adj : capable of being drawn back or in <~ claws>

¹re·tread \(ˌ)rē-'tred\ vb re·tread·ed; re·tread·ing : to put a new tread on (a worn tire)

²re·tread \'rē-ˌtred\ n 1 : a retreaded tire 2 : one pressed into service again; also : REMAKE

¹re·treat \ri-'trēt\ n 1 : an act of withdrawing esp. from something dangerous, difficult, or disagreeable 2 : a military signal for withdrawal; also : a military flag-lowering ceremony 3 : a place of privacy or safety : REFUGE 4 : a group withdrawal for prayer, meditation, or study

²retreat vb 1 : to make a retreat : WITHDRAW 2 : to slope backward

re·trench \ri-'trench\ vb [obs. F retrencher (now retrancher), fr. MF retrenchier, fr. re- + trenchier to cut] 1 : to cut down or pare away : REDUCE, CURTAIL 2 : to cut down expenses : ECONOMIZE <the company had to ~> — **re·trench·ment** n

ret·ri·bu·tion \ˌre-trə-'byü-shən\ n : something administered or exacted in recompense; esp : PUNISHMENT ♦ **Synonyms** REPRISAL, VENGEANCE, REVENGE, RETALIATION — **re·trib·u·tive** \ri-'tri-byə-tiv\ adj — **re·trib·u·to·ry** \-byə-ˌtȯr-ē\ adj

re·trieve \ri-'trēv\ vb re·trieved; re·triev·ing 1 : to search about for and bring in (killed or wounded game) 2 : RECOVER, RESTORE — **re·triev·able** adj — **re·triev·al** \-'trē-vəl\ n

re·triev·er \ri-'trē-vər\ n : one that retrieves; esp : a dog of any of several breeds used esp. for retrieving game

ret·ro \'re-trō\ adj : relating to or being the styles and fashions of the past <~ clothing>

ret·ro·ac·tive \ˌre-trō-'ak-tiv\ adj : made effective as of a date prior to enactment <a ~ pay raise> — **ret·ro·ac·tive·ly** adv

ret·ro·fit \'re-trō-ˌfit, ˌre-trō-'fit\ vb 1 : to furnish (as an aircraft) with newly available equipment 2 : to adapt to a new purpose or need : MODIFY — **ret·ro·fit** \'re-trō-ˌfit\ n

¹ret·ro·grade \'re-trə-ˌgrād\ adj 1 : moving or tending backward 2 : tending toward or resulting in a worse condition

²retrograde vb 1 : RETREAT 2 : DETERIORATE, DEGENERATE

ret·ro·gres·sion \ˌre-trə-'gre-shən\ n : return to a former and less complex level of development or organization — **ret·ro·gress** \ˌre-trə-'gres\ vb — **ret·ro·gres·sive** \ˌre-trə-'gre-siv\ adj

ret·ro·rock·et \'re-trō-ˌrä-kət\ n : an auxiliary rocket engine (as on a spacecraft) used to slow forward motion

ret·ro·spect \'re-trə-ˌspekt\ n : a review of past events — **ret·ro·spec·tion** \ˌre-trə-'spek-shən\ n

ret·ro·spec·tive \ˌre-trə-'spek-tiv\ n 1 : a comprehensive examination of an artist's work over many years 2 : REVIEW 4 <a

---

| | | |
|---|---|---|
| retaste | retransmission | retrial |
| retell | retrain | |
| | retransmit | |

war ~⟩ — **retrospective** *adj* — **ret·ro·spec·tive·ly** *adv*

**ret·ro·vi·rus** \'re-tō-,vī-rəs\ *n* : any of a group of RNA-containing viruses (as HIV) that make DNA using RNA instead of the reverse — **re·tro·vi·ral** \-rəl\ *adj*

¹**re·turn** \ri-'tərn\ *vb* **1** : to go or come back **2** : to pass, give, or send back to an earlier possessor **3** : to put back to or in a former place or state **4** : REPLY, AN-SWER **5** : to report esp. officially **6** : to elect to office **7** : to bring in (as profit) : YIELD **8** : to give or perform in return ⟨~ a favor⟩ — **re·turn·er** *n*

²**return** *n* **1** : an act of coming or going back to or from a former place or state **2** : RECURRENCE **3** : a report of the results of balloting **4** : a formal statement of taxable income **5** : the profit from labor, investment, or business : YIELD **6** : the act of returning something **7** : something that returns or is returned; *also* : a means for conveying something (as water) back to its starting point **8** : something given in repayment or reciprocation; *also* : AN-SWER, RETORT **9** : an answering play — **return** *adj*

¹**re·turn·able** \ri-'tər-nə-bəl\ *adj* : capable of being returned (as for reuse); *also* : permitted to be returned

²**returnable** *n* : a returnable beverage container

**re·turn·ee** \ri-,tər-'nē\ *n* : one who returns

**re·union** \rē-'yün-yən\ *n* **1** : an act of reuniting : the state of being reunited **2** : a meeting of persons after separation

¹**rev** \'rev\ *n* : a revolution of a motor

²**rev** *vb* **revved; rev·ving 1** : to increase the revolutions per minute of (a motor) **2** : STIMULATE, EXCITE

³**rev** *abbr* **1** revenue **2** reverse **3** review; reviewed **4** revised; revision **5** revolution

**Rev** *abbr* **1** Revelation **2** Reverend

**re·vamp** \(,)rē-'vamp\ *vb* : RECON-STRUCT, REVISE; *also* : RENOVATE

**re·vanche** \rə-'vänsh\ *n* [F] : REVENGE; *esp* : a usu. political policy designed to recover lost territory or status

**re·veal** \ri-'vēl\ *vb* **1** : to make known **2** : to show plainly : open up to view

**rev·eil·le** \'re-və-lē\ *n* [modif. of F *réveillez*, imper. pl. of *réveiller* to awaken, fr. MF *eveiller* to awaken, fr. VL *exvigilare*, fr. L *vigilare* to keep watch, stay awake] : a military signal sounded at about sunrise

¹**rev·el** \'re-vəl\ *vb* **-eled** *or* **-elled; -el·ing** *or* **-el·ling 1** : to take part in a revel **2** : to take great pleasure or satisfaction ⟨~ed in the quiet⟩ — **rev·el·er** *or* **rev·el·ler** *n* — **rev·el·ry** \-vəl-rē\ *n*

²**revel** *n* : a usu. wild party or celebration

**rev·e·la·tion** \,re-və-'lā-shən\ *n* **1** : an act of revealing **2** : something revealed; *esp* : an enlightening or astonishing disclosure

**Revelation** *n* — see BIBLE table

¹**re·venge** \ri-'venj\ *vb* **re·venged; re·veng·ing** : to inflict harm or injury in return for (a wrong) : AVENGE — **re·veng·er** *n*

²**revenge** *n* **1** : a desire for revenge **2** : an act or instance of retaliation to get even **3** : an opportunity for getting satisfaction
♦ *Synonyms* VENGEANCE, RETRIBU-TION, REPRISAL — **re·venge·ful** *adj*

**rev·e·nue** \'re-və-,nü, -,nyü\ *n* [ME, return, revenue, fr. AF, fr. *revenir* to return, fr. L *revenire*, fr. *re-* back + *venire* to come] **1** : investment income **2** : money collected by a government (as through taxes)

**rev·e·nu·er** \'re-və-,nü-ər, -,nyü\ *n* : a revenue officer or boat

**re·verb** \ri-'vərb, 'rē-,vərb\ *n* : an electronically produced echo effect in recorded music; *also* : a device for producing reverb

**re·ver·ber·ate** \ri-'vər-bə-,rāt\ *vb* **-at·ed; -at·ing 1** : REFLECT ⟨~ light or heat⟩ **2** : to resound in or as if in a series of echoes — **re·ver·ber·a·tion** \-,vər-bə-'rā-shən\ *n*

**re·vere** \ri-'vir\ *vb* **re·vered; re·ver·ing** : to show honor and devotion to : VENER-ATE ⟨a teacher *revered* by students⟩
♦ *Synonyms* REVERENCE, WORSHIP, ADORE

¹**rev·er·ence** \'re-vrəns, -və-rəns\ *n* **1** : honor or respect felt or shown **2** : a gesture (as a bow or curtsy) of respect

²**reverence** *vb* **-enced; -enc·ing** : to regard or treat with reverence

¹**rev·er·end** \'re-vrənd, -və-rənd\ *adj* **1** : worthy of reverence : REVERED **2** : being a member of the clergy — used as a title

²**reverend** *n* : a member of the clergy

**rev·er·ent** \'re-vrənt, -və-rənt\ *adj* : expressing reverence — **rev·er·ent·ly** *adv*

**rev·er·en·tial** \,re-və-'ren-chəl\ *adj* : REV-ERENT

**rev·er·ie** *also* **rev·ery** \'re-və-rē\ *n, pl* **-er·ies** [F *rêverie*, fr. MF, delirium, fr. *resver, rever* to wander, be delirious] **1** : DAY-DREAM **2** : the state of being lost in thought

**re·ver·sal** \ri-'vər-səl\ *n* : an act or process of reversing

¹**re·verse** \ri-'vərs\ *adj* **1** : opposite to a previous or normal condition ⟨in ~ order⟩ **2** : acting or working in a manner opposite the usual **3** : bringing about reverse movement ⟨~ gear⟩ — **re·verse·ly** *adv*

²**reverse** *vb* **re·versed; re·vers·ing 1** : to turn upside down or completely about in position or direction **2** : to set aside or change (as a legal decision) **3** : to change to the contrary ⟨~ a policy⟩ **4** : to go or cause to go in the opposite direction **5** : to put (as a car) in reverse — **re·vers·ible** \-'vər-sə-bəl\ *adj*

³**reverse** *n* **1** : something contrary to

| | | |
|---|---|---|
| reunification | reusable | revaluation |
| reunify | reuse | revalue |
| reunite | revaluate | |

something else : OPPOSITE **2** : an act or instance of reversing; *esp* : a change for the worse **3** : the back side of something (as a coin or card) **4** : a gear that reverses something

**reverse engineer** *vb* : to disassemble or analyze in detail in order to discover concepts involved in manufacture — **reverse engineering** *n*

**re·ver·sion** \ri-'vər-zhən\ *n* **1** : the right of succession or future possession (as to a title or property) **2** : return toward some former or ancestral condition; *also* : a product of this — **re·ver·sion·ary** \-zhə-ˌner-ē\ *adj*

**re·vert** \ri-'vərt\ *vb* **1** : to come or go back ⟨~ed to savagery⟩ **2** : to return to a proprietor or his or her heirs **3** : to return to an ancestral type

**¹re·view** \ri-'vyü\ *n* **1** : an act of revising **2** : a formal military inspection **3** : a general survey **4** : INSPECTION, EXAMINATION; *esp* : REEXAMINATION **5** : a critical evaluation (as of a book) **6** : a magazine devoted to reviews and essays **7** : a renewed study of previously studied material **8** : REVUE

**²re·view** \ri-'vyü, *1 also* 'rē-\ *vb* **1** : to examine or study again; *esp* : to reexamine judicially **2** : to hold a review of ⟨~ troops⟩ **3** : to write a critical examination of ⟨~ a novel⟩ **4** : to look back over ⟨~ed her accomplishments⟩ **5** : to study material again

**re·view·er** \ri-'vyü-ər\ *n* : one that reviews; *esp* : a writer of critical reviews

**re·vile** \ri-'vī(-ə)l\ *vb* **re·viled; re·vil·ing** : to abuse verbally : rail at ♦ *Synonyms* VITUPERATE, BERATE, RATE, UPBRAID, SCOLD — **re·vile·ment** *n* — **re·vil·er** *n*

**re·vise** \ri-'vīz\ *vb* **re·vised; re·vis·ing 1** : to look over something written in order to correct or improve ⟨~ an essay⟩ **2** : to make a new version of ⟨~ an almanac⟩ — **re·vis·able** *adj* — **re·vise** *n* — **re·vis·er** *or* **re·vi·sor** \-'vī-zər\ *n* — **re·vi·sion** \-'vi-zhən\ *n*

**re·vi·tal·ise** *Brit var of* REVITALIZE

**re·vi·tal·ize** \ˌrē-'vīt-ə-ˌlīz\ *vb* **-ized; -iz·ing** : to give new life or vigor to ⟨~ the shopping district⟩ — **re·vi·tal·i·za·tion** \(ˌ)rē-ˌvī-tə-lə-'zā-shən\ *n*

**re·viv·al** \ri-'vī-vəl\ *n* **1** : an act of reviving : the state of being revived **2** : a new publication or presentation (as of a book or play) **3** : an evangelistic meeting or series of meetings

**re·vive** \ri-'vīv\ *vb* **re·vived; re·viv·ing 1** : to bring back to life, consciousness, or activity : make or become fresh or strong again **2** : to bring back into use ⟨revived its native language⟩ — **re·viv·er** *n*

**re·viv·i·fy** \rē-'vi-və-ˌfī\ *vb* : REVIVE — **re·viv·i·fi·ca·tion** \-ˌvi-və-fə-'kā-shən\ *n*

**re·vo·ca·ble** \'re-və-kə-bəl *also* ri-'vō-kə-bəl\ *adj* : capable of being revoked

**re·vo·ca·tion** \ˌre-və-'kā-shən\ *n* : an act or instance of revoking

**re·voke** \ri-'vōk\ *vb* **re·voked; re·vok-**

ing **1** : to annul by recalling or taking back : REPEAL, RESCIND ⟨~ a license⟩ **2** : RENEGE ⟨~⟩ — **re·vok·er** *n*

**¹re·volt** \ri-'vōlt\ *vb* [MF *revolter*, fr. It *rivoltare* to overthrow, fr. VL *revolvitare*, fr. L *revolvere* to revolve, roll back] **1** : to throw off allegiance to a ruler or government : REBEL **2** : to experience disgust or shock **3** : to turn or cause to turn away with disgust or abhorrence ⟨violence ~ed her⟩ — **re·volt·er** *n*

**²revolt** *n* : REBELLION, INSURRECTION

**re·volt·ing** *adj* : extremely offensive ⟨a ~ odor⟩ — **re·volt·ing·ly** *adv*

**rev·o·lu·tion** \ˌre-və-'lü-shən\ *n* **1** : the action by a heavenly body of going round in an orbit **2** : ROTATION **3** : a sudden, radical, or complete change; *esp* : the overthrow or renunciation of one ruler or government and substitution of another by the governed

**¹rev·o·lu·tion·ary** \-shə-ˌner-ē\ *adj* **1** : of or relating to revolution **2** : tending to or promoting revolution **3** : constituting or bringing about a major change

**²revolutionary** *n, pl* **-ar·ies** : one who takes part in a revolution or who advocates revolutionary doctrines

**rev·o·lu·tion·ise** *Brit var of* REVOLUTIONIZE

**rev·o·lu·tion·ist** \ˌre-və-'lü-shə-nist\ *n* : REVOLUTIONARY — **revolutionist** *adj*

**rev·o·lu·tion·ize** \-ˌnīz\ *vb* **-ized; -iz·ing** : to change fundamentally or completely ⟨~ an industry⟩ — **rev·o·lu·tion·iz·er** *n*

**re·volve** \ri-'välv\ *vb* **re·volved; re·volv·ing 1** : to turn over in the mind : reflect upon : PONDER **2** : to move in an orbit; *also* : ROTATE **3** : to have a specified focus ⟨the debate *revolved* around taxes⟩ — **re·volv·able** *adj*

**re·volv·er** \ri-'väl-vər\ *n* : a pistol with a revolving cylinder of several chambers

**re·vue** \ri-'vyü\ *n* : a theatrical production consisting typically of brief often satirical sketches and songs

**re·vul·sion** \ri-'vəl-shən\ *n* **1** : a strong sudden reaction or change of feeling **2** : a feeling of complete distaste or repugnance

**revved** *past and past part of* REV

**revving** *pres part of* REV

**¹re·ward** \ri-'word\ *vb* **1** : to give a reward to or for **2** : RECOMPENSE

**²reward** *n* **1** : something given in return for good or evil done or received or for some service or attainment **2** : a stimulus that is administered to an organism after a response and that increases the probability of occurrence of the response ♦ *Synonyms* PREMIUM, PRIZE, AWARD

**¹re·wind** \(ˌ)rē-'wīnd\ *vb* **-wound; -wind·ing 1** : to wind again **2** : to reverse the winding of (as film)

**²re·wind** \'rē-ˌwīnd\ *n* **1** : something that rewinds **2** : an act of rewinding **3** : a function of an electronic device that reverses a recording to a previous portion

---

| | | | |
|---|---|---|---|
| revisit | rewash | rewed | rewire |
| rewarm | reweave | reweigh | rezone |

**re·work** \(ˌ)rē-ˈwərk\ *vb* **1** : REVISE **2** : to reprocess for further use

¹**re·write** \(ˌ)rē-ˈrīt\ *vb* **-wrote; -writ·ten; -writ·ing** : to make a revision of : REVISE

²**re·write** \ˈrē-ˌrīt\ *n* : an instance or a piece of rewriting

**RF** *abbr* radio frequency

**RFD** *abbr* rural free delivery

**Rg** *abbr* roentgenium

**Rh** *symbol* rhodium

**RH** *abbr* right hand

**rhap·so·dy** \ˈrap-sə-dē\ *n, pl* **-dies** [L *rhapsodia* portion of an epic poem adapted for recitation, fr. Gk *rhapsōidia* recitation of selections from epic poetry, ultim. fr. *rhaptein* to sew, stitch together + *aidein* to sing] **1** : an expression of extravagant praise or ecstasy **2** : a musical composition of irregular form — **rhap·sod·ic** \rap-ˈsä-dik\ *adj* — **rhap·sod·i·cal·ly** \-di-k(ə-)lē\ *adv* — **rhap·so·dize** \ˈrap-sə-ˌdīz\ *vb*

**rhea** \ˈrē-ə\ *n* : either of two large flightless 3-toed So. American birds that resemble but are smaller than the African ostrich

**rhe·ni·um** \ˈrē-nē-əm\ *n* : a rare heavy metallic chemical element

**rheo·stat** \ˈrē-ə-ˌstat\ *n* : a resistor for regulating an electric current by means of variable resistances — **rheo·stat·ic** \ˌrē-ə-ˈsta-tik\ *adj*

**rhe·sus monkey** \ˈrē-səs-\ *n* : a pale brown Asian monkey often used in medical research

**rhet·o·ric** \ˈre-tə-rik\ *n* [ME *rethorik*, fr. AF *rethorique*, fr. L *rhetorica*, fr. Gk *rhētorikē*, lit., art of oratory, fr. *rhētōr* public speaker, fr. *eirein* to speak] : the art of speaking or writing effectively — **rhet·o·ri·cian** \ˌre-tə-ˈri-shən\ *n*

**rhe·tor·i·cal** \ri-ˈtòr-i-kəl\ *adj* **1** : of or relating to rhetoric **2** : asked merely for effect with no answer expected ⟨a ~ question⟩

**rheum** \ˈrüm\ *n* : a watery discharge from the mucous membranes esp. of the eyes or nose — **rheumy** *adj*

**rheu·mat·ic fever** \rü-ˈma-tik-\ *n* : an acute disease chiefly of children and young adults that is characterized by fever, by inflammation and pain in and around the joints, and by inflammation of the membranes surrounding the heart and the heart valves

**rheu·ma·tism** \ˈrü-mə-ˌti-zəm, ˈrù-\ *n* **1** : any of various conditions marked by stiffness, pain, or swelling in muscles or joints **2** : RHEUMATOID ARTHRITIS — **rheu·mat·ic** \rù-ˈma-tik\ *adj*

**rheu·ma·toid arthritis** \-ˌtòid-\ *n* : a usu. chronic progressive autoimmune disease characterized by inflammation and swelling of joint structures

**rheu·ma·tol·o·gy** \ˌrü-mə-ˈtä-lə-jē, ˌrù-\ *n* : a medical science dealing with rheumatic diseases — **rheu·ma·tol·o·gist** \-jist\ *n*

**Rh factor** \ˌär-ˈāch-\ *n* [*rhesus* monkey (in which it was first detected)] : any of one or more inherited substances in red blood cells that may cause dangerous reactions in some infants or in transfusions

**rhine·stone** \ˈrīn-ˌstōn\ *n* : a colorless imitation stone of high luster made of glass, paste, or gem quartz

**rhi·no** \ˈrī-nō\ *n, pl* **rhinos** *also* **rhino** : RHINOCEROS

**rhi·noc·er·os** \rī-ˈnä-sə-rəs\ *n, pl* **-noc·er·os·es** *also* **-noc·er·os** *or* **-noc·eri** \-ˈnäsə-ˌrī\ [ME *rinoceros*, fr. AF, fr. L *rhinoceros*, fr. Gk *rhinokerōs*, fr. *rhin-, rhis* nose + *keras* horn] : any of a family of large thick-skinned mammals of Africa and Asia with one or two upright horns of keratin on the snout and three toes on each foot

**rhi·zome** \ˈrī-ˌzōm\ *n* : a fleshy, rootlike, and usu. horizontal underground plant stem that forms shoots above and roots below — **rhi·zom·a·tous** \rī-ˈzä-mə-təs\ *adj*

**Rh-neg·a·tive** \ˌär-ˌāch-ˈne-gə-tiv\ *adj* : lacking Rh factors in the red blood cells

**rho** \ˈrō\ *n* : the 17th letter of the Greek alphabet — P or ρ

**rho·di·um** \ˈrō-dē-əm\ *n* : a rare hard ductile metallic chemical element

**rho·do·den·dron** \ˌrō-də-ˈden-drən\ *n* : any of a genus of shrubs or trees of the heath family with clusters of large bright flowers

**rhom·boid** \ˈräm-ˌbòid\ *n* : a parallelogram with unequal adjacent sides and angles that are not right angles — **rhom·boid** *or* **rhom·boi·dal** \räm-ˈbòi-dᵊl\ *adj*

**rhom·bus** \ˈräm-bəs\ *n, pl* **rhom·bus·es** *or* **rhom·bi** \-ˌbī\ : a parallelogram having all four sides equal

**Rh-pos·i·tive** \ˌär-ˌāch-ˈpä-zə-tiv\ *adj* : containing one or more Rh factors in the red blood cells

**rhu·barb** \ˈrü-ˌbärb\ *n* [ME *rubarbe*, fr. AF *reubarbe*, fr. ML *reubarbarum*, alter. of *rha barbarum*, lit., barbarian rhubarb] : a garden plant related to the buckwheat having leaves with thick juicy edible pink and red stems

¹**rhyme** *also* **rime** \ˈrīm\ *n* **1** : a composition in verse that rhymes; *also* : POETRY **2** : correspondence in terminal sounds (as of two lines of verse)

²**rhyme** *also* **rime** *vb* **rhymed** *also* **rimed; rhym·ing** *also* **rim·ing 1** : to make rhymes; *also* : to write poetry **2** : to have rhymes : be in rhyme

**rhythm** \ˈri-thəm\ *n* **1** : regular rise and fall in the flow of sound in speech **2** : a movement or activity in which some action or element recurs regularly — **rhyth·mic** \ˈrith-mik\ *or* **rhyth·mi·cal** \-mi-kəl\ *adj* — **rhyth·mi·cal·ly** \-k(ə-)lē\ *adv*

**rhythm and blues** *n* : popular music based on blues and black folk music

**rhythm method** *n* : birth control by refraining from sexual intercourse during the time when ovulation is most likely to occur

**RI** *abbr* Rhode Island

**ri·al** \rē-ˈòl, -ˈäl\ *n* — see MONEY table

¹**rib** \ˈrib\ *n* **1** : any of the series of curved bones of the chest of most vertebrates

that are joined to the backbone in pairs and help to support the body wall and protect the organs inside **2** : something resembling a rib in shape or function **3** : an elongated ridge (as in fabric)

²**rib** vb **ribbed; rib·bing 1** : to furnish or strengthen with ribs **2** : to knit so as to form ridges

³**rib** vb **ribbed; rib·bing** : to poke fun at : TEASE — **rib·ber** n

**rib·ald** \'ri-bəld\ adj : coarse or indecent esp. in language ⟨~ jokes⟩ — **rib·ald·ry** \-bəl-drē\ n

**rib·and** \'ri-bənd\ n : RIBBON

**rib·bon** \'ri-bən\ n **1** : a narrow fabric typically of silk or velvet used for trimming and for badges **2** : a strip of inked cloth (as in a typewriter) **3** : TATTER, SHRED ⟨torn to ~s⟩

**ri·bo·fla·vin** \,rī-bə-'flā-vən, 'rī-bə-,flā-vən\ n : a growth-promoting vitamin of the vitamin B complex occurring esp. in milk and liver

**ri·bo·nu·cle·ic acid** \,rī-bō-nù-'klē-ik-, -nyù-, -,klā-\ n : RNA

**ri·bose** \'rī-,bōs\ n : a sugar with five carbon atoms and five oxygen atoms in each molecule that is part of RNA

**ri·bo·some** \'rī-bə-,sōm\ n : any of the RNA-rich cytoplasmic granules in a cell that are sites of protein synthesis — **ri·bo·som·al** \,rī-bə-'sō-məl\ adj

**rice** \'rīs\ n : the starchy seeds of an annual grass that are cooked and used for food; also : this widely cultivated grass of warm wet areas

**rich** \'rich\ adj **1** : possessing or controlling great wealth : WEALTHY **2** : COSTLY, VALUABLE **3** : deep and pleasing in color or tone **4** : ABUNDANT **5** : containing much sugar, fat, or seasoning; also : high in combustible content **6** : FRUITFUL, FERTILE — **rich·ly** adv — **rich·ness** n

**rich·es** \'ri-chəz\ n pl [ME, sing. or pl., fr. richesse wealth, fr. AF richesce, fr. riche rich] : things that make one rich : WEALTH

**Rich·ter scale** \'rik-tər-\ n : a scale for expressing the magnitude of a seismic disturbance (as an earthquake) in terms of the energy dissipated in it

**rick** \'rik\ n : a large stack (as of hay) in the open air

**rick·ets** \'ri-kəts\ n : a childhood deficiency disease marked esp. by soft deformed bones and caused by lack of vitamin D

**rick·ett·sia** \ri-'ket-sē-ə\ n, pl **-si·as** or **-si·ae** \-sē-,ē\ : any of a group of usu. rod-shaped bacteria that cause various diseases (as typhus)

**rick·ety** \'ri-kə-tē\ adj **1** : affected with rickets **2** : SHAKY; also : in unsound physical condition ⟨~ stairs⟩

**rick·shaw** also **rick·sha** \'rik-,shò\ n : a small covered 2-wheeled carriage pulled by one person and used orig. in Japan

¹**ric·o·chet** \'ri-kə-,shā, Brit also -,shet\ n [F] : a bouncing off at an angle (as of a bullet off a wall); also : an object that ricochets

²**ricochet** vb **-cheted** \-,shād\ also **-chet-**

**ted** \-,she-təd\; **-chet·ing** \-,shā-iŋ\ or **-chet·ting** \-,she-tiŋ\ : to bounce or skip with or as if with a glancing rebound

**ri·cot·ta** \ri-'kä-tə, -'kò-\ n : a white unripened whey cheese of Italy that resembles cottage cheese

**rid** \'rid\ vb **rid** also **rid·ded; rid·ding** : to make free : CLEAR, RELIEVE ⟨~ the house of mice⟩ — **rid·dance** \'ri-dᵊns\ n

**rid·den** \'ri-dᵊn\ adj **1** : harassed, oppressed, or obsessed by ⟨debt-ridden⟩ **2** : excessively full of or supplied with ⟨slum-ridden⟩

¹**rid·dle** \'ri-dᵊl\ n : a puzzling question to be solved or answered by guessing

²**riddle** vb **rid·dled; rid·dling 1** : EXPLAIN, SOLVE **2** : to speak in riddles

³**riddle** n : a coarse sieve

⁴**riddle** vb **rid·dled; rid·dling 1** : to sift with a riddle **2** : to pierce with many holes **3** : PERMEATE

¹**ride** \'rīd\ vb **rode** \'rōd\; **rid·den** \'ri-dᵊn\; **rid·ing 1** : to go on an animal's back or in a conveyance (as a boat, car, or airplane); also : to sit on and control so as to be carried along ⟨~ a bicycle⟩ **2** : to float or move on water ⟨~ at anchor⟩; also : to move like a floating object **3** : to bear along : CARRY ⟨rode her on their shoulders⟩ **4** : to travel over a surface ⟨the car ~s well⟩ **5** : to proceed over on horseback **6** : to torment by nagging or teasing

²**ride** n **1** : an act of riding; esp : a trip on horseback or by vehicle **2** : a way (as a road or path) suitable for riding **3** : a mechanical device (as a merry-go-round) for riding on **4** : a means of transportation

**rid·er** \'rī-dər\ n **1** : one that rides **2** : an addition to a document often attached on a separate piece of paper **3** : a clause dealing with an unrelated matter attached to a legislative bill during passage — **rid·er·less** adj

¹**ridge** \'rij\ n [ME rigge, fr. OE hrycg] **1** : an elevated body part or structure **2** : a range of hills **3** : a raised line or strip **4** : the line made where two sloping surfaces (as of a roof) meet — **ridgy** adj

²**ridge** vb **ridged; ridg·ing 1** : to form into a ridge **2** : to extend in ridges

¹**rid·i·cule** \'ri-də-,kyül\ n : the act of ridiculing : DERISION, MOCKERY

²**ridicule** vb **-culed; -cul·ing** : to laugh at or make fun of mockingly or contemptuously ⟨was ridiculed by his peers⟩

♦ **Synonyms** DERIDE, TAUNT, TWIT, MOCK

**ri·dic·u·lous** \rə-'di-kyə-ləs\ adj : arousing or deserving ridicule : ABSURD, PREPOSTEROUS ♦ **Synonyms** LAUGHABLE, LUDICROUS, FARCICAL, RISIBLE — **ri·dic·u·lous·ly** adv — **ri·dic·u·lous·ness** n

**rid·ley** \'rid-lē\ n : either of two relatively small sea turtles

**ri·el** \rē-'el\ n — see MONEY table

**Ries·ling** \'rēz-liŋ, 'rēs-\ n : a sweet to very dry white wine made from a single variety of grape orig. grown in Germany

**RIF** abbr reduction in force

**rife** \'rīf\ *adj* : WIDESPREAD, PREVALENT, ABOUNDING — **rife** *adv* — **rife·ly** *adv*

¹**riff** \'rif\ *n* **1** : a repeated phrase in jazz typically supporting a solo improvisation; *also* : a piece based on such a phrase **2** : a usu. witty or improvised remark or outpouring **3** : a distinct variation : TAKE — **riff** *vb*

**riff-raff** \'rif-,raf\ *n* [ME *riffe raffe*, fr. *rif and raf* every single one, fr. AF *rif et raf* altogether] **1** : RABBLE ⟨did not associate with the ∼⟩ **2** : REFUSE, RUBBISH

¹**ri·fle** \'rī-fəl\ *vb* **ri·fled; ri·fling** : to ransack esp. with the intent to steal — **ri·fler** *n*

²**rifle** *vb* **ri·fled; ri·fling** : to cut spiral grooves into the bore of ⟨*rifled* pipe⟩ — **rifling** *n*

³**rifle** *n* **1** : a shoulder weapon with a rifled bore **2** *pl* : soldiers armed with rifles — **ri·fle·man** \-fəl-mən\ *n*

**rift** \'rift\ *n* **1** : CLEFT, FISSURE **2** : FAULT 6 **3** : ESTRANGEMENT, SEPARATION ⟨a ∼ between spouses⟩ — **rift** *vb*

¹**rig** \'rig\ *vb* **rigged; rig·ging 1** : to fit out (as a ship) with rigging **2** : CLOTHE, DRESS **3** : EQUIP **4** : to set up esp. as a makeshift ⟨∼ up a shelter⟩

²**rig** *n* **1** : the distinctive shape, number, and arrangement of sails and masts of a ship **2** : a carriage with its horse **3** : CLOTHING, DRESS **4** : EQUIPMENT

³**rig** *vb* **rigged; rig·ging 1** : to manipulate or control esp. by deceptive or dishonest means **2** : to fix in advance for a desired result — **rig·ger** *n*

**rig·ging** \'ri-giṇ, -gən\ *n* **1** : the ropes and chains that hold and move masts, sails, and spars of a ship **2** : a network (as in theater scenery) used for support and manipulation

¹**right** \'rīt\ *adj* **1** : RIGHTEOUS, UPRIGHT **2** : JUST, PROPER **3** : conforming to truth or fact : CORRECT **4** : APPROPRIATE, SUITABLE **5** : STRAIGHT ⟨a ∼ line⟩ **6** : GENUINE, REAL **7** : of, relating to, or being the side of the body which is away from the side on which the heart is mostly located **8** : located nearer to the right hand; *esp* : being on the right when facing in the same direction as the observer **9** : made to be placed or worn outward ⟨∼ side of a rug⟩ **10** : NORMAL, SOUND ⟨not in her ∼ mind⟩ ♦ *Synonyms* CORRECT, ACCURATE, EXACT, PRECISE, NICE — **right·ness** *n*

²**right** *n* **1** : qualities that constitute what is correct, just, proper, or honorable **2** : something (as a power or privilege) to which one has a just or lawful claim **3** : just action or decision : the cause of justice **4** : the side or part that is on or toward the right side **5** *cap* : political conservatives **6** *often cap* : a conservative position — **right·ward** \-wərd\ *adj or adv*

³**right** *adv* **1** : according to what is right ⟨live ∼⟩ **2** : EXACTLY, PRECISELY ⟨∼ here and now⟩ **3** : DIRECTLY ⟨went ∼ home⟩ **4** : according to fact or truth ⟨guess ∼⟩ **5** : all the way : COMPLETELY ⟨∼ to the end⟩ **6** : IMMEDIATELY ⟨∼ after lunch⟩ **7** : QUITE, VERY ⟨∼ nice

weather⟩ **8** : on or to the right ⟨looked ∼ and left⟩

⁴**right** *vb* **1** : to relieve from wrong **2** : to adjust or restore to a proper state or position **3** : to bring or restore to an upright position **4** : to become upright — **right·er** *n*

**right angle** *n* : an angle whose measure is 90° : an angle whose sides are perpendicular to each other — **right–an·gled** \'rīt-'aṇ-gəld\ *or* **right–an·gle** \-gəl\ *adj*

**right·eous** \'rī-chəs\ *adj* : acting or being in accordance with what is just, honorable, and free from guilt or wrong : UPRIGHT ♦ *Synonyms* VIRTUOUS, NOBLE, MORAL, ETHICAL — **right·eous·ly** *adv* — **right·eous·ness** *n*

**right·ful** \'rīt-fəl\ *adj* **1** : JUST; *also* : FITTING **2** : having or held by a legally just claim — **right·ful·ly** *adv* — **right·ful·ness** *n*

**right–hand** \'rīt-,hand\ *adj* **1** : situated on the right **2** : RIGHT-HANDED **3** : chiefly relied on ⟨his ∼ man⟩

**right–hand·ed** \-'han-dəd\ *adj* **1** : using the right hand habitually or better than the left **2** : designed for or done with the right hand **3** : CLOCKWISE ⟨a ∼ twist⟩ — **right–handed** *adv* — **right–hand·ed·ly** *adv* — **right–hand·ed·ness** *n*

**right·ly** \'rīt-lē\ *adv* **1** : FAIRLY, JUSTLY **2** : PROPERLY **3** : CORRECTLY, EXACTLY

**right–of–way** *n, pl* **rights–of–way 1** : a legal right of passage over another person's ground **2** : the area over which a right-of-way exists **3** : the land on which a public road is built **4** : the land occupied by a railroad **5** : the land used by a public utility **6** : the right of traffic to take precedence over other traffic

**right on** *interj* — used to express agreement or give encouragement

**right–to–life** *adj* : ANTIABORTION — **right–to–lifer** *n*

**right triangle** *n* : a triangle having one right angle

**right whale** *n* : any of a family of large baleen whales having a very large head on a stocky body

**rig·id** \'ri-jəd\ *adj* **1** : lacking flexibility **2** : strictly observed ♦ *Synonyms* SEVERE, STERN, RIGOROUS, STRINGENT — **ri·gid·i·ty** \rə-'ji-də-tē\ *n* — **rig·id·ly** *adv*

**rig·ma·role** \'ri-gə-mə-,rōl\ *n* [alter. of obs. *ragman roll* long list, catalog] **1** : confused or senseless talk **2** : a complex and ritualistic procedure

**rig·or** \'ri-gər\ *n* **1** : the quality of being inflexible or unyielding : STRICTNESS **2** : HARSHNESS, SEVERITY **3** : a tremor caused by a chill **4** : strict precision : EXACTNESS ⟨scientific ∼⟩ — **rig·or·ous** *adj* — **rig·or·ous·ly** *adv*

**rig·or mor·tis** \,ri-gər-'mȯr-təs\ *n* [NL, stiffness of death] : temporary rigidity of muscles occurring after death

**rig·our** *chiefly Brit var of* RIGOR

**rile** \'rī(-ə)l\ *vb* **riled; ril·ing 1** : to make angry **2** : ROIL 1

**rill** \'ril\ *n* : a very small brook

¹**rim** \'rim\ *n* **1** : the outer part of a wheel

2 : an outer edge esp. of something curved : BORDER, MARGIN

²rim vb rimmed; rim·ming 1 : to serve as a rim for : BORDER 2 : to run around the rim of

¹rime \'rīm\ n : FROST 2 — rimy \'rī-mē\ adj

²rime var of RHYME

rind \'rīnd\ n : a usu. hard or tough outer layer ⟨lemon ∼⟩

¹ring \'riŋ\ n 1 : a circular band worn as an ornament or token or used for holding or fastening ⟨wedding ∼⟩ ⟨key ∼⟩ 2 : something circular in shape ⟨smoke ∼⟩ 3 : a place for contest or display ⟨boxing ∼⟩; also : PRIZEFIGHTING 4 : ANNUAL RING 5 : a group of people who work together for selfish or dishonest purposes ⟨a ∼ of smugglers⟩ — ringed adj — ring·like \'riŋ-,līk\ adj

²ring vb ringed; ring·ing \'riŋ-iŋ\ 1 : EN-CIRCLE 2 : to throw a ring over (a mark) in a game (as quoits) 3 : to move in a ring or spirally

³ring \'riŋ\ vb rang \'raŋ\; rung \'rəŋ\; ring·ing \'riŋ-iŋ\ 1 : to sound resonantly when struck; also : to feel as if filled with such sound 2 : to cause to make a clear metallic sound by striking 3 : to announce or call by or as if by striking a bell ⟨∼ an alarm⟩ 4 : to repeat loudly and persistently 5 : to summon esp. by a bell ⟨∼ for the butler⟩ — ring a bell : to arouse a response ⟨that name rings a bell⟩

⁴ring n 1 : a set of bells 2 : the clear resonant sound of vibrating metal 3 : resonant tone : SONORITY 4 : a sound or character expressive of a particular quality 5 : an act or instance of ringing; esp : a telephone call

¹ring·er \'riŋ-ər\ n 1 : one that sounds by ringing 2 : one that enters a competition under false representations 3 : one that closely resembles another

²ringer n : one that encircles or puts a ring around

ring finger n : the third finger of the left hand counting the index finger as the first

ring·git \'riŋ-git\ n — see MONEY table

ring·lead·er \'riŋ-,lē-dər\ n : a leader esp. of a group of troublemakers

ring·let \-lət\ n : a long curl

ring·mas·ter \-,mas-tər\ n : one in charge of performances in a circus ring

ring up vb 1 : to total and record esp. by means of a cash register 2 : ACHIEVE ⟨rang up many triumphs⟩

ring·worm \'riŋ-,wərm\ n : any of several contagious skin diseases caused by fungi and marked by ring-shaped discolored patches

rink \'riŋk\ n : a level extent of ice marked off for skating or various games; also : a similar surface (as of wood) marked off or enclosed for a sport or game ⟨roller-skating ∼⟩

¹rinse \'rins\ vb rinsed; rins·ing [ME rincen, AF rincer, alter. of OF recincier, fr. VL *recentiare, fr. L recent-, recens fresh, recent] 1 : to wash lightly or in water only 2 : to cleanse (as of soap) with

clear water 3 : to treat (hair) with a rinse — rins·er n

²rinse n 1 : an act of rinsing 2 : a liquid used for rinsing 3 : a solution that temporarily tints hair

ri·ot \'rī-ət\ n 1 archaic : disorderly behavior 2 : disturbance of the public peace; esp : a violent public disorder 3 : random or disorderly profusion ⟨a ∼ of color⟩ 4 : one that is wildly amusing ⟨the comedy is a ∼⟩ — riot vb — ri·ot·er n — ri·ot·ous adj

¹rip \'rip\ vb ripped; rip·ping 1 : to cut or tear open 2 : to saw or split (wood) with the grain 3 : CRITICIZE, DISPARAGE ⟨ripped into the team⟩ — rip·per n

²rip n : a rent made by ripping

RIP abbr [L requiescat in pace] may he rest in peace, may she rest in peace; [L requiescant in pace] may they rest in peace

ri·par·i·an \rə-'per-ē-ən\ adj : of or relating to the bank of a stream, river, or lake ⟨∼ trees⟩

rip cord n : a cord that is pulled to release a parachute out of its container

ripe \'rīp\ adj rip·er; rip·est 1 : fully grown and developed : MATURE ⟨∼ fruit⟩ 2 : fully prepared : READY ⟨slaves ∼ for a revolt⟩ — ripe·ly adv — ripe·ness n

rip·en \'rī-pən\ vb rip·ened; rip·en·ing 1 : to grow or make ripe 2 : to bring to completeness or perfection; also : to age or cure (cheese) to develop characteristic flavor, odor, body, texture, and color

rip-off \'rip-,óf\ n 1 : an act of stealing : THEFT 2 : a cheap imitation — rip off vb

ri·poste \ri-'pōst\ n [F, modif. of It risposta, lit., answer] 1 : a fencer's return thrust after a parry 2 : a retaliatory maneuver or response; esp : a quick retort — riposte vb

ripped \'ript\ adj : having high muscle definition ⟨a ∼ body⟩

rip·ple \'ri-pəl\ vb rip·pled; rip·pling 1 : to become lightly ruffled on the surface 2 : to make a sound like that of rippling water — ripple n

rip·saw \'rip-,só\ n : a coarse-toothed saw used to cut wood in the direction of the grain

rip·stop \'rip-,stäp\ adj : being a fabric woven in such a way that small tears do not spread ⟨∼ nylon⟩ — ripstop n

¹rise \'rīz\ vb rose \'rōz\; ris·en \'riz-ən\; ris·ing 1 : to get up from sitting, kneeling, or lying 2 : to get up from sleep or from one's bed 3 : to return from death 4 : to take up arms 5 : to end a session : ADJOURN 6 : to appear above the horizon 7 : to move upward : ASCEND 8 : to extend above other objects 9 : to attain a higher level or rank 10 : to increase in quantity, intensity, or pitch 11 : to come into being : HAPPEN, BEGIN, ORIGINATE

²rise n 1 : a spot higher than surrounding ground 2 : an upward slope 3 : an act of rising : a state of being risen 4 : BEGINNING, ORIGIN 5 : the elevation of one point above another 6 : an increase in

amount, number, or volume **7** : an angry reaction ⟨tried to get a ~ out of me⟩

**ris·er** \'rī-zər\ *n* **1** : one that rises **2** : the upright part between stair treads

**ris·i·bil·i·ty** \,ri-zə-'bi-lə-tē\ *n, pl* **-ties** : the ability or inclination to laugh — often used in pl.

**ris·i·ble** \'ri-zə-bəl\ *adj* **1** : able or inclined to laugh **2** : arousing laughter; *esp* : amusingly ridiculous

**¹risk** \'risk\ *n* **1** : exposure to possible loss or injury : DANGER, PERIL ⟨health ~s⟩ **2** : the chance that an investment will lose value — **risk·i·ness** \'ris-kē-nəs\ *n* — **risky** *adj*

**²risk** *vb* **1** : to expose to danger ⟨~ed his life⟩ **2** : to incur the danger of

**ri·sot·to** \ri-'sò-tō, -'zò-\ *n, pl* **-tos** : rice cooked usu. in meat or seafood stock and seasoned

**ris·qué** \ris-'kā\ *adj* [F] : verging on impropriety or indecency ⟨~ jokes⟩

**ri·tard** \ri-'tärd\ *adv or adj* : with a gradual slackening in tempo — used as a direction in music

**rite** \'rīt\ *n* **1** : a set form for conducting a ceremony **2** : the liturgy of a church **3** : a ceremonial act or action

**rit·u·al** \'ri-chə-wəl\ *n* **1** : the established form esp. for a religious ceremony **2** : a system of rites **3** : a ceremonial act or action **4** : an act or series of acts regularly repeated in a precise manner — **rit·ual** *adj* — **rit·u·al·ism** \-wə-,li-zəm\ *n* — **rit·u·al·is·tic** \,ri-chə-wə-'lis-tik\ *adj* — **rit·u·al·is·ti·cal·ly** \-ti-k(ə-)lē\ *adv* — **rit·u·al·ly** *adv*

**ritzy** \'rit-sē\ *adj* **ritz·i·er; -est** : showily elegant : POSH

**riv** *abbr* river

**¹ri·val** \'rī-vəl\ *n* [MF or L; MF, fr. L *rivalis* one using the same stream as another, rival in love, fr. *rivalis* of a stream, fr. *rivus* stream] **1** : one of two or more trying to get what only one can have **2** : one striving for competitive advantage **3** : one that equals another esp. in desired qualities : MATCH, PEER

**²rival** *adj* : COMPETING

**³rival** *vb* **-valed** *or* **-valled; -val·ing** *or* **-val·ling** **1** : to be in competition with **2** : to try to equal or excel **3** : to have qualities that approach or equal another's

**ri·val·ry** \'rī-vəl-rē\ *n, pl* **-ries** : COMPETITION

**rive** \'rīv\ *vb* **rived** \'rīvd\; **riv·en** \'ri-vən\ *also* **rived; riv·ing 1** : SPLIT, REND **2** : SHATTER ⟨nations *riven* by war⟩

**riv·er** \'ri-vər\ *n* **1** : a natural stream larger than a brook **2** : a large stream or flow

**riv·er·bank** \-,baŋk\ *n* : the bank of a river

**riv·er·bed** \-,bed\ *n* : the channel occupied by a river

**riv·er·boat** \-,bōt\ *n* : a boat for use on a river

**riv·er·front** \-,frənt\ *n* : the land or area along a river

**riv·er·side** \-,sīd\ *n* : the side or bank of a river

**¹riv·et** \'ri-vət\ *n* : a metal bolt with a head at one end used to join parts by being put through holes in them and then being flattened on the plain end to make another head

**²rivet** *vb* : to fasten with or as if with a rivet — **riv·et·er** *n*

**riv·u·let** \'ri-vyə-lət, -və-\ *n* : a small stream

**ri·yal** *also* **ri·al** \rē-'äl, -'al\ *n* — see MONEY table

**rm** *abbr* room

**Rn** *symbol* radon

**¹RN** \,är-'en\ *n* : REGISTERED NURSE

**²RN** *abbr* Royal Navy

**RNA** \,är-(,)en-'ā\ *n* : any of various nucleic acids (as messenger RNA) that are found esp. in the cytoplasm of cells, have ribose as the 5-carbon sugar, and are associated with the control of cellular chemical activities

**rnd** *abbr* round

**¹roach** \'rōch\ *n, pl* **roach** *also* **roach·es** : any of various bony fishes related to the carp; *also* : any of several sunfishes

**²roach** *n* **1** : COCKROACH **2** : the butt of a marijuana cigarette

**road** \'rōd\ *n* [ME *rode*, fr. OE *rād* ride, journey] **1** : ROADSTEAD — often used in pl. **2** : an open way for vehicles, persons, and animals : HIGHWAY **3** : a way to a conclusion or end ⟨the ~ to success⟩ **4** : a series of scheduled visits (as games or performances) in several locations or the travel necessary to make these visits ⟨the team is on the ~⟩

**road·bed** \'rōd-,bed\ *n* **1** : the foundation of a road or railroad **2** : the part of the surface of a road on which vehicles travel

**road·block** \-,bläk\ *n* **1** : a barricade on the road ⟨a police ~⟩ **2** : an obstruction to progress

**road·ie** \'rō-dē\ *n* : a person who works for traveling entertainers

**road·kill** \'rōd-,kil\ *n* **1** : the remains of an animal that has been killed on a road by a motor vehicle **2** : one that falls victim to intense competition ⟨political ~⟩

**road·run·ner** \-,rə-nər\ *n* : a largely terrestrial bird of the southwestern U.S. and Mexico that is a speedy runner

**road·side** \'rōd-,sīd\ *n* : the strip of land along a road — **roadside** *adj*

**road·stead** \-,sted\ *n* : an anchorage for ships usu. less sheltered than a harbor

**road·ster** \'rōd-stər\ *n* **1** : a driving horse **2** : an open automobile that seats two often with a storage compartment or rumble seat in the rear

**road·way** \-,wā\ *n* : ROAD; *esp* : ROADBED

**road·work** \-,wərk\ *n* **1** : work done in constructing or repairing roads **2** : conditioning for an athletic contest (as a boxing match) consisting mainly of long runs

**roam** \'rōm\ *vb* **1** : WANDER, ROVE **2** : to range or wander over or about **3** : to use a cell phone outside one's local calling area

**¹roan** \'rōn\ *adj* : of dark color (as black, red, or brown) sprinkled with white ⟨a ~ horse⟩

**²roan** *n* : an animal (as a horse) with a roan coat; *also* : its color

¹**roar** \'rȯr\ *vb* **1** : to utter a full loud prolonged sound **2** : to make a loud confused sound (as of wind or waves) — **roar·er** *n*

²**roar** *n* : a sound of roaring

¹**roast** \'rōst\ *vb* **1** : to cook by exposure to dry heat or an open flame **2** : to criticize severely or kiddingly

²**roast** *n* **1** : a piece of meat suitable for roasting **2** : an outing at which food is roasted ⟨corn ⁓⟩ **3** : severe criticism or kidding

³**roast** *adj* : ROASTED

**roast·er** \'rō-stər\ *n* **1** : one that roasts **2** : a device for roasting **3** : something (as a young chicken) fit for roasting

**rob** \'räb\ *vb* **robbed; rob·bing 1** : to steal from **2** : to deprive of something due or expected **3** : to commit robbery — **rob·ber** *n*

**robber fly** *n* : any of a family of predaceous flies resembling bumblebees

**rob·bery** \'rä-bə-rē\ *n, pl* **-ber·ies** : the act or practice of robbing; *esp* : theft of something from a person by use of violence or threat

¹**robe** \'rōb\ *n* **1** : a long flowing outer garment; *esp* : one used for ceremonial occasions **2** : a wrap or covering for the lower body (as for sitting outdoors)

²**robe** *vb* **robed; rob·ing 1** : to clothe with or as if with a robe **2** : DRESS

**rob·in** \'rä-bən\ *n* **1** : a small chiefly European thrush with a somewhat orange face and breast **2** : a large No. American thrush with a grayish back, a streaked throat, and a chiefly dull reddish breast

**ro·bo·call** \'rō-bō-ˌkȯl\ *n* : a telephone call from an automated source that delivers a message to a large number of people

**ro·bot** \'rō-ˌbät, -bət\ *n* [Czech, fr. *robota* compulsory labor] **1** : a machine that looks and acts like a human being **2** : an efficient but insensitive person **3** : a device that automatically performs esp. repetitive tasks **4** : something guided by automatic controls — **ro·bot·ic** \rō-'bä-tik\ *adj*

**ro·bot·ics** \rō-'bä-tiks\ *n* : technology dealing with the design, construction, and operation of robots

**ro·bust** \rō-'bəst, 'rō-(ˌ)bəst\ *adj* [L *robustus* oaken, strong, fr. *robur* oak, strength] **1** : strong and vigorously healthy **2** : capable of performing without failure under a wide range of conditions ⟨⁓ software⟩ — **ro·bust·ly** *adv* — **ro·bust·ness** *n*

**ROC** *abbr* Republic of China (Taiwan)

¹**rock** \'räk\ *vb* **1** : to move back and forth in or as if in a cradle **2** : to sway or cause to sway back and forth **3** : to arouse to excitement (as with rock music) ⟨⁓ed the crowd⟩ **4** *slang* : to be extremely enjoyable or effective ⟨this car ⁓s⟩

²**rock** *n* **1** : a rocking movement **2** : popular music usu. played on electric instruments and characterized by a strong beat and much repetition

³**rock** *n* **1** : a mass of stony material; *also* : broken pieces of stone **2** : solid mineral deposits **3** : something like a rock in

firmness **4** : GEM; *esp* : DIAMOND — **rock** *adj* — **rock·like** *adj* — **rocky** *adj* — **on the rocks 1** : in a state of ruin ⟨a marriage *on the rocks*⟩ **2** : on ice cubes ⟨bourbon *on the rocks*⟩

**rock and roll** *n* : ²ROCK 2

**rock·bound** \'räk-ˌbau̇nd\ *adj* : fringed or covered with rocks

**rock·er** \'rä-kər\ *n* **1** : one of the curved pieces on which something (as a chair or cradle) rocks **2** : a chair that rocks on rockers **3** : a device that works with a rocking motion **4** : a rock performer, song, or enthusiast

¹**rock·et** \'rä-kət\ *n* [It *rocchetta*, lit., small distaff] **1** : a firework that is propelled through the air by the discharge of gases produced by a burning substance **2** : a jet engine that operates on the same principle as a firework rocket but carries the oxygen needed for burning its fuel **3** : a rocket-propelled bomb or missile

²**rocket** *vb* **1** : to convey by means of a rocket **2** : to rise abruptly and rapidly

**rock·et·ry** \'rä-kə-trē\ *n* : the study or use of rockets

**rocket ship** *n* : a rocket-propelled spacecraft

**rock·fall** \'räk-ˌfȯl\ *n* : a mass of falling or fallen rocks

**rock·fish** \-ˌfish\ *n* : any of various bony fishes that live among rocks or on rocky bottoms

**rock salt** *n* : common salt in rocklike masses or large crystals

**Rocky Mountain sheep** *n* : BIGHORN

**ro·co·co** \rə-'kō-kō\ *adj* [F, irreg. fr. *rocaille* style of ornament, lit., stone debris] : of or relating to an artistic style esp. of the 18th century marked by fanciful curved forms and elaborate ornamentation — **rococo** *n*

**rod** \'räd\ *n* **1** : a straight slender stick **2** : a stick or bundle of twigs used in punishing a person; *also* : PUNISHMENT **3** : a staff borne to show rank **4** — see WEIGHT table **5** : any of the rod-shaped receptor cells of the retina that are sensitive to faint light **6** *slang* : HANDGUN

**rode** *past of* RIDE

**ro·dent** \'rō-dᵊnt\ *n* [ultim. fr. L *rodent-, rodens*, prp. of *rodere* to gnaw] : any of an order of relatively small mammals (as mice, squirrels, and beavers) with sharp front teeth used for gnawing

**ro·deo** \'rō-dē-ˌō, rə-'dā-ō\ *n, pl* **ro·de·os** [Sp, fr. *rodear* to surround, fr. *rueda* wheel, fr. L *rota*] **1** : ROUNDUP 1 **2** : a public performance featuring cowboy skills (as riding and roping)

¹**roe** \'rō\ *n, pl* **roe** *or* **roes** : DOE

²**roe** *n* : the eggs of a fish esp. while bound together in a mass

**roe·buck** \'rō-ˌbək\ *n, pl* **roebuck** *or* **roebucks** : a male roe deer

**roe deer** *n* : either of two small nimble European or Asian deers

**roent·gen** \'rent-gən, 'rənt-, -jən\ *n* : the international unit of measurement for X-rays and gamma rays

**roent·gen·i·um** \rent-'ge-nē-əm, rənt-,

-'je-\ *n* : a short-lived radioactive chemical element

**rog·er** \'rä-jər\ *interj* — used esp. in radio and signaling to indicate that a message has been received and understood

¹**rogue** \'rōg\ *n* **1** : a dishonest person : SCOUNDREL **2** : a mischievous person : SCAMP — **rogu·ery** \'rō-gə-rē\ *n* — **rogu·ish** *adj* — **rogu·ish·ly** *adv* — **rogu·ish·ness** *n*

²**rogue** *adj* **1** : CORRUPT, DISHONEST ⟨~ cops⟩ **2** : of or being a nation whose leaders defy international law or norms

**roil** \'rȯi(-ə)l, *for 2 also* 'rī(-ə)l\ *vb* **1** : to make cloudy or muddy by stirring up **2** : RILE **1** — **roily** \'rȯi-lē\ *adj*

**rois·ter** \'rȯi-stər\ *vb* **rois·tered; rois·ter·ing** : to engage in noisy revelry : CAROUSE — **rois·ter·er** *n* — **rois·ter·ous** \-stə-rəs\ *adj*

**ROK** *abbr* Republic of Korea (South Korea)

**role** *also* **rôle** \'rōl\ *n* **1** : an assigned or assumed character; *also* : a part played (as by an actor) **2** : FUNCTION

**role model** *n* : a person whose behavior in a particular role is imitated by others

¹**roll** \'rōl\ *n* [ME *rolle* scroll, fr. AF, fr. ML *rolla*, alter. of *rotula*, fr. L, dim. of *rota* wheel] **1** : a document containing an official record **2** : an official list of names **3** : bread baked in a small rounded mass **4** : something that rolls : ROLLER

²**roll** *vb* **1** : to move by turning over and over ⟨~ dice⟩ ⟨~ed her eyes⟩ **2** : to press with a roller ⟨~ dough⟩ **3** : to move on wheels **4** : to sound with a full reverberating tone **5** : to make a continuous beating sound (as on a drum) **6** : to utter with a trill **7** : to move onward as if by completing a revolution ⟨years ~ed by⟩ **8** : to flow or seem to flow in a continuous stream or with a rising and falling motion ⟨the river ~ed on⟩ **9** : to swing or sway from side to side **10** : to shape or become shaped in rounded form ⟨~ up the paper⟩ **11** : to move by or as if by turning a crank ⟨~ down the window⟩

³**roll** *n* **1** : a sound produced by rapid strokes on a drum **2** : a heavy reverberating sound **3** : a rolling movement or action **4** : a swaying movement (as of a ship) **5** : a somersault made in contact with the ground

**roll·back** \'rōl-ˌbak\ *n* : the act or an instance of rolling back

**roll back** *vb* **1** : to reduce (as a commodity price) on a national scale **2** : to cause to withdraw : push back

**roll bar** *n* : an overhead metal bar on an automobile designed to protect riders in case the automobile overturns

**roll call** *n* : the act or an instance of calling off a list of names (as of soldiers); *also* : a time for a roll call

**roll·er** \'rō-lər\ *n* **1** : a revolving cylinder used for moving, pressing, shaping, applying, or smoothing something **2** : a rod on which something is rolled up **3** : a long heavy ocean wave

**roller coast·er** \'rō-lər-ˌkō-stər\ *n* : an

amusement ride consisting of an elevated railway having sharp curves and steep slopes

**roller skate** *n* : a skate with wheels instead of a runner — **roller-skate** *vb* — **roller skater** *n*

**rol·lick** \'rä-lik\ *vb* : ROMP, FROLIC

**rol·lick·ing** *adj* : full of fun and good spirits ⟨a ~ good time⟩

**roly-poly** \ˌrō-lē-'pō-lē\ *adj* : ROTUND

**Rom** *abbr* **1** Roman **2** Romance **3** Romania; Romanian **4** Romans

**ROM** \'räm\ *n* : a computer memory that contains special-purpose information (as a program) which cannot be altered

**ro·maine** \rō-'mān\ *n* [F, lit., Roman] : a garden lettuce with a tall loose head of long crisp leaves

¹**Ro·man** \'rō-mən\ *n* **1** : a native or resident of Rome **2** *not cap* : roman letters or type

²**Roman** *adj* **1** : of or relating to Rome or the Romans and esp. the ancient Romans **2** *not cap* : relating to type in which the letters are upright **3** : of or relating to the Roman Catholic Church

**Roman candle** *n* : a cylindrical firework that discharges balls of fire

**Roman Catholic** *adj* : of, relating to, or being a Christian church led by the pope and having a liturgy centered in the Mass — **Roman Catholicism** *n*

¹**ro·mance** \rō-'mans, 'rō-ˌmans\ *n* [ME *romauns*, fr. AF *romanz* French, something written in French, tale in verse, fr. ML *Romanice* in a vernacular language, ultim. fr. L *Romanus* Roman] **1** : a medieval tale of knightly adventure **2** : a prose narrative dealing with heroic or mysterious events set in a remote time or place **3** : a love story **4** : a romantic attachment or episode between lovers — **ro·manc·er** *n*

²**romance** *vb* **ro·manced; ro·manc·ing 1** : to exaggerate or invent detail or incident **2** : to have romantic fancies **3** : to carry on a romantic episode with

**Ro·mance** \rō-'mans, 'rō-ˌmans\ *adj* : of or relating to any of several languages developed from Latin

**Ro·ma·nian** \ru̇-'mā-nē-ən, rō-, -nyən\ *also* **Ru·ma·nian** \ru̇-\ *n* **1** : a native or inhabitant of Romania **2** : the language of the Romanians

**Roman numeral** *n* : a numeral in a system of notation that is based on the ancient Roman system

**Ro·ma·no** \rō-'mä-nō\ *n* : a hard Italian cheese that is sharper than Parmesan

**Ro·mans** \'rō-mənz\ *n* — see BIBLE table

¹**ro·man·tic** \rō-'man-tik\ *adj* **1** : IMAGINARY **2** : VISIONARY **3** : having an imaginative or emotional appeal **4** : of, relating to, or having the characteristics of romanticism — **ro·man·ti·cal·ly** \-ti-k(ə-)lē\ *adv*

²**romantic** *n* : a romantic person; *esp* : a romantic writer, composer, or artist

**ro·man·ti·cism** \rō-'man-tə-ˌsi-zəm\ *n*, *often cap* : a literary movement (as in early 19th century England) marked esp. by emphasis on the imagination and the emotions and by the use of autobiographical material — **ro·man·ti·cist** \-sist\ *n, often cap*

**ro·man·ti·cize** \-'man-tə-,sīz\ *vb* -**cized**; -**ciz·ing** 1 : to make romantic 2 : to have romantic ideas

**romp** \'rämp\ *vb* 1 : to play actively and noisily 2 : to win a contest easily — **romp** *n*

**romp·er** \'räm-pər\ *n* 1 : one that romps 2 : a jumpsuit usu. for infants — usu. used in pl.

**rood** \'rüd\ *n* : CROSS, CRUCIFIX

¹**roof** \'rüf, 'ru̇f\ *n, pl* **roofs** \'rüfs, 'ru̇fs; 'rüvz, 'ru̇vz\ 1 : the upper covering part of a building 2 : something suggesting a roof of a building — **roofed** \'rüft, 'ru̇ft\ *adj* — **roof·ing** *n* — **roof·less** *adj* — **through the roof** : to an extremely high level ⟨prices went *through the roof*⟩

²**roof** *vb* : to cover with a roof

**roof·top** \-,täp\ *n* : a roof esp. of a house

¹**rook** \'ru̇k\ *n* : a crow that nests and roosts in usu. treetop colonies

²**rook** *vb* : CHEAT, SWINDLE

³**rook** *n* : a chess piece that can move parallel to the sides of the board across any number of unoccupied squares

**rook·ery** \'ru̇-kə-rē\ *n, pl* -**er·ies** : a breeding ground or haunt of gregarious birds or mammals; *also* : a colony of such birds or mammals

**rook·ie** \'ru̇-kē\ *n* : BEGINNER, RECRUIT; *esp* : a first-year player in a professional sport

¹**room** \'rüm, 'ru̇m\ *n* 1 : an extent of space occupied by or sufficient or available for something 2 : a partitioned part of a building : CHAMBER; *also* : the people in a room 3 : OPPORTUNITY, CHANCE ⟨∼ to develop his talents⟩ — **room·ful** *n* — **roomy** *adj*

²**room** *vb* : to occupy or share lodgings : LODGE — **room·er** *n*

**room·ette** \rü-'met, ru̇-\ *n* : a small private room on a railroad sleeping car

**room·mate** \'rüm-,māt, 'ru̇m-\ *n* : one of two or more persons sharing the same room or dwelling

¹**roost** \'rüst\ *n* : a support on which or a place where birds perch

²**roost** *vb* : to settle on or as if on a roost

**roost·er** \'rüs-tər, 'ru̇s-\ *n* : an adult male domestic chicken : COCK

¹**root** \'rüt, 'ru̇t\ *n* 1 : the leafless usu. underground part of a seed plant that functions in absorption, aeration, and storage or as a means of anchorage; *also* : an underground plant part esp. when fleshy and edible 2 : something (as the basal part of a tooth or hair) resembling a root 3 : SOURCE, ORIGIN; *esp* : ANCESTRY — usu. used in pl. 4 : the essential core : HEART ⟨get to the ∼ of the matter⟩ 5 : a number that when taken as a factor an indicated number of times gives a specified number 6 : the lower part — **root·less** *adj* — **root·like** *adj*

²**root** *vb* 1 : to form roots 2 : to fix or become fixed by or as if by roots : ESTABLISH 3 : UPROOT

³**root** *vb* 1 : to turn up or dig with the

snout ⟨pigs ∼*ing*⟩ 2 : to poke or dig around (as in search of something)

⁴**root** \'rüt\ *vb* 1 : to applaud or encourage noisily : CHEER 2 : to wish success or lend support to — **root·er** *n*

**root beer** *n* : a sweetened carbonated beverage flavored with extracts of roots and herbs

**root canal** *n* : a dental operation to save a tooth by removing the pulp in the root of the tooth and filling the cavity with a protective substance

**root·let** \'rüt-lət, 'ru̇t-\ *n* : a small root

**root·stock** \-,stäk\ *n* : an underground part of a plant that resembles a rhizome

¹**rope** \'rōp\ *n* 1 : a large strong cord made of strands of fiber 2 : a hangman's noose 3 : a thick string (as of pearls) made by twisting or braiding

²**rope** *vb* **roped**; **rop·ing** 1 : to bind, tie, or fasten together with a rope 2 : to separate or divide by means of a rope 3 : LASSO

**Ror·schach test** \'rȯr-,shäk-\ *n* : a psychological test in which a subject interprets ink-blot designs in terms that reveal intellectual and emotional factors

**ro·sa·ry** \'rō-zə-rē\ *n, pl* -**ries** 1 *often cap* : a Roman Catholic devotion consisting of meditation on sacred mysteries during recitation of Hail Marys 2 : a string of beads used in praying

¹**rose** *past of* RISE

²**rose** \'rōz\ *n* 1 : any of a genus of usu. prickly often climbing shrubs with divided leaves and bright often fragrant flowers; *also* : one of these flowers 2 : something resembling a rose in form 3 : a moderate purplish red color — **rose** *adj*

**ro·sé** \rō-'zā\ *n* [F] : a light pink wine

**ro·se·ate** \'rō-zē-ət, -zē-,āt\ *adj* 1 : resembling a rose esp. in color 2 : OPTIMISTIC ⟨a ∼ view of the future⟩

**rose·bud** \'rōz-,bəd\ *n* : the flower of a rose when it is at most partly open

**rose·bush** \-,bu̇sh\ *n* : a shrubby rose

**rose·mary** \'rōz-,mer-ē\ *n, pl* -**mar·ies** [ME *rosmarine,* fr. AF *rosmarin,* fr. L *rosmarinus,* fr. *ros* dew + *marinus* of the sea, fr. *mare* sea] : a fragrant shrubby Mediterranean mint; *also* : its leaves used as a seasoning

**ro·sette** \rō-'zet\ *n* [F] 1 : a usu. small badge or ornament of ribbon gathered in the shape of a rose 2 : a circular ornament filled with representations of leaves

**rose wa·ter** \'rōz-,wȯ-tər, -,wä-\ *n* : a watery solution of the fragrant constituents of the rose used as a perfume

**rose·wood** \-,wu̇d\ *n* : any of various tropical trees with dark red wood streaked with black; *also* : this wood

**Rosh Ha·sha·nah** \,räsh-hə-'shä-nə, ,rōsh-, -'shō-\ *n* [Heb *rōsh hashshānāh,* lit., beginning of the year] : the Jewish New Year observed as a religious holiday in September or October

**ros·in** \'rä-zⁿn\ *n* : a brittle resin obtained esp. from pine trees and used esp. in varnishes and on violin bows

**ros·ter** \'räs-tər\ *n* 1 : a list of personnel;

*also* : the persons listed on a roster **2** : an itemized list

**ros·trum** \'räs-trəm\ *n, pl* **rostrums** *or* **ros·tra** \-trə\ [L *Rostra*, pl., a platform for speakers in the Roman Forum decorated with the beaks of captured ships, fr. pl. of *rostrum* beak, ship's beak, fr. *rodere* to gnaw] : a stage or platform for public speaking

**rosy** \'rō-zē\ *adj* **ros·i·er; -est 1** : of the color rose **2** : HOPEFUL, PROMISING ⟨a ~ outlook⟩ — **ros·i·ly** \'rō-zə-lē\ *adv* — **ros·i·ness** \-zē-nəs\ *n*

¹**rot** \'rät\ *vb* **rot·ted; rot·ting** : to undergo decomposition : DECAY

²**rot** *n* **1** : DECAY **2** : any of various diseases of plants or animals in which tissue breaks down **3** : NONSENSE

¹**ro·ta·ry** \'rō-tə-rē\ *adj* **1** : turning on an axis like a wheel **2** : having a rotating part ⟨a ~ telephone⟩

²**rotary** *n, pl* **-ries 1** : a rotary machine **2** : a one-way circular road junction

**ro·tate** \'rō-ˌtāt\ *vb* **ro·tat·ed; ro·tat·ing 1** : to turn or cause to turn about an axis or a center : REVOLVE **2** : to alternate in a series ♦ *Synonyms* TURN, CIRCLE, SPIN, WHIRL, TWIRL — **ro·ta·tion** \rō-'tā-shən\ *n* — **ro·ta·tor** \'rō-ˌtā-tər\ *n* — **ro·ta·to·ry** \'rō-tə-ˌtōr-ē\ *adj*

**ROTC** *abbr* Reserve Officers' Training Corps

**rote** \'rōt\ *n* **1** : repetition from memory often without attention to meaning ⟨learn by ~⟩ **2** : mechanical or unthinking routine or repetition — **rote** *adj*

**ro·tis·se·rie** \rō-'tis-ə-rē\ *n* [F] **1** : a restaurant specializing in broiled and barbecued meats **2** : an appliance fitted with a spit on which food is rotated before or over a source of heat

**ro·to·gra·vure** \ˌrō-tə-grə-'vyůr\ *n* : PHOTOGRAVURE

**ro·tor** \'rō-tər\ *n* **1** : a part that rotates; *esp* : the rotating part of an electrical machine **2** : a system of rotating horizontal blades for supporting a helicopter

**ro·to·till·er** \'rō-tō-ˌti-lər\ *n* : an engine-powered machine with rotating blades used to lift and turn over soil

**rot·ten** \'rä-t²n\ *adj* **1** : having rotted **2** : CORRUPT **3** : extremely unpleasant or inferior — **rot·ten·ness** *n*

**rot·ten·stone** \'rä-t²n-ˌstōn\ *n* : a decomposed siliceous limestone used for polishing

**rott·wei·ler** \'rät-ˌwī-lər\ *n, often cap* : any of a breed of tall powerful black-and-tan short-haired dogs

**ro·tund** \rō-'tənd\ *adj* : rounded out ♦ *Synonyms* PLUMP, CHUBBY, PORTLY, STOUT — **ro·tun·di·ty** \-'tən-də-tē\ *n*

**ro·tun·da** \rō-'tən-də\ *n* **1** : a round building; *esp* : one covered by a dome **2** : a large round room

**rouble** *var of* RUBLE

**roué** \rü-'ā\ *n* [F, lit., broken on the wheel, fr. pp. of *rouer* to break on the wheel, fr. ML *rotare*, fr. L, to rotate; fr. the feeling that such a person deserves this punishment] : a man devoted to a life of sensual pleasure : RAKE

**rouge** \'rüzh, 'rüj\ *n* [F, lit., red] : a cosmetic used to give a red color to cheeks and lips — **rouge** *vb*

¹**rough** \'rəf\ *adj* **rough·er; rough·est 1** : uneven in surface : not smooth **2** : SHAGGY **3** : not calm : TURBULENT, TEMPESTUOUS **4** : marked by harshness or violence **5** : DIFFICULT, TRYING **6** : coarse or rugged in character or appearance **7** : marked by lack of refinement **8** : CRUDE, UNFINISHED **9** : done or made hastily or tentatively ⟨a ~ estimate⟩ — **rough·ly** *adv* — **rough·ness** *n*

²**rough** *n* **1** : uneven ground covered with high grass esp. along a golf fairway **2** : a crude, unfinished, or preliminary state; *also* : something in such a state **3** : ROWDY, TOUGH

³**rough** *vb* **1** : ROUGHEN **2** : MANHANDLE **3** : to make or shape roughly esp. in a preliminary way — **rough·er** *n*

**rough·age** \'rə-fij\ *n* : FIBER **2**; *also* : food containing much indigestible material acting as fiber

**rough–and–ready** \ˌrə-fən-'re-dē\ *adj* : rude or unpolished in nature, method, or manner but effective in action or use ⟨a ~ solution⟩

**rough–and–tum·ble** \-'təm-bəl\ *n* : rough unrestrained fighting or struggling — **rough–and–tumble** *adj*

**rough·en** \'rə-fən\ *vb* **rough·ened; rough·en·ing** : to make or become rough

**rough–hewn** \'rəf-'hyün\ *adj* **1** : being rough and unfinished ⟨~ beams⟩ **2** : lacking smooth manners or social grace — **rough–hew** \-'hyü\ *vb*

**rough·house** \'rəf-ˌhau̇s\ *vb* **rough·housed; rough·hous·ing** : to participate in rough noisy behavior — **rough·house** *n*

**rough·neck** \'rəf-ˌnek\ *n* **1** : ROWDY, TOUGH **2** : a worker on a crew drilling oil wells

**rough·shod** \'rəf-ˌshäd\ *adv* : in a roughly forceful manner ⟨rode ~ over the opposition⟩

**rou·lette** \rü-'let\ *n* [F, lit., small wheel] **1** : a gambling game in which a whirling wheel is used **2** : a wheel or disk with teeth around the outside

¹**round** \'rau̇nd\ *adj* **1** : having every part of the surface or circumference the same distance from the center **2** : CYLINDRICAL **3** : COMPLETE, FULL **4** : approximately correct; *esp* : exact only to a specific decimal or place ⟨~ numbers⟩ **5** : liberal or ample in size or amount **6** : BLUNT, OUTSPOKEN **7** : moving in or forming a circle **8** : having curves rather than angles — **round·ish** *adj* — **round·ness** *n*

²**round** *prep or adv* : AROUND

³**round** *n* **1** : something round (as a circle, globe, or ring) **2** : a curved or rounded part (as a rung of a ladder) **3** : an indirect path or course; *also* : a regularly covered route (as of a security guard) **4** : a series or cycle of recurring actions or events **5** : one shot fired by a soldier or a gun; *also* : ammunition for one shot **6** : a period of

time or a unit of play in a game or contest **7** : a cut of meat (as beef) esp. between the rump and the lower leg — **in the round 1** : FREESTANDING **2** : with a center stage surrounded by an audience ⟨theater *in the round*⟩

⁴**round** *vb* **1** : to make or become round **2** : to go or pass around or part way around **3** : COMPLETE, FINISH **4** : to become plump or shapely **5** : to express as a round number — often used with *off* **6** : to follow a winding course : BEND

¹**round·about** \'raún-də-ˌbaút\ *adj* : INDIRECT, CIRCUITOUS ⟨a ~ explanation⟩

²**roundabout** *n* **1** *Brit* : MERRY-GO-ROUND **2** *Brit* : ROTARY 2

**roun·de·lay** \'raún-də-ˌlā\ *n* **1** : a simple song with a refrain **2** : a poem with a recurring refrain

**round·house** \'raúnd-ˌhaús\ *n* **1** : a circular building for housing and repairing locomotives **2** : a blow with the hand made with a wide swing — **roundhouse** *adj*

**round·ly** \'raúnd-lē\ *adv* **1** : in a complete manner; *also* : WIDELY **2** : in a blunt way **3** : with vigor

**round–rob·in** \'raúnd-ˌrä-bən\ *n* : a tournament in which each contestant meets every other contestant in turn

**round–shoul·dered** \-ˌshōl-dərd\ *adj* : having the shoulders stooping or rounded

**round–trip** *n* : a trip to a place and back

**round·up** \'raúnd-ˌəp\ *n* **1** : the gathering together of cattle on the range by riding around them and driving them in; *also* : the ranch hands and horses engaged in a roundup **2** : a gathering in of scattered persons or things : SUMMARY ⟨news ~⟩ — **round up** *vb*

**round·worm** \-ˌwərm\ *n* : NEMATODE

**rouse** \'raúz\ *vb* **roused; rous·ing 1** : to excite to activity : stir up **2** : to wake from sleep — **rous·er** *n*

**roust·about** \'raús-tə-ˌbaút\ *n* **1** : one who does heavy unskilled labor on a dock or in an oil field) **2** : a laborer at a circus **3** : a person with no established home or occupation

¹**rout** \'raút\ *n* **1** : MOB 1, 2 **2** : DISTURBANCE **3** : a fashionable gathering

²**rout** *vb* **1** : RUMMAGE **2** : to gouge out **3** : to expel by force ⟨~ed out of their homes⟩

³**rout** *n* **1** : a state of wild confusion or disorderly retreat **2** : a disastrous defeat

⁴**rout** *vb* **1** : to put to flight **2** : to defeat decisively

¹**route** \'rüt, 'raút\ *n* [ME, fr. AF *rute*, fr. VL *\*rupta (via)*, lit., broken way] **1** : a traveled way **2** : CHANNEL **3** : a line of travel

²**route** *vb* **rout·ed; rout·ing** : to send by a selected route : DIRECT

**route·man** \-mən, -ˌman\ *n* : a person who sells and makes deliveries on an assigned route

**rout·er** \'raú-tər\ *n* : a machine with a revolving spindle and cutter for shaping a surface (as of wood)

**rou·tine** \rü-'tēn\ *n* [F, fr. MF, fr. *route*

traveled way] **1** : a regular course of procedure **2** : an often repeated speech or formula **3** : a part fully worked out ⟨a comedy ~⟩ **4** : a set of computer instructions that will perform a certain task — **routine** *adj* — **rou·tine·ly** *adv* — **rou·tin·ize** \-'tē-ˌnīz\ *vb*

¹**rove** \'rōv\ *vb* **roved; rov·ing** : to wander over or through — **rov·er** *n*

²**rove** *past and past part of* REEVE

¹**row** \'rō\ *vb* **1** : to propel a boat with oars **2** : to transport in a rowboat **3** : to pull an oar in a crew — **row·er** \'rō-ər\ *n*

²**row** *n* : an act or instance of rowing

³**row** *n* **1** : a number of objects in an orderly sequence **2** : WAY, STREET

⁴**row** \'raú\ *n* : a noisy quarrel

⁵**row** \'raú\ *vb* : to engage in a row

**row·boat** \'rō-ˌbōt\ *n* : a small boat designed to be rowed

**row·dy** \'raú-dē\ *adj* **row·di·er; -est** : coarse or boisterous in behavior : ROUGH ⟨a ~ crowd⟩ — **row·di·ness** \'raú-dē-nəs\ *n* — **rowdy** *n* — **row·dy·ish** *adj* — **row·dy·ism** *n*

**row·el** \'raú-(ə)l\ *n* : a small pointed wheel on a rider's spur — **rowel** *vb*

¹**roy·al** \'rói-(ə)l\ *adj* [ME *roial*, fr. AF *real, roial*, fr. L *regalis*, fr. *reg-, rex* king] **1** : of or relating to a sovereign : REGAL **2** : fit for a king or queen ⟨a ~ welcome⟩ — **roy·al·ly** *adv*

²**royal** *n* : a person of royal blood

**royal flush** *n* : a straight flush having an ace as the highest card

**roy·al·ist** \'rói-ə-list\ *n* : an adherent of a king or of monarchical government

**roy·al·ty** \'rói-əl-tē\ *n, pl* **-ties 1** : the state of being royal **2** : royal persons **3** : a share of a product or profit (as of a mine or oil well) claimed by the owner for allowing another person to use the property **4** : a payment made to an author or composer for each copy of a work sold or to an inventor for each article sold under a patent

**RP** *abbr* **1** relief pitcher **2** Republic of the Philippines

**rpm** *abbr* revolutions per minute

**rps** *abbr* revolutions per second

**rpt** *abbr* **1** repeat **2** report

**RR** *abbr* **1** railroad **2** rural route

**RS** *abbr* **1** recording secretary **2** revised statutes **3** Royal Society

**RSV** *abbr* Revised Standard Version

**RSVP** *abbr* [F *répondez s'il vous plaît*] please reply

**rt** *abbr* **1** right **2** route

**RT** *abbr* round-trip

**rte** *abbr* route

**Ru** *symbol* ruthenium

¹**rub** \'rəb\ *vb* **rubbed; rub·bing 1** : to use pressure and friction on a body or object **2** : to fret or chafe with friction **3** : to scour, polish, erase, or smear by pressure and friction

²**rub** *n* **1** : DIFFICULTY, OBSTRUCTION **2** : something grating to the feelings

¹**rub·ber** \'rə-bər\ *n* **1** : one that rubs **2** : ERASER **3** : a flexible waterproof elastic substance made from the milky juice of various tropical plants or made syntheti-

cally; *also* : something made of this material   **4** : CONDOM — **rubber** *adj* — **rubber·ize** \'rə-bə-ˌrīz\ *vb* — **rub·bery** *adj*

²**rubber** *n*   **1** : a contest that consists of an odd number of games and is won by the side that takes a majority   **2** : an extra game played to decide a tie

¹**rub·ber·neck** \-ˌnek\ *n*   **1** : an idly or overly inquisitive person   **2** : a person on a guided tour

²**rubberneck** *vb* : to look about, stare, or listen with excessive curiosity ⟨*~ing* drivers⟩ — **rub·ber·neck·er** *n*

**rub·bish** \'rə-bish\ *n*   **1** : useless waste or rejected matter : TRASH   **2** : something worthless or nonsensical

**rub·ble** \'rə-bəl\ *n* : broken fragments esp. of a destroyed building

**ru·bel** *or* **ru·ble** \'rü-bəl\ — see MONEY table

**ru·bel·la** \rü-'be-lə\ *n* : GERMAN MEASLES

**ru·bi·cund** \'rü-bi-(ˌ)kənd\ *adj* : RED, RUDDY ⟨a *~* face⟩

**ru·bid·i·um** \rü-'bi-dē-əm\ *n* : a soft silvery metallic chemical element

**ru·ble** *also* **rou·ble** \'rü-bəl\ *n* — see MONEY table

**ru·bric** \'rü-brik\ *n* [ME *rubrike* red ocher, heading in red letters of part of a book, fr. AF, fr. L *rubrica*, fr. *ruber* red]   **1** : HEADING, TITLE; *also* : CLASS, CATEGORY   **2** : a rule esp. for the conduct of a religious service

**ru·by** \'rü-bē\ *n, pl* **rubies** : a clear red precious stone — **ruby** *adj*

**ru·by–throat·ed hummingbird** \'rü-bē-ˌthrō-təd-\ *n* : a bright green and whitish hummingbird of eastern No. America with a red throat in the male

**ruck·us** \'rə-kəs\ *n* : ROW, DISTURBANCE

**rud·der** \'rə-dər\ *n* : a movable flat piece attached at the rear of a ship or aircraft for steering

**rud·dy** \'rə-dē\ *adj* **rud·di·er; -est** : REDDISH; *esp* : of a healthy reddish complexion — **rud·di·ness** \'rə-dē-nəs\ *n*

**rude** \'rüd\ *adj* **rud·er; rud·est**   **1** : roughly made : CRUDE   **2** : UNDEVELOPED, PRIMITIVE   **3** : IMPOLITE   **4** : UNSKILLED — **rude·ly** *adv* — **rude·ness** *n*

**ru·di·ment** \'rü-də-mənt\ *n*   **1** : an elementary principle or basic skill — usu. used in pl. ⟨the *~s* of mathematics⟩   **2** : something not fully developed — usu. used in pl. ⟨the *~s* of a plan⟩ — **ru·di·men·ta·ry** \ˌrü-də-'men-tə-rē\ *adj*

¹**rue** \'rü\ *vb* **rued; ru·ing** : to feel regret, remorse, or penitence for ⟨*~s* his decision⟩

²**rue** *n* : REGRET, SORROW — **rue·ful** \-fəl\ *adj* — **rue·ful·ly** *adv* — **rue·ful·ness** *n*

³**rue** *n* : a European strong-scented woody herb with bitter-tasting leaves

**ruff** \'rəf\ *n*   **1** : a large round pleated collar worn about 1600   **2** : a fringe of long hair or feathers around the neck of an animal — **ruffed** \'rəft\ *adj*

**ruf·fi·an** \'rə-fē-ən\ *n* : a brutal person — **ruf·fi·an·ly** *adj*

¹**ruf·fle** \'rə-fəl\ *vb* **ruf·fled; ruf·fling**   **1** : to roughen the surface of   **2** : IRRITATE,

VEX   **3** : to erect (as hair or feathers) in or like a ruff   **4** : to flip through (as pages)   **5** : to draw into or provide with plaits or folds

²**ruffle** *n*   **1** : a strip of fabric gathered or pleated on one edge   **2** : RUFF   **3** : RIPPLE — **ruf·fly** \'rə-fə-lē, -flē\ *adj*

**ru·fi·yaa** \'rü-fē-ˌyä\ *n, pl* **rufiyaa** — see MONEY table

**RU–486** \ˌär-ˌyü-ˌför-ˌā-tē-'siks\ *n* : a drug taken orally to induce abortion esp. early in pregnancy

**rug** \'rəg\ *n*   **1** : a covering for the legs, lap, and feet   **2** : a piece of heavy fabric usu. with a nap or pile used as a floor covering

**rug·by** \'rəg-bē\ *n, often cap* [*Rugby* School, Rugby, England, where it was first played] : a football game in which play is continuous and interference and forward passing are not permitted

**rug·ged** \'rə-gəd\ *adj*   **1** : having a rough uneven surface   **2** : TURBULENT, STORMY   **3** : HARSH, STERN   **4** : ROBUST, STURDY — **rug·ged·ize** \'rə-gə-ˌdīz\ *vb* — **rug·ged·ly** *adv* — **rug·ged·ness** *n*

¹**ru·in** \'rü-ən\ *n*   **1** : complete collapse or destruction   **2** : the remains of something destroyed — usu. used in pl.   **3** : a cause of destruction   **4** : the action of destroying

²**ruin** *vb*   **1** : DESTROY   **2** : to damage beyond repair   **3** : BANKRUPT

**ru·in·ation** \ˌrü-ə-'nā-shən\ *n* : RUIN, DESTRUCTION

**ru·in·ous** \'rü-ə-nəs\ *adj*   **1** : RUINED, DILAPIDATED   **2** : causing ruin ⟨*~* conflicts⟩ — **ru·in·ous·ly** *adv*

¹**rule** \'rül\ *n* [ME *reule*, fr. AF, fr. L *regula* straightedge, rule, fr. *regere* to keep straight, direct]   **1** : a guide or principle for governing action : REGULATION   **2** : the usual way of doing something   **3** : the exercise of authority or control : GOVERNMENT   **4** : RULER 2

²**rule** *vb* **ruled; rul·ing**   **1** : CONTROL; *also* : GOVERN   **2** : to be supreme or outstanding in   **3** : to give or state as a considered decision   **4** : to mark on paper with or as if with a ruler   **5** *slang* : to be extremely cool or popular

**rul·er** \'rü-lər\ *n*   **1** : SOVEREIGN   **2** : a straight strip of material (as wood or metal) marked off in units and used for measuring or as a straightedge

**rum** \'rəm\ *n*   **1** : an alcoholic liquor made from sugarcane products (as molasses)   **2** : alcoholic liquor

**Ru·ma·nian** *var of* ROMANIAN

**rum·ba** \'rəm-bə, 'rüm-\ *n* : a dance of Cuban origin marked by strong rhythmic movements

¹**rum·ble** \'rəm-bəl\ *vb* **rum·bled; rum·bling** : to make a low heavy rolling sound; *also* : to move along with such a sound — **rum·bler** *n*

²**rumble** *n*   **1** : a low heavy rolling sound   **2** : a street fight esp. among gangs

**rumble seat** *n* : a folding seat in the back of an automobile that is not covered by the top

**rum·bling** \'rəm-bliŋ\ *n*   **1** : RUMBLE 2

: widespread talk or complaints — usu. used in pl.

**ru·men** \'rü-mən\ *n, pl* **ru·mi·na** \-mə-nə\ *or* **rumens** : the large first compartment of the stomach of a ruminant (as a cow)

**¹ru·mi·nant** \'rü-mə-nənt\ *n* : a ruminant mammal

**²ruminant** *adj* **1** : chewing the cud; *also* : of or relating to a group of hoofed mammals (as cattle, deer, and camels) that chew the cud and have a complex 3- or 4-chambered stomach **2** : MEDITATIVE

**ru·mi·nate** \'rü-mə-ˌnāt\ *vb* **-nat·ed; -nat·ing** [L *ruminari* to chew the cud, muse upon, fr. *rumin-, rumen* first stomach chamber of a ruminant] **1** : MEDITATE, MUSE **2** : to chew the cud — **ru·mi·na·tion** \ˌrü-mə-ˈnā-shən\ *n*

**¹rum·mage** \'rə-mij\ *vb* **rum·maged; rum·mag·ing** : to search thoroughly ⟨*rummaged* the room for his key⟩ — **rum·mag·er** *n*

**²rummage** *n* **1** : a miscellaneous collection **2** : act of rummaging

**rum·my** \'rə-mē\ *n* : any of several card games for two or more players

**ru·mor** \'rü-mər\ *n* **1** : common talk **2** : a statement or report current but not authenticated — **rumor** *vb*

**ru·mour** *chiefly Brit var of* RUMOR

**rump** \'rəmp\ *n* **1** : the rear part of an animal; *also* : a cut of meat (as beef) behind the upper sirloin **2** : a small or inferior remnant (as of a group)

**rum·ple** \'rəm-pəl\ *vb* **rum·pled; rum·pling** : TOUSLE, MUSS, WRINKLE — **rumple** *n* — **rum·ply** \'rəm-pə-lē\ *adj*

**rum·pus** \'rəm-pəs\ *n* : DISTURBANCE, RUCKUS

**rumpus room** *n* : a room usu. in the basement of a home that is used for games, parties, and recreation

**¹run** \'rən\ *vb* **ran** \'ran\; **run; run·ning** **1** : to go faster than a walk **2** : to take to flight : FLEE **3** : to go without restraint ⟨let chickens ∼ loose⟩ **4** : to go rapidly or hurriedly : HASTEN, RUSH **5** : to make a quick or casual trip or visit **6** : to contend in a race; *esp* : to enter an election ⟨∼ for mayor⟩ **7** : to put forward as a candidate for office **8** : to move on or as if on wheels : pass or slide freely **9** : to go back and forth : PLY **10** : to move in large numbers esp. to a spawning ground ⟨shad are *running*⟩ **11** : FUNCTION, OPERATE ⟨∼s on gasoline⟩ ⟨software that ∼s on her computer⟩ **12** : to continue in force ⟨two years to ∼⟩ **13** : to flow rapidly or under pressure : MELT, FUSE, DISSOLVE; *also* : DISCHARGE ⟨my nose is *running*⟩ **14** : to tend to produce or to recur ⟨family ∼s to blonds⟩ ⟨stubbornness ∼s in the family⟩ **15** : to take a certain direction **16** : to be worded or written **17** : to be current ⟨rumors *running* wild⟩ **18** : to cause to produce a flow ⟨*ran* the faucet⟩ **19** : TRACE ⟨∼ down a rumor⟩ **20** : to perform or bring about by running **21** : to cause to pass ⟨∼ a wire from the antenna⟩ **22** : to cause to collide **23** : SMUGGLE **24**

: MANAGE, CONDUCT, OPERATE ⟨∼ a business⟩ **25** : INCUR ⟨∼ a risk⟩ **26** : to permit to accumulate before settling ⟨∼ up a bill⟩ **27** : PRINT, PUBLISH ⟨∼ a news story⟩

**²run** *n* **1** : an act or the action of running **2** : a migration of fish; *also* : the migrating fish **3** : a score in baseball **4** : BROOK, CREEK **5** : a continuous series esp. of similar things **6** : persistent heavy demands from depositors, creditors, or customers **7** : the quantity of work turned out in a continuous operation; *also* : a period of operation (as of a machine or plant) **8** : the usual or normal kind ⟨the ordinary ∼ of students⟩ **9** : the distance covered in continuous travel or sailing **10** : a regular course or trip **11** : freedom of movement in a place or area ⟨has the ∼ of the house⟩ **12** : an enclosure for animals **13** : an inclined course (as for skiing) **14** : a lengthwise ravel (as in a stocking) — **run·less** *adj*

**run·about** \'rə-nə-ˌbaut\ *n* : a light wagon, automobile, or motorboat

**run·a·gate** \'rə-nə-ˌgāt\ *n* **1** : VAGABOND **2** : FUGITIVE

**run·around** \'rə-nə-ˌraund\ *n* : evasive or delaying action esp. in response to a request

**¹run·away** \'rə-nə-ˌwā\ *n* **1** : one that runs away : FUGITIVE **2** : the act of running away out of control; *also* : something (as a horse) that is running out of control

**²runaway** *adj* **1** : FUGITIVE **2** : won by a long lead; *also* : extremely successful **3** : subject to uncontrolled changes ⟨∼ inflation⟩ **4** : operating out of control ⟨∼ locomotive⟩

**run·down** \'rən-ˌdaun\ *n* : an item-by-item report or review : SUMMARY

**run—down** \'rən-ˈdaun\ *adj* **1** : EXHAUSTED, WORN-OUT ⟨that ∼ feeling⟩ **2** : being in poor repair ⟨a ∼ farm⟩

**run down** *vb* **1** : to collide with and knock down **2** : to chase until exhausted or captured **3** : to find by search **4** : DISPARAGE **5** : to cease to operate for lack of motive power **6** : to decline in physical condition

**rune** \'rün\ *n* **1** : any of the characters of any of several alphabets formerly used by the Germanic peoples **2** : MYSTERY, MAGIC **3** : a poem esp. in Finnish or Old Norse — **ru·nic** \'rü-nik\ *adj*

**¹rung** *past part of* RING

**²rung** \'rəŋ\ *n* **1** : a rounded crosspiece between the legs of a chair **2** : one of the crosspieces of a ladder

**run—in** \'rən-ˌin\ *n* **1** : ALTERCATION, QUARREL **2** : something run in

**run in** *vb* **1** : to insert as additional matter **2** : to arrest esp. for a minor offense **3** : to pay a casual visit

**run·nel** \'rə-nᵊl\ *n* : BROOK, STREAMLET

**run·ner** \'rə-nər\ *n* **1** : one that runs **2** : BASE RUNNER **3** : BALLCARRIER **4** : a thin piece or part on which something (as a sled or an ice skate) slides **5** : the support of a drawer or a sliding door **6** : a horizontal branch from the base of a plant that produces new plants **7** : a plant producing runners **8** : a long narrow carpet **9** : a narrow decorative cloth cover for a table or dresser top

**run·ner-up** \'rə-nər-ˌəp\ *n, pl* **runners-up** *also* **runner-ups** : the competitor in a contest who finishes second

¹**run·ning** *adj* **1** : FLOWING **2** : FLUID, RUNNY **3** : CONTINUOUS, INCESSANT **4** : measured in a straight line ⟨cost per ∼ foot⟩ **5** : of or relating to an act of running **6** : made or trained for running ⟨∼ horse⟩ ⟨∼ shoes⟩

²**running** *adv* : in succession

**running light** *n* : any of the lights carried by a vehicle (as a ship) at night

**run·ny** \'rə-nē\ *adj* : having a tendency to run ⟨a ∼ dough⟩ ⟨a ∼ nose⟩

**run·off** \'rən-ˌȯf\ *n* : a final contest (as an election) to decide a previous indecisive contest

**run-of-the-mill** *adj* : not outstanding : AVERAGE ⟨a ∼ performance⟩

**run on** *vb* **1** : to talk at length **2** : to continue (matter in type) without a break or a new paragraph **3** : to place or add (as an entry in a dictionary) at the end of a paragraphed item — **run–on** \'rən-ˌȯn, -ˌän\ *n*

**run out** *vb* : to use up or exhaust a supply ⟨*ran out* of gas⟩

**runt** \'rənt\ *n* : an unusually small person or animal : DWARF — **runty** *adj*

**run·way** \'rən-ˌwā\ *n* **1** : a beaten path made by animals; *also* : a passage for animals **2** : a paved strip of ground for the landing and takeoff of aircraft **3** : a narrow platform from a stage into an auditorium **4** : a support (as a track) on which something runs

**ru·pee** \rü-'pē, 'rü-ˌpē\ *n* — see MONEY table

**ru·pi·ah** \rü-'pē-ə\ *n, pl* **rupiah** *or* **rupiahs** — see MONEY table

¹**rup·ture** \'rəp-chər\ *n* : a breaking or tearing apart; *also* : HERNIA

²**rupture** *vb* **rup·tured; rup·tur·ing** : to cause or undergo rupture

**ru·ral** \'rur-əl\ *adj* : of or relating to the country, country people, or agriculture

**ruse** \'rüs, 'rüz\ *n* : a wily subterfuge : TRICK, ARTIFICE

¹**rush** \'rəsh\ *n* : any of various often tufted and hollow-stemmed grasslike marsh plants — **rushy** *adj*

²**rush** *vb* [ME *russhen*, fr. AF *reuser, ruser, russher* to drive back, repulse, fr. L *recusare* to oppose] **1** : to move forward or act with too great haste or eagerness or without preparation **2** : to perform in a short time or at high speed **3** : ATTACK, CHARGE **4** : to advance a football by running — **rush·er** *n*

³**rush** *n* **1** : a violent forward motion **2** : unusual demand or activity **3** : a crowding of people to one place **4** : a running

play in football **5** : a sudden feeling of pleasure

⁴**rush** *adj* : requiring or marked by special speed or urgency ⟨∼ orders⟩

**rush hour** *n* : a time when the amount of traffic or business is at a peak

**rusk** \'rəsk\ *n* : a sweet or plain bread baked, sliced, and baked again until dry and crisp

**rus·set** \'rə-sət\ *n* **1** : a coarse reddish brown cloth **2** : a reddish brown **3** : a baking potato — **russet** *adj*

**Rus·sian** \'rə-shən\ *n* **1** : a native or inhabitant of Russia **2** : a Slavic language of the Russian people — **Russian** *adj*

**rust** \'rəst\ *n* **1** : a reddish coating formed on iron when it is exposed to esp. moist air **2** : any of numerous plant diseases characterized by usu. reddish spots; *also* : a fungus causing rust **3** : a strong reddish brown — **rust** *vb* — **rusty** *adj*

¹**rus·tic** \'rəs-tik\ *adj* : of, relating to, or suitable for the country or country people ⟨a ∼ inn⟩ — **rus·ti·cal·ly** \-ti-k(ə-)lē\ *adv* — **rus·tic·i·ty** \ˌrəs-'ti-sə-tē\ *n*

²**rustic** *n* : a rustic person

**rus·ti·cate** \'rəs-ti-ˌkāt\ *vb* **-cat·ed; -cat·ing** : to go into or reside in the country — **rus·ti·ca·tion** \ˌrəs-ti-'kā-shən\ *n*

¹**rus·tle** \'rə-səl\ *vb* **rus·tled; rus·tling** **1** : to make or cause a rustle **2** : to cause to rustle ⟨∼ a newspaper⟩ **3** : to act or move with energy or speed; *also* : to procure in this way **4** : to forage food **5** : to steal cattle from the range — **rus·tler** *n*

²**rustle** *n* : a quick series of small sounds ⟨∼ of leaves⟩

¹**rut** \'rət\ *n* : state or period of sexual excitement esp. in male deer — **rut** *vb*

²**rut** *n* **1** : a track worn by wheels or by habitual passage of something **2** : a usual or fixed routine

**ru·ta·ba·ga** \ˌrü-tə-'bā-gə, ˌrü-\ *n* : a turnip with a large yellowish root

**Ruth** \'rüth\ *n* — see BIBLE table

**ru·the·ni·um** \rü-'thē-nē-əm\ *n* : a rare hard metallic chemical element

**ruth·er·for·di·um** \ˌrə-thər-'fȯr-dē-əm\ *n* : an artifically produced radioactive chemical element

**ruth·less** \'rüth-ləs\ *adj* [fr. *ruth* compassion, pity, fr. ME *ruthe*, fr. *ruen* to rue, fr. OE *hrēowan*] : having no pity : MERCILESS, CRUEL ⟨a ∼ tyrant⟩ — **ruth·less·ly** *adv* — **ruth·less·ness** *n*

¹**RV** \ˌär-'vē\ *n* : RECREATIONAL VEHICLE

²**RV** *abbr* Revised Version

**R–value** \'är-ˌval-yü\ *n* : a measure of resistance to the flow of heat through a substance (as insulation)

**RW** *abbr* **1** right worshipful **2** right worthy

**rwy** *or* **ry** *abbr* railway

**-ry** *n suffix* : ERY ⟨bigot*ry*⟩

**rye** \'rī\ *n* **1** : a hardy annual grass grown for grain or as a cover crop; *also* : its seed **2** : a whiskey distilled from a rye mash

¹**s** \'es\ *n, pl* **s's** *or* **ss** \'e-səz\ *often cap*
: the 19th letter of the English alphabet

²**s** *abbr, often cap* **1** saint **2** second **3** senate **4** series **5** shilling **6** singular **7** small
**8** son **9** south; southern

¹**-s** \s *after sounds* f, k, k̲, p, t, th; əz *after
sounds* ch, j, s, sh, z, zh; z *after other
sounds*\ *n pl suffix* — used to form the
plural of most nouns that do not end in *s,
z, sh,* or *ch* or *y* following a consonant
⟨heads⟩ ⟨books⟩ ⟨boys⟩ ⟨beliefs⟩, to
form the plural of proper nouns that end
in *y* following a consonant ⟨Marys⟩, and
with or without a preceding apostrophe
to form the plural of abbreviations, numbers, letters, and symbols used as nouns
⟨MCs⟩ ⟨4s⟩ ⟨#s⟩ ⟨B's⟩

²**-s** *adv suffix* — used to form adverbs denoting usual or repeated action or state
⟨works nights⟩

³**-s** *vb suffix* — used to form the third person singular present of most verbs that
do not end in *s, z, sh,* or *ch* or *y* following
a consonant ⟨falls⟩ ⟨takes⟩ ⟨plays⟩

**S** *symbol* sulfur

**SA** *abbr* **1** Salvation Army **2** seaman apprentice **3** sex appeal **4** [L *sine anno*
*without year*] without date **5** South Africa **6** South America **7** subject to approval

**Saami** *var of* SAMI

**Sab·bath** \'sa-bəth\ *n* [ME *sabat,* fr. AF
& OE, fr. L *sabbatum,* fr. Gk *sabbaton,*
fr. Heb *shabbāth,* lit., rest] **1** : the 7th day
of the week observed as a day of worship
by Jews and some Christians **2** : Sunday
observed among Christians as a day of
worship

**sab·bat·i·cal** \sə-'ba-ti-kəl\ *n* : a leave often with pay granted (as to a college professor) usu. every 7th year for rest, travel,
or research

**sa·ber** *or* **sa·bre** \'sā-bər\ *n* [F *sabre*] : a
cavalry sword with a curved blade and
thick back

**saber saw** *n* : a portable electric saw with
a pointed reciprocating blade; *esp* : JIGSAW

**sa·ble** \'sā-bəl\ *n, pl* **sables** **1** : the color
black **2** *pl* : mourning garments **3** : a
dark brown mammal chiefly of northern
Asia related to the weasels; *also* : its fur
or pelt

¹**sab·o·tage** \'sa-bə-ˌtäzh\ *n* [F] **1** : deliberate destruction of an employer's property or hindering of production by workers **2** : destructive or hampering action
by enemy agents or sympathizers in time
of war

²**sabotage** *vb* **-taged; -tag·ing** : to practice sabotage on : WRECK

**sab·o·teur** \ˌsa-bə-'tər\ *n* : a person who
practices sabotage

**sac** \'sak\ *n* : a pouch in an animal or
plant often containing a fluid

**SAC** *abbr* Strategic Air Command

**sac·cha·rin** \'sa-kə-rən\ *n* : a white crystalline compound used as an artificial
calorie-free sweetener

**sac·cha·rine** \'sa-kə-rən\ *adj* : nauseatingly sweet ⟨~ poetry⟩

**sac·er·do·tal** \ˌsa-sər-'dō-t°l, -kər-\ *adj*
: PRIESTLY

**sac·er·do·tal·ism** \-tə-ˌli-zəm\ *n* : a religious belief emphasizing the powers of
priests as essential mediators between
God and man

**sa·chem** \'sā-chəm\ *n* [Narragansett
*sâchim*] : a No. American Indian chief

**sa·chet** \sa-'shā\ *n* [MF, fr. OF, dim. of
*sac* bag] : a small bag filled with perfumed powder for scenting clothes

¹**sack** \'sak\ *n* **1** : a usu. rectangular-shaped bag (as of paper or burlap) **2** : a
loose jacket or short coat

²**sack** *vb* : DISMISS, FIRE

³**sack** *n* [modif. of MF *sec* dry, fr. L *siccus*]
: a white wine popular in England in the
16th and 17th centuries

⁴**sack** *vb* : to plunder a captured town

**sack·cloth** \-ˌklòth\ *n* : a rough garment
worn as a sign of penitence

**sac·ra·ment** \'sa-krə-mənt\ *n* **1** : a formal religious act or rite; *esp* : one (as baptism or the Eucharist) held to have been
instituted by Christ **2** : the elements of
the Eucharist — **sac·ra·men·tal** \ˌsa-krə-'men-t°l\ *adj*

**sa·cred** \'sā-krəd\ *adj* **1** : set apart for
the service or worship of deity **2** : devoted exclusively to one service or use **3**
: worthy of veneration or reverence **4**
: of or relating to religion : RELIGIOUS
♦ **Synonyms** BLESSED, DIVINE, HALLOWED, HOLY, SANCTIFIED — **sa·cred·ly** *adv* — **sa·cred·ness** *n*

**sacred cow** *n* : one that is often unreasonably immune from criticism

¹**sac·ri·fice** \'sa-krə-ˌfīs\ *n* **1** : the offering
of something precious to deity **2** : something offered in sacrifice **3** : LOSS, DEPRIVATION **4** : a bunt allowing a base runner
to advance while the batter is put out;
*also* : a fly ball allowing a runner to score
after the catch — **sac·ri·fi·cial** \ˌsa-krə-'fi-shəl\ *adj* — **sac·ri·fi·cial·ly** *adv*

²**sac·ri·fice** *vb* **-ficed; -fic·ing** **1** : to offer
up or kill as a sacrifice **2** : to accept the
loss or destruction of for an end, cause,
or ideal ⟨*sacrificed* her career for her
family⟩ **3** : to make a sacrifice in baseball

**sac·ri·lege** \'sa-krə-lij\ *n* [ME, fr. AF, fr.
L *sacrilegium,* fr. *sacrilegus* one who robs
sacred property fr. *sacr-, sacer* sacred +
*legere* to gather, steal] **1** : violation of
something consecrated to God **2** : gross
irreverence toward a hallowed person,
place, or thing — **sac·ri·le·gious** \ˌsa-

krə-'li-jəs, -'lē-\ adj — **sac·ri·le·gious·ly** adv

**sac·ris·tan** \'sa-krə-stən\ n 1 : a church officer in charge of the sacristy 2 : SEXTON

**sac·ris·ty** \'sa-krə-stē\ n, pl -ties : VESTRY

**sac·ro·il·i·ac** \,sa-krō-'i-lē-,ak\ n : the joint between the upper part of the hipbone and the sacrum

**sac·ro·sanct** \'sa-krō-,saŋkt\ adj : SACRED, INVIOLABLE

**sa·crum** \'sa-krəm, 'sā-\ n, pl **sa·cra** \'sa-krə, 'sā-\ : the part of the vertebral column that is directly connected with or forms a part of the pelvis and in humans consists of five fused vertebrae

**sad** \'sad\ adj **sad·der; sad·dest** 1 : GRIEVING, MOURNFUL, DOWNCAST 2 : causing sorrow 3 : DULL, SOMBER — **sad·ly** adv — **sad·ness** n

**sad·den** \'sa-dᵊn\ vb : to make sad

¹**sad·dle** \'sa-dᵊl\ n : a usu. padded leather-covered seat (as for a rider on horseback)

²**saddle** vb **sad·dled; sad·dling** 1 : to put a saddle on 2 : OPPRESS, BURDEN

**sad·dle·bow** \'sa-dᵊl-,bō\ n : the arch in the front of a saddle

**saddle horse** n : a horse suited for or trained for riding

**Sad·du·cee** \'sa-jə-,sē, 'sa-dyə-\ n : a member of an ancient Jewish sect consisting of a ruling class of priests and rejecting certain doctrines — **Sad·du·ce·an** \,sa-jə-'sē-ən, ,sa-dyə-\ adj

**sad·iron** \'sa-,dī-ərn\ n : a flatiron with a removable handle

**sa·dism** \'sā-,di-zəm, 'sa-\ n : a sexual perversion in which gratification is obtained by inflicting physical or mental pain on others — **sa·dist** \'sā-dist, 'sa-\ n — **sa·dis·tic** \sə-'dis-tik\ adj — **sa·dis·ti·cal·ly** \-ti-k(ə-)lē\ adv

**sa·do·mas·och·ism** \,sā-(,)dō-'ma-sə-,ki-zəm, ,sa-, -'ma-zə-\ n : the derivation of pleasure from the infliction of physical or mental pain either on others or on oneself — **sa·do·mas·och·is·tic** \-,ma-sə-'kis-tik, -,ma-zə-\ adj

**SAE** abbr 1 self-addressed envelope 2 Society of Automotive Engineers 3 stamped addressed envelope

**sa·fa·ri** \sə-'fär-ē, -'fär-ē\ n [Swahili, trip, fr. Ar safarī of a trip] 1 : a hunting expedition esp. in eastern Africa 2 : JOURNEY, TRIP

¹**safe** \'sāf\ adj **saf·er; saf·est** 1 : free from harm or risk 2 : affording safety; also : secure from danger or loss 3 : RELIABLE — **safe·ly** adv

²**safe** n : a container for keeping articles (as valuables) safe

**safe·con·duct** \-'kän-(,)dəkt\ n : a pass permitting a person to go through enemy lines

¹**safe·guard** \-,gärd\ n : a measure or device for preventing accident

²**safeguard** vb : to provide a safeguard for : PROTECT ⟨~ your valuables⟩

**safe·keep·ing** \'sāf-'kē-piŋ\ n : a keeping or being kept in safety

**safer sex** n : SAFE SEX

**safe sex** n : sexual activity and esp. sexual intercourse in which various measures (as the use of latex condoms) are taken to avoid disease (as AIDS) transmitted by sexual contact

**safe·ty** \'sāf-tē\ n, pl **safeties** 1 : freedom from danger 2 : a protective device 3 : a football play in which the ball is downed by the offensive team behind its own goal line 4 : a defensive football back in the deepest position — **safety** adj

**safety glass** n : shatter-resistant material formed of two sheets of glass with a sheet of clear plastic between them

**safety match** n : a match that ignites only when struck on a special surface

**saf·flow·er** \'sa-,flaù-(-ə)r\ n : a widely grown Old World herb related to the daisies that has large orange or red flower heads yielding a dyestuff and seeds rich in edible oil

**saf·fron** \'sa-frən\ n : a deep orange powder from the flower of a crocus used to color and flavor foods

**sag** \'sag\ vb **sagged; sag·ging** 1 : to droop or settle from or as if from pressure ⟨a sagging mattress⟩ 2 : to lose firmness or vigor — **sag** n

**sa·ga** \'sä-gə\ n [ON] : a narrative of heroic deeds; esp : one recorded in Iceland in the 12th and 13th centuries

**sa·ga·cious** \sə-'gā-shəs\ adj : of keen mind : SHREWD ⟨a ~ counselor⟩ — **sa·gac·i·ty** \-'ga-sə-tē\ n

**sag·a·more** \'sa-gə-,mór\ n : a subordinate No. American Indian chief

¹**sage** \'sāj\ adj [ME, fr. AF, fr. VL *sapius, fr. L sapere to taste, have good taste, be wise] : WISE, PRUDENT — **sage·ly** adv

²**sage** n : one who is distinguished for wisdom

³**sage** n [ME, fr. AF sage, salge, fr. L salvia, fr. salvus healthy; fr. its use as a medicinal herb] 1 : a perennial mint with aromatic leaves used in flavoring; also : its leaves 2 : SAGEBRUSH 3 : a light grayish green

**sage·brush** \'sāj-,brəsh\ n : any of several low shrubby No. American composite plants; esp : one of the western U.S. with a sagelike odor

**Sag·it·tar·i·us** \,sa-jə-'ter-ē-əs\ n [L, lit., archer] 1 : a zodiacal constellation between Scorpio and Capricorn usu. pictured as a centaur archer 2 : the 9th sign of the zodiac in astrology; also : one born under this sign

**sa·go** \'sā-gō\ n, pl **sagos** : a dry granulated starch esp. from the pith of various tropical palms (sago palm)

**sa·gua·ro** \sə-'wär-ə, -'gwär-, -ō\ n, pl -ros [MexSp] : a tall columnar usu. sparsely-branched cactus of dry areas of the southwestern U.S. and Mexico that may attain a height of up to 50 feet (16 meters)

**said** past and past part of SAY

¹**sail** \'sāl\ n 1 : a piece of fabric by means of which the wind is used to propel a ship 2 : a sailing ship 3 : something resembling a sail 4 : a trip on a sailboat

²**sail** vb 1 : to travel on a sailing ship 2 : to

pass over in a ship **3** : to manage or direct the course of a ship **4** : to move with ease, grace, or nonchalance

**sail·board** \'sāl-ˌbȯrd\ *n* : a modified surfboard having a mast and sailed by a standing person

**sail·boat** \-ˌbōt\ *n* : a boat propelled primarily by sail

**sail·cloth** \-ˌklȯth\ *n* : a heavy canvas used for sails, tents, or upholstery

**sail·fish** \-ˌfish\ *n* : any of a genus of large marine bony fishes with a large dorsal fin that are related to marlins

**sail·ing** *n* : the sport of handling or riding in a sailboat

**sail·or** \'sā-lər\ *n* : one that sails; *esp* : a member of a ship's crew

**sail·plane** \'sāl-ˌplān\ *n* : a glider designed to rise in an upward air current

**saint** \'sānt, *before a name* (ˌ)sānt *or* sənt\ *n* **1** : one officially recognized as preeminent for holiness **2** : one of the spirits of the departed in heaven **3** : a holy or godly person — **saint·ed** \'-sān-təd\ *adj* — **saint·hood** \-ˌhu̇d\ *n*

**Saint Ber·nard** \-bər-ˈnärd\ *n* : any of a Swiss alpine breed of tall powerful working dogs used esp. formerly in aiding lost travelers

**Saint–John's–wort** \'sānt-ˈjänz-ˌwȯrt, -ˌwȯrt\ *n* **1** : any of a genus of herbs and shrubs with showy yellow flowers **2** : the dried aerial parts of a Saint-John's-wort used esp. in herbal remedies

**saint·ly** \'sānt-lē\ *adj* : relating to, resembling, or befitting a saint ⟨~ zeal⟩ — **saint·li·ness** \-lē-nəs\ *n*

**Saint Val·en·tine's Day** \-'va-lən-ˌtīnz-\ *n* : VALENTINE'S DAY

**¹sake** \'sāk\ *n* **1** : END, PURPOSE **2** : personal or social welfare, safety, or well-being

**²sa·ke** *or* **sa·ki** \'sä-kē\ *n* : a Japanese alcoholic beverage of fermented rice

**sa·laam** \sə-ˈläm\ *n* [Ar *salām*, lit., peace] **1** : a salutation or ceremonial greeting in the East **2** : an obeisance performed by bowing very low and placing the right palm on the forehead — **salaam** *vb*

**sa·la·cious** \sə-ˈlā-shəs\ *adj* **1** : arousing sexual desire or imagination **2** : LUSTFUL — **sa·la·cious·ly** *adv* — **sa·la·cious·ness** *n*

**sal·ad** \'sa-ləd\ *n* : a cold dish (as of lettuce, vegetables, fish, eggs, or fruit) served with dressing

**sal·a·man·der** \'sa-lə-ˌman-dər\ *n* : any of numerous amphibians that look like lizards but have scaleless usu. smooth moist skin

**sa·la·mi** \sə-ˈlä-mē\ *n* [It] : a highly seasoned sausage of pork and beef

**sal·a·ry** \'sa-lə-rē\ *n, pl* **-ries** [ME *salarie*, fr. AF, fr. L *salarium* pension, salary, fr. neut. of *salarius* of salt, fr. *sal* salt] : payment made at regular intervals for services

**sale** \'sāl\ *n* **1** : transfer of ownership of property from one person to another in return for money **2** : ready market : DEMAND **3** : AUCTION **4** : a selling of goods at bargain prices — **sal·able** *or* **sale·able** \'sā-lə-bəl\ *adj*

**sales·girl** \'sālz-ˌgərl\ *n* : SALESWOMAN

**sales·man** \-mən\ *n* : a person who sells in a store or to outside customers — **sales·man·ship** *n*

**sales·per·son** \-ˌpər-sən\ *n* : a salesman or saleswoman

**sales·wom·an** \-ˌwu̇-mən\ *n* : a woman who sells merchandise

**sal·i·cyl·ic acid** \ˌsa-lə-ˈsi-lik-\ *n* : a crystalline organic acid used in making aspirin and other medicinal preparations (as skin lotions)

**¹sa·lient** \'sāl-yənt, 'sā-lē-ənt\ *adj* : jutting forward beyond a line; *also* : PROMINENT ⟨a ~ feature⟩ **♦ Synonyms** CONSPICUOUS, STRIKING, NOTICEABLE

**²salient** *n* : a projecting part in a line of defense

**¹sa·line** \'sā-ˌlēn, -ˌlīn\ *adj* : consisting of or containing salt : SALTY — **sa·lin·i·ty** \sā-ˈli-nə-tē, sə-\ *n*

**²saline** *n* **1** : a metallic salt esp. with a purgative action **2** : a saline solution

**sa·li·va** \sə-ˈlī-və\ *n* : a liquid secreted into the mouth that helps digestion — **sal·i·vary** \'sa-lə-ˌver-ē\ *adj*

**sal·i·vate** \'sa-lə-ˌvāt\ *vb* **-vat·ed; -vat·ing** : to produce saliva esp. in excess — **sal·i·va·tion** \ˌsa-lə-ˈvā-shən\ *n*

**sal·low** \'sa-lō\ *adj* : of a yellowish sickly color ⟨a ~ face⟩

**sal·ly** \'sa-lē\ *n, pl* **sallies 1** : a rushing attack on besiegers by troops of a besieged place **2** : a witty remark or retort **3** : a brief excursion — **sally** *vb*

**salm·on** \'sa-mən\ *n, pl* **salmon** *also* **salmons 1** : any of several bony fishes with pinkish flesh that are used for food and are related to the trouts **2** : a strong yellowish pink color

**sal·mo·nel·la** \ˌsal-mə-ˈne-lə\ *n, pl* **-nel·lae** \-ˈne-(ˌ)lē, -ˌlī\ *or* **-nellas** *or* **-nella** : any of a genus of rod-shaped bacteria that cause various illnesses (as food poisoning)

**sa·lon** \sə-ˈlän, 'sa-ˌlän, sa-ˈlōⁿ\ *n* [F] : an elegant drawing room; *also* : a fashionable shop ⟨beauty ~⟩

**sa·loon** \sə-ˈlün\ *n* **1** : a large public cabin on a ship **2** : a place where liquors are sold and drunk : BARROOM **3** *Brit* : SEDAN 2

**sal·sa** \'sȯl-sə, 'säl-\ *n* : a spicy sauce of tomatoes, onions, and hot peppers

**¹salt** \'sȯlt\ *n* **1** : a white crystalline substance that consists of sodium and chlorine and is used in seasoning foods **2** : a saltlike cathartic substance (as Epsom salts) **3** : a compound formed usu. by action of an acid on metal **4** : SAILOR — **salt·i·ness** \'sȯl-tē-nəs\ *n* — **salty** \'sȯl-tē\ *adj*

**²salt** *vb* : to preserve, season, or feed with salt

**³salt** *adj* : preserved or treated with salt ⟨~ pork⟩; *also* : SALTY

**SALT** *abbr* Strategic Arms Limitation Talks

**salt away** *vb* : to lay away safely : SAVE

**salt·box** \'sȯlt-ˌbäks\ *n* : a frame dwelling

with two stories in front and one behind and a long sloping roof

**salt·cel·lar** \-ˌsel-ər\ n : a small container for holding salt at the table

**sal·tine** \sȯl-ˈtēn\ n : a thin crisp cracker sprinkled with salt

**salt lick** n : LICK 5

**salt·pe·ter** \ˈsȯlt-ˈpē-tər\ n [ME salt petre, alter. of salpetre, fr. ML sal petrae, lit., salt of the rock] 1 : POTASSIUM NITRATE 2 : SODIUM NITRATE

**salt·wa·ter** \-ˌwȯ-tər, -ˌwä-\ adj : of, relating to, or living in salt water

**sa·lu·bri·ous** \sə-ˈlü-brē-əs\ adj : favorable to health ⟨a ~ climate⟩

**sal·u·tary** \ˈsal-yə-ˌter-ē\ adj : health-giving; also : BENEFICIAL ⟨~ effects⟩

**sal·u·ta·tion** \ˌsal-yə-ˈtā-shən\ n : an expression of greeting, goodwill, or courtesy usu. by word or gesture

**sa·lu·ta·to·ri·an** \sə-ˌlü-tə-ˈtȯr-ē-ən\ n : the student having the 2d highest rank in a graduating class who delivers the salutatory address

**sa·lu·ta·to·ry** \sə-ˈlü-tə-ˌtȯr-ē\ adj : relating to or being the welcoming oration delivered at an academic commencement

¹**sa·lute** \sə-ˈlüt\ vb **sa·lut·ed; sa·lut·ing** 1 : GREET 2 : to honor by special ceremonies 3 : to show respect to (a superior officer) by a formal position of hand, rifle, or sword

²**salute** n 1 : GREETING 2 : the formal position assumed in saluting a superior

¹**sal·vage** \ˈsal-vij\ n 1 : money paid for saving a ship, its cargo, or passengers when the ship is wrecked or in danger 2 : the saving of a ship 3 : the saving of possessions in danger of being lost 4 : things saved from loss or destruction (as by a wreck or fire)

²**salvage** vb **sal·vaged; sal·vag·ing** : to rescue from destruction

**sal·va·tion** \sal-ˈvā-shən\ n 1 : the saving of a person from sin or its consequences esp. in the life after death 2 : the saving from danger, difficulty, or evil 3 : something that saves ⟨tourism has been the island's ~⟩

¹**salve** \ˈsav, ˈsäv\ n 1 : a medicinal substance applied to the skin 2 : a soothing influence

²**salve** vb **salved; salv·ing** : EASE, SOOTHE

**sal·ver** \ˈsal-vər\ n [F salve, fr. Sp salva sampling of food to detect poison, tray, fr. salvar to save, sample food to detect poison, fr. LL salvare to save, fr. L salvus safe] : a small serving tray

**sal·vo** \ˈsal-vō\ n, pl **salvos** or **salvoes** : a simultaneous discharge of guns

**Sam or Saml** abbr Samuel

**SAM** \ˈsam, ˌes-ˌā-ˈem\ n [surface-to-air missile] : a guided missile for use against aircraft by ground units

**Sa·mar·i·tan** \sə-ˈmer-ə-tən\ n 1 : a native or inhabitant of Samaria 2 : a person who is generous in helping those in distress

**sa·mar·i·um** \sə-ˈmer-ē-əm\ n : a silvery-white lustrous rare metallic chemical element

¹**same** \ˈsām\ adj 1 : being the one referred to : not different 2 : SIMILAR

**same·ness** n

²**same** pron : the same one or ones

³**same** adv : in the same manner

**Sa·mi** also **Saa·mi** \ˈsä-mē\ n, pl **Sami** or **Samis** also **Saami** or **Saamis** : a member of a people of northern Scandinavia, Finland, and the Kola Peninsula of Russia

**Sa·mo·an** \sə-ˈmō-ən\ n : a native or inhabitant of Samoa — **Samoan** adj

**sa·mo·sa** \sə-ˈmō-sə\ n : a small triangular pastry filled with spiced meat or vegetables and fried

**sam·o·var** \ˈsa-mə-ˌvär\ n [Russ, fr. samo-self + varit' to boil] : an urn with a spigot at the base used esp. in Russia to boil water for tea

**sam·pan** \ˈsam-ˌpan\ n : a flat-bottomed skiff of eastern Asia usu. propelled by two short oars

¹**sam·ple** \ˈsam-pəl\ n : a representative piece, item, or set of individuals that shows the quality or nature of the whole from which it was taken : EXAMPLE, SPECIMEN

²**sample** vb **sam·pled; sam·pling** : to judge the quality of by a sample

**sam·pler** \ˈsam-plər\ n 1 : a piece of needlework; esp : one testing skill in embroidering 2 : a collection of various examples of something ⟨a chocolate ~⟩

**Sam·u·el** \ˈsam-yə-wəl\ n — see BIBLE table

**sam·u·rai** \ˈsa-mə-ˌrī, ˈsam-yə-\ n, pl **samurai** : a military retainer of a Japanese feudal lord who adhered to strict principles of honor and duty

**san·a·to·ri·um** \ˌsa-nə-ˈtȯr-ē-əm\ n, pl **-ri·ums** or **-ria** \-ē-ə\ 1 : a health resort 2 : an establishment for the care esp. of convalescents or the chronically ill

**sanc·ti·fy** \ˈsaŋk-tə-ˌfī\ vb **-fied; -fy·ing** 1 : to make holy : CONSECRATE 2 : to free from sin — **sanc·ti·fi·ca·tion** \ˌsaŋk-tə-fə-ˈkā-shən\ n

**sanc·ti·mo·nious** \ˌsaŋk-tə-ˈmō-nē-əs\ adj : hypocritically pious ⟨~ politicians⟩ — **sanc·ti·mo·nious·ly** adv

¹**sanc·tion** \ˈsaŋk-shən\ n 1 : authoritative approval 2 : a measure (as a threat or fine) designed to enforce a law or standard ⟨economic ~s⟩

²**sanction** vb : to give approval to : RATIFY

♦ **Synonyms** ENDORSE, ACCREDIT, CERTIFY, APPROVE

**sanc·ti·ty** \ˈsaŋk-tə-tē\ n, pl **-ties** 1 : GODLINESS 2 : SACREDNESS

**sanc·tu·ary** \ˈsaŋk-chə-ˌwer-ē\ n, pl **-ar·ies** 1 : a consecrated place (as the part of a church in which the altar is placed) 2 : a place of refuge ⟨bird ~⟩

**sanc·tum** \ˈsaŋk-təm\ n, pl **sanctums** also **sanc·ta** \-tə\ : a private office or study : DEN ⟨an editor's ~⟩

¹**sand** \ˈsand\ n : loose particles of hard broken rock — **sandy** adj

²**sand** vb 1 : to cover or fill with sand 2 : to scour, smooth, or polish with an abrasive (as sandpaper) — **sand·er** n

**san·dal** \ˈsan-dᵊl\ n : a shoe consisting of

a sole strapped to the foot; *also* : a low or open slipper or rubber overshoe

**san·dal·wood** \-₁wu̇d\ *n* : the fragrant yellowish heartwood of a parasitic tree of southern Asia that is much used in ornamental carving and cabinetwork; *also* : the tree

**sand·bag** \'sand-₁bag\ *n* : a bag filled with sand and used in fortifications, as ballast, or as a weapon

**sand·bank** \-₁baŋk\ *n* : a deposit of sand (as in a bar or shoal)

**sand·bar** \-₁bär\ *n* : a ridge of sand formed in water by tides or currents

**sand·blast** \-₁blast\ *vb* : to treat with a stream of sand blown (as for cleaning stone) by compressed air — **sand·blast·er** *n*

**sand dollar** *n* : any of numerous flat circular sea urchins living chiefly on sandy bottoms in shallow water

**S & H** *abbr* shipping and handling

**sand·hog** \'sand-₁hȯg, -₁häg\ *n* : a laborer who builds underwater tunnels

**sand·lot** \-₁lät\ *n* : a vacant lot esp. when used for the unorganized sports of children — **sand·lot** *adj* — **sand·lot·ter** *n*

**sand·man** \-₁man\ *n* : the genie of folklore who makes children sleepy

**sand·pa·per** \-₁pā-pər\ *n* : paper with abrasive (as sand) glued on one side used in smoothing and polishing surfaces — **sandpaper** *vb*

**sand·pip·er** \-₁pī-pər\ *n* : any of various shorebirds with a soft-tipped bill longer than that of the related plovers

**sand·stone** \-₁stōn\ *n* : rock made of sand united by a natural cement

**sand·storm** \-₁sto̊rm\ *n* : a windstorm that drives clouds of sand

**sand trap** *n* : a hazard on a golf course consisting of a hollow containing sand

¹**sand·wich** \'sand-(₁)wich\ *n* [after John Montagu, 4th Earl of *Sandwich* †1792 Eng. diplomat] **1** : two or more slices of bread with a layer (as of meat or cheese) spread between them **2** : something resembling a sandwich

²**sandwich** *vb* : to squeeze or crowd in

**sane** \'sān\ *adj* **san·er; -est** : mentally sound and healthy; *also* : SENSIBLE, RATIONAL — **sane·ly** *adv*

**sang** *past of* SING

**sang·froid** \'sän-'frwä\ *n* [F *sang-froid*, lit., cold blood] : self-possession or an imperturbable state esp. under strain

**san·gui·nary** \'saŋ-gwə-₁ner-ē\ *adj* : BLOODY ⟨~ battle⟩

**san·guine** \'saŋ-gwən\ *adj* **1** : RUDDY **2** : CHEERFUL, HOPEFUL ⟨a ~ disposition⟩

**sanit** *abbr* sanitary; sanitation

**san·i·tar·i·an** \₁sa-nə-'ter-ē-ən\ *n* : a specialist in sanitation and public health

**san·i·tar·i·um** \₁sa-nə-'ter-ē-əm\ *n, pl* **-i·ums** *or* **-ia** \-ē-ə\ : SANATORIUM

**san·i·tary** \'sa-nə-₁ter-ē\ *adj* **1** : of or relating to health : HYGIENIC **2** : free from filth or infective matter

**sanitary napkin** *n* : a disposable absorbent pad used to absorb uterine flow (as during menstruation)

**san·i·ta·tion** \₁sa-nə-'tā-shən\ *n* : the act

or process of making sanitary; *also* : protection of health by maintenance of sanitary conditions

**san·i·tize** \'sa-nə-₁tīz\ *vb* **-tized; -tiz·ing** **1** : to make sanitary **2** : to make more acceptable by removing unpleasant features

**san·i·ty** \'sa-nə-tē\ *n* : soundness of mind

**sank** *past of* SINK

**sans** \'sanz\ *prep* : WITHOUT

**San·skrit** \'san-₁skrit\ *n* : an ancient language that is the classical language of India and of Hinduism — **Sanskrit** *adj*

**San·ta Ana** \₁san-tə-'a-nə\ *n* [*Santa Ana* Mountains in southern Calif.] : a hot dry wind from the north, northeast, or east in southern California

**san·tims** \'sän-₁tims\ *n, pl* **san·ti·mi** \-ti-mē\ : a monetary unit equal to ¹⁄₁₀₀ lats formerly used in Latvia

¹**sap** \'sap\ *n* **1** : a vital fluid; *esp* : a watery fluid that circulates through a vascular plant **2** : a foolish gullible person — **sap·less** *adj*

²**sap** *vb* **sapped; sap·ping** **1** : UNDERMINE **2** : to weaken gradually

**sap·id** \'sa-pəd\ *adj* : FLAVORFUL

**sa·pi·ent** \'sā-pē-ənt, 'sa-\ *adj* : WISE, DISCERNING — **sa·pi·ence** \-əns\ *n*

**sap·ling** \'sa-pliŋ\ *n* : a young tree

**sap·phire** \'sa-₁fī(-ə)r\ *n* : a hard transparent usu. rich blue gem

**sap·py** \'sa-pē\ *adj* **sap·pi·er; -est** **1** : full of sap **2** : overly sentimental ⟨a ~ movie⟩ **3** : SILLY, FOOLISH

**sap·ro·phyte** \'sa-prə-₁fīt\ *n* : a living thing and esp. a plant living on dead or decaying organic matter — **sap·ro·phyt·ic** \₁sa-prə-'fi-tik\ *adj*

**sap·suck·er** \'sap-₁sə-kər\ *n* : any of a genus of No. American woodpeckers

**sap·wood** \-₁wu̇d\ *n* : the younger active and usu. lighter and softer outer layer of wood (as of a tree trunk)

**sar·casm** \'sär-₁ka-zəm\ *n* **1** : a cutting or contemptuous remark **2** : ironic criticism or reproach — **sar·cas·tic** \sär-'kas-tik\ *adj* — **sar·cas·ti·cal·ly** \-ti-k(ə-)lē\ *adv*

**sar·co·ma** \sär-'kō-mə\ *n, pl* **-mas** *also* **-ma·ta** \-mə-tə\ : a malignant tumor esp. of connective tissue, bone, cartilage, or striated muscle

**sar·coph·a·gus** \sär-'kä-fə-gəs\ *n, pl* **-gi** \-₁gī, -₁jī\ *also* **-gus·es** [L *sarcophagus* (*lapis*) limestone used for coffins, fr. Gk (*lithos*) *sarkophagos*, lit., flesh-eating stone, fr. *sark-, sarx* flesh + *phagein* to eat] : a large stone coffin

**sar·dine** \sär-'dēn\ *n, pl* **sardines** *also* **sardine** : a young or small fish preserved for use as food

**sar·don·ic** \sär-'dä-nik\ *adj* : disdainfully or skeptically humorous : derisively mocking ◆ **Synonyms** IRONIC, SATIRIC, SARCASTIC — **sar·don·i·cal·ly** \-ni-k(ə-)lē\ *adv*

**sa·ri** *also* **sa·ree** \'sär-ē\ *n* [Hindi *sāṛī*] : a garment worn by women in southern Asia that consists of a long cloth draped around the body and head or shoulder

**sa·rin** \'sär-ən, zä-'rēn\ *n* : an extremely

toxic chemical weapon used as a lethal nerve gas

**sa·rong** \sə-'rȯṅ, -'räṅ\ *n* : a loose garment wrapped around the body and worn by men and women of the Malay Archipelago and the Pacific islands

**sar·sa·pa·ril·la** \ˌsas-pə-'ri-lə, ˌsärs-\ *n* **1** : the dried roots of a tropical American smilax used esp. for flavoring; *also* : the plant **2** : a sweetened carbonated beverage flavored with sassafras and an oil from a birch

**sar·to·ri·al** \sär-'tȯr-ē-əl\ *adj* : of or relating to a tailor or tailored clothes — **sar·to·ri·al·ly** *adv*

**SASE** *abbr* self-addressed stamped envelope

**¹sash** \'sash\ *n* : a broad band worn around the waist or over the shoulder

**²sash** *n, pl* **sash** *also* **sash·es** : a frame for panes of glass in a door or window; *also* : the movable part of a window

**sa·shay** \sa-'shā\ *vb* **1** : WALK, GLIDE, GO **2** : to strut or move about in an ostentatious manner **3** : to proceed in a diagonal or sideways manner

**Sask** *abbr* Saskatchewan

**Sas·quatch** \'sas-ˌkwäch, -ˌkwäch\ *n* [Halkomelem (American Indian language of British Columbia) *sésq̓əc*] : a large hairy humanlike creature reported to exist in the northwestern U.S. and western Canada

**sas·sa·fras** \'sa-sə-ˌfras\ *n* [Sp *sasafrás*] : an aromatic No. American tree related to the laurel; *also* : its carcinogenic dried root bark

**sassy** \'sa-sē\ *adj* **sass·i·er; -est** : SAUCY

**¹sat** *past and past part of* SIT

**²sat** *abbr* **1** satellite **2** saturated

**Sat** *abbr* Saturday

**Sa·tan** \'sā-t²n\ *n* : DEVIL

**sa·tang** \sä-'täṅ\ *n, pl* **satang** *or* **satangs** — see *baht* at MONEY table

**sa·tan·ic** \sə-'ta-nik, sā-\ *adj* **1** : of or characteristic of Satan **2** : extremely malicious or wicked — **sa·tan·i·cal·ly** \-ni-k(ə-)lē\ *adv*

**satch·el** \'sa-chəl\ *n* : SUITCASE

**sate** \'sāt\ *vb* **sat·ed; sat·ing** : to satisfy to the full; *also* : SURFEIT, GLUT

**sa·teen** \sa-'tēn, sə-\ *n* : a cotton cloth finished to resemble satin

**sat·el·lite** \'sa-tə-ˌlīt\ *n* [MF, fr. L *satelles* attendant] **1** : an obsequious follower of a distinguished person : TOADY **2** : a celestial body that orbits a larger body **3** : a manufactured object that orbits a celestial body

**satellite dish** *n* : a microwave dish for receiving usu. television transmissions from an orbiting satellite

**sa·ti·ate** \'sā-shē-ˌāt\ *vb* **-at·ed; -at·ing** : to satisfy fully or to excess

**sa·ti·ety** \sə-'tī-ə-tē\ *n* : fullness to the point of excess

**sat·in** \'sa-t²n\ *n* : a fabric (as of silk) with a glossy surface — **sat·iny** *adj*

**sat·in·wood** \'sa-t²n-ˌwu̇d\ *n* : a hard yellowish brown wood of satiny luster; *also* : a tree yielding this wood

**sat·ire** \'sa-ˌtī(-ə)r\ *n* : biting wit, irony, or

sarcasm used to expose vice or folly; *also* : a literary work having these qualities — **sa·tir·ic** \sə-'tir-ik\ *or* **sa·tir·i·cal** \-i-kəl\ *adj* — **sa·tir·i·cal·ly** *adv* — **sat·i·rist** \'sa-tə-rist\ *n* — **sat·i·rize** \-tə-ˌrīz\ *vb*

**sat·is·fac·tion** \ˌsa-təs-'fak-shən\ *n* **1** : payment through penance of punishment incurred by sin **2** : CONTENTMENT, GRATIFICATION **3** : reparation for an insult **4** : settlement of a claim

**sat·is·fac·to·ry** \-'fak-tə-rē\ *adj* : giving satisfaction : ADEQUATE — **sat·is·fac·to·ri·ly** \-'fak-tə-rə-lē\ *adv*

**sat·is·fy** \'sa-təs-ˌfī\ *vb* **-fied; -fy·ing** **1** : to answer or discharge (a claim) in full **2** : to make happy : GRATIFY **3** : to pay what is due to **4** : CONVINCE **5** : to meet the requirements of — **sat·is·fy·ing·ly** *adv*

**sa·trap** \'sā-ˌtrap, 'sa-\ *n* [ME, fr. L *satrapes*, fr. Gk *satrapēs*, fr. OPers *khshathrapāvan*, lit., protector of the dominion] : a petty prince : a subordinate ruler

**sat·u·rate** \'sa-chə-ˌrāt\ *vb* **-rat·ed; -rat·ing** **1** : to soak thoroughly **2** : to treat or charge with something to the point where no more can be absorbed, dissolved, or retained — **sat·u·ra·ble** \'sa-chə-rə-bəl\ *adj* — **sat·u·ra·tion** \ˌsa-chə-'rā-shən\ *n*

**saturated** *adj* **1** : full of moisture **2** : having no double or triple bonds between carbon atoms ⟨~ fats⟩

**Sat·ur·day** \'sa-tər-dē, -ˌdā\ *n* : the 7th day of the week

**Saturday night special** *n* : a cheap easily concealed handgun

**Sat·urn** \'sa-tərn\ *n* : the planet 6th in order from the sun

**sat·ur·nine** \'sa-tər-ˌnīn\ *adj* : SULLEN, SARDONIC

**sa·tyr** \'sā-tər\ *n* **1** *often cap* : a woodland deity in Greek mythology having certain characteristics of a horse or goat **2** : a lecherous man

**¹sauce** \'sȯs, 3 *usu* 'sas\ *n* **1** : a fluid dressing or topping for food **2** : stewed fruit **3** : IMPUDENCE

**²sauce** \'sȯs, 2 *usu* 'sas\ *vb* **sauced; sauc·ing** **1** : to put sauce on; *also* : to add zest to **2** : to be impudent to

**sauce·pan** \'sȯs-ˌpan\ *n* : a small deep cooking pan with a handle

**sau·cer** \'sȯ-sər\ *n* : a rounded shallow dish for use under a cup

**saucy** \'sa-sē, 'sȯ-\ *adj* **sauc·i·er; -est** : IMPUDENT, PERT — **sauc·i·ly** \-sə-lē\ *adv* — **sauc·i·ness** \-sē-nəs\ *n*

**Sau·di** \'saü-dē, 'sȯ-; sä-'ü-dē\ *n* : SAUDI ARABIAN — **Saudi** *adj*

**Saudi Arabian** *n* : a native or inhabitant of Saudi Arabia — **Saudi Arabian** *adj*

**sau·er·kraut** \'saü-(ə)r-ˌkraüt\ *n* [G, fr. *sauer* sour + *Kraut* greens] : finely cut cabbage fermented in brine

**Sauk** \'sȯk\ *or* **Sac** \'sak, 'sȯk\ *n, pl* **Sauk** *or* **Sauks** *or* **Sac** *or* **Sacs** : a member of an American Indian people formerly living in what is now Wisconsin

**sau·na** \'sȯ-nə, 'saü-nə\ *n* **1** : a Finnish steam bath in which the steam is provided by water thrown on hot stones **2** : a dry heat bath; *also* : a room or cabinet used for such a bath

**saun·ter** \'sȯn-tər, 'sän-\ *vb* : STROLL

**sau·ro·pod** \'sȯr-ə-ˌpäd\ *n* : any of a suborder of plant-eating dinosaurs (as a brontosaurus) with a long neck and tail and a small head — **sauropod** *adj*

**sau·sage** \'sȯ-sij\ *n* [ME *sausige*, fr. AF *sauseche*, fr. LL *salsicia*, fr. L *salsus* salted] : minced and highly seasoned meat (as pork) usu. enclosed in a tubular casing

**S Aust** *abbr* South Australia

**sau·té** \sȯ-'tā, sō-\ *vb* **sau·téed** *or* **sau·téd**; **sau·té·ing** [F] : to fry lightly in a little fat — **sauté** *n*

**sau·terne** \sō-'tərn, sȯ-\ *n, often cap* : a usu. semisweet American white wine

¹**sav·age** \'sa-vij\ *adj* [ME, fr. AF *salvage*, *savage*, fr. LL *salvaticus*, alter. of L *silvaticus* of the woods, wild, fr. *silva* forest] 1 : WILD, UNTAMED 2 : UNCIVILIZED, BARBAROUS 3 : CRUEL, FIERCE — **sav·age·ly** *adv* — **sav·age·ness** *n* — **sav·age·ry** \-rē\ *n*

²**savage** *n* 1 : a member of a primitive human society 2 : a rude, unmannerly, or brutal person

**sa·van·na** *or* **sa·van·nah** \sə-'va-nə\ *n* [Sp *zavana*] : grassland containing scattered trees

**sa·vant** \sa-'vänt, sə-, 'sa-vənt\ *n* : a learned person : SCHOLAR

¹**save** \'sāv\ *vb* **saved**; **sav·ing** 1 : to redeem from sin 2 : to rescue from danger 3 : to preserve or guard from destruction or loss; *also* : to store (data) in a computer or on a storage device 4 : to put aside as a store or reserve — **sav·er** *n*

²**save** *n* : a play that prevents an opponent from scoring or winning

³**save** *prep* : EXCEPT

⁴**save** *conj* : BUT

**savings and loan association** *n* : a cooperative association that holds savings of members in the form of dividend-bearing shares and that invests chiefly in mortgage loans

**savings bank** *n* : a bank that holds funds of individual depositors in interest-bearing accounts and makes long-term investments (as mortgage loans)

**savings bond** *n* : a registered U.S. bond issued in denominations of $50 to $10,000

**sav·ior** *or* **sav·iour** \'sāv-yər\ *n* 1 : one who saves 2 *cap* : Jesus Christ

**sa·voir faire** \ˌsav-ˌwär-'fer\ *n* [F *savoir-faire*, lit., knowing how to do] : sureness in social behavior

¹**sa·vor** *also* **sa·vour** \'sā-vər\ *n* 1 : the taste and odor of something 2 : a special flavor or quality — **sa·vory** *adj*

²**savor** *also* **savour** *vb* 1 : to have a specified taste, smell, or quality 2 : to taste with pleasure ⟨~ed every morsel⟩

**sa·vo·ry** \'sā-və-rē\ *n, pl* **-ries** : either of two aromatic mints used in cooking

¹**sav·vy** \'sa-vē\ *vb* **sav·vied**; **sav·vy·ing** : UNDERSTAND, COMPREHEND

²**savvy** *n* : practical know-how ⟨political ~⟩ — **savvy** *adj*

¹**saw** *past of* SEE

²**saw** \'sȯ\ *n* : a cutting tool with a blade having a line of teeth along its edge

³**saw** *vb* **sawed** \'sȯd\; **sawed** *or* **sawn** \'sȯn\; **saw·ing** : to cut or shape with or as if with a saw

⁴**saw** *n* : a common saying : MAXIM

**saw·dust** \'sȯ-(ˌ)dəst\ *n* : fine particles made by a saw in cutting

**saw·fly** \-ˌflī\ *n* : any of numerous insects belonging to the same order as bees and wasps and including many whose larvae are plant-feeding pests

**saw·horse** \-ˌhȯrs\ *n* : a rack on which wood is rested while being sawed by hand

**saw·mill** \-ˌmil\ *n* : a mill for sawing logs

**saw palmetto** *n* 1 : any of several shrubby palms with spiny-toothed petioles 2 : the fruit of a saw palmetto used esp. in herbal remedies

**saw·yer** \'sȯ-yər\ *n* : a person who saws timber

**sax** \'saks\ *n* : SAXOPHONE

**sax·i·frage** \'sak-sə-frij, -ˌfrāj\ *n* [ME, fr. AF, fr. LL *saxifraga*, fr. L, fem. of *saxifragus*, breaking rocks] : any of a genus of plants with showy flowers and usu. with leaves growing in tufts close to the ground

**sax·o·phone** \'sak-sə-ˌfōn\ *n* : a musical instrument having a conical metal tube with a reed mouthpiece and finger keys — **sax·o·phon·ist** \-ˌfō-nist\ *n*

¹**say** \'sā\ *vb* **said** \'sed\; **say·ing**; **says** \'sez\ 1 : to express in words ⟨~ what you mean⟩ 2 : to state as opinion or belief 3 : PRONOUNCE; *also* : RECITE, REPEAT ⟨~ your prayers⟩ 4 : INDICATE ⟨the clock ~s noon⟩

²**say** *n, pl* **says** \'sāz\ 1 : an expression of opinion 2 : power of decision

**say·ing** *n* : a commonly repeated statement

**say–so** \'sā-(ˌ)sō\ *n* : an esp. authoritative assertion or decision; *also* : the right to decide ⟨he has the ~ on this matter⟩

**sb** *abbr* substantive

**Sb** *symbol* [L *stibium*] antimony

**SB** *abbr* [NL *scientiae baccalaureus*] bachelor of science

**SBA** *abbr* Small Business Administration

**sc** *abbr* 1 scene 2 science

**Sc** *symbol* scandium

**SC** *abbr* 1 South Carolina 2 supreme court

¹**scab** \'skab\ *n* 1 : scabies of domestic animals 2 : a crust of hardened blood forming over a wound 3 : a worker who replaces a striker or works under conditions not authorized by a union 4 : any of various bacterial or fungus plant diseases marked by crusted spots on stems or leaves — **scab·by** *adj*

²**scab** *vb* **scabbed**; **scab·bing** 1 : to become covered with a scab 2 : to work as a scab

**scab·bard** \'ska-bərd\ *n* : a sheath for the blade of a weapon (as a sword)

**sca·bies** \'skā-bēz\ *n* [L] : contagious itch or mange caused by mites living as parasites under the skin

**sca·brous** \'ska-brəs, 'skā-\ *adj* 1 : DIFFICULT, KNOTTY 2 : rough to the touch

: SCALY, SCURFY ⟨a ~ leaf⟩  3 : dealing with suggestive, indecent, or scandalous themes ⟨~ lyrics⟩; *also* : SQUALID

**scad** \'skad\ *n* : a large number or quantity — usu. used in pl.

**scaf·fold** \'ska-fəld, -ˌfōld\ *n*  1 : a raised platform for workers to sit or stand on  2 : a platform on which a criminal is executed (as by hanging)

**scaf·fold·ing** *n* : a system of scaffolds; *also* : materials for scaffolds

**scal·a·wag** *or* **scal·ly·wag** \'ska-li-ˌwag\ *n* : RASCAL

¹**scald** \'skóld\ *vb*  1 : to burn with or as if with hot liquid or steam  2 : to heat to just below the boiling point

²**scald** *n* : a burn caused by scalding

¹**scale** \'skāl\ *n*  1 : either pan of a balance  2 : BALANCE — usu. used in pl.  3 : a weighing instrument

²**scale** *vb* **scaled; scal·ing** : WEIGH

³**scale** *n*  1 : one of the small thin plates that cover the body esp. of a fish or reptile  2 : a thin plate or flake  3 : a thin coating, layer, or incrustation  4 : SCALE INSECT — **scaled** \'skāld\ *adj* — **scale·less** \'skāl-ləs\ *adj* — **scaly** *adj*

⁴**scale** *vb* **scaled; scal·ing** : to strip of scales

⁵**scale** *n* [ME, fr. LL *scala* ladder, staircase, fr. L *scalae*, pl., stairs, rungs, ladder]  1 : something divided into regular spaces as a help in drawing or measuring  2 : a graduated series  3 : the size of a sample (as a model) in proportion to the size of the actual thing  4 : a standard of estimation or judgment  5 : a series of musical tones going up or down in pitch according to a specified scheme

⁶**scale** *vb* **scaled; scal·ing**  1 : to climb by or as if by a ladder  2 : to arrange in a graded series

**scale insect** *n* : any of numerous small insects with wingless scale-covered females that are related to aphids and feed on and are often pests of plants

**scale-pan** \'skāl-ˌpan\ *n* : ¹SCALE 1

**scal·lion** \'skal-yən\ *n* [ultim. fr. L *ascalonia (caepa)* onion of Ascalon (seaport in Palestine)] : an onion without an enlarged bulb; *also* : GREEN ONION

¹**scal·lop** \'skä-ləp, 'ska-\ *n*  1 : any of numerous marine bivalve mollusks with radially ridged shells; *also* : a large edible muscle of this mollusk  2 : one of a continuous series of rounded projections forming an edge

²**scallop** *vb*  1 : to bake in a casserole ⟨~ed potatoes⟩  2 : to shape, cut, or finish in scallops ⟨~ed edges⟩

¹**scalp** \'skalp\ *n* : the part of the skin and flesh of the head usu. covered with hair

²**scalp** *vb*  1 : to remove the scalp from  2 : to resell at greatly increased prices ⟨~ tickets⟩ — **scalp·er** *n*

**scal·pel** \'skal-pəl\ *n* : a small straight knife with a thin blade used esp. in surgery

**scam** \'skam\ *n* : a fraudulent or deceptive act or operation

**scamp** \'skamp\ *n* : RASCAL

**scam·per** \'skam-pər\ *vb* : to run nimbly and playfully — **scamper** *n*

**scam·pi** \'skam-pē\ *n, pl* **scampi** [It] : a usu. large shrimp; *also* : large shrimp prepared with a garlic-flavored sauce

¹**scan** \'skan\ *vb* **scanned; scan·ning**  1 : to read (verses) so as to show metrical structure  2 : to examine closely  3 : to input or examine systematically in order to obtain data esp. for display or storage  4 : to make a scan of (as the human body) — **scan·ner** *n*

²**scan** *n*  1 : the act or process of scanning  2 : a picture of the distribution of radioactive material in something; *also* : an image of a bodily part produced (as by computer) by combining radiographic data obtained from several angles or sections

**Scand** *abbr* Scandinavia

**scan·dal** \'skan-d°l\ *n* [ME, fr. LL *scandalum* stumbling block, offense, fr. Gk *skandalon*]  1 : DISGRACE, DISHONOR  2 : malicious gossip : SLANDER — **scan·dal·ize** *vb* — **scan·dal·ous** *adj* — **scan·dal·ous·ly** *adv*

**scan·dal·mon·ger** \-ˌmən-gər, -ˌmän-\ *n* : a person who circulates scandal

**Scan·di·na·vian** \ˌskan-də-'nā-vē-ən\ *n* : a native or inhabitant of Scandinavia — **Scandinavian** *adj*

**scan·di·um** \'skan-dē-əm\ *n* : a silvery-white metallic chemical element

**scan·ner** \'ska-nər\ *n*  1 : a radio receiver that sequentially scans a range of frequencies for a signal  2 : a device that scans an image or document esp. for use or storage on a computer

¹**scant** \'skant\ *adj*  1 : barely sufficient ⟨food is in ~ supply⟩  2 : having scarcely enough ♦ *Synonyms* SCANTY, SKIMPY, MEAGER, SPARSE, EXIGUOUS

²**scant** *vb*  1 : SKIMP  2 : STINT

**scant·ling** \'skant-liŋ\ *n* : a small piece of lumber (as an upright in a house)

**scanty** \'skan-tē\ *adj* **scant·i·er; -est** : barely sufficient : SCANT ⟨wore ~ outfits⟩ — **scant·i·ly** \'skan-tə-lē\ *adv* — **scant·i·ness** \-tē-nəs\ *n*

**scape·goat** \'skāp-ˌgōt\ *n* : one that bears the blame for others

**scape·grace** \-ˌgrās\ *n* [*scape* (escape)] : an incorrigible rascal

**scap·u·la** \'ska-pyə-lə\ *n, pl* **-lae** \-ˌlē\ *or* **-las** [L] : SHOULDER BLADE

**scap·u·lar** \-lər\ *n* : a pair of small cloth squares worn on the breast and back under the clothing esp. for religious purposes

**scar** \'skär\ *n* : a mark left after injured tissue has healed — **scar** *vb*

**scar·ab** \'ska-rəb\ *n* [MF *scarabee*, fr. L *scarabaeus*] : any of a family of large stout beetles; *also* : an ornament (as a gem) representing such a beetle

**scarce** \'skers\ *adj* **scarc·er; scarc·est**  1 : deficient in quantity or number : not plentiful  2 : intentionally absent ⟨made himself ~ at inspection time⟩ — **scar·ci·ty** \'sker-sə-tē\ *n*

**scarce·ly** \-lē\ *adv*  1 : BARELY ⟨can ~

see them⟩ 2 : almost not 3 : very probably not

**¹scare** \'sker\ vb **scared; scar·ing** : FRIGHTEN, STARTLE

**²scare** n : FRIGHT — **scary** adj

**scare-crow** \'sker-ˌkrō\ n : a crude figure set up to scare birds away from crops

**¹scarf** \'skärf\ n, pl **scarves** \'skärvz\ or **scarfs** 1 : a broad band (as of cloth) worn about the shoulders, around the neck, over the head, or about the waist 2 : a long narrow cloth cover for a table or dresser top

**²scarf** vb [alter. of earlier scoff eat greedily] : to eat greedily ⟨~ed down his lunch⟩

**scar·i·fy** \'sker-ə-ˌfī\ vb **-fied; -fy·ing** 1 : to make scratches or small cuts in ⟨~ skin for vaccination⟩ ⟨~ seeds to help them germinate⟩ 2 : to lacerate the feelings of 3 : to break up and loosen the surface of (as a road) — **scar·i·fi·ca·tion** \ˌskar-ə-fə-ˈkā-shən\ n

**scar·let** \'skär-lət\ n : a bright red color — **scarlet** adj

**scarlet fever** n : an acute contagious disease marked by fever, sore throat, and red rash and caused by certain streptococci

**scarp** \'skärp\ n : a line of cliffs produced by faulting or erosion

**scath·ing** \'skā-thiŋ\ adj : bitterly severe ⟨a ~ condemnation⟩

**scat·o·log·i·cal** \ˌska-tə-ˈlä-ji-kəl\ adj : concerned with obscene matters

**scat·ter** \'ska-tər\ vb 1 : to distribute or strew about irregularly 2 : DISPERSE

**scat·ter·brain** \'ska-tər-ˌbrān\ n : a silly careless person — **scat·ter·brained** \-ˌbrānd\ adj

**scav·enge** \'ska-vənj\ vb **scav·enged; scav·eng·ing** : to work or function as a scavenger

**scav·en·ger** \'ska-vən-jər\ n [alter. of earlier scavager, fr. AF scawageour collector of scavage (duty imposed on nonresident street merchants), fr. scawage scavage, fr. MF dial. (Flanders) escauver to inspect, fr. MD scouwen] : a person or animal that collects, eats, or disposes of refuse or waste

**sce·nar·io** \sə-ˈner-ē-ˌō\ n, pl **-i·os** : the plot or outline of a dramatic work; also : an account of a possible action

**scene** \'sēn\ n [MF, stage, fr. L scena, scaena stage, scene, prob. fr. Etruscan, fr. Gk skēnē temporary shelter, tent, building forming the background for a dramatic performance, stage] 1 : a division of one act of a play 2 : a single situation or sequence in a play or motion picture 3 : a stage setting 4 : VIEW, PROSPECT 5 : the place of an occurrence or action 6 : a display of strong feeling and esp. anger 7 : a sphere of activity ⟨the fashion ~⟩ — **sce·nic** \'sē-nik\ adj

**scen·ery** \'sē-nə-rē\ n, pl **-er·ies** 1 : the painted scenes or hangings and accessories used on a theater stage 2 : a picturesque view or landscape

**¹scent** \'sent\ n 1 : ODOR, SMELL 2 : sense of smell 3 : course of pursuit

: TRACK 4 : PERFUME 2 — **scent·ed** \'sen-təd\ adj — **scent·less** adj

**²scent** vb 1 : SMELL 2 : to imbue or fill with odor

**scep·ter** \'sep-tər\ n : a staff borne by a sovereign as an emblem of authority

**scep·tic** var of SKEPTIC

**scep·tre** Brit var of SCEPTER

**sch** abbr school

**¹sched·ule** \'ske-jül, esp Brit 'she-dyül\ n 1 : a list of items or details 2 : TIMETABLE

**²schedule** vb **sched·uled; sched·ul·ing** 1 : to appoint, assign, or designate for a fixed time 2 : to make a schedule of; also : to enter on a schedule

**sche·ma** \'skē-mə\ n, pl **sche·ma·ta** \-mə-tə\ also **schemas** : a diagrammatic presentation or plan : OUTLINE

**sche·mat·ic** \ski-ˈma-tik\ adj : of or relating to a scheme or diagram : DIAGRAMMATIC — **schematic** n — **sche·mat·i·cal·ly** \-ti-k(ə-)lē\ adv

**¹scheme** \'skēm\ n 1 : a plan for doing something; esp : a crafty plot 2 : a systematic design ⟨a color ~⟩

**²scheme** vb **schemed; schem·ing** : to form a plot : INTRIGUE — **schem·er** n

**schil·ling** \'shil-iŋ\ n : a former basic monetary unit of Austria

**schism** \'si-zəm, 'ski-\ n 1 : DIVISION, SPLIT; also : DISCORD, DISSENSION 2 : a formal division in or separation from a religious body

**schis·mat·ic** \siz-ˈma-tik, ski-\ n : one who creates or takes part in schism — **schismatic** adj

**schist** \'shist\ n : a metamorphic crystalline rock

**schizo·phre·nia** \ˌskit-sə-ˈfrē-nē-ə\ n [NL, fr. Gk schizein to split + phrēn diaphragm, mind] : a psychotic mental illness that is characterized by a distorted view of the real world, by a greatly reduced ability to carry out one's daily tasks, and by abnormal ways of thinking, feeling, perceiving, and behaving — **schiz·oid** \'skit-ˌsȯid\ adj or n — **schizo·phren·ic** \ˌskit-sə-ˈfre-nik\ adj or n

**schle·miel** also **shle·miel** \shlə-ˈmēl\ n : an unlucky bungler : CHUMP

**schlep** or **schlepp** \'shlep\ vb [Yiddish shlepn] 1 : DRAG, HAUL 2 : to move slowly or awkwardly

**schlock** \'shläk\ or **schlocky** \'shlä-kē\ adj : of low quality or value — **schlock** n

**schlub** also **shlub** \'shləb\ n [Yiddish zhlob, zhlub yokel, boor] slang : a stupid, ineffectual, or unattractive person

**schmaltz** also **schmalz** \'shmȯlts, 'shmälts\ n [Yiddish shmalts, lit., rendered fat] : sentimental or florid music or art — **schmaltzy** adj

**schmooze** or **shmooze** \'shmüz\ vb : to chat informally esp. to gain favor — **schmooze** n

**schnapps** \'shnaps\ n, pl **schnapps** : a liquor (as gin) of high alcoholic content

**schnau·zer** \'shnau̇-zər, 'shnaut-sər\ n [G, fr. Schnauze snout] : a dog of any of three breeds that are characterized by a wiry coat, long head, pointed ears, heavy eyebrows, and long hair on the muzzle

**schol·ar** \'skä-lər\ n **1** : STUDENT, PUPIL **2** : a learned person : SAVANT — **schol·ar·ly** adj

**schol·ar·ship** \-,ship\ n **1** : the qualities or learning of a scholar **2** : money awarded to a student to help pay for further education

**scho·las·tic** \skə-'las-tik\ adj : of or relating to schools, scholars, or scholarship

**¹school** \'skül\ n **1** : an institution for teaching and learning; also : the pupils in attendance **2** : a body of persons of like opinions or beliefs ⟨the radical ~⟩

**²school** vb : TEACH, TRAIN, DRILL

**³school** n : a large number of one kind of water animal swimming and feeding together

**school·boy** \-,bȯi\ n : a boy attending school

**school·fel·low** \-,fe-lō\ n : SCHOOLMATE

**school·girl** \-,gərl\ n : a girl attending school

**school·house** \-,haȯs\ n : a building used as a school

**school·marm** \-,märm\ or **school·ma'am** \-,mäm, -,mam\ n **1** : a woman who is a schoolteacher **2** : a person who exhibits characteristics popularly attributed to schoolteachers

**school·mas·ter** \-,mas-tər\ n : a man who is a schoolteacher

**school·mate** \-,māt\ n : a school companion

**school·mis·tress** \-,mis-trəs\ n : a woman who is a schoolteacher

**school·room** \-,rüm, -,rüm\ n : CLASSROOM

**school·teach·er** \-,tē-chər\ n : one who teaches in a school

**schoo·ner** \'skü-nər\ n : a fore-and-aft rigged sailing ship

**schtick** var of SHTICK

**schuss** \'shús, 'shüs\ vb [G Schuss, n., lit., shot] : to ski down a slope at high speed — **schuss** n

**sci** abbr science; scientific

**sci·at·i·ca** \sī-'a-ti-kə\ n : pain in the region of the hips or along the course of the nerve at the back of the thigh

**sci·ence** \'sī-əns\ n [ME, fr. AF, fr. L scientia, fr. scient-, sciens having knowledge, fr. prp. of scire to know] **1** : an area of knowledge that is an object of study; esp : NATURAL SCIENCE **2** : knowledge covering general truths or the operation of general laws especially as obtained and tested through the scientific method — **sci·en·tif·ic** \,sī-ən-'ti-fik\ adj — **sci·en·tif·i·cal·ly** \-fi-k(ə-)lē\ adv — **sci·en·tist** \'sī-ən-tist\ n

**science fiction** n : fiction dealing principally with the impact of actual or imagined science on society or individuals

**scientific method** n : the rules and methods for the pursuit of knowledge involving the finding and stating of a problem, the collection of facts through observation and experiment, and the making and testing of ideas that need to be proven right or wrong

**scim·i·tar** \'si-mə-tər\ n : a curved sword used chiefly by Arabs and Turks

**scin·til·la** \sin-'ti-lə\ n : SPARK, TRACE ⟨isn't a ~ of evidence⟩

**scin·til·late** \'sin-tə-,lāt\ vb -lat·ed; -lat·ing : SPARKLE, GLEAM — **scin·til·la·tion** \,sin-tə-'lā-shən\ n

**sci·on** \'sī-ən\ n **1** : a shoot of a plant joined to a stock in grafting **2** : DESCENDANT ⟨a ~ of a powerful family⟩

**scis·sors** \'si-zərz\ n pl : a cutting instrument like shears but usu. smaller

**scissors kick** n : a swimming kick in which the legs move like scissors

**scle·ro·der·ma** \,sklēr-ə-'dər-mə\ n : a chronic disease characterized by the usu. progressive hardening and thickening of the skin

**scle·ro·sis** \sklə-'rō-səs\ n : abnormal hardening of tissue (as of an artery); also : a disease characterized by this — **scle·rot·ic** \-'rä-tik\ adj

**scoff** \'skäf\ vb : MOCK, JEER ⟨~ed at his proposal⟩ — **scoff·er** n

**scoff·law** \-,lȯ\ n : a contemptuous law violator

**¹scold** \'skōld\ n : a person who scolds

**²scold** vb : to censure severely or angrily

**sconce** \'skäns\ n : a candlestick or an electric light fixture fastened to a wall

**scone** \'skōn, 'skän\ n : a biscuit (as of oatmeal) baked on a griddle

**¹scoop** \'sküp\ n **1** : a large shovel; also : a utensil with a shovellike or rounded end **2** : the amount contained by a scoop **3** : an act of scooping **4** : information of immediate interest

**²scoop** vb **1** : to take out or up or empty with or as if with a scoop **2** : to make hollow **3** : to report a news item in advance of ⟨~ed the other newspapers⟩

**scoot** \'sküt\ vb : to move swiftly

**scoot·er** \'skü-tər\ n **1** : a child's vehicle consisting of a narrow board mounted between two wheels tandem with an upright steering handle attached to the front wheel **2** : MOTOR SCOOTER

**¹scope** \'skōp\ n [It scopo purpose, goal, fr. Gk skopos] **1** : space or opportunity for action or thought **2** : extent covered : RANGE ⟨is beyond the ~ of this essay⟩

**²scope** n : an instrument (as a microscope or telescope) for viewing

**scorch** \'skȯrch\ vb : to burn the surface of; also : to dry or shrivel with heat ⟨~ed lawns⟩

**¹score** \'skȯr\ n, pl **scores 1** or pl **score** : TWENTY **2** : CUT, SCRATCH, SLASH **3** : a record of points made (as in a game) **4** : DEBT **5** : REASON, GROUND **6** : the music of a composition or arrangement with different parts indicated **7** : success in obtaining something (as drugs) esp. illegally

**²score** vb **scored; scor·ing 1** : RECORD **2** : to keep score in a game **3** : to mark with lines, grooves, scratches, or notches **4** : to gain or tally in or as if in a game ⟨scored a point⟩ **5** : to assign a grade or score to ⟨~ the tests⟩ **6** : to compose a score for **7** : SUCCEED **8** : ACQUIRE

⟨*scored* tickets to the game⟩ — **score·less** *adj* — **scor·er** *n*

¹**scorn** \\'skȯrn\ *n* : an emotion involving both anger and disgust : CONTEMPT — **scorn·ful** \-fəl\ *adj* — **scorn·ful·ly** *adv*

²**scorn** *vb* : to hold in contempt : DISDAIN ⟨were ~*ed* as fanatics⟩ — **scorn·er** *n*

**Scor·pio** \\'skȯr-pē-ˌō\ *n* [L, lit., scorpion] **1** : a zodiacal constellation between Libra and Sagittarius usu. pictured as a scorpio **2** : the 8th sign of the zodiac in astrology; *also* : one born under this sign

**scor·pi·on** \\'skȯr-pē-ən\ *n* : any of an order of arthropods related to the spiders that have a poisonous stinger at the tip of a long jointed tail

¹**Scot** \\'skät\ *n* : a native or inhabitant of Scotland

²**Scot** *abbr* Scotland; Scottish

**Scotch** \\'skäch\ *n* **1** : SCOTS **2** Scotch *pl* : the people of Scotland **3** : a whiskey distilled in Scotland esp. from malted barley — **Scotch** *adj* — **Scotch·man** \-mən\ *n* — **Scotch·wom·an** \-ˌwu̇-mən\ *n*

**Scotch bonnet** *n* : a small roundish very hot chili pepper esp. of the Caribbean

**Scotch pine** *n* : a pine that is naturalized in the U.S. from northern Europe and Asia and is a valuable timber tree

**Scotch terrier** *n* : SCOTTISH TERRIER

**scot–free** \\'skät-ˈfrē\ *adj* : free from obligation, harm, or penalty

**Scots** \\'skäts\ *n* : the English language of Scotland

**Scots·man** \\'skäts-mən\ *n* : SCOT

**Scots·wom·an** \-ˌwu̇-mən\ *n* : a woman who is a Scot

**Scot·tie** \\'skä-tē\ *n* : SCOTTISH TERRIER

**Scot·tish** \\'skä-tish\ *adj* : of, relating to, or characteristic of Scotland, Scots, or the Scots

**Scottish terrier** *n* : any of an old Scottish breed of terrier with short legs, a long head with small erect ears, a broad deep chest, and a thick rough coat

**scoun·drel** \\'skau̇n-drəl\ *n* : a disreputable person : VILLAIN

¹**scour** \\'skau̇(-ə)r\ *vb* **1** : to rub (as with a gritty substance) in order to clean **2** : to cleanse by or as if by rubbing

²**scour** *vb* **1** : to move rapidly through : RUSH **2** : to examine thoroughly

¹**scourge** \\'skərj\ *n* **1** : LASH, WHIP **2** : PUNISHMENT; *also* : a cause of affliction (as a plague)

²**scourge** *vb* **scourged; scourg·ing 1** : LASH, FLOG **2** : to punish severely

¹**scout** \\'skau̇t\ *vb* [ME, fr. AF *escuter* to listen, fr. L *auscultare*] **1** : to look around : RECONNOITER **2** : to inspect or observe to get information

²**scout** *n* **1** : a person sent out to get information; *also* : a soldier, airplane, or ship sent out to reconnoiter **2** : BOY SCOUT **3** : GIRL SCOUT — **scout·mas·ter** \-ˌmas-tər\ *n*

³**scout** *vb* : SCORN, SCOFF

**scow** \\'skau̇\ *n* : a large flat-bottomed boat with square ends

**scowl** \\'skau̇(-ə)l\ *vb* : to make a frowning expression of displeasure — **scowl** *n*

**SCPO** *abbr* senior chief petty officer

**scrab·ble** \\'skra-bəl\ *vb* **scrab·bled; scrab·bling 1** : SCRAPE, SCRATCH **2** : CLAMBER, SCRAMBLE ⟨*scrabbled* on the slippery rocks⟩ **3** : to work hard and long **4** : SCRIBBLE — **scrabble** *n* — **scrab·bler** *n*

**scrag·gly** \\'skra-glē\ *adj* : IRREGULAR; *also* : RAGGED, UNKEMPT ⟨a ~ beard⟩

**scram** \\'skram\ *vb* **scrammed; scram·ming** : to go away at once

**scram·ble** \\'skram-bəl\ *vb* **scram·bled; scram·bling 1** : to clamber clumsily around **2** : to struggle for or as if for possession of something **3** : to spread irregularly **4** : to mix together **5** : to cook (eggs) by stirring during frying — **scramble** *n*

¹**scrap** \\'skrap\ *n* **1** : FRAGMENT, PIECE **2** : discarded material : REFUSE

²**scrap** *vb* **scrapped; scrap·ping 1** : to make into scrap ⟨~ a battleship⟩ **2** : to get rid of as useless ⟨*scrapped* the plans⟩

³**scrap** *n* : FIGHT

⁴**scrap** *vb* **scrapped; scrap·ping** : FIGHT, QUARREL — **scrap·per** *n*

**scrap·book** \\'skrap-ˌbu̇k\ *n* : a blank book in which mementos are kept

¹**scrape** \\'skrāp\ *vb* **scraped; scrap·ing 1** : to remove by drawing a knife over; *also* : to clean or smooth by rubbing off the covering **2** : to damage or injure the surface of by contact with something rough **3** : to draw across a surface with a grating sound **4** : to get together (money) by strict economy **5** : to get along with difficulty ⟨barely *scraping* by on her income⟩ — **scrap·er** *n*

²**scrape** *n* **1** : the act or the effect of scraping **2** : a bow accompanied by a drawing back of the foot **3** : an unpleasant predicament

**scra·pie** \\'skrā-pē\ *n* : a usu. fatal degenerative disease of the brain esp. of sheep that is related to mad cow disease

¹**scrap·py** \\'skra-pē\ *adj* **scrap·pi·er; -est** : DISCONNECTED, FRAGMENTARY

²**scrappy** *adj* **scrap·pi·er; -est 1** : QUARRELSOME **2** : having an aggressive and determined spirit ⟨a ~ competitor⟩

¹**scratch** \\'skrach\ *vb* **1** : to scrape, dig, or rub with or as if with claws or nails ⟨a dog ~*ing* at the door⟩ ⟨~*ed* my arm⟩ **2** : SCRAPE **3** ⟨~*ed* his nails across the blackboard⟩ **3** : SCRAPE **4 4** : to cancel or erase by or as if by drawing a line through **5** : to withdraw from a contest — **scratchy** *adj* — **scratch one's head** : to become confused or perplexed

²**scratch** *n* **1** : a mark or injury made by or as if by scratching; *also* : a sound so made **2** : the starting line in a race — **from scratch** : with no steps completed or ingredients prepared ahead of time ⟨built from ~⟩

³**scratch** *adj* **1** : made or done by chance ⟨a ~ hit⟩ **2** : made as or used for a trial attempt ⟨~ paper⟩

**scratch card** *n* : a card with a small area covered by an opaque coating which may be scraped away to reveal hidden information

**scrawl** \\'skrȯl\\ vb : to write hastily and carelessly — **scrawl** n

**scraw·ny** \\'skrȯ-nē\\ adj **scraw·ni·er; -est** : very thin : SKINNY

¹**scream** \\'skrēm\\ vb : to cry out loudly and shrilly

²**scream** n : a loud shrill cry

**scream·ing** \\'skrē-miŋ\\ adj : so striking as to attract notice as if by screaming ⟨~ headlines⟩

**screech** \\'skrēch\\ vb : SHRIEK — **screech** n — **screechy** \\'skrē-chē\\ adj

**screech·ing** \\'skrē-chiŋ\\ adj : ABRUPT ⟨came to a ~ halt⟩

¹**screen** \\'skrēn\\ n 1 : a device or partition used to hide, restrain, protect, or decorate ⟨a window ~⟩; also : something that shelters, protects, or conceals 2 : a sieve or perforated material for separating finer from coarser parts (as of sand) 3 : a surface on which an image is made to appear (as in television); also : the information displayed on a computer screen at one time 4 : the motion-picture industry

²**screen** vb 1 : to shield with or as if with a screen 2 : to separate with a screen; also : to select or categorize methodically ⟨~ contestants⟩ 3 : to present (as a motion picture) on the screen

**screen·ing** \\'skrē-niŋ\\ n 1 : metal or plastic mesh (as for window screens) 2 : a showing of a motion picture

**screen saver** n : a computer program that displays something (as images) on the screen of a computer that is on but not in use

¹**screw** \\'skrü\\ n [ME, fr. MF escroe female screw, nut, fr. ML scrofa, fr. L, sow] 1 : a machine consisting of a solid cylinder with a spiral groove around it and a corresponding hollow cylinder into which it fits 2 : a naillike metal piece with a spiral groove and a head with a slot that is inserted into material by rotating and is used to fasten pieces of solid material together 3 : PROPELLER

²**screw** vb 1 : to fasten or close by means of a screw 2 : to operate or adjust by means of a screw 3 : to move or cause to move spirally; also : to close or set in position by such an action

**screw·ball** \\'skrü-,bȯl\\ n 1 : a baseball pitch breaking in a direction opposite to a curve 2 : a whimsical, eccentric, or crazy person

**screw·driv·er** \\-,drī-vər\\ n 1 : a tool for turning screws 2 : a drink made of vodka and orange juice

**screw·worm** \\'skrü-,wərm\\ n : an American blowfly of warm regions whose larva matures in wounds or sores of mammals and may cause disease or death; esp : its larva

**screwy** \\'skrü-ē\\ adj **screw·i·er; -est** 1 : crazily absurd, eccentric, or unusual ⟨a ~ idea⟩ 2 : CRAZY, INSANE

**scrib·ble** \\'skri-bəl\\ vb **scrib·bled; scrib·bling** : to write hastily or carelessly — **scribble** n — **scrib·bler** n

**scribe** \\'skrīb\\ n 1 : a scholar of Jewish law in New Testament times 2 : a person

whose business is the copying of writing 3 : JOURNALIST

**scrim** \\'skrim\\ n : a light loosely woven cotton or linen cloth

**scrim·mage** \\'skri-mij\\ n : the play between two football teams beginning with the snap of the ball; also : practice play between two teams — **scrimmage** vb

**scrimp** \\'skrimp\\ vb : to economize greatly ⟨~ and save⟩

**scrim·shaw** \\'skrim-,shȯ\\ n : carved or engraved articles made orig. by American whalers usu. from baleen or whale ivory — **scrimshaw** vb

**scrip** \\'skrip\\ n 1 : a certificate showing its holder is entitled to something (as stock or land) 2 : paper money issued for temporary use in an emergency

¹**script** \\'skript\\ n 1 : written matter (as lines for a play or broadcast) 2 : HANDWRITING

²**script** abbr scripture

**scrip·ture** \\'skrip-chər\\ n 1 cap : the books of the Bible — often used in pl. 2 : the sacred writings of a religion — **scrip·tur·al** \\'skrip-chə-rəl\\ adj — **scrip·tur·al·ly** adv

**scriv·en·er** \\'skri-və-nər\\ n : SCRIBE, COPYIST, WRITER

**scrod** \\'skräd\\ n [prob. fr. Brit. dial. (Cornwall) scrawed, pp. of scraw, scrod to split, salt, and dry (young fish)] : a young fish (as a cod or haddock); esp : one split and boned for cooking

**scrof·u·la** \\'skrȯ-fyə-lə\\ n : tuberculosis of lymph nodes esp. in the neck

¹**scroll** \\'skrōl\\ n : a roll of paper or parchment for writing a document; also : a spiral or coiled ornamental form suggesting a loosely or partly rolled scroll

²**scroll** vb : to move or cause to move text or graphics up, down, or across a display screen

**scroll saw** n 1 : FRETSAW 2 : a machine saw with a narrow vertically reciprocating blade for cutting curved lines or openwork

**scro·tum** \\'skrō-təm\\ n, pl **scro·ta** \\-tə\\ or **scrotums** [L] : a pouch that in most male mammals contains the testes

**scrounge** \\'skraúnj\\ vb **scrounged; scroung·ing** : to collect by or as if by foraging

¹**scrub** \\'skrəb\\ n 1 : a thick growth of stunted trees or shrubs; also : an area of land covered with scrub 2 : an inferior domestic animal 3 : a person of insignificant size or standing 4 : a player not on the first team — **scrub** adj — **scrub·by** adj

²**scrub** vb **scrubbed; scrub·bing** 1 : to clean or wash by rubbing ⟨~ clothes⟩ ⟨~ out a spot⟩ 2 : CANCEL

³**scrub** n 1 : an act or instance of scrubbing ⟨gave the clothes a good ~⟩ 2 pl : loose-fitting clothing worn by hospital staff ⟨surgical ~s⟩

**scrub·ber** \\'skrə-bər\\ n : one that scrubs; esp : an apparatus for removing impurities esp. from gases

**scruff** \\'skrəf\\ n : the loose skin of the back of the neck : NAPE

**scruffy** \'skrə-fē\ adj **scruff·i·er; -est** : UNKEMPT, SLOVENLY ⟨a ~ tramp⟩

**scrump·tious** \'skrəmp-shəs\ adj : DELIGHTFUL, EXCELLENT; esp : DELICIOUS ⟨a ~ cake⟩ — **scrump·tious·ly** adv

**scrunch·ie** or **scrunchy** \'skrən-chē, 'skrun-\ n : a fabric-covered elastic for the hair

¹**scru·ple** \'skrü-pəl\ n [ME scrupil, scriple, fr. AF scruble, fr. L scrupulus, dim. of scrupus source of uneasiness, lit., sharp stone] **1** : a point of conscience or honor **2** : hesitation due to ethical considerations

²**scruple** vb **scru·pled; scru·pling** : to be reluctant on grounds of conscience : HESITATE

**scru·pu·lous** \'skrü-pyə-ləs\ adj **1** : having moral integrity **2** : PAINSTAKING ⟨was ~ about her work⟩ — **scru·pu·lous·ly** adv — **scru·pu·lous·ness** n

**scru·ti·nise** Brit var of SCRUTINIZE

**scru·ti·nize** \'skrü-tə-ˌnīz\ vb **-nized; -niz·ing** : to examine closely

**scru·ti·ny** \'skrü-tə-nē\ n, pl **-nies** [L scrutinium, fr. scrutari to search, examine, prob. fr. scruta trash] : a careful looking over ♦ **Synonyms** INSPECTION, EXAMINATION, ANALYSIS

**scu·ba** \'skü-bə\ n [self-contained underwater breathing apparatus] : an apparatus for breathing while swimming underwater

**scuba diver** n : one who swims underwater with the aid of scuba gear

¹**scud** \'skəd\ vb **scud·ded; scud·ding** : to move speedily

²**scud** n : light clouds driven by the wind

¹**scuff** \'skəf\ vb **1** : to scrape the feet while walking : SHUFFLE **2** : to scratch or become scratched or worn away

²**scuff** n **1** : a mark or injury caused by scuffing **2** : a flat-soled slipper without heel strap

**scuf·fle** \'skə-fəl\ vb **scuf·fled; scuffling** **1** : to struggle confusedly at close quarters ⟨scuffled with the police⟩ **2** : to shuffle one's feet — **scuffle** n

¹**scull** \'skəl\ n **1** : an oar for use in sculling; also : one of a pair of short oars for a single oarsman **2** : a racing shell propelled by one or two persons using sculls

²**scull** vb : to propel (a boat) by an oar over the stern

**scul·lery** \'skə-lə-rē\ n, pl **-ler·ies** [ME squilerie, sculerie department of household in charge of dishes, fr. AF esquilerie, fr. escuele bowl, fr. L scutella drinking bowl] : a small room near the kitchen used for cleaning dishes, cooking utensils, and vegetables

**scul·lion** \'skəl-yən\ n : a kitchen helper

**sculpt** \'skəlpt\ vb : CARVE, SCULPTURE

**sculp·tor** \'skəlp-tər\ n : a person who produces works of sculpture

¹**sculp·ture** \'skəlp-chər\ n : the act, process, or art of carving or molding material (as stone, wood, or plastic); also : work produced this way — **sculp·tur·al** \'skəlp-chə-rəl\ adj

²**sculpture** vb **sculp·tured; sculp·tur·ing**

: to form or alter as or as if a work of sculpture ⟨sculptured hedges⟩

**scum** \'skəm\ n **1** : a slimy or filmy covering on the surface of a liquid **2** : waste matter **3** : RABBLE

**scup·per** \'skə-pər\ n [ME skopper-, perh. fr. AF *escopoir, fr. escopir to spit out] : an opening in the side of a ship through which water on deck is drained overboard

**scurf** \'skərf\ n : thin scales of skin (as dandruff); also : a scaly deposit or covering — **scurfy** \'skər-fē\ adj

**scur·ri·lous** \'skər-ə-ləs\ adj : coarsely jesting : OBSCENE, VULGAR

**scur·ry** \'skər-ē\ vb **scur·ried; scur·ry·ing** : SCAMPER ⟨scurried for cover⟩

¹**scur·vy** \'skər-vē\ n : a disease caused by a lack of vitamin C and characterized by spongy gums, loosened teeth, and bleeding under the skin

²**scurvy** adj : MEAN, CONTEMPTIBLE — **scur·vi·ly** \'skər-və-lē\ adv

**scutch·eon** \'skə-chən\ n : ESCUTCHEON

¹**scut·tle** \'skə-t²l\ n : a pail for carrying coal

²**scuttle** n : a small opening with a lid esp. in the deck, side, or bottom of a ship

³**scuttle** vb **scut·tled; scut·tling** : to cut a hole in the deck, side, or bottom of (a ship) in order to sink

⁴**scuttle** vb **scut·tled; scut·tling** : SCURRY, SCAMPER

**scut·tle·butt** \'skə-t²l-ˌbət\ n : GOSSIP

**scythe** \'sīth\ n : an implement for mowing (as grass or grain) by hand — **scythe** vb

**SD** abbr **1** South Dakota **2** special delivery

**S Dak** abbr South Dakota

**SDI** abbr Strategic Defense Initiative

**Se** symbol selenium

**SE** abbr southeast

¹**sea** \'sē\ n **1** : a large body of salt water **2** : OCEAN **3** : rough water; also : a large wave **4** : something likened to the sea esp. in vastness ⟨a ~ of wheat⟩ — **sea** adj — **at sea** : LOST, BEWILDERED

**sea anemone** n : any of numerous coelenterate polyps whose form, bright and varied colors, and cluster of tentacles superficially resemble a flower

**sea·bird** \'sē-ˌbərd\ n : a bird (as a gull) frequenting the open ocean

**sea·board** \-ˌbȯrd\ n : SEACOAST; also : the land bordering a coast

**sea·bor·gi·um** \sē-ˈbȯr-gē-əm\ n : a short-lived radioactive chemical element produced artificially

**sea·coast** \-ˌkōst\ n : the shore of the sea

**sea·far·er** \-ˌfer-ər\ n : SEAMAN 1

**sea·far·ing** \-ˌfer-iŋ\ n : the use of the sea for travel or transportation — **seafaring** adj

**sea·food** \-ˌfüd\ n : edible marine fish and shellfish

**sea·go·ing** \-ˌgō-iŋ\ adj : OCEANGOING

**sea·gull** \'sē-ˌgəl\ n : GULL

**sea horse** n : any of a genus of small marine fishes with the head and forepart of the body sharply flexed like the head and neck of a horse

**¹seal** \'sēl\ *n, pl* **seals** *also* **seal** [ME *sele,* fr. OE *seolh*] **1** : any of numerous large carnivorous sea mammals occurring chiefly in cold regions and having limbs adapted for swimming **2** : the pelt of a seal

**²seal** *vb* : to hunt seals

**³seal** *n* [ME *sele, seel,* fr. AF *seal, sel,* fr. L *sigillum,* fr. dim. of *signum* sign, seal] **1** : GUARANTEE, PLEDGE **2** : a device having a raised design that can be stamped on clay or wax; *also* : the impression made by stamping with such a device **3** : something that seals or closes up ⟨safety ∼⟩

**⁴seal** *vb* **1** : to affix a seal to; *also* : AUTHENTICATE **2** : to fasten with or as if with a seal to prevent tampering **3** : to close or make secure against access, leakage, or passage **4** : to determine irrevocably ⟨∼ed his fate⟩

**sea–lane** \'sē-,lān\ *n* : an established sea route

**seal·ant** \'sē-lənt\ *n* : a sealing agent

**seal·er** \'sē-lər\ *n* : a coat applied to prevent subsequent coats of paint or varnish from sinking in

**sea level** *n* : the level of the surface of the sea esp. at its mean midway between mean high and low water

**sea·lift** \'sē-,lift\ *n* : transport of military personnel and equipment by ship

**sea lion** *n* : any of several large Pacific seals with small external ears

**seal·skin** \'sēl-,skin\ *n* **1** : ¹SEAL 2 **2** : a garment of sealskin

**¹seam** \'sēm\ *n* **1** : the line of junction of two edges and esp. of edges of fabric sewn together **2** : a layer of mineral matter **3** : WRINKLE

**²seam** *vb* **1** : to join by or as if by sewing **2** : WRINKLE, FURROW

**sea·man** \'sē-mən\ *n* **1** : one who assists in the handling of ships : MARINER **2** : an enlisted person in the navy ranking next below a petty officer third class

**seaman apprentice** *n* : an enlisted person in the navy ranking next below a seaman

**seaman recruit** *n* : an enlisted person of the lowest rank in the navy

**sea·man·ship** \'sē-mən-,ship\ *n* : the art or skill of handling a ship

**seam·less** \'sēm-ləs\ *adj* : having no flaws or interruptions ⟨a ∼ transition⟩ — **seam·less·ly** *adv*

**sea·mount** \'sē-,maůnt\ *n* : an underwater mountain

**seam·stress** \'sēm-strəs\ *n* : a woman who does sewing

**seamy** \'sē-mē\ *adj* **seam·i·er; -est 1** : UNPLEASANT **2** : DEGRADED, SORDID ⟨the ∼ part of town⟩

**sé·ance** \'sā-,äns\ *n* [F] : a meeting to receive communications from spirits

**sea·plane** \'sē-,plān\ *n* : an airplane that can take off from and land on water

**sea·port** \-,pōrt\ *n* : a port for oceangoing ships

**sear** \'sir\ *vb* **1** : WITHER **2** : to cook, burn, or scorch esp. on the surface; *also* : BRAND — **sear** *n*

**¹search** \'sərch\ *vb* [ME *cerchen,* fr. AF *cercher* to travel about, investigate, search, fr. LL *circare* to go about, fr. L *circum* round about] **1** : to look through in trying to find something **2** : SEEK **3** : PROBE — **search·er** *n*

**²search** *n* : the act of searching

**search engine** *n* : computer software or a website used to search data (as text or other websites) for specified information

**search·light** \-,līt\ *n* : an apparatus for projecting a powerful beam of light; *also* : the light projected

**sear·ing** \'sir-in\ *adj* : very sharp, harsh or intense ⟨∼ pain⟩ ⟨a ∼ review⟩

**sea scallop** *n* : a large scallop of the Atlantic coast of No. America that is harvested for food

**sea·scape** \'sē-,skāp\ *n* **1** : a view of the sea **2** : a picture representing a scene at or of the sea

**sea·shell** \'sē-,shel\ *n* : the shell of a marine animal and esp. a mollusk

**sea·shore** \-,shōr\ *n* : the shore of a sea

**sea·sick** \-,sik\ *adj* : nauseated by or as if by the motion of a ship — **sea·sick·ness** *n*

**sea·side** \'sē-,sīd\ *n* : SEASHORE

**¹sea·son** \'sē-zən\ *n* [ME *sesoun,* fr. AF *seison* natural season, appropriate time, fr. L *sation-, satio* action of sowing, fr. *serere* to sow] **1** : one of the divisions of the year (as spring or summer) **2** : a period of the year associated with a particular activity, event, or holiday ⟨the Easter ∼⟩ ⟨hunting ∼⟩ — **sea·son·al** \-zə-nəl\ *adj* — **sea·son·al·ly** *adv*

**²season** *vb* **1** : to make pleasant to the taste by use of salt, pepper, or spices **2** : to make (as by aging or drying) suitable for use **3** : to accustom or habituate to something (as hardship) ♦ *Synonyms* HARDEN, INURE, ACCLIMATE, TOUGHEN — **sea·son·er** *n*

**sea·son·able** \'sē-zə-nə-bəl\ *adj* : occurring at a good or proper time ⟨∼ weather⟩ ♦ *Synonyms* TIMELY, PROPITIOUS, OPPORTUNE — **sea·son·ably** \-blē\ *adv*

**seasonal affective disorder** *n* : depression that recurs as the days grow shorter during the fall and winter

**sea·son·ing** *n* : something that seasons : CONDIMENT

**¹seat** \'sēt\ *n* **1** : a chair, bench, or stool for sitting on **2** : a place which serves as a capital or center

**²seat** *vb* **1** : to place in or on a seat **2** : to provide seats for

**seat belt** *n* : straps designed to hold a person in a seat

**SEATO** \'sē-,tō\ *abbr* Southeast Asia Treaty Organization

**seat–of–the–pants** *adj* : employing or based on personal experience, judgment, and effort rather than technological aids ⟨∼ navigation⟩

**sea turtle** *n* : any of two families of marine turtles that have the feet modified into paddles

**sea urchin** *n* : any of numerous spiny marine echinoderms having thin brittle globular shells

**sea·wall** \'sē-,wȯl\ *n* : an embankment to protect the shore from erosion

¹**sea·ward** \'sē-wərd\ *n* : the direction or side away from land and toward the open sea

²**seaward** *also* **sea·wards** \-wərdz\ *adv* : toward the sea

³**seaward** *adj* **1** : directed or situated toward the sea **2** : coming from the sea

**sea·wa·ter** \'sē-,wȯ-tər, -,wä-\ *n* : water in or from the sea

**sea·way** \-,wā\ *n* : an inland waterway that admits ocean shipping

**sea·weed** \-,wēd\ *n* : a marine alga (as a kelp); *also* : a mass of marine algae

**sea·wor·thy** \-,wər-thē\ *adj* : fit for a sea voyage ⟨a ∼ ship⟩

**se·ba·ceous** \si-'bā-shəs\ *adj* : of, relating to, or secreting fatty material

**sec** *abbr* **1** second; secondary **2** secretary **3** section **4** [L *secundum*] according to

**SEC** *abbr* Securities and Exchange Commission

**se·cede** \si-'sēd\ *vb* **se·ced·ed; se·ced·ing** : to withdraw from an organized body and esp. from a political body

**se·ces·sion** \si-'se-shən\ *n* : the act of seceding — **se·ces·sion·ist** *n*

**se·clude** \si-'klüd\ *vb* **se·clud·ed; se·clud·ing** : to keep or shut away from others ⟨*secluded* herself in her room⟩

**se·clu·sion** \si-'klü-zhən\ *n* : the act of secluding : the state of being secluded — **se·clu·sive** \-siv\ *adj*

¹**sec·ond** \'se-kənd\ *adj* [ME, fr. AF *secund*, fr. L *secundus* second, following, favorable, fr. *sequi* to follow] **1** : being number two in a countable series **2** : next after the first **3** : ALTERNATE ⟨every ∼ year⟩ — **second** *or* **sec·ond·ly** *adv*

²**second** *n* **1** : one that is second **2** : one who assists another (as in a duel) **3** : an inferior or flawed article **4** : the second forward gear in a motor vehicle

³**second** *n* [ME *seconde*, fr. ML *secunda*, fr. L, fem. of *secundus* second; fr. its being the second division of a unit into 60 parts, as a minute is the first] **1** : the 60th part of a minute of time or angular measure **2** : an instant of time

⁴**second** *vb* **1** : to encourage or give support to **2** : to act as a second to **3** : to support (a motion) by adding one's voice to that of a proposer

¹**sec·ond·ary** \'se-kən-,der-ē\ *adj* **1** : second in rank, value, or occurrence : LESSER **2** : belonging to a second or later stage of development **3** : coming after the primary or elementary ⟨∼ schools⟩
♦ *Synonyms* SUBORDINATE, COLLATERAL, DEPENDENT

²**secondary** *n, pl* **-ar·ies** : the defensive backfield of a football team

**secondary sex characteristic** *n* : a physical characteristic that appears in members of one sex at puberty or in seasonal breeders at breeding season and is not directly concerned with reproduction

**second fiddle** *n* : one that plays a supporting or subservient role

**sec·ond–guess** \,se-kənd-'ges\ *vb* **1** : to think out other strategies or explanations for after the event **2** : to seek to anticipate or predict ⟨∼ the stock market⟩

**sec·ond·hand** \-'hand\ *adj* **1** : not original **2** : not new : USED ⟨∼ clothes⟩ **3** : dealing in used goods

**secondhand smoke** *n* : tobacco smoke that is exhaled by smokers or is given off by burning tobacco and is inhaled by persons nearby

**second lieutenant** *n* : a commissioned officer (as in the army) ranking next below a first lieutenant

**sec·ond–rate** \,se-kənd-'rāt\ *adj* : INFERIOR ⟨∼ hotels⟩

**sec·ond–string** \'se-kənd-'striŋ\ *adj* : being a substitute (as on a team)

**se·cre·cy** \'sē-krə-sē\ *n, pl* **-cies** **1** : the habit or practice of being secretive **2** : the condition of being hidden or concealed

¹**se·cret** \'sē-krət\ *adj* **1** : HIDDEN, CONCEALED ⟨a ∼ staircase⟩ **2** : COVERT, STEALTHY; *also* : engaged in detecting or spying ⟨a ∼ agent⟩ **3** : kept from general knowledge — **se·cret·ly** *adv*

²**secret** *n* **1** : MYSTERY **2** : something kept from the knowledge of others

**sec·re·tar·i·at** \,se-krə-'ter-ē-ət\ *n* **1** : the office of a secretary **2** : the secretarial staff in an office **3** : the administrative department of a governmental organization ⟨the UN ∼⟩

**sec·re·tary** \'se-krə-,ter-ē\ *n, pl* **-tar·ies** **1** : a person employed to handle records, correspondence, and routine work for another person **2** : an officer of a corporation or business who is in charge of correspondence and records **3** : an official at the head of a department of government **4** : a writing desk — **sec·re·tar·i·al** \,se-krə-'ter-ē-əl\ *adj* — **sec·re·tary·ship** \'se-krə-,ter-ē-,ship\ *n*

¹**se·crete** \si-'krēt\ *vb* **se·cret·ed; se·cret·ing** : to form and give off (a secretion)

²**se·crete** \si-'krēt, 'sē-krət\ *vb* **se·cret·ed; se·cret·ing** : HIDE, CONCEAL

**se·cre·tion** \si-'krē-shən\ *n* **1** : the process of secreting something **2** : a product of glandular activity; *esp* : one (as a hormone) useful in the organism **3** : the act of hiding something — **se·cre·to·ry** \'sē-krə-,tȯr-ē\ *adj*

**se·cre·tive** \'sē-krə-tiv, si-'krē-\ *adj* : tending to keep secrets or to act secretly ⟨∼ about his work⟩ — **se·cre·tive·ly** *adv* — **se·cre·tive·ness** *n*

¹**sect** \'sekt\ *n* **1** : a dissenting religious body **2** : a religious denomination **3** : a group adhering to a distinctive doctrine or to a leader

²**sect** *abbr* section; sectional

¹**sec·tar·i·an** \sek-'ter-ē-ən\ *adj* **1** : of or relating to a sect or sectarian **2** : limited in character or scope — **sec·tar·i·an·ism** *n*

²**sectarian** *n* **1** : an adherent of a sect **2** : a narrow or bigoted person

**sec·ta·ry** \'sek-tə-rē\ *n, pl* **-ries** : a member of a sect

¹**sec·tion** \'sek-shən\ *n* **1** : a part cut off or

separated **2** : a distinct part **3** : the appearance that a thing has or would have if cut straight through

²**section** *vb* **1** : to separate or become separated into sections ⟨~ an orange⟩ **2** : to represent in sections

**sec·tion·al** \'sek-shə-nəl\ *adj* **1** : of, relating to, or characteristic of a section **2** : local or regional rather than general in character **3** : divided into sections — **sec·tion·al·ism** *n*

**sec·tor** \'sek-tər\ *n* **1** : a part of a circle between two radii **2** : an area assigned to a military leader to defend **3** : a subdivision of society

**sec·u·lar** \'se-kyə-lər\ *adj* **1** : not sacred or ecclesiastical **2** : not bound by monastic vows ⟨a ~ priest⟩

**sec·u·lar·ise** *Brit var of* SECULARIZE

**sec·u·lar·ism** \'se-kyə-lə-,ri-zəm\ *n* : indifference to or exclusion of religion — **sec·u·lar·ist** \-rist\ *n* — **secularist** *also* **sec·u·lar·is·tic** \-se-kyə-lə-'ris-tik\ *adj*

**sec·u·lar·ize** \'se-kyə-lə-,rīz\ *vb* **-ized; -iz·ing 1** : to make secular **2** : to transfer from ecclesiastical to civil or lay use, possession, or control — **sec·u·lar·i·za·tion** \,se-kyə-lə-rə-'zā-shən\ *n* — **sec·u·lar·iz·er** \'se-kyə-lə-,rī-zər\ *n*

¹**se·cure** \si-'kyùr\ *adj* **se·cur·er; -est** [L *securus* safe, secure, fr. *se* without + *cura* care] **1** : easy in mind : free from fear **2** : free from danger or risk of loss : SAFE **3** : CERTAIN, SURE — **se·cure·ly** *adv*

²**secure** *vb* **se·cured; se·cur·ing 1** : to make safe : GUARD **2** : to assure payment of by giving a pledge or collateral **3** : to fasten safely ⟨~ a door⟩ **4** : GET, ACQUIRE ⟨~ permission⟩

**se·cu·ri·ty** \si-'kyùr-ə-tē\ *n, pl* **-ties 1** : SAFETY **2** : freedom from worry **3** : something given as pledge of payment ⟨a ~ deposit⟩ **4** *pl* : bond or stock certificates **5** : PROTECTION

**secy** *abbr* secretary

**se·dan** \si-'dan\ *n* **1** : a covered chair borne on poles by two men **2** : an automobile seating four or more people and usu. having a permanent top

¹**se·date** \si-'dāt\ *adj* : quiet and dignified in behavior ♦ *Synonyms* STAID, SOBER, SERIOUS, SOLEMN — **se·date·ly** *adv*

²**sedate** *vb* **se·dat·ed; se·dat·ing** : to dose with sedatives — **se·da·tion** \si-'dā-shən\ *n*

¹**sed·a·tive** \'se-də-tiv\ *adj* : serving or tending to relieve tension

²**sedative** *n* : a sedative drug

**sed·en·tary** \'se-dᵊn-,ter-ē\ *adj* : characterized by or requiring much sitting

**sedge** \'sej\ *n* : any of a family of plants esp. of marshy areas that differ from the related grasses esp. in having solid stems — **sedgy** \'se-jē\ *adj*

**sed·i·ment** \'se-də-mənt\ *n* **1** : the material that settles to the bottom of a liquid **2** : material (as stones and sand) deposited by water, wind, or a glacier — **sed·i·men·ta·ry** \,se-də-'men-tə-rē\ *adj* — **sed·i·men·ta·tion** \-mən-'tā-shən, -,men-\ *n*

**se·di·tion** \si-'di-shən\ *n* : the causing of discontent, insurrection, or resistance against a government — **se·di·tious** \-shəs\ *adj*

**se·duce** \si-'düs, -'dyüs\ *vb* **se·duced; se·duc·ing 1** : to persuade to disobedience or disloyalty **2** : to lead astray **3** : to entice to sexual intercourse ♦ *Synonyms* TEMPT, ENTICE, INVEIGLE, LURE — **se·duc·er** *n* — **se·duc·tion** \-'dək-shən\ *n* — **se·duc·tive** \-tiv\ *adj*

**sed·u·lous** \'se-jə-ləs\ *adj* [L *sedulus,* fr. *sedulo* sincerely, diligently, fr. *se* without + *dolus* guile] : DILIGENT, PAINSTAKING

¹**see** \'sē\ *vb* **saw** \'sò\; **seen** \'sēn\; **see·ing 1** : to perceive by the eye; *also* : to have the power of sight **2** : EXPERIENCE **3** : UNDERSTAND **4** : to make sure ⟨~ that order is kept⟩ **5** : to meet with **6** : to keep company with esp. in dating **7** : ACCOMPANY, ESCORT ⟨~ the guests to the door⟩ ♦ *Synonyms* BEHOLD, DESCRY, ESPY, VIEW, OBSERVE, NOTE, DISCERN — **see red** : to become very angry — **see the light** : to realize an obscured truth

²**see** *n* : the authority or jurisdiction of a bishop

¹**seed** \'sēd\ *n, pl* **seed** *or* **seeds 1** : the grains of plants used for sowing **2** : a ripened ovule of a flowering plant that may develop into a new plant; *also* : a plant structure (as a spore or small dry fruit) capable of producing a new plant **3** : DESCENDANTS **4** : SOURCE, ORIGIN **5** : a competitor seeded in a tournament — **seed·less** *adj* — **go to seed** *or* **run to seed 1** : to develop seed **2** : DECAY, DETERIORATE

²**seed** *vb* **1** : SOW, PLANT ⟨~ land with grass⟩ **2** : to bear or shed seeds **3** : to remove seeds from **4** : to rank or schedule (contestants) in a tournament — **seed·er** *n*

**seed·bed** \-,bed\ *n* : soil or a bed of soil prepared for planting seed

**seed·ling** \'sēd-liŋ\ *n* **1** : a young plant grown from seed **2** : a young tree before it becomes a sapling

**seed·time** \'sēd-,tīm\ *n* : the season for sowing

**seedy** \'sē-dē\ *adj* **seed·i·er; -est 1** : containing or full of seeds **2** : SHABBY

**seek** \'sēk\ *vb* **sought** \'sòt\; **seek·ing 1** : to search for **2** : to try to reach or obtain **3** : ATTEMPT — **seek·er** *n*

**seem** \'sēm\ *vb* **1** : to appear to the observation or understanding **2** : to give the impression of being : APPEAR

**seem·ing** *adj* : outwardly apparent ⟨~ indifference⟩ — **seem·ing·ly** *adv*

**seem·ly** \'sēm-lē\ *adj* **seem·li·er; -est 1** : conventionally proper **2** : FIT

**seep** \'sēp\ *vb* : to flow or pass slowly through fine pores or cracks — **seep·age** \'sē-pij\ *n*

**seer** \'sir\ *n* : a person who foresees or predicts events : PROPHET

**seer·suck·er** \'sir-,sə-kər\ *n* [Hindi *śīrsakar,* fr. Pers *shīr-o-shakar,* lit., milk and sugar] : a light fabric of linen, cotton, or rayon usu. striped and slightly puckered

**see·saw** \'sē-,só\ *n* 1 : a contest in which each side assumes then relinquishes the lead 2 : a children's sport of riding up and down on the ends of a plank supported in the middle; *also* : the plank so used — **seesaw** *vb*

**seethe** \'sēth\ *vb* **seethed; seeth·ing** [archaic *seethe* boil] : to become violently agitated ⟨~ with jealousy⟩

**seg·ment** \'seg-mənt\ *n* 1 : a part cut off from a geometrical figure (as a circle) by one or more points, lines, or planes 2 : a division of a thing : SECTION — **seg·men·tal** \seg-'men-tᵊl\ *adj* — **seg·men·ta·tion** \,seg-mən-'tā-shən\ *n* — **seg·ment·ed** \'seg-,men-təd\ *adj*

**seg·re·gate** \'se-gri-,gāt\ *vb* **-gat·ed; -gat·ing** [L *segregare*, fr. *se-* apart + *greg-, grex* herd, flock] : to cut off from others; *esp* : to separate esp. by races or ethnic groups — **seg·re·ga·tion** \,se-gri-'gā-shən\ *n*

**seg·re·ga·tion·ist** \,se-gri-'gā-shə-nist\ *n* : one who believes in or practices the segregation of races

¹**se·gue** \'se-(,)gwā, 'sā-\ *vb* **se·gued; se·gue·ing** 1 : to proceed without pause from one musical number to another 2 : to make a transition without interruption from one activity, topic, scene, or part to another

²**segue** *n* : the act or an instance of segueing

**sei·gneur** \sān-'yər\ *n, often cap* [MF, fr. ML *senior*, fr. L, adj., elder] : a feudal lord

¹**seine** \'sān\ *n* : a large weighted fishing net

²**seine** *vb* **seined; sein·ing** : to fish or catch with a seine — **sein·er** *n*

**seis·mic** \'sīz-mik, 'sīs-\ *adj* : of, relating to, resembling, or caused by an earthquake — **seis·mi·cal·ly** \-mi-k(ə-)lē\ *adv* — **seis·mic·i·ty** \sīz-'mi-sə-tē, sīs-\ *n*

**seis·mo·gram** \'sīz-mə-,gram, 'sīs-\ *n* : the record of an earth tremor made by a seismograph

**seis·mo·graph** \-,graf\ *n* : an apparatus to measure and record seismic vibrations — **seis·mo·graph·ic** \,sīz-mə-'gra-fik, ,sīs-\ *adj* — **seis·mog·ra·phy** \sīz-'mä-grə-fē, sīs-\ *n*

**seis·mol·o·gy** \sīz-'mä-lə-jē, sīs-\ *n* : a science that deals with earthquakes — **seis·mo·log·i·cal** \,sīz-mə-'lä-ji-kəl, ,sīs-\ *adj* — **seis·mol·o·gist** \sīz-'mä-lə-jist, sīs-\ *n*

**seis·mom·e·ter** \sīz-'mä-mə-tər, sīs-\ *n*

: a seismograph measuring the actual movement of the ground

**seize** \'sēz\ *vb* **seized; seiz·ing** 1 : to lay hold of or take possession of by force 2 : ARREST 3 : UNDERSTAND 4 : to attack or overwhelm physically : AFFLICT ⟨*seized* by panic⟩ ♦ *Synonyms* TAKE, GRASP, CLUTCH, SNATCH, GRAB

**sei·zure** \'sē-zhər\ *n* 1 : the act of seizing : the state of being seized 2 : a sudden attack (as of disease)

**sel** *abbr* select; selected; selection

**sel·dom** \'sel-dəm\ *adv* : not often : RARELY

¹**se·lect** \sə-'lekt\ *adj* 1 : CHOSEN, PICKED; *also* : CHOICE 2 : judicious or restrictive in choice : DISCRIMINATING

²**select** *vb* : to choose from a number or group : pick out

**se·lec·tion** \sə-'lek-shən\ *n* 1 : the act or process of selecting 2 : something selected : CHOICE 3 : a natural or artificial process that tends to favor the survival and reproduction of individuals with certain traits but not those with others

**se·lec·tive** \sə-'lek-tiv\ *adj* : of or relating to selection : selecting or tending to select ⟨~ shoppers⟩

**selective service** *n* : a system for calling men up for military service : DRAFT

**se·lect·man** \si-'lekt-,man, -mən\ *n* : one of a board of officials elected in towns of most New England states to administer town affairs

**se·le·ni·um** \sə-'lē-nē-əm\ *n* : a photosensitive chemical element

**self** \'self\ *n, pl* **selves** \'selvz\ 1 : the essential person distinct from all other persons in identity 2 : a particular side of a person's character 3 : personal interest : SELFISHNESS ⟨put service before ~⟩

**self-** *comb form* 1 : oneself : itself 2 : of oneself or itself 3 : by oneself or itself; *also* : automatic 4 : to, for, or toward oneself

**self–cen·tered** \'self-'sen-tərd\ *adj* : concerned only with one's own self — **self–cen·tered·ness** *n*

**self–com·posed** \,self-kəm-'pōzd\ *adj* : having control over one's emotions

**self–con·scious** \'self-'kän-chəs\ *adj* : uncomfortably conscious of oneself as an object of observation by others — **self–con·scious·ly** *adv* — **self–con·scious·ness** *n*

**self–con·tained** \,self-kən-'tānd\ *adj* 1 : complete in itself 2 : showing self-control; *also* : reserved in manner

| | | | |
|---|---|---|---|
| self–abasement | self–aggrandizing | self–cleaning | self–contempt |
| self–absorbed | self–analysis | self–closing | self–contradiction |
| self–absorption | self–anointed | self–complacent | self–contradictory |
| self–acceptance | self–appointed | self–conceit | self–control |
| self–accusation | self–appraisal | self–concern | self–correcting |
| self–acting | self–asserting | self–condemned | self–created |
| self–addressed | self–assertion | self–confessed | self–criticism |
| self–adjusting | self–assertive | self–confidence | self–cultivation |
| self–administer | self–assurance | self–confident | self–deceit |
| self–advancement | self–assured | self–congratulation | self–deception |
| self–aggrandize-ment | self–awareness | self–congratulatory | self–defeating |
| | self–betrayal | self–constituted | |

**self–de·fense** \'self-di-'fens\ *n* **1** : a plea of justification for the use of force or for homicide **2** : the act of defending oneself, one's property, or a close relative

**self–ef·fac·ing** \-ə-'fā-siŋ\ *adj* : RETIRING, SHY ⟨is quiet and ∼⟩

**self–ev·i·dent** \'self-'e-və-dənt\ *adj* : evident without proof or reasoning

**self–fer·til·i·za·tion** \,self-,fər-tə-lə-'zā-shən\ *n* : fertilization of a plant or animal by its own pollen or sperm

**self–ful·fill·ing** \,self-fül-'fi-liŋ\ *adj* : becoming real or true by virtue of having been predicted or expected ⟨a ∼ prophecy⟩

**self–help** \'self-'help\ *n* : the process of bettering oneself or coping with one's problems without the aid of others — **self–help** *adj*

**self·ish** \'sel-fish\ *adj* : concerned with one's own welfare excessively or without regard for others — **self·ish·ly** *adv* — **self·ish·ness** *n*

**self·less** \'self-ləs\ *adj* : UNSELFISH ⟨∼ dedication⟩ — **self·less·ness** *n*

**self–made** \'self-'mād\ *adj* : having achieved success or prominence by one's own efforts ⟨a ∼ man⟩

**self–pol·li·na·tion** \,self-,pä-lə-'nā-shən\ *n* : pollination of a flower by its own pollen or sometimes by pollen from another flower on the same plant

**self–reg·u·lat·ing** \'self-'re-gyə-,lā-tiŋ\ *adj* : AUTOMATIC

**self–righ·teous** \-'rī-chəs\ *adj* : strongly convinced of one's own righteousness — **self–righ·teous·ly** *adv*

**self·same** \'self-,sām\ *adj* : precisely the same : IDENTICAL

**self–seal·ing** \'self-'sē-liŋ\ *adj* : capable of sealing itself (as after puncture)

**self–seek·ing** \'self-'sē-kiŋ\ *adj* : seeking only to further one's own interests — **self–seeking** *n*

**self–start·er** \-'stär-tər\ *n* : a person who has initiative

**self–will** \'self-'wil\ *n* : OBSTINACY

**sell** \'sel\ *vb* **sold** \'sōld\; **sell·ing** **1** : to transfer (property) in return for money or something else of value **2** : to deal in as a business **3** : to be sold ⟨cars are ∼ing well⟩ — **sell·er** *n*

**sell out** *vb* **1** : to dispose of entirely by sale; *esp* : to sell one's business **2** : BETRAY — **sell·out** \'sel-,aút\ *n*

**selt·zer** \'selt-sər\ *n* [modif. of G *Selterser (Wasser)* water of Selters, fr. Nieder *Selters,* Germany] : artificially carbonated water

**sel·vage** *or* **sel·vedge** \'sel-vij\ *n* : the edge of a woven fabric so formed as to prevent raveling

**selves** *pl of* SELF

**sem** *abbr* **1** semicolon **2** seminar **3** seminary

**se·man·tic** \si-'man-tik\ *also* **se·man·ti·cal** \-ti-kəl\ *adj* : of or relating to meaning in language ⟨∼ change⟩

**se·man·tics** \si-'man-tiks\ *n sing or pl* : the study of meanings in language

**sema·phore** \'se-mə-,fór\ *n* **1** : a visual signaling apparatus with movable arms **2** : signaling by hand-held flags

**sem·blance** \'sem-bləns\ *n* **1** : outward appearance **2** : IMAGE, LIKENESS

**se·men** \'sē-mən\ *n* [NL, fr. L, seed] : a sticky whitish fluid of the male reproductive tract that contains the sperm

**se·mes·ter** \sə-'mes-tər\ *n* [G, fr. L *semestris* half-yearly, fr. *sex* six + *mensis* month] **1** : half a year **2** : one of the two terms into which many colleges divide the school year

**semi** \'se-,mī\ *n, pl* **sem·is** : SEMITRAILER

**semi–** \'se-mi, -,mī\ *prefix* **1** : precisely half of **2** : half in quantity or value; *also* : half of or occurring halfway through a specified period **3** : partly : incompletely **4** : partial : incomplete **5** : having some of the characteristics of

**semi·au·to·mat·ic** \,se-mē-,ó-tə-'ma-tik\ *adj, of a firearm* : able to fire repeatedly

| | | | |
|---|---|---|---|
| self–definition | self–explaining | self–limiting | self–renewing |
| self–delusion | self–explanatory | self–love | self–reproach |
| self–denial | self–expression | self–lubricating | self–respect |
| self–denying | self–forgetful | self–luminous | self–respecting |
| self–deprecating | self–giving | self–operating | self–restraint |
| self–deprecation | self–governing | self–perception | self–revelation |
| self–depreciation | self–government | self–perpetuating | self–rule |
| self–described | self–hate | self–pity | self–sacrifice |
| self–despair | self–hypnosis | self–portrait | self–sacrificing |
| self–destruct | self–identity | self–possessed | self–satisfaction |
| self–destruction | self–image | self–possession | self–satisfied |
| self–destructive | self–importance | self–preservation | self–service |
| self–determination | self–important | self–proclaimed | self–serving |
| self–directed | self–imposed | self–professed | self–starting |
| self–discipline | self–improvement | self–promotion | self–styled |
| self–distrust | self–incrimination | self–propelled | self–sufficiency |
| self–doubt | self–induced | self–propelling | self–sufficient |
| self–educated | self–indulgence | self–protection | self–supporting |
| self–employed | self–indulgent | self–realization | self–sustaining |
| self–employment | self–inflicted | self–referential | self–taught |
| self–enhancement | self–instruction | self–regard | self–torment |
| self–esteem | self–interest | self–reliance | self–winding |
| self–examination | self–knowledge | self–reliant | self–worth |

| | |
|---|---|
| semiannual | semiarid |

but requiring release and another press of the trigger for each successive shot

**semi·co·lon** \'se-mi-ˌkō-lən\ *n* : a punctuation mark ; used esp. to separate major sentence elements

**semi·con·duc·tor** \ˌse-mi-kən-'dək-tər\ *n* : a substance whose electrical conductivity is between that of a conductor and an insulator — **semi·con·duct·ing** *adj*

¹**semi·fi·nal** \ˌse-mi-'fī-nᵊl\ *adj* : being next to the last in an elimination tournament

²**semi·fi·nal** \ˌse-mi-ˌfī-nᵊl\ *n* : a semifinal round or match — **semi·fi·nal·ist** \-ist\ *n*

**semi·lu·nar** \-'lü-nər\ *adj* : LUNATE

**semi·nal** \'se-mə-nᵊl\ *adj* **1** : of, relating to, or consisting of seed or semen **2** : containing or contributing the seeds of later development : CREATIVE, ORIGINAL — **semi·nal·ly** *adv*

**sem·i·nar** \'se-mə-ˌnär\ *n* **1** : a course of study pursued by a group of advanced students doing original research under a professor **2** : CONFERENCE

**sem·i·nary** \'se-mə-ˌner-ē\ *n, pl* **-nar·ies** [ME, seedbed, nursery, fr. L *seminarium*, fr. *semen* seed] : an educational institution; *esp* : one that gives theological training — **sem·i·nar·i·an** \ˌse-mə-'ner-ē-ən\ *n*

**Sem·i·nole** \'se-mə-ˌnōl\ *n, pl* **Seminoles** *or* **Seminole** : a member of an American Indian people of Florida

**semi·per·me·able** \ˌse-mi-'pər-mē-ə-bəl\ *adj* : partially but not freely or wholly permeable; *esp* : permeable to some usu. small molecules but not to other usu. larger particles ⟨a ~ membrane⟩ — **semi·per·me·abil·i·ty** \-ˌpər-mē-ə-'bi-lə-tē\ *n*

**Sem·ite** \'se-ˌmīt\ *n* : a member of any of a group of peoples (as the Hebrews or Arabs) of southwestern Asia — **Se·mit·ic** \sə-'mi-tik\ *adj*

**semi·trail·er** \'se-mi-ˌtrā-lər, -ˌmī-\ *n* : a freight trailer that when attached is supported at its forward end by the truck tractor; *also* : a semitrailer with attached tractor

**sem·o·li·na** \ˌse-mə-'lē-nə\ *n* : the purified hard grains produced from the milling of wheat and used esp. for pasta

**sempstress** *var of* SEAMSTRESS

¹**sen** \'sen\ *n, pl* **sen** — see *yen* at MONEY table

²**sen** *n, pl* **sen** — see *dollar, ringgit, rupiah* at MONEY table

³**sen** *n, pl* **sen** — see *riel* at MONEY table

⁴**sen** *abbr* **1** senate; senator **2** senior

**sen·ate** \'se-nət\ *n* : the second of two chambers of a legislature

**sen·a·tor** \'se-nə-tər\ *n* : a member of a senate — **sen·a·to·ri·al** \ˌse-nə-'tȯr-ē-əl\ *adj*

**send** \'send\ *vb* **sent** \'sent\; **send·ing** **1** : to cause to go **2** : EMIT **3** : to propel or drive esp. with force **4** : to put or bring into a certain condition ⟨*sent* them into a rage⟩ **5** : to convey or transmit by an agent — **send·er** *n*

**send-off** \'send-ˌȯf\ *n* : a demonstration of goodwill and enthusiasm at the start of a new venture (as a trip)

**send-up** \'send-ˌəp\ *n* : PARODY

**se·ne** \'sā-(ˌ)nā\ *n, pl* **sene** — see *tala* at MONEY table

**Sen·e·ca** \'se-ni-kə\ *n, pl* **Seneca** *or* **Senecas** : a member of an American Indian people of western New York

**Sen·e·ga·lese** \ˌse-ni-gə-'lēz, -'lēs\ *n, pl* **Senegalese** : a native or inhabitant of Senegal — **Senegalese** *adj*

**se·nes·cence** \si-'ne-sᵊns\ *n* : the state of being old; *also* : the process of becoming old — **se·nes·cent** \-ᵊnt\ *adj*

**se·nile** \'sē-ˌnī(-ə)l, 'se-\ *adj* : OLD, AGED; *esp* : exhibiting a loss of cognitive abilities associated with old age — **se·nil·i·ty** \si-'ni-lə-tē\ *n*

¹**se·nior** \'sē-nyər\ *n* **1** : a person older or of higher rank than another **2** : a member of the graduating class of a high school or college

²**senior** *adj* [ME, fr. L, older, elder, compar. of *senex* old] **1** : ELDER **2** : more advanced in dignity or rank **3** : belonging to the final year of a school or college course

**senior airman** *n* : an enlisted person in the air force ranking next below a staff sergeant

**senior chief petty officer** *n* : a petty officer in the navy or coast guard ranking next below a master chief petty officer

**senior citizen** *n* : an elderly person; *esp* : one who has retired

**senior high school** *n* : a school usu. including grades 10 to 12

**se·nior·i·ty** \sēn-'yȯr-ə-tē\ *n* **1** : the quality or state of being senior **2** : a privileged status owing to length of continuous service

**senior master sergeant** *n* : a noncommissioned officer in the air force ranking next below a chief master sergeant

**sen·i·ti** \'se-nə-tē\ *n, pl* **seniti** — see *pa'anga* at MONEY table

**sen·na** \'se-nə\ *n* **1** : CASSIA 2; *esp* : one used medicinally **2** : the dried leaflets or pods of a cassia used as a purgative

**sen·sa·tion** \sen-'sā-shən\ *n* **1** : awareness (as of noise or heat) or a mental process (as seeing or hearing) due to stimulation of a sense organ; *also* : an indefinite bodily feeling **2** : a condition of excitement; *also* : the thing that causes this condition

| | | | |
|---|---|---|---|
| semicentennial | semiformal | semipermanent | semiskilled |
| semicircle | semigloss | semipolitical | semisoft |
| semicircular | semi–independent | semiprecious | semisolid |
| semicivilized | semiliquid | semiprivate | semisweet |
| semiclassical | semiliterate | semiprofessional | semitransparent |
| semiconscious | semimonthly | semireligious | semiweekly |
| semidarkness | semiofficial | semiretired | semiyearly |
| semidivine | | | |

**sen·sa·tion·al** \-shə-nəl\ adj 1 : of or relating to sensation or the senses 2 : arousing an intense and usu. superficial interest or emotional reaction — **sen·sa·tion·al·ly** adv

**sen·sa·tion·al·ise** Brit var of SENSATIONALIZE

**sen·sa·tion·al·ism** \-nə-ˌli-zəm\ n : the use or effect of sensational subject matter or treatment — **sen·sa·tion·al·ist** \-nə-list\ adj or n — **sen·sa·tion·al·is·tic** \-ˌsā-shə-nə-ˈlis-tik\ adj

**sen·sa·tion·al·ize** \-nə-ˌlīz\ vb -ized; -izing : to present in a sensational manner

¹**sense** \ˈsens\ n 1 : semantic content : MEANING 2 : the faculty of perceiving by means of sense organs; also : a bodily function or mechanism (as sight, hearing, or smell) involving the action and effect of a stimulus on a sense organ 3 : SENSATION, AWARENESS 4 : INTELLIGENCE, JUDGMENT 5 : OPINION ⟨the ~ of the meeting⟩ — **sense·less** adj — **sense·less·ly** adv — **sense·less·ness** n

²**sense** vb **sensed; sens·ing** 1 : to be or become aware of ⟨~ danger⟩; also : to perceive by the senses 2 : to detect (as radiation) automatically

**sense organ** n : a bodily structure (as an eye or ear) that receives stimuli (as heat or light) which excite neurons to send information to the brain

**sen·si·bil·i·ty** \ˌsen-sə-ˈbi-lə-tē\ n, pl -ties : delicacy of feeling : SENSITIVITY

**sen·si·ble** \ˈsen-sə-bəl\ adj 1 : capable of being perceived by the senses or the mind; also : capable of receiving sense impressions 2 : AWARE, CONSCIOUS 3 : REASONABLE, RATIONAL ⟨a ~ decision⟩ — **sen·si·bly** \-blē\ adv

**sen·si·tive** \ˈsen-sə-tiv\ adj 1 : subject to excitation by or responsive to stimuli 2 : having power of feeling 3 : of such a nature as to be easily affected 4 : TOUCHY ⟨a ~ issue⟩ — **sen·si·tive·ly** adv — **sen·si·tive·ness** n — **sen·si·tiv·i·ty** \ˌsen-sə-ˈti-və-tē\ n

**sensitive plant** n : any of several mimosas with leaves that fold or droop when touched

**sen·si·tize** \ˈsen-sə-ˌtīz\ vb -tized; -tiz·ing : to make or become sensitive or hypersensitive — **sen·si·ti·za·tion** \ˌsen-sə-tə-ˈzā-shən\ n

**sen·sor** \ˈsen-ˌsȯr, -sər\ n : a device that responds to a physical stimulus

**sen·so·ry** \ˈsen-sə-rē\ adj 1 : of or relating to sensation or the senses ⟨~ perception⟩ 2 : AFFERENT

**sen·su·al** \ˈsen-shə-wəl\ adj 1 : relating to gratification of the senses 2 : devoted to the pleasures of the senses — **sen·su·al·ist** n — **sen·su·al·i·ty** \ˌsen-shə-ˈwa-lə-tē\ n — **sen·su·al·ly** adv

**sen·su·ous** \ˈsen-shə-wəs\ adj 1 : relating to the senses or to things that can be perceived by the senses 2 : VOLUPTUOUS ⟨~ lips⟩ — **sen·su·ous·ly** adv — **sen·su·ous·ness** n

¹**sent** past and past part of SEND

²**sent** \ˈsent\ n, pl **sen·ti** \ˈsen-tē\ : a monetary unit equal to ¹⁄₁₀₀ kroon formerly used in Estonia

**sen·te** \ˈsen-tē\ n, pl **li·cen·te** or **li·sen·te** \li-ˈsen-tē\ — see loti at MONEY table

¹**sen·tence** \ˈsen-təns, -tən(t)s\ n [ME, fr. AF, fr. L sententia, lit., feeling, opinion, fr. sentire to feel] 1 : the punishment set by a court 2 : a grammatically self-contained speech unit that expresses an assertion, a question, a command, a wish, or an exclamation

²**sentence** vb **sen·tenced; sen·tenc·ing** : to impose a sentence on

**sen·ten·tious** \sen-ˈten-chəs\ adj : using wise sayings or proverbs; also : using pompous language — **sen·ten·tious·ly** adv — **sen·ten·tious·ness** n

**sen·tient** \ˈsen-chənt, -chē-ənt\ adj : capable of feeling : having perception

**sen·ti·ment** \ˈsen-tə-mənt\ n 1 : FEELING; also : thought and judgment influenced by feeling : emotional attitude 2 : OPINION, NOTION

**sen·ti·men·tal** \ˌsen-tə-ˈmen-tᵊl\ adj 1 : influenced by tender feelings 2 : affecting the emotions ◆ Synonyms BATHETIC, MAUDLIN, MAWKISH, MUSHY — **sen·ti·men·tal·ism** n — **sen·ti·men·tal·ist** n — **sen·ti·men·tal·i·ty** \-ˌmen-ˈta-lə-tē, -mən-\ n — **sen·ti·men·tal·ly** adv

**sen·ti·men·tal·ise** Brit var of SENTIMENTALIZE

**sen·ti·men·tal·ize** \-ˈmen-tə-ˌlīz\ vb -ized; -iz·ing 1 : to indulge in sentiment 2 : to look upon or imbue with sentiment ⟨~s the past⟩ — **sen·ti·men·tal·i·za·tion** \-ˌmen-tə-lə-ˈzā-shən\ n

**sen·ti·mo** \sen-ˈtē-(ˌ)mō\ n, pl -mos — see peso at MONEY table

**sen·ti·nel** \ˈsen-tᵊn-əl\ n [MF sentinelle, fr. It sentinella, fr. sentina vigilance, fr. sentire to perceive, fr. L] : SENTRY

**sen·try** \ˈsen-trē\ n, pl **sentries** : a guard at a point of passage

**sep** abbr separate, separated

**Sep** abbr September

**SEP** abbr simplified employee pension

**se·pal** \ˈsē-pəl, ˈse-\ n : one of the modified leaves comprising a flower calyx

**sep·a·ra·ble** \ˈse-pə-rə-bəl\ adj : capable of being separated — **sep·a·ra·bil·i·ty** \ˌse-pə-rə-ˈbi-lə-tē\

¹**sep·a·rate** \ˈse-pə-ˌrāt\ vb -rat·ed; -rat·ing 1 : to set or keep apart : DISCONNECT, SEVER 2 : to keep apart by something intervening 3 : to cease to be together : PART ⟨the couple decided to ~⟩

²**sep·a·rate** \ˈse-prət, ˈse-pə-rət\ adj 1 : not connected 2 : divided from each other 3 : SINGLE, PARTICULAR ⟨the ~ pieces of the puzzle⟩ — **sep·a·rate·ly** adv

³**sep·a·rate** \ˈse-prət, -pə-rət\ n : an article of dress designed to be worn interchangeably with others to form various combinations

**sep·a·ra·tion** \ˌse-pə-ˈrā-shən\ n 1 : the act or process of separating : the state of being separated 2 : a point, line, means, or area of division 3 : a formal separating of a married couple by agreement but without divorce

**sep·a·rat·ist** \ˈse-prə-tist, ˈse-pə-ˌrā-\ n

: an advocate of separation (as from a political body) — **sep·a·rat·ism** \'se-prə-ˌti-zəm\ *n*

**sep·a·ra·tive** \'se-pə-ˌrā-tiv, 'se-prə-tiv\ *adj* : tending toward, causing, or expressing separation ⟨∼ influences⟩

**sep·a·ra·tor** \'se-pə-ˌrā-tər\ *n* : one that separates; *esp* : a device for separating cream from milk

**se·pia** \'sē-pē-ə\ *n* : a brownish gray to dark brown color

**sep·sis** \'sep-səs\ *n, pl* **sep·ses** \'sep-ˌsēz\ : a toxic condition due to spread of bacteria or their toxic products in the body

**Sept** *abbr* September

**Sep·tem·ber** \sep-'tem-bər\ *n* [ME *Septembre*, fr. AF & OE, both fr. L *September* (seventh month), fr. *septem* seven] : the 9th month of the year having 30 days

**sep·tic** \'sep-tik\ *adj* 1 : PUTREFACTIVE 2 : relating to or involving sepsis 3 : of, relating to, or used for sewage treatment and disposal

**sep·ti·ce·mia** \ˌsep-tə-'sē-mē-ə\ *n* : BLOOD POISONING

**septic tank** *n* : a tank in which sewage is disintegrated by bacteria

**sep·tu·a·ge·nar·i·an** \ˌsep-ˌtü-ə-jə-'ner-ē-ən, -ˌtyü-\ *n* : a person whose age is in the seventies — **septuagenarian** *adj*

**Sep·tu·a·gint** \sep-'tü-ə-jənt, -'tyü-\ *n* : a Greek version of the Old Testament prepared in the 3d and 2d centuries B.C. by Jewish scholars

**sep·tum** \'sep-təm\ *n, pl* **sep·ta** \-tə\ : a dividing wall or membrane between bodily spaces or masses of soft tissue

**se·pul·chral** \sə-'pəl-krəl\ *adj* 1 : relating to burial or the grave 2 : GLOOMY

¹**sep·ul·chre** *or* **sep·ul·cher** \'se-pəl-kər\ *n* : a burial vault : TOMB

²**sepulchre** *or* **sepulcher** *vb* **-chred** *or* **-chered; -chring** *or* **-chering** : BURY, ENTOMB

**sep·ul·ture** \'se-pəl-ˌchùr\ *n* 1 : BURIAL 2 : SEPULCHRE

**se·quel** \'sē-kwəl\ *n* 1 : logical consequence 2 : a literary or cinematic work continuing a story begun in a preceding one

¹**se·quence** \'sē-kwəns\ *n* 1 : SERIES 2 : chronological order of events 3 : RESULT, SEQUEL ♦ *Synonyms* SUCCESSION, CHAIN, PROGRESSION, TRAIN — **se·quen·tial** \si-'kwen-chəl\ *adj* — **se·quen·tial·ly** *adv*

²**sequence** *vb* **se·quenced; se·quenc·ing** 1 : to arrange in a sequence 2 : to determine the sequence of chemical constituents in ⟨∼ DNA⟩

**se·quent** \'sē-kwənt\ *adj* 1 : SUCCEEDING, CONSECUTIVE 2 : RESULTANT

**se·ques·ter** \si-'kwes-tər\ *vb* : to set apart : SEGREGATE ⟨∼ a jury⟩

**se·ques·trate** \'sē-kwəs-ˌtrāt, si-'kwes-\ *vb* **-trat·ed; -trat·ing** : SEQUESTER — **se·ques·tra·tion** \ˌsē-kwəs-'trā-shən, ˌse-\ *n*

**se·quin** \'sē-kwən\ *n* 1 : an old gold coin of Turkey and Italy 2 : a small metal or plastic plate used for ornamentation esp.

on clothing — **se·quined** *or* **se·quinned** \-kwənd\ *adj*

**se·quoia** \si-'kwòi-ə\ *n* : either of two huge California coniferous trees

**ser** *abbr* 1 serial 2 series 3 service

**sera** *pl of* SERUM

**se·ra·glio** \sə-'ral-yō\ *n, pl* **-glios** [It *seraglio*] : HAREM

**se·ra·pe** \sə-'rä-pē\ *n* : a colorful woolen shawl worn over the shoulders esp. by Mexican men

**ser·aph** \'ser-əf\ *n, pl* **ser·a·phim** \-ə-ˌfim, -ˌfēm\ *or* **seraphs** : one of the 6-winged angels standing in the presence of God

**ser·a·phim** \'ser-ə-ˌfim, -ˌfēm\ *n pl* 1 : the highest order of angels 2 *sing, pl* **seraphim** : SERAPH — **se·raph·ic** \sə-'ra-fik\ *adj*

**Ser·bi·an** \'sər-bē-ən\ *n* 1 : SERB 2 : a south Slavic language spoken by the Serbian people — **Serbian** *adj*

**Ser·bo–Cro·a·tian** \ˌsər-(ˌ)bō-krō-'ā-shən\ *n* : the Serbian and Croatian languages together with the Slavic speech of Bosnia, Herzegovina, and Montenegro taken as a single language with regional variants

**sere** \'sir\ *adj* : DRY, WITHERED

¹**ser·e·nade** \ˌser-ə-'nād\ *n* [F, fr. It *serenata*, fr. *sereno* clear, calm (of weather) fr. L *serenus*] : music sung or played as a compliment esp. outdoors at night for a woman being courted

²**serenade** *vb* **-nad·ed; -nad·ing** : to entertain with or perform a serenade

**ser·en·dip·i·ty** \ˌser-ən-'di-pə-tē\ *n* [fr. its possession by the heroes of the Persian fairy tale *The Three Princes of Serendip*] : the gift of finding valuable or agreeable things not sought for — **ser·en·dip·i·tous** \-təs\ *adj* — **ser·en·dip·i·tous·ly** *adv*

**se·rene** \sə-'rēn\ *adj* 1 : CLEAR ⟨∼ skies⟩ 2 : QUIET, CALM ♦ *Synonyms* TRANQUIL, PEACEFUL, PLACID — **se·rene·ly** *adv* — **se·ren·i·ty** \sə-'re-nə-tē\ *n*

**serf** \'sərf\ *n* : a member of a servile class bound to the land and subject to the will of the landowner — **serf·dom** \-dəm\ *n*

**serge** \'sərj\ *n* : a twilled woolen cloth

**ser·geant** \'sär-jənt\ *n* [ME, servant, attendant, sergeant, fr. AF *sergant, serjant,* fr. L *servient-, serviens,* prp. of *servire* to serve] 1 : a noncommissioned officer (as in the army) ranking next below a staff sergeant 2 : an officer in a police force

**sergeant at arms** : an officer of an organization who preserves order and executes commands

**sergeant first class** *n* : a noncommissioned officer in the army ranking next below a master sergeant

**sergeant major** *n, pl* **sergeants major** *or* **sergeant majors** 1 : a noncommissioned officer in the army or marine corps serving as chief administrative assistant in a headquarters 2 : a noncommissioned officer in the marine corps ranking above a first sergeant

¹**se·ri·al** \'sir-ē-əl\ *adj* 1 : appearing in parts that follow regularly ⟨a ∼ story⟩ 2

: performing a series of similar acts over a period of time ⟨a ∼ killer⟩; *also* : occurring in such a series — **se·ri·al·ly** *adv*

²**serial** *n* : a serial story or other writing — **se·ri·al·ist** \-ə-list\ *n*

**se·ries** \'sir-ēz\ *n, pl* **series** : a number of things or events arranged in order and connected by being alike in some way ◆ **Synonyms** SUCCESSION, PROGRESSION, SEQUENCE, CHAIN, TRAIN, STRING

**seri·graph** \'ser-ə-ˌgraf\ *n* : an original silk-screen print — **se·rig·ra·pher** \sə-'ri-grə-fər\ *n* — **se·rig·ra·phy** \-fē\ *n*

**se·ri·ous** \'sir-ē-əs\ *adj* **1** : thoughtful or subdued in appearance or manner : SOBER **2** : requiring much thought or work **3** : EARNEST, DEVOTED **4** : DANGEROUS, HARMFUL ⟨a ∼ illness⟩ **5** : excessive or impressive in quantity or degree ⟨making ∼ money⟩ ◆ **Synonyms** GRAVE, SEDATE, STAID — **se·ri·ous·ly** *adv* — **se·ri·ous·ness** *n*

**ser·mon** \'sər-mən\ *n* [ME, fr. AF *sermun*, fr. ML *sermon, sermo*, fr. L, speech, conversation, fr. *serere* to link together] **1** : a religious discourse esp. as part of a worship service **2** : a lecture on conduct or duty

**ser·mon·ize** \'sər-mə-ˌnīz\ *vb* **-ized; -iz·ing 1** : to compose or deliver a sermon **2** : to preach to or on at length

**se·rol·o·gy** \sə-'rä-lə-jē\ *n* : a science dealing with serums and esp. their reactions and properties — **se·ro·log·i·cal** \ˌsir-ə-'lä-ji-kəl\ *or* **se·ro·log·ic** \-jik\ *adj* — **se·ro·log·i·cal·ly** \-ji-k(ə-)lē\ *adv*

**se·ro·to·nin** \ˌsir-ə-'tō-nən, ˌser-\ *n* : a neurotransmitter that is a powerful vasoconstrictor

**se·rous** \'sir-əs\ *adj* : of, relating to, resembling, or producing serum; *esp* : of thin watery constitution

**ser·pent** \'sər-pənt\ *n* : SNAKE

¹**ser·pen·tine** \'sər-pən-ˌtēn, -ˌtīn\ *adj* **1** : SLY, CRAFTY **2** : WINDING, TURNING

²**ser·pen·tine** \-ˌtēn\ *n* : a dull-green mineral having a mottled appearance

**ser·rate** \'ser-ˌāt\ *adj* : having a saw-toothed edge ⟨a ∼ leaf⟩

**ser·ried** \'ser-ēd\ *adj* : crowded together

**se·rum** \'sir-əm\ *n, pl* **serums** *or* **se·ra** \-ə\ [L, whey, wheylike fluid] : the clear yellowish antibody-containing fluid that can be separated from blood when it clots; *also* : a preparation of animal serum containing specific antibodies and used to prevent or cure disease

**serv** *abbr* service

**ser·vant** \'sər-vənt\ *n* : one that serves others; *esp* : a person employed for domestic or personal work

¹**serve** \'sərv\ *vb* **served; serv·ing 1** : to work as a servant **2** : to render obedience and worship to (God) **3** : to comply with the commands or demands of **4** : to work through or perform a term of service (as in the navy) **5** : PUT IN ⟨*served* five years in jail⟩ **6** : to be of use : ANSWER ⟨pine boughs *served* for a bed⟩ **7** : BENEFIT **8** : to prove adequate or satisfactory for ⟨a pie that ∼s eight people⟩ **9** : to make ready and pass out ⟨∼ drinks⟩ **10** : to

furnish or supply with something ⟨one power company *serving* the whole state⟩ **11** : to wait on ⟨∼ a customer⟩ **12** : to treat or act toward in a specified way ⟨*served* as her maid⟩ **13** : to put the ball in play (as in tennis)

²**serve** *n* : the act of serving a ball (as in tennis)

**serv·er** \'sər-vər\ *n* **1** : one that serves **2** : a computer in a network that is used to provide services (as access to files) to other computers in the network

¹**ser·vice** \'sər-vəs\ *n* **1** : the occupation of a servant **2** : HELP, BENEFIT **3** : a meeting for worship; *also* : a form followed in worship or in a ceremony ⟨burial ∼⟩ **4** : the act, fact, or means of serving **5** : performance of official or professional duties **6** : SERVE **7** : a set of dishes or silverware **8** : a branch of public employment; *also* : the persons in it ⟨civil ∼⟩ **9** : military or naval duty

²**service** *vb* **ser·viced; ser·vic·ing** : to do maintenance or repair work on or for

**ser·vice·able** \'sər-və-sə-bəl\ *adj* : prepared for service : USEFUL, USABLE

**ser·vice·man** \'sər-vəs-ˌman, -mən\ *n* **1** : a man who is a member of the armed forces **2** : a man employed to repair or maintain equipment

**service mark** *n* : a mark or device used to identify a service (as transportation or insurance) offered to customers

**service station** *n* : GAS STATION

**ser·vice·wom·an** \'sər-vəs-ˌwu̇-mən\ *n* : a woman who is a member of the armed forces

**ser·vile** \'sər-vəl, -ˌvī(-ə)l\ *adj* **1** : befitting a slave or servant **2** : behaving like a slave : SUBMISSIVE — **ser·vile·ly** *adv* — **ser·vil·i·ty** \ˌsər-'vi-lə-tē\ *n*

**serv·ing** \'sər-viŋ\ *n* : HELPING

**ser·vi·tor** \'sər-və-tər\ *n* : a male servant

**ser·vi·tude** \'sər-və-ˌtüd, -ˌtyüd\ *n* : SLAVERY, BONDAGE

**ser·vo** \'sər-vō\ *n, pl* **servos 1** : SERVOMOTOR **2** : SERVOMECHANISM

**ser·vo·mech·a·nism** \'sər-vō-ˌmc-kə-ˌni-zəm\ *n* : a device for automatically correcting the performance of a mechanism

**ser·vo·mo·tor** \-ˌmō-tər\ *n* : a mechanism that supplements a primary control

**ses·a·me** \'se-sə-mē\ *n* : a widely cultivated annual herb of warm regions; *also* : its seeds that yield an edible oil (**sesame oil**) and are used in flavoring

**ses·qui·cen·ten·ni·al** \ˌses-kwi-sen-'te-nē-əl\ *n* [L *sesqui-* one and a half, half again] : a 150th anniversary or its celebration — **sesquicentennial** *adj*

**ses·qui·pe·da·lian** \ˌses-kwə-pə-'dāl-yən\ *adj* **1** : having many syllables : LONG **2** : using long words

**ses·sile** \'se-sī(-ə)l, -səl\ *adj* : permanently attached and not free to move about

**ses·sion** \'se-shən\ *n* **1** : a meeting or series of meetings of a body (as a court or legislature) for the transaction of business **2** : a meeting or period devoted to a particular activity

¹**set** \'set\ *vb* **set; set·ting 1** : to cause to sit **2** : PLACE **3** : ARRANGE, ADJUST **4**

: to cause to be or do   **5** : SETTLE, DE-
CREE   **6** : to fix in a frame   **7** : to fix at a
certain amount   **8** : WAGER, STAKE   **9** : to
make or become fast or rigid   **10** : to
adapt (as words) to something (as music)
**11** : to become fixed or firm or solid   **12**
: to be suitable : FIT   **13** : BROOD   **14** : to
have a certain direction   **15** : to pass below the horizon   **16** : to defeat in bridge
— **set about** : to begin to do — **set
forth** : to begin a trip — **set off 1** : to
start out on a course or a trip   **2** : to cause
to explode — **set out 1** : to begin a trip or
undertaking — **set sail** : to begin a voyage — **set upon** : to attack usu. with violence

²**set** *n* **1** : a setting or a being set   **2** : DI-
RECTION, COURSE; *also* : TENDENCY   **3**
: FORM, BUILD   **4** : the fit of something
(as a coat)   **5** : an artificial setting for the
scene of a play or motion picture   **6** : a
group of tennis games in which one side
wins at least six   **7** : a group of persons or
things of the same kind or having a common characteristic usu. classed together
**8** : a collection of things and esp. of
mathematical elements (as numbers or
points)   **9** : an electronic apparatus ⟨a
television ~⟩

³**set** *adj* **1** : DELIBERATE, INTENT   **2** : fixed
by authority or custom ⟨a ~ price⟩   **3**
: RIGID ⟨a ~ frown⟩   **4** : PERSISTENT

**set·back** \'set-ˌbak\ *n* : a temporary defeat : REVERSE

**set back** *vb* **1** : HINDER, DELAY; *also*
: REVERSE   **2** : COST

**set piece 1** : a composition (as in literature or music) executed in fixed or ideal
form often with brilliant effect   **2** : a
scene, depiction, speech, or event obviously designed to have an imposing effect

**set·screw** \'set-ˌskrü\ *n* : a screw screwed
through one part tightly upon or into another part to prevent relative movement

**set·tee** \se-'tē\ *n* : a bench or sofa with a
back and arms

**set·ter** \'se-tər\ *n* : a large long-coated
hunting dog

**set·ting** \'se-tin\ *n* **1** : the frame in which
a gem is set   **2** : the time, place, and circumstances in which something occurs
or develops; *also* : SCENERY   **3** : music
written for a text (as of a poem)   **4** : the
eggs that a fowl sits on for hatching at
one time

**set·tle** \'se-t⁰l\ *vb* **set·tled; set·tling** [ME
*settlen* to seat, bring to rest, come to rest,
fr. OE *setlan*, fr. *setl* seat]   **1** : to place so
as to stay   **2** : to establish in residence;
*also* : COLONIZE   **3** : to make compact   **4**
: QUIET, CALM   **5** : to establish or secure
permanently   **6** : to direct one's efforts   **7**
: to fix by agreement   **8** : to give legally   **9**
: ADJUST, ARRANGE   **10** : DECIDE, DE-
TERMINE   **11** : to make a final disposition
of ⟨~ an account⟩   **12** : to come to rest
**13** : to reach an agreement on   **14** : to
sink gradually to a lower level   **15** : to
become clear by depositing sediment —
**set·tler** *n*

**set·tle·ment** \'se-t⁰l-mənt\ *n* **1** : the act
or process of settling   **2** : BESTOWAL ⟨a

marriage ~⟩   **3** : payment or adjustment
of an account   **4** : COLONY   **5** : a small
village   **6** : an institution providing various community services esp. to large city
populations   **7** : adjustment of doubts and
differences

**set–to** \'set-ˌtü\ *n, pl* **set–tos** : FIGHT

**set·up** \'set-ˌəp\ *n* **1** : the manner or act
of arranging   **2** : glass, ice, and nonalcoholic beverage for mixing served to patrons who supply their own liquor   **3**
: something (as a plot) that has been constructed or contrived; *also* : FRAME-UP

**set up** *vb* **1** : to place in position; *also*
: ASSEMBLE   **2** : CAUSE   **3** : FOUND, ES-
TABLISH ⟨*set up* a school⟩   **4** : FRAME   **5**

**sev·en** \'se-vən\ *n* **1** : one more than six
**2** : the 7th in a set or series   **3** : something
having seven units — **seven** *adj or pron*
— **sev·enth** \-vənth\ *adj or n*

**sev·en·teen** \ˌse-vən-'tēn\ *n* : one more
than 16 — **seventeen** *adj or pron* —
**sev·en·teenth** \-'tēnth\ *adj or n*

**seventeen–year locust** *n* : a cicada of
the U.S. that has in the North a life of 17
years and in the South of 13 years of
which most is spent underground as a
nymph and only a few weeks as a winged
adult

**sev·en·ty** \'se-vən-tē\ *n, pl* **-ties** : seven
times 10 — **sev·en·ti·eth** \-tē-əth\ *adj or
n* — **seventy** *adj or pron*

**sev·er** \'se-vər\ *vb* **sev·ered; sev·er·ing**
: DIVIDE; *esp* : to separate by or as if by
cutting ⟨~ed ties with his brother⟩ —
**sev·er·ance** \'sev-rəns, 'se-və-\ *n*

**sev·er·al** \'sev-rəl, 'se-və-\ *adj* [ME, fr.
AF, fr. ML *separalis*, fr. L *separ* separate,
fr. *separare* to separate]   **1** : INDIVIDUAL,
DISTINCT ⟨federal union of the ~ states⟩
**2** : consisting of an indefinite number but
yet not very many ⟨ate ~ cookies⟩ —
**sev·er·al·ly** *adv*

**severance pay** *n* : extra pay given an employee on termination of employment

**se·vere** \sə-'vir\ *adj* **se·ver·er; -est** **1**
: marked by strictness or sternness : AUS-
TERE   **2** : strict in discipline   **3** : causing
distress and esp. physical discomfort or
pain ⟨~ weather⟩ ⟨a ~ wound⟩   **4**
: hard to endure ⟨~ trials⟩   **5** : SERIOUS
⟨~ depression⟩   ♦ **Synonyms** STERN,
ASCETIC, ASTRINGENT — **se·vere·ly** *adv*
— **se·ver·i·ty** \-'ver-ə-tē\ *n*

**sew** \'sō\ *vb* **sewed; sewn** \'sōn\ *or*
**sewed; sew·ing**   **1** : to unite or fasten by
stitches   **2** : to engage in sewing

**sew·age** \'sü-ij\ *n* : waste materials carried off by sewers

¹**sew·er** \'sō-ər\ *n* : one that sews

²**sew·er** \'sü-ər\ *n* : an artificial pipe or
channel to carry off waste matter

**sew·er·age** \'sü-ə-rij\ *n* **1** : a system of
sewers   **2** : SEWAGE

**sew·ing** *n* **1** : the activity of one who
sews   **2** : material that has been or is to be
sewed

**sex** \'seks\ *n* **1** : either of the two major
forms that occur in many living things
and are designated male or female according to their role in reproduction; *also*
: the qualities by which these sexes are

differentiated and which directly or indirectly function in reproduction involving two parents **2** : sexual activity or behavior; *also* : SEXUAL INTERCOURSE — **sexed** \'sekst\ *adj* — **sex·less** *adj*

**sex·a·ge·nar·i·an** \ˌsek-sə-jə-'ner-ē-ən\ *n* : a person whose age is in the sixties — **sexagenarian** *adj*

**sex appeal** *n* : personal appeal or physical attractiveness esp. for members of the opposite sex

**sex cell** *n* : an egg cell or sperm cell

**sex chromosome** *n* : one of usu. a pair of chromosomes that are usu. similar in one sex but different in the other sex and are concerned with the inheritance of sex

**sex hormone** *n* : a steroid hormone (as estrogen or testosterone) that is produced esp. by the gonads or adrenal cortex and chiefly affects the growth or function of the reproductive organs

**sex·ism** \'sek-ˌsi-zəm\ *n* : prejudice or discrimination based on sex; *esp* : discrimination against women — **sex·ist** \'sek-sist\ *adj or n*

**sex·ol·o·gy** \sek-'sä-lə-je\ *n* : the study of sex or of the interactions of the sexes — **sex·ol·o·gist** \-jist\ *n*

**sex·pot** \'seks-ˌpät\ *n* : a conspicuously sexy woman

**sex symbol** *n* : a usu. renowned person (as an entertainer) noted and admired for conspicuous attractiveness

**sex·tant** \'sek-stənt\ *n* [NL *sextant-*, *sextans* sixth part of a circle, fr. L, sixth part, fr. *sextus* sixth] : a navigational instrument for determining latitude

**sex·tet** \sek-'stet\ *n* **1** : a musical composition for six voices or instruments; *also* : the performers of such a composition **2** : a group or set of six

**sex·ton** \'sek-stən\ *n* : one who takes care of church property

**sex·u·al** \'sek-shə-wəl\ *adj* : of, relating to, or involving sex or the sexes ⟨a ∼ spore⟩ ⟨∼ relations⟩ — **sex·u·al·i·ty** \ˌsek-shə-'wa-lə-tē\ *n* — **sex·u·al·ly** \'sek-shə-wə-lē\ *adv*

**sexual intercourse** *n* **1** : intercourse between a male and a female in which the penis is inserted into the vagina **2** : intercourse between individuals involving genital contact other than insertion of the penis into the vagina

**sexually transmitted disease** *n* : a disease (as syphilis, gonorrhea, AIDS, or the genital form of herpes simplex) that is caused by a microorganism or virus usu. or often transmitted by direct sexual contact

**sexual relations** *n pl* : SEXUAL INTERCOURSE

**sexy** \'sek-sē\ *adj* **sex·i·er**; **-est** : sexually suggestive or stimulating : EROTIC — **sex·i·ly** \-sə-lē\ *adv* — **sex·i·ness** \-sē-nəs\ *n*

**SF** *abbr* **1** sacrifice fly **2** science fiction **3** square feet

**SFC** *abbr* sergeant first class

**¹SG** *abbr* **1** sergeant **2** solicitor general **3** surgeon general

**²SG** *symbol* seaborgium

**sgd** *abbr* signed

**Sgt** *abbr* sergeant

**Sgt Maj** *abbr* sergeant major

**sh** *abbr* share

**shab·by** \'sha-bē\ *adj* **shab·bi·er**; **-est** **1** : dressed in worn clothes **2** : threadbare and faded from wear **3** : DESPICABLE, MEAN; *also* : UNFAIR ⟨∼ treatment⟩ — **shab·bi·ly** \'sha-bə-lē\ *adv* — **shab·bi·ness** \-bē-nəs\ *n*

**shack** \'shak\ *n* : HUT, SHANTY

**¹shack·le** \'sha-kəl\ *n* **1** : something (as a manacle or fetter) that confines the legs or arms **2** : a check on free action made as if by fetters **3** : a device for making something fast or secure

**²shackle** *vb* **shack·led**; **shack·ling** : to bind or fasten with shackles

**shad** \'shad\ *n, pl* **shad** : any of several sea fishes related to the herrings that swim up rivers to spawn and include some important food fishes

**¹shade** \'shād\ *n* **1** : partial obscurity **2** : space sheltered from the light esp. of the sun **3** : PHANTOM **4** : something that shelters from or intercepts light or heat; *also, pl* : SUNGLASSES **5** : a dark color or a variety of a color **6** : a small difference

**²shade** *vb* **shad·ed**; **shad·ing** **1** : to shelter from light and heat **2** : DARKEN, OBSCURE **3** : to mark with degrees of light or color **4** : to show slight differences esp. in color or meaning

**shad·ing** *n* : the color and lines representing darkness or shadow in a drawing or painting

**¹shad·ow** \'sha-dō\ *n* **1** : partial darkness in a space from which light rays are cut off **2** : SHELTER **3** : shade cast upon a surface by something intercepting rays from a light ⟨the ∼ of a tree⟩ **4** : PHANTOM **5** : a shaded portion of a picture **6** : a small portion or degree : TRACE ⟨a ∼ of doubt⟩ **7** : a source of gloom or unhappiness — **shad·owy** *adj*

**²shadow** *vb* **1** : to cast a shadow on **2** : to represent faintly or vaguely **3** : to follow and watch closely : TRAIL

**shad·ow·box** \'sha-dō-ˌbäks\ *vb* : to box with an imaginary opponent esp. for training

**shady** \'shā-dē\ *adj* **shad·i·er**; **-est** **1** : affording shade **2** : of questionable honesty or reputation ⟨a ∼ politician⟩

**¹shaft** \'shaft\ *n, pl* **shafts 1** : the long handle of a spear or lance **2** : SPEAR, LANCE **3** *or pl* **shaves** \'shavz\ : POLE; *esp* : one of two poles between which a horse is hitched to pull a vehicle **4** : something (as a column) long and slender **5** : a bar to support a rotating piece or to transmit power by rotation **6** : an inclined opening in the ground (as for finding or mining ore) **7** : a vertical opening (as for an elevator) through the floors of a building **8** : harsh or unfair treatment — usu. used with *the*

**²shaft** *vb* **1** : to fit with a shaft **2** : to treat unfairly or harshly

**shag** \'shag\ *n* : a shaggy tangled mass or covering (as of wool) : long coarse or matted fiber, nap, or pile

**shag·gy** \'sha-gē\ *adj* **shag·gi·er; -est 1** : rough with or as if with long hair or wool **2** : tangled or rough in surface

**shah** \'shä, 'shȯ\ *n, often cap* : a sovereign of Iran

**Shak** *abbr* Shakespeare

¹**shake** \'shāk\ *vb* **shook** \'shu̇k\; **shak·en** \'shā-kən\; **shak·ing 1** : to move or cause to move jerkily or irregularly **2** : BRANDISH, WAVE ⟨*shaking* his fist⟩ **3** : to disturb emotionally ⟨*shaken* by her death⟩ **4** : WEAKEN ⟨*shook* his faith⟩ **5** : to bring or come into a certain position, condition, or arrangement by or as if by moving jerkily **6** : to clasp (hands) in greeting or as a sign of goodwill or agreement ◆ *Synonyms* TREMBLE, QUAKE, QUAVER, SHIVER, QUIVER — **shak·able** *or* **shake·able** \'shā-kə-bəl\ *adj*

²**shake** *n* **1** : the act or a result of shaking **2** : DEAL, TREATMENT ⟨a fair ∼⟩

**shake·down** \'shāk-ˌdau̇n\ *n* **1** : an improvised bed **2** : EXTORTION ⟨was a victim of a ∼⟩ **3** : a process or period of adjustment **4** : a test (as of a new ship or airplane) under operating conditions

**shake down** *vb* **1** : to take up temporary quarters **2** : to occupy a makeshift bed **3** : to become accustomed esp. to new surroundings or duties **4** : to settle down **5** : to give a shakedown test to **6** : to obtain money from in a deceitful or illegal manner **7** : to bring about a reduction of

**shak·er** \'shā-kər\ *n* **1** : one that shakes ⟨pepper ∼⟩ **2** *cap* : a member of a religious sect founded in England in 1747

**Shake·spear·ean** *or* **Shake·spear·ian** \shāk-'spir-ē-ən\ *adj* : of, relating to, or having the characteristics of Shakespeare or his writings

**shake-up** \'shāk-ˌəp\ *n* : an extensive often drastic reorganization

**shaky** \'shā-kē\ *adj* **shak·i·er; -est** : UNSOUND, WEAK ⟨a ∼ ladder⟩ — **shak·i·ly** \'shā-kə-lē\ *adv* — **shak·i·ness** \-kē-nəs\ *n*

**shale** \'shāl\ *n* : a finely layered rock formed from clay, mud, or silt

**shall** \shəl, 'shal\ *vb, past* **should** \shəd, 'shu̇d\ *pres sing & pl* **shall** — used as an auxiliary to express a command, what seems inevitable or likely in the future, simple futurity, or determination

**shal·lop** \'sha-ləp\ *n* : a light open boat

**shal·lot** \'sha-lät, 'sha-lət\ *n* [modif. of F *échalote*] **1** : a small clustered bulb that is used in seasoning and is produced by a perennial herb belonging to a subspecies of the onion; *also* : this herb **2** : GREEN ONION

¹**shal·low** \'sha-lō\ *adj* **1** : not deep **2** : not intellectually profound

²**shallow** *n* : a shallow place in a body of water — usu. used in pl.

¹**sham** \'sham\ *n* **1** : an ornamental covering for a pillow **2** : COUNTERFEIT, IMITATION **3** : a person who shams

²**sham** *vb* **shammed; sham·ming** : FEIGN, PRETEND — **sham·mer** *n*

³**sham** *adj* : not genuine : FALSE, FEIGNED

**sha·man** \'shä-mən, 'shā-\ *n* [ultim. fr. Evenki (a language of Siberia) *šamán*] : a priest or priestess who uses magic to cure the sick, to divine the hidden, and to control events

**sham·ble** \'sham-bəl\ *vb* **sham·bled; sham·bling** : to shuffle along — **shamble** *n*

**sham·bles** \'sham-bəlz\ *n* **1** : a scene of great slaughter **2** : a scene or state of great destruction or disorder; *also* : MESS

¹**shame** \'shām\ *n* **1** : a painful sense of having done something wrong, improper, or immodest **2** : DISGRACE, DISHONOR **3** : a cause of feeling shame **4** : something to be regretted ⟨it's a ∼ you'll miss the party⟩ — **shame·ful** \-fəl\ *adj* — **shame·ful·ly** *adv* — **shame·less** *adj* — **shame·less·ly** *adv*

²**shame** *vb* **shamed; sham·ing 1** : DISGRACE **2** : to make ashamed

**shame·faced** \'shām-ˌfāst\ *adj* : ASHAMED, ABASHED — **shame·faced·ly** \-ˌfā-səd-lē, -ˌfāst-lē\ *adv*

¹**sham·poo** \sham-'pü\ *vb* [Hindi *cāpo*, imper. of *cāpnā* to press, shampoo] : to wash (as the hair) with soap and water or with a special preparation; *also* : to clean (as a rug) similarly

²**shampoo** *n, pl* **shampoos 1** : the act or an instance of shampooing **2** : a preparation for use in shampooing

**sham·rock** \'sham-ˌräk\ *n* [Ir *seamróg*, dim. of *seamar* clover] : a plant of folk legend with leaves composed of three leaflets that is associated with St. Patrick and Ireland

**shang·hai** \shaŋ-'hī\ *vb* **shang·haied; shang·hai·ing** [*Shanghai*, China] : to force aboard a ship for service as a sailor; *also* : to trick or force into an undesirable position

**Shan·gri-la** \ˌshaŋ-gri-'lä\ *n* [*Shangri-La*, imaginary land depicted in the novel *Lost Horizon* (1933) by James Hilton] : a remote idyllic hideaway

**shank** \'shaŋk\ *n* **1** : the part of the leg between the knee and the human ankle or a corresponding part of a quadruped **2** : a cut of meat from the leg **3** : the narrow part of the sole of a shoe beneath the instep **4** : the part of a tool or instrument (as a key or anchor) connecting the functioning part with a part by which it is held or moved

**shan·tung** \shan-'təŋ\ *n* : a fabric in plain weave having a slightly irregular surface

**shan·ty** \'shan-tē\ *n, pl* **shanties** [prob. fr. CanF *chantier* lumber camp, hut, fr. F, builder's yard, ways, support for barrels, fr. OF, support, fr. L *cantherius* rafter, trellis] : a small roughly built shelter or dwelling

¹**shape** \'shāp\ *vb* **shaped; shap·ing 1** : to form esp. in a particular shape **2** : DESIGN **3** : ADAPT, ADJUST **4** : REGULATE ◆ *Synonyms* MAKE, FASHION, FABRICATE, MANUFACTURE, FRAME, MOLD

²**shape** *n* **1** : APPEARANCE ⟨the ∼ of an apple⟩ **2** : surface configuration : FORM **3** : bodily contour apart from the head

and face : FIGURE **4** : PHANTOM **5** : CONDITION ⟨was in fine ∼⟩ — **shaped** *adj*

**shape·less** \'shā-pləs\ *adj* **1** : having no definite shape **2** : not shapely — **shape·less·ly** *adv* — **shape·less·ness** *n*

**shape·ly** \'shā-plē\ *adj* **shape·li·er; -est** : having a pleasing shape ⟨a ∼ model⟩ — **shape·li·ness** *n*

**shape–shift·er** \'shāp-ˌshif-tər\ *n* : one that seems able to change form or identity at will

**chard** \'shärd\ *also* **shcrd** \'shərd\ *n* : a broken piece : FRAGMENT

**¹share** \'sher\ *n* : PLOWSHARE

**²share** *n* **1** : a portion belonging to one person or group **2** : any of the equal interests into which the capital stock of a corporation is divided

**³share** *vb* **shared; shar·ing 1** : APPORTION **2** : to use or enjoy with others **3** : PARTICIPATE — **shar·er** *n*

**share·crop·per** \-ˌkrä-pər\ *n* : a farmer who works another's land in return for a share of the crop — **share·crop** *vb*

**share·hold·er** \-ˌhōl-dər\ *n* : STOCKHOLDER

**share·ware** \'sher-ˌwer\ *n* : software available for usu. limited trial use at little or no cost but that can be upgraded for a fee

**¹shark** \'shärk\ *n* : any of various active, usu. predatory, and mostly large marine cartilaginous fishes

**²shark** *n* : a greedy crafty person

**shark·skin** \-ˌskin\ *n* **1** : the hide of a shark or leather made from it **2** : a fabric woven from strands of many fine threads and having a sleek appearance and silky feel

**¹sharp** \'shärp\ *adj* **1** : having a thin cutting edge or fine point : not dull or blunt **2** : COLD, NIPPING ⟨a ∼ wind⟩ **3** : keen in intellect, perception, or attention **4** : BRISK, ENERGETIC **5** : IRRITABLE ⟨a ∼ temper⟩ **6** : causing intense distress ⟨a ∼ pain⟩ **7** : HARSH, CUTTING ⟨a ∼ rebuke⟩ **8** : affecting the senses as if cutting or piercing ⟨a ∼ sound⟩ ⟨a ∼ smell⟩ **9** : not smooth or rounded ⟨∼ features⟩ **10** : involving an abrupt or extreme change ⟨a ∼ turn⟩ **11** : CLEAR, DISTINCT ⟨mountains in ∼ relief⟩; *also* : easy to perceive ⟨a ∼ contrast⟩ **12** : higher than the true pitch; *also* : raised by a half step **13** : STYLISH ⟨a ∼ dresser⟩

♦ *Synonyms* KEEN, ACUTE, QUICK-WITTED, PENETRATIVE — **sharp·ly** *adv* — **sharp·ness** *n*

**²sharp** *adv* **1** : in a sharp manner **2** : EXACTLY, PRECISELY ⟨left at 8 ∼⟩

**³sharp** *n* **1** : a sharp edge or point **2** : a character **#** which indicates that a specified note is to be raised by a half step; *also* : the resulting note **3** : SHARPER

**⁴sharp** *vb* : to raise in pitch by a half step

**shar–pei** \'shär-'pā, ˌshär-\ *n, pl* **sharpeis** *often cap S&P* [Chin (Guangdong dial.) *sà* sand + *péi* fur] : any of a Chinese breed of dogs that have loose wrinkled skin esp. when young

**sharp·en** \'shär-pən\ *vb* : to make or become sharp — **sharp·en·er** *n*

**sharp·er** \'shär-pər\ *n* : SWINDLER; *esp* : a cheating gambler

**sharp·ie** *or* **sharpy** \'shär-pē\ *n, pl* **sharp·ies 1** : SHARPER **2** : a person who is exceptionally alert

**sharp·shoot·er** \'shärp-ˌshü-tər\ *n* : a proficient marksman — **sharp·shoot·ing** *n*

**shat·ter** \'sha-tər\ *vb* : to dash or burst into fragments — **shat·ter·proof** \'sha-tər-ˌprüf\ *adj*

**¹shave** \'shāv\ *vb* **shaved; shaved** *or* **shav·en** \'shā-vən\; **shav·ing 1** : to slice in thin pieces **2** : to make bare or smooth by cutting the hair from **3** : to cut or pare off by the sliding movement of a razor **4** : to skim along or near the surface of

**²shave** *n* **1** : any of various tools for cutting thin slices **2** : an act or process of shaving

**shav·er** \'shā-vər\ *n* **1** : an electric razor **2** : BOY, YOUNGSTER

**shaves** *pl of* SHAFT

**shaving** *n* **1** : the act of one that shaves **2** : something shaved off

**shawl** \'shól\ *n* : a square or oblong piece of fabric used esp. by women as a loose covering for the head or shoulders

**Shaw·nee** \shó-'nē, shä-\ *n, pl* **Shawnee** *or* **Shawnees** : a member of an American Indian people orig. of the central Ohio valley; *also* : their language

**shd** *abbr* should

**she** \'shē\ *pron* : that female one ⟨who is ∼⟩; *also* : that one regarded as feminine ⟨∼'s a fine ship⟩

**sheaf** \'shēf\ *n, pl* **sheaves** \'shēvz\ **1** : a bundle of stalks and ears of grain **2** : a group of things bound together

**¹shear** \'shir\ *vb* **sheared; sheared** *or* **shorn** \'shórn\; **shear·ing 1** : to cut the hair or wool from : CLIP, TRIM **2** : to deprive by or as if by cutting ⟨a tyrant *shorn* of power⟩ **3** : to cut or break sharply

**²shear** *n* **1** : any of various cutting tools that consist of two blades fastened together so that the edges slide one by the other — usu. used in pl. **2** *chiefly Brit* : the act, an instance, or the result of shearing **3** : an action or stress caused by applied forces that causes two parts of a body to slide on each other

**shear·wa·ter** \'shir-ˌwó-tər, -ˌwä-\ *n* : any of several seabirds related to the petrels that often skim along waves in flight

**sheath** \'shēth\ *n, pl* **sheaths** \'shēthz, 'shēths\ **1** : a case for a blade (as of a knife); *also* : an anatomical covering suggesting such a case **2** : a close-fitting dress usu. worn without a belt

**sheathe** \'shēth\ *also* **sheath** \'shēth\ *vb* **sheathed; sheath·ing 1** : to put into a sheath **2** : to cover with something that guards or protects

**sheath·ing** \'shē-thiŋ, -thin\ *n* : material used to sheathe something; *esp* : the first covering of boards or of waterproof material on the outside wall of a frame house or on a timber roof

**sheave** \'shiv, 'shēv\ *n* : a grooved wheel or pulley (as on a pulley block)

**she-bang** \shi-'baŋ\ *n* : everything involved in what is under consideration ⟨sold the whole ∼⟩

¹**shed** \'shed\ *vb* **shed; shed·ding** **1** : to cause to flow from a cut or wound ⟨∼ blood⟩ **2** : to pour down in drops ⟨∼ tears⟩ **3** : to give out (as light) : DIFFUSE **4** : to throw off (as a natural covering) : DISCARD ⟨∼ skin⟩

²**shed** *n* : a slight structure built for shelter or storage

**sheen** \'shēn\ *n* : a subdued luster

**sheep** \'shēp\ *n, pl* **sheep** **1** : any of various cud-chewing mammals that are stockier than the related goats and lack a beard in the male; *esp* : one raised for meat or for its wool or skin **2** : a timid or defenseless person **3** : SHEEPSKIN

**sheep·dog** \'shēp-ˌdȯg\ *n* : a dog used to tend, drive, or guard sheep

**sheep·fold** \'shēp-ˌfōld\ *n* : a pen or shelter for sheep

**sheep·herd·er** \-ˌhər-dər\ *n* : a worker in charge of sheep esp. on open range — **sheep·herd·ing** *n*

**sheep·ish** \'shē-pish\ *adj* : BASHFUL, TIMID; *esp* : embarrassed by consciousness of a fault — **sheep·ish·ly** *adv*

**sheep·skin** \'shēp-ˌskin\ *n* **1** : the hide of a sheep or leather prepared from it; *also* : PARCHMENT **2** : DIPLOMA

¹**sheer** \'shir\ *vb* : to turn from a course

²**sheer** *adj* **1** : very thin or transparent **2** : UNQUALIFIED ⟨∼ folly⟩ **3** : very steep
◆ *Synonyms* PURE, SIMPLE, ABSOLUTE, UNADULTERATED, UNMITIGATED — **sheer** *adv*

¹**sheet** \'shēt\ *n* **1** : a broad piece of cloth (as for a bed); *also* : SAIL **2** : a single piece of paper **3** : a broad flat surface ⟨a ∼ of ice⟩ **4** : something broad and long and relatively thin

²**sheet** *n* : a rope used to trim a sail

**sheet·ing** \'shē-tiŋ\ *n* : material in the form of sheets or suitable for forming into sheets

**sheikh** *or* **sheik** \'shēk, 'shāk\ *n* : an Arab chief — **sheikh·dom** *or* **sheik·dom** \-dəm\ *n*

**shek·el** \'she-kəl\ *n* — see MONEY table

**shelf** \'shelf\ *n, pl* **shelves** \'shelvz\ **1** : a thin flat usu. long and narrow structure fastened horizontally (as on a wall) above the floor to hold things **2** : something (as a sandbar) that suggests a shelf

**shelf life** *n* : the period of storage time during which a material will remain useful

¹**shell** \'shel\ *n* **1** : a hard or tough often thin outer covering of an animal (as a beetle, turtle, or mollusk) or of an egg or a seed or fruit (as a nut); *also* : something that resembles a shell ⟨a pastry ∼⟩ **2** : a light narrow racing boat propelled by oarsmen **3** : a case holding an explosive and designed to be fired from a cannon; *also* : a case holding the charge of powder and shot or bullet for small arms **4** : a plain usu. sleeveless blouse or sweater —

**shelled** \'sheld\ *adj* — **shelly** \'she-lē\ *adj*

²**shell** *vb* **1** : to remove from a shell or husk **2** : BOMBARD — **shell·er** *n*

¹**shel·lac** \shə-'lak\ *n* : a purified lac **2** : lac dissolved in alcohol and used as a wood filler or finish

²**shellac** *vb* **shel·lacked; shel·lack·ing** **1** : to coat or treat with shellac **2** : to defeat decisively ⟨*shellacked* their opponents⟩

**shellacking** *n* : a sound drubbing

**shell bean** *n* : a bean grown esp. for its edible seeds; *also* : its edible seed

**shell·fish** \-ˌfish\ *n* : an invertebrate water animal (as an oyster or lobster) with a shell

**shell out** *vb* : PAY

**shell shock** *n* : COMBAT FATIGUE — **shell–shocked** \'shel-ˌshäkt\ *adj*

¹**shel·ter** \'shel-tər\ *n* : something that gives protection : REFUGE

²**shelter** *vb* **shel·tered; shel·ter·ing** : to give protection or refuge to

**shelve** \'shelv\ *vb* **shelved; shelv·ing** **1** : to slope gradually **2** : to store on shelves **3** : to dismiss from service or use **4** : to put aside : DEFER ⟨∼ a proposal⟩

**shelv·ing** \'shel-viŋ\ *n* : material for shelves; *also* : SHELVES

**she·nan·i·gan** \shə-'na-ni-gən\ *n* **1** : an underhand trick **2** : questionable conduct — usu. used in pl. **3** : high-spirited or mischievous activity — usu. used in pl.

¹**shep·herd** \'she-pərd\ *n* **1** : one who tends sheep **2** : GERMAN SHEPHERD

²**shepherd** *vb* : to tend as or in the manner of a shepherd

**shep·herd·ess** \'she-pər-dəs\ *n* : a woman who tends sheep

**shepherd's pie** *n* : a meat pie with a mashed potato crust

**sheqel** *n, pl* **sheqalim** *var of* SHEKEL

**sher·bet** \'shər-bət\ *n* [Turk *şerbet,* fr. Pers *sharbat,* fr. Ar *sharba* drink] **1** : a drink of sweetened diluted fruit juice **2** *also* **sher·bert** \-bərt\ : a frozen dessert of fruit juices, sugar, milk or water, and egg whites or gelatin

**sherd** *var of* SHARD

**sher·iff** \'sher-əf\ *n* [ME *shirreve,* fr. OE *scīrgerēfa,* lit., shire reeve (local official)] : a county officer charged with the execution of the law and the preservation of order

**sher·ry** \'sher-ē\ *n, pl* **sherries** [alter. of earlier *sherris* (taken as pl.), fr. *Xeres* (now *Jerez*), Spain] : a fortified wine with a nutty flavor

**Shet·land pony** \'shet-lənd-\ *n* : any of a breed of small stocky hardy ponies

**shew** \'shō\ *Brit var of* SHOW

**shi·at·su** *also* **shi·at·zu** \shē-'ät-sü\ *n* : a form of acupressure originating in Japan

**shib·bo·leth** \'shi-bə-ləth\ *n* [Heb *shibbōleth* stream; fr. the use of this word as a test to distinguish the men of Gilead from members of the tribe of Ephraim (Judges 12:5, 6)] **1** : CATCHPHRASE **2** : language that is a criterion for distinguishing members of a group

¹**shield** \'shēld\ *n* **1** : a broad piece of de-

fensive armor carried on the arm **2**
: something that protects or hides **3** : a
police officer's badge
²**shield** *vb* : to protect or hide with a shield
♦ **Synonyms** PROTECT, GUARD, SAFE-
GUARD

**shier** *comparative of* SHY
**shiest** *superlative of* SHY

¹**shift** \'shift\ *vb* **1** : EXCHANGE, REPLACE
**2** : to change place, position, or direction
: MOVE; *also* : to change gears **3** : GET BY,
MANAGE

²**shift** *n* **1** : SCHEME, TRICK **2** : a woman's
slip or loose-fitting dress **3** : a change in
direction, emphasis, or attitude **4** : a
group working together alternating with
other groups **5** : TRANSFER **6** : GEAR-
SHIFT

**shift·less** \'shift-ləs\ *adj* : LAZY, INEFFI-
CIENT — **shift·less·ness** *n*

**shifty** \'shif-tē\ *adj* **shift·i·er; -est** **1**
: TRICKY; *also* : ELUSIVE **2** : indicative of
a tricky nature ⟨~ eyes⟩

**shih tzu** \'shēd-'zü, 'shēt-'sü\ *n, pl* **shih
tzus** *also* **shih tzu** *often cap S&T* [Chin
(Beijing) *shīzi (gǒu)*, fr. *shīzi* lion + *gǒu*
dog] : any of a breed of small short-
legged dogs of Chinese origin that have a
short muzzle and a long dense coat

**shii·ta·ke** \shē-'tä-kē\ *n* [Jp] : a dark
Asian mushroom widely cultivated for its
edible cap

**shill** \'shil\ *n* : one who acts as a decoy (as
for a pitchman) — **shill** *vb*

**shil·le·lagh** *also* **shil·la·lah** \shə-'lä-lē\ *n*
[*Shillelagh*, town in Ireland] : CUDGEL,
CLUB

**shil·ling** \'shi-liŋ\ *n* — see MONEY table

**shil·ly–shal·ly** \'shi-lē-,sha-lē\ *vb* **shilly–
shall·ied; shilly–shally·ing** **1** : to show
hesitation or lack of decisiveness **2** : to
waste time

**shim** \'shim\ *n* : a thin often tapered piece
of wood, metal, or stone used (as in leveling) to fill in space

**shim·mer** \'shi-mər\ *vb* : to shine waver-
ingly or tremulously : GLIMMER ⟨~ing
light⟩ ♦ **Synonyms** FLASH, GLEAM,
GLINT, SPARKLE, GLITTER — **shimmer** *n*
— **shim·mery** *adj*

**shim·my** \'shi-mē\ *n, pl* **shimmies** : an
abnormal vibration esp. in the front
wheels of a motor vehicle — **shimmy** *vb*

¹**shin** \'shin\ *n* : the front part of the leg
below the knee

²**shin** *vb* **shinned; shin·ning** : to climb (as
a pole) by gripping alternately with arms
or hands and legs

**shin·bone** \'shin-,bōn\ *n* : TIBIA

¹**shine** \'shīn\ *vb* **shone** \'shōn\ *or*
**shined; shin·ing** **1** : to give or cause to
give light **2** : GLEAM, GLITTER **3** : to be
eminent, conspicuous, or distinguished
⟨gave her a chance to ~⟩ **4** : POLISH ⟨~
your shoes⟩

²**shine** *n* **1** : BRIGHTNESS, RADIANCE **2**
: LUSTER, BRILLIANCE **3** : fair weather
: SUNSHINE ⟨rain or ~⟩ **4** : LIKING,
FANCY ⟨took a ~ to them⟩ **5** : a polish
given to shoes

**shin·er** \'shī-nər\ *n* **1** : a silvery fish; *esp*
: any of numerous small freshwater

American fishes related to the carp **2**
: BLACK EYE

¹**shin·gle** \'shiŋ-gəl\ *n* **1** : a small thin
piece of building material used in overlapping rows for covering a roof or outside wall **2** : a small sign

²**shingle** *vb* **shin·gled; shin·gling** : to
cover with shingles

³**shingle** *n* : a beach strewn with gravel;
*also* : coarse gravel (as on a beach)

**shin·gles** \'shiŋ-gəlz\ *n* : an acute inflammation of the spinal and cranial nerves
caused by reactivation of the chicken
pox virus and associated with eruptions
and pain along the course of the affected
nerves

**shin·ny** \'shi-nē\ *vb* **shin·nied; shin·ny-
ing** : SHIN

**shin splints** *n sing or pl* : a condition
marked by pain and sometimes tenderness and swelling in the shin caused by
repeated small injuries to muscles and associated tissue esp. from running

**Shin·to** \'shin-,tō\ *n* : the indigenous religion of Japan consisting esp. in reverence
of the spirits of natural forces and imperial ancestors — **Shin·to·ism** *n* — **Shin-
to·ist** *n or adj*

**shiny** \'shī-nē\ *adj* **shin·i·er; -est**
: BRIGHT, RADIANT; *also* : POLISHED

¹**ship** \'ship\ *n* **1** : a large oceangoing boat
**2** : a ship's officers and crew **3** : AIRSHIP,
AIRCRAFT, SPACECRAFT

²**ship** *vb* **shipped; ship·ping** **1** : to put or
receive on board a ship for transporta-
tion **2** : to have transported by a carrier
**3** : to take or draw into a boat ⟨~ oars⟩
⟨~ water⟩ **4** : to engage to serve on a
ship — **ship·per** *n*

-**ship** \,ship\ *n suffix* **1** : state : condition
: quality ⟨friendship⟩ **2** : office : dignity
: profession ⟨lordship⟩ ⟨clerkship⟩ **3**
: art : skill ⟨horsemanship⟩ **4** : something
showing, exhibiting, or embodying a
quality or state ⟨township⟩ **5** : one entitled to a (specified) rank, title, or appellation ⟨his Lordship⟩ **6** : the body of persons engaged in a specified activity
⟨readership⟩

**ship·board** \'ship-,bōrd\ *n* : SHIP

**ship·build·er** \-,bil-dər\ *n* : one who designs or builds ships

**ship·fit·ter** \-,fi-tər\ *n* **1** : one who constructs ships **2** : a naval enlisted person
who works as a plumber

**ship·mate** \-,māt\ *n* : a fellow sailor

**ship·ment** \-mənt\ *n* : the process of shipping; *also* : the goods shipped

**shipping** *n* **1** : SHIPS; *esp* : ships in one
port or belonging to one country **2**
: transportation of goods

**ship·shape** \'ship-,shāp\ *adj* : TRIM, TIDY
⟨kept the garage ~⟩

**ship·worm** \-,wərm\ *n* : any of various
wormlike marine clams that have a shell
used for burrowing in wood and damage
wooden ships and wharves

¹**ship·wreck** \-,rek\ *n* **1** : a wrecked ship
**2** : destruction or loss of a ship **3** : total
loss or failure : RUIN

²**shipwreck** *vb* : to cause or meet disaster
at sea through destruction or foundering

**ship·wright** \'ship-ˌrīt\ *n* : a carpenter skilled in ship construction and repair

**ship·yard** \-ˌyärd\ *n* : a place where ships are built or repaired

**shire** \'shī(-ə)r, *in place-name compounds* ˌshir, shər\ *n* : a county in Great Britain

**shirk** \'shərk\ *vb* : to avoid performing (duty or work) — **shirk·er** *n*

**shirr** \'shər\ *vb* 1 : to make shirring in 2 : to bake (eggs removed from the shell) until set

**shirr·ing** \'shər-iŋ\ *n* : a decorative gathering in cloth made by drawing up parallel lines of stitches

**shirt** \'shərt\ *n* 1 : a loose cloth garment usu. having a collar, sleeves, a front opening, and a tail long enough to be tucked inside pants or a skirt 2 : UNDERSHIRT — **shirt·less** *adj*

**shirt·ing** \'shər-tiŋ\ *n* : cloth suitable for making shirts

**shish ke·bab** \'shish-kə-ˌbäb\ *n* [Turk *şiş kebabı*, fr. *şiş* spit + *kebap* roast meat] : kebab cooked on skewers

**shiv** \'shiv\ *n, slang* : KNIFE

¹**shiv·er** \'shi-vər\ *vb* : TREMBLE, QUIVER
♦ **Synonyms** SHUDDER, QUAVER, SHAKE, QUAKE

²**shiver** *n* : an instance of shivering — **shiv·ery** *adj*

**shlemiel** *var of* SCHLEMIEL

**shlub** *var of* SCHLUB

**shmooze** *var of* SCHMOOZE

**Sho·ah** \'shō-ə, -ˌä\ *n* : HOLOCAUST 2

¹**shoal** \'shōl\ *n* 1 : SHALLOW 2 : a sandbank or bar creating a shallow

²**shoal** *n* : a large group (as of fish)

**shoat** \'shōt\ *n* : a weaned young pig

¹**shock** \'shäk\ *n* : a pile of sheaves of grain or cornstalks set up in a field

²**shock** *n* [MF *choc*, fr. *choquer* to strike against] 1 : a sharp impact or violent shake or jar 2 : a sudden violent mental or emotional disturbance 3 : a state of bodily collapse that is often marked by a drop in blood pressure and volume and that is caused esp. by crushing wounds, blood loss, or burns 4 : the effect of a charge of electricity passing through the body 5 : SHOCK ABSORBER — **shock·proof** \-ˌprüf\ *adj*

³**shock** *vb* 1 : to strike with surprise, horror, or disgust 2 : to subject to the action of an electrical discharge

⁴**shock** *n* : a thick bushy mass (as of hair)

**shock absorber** *n* : any of several devices for absorbing the energy of sudden shocks in machinery

**shock·er** \'shä-kər\ *n* : one that shocks; *esp* : a sensational work of fiction or drama

**shock·ing** \'shä-kiŋ\ *adj* : extremely startling and offensive — **shock·ing·ly** *adv*

**shock therapy** *n* : the treatment of mental disorder by induction of coma or convulsions by drugs or electricity

**shock wave** *n* : a wave formed by the sudden violent compression of the medium through which it travels

¹**shod·dy** \'shä-dē\ *n* 1 : wool reclaimed from old rags; *also* : a fabric made from it 2 : inferior or imitation material

²**shoddy** *adj* **shod·di·er; -est** 1 : made of shoddy 2 : poorly done or made ⟨~ workmanship⟩ — **shod·di·ly** \'shä-də-lē\ *adv* — **shod·di·ness** \-dē-nəs\ *n*

¹**shoe** \'shü\ *n* 1 : a covering for the human foot 2 : HORSESHOE 3 : the part of a brake that presses on the wheel

²**shoe** *vb* **shod** \'shäd\ *also* **shoed** \'shüd\; **shoe·ing** : to put a shoe or shoes on

**shoe·horn** \-ˌhörn\ *n* : a curved implement (as of horn or plastic) used in putting on a shoe

**shoe·lace** \'shü-ˌlās\ *n* : a lace or string for fastening a shoe

**shoe·mak·er** \-ˌmā-kər\ *n* : one who makes or repairs shoes

**shoe·string** \-ˌstriŋ\ *n* 1 : SHOELACE 2 : a small sum of money

**sho·gun** \'shō-gən\ *n* [Jp *shōgun* general] : any of a line of military governors ruling Japan until the revolution of 1867–68 — **sho·gun·ate** \'shō-gə-nət, -ˌnāt\ *n*

**shone** *past and past part of* SHINE

**shook** *past of* SHAKE

**shook-up** \(ˌ)shúk-'əp\ *adj* : nervously upset : AGITATED

¹**shoot** \'shüt\ *vb* **shot** \'shät\; **shoot·ing** 1 : to drive (as an arrow or bullet) forward quickly or forcibly 2 : to hit, kill, or wound with a missile 3 : to cause a missile to be driven forth or forth from ⟨~ a gun⟩ 4 : to send forth (as a ray of light) 5 : to thrust forward or out 6 : to pass rapidly along ⟨~ the rapids⟩ 7 : PHOTOGRAPH, FILM 8 : to move swiftly : DART 9 : to grow by or as if by sending out shoots; *also* : MATURE, DEVELOP — **shoot·er** *n*

²**shoot** *n* 1 : a plant stem with its leaves and branches esp. when not yet mature 2 : an act of shooting 3 : a shooting match

**shooting iron** *n* : FIREARM

**shooting star** *n* : METEOR 2

**shoot up** *vb* : to inject a narcotic into a vein

¹**shop** \'shäp\ *n* [ME *shoppe*, fr. OE *sceoppa* booth] 1 : a place where things are made or worked on : FACTORY, MILL 2 : a retail store ⟨dress ~⟩

²**shop** *vb* **shopped; shop·ping** : to visit stores for purchasing or examining goods — **shop·per** *n*

**shop·keep·er** \'shäp-ˌkē-pər\ *n* : a retail merchant

**shop·lift** \-ˌlift\ *vb* : to steal goods on display from a store — **shop·lift·er** *n*

**shop·talk** \-ˌtök\ *n* : talk about one's business or special interests

**shop·worn** \-ˌwörn\ *adj* : soiled or frayed from much handling in a store

¹**shore** \'shōr\ *n* : land along the edge of a body of water — **shore·less** *adj*

²**shore** *vb* **shored; shor·ing** : to give support to : BRACE

³**shore** *n* : ¹PROP

**shore·bird** \-ˌbərd\ *n* : any of a suborder of birds (as the plovers and sandpipers) found mostly along the seashore

**shore patrol** *n* : a branch of a navy that exercises guard and police functions

**shor·ing** \'shōr-iŋ\ *n* : a group of things that shore something up

**shorn** *past part of* SHEAR

¹**short** \'short\ *adj* **1** : not long or tall **2** : not great in distance **3** : brief in time **4** : not coming up to standard or to an expected amount **5** : CURT, ABRUPT ⟨was ~ with the busybody⟩ **6** : insufficiently supplied ⟨~ of cash⟩ **7** : made with shortening : FLAKY **8** : consisting of or relating to a sale of securities or commodities that the seller does not possess or has not contracted for at the time of the sale ⟨~ sale⟩ — **short·ness** *n*

²**short** *adv* **1** : ABRUPTLY, CURTLY **2** : at some point before a goal aimed at

³**short** *n* **1** : something shorter than normal or standard **2** *pl* : drawers or pants of less than knee length **3** : SHORT CIRCUIT

⁴**short** *vb* : SHORT-CIRCUIT

**short·age** \'shor-tij\ *n* : LACK, DEFICIT

**short·cake** \'short-,kāk\ *n* : a dessert consisting of short biscuit spread with sweetened fruit

**short·change** \-'chānj\ *vb* : to cheat esp. by giving less than the correct amount of change

**short circuit** *n* : a connection made between points in an electric circuit where current is not intended to flow — **short-circuit** *vb*

**short·com·ing** \'short-,kə-miŋ\ *n* : FAULT 1, FLAW

**short·cut** \-,kət\ *n* **1** : a route more direct than that usu. taken **2** : a quicker way of doing something

**short·en** \'shor-tᵊn\ *vb* : to make or become short ✦ *Synonyms* CURTAIL, ABBREVIATE, ABRIDGE, RETRENCH

**short·en·ing** \'shor-tᵊn-iŋ\ *n* : a substance (as lard or butter) that makes pastry tender and flaky

**short·hand** \'short-,hand\ *n* : a method of writing rapidly by using symbols and abbreviations for letters, words, or phrases : STENOGRAPHY

**short·hand·ed** \,short-'han-dəd\ *adj* : short of the needed number of people

**short·horn** \'short-,horn\ *n*, *often cap* : any of a breed of red, roan, or white cattle of English origin

**short hundredweight** *n* — see WEIGHT table

**short–lived** \'short-,livd, -'līvd\ *adj* : of short life or duration

**short·ly** \'short-lē\ *adv* **1** : in a few words **2** : in a short time : SOON

**short–or·der** \'short-,or-dər\ *adj* : preparing or serving food that can be quickly cooked ⟨a ~ cook⟩

**short shrift** *n* **1** : a brief respite from death **2** : little consideration

**short·sight·ed** \'short-,sī-təd\ *adj* **1** : lacking foresight **2** : NEARSIGHTED — **short·sight·ed·ness** *n*

**short·stop** \-,stäp\ *n* : a baseball player defending the area between second and third base

**short story** *n* : a short work of fiction usu. dealing with a few characters and a single event

**short–tem·pered** \,short-'tem-pərd\ *adj* : having a quick temper

**short–term** \'short-,tərm\ *adj* **1** : occurring over or involving a relatively short period of time **2** : of or relating to a financial transaction based on a term usu. of less than a year

**short ton** *n* — see WEIGHT table

**short·wave** \'short-,wāv\ *n* : a radio wave with a wavelength between 10 and 100 meters

**Sho·sho·ne** *or* **Sho·sho·ni** \shə-'shō-nē\ *n*, *pl* **Shoshones** *or* **Shoshoni** : a member of an American Indian people orig. ranging through California, Idaho, Nevada, Utah, and Wyoming

¹**shot** \'shät\ *n* **1** : an act of shooting **2** : a stroke or throw in some games **3** : something that is shot : MISSILE, PROJECTILE; *esp* : small pellets forming a charge for a shotgun **4** : a metal sphere that is thrown for distance in the shot put **5** : RANGE, REACH **6** : MARKSMAN **7** : a single photographic exposure **8** : a single sequence of a motion picture or a television program made by one camera **9** : an injection (as of medicine) into the body **10** : a small serving of undiluted liquor or other beverage

²**shot** *past and past part of* SHOOT

**shot·gun** \'shät-,gən\ *n* : a gun with a smooth bore used to fire shot at short range

**shot put** *n* : a field event in which a shot is heaved for distance

**should** \'shud, shəd\ *past of* SHALL — used as an auxiliary to express condition, obligation or propriety, probability, or futurity from a point of view in the past

¹**shoul·der** \'shōl-dər\ *n* **1** : the part of the body of a person or animal where the arm or foreleg joins the body **2** : either edge of a roadway **3** : a rounded or sloping part (as of a bottle) where the neck joins the body

²**shoulder** *vb* **1** : to push or thrust with the shoulder **2** : to bear on the shoulder **3** : to take the responsibility of

**shoulder belt** *n* : an automobile safety belt worn across the torso and over the shoulder

**shoulder blade** *n* : a flat triangular bone at the back of each shoulder

**shout** \'shaut\ *vb* : to utter a sudden loud cry — **shout** *n*

**shove** \'shəv\ *vb* **shoved; shov·ing** : to push along, aside, or away — **shove** *n*

¹**shov·el** \'shə-vəl\ *n* **1** : a broad long-handled scoop used to lift and throw material **2** : the amount a shovel will hold — **shov·el·ful** \'shə-vəl-,fúl\ *n*

²**shovel** *vb* **-eled** *or* **-elled; -el·ing** *or* **-el·ling** **1** : to take up and throw with a shovel **2** : to dig or clean out with a shovel

¹**show** \'shō\ *vb* **showed** \'shōd\; **shown** \'shōn\ *or* **showed; show·ing** **1** : to cause or permit to be seen : EXHIBIT ⟨~ anger⟩ **2** : CONFER, BESTOW ⟨~ mercy⟩ **3** : REVEAL, DISCLOSE ⟨~ed courage in battle⟩ **4** : INSTRUCT ⟨~ me how⟩ **5** : PROVE ⟨~s he was guilty⟩ **6** : APPEAR **7** : to be noticeable **8** : to be third in a horse race

²**show** n  1 : a demonstrative display  2 : outward appearance ⟨a ~ of resistance⟩  3 : SPECTACLE  4 : a theatrical presentation  5 : a radio or television program  6 : third place in a horse race

¹**show•case** \'shō-ˌkās\ n : a cabinet for displaying items (as in a store)

²**showcase** vb **show•cased; show•cas•ing** : EXHIBIT

**show•down** \'shō-ˌdaún\ n : a decisive confrontation or contest; esp : the showing of poker hands to determine the winner of a pot

¹**show•er** \'shaú(-ə)r\ n  1 : a brief fall of rain  2 : a party given by friends who bring gifts  3 : a bath in which water is showered on the person; also : a facility (as a stall) for such a bath — **show•ery** adj

²**shower** vb  1 : to rain or fall in a shower  2 : to bathe in a shower

**show•man** \'shō-mən\ n : a notably spectacular, dramatic, or effective performer — **show•man•ship** n

**show–off** \'shō-ˌȯf\ n : one that seeks to attract attention by conspicuous behavior

**show off** vb  1 : to display proudly  2 : to act as a show-off

**show•piece** \'shō-ˌpēs\ n : an outstanding example used for exhibition

**show•place** \-ˌplās\ n : an estate or building that is a showpiece

**show up** vb : ARRIVE

**showy** \'shō-ē\ adj **show•i•er; -est** : superficially impressive or striking ⟨a ~ orchid⟩ — **show•i•ly** \'shō-ə-lē\ adv — **show•i•ness** \-ē-nəs\ n

**shpt** abbr shipment

**shrap•nel** \'shrap-nəl\ n, pl **shrapnel** [Henry *Shrapnel* †1842 Eng. artillery officer] : bomb, mine, or shell fragments

¹**shred** \'shred\ n : a narrow strip cut or torn off : a small fragment

²**shred** vb **shred•ded; shred•ding** : to cut or tear into shreds

**shrew** \'shrü\ n  1 : any of a family of very small mammals with short velvety fur that are related to the moles  2 : a scolding woman

**shrewd** \'shrüd\ adj : CLEVER, ASTUTE — **shrewd•ly** adv — **shrewd•ness** n

**shrew•ish** \'shrü-ish\ adj : having an irritable disposition : ILL-TEMPERED — **shrew•ish•ly** adv — **shrew•ish•ness** n

**shriek** \'shrēk\ n : a shrill cry : SCREAM, YELL — **shriek** vb

**shrift** \'shrift\ n, archaic : the act of shriving : CONFESSION

**shrike** \'shrīk\ n : any of numerous usu. largely grayish or brownish birds that often impale their usu. insect prey upon thorns before devouring it

¹**shrill** \'shril\ vb : to make a high-pitched piercing sound

²**shrill** adj : high-pitched : PIERCING ⟨~ whistle⟩ — **shril•ly** adv

**shrimp** \'shrimp\ n, pl **shrimps** or **shrimp**  1 : any of various small marine crustaceans related to the lobsters  2 : a small or puny person

**shrine** \'shrīn\ n [ME, receptacle for the relics of a saint, fr. OE *scrīn*, fr. L *scrinium* case, chest]  1 : the tomb of a saint; also : a place where devotion is paid to a saint or deity  2 : a place or object hallowed by its associations

**shrink** \'shriŋk\ vb **shrank** \'shraŋk\ or **shrunk** \'shrəŋk\; **shrunk** or **shrunk•en** \'shrəŋ-kən\; **shrink•ing**  1 : to draw back or away  2 : to become smaller or more compact  3 : to lessen in value

♦ **Synonyms** CONTRACT, CONSTRICT, COMPRESS, CONDENSE — **shrink•able** adj

²**shrink** n : a clinical psychiatrist or psychologist

**shrink•age** \'shriŋ-kij\ n  1 : the act of shrinking  2 : the amount lost by shrinkage

**shrive** \'shrīv\ vb **shrived** or **shrove** \'shrōv\; **shriv•en** \'shri-vən\ or **shrived** [ME, fr. OE *scrīfan* to prescribe, allot, shrive, fr. L *scribere* to write] : to administer the sacrament of reconciliation to

**shriv•el** \'shri-vəl\ vb **-eled** or **-elled; -el•ing** or **-el•ling** : to shrink and draw into wrinkles : DWINDLE

¹**shroud** \'shraúd\ n  1 : something that covers or screens  2 : a cloth placed over a dead body  3 : any of the ropes leading from the masthead of a ship to the side to support the mast

²**shroud** vb : to veil or screen from view

**shrub** \'shrəb\ n : a low usu. several-stemmed woody plant — **shrub•by** adj

**shrub•bery** \'shrə-bə-rē\ n, pl **-ber•ies** : a planting or growth of shrubs

**shrug** \'shrəg\ vb **shrugged; shrug•ging** : to hunch (the shoulders) up to express aloofness, indifference, or uncertainty — **shrug** n

**shrug off** vb  1 : to brush aside : MINIMIZE ⟨she *shrugged* off their concerns⟩  2 : to shake off  3 : to remove (a garment) by wriggling out

**shtick** also **schtick** or **shtik** \'shtik\ n [Yiddish *shtik* pranks, lit., piece]  1 : a usu. comic or repetitious performance or routine  2 : one's special trait, interest, or activity

¹**shuck** \'shək\ n : SHELL, HUSK

²**shuck** vb : to strip of shucks

**shud•der** \'shə-dər\ vb : TREMBLE, QUAKE — **shudder** n

**shuf•fle** \'shə-fəl\ vb **shuf•fled; shuf•fling**  1 : to mix in a disorderly mass  2 : to rearrange the order of (cards in a pack) by mixing two parts of the pack together  3 : to shift from place to place  4 : to move with a sliding or dragging gait  5 : to dance in a slow lagging manner — **shuffle** n

**shuf•fle•board** \'shə-fəl-ˌbȯrd\ n : a game in which players use long-handled cues to shove disks into scoring areas marked on a smooth surface

**shun** \'shən\ vb **shunned; shun•ning** : to avoid deliberately or habitually

♦ **Synonyms** EVADE, ELUDE, ESCAPE, DUCK

¹**shunt** \'shənt\ vb [ME, to turn away] : to turn off to one side; esp : to switch (a train) from one track to another

²**shunt** *n* **1** : a method or device for turning or thrusting aside **2** : a conductor joining two points in an electrical circuit forming an alternate path through which a portion of the current may pass

**shut** \'shət\ *vb* **shut; shut·ting 1** : CLOSE **2** : to forbid entrance into **3** : to lock up **4** : to fold together ⟨~ a penknife⟩ **5** : to cease or suspend activity ⟨~ down an assembly line⟩

**shut·down** \-ˌdau̇n\ *n* : a temporary cessation of activity (as in a factory)

**shut–in** \'shət-ˌin\ *n* : a person confined to home, a room, or bed because of illness or incapacity

**shut·out** \'shət-ˌau̇t\ *n* : a game or contest in which one side fails to score

**shut out** *vb* **1** : EXCLUDE **2** : to prevent (an opponent) from scoring in a game or contest

**shut·ter** \'shə-tər\ *n* **1** : a movable cover for a door or window : BLIND **2** : the part of a camera that opens and closes to allow light to enter

**shut·ter·bug** \'shə-tər-ˌbəg\ *n* : a photography enthusiast

¹**shut·tle** \'shə-tᵊl\ *n* **1** : an instrument used in weaving for passing the horizontal threads between the vertical threads **2** : a vehicle traveling back and forth over a short route ⟨a ~ bus⟩ **3** : SPACE SHUTTLE

²**shuttle** *vb* **shut·tled; shut·tling** : to move back and forth frequently

**shut·tle·cock** \'shə-tᵊl-ˌkäk\ *n* : a light conical object (as of cork or plastic) used in badminton

**shut up** *vb* : to cease or cause to cease talking

¹**shy** \'shī\ *adj* **shi·er** *or* **shy·er** \'shī-ər\; **shi·est** *or* **shy·est** \'shī-əst\ **1** : easily frightened : TIMID **2** : WARY **3** : BASHFUL **4** : DEFICIENT, LACKING ⟨a nickel ~ of a quarter⟩ — **shy·ly** *adv* — **shy·ness** *n*

²**shy** *vb* **shied; shy·ing 1** : to show a dislike ; RECOIL **2** : to start suddenly aside through fright ⟨the horse *shied*⟩

**shy·ster** \'shīs-tər\ *n* : an unscrupulous lawyer or politician

**Si** *symbol* silicon

**SI** *abbr* [F *Système International d'Unités*] International System of Units

**Si·a·mese** \ˌsī-ə-ˈmēz, -ˈmēs\ *n, pl* **Siamese** : THAI — **Siamese** *adj*

**Siamese cat** *n* : any of a breed of slender blue-eyed short-haired domestic cats of Asian origin

**Siamese twin** *n* [fr. Chang †1874 and Eng †1874 twins born in Siam with bodies united] : one of a pair of twins with bodies joined together at birth

**Siberian husky** *n* : any of a breed of thick-coated compact dogs orig. developed in Siberia to pull sleds

¹**sib·i·lant** \'si-bə-lənt\ *adj* : having, containing, or producing the sound of or a sound resembling that of the *s* or the *sh* in *sash* — **sib·i·lant·ly** *adv*

²**sibilant** *n* : a sibilant speech sound (as English \s\, \z\, \sh\, \zh\, \ch (=tsh)\, or \j (=dzh)\)

**sib·ling** \'si-bliŋ\ *n* : a brother or sister considered irrespective of sex; *also* : one of two or more offspring having one common parent

**sib·yl** \'si-bəl\ *n, often cap* : PROPHETESS — **sib·yl·line** \-bə-ˌlīn, -ˌlēn\ *adj*

**sic** \'sik, 'sēk\ *adv* : intentionally so written — used after a printed word or passage to indicate that it exactly reproduces an original ⟨said he seed [~] it all⟩

**sick** \'sik\ *adj* **1** : not in good health : ILL; *also* : of, relating to, or intended for use in sickness ⟨~ pay⟩ **2** : NAUSEATED **3** : DISGUSTED **4** : PINING **5** : mentally or emotionally unsound **6** : MACABRE, SADISTIC ⟨~ jokes⟩ — **sick·ly** *adj*

**sick·bed** \'sik-ˌbed\ *n* : a bed on which one lies sick

**sick·en** \'si-kən\ *vb* : to make or become sick — **sick·en·ing·ly** *adv*

**sick·le** \'si-kəl\ *n* : a cutting tool consisting of a curved metal blade with a short handle

**sickle–cell anemia** *n* : an inherited anemia in which red blood cells tend to become crescent-shaped and clog small blood vessels and which occurs esp. in individuals of African, Mediterranean, or southwest Asian ancestry

**sick·ness** \'sik-nəs\ *n* **1** : ill health; *also* : a specific disease **2** : NAUSEA

**side** \'sīd\ *n* **1** : the right or left part of the trunk of a body **2** : a place away from a central point or line **3** : a border of an object; *esp* : one of the longer borders as contrasted with an end **4** : an outer surface of an object **5** : a position regarded as opposite to another **6** : a body of contestants — **side** *adj* — **on the side** : in addition to the main portion

**side·arm** \-ˌärm\ *adj* : made with a sideways sweep of the arm ⟨a ~ pitch⟩ — **sidearm** *adv*

**side arm** *n* : a weapon worn at the side or in the belt

**side·bar** \'sīd-ˌbär\ *n* : a short news story accompanying a major story and presenting related information

**side·board** \-ˌbȯrd\ *n* : a piece of dining-room furniture for holding articles of table service

**side·burns** \-ˌbərnz\ *n pl* : whiskers on the side of the face in front of the ears

**side by side** *adv* **1** : beside one another **2** : in the same place, time, or circumstance — **side–by–side** *adj*

**side·car** \-ˌkär\ *n* : a one-wheeled passenger car attached to the side of a motorcycle

**side effect** *n* : a secondary and usu. adverse effect (as of a drug)

**side·kick** \'sīd-ˌkik\ *n* : PAL, PARTNER

**side·line** \'sīd-ˌlīn\ *n* **1** : an activity pursued in addition to one's regular occupation **2** : the space immediately outside the lines of an athletic field or court **3** : a sphere of little or no participation — usu. used in pl.

¹**side·long** \'sīd-ˌlȯŋ\ *adv* : in the direction of or along the side : OBLIQUELY

²**sidelong** *adj* : directed to one side ⟨~ look⟩

**side·man** \'sīd-,man\ n : a member of a jazz or swing orchestra

**side-piece** \-,pēs\ n : a piece forming or contained in the side of something

**si·de·re·al** \sī-'dir-ē-əl, sə-\ adj [L *sidereus*, fr. *sider-, sidus* star, constellation] 1 : of or relating to the stars 2 : measured by the apparent motion of the stars

**side-sad·dle** \'sīd-,sa-d°l\ n : a saddle for women on which the rider sits with both legs on the same side of the horse — **sidesaddle** adv

**side-show** \'sīd-,shō\ n 1 : a minor show offered in addition to a main exhibition (as of a circus) 2 : an incidental diversion

**side-step** \-,step\ vb 1 : to step aside 2 : AVOID, EVADE ⟨sidestepped the question⟩

**side-stroke** \-,strōk\ n : a swimming stroke which is executed on the side and in which the arms are swept backward and downward and the legs do a scissors kick

**side-swipe** \-,swīp\ vb : to strike with a glancing blow along the side — **side-swipe** n

¹**side-track** \-,trak\ n : SIDING 1

²**sidetrack** vb 1 : to switch from a main railroad line to a siding 2 : to turn aside from a purpose

**side-walk** \'sīd-,wȯk\ n : a paved walk at the side of a road or street

**side-wall** \-,wȯl\ n 1 : a wall forming the side of something 2 : the side of an automobile tire

**side-ways** \-,wāz\ adv or adj 1 : from the side 2 : with one side to the front 3 : to, toward, or at one side

**side-wind·er** \-,wīn-dər\ n : a small pale-colored desert rattlesnake of the southwestern U.S.

**sid·ing** \'sī-diŋ\ n 1 : a short railroad track connected with the main track 2 : material (as boards) covering the outside of frame buildings

**si·dle** \'sī-d°l\ vb **si·dled; si·dling** : to move sideways with one side foremost

**SIDS** abbr sudden infant death syndrome

**siege** \'sēj\ n 1 : the placing of an army around or before a fortified place to force its surrender 2 : a persistent attack (as of illness)

**sie·mens** \'sē-mənz, 'zē-\ n : a unit of conductance equivalent to one ampere per volt

**si·er·ra** \sē-'er-ə\ n [Sp, lit., saw, fr. L *serra*] : a range of mountains esp. with jagged peaks

**si·es·ta** \sē-'es-tə\ n [Sp, fr. L *sexta (hora)* noon, lit., sixth hour] : a midday rest or nap

**sieve** \'siv\ n : a utensil with meshes or holes to separate finer particles from coarser or solids from liquids

**sift** \'sift\ vb 1 : to pass through a sieve 2 : to separate with or as if with a sieve 3 : to examine carefully 4 : to scatter by or as if by passing through a sieve — **sift·er** n

**sig** abbr signature

**SIG** abbr special interest group

**sigh** \'sī\ vb 1 : to let out a deep audible breath (as in weariness or sorrow) 2 : GRIEVE, YEARN — **sigh** n

¹**sight** \'sīt\ n 1 : something seen or worth seeing 2 : the process or power of seeing; esp : the sense of which the eye is the receptor and by which qualities of appearance (as position, shape, and color) are perceived 3 : INSPECTION 4 : a device (as a small bead on a gun barrel) that aids the eye in aiming 5 : VIEW, GLIMPSE 6 : the range of vision — **sight·less** adj

²**sight** vb 1 : to get sight of 2 : to aim by means of a sight

**sight·ed** \'sī-təd\ adj : having sight

**sight·ly** \-lē\ adj : pleasing to the sight

**sight-see·ing** \'sīt-,sē-iŋ\ adj : engaged in or used for seeing sights of interest — **sight-seer** \-,sē-ər\ n

**sig·ma** \'sig-mə\ n : the 18th letter of the Greek alphabet — Σ or σ or ς

¹**sign** \'sīn\ n 1 : a gesture expressing a command, wish, or thought 2 : SYMBOL 3 : a notice publicly displayed for advertising purposes or for giving direction or warning 4 : OMEN, PORTENT 5 : TRACE, VESTIGE ⟨left without a ∼⟩

²**sign** vb 1 : to mark with a sign 2 : to represent by a sign 3 : to make a sign or signal 4 : to write one's name on in token of assent or obligation 5 : to assign legally 6 : to use sign language — **sign·er** n

¹**sig·nal** \'sig-nəl\ n 1 : a sign agreed on as the start of some joint action 2 : a sign giving warning or notice of something 3 : the message, sound, or image transmitted in electronic communication (as radio)

²**signal** vb **-naled** or **-nalled; -nal·ing** or **-nal·ling** 1 : to notify by a signal 2 : to communicate by signals

³**signal** adj : DISTINGUISHED ⟨a ∼ honor⟩ — **sig·nal·ly** adv

**sig·nal·ize** \'sig-nə-,līz\ vb **-ized; -iz·ing** : to point out or make conspicuous — **sig·nal·i·za·tion** \,sig-nə-lə-'zā-shən\ n

**sig·nal·man** \'sig-nəl-mən, -,man\ n : a person who signals or works with signals

**sig·na·to·ry** \'sig-nə-,tȯr-ē\ n, pl **-ries** : a person or government that signs jointly with others — **signatory** adj

**sig·na·ture** \'sig-nə-,chúr\ n 1 : the name of a person written by himself or herself 2 : the sign placed after the clef to indicate the key or the meter of a piece of music

**sign·board** \'sīn-,bȯrd\ n : a board bearing a sign or notice

**sig·net** \'sig-nət\ n : a small intaglio seal (as in a ring)

**sig·nif·i·cance** \sig-'ni-fi-kəns\ n 1 : something signified : MEANING 2 : SUGGESTIVENESS 3 : CONSEQUENCE, IMPORTANCE ⟨the ∼ of the treaty⟩

**sig·nif·i·cant** \-kənt\ adj 1 : having meaning; esp : having a hidden or special meaning 2 : having or likely to have considerable influence or effect : IMPORTANT — **sig·nif·i·cant·ly** adv

**sig·ni·fy** \'sig-nə-,fī\ vb **-fied; -fy·ing** 1 : to show by a sign 2 : MEAN, IMPORT 3

: to have significance    **sig·ni·fi·ca·tion** \ˌsig-nə-fə-ˈkā-shən\ n

**sign in** vb : to make a record of arrival (as by signing a register)

**sign language** n : a formal system of hand gestures used for communication (as by the deaf)

**sign off** vb : to announce the end (as of a program or broadcast)

**sign of the cross** : a gesture of the hand forming a cross (as to invoke divine blessing)

**sign on** vb **1** : ENLIST **2** : to announce the start of broadcasting for the day

**sign out** vb : to make a record of departure (as by signing a register)

**sign·post** \ˈsīn-ˌpōst\ n : a post bearing a sign

**sign up** vb : to sign one's name in order to obtain, do, or join something

**Sikh** \ˈsēk\ n : an adherent of a religion of India marked by rejection of caste — **Sikh·ism** n

**si·lage** \ˈsī-lij\ n : fodder fermented (as in a silo) to produce a rich moist animal feed

**¹si·lence** \ˈsī-ləns\ n **1** : the state of being silent **2** : STILLNESS **3** : SECRECY

**²silence** vb **si·lenced; si·lenc·ing 1** : to reduce to silence : STILL **2** : to cause to cease hostile firing or criticism

**si·lenc·er** \ˈsī-lən-sər\ n : a device for muffling the noise of a gunshot

**si·lent** \ˈsī-lənt\ adj **1** : not speaking : MUTE; also : TACITURN **2** : STILL, QUIET **3** : performed or borne without utterance ⟨a ∼ prayer⟩ ♦ **Synonyms** RETICENT, RESERVED, CLOSEMOUTHED, CLOSE — **si·lent·ly** adv

**¹sil·hou·ette** \ˌsi-lə-ˈwet\ n [F] **1** : a representation of the outlines of an object filled in with black or some other uniform color **2** : OUTLINE ⟨∼ of a ship⟩

**²silhouette** vb **-ett·ed; -ett·ing** : to represent by a silhouette; also : to show against a light background

**sil·i·ca** \ˈsi-li-kə\ n : a mineral that consists of silicon and oxygen

**sil·i·cate** \ˈsi-lə-ˌkāt, ˈsi-li-kət\ n : a chemical salt that consists of a metal combined with silicon and oxygen

**si·li·ceous** also **si·li·cious** \sə-ˈli-shəs\ adj : of, relating to, or containing silica or a silicate

**sil·i·con** \ˈsi-li-kən, ˈsi-lə-ˌkän\ n : a nonmetallic chemical element that occurs in combination as the most abundant element next to oxygen in the earth's crust and is used esp. in alloys and semiconductors

**sil·i·cone** \ˈsi-lə-ˌkōn\ n : an organic silicon compound used esp. for lubricants and varnishes

**sil·i·co·sis** \ˌsi-lə-ˈkō-səs\ n : a lung disease caused by prolonged inhaling of silica dusts

**silk** \ˈsilk\ n **1** : a fine strong lustrous protein fiber produced by insect larvae usu. for their cocoons; esp : one from moth larvae (**silk·worms** \-ˌwərmz\) used for cloth **2** : thread or cloth made from silk — **silk·en** \ˈsil-kən\ adj — **silky** adj

**silk screen** n : a stencil process in which coloring matter is forced through the meshes of a prepared silk or organdy screen; also : a print made by this process — **silk–screen** vb

**sill** \ˈsil\ n : a heavy crosspiece (as of wood or stone) that forms the bottom member of a window frame or a doorway; also : a horizontal supporting piece at the base of a structure

**sil·ly** \ˈsi-lē\ adj **sil·li·er; -est** [ME *sely, silly* happy, innocent, pitiable, feeble, fr. OE *sǣlig*, fr. *sǣl* happiness] **1** : FOOLISH, ABSURD, STUPID — **sil·li·ness** n

**si·lo** \ˈsī-lō\ n, pl **silos** [Sp] **1** : a trench, pit, or esp. a tall cylinder for making and storing silage **2** : an underground structure for housing a guided missile

**¹silt** \ˈsilt\ n **1** : fine earth; esp : particles of such soil floating in rivers, ponds, or lakes **2** : a deposit (as by a river) of silt — **silty** adj

**²silt** vb : to obstruct or cover with silt — **silt·ation** \sil-ˈtā-shən\ n

**Si·lu·ri·an** \sī-ˈlu̇r-ē-ən\ adj : of, relating to, or being the period of the Paleozoic era between the Ordovician and the Devonian marked by the appearance of the first land plants — **Silurian** n

**¹sil·ver** \ˈsil-vər\ n **1** : a white ductile metallic chemical element that takes a high polish and is a better conductor of heat and electricity than any other substance **2** : coin made of silver **3** : FLATWARE **4** : a grayish white color — **sil·very** adj

**²silver** adj **1** : relating to, made of, or coated with silver **2** : SILVERY

**³silver** vb **sil·vered; sil·ver·ing** : to coat with or as if with silver — **sil·ver·er** n

**silver bromide** n : a light-sensitive compound used esp. in photography

**sil·ver·fish** \ˈsil-vər-ˌfish\ n : any of various small wingless insects found in houses and sometimes injurious esp. to sized paper and starched clothes

**silver iodide** n : a light-sensitive compound used in photography, rainmaking, and medicine

**silver maple** n : a No. American maple with deeply cut leaves that are green above and silvery white below

**silver nitrate** n : a soluble compound used in photography and as an antiseptic

**sil·ver·ware** \ˈsil-vər-ˌwer\ n : FLATWARE

**sim** abbr simulation; simulator

**sim·i·an** \ˈsi-mē-ən\ n : MONKEY, APE — **simian** adj

**simian immunodeficiency virus** n : SIV

**sim·i·lar** \ˈsi-mə-lər\ adj : marked by correspondence or resemblance ♦ **Synonyms** ALIKE, AKIN, COMPARABLE, PARALLEL — **sim·i·lar·i·ty** \ˌsi-mə-ˈler-ə-tē\ n — **sim·i·lar·ly** adv

**sim·i·le** \ˈsi-mə-(ˌ)lē\ n [ME, fr. L, likeness, comparison, fr. neut. of *similis* like, similar] : a figure of speech in which two dissimilar things are compared by the use of *like* or *as* (as in "cheeks like roses")

**si·mil·i·tude** \sə-ˈmi-lə-ˌtüd, -ˌtyüd\ n : LIKENESS, RESEMBLANCE

**sim·mer** \ˈsi-mər\ vb **sim·mered; sim·mer·ing 1** : to stew at or just below the boiling point **2** : to be on the point of bursting out with violence or emotional disturbance — **simmer** *n*

**simmer down** *vb* : to become calm or peaceful

**si·mo·nize** \'sī-mə-ˌnīz\ *vb* **-nized; -niz·ing** : to polish with or as if with wax

**si·mo·ny** \'sī-mə-nē, 'si-\ *n* [ME *symonie*, fr. AF *simonie*, fr. LL *simonia*, fr. *Simon* Magus sorcerer of Samaria in Acts 8:9–24] : the buying or selling of a church office

**sim·pa·ti·co** \sim-'pä-ti-ˌkō, -'pa-\ *adj* : CONGENIAL, LIKABLE

**sim·per** \'sim-pər\ *vb* : to smile in a silly manner — **simper** *n*

**sim·ple** \'sim-pəl\ *adj* **sim·pler** \-pə-lər\; **sim·plest** \-pə-ləst\ [ME, fr. AF, plain, uncomplicated, artless, fr. L *simplus, simplex*, lit., single; L *simplex* fr. *sim-* one + *-plus* multiplied by; L *simplex* fr. *sim-* + *-plex* -fold] **1** : free from dishonesty or vanity : INNOCENT **2** : free from ostentation **3** : of humble origin or modest position **4** : STUPID **5** : not complex : PLAIN ⟨a ∼ melody⟩ ⟨∼ directions⟩ **6** : lacking education, experience, or intelligence **7** : developing from a single ovary ⟨a ∼ fruit⟩ ♦ **Synonyms** EASY, FACILE, LIGHT, EFFORTLESS — **sim·ple·ness** *n* — **sim·ply** *adv*

**simple interest** *n* : interest paid or computed on the original principal only of a loan or on the amount of an account

**sim·ple·ton** \'sim-pəl-tən\ *n* : FOOL

**sim·plic·i·ty** \sim-'pli-sə-tē\ *n, pl* **-ties 1** : lack of complication : CLEARNESS ⟨the ∼ of his reasoning⟩ **2** : CANDOR, ARTLESSNESS **3** : plainness in manners or way of life **4** : SILLINESS, FOLLY

**sim·pli·fy** \'sim-plə-ˌfī\ *vb* **-fied; -fy·ing** : to make less complex — **sim·pli·fi·ca·tion** \ˌsim-plə-fə-'kā-shən\ *n*

**sim·plis·tic** \sim-'plis-tik\ *adj* : excessively simple : tending to overlook complexities ⟨a ∼ solution⟩

**sim·u·late** \'sim-yə-ˌlāt\ *vb* **-lat·ed; -lat·ing** : to give or create the effect or appearance of : IMITATE; *also* : to make a simulation of — **sim·u·la·tor** \'sim-yə-ˌlā-tər\ *n*

**sim·u·la·tion** \ˌsim-yə-'lā-shən\ *n* **1** : the act or process of simulating **2** : an object that is not genuine **3** : the imitation by one system or process of the way in which another system or process works

**si·mul·ta·ne·ous** \ˌsī-məl-'tā-nē-əs, ˌsi-\ *adj* : occurring or operating at the same time — **si·mul·ta·ne·ous·ly** *adv* — **si·mul·ta·ne·ous·ness** *n*

**¹sin** \'sin\ *n* **1** : an offense esp. against God **2** : FAULT **3** : a weakened state of human nature in which the self is estranged from God — **sin·less** *adj*

**²sin** *vb* **sinned; sin·ning** : to commit a sin — **sin·ner** *n*

**³sin** *abbr* sine

**¹since** \'sins\ *adv* **1** : from a past time until now **2** : backward in time : AGO **3** : after a time in the past

**²since** *conj* **1** : from the time when **2** : seeing that : BECAUSE

**³since** *prep* **1** : in the period after ⟨changes made ∼ the war⟩ **2** : continuously from ⟨has been here ∼ 1980⟩

**sin·cere** \sin-'sir\ *adj* **sin·cer·er; sin·cer·est 1** : free from hypocrisy : HONEST **2** : GENUINE, REAL — **sin·cere·ly** *adv* — **sin·cer·i·ty** \-'ser-ə-tē\ *n*

**sine** \'sīn\ *n* [ML *sinus*, fr. L, curve] : the trigonometric function that is the ratio between the side opposite an acute angle in a right triangle and the hypotenuse

**si·ne·cure** \'sī-ni-ˌkyur, 'si-\ *n* : a paying job that requires little or no work

**si·ne die** \ˌsī-ni-'dī-ˌē, ˌsi-nā-'dē-ˌā\ *adv* [L, without day] : INDEFINITELY ⟨the meeting adjourned *sine die*⟩

**si·ne qua non** \ˌsi-ni-ˌkwä-'nän, -'nōn\ *n, pl* **sine qua nons** *also* **sine qui·bus non** \-ˌkwi-(ˌ)bùs-\ [LL, without which not] : something indispensable or essential

**sin·ew** \'sin-yü\ *n* **1** : TENDON **2** : physical strength — **sin·ewy** *adj*

**sin·ful** \'sin-fəl\ *adj* : marked by or full of sin : WICKED — **sin·ful·ly** *adv* — **sin·ful·ness** *n*

**¹sing** \'siŋ\ *vb* **sang** \'saŋ\ *or* **sung** \'səŋ\; **sung; sing·ing 1** : to produce musical tones with the voice; *also* : to utter with musical tones **2** : to make a prolonged shrill sound ⟨locusts ∼*ing*⟩ **3** : to produce sustained musical sounds ⟨birds ∼*ing*⟩ **4** : CHANT, INTONE **5** : to write poetry; *also* : to celebrate in song or verse **6** : to give information or evidence — **sing·er** *n*

**²sing** *abbr* singular

**singe** \'sinj\ *vb* **singed; singe·ing** : to scorch lightly the outside of; *esp* : to remove the hair or down from usu. by passing over a flame

**¹sin·gle** \'siŋ-gəl\ *adj* **1** : UNMARRIED **2** : being alone : being the only one **3** : having only one feature or part **4** : made for one person ♦ **Synonyms** SOLE, UNIQUE, LONE, SOLITARY, SEPARATE, PARTICULAR — **sin·gle·ness** *n* — **sin·gly** *adv*

**²single** *n* **1** : a separate person or thing; *also* : an unmarried person **2** : a hit in baseball that enables the batter to reach first base **3** *pl* : a tennis match with one player on each side

**³single** *vb* **sin·gled; sin·gling 1** : to select (one) from a group **2** : to hit a single

**single bond** *n* : a chemical bond in which one pair of electrons is shared by two atoms in a molecule

**single–lens reflex** *n* : a camera having a single lens that forms an image which is reflected to the viewfinder or recorded on film

**sin·gle–mind·ed** \ˌsiŋ-gəl-'mīn-dəd\ *adj* : having one driving purpose or resolve ⟨∼ determination⟩ — **sin·gle–mind·ed·ly** *adv* — **sin·gle–mind·ed·ness** *n*

**sing·song** \'siŋ-ˌsoŋ\ *n* **1** : verse with marked and regular rhythm and rhyme **2** : a voice delivery marked by monotonous rhythm — **sing·songy** \-ˌsoŋ-ē\ *adj*

**sin·gu·lar** \'siŋ-gyə-lər\ *adj* **1** : of, relating to, or constituting a word form denoting one person, thing, or instance **2** : OUTSTANDING, EXCEPTIONAL **3** : of unusual quality **4** : ODD, PECULIAR — **singular** n — **sin·gu·lar·i·ty** \ˌsiŋ-gyə-ˈler-ə-tē\ n — **sin·gu·lar·ly** adv

**sin·is·tor** \ˈsi-nəs-tər\ adj [ME sinistre, fr. AF senestre on the left, fr. L sinister on the left side, inauspicious] **1** : singularly evil or productive of evil **2** : accompanied by or leading to disaster ♦ **Synonyms** BALEFUL, MALIGN, MALEFIC, MALEFICENT — **sin·is·ter·ly** adv

¹**sink** \ˈsiŋk\ vb **sank** \ˈsaŋk\ or **sunk** \ˈsəŋk\; **sunk; sink·ing 1** : SUBMERGE **2** : to descend lower and lower **3** : to grow less in volume or height **4** : to slope downward **5** : to penetrate downward **6** : to fail in health or strength **7** : LAPSE, DEGENERATE **8** : to cause (a ship) to descend to the bottom **9** : to make (a hole or shaft) by digging, boring, or cutting **10** : INVEST — **sink·able** adj

²**sink** n **1** : DRAIN, SEWER **2** : a basin connected with a drain **3** : an extensive depression in the land surface

**sink·er** \ˈsiŋ-kər\ n : a weight for sinking a fishing line or net

**sink·hole** \ˈsiŋk-ˌhōl\ n : a hollow place in which drainage collects

**si·nol·o·gy** \sī-ˈnä-lə-jē\ n, often cap : the study of the Chinese and esp. their language, history, and culture — **si·no·log·i·cal** \ˌsī-nə-ˈlä-ji-kəl\ adj, often cap — **si·nol·o·gist** \sī-ˈnä-lə-jist\ n, often cap

**sin tax** n : a tax on substances or activities considered sinful or harmful

**sin·u·ous** \ˈsin-yə-wəs\ adj : bending in and out : WINDING — **sin·u·os·i·ty** \ˌsin-yə-ˈwä-sə-tē\ n — **sin·u·ous·ly** adv

**si·nus** \ˈsī-nəs\ n [ME, fr. ML, fr. L, curve, hollow] **1** : any of several cavities of the skull usu. connecting with the nostrils **2** : a space forming a channel (as for the passage of blood)

**si·nus·itis** \ˌsī-nə-ˈsī-təs\ n : inflammation of a sinus of the skull

**Sioux** \ˈsü\ n, pl **Sioux** \same or ˈsüz\ [AmerF, short for Nadouessioux, fr. Ojibwa na towe ssiw-, prob. fr. Algonquian *aˈtowe*- speak another language] : DAKOTA

**sip** \ˈsip\ vb **sipped; sip·ping** : to drink in small quantities — **sip** n

¹**si·phon** also **sy·phon** \ˈsī-fən\ n **1** : a bent tube through which a liquid can be transferred by means of air pressure up and over the edge of one container and into another container placed at a lower level **2** usu **sy·phon** : a bottle that ejects soda water through a tube when a valve is opened

²**siphon** also **syphon** vb **si·phoned** also **sy·phoned; si·phon·ing** also **sy·phon·ing** : to draw off by means of a siphon

**sip·py cup** \ˈsi-pē-\ n : a cup having a lid with a perforated spout for a young child

**sir** \ˈsər\ n [ME sir, sire, fr. AF, lord, feudal superior, fr. VL *seior*, alter. of L senior, compar. of senex old, old man] **1** : a man of rank or position — used as a title before the given name of a knight or baronet **2** — used as a usu. respectful form of address

**Si·rach** \ˈsī-rak, sə-ˈräk\ n — see BIBLE table

¹**sire** \ˈsī(-ə)r\ n **1** : FATHER; also, archaic : FOREFATHER **2** archaic : LORD — used as a form of address and a title **3** : the male parent of an animal (as a horse or dog)

²**sire** vb **sired; sir·ing** : BEGET

**si·ren** \ˈsī-rən\ n **1** : a seductive or alluring woman **2** : an electrically operated device for producing a loud shrill warning signal — **siren** adj

**sir·loin** \ˈsər-ˌlóin\ n [alter. of earlier surloin, modif. of MF surlonge, fr. sur over (fr. L super) + longe loin] : a cut of beef taken from the part in front of the round

**sirup** var of SYRUP

**si·sal** \ˈsī-səl, -zəl\ n : a strong cordage fiber from an agave; also : this agave

**sis·sy** \ˈsi-sē\ n, pl **sissies** : an effeminate boy or man; also : a timid or cowardly person

**sis·ter** \ˈsis-tər\ n **1** : a female having one or both parents in common with another individual **2** : a member of a religious order of women : NUN **3** chiefly Brit : NURSE **4 a** : a girl or woman regarded as a comrade **b** : a girl or woman that shares with another a common national or racial origin — **sis·ter·ly** adj

**sis·ter·hood** \-ˌhúd\ n **1** : the state of being a sister **2** : a community or society of sisters **3** : the solidarity of women based on shared conditions

**sis·ter–in–law** \ˈsis-tə-rən-ˌlò\ n, pl **sis·ters–in–law** : the sister of one's spouse; also : the wife of one's brother

**sit** \ˈsit\ vb **sat** \ˈsat\; **sit·ting 1** : to rest upon the buttocks or haunches **2** : ROOST, PERCH **3** : to occupy a seat **4** : to hold a session **5** : to cover eggs for hatching : BROOD **6** : to pose for a portrait **7** : to remain quiet or inactive **8** : FIT **9** : to cause (oneself) to be seated **10** : to place in position **11** : to keep one's seat on (~ a horse) **12** : BABYSIT — **sit·ter** n

**si·tar** \si-ˈtär\ n [Hindi & Urdu sitār] : an Indian lute with a long neck and a varying number of strings

**sit·com** \ˈsit-ˌkäm\ n : SITUATION COMEDY

**site** \ˈsīt\ n **1** : LOCATION **2** : WEBSITE

**sit–in** \ˈsit-ˌin\ n : an act of sitting in the seats or on the floor of an establishment as a means of organized protest

**sit·u·at·ed** \ˈsi-chə-ˌwä-təd\ adj : LOCATED, PLACED

**sit·u·a·tion** \ˌsi-chə-ˈwä-shən\ n **1** : LOCATION, SITE **2** : JOB **3** : CONDITION, CIRCUMSTANCES — **sit·u·a·tion·al** \-shə-nəl\ adj

**situation comedy** n : a radio or television comedy series that involves a continuing cast of characters in a succession of episodes

**sit–up** \ˈsit-ˌəp\ n : an exercise performed from a supine position by raising the torso to a sitting position and returning to the original position without lifting the feet

**SIV** \ˌes-ˌī-ˈvē\ n [simian immunodeficiency

virus] : a retrovirus related to HIV that causes a disease in monkeys similar to AIDS

**six** \'siks\ *n* **1** : one more than five **2** : the 6th in a set or series **3** : something having six units — **six** *adj or pron* — **sixth** \'siksth\ *adj or adv or n*

**six–gun** \'siks-ˌgən\ *n* : a 6-chambered revolver

**six–pack** \-ˌpak\ *n* : six bottles or cans (as of beer) packaged and purchased together; *also* : the contents of a six-pack

**six·pence** \-pəns, *US also* -ˌpens\ *n* : the sum of six pence; *also* : an English silver coin of this value

**six–shoot·er** \'siks-ˌshü-tər\ *n* : SIX-GUN

**six·teen** \siks-'tēn\ *n* : one more than 15 — **sixteen** *adj or pron* — **six·teenth** \-'tēnth\ *adj or n*

**six·ty** \'siks-tē\ *n, pl* **sixties** : six times 10 — **six·ti·eth** \'siks-tē-əth\ *adj or n* — **sixty** *adj or pron*

**siz·able** *or* **size·able** \'sī-zə-bəl\ *adj* : quite large — **siz·ably** \-blē\ *adv*

**¹size** \'sīz\ *n* [ME *sise* assize, judgment, quantity, fr. AF, short for *assise* assize] : physical extent or bulk : DIMENSIONS; *also* : considerable proportions — **sized** \'sīzd\ *adj*

**²size** *vb* **sized; siz·ing 1** : to grade or classify according to size **2** : to form a judgment of ⟨~ up the situation⟩

**³size** *n* : a gluey material used for filling the pores in paper, plaster, or textiles — **siz·ing** *n*

**⁴size** *vb* **sized; siz·ing** : to cover, stiffen, or glaze with size

**siz·zle** \'sj-zəl\ *vb* **siz·zled; siz·zling** : to fry or shrivel up with a hissing sound — **sizzle** *n*

**SJ** *abbr* Society of Jesus

**SK** *abbr* Saskatchewan

**ska** \'skä\ *n* : popular music of Jamaican origin combining traditional Caribbean rhythms and jazz

**¹skate** \'skāt\ *n, pl* **skates** *also* **skate** : any of a family of rays with thick broad winglike fins

**²skate** *n* **1** : a metal frame and runner attached to a shoe and used for gliding over ice **2** : ROLLER SKATE; *esp* : IN-LINE SKATE — **skate** *vb* — **skat·er** *n*

**skate·board** \'skāt-ˌbȯrd\ *n* : a short board mounted on small wheels — **skateboard** *vb* — **skate·board·er** *n*

**skeet** \'skēt\ *n* : trapshooting in which clay targets are thrown in such a way that their angle of flight simulates that of a flushed game bird

**skein** \'skān\ *n* : a loosely twisted quantity of yarn or thread wound on a reel

**skel·e·ton** \'ske-lə-tᵊn\ *n* **1** : a usu. bony supporting framework of an animal body **2** : a bare minimum **3** : FRAMEWORK — **skel·e·tal** \-lə-tᵊl\ *adj*

**skep·tic** \'skep-tik\ *n* **1** : one who believes in skepticism **2** : a person disposed to skepticism esp. regarding religion — **skep·ti·cal** \-ti-kəl\ *adj* — **skep·ti·cal·ly** \-k(ə-)lē\ *adv*

**skep·ti·cism** \'skep-tə-ˌsi-zəm\ *n* **1** : a doubting state of mind **2** : a doctrine that

certainty of knowledge cannot be attained **3** : doubt concerning religion

**sketch** \'skech\ *n* [D *schets*, fr. It *schizzo*, lit., splash] **1** : a rough drawing or outline **2** : a short or light literary composition (as a story or essay); *also* : a short comedy piece — **sketch** *vb* — **sketchy** *adj*

**¹skew** \'skyü\ *vb* : TWIST, SWERVE

**²skew** *n* : SLANT

**skew·er** \'skyü-ər\ *n* : a long pin for holding small pieces of meat and vegetables for broiling — **skewer** *vb*

**¹ski** \'skē\ *n, pl* **skis** [Norw. fr. ON *skīth* stick of wood, ski] : one of a pair of long strips (as of wood, metal or plastic) curving upward in front that are used for gliding over snow or water

**²ski** *vb* **skied** \'skēd\; **ski·ing** : to glide on skis — **ski·able** \'skē-ə-bəl\ *adj* — **ski·er** *n*

**¹skid** \'skid\ *n* **1** : a plank for supporting something above the ground **2** : a device placed under a wheel to prevent turning **3** : a timber or rail over or on which something is slid or rolled **4** : the act of skidding **5** : a runner on the landing gear of an aircraft *sic* : ²PALLET

**²skid** *vb* **skid·ded; skid·ding 1** : to slide without rotating ⟨a *skidding* wheel⟩ **2** : to slide sideways on the road ⟨the car *skidded* on ice⟩ **3** : SLIDE, SLIP

**skid row** *n* : a district of cheap saloons frequented by vagrants and alcoholics

**skiff** \'skif\ *n* : a small boat

**ski jump** *n* : a jump made by a person wearing skis; *also* : a course or track prepared for such jumping — **ski jump** *vb* — **ski jumper** *n*

**skil·ful** *chiefly Brit var of* SKILLFUL

**ski lift** *n* : a mechanical device (as a chairlift) for carrying skiers up a long slope

**skill** \'skil\ *n* **1** : ability to use one's knowledge effectively in doing something **2** : developed or acquired ability ♦ *Synonyms* ART, CRAFT, CUNNING, DEXTERITY, EXPERTISE, KNOW-HOW — **skilled** \'skild\ *adj*

**skil·let** \'ski-lət\ *n* : a frying pan

**skill·ful** \'skil-fəl\ *adj* **1** : having or displaying skill : EXPERT **2** : accomplished with skill — **skill·ful·ly** *adv* — **skill·ful·ness** *n*

**¹skim** \'skim\ *vb* **skimmed; skim·ming** : to take off from the top of a liquid; *also* : to remove (scum or cream) from ⟨~ milk⟩ **2** : to read rapidly and superficially **3** : to pass swiftly over — **skim·mer** *n*

**²skim** *adj* : having the cream removed

**skimp** \'skimp\ *vb* : to give insufficient attention, effort, or funds; *also* : to save by skimping

**skimpy** \'skim-pē\ *adj* **skimp·i·er; -est** : deficient in supply or execution — **skimp·i·ly** \-pə-lē\ *adv*

**skin** \'skin\ *n* **1** : the outer limiting layer of an animal body; *also* : the usu. thin tough tissue of which this is made **2** : an outer or surface layer (as a rind or peel) — **skin·less** *adj* — **skinned** *adj*

**²skin** vb **skinned; skin·ning** : to free from skin : remove the skin of ⟨~ a rabbit⟩

**³skin** adj : devoted to showing nudes ⟨~ magazines⟩

**skin diving** n : the sport of swimming under water with a face mask and flippers and esp. without a portable breathing device — **skin–dive** vb — **skin diver** n

**skin·flint** \'skin-ˌflint\ n : a very stingy person

**skin graft** n : a piece of skin surgically removed from one area to replace skin in another area — **skin grafting** n

**skin·head** \'skin-ˌhed\ n : a person whose hair is cut very short

**¹skin·ny** \'ski-nē\ adj **skin·ni·er; -est** 1 : resembling skin 2 : very thin

**²skinny** n : inside information

**skin·ny–dip** \'ski-nē-ˌdip\ vb : to swim in the nude — **skin·ny–dip·per** \-ˌdi-pər\ n

**skin·tight** \'skin-'tīt\ adj : closely fitted to the figure ⟨~ pants⟩

**¹skip** \'skip\ vb **skipped; skip·ping** 1 : to move with leaps and bounds 2 : to leap lightly over 3 : to pass from point to point (as in reading) disregarding what is in between 4 : to pass over without notice or mention

**²skip** n : a light bouncing step; also : a gait of alternate hops and steps

**skip·jack** \'skip-ˌjak\ n : a small sailboat with vertical sides and a bottom similar to a flat V

**skip·per** \'ski-pər\ n [ME, fr. MD schipper, fr. schip ship] : the master of a ship; also : the manager of a baseball team — **skipper** vb

**skir·mish** \'skər-mish\ n : a minor engagement in war; also : a minor dispute or contest — **skirmish** vb

**¹skirt** \'skərt\ n : a free-hanging garment or part of a garment extending from the waist down

**²skirt** vb 1 : to pass around the outer edge of 2 : BORDER 3 : EVADE ⟨~ the issue⟩

**skit** \'skit\ n : a brief dramatic sketch

**ski tow** n : SKI LIFT

**skit·ter** \'ski-tər\ vb : to glide or skip lightly or quickly : skim along a surface

**skit·tish** \'ski-tish\ adj 1 : CAPRICIOUS 2 : easily frightened ⟨a ~ horse⟩; also : WARY ⟨~ investors⟩

**ski·wear** \'skē-ˌwer\ n : clothing suitable for wear while skiing

**skosh** \'skōsh\ n [Jp sukoshi] : a small amount : BIT ⟨has a ~ more room⟩

**skul·dug·gery** or **skull·dug·gery** \ˌskəl-'də-gə-rē\ n, pl **-ger·ies** : underhanded or unscrupulous behavior

**skulk** \'skəlk\ vb : to move furtively : SNEAK, LURK — **skulk·er** n

**skull** \'skəl\ n : the skeleton of the head of a vertebrate that protects the brain and supports the jaws

**skull and crossbones** n, pl **skulls and crossbones** : a depiction of a human skull over crossbones usu. indicating a danger

**skull·cap** \'skəl-ˌkap\ n : a close-fitting brimless cap

**¹skunk** \'skəŋk\ n, pl **skunks** also **skunk** 1 : any of various black-and-white New World mammals related to the weasels that can forcibly eject an ill-smelling fluid when startled 2 : a contemptible person

**²skunk** vb : to defeat decisively; esp : to prevent entirely from scoring in a game

**skunk cabbage** n : either of two No. American perennial herbs related to the arums that occur in shaded wet to swampy areas and have a fetid odor suggestive of a skunk

**sky** \'skī\ n, pl **skies** [ME, sky, cloud, fr. ON skȳ cloud] 1 : the upper air 2 : HEAVEN — **sky·ey** \'skī-ē\ adj

**sky·cap** \-ˌkap\ n : a person employed to carry luggage at an airport

**sky·div·ing** \-ˌdī-viŋ\ n : the sport of jumping from an airplane and executing various body maneuvers before opening a parachute — **skydiver** n

**sky·jack** \-ˌjak\ vb : to commandeer an airplane in flight by threat of violence — **sky·jack·er** — **sky·jack·ing** n

**¹sky·lark** \-ˌlärk\ n : a European lark noted for singing during flight

**²skylark** vb : FROLIC, SPORT

**sky·light** \'skī-ˌlīt\ n : a window in a roof or ceiling — **sky·light·ed** \-ˌlī-təd\ adj

**sky·line** \-ˌlīn\ n 1 : HORIZON 2 : an out line (as of buildings) against the sky

**¹sky·rock·et** \-ˌrä-kət\ n : ROCKET 1

**²skyrocket** vb : ROCKET 2

**sky·scrap·er** \-ˌskrā-pər\ n : a very tall building

**sky·surf·ing** \-ˌsər-fiŋ\ n : skydiving with a short modified surfboard attached to the feet — **sky·surf·er** \-fər\ n

**sky·walk** \-ˌwȯk\ n : an aerial walkway connecting two buildings

**sky·ward** \-wərd\ adv : toward the sky

**sky·writ·ing** \-ˌrī-tiŋ\ n : writing in the sky formed by smoke emitted from an airplane — **sky·writ·er** n

**sl** abbr 1 slightly 2 slip 3 slow

**slab** \'slab\ n : a thick flat piece or slice

**¹slack** \'slak\ adj 1 : CARELESS, NEGLIGENT 2 : SLUGGISH, LISTLESS 3 : not taut : LOOSE 4 : not busy or active ⟨a ~ season⟩ ♦ **Synonyms** LAX, REMISS, NEGLECTFUL, DELINQUENT, DERELICT — **slack·ly** adv — **slack·ness** n

**²slack** vb 1 : to make or become slack : LOOSEN, RELAX 2 : SLAKE 2

**³slack** n 1 : cessation of movement or flow : LETUP 2 : a part that hangs loose without strain ⟨~ of a rope⟩ 3 : pants esp. for casual wear — usu. used in pl.

**slack·en** \'sla-kən\ vb : to make or become slack

**slack·er** \'sla-kər\ n 1 : one that shirks work or evades military duty 2 : a young person perceived to be disaffected, apathetic, cynical, or lacking ambition

**slag** \'slag\ n : the waste left after the melting of ores and the separation of metal from them

**slain** past part of SLAY

**slake** \'slāk, for 2 also 'slak\ vb **slaked; slak·ing** 1 : to relieve or satisfy with or as if with refreshing drink ⟨~ thirst⟩ 2 : to cause (lime) to crumble by mixture with water

**sla·lom** \'slä-ləm\ *n* [Norw *slalam*, lit., sloping track] : skiing in a zigzag course between obstacles

**¹slam** \'slam\ *n* : the winning of every trick or of all tricks but one in bridge

**²slam** *n* **1** : a heavy jarring impact : BANG **2** : harsh criticism **3** : a poetry competition

**³slam** *vb* **slammed; slam·ming 1** : to shut violently and noisily **2** : to throw or strike with a loud impact **3** : to criticize harshly ⟨was *slammed* in the press⟩

**slam·mer** \'sla-mər\ *n* : JAIL, PRISON

**¹slan·der** \'slan-dər\ *vb* : to utter slander against : DEFAME — **slan·der·er** *n*

**²slander** *n* [ME *sclaundre, slaundre*, fr. AF *esclandre*, alter. of *escandle*, fr. LL *scandalum* stumbling block, offense] : a false report maliciously uttered and tending to injure the reputation of a person — **slan·der·ous** *adj*

**slang** \'slaŋ\ *n* : an informal nonstandard vocabulary composed typically of invented words, arbitrarily changed words, and extravagant figures of speech — **slangy** *adj*

**¹slant** \'slant\ *n* **1** : a sloping direction, line, or plane **2** : a particular or personal viewpoint ⟨has a liberal ∼⟩ — **slant** *adj* — **slant·wise** \-,wīz\ *adv or adj*

**²slant** *vb* **1** : SLOPE **2** : to interpret or present in accordance with a special viewpoint or bias ⟨∼ed the story for their benefit⟩ ♦ *Synonyms* INCLINE, LEAN, LIST, TILT, HEEL — **slant·ing·ly** *adv*

**slap** \'slap\ *vb* **slapped; slap·ping 1** : to strike sharply with the open hand **2** : REBUFF, INSULT — **slap** *n*

**slap·stick** \-,stik\ *n* : comedy stressing horseplay

**¹slash** \'slash\ *vb* **1** : to cut with sweeping strokes **2** : to cut slits in (a garment) **3** : to reduce sharply ⟨∼ed prices⟩ — **slash·er** \'sla-shər\ *n*

**²slash** *n* **1** : GASH **2** : an ornamental slit in a garment **3** : a mark / used to denote "or" (as in *and/or*), "and or" (as in *straggler/deserter*), or "per" (as in *feet/second*)

**slat** \'slat\ *n* : a thin narrow flat strip

**¹slate** \'slāt\ *n* **1** : a dense fine-grained rock that splits into thin layers **2** : a roofing tile or a writing tablet made from this rock **3** : a written or unwritten record ⟨start with a clean ∼⟩ **4** : a list of candidates for election

**²slate** *vb* **slat·ed; slat·ing 1** : to cover with slate **2** : to designate for action or appointment ⟨is *slated* to open soon⟩

**slath·er** \'sla-thər\ *vb* : to spread with or on thickly or lavishly

**slat·tern** \'sla-tərn\ *n* : a slovenly woman — **slat·tern·ly** *adj*

**¹slaugh·ter** \'slȯ-tər\ *n* **1** : the butchering of livestock for market **2** : great destruction of lives esp. in battle

**²slaughter** *vb* **1** : to kill (animals) for food : BUTCHER **2** : to kill in large numbers or in a bloody way : MASSACRE

**slaugh·ter·house** \-,hau̇s\ *n* : an establishment where animals are butchered

**Slav** \'släv, 'slav\ *n* : a person speaking a Slavic language

**¹slave** \'slāv\ *n* [ME *sclave*, fr. AF or ML; AF *esclave*, fr. ML *sclavus*, fr. *Sclavus* Slav; fr. the enslavement of Slavs in central Europe in the Middle Ages] **1** : a person held in servitude as property **2** : a device (as the printer of a computer) that is directly responsive to another — **slave** *adj*

**²slave** *vb* **slaved; slav·ing** : to work like a slave : DRUDGE ⟨*slaved* away at his work⟩

**¹sla·ver** \'sla-vər, 'slä-\ *n* : SLOBBER — **slaver** *vb*

**²slav·er** \'slā-vər\ *n* : a ship or a person engaged in transporting slaves

**slav·ery** \'slāv-rē, 'slā-və-\ *n* **1** : wearisome drudgery **2** : the condition of being a slave **3** : the practice of owning slaves ♦ *Synonyms* SERVITUDE, BONDAGE, ENSLAVEMENT

**¹Slav·ic** \'sla-vik, 'slä-\ *n* : a branch of the Indo-European language family including various languages (as Russian or Polish) of eastern Europe

**²Slavic** *adj* : of or relating to the Slavs or their languages

**slav·ish** \'slā-vish\ *adj* **1** : SERVILE **2** : obeying or imitating with no freedom of judgment or choice — **slav·ish·ly** *adv*

**slaw** \'slȯ\ *n* : COLESLAW

**slay** \'slā\ *vb* **slew** \'slü\; **slain** \'slān\; **slay·ing** : KILL — **slay·er** *n*

**SLBM** *abbr* submarine-launched ballistic missile

**sleaze** \'slēz\ *n* : a sleazy quality, appearance, or behavior

**slea·zy** \'slē-zē\ *adj* **slea·zi·er; -est 1** : FLIMSY, SHODDY **2** : marked by low character or quality ⟨a ∼ lawyer⟩

**¹sled** \'sled\ *n* : a vehicle usu. on runners adapted esp. for sliding on snow

**²sled** *vb* **sled·ded; sled·ding** : to ride or carry on a sled

**¹sledge** \'slej\ *n* : SLEDGEHAMMER

**²sledge** *n* : a strong heavy sled

**sledge·ham·mer** \'slej-,ha-mər\ *n* : a large heavy hammer wielded with both hands — **sledgehammer** *adj or vb*

**¹sleek** \'slēk\ *vb* **1** : to make smooth or glossy **2** : to gloss over

**²sleek** *adj* **1** : having a smooth well-groomed look **2** : trim and graceful in design ⟨a ∼ car⟩

**¹sleep** \'slēp\ *n* **1** : the natural periodic suspension of consciousness during which bodily powers are restored **2** : a state (as death or coma) suggesting sleep — **sleep·less** *adj* — **sleep·less·ness** *n*

**²sleep** *vb* **slept** \'slept\; **sleep·ing 1** : to rest or be in a state of sleep; *also* : to spend in sleep **2** : to have sexual intercourse — usu. used with *with* **3** : to provide sleeping space for

**sleep·er** \'slē-pər\ *n* **1** : one that sleeps **2** : a horizontal beam to support something on or near ground level **3** : SLEEPING CAR **4** : someone or something unpromising or unnoticed that suddenly attains prominence or value

**sleep·ing bag** *n* : a warmly lined bag for sleeping esp. outdoors

**sleeping car** *n* : a railroad car with berths for sleeping

**sleeping pill** *n* : a drug in tablet or capsule form taken to induce sleep

**sleeping sickness** *n* : a serious disease of tropical Africa that is marked by fever, lethargy, confusion, and sleep disturbances and is caused by protozoans transmitted by the tsetse fly

**sleep·over** \'slēp-ˌō-vər\ *n* : an overnight stay (as at another's home)

**sleep·walk·er** \'slēp-ˌwȯ-kər\ *n* : one that walks while or as if while asleep — **sleep·walk** \-ˌwȯk\ *vb*

**sleepy** \'slē-pē\ *adj* **sleep·i·er; -est** : 1 : ready for sleep 2 : quietly inactive — **sleep·i·ly** \'slē-pə-lē\ *adv* — **sleep·i·ness** \-pē-nəs\ *n*

**sleet** \'slēt\ *n* : frozen or partly frozen rain — **sleet** *vb* — **sleety** *adj*

**sleeve** \'slēv\ *n* 1 : a part of a garment covering an arm 2 : a tubular part designed to fit over another part — **sleeved** *adj* — **sleeve·less** *adj*

**¹sleigh** \'slā\ *n* : an open usu. horse-drawn vehicle on runners for use on snow or ice

**²sleigh** *vb* : to drive or travel in a sleigh

**sleight** \'slīt\ *n* 1 : TRICK 2 : DEXTERITY

**sleight of hand** : a trick requiring skillful manual manipulation

**slen·der** \'slen-dər\ *adj* 1 : SLIM, THIN 2 : WEAK, SLIGHT 3 : MEAGER, INADEQUATE ⟨~ opportunities⟩

**slen·der·ize** \-də-ˌrīz\ *vb* **-ized; -iz·ing** : to make slender

**sleuth** \'slüth\ *n* [short for *sleuthhound* bloodhound, fr. ME (Sc) *sleuth hund*, fr. ME *sleuth, sloith, sloth* track of an animal or person, fr. ON *slōth*] : DETECTIVE

**¹slew** \'slü\ *past of* SLAY

**²slew** *vb* : TURN, VEER, SKID

**¹slice** \'slīs\ *vb* **sliced; slic·ing** 1 : to cut a slice from; *also* : to cut into slices 2 : to hit (a ball) so that it curves to the side

**²slice** *n* 1 : a thin flat piece cut from something 2 : a flight of a ball (as in golf) that curves in the direction of the dominant hand of the player hitting it

**¹slick** \'slik\ *vb* : to make smooth or sleek

**²slick** *adj* 1 : very smooth : SLIPPERY 2 : CLEVER, SMART ⟨a ~ salesperson⟩

**³slick** *n* 1 : a smooth patch of water covered with a film of oil 2 : a popular magazine printed on coated paper

**slick·er** \'sli-kər\ *n* 1 : a long loose raincoat 2 : a sly tricky person 3 : a city dweller esp. of natty appearance or sophisticated mannerisms

**¹slide** \'slīd\ *vb* **slid** \'slid\; **slid·ing** \'slī-diŋ\ 1 : to move smoothly along a surface 2 : to fall by a loss of support 3 : to pass unobtrusively 4 : to move or pass smoothly; *also* : to pass unnoticed ⟨let it ~ by⟩ 5 : to fall or dive toward a base in baseball

**²slide** *n* 1 : an act or instance of sliding 2 : something (as a cover or fastener) that operates by sliding 3 : a fall of a mass of earth or snow down a hillside 4 : a surface on which something slides 5 : a glass plate on which a specimen is mounted for examination under a microscope 6 : a small transparent photograph that can be projected on a screen

**slid·er** \'slī-dər\ *n* 1 : one that slides 2 : a baseball pitch that looks like a fastball but curves slightly 3 : a small hamburger

**slide rule** *n* : a manual device for calculation consisting of a ruler and a movable middle piece graduated with logarithmic scales

**slier** *comparative of* SLY

**sliest** *superlative of* SLY

**¹slight** \'slīt\ *adj* 1 : SLENDER; *also* : FRAIL 2 : UNIMPORTANT ⟨a ~ movie⟩ 3 : small of its kind or in amount ⟨a ~ odor⟩ — **slight·ly** *adv*

**²slight** *vb* 1 : to treat as unimportant 2 : to ignore discourteously ⟨~ed the mayor⟩ 3 : to perform or attend to carelessly

**³slight** *n* : a humiliating discourtesy

**¹slim** \'slim\ *adj* **slim·mer; slim·mest** [D, bad, inferior, fr. MD, *slimp* crooked, bad] 1 : SLENDER, SLIGHT, THIN 2 : SMALL, SLIGHT ⟨a ~ chance⟩

**²slim** *vb* **slimmed; slim·ming** : to make or become slimmer

**slime** \'slīm\ *n* 1 : sticky mud 2 : a slippery substance (as on the skin of a slug or catfish) — **slimy** *adj*

**¹sling** \'sliŋ\ *vb* **slung** \'sləŋ\; **sling·ing** : to throw forcibly : FLING 2 : to hurl with or as if with a sling

**²sling** *n* 1 : a short strap with strings attached for hurling stones or shot 2 : something (as a rope or chain) used to hoist, lower, support, or carry; *esp* : a bandage hanging from the neck to support an arm or hand

**sling·shot** \'sliŋ-ˌshät\ *n* : a forked stick with elastic bands for shooting small stones or shot

**slink** \'sliŋk\ *vb* **slunk** \'sləŋk\ *also* **slinked** \'sliŋkt\; **slink·ing** 1 : to move stealthily or furtively 2 : to move sinuously — **slinky** *adj*

**¹slip** \'slip\ *vb* **slipped; slip·ping** 1 : to escape quietly or secretly 2 : to slide along or cause to slide along smoothly 3 : to make a mistake 4 : to pass unnoticed or undone 5 : to fall off from a standard or level

**²slip** *n* 1 : a ramp for repairing ships 2 : a ship's berth between two piers 3 : secret or hurried departure, escape, or evasion 4 : BLUNDER 5 : a sudden mishap 6 : a woman's one-piece garment worn under a dress 7 : PILLOWCASE

**³slip** *n* 1 : a shoot or twig from a plant for planting or grafting 2 : a long narrow strip; *esp* : one of paper used for a record ⟨deposit ~⟩

**⁴slip** *vb* **slipped; slip·ping** : to take slips from (a plant)

**slip·knot** \'slip-ˌnät\ *n* : a knot that slips along the rope around which it is made

**slipped disk** *n* : a protrusion of one of the disks of cartilage between vertebrae with pressure on spinal nerves resulting esp. in low back pain

**slip·per** \'sli-pər\ *n* : a light low shoe that may be easily slipped on and off

# slippery • slum

**slip·pery** \ˈsli-pə-rē\ *adj* **slip·per·i·er; -est** **1** : icy, wet, smooth, or greasy enough to cause one to fall or lose one's hold **2** : not to be trusted : TRICKY ⟨a ~ salesman⟩ — **slip·per·i·ness** *n*

**slip·shod** \ˈslip-ˈshäd\ *adj* : SLOVENLY, CARELESS ⟨~ work⟩

**slip·stream** \ˈslip-ˌstrēm\ *n* : a stream (as of air) driven aft by a propeller

**slip–up** \ˈslip-ˌəp\ *n* **1** : MISTAKE **2** : ACCIDENT

**¹slit** \ˈslit\ *vb* **slit; slit·ting** **1** : SLASH **2** : to cut off or away

**²slit** *n* : a long narrow cut or opening

**slith·er** \ˈsli-thər\ *vb* : to slip or glide along like a snake — **slith·ery** *adj*

**sliv·er** \ˈsli-vər\ *n* : SPLINTER

**slob** \ˈsläb\ *n* : a slovenly or boorish person

**slob·ber** \ˈslä-bər\ *vb* **slob·bered; slob·ber·ing** : to dribble saliva — **slobber** *n*

**sloe** \ˈslō\ *n* : the fruit of the blackthorn

**slog** \ˈsläg\ *vb* **slogged; slog·ging** **1** : to hit hard : BEAT **2** : to work hard and steadily

**slo·gan** \ˈslō-gən\ *n* [alter. of earlier *slogorn*, fr. ScGael *sluagh-ghairm*, fr. *sluagh* army, host + *gairm* cry] : a word or phrase expressing the spirit or aim of a party, group, or cause

**slo–mo** \ˈslō-ˌmō\ *n* : SLOW MOTION — **slo–mo** *adj*

**sloop** \ˈslüp\ *n* [D *sloep*] : a single-masted sailboat with a jib and a fore-and-aft mainsail

**¹slop** \ˈsläp\ *n* **1** : thin tasteless drink or liquid food — usu. used in pl. **2** : food waste for animal feed : SWILL **3** : excreted body waste — usu. used in pl.

**²slop** *vb* **slopped; slop·ping** **1** : SPILL **2** : to feed with slop ⟨~ hogs⟩

**¹slope** \ˈslōp\ *vb* **sloped; slop·ing** : SLANT, INCLINE

**²slope** *n* **1** : upward or downward slant or degree of slant **2** : ground that forms an incline **3** : the part of a landmass draining into a particular ocean

**slop·py** \ˈslä-pē\ *adj* **slop·pi·er; -est** **1** : MUDDY, SLUSHY **2** : SLOVENLY, MESSY

**sloppy joe** \-ˈjō\ *n* : ground beef cooked in a thick spicy sauce and usu. served on a bun

**slosh** \ˈsläsh\ *vb* **1** : to flounder through or splash about in or with water, mud, or slush **2** : to move with a splashing motion

**slot** \ˈslät\ *n* **1** : a long narrow opening or groove **2** : a position in a sequence

**slot car** *n* : an electric toy racing car that runs on a grooved track

**sloth** \ˈslȯth\ *n, pl* **sloths** \ˈslȯths, ˈslȯthz\ **1** : LAZINESS, INDOLENCE **2** : any of several slow-moving plant-eating arboreal mammals of So. and Central America — **sloth·ful** *adj*

**slot machine** *n* **1** : a machine whose operation is begun by dropping a coin into a slot **2** : a coin-operated gambling machine that pays off according to the matching of symbols on wheels spun by a handle

**¹slouch** \ˈslau̇ch\ *n* **1** : a lazy or incompetent person **2** : a loose or drooping gait or posture

**²slouch** *vb* : to walk, stand, or sit with a slouch : SLUMP

**¹slough** \ˈslü, *2 usu* ˈslau̇\ *n* **1** : a wet and marshy or muddy place (as a swamp) **2** : a discouraged state of mind

**²slough** \ˈsləf\ *also* **sluff** *n* : something that may be or may be shed or cast off

**³slough** \ˈsləf\ *also* **sluff** *vb* : to cast off

**Slo·vak** \ˈslō-ˌväk, -ˌvak\ *n* **1** : a member of a Slavic people of Slovakia **2** : the language of the Slovaks — **Slovak** *adj* — **Slo·va·ki·an** \slō-ˈvä-kē-ən, -ˈva-\ *adj or n*

**slov·en** \ˈslə-vən\ *n* [ME *sloveyn* slut, rascal, perh. fr. MD *slof* negligent] : an untidy person

**Slo·vene** \ˈslō-ˌvēn\ *n* **1** : a member of a Slavic people living largely in Slovenia **2** : the language of the Slovenes — **Slovene** *adj* — **Slo·ve·nian** \slō-ˈvē-nē-ən\ *adj or n*

**slov·en·ly** \ˈslə-vən-lē\ *adj* **1** : untidy in dress or person **2** : lazily or carelessly done : SLIPSHOD ⟨~ thinking⟩

**¹slow** \ˈslō\ *adj* **1** : SLUGGISH; *also* : dull in mind : STUPID **2** : moving, flowing, or proceeding at less than the usual speed **3** : taking more than the usual time **4** : registering behind the correct time **5** : not lively : BORING ♦ *Synonyms* DILATORY, LAGGARD, DELIBERATE, LEISURELY — **slow** *adv* — **slow·ly** *adv* — **slow·ness** *n*

**²slow** *vb* **1** : to make slow : hold back **2** : to go slower

**slow motion** *n* : motion-picture action photographed so as to appear much slower than normal — **slow–motion** *adj*

**SLR** *abbr* single-lens reflex

**sludge** \ˈsləj\ *n* : a slushy mass : OOZE; *esp* : solid matter produced by sewage treatment processes

**slue** *var of* ²SLEW

**¹slug** \ˈsləg\ *n* **1** : a small mass of metal; *esp* : BULLET **2** : a metal disk for use (as in a slot machine) in place of a coin **3** : any of numerous wormlike mollusks related to the snails **4** : a quantity of liquor drunk

**²slug** *vb* **slugged; slug·ging** : to strike forcibly and heavily — **slug·ger** *n*

**slug·gard** \ˈslə-gərd\ *n* : a lazy person

**slug·gish** \ˈslə-gish\ *adj* **1** : SLOTHFUL, LAZY **2** : slow in movement, flow, or growth ⟨a ~ economy⟩ **3** : STAGNANT, DULL — **slug·gish·ly** *adv* — **slug·gish·ness** *n*

**¹sluice** \ˈslüs\ *n* [ME *sluse, scluse*, fr. AF *escluse*, fr. LL *exclusa*, fr. L, fem. of *exclusus*, pp. of *excludere* to shut out, exclude] **1** : an artificial passage for water with a gate for controlling the flow; *also* : the gate so used **2** : a channel that carries off surplus water **3** : an inclined trough or flume for washing ore or floating logs

**²sluice** *vb* **sluiced; sluic·ing** **1** : to draw off through a sluice **2** : to wash with running water : FLUSH

**¹slum** \ˈsləm\ *n* : a thickly populated area

marked by poverty and dirty or deteriorated houses — **slum·my** \'slə-mē\ adj

²**slum** vb **slummed; slum·ming** : to visit slums esp. out of curiosity; also : to go somewhere or do something that might be considered beneath one's station

¹**slum·ber** \'sləm-bər\ vb **slum·bered; slum·ber·ing 1** : DOZE; also : SLEEP **2** : to be in a sluggish or torpid state

²**slumber** n : SLEEP

**slum·ber·ous** \'sləm-bə-rəs\ or **slum·brous** \-brəs\ adj **1** : SLUMBERING, SLEEPY **2** : PEACEFUL, INACTIVE

**slum·lord** \'sləm-ˌlȯrd\ n : a landlord who receives unusually large profits from substandard properties

**slump** \'sləmp\ vb **1** : to sink down suddenly : COLLAPSE **2** : SLOUCH **3** : to decline sharply — **slump** n

**slung** past and past part of SLING

**slunk** past and past part of SLINK

¹**slur** \'slər\ n : a slighting remark : ASPERSION — **slur** vb

²**slur** vb **slurred; slur·ring 1** : to slide or slip over without due mention or emphasis **2** : to perform two or more successive notes of different pitch in a smooth or connected way

³**slur** n : a curved line connecting notes to be slurred; also : a group of slurred notes

**slurp** \'slərp\ vb : to eat or drink noisily — **slurp** n

**slur·ry** \'slər-ē\ n, pl **slur·ries** : a watery mixture of insoluble matter

**slush** \'sləsh\ n **1** : partly melted or watery snow **2** : soft mud — **slushy** adj

**slush fund** n : an unregulated fund often for illicit purposes

**slut** \'slət\ n **1** : a slovenly woman **2** : a promiscuous woman — **slut·tish** adj

**sly** \'slī\ adj **sly·er** also **sli·er** \'slī-ər\; **sly·est** also **sli·est** \'slī-əst\ **1** : CRAFTY, CUNNING **2** : SECRETIVE, FURTIVE **3** : ROGUISH ♦ **Synonyms** TRICKY, WILY, ARTFUL, FOXY, GUILEFUL — **sly·ly** also **sli·ly** adv — **sly·ness** n

**sm** abbr small

**Sm** symbol samarium

**SM** abbr **1** master of science **2** sergeant major **3** service mark **4** stage manager

**SMA** abbr sergeant major of the army

¹**smack** \'smak\ n : characteristic flavor; also : a slight trace

²**smack** vb **1** : to have a taste **2** : to have a trace or suggestion ⟨~s of treason⟩

³**smack** vb **1** : to move (the lips) so as to make a sharp noise **2** : to kiss or slap with a loud noise

⁴**smack** n **1** : a sharp noise made by the lips **2** : a loud kiss or slap

⁵**smack** adv : squarely and sharply

⁶**smack** n : a sailing ship used in fishing

⁷**smack** n, slang : HEROIN

**smack·down** \'smak-ˌdau̇n\ n **1** : the act of knocking down an opponent **2** : a wrestling match **3** : a decisive defeat **4** : a competition between rivals

**SMaj** abbr sergeant major

¹**small** \'smȯl\ adj **1** : little in size or amount **2** : operating on a limited scale **3** : little or close to zero (as in number or value) **4** : made up of little things **5**

: TRIFLING, UNIMPORTANT **6** : MEAN, PETTY ♦ **Synonyms** DIMINUTIVE, PETITE, WEE, TINY, MINUTE — **small·ish** adj — **small·ness** n

²**small** n : a small part or product ⟨the ~ of the back⟩

**small·pox** \'smȯl-ˌpäks\ n : a contagious virus disease of humans formerly common but now eradicated

**small talk** n : light or casual conversation

**small–time** \'smȯl-ˈtīm\ adj : insignificant in performance and standing : MINOR — **small–tim·er** n

**smarmy** \'smär-mē\ adj **smarm·i·er; -est** : marked by a smug, ingratiating, or false earnestness ⟨~ politeness⟩

¹**smart** \'smärt\ adj **1** : making one smart ⟨a ~ blow⟩ **2** : mentally quick : BRIGHT **3** : WITTY, CLEVER **4** : STYLISH **5** : being a guided missile **6** : containing a microprocessor for limited computing capability ⟨~ terminal⟩ ♦ **Synonyms** KNOWING, QUICK-WITTED, INTELLIGENT, BRAINY, SHARP — **smart·ly** adv — **smart·ness** n

²**smart** vb **1** : to cause or feel a stinging pain **2** : to feel or endure distress — **smart** n

**smart al·eck** \'smärt-ˌa-lik\ n : a person given to obnoxious cleverness

**smart card** n : a small plastic card that has a built-in microprocessor to store and handle data

**smart·en** \'smär-tᵊn\ vb : to make smart or smarter — usu. used with up

**smart phone** n : a cell phone that includes additional software functions (as e-mail or an Internet browser)

¹**smash** \'smash\ n **1** : a smashing blow **2** : a hard, overhand stroke in tennis **3** : the act or sound of smashing **4** : collision of vehicles : CRASH **5** : COLLAPSE, RUIN; esp : BANKRUPTCY **6** : a striking success : HIT — **smash** adj

²**smash** vb **1** : to break or be broken into pieces **2** : to move forward with force and shattering effect **3** : to destroy utterly : WRECK

**smat·ter·ing** \'sma-tə-riŋ\ n **1** : superficial knowledge **2** : a small scattered number or amount

¹**smear** \'smir\ n **1** : a spot left by an oily or sticky substance **2** : material smeared on a surface (as of a microscope slide)

²**smear** vb **1** : to overspread esp. with something oily or sticky : SMUDGE, SOIL **3** : to injure by slander or insults

¹**smell** \'smel\ vb **smelled** \'smeld\ or **smelt** \'smelt\; **smell·ing 1** : to perceive the odor of by sense organs of the nose; also : to detect or seek with or as if with these organs **2** : to have or give off an odor

²**smell** n **1** : ODOR, SCENT **2** : the process or power of perceiving odor; also : the sense by which one perceives odor **3** : an act of smelling — **smelly** adj

**smelling salts** n pl : an aromatic preparation used as a stimulant and restorative (as to relieve faintness)

¹**smelt** \'smelt\ n, pl **smelts** or **smelt** : any of a family of small food fishes of coastal

or fresh waters that are related to the trouts and salmons

²**smelt** vb : to melt or fuse (ore) in order to separate the metal; also : REFINE

**smelt·er** \'smel-tər\ n 1 : one that smelts 2 : an establishment for smelting

**smid·gen** also **smid·geon** or **smid·gin** \'smi-jən\ n : a small amount : BIT

**smi·lax** \'smī-ˌlaks\ n 1 : any of various mostly climbing and prickly plants related to the lilies 2 : an ornamental plant related to the asparagus

¹**smile** \'smī(-ə)l\ vb smiled; smil·ing 1 : to look with a smile 2 : to be favorable 3 : to express by a smile

²**smile** n : a change of facial expression to express amusement, pleasure, or affection — **smile·less** \'smī(-ə)l-ləs\ adj

**smil·ey** \'smī-lē\ adj : exhibiting a smile : frequently smiling

**smiley face** n : a line drawing that symbolizes a smiling face

**smirch** \'smərch\ vb 1 : to make dirty or stained 2 : to bring disgrace on — **smirch** n

**smirk** \'smərk\ vb : to smile in an affected or smug manner : SIMPER — **smirk** n

**smite** \'smīt\ vb smote \'smōt\; smit·ten \'smi-tᵊn\ or smote; smit·ing \'smī-tiŋ\ 1 : to strike heavily; also : to kill by striking 2 : to affect as if by a heavy blow

**smith** \'smith\ n : a worker in metals; esp : BLACKSMITH

**smith·er·eens** \ˌsmi-thə-'rēnz\ n pl [perh. fr. Ir smidiríní] : FRAGMENTS, BITS

**smithy** \'smi-thē\ n, pl smith·ies 1 : a smith's workshop 2 : BLACKSMITH

¹**smock** \'smäk\ n : a loose garment worn over other clothes as a protection

²**smock** vb : to gather (cloth) in regularly spaced tucks — **smock·ing** n

**smog** \'smäg, 'smȯg\ n [blend of smoke and fog] : a thick haze caused by the action of sunlight on air polluted by smoke and automobile exhaust fumes — **smog·gy** adj

¹**smoke** \'smōk\ n 1 : the gas from burning material (as coal, wood, or tobacco) in which are suspended particles of soot 2 : a mass or column of smoke 3 : something (as a cigarette) to smoke; also : the act of smoking — **smoke·less** adj — **smoky** adj

²**smoke** vb smoked; smok·ing 1 : to emit smoke 2 : to inhale and exhale the fumes of burning tobacco; also : to use in smoking ⟨∼ a pipe⟩ 3 : to stupefy or drive away by smoke 4 : to discolor with smoke 5 : to cure (as meat) with smoke — **smok·er** n

**smoke detector** n : an alarm that sounds automatically when it detects smoke

**smoke jumper** n : a forest firefighter who parachutes to locations otherwise difficult to reach

**smoke screen** n 1 : a screen of smoke to hinder enemy observation 2 : something designed to obscure, confuse, or mislead

**smoke·stack** \'smōk-ˌstak\ n : a pipe or funnel through which smoke and gases are discharged

**smol·der** or **smoul·der** \'smōl-dər\ vb

**smol·dered** or **smoul·dered**; **smol·der·ing** or **smoul·der·ing** 1 : to burn and smoke without flame 2 : to burn inwardly — **smolder** n

**smooch** \'smüch\ vb : KISS, PET — **smooch** n

¹**smooth** \'smüth\ adj 1 : not rough or uneven 2 : not jarring or jolting 3 : BLAND, MILD 4 : fluent in speech and agreeable in manner — **smooth·ly** adv — **smooth·ness** n

²**smooth** vb 1 : to make smooth 2 : to free from trouble or difficulty

**smooth muscle** n : muscle with no cross striations that is typical of visceral organs (as the stomach and bladder) and is not under voluntary control

**smoothy** or **smooth·ie** \'smü-thē\ n, pl **smooth·ies** 1 : an artfully suave person 2 smoothie : a creamy beverage of fruit blended with juice, milk, or yogurt

**s'more** \'smȯr\ n : a dessert of marshmallow and pieces of chocolate sandwiched between graham crackers

**smor·gas·bord** \'smȯr-gəs-ˌbȯrd\ n [Sw smörgasbord, fr. smörgas open sandwich + bord table] : a luncheon or supper buffet consisting of many foods

**smote** past and past part of SMITE

¹**smoth·er** \'smə-thər\ n 1 : thick stifling smoke 2 : a dense cloud (as of fog or dust) 3 : a confused multitude of things

²**smother** vb smoth·ered; smoth·er·ing 1 : to be overcome by or die from lack of air 2 : to kill by depriving of air 3 : SUPPRESS 4 : to cover thickly

**SMSgt** abbr senior master sergeant

¹**smudge** \'sməj\ vb smudged; smudg·ing : to soil or blur by rubbing or smearing ⟨his face was smudged with grease⟩

²**smudge** n : a dirty or blurred spot — **smudgy** adj

**smug** \'sməg\ adj smug·ger; smug·gest : conscious of one's virtue and importance : SELF-SATISFIED ⟨was ∼ about her victory⟩ — **smug·ly** adv — **smug·ness** n

**smug·gle** \'smə-gəl\ vb smug·gled; smug·gling 1 : to import or export secretly, illegally, or without paying the duties required by law 2 : to convey secretly — **smug·gler** \'smə-glər\ n

**smut** \'smət\ n 1 : something (as soot) that smudges; also : SMUDGE, SPOT 2 : any of various destructive diseases of plants caused by fungi; also : a fungus causing smut 3 : indecent language or matter — **smut·ty** adj

**smutch** \'sməch\ n : SMUDGE

**Sn** symbol [LL stannum] tin

**SN** abbr seaman

**snack** \'snak\ n : a light meal : BITE — **snack** vb

**snaf·fle** \'sna-fəl\ n : a simple jointed bit for a horse's bridle

¹**snag** \'snag\ n 1 : a stump or piece of a tree esp. when under water 2 : an unexpected difficulty ♦ *Synonyms* OBSTACLE, OBSTRUCTION, IMPEDIMENT, BAR

²**snag** vb snagged; snag·ging 1 : to become caught on or as if on a snag 2 : to seize quickly : SNATCH

**snail** \\'snāl\\ *n* : any of numerous small gastropod mollusks with a spiral shell into which they can withdraw

**snail mail** *n* **1** : mail delivered by a postal system **2** : MAIL 2

**snake** \\'snāk\\ *n* **1** : any of numerous long-bodied limbless reptiles **2** : a treacherous person **3** : something that resembles a snake — **snake·like** \\-,līk\\ *adj* — **snaky** *adj*

**snake·bite** \\-,bīt\\ *n* : the bite of a snake and esp. a venomous snake

**¹snap** \\'snap\\ *vb* **snapped; snap·ping 1** : to grasp or slash at something with the teeth **2** : to get or buy quickly **3** : to utter sharp or angry words **4** : to break suddenly with a sharp sound **5** : to give a sharp cracking noise **6** : to throw with a quick motion **7** : FLASH ⟨her eyes *snapped*⟩ **8** : to put a football into play — **snap·per** *n* — **snap·pish** *adj*

**²snap** *n* **1** : the act or sound of snapping **2** : something very easy to do : CINCH **3** : a short period of cold weather **4** : a catch or fastening that closes with a click **5** : a thin brittle cookie **6** : ENERGY, VIM; *also* : smartness of movement **7** : the putting of the ball into play in football

**snap bean** *n* : a bean grown primarily for its long pods that are cooked as a vegetable when young and as dried seeds

**snap·drag·on** \\'snap-,dra-gən\\ *n* : any of a genus of herbs with long spikes of showy flowers

**snapping turtle** *n* : either of two large American turtles with powerful jaws and a strong musky odor

**snap·py** \\'sna-pē\\ *adj* **1** : quickly made or done **2** : marked by vigor **3** : STYLISH ⟨a ~ dresser⟩

**snap·shot** \\'snap-,shat\\ *n* : a photograph taken usu. with an inexpensive hand-held camera

**snare** \\'sner\\ *n* : a trap often consisting of a noose for catching birds or mammals — **snare** *vb*

**¹snarl** \\'snärl\\ *vb* : to cause to become knotted and intertwined

**²snarl** *n* : TANGLE — **snarly** \\'snär-lē\\ *adj*

**³snarl** *vb* : to growl angrily or threateningly

**⁴snarl** *n* : an angry ill-tempered growl

**¹snatch** \\'snach\\ *vb* **1** : to try to grasp something suddenly **2** : to seize or take away suddenly ♦ *Synonyms* CLUTCH, SEIZE, GRAB, NAB

**²snatch** *n* **1** : a short period **2** : an act of snatching **3** : something brief or fragmentary ⟨~*es* of song⟩

**¹sneak** \\'snēk\\ *vb* **sneaked** \\'snēkt\\ *or* **snuck** \\'snək\\; **sneak·ing** : to move, act, or take in a furtive manner ⟨~*ed* past the guard⟩ — **sneak·ing·ly** *adv*

**²sneak** *n* **1** : one who acts in a furtive or shifty manner **2** : a stealthy or furtive move or escape — **sneak·i·ly** \\'snē-kə-lē\\ *adv* — **sneaky** *adj*

**sneak·er** \\'snē-kər\\ *n* : a sports shoe with a pliable rubber sole

**sneer** \\'snir\\ *vb* : to show scorn or contempt by curling the lip or by a jeering tone — **sneer** *n*

**sneeze** \\'snēz\\ *vb* **sneezed; sneez·ing** [ME *snesen*, alter. of *fnesen*, fr. OE *fnēosan*] : to force the breath out suddenly and violently as a reflex act — **sneeze** *n*

**SNF** *abbr* skilled nursing facility

**snick·er** \\'sni-kər\\ *n* : a partly suppressed laugh — **snicker** *vb*

**snide** \\'snīd\\ *adj* **1** : MEAN, LOW ⟨a ~ trick⟩ **2** : slyly disparaging ⟨a ~ remark⟩ — **snide·ly** *adv* — **snide·ness** *n*

**sniff** \\'snif\\ *vb* **1** : to draw air audibly up the nose esp. for smelling **2** : to show disdain or scorn **3** : to detect by or as if by smelling — **sniff** *n*

**snif·fle** \\'sni-fəl\\ *n* **1** *pl* : a head cold marked by nasal discharge **2** : SNUFFLE — **sniffle** *vb*

**¹snip** \\'snip\\ *n* **1** : a fragment snipped off **2** : a simple stroke of the scissors or shears

**²snip** *vb* **snipped; snip·ping** : to cut off by bits : CLIP; *also* : to remove by cutting off ⟨~ a flower⟩

**¹snipe** \\'snīp\\ *n*, *pl* **snipes** *or* **snipe** : any of several long-billed game birds esp. of marshy areas that belong to the same family as the sandpipers

**²snipe** *vb* **sniped; snip·ing** : to shoot at an exposed enemy from a concealed position — **snip·er** *n*

**snip·py** \\'sni-pē\\ *adj* **snip·pi·er; -est** : CURT, SNAPPISH ⟨~ comments⟩ — **snip·pi·ly** \\'sni-pə-lē\\ *adv*

**snips** \\'snips\\ *n pl* : hand shears used esp. for cutting sheet metal ⟨tin ~⟩

**snitch** \\'snich\\ *vb* **1** : INFORM, TATTLE **2** : PILFER, SNATCH — **snitch** *n*

**sniv·el** \\'sni-vəl\\ *vb* **-eled** *or* **-elled; -el·ing** *or* **-el·ling 1** : to have a running nose; *also* : SNUFFLE **2** : to whine in a snuffling manner — **snivel** *n*

**snob** \\'snäb\\ *n* : one who seeks association with persons of higher social position and looks down on those considered inferior — **snob·bish** *adj* — **snob·bish·ly** *adv* — **snob·bish·ness** *n* — **snob·by** \\'snä-bē\\ *adj*

**snob·bery** \\'snä-bə-rē\\ *n*, *pl* **-ber·ies** : snobbish conduct

**¹snoop** \\'snüp\\ *vb* [D *snoepen* to buy or eat on the sly] : to pry in a furtive or meddlesome way

**²snoop** *n* : a prying meddlesome person

**snoopy** \\'snü-pē\\ *adj* **snoop·i·er; -est** : given to snooping

**snooty** \\'snü-tē\\ *adj* **snoot·i·er; -est** : DISDAINFUL, SNOBBISH ⟨~ rich people⟩ — **snoot·i·ly** \\'snü-tə-lē\\ *adv*

**snooze** \\'snüz\\ *vb* **snoozed; snooz·ing** : to take a nap : DOZE — **snooze** *n*

**snore** \\'snȯr\\ *vb* **snored; snor·ing** : to breathe with a rough hoarse noise while sleeping — **snore** *n*

**snor·kel** \\'snȯr-kəl\\ *n* [G *Schnorchel*] : a tube projecting above the water used by swimmers for breathing with the face under water — **snorkel** *vb*

**snort** \\'snȯrt\\ *vb* **1** : to force air violently and noisily through the nose ⟨his horse ~*ed*⟩ **2** : to inhale (a drug) through the nostrils — **snort** *n*

**snot** \\'snät\\ *n* : nasal mucus

**snot·ty** \'snä-tē\ adj **snot·ti·er; -est** 1 : soiled with snot 2 : meanly contemptible ⟨a ~ reply⟩

**snout** \'snaůt\ n 1 : a long projecting muzzle (as of a pig) 2 : a usu. large or grotesque nose

¹**snow** \'snō\ n 1 : crystals of ice formed from water vapor in the air 2 : a descent or shower of snow crystals

²**snow** vb 1 : to fall or cause to fall in or as snow 2 : to cover or shut in with or as if with snow

**snow·ball** \'snō-,ból\ n : a round mass of snow pressed into shape in the hand for throwing

²**snowball** vb 1 : to throw snowballs at 2 : to increase or expand at a rapidly accelerating rate

**snow·bank** \-,baŋk\ n : a mound or slope of snow

**snow·belt** \-,belt\ n, often cap : a region that receives an appreciable amount of annual snowfall

**snow·blow·er** \-,blō-ər\ n : a machine in which a rotating spiral blade picks up and propels snow aside

**snow·board** \-,bórd\ n : a board like a wide ski ridden in a surfing position downhill over snow

**snow·drift** \-,drift\ n : a bank of drifted snow

**snow·drop** \-,dräp\ n : a plant with narrow leaves and a nodding white flower that blooms early in the spring

**snow·fall** \-,fól\ n : a fall of snow

**snow fence** n : a fence across the path of prevailing winds to protect something (as a road) from drifting snow

**snow·field** \'snō-,fēld\ n : a mass of perennial snow at the head of a glacier

**snow·mo·bile** \'snō-mō-,bēl\ n : any of various automotive vehicles for travel on snow — **snow·mo·bil·er** \-,bē-lər\ n — **snow·mo·bil·ing** \-liŋ\ n

**snow pea** n : a cultivated pea with flat edible pods

**snow·plow** \'snō-,plaů\ n 1 : a device for clearing away snow 2 : a skiing maneuver in which the heels of both skis are slid outward for slowing down or stopping

¹**snow·shoe** \-,shü\ n : a lightweight platform for the foot designed to enable a person to walk on soft snow without sinking

²**snowshoe** vb **snow·shoed; snow·shoe·ing** : to travel on snowshoes

**snow·storm** \-,stórm\ n : a storm of falling snow

**snow thrower** n : SNOWBLOWER

**snowy** \'snō-ē\ adj **snow·i·er; -est** 1 : marked by snow 2 : white as snow

**snowy egret** n : a white American egret with a slender black bill

**snub** \'snəb\ vb **snubbed; snub·bing** : to treat with disdain : SLIGHT — **snub** n

**snub–nosed** \'snəb-,nōzd\ adj : having a nose slightly turned up at the end

**snuck** past and past part of SNEAK

¹**snuff** \'snəf\ vb 1 : to pinch off the charred end of (a candle) 2 : to put out (a candle) — **snuff·er** n

²**snuff** vb 1 : to draw forcibly into or through the nose 2 : SMELL

³**snuff** n : SNIFF

⁴**snuff** n : pulverized tobacco

**snuf·fle** \'snə-fəl\ vb **snuf·fled; snuf·fling** 1 : to snuff or sniff audibly and repeatedly 2 : to breathe with a sniffing sound — **snuf·fle** n

**snug** \'snəg\ adj **snug·ger; snug·gest** 1 : fitting closely and comfortably 2 : CONCEALED ⟨a ~ position⟩ — **snug·ly** adv — **snug·ness** n

**snug·gle** \'snə-gəl\ vb **snug·gled; snug·gling** : to curl up or draw close comfortably : NESTLE

¹**so** \'sō\ adv 1 : in the manner indicated 2 : in the same way ⟨he's hungry and ~ am I⟩ 3 : THUS 4 : FINALLY 5 : to an indicated or great extent ⟨I'm ~ bored⟩ 6 : THEREFORE

²**so** conj : for that reason ⟨he wanted it, ~ he took it⟩

³**so** pron 1 : the same ⟨became chairman and remained ~⟩ 2 : approximately that ⟨a dozen or ~⟩

⁴**so** abbr south; southern

**SO** abbr strikeout

¹**soak** \'sōk\ vb 1 : to remain in a liquid 2 : WET, SATURATE 3 : to draw in by or as if by absorption ⟨~ up the sunshine⟩ ♦ Synonyms DRENCH, STEEP, IMPREGNATE

²**soak** n 1 : the act of soaking 2 : the liquid in which something is soaked 3 : DRUNKARD

**soap** \'sōp\ n : a cleansing substance made usu. by action of alkali on fat — **soap** vb — **soapy** adj

**soap·box** \'sōp-,bäks\ n : an improvised platform used for delivering informal speeches

**soap opera** n [fr. its sponsorship by soap manufacturers] : a radio or television daytime serial drama

**soap·stone** \'sōp-,stōn\ n : a soft talc-containing stone with a soapy feel

**soar** \'sór\ vb : to fly upward or at a height on or as if on wings

**sob** \'säb\ vb **sobbed; sob·bing** : to weep with convulsive heavings of the chest or contractions of the throat — **sob** n

**so·ba** \'sō-bə\ n [Jp] : a Japanese noodle made from buckwheat flour

**so·ber** \'sō-bər\ adj **so·ber·er** \-bər-ər\; **so·ber·est** \-bə-rəst\ 1 : temperate in the use of liquor 2 : not drunk 3 : serious or grave in mood or disposition 4 : having a quiet tone or color ♦ Synonyms SOLEMN, EARNEST, STAID, SEDATE — **so·ber·ly** adv — **so·ber·ness** n

**so·bri·ety** \sə-'brī-ə-tē\ n : the quality or state of being sober

**so·bri·quet** \'sō-bri-,kā, -,ket\ n [F] : NICKNAME

**soc** abbr 1 social; society 2 sociology

**so·ca** \'sō-kə, -kä\ n : soul music blended with calypso

**so–called** \'sō-'kóld\ adj : commonly but often inaccurately so termed

**soc·cer** \'sä-kər\ n [by shortening & alter. fr. association football] : a game played on a field by two teams with a round inflated ball that is kicked or hit with any body part other than the hands or arms

¹**so·cia·ble** \'sō-shə-bəl\ *adj* **1** : liking companionship : FRIENDLY **2** : characterized by pleasant social relations ♦ *Synonyms* GRACIOUS, CORDIAL, AFFABLE, GENIAL — **so·cia·bil·i·ty** \ˌsō-shə-'bi-lə-tē\ *n* — **so·cia·bly** \'sō-shə-blē\ *adv*

²**sociable** *n* : SOCIAL

¹**so·cial** \'sō-shəl\ *adj* **1** : marked by pleasant companionship with one's friends **2** : naturally living and breeding in organized communities ⟨~ insects⟩ **3** : of or relating to human society ⟨~ institutions⟩ **4** : of, relating to, or based on rank in a particular society ⟨~ circles⟩; *also* : of or relating to fashionable society — **so·cial·ly** *adv*

²**social** *n* : a social gathering

**so·cial·ise** *Brit var of* SOCIALIZE

**so·cial·ism** \'sō-shə-ˌli-zəm\ *n* : any of various social systems based on shared or government ownership and administration of the means of production and distribution of goods — **so·cial·ist** \'sō-shə-list\ *n or adj* — **so·cial·is·tic** \ˌsō-shə-'lis-tik\ *adj*

**so·cial·ite** \'sō-shə-ˌlīt\ *n* : a person prominent in fashionable society

**so·cial·ize** \'sō-shə-ˌlīz\ *vb* **-ized; -iz·ing** **1** : to regulate according to the theory and practice of socialism **2** : to adapt to social needs or uses **3** : to participate actively in a social gathering — **so·cial·i·za·tion** \ˌsō-shə-lə-'zā-shən\ *n*

**social media** *n pl* : forms of electronic communication (as websites) for sharing information or videos with other users

**social science** *n* : a science (as economics or political science) dealing with a particular aspect of human society — **social scientist** *n*

**social work** *n* : services, activities, or methods providing social services esp. to the economically or socially disadvantaged — **social worker** *n*

**so·ci·e·ty** \sə-'sī-ə-tē\ *n, pl* **-ties** [MF *société*, fr. L *societat-, societas*, fr. *socius* companion] **1** : COMPANIONSHIP **2** : a voluntary association of persons for common ends **3** : a part of a community bound together by common interests and standards; *esp* : the group or set of fashionable people

**so·cio·eco·nom·ic** \ˌsō-sē-ō-ˌe-kə-'nä-mik, -ˌsō-shē-, -ˌē-kə-\ *adj* : of, relating to, or involving both social and economic factors

**sociol** *abbr* sociologist; sociology

**so·ci·ol·o·gy** \ˌsō-sē-'ä-lə-jē, ˌsō-shē-\ *n* : the science of society, social institutions, and social relationships — **so·cio·log·i·cal** \ˌsō-sē-ə-'lä-ji-kəl, ˌsō-shē-\ *adj* — **so·ci·ol·o·gist** \-'ä-lə-jist\ *n*

**so·cio·path** \'sō-sē-ə-ˌpath, 'sō-shē-\ *n* : a person exhibiting antisocial behavior : PSYCHOPATH — **so·cio·path·ic** \ˌsō-sē-ə-'pa-thik, ˌsō-shē-\ *adj*

¹**sock** \'säk\ *n, pl* **socks** *or* **sox** \'säks\ : a stocking with a short leg

²**sock** *vb* : to hit, strike, or apply forcefully

³**sock** *n* : a vigorous blow : PUNCH

**sock·et** \'sä-kət\ *n* : an opening or hollow that forms a holder for something

**socket wrench** *n* : a wrench usu. in the form of a bar and removable socket made to fit a bolt or nut

**sock·eye salmon** \'säk-ˌī-\ *n* : a commercially important Pacific salmon

¹**sod** \'säd\ *n* : TURF 1

²**sod** *vb* **sod·ded; sod·ding** : to cover with sod

**so·da** \'sō-də\ *n* **1** : SODIUM CARBONATE **2** : SODIUM BICARBONATE **3** : SODIUM **4** : SODA WATER **5** : SODA POP **6** : a sweet drink of soda water, flavoring, and often ice cream

**soda pop** *n* : a carbonated, sweetened, and flavored soft drink

**soda water** *n* : a beverage of water charged with carbon dioxide

**sod·den** \'sä-dᵊn\ *adj* **1** : lacking spirit : DULLED **2** : SOAKED, DRENCHED **3** : heavy or doughy from being improperly cooked ⟨~ biscuits⟩

**so·di·um** \'sō-dē-əm\ *n* : a soft waxy silver white metallic chemical element occurring in nature in combined form (as in salt)

**sodium bicarbonate** *n* : a white weakly alkaline salt used esp. in baking powders, fire extinguishers, and medicine

**sodium carbonate** *n* : a carbonate of sodium used esp. in washing and bleaching textiles

**sodium chloride** *n* : SALT 1

**sodium fluoride** *n* : a salt used chiefly in tiny amounts (as in fluoridation) to prevent tooth decay

**sodium hydroxide** *n* : a white brittle caustic substance used in making soap and rayon and in bleaching

**sodium nitrate** *n* : a crystalline salt used as a fertilizer and in curing meat

**sodium thiosulfate** *n* : a hygroscopic crystalline salt used as a photographic fixing agent

**sod·omy** \'sä-də-mē\ *n* : anal or oral sexual intercourse with a member of the same or opposite sex; *also* : sexual intercourse with an animal — **sod·om·ize** \'sä-də-ˌmīz\ *vb*

**so·ev·er** \sō-'e-vər\ *adv* **1** : in any degree or manner ⟨how bad ~⟩ **2** : at all : of any kind ⟨any help ~⟩

**so·fa** \'sō-fə\ *n* [earlier, raised carpeted floor, fr. It *sofà*, fr. Turk *sofa*, fr. Ar *suffa* carpet, divan] : a couch usu. with upholstered back and arms

**soft** \'sóft\ *adj* **1** : not hard or rough : NONVIOLENT **2** : RESTFUL, GENTLE, SOOTHING **3** : emotionally susceptible **4** : not prepared to endure hardship **5** : not containing certain salts that prevent lathering ⟨~ water⟩ **6** : occurring at such a speed as to avoid destructive impact ⟨~ landing of a spacecraft on the moon⟩ **7** : BIODEGRADABLE ⟨a ~ pesticide⟩ **8** : not alcoholic ⟨~ drinks⟩ **9** : less detrimental than a hard narcotic ⟨∼ drugs⟩ — **soft·ly** adv — **soft·ness** n

**soft·ball** \'sȯft-ˌbȯl\ n : a game similar to baseball played with a ball larger and softer than a baseball; also : the ball used in this game

**soft·bound** \-ˌbau̇nd\ adj : not bound in hard covers ⟨∼ books⟩

**soft coal** n : BITUMINOUS COAL

**soft·en** \'sȯf-fən\ vb : to make or become soft — **soft·en·er** n

**soft palate** n : the fold at the back of the hard palate that partially separates the mouth from the pharynx

**soft·ware** \'sȯft-ˌwer\ n : the entire set of programs, procedures, and related documentation associated with a system; esp : computer programs

**soft·wood** \-ˌwu̇d\ n 1 : the wood of a coniferous tree as compared to that of a broad-leaved deciduous tree 2 : a tree yielding softwood — **softwood** adj

**sog·gy** \'sä-gē\ adj **sog·gi·er; -est** : heavy with water or moisture — **sog·gi·ly** \'sä-gə-lē\ adv — **sog·gi·ness** \-gē-nəs\ n

**soi·gné** or **soi·gnée** \swän-'yā\ adj : elegantly maintained; esp : WELL-GROOMED

¹**soil** \'sȯi(-ə)l\ vb 1 : CORRUPT, POLLUTE 2 : to make or become dirty 3 : STAIN, DISGRACE ⟨∼ed his reputation⟩

²**soil** n 1 : STAIN, DEFILEMENT 2 : EXCREMENT, WASTE

³**soil** n 1 : firm land : EARTH 2 : the upper layer of earth in which plants grow 3 : COUNTRY, REGION

**soi·ree** or **soi·rée** \swä-'rā\ n [F soirée evening period, evening party, fr. MF, fr. soir evening, fr. L sero at a late hour] : an evening party

**so·journ** \'sō-ˌjərn, sō-'jərn\ vb : to dwell in a place temporarily — **sojourn** n — **so·journ·er** n

¹**sol** \'säl, 'sȯl\ n — see MONEY table

²**sol** n : a fluid colloidal system

³**sol** abbr 1 solicitor 2 soluble 3 solution

**Sol** \'säl\ n : SUN

¹**sol·ace** \'sä-ləs\ n : COMFORT

²**solace** vb **so·laced; so·lac·ing** : to give solace to : CONSOLE

**so·lar** \'sō-lər\ adj 1 : of, derived from, or relating to the sun 2 : measured by the earth's course in relation to the sun ⟨the ∼ year⟩ 3 : operated by or using the sun's light or heat ⟨∼ energy⟩

**solar cell** n : a photoelectric cell used as a power source

**solar collector** n : a device for the absorption of solar radiation for the heating of water or buildings or the production of electricity

**solar flare** n : a sudden temporary outburst of energy from a small area of the sun's surface

**so·lar·i·um** \sō-'ler-ē-əm\ n, pl **-ia** \-ē-ə\ also **-i·ums** : a room exposed to the sun; esp : a room (as in a hospital) for exposure of the body to sunshine

**solar mass** n : a unit of mass equal to the mass of the sun or about $2 \times 10^{30}$ kilograms

**solar plexus** n : the general area of the stomach below the sternum

**solar system** n : the sun together with the group of celestial bodies that revolve around it

**solar wind** n : plasma continuously ejected from the sun's surface

**sold** past and past part of SELL

**sol·der** \'sä-dər, 'sȯ-\ n : a metallic alloy used when melted to mend or join metallic surfaces — **solder** vb

**soldering iron** n : a metal device for applying heat in soldering

¹**sol·dier** \'sōl-jər\ n [ME soudeour, fr. AF, mercenary, fr. soudee shilling's worth, wage, fr. sou, soud shilling, fr. LL solidus a Roman coin, fr. L, solid] : a person in military service; esp : an enlisted man or woman — **sol·dier·ly** adj or adv

²**soldier** vb **sol·diered; sol·dier·ing** 1 : to serve as a soldier 2 : to pretend to work while actually doing nothing

**soldier of fortune** : ADVENTURER 2

**sol·diery** \'sōl-jə-rē\ n : a body of soldiers

¹**sole** \'sōl\ n : any of various flatfishes including some used for food

²**sole** n 1 : the undersurface of the foot 2 : the bottom of a shoe

³**sole** vb **soled; sol·ing** : to furnish (a shoe) with a sole

⁴**sole** adj : SINGLE, ONLY ⟨the ∼ survivor⟩ — **sole·ly** \'sōl-lē\ adv

**so·le·cism** \'sä-lə-ˌsi-zəm, 'sō-\ n 1 : a mistake in grammar 2 : a breach of etiquette

**sol·emn** \'sä-ləm\ adj 1 : marked by or observed with full religious ceremony ⟨a ∼ oath⟩ 2 : FORMAL, CEREMONIOUS 3 : highly serious : GRAVE ⟨a ∼ gathering⟩ 4 : SOMBER, GLOOMY ⟨a ∼ city⟩ — **so·lem·ni·ty** \sə-'lem-nə-tē\ n — **sol·emn·ly** \'sä-ləm-lē\ adv

**sol·em·nize** \'sä-ləm-ˌnīz\ vb **-nized; -niz·ing** 1 : to observe or honor with solemnity 2 : to celebrate (a marriage) with religious rites — **sol·em·ni·za·tion** \ˌsä-ləm-nə-'zā-shən\ n

**so·le·noid** \'sō-lə-ˌnȯid, 'sä-\ n : a coil of wire usu. in cylindrical form that when carrying a current acts like a magnet

**so·lic·it** \sə-'li-sət\ vb 1 : ENTREAT, BEG 2 : to approach with a request or plea 3 : TEMPT, LURE 4 : to try to obtain by request ⟨∼ donations⟩ — **so·lic·i·ta·tion** \-ˌli-sə-'tā-shən\ n

**so·lic·i·tor** \sə-'li-sə-tər\ n 1 : one that solicits 2 : LAWYER; esp : a legal official of a city or state

**so·lic·i·tous** \sə-'li-sə-təs\ adj 1 : WORRIED, CONCERNED 2 : EAGER, WILLING ♦ Synonyms AVID, IMPATIENT, KEEN, ANXIOUS — **so·lic·i·tous·ly** adv

**so·lic·i·tude** \sə-'li-sə-ˌtüd, -ˌtyüd\ n : CONCERN, ANXIETY

¹**sol·id** \'sä-ləd\ adj 1 : not hollow; also : written as one word without a hyphen ⟨a ∼ compound⟩ 2 : having, involving, or dealing with three dimensions or with solids ⟨∼ geometry⟩ 3 : not loose or spongy : COMPACT ⟨a ∼ mass of rock⟩; also : neither gaseous nor liquid : HARD, RIGID ⟨∼ ice⟩ 4 : of good substantial

quality or kind ⟨∼ comfort⟩ **5** : thoroughly dependable : RELIABLE ⟨a ∼ citizen⟩; *also* : serious in purpose or character ⟨∼ reading⟩ **6** : UNANIMOUS, UNITED ⟨∼ for pay increases⟩ **7** : of one substance or character — **solid** *adv* — **so·lid·i·ty** \sə-'li-də-tē\ *n* — **sol·id·ly** *adv* — **sol·id·ness** *n*

²**solid** *n* **1** : a geometrical figure (as a cube or sphere) having three dimensions **2** : a solid substance

**sol·i·dar·i·ty** \,sä-lə-'der-ə-tē\ *n* : unity based on shared interests, objectives, or standards

**so·lid·i·fy** \sə-'li-də-,fī\ *vb* -**fied**; -**fy·ing** : to make or become solid — **so·lid·i·fi·ca·tion** \-,li-də-fə-'kā-shən\ *n*

**solid–state** *adj* **1** : relating to the structure and properties of solid material **2** : using semiconductor devices rather than vacuum tubes

**so·lil·o·quize** \sə-'li-lə-,kwīz\ *vb* -**quized**; -**quiz·ing** : to talk to oneself : utter a soliloquy

**so·lil·o·quy** \sə-'li-lə-kwē\ *n, pl* -**quies** [LL *soliloquium,* fr. L *solus* alone + *loqui* to speak] **1** : the act of talking to oneself **2** : a dramatic monologue that represents unspoken reflections by a character

**sol·i·taire** \'sä-lə-,ter\ *n* **1** : a single gem (as a diamond) set alone **2** : a card game for one person

**sol·i·tary** \'sä-lə-,ter-ē\ *adj* **1** : being or living apart from others **2** : LONELY, SECLUDED **3** : SOLE, ONLY ⟨a ∼ example⟩

**sol·i·tude** \'sä-lə-,tüd, -,tyüd\ *n* **1** : the state of being alone : SECLUSION ⟨worked in ∼⟩ **2** : a lonely place

**soln** *abbr* solution

¹**so·lo** \'sō-lō\ *n, pl* **solos** [It, fr. *solo* alone, fr. L *solus*] **1** : a piece of music for a single voice or instrument with or without accompaniment **2** : an action in which there is only one performer — **solo** *adj or vb* — **so·lo·ist** *n*

²**solo** *adv* : without a companion : ALONE

**so·lon** \'sō-lən\ *n* **1** : a wise and skillful lawgiver **2** : a member of a legislative body

**sol·stice** \'säl-stəs, 'sōl-\ *n* [ME, fr. L *solstitium,* fr. *sol* sun + *-stit-, -stes* standing] : the time of the year when the sun is farthest north of the equator (**summer solstice**) about June 22 or farthest south (**winter solstice**) about Dec. 22 — **sol·sti·tial** \säl-'sti-shəl, sōl-\ *adj*

**sol·u·ble** \'säl-yə-bəl\ *adj* **1** : capable of being dissolved in or as if in a liquid **2** : capable of being solved or explained — **sol·u·bil·i·ty** \,säl-yə-'bi-lə-tē\ *n*

**sol·ute** \'säl-,yüt\ *n* : a dissolved substance

**so·lu·tion** \sə-'lü-shən\ *n* **1** : an action or process of solving a problem; *also* : an answer to a problem **2** : an act or the process by which one substance is homogeneously mixed with another usu. liquid substance; *also* : a mixture thus formed

**solve** \'sälv\ *vb* **solved**; **solv·ing** : to find the answer to or a solution for — **solvable** *adj*

**sol·ven·cy** \'säl-vən-sē\ *n* : the condition of being solvent

¹**sol·vent** \-vənt\ *adj* **1** : able or sufficient to pay all legal debts **2** : dissolving or able to dissolve

²**solvent** *n* : a usu. liquid substance capable of dissolving or dispersing one or more other substances

**som** \'sōm\ *n* **1** *pl* **som** — see MONEY table **2** *or* **sum** *pl* **soms** *or* **sums** — see MONEY table

**so·mat·ic** \sō-'ma-tik\ *adj* : of, relating to, or affecting the body in contrast to the mind or the sex cells and their precursors

**som·ber** *or* **som·bre** \'säm-bər\ *adj* **1** : DARK, GLOOMY **2** : GRAVE, MELANCHOLY ⟨a ∼ mood⟩ — **som·ber·ly** *adv*

**som·bre·ro** \səm-'brer-ō\ *n, pl* -**ros** [Sp, fr. *sombra* shade] : a broad-brimmed felt hat worn esp. in the Southwest and in Mexico

¹**some** \'səm\ *adj* **1** : one unspecified ⟨∼ man called⟩ **2** : an unspecified or indefinite number of ⟨∼ berries are ripe⟩ **3** : at least a few or a little ⟨∼ years ago⟩

²**some** *pron* : a certain number or amount ⟨∼ of the berries are ripe⟩ ⟨∼ of it is missing⟩

¹**-some** \səm\ *adj suffix* : characterized by a (specified) thing, quality, state, or action ⟨awe*some*⟩ ⟨burden*some*⟩

²**-some** *n suffix* : a group of (so many) members and esp. persons ⟨four*some*⟩

**some·body** \'səm-,bä-dē, -bə-\ *pron* : some person

²**somebody** *n* : a person of importance

**some·day** \'səm-,dā\ *adv* : at some future time

**some·how** \-,haù\ *adv* : by some means

**some·one** \-,(,)wən\ *pron* : some person

**som·er·sault** *also* **som·er·set** \'sə-mər-,sòlt\ *n* [MF *sombresaut* leap, ultim. fr. L *super* over + *saltus* leap, fr. *salire* to jump] : a leap or roll in which a person turns heels over head — **somersault** *vb*

**som·er·set** \-,set\ *n or vb* : SOMERSAULT

**some·thing** \'səm-thiŋ\ *pron* : some undetermined or unspecified thing

**some·time** \-,tīm\ *adv* **1** : at a future time **2** : at an unknown or unnamed time

**some·times** \-,tīmz\ *adv* : OCCASIONALLY

¹**some·what** \-,hwät, -,hwət\ *pron* : SOMETHING

²**somewhat** *adv* : in some degree

**some·where** \-,hwer\ *adv* : in, at, or to an unknown or unnamed place

**som·nam·bu·lism** \säm-'nam-byə-,li-zəm\ *n* : performance of motor acts (as walking) during sleep; *also* : an abnormal condition of sleep characterized by this — **som·nam·bu·list** \-list\ *n*

**som·no·lent** \'säm-nə-lənt\ *adj* : SLEEPY, DROWSY — **som·no·lence** \-ləns\ *n*

**so·mo·ni** \,sō-mō-'nē\ *n, pl* **somoni** — see MONEY table

**son** \'sən\ *n* **1** : a male offspring or descendant **2** *cap* : Jesus Christ **3** : a person deriving from a particular source (as a country, race, or school)

**so·nar** \'sō-,när\ *n* [*sound navigation ranging*] : a method or device for detecting and locating submerged objects (as submarines) by sound waves

**so-na-ta** \sə-ˈnä-tə\ n [It] : an instrumental composition with three or four movements differing in rhythm and mood but related in key

**son-a-ti-na** \ˌsä-nə-ˈtē-nə\ n [It, dim. of *sonata*] : a short usu. simplified sonata

**song** \ˈsȯŋ\ n 1 : vocal music; *also* : a short composition of words and music 2 : poetic composition 3 : a distinctive or characteristic sound (as of a bird) 4 : a small amount ⟨sold for a ~⟩

**song-bird** \ˈsȯŋ-ˌbərd\ n : a bird that utters a series of musical tones

**Song of Sol-o-mon** \-ˈsä-lə-mən\ — see BIBLE table

**Song of Songs** — see BIBLE table

**song-ster** \ˈsȯŋ-stər\ n : one that sings

**song-stress** \-strəs\ n : a girl or woman who is a singer

**son-ic** \ˈsä-nik\ adj : of or relating to sound waves or the speed of sound

**sonic boom** n : an explosive sound produced by an aircraft traveling at supersonic speed

**son-in-law** \ˈsən-ən-ˌlȯ\ n, pl **sons-in-law** : the husband of one's daughter

**son-net** \ˈsä-nət\ n : a poem of 14 lines usu. in iambic pentameter with a definite rhyme scheme

**son of a gun** n, pl **sons of guns** : an offensive or disagreeable person

**so-no-rous** \sə-ˈnȯr-əs, ˈsä-nə-rəs\ adj 1 : giving out sound when struck 2 : loud, deep, or rich in sound : RESONANT ⟨a ~ voice⟩ 3 : high-sounding : IMPRESSIVE — **so-nor-i-ty** \sə-ˈnȯr-ə-tē\ n

**soon** \ˈsün\ adv 1 : before long 2 : PROMPTLY, QUICKLY 3 *archaic* : EARLY 4 : WILLINGLY, READILY

**soot** \ˈsut̩, ˈsət, ˈsüt\ n : a fine black powder consisting chiefly of carbon that is formed when something burns and that colors smoke — **sooty** adj

**sooth** \ˈsüth\ n, *archaic* : TRUTH

**soothe** \ˈsüth\ vb **soothed; sooth-ing** 1 : to please by flattery or attention 2 : RELIEVE, ALLEVIATE ⟨~ a burn⟩ 3 : to calm down : COMFORT ⟨~ a child⟩ — **sooth-er** n — **sooth-ing-ly** adv

**sooth-say-er** \ˈsüth-ˌsā-ər\ n : one who foretells events — **sooth-say-ing** n

¹**sop** \ˈsäp\ n : a conciliatory bribe, gift, or concession

²**sop** vb **sopped; sop-ping** 1 : to steep or dip in or as if in a liquid 2 : to wet thoroughly : SOAK; *also* : to mop up (a liquid)

**SOP** abbr standard operating procedure; standing operating procedure

**soph** abbr sophomore

**soph-ism** \ˈsä-ˌfi-zəm\ n 1 : an argument correct in form but embodying a subtle fallacy 2 : SOPHISTRY

**soph-ist** \ˈsä-fist\ n : PHILOSOPHER; *esp* : a captious or fallacious reasoner

**so-phis-tic** \sä-ˈfis-tik, sə-\ *or* **so-phis-ti-cal** \-ti-kəl\ adj : of or characteristic of sophists or sophistry ♦ **Synonyms** FALLACIOUS, ILLOGICAL, UNREASONABLE, SPECIOUS

**so-phis-ti-cat-ed** \sə-ˈfis-tə-ˌkā-təd\ adj 1

: COMPLEX ⟨~ instruments⟩ 2 : made worldly-wise by wide experience 3 : intellectually appealing ⟨a ~ novel⟩ — **so-phis-ti-ca-tion** \-ˌfis-tə-ˈkā-shən\ n

**soph-o-more** \ˈsäf-ˌmȯr, ˈsä-fə-\ n : a student in the second year of high school or college

**soph-o-mor-ic** \ˌsäf-ˈmȯr-ik, ˌsä-fə-\ adj 1 : being overconfident of knowledge but poorly informed and immature ⟨~ reasoning⟩ 2 : of, relating to, or characteristic of a sophomore ⟨~ humor⟩

**So-pho-ni-as** \ˌsä-fə-ˈnī-əs, ˌsō-\ n : ZEPHANIAH

**sop-o-rif-ic** \ˌsä-pə-ˈri-fik\ adj 1 : causing sleep or drowsiness 2 : LETHARGIC

**so-pra-no** \sə-ˈpra-nō, -ˈprä-\ n, pl **-nos** [It, fr. *sopra* above, fr. L *supra*] 1 : the highest singing voice; *also* : a singer with this voice 2 : the highest part in a 4-part chorus — **soprano** adj

**sor-bet** \sȯr-ˈbā\ n : a usu. fruit-flavored ice served for dessert or between courses as a palate refresher

**sor-cery** \ˈsȯr-sə-rē\ n [ME *sorcerie*, fr. AF, fr. *sorcer* sorcerer, fr. ML *sortiarius*, fr. L *sort-, sors* chance, lot] : the use of magic : WITCHCRAFT — **sor-cer-er** \-rər\ n — **sor-cer-ess** \-rəs\ n

**sor-did** \ˈsȯr-dəd\ adj 1 : marked by baseness or grossness : VILE 2 : DIRTY, SQUALID ⟨~ living conditions⟩ — **sor-did-ly** adv — **sor-did-ness** n

¹**sore** \ˈsȯr\ adj **sor-er; sor-est** 1 : causing pain or distress ⟨a ~ bruise⟩ 2 : painfully sensitive ⟨~ muscles⟩ 3 : SEVERE, INTENSE 4 : IRRITATED, ANGRY — **sore-ly** adv — **sore-ness** n

²**sore** n 1 : a sore spot on the body; *esp* : one (as an ulcer) with the tissues broken and usu. infected 2 : a source of pain or vexation

**sore-head** \ˈsȯr-ˌhed\ n : a person easily angered or discontented

**sore throat** n : painful throat due to inflammation of the fauces and pharynx

**sor-ghum** \ˈsȯr-gəm\ n : a tall variable Old World tropical grass grown widely for its edible seed, for forage, or for its sweet juice which yields a syrup

**so-ror-i-ty** \sə-ˈrȯr-ə-tē\ n, pl **-ties** [ML *sororitas* sisterhood, fr. L *soror* sister] : a club or organization usu. of female students for social purposes

¹**sor-rel** \ˈsȯr-əl\ n : a brownish orange to light brown color; *also* : a sorrel-colored animal (as a horse)

²**sorrel** n : any of various herbs having a sour juice

**sor-row** \ˈsär-ō\ n 1 : deep distress, sadness, or regret; *also* : resultant unhappy or unpleasant state 2 : a cause of grief or sadness 3 : a display of grief or sadness — **sorrow** vb — **sor-row-ful** \-fəl\ adj — **sor-row-ful-ly** \-f(ə)-lē\ adv

**sor-ry** \ˈsär-ē\ adj **sor-ri-er; -est** 1 : feeling sorrow, regret, or penitence ⟨~ for yelling at her⟩ 2 : MOURNFUL, SAD 3 : causing sorrow, pity, or scorn : PITIFUL ⟨a ~ lot of ragamuffins⟩

**¹sort** \\'sòrt\ *n* **1** : a group of persons or things that have similar characteristics : CLASS **2** : QUALITY, NATURE **3** : an instance of sorting — **all sorts of** : many different — **out of sorts 1** : somewhat ill **2** : GROUCHY, IRRITABLE

**²sort** *vb* **1** : to put in a certain place according to kind, class, or nature **2** : to be in accord : AGREE **3** : SEARCH ⟨~ through this mess⟩ — **sort·er** *n*

**sor·tie** \\'sòr-tē, sòr-'tē\ *n* **1** : a sudden issuing of troops from a defensive position against the enemy **2** : one mission or attack by one airplane

**sort of** *adv* : to a moderate degree

**SOS** \\,es-(,)ō-'es\ *n* : a call or request for help or rescue

**so-so** \\'sō-'sō\ *adv or adj* : PASSABLY

**sot** \\'sät\ *n* : a habitual drunkard — **sot·tish** *adj* — **sot·tish·ly** *adv*

**souf·flé** \sü-'flā\ *n* [F, fr. *soufflé*, pp. of *souffler* to blow, puff up, fr. OF *sufler*, fr. L *sufflare*, fr. *sub-* up + *flare* to blow] : a spongy dish made light in baking by stiffly beaten egg whites

**sough** \\'saú, 'sóf\ *vb* : to make a moaning or sighing sound — **sough** *n*

**sought** *past and past part of* SEEK

**¹soul** \\'sōl\ *n* **1** : the immaterial essence of an individual life **2** : the spiritual principle embodied in human beings or the universe **3** : an active or essential part **4** : the moral and emotional nature of human beings **5** : spiritual or moral force **6** : PERSON ⟨a kindly ~⟩ **7** : a strong, positive feeling (as of intense sensitivity and emotional fervor) conveyed esp. by African-American performers **8** : SOUL MUSIC — **souled** \\'sōld\ *adj* — **soul·less** \\'sōl-ləs\ *adj*

**²soul** *adj* **1** : of, relating to, or characteristic of African-Americans or their culture ⟨~ food⟩ **2** : designed for or controlled by African Americans ⟨~ radio stations⟩

**soul brother** *n* : an African-American male

**soul·ful** \\'sōl-fəl\ *adj* : full of or expressing deep feeling ⟨a ~ ballad⟩ — **soul·ful·ly** *adv*

**soul music** *n* : music that is closely related to rhythm and blues and characterized by intensity of feeling

**¹sound** \\'saúnd\ *adj* **1** : not diseased or sickly **2** : free from flaw or defect ⟨a ~ structure⟩ **3** : FIRM, STRONG **4** : free from error or fallacy : RIGHT ⟨~ logic⟩ **5** : LEGAL, VALID **6** : THOROUGH **7** : UNDISTURBED ⟨~ sleep⟩ **8** : showing good judgment ⟨~ reasoning⟩ — **sound·ly** *adv* — **sound·ness** *n*

**²sound** *n* **1** : the sensation of hearing; *also* : mechanical energy transmitted by longitudinal pressure waves (**sound waves**) (as in air) that is the stimulus to hearing **2** : something heard : NOISE, TONE; *also* : hearing distance : EARSHOT **3** : a musical style ⟨the band's ~⟩ — **sound·less** *adj* — **sound·less·ly** *adv* — **sound·proof** \-,prüf\ *adj or vb*

**³sound** *vb* **1** : to make or cause to make a sound **2** : to order or proclaim by a

sound ⟨~ the alarm⟩ **3** : to convey a certain impression : SEEM ⟨that ~s like fun⟩ **4** : to examine the condition of by causing to give out sounds — **sound·able** \\'saún-də-bəl\ *adj*

**⁴sound** *n* : a long passage of water wider than a strait often connecting two larger bodies of water

**⁵sound** *vb* **1** : to measure the depth of (water) esp. by a weighted line dropped from the surface : FATHOM **2** : PROBE **3** : to dive down suddenly ⟨the hooked fish ~ed⟩ — **sound·ing** *n*

**sound bite** *n* : a brief recorded statement broadcast esp. on a news program — **sound–bite** *adj*

**sound card** *n* : a circuit board in a computer system designed to produce or reproduce sound

**sound·er** \\'saún-dər\ *n* : one that sounds; *esp* : a device for making soundings

**sound·stage** \\'saúnd-,stāj\ *n* : the part of a motion-picture studio in which a production is filmed

**sound·track** \\'saún(d)-,trak\ *n* : music recorded to accompany a film or videotape

**soup** \\'süp\ *n* **1** : a liquid food with stock as its base and often containing pieces of solid food **2** : something having the consistency of soup **3** : an unfortunate predicament ⟨in the ~⟩

**soup·çon** \süp-'sōⁿ\ *n* [F, lit., suspicion] : a little bit : ¹TRACE 2 ⟨a ~ of garlic⟩

**soup up** *vb* : to increase the power of — **souped–up** \\'süpt-'əp\ *adj*

**soupy** \\'sü-pē\ *adj* **soup·i·er; -est** **1** : having the consistency of soup **2** : densely foggy or cloudy

**¹sour** \\'saú(-ə)r\ *adj* **1** : having an acid or tart taste ⟨~ as vinegar⟩ **2** : SPOILED, PUTRID ⟨a ~ odor⟩ **3** : UNPLEASANT, DISAGREEABLE ⟨~ disposition⟩ — **sour·ish** *adj* — **sour·ly** *adv* — **sour·ness** *n*

**²sour** *vb* : to become or make sour

**source** \\'sòrs\ *n* **1** : ORIGIN, BEGINNING **2** : a supplier of information **3** : the beginning of a stream of water

**source code** *n* : a computer program in its original programming language and before translation (as by a compiler)

**¹souse** \\'saús\ *vb* **soused; sous·ing** **1** : PICKLE **2** : to plunge into a liquid **3** : DRENCH **4** : to make drunk

**²souse** *n* **1** : something (as pigs' feet) steeped in pickle **2** : a soaking in liquid **3** : DRUNKARD

**¹south** \\'saúth\ *adv* : to or toward the south; *also* : into a state of decline

**²south** *adj* **1** : situated toward or at the south **2** : coming from the south

**³south** *n* **1** : the direction to the right of one facing east **2** : the compass point directly opposite to north **3** *cap* : regions or countries south of a specified or implied point; *esp* : the southeastern part of the U.S. — **south·er·ly** \\'sə-thər-lē\ *adj or adv* — **south·ern** \\'sə-thərn\ *adj* — **South·ern·er** *n* — **south·ern·most** \-,mōst\ *adj* — **south·ward** \\'saúth-wərd\ *adv or adj* — **south·wards** \-wərdz\ *adv*

**south·east** \saù-'thēst, *naut* saù-'ēst\ *n* **1** : the general direction between south and east **2** : the compass point midway between south and east **3** *cap* : regions or countries southeast of a specified or implied point — **southeast** *adj or adv* — **south·east·er·ly** *adv or adj* — **south·east·ern** \-'ēs-tərn\ *adj*

**south·paw** \'saùth-,pȯ\ *n* : a left-handed person; *esp* : a left-handed baseball pitcher — **southpaw** *adj*

**south pole** *n, often cap S&P* : the southernmost point of the earth

**south·west** \saùth-'west, *naut* saù-'west\ *n* **1** : the general direction between south and west **2** : the compass point midway between south and west **3** *cap* : regions or countries southwest of a specified or implied point — **southwest** *adj or adv* — **south·west·er·ly** *adv or adj* — **south·west·ern** \-'wes-tərn\ *adj*

**sou·ve·nir** \,sü-və-'nir\ *n* [F] : something serving as a reminder

**sou'·west·er** \saù-'wes-tər\ *n* : a long waterproof coat worn at sea in stormy weather; *also* : a waterproof hat

**¹sov·er·eign** \'sä-vrən, -və-rən\ *n* **1** : one possessing the supreme power and authority in a state **2** : a gold coin of the United Kingdom

**²sovereign** *adj* **1** : EXCELLENT, FINE **2** : supreme in power or authority **3** : CHIEF, HIGHEST **4** : having independent authority ♦ **Synonyms** DOMINANT, PREDOMINANT, PARAMOUNT, PREPONDERANT

**sov·er·eign·ty** \-tē\ *n, pl* **-ties** **1** : supremacy in rule or power **2** : power to govern without external control **3** : the supreme political power in a state

**so·vi·et** \'sō-vē-,et, 'sä-, -ət\ *n* **1** : an elected governmental council in a Communist country **2** *pl, cap* : the people and esp. the leaders of the U.S.S.R. — **soviet** *adj, often cap* — **so·vi·et·ize** *vb, often cap*

**¹sow** \'saù\ *n* : an adult female swine

**²sow** \'sō\ *vb* **sowed; sown** \'sōn\ *or* **sowed; sow·ing** **1** : to plant seed for growing esp. by scattering **2** : to strew with seed **3** : to scatter abroad — **sow·er** \'sō-ər\ *n*

**sow bug** \'saù-\ *n* : WOOD LOUSE

**sox** *pl of* SOCK

**soy** \'sȯi\ *n* : a sauce made from soybeans fermented in brine

**soy·bean** \'sȯi-,bēn\ *n* : an Asian legume widely grown for forage and for its edible seeds that yield a valuable oil (**soybean oil**); *also* : its seed

**sp** *abbr* **1** special **2** species **3** specimen **4** spelling **5** spirit

**Sp** *abbr* Spain

**SP** *abbr* **1** shore patrol; shore patrolman **2** shore police **3** specialist

**spa** \'spä\ *n* [*Spa*, watering place in Belgium] **1** : a mineral spring; *also* : a resort with mineral springs **2** : a health and fitness facility **3** : a hot tub with a whirlpool device

**¹space** \'spās\ *n* **1** : a period of time **2** : some small measurable distance, area, or volume **3** : the limitless area in which all things exist and move **4** : an empty place **5** : the region beyond the earth's atmosphere **6** : a definite place (as a seat on a train or ship) **7** : the distance from others that a person needs for comfort

**²space** *vb* **spaced; spac·ing** : to place at intervals — **spac·er** *n*

**space–age** \'spās-,āj\ *adj* : of or relating to the age of space exploration

**space·craft** \-,kraft\ *n* : a vehicle for travel beyond the earth's atmosphere

**space·flight** \-,flīt\ *n* : flight beyond the earth's atmosphere

**space heater** *n* : a usu. portable device for heating a relatively small area

**space·man** \'spās-,man, -mən\ *n* : one who travels outside the earth's atmosphere

**space out** *vb* : to become distracted or inattentive

**space·ship** \-,ship\ *n* : a vehicle used for space travel

**space shuttle** *n* : a reusable spacecraft designed to transport people and cargo between earth and space

**space station** *n* : a large artificial satellite serving as a base (as for scientific observation)

**space suit** *n* : a suit equipped to make life in space possible for its wearer

**space walk** *n* : a period of activity outside a spacecraft by an astronaut in space — **space·walk** \'spās-,wȯk\ *vb* — **space·walk·er** *n*

**spa·cious** \'spā-shəs\ *adj* : very large in extent : ROOMY ♦ **Synonyms** COMMODIOUS, CAPACIOUS, AMPLE — **spa·cious·ly** *adv* — **spa·cious·ness** *n*

**¹spade** \'spād\ *n* : a shovel with a blade for digging — **spade·ful** *n*

**²spade** *vb* **spad·ed; spad·ing** : to dig with a spade — **spad·er** *n*

**³spade** *n* : any of a suit of playing cards marked with a black figure resembling an inverted heart with a short stem at the bottom

**spa·dix** \'spā-diks\ *n, pl* **spa·di·ces** \'spā-də-,sēz\ : a floral spike with a fleshy or succulent axis usu. enclosed in a spathe

**spa·ghet·ti** \spə-'ge-tē\ *n* [It, fr. pl. of *spaghetto*, dim. of *spago* cord, string] : pasta made in thin solid strings

**spam** \'spam\ *n* : unsolicited usu. commercial e-mail sent to a large number of addresses — **spam** *vb*

**¹span** \'span\ *n* **1** : an English unit of length equal to nine inches (about 23 centimeters) **2** : a limited portion of time **3** : the spread (as of an arch) from one support to another

**²span** *vb* **spanned; span·ning** **1** : MEASURE **2** : to extend across

**³span** *n* : a pair of animals (as mules) driven together

**Span** *abbr* Spanish

**span·dex** \'span-,deks\ *n* : any of various elastic synthetic textile fibers

**span·gle** \'span-gəl\ *n* : a small disk of shining metal or plastic used esp. on a dress for ornament — **spangle** *vb*

**Span·glish** \'span-glish\ *n* : Spanish with many English words included; *also* : a combination of English and Spanish

**Span·lard** \'span-yərd\ *n* : a native or inhabitant of Spain

**span·iel** \'span-yəl\ *n* [ME *spaynel*, *spaniell*, fr. AF *espainnel*, alter. of *espaignol*, Spaniard] : a dog of any of several breeds of mostly small and short-legged dogs usu. with long wavy hair and large drooping ears

**Span·ish** \'spa-nish\ *n* 1 : the chief language of Spain and of the countries colonized by the Spanish 2 **Spanish** *pl* : the people of Spain — **Spanish** *adj*

**Spanish American** *n* : a resident of the U.S. whose native language is Spanish; *also* : a native or inhabitant of one of the countries of America in which Spanish is the national language — **Spanish–American** *adj*

**Spanish fly** *n* : a toxic preparation of dried green European beetles that causes the skin to blister and is thought to be an aphrodisiac

**Spanish moss** *n* : a plant related to the pineapple that grows in pendent tufts of grayish green filaments on trees from the southern U.S. to Argentina

**Spanish onion** *n* : a large mild-flavored onion

**spank** \'spaŋk\ *vb* : to hit on the buttocks with the open hand — **spank** *n*

**spank·ing** \'spaŋ-kiŋ\ *adj* : BRISK, LIVELY ⟨~ breeze⟩ — **spanking** *adv*

¹**spar** \'spär\ *n* : a rounded wood or metal piece (as a mast, yard, boom, or gaff) for supporting sail rigging

²**spar** *vb* **sparred; spar·ring** : to box for practice without serious hitting; *also* : SKIRMISH, WRANGLE

¹**spare** \'sper\ *vb* **spared; spar·ing** 1 : to refrain from punishing or injuring : show mercy to 2 : to exempt from something 3 : to get along without ⟨can you ~ ten dollars?⟩ 4 : to use frugally or rarely

²**spare** *adj* **spar·er; spar·est** 1 : held in reserve 2 : SUPERFLUOUS 3 : not liberal or profuse 4 : LEAN, THIN 5 : SCANTY ◆ **Synonyms** MEAGER, SPARSE, SKIMPY, EXIGUOUS, SCANT — **spare·ness** *n*

³**spare** *n* 1 : a duplicate kept in reserve; *esp* : a spare tire 2 : the knocking down of all the bowling pins with the first two balls

**sparing** *adj* : SAVING, FRUGAL ◆ **Synonyms** THRIFTY, ECONOMICAL, PROVIDENT — **spar·ing·ly** *adv*

¹**spark** \'spärk\ *n* 1 : a small particle of a burning substance or a hot glowing particle struck from a mass (as by steel on flint) 2 : a short bright flash of electricity between two points 3 : SPARKLE 4 : a particle capable of being kindled or developed : GERM

²**spark** *vb* 1 : to emit or produce sparks 2 : to stir to activity : INCITE

³**spark** *vb* : WOO, COURT

¹**spar·kle** \'spär-kəl\ *vb* **spar·kled; spar·kling** 1 : FLASH, GLEAM 2 : to perform brilliantly 3 : EFFERVESCE ⟨sparkling wine⟩ — **spar·kler** *n*

²**sparkle** *n* 1 : GLEAM 2 : ANIMATION

**spark plug** *n* : a device that produces a spark to ignite the fuel mixture in an engine cylinder

**spar·row** \'spa-rō\ *n* : any of several small dull-colored singing birds

**sparse** \'spärs\ *adj* **spars·er; spars·est** : thinly scattered : SCANTY ⟨~ vegetation⟩ ◆ **Synonyms** MEAGER, SPARE, SKIMPY, EXIGUOUS, SCANT — **sparse·ly** *adv* — **sparse·ness** *n*

¹**Spar·tan** \'spär-t³n\ *n* 1 : a native or inhabitant of ancient Sparta 2 : a person of great courage and self-discipline

²**Spartan** *adj* 1 : of or relating to Sparta or Spartans 2 *often not cap* : marked by simplicity, frugality, or avoidance of luxury and comfort ⟨a ~ room⟩

**spasm** \'spa-zəm\ *n* 1 : an involuntary and abnormal muscular contraction 2 : a sudden, violent, and temporary effort, emotion, or sensation — **spas·mod·ic** \spaz-'mä-dik\ *adj* — **spas·mod·i·cal·ly** \-di-k(ə-)lē\ *adv*

**spas·tic** \'spas-tik\ *adj* : of, relating to, marked by, or affected with muscular spasm ⟨~ paralysis⟩ — **spastic** *n*

¹**spat** \'spat\ *past and past part of* SPIT

²**spat** *n, pl* **spat** *or* **spats** : a young bivalve mollusk (as an oyster)

³**spat** *n* : a gaiter covering instep and ankle

⁴**spat** *n* : a brief petty quarrel : DISPUTE

⁵**spat** *vb* **spat·ted; spat·ting** : to quarrel briefly

**spate** \'spāt\ *n* : a sudden outburst

**spathe** \'spāth\ *n* : a sheathing bract or pair of bracts enclosing an inflorescence (as of the calla lily) and esp. a spadix on the same axis

**spa·tial** \'spā-shəl\ *adj* : of or relating to space or to the facility to perceive objects in space — **spa·tial·ly** *adv*

**spat·ter** \'spa-tər\ *vb* 1 : to splash with drops of liquid ⟨clothes ~ed with paint⟩ 2 : to sprinkle around — **spatter** *n*

**spat·u·la** \'spa-chə-lə\ *n* : a flexible knife-like implement for scooping, spreading, or mixing soft substances

**spav·in** \'spa-vən\ *n* : a bony enlargement of the hock of a horse — **spav·ined** \-vənd\ *adj*

¹**spawn** \'spȯn\ *vb* [ME, fr. AF *espandre* to spread out, shed, scatter, spawn, fr. L *expandere*, fr. *ex-* out + *pandere* to spread] 1 : to produce eggs or offspring esp. in large numbers 2 : GENERATE ⟨~ed much protest⟩ — **spawn·er** *n*

²**spawn** *n* 1 : the eggs of water animals (as fishes or oysters) that lay many small eggs 2 : offspring esp. when produced in great numbers

**spay** \'spā\ *vb* **spayed; spay·ing** : to remove the ovaries of (a female animal)

**SPCA** *abbr* Society for the Prevention of Cruelty to Animals

**SPCC** *abbr* Society for the Prevention of Cruelty to Children

**speak** \'spēk\ *vb* **spoke** \'spōk\; **spo·ken** \'spō-kən\; **speak·ing** 1 : to utter words 2 : to express orally 3 : to mention in speech or writing 4 : to address an audience 5 : to use or be able to use (a language) in talking — **to speak of** : worthy of mention ⟨no progress *to speak of*⟩

**speak·eas·y** \'spēk-ˌē-zē\ *n, pl* **-eas·ies** : an illicit drinking place

**speak·er** \'spē-kər\ *n* **1** : one that speaks **2** : the presiding officer of a deliberative assembly **3** : LOUDSPEAKER

**¹spear** \'spir\ *n* **1** : a long-shafted weapon with a sharp point for thrusting or throwing **2** : a sharp-pointed instrument with barbs used in spearing fish — **spear·man** \-mən\ *n*

**²spear** *vb* : to strike or pierce with or as if with a spear — **spear·er** *n*

**³spear** *n* : a usu. young blade, shoot, or sprout (as of asparagus)

**spear·head** \-ˌhed\ *n* : a leading force, element, or influence — **spearhead** *vb*

**spear·mint** \-ˌmint\ *n* : a common highly aromatic garden mint

**¹spec** *abbr* **1** special; specialist **2** specifically

**²spec** \'spek\ *n* : SPECIFICATION 2 — usu. used in pl.

**spe·cial** \'spe-shəl\ *adj* **1** : UNCOMMON, NOTEWORTHY **2** : particularly favored **3** : INDIVIDUAL, UNIQUE **4** : EXTRA, ADDITIONAL **5** : confined to or designed for a definite field of action, purpose, or occasion ⟨a ~ assignment⟩ — **special** *n*

**special delivery** *n* : delivery of mail by messenger for an extra fee

**special effects** *n pl* : visual or sound effects introduced into a motion picture, video recording, or taped television production

**Special Forces** *n pl* : a branch of the army composed of soldiers specially trained in guerrilla warfare

**spe·cial·ise** *Brit var of* SPECIALIZE

**spe·cial·ist** \'spe-shə-list\ *n* **1** : a person who specializes in a particular branch of learning or activity **2** : a rank in the U.S. Army corresponding to that of corporal

**spe·cial·ize** \'spe-shə-ˌlīz\ *vb* **-ized; -iz·ing** : to concentrate one's efforts in a special activity or field; *also* : to change in an adaptive manner — **spe·cial·i·za·tion** \ˌspe-shə-lə-'zā-shən\ *n*

**spe·cial·ly** \'spe-shə-lē\ *adv* **1** : in a special manner **2** : for a special purpose : in particular

**spe·cial·ty** \'spe-shəl-tē\ *n, pl* **-ties 1** : a particular quality or detail **2** : a product of a special kind or of special excellence **3** : a skill or discipline in which one specializes ⟨the doctor's ~ is dermatology⟩

**spe·cie** \'spē-shē, -sē\ *n* : money in coin

**spe·cies** \'spē-shēz, -sēz\ *n, pl* **species** [ME, fr. L, appearance, kind, species, fr. *specere* to look] **1** : SORT, KIND **2** : a category of biological classification ranking just below the genus or subgenus and comprising closely related organisms potentially able to breed with one another

**specif** *abbr* specific; specifically

**¹spe·cif·ic** \spi-'si-fik\ *adj* **1** : having a unique effect or influence or reacting in only one way or with only one thing ⟨~ antibodies⟩ ⟨~ enzymes⟩ **2** : DEFINITE, EXACT ⟨a ~ agreement⟩ **3** : of, relating to, or constituting a species — **spe·cif·i-**

**cal·ly** \-fi-k(ə-)lē\ *adv* — **spec·i·fic·i·ty** \ˌspe-sə-'fi-sə-tē\ *n*

**²specific** *n* : something specific : DETAIL, PARTICULAR — usu. used in pl.

**spec·i·fi·ca·tion** \ˌspe-sə-fə-'kā-shən\ *n* **1** : the act or process of specifying **2** : a description of work to be done and materials to be used (as in building) — usu. used in pl.

**specific gravity** *n* : the ratio of the density of a substance to the density of some substance (as water) taken as a standard when both densities are obtained by weighing in air

**spec·i·fy** \'spe-sə-ˌfī\ *vb* **-fied; -fy·ing** : to mention or name explicitly

**spec·i·men** \'spe-sə-mən\ *n* : an item or part typical of a group or whole

**spe·cious** \'spē-shəs\ *adj* : seeming to be genuine, correct, or beautiful but not really so ⟨~ reasoning⟩

**speck** \'spek\ *n* **1** : a small spot or blemish **2** : a small particle — **speck** *vb*

**speck·le** \'spe-kəl\ *n* : a little speck — **speckle** *vb*

**specs** \'speks\ *n pl* : GLASSES

**spec·ta·cle** \'spek-ti-kəl\ *n* **1** : an unusual or impressive public display **2** *pl* : GLASSES — **spec·ta·cled** \-kəld\ *adj*

**spec·tac·u·lar** \spek-'ta-kyə-lər\ *adj* : exciting to see : SENSATIONAL

**spec·ta·tor** \'spek-ˌtā-tər\ *n* : a person who looks on (as at a sports event)
♦ *Synonyms* OBSERVER, WITNESS, BYSTANDER, ONLOOKER, EYEWITNESS

**spec·ter** *or* **spec·tre** \'spek-tər\ *n* : a visible disembodied spirit : GHOST

**spec·tral** \'spek-trəl\ *adj* **1** : of, relating to, or resembling a specter **2** : of, relating to, or made by a spectrum

**spec·tro·gram** \'spek-trə-ˌgram\ *n* : a photograph, image, or diagram of a spectrum

**spec·tro·graph** \-ˌgraf\ *n* : an instrument for dispersing radiation into a spectrum and recording or mapping the spectrum — **spec·tro·graph·ic** \ˌspek-trə-'gra-fik\ *adj* — **spec·tro·graph·i·cal·ly** \-fi-k(ə-)lē\ *adv*

**spec·trom·e·ter** \spek-'trä-mə-tər\ *n* : an instrument for measuring spectra — **spec·tro·met·ric** \ˌspek-trə-'me-trik\ *adj* — **spec·trom·e·try** \spek-'trä-mə-trē\ *n*

**spec·tro·scope** \'spek-trə-ˌskōp\ *n* : an instrument that produces spectra esp. of visible electromagnetic radiation — **spec·tro·scop·ic** \ˌspek-trə-'skä-pik\ *adj* — **spec·tro·scop·i·cal·ly** \-pi-k(ə-)lē\ *adv* — **spec·tros·co·pist** \spek-'träs-kə-pist\ *n* — **spec·tros·co·py** \-pē\ *n*

**spec·trum** \'spek-trəm\ *n, pl* **spec·tra** \-trə\ *or* **spectrums** [NL, fr. L, appearance, fr. *specere* to look] **1** : a series of colors formed when a beam of white light is dispersed (as by a prism) so that its parts are arranged in the order of their wavelengths **2** : a series of radiations arranged in regular order **3** : a continuous sequence or range ⟨a wide ~ of political opinions⟩

**spec·u·late** \'spe-kyə-ˌlāt\ *vb* **-lat·ed; -lat·ing** [L *speculari* to spy out, examine, fr. *specula* lookout post, fr. *specere* to look, look at] **1** : to think or wonder about a subject **2** : to take a business risk in hope of gain ✦ *Synonyms* REASON, THINK, DELIBERATE, COGITATE — **spec·u·la·tion** \spe-kyə-'lā-shən\ *n* — **spec·u·la·tive** \'spe-kyə-ˌlā-tiv\ *adj* — **spec·u·la·tive·ly** *adv* — **spec·u·la·tor** \-ˌlā-tər\ *n*

**speech** \'spēch\ *n* **1** : the act of speaking **2** : TALK, CONVERSATION **3** : a public talk or lecture **4** : LANGUAGE, DIALECT **5** : an individual manner of speaking **6** : the power of speaking — **speech·less** *adj*

¹**speed** \'spēd\ *n* **1** *archaic* : SUCCESS **2** : SWIFTNESS, RAPIDITY **3** : rate of motion or performance **4** : a transmission gear (as of a bicycle) **5** : METHAMPHETAMINE; *also* : a related drug ✦ *Synonyms* HASTE, HURRY, DISPATCH, CELERITY — **speed·i·ly** \'spē-də-lē\ *adv* — **speedy** *adj*

²**speed** *vb* **sped** \'sped\ *or* **speed·ed; speed·ing 1** *archaic* : PROSPER; *also* : GET ALONG, FARE **2** : to go fast; *esp* : to go at an excessive or illegal speed **3** : to cause to go faster — **speed·er** *n*

**speed·boat** \-ˌbōt\ *n* : a fast motorboat

**speed bump** *n* : a low raised ridge across a roadway (as in a parking lot) to limit vehicle speed

**speed of light** : a fundamental physical constant that is the speed of electromagnetic radiation propagation in a vacuum and has the value of 299,792,458 meters per second

**speed·om·e·ter** \spi-'dä-mə-tər\ *n* : an instrument for indicating speed

**speed·up** \'spēd-ˌəp\ *n* : ACCELERATION

**speed·way** \-ˌwā\ *n* : a racecourse for motor vehicles

**speed·well** \'spēd-ˌwel\ *n* : VERONICA

¹**spell** \'spel\ *vb* **spelled** \'speld, 'spelt\; **spell·ing** [ME, to signify, read by spelling out, fr. AF *espeleir*, of Gmc origin] **1** : to name, write, or print in order the letters of a word **2** : MEAN ⟨another drought may ∼ famine⟩

²**spell** *n* [ME, talk, tale, fr. OE] **1** : a magic formula : INCANTATION **2** : a compelling influence ⟨under the ∼ of a guru⟩

³**spell** *n* **1** : one's turn at work or duty **2** : a stretch of a specified kind of weather **3** : a period of bodily or mental distress or disorder : ATTACK ⟨a dizzy ∼⟩

⁴**spell** *vb* **spelled** \'speld\; **spell·ing** : to take the place of for a time in work or duty : RELIEVE

**spell·bind·er** \-ˌbīn-dər\ *n* : a speaker of compelling eloquence; *also* : one that compels attention

**spell·bound** \-ˌbaund\ *adj* : held by or as if by a spell : FASCINATED

**spell–check·er** \'spel-ˌche-kər\ *n* : a computer program that identifies possible misspellings in a block of text — **spell–check** \-ˌchek\ *vb*

**spell·er** \'spe-lər\ *n* **1** : one who spells words **2** : a book with exercises for teaching spelling

**spelt** \'spelt\ *chiefly Brit past and past part of* ¹SPELL

**spe·lunk·er** \spi-'ləŋ-kər, 'spē-ˌləŋ-kər\ *n* [L *spelunca* cave, fr. Gk *spēlynx*] : one who makes a hobby of exploring caves — **spe·lunk·ing** *n*

**spend** \'spend\ *vb* **spent** \'spent\; **spend·ing 1** : to pay out : EXPEND **2** : WEAR OUT, EXHAUST; *also* : to consume wastefully **3** : to cause or permit to elapse : PASS — **spend·er** *n*

**spend·thrift** \'spend-ˌthrift\ *n* : one who spends wastefully or recklessly

**spent** \'spent\ *adj* : drained of energy

**sperm** \'spərm\ *n, pl* **sperm** *or* **sperms 1** : SEMEN **2** : a male gamete

**sper·ma·to·zo·on** \(ˌ)spər-ˌma-tə-'zō-ˌän, -'zō-ən\ *n, pl* **-zoa** \-'zō-ə\ : a motile male gamete of an animal usu. with a rounded or elongated head and a long posterior flagellum

**sperm cell** *n* : SPERM 2

**sper·mi·cide** \'spər-mə-ˌsīd\ *n* : a preparation or substance used to kill sperm — **sper·mi·cid·al** \ˌspər-mə-'sī-dəl\ *adj*

**sperm whale** *n* : a large whale with a massive square-shaped head containing a fluid-filled cavity

**spew** \'spyü\ *vb* : VOMIT

**SPF** *abbr* sun protection factor

**sp gr** *abbr* specific gravity

**sphag·num** \'sfag-nəm\ *n* : any of a genus of atypical mosses that grow in wet acid areas where their remains become compacted with other plant debris to form peat; *also* : a mass of these mosses

**sphere** \'sfir\ *n* [ME *spere* celestial sphere, fr. AF *espere*, fr. L *sphaera*, fr. Gk *sphaira*, lit., ball] **1** : a globe-shaped body **2** : a celestial body **3** : a solid figure so shaped that every point on its surface is an equal distance from the center **4** : range of action or influence — **spher·i·cal** \'sfir-i-kəl, 'sfer-\ *adj* — **spher·i·cal·ly** \-i k(ə-)lē\ *adv*

**spher·oid** \'sfir-ˌȯid, 'sfer-\ *n* : a figure similar to a sphere but not perfectly round — **sphe·roi·dal** \sfir-'ȯi-dəl\ *adj*

**sphinc·ter** \'sfiŋk-tər\ *n* : a muscular ring that closes a bodily opening

**sphinx** \'sfiŋks\ *n, pl* **sphinx·es** *or* **sphin·ges** \'sfin-ˌjēz\ **1** : a winged monster in Greek mythology having a woman's head and a lion's body and noted for killing anyone unable to answer its riddle **2** : an enigmatic or mysterious person **3** : an ancient Egyptian image having the body of a lion and the head of a man, ram, or hawk

**spice** \'spīs\ *n* **1** : any of various aromatic plant products (as pepper or nutmeg) used to season or flavor foods **2** : something that adds interest and relish — **spice** *vb* — **spicy** *adj*

**spick–and–span** *or* **spic–and–span** \ˌspik-ənd-'span\ *adj* : quite new; *also* : spotlessly clean

**spic·ule** \'spi-kyül\ *n* : a slender pointed body esp. of calcium or silica ⟨sponge ∼s⟩

**spi·der** \'spī-dər\ *n* **1** : any of an order of arachnids that have a 2-part body, eight legs, and two or more pairs of abdominal organs for spinning threads of silk used esp. in making webs for catching prey **2** : a cast-iron frying pan — **spi·dery** *adj*

**spider mite** *n* : any of various small web-spinning mites that feed on and are pests of plants

**spider plant** *n* : a houseplant of the lily family having long green leaves usu. striped with white and producing tufts of small plants on long hanging stems

**spi·der·web** \'spī-dər-ˌweb\ *n* : the web spun by a spider

**spiel** \'spēl\ *vb* : to talk in a fast, smooth, and usu. colorful manner — **spiel** *n*

**spig·ot** \'spi-gət, -kət\ *n* : FAUCET

¹**spike** \'spīk\ *n* **1** : a very large nail **2** : any of various pointed projections (as on the sole of a shoe to prevent slipping) — **spiky** *adj*

²**spike** *vb* **spiked; spik·ing 1** : to fasten with spikes **2** : to put an end to : QUASH ⟨∼ a rumor⟩ **3** : to pierce with or impale on a spike **4** : to add alcoholic liquor to (a drink)

³**spike** *n* **1** : an ear of grain **2** : a long cluster of usu. stemless flowers

¹**spill** \'spil\ *vb* **spilled** \'spild, 'spilt\ *also* **spilt** \'spilt\; **spill·ing 1** : to cause or allow to fall, flow, or run out esp. unintentionally **2** : to cause (blood) to be lost by wounding **3** : to run out or over with resulting loss or waste **4** : to let out : DIVULGE — **spill·able** *adj*

²**spill** *n* **1** : an act of spilling; *also* : a fall from a horse or vehicle or an erect position **2** : something spilled

**spill·way** \-ˌwā\ *n* : a passage for surplus water to run over or around an obstruction (as a dam)

¹**spin** \'spin\ *vb* **spun** \'spən\; **spin·ning 1** : to draw out (fiber) and twist into thread; *also* : to form (thread) by such means **2** : to form thread by extruding a sticky quickly hardening fluid; *also* : to construct from such thread ⟨spiders ∼ their webs⟩ **3** : to produce slowly and by degrees ⟨∼ a story⟩ **4** : TWIRL **5** : WHIRL, REEL ⟨my head is *spinning*⟩ **6** : to move rapidly along **7** : to present (as information) with a particular spin — **spin·ner** *n*

²**spin** *n* **1** : a rapid rotating motion **2** : an excursion in a wheeled vehicle **3** : a particular point of view, emphasis, or interpretation

**spi·na bif·i·da** \ˌspī-nə-'bi-fə-də\ *n* : a birth defect in which the spinal column has a fissure

**spin·ach** \'spi-nich\ *n* : a dark green herb grown for its edible leaves

**spi·nal** \'spī-n²l\ *adj* : of or relating to the backbone or spinal cord — **spi·nal·ly** *adv*

**spinal column** *n* : BACKBONE 1

**spinal cord** *n* : the thick cord of nervous tissue that extends from the brain along the back in the cavity of the backbone and carries nerve impulses to and from the brain

**spinal nerve** *n* : any of the paired nerves which arise from the spinal cord and pass to various parts of the body and of which there are normally 31 pairs in human beings

**spin control** *n* : the act or practice of attempting to manipulate the way an event is interpreted

**spin·dle** \'spin-d²l\ *n* **1** : a round tapering stick or rod by which fibers are twisted in spinning **2** : a turned part of a piece of furniture ⟨the ∼s of a chair⟩ **3** : a slender pin or rod which turns or on which something else turns

**spin·dling** \'spind-liŋ\ *adj* : SPINDLY

**spin·dly** \'spind-lē\ *adj* : being long or tall and thin and usu. weak

**spin·drift** \'spin-ˌdrift\ *n* : spray blown from waves

**spine** \'spīn\ *n* **1** : BACKBONE **2** : a stiff sharp process esp. on a plant or animal **3** : the part of a book where the pages are attached — **spiny** *adj*

**spi·nel** \spə-'nel\ *n* : a hard crystalline mineral of variable color used as a gem

**spine·less** \'spīn-ləs\ *adj* **1** : having no spines, thorns, or prickles **2** : lacking a backbone **3** : lacking courage or determination ⟨a ∼ politician⟩

**spin·et** \'spi-nət\ *n* **1** : an early harpsichord having a single keyboard and only one string for each note **2** : a small upright piano

**spin·na·ker** \'spi-ni-kər\ *n* : a large triangular sail set on a long light pole

**spinning jen·ny** \-'je-nē\ *n* : an early multiple-spindle machine for spinning wool or cotton

**spinning wheel** *n* : a small machine for spinning thread or yarn in which a large wheel drives a single spindle

**spin-off** \'spin-ˌȯf\ *n* **1** : a usu. useful by-product **2** : something (as a TV show) derived from an earlier work — **spin off** *vb*

**spin·ster** \'spin-stər\ *n* : an unmarried woman past the common age for marrying — **spin·ster·hood** \-ˌhu̇d\ *n*

**spiny lobster** *n* : any of several edible crustaceans differing from the related lobsters in lacking the large front claws and in having a spiny carapace

¹**spi·ral** \'spī-rəl\ *adj* : winding or coiling around a center or axis and usu. getting closer to or farther away from it — **spi·ral·ly** *adv*

²**spiral** *n* **1** : something that has a spiral form; *also* : a single turn in a spiral object **2** : a continuously spreading and accelerating increase or decrease

³**spiral** *vb* **-raled** *or* **-ralled; -ral·ing** *or* **-ral·ling 1** : to move and esp. to rise or fall in a spiral course **2** : to form into a spiral

**spi·rant** \'spī-rənt\ *n* : a consonant (as \f\, \s\, \sh\) uttered with decided friction of the breath against some part of the oral passage — **spirant** *adj*

**spire** \'spī(-ə)r\ *n* **1** : a slender tapering stalk (as of grass) **2** : a pointed tip (as of an antler) **3** : STEEPLE — **spiry** *adj*

**spi·rea** *or* **spi·raea** \spī-'rē-ə\ *n* : any of a genus of shrubs related to the roses with dense clusters of small usu. white or pink flowers

¹**spir·it** \'spir-ət\ *n* [ME, fr. AF or L; AF, fr. L *spiritus*, lit., breath, fr. *spirare* to blow,

breathe] **1** : a life-giving force; *also* : the animating principle : SOUL  **2** *cap* : HOLY SPIRIT  **3** : SPECTER, GHOST  **4** : PERSON ⟨a bold ∼⟩  **5** : DISPOSITION, MOOD ⟨in good ∼*s*⟩  **6** : VIVACITY, ARDOR  **7** : essential or real meaning : INTENT  **8** : distilled alcoholic liquor  **9** : LOYALTY ⟨school ∼⟩ — **spir·it·less** *adj*

²**spirit** *vb* : to carry off secretly or mysteriously

**spir·it·ed** \'spir-ə-təd\ *adj* : full of energy, animation, or courage

¹**spir·i·tu·al** \'spir-i-chəl, -chə-wəl\ *adj* **1** : of, relating to, consisting of, or affecting the spirit : INCORPOREAL ⟨∼ needs⟩  **2** : of or relating to sacred matters  **3** : ecclesiastical rather than lay or temporal — **spir·i·tu·al·i·ty** \ˌspir-i-chə-'wa-lə-tē\ *n* — **spir·i·tu·al·ize** \'spir-i-chə-ˌlīz, -chə-wə-\ *vb* — **spir·i·tu·al·ly** *adv*

²**spiritual** *n* : a religious song originating among African-Americans of the southern U.S.

**spir·i·tu·al·ism** \'spir-i-chə-ˌli-zəm, -chə-wə-\ *n* : a belief that spirits of the dead communicate with the living usu. through a medium — **spir·i·tu·al·ist** \-list\ *n, often cap* — **spir·i·tu·al·is·tic** \ˌspir-i-chə-'lis-tik, -chə-wə-\ *adj*

**spir·i·tu·ous** \'spir-i-chəs, -chə-wəs; 'spir-ə-təs\ *adj* : containing alcohol

**spi·ro·chete** *also* **spi·ro·chaete** \'spī-rə-ˌkēt\ *n* : any of an order of spirally undulating bacteria including those causing syphilis and Lyme disease

**spirt** *var of* SPURT

¹**spit** \'spit\ *n* **1** : a thin pointed rod for holding meat over a fire  **2** : a point of land that runs out into the water

²**spit** *vb* **spit·ted; spit·ting** : to pierce with or as if with a spit

³**spit** *vb* **spit** *or* **spat** \'spat\; **spit·ting 1** : to eject (saliva) from the mouth  **2** : to express by or as if by spitting  **3** : to rain or snow lightly

⁴**spit** *n* **1** : SALIVA  **2** : perfect likeness ⟨∼ and image of his father⟩

**spit·ball** \'spit-ˌbȯl\ *n* **1** : paper chewed and rolled into a ball to be thrown as a missile  **2** : a baseball pitch delivered after the ball has been moistened with saliva or sweat

¹**spite** \'spīt\ *n* : ill will with a wish to annoy, anger, or frustrate : petty malice  ♦ **Synonyms**  MALIGNITY,  SPLEEN, GRUDGE, MALEVOLENCE — **spite·ful** \-fəl\ *adj* — **spite·ful·ly** *adv* — **spite·ful·ness** *n* — **in spite of** : in defiance or contempt of : NOTWITHSTANDING

²**spite** *vb* **spit·ed; spit·ing** : to treat maliciously : ANNOY, OFFEND

**spit·tle** \'spi-tᵊl\ *n* : SALIVA

**spit·tle·bug** \-ˌbəg\ *n* : any of a family of leaping insects with froth-secreting larvae that are related to aphids

**spit·toon** \spi-'tün\ *n* : a receptacle for spit

**splash** \'splash\ *vb* **1** : to dash a liquid about  **2** : to scatter a liquid on : SPATTER  **3** : to fall or strike with a splashing noise  ♦ **Synonyms** SPRINKLE, BESPATTER, DOUSE, SPLATTER — **splash** *n*

**splash·down** \'splash-ˌdaun\ *n* : the landing of a manned spacecraft in the ocean — **splash down** *vb*

**splashy** \'spla-shē\ *adj* **splash·i·er; -est** : conspicuously showy : OSTENTATIOUS

¹**splat·ter** \'spla-tər\ *vb* : SPATTER — **splatter** *n*

²**splatter** *adj* : extremely gory or violent ⟨a ∼ movie⟩

¹**splay** \'splā\ *vb* : to spread outward or apart ⟨∼ed out her fingers⟩ — **splay** *n*

²**splay** *adj* **1** : spread out : turned outward  **2** : AWKWARD, CLUMSY

**spleen** \'splēn\ *n* **1** : a vascular organ located near the stomach in most vertebrates that is concerned esp. with the filtration and storage of blood, destruction of red blood cells, and production of lymphocytes  **2** : SPITE, MALICE  ♦ **Synonyms** MALIGNITY, GRUDGE, MALEVOLENCE, ILL WILL, SPITEFULNESS

**splen·did** \'splen-dəd\ *adj* [L *splendidus*, fr. *splendēre* to shine]  **1** : SHINING, BRILLIANT  **2** : SHOWY, GORGEOUS  **3** : ILLUSTRIOUS  **4** : EXCELLENT ⟨a ∼ opportunity⟩  ♦ **Synonyms**  RESPLENDENT, GLORIOUS, SUBLIME, SUPERB — **splen·did·ly** *adv*

**splen·dor** \'splen-dər\ *n* **1** : BRILLIANCE ⟨the ∼ of the sun⟩  **2** : POMP, MAGNIFICENCE

**splen·dour** \'splen-dər\ *chiefly Brit var of* SPLENDOR

**sple·net·ic** \spli-'ne-tik\ *adj* : marked by bad temper or spleen

**splen·ic** \'sple-nik\ *adj* : of, relating to, or located in the spleen

**splice** \'splīs\ *vb* **spliced; splic·ing 1** : to unite (as two ropes) by weaving the strands together  **2** : to unite (as two lengths of film) by connecting the ends together — **splice** *n*

**splint** \'splint\ *n* **1** : a thin strip of wood interwoven with others to make something (as a basket)  **2** : material or a device used to protect and keep in place an injured body part (as a broken arm)

¹**splin·ter** \'splin-tər\ *n* : a thin piece of something split off lengthwise : SLIVER

²**splinter** *vb* : to split into splinters

**split** \'split\ *vb* **split; split·ting 1** : to divide lengthwise or along a grain or seam  **2** : to burst or break in pieces  **3** : to divide into parts or sections  **4** : LEAVE ⟨∼ the party⟩  ♦ **Synonyms** REND, CLEAVE, RIP, TEAR — **split** *n*

**split-lev·el** \'split-'le-vəl\ *n* : a house divided so that the floor in one part is about halfway between two floors in the other

**split personality** *n* : SCHIZOPHRENIA; *also* : MULTIPLE PERSONALITY DISORDER

**split–second** \'split-'se-kənd\ *adj* **1** : occurring in a very brief time  **2** : extremely precise ⟨∼ timing⟩

**split·ting** *adj* : causing a piercing sensation ⟨a ∼ headache⟩

**splotch** \'spläch\ *n* : BLOTCH

**splurge** \'splərj\ *vb* **splurged; splurg·ing** : to spend more than usual esp. on oneself — **splurge** *n*

**splut·ter** \'splə-tər\ *n* : SPUTTER — **splut·ter** *vb*

¹**spoil** \'spȯi(-ə)l\ *n* : PLUNDER ⟨∼s of war⟩

²**spoil** *vb* **spoiled** \'spȯi(-ə)ld, 'spȯi(-ə)lt\ *or* **spoilt** \'spȯi(-ə)lt\; **spoil·ing** **1** : ROB, PILLAGE **2** : to damage seriously : RUIN **3** : to impair the quality or effect of **4** : to damage the disposition of by pampering; *also* : INDULGE, CODDLE **5** : DECAY, ROT **6** : to have an eager desire ⟨∼*ing* for a fight⟩ ♦ **Synonyms** INJURE, HARM, HURT, MAR — **spoil·age** \'spȯi-lij\ *n*

**spoil·er** \'spȯi-lər\ *n* **1** : one that spoils **2** : a device (as on an airplane or automobile) used to disrupt airflow and decrease lift **3** : information about a movie or TV plot that can spoil a viewer's sense of surprise or suspense

**spoil·sport** \'spȯi(-ə)l-ˌspȯrt\ *n* : one who spoils the fun of others

¹**spoke** \'spōk\ *past & archaic past part of* SPEAK

²**spoke** *n* : any of the rods extending from the hub of a wheel to the rim

**spo·ken** \'spō-kən\ *past part of* SPEAK

**spokes·man** \'spōks-mən\ *n* : a person who speaks as the representative of another or others

**spokes·mod·el** \-ˌmä-dᵊl\ *n* : a model who is a spokesman or spokeswoman

**spokes·per·son** \-ˌpər-sən\ *n* : SPOKESMAN

**spokes·wom·an** \-ˌwu̇-mən\ *n* : a woman who speaks as the representative of another or others

**spo·li·a·tion** \ˌspō-lē-ˈā-shən\ *n* : the act of plundering : the state of being plundered

¹**sponge** \'spənj\ *n* **1** : an elastic porous water-absorbing mass of fibers that forms the skeleton of various primitive sea animals; *also* : any of a phylum of chiefly marine sea animals that are the source of natural sponges **2** : a spongelike or porous mass or material — **spongy** \'spən-jē\ *adj*

²**sponge** *vb* **sponged; spong·ing** **1** : to bathe or wipe with a sponge **2** : to live at another's expense **3** : to gather sponges — **spong·er** *n*

**sponge cake** *n* : a light cake made without shortening

**sponge rubber** *n* : a cellular rubber resembling natural sponge

**spon·sor** \'spän-sər\ *n* [LL, fr. L, guarantor, surety, fr. *spondēre* to promise] **1** : one who takes the responsibility for some other person or thing : SURETY **2** : GODPARENT **3** : a business firm that pays the cost of a radio or television program usu. in return for advertising time during its course — **sponsor** *vb* — **spon·sor·ship** *n*

**spon·ta·ne·ous** \spän-ˈtā-nē-əs\ *adj* [LL *spontaneus*, fr. L *sponte* of one's free will, voluntarily] **1** : done or produced freely or naturally **2** : acting or taking place without external force or cause ♦ **Synonyms** IMPULSIVE, INSTINCTIVE, AUTOMATIC, UNPREMEDITATED — **spon·ta·**

ne·ity \ˌspän-tə-ˈnē-ə-tē, -ˈnā-\ *n* — **spon·ta·ne·ous·ly** *adv*

**spontaneous combustion** *n* : a bursting into flame of material through heat produced within itself by chemical action (as oxidation)

**spoof** \'spüf\ *vb* **1** : DECEIVE, HOAX **2** : to make good-natured fun of ⟨the movie ∼s horror films⟩ — **spoof** *n*

¹**spook** \'spük\ *n* **1** : GHOST, APPARITION **2** : SPY **2** — **spooky** *adj*

²**spook** *vb* : FRIGHTEN

¹**spool** \'spül\ *n* : a cylinder on which flexible material (as thread) is wound

²**spool** *vb* **1** : to wind on a spool **2** : to regulate data flow by means of a spooler

**spool·er** \'spü-lər\ *n* : a computer program or routine for regulating data flow

**spoon** \'spün\ *n* [ME, fr. OE *spōn* splinter, chip] **1** : an eating or cooking implement consisting of a small shallow bowl with a handle **2** : a metal piece used on a fishing line as a lure — **spoon** *vb* — **spoon·ful** *n*

**spoon·bill** \'spün-ˌbil\ *n* : any of several wading birds related to the ibises that have a bill with a broad flat tip

**spoon–feed** \-ˌfēd\ *vb* **-fed** \-ˌfed\; **-feed·ing** : to feed by means of a spoon

**spoor** \'spu̇r, 'spȯr\ *n, pl* **spoor** *or* **spoors** : a track, a trail, a scent, or droppings esp. of a wild animal

**spo·rad·ic** \spə-ˈra-dik\ *adj* : occurring now and then ⟨∼ outbreaks of disease⟩ ♦ **Synonyms** OCCASIONAL, RARE, SCARCE, INFREQUENT, UNCOMMON — **spo·rad·i·cal·ly** \-di-k(ə-)lē\ *adv*

**spore** \'spȯr\ *n* : a primitive usu. one-celled often environmentally resistant dormant or reproductive body produced by plants, fungi, and some microorganisms

¹**sport** \'spȯrt\ *vb* [ME, to divert, amuse, short for *disporten*, fr. AF *desporter* to carry away, comfort, entertain, fr. *des-* (fr. L *dis-* apart) + *porter* to carry, fr. L *portare*] **1** : to amuse oneself : FROLIC **2** : SHOW OFF **1** ⟨∼*ing* new shoes⟩ — **sport·ive** *adj*

²**sport** *n* **1** : a source of diversion : PASTIME **2** : physical activity engaged in for pleasure **3** : JEST **4** : MOCKERY ⟨make ∼ of his efforts⟩ **5** : BUTT, LAUGHINGSTOCK **6** : one who accepts results cheerfully whether favorable or not **7** : an individual exhibiting marked deviation from its normal type esp. as a result of mutation ♦ **Synonyms** PLAY, FROLIC, FUN, RECREATION — **sporty** *adj*

³**sport** *or* **sports** *adj* : of, relating to, or suitable for sport or casual wear ⟨∼ coats⟩

**sport fish** *n* : a fish noted for the sport it affords anglers

**sports·cast** \'spȯrts-ˌkast\ *n* : a broadcast dealing with sports events — **sports·cast·er** \-ˌkas-tər\ *n*

**sports·man** \'spȯrts-mən\ *n* **1** : a person who engages in sports (as in hunting or fishing) **2** : one who plays fairly and wins or loses gracefully — **sports·man·like** \-ˌlīk\ *adj* — **sports·man·ship** *n*

**sports medicine** *n* : a field of medicine dealing with the prevention and treatment of sports-related injuries

**sports·wom·an** \-ˌwú-mən\ *n* : a woman who engages in sports

**sports·writ·er** \-ˌrī-tər\ *n* : one who writes about sports esp. for a newspaper — **sports·writ·ing** *n*

**sport–util·i·ty vehicle** \ˈspȯrt-yü-ˈti-lə-tē-\ *n* : SUV

¹**spot** \ˈspät\ *n* **1** : STAIN, BLEMISH **2** : a small part different (as in color) from the main part **3** : LOCATION, SITE — **spot·less** *adj* — **spot·less·ly** *adv* — **on the spot 1** : at the place of action **2** : in difficulty or danger

²**spot** *vb* **spot·ted; spot·ting 1** : to mark or disfigure with spots **2** : to pick out **3** : RECOGNIZE, IDENTIFY

³**spot** *adj* **1** : being, done, or originating on the spot ⟨a ∼ broadcast⟩ **2** : paid upon delivery **3** : made at random or at a few key points ⟨a ∼ check⟩

**spot–check** \ˈspät-ˌchek\ *vb* : to make a spot check of

**spot·light** \-ˌlīt\ *n* **1** : a circle of brilliant light projected upon a particular area, person, or object (as on a stage); *also* : the device that produces this light **2** : public notice — **spotlight** *vb*

**spot–on** \ˈspät-ˈän\ *adj* : exactly correct ⟨a ∼ forecast⟩

**spotted owl** *n* : a rare large dark brown dark-eyed owl of humid old growth forests and thickly wooded canyons from British Columbia to southern California and central Mexico

**spot·ter** \ˈspä-tər\ *n* **1** : one that keeps watch : OBSERVER **2** : one that removes spots

**spot·ty** \ˈspä-tē\ *adj* **spot·ti·er; -est** : uneven in quality; *also* : sparsely distributed ⟨∼ attendance⟩

**spou·sal** \ˈspau̇-zəl, -səl\ *n* : MARRIAGE 2, WEDDING — usu. used in pl.

**spouse** \ˈspau̇s\ *n* : one's husband or wife — **spou·sal** \ˈspau̇-zəl, -səl\ *adj*

¹**spout** \ˈspau̇t\ *vb* **1** : to eject or issue forth forcibly and freely ⟨wells ∼ing oil⟩ **2** : to speak pompously

²**spout** *n* **1** : a pipe or hole through which liquid spouts **2** : a jet of liquid; *esp* : WATERSPOUT 2

**spp** *abbr* species (*pl*)

¹**sprain** \ˈsprān\ *n* : a sudden or severe twisting of a joint with stretching or tearing of ligaments; *also* : a sprained condition

²**sprain** *vb* : to subject to sprain

**sprat** \ˈsprat\ *n* : a small European fish related to the herring; *also* : SARDINE

**sprawl** \ˈsprȯl\ *vb* **1** : to lie or sit with limbs spread out awkwardly **2** : to spread out irregularly — **sprawl** *n*

¹**spray** \ˈsprā\ *n* : a usu. flowering branch; *also* : a decorative arrangement of flowers and foliage

²**spray** *n* **1** : liquid flying in small drops like water blown from a wave **2** : a jet of fine vapor (as from an atomizer) **3** : an instrument (as an atomizer) for scattering fine liquid

³**spray** *vb* **1** : to discharge spray on or into **2** : to scatter or let fall in a spray — **spray·er** *n*

**spray can** *n* : a pressurized container from which aerosols are sprayed

**spray gun** *n* : a device for spraying liquids (as paint or insecticide)

¹**spread** \ˈspred\ *vb* **spread; spread·ing 1** : to scatter over a surface **2** : to flatten out : open out **3** : to distribute over a period of time or among many persons **4** : to cover something with ⟨∼ rugs on the floor⟩ **5** : to prepare for a meal ⟨∼ a table⟩ **6** : to pass on from person to person **7** : to stretch, force, or push apart ⟨a bird ∼ing its wings⟩ — **spread·er** *n*

²**spread** *n* **1** : the act or process of spreading **2** : EXPANSE, EXTENT **3** : a prominent display in a periodical **4** : a food to be spread on bread or crackers **5** : a cloth cover for a bed **6** : distance between two points : GAP

**spread·sheet** \ˈspred-ˌshēt\ *n* : an accounting program for a computer

**spree** \ˈsprē\ *n* : an unrestrained outburst ⟨buying ∼⟩; *also* : a drinking bout

**sprig** \ˈsprig\ *n* : a small shoot or twig

**spright·ly** \ˈsprīt-lē\ *adj* **spright·li·er; -est** : LIVELY, SPIRITED ⟨a ∼ musical⟩ **♦ Synonyms** ANIMATED, VIVACIOUS, GAY — **spright·li·ness** *n*

¹**spring** \ˈspriŋ\ *vb* **sprang** \ˈspraŋ\ *or* **sprung** \ˈsprəŋ\; **sprung; spring·ing 1** : to move suddenly upward or forward **2** : to grow quickly ⟨weeds *sprang* up overnight⟩ **3** : to come from by birth or descent **4** : to move quickly by elastic force **5** : WARP **6** : to develop (a leak) through the seams **7** : to cause to close suddenly ⟨∼ a trap⟩ **8** : to make known suddenly ⟨∼ a surprise⟩ **9** : to make lame : STRAIN ⟨*sprang* a leg muscle⟩

²**spring** *n* **1** : a source of supply; *esp* : an issuing of water from the ground **2** : SOURCE, ORIGIN; *also* : MOTIVE **3** : the season between winter and summer **4** : an elastic body or device that recovers its original shape when it is released after being distorted **5** : the act or an instance of leaping up or forward **6** : RESILIENCE — **springy** *adj*

**spring·board** \ˈspriŋ-ˌbȯrd\ *n* : a springy board used in jumping or vaulting or for diving

**spring fever** *n* : a lazy or restless feeling often associated with the onset of spring

**spring tide** *n* : a tide of greater-than-average range that occurs at each new moon and full moon

**spring·time** \ˈspriŋ-ˌtīm\ *n* : the season of spring

¹**sprin·kle** \ˈspriŋ-kəl\ *vb* **sprin·kled; sprin·kling** : to scatter in small drops or particles — **sprin·kler** *n*

²**sprinkle** *n* : a light rainfall

**sprin·kling** *n* : SMATTERING

¹**sprint** \ˈsprint\ *vb* : to run at top speed esp. for a short distance — **sprint·er** *n*

²**sprint** *n* **1** : a short run at top speed **2** : a short distance race

**sprite** \ˈsprīt\ *n* **1** : GHOST, SPIRIT **2** : ELF, FAIRY

**spritz** \'sprits, 'shpritz\ *vb* : SPRAY 〈~ the plants〉 — **spritz** *n*

**sprock·et** \'sprä-kət\ *n* : a toothed wheel whose teeth engage the links of a chain

¹**sprout** \'spraůt\ *vb* : to send out new growth 〈~*ing* seeds〉

²**sprout** *n* : a usu. young and growing plant shoot (as from a seed)

¹**spruce** \'sprüs\ *vb* **spruced; spruc·ing** : to make or become spruce

²**spruce** *adj* **spruc·er; spruc·est** : neat and smart in appearance ♦ *Synonyms* STYLISH, FASHIONABLE, MODISH, DAPPER, NATTY

³**spruce** *n, pl* **spruc·es** *also* **spruce** : any of a genus of evergreen pyramid-shaped trees related to the pines and having soft light wood; *also* : the wood of a spruce

**sprung** *past and past part of* SPRING

**spry** \'sprī\ *adj* **spri·er** *or* **spry·er** \'sprī-ər\; **spri·est** *or* **spry·est** \'sprī-əst\ : NIMBLE, ACTIVE 〈a ~ 75-year-old〉 ♦ *Synonyms* AGILE, BRISK, LIVELY, SPRIGHTLY

**spud** \'spəd\ *n* **1** : a sharp narrow spade **2** : POTATO

**spume** \'spyüm\ *n* : frothy matter on liquids : FOAM — **spumy** \'spyü-mē\ *adj*

**spu·mo·ni** *also* **spu·mo·ne** \spü-'mō-nē\ *n* [It *spumone*, fr. *spuma* foam] : ice cream in layers of different colors, flavors, and textures often with candied fruits and nuts

**spun** *past and past part of* SPIN

**spun glass** *n* : FIBERGLASS

**spunk** \'spəŋk\ *n* [fr. *spunk* tinder, fr. ScGael *spong* sponge, tinder, fr. Middle Irish *sponge*, fr. L *spongia* sponge] : PLUCK, COURAGE — **spunky** *adj*

¹**spur** \'spər\ *n* **1** : a pointed device fastened to a rider's boot and used to urge on a horse **2** : something that urges to action **3** : a stiff sharp spine (as on the leg of a cock); *also* : a hollow projecting appendage of a flower (as a columbine) **4** : a ridge extending sideways from a mountain **5** : a branch of railroad track extending from the main line ♦ *Synonyms* GOAD, MOTIVE, IMPULSE, INCENTIVE, INDUCEMENT — **spurred** \'spərd\ *adj* — **on the spur of the moment** : on hasty impulse

²**spur** *vb* **spurred; spur·ring 1** : to urge a horse on with spurs **2** : INCITE

**spurge** \'spərj\ *n* : any of a family of herbs and woody plants with a bitter milky juice

**spu·ri·ous** \'spyůr-ē-əs\ *adj* [LL *spurius* false, fr. L *spurius*, n., son of an unknown father] : not genuine : FALSE 〈~ eminence〉

**spurn** \'spərn\ *vb* **1** : to kick away or trample on **2** : to reject with disdain

¹**spurt** \'spərt\ *vb* **1** : to gush out : SPOUT

²**spurt** *n* : a sudden gushing or spouting

³**spurt** *n* **1** : a sudden brief burst of effort, speed, or development **2** : a sharp increase of activity 〈~ in sales〉

⁴**spurt** *vb* : to make a spurt

**sput·ter** \'spə-tər\ *vb* **1** : to spit small scattered particles : SPLUTTER **2** : to utter words hastily or explosively in excitement or confusion **3** : to make small popping sounds — **sputter** *n*

**spu·tum** \'spyü-təm\ *n, pl* **spu·ta** \-tə\ [L] : material (as phlegm) that is spit out or coughed up esp. during illness

¹**spy** \'spī\ *vb* **spied; spy·ing 1** : to watch or search for information secretly : act as a spy **2** : to get a momentary or quick glimpse of : SEE

²**spy** *n, pl* **spies 1** : one who secretly watches others **2** : a secret agent who tries to get information for one country in the territory of an enemy

**spy·glass** \-ˌglas\ *n* : a small telescope

**sq** *abbr* **1** squadron **2** square

**squab** \'skwäb\ *n, pl* **squabs** *or* **squab** : a young bird and esp. a pigeon

**squab·ble** \'skwä-bəl\ *n* : a noisy altercation : WRANGLE ♦ *Synonyms* QUARREL, SPAT, ROW, TIFF — **squabble** *vb*

**squad** \'skwäd\ *n* **1** : a small organized group of military personnel **2** : a small group engaged in a common effort

**squad car** *n* : a police car connected by two-way radio with headquarters

**squad·ron** \'skwä-drən\ *n* : any of several units of military organization

**squal·id** \'skwä-ləd\ *adj* **1** : filthy or degraded through neglect or poverty **2** : SORDID, DEBASED 〈a ~ political ploy〉 ♦ *Synonyms* NASTY, FOUL, DIRTY, GRUBBY

**squall** \'skwȯl\ *n* : a sudden violent gust of wind often with rain or snow — **squally** *adj*

**squa·lor** \'skwä-lər\ *n* : the quality or state of being squalid

**squa·mous cell** \'skwä-məs-\ *n* : a scalelike cell of the outer layers of the skin from which a type of carcinoma arises

**squan·der** \'skwän-dər\ *vb* : to spend wastefully or foolishly

¹**square** \'skwer\ *n* **1** : an instrument used to lay out or test right angles **2** : a rectangle with all four sides equal **3** : something square **4** : the product of a number multiplied by itself **5** : an area bounded by four streets **6** : an open area in a city where streets meet **7** : a highly conventional person

²**square** *adj* **squar·er; squar·est 1** : having four equal sides and four right angles **2** : forming a right angle 〈cut a ~ corner〉 **3** : multiplied by itself : SQUARED 〈x² is the symbol for x ~〉 **4** : being a unit of square measure equal to a square each side of which measures one unit 〈a ~ foot〉 **5** : being of a specified length in each of two dimensions 〈an area 10 feet ~〉 **6** : exactly adjusted **7** : JUST, FAIR 〈a ~ deal〉 **8** : leaving no balance 〈make accounts ~〉 **9** : SUBSTANTIAL 〈a ~ meal〉 **10** : highly conservative or conventional — **square·ly** *adv*

³**square** *vb* **squared; squar·ing 1** : to form with four equal sides and right angles or with flat surfaces 〈~ a timber〉 **2** : to multiply (a number) by itself **3** : CONFORM, AGREE **4** : BALANCE, SETTLE 〈~ an account〉

**square dance** *n* : a dance for four couples arranged to form a square

**square measure** *n* : a unit or system of units for measuring area — see METRIC SYSTEM table, WEIGHT table

**square–rigged** \'skwer-'rigd\ *adj* : having the chief sails extended on yards that are fastened to the masts horizontally and at their center

**square–rig·ger** \-ˌri-gər\ *n* : a square-rigged craft

**square root** *n* : either of the two numbers whose squares are equal to a given number ⟨the *square root* of 9 is +3 or −3⟩

¹**squash** \'skwäsh, 'skwósh\ *vb* **1** : to beat or press into a pulp or flat mass **2** : QUASH, SUPPRESS ⟨∼ a revolt⟩

²**squash** *n* **1** : the impact of something soft and heavy; *also* : the sound of such impact **2** : a crushed mass **3** : a game played on a 4-wall court with a racket and rubber ball

³**squash** *n, pl* **squash·es** *or* **squash** : any of various fruits of plants of the gourd family that are used esp. as vegetables; *also* : a plant and esp. a vine bearing squashes

**squash racquets** *n* : SQUASH 3

¹**squat** \'skwät\ *vb* **squat·ted; squat·ting** [ME *squatten* to crush, crouch in hiding, fr. MF (dial. of Picardy) *esquatir, escuatir,* fr. OF *es-* ex- + *quatir* to hide, fr. VL \**coactire* to squeeze, alter. of L *coactare* to compel, fr. *cogere* to compel] **1** : to sit down upon the hams or heels **2** : to settle on land without right or title; *also* : to settle on public land with a view to acquiring title — **squat·ter** *n*

²**squat** *adj* **squat·ter; squat·test** : low to the ground; *also* : short and thick in stature ◆ *Synonyms* THICKSET, STOCKY, HEAVYSET, STUBBY

³**squat** *n* : the act or posture of squatting

**squawk** \'skwók\ *n* : a harsh loud cry; *also* : a noisy protest — **squawk** *vb*

**squeak** \'skwēk\ *vb* **1** : to utter or speak in a weak shrill tone **2** : to make a thin high-pitched sound ⟨the door ∼s⟩ — **squeak** *n* — **squeaky** *adj*

¹**squeal** \'skwēl\ *vb* **1** : to make a shrill sound or cry **2** : to betray a secret or turn informer **3** : COMPLAIN, PROTEST

²**squeal** *n* : a shrill sharp cry or noise

**squea·mish** \'skwē-mish\ *adj* **1** : easily nauseated; *also* : NAUSEATED **2** : easily disgusted ◆ *Synonyms* FUSSY, NICE, DAINTY, FASTIDIOUS, PERSNICKETY — **squea·mish·ness** *n*

**squee·gee** \'skwē-ˌjē\ *n* : a blade set crosswise on a handle and used for spreading and wiping liquid on, across, or off a surface — **squeegee** *vb*

¹**squeeze** \'skwēz\ *vb* **squeezed; squeez·ing** **1** : to exert pressure on the opposite sides or parts of **2** : to obtain by pressure ⟨∼ juice from a lemon⟩ **3** : to force or move into a small space ⟨*squeezed* into her jeans⟩ — **squeez·er** *n*

²**squeeze** *n* **1** : an act of squeezing **2** : a quantity squeezed out

**squeeze bottle** *n* : a flexible plastic bottle that dispenses its contents when it is squeezed

**squelch** \'skwelch\ *vb* **1** : to suppress completely : CRUSH ⟨∼ resistance⟩ **2** : to move in soft mud — **squelch** *n*

**squib** \'skwib\ *n* : a brief witty writing or speech

**squid** \'skwid\ *n, pl* **squid** *or* **squids** : any of an order of long-bodied sea mollusks having eight short arms and two longer tentacles and usu. a slender internal shell

**squint** \'skwint\ *vb* **1** : to look or aim obliquely **2** : to look or peer with the eyes partly closed ⟨∼ing into the sun⟩ **3** : to be cross-eyed — **squint** *n or adj*

¹**squire** \'skwi(-ə)r\ *n* [ME *squier,* fr. AF *esquier,* fr. LL *scutarius,* fr. L *scutum* shield] **1** : an armor-bearer of a knight **2** : a man gallantly devoted to a lady **3** : a member of the British gentry ranking below a knight and above a gentleman; *also* : a prominent landowner **4** : a local magistrate

²**squire** *vb* **squired; squir·ing** : to attend as a squire or escort

**squirm** \'skwərm\ *vb* : to twist about like a worm : WRIGGLE

¹**squir·rel** \'skwər-əl\ *n, pl* **squirrels** *also* **squirrel** [ME *squirel,* fr. AF *escurel, esquirel,* fr. VL \**scuriolus,* dim. of \**scurius,* alter. of L *sciurus,* fr. Gk *skiouros,* prob. fr. *skia* shadow + *oura* tail] : any of various rodents usu. with a long bushy tail and strong hind legs; *also* : the fur of a squirrel

²**squirrel** *vb* **-reled** *or* **-relled; -rel·ing** *or* **-rel·ling** : to store up for future use

¹**squirt** \'skwərt\ *vb* : to eject liquid in a thin spurt

²**squirt** *n* **1** : an instrument (as a syringe) for squirting **2** : a small forcible jet of liquid

¹**Sr** *abbr* **1** senior **2** sister

²**Sr** *symbol* strontium

**SR** *abbr* seaman recruit

¹**SRO** \ˌes-(ˌ)är-'ō\ *n* [single-room occupancy] : a house or apartment building in which low-income tenants live in single rooms

²**SRO** *abbr* standing room only

**SS** *abbr* **1** saints **2** Social Security **3** steamship **4** sworn statement

**SSA** *abbr* Social Security Administration

**SSE** *abbr* south-southeast

**SSG** *or* **SSgt** *abbr* staff sergeant

**SSI** *abbr* supplemental security income

**SSM** *abbr* staff sergeant major

**SSN** *abbr* Social Security Number

**ssp** *abbr* subspecies

**SSR** *abbr* Soviet Socialist Republic

**SSS** *abbr* Selective Service System

**SST** \ˌes-(ˌ)es-'tē\ *n* [supersonic transport] : a supersonic passenger airplane

**SSW** *abbr* south-southwest

**st** *abbr* **1** stanza **2** state **3** stitch **4** stone **5** street

**St** *abbr* saint

**ST** *abbr* **1** short ton **2** standard time

**-st** — see -EST

**sta** *abbr* station; stationary

¹**stab** \'stab\ *n* **1** : a wound produced by a pointed weapon **2** : a quick thrust **3** : a brief attempt

²**stab** *vb* **stabbed; stab·bing** : to pierce or

wound with or as if with a pointed weapon; *also* : THRUST, DRIVE

**sta·bile** \'stā-ˌbēl\ *n* : an abstract sculpture or construction similar to a mobile but made to be stationary

**sta·bi·lize** \'stā-bə-ˌlīz\ *vb* **-lized; -liz·ing** **1** : to make stable **2** : to hold steady ⟨~ prices⟩ — **sta·bi·li·za·tion** \ˌstā-bə-lə-ˈzā-shən\ *n* — **sta·bi·liz·er** \'stā-bə-ˌlī-zər\ *n*

¹**sta·ble** \'stā-bəl\ *n* : a building in which domestic animals are sheltered and fed — **sta·ble·man** \-mən, -ˌman\ *n*

²**stable** *vb* **sta·bled; sta·bling** : to put or keep in a stable

³**stable** *adj* **sta·bler; sta·blest 1** : firmly established; *also* : mentally and emotionally healthy **2** : steady in purpose : CONSTANT **3** : DURABLE, ENDURING ⟨~ civilizations⟩ **4** : resistant to chemical or physical change ♦ *Synonyms* LASTING, PERMANENT, PERPETUAL, PERDURABLE — **sta·bil·i·ty** \stə-ˈbi-lə-tē\ *n*

**stac·ca·to** \stə-ˈkä-tō\ *adj or adv* [It] : cut short so as not to sound connected ⟨~ notes⟩

¹**stack** \'stak\ *n* **1** : a large pile (as of hay or grain) **2** : an orderly pile (as of poker chips) **3** : a large quantity **4** : a vertical pipe : SMOKESTACK **5** : a rack with shelves for storing books ⟨library ~s⟩

²**stack** *vb* **1** : to pile up **2** : to arrange (cards) secretly for cheating

**stack up** *vb* : MEASURE UP ⟨how do they *stack up* against the competition?⟩

**sta·di·um** \'stā-dē-əm\ *n, pl* **-dia** \-dē-ə\ *or* **-di·ums** : a structure with tiers of seats for spectators built around a field for sports events

¹**staff** \'staf\ *n, pl* **staffs** \'stafs, 'stavz\ *or* **staves** \'stavz, 'stāvz\ **1** : a pole, stick, rod, or bar used for supporting, for measuring, or as a symbol of authority; *also* : CLUB, CUDGEL **2** : something that sustains ⟨bread is the ~ of life⟩ **3** : the five horizontal lines on which music is written **4** : a body of assistants to an executive **5** : a group of officers holding no command but having duties concerned with planning and managing

²**staff** *vb* : to supply with a staff or with workers ⟨~ a hotel⟩

**staff·er** \'sta-fər\ *n* : a member of a staff (as of a newspaper)

**staff sergeant** *n* : a noncommissioned officer ranking in the army next below a sergeant first class, in the air force next below a technical sergeant, and in the marine corps next below a gunnery sergeant

¹**stag** \'stag\ *n, pl* **stags** *or* **stag** : an adult male of various large deer

²**stag** *adj* : restricted to or intended for men ⟨a ~ party⟩ ⟨~ movies⟩

³**stag** *adv* : unaccompanied by a date

¹**stage** \'stāj\ *n* [ME, fr. AF *estage* abode, story of a building, stage, fr. VL *staticum*, fr. L *stare* to stand] **1** : a raised platform on which an orator may speak or a play may be presented **2** : the acting profession : THEATER **3** : the scene of a notable action or event **4** : a station or rest-

ing place on a traveled road **5** : STAGECOACH **6** : a degree of advance in an undertaking, process, or development **7** : a propulsion unit in a rocket — **stagy** \'stā-jē\ *adj*

²**stage** *vb* **staged; stag·ing** : to produce or perform on or as if on a stage ⟨~ a play⟩ — **stage·able** *adj*

**stage·coach** \'stāj-ˌkōch\ *n* : a horse-drawn coach that runs regularly between stations

**stage manager** *n* : one who supervises the physical aspects of a stage production

**stag·fla·tion** \ˌstag-ˈflā-shən\ *n* : inflation with stagnant economic activity and high unemployment

¹**stag·ger** \'sta-gər\ *vb* **1** : to reel from side to side : TOTTER **2** : to begin to doubt : WAVER **3** : to cause to reel or waver **4** : to arrange in overlapping or alternating positions or times ⟨~ working hours⟩ **5** : ASTONISH ⟨their indifference ~s me⟩ — **stag·ger·ing·ly** *adv*

²**stagger** *n* **1** *sing or pl* : an abnormal condition of domestic animals associated with damage to the central nervous system and marked by lack of coordination and a reeling unsteady gait **2** : a reeling or unsteady gait or stance

**stag·ing** \'stā-jiŋ\ *n* **1** : SCAFFOLDING **2** : the assembling of troops and matériel in transit in a particular place

**staging post** *n* : STOPOVER 2

**stag·nant** \'stag-nənt\ *adj* **1** : not flowing : MOTIONLESS ⟨~ water in a pond⟩ **2** : DULL, INACTIVE ⟨~ business⟩

**stag·nate** \'stag-ˌnāt\ *vb* **stag·nat·ed; stag·nat·ing** : to be or become stagnant — **stag·na·tion** \stag-ˈnā-shən\ *n*

**staid** \'stād\ *adj* : SOBER, SEDATE ♦ *Synonyms* GRAVE, SERIOUS, EARNEST

¹**stain** \'stān\ *vb* **1** : DISCOLOR, SOIL **2** : TAINT, CORRUPT **3** : DISGRACE **4** : to color (as wood, paper, or cloth) by processes affecting the material itself

²**stain** *n* **1** : a small soiled or discolored area **2** : a taint of guilt : STIGMA **3** : a preparation (as a dye or pigment) used in staining — **stain·less** *adj*

**stainless steel** *n* : steel alloyed with chromium that is highly resistant to stain, rust, and corrosion

**stair** \'ster\ *n* **1** : a series of steps or flights of steps for passing from one level to another — often used in pl. **2** : one step of a stairway

**stair·case** \-ˌkās\ *n* : a flight of steps with their supporting framework, casing, and balusters

**stair·way** \-ˌwā\ *n* : one or more flights of stairs with connecting landings

**stair·well** \-ˌwel\ *n* : a vertical shaft in which stairs are located

¹**stake** \'stāk\ *n* **1** : a pointed piece of material (as of wood) driven into the ground as a marker or a support **2** : a post to which a person is bound for death by burning; *also* : execution by burning at the stake **3** : something that is staked for gain or loss **4** : the prize in a contest

²**stake** *vb* **staked; stak·ing** **1** : to mark the limits of by or as if by stakes **2** : to tie

to a stake  **3** : to support or secure with stakes  **4** : BET, WAGER

**stake·out** \'stāk-ˌau̇t\ *n* : a surveillance by police (as of a suspected criminal)

**sta·lac·tite** \stə-'lak-ˌtīt\ *n* [NL *stalactites*, fr. Gk *stalaktos* dripping, fr. *stalassein* to let drip] : an icicle-shaped deposit hanging from the roof or sides of a cavern

**sta·lag·mite** \stə-'lag-ˌmīt\ *n* [NL *stalagmites*, fr. Gk *stalagma* drop or *stalagmos* dripping, fr. *stalassein* to let drip] : a deposit resembling an inverted stalactite rising from the floor of a cavern

**stale** \'stāl\ *adj* **stal·er; stal·est** **1** : having lost good taste and quality from age ⟨~ bread⟩  **2** : used or heard so often as to be dull ⟨~ news⟩  **3** : not as strong or effective as before ⟨~ from lack of practice⟩ — **stale·ness** *n*

**stale·mate** \'stāl-ˌmāt\ *n* : a drawn contest : DEADLOCK — **stalemate** *vb*

**¹stalk** \'stȯk\ *n* : a plant stem; *also* : any slender usu. upright supporting or connecting part — **stalked** \'stȯkt\ *adj*

**²stalk** *vb* **1** : to pursue (game) stealthily **2** : to walk stiffly or haughtily  **3** : to follow (a person) obsessively

**¹stall** \'stȯl\ *n* **1** : a compartment in a stable or barn for one animal  **2** : a booth or counter where articles may be displayed for sale  **3** : a seat in a church choir; *also* : a church pew  **4** *chiefly Brit* : a front orchestra seat in a theater

**²stall** *vb* : to bring or come to a standstill unintentionally ⟨~ an engine⟩

**³stall** *n* : the condition of an airfoil or aircraft in which lift is lost and the airfoil or aircraft tends to drop

**⁴stall** *n* [alter. of *stale* lure] : a ruse to deceive or delay

**⁵stall** *vb* : to hold off, divert, or delay by evasion or deception

**stal·lion** \'stal-yən\ *n* : a male horse

**stal·wart** \'stȯl-wərt\ *adj* : STOUT, STRONG; *also* : BRAVE, VALIANT

**sta·men** \'stā-mən\ *n* : an organ of a flower that produces pollen

**stam·i·na** \'sta-mə-nə\ *n* [L, pl. of *stamen* warp, thread of life spun by the Fates] : VIGOR, ENDURANCE ⟨had the ~ to win⟩

**sta·mi·nate** \'stā-mə-nət, 'sta-mə-, -ˌnāt\ *adj* **1** : having or producing stamens **2** : having stamens but no pistils

**stam·mer** \'sta-mər\ *vb* : to hesitate or stumble in speaking — **stammer** *n* — **stam·mer·er** *n*

**¹stamp** \'stamp; *for 2 also* 'stämp *or* 'stȯmp\ *vb* **1** : to pound or crush with a heavy instrument  **2** : to strike or beat with the bottom of the foot  **3** : IMPRESS, IMPRINT ⟨~ "paid" on the bill⟩  **4** : to cut out or indent with a stamp or die  **5** : to attach a postage stamp to

**²stamp** *n* **1** : a device or instrument for stamping  **2** : the mark made by stamping; *also* : a distinctive mark or quality  **3** : the act of stamping  **4** : a stamped or printed paper affixed to show that a charge has been paid ⟨postage ~⟩ ⟨tax ~⟩

**¹stam·pede** \stam-'pēd\ *n* : a wild headlong rush or flight esp. of frightened animals

**²stampede** *vb* **stam·ped·ed; stam·ped·ing** **1** : to flee or cause to flee in panic **2** : to act or cause to act together suddenly and heedlessly

**stance** \'stans\ *n* : a way of standing

**¹stanch** \'stȯnch, 'stänch, 'stanch\ *or* **staunch** \'stȯnch, 'stänch\ *vb* : to check the flowing of (as blood); *also* : to cease flowing or bleeding

**²stanch** *var of* ²STAUNCH

**stan·chion** \'stan-chən\ *n* : an upright bar, post, or support

**¹stand** \'stand\ *vb* **stood** \'stu̇d\; **standing** **1** : to take or be at rest in an upright or firm position  **2** : to assume a specified position  **3** : to remain stationary or unchanged  **4** : to be steadfast  **5** : to act in resistance ⟨~ against a foe⟩  **6** : to maintain a relative position or rank  **7** : to gather slowly and remain ⟨tears *stood* in her eyes⟩  **8** : to set upright  **9** : ENDURE, TOLERATE ⟨I won't ~ for that⟩  **10** : to submit to ⟨~ trial⟩ — **stand pat** : to oppose or resist change

**²stand** *n* **1** : an act of standing, staying, or resisting  **2** : a stop made to give a performance  **3** : POSITION, VIEWPOINT  **4** : a place taken by a witness to testify in court  **5** *pl* : tiered seats for spectators  **6** : a raised platform (as for speakers)  **7** : a structure for a small retail business  **8** : a structure for supporting or holding something upright ⟨music ~⟩  **9** : a group of plants growing in a continuous area

**stand–alone** \'stan-də-ˌlōn\ *adj* : SELF-CONTAINED; *esp* : capable of operation independent of a computer system

**¹stan·dard** \'stan-dərd\ *n* **1** : a figure adopted as an emblem by a people **2** : the personal flag of a ruler; *also* : FLAG **3** : something set up as a rule for measuring or as a model to be followed  **4** : an upright support ⟨lamp ~⟩

**²standard** *adj* **1** : used as or meeting a standard established by law or custom  **2** : regularly and widely used ⟨a ~ practice⟩  **3** : well established by usage in speech or writing

**stan·dard–bear·er** \-ˌber-ər\ *n* : the leader of a cause

**standard deviation** *n* : a measure of dispersion in a set of data

**stan·dard·ise** *Brit var of* STANDARDIZE

**stan·dard–is·sue** \'stan-dərd-'i-shü\ *adj* : STANDARD, TYPICAL ⟨a ~ blue suit⟩

**stan·dard·ize** \'stan-dər-ˌdīz\ *vb* **-ized; -iz·ing** : to make standard or uniform — **stan·dard·i·za·tion** \ˌstan-dər-də-'zā-shən\ *n*

**standard of living** *n* : the necessities, comforts, and luxuries that a person or group is accustomed to

**standard time** *n* : the time established by law or by general usage over a region or country

**¹stand·by** \'stand-ˌbī\ *n, pl* **stand·bys** \-ˌbīz\ **1** : one that can be relied on  **2** : a substitute in reserve — **on standby**

: ready or available for immediate action or use

²**standby** *adj* **1** : ready for use **2** : relating to airline travel in which the passenger must wait for an available unreserved seat — **standby** *adv*

**stand-in** \'stan-ˌdin\ *n* **1** : someone employed to occupy an actor's place while lights and camera are readied **2** : SUBSTITUTE

¹**stand-ing** \'stan-diŋ\ *adj* **1** : ERECT ⟨~ timber⟩ **2** : not flowing : STAGNANT **3** : remaining at the same level or amount for an indefinite period ⟨~ offer⟩ **4** : PERMANENT ⟨a ~ army⟩ **5** : done from a standing position ⟨a ~ jump⟩

²**standing** *n* **1** : length of service; *also* : relative position in society or in a profession : RANK **2** : DURATION ⟨a custom of long ~⟩

**stand-off** \'stan-ˌdof\ *n* : TIE, DRAW

**stand-off-ish** \stan-'do-fish\ *adj* : somewhat cold and reserved

**stand-out** \'stan-ˌdaut\ *n* : something conspicuously excellent

**stand-pipe** \'stand-ˌpip\ *n* : a high vertical pipe or reservoir for water used to produce a uniform pressure

**stand-point** \-ˌpoint\ *n* : a position from which objects or principles are judged

**stand-still** \-ˌstil\ *n* : a state of rest

**stand-up** \'stan-ˌdəp\ *adj* : done or performing in a standing position ⟨a ~ comic⟩ ⟨~ comedy⟩

**stank** *past of* STINK

**stan-za** \'stan-zə\ *n* [It] : a group of lines forming a division of a poem

**sta-pes** \'stā-ˌpēz\ *n, pl* **stapes** *or* **sta-pe-des** \'stā-pə-ˌdēz\ : the innermost bone of the middle ear of mammals

**staph** \'staf\ *n* : STAPHYLOCOCCUS

**staph-y-lo-coc-cus** \ˌsta-fə-lō-'kä-kəs\ *n, pl* **-coc-ci** \-'kä-ˌkī, -'käk-ˌsī\ : any of a genus of spherical bacteria including some pathogens of skin and mucous membranes — **staph-y-lo-coc-cal** \-'kä-kəl\ *adj*

¹**sta-ple** \'stā-pəl\ *n* : a U-shaped piece of metal or wire with sharp points to be driven into a surface or through thin layers (as paper) for attaching or holding together — **staple** *vb* — **sta-pler** *n*

²**staple** *n* **1** : a chief commodity or product **2** : a chief part of something ⟨a ~ of their diet⟩ **3** : unmanufactured or raw material **4** : a textile fiber suitable for spinning into yarn

³**staple** *adj* **1** : regularly produced in large quantities **2** : PRINCIPAL, MAIN ⟨the ~ crop⟩

¹**star** \'stär\ *n* **1** : a celestial body that appears as a fixed point of light; *esp* : such a body that is gaseous, self-luminous, and of great mass **2** : a planet or configuration of planets that is held in astrology to influence one's fortune — usu. used in pl. **3** *obs* : DESTINY **4** : a conventional figure representing a star; *esp* : ASTERISK **5** : an actor or actress playing the leading role **6** : a brilliant performer — **star-dom** \'stär-dəm\ *n* — **star-less** *adj* — **star-like** *adj* — **star-ry** *adj*

²**star** *vb* **starred; star-ring** **1** : to adorn with stars **2** : to mark with an asterisk **3** : to play the leading role

**star anise** *n* : the small brown star-shaped fruit of an Asian tree used as a spice esp. in Chinese cooking

**star-board** \'stär-bərd\ *n* [ME sterbord, fr. OE stēorbord, fr. stēor- steering oar + bord ship's side] : the right side of a ship or airplane looking forward — **star-board** *adj*

**star-burst** \'stär-bərst\ *n* : a pattern that resembles diverging rays of light

¹**starch** \'stärch\ *vb* : to stiffen with or as if with starch

²**starch** *n* : a complex carbohydrate that is stored in plants, is an important foodstuff, and is used in adhesives and sizes, in laundering, and in pharmacy — **starchy** *adj*

**stare** \'ster\ *vb* **stared; star-ing** : to look fixedly with wide-open eyes ⟨stared in disbelief⟩ — **stare** *n* — **star-er** *n*

**star-fish** \'stär-ˌfish\ *n* : any of a class of echinoderms that have usu. five arms arranged around a central disk and feed largely on mollusks

**star fruit** *n* : CARAMBOLA 1

¹**stark** \'stärk\ *adj* **1** : rigid as if in death; *also* : STRICT **2** *archaic* : STRONG, ROBUST **3** : SHEER, UTTER ⟨~ nonsense⟩ **4** : BARREN, DESOLATE ⟨~ landscape⟩; *also* : UNADORNED ⟨~ realism⟩ **5** : sharply delineated — **stark-ly** *adv*

²**stark** *adv* : WHOLLY, ABSOLUTELY ⟨~ naked⟩

**star-light** \'stär-ˌlīt\ *n* : the light given by the stars

**star-ling** \'stär-liŋ\ *n* : a dark brown or in summer glossy greenish black European bird that is naturalized nearly worldwide and often considered a pest

¹**start** \'stärt\ *vb* **1** : to give an involuntary twitch or jerk (as from surprise) **2** : BEGIN, COMMENCE **3** : to set going ⟨~ an engine⟩ **4** : to enter or cause to enter a game or contest; *also* : to be in the starting lineup — **start-er** *n*

²**start** *n* **1** : a sudden involuntary motion : LEAP **2** : a spasmodic and brief effort or action **3** : BEGINNING; *also* : the place of beginning

**start-er** \'stär-tər\ *adj* : being an item acquired with the expectation that a more elaborate one will be acquired in the future ⟨a ~ home⟩

**star-tle** \'stär-t⁴l\ *vb* **star-tled; star-tling** : to frighten or surprise suddenly : cause to start ⟨the noise startled the dog⟩

**star-tling** *adj* : causing sudden fear, surprise, or anxiety — **star-tling-ly** *adv*

**starve** \'stärv\ *vb* **starved; starv-ing** [ME sterven to die, fr. OE steorfan] **1** : to die or cause to die from hunger **2** : to suffer extreme hunger or deprivation ⟨starving for affection⟩ **3** : to subdue by famine — **star-va-tion** \stär-'vā-shən\ *n*

**starve-ling** \'stärv-liŋ\ *n* : one that is thin from lack of nourishment

**stash** \'stash\ *vb* : to store in a secret place for future use — **stash** *n*

**sta-sis** \'stā-səs, 'sta-\ *n, pl* **sta-ses** \'stā-

,sēz, 'stå-\ **1** : a stoppage or slowing of the normal flow of a bodily fluid (as blood)　**2** : a state of static balance : STAGNATION

**¹stat** \'stat\ *adv* [L *statim*] : without delay : IMMEDIATELY

**²stat** *abbr* statute

**¹state** \'stāt\ *n* [ME *stat*, fr. AF & L; AF *estat*, fr. L *status*, fr. *stare* to stand] **1** : mode or condition of being ⟨the four ~s of matter⟩ **2** : condition of mind **3** : social position **4** : a body of people occupying a territory and organized under one government; *also* : the government of such a body of people **5** : one of the constituent units of a nation having a federal government — **state·hood** \-,hùd\ *n*

**²state** *vb* **stat·ed; stat·ing** **1** : to set by regulation or authority **2** : to express in words

**state·craft** \'stāt-,kraft\ *n* : the art of conducting state affairs

**state·house** \-,haùs\ *n* : the building in which a state legislature meets

**state·ly** \'stāt-lē\ *adj* **state·li·er; -est** **1** : having lofty dignity : HAUGHTY **2** : IMPRESSIVE, MAJESTIC ⟨~ homes⟩ ♦ *Synonyms* MAGNIFICENT, IMPOSING, AUGUST — **state·li·ness** *n*

**state·ment** \'stāt-mǝnt\ *n* **1** : the act or result of presenting in words **2** : a summary of a financial account

**state·room** \'stāt-,rüm, -,rùm\ *n* : a private room on a ship or railroad car

**state·side** \'stāt-,sīd\ *adj* : of or relating to the U.S. as regarded from outside its continental limits — **stateside** *adv*

**states·man** \'stāts-mǝn\ *n* : a person engaged in fixing the policies and conducting the affairs of a government; *esp* : one wise and skilled in such matters — **states·man·like** *adj* — **states·man·ship** *n*

**¹stat·ic** \'sta-tik\ *adj* **1** : acting by mere weight without motion ⟨~ pressure⟩ **2** : relating to bodies at rest or forces in equilibrium **3** : showing little change **4** : not moving : not active **5** : of or relating to stationary charges of electricity **6** : of, relating to, or caused by radio static

**²static** *n* : noise produced in a radio or television receiver by atmospheric or other electrical disturbances

**stat·in** \'sta-tᵊn\ *n* : any of a group of drugs that inhibit the synthesis of cholesterol

**¹sta·tion** \'stā-shǝn\ *n* **1** : the place where a person or thing stands or is assigned to remain **2** : a regular stopping place on a transportation route : DEPOT **3** : a place where a fleet is assigned for duty **4** : a stock farm or ranch esp. in Australia or New Zealand **5** : social standing **6** : a complete assemblage of radio or television equipment for sending or receiving

**²station** *vb* : to assign to a station

**sta·tion·ary** \'stā-shǝ-,ner-ē\ *adj* **1** : fixed in a station, course, or mode **2** : unchanging in condition ⟨a ~ population⟩

**stationary front** *n* : the boundary between two air masses neither of which is advancing

**station break** *n* : a pause in a radio or television broadcast to announce the identity of the network or station

**sta·tio·ner** \'stā-shǝ-nǝr\ *n* : one that sells stationery

**sta·tio·nery** \'stā-shǝ-,ner-ē\ *n* : materials (as paper, pens, or ink) for writing; *esp* : letter paper with envelopes

**station wagon** *n* : an automobile having a long interior, one or more folding or removable rear seats, and usu. a door at the rear

**sta·tis·tic** \stǝ-'tis-tik\ *n* **1** : a single term or datum in a collection of statistics **2** : a quantity (as the mean) that is computed from a sample

**sta·tis·tics** \-tiks\ *n sing or pl* [G *Statistik* study of political facts and figures, fr. NL *statisticus* of politics, fr. L *status* state] : a branch of mathematics dealing with the collection, analysis, and interpretation of masses of numerical data; *also* : a collection of such numerical data — **sta·tis·ti·cal** \-ti-kǝl\ *adj* — **sta·tis·ti·cal·ly** \-ti-k(ǝ-)lē\ *adv* — **stat·is·ti·cian** \,sta-tǝ-'sti-shǝn\ *n*

**stat·u·ary** \'sta-chǝ-,wer-ē\ *n, pl* **-ar·ies** **1** : the art of making statues **2** : STATUES

**stat·ue** \'sta-chü\ *n* : a likeness (as of a person or animal) sculptured, modeled, or cast in a solid substance

**stat·u·esque** \,sta-chǝ-'wesk\ *adj* : tall and shapely

**stat·u·ette** \,sta-chǝ-'wet\ *n* : a small statue

**stat·ure** \'sta-chǝr\ *n* **1** : natural height (as of a person) **2** : quality or status gained (as by achievement)

**sta·tus** \'stā-tǝs, 'sta-\ *n* **1** : the condition of a person in the eyes of others or of the law **2** : state or condition with respect to circumstances

**sta·tus quo** \-'kwō\ *n* [L, state in which] : the existing state of affairs

**stat·ute** \'sta-chüt\ *n* : a law enacted by a legislative body

**stat·u·to·ry** \'sta-chǝ-,tòr-ē\ *adj* : imposed by statute : LAWFUL

**statutory rape** *n* : sexual intercourse with a person who is below the statutory age of consent

**¹staunch** *var of* ¹STANCH

**²staunch** \'stònch, 'stänch\ *adj* **1** : WATERTIGHT ⟨a ~ ship⟩ **2** : FIRM, STRONG; *also* : STEADFAST, LOYAL ⟨a ~ supporter⟩ ♦ *Synonyms* RESOLUTE, CONSTANT, TRUE, FAITHFUL — **staunch·ly** *adv*

**¹stave** \'stāv\ *n* **1** : CUDGEL, STAFF **2** : any of several narrow strips of wood placed edge to edge to make something (as a barrel) **3** : STANZA

**²stave** *vb* **staved** *or* **stove** \'stōv\; **stav·ing** **1** : to break in the staves of; *also* : to break a hole in **2** : to drive or thrust away ⟨~ off hunger⟩

**staves** *pl of* STAFF

**¹stay** \'stā\ *n* **1** : a strong rope or wire used to support a mast **2** : ¹GUY

**²stay** *vb* **stayed** \'stād\ *also* **staid** \'stād\;

**stay·ing 1** : PAUSE, WAIT **2** : REMAIN **3** : to stand firm **4** : LIVE, DWELL **5** : DELAY, POSTPONE **6** : to last out (as a race) **7** : STOP, CHECK **8** : to satisfy (as hunger) for a time ♦ *Synonyms* REMAIN, ABIDE, LINGER, TARRY

³**stay** *n* **1** : STOP, HALT **2** : a residence or sojourn in a place

⁴**stay** *n* **1** : PROP, SUPPORT **2** : CORSET — usu. used in pl.

⁵**stay** *vb* : to hold up : PROP

**staying power** *n* : STAMINA

**stbd** *abbr* starboard

**std** *abbr* standard

**STD** \ˌes-ˌtē-ˈdē\ *n* : SEXUALLY TRANSMITTED DISEASE

**Ste** *abbr* [F *sainte*] saint (female)

**stead** \ˈsted\ *n* **1** : ADVANTAGE ⟨stood him in good ~⟩ **2** : the place or function ordinarily occupied or carried on by another ⟨acted in her brother's ~⟩

**stead·fast** \ˈsted-ˌfast\ *adj* **1** : firmly fixed in place **2** : not subject to change **3** : firm in belief, determination, and adherence : LOYAL ♦ *Synonyms* RESOLUTE, TRUE, FAITHFUL, STAUNCH — **stead·fast·ly** *adv* — **stead·fast·ness** *n*

¹**steady** \ˈste-dē\ *adj* **stead·i·er; -est 1** : direct or sure in movement; *also* : CALM **2** : FIRM, FIXED ⟨held the pole ~⟩ **3** : STABLE ⟨~ prices⟩ **4** : not easily disturbed **5** : RELIABLE ⟨~ friends⟩ **6** : temperate in character or demeanor ♦ *Synonyms* UNIFORM, EVEN — **stead·i·ly** \-də-lē\ *adv* — **stead·i·ness** \-dē-nəs\ *n* — **steady** *adv*

²**steady** *vb* **stead·ied; steady·ing** : to make or become steady

**steak** \ˈstāk\ *n* : a slice of meat and esp. beef; *also* : a slice of a large fish

¹**steal** \ˈstēl\ *vb* **stole** \ˈstōl\; **sto·len** \ˈstō-lən\; **steal·ing 1** : to take and carry away without right or permission **2** : to come or go secretly or gradually **3** : to get for oneself slyly or by skill and daring ⟨~ a kiss⟩ ⟨~ the ball in basketball⟩ **4** : to gain or attempt to gain a base in baseball by running without the aid of a hit or an error ♦ *Synonyms* PILFER, FILCH, PURLOIN, SWIPE

²**steal** *n* : an act of stealing : BARGAIN

¹**stealth** \ˈstelth\ *n* **1** : secret or unobtrusive procedure **2** : an aircraft design intended to produce a weak radar return

²**stealth** *adj* : STEALTHY

**stealthy** \ˈstel-thē\ *adj* **stealth·i·er; -est** : done by stealth : FURTIVE, SLY ⟨a ~ burglar⟩ ♦ *Synonyms* SECRET, COVERT, CLANDESTINE, SURREPTITIOUS, UNDERHANDED — **stealth·i·ly** \ˈstel-thə-lē\ *adv*

¹**steam** \ˈstēm\ *n* **1** : the vapor into which water is changed when heated to the boiling point **2** : water vapor when compressed so that it supplies heat and power **3** : POWER, FORCE, ENERGY — **steamy** *adj*

²**steam** *vb* **1** : to pass off as vapor **2** : to emit vapor **3** : to move by or as if by the agency of steam — **steam·er** *n*

**steam·boat** \ˈstēm-ˌbōt\ *n* : a boat driven by steam

**steam engine** *n* : a reciprocating engine having a piston driven by steam

**steam·fit·ter** \ˈstēm-ˌfi-tər\ *n* : a worker who puts in or repairs equipment (as steam pipes) for heating, ventilating, or refrigerating systems

**steam·punk** \ˈstēm-ˌpəŋk\ *n* : science fiction involving historical or imagined steam-powered technology

**steam·roll·er** \-ˌrō-lər\ *n* : a machine for compacting roads or pavements — **steam·roll·er** *also* **steam·roll** \-ˌrōl\ *vb*

**steam·ship** \-ˌship\ *n* : a ship driven by steam

**steed** \ˈstēd\ *n* : HORSE

¹**steel** \ˈstēl\ *n* **1** : iron treated with intense heat and mixed with carbon to make it hard and tough **2** : an article made of steel **3** : a quality (as hardness of mind) that suggests steel — **steel** *adj* — **steely** *adj*

²**steel** *vb* : to fill with courage or determination ⟨~ed himself for her rage⟩

**steel wool** *n* : long fine steel shavings used esp. for cleaning and polishing

¹**steep** \ˈstēp\ *adj* **1** : having a very sharp slope : PRECIPITOUS **2** : too high ⟨~ prices⟩ — **steep·ly** *adv* — **steep·ness** *n*

²**steep** *n* : a steep slope

³**steep** *vb* **1** : to soak in a liquid; *esp* : to extract the essence of by soaking ⟨~ tea⟩ **2** : SATURATE ⟨~ed in learning⟩

**stee·ple** \ˈstē-pəl\ *n* : a tall tapering structure built on top of a church tower; *also* : a church tower

**stee·ple·chase** \-ˌchās\ *n* [fr. the use of church steeples as landmarks to guide the riders] : a horse race across country; *also* : a race over a course obstructed by hurdles

¹**steer** \ˈstir\ *n* : a male bovine animal castrated before sexual maturity and usu. raised for beef

²**steer** *vb* **1** : to direct the course of (as by a rudder or wheel) **2** : GUIDE, CONTROL **3** : to pursue a course of action **4** : to be subject to guidance or direction — **steers·man** \ˈstirz-mən\ *n*

**steer·age** \ˈstir-ij\ *n* **1** : DIRECTION, GUIDANCE **2** : a section in a passenger ship for passengers paying the lowest fares

**stego·sau·rus** \ˌste-gə-ˈsȯr-əs\ *n* : any of a genus of plant-eating armored dinosaurs with a series of bony plates along the backbone

**stein** \ˈstīn\ *n* : an earthenware mug

**stel·lar** \ˈste-lər\ *adj* : of or relating to stars : resembling a star

¹**stem** \ˈstem\ *n* **1** : the main stalk of a plant; *also* : a plant part that supports another part (as a leaf or fruit) **2** : the bow of a ship **3** : a line of ancestry : STOCK **4** : that part of an inflected word which remains unchanged throughout a given inflection **5** : something resembling the stem of a plant — **stem·less** *adj* — **stemmed** \ˈstemd\ *adj*

²**stem** *vb* **stemmed; stem·ming** : to have a specified source : DERIVE

³**stem** *vb* **stemmed; stem·ming** : to make headway against ⟨~ the tide⟩

**⁴stem** *vb* **stemmed; stem·ming :** to stop or check by or as if by damming

**STEM** *abbr* science, technology, engineering, and math

**stem cell** *n* : an undifferentiated cell that may give rise to many different types of cells

**stench** \'stench\ *n* : STINK

**sten·cil** \'sten-səl\ *n* [prob. ultim. fr. ME *stanseld* brightly ornamented, fr. AF *estenceléd* spangled, pp. of *estenceler* to sparkle, fr. *estencele* spark, fr. VL *stincilla*, alter. of L *scintilla*] : an impervious material (as metal or paper) perforated with lettering or a design through which a substance (as ink or paint) is applied to a surface to be printed — **stencil** *vb*

**ste·nog·ra·phy** \stə-'nä-grə-fē\ *n* : the art or process of writing in shorthand — **ste·nog·ra·pher** \-fər\ *n* — **steno·graph·ic** \ˌste-nə-'gra-fik\ *adj*

**ste·no·sis** \stə-'nō-səs\ *n, pl* **-no·ses** \-ˌsēz\ : a narrowing of a bodily passage or orifice

**stent** \'stent\ *n* : a short narrow tube inserted into an anatomical vessel esp. to keep a passage open

**sten·to·ri·an** \sten-'tȯr-ē-ən\ *adj* : extremely loud ⟨~ tones⟩

**¹step** \'step\ *n* **1 :** a rest for the foot in ascending or descending : STAIR  **2 :** an advance made by raising one foot and putting it down elsewhere  **3 :** manner of walking  **4 :** a small space or distance  **5 :** a degree, rank, or plane in a series  **6 :** a sequential measure leading to a result

**²step** *vb* **stepped; step·ping  1 :** to advance or recede by steps  **2 :** to go on foot : WALK  **3 :** to move along briskly  **4 :** to press down with the foot  **5 :** to measure by steps  **6 :** to construct or arrange in or as if in steps

**step aerobics** *n sing or pl* : aerobics that involves repeatedly stepping on and off a raised platform

**step aside** *vb* : STEP DOWN 1

**step·broth·er** \'step-ˌbrə-ᵗʰər\ *n* : the son of one's stepparent by a former marriage

**step·child** \-ˌchī(-ə)ld\ *n* : a child of one's husband or wife by a former marriage

**step·daugh·ter** \-ˌdȯ-tər\ *n* : a daughter of one's wife or husband by a former marriage

**step down** *vb* **1 :** to give up a position : RETIRE, RESIGN  **2 :** to lower (a voltage) by means of a transformer

**step·fa·ther** \-ˌfä-ᵗʰər\ *n* : the husband of one's mother when distinct from one's natural or legal father

**step·lad·der** \'step-ˌla-dər\ *n* : a light portable set of steps in a hinged frame

**step·moth·er** \-ˌmə-ᵗʰər\ *n* : the wife of one's father when distinct from one's natural or legal mother

**step·par·ent** \-ˌper-ənt\ *n* : a person who is a stepfather or stepmother

**steppe** \'step\ *n* [Russ *step'*] : dry level grass-covered treeless land in regions of wide temperature range esp. in southeastern Europe and Asia

**step·sis·ter** \'step-ˌsis-tər\ *n* : the daughter of one's stepparent by a former marriage

**step·son** \-ˌsən\ *n* : a son of one's wife or husband by a former marriage

**step up** *vb* **1 :** to increase (a voltage) by means of a transformer  **2 :** INCREASE, ACCELERATE  **3 :** to come forward — **step-up** \'step-ˌəp\ *n*

**ster** *abbr* sterling

**ste·reo** \'ster-ē-ˌo, 'stir-\ *n, pl* **ste·re·os  1 :** stereophonic reproduction  **2 :** a stereophonic sound system — **stereo** *adj*

**ste·reo·phon·ic** \ˌster-ē-ə-'fä-nik, ˌstir-\ *adj* : of or relating to sound reproduction designed to create the effect of listening to the original — **ste·reo·phon·i·cal·ly** \-'fä-ni-k(ə-)lē\ *adv*

**ste·reo·scope** \'ster-ē-ə-ˌskōp, 'stir-\ *n* [Gk *stereos* solid + *-skopion* means for viewing] : an optical instrument that blends two slightly different pictures of the same subject to give the effect of depth

**ste·reo·scop·ic** \ˌster-ē-ə-'skä-pik, ˌstir-\ *adj* **1 :** of or relating to the stereoscope  **2 :** characterized by the seeing of objects in three dimensions ⟨~ vision⟩ — **ste·reo·scop·i·cal·ly** \-'skä-pi-k(ə-)lē\ *adv* — **ste·re·os·co·py** \ˌster-ē-'äs-kə-pē, ˌstir-\ *n*

**ste·reo·type** \'ster-ē-ə-ˌtīp, 'stir-\ *n* **1 :** a metal printing plate cast from a mold made from set type  **2 :** something agreeing with a pattern; *esp* : an idea that many people have about a thing or a group and that may often be untrue or only partly true — **stereotype** *vb* — **ste·reo·typ·i·cal** \ˌster-ē-ə-'ti-pi-kəl\ *adj* — **ste·reo·typ·i·cal·ly** \-pi-k(ə-)lē\ *adv*

**ste·reo·typed** \-ˌtīpt\ *adj* : lacking originality or individuality  ♦ **Synonyms** TRITE, CLICHÉD, COMMONPLACE, HACKNEYED, STALE, THREADBARE

**ster·ile** \'ster-əl\ *adj* **1 :** unable to bear fruit, crops, or offspring  **2 :** free from living things and esp. germs — **ste·ril·i·ty** \stə-'ri-lə-tē\ *n*

**ster·il·ize** \'ster-ə-ˌlīz\ *vb* **-ized; -iz·ing** : to make sterile; *esp* : to free from germs — **ster·il·i·za·tion** \ˌster-ə-lə-'zā-shən\ *n* — **ster·il·iz·er** \'ster-ə-ˌlī-zər\ *n*

**¹ster·ling** \'stər-liŋ\ *n* **1 :** British money  **2 :** sterling silver

**²sterling** *adj* **1 :** of, relating to, or calculated in terms of British sterling  **2 :** having a fixed standard of purity represented by an alloy of 925 parts of silver with 75 parts of copper  **3 :** made of sterling silver  **4 :** EXCELLENT ⟨a ~ record of achievement⟩

**¹stern** \'stərn\ *adj* **1 :** SEVERE, AUSTERE ⟨~ taskmasters⟩  **2 :** STOUT, STURDY ⟨~ resolve⟩ — **stern·ly** *adv* — **stern·ness** *n*

**²stern** *n* : the rear end of a boat

**ster·num** \'stər-nəm\ *n, pl* **sternums** or **ster·na** \-nə\ : a long flat bone or cartilage at the center front of the chest connecting the ribs of the two sides

**ste·roid** \'stir-ˌȯid, 'ster-\ *n* : any of various compounds including numerous hormones (as anabolic steroids) and sugar derivatives — **steroid** or **ste·roi·dal** \stə-ˈròi-dᵊl\ adj

**stetho·scope** \ˈste-thə-ˌskōp\ n : an instrument used to detect and listen to sounds produced in the body

**ste·ve·dore** \ˈstē-və-ˌdòr\ n [Sp estibador, fr. estibar to pack, fr. L stipare to press together] : one who works at loading and unloading ships

**ste·via** \ˈstē-vē-ə\ n [NL, plant from which it is derived, fr. Petrus Stevus †1555 Sp. botanist] : a plant-derived powder used as a noncaloric sweetener

¹**stew** \ˈstü, ˈstyü\ n 1 : a dish of stewed meat and vegetables served in gravy 2 : a state of agitation, worry, or resentment

²**stew** vb 1 : to boil slowly : SIMMER 2 : to be in a state of agitation, worry, or resentment 〈~ed about her predicament〉

**stew·ard** \ˈstü-ərd, ˈstyü-\ n [ME, fr. OE stīweard, fr. stī, stig hall, sty + weard ward] 1 : one employed on a large estate to manage domestic concerns 2 : one who supervises the provision and distribution of food (as on a ship); also : an employee on a ship or airplane who serves passengers 3 : one actively concerned with the direction of the affairs of an organization — **stew·ard·ship** n

**stew·ard·ess** \ˈstü-ər-dəs, ˈstyü-\ n : a woman who is a steward esp. on an airplane

**stg** abbr sterling

¹**stick** \ˈstik\ n 1 : a cut or broken branch or twig; also : a long slender piece of wood 2 : ROD, STAFF 3 : something resembling a stick 4 : a dull uninteresting person 5 pl : remote usu. rural areas

²**stick** vb **stuck** \ˈstək\; **stick·ing** 1 : STAB, PRICK 2 : IMPALE 3 : ATTACH, FASTEN 4 : to thrust or project in some direction or manner 5 : to be unable to proceed or move freely 6 : to hold fast by or as if by gluing : ADHERE 7 : to hold to something firmly or closely : CLING 8 : to become jammed or blocked 〈the door always ~s〉

**stick·er** \ˈsti-kər\ n : one that sticks (as a bur) or causes sticking (as glue); esp : an adhesive label

**sticker shock** n : astonishment and dismay on being informed of a product's unexpectedly high price

**stick insect** n : any of various usu. wingless insects with a long round body resembling a stick

**stick·ler** \ˈsti-klər, -kə-lər\ n : one who insists on exactness or completeness

**stick shift** n : a manually operated automobile gearshift usu. mounted on the floor

**stick–to–it·ive·ness** \stik-ˈtü-ə-tiv-nəs\ n : dogged perseverance : TENACITY

**stick up** vb : to rob at gunpoint — **stick-up** \ˈstik-ˌəp\ n

**sticky** \ˈsti-kē\ adj **stick·i·er; -est** 1 : ADHESIVE 2 : VISCOUS, GLUEY 3 : tending to stick 〈~ valve〉 4 : DIFFICULT 〈a ~ problem〉

¹**stiff** \ˈstif\ adj 1 : not pliant : RIGID 2 : not limber 〈~ joints〉; also : TENSE, TAUT 3 : not flowing or working easily 〈~ paste〉 4 : not natural and easy : FORMAL 5 : STRONG, FORCEFUL 〈a ~ breeze〉 6 : HARSH, SEVERE 〈a ~ penalty〉 ♦ Synonyms INFLEXIBLE, INELASTIC — **stiff·ly** adv — **stiff·ness** n

²**stiff** vb : to refuse to pay or tip

**stiff–arm** \ˈstif-ˌärm\ vb : to treat with disdain or neglect 〈~ed her advice〉

**stiff·en** \ˈsti-fən\ vb : to make or become stiff — **stiff·en·er** n

**stiff–necked** \ˈstif-ˈnekt\ adj : STUBBORN, HAUGHTY 〈too ~ to ask for help〉

**sti·fle** \ˈstī-fəl\ vb **sti·fled; sti·fling** 1 : to kill by depriving of or the dying from lack of oxygen or air : SMOTHER 2 : to keep in check by effort : SUPPRESS 〈~ a sneeze〉 — **sti·fling·ly** adv

**stig·ma** \ˈstig-mə\ n, pl **stig·ma·ta** \stig-ˈmä-tə, ˈstig-mə-tə\ or **stigmas** [L] 1 : a mark of disgrace or discredit 2 **stigmata** pl : bodily marks resembling the wounds of the crucified Jesus 3 : the upper part of the pistil of a flower that receives the pollen in fertilization — **stig·mat·ic** \stig-ˈma-tik\ adj

**stig·ma·tize** \ˈstig-mə-ˌtīz\ vb **-tized; -tizing** 1 : to mark with a stigma 2 : to characterize as disgraceful 〈was stigmatized by the scandal〉

**stile** \ˈstī(-ə)l\ n : steps used for crossing a fence or wall

**sti·let·to** \stə-ˈle-tō\ n, pl **-tos** or **-toes** [It, dim. of stilo stylus, dagger] : a slender dagger

¹**still** \ˈstil\ adj 1 : MOTIONLESS 2 : making no sound : SILENT — **still·ness** n

²**still** vb : to make or become still

³**still** adv 1 : without motion 〈sit ~〉 2 : up to and during this or that time 3 : in spite of that : NEVERTHELESS 4 : EVEN 〈ran ~ faster〉 5 : YET 〈has ~ to be recognized〉

⁴**still** n 1 : STILLNESS, SILENCE 2 : a static photograph esp. from a motion picture

⁵**still** n 1 : DISTILLERY 2 : apparatus used in distillation

**still·birth** \ˈstil-ˌbərth\ n : the birth of a dead fetus

**still·born** \-ˈbòrn\ adj : born dead

**still life** n, pl **still lifes** : a picture of inanimate objects

**stilt** \ˈstilt\ n : one of a pair of poles for walking with each having a step or loop for the foot to elevate the wearer above the ground; also : a polelike support of a structure above ground or water level

**stilt·ed** \ˈstil-təd\ adj : not easy and natural 〈~ language〉

**Stil·ton** \ˈstil-tᵊn\ n : a blue cheese of English origin

**stim·u·lant** \ˈsti-myə-lənt\ n 1 : an agent (as a drug) that temporarily increases the activity of an organism or any of its parts 2 : STIMULUS 3 : an alcoholic beverage — **stimulant** adj

**stim·u·late** \-ˌlāt\ vb **-lat·ed; -lat·ing** : to make active or more active : ANIMATE, AROUSE 〈~ interest〉 ♦ Synonyms EXCITE, PROVOKE, MOTIVATE, QUICKEN — **stim·u·la·tion** \ˌsti-myə-ˈlā-shən\ n — **stim·u·la·tive** \ˈsti-myə-ˌlā-tiv\ adj —

**stim·u·la·tor** \-ˌlā-tər\ n — **stim·u·la·to·ry** \-lə-ˌtȯr-ē\ adj

**stim·u·lus** \'sti-myə-ləs\ n, pl **-li** \-ˌlī\ [L] **1** : something that moves to activity **2** : an agent that directly influences the activity of a living organism or one of its parts

**¹sting** \'stiŋ\ vb **stung** \'stəŋ\; **sting·ing 1** : to prick painfully esp. with a sharp or poisonous process **2** : to cause to suffer acutely — **sting·er** n

**²sting** n **1** : an act of stinging; also : a resultant wound, sore, or pain **2** : a pointed often venom-bearing organ (as of a bee) : STINGER **3** : an elaborate confidence game; esp : one worked by undercover police to trap criminals

**sting·ray** \'stiŋ-ˌrā\ n : any of numerous rays with sharp stinging spines on a whip-like tail

**stin·gy** \'stin-jē\ adj **stin·gi·er; -est** : not generous : giving or spending as little as possible — **stin·gi·ness** n

**stink** \'stiŋk\ vb **stank** \'staŋk\ or **stunk** \'stəŋk\; **stunk; stink·ing** : to give forth a strong and offensive smell; also : to be extremely bad in quality or repute — **stink** n — **stink·er** n

**stink·bug** \'stiŋk-ˌbəg\ n : any of various true bugs that emit a disagreeable odor

**¹stint** \'stint\ vb **1** : to be sparing or frugal **2** : to cut short in amount

**²stint** n **1** : an assigned amount of work **2** : RESTRAINT, LIMITATION **3** : a period of time spent at a particular activity

**sti·pend** \'stī-ˌpend, -pənd\ n [ME, alter. of stipendy, fr. L stipendium, fr. stips gift + pendere to weigh, pay] : a fixed sum of money paid periodically for services or to defray expenses

**stip·ple** \'sti-pəl\ vb **stip·pled; stip·pling 1** : to engrave by means of dots and light strokes **2** : to apply (as paint or ink) with small short touches — **stipple** n

**stip·u·late** \'sti-pyə-ˌlāt\ vb **-lat·ed; -lat·ing** : to make an agreement; esp : to make a special demand for something as a condition in an agreement — **stip·u·la·tion** \ˌsti-pyə-'lā-shən\ n

**¹stir** \'stər\ vb **stirred; stir·ring 1** : to move slightly **2** : AROUSE, EXCITE **3** : to mix, dissolve, or make by continued circular movement ⟨~ eggs into cake batter⟩ **4** : to move to activity (as by pushing, beating, or prodding)

**²stir** n **1** : a state of agitation or activity **2** : an act of stirring

**stir–fry** \'stər-ˌfrī\ vb : to fry quickly over high heat while stirring continuously — **stir–fry** n

**¹stir·ring** \'stər-in\ adj **1** : ACTIVE, BUSTLING **2** : ROUSING, INSPIRING ⟨a ~ speech⟩

**²stirring** n : a beginning of activity ⟨the first ~s of revolution⟩

**stir·rup** \'stər-əp\ n [ME stirop, fr. OE sti·grāp, lit., mounting rope] **1** : a light frame hung from a saddle to support the rider's foot **2** : STAPES

**¹stitch** \'stich\ n **1** : a sudden sharp pain esp. in the side **2** : one of the series of loops formed by or over a needle in sewing

**²stitch** vb **1** : to fasten or join with stitches **2** : to make (as a design) with stitches **3** : SEW

**stk** abbr stock

**stoat** \'stōt\ n, pl **stoats** also **stoat** : the common Old and New World ermine esp. in its brown summer coat

**¹stock** \'stäk\ n **1** archaic : a block of wood **2** : a stupid person **3** : a wooden part of a thing serving as its support, frame, or handle **4** pl : a device for publicly punishing offenders consisting of a wooden frame with holes in which the feet and hands can be locked **5** : the original from which others derive; also : a group having a common origin : FAMILY **6** : LIVESTOCK **7** : a supply of goods **8** : the ownership element in a corporation divided to give the owners an interest and usu. voting power **9** : a company of actors playing at a particular theater and presenting a series of plays **10** : liquid in which meat, fish, or vegetables have been simmered that is used as a basis for soup, gravy, or sauce

**²stock** vb : to provide with stock

**³stock** adj : kept regularly for sale or use; also : commonly used : STANDARD

**stock·ade** \stä-'kād\ n [Sp estacada, fr. estaca stake, pale, of Gmc origin] : an enclosure (as of posts and stakes) for defense or confinement

**stock·bro·ker** \-ˌbrō-kər\ n : one who executes orders to buy and sell securities

**stock car** n : a racing car that is similar to a regular car

**stock exchange** n : a place where the buying and selling of securities is conducted

**stock·hold·er** \'stäk-ˌhōl-dər\ n : one who owns corporate stock

**stock·i·nette** or **stock·i·net** \ˌstä-kə-'net\ n : an elastic knitted fabric used esp. for infants' wear and bandages

**stock·ing** \'stä-kin\ n : a close-fitting knitted covering for the foot and leg

**stock market** n **1** : STOCK EXCHANGE **2** : a market for stocks

**stock·pile** \'stäk-ˌpī(-ə)l\ n : a reserve supply esp. of something essential — **stockpile** vb

**stocky** \'stä-kē\ adj **stock·i·er; -est** : being short and relatively thick : STURDY ◆ **Synonyms** THICKSET, SQUAT, HEAVY-SET, STUBBY

**stock·yard** \'stäk-ˌyärd\ n : a yard for stock; esp : one for livestock about to be slaughtered or shipped

**stodgy** \'stä-jē\ adj **stodg·i·er; -est 1** : thick in texture : HEAVY ⟨~ bread⟩ **2** : not interesting : DULL ⟨a ~ accountant⟩ **3** : extremely old-fashioned

**¹sto·ic** \'stō-ik\ n [ME, fr. L stoicus, fr. Gk stōïkos, lit., of the portico, fr. Stoa (Poikilē) the Painted Portico, portico at Athens where the philosopher Zeno taught] : one who suffers without complaining

**²stoic** or **sto·i·cal** \-i-kəl\ adj : not affected by passion or feeling; esp : showing indifference to pain ◆ **Synonyms**

IMPASSIVE, PHLEGMATIC, APATHETIC, STOLID — **sto·i·cal·ly** \-i-k(ə-)lē\ *adv* — **sto·i·cism** \'stō-ə-ˌsi-zəm\ *n*

**stoke** \'stōk\ *vb* **stoked; stok·ing 1** : to stir up a fire **2** : to tend and supply fuel to a furnace — **stok·er** *n*

**STOL** *abbr* short takeoff and landing

¹**stole** *past of* STEAL

²**stole** \'stōl\ *n* **1** : a long narrow band worn round the neck by some members of the clergy **2** : a long wide scarf or similar covering worn by women

**stolen** *past part of* STEAL

**stol·id** \'stä-ləd\ *adj* : not easily aroused or excited : showing little or no emotion ⟨a ∼ face⟩ ♦ *Synonyms* PHLEGMATIC, APATHETIC, IMPASSIVE, STOIC — **sto·lid·i·ty** \stä-'li-də-tē\ *n* — **stol·id·ly** *adv*

**sto·lon** \'stō-lən, -ˌlän\ *n* : RUNNER 6

¹**stom·ach** \'stə-mək\ *n* **1** : a saclike digestive organ of a vertebrate into which food goes from the mouth by way of the throat and which opens below into the intestine **2** : a cavity in an invertebrate animal that is analogous to a stomach **3** : ABDOMEN **4** : desire for food caused by hunger : APPETITE **5** : INCLINATION, DESIRE ⟨had no ∼ for an argument⟩

²**stomach** *vb* : to bear without open resentment : put up with

**stom·ach·ache** \-ˌāk\ *n* : pain in or in the region of the stomach

**stom·ach·er** \'stə-mi-kər, -chər\ *n* : the front of a bodice often appearing between the laces of an outer garment (as in 16th century costume)

**stomp** \'stämp, 'stȯmp\ *vb* : STAMP — **stomp** *n*

¹**stone** \'stōn\ *n* **1** : hardened earth or mineral matter : ROCK **2** : a small piece of rock **3** : a precious stone : GEM **4** : CALCULUS **3 5** : a hard stony seed (as of a date) or one (as of a plum) with a stony covering **6** *pl usu* **stone** : a British unit of weight equal to 14 pounds — **stony** *also* **ston·ey** \'stō-nē\ *adj*

²**stone** *vb* **stoned; ston·ing 1** : to pelt or kill with stones **2** : to remove the stones of (a fruit)

**Stone Age** *n* : the first known period of prehistoric human culture characterized by the use of stone tools

**stoned** \'stōnd\ *adj* **1** : DRUNK **2** : being under the influence of a drug

**stone·wall** \'stōn-ˌwȯl\ *vb* : to refuse to comply or cooperate with

**stone-washed** \'stōn-ˌwȯsht, -ˌwäsht\ *adj* : having been washed with stones during manufacture to create a softer fabric ⟨∼ jeans⟩

**stood** *past and past part of* STAND

**stooge** \'stüj\ *n* **1** : a person who plays a subordinate or compliant role to a principal **2** : STRAIGHT MAN

**stool** \'stül\ *n* **1** : a seat usu. without back or arms **2** : FOOTSTOOL **3** : a seat used while urinating or defecating **4** : a discharge of fecal matter

**stool pigeon** *n* : DECOY, INFORMER

¹**stoop** \'stüp\ *vb* **1** : to bend forward and downward **2** : CONDESCEND **3** : to lower oneself morally ⟨∼ to lying⟩

²**stoop** *n* **1** : an act of bending forward **2** : a bent position of head and shoulders

³**stoop** *n* [D *stoep*] : a porch, platform, or entrance stairway at a house door

¹**stop** \'stäp\ *vb* **stopped; stop·ping 1** : to close (an opening) by filling or covering closely **2** : BLOCK, HALT **3** : to cease to go on **4** : to bring activity or operation to an end **5** : STAY, TARRY ♦ *Synonyms* QUIT, DISCONTINUE, DESIST, CEASE

²**stop** *n* **1** : END, CESSATION **2** : a set of organ pipes of one tone quality; *also* : a control knob for such a set **3** : OBSTRUCTION **4** : PLUG, STOPPER **5** : an act of stopping : CHECK **6** : a delay in a journey : STAY **7** : a place for stopping **8** *chiefly Brit* : any of several punctuation marks **9** : a function of an electronic device that stops a recording

**stop-ac·tion** \'stäp-'ak-shən\ *n* : STOP-MOTION

**stop-gap** \'stäp-ˌgap\ *n* : something that serves as a temporary expedient

**stop·light** \-ˌlīt\ *n* : TRAFFIC LIGHT

**stop-mo·tion** \'stäp-'mō-shən\ *n* : a filming technique in which successive positions of objects are photographed to produce the appearance of movement

**stop·over** \'stäp-ˌō-vər\ *n* **1** : a stop at an intermediate point in one's journey **2** : a stopping place on a journey

**stop·page** \'stä-pij\ *n* : the act of stopping : the state of being stopped

**stop·per** \'stä-pər\ *n* : something (as a cork) for sealing an opening

**stop·watch** \'stäp-ˌwäch\ *n* : a watch that can be started or stopped at will for exact timing

**stor·age** \'stȯr-ij\ *n* **1** : space for storing; *also* : cost of storing **2** : MEMORY 6 **3** : the act of storing; *esp* : the safekeeping of goods (as in a warehouse)

**storage battery** *n* : a group of connected rechargeable electrochemical cells used to provide electric current

¹**store** \'stȯr\ *vb* **stored; stor·ing 1** : to place or leave in a safe location for preservation or future use **2** : to provide esp. for a future need ⟨∼ information⟩

²**store** *n* **1** : something accumulated and kept for future use **2** : a large or ample quantity **3** : STOREHOUSE **4** : a retail business establishment

**store·house** \-ˌhau̇s\ *n* : a building for storing goods or supplies; *also* : an abundant source or supply

**store·keep·er** \-ˌkē-pər\ *n* : one who operates a retail store

**store·room** \-ˌrüm, -ˌru̇m\ *n* : a room for storing goods or supplies

**sto·ried** \'stȯr-ēd\ *adj* : celebrated in story or history ⟨a ∼ career⟩

**stork** \'stȯrk\ *n* : any of various large stout-billed Old World wading birds related to the herons and ibises

¹**storm** \'stȯrm\ *n* **1** : a heavy fall of rain, snow, or hail with high wind **2** : a violent outbreak or disturbance **3** : a mass attack on a defended position — **storm·i·ly** \'stȯr-mə-lē\ *adv* — **storm·i·ness** \-mē-nəs\ *n* — **stormy** *adj*

²**storm** *vb* **1** : to blow with violence; *also*

: to rain, snow, or hail heavily **2** : to make a mass attack against **3** : to be violently angry : RAGE **4** : to rush along furiously ⟨~ed out of the room⟩

¹**sto·ry** \'stȯr-ē\ *n, pl* **stories 1** : NARRATIVE, ACCOUNT **2** : REPORT, STATEMENT **3** : ANECDOTE **4** : SHORT STORY **5** : LIE, FALSEHOOD **6** : a news article or broadcast ♦ *Synonyms* UNTRUTH, TALE, CANARD

²**story** *also* **sto·rey** \'stȯr-ē\ *n, pl* **stories** *also* **storeys** : a floor of a building or the space between two adjacent floor levels

**sto·ry·tell·er** \-ˌte-lər\ *n* : a teller of stories

**sto·tin** \'stȯ-ˌtēn\ *n, pl* **sto·ti·nov** \stō-'tē-ˌnȯv\ : a monetary unit equal to ¹⁄₁₀₀ tolar formerly used in Slovenia

**sto·tin·ka** \stō-'tiŋ-kə\ *n, pl* **-tin·ki** \-kē\ — see *lev* at MONEY table

¹**stout** \'staút\ *adj* **1** : BRAVE **2** : FIRM ⟨a ~ refusal⟩ **3** : STURDY **4** : STAUNCH, ENDURING ⟨~ loyalty⟩ **5** : SOLID **6** : FORCEFUL, VIOLENT ⟨a ~ attack⟩ ⟨a ~ wind⟩ **7** : BULKY, THICKSET ♦ *Synonyms* FLESHY, FAT, PORTLY, CORPULENT, OBESE, PLUMP — **stout·ly** *adv* — **stout·ness** *n*

²**stout** *n* : a dark heavy ale

¹**stove** \'stōv\ *n* : an apparatus that burns fuel or uses electricity to provide heat (as for cooking or heating)

²**stove** *past and past part of* STAVE

**stow** \'stō\ *vb* **1** : HIDE, STORE ⟨~ baggage⟩ **2** : to pack in a compact mass

**stow·away** \'stō-ə-ˌwā\ *n* : one who hides on a vehicle to ride free

**STP** *abbr* standard temperature and pressure

**strad·dle** \'stra-dᵊl\ *vb* **strad·dled; strad·dling 1** : to stand, sit, or walk with legs spread apart **2** : to favor or seem to favor two apparently opposite sides — **strad·dle** *n*

**strafe** \'strāf\ *vb* **strafed; straf·ing** [G *Gott strafe England* may God punish England, propaganda slogan during World War I] : to fire upon with machine guns from a low-flying airplane

**strag·gle** \'stra-gəl\ *vb* **strag·gled; strag·gling 1** : to wander from the direct course : ROVE, STRAY **2** : to become separated from others of the same kind — **strag·gler** *n* — **strag·gly** \'stra-g(ə-)lē\ *adj*

¹**straight** \'strāt\ *adj* **1** : free from curves, bends, angles, or irregularities **2** : not wandering from the main point or proper course ⟨~ thinking⟩ **3** : HONEST ⟨a ~ answer⟩ **4** : having the elements in correct order **5** : UNMIXED, UNDILUTED ⟨~ whiskey⟩ **6** : CONVENTIONAL, SQUARE **7** : HETEROSEXUAL

²**straight** *adv* : in a straight manner

³**straight** *n* **1** : a straight line, course, or arrangement **2** : the part of a racetrack between the last turn and the finish **3** : a sequence of five cards in a poker hand

**straight–arm** \'strāt-ˌärm\ *n* : an act of warding off a person with the arm fully extended — **straight–arm** *vb*

**straight·away** \'strā-tə-ˌwā\ *n* : a straight stretch (as at a racetrack)

**straight–edge** \'strāt-ˌej\ *n* : a piece of material with a straight edge for testing straight lines and surfaces or for cutting along or drawing straight lines

**straight·en** \'strā-tᵊn\ *vb* : to make or become straight

**straight flush** *n* : a poker hand containing five cards of the same suit in sequence

**straight·for·ward** \strāt-'fȯr-wərd\ *adj* **1** : FRANK, CANDID, HONEST ⟨a ~ account⟩ **2** : proceeding in a straight course or manner

**straight man** *n* : an entertainer who feeds lines to a comedian who replies with usu. humorous quips

**straight shooter** *n* : a thoroughly upright straightforward person

**straight·way** \'strāt-'wā, -ˌwā\ *adv* : IMMEDIATELY ⟨get ~ to work⟩

¹**strain** \'strān\ *n* [ME *streen* progeny, lineage, fr. OE *strēon* gain, acquisition] **1** : LINEAGE, ANCESTRY **2** : a group (as of people or plants) of presumed common ancestry **3** : an inherited or inherent character or quality ⟨a ~ of madness in the family⟩ **4** : STREAK, TRACE ⟨a ~ of fanaticism⟩ **5** : MELODY **6** : the general style or tone

²**strain** *vb* [ME, fr. AF *estreindre*, fr. L *stringere* to bind or draw tight, press together] **1** : to draw taut **2** : to exert to the utmost **3** : to strive violently **4** : to injure by improper or excessive use **5** : to filter or remove by filtering **6** : to stretch beyond a proper limit — **strain·er** *n*

³**strain** *n* **1** : excessive tension or exertion (as of body or mind) **2** : bodily injury from excessive tension, effort, or use; *esp* : one in which muscles or ligaments are unduly stretched usu. from a wrench or twist **3** : deformation of a material body under the action of applied forces

¹**strait** \'strāt\ *adj* [ME, fr. AF *estreit*, fr. L *strictus* strait, strict, fr. pp. of *stringere*] **1** *archaic* : STRICT **2** *archaic* : NARROW **3** *archaic* : CONSTRICTED **4** : DIFFICULT, STRAITENED

²**strait** *n* **1** : a narrow channel connecting two bodies of water **2** *pl* : DISTRESS

**strait·en** \'strā-tᵊn\ *vb* **1** : to hem in : CONFINE **2** : to subject to distress or difficulty ⟨~ed by misfortune⟩

**strait·jack·et** *also* **straight·jack·et** \'strāt-ˌja-kət\ *n* : a cover or garment of strong material (as canvas) used to bind the body and esp. the arms closely in restraining a violent prisoner or patient — **straitjacket** *vb*

**strait·laced** *or* **straight·laced** \-'lāst\ *adj* : strict in manners, morals, or opinion

¹**strand** \'strand\ *n* : SHORE, BEACH

²**strand** *vb* **1** : to run, drift, or drive upon the shore ⟨a ~ed ship⟩ **2** : to place or leave in a helpless position

³**strand** *n* **1** : one of the fibers twisted or plaited together into a cord, rope, or cable; *also* : a cord, rope, or cable made up of such fibers **2** : a twisted or plaited

ropelike mass ⟨a ∼ of pearls⟩ — **strand-ed** \'stran-dəd\ adj

¹**strange** \'strānj\ adj **strang·er; strang·est** [ME, fr. AF *estrange*, fr. L *extraneus*, lit., external, fr. *extra* outside] **1** : of external origin, kind, or character **2** : NEW, UNFAMILIAR ⟨moved to a ∼ neighborhood⟩ **3** : DISTANT 6 **4** : UNACCUSTOMED, INEXPERIENCED ⟨she was ∼ to his ways⟩ ♦ **Synonyms** SINGULAR, PECULIAR, ECCENTRIC, ERRATIC, ODD, QUEER, QUAINT, CURIOUS — **strange·ly** adv — **strange·ness** n

²**strange** n : a quark with a charge of −¹⁄₃ and a measured energy of approximately 150 million electron volts

**strang·er** \'strān-jər\ n **1** : FOREIGNER **2** : INTRUDER **3** : a person with whom one is unacquainted

**stran·gle** \'straŋ-gəl\ vb **stran·gled; stran·gling 1** : to choke to death : THROTTLE **2** : STIFLE, SUPPRESS ⟨repression ∼s free speech⟩ — **stran·gler** n

**strangler fig** n : any of several figs that begin life atop a host tree and then send down roots that surround it

**stran·gu·late** \'straŋ-gyə-ˌlāt\ vb **-lat·ed; -lat·ing 1** : STRANGLE, CONSTRICT **2** : to become so constricted as to stop circulation

**stran·gu·la·tion** \ˌstraŋ-gyə-'lā-shən\ n : the act or process of strangling or strangulating; also : the state of being strangled or strangulated

¹**strap** \'strap\ n : a narrow strip of flexible material used esp. for fastening, holding together, or wrapping

²**strap** vb **strapped; strap·ping 1** : to secure with a strap **2** : BIND, CONSTRICT **3** : to flog with a strap **4** : STROP

**strap·less** \-ləs\ adj : having no straps; esp : having no shoulder straps

¹**strap·ping** adj : LARGE, STRONG, HUSKY

²**strap·ping** n : material for a strap

**strat·a·gem** \'stra-tə-jəm, -ˌjem\ n **1** : a trick to deceive or outwit the enemy; also : a deceptive scheme **2** : skill in deception

**strat·e·gy** \'stra-tə-jē\ n, pl **-gies** [Gk *stratēgia* generalship, fr. *stratēgos* general, fr. *stratos* camp, army + *agein* to lead] **1** : the science and art of military command aimed at meeting the enemy under conditions advantageous to one's own force **2** : a careful plan or method esp. for achieving an end — **strat·e·gic** \strə-'tē-jik\ adj — **strat·e·gist** \'stra-tə-jist\ n

**strat·i·fy** \'stra-tə-ˌfī\ vb **-fied; -fy·ing** : to form or arrange in layers — **strat·i·fi·ca·tion** \ˌstra-tə-fə-'kā-shən\ n

**stra·tig·ra·phy** \strə-'ti-grə-fē\ n : geology that deals with rock strata — **strati·graph·ic** \ˌstra-tə-'gra-fik\ adj

**strato·sphere** \'stra-tə-ˌsfir\ n : the part of the earth's atmosphere between about 7 miles (11 kilometers) and 31 miles (50 kilometers) above the earth — **strato·spher·ic** \ˌstra-tə-'sfir-ik, -'sfer-\ adj

**stra·tum** \'strā-təm, 'stra-\ n, pl **stra·ta** \'strā-tə, 'stra-\ [NL, fr. L, spread, bed, fr. neut. of *stratus*, pp. of *sternere* to spread out] **1** : a bed, layer, or sheetlike mass (as

of one kind of rock lying between layers of other kinds of rock) **2** : a level of culture; also : a group of people representing one stage in cultural development

¹**straw** \'strȯ\ n **1** : stalks of grain after threshing; also : a single coarse dry stem (as of a grass) **2** : a thing of small worth : TRIFLE **3** : a tube (as of paper or plastic) for sucking up a beverage

²**straw** adj **1** : made of straw **2** : having no real force or validity ⟨a ∼ vote⟩

**straw·ber·ry** \'strȯ-ˌber-ē, -bə-rē\ n : an edible juicy usu. red pulpy fruit of any of several low herbs with white flowers and long slender runners; also : one of these herbs

**straw boss** n : a foreman of a small group of workers

**straw·flow·er** \'strȯ-ˌflaȯ(-ə)r\ n : any of several plants whose flowers can be dried with little loss of form or color

¹**stray** \'strā\ n **1** : a domestic animal wandering at large or lost **2** : WAIF

²**stray** vb **1** : to wander or roam without purpose **2** : DEVIATE ⟨∼ed from the topic⟩

³**stray** adj **1** : having strayed : separated from the group or the main body **2** : occurring at random ⟨∼ remarks⟩

¹**streak** \'strēk\ n **1** : a line or mark of a different color or texture from its background **2** : a narrow band of light; also : a lightning bolt **3** : a slight admixture : TRACE **4** : a brief run (as of luck); also : an unbroken series ⟨a winning ∼⟩

²**streak** vb **1** : to form streaks in or on **2** : to move very swiftly

¹**stream** \'strēm\ n **1** : a body of water (as a river) flowing on the earth; also : any body of flowing fluid (as water or gas) **2** : a continuous procession ⟨a ∼ of traffic⟩

²**stream** vb **1** : to flow in or as if in a stream **2** : to pour out streams of liquid **3** : to trail out in length **4** : to move forward in a steady stream

**stream·bed** \'strēm-ˌbed\ n : the channel occupied by a stream

**stream·er** \'strē-mər\ n **1** : a long narrow ribbonlike flag **2** : a long ribbon on a dress or hat **3** : a newspaper headline that runs across the entire sheet **4** pl : AURORA

**stream·ing** \'strē-miŋ\ adj : relating to or being the transfer of data (as music or videos) in a continuous stream esp. for immediate processing or playback

**stream·let** \'strēm-lət\ n : a small stream

**stream·lined** \-ˌlīnd\ adj **1** : made with contours to reduce resistance to motion through water or air **2** : SIMPLIFIED **3** : MODERNIZED — **stream·line** vb

**street** \'strēt\ n [ME *strete*, fr. OE *strǣt*, fr. LL *strata* paved road, fr. L, fem. of *stratus*, pp. of *sternere* to spread out] **1** : a thoroughfare esp. in a city, town, or village **2** : the occupants of the houses on a street ⟨the whole ∼ objects to the proposal⟩

**street·car** \-ˌkär\ n : a passenger vehicle running on rails on city streets

**street fighter** *n* : a tough belligerent person

**street hockey** *n* : a game resembling ice hockey played on a hard surface with hockey sticks and a small ball

**street railway** *n* : a company operating streetcars or buses

**street·walk·er** \'strēt-ˌwȯ-kər\ *n* : PROSTITUTE

**strength** \'streṇth\ *n* **1** : the quality of being strong : ability to do or endure : POWER **2** : TOUGHNESS, SOLIDITY **3** : power to resist attack **4** : INTENSITY **5** : force as measured in numbers ⟨the ~ of an army⟩

**strength·en** \'streṇ-thən\ *vb* : to make or become stronger — **strength·en·er** *n*

**stren·u·ous** \'stren-yə-wəs\ *adj* **1** : VIGOROUS, ENERGETIC **2** : requiring energy or stamina — **stren·u·ous·ly** *adv*

**strep** \'strep\ *n* : STREPTOCOCCUS

**strep throat** *n* : an inflammatory sore throat caused by streptococci and marked by fever, prostration, and toxemia

**strep·to·coc·cus** \ˌstrep-tə-'kä-kəs\ *n, pl* **-coc·ci** \-'kä-ˌkī, -'käk-ˌsī, -'kä-ˌkē, -'käk-ˌsē\ : any of various spherical bacteria that usu. grow in chains and include some causing serious diseases — **strep·to·coc·cal** \-kəl\ *adj*

**strep·to·my·cin** \-'mī-sʲn\ *n* : an antibiotic produced by soil bacteria and used esp. in treating tuberculosis

**¹stress** \'stres\ *n* **1** : PRESSURE, STRAIN; *esp* : a force that tends to distort a body **2** : a factor that induces bodily or mental tension; *also* : a state induced by such a stress **3** : EMPHASIS **4** : relative prominence of sound **5** : ACCENT; *also* : any syllable carrying the accent — **stress·ful** \'stres-fəl\ *adj*

**²stress** *vb* **1** : to put pressure or strain on **2** : to put emphasis on : ACCENT

**¹stretch** \'strech\ *vb* **1** : to spread or reach out : EXTEND ⟨~ed out her arm⟩ **2** : to draw out in length or breadth : EXPAND **3** : to make tense : STRAIN **4** : EXAGGERATE ⟨~ed the truth⟩ **5** : to become extended without breaking ⟨rubber ~es easily⟩ — **stretchy** \'stre-chē\ *adj*

**²stretch** *n* **1** : an act of extending or drawing out beyond ordinary or normal limits **2** : a continuous extent in length, area, or time **3** : the extent to which something may be stretched **4** : either of the straight sides of a racecourse

**³stretch** *adj* : easily stretched ⟨~ pants⟩

**¹stretch·er** \'stre-chər\ *n* **1** : one that stretches **2** : a device for carrying a sick, injured, or dead person

**²stretcher** *vb* : to carry or transport on a stretcher

**stretch marks** *n pl* : striae on the skin (as of the abdomen) due to excessive stretching and rupture of elastic fibers (as from pregnancy)

**strew** \'strü\ *vb* **strewed**; **strewed** *or* **strewn** \'strün\; **strew·ing 1** : to spread by scattering **2** : to cover by or as if by scattering something over or on ⟨a floor *strewn* with toys⟩ **3** : DISSEMINATE

**stria** \'strī-ə\ *n, pl* **stri·ae** \'strī-ˌē\ **1** : STRIATION 3 **2** : a stripe or line (as in the skin)

**stri·at·ed muscle** \'strī-ˌā-təd-\ *n* : muscle tissue made up of long thin cells with many nuclei and alternate light and dark stripes that includes esp. the muscle of the heart and muscle that moves the vertebrate skeleton and is mostly under voluntary control

**stri·a·tion** \strī-'ā-shən\ *n* **1** : the state of being marked with stripes or lines **2** : arrangement of striations or striae **3** : a minute groove, scratch, or channel esp. when one of a parallel series

**strick·en** \'stri-kən\ *adj* **1** : afflicted by or as if by disease, misfortune, or sorrow **2** : WOUNDED ⟨was ~ by an arrow⟩

**strict** \'strikt\ *adj* **1** : allowing no evasion or escape : RIGOROUS ⟨~ discipline⟩ **2** : ACCURATE, PRECISE ⟨the ~ sense of the word⟩ ♦ *Synonyms* STRINGENT, RIGID — **strict·ly** *adv* — **strict·ness** *n*

**stric·ture** \'strik-chər\ *n* **1** : an abnormal narrowing of a bodily passage; *also* : the narrowed part **2** : hostile criticism : a critical remark

**¹stride** \'strīd\ *vb* **strode** \'strōd\; **strid·den** \'stri-dʲn\; **strid·ing** : to walk or run with long regular steps — **strid·er** *n*

**²stride** *n* **1** : a long step **2** : a stage of progress **3** : manner of striding : GAIT

**stri·dent** \'strī-dʲnt\ *adj* : harsh sounding : GRATING, SHRILL ⟨a ~ voice⟩

**strife** \'strīf\ *n* : CONFLICT, FIGHT, STRUGGLE ♦ *Synonyms* DISCORD, CONTENTION, DISSENSION

**¹strike** \'strīk\ *vb* **struck** \'strək\; **struck** *also* **strick·en** \'stri-kən\; **strik·ing 1** : to take a course : GO ⟨*struck* off through the brush⟩ **2** : to touch or hit sharply; *also* : to deliver a blow **3** : to produce by or as if by a blow ⟨*struck* terror in the foe⟩ **4** : to lower (as a flag or sail) **5** : to collide with; *also* : to injure or destroy by collision **6** : DELETE, CANCEL **7** : to produce by impressing ⟨*struck* a medal⟩; *also* : COIN ⟨~ a new cent⟩ **8** : to cause to sound ⟨~ a bell⟩ **9** : to afflict suddenly : lay low ⟨*stricken* with a high fever⟩ **10** : to appear to; *also* : to appear to as remarkable : IMPRESS **11** : to reach by reckoning ⟨~ an average⟩ **12** : to stop work in order to obtain a change in conditions of employment **13** : to cause (a match) to ignite by rubbing **14** : to come upon ⟨~ gold⟩ **15** : TAKE ON, ASSUME ⟨~ a pose⟩ — **strik·er** *n*

**²strike** *n* **1** : an act or instance of striking **2** : a sudden discovery of rich ore or oil deposits **3** : a pitched baseball that is swung at but not hit **4** : the knocking down of all the bowling pins with the 1st ball **5** : a military attack

**strike·break·er** \-ˌbrā-kər\ *n* : a person hired to replace a striking worker

**strike-out** \-ˌaút\ *n* : an out in baseball as a result of a batter's being charged with three strikes

**strike out** *vb* **1** : to enter upon a course of action **2** : to start out vigorously **3** : to make an out in baseball by a strikeout

**strike–slip** \'strīk-ˌslip\ *n* : a fault about which movement is predominantly horizontal

**strike up** *vb* **1** : to begin or cause to begin to sing or play ⟨*strike up* the band⟩ **2** : BEGIN ⟨~ a conversation⟩

**strike zone** *n* : the area over home plate through which a pitched baseball must pass to be called a strike

**striking** *adj* : attracting attention : very noticeable ♦ **Synonyms** ARRESTING, SALIENT, CONSPICUOUS, OUTSTANDING, REMARKABLE, PROMINENT — **strik·ing·ly** *adv*

¹**string** \'striŋ\ *n* **1** : a line usu. composed of twisted threads **2** : a series of things arranged as if strung on a cord **3** : a plant fiber (as a leaf vein) **4** *pl* : the stringed instruments of an orchestra ♦ **Synonyms** SUCCESSION, PROGRESSION, SEQUENCE, CHAIN, TRAIN

²**string** *vb* **strung** \'strəŋ\; **string·ing 1** : to provide with strings ⟨~ a racket⟩ **2** : to make tense **3** : to thread on or as if on a string ⟨~ pearls⟩ **4** : to hang, tie, or fasten by a string **5** : to take the strings out of ⟨~ beans⟩ **6** : to extend like a string

**string bean** *n* : a bean of one of the older varieties of kidney bean that have stringy fibers on the lines of separation of the pods; *also* : SNAP BEAN

**string bikini** *n* : a scanty bikini

**string cheese** *n* : cheese that can be pulled apart in narrow strips

**stringed** \'striŋd\ *adj* **1** : having strings ⟨~ instruments⟩ **2** : produced by strings

**strin·gen·cy** \'strin-jən-sē\ *n* **1** : STRICTNESS, SEVERITY **2** : SCARCITY ⟨~ of money⟩ — **strin·gent** \-jənt\ *adj*

**string·er** \'striŋ-ər\ *n* **1** : a long horizontal member in a framed structure or a bridge **2** : a news correspondent paid by the amount of copy

**stringy** \'striŋ-ē\ *adj* **string·i·er; -est 1** : resembling string esp. in tough, fibrous, or disordered quality ⟨~ meat⟩ ⟨~ hair⟩ **2** : lean and sinewy in build

¹**strip** \'strip\ *vb* **stripped** \'stript\ *also* **stript; strip·ping 1** : to take the covering or clothing from **2** : to take off one's clothes **3** : to pull or tear off **4** : to make bare or clear (as by cutting or grazing) **5** : PLUNDER, PILLAGE ♦ **Synonyms** DIVEST, DENUDE, DEPRIVE, DISMANTLE — **strip·per** *n*

²**strip** *n* **1** : a long narrow flat piece **2** : AIRSTRIP

¹**stripe** \'strīp\ *vb* **striped** \'strīpt\; **strip·ing** : to make stripes on

²**stripe** *n* **1** : a line or long narrow division having a different color from the background **2** : a strip of braid (as on a sleeve) indicating military rank or length of service **3** : TYPE, CHARACTER — **striped** \'strīpt, 'strī-pəd\ *adj*

**striped bass** *n* : a large black-striped marine bony fish that occurs along the Atlantic and Pacific coasts of the U.S. and is an excellent food and sport fish

**strip·ling** \'stri-pliŋ\ *n* : YOUTH, LAD

**strip mall** *n* : a long building or group of buildings housing several retail stores or service establishments

**strip mine** *n* : a mine that is worked from the earth's surface by the stripping of the topsoil — **strip–mine** *vb*

**strip-tease** \'strip-ˌtēz\ *n* : a burlesque act in which a performer removes clothing piece by piece — **strip-teas·er** *n*

**strive** \'strīv\ *vb* **strove** \'strōv\ *also* **strived** \'strīvd\; **striv·en** \'stri-vən\ *or* **strived; striv·ing 1** : to make effort : labor hard **2** : to struggle in opposition : CONTEND ♦ **Synonyms** ENDEAVOR, ATTEMPT, TRY, ASSAY

**strobe** \'strōb\ *n* **1** : STROBOSCOPE **2** : a device for high-speed intermittent illumination (as in photography)

**stro·bo·scope** \'strō-bə-ˌskōp\ *n* : an instrument for studying rapid motion by means of a rapidly flashing light

**strode** *past of* STRIDE

¹**stroke** \'strōk\ *vb* **stroked; strok·ing 1** : to rub gently **2** : to flatter in a manner designed to persuade

²**stroke** *n* **1** : the act of striking : BLOW, KNOCK **2** : a sudden action or process producing an impact ⟨~ of lightning⟩; *also* : an unexpected result **3** : sudden weakening or loss of consciousness or the power to move or feel caused by rupture or obstruction (as by a clot) of a blood vessel of the brain **4** : one of a series of movements against air or water to get through or over it ⟨the ~ of a bird's wing⟩ **5** : a rower who sets the pace for a crew **6** : a vigorous effort **7** : the sound of striking (as of a clock) **8** : a single movement with or as if with a tool or implement (as a pen)

**stroll** \'strōl\ *vb* : to walk in a leisurely or idle manner — **stroll** *n* — **stroll·er** *n*

**strong** \'strȯŋ\ *adj* **stron·ger** \'strȯŋ-gər\; **stron·gest** \'strȯŋ-gəst\ **1** : POWERFUL, VIGOROUS **2** : HEALTHY, ROBUST **3** : of a specified number ⟨an army 10 thousand ~⟩ **4** : not mild or weak **5** : VIOLENT ⟨~ wind⟩ **6** : ZEALOUS ⟨a ~ supporter⟩ **7** : not easily broken **8** : FIRM, SOLID ⟨~ beliefs⟩ ♦ **Synonyms** STOUT, STURDY, STALWART, TOUGH — **strong·ly** *adv*

**strong–arm** \'strȯŋ-ˌärm\ *adj* : having or using undue force ⟨~ operatives⟩

**strong force** *n* : the physical force responsible for binding together nucleons in the atomic nucleus

**strong·hold** \-ˌhōld\ *n* : a fortified place : FORTRESS

**strong·man** \-ˌman\ *n* : one who leads or controls by force of will and character or by military strength

**stron·tium** \'strän-chē-əm, 'strän-tē-əm\ *n* : a soft malleable metallic chemical element

¹**strop** \'sträp\ *n* : STRAP; *esp* : one for sharpening a razor

²**strop** *vb* **stropped; strop·ping** : to sharpen a razor on a strop

**stro·phe** \'strō-fē\ *n* [Gk *strophē*, lit., act of turning] : a division of a poem — **stroph·ic** \'strä-fik\ *adj*

**strove** *past of* STRIVE

**struck** *past and past part of* STRIKE

¹**struc·ture** \'strək-chər\ *n* [ME, fr. L *structura,* fr. *structus,* pp. of *struere* to heap up, build] **1** : the action of building : CONSTRUCTION **2** : something built (as a house or a dam); *also* : something made up of interdependent parts in a definite pattern of organization **3** : arrangement or relationship of elements (as particles, parts, or organs) in a substance, body, or system — **struc·tur·al** *adj*

²**structure** *vb* **struc·tured; struc·tur·ing** : to make into a structure

**stru·del** \'strüd-ᵊl, 'shtrü-\ *n* [G, lit., whirlpool] : a pastry made of a thin sheet of dough rolled up with filling and baked 〈apple ∼〉

¹**strug·gle** \'strə-gəl\ *vb* **strug·gled; strug·gling** **1** : to make strenuous efforts against opposition : STRIVE **2** : to proceed with difficulty or with great effort ♦ **Synonyms** ENDEAVOR, ATTEMPT, TRY, ASSAY

²**struggle** *n* **1** : CONTEST, STRIFE **2** : a violent effort or exertion

**strum** \'strəm\ *vb* **strummed; strumming** : to play on a stringed instrument by brushing the strings with the fingers 〈∼ a guitar〉

**strum·pet** \'strəm-pət\ *n* : PROSTITUTE

**strung** \'strəŋ\ *past and past part of* STRING

¹**strut** \'strət\ *vb* **strut·ted; strut·ting** : to walk with an affectedly proud gait

²**strut** *n* **1** : a bar or rod for resisting lengthwise pressure **2** : a haughty or pompous gait

**strych·nine** \'strik-ˌnīn, -nən, -ˌnēn\ *n* : a bitter poisonous plant alkaloid used as a poison (as for rats) and medicinally as a stimulant of the central nervous system

¹**stub** \'stəb\ *n* **1** : STUMP **2** : a short blunt end **3** : a small part of each leaf (as of a checkbook) kept as a memorandum of the items on the detached part

²**stub** *vb* **stubbed; stub·bing** : to strike (as one's toe) against something

**stub·ble** \'stə-bəl\ *n* **1** : the cut stem ends of herbs and grasses left in the soil after harvest **2** : a rough surface or growth resembling stubble 〈his face covered with ∼〉 — **stub·bly** \-b(ə-)lē\ *adj*

**stub·born** \'stə-bərn\ *adj* **1** : FIRM, DETERMINED **2** : done or continued in a willful, unreasonable, or persistent manner **3** : not easily controlled or remedied 〈a ∼ cold〉 — **stub·born·ly** *adv* — **stub·born·ness** *n*

**stub·by** \'stə-bē\ *adj* : short, blunt, and thick like a stub 〈∼ fingers〉

**stuc·co** \'stə-kō\ *n, pl* **stuccos** *or* **stuccoes** [It] : plaster for coating exterior walls — **stuc·coed** \-kōd\ *adj*

**stuck** *past and past part of* STICK

¹**stud** \'stəd\ *n* **1** : a male animal and esp. a horse (**stud·horse** \-ˌhȯrs\) kept for breeding

²**stud** *n* **1** : one of the smaller uprights in a building to which the wall materials are fastened **2** : a removable device like a button used as a fastener or ornament

〈shirt ∼s〉 **3** : a projecting nail, pin, or rod

³**stud** *vb* **stud·ded; stud·ding** **1** : to supply with or adorn with studs **2** : DOT 〈the sky was *studded* with stars〉

⁴**stud** *abbr* student

**stud·book** \'stəd-ˌbu̇k\ *n* : an official record of the pedigree of purebred animals (as horses or dogs)

**studding** *n* : the studs in a building or wall

**stu·dent** \'stü-dᵊnt, 'styü-\ *n* : SCHOLAR, PUPIL; *esp* : one who attends a school

**stud·ied** \'stə-dēd\ *adj* : INTENTIONAL 〈a ∼ insult〉 ♦ **Synonyms** DELIBERATE, CONSIDERED, PREMEDITATED, DESIGNED

**stu·dio** \'stü-dē-ˌō, 'styü-\ *n, pl* **-dios** **1** : a place where an artist works; *also* : a place for the study of an art **2** : a place where motion pictures are made **3** : a place equipped for the transmission of radio or television programs

**stu·di·ous** \'stü-dē-əs, 'styü-\ *adj* : devoted to study — **stu·di·ous·ly** *adv*

¹**study** \'stə-dē\ *n, pl* **stud·ies** **1** : the use of the mind to gain knowledge **2** : the act or process of learning about something **3** : careful examination **4** : INTENT, PURPOSE **5** : a branch of learning **6** : a room esp. for reading and writing

²**study** *vb* **stud·ied; study·ing** **1** : to engage in study or the study of **2** : to consider attentively or in detail ♦ **Synonyms** CONSIDER, CONTEMPLATE, WEIGH

¹**stuff** \'stəf\ *n* [ME, fr. AF *estuffes* goods, fr. *estuffer* to fill in (with rubble), furnish, equip, of Gmc origin] **1** : personal property **2** : raw material **3** : a finished textile fabric; *esp* : a worsted fabric **4** : writing, talk, or ideas of little or transitory worth **5** : an unspecified material substance or aggregate of matter **6** : fundamental material **7** : special knowledge or capability

²**stuff** *vb* **1** : to fill by packing things in : CRAM **2** : to eat greedily : GORGE **3** : to prepare (as meat) by filling with a stuffing **4** : to fill (as a cushion) with a soft material **5** : to stop up : PLUG

**stuffed shirt** \'stəft-\ *n* : a smug, conceited, and usu. pompous and inflexibly conservative person

**stuff·ing** *n* : material used to fill tightly; *esp* : a mixture of bread crumbs and spices used to stuff food

**stuffy** \'stə-fē\ *adj* **stuff·i·er; -est** **1** : STODGY **2** : lacking fresh air : CLOSE; *also* : blocked up 〈a ∼ nose〉

**stul·ti·fy** \'stəl-tə-ˌfī\ *vb* **-fied; -fy·ing** **1** : to cause to appear foolish or stupid **2** : to impair, invalidate, or make ineffective **3** : to have a dulling effect on — **stul·ti·fi·ca·tion** \ˌstəl-tə-fə-'kā-shən\ *n*

**stum·ble** \'stəm-bəl\ *vb* **stum·bled; stum·bling** **1** : to blunder morally **2** : to trip in walking or running **3** : to walk unsteadily; *also* : to speak or act in a blundering or clumsy manner **4** : to happen by chance — **stumble** *n*

**stumbling block** *n* : an obstacle to belief, understanding, or progress

¹**stump** \'stəmp\ *n* **1** : the base of a bodily part (as a leg or tooth) left after the rest is removed **2** : the part of a plant and esp. a tree remaining with the root after the trunk is cut off **3** : a place or occasion for political public speaking — **stumpy** *adj*

²**stump** *vb* **1** : BAFFLE, PERPLEX **2** : to clear (land) of stumps **3** : to tour (a region) making political speeches **4** : to walk clumsily and heavily

**stun** \'stən\ *vb* **stunned**; **stun·ning 1** : to make senseless or dizzy by or as if by a blow **2** : BEWILDER, STUPEFY ⟨*stunned* by the news⟩

**stung** *past and past part of* STING

**stunk** *past and past part of* STINK

**stun·ning** *adj* **1** : causing astonishment or disbelief **2** : strikingly beautiful — **stun·ning·ly** *adv*

¹**stunt** \'stənt\ *vb* : to hinder the normal growth or progress of

²**stunt** *n* : an unusual or spectacular feat

**stu·pe·fy** \'stü-pə-ˌfī, 'styü-\ *vb* **-fied**; **-fy·ing 1** : to make stupid, groggy, or insensible **2** : ASTONISH — **stu·pe·fac·tion** \ˌstü-pə-'fak-shən, ˌstyü-\ *n*

**stu·pen·dous** \stü-'pen-dəs, styü-\ *adj* : causing astonishment esp. because of great size or height ♦ *Synonyms* TREMENDOUS, PRODIGIOUS, MONUMENTAL, MONSTROUS — **stu·pen·dous·ly** *adv*

**stu·pid** \'stü-pəd, 'styü-\ *adj* [MF *stupide*, fr. L *stupidus*, fr. *stupēre* to be numb, be astonished] **1** : very dull in mind **2** : showing or resulting from dullness of mind — **stu·pid·i·ty** \stü-'pi-də-tē, styü-\ *n* — **stu·pid·ly** *adv*

**stu·por** \'stü-pər, 'styü-\ *n* **1** : a condition of greatly dulled or completely suspended sense or feeling **2** : a state of extreme apathy or torpor often following stress or shock — **stu·por·ous** *adj*

**stur·dy** \'stər-dē\ *adj* **stur·di·er; -est** [ME, brave, stubborn, fr. AF *esturdi* stunned, fr. pp. of *esturdir* to stun, fr. VL *exturdire*, fr. L *ex-* + VL *turdus* simpleton, fr. L *turdus* thrush] **1** : STRONG, ROBUST **2** : RESOLUTE, UNYIELDING ♦ *Synonyms* STOUT, STALWART, TOUGH, TENACIOUS — **stur·di·ly** \-də-lē\ *adv* — **stur·di·ness** \-dē-nəs\ *n*

**stur·geon** \'stər-jən\ *n* : any of a family of large bony fishes including some whose roe are made into caviar

**stut·ter** \'stə-tər\ *vb* : to speak with involuntary disruption or blocking of sounds — **stutter** *n* — **stut·ter·er** *n*

**stutter step** *n* : a move made by a runner (as in football) done to fake a defender out of position

¹**sty** \'stī\ *n, pl* **sties** : PIGPEN

²**sty** *or* **stye** *n, pl* **sties** *or* **styes** : an inflamed swelling of a skin gland on the edge of an eyelid

¹**style** \'stī(-ə)l\ *n* **1** : mode of address : TITLE **2** : a way of speaking or writing; *esp* : one characteristic of an individual, period, school, or nation ⟨ornate ~⟩ **3** : manner or method of acting, making, or performing; *also* : a distinctive or characteristic manner **4** : a slender pointed instrument or process; *esp* : STYLUS **5** : a fashionable manner or mode **6** : overall excellence, skill, or grace in performance, manner, or appearance **7** : the custom followed in spelling, capitalization, punctuation, and typography — **sty·lis·tic** \stī-'lis-tik\ *adj*

²**style** *vb* **styled**; **styl·ing 1** : NAME, DESIGNATE **2** : to make or design in accord with a prevailing mode ⟨~ hair⟩

**styling** *n* : the way in which something is styled

**styl·ise** *Brit var of* STYLIZE

**styl·ish** \'stī-lish\ *adj* : conforming to current fashion ♦ *Synonyms* MODISH, SMART, CHIC — **styl·ish·ly** *adv* — **styl·ish·ness** *n*

**styl·ist** \'stī-list\ *n* **1** : one (as a writer) noted for a distinctive style **2** : a developer or designer of styles

**styl·ize** \'stī-ˌlīz, 'stī-ə-\ *vb* **styl·ized**; **styl·iz·ing** : to conform to a style; *esp* : to represent or design according to a pattern or style rather than according to nature or tradition ⟨*stylized* flower prints⟩ — **styl·i·za·tion** \ˌstī-lə-'zā-shən\ *n*

**sty·lus** \'stī-ləs\ *n, pl* **styl·li** \stī-ˌlī\ *also* **sty·lus·es** \'stī-lə-səz\ [L *stylus*, *stilus* spike, stylus] **1** : a pointed implement used by the ancients for writing on wax **2** : a phonograph needle **3** : a pen-shaped pointing device for entering data into a computer

**sty·mie** \'stī-mē\ *vb* **sty·mied**; **sty·mie·ing** : BLOCK, FRUSTRATE ⟨managed to ~ the opposition⟩

**styp·tic** \'stip-tik\ *adj* : tending to check bleeding — **styptic** *n*

**suave** \'swäv\ *adj* [F, fr. MF, pleasant, sweet, fr. L *suavis*] : persuasively pleasing : smoothly agreeable ♦ *Synonyms* URBANE, SMOOTH, BLAND — **suave·ly** *adv* — **sua·vi·ty** \'swä-və-tē\ *n*

¹**sub** \'səb\ *n* : SUBSTITUTE — **sub** *vb*

²**sub** *n* : SUBMARINE

³**sub** *abbr* **1** subtract **2** suburb

**sub-** \'səb\ *prefix* **1** : under : beneath **2** : subordinate : secondary **3** : subordinate portion of : subdivision of **4** : with repetition of a process described in a simple verb so as to form, stress, or deal with subordinate parts or relations **5** : somewhat **6** : falling nearly in the category of : bordering on

**sub·al·pine** \ˌsəb-'al-ˌpīn\ *adj* **1** : of or relating to the region about the foot and lower slopes of the Alps **2** : of, relating to, or inhabiting high upland slopes esp. just below the timberline

**sub·al·tern** \sə-'bȯl-tərn\ *n* : SUBORDINATE; *esp* : a junior officer (as in the British army)

**sub·as·sem·bly** \ˌsəb-ə-'sem-blē\ *n* : an

assembled unit to be incorporated with other units in a finished product

**sub·atom·ic** \ˌsəb-ə-ˈtä-mik\ *adj* : of or relating to the inside of the atom or to particles smaller than atoms

**sub·clin·i·cal** \ˌsəb-ˈkli-nə-kəl\ *adj* : not detectable by the usual clinical tests ⟨ ~ infection⟩

**sub·com·pact** \ˈsəb-ˈkäm-ˌpakt\ *n* : an automobile smaller than a compact

**¹sub·con·scious** \ˌsəb-ˈkän-chəs, ˈsəb-\ *adj* : existing in the mind without entering conscious awareness — **sub·con·scious·ly** *adv* — **sub·con·scious·ness** *n*

**²subconscious** *n* : mental activities just below the threshold of consciousness

**sub·con·ti·nent** \ˈsəb-ˈkän-tə-nənt\ *n* : a major subdivision of a continent — **sub·con·ti·nen·tal** \ˌsəb-ˌkän-tə-ˈnen-t°l\ *adj*

**sub·di·vide** \ˌsəb-də-ˈvīd, ˈsəb-də-ˌvīd\ *vb* : to divide the parts of into more parts; *esp* : to divide (a tract of land) into building lots — **sub·di·vi·sion** \-ˈvi-zhən, -ˌvi-\ *n*

**sub·duc·tion** \səb-ˈdək-shən\ *n* : the descent of the edge of one crustal plate beneath the edge of an adjacent plate

**sub·due** \səb-ˈdü, -ˈdyü\ *vb* **sub·dued; sub·du·ing 1** : to bring into subjection : VANQUISH **2** : to bring under control : CURB **3** : to reduce the intensity of

**subj** *abbr* **1** subject **2** subjunctive

**¹sub·ject** \ˈsəb-jikt\ *n* [ME *suget, subget*, fr. AF, fr. L *subjectus* one under authority & *subjectum* subject of a proposition, fr. *subicere* to subject, lit., to throw under, fr. *sub-* under + *jacere* to throw] **1** : a person under the authority of another **2** : a person subject to a sovereign **3** : an individual that is studied or experimented on **4** : the person or thing discussed or treated : TOPIC, THEME **5** : a word or word group denoting that of which something is predicated

**²subject** *adj* **1** : being under the power or rule of another **2** : LIABLE, EXPOSED ⟨ ~ to floods⟩ **3** : dependent on some act or condition ⟨appointment ~ to senate approval⟩ ♦ *Synonyms* SUBORDINATE, SECONDARY, TRIBUTARY, COLLATERAL, DEPENDENT

**³sub·ject** \səb-ˈjəkt\ *vb* **1** : to bring under control : CONQUER **2** : to make liable **3** : to cause to undergo or endure — **sub·jec·tion** \-ˈjek-shən\ *n*

**sub·jec·tive** \ˌsəb-ˈjek-tiv\ *adj* **1** : of, relating to, or constituting a subject **2** : of, relating to, or arising within one's self or mind in contrast to what is outside : PERSONAL ⟨ ~ judgments⟩ ⟨a ~ sensation⟩ — **sub·jec·tive·ly** *adv* — **sub·jec·tiv·i·ty** \-ˌjek-ˈti-və-tē\ *n*

**subject matter** *n* : matter presented for consideration, discussion, or study

**sub·join** \ˌsəb-ˈjoin\ *vb* : APPEND ⟨ ~ed a statement of expenses to her report⟩

**sub ju·di·ce** \ˌsüb-ˈyü-di-ˌkā, ˈsəb-ˈjü-də-ˌsē\ *adv* [L] : before a judge or court : not yet legally decided

**sub·ju·gate** \ˈsəb-ji-ˌgāt\ *vb* **-gat·ed; -gat·ing** : CONQUER, SUBDUE; *also* : ENSLAVE ♦ *Synonyms* REDUCE, OVERCOME, OVERTHROW, VANQUISH, DEFEAT, BEAT — **sub·ju·ga·tion** \ˌsəb-ji-ˈgā-shən\ *n*

**sub·junc·tive** \səb-ˈjəŋk-tiv\ *adj* : of, relating to, or constituting a verb form that represents an act or state as contingent or possible or viewed emotionally (as with desire) ⟨the ~ mood⟩ — **subjunctive** *n*

**sub·lease** \ˈsəb-ˌlēs, -ˈlēs\ *n* : a lease by a lessee of part or all of leased premises to another person with the original lessee retaining some right under the original lease — **sublease** *vb*

**¹sub·let** \ˈsəb-ˈlet\ *vb* **-let; -let·ting** : to let all or a part of (a leased property) to another; *also* : to rent (a property) from a lessee

**²sublet** \-ˌlet\ *n* : property esp. housing obtained through or available through a sublease

**sub·li·mate** \ˈsə-blə-ˌmāt\ *vb* **-mat·ed; -mat·ing 1** : SUBLIME **2** : to direct the expression of (as a desire or impulse) from a primitive to a more socially and culturally acceptable form — **sub·li·ma·tion** \ˌsə-blə-ˈmā-shən\ *n*

**¹sub·lime** \sə-ˈblīm\ *vb* **sub·limed; sub·lim·ing** : to pass or cause to pass directly from the solid to the vapor state

**²sublime** *adj* **1** : EXALTED, NOBLE **2** : having awe-inspiring beauty or grandeur ♦ *Synonyms* GLORIOUS, SPLENDID, SUPERB, RESPLENDENT, GORGEOUS — **sub·lime·ly** *adv* — **sub·lim·i·ty** \-ˈbli-mə-tē\ *n*

**sub·lim·i·nal** \ˌsəb-ˈli-mə-n°l, ˈsəb-\ *adj* [*sub-* + L *limin-, limen* threshold] **1** : inadequate to produce a sensation or mental awareness ⟨ ~ stimuli⟩ **2** : existing or functioning below the threshold of consciousness ⟨the ~ mind⟩ ⟨ ~ advertising⟩

**sub·ma·chine gun** \ˌsəb-mə-ˈshēn-ˌgən\ *n* : an automatic firearm fired from the shoulder or hip

**¹sub·ma·rine** \ˈsəb-mə-ˌrēn, ˌsəb-mə-ˈrēn\ *adj* : UNDERWATER; *esp* : UNDERSEA

**²submarine** *n* **1** : a naval vessel designed to operate underwater **2** : a large sandwich made from a long split roll with any of a variety of fillings

**sub·merge** \səb-ˈmərj\ *vb* **sub·merged; sub·merg·ing 1** : to put or plunge under the surface of water **2** : INUNDATE — **sub·mer·gence** \-ˈmər-jəns\ *n*

**sub·merse** \səb-ˈmərs\ *vb* **sub·mersed;**

| | | | |
|---|---|---|---|
| subatmospheric | subclassify | subentry | subhead |
| subaverage | subcommittee | subfamily | subheading |
| subbasement | subcontract | subfield | subhuman |
| subcategory | subcontractor | subfreezing | subkingdom |
| subcellular | subculture | subgenre | sublethal |
| subchapter | subcutaneous | subgenus | subliterate |
| subclass | subdiscipline | subgroup | |

**sub·mers·ing** : SUBMERGE — **sub·mer·sion** \-'mər-zhən\ n

¹**sub·mers·ible** \səb-'mər-sə-bəl\ adj : capable of being submerged

²**submersible** n : something that is submersible; esp : a small underwater craft used for deep-sea research

**sub·mi·cro·scop·ic** \ˌsəb-ˌmī-krə-'skä-pik\ adj : too small to be seen in an ordinary light microscope

**sub·min·ia·ture** \ˌsəb-'mi-nē-ə-ˌchùr, 'səb-, -'mi-ni-ˌchùr, -chər\ adj : very small

**sub·mit** \səb-'mit\ vb **sub·mit·ted; sub·mit·ting 1** : to commit to the discretion or decision of another or of others **2** : YIELD, SURRENDER **3** : to put forward as an opinion — **sub·mis·sion** \-'mi-shən\ n — **sub·mis·sive** \-'mi-siv\ adj

**sub·nor·mal** \ˌsəb-'nor-məl\ adj : falling below what is normal; also : having less of something and esp. intelligence than is normal — **sub·nor·mal·i·ty** \ˌsəb-nor-'ma-lə-tē\ n

**sub·or·bit·al** \ˌsəb-'or-bə-t'l, 'səb-\ adj : being at or involving less than one orbit

¹**sub·or·di·nate** \sə-'bor-də-nət\ adj **1** : of lower class or rank ⟨a ~ officer⟩ **2** : INFERIOR **3** : submissive to authority **4** : subordinated to other elements in a sentence : DEPENDENT ⟨~ clause⟩ ♦ **Synonyms** SECONDARY, SUBJECT, TRIBUTARY, COLLATERAL

²**subordinate** n : one that is subordinate

³**sub·or·di·nate** \sə-'bor-də-ˌnāt\ vb **-nat·ed; -nat·ing 1** : SUBDUE **2** : to place in a lower rank or class — **sub·or·di·na·tion** \-ˌbor-də-'nā-shən\ n

**sub·orn** \sə-'bórn\ vb **1** : to induce secretly to do an unlawful thing **2** : to induce to commit perjury — **sub·or·na·tion** \ˌsə-ˌbor-'nā-shən\ n

¹**sub·poe·na** \sə-'pē-nə\ n [ME suppena, fr. L sub poena under penalty] : a writ commanding the person named in it to attend court under penalty for failure to do so

²**subpoena** vb **-naed; -na·ing** : to summon with a subpoena

**sub–Sa·ha·ran** \ˌsəb-sə-'her-ən\ adj : of, relating to, or being the part of Africa south of the Sahara

**sub·scribe** \səb-'skrīb\ vb **sub·scribed; sub·scrib·ing 1** : to sign one's name to a document **2** : to give consent by or as if by signing one's name **3** : to promise to contribute by signing one's name with the amount promised **4** : to place an order by signing **5** : to receive a periodical or service regularly on order **6** : FAVOR, APPROVE ⟨~ to the theory⟩ ♦ **Synonyms** AGREE, ACQUIESCE, ASSENT, ACCEDE — **sub·scrib·er** n

**sub·script** \'səb-ˌskript\ n : a symbol (as a letter or number) immediately below or below and to the right or left of another written character — **subscript** adj

**sub·scrip·tion** \səb-'skrip-shən\ n **1** : the act of subscribing : SIGNATURE **2** : a purchase by signed order

**sub·se·quent** \'səb-si-kwənt, -sə-ˌkwent\ adj : following after : SUCCEEDING ⟨~ events⟩ — **sub·se·quent·ly** adv

**sub·ser·vi·ence** \ˌsəb-'sər-vē-əns\ n **1** : a subordinate place or condition **2** : SERVILITY — **sub·ser·vi·en·cy** \-ən-sē\ n — **sub·ser·vi·ent** \-ənt\ adj

**sub·set** \'səb-ˌset\ n : a set each of whose elements is an element of an inclusive set

**sub·side** \səb-'sīd\ vb **sub·sid·ed; sub·sid·ing** [L subsidere, fr. sub- under + sidere to sit down, sink] **1** : to settle to the bottom of a liquid **2** : to tend downward : DESCEND **3** : SINK, SUBMERGE ⟨subsided into a chair⟩ **4** : to become quiet and tranquil ♦ **Synonyms** ABATE, WANE, MODERATE, SLACKEN — **sub·sid·ence** \səb-'sī-d'ns, 'səb-sə-dəns\ n

¹**sub·sid·iary** \səb-'si-dē-ˌer-ē\ adj **1** : furnishing aid or support **2** : of secondary importance **3** : of or relating to a subsidy ♦ **Synonyms** AUXILIARY, CONTRIBUTORY, SUBSERVIENT, ACCESSORY

²**subsidiary** n, pl **-iar·ies** : one that is subsidiary; esp : a company controlled by another

**sub·si·dise** Brit var of SUBSIDIZE

**sub·si·dize** \'səb-sə-ˌdīz\ vb **-dized; -diz·ing** : to aid or furnish with a subsidy

**sub·si·dy** \'səb-sə-dē\ n, pl **-dies** [ME, subsidie, fr. AF, fr. L subsidium reserve troops, support, assistance, fr. sub- near + sedēre to sit] : a gift of public money to a private person or company or to another government

**sub·sist** \səb-'sist\ vb **1** : EXIST, PERSIST **2** : to have the means (as food and clothing) of maintaining life; esp : to nourish oneself

**sub·sis·tence** \səb-'sis-təns\ n **1** : EXISTENCE **2** : means of subsisting : the minimum (as of food and clothing) necessary to support life

**sub·son·ic** \ˌsəb-'sä-nik, 'səb-\ adj : being or relating to a speed less than that of sound; also : moving at such a speed

**sub·spe·cies** \'səb-ˌspē-shēz, -sēz\ n : a subdivision of a species; esp : a category in biological classification ranking just below a species that designates a geographic population genetically distinct from other such populations and potentially able to breed with them where its range overlaps theirs

**sub·stance** \'səb-stəns\ n **1** : essential nature : ESSENCE ⟨divine ~⟩; also : the fundamental or essential part or quality ⟨the ~ of the speech⟩ **2** : physical material from which something is made or which has discrete existence; also : matter of particular or definite chemical constitution **3** : something (as drugs or alcohol) deemed harmful and usu. subject to

| | | | |
|---|---|---|---|
| subminimal | subparallel | subprofessional | subsense |
| subminimum | subphylum | subprogram | subsoil |
| suboptimal | subplot | subregion | substage |
| suborder | subpopulation | subroutine | |
| subparagraph | subproblem | subsection | |

legal restriction ⟨~ abuse⟩ 4 : material possessions : PROPERTY, WEALTH

**sub·stan·dard** \ˌsəb-'stan-dərd\ *adj* : falling short of a standard or norm

**sub·stan·tial** \səb-'stan-chəl\ *adj* 1 : existing as or in substance : MATERIAL; *also* : not illusory : REAL 2 : IMPORTANT, ESSENTIAL ⟨a ~ difference in the stories⟩ 3 : NOURISHING, SATISFYING ⟨~ meal⟩ 4 : having means : WELL-TO-DO 5 : CONSIDERABLE ⟨~ profit⟩ 6 : STRONG, FIRM — **sub·stan·tial·ly** *adv*

**sub·stan·ti·ate** \səb-'stan-chē-ˌāt\ *vb* **-at·ed; -at·ing** 1 : to give substance or body to 2 : VERIFY, PROVE ⟨~ a charge⟩ — **sub·stan·ti·a·tion** \-ˌstan-chē-'ā-shən\ *n*

¹**sub·stan·tive** \'səb-stən-tiv\ *n* : NOUN; *also* : a word or phrase used as a noun

²**substantive** *adj* : having substance : REAL ⟨~ changes⟩

¹**sub·sti·tute** \'səb-stə-ˌtüt, -ˌtyüt\ *n* : a person or thing replacing another — **substitute** *adj*

²**substitute** *vb* **-tut·ed; -tut·ing** 1 : to put or use in the place of another 2 : to serve as a substitute — **sub·sti·tu·tion** \ˌsəb-stə-'tü-shən, -'tyü-\ *n*

**sub·strate** \'səb-ˌstrāt\ *n* 1 : the base on which a plant or animal lives 2 : a substance acted upon (as by an enzyme)

**sub·stra·tum** \'səb-ˌstrā-təm, -ˌstrā-\ *n, pl* **-stra·ta** \-tə\ : the layer or structure (as subsoil) lying underneath

**sub·struc·ture** \'səb-ˌstrək-chər\ *n* : FOUNDATION, GROUNDWORK

**sub·sume** \səb-'süm\ *vb* **sub·sumed; sub·sum·ing** : to include or place within something larger or more comprehensive

**sub·sur·face** \'səb-ˌsər-fəs\ *n* : earth material near the surface of the ground — **subsurface** *adj*

**sub·ter·fuge** \'səb-tər-ˌfyüj\ *n* : a trick or device used in order to conceal, escape, or evade ♦ **Synonyms** FRAUD, DECEPTION, TRICKERY

**sub·ter·ra·nean** \ˌsəb-tə-'rā-nē-ən\ *adj* 1 : lying or being underground 2 : SECRET, HIDDEN ⟨a ~ network of criminals⟩

**sub·tile** \'sə-t°l\ *adj* **sub·til·er** \'sə-t°l-ər\; **sub·til·est** \'sə-t°l-əst\ : SUBTLE ⟨a ~ aroma⟩

**sub·ti·tle** \'səb-ˌtī-t°l\ *n* 1 : a secondary or explanatory title (as of a book) 2 : printed matter projected on a motion-picture screen during or between the scenes

**sub·tle** \'sə-t°l\ *adj* **sub·tler** \'sə-t°l-ər\; **sub·tlest** \'sə-t°l-əst\ 1 : hardly noticeable ⟨~ differences⟩ 2 : SHREWD, PERCEPTIVE ⟨a ~ mind⟩ 3 : CLEVER, SLY ⟨a ~ rogue⟩ — **sub·tle·ty** \-tē\ *n* — **sub·tly** \'sə-t°l-ē\ *adv*

**sub·tract** \səb-'trakt\ *vb* : to take away (as one part or number) from another; *also* : to perform the operation of deducting one number from another — **sub·trac·tion** \-'trak-shən\ *n*

**sub·tra·hend** \'səb-trə-ˌhend\ *n* : a number that is to be subtracted from another

**sub·trop·i·cal** \ˌsəb-'trä-pi-kəl, 'səb-\ *also* **sub·trop·ic** \-pik\ *adj* : of, relating to, or being regions bordering on the tropical zone ⟨a ~ environment⟩ — **sub·trop·ics** \-piks\ *n pl*

**sub·urb** \'sə-ˌbərb\ *n* 1 : an outlying part of a city; *also* : a small community adjacent to a city 2 *pl* : a residential area adjacent to a city — **sub·ur·ban** \sə-'bər-bən\ *adj or n* — **sub·ur·ban·ite** \sə-'bər-bə-ˌnīt\ *n*

**sub·ur·bia** \sə-'bər-bē-ə\ *n* 1 : SUBURBS 2 : suburban people or customs

**sub·ven·tion** \səb-'ven-chən\ *n* : SUBSIDY, ENDOWMENT

**sub·vert** \səb-'vərt\ *vb* 1 : OVERTHROW, RUIN 2 : CORRUPT ⟨~ the rule of law⟩ — **sub·ver·sion** \-'vər-zhən\ *n* — **sub·ver·sive** \-'vər-siv\ *adj*

**sub·way** \'səb-ˌwā\ *n* : an underground way; *esp* : an underground electric railway

**sub·woof·er** \'səb-ˌwu̇-fər\ *n* : a loudspeaker responsive only to the lowest acoustic frequencies

**suc·ceed** \sək-'sēd\ *vb* 1 : to follow next in order or next after another; *esp* : to inherit sovereignty, rank, title, or property 2 : to attain a desired object or end : be successful

**suc·cess** \sək-'ses\ *n* 1 : favorable or desired outcome 2 : the gaining of wealth and fame 3 : one that succeeds — **suc·cess·ful** \-fəl\ *adj* — **suc·cess·ful·ly** *adv*

**suc·ces·sion** \sək-'se-shən\ *n* 1 : the order, act, or right of succeeding to a property, title, or throne 2 : the act or process of following in order 3 : a series of persons or things that follow one after another ♦ **Synonyms** PROGRESSION, SEQUENCE, CHAIN, TRAIN, STRING

**suc·ces·sive** \sək-'se-siv\ *adj* : following in order : CONSECUTIVE ⟨three ~ days⟩ — **suc·ces·sive·ly** *adv*

**suc·ces·sor** \sək-'se-sər\ *n* : one that succeeds (as to a throne, title, estate, or office)

**suc·cinct** \(ˌ)sək-'siŋkt, sə-'siŋkt\ *adj* : BRIEF, CONCISE ⟨a ~ description⟩ ♦ **Synonyms** TERSE, LACONIC, SUMMARY, CURT, SHORT — **suc·cinct·ly** *adv* — **suc·cinct·ness** *n*

**suc·cor** \'sə-kər\ *n* [ME *socour, sucurs* (taken as pl.), fr. AF *sucur, sucors*, fr. ML *succursus*, fr. L *succurrere* to run to the rescue, bring aid] : AID, HELP, RELIEF — **succor** *vb*

**suc·co·tash** \'sə-kə-ˌtash\ *n* [Narragansett *msíckquatash* boiled corn kernels] : beans and corn kernels cooked together

**suc·cour** *chiefly Brit var of* SUCCOR

¹**suc·cu·lent** \'sə-kyə-lənt\ *adj* : full of juice : JUICY; *also* : having fleshy tissues

| | | | |
|---|---|---|---|
| substation | subthreshold | subtreasury | subvariety |
| subsystem | subtopic | subtype | subvisible |
| subteen | subtotal | subunit | subzero |

that conserve moisture ⟨∼ plants⟩ — **suc·cu·lence** \-ləns\ n

²**succulent** n : a succulent plant (as a cactus or an aloe)

**suc·cumb** \sə-'kəm\ vb **1** : to yield to superior strength or force or overpowering appeal or desire **2** : DIE ♦ *Synonyms* SUBMIT, CAPITULATE, RELENT, DEFER

¹**such** \'səch, 'sich\ adj **1** : of this or that kind **2** : having a quality just specified or to be specified

²**such** pron **1** : such a one or ones ⟨he's a star, and acted as ∼⟩ **2** : that or those similar or related thereto ⟨boards and nails and ∼⟩

³**such** adv : to that degree : so

**such·like** \'səch-ˌlīk\ adj : SIMILAR

¹**suck** \'sək\ vb **1** : to draw in liquid and esp. mother's milk with the mouth **2** : to draw liquid from by action of the mouth ⟨∼ an orange⟩ **3** : to take in or up or remove by or as if by suction **4** slang : to be objectionable

²**suck** n **1** : a sucking movement or force **2** : the act of sucking

**suck·er** \'sə-kər\ n **1** : one that sucks **2** : a part of an animal's body used for sucking or for clinging **3** : any of numerous freshwater fishes with thick soft lips for sucking in food **4** : a shoot from the roots or lower part of a plant **5** : a person easily deceived **6** — used as a generalized term of reference ⟨see if you can get that ∼ working again⟩

**suck·le** \'sə-kəl\ vb **suck·led; suck·ling** : to give or draw milk from the breast or udder; also : NURTURE

**suck·ling** \'sə-kliŋ\ n : a young unweaned mammal

**suck–up** \'sək-ˌəp\ n : a person who seeks to gain favor by flattery ⟨a ∼ to the teacher⟩

**su·cre** \'sü-(ˌ)krā\ n : the basic monetary unit of Ecuador until 2000

**su·crose** \'sü-ˌkrōs, -ˌkrōz\ n : a sweet sugar obtained commercially esp. from sugarcane or sugar beets

**suc·tion** \'sək-shən\ n **1** : the act of sucking **2** : the act or process of drawing something (as liquid or dust) into a space (as in a vacuum cleaner or a pump) by partially exhausting the air in the space — **suc·tion·al** \-shə-nəl\ adj

**suction cup** n : a cup-shaped device in which a partial vacuum is produced when applied to a surface

**sud·den** \'sə-dᵊn\ adj [ME sodain, fr. AF sudain, fr. L subitaneus, fr. subitus sudden, fr. pp. of subire to come up] **1** : happening or coming unexpectedly ⟨∼ shower⟩; also : changing angle or character all at once ⟨∼ turn⟩ ⟨∼ descent⟩ **2** : HASTY, RASH ⟨∼ decision⟩ **3** : made or brought about in a short time : PROMPT ⟨∼ cure⟩ ♦ *Synonyms* PRECIPITATE, HEADLONG, IMPETUOUS — **sud·den·ly** adv — **sud·den·ness** n

**sudden infant death syndrome** n : death due to unknown causes of an apparently healthy infant usu. before one year of age and esp. during sleep

**su·do·ku** \sü-'dō-kü\ n [Jp sūdoku, short

for sūji wa dokushin ni kagiru "the numerals must remain single"] : a puzzle in which several numbers are to be filled into a 9x9 grid of squares so that every row, every column, and every 3x3 box contains the numbers 1 through 9

**suds** \'sədz\ n pl : soapy water esp. when frothy — **sudsy** \'səd-zē\ adj

**sue** \'sü\ vb **sued; su·ing** [ME sewen, siuen to follow, strive for, petition, fr. AF sivre, siure, fr. VL *sequere, fr. L sequi to follow] **1** : PETITION, SOLICIT ⟨sued for peace⟩ **2** : to seek justice or right by bringing legal action ⟨sued the company⟩

**suede** also **suède** \'swād\ n [F gants de Suède Swedish gloves] **1** : leather with a napped surface **2** : a fabric with a suede-like nap

**su·et** \'sü-ət\ n : the hard fat from beef and mutton that yields tallow

**suff** abbr **1** sufficient **2** suffix

**suf·fer** \'sə-fər\ vb **suf·fered; suf·fer·ing** **1** : to feel or endure pain **2** : EXPERIENCE, UNDERGO ⟨∼ a defeat⟩ **3** : to bear loss, damage, or injury **4** : ALLOW, PERMIT ♦ *Synonyms* ENDURE, ABIDE, TOLERATE, STAND, BROOK, STOMACH — **suf·fer·able** \'sə-fə-rə-bəl\ adj — **suf·fer·er** n

**suf·fer·ance** \'sə-frəns, -fə-rəns\ n **1** : consent or approval implied by lack of interference or resistance **2** : ENDURANCE, PATIENCE

**suf·fer·ing** \'sə-friŋ, -fə-riŋ\ n : PAIN, MISERY, HARDSHIP ⟨human ∼⟩

**suf·fice** \sə-'fīs\ vb **suf·ficed; suf·fic·ing** **1** : to satisfy a need : be sufficient **2** : to be capable or competent

**suf·fi·cien·cy** \sə-'fi-shən-sē\ n **1** : a sufficient quantity to meet one's needs **2** : ADEQUACY

**suf·fi·cient** \sə-'fi-shənt\ adj : adequate to accomplish a purpose or meet a need — **suf·fi·cient·ly** adv

¹**suf·fix** \'sə-ˌfiks\ n : an affix occurring at the end of a word

²**suf·fix** \'sə-ˌfiks, (ˌ)sə-'fiks\ vb : to attach as a suffix — **suf·fix·ation** \ˌsə-ˌfik-'sā-shən\ n

**suf·fo·cate** \'sə-fə-ˌkāt\ vb **-cat·ed; -cat·ing** : STIFLE, SMOTHER, CHOKE — **suf·fo·cat·ing·ly** adv — **suf·fo·ca·tion** \ˌsə-fə-'kā-shən\ n

**suf·fra·gan** \'sə-fri-gən\ n : an assistant bishop; esp : one not having the right of succession — **suffragan** adj

**suf·frage** \'sə-frij\ n [L suffragium] **1** : VOTE **2** : the right to vote : FRANCHISE

**suf·frag·ette** \ˌsə-fri-'jet\ n : a woman who advocates suffrage for women

**suf·frag·ist** \'sə-fri-jist\ n : one who advocates extension of the suffrage esp. to women

**suf·fuse** \sə-'fyüz\ vb **suf·fused; suf·fus·ing** : to spread over or through in the manner of a fluid or light ♦ *Synonyms* INFUSE, IMBUE, INGRAIN, STEEP — **suf·fu·sion** \-'fyü-zhən\ n

¹**sug·ar** \'shu-gər\ n **1** : a sweet substance that is colorless or white when pure and is chiefly sucrose from sugarcane or sugar beets **2** : a water-soluble compound

(as glucose) similar to sucrose — **sug·ary** *adj*

²**sugar** *vb* **sug·ared; sug·ar·ing** **1** : to mix, cover, or sprinkle with sugar **2** : SWEETEN ⟨~ advice with flattery⟩ **3** : to form sugar ⟨a syrup that ~*s*⟩ **4** : GRANULATE

**sugar beet** *n* : a large beet with a white root from which sugar is made

**sug·ar·cane** \'shu̇-gər-ˌkan\ *n* : a tall grass widely grown in warm regions for the sugar in its stalks

**sugar daddy** *n* **1** : a well-to-do usu. older man who supports or spends lavishly on a mistress or girlfriend **2** : a generous benefactor of a cause

**sugar maple** *n* : a maple with a sweet sap; *esp* : one of eastern No. America with sap that is the chief source of maple syrup and maple sugar

**sugar pea** *n* : SNOW PEA

**sug·ar·plum** \'shu̇-gər-ˌpləm\ *n* : a small ball of candy

**sug·gest** \səg-'jest, sə-\ *vb* **1** : to put (as a thought, plan, or desire) into a person's mind **2** : to remind or evoke by association of ideas ♦ *Synonyms* IMPLY, HINT, INTIMATE, INSINUATE, CONNOTE

**sug·gest·ible** \səg-'jes-tə-bəl, sə-\ *adj* : easily influenced by suggestion

**sug·ges·tion** \-'jes-chən\ *n* **1** : an act or instance of suggesting; *also* : something suggested **2** : a slight indication

**sug·ges·tive** \-'jes-tiv\ *adj* : tending to suggest something; *esp* : suggesting something improper or indecent — **sug·ges·tive·ly** *adv* — **sug·ges·tive·ness** *n*

¹**sui·cide** \'su̇-ə-ˌsīd\ *n* **1** : the act of killing oneself purposely **2** : one that commits or attempts suicide — **sui·cid·al** \ˌsü-ə-'sī-dᵊl\ *adj*

²**suicide** *adj* : being or performing a deliberate act resulting in the voluntary death of the person who does it ⟨a ~ mission⟩ ⟨a ~ bomber⟩

**sui ge·ner·is** \ˌsü-ˌī-'je-nə-rəs, ˌsü-ē-\ *adj* [L, of its own kind] : being in a class by itself : UNIQUE

¹**suit** \'sü̇t\ *n* **1** : an action in court to recover a right or claim **2** : an act of suing or entreating; *esp* : COURTSHIP **3** : a number of things used together ⟨~ of clothes⟩ **4** : all the playing cards in a pack bearing the same symbol

²**suit** *vb* **1** : to be appropriate or fitting **2** : to be becoming to **3** : to meet the needs or desires of : PLEASE

**suit·able** \'sü-tə-bəl\ *adj* : FITTING, PROPER, APPROPRIATE ⟨~ dress⟩ ♦ *Synonyms* FIT, MEET, APT, HAPPY — **suit·abil·i·ty** \ˌsü-tə-'bi-lə-tē\ *n* — **suit·able·ness** \'sü-tə-bəl-nəs\ *n* — **suit·ably** \-tə-blē\ *adv*

**suit·case** \'süt-ˌkās\ *n* : a portable case designed to hold a traveler's clothing and personal articles

**suite** \'swēt, *for 4 also* 'süt\ *n* **1** : RETINUE **2** : a group of rooms occupied as a unit **3** : a modern instrumental composition in several movements of different character; *also* : a long orchestral concert arrangement in suite form of material

drawn from a longer work **4** : a set of matched furniture for a room

**suit·ing** \'sü-tiŋ\ *n* : fabric for suits of clothes

**suit·or** \'sü-tər\ *n* **1** : one who sues or petitions **2** : one who courts a woman or seeks to marry her

**su·ki·ya·ki** \skē-'yä-kē, ˌsu̇-kē-'yä-\ *n* : thin slices of meat, tofu, and vegetables cooked in soy sauce and sugar

**sul·fa drug** \'səl-fə-\ *n* : any of various synthetic organic bacteria-inhibiting drugs

**sul·fate** \'səl-ˌfāt\ *n* : a salt or ester of sulfuric acid

**sul·fide** \'səl-ˌfīd\ *n* : a compound of sulfur

**sul·fur** *also* **sul·phur** \'səl-fər\ *n* : a nonmetallic chemical element used esp. in the chemical and paper industries and in vulcanizing rubber

**sulfur di·ox·ide** \-dī-'äk-ˌsīd\ *n* : a heavy pungent toxic gas that is used esp. in bleaching, as a preservative, and as a refrigerant, and is a major air pollutant

**sul·fu·ric** \ˌsəl-'fyu̇r-ik\ *adj* : of, relating to, or containing sulfur

**sulfuric acid** *or* **sul·phu·ric acid** \ˌsəl-'fyu̇r-ik-\ *n* : a heavy corrosive oily strong acid

**sul·fu·rous** *also* **sul·phu·rous** \'səl-fə-rəs, -fyə-, *also esp for 1* ˌsəl-'fyu̇r-əs\ *adj* **1** : of, relating to, or containing sulfur **2** : of or relating to brimstone or the fire of hell : INFERNAL **3** : FIERY, INFLAMED ⟨~ sermons⟩

¹**sulk** \'səlk\ *vb* : to be or become moodily silent or irritable

²**sulk** *n* : a sulky mood or spell

¹**sulky** \'səl-kē\ *adj* **sulk·i·er; -est** : inclined to sulk : MOROSE, MOODY ⟨a ~ mood⟩ ♦ *Synonyms* SURLY, GLUM, SULLEN, GLOOMY — **sulk·i·ly** \'səl-kə-lē\ *adv* — **sulk·i·ness** \-kē-nəs\ *n*

²**sulky** *n, pl* **sulkies** : a light 2-wheeled horse-drawn vehicle with a seat for the driver and usu. no body

**sul·len** \'sə-lən\ *adj* **1** : gloomily silent : MOROSE **2** : DISMAL, GLOOMY ⟨a ~ sky⟩ ♦ *Synonyms* GLUM, SURLY, DOUR, SATURNINE — **sul·len·ly** *adv* — **sul·len·ness** *n*

**sul·ly** \'sə-lē\ *vb* **sul·lied; sul·ly·ing** : SOIL, SMIRCH, DEFILE ⟨~ his name⟩

**sul·tan** \'səl-tᵊn\ *n* : a sovereign esp. of a Muslim state — **sul·tan·ate** \-ˌāt\ *n*

**sul·ta·na** \ˌsəl-'ta-nə\ *n* **1** : a female member of a sultan's family **2** : a pale seedless grape; *also* : a raisin of this grape

**sul·try** \'səl-trē\ *adj* **sul·tri·er; -est** [obs. E *sulter* to swelter, alter. of E *swelter*] : very hot and moist : SWELTERING; *also* : exciting sexual desire ⟨a ~ look⟩

¹**sum** \'səm\ *n* [ME *summe*, fr. AF *sume*, *somme*, fr. L *summa*, fr. fem. of *summus* highest] **1** : a quantity of money **2** : the whole amount **3** : GIST ⟨the ~ of an argument⟩ **4** : the result obtained by adding numbers **5** : a problem in arithmetic

²**sum** *vb* **summed; sum·ming** : to find the sum of by adding or counting

³**sum** *n* : the som of Uzbekistan

**su·mac** *also* **su·mach** \'sü-ˌmak, 'shü-\ *n* : any of a genus of trees, shrubs, and woody vines having spikes or loose clusters of red or whitish berries

**sum·ma·rise** *Brit var of* SUMMARIZE

**sum·ma·rize** \'sə-mə-ˌrīz\ *vb* **-rized; -riz·ing** : to tell in a summary

¹**sum·ma·ry** \'sə-mə-rē\ *adj* **1** : covering the main points briefly : CONCISE **2** : done without delay or formality ⟨~ punishment⟩ ♦ **Synonyms** TERSE, SUCCINCT, LACONIC — **sum·mar·i·ly** \(ˌ)sə-'mer-ə-lē, 'sə-mə-rə-lē\ *adv*

²**summary** *n, pl* **-ries** : a concise statement of the main points

**sum·ma·tion** \(ˌ)sə-'mā-shən\ *n* : a summing up; *esp* : a speech in court summing up the arguments in a case

**sum·mer** \'sə-mər\ *n* : the season of the year in a region in which the sun shines most directly : the warmest period of the year — **sum·mery** *adj*

**sum·mer·house** \'sə-mər-ˌhaús\ *n* : a covered structure in a garden or park to provide a shady retreat

**summersault** *var of* SOMERSAULT

**summer squash** *n* : any of various squashes (as zucchini) used as a vegetable while immature

**sum·mit** \'sə-mət\ *n* **1** : the highest point **2** : a conference of highest-level officials ⟨an economic ~⟩

**sum·mon** \'sə-mən\ *vb* [ME *somnen, somonen,* fr. AF *somondre,* fr. VL *summonere,* alter. of L *summonēre* to remind secretly] **1** : to call to a meeting : CONVOKE **2** : to send for; *also* : to order to appear in court **3** : to evoke esp. by an act of the will ⟨~ up courage⟩ — **sum·mon·er** *n*

**sum·mons** \'sə-mənz\ *n, pl* **sum·mons·es 1** : an authoritative call to appear at a designated place or to attend to a duty **2** : a warning or citation to appear in court at a specified time to answer charges

**sump·tu·ous** \'səmp-shə-wəs, -chə-\ *adj* : LAVISH, LUXURIOUS ⟨a ~ banquet⟩ ⟨a ~ residence⟩

**sum up** *vb* : SUMMARIZE

¹**sun** \'sən\ *n* **1** : the shining celestial body around which the earth and other planets revolve and from which they receive light and heat **2** : a celestial body like the sun **3** : SUNSHINE — **sun·less** *adj* — **sun·ny** *adj*

²**sun** *vb* **sunned; sun·ning 1** : to expose to or as if to the rays of the sun **2** : to sun oneself

**Sun** *abbr* Sunday

**sun·bath** \'sən-ˌbath, -ˌbäth\ *n* : an exposure to sunlight or a sunlamp — **sun·bathe** \-ˌbāth\ *vb*

**sun·beam** \-ˌbēm\ *n* : a ray of sunlight

**sun·block** \'sən-ˌbläk\ *n* : a preparation used on the skin to prevent sunburn (as by blocking ultraviolet radiation)

**sun·bon·net** \-ˌbä-nət\ *n* : a bonnet with a wide brim to shield the face and neck from the sun

¹**sun·burn** \-ˌbərn\ *vb* **-burned** \-ˌbərnd\ *or* **-burnt** \-ˌbərnt\; **-burn·ing** : to cause or become affected with sunburn

²**sunburn** *n* : a skin inflammation caused by overexposure to ultraviolet radiation esp. from sunshine

**sun·dae** \'sən-(ˌ)dā, -dē\ *n* : ice cream served with topping

**Sun·day** \'sən-ˌdā, -dē\ *n* : the 1st day of the week : the Christian Sabbath

**sun·der** \'sən-dər\ *vb* : to force apart ⟨a family ~ed by scandal⟩ ♦ **Synonyms** SEVER, PART, DISJOIN, DISUNITE

**sun·di·al** \'sən-ˌdī(-ə)l\ *n* : a device for showing the time of day from the shadow cast on a plate by an object with a straight edge

**sun·down** \-ˌdaún\ *n* : SUNSET 2

**sun·dries** \'sən-drēz\ *n pl* : various small articles or items

**sun·dry** \'sən-drē\ *adj* : SEVERAL, DIVERS, VARIOUS ⟨for ~ reasons⟩

**sun·fish** \'sən-ˌfish\ *n* **1** : a large marine fish with a deep flattened body **2** : any of numerous often brightly colored No. American freshwater fishes related to the perches and usu. having the body flattened from side to side

**sun·flow·er** \-ˌflaú(-ə)r\ *n* : any of a genus of tall New World plants related to the daisies and often grown for the oil-rich seeds of their yellow-petaled dark-centered flower heads

**sung** *past and past part of* SING

**sun·glasses** \'sən-ˌgla-səz\ *n pl* : glasses to protect the eyes from the sun

**sunk** *past and past part of* SINK

**sunk·en** \'sən-kən\ *adj* **1** : SUBMERGED ⟨~ ships⟩ **2** : fallen in : HOLLOW ⟨~ cheeks⟩ **3** : lying in a depression ⟨~ garden⟩; *also* : constructed below the general floor level ⟨a ~ living room⟩

**sun·lamp** \'sən-ˌlamp\ *n* : an electric lamp designed to emit radiation of wavelengths from ultraviolet to infrared

**sun·light** \-ˌlīt\ *n* : SUNSHINE

**sun·lit** \-ˌlit\ *adj* : lighted by or as if by the sun

**sun protection factor** *n* : a number that is the factor by which the time required for unprotected skin to become sunburned is increased when a sunscreen is used

**sun·rise** \-ˌrīz\ *n* **1** : the apparent rising of the sun above the horizon **2** : the time at which the sun rises

**sun·roof** \-ˌrüf, -ˌrúf\ *n* : a panel in an automobile roof that can be opened

**sun·screen** \-ˌskrēn\ *n* : a preparation on the skin to prevent sunburn (as by absorbing ultraviolet radiation)

**sun·set** \-ˌset\ *n* **1** : the apparent descent of the sun below the horizon **2** : the time at which the sun sets

**sun·shade** \'sən-ˌshād\ *n* : something (as a parasol or awning) used as a protection from the sun's rays

**sun·shine** \-ˌshīn\ *n* : the direct light of the sun — **sun·shiny** *adj*

**sun·spot** \-ˌspät\ *n* : any of the dark spots that appear at times on the sun's surface

**sun·stroke** \-ˌströk\ *n* : heatstroke caused by direct exposure to the sun

**sun·tan** \-ˌtan\ *n* : a browning of the skin from exposure to the sun's rays

**sun·up** \-ˌəp\ *n* : SUNRISE 2

**¹sup** \'səp\ *vb* **supped; sup·ping** : to take or drink in swallows or gulps

**²sup** *n* : a mouthful esp. of liquor or broth; *also* : a small quantity of liquid

**³sup** *vb* **supped; sup·ping** 1 : to eat the evening meal 2 : to make one's supper ⟨*supped* on roast beef⟩

**⁴sup** *abbr* 1 superior 2 supplement; supplementary 3 supply 4 supra

**¹su·per** \'sü-pər\ *adj* 1 : very fine : EXCELLENT 2 : EXTREME, EXCESSIVE ⟨∼ secrecy⟩

**²super** *n* : SUPERINTENDENT

**super-** \ˌsü-pər\ *prefix* 1 : over and above : higher in quantity, quality, or degree than : more than 2 : in addition : extra 3 : exceeding a norm 4 : in excessive degree or intensity 5 : surpassing all or most others of its kind 6 : situated above, on, or at the top of 7 : next above or higher 8 : more inclusive than 9 : superior in status or position

**su·per·abun·dant** \ˌsü-pər-ə-'bən-dənt\ *adj* : more than ample — **su·per·abun·dance** \-dəns\ *n*

**su·per·an·nu·ate** \ˌsü-pər-'an-yə-ˌwāt\ *vb* **-at·ed; -at·ing** 1 : to make out-of-date 2 : to retire and pension because of age or infirmity — **su·per·an·nu·at·ed** *adj*

**su·perb** \su̇-'pərb\ *adj* [L *superbus* excellent, proud, fr. *super* above] : marked to the highest degree by excellence, brilliance, or competence ♦ *Synonyms* RESPLENDENT, GLORIOUS, GORGEOUS, SUBLIME — **su·perb·ly** *adv*

**su·per·charg·er** \'sü-pər-ˌchär-jər\ *n* : a device for increasing the amount of air supplied to an internal combustion engine

**su·per·cil·ious** \ˌsü-pər-'si-lē-əs\ *adj* [L *superciliosus*, fr. *supercilium* eyebrow, haughtiness] : haughtily contemptuous ♦ *Synonyms* DISDAINFUL, OVERBEARING, ARROGANT, LORDLY, SUPERIOR

**su·per·com·put·er** \'sü-pər-kəm-ˌpyü-tər\ *n* : a large very fast mainframe

**su·per·con·duc·tiv·i·ty** \ˌsü-pər-ˌkän-ˌdək-'ti-və-tē\ *n* : a complete disappearance of electrical resistance in a substance esp. at very low temperatures — **su·per·con·duc·tive** \-kən-'dək-tiv\ *adj* — **su·per·con·duc·tor** \-'dək-tər\ *n*

**su·per·con·ti·nent** \'sü-pər-ˌkän-tə-nənt\ *n* : a former large continent from which other continents are held to have broken off and drifted away

**su·per·ego** \ˌsü-pər-'ē-gō\ *n* : the one of the three divisions of the psyche in psychoanalytic theory that functions to reward and punish through a system of moral attitudes, conscience, and a sense of guilt

**su·per·fi·cial** \ˌsü-pər-'fi-shəl\ *adj* 1 : of or relating to the surface or appearance only 2 : not thorough : SHALLOW ⟨a ∼

analysis⟩ — **su·per·fi·ci·al·i·ty** \-ˌfi-shē-'a-lə-tē\ *n* — **su·per·fi·cial·ly** *adv*

**su·per·flu·ous** \su̇-'pər-flə-wəs\ *adj* : exceeding what is sufficient or necessary : SURPLUS ⟨∼ details⟩ ♦ *Synonyms* EXTRA, SPARE, SUPERNUMERARY — **su·per·flu·i·ty** \ˌsü-pər-'flü-ə-tē\ *n*

**su·per·high·way** \ˌsü-pər-'hī-ˌwā\ *n* : a broad highway designed for high-speed traffic

**su·per·im·pose** \ˌsü-pər-im-'pōz\ *vb* : to lay (one thing) over or above something else

**su·per·in·tend** \ˌsü-pə-rin-'tend\ *vb* : to have or exercise the charge and oversight of : DIRECT ⟨∼ed the school system⟩ — **su·per·in·ten·dence** \-'ten-dəns\ *n* — **su·per·in·ten·den·cy** \-dən-sē\ *n* — **su·per·in·ten·dent** \-dənt\ *n*

**¹su·pe·ri·or** \su̇-'pir-ē-ər\ *adj* 1 : situated higher up, over, or near the top; *also* : higher in rank or numbers 2 : of greater value or importance 3 : courageously indifferent (as to pain or misfortune) 4 : better than most others of its kind 5 : ARROGANT, HAUGHTY — **su·pe·ri·or·i·ty** \-ˌpir-ē-'ȯr-ə-tē\ *n*

**²superior** *n* 1 : one who is above another in rank, office, or station; *esp* : the head of a religious house or order 2 : one higher in quality or merit

**¹su·per·la·tive** \su̇-'pər-lə-tiv\ *adj* 1 : of, relating to, or constituting the degree of grammatical comparison that denotes an extreme or unsurpassed level or extent 2 : surpassing others : SUPREME ♦ *Synonyms* PEERLESS, INCOMPARABLE, SUPERB — **su·per·la·tive·ly** *adv*

**²superlative** *n* 1 : the superlative degree or a superlative form in a language 2 : the utmost degree : ACME

**su·per·mar·ket** \'sü-pər-ˌmär-kət\ *n* : a self-service retail market selling foods and household merchandise

**su·per·mod·el** \'sü-pər-ˌmä-d°l\ *n* : a famous and successful fashion model

**su·per·mom** \'sü-pər-ˌmäm\ *n* : an exemplary mother; *also* : a woman who performs the duties of housekeeping and raising children while also having a full-time job

**su·per·nal** \su̇-'pər-nəl\ *adj* 1 : being or coming from on high 2 : of heavenly or spiritual character

**su·per·nat·u·ral** \ˌsü-pər-'na-chə-rəl\ *adj* : of or relating to phenomena beyond or outside of nature; *esp* : relating to or attributed to a divinity, ghost, or devil — **su·per·nat·u·ral·ly** *adv*

**su·per·no·va** \ˌsü-pər-'nō-və\ *n* : the explosion of a very large star

**¹su·per·nu·mer·ary** \ˌsü-pər-'nü-mə-ˌrer-ē, -'nyü-\ *adj* : exceeding the usual or required number : EXTRA ♦ *Synonyms* SURPLUS, SUPERFLUOUS, SPARE

**²supernumerary** *n, pl* **-ar·ies** : an extra

| | | | |
|---|---|---|---|
| superabsorbent | supercity | superheat | superindividual |
| superachiever | superclean | superheavy | superliner |
| superagency | superexpensive | superhero | superman |
| superblock | superfast | superhuman | supernormal |
| superbomb | superfine | superhumanly | |

person or thing; *esp* : an actor hired for a nonspeaking part

**su·per·pose** \ˌsü-pər-ˈpōz\ *vb* **-posed; -pos·ing** : SUPERIMPOSE — **su·per·po·si·tion** \-pə-ˈzi-shən\ *n*

**su·per·pow·er** \ˈsü-pər-ˌpaů(-ə)r\ *n* 1 : excessive or superior power 2 : one of a few politically and militarily dominant nations

**su·per·sat·u·rat·ed** \-ˈsa-chə-ˌrā-təd\ *adj* : containing an amount of a substance greater than that required for saturation

**su·per·scribe** \ˈsü-pər-ˌskrīb, ˌsü-pər-ˈskrīb\ *vb* **-scribed; -scrib·ing** : to write on the top or outside : ADDRESS — **su·per·scrip·tion** \ˌsü-pər-ˈskrip-shən\ *n*

**su·per·script** \ˈsü-pər-ˌskript\ *n* : a symbol (as a numeral or letter) written immediately above or above and to one side of another character

**su·per·sede** \ˌsü-pər-ˈsēd\ *vb* **-sed·ed; -sed·ing** [ME (Sc) *superceden* to defer, fr. MF *superceder*, fr. L *supersedēre* to be superior to, refrain from, fr. *super-* above + *sedēre* to sit] : to take the place of : REPLACE ⟨this edition *—s* the previous one⟩

**su·per·son·ic** \-ˈsä-nik\ *adj* 1 : ULTRASONIC 2 : being or relating to speeds from one to five times the speed of sound; *also* : capable of moving at such a speed ⟨a *~* airplane⟩

**su·per·sti·tion** \ˌsü-pər-ˈsti-shən\ *n* 1 : beliefs or practices resulting from ignorance, fear of the unknown, or trust in magic or chance 2 : an unreasoning fear of nature, the unknown, or God resulting from superstition — **su·per·sti·tious** \-shəs\ *adj*

**su·per·struc·ture** \ˈsü-pər-ˌstrək-chər\ *n* : something built on a base or as a vertical extension

**su·per·ti·tle** \ˈsü-pər-ˌtī-t²l\ *n* : a translation of foreign-language dialogue displayed above a screen or performance

**su·per·vene** \ˌsü-pər-ˈvēn\ *vb* **-vened; -ven·ing** : to occur as something additional or unexpected

**su·per·vise** \ˈsü-pər-ˌvīz\ *vb* **-vised; -vis·ing** : OVERSEE, SUPERINTEND — **su·per·vi·sion** \ˌsü-pər-ˈvi-zhən\ *n* — **su·per·vi·sor** \ˈsü-pər-ˌvī-zər\ *n* — **su·per·vi·so·ry** \ˌsü-pər-ˈvī-zə-rē\ *adj*

**su·pine** \sü-ˈpīn\ *adj* 1 : lying on the back or with the face upward 2 : LETHARGIC, SLUGGISH; *also* : ABJECT ⟨a *~* legislature⟩ ♦ **Synonyms** INACTIVE, INERT, PASSIVE, IDLE

**supp** *or* **suppl** *abbr* supplement; supplementary

**sup·per** \ˈsə-pər\ *n* : the evening meal esp. when dinner is taken at midday — **sup·per·time** \-ˌtīm\ *n*

**sup·plant** \sə-ˈplant\ *vb* 1 : to take the place of (another) esp. by force or trickery 2 : REPLACE

**sup·ple** \ˈsə-pəl\ *adj* **sup·pler; sup·plest** 1 : COMPLIANT, ADAPTABLE 2 : capable of bending without breaking or creasing : LIMBER ♦ **Synonyms** RESILIENT, ELASTIC, FLEXIBLE

¹**sup·ple·ment** \ˈsə-plə-mənt\ *n* 1 : something that supplies a want or makes an addition 2 : DIETARY SUPPLEMENT 3 : a continuation (as of a book) containing corrections or additional material — **sup·ple·men·tal** \ˌsə-plə-ˈmen-t²l\ *adj* — **sup·ple·men·ta·ry** \-ˈmen-tə-rē\ *adj*

²**sup·ple·ment** \ˈsə-plə-ˌment\ *vb* : to fill up the deficiencies of : add to — **sup·ple·men·ta·tion** \ˌsə-plə-ˌmen-ˈtā-shən, -mən-\ *n*

**sup·pli·ant** \ˈsə-plē-ənt\ *n* : one who supplicates : PETITIONER, PLEADER

**sup·pli·cant** \ˈsə-pli-kənt\ *n* : SUPPLIANT

**sup·pli·cate** \ˈsə-plə-ˌkāt\ *vb* **-cat·ed; -cat·ing** 1 : to make a humble entreaty; *esp* : to pray to God 2 : to ask earnestly and humbly : BESEECH ♦ **Synonyms** IMPLORE, BEG, ENTREAT, PLEAD — **sup·pli·ca·tion** \ˌsə-plə-ˈkā-shən\ *n*

¹**sup·ply** \sə-ˈplī\ *vb* **sup·plied; sup·ply·ing** [ME *supplien*, to complete, compensate for, fr. MF *souplier* fr. L *supplēre* to fill up, supplement, supply, fr. *sub-* under, up to + *plēre* to fill] 1 : to add as a supplement 2 : to satisfy the needs of 3 : FURNISH, PROVIDE — **sup·pli·er** *n*

²**supply** *n, pl* **supplies** 1 : the quantity or amount (as of a commodity) needed or available; *also* : PROVISIONS, STORES — usu. used in pl. 2 : the act or process of filling a want or need : PROVISION 3 : the quantities of goods or services offered for sale at a particular time or at one price

**sup·ply-side** \sə-ˈplī-ˌsīd\ *adj* : of, relating to, or being an economic theory that recommends the reduction of tax rates to expand economic activity

¹**sup·port** \sə-ˈpórt\ *vb* 1 : BEAR, TOLERATE 2 : to take sides with : BACK, ASSIST 3 : to provide with food, clothing, and shelter 4 : to hold up or serve as a foundation for ♦ **Synonyms** UPHOLD, ADVOCATE, CHAMPION — **sup·port·able** *adj* — **sup·port·er** *n* — **sup·port·ive** \-ˈpór-tiv\ *adj*

²**support** *n* 1 : the act of supporting : the state of being supported 2 : one that supports : PROP, BASE

**support group** *n* : a group of people with common experiences and concerns who provide emotional and moral support for one another

**sup·pose** \sə-ˈpōz\ *vb* **sup·posed; sup·pos·ing** 1 : to assume to be true (as for the sake of argument) 2 : EXPECT ⟨I am *supposed* to go⟩ 3 : to think probable ⟨I *~* so⟩ — **sup·pos·al** *n*

**sup·posed** \sə-'pōzd, -'pō-zəd\ *adj* : BE-LIEVED; *also* : mistakenly believed ⟨a ~ cure⟩ — **sup·pos·ed·ly** \-'pō-zəd-lē, -'pōzd-lē\ *adv*

**sup·pos·ing** *conj* : if by way of hypothesis : on the assumption that ⟨~ I did agree with you⟩

**sup·po·si·tion** \ˌsə-pə-'zi-shən\ *n* 1 : something that is supposed : HYPOTHESIS 2 : the act of supposing

**sup·pos·i·to·ry** \sə-'pä-zə-ˌtȯr-ē\ *n, pl* -ries [ME *suppositorie*, fr. AF, fr. ML *suppositorium*, fr. LL, neut. of *suppositorius* placed beneath] : a small easily melted mass of usu. medicated material for insertion (as into the rectum)

**sup·press** \sə-'pres\ *vb* 1 : to put down by authority or force : SUBDUE ⟨~ a revolt⟩ 2 : to keep from being known; *also* : to stop the publication or circulation of 3 : to hold back : REPRESS ⟨~ anger⟩ ⟨~ a cough⟩ — **sup·press·ible** \-'pre-sə-bəl\ *adj* — **sup·pres·sion** \-'pre-shən\ *n* — **sup·pres·sor** \-'pre-sər\ *n*

**sup·pres·sant** \sə-'pre-sᵊnt\ *n* : an agent (as a drug) suppressing rather than eliminating something ⟨a cough ~⟩

**sup·pu·rate** \'sə-pyə-ˌrāt\ *vb* -rat·ed; -rat·ing : to form or give off pus — **sup·pu·ra·tion** \ˌsə-pyə-'rā-shən\ *n*

**su·pra** \'sü-prə, -ˌprä\ *adv* : earlier in this writing : ABOVE

**su·pra·na·tion·al** \ˌsü-prə-'na-shə-nəl, -ˌprä-\ *adj* : going beyond national boundaries, authority, or interests ⟨~ organizations⟩

**su·prem·a·cist** \su̇-'pre-mə-sist\ *n* : an advocate of group supremacy

**su·prem·a·cy** \su̇-'pre-mə-sē\ *n, pl* -cies : supreme rank, power, or authority

**su·preme** \su̇-'prēm\ *adj* [L *supremus*, superl. of *superus* upper, fr. *super* over, above] 1 : highest in rank or authority 2 : highest in degree or quality ⟨~ among poets⟩ 3 : ULTIMATE ⟨the ~ sacrifice⟩ ♦ **Synonyms** SUPERLATIVE, SURPASSING, PEERLESS, INCOMPARABLE — **su·preme·ly** *adv* — **su·preme·ness** *n*

**Supreme Being** *n* : GOD 1

**supt** *abbr* superintendent

**sur·cease** \'sər-ˌsēs\ *n* : CESSATION, RESPITE ⟨a ~ from pain⟩

¹**sur·charge** \'sər-ˌchärj\ *vb* 1 : to fill to excess : OVERLOAD 2 : to apply a surcharge to (postage stamps)

²**surcharge** *n* 1 : an extra fee or cost 2 : an excessive load or burden 3 : something officially printed on a postage stamp esp. to change its value

**sur·cin·gle** \'sər-ˌsiŋ-gəl\ *n* : a band put around a horse's body to make something (as a saddle) fast

¹**sure** \'shu̇r\ *adj* **sur·er; sur·est** [ME, *seur, sure*, fr. AF *seur*, fr. L *securus* secure] 1 : firmly established 2 : TRUSTWORTHY, RELIABLE ⟨a ~ friend⟩ 3 : CONFIDENT ⟨I'm ~ I'm right⟩ 4 : not to be disputed : UNDOUBTED 5 : bound to happen 6 : careful to remember or attend to something ⟨be ~ to lock the door⟩ ♦ **Synonyms** CERTAIN, COCKSURE, POSITIVE — **sure·ness** *n*

²**sure** *adv* : SURELY

**sure·fire** \'shu̇r-'fī(-ə)r\ *adj* : certain to get results : DEPENDABLE

**sure·ly** \'shu̇r-lē\ *adv* 1 : in a sure manner 2 : without doubt 3 : INDEED, REALLY ⟨~, you don't believe that⟩

**sure·ty** \'shu̇r-ə-tē\ *n, pl* -ties 1 : SURENESS, CERTAINTY 2 : something that makes sure : GUARANTEE 3 : one who is a guarantor for another person

¹**surf** \'sərf\ *n* : waves that break upon the shore; *also* : the sound or foam of breaking waves

²**surf** *vb* 1 : to ride the surf (as on a surfboard) 2 : to scan the offerings of (as television or the Internet) for something of interest — **surf·er** *n* — **surf·ing** *n*

¹**sur·face** \'sər-fəs\ *n* 1 : the outside of an object or body 2 : outward aspect or appearance — **surface** *adj*

²**surface** *vb* **sur·faced; sur·fac·ing** 1 : to give a surface to : make smooth 2 : to rise to the surface

**surf·board** \'sərf-ˌbȯrd\ *n* : a buoyant board used in surfing

¹**sur·feit** \'sər-fət\ *n* 1 : EXCESS, SUPERABUNDANCE 2 : excessive indulgence (as in food or drink) 3 : disgust caused by excess

²**surfeit** *vb* : to feed, supply, or indulge to the point of surfeit : CLOY

**surg** *abbr* surgeon; surgery; surgical

¹**surge** \'sərj\ *vb* **surged; surg·ing** 1 : to rise and fall actively : TOSS 2 : to move in waves 3 : to rise suddenly to an excessive or abnormal value

²**surge** *n* 1 : a sweeping onward like a wave of the sea ⟨a ~ of emotion⟩ 2 : a large billow 3 : a transient sudden increase of current or voltage in an electrical circuit

**sur·geon** \'sər-jən\ *n* : a physician who specializes in surgery

**sur·gery** \'sər-jə-rē\ *n, pl* -ger·ies [ME *surgerie*, fr. AF *cirurgerie, surgerie*, fr. L *chirurgia*, fr. Gk *cheirourgia*, fr. *cheirourgos* surgeon, fr. *cheirourgos* doing by hand, fr. *cheir* hand + *ergon* work] 1 : a branch of medicine concerned with the correction of physical defects, the repair of injuries, and the treatment of disease esp. by operations 2 : a room or area where surgery is performed 3 : the work done by a surgeon

**sur·gi·cal** \'sər-ji-kəl\ *adj* : of, relating to, or associated with surgeons or surgery — **sur·gi·cal·ly** \-k(ə-)lē\ *adv*

**sur·ly** \'sər-lē\ *adj* **sur·li·er; -est** [alter. of ME *serreli* lordly, imperious, prob. fr. *sire, ser* sire] : having a rude unfriendly disposition ⟨a ~ customer⟩ ♦ **Synonyms** MOROSE, GLUM, SULLEN, SULKY, GLOOMY — **sur·li·ness** \-lē-nəs\ *n*

**sur·mise** \sər-'mīz\ *vb* **sur·mised; sur·mis·ing** : to form a notion of from scanty evidence ♦ **Synonyms** CONJECTURE, PRESUME, SUPPOSE — **surmise** *n*

**sur·mount** \sər-'maȯnt\ *vb* 1 : to prevail over : OVERCOME ⟨~ a problem⟩ 2 : to get to or lie at the top of

**sur·name** \'sər-ˌnām\ *n* 1 : NICKNAME 2

: the name borne in common by members of a family

**sur·pass** \sər-'pas\ *vb* **1** : to be superior to in quality, degree, or performance : EXCEL **2** : to go beyond the reach or powers of ♦ *Synonyms* TRANSCEND, OUTDO, OUTSTRIP, EXCEED — **sur·pass·ing·ly** *adv*

**sur·plice** \'sər-pləs\ *n* : a loose white outer vestment usu. of knee length

**sur·plus** \'sər-(,)pləs\ *n* **1** : quantity left over : EXCESS **2** : the excess of assets over liabilities ♦ *Synonyms* SUPERFLUITY, OVERABUNDANCE, SURFEIT

**¹sur·prise** \sər-'prīz\ *n* **1** : an attack made without warning **2** : a taking unawares **3** : something that surprises **4** : AMAZEMENT, ASTONISHMENT

**²surprise** *vb* **sur·prised; sur·pris·ing 1** : to come upon and attack unexpectedly **2** : to take unawares **3** : AMAZE ⟨his conduct *surprised* me⟩ **4** : to cause astonishment or surprise ⟨her success didn't ∼⟩ ♦ *Synonyms* ASTONISH, ASTOUND, DUMBFOUND — **sur·pris·ing** *adj*

**sur·pris·ing·ly** \-'prī-ziŋ-lē\ *adv* **1** : in a surprising manner or degree **2** : it is surprising that ⟨∼, voter turnout was high⟩

**sur·re·al** \sə-'rē-əl, -'rēl\ *adj* **1** : having the intense irrational reality of a dream **2** : of or relating to surrealism ⟨∼ art⟩ — **sur·re·al·ly** *adv*

**sur·re·al·ism** \sə-'rē-ə,li-zəm\ *n* : art, literature, or theater characterized by fantastic or incongruous imagery or effects produced by unnatural juxtapositions and combinations — **sur·re·al·ist** \-list\ *n or adj* — **sur·re·al·is·tic** \sə-,rē-ə-'lis-tik\ *adj* — **sur·re·al·is·ti·cal·ly** \-ti-k(ə-)lē\ *adv*

**¹sur·ren·der** \sə-'ren-dər\ *vb* **1** : to yield to the power of another : give up under compulsion **2** : RELINQUISH

**²surrender** *n* : the act of giving up or yielding oneself or the possession of something to another

**sur·rep·ti·tious** \,sər-əp-'ti-shəs\ *adj* : done, made, or acquired by stealth : CLANDESTINE ⟨a ∼ relationship⟩ ♦ *Synonyms* UNDERHAND, COVERT, FURTIVE — **sur·rep·ti·tious·ly** *adv*

**sur·rey** \'sər-ē\ *n, pl* **surreys** : a 2-seated horse-drawn carriage

**sur·ro·ga·cy** \'sər-ə-gə-sē\ *n* : SURROGATE MOTHERHOOD

**sur·ro·gate** \'sər-ə,gāt, -gət\ *n* **1** : DEPUTY, SUBSTITUTE **2** : a law officer in some states with authority in the probate of wills, the settlement of estates, and the appointment of guardians **3** : SURROGATE MOTHER

**surrogate mother** *n* : a woman who becomes pregnant (as by surgical implantation of a fertilized egg) in order to carry the fetus for another woman — **surrogate motherhood** *n*

**sur·round** \sə-'raůnd\ *vb* **1** : to enclose on all sides : ENCIRCLE **2** : to enclose so as to cut off retreat or escape

**sur·round·ings** \sə-'raůn-diŋz\ *n pl* : conditions by which one is surrounded

**surround sound** *n* : sound reproduction that uses three or more transmission channels

**sur·tax** \'sər-,taks\ *n* : an additional tax over and above a normal tax

**sur·tout** \(,)sər-'tü\ *n* [F, fr. *sur* over + *tout* all] : a man's long close-fitting overcoat

**surv** *abbr* survey; surveying; surveyor

**sur·veil·lance** \sər-'vā-ləns\ *n* [F] : close watch; *also* : SUPERVISION

**¹sur·vey** \sər-'vā\ *vb* **sur·veyed; sur·vey·ing** [ME, fr. AF *surveer* to look over, fr. *sur-* over + *veer* to see, fr. L *vidēre*] **1** : to look over and examine closely **2** : to find and represent the contours, measurements, and position of a part of the earth's surface (as a tract of land) **3** : to view or study something as a whole ♦ *Synonyms* SCRUTINIZE, EXAMINE, INSPECT, STUDY — **sur·vey·or** \-ər\ *n*

**²sur·vey** \'sər-,vā\ *n, pl* **surveys** : the act or an instance of surveying; *also* : something that is surveyed

**sur·viv·al·ism** \sər-'vī-və-,li-zəm\ *n* : an attitude, policy, or practice based on the primacy of survival as a value — **sur·viv·al·ist** \-və-list\ *n or adj*

**sur·vive** \sər-'vīv\ *vb* **sur·vived; sur·viv·ing 1** : to remain alive or existent **2** : OUTLIVE, OUTLAST — **sur·viv·al** *n* — **sur·vi·vor** \-'vī-vər\ *n*

**sus·cep·ti·ble** \sə-'sep-tə-bəl\ *adj* **1** : of such a nature as to permit ⟨words ∼ of being misunderstood⟩ **2** : having little resistance to a stimulus or agency ⟨∼ to colds⟩ **3** : IMPRESSIONABLE, RESPONSIVE ⟨a ∼ mind⟩ ♦ *Synonyms* SENSITIVE, SUBJECT, EXPOSED, PRONE, LIABLE, OPEN — **sus·cep·ti·bil·i·ty** \-,sep-tə-'bi-lə-tē\ *n*

**su·shi** \'sü-shē\ *n* [Jp] : cold rice formed into various shapes and garnished esp. with bits of raw fish or seafood

**¹sus·pect** \'səs-,pekt, sə-'spekt\ *adj* : regarded with suspicion; *also* : QUESTIONABLE ⟨his claim is ∼⟩

**²sus·pect** \'səs-,pekt\ *n* : one who is suspected (as of a crime)

**³sus·pect** \sə-'spekt\ *vb* **1** : to have doubts of : MISTRUST **2** : to imagine to be guilty without proof **3** : SURMISE

**sus·pend** \sə-'spend\ *vb* **1** : to bar temporarily from a privilege, office, or function **2** : to stop temporarily : make inactive for a time **3** : to withhold (judgment) for a time **4** : HANG; *esp* : to hang so as to be free except at one point **5** : to put or hold in suspension **6** : to keep from falling or sinking by some invisible support

**sus·pend·er** \sə-'spen-dər\ *n* : one of two supporting straps which pass over the shoulders and to which the pants are fastened

**sus·pense** \sə-'spens\ *n* **1** : SUSPENSION **2** : mental uncertainty : ANXIETY **3** : excitement as to an outcome — **sus·pense·ful** *adj*

**sus·pen·sion** \sə-'spen-chən\ *n* **1** : the act of suspending : the state or period of being suspended **2** : the state of a substance when its particles are mixed with but undissolved in a fluid or solid; *also* : a substance in this state **3** : something suspended **4** : the system of devices supporting the upper part of a vehicle on the axles

**sus·pen·so·ry** \sə-'spen-sə-rē\ *adj* **1** : SUSPENDED; *also* : fitted or serving to suspend something **2** : temporarily leaving undetermined

**sus·pi·cion** \sə-'spi-shən\ *n* **1** : the act or an instance of suspecting something wrong without proof **2** : TRACE, SOUPÇON ⟨a ~ of garlic⟩ ♦ *Synonyms* MISTRUST, UNCERTAINTY, DOUBT, SKEPTICISM

**sus·pi·cious** \sə-'spi-shəs\ *adj* **1** : open to or arousing suspicion **2** : inclined to suspect **3** : showing suspicion ⟨is ~ of strangers⟩ — **sus·pi·cious·ly** *adv*

**sus·tain** \sə-'stān\ *vb* **1** : to provide with nourishment **2** : to keep going : PROLONG ⟨~ed effort⟩ **3** : to hold up : PROP **4** : to hold up under : ENDURE **5** : SUFFER ⟨a broken arm⟩ **6** : to support as true, legal, or valid ⟨the objection was ~ed⟩ **7** : PROVE, CORROBORATE — **sus·tain·able** \səs-'tā-nə-bəl\ *adj*

**sus·te·nance** \'səs-tə-nəns\ *n* **1** : FOOD, NOURISHMENT **2** : a supplying with the necessities of life **3** : something that sustains or supports

**su·ture** \'sü-chər\ *n* **1** : material or a stitch for sewing a wound together **2** : a seam or line along which two things or parts are joined by or as if by sewing

**SUV** \es-,yü-'vē\ *n* [*sport-utility vehicle*] : a vehicle similar to a station wagon but built on a light-truck chassis

**su·ze·rain** \'sü-zə-rən, -,rān\ *n* [F] **1** : a feudal lord **2** : a nation that has political control over the foreign relations of another nation — **su·ze·rain·ty** \-tē\ *n*

**svc** *or* **svce** *abbr* service

**svelte** \'sfelt\ *adj* **svelt·er; svelt·est** [F, fr. It *svelto*, fr. pp. of *svellere* to pluck out, modif. of L *evellere*, fr. *e-* out + *vellere* to pluck] : SLENDER, LITHE ⟨a ~ figure⟩

**svgs** *abbr* savings

**SW** *abbr* **1** shortwave **2** southwest

**¹swab** \'swäb\ *n* **1** : MOP **2** : a wad of absorbent material esp. for applying medicine or for cleaning; *also* : a sample taken with a swab **3** : SAILOR

**²swab** *vb* **swabbed; swab·bing** : to use a swab on : MOP

**swad·dle** \'swä-d⁰l\ *vb* **swad·dled; swad·dling 1** : to bind (an infant) in bands of cloth **2** : to wrap up : SWATHE

**swaddling clothes** *n pl* : bands of cloth wrapped around an infant

**swag** \'swag\ *n* : stolen goods : LOOT

**swag·ger** \'swa-gər\ *vb* **1** : to walk with a conceited swing or strut **2** : BOAST, BRAG — **swagger** *n*

**Swa·hi·li** \swä-'hē-lē\ *n* : a language that is a trade and governmental language over much of eastern Africa and the Congo region

**swain** \'swān\ *n* [ME *swein* boy, servant, fr. ON *sveinn*] **1** : RUSTIC; *esp* : SHEPHERD **2** : ADMIRER, SUITOR

**SWAK** *abbr* sealed with a kiss

**¹swal·low** \'swä-lō\ *n* : any of numerous small long-winged migratory birds that often have a deeply forked tail

**²swallow** *vb* **1** : to take into the stomach through the throat **2** : to envelop or take in as if by swallowing **3** : to accept or believe without question, protest, or anger

**³swallow** *n* **1** : an act of swallowing **2** : an amount that can be swallowed at one time

**swal·low·tail** \'swä-lō-,tāl\ *n* **1** : a deeply forked and tapering tail like that of a swallow **2** : TAILCOAT **3** : any of various large butterflies with the border of each hind wing usu. drawn out into a process resembling a tail — **swal·low–tailed** \-,tāld\ *adj*

**swam** *past of* SWIM

**swa·mi** \'swä-mē\ *n* [Hindi *svāmī*, fr. Skt *svāmin* owner, lord] : a Hindu ascetic or religious teacher

**¹swamp** \'swämp\ *n* : a spongy wetland — **swamp** *adj* — **swampy** *adj*

**²swamp** *vb* **1** : to fill or become filled with or as if with water **2** : OVERWHELM **3**

**swamp·land** \-,land\ *n* : SWAMP

**swan** \'swän\ *n, pl* **swans** *also* **swan** : any of various heavy-bodied long-necked mostly pure white swimming birds related to the geese

**¹swank** \'swaŋk\ *or* **swanky** \'swaŋ-kē\ *adj* **swank·er** *or* **swank·i·er; -est** : showily smart and dashing; *also* : fashionably elegant ⟨a ~ hotel⟩

**²swank** *n* **1** : PRETENTIOUSNESS **2** : ELEGANCE

**swans·down** \'swänz-,daun\ *n* **1** : the very soft down of a swan used esp. for trimming **2** : a soft thick cotton flannel

**swan song** *n* : a farewell appearance, act, or pronouncement

**swap** \'swäp\ *vb* **swapped; swap·ping** : TRADE, EXCHANGE — **swap** *n*

**sward** \'sword\ *n* : the grassy surface of land

**¹swarm** \'sworm\ *n* **1** : a great number of honeybees leaving together from a hive with a queen to start a new colony; *also* : a hive of bees **2** : a large crowd

**²swarm** *vb* **1** : to form in a swarm and depart from a hive **2** : to throng together : gather in great numbers

**swart** \'swort\ *adj* : SWARTHY

**swar·thy** \'swor-thē, -thē\ *adj* **swar·thi·er; -est** : dark in color or complexion : dark-skinned

**swash** \'swäsh\ *vb* : to move about with a splashing sound — **swash** *n*

**swash·buck·ler** \-,bə-klər\ *n* : a swaggering or daring soldier or adventurer — **swash·buck·ling** *adj*

**swas·ti·ka** \'swäs-ti-kə\ *n* [Skt *svastika*, fr. *svasti* well-being, fr. *su-* well + *as-* to be] : a symbol or ornament in the form of a cross with the ends of the arms bent at right angles

**swat** \'swät\ *vb* **swat·ted; swat·ting** : to hit sharply ⟨~ a fly⟩ ⟨~ a ball⟩ — **swat** *n* — **swat·ter** *n*

**SWAT** *abbr* Special Weapons and Tactics

**swatch** \'swäch\ *n* : a sample piece (as of fabric) or a collection of samples

**swath** \'swäth, 'swȯth\ *or* **swathe** \'swäth, 'swȯth, 'swāth\ *n* [ME, fr. OE *swæth* footstep, trace] **1** : a row of cut grass or grain **2** : the sweep of a scythe or mowing machine or the path cut in mowing

**swathe** \'swäth, 'swȯth, 'swāth\ *vb* **swathed; swath·ing** : to bind or wrap with or as if with a bandage

**¹sway** \'swā\ *n* **1** : a gentle swinging from side to side **2** : controlling influence or power : DOMINION

**²sway** *vb* **1** : to swing gently from side to side **2** : RULE, GOVERN **3** : to cause to swing from side to side **4** : BEND, SWERVE; *also* : INFLUENCE ⟨tried to ~ the jury⟩ ♦ *Synonyms* OSCILLATE, FLUCTUATE, VIBRATE, WAVER

**sway·backed** \'swā-,bakt\ *also* **sway·back** \-,bak\ *adj* : having an abnormally sagging back ⟨a ~ mare⟩ — **swayback** *n*

**swear** \'swer\ *vb* **swore** \'swȯr\; **sworn** \'swȯrn\; **swear·ing 1** : to make a solemn statement or promise under oath **2** : to assert or promise emphatically or earnestly **3** : to administer an oath to **4** : to bind by or as if by an oath **5** : to use profane or obscene language — **swear·er** *n*

**swear in** *vb* : to induct into office by administering of an oath

**sweat** \'swet\ *vb* **sweat** *or* **sweat·ed; sweat·ing 1** : to excrete salty moisture from glands of the skin : PERSPIRE **2** : to form drops of moisture on the surface **3** : to work so that one sweats : TOIL **4** : to cause to sweat **5** : to draw out or get rid of by or as if by sweating **6** : to make a person overwork — **sweat** *n* — **sweaty** *adj*

**sweat·er** \'swe-tər\ *n* **1** : one that sweats **2** : a knitted or crocheted jacket or pullover

**sweat·shirt** \'swet-,shərt\ *n* : a loose collarless pullover or jacket usu. of heavy cotton jersey

**sweat·shop** \'swet-,shäp\ *n* : a shop or factory in which workers are employed for long hours at low wages and under unhealthy conditions

**Swed** *abbr* Sweden

**swede** \'swēd\ *n* **1** *cap* : a native or inhabitant of Sweden **2** *chiefly Brit* : RUTABAGA

**Swed·ish** \'swē-dish\ *n* **1** : the language of Sweden **2 Swedish** *pl* : the people of Sweden — **Swedish** *adj*

**¹sweep** \'swēp\ *vb* **swept** \'swept\; **sweep·ing 1** : to remove or clean by or as if by brushing **2** : to destroy completely; *also* : to remove or take with a single swift movement **3** : to remove from sight or consideration **4** : to move over with speed and force ⟨the tide *swept* over the shore⟩ **5** : to win in an overwhelming victory in; *also* : to win all the games or contests of **6** : to move or extend in a wide curve — **sweep·er** *n*

**²sweep** *n* **1** : something (as a long oar) that operates with a sweeping motion **2** : a clearing off or away **3** : a winning of all the contests or prizes in a competition **4** : a sweeping movement **5** : CURVE, BEND **6** : RANGE, SCOPE

**sweeping** *adj* : EXTENSIVE ⟨~ reforms⟩; *also* : indiscriminately inclusive ⟨~ generalities⟩

**sweep·ings** \'swē-piŋz\ *n pl* : things collected by sweeping

**sweep–sec·ond hand** \'swēp-,se-kənd-\ *n* : a hand marking seconds on a timepiece

**sweep·stakes** \'swēp-,stāks\ *also* **sweep·stake** \-,stāk\ *n, pl* **sweepstakes 1** : a race or contest in which the entire prize may go to the winner **2** : any of various lotteries

**¹sweet** \'swēt\ *adj* **1** : being or causing the one of the four basic taste sensations that is caused esp. by table sugar and is identified esp. by the taste buds at the front of the tongue; *also* : pleasing to the taste **2** : AGREEABLE ⟨how ~ it is⟩ **3** : pleasing to a sense other than taste ⟨a ~ smell⟩ ⟨~ music⟩ **4** : not stale or spoiled : WHOLESOME ⟨~ milk⟩ **5** : not salted ⟨~ butter⟩ — **sweet·ish** *adj* — **sweet·ly** *adv* — **sweet·ness** *n*

**²sweet** *n* **1** : something sweet : CANDY **2** : DARLING

**sweet·bread** \'swēt-,bred\ *n* : the pancreas or thymus of an animal (as a calf or lamb) used for food

**sweet·bri·ar** *or* **sweet·bri·er** \-,brī-ər\ *n* : a thorny Old World rose with fragrant white to deep pink flowers

**sweet clover** *n* : any of a genus of erect legumes widely grown for soil improvement or hay

**sweet corn** *n* : corn of a variety having soft kernels containing a high percentage of sugar

**sweet·en** \'swē-tᵊn\ *vb* **sweet·ened; sweet·en·ing** : to make sweet — **sweet·en·er** *n* — **sweet·en·ing** *n*

**sweet·heart** \'swēt-,härt\ *n* : one who is loved

**sweet·meat** \-,mēt\ *n* : CANDY 1

**sweet pea** *n* : a garden plant of the legume family with climbing stems and fragrant flowers of many colors; *also* : its flower

**sweet pepper** *n* : any of various large mild thick-walled fruits of a pepper; *also* : a plant bearing sweet peppers

**sweet potato** *n* : a tropical vine related to the morning glory; *also* : its large sweet edible root

**sweet–talk** \'swēt-,tȯk\ *vb* : FLATTER, COAX — **sweet talk** *n*

**sweet tooth** *n* : a craving or fondness for sweet food

**sweet wil·liam** \,swēt-'wil-yəm\ *n, often cap W* : a widely cultivated Old World pink with small white to deep red or purple flowers often showily spotted, banded, or mottled

**¹swell** \'swel\ *vb* **swelled; swelled** *or* **swol·len** \'swō-lən\; **swell·ing 1** : to grow big or make bigger **2** : to expand or distend abnormally or excessively ⟨a *swollen* joint); *also* : BULGE **3** : to fill or be filled with emotion (as pride) ◆ *Synonyms* EXPAND, AMPLIFY, DISTEND, INFLATE, DILATE — **swell·ing** *n*

²**swell** *n* **1** : a long crestless wave or series of waves in the open sea **2** : the condition of being protuberant **3** : a person dressed in the height of fashion; *also* : a person of high social position

³**swell** *adj* **1** : STYLISH; *also* : socially prominent **2** : EXCELLENT (a ~ party)

**swelled head** *n* : an exaggerated opinion of oneself : SELF-CONCEIT

**swel·ter** \'swel-tər\ *vb* [ME *sweltren*, fr. *swelten* to die, be overcome by heat, fr. OE *sweltan* to die] **1** : to be faint or oppressed with the heat **2** : to become exceedingly hot — **swel·ter·ing** \-tə-riŋ\ *adj*

**swept** *past and past part of* SWEEP

**swerve** \'swərv\ *vb* **swerved; swerv·ing** : to move abruptly aside from a straight line or course — **swerve** *n*

¹**swift** \'swift\ *adj* **1** : moving or capable of moving with great speed **2** : occurring suddenly **3** : READY, ALERT (~ for vengeance) — **swift·ly** *adv* — **swift·ness** *n*

²**swift** *n* : any of numerous small insect-eating birds with long narrow wings

**swig** \'swig\ *vb* **swigged; swig·ging** : to drink in long drafts — **swig** *n*

¹**swill** \'swil\ *vb* **1** : to swallow greedily : GUZZLE **2** : to feed (as hogs) on swill

²**swill** *n* **1** : food for animals composed of edible refuse mixed with liquid **2** : GARBAGE

¹**swim** \'swim\ *vb* **swam** \'swam\; **swum** \'swəm\; **swim·ming** **1** : to propel oneself along in water by natural means (as by hands and legs, by tail, or by fins) **2** : to glide smoothly along **3** : FLOAT **4** : to be covered with or as if with a liquid **5** : to be dizzy (his head *swam*) **6** : to cross or go over by swimming (*swam* the river) — **swim·mer** *n*

²**swim** *n* **1** : an act of swimming **2** : the main current of activity (in the ~)

**swim·ming** *n* : the action, art, or sport of swimming and diving

**swimming pool** *n* : a tank (as of concrete or plastic) designed for swimming

**swim·suit** \'swim-ˌsüt\ *n* : a suit for swimming or bathing

**swim·wear** \'swim-ˌwer\ *n* : clothing for wear while swimming or bathing

**swin·dle** \'swin-dᵊl\ *vb* **swin·dled; swin·dling** [fr. *swindler*, fr. G *Schwindler* giddy person, fr. *schwindeln* to be dizzy] : CHEAT, DEFRAUD — **swindle** *n* — **swin·dler** *n*

**swine** \'swin\ *n, pl* **swine** **1** : any of a family of stout short-legged hoofed mammals with bristly skin and a long flexible snout; *esp* : one widely raised as a meat animal **2** : a contemptible person — **swin·ish** *adj*

¹**swing** \'swiŋ\ *vb* **swung** \'swəŋ\; **swing·ing** **1** : to move or cause to move rapidly in an arc **2** : to sway or cause to sway back and forth **3** : to hang so as to move freely back and forth or in a curve **4** : to be executed by hanging **5** : to move or

turn on a hinge or pivot **6** : to manage or handle successfully **7** : to march or walk with free swaying movements **8** : to have a steady pulsing rhythm; *also* : to play swing music **9** : to be lively and up-to-date; *also* : to engage freely in sex ◆ *Synonyms* WIELD, MANIPULATE, PLY, MANEUVER — **swing·er** *n* — **swing·ing** *adj*

²**swing** *n* **1** : the act of swinging **2** : a swinging blow, movement, or rhythm **3** : the distance through which something swings : FLUCTUATION **4** : progression of an activity or process (in full ~) **5** : a seat suspended by a rope or chain for swinging back and forth for pleasure **6** : jazz music played esp. by a large band and marked by a steady lively rhythm, simple harmony, and a basic melody often submerged in improvisation

³**swing** *adj* **1** : of or relating to musical swing **2** : that may swing decisively either way (as on an issue) (~ voters)

¹**swipe** \'swīp\ *n* : a strong sweeping blow

²**swipe** *vb* **swiped; swip·ing** **1** : to strike or wipe with a sweeping motion **2** : PILFER, SNATCH **3** : to slide (a card having a magnetic code) through a reading device

**swirl** \'swərl\ *vb* : to move or cause to move with a whirling motion — **swirl** *n* — **swirly** \'swər-lē\ *adj*

**swish** \'swish\ *n* **1** : a prolonged hissing sound **2** : a light sweeping or brushing sound — **swish** *vb*

**Swiss** \'swis\ *n* **1** *pl* **Swiss** : a native or inhabitant of Switzerland **2** : a hard cheese with large holes — **Swiss** *adj*

**Swiss chard** *n* : a beet having large leaves and succulent stalks often cooked as a vegetable

¹**switch** \'swich\ *n* **1** : a slender flexible whip, rod, or twig **2** : a blow with a switch **3** : a shift from one thing to another; *also* : change from the usual **4** : a device for adjusting the rails of a track so that a locomotive or train may be turned from one track to another; *also* : a railroad siding **5** : a device for making, breaking, or changing the connections in an electrical circuit **6** : a heavy strand of hair often used in addition to a person's own hair for some coiffures

²**switch** *vb* **1** : to punish or urge on with a switch **2** : WHISK (a cow ~*ing* her tail) **3** : to shift or turn by operating a switch **4** : CHANGE, EXCHANGE

**switch·back** \'swich-ˌbak\ *n* : a zigzag road, trail, or section of railroad tracks for climbing a steep hill

**switch·blade** \-ˌblād\ *n* : a pocket-knife with a spring-operated blade

**switch·board** \-ˌbȯrd\ *n* : a panel for controlling the operation of a number of electric circuits; *esp* : one used to make and break telephone connections

**switch-hit·ter** \-'hi-tər\ *n* : a baseball player who bats either right-handed or left-handed — **switch-hit** \-'hit\ *vb*

**switch·man** \'swich-mən\ *n* : one who attends a railroad switch

**Switz** *abbr* Switzerland

¹**swiv·el** \\'swi-vəl\\ n : a device joining two parts so that one or both can turn freely

²**swivel** vb -eled or -elled; -el·ing or -el·ling : to swing or turn on or as if on a swivel

**swiv·et** \\'swi-vət\\ n : an agitated state

**swiz·zle stick** \\'swi-zəl-\\ n : a stick used to stir mixed drinks

**swollen** past part of SWELL

**swoon** \\'swün\\ vb : FAINT — swoon n

**swoop** \\'swüp\\ vb : to move with a sweep ⟨the eagle ∼ed down on its prey⟩ — swoop n

**swoopy** \\'swü-pē\\ adj : having lines that extend in a wide curve ⟨a ∼ silhouette⟩

**swop** chiefly Brit var of SWAP

**sword** \\'sórd\\ n 1 : a weapon with a long blade for cutting or thrusting 2 : the use of force

**sword·fish** \\-,fish\\ n : a very large ocean fish used for food that has the upper jaw prolonged into a long swordlike beak

**sword·play** \\-,plā\\ n : the art or skill of wielding a sword

**swords·man** \\'sórdz-mən\\ n : one skilled in swordplay; esp : FENCER

**sword·tail** \\'sórd-,tāl\\ n : a small brightly marked Central American fish often kept in aquariums

**swore** past of SWEAR

**sworn** past part of SWEAR

**swum** past part of SWIM

**swung** past and past part of SWING

**syb·a·rite** \\'si-bə-,rīt\\ n : a lover of luxury : VOLUPTUARY — **syb·a·rit·ic** \\,si-bə-ˈri-tik\\ adj

**syc·a·more** \\'si-kə-,mòr\\ n : a large spreading tree chiefly of the eastern and central U.S. that has light brown flaky bark and small round fruits hanging on long stalks

**sy·co·phant** \\'si-kə-fənt\\ n : a servile flatterer — **sy·co·phan·cy** \\'si-kə-fən-sē\\ n — **sy·co·phan·tic** \\,si-kə-ˈfan-tik\\ adj

**syl** or **syll** abbr syllable

**syl·lab·i·ca·tion** \\,sə-,la-bə-ˈkā-shən\\ n : the division of words into syllables

**syl·lab·i·fy** \\sə-ˈla-bə-,fī\\ vb -fied; -fy·ing : to form or divide into syllables — **syl·lab·i·fi·ca·tion** \\-,la-bə-fə-ˈkā-shən\\ n

**syl·la·ble** \\'si-lə-bəl\\ n [ME, fr. AF sillabe, silable, fr. L syllaba, fr. Gk syllabē, fr. syllambanein to gather together, fr. syn- with + lambanein to take] : a unit of spoken language consisting of an uninterrupted utterance and forming either a whole word (as cat) or a commonly recognized division of a word (as syl in syl·la-ble); also : one or more letters representing such a unit — **syl·lab·ic** \\sə-ˈla-bik\\ adj

**syl·la·bus** \\'si-lə-bəs\\ n, pl -bi \\-,bī\\ or -bus·es : a summary containing the heads or main topics of a speech, book, or course of study

**syl·lo·gism** \\'si-lə-,ji-zəm\\ n : a logical scheme of a formal argument consisting of a major and a minor premise and a conclusion which must logically be true if the premises are true — **syl·lo·gis·tic** \\,si-lə-ˈjis-tik\\ adj

**sylph** \\'silf\\ n 1 : an imaginary being inhabiting the air 2 : a slender graceful woman

**syl·van** \\'sil-vən\\ adj 1 : living or located in a wooded area; also : of, relating to, or characteristic of forest 2 : abounding in woods or trees

**sym** abbr 1 symbol 2 symmetrical

**sym·bi·o·sis** \\,sim-,bī-ˈō-səs, -bē-\\ n, pl -o·ses \\-,sēz\\ : the living together in close association of two dissimilar organisms esp. when mutually beneficial — **sym·bi·ot·ic** \\-ˈä-tik\\ adj

**sym·bol** \\'sim-bəl\\ n 1 : something that stands for something else; esp : something concrete that represents or suggests another thing that cannot in itself be pictured ⟨the lion is a ∼ of bravery⟩ 2 : a letter, character, or sign used in writing or printing to represent operations, quantities, elements, sounds, or other ideas — **sym·bol·ic** \\sim-ˈbä-lik\\ also **sym·bol·i·cal** \\-li-kəl\\ adj — **sym·bol·i·cal·ly** \\-k(ə-)lē\\ adv

**sym·bol·ise** Brit var of SYMBOLIZE

**sym·bol·ism** \\'sim-bə-,li-zəm\\ n : representation of abstract or intangible things by means of symbols

**sym·bol·ize** \\'sim-bə-,līz\\ vb -ized; -iz·ing 1 : to serve as a symbol of 2 : to represent by symbols — **sym·bol·i·za·tion** \\,sim-bə-lə-ˈzā-shən\\ n

**sym·me·try** \\'si-mə-trē\\ n, pl -tries 1 : an arrangement marked by regularity and balanced proportions 2 : correspondence in size, shape, and position of parts that are on opposite sides of a dividing line or center — **sym·met·ri·cal** \\sə-ˈme-tri-kəl\\ or **sym·met·ric** \\sə-ˈme-trik\\ adj — **sym·met·ri·cal·ly** \\-k(ə-)lē\\ adv

**sympathetic nervous system** n : the part of the autonomic nervous system that is concerned esp. with the body's response to stress and that tends to decrease the tone and contractility of smooth muscle and increase blood pressure and the activity of the heart

**sym·pa·thise** chiefly Brit var of SYMPATHIZE

**sym·pa·thize** \\'sim-pə-,thīz\\ vb -thized; -thiz·ing : to feel or show sympathy — **sym·pa·thiz·er** n

**sym·pa·thy** \\'sim-pə-thē\\ n, pl -thies 1 : a relationship between persons or things wherein whatever affects one similarly affects the other 2 : harmony of interests and aims 3 : FAVOR, SUPPORT 4 : the capacity for entering into and sharing the feelings or interests of another; also : COMPASSION, PITY 5 : an expression of sorrow for another's loss, grief, or misfortune — **sym·pa·thet·ic** \\,sim-pə-ˈthe-tik\\ adj — **sym·pa·thet·i·cal·ly** \\-ti-k(ə-)lē\\ adv

**sym·pho·ny** \\'sim-fə-nē\\ n, pl -nies 1 : harmony of sounds 2 : a large and complex composition for a full orchestra 3 : a large orchestra of a kind that plays symphonies — **sym·phon·ic** \\sim-ˈfä-nik\\ adj

**sym·po·sium** \\sim-ˈpō-zē-əm\\ n, pl -sia \\-zē-ə\\ or -siums : a conference at which a particular topic is discussed by various speakers; *also* : a collection of opinions about a subject

**symp·tom** \'simp-təm\ *n* [LL *symptoma*, fr. Gk *symptōma* happening, attribute, symptom, fr. *sympiptein* to happen, fr. *syn-* with + *piptein* to fall] **1** : something that indicates the presence of disease or abnormality; *esp* : something (as a headache) that can be sensed only by the individual affected **2** : SIGN, INDICATION ⟨∼s of inner turmoil⟩ — **symp·tom·at·ic** \,simp-tə-'ma-tik\ *adj*

**syn** *abbr* synonym; synonymous; synonymy

**syn·a·gogue** *also* **syn·a·gog** \'si-nə-,gäg\ *n* [ME *synagoge*, fr. AF, fr. LL *synagoga*, fr. Gk *synagōgē* assembly, synagogue, fr. *synagein* to bring together] **1** : a Jewish congregation **2** : the house of worship of a Jewish congregation

**syn·apse** \'si-,naps, sə-'naps\ *n* : the point at which a nervous impulse passes from one neuron to another — **syn·ap·tic** \sə-'nap-tik\ *adj*

**¹sync** *also* **synch** \'siŋk\ *vb* **synced** *also* **synched** \'siŋkt\; **sync·ing** *also* **synch·ing** \'siŋ-kiŋ\ : SYNCHRONIZE

**²sync** *also* **synch** *n* : SYNCHRONIZATION, SYNCHRONISM — **sync** *adj*

**syn·chro·ni·sa·tion, syn·chro·nise** *Brit var of* SYNCHRONIZATION, SYNCHRONIZE

**syn·chro·nize** \'siŋ-krə-,nīz, 'sin-\ *vb* **-nized; -niz·ing 1** : to occur or cause to occur at the same instant **2** : to represent, arrange, or tabulate according to dates or time **3** : to cause to agree in time **4** : to make synchronous in operation — **syn·chro·nism** \-,ni-zəm\ *n* — **syn·chro·ni·za·tion** \,siŋ-krə-nə-'zā-shən, ,sin-\ *n* — **syn·chro·niz·er** *n*

**syn·chro·nous** \'siŋ-krə-nəs, 'sin-\ *adj* **1** : happening at the same time : CONCURRENT **2** : working, moving, or occurring together at the same rate and at the proper time

**syn·co·pa·tion** \,siŋ-kə-'pā-shən, ,sin-\ *n* : a shifting of the regular musical accent : occurrence of accented notes on the weak beat — **syn·co·pate** \'siŋ-kə-,pāt, 'sin-\ *vb*

**syn·co·pe** \'siŋ-kə-(,)pē, 'sin-\ *n* : the loss of one or more sounds or letters in the interior of a word (as in *fo'c'sle* for *forecastle*)

**¹syn·di·cate** \'sin-di-kət\ *n* **1** : a group of persons who combine to carry out a financial or industrial undertaking **2** : a loose association of racketeers **3** : a business concern that sells materials for publication in many newspapers and periodicals at the same time

**²syn·di·cate** \-də-,kāt\ *vb* **-cat·ed; -cat·ing 1** : to combine into or manage as a syndicate **2** : to publish through a syndicate — **syn·di·ca·tion** \,sin-də-'kā-shən\ *n*

**syn·drome** \'sin-,drōm\ *n* : a group of signs and symptoms that occur together and characterize a particular abnormality or condition

**syn·er·gism** \'sin-ər-,ji-zəm\ *n* : interaction of discrete agencies (as industrial firms), agents (as drugs), or conditions such that the total effect is greater than the sum of the individual effects — **syn·er·gist** \-jist\ *n* — **syn·er·gis·tic** \,si-nər-'jis-tik\ *adj* — **syn·er·gis·ti·cal·ly** \-ti-k(ə-)lē\ *adv*

**syn·er·gy** \'si-nər-jē\ *n, pl* **-gies** : SYNERGISM

**syn·fuel** \'sin-,fyül\ *n* [*synthetic*] : a fuel derived esp. from a fossil fuel

**syn·od** \'si-nəd\ *n* **1** : COUNCIL, ASSEMBLY; *esp* : a religious governing body — **syn·od·al** \-nə-d°l, -,nä-d°l\ *adj* — **syn·od·ic** \sə-'nä-dik\ *or* **syn·od·i·cal** \-di-kəl\ *adj*

**syn·onym** \'si-nə-,nim\ *n* : one of two or more words in the same language which have the same or very nearly the same meaning — **syn·on·y·mous** \sə-'nä-nə-məs\ *adj* — **syn·on·y·mous·ly** *adv* — **syn·on·y·my** \-mē\ *n*

**syn·op·sis** \sə-'näp-səs\ *n, pl* **-op·ses** \-,sēz\ : a condensed statement or outline (as of a treatise) : ABSTRACT

**syn·op·tic** \sə-'näp-tik\ *also* **syn·op·ti·cal** \-ti-kəl\ *adj* : characterized by or affording a comprehensive view

**syn·tax** \'sin-,taks\ *n* : the way in which words are put together to form phrases, clauses, or sentences — **syn·tac·tic** \sin-'tak-tik\ *or* **syn·tac·ti·cal** \-ti-kəl\ *adj*

**syn·the·sis** \'sin-thə-səs\ *n, pl* **-the·ses** \-,sēz\ : the combination of parts or elements into a whole; *esp* : the production of a substance by union of chemically simpler substances — **syn·the·size** \-,sīz\ *vb* — **syn·the·siz·er** *n*

**syn·thet·ic** \sin-'the-tik\ *adj* : produced artificially esp. by chemical means; *also* : not genuine — **synthetic** *n* — **syn·thet·i·cal·ly** \-ti-k(ə-)lē\ *adv*

**syph·i·lis** \'si-fə-ləs\ *n* [NL, fr. *Syphilus*, hero of the poem *Syphilis sive Morbus Gallicus* (*Syphilis or the French disease*) (1530) by Girolamo Fracastoro †1553 Ital. physician] : an infectious usu. venereal disease caused by a spirochete — **syph·i·lit·ic** \,si-fə-'li-tik\ *adj or n*

**syphon** *var of* SIPHON

**Sy·rah** \sē-'rä\ *n* : a red wine

**¹sy·ringe** \sə-'rinj\ *n* : a device used esp. for injecting liquids into or withdrawing them from the body

**²syringe** *vb* **sy·ringed; sy·ring·ing** : to flush or cleanse with or as if with a syringe

**syr·up** *also* **sir·up** \'sər-əp, 'sir-əp\ *n* **1** : a thick sticky solution of sugar and water often flavored or medicated **2** : the concentrated juice of a fruit or plant — **syr·upy** *adj*

**syst** *abbr* system

**sys·tem** \'sis-təm\ *n* **1** : a group of units so combined as to form a whole and to operate in unison **2** : the body as a functioning whole; *also* : a group of bodily organs (as the nervous system) that together carry on some vital function **3** : a definite scheme or method of procedure or classification **4** : regular method or order — **sys·tem·at·ic** \,sis-tə-'ma-tik\ — **sys·tem·at·i·cal·ly** \-ti-k(ə-)lē\ *adv*

**sys·tem·a·tise** Brit var of SYSTEMATIZE

**sys·tem·a·tize** \'sis-tə-mə-ˌtīz\ vb **-tized;**
**-tiz·ing** : to make into a system : arrange
methodically

¹**sys·tem·ic** \sis-'te-mik\ adj **1** : of, relating
to, or affecting the whole body ⟨~ dis-
ease⟩ **2** : of, relating to, or being a pesticide that when absorbed into the sap or
bloodstream makes the entire plant or animal toxic to a pest (as an insect or fungus)

²**systemic** n : a systemic pesticide

**systemic lupus er·y·the·ma·to·sus** \ˌer-
ə-ˌthē-mə-'tō-səs\ n : a systemic disease
esp. of women characterized by fever,
skin rash, and arthritis, often by anemia,
by small hemorrhages of the skin and
mucous membranes, and in serious cases
by involvement of internal organs

**sys·tem·ize** \'sis-tə-ˌmīz\ vb **-ized; -iz-**
**ing** : SYSTEMATIZE

**systems analyst** n : a person who studies a procedure or business to determine
its goals or purposes and to discover the
best ways to accomplish them — **sys-**
**tems analysis** n

**sys·to·le** \'sis-tə-(ˌ)lē\ n : a rhythmically
recurrent contraction of the heart —
**sys·tol·ic** \sis-'tä-lik\ adj

¹**t** \'tē\ n, pl **t's** or **ts** \'tēz\ often cap : the
20th letter of the English alphabet

²**t** abbr, often cap **1** tablespoon **2** teaspoon
**3** temperature **4** ton **5** transitive **6** troy
**7** true

**T** abbr **1** toddler **2** T-shirt

**Ta** symbol tantalum

**TA** abbr teaching assistant

¹**tab** \'tab\ n **1** : a short projecting flap,
loop, or tag; also : a small insert or addition **2** : close surveillance : WATCH ⟨keep
~s on him⟩ **3** : BILL, CHECK **4** : a key
on a keyboard esp. for putting data in
columns

²**tab** vb **tabbed; tab·bing** : DESIGNATE

**tab·by** \'ta-bē\ n, pl **tabbies** : a usu.
striped or mottled domestic cat; also : a
female domestic cat

**tab·er·na·cle** \'ta-bər-ˌna-kəl\ n [ME, fr.
AF, fr. LL tabernaculum, fr. L, tent, fr.
taberna hut] **1** often cap : a tent sanctu-
ary used by the Israelites during the Exodus **2** : a receptacle for the consecrated
elements of the Eucharist **3** : a house of
worship

¹**ta·ble** \'tā-bəl\ n **1** : TABLET 1 **2** : a piece
of furniture consisting of a smooth flat
top fixed on legs **3** : a supply of food
: BOARD, FARE **4** : a group of people assembled at or as if at a table **5** : an orderly arrangement of data usu. in rows
and columns **6** : a short list ⟨~ of con-
tents⟩ — **ta·ble·top** \-ˌtäp\ n

²**table** vb **ta·bled; ta·bling 1** Brit : to place
on the agenda **2** : to remove (a parliamentary motion) from consideration indefinitely

**tab·leau** \'ta-ˌblō\ n, pl **tab·leaux** \-ˌblōz\
also **tableaus** [F] : a scene or event usu.
presented on a stage by silent and motionless costumed participants

**ta·ble·cloth** \'tā-bəl-ˌklȯth\ n : a covering
spread over a dining table before the table is set

**ta·ble d'hôte** \ˌtä-bəl-'dōt\ n [F, lit., host's
table] : a complete meal of several courses offered at a fixed price

**ta·ble·land** \'tā-bəl-ˌland\ n : PLATEAU

**ta·ble·spoon** \-ˌspün\ n **1** : a large spoon
used esp. for serving **2** : a unit of measure equal to ½ fluid ounce (15 milliliters)

**ta·ble·spoon·ful** \-ˌfúl\ n, pl **-spoonfuls**
\-ˌfúlz\ also **-spoons·ful** \-ˌspünz-ˌfúl\
: TABLESPOON 2

**tab·let** \'ta-blət\ n **1** : a flat slab suited for
or bearing an inscription **2** : a collection
of sheets of paper glued together at one
edge **3** : a compressed or molded block
of material; esp : a usu. disk-shaped medicated mass

**table tennis** n : a game resembling tennis
played on a tabletop with wooden paddles and a small hollow plastic ball

**ta·ble·ware** \'tā-bəl-ˌwer\ n : utensils (as
of china or silver) for table use

¹**tab·loid** \'ta-ˌblȯid\ adj : condensed into
small scope

²**tabloid** n : a newspaper marked by small
pages, condensation of the news, and
usu. many photographs

¹**ta·boo** also **ta·bu** \tə-'bü, ta-\ adj [Tongan
(a Polynesian language) tabu] : prohibited by a taboo

²**taboo** also **tabu** n, pl **taboos** also **tabus**
**1** : a prohibition against touching, saying,
or doing something for fear of immediate
harm from a supernatural force **2** : a
prohibition imposed by social custom

**ta·bor** also **ta·bour** \'tā-bər\ n : a small
drum used to accompany a pipe or fife
played by the same person

**tab·u·lar** \'ta-byə-lər\ adj **1** : having a flat
surface **2** : arranged in a table; esp : set
up in rows and columns **3** : computed by
means of a table

**tab·u·late** \-ˌlāt\ vb **-lat·ed; -lat·ing** : to
put into tabular form — **tab·u·la·tion**
\ˌta-byə-'lā-shən\ n — **tab·u·la·tor** \'ta-
byə-ˌlā-tər\ n

**TAC** \'tak\ abbr Tactical Air Command

**tach** \'tak\ n : TACHOMETER

**ta·chom·e·ter** \ta-'kä-mə-tər, tə-\ n [ul-
tim. fr. Gk tachos speed] : a device to indicate speed of rotation

**tachy·car·dia** \ˌta-ki-'kär-dē-ə\ n : relatively rapid heart action

**tachy·on** \'ta-kē-ˌän\ *n* : a hypothetical particle held to travel faster than light

**tac·it** \'ta-sət\ *adj* [F or L; F *tacite*, fr. L *tacitus* silent, fr. *tacēre* to be silent] **1** : expressed without words or speech **2** : implied or indicated but not actually expressed ⟨~ consent⟩ — **tac·it·ly** *adv* — **tac·it·ness** *n*

**tac·i·turn** \'ta-sə-ˌtərn\ *adj* : disinclined to talk ✦ *Synonyms* UNCOMMUNICATIVE, RESERVED, RETICENT, CLOSEMOUTHED — **tac·i·tur·ni·ty** \ˌta-sə-'tər-nə-tē\ *n*

**¹tack** \'tak\ *vb* **1** : to fasten with tacks; *also* : to add on **2** : to change the direction of (a sailing ship) from one tack to another **3** : to follow a zigzag course

**²tack** *n* **1** : a small sharp nail with a broad flat head **2** : the direction toward the wind that a ship is sailing ⟨starboard ~⟩; *also* : the run of a ship on one tack **3** : a change of course from one tack to another **4** : a zigzag course **5** : a course of action

**³tack** *n* : gear for harnessing a horse

**¹tack·le** \'ta-kəl, *naut often* 'tā-\ *n* **1** : GEAR, APPARATUS, EQUIPMENT **2** : the rigging of a ship **3** : an arrangement of ropes and pulleys for hoisting or pulling heavy objects **4** : the act or an instance of tackling; *also* : a football lineman playing between guard and end

**²tackle** *vb* **tack·led; tack·ling 1** : to attach and secure with or as if with tackle **2** : to seize, grapple with, or throw down with the intention of subduing or stopping **3** : to set about dealing with ⟨~ a problem⟩ — **tack·ler** *n*

**¹tacky** \'ta-kē\ *adj* **tack·i·er; -est** : sticky to the touch

**²tacky** *adj* **tack·i·er; -est 1** : SHABBY, SEEDY **2** : marked by lack of style or good taste; *also* : cheaply showy ⟨a ~ publicity stunt⟩ ⟨a ~ outfit⟩

**ta·co** \'tä-kō\ *n, pl* **tacos** \-kōz\ [MexSp] : a usu. fried tortilla rolled up with or folded over a filling

**tact** \'takt\ *n* [F, sense of touch, fr. L *tactus*, fr. *tangere* to touch] : a keen sense of what to do or say to keep good relations with others ⟨a diplomat with ~⟩ — **tact·ful** \-fəl\ *adj* — **tact·ful·ly** *adv* — **tact·less** *adj* — **tact·less·ly** *adv*

**tac·tic** \'tak-tik\ *n* : a planned action for accomplishing an end

**tac·tics** \'tak-tiks\ *n sing or pl* **1** : the science of maneuvering forces in combat **2** : the skill of using available means to accomplish an end — **tac·ti·cal** \-ti-kəl\ *adj* — **tac·ti·cian** \tak-'ti-shən\ *n*

**tac·tile** \'tak-tᵊl, 'tak-ˌtī(-ə)l\ *adj* : of, relating to, or perceptible through the sense of touch

**tad·pole** \'tad-ˌpōl\ *n* [ME *taddepol*, fr. *tode* toad + *polle* head] : an aquatic larva of a frog or toad that has a tail and gills

**tae kwon do** \'tī-'kwän-'dō\ *n* : a Korean martial art of self-defense

**taf·fe·ta** \'ta-fə-tə\ *n* : a crisp lustrous fabric (as of silk or rayon)

**taff·rail** \'taf-ˌrāl, -rəl\ *n* : the rail around a ship's stern

**taf·fy** \'ta-fē\ *n, pl* **taffies** : a candy usu. of molasses or brown sugar stretched until porous and light-colored

**¹tag** \'tag\ *n* **1** : a metal or plastic binding on an end of a shoelace **2** : a piece of hanging or attached material **3** : a hackneyed quotation or saying **4** : a descriptive or identifying epithet

**²tag** *vb* **tagged; tag·ging 1** : to provide or mark with or as if with a tag; *esp* : IDENTIFY **2** : to attach as an addition **3** : to follow closely and persistently ⟨~s along everywhere we go⟩ **4** : to hold responsible for something

**³tag** *n* : a game in which one player chases others and tries to touch one of them

**⁴tag** *vb* **tagged; tag·ging 1** : to touch in or as if in a game of tag **2** : SELECT

**TAG** *abbr* the adjutant general

**tag sale** *n* : GARAGE SALE

**Ta·hi·tian** \tə-'hē-shən\ *n* **1** : a native or inhabitant of Tahiti **2** : the Polynesian language of the Tahitians — **Tahitian** *adj*

**tai·ga** \'tī-gə\ *n* [Russ *taiga*] : a moist coniferous subarctic forest extending south from the tundra

**¹tail** \'tāl\ *n* **1** : the rear end or a process extending from the rear end of an animal **2** : something resembling an animal's tail **3** *pl* : full evening dress for men **4** : the back, last, lower, or inferior part of something; *esp* : the reverse of a coin — usu. used in pl. ⟨~s, I win⟩ **5** : one who follows or keeps watch on someone — **tailed** \'tāld\ *adj* — **tail·less** \'tāl-ləs\ *adj*

**²tail** *vb* : FOLLOW; *esp* : to follow for the purpose of surveillance

**tail·coat** \-'kōt\ *n* : a coat with tails; *esp* : a man's full-dress coat with two long tapering skirts at the back

**¹tail·gate** \-ˌgāt\ *n* : a board or gate at the back end of a vehicle that can be let down (as for loading)

**²tailgate** *vb* **tail·gat·ed; tail·gat·ing 1** : to drive dangerously close behind another vehicle **2** : to hold a tailgate picnic

**³tailgate** *adj* : relating to or being a picnic set up on a tailgate ⟨a ~ party⟩

**tail·light** \-ˌlīt\ *n* : a usu. red warning light mounted at the rear of a vehicle

**¹tai·lor** \'tā-lər\ *n* [ME *taillour*, fr. AF *taillur*, fr. *tailler* to cut, fr. LL *taliare*, fr. L *talea* twig, cutting] : a person whose occupation is making or altering garments

**²tailor** *vb* **1** : to make or fashion as the work of a tailor **2** : to make or adapt to suit a special purpose

**tail·pipe** \'tāl-ˌpīp\ *n* : an outlet by which engine exhaust gases are expelled from a vehicle (as an automobile)

**tail·spin** \'tāl-ˌspin\ *n* : a rapid descent or downward spiral

**tail·wind** \'tāl-ˌwind\ *n* : a wind blowing in the same general direction as a course of movement (as of an aircraft)

**¹taint** \'tānt\ *vb* **1** : CORRUPT, CONTAMINATE **2** : to affect or become affected with something bad (as putrefaction)

**²taint** *n* : a contaminating mark or influence

**ta·ka** \'tä-kə\ *n* — see MONEY table

**take** \'tāk\ *vb* **took** \'tuk\; **tak·en** \'tā-kən\; **tak·ing** [ME, fr. OE *tacan*, fr. ON

# take • tamale

*taka*] **1** : to get into one's hands or possession : GRASP, SEIZE **2** : CAPTURE; *also* : DEFEAT **3** : to obtain or secure for use **4** : to catch or attack through the effect of a sudden force or influence ⟨*taken* ill⟩ **5** : CAPTIVATE, DELIGHT **6** : to bring into a relation ⟨∼ a wife⟩ **7** : REMOVE, SUBTRACT ⟨∼ three from eight⟩ **8** : to pick out : CHOOSE **9** : ASSUME, UNDERTAKE **10** : RECEIVE, ACCEPT **11** : to use for transportation ⟨∼ a bus⟩ **12** : to become impregnated with : ABSORB ⟨∼s a dye⟩ **13** : to receive into one's body (as by swallowing) ⟨∼ a pill⟩ **14** : ENDURE, UNDERGO ⟨∼ a cut in pay⟩ **15** : to lead, carry, or cause to go along to another place **16** : NEED, REQUIRE ⟨∼s a size nine shoe⟩ **17** : to obtain as the result of a special procedure ⟨∼ a snapshot⟩ **18** : to undertake and do, make, or perform ⟨∼ a walk⟩ **19** : to take effect : ACT, OPERATE ♦ *Synonyms* GRAB, CLUTCH, SNATCH, SEIZE, NAB, GRAPPLE — **tak·er** *n* — **take advantage of 1** : to profit by **2** : EXPLOIT — **take after** : RESEMBLE — **take care** : to be careful — **take care of** : to attend to — **take effect** : to become operative — **take exception** : OBJECT — **take for** : to suppose to be; *esp* : to mistake for — **take place** : HAPPEN — **take to 1** : to go to **2** : to apply or devote oneself to **3** : to conceive a liking for

**²take** *n* **1** : the number or quantity taken; *also* : PROCEEDS, RECEIPTS **2** : an act or the action of taking **3** : a television or movie scene filmed or taped at one time; *also* : a sound recording made at one time **4** : a distinct or personal point of view

**take·off** \'tāk-ˌȯf\ *n* **1** : IMITATION; *esp* : PARODY ⟨did a ∼ of the president⟩ **2** : an act or instance of taking off

**take off** *vb* **1** : REMOVE **2** : DEDUCT **3** : to set out : go away **4** : to begin flight

**take on** *vb* **1** : to begin to perform or deal with; *also* : to contend with as an opponent **2** : ENGAGE, HIRE **3** : to assume or acquire as or as if one's own **4** : to make an unusual show of one's feelings esp. of grief or anger

**take over** *vb* : to assume control or possession of or responsibility for ⟨*took over* the company⟩ — **take·over** \'tāk-ˌō-vər\ *n*

**take up** *vb* **1** : PICK UP **2** : to begin to occupy (land) **3** : to absorb or incorporate into itself ⟨plants *taking up* nutrients⟩ **4** : to begin to engage in ⟨*took up* jogging⟩ **5** : to make tighter or shorter ⟨*take up* the slack⟩

**tak·ings** \'tā-kiŋz\ *n pl, chiefly Brit* : receipts esp. of money

**ta·la** \'tä-lə\ *n, pl* tala — see MONEY table

**talc** \'talk\ *n* : a soft mineral with a soapy feel used esp. in making a soothing powder (**tal·cum powder** \'tal-kəm-\) for the skin

**tale** \'tāl\ *n* **1** : a relation of a series of events **2** : a report of a confidential matter **3** : idle talk; *esp* : harmful gossip **4** : a usu. imaginative narrative **5** : FALSEHOOD **6** : COUNT, TALLY

**tal·ent** \'ta-lənt\ *n* **1** : an ancient unit of

weight and value **2** : the natural endowments of a person **3** : a special often creative or artistic aptitude **4** : mental power : ABILITY **5** : a person of talent ♦ *Synonyms* GENIUS, GIFT, FACULTY, APTITUDE, KNACK — **tal·ent·ed** *adj*

**ta·ler** \'tä-lər\ *n* : any of numerous silver coins issued by German states from the 15th to the 19th centuries

**tales·man** \'tālz-mən\ *n* : a person summoned for jury duty

**tal·is·man** \'ta-ləs-mən, -ləz-\ *n, pl* **-mans** [F *talisman* or Sp *talismán* or It *talismano*, fr. Ar *tilsam*, fr. MGk *telesma*, fr. Gk, consecration, fr. *telein* to initiate into the mysteries, complete, fr. *telos* end] : an object thought to act as a charm

**¹talk** \'tȯk\ *vb* **1** : to express in speech : utter words : SPEAK **2** : DISCUSS ⟨∼ business⟩ **3** : to influence or cause by talking ⟨∼ed him into going⟩ **4** : to use (a language) for communicating **5** : CONVERSE **6** : to reveal confidential information; *also* : GOSSIP **7** : to give a talk : LECTURE — **talk·er** *n* — **talk back** : to answer impertinently

**²talk** *n* **1** : the act of talking **2** : a way of speaking **3** : a formal discussion **4** : REPORT, RUMOR **5** : the topic of comment or gossip ⟨the ∼ of the town⟩ **6** : an informal address or lecture

**talk·ative** \'tȯ-kə-tiv\ *adj* : given to talking ♦ *Synonyms* LOQUACIOUS, CHATTY, GABBY, GARRULOUS — **talk·ative·ly** *adv* — **talk·ative·ness** *n*

**talk·ing-to** \'tȯ-kiŋ-ˌtü\ *n* : REPRIMAND, REPROOF

**talk radio** *n* : radio programming consisting of call-in shows

**tall** \'tȯl\ *adj* **1** : high in stature; *also* : of a specified height ⟨six feet ∼⟩ **2** : LARGE, FORMIDABLE ⟨a ∼ order⟩ **3** : UNBELIEVABLE, IMPROBABLE ⟨a ∼ story⟩ — **tall·ness** *n*

**tal·low** \'ta-lō\ *n* : a hard white fat rendered usu. from cattle or sheep tissues and used esp. in candles

**¹tal·ly** \'ta-lē\ *n, pl* **tallies 1** : a device for visibly recording or accounting esp. business transactions **2** : a recorded account **3** : a corresponding part; *also* : CORRESPONDENCE

**²tally** *vb* **tal·lied; tal·ly·ing 1** : to mark on or as if on a tally **2** : to make a count of : RECKON; *also* : SCORE **3** : CORRESPOND, MATCH ♦ *Synonyms* SQUARE, ACCORD, HARMONIZE, CONFORM, JIBE

**tal·ly·ho** \ˌta-lē-ˈhō\ *n, pl* **-hos** : a call of a huntsman at sight of the fox

**Tal·mud** \'täl-ˌmud, 'tal-məd\ *n* [Late Heb *talmūdh*, lit., instruction] : the authoritative body of Jewish tradition — **Tal·mu·dic** \tal-ˈmü-dik, -ˈmyü-, -ˈmə-; täl-ˈmu-\ *adj* — **Tal·mud·ist** \'täl-ˌmu-dist, 'tal-mə-\ *n*

**tal·on** \'ta-lən\ *n* : the claw of an animal and esp. of a bird of prey

**ta·lus** \'tā-ləs, 'ta-\ *n* : rock debris at the base of a cliff

**tam** \'tam\ *n* : TAM-O'-SHANTER

**ta·ma·le** \tə-ˈmä-lē\ *n* [MexSp *tamales*, pl. of *tamal* tamale, fr. Nahuatl *tamalli* steamed cornmeal dough] : ground meat seasoned with chili, rolled in cornmeal dough, wrapped in corn husks, and steamed

**tam·a·rack** \'ta-mə-ˌrak\ n : a larch of northern No. America; also : its hard resinous wood

**tam·a·rin** \'ta-mə-rən\ n : any of several small So. American monkeys related to the marmosets

**tam·a·rind** \'ta-mə-rənd, -ˌrind\ n [Sp & Pg tamarindo, fr. Ar tamr hindī, lit., Indian date] : a tropical tree of the legume family with hard yellowish wood and feathery leaves; also : its acid fruit

**tam·ba·la** \täm-'bä-lə\ n, pl -la or -las — see kwacha at MONEY table

**tam·bou·rine** \ˌtam-bə-'rēn\ n : a small shallow drum with loose disks at the sides played by shaking or striking with the hand

**¹tame** \'tām\ adj tam·er; tam·est 1 : reduced from a state of native wildness esp. so as to be useful to humans : DOMESTICATED 2 : made docile : SUBDUED 3 : lacking spirit or interest : INSIPID ♦ Synonyms SUBMISSIVE, DOMESTIC, DOMESTICATED — tame·ly adv — tameness n

**²tame** vb tamed; tam·ing 1 : to make or become tame; also : to subject (land) to cultivation 2 : HUMBLE, SUBDUE — tam·able or tame·able \'tā-mə-bəl\ adj — tame·less adj — tam·er n

**tam-o'-shan·ter** \'ta-mə-ˌshan-tər\ n [fr. poem Tam o' Shanter (1790) by Robert Burns †1796 Scot. poet] : a Scottish woolen cap with a wide flat circular crown and usu. a pom-pom in the center

**ta·mox·i·fen** \tə-'mäk-sə-ˌfen\ n : a drug used esp. to treat breast cancer

**tamp** \'tamp\ vb : to drive down or in by a series of light blows

**tam·per** \'tam-pər\ vb 1 : to carry on underhand negotiations (as by bribery) ⟨~ with a witness⟩ 2 : to interfere so as to weaken or change for the worse ⟨~ with a document⟩ 3 : to try foolish or dangerous experiments

**tam·pon** \'tam-ˌpän\ n [F, lit., plug] : a plug (as of cotton) introduced into a body cavity usu. to absorb secretions (as from menstruation) or to arrest bleeding

**¹tan** \'tan\ vb tanned; tan·ning 1 : to change (hide) into leather esp. by soaking in a liquid containing tannin 2 : to make or become brown (as by exposure to the sun) 3 : WHIP, THRASH

**²tan** n 1 : a brown skin color induced by sun or weather 2 : a light yellowish brown color

**³tan** abbr tangent

**tan·a·ger** \'ta-ni-jər\ n : any of numerous American birds that are often brightly colored

**tan·bark** \'tan-ˌbärk\ n : bark (as of oak or sumac) that is rich in tannin and used in tanning

**¹tan·dem** \'tan-dəm\ n [L, at last, at length (taken to mean "lengthwise"), fr. tam so] 1 : a 2-seated carriage with horses hitched tandem; also : its team 2 : a bicycle for

two persons sitting one behind the other — **in tandem** : in a tandem arrangement

**²tandem** adv : one behind another

**³tandem** adj 1 : consisting of things arranged one behind the other 2 : working in conjunction with each other

**tang** \'taŋ\ n 1 : a part in a tool that connects the blade with the handle 2 : a sharp distinctive flavor; also : a pungent odor — **tangy** adj

**¹tan·gent** \'tan-jənt\ adj [L tangent-, tangens, prp. of tangere to touch] : TOUCHING; esp : touching a circle or sphere at only one point

**²tangent** n 1 : the trigonometric function that is the ratio between the side opposite and the side adjacent to an acute angle in a right triangle 2 : a tangent line, curve, or surface 3 : an abrupt change of course

**tan·gen·tial** \tan-'jen-chəl\ adj 1 : TANGENT 2 : touching lightly : INCIDENTAL ⟨~ involvement⟩ — **tan·gen·tial·ly** adv

**tan·ger·ine** \'tan-jə-ˌrēn, ˌtan-jə-'rēn\ n : a deep orange loose-skinned citrus fruit; also : a tree that bears tangerines

**¹tan·gi·ble** \'tan-jə-bəl\ adj 1 : perceptible esp. by the sense of touch : PALPABLE 2 : substantially real : MATERIAL ⟨~ rewards⟩ 3 : capable of being appraised ⟨~ assets⟩ ♦ Synonyms APPRECIABLE, PERCEPTIBLE, SENSIBLE, DISCERNIBLE — **tan·gi·bil·i·ty** \ˌtan-jə-'bi-lə-tē\ n

**²tangible** n : something tangible; esp : a tangible asset

**¹tan·gle** \'taŋ-gəl\ vb tan·gled; tan·gling 1 : to involve so as to hamper or embarrass; also : ENTRAP 2 : to unite or knit together in intricate confusion : ENTANGLE

**²tangle** n 1 : a tangled twisted mass 2 : a confusedly complicated state : MUDDLE

**tan·go** \'taŋ-gō\ n, pl tangos : a dance of Latin-American origin — **tango** vb

**tank** \'taŋk\ n 1 : a large artificial receptacle for liquids 2 : a heavily armed and armored combat vehicle that moves on tracks — **tank·ful** n

**tan·kard** \'taŋ-kərd\ n : a tall one-handled drinking vessel

**tank·er** \'taŋ-kər\ n : a vehicle equipped for transporting a liquid

**tank top** n : a sleeveless collarless pullover shirt with shoulder straps

**tank town** n : a small town

**tan·ner** \'ta-nər\ n : one that tans hides

**tan·nery** \'ta-nə-rē\ n, pl -ner·ies : a place where tanning is carried on

**tan·nic acid** \'ta-nik-\ n : TANNIN

**tan·nin** \'ta-nən\ n : any of various plant substances used esp. in tanning and dyeing, in inks, and as astringents

**tan·sy** \'tan-zē\ n, pl tansies : a common weedy herb related to the daisies with an aromatic odor and bitter-tasting finely divided leaves

**tan·ta·lise** Brit var of TANTALIZE

**tan·ta·lize** \'tan-tə-ˌlīz\ vb -lized; -liz·ing [fr. Tantalus, king of Greek myth punished in Hades by having to stand up to his chin in water that receded as he bent to drink] : to tease or torment by presenting something desirable but keeping it out of reach — **tan·ta·liz·er** *n* — **tan·ta·liz·ing·ly** *adv*

**tan·ta·lum** \'tan-tə-ləm\ *n* : a gray-white ductile metallic chemical element

**tan·ta·mount** \'tan-tə-ˌmaůnt\ *adj* : equivalent in value or meaning ⟨a relationship ~ to marriage⟩

**tan·trum** \'tan-trəm\ *n* : a fit of bad temper

**Tao·ism** \'taů-ˌi-zəm, 'daů-\ *n* : a Chinese mystical philosophy; *also* : a religion developed from Taoist philosophy and Buddhism — **Tao·ist** \-ist\ *adj or n*

¹**tap** \'tap\ *n* **1** : FAUCET, COCK **2** : liquor drawn through a tap **3** : the removing of fluid from a container or cavity by tapping **4** : a tool for forming an internal screw thread **5** : a point in an electric circuit where a connection may be made

²**tap** *vb* **tapped; tap·ping 1** : to release or cause to flow by piercing or by drawing a plug from a container or cavity **2** : to pierce so as to let out or draw off a fluid **3** : to draw from ⟨~ resources⟩ **4** : to cut in on (as a telephone signal) to get information **5** : to form an internal screw thread in by means of a tap **6** : to connect (as a gas or water main) with a local supply — **tap·per** *n*

³**tap** *vb* **tapped; tap·ping 1** : to rap lightly **2** : to bring about by repeated light blows **3** : SELECT; *esp* : to elect to membership

⁴**tap** *n* **1** : a light blow or stroke; *also* : its sound **2** : a small metal plate for the sole or heel of a shoe

**ta·pa** \'tä-pə, 'ta-\ *n* [Sp, lit., cover, lid] : an hors d'oeuvre served with drinks esp. in Spanish bars — usu. used in pl.

¹**tape** \'tāp\ *n* **1** : a narrow flexible band or strip (as of woven fabric) **2** : MAGNETIC TAPE; *also* : CASSETTE

²**tape** *vb* **taped; tap·ing 1** : to fasten or support with tape **2** : to record on magnetic tape

**tape deck** *n* : a device used to play back cassette tapes that usu. has to be connected to an audio system

**tape measure** *n* : a tape marked off in units (as inches) for measuring

¹**ta·per** \'tā-pər\ *n* **1** : a slender wax candle; *also* : a long waxed wick **2** : a gradual lessening of thickness or width in a long object

²**taper** *vb* **ta·pered; ta·per·ing 1** : to make or become gradually smaller toward one end **2** : to diminish gradually

**tape–re·cord** \ˌtāp-ri-'kȯrd\ *vb* : to make a recording of on magnetic tape — **tape recorder** *n* — **tape recording** *n*

**tap·es·try** \'ta-pə-strē\ *n, pl* **-tries** : a heavy reversible textile that has designs or pictures woven into it and is used esp. as a wall hanging

**tape·worm** \'tāp-ˌwərm\ *n* : any of a class of long flat segmented worms parasitic esp. in vertebrate intestines

**tap·i·o·ca** \ˌta-pē-'ō-kə\ *n* : a usu. granular preparation of cassava starch used esp. in puddings; *also* : a dish (as pudding) that contains tapioca

**ta·pir** \'tā-pər\ *n, pl* **tapirs** *also* **tapir** [Pg *tapir, tapira*, fr. Tupinambà (American Indian language of Brazil)] *tapiʔíra*] : any of a genus of large herbivorous hoofed mammals of tropical America and southeastern Asia

**tap·pet** \'ta-pət\ *n* : a lever or projection moved by some other piece (as a cam) or intended to move something else

**tap·room** \'tap-ˌrüm, -ˌrům\ *n* : BARROOM

**tap·root** \-ˌrüt, -ˌrůt\ *n* : a large main root growing straight down and giving off small side roots

**taps** \'taps\ *n sing or pl* : the last bugle call at night blown as a signal that lights are to be put out; *also* : a similar call blown at military funerals and memorial services

**tap·ster** \'tap-stər\ *n* : BARTENDER

¹**tar** \'tär\ *n* **1** : a thick dark sticky liquid distilled from organic material (as wood or coal) **2** : SAILOR, SEAMAN

²**tar** *vb* **tarred; tar·ring** : to cover or smear with or as if with tar

**tar·an·tel·la** \ˌtä-rən-'te-lə\ *n* : a lively folk dance of southern Italy in 6/8 time

**ta·ran·tu·la** \tə-'ran-chə-lə, -tə-lə\ *n, pl* **tarantulas** *also* **ta·ran·tu·lae** \-'ran-chə-ˌlē, -tə-ˌlē\ : any of a family of large hairy American spiders with a sharp bite that is not very poisonous to human beings

**tar·dy** \'tär-dē\ *adj* **tar·di·er; -est 1** : moving slowly : SLUGGISH **2** : LATE ⟨was ~ to work⟩ ♦ **Synonyms** BEHINDHAND, OVERDUE, BELATED — **tar·di·ly** \-də-lē\ *adv* — **tar·di·ness** \-dē-nəs\ *n*

¹**tare** \'ter\ *n* : a weed of grain fields

²**tare** *n* : a deduction from the gross weight of a substance and its container made in allowance for the weight of the container — **tare** *vb*

¹**tar·get** \'tär-gət\ *n* [ME, fr. MF *targette*, dim. of *targe* light shield, of Gmc origin] **1** : a mark to shoot at **2** : an object of ridicule or criticism **3** : a goal to be achieved

²**target** *vb* : to make a target of

**tar·iff** \'ta-rəf\ *n* [It *tariffa*, fr. Ar *ta'rīf* notification] **1** : a schedule of duties imposed by a government esp. on imported goods; *also* : a duty or rate of duty imposed in such a schedule **2** : a schedule of rates or charges

**tar·mac** \'tär-ˌmak\ *n* : a surface paved with crushed stone covered with tar

**tarn** \'tärn\ *n* : a small mountain lake

**tar·nish** \'tär-nish\ *vb* : to make or become dull or discolored — **tarnish** *n*

**ta·ro** \'tär-ō, 'ter-\ *n, pl* **taros** : a large-leaved tropical plant related to the arums that is grown for its edible starchy corms; *also* : its corms

**tar·ot** \'ter-ō, 'ta-rō\ *n* : one of a set of usu. 78 playing cards used esp. for fortune-telling

**tar·pau·lin** \tär-'pȯ-lən, 'tär-pə-\ *n* : a piece of material (as durable plastic) used for protecting exposed objects

**tar·pon** \'tär-pən\ *n, pl* **tarpon** *or* **tar·pons** : a large silvery bony fish often caught for sport in the warm coastal waters of the Atlantic esp. off Florida

**tar·ra·gon** \'ter-ə-gən\ [MF *targon*, ultim. fr. Ar *ṭarkhūn*] : a small widely cultivated perennial wormwood with aromatic leaves used as a seasoning; *also* : its leaves

¹**tar·ry** \'ta-rē\ *vb* **tar·ried; tar·ry·ing** 1 : to be tardy : DELAY; *esp* : to be slow in leaving 2 : to stay in or at a place : SOJOURN ♦ *Synonyms* REMAIN, WAIT, LINGER, ABIDE

²**tar·ry** \'tär-ē\ *adj* : of, resembling, or smeared with tar

**tar sand** *n* : sand or sandstone that is naturally soaked with the heavy sticky portions of petroleum

**tar·sus** \'tär-səs\ *n, pl* **tar·si** \-ˌsī\ [NL] : the part of a vertebrate foot between the metatarsus and the leg; *also* : the small bones that support this part — **tar·sal** \-səl\ *adj or n*

¹**tart** \'tärt\ *adj* 1 : agreeably sharp to the taste : PUNGENT 2 : BITING, CAUSTIC ⟨~ comments⟩ — **tart·ly** *adv* — **tart·ness** *n*

²**tart** *n* 1 : a small pie or pastry shell containing jelly, custard, or fruit 2 : PROSTITUTE

**tar·tan** \'tärt-ᵊn\ *n* : a plaid textile design of Scottish origin usu. distinctively patterned to designate a particular clan

**tar·tar** \'tär-tər\ *n* 1 : a substance in the juice of grapes deposited (as in wine casks) as a reddish crust or sediment 2 : a crust on the teeth formed from plaque hardened by calcium salts

**tar·tar sauce** *or* **tar·tare sauce** \'tär-tər-\ *n* : mayonnaise with chopped pickles, olives, or capers

¹**task** \'task\ *n* [ME *taske*, fr. MF dial. *tasque*, fr. ML *tasca* tax or service imposed by a feudal superior, fr. *taxare* to tax] : a piece of assigned work ♦ *Synonyms* JOB, DUTY, CHORE, STINT, ASSIGNMENT

²**task** *vb* : to oppress with great labor

**task force** *n* : a temporary grouping to accomplish a particular objective

**task·mas·ter** \'task-ˌmas-tər\ *n* : one that imposes a task or burdens another with labor

¹**tas·sel** \'ta-səl, 'tä-\ *n* 1 : a hanging ornament made of a bunch of cords of even length fastened at one end 2 : something suggesting a tassel; *esp* : a male flower cluster of corn

²**tassel** *vb* **-seled** *or* **-selled; -sel·ing** *or* **-sel·ling** : to adorn with or put forth tassels

¹**taste** \'tāst\ *vb* **tast·ed; tast·ing** 1 : EXPERIENCE, UNDERGO 2 : to try or determine the flavor of by taking a bit into the mouth 3 : to eat or drink esp. in small quantities : SAMPLE 4 : to have a specific flavor ⟨the milk ~s sour⟩

²**taste** *n* 1 : a small amount tasted 2 : BIT; *esp* : a sample of experience 3 : the special sense that perceives and identifies sweet, sour, bitter, or salty qualities and is mediated by taste buds on the tongue 4 : a quality perceptible to the sense of taste; *also* : the sensation obtained from a substance in the mouth : FLAVOR 5 : individual preference 6 : critical judgment, discernment, or appreciation; *also* : aesthetic quality ♦ *Synonyms* TANG, REL-ISH, FLAVOR, SAVOR — **taste·ful** \-fəl\ *adj* — **taste·ful·ly** *adv* — **taste·less** *adj* — **taste·less·ly** *adv* — **tast·er** *n*

**taste bud** *n* : a sense organ mediating the sensation of taste

**tasty** \'tā-stē\ *adj* **tast·i·er; -est** : pleasing to the taste : SAVORY ⟨a very ~ meal⟩ ♦ *Synonyms* PALATABLE, APPETIZING, TOOTHSOME, FLAVORSOME — **tast·i·ness** \'tā-stē-nəs\ *n*

**tat** \'tat\ *vb* **tat·ted; tat·ting** : to work at or make tatting

¹**tat·ter** \'ta-tər\ *vb* : to make or become ragged

²**tatter** *n* 1 : a part torn and left hanging 2 *pl* : tattered clothing

**tat·ter·de·ma·lion** \ˌta-tər-di-'māl-yən\ *n* : one that is ragged or disreputable

**tat·ter·sall** \'ta-tər-ˌsȯl, -səl\ *n* : a pattern of colored lines forming squares on solid background; *also* : a fabric in a tattersall pattern

**tat·ting** \'ta-tiŋ\ *n* : a delicate handmade lace formed usu. by looping and knotting with a single thread and a small shuttle; *also* : the act or process of making such lace

**tat·tle** \'ta-tᵊl\ *vb* **tat·tled; tat·tling** 1 : CHATTER, PRATE 2 : to tell secrets; *also* : to inform against another — **tat·tler** *n*

**tat·tle·tale** \'ta-tᵊl-ˌtāl\ *n* : one that tattles : INFORMER

¹**tat·too** \ta-'tü\ *n, pl* **tattoos** [alter. of earlier *taptoo*, fr. D *taptoe*, fr. the phrase *tap toe!* taps shut!] 1 : a call sounded before taps as notice to go to quarters 2 : a rapid rhythmic rapping

²**tattoo** *vb* : to mark (the skin) with tattoos

³**tattoo** *n, pl* **tattoos** [Tahitian *tatau*] : an indelible figure fixed upon the body esp. by insertion of pigment under the skin

**tau** \'taů, 'tȯ\ *n* : the 19th letter of the Greek alphabet — T or τ

**taught** *past and past part of* TEACH

¹**taunt** \'tȯnt\ *n* : a sarcastic challenge or insult

²**taunt** *vb* : to reproach or challenge in a mocking manner : jeer at ⟨the boys ~ed each other⟩ ♦ *Synonyms* MOCK, DERIDE, RIDICULE, TWIT — **taunt·er** *n*

**taupe** \'tōp\ *n* : a brownish gray

**Tau·rus** \'tȯr-əs\ *n* [L, lit., bull] 1 : a zodiacal constellation between Aries and Gemini usu. pictured as a bull 2 : the 2d sign of the zodiac in astrology; *also* : one born under this sign

**taut** \'tȯt\ *adj* 1 : tightly drawn : not slack 2 : extremely nervous : TENSE 3 : TRIM, TIDY ⟨a ~ ship⟩ — **taut·ly** *adv* — **taut·ness** *n*

**tau·tol·o·gy** \tȯ-'tä-lə-jē\ *n, pl* **-gies** : needless repetition of an idea, statement, or word; *also* : an instance of such repetition — **tau·to·log·i·cal** \ˌtȯ-tə-'lä-ji-kəl\ *adj* — **tau·to·log·i·cal·ly** \-ji-k(ə-)lē\ *adv* — **tau·tol·o·gous** \tȯ-'tä-lə-gəs\ *adj* — **tau·tol·o·gous·ly** *adv*

**tav·ern** \'ta-vərn\ *n* [ME *taverne*, fr. AF, fr. L *taberna* hut, shop] 1 : an establishment where alcoholic liquors are sold to be drunk on the premises 2 : INN

**taw** \'tȯ\ *n* **1** : a marble used as a shooter **2** : the line from which players shoot at marbles

**taw·dry** \'tȯ-drē\ *adj* **taw·dri·er; -est** [*tawdry lace* a tie of lace for the neck, fr. *St. Audrey* (St. Etheldreda) †679 queen of Northumbria] : cheap and gaudy in appearance and quality ⟨∼ decorations⟩ ♦ **Synonyms** GARISH, FLASHY, CHINTZY, MERETRICIOUS — **taw·dri·ly** *adv*

**taw·ny** \'tȯ-nē\ *adj* **taw·ni·er; -est** : of a brownish orange color

**¹tax** \'taks\ *vb* **1** : to levy a tax on **2** : CHARGE, ACCUSE **3** : to put under pressure — **tax·able** \'tak-sə-bəl\ *adj* — **tax·a·tion** \tak-'sā-shən\ *n*

**²tax** *n* **1** : a charge usu. of money imposed by authority on persons or property for public purposes **2** : a heavy charge : STRAIN

**¹taxi** \'tak-sē\ *n, pl* **tax·is** \-sēz\ *also* **tax·ies** : TAXICAB; *also* : a similarly operated boat or aircraft

**²taxi** *vb* **tax·ied; taxi·ing** *or* **taxy·ing; tax·is** *or* **tax·ies** **1** : to move along the ground or on the water under an aircraft's own power when starting or after a landing **2** : to go by taxicab

**taxi·cab** \'tak-sē-,kab\ *n* : an automobile that carries passengers for a fare usu. based on the distance traveled

**taxi·der·my** \'tak-sə-,dər-mē\ *n* : the skill or occupation of preparing, stuffing, and mounting skins of animals — **taxi·der·mist** \-mist\ *n*

**tax·on** \'tak-,sän\ *n, pl* **taxa** \-sə\; *also* **taxons** : a taxonomic group or entity

**tax·on·o·my** \tak-'sä-nə-mē\ *n* : classification esp. of animals or plants according to natural relationships — **tax·o·nom·ic** \,tak-sə-'nä-mik\ *adj* — **tax·on·o·mist** \tak-'sä-nə-mist\ *n*

**tax·pay·er** \'taks-,pā-ər\ *n* : one who pays or is liable for a tax — **tax·pay·ing** *adj*

**Tay–Sachs disease** \'tā-'saks-\ *n* : a hereditary disorder caused by the absence of an enzyme needed to break down fatty material, marked by buildup of lipids in nervous tissue, and causing death in childhood

**tb** *abbr* tablespoon; tablespoonful

**Tb** *symbol* terbium

**TB** \,tē-'bē\ *n* : TUBERCULOSIS

**TBA** *abbr, often not cap* to be announced

**T–bar** \'tē-,bär\ *n* : a ski lift with a series of T-shaped bars

**tbs** *or* **tbsp** *abbr* tablespoon; tablespoonful

**Tc** *symbol* technetium

**TC** *abbr* teachers college

**T cell** *n* : any of several lymphocytes (as a helper T cell) specialized esp. for activity in and control of immunity and the immune response

**TCP/IP** \,tē-(,)sē-'pē-,ī-'pē\ *n* [*transmission control protocol/Internet protocol*] : a set of communications protocols used over networks and esp. the Internet

**TD** *abbr* **1** touchdown **2** Treasury Department

**TDD** *abbr* telecommunications device for the deaf

**TDY** *abbr* temporary duty

**Te** *symbol* tellurium

**tea** \'tē\ *n* [Chin (dialect of Fujian province) *dé*] **1** : the cured leaves and leaf buds of a shrub grown chiefly in China, Japan, India, and Sri Lanka; *also* : this shrub **2** : a drink made by steeping tea in boiling water **3** : refreshments usu. including tea served in late afternoon; *also* : a reception at which tea is served

**teach** \'tēch\ *vb* **taught** \'tȯt\; **teach·ing** **1** : to cause to know something : act as a teacher **2** : to show how ⟨∼ a child to swim⟩ **3** : to make to know the disagreeable consequences of an action **4** : to guide the studies of **5** : to impart the knowledge of ⟨∼ algebra⟩ — **teach·able** *adj* — **teach·er** *n*

**teach·ing** *n* **1** : the act, practice, or profession of a teacher **2** : something taught; *esp* : DOCTRINE

**tea·cup** \'tē-,kəp\ *n* : a small cup used with a saucer for hot beverages

**teak** \'tēk\ *n* : the hard durable yellowish brown wood of a tall tropical Asian timber tree related to the vervains; *also* : this tree

**tea·ket·tle** \'tē-,ke-t³l\ *n* : a covered kettle with a handle and spout for boiling water

**teal** \'tēl\ *n, pl* **teal** *or* **teals** **1** : any of various small short-necked wild ducks **2** : a dark greenish blue color

**¹team** \'tēm\ *n* [ME *teme*, fr. OE *tēam* offspring, lineage, group of draft animals] **1** : two or more draft animals harnessed to the same vehicle or implement **2** : a number of persons associated in work or activity; *esp* : a group on one side in a match

**²team** *adj* : of or performed by a team; *also* : marked by devotion to teamwork ⟨a ∼ player⟩

**³team** *vb* **1** : to haul with or drive a team **2** : to form a team : join forces

**team·mate** \-,māt\ *n* : a fellow member of a team

**team·ster** \'tēm-stər\ *n* : one who drives a team or truck

**team·work** \-,wərk\ *n* : the work or activity of a number of persons acting in close association as members of a unit

**tea·pot** \'tē-,pät\ *n* : a vessel with a spout for brewing and serving tea

**¹tear** \'tir\ *n* : a drop of the salty liquid that moistens the eye and inner side of the eyelids; *also, pl* : an act of weeping or grieving — **tear·ful** \-fəl\ *adj* — **tear·ful·ly** *adv* — **teary** \'tir-ē\ *adj*

**²tear** \'tir\ *vb* : to fill with or shed tears ⟨eyes ∼*ing* in the wind⟩

**³tear** \'ter\ *vb* **tore** \'tȯr\; **torn** \'tȯrn\; **tear·ing** **1** : to separate parts of or pull apart by force : REND **2** : LACERATE **3** : to disrupt by the pull of contrary forces **4** : to remove by force : WRENCH ⟨∼ down a house⟩ **5** : to move or act with violence, haste, or force ♦ **Synonyms** RIP, SPLIT, CLEAVE, SLIT

**⁴tear** \'ter\ *n* **1** : the act of tearing **2** : a hole or flaw made by tearing : RENT

**tear gas** \'tir-\ *n* : a substance that on dispersion in the atmosphere blinds the eyes with tears — **tear gas** *vb*

**tear·jerk·er** \'tir-ˌjər-kər\ *n* : an extravagantly pathetic story, song, play, movie, or broadcast

¹**tease** \'tēz\ *vb* **teased; teas·ing 1** : to disentangle and lay parallel by combing or carding ⟨∼ wool⟩ **2** : to scratch the surface of (cloth) so as to raise a nap **3** : to annoy persistently esp. in fun by goading, coaxing, or tantalizing ⟨stop *teasing* the dog⟩ **4** : to comb (hair) by taking a strand and pushing the short hairs toward the scalp with the comb ◆ **Synonyms** HARASS, WORRY, PESTER, ANNOY

²**tease** *n* **1** : the act of teasing or state of being teased **2** : one that teases

**tea·sel** \'tē-zəl\ *n* : a prickly herb or its flower head covered with stiff hooked bracts and used to raise the nap on cloth; *also* : an artificial device used for this purpose

**tea·spoon** \'tē-ˌspün\ *n* **1** : a small spoon suitable for stirring beverages **2** : a unit of measure equal to ⅙ fluid ounce (5 milliliters)

**tea·spoon·ful** \-ˌfül\ *n, pl* **-spoonfuls** *also* **-spoons·ful** \-ˌspünz-ˌfül\ : TEASPOON 2

**teat** \'tit, 'tēt\ *n* : the protuberance through which milk is drawn from an udder or breast

**tech** *abbr* **1** technical; technically; technician **2** technological

**tech·ne·tium** \tek-'nē-shē-əm\ *n* : a radioactive metallic chemical element

**tech·nic** \'tek-nik, tek-'nēk\ *n* : TECHNIQUE 1

**tech·ni·cal** \'tek-ni-kəl\ *adj* [Gk *technikos* of art, skillful, fr. *technē* art, craft, skill] **1** : having special knowledge esp. of a mechanical or scientific subject ⟨∼ experts⟩ **2** : of or relating to a particular and esp. a practical or scientific subject ⟨∼ training⟩ **3** : according to a strict interpretation of the rules **4** : of or relating to technique — **tech·ni·cal·ly** \-k(ə-)lē\ *adv*

**tech·ni·cal·i·ty** \ˌtek-nə-'ka-lə-tē\ *n, pl* **-ties 1** : a detail meaningful only to a specialist **2** : the quality or state of being technical

**technical sergeant** *n* : a noncommissioned officer in the air force ranking next below a master sergeant

**tech·ni·cian** \tek-'ni-shən\ *n* : a person who has acquired the technique of a specialized skill or subject

**tech·nique** \tek-'nēk\ *n* [F] **1** : the manner in which technical details are treated or basic physical movements are used **2** : technical methods

**tech·no** \'tek-nō\ *n* : dance music featuring a fast beat and electronically created sounds usu. without vocals

**tech·noc·ra·cy** \tek-'nä-krə-sē\ *n* : management of society by technical experts — **tech·no·crat** \'tek-nə-ˌkrat\ *n* — **tech·no·crat·ic** \ˌtek-nə-'kra-tik\ *adj*

**tech·nol·o·gy** \tek-'nä-lə-jē\ *n, pl* **-gies**

: ENGINEERING; *also* : a manner of accomplishing a task using technical methods or knowledge — **tech·no·log·i·cal** \ˌtek-nə-'lä-ji-kəl\ *adj*

**tec·ton·ics** \tek-'tä-niks\ *n sing or pl* **1** : geological structural features **2** : geology dealing esp. with the faulting and folding of a planet or moon — **tec·ton·ic** \-nik\ *adj*

**ted·dy bear** \'te-dē-ˌber\ *n* [*Teddy* Roosevelt; fr. a cartoon depicting the president sparing the life of a bear cub while hunting] : a stuffed toy bear

**te·dious** \'tē-dē-əs\ *adj* : tiresome because of length or dullness ⟨a ∼ speech⟩ ◆ **Synonyms** BORING, TIRING, IRKSOME — **te·dious·ly** *adv* — **te·dious·ness** *n*

**te·di·um** \'tē-dē-əm\ *n* : TEDIOUSNESS; *also* : BOREDOM

¹**tee** \'tē\ *n* : a small mound or peg on which a golf ball is placed to be hit at the beginning of play on a hole; *also* : the area from which the ball is hit to begin play

²**tee** *vb* **teed; tee·ing** : to place (a ball) on a tee

**teem** \'tēm\ *vb* : to become filled to overflowing : ABOUND ◆ **Synonyms** SWARM, CRAWL, FLOW

**teen** *adj* : TEENAGE

**teen·age** \'tē-ˌnāj\ *or* **teen-aged** \-ˌnājd\ *adj* : of, being, or relating to people in their teens — **teen·ag·er** \-ˌnā-jər\ *n*

**teens** \'tēnz\ *n pl* : the numbers 13 to 19 inclusive; *esp* : the years 13 to 19 in a person's life

**tee·ny** \'tē-nē\ *adj* **tee·ni·er; -est** : TINY

**teepee** *var of* TEPEE

**tee shirt** *var of* T-SHIRT

**tee·ter** \'tē-tər\ *vb* **1** : to move unsteadily **2** : SEESAW — **teeter** *n*

**teeth** *pl of* TOOTH

**teethe** \'tēth\ *vb* **teethed; teeth·ing** : to experience the rising of one's teeth through the gums : to grow teeth

**teething** *n* : growth of the first set of teeth through the gums with its accompanying phenomena

**tee·to·tal·er** *or* **tee·to·tal·ler** \'tē-'tō-tᵊl-ər\ *n* : a person who practices complete abstinence from alcoholic drinks — **tee·to·tal** \'tē-'tō-tᵊl, -ˌtō-\ *adj* — **tee·to·tal·ism** \-tᵊl-ˌi-zəm\ *n*

**TEFL** *abbr* teaching English as a foreign language

**Te·ja·no** \tā-'hä-(ˌ)nō\ *n, pl* **-nos** [Mex Sp, fr. *Tejas* Texas] : a Texan of Hispanic descent

**tek·tite** \'tek-ˌtīt\ *n* : a glassy body of probably meteoric origin

**tel** *abbr* **1** telegram **2** telegraph **3** telephone

**tele·cast** \'te-li-ˌkast\ *vb* **-cast** *also* **-cast·ed; -cast·ing** : to broadcast by television — **telecast** *n* — **tele·cast·er** *n*

**tel·e·com** \'te-li-ˌkäm\ *n* : TELECOMMUNICATION; *also* : the telecommunications industry

**tele·com·mu·ni·ca·tion** \ˌte-li-kə-ˌmyü-nə-'kā-shən\ *n* : communication at a distance (as by telephone or radio)

**tele·com·mute** \'te-li-kə-ˌmyüt\ *vb* : to

work at home by the use of an electronic linkup with a central office

**tele·con·fer·ence** \'te-li-ˌkän-fə-rəns\ *n* : a conference among people remote from one another held using telecommunications — **tele·con·fer·enc·ing** *n*

**teleg** *abbr* telegraphy

**tele·gen·ic** \ˌte-lə-'je-nik, -'jē-\ *adj* : markedly attractive to television viewers

**tele·gram** \'te-lə-ˌgram\ *n* : a message sent by telegraph

¹**tele·graph** \-ˌgraf\ *n* : an electric apparatus or system for sending messages by a code over wires — **tele·graph·ic** \ˌte-lə-'gra-fik\ *adj*

²**telegraph** *vb* : to send or communicate by or as if by telegraph — **te·leg·ra·pher** \tə-'le-grə-fər\ *n*

**te·leg·ra·phy** \tə-'le-grə-fē\ *n* : the use or operation of a telegraph apparatus or system

**tele·mar·ket·ing** \ˌte-lə-'mär-kə-tin\ *n* : the marketing of goods or services by telephone — **tele·mar·ket·er** \-tər\ *n*

**tele·med·i·cine** \ˌte-lə-'me-də-sən\ *n* : the practice of medicine using two-way voice and visual communication

**te·lem·e·try** \tə-'le-mə-trē\ *n* : the transmission esp. by radio of measurements made by automatic instruments to a distant station — **tele·me·ter** \'te-lə-ˌmē-tər\ *n*

**tel·e·no·vela** \ˌte-lə-nō-'ve-lə\ *n* : a soap opera televised in or from many Latin-American countries

**te·lep·a·thy** \tə-'le-pə-thē\ *n* : apparent communication from one mind to another by extrasensory means — **tele·path·ic** \ˌte-lə-'pa-thik\ *adj* — **tele·path·i·cal·ly** \-thi-k(ə-)lē\ *adv*

¹**tele·phone** \'te-lə-ˌfōn\ *n* : an instrument for sending and receiving sounds over long distances by electricity

²**telephone** *vb* **-phoned; -phon·ing** **1** : to send or communicate by telephone **2** : to speak to (a person) by telephone — **tele·phon·er** *n*

**te·le·pho·ny** \tə-'le-fə-nē, 'te-lə-ˌfō-\ *n* : use or operation of an apparatus for transmission of sounds as electrical signals between distant points — **tele·phon·ic** \ˌte-lə-'fä-nik\ *adj*

**tele·pho·to** \ˌte-lə-'fō-tō\ *adj* : being a camera lens giving a large image of a distant object — **tele·pho·tog·ra·phy** \-fə-'tä-grə-fē\ *n*

**tele·play** \'te-li-ˌplā\ *n* : a story prepared for television production

**tele·print·er** \'te-lə-ˌprin-tər\ *n* : TELETYPEWRITER

**tele·prompt·er** \'te-lə-ˌprämp-tər\ *n* : a device for displaying prepared text to a speaker or performer

¹**tele·scope** \'te-lə-ˌskōp\ *n* **1** : a cylindrical instrument equipped with lenses or mirrors for viewing distant objects **2** : RADIO TELESCOPE

²**telescope** *vb* **-scoped; -scop·ing 1** : to slide or pass or cause to slide or pass one within another like the sections of a collapsible hand telescope **2** : COMPRESS, CONDENSE

**tele·scop·ic** \ˌte-lə-'skä-pik\ *adj* **1** : of or relating to a telescope **2** : seen only by a telescope **3** : able to discern objects at a distance **4** : having parts that telescope — **tele·scop·i·cal·ly** \-pi-k(ə-)lē\ *adv*

**tele·text** \'te-lə-ˌtekst\ *n* : a system for broadcasting text over a television signal and displaying it on a decoder-equipped television

**tele·thon** \'te-lə-ˌthän\ *n* : a long television program usu. to solicit funds for a charity

**tele·type·writ·er** \ˌte-lə-'tīp-ˌrī-tər\ *n* : a printing device resembling a typewriter used to send and receive signals over telephone lines

**tele·vise** \'te-lə-ˌvīz\ *vb* **-vised; -vis·ing** : to broadcast by television

**tele·vi·sion** \'te-lə-ˌvi-zhən\ *n* [F *télévision,* fr. Gk *tēle* far, at a distance + F *vision* vision] : a system for transmitting images and sound by converting them into electrical or radio waves which are converted back into images and sound by a receiver; *also* : a television receiving set

**tell** \'tel\ *vb* **told** \'tōld\; **tell·ing 1** : COUNT, ENUMERATE **2** : to relate in detail : NARRATE ⟨*told* us what happened⟩ **3** : SAY, UTTER **4** : to make known : REVEAL **5** : to report to : INFORM ⟨*told* me her name⟩ **6** : ORDER, DIRECT **7** : to find out by observing ⟨can ~ the difference⟩ **8** : to have a marked effect **9** : to serve as evidence ♦ **Synonyms** DISCLOSE, DISCOVER, BETRAY

**tell·er** \'te-lər\ *n* **1** : one that relates : NARRATOR **2** : one that counts **3** : a bank employee handling money received or paid out

**tell·ing** \'te-lin\ *adj* : producing a marked effect : EFFECTIVE ⟨~ evidence⟩ ♦ **Synonyms** COGENT, CONVINCING, SOUND

**tell off** *vb* : REPRIMAND, SCOLD

**tell·tale** \'tel-ˌtāl\ *n* **1** : INFORMER, TATTLETALE **2** : something that serves to disclose : INDICATION — **telltale** *adj*

**tel·lu·ri·um** \tə-'lur-ē-əm\ *n* : a chemical element used esp. in alloys

**tel·net** \'tel-ˌnet\ *n* : a telecommunications protocol for accessing and using a remote computer via a local computer — **telnet** *vb*

**tem·blor** \'tem-blər\ *n* [Sp, lit., trembling] : EARTHQUAKE

**te·mer·i·ty** \tə-'mer-ə-tē\ *n, pl* **-ties** : rash or presumptuous daring : BOLDNESS ♦ **Synonyms** AUDACITY, EFFRONTERY, GALL, NERVE, CHEEK

¹**temp** \'temp\ *n* **1** : TEMPERATURE **2** : a temporary worker

²**temp** *abbr* temporary

¹**tem·per** \'tem-pər\ *vb* **1** : to dilute or soften by the addition of something else ⟨~ justice with mercy⟩ **2** : to bring (as steel) to a desired hardness by reheating and cooling **3** : to toughen (glass) by gradual heating and cooling **4** : TOUGHEN **5** : TUNE

²**temper** *n* **1** : characteristic tone : TEN-

DENCY **2** : the hardness or toughness of a substance ⟨the ~ of a knife blade⟩ **3** : a characteristic frame of mind : DISPOSITION **4** : calmness of mind : COMPOSURE **5** : state of feeling or frame of mind at a particular time **6** : heat of mind or emotion ♦ *Synonyms* TEMPERAMENT, CHARACTER, PERSONALITY, MAKEUP — **tem·pered** \'tem-pərd\ *adj*

**tem·pera** \'tem-pə-rə\ *n* [It] : a painting process using an albuminous or colloidal medium as a vehicle; *also* : a painting done in tempera

**tem·per·a·ment** \'tem-prə-mənt, -pər-mənt\ *n* **1** : characteristic or habitual inclination or mode of emotional response : DISPOSITION ⟨nervous ~⟩ **2** : excessive sensitiveness or irritability ♦ *Synonyms* CHARACTER, PERSONALITY, NATURE, MAKEUP — **tem·per·a·men·tal** \,tem-prə-'men-tᵊl, -pər-'ment-\ *adj*

**tem·per·ance** \'tem-prəns, -pə-rəns\ *n* : habitual moderation in the indulgence of the appetites or passions; *esp* : moderation in or abstinence from the use of alcoholic beverages

**tem·per·ate** \'tem-prət, -pə-rət\ *adj* **1** : not extreme or excessive : MILD **2** : moderate in indulgence of appetite or desire **3** : moderate in the use of alcoholic beverages **4** : having a moderate climate ♦ *Synonyms* SOBER, CONTINENT, ABSTEMIOUS

**temperate zone** *n, often cap T&Z* : the region between the Tropic of Cancer and the arctic circle or between the Tropic of Capricorn and the antarctic circle

**tem·per·a·ture** \'tem-pər-,chùr, -prə-,chùr, -chər\ *n* **1** : degree of hotness or coldness of something (as air, water, or the body) as shown by a thermometer **2** : FEVER 1

**tem·pest** \'tem-pəst\ *n* [ME *tempeste*, fr. AF, ultim. fr. L *tempestas* season, weather, storm, fr. *tempus* time] : a violent storm

**tempest in a teapot** : a great commotion over an unimportant matter

**tem·pes·tu·ous** \tem-'pes-chə-wəs\ *adj* : of, involving, or resembling a tempest : STORMY — **tem·pes·tu·ous·ly** *adv* — **tem·pes·tu·ous·ness** *n*

**tem·plate** \'tem-plət\ *n* : a gauge, mold, or pattern that functions as a guide to the form or structure of something being made

¹**tem·ple** \'tem-pəl\ *n* **1** : a building reserved for religious practice **2** : a place devoted to a special or exalted purpose ⟨a ~ of cuisine⟩

²**temple** *n* : the flattened space on each side of the forehead esp. of humans

**tem·po** \'tem-pō\ *n, pl* **tem·pi** \-(,)pē\ *or* **tempos** [It, lit., time] **1** : the rate of speed of a musical piece or passage **2** : rate of motion or activity : PACE

¹**tem·po·ral** \'tem-pə-rəl\ *adj* **1** : of, relating to, or limited by time ⟨~ and spatial bounds⟩ **2** : of or relating to earthly life or secular concerns ⟨~ power⟩

²**temporal** *adj* : of or relating to the temples or the sides of the skull

¹**tem·po·rary** \'tem-pə-,rer-ē\ *adj* : lasting for a limited only : TRANSITORY ♦ *Synonyms* TRANSIENT, EPHEMERAL, MOMENTARY, IMPERMANENT — **tem·po·rar·i·ly** \,tem-pə-'rer-ə-lē\ *adv*

²**temporary** *n, pl* **-rar·ies** : one serving for a limited time

**tem·po·rise** *Brit var of* TEMPORIZE

**tem·po·rize** \'tem-pə-,rīz\ *vb* **-rized; -riz·ing** **1** : to adapt one's actions to the time or the dominant opinion : COMPROMISE **2** : to draw out matters so as to gain time — **tem·po·riz·er** *n*

**tempt** \'tempt\ *vb* **1** : to entice to do wrong by promise of pleasure or gain : PROVOKE ⟨~ fate⟩ **2** : to risk the dangers of **3** : to induce to do something : INCITE ♦ *Synonyms* INVEIGLE, DECOY, SEDUCE, LURE — **tempt·er** *n* — **tempt·ing·ly** *adv*

**temp·ta·tion** \temp-'tā-shən\ *n* **1** : the act of tempting : the state of being tempted **2** : something that tempts

**tempt·ress** \'temp-trəs\ *n* : a woman who tempts

**ten** \'ten\ *n* **1** : one more than nine **2** : the 10th in a set or series **3** : something having 10 units — **ten** *adj or pron* — **tenth** \'tenth\ *adj or adv or n*

**ten·a·ble** \'te-nə-bəl\ *adj* : capable of being held, maintained, or defended — **ten·a·bil·i·ty** \,te-nə-'bi-lə-tē\ *n*

**te·na·cious** \tə-'nā-shəs\ *adj* **1** : not easily pulled apart : COHESIVE, TOUGH ⟨a ~ metal⟩ **2** : holding fast ⟨~ of his rights⟩ **3** : RETENTIVE ⟨a ~ memory⟩ — **te·na·cious·ly** *adv* — **te·nac·i·ty** \tə-'na-sə-tē\ *n*

**ten·an·cy** \'te-nən-sē\ *n, pl* **-cies** : the temporary possession or occupancy of something (as a house) that belongs to another; *also* : the period of a tenant's occupancy

**ten·ant** \'te-nənt\ *n* **1** : one who rents or leases (as a house) from a landlord **2** : DWELLER, OCCUPANT — **tenant** *vb* — **ten·ant·less** *adj*

**tenant farmer** *n* : a farmer who works land owned by another and pays rent either in cash or in shares of produce

**ten·ant·ry** \'te-nən-trē\ *n, pl* **-ries** : the body of tenants esp. on an estate

**Ten Commandments** *n pl* : the commandments of God given to Moses on Mount Sinai

¹**tend** \'tend\ *vb* **1** : to apply oneself ⟨~ to your affairs⟩ **2** : to take care of ⟨~ a plant⟩ **3** : to manage the operations of ⟨~ a machine⟩

²**tend** *vb* **1** : to move or develop one's course in a particular direction **2** : to show an inclination or tendency

**ten·den·cy** \'ten-dən-sē\ *n, pl* **-cies** **1** : DRIFT, TREND **2** : a proneness to or readiness for a particular kind of thought or action : PROPENSITY ⟨a ~ to overreact⟩ ♦ *Synonyms* BENT, LEANING, DISPOSITION, INCLINATION

**ten·den·tious** \ten-'den-chəs\ *adj* : marked by a tendency in favor of a particular point of view : BIASED ⟨∼ remarks⟩ — **ten·den·tious·ly** *adv* — **ten·den·tious·ness** *n*

¹**ten·der** \'ten-dər\ *adj* [ME, fr. AF *tendre*, fr. L *tener*] **1** : having a soft texture : easily broken, chewed, or cut **2** : physically weak : DELICATE; *also* : IMMATURE **3** : expressing or responsive to love or sympathy : LOVING, COMPASSIONATE ⟨a ∼ smile⟩ **4** : SENSITIVE, TOUCHY ⟨an ∼ ego⟩ ♦ **Synonyms** SYMPATHETIC, WARM, WARMHEARTED — **ten·der·ly** *adv* — **ten·der·ness** *n*

²**tender** *n* [AF *tendre*, fr. *tendre*, v., to stretch, hold out, offer, fr. L *tendere* to stretch, direct] **1** : an offer or proposal made for acceptance; *esp* : an offer of a bid for a contract **2** : something (as money) that may be offered in payment

³**tender** *vb* : to present for acceptance

⁴**tend·er** \'ten-dər\ *n* **1** : one that tends or takes care **2** : a boat carrying passengers and freight to a larger ship **3** : a car attached to a steam locomotive for carrying fuel and water

⁵**tender** *n* [prob. short for *tenderloin*] : a strip of meat (as chicken) often breaded

**ten·der·foot** \'ten-dər-ˌfu̇t\ *n, pl* **-feet** \-ˌfēt\ *also* **-foots** \-ˌfu̇ts\ **1** : one not hardened to frontier or rough outdoor life **2** : an inexperienced beginner

**ten·der·heart·ed** \ˌten-dər-ˈhär-təd\ *adj* : easily moved to love, pity, or sorrow

**ten·der·ize** \'ten-də-ˌrīz\ *vb* **-ized; -iz·ing** : to make (meat) tender — **ten·der·iz·er** \'ten-də-ˌrī-zər\ *n*

**ten·der·loin** \'ten-dər-ˌlȯin\ *n* **1** : a tender strip of beef or pork from near the backbone **2** : a district of a city largely devoted to vice

**ten·di·ni·tis** *or* **ten·don·itis** \ˌten-də-ˈnī-təs\ *n* : inflammation of a tendon

**ten·don** \'ten-dən\ *n* : a tough cord of dense white fibrous tissue uniting a muscle with another part (as a bone) — **ten·di·nous** \-də-nəs\ *adj*

**ten·dril** \'ten-drəl\ *n* : a slender coiling organ by which some climbing plants attach themselves to a support

**ten·e·brous** \'te-nə-brəs\ *adj* : shut off from the light : GLOOMY, OBSCURE

**ten·e·ment** \'te-nə-mənt\ *n* **1** : a house used as a dwelling **2** : a building divided into apartments for rent to families; *esp* : one meeting only minimum standards of safety and comfort **3** : APARTMENT, FLAT

**te·net** \'te-nət\ *n* [L, he holds, fr. *tenēre* to hold] : one of the principles or doctrines held in common by members of a group (as a church or profession) ♦ **Synonyms** DOCTRINE, DOGMA, BELIEF

**ten·fold** \'ten-ˌfōld, -ˈfōld\ *adj* : being 10 times as great or as many — **ten·fold** \-ˈfōld\ *adv*

**tenge** \'teŋ-ˌgä\ *n, pl* **tenge** — see MONEY table

**ten–gallon hat** *n* : a wide-brimmed hat with a large soft crown

**Tenn** *abbr* Tennessee

**ten·ne** \'ten-ā\ *n, pl* **ten·e·si** \'teŋ-ə-sē\ *or*

**tenne** *or* **ten·ne·si** \'teŋ-ə-sē\ — see *manat* at MONEY table

**ten·nis** \'te-nəs\ *n* : a game played with a ball and racket on a court divided by a net

**ten·on** \'te-nən\ *n* : a projecting part in a piece of material (as wood) for insertion into a mortise to make a joint

**ten·or** \'te-nər\ *n* **1** : the general drift of something spoken or written ⟨his speech had an angry ∼⟩ **2** : the highest natural adult male voice; *also* : a singer having this voice **3** : a continuing in a course, movement, or activity ⟨the ∼ of my life⟩

**tenpenny nail** *n* : a nail three inches (about 7.6 centimeters) long

**ten·pin** \'ten-ˌpin\ *n* : a bottle-shaped bowling pin set in groups of 10 and bowled at in a game (**tenpins**)

¹**tense** \'tens\ *n* [ME *tens* time, tense, fr. AF, fr. L *tempus*] : distinction of form of a verb to indicate the time of the action or state

²**tense** *adj* **tens·er; tens·est** [L *tensus*, fr. pp. of *tendere* to stretch] **1** : stretched tight : TAUT **2** : feeling or showing nervous tension ⟨a ∼ smile⟩ ♦ **Synonyms** STIFF, RIGID, INFLEXIBLE — **tense·ly** *adv* — **tense·ness** *n* — **ten·si·ty** \'ten-sə-tē\ *n*

³**tense** *vb* **tensed; tens·ing** : to make or become tense

**ten·sile** \'ten-səl, -ˌsī(-ə)l\ *adj* : of or relating to tension ⟨∼ strength⟩

**ten·sion** \'ten-chən\ *n* **1** : the act of straining or stretching; *also* : the condition of being strained or stretched **2** : a state of mental unrest often with signs of bodily stress **3** : a state of latent hostility or opposition

**ten–speed** \'ten-ˌspēd\ *n* : a bicycle with a derailleur having 10 possible combinations of gears

¹**tent** \'tent\ *n* **1** : a collapsible shelter of material stretched and supported by poles **2** : a canopy placed over the head and shoulders to retain vapors or oxygen given for medical reasons

²**tent** *vb* **1** : to lodge in tents **2** : to cover with or as if with a tent

**ten·ta·cle** \'ten-ti-kəl\ *n* : any of various long flexible projections about the head or mouth (as of an insect, mollusk, or fish) — **ten·ta·cled** \-kəld\ *adj* — **ten·tac·u·lar** \ten-ˈta-kyə-lər\ *adj*

**ten·ta·tive** \'ten-tə-tiv\ *adj* **1** : not fully worked out or developed ⟨∼ plans⟩ **2** : HESITANT, UNCERTAIN ⟨a ∼ smile⟩ — **ten·ta·tive·ly** *adv* — **ten·ta·tive·ness** *n*

**ten·u·ous** \'ten-yə-wəs\ *adj* **1** : not dense : RARE ⟨a ∼ fluid⟩ **2** : not thick : SLENDER ⟨a ∼ rope⟩ **3** : having little substance : FLIMSY, WEAK ⟨∼ influences⟩ **4** : lacking stability : SHAKY ⟨∼ reasoning⟩ — **te·nu·i·ty** \te-ˈnü-ə-tē, tə-, -ˈnyü-\ *n* — **ten·u·ous·ly** *adv* — **ten·u·ous·ness** *n*

**ten·ure** \'ten-yər\ *n* : the act, right, manner, or period of holding something (as a landed property, an office, or a position)

**ten·ured** \'ten-yərd\ *adj* : having tenure ⟨∼ faculty members⟩

**te·o·sin·te** \ˌtā-ō-ˈsin-tē\ *n* : a tall annual

grass of Mexico that is closely related to and usu. considered ancestral to corn

**te·pee** *or* **tee·pee** \'tē-(,)pē\ *n* [Dakota *t<sup>h</sup>ipi*, fr. *t<sup>h</sup>i*- to dwell] : an American Indian conical tent usu. of skins

**tep·id** \'te-pəd\ *adj* **1** : moderately warm : LUKEWARM **2** : HALFHEARTED

**te·qui·la** \tə-'kē-lə, tā-\ *n* : a Mexican liquor distilled from an agave's sap

**ter** *abbr* **1** terrace **2** territory

**tera·byte** \'ter-ə-,bīt\ *n* [*tera*- trillion (10¹²), fr. Gk *terat-, teras* monster] : 1024 gigabytes; *also* : one trillion bytes

**ter·bi·um** \'tər-bē-əm\ *n* : a metallic chemical element

**ter·cen·te·na·ry** \,tər-,sen-'tc-nə-rē, tər-'sen-tə-,ner-ē\ *n, pl* **-ries** : a 300th anniversary or its celebration — **tercentenary** *adj*

**ter·cen·ten·ni·al** \,tər-,sen-'te-nē-əl\ *adj or n* : TERCENTENARY

**te·re·do** \tə-'rē-dō, -'rā-\ *n, pl* **-dos** [L] : SHIPWORM

**ter·i·ya·ki** \,ter-ē-'yä-kē\ *n* [Jp] : a Japanese dish of meat or fish soaked in a soy marinade and cooked

**¹term** \'tərm\ *n* **1** : END, TERMINATION **2** : DURATION; *esp* : a period of time fixed esp. by law or custom **3** : a mathematical expression connected with another by a plus or minus sign; *also* : an element (as a numerator) of a fraction or proportion **4** : a word or expression that has a precise meaning in some uses or is limited to a particular subject or field **5** *pl* : PROVISIONS, CONDITIONS ⟨~s of a contract⟩ **6** *pl* : mutual relationship ⟨on good ~s⟩ **7** : AGREEMENT, CONCORD **8** : a state of acceptance ⟨come to ~s with his grief⟩

**²term** *vb* : to apply a term to : CALL

**ter·ma·gant** \'tər-mə-gənt\ *n* : an overbearing or nagging woman : SHREW

**¹ter·mi·nal** \'tər-mə-n°l\ *adj* **1** : of, relating to, or forming an end, limit, or terminus **2** : FATAL 2 ⟨~ cancer⟩; *also* : being in or relating to the final stages of a fatal disease ⟨a ~ patient⟩ ♦ *Synonyms* FINAL, CONCLUDING, LAST, LATEST — **ter·mi·nal·ly** *adv*

**²terminal** *n* **1** : EXTREMITY, END **2** : a device at the end of a wire or on electrical equipment for making a connection **3** : either end of a transportation line (as a railroad) with its offices and freight and passenger stations; *also* : a freight or passenger station **4** : a device (as in a computer system) for data entry and display

**ter·mi·nate** \'tər-mə-,nāt\ *vb* **-nat·ed; -nat·ing** : to bring or come to an end ♦ *Synonyms* CONCLUDE, FINISH, COMPLETE — **ter·mi·na·ble** \-nə-bəl\ *adj* — **ter·mi·na·tion** \,tər-mə-'nā-shən\ *n* — **ter·mi·na·tor** \'tər-mə-,nā-tər\ *n*

**ter·mi·nol·o·gy** \,tər-mə-'nä-lə-jē\ *n, pl* **-gies** : the technical or special terms used in a business, art, science, or subject

**ter·mi·nus** \'tər-mə-nəs\ *n, pl* **-ni** \-,nī\ *or* **-nus·es** [L] **1** : final goal : END **2** : either end of a transportation line or travel route; *also* : the station or city at such a place

**ter·mite** \'tər-,mīt\ *n* : any of numerous pale soft-bodied social insects that feed on wood

**tern** \'tərn\ *n* : any of various chiefly marine birds with narrow wings and often a forked tail

**ter·na·ry** \'tər-nə-rē\ *adj* **1** : of, relating to, or proceeding by threes **2** : having three elements or parts

**terr** *abbr* territory

**¹ter·race** \'ter-əs\ *n* **1** : a flat roof or open platform **2** : a level area next to a building **3** : an embankment with level top **4** : a bank or ridge on a slope to conserve moisture and soil **5** : a row of houses on raised land; *also* : a street with such a row of houses **6** : a strip of park in the middle of a street

**²terrace** *vb* **ter·raced; ter·rac·ing** : to form into a terrace or supply with terraces

**ter·ra–cot·ta** \,ter-ə-'kä-tə\ *n* [It *terra cotta,* lit., baked earth] : a reddish brown earthenware

**terra fir·ma** \-'fər-mə\ *n* [NL] : solid ground

**ter·rain** \tə-'rān\ *n* : the surface features of an area of land ⟨a rough ~⟩

**ter·ra in·cog·ni·ta** \'ter-ə-,in-,käg-'nē-tə\ *n, pl* **ter·rae in·cog·ni·tae** \'ter-,ī-,in-,käg-'nē-tī\ [L] : an unexplored area or field of knowledge

**ter·ra·pin** \'ter-ə-pən\ *n* : any of various turtles of fresh or brackish water

**ter·rar·i·um** \tə-'rer-ē-əm\ *n, pl* **-ia** \-ē-ə\ *or* **-i·ums** : a usu. transparent enclosure for keeping or raising plants or small animals indoors

**ter·res·tri·al** \tə-'res-trē-əl\ *adj* **1** : of or relating to the earth or its inhabitants **2** : living or growing on land ⟨~ plants⟩ ♦ *Synonyms* MUNDANE, EARTHLY, WORLDLY

**ter·ri·ble** \'ter-ə-bəl\ *adj* **1** : exciting terror : FEARFUL, DREADFUL ⟨~ weapons⟩ **2** : hard to bear : DISTRESSING ⟨a ~ situation⟩ **3** : extreme in degree : INTENSE ⟨~ heat⟩ **4** : of very poor quality : AWFUL ⟨a ~ play⟩ ♦ *Synonyms* FRIGHTFUL, HORRIBLE, SHOCKING, APPALLING — **ter·ri·bly** \-blē\ *adv*

**ter·ri·er** \'ter-ē-ər\ *n* [ME *terryer, terrer,* fr. AF (*chen*) *terrer,* lit., earth dog, fr. *terre* earth, fr. L *terra*] : any of various usu. small energetic dogs orig. used by hunters to drive small game animals from their holes

**ter·rif·ic** \tə-'ri-fik\ *adj* **1** : exciting terror ⟨a ~ explosion⟩ **2** : EXTRAORDINARY, ASTOUNDING ⟨~ speed⟩ **3** : MAGNIFICENT ⟨makes ~ chili⟩

**ter·ri·fy** \'ter-ə-,fī\ *vb* **-fied; -fy·ing** : to fill with terror : FRIGHTEN ♦ *Synonyms* SCARE, TERRORIZE, STARTLE, ALARM — **ter·ri·fy·ing·ly** *adv*

**ter·ri·to·ri·al·i·ty** \,ter-ə-,tòr-ē-'a-lə-tē\ *n* : persistent attachment to a specific territory ⟨~ in bears⟩

**ter·ri·to·ry** \'ter-ə-,tòr-ē\ *n, pl* **-ries** **1** : a geographic area belonging to or under the jurisdiction of a governmental authority **2** : a part of the U.S. not included within any state but organized with a separate legislature 3 : REGION, DISTRICT; *also* : a region in which one feels at home 4 : a field of knowledge or interest 5 : an assigned area 6 : an area occupied and defended by one or a group of animals — **ter·ri·to·ri·al** \ˌter-ə-ˈtȯr-ē-əl\ *adj* — **go with the territory** *or* **come with the territory** : to accompany a situation naturally

**ter·ror** \ˈter-ər\ *n* 1 : a state of intense fear : FRIGHT 2 : one that inspires fear 3 : violent or destructive acts committed to intimidate a people or government ♦ *Synonyms* PANIC, CONSTERNATION, DREAD, ALARM, DISMAY, HORROR, TREPIDATION

**ter·ror·ism** \ˈter-ər-ˌi-zəm\ *n* : the systematic use of terror esp. as a means of coercion — **ter·ror·ist** \-ist\ *adj or n*

**ter·ror·ize** \ˈter-ər-ˌīz\ *vb* **-ized; -iz·ing** 1 : to fill with terror : SCARE 2 : to coerce by threat or violence ♦ *Synonyms* TERRIFY, FRIGHTEN, ALARM, STARTLE

**ter·ry** \ˈter-ē\ *n, pl* **terries** : an absorbent fabric with a loose pile of uncut loops

**terse** \ˈtərs\ *adj* **ters·er; ters·est** [L *tersus* clean, neat, fr. pp. of *tergēre* to wipe off] : effectively brief : CONCISE — **terse·ly** *adv* — **terse·ness** *n*

**ter·tia·ry** \ˈtər-shē-ˌer-ē\ *adj* 1 : of third rank, importance, or value 2 *cap* : of, relating to, or being the earlier period of the Cenozoic era 3 : occurring in or being the third stage ⟨~ medical care⟩

**Tertiary** *n* : the Tertiary period

**TESL** *abbr* teaching English as a second language

**TESOL** *abbr* Teachers of English to Speakers of Other Languages

¹**test** \ˈtest\ *n* [ME, vessel in which metals were assayed, potsherd, fr. AF, pot, fr. L *testum* earthen vessel] 1 : a critical examination or evaluation : TRIAL 2 : a means or result of testing

²**test** *vb* 1 : to put to test : TRY, EXAMINE 2 : to undergo or score on tests

³**test** *adj* : relating to or used in testing ⟨a ~ group⟩

**tes·ta·ment** \ˈtes-tə-mənt\ *n* 1 *cap* : either of two main divisions of the Bible 2 : EVIDENCE, WITNESS 3 : CREED 4 : the legal instructions for the disposition of one's property after death : WILL — **tes·ta·men·ta·ry** \ˌtes-tə-ˈmen-tə-rē\ *adj*

**tes·tate** \ˈtes-ˌtāt, -tət\ *adj* : having left a valid will

**tes·ta·tor** \ˈtes-ˌtā-tər, tes-ˈtā-\ *n* : a person who dies leaving a valid will

**tes·ta·trix** \tes-ˈtā-triks\ *n* : a woman who is a testator

¹**tes·ter** \ˈtēs-tər, ˈtes-\ *n* : a canopy over a bed, pulpit, or altar

²**test·er** \ˈtes-tər\ *n* : one that tests

**tes·ti·cle** \ˈtes-ti-kəl\ *n* : TESTIS; *esp* : one of a mammal usu. with its enclosing structures — **tes·tic·u·lar** *adj*

**tes·ti·fy** \ˈtes-tə-ˌfī\ *vb* **-fied; -fy·ing** 1 : to make a statement based on personal knowledge or belief : bear witness 2 : to serve as evidence or proof

**tes·ti·mo·ni·al** \ˌtes-tə-ˈmō-nē-əl\ *n* 1 : a

statement testifying to benefits received; *also* : a character reference 2 : an expression of appreciation : TRIBUTE — **testimonial** *adj*

**tes·ti·mo·ny** \ˈtes-tə-ˌmō-nē\ *n, pl* **-nies** 1 : evidence based on observation or knowledge 2 : an outward sign : SYMBOL 3 : a solemn declaration made by a witness under oath esp. in a court ♦ *Synonyms* EVIDENCE, CONFIRMATION, PROOF, TESTAMENT

**tes·tis** \ˈtes-təs\ *n, pl* **tes·tes** \ˈtes-ˌtēz\ [L, witness, testis] : a typically paired male reproductive gland that produces sperm and testosterone and that in most mammals is contained within the scrotum at sexual maturity

**tes·tos·ter·one** \te-ˈstäs-tə-ˌrōn\ *n* : a male sex hormone causing development of the male reproductive system and secondary sex characteristics

**test–tube** *adj* 1 : IN VITRO ⟨~ experiments⟩ 2 : produced by in vitro fertilization ⟨~ babies⟩

**test tube** *n* : a glass tube closed at one end and used esp. in chemistry and biology

**tes·ty** \ˈtes-tē\ *adj* **tes·ti·er; -est** [ME *testif*, fr. AF, headstrong, fr. *teste* head, fr. LL *testa* skull, fr. L, shell] : easily annoyed; *also* : marked by ill humor

**tet·a·nus** \ˈtet-ə-nəs\ *n* : an infectious disease caused by bacterial poisons and marked by muscle stiffness and spasms esp. of the jaws — **tet·a·nal** \-əl\ *adj*

**tetchy** \ˈte-chē\ *adj* **tetchi·er; -est** : irritably or peevishly sensitive

¹**tête–à–tête** \ˈtāt-ə-ˌtāt\ *n* [F, lit., head to head] : a private conversation between two persons

²**tête–à–tête** \ˌtāt-ə-ˈtāt\ *adv* : in private

³**tête–à–tête** \ˈtāt-ə-ˌtāt\ *adj* : being face-to-face : PRIVATE

¹**teth·er** \ˈte-thər\ *n* 1 : something (as a rope) by which an animal is fastened 2 : the limit of one's strength or resources

²**tether** *vb* : to fasten or restrain by or as if by a tether

**tet·ra·eth·yl lead** \ˌte-trə-ˈe-thəl-\ *n* : a heavy oily poisonous liquid used esp. formerly as an antiknock agent in gasoline

**tet·ra·he·dron** \-ˈhē-drən\ *n, pl* **-drons** *or* **-dra** \-drə\ : a polyhedron that has four faces — **tet·ra·he·dral** \-drəl\ *adj*

**tet·ra·hy·dro·can·nab·i·nol** \-ˌhī-drə-kə-ˈna-bə-ˌnȯl, -ˌnōl\ *n* : THC

**te·tram·e·ter** \te-ˈtra-mə-tər\ *n* : a line of verse consisting of four metrical feet

**tet·ri** \ˈte-trē\ *n, pl* **tetri** — see *lari* at MONEY table

**Teu·ton·ic** \tü-ˈtä-nik, tyü-\ *adj* : GERMANIC

**Tex** *abbr* Texas

**Tex–Mex** \ˈteks-ˈmeks\ *adj* : characteristic of Mexican-American culture and esp. that of southern Texas

¹**text** \ˈtekst\ *n* 1 : the actual words of an author's work 2 : the main body of printed or written matter on a page 3 : a scriptural passage chosen as the subject esp. of a sermon 4 : THEME, TOPIC 5

: TEXTBOOK   **6** : TEXT MESSAGE — **tex·tu·al** \'teks-chə-wəl\ *adj*

²**text** *vb* : to send a text message from one cell phone to another

**text·book** \'tekst-ˌbu̇k\ *n* : a book used in the study of a subject

**tex·tile** \'tek-ˌstī(-ə)l, 'teks-tᵊl\ *n* : CLOTH; *esp* : a woven or knit cloth

**text message** *n* : a short message sent electronically to a cell phone or other device

**tex·ture** \'teks-chər\ *n*   **1** : the visual or tactile surface characteristics and appearance of something ⟨a coarse ∼⟩   **2** : essential part   **3** : basic scheme or structure : FABRIC   **4** : overall structure — **tex·tur·al** \-chə-rəl\ *adj*

**TGIF** *abbr* thank God it's Friday

¹**Th** *abbr* Thursday

²**Th** *symbol* thorium

¹**-th** — see ¹-ETH

²**-th** *or* **-eth** *adj suffix* — used in forming ordinal numbers ⟨hundred*th*⟩

³**-th** *n suffix* **1** : act or process **2** : state or condition ⟨dear*th*⟩

**Thai** \'tī\ *n, pl* **Thai** *or* **Thais** **1** : a native or inhabitant of Thailand   **2** : the official language of Thailand — **Thai** *adj*

**thal·a·mus** \'tha-lə-məs\ *n, pl* **-mi** \-ˌmī\ [NL] : a subdivision of the brain that serves as a relay station to and from the cerebral cortex and functions in arousal and the integration of sensory information — **tha·lam·ic** \thə-'la-mik\ *adj*

**thal·as·se·mia** \ˌtha-lə-'sē-mē-ə\ *n* : any of a group of inherited disorders of hemoglobin synthesis

**tha·las·so·ther·a·py** \thə-ˌla-sō-'ther-ə-pē\ *n* [Gk *thalassa* sea] : the use of seawater or sea products (as seaweed) for the benefit of health or beauty

**thal·li·um** \'tha-lē-əm\ *n* : a poisonous metallic chemical element

¹**than** \'than, 'thən\ *conj* **1** — used after a comparative adjective or adverb to introduce the second part of a comparison expressing inequality ⟨older ∼ I am⟩   **2** — used after *other* or a word of similar meaning to express a difference of kind, manner, or identity ⟨adults other ∼ parents⟩

²**than** *prep* : in comparison with ⟨older ∼ me⟩

**thane** \'thān\ *n* **1** : a free retainer of an Anglo-Saxon lord   **2** : a Scottish feudal lord

**thank** \'thaŋk\ *vb* : to express gratitude to ⟨∼*ed* them for the present⟩

**thank·ful** \'thaŋk-fəl\ *adj* **1** : conscious of benefit received **2** : expressive of thanks **3** : GLAD — **thank·ful·ness** *n*

**thank·ful·ly** \-fə-lē\ *adv* **1** : in a thankful manner **2** : as makes one thankful

**thank·less** \'thaŋk-ləs\ *adj* **1** : UNAPPRECIATED **2** : UNGRATEFUL

**thanks** \'thaŋks\ *n pl* : an expression of gratitude

**thanks·giv·ing** \thaŋks-'gi-viŋ\ *n* **1** : the act of giving thanks **2** : a prayer expressing gratitude **3** *cap* : the 4th Thursday in November observed as a legal holiday for giving thanks for divine goodness

¹**that** \'that, thət\ *pron, pl* **those** \'thōz\ **1** : the one indicated, mentioned, or understood ⟨∼ is my house⟩ **2** : the one farther away or first mentioned ⟨this is an elm, ∼'s a maple⟩ **3** : what has been indicated or mentioned ⟨after ∼, we left⟩ **4** : the one or ones : IT, THEY ⟨*those* who wish to leave may do so⟩

²**that** \thət, 'that\ *conj* **1** : the following, namely ⟨he said ∼ he would⟩; *also* : which is, namely ⟨there's a chance ∼ it may fail⟩ **2** : to this end or purpose ⟨shouted ∼ all might hear⟩ **3** : as to result in the following, namely ⟨so heavy ∼ it can't be moved⟩ **4** : for this reason, namely : BECAUSE ⟨we're glad ∼ you came⟩

³**that** *adj, pl* **those** **1** : being the one mentioned, indicated, or understood ⟨∼ boy⟩ ⟨*those* people⟩ **2** : being the one farther away or less immediately under discussion ⟨this chair or ∼ one⟩

⁴**that** \thət, 'that\ *pron* **1** : WHO, WHOM, WHICH ⟨the man ∼ saw you⟩ ⟨the man ∼ you saw⟩ ⟨the money ∼ was spent⟩ **2** : in, on, or at which ⟨the way ∼ he drives⟩ ⟨the day ∼ it rained⟩

⁵**that** \'that\ *adv* : to such an extent or degree ⟨I like it, but not ∼ much⟩

¹**thatch** \'thach\ *vb* : to cover with or as if with thatch — **thatch·er** *n*

²**thatch** *n* **1** : plant material (as straw) for use as roofing **2** : a mat of grass clippings accumulated next to the soil on a lawn **3** : a covering of or as if of thatch ⟨a ∼ of white hair⟩

**thaw** \'thȯ\ *vb* **1** : to melt or cause to melt **2** : to become so warm as to melt ice or snow **3** : to abandon aloofness or hostility — **thaw** *n*

**THC** \ˌtē-(ˌ)āch-'sē\ *n* [*tetrahydrocannabinol*] : a physiologically active chemical from hemp plant resin that is the chief intoxicant in marijuana

¹**the** \thə, before vowel sounds usu thē\ *definite article* **1** : that in particular **2** — used before adjectives functioning as nouns ⟨a word to ∼ wise⟩

²**the** *adv* **1** : to what extent ⟨∼ sooner, ∼ better⟩ **2** : to that extent ⟨the sooner, ∼ better⟩

**theat** *abbr* theater; theatrical

**the·ater** *or* **the·atre** \'thē-ə-tər\ *n* [ME *theatre*, fr. MF, fr. L *theatrum*, fr. Gk *theatron*, fr. *theasthai* to view, fr. *thea* act of seeing] **1** : a building or area for dramatic performances; *also* : a building or area for showing motion pictures **2** : a place of enactment of significant events ⟨∼ of war⟩ **3** : a place (as a lecture room) resembling a theater **4** : dramatic literature or performance

**theater–in–the–round** *n* : a theater with the stage in the center of the auditorium

**the·at·ri·cal** \thē-'a-tri-kəl\ *also* **the·at·ric** \-trik\ *adj* **1** : of or relating to the theater **2** : marked by artificiality of emotion : HISTRIONIC ⟨a ∼ gesture⟩ **3** : marked by extravagant display : SHOWY

**the·at·ri·cals** \-kəlz\ *n pl* : the performance of plays

**the·at·rics** \thē-'a-triks\ *n pl* 1 : THEAT-
RICALS 2 : staged or contrived effects
**the·be** \'thä-bā\ *n, pl* thebe — see *pula* at
MONEY table
**thee** \'thē\ *pron, archaic objective case of*
THOU
**theft** \'theft\ *n* : the act of stealing
**thegn** \'thān\ *n* : THANE 1
**their** \thər, 'ther\ *adj* : of or relating to
them or themselves
**theirs** \'therz\ *pron* : their one : their ones
**the·ism** \'thē-ˌi-zəm\ *n* : belief in the existence of a god or gods — **the·ist** \-ist\ *n
or adj* — **the·is·tic** \thē-'is-tik\ *adj*
**them** \thəm, 'them\ *pron, objective case of*
THEY
**theme** \'thēm\ *n* 1 : a subject or topic of
discourse or of artistic representation 2
: a written exercise : COMPOSITION 3 : a
melodic subject of a musical composition
or movement — **the·mat·ic** \thi-'ma-tik\
*adj*
**them·selves** \thəm-'selvz, them-\ *pron pl*
: THEY, THEM — used reflexively, for emphasis, or in absolute constructions ⟨they
govern ∼⟩ ⟨they ∼ came⟩ ⟨∼ busy,
they sent me⟩
**¹then** \'then\ *adv* 1 : at that time 2 : soon
after that : NEXT 3 : in addition : BE-
SIDES 4 : in that case 5 : CONSEQUENT-
LY
**²then** *n* : that time ⟨since ∼⟩
**³then** *adj* : existing or acting at that time
⟨the ∼ attorney general⟩
**thence** \'thens, 'thens\ *adv* 1 : from that
place 2 *archaic* : THENCEFORTH 3
: from that fact : THEREFROM
**thence·forth** \-ˌfōrth\ *adv* : from that
time forward : THEREAFTER
**thence·for·ward** \thens-'fōr-wərd,
thens-\ *also* **thence·for·wards** \-wərdz\
*adv* : onward from that place or time
**the·oc·ra·cy** \thē-'ä-krə-sē\ *n, pl* -cies 1
: government by officials regarded as divinely inspired 2 : a state governed by a
theocracy — **the·o·crat·ic** \ˌthē-ə-'kra-
tik\ *adj*
**theol** *abbr* theological; theology
**the·ol·o·gy** \thē-'ä-lə-jē\ *n, pl* -gies 1
: the study of religious faith, practice,
and experience; *esp* : the study of God
and of God's relation to the world 2 : a
theory or system of theology — **the·o·lo·
gian** \ˌthē-ə-'lō-jən\ *n* — **the·o·log·i·cal**
\-'lä-ji-kəl\ *adj*
**the·o·rem** \'thē-ə-rəm, 'thir-əm\ *n* 1 : a
statement esp. in mathematics that has
been or is to be proved 2 : an idea accepted or proposed as a demonstrable
truth : PROPOSITION
**the·o·ret·i·cal** \ˌthē-ə-'re-ti-kəl\ *also* the-
**o·ret·ic** \-tik\ *adj* 1 : relating to or having the character of theory 2 : existing
only in theory : HYPOTHETICAL — **the·o·
ret·i·cal·ly** \-ti-k(ə-)lē\ *adv*
**the·o·rise** *Brit var of* THEORIZE
**the·o·rize** \'thē-ə-ˌrīz\ *vb* -rized; -riz·ing
: to form a theory : SPECULATE — **the·o·
rist** \-rist\ *n*
**the·o·ry** \'thē-ə-rē, 'thir-ē\ *n, pl* -ries 1
: abstract thought 2 : the general principles of a subject 3 : a plausible or scien-

tifically acceptable general principle offered to explain observed facts 4 : HY-
POTHESIS, CONJECTURE
**theory of games** : GAME THEORY
**the·os·o·phy** \thē-'ä-sə-fē\ *n* : belief
about God and the world held to be
based on mystical insight — **theo·soph·
i·cal** \ˌthē-ə-'sä-fi-kəl\ *adj* — **the·os·o·
phist** \thē-'ä-sə-fist\ *n*
**ther·a·peu·tic** \ˌther-ə-'pyü-tik\ *adj* [Gk
*therapeutikos*, fr. *therapeuein* to attend,
treat, fr. *theraps* attendant] : of, relating
to, or dealing with healing and esp. with
remedies for diseases — **ther·a·peu·ti·
cal·ly** \-ti-k(ə-)lē\ *adv*
**ther·a·peu·tics** \ˌther-ə-'pyü-tiks\ *n* : a
branch of medical or dental science dealing with the use of remedies
**ther·a·py** \'ther-ə-pē\ *n, pl* -pies : treatment of bodily, mental, or behavioral
disorders — **ther·a·pist** \-pist\ *n*
**¹there** \'ther\ *adv* 1 : in or at that place —
often used interjectionally 2 : to or into
that place ⟨went ∼ after work⟩ 3 : in
that matter or respect
**²there** \'ther, thər\ *pron* — used as a function word to introduce a sentence or
clause ⟨∼'s a pen here⟩
**³there** \'ther\ *n* 1 : that place ⟨get away
from ∼⟩ 2 : that point ⟨you take it from
∼⟩
**there·abouts** \ˌthr-ə-'bauts, 'ther-ə-
ˌbauts\ *or* there·about \-'baut, -ˌbaut\
*adv* 1 : near that place or time 2 : near
that number, degree, or quantity
**there·af·ter** \ther-'af-tər\ *adv* : after that
: AFTERWARD
**there·at** \-'at\ *adv* 1 : at that place 2 : at
that occurrence : on that account
**there·by** \ther-'bī, 'ther-ˌbī\ *adv* 1 : by
that : by that means 2 : connected with
or with reference to that
**there·for** \ther-'fōr\ *adv* : for or in return
for that ⟨wanted a refund ∼⟩
**there·fore** \'ther-ˌfōr\ *adv* : for that reason : CONSEQUENTLY
**there·from** \ther-'frəm\ *adv* : from that
or it
**there·in** \ther-'in\ *adv* 1 : in or into that
place, time, or thing 2 : in that respect
**there·of** \-'əv, -'äv\ *adv* 1 : of that or it 2
: from that : THEREFROM
**there·on** \-'ön, -'än\ *adv* 1 : on that 2
*archaic* : THEREUPON 3
**there·to** \ther-'tü\ *adv* : to that
**there·un·to** \ˌther-'ən-(ˌ)tü, ˌther-ən-'tü\
*adv, archaic* : THERETO
**there·upon** \'ther-ə-ˌpön, -ˌpän; ˌther-ə-
'pön, -'pän\ *adv* 1 : on that matter 2
: THEREFORE 3 : immediately after that
: at once
**there·with** \ther-'with -with\ *adv* 1 : with
that 2 *archaic* : THEREUPON, FORTH-
WITH
**there·with·al** \'ther-wi-ˌthöl, -ˌthöl\ *adv* 1
*archaic* : BESIDES 2 : THEREWITH
**therm** *abbr* thermometer
**ther·mal** \'thər-məl\ *adj* 1 : of, relating
to, or caused by heat 2 : designed to prevent the loss of body heat ⟨∼ under-
wear⟩ — **ther·mal·ly** *adv*
**thermal pollution** *n* : the discharge of

heated liquid (as waste water from a factory) into natural waters at a temperature harmful to the environment

**therm·is·tor** \'thər ˌmis-tər\ *n* : an electrical resistor whose resistance varies sharply with temperature

**ther·mo·cline** \'thər-mə-ˌklīn\ *n* : the region in a thermally stratified body of water that separates warmer surface water from cold deep water

**ther·mo·cou·ple** \'thər-mə-ˌkə-pəl\ *n* : a device for measuring temperature by measuring the temperature-dependent potential difference created at the junction of two dissimilar metals

**ther·mo·dy·nam·ics** \ˌthər-mō-dī-ˈna-miks\ *n* : physics that deals with the mechanical action or relations of heat — **ther·mo·dy·nam·ic** \-mik\ *adj* — **ther·mo·dy·nam·i·cal·ly** \-mi-k(ə-)lē\ *adv*

**ther·mom·e·ter** \thər-ˈmä-mə-tər\ *n* [F *thermomètre*, fr. Gk *thermē* heat + *metron* measure] : an instrument for measuring temperature typically by the rise or fall of a liquid (as mercury) in a thin glass tube — **ther·mo·met·ric** \ˌthər-mə-ˈme-trik\ *adj* — **ther·mo·met·ri·cal·ly** \-tri-k(ə-)lē\ *adv*

**ther·mo·nu·cle·ar** \ˌthər-mō-ˈnü-klē-ər, -ˈnyü-\ *adj* 1 : of or relating to changes in the nucleus of atoms of low atomic weight (as hydrogen) that require a very high temperature (as in the hydrogen bomb) 2 : utilizing or relating to a thermonuclear bomb ⟨~ war⟩

**ther·mo·plas·tic** \ˌthər-mə-ˈplas-tik\ *adj* : capable of softening when heated and of hardening again when cooled ⟨~ resins⟩ — **thermoplastic** *n*

**ther·mos** \'thər-məs\ *n* : a cylindrical container with a vacuum between an inner and an outer wall used to keep liquids hot or cold

**ther·mo·sphere** \'thər-mə-ˌsfir\ *n* : the part of the earth's atmosphere that lies above the mesosphere and that is characterized by steadily increasing temperature with height

**ther·mo·stat** \'thər-mə-ˌstat\ *n* : a device that automatically controls temperature — **ther·mo·stat·ic** \ˌthər-mə-ˈsta-tik\ *adj* — **ther·mo·stat·i·cal·ly** \-ti-k(ə-)lē\ *adv*

**the·sau·rus** \thi-ˈsȯr-əs\ *n, pl* **-sau·ri** \-ˈsȯr-ˌī\ *or* **-sau·rus·es** \-ˈsȯr-ə-səz\ [NL, fr. L; treasure, collection, fr. Gk *thēsauros*] : a book of words and their synonyms — **the·sau·ral** \-ˈsȯr-əl\ *adj*

**these** *pl of* THIS

**the·sis** \'thē-səs\ *n, pl* **the·ses** \'thē-ˌsēz\ 1 : a proposition that a person advances and offers to maintain by argument 2 : an essay embodying results of original research; *esp* : one written for an academic degree

¹**thes·pi·an** \'thes-pē-ən\ *adj, often cap* [fr. *Thespis*, 6th cent. B.C. Greek poet and reputed originator of tragedy] : relating to the drama : DRAMATIC

²**thespian** *n* : ACTOR

**Thess** *abbr* Thessalonians

**Thes·sa·lo·nians** \ˌthe-sə-ˈlō-nyənz, -nē-ənz\ *n* — see BIBLE table

**the·ta** \'thā-tə\ *n* : the 8th letter of the Greek alphabet — Θ or θ

**thew** \'thü, 'thyü\ *n* : MUSCLE, SINEW — usu used in pl.

**they** \'thā\ *pron* 1 : those individuals under discussion : the ones previously mentioned or referred to 2 : unspecified persons : PEOPLE

**thi·a·mine** \'thī-ə-mən, -ˌmēn\ *also* **thi·a·min** \-mən\ *n* : a vitamin of the vitamin B complex essential to normal metabolism and nerve function

¹**thick** \'thik\ *adj* 1 : having relatively great depth or extent from one surface to its opposite ⟨a ~ plank⟩; *also* : heavily built : THICKSET 2 : densely massed : CROWDED; *also* : FREQUENT, NUMEROUS 3 : dense or viscous in consistency ⟨~ syrup⟩ 4 : marked by haze, fog, or mist ⟨~ weather⟩ 5 : measuring in thickness ⟨one meter ~⟩ 6 : imperfectly articulated : INDISTINCT ⟨~ speech⟩ 7 : STUPID, OBTUSE 8 : associated on close terms : INTIMATE 9 : EXCESSIVE ♦ **Synonyms** COMPACT, CLOSE, TIGHT — **thick·ly** *adv*

²**thick** *n* 1 : the most crowded or active part 2 : the part of greatest thickness

**thick and thin** *n* : every difficulty and obstacle ⟨was loyal through *thick and thin*⟩

**thick·en** \'thi-kən\ *vb* : to make or become thick — **thick·en·er** *n*

**thick·et** \'thi-kət\ *n* : a dense growth of bushes or small trees

**thick·ness** \-nəs\ *n* 1 : the smallest of three dimensions ⟨length, width, and ~⟩ 2 : the quality or state of being thick 3 : LAYER, SHEET ⟨a single ~ of canvas⟩

**thick·set** \'thik-ˈset\ *adj* 1 : closely placed or planted 2 : having a thick body : BURLY

**thick-skinned** \-ˈskind\ *adj* 1 : having a thick skin 2 : not easily bothered by criticism or insult ⟨a ~ politician⟩

**thief** \'thēf\ *n, pl* **thieves** \'thēvz\ : one that steals esp. secretly

**thieve** \'thēv\ *vb* **thieved; thiev·ing** : STEAL, ROB ♦ **Synonyms** FILCH, PILFER, PURLOIN, SWIPE

**thiev·ery** \'thē-və-rē\ *n, pl* **-er·ies** : the act of stealing : THEFT

**thigh** \'thī\ *n* : the part of the vertebrate hind or lower limb between the knee and the hip

**thigh·bone** \'thī-ˌbōn\ *n* : FEMUR

**thim·ble** \'thim-bəl\ *n* : a cap or guard worn on the finger to push the needle in sewing — **thim·ble·ful** *n*

¹**thin** \'thin\ *adj* **thin·ner; thin·nest** 1 : having little extent from one surface through to its opposite : not thick : SLENDER 2 : not closely set or placed : SPARSE ⟨~ hair⟩ 3 : not dense or not dense enough : more fluid or rarefied than normal ⟨~ air⟩ ⟨~ syrup⟩ 4 : lacking substance, fullness, or strength ⟨~ broth⟩ 5 : FLIMSY ⟨a ~ excuse⟩ — **thin·ly** *adv* — **thin·ness** *n*

²**thin** *vb* **thinned; thin·ning** : to make or become thin

**thine** \'thīn\ *pron, archaic* : one or the ones belonging to thee

**thing** \'thiŋ\ *n* **1** : a matter of concern : AFFAIR ⟨∼s to do⟩ **2** *pl* : state of affairs ⟨∼s are improving⟩ **3** : EVENT, CIRCUMSTANCE ⟨the crime was a terrible ∼⟩ **4** : DEED, ACT ⟨expected great ∼s of him⟩ **5** : a distinct entity : OBJECT **6** : an inanimate object distinguished from a living being **7** *pl* : POSSESSIONS, EFFECTS **8** : an article of clothing **9** : DETAIL, POINT ⟨checks every little ∼⟩ **10** : IDEA, NOTION ⟨says the first ∼ he thinks of⟩ **11** : something one likes to do : SPECIALTY ⟨doing her ∼⟩

**think** \'thiŋk\ *vb* **thought** \'thȯt\; **thinking 1** : to form or have in the mind **2** : to have as an opinion : BELIEVE **3** : to reflect on : PONDER **4** : to call to mind : REMEMBER **5** : REASON **6** : to form a mental picture of : IMAGINE **7** : to devise by thinking ⟨*thought* up a plan to escape⟩ ♦ **Synonyms** CONCEIVE, FANCY, REALIZE, ENVISAGE — **think·er** *n*

**think tank** *n* : an institute, corporation, or group organized for interdisciplinary research (as in technological or social problems)

**thin·ner** \'thi-nər\ *n* : a volatile liquid (as turpentine) used to thin paint

**thin–skinned** \'thin-'skind\ *adj* **1** : having a thin skin or rind **2** : extremely sensitive to criticism or insult

**¹third** \'thərd\ *adj* : next after the second — **third** *or* **third·ly** *adv*

**²third** *n* **1** : one of three equal parts of something **2** : one that is number three in a countable series **3** : the 3d forward gear in an automotive vehicle

**third degree** *n* : the subjection of a prisoner to mental or physical torture to force a confession

**third dimension** *n* **1** : thickness, depth, or apparent thickness or depth that confers solidity on an object **2** : a quality that confers reality — **third–dimensional** *adj*

**third world** *n, often cap T&W* : the aggregate of the underdeveloped nations of the world

**¹thirst** \'thərst\ *n* **1** : a feeling of dryness in the mouth and throat associated with a desire to drink; *also* : a bodily condition producing this **2** : an ardent desire : CRAVING ⟨a ∼ for knowledge⟩ — **thirsty** *adj*

**²thirst** *vb* **1** : to need drink : suffer thirst **2** : to have a strong desire : CRAVE

**thir·teen** \,thər-'tēn\ *n* : one more than 12 — **thirteen** *adj or pron* — **thir·teenth** \-'tēnth\ *adj or n*

**thir·ty** \'thər-tē\ *n, pl* **thirties** : three times 10 — **thir·ti·eth** \-tē-əth\ *adj or n* — **thirty** *adj or pron*

**¹this** \'this\ *pron, pl* **these** \'thēz\ **1** : the one close or closest in time or space ⟨∼ is your book⟩ **2** : what is in the present or under immediate observation or discussion ⟨∼ is a mess⟩; *also* : what is happening or being done now ⟨after ∼ we'll leave⟩

**²this** *adj, pl* **these 1** : being the one near, present, just mentioned, or more immediately under observation ⟨∼ book⟩ **2**

: constituting the immediate past or future ⟨friends all *these* years⟩

**³this** *adv* : to such an extent or degree ⟨didn't expect to wait ∼ long⟩

**this·tle** \'thi-səl\ *n* : any of various tall prickly composite plants with often showy heads of tightly packed tubular flowers

**this·tle·down** \-,daun\ *n* : the down from the ripe flower head of a thistle

**¹thith·er** \'thi-thər\ *adv* : to that place

**²thither** *adj* : being on the farther side

**thith·er·ward** \-wərd\ *adv* : toward that place : THITHER

**thong** \'thȯŋ\ *n* **1** : a strip esp. of leather or hide **2** : a sandal held on the foot by a thong between the toes **3** : a narrow strip of swimwear or underwear that passes between the thighs

**tho·rax** \'thȯr-,aks\ *n, pl* **tho·rax·es** *or* **tho·ra·ces** \'thȯr-ə-,sēz\ **1** : the part of the body of a mammal between the neck and the abdomen; *also* : its cavity containing the heart and lungs **2** : the middle of the three main divisions of the body of an insect — **tho·rac·ic** \thə-'ra-sik\ *adj*

**tho·ri·um** \'thȯr-ē-əm\ *n* : a radioactive metallic chemical element

**thorn** \'thȯrn\ *n* **1** : a woody plant bearing sharp processes **2** : a sharp rigid plant process that is usu. a modified leafless branch **3** : something that causes distress — **thorny** *adj*

**thor·ough** \'thər-ō\ *adj* **1** : COMPLETE, EXHAUSTIVE ⟨a ∼ search⟩ **2** : very careful : PAINSTAKING ⟨a ∼ scholar⟩ **3** : having full mastery — **thor·ough·ly** *adv* — **thor·ough·ness** *n*

**¹thor·ough·bred** \'thər-ə-,bred\ *adj* **1** : bred from the best blood through a long line **2** *cap* : of or relating to the Thoroughbred breed of horses **3** : marked by high-spirited grace

**²thoroughbred** *n* **1** *cap* : any of an English breed of light speedy horses kept chiefly for racing **2** : one (as a pedigreed animal) of excellent quality

**thor·ough·fare** \-,fer\ *n* : a public road or street

**thor·ough·go·ing** \,thər-ə-'gō-iŋ\ *adj* : marked by thoroughness or zeal

**thorp** \'thȯrp\ *n, archaic* : VILLAGE

**those** *pl of* THAT

**¹thou** \'thau\ *pron, archaic* : the person addressed

**²thou** \'thau\ *n, pl* **thou** : a thousand of something (as dollars)

**¹though** \'thō\ *conj* **1** : despite the fact that ⟨∼ the odds are hopeless, they fight on⟩ **2** : granting that ⟨∼ it may look bad, still, all is not lost⟩

**²though** *adv* : HOWEVER, NEVERTHELESS ⟨not for long, ∼⟩

**¹thought** \'thȯt\ *past and past part of* THINK

**²thought** *n* **1** : the process of thinking **2** : serious consideration : REGARD **3** : reasoning power **4** : the power to imagine : CONCEPTION **5** : IDEA, NOTION **6** : OPINION, BELIEF ⟨spoke his ∼s freely⟩

**thought·ful** \'thȯt-fəl\ *adj* **1** : absorbed in thought **2** : marked by careful thinking

⟨a ∼ essay⟩ **3** : considerate of others ⟨a ∼ host⟩ — **thought·ful·ly** adv — **thought·ful·ness** n

**thought·less** \-ləs\ adj **1** : insufficiently alert : CARELESS ⟨a ∼ worker⟩ **2** : RECKLESS ⟨a ∼ act⟩ **3** : lacking concern for others : INCONSIDERATE ⟨∼ remarks⟩ — **thought·less·ly** adv — **thought·less·ness** n

**thou·sand** \'thaủz-ᵊnd\ n, pl **thousands** or **thousand** : 10 times 100 — **thousand** adj — **thou·sandth** \-ᵊnth\ adj or n

**thousands place** n : the place four to the left of the decimal point in an Arabic number

**thrall** \'thrȯl\ n **1** : SLAVE, BONDMAN **2** : a state of servitude — **thrall·dom** or **thral·dom** \'thrȯl-dəm\ n

**¹thrash** \'thrash\ vb **1** : THRESH 1 **2** : BEAT, WHIP; also : DEFEAT **3** : to move about violently **4** : to go over again and again ⟨∼ over the matter⟩; also : to hammer out ⟨∼ out a plan⟩

**²thrash** n : rock music that is extremely fast and loud

**¹thrash·er** \'thra-shər\ n : one that thrashes or threshes

**²thrasher** n : any of various long-tailed American songbirds related to the mockingbird

**¹thread** \'thred\ n **1** : a thin continuous strand of spun and twisted textile fibers **2** : something resembling a textile thread **3** : the ridge or groove that winds around a screw **4** : a line of reasoning or train of thought **5** : a continuing element **6** : a tenuous or feeble support

**²thread** vb **1** : to pass a thread through the eye of (a needle) **2** : to pass (as film) through something **3** : to make one's way through or between **4** : to put together on a thread ⟨∼ beads⟩ **5** : to form a screw thread on or in

**thread·bare** \-ˌber\ adj **1** : having the nap worn off so that the thread shows : SHABBY **2** : TRITE ⟨∼ excuses⟩

**thready** \'thre-dē\ adj **1** : consisting of or bearing fibers of filaments ⟨a ∼ bark⟩ **2** : lacking in fullness, body, or vigor ⟨a ∼ voice⟩

**threat** \'thret\ n **1** : an expression of intent to do harm **2** : one that threatens

**threat·en** \'thre-tᵊn\ vb **1** : to utter threats against **2** : to give signs or warning of : PORTEND **3** : to hang over as a threat : MENACE **4** : to cause to feel insecure or anxious — **threat·en·ing·ly** adv

**threat·ened** \-tᵊnd\ adj : having an uncertain chance of continued survival; esp : likely to become an endangered species

**three** \'thrē\ n **1** : one more than two **2** : the 3d in a set or series **3** : something having three units — **three** adj or pron

**3–D** \'thrē-'dē\ n : a three-dimensional form or picture

**three–dimensional** adj **1** : relating to or having three dimensions **2** : giving the illusion of varying distances ⟨a ∼ picture⟩

**three·fold** \'thrē-ˌfōld, -'fōld\ adj **1** : having three parts : TRIPLE **2** : being three

times as great or as many — **three·fold** \-'fōld\ adv

**three·pence** \'thre-pəns, 'thri-, 'thrə , US also 'thrē-pens\ n **1** pl **threepence** or **three·penc·es** : a coin worth three pennies **2** : the sum of three British pennies

**three·score** \'thrē-'skȯr\ adj : being three times twenty : SIXTY

**three·some** \'thrē-səm\ n : a group of three persons or things

**thren·o·dy** \'thre-nə-dē\ n, pl **-dies** : a song of lamentation : ELEGY

**thresh** \'thresh, 'thrash\ vb **1** : to separate (as grain from straw) mechanically **2** : THRASH — **thresh·er** n

**thresh·old** \'thresh-ˌhōld\ n **1** : the sill of a door **2** : a point or place of beginning or entering : OUTSET ⟨on the ∼ of a new era⟩ **3** : a point at which a physiological or psychological effect begins to be produced ⟨pain ∼s⟩

**threw** past of THROW

**thrice** \'thrīs\ adv **1** : three times **2** : in a threefold manner or degree

**thrift** \'thrift\ n [ME, fr. ON, prosperity, fr. thrīfask to thrive] : careful management esp. of money : FRUGALITY — **thrift·i·ly** \'thrif-tə-lē\ adv — **thrift·less** adj — **thrifty** adj

**thrill** \'thril\ vb [ME thirlen, thrillen to pierce, fr. OE thyrlian, fr. thyrel hole, fr. thurh through] **1** : to have or cause to have sudden sharp feeling of excitement ⟨was thrilled by their decision⟩; also : TINGLE, SHIVER **2** : TREMBLE, VIBRATE — **thrill** n — **thrill·er** n — **thrill·ing·ly** adv

**thrips** \'thrips\ n, pl **thrips** : any of an order of minute sucking insects including many plant-feeding pests

**thrive** \'thrīv\ vb **thrived** or **throve** \'thrōv\; **thrived** also **thriv·en** \'thri-vən\; **thriv·ing 1** : to grow luxuriantly : FLOURISH **2** : to gain in wealth or possessions : PROSPER ⟨her business ∼s⟩

**throat** \'thrōt\ n : the part of the neck in front of the spinal column; also : the passage through it to the stomach and lungs — **throat·ed** adj

**throaty** \'thrō-tē\ adj **throat·i·er; -est 1** : uttered or produced from low in the throat ⟨a ∼ voice⟩ **2** : heavy, thick, or deep as if from the throat ⟨∼ notes of a horn⟩ — **throat·i·ly** \-tə-lē\ adv — **throat·i·ness** \-tē-nəs\ n

**¹throb** \'thräb\ vb **throbbed; throb·bing** : to pulsate or pound esp. with abnormal force or rapidity : BEAT, VIBRATE

**²throb** n : BEAT, PULSE

**throe** \'thrō\ n **1** : PANG, SPASM ⟨death ∼s⟩ **2** pl : a hard or painful struggle

**throm·bo·lyt·ic** \ˌthräm-bə-'li-tik\ adj : destroying or breaking up a thrombus — **thrombolytic** n

**throm·bo·sis** \thräm-'bō-səs\ n, pl **-bo·ses** \-ˌsēz\ : the formation or presence of a clot in a blood vessel — **throm·bot·ic** \-'bä-tik\ adj

**throm·bus** \'thräm-bəs\ n, pl **throm·bi** \-ˌbī\ [NL, fr. Gk thrombos lump, clot] : a clot of blood formed within a blood vessel and remaining attached to its place of origin

**throne** \'thrōn\ *n* **1** : the chair of state of a sovereign or high dignitary **2** : royal power : SOVEREIGNTY

**¹throng** \'thrȯŋ\ *n* **1** : MULTITUDE **2** : a crowding together of many persons

**²throng** *vb* **thronged; throng·ing** : CROWD

**¹throt·tle** \'thrä-t²l\ *vb* **throt·tled; throt·tling** [ME *throtlen,* fr. *throte* throat] **1** : CHOKE, STRANGLE **2** : SUPPRESS ⟨policies that ∼ creativity⟩ **3** : to reduce the speed of (an engine) by closing the throttle — **throt·tler** *n*

**²throttle** *n* : a valve regulating the flow of steam or fuel to an engine; *also* : the lever controlling this valve

**¹through** \'thrü\ *prep* **1** : into at one side and out at the other side of ⟨go ∼ the door⟩ **2** : by way of ⟨entered ∼ a skylight⟩ **3** : in the midst of ⟨a path ∼ the trees⟩ **4** : by means of ⟨succeeded ∼ hard work⟩ **5** : over the whole of ⟨rumors swept ∼ the office⟩ **6** : during the whole of ⟨∼ the night⟩ **7** : to and including ⟨Monday ∼ Friday⟩

**²through** *adv* **1** : from one end or side to the other **2** : from beginning to end : to completion ⟨see it ∼⟩ **3** : to the core : THOROUGHLY ⟨he was wet ∼⟩ **4** : into the open : OUT ⟨break ∼⟩

**³through** *adj* **1** : permitting free passage ⟨a ∼ street⟩ **2** : going from point of origin to destination without change or transfer ⟨a ∼ train⟩ **3** : coming from or going to points outside a local area ⟨∼ traffic⟩ **4** : FINISHED ⟨∼ with the job⟩

**¹through·out** \thrü-'aȯt\ *adv* **1** : EVERYWHERE **2** : from beginning to end

**²throughout** *prep* **1** : in or to every part of **2** : during the whole period of

**through·put** \'thrü-,pu̇t\ *n* : OUTPUT, PRODUCTION ⟨the ∼ of a computer⟩

**throve** *past of* THRIVE

**¹throw** \'thrō\ *vb* **threw** \'thrü\; **thrown** \'thrōn\; **throw·ing** [ME, to cause to twist, throw, fr. OE *thrāwan* to cause to twist] **1** : to propel through the air esp. with a forward motion of the hand and arm ⟨∼ a ball⟩ **2** : to cause to fall or fall off **3** : to put suddenly in a certain position or condition ⟨∼ into panic⟩ **4** : to put on or take off hastily ⟨∼ on a coat⟩ **5** : to lose intentionally ⟨∼ a game⟩ **6** : to move (a lever) so as to connect or disconnect parts of something (as a clutch) **7** : to put (an automobile) into a different gear **8** : to act as host for ⟨∼ a party⟩ ♦ **Synonyms** TOSS, FLING, PITCH, SLING — **throw·er** *n*

**²throw** *n* **1** : an act of throwing, hurling, or flinging; *also* : CAST **2** : the distance a missile may be thrown **3** : a light coverlet **4** : a woman's scarf or light wrap

**¹throw·away** \'thrō-ə-,wā\ *n* : something that is or is designed to be thrown away esp. after one use

**²throwaway** *adj* : overly wasteful ⟨a ∼ society⟩

**throw·back** \-,bak\ *n* : reversion to an earlier type or phase; *also* : an instance or product of this

**throw up** *vb* **1** : to build hurriedly **2** : VOMIT

**thrum** \'thrəm\ *vb* **thrummed; thrumming** : to play or pluck a stringed instrument idly : STRUM

**thrush** \'thrəsh\ *n* : any of numerous small or medium-sized songbirds that are mostly of a plain color often with spotted underparts

**¹thrust** \'thrəst\ *vb* **thrust; thrust·ing** **1** : to push or drive with force : SHOVE **2** : STAB, PIERCE **3** : INTERJECT **4** : to press the acceptance of upon someone

**²thrust** *n* **1** : a lunge with a pointed weapon **2** : ATTACK **3** : the pressure of one part of a construction against another (as of an arch against an abutment) **4** : the force produced by a propeller or jet or rocket engine that drives a vehicle (as an aircraft) forward **5** : a violent push : SHOVE **6** : prominent or essential element ⟨the ∼ of the argument⟩

**thrust·er** *also* **thrust·or** \'thrəs-tər\ *n* : one that thrusts; *esp* : a rocket engine

**thru·way** \'thrü-,wā\ *n* : EXPRESSWAY

**¹thud** \'thəd\ *n* **1** : ⁴BLOW **2** : a dull sound

**²thud** *vb* **thud·ded; thud·ding** : to move or strike so as to make a thud

**thug** \'thəg\ *n* [Hindi & Urdu *thag,* lit., thief] : a brutal ruffian or assassin — **thug·gish** *adj*

**thu·li·um** \'thü-lē-əm, 'thyü-\ *n* : a rare metallic chemical element

**¹thumb** \'thəm\ *n* **1** : the short thick first digit of the human hand or a corresponding digit of a lower animal **2** : the part of a glove or mitten that covers the thumb

**²thumb** *vb* **1** : to leaf through (pages) with the thumb **2** : to wear or soil with the thumb by frequent handling **3** : to request or obtain (a ride) in a passing automobile by signaling with the thumb

**¹thumb·nail** \'thəm-,nāl\ *n* : the nail of the thumb

**²thumbnail** *adj* : BRIEF, CONCISE ⟨a ∼ description⟩ ⟨a ∼ picture⟩

**thumb·print** \-,print\ *n* : an impression made by the thumb

**thumb·screw** \-,skrü\ *n* **1** : a device of torture for squeezing the thumb **2** : a screw with a head that may be turned by the thumb and index finger

**thumb·tack** \-,tak\ *n* : a tack with a broad flat head for pressing with one's thumb into a board or wall

**¹thump** \'thəmp\ *vb* **1** : to strike with or as if with something thick or heavy so as to cause a dull sound **2** : POUND

**²thump** *n* : a blow with or as if with something blunt or heavy; *also* : the sound made by such a blow

**¹thun·der** \'thən-dər\ *n* **1** : the sound following a flash of lightning; *also* : a noise like such a sound **2** : a loud utterance or threat

**²thunder** *vb* **1** : to produce thunder **2** : ROAR, SHOUT ⟨jets ∼ed overhead⟩

**thun·der·bolt** \-,bōlt\ *n* : a flash of lightning with its accompanying thunder

**thun·der·clap** \-ˌklap\ n : a crash of thunder

**thun·der·cloud** \-ˌklaůd\ n : a cloud charged with electricity and producing lightning and thunder

**thun·der·head** \-ˌhed\ n : a large cumulus or cumulonimbus cloud often appearing before a thunderstorm

**thun·der·ous** \ˈthən-də-rəs\ adj : producing thunder; also : making a noise like thunder — **thun·der·ous·ly** adv

**thun·der·show·er** \ˈthən-dər-ˌshaů(-ə)r\ n : a shower accompanied by thunder and lightning

**thun·der·storm** \-ˌstȯrm\ n : a storm accompanied by thunder and lightning

**thun·der·struck** \-ˌstrək\ adj : stunned as if struck by a thunderbolt

**Thurs** or **Thu** abbr Thursday

**Thurs·day** \ˈthərz-dā, -dē\ n [ME, fr. OE thursdæg, fr. ON thōrsdagr, lit., day of Thor (Norse god)] : the 5th day of the week

**thus** \ˈthəs\ adv 1 : in this or that manner 2 : to this degree or extent : SO 3 : because of this or that : HENCE

¹**thwack** \ˈthwak\ vb : to strike with or as if with something flat or heavy

²**thwack** n : a heavy blow : WHACK

¹**thwart** \ˈthwȯrt\ vb 1 : FOIL, BAFFLE 2 : BLOCK, DEFEAT ⟨∼ed the attack⟩
♦ **Synonyms** BALK, OUTWIT, FRUSTRATE

²**thwart** \ˈthwȯrt, naut often ˈthȯrt\ adv : ATHWART

³**thwart** adj : situated or placed across something else

⁴**thwart** n : a seat extending across a boat

**thy** \ˈthī\ adj, archaic : of, relating to, or done by or to thee or thyself

**thyme** \ˈtīm, ˈthīm\ n [ME, fr. AF time, fr. L thymum, fr. Gk thymon, prob. fr. thyein to make a burnt offering, sacrifice] : a garden mint with small aromatic leaves used esp. in seasoning; also : its leaves so used

**thy·mine** \ˈthī-ˌmēn\ n : a pyrimidine base that is one of the four bases coding genetic information in the molecular chain of DNA

**thy·mus** \ˈthī-məs\ n, pl **thy·mus·es** : a glandular organ of the neck region that is composed largely of lymphoid tissue, functions esp. in the development of the immune system, and tends to atrophy in the adult

**thy·ris·tor** \thī-ˈris-tər\ n : a semiconductor device that acts as a switch, rectifier, or voltage regulator

**thy·roid** \ˈthī-ˌrȯid\ n [NL thyroides, fr. Gk thyreoeidēs shield-shaped, thyroid, fr. thyreos shield shaped like a door, fr. thyra door] : a large 2-lobed endocrine gland that lies at the base of the neck and produces several iodine-containing hormones that affect growth, development, and metabolism — **thyroid** also **thy·roi·dal** \thī-ˈrȯi-dᵊl\ adj

**thy·rox·ine** or **thy·rox·in** \thī-ˈräk-ˌsēn, -sən\ n : an iodine-containing hormone that is produced by the thyroid gland, increases metabolic rate, and is used to treat thyroid disorders

**thy·self** \thī-ˈself\ pron, archaic : YOURSELF

**Ti** symbol titanium

**ti·ara** \tē-ˈer-ə, -ˈär-\ n 1 : a 3-tiered crown worn by the pope 2 : a decorative headband or semicircle for formal wear by women

**Ti·bet·an** \tə-ˈbe-tᵊn\ n 1 : the language of the Tibetan people 2 : a native or inhabitant of Tibet — **Tibetan** adj

**tib·ia** \ˈti-bē-ə\ n, pl **-i·ae** \-bē-ˌē\ also **-i·as** [L] : the inner of the two bones of the vertebrate hind or lower limb between the knee and the ankle

**tic** \ˈtik\ n : a local and habitual twitching of muscles esp. of the face

**ti·cal** \ti-ˈkäl, ˈti-kəl\ n, pl **ticals** or **tical** : BAHT

¹**tick** \ˈtik\ n : any of a large group of small bloodsucking arachnids

²**tick** n : the fabric case of a mattress or pillow; also : a mattress consisting of a tick and its filling

³**tick** n 1 : a light rhythmic audible tap or beat 2 : a small mark used to draw attention to or check something

⁴**tick** vb 1 : to make the sound of a tick or series of ticks 2 : to mark, count, or announce by or as if by ticking beats 3 : to mark or check with a tick 4 : to function as an operating mechanism : RUN

⁵**tick** n, chiefly Brit : CREDIT; also : a credit account

**tick·er** \ˈti-kər\ n 1 : something (as a watch) that ticks 2 : a telegraph instrument that prints information (as stock prices) on paper tape 3 slang : HEART

**ticker tape** n : the paper ribbon on which a telegraphic ticker prints

¹**tick·et** \ˈti-kət\ n [MF etiquet, estiquette notice attached to something, fr. MF dial. estiquier to attach, fr. MD steken to stick] 1 : CERTIFICATE, LICENSE, PERMIT; esp : a certificate or token showing that a fare or admission fee has been paid 2 : TAG, LABEL 3 : SLATE 4 : a summons issued to a traffic offender

²**ticket** vb 1 : to attach a ticket to 2 : to furnish or serve with a ticket

**tick·ing** \ˈti-kiŋ\ n : a strong fabric used in upholstering and as a mattress covering

**tick·le** \ˈti-kəl\ vb **tick·led; tick·ling** 1 : to excite or stir up agreeably : PLEASE, AMUSE 2 : to have a tingling sensation 3 : to touch (as a body part) lightly so as to cause uneasiness, laughter, or spasmodic movements ⟨tickled her under the chin⟩ — **tickle** n — **tick·ler** n

**tick·lish** \-kə-lish\ adj 1 : OVERSENSITIVE, TOUCHY 2 : UNSTABLE ⟨a ∼ foothold⟩ 3 : requiring delicate handling ⟨∼ subject⟩ 4 : sensitive to tickling — **tick·lish·ly** adv — **tick·lish·ness** n

**tidal wave** n 1 : an unusually high sea wave that sometimes follows an earthquake 2 : an unusual rise of water along-shore due to strong winds

**tid·bit** \ˈtid-ˌbit\ n : a choice morsel

¹**tide** \ˈtīd\ n [ME, time, fr. OE tīd] 1 : the

alternate rising and falling of the surface of the ocean **2** : something that fluctuates like the tides of the sea ⟨the ~ of public opinion⟩ — **tid·al** \'tī-dᵊl\ adj

²**tide** vb **tid·ed; tid·ing** : to carry through or help along as if by the tide ⟨a loan to ~ us over⟩

**tide·land** \'tīd-ₗland, -lənd\ n **1** : land overflowed during flood tide **2** : land under the ocean within a nation's territorial waters — often used in pl.

**tide·wa·ter** \-ₗwȯ-tər, -ₗwä-\ n **1** : water overflowing land at flood tide **2** : low-lying coastal land

**tid·ings** \'tī-diŋz\ n pl : NEWS, MESSAGE

¹**ti·dy** \'tī-dē\ adj **ti·di·er; -est 1** : well ordered and cared for : NEAT **2** : LARGE, SUBSTANTIAL ⟨a ~ sum⟩ — **ti·di·ness** \'tī-dē-nəs\ n

²**tidy** vb **ti·died; ti·dy·ing 1** : to put in order **2** : to make things tidy

³**tidy** n, pl **tidies** : a decorated covering used to protect the back or arms of a chair from wear or soil

¹**tie** \'tī\ n **1** : a line, ribbon, or cord used for fastening, uniting, or closing **2** : a structural element (as a beam or rod) holding two pieces together **3** : one of the cross supports to which railroad rails are fastened **4** : a connecting link : BOND ⟨family ~s⟩ **5** : an equality in number (as of votes or scores); also : an undecided or deadlocked contest **6** : NECKTIE

²**tie** vb **tied; ty·ing** or **tie·ing 1** : to fasten, attach, or close by means of a tie **2** : to bring together firmly : UNITE **3** : to form a knot or bow in ⟨~ a scarf⟩ **4** : to restrain from freedom of action : CONSTRAIN **5** : to make or have an equal score with

**tie·back** \'tī-ₗbak\ n : a decorative strip for draping a curtain to the side of a window

**tie–dye·ing** \'tī-ₗdī-iŋ\ n : a method of producing patterns in textiles by tying parts of the fabric so that they will not absorb the dye — **tie–dyed** \-ₗdīd\ adj

**tie–in** \'tī-ₗin\ n : CONNECTION

**tier** \'tir\ n : ROW, LAYER; esp : one of two or more rows arranged one above another — **tiered** \'tird\ adj

**tie–rod** \'tī-ₗräd\ n : a rod used as a connecting member or brace

**tie–up** \-ₗəp\ n **1** : a slowing or stopping of traffic or business **2** : CONNECTION

**tiff** \'tif\ n : a petty quarrel — **tiff** vb

**Tif·fa·ny** \'ti-fə-nē\ adj : made of pieces of stained glass ⟨a ~ lamp⟩

**ti·ger** \'tī-gər\ n : a very large tawny black-striped Asian cat — **ti·ger·ish** adj

¹**tight** \'tīt\ adj **1** : so close in structure as to prevent passage of a liquid or gas **2** : strongly fixed or held : SECURE **3** : TAUT **4** : fitting usu. too closely ⟨~ shoes⟩ **5** : set close together : COMPACT ⟨a ~ formation⟩ **6** : DIFFICULT, TRYING ⟨get in a ~ spot⟩ **7** : STINGY, MISERLY **8** : evenly contested : CLOSE **9** : INTOXICATED **10** : low in supply : hard to get ⟨money is ~⟩ — **tight·ly** adv — **tight·ness** n

²**tight** adv **1** : TIGHTLY, FIRMLY **2** : SOUNDLY ⟨sleep ~⟩

**tight·en** \'tī-tᵊn\ vb : to make or become tight

**tight·fist·ed** \'tīt-'fis-təd\ adj : STINGY

**tight·rope** \-ₗrōp\ n : a taut rope or wire for acrobats to perform on

**tights** \'tīts\ n pl : skintight garments covering the body esp. below the waist; also, Brit : PANTY HOSE

**tight·wad** \'tīt-ₗwäd\ n : a stingy person

**ti·gress** \'tī-grəs\ n : a female tiger

**ti·la·pia** \tə-'lä-pē-ə, -'lā-\ n, pl **tilapia** also **ti·la·pi·as** : any of numerous chiefly African freshwater fishes widely raised for food

**til·de** \'til-də\ n [Sp, fr. ML titulus tittle] : a mark ⁓ placed esp. over the letter n (as in Spanish señor sir) to denote the sound \nʸ\ or over vowels (as in Portuguese irmã sister) to indicate nasal quality

¹**tile** \'tī(-ə)l\ n **1** : a flat or curved piece of fired clay, stone, or concrete used for roofs, floors, or walls; also : a pipe of earthenware or concrete used for a drain **2** : a thin piece (as of linoleum) used for covering walls or floors — **til·ing** \'tī-liŋ\ n

²**tile** vb **tiled; til·ing** : to cover with tiles — **til·er** n

¹**till** \'til\ prep or conj : UNTIL

²**till** vb : to work by plowing, sowing, and raising crops : CULTIVATE — **till·able** adj

³**till** n : DRAWER; esp : a money drawer in a store or bank

**till·age** \'ti-lij\ n **1** : the work of tilling land **2** : cultivated land

¹**til·ler** \'ti-lər\ n [OE telgor, telgra twig, shoot] : a sprout or stalk esp. from the base or lower part of a plant

²**till·er** \'ti-lər\ n : one that tills

³**till·er** \'ti-lər\ n [ME tiler stock of a crossbow, tiller, fr. AF teiler stock of a crossbow] : a lever used for turning a boat's rudder from side to side

¹**tilt** \'tilt\ n **1** : a contest in which two combatants charging usu. with lances try to unhorse each other : JOUST; also : a tournament of tilts **2** : a verbal contest : DISPUTE **3** : a sloping surface : SLANT

²**tilt** vb **1** : to move or shift so as to incline : TIP **2** : to engage in or as if in combat with lances : JOUST, ATTACK

**tilth** \'tilth\ n **1** : TILLAGE **2** : the state of a soil esp. in relation to the suitability of its particle size and structure for growing crops

**Tim** abbr Timothy

**tim·ber** \'tim-bər\ n [ME, fr. OE, building, wood] **1** : growing trees or their wood — often used interjectionally to warn of a falling tree **2** : wood for use in making something **3** : a usu. large squared or dressed piece of wood

**tim·bered** \'tim-bərd\ adj : having walls framed by exposed timbers

**tim·ber·land** \'tim-bər-ₗland\ n : wooded land

**tim·ber·line** \'tim-bər-ₗlīn\ n : the upper limit of tree growth in mountains or high latitudes

**timber rattlesnake** *n* : a widely distributed rattlesnake of the eastern U.S.

**timber wolf** *n* : GRAY WOLF

**tim·bre** *also* **tim·ber** \'tam-bər, 'tim-\ *n* [F, fr. MF, bell struck by a hammer, fr. OF, drum, fr. MGk *tymbanon* kettledrum, fr. Gk *tympanon*] : the distinctive quality given to a sound by its overtones

**tim·brel** \'tim-brəl\ *n* : a small hand drum or tambourine

¹**time** \'tīm\ *n* 1 : a period during which an action, process, or condition exists or continues ⟨gone a long ∼⟩ 2 : LEISURE ⟨found ∼ to read⟩ 3 : a point or period when something occurs : OCCASION ⟨the last ∼ we met⟩ 4 : a set or customary moment or hour for something to occur ⟨arrived on ∼⟩ 5 : AGE, ERA 6 : state of affairs : CONDITIONS ⟨hard ∼s⟩ 7 : a rate of speed : TEMPO 8 : a moment, hour, day, or year as indicated by a clock or calendar ⟨what ∼ is it⟩ 9 : a system of reckoning time ⟨solar ∼⟩ 10 : one of a series of recurring instances; *also, pl* : added or accumulated quantities or examples ⟨five ∼s greater⟩ 11 : a person's experience during a particular period ⟨had a good ∼⟩ 12 : the hours or days of one's work; *also* : an hourly pay rate ⟨straight ∼⟩ 13 : TIME-OUT 1

²**time** *vb* **timed; tim·ing** 1 : to arrange or set the time of : SCHEDULE ⟨∼s his calls conveniently⟩ 2 : to set the tempo or duration of ⟨∼ a performance⟩ 3 : to cause to keep time with 4 : to determine or record the time, duration, or rate of ⟨∼ a sprinter⟩ — **tim·er** *n*

**time bomb** *n* 1 : a bomb so made as to explode at a predetermined time 2 : something with a potentially dangerous delayed reaction

**time clock** *n* : a clock that records the time workers arrive and depart

**time frame** *n* : a period of time esp. with respect to some action or project

**time–hon·ored** \'tīm-ˌä-nərd\ *adj* : honored because of age or long usage

**time·keep·er** \-ˌkē-pər\ *n* 1 : a clerk who keeps records of the time worked by employees 2 : one appointed to mark and announce the time in an athletic game or contest

**time·less** \-ləs\ *adj* 1 : ETERNAL 2 : not limited or affected by time ⟨∼ works of art⟩ — **time·less·ly** *adv* — **time·less·ness** *n*

**time·ly** \-lē\ *adj* **time·li·er; -est** 1 : coming early or at the right time ⟨a ∼ decision⟩ ⟨∼ payment⟩ 2 : appropriate to the time ⟨a ∼ book⟩ — **time·li·ness** *n*

**time–out** \'tīm-'aút\ *n* 1 : a brief suspension of activity esp. in an athletic game 2 : a quiet period used esp. as a disciplinary measure for a child

**time·piece** \-ˌpēs\ *n* : a device (as a clock) to show the passage of time

**times** \'tīmz\ *prep* : multiplied by ⟨2 ∼ 2 is 4⟩

**time–shar·ing** \'tīm-ˌsher-iŋ\ *n* 1 : simultaneous use of a computer by many users 2 *or* **time–share** \-ˌsher\ : joint ownership or rental of a vacation lodging by

several persons with each taking turns using the place

**times sign** *n* : the symbol × used to indicate multiplication

**time·ta·ble** \'tīm-ˌtā-bəl\ *n* 1 : a table of the departure and arrival times (as of trains) 2 : a schedule showing a planned order or sequence

**time warp** *n* : an anomaly, discontinuity, or suspension held to occur in the progress of time

**time–worn** \-ˌwórn\ *adj* 1 : worn by time 2 : HACKNEYED, STALE ⟨a ∼ joke⟩

**tim·id** \'ti-məd\ *adj* : lacking in courage or self-confidence : FEARFUL — **ti·mid·i·ty** \tə-'mi-də-tē\ *n* — **tim·id·ly** *adv*

**tim·o·rous** \'ti-mə-rəs\ *adj* : of a timid disposition : AFRAID ⟨a ∼ kitten⟩ — **tim·o·rous·ly** *adv* — **tim·o·rous·ness** *n*

**tim·o·thy** \'ti-mə-thē\ *n* : a perennial grass with long cylindrical spikes widely grown for hay in the U.S.

**Tim·o·thy** \'ti-mə-thē\ *n* — see BIBLE table

**tim·pa·ni** \'tim-pə-nē\ *n sing or pl* [It] : a set of kettledrums played by one performer in an orchestra — **tim·pa·nist** \-nist\ *n*

¹**tin** \'tin\ *n* 1 : a soft white crystalline metallic chemical element malleable at ordinary temperatures that is used esp. in solders and alloys 2 : a container (as a can) made of metal (as tinplate)

²**tin** *vb* **tinned; tin·ning** 1 : to cover or plate with tin 2 : to pack in tins

**TIN** *abbr* taxpayer identification number

**tinct** \'tiŋkt\ *n* : TINCTURE, TINGE

¹**tinc·ture** \'tiŋk-chər\ *n* 1 *archaic* : a substance that colors 2 : a slight admixture : TRACE 3 : an alcoholic solution of a medicinal substance ♦ **Synonyms** TOUCH, SUGGESTION, SUSPICION, TINGE

²**tincture** *vb* **tinc·tured; tinc·tur·ing** 1 : COLOR, TINGE 2 : AFFECT

**tin·der** \'tin-dər\ *n* 1 : a very flammable substance used as kindling 2 : something serving to incite or inflame

**tin·der·box** \'tin-dər-ˌbäks\ *n* 1 : a metal box for holding tinder and usu. flint and steel for striking a spark 2 : a highly flammable object or place

**tine** \'tīn\ *n* : a slender pointed part (as of a fork or an antler) : PRONG

**tin·foil** \'tin-ˌfói(-ə)l\ *n* : a thin metal sheeting usu. of aluminum or tin-lead alloy

¹**tinge** \'tinj\ *vb* **tinged; tinge·ing** *or* **ting·ing** 1 : to color slightly : TINT 2 : to affect or modify esp. with a slight odor or taste

²**tinge** *n* : a slight coloring, flavor, or quality : TRACE ⟨a ∼ of color⟩ ⟨a ∼ of regret⟩ ♦ **Synonyms** TOUCH, SUGGESTION, SUSPICION, TINCTURE, SOUPÇON

**tin·gle** \'tiŋ-gəl\ *vb* **tin·gled; tin·gling** 1 : to feel a prickling or thrilling sensation 2 : TINKLE — **tingle** *n*

¹**tin·ker** \'tiŋ-kər\ *n* 1 : a usu. itinerant mender of household utensils 2 : an unskillful mender : BUNGLER

²**tinker** *vb* : to repair or adjust something

in an unskillful or experimental manner — **tin·ker·er** *n*

¹**tin·kle** \'tiŋ-kəl\ *vb* **tin·kled; tin·kling** : to make or cause to make a tinkle

²**tinkle** *n* : a series of short high ringing or clinking sounds

**tin·ni·tus** \'tī-nə-təs, tə-'nī-təs\ *n* : a sensation of noise (as ringing or roaring) in the ears

**tin·ny** \'ti-nē\ *adj* **tin·ni·er; -est** **1** : abounding in or yielding tin **2** : resembling tin; *also* : LIGHT, CHEAP **3** : thin in tone ⟨a ~ voice⟩ — **tin·ni·ly** \-nə-lē\ *adv* — **tin·ni·ness** \-nē-nəs\ *n*

**tin·plate** \'tin-'plāt\ *n* : thin sheet iron or steel coated with tin — **tin—plate** *vb*

**tin·sel** \'tin-səl\ *n* [ME *tyneseyle* cloth interwoven with metallic thread, prob. fr. AF *tencelé*, pp. of *tenceler, estenceler* to sparkle] **1** : threads, strips, or sheets of metal, paper, or plastic used to produce a glittering appearance **2** : something superficially attractive but of little worth

**tin·smith** \'tin-,smith\ *n* : one that works with sheet metal (as tinplate)

¹**tint** \'tint\ *n* **1** : a slight or pale coloration : HUE **2** : any of various shades of a color

²**tint** *vb* : to impart a tint to : COLOR

**tin·tin·nab·u·la·tion** \,tin-tə-,na-byə-'lā-shən\ *n* **1** : the ringing of bells **2** : a tinkling or jingling sound as if of bells

**tin·ware** \'tin-,wer\ *n* : articles and esp. utensils made of tinplate

**ti·ny** \'tī-nē\ *adj* **ti·ni·er; -est** : very small : MINUTE ♦ *Synonyms* MINIATURE, DIMINUTIVE, WEE, LILLIPUTIAN

¹**tip** \'tip\ *vb* **tipped; tip·ping** **1** : OVERTURN, UPSET **2** : LEAN, SLANT; *also* : to raise and tilt forward ⟨*tipped* his hat⟩

²**tip** *n* : the act or an instance of tipping

³**tip** *vb* **tipped; tip·ping** : to furnish with a tip **2** : to cover or adorn the tip of

⁴**tip** *n* **1** : the usu. pointed end of something **2** : a small piece or part serving as an end, cap, or point

⁵**tip** *n* : a light touch or blow

⁶**tip** *vb* **tipped; tip·ping** : to strike lightly : TAP

⁷**tip** *n* : a piece of advice or expert or confidential information : HINT

⁸**tip** *vb* **tipped; tip·ping** : to impart a piece of information about or to

⁹**tip** *vb* **tipped; tip·ping** : to give a gratuity to — **tip·per** *n*

¹⁰**tip** *n* : a gift or small sum given for a service performed or anticipated

**tip—off** \'tip-,óf\ *n* : WARNING, TIP

**tip·pet** \'ti-pət\ *n* : a long scarf or shoulder cape

**tipping point** *n* : the critical point in a situation or process beyond which a significant effect takes place

**tip·ple** \'ti-pəl\ *vb* **tip·pled; tip·pling** : to drink intoxicating liquor esp. habitually or excessively — **tipple** *n* — **tip·pler** *n*

**tip·ster** \'tip-stər\ *n* : a person who gives or sells tips esp. for gambling

**tip·sy** \'tip-sē\ *adj* **tip·si·er; -est** : unsteady or foolish from the effects of alcohol — **tip·si·ly** \-sə-lē\ *adv* — **tip·si·ness** \-sē-nəs\ *n*

¹**tip·toe** \'tip-,tō\ *n* : the position of being balanced on the balls of the feet and toes with the heels raised; *also* : the ends of the toes

²**tiptoe** *adv or adj* : on or as if on tiptoe

³**tiptoe** *vb* **tip·toed; tip·toe·ing** : to walk or proceed on or as if on tiptoe ⟨~ around the issue⟩

¹**tip—top** \'tip-'täp\ *n* : the highest point

²**tip—top** *adj* : EXCELLENT, FIRST-RATE

**ti·rade** \'tī-,rād\ *n* [F, shot, tirade, fr. MF, fr. It *tirata*, fr. *tirare* to draw, shoot] : a prolonged speech of abuse or condemnation

**tir·a·mi·su** \,tir-ə-'mē-sü, -,mē-'sü\ *n* [It *tiramisù*] : a dessert made with ladyfingers, mascarpone, and espresso

¹**tire** \'tī(-ə)r\ *vb* **tired; tir·ing** **1** : to make or become weary : FATIGUE **2** : to wear out the patience of : BORE

²**tire** *n* **1** : a metal hoop that forms the tread of a wheel **2** : a rubber cushion usu. containing compressed air that encircles a wheel (as of a bike)

**tired** *adj* **1** : WEARY, FATIGUED **2** : HACKNEYED — **tired·ness** *n*

**tire·less** \'tī(-ə)r-ləs\ *adj* : not tiring : UNTIRING, INDEFATIGABLE ⟨~ workers⟩ — **tire·less·ly** *adv* — **tire·less·ness** *n*

**tire·some** \-səm\ *adj* : tending to bore : WEARISOME, TEDIOUS ⟨~ lectures⟩ — **tire·some·ly** *adv* — **tire·some·ness** *n*

**ti·ro** *chiefly Brit var of* TYRO

**tis·sue** \'ti-shü\ *n* [ME *tysshewe, tyssew*, a rich fabric, fr. AF, fr. *tistre* to weave, fr. L *texere*] **1** : a fine lightweight often sheer fabric **2** : NETWORK, WEB ⟨a ~ of lies⟩ **3** : a soft absorbent paper **4** : a mass or layer of cells forming a basic structural material of an animal or plant

¹**tit** \'tit\ *n* : TEAT

²**tit** *n* : any of various small plump Old World songbirds related to the titmice

**Tit** *abbr* Titus

**ti·tan** \'tī-t³n\ *n* **1** *cap* : one of a family of giants overthrown by the gods in Greek mythology **2** : one gigantic in size or power ⟨a media ~⟩

**ti·tan·ic** \tī-'ta-nik\ *adj* : enormous in size, force, or power ♦ *Synonyms* IMMENSE, GIGANTIC, GIANT, COLOSSAL, MAMMOTH

**ti·ta·ni·um** \tī-'tā-nē-əm\ *n* : a gray light strong metallic chemical element used esp. in alloys

**titbit** *var of* TIDBIT

**tithe** \'tīth\ *n* [ME, fr. OE *teogotha* tenth] : a 10th part paid or given esp. for the support of a church — **tithe** *vb* — **tith·er** *n*

**tit·il·late** \'ti-t³l-,āt\ *vb* **-lat·ed; -lat·ing** **1** : to excite pleasurably **2** : TICKLE **3** — **tit·il·la·tion** \,ti-t³l-'lā-shən\ *n*

**tit·i·vate** *or* **tit·ti·vate** \'ti-tə-,vāt\ *vb* **-vat·ed; -vat·ing** : to dress up : spruce up — **tit·i·va·tion** \,ti-tə-'vā-shən\ *n*

**ti·tle** \'tī-t³l\ *n* **1** : CLAIM, RIGHT; *esp* : a legal right to the ownership of property **2** : the distinguishing name of a written, filmed, or musical production or a work of art **3** : an appellation of honor, rank, or office **4** : CHAMPIONSHIP ♦ *Synonyms* DESIGNATION, DENOMINATION, APPELLATION

**ti·tled** \'tī-t°ld\ *adj* : having a title esp. of nobility

**title page** *n* : a page of a book bearing the title and usu. the names of the author and publisher

**tit·mouse** \'tit-ˌmaus\ *n*, *pl* **tit·mice** \-ˌmīs\ : any of several small long-tailed No. American songbirds related to the chickadees

**ti·tra·tion** \tī-'trā-shən\ *n* : a process of finding the concentration of a solution (as of an acid) by adding small portions of a second solution of known concentration (as of a base) to a fixed amount of the first until an expected change (as in color) occurs

**tit·ter** \'ti-tər\ *vb* : to laugh in an affected or in a nervous or half suppressed manner : GIGGLE — **titter** *n*

**tit·tle** \'ti-t°l\ *n* : a tiny part

**tit·tle–tat·tle** \'ti-t°l-ˌta-t°l\ *n* : idle talk : GOSSIP — **tittle–tattle** *vb*

**tit·u·lar** \'ti-chə-lər\ *adj* **1** : existing in title only : NOMINAL ⟨~ ruler⟩ **2** : of, relating to, or bearing a title ⟨~ role⟩

**Ti·tus** \'tī-təs\ *n* — see BIBLE table

**ti·yin** \tē-'ēn\ *n* **1** *pl* **ti·yins** — see *tenge* at MONEY table **2** *pl* **tiyin** or **tiyins** — see *som* at MONEY table

**tiz·zy** \'ti-zē\ *n*, *pl* **tizzies** : a highly excited and distracted state of mind

**tk** *abbr* **1** tank **2** truck

**TKO** \ˌtē-ˌkā-'ō\ *n* [*technical knockout*] : the termination of a boxing match when a boxer is declared unable to continue the fight

**tkt** *abbr* ticket

**Tl** *symbol* thallium

**TLC** *abbr* tender loving care

**T lymphocyte** *n* : T CELL

**Tm** *symbol* thulium

**TM** *abbr* trademark

**T–man** \'tē-ˌman\ *n* : a special agent of the U.S. Treasury Department

**tn** *abbr* **1** ton **2** town

**TN** *abbr* Tennessee

**tng** *abbr* training

**tnpk** *abbr* turnpike

**TNT** \ˌtē-(ˌ)en-'tē\ *n* : a flammable toxic compound used as a high explosive and in chemical synthesis

**¹to** \tə, 'tü\ *prep* **1** : in the direction of and reaching ⟨drove ~ town⟩ **2** : in the direction of : TOWARD **3** : ON, AGAINST ⟨apply salve ~ a burn⟩ **4** : as far as ⟨can pay up ~ a dollar⟩ **5** : so as to become or bring about ⟨beaten ~ death⟩ ⟨broken ~ pieces⟩ **6** : BEFORE ⟨it's five minutes ~ six⟩ **7** : UNTIL ⟨from May ~ December⟩ **8** : fitting or being a part of : FOR ⟨key ~ the lock⟩ **9** : with the accompaniment of ⟨sing ~ the music⟩ **10** : in relation or comparison with ⟨similar ~ that one⟩ ⟨won 10 ~ 6⟩ **11** : in accordance with ⟨add salt ~ taste⟩ **12** : within the range of ⟨~ my knowledge⟩ **13** : contained, occurring, or included in ⟨two pints ~ a quart⟩ **14** : as regards ⟨agreeable ~ everyone⟩ **15** : affecting as the receiver or beneficiary ⟨whispered ~ her⟩ ⟨gave it ~ me⟩ **16** : for no one except ⟨a room ~ myself⟩ **17** : into the

action of ⟨we got ~ talking⟩ **18** — used for marking the following verb as an infinitive ⟨wants ~ go⟩ and often used by itself at the end of a clause in place of an infinitive suggested by the preceding context ⟨goes to town whenever he wants ~⟩ ⟨can leave if you'd like ~⟩

**²to** \'tü\ *adv* **1** : in a direction toward ⟨run ~ and fro⟩ **2** : into contact esp. with the frame of a door ⟨the door slammed ~⟩ **3** : to the matter in hand ⟨fell ~ and ate heartily⟩ **4** : to a state of consciousness or awareness ⟨came ~ hours after the accident⟩

**TO** *abbr* turn over

**toad** \'tōd\ *n* : any of numerous tailless leaping amphibians differing typically from the related frogs in having a shorter stockier build, rough dry warty skin, and less aquatic habits

**toad·stool** \-ˌstül\ *n* : MUSHROOM; *esp* : one that is poisonous or inedible

**toady** \'tō-dē\ *n*, *pl* **toad·ies** : a person who flatters in the hope of gaining favors : SYCOPHANT — **toady** *vb*

**to–and–fro** \ˌtü-ən-'frō\ *adj* : forward and backward — **to**–and–**fro** *n*

**¹toast** \'tōst\ *vb* **1** : to warm thoroughly **2** : to make (as bread) crisp, hot, and brown by heat **3** : to become toasted

**²toast** *n* **1** : sliced toasted bread **2** : someone or something in whose honor persons drink **3** : an act of drinking in honor of a toast

**³toast** *vb* : to propose or drink to as a toast

**toast·er** \'tō-stər\ *n* : an electrical appliance for toasting

**toaster oven** *n* : a portable electrical appliance that bakes, broils, and toasts

**toast·mas·ter** \'tōst-ˌmas-tər\ *n* : a person who presides at a banquet and introduces the after-dinner speakers

**toast·mis·tress** \-ˌmis-trəs\ *n* : a woman who acts as toastmaster

**toasty** \'tō-stē\ *adj* **toast·i·er; -est** : pleasantly warm

**Tob** *abbr* Tobit

**to·bac·co** \tə-'ba-kō\ *n*, *pl* **-cos** [Sp *tabaco*] **1** : a tall broad-leaved herb related to the potato; *also* : its leaves prepared for smoking or chewing or as snuff **2** : manufactured tobacco products; *also* : smoking as a practice

**to·bac·co·nist** \tə-'ba-kə-nist\ *n* : a dealer in tobacco

**To·bi·as** \tō-'bī-əs\ *n* : TOBIT

**To·bit** \'tō-bət\ *n* — see BIBLE table

**¹to·bog·gan** \tə-'bä-gən\ *n* : a long flat-bottomed light sled made of thin boards curved up at one end

**²toboggan** *vb* **1** : to coast on or as if on a toboggan **2** : to decline suddenly (as in value) — **to·bog·gan·er** *n*

**toc·sin** \'täk-sən\ *n* **1** : an alarm bell **2** : a warning signal

**¹to·day** \tə-'dā\ *adv* **1** : on or for this day **2** : at the present time

**²today** *n* : the present day, time, or age

**tod·dle** \'täd-°l\ *vb* **tod·dled; tod·dling** : to walk with short tottering steps in the manner of a young child — **toddle** *n* — **tod·dler** *n*

**tod·dy** \\'tä-dē\\ *n, pl* **toddies** [Hindi & Urdu *tāṛī* juice of a palm, fr. *tāṛ* a palm, fr. Skt *tāla*] : a drink made of liquor, sugar, spices, and hot water

**to–do** \\tə-'dü\\ *n, pl* **to–dos** \\-'düz\\ : BUSTLE, STIR, FUSS

¹**toe** \\'tō\\ *n* **1** : one of the jointed parts of the front end of the vertebrate foot **2** : the front part of a foot or hoof

²**toe** *vb* **toed; toe·ing** : to touch, reach, or drive with the toes

**toea** \\'tō-ə\\ *n* — see *kina* at MONEY table

**toe·hold** \\'tō-,hōld\\ *n* **1** : a place of support for the toes **2** : a slight footing

**toe·nail** \\'tō-,nāl\\ *n* : a nail of a toe

**tof·fee** *or* **tof·fy** \\'tò-fē, 'tä-\\ *n, pl* **toffees** *or* **toffies** : candy of brittle but tender texture made by boiling sugar and butter together

**to·fu** \\'tō-(,)fü\\ *n* [Jp *tōfu*] : a soft white food product made from soybeans

**tog** \\'täg, 'tòg\\ *vb* **togged; tog·ging** : to put togs on : DRESS

**to·ga** \\'tō-gə\\ *n* : the loose outer garment worn in public by citizens of ancient Rome — **to·gaed** \\-gəd\\ *adj*

¹**to·geth·er** \\tə-'ge-thər\\ *adv* **1** : in or into one place or group **2** : in or into contact or association ⟨mix ∼⟩ **3** : at one time : SIMULTANEOUSLY ⟨talk and work ∼⟩ **4** : in succession ⟨for days ∼⟩ **5** : in or into harmony or coherence ⟨get ∼ on a plan⟩ **6** : as a group : JOINTLY — **to·geth·er·ness** *n*

²**together** *adj* : composed in mind or manner

**together with** *prep* : in addition to : in association with

**tog·gery** \\'tä-gə-rē, 'tò-\\ *n* : CLOTHING

**tog·gle** \\'tä-gəl\\ *vb* : to switch between two options esp. of an electronic device

**toggle switch** *n* : an electric switch operated by pushing a projecting lever through a small arc

**togs** \\'tägz, 'tògz\\ *n pl* : CLOTHING; *esp* : clothes for a specified use ⟨riding ∼⟩

¹**toil** \\'tòi(-ə)l\\ *n* **1** : laborious effort **2** : long fatiguing labor : DRUDGERY — **toil·ful** \\-fəl\\ *adj* — **toil·some** *adj*

²**toil** *vb* [ME, to argue, struggle, fr. AF *toiller* to make dirty, fight, wrangle, fr. L *tudiculare* to crush, grind, fr. *tudicula* machine for crushing olives, dim. of *tudes* hammer] **1** : to work hard and long **2** : to proceed with great effort : PLOD — **toil·er** *n*

³**toil** *n* [ME *toile* cloth, net, fr. OF *teile*, fr. L *tela* cloth on a loom] : NET, TRAP — usu. used in pl. ⟨caught in the ∼s of the law⟩

**toi·let** \\'tòi-lət\\ *n* **1** : the act or process of dressing and grooming oneself **2** : BATHROOM **3** : a fixture for use in urinating and defecating; *esp* : one consisting essentially of a water-flushed bowl and seat — **toilet** *vb*

**toi·let·ry** \\'tòi-lə-trē\\ *n, pl* **-ries** : an article or preparation used in cleaning or grooming oneself — usu. used in pl.

**toi·lette** \\twä-'let\\ *n* **1** : TOILET **1 2** : formal attire; *also* : a particular costume

**toilet training** *n* : the process of training a child to control bladder and bowel movements and to use the toilet — **toilet train** *vb*

**toil·worn** \\'tòi(-ə)l-,wòrn\\ *adj* : showing the effects of toil

**To·kay** \\tō-'kā\\ *n* : naturally sweet wine from Hungary

**toke** \\'tōk\\ *n, slang* : a puff on a marijuana cigarette or pipe

¹**to·ken** \\'tō-kən\\ *n* **1** : an outward sign **2** : SYMBOL, EMBLEM **3** : SOUVENIR, KEEPSAKE **4** : a small part representing the whole **5** : a piece resembling a coin issued as money or for use by a particular group on specified terms

²**token** *adj* **1** : done or given as a token esp. in partial fulfillment of an obligation **2** : representing only a symbolic effort : MINIMAL, PERFUNCTORY

**to·ken·ism** \\'tō-kə-,ni-zəm\\ *n* : the policy or practice of making only a symbolic effort (as to desegregate)

**tolar** \\'tō-lär\\ *n, pl* **to·lar·ja** \\'tō-lär-,yä\\ *or* **to·lar·jev** \\'tō-lär-,yev\\ *or* **tolars** : the basic monetary unit of Slovenia from 1992 to 2007

**told** *past and past part of* TELL

**tole** \\'tōl\\ *n* : sheet metal and esp. tinplate for use in domestic and ornamental wares

**tol·er·a·ble** \\'tä-lə-rə-bəl\\ *adj* **1** : capable of being borne or endured **2** : moderately good : PASSABLE — **tol·er·a·bly** \\-blē\\ *adv*

**tol·er·ance** \\'tä-lə-rəns\\ *n* **1** : the act or practice of tolerating; *esp* : sympathy or indulgence for beliefs or practices differing from one's own **2** : the allowable deviation from a standard (as of size) **3** : the body's capacity to become less responsive over time to something (as a drug used repeatedly) — **tol·er·ant** *adj* — **tol·er·ant·ly** *adv*

**tol·er·ate** \\'tä-lə-,rāt\\ *vb* **-at·ed; -at·ing 1** : to exhibit physiological tolerance for (as a drug) **2** : to allow to be or to be done without hindrance ♦ *Synonyms* ABIDE, BEAR, SUFFER, STAND, BROOK — **tol·er·a·tion** \\,tä-lə-'rā-shən\\ *n*

¹**toll** \\'tōl\\ *n* **1** : a tax paid for a privilege (as for passing over a bridge) **2** : a charge for a service (as for a long-distance telephone call) **3** : the cost in life, health, loss, or suffering

²**toll** *vb* **1** : to cause the slow regular sounding of (a bell) esp. by pulling a rope **2** : to give signal of : SOUND **3** : to sound with slow measured strokes **4** : to announce by tolling

³**toll** *n* : the sound of a tolling bell

**toll·booth** \\'tōl-,büth\\ *n* : a booth where tolls are paid

**toll·gate** \\-,gāt\\ *n* : a point where vehicles stop to pay a toll

**toll·house** \\-,haùs\\ *n* : a house or booth where tolls are paid

**tol·u·ene** \\'täl-yə-,wēn\\ *n* : a liquid hydrocarbon used esp. as a solvent

**tom** \\'täm\\ *n* : the male of various animals (as a cat or turkey)

¹**tom·a·hawk** \\'tä-mə-,hòk\\ *n* : a light ax

used as a missile and as a hand weapon esp. by No. American Indians

²**tomahawk** *vb* : to strike or kill with a tomahawk

**to·ma·til·lo** \ˌtō-mə-ˈtē-(ˌ)yō\ *n, pl* **-los** : a small round usu. pale green edible fruit of a Mexican herb related to the tomato; *also* : this herb

**to·ma·to** \tə-ˈmā-tō, -ˈmä-\ *n, pl* **-toes** [alter. of earlier *tomate*, fr. Sp, fr. Nahuatl *tomatl*] : a usu. large, rounded, and red or yellow pulpy edible berry of a widely grown tropical herb related to the potato; *also* : this herb

**tomb** \ˈtüm\ *n* **1** : a place of burial : GRAVE **2** : a house, chamber, or vault for the dead — **tomb** *vb*

**tom·boy** \ˈtäm-ˌbȯi\ *n* : a girl who behaves in a manner usu. considered boyish — **tom·boy·ish** *adj*

**tomb·stone** \ˈtüm-ˌstōn\ *n* : a stone marking a grave

**tom·cat** \ˈtäm-ˌkat\ *n* : a male domestic cat

**Tom Col·lins** \ˈtäm-ˈkä-lənz\ *n* : a tall iced drink with a base of gin

**tome** \ˈtōm\ *n* : BOOK; *esp* : a large or weighty one

**tom·fool·ery** \täm-ˈfü-lə-rē\ *n* : playful or foolish behavior

**tom·my gun** \ˈtä-mē-ˌgən\ *n* : SUBMACHINE GUN — **tommy–gun** *vb*

**to·mog·ra·phy** \tō-ˈmä-grə-fē\ *n* : a method of producing a three-dimensional image of the internal structures of a solid object (as the human body or the earth) — **to·mo·graph·ic** \ˌtō-mə-ˈgra-fik\ *adj*

**to·mor·row** \tə-ˈmär-ō\ *adv* : on or for the day after today — **tomorrow** *n*

**tom–tom** \ˈtäm-ˌtäm\ *n* : a small-headed drum beaten with the hands

**ton** \ˈtən\ *n, pl* **tons** *also* **ton** — see WEIGHT table : a unit equal to the volume of a long ton weight of seawater used in reckoning the displacement of ships and equal to 35 cubic feet

**to·nal·i·ty** \tō-ˈna-lə-tē\ *n, pl* **-ties** : tonal quality

¹**tone** \ˈtōn\ *n* [ME, fr. L *tonus* tension, tone, fr. Gk *tonos*, lit., act of stretching; fr. the dependence of the pitch of a musical string on its tension] **1** : vocal or musical sound; *esp* : sound quality **2** : a sound of definite pitch **3** : WHOLE STEP **4** : accent or inflection expressive of an emotion **5** : the pitch of a word often used to express differences of meaning **6** : style or manner of expression **7** : color quality; *also* : SHADE, TINT **8** : the effect in painting of light and shade together with color **9** : healthy and vigorous condition of a living body or bodily part; *also* : the state of partial contraction characteristic of normal muscle **10** : general character, quality, or trend ♦ **Synonyms** ATMOSPHERE, FEELING, MOOD, VEIN — **ton·al** \ˈtō-nᵊl\ *adj*

²**tone** *vb* **toned; ton·ing 1** : to give a particular intonation or inflection to **2** : to impart tone to **3** : SOFTEN, MELLOW ⟨∼ down your language⟩ **4** : to harmonize in color : BLEND

**tone·arm** *n* : the movable part of a record player that carries the pickup and the needle

**to·ney** *var of* TONY

**tong** \ˈtäŋ, ˈtȯŋ\ *n* : a Chinese secret society in the U.S.

**tongs** \ˈtäŋz, ˈtȯŋz\ *n pl* : a grasping device consisting of two pieces joined at one end by a pivot or hinged like scissors — **tong** *vb*

¹**tongue** \ˈtəŋ\ *n* **1** : a fleshy movable process of the floor of the mouth used in tasting and in taking and swallowing food and in humans as a speech organ **2** : the flesh of a tongue (as of the ox) used as food **3** : the power of communication **4** : LANGUAGE **1 5** : manner or quality of utterance; *also* : intended meaning **6** : ecstatic usu. unintelligible utterance accompanying religious excitement — usu. used in pl. **7** : something resembling an animal's tongue esp. in being elongated and fastened at one end only — **tongued** \ˈtəŋd\ *adj* — **tongue·less** *adj*

²**tongue** *vb* **tongued; tongu·ing 1** : to touch or lick with the tongue **2** : to articulate notes on a wind instrument

**tongue-in-cheek** *adj* : characterized by insincerity, irony, or whimsical exaggeration — **tongue in cheek** *adv*

**tongue–lash** \ˈtəŋ-ˌlash\ *vb* : CHIDE, REPROVE — **tongue–lash·ing** \-iŋ\ *n*

**tongue–tied** \-ˌtīd\ *adj* : unable or disinclined to speak clearly or freely (as from shyness or a tongue impairment)

**tongue twister** *n* : an utterance that is difficult to articulate because of a succession of similar consonants

¹**ton·ic** \ˈtä-nik\ *adj* **1** : of, relating to, or producing a healthy physical or mental condition : INVIGORATING **2** : relating to or based on the 1st tone of a scale — **to·nic·i·ty** \tō-ˈni-sə-tē\ *n*

²**tonic** *n* **1** : the 1st degree of a musical scale **2** : something that invigorates, restores, or refreshes

**tonic water** *n* : a carbonated beverage flavored with a bit of quinine, lemon, and lime

¹**to·night** \tə-ˈnīt\ *adv* : on this present night or the coming night

²**tonight** *n* : the present or the coming night

**ton·nage** \ˈtə-nij\ *n* **1** : a duty on ships based on tons carried **2** : ships in terms of the number of tons registered or carried **3** : total weight in tons shipped, carried, or mined

**ton·sil** \ˈtän-səl\ *n* : either of a pair of oval masses of lymphoid tissue that lie one on each side of the throat at the back of the mouth

**ton·sil·lec·to·my** \ˌtän-sə-ˈlek-tə-mē\ *n, pl* **-mies** : the surgical removal of the tonsils

**ton·sil·li·tis** \-ˈlī-təs\ *n* : inflammation of the tonsils

**ton·so·ri·al** \tän-ˈsȯr-ē-əl\ *adj* : of or relating to a barber or a barber's work

**ton·sure** \ˈtän-chər\ *n* [ME, fr. AF, ML *tonsura*, fr. L, act of shearing, fr. *tonsus*, pp. of *tondēre* to shear] **1** : the rite of admission to the clerical state by the clipping or shaving of the head 2 : the shaven crown or patch worn by clerics (as monks) — **tonsure** vb

**tony** also **ton·ey** \'tō-nē\ adj **ton·i·er; -est** : marked by an aristocratic manner or style

**too** \'tü\ adv 1 : in addition : ALSO 2 : EXCESSIVELY ⟨the music is ~ loud⟩ 3 : to such a degree as to be regrettable 4 : VERY ⟨didn't seem ~ interested⟩

**took** past of TAKE

¹**tool** \'tül\ n 1 : a hand instrument that aids in accomplishing a task 2 : the cutting or shaping part in a machine; also : a machine for shaping metal in any way 3 : something used in doing a job ⟨a scholar's books are his ~s⟩; also : a means to an end 4 : a person used by another : DUPE 5 pl : natural ability

²**tool** vb 1 : to shape, form, or finish with a tool; esp : to letter or decorate (as a book cover) by means of hand tools 2 : to equip a plant or industry with machines and tools for production 3 : DRIVE, RIDE ⟨~ing along at 60 miles per hour⟩

**tool bar** n : a strip of icons on a computer display providing quick access to the pictured functions

¹**toot** \'tüt\ vb 1 : to sound or cause to sound in short blasts 2 : to blow an instrument (as a horn) — **toot·er** n

²**toot** n : a short blast (as on a horn)

**tooth** \'tüth\ n, pl **teeth** \'tēth\ 1 : one of the hard bony structures borne esp. on the jaws of vertebrates and used for seizing and chewing food and as weapons; also : a hard sharp structure esp. around the mouth of an invertebrate 2 : something resembling an animal's tooth 3 : any of the projections on the edge of a wheel that fits into corresponding projections on another wheel 4 pl : effective means of enforcement — **toothed** \'tütht\ adj — **tooth·less** adj

**tooth·ache** \'tüth-ˌāk\ n : pain in or about a tooth

**tooth·brush** \-ˌbrəsh\ n : a brush for cleaning the teeth

**tooth·paste** \-ˌpāst\ n : a paste for cleaning the teeth

**tooth·pick** \-ˌpik\ n : a pointed instrument for removing food particles caught between the teeth

**tooth powder** n : a powder for cleaning the teeth

**tooth·some** \'tüth-səm\ adj 1 : AGREEABLE, ATTRACTIVE 2 : pleasing to the taste : DELICIOUS ♦ **Synonyms** PALATABLE, APPETIZING, SAVORY, TASTY

**toothy** \'tü-thē\ adj **tooth·i·er; -est** : having or showing prominent teeth

¹**top** \'täp\ n 1 : the highest part, point, or level of something 2 : the part of a plant with edible roots lying above the ground ⟨beet ~s⟩ 3 : the upper end, edge, or surface ⟨the ~ of a page⟩ 4 : an upper piece, lid, or covering 5 : the highest degree, pitch, or rank 6 : a quark with a charge of +⅔ and a measured energy of approximately 175 billion electron volts

²**top** vb **topped; top·ping** 1 : to remove or trim the top of : PRUNE ⟨~ a tree⟩ 2 : to cover with a top or on the top : CROWN, CAP 3 : to be superior to : EXCEL, SURPASS 4 : to go over the top of 5 : to strike (a ball) above the center 6 : to make an end or conclusion ⟨~ off a meal with coffee⟩

³**top** adj 1 : of, relating to, or being at the top : HIGHEST ⟨is ~ in her class⟩ 2 : CHIEF

⁴**top** n : a toy that has a tapering point on which it is made to spin

**to·paz** \'tō-ˌpaz\ n : a hard silicate of aluminum; esp : a yellow transparent topaz used as a gem

**top·coat** \'täp-ˌkōt\ n 1 : a lightweight overcoat 2 : a protective coating (as of paint)

**top dollar** n : the highest amount being paid for a commodity or service

**top–dress** \-ˌdres\ vb : to apply material to (as land) without working it in; esp : to scatter fertilizer over

**top–dress·ing** \-ˌdre-siŋ\ n : a material used to top-dress soil

**top–end** \'täp-ˈend\ adj : TOPFLIGHT

**top·flight** \'täp-ˈflīt\ adj : of, relating to, or being the highest level of excellence or rank ⟨a ~ staff⟩ — **top flight** n

**top hat** n : a tall-crowned hat usu. of beaver or silk

**top–heavy** \'täp-ˌhe-vē\ adj : having the top part too heavy for the lower part

**to·pi·ary** \'tō-pē-ˌer-ē\ n, pl **-ar·ies** : the art of training and trimming trees or shrubs with decorative shapes — **topiary** adj

**top·ic** \'tä-pik\ n 1 : a heading in an outlined argument 2 : the subject of a discourse or a section of it : THEME

**top·i·cal** \-pi-kəl\ adj 1 : of, relating to, or arranged by topics ⟨a ~ outline⟩ 2 : relating to current or local events 3 : designed to be applied to or to work on a part (as of the body) — **top·i·cal·ly** \-k(ə-)lē\ adv

**top·knot** \'täp-ˌnät\ n 1 : an ornament (as a knot of ribbons) forming a headdress 2 : a crest of feathers or tuft of hair on the top of the head

**top·less** \-ləs\ adj 1 : wearing no clothing on the upper body 2 : featuring topless waitresses or entertainers

**top·mast** \'täp-ˌmast, -məst\ n : the 2d mast above a ship's deck

**top·most** \'täp-ˌmōst\ adj : highest of all : UPPERMOST

**top–notch** \-ˈnäch\ adj : of the highest quality : FIRST-RATE

**top–of–the–line** adj : being or belonging to the highest or most expensive class

**to·pog·ra·phy** \tə-ˈpä-grə-fē\ n 1 : the art of showing in detail on a map or chart the physical features of a place or region 2 : the outline of the form of a place showing its relief and the position of features (as rivers, roads, or cities) — **to·pog·ra·pher** \-fər\ n — **top·o·graph·ic** \ˌtä-pə-ˈgra-fik\ or **top·o·graph·i·cal** \-fi-kəl\ adj

**top·ping** *n* : a food served on top of another to make it look or taste better

**top·ple** \'tä-pəl\ *vb* **top·pled; top·pling**
**1** : to fall from or as if from being top-heavy **2** : to push over : OVERTURN; *also*
: OVERTHROW ⟨*toppled* the dictator⟩

**¹tops** \'täps\ *adj* : topmost in quality or importance ⟨∼ in his field⟩

**²tops** *adv* : at the very most

**top·sail** \'täp-,säl, -səl\ *also* **top·s'l** \-səl\
*n* : the sail next above the lowest sail on a mast in a square-rigged ship

**top secret** *adj* : demanding extreme secrecy among those concerned

**top·side** \'täp-'sīd\ *adv or adj* **1** : to or on the top or surface **2** : on deck

**top·sides** \-'sīdz\ *n pl* : the top portion of the outer surface of a ship on each side above the waterline

**top·soil** \'täp-,soi(-ə)l\ *n* : surface soil usu. including the organic layer in which plants have most of their roots

**top·sy-tur·vy** \,täp-sē-'tər-vē\ *adv* **1** : in utter confusion **2** : UPSIDE DOWN — **topsy-turvy** *adj*

**toque** \'tōk\ *n* : a woman's small hat without a brim

**tor** \'tòr\ *n* : a high craggy hill

**To·rah** \'tòr-ə\ *n* **1** : a scroll of the first five books of the Old Testament used in a synagogue; *also* : these five books **2** : the body of divine knowledge and law found in the Jewish scriptures and tradition

**¹torch** \'tòrch\ *n* **1** : a flaming light made of something that burns brightly and usu. carried in the hand **2** : something that resembles a torch in giving light, heat, or guidance **3** : a portable burner for producing a hot flame **4** *chiefly Brit* : FLASHLIGHT

**²torch** *vb* : to set fire to

**torch·bear·er** \'tòrch-,ber-ər\ *n* **1** : a person who carries a torch **2** : one in the forefront (as of a political campaign)

**torch·light** \-,līt\ *n* : light given by torches

**torch song** *n* : a popular sentimental song of unrequited love

**tore** *past of* TEAR

**to·re·ador** \'tòr-ē-ə-,dòr\ *n* : BULLFIGHTER

**to·re·ro** \tə-'rer-ō\ *n, pl* **-ros** [Sp] : BULLFIGHTER

**¹tor·ment** \'tòr-,ment\ *n* **1** : extreme pain or anguish of body or mind **2** : a source of vexation or pain

**²tor·ment** \tòr-'ment\ *vb* **1** : to cause severe suffering of body or mind to **2** : DISTORT, TWIST ♦ *Synonyms* RACK, AFFLICT, TRY, TORTURE — **tor·men·tor** \-'men-tər\ *n*

**torn** *past part of* TEAR

**tor·na·do** \tòr-'nā-dō\ *n, pl* **-does** *or* **-dos** [modif of Sp *tronada* thunderstorm, fr. *tronar* to thunder, fr. L *tonare*] : a violent destructive whirling wind accompanied by a funnel-shaped cloud that moves over a narrow path

**¹tor·pe·do** \tòr-'pē-dō\ *n, pl* **-does** : a thin cylindrical self-propelled underwater weapon

**²torpedo** *vb* **tor·pe·doed; tor·pe·do·ing**
: to hit or destroy with or as if with a torpedo

**torpedo boat** *n* : a small very fast boat for firing torpedoes

**tor·pid** \'tòr-pəd\ *adj* **1** : having lost motion or the power of exertion : DORMANT
**2** : SLUGGISH **3** : lacking vigor — **tor·pid·i·ty** \tòr-'pi-də-tē\ *n*

**tor·por** \'tòr-pər\ *n* **1** : DULLNESS, APATHY **2** : extreme sluggishness : STAGNATION ♦ *Synonyms* STUPOR, LETHARGY, LANGUOR, LASSITUDE

**¹torque** \'tòrk\ *n* : a force that produces or tends to produce rotation or torsion

**²torque** *vb* **torqued; torqu·ing** : to impart torque to : cause to twist (as about an axis)

**tor·rent** \'tòr-ənt\ *n* [F, fr. L *torrent-, torrens*, fr. *torrent-, torrens* burning, seething, rushing, fr. prp. of *torrēre* to parch, burn] **1** : a tumultuous outburst **2** : a rushing stream (as of water)

**tor·ren·tial** \tò-'ren-chəl\ *adj* : relating to or resembling a torrent ⟨∼ rains⟩

**tor·rid** \'tòr-əd\ *adj* **1** : parched with heat esp. of the sun : HOT **2** : ARDENT

**torrid zone** *n* : the region of the earth between the Tropic of Cancer and the Tropic of Capricorn

**tor·sion** \'tòr-shən\ *n* **1** : a wrenching by which one part of a body is under pressure to turn about a longitudinal axis while the other part is held fast or is under pressure to turn in the opposite direction **2** : a twisting of a bodily organ or part on its own axis — **tor·sion·al** \'tòr-shə-nəl\ *adj* — **tor·sion·al·ly** *adv*

**tor·so** \'tòr-sō\ *n, pl* **torsos** *or* **tor·si** \'tòr-,sē\ [It, lit., stalk] : the trunk of the human body

**tort** \'tòrt\ *n* : a wrongful act which does not involve a breach of contract and for which the injured party can recover damages in a civil action

**tor·ti·lla** \tòr-'tē-ə\ *n* : a round thin cake of unleavened cornmeal or wheat flour bread

**tor·toise** \'tòr-təs\ *n* : TURTLE; *esp* : any of a family of land turtles

**tor·toise·shell** \-,shel\ *n* : the mottled horny substance of the shell of some turtles used in inlaying and in making various ornamental articles — **tortoiseshell** *adj*

**tor·to·ni** \tòr-'tō-nē\ *n* : rich ice cream often made with minced almonds and chopped cherries and flavored with rum

**tor·tu·ous** \'tòr-chə-wəs\ *adj* **1** : marked by twists or turns : WINDING ⟨a ∼ path⟩
**2** : DEVIOUS, TRICKY

**¹tor·ture** \'tòr-chər\ *n* **1** : anguish of body or mind **2** : the infliction of severe pain esp. to punish or coerce — **tor·tur·ous** \'tòrch-rəs, 'tòr-chə-\ *adj*

**²torture** *vb* **tor·tured; tor·tur·ing 1** : to cause intense suffering to : TORMENT **2** : to punish or coerce by inflicting severe pain **3** : TWIST, DISTORT ♦ *Synonyms* RACK, HARROW, AFFLICT, TRY — **tor·tur·er** *n*

**To·ry** \'tòr-ē\ *n, pl* **Tories 1** : a member of a chiefly 18th century British party upholding the established church and the traditional political structure **2** : an American supporter of the British during the American Revolution **3** *often not cap* : an extreme conservative — **Tory** *adj*

**¹toss** \ˈtȯs, ˈtäs\ *vb* **1** : to fling to and fro or up and down **2** : to throw with a quick light motion; *also* : BANDY **3** : to fling or lift with a sudden motion ⟨~ed her head angrily⟩ **4** : to move restlessly or turbulently ⟨~es on the waves⟩ **5** : to twist and turn repeatedly **6** : FLOUNCE **7** : to accomplish readily ⟨~ off an article⟩ **8** : to decide an issue by flipping a coin

**²toss** *n* : an act or instance of tossing; *esp* : TOSS-UP 1

**toss–up** \ˌəp\ *n* **1** : a deciding by flipping a coin **2** : an even chance **3** : something that offers no clear basis for choice

**¹tot** \ˈtät\ *n* **1** : a small child **2** : a small drink of alcoholic liquor : SHOT

**²tot** *vb* **tot·ted; tot·ting** : to add up

**³tot** *abbr* total

**¹to·tal** \ˈtōt-ᵊl\ *adj* **1** : making up a whole : ENTIRE ⟨~ amount⟩ **2** : COMPLETE, UTTER ⟨a ~ failure⟩ ⟨a ~ stranger⟩ **3** : involving a complete and unified effort esp. to achieve a desired effect — **to·tal·ly** *adv*

**²total** *n* **1** : SUM 4 **2** : the entire amount ♦ *Synonyms* AGGREGATE, WHOLE, GROSS, TOTALITY

**³total** *vb* **to·taled** *or* **to·talled; to·tal·ing** *or* **to·tal·ling 1** : to add up : COMPUTE **2** : to amount to : NUMBER **3** : to make a total wreck of ⟨a car⟩

**to·tal·i·tar·i·an** \tō-ˌta-lə-ˈter-ē-ən\ *adj* : of, relating to, or advocating a political regime based on subordination of the individual to the state and strict control of all aspects of life esp. by coercive measures — **totalitarian** *n* — **to·tal·i·tar·i·an·ism** \-ē-ə-ˌni-zəm\ *n*

**to·tal·i·ty** \tō-ˈta-lə-tē\ *n, pl* **-ties 1** : an aggregate amount : SUM, WHOLE **2** : ENTIRETY, WHOLENESS

**to·tal·iza·tor** *or* **to·tal·isa·tor** \ˈtō-tᵊl-ə-ˌzā-tər\ *n* : a machine for registering and indicating the number of bets and the odds on a horse or dog race

**¹tote** \ˈtōt\ *vb* **tot·ed; tot·ing** : CARRY

**²tote** *vb* **tot·ed; tot·ing** : ADD, TOTAL — usu. used with *up*

**to·tem** \ˈtō-təm\ *n* [Ojibwa *oto·te·man* his totem] : an object (as an animal or plant) serving as the emblem of a family or clan and often as a reminder of its ancestry; *also* : something usu. carved or painted to represent such an object

**totem pole** *n* : a pole that is carved with a series of totems and is erected before the houses of some northwest American Indians

**tot·ter** \ˈtä-tər\ *vb* **1** : to tremble or rock as if about to fall : SWAY **2** : to move unsteadily : STAGGER

**tou·can** \ˈtü-ˌkan\ *n* [F, fr. Pg *tucano*, fr. Tupinambá (American Indian language of Brazil) *tukána*] : any of a family of chiefly fruit-eating birds of tropical America with brilliant coloring and a very large bill

**¹touch** \ˈtəch\ *vb* **1** : to bring a bodily part (as the hand) into contact with so as to feel **2** : to be or cause to be in contact **3** : to strike or push lightly esp. with the hand or foot **4** : DISTURB, HARM **5** : to make use of ⟨never ~es alcohol⟩ **6** : to induce to give or lend **7** : to get to : REACH **8** : to refer to in passing : MENTION **9** : to affect the interest of : CONCERN **10** : to leave a mark on; *also* : BLEMISH **11** : to move to sympathetic feeling **12** : to come close : VERGE **13** : to have a bearing : RELATE **14** : to make a usu. brief or incidental stop in port ♦ *Synonyms* AFFECT, INFLUENCE, IMPRESS, STRIKE, SWAY

**²touch** *n* **1** : a light stroke or tap **2** : the act or fact of touching or being touched **3** : the sense by which pressure or traction on the skin or mucous membrane is perceived; *also* : a particular sensation conveyed by this sense **4** : mental or moral sensitiveness : TACT **5** : a small quantity : HINT ⟨a ~ of spring in the air⟩ **6** : a manner of striking or touching esp. the keys of a keyboard instrument **7** : an improving detail ⟨add a few ~es to the painting⟩ **8** : distinctive manner or skill ⟨the ~ of a master⟩ **9** : the state of being in contact ⟨keep in ~⟩ ♦ *Synonyms* SUGGESTION, SUSPICION, TINCTURE, TINGE

**touch·down** \ˈtəch-ˌdau̇n\ *n* : the act of scoring six points in American football by being lawfully in possession of the ball on, above, or behind an opponent's goal line

**tou·ché** \tü-ˈshā\ *interj* [F] — used to acknowledge a hit in fencing or the success of an argument, an accusation, or a witty point

**touch football** *n* : football in which touching is substituted for tackling

**touch·ing** \ˈtə-chiŋ\ *adj* : capable of stirring emotions ♦ *Synonyms* MOVING, IMPRESSIVE, POIGNANT, AFFECTING

**touch off** *vb* **1** : to describe with precision **2** : to start by or as if by touching with fire ⟨*touched off* a riot⟩

**touch·stone** \ˈtəch-ˌstōn\ *n* : a test or criterion of genuineness or quality ♦ *Synonyms* STANDARD, GAUGE, BENCHMARK, YARDSTICK

**touch–tone** \ˈtəch-ˌtōn\ *adj* : of, relating to, or being a telephone having push buttons that produce tones corresponding to numbers

**touch up** *vb* : to improve or perfect by small additional strokes or alterations ⟨*touch up* a photo⟩ — **touch–up** \ˈtəch-ˌəp\ *n*

**touchy** \ˈtə-chē\ *adj* **touch·i·er; -est 1** : easily offended : PEEVISH **2** : calling for tact in treatment ⟨a ~ subject⟩ ♦ *Synonyms* IRASCIBLE, CRANKY, CROSS, TETCHY, TESTY

**¹tough** \ˈtəf\ *adj* **1** : strong or firm in texture but flexible and not brittle **2** : not easily chewed **3** : characterized by severity and determination ⟨a ~ policy⟩ **4** : capable of enduring strain or hardship : ROBUST **5** : hard to influence : STUB-

BORN **6** : difficult to accomplish, resolve, or cope with ⟨a ~ problem⟩ **7** : ROWDYISH ♦ *Synonyms* TENACIOUS, STOUT, STURDY, STALWART — **tough·ly** *adv* — **tough·ness** *n*

²**tough** *n* : a tough person : ROWDY

**tough·en** \'tə-fən\ *vb* **tough·ened**; **tough·en·ing** : to make or become tough ⟨training ~ed him up⟩

**tou·pee** \tü-'pā\ *n* [F *toupet* forelock] : a small wig for a bald spot

¹**tour** \'tùr, *1 is also* 'taù-(ə)r\ *n* **1** : one's turn : SHIFT **2** : a journey in which one returns to the starting point

²**tour** *vb* : to make a tour

**tour de force** \,tùr-də-'fòrs\ *n, pl* **tours de force** \*same*\ [F] : a feat or display of strength, skill, or ingenuity

**Tou·rette's syndrome** \tu-'rets-\ *n* : a familial neurological disorder marked by recurrent involuntary tics and vocal sounds

**tour·ism** \'tùr-,i-zəm\ *n* **1** : the practice of traveling for recreation **2** : promotion of touring **3** : accommodation of tourists — **tour·ist** \-ist\ *n*

**tourist class** *n* : economy accommodations (as on a ship)

**tour·ma·line** \'tùr-mə-lən, -,lēn\ *n* : a mineral that when transparent is valued as a gem

**tour·na·ment** \'tùr-nə-mənt, 'tər-\ *n* **1** : a medieval sport in which mounted armored knights contended with blunted lances or swords **2** : a championship series of games or athletic contests

**tour·ney** \-nē\ *n, pl* **tourneys** : TOURNAMENT

**tour·ni·quet** \'tùr-ni-kət, 'tər-\ *n* : a device (as a tight bandage) to check bleeding or blood flow

**tou·sle** \'taù-zəl\ *vb* **tou·sled**; **tou·sling** : to disorder by rough handling : DISHEVEL, MUSS ⟨*tousled* his hair⟩

**tout** \'taùt, *2 is also* 'tüt\ *vb* **1** : to give a tip or solicit bets on a racehorse **2** : to praise or publicize loudly — **tout** *n*

¹**tow** \'tō\ *vb* : to draw or pull along behind

²**tow** *n* **1** : an act of towing or condition of being towed **2** : something (as a barge) that is towed

³**tow** *n* : short or broken fiber (as of flax or hemp) used esp. for yarn, twine, or stuffing

**to·ward** \'tōrd, 'tō-ərd, tə-'wórd\ *or* **to·wards** \'tōrdz, 'tō-ərdz, tə-'wórdz\ *prep* **1** : in the direction of ⟨heading ~ the river⟩ **2** : along a course leading to ⟨efforts ~ reconciliation⟩ **3** : in regard to ⟨tolerance ~ minorities⟩ **4** : so as to face ⟨turn the chair ~ the window⟩ **5** : close upon ⟨it was getting along ~ sundown⟩ **6** : for part payment of ⟨here's $100 ~ your tuition⟩

**tow·boat** \'tō-,bōt\ *n* : TUGBOAT

**tow·el** \'taù(-ə)l\ *n* : an absorbent cloth or paper for wiping or drying

**tow·el·ing** *or* **tow·el·ling** *n* : a cotton or linen fabric for making towels

¹**tow·er** \'taù-(ə)r\ *n* **1** : a tall structure either isolated or built upon a larger structure ⟨an observation ~⟩ **2** : a towering citadel **3** : a personal computer case that stands in an upright position — **tow·ered** *adj*

²**tower** *vb* : to reach or rise to a great height

**tow·er·ing** \'taù(-ə)-riŋ\ *adj* **1** : LOFTY ⟨~ pines⟩ **2** : reaching high intensity ⟨a ~ rage⟩ **3** : EXCESSIVE ⟨~ ambition⟩

**tow·head** \'tō-,hed\ *n* : a person having whitish blond hair — **tow·head·ed** \-,he-dəd\ *adj*

**to·whee** \'tō-,hē, 'tō-(,)ē, tō-'hē\ *n* : a common finch of eastern No. America having the male black, white, and reddish; *also* : any of several closely related finches

**to wit** *adv* : NAMELY

**town** \'taùn\ *n* **1** : a compactly settled area usu. larger than a village but smaller than a city **2** : CITY **3** : the inhabitants of a town **4** : a New England territorial and political unit usu. containing both rural and urban areas; *also* : a New England community in which matters of local government are decided by a general assembly (**town meeting**) of qualified voters

**town house** *n* **1** : the city residence of a person having a country home **2** : a single-family house of two or sometimes three stories connected to another house by a common wall

**town·ie** *or* **towny** \'taù-nē\ *n, pl* **townies** : a permanent resident of a town as distinguished from a member of another group

**towns·folk** \'taùnz-,fōk\ *n pl* : TOWNSPEOPLE

**town·ship** \'taùn-,ship\ *n* **1** : TOWN 4 **2** : a unit of local government in some states **3** : an unorganized subdivision of a county **4** : a division of territory in surveys of U.S. public land containing 36 square miles **5** : an area in the Republic of South Africa segregated for occupation by persons of non-European descent

**towns·man** \'taùnz-mən\ *n* **1** : a native or resident of a town or city **2** : a fellow citizen of a town

**towns·peo·ple** \-,pē-pəl\ *n pl* **1** : the inhabitants of a town or city **2** : town-bred persons

**towns·wom·an** \-,wù-mən\ *n* **1** : a woman who is a native or resident of a town or city **2** : a woman who is a fellow citizen of a town

**tow·path** \'tō-,path, -,päth\ *n* : a path (as along a canal) traveled esp. by draft animals towing boats

**tow truck** *n* : a truck equipped for towing vehicles

**tox·emia** \täk-'sē-mē-ə\ *n* : a bodily disorder associated with the presence of toxic substances in the blood

**tox·ic** \'täk-sik\ *adj* [LL *toxicus*, fr. L *toxicum* poison, fr. Gk *toxikon* arrow poison, fr. neut. of *toxikos* of a bow, fr. *toxon* bow, arrow] : of, relating to, or caused by poison or a toxin : POISONOUS — **tox·ic·i·ty** \'täk-'si-sə-tē\ *n*

**tox·i·col·o·gy** \,täk-si-'kä-lə-jē\ *n* : a science that deals with poisons and esp. with

**tox·i·co·log·i·cal** \-kə-'lä-ji-kəl\ *also* **tox·i·co·log·ic** \-kə-'läj-ik\ *adj* — **tox·i·col·o·gist** \-'kä-lə-jist\ *n*

**toxic shock syndrome** *n* : an acute disease associated with the presence of a bacterium that is characterized by fever, diarrhea, nausea, diffuse erythema, and shock and occurs esp. in menstruating females using tampons

**tox·in** \'täk-sən\ *n* : a poisonous substance produced by metabolic activities of a living organism that is usu. unstable, very toxic when introduced into the tissues, and usu. capable of inducing antibodies

¹**toy** \'tȯi\ *n* **1** : something trifling **2** : a small ornament : BAUBLE **3** : something for a child to play with

²**toy** *vb* **1** : to deal with something lightly : TRIFLE **2** : FLIRT **3** : to amuse oneself as if with a plaything

³**toy** *adj* **1** : DIMINUTIVE ⟨a ~ dog⟩ **2** : designed for use as a toy

**tp** *abbr* **1** title page **2** township

**tpk** *or* **tpke** *abbr* turnpike

**tr** *abbr* **1** translated; translation; translator **2** transpose **3** troop

¹**trace** \'träs\ *n* **1** : a mark (as a footprint or track) left by something that has passed **2** : a minute or barely detectable amount ⟨disappeared without a ~⟩

²**trace** *vb* **traced; trac·ing** **1** : to mark out : SKETCH **2** : to form (as letters) carefully **3** : to copy (a drawing) by marking lines on transparent paper laid over the drawing to be copied **4** : to follow the trail of : track down **5** : to study out and follow the development of ⟨~ed his family's history⟩ — **trace·able** *adj*

³**trace** *n* : either of two lines of a harness for fastening a draft animal to a vehicle

**trac·er** \'trā-sər\ *n* **1** : one that traces **2** : ammunition containing a chemical to mark the flight of projectiles by a trail of smoke or light

**trac·ery** \'trā-sə-rē\ *n, pl* **-er·ies** : ornamental work having a design with branching or interlacing lines

**tra·chea** \'trā-kē-ə\ *n, pl* **-che·ae** \-kē-ē\ *also* **-che·as** *or* **-chea** : the main tube by which air passes from the larynx to the lungs of vertebrates — **tra·che·al** \-kē-əl\ *adj*

**tra·che·ot·o·my** \ˌtrā-kē-'ä-tə-mē\ *n, pl* **-mies** : the surgical operation of cutting into the trachea esp. through the skin

**tracing** *n* **1** : the act of one that traces **2** : something that is traced **3** : a graphic record made by an instrument for measuring vibrations or pulsations

¹**track** \'trak\ *n* **1** : a mark left in passing **2** : PATH, ROUTE, TRAIL **3** : a course laid out for racing; *also* : track-and-field sports **4** : one of a series of paths along which material (as music) is recorded (as on a CD or magnetic tape) **5** : the course along which something moves; *esp* : a way made by two parallel lines of metal rails **6** : awareness of a fact or progression ⟨lost ~ of time⟩ **7** : either of two

endless metal belts on which a vehicle (as a bulldozer) travels

²**track** *vb* **1** : to follow the tracks or traces of : TRAIL **2** : to observe the moving path of (as a missile) **3** : to make tracks on **4** : to carry (as mud) on the feet and deposit — **track·er** *n*

**track·age** \'tra-kij\ *n* : lines of railway track

**track–and–field** *adj* : of or relating to athletic contests held on a running track or on the adjacent field

¹**tract** \'trakt\ *n* **1** : an area without precise boundaries ⟨huge ~s of land⟩ **2** : a defined area of land **3** : a system of body parts or organs that act together to perform some function ⟨the digestive ~⟩

²**tract** *n* : a pamphlet of political or religious propaganda

**trac·ta·ble** \'trak-tə-bəl\ *adj* : easily controlled : DOCILE ♦ *Synonyms* AMENABLE, OBEDIENT, BIDDABLE

**tract house** *n* : any of many similar houses built on a tract of land

**trac·tion** \'trak-shən\ *n* **1** : the act of drawing : the state of being drawn **2** : the drawing of a vehicle by motive power; *also* : the particular form of motive power used **3** : the adhesive friction of a body on a surface on which it moves **4** : a pulling force applied to a skeletal structure (as a broken bone) by means of a special device; *also* : a state of tension created by such a pulling force ⟨a leg in ~⟩ — **trac·tion·al** \-shə-nəl\ *adj* — **trac·tive** \'trak-tiv\ *adj*

**trac·tor** \'trak-tər\ *n* **1** : an automotive vehicle used esp. for drawing farm equipment **2** : a truck for hauling a trailer

¹**trade** \'trād\ *n* **1** : one's regular business or work : OCCUPATION **2** : an occupation requiring manual or mechanical skill **3** : the persons engaged in a business or industry **4** : the business of buying and selling or bartering commodities **5** : an act of trading : TRANSACTION

²**trade** *vb* **trad·ed; trad·ing** **1** : to give in exchange for another commodity : BARTER **2** : to engage in the exchange, purchase, or sale of goods **3** : to deal regularly as a customer — **trade on** : EXPLOIT ⟨trades on his family name⟩

**trade–in** \'trād-ˌin\ *n* : an item of merchandise traded in

**trade in** *vb* : to turn in as part payment for a purchase

¹**trade·mark** \'trād-ˌmärk\ *n* : a device (as a word or mark) that points distinctly to the origin or ownership of merchandise to which it is applied and that is legally reserved for the exclusive use of the owner; *also* : something that identifies a person or thing

²**trademark** *vb* : to secure the trademark rights for ⟨that name is ~ed⟩

**trade name** *n* : a name that is given by a manufacturer or merchant to a product to distinguish it as made or sold by him and that may be used and protected as a trademark

**trad·er** \'trā-dər\ *n* **1** : a person whose

business is buying or selling  **2** : a ship engaged in trade

**trades·man** \'trādz-mən\ *n* **1** : one who runs a retail store : SHOPKEEPER  **2** : CRAFTSMAN

**trades·peo·ple** \-ˌpē-pəl\ *n pl* : people engaged in trade

**trade union** *n* : LABOR UNION

**trade wind** *n* : a wind blowing almost constantly in one direction

**trading stamp** *n* : a printed stamp given as a premium to a retail customer that when accumulated may be redeemed for merchandise

**tra·di·tion** \trə-'di-shən\ *n* **1** : an inherited, established, or customary pattern of thought or action  **2** : the handing down of beliefs and customs by word of mouth or by example without written instruction; *also* : a belief or custom thus handed down — **tra·di·tion·al** \-ˌdi-shə-nəl\ *adj* — **tra·di·tion·al·ly** *adv*

**tra·duce** \trə-'dūs, -'dyūs\ *vb* **tra·duced**; **tra·duc·ing** : to lower the reputation of : DEFAME, SLANDER ⟨he was *traduced* in the past⟩ ♦ *Synonyms* MALIGN, LIBEL, CALUMNIATE — **tra·duc·er** *n*

¹**traf·fic** \'tra-fik\ *n* **1** : the business of bartering or buying and selling  **2** : communication or dealings between individuals or groups  **3** : the movement (as of vehicles) along a route; *also* : the vehicles, people, ships, or planes moving along a route  **4** : the passengers or cargo carried by a transportation system

²**traffic** *vb* **traf·ficked**; **traf·fick·ing** **1** : to carry on business dealings  **2** : DEAL, TRADE ⟨*trafficked* in illegal drugs⟩ — **traf·fick·er** *n*

**traffic circle** *n* : ROTARY 2

**traffic light** *n* : a visual signal (as a system of lights) for controlling traffic

**tra·ge·di·an** \trə-'jē-dē-ən\ *n* **1** : a writer of tragedies  **2** : an actor who plays tragic roles

**tra·ge·di·enne** \trə-ˌjē-dē-'en\ *n* [F] : an actress who plays tragic roles

**trag·e·dy** \'tra-jə-dē\ *n, pl* **-dies** [ME *tragedie*, fr. MF, fr. L *tragoedia*, fr. Gk *tragōidia*, fr. *tragos* goat + *aeidein* to sing] **1** : a serious drama with a sorrowful or disastrous conclusion : CALAMITY; *also* **2** : MISFORTUNE  **3** : tragic quality or element ⟨the ~ of life⟩

**trag·ic** \'tra-jik\ *also* **trag·i·cal** \-ji-kəl\ *adj* **1** : of, relating to, or expressive of tragedy  **2** : appropriate to tragedy  **3** : LAMENTABLE, UNFORTUNATE ⟨a ~ mistake⟩ — **trag·i·cal·ly** \-ji-k(ə-)lē\ *adv*

¹**trail** \'trāl\ *vb* **1** : to hang down so as to drag along or sweep the ground  **2** : to draw or drag along behind  **3** : to extend over a surface in a straggling manner  **4** : to lag behind  **5** : to follow the track of : PURSUE  **6** : DWINDLE ⟨her voice ~ed off⟩

²**trail** *n* **1** : something that trails or is trailed ⟨a ~ of smoke⟩  **2** : a trace or mark left by something that has passed or been drawn along : SCENT, TRACK ⟨a ~ of blood⟩  **3** : a beaten path; *also* : a marked path through woods

**trail bike** *n* : a small motorcycle for off-road use

**trail·blaz·er** \-ˌblā-zər\ *n* : PATHFINDER, PIONEER — **trail·blaz·ing** *adj or n*

**trail·er** \'trā-lər\ *n* **1** : one that trails; *esp* : a creeping plant (as an ivy)  **2** : a vehicle that is hauled by another (as a tractor)  **3** : a vehicle equipped to serve wherever parked as a dwelling or place of business  **4** : PREVIEW 3

**trailer park** *n* : a site equipped to accommodate mobile homes

**trailing arbutus** *n* : a creeping spring-flowering plant of the heath family with fragrant pink or white flowers

¹**train** \'trān\ *n* [ME, fr. AF, fr. *trainer* to draw, drag]  **1** : a part of a gown that trails behind the wearer  **2** : RETINUE  **3** : a moving file of persons, vehicles, or animals  **4** : a connected series ⟨a ~ of thought⟩  **5** : AFTERMATH  **6** : a connected line of railroad cars usu. hauled by a locomotive ♦ *Synonyms* SUCCESSION, SEQUENCE, PROCESSION, CHAIN

²**train** *vb* [ME, to trail, drag, train, fr. AF *trainer*]  **1** : to cause to grow as desired ⟨~ a vine on a trellis⟩  **2** : to form by instruction, discipline, or drill  **3** : to make or become prepared (as by exercise) for a test of skill  **4** : to aim or point at an object ⟨~ guns on a fort⟩ ♦ *Synonyms* DISCIPLINE, SCHOOL, EDUCATE, INSTRUCT — **train·er** *n*

**train·ee** \trā-'nē\ *n* : one who is being trained esp. for a job

**train·ing** \'trā-nin\ *n* **1** : the act, process, or method of one who trains  **2** : the skill, knowledge, or experience gained by one who trains

**train·man** \-mən\ *n* : a member of a train crew

**traipse** \'trāps\ *vb* **traipsed**; **traips·ing** : TRAMP, WALK ⟨~ the countryside⟩

**trait** \'trāt\ *n* **1** : a distinguishing quality (as of personality)  **2** : an inherited characteristic

**trai·tor** \'trā-tər\ *n* [ME *traytour*, fr. AF *traitre*, fr. L *traditor*, fr. *tradere* to hand over, deliver, betray, fr. *trans-* across + *dare* to give]  **1** : one who betrays another's trust or is false to an obligation  **2** : one who commits treason — **trai·tor·ous** *adj*

**tra·jec·to·ry** \trə-'jek-tə-rē\ *n, pl* **-ries** : the curve that a body (as a planet in its orbit) describes in space

**tram** \'tram\ *n* **1** : a boxlike car running on rails (as in a mine)  **2** *chiefly Brit* : STREETCAR  **3** : an overhead cable car

¹**tram·mel** \'tra-məl\ *n* [ME *tramayle*, a kind of net, fr. OF *tramail*, fr. LL *tremaculum*, fr. L *tres* three + *macula* mesh, spot] : something impeding activity, progress, or freedom — usu. used in pl.

²**trammel** *vb* **-meled** *or* **-melled**; **-mel·ing** *or* **-mel·ling** **1** : to catch and hold in or as if in a net  **2** : HAMPER ♦ *Synonyms* CLOG, FETTER, SHACKLE, HOBBLE

¹**tramp** \'tramp, *1 & 3 are also* 'trämp, 'trȯmp\ *vb* **1** : to walk, tread, or step heavily  **2** : to walk about or through;

*also* : HIKE ⟨~ed through the woods⟩ **3** : to tread on forcibly and repeatedly

**²tramp** \'tramp, *5 also* 'trämp, 'trômp\ *n* **1** : a begging or thieving vagrant **2** : a foot traveler **3** : an immoral woman; *esp* : PROSTITUTE **4** : a walking trip : HIKE **5** : the succession of sounds made by the beating of feet on a road **6** : a ship that does not follow a regular course but takes cargo to any port — **trampy** \'tram-pē\ *adj*

**tram·ple** \'tram-pəl\ *vb* **tram·pled; tram·pling 1** : to tread heavily so as to bruise, crush, or injure **2** : to inflict injury or destruction **3** : to press down or crush by or as if by treading — **trample** *n* — **tram·pler** *n*

**tram·po·line** \ˌtram-pə-'lēn, 'tram-pə-ˌlēn\ *n* [It *trampolino* springboard] : a resilient sheet or web (as of nylon) supported by springs in a metal frame and used as a springboard in tumbling — **tram·po·lin·ist** \-'lē-nist, -ˌlē-\ *n*

**trance** \'trans\ *n* [ME, fr. AF *transe*, death, coma, rapture, fr. *transir* to depart, die, fr. L *transire* to cross, pass by, fr. *trans-* across + *ire* to go] **1** : STUPOR, DAZE **2** : a sleeplike state of altered consciousness (as of deep hypnosis) **3** : a state of very deep absorption — **trance·like** \-ˌlīk\ *adj*

**tran·quil** \'traŋ-kwəl, 'tran-\ *adj* : free from agitation or disturbance : QUIET ♦ **Synonyms** SERENE, PLACID, PEACEFUL — **tran·quil·li·ty** *or* **tran·quil·i·ty** \tran-'kwi-lə-tē, traŋ-\ *n* — **tran·quil·ly** *adv*

**tran·quil·ize** *also* **tran·quil·lize** \'traŋ-kwə-ˌlīz, 'tran-\ *vb* **-ized** *also* **-lized; -iz·ing** *also* **-liz·ing** : to make or become tranquil; *esp* : to relieve of mental tension and anxiety by means of drugs

**tran·quil·iz·er** *also* **tran·quil·liz·er** \-ˌlī-zər\ *n* : a drug used to relieve mental disturbance (as tension and anxiety)

**¹trans** \'tranz\ *adj* : TRANSGENDER, TRANSSEXUAL

**²trans** *abbr* **1** transaction **2** transitive **3** translated; translation; translator **4** transmission **5** transportation **6** transverse

**trans·act** \tran-'zakt, -'sakt\ *vb* : CARRY OUT, PERFORM; *also* : CONDUCT

**trans·ac·tion** \-'zak-shən, -'sak-\ *n* **1** : something transacted; *esp* : a business deal **2** : an act or process of transacting **3** *pl* : the records of the proceedings of a society or organization — **trans·ac·tion·al** \-shnəl, -shə-nᵊl\ *adj*

**trans·at·lan·tic** \ˌtrans-ət-'lan-tik, ˌtranz-\ *adj* : crossing or extending across or situated beyond the Atlantic Ocean ⟨a ~ flight⟩

**trans·ax·le** \trans-'ak-səl\ *n* : a unit combining the transmission and differential gear of a front-wheel-drive automobile

**trans·ceiv·er** \tran-'sē-vər\ *n* : a radio transmitter-receiver that uses many of the same components for both transmission and reception

**tran·scend** \tran-'send\ *vb* **1** : to rise above the limits of ⟨music that ~s cultural boundaries⟩ **2** : SURPASS ♦ **Synonyms** EXCEED, OUTDO, OUTSHINE, OUTSTRIP

**tran·scen·dent** \-'sen-dənt\ *adj* **1** : exceeding usual limits : SURPASSING **2** : transcending material existence ♦ **Synonyms** SUPERLATIVE, SUPREME, PEERLESS, INCOMPARABLE

**tran·scen·den·tal** \ˌtran-ˌsen-'den-tᵊl, -sən-\ *adj* **1** : TRANSCENDENT 2 **2** : of, relating to, or characteristic of transcendentalism; *also* : ABSTRUSE

**tran·scen·den·tal·ism** \-tə-ˌli-zəm\ *n* : a philosophy holding that ultimate reality is unknowable or asserting the primacy of the spiritual over the material and empirical — **tran·scen·den·tal·ist** \-tə-list\ *adj or n*

**tran·con·ti·nen·tal** \ˌtrans-ˌkän-tə-'nen-tᵊl\ *adj* : extending or going across a continent ⟨a ~ railroad⟩

**tran·scribe** \tran-'skrīb\ *vb* **tran·scribed; tran·scrib·ing 1** : to write a copy of **2** : to make a copy of (dictated or recorded matter) in longhand or on a typewriter **3** : to represent (speech sounds) by means of phonetic symbols; *also* : to make a musical transcription of

**tran·script** \'tran-ˌskript\ *n* **1** : a written, printed, or typed copy **2** : an official copy esp. of a student's educational record

**tran·scrip·tion** \tran-'skrip-shən\ *n* **1** : an act or process of transcribing **2** : COPY, TRANSCRIPT **3** : an arrangement of a musical composition for some instrument or voice other than the original **4** : the process of constructing a messenger RNA molecule using a DNA molecule as a template

**tran·scrip·tion·ist** \-shə-nist\ *n* : one that transcribes; *esp* : a typist who transcribes medical reports

**trans·der·mal** \trans-'dər-məl, 'tranz-\ *adj* : relating to, being, or supplying a medication in a form for absorption through the skin ⟨~ nicotine patch⟩

**trans·duc·er** \trans-'dü-sər, tranz-, -'dyü-\ *n* : a device that is actuated by power from one system and supplies power usu. in another form to a second system

**tran·sept** \'tran-ˌsept\ *n* : the part of a cruciform church that crosses at right angles to the greatest length; *also* : either of the projecting ends

**trans fat** \'tran(t)s-, 'tranz-\ *n* : a fat containing unsaturated fatty acids (**trans–fatty acids**) that have been linked to an increase in blood cholesterol

**¹trans·fer** \trans-'fər, 'trans-ˌfər\ *vb* **transferred; trans·fer·ring 1** : to pass or cause to pass from one person, place, or situation to another : MOVE, TRANSMIT **2** : to make over the possession of : CONVEY **3** : to print or copy from one surface to another by contact **4** : to change from one vehicle or transportation line to another — **trans·fer·able** \trans-'fər-ə-bəl\ *adj* — **trans·fer·al** \-'əl\ *n*

**²trans·fer** \'trans-ˌfər\ *n* **1** : conveyance of right, title, or interest in property from one person to another **2** : an act or process of transferring **3** : one that transfers or is transferred **4** : a ticket entitling a passenger to continue a trip on another route

**trans·fer·ence** \trans-ˈfər-əns\ *n* : an act, process, or instance of transferring

**trans·fig·ure** \trans-ˈfi-gyər\ *vb* **-ured; -ur·ing 1** : to change the form or appearance of **2** : EXALT, GLORIFY — **trans·fig·u·ra·tion** \trans-ˌfi-gyə-ˈrā-shən, -gə-\ *n*

**trans·fix** \trans-ˈfiks\ *vb* **1** : to pierce through with or as if with a pointed weapon **2** : to hold motionless by or as if by piercing ⟨stood ∼ed by her gaze⟩

**trans·form** \trans-ˈfȯrm\ *vb* : to change in structure, appearance, or character ♦ *Synonyms* TRANSMUTE, TRANSFIGURE, TRANSMOGRIFY — **trans·for·ma·tion** \ˌtrans-fər-ˈmā-shən\ *n* — **trans·for·ma·tive** \trans-ˈfȯr-mə-tiv\ *adj*

**trans·form·er** \trans-ˈfȯr-mər\ *n* : one that transforms; *esp* : a device for converting variations of current in one circuit into variations of voltage and current in another circuit

**trans·fuse** \trans-ˈfyüz\ *vb* **trans·fused; trans·fus·ing 1** : to cause to pass from one to another **2** : to diffuse into or through **3** : to transfer (as blood) into a vein or an artery of a person or animal — **trans·fu·sion** \-ˈfyü-zhən\ *n*

**trans·gen·der** \tranz-ˈjen-dər\ *or* **trans·gen·dered** \-dərd\ *adj* : having physical or behavioral characteristics transcending traditional gender boundaries ⟨a ∼ person⟩

**trans·gen·ic** \tran(t)s-ˈje-nik\ *adj* : being or used to produce an organism or cell with genes introduced from another species of organism ⟨∼ crops⟩

**trans·gress** \trans-ˈgres, tranz-\ *vb* [ME, fr. MF *transgresser*, fr. L *transgressus*, pp. of *transgredi* to step beyond or across, fr. *trans-* across + *gradi* to step] **1** : to go beyond the limits set by ⟨∼ the divine law⟩ **2** : to go beyond : EXCEED **3** : SIN — **trans·gres·sion** \-ˈgre-shən\ *n* — **trans·gres·sor** \-ˈgre-sər\ *n*

**¹tran·sient** \ˈtran-shənt; -sē-ənt, -shē-, -zē-\ *adj* **1** : not lasting long : SHORT-LIVED ⟨∼ optimism⟩ **2** : passing through a place with only a brief stay ⟨∼visitors⟩ ♦ *Synonyms* TRANSITORY, PASSING, MOMENTARY, FLEETING — **tran·sient·ly** *adv*

**²transient** *n* : one that is transient; *esp* : a transient guest

**tran·sis·tor** \tran-ˈzis-tər, -ˈsis-\ *n* [*transfer* + *resistor*; fr. its transferring an electrical signal across a resistor] **1** : a small electronic semiconductor device used in electronic equipment **2** : a radio having transistors

**tran·sis·tor·ized** \-tə-ˌrīzd\ *adj* : having or using transistors

**tran·sit** \ˈtran-sət, -zət\ *n* **1** : a passing through, across, or over : PASSAGE **2** : conveyance of persons or things from one place to another **3** : usu. local transportation esp. of people by public con-

veyance **4** : a surveyor's instrument for measuring angles

**tran·si·tion** \tran-ˈsi-shən, -ˈzi-\ *n* : passage from one state, place, stage, or subject to another : CHANGE — **tran·si·tion·al** \-ˈsi-shə-nəl, -ˈzi\ *adj*

**tran·si·tive** \ˈtran-sə-tiv, -zə-\ *adj* **1** : having or containing an object required to complete the meaning ⟨a ∼ verb⟩ **2** : TRANSITIONAL — **tran·si·tive·ly** *adv* — **tran·si·tive·ness** *n* — **tran·si·tiv·i·ty** \ˌtran-sə-ˈti-və-tē, -zə-\ *n*

**tran·si·to·ry** \ˈtran-sə-ˌtȯr-ē, -zə-\ *adj* : of brief duration : SHORT-LIVED, TEMPORARY ♦ *Synonyms* TRANSIENT, PASSING, MOMENTARY, FLEETING

**transl** *abbr* translated; translation

**trans·late** \trans-ˈlāt, tranz-\ *vb* **trans·lat·ed; trans·lat·ing 1** : to change from one place, state, or form to another **2** : to convey to heaven without death **3** : to turn into one's own or another language — **trans·lat·able** *adj* — **trans·la·tor** \-ˈlā-tər\ *n*

**trans·la·tion** \tran(t)s-ˈlā-shən, tranz-\ *n* **1** : an act, process, or instance of translating **2** : the process of forming a protein molecule from information in messenger RNA — **trans·la·tion·al** \-shnəl, -shə-nᵊl\ *adj*

**trans·lit·er·ate** \trans-ˈli-tə-ˌrāt, tranz-\ *vb* **-at·ed; -at·ing** : to represent or spell in the characters of another alphabet — **trans·lit·er·a·tion** \ˌtrans-ˌli-tə-ˈrā-shən, ˌtranz-\ *n*

**trans·lu·cent** \trans-ˈlü-sᵊnt, tranz-\ *adj* : not transparent but clear enough to allow light to pass through — **trans·lu·cence** \-sᵊns\ *n* — **trans·lu·cen·cy** \-sᵊn-sē\ *n* — **trans·lu·cent·ly** *adv*

**trans·mi·grate** \ˈtranz-ˌmī-ˌgrāt\ *vb* : to pass at death from one body or being to another — **trans·mi·gra·tion** \ˌtranz-ˌmī-ˈgrā-shən, ˌtranz-\ *n* — **trans·mi·gra·to·ry** \ˌtranz-ˈmī-grə-ˌtȯr-ē\ *adj*

**trans·mis·sion** \-ˈmi-shən\ *n* **1** : an act or process of transmitting **2** : the passage of radio waves between transmitting stations and receiving stations **3** : the gears by which power is transmitted from the engine of an automobile to the axle that propels the vehicle **4** : something transmitted

**trans·mit** \-ˈmit\ *vb* **trans·mit·ted; trans·mit·ting 1** : to transfer from one person or place to another : FORWARD **2** : to pass on by or as if by inheritance **3** : to cause or allow to spread abroad or to another ⟨∼ a disease⟩ **4** : to cause (as light, electricity, or force) to pass through space or a medium **5** : to send out (radio or television signals) ♦ *Synonyms* CONVEY, COMMUNICATE, IMPART — **trans·mis·si·ble** \-ˈmi-sə-bəl\ *adj* — **trans·mit·ta·ble** \-ˈmi-tə-bəl\ *adj* — **trans·mit·tal** \-ˈmit-ᵊl\ *n*

**trans·mit·ter** \-ˈmi-tər\ *n* : one that transmits; *esp* : an apparatus for transmitting telegraph, radio, or television signals

**trans·mog·ri·fy** \trans-ˈmä-grə-ˌfī, tranz-\ *vb* **-fied; -fy·ing** : to change or alter often with grotesque or humorous effect —

**trans·mog·ri·fi·ca·tion** \-ˌmä-grə-fə-ˈkā-shən\ *n*

**trans·mute** \-ˈmyüt\ *vb* **trans·muted; trans·mut·ing** : to change or alter in form, appearance, or nature ♦ *Synonyms* TRANSFORM, CONVERT, TRANSFIGURE, METAMORPHOSE — **trans·mu·ta·tion** \ˌtrans-myü-ˈtā-shən, ˌtranz-\ *n*

**trans·na·tion·al** \-ˈna-shə-nəl\ *adj* : extending beyond national boundaries

**trans·oce·an·ic** \ˌtrans-ˌō-shē-ˈa-nik, ˌtranz-\ *adj* 1 : lying or dwelling beyond the ocean 2 : crossing or extending across the ocean

**tran·som** \ˈtran-səm\ *n* 1 : a piece (as a crossbar in the frame of a window or door) that lies crosswise in a structure 2 : a window above an opening (as a door) built on and often hinged to a horizontal crossbar

**tran·son·ic** *also* **trans–son·ic** \trans-ˈsä-nik\ *adj* : being or relating to speeds near that of sound in air or about 741 miles (1185 kilometers) per hour

**trans·pa·cif·ic** \ˌtrans-pə-ˈsi-fik\ *adj* : crossing, extending across, or situated beyond the Pacific Ocean

**trans·par·ent** \trans-ˈper-ənt\ *adj* 1 : clear enough to be seen through 2 : SHEER, DIAPHANOUS ⟨a ∼ fabric⟩ 3 : readily understood : CLEAR; *also* : easily detected ⟨a ∼ lie⟩ ♦ *Synonyms* LUCID, TRANSLUCENT, LUCENT — **trans·par·en·cy** \-ən-sē\ *n* — **trans·par·ent·ly** *adv*

**tran·spire** \trans-ˈpī(-ə)r\ *vb* **trans·pired; tran·spir·ing** [MF *transpirer*, fr. ML *transpirare*, fr. L *trans-* across + *spirare* to breathe] 1 : to pass or give off (as water vapor) through pores or a membrane 2 : to become known 3 : to take place : HAPPEN — **tran·spi·ra·tion** \ˌtrans-pə-ˈrā-shən\ *n*

¹**trans·plant** \trans-ˈplant\ *vb* 1 : to dig up and plant elsewhere 2 : to remove from one place and settle or introduce elsewhere : TRANSPORT 3 : to transfer (an organ or tissue) from one part or individual to another — **trans·plan·ta·tion** \ˌtrans-ˌplan-ˈtā-shən\ *n*

²**trans·plant** \ˈtrans-ˌplant\ *n* 1 : a person or thing transplanted 2 : the act or process of transplanting

**trans·po·lar** \trans-ˈpō-lər\ *adj* : going or extending across either of the polar regions

**transponder** \tran-ˈspän-dər\ *n* [*transmitter* + re*sponder*] : a radio or radar set that upon receiving a certain signal emits a radio signal and that is used to locate and identify objects and in satellites to relay communications signals

¹**trans·port** \trans-ˈpȯrt\ *vb* 1 : to convey from one place to another : CARRY 2 : to carry away by strong emotion : ENRAPTURE 3 : to send to a penal colony overseas ♦ *Synonyms* BEAR, FERRY — **trans·por·ta·tion** \ˌtrans-pər-ˈtā-shən\ *n* — **trans·port·er** *n*

²**trans·port** \ˈtrans-ˌpȯrt\ *n* 1 : an act of transporting 2 : strong or intensely pleasurable emotion ⟨∼s of joy⟩ 3 : a ship used in transporting troops or supplies;

*also* : a vehicle (as a truck or plane) used to transport persons or goods

**trans·pose** \trans-ˈpōz\ *vb* **trans·posed; trans·pos·ing** 1 : to change the position or sequence of ⟨∼ the letters in a word⟩ 2 : to write or perform (a musical composition) in a different key — **trans·po·si·tion** \ˌtrans-pə-ˈzi-shən\ *n*

**trans·sex·u·al** \(ˌ)trans-ˈsek-shə-wəl\ *n* : a person who psychologically identifies with the opposite sex and may seek to live as a member of this sex esp. by undergoing surgery to modify the external sex organs

**trans·ship** \tran-ˈship, trans-\ *vb* : to transfer for further transportation from one ship or conveyance to another — **trans·ship·ment** *n*

**tran·sub·stan·ti·a·tion** \ˌtran-səb-ˌstan-chē-ˈā-shən\ *n* : the change in the eucharistic elements from the substance of bread and wine to the substance of the body of Christ with only the appearances of bread and wine remaining

**trans·verse** \trans-ˈvərs, tranz-\ *adj* : lying across : set crosswise — **transverse** \ˈtrans-ˌvərs, ˈtranz-\ *n* — **trans·verse·ly** *adv*

**trans·ves·tite** \trans-ˈves-ˌtīt, tranz-\ *n* : a person and esp. a male who adopts the dress and often the behavior of the opposite sex — **transvestite** *adj* — **trans·ves·tism** \-ˌti-zəm\ *n*

¹**trap** \ˈtrap\ *n* 1 : a device for catching animals 2 : something by which one is caught unawares; *also* : a situation from which escape is difficult or impossible 3 : a machine for throwing clay pigeons into the air; *also* : SAND TRAP 4 : a light one-horse carriage on springs 5 : a device to allow some one thing to pass through while keeping other things out ⟨a ∼ in a drainpipe⟩ 6 *pl* : a group of percussion instruments (as in a dance orchestra)

²**trap** *vb* **trapped; trap·ping** 1 : to catch in or as if in a trap; *also* : CONFINE 2 : to provide or set (a place) with traps 3 : to set traps for animals esp. as a business ♦ *Synonyms* SNARE, ENTRAP, ENSNARE, BAG, LURE, DECOY — **trap·per** *n*

**trap·door** \ˈtrap-ˈdȯr\ *n* : a lifting or sliding door covering an opening in a floor or roof

**tra·peze** \tra-ˈpēz\ *n* : a gymnastic apparatus consisting of a horizontal bar suspended by two parallel ropes

**trap·e·zoid** \ˈtra-pə-ˌzȯid\ *n* [NL *trapezoides*, fr. Gk *trapezoeidēs* trapezoidal, fr. *trapeza* table, fr. *tra-* four + *peza* foot] : a 4-sided polygon with exactly two sides parallel — **trap·e·zoi·dal** \ˌtra-pə-ˈzȯi-dəl\ *adj*

**trap·pings** \ˈtra-piŋz\ *n pl* 1 : CAPARISON 1 2 : outward decoration or dress; *also* : outward sign ⟨∼ of success⟩

**traps** \ˈtraps\ *n pl* : personal belongings : LUGGAGE

**trap·shoot·ing** \ˈtrap-ˌshü-tiŋ\ *n* : shooting at clay pigeons sprung from a trap into the air away from the shooter

¹**trash** \ˈtrash\ *n* 1 : something of little

worth : RUBBISH **2** : empty or disparaging talk **3** : a worthless person; *also* : such persons as a group : RIFFRAFF — **trash•y** *adj*

**²trash** *vb* **1** : to dispose of : DISCARD ⟨~*ed* the plans⟩ **2** : VANDALIZE, DESTROY **3** : ATTACK **4** : SPOIL, RUIN **5** : to criticize or disparage harshly

**trau•ma** \'traù-mə, 'trò-\ *n, pl* **traumas** *also* **trau•ma•ta** \-mə-tə\ [Gk, wound] : a bodily or mental injury usu. caused by an external agent; *also* : a cause of trauma — **trau•mat•ic** \trə-'ma-tik, trò-, traù-\ *adj*

**trau•ma•tize** \-‚tīz\ *vb* **-tized; -tiz•ing** : to inflict trauma upon

**¹tra•vail** \trə-'vāl, 'tra-‚vāl\ *n* **1** : painful work or exertion : TOIL **2** : AGONY, TORMENT **3** : CHILDBIRTH, LABOR

**²travail** *vb* : to labor hard : TOIL

**¹trav•el** \'tra-vəl\ *vb* **-eled** *or* **-elled; -el•ing** *or* **-el•ling** [ME *travailen* to torment, labor, journey, fr. AF *travailler* strive, fr. VL *\*trepaliare* to torture, fr. LL *trepalium* instrument of torture] **1** : to go on or as if on a trip or tour : JOURNEY **2** : to move as if by traveling ⟨news ~s fast⟩ **3** : ASSOCIATE **4** : to go from place to place as a sales representative **5** : to move from point to point ⟨light waves ~ very fast⟩ **6** : to journey over or through ⟨~*ing* the highways⟩ **7** : to take excessive steps while holding a basketball — **trav•el•er** *or* **trav•el•ler** *n*

**²travel** *n* **1** : the act of traveling : PASSAGE **2** : JOURNEY, TRIP — often used in pl. **3** : the number traveling : TRAFFIC **4** : the motion of a piece of machinery and esp. when to and fro

**traveler's check** *n* : a check paid for in advance that is signed when bought and signed again when cashed

**traveling bag** *n* : SUITCASE

**trav•el•ogue** *or* **trav•el•og** \'tra-və-‚lòg, -‚läg\ *n* : a usu. illustrated lecture on travel

**¹tra•verse** \'tra-vərs\ *n* : something that crosses or lies across

**²tra•verse** \trə-'vərs, tra-'vərs *or* 'tra-vərs\ *vb* **tra•versed; tra•vers•ing 1** : to go or travel across or over **2** : to move or pass along or through **3** : to extend over **4** : SWIVEL

**³tra•verse** \'tra-‚vərs\ *adj* : TRANSVERSE

**trav•er•tine** \'tra-vər-‚tēn, -tən\ *n* : a crystalline mineral formed by deposition from spring waters

**¹trav•es•ty** \'tra-və-stē\ *vb* **-tied; -ty•ing** : to make a travesty of

**²travesty** *n, pl* **-ties** [obs. E *travesty* disguised, parodied, fr. F *travesti*, pp. of *travestir* to disguise, fr. It *travestire*, fr. *tra-* across (fr. L *trans-*) + *vestire* to dress] : an imitation that makes crude fun of something; *also* : an inferior imitation

**¹trawl** \'tròl\ *vb* : to fish or catch with a trawl — **trawl•er** *n*

**²trawl** *n* **1** : a large conical net dragged along the sea bottom in fishing **2** : a long heavy fishing line equipped with many hooks in series

**tray** \'trā\ *n* : an open receptacle with flat

---

bottom and low rim for holding, carrying, or exhibiting articles

**treach•er•ous** \'tre-chə-rəs\ *adj* **1** : characterized by treachery **2** : UNTRUSTWORTHY, UNRELIABLE ⟨a ~ coworker⟩ **3** : providing insecure footing or support ⟨a ~ slope⟩ ♦ **Synonyms** TRAITOROUS, FAITHLESS, FALSE, DISLOYAL — **treach•er•ous•ly** *adv*

**treach•ery** \'tre-chə-rē\ *n, pl* **-er•ies** : violation of allegiance or trust

**trea•cle** \'trē-kəl\ *n* [ME *triacle* a medicinal compound, fr. AF, fr. L *theriaca*, fr. Gk *thēriakē* antidote against a poisonous bite, fr. *thērion* wild animal] *chiefly Brit* : MOLASSES — **trea•cly** \-k(ə-)lē\ *adj*

**¹tread** \'tred\ *vb* **trod** \'träd\; **trod•den** \'trä-d⁰n\ *or* **trod; tread•ing 1** : to step or walk on or over **2** : to move on foot : WALK; *also* : DANCE **3** : to beat or press with the feet — **tread water** : to stay afloat and upright in water by sustaining a walking motion

**²tread** *n* **1** : a mark made by or as if by treading **2** : the manner or sound of stepping **3** : the part of a wheel that makes contact with a road **4** : the horizontal part of a step

**trea•dle** \'tre-d⁰l\ *n* : a lever device pressed by the foot to drive a machine — **treadle** *vb*

**tread•mill** \'tred-‚mil\ *n* **1** : a mill worked by persons who tread on steps around the edge of a wheel or by animals that walk on an endless belt **2** : a device with an endless belt on which a person walks or runs in place **3** : a wearisome routine

**treas** *abbr* treasurer; treasury

**trea•son** \'trē-z⁰n\ *n* : the offense of attempting to overthrow the government of one's country or of assisting its enemies in war — **trea•son•able** \-z⁰n-ə-bəl\ *adj* — **trea•son•ous** \-z⁰n-əs\ *adj*

**¹trea•sure** \'tre-zhər, 'trā-\ *n* [ME *tresor*, fr. AF, fr. L *thesaurus*, fr. Gk *thēsauros*] **1** : wealth stored up or held in reserve **2** : something of great value

**²treasure** *vb* **trea•sured; trea•sur•ing 1** : HOARD **2** : to keep as precious : CHERISH ♦ **Synonyms** PRIZE, VALUE, APPRECIATE, ESTEEM

**trea•sur•er** \'tre-zhə-rər, 'trā-\ *n* : an officer of a club, business, or government who has charge of money taken in and paid out

**treasure trove** \-‚trōv\ *n* **1** : treasure of unknown ownership found buried or hidden **2** : a valuable discovery

**trea•sury** \'tre-zhə-rē, 'trā-\ *n, pl* **-sur•ies 1** : a place in which stores of wealth are kept **2** : the place where collected funds are stored and paid out **3** *cap* : a governmental department in charge of finances

**¹treat** \'trēt\ *vb* **1** : NEGOTIATE **2** : to deal with esp. in writing; *also* : HANDLE **3** : to pay for the food or entertainment of **4** : to behave or act toward ⟨~ them well⟩ **5** : to regard in a specified manner ⟨~ as inferiors⟩ **6** : to give medical or surgical care to **7** : to subject to some action ⟨~ soil with lime⟩

**²treat** *n* **1** : an entertainment given free to

those invited; *also* : food, drink, or entertainment provided at another's expense **2** : a source of joy or amusement

**trea·tise** \'trē-təs\ *n* : a systematic written exposition or argument

**treat·ment** \'trēt-mənt\ *n* : the act or manner or an instance of treating someone or something; *also* : a substance or method used in treating

**trea·ty** \'trēt-ē\ *n, pl* **treaties** : an agreement made by negotiation or diplomacy esp. between two or more states or governments

¹**tre·ble** \'tre-bəl\ *n* **1** : the highest of the four voice parts in vocal music : SOPRANO **2** : a high-pitched or shrill voice or sound **3** : the upper half of the musical pitch range

²**treble** *adj* **1** : triple in number or amount **2** : relating to or having the range of a musical treble **3** : high-pitched : SHRILL — **tre·bly** *adv*

³**treble** *vb* **tre·bled; tre·bling** : to make or become three times the size, amount, or number

¹**tree** \'trē\ *n* **1** : a woody perennial plant usu. with a single main stem and a head of branches and leaves at the top **2** : a piece of wood adapted to a particular use ⟨a shoe ∼⟩ **3** : something resembling a tree ⟨a genealogical ∼⟩ — **tree·less** *adj*

²**tree** *vb* **treed; tree·ing** : to drive to or up a tree ⟨∼ a raccoon⟩

**tree farm** *n* : an area of forest land managed to ensure continuous commercial production

**tree frog** *n* : any of numerous small usu. tree-dwelling amphibians with adhesive disks on the toes

**tree line** *n* : TIMBERLINE

**tree of heaven** : a Chinese ailanthus widely grown as an ornamental tree

**tree surgery** *n* : operative treatment of diseased trees esp. for control of decay — **tree surgeon** *n*

**tre·foil** \'trē-ˌfȯi(-ə)l, 'tre-\ *n* **1** : an herb (as a clover) with leaves that have three leaflets **2** : a decorative design with three leaflike parts

¹**trek** \'trek\ *vb* **trekked; trek·king** **1** *chiefly southern Africa* : to travel or migrate by ox wagon **2** : to make one's way arduously

²**trek** *n* **1** *chiefly southern Africa* : a migration esp. of settlers by ox wagon **2** : a slow or difficult journey

¹**trel·lis** \'tre-ləs\ *n* [ME *trelis*, fr. AF *treleis*, fr. OF *treille* arbor, fr. L *trichila* summerhouse] : a frame of latticework used esp. to support climbing plants

²**trellis** *vb* : to provide with a trellis; *esp* : to train (as a vine) on a trellis

**trem·a·tode** \'tre-mə-ˌtōd\ *n* : any of a class of parasitic worms

¹**trem·ble** \'trem-bəl\ *vb* **trem·bled; trembling** **1** : to shake involuntarily (as with fear or cold) : SHIVER **2** : to move, sound, pass, or come to pass as if shaken or tremulous or to be affected with fear or doubt

²**tremble** *n* : a spell of shaking or quivering

**tre·men·dous** \tri-'men-dəs\ *adj* **1**

: causing dread, awe, or terror : TERRIFYING **2** : unusually large, powerful, great, or excellent ⟨∼ strength⟩ ♦ *Synonyms* STUPENDOUS, MONUMENTAL, MONSTROUS — **tre·men·dous·ly** *adv*

**trem·o·lo** \'tre-mə-ˌlō\ *n, pl* **-los** [It] : a rapid fluttering of a tone or alternating tones

**trem·or** \'tre-mər\ *n* **1** : a trembling or shaking esp. from weakness, emotional stress, or disease **2** : a quivering motion of the earth (as during an earthquake)

**trem·u·lous** \'trem-yə-ləs\ *adj* **1** : marked by trembling or tremors : QUIVERING ⟨∼ hands⟩ **2** : TIMOROUS, TIMID — **trem·u·lous·ly** *adv*

¹**trench** \'trench\ *n* [ME *trenche* track cut through a wood, fr. AF, act of cutting, fr. *trencher* to cut, prob. fr. VL *trinicare* to cut in three, fr. L *trini* three each] **1** : a long narrow cut in the ground : DITCH; *esp* : a ditch protected by banks of earth and used to shelter soldiers **2** *pl* : a place or situation likened to warfare conducted from trenches **3** : a long narrow steep-sided depression in the ocean floor

²**trench** *vb* **1** : to cut or dig trenches in **2** : to protect (troops) with trenches **3** : to come close : VERGE

**tren·chant** \'tren-chənt\ *adj* **1** : vigorously effective; *also* : CAUSTIC ⟨∼ comments⟩ **2** : sharply perceptive : KEEN ⟨a ∼ wit⟩ **3** : CLEAR-CUT, DISTINCT

**tren·cher** \'tren-chər\ *n* : a wooden platter for serving food

**tren·cher·man** \'tren-chər-mən\ *n* : a hearty eater

**trench foot** *n* : a painful foot disorder resembling frostbite and resulting from exposure to cold and wet

**trench mouth** *n* : a progressive painful bacterial infection of the mouth and adjacent parts marked by ulceration, bleeding gums, and foul breath

¹**trend** \'trend\ *vb* **1** : to have or take a general direction : TEND **2** : to show a tendency : INCLINE

²**trend** *n* **1** : a general direction taken (as by a stream or mountain range) **2** : a prevailing tendency : DRIFT **3** : a current style or preference : VOGUE

**trendy** \'tren-dē\ *adj* **trend·i·er; -est** : very fashionable; *also* : marked by superficial or faddish appeal or taste

**trep·i·da·tion** \ˌtre-pə-'dā-shən\ *n* : nervous agitation : APPREHENSION ♦ *Synonyms* HORROR, TERROR, PANIC, CONSTERNATION, DREAD, FRIGHT, DISMAY

¹**tres·pass** \'tres-pəs, -ˌpas\ *n* **1** : SIN, OFFENSE **2** : unlawful entry on someone else's land ♦ *Synonyms* TRANSGRESSION, VIOLATION, INFRACTION, INFRINGEMENT

²**trespass** *vb* **1** : to commit an offense : ERR, SIN **2** : INTRUDE, ENCROACH; *esp* : to enter unlawfully upon the land of another — **tres·pass·er** *n*

**tress** \'tres\ *n* : a long lock of hair — usu. used in pl.

**tres·tle** *also* **tres·sel** \'tre-səl\ *n* **1** : a supporting framework consisting usu. of a horizontal piece with spreading legs at each end **2** : a braced framework of timbers, piles, or steel for carrying a road or railroad over a depression

**T. rex** \'tē-'rcks\ *n* : TYRANNOSAUR

**trey** \'trā\ *n, pl* **treys** : a card or the side of a die with three spots

**tri·ad** \'trī-,ad, -əd\ *n* : a union or group of three usu. closely related persons or things

**tri·age** \trē-'äzh, 'trē-,äzh\ *n* [F, sorting] : the sorting of and allocation of treatment to patients and esp. battle or disaster victims according to a system of priorities designed to maximize the number of survivors

**tri·al** \'trī-əl\ *n* **1** : the action or process of trying or putting to the proof : TEST **2** : the hearing and judgment of a matter in issue before a competent tribunal **3** : a source of vexation or annoyance **4** : an experiment to test quality, value, or usefulness **5** : EFFORT, ATTEMPT ♦ **Synonyms** CROSS, ORDEAL, TRIBULATION, AFFLICTION — **trial** *adj*

**tri·an·gle** \'trī-,aŋ-gəl\ *n* **1** : a polygon that has three sides **2** : something shaped like a triangle — **tri·an·gu·lar** \trī-'aŋ-gyə-lər\ *adj* — **tri·an·gu·lar·ly** *adv*

**tri·an·gu·la·tion** \(,)trī-,aŋ-gyə-'lā-shən\ *n* : a method using trigonometry to find the location of a point using bearings from two fixed points a known distance apart — **tri·an·gu·late** \(,)trī-'aŋ-gyə-,lāt\ *vb*

**Tri·as·sic** \trī-'a-sik\ *adj* : of, relating to, or being the earliest period of the Mesozoic era marked by the first appearance of the dinosaurs — **Triassic** *n*

**tri·ath·lon** \trī-'ath-lən, -,län\ *n* : an athletic contest consisting of three phases (as swimming, bicycling, and running)

**trib** *abbr* tributary

**tribe** \'trīb\ *n* **1** : a social group comprising numerous families, clans, or generations **2** : a group of persons having a common character, occupation, or interest **3** : a group of related plants or animals ⟨the cat ∼⟩ — **trib·al** \'trī-bəl\ *adj*

**tribes·man** \'trībz-mən\ *n* : a member of a tribe

**trib·u·la·tion** \,tri-byə-'lā-shən\ *n* [ME *tribulacion*, fr. AF, fr. L *tribulatio*, fr. *tribulare* to press, oppress, fr. *tribulum* drag used in threshing] : distress or suffering resulting from oppression or persecution; *also* : a trying experience ♦ **Synonyms** TRIAL, AFFLICTION, CROSS, ORDEAL

**tri·bu·nal** \trī-'byü-nᵊl, tri-\ *n* **1** : the seat of a judge **2** : a court of justice **3** : something that decides or determines ⟨the ∼ of public opinion⟩

**tri·bune** \'tri-,byün, tri-'byün\ *n* **1** : an official in ancient Rome with the function of protecting the interests of plebeian citizens from the patricians **2** : a defender of the people

¹**trib·u·tary** \'tri-byə-,ter-ē\ *adj* **1** : paying tribute : SUBJECT **2** : flowing into a larger stream or a lake ♦ **Synonyms** SUBORDINATE, SECONDARY, DEPENDENT

²**tributary** *n, pl* **-tar·ies** **1** : a ruler or state that pays tribute **2** : a tributary stream

**trib·ute** \'tri-(,)byüt, -byət\ *n* **1** : a payment by one ruler or nation to another as an act of submission or price of protection **2** : a usu. excessive tax, rental, or levy exacted by a sovereign or superior **3** : a gift or service showing respect, gratitude, or affection; *also* : PRAISE ♦ **Synonyms** EULOGY, CITATION, ENCOMIUM, PANEGYRIC

**trice** \'trīs\ *n* : INSTANT, MOMENT

**tri·ceps** \'trī-,seps\ *n, pl* **triceps** : a large muscle along the back of the upper arm that is attached at its upper end by three main parts and acts to extend the forearm at the elbow joint

**tri·cer·a·tops** \(,)trī-'ser-ə-,täps\ *n, pl* **-tops** *also* **-tops·es** [NL, fr. Gk *tri-* three + *kerat-, keras* horn + *ōps* face] : any of a genus of large plant-eating Cretaceous dinosaurs with three horns, a bony crest on the neck, and hoofed toes

**tri·chi·na** \tri-'kī-nə\ *n, pl* **-nae** \-(,)nē\ *also* **-nas** : a small slender nematode worm that in the larval state is parasitic in the striated muscles of flesh-eating mammals (as humans)

**trich·i·no·sis** \,tri-kə-'nō-səs\ *n* : infestation with or disease caused by trichinae and marked esp. by muscular pain, fever, and swelling

¹**trick** \'trik\ *n* **1** : a crafty procedure meant to deceive **2** : a mischievous action : PRANK **3** : a childish action **4** : a deceptive or ingenious feat designed to puzzle or amuse **5** : PECULIARITY, MANNERISM **6** : a quick or artful way of getting a result : KNACK ⟨∼s of the trade⟩ **7** : the cards played in one round of a card game **8** : a tour of duty : SHIFT ♦ **Synonyms** RUSE, MANEUVER, ARTIFICE, WILE, FEINT

²**trick** *vb* **1** : to deceive by cunning or artifice : CHEAT **2** : to dress ornately

**trick·ery** \'tri-kə-rē\ *n* : deception by tricks and strategems

**trick·le** \'tri-kəl\ *vb* **trick·led; trick·ling** **1** : to run or fall in drops **2** : to flow in a thin gentle stream — **trickle** *n*

**trick·ster** \'trik-stər\ *n* : one who tricks or cheats

**tricky** \'tri-kē\ *adj* **trick·i·er; -est** **1** : inclined to trickery or deception **2** : requiring skill or caution ⟨a ∼ situation to handle⟩ **3** : UNRELIABLE ⟨a ∼ lock⟩

**tri·col·or** \'trī-,kə-lər\ *n* : a flag of three colors ⟨the French ∼⟩

**tri·cy·cle** \'trī-,si-kəl\ *n* : a 3-wheeled vehicle usu. propelled by pedals

**tri·dent** \'trī-dᵊnt\ *n* [L *trident-, tridens*, fr. *tri-* three + *dent-, dens* tooth] : a 3-pronged spear

**tried** \'trīd\ *adj* **1** : found trustworthy through testing **2** : subjected to trials

**tri·en·ni·al** \trī-'e-nē-əl\ *adj* **1** : occurring or being done every three years **2** : lasting for three years — **triennial** *n*

¹**tri·fle** \'trī-fəl\ *n* **1** : something of little value or importance **2** : a dessert of cake soaked with liqueur and served with toppings (as fruit or cream)

²**trifle** *vb* **tri·fled; tri·fling** **1** : to talk in a jesting or mocking manner **2** : to treat

someone or something as unimportant **3**
: DALLY, FLIRT **4** : to handle idly : TOY
— **tri·fler** *n*

**tri·fling** \ˈtrī-fliŋ\ *adj* **1** : FRIVOLOUS **2**
: TRIVIAL, INSIGNIFICANT ⟨~ details⟩
♦ *Synonyms* PETTY, PALTRY, MEASLY,
INCONSEQUENTIAL

**tri·fo·cals** \trī-ˈfō-kəlz\ *n pl* : eyeglasses
with lenses having one part for close focus, one for intermediate focus, and one
for distant focus

**tri·fo·li·ate** \trī-ˈfō-lē-ət\ *adj* : having
three leaves or leaflets

**¹trig** \ˈtrig\ *adj* : stylishly trim : SMART

**²trig** *n* : TRIGONOMETRY

**¹trig·ger** \ˈtri-gər\ *n* [alter. of earlier *trick-
er*, fr. D *trekker*, fr. MD *trecker* one that
pulls, fr. *trecken* to pull] : a movable lever
that activates a device when it is
squeezed; *esp* : the part of a firearm lock
moved by the finger to fire a gun — **trigger** *adj* — **trig·gered** *adj*

**²trigger** *vb* **1** : to fire by pulling a trigger
**2** : to initiate, actuate, or set off as if by a
trigger ⟨remarks that ~ed a fight⟩

**tri·glyc·er·ide** \trī-ˈgli-sə-ˌrīd\ *n* : any of a
group of lipids that are formed from
glycerol and fatty acids and are widespread in animal tissue

**trig·o·nom·e·try** \ˌtri-gə-ˈnä-mə-trē\ *n*
: the branch of mathematics dealing with
the properties of triangles and esp. with
finding unknown angles or sides given
the size or length of some angles or sides
— **trig·o·no·met·ric** \-nə-ˈme-trik\ *also*
**trig·o·no·met·ri·cal** \-tri-kəl\ *adj*

**trike** \ˈtrīk\ *n* : TRICYCLE

**¹trill** \ˈtril\ *n* **1** : the alternation of two musical tones a scale degree apart **2** : WAR-
BLE **3** : the rapid vibration of one speech
organ against another (as of the tip of the
tongue against the teeth)

**²trill** *vb* : to utter as or with a trill

**tril·lion** \ˈtril-yən\ *n* **1** : a thousand billions **2** *Brit* : a million billions — **trillion**
*adj* — **tril·lionth** \-yənth\ *adj or n*

**tril·li·um** \ˈtri-lē-əm\ *n* : any of a genus of
spring-blooming herbs that are related to
the lilies and have an erect stem bearing
a whorl of three leaves and a solitary
flower

**tril·o·gy** \ˈtri-lə-jē\ *n, pl* **-gies** : a series of
three dramas or literary or musical compositions that are closely related and develop one theme

**¹trim** \ˈtrim\ *vb* **trimmed; trim·ming** [OE
*tryman, trymman* to strengthen, arrange,
fr. *trum* strong, firm] **1** : to put ornaments on : ADORN **2** : to defeat esp. re-
soundingly **3** : to make trim, neat, regular, or less bulky by or as if by cutting
⟨~ a beard⟩ ⟨~ a budget⟩ **4** : to cause
(a boat) to assume a desired position in
the water by arrangement of the load;
*also* : to adjust (as a submarine or airplane) esp. for horizontal motion **5** : to
adjust (a sail) to a desired position **6** : to
change one's views for safety or expedi-
ency — **trim·ly** *adv* — **trim·mer** *n* —
**trim·ness** *n*

**²trim** *adj* **trim·mer; trim·mest** : showing
neatness, good order, or compactness ⟨a

~ figure⟩ ♦ *Synonyms* TIDY, TRIG,
SMART, SPRUCE, SHIPSHAPE

**³trim** *n* **1** : good condition : FITNESS **2**
: material used for ornament or trim-
ming; *esp* : the woodwork in the finish of
a house esp. around doors and windows
**3** : the position of a ship or boat esp. with
reference to the horizontal; *also* : the relation between the plane of a sail and the
direction of a ship **4** : the position of an
airplane at which it will continue in level
flight with no adjustments to the controls
**5** : something that is trimmed off

**tri·ma·ran** \ˈtrī-mə-ˌran, ˌtrī-mə-ˈran\ *n* : a
sailboat with three hulls

**tri·mes·ter** \trī-ˈmes-tər, ˈtrī-ˌmes-tər\ *n* **1**
: a period of three or about three months
(as in pregnancy) **2** : one of three terms
into which an academic year is sometimes divided

**trim·e·ter** \ˈtri-mə-tər\ *n* : a line of verse
consisting of three metrical feet

**trim·ming** \ˈtri-miŋ\ *n* **1** : DEFEAT **2** : the
action of one that trims **3** : something
that trims, ornaments, or completes

**tri·month·ly** \trī-ˈmənth-lē\ *adj* : occurring every three months

**trine** \ˈtrīn\ *adj* : THREEFOLD, TRIPLE

**Trin·i·da·di·an** \ˌtri-nə-ˈdā-dē-ən, -ˈda-\ *n*
: a native or inhabitant of the island of
Trinidad — **Trinidadian** *adj*

**Trin·i·tar·i·an** \ˌtri-nə-ˈter-ē-ən\ *n* : a believer in the doctrine of the Trinity —
**Trin·i·tar·i·an·ism** \-ē-ə-ˌni-zəm\ *n*

**Trin·i·ty** \ˈtri-nə-tē\ *n* **1** : the unity of Father, Son, and Holy Spirit as three per-
sons in one Godhead **2** *not cap* : TRIAD

**trin·ket** \ˈtriŋ-kət\ *n* **1** : a small ornament
(as a jewel or ring) **2** : TRIFLE I

**trio** \ˈtrē-ō\ *n, pl* **tri·os 1** : a musical composition for three voices or three instruments **2** : the performers of a trio **3** : a
group or set of three

**¹trip** \ˈtrip\ *vb* **tripped; trip·ping 1** : to
move with light quick steps **2** : to catch
the foot against something so as to stumble or cause to stumble **3** : to make a
mistake : SLIP; *also* : to detect in a mis-
step : EXPOSE **4** : to release (as a spring
or switch) by moving a catch; *also* : ACTI-
VATE ⟨~ an alarm⟩ **5** : to get high on a
usu. hallucinatory drug

**²trip** *n* **1** : JOURNEY, VOYAGE **2** : a quick
light step **3** : a false step : STUMBLE; *also*
: ERROR **4** : the action of tripping mechanically; *also* : a device for tripping **5**
: an intense experience; *esp* : one trig-
gered by a hallucinatory drug **6** : absorption in an attitude or state of mind ⟨an
ego ~⟩

**tri·par·tite** \trī-ˈpär-ˌtīt\ *adj* **1** : divided
into three parts **2** : having three corresponding parts or copies **3** : made between three parties ⟨a ~ treaty⟩

**tripe** \ˈtrīp\ *n* **1** : stomach tissue esp. of a
ruminant (as an ox) used as food **2**
: something poor, worthless, or offensive
: TRASH

**¹tri·ple** \ˈtri-pəl\ *vb* **tri·pled; tri·pling 1**
: to make or become three times as great
or as many **2** : to hit a triple

**triple** *n* **1** : a triple quantity **2** : a group

of three **3** : a hit in baseball that lets the batter reach third base

³**triple** *adj* **1** : being three times as great or as many **2** : having three units or members **3** : repeated three times

**triple bond** *n* : a chemical bond in which three pairs of electrons are shared by two atoms in a molecule

**triple point** *n* : the condition of temperature and pressure under which the gaseous, liquid, and solid forms of a substance can exist in equilibrium

**trip·let** \'tri-plət\ *n* **1** : a unit of three lines of verse **2** : a group of three of a kind **3** : one of three offspring born at one birth

**tri·plex** \'tri-ˌpleks, 'trī-\ *adj* : THREE-FOLD, TRIPLE

¹**trip·li·cate** \'tri-pli-kət\ *adj* : made in three identical copies

²**trip·li·cate** \-plə-ˌkāt\ *vb* -cat·ed; -cat·ing **1** : TRIPLE **2** : to provide three copies of ⟨∼ a document⟩

³**trip·li·cate** \-pli-kət\ *n* : three copies all alike — used with *in* ⟨typed in ∼⟩

**tri·ply** \'tri-plē, 'tri-pə-lē\ *adv* : in a triple degree, amount, or manner

**tri·pod** \'trī-ˌpäd\ *n* : something (as a caldron, stool, or camera stand) that rests on three legs — **tripod** *or* **tri·po·dal** \'tri-pə-dᵊl, 'trī-ˌpä-\ *adj*

**trip·tych** \'trip-tik\ *n* : a picture or carving in three panels side by side

**tri·reme** \'trī-ˌrēm\ *n* : an ancient galley having three banks of oars

**tri·sect** \'trī-ˌsekt, trī-'sekt\ *vb* : to divide into three usu. equal parts — **tri·sec·tion** \'trī-ˌsek-shən\ *n*

**trite** \'trīt\ *adj* **trit·er; trit·est** [L *tritus*, fr. pp. of *terere* to rub, wear away] : used so commonly that the novelty is worn off : STALE ♦ *Synonyms* HACKNEYED, STEREOTYPED, COMMONPLACE, CLICHÉD

**tri·ti·um** \'tri-tē-əm, 'tri-shē-\ *n* : a radioactive form of hydrogen with one proton and two neutrons in its nucleus and three times the mass of ordinary hydrogen

**tri·ton** \'trī-tᵊn\ *n* : any of various large marine gastropod mollusks with a heavy elongated conical shell; *also* : the shell of a triton

**trit·u·rate** \'tri-chə-ˌrāt\ *vb* -rat·ed; -rat·ing : to rub or grind to a fine powder

¹**tri·umph** \'trī-əmf\ *n* **1** : the joy or exultation of victory or success **2** : VICTORY, CONQUEST — **tri·um·phal** \trī-'əm-fəl\ *adj*

²**triumph** *vb* **1** : to obtain victory : PREVAIL **2** : to celebrate victory or success exultantly — **tri·um·phant** \trī-'əm-fənt\ *adj* — **tri·um·phant·ly** *adv*

**tri·um·vir** \trī-'əm-vər\ *n, pl* -**virs** *also* -**vi·ri** \-və-ˌrī\ : a member of a triumvirate

**tri·um·vi·rate** \-və-rət\ *n* : a ruling body of three persons

**tri·une** \'trī-ˌün, -ˌyün\ *adj* : being three in one ⟨the ∼ God⟩

**triv·et** \'tri-vət\ *n* **1** : a 3-legged stand : TRIPOD **2** : a usu. metal stand with short feet for use under a hot dish

**triv·ia** \'tri-vē-ə\ *n sing or pl* : unimportant

matters : obscure facts or details ⟨movie ∼⟩

**triv·i·al** \'tri-vē-əl\ *adj* [L *trivialis* found everywhere, commonplace, fr. *trivium* crossroads, fr. *tri-* three + *via* way] : of little importance — **triv·i·al·i·ty** \ˌtri-vē-'a-lə-tē\ *n*

**triv·i·um** \'tri-vē-əm\ *n, pl* **triv·ia** \-vē-ə\ : the three liberal arts of grammar, rhetoric, and logic in a medieval university

**tri·week·ly** \trī-'wē-klē\ *adj* **1** : occurring or appearing three times a week **2** : occurring or appearing every three weeks — **triweekly** *adv*

**tro·che** \'trō-kē\ *n* : LOZENGE 2

**tro·chee** \'trō-(ˌ)kē\ *n* : a metrical foot of one accented syllable followed by one unaccented syllable — **tro·cha·ic** \trō-'kā-ik\ *adj*

**trod** *past and past part of* TREAD

**trodden** *past part of* TREAD

**troi·ka** \'troi-kə\ *n* [Russ *troĭka*, fr. *troe* three] : a group of three; *esp* : an administrative or ruling body of three

¹**troll** \'trōl\ *vb* **1** : to sing the parts of (a song) in succession **2** : to fish by trailing a lure or baited hook from a moving boat **3** : to sing or play jovially

²**troll** *n* : a lure used in trolling; *also* : the line with its lure

³**troll** *n* : a dwarf or giant in Scandinavian folklore inhabiting caves or hills

**trol·ley** *also* **trol·ly** \'trä-lē\ *n, pl* **trolleys** *also* **trollies** **1** : a device (as a grooved wheel on the end of a pole) to carry current from a wire to an electrically driven vehicle **2** : a streetcar powered electrically by overhead wires **3** : a wheeled carriage running on an overhead rail or track

**trol·ley·bus** \'trä-lē-ˌbəs\ *n* : a bus powered electrically by overhead wires

**trolley car** *n* : TROLLEY 2

**trol·lop** \'trä-ləp\ *n* : a disreputable woman; *esp* : one who engages in sex promiscuously

**trom·bone** \träm-'bōn, 'träm-ˌbōn\ *n* [It, fr. *tromba* trumpet] : a brass wind instrument that consists of a long metal tube with two turns and a flaring end and that usu. has a movable slide to vary the pitch — **trom·bon·ist** \-'bō-nist, -ˌbō-\ *n*

**tromp** \'trämp, 'trȯmp\ *vb* **1** : TRAMP, MARCH **2** : to stamp with the foot **3** : to defeat decisively

**trompe l'oeil** \(ˌ)trȯmp-'lə-ē, trȯ[n]p-'lœi\ *n* [F *trompe-l'oeil*, lit., deceives the eye] : a style of painting in which objects are depicted with photographic detail

¹**troop** \'trüp\ *n* **1** : a cavalry unit corresponding to an infantry company **2** *pl* : armed forces : SOLDIERS **3** : a collection of people, animals, or things **4** : a unit of Girl Scouts or Boy Scouts under an adult leader

²**troop** *vb* : to move or gather in crowds

**troop·er** \'trü-pər\ *n* **1** : an enlisted cavalryman; *also* : a cavalry horse **2** : a mounted or a state police officer

**troop·ship** \'trüp-ˌship\ *n* : a ship or aircraft for carrying troops

**trope** \'trōp\ *n* : a word or expression used in a figurative sense

**tro·phic** \'trō-fik\ *adj* : of or relating to nutrition

**tro·phy** \'trō-fē\ *n, pl* **trophies** : something gained or given in conquest or victory esp. when preserved or mounted as a memorial

**trop·ic** \'trä-pik\ *n* [ME *tropik*, fr. L *tropicus* of the solstice, fr. Gk *tropikos*, fr. *tropē* turn] **1** : either of the two parallels of latitude approximately 23½ degrees north (**Tropic of Can·cer**) or south (**Tropic of Cap·ri·corn**) of the equator where the sun is directly overhead when it reaches its most northerly or southerly point in the sky **2** *pl, often cap* : the region lying between the tropics — **trop·i·cal** \-pi-kəl\ *or* **tropic** *adj*

**tro·pism** \'trō-,pi-zəm\ *n* : an automatic movement by an organism in response to a source of stimulation; *also* : a reflex reaction involving this

**tro·po·sphere** \'trō-pə-,sfir, 'trä-\ *n* : the part of the atmosphere between the earth's surface and the stratosphere in which most weather changes occur — **tro·po·spher·ic** \,trō-pə-'sfir-ik, ,trä-, -'sfer-\ *adj*

**¹trot** \'trät\ *n* **1** : a moderately fast gait of a 4-footed animal (as a horse) in which the legs move in diagonal pairs **2** : a human jogging gait between a walk and a run

**²trot** *vb* **trot·ted; trot·ting** **1** : to ride, drive, or go at a trot **2** : to proceed briskly : HURRY — **trot·ter** *n*

**troth** \'träth, 'trōth, 'trȯth\ *n* **1** : pledged faithfulness **2** : one's pledged word; *also* : BETROTHAL

**trou·ba·dour** \'trü-bə-,dȯr\ *n* [F, fr. Old Occitan *trobador*, fr. *trobar* to compose] : any of a class of poet-musicians flourishing esp. in southern France and northern Italy during the 11th, 12th, and 13th centuries

**¹trou·ble** \'trə-bəl\ *vb* **trou·bled; trou·bling** **1** : to agitate mentally or spiritually : DISTURB, WORRY **2** : to produce physical disorder in : AFFLICT **3** : to put to inconvenience **4** : RUFFLE ⟨~ the waters⟩ **5** : to make an effort ♦ **Synonyms** DISTRESS, AIL, UPSET — **trou·ble·some** *adj* — **trou·ble·some·ly** *adv* — **trou·blous** \-bə-ləs\ *adj*

**²trouble** *n* **1** : the quality or state of being troubled esp. mentally **2** : an instance of distress or annoyance **3** : DISEASE, AILMENT ⟨heart ~⟩ **4** : EXERTION, PAINS ⟨took the ~ to phone⟩ **5** : a cause of disturbance or distress

**trou·ble·mak·er** \-,mā-kər\ *n* : a person who causes trouble

**trou·ble·shoot·er** \-,shü-tər\ *n* **1** : a worker employed to locate trouble and make repairs in equipment **2** : an expert in resolving disputes or problems — **trou·ble·shoot** *vb*

**trough** \'trȯf, 'trȯth\ *n, pl* **troughs** \'trȯfs, 'trȯvz; 'trȯths, 'trȯthz\ **1** : a long shallow open boxlike container esp. for water or feed for livestock **2** : a gutter along the eaves of a house **3** : a long channel or depression (as between waves or hills) **4** : an elongated area of low barometric pressure

**trounce** \'traúns\ *vb* **trounced; trouncing** **1** : to thrash or punish severely **2** : to defeat decisively

**troupe** \'trüp\ *n* : COMPANY; *esp* : a group of performers on the stage — **troup·er** *n*

**trou·sers** \'traú-zərz\ *n pl* [alter. of earlier *trouse*, fr. ScGael *triubhas*] : PANTS — **trouser** *adj*

**trous·seau** \'trü-sō, trü-'sō\ *n, pl* **trousseaux** \-sōz, -'sōz\ *or* **trous·seaus** [F] : the personal outfit of a bride

**trout** \'traút\ *n, pl* **trout** *also* **trouts** [ME, fr. OE *trüht*, fr. LL *tructa*, a fish with sharp teeth, fr. Gk *trōktēs*, lit., gnawer] : any of various mostly freshwater food and game fishes usu. smaller than the related salmons

**trow** \'trō\ *vb, archaic* : THINK, SUPPOSE

**trow·el** \'traú(-ə)l\ *n* **1** : a hand tool used for spreading, shaping, or smoothing loose or plastic material (as mortar or plaster) **2** : a scoop-shaped tool used in gardening — **trowel** *vb*

**troy** \'trȯi\ *adj* : expressed in troy weight ⟨~ ounce⟩

**troy weight** *n* : a system of weights based on a pound of 12 ounces and an ounce of 480 grains (31 grams) — see WEIGHT table

**tru·ant** \'trü-ənt\ *n* [ME, vagabond, idler, fr. AF, of Celt origin] : a student who stays out of school without permission — **tru·an·cy** \-ən-sē\ *n* — **truant** *adj*

**truce** \'trüs\ *n* **1** : ARMISTICE **2** : a respite esp. from something unpleasant

**¹truck** \'trək\ *vb* **1** : EXCHANGE, BARTER **2** : to have dealings : TRAFFIC

**²truck** *n* **1** : BARTER **2** : DEALINGS **3** : small goods or merchandise; *esp* : vegetables grown for market

**³truck** *n* **1** : a wheeled vehicle (as a strong heavy automobile) designed for carrying heavy articles or hauling a trailer **2** : a swiveling frame with springs and one or more pairs of wheels used to carry and guide one end of a locomotive or railroad car

**⁴truck** *vb* **1** : to transport on a truck ⟨~s vegetables⟩ **2** : to be employed in driving a truck — **truck·er** *n*

**truck farm** *n* : a farm growing vegetables for market — **truck farmer** *n*

**truck·le** \'trə-kəl\ *vb* **truck·led; truck·ling** : to yield slavishly to the will of another : SUBMIT ♦ **Synonyms** FAWN, TOADY, CRINGE, COWER

**truc·u·lent** \'trə-kyə-lənt\ *adj* **1** : feeling or showing ferocity : SAVAGE **2** : aggressively self-assertive : BELLIGERENT — **truc·u·lence** \-ləns\ *n* — **truc·u·len·cy** \-lən-sē\ *n* — **truc·u·lent·ly** *adv*

**trudge** \'trəj\ *vb* **trudged; trudg·ing** : to walk or march steadily and usu. laboriously ⟨*trudged* through the snow⟩

**¹true** \'trü\ *adj* **tru·er; tru·est** **1** : STEADFAST, LOYAL **2** : agreeing with facts or reality ⟨a ~ description⟩ **3** : CONSISTENT ⟨~ to expectations⟩ **4** : properly so called ⟨~ love⟩ **5** : RIGHTFUL ⟨~ and lawful king⟩ **6** : conformable to a standard or pattern; *also* : placed or formed accurately ◆ **Synonyms** CONSTANT, STAUNCH, RESOLUTE, STEADFAST

²**true** *adv* **1** : TRUTHFULLY **2** : ACCURATELY ⟨the bullet flew straight and ~⟩; *also* : without variation from type ⟨breed ~⟩

³**true** *n* **1** : TRUTH, REALITY — usu. used with *the* **2** : the state of being accurate (as in alignment) ⟨out of ~⟩

⁴**true** *vb* **trued; true·ing** *also* **tru·ing** : to bring or restore to a desired precision

**true–blue** *adj* : marked by unswerving loyalty ⟨a ~ patriot⟩

**true bug** *n* : BUG 2

**true·heart·ed** \'trü-¸här-təd\ *adj* : FAITHFUL, LOYAL ⟨a ~ soldier⟩

**truf·fle** \'trə-fəl, 'trü-\ *n* **1** : the dark or light edible spore-bearing organ of any of several European fungi that grow underground; *also* : one of these fungi **2** : a candy made of chocolate, butter, and sugar shaped into balls and coated with cocoa

**tru·ism** \'trü-¸i-zəm\ *n* : an undoubted or self-evident truth ◆ **Synonyms** COMMONPLACE, PLATITUDE, CLICH

**tru·ly** \'trü-lē\ *adv* **1** : in all sincerity ⟨is ~ sorry⟩ **2** : in agreement with fact ⟨report it ~⟩ **3** : ACCURATELY **4** : in a proper or suitable manner

¹**trump** \'trəmp\ *n* : TRUMPET

²**trump** *n* : a card of a designated suit any of whose cards will win over a card that is not of this suit; *also* : the suit itself — often used in pl.

³**trump** *vb* : to take with a trump

**trumped–up** \'trəmpt-'əp\ *adj* : fraudulently concocted : SPURIOUS ⟨~ charges⟩

**trum·pery** \'trəm-pə-rē\ *n* **1** : NONSENSE **2** : trivial articles : JUNK

¹**trum·pet** \'trəm-pət\ *n* **1** : a wind instrument consisting of a long curved metal tube flaring at one end and with a cupshaped mouthpiece at the other **2** : something that resembles a trumpet or its tonal quality **3** : a funnel-shaped instrument for collecting, directing, or intensifying sound

²**trumpet** *vb* **1** : to blow a trumpet **2** : to proclaim on or as if on a trumpet ⟨~ the news⟩ — **trum·pet·er** *n*

¹**trun·cate** \'trən-¸kāt, 'trən-\ *adj* : having the end square or blunt

²**truncate** *vb* **trun·cat·ed; trun·cat·ing** : to shorten by or as if by cutting : LOP — **trun·ca·tion** \¸trən-'kā-shən\ *n*

**trun·cheon** \'trən-chən\ *n* : a police officer's billy club

**trun·dle** \'trən-d⁰l\ *vb* **trun·dled; trundling** : to roll along : WHEEL

**trundle bed** *n* : a low bed that can be stored under a higher bed

**trunk** \'trəŋk\ *n* **1** : the main stem of a tree **2** : the body of a person or animal apart from the head and limbs **3** : the main or central part of something **4** : a box or chest used to hold valuables, clothes or personal effects (as of a traveler); *also* : the enclosed luggage space in the rear of

an automobile **5** : the long muscular nose of an elephant **6** *pl* : men's shorts worn chiefly for sports ⟨swimming ~s⟩ **7** : a usu. major channel or passage

**trunk line** *n* : a transportation system handling long-distance through traffic

¹**truss** \'trəs\ *vb* **1** : to secure tightly : BIND **2** : to arrange for cooking by binding close the wings or legs of (a fowl) **3** : to support, strengthen, or stiffen by or as if by a truss

²**truss** *n* **1** : a collection of structural parts (as beams) forming a rigid framework (as in bridge or building construction) **2** : a device worn to reduce a hernia by pressure

¹**trust** \'trəst\ *n* **1** : assured reliance on the character, strength, or truth of someone or something **2** : a basis of reliance, faith, or hope **3** : confident hope **4** : financial credit **5** : a property interest held by one person for the benefit of another **6** : a combination of firms formed by a legal agreement; *esp* : one that reduces competition **7** : something entrusted to one to be cared for in the interest of another **8** : CARE, CUSTODY ◆ **Synonyms** CONFIDENCE, DEPENDENCE, FAITH, RELIANCE

²**trust** *vb* **1** : to place confidence : DEPEND **2** : to be confident : HOPE **3** : ENTRUST **4** : to permit to stay or go or to do something without fear or misgiving **5** : to rely on or on the truth of : BELIEVE **6** : to extend credit to

**trust·ee** \¸trəs-'tē\ *n* **1** : a person to whom property is legally committed in trust **2** : a country charged with the supervision of a trust territory

**trust·ee·ship** \¸trəs-'tē-¸ship\ *n* **1** : the office or function of a trustee **2** : supervisory control by one or more nations over a trust territory

**trust·ful** \'trəst-fəl\ *adj* : full of trust : CONFIDING — **trust·ful·ly** *adv* — **trust·ful·ness** *n*

**trust territory** *n* : a non-self-governing territory placed under a supervisory authority by the Trusteeship Council of the United Nations

**trust·wor·thy** \-¸wər-thē\ *adj* : worthy of confidence : DEPENDABLE ⟨a ~ assistant⟩ ◆ **Synonyms** TRUSTY, TRIED, RELIABLE — **trust·wor·thi·ness** *n*

¹**trusty** \'trəs-tē\ *adj* **trust·i·er; -est** : TRUSTWORTHY, DEPENDABLE ⟨a ~ friend⟩

²**trusty** \'trəs-tē, ¸trəs-'tē\ *n, pl* **trust·ies** : a trusted person; *esp* : a convict considered trustworthy and allowed special privileges

**truth** \'trüth\ *n, pl* **truths** \'trüthz, 'trüths\ **1** : TRUTHFULNESS, HONESTY **2** : the real state of things : FACT **3** : the body of real events or facts : ACTUALITY **4** : a true or accepted statement or proposition ⟨the ~s of science⟩ **5** : agreement with fact or reality : CORRECTNESS ◆ **Synonyms** VERACITY, VERITY

**truth·ful** \'trüth-fəl\ *adj* : telling or disposed to tell the truth — **truth·ful·ly** *adv* — **truth·ful·ness** *n*

**truth serum** *n* : a drug held to induce a subject under questioning to talk freely

¹**try** \'trī\ *vb* **tried; try·ing** [ME *trien,* fr. AF *trier* to select, sort, examine, prob. fr. LL *tritare* to grind] **1** : to examine or investigate judicially **2** : to conduct the trial of **3** : to put to test or trial **4** : to subject to strain, affliction, or annoyance **5** : to extract or clarify (as lard) by melting **6** : to make an effort to do something : ATTEMPT, ENDEAVOR ♦ **Synonyms** ESSAY, ASSAY, STRIVE, STRUGGLE

²**try** *n, pl* **tries** : an experimental trial

**try·ing** *adj* : severely straining the powers of endurance

**try on** *vb* : to put on (a garment) to test the fit and looks

**try out** *vb* : to participate in competition esp. for a position on an athletic team or a part in a play — **try·out** \'trī-ˌaùt\ *n*

**tryp·to·phan** \'trip-tə-ˌfan\ *n* : a crystalline essential amino acid that is widely distributed in proteins

**tryst** \'trist\ *n* **1** : an agreement (as between lovers) to meet **2** : an appointed meeting or meeting place — **tryst** *vb* — **tryst·er** *n*

**TSA** *abbr* Transportation Security Administration

**tsar, tsarist** *var of* CZAR, CZARIST

**tsarina** *var of* CZARINA

**tset·se fly** \'tset-sē-, 'tsēt-, 'tet-, 'tēt-, 'set-, 'sēt-\ *n* : any of several sub-Saharan African dipteran flies including the vector of sleeping sickness

**TSgt** *abbr* technical sergeant

**T–shirt** \'tē-ˌshərt\ *n* : a collarless short-sleeved or sleeveless cotton undershirt; *also* : an outer shirt of similar design — **T–shirt·ed** \-ˌshər-təd\ *adj*

**tsk** \*a click; often read as* 'tisk\ *interj* — used to express disapproval

**tsp** *abbr* teaspoon; teaspoonful

**T square** *n* : a ruler with a crosspiece at one end for making parallel lines

**tsu·na·mi** \sù-'nä-mē, tsù-\ *n* [Jp] : a tidal wave caused esp. by an underwater earthquake or volcanic eruption

**TT** *abbr* Trust Territories

**TTY** *abbr* teletypewriter

**Tu** *abbr* Tuesday

**tub** \'təb\ *n* **1** : a wide low bucketlike vessel **2** : BATHTUB; *also* : BATH **3** : the amount that a tub will hold

**tu·ba** \'tü-bə, 'tyü-\ *n* : a large low-pitched brass wind instrument

**tub·al** \'tü-bəl, 'tyü-\ *adj* : of, relating to, or involving a tube and esp. a fallopian tube ⟨~ infection⟩

**tube** \'tüb, 'tyüb\ *n* **1** : any of various usu. cylindrical structures or devices; *esp* : one to convey fluids **2** : a slender hollow anatomical part (as a fallopian tube) functioning as a channel in a plant or animal body : DUCT **3** : a soft round container from which a paste is squeezed **4** : a tunnel for vehicular or rail travel **5** *Brit* : SUBWAY **6** : INNER TUBE **7** : ELECTRON TUBE **8** : TELEVISION — **tubed** \'tübd, 'tyübd\ *adj* — **tube·less** *adj* — **tube·like** \'tüb-ˌlīk, 'tyüb-\ *adj*

**tu·ber** \'tü-bər, 'tyü-\ *n* : a short fleshy usu. underground stem (as of a potato plant) bearing minute scalelike leaves each with a bud at its base

**tu·ber·cle** \'tü-bər-kəl, 'tyü-\ *n* **1** : a small knobby prominence or outgrowth esp. on an animal or plant **2** : a small abnormal lump in an organ or on the skin; *esp* : one caused by tuberculosis

**tubercle bacillus** *n* : a bacterium that is the cause of tuberculosis

**tu·ber·cu·lar** \tù-'bər-kyə-lər, tyù-\ *adj* **1** : TUBERCULOUS **2** : of, resembling, or being a tubercle

**tu·ber·cu·lin** \tù-'bər-kyə-lən, tyù-\ *n* : a sterile liquid extracted from the tubercle bacillus and used in the diagnosis of tuberculosis esp. in children and cattle

**tu·ber·cu·lo·sis** \tù-ˌbər-kyə-'lō-səs, tyù-\ *n, pl* **-lo·ses** \-ˌsēz\ : a communicable bacterial disease that affects esp. the lungs and is typically marked by fever, cough, difficulty in breathing, and formation of tubercles — **tu·ber·cu·lous** \-'bər-kyə-ləs\ *adj*

**tube·rose** \'tüb-ˌrōz, 'tyüb-\ *n* : a bulbous herb related to the agaves and often grown for its spike of fragrant waxy-white flowers

**tu·ber·ous** \'tü-bə-rəs, 'tyü-\ *adj* : of, resembling, or being a tuber

**tub·ing** \'tü-biŋ, 'tyü-\ *n* **1** : material in the form of a tube; *also* : a length of tube **2** : a series or system of tubes

**tu·bu·lar** \'tü-byə-lər, 'tyü-\ *adj* : having the form of or consisting of a tube; *also* : made with tubes

**tu·bule** \'tü-byül, 'tyü-\ *n* : a small tube

¹**tuck** \'tək\ *vb* **1** : to pull up into a fold ⟨~ed up her skirt⟩ **2** : to make tucks in **3** : to put into a snug often concealing place ⟨~ a book under the arm⟩ **4** : to secure in place by pushing the edges under ⟨~ in a blanket⟩ **5** : to cover by tucking in bedclothes

²**tuck** *n* **1** : a fold stitched into cloth to shorten, decorate, or control fullness **2** : a cosmetic surgical operation for the removal of excess skin or fat ⟨a tummy ~⟩

**tuck·er** \'tə-kər\ *vb* **tuck·ered; tuck·er·ing** : EXHAUST, FATIGUE ⟨was ~ed out after a long day's work⟩

**Tues** *or* **Tue** *abbr* Tuesday

**Tues·day** \'tüz-dē, 'tyüz-, -dā\ *n* : the 3d day of the week

**tu·fa** \'tü-fə, 'tyü-\ *n* : a porous rock (as travertine) formed as a deposit from springs or streams

**tuff** \'təf\ *n* : a rock composed of volcanic detritus

¹**tuft** \'təft\ *n* **1** : a small cluster of long flexible outgrowths (as hairs); *also* : a bunch of soft fluffy threads cut off short and used as ornament **2** : CLUMP, CLUSTER — **tuft·ed** *adj*

²**tuft** *vb* **1** : to provide or adorn with a tuft **2** : to make (as a mattress) firm by stitching at intervals and sewing on tufts — **tuft·er** *n*

¹**tug** \'təg\ *vb* **tugged; tug·ging** **1** : to pull hard **2** : to struggle in opposition : CON-

TEND **3** : to move by pulling hard : HAUL **4** : to tow with a tugboat

²**tug** n **1** : a harness trace **2** : an act of tugging : PULL **3** : a straining effort **4** : a struggle between opposing people or forces **5** : TUGBOAT

**tug·boat** \-ˌbōt\ n : a strongly built boat used for towing or pushing

**tug–of–war** \ˌtəg-əv-ˈwȯr\ n, pl **tugs–of–war 1** : a struggle for supremacy **2** : an athletic contest in which two teams pull against each other at opposite ends of a rope

**tu·grik** or **tu·ghrik** \ˈtü-grik\ n — see MONEY table

**tu·ition** \tü-ˈi-shən, tyü-\ n : money paid for instruction ⟨college ~⟩

**tu·la·re·mia** \ˌtü-lə-ˈrē-mē-ə, ˌtyü-\ n : an infectious bacterial disease esp. of wild rabbits, rodents, humans, and some domestic animals that in humans is marked by symptoms (as fever) similar to those of influenza

**tu·lip** \ˈtü-ləp, ˈtyü-\ n [NL *tulipa*, fr. Turk *tülbent* turban] : any of a genus of Eurasian bulbous herbs related to the lilies and grown for their large showy erect cup-shaped flowers; *also* : a flower or bulb of a tulip

**tulip tree** n : a tall No. American timber tree that is related to the magnolias and has greenish tulip-shaped flowers and soft white wood

**tulle** \ˈtül\ n : a sheer often stiffened silk, rayon, or nylon net ⟨a veil of ~⟩

¹**tum·ble** \ˈtəm-bəl\ vb **tum·bled; tum·bling** [ME, fr. *tumben* to dance, fr. OE *tumbian*] **1** : to fall or cause to fall suddenly and helplessly **2** : to fall into ruin **3** : to perform gymnastic feats of rolling and turning **4** : to roll over and over : TOSS **5** : to issue forth hurriedly and confusedly **6** : to come to understand **7** : to throw together in a confused mass

²**tumble** n **1** : a disorderly state **2** : an act or instance of tumbling

**tum·ble–down** \ˈtəm-bəl-ˈdaun\ adj : DILAPIDATED, RAMSHACKLE ⟨a ~ shack⟩

**tum·bler** \ˈtəm-blər\ n **1** : one that tumbles; *esp* : ACROBAT **2** : a drinking glass without foot or stem **3** : a movable obstruction in a lock that must be adjusted to a particular position (as by a key) before the bolt can be thrown

**tum·ble·weed** \ˈtəm-bəl-ˌwēd\ n : a plant that breaks away from its roots in autumn and is driven about by the wind

**tum·brel** or **tum·bril** \ˈtəm-brəl\ n **1** : CART **2** : a vehicle carrying condemned persons (as during the French Revolution) to a place of execution

**tu·mid** \ˈtü-məd, ˈtyü-\ adj **1** : SWOLLEN, DISTENDED **2** : BOMBASTIC, TURGID

**tum·my** \ˈtə-mē\ n, pl **tummies** : BELLY, ABDOMEN, STOMACH

**tu·mor** \ˈtü-mər, ˈtyü-\ n : an abnormal and functionless new growth of tissue that arises from uncontrolled cellular proliferation — **tu·mor·ous** adj

**tu·mour** chiefly Brit var of TUMOR

**tu·mult** \ˈtü-ˌməlt, ˈtyü-\ n **1** : UPROAR **2** : violent agitation of mind or feelings

**tu·mul·tu·ous** \tu-ˈməl-chə-wəs, tyu-, -chəs\ adj **1** : marked by tumult ⟨~ applause⟩ **2** : tending to incite a tumult **3** : marked by violent upheaval ⟨~ war years⟩

**tun** \ˈtən\ n : a large cask

**tu·na** \ˈtü-nə, ˈtyü-\ n, pl **tuna** or **tunas** : any of several mostly large marine fishes related to the mackerels and caught for food and sport; *also* : the flesh of a tuna

**tun·able** \ˈtü-nə-bəl, ˈtyü-\ adj : capable of being tuned — **tun·abil·i·ty** \ˌtü-nə-ˈbi-lə-tē, ˌtyü-\ n

**tun·dra** \ˈtən-drə\ n [Russ] : a treeless plain of arctic and subarctic regions

¹**tune** \ˈtün, ˈtyün\ n **1** : a succession of pleasing musical tones : MELODY **2** : correct musical pitch **3** : harmonious relationship : AGREEMENT ⟨in ~ with the times⟩ **4** : general attitude ⟨changed his ~⟩ **5** : AMOUNT, EXTENT ⟨in debt to the ~ of millions⟩

²**tune** vb **tuned; tun·ing 1** : to adjust in musical pitch **2** : to bring or come into harmony : ATTUNE **3** : to put in good working order **4** : to adjust a radio or television receiver so as to receive a broadcast **5** : to adjust the frequency of the output of (a device) to a chosen frequency — **tun·er** n

**tune·ful** \-fəl\ adj : MELODIOUS, MUSICAL ⟨a ~ ballad⟩ — **tune·ful·ly** adv — **tune·ful·ness** n

**tune·less** \-ləs\ adj **1** : UNMELODIOUS **2** : not producing music — **tune·less·ly** adv

**tune–up** \ˈtün-ˌəp, ˈtyün-\ n : an adjustment to ensure efficient functioning ⟨an engine ~⟩

**tung·sten** \ˈtəŋ-stən\ n [Sw, fr. *tung* heavy + *sten* stone] : a gray-white hard heavy ductile metallic chemical element used esp. in carbide materials, electrical components, and alloys

**tu·nic** \ˈtü-nik, ˈtyü-\ n **1** : a usu. knee-length belted garment worn by ancient Greeks and Romans **2** : a hip-length or longer blouse or jacket

**tuning fork** n : a 2-pronged metal implement that gives a fixed tone when struck and is useful for tuning musical instruments

¹**tun·nel** \ˈtə-nᵊl\ n : an enclosed passage (as a tube or conduit); *esp* : one underground (as in a mine)

²**tunnel** vb **-neled** or **-nelled; -nel·ing** or **-nel·ling** : to make a tunnel through or under — **tun·nel·er** \ˈtən-lər, ˈtə-nᵊl-ər\ n

**tun·ny** \ˈtə-nē\ n, pl **tunnies** also **tunny** : TUNA

**tuque** \ˈtük, ˈtyük\ n [CanF] : a warm knitted cone-shaped cap

**tur·ban** \ˈtər-bən\ n **1** : a headdress worn esp. by Muslims and made of a cap around which is wound a long cloth **2** : a headdress resembling a turban; *esp* : a woman's close-fitting hat without a brim

**tur·bid** \ˈtər-bəd\ adj [L *turbidus* confused, turbid, fr. *turba* confusion, crowd] **1** : cloudy or discolored by suspended particles ⟨a ~ stream⟩ **2** : CONFUSED,

MUDDLED — **tur·bid·i·ty** \ˌtər-ˈbi-də-tē\ *n*

**tur·bine** \ˈtər-bən, -ˌbīn\ *n* [F, fr. L *turbin-, turbo* top, whirlwind, whirl] : an engine whose central driveshaft is fitted with curved vanes spun by the pressure of water, steam, or gas

**tur·bo·fan** \ˈtər-bō-ˌfan\ *n* : a jet engine having a fan driven by a turbine for supplying air for combustion

**tur·bo·jet** \-ˌjet\ *n* : an airplane powered by a jet engine (**turbojet engine**) having a turbine-driven air compressor supplying compressed air to the combustion chamber

**tur·bo·prop** \-ˌpräp\ *n* : an airplane powered by a jet engine (**turboprop engine**) having a turbine-driven propeller

**tur·bot** \ˈtər-bət\ *n, pl* **turbot** *also* **tur·bots** : a European flatfish that is a popular food fish; *also* : any of several similar flatfishes

**tur·bu·lence** \ˈtər-byə-ləns\ *n* : the quality or state of being turbulent

**tur·bu·lent** \-lənt\ *adj* **1** : causing violence or disturbance **2** : marked by agitation or tumult : TEMPESTUOUS ⟨a ~ marriage⟩ — **tur·bu·lent·ly** *adv*

**tu·reen** \tə-ˈrēn, tyů-\ *n* [F *terrine*, fr. MF, fr. fem. of *terrin* of earth] : a deep bowl from which foods (as soup) are served at the table

**¹turf** \ˈtərf\ *n, pl* **turfs** \ˈtərfs\ *also* **turves** \ˈtərvz\ **1** : the upper layer of soil bound by grass and roots into a close mat; *also* : a piece of this **2** : an artificial substitute for turf (as on a playing field) **3** : a piece of peat dried for fuel **4** : a track or course for horse racing; *also* : horse racing as a sport or business

**²turf** *vb* : to cover with turf

**tur·gid** \ˈtər-jəd\ *adj* **1** : being in a swollen state **2** : excessively embellished in style or language : BOMBASTIC ⟨~ writing⟩ — **tur·gid·i·ty** \ˌtər-ˈji-də-tē\ *n*

**tur·key** \ˈtər-kē\ *n, pl* **turkeys** [*Turkey*, country in western Asia and southeastern Europe; fr. confusion with the guinea fowl, supposed to be imported from Turkish territory] : a large No. American bird related to the domestic chicken and widely raised for food

**turkey buzzard** *n* : TURKEY VULTURE

**turkey vulture** *n* : an American vulture with a red head and whitish bill

**Turk·ish** \ˈtər-kish\ *n* : the language of Turkey — **Turkish** *adj*

**tur·mer·ic** \ˈtər-mə-rik\ *n* : a spice or dyestuff obtained from the large aromatic deep-yellow rhizome of an Indian perennial herb related to the ginger; *also* : this herb

**tur·moil** \ˈtər-ˌmòi(-ə)l\ *n* : an extremely confused or agitated condition

**¹turn** \ˈtərn\ *vb* **1** : to move around an axis or center : ROTATE, REVOLVE ⟨~ a wheel⟩ **2** : to effect a desired end by turning something ⟨~ the oven on⟩ **3** : WRENCH ⟨~ an ankle⟩ **4** : to change or cause to change position by moving through an arc of a circle ⟨~ed her chair to the fire⟩ **5** : to cause to move around a center so as to show another side of ⟨~ a page⟩ **6** : to revolve mentally : PONDER **7** : to become dizzy : REEL **8** : to reverse the sides or surfaces of ⟨~ a pancake⟩ **9** : UPSET, DISORDER ⟨things were ~ed topsy-turvy⟩ **10** : to set in another esp. contrary direction **11** : to change one's course or direction **12** : to go around ⟨~ a corner⟩ **13** : BECOME ⟨my hair ~ed gray⟩ ⟨~ed twenty-one⟩ **14** : to direct toward or away from something; *also* : DEVOTE, APPLY **15** : to have recourse **16** : to become or make hostile **17** : to cause to become of a specified nature or appearance ⟨~s the leaves yellow⟩ **18** : to make or become spoiled : SOUR **19** : to pass from one state to another ⟨water ~s to ice⟩ **20** : CONVERT, TRANSFORM **21** : TRANSLATE, PARAPHRASE **22** : to give a rounded form to; *esp* : to shape by means of a lathe **23** : to gain by passing in trade ⟨~ a quick profit⟩ — **turn·able** \ˈtər-nə-bəl\ *adj* — **turn color 1** : BLUSH **2** : to become pale — **turn loose** : to set free

**²turn** *n* **1** : a turning about a center or axis : REVOLUTION, ROTATION **2** : the action or an act of giving or taking a different direction ⟨make a left ~⟩ **3** : a change of course or tendency ⟨a ~ for the better⟩ **4** : a place at which something turns : BEND, CURVE **5** : a short walk or trip round about ⟨take a ~ around the block⟩ **6** : an act affecting another ⟨did him a good ~⟩ **7** : a place, time, or opportunity accorded in a scheduled order ⟨waited his ~ in line⟩ **8** : a period of duty : SHIFT **9** : a short act esp. in a variety show **10** : a special purpose or requirement ⟨the job serves his ~⟩ **11** : a skillful fashioning ⟨neat ~ of phrase⟩ **12** : a single round (as of rope passed around an object) **13** : natural or special aptitude **14** : a usu. sudden and brief disorder of body or spirits; *esp* : a spell of nervous shock or faintness

**turn·about** \ˈtərn-ə-ˌbaůt\ *n* **1** : a reversal of direction, trend, or policy **2** : RETALIATION

**turn·buck·le** \ˈtərn-ˌbə-kəl\ *n* : a link with a screw thread at one or both ends for tightening a rod or stay

**turn·coat** \-ˌkōt\ *n* : one who switches to an opposing side or party : TRAITOR

**turn down** *vb* : to decline to accept : REJECT — **turn·down** \ˈtərn-ˌdaůn\ *n*

**turn·er** \ˈtər-nər\ *n* **1** : one that turns or is used for turning **2** : one that forms articles with a lathe

**turn·ery** \ˈtər-nə-rē\ *n, pl* **-er·ies** : the work, products, or shop of a turner

**turn in** *vb* **1** : to deliver up **2** : to inform on **3** : to acquit oneself of ⟨*turn in* a good job⟩ **4** : to go to bed

**turn·ing** \ˈtər-niŋ\ *n* **1** : the act or course of one that turns **2** : a place of a change of direction

**tur·nip** \ˈtər-nəp\ *n* **1** : a garden herb related to the cabbage with a thick edible usu. white root **2** : RUTABAGA **3** : the root of a turnip

**turn·key** \'tərn ˌkē\ *n, pl* **turnkeys** : one who has charge of a prison's keys

**turn-off** \'tərn-ˌȯf\ *n* : a place for turning off esp. from an expressway

**turn off** *vb* **1** : to deviate from a straight course or a main road **2** : to stop the functioning or flow of **3** : to cause to lose interest; *also* : to evoke a negative feeling in ⟨violence on TV *turns* her *off*⟩

**turn on** *vb* **1** : to cause to flow, function, or operate **2** : to get high or cause to get high as a result of using a drug (as marijuana) **3** : EXCITE, STIMULATE

**turn-out** \'tərn-ˌau̇t\ *n* **1** : an act of turning out **2** : the number of people who participate or attend an event **3** : a widened place in a highway for vehicles to pass or park **4** : manner of dress **5** : net yield : OUTPUT

**turn out** *vb* **1** : EXPEL, EVICT **2** : PRODUCE **3** : to cause to stop functioning by turning a switch **4** : to come forth and assemble **5** : to get out of bed **6** : to prove to be in the end

¹**turn·over** \'tərn-ˌō-vər\ *n* **1** : UPSET **2** : SHIFT, REVERSAL **3** : a filled pastry made by turning half of the crust over the other half **4** : the volume of business done **5** : movement (as of goods or people) into, through, and out of a place **6** : the number of persons hired within a period to replace those leaving or dropped **7** : an instance of a team's losing possession of the ball esp. through error

²**turnover** *adj* : capable of being turned over

**turn over** *vb* : TRANSFER ⟨*turn* the job *over* to her⟩

**turn·pike** \'tərn-ˌpīk\ *n* [ME *turnepike* revolving frame bearing spikes and serving as a barrier, fr. *turnen* to turn + *pike*] **1** : TOLLGATE; *also* : an expressway on which tolls are charged **2** : a main road

**turn·stile** \-ˌstī(-ə)l\ *n* : a post with arms pivoted on the top set in a passageway so that persons can pass through only on foot one by one

**turn·ta·ble** \-ˌtā-bəl\ *n* : a circular platform that revolves (as for turning a locomotive or a phonograph record)

**turn to** *vb* : to apply oneself to work

**turn up** *vb* **1** : to come to light or bring to light : DISCOVER, APPEAR **2** : to raise or increase by or as if by turning a control **3** : to arrive at an appointed time or place **4** : to happen unexpectedly

**tur·pen·tine** \'tər-pən-ˌtīn\ *n* **1** : a mixture of oil and resin obtained from various cone-bearing trees (as pines) **2** : an oil distilled from turpentine or pine wood and used as a solvent and paint thinner

**tur·pi·tude** \'tər-pə-ˌtüd, -ˌtyüd\ *n* : inherent baseness : DEPRAVITY

**tur·quoise** *also* **tur·quois** \'tər-ˌkȯiz, -ˌkwȯiz\ *n* [ME *turkeys*, fr. AF *turkeise*, fr. fem. of *turkeis* Turkish, fr. *Turc* Turk] **1** : a blue, bluish green, or greenish gray mineral that is valued as a gem **2** : a light greenish blue color

**tur·ret** \'tər-ət\ *n* **1** : a little ornamental tower often at a corner of a building **2** : a low usu. revolving structure (as on a tank or warship) in which one or more guns are mounted — **tur·ret·ed** \'tər-ə-təd\ *adj*

¹**tur·tle** \'tər-t⁹l\ *n, archaic* : TURTLEDOVE

²**turtle** *n, pl* **turtles** *also* **turtle** : any of an order of horny-beaked land, freshwater, or sea reptiles with the trunk enclosed in a bony shell

**tur·tle·dove** \'tər-t⁹l-ˌdəv\ *n* : any of several small pigeons noted for plaintive cooing

**tur·tle·neck** \-ˌnek\ *n* : a high close-fitting turnover collar (as on a sweater); *also* : a sweater or shirt with a turtleneck — **tur·tle·necked** \-ˌnekt\ *adj*

**turves** *pl of* TURF

**Tus·ca·ro·ra** \ˌtəs-kə-ˈrȯr-ə\ *n, pl* **Tuscarora** *or* **Tuscaroras** : a member of an American Indian people of No. Carolina and later of New York and Ontario

**tusk** \'təsk\ *n* : a long enlarged protruding tooth (as of an elephant, walrus, or boar) used esp. to dig up food or as a weapon — **tusked** \'təskt\ *adj*

**tusk·er** \'təs-kər\ *n* : an animal with tusks; *esp* : a male elephant with two normally developed tusks

**tus·sle** \'tə-səl\ *n* **1** : a physical struggle : SCUFFLE **2** : an intense argument, controversy, or struggle

²**tussle** *vb* **tus·sled; tus·sling** : to struggle roughly ⟨players *tussled* for the ball⟩

**tus·sock** \'tə-sək\ *n* : a dense tuft esp. of grass or sedge; *also* : a hummock in a marsh or bog bound together by roots — **tus·socky** *adj*

**tu·te·lage** \'tü-t⁹l-ij, 'tyü-\ *n* **1** : an act of guarding or protecting **2** : the state of being under a guardian or tutor **3** : instruction esp. of an individual

**tu·te·lary** \'tü-tə-ˌler-ē, 'tyü-\ *adj* : acting as a guardian ⟨~ deity⟩

¹**tu·tor** \'tü-tər, 'tyü-\ *n* **1** : a person charged with the instruction and guidance of another **2** : a private teacher

²**tutor** *vb* **1** : to have the guardianship of **2** : to teach or guide individually : COACH ⟨~*ed* her in Latin⟩ **3** : to receive instruction esp. privately

**tu·to·ri·al** \tü-ˈtȯr-ē-əl, tyü-\ *n* : a class conducted by a tutor for one student or a small number of students

**tut·ti** \'tü-tē, 'tu̇-, -ˌtē\ *adj or adv* [It, pl. of *tutto* all] : with all voices and instruments playing together — used as a direction in music

**tut·ti-frut·ti** \ˌtü-ti-ˈfrü-tē, ˌtu̇-\ *n* [It, lit., all fruits] : a confection or ice cream containing chopped usu. candied fruits

**tu·tu** \'tü-(ˌ)tü\ *n* [F] : a short projecting skirt worn by a ballerina

**tux·e·do** \ˌtək-ˈsē-dō\ *n, pl* **-dos** *or* **-does** [*Tuxedo* Park, N.Y.] **1** : a usu. black or blackish blue jacket **2** : a semiformal evening suit for men

**TV** \'tē-ˈvē\ *n* : TELEVISION

**TVA** *abbr* Tennessee Valley Authority

**TV dinner** *n* : a frozen packaged dinner that needs only heating before serving

**twad·dle** \'twä-d⁹l\ *n* : silly idle talk : DRIVEL — **twaddle** *vb*

**twain** \'twān\ *n* **1** : TWO **2** : PAIR

**¹twang** \'twaŋ\ *n* **1** : a harsh quick ringing sound like that of a plucked bowstring **2** : nasal speech or resonance **3** : the characteristic speech of a region

**²twang** *vb* **twanged; twang·ing 1** : to sound or cause to sound with a twang **2** : to speak with a nasal twang

**tweak** \'twēk\ *vb* **1** : to pinch and pull with a sudden jerk and twitch **2** : to make small adjustments to — **tweak** *n*

**tweed** \'twēd\ *n* **1** : a rough woolen fabric made usu. in twill weaves **2** *pl* : tweed clothing; *esp* : a tweed suit

**tweedy** \'twē-dē\ *adj* **tweed·i·er; -est 1** : of or resembling tweed **2** : given to wearing tweeds **3** : suggestive of the outdoors in taste or habits **4** : ACADEMIC, SCHOLARLY

**tween** \'twēn\ *prep* : BETWEEN

**¹tweet** \'twēt\ *n* **1** : a chirping note **2** : a short message posted on the Twitter online service

**²tweet** *vb* **1** : to make a chirping sound **2** : to post a tweet

**tweet·er** \'twē-tər\ *n* : a small loudspeaker that reproduces sounds of high pitch

**twee·zers** \'twē-zərz\ *n pl* [obs. E *tweeze*, n., case for small implements, short for obs. E *etweese*, fr. pl. of obs. E *etwee*, fr. F *étui*] : a small pincerlike implement usu. held between the thumb and index finger and used for grasping something

**twelve** \'twelv\ *n* **1** : one more than 11 **2** : the 12th in a set or series **3** : something having 12 units — **twelfth** \'twelfth\ *adj or n* — **twelve** *adj or pron*

**twelve·month** \-ˌmənth\ *n* : YEAR

**12–step** \'twelv-ˌstep\ *adj* : of, relating to, or being a program designed esp. to help someone overcome a problem (as an addiction) by following 12 tenets

**twen·ty** \'twen-tē\ *n, pl* **twenties** : two times 10 — **twen·ti·eth** \-tē-əth\ *adj or n* — **twenty** *adj or pron*

**twenty–twenty** *or* **20/20** \ˌtwen-tē-'twen-tē\ *adj* : characterized by a visual capacity for seeing detail that is normal for the human eye ⟨~ vision⟩

**twice** \'twīs\ *adv* **1** : on two occasions **2** : two times ⟨~ two is four⟩

**¹twid·dle** \'twi-dᵊl\ *vb* **twid·dled; twid·dling 1** : to be busy with trifles; *also* : to play idly with something **2** : to rotate lightly or idly

**²twiddle** *n* : TURN, TWIST

**twig** \'twig\ *n* : a small branch — **twig·gy** *adj*

**twi·light** \'twī-ˌlīt\ *n* **1** : the light from the sky between full night and sunrise or between sunset and full night **2** : a state of imperfect clarity **3** : a period of decline

**twilight zone** *n* **1** : an area just beyond ordinary legal or ethical limits **2** : TWILIGHT 2 **3** : a world of fantasy or unreality

**twill** \'twil\ *n* [ME *twyll*, fr. OE *twilic* having a double thread, part trans. of L *bi-lic-, bilix*, fr. *bi-* two + *licium* thread] **1** : a fabric with a twill weave **2** : a textile weave that gives an appearance of diagonal lines

**twilled** \'twild\ *adj* : made with a twill weave

**¹twin** \'twin\ *n* **1** : either of two offspring produced at a birth **2** : one of two persons or things closely related to or resembling each other

**²twin** *vb* **twinned; twin·ning 1** : to be coupled with another **2** : to bring forth twins

**³twin** *adj* **1** : born with one other or as a pair at one birth ⟨~ brother⟩ ⟨~ girls⟩ **2** : made up of two similar or related members or parts **3** : being one of a pair ⟨~ city⟩

**¹twine** \'twīn\ *n* **1** : a strong thread of two or three strands twisted together **2** : an act of entwining or interlacing — **twiny** *adj*

**²twine** *vb* **twined; twin·ing 1** : to twist together; *also* : to form by twisting **2** : INTERLACE, WEAVE **3** : to coil about a support **4** : to stretch or move in a sinuous manner — **twin·er** *n*

**¹twinge** \'twinj\ *vb* **twinged; twing·ing** *or* **twinge·ing** : to affect with or feel a sharp sudden pain

**²twinge** *n* : a sudden sharp stab (as of pain or distress)

**twin·kle** \'twiŋ-kəl\ *vb* **twin·kled; twin·kling 1** : to shine or cause to shine with a flickering or sparkling light **2** : to appear bright with merriment **3** : to flutter or flit rapidly — **twin·kler** *n*

**²twinkle** *n* **1** : a wink of the eyelids; *also* : the duration of a wink **2** : an intermittent radiance **3** : a rapid flashing motion — **twin·kly** \'twiŋ-klē\ *adj*

**twin·kling** \'twiŋ-kliŋ\ *n* : the time required for a wink : INSTANT

**¹twirl** \'twərl\ *vb* : to turn or cause to turn rapidly ⟨~ a baton⟩ ♦ **Synonyms** REVOLVE, ROTATE, CIRCLE, SPIN, SWIRL, PIROUETTE — **twirl·er** *n*

**²twirl** *n* **1** : an act of twirling **2** : COIL, WHORL — **twirly** \'twər-lē\ *adj*

**twist** \'twist\ *vb* **1** : to unite by winding one thread or strand round another **2** : WREATHE, TWINE **3** : to turn so as to hurt : SPRAIN ⟨~ed my ankle⟩ **4** : to twirl into spiral shape **5** : to subject (as a shaft) to torsion **6** : to turn from the true form or meaning **7** : to pull off or break by torsion **8** : to follow a winding course **9** : to turn around

**²twist** *n* **1** : something formed by twisting or winding **2** : an act of twisting : the state of being twisted **3** : a spiral turn or curve; *also* : SPIN **4** : a turning aside **5** : ECCENTRICITY **6** : a distortion of meaning **7** : an unexpected turn or development **8** : DEVICE, TRICK **9** : a variant approach or method

**twist·er** \'twis-tər\ *n* : one that twists; *esp* : a ball with a forward and spinning motion **2** : TORNADO; *also* : WATERSPOUT 2

**¹twit** \'twit\ *n* : a silly or foolish person

**²twit** *vb* **twit·ted; twit·ting** : to ridicule as a fault; *also* : TAUNT ♦ **Synonyms** DERIDE, MOCK, RAZZ

**¹twitch** \'twich\ *vb* **1** : to move or pull

with a sudden motion : JERK **2** : to move jerkily : QUIVER **3** : to have a twitch

**²twitch** *n* **1** : an act or movement of twitching **2** : a brief spasmodic contraction of muscle fibers

**¹twit·ter** \'twi-tər\ *vb* **1** : to make a succession of chirping noises **2** : to talk in a chattering fashion **3** : to tremble with agitation : FLUTTER

**²twitter** *n* **1** : a slight agitation of the nerves **2** : a small tremulous intermittent noise (as made by a swallow) **3** : a light chattering

**twixt** \'twikst\ *prep* : BETWEEN ⟨~ the two extremes⟩

**two** \'tü\ *n, pl* **twos 1** : one more than one **2** : the second in a set or series **3** : something having two units — **two** *adj or pron*

**two cents** *n* **1** *or* **two cents' worth** : an opinion offered on a topic under discussion **2** : a sum or object of very small value

**two–faced** \'tü-'fāst\ *adj* **1** : DOUBLE-DEALING, FALSE **2** : having two faces

**two·fold** \'tü-,fōld, -'fōld\ *adj* **1** : having two units or members **2** : being twice as much or as many — **twofold** \-'fōld\ *adv*

**2,4–D** \,tü-,fōr-'dē\ *n* : an irritant compound used esp. as a weed killer

**2,4,5–T** \-,fīv-'tē\ *n* : an irritant compound used esp. as an herbicide and defoliant

**two·pence** \'tə-pəns, *US also* 'tü-,pens\ *n* : the sum of two pence

**two·pen·ny** \'tə-pə-nē, *US also* 'tü-,pe-nē\ *adj* : of the value of or costing twopence

**two–ply** \'tü-'plī\ *adj* **1** : woven as a double cloth **2** : consisting of two strands or thicknesses (~ toilet paper)

**two·some** \'tü-səm\ *n* **1** : a group of two persons or things : COUPLE **2** : a golf match between two players

**two–step** \'tü-,step\ *n* : a ballroom dance performed with a sliding step in march or polka time; *also* : a piece of music for this dance — **two–step** *vb*

**two–time** \'tü-,tīm\ *vb* : to betray (a spouse or lover) by secret lovemaking with another — **two–tim·er** *n*

**two–way** *adj* : involving two elements or allowing movement or use in two directions or manners

**2WD** *abbr* two-wheel drive

**twp** *abbr* township

**TWX** *abbr* teletypewriter exchange

**TX** *abbr* Texas

**ty·coon** \tī-'kün\ *n* [Jp *taikun* feudal lord] **1** : a masterful leader (as in politics) **2** : a powerful businessman or industrialist

**tying** *pres part of* TIE

**ty·iyn** \tē-'ɛn\ *n, pl* **tyiyn** — see *som* at MONEY table

**tyke** \'tīk\ *n* : a small child

**tym·pan·ic membrane** \tim-'pa-nik-\ *n* : EARDRUM

**tym·pa·num** \'tim-pə-nəm\ *n, pl* **-na** \-nə\ *also* **-nums** : EARDRUM; *also* : MIDDLE EAR — **tym·pan·ic** \tim-'pa-nik\ *adj*

**¹type** \'tīp\ *n* [ME, fr. LL *typus*, fr. L & Gk; L *typus* image, fr. Gk *typos* blow, impression, model, fr. *typtein* to strike, beat] **1**

: a person, thing, or event that foreshadows another to come : TOKEN, SYMBOL **2** : MODEL, EXAMPLE **3** : a distinctive stamp, mark, or sign : EMBLEM **4** : rectangular blocks usu. of metal each having a face so shaped as to produce a character when printed **5** : the letters or characters printed from or as if from type **6** : general character or form common to a number of individuals and setting them off as a distinguishable class ⟨horses of draft ~⟩ **7** : a class, kind, or group set apart by common characteristics ⟨a seedless ~ of orange⟩; *also* : something distinguishable as a variety ⟨reactions of this ~⟩ ♦ **Synonyms** SORT, NATURE, CHARACTER, DESCRIPTION

**²type** *vb* **typed; typ·ing 1** : to represent beforehand as a type **2** : to produce a copy of; *also* : REPRESENT, TYPIFY **3** : to write with a typewriter or computer keyboard **4** : to identify as belonging to a type **5** : TYPECAST

**type A** *adj* : relating to, having, or being a personality marked esp. by impatience and aggressiveness

**type·cast** \-,kast\ *vb* **-cast; -cast·ing 1** : to cast (an actor) in a part calling for characteristics possessed by the actor **2** : to cast repeatedly in the same type of role

**type·face** \-,fās\ *n* : all type of a single design

**type 1 diabetes** \'tīp-'wən-\ *n* : a form of diabetes mellitus usu. developing before adulthood and marked by severe insulin deficiency

**type·script** \'tīp-,skript\ *n* : typewritten matter

**type·set** \-,set\ *vb* **-set; -set·ting** : to set in type : COMPOSE — **type·set·ter** *n*

**type 2 diabetes** \'tü\ *n* : a form of diabetes mellitus developing esp. in adults and usu. in obese individuals and marked by excess sugar in the blood

**type·write** \-,rīt\ *vb* **-wrote** \-,rōt\; **-writ·ten** \-,ri-t²n\ : TYPE **3**

**type·writ·er** \-,rī-tər\ *n* **1** : a machine for writing in characters similar to those produced by printers' type by means of types striking a ribbon to transfer ink or carbon impressions onto paper **2** : TYPIST

**type·writ·ing** \-,rī-tin\ *n* : the use of a typewriter ⟨teach ~⟩; *also* : writing produced with a typewriter

**¹ty·phoid** \'tī-,fōid, tī-'fōid\ *adj* : of, relating to, or being a communicable bacterial disease (**typhoid fever**) marked by fever, diarrhea, prostration, and intestinal inflammation

**²typhoid** *n* : TYPHOID FEVER

**ty·phoon** \tī-'fün\ *n* : a hurricane occurring esp. in the region of the Philippines or the China sea

**ty·phus** \'tī-fəs\ *n* : a severe infectious disease transmitted esp. by body lice, caused by a rickettsia, and marked by high fever, stupor and delirium, intense headache, and a dark red rash

**typ·i·cal** \'ti-pi-kəl\ *adj* **1** : being or having the nature of a type **2** : exhibiting the essential characteristics of a group **3**

: conforming to a type — **typ·i·cal·i·ty** \ˌti-pə-ˈka-lə-tē\ n — **typ·i·cal·ness** n

**typ·i·cal·ly** \-pi-k(ə-)lē\ adv **1** : in a typical manner **2** : in typical circumstances

**typ·i·fy** \ˈti-pə-ˌfī\ vb **-fied; -fy·ing 1** : to represent by an image, form, model, or resemblance **2** : to embody the essential or common characteristics of

**typ·ist** \ˈtī-pist\ n : a person who types esp. as a job

**ty·po** \ˈtī-pō\ n, pl **typos** : an error (as of spelling) in typed or typeset material

**ty·pog·ra·pher** \tī-ˈpä-grə-fər\ n : one who designs or arranges printing

**ty·pog·ra·phy** \tī-ˈpä-grə-fē\ n : the art of printing with type; also : the style, arrangement, or appearance of printed matter — **ty·po·graph·ic** \ˌtī-pə-ˈgra-fik\ or **ty·po·graph·i·cal** \-fi-kəl\ adj — **ty·po·graph·i·cal·ly** adv

**ty·ran·ni·cal** \tə-ˈra-ni-kəl, tī-\ also **ty·ran·nic** \-nik\ adj : of or relating to a tyrant : DESPOTIC ✦ **Synonyms** ARBITRARY, ABSOLUTE, AUTOCRATIC — **ty·ran·ni·cal·ly** \-ni-k(ə-)lē\ adv

**tyr·an·nise** Brit var of TYRANNIZE

**tyr·an·nize** \ˈtir-ə-ˌnīz\ vb **-nized; -niz·ing** : to act as a tyrant : rule with unjust severity — **tyr·an·niz·er** n

**ty·ran·no·saur** \tə-ˈra-nə-ˌsòr\ n : a massive American flesh-eating dinosaur of the Cretaceous that had small forelegs and walked on its hind legs

**ty·ran·no·sau·rus** \tə-ˌra-nə-ˈsòr-əs\ n : TYRANNOSAUR

**tyr·an·nous** \ˈtir-ə-nəs\ adj : unjustly severe — **tyr·an·nous·ly** adv

**tyr·an·ny** \ˈtir-ə-nē\ n, pl **-nies 1** : oppressive power **2** : the rule or authority of a tyrant : government in which absolute power is vested in a single ruler **3** : a tyrannical act

**ty·rant** \ˈtī-rənt\ n **1** : an absolute ruler : DESPOT **2** : a ruler who governs oppressively or brutally **3** : one who uses authority or power harshly

**tyre** chiefly Brit var of ²TIRE

**ty·ro** \ˈtī-rō\ n, pl **tyros** [ML, fr. L tiro young soldier, tyro] : a beginner in learning : NOVICE

**tzar, tzarist** var of CZAR, CZARIST

**¹u** \ˈyü\ n, pl **u's** or **us** \ˈyüz\ often cap : the 21st letter of the English alphabet

**²u** abbr, often cap unit

**¹U** \ˈyü\ adj : characteristic of the upper classes

**²U 1** [abbr. of Union of Orthodox Hebrew Congregations] kosher certification — often enclosed in a circle **2** university **3** unsatisfactory

**³U** symbol uranium

**UAE** abbr United Arab Emirates

**UAR** abbr United Arab Republic

**UAW** abbr United Automobile Workers

**ubiq·ui·tous** \yü-ˈbi-kwə-təs\ adj : existing or being everywhere at the same time : OMNIPRESENT — **ubiq·ui·tous·ly** adv — **ubiq·ui·ty** \-kwə-tē\ n

**U-boat** \ˈyü-ˌbōt\ n [trans. of G U-boot, short for Unterseeboot, lit., undersea boat] : a German submarine

**UC** abbr uppercase

**ud·der** \ˈə-dər\ n : an organ (as of a cow) consisting of two or more milk glands enclosed in a large hanging sac and each provided with a nipple

**UFO** \ˌyü-(ˌ)ef-ˈō\ n, pl **UFO's** or **UFOs** \-ˈōz\ : an unidentified flying object; esp : FLYING SAUCER

**ug·ly** \ˈə-glē\ adj **ug·li·er; -est** [ME, fr. ON ugglig, fr. uggr fear] **1** : FRIGHTFUL, DIRE **2** : offensive to the sight : HIDEOUS **3** : offensive or unpleasant to any sense **4** : morally objectionable : REPULSIVE **5** : likely to cause inconvenience or discomfort **6** : SURLY, QUARRELSOME ⟨an ∼ disposition⟩ — **ug·li·ness** \-glē-nəs\ n

**UHF** abbr ultrahigh frequency

**UK** abbr United Kingdom

**ukase** \yü-ˈkās, -ˈkāz\ n [F & Russ; F, fr. Russ ukaz, fr. ukazat' to show, order] : an edict esp. of a Russian emperor or government

**Ukrai·ni·an** \yü-ˈkrā-nē-ən\ n **1** : a native or inhabitant of Ukraine **2** : a Slavic language of the Ukrainian people — **Ukrainian** adj

**uku·le·le** also **uke·le·le** \ˌyü-kə-ˈlā-lē\ n [Hawaiian ʻukulele, fr. ʻuku flea + lele jumping] : a small usu. 4-stringed guitar popularized in Hawaii

**ul·cer** \ˈəl-sər\ n **1** : an open eroded sore of skin or mucous membrane often discharging pus **2** : something that festers and corrupts like an open sore — **ul·cer·ous** adj

**ul·cer·ate** \ˈəl-sə-ˌrāt\ vb **-at·ed; -at·ing** : to become affected with an ulcer — **ul·cer·a·tive** \ˈəl-sə-ˌrā-tiv\ adj

**ul·cer·a·tion** \ˌəl-sə-ˈrā-shən\ n **1** : the process of forming or state of having an ulcer **2** : ULCER 1

**ul·na** \ˈəl-nə\ n : the bone on the little-finger side of the human forearm; also : a corresponding bone of the forelimb of vertebrates above fishes

**ul·ster** \ˈəl-stər\ n : a long loose overcoat

**ult** abbr **1** ultimate **2** ultimo

**ul·te·ri·or** \ˌəl-ˈtir-ē-ər\ adj **1** : lying farther away : more remote **2** : situated beyond or on the farther side **3** : going beyond what is openly said or shown : HIDDEN ⟨∼ motives⟩

¹**ul·ti·mate** \ˈəl tə mət\ adj **1** : most remote in space or time : FARTHEST **2** : last in a progression : FINAL **3** : the best or most extreme of its kind **4** : arrived at as the last resort **5** : FUNDAMENTAL, ABSOLUTE, SUPREME ⟨~ reality⟩ **6** : incapable of further analysis or division : ELEMENTAL **7** : MAXIMUM ♦ *Synonyms* CONCLUDING, EVENTUAL, LATEST, TERMINAL — **ul·ti·mate·ly** adv

²**ultimate** n : something ultimate

**ul·ti·ma·tum** \ˌəl-tə-ˈmā-təm, -ˈmä-\ n, pl **-tums** or **-ta** \-tə\ : a final condition or demand whose rejection will bring about a resort to forceful action

**ul·ti·mo** \ˈəl-tə-ˌmō\ adj [L *ultimo mense* in the last month] : of or occurring in the month preceding the present

¹**ul·tra** \ˈəl-trə\ adj : going beyond others or beyond due limits : EXTREME

²**ultra** n : EXTREMIST

**ul·tra·con·ser·va·tive** \-kən-ˈsər-və-tiv\ adj : extremely conservative

**ul·tra·high frequency** \ˈhī-\ n : a radio frequency between 300 and 3000 megahertz

¹**ul·tra·light** \ˈəl-trə-ˌlīt\ adj : extremely light esp. in weight

²**ultralight** n : a very light recreational aircraft typically carrying only one person

**ul·tra·ma·rine** \ˌəl-trə-mə-ˈrēn\ n **1** : a deep blue pigment **2** : a very bright deep blue color

**ul·tra·mi·cro·scop·ic** \-ˌmī-krə-ˈskä-pik\ adj : too small to be seen with an ordinary microscope

**ul·tra·mod·ern** \-ˈmä-dərn\ adj : extremely or excessively modern in idea, style, or tendency

**ul·tra·mon·tane** \-ˈmän-ˌtān, -ˌmän-ˈtān\ adj **1** : of or relating to countries or peoples beyond the mountains (as the Alps) **2** : favoring greater or absolute supremacy of papal over national or diocesan authority in the Roman Catholic Church — **ultramontane** n, often cap — **ul·tra·mon·tan·ism** \-ˈmän-tə-ˌni-zəm\ n

**ul·tra·pure** \-ˈpyür\ adj : of the utmost purity

**ul·tra·short** \-ˈshȯrt\ adj **1** : having a wavelength below 10 meters **2** : very short in duration

**ul·tra·son·ic** \ˌəl-trə-ˈsä-nik\ adj : having a frequency too high to be heard by the human ear — **ul·tra·son·i·cal·ly** \-ni-k(ə-)lē\ adv

**ul·tra·son·ics** \-ˈsä-niks\ n sing or pl **1** : ultrasonic vibrations **2** : the science of ultrasonic phenomena

**ul·tra·sound** \-ˌsaund\ n **1** : ultrasonic vibrations **2** : the diagnostic or therapeutic use of ultrasound and esp. a technique involving the formation of a two-dimensional image of internal body structures **3** : a diagnostic examination using ultrasound

**ul·tra·vi·o·let** \-ˈvī-ə-lət\ adj : having a

wavelength shorter than those of visible light and longer than those of X-rays ⟨~ radiation⟩; also : producing or employing ultraviolet radiation — **ultraviolet** n

**ul·tra vi·res** \ˈəl-trə-ˈvī-rēz\ adv or adj [NL, lit., beyond power] : beyond the scope of legal power or authority

**ul·u·late** \ˈəl-yə-ˌlāt\ vb **-lat·ed; -lat·ing** : HOWL, WAIL

**uma·mi** \ü-ˈmä-mē\ n [Jp, flavor] : a meaty or savory taste sensation produced esp. by monosodium glutamate

**um·bel** \ˈəm-bəl\ n : a flat-topped or rounded flower cluster in which the individual flower stalks all arise near one point on the main stem

**um·ber** \ˈəm-bər\ n : a brown earthy substance valued as a pigment either in its raw state or burnt — **umber** adj

**umbilical cord** n : a cord containing blood vessels that connects the navel of a fetus with the placenta of its mother

**um·bi·li·cus** \ˌəm-ˈbi-li-kəs, ˌəm-bə-ˈlī-\ n, pl **um·bi·li·ci** \ˌəm-ˈbi-lə-ˌkī, ˌəm-bə-ˈlī-ˌkī, -ˌsī\ or **um·bi·li·cus·es** : NAVEL — **um·bil·i·cal** \ˌəm-ˈbi-li-kəl\ adj

**um·bra** \ˈəm-brə\ n, pl **umbras** or **umbrae** \-(ˌ)brē, -ˌbrī\ **1** : SHADE, SHADOW **2** : the conical part of the shadow of a celestial body from which the sun's light is completely blocked

**um·brage** \ˈəm-brij\ n **1** : SHADE; also : FOLIAGE **2** : RESENTMENT, OFFENSE ⟨take ~ at a remark⟩

**um·brel·la** \ˌəm-ˈbre-lə\ n **1** : a collapsible shade for protection against weather consisting of fabric stretched over hinged ribs radiating from a center pole **2** : something that provides protection **3** : something that covers a range of elements

**umi·ak** \ˈü-mē-ˌak\ n : an open Inuit boat made of a wooden frame covered with skins

**ump** \ˈəmp\ n : UMPIRE

**um·pire** \ˈəm-ˌpī(-ə)r\ n [ME *oumpere*, alter. of *noumpere* (the phrase *a noumpere* being understood as *an oumpere*), fr. AF *nounpier* single, odd, fr. *non* not + *per* equal, fr. L *par*] **1** : one having authority to decide finally a controversy or question between parties **2** : an official in a sport who rules on plays — **umpire** vb

**ump·teen** \ˈəmp-ˌtēn\ adj : very many : indefinitely numerous — **ump·teenth** \-ˌtēnth\ adj

**UN** abbr United Nations

**un-** \ˌən, ˈən\ prefix **1** : not : IN-, NON- **2** : opposite of : contrary to

**un·able** \ˌən-ˈā-bəl\ adj **1** : not able **2** : UNQUALIFIED, INCOMPETENT

**un·abridged** \ˌən-ə-ˈbrijd\ adj **1** : not abridged ⟨an ~ edition of Shakespeare⟩ **2** : complete of its class : not based on one larger ⟨an ~ dictionary⟩

**un·ac·com·pa·nied** \ˌən-ə-ˈkəm-pə-nēd\

| | | |
|---|---|---|
| unabashed | unabsorbent | unaccented | unacclimatized |
| unabated | unacademic | unacceptable | unaccommodating |
| unabsorbed | | | |

*adj* : not accompanied; *esp* : being without instrumental accompaniment

**un·ac·count·able** \ˌən-ə-ˈkaún-tə-bəl\ *adj* **1** : not to be accounted for : INEXPLICABLE **2** : not responsible — **un·ac·count·ably** \-blē\ *adv*

**un·ac·count·ed** \-ˈkaún-təd\ *adj* : not accounted ⟨the loss was ∼ for⟩

**un·ac·cus·tomed** \ˌən-ə-ˈkəs-təmd\ *adj* **1** : not customary : not usual or common **2** : not accustomed or habituated ⟨∼ to noise⟩

**un·adul·ter·at·ed** \ˌən-ə-ˈdəl-tə-ˌrā-təd\ *adj* : PURE, UNMIXED ⟨∼ meat⟩ ♦ **Synonyms** ABSOLUTE, SHEER, SIMPLE, UNALLOYED, UNDILUTED, UNMITIGATED

**un·af·fect·ed** \ˌən-ə-ˈfek-təd\ *adj* **1** : not influenced or changed mentally, physically, or chemically **2** : free from affectation : NATURAL, GENUINE — **un·af·fect·ed·ly** *adv*

**un·alien·able** \-ˈāl-yə-nə-bəl, -ˈā-lē-ə-\ : INALIENABLE

**un·aligned** \ˌən-ə-ˈlīnd\ *adj* : not associated with any one of competing international blocs ⟨∼ nations⟩

**un·al·loyed** \ˌən-ə-ˈlȯid\ *adj* : UNMIXED, UNQUALIFIED, PURE ⟨∼ happiness⟩

**un·al·ter·able** \ˌən-ˈȯl-tə-rə-bəl\ *adj* : not capable of being altered or changed ⟨an ∼ rule⟩ — **un·al·ter·ably** \-blē\ *adv*

**un–Amer·i·can** \ˌən-ə-ˈmer-ə-kən\ *adj* : not characteristic of or consistent with American customs or principles

**unan·i·mous** \yü-ˈna-nə-məs\ *adj* [L *unanimus*, fr. *unus* one + *animus* mind] **1** : being of one mind : AGREEING **2** : formed with or indicating the agreement of all — **una·nim·i·ty** \yü-nə-ˈni-mə-tē\ *n* — **unan·i·mous·ly** *adv*

**un·arm** \ˌən-ˈärm\ *vb* : DISARM

**un·armed** \-ˈärmd\ *adj* : not armed or armored ⟨∼ civilians⟩

**un·as·sail·able** \ˌən-ə-ˈsā-lə-bəl\ *adj* : not liable to doubt, attack, or question ⟨an ∼ argument⟩

**un·as·sum·ing** \ˌən-ə-ˈsü-miŋ\ *adj* : MODEST ⟨an ∼ librarian⟩ ⟨an ∼ manner⟩ ⟨an ∼ neighborhood⟩ ♦ **Synonyms** HUMBLE, LOWLY, MEEK

**un·at·tached** \ˌən-ə-ˈtacht\ *adj* **1** : not married or engaged **2** : not joined or united

**un·avail·ing** \ˌən-ə-ˈvā-liŋ\ *adj* : being of no avail — **un·avail·ing·ly** *adv*

**un·avoid·able** \ˌən-ə-ˈvȯi-də-bəl\ *adj* : not avoidable : INEVITABLE ⟨an ∼ fact⟩

♦ **Synonyms** CERTAIN, INELUCTABLE, INESCAPABLE, NECESSARY — **un·avoid·ably** \-blē\ *adv*

**¹un·aware** \ˌən-ə-ˈwer\ *adv* : UNAWARES

**²unaware** *adj* : not aware : IGNORANT ⟨∼ of the danger⟩ — **un·aware·ness** *n*

**un·awares** \-ˈwerz\ *adv* **1** : without knowing : UNINTENTIONALLY **2** : without warning : by surprise ⟨taken ∼⟩

**un·bal·anced** \ˌən-ˈba-lənst\ *adj* **1** : not in a state of balance **2** : mentally disordered **3** : not adjusted so as to make credits equal to debits

**un·bar** \-ˈbär\ *vb* : UNBOLT, OPEN

**un·bear·able** \ˌən-ˈber-ə-bəl\ *adj* : greater than can be borne ⟨∼ pain⟩ ♦ **Synonyms** INSUFFERABLE, INSUPPORTABLE, INTOLERABLE, UNENDURABLE, UNSUPPORTABLE — **un·bear·ably** \-blē\ *adv*

**un·beat·able** \-ˈbē-tə-bəl\ *adj* : not capable of being defeated ♦ **Synonyms** INDOMITABLE, INVINCIBLE, INVULNERABLE, UNCONQUERABLE

**un·beat·en** \-ˈbē-tᵊn\ *adj* **1** : not pounded, beaten, or whipped **2** : UNTRODDEN **3** : UNDEFEATED

**un·be·com·ing** \ˌən-bi-ˈkə-miŋ\ *adj* : not becoming : UNSUITABLE, IMPROPER ⟨conduct ∼ an officer⟩ ♦ **Synonyms** INDECOROUS, INDECENT, INDELICATE, UNSEEMLY — **un·be·com·ing·ly** *adv*

**un·be·knownst** \ˌən-bi-ˈnōnst\ *also* **un·be·known** \-ˈnōn\ *adj* : happening or existing without one's knowledge

**un·be·lief** \ˌən-bə-ˈlēf\ *n* : the withholding or absence of belief : DOUBT — **un·be·liev·ing** \-ˈlē-viŋ\ *adj*

**un·be·liev·able** \-ˈlē-və-bəl\ *adj* : too improbable for belief; *also* : of such a superlative degree as to be hard to believe ⟨an ∼ catch for a touchdown⟩ ♦ **Synonyms** INCONCEIVABLE, UNIMAGINABLE, UNTHINKABLE — **un·be·liev·ably** \-blē\ *adv*

**un·be·liev·er** \-ˈlē-vər\ *n* **1** : INFIDEL **2** : DOUBTER

**un·bend** \-ˈbend\ *vb* **-bent** \-ˈbent\; **-bend·ing** **1** : to free from being bent : make or become straight **2** : UNTIE **3** : to make or become less stiff or more affable : RELAX

**un·bend·ing** *adj* : formal and distant in manner : INFLEXIBLE

**un·bi·ased** \ˌən-ˈbī-əst\ *adj* : free from bias; *esp* : UNPREJUDICED ⟨an ∼ opinion⟩ ♦ **Synonyms** DISINTERESTED, DIS-

| | | | |
|---|---|---|---|
| unaccredited | unaltered | unappreciated | unattainable |
| unacknowledged | unambiguous | unappreciative | unattended |
| unacquainted | unambiguously | unapproachable | unattested |
| unadapted | unambitious | unappropriated | unattractive |
| unadjusted | unanchored | unapproved | unauthentic |
| unadorned | unannounced | unarguable | unauthorized |
| unadventurous | unanswerable | unarguably | unavailable |
| unadvertised | unanswered | unarmored | unavowed |
| unaesthetic | unanticipated | unartistic | unawakened |
| unaffiliated | unapologetic | unashamed | unbaked |
| unafraid | unapparent | unasked | unbaptized |
| unaggressive | unappealing | unassertive | unbeloved |
| unaided | unappeased | unassisted | |
| unalike | unappetizing | unathletic | |

PASSIONATE, IMPARTIAL, NONDISCRIMI-
NATORY, NONPARTISAN, OBJECTIVE, UN-
COLORED

**un·bid·den** \-'bi-d°n\ *also* **un·bid** \ 'bid\ *adj* : not bidden : UNASKED

**un·bind** \-'bīnd\ *vb* **-bound** \-'baùnd\; **-bind·ing** **1** : to remove bindings from : UNTIE **2** : RELEASE

**un·blessed** *also* **un·blest** \ˌən-'blest\ *adj* **1** : not blessed **2** : EVIL

**un·block** \-'bläk\ *vb* : to free from being blocked

**un·blush·ing** \-'blə-shiŋ\ *adj* **1** : not blushing 〈~ greed〉 — **un·blush·ing·ly** *adv*

**un·bod·ied** \-'bä-dēd\ *adj* **1** : having no body; *also* : DISEMBODIED **2** : FORMLESS

**un·bolt** \ˌən-'bōlt\ *vb* : to open or unfasten by withdrawing a bolt

**un·bolt·ed** \-'bōl-təd\ *adj* : not fastened by bolts

**un·born** \-'bórn\ *adj* : not yet born

**un·bos·om** \-'bú-zəm, -'bü-\ *vb* **1** : DIS-CLOSE, REVEAL **2** : to disclose the thoughts or feelings of oneself

**un·bound·ed** \-'baùn-dəd\ *adj* : having no bounds or limits 〈~ enthusiasm〉 ♦ *Synonyms* BOUNDLESS, ENDLESS, IM-MEASURABLE, LIMITLESS, MEASURELESS, UNLIMITED

**un·bowed** \ˌən-'baùd\ *adj* **1** : not bowed down **2** : UNSUBDUED 〈~ by failure〉

**un·bri·dled** \-'brī-d°ld\ *adj* **1** : UNRE-STRAINED 〈~ enthusiasm〉 **2** : not confined by a bridle

**un·bro·ken** \-'brō-kən\ *adj* **1** : not damaged **2** : not subdued or tamed **3** : not interrupted : CONTINUOUS

**un·buck·le** \-'bə-kəl\ *vb* : to loose the buckle of 〈~ a belt〉

**un·bur·den** \-'bər-d°n\ *vb* **1** : to free or relieve from a burden **2** : to relieve one-self of (as cares or worries)

**un·but·ton** \-'bə-t°n\ *vb* : to unfasten the buttons of 〈~ your coat〉

**un·called–for** \ˌən-'kóld-ˌfòr\ *adj* : not called for, needed, or wanted

**un·can·ny** \-'ka-nē\ *adj* **1** : GHOSTLY, MYSTERIOUS, EERIE **2** : suggesting super-human or supernatural powers ♦ *Syn-onyms* SPOOKY, UNEARTHLY, WEIRD — **un·can·ni·ly** \-'ka-nə-lē\ *adv*

**un·ceas·ing** \-'sē-siŋ\ *adj* : never ceasing ♦ *Synonyms* CEASELESS, CONTINUOUS, ENDLESS, INTERMINABLE, UNENDING, UNREMITTING — **un·ceas·ing·ly** *adv*

**un·cer·e·mo·ni·ous** \ˌən-ˌser-ə-'mō-nē-əs\ *adj* : acting without or lacking ordi-nary courtesy : ABRUPT 〈his ~ dismiss-al〉 — **un·cer·e·mo·ni·ous·ly** *adv*

**un·cer·tain** \ˌən-'sər-t°n\ *adj* **1** : not de-termined or fixed 〈an ~ quantity〉 **2** : subject to chance or change : not de-pendable 〈~ weather〉 **3** : not definitely known **4** : not sure 〈~ of the truth〉 — **un·cer·tain·ly** *adv*

**un·cer·tain·ty** \-t°n-tē\ *n* **1** : lack of cer-tainty : DOUBT **2** : something that is un-certain ♦ *Synonyms* CONCERN, DOUBT, DUBIETY, INCERTITUDE, SKEPTICISM, SUSPICION

**un·chain** \ˌən-'chān\ *vb* : to free by or as if by removing a chain

**un·charged** \ˌən-'chärjd\ *adj* : having no electrical charge

**un·char·i·ta·ble** \-'cha-rə-tə-bəl\ *adj* : not charitable; *esp* : severe in judging others — **un·char·i·ta·ble·ness** *n* — **un·char·i·ta·bly** \-blē\ *adv*

**un·chart·ed** \-'chär-təd\ *adj* **1** : not re-corded on a map, chart, or plan **2** : UN-KNOWN 〈discussion moving into ~ terri-tory〉

**un·chris·tian** \-'kris-chən\ *adj* **1** : not of the Christian faith **2** : contrary to the Christian spirit

**un·churched** \-'chərcht\ *adj* : not belong-ing to or connected with a church

**un·cial** \'ən-shəl, -chəl; 'ən-sē-əl\ *adj* : re-lating to or written in a form of script with rounded letters used esp. in early Greek and Latin manuscripts — **uncial** *n*

**un·cir·cu·lat·ed** \ˌən-'sər-kyə-ˌlā-təd\ *adj* : issued for use as money but kept out of circulation

**un·cir·cum·cised** \ˌən-'sər-kəm-ˌsīzd\ *adj* **1** : not circumcised **2** : HEATHEN

**un·civ·il** \ˌən-'si-vəl\ *adj* **1** : not civilized : BARBAROUS **2** : DISCOURTEOUS, ILL-MANNERED, IMPOLITE 〈~ remarks〉

**un·civ·i·lized** \-'si-və-ˌlīzd\ *adj* **1** : not civilized : BARBAROUS **2** : remote from civilization : WILD

**un·clasp** \-'klasp\ *vb* : to open by or as if by loosing the clasp

**un·cle** \'əŋ-kəl\ *n* [ME, fr. AF, fr. L *avun-culus* mother's brother] **1** : the brother of one's father or mother **2** : the husband of one's aunt

**un·clean** \ˌən-'klēn\ *adj* **1** : morally or spiritually impure **2** : prohibited by ritu-al law for use or contact **3** : DIRTY, SOILED — **un·clean·li·ness** \-lē-nəs\ *n* — **un·clean·ly** *adj* — **un·clean·ness** *n*

**un·clench** \-'klench\ *vb* : to open from a clenched position : RELAX

**Uncle Tom** \-'täm\ *n* [fr. *Uncle Tom*, faith-ful slave in Harriet Beecher Stowe's novel *Uncle Tom's Cabin* (1851-52)] : a black

| | | | |
|---|---|---|---|
| unbleached | unburied | unchallenged | unchivalrous |
| unblemished | unburned | unchangeable | unchristened |
| unblinking | uncanceled | unchanged | unclad |
| unbound | uncanonical | unchanging | unclaimed |
| unbranched | uncap | unchaperoned | unclassified |
| unbranded | uncapitalized | uncharacteristic | uncleaned |
| unbreakable | uncared–for | unchaste | unclear |
| unbridgeable | uncataloged | unchastely | uncleared |
| unbruised | uncaught | unchasteness | |
| unbrushed | uncensored | unchastity | |
| unbudging | uncensured | unchecked | |

who is eager to win the approval of whites

**un·cloak** \ən-ˈklōk\ *vb* **1** : to remove a cloak or cover from **2** : UNMASK, REVEAL ⟨∼ an impostor⟩

**un·clog** \-ˈkläg\ *vb* : to remove an obstruction from

**un·close** \-ˈklōz\ *vb* : OPEN — **un·closed** \-ˈklōzd\ *adj*

**un·clothe** \-ˈklōth\ *vb* : to strip of clothes or a covering — **un·clothed** \-ˈklōthd\ *adj*

**un·coil** \ˌən-ˈkȯi(-ə)l\ *vb* : to release or become released from a coiled state

**un·com·fort·able** \ˌən-ˈkəmf-tə-bəl, -ˈkəm-fər-tə-\ *adj* **1** : causing discomfort **2** : feeling discomfort — **un·com·fort·ably** \-blē\ *adv*

**un·com·mit·ted** \ˌən-kə-ˈmi-təd\ *adj* : not committed; *esp* : not pledged to a particular belief, allegiance, or program ⟨∼ voters⟩

**un·com·mon** \ˌən-ˈkä-mən\ *adj* **1** : not ordinarily encountered : UNUSUAL, RARE **2** : REMARKABLE, EXCEPTIONAL ⟨a soldier of ∼ courage⟩ ♦ **Synonyms** EXTRAORDINARY, PHENOMENAL, SINGULAR, UNIQUE — **un·com·mon·ly** *adv*

**un·com·mu·ni·ca·tive** \ˌən-kə-ˈmyü-nə-ˌkā-tiv, -ni-kə-\ *adj* : not inclined to talk or impart information : RESERVED ♦ **Synonyms** CLOSEMOUTHED, RETICENT, SILENT, TACITURN

**un·com·pro·mis·ing** \ˌən-ˈkäm-prə-ˌmī-ziŋ\ *adj* : not making or accepting a compromise : UNYIELDING ♦ **Synonyms** ADAMANT, INFLEXIBLE, OBDURATE, RIGID, UNBENDING

**un·con·cern** \ˌən-kən-ˈsərn\ *n* **1** : lack of care or interest : INDIFFERENCE **2** : freedom from excessive concern

**un·con·cerned** \-ˈsərnd\ *adj* **1** : not having any part or interest **2** : not anxious or upset : free of worry ♦ **Synonyms** ALOOF, DETACHED, INCURIOUS, REMOTE, UNCURIOUS, UNINTERESTED — **un·con·cern·ed·ly** \-ˈsər-nəd-lē\ *adv*

**un·con·di·tion·al** \ˌən-kən-ˈdi-shə-nəl\ *adj* : not limited in any way ⟨∼ surrender⟩ — **un·con·di·tion·al·ly** *adv*

**un·con·di·tioned** \-ˈdi-shənd\ *adj* **1** : not subject to conditions **2** : not acquired or learned : NATURAL ⟨∼ responses⟩ **3** : producing an unconditioned response ⟨∼ stimuli⟩

**un·con·quer·able** \ˌən-ˈkäŋ-kə-rə-bəl\ *adj* : incapable of being conquered or overcome : INDOMITABLE

**un·con·scio·na·ble** \-ˈkän-shə-nə-bəl\ *adj* **1** : not guided or controlled by conscience **2** : not in accordance with what is right or just ⟨∼ sales practices⟩ ♦ **Synonyms** UNREASONABLE, UNDUE, UNJUSTIFIABLE, UNWARRANTABLE, UNWARRANTED — **un·con·scio·na·bly** \-blē\ *adv*

¹**un·con·scious** \ˌən-ˈkän-chəs, -shəs\ *adj* **1** : not knowing or perceiving : not aware **2** : not done consciously or on purpose **3** : having lost consciousness **4** : of or relating to the unconscious — **un·con·scious·ly** *adv* — **un·con·scious·ness** *n*

²**unconscious** *n* : the part of one's mental life of which one is not ordinarily aware but which is often a powerful force in influencing behavior

**un·con·sti·tu·tion·al** \ˌən-ˌkän-stə-ˈtü-shə-nəl, -ˈtyü-\ *adj* : not according to or consistent with the constitution of a state or society — **un·con·sti·tu·tion·al·i·ty** \-ˌtü-shə-ˈna-lə-tē, -ˌtyü-\ *n* — **un·con·sti·tu·tion·al·ly** \-ˈtü-shə-nə-lē, -ˈtyü-\ *adv*

**un·con·trol·la·ble** \ˌən-kən-ˈtrō-lə-bəl\ *adj* : incapable of being controlled : UNGOVERNABLE — **un·con·trol·la·bly** \-blē\ *adv*

**un·con·ven·tion·al** \-ˈven-chə-nəl\ *adj* : not conventional : being out of the ordinary — **un·con·ven·tion·al·i·ty** \-ˌven-chə-ˈna-lə-tē\ *n* — **un·con·ven·tion·al·ly** \-ˈven-chə-nə-lē\ *adv*

**un·cork** \ˌən-ˈkȯrk\ *vb* **1** : to draw a cork from **2** : to release from a sealed or pent-up state; *also* : to let go

**un·count·ed** \-ˈkaun-təd\ *adj* **1** : not counted **2** : INNUMERABLE

**un·cou·ple** \-ˈkə-pəl\ *vb* : DISCONNECT ⟨∼ railroad cars⟩

**un·couth** \-ˈküth\ *adj* [ME, unfamiliar, fr. OE *uncūth*, fr. *un-* + *cūth* known] **1** : strange, awkward, and clumsy in shape or appearance **2** : vulgar in conduct or speech : RUDE ♦ **Synonyms** DISCOURTEOUS, ILL-MANNERED, IMPOLITE, UNGRACIOUS, UNMANNERED, UNMANNERLY

**un·cov·er** \-ˈkə-vər\ *vb* **1** : to make known : DISCLOSE, REVEAL **2** : to expose to view by removing some covering **3** : to take the cover from **4** : to remove the hat from; *also* : to take off the hat as a token of respect — **un·cov·ered** *adj*

**un·crit·i·cal** \ˌən-ˈkri-ti-kəl\ *adj* **1** : not critical : lacking in discrimination **2** : showing lack or improper use of critical standards or procedures — **un·crit·i·cal·ly** \-k(ə-)lē\ *adv*

**un·cross** \-ˈkrȯs\ *vb* : to change from a crossed position ⟨∼ed his legs⟩

| | | | |
|---|---|---|---|
| unclouded | uncompleted | unconsecrated | uncooked |
| uncluttered | uncomplicated | unconsidered | uncooperative |
| uncoated | uncomplimentary | unconsolidated | uncoordinated |
| uncollected | uncompounded | unconstrained | uncorrected |
| uncolored | uncomprehending | unconsumed | uncorroborated |
| uncombed | unconcealed | unconsummated | uncountable |
| uncombined | unconfined | uncontaminated | uncreative |
| uncomely | unconfirmed | uncontested | uncredited |
| uncomic | unconformable | uncontrolled | uncropped |
| uncommercial | uncongenial | uncontroversial | uncrowded |
| uncompensated | unconnected | unconverted | uncrowned |
| uncomplaining | unconquered | unconvincing | uncrystallized |

**unc·tion** \ˈəŋk-shən\ *n* **1** : the act of anointing as a rite of consecration or healing **2** : exaggerated or insincere earnestness of language or manner

**unc·tu·ous** \ˈəŋk-chə-wəs\ *adj* [ME, fr. MF or ML; MF *unctueus*, fr. ML *unctuosus*, fr. L *unctus* act of anointing, fr. *unguere* to anoint] **1** : FATTY, OILY **2** : insincerely smooth in speech and manner ⟨an ∼ politician⟩ — **unc·tu·ous·ly** *adv*

**un·curl** \ˌən-ˈkərl\ *vb* : to make or become straightened out from a curled or coiled position

**un·cut** \ˌən-ˈkət\ *adj* **1** : not cut down or into **2** : not shaped by cutting ⟨an ∼ diamond⟩ **3** : not having the folds of the leaves slit ⟨an ∼ book⟩ **4** : not abridged or curtailed ⟨the ∼ version of the film⟩ **5** : not diluted ⟨∼ heroin⟩

**un·daunt·ed** \-ˈdȯn-təd\ *adj* : not daunted : not discouraged or dismayed ♦ *Synonyms* BOLD, BRAVE, DAUNTLESS, FEARLESS, INTREPID, VALIANT — **un·daunt·ed·ly** *adv*

**un·de·ceive** \ˌən-di-ˈsēv\ *vb* : to free from deception, illusion, or error

**un·de·mon·stra·tive** \ˌən-di-ˈmän-strə-tiv\ *adj* : restrained in expression of feeling : RESERVED

**un·de·ni·able** \ˌən-di-ˈnī-ə-bəl\ *adj* **1** : plainly true : INCONTESTABLE **2** : unquestionably excellent or genuine ♦ *Synonyms* INCONTROVERTIBLE, INDISPUTABLE, INDUBITABLE, UNQUESTIONABLE — **un·de·ni·ably** \-blē\ *adv*

**¹un·der** \ˈən-dər\ *adv* **1** : in or into a position below or beneath something **2** : below some quantity, level, or limit ⟨$10 or ∼⟩ **3** : in or into a condition of subjection, subordination, or unconsciousness ⟨the ether put him ∼⟩

**²un·der** \ˈən-dər, ˈən-\ *prep* **1** : lower than and overhung, surmounted, or sheltered by ⟨∼ a tree⟩ **2** : subject to the authority or guidance of ⟨served ∼ him⟩ ⟨was ∼ contract⟩ **3** : subject to the action or effect of ⟨∼ the influence of alcohol⟩ **4** : within the division or grouping of ⟨items ∼ this heading⟩ **5** : less or lower than (as in size, amount, or rank) ⟨earns ∼ $5000⟩

**³under** \ˈən-dər\ *adj* **1** : lying below, beneath, or on the ventral side **2** : facing or protruding downward **3** : SUBORDINATE **4** : lower than usual, proper, or desired in amount, quality, or degree

**un·der·achiev·er** \ˌən-dər-ə-ˈchē-vər\ *n* : one (as a student) who performs below an expected level of proficiency

**un·der·act** \-ˈakt\ *vb* : to perform feebly or with restraint

**un·der·ac·tive** \-ˈak-tiv\ *adj* : characterized by abnormally low activity ⟨an ∼ thyroid gland⟩ — **un·der·ac·tiv·i·ty** \-ˌak-ˈti-və-tē\ *n*

**un·der·age** \-ˈāj\ *adj* : of less than mature or legal age

**un·der·arm** \-ˈärm\ *adj* **1** : UNDERHAND **2** ⟨an ∼ throw⟩ **2** : placed under or on the underside of the arms ⟨∼ seams⟩ — **underarm** *adv* or *n*

**un·der·bel·ly** \ˈən-dər-ˌbe-lē\ *n* **1** : a vulnerable area **2** : the underside of a body or mass

**un·der·bid** \ˌən-dər-ˈbid\ *vb* **-bid; -bidding** **1** : to bid less than another **2** : to bid too low

**un·der·body** \ˈən-dər-ˌbä-dē\ *n* : the lower parts of the body of a vehicle

**un·der·bred** \ˌən-dər-ˈbred\ *adj* : marked by lack of good breeding

**un·der·brush** \ˈən-dər-ˌbrəsh\ *n* : shrubs, bushes, or small trees growing beneath large trees

**un·der·car·riage** \-ˌka-rij\ *n* **1** : a supporting framework or underside (as of an automobile) **2** : the landing gear of an airplane

**un·der·charge** \ˌən-dər-ˈchärj\ *vb* : to charge (as a person) too little — **undercharge** \ˈən-dər-ˌchärj\ *n*

**un·der·class** \ˈən-dər-ˌklas\ *n* : LOWER CLASS

**un·der·class·man** \ˌən-dər-ˈklas-mən\ *n* : a member of the freshman or sophomore class

**un·der·clothes** \ˈən-dər-ˌklōthz\ *n pl* : UNDERWEAR

**un·der·cloth·ing** \-ˌklō-thiŋ\ *n* : UNDERWEAR

**un·der·coat** \-ˌkōt\ *n* **1** : a coat worn under another **2** : a growth of short hair or fur partly concealed by the longer and usu. coarser hairs of a mammal **3** : a coat of paint under another

**un·der·coat·ing** \-ˌkō-tiŋ\ *n* : a special waterproof coating applied to the underside of a vehicle

**un·der·cov·er** \ˌən-dər-ˈkə-vər\ *adj* : acting or executed in secret; *esp* : employed or engaged in secret investigation ⟨an ∼ agent⟩

**un·der·croft** \ˈən-dər-ˌkrȯft\ *n* [ME, fr. *under* + *crofte* crypt, fr. MD, fr. ML *crupta*, fr. L *crypta*] : a vaulted chamber under a church

**un·der·cur·rent** \-ˌkər-ənt\ *n* **1** : a current below the surface **2** : a hidden tendency of feeling or opinion ⟨an ∼ of dread⟩

**un·der·cut** \ˌən-dər-ˈkət\ *vb* **-cut; -cutting** **1** : to cut away the underpart of **2** : to offer to sell or to work at a lower rate than **3** : to strike (the ball) obliquely downward so as to give a backward spin or elevation to the shot — **un·der·cut** \ˈən-dər-ˌkət\ *n*

**un·der·de·vel·oped** \ˌən-dər-di-ˈve-ləpt\ *adj* **1** : not normally or adequately developed ⟨∼ muscles⟩ **2** : having a relatively

| | | | |
|---|---|---|---|
| uncultivated | undamaged | undecorated | undemanding |
| uncultured | undamped | undefeated | undemocratic |
| uncured | undated | undefended | undenominational |
| uncurious | undecided | undefiled | undependable |
| uncurtained | undecipherable | undefinable | |
| uncustomary | undeclared | undefined | |

low level of economic development ⟨the ~ nations⟩

**un·der·dog** \'ən-dər-ˌdȯg\ n : the loser or predicted loser in a struggle

**un·der·done** \ˌən-dər-'dən\ adj : not thoroughly done or cooked : RARE

**un·der·draw·ers** \'ən-dər-ˌdrȯrz, -ˌdrȯ-ərz\ n pl : UNDERPANTS

**un·der·draw·ing** \'ən-dər-ˌdrȯ-iŋ\ n : a preliminary sketch made prior to painting

**un·der·em·pha·size** \ˌən-dər-'em-fə-ˌsīz\ vb : to emphasize inadequately — **un·der·em·pha·sis** \-səs\ n

**un·der·em·ployed** \-im-'plȯid\ adj : having less than full-time or adequate employment

**un·der·es·ti·mate** \-'es-tə-ˌmāt\ vb : to set too low a value on

**un·der·ex·pose** \-ik-'spōz\ vb : to expose (a photographic plate or film) for less time than is needed — **un·der·ex·po·sure** \-'spō-zhər\ n

**un·der·feed** \ˌən-dər-'fēd\ vb -fed \-'fed\; -feed·ing : to feed with too little food

**un·der·foot** \-'fu̇t\ adv 1 : under the feet ⟨flowers trampled ~⟩ 2 : close about one's feet : in the way

**un·der·fur** \'ən-dər-ˌfər\ n : an undercoat of fur esp. when thick and soft

**un·der·gar·ment** \-ˌgär-mənt\ n : a garment to be worn under another

**un·der·gird** \ˌən-dər-'gərd\ vb : to brace up : STRENGTHEN

**un·der·go** \ˌən-dər-'gō\ vb -went \-'went\; -gone \-'gȯn, -'gän\; -go·ing 1 : to submit to : ENDURE 2 : to go through : EXPERIENCE ⟨~ a change⟩

**un·der·grad** \'ən-dər-ˌgrad\ n : UNDERGRADUATE

**un·der·grad·u·ate** \ˌən-dər-'gra-jə-wət, -jə-ˌwāt\ n : a student at a university or college who has not received a first degree

¹**un·der·ground** \ˌən-dər-'grau̇nd\ adv 1 : beneath the surface of the earth 2 : in or into hiding or secret operation

²**un·der·ground** \'ən-dər-ˌgrau̇nd\ n 1 : a space under the surface of the ground; esp : SUBWAY 2 : a secret political movement or group; esp : an organized body working in secret to overthrow a government or an occupying power 3 : an avant-garde group or movement that operates outside the establishment

³**underground** \'ən-dər-ˌgrau̇nd\ adj 1 : being, growing, operating, or located below the surface of the ground ⟨~ stems⟩ 2 : conducted by secret means 3 : produced or published by the underground ⟨~ publications⟩; also : of or relating to the avant-garde underground

**un·der·growth** \'ən-dər-ˌgrōth\ n : low growth (as of herbs and shrubs) on the floor of a forest

¹**un·der·hand** \'ən-dər-ˌhand\ adv 1 : in an underhanded or secret manner 2 : with an underhand motion

²**underhand** adj 1 : UNDERHANDED 2 : made with the hand kept below the level of the shoulder ⟨an ~ pitch⟩

¹**un·der·hand·ed** \ˌən-dər-'han-dəd\ adv : UNDERHAND

²**underhanded** adj : marked by secrecy and

deception ⟨~ tactics⟩ — **un·der·hand·ed·ly** adv — **un·der·hand·ed·ness** n

**un·der·lie** \-'lī\ vb -lay \-'lā\; -lain \-'lān\; -ly·ing \-'lī-iŋ\ 1 : to lie or be situated under 2 : to be at the basis of : form the foundation of : SUPPORT

**un·der·line** \'ən-dər-ˌlīn\ vb 1 : to draw a line under 2 : EMPHASIZE, STRESS — **underline** n

**un·der·ling** \'ən-dər-liŋ\ n : SUBORDINATE, INFERIOR

**un·der·lip** \ˌən-dər-'lip\ n : the lower lip

**un·der·ly·ing** \ˌən-dər-'lī-iŋ\ adj 1 : lying under or below 2 : FUNDAMENTAL, BASIC ⟨~ principles⟩

**un·der·mine** \-'mīn\ vb 1 : to excavate beneath 2 : to weaken or wear away secretly or gradually ⟨~ authority⟩

**un·der·most** \'ən-dər-ˌmōst\ adj : lowest in relative position — **undermost** adv

¹**un·der·neath** \ˌən-dər-'nēth\ prep 1 : directly under 2 : under subjection to

²**underneath** adv 1 : below a surface or object : BENEATH 2 : on the lower side

**un·der·nour·ished** \ˌən-dər-'nər-isht\ adj : supplied with insufficient nourishment — **un·der·nour·ish·ment** \-'nər-ish-mənt\ n

**un·der·pants** \'ən-dər-ˌpants\ n pl : a usu. short undergarment for the lower trunk : DRAWERS

**un·der·part** \-ˌpärt\ n : a part lying on the lower side (as of a bird or mammal)

**un·der·pass** \-ˌpas\ n : a crossing of a highway and another way (as a road) at different levels; also : the lower level

**un·der·pay** \ˌən-dər-'pā\ vb : to pay less than what is normal or required

**un·der·pin·ning** \'ən-dər-ˌpi-niŋ\ n : the material and construction (as a foundation) used for support of a structure — **un·der·pin** \ˌən-dər-'pin\ vb

**un·der·play** \ˌən-dər-'plā\ vb : to treat or handle with restraint; esp : to play a role with subdued force

**un·der·pop·u·lat·ed** \ˌən-dər-'pä-pyə-ˌlā-təd\ adj : having a lower than normal or desirable density of population

**un·der·priv·i·leged** \-'priv-lijd, -'pri-və-lijd\ adj : having fewer esp. economic and social privileges than others

**un·der·pro·duc·tion** \ˌən-dər-prə-'dək-shən\ n : the production of less than enough to satisfy the demand or of less than the usual supply

**un·der·rate** \-'rāt\ vb : to rate or value too low

**un·der·rep·re·sent·ed** \-ˌre-pri-'zen-təd\ adj : inadequately represented

**un·der·score** \'ən-dər-ˌskȯr\ vb 1 : to draw a line under : UNDERLINE 2 : EMPHASIZE — **underscore** n

¹**un·der·sea** \ˌən-dər-'sē\ adj : being, carried on, or used beneath the surface of the sea

²**undersea** or **un·der·seas** \-'sēz\ adv : beneath the surface of the sea

**un·der·sec·re·tary** \ˌən-dər-'se-krə-ˌter-ē\ n : a secretary immediately subordinate to a principal secretary ⟨~ of state⟩

**un·der·sell** \-'sel\ vb -sold \-'sōld\; -sell·ing : to sell articles cheaper than

**un·der·sexed** \-'sekst\ *adj* : deficient in sexual desire

**un·der·shirt** \'ən-dər-ˌshərt\ *n* : a collarless undergarment with or without sleeves

**un·der·shoot** \ˌən-dər-'shüt\ *vb* **-shot** \-'shät\; **-shoot·ing** 1 : to shoot short of or below (a target) 2 : to fall short of (a runway) in landing an airplane

**un·der·shorts** \'ən-dər-ˌshôrts\ *n pl* : underpants for men or boys

**un·der·shot** \'ən-dər-ˌshät\ *adj* 1 : moved by water passing beneath ⟨an ~ waterwheel⟩ 2 : having the lower front teeth projecting beyond the upper when the mouth is closed

**un·der·side** \'ən-dər-ˌsīd, ˌən-dər-'sīd\ *n* : the side or surface lying underneath

**un·der·signed** \'ən-dər-ˌsīnd\ *n, pl* **undersigned** : one whose name is signed at the end of a document

**un·der·sized** \ˌən-dər-'sīzd\ *also* **un·der·size** \-'sīz\ *adj* : of a size less than is common, proper, or normal

**un·der·skirt** \'ən-dər-ˌskərt\ *n* : a skirt worn under an outer skirt; *esp* : PETTICOAT

**un·der·staffed** \ˌən-dər-'staft\ *adj* : inadequately staffed

**un·der·stand** \ˌən-dər-'stand\ *vb* **-stood** \-'stud\; **-stand·ing** 1 : to grasp the meaning of : COMPREHEND 2 : to have thorough or technical acquaintance with or expertness in ⟨~ finance⟩ 3 : to have reason to believe ⟨I ~ you are leaving tomorrow⟩ 4 : INTERPRET ⟨we ~ this to be a refusal⟩ 5 : to have a sympathetic attitude 6 : to accept as settled ⟨it is *understood* that he will pay the expenses⟩ — **un·der·stand·able** \-'stan-də-bəl\ *adj*

**un·der·stand·ably** \-blē\ *adv* : as can be easily understood

¹**un·der·stand·ing** \ˌən-dər-'stan-diŋ\ *n* 1 : knowledge and ability to judge : INTELLIGENCE ⟨a person of ~⟩ 2 : agreement of opinion or feeling 3 : a mutual agreement informally or tacitly entered into

²**understanding** *adj* : endowed with understanding : TOLERANT, SYMPATHETIC

**un·der·state** \ˌən-dər-'stāt\ *vb* 1 : to represent as less than is the case 2 : to state with restraint esp. for effect — **un·der·state·ment** *n*

**un·der·stood** \ˌən-dər-'stud\ *adj* 1 : agreed upon 2 : IMPLICIT

**un·der·sto·ry** \'ən-dər-ˌstôr-ē\ *n* : the vegetative layer between the top layer of a forest and the ground cover

**un·der·study** \'ən-dər-ˌstə-dē\ *n* : one who is prepared to act another's part or take over another's duties — **under·study** \'ən-dər-ˌstə-dē, ˌən-dər-'stə-dē\ *vb*

**un·der·sur·face** \'ən-dər-ˌsər-fəs\ *n* : UNDERSIDE

**un·der·take** \ˌən-dər-'tāk\ *vb* **-took** \-'tuk\; **-tak·en** \-'tā-kən\; **-tak·ing** 1 : to take upon oneself : set about ⟨~ a task⟩ 2 : to put oneself under obligation 3 : GUARANTEE, PROMISE

**un·der·tak·er** \'ən-dər-ˌtā-kər\ *n* : one whose business is to prepare the dead for burial and to arrange and manage funerals

**un·der·tak·ing** \'ən-dər-ˌtā-kiŋ, ˌən-dər-'tā-kiŋ *only*\ *n* 1 : the act of one who undertakes or engages in any project 2 : the business of an undertaker 3 : something undertaken 4 : PROMISE, GUARANTEE

**under–the–counter** *adj* : UNLAWFUL, ILLICIT ⟨~ sale of drugs⟩

**un·der·tone** \'ən-dər-ˌtōn\ *n* 1 : a low or subdued tone or utterance 2 : a subdued color (as seen through and modifying another color)

**un·der·tow** \-ˌtō\ *n* : the current beneath the surface that flows seaward when waves are breaking upon the shore

**un·der·val·ue** \ˌən-dər-'val-yü\ *vb* 1 : to value or estimate below the real worth 2 : to esteem lightly

**un·der·wa·ter** \ˌən-dər-'wȯ-tər, -'wä-\ *adj* : lying, growing, worn, or operating below the surface of the water ⟨an ~ camera⟩ — **un·der·wa·ter** *adv*

**under way** \-'wā\ *adv* 1 : into motion from a standstill 2 : in progress

**un·der·wear** \'ən-dər-ˌwer\ *n* : clothing or a garment worn next to the skin and under other clothing

**un·der·weight** \'ən-dər-ˌwāt\ *adj* : weighing below what is normal, average, or necessary — **underweight** *n*

**un·der·wire** \'ən-dər-ˌwī(-ə)r\ *n* : a wire running through the bottom of a brassiere to aid in support

**un·der·world** \'ən-dər-ˌwərld\ *n* 1 : the place of departed souls : HADES 2 : the side of the world opposite to one 3 : the world of organized crime

**un·der·write** \'ən-dər-ˌrīt, ˌən-dər-'rīt\ *vb* **-wrote** \-ˌrōt, -'rōt\; **-writ·ten** \-ˌri-tᵊn, -'ri-tᵊn\; **-writ·ing** 1 : to write under or at the end of something else 2 : to set one's name to an insurance policy and thereby become answerable for a designated loss or damage 3 : to subscribe to : agree to 4 : to guarantee financial support of — **un·der·writ·er** *n*

**un·de·sign·ing** \ˌən-di-'zī-niŋ\ *adj* : having no artful, ulterior, or fraudulent purpose : SINCERE

**un·de·sir·able** \-'zī-rə-bəl\ *adj* : not desirable — **undesirable** *n*

**un·de·vi·at·ing** \ˌən-'dē-vē-ˌā-tiŋ\ *adj* : keeping a true course

**un·dies** \'ən-dēz\ *n pl* : UNDERWEAR; *esp* : women's underwear

| | | | |
|---|---|---|---|
| undeserved | undifferentiated | undirected | undisputed |
| undeserving | undigested | undisciplined | undissolved |
| undesired | undignified | undisclosed | undistinguished |
| undetected | undiluted | undiscovered | undistributed |
| undetermined | undiminished | undiscriminating | undisturbed |
| undeterred | undimmed | undisguised | undivided |
| undeveloped | undiplomatic | undismayed | |

**un·do** \ˌən-ˈdü\ *vb* **-did** \-ˈdid\; **-done** \-ˈdən\; **-do·ing** 1 : to make or become unfastened or loosened : OPEN 2 : to make null or as if not done : REVERSE 3 : to bring to ruin; *also* : UPSET

**un·doc·u·ment·ed** \ˌən-ˈdä-kyə-ˌmen-təd\ *adj* 1 : not supported by documentary evidence 2 : lacking documents required for legal immigration

**un·do·ing** *n* : a cause of ruin

**un·doubt·ed** \-ˈdau̇-təd\ *adj* : not doubted or called into question : CERTAIN — **un·doubt·ed·ly** *adv*

¹**un·dress** \ˌən-ˈdres\ *vb* : to remove the clothes or covering of : STRIP, DISROBE

²**undress** *n* 1 : informal dress; *esp* : a loose robe or dressing gown 2 : ordinary dress 3 : NUDITY

**un·due** \-ˈdü, -ˈdyü\ *adj* 1 : not due 2 : exceeding or violating propriety or fitness : EXCESSIVE ⟨~ force⟩

**un·du·lant** \ˈən-jə-lənt, ˈən-də-, -dyə-\ *adj* : rising and falling in waves ⟨~ hills⟩

**undulant fever** *n* : a human disease caused by bacteria from infected domestic animals or their products and marked by intermittent fever, chills, headache, weakness, and weight loss

**un·du·late** \-ˌlāt\ *vb* **-lat·ed; -lat·ing** [LL *undula* small wave, fr. L *unda* wave] 1 : to have a wavelike motion or appearance 2 : to rise and fall in pitch or volume ⟨*undulating* music⟩

**un·du·la·tion** \ˌən-jə-ˈlā-shən, ˌən-də-, -dyə-\ *n* 1 : wavy or wavelike motion 2 : pulsation of sound 3 : a wavy appearance or outline — **un·du·la·to·ry** \ˈən-jə-lə-ˌtȯr-ē, ˈən-də-, -dyə-\ *adj*

**un·du·ly** \ˌən-ˈdü-lē, ˈən-, -ˈdyü-\ *adv* : in an undue manner : EXCESSIVELY

**un·dy·ing** \-ˈdī-iŋ\ *adj* : not dying : IMMORTAL, PERPETUAL

**un·earned** \-ˈərnd\ *adj* : not earned by labor, service, or skill ⟨~ income⟩

**un·earth** \ˌən-ˈərth\ *vb* 1 : to dig up out of or as if out of the earth ⟨~ buried treasure⟩ 2 : to bring to light : DISCOVER ⟨~ a secret⟩

**un·earth·ly** \-lē\ *adj* 1 : not of or belonging to the earth 2 : SUPERNATURAL, WEIRD; *also* : ABSURD

**un·easy** \ˌən-ˈē-zē\ *adj* 1 : AWKWARD, EMBARRASSED ⟨~ among strangers⟩ 2 : disturbed by pain or worry; *also* : RESTLESS 3 : UNSTABLE ⟨an ~ truce⟩ — **un·eas·i·ly** \-ˈē-zə-lē\ *adv* — **un·eas·i·ness** \-ˈē-zē-nəs\ *n*

**un·em·ployed** \ˌən-im-ˈplȯid\ *adj* : not being used; *also* : having no job

**un·em·ploy·ment** \-ˈplȯi-mənt\ *n* 1 : lack of employment 2 : money paid at regular intervals (as by a government agency) to an unemployed person

**un·end·ing** \ˌən-ˈen-diŋ\ *adj* : having no ending : ENDLESS

**un·equal** \ˌən-ˈē-kwəl\ *adj* 1 : not alike (as in size, amount, number, or value) 2 : not uniform : VARIABLE 3 : badly balanced or matched 4 : INADEQUATE, INSUFFICIENT ⟨~ to the task⟩ — **un·equal·ly** *adv*

**un·equaled** *or* **un·equalled** \-kwəld\ *adj* : not equaled : UNPARALLELED ⟨an artist of ~ talent⟩

**un·equiv·o·cal** \ˌən-i-ˈkwi-və-kəl\ *adj* : leaving no doubt : CLEAR — **un·equiv·o·cal·ly** *adv*

**un·err·ing** \ˌən-ˈer-iŋ, -ˈər-\ *adj* : making no errors : CERTAIN, UNFAILING ⟨~ accuracy⟩ — **un·err·ing·ly** *adv*

**UNES·CO** \yu̇-ˈnes-kō\ *abbr* United Nations Educational, Scientific, and Cultural Organization

**un·even** \ˌən-ˈē-vən\ *adj* 1 : ODD 3 2 : not even : not level or smooth : RUGGED, RAGGED 3 : IRREGULAR; *also* : varying in quality — **un·even·ly** *adv* — **un·even·ness** *n*

**un·event·ful** \ˌən-i-ˈvent-fəl\ *adj* : lacking interesting or noteworthy incidents — **un·event·ful·ly** *adv*

**un·evolved** \ˌən-i-ˈvälvd\ *adj* 1 : not fully developed ⟨an ~ wine⟩ 2 : lacking cultural refinement

**un·ex·am·pled** \ˌən-ig-ˈzam-pəld\ *adj* : UNPRECEDENTED, UNPARALLELED ⟨fought with ~ passion⟩

**un·ex·cep·tion·able** \ˌən-ik-ˈsep-shə-nə-bəl\ *adj* : not open to exception or objection : beyond reproach

**un·ex·pect·ed** \ˌən-ik-ˈspek-təd\ *adj* : not expected : UNFORESEEN — **un·ex·pect·ed·ly** *adv*

**un·fail·ing** \ˌən-ˈfā-liŋ\ *adj* 1 : not failing, flagging, or waning : CONSTANT 2 : INEXHAUSTIBLE ⟨a subject of ~ interest⟩ 3 : INFALLIBLE, SURE ⟨an ~ test⟩ — **un·fail·ing·ly** *adv*

**un·fair** \-ˈfer\ *adj* 1 : marked by injustice, partiality, or deception : UNJUST 2 : not equitable in business dealings — **un·fair·ly** *adv* — **un·fair·ness** *n*

**un·faith·ful** \ˌən-ˈfāth-fəl\ *adj* 1 : not observant of vows, allegiance, or duty : DISLOYAL 2 : INACCURATE, UNTRUST-

| | | | |
|---|---|---|---|
| undogmatic | uneatable | unenforceable | unexciting |
| undomesticated | uneaten | unenforced | unexpired |
| undone | uneconomic | unenlightened | unexplained |
| undoubled | uneconomical | unenterprising | unexploded |
| undramatic | unedifying | unenthusiastic | unexplored |
| undraped | unedited | unenviable | unexposed |
| undreamed | uneducated | unequipped | unexpressed |
| undressed | unembarrassed | unessential | unexpurgated |
| undrinkable | unemotional | unethical | unfading |
| undulled | unemphatic | unexamined | unfaltering |
| undutiful | unenclosed | unexcelled | |
| undyed | unencumbered | unexceptional | |
| uneager | unendurable | unexcited | |

WORTHY ⟨an ~ copy of a document⟩ — **un·faith·ful·ly** adv   **un·faith·ful·ness** n

**un·fa·mil·iar** \ˌən-fə-'mil-yər\ adj 1 : not well-known : STRANGE ⟨an ~ place⟩ 2 : not well acquainted ⟨~ with the subject⟩ — **un·fa·mil·iar·i·ty** \-ˌmi-lē-'er-, -'yer-\ n

**un·fas·ten** \ˌən-'fa-sᵊn\ vb : to make or become loose : UNDO, DETACH

**un·feel·ing** \-'fē-liŋ\ adj 1 : lacking feeling : INSENSATE 2 : HARDHEARTED, CRUEL — **un·feel·ing·ly** adv

**un·feigned** \-'fānd\ adj : not feigned : not hypocritical : GENUINE

**un·fet·ter** \-'fe-tər\ vb 1 : to free from fetters 2 : LIBERATE

**un·fil·ial** \ˌən-'fi-lē-əl, -'fil-yəl\ adj : not observing the obligations of a child to a parent : UNDUTIFUL

**un·fin·ished** \ˌən-'fi-nisht\ adj 1 : not brought to an end 2 : being in a rough or unpolished state

¹**un·fit** \-'fit\ adj : not fit or suitable; esp : physically or mentally unsound ⟨~ for army service⟩ — **un·fit·ness** n

²**unfit** vb : to make unfit : DISQUALIFY

**un·fix** \-'fiks\ vb 1 : to loosen from a fastening : DETACH 2 : UNSETTLE

**un·flap·pa·ble** \-'fla-pə-bəl\ adj : not easily upset or panicked — **un·flap·pa·bly** adv

**un·fledged** \ˌən-'flejd\ adj : not feathered or ready for flight; also : IMMATURE, CALLOW

**un·flinch·ing** \-'flin-chiŋ\ adj : not flinching or shrinking : STEADFAST — **un·flinch·ing·ly** adv

**un·fold** \-'fōld\ vb 1 : to open the folds of : open up 2 : to lay open to view : DISCLOSE 3 : BLOSSOM, DEVELOP

**un·for·get·ta·ble** \ˌən-fər-'ge-tə-bəl\ adj : incapable of being forgotten ⟨an ~ event⟩ — **un·for·get·ta·bly** \-blē\ adv

**un·formed** \-'fȯrmd\ adj : not regularly formed or ordered : UNDEVELOPED

**un·for·tu·nate** \-'fȯr-chə-nət\ adj 1 : not fortunate : UNLUCKY 2 : attended with misfortune 3 : UNSUITABLE ⟨an ~ choice of words⟩ — **unfortunate** n

**un·for·tu·nate·ly** \-nət-lē\ adv 1 : in an unfortunate manner 2 : it is unfortunate

**un·found·ed** \ˌən-'faȯn-dəd\ adj : lacking a sound basis : GROUNDLESS

**un·freeze** \-'frēz\ vb **-froze** \-'frōz\; **-fro·zen** \-'frō-zᵊn\; **-freez·ing** 1 : to cause to thaw 2 : to remove from a freeze ⟨~ prices⟩

**un·fre·quent·ed** \ˌən-frē-'kwen-təd; ˌən-

'frē-kwən-\ adj : seldom visited or traveled over

**un·friend·ly** \ˌən-'frend-lē\ adj 1 : not friendly or kind : HOSTILE 2 : UNFAVORABLE ⟨~ to new business⟩ — **un·friend·li·ness** \-lē-nəs\ n

**un·frock** \-'fräk\ vb : DEFROCK

**un·fruit·ful** \-'früt-fəl\ adj 1 : not producing fruit or offspring : BARREN 2 : yielding no valuable result : UNPROFITABLE — **un·fruit·ful·ness** n

**un·furl** \-'fərl\ vb : to loose from a furled state : UNFOLD

**un·gain·ly** \-'gān-lē\ adj [un- + obs. gainly proper, becoming, fr. gain direct, handy, fr. ME geyn, fr. OE gen, fr. ON gegn against] : CLUMSY, AWKWARD — **un·gain·li·ness** \-lē-nəs\ n

**un·gen·er·ous** \ˌən-'je-nə-rəs\ adj : not generous or liberal : STINGY

**un·glued** \ˌən-'glüd\ adj : UPSET, DISORDERED ⟨became ~ when she was refused⟩

**un·god·ly** \ˌən-'gäd-lē, -'gȯd-\ adj 1 : IMPIOUS, IRRELIGIOUS 2 : SINFUL, WICKED 3 : OUTRAGEOUS ⟨an ~ hour⟩ — **un·god·li·ness** \-lē-nəs\ n

**un·gov·ern·able** \-'gə-vər-nə-bəl\ adj : not capable of being governed, guided, or restrained : UNRULY

**un·gra·cious** \-'grā-shəs\ adj 1 : not courteous : RUDE 2 : not pleasing : DISAGREEABLE ⟨an ~ task⟩

**un·grate·ful** \ˌən-'grāt-fəl\ adj 1 : not thankful for favors 2 : DISAGREEABLE; also : THANKLESS — **un·grate·ful·ly** adv — **un·grate·ful·ness** n

**un·guard·ed** \-'gär-dəd\ adj 1 : UNPROTECTED 2 : DIRECT, INCAUTIOUS ⟨~ remarks⟩

**un·guent** \'əŋ-gwənt, 'ən-\ n : a soothing or healing salve : OINTMENT

¹**un·gu·late** \'əŋ-gyə-lət, 'ən-, -ˌlāt\ adj [LL ungulatus, fr. L ungula hoof, fr. unguis nail, hoof] : having hoofs

²**ungulate** n : a hoofed mammal (as a cow, horse, or rhinoceros)

**un·hal·lowed** \ˌən-'ha-lōd\ adj 1 : not consecrated : UNHOLY 2 : IMPIOUS, PROFANE 3 : contrary to accepted standards : IMMORAL

**un·hand** \ˌən-'hand\ vb : to remove the hand from : let go

**un·hand·some** \-'han-səm\ adj 1 : not beautiful or handsome : HOMELY 2 : UNBECOMING 3 : DISCOURTEOUS, RUDE

**un·handy** \-'han-dē\ adj : INCONVENIENT; also : AWKWARD

**un·hap·py** \-'ha-pē\ adj 1 : UNLUCKY,

---

| | | | |
|---|---|---|---|
| unfashionable | unfitted | unfortified | unglazed |
| unfashionably | unflagging | unframed | ungoverned |
| unfathomable | unflattering | unfree | ungraceful |
| unfavorable | unflavored | unfulfilled | ungracefully |
| unfavorably | unfocused | unfunded | ungraded |
| unfeasible | unfolded | unfunny | ungrammatical |
| unfeminine | unforced | unfurnished | unground |
| unfenced | unforeseeable | unfussy | ungrudging |
| unfermented | unforeseen | ungentle | unguided |
| unfertilized | unforgivable | ungentlemanly | unhackneyed |
| unfilled | unforgiving | ungerminated | unhampered |
| unfiltered | unformulated | unglamorous | |

UNFORTUNATE ⟨an ∼ coincidence⟩ **2** : SAD, MISERABLE **3** : INAPPROPRIATE ⟨an ∼ choice⟩ — **un·hap·pi·ly** \-'ha-pə-lē\ adv — **un·hap·pi·ness** \-pē-nəs\ n

**un·har·ness** \-'här-nəs\ vb : to remove the harness from (as a horse)

**un·healthy** \-'hel-thē\ adj **1** : not conducive to health : UNWHOLESOME ⟨∼ foods⟩ **2** : SICKLY, DISEASED

**un·heard** \-'hərd\ adj **1** : not heard **2** : not granted a hearing

**unheard–of** adj : previously unknown; esp : UNPRECEDENTED ⟨moving at ∼ speeds⟩

**un·hinge** \,ən-'hinj\ vb **1** : to make unstable esp. mentally ⟨∼ by grief⟩ **2** : to take from the hinges

**un·hitch** \-'hich\ vb : UNFASTEN, LOOSE

**un·ho·ly** \-'hō-lē\ adj **1** : not holy : PROFANE, WICKED **2** : very unpleasant ⟨an ∼ mess⟩ — **un·ho·li·ness** \-lē-nəs\ n

**un·hook** \-'huk\ vb : to loose from a hook

**un·horse** \-'hȯrs\ vb : to dislodge from or as if from a horse

**uni·cam·er·al** \,yü-ni-'ka-mə-rəl\ adj : having a single legislative house or chamber

**UNI·CEF** \'yü-nə-,sef\ abbr [United Nations International Children's Emergency Fund, its former name] United Nations Children's Fund

**uni·cel·lu·lar** \,yü-ni-'sel-yə-lər\ adj : having or consisting of a single cell

**uni·corn** \'yü-nə-,kȯrn\ n [ME unicorne, fr. AF, fr. LL unicornis, fr. L, having one horn, fr. unus one + cornu horn] : a mythical animal with one horn in the middle of the forehead

**uni·cy·cle** \'yü-ni-,sī-kəl\ n : a vehicle that has a single wheel and is usu. propelled by pedals

**uni·di·rec·tion·al** \,yü-ni-də-'rek-shə-nəl, -dī-\ adj : having, moving in, or responsive in a single direction

**uni·fi·ca·tion** \,yü-nə-fə-'kā-shən\ n : the act, process, or result of unifying : the state of being unified

**¹uni·form** \'yü-nə-,fȯrm\ adj **1** : not varying ⟨∼ procedures⟩ **2** : of the same form with others — **uni·form·ly** adv

**²uniform** vb : to clothe with a uniform

**³uniform** n : distinctive dress worn by members of a particular group (as an army or a police force)

**uni·for·mi·ty** \,yü-nə-'fȯr-mə-tē\ n, pl **-ties** : the state of being uniform

**uni·fy** \'yü-nə-,fī\ vb **-fied; -fy·ing** : to make into a coherent whole : UNITE

**uni·lat·er·al** \,yü-nə-'la-tə-rəl\ adj : of, having, affecting, or done by one side only — **uni·lat·er·al·ly** adv

**un·im·peach·able** \,ən-im-'pē-chə-bəl\ adj : not liable to accusation : IRREPROACHABLE ⟨an ∼ reputation⟩

**un·in·hib·it·ed** \,ən-in-'hi-bə-təd\ adj : free from inhibition; also : boisterously informal — **un·in·hib·it·ed·ly** adv

**un·in·stall** \,ən-in-'stȯl\ vb : to remove (software) from a computer system

**un·in·tel·li·gent** \-'te-lə-jənt\ adj : lacking intelligence

**un·in·tel·li·gi·ble** \-jə-bəl\ adj : not intelligible : OBSCURE ⟨an ∼ voice mail⟩ — **un·in·tel·li·gi·bly** \-blē\ adv

**un·in·ter·est·ed** \,ən-'in-trəs-təd, -tə-rəs-, -tə-,res-\ adj : not interested : not having the mind or feelings engaged or aroused

**un·in·ter·rupt·ed** \,ən-,in-tə-'rəp-təd\ adj : not interrupted : CONTINUOUS

**union** \'yün-yən\ n **1** : an act or instance of uniting two or more things into one : the state of being so united : COMBINATION, JUNCTION **2** : a uniting in marriage **3** : something formed by a combining of parts or members; esp : a confederation of independent individuals (as nations or persons) for some common purpose **4** : an organization of workers (as a labor union or a trade union) formed to advance its members' interests esp. in respect to wages and working conditions **5** : a device emblematic of union used on or as a national flag; also : the upper inner corner of a flag **6** : a device for connecting parts (as of a machine); esp : a coupling for pipes

**union·ise** Brit var of UNIONIZE

**union·ism** \'yün-yə-,ni-zəm\ n **1** : the principle or policy of forming or adhering to a union; esp, cap : adherence to the policy of a firm federal union before or during the U.S. Civil War **2** : the principles or system of trade unions — **union·ist** n

**union·ize** \'yün-yə-,nīz\ vb **-ized; -iz·ing** : to form into or cause to join a labor union — **union·i·za·tion** \,yün-yə-nə-'zā-shən\ n

**union jack** n **1** : a flag consisting of the part of a national flag that signifies union **2** cap U&J : the national flag of the United Kingdom

**unique** \yu-'nēk\ adj **1** : being the only one of its kind : SINGLE, SOLE ⟨each snow-

| | | | |
|---|---|---|---|
| unhardened | unhonored | unimposing | unimpressed |
| unharmed | unhoused | unimpressed | uninstructed |
| unharvested | unhurried | unimpressive | uninstructive |
| unhatched | unhurt | unimproved | uninsured |
| unhealed | unhygienic | unincorporated | unintelligent |
| unhealthful | unidentifiable | uninfected | unintelligible |
| unheated | unidentified | uninfluenced | unintelligibly |
| unheeded | unidiomatic | uninformative | unintended |
| unhelpful | unimaginable | uninformed | unintentional |
| unheralded | unimaginative | uninhabitable | unintentionally |
| unheroic | unimpaired | uninhabited | uninteresting |
| unhesitating | unimpassioned | uninitiated | uninterrupted |
| unhindered | unimpeded | uninjured | uninvited |
| unhistorical | unimportant | uninspired | uninviting |

flake is ~〉 **2** : very unusual : NOTABLE — **unique·ly** adv — **unique·ness** n

**uni·sex** \'yü-,seks\ adj : not distinguishable as male or female; also : suitable or designed for both males and females ⟨a ~ clothing⟩ — **unisex** n

**uni·sex·u·al** \,yü-nə-'sek-shə-wəl\ adj **1** : having only male or only female sex organs **2** : UNISEX

**uni·son** \'yü-nə-sən, -zən\ n [ME unisoun, fr. MF unisson, fr. ML unisonus having the same sound, fr. L unus one + sonus sound] **1** : sameness or identity in musical pitch **2** : the condition of being tuned or sounded at the same pitch or in octaves ⟨sing in ~⟩ **3** : harmonious agreement or union : ACCORD

**unit** \'yü-nət\ n **1** : the smallest whole number greater than zero : ONE **2** : a definite amount or quantity used as a standard of measurement **3** : a single thing, person, or group that is a constituent of a whole; also : a part of a military establishment that has a prescribed organization — **unit** adj

**Uni·tar·i·an** \,yü-nə-'ter-ē-ən\ n : a member of a religious denomination stressing individual freedom of belief — **Uni·tar·i·an·ism** n

**uni·tary** \'yü-nə-,ter-ē\ adj **1** : of or relating to a unit **2** : not divided — **uni·tar·i·ly** \,yü-nə-'ter-ə-lē\ adv

**unite** \yù-'nīt\ vb **unit·ed; unit·ing 1** : to put or join together so as to make one : COMBINE, COALESCE **2** : to join by a legal or moral bond; also : to join in interest or fellowship **3** : AMALGAMATE, CONSOLIDATE **4** : to act in concert

**unit·ed** \yù-'nī-təd\ adj **1** : made one : COMBINED **2** : relating to or produced by joint action **3** : being in agreement : HARMONIOUS

**unit·ize** \'yü-nə-,tīz\ vb **-ized; -iz·ing 1** : to form or convert into a unit **2** : to divide into units

**uni·ty** \'yü-nə-tē\ n, pl **-ties 1** : the quality or state of being or being made one : ONENESS **2** : a definite quantity or combination of quantities taken as one or for which 1 is made to stand in calculation **3** : CONCORD, ACCORD, HARMONY **4** : continuity without change ⟨~ of purpose⟩ **5** : reference of all the parts of a literary or artistic composition to a single main idea **6** : totality of related parts ♦ **Synonyms** SOLIDARITY, UNION, INTEGRITY

**univ** abbr **1** universal **2** university

**uni·valve** \'yü-ni-,valv\ n : a mollusk having a shell with only one piece; esp : GASTROPOD — **univalve** adj

**uni·ver·sal** \,yü-nə-'vər-səl\ adj **1** : including, covering, or affecting the whole without limit or exception : available or applying to everyone ⟨~ privileges⟩ ⟨a ~ rule⟩ **2** : present or occurring everywhere **3** : used or for use among all ⟨a ~

language⟩ **4** : adaptable for various purposes ⟨a ~ remote control⟩ — **uni·ver·sal·ly** adv

**uni·ver·sal·i·ty** \-,vər-'sa-lə-tē\ n : the quality or state of being universal

**uni·ver·sal·ize** \-'vər-sə-,līz\ vb **-ized; -iz·ing** : to make universal : GENERALIZE ⟨would ~ equal rights⟩ — **uni·ver·sal·i·za·tion** \-,vər-sə-lə-'zā-shən\ n

**universal joint** n : a shaft coupling for transmitting rotation from one shaft to another not in a straight line with it

**Universal Product Code** n : a combination of a bar code and numbers by which a scanner can identify a product and usu. assign a price

**uni·verse** \'yü-nə-,vərs\ n [ME, fr. L universum, fr. neut. of universus entire, whole, fr. unus one + versus turned toward, fr. pp. of vertere to turn] : the whole body of things observed or assumed : COSMOS

**uni·ver·si·ty** \,yü-nə-'vər-sə-tē\ n, pl **-ties** : an institution of higher learning authorized to confer degrees in various special fields (as theology, law, and medicine) as well as in the arts and sciences generally

**un·just** \,ən-'jəst\ adj : characterized by injustice — **un·just·ly** adv

**un·kempt** \-'kempt\ adj **1** : lacking order or neatness; also : ROUGH, UNPOLISHED **2** : not combed : DISHEVELED

**un·kind** \-'kīnd\ adj : not kind or sympathetic ⟨an ~ remark⟩ — **un·kind·ly** adv — **un·kind·ness** n

**un·kind·ly** \-'kīnd-lē\ adj : UNKIND — **un·kind·li·ness** n

**un·know·ing** \,ən-'nō-iŋ\ adj : not knowing — **un·know·ing·ly** adv

**un·known** \-'nōn\ adj : not known or not well-known — **unknown** n

**un·lace** \,ən-'lās\ vb : to loose by undoing a lace

**un·lade** \-'lād\ vb **lad·ed; -laded** or **-laden** \-'lā-dᵊn\; **-lad·ing** : to take the load or cargo from : UNLOAD

**un·latch** \-'lach\ vb **1** : to open or loose by lifting the latch **2** : to become loosed or opened

**un·law·ful** \,ən-'lò-fəl\ adj **1** : not lawful : ILLEGAL **2** : ILLEGITIMATE — **un·law·ful·ly** adv

**un·lead·ed** \-'le-dəd\ adj : not treated or mixed with lead or lead compounds

**un·learn** \-'lərn\ vb : to put out of one's knowledge or memory; also : to discard the habit of

**un·learned** \-'lər-nəd for 1; -'lərnd for 2\ adj **1** : UNEDUCATED, ILLITERATE **2** : not gained by study or training

**un·leash** \-'lēsh\ vb : to free from or as if from a leash : let loose

**un·less** \ən-'les, 'ən-,les\ conj : except on condition that ⟨won't go ~ you do⟩

**un·let·tered** \,ən-'le-tərd\ adj : not educated : ILLITERATE

**¹un·like** \-'līk\ adj **1** : not like : DISSIMI-

---

| | | | |
|---|---|---|---|
| unjointed | unknowable | unladylike | unlicensed |
| unjustifiable | unknowledgeable | unlamented | unlighted |
| unjustified | unlabeled | unleavened | unlikable |
| unkept | | | |

LAR, DIFFERENT **2** : UNEQUAL — **un·like·ness** *n*

²**unlike** *prep* **1** : different from ⟨she's quite ∼ her sister⟩ **2** : unusual for ⟨it's ∼ you to be late⟩ **3** : differently from ⟨behaves ∼ his brother⟩

**un·like·li·hood** \ˌən-ˈlī-klē-ˌhùd\ *n* : IMPROBABILITY

**un·like·ly** \-ˈli-klē\ *adj* **1** : not likely : IMPROBABLE **2** : likely to fail

**un·lim·ber** \ˌən-ˈlim-bər\ *vb* : to get ready for action

**un·list·ed** \ˌən-ˈlis-təd\ *adj* **1** : not appearing on a list; *esp* : not appearing in a telephone book **2** : not listed on a stock exchange

**un·load** \-ˈlōd\ *vb* **1** : to take away or off : REMOVE ⟨∼ cargo from a hold⟩; *also* : to get rid of **2** : to take a load from ⟨∼ the ship⟩; *also* : to relieve or set free : UNBURDEN ⟨∼ one's mind of worries⟩ **3** : to draw the charge from ⟨∼ed the gun⟩ **4** : to sell in volume

**un·lock** \-ˈläk\ *vb* **1** : to open or unfasten through release of a lock **2** : RELEASE ⟨∼ a flood of emotions⟩ **3** : DISCLOSE, REVEAL ⟨∼ nature's secrets⟩

**un·looked-for** \-ˈlùkt-ˌfòr\ *adj* : UNEXPECTED

**un·loose** \ˌən-ˈlüs\ *vb* **1** : to relax the strain of : set free; *also* : UNTIE

**un·loos·en** \-ˈlü-sᵊn\ *vb* : UNLOOSE

**un·love·ly** \-ˈləv-lē\ *adj* : having no charm or appeal : not amiable

**un·luck·i·ly** \-ˈlə-kə-lē\ *adv* : UNFORTUNATELY

**un·lucky** \-ˈlə-kē\ *adj* **1** : UNFORTUNATE, ILL-FATED **2** : likely to bring misfortune : INAUSPICIOUS **3** : REGRETTABLE

**un·man** \ˌən-ˈman\ *vb* **1** : to deprive of manly courage **2** : CASTRATE

**un·man·ly** \-ˈman-lē\ *adj* : not manly : COWARDLY; *also* : EFFEMINATE

**un·man·ner·ly** \-ˈma-nər-lē\ *adj* : RUDE, IMPOLITE — **unmannerly** *adv*

**un·mask** \ˌən-ˈmask\ *vb* **1** : to strip of a mask or a disguise : EXPOSE **2** : to remove one's mask

**un·mean·ing** \-ˈmē-niŋ\ *adj* : having no meaning : SENSELESS

**un·me·di·at·ed** \ˌən-ˈmē-dē-ˌā-təd\ *adj* : not mediated : not communicated or transformed by an intervening agency

**un·meet** \-ˈmēt\ *adj* : not meet or fit : UNSUITABLE, IMPROPER

**un·men·tion·able** \-ˈmen-chə-nə-bəl\ *adj* : not fit or proper to be talked about ⟨an ∼ topic⟩

**un·mer·ci·ful** \-ˈmər-si-fəl\ *adj* : not merciful : CRUEL, MERCILESS — **un·mer·ciful·ly** *adv*

**un·mind·ful** \-ˈmīnd-fəl\ *adj* : not mindful : CARELESS, UNAWARE

**un·mis·tak·able** \ˌən-mə-ˈstā-kə-bəl\ *adj* : not capable of being mistaken or misunderstood : CLEAR, OBVIOUS — **un·mistak·ably** \-blē\ *adv*

**un·mit·i·gat·ed** \ˌən-ˈmi-tə-ˌgā-təd\ *adj* **1** : not softened or lessened **2** : ABSOLUTE, DOWNRIGHT ⟨an ∼ liar⟩

**un·moor** \-ˈmùr\ *vb* : to loose from or as if from moorings

**un·mor·al** \-ˈmòr-əl\ *adj* : having no moral perception or quality : AMORAL — **unmo·ral·i·ty** \ˌən-mə-ˈra-lə-tē\ *n*

**un·muz·zle** \-ˈmə-zəl\ *vb* : to remove a muzzle from

**un·nat·u·ral** \ˌən-ˈna-chə-rəl\ *adj* : contrary to or acting contrary to nature or natural instincts; *also* : ABNORMAL — **un·nat·u·ral·ly** *adv* — **un·nat·u·ralness** *n*

**un·nec·es·sar·i·ly** \ˌən-ˌne-sə-ˈser-ə-lē\ *adv* **1** : not by necessity **2** : to an unnecessary degree ⟨∼ harsh⟩

**un·nerve** \ˌən-ˈnərv\ *vb* : to deprive of courage, strength, or steadiness ⟨fear *unnerved* them⟩; *also* : UPSET

**un·num·bered** \ˌən-ˈnəm-bərd\ *adj* : not numbered or counted : INNUMERABLE

**un·ob·tru·sive** \ˌən-əb-ˈtrü-siv\ *adj* : not obtrusive or forward : not bold : INCONSPICUOUS — **un·ob·tru·sive·ly** *adv*

**un·oc·cu·pied** \ˌən-ˈä-kyə-ˌpīd\ *adj* **1** : not busy : UNEMPLOYED **2** : not occupied : EMPTY, VACANT

**un·or·ga·nized** \ˌən-ˈòr-gə-ˌnīzd\ *adj* **1** : not formed or brought into an integrated or ordered whole **2** : not organized into unions ⟨∼ labor⟩

**un·pack** \ˌən-ˈpak\ *vb* **1** : to separate and remove things packed **2** : to open and remove the contents of

**un·par·al·leled** \ˌən-ˈpa-rə-ˌleld\ *adj* : having no parallel; *esp* : having no equal or match ⟨an ∼ achievement⟩

**un·par·lia·men·ta·ry** \ˌən-ˌpär-lə-ˈmentə-rē\ *adj* : contrary to parliamentary practice

| | | | |
|---|---|---|---|
| unlimited | unmasculine | unmoved | unopened |
| unlined | unmatched | unmusical | unopposed |
| unlit | unmeant | unnameable | unoriginal |
| unliterary | unmeasurable | unnamed | unorthodox |
| unlivable | unmeasured | unnecessary | unorthodoxy |
| unlovable | unmelodious | unneeded | unostentatious |
| unloved | unmentioned | unnewsworthy | unowned |
| unloving | unmerited | unnoticeable | unpaged |
| unmade | unmilitary | unnoticed | unpaid |
| unmalicious | unmilled | unobjectionable | unpainted |
| unmanageable | unmixed | unobservant | unpaired |
| unmanned | unmodified | unobserved | unpalatable |
| unmapped | unmolested | unobstructed | unpardonable |
| unmarked | unmotivated | unobtainable | unpasteurized |
| unmarketable | unmounted | unofficial | unpatriotic |
| unmarred | unmovable | unofficially | unpaved |
| unmarried | | | |

**un·peg** \ˌən-ˈpeg\ *vb* **1** : to remove a peg from **2** : to unfasten by or as if by removing a peg

**un·per·son** \ˈən-ˌpər-sᵊn, -ˌpər-\ *n* : a person who usu. for political or ideological reasons is removed from recognition or consideration

**un·pile** \ˌən-ˈp(-ə)l\ *vb* : to take or disentangle from a pile

**un·pin** \-ˈpin\ *vb* : to remove a pin from : UNFASTEN

**un·pleas·ant** \-ˈple-zᵊnt\ *adj* : not pleasant : DISAGREEABLE — **un·pleas·ant·ly** *adv* — **un·pleas·ant·ness** *n*

**un·plug** \ˌən-ˈpləg\ *vb* **1** : UNCLOG **2** : to remove (a plug) from a receptacle; *also* : to disconnect from an electric circuit by removing a plug

**un·plumbed** \-ˈpləmd\ *adj* **1** : not tested or measured with a plumb line **2** : not thoroughly explored

**un·pop·u·lar** \ˌən-ˈpä-pyə-lər\ *adj* : not popular : looked upon or received unfavorably — **un·pop·u·lar·i·ty** \ˌən-ˌpä-pyə-ˈla-rə-tē\ *n*

**un·prec·e·dent·ed** \ˌən-ˈpre-sə-ˌden-təd\ *adj* : having no precedent : NOVEL

**un·pre·ten·tious** \ˌən-pri-ˈten-chəs\ *adj* : not pretentious : MODEST

**un·prin·ci·pled** \ˌən-ˈprin-sə-pəld\ *adj* : lacking sound or honorable principles : UNSCRUPULOUS ⟨an ~ criminal⟩

**un·print·able** \-ˈprin-tə-bəl\ *adj* : unfit or too offensive to be printed ⟨~ remarks⟩

**un·prof·it·able** \ˌən-ˈprä-fə-tə-bəl\ *adj* : not profitable : USELESS, VAIN

**un·pro·tect·ed** \ˌən-prə-ˈtek-təd\ *adj* **1** : lacking protection **2** : performed without measures to prevent pregnancy or sexually transmitted disease ⟨~ sex⟩

**un·qual·i·fied** \ˌən-ˈkwä-lə-ˌfīd\ *adj* **1** : not having requisite qualifications **2** : not modified or restricted by reservations : COMPLETE — **un·qual·i·fied·ly** \-ˌfī-əd-lē\ *adv*

**un·ques·tion·able** \-ˈkwes-chə-nə-bəl\ *adj* : not questionable : INDISPUTABLE — **un·ques·tion·ably** \-blē\ *adv*

**un·ques·tion·ing** \-chə-niŋ\ *adj* : not questioning : accepting without examina-

tion or hesitation ⟨~ obedience⟩ — **un·ques·tion·ing·ly** *adv*

**un·qui·et** \-ˈkwī-ət\ *adj* **1** : not quiet : AGITATED, DISTURBED **2** : physically, emotionally, or mentally restless : UNEASY

**un·quote** \ˈən-ˌkwōt\ *n* — used orally to indicate the end of a direct quotation

**un·rav·el** \ˌən-ˈra-vəl\ *vb* **1** : to separate the threads of **2** : SOLVE ⟨~ a mystery⟩ **3** : to become unraveled

**un·read** \-ˈred\ *adj* **1** : not read; *also* : left unexamined **2** : lacking the benefits or the experience of reading

**un·re·al** \-ˈrēl\ *adj* : lacking in reality, substance, or genuineness — **un·re·al·i·ty** \ˌən-ˌrē-ˈa-lə-tē\ *n*

**un·rea·son·able** \-ˈrē-zᵊn-ə-bəl\ *adj* **1** : not governed by or acting according to reason; *also* : not conformable to reason : ABSURD **2** : exceeding the bounds of reason or moderation — **un·rea·son·able·ness** *n* — **un·rea·son·ably** *adv*

**un·rea·soned** \-ˈrē-zᵊnd\ *adj* : not based on reason or reasoning ⟨~ fears⟩

**un·rea·son·ing** \-ˈrē-zᵊn-iŋ\ *adj* : not using or showing the use of reason as a guide or control

**un·re·con·struct·ed** \ˌən-ˌrē-kən-ˈstrək-təd\ *adj* : not reconciled to some political, economic, or social change; *esp* : holding stubbornly to a particular belief, view, place, or style

**un·reel** \ˌən-ˈrēl\ *vb* **1** : to unwind from or as if from a reel **2** : to perform successfully

**un·re·gen·er·ate** \ˌən-ri-ˈje-nə-rət\ *adj* : not regenerated or reformed

**un·re·lent·ing** \-ˈlen-tiŋ\ *adj* **1** : not yielding in determination : STERN ⟨~ leader⟩ **2** : not letting up or weakening in vigor or pace : CONSTANT — **un·re·lent·ing·ly** *adv*

**un·re·mit·ting** \-ˈmi-tiŋ\ *adj* : CONSTANT, INCESSANT ⟨~ pain⟩ — **un·re·mit·ting·ly** *adv*

**un·re·quit·ed** \ˌən-ri-ˈkwī-təd\ *adj* : not requited or not reciprocated or returned in kind ⟨~ love⟩

**un·re·served** \-ˈzərvd\ *adj* **1** : not limited or partial ⟨~ enthusiasm⟩ **2** : not cautious or reticent : FRANK, OPEN **3** : not set aside for special use — **un·re·serv·ed·ly** \-ˈzər-vəd-lē\ *adv*

---

| | | | |
|---|---|---|---|
| unpeeled | unpremeditated | unprovoked | unreflective |
| unperceived | unprepared | unpublished | unregistered |
| unperceptive | unpreparedness | unpunished | unregulated |
| unperformed | unprepossessing | unquenchable | unrehearsed |
| unpersuaded | unpressed | unquestioned | unrelated |
| unpersuasive | unpretending | unraised | unreliable |
| unperturbed | unpretty | unrated | unrelieved |
| unplanned | unprivileged | unratified | unremarkable |
| unplanted | unprocessed | unreachable | unremembered |
| unpleasing | unproductive | unreadable | unremovable |
| unplowed | unprofessed | unready | unrepentant |
| unpoetic | unprofessional | unrealistic | unreported |
| unpolished | unprogrammed | unrealized | unrepresentative |
| unpolitical | unprogressive | unrecognizable | unrepresented |
| unpolluted | unpromising | unrecognized | unrepressed |
| unposed | unprompted | unrecorded | unresistant |
| unpractical | unpronounceable | unrecoverable | unresisting |
| unpredictability | unpropitious | unredeemable | unresolved |
| unpredictable | unproven | unrefined | unresponsive |
| unprejudiced | unprovided | unreflecting | unresponsiveness |

**un·rest** \ˌən-'rest\ *n* : a disturbed or un-easy state : TURMOIL

**un·re·strained** \ˌən-ri-'strānd\ *adj* 1 : IM-MODERATE, UNCONTROLLED ⟨∼ anger⟩ 2 : SPONTANEOUS

**un·re·straint** \-ri-'strānt\ *n* : lack of re-straint

**un·rid·dle** \ˌən-'ri-dᵊl\ *vb* : to find the ex-planation of : SOLVE

**un·righ·teous** \-'rī-chəs\ *adj* 1 : SINFUL, WICKED 2 : UNJUST — **un·righ·teous·ness** *n*

**un·ripe** \-'rīp\ *adj* : not ripe : IMMATURE

**un·ri·valed** *or* **un·ri·valled** \ˌən-'rī-vəld\ *adj* : having no rival : SUPREME

**un·robe** \-'rōb\ *vb* : DISROBE, UNDRESS

**un·roll** \-'rōl\ *vb* 1 : to unwind a roll of : open out 2 : DISPLAY, DISCLOSE 3 : to become unrolled or spread out

**un·roof** \-'rüf, -'rüf\ *vb* : to strip off the roof or covering of

**un·ruf·fled** \ˌən-'rə-fəld\ *adj* 1 : not agi-tated or upset 2 : not ruffled : SMOOTH ⟨∼ water⟩

**un·ruly** \-'rü-lē\ *adj* [ME *unreuly*, fr. *un-* + *reuly* disciplined, fr. *reule* rule, fr. AF, fr. L *regula* straightedge, rule, fr. *regere* to direct] : not submissive to rule or re-straint : TURBULENT ⟨∼ passions⟩ — **un·rul·i·ness** \-'rü-lē-nəs\ *n*

**un·sad·dle** \ˌən-'sa-dᵊl\ *vb* 1 : to remove the saddle from a horse 2 : UNHORSE

**un·sat·u·rat·ed** \-'sa-chə-ˌrā-təd\ *adj* 1 : capable of absorbing or dissolving more of something 2 : containing double or triple bonds between carbon atoms ⟨∼ fat⟩ — **un·sat·u·rate** \-rət\ *n*

**un·saved** \ˌən-'sāvd\ *adj* : not saved; *esp* : not rescued from eternal punishment

**un·sa·vory** \-'sā-və-rē\ *adj* 1 : TASTELESS 2 : unpleasant to taste or smell 3 : mor-ally offensive ⟨∼ characters⟩

**un·say** \-'sā\ *vb* **-said** \-'sed\; **-say·ing** : to take back (something said) : RE-TRACT, WITHDRAW

**un·scathed** \-'skāthd\ *adj* : wholly un-harmed : not injured

**un·schooled** \-'sküld\ *adj* : not schooled : UNTAUGHT, UNTRAINED

**un·sci·en·tif·ic** \ˌən-ˌsī-ən-'ti-fik\ *adj* : not scientific : not in accord with the principles and methods of science

**un·scram·ble** \ˌən-'skram-bəl\ *vb* 1 : RE-SOLVE, CLARIFY 2 : to restore (as a radio message) to intelligible form

**un·screw** \-'skrü\ *vb* 1 : to draw the screws from 2 : to loosen by turning

**un·scru·pu·lous** \-'skrü-pyə-ləs\ *adj* : not scrupulous : UNPRINCIPLED — **un·scru·pu·lous·ly** *adv* — **un·scru·pu·lous·ness** *n*

**un·seal** \-'sēl\ *vb* : to break or remove the seal of : OPEN

**un·search·able** \-'sər-chə-bəl\ *adj* : not capable of being searched or explored ⟨∼ forests⟩

**un·sea·son·able** \-'sē-zᵊn-ə-bəl\ *adj* : not seasonable : happening or coming at the wrong time : UNTIMELY — **un·sea·son·ably** \-blē\ *adv*

**un·seat** \-'sēt\ *vb* 1 : to throw from one's seat esp. on horseback 2 : to remove from political office

**un·seem·ly** \-'sēm-lē\ *adj* : not according with established standards of good form or taste ⟨∼ behavior⟩; *also* : not suitable — **un·seem·li·ness** *n*

**un·seen** \ˌən-'sēn\ *adj* : not seen : INVISI-BLE ⟨∼ dangers⟩

**un·seg·re·gat·ed** \-'se-gri-ˌgā-təd\ *adj* : not segregated; *esp* : free from racial segregation

**un·self·ish** \-'sel-fish\ *adj* : not selfish : GENEROUS — **un·self·ish·ly** *adv* — **un·self·ish·ness** *n*

**un·set·tle** \ˌən-'se-tᵊl\ *vb* : to move or loosen from a settled position : DIS-PLACE, DISTURB

**un·set·tled** \-'se-tᵊld\ *adj* 1 : not settled : not fixed (as in position or character) 2 : not calm : DISTURBED 3 : not decided in mind : UNRESOLVED 4 : not paid ⟨∼ accounts⟩ 5 : not occupied by settlers

**un·shack·le** \-'sha-kəl\ *vb* : to free from shackles

**un·shaped** \-'shāpt\ *adj* : not shaped; *esp* : not being in finished, final, or perfect form ⟨∼ ideas⟩ ⟨∼ timber⟩

**un·sheathe** \ˌən-'shēth\ *vb* : to draw from or as if from a sheath

**un·ship** \-'ship\ *vb* 1 : to remove from a ship 2 : to remove or become removed from position ⟨∼ an oar⟩

**un·shod** \ˌən-'shäd\ *adj* : not wearing or provided with shoes

**un·sight·ly** \ˌən-'sīt-lē\ *adj* : unpleasant to the sight : UGLY ⟨an ∼ mess⟩

**un·skilled** \-'skild\ *adj* 1 : not skilled : not skilled in a specified branch of work 2 : not requiring skill

**un·skill·ful** \-'skil-fəl\ *adj* : lacking in skill or proficiency — **un·skill·ful·ly** *adv*

**un·sling** \-'sliŋ\ *vb* **-slung** \-'sləŋ\; **-sling·ing** : to remove from being slung

**un·snap** \-'snap\ *vb* : to loosen or free by or as if by undoing a snap

**un·snarl** \-'snärl\ *vb* : to remove snarls from : UNTANGLE

---

| | | | |
|---|---|---|---|
| unrestful | unsalted | unself–conscious | unshorn |
| unrestricted | unsanctioned | unself–consciously | unsifted |
| unreturnable | unsanitary | unsensational | unsigned |
| unrewarding | unsatisfactory | unsentimental | unsinkable |
| unrhymed | unsatisfied | unserious | unsmiling |
| unrhythmic | unscented | unserviceable | unsociable |
| unripened | unscheduled | unsexual | unsoiled |
| unromantic | unscholarly | unshaded | unsold |
| unromantically | unsealed | unshakable | unsoldierly |
| unsafe | unseasoned | unshaken | unsolicited |
| unsaid | unseaworthy | unshapely | unsolvable |
| unsalable | unsegmented | unshaven | unsolved |

**un·so·phis·ti·cat·ed** \ˌən-sə-ˈfis-tə-ˌkā-təd\ *adj* **1** : not worldly-wise : lacking sophistication **2** : SIMPLE ⟨~ designs⟩

**un·sought** \ˌən-ˈsȯt\ *adj* : not sought : not searched for or asked for : not obtained by effort ⟨~ honors⟩

**un·sound** \-ˈsau̇nd\ *adj* **1** : not healthy or whole; *also* : not mentally normal ⟨of ~ mind⟩ **2** : not valid **3** : not firmly made or fixed ⟨structurally ~⟩ — **un·sound·ly** *adv* — **un·sound·ness** *n*

**un·spar·ing** \ˈsper-iŋ\ *adj* **1** : HARD, RUTHLESS ⟨~ criticism⟩ **2** : not frugal : LIBERAL, PROFUSE ⟨~ generosity⟩

**un·speak·able** \-ˈspē-kə-bəl\ *adj* **1** : impossible to express in words **2** : extremely bad ⟨~ offenses⟩ — **un·speak·ably** \-blē\ *adv*

**un·spool** \ˌən-ˈspül\ *vb* **1** : to unwind from a spool **2** : to present artfully ⟨~ a new film⟩

**un·spot·ted** \-ˈspä-təd\ *adj* : not spotted or stained; *esp* : free from moral stain

**un·sprung** \-ˈsprəŋ\ *adj* : not sprung; *esp* : not equipped with springs

**un·sta·ble** \-ˈstā-bəl\ *adj* **1** : not stable **2** : FICKLE, VACILLATING; *also* : lacking effective emotional control **3** : readily changing (as by decomposing) in chemical or physical composition or in biological activity ⟨an ~ atomic nucleus⟩

**un·steady** \ˌən-ˈste-dē\ *adj* : not steady : UNSTABLE — **un·stead·i·ly** \-ˈste-də-lē\ *adv* — **un·stead·i·ness** \-ˈste-dē-nəs\ *n*

**un·stint·ing** \-ˈstin-tiŋ\ *adj* **1** : not restricting or holding back **2** : giving or being given freely or generously ⟨~ praise⟩

**un·stop** \-ˈstäp\ *vb* **1** : UNCLOG **2** : to remove a stopper from

**un·stop·pa·ble** \ˌən-ˈstä-pə-bəl\ *adj* : incapable of being stopped

**un·strap** \-ˈstrap\ *vb* : to remove or loose a strap from

**un·stressed** \ˌən-ˈstrest\ *adj* : not stressed; *esp* : not bearing a stress or accent ⟨~ syllables⟩

**un·strung** \-ˈstrəŋ\ *adj* **1** : having the strings loose or detached **2** : made weak, disordered, or unstable

**un·stud·ied** \-ˈstə-dēd\ *adj* **1** : not acquired by study **2** : NATURAL, UNFORCED ⟨moved with ~ grace⟩

**un·sub·stan·tial** \ˌən-səb-ˈstan-chəl\ *adj* : INSUBSTANTIAL

**un·sung** \ˌən-ˈsəŋ\ *adj* **1** : not sung **2** : not celebrated in song or verse ⟨~ heroes⟩

**un·swerv·ing** \ˌən-ˈswər-viŋ\ *adj* **1** : not swerving or turning aside **2** : STEADY

**un·tan·gle** \-ˈtaŋ-gəl\ *vb* **1** : DISENTANGLE **2** : to straighten out : RESOLVE ⟨~ a problem⟩

**un·taught** \-ˈtȯt\ *adj* **1** : not instructed or taught : IGNORANT **2** : NATURAL, SPONTANEOUS ⟨~ kindness⟩

**un·think·able** \-ˈthiŋ-kə-bəl\ *adj* : not to be thought of or considered as possible ⟨~ cruelty⟩

**un·think·ing** \ˌən-ˈthiŋ-kiŋ\ *adj* : not thinking; *esp* : THOUGHTLESS, HEEDLESS ⟨~ remarks⟩ — **un·think·ing·ly** *adv*

**un·thought** \ˌən-ˈthȯt\ *adj* : not anticipated : UNEXPECTED — often used with *of* ⟨*unthought*-of development⟩

**un·tie** \-ˈtī\ *vb* **-tied; -ty·ing** *or* **-tie·ing** **1** : to free from something that ties, fastens, or restrains : UNBIND **2** : DISENTANGLE, RESOLVE **3** : to become loosened or unbound

**¹un·til** \ˌən-ˈtil\ *prep* : up to the time of ⟨worked ~ 5 o'clock⟩

**²until** *conj* **1** : up to the time that ⟨wait ~ he calls⟩ **2** : to the point or degree that ⟨ran ~ she was breathless⟩

**¹un·time·ly** \ˌən-ˈtīm-lē\ *adv* : at an inopportune time : UNSEASONABLY; *also* : PREMATURELY

**²untimely** *adj* **1** : PREMATURE ⟨~ death⟩; *also* : INOPPORTUNE, UNSEASONABLE

**un·tir·ing** \ˌən-ˈtī-riŋ\ *adj* : not becoming tired : INDEFATIGABLE ⟨an ~ worker⟩ — **un·tir·ing·ly** *adv*

**un·to** \ˈən-ˌtü\ *prep* : TO

**un·told** \ˌən-ˈtōld\ *adj* **1** : too great or numerous to count **2** : not told : not revealed

**¹un·touch·able** \ˌən-ˈtə-chə-bəl\ *adj* : forbidden to the touch

**²untouchable** *n* : a member of the lowest social class in India having in traditional Hindu belief the quality of defiling by contact a member of a higher caste

**un·touched** \ˌən-ˈtəcht\ *adj* **1** : not subjected to touching **2** : not described or dealt with **3** : not tasted **4** : being in a primeval state or condition **5** : UNAFFECTED ⟨~ by scandals⟩

**un·tow·ard** \ˌən-ˈtȯrd, -ˈtō-ərd; ˌən-tə-ˈwȯrd\ *adj* **1** : difficult to manage : STUBBORN, WILLFUL ⟨an ~ child⟩ **2** : INCONVENIENT, TROUBLESOME ⟨an ~ encounter⟩

---

| | | | |
|---|---|---|---|
| unsorted | unsuccessful | unsweetened | untended |
| unspecified | unsuccessfully | unsymmetrical | untested |
| unspectacular | unsuitable | unsympathetic | unthrifty |
| unspent | unsuited | unsystematic | untidy |
| unspiritual | unsullied | untactful | untilled |
| unspoiled | unsupervised | untainted | untitled |
| unspoken | unsupportable | untalented | untraceable |
| unsportsmanlike | unsupported | untamed | untraditional |
| unstained | unsure | untanned | untrained |
| unstated | unsurpassed | untapped | untrammeled |
| unsterile | unsurprising | untarnished | untranslatable |
| unstructured | unsurprisingly | untaxed | untranslated |
| unstylish | unsuspected | unteachable | untraveled |
| unsubdued | unsuspecting | untenable | untraversed |
| unsubstantiated | unsuspicious | untenanted | untreated |
| unsubtle | | | |

**un·tried** \ˌən-ˈtrīd\ *adj* : not tested or proved by experience or trial; *also* : not tried in court

**un·true** \-ˈtrü\ *adj* **1** : not faithful : DISLOYAL **2** : not according with a standard of correctness **3** : FALSE

**un·truth** \ˌən-ˈtrüth, ˈən-ˌtrüth\ *n* **1** : lack of truthfulness **2** : FALSEHOOD

**un·tune** \-ˈtün, -ˈtyün\ *vb* **1** : to put out of tune **2** : DISARRANGE, DISCOMPOSE

**un·tu·tored** \-ˈtü-tərd, -ˈtyü-\ *adj* : UNTAUGHT, UNLEARNED, IGNORANT

**un·twine** \-ˈtwīn\ *vb* : UNWIND, DISENTANGLE

**un·twist** \ˌən-ˈtwist\ *vb* **1** : to separate the twisted parts of : UNTWINE **2** : to become untwined

**un·used** \-ˈyüst, -ˈyüzd *for 1;* -ˈyüzd *for 2*\ *adj* **1** : UNACCUSTOMED ⟨~ to such treatment⟩ **2** : not used

**un·usu·al** \-ˈyü-zhə-wəl\ *adj* : not usual : UNCOMMON, RARE — **un·usu·al·ly** *adv*

**un·ut·ter·able** \ˌən-ˈə-tə-rə-bəl\ *adj* : being beyond the powers of description : INEXPRESSIBLE ⟨~ shame⟩ — **un·ut·ter·ably** \-blē\ *adv*

**un·var·nished** \-ˈvär-nisht\ *adj* **1** : not varnished **2** : not embellished : PLAIN ⟨the ~ truth⟩

**un·veil** \ˌən-ˈvāl\ *vb* **1** : to remove a veil or covering from : DISCLOSE **2** : to remove a veil : reveal oneself

**un·voiced** \-ˈvȯist\ *adj* **1** : not verbally expressed : UNSPOKEN **2** : VOICELESS

**un·war·rant·able** \-ˈwȯr-ən-tə-bəl\ *adj* : not justifiable : INEXCUSABLE — **un·war·rant·ably** \-blē\ *adv*

**un·weave** \ˌən-ˈwēv\ *vb* **-wove** \-ˈwōv\; **-wo·ven** \-ˈwō-vən\; **-weav·ing** : DISENTANGLE, RAVEL

**un·well** \ˌən-ˈwel\ *adj* : SICK, AILING

**un·whole·some** \-ˈhōl-səm\ *adj* **1** : harmful to physical, mental, or moral well-being ⟨~ food⟩ **2** : CORRUPT, UNSOUND ⟨~ deals⟩; *also* : offensive to the senses : LOATHSOME ⟨an ~ stench⟩

**un·wieldy** \-ˈwēl-dē\ *adj* : not easily managed, handled, or used (as because of bulk, weight, or complexity) : AWKWARD ⟨an ~ tool⟩

**un·wind** \-ˈwīnd\ *vb* **-wound** \-ˈwaůnd\; **-wind·ing** **1** : to undo something that is wound : loose from coils **2** : to become unwound : be capable of being unwound **3** : RELAX ⟨~ after work⟩

**un·wise** \ˌən-ˈwīz\ *adj* : not wise : FOOLISH — **un·wise·ly** *adv*

**un·wit·ting** \-ˈwi-tiŋ\ *adj* **1** : not knowing : UNAWARE **2** : not intended : INADVERTENT ⟨~ mistake⟩ — **un·wit·ting·ly** *adv*

**un·wont·ed** \-ˈwȯn-təd, -ˈwōn-\ *adj* **1** : RARE, UNUSUAL **2** : not accustomed by experience — **un·wont·ed·ly** *adv*

**un·world·ly** \-ˈwərld-lē\ *adj* **1** : not of this world; *esp* : SPIRITUAL **2** : NAIVE **3** : not swayed by worldly considerations — **un·world·li·ness** \-lē-nəs\ *n*

**un·wor·thy** \ˌən-ˈwər-t͟hē\ *adj* **1** : BASE, DISHONORABLE **2** : not meritorious : not worthy : UNDESERVING **3** : not deserved : UNMERITED ⟨~ treatment⟩ — **un·wor·thi·ly** \-t͟hə-lē\ *adv* — **un·wor·thi·ness** \-t͟hē-nəs\ *n*

**un·wrap** \-ˈrap\ *vb* : to remove the wrapping from : DISCLOSE

**un·writ·ten** \-ˈri-t͟ᵊn\ *adj* **1** : not in writing : ORAL, TRADITIONAL ⟨an ~ law⟩ **2** : containing no writing : BLANK

**un·yield·ing** \ˌən-ˈyēl-diŋ\ *adj* **1** : characterized by lack of softness or flexibility **2** : characterized by firmness or obduracy ⟨~ opposition⟩

**un·yoke** \-ˈyōk\ *vb* : to remove a yoke from; *also* : SEPARATE, DISCONNECT

**un·zip** \-ˈzip\ *vb* : to zip open : open by means of a zipper

**¹up** \ˈəp\ *adv* **1** : in or to a higher position or level; *esp* : away from the center of the earth **2** : from beneath a surface (as ground or water) **3** : from below the horizon **4** : in or into an upright position; *esp* : out of bed **5** : with greater intensity ⟨speak ~⟩ **6** : to or at a greater rate or amount ⟨prices went ~⟩ **7** : in or into a better or more advanced state or a state of greater intensity or activity ⟨stir ~ a fire⟩ **8** : into existence, evidence, or knowledge ⟨the missing book turned ~⟩ **9** : into consideration ⟨brought the matter ~⟩ **10** : to or at bat **11** : into possession or custody ⟨gave himself ~⟩ **12** : ENTIRELY, COMPLETELY ⟨eat it ~⟩ **13** — used for emphasis ⟨clean ~ a room⟩ **14** : ASIDE, BY ⟨lay ~ supplies⟩ **15** : so as to arrive or approach ⟨ran ~ the path⟩ **16** : in a direction opposite to down **17** : in or into parts ⟨tear ~ paper⟩ **18** : to a stop ⟨pull ~ at the curb⟩ **19** : for each side ⟨the score was 15 ~⟩

**²up** *adj* **1** : risen above the horizon ⟨the sun is ~⟩ **2** : being out of bed ⟨~ by 6 o'clock⟩ **3** : relatively high ⟨prices are ~⟩ **4** : RAISED, LIFTED ⟨windows are ~⟩ **5** : BUILT, CONSTRUCTED ⟨the house is ~⟩ **6** : grown above a surface ⟨the corn is ~⟩ **7** : moving, inclining, or directed upward **8** : marked by agitation, excitement, or activity **9** : READY; *esp* : highly prepared **10** : going on : taking place ⟨find out what is ~⟩ **11** : EXPIRED, ENDED ⟨the time is ~⟩ **12** : extensively aware or informed ⟨~ on the news⟩ **13** : being ahead or in advance of

| | | | |
|---|---|---|---|
| untrimmed | unvarying | unwashed | unwillingly |
| untrod | unventilated | unwavering | unwillingness |
| untrodden | unverifiable | unweaned | unwomanly |
| untroubled | unverified | unwearable | unworkable |
| untrustworthy | unversed | unwearied | unworn |
| untruthful | unvisited | unweathered | unworried |
| untypical | unwarranted | unwed | unwounded |
| unusable | unwarranted | unwelcome | unwoven |
| unvaried | unwary | unwilling | |

an opponent ⟨one hole ~ in a match⟩
**14** : presented for or being under consideration ⟨~ for promotion⟩ **15** : charged before a court ⟨~ for robbery⟩

³**up** *prep* **1** : to, toward, or at a higher point of ⟨~ a ladder⟩ **2** : to or toward the source of ⟨~ the river⟩ **3** : to or toward the northern part of ⟨~ the coast⟩ **4** : to or toward the interior of ⟨traveling ~ the country⟩ **5** : ALONG ⟨walk ~ the street⟩

⁴**up** *n* **1** : an upward course or slope **2** : a period or state of prosperity or success ⟨he had his ~s and downs⟩ **3** : a quark with a charge of +⅔ that is one of the constituents of the proton and neutron

⁵**up** *vb* **upped** \'əpt\ *or in 2* **up**; **upped**; **up·ping**; **ups** *or in 2* **up** **1** : to rise from a lying or sitting position **2** : to act abruptly or surprisingly ⟨she *upped* and left home⟩ **3** : to move or cause to move upward ⟨*upped* the prices⟩

**Upa·ni·shad** \ü-'pän-i-ˌshäd\ *n* : one of a set of Vedic philosophical treatises

¹**up·beat** \'əp-ˌbēt\ *n* : an unaccented beat in a musical measure; *esp* : the last beat of the measure

²**upbeat** *adj* : OPTIMISTIC, CHEERFUL

**up·braid** \ˌəp-'brād\ *vb* : to criticize, reproach, or scold severely

**up·bring·ing** \'əp-ˌbriŋ-iŋ\ *n* : the process of bringing up and training

**UPC** *abbr* Universal Product Code

**up·chuck** \'əp-ˌchək\ *vb* : VOMIT

**up·com·ing** \'əp-ˌkə-miŋ\ *adj* : FORTHCOMING, APPROACHING ⟨the ~ election⟩

**up·coun·try** \'əp-ˌkən-trē\ *adj* : of or relating to the interior of a country or a region — **up·country** \ˌəp-'kən-\ *adv*

**up·date** \ˌəp-'dāt\ *vb* : to bring up to date — **update** \'əp-ˌdāt\ *n*

**up·draft** \'əp-ˌdraft, -ˌdräft\ *n* : an upward movement of gas (as air)

**up·end** \ˌəp-'end\ *vb* : to set, stand, or rise on end; *also* : OVERTURN

¹**up·front** \'əp-ˌfrənt, ˌəp-'frənt\ *adj* **1** : HONEST, CANDID ⟨an ~ answer⟩ **2** : ADVANCE ⟨~ payment⟩

**up front** *adv* : in advance ⟨paid *up front*⟩

¹**up·grade** \'əp-ˌgrād\ *n* **1** : an upward grade or slope **2** : INCREASE, RISE

²**up·grade** \'əp-ˌgrād, ˌəp-'grād\ *vb* **1** : to raise to a higher grade or position; *esp* : to advance to a job requiring a higher level of skill **2** : to improve or replace (as software or a device) for increased usefulness

**up·growth** \'əp-ˌgrōth\ *n* : the process of growing upward : DEVELOPMENT; *also* : a product or result of this

**up·heav·al** \ˌəp-'hē-vəl\ *n* **1** : the action or an instance of uplifting esp. of part of the earth's crust **2** : a violent agitation or change

¹**up·hill** \'əp-'hil\ *adv* : upward on a hill or incline; *also* : against difficulties

²**up·hill** \-ˌhil\ *adj* **1** : situated on elevated ground **2** : ASCENDING **3** : DIFFICULT, LABORIOUS ⟨an ~ struggle⟩

**up·hold** \ˌəp-'hōld\ *vb* **-held** \-'held\; **-hold·ing** **1** : to give support to ⟨the ~

law⟩ **2** : to support against an opponent **3** : to keep elevated — **up·hold·er** *n*

**up·hol·ster** \ˌəp-'hōl-stər\ *vb* : to furnish with or as it with upholstery — **up·hol·ster·er** *n*

**up·hol·stery** \-stə-rē\ *n, pl* **-ster·ies** [ME *upholdester* upholsterer, fr. *upholden* to uphold, fr. *up* + *holden* to hold] : materials (as fabrics, padding, and springs) used to make a soft covering esp. for a seat

**UPI** *abbr* United Press International

**up·keep** \'əp-ˌkēp\ *n* : the act or cost of keeping up or maintaining; *also* : the state of being maintained

**up·land** \'əp-lənd, -ˌland\ *n* : high land esp. at some distance from the sea — **upland** *adj*

¹**up·lift** \ˌəp-'lift\ *vb* **1** : to lift or raise up **2** : ELEVATE **2** : to improve the condition of esp. morally, socially, or intellectually

²**up·lift** \'əp-ˌlift\ *n* **1** : a lifting up; *esp* : an upheaval of the earth's surface **2** : moral or social improvement ⟨spiritual ~⟩; *also* : a movement to make such improvement

**up·mar·ket** \ˌəp-'mär-kət\ *adj* : appealing to wealthy consumers

**up·most** \'əp-ˌmōst\ *adj* : UPPERMOST

**up·on** \ə-'pȯn, -'pän\ *prep* : ON

¹**up·per** \'ə-pər\ *adj* **1** : higher in physical position, rank, or order ⟨~ management⟩ **2** : constituting the smaller and more restricted branch of a bicameral legislature **3** *cap* : being a later part or formation of a specific geological period **4** : being toward the interior ⟨the ~ Amazon⟩ **5** : NORTHERN ⟨~ Minnesota⟩

²**upper** *n* : one that is upper; *esp* : the parts of a shoe or boot above the sole

**up·per·case** \ˌə-pər-'kās\ *adj* : CAPITAL 1 — **uppercase** *n*

**upper class** *n* : a social class occupying a position above the middle class and having the highest status in a society — **upper–class** *adj*

**up·per·class·man** \ˌə-pər-'klas-mən\ *n* : a junior or senior in a college or high school

**upper crust** *n* : the highest social class or group; *esp* : the highest circle of the upper class

**up·per·cut** \'ə-pər-ˌkət\ *n* : a short swinging punch delivered (as in boxing) in an upward direction usu. with a bent arm

**upper hand** *n* : MASTERY, ADVANTAGE

**up·per·most** \'ə-pər-ˌmōst\ *adv* : in or into the highest or most prominent position — **uppermost** *adj*

**up·pish** \'ə-pish\ *adj* : UPPITY

**up·pi·ty** \'ə-pə-tē\ *adj* : ARROGANT, PRESUMPTUOUS ⟨an ~ sales clerk⟩

**up·raise** \ˌəp-'rāz\ *vb* : to lift up : ELEVATE

¹**up·right** \'əp-ˌrīt\ *adj* **1** : PERPENDICULAR, VERTICAL **2** : erect in carriage or posture **3** : morally correct : JUST ⟨an ~ family man⟩ — **upright** *adv* — **up·right·ly** *adv* — **up·right·ness** *n*

²**upright** *n* **1** : the state of being upright : a vertical position **2** : something that stands upright

**upright piano** *n* : a piano whose strings run vertically

**up·ris·ing** \'əp-₁rī-ziŋ\ *n* : INSURRECTION, REVOLT, REBELLION

**up·riv·er** \'əp-'ri-vər\ *adv or adj* : toward or at a point nearer the source of a river

**up·roar** \'əp-₁rȯr\ *n* [D *oproer*, fr. MD, fr. *op* up + *roer* motion] : a state of commotion, excitement, or violent disturbance

**up·roar·i·ous** \₁əp-'rȯr-ē-əs\ *adj* **1** : marked by uproar **2** : extremely funny — **up·roar·i·ous·ly** *adv*

**up·root** \₁əp-'rüt, -'rut\ *vb* **1** : to remove by or as if by pulling up by the roots **2** : DISPLACE 1 ⟨families were ~*ed*⟩

**¹up·set** \₁əp-'set\ *vb* **-set; -set·ting** **1** : to force or be forced out of the usual upright, level, or proper position **2** : to disturb emotionally : WORRY; *also* : to make somewhat ill **3** : UNSETTLE, DISARRANGE **4** : to defeat unexpectedly

**²up·set** \'əp-₁set\ *n* **1** : an upsetting or being upset; *esp* : a minor illness **2** : a derangement of plans or ideas **3** : an unexpected defeat

**³up·set** \(₁)əp-'set\ *adj* : emotionally disturbed or agitated ⟨~ about the divorce⟩

**up·shot** \'əp-₁shät\ *n* : the final result

**¹up·side** \'əp-₁sīd\ *n* **1** : the upper side **2** : a positive aspect **3** : PROMISE ⟨rookies with much ~⟩

**²up·side** \₁əp-'sīd\ *prep* : up on or against the side of ⟨knocked him ~ the head⟩

**up·side down** \₁əp-₁sīd-'daùn\ *adv* **1** : with the upper and the lower parts reversed in position **2** : in or into confusion or disorder — **upside-down** *adj*

**up·si·lon** \'üp-sə-₁län, 'yüp-, 'əp-\ *n* : the 20th letter of the Greek alphabet — Υ or υ

**¹up·stage** \'əp-'stāj\ *adv or adj* : toward or at the rear of a theatrical stage

**²up·stage** \₁əp-'stāj\ *vb* : to draw attention away from (as an actor)

**¹up·stairs** \'əp-'sterz\ *adv* **1** : up the stairs : to or on a higher floor **2** : to or at a higher position

**²up·stairs** \'əp-'sterz\ *adj* : situated above the stairs esp. on an upper floor ⟨~ bedroom⟩

**³up·stairs** \'əp-'sterz, 'əp-₁sterz\ *n sing or pl* : the part of a building above the ground floor

**up·stand·ing** \₁əp-'stan-diŋ, 'əp-\ *adj* **1** : ERECT **2** : STRAIGHTFORWARD, HONEST ⟨~ citizens⟩

**¹up·start** \₁əp-'stärt\ *vb* : to jump up suddenly

**²up·start** \'əp-₁stärt\ *n* : one that has risen suddenly; *esp* : one that claims more personal importance than is warranted — **up·start** \-'stärt\ *adj*

**up·state** \'əp-'stāt\ *adj* : of, relating to, or characteristic of a part of a state away from a large city and esp. to the north — **upstate** *adv* — **upstate** *n*

**up·stream** \'əp-'strēm\ *adv* : at or toward the source of a stream — **upstream** *adj*

**up·stroke** \'əp-₁strōk\ *n* : an upward stroke (as of a pen)

**up·surge** \-₁sərj\ *n* : a rapid or sudden rise ⟨an ~ in interest⟩

**up·swept** \'əp-₁swept\ *adj* : swept upward ⟨~ hairdo⟩

**up·swing** \'əp-₁swiŋ\ *n* : an upward swing; *esp* : a marked increase or rise (as in activity)

**up·take** \'əp-₁tāk\ *n* **1** : UNDERSTANDING, COMPREHENSION ⟨quick on the ~⟩ **2** : an act or instance of absorbing and incorporating esp. into a living organism, tissue, or cell

**up·thrust** \'əp-₁thrəst\ *n* : an upward thrust (as of the earth's crust) — **upthrust** *vb*

**up·tight** \'əp-'tīt\ *adj* **1** : TENSE, NERVOUS, UNEASY; *also* : ANGRY, INDIGNANT **2** : rigidly conventional

**up-to-date** *adj* **1** : extending up to the present time **2** : abreast of the times : MODERN — **up-to-date·ness** *n*

**up·town** \'əp-₁taùn\ *n* : the upper part of a town or city; *esp* : the residential district — **up·town** \'əp-'taùn\ *adj or adv*

**¹up·turn** \'əp-₁tərn, ₁əp-'tərn\ *vb* **1** : to turn (as earth) up or over **2** : to turn or direct upward

**²up·turn** \'əp-₁tərn\ *n* : an upward turn esp. toward better conditions or higher prices

**¹up·ward** \'əp-wərd\ *or* **up·wards** \-wərdz\ *adv* **1** : in a direction from lower to higher **2** : toward a higher or better condition **3** : toward a greater amount or higher number, degree, or rate

**²upward** *adj* : directed or moving toward or situated in a higher place or level : ASCENDING — **up·ward·ly** *adv*

**upwards** *also* **upward** *of adv* : more than : in excess of ⟨they cost *upwards* of $25 each⟩

**up·well** \₁əp-'wel\ *vb* : to move or flow upward

**up·well·ing** \-'we-liŋ\ *n* : a rising or an appearance of rising to the surface and flowing outward; *esp* : the movement of deep cold usu. nutrient-rich ocean water to the surface

**up·wind** \'əp-'wind\ *adv or adj* : in the direction from which the wind is blowing

**ura·cil** \'yùr-ə-₁sil\ *n* : a pyrimidine base that is one of the four bases coding genetic information in the molecular chain of RNA

**ura·ni·um** \yù-'rā-nē-əm\ *n* : a silvery heavy radioactive metallic chemical element used as a source of atomic energy

**Ura·nus** \'yùr-ə-nəs, yù-'rā-\ *n* [LL, the sky personified as a god, fr. Gk *Ouranos*, fr. *ouranos* sky, heaven] : the planet 7th in order from the sun

**ur·ban** \'ər-bən\ *adj* : of, relating to, characteristic of, or constituting a city

**ur·bane** \₁ər-'bān\ *adj* [L *urbanus* urban, urbane, fr. *urbs* city] : very polite and polished in manner : SUAVE

**ur·ban·ite** \'ər-bə-₁nīt\ *n* : a person who lives in a city

**ur·ban·i·ty** \₁ər-'ba-nə-tē\ *n, pl* **-ties** : the quality or state of being urbane

**ur·ban·ize** \'ər-bə-₁nīz\ *vb* **-ized; -iz·ing** : to cause to take on urban characteristics — **ur·ban·i·za·tion** \₁ər-bə-nə-'zā-shən\ *n*

**ur·chin** \'ər-chən\ *n* [ME, hedgehog, fr. AF *hericun, hirechoun*, ultim. fr. L *ericius*] : a pert or mischievous youngster

**Ur·du** \'ur-dü, 'ər-\ *n* [Hindi & Urdu *urdū*, fr. Pers *zabān-e-urdū-e-muallā* language of the Exalted Comp (the imperial bazaar in Delhi)] : an Indo-Aryan language that is the official language of Pakistan and that is widely used by Muslims in urban areas of India

**urea** \yu̇-'rē-ə\ *n* : a soluble nitrogenous compound that is the chief solid constituent of mammalian urine

**ure·mia** \yu̇-'rē-mē-ə\ *n* : accumulation in the blood of materials normally passed off in the urine resulting in a poisoned condition — **ure·mic** \-mik\ *adj*

**ure·ter** \'yu̇r-ə-tər\ *n* : a duct that carries the urine from a kidney to the bladder

**ure·thra** \yu̇-'rē-thrə\ *n, pl* **-thras** *or* **-thrae** \-(,)thrē\ : the canal that in most mammals carries off the urine from the bladder and in the male also serves to carry semen from the body — **ure·thral** \-thrəl\ *adj*

**ure·thri·tis** \yu̇r-i-'thrī-təs\ *n* : inflammation of the urethra

¹**urge** \'ərj\ *vb* **urged; urg·ing** **1** : to present, advocate, or demand earnestly **2** : to try to persuade or sway ⟨~ a guest to stay⟩ **3** : to serve as a motive or reason for **4** : to impress or impel to some course or activity ⟨the dog *urged* the sheep onward⟩

²**urge** *n* **1** : the act or process of urging **2** : a force or impulse that urges or drives

**ur·gent** \'ər-jənt\ *adj* **1** : calling for immediate attention : PRESSING **2** : urging insistently — **ur·gen·cy** \-jən-sē\ *n* — **ur·gent·ly** *adv*

**uric** \'yu̇r-ik\ *adj* : of, relating to, or found in urine

**uric acid** *n* : a nearly insoluble acid that is the chief nitrogenous excretory product of birds but is present in only small amounts in mammalian urine

**uri·nal** \'yu̇r-ə-n³l\ *n* **1** : a receptacle for urine **2** : a place for urinating

**uri·nal·y·sis** \yu̇r-ə-'na-lə-səs\ *n* : chemical analysis of urine

**uri·nary** \'yu̇r-ə-,ner-ē\ *adj* **1** : relating to, occurring in, or being organs for the formation and discharge of urine **2** : of, relating to, or for urine

**urinary bladder** *n* : a membranous sac in many vertebrates that serves for the temporary retention of urine and discharges by the urethra

**uri·nate** \'yu̇r-ə-,nāt\ *vb* **-nat·ed; -nat·ing** : to release or give off urine — **uri·na·tion** \yu̇r-ə-'nā-shən\ *n*

**urine** \'yu̇r-ən\ *n* : a waste material from the kidneys that is usu. a yellowish watery liquid in mammals but is semisolid in birds and reptiles

**URL** \,yü-(,)är-'el, 'ər(-ə)l\ *n* [*uniform* (or *universal*) *resource locator*] : a series of usu. alphanumeric characters that specifies the storage location of a resource on the Internet

**urn** \'ərn\ *n* **1** : a vessel that typically has the form of a vase on a pedestal and often

is used to hold the ashes of the dead **2** : a closed vessel usu. with a spout for serving a hot beverage

**uro·gen·i·tal** \,yu̇r-ō-'je-nə-t³l\ *adj* : of, relating to, or being the excretory and reproductive organs or functions

**urol·o·gy** \yu̇-'rä-lə-jē\ *n* : a branch of medical science dealing with the urinary or urogenital tract and its disorders — **uro·log·i·cal** \,yu̇r-ə-'lä-ji-kəl\ *also* **uro·log·ic** \-jik\ *adj* — **urol·o·gist** \yu̇-'rä-lə-jist\ *n*

**Ur·sa Ma·jor** \,ər-sə-'mā-jər\ *n* [L, lit., greater bear] : the northern constellation that contains the stars which form the Big Dipper

**Ursa Mi·nor** \-'mī-nər\ *n* [L, lit., lesser bear] : the constellation including the north pole of the heavens and the stars that form the Little Dipper with the North Star at the tip of the handle

**ur·sine** \'ər-,sīn\ *adj* : of, relating to, or resembling a bear

**ur·ti·car·ia** \,ər-tə-'ker-ē-ə\ *n* [NL, fr. L *urtica* nettle] : HIVES

**us** \'əs\ *pron, objective case of* WE

**US** *abbr* United States

**USA** *abbr* **1** United States Army **2** United States of America

**us·able** *also* **use·able** \'yü-zə-bəl\ *adj* : suitable or fit for use — **us·abil·i·ty** \,yü-zə-'bi-lə-tē\ *n*

**USAF** *abbr* United States Air Force

**us·age** \'yü-sij, -zij\ *n* **1** : habitual or customary practice or procedure **2** : the way in which words and phrases are actually used **3** : the action or mode of using **4** : manner of treating

**USB** \,yü-(,)es-'bē\ *n* [*universal serial bus*] : a standardized computer interface for attaching peripherals

**USCG** *abbr* United States Coast Guard

**USDA** *abbr* United States Department of Agriculture

¹**use** \'yüs\ *n* **1** : the act or practice of using or employing something : EMPLOYMENT, APPLICATION **2** : the fact or state of being used **3** : the way of using **4** : USAGE, CUSTOM **5** : the privilege or benefit of using something **6** : the ability or power to use something (as a limb) **7** : the legal enjoyment of property that consists in its employment, occupation, or exercise; *also* : the benefit or profit esp. from property held in trust **8** : USEFULNESS, UTILITY; *also* : the end served : OBJECT, FUNCTION **9** : something useful or beneficial ⟨it's no ~ arguing⟩ **10** : the occasion or need to employ ⟨he had no more ~ for it⟩ **11** : ESTEEM, LIKING ⟨had no ~ for modern art⟩

²**use** \'yüz\ *vb* **used** \'yüzd; "used to" usu 'yüs-tə\; **us·ing** \'yü-ziŋ\ **1** : to put into action or service : EMPLOY **2** : to consume or take (as drugs) regularly **3** : UTILIZE ⟨~ tact⟩; *also* : MANIPULATE ⟨*used* his friends to get ahead⟩ **4** : to expend or consume by putting to use **5** : to behave toward : TREAT ⟨*used* the horse cruelly⟩ **6** : to benefit from ⟨house could ~ a coat of paint⟩ **7** — used in the past with *to* to indicate a former practice, fact, or

state ⟨we *used* to work harder⟩ — **us·er** *n*

**used** \'yüzd\ *adj* **1** : having been used by another : SECONDHAND ⟨∼ cars⟩ **2** : ACCUSTOMED, HABITUATED ⟨∼ to the heat⟩

**use·ful** \'yüs-fəl\ *adj* : capable of being put to use : ADVANTAGEOUS; *esp* : serviceable for a beneficial end — **use·ful·ly** *adv* — **use·ful·ness** *n*

**use·less** \-ləs\ *adj* : having or being of no use : WORTHLESS, INEFFECTUAL — **useless·ly** *adv* — **use·less·ness** *n*

**USES** *abbr* United States Employment Service

**use up** *vb* : to consume completely

¹**ush·er** \'ə-shər\ *n* [ME *ussher*, fr. AF *ussier, usscher*, fr. VL *\*ustiarius* doorkeeper, fr. L *ostium, ustium* door, mouth of a river] **1** : an officer who walks before a person of rank **2** : one who escorts people to their seats (as in a church or theater)

²**usher** *vb* **1** : to conduct to a place **2** : to precede as an usher, forerunner, or harbinger **3** : INAUGURATE, INTRODUCE ⟨∼ in a new era⟩

**ush·er·ette** \,ə-shə-'ret\ *n* : a girl or woman who is an usher (as in a theater)

**USIA** *abbr* United States Information Agency

**USMC** *abbr* United States Marine Corps

**USN** *abbr* United States Navy

**USO** *abbr* United Service Organizations

**USP** *abbr* United States Pharmacopeia

**USPS** *abbr* United States Postal Service

**USS** *abbr* United States ship

**USSR** *abbr* Union of Soviet Socialist Republics

**usu** *abbr* usual; usually

**usu·al** \'yü-zhə-wəl\ *adj* **1** : accordant with usage, custom, or habit : NORMAL **2** : commonly or ordinarily used **3** : ORDINARY ♦ **Synonyms** CUSTOMARY, HABITUAL, ACCUSTOMED, ROUTINE — **usual·ly** \'yü-zhə-wə-lē, 'yü-zhə-lē\ *adv*

**usu·fruct** \'yü-zə-,frəkt\ *n* [L *ususfructus*, fr. *usus et fructus* use and enjoyment] : the legal right to use and enjoy the benefits and profits of something belonging to another

**usu·rer** \'yü-zhər-ər\ *n* : one that lends money esp. at an exorbitant rate

**usu·ri·ous** \yü-'zhùr-ē-əs\ *adj* : practicing, involving, or constituting usury ⟨a ∼ rate of interest⟩

**usurp** \yù-'sərp, -'zərp\ *vb* [ME, fr. AF *usorper*, fr. L *usurpare*, to take possession of without legal claim, fr. *usu* (abl. of *usus* use) + *rapere* to seize] : to seize and hold by force or without right ⟨∼ a throne⟩ — **usur·pa·tion** \,yü-sər-'pāshən, -zər-\ *n* — **usurp·er** \yù-'sər-pər, -'zər-\ *n*

**usu·ry** \'yü-zhə-rē\ *n, pl* **-ries** **1** : the lending of money with an interest charge for its use **2** : an excessive rate or amount of interest charged; *esp* : interest above an established legal rate

**UT** *abbr* Utah

**Ute** \'yüt\ *n, pl* **Ute** *or* **Utes** : a member of an American Indian people orig. ranging through Utah, Colorado, Arizona, and New Mexico

**uten·sil** \yù-'ten-səl\ *n* [ME, vessels for domestic use, fr. MF *utensile*, fr. L *utensilia*, fr. neut. pl. of *utensilis* useful, fr. *uti* to use] **1** : an instrument or vessel used in a household and esp. a kitchen **2** : a useful tool

**uter·us** \'yü-tə-rəs\ *n, pl* **uter·us·es** *or* **uteri** \'yü-tə-,rī\ : the muscular organ of a female mammal in which the young develop before birth — **uter·ine** \-,rīn, -rən\ *adj*

**utile** \'yüt-ᵊl, 'yü-,tī(-ə)l\ *adj* : USEFUL

**uti·lise** *Brit var of* UTILIZE

¹**util·i·tar·i·an** \yù-,ti-lə-'ter-ē-ən\ *n* : a person who believes in utilitarianism

²**utilitarian** *adj* **1** : of or relating to utilitarianism **2** : of or relating to utility : aiming at usefulness rather than beauty; *also* : serving a useful purpose

**util·i·tar·i·an·ism** \yù-,ti-lə-'ter-ē-ə-,ni-zəm\ *n* : a theory that the greatest good for the greatest number should be the main consideration in making a choice of actions

¹**util·i·ty** \yù-'ti-lə-tē\ *n, pl* **-ties** **1** : USEFULNESS **2** : something useful or designed for use **3** : a business organization performing a public service and subject to special governmental regulation **4** : a public service or a commodity (as electricity or water) provided by a public utility; *also* : equipment to provide such or a similar service

²**utility** *adj* **1** : capable of serving esp. as a substitute in various uses or positions ⟨a ∼ outfielder⟩ ⟨a ∼ cord⟩ **2** : being of a usable but poor quality ⟨∼ beef⟩

**utility knife** *n* : a knife designed for general use; *esp* : one with a retractable blade

**uti·lize** \'yü-tə-,līz\ *vb* **-lized; -liz·ing** : to make use of : turn to profitable account or use — **uti·li·za·tion** \,yü-tə-lə-'zāshən\ *n*

**ut·most** \'ət-,mōst\ *adj* **1** : situated at the farthest or most distant point : EXTREME **2** : of the greatest or highest degree, quantity, number, or amount — **utmost** *n*

**uto·pia** \yù-'tō-pē-ə\ *n* [*Utopia*, imaginary island described in Sir Thomas More's *Utopia*, fr. Gk *ou* not, no + *topos* place] *often cap* **1** : a place of ideal perfection esp. in laws, government, and social conditions **2** : an impractical scheme for social improvement

¹**uto·pi·an** \-pē-ən\ *adj, often cap* **1** : of, relating to, or resembling a utopia **2** : proposing ideal social and political schemes that are impractical **3** : VISIONARY

²**utopian** *n* **1** : a believer in the perfectibility of human society **2** : one who proposes or advocates utopian schemes

¹**ut·ter** \'ə-tər\ *adj* [ME, remote, fr. OE *ūtera* outer, compar. adj. fr. *ūt* out, adv.] : ABSOLUTE, TOTAL ⟨∼ ruin⟩ — **ut·ter·ly** *adv*

²**utter** *vb* [ME *uttren*, fr. *utter* outside, adv., fr. OE *ūtor*, compar. of *ūt* out] **1** : to send forth as a sound : express in usu. spoken

words : PRONOUNCE, SPEAK 2 : to put (as currency) into circulation — **ut·ter·er** n

**ut·ter·ance** \'ə-tə-rəns\ n 1 : something uttered; esp : an oral or written statement 2 : the action of uttering with the voice : SPEECH 3 : power, style, or manner of speaking

**ut·ter·most** \'ə-tər-ˌmōst\ adj : EXTREME, UTMOST ⟨the ~ parts of the earth⟩ — **uttermost** n

**U–turn** \'yü-ˌtərn\ n : a turn resembling the letter U; esp : a 180-degree turn made by a vehicle in a road

**UV** abbr ultraviolet

**uvu·la** \'yü-vyə-lə\ n, pl **-las** or **-lae** \-ˌlē, -ˌlī\ : the fleshy lobe hanging at the back of the roof of the mouth — **uvu·lar** \-lər\ adj

**UW** abbr underwriter

**ux·o·ri·ous** \ˌək-'sȯr-ē-əs, ˌəg-'zȯr-\ adj : excessively devoted or submissive to a wife

**¹v** \'vē\ n, pl **v's** or **vs** \'vēz\ often cap : the 22d letter of the English alphabet

**²v** abbr, often cap 1 vector 2 velocity 3 verb 4 verse 5 versus 6 very 7 victory 8 vide 9 voice 10 voltage 11 volume 12 vowel

**V** symbol 1 vanadium 2 volt

**Va** abbr Virginia

**VA** abbr 1 Veterans Administration 2 vice admiral 3 Virginia

**va·can·cy** \'vā-kən-sē\ n, pl **-cies** 1 : a vacating esp. of an office, position, or piece of property 2 : a vacant office, position, or tenancy; also : the period during which it stands vacant 3 : empty space : VOID 4 : the state of being vacant

**va·cant** \'vā-kənt\ adj 1 : not occupied ⟨~ seat⟩ ⟨~ room⟩ 2 : EMPTY ⟨~ space⟩ 3 : free from business or care ⟨a few ~ hours⟩ 4 : devoid of thought, reflection, or expression ⟨a ~ smile⟩ — **va·cant·ly** adv

**va·cate** \'vā-ˌkāt\ vb **va·cat·ed; va·cat·ing** 1 : to make void : ANNUL 2 : to make vacant (as an office or house); also : to give up the occupancy of

**¹va·ca·tion** \vā-'kā-shən, və-\ n : a period of rest from work : HOLIDAY

**²vacation** vb : to take or spend a vacation — **va·ca·tion·er** n

**va·ca·tion·ist** \-shə-nist\ n : a person taking a vacation

**va·ca·tion·land** \-shən-ˌland\ n : an area with recreational attractions and facilities for vacationists

**vac·ci·nate** \'vak-sə-ˌnāt\ vb **-nat·ed; -nat·ing** : to administer a vaccine to usu. by injection

**vac·ci·na·tion** \ˌvak-sə-'nā-shən\ n 1 : the act of vaccinating 2 : the scar left by vaccinating

**vac·cine** \vak-'sēn, 'vak-ˌsēn\ n [F vaccin, fr. vaccine cowpox, fr. NL vaccina (in variolae vaccinae cowpox), fr. L, fem. of vaccinus of or from cows, fr. vacca cow] : a preparation of material (as of killed or weakened viruses or bacteria) used in vaccinating to produce or increase immunity to a disease

**vac·cin·ia** \vak-'si-nē-ə\ n : COWPOX

**vac·il·late** \'va-sə-ˌlāt\ vb **-lat·ed; -lat·ing** 1 : SWAY, TOTTER; also : FLUCTUATE 2 : to incline first to one course or opinion and then to another : WAVER — **vac·il·la·tion** \ˌva-sə-'lā-shən\ n

**va·cu·ity** \va-'kyü-ə-tē\ n, pl **-ities** 1 : an empty space 2 : the state, fact, or quality of being vacuous 3 : something that is vacuous

**vac·u·ole** \'va-kyə-ˌwōl\ n : a usu. fluid-filled cavity esp. in the cytoplasm of an individual cell — **vac·u·o·lar** \ˌva-kyə-'wō-lər, -ˌlär\ adj

**vac·u·ous** \'va-kyə-wəs\ adj 1 : EMPTY, VACANT, BLANK 2 : DULL, STUPID, INANE ⟨~ movies⟩ — **vac·u·ous·ly** adv — **vac·u·ous·ness** n

**¹vac·u·um** \'va-(ˌ)kyüm, -kyəm\ n, pl **vac·uums** or **vac·ua** \-kyə-wə\ [L, fr. neut. of vacuus empty] 1 : a space entirely empty of matter 2 : a space from which most of the air has been removed (as by a pump) 3 : VOID, GAP 4 : VACUUM CLEANER — **vacuum** adj

**²vacuum** vb : to use a vacuum device (as a vacuum cleaner) on ⟨~ the den⟩

**vacuum bottle** n : THERMOS

**vacuum cleaner** n : a household appliance for cleaning (as floors or rugs) by suction

**vacuum–packed** adj : having much of the air removed before being hermetically sealed ⟨~ fish⟩

**vacuum tube** n : an electron tube from which most of the air has been removed

**va·de me·cum** \ˌvā-dē-'mē-kəm, ˌvä-dē-'mā-\ n, pl **vade mecums** [L, go with me] : something (as a handbook or manual) regularly carried about

**VADM** abbr vice admiral

**¹vag·a·bond** \'va-gə-ˌbänd\ adj 1 : WANDERING, HOMELESS 2 : of, characteristic of, or leading the life of a vagrant or tramp 3 : leading an unsettled or irresponsible life

**²vagabond** n : one leading a vagabond life; esp : VAGRANT, TRAMP

**va·gar·i·ous** \vā-'ger-ē-əs\ adj : marked by vagaries : CAPRICIOUS ⟨~ leadership⟩ — **va·gar·i·ous·ly** adv

**va·ga·ry** \'vā-gə-rē, və-'ger-ē\ n, pl **-ries** : an odd or eccentric idea or action : WHIM, CAPRICE ⟨vagaries of the weather⟩

**va·gi·na** \və-'jī-nə\ *n, pl* **-nae** \-(ˌ)nē\ *or* **-nas** [L, lit., sheath] : a canal that leads from the uterus to the external opening of the female sex organs — **vag·i·nal** \'va-jə-nᵊl\ *adj* — **vag·i·nal·ly** \-nᵊl-ē\ *adv*

**vag·i·ni·tis** \ˌva-jə-'nī-təs\ *n* : inflammation of the vagina

**va·gran·cy** \'vā-grən-sē\ *n, pl* **-cies** 1 : the quality or state of being vagrant; *also* : a vagrant act or notion 2 : the offense of being a vagrant

¹**va·grant** \'vā-grənt\ *n* : a person who has no job and wanders from place to place

²**vagrant** *adj* 1 : of, relating to, or characteristic of a vagrant 2 : following no fixed course : RANDOM, CAPRICIOUS ⟨~ thoughts⟩ — **va·grant·ly** *adv*

**vague** \'vāg\ *adj* **vagu·er; vagu·est** [MF, fr. L *vagus*, lit., wandering] 1 : not clear, definite, or distinct ⟨a ~ plan⟩ ⟨~ silhouettes⟩ 2 : not clearly felt or analyzed ⟨a ~ unrest⟩ ♦ *Synonyms* OBSCURE, DARK, ENIGMATIC, AMBIGUOUS, EQUIVOCAL — **vague·ly** *adv* — **vague·ness** *n*

**vain** \'vān\ *adj* [ME, fr. AF, empty, futile, fr. L *vanus*] 1 : of no real value : IDLE, WORTHLESS 2 : FUTILE, UNSUCCESSFUL 3 : proud of one's looks or abilities ♦ *Synonyms* CONCEITED, NARCISSISTIC, VAINGLORIOUS — **vain·ly** *adv* — **in vain** 1 : without success ⟨her efforts were *in vain*⟩ 2 : in a blasphemous manner ⟨took the Lord's name *in vain*⟩

**vain·glo·ri·ous** \ˌvān-'glȯr-ē-əs\ *adj* : marked by vainglory : BOASTFUL

**vain·glo·ry** \'vān-ˌglȯr-ē\ *n* 1 : excessive or ostentatious pride esp. in one's own achievements 2 : vain display : VANITY

**val** *abbr* value; valued

**va·lance** \'va-ləns, 'vā-\ *n* 1 : drapery hanging from an edge (as of an altar, table, or bed) 2 : a drapery or a decorative frame across the top of a window

**vale** \'vāl\ *n* : VALLEY, DALE

**vale·dic·tion** \ˌva-lə-'dik-shən\ *n* [L *valedicere* to say farewell, fr. *vale* farewell + *dicere* to say] : an act or utterance of leave-taking : FAREWELL

**vale·dic·to·ri·an** \-ˌdik-'tȯr-ē-ən\ *n* : the student usu. of the highest rank in a graduating class who delivers the valedictory address at commencement

**vale·dic·to·ry** \-'dik-tə-rē\ *adj* : bidding farewell : delivered as a valediction ⟨a ~ address⟩ — **valedictory** *n*

**va·lence** \'vā-ləns\ *n* [LL *valentia* power, capacity, fr. L *valēre* to be strong] : the combining power of an atom as shown by the number of its electrons that are lost, gained, or shared in the formation of chemical bonds

**Va·len·ci·ennes** \və-ˌlen-sē-'en, ˌva-lən-sē-, -'enz\ *n* : a fine handmade lace

**val·en·tine** \'va-lən-ˌtīn\ *n* : a sweetheart chosen or complimented on Valentine's Day; *also* : a gift or greeting given on this day

**Valentine's Day** *also* **Valentine Day** *n* : February 14 observed in honor of St. Valentine and as a time for exchanging valentines

¹**va·let** \'va-lət, -(ˌ)lā; va-'lā\ *n* 1 : a male servant who takes care of a man's clothes and performs personal services 2 : an attendant in a hotel or restaurant who performs personal services (as parking cars) for customers

²**valet** *vb* : to serve as a valet

**val·e·tu·di·nar·i·an** \ˌva-lə-ˌtü-də-'ner-ē-ən, -ˌtyü-\ *n* : a person of a weak or sickly constitution; *esp* : one whose chief concern is his or her ill health — **val·e·tu·di·nar·i·an·ism** \-ē-ə-ˌni-zəm\ *n*

**val·iant** \'val-yənt\ *adj* : having or showing valor : BRAVE, HEROIC ♦ *Synonyms* VALOROUS, DOUGHTY, COURAGEOUS, BOLD, AUDACIOUS, DAUNTLESS, UNDAUNTED, INTREPID — **val·iant·ly** *adv*

**val·id** \'va-ləd\ *adj* 1 : having legal force ⟨a ~ contract⟩ 2 : founded on truth or fact : capable of being justified or defended : SOUND ⟨a ~ argument⟩ ⟨~ reasons⟩ — **va·lid·i·ty** \və-'li-də-tē\ *n* — **val·id·ly** *adv*

**val·i·date** \'va-lə-ˌdāt\ *vb* **-dat·ed; -dat·ing** 1 : to make legally valid 2 : to confirm the validity of 3 : VERIFY — **val·i·da·tion** \ˌva-lə-'dā-shən\ *n*

**va·lise** \və-'lēs\ *n* [F] : SUITCASE

**val·ley** \'va-lē\ *n, pl* **valleys** : a long depression between ranges of hills or mountains

**val·or** \'va-lər\ *n* [ME *valour*, worth, worthiness, bravery, fr. AF, fr. ML *valor*, fr. L *valēre* to be strong] : personal bravery ♦ *Synonyms* HEROISM, PROWESS, GALLANTRY — **val·or·ous** \'va-lə-rəs\ *adj*

**val·o·ri·za·tion** \ˌva-lə-rə-'zā-shən\ *n* : the support of commodity prices by any of various forms of government subsidy — **val·o·rize** \'va-lə-ˌrīz\ *vb*

**val·our** *chiefly Brit var of* VALOR

**valu·able** \'val-yə-bəl, -yə-wə-bəl\ *adj* 1 : having money value 2 : having great money value 3 : of great use or service ♦ *Synonyms* INVALUABLE, PRICELESS, COSTLY, EXPENSIVE, DEAR, PRECIOUS

²**valuable** *n* : a usu. personal possession of considerable value ⟨their ~s were stolen⟩

**val·u·ate** \'val-yə-ˌwāt\ *vb* **-at·ed; -at·ing** : to place a value on : APPRAISE — **val·u·a·tor** \-ˌwā-tər\ *n*

**val·u·a·tion** \ˌval-yə-'wā-shən\ *n* 1 : the act or process of valuing; *esp* : appraisal of property 2 : the estimated or determined market value of a thing

¹**val·ue** \'val-yü\ *n* 1 : a fair return or equivalent in money, goods, or services for something exchanged 2 : the monetary worth of a thing; *also* : relative worth, utility, or importance ⟨nothing of ~ to say⟩ 3 : an assigned or computed numerical quantity ⟨the ~ of *x* in an equation⟩ 4 : relative lightness or darkness of a color : LUMINOSITY 5 : the relative length of a tone or note 6 : something (as a principle or ideal) intrinsically valuable or desirable ⟨human rather than material ~s⟩ — **val·ue·less** *adj*

²**value** *vb* **val·ued; valu·ing** 1 : to estimate the monetary worth of : APPRAISE

**2** : to rate in usefulness, importance, or general worth **3** : to consider or rate highly : PRIZE, ESTEEM ⟨*valued* your opinions⟩ — **val·u·er** *n*

**val·ue–add·ed tax** *n* : an incremental excise tax that is levied on the value added at each stage of the processing of a raw material or the production and distribution of a commodity

**valve** \'valv\ *n* **1** : a structure (as in a vein) that temporarily closes a passage or that permits movement in one direction only **2** : a device by which the flow of a fluid material may be regulated by a movable part; *also* : the movable part of such a device **3** : a device in a brass wind instrument for quickly varying the tube length in order to change the fundamental tone by some definite interval **4** : one of the separate usu. hinged pieces of which the shell of some animals and esp. bivalve mollusks consists **5** : one of the pieces into which a ripe seed capsule or pod separates — **valved** \'valvd\ *adj* — **valve·less** *adj*

**val·vu·lar** \'val-vyə-lər\ *adj* : of, relating to, or affecting a valve esp. of the heart ⟨*∼* heart disease⟩

**va·moose** \va-'müs, va-\ *vb* **va·moosed; va·moos·ing** [Sp *vamos* let us go] : to leave or go away quickly

**¹vamp** *n* **1** : the part of a boot or shoe upper covering esp. the front part of the foot **2** : a short introductory musical passage often repeated

**²vamp** \'vamp\ *vb* **1** : to provide with a new vamp **2** : to patch up with a new part : INVENT, IMPROVISE ⟨*∼* up an excuse⟩

**³vamp** *n* : a woman who uses her charm or wiles to seduce and exploit men

**⁴vamp** *vb* : to practice seductive wiles on : to act like a vamp

**vam·pire** \'vam-ˌpī(-ə)r\ *n* [F, fr. G *Vampir,* fr. Serbian *vampir*] **1** : a reanimated corpse of folklore that bites and sucks the blood of the living **2** : a person who preys on other people; *esp* : a woman who exploits and ruins her lover **3** : VAMPIRE BAT

**vampire bat** *n* : any of various bats of Central and South America that feed on the blood of animals; *also* : any of several bats that do not feed on blood but are sometimes reputed to do so

**¹van** \'van\ *n* : VANGUARD

**²van** *n* : a usu. enclosed wagon or motortruck for moving goods or animals; *also* : a versatile enclosed box-like motor vehicle

**va·na·di·um** \və-'nā-dē-əm\ *n* : a soft grayish ductile metallic chemical element used esp. to form alloys

**Van Al·len belt** \van-'a-lən-\ *n* : a belt of intense radiation in the magnetosphere composed of charged particles trapped by earth's magnetic field

**van·co·my·cin** \ˌvan-kə-'mī-sᵊn\ *n* : an antibiotic used esp. against staphylococci

**van·dal** \'van-dᵊl\ *n* **1** *cap* : a member of a Germanic people who sacked Rome in A.D. 455 **2** : a person who willfully mars or destroys property

**van·dal·ise** *Brit var of* VANDALIZE

**van·dal·ism** \'van-də-ˌli-zəm\ *n* : willful or malicious destruction or defacement of public or private property

**van·dal·ize** \-ˌlīz\ *vb* **-ized; -iz·ing** : to subject to vandalism : DAMAGE

**Van·dyke** \van-'dīk\ *n* : a trim pointed beard

**vane** \'vān\ *n* [ME, fr. OE *fana* banner] **1** : a movable device attached to a high object for showing wind direction **2** : a thin flat or curved object that is rotated about an axis by a flow of fluid or that rotates to cause a fluid to flow or that redirects a flow of fluid ⟨the *∼s* of a windmill⟩ **3** : a feather fastened near the back end of an arrow for stability in flight

**van·guard** \'van-ˌgärd\ *n* **1** : the troops moving at the front of an army **2** : the forefront of an action or movement

**va·nil·la** \və-'ni-lə\ *n* [NL, genus name, fr. Sp *vainilla* vanilla (plant and fruit), dim. of *vaina* sheath, fr. L *vagina*] : a flavoring extract made synthetically or obtained from the long beanlike pods (**vanilla beans**) of a tropical American climbing orchid; *also* : this orchid

**van·ish** \'va-nish\ *vb* : to pass from sight or existence : disappear completely — **van·ish·er** *n*

**van·i·ty** \'va-nə-tē\ *n, pl* **-ties** **1** : something that is vain, empty, or useless **2** : the quality or fact of being useless or futile : FUTILITY **3** : undue pride in oneself or one's appearance : CONCEIT **4** : a small case for cosmetics : COMPACT

**vanity plate** *n* : an automobile license plate bearing distinctive letters or numbers designated by the owner

**van·quish** \'vaŋ-kwish, 'van-\ *vb* **1** : to overcome in battle or in a contest **2** : to gain mastery over (as an emotion)

**van·tage** \'van-tij\ *n* **1** : superiority in a contest **2** : a position giving a strategic advantage or a commanding perspective

**va·pid** \'va-pəd, 'vā-\ *adj* : lacking spirit, liveliness, or zest : FLAT, INSIPID ⟨*∼* gossip⟩ — **va·pid·i·ty** \va-'pi-də-tē\ *n* — **vap·id·ly** *adv* — **vap·id·ness** *n*

**va·por** \'vā-pər\ *n* **1** : fine separated particles (as fog or smoke) floating in the air and clouding it **2** : a substance in the gaseous state; *esp* : one that is liquid under ordinary conditions **3** : something insubstantial or fleeting **4** *pl* : a depressed or hysterical nervous condition

**va·por·ing** \'vā-pə-riŋ\ *n* : an idle, boastful, or high-flown expression or speech — usu. used in pl. ⟨political *∼s*⟩

**va·por·ise** *Brit var of* VAPORIZE

**va·por·ize** \'vā-pə-ˌrīz\ *vb* **-ized; -iz·ing** **1** : to convert into vapor **2** : to destroy as if by converting to vapor ⟨*vaporized* enemy tanks⟩ — **va·por·i·za·tion** \ˌvā-pə-rə-'zā-shən\ *n*

**va·por·iz·er** \-ˌrī-zər\ *n* : a device that vaporizes something (as a medicated liquid)

**vapor lock** *n* : an interruption of flow of a fluid (as fuel in an engine) caused by the formation of vapor in the feeding system

**va·por·ous** \'vā-pə-rəs\ adj 1 : full of vapors : FOGGY, MISTY 2 : UNSUBSTANTIAL, VAGUE ⟨∼ speculations⟩ — **va·por·ous·ly** adv — **va·por·ous·ness** n

**va·pory** \'vā-pə-rē\ adj : MISTY

**va·pour** chiefly Brit var of VAPOR

**va·que·ro** \vä-'ker-ō\ n, pl **-ros** [Sp, fr. vaca cow, fr. L vacca] : a ranch hand : COWBOY

**var** abbr 1 variable 2 variant; variation 3 variety 4 various

**¹vari·able** \'ver-ē-ə-bəl\ adj 1 : able or apt to vary : CHANGEABLE 2 : FICKLE 3 : not true to type : ABERRANT ⟨a ∼ wheat⟩ — **var·i·abil·i·ty** \,ver-ē-ə-'bi-lə-tē,\ var-\ n — **vari·ably** \-blē\ adv

**²variable** n 1 : a quantity that may take on any of a set of values; also : a mathematical symbol representing a variable 2 : something that is variable

**var·i·ance** \'ver-ē-əns\ n 1 : variation or a degree of variation : DEVIATION 2 : DISAGREEMENT, DISPUTE 3 : a license to do something contrary to the usual rule ⟨a zoning ∼⟩ 4 : the square of the standard deviation ♦ **Synonyms** DISCORD, CONTENTION, DISSENSION, STRIFE, CONFLICT

**¹vari·ant** \'ver-ē-ənt\ adj 1 : differing from others of its kind or class 2 : varying usu. slightly from the standard or type

**²variant** n 1 : one that exhibits variation from a type or norm 2 : one of two or more different spellings or pronunciations of a word

**var·i·a·tion** \,ver-ē-'ā-shən\ n 1 : the act, process, or an instance of varying : a change in form, position, or condition : MODIFICATION, ALTERATION 2 : extent of change or difference 3 : divergence in the characteristics of an organism from those typical or usual for its group; also : one exhibiting such variation 4 : repetition of a musical theme with modification in rhythm, tune, harmony, or key

**vari·col·ored** \'ver-i-,kə-lərd\ adj : having various colors : VARIEGATED

**var·i·cose** \'va-rə-,kōs\ adj : abnormally swollen and dilated ⟨∼ veins⟩ — **vari·cos·i·ty** \,va-rə-'kä-sə-tē\ n

**var·ied** \'ver-ēd\ adj 1 : having many forms or types : DIVERSE ⟨∼ interests⟩ 2 : VARIEGATED — **var·ied·ly** adv

**var·ie·gat·ed** \'ver-ē-ə-,gā-təd\ adj 1 : having patches, stripes, or marks of different colors ⟨∼ flowers⟩ 2 : VARIED 1 — **var·ie·gate** \-,gāt\ vb — **var·ie·ga·tion** \,ver-ē-ə-'gā-shən\ n

**¹va·ri·etal** \və-'rī-ə-t⁹l\ adj : of or relating to a variety; esp : of, relating to, or producing a varietal

**²varietal** n : a wine bearing the name of the principal grape from which it is made

**va·ri·ety** \və-'rī-ə-tē\ n, pl **-eties 1** : the state of being varied or various : DIVERSITY 2 : a collection of different things : ASSORTMENT 3 : something varying from others of the same general kind 4 : any of various groups of plants or animals within a species distinguished by characteristics insufficient to separate species : SUBSPECIES 5 : entertainment such as is given in a stage presentation comprising a series of performances (as songs, dances, or acrobatic acts)

**var·i·o·rum** \,ver-ē-'ȯr-əm\ n : an edition or text of a work containing notes by various persons or variant readings of the text

**var·i·ous** \'ver-ē-əs\ adj 1 : VARICOLORED 2 : of differing kinds : MULTIFARIOUS 3 : UNLIKE ⟨animals as ∼ as the jaguar and the sloth⟩ 4 : having a number of different aspects 5 : NUMEROUS, MANY 6 : INDIVIDUAL, SEPARATE ♦ **Synonyms** DIVERGENT, DISPARATE, DIFFERENT, DISSIMILAR, DIVERSE, UNALIKE — **var·i·ous·ly** adv

**var·let** \'vär-lət\ n 1 : ATTENDANT 2 : SCOUNDREL, KNAVE

**var·mint** \'vär-mənt\ n [alter. of vermin] 1 : an animal considered a pest; esp : one classed as vermin and unprotected by game law 2 : a contemptible person : RASCAL

**¹var·nish** \'vär-nish\ n 1 : a liquid preparation that is applied to a surface and dries into a hard glossy coating; also : the glaze of this coating 2 : something suggesting varnish by its gloss 3 : outside show : deceptive or superficial appearance

**²varnish** vb 1 : to cover with varnish 2 : to cover or conceal with something that gives a fair appearance : GLOSS

**var·si·ty** \'vär-sə-tē\ n, pl **-ties** [by shortening & alter. fr. university] 1 Brit : UNIVERSITY 2 : the principal team representing a college, school, or club

**vary** \'ver-ē\ vb **var·ied; vary·ing 1** : ALTER, CHANGE 2 : to make or be of different kinds : introduce or have variety : DIVERSIFY, DIFFER 3 : DEVIATE, SWERVE 4 : to change in bodily structure or function away from what is usual for members of a group

**vas·cu·lar** \'vas-kyə-lər\ adj [NL vascularis, fr. L vasculum small vessel, dim. of vas vase, vessel] : of or relating to a channel or system of channels for the conveyance of a body fluid (as blood or sap); also : supplied with or containing such vessels and esp. blood vessels ⟨the ∼ system⟩

**vascular plant** n : a plant having a specialized system for carrying fluids that includes xylem and phloem

**vas def·er·ens** \'vas-'de-fə-rənz\ n, pl **va·sa def·er·en·tia** \'vā-zə-,de-fə-'ren-shē-ə\ : a sperm-carrying duct of the testis

**vase** \'vās, 'vāz\ n : a usu. round vessel of greater depth than width used chiefly for ornament or for flowers

**va·sec·to·my** \və-'sek-tə-mē, vā-'zek-\ n, pl **-mies** : surgical excision of all or part of the vas deferens usu. to induce sterility

**va·so·con·stric·tion** \,vā-zō-kən-'strik-shən\ n : narrowing of the interior diameter of blood vessels

**va·so·con·stric·tor** \-tər\ n : an agent (as

a nerve fiber or a drug) that initiates or induces vasoconstriction

**vas·sal** \'va-səl\ *n* **1** : a person under the protection of a feudal lord to whom he owes homage and loyalty : a feudal tenant **2** : one occupying a dependent or subordinate position — **vassal** *adj*

**vas·sal·age** \-sə-lij\ *n* **1** : the state of being a vassal **2** : the homage and loyalty due from a vassal **3** : SERVITUDE, SUBJECTION

**¹vast** \'vast\ *adj* : very great in size, amount, degree, intensity, or esp. extent ⟨~ plains⟩ ⟨~ knowledge⟩ ♦ *Synonyms* ENORMOUS, HUGE, GIGANTIC, COLOSSAL, MAMMOTH — **vast·ly** *adv* — **vast·ness** *n*

**²vast** *n* : a great expanse : IMMENSITY
**vast·ly** \'vast-lē\ *adj* : VAST, IMMENSE

**vat** \'vat\ *n* : a large vessel (as a tub or barrel) esp. for holding liquids in manufacturing processes

**VAT** *abbr* value-added tax

**vat·ic** \'va-tik\ *adj* : PROPHETIC, ORACULAR ⟨~ pronouncements⟩

**Vat·i·can** \'va-ti-kən\ *n* **1** : the papal headquarters in Rome **2** : the papal government

**va·tu** \'vä-,tü\ *n, pl* **vatu** — see MONEY table

**vaude·ville** \'vod-vəl, 'väd-, 'vōd-, -,vil\ *n* [F, fr. MF, satirical song, alter. of *vaudevire*, fr. *vau-de-Vire* valley of Vire, town in northwest France where such songs were composed] : a stage entertainment consisting of unrelated acts (as of acrobats, comedians, dancers, or singers)

**¹vault** \'volt\ *n* **1** : an arched masonry structure usu. forming a ceiling or roof; *also* : something (as the sky) resembling a vault **2** : a room or space covered by a vault esp. when underground **3** : a room or compartment for the safekeeping of valuables **4** : a burial chamber; *also* : a usu. metal or concrete case in which a casket is enclosed at burial — **vaulty** *adj*

**²vault** *vb* : to form or cover with a vault

**³vault** *vb* : to leap vigorously esp. by aid of the hands or a pole — **vault·er** *n*

**⁴vault** *n* : an act of vaulting : LEAP

**vault·ed** \'vol-təd\ *adj* **1** : built in the form of a vault : ARCHED **2** : covered with a vault

**vault·ing** \-tiŋ\ *adj* : reaching for the heights ⟨~ ambition⟩

**vaunt** \'vont\ *vb* [ME, fr. AF *vanter*, fr. LL *vanitare*, ultim. fr. L *vanus* vain] : to boast of ⟨~s his successes⟩ — **vaunt** *n*

**vaunt·ed** \'von-təd\ *adj* : much praised or boasted of

**vb** *abbr* verb; verbal

**V–chip** \'vē-,chip\ *n* : a computer chip in a television set used to block based on content the viewing of certain programs

**VCR** \,vē-(,)sē-'är\ *n* [videocassette recorder] : a device that records and plays back videotapes

**VD** *abbr* venereal disease

**VDT** *abbr* video display terminal

**veal** \'vēl\ *n* : the flesh of a young calf

**vec·tor** \'vek-tər\ *n* **1** : a quantity that has magnitude and direction **2** : an organism (as a fly or tick) that transmits a pathogen

**Ve·da** \'vā-də\ *n* [Skt, lit., knowledge] : any of a class of Hindu sacred writings — **Ve·dic** \'vā-dik\ *adj*

**Ve·dan·ta** \vā-'dän-tə, və-, 'dan-\ *n* : an orthodox Hindu philosophy based on the Upanishads

**vee·jay** \'vē-jā\ *n* : an announcer of a program featuring music videos

**veep** \'vēp\ *n* : VICE PRESIDENT

**veer** \'vir\ *vb* : to shift from one direction or course to another ♦ *Synonyms* TURN, AVERT, DEFLECT, DIVERT — **veer** *n*

**veg·an** \'vē-gən, 'vä-; 've-jən, -jan\ *n* : a strict vegetarian who consumes no animal food or dairy products — **veg·an·ism** \'vē-gə-,ni-zəm, 'vä-, 've-\ *n*

**¹veg·e·ta·ble** \'vej-tə-bəl, 've-jə-\ *adj* [ME, fr. ML *vegetabilis* vegetative, fr. *vegetare* to grow, fr. L, to animate, fr. *vegetus* lively, fr. *vegēre* to enliven] **1** : of, relating to, or growing like plants ⟨the ~ kingdom⟩ **2** : made from, obtained from, or containing plants or plant products ⟨~ oils⟩ **3** : suggesting that of a plant (as in inertness) ⟨a ~ existence⟩

**²vegetable** *n* **1** : PLANT 1 **2** : a usu. herbaceous plant grown for an edible part that is usu. eaten as part of a meal; *also* : such an edible part

**veg·e·tal** \'ve-jə-t³l\ *adj* **1** : VEGETABLE **2** : VEGETATIVE

**veg·e·tar·i·an** \,ve-jə-'ter-ē-ən\ *n* : one that believes in or practices living on a diet of vegetables, fruits, grains, nuts, and sometimes animal products (as milk and cheese) — **vegetarian** *adj* — **veg·e·tar·i·an·ism** \-ē-ə-,ni-zəm\ *n*

**veg·e·tate** \'ve-jə-,tāt\ *vb* **-tat·ed; -tat·ing** : to live or grow in the manner of a plant; *esp* : to lead a dull inert life

**veg·e·ta·tion** \,ve-jə-'tā-shən\ *n* **1** : the act or process of vegetating; *also* : inert existence **2** : plant life or cover (as of an area) — **veg·e·ta·tion·al** \-shə-nəl\ *adj*

**veg·e·ta·tive** \'ve-jə-,tā-tiv\ *adj* **1** : of or relating to nutrition and growth esp. as contrasted with reproduction **2** : of, relating to, or composed of vegetation ⟨~ cover⟩ **3** : VEGETABLE 3

**veg out** \'vej-\ *vb* **vegged out; vegging out** [short for *vegetate*] : to spend time idly or passively

**ve·he·ment** \'vē-ə-mənt\ *adj* **1** : marked by great force or energy **2** : marked by strong feeling or expression : PASSIONATE, FERVID ⟨~ opposition⟩ — **ve·he·mence** \-məns\ *n* — **ve·he·ment·ly** *adv*

**ve·hi·cle** \'vē-ə-kəl, 'vē-,hi-\ *n* **1** : a medium by which a thing is applied or administered ⟨linseed oil is a ~ for pigments⟩ **2** : a medium through or by means of which something is conveyed or expressed **3** : a means of transporting persons or goods ♦ *Synonyms* INSTRUMENT, AGENT, AGENCY, ORGAN, CHANNEL — **ve·hic·u·lar** \vē-'hi-kyə-lər\ *adj*

**¹veil** \'vāl\ *n* **1** : a piece of often sheer or diaphanous material used to screen or curtain something or to cover the head or face **2** : the life of a nun ⟨take the ∼⟩ **3** : something that hides or obscures like a veil ⟨a ∼ of secrecy⟩

²**veil** vb : to cover with or as if with a veil : wear a veil

¹**vein** \'vān\ n **1** : a fissure in rock filled with mineral matter; also : a bed of useful mineral matter **2** : any of the tubular branching vessels that carry blood from the capillaries toward the heart **3** : any of the bundles of vascular vessels forming the framework of a leaf **4** : any of the thickened ribs that stiffen the wings of an insect **5** : something (as a wavy variegation in marble) suggesting veins **6** : a distinctive style of expression **7** : a distinctive element or quality : STRAIN **8** : MOOD, HUMOR — **veined** \'vānd\ adj

²**vein** vb : to pattern with or as if with veins — **vein·ing** n

**vel** abbr velocity

**ve·lar** \'vē-lər\ adj : of or relating to a velum and esp. that of the soft palate

**veld** or **veldt** \'velt, 'felt\ n [Afrikaans veld, fr. D. field] : an open grassland esp. in southern Africa usu. with scattered shrubs or trees

**vel·lum** \'ve-ləm\ n [ME velym, fr. AF velim, veeslin, fr. *veelin, adj., of a calf, fr. veel calf] **1** : a fine-grained lambskin, kidskin, or calfskin prepared for writing on or for binding books **2** : a strong cream-colored paper — **vellum** adj

**ve·loc·i·pede** \və-'lä-sə-ˌpēd\ n : an early bicycle

**ve·loc·i·rap·tor** \və-'lä-sə-ˌrap-tər\ n : any of a genus of agile flesh-eating bipedal dinosaurs of the Cretaceous having a sickle-shaped claw on each foot

**ve·loc·i·ty** \və-'lä-sə-tē\ n, pl **-ties** : quickness of motion : SPEED ⟨the ∼ of light⟩

**ve·lour** or **ve·lours** \və-'lůr\ n, pl **ve·lours** \-'lůrz\ : any of various textile fabrics with pile like that of velvet

**ve·lum** \'vē-ləm\ n, pl **ve·la** \-lə\ : a membranous body part (as the soft palate) resembling a veil

**vel·vet** \'vel-vət\ n [ME veluet, velvet, fr. AF, fr. velu shaggy, ultim. fr. L villus shaggy hair] **1** : a fabric having a short soft dense warp pile **2** : something resembling or suggesting velvet (as in softness or luster) **3** : the soft skin covering the growing antlers of a deer — **velvet** adj — **velvety** adj

**vel·ve·teen** \ˌvel-və-'tēn\ n **1** : a fabric woven usu. of cotton in imitation of velvet **2** pl : clothes made of velveteen

**Ven** abbr venerable

**ve·nal** \'vē-n°l\ adj : capable of being bought or bribed : MERCENARY, CORRUPT ⟨∼ legislators⟩ — **ve·nal·i·ty** \vi-'na-lə-tē\ n — **ve·nal·ly** \'vē-n°l-ē\ adv

**ve·na·tion** \ve-'nā-shən, vē-\ n : an arrangement or system of veins ⟨the ∼ of the hand⟩ ⟨leaf ∼⟩

**vend** \'vend\ vb : SELL; esp : to sell as a hawker or peddler — **vend·ible** adj

**vend·ee** \ven-'dē\ n : one to whom a thing is sold : BUYER

**ven·det·ta** \ven-'de-tə\ n : a feud marked by acts of revenge

**vending machine** n : a coin-operated machine for selling merchandise

**ven·dor** \'ven-dər, for 1 also ven-'dȯr\ n **1** : one that vends : SELLER **2** : VENDING MACHINE

¹**ve·neer** \və-'nir\ n [G Furnier, fr. furnieren to veneer, fr. F fournir to furnish] **1** : a thin usu. superficial layer of material ⟨brick ∼⟩; esp : a thin layer of fine wood glued over a cheaper wood **2** : superficial display : GLOSS

²**veneer** vb : to overlay with a veneer

**ven·er·a·ble** \'ve-nə-rə-bəl\ adj **1** : deserving to be venerated — often used as a religious title **2** : made sacred by association

**ven·er·ate** \'ve-nə-ˌrāt\ vb **-at·ed; -at·ing** : to regard with reverential respect

♦ **Synonyms** ADORE, REVERE, REVERENCE, WORSHIP — **ven·er·a·tion** \ˌve-nə-'rā-shən\ n

**ve·ne·re·al** \və-'nir-ē-əl\ adj : of or relating to sexual intercourse or to diseases transmitted by it ⟨a ∼ infection⟩

**venereal disease** n : a contagious disease (as gonorrhea or syphilis) usu. acquired by having sexual intercourse with someone who already has it

**ve·ne·tian blind** \və-'nē-shən-\ n : a blind having thin horizontal parallel slats that can be adjusted to admit a desired amount of light

**ven·geance** \'ven-jəns\ n : punishment inflicted in retaliation for an injury or offense : REVENGE

**venge·ful** \'venj-fəl\ adj : filled with a desire for revenge : VINDICTIVE ⟨a ∼ former employee⟩ — **venge·ful·ly** adv

**ve·nial** \'vē-nē-əl\ adj : capable of being forgiven : EXCUSABLE ⟨∼ sin⟩

**ve·ni·re** \və-'nī-rē\ n : a panel from which a jury is drawn

**ve·ni·re fa·ci·as** \-'fā-shē-əs\ n [ME, fr. ML, you should cause to come] : a writ summoning persons to appear in court to serve as jurors

**ve·ni·re·man** \və-'nī-rē-mən, -'nir-ē-\ n : a member of a venire

**ven·i·son** \'ve-nə-sən, -zən\ n, pl **venisons** also **venison** [ME, fr. AF veneisun game, venison, fr. L venatio, fr. venari to hunt, pursue] : the edible flesh of a deer

**ven·om** \'ve-nəm\ n [ME venim, fr. AF, ultim. fr. L venenum magic charm, drug, poison] **1** : poisonous material secreted by some animals (as snakes, spiders, or bees) and transmitted usu. by biting or stinging **2** : ILL WILL, MALEVOLENCE

**ven·om·ous** \'ve-nə-məs\ adj **1** : full of venom : POISONOUS **2** : SPITEFUL, MALEVOLENT ⟨∼ comments⟩ **3** : secreting and using venom ⟨∼ snakes⟩ — **ven·om·ous·ly** adv

**ve·nous** \'vē-nəs\ adj **1** : of, relating to, or full of veins **2** : being purplish red oxygen-deficient blood rich in carbon dioxide that is present in most veins

¹**vent** \'vent\ vb **1** : to provide with a vent **2** : to serve as a vent for **3** : EXPEL, DISCHARGE **4** : to relieve oneself by vigorous or emotional expression

²**vent** n **1** : an opportunity or way of es-

cape or passage : OUTLET **2** : an opening for the escape of a gas or liquid or for the relief of pressure

**³vent** *n* : a slit in a garment esp. in the lower part of a seam (as of a jacket or skirt)

**ven·ti·late** \'ven-tə-ˌlāt\ *vb* **-lat·ed; -lat·ing** **1** : to discuss freely and openly ⟨∼ a question⟩ **2** : to give vent to ⟨∼ one's grievances⟩ **3** : to cause fresh air to circulate through (as a room or mine) so as to replace foul air **4** : to provide with a vent or outlet ♦ *Synonyms* EXPRESS, VENT, AIR, UTTER, VOICE, BROACH — **ven·ti·la·tor** \-lə-tər\ *n*

**ven·ti·la·tion** \ˌven-tə-ˈlā-shən\ *n* **1** : the act or process of ventilating **2** : circulation of air in a room **3** : a system or means of providing fresh air

**ven·tral** \'ven-trəl\ *adj* **1** : of or relating to the belly : ABDOMINAL **2** : of, relating to, or located on or near the surface of the body that in humans is the front but in most other animals is the lower surface — **ven·tral·ly** *adv*

**ven·tri·cle** \'ven-tri-kəl\ *n* **1** : a chamber of the heart that receives blood from the atrium of the same side and pumps it into the arteries **2** : any of the communicating cavities of the brain that are continuous with the central canal of the spinal cord — **ven·tric·u·lar** \ven-ˈtri-kyə-lər\ *adj*

**ven·tril·o·quism** \ven-ˈtri-lə-ˌkwi-zəm\ *n* [LL *ventriloquus* ventriloquist, fr. L *venter* belly + *loqui* to speak; fr. the belief that the voice is produced from the ventriloquist's stomach] : the production of the voice in such a manner that the sound appears to come from a source other than the speaker — **ven·tril·o·quist** \-kwist\ *n*

**ven·tril·o·quy** \-kwē\ *n* : VENTRILOQUISM

**¹ven·ture** \'ven-chər\ *vb* **ven·tured; ven·tur·ing** **1** : to expose to hazard : RISK **2** : to undertake the risks of : BRAVE **3** : to offer at the risk of rebuff, rejection, or censure ⟨∼ an opinion⟩ **4** : to proceed despite danger : DARE

**²venture** *n* **1** : an undertaking involving chance or risk; *esp* : a speculative business enterprise **2** : something risked in a speculative venture : STAKE

**ven·ture·some** \'ven-chər-səm\ *adj* **1** : involving risk : DANGEROUS, HAZARDOUS **2** : inclined to venture : BOLD, DARING ♦ *Synonyms* ADVENTUROUS, VENTUROUS, RASH, RECKLESS, FOOLHARDY — **ven·ture·some·ly** *adv* — **ven·ture·some·ness** *n*

**ven·tur·ous** \'ven-chə-rəs\ *adj* : VENTURESOME — **ven·tur·ous·ly** *adv* — **ven·tur·ous·ness** *n*

**ven·ue** \'ven-yü\ *n* [AF, alter. of *vinné, visné,* lit., neighborhood, neighbors, ultim. fr. L *vicinitas* vicinity] **1** : the place from which the jury is taken and where the trial is held **2** : the place in which the alleged events from which a legal action arises took place **3** : a place where events are held ⟨music ∼s⟩

**Ve·nus** \'vē-nəs\ *n* : the planet 2d in order from the sun

**Venus fly·trap** *or* **Ve·nus's–fly·trap** \'vē-nə-səz-ˈflī-ˌtrap\ *n* : an insect-eating plant of the Carolina coast that has the leaf tip modified into an insect trap

**Ve·nu·sian** \vi-ˈnü-zhən, -ˈnyü-\ *adj* : of or relating to the planet Venus

**ve·ra·cious** \və-ˈrā-shəs\ *adj* **1** : TRUTHFUL, HONEST **2** : TRUE, ACCURATE ⟨∼ details⟩ — **ve·ra·cious·ly** *adv*

**ve·rac·i·ty** \və-ˈra-sə-tē\ *n, pl* **-ties** **1** : devotion to truth : TRUTHFULNESS **2** : conformity with fact : ACCURACY **3** : something true

**ve·ran·da** *or* **ve·ran·dah** \və-ˈran-də\ *n* : a long open usu. roofed porch

**verb** \'vərb\ *n* : a word that is the grammatical center of a predicate and expresses an act, occurrence, or mode of being

**¹ver·bal** \'vər-bəl\ *adj* **1** : of, relating to, or consisting of words; *esp* : having to do with words rather than with the ideas to be conveyed **2** : expressed in usu. spoken words : not written : ORAL ⟨a ∼ contract⟩ **3** : of, relating to, or formed from a verb ⟨a ∼ adjective⟩ **4** : LITERAL, VERBATIM — **ver·bal·ly** *adv*

**²verbal** *n* : a word that combines characteristics of a verb with those of a noun or adjective

**verbal auxiliary** *n* : an auxiliary verb

**ver·bal·ize** \'vər-bə-ˌlīz\ *vb* **-ized; -iz·ing** **1** : to speak or write in wordy or empty fashion **2** : to express something in words : describe verbally ⟨*verbalized* her feelings⟩ **3** : to convert into a verb — **ver·bal·i·za·tion** \ˌvər-bə-lə-ˈzā-shən\ *n*

**verbal noun** *n* : a noun derived directly from a verb or verb stem and in some uses having the sense and constructions of a verb

**ver·ba·tim** \(ˌ)vər-ˈbā-təm\ *adv or adj* : in the same words : word for word

**ver·be·na** \(ˌ)vər-ˈbē-nə\ *n* : VERVAIN; *esp* : any of several garden vervains of hybrid origin with showy spikes of bright often fragrant flowers

**ver·biage** \'vər-bē-ij, -bij\ *n* **1** : superfluity of words usu. of little or obscure content **2** : DICTION, WORDING

**ver·bose** \(ˌ)vər-ˈbōs\ *adj* : using more words than are needed : WORDY ♦ *Synonyms* PROLIX, DIFFUSE, REDUNDANT, WINDY — **ver·bos·i·ty** \-ˈbä-sə-tē\ *n*

**ver·bo·ten** \vər-ˈbō-tᵊn, fər-\ *adj* [G] : forbidden usu. by dictate

**ver·dant** \'vər-dᵊnt\ *adj* : green with growing plants — **ver·dant·ly** *adv*

**ver·dict** \'vər-(ˌ)dikt\ *n* [ME *verdit, verdict,* fr. AF *veirdit,* fr. *veir* true (fr. L *verus*) + *dit* saying, dictum, fr. L *dictum,* fr. *dicere* to say] **1** : the finding or decision of a jury **2** : DECISION, JUDGMENT

**ver·di·gris** \'vər-də-ˌgrēs, -ˌgris\ *n* : a green or bluish deposit that forms on copper, brass, or bronze surfaces

**ver·dure** \'vər-jər\ *n* : the greenness of growing vegetation; *also* : such vegetation

**¹verge** \'vərj\ *n* [[ME, rod, measuring rod, margin, fr. AF, rod, area of jurisdiction, fr. L *virga* twig, rod, line] **1** : a staff carried as an emblem of authority or office **2** : something that borders or bounds : EDGE, MARGIN **3** : BRINK, THRESHOLD ⟨on the ~ of collapse⟩

²**verge** *vb* **verged; verg·ing 1** : to be contiguous **2** : to be on the verge

³**verge** *vb* **verged; verg·ing 1** : to move or extend in some direction or toward some condition : INCLINE **2** : to be in transition or change

**verg·er** \'vər-jər\ *n* **1** *chiefly Brit* : an attendant who carries a verge (as before a bishop) **2** : SEXTON

**ve·rid·i·cal** \və-'ri-di-kəl\ *adj* **1** : TRUTHFUL **2** : not illusory : GENUINE

**ver·i·fy** \'ver-ə-ˌfī\ *vb* **-fied; -fy·ing 1** : to confirm in law by oath **2** : to establish the truth, accuracy, or reality of ⟨~ the claim⟩ ◆ **Synonyms** AUTHENTICATE, CORROBORATE, SUBSTANTIATE, VALIDATE — **ver·i·fi·able** *adj* — **ver·i·fi·ca·tion** \ˌver-ə-fə-'kā-shən\ *n*

**ver·i·ly** \'ver-ə-lē\ *adv* **1** : in very truth : CERTAINLY **2** : TRULY, CONFIDENTLY

**veri·si·mil·i·tude** \ˌver-ə-sə-'mi-lə-ˌtüd, -ˌtyüd\ *n* : the quality or state of appearing to be true or real

**ver·i·ta·ble** \'ver-ə-tə-bəl\ *adj* : ACTUAL, GENUINE, TRUE — **ver·i·ta·bly** *adv*

**ver·i·ty** \'ver-ə-tē\ *n, pl* **-ties 1** : the quality or state of being true or real : TRUTH, REALITY **2** : something (as a statement) that is true **3** : HONESTY, VERACITY

**ver·meil 1** [MF] **1** \'vər-məl, -ˌmāl\ : VERMILION **2** \ver-'mā\ : gilded silver

**ver·mi·cel·li** \ˌvər-mə-'che-lē, -'se-\ *n* [It, fr. pl. of *vermicello,* dim. of *verme* worm] : a pasta made in thinner strings than spaghetti

**ver·mic·u·lite** \vər-'mi-kyə-ˌlīt\ *n* : any of various lightweight water-absorbent minerals derived from mica

**ver·mi·form appendix** \'vər-mə-ˌform-\ *n* : APPENDIX 2

**ver·mil·ion** *also* **ver·mil·lion** \vər-'mil-yən\ *n* : a bright reddish orange color; *also* : any of various red pigments

**ver·min** \'vər-mən\ *n, pl* **vermin 1** : small common harmful or objectionable animals (as lice or mice) that are difficult to get rid of **2** : birds and mammals that prey on game — **ver·min·ous** *adj*

**ver·mouth** \vər-'müth\ *n* [F *vermout,* fr. G *Wermut* wormwood] : a dry or sweet wine flavored with herbs and often used in mixed drinks

¹**ver·nac·u·lar** \vər-'na-kyə-lər\ *adj* [L *vernaculus* native, fr. *verna* slave born in the master's house, native] **1** : of, relating to, or being a language or dialect native to a region or country rather than a literary, cultured, or foreign language **2** : of, relating to, or being the normal spoken form of a language **3** : applied to a plant or animal in common speech as distinguished from biological nomenclature ⟨~ names⟩

²**vernacular** *n* **1** : a vernacular language **2** : the mode of expression of a group or class **3** : a vernacular name of a plant or animal

**ver·nal** \'vər-nᵊl\ *adj* : of, relating to, or occurring in the spring ⟨~ equinox⟩

**ver·ni·er** \'vər-nē-ər\ *n* : a short scale made to slide along the divisions of a graduated instrument to indicate parts of divisions

**ve·ron·i·ca** \və-'rä-ni-kə\ *n* : any of a genus of herbs related to the snapdragons that have small usu. bluish flowers

**ver·sa·tile** \'vər-sə-tᵊl\ *adj* : turning with ease from one thing or position to another; *esp* : having many aptitudes — **ver·sa·til·i·ty** \ˌvər-sə-'ti-lə-tē\ *n*

¹**verse** \'vərs\ *n* **1** : a line of poetry; *also* : STANZA **2** : metrical writing distinguished from poetry esp. by its lower level of intensity **3** : POETRY **4** : POEM **5** : one of the short divisions of a chapter in the Bible

²**verse** *vb* **versed; vers·ing** : to familiarize by experience, study, or practice ⟨well *versed* in the theater⟩

**ver·si·cle** \'vər-si-kəl\ *n* : a verse or sentence said or sung by a leader in public worship and followed by a response from the people

**ver·si·fi·ca·tion** \ˌvər-sə-fə-'kā-shən\ *n* **1** : the making of verses **2** : metrical structure

**ver·si·fy** \'vər-sə-ˌfī\ *vb* **-fied; -fy·ing 1** : to write verse **2** : to turn into verse — **ver·si·fi·er** \-ˌfī-ər\ *n*

**ver·sion** \'vər-zhən\ *n* **1** : TRANSLATION; *esp* : a translation of the Bible **2** : an account or description from a particular point of view esp. as contrasted with another **3** : a form or variant of a type or original

**vers li·bre** \ˌver-'lēbrᵊ\ *n, pl* **vers li·bres** \*same*\ [F] : FREE VERSE

**ver·so** \'vər-sō\ *n, pl* **versos** : a left-hand page

**ver·sus** \'vər-səs\ *prep* **1** : AGAINST 1 ⟨the champion ~ the challenger⟩ **2** : in contrast or as an alternative to ⟨free trade ~ protection⟩

**vert** *abbr* vertical

**ver·te·bra** \'vər-tə-brə\ *n, pl* **-brae** \-ˌbrā, -ˌbrē\ *or* **-bras** [L] : one of the segments of bone or cartilage making up the backbone

**ver·te·bral** \(ˌ)vər-'tē-brəl, 'vər-tə-\ *adj* : of, relating to, or made up of vertebrae : SPINAL

**vertebral column** *n* : BACKBONE 1

¹**ver·te·brate** \'vər-tə-brət, -ˌbrāt\ *adj* **1** : having a backbone **2** : of or relating to the vertebrates

²**vertebrate** *n* : any of a large group of animals (as mammals, birds, reptiles, amphibians, or fishes) that have a backbone or in some primitive forms (as a lamprey) a flexible rod of cells and that have a tubular nervous system arranged along the back and divided into a brain and spinal cord

**ver·tex** \'vər-ˌteks\ *n, pl* **ver·ti·ces** \'vər-tə-ˌsēz\ *also* **ver·tex·es** [ME, top of the head, fr. L *vertex, vortex* whirl, whirlpool, top of the head, summit, fr. *vertere* to turn] **1** : the point opposite to and farthest from the base of a geometrical figure **2** : the point where the sides of an angle or three or more edges of a polyhedron (as a cube) meet **3** : the highest point : TOP, SUMMIT

**ver·ti·cal** \'vər-ti-kəl\ *adj* **1** : of, relating to, or located at the vertex : directly overhead **2** : rising perpendicularly from a level surface : UPRIGHT — **vertical** *n* — **ver·ti·cal·i·ty** \ˌvər-tə-'ka-lə-tē\ *n* — **ver·ti·cal·ly** \-k(ə-)lē\ *adv*

**ver·tig·i·nous** \ˌ(ˌ)vər-'ti-jə-nəs\ *adj* : marked by, affected with, or tending to cause dizziness

**ver·ti·go** \'vər-ti-ˌgō\ *n, pl* **-goes** *or* **-gos** : DIZZINESS, GIDDINESS

**vertu** *var of* VIRTU

**ver·vain** \'vər-ˌvān\ *n* : any of a genus of chiefly American herbs or low woody plants with often showy heads or spikes of tubular flowers

**verve** \'vərv\ *n* : liveliness of imagination; *also* : VIVACITY

¹**very** \'ver-ē\ *adj* **veri·er; -est** [ME *verray, verry,* fr. AF *verai,* ultim. fr. L *verax* truthful, fr. *verus* true] **1** : EXACT, PRECISE ⟨the ∼ heart of the city⟩ **2** : exactly suitable ⟨the ∼ tool for the job⟩ **3** : ABSOLUTE, UTTER ⟨the *veriest* nonsense⟩ **4** — used as an intensive esp. to emphasize identity ⟨before my ∼ eyes⟩ **5** : MERE, BARE ⟨the ∼ idea scared him⟩ **6** : SELFSAME, IDENTICAL ⟨the ∼ man I saw⟩

²**very** *adv* **1** : in actual fact : TRULY **2** : to a high degree : EXTREMELY

**very high frequency** *n* : a radio frequency of between 30 and 300 megahertz

**ves·i·cant** \'ve-si-kənt\ *n* : an agent that causes blistering — **vesicant** *adj*

**ves·i·cle** \'ve-si-kəl\ *n* : a membranous and usu. fluid-filled cavity in a plant or animal; *also* : BLISTER — **ve·sic·u·lar** \və-'si-kyə-lər\ *adj*

¹**ves·per** \'ves-pər\ *n* **1** *cap, archaic* : EVENING STAR **2** : a vesper bell **3** *archaic* : EVENING, EVENTIDE

²**vesper** *adj* : of or relating to vespers or the evening ⟨a ∼ service⟩

**ves·pers** \-pərz\ *n pl, often cap* : a late afternoon or evening worship service

**ves·sel** \'ve-səl\ *n* **1** : a container (as a barrel, bottle, bowl, or cup) for holding something **2** : a person held to be the recipient of a quality (as grace) **3** : a craft bigger than a rowboat **4** : a tube in which a body fluid (as blood or sap) is contained and circulated

¹**vest** \'vest\ *vb* **1** : to place or give into the possession or discretion of some person or authority **2** : to grant or endow with a particular authority, right, or property **3** : to become legally vested **4** : to clothe with or as if with a garment; *esp* : to garb in ecclesiastical vestments

²**vest** *n* **1** : a sleeveless garment for the upper body usu. worn over a shirt **2** *chiefly Brit* : a man's sleeveless undershirt **3** : a front piece of a dress resembling the front of a vest

¹**ves·tal** \'ves-t²l\ *adj* : CHASTE

²**vestal** *n* : VESTAL VIRGIN

**vestal virgin** *n* **1** : a virgin consecrated to the Roman goddess Vesta and to the ser-

vice of watching the sacred fire perpetually kept burning on her altar **2** : a chaste woman

**vest·ed** \'ves-təd\ *adj* : fully and unconditionally guaranteed as a legal right, benefit, or privilege

**vested interest** *n* : an interest (as in an existing political, economic, or social arrangement) to which the holder has a strong commitment; *also* : one (as a corporation) having a vested interest

**ves·ti·bule** \'ves-tə-ˌbyül\ *n* **1** : a passage or room between the outer door and the interior of a building **2** : any of various bodily cavities forming or suggesting an entrance to some other cavity or space — **ves·tib·u·lar** \ve-'sti-byə-lər\ *adj*

**ves·tige** \'ves-tij\ *n* [F, fr. L *vestigium* footprint, track, vestige] : a trace or visible sign left by something lost or vanished; *also* : a minute remaining amount — **ves·ti·gial** \ve-'sti-jē-əl, -jəl\ *adj* — **ves·ti·gial·ly** *adv*

**vest·ing** \'ves-tiŋ\ *n* : the conveying to an employee of inalienable rights to share in a pension fund; *also* : the right so conveyed

**vest·ment** \'vest-mənt\ *n* **1** : an outer garment; *esp* : a ceremonial or official robe **2** *pl* : CLOTHING, GARB **3** : a garment or insignia worn by a cleric when officiating or assisting at a religious service

**vest–pocket** *adj* : very small ⟨a ∼ park⟩

**ves·try** \'ves-trē\ *n, pl* **vestries** **1** : a room in a church for vestments, altar linens, and sacred vessels **2** : a room used for church meetings and classes **3** : a body administering the temporal affairs of an Episcopal parish

**ves·try·man** \-mən\ *n* : a member of a vestry

**ves·ture** \'ves-chər\ *n* **1** : a covering garment **2** : CLOTHING, APPAREL

¹**vet** \'vet\ *n* : VETERINARIAN

²**vet** *adj or n* : VETERAN

³**vet** *vb* : to evaluate for appraisal or acceptance ⟨∼ a manuscript⟩

**vetch** \'vech\ *n* : any of a genus of twining leguminous herbs including some grown for fodder and green manure

**vet·er·an** \'ve-trən, -tə-rən\ *n* [L *veteranus,* fr. *veteranus* old, of long experience, fr. *veter-, vetus* old] **1** : an old soldier of long service **2** : a former member of the armed forces **3** : a person of long experience usu. in an occupation or skill — **veteran** *adj*

**Veterans Day** *n* : November 11 observed as a legal holiday in commemoration of the end of hostilities in 1918 and 1945

**vet·er·i·nar·i·an** \ˌve-trə-'ner-ē-ən, ˌve-tə-rə-\ *n* : one qualified and authorized to practice veterinary medicine

¹**vet·er·i·nary** \'ve-trə-ˌner-ē, 've-tə-rə-\ *adj* : of, relating to, or being the medical care of animals and esp. domestic animals

²**veterinary** *n, pl* **-nar·ies** : VETERINARIAN

¹**ve·to** \'vē-tō\ *n, pl* **vetoes** [L, I forbid] **1** : an authoritative prohibition **2** : a power of one part of a government to forbid the

carrying out of projects attempted by another part; *esp* : a power vested in a chief executive to prevent the carrying out of measures adopted by a legislature **3** : the exercise of the power of veto

²**veto** *vb* **1** : FORBID, PROHIBIT **2** : to refuse assent to (a legislative bill) so as to prevent enactment or cause reconsideration — **ve·to·er** *n*

**vex** \'veks\ *vb* **vexed** *also* **vext**; **vex·ing 1** : to bring trouble, distress, or agitation to ⟨a ~*ing* problem⟩ **2** : to annoy continually with little irritations

**vex·a·tion** \vek-'sā-shən\ *n* **1** : the act of vexing **2** : the quality or state of being vexed : IRRITATION **3** : a cause of trouble or annoyance

**vex·a·tious** \-shəs\ *adj* **1** : causing vexation : ANNOYING **2** : full of distress or annoyance : TROUBLED — **vex·a·tious·ly** *adv* — **vex·a·tious·ness** *n*

**vexed** \'vekst\ *adj* : fully debated or discussed ⟨a ~ question⟩

**VF** *abbr* **1** video frequency **2** visual field

**VFD** *abbr* volunteer fire department

**VFW** *abbr* Veterans of Foreign Wars

**VG** *abbr* **1** very good **2** vicar-general

**VHF** *abbr* very high frequency

**VI** *abbr* Virgin Islands

**via** \'vī-ə, 'vē-ə\ *prep* **1** : by way of **2** : by means of

**vi·a·ble** \'vī-ə-bəl\ *adj* **1** : capable of living; *esp* : sufficiently developed as to be capable of surviving outside the mother's womb ⟨a ~ fetus⟩ **2** : capable of growing and developing ⟨~ seeds⟩ **3** : capable of being put into practice : WORKABLE **4** : having a reasonable chance of succeeding ⟨a ~ candidate⟩ — **vi·a·bil·i·ty** \,vī-ə-'bi-lə-tē\ *n* — **vi·a·bly** \'vī-ə-blē\ *adv*

**via·duct** \'vī-ə-,dəkt\ *n* : a long elevated roadway usu. consisting of a series of short spans supported on arches, piers, or columns

**vi·al** \'vī-əl\ *n* : a small vessel for liquids

**vi·and** \'vī-ənd\ *n* : an article of food

**vi·at·i·cum** \vī-'a-ti-kəm, vē-\ *n, pl* **-cums** *or* **-ca** \-kə\ **1** : the Christian Eucharist given to a person in danger of death **2** : an allowance esp. in money for traveling needs and expenses

**vibes** \'vībz\ *n pl* **1** : VIBRAPHONE **2** : VIBRATIONS

**vi·brant** \'vī-brənt\ *adj* **1** : VIBRATING, PULSATING **2** : pulsating with vigor or activity ⟨a ~ personality⟩ **3** : readily set in vibration : RESPONSIVE **4** : sounding from vibration **5** : BRIGHT ⟨~ colors⟩ — **vi·bran·cy** \-brən-sē\ *n*

**vi·bra·phone** \'vī-brə-,fōn\ *n* : a percussion instrument like the xylophone but with metal bars and motor-driven resonators

**vi·brate** \'vī-,brāt\ *vb* **vi·brat·ed; vi·brat·ing 1** : OSCILLATE **2** : to set in vibration **3** : to be in vibration **4** : WAVER, FLUCTUATE **5** : to respond sympathetically : THRILL

**vi·bra·tion** \vī-'brā-shən\ *n* : a rapid to-and-fro motion of the particles of an elastic body or medium (as a stretched cord)

that produces sound **2** : an act of vibrating : a state of being vibrated : OSCILLATION **3** : a trembling motion **4** : VACILLATION **5** : a feeling or impression that someone or something gives off — usu. used in pl. ⟨good ~s⟩ — **vi·bra·tion·al** \-shə-nəl\ *adj*

**vi·bra·to** \vi-'brä-tō\ *n, pl* **-tos** [It] : a slightly tremulous effect imparted to vocal or instrumental music

**vi·bra·tor** \'vī-,brā-tər\ *n* : one that vibrates or causes vibration; *esp* : a vibrating electrical device used in massage or for sexual stimulation

**vi·bra·to·ry** \'vī-brə-,tór-ē\ *adj* : consisting of, capable of, or causing vibration

**vi·bur·num** \vī-'bər-nəm\ *n* : any of a genus of widely distributed shrubs or small trees related to the honeysuckle and bearing small usu. white flowers in broad clusters

**vic** *abbr* vicinity

**Vic** *abbr* Victoria

**vic·ar** \'vi-kər\ *n* **1** : an administrative deputy **2** : a minister in charge of a church who serves under the authority of another minister — **vi·car·i·ate** \vī-'ker-ē-ət\ *n*

**vic·ar·age** \'vi-kə-rij\ *n* : a vicar's home

**vicar–general** *n, pl* **vicars–general** : an administrative deputy (as of a Roman Catholic or Anglican bishop)

**vi·car·i·ous** \vī-'ker-ē-əs\ *adj* [L *vicarius*, fr. *vicis* change, alternation, stead] **1** : acting for another **2** : done or suffered by one person on behalf of another or others ⟨a ~ sacrifice⟩ **3** : sharing in someone else's experience through the use of the imagination or sympathetic feelings ⟨~ thrills⟩ — **vi·car·i·ous·ly** *adv* — **vi·car·i·ous·ness** *n*

¹**vice** \'vīs\ *n* **1** : DEPRAVITY, WICKEDNESS **2** : a moral fault or failing **3** : a habitual usu. trivial fault **4** : an undesirable behavior pattern in a domestic animal

²**vice** *chiefly Brit var of* VISE

³**vi·ce** \'vī-sē\ *prep* : in the place of; *also* : rather than

**vice admiral** *n* : a commissioned officer in the navy or coast guard ranking above a rear admiral

**vice·ge·rent** \'vīs-'jir-ənt\ *n* : an administrative deputy of a king or magistrate — **vice·ge·ren·cy** \-ən-sē\ *n*

**vi·cen·ni·al** \vī-'se-nē-əl\ *adj* : occurring once every 20 years

**vice presidency** *n* : the office of vice president

**vice president** *n* **1** : an officer ranking next to a president and usu. empowered to act for the president during an absence or disability **2** : any of several of a president's deputies

**vice·re·gal** \'vīs-'rē-gəl\ *adj* : of or relating to a viceroy

**vice·roy** \'vīs-,ról\ *n* : the governor of a country or province who rules as representative of the sovereign — **vice·roy·al·ty** \-əl-tē\ *n*

**vice ver·sa** \,vī-si-'vər-sə, 'vīs-'vər-\ *adv* : with the order reversed

**vi·chys·soise** \,vi-shē-'swäz, ,vē-\ *n* [F]

: a soup made esp. from leeks or onions and potatoes, cream, and chicken stock and usu. served cold

**vic·i·nage** \'vis-ə-nij\ n : a neighboring or surrounding district : VICINITY

**vi·cin·i·ty** \və-'si-nə-tē\ n, pl **-ties** [MF vicinité, fr. L vicinitas, fr. vicinus neighboring, fr. vicus row of houses, village] 1 : NEARNESS, PROXIMITY 2 : a surrounding area : NEIGHBORHOOD

**vi·cious** \'vi-shəs\ adj 1 : having the quality of vice : WICKED, DEPRAVED 2 : DEFECTIVE, FAULTY; also : INVALID 3 : IMPURE, FOUL 4 : having a savage disposition; also : marked by violence or ferocity ⟨a ~ attack⟩ 5 : MALICIOUS, SPITEFUL ⟨~ gossip⟩ 6 : worsened by internal causes that augment each other ⟨~ wage price spiral⟩ — **vi·cious·ly** adv — **vi·cious·ness** n

**vi·cis·si·tude** \və-'si-sə-,tüd, vī-, -,tyüd\ n : an irregular, unexpected, or surprising change ⟨the ~s of business⟩

**vic·tim** \'vik-təm\ n 1 : a living being offered as a sacrifice in a religious rite 2 : an individual injured or killed (as by disease or accident) 3 : a person cheated, fooled, or injured ⟨a ~ of circumstances⟩

**vic·tim·ise** Brit var of VICTIMIZE

**vic·tim·ize** \'vik-tə-,mīz\ vb **-ized; -iz·ing** : to make a victim of — **vic·tim·i·za·tion** \,vik-tə-mə-'zā-shən\ n — **vic·tim·iz·er** \'vik-tə-,mī-zər\ n

**vic·tim·less** \'vik-təm-ləs\ adj : having no victim ⟨considered gambling to be a ~ crime⟩

**vic·tor** \'vik-tər\ n : WINNER, CONQUEROR

**vic·to·ria** \vik-'tȯr-ē-ə\ n : a low 4-wheeled carriage with a folding top and a raised driver's seat in front

**¹Vic·to·ri·an** \vik-'tȯr-ē-ən\ adj 1 : of or relating to the reign of Queen Victoria of England or the art, letters, or tastes of her time 2 : typical of the standards, attitudes, or conduct of the age of Victoria esp. when considered prudish or narrow

**²Victorian** n 1 : a person and esp. an author of the Victorian period 2 : a typically large ornate house built during Queen Victoria's reign

**vic·to·ri·ous** \vik-'tȯr-ē-əs\ adj 1 : having won a victory 2 : of, relating to, or characteristic of victory ⟨~ exuberance⟩ — **vic·to·ri·ous·ly** adv

**vic·to·ry** \'vik-tə-rē\ n, pl **-ries** 1 : the overcoming of an enemy or an antagonist 2 : achievement of mastery or success in a struggle or endeavor

**¹vict·ual** \'vi-t²l\ n [ME vitaille, victuayle, fr. AF, fr. LL victualia, pl., provisions, food, fr. neut. pl. of victualis of nourishment, fr. L victus nourishment, way of living, fr. vivere to live] 1 : food fit for humans 2 pl : food supplies

**²victual** vb **-ualed** or **-ualled; -ual·ing** or **-ual·ling** 1 : to supply with food 2 : to store up provisions

**vict·ual·ler** or **vict·ual·er** \'vi-t²l-ər\ n : one that supplies provisions (as to an army or a ship)

**vi·cu·ña** or **vi·cu·na** \vi-'kün-yə, vī-; vī-'kün-ə, -'kyü-\ n 1 : a So. American wild mammal related to the llama and alpaca; also : its wool 2 : a soft fabric woven from the wool of the vicuña; also : a sheep's wool imitation of this

**vi·de** \'vī-dē, 'vē-,dā\ vb imper [L] : SEE — used to direct a reader to another item

**vi·de·li·cet** \və-'de-lə-,set, vī-; vi-'dā-li-,ket\ adv [ME, fr. L, fr. vidēre to see + licet it is permitted] : that is to say : NAMELY

**¹vid·eo** \'vi-dē-,ō\ n 1 : TELEVISION 2 : VIDEOTAPE; also : a recording similar to a videotape but stored in digital form 3 : a videotaped performance ⟨music ~s⟩

**²video** adj 1 : relating to or used in transmission or reception of the television image 2 : relating to or being images on a television screen or computer display ⟨a ~ terminal⟩

**video camera** n : a camera that records visual images and usu. sound; esp : CAMCORDER

**vid·eo·cas·sette** \,vi-dē-ō-kə-'set\ n 1 : a case containing videotape for use with a VCR 2 : a recording (as of a movie) on a videocassette

**videocassette recorder** n : VCR

**vid·eo·disc** or **vid·eo·disk** \'vi-dē-ō-,disk\ n 1 : OPTICAL DISK 2 : a recording (as of a movie) on a videodisc

**video game** n : an electronic game played on a video screen

**vid·e·o·gen·ic** \,vi-dē-ō-'je-nik\ adj : TELEGENIC

**vid·eo·phone** \'vi-dē-ə-,fōn\ n : a telephone for transmitting both audio and video signals

**¹vid·eo·tape** \'vi-dē-ō-,tāp\ n : a recording of visual images and sound made on magnetic tape; also : the magnetic tape used for such a recording

**²videotape** vb : to make a videotape of

**videotape recorder** n : a device for recording and playing back videotapes

**vie** \'vī\ vb **vied; vy·ing** \'vī-iŋ\ : to compete for superiority : CONTEND ⟨~ for⟩ — **vi·er** \'vī-ər\ n

**Viet·cong** \vē-'et-'käŋ, vē-ət-, -'kȯŋ\ n, pl **Vietcong** : a guerrilla member of the Vietnamese communist movement

**¹view** \'vyü\ n 1 : the act of seeing or examining : INSPECTION; also : SURVEY 2 : a way of looking at or regarding something 3 : ESTIMATE, JUDGMENT ⟨stated his ~s⟩ 4 : a sight (as of a landscape) regarded for its pictorial quality 5 : extent or range of vision ⟨within ~⟩ 6 : OBJECT, PURPOSE ⟨done with a ~ to promotion⟩ 7 : a picture of a scene

**²view** vb 1 : to look at attentively : EXAMINE 2 : SEE, WATCH ⟨~ a film⟩ 3 : to examine mentally : CONSIDER ⟨~ a problem⟩ — **view·er** n

**view·er·ship** \'vyü-ər-,ship\ n : a television audience esp. with respect to size or makeup

**view·find·er** \'vyü-,fīn-dər\ n : a device on a camera for showing the view to be included in the picture

**view·point** \-ˌpȯint\ n : POINT OF VIEW, STANDPOINT

**vi·ges·i·mal** \vī-ˈje-sə-məl\ adj : based on the number 20

**vig·il** \ˈvi-jəl\ n 1 : a religious observance formerly held on the night before a religious feast 2 : the day before a religious feast observed as a day of spiritual preparation 3 : evening or nocturnal devotions or prayers — usu. used in pl. 4 : an act or a time of keeping awake when sleep is customary; esp : WATCH 1

**vigilance committee** n : a committee of vigilantes

**vig·i·lant** \ˈvi-jə-lənt\ adj : alertly watchful esp. to avoid danger — **vig·i·lance** \-ləns\ n — **vig·i·lant·ly** adv

**vig·i·lan·te** \ˌvi-jə-ˈlan-tē\ n : a member of a volunteer committee organized to suppress and punish crime summarily (as when the processes of law are viewed as inadequate); also : a self-appointed doer of justice — **vig·i·lan·tism** \-ˈlan-ˌti-zəm\ n

**¹vi·gnette** \vin-ˈyet\ n [F, fr. MF vignete, fr. dim. of vigne vine] 1 : a small decorative design 2 : a picture (as an engraving or a photograph) that shades off gradually into the surrounding ground 3 : a short descriptive literary sketch

**²vignette** vb **vi·gnett·ed; vi·gnett·ing** 1 : to finish (as a photograph) like a vignette 2 : to describe briefly

**vig·or** \ˈvi-gər\ n 1 : active strength or energy of body or mind 2 : INTENSITY, FORCE ⟨the ~ of their quarrel⟩

**vig·or·ous** \ˈvi-gə-rəs\ adj 1 : having vigor : ROBUST 2 : done with force and energy ⟨a ~ debate⟩ — **vig·or·ous·ly** adv — **vig·or·ous·ness** n

**vig·our** chiefly Brit var of VIGOR

**Vi·king** \ˈvī-kiŋ\ n [ON vīkingr] : any of the pirate Norsemen who raided or invaded the coasts of Europe in the 8th to 10th centuries

**vile** \ˈvī(-ə)l\ adj **vil·er; vil·est** 1 : morally despicable 2 : physically repulsive : FOUL 3 : of little worth 4 : DEGRADING, IGNOMINIOUS 5 : utterly bad or contemptible ⟨~ weather⟩ — **vile·ly** \ˈvī(-ə)l-lē\ adv — **vile·ness** n

**vil·i·fy** \ˈvi-lə-ˌfī\ vb **-fied; -fy·ing** : to blacken the character of with abusive language : DEFAME ♦ Synonyms MALIGN, CALUMNIATE, SLANDER, LIBEL, TRADUCE — **vil·i·fi·ca·tion** \ˌvi-lə-fə-ˈkā-shən\ n — **vil·i·fi·er** \ˈvi-lə-ˌfī-ər\ n

**vil·la** \ˈvi-lə\ n 1 : a country estate 2 : the rural or suburban residence of a wealthy person

**vil·lage** \ˈvi-lij\ n [ME, fr. AF vilage, fr. vile manorial estate, farmstead, fr. L villa] 1 : a settlement usu. larger than a hamlet and smaller than a town 2 : an incorporated minor municipality 3 : the people of a village

**vil·lag·er** \ˈvi-li-jər\ n : an inhabitant of a village

**vil·lain** \ˈvi-lən\ n 1 : VILLEIN 2 : an evil person : SCOUNDREL

**vil·lain·ess** \-lə-nəs\ n : a woman who is a villain

**vil·lain·ous** \-lə-nəs\ adj 1 : befitting a villain : WICKED, EVIL 2 : highly objectionable : DETESTABLE ♦ Synonyms VICIOUS, INIQUITOUS, NEFARIOUS, INFAMOUS, CORRUPT, DEGENERATE — **vil·lain·ous·ly** adv — **vil·lain·ous·ness** n

**vil·lainy** \-lə-nē\ n, pl **-lain·ies** 1 : villainous conduct; also : a villainous act 2 : villainous character or nature

**vil·lein** \ˈvi-lən, -ˌlān\ n 1 : a free villager of Anglo-Saxon times 2 : an unfree peasant having the status of a slave to a feudal lord

**vil·len·age** \ˈvil-ə-nij\ n 1 : the holding of land at the will of a feudal lord 2 : the status of a villein

**vil·lous** \ˈvi-ləs\ adj : covered with fine hairs or villi

**vil·lus** \ˈvi-ləs\ n, pl **vil·li** \-ˌlī, -ˌ(ˌ)lē\ : a slender usu. vascular process; esp : one of the tiny projections of the mucous membrane of the small intestine that function in the absorption of food

**vim** \ˈvim\ n : robust energy and enthusiasm : VITALITY

**VIN** abbr vehicle identification number

**vin·ai·grette** \ˌvi-ni-ˈgret\ n [F] : a sauce made typically of oil, vinegar, and seasonings

**vin·ci·ble** \ˈvin-sə-bəl\ adj : capable of being overcome or subdued

**vin·di·cate** \ˈvin-də-ˌkāt\ vb **-cat·ed; -cat·ing** 1 : AVENGE 2 : EXONERATE, ABSOLVE 3 : CONFIRM, SUBSTANTIATE 4 : to provide defense for : JUSTIFY 5 : to maintain a right to : ASSERT — **vin·di·ca·tor** \-ˌkā-tər\ n

**vin·di·ca·tion** \ˌvin-də-ˈkā-shən\ n : the act of vindicating or the state of being vindicated; esp : justification against denial or censure : DEFENSE

**vin·dic·tive** \vin-ˈdik-tiv\ adj 1 : disposed to revenge 2 : intended for or involving revenge ⟨~ punishment⟩ 3 : VICIOUS, SPITEFUL — **vin·dic·tive·ly** adv — **vin·dic·tive·ness** n

**vine** \ˈvīn\ n [ME, fr. AF vigne, fr. L vinea vine, vineyard, fr. fem. of vineus of wine, fr. vinum wine] 1 : GRAPE 2 2 : a plant whose stem requires support and which climbs (as by tendrils) or trails along the ground; also : the stem of such a plant

**vin·e·gar** \ˈvi-ni-gər\ n [ME vinegre, fr. AF vin egre, lit., sour wine] : a sour liquid obtained by fermentation (as of cider, wine, or malt) and used to flavor or preserve foods

**vin·e·gary** \-gə-rē\ adj 1 : resembling vinegar : SOUR 2 : disagreeable in manner or disposition : CRABBED

**vine·yard** \ˈvin-yərd\ n 1 : a field of grapevines esp. to produce grapes for wine production 2 : a sphere of activity : field of endeavor

**vi·nous** \ˈvī-nəs\ adj 1 : of, relating to, or made with wine ⟨~ medications⟩ 2 : showing the effects of the use of wine ⟨~ bloodshot eyes⟩

**¹vin·tage** \ˈvin-tij\ n 1 : a season's yield of grapes or wine 2 : WINE; esp : a usu. superior wine which comes from a single year 3 : the act or period of gathering grapes or making wine **4** : a period of origin ⟨clothes of 1890 ~⟩

²**vintage** *adj* **1** : of, relating to, or produced in a particular vintage **2** : of old, recognized, and enduring interest, importance, or quality : CLASSIC ⟨~ cars⟩ **3** : of the best and most characteristic — used with a proper noun

**vint·ner** \'vint-nər\ *n* : a dealer in wines

**vi·nyl** \'vī-nᵊl\ *n* **1** : a chemical derived from ethylene by the removal of one hydrogen atom **2** : a polymer of a vinyl compound or a product (as a textile fiber) made from one

**vinyl chloride** *n* : a flammable gaseous carcinogenic compound used esp. to make vinyl resins

**vi·ol** \'vī-əl\ *n* : a bowed stringed instrument chiefly of the 16th and 17th centuries having a fretted neck and usu. six strings

¹**vi·o·la** \vī-'ō-lə, 'vī-ə-lə\ *n* : VIOLET 1; *esp* : any of various hybrid garden plants with white, yellow, purple, or variously colored flowers that resemble but are smaller than those of the related pansies

²**vi·o·la** \vē-'ō-lə\ *n* : an instrument of the violin family slightly larger and tuned lower than a violin — **vi·o·list** \-list\ *n*

**vi·o·la·ble** \'vī-ə-lə-bəl\ *adj* : capable of being violated ⟨~ boundaries⟩

**vi·o·late** \'vī-ə-ˌlāt\ *vb* **-lat·ed; -lat·ing 1** : BREAK, DISREGARD ⟨~ a law⟩ ⟨~ a frontier⟩ **2** : RAPE **3** : PROFANE, DESECRATE **4** : INTERRUPT, DISTURB ⟨*violated* his privacy⟩ — **vi·o·la·tor** \-ˌlā-tər\ *n*

**vi·o·la·tion** \ˌvī-ə-'lā-shən\ *n* : an act or instance of violating : the state of being violated ♦ **Synonyms** BREACH, INFRACTION, TRESPASS, INFRINGEMENT, TRANSGRESSION

**vi·o·lence** \'vī-ləns, 'vī-ə-\ *n* **1** : exertion of physical force so as to injure or abuse **2** : injury by or as if by infringement or profanation **3** : intense or furious often destructive action or force **4** : vehement feeling or expression : INTENSITY **5** : jarring quality : DISCORDANCE ♦ **Synonyms** COMPULSION, COERCION, DURESS, CONSTRAINT

**vi·o·lent** \-lənt\ *adj* **1** : marked by extreme force or sudden intense activity **2** : caused by or showing strong feeling ⟨~ words⟩ **3** : EXTREME, INTENSE ⟨~ pain⟩ ⟨~ colors⟩ **4** : emotionally agitated to the point of loss of self-control **5** : caused by force : not natural ⟨~ death⟩ — **vi·o·lent·ly** *adv*

**vi·o·let** \'vī-ə-lət\ *n* **1** : any of a genus of herbs or small shrubs usu. with heart=shaped leaves and both aerial and underground flowers; *esp* : one with small usu. solid-colored flowers **2** : a reddish blue color

**vi·o·lin** \ˌvī-ə-'lin\ *n* : a bowed stringed instrument with four strings that has a shallow body, a fingerboard without frets, and a curved bridge — **vi·o·lin·ist** \-'li-nist\ *n*

**vi·o·lon·cel·lo** \ˌvī-ə-lən-'che-lō\ *n* [It] : CELLO — **vi·o·lon·cel·list** \-list\ *n*

**VIP** \ˌvē-ˌī-'pē\ *n, pl* **VIPs** \-'pēz\ [*very im-*

portant person] : a person of great influence or prestige; *esp* : a high official with special privileges

**vi·per** \'vī-pər\ *n* **1** : a common stout=bodied Eurasian venomous snake having a bite only rarely fatal to humans; *also* : any snake (as a pit viper) of the same family as the viper **2** : any venomous or reputedly venomous snake **3** : a vicious or treacherous person — **vi·per·ine** \-pə-ˌrīn\ *adj*

**vi·ra·go** \və-'rä-gō, -'rā-\ *n, pl* **-goes** or **-gos** [ME, fr. L, strong or heroic woman, fr. *vir* man] **1** : a loud overbearing woman **2** : a woman of great strength and courage

**vi·ral** \'vī-rəl\ *adj* : of, relating to, or caused by a virus ⟨a ~ infection⟩ — **vi·ral·ly** *adv*

**vi·reo** \'vir-ē-ˌō\ *n, pl* **-e·os** [L, a small bird, fr. *virēre* to be green] : any of various small insect-eating American songbirds mostly olive green and grayish in color

¹**vir·gin** \'vər-jən\ *n* **1** : an unmarried woman devoted to religion **2** : an unmarried girl or woman **3** *cap* : the mother of Jesus **4** : a person who has not had sexual intercourse

²**virgin** *adj* **1** : free from stain : PURE, SPOTLESS **2** : CHASTE **3** : befitting a virgin : MODEST **4** : FRESH, UNSPOILED; *esp* : not altered by human activity ⟨~ forest⟩ **5** : INITIAL, FIRST

¹**vir·gin·al** \'vər-jə-nᵊl\ *adj* : of, relating to, or characteristic of a virgin or virginity ⟨~ innocence⟩ — **vir·gin·al·ly** *adv*

²**virginal** *n* : a small rectangular spinet without legs popular in the 16th and 17th centuries

**Vir·gin·ia creeper** \vər-'jin-yə-\ *n* : a No. American vine related to the grapes that has leaves with five leaflets and bluish=black berries

**Virginia reel** *n* : an American country=dance

**vir·gin·i·ty** \vər-'ji-nə-tē\ *n, pl* **-ties 1** : the quality or state of being virgin; *esp* : MAIDENHOOD **2** : the unmarried life : CELIBACY

**Vir·go** \'vər-ˌgō\ *n* [L, lit., virgin] **1** : a zodiacal constellation between Leo and Libra usu. pictured as a young woman **2** : the 6th sign of the zodiac in astrology; *also* : one born under this sign

**vir·gule** \'vər-gyül\ *n* : ²SLASH 3

**vir·i·des·cent** \ˌvir-ə-'de-sᵊnt\ *adj* : slightly green : GREENISH

**vir·ile** \'vir-əl\ *adj* **1** : having the nature, powers, or qualities of a man **2** : MASCULINE, MALE **3** : MASTERFUL, FORCEFUL — **vi·ril·i·ty** \və-'ri-lə-tē\ *n*

**vi·ri·on** \'vī-rē-ˌän, 'vir-ē-\ *n* : a complete virus particle consisting of an RNA or DNA core with a protein coat

**vi·rol·o·gy** \vī-'rä-lə-jē\ *n* : a branch of science that deals with viruses and viral diseases — **vi·rol·o·gist** \-jist\ *n*

**vir·tu** \vər-'tü, vir-\ or **ver·tu** \vər-, ˌver-\ *n* [It *virtù*, lit., virtue] **1** : a love of or taste for objects of art **2** : objects of art (as curios and antiques)

**vir·tu·al** \'vər-chə-wəl\ adj 1 : being in essence or in effect though not formally recognized or admitted ⟨a ~ dictator⟩ 2 : being on or simulated on a computer or computer network ⟨~ shopping⟩

**vir·tu·al·ly** \'vər-chə-wə-lē\ adv 1 : almost entirely : NEARLY 2 : for all practical purposes ⟨~ unknown⟩

**virtual reality** n : an artificial environment that is experienced through sensory stimuli (as sights and sounds) provided by an interactive computer program; also : the technology used to create or access a virtual reality

**vir·tue** \'vər-chü\ n [ME vertu, fr. AF, fr. L virtus strength, manliness, virtue, fr. vir man] 1 : conformity to a standard of right : MORALITY 2 : a particular moral excellence 3 : manly strength or courage : VALOR 4 : a commendable quality : MERIT 5 : active power to accomplish a given effect : POTENCY, EFFICACY 6 : chastity esp. in a woman

**vir·tu·os·i·ty** \,vər-chə-'wä-sə-tē\ n, pl -ties : great technical skill in the practice of a fine art

**vir·tu·o·so** \,vər-chə-'wō-sō, -zō\ n, pl -sos or -si \-sē, -zē\ [It] 1 : one skilled in or having a taste for the fine arts 2 : one who excels in the technique of an art; esp : a highly skilled musical performer ♦ Synonyms EXPERT, ADEPT, ARTIST, DOYEN, MASTER — **virtuoso** adj

**vir·tu·ous** \'vər-chə-wəs\ adj 1 : having or showing virtue and esp. moral virtue 2 : CHASTE — **vir·tu·ous·ly** adv

**vir·u·lent** \'vir-ə-lənt, 'vir-yə-\ adj 1 : highly infectious ⟨a ~ germ⟩; also : marked by a rapid, severe, and often deadly course ⟨a ~ disease⟩ 2 : extremely poisonous or venomous : NOXIOUS 3 : full of malice : MALIGNANT — **vir·u·lence** \-ləns\ n — **vir·u·lent·ly** adv

**vi·rus** \'vī-rəs\ n, pl **vi·rus·es** [L, venom, poisonous emanation] 1 : any of a large group of submicroscopic infectious agents that have an outside coat of protein around a core of RNA or DNA, that can grow and multiply only in living cells, and that cause important diseases in human beings, lower animals, and plants; also : a disease caused by a virus 2 : something (as a corrupting influence) that poisons the mind or spirit 3 : a computer program that is usu. hidden within another program and that reproduces itself and inserts the copies into other programs and usu. performs a malicious action (as destroying data)

**vis** abbr 1 visibility 2 visual

**¹vi·sa** \'vē-zə, -sə\ n [F] 1 : an endorsement by the proper authorities on a passport to show that it has been examined and the bearer may proceed 2 : a signature by a superior official signifying approval of a document

**²visa** vb **vi·saed** \-zəd, -səd\; **vi·sa·ing** \-zə-iŋ, -sə-\ : to give a visa to (a passport)

**vis·age** \'vi-zij\ n : the face or countenance of a person or sometimes an animal; also : LOOK, APPEARANCE

**¹vis-à-vis** \,vēz-ə-'vē, ,vēs-\ prep [F, lit., face-to-face] 1 : face-to-face with : OPPOSITE 2 : in relation to 3 : as compared with

**²vis-à-vis** n, pl **vis-à-vis** \same or -'vēz\ 1 : one that is face-to-face with another 2 : ESCORT 3 : COUNTERPART 4 : TÊTE-À-TÊTE

**³vis-à-vis** adv : in company : TOGETHER

**viscera** pl of VISCUS

**vis·cer·al** \'vi-sə-rəl\ adj 1 : felt in or as if in the viscera 2 : not intellectual : INSTINCTIVE 3 : of or relating to the viscera — **vis·cer·al·ly** adv

**vis·cid** \'vi-səd\ adj : VISCOUS — **vis·cid·i·ty** \vi-'si-də-tē\ n

**vis·cos·i·ty** \vis-'kä-sə-tē\ n, pl -ties : the quality of being viscous; esp : the property of resistance to flow in a fluid

**vis·count** \'vī-,kaunt\ n : a member of the British peerage ranking below an earl and above a baron

**vis·count·ess** \-,kaun-təs\ n 1 : the wife or widow of a viscount 2 : a woman who holds the rank of viscount in her own right

**vis·cous** \'vis-kəs\ adj [ME viscouse, fr. AF viscos, fr. LL viscosus full of birdlime, viscous, fr. L viscum mistletoe, birdlime] 1 : having the sticky consistency of glue 2 : having or characterized by viscosity

**vis·cus** \'vis-kəs\ n, pl **vis·cera** \'vi-sə-rə\ : an internal organ of the body; esp : one (as the heart or liver) located in the cavity of the trunk

**vise** \'vīs\ n [ME vys, vice screw, fr. AF vyz, fr. L vitis vine] : a tool with two jaws for holding work that typically close by a screw or lever

**vis·i·bil·i·ty** \,vi-zə-'bi-lə-tē\ n, pl -ties 1 : the quality, condition, or degree of being visible 2 : the degree of clearness of the atmosphere

**vis·i·ble** \'vi-zə-bəl\ adj : capable of being seen ⟨~ stars⟩; also : MANIFEST, APPARENT ⟨has no ~ means of support⟩ — **vis·i·bly** \-blē\ adv

**¹vi·sion** \'vi-zhən\ n 1 : something seen otherwise than by ordinary sight (as in a dream or trance) 2 : a vivid picture created by the imagination ⟨~s of fame and fortune⟩ 3 : the act or power of imagination 4 : unusual wisdom in foreseeing what is going to happen 5 : the act or power of seeing : SIGHT 6 : something seen; esp : a lovely sight

**²vision** vb : IMAGINE, ENVISION

**¹vi·sion·ary** \'vi-zhə-,ner-ē\ adj 1 : of the nature of a vision : ILLUSORY, UNREAL 2 : not practical : UTOPIAN 3 : seeing or likely to see visions : given to dreaming or imagining ♦ Synonyms IMAGINARY, FANTASTIC, CHIMERICAL, QUIXOTIC

**²visionary** n, pl -ar·ies 1 : one whose ideas or projects are impractical : DREAMER 2 : one who sees visions

**¹vis·it** \'vi-zət\ vb 1 : to go to see in order to comfort or help 2 : to call on either as an act of courtesy or friendship 3 : to dwell with for a time as a guest 4 : to come to or upon as a reward, affliction, or punishment 5 : INFLICT ⟨~ed his wrath upon them⟩ 6 : to make a visit or regular or frequent visits **7** : CHAT, CONVERSE ⟨enjoys ~*ing* with the neighbors⟩ — **vis·it·able** *adj*

²**visit** *n* **1** : a short stay : CALL **2** : a brief residence as a guest **3** : a journey to and stay at a place **4** : a formal or professional call (as by a doctor)

**vis·i·tant** \'vi-zə-tənt\ *n* : VISITOR

**vis·i·ta·tion** \ˌvi-zə-'tā-shən\ *n* **1** : VISIT; *esp* : an official visit **2** : a special dispensation of divine favor or wrath; *also* : a severe trial

**visiting nurse** *n* : a nurse employed to visit sick persons or perform public health services in a community

**vis·i·tor** \'vi-zə-tər\ *n* : one that visits

**vi·sor** \'vī-zər\ *n* **1** : the front piece of a helmet; *esp* : a movable upper piece **2** : VIZARD **3** : a projecting part (as on a cap) to shade the eyes — **vi·sored** \-zərd\ *adj*

**vis·ta** \'vis-tə\ *n* **1** : a distant view through or along an avenue or opening **2** : an extensive mental view over a series of years or events

**VISTA** *abbr* Volunteers in Service to America

¹**vi·su·al** \'vi-zhə-wəl\ *adj* **1** : of, relating to, or used in vision ⟨~ organs⟩ **2** : perceived by vision ⟨a ~ impression⟩ **3** : VISIBLE ⟨~ objects⟩ **4** : done by sight only ⟨~ navigation⟩ **5** : of or relating to instruction by means of sight ⟨~ aids⟩ — **vi·su·al·ly** *adv*

²**visual** *n* : something (as a graphic) that appeals to the sight and is used for illustration, demonstration, or promotion — usu. used in pl.

**vi·su·al·ize** \'vi-zhə-wə-ˌlīz\ *vb* **-ized; -iz·ing** : to make visible; *esp* : to form a mental image of — **vi·su·al·i·za·tion** \ˌvi-zhə-wə-lə-'zā-shən\ *n* — **vi·su·al·iz·er** *n*

**vi·ta** \'vē-tə, 'vī-\ *n, pl* **vi·tae** \'vē-ˌtī, 'vī-tē\ [L, lit., life] : a brief autobiographical sketch

**vi·tal** \'vī-tᵊl\ *adj* **1** : concerned with or necessary to the maintenance of life ⟨~ organs⟩ **2** : full of life and vigor : ANIMATED **3** : of, relating to, or characteristic of life or living beings **4** : FATAL, MORTAL ⟨~ wound⟩ **5** : FUNDAMENTAL, INDISPENSABLE — **vi·tal·ly** *adv*

**vi·tal·i·ty** \vī-'ta-lə-tē\ *n, pl* **-ties** **1** : the property distinguishing the living from the nonliving **2** : mental and physical vigor **3** : enduring quality **4** : ANIMATION, LIVELINESS ⟨the ~ of youth⟩

**vi·tal·ize** \'vī-tə-ˌlīz\ *vb* **-ized; -iz·ing** : to impart life or vigor to : ANIMATE — **vi·tal·i·za·tion** \ˌvī-tə-lə-'zā-shən\ *n*

**vi·tals** \'vī-tᵊlz\ *n pl* **1** : vital organs (as the heart and brain) **2** : essential parts

**vital signs** *n pl* : the pulse rate, respiratory rate, body temperature, and often blood pressure of a person

**vital statistics** *n pl* : statistics dealing with births, deaths, marriages, health, and disease

**vi·ta·min** \'vī-tə-mən\ *n* : any of various organic substances that are essential in tiny amounts to the nutrition of most animals and some plants and are mostly obtained from foods

**vitamin A** *n* : any of several vitamins (as from egg yolk or fish-liver oils) required esp. for good vision

**vitamin B** *n* **1** : VITAMIN B COMPLEX **2** *or* **vitamin B₁** : THIAMINE

**vitamin B complex** *n* : a group of vitamins that are found widely in foods and are essential for normal function of certain enzymes and for growth

**vitamin B₆** \-'bē-ˌsiks\ *n* : any of several compounds that are considered essential to vertebrate nutrition

**vitamin B₁₂** \-'bē-'twelv\ *n* : a complex cobalt-containing compound that occurs esp. in liver and is essential to normal blood formation, neural function, and growth; *also* : any of several compounds of similar action

**vitamin C** *n* : a vitamin found esp. in fruits and vegetables that is needed by the body to prevent scurvy

**vitamin D** *n* : any or all of several vitamins that are needed for normal bone and tooth structure and are found esp. in fish-liver oils, egg yolk, and milk or are produced by the body in response to ultraviolet light

**vitamin E** *n* : any of various oily fat-soluble liquid vitamins whose absence in the body is associated with such ailments as infertility, the breakdown of muscles, and vascular problems and which are found esp. in leaves and in seed germ oils

**vitamin K** *n* : any of several vitamins needed for blood to clot properly

**vi·ti·ate** \'vi-shē-ˌāt\ *vb* **-at·ed; -at·ing** **1** : CONTAMINATE, POLLUTE; *also* : DEBASE, PERVERT **2** : to make legally ineffective : INVALIDATE ⟨~ a contract⟩ — **vi·ti·a·tion** \ˌvi-shē-'ā-shən\ *n* — **vi·ti·a·tor** \'vi-shē-ˌā-tər\ *n*

**vi·ti·cul·ture** \'vi-tə-ˌkəl-chər\ *n* : the growing of grapes — **vi·ti·cul·tur·al** \ˌvi-tə-'kəl-chə-rəl\ *adj* — **vi·ti·cul·tur·ist** \-rist\ *n*

**vit·re·ous** \'vi-trē-əs\ *adj* **1** : of, relating to, or resembling glass : GLASSY ⟨~ rocks⟩ **2** : of, relating to, or being the clear colorless transparent jelly (**vitreous humor**) behind the lens in the eyeball

**vit·ri·ol** \'vi-trē-əl\ *n* : something resembling acid in being caustic, corrosive, or biting — **vit·ri·ol·ic** \ˌvi-trē-'ä-lik\ *adj*

**vit·tles** \'vi-tᵊlz\ *n pl* : VICTUALS

**vi·tu·per·ate** \vī-'tü-pə-ˌrāt, və-, -'tyü-\ *vb* **-at·ed; -at·ing** : to abuse in words : SCOLD ♦ **Synonyms** REVILE, BERATE, RATE, UPBRAID, RAIL, LASH — **vi·tu·per·a·tive** \-'tü-pə-rə-tiv, -'tyü-, -ˌrā-\ *adj* — **vi·tu·per·a·tive·ly** *adv*

**vi·tu·per·a·tion** \(ˌ)vī-tü-pə-'rā-shən, və-, -tyü-\ *n* : lengthy harsh criticism or abuse

**vi·va** \'vē-və\ *interj* [It & Sp, long live] — used to express goodwill or approval

**vi·va·ce** \vē-'vä-chā\ *adv or adj* [It] : in a brisk spirited manner — used as a direction in music

**vi·va·cious** \və-'vā-shəs, vī-\ *adj* : lively in temper, conduct, or spirit : SPRIGHTLY ⟨a

~ personality) — **vi·va·cious·ly** adv — **vi·va·cious·ness** n

**vi·vac·i·ty** \-'va-sə-tē\ n : the quality or state of being vivacious

**vi·va vo·ce** \ˌvī-və-'vō-sē, ˌvē-və-'vō-ˌchā\ adj [ML, with the living voice] : expressed or conducted by word of mouth : ORAL — **viva voce** adv

**viv·id** \'vi-vəd\ adj **1** : BRILLIANT, INTENSE ⟨a ~ red⟩ **2** : having the appearance of vigorous life **3** : producing a strong impression on the senses; esp : producing distinct mental pictures ⟨a ~ description⟩ — **viv·id·ly** adv — **viv·id·ness** n

**viv·i·fy** \'vi-və-ˌfī\ vb **-fied; -fy·ing 1** : to put life into : ANIMATE ⟨details that ~ a story⟩ **2** : to make vivid — **viv·i·fi·ca·tion** \ˌvi-və-fə-'kā-shən\ n — **viv·i·fi·er** n

**vi·vip·a·rous** \vī-'vi-pə-rəs, və-\ adj : producing living young from within the body rather than from eggs — **vi·vi·par·i·ty** \ˌvī-və-'pa-rə-tē, ˌvi-\ n

**viv·i·sec·tion** \ˌvi-və-'sek-shən, 'vi-və-ˌsek-\ n : the cutting of or operation on a living animal; also : animal experimentation esp. if causing distress to the subject

**vix·en** \'vik-sən\ n **1** : an ill-tempered scolding woman **2** : a female fox

**viz** abbr videlicet

**viz·ard** \'vi-zərd\ n : a mask for disguise or protection

**vi·zier** \və-'zir\ n : a high executive officer of many Muslim countries

**VJ** abbr veejay

**vlog** \'vlȯg, 'vläg\ n [video + blog] : a blog that contains video material — **vlog** vb — **vlog·ger** n

**VOA** abbr Voice of America

**voc** abbr **1** vocational **2** vocative

**vocab** abbr vocabulary

**vo·ca·ble** \'vō-kə-bəl\ n : TERM, NAME; esp : a word as such without regard to its meaning

**vo·cab·u·lary** \vō-'ka-byə-ˌler-ē\ n, pl **-lar·ies 1** : a list or collection of words usu. alphabetically arranged and defined or explained : LEXICON **2** : a stock of words in a language used by a class or individual or in relation to a subject

**vocabulary entry** n : a word (as the noun book), hyphened or open compound (as the verb cross-refer or the noun boric acid), word element (as the affix -an), abbreviation (as agt), verbalized symbol (as Na), or term (as master of ceremonies) entered alphabetically in a dictionary for the purpose of definition or identification or expressly included as an inflected form (as the noun mice or the verb saw) or as a derived form (as the noun godlessness or the adverb globally) or related phrase (as in spite of) run on at its base word and usu. set in a type (as boldface) readily distinguishable from that of the lightface running text which defines, explains, or identifies the entry

**¹vo·cal** \'vō-kəl\ adj **1** : uttered by the voice : ORAL **2** : relating to, composed or arranged for, or sung by the human voice ⟨~ music⟩ **3** : given to expressing oneself freely or insistently : OUTSPOKEN ⟨a ~ critic⟩ **4** : of or relating to the voice

**²vocal** n **1** : a vocal sound **2** : a vocal composition or its performance

**vocal cords** n pl : either of two pairs of elastic folds of mucous membrane that project into the cavity of the larynx and function in the production of vocal sounds

**vo·cal·ic** \vō-'ka-lik\ adj : of, relating to, or functioning as a vowel

**vo·cal·ise** Brit var of VOCALIZE

**vo·cal·ist** \'vō-kə-list\ n : SINGER

**vo·cal·ize** \-ˌlīz\ vb **-ized; -iz·ing 1** : to give vocal expression to : UTTER; esp : SING **2** : to make voiced rather than voiceless — **vo·cal·iz·er** n

**vo·ca·tion** \vō-'kā-shən\ n **1** : a summons or strong inclination to a particular state or course of action ⟨religious ~⟩ **2** : regular employment : OCCUPATION, PROFESSION — **vo·ca·tion·al** \-shə-nəl\ adj

**vo·ca·tion·al·ism** \-shə-nə-ˌli-zəm\ n : emphasis on vocational training in education

**voc·a·tive** \'vä-kə-tiv\ adj : of, relating to, or constituting a grammatical case marking the one addressed — **vocative** n

**vo·cif·er·ate** \vō-'si-fə-ˌrāt\ vb **-at·ed; -at·ing** [L vociferari, fr. voc-, vox voice + ferre to bear] : to cry out loudly : CLAMOR, SHOUT — **vo·cif·er·a·tion** \-ˌsi-fə-'rā-shən\ n

**vo·cif·er·ous** \vō-'si-fə-rəs\ adj : making or given to loud outcry — **vo·cif·er·ous·ly** adv — **vo·cif·er·ous·ness** n

**vod·ka** \'väd-kə\ n [Russ, fr. voda water] : a colorless liquor distilled from a mash (as of rye or wheat)

**vogue** \'vōg\ n [MF, action of rowing, course, fashion, fr. voguer to sail, fr. OF, fr. OIt vogare to row] **1** : popular acceptance or favor : POPULARITY **2** : a period of popularity **3** : one that is in fashion at a particular time ♦ **Synonyms** MODE, FAD, RAGE, CRAZE, TREND, FASHION

**vogu·ish** \'vō-gish\ adj **1** : FASHIONABLE, SMART **2** : suddenly or temporarily popular ⟨~ expressions⟩

**¹voice** \'vȯis\ n **1** : sound produced through the mouth by vertebrates and esp. by human beings (as in speaking or singing) **2** : musical sound produced by the vocal cords : the power to produce such sound; also : one of the melodic parts in a vocal or instrumental composition **3** : the vocal organs as a means of tone production ⟨train the ~⟩ **4** : sound produced by vibration of the vocal cords as heard in vowels and some consonants **5** : the power of speaking **6** : a sound suggesting a voice ⟨the ~ of the sea⟩ **7** : an instrument or medium of expression **8** : a choice, opinion, or wish openly expressed; also : right of expression **9** : distinction of form of a verb to indicate the relation of the subject to the action expressed by the verb

**²voice** vb **voiced; voic·ing** : to give voice or expression to : UTTER ⟨~ a complaint\   ◆ *Synonyms* EXPRESS, VENT, AIR, VENTILATE

**voice box** *n* : LARYNX

**voiced** \'vȯist\ *adj* **1** : having a voice <soft-*voiced*> **2** : uttered with voice <a ~ consonant> — **voiced·ness** \'vȯist-nəs, 'vȯi-səd-nəs\ *n*

**voice·less** \'vȯis-ləs\ *adj* **1** : having no voice **2** : not pronounced with voice — **voice·less·ly** *adv* — **voice·less·ness** *n*

**voice mail** *n* : an electronic communication system in which spoken messages are recorded for later playback to the intended recipient; *also* : such a message

**voice–over** *n* : the voice in a film or television program of a person who is heard but not seen or not seen talking

**voice·print** \'vȯis-ˌprint\ *n* : an individually distinctive pattern of voice characteristics that is spectrographically produced

¹**void** \'vȯid\ *adj* **1** : UNOCCUPIED, VACANT <a ~ bishopric> **2** : containing nothing : EMPTY **3** : LACKING, DEVOID <proposals ~ of sense> **4** : VAIN, USELESS **5** : of no legal force or effect : NULL

²**void** *n* **1** : empty space : EMPTINESS, VACUUM **2** : a feeling of want or hollowness

³**void** *vb* **1** : to make or leave empty; *also* : VACATE, LEAVE **2** : DISCHARGE, EMIT <~ urine> **3** : to render void : ANNUL, NULLIFY <~ a contract> — **void·able** *adj* — **void·er** *n*

**voi·là** \vwä-'lä\ *interj* [F] — used to call attention or to express satisfaction or approval

**voile** \'vȯi(-ə)l\ *n* : a sheer fabric used for women's clothing and curtains

**vol** *abbr* **1** volume **2** volunteer

**vol·a·tile** \'vä-lə-t⁹l\ *adj* **1** : readily becoming a vapor at a relatively low temperature <a ~ liquid> **2** : tending to erupt into violence **3** : likely to change suddenly — **vol·a·til·i·ty** \ˌvä-lə-'ti-lə-tē\ *n* — **vol·a·til·ize** \'vä-lə-tə-ˌlīz\ *vb*

**vol·ca·nic** \väl-'ka-nik\ *adj* **1** : of, relating to, or produced by a volcano **2** : explosively violent <~ emotions>

**vol·ca·nism** \'väl-kə-ˌni-zəm\ *n* : volcanic action or activity

**vol·ca·no** \väl-'kā-nō\ *n, pl* **-noes** *or* **-nos** [It or Sp; It *vulcano*, fr. Sp *vulcán*, ultim. fr. L *Volcanus*, Vulcan, Roman god of fire and metalworking] : an opening in the crust of the earth, a planet, or a moon from which molten rock and steam issue; *also* : a hill or mountain composed of the ejected material

**vol·ca·nol·o·gy** \ˌväl-kə-'nä-lə-jē\ *n* : a branch of geology that deals with volcanic phenomena — **vol·ca·nol·o·gist** \-kə-'nä-lə-jist\ *n*

**vole** \'vōl\ *n* : any of various small rodents that are closely related to the lemmings and muskrats

**vo·li·tion** \vō-'li-shən\ *n* **1** : the act or the power of making a choice or decision : WILL **2** : a choice or decision made — **vo·li·tion·al** \-'li-shə-nəl\ *adj*

¹**vol·ley** \'vä-lē\ *n, pl* **volleys** **1** : a flight of missiles (as arrows) **2** : simultaneous discharge of a number of missile weapons **3** : an act of volleying **4** : a burst of many things at once <a ~ of angry letters>

²**volley** *vb* **vol·leyed; vol·ley·ing** **1** : to discharge or become discharged in or as if in a volley **2** : to hit an object of play (as a ball) in the air before it touches the ground

**vol·ley·ball** \-ˌbȯl\ *n* : a game played by volleying an inflated ball over a net; *also* : the ball used in this game

**volt** \'vōlt\ *n* : the meter-kilogram-second unit of electrical potential difference and electromotive force equal to the difference in potential between two points in a wire carrying a constant current of one ampere when the power dissipated between the points is equal to one watt

**volt·age** \'vōl-tij\ *n* : potential difference measured in volts

**vol·ta·ic** \väl-'tā-ik, vōl-\ *adj* : of, relating to, or producing direct electric current by chemical action

**volte–face** \ˌvȯlt-'fäs, ˌvōl-tə-\ *n* : a reversal in policy : ABOUT-FACE

**volt·me·ter** \'vōlt-ˌmē-tər\ *n* : an instrument for measuring in volts the difference in potential between different points of an electrical circuit

**vol·u·ble** \'väl-yə-bəl\ *adj* : fluent and smooth in speech : GLIB   ◆ *Synonyms* GARRULOUS, LOQUACIOUS, TALKATIVE — **vol·u·bil·i·ty** \ˌväl-yə-'bi-lə-tē\ *n* — **vol·u·bly** \'väl-yə-blē\ *adv*

**vol·ume** \'väl-yəm, -(ˌ)yüm\ *n* [ME, fr. AF, fr. L *volumen* roll, scroll, fr. *volvere* to roll] **1** : a series of printed sheets bound typically in book form; *also* : an arbitrary number of issues of a periodical **2** : space occupied as measured by cubic units <the ~ of a cylinder> **3** : sufficient matter to fill a book <her glance spoke ~s> **4** : AMOUNT <increasing ~ of business> **5** : the degree of loudness of a sound   ◆ *Synonyms* BODY, BULK, MASS

**vo·lu·mi·nous** \və-'lü-mə-nəs\ *adj* : having or marked by great volume or bulk : LARGE — **vo·lu·mi·nous·ly** *adv* — **vo·lu·mi·nous·ness** *n*

¹**vol·un·tary** \'vä-lən-ˌter-ē\ *adj* **1** : done, made, or given freely and without compulsion <a ~ sacrifice> **2** : done on purpose : INTENTIONAL <~ manslaughter> **3** : of, relating to, or regulated by the will <~ behavior> **4** : having power of free choice **5** : provided or supported by voluntary action <a ~ organization>   ◆ *Synonyms* DELIBERATE, WILLFUL, WILLING, WITTING — **vol·un·tar·i·ly** \ˌvä-lən-'ter-ə-lē\ *adv*

²**voluntary** *n, pl* **-tar·ies** : an organ solo played in a religious service

**voluntary muscle** *n* : muscle (as most striated muscle) under voluntary control

¹**vol·un·teer** \ˌvä-lən-'tir\ *n* **1** : a person who voluntarily undertakes a service or duty **2** : a plant growing spontaneously esp. from seeds lost from a previous crop

²**volunteer** *vb* **1** : to offer or give voluntarily **2** : to offer oneself as a volunteer

**vo·lup·tu·ary** \və-'ləp-chə-ˌwer-ē\ *n, pl*

-ar·ies : a person whose chief interest in life is the indulgence of sensual appetites

**vo·lup·tu·ous** \-chə-wəs\ *adj* 1 : giving sensual gratification 2 : given to or spent in enjoyment of luxury or pleasure ♦ *Synonyms* LUXURIOUS, EPICUREAN, SENSUOUS — **vo·lup·tu·ous·ly** *adv* — **vo·lup·tu·ous·ness** *n*

**vo·lute** \və-ˈlüt\ *n* : a spiral or scroll-shaped decoration

¹**vom·it** \ˈvä-mət\ *n* : an act or instance of throwing up the contents of the stomach through the mouth; *also* : the matter thrown up

²**vomit** *vb* 1 : to throw up the contents of the stomach through the mouth 2 : to belch forth : GUSH

**voo·doo** \ˈvü-dü\ *n, pl* **voodoos** 1 : a religion that is derived from African polytheism and is practiced chiefly in Haiti 2 : a person who deals in spells and necromancy 3 : a charm used in voodoo; *also* : ²SPELL 1 — **voodoo** *adj*

**voo·doo·ism** \-ˌi-zəm\ *n* 1 : VOODOO 1 2 : the practice of witchcraft

**vo·ra·cious** \vȯ-ˈrā-shəs, və-\ *adj* 1 : having a huge appetite : RAVENOUS 2 : very eager ⟨a ~ reader⟩ ♦ *Synonyms* GLUTTONOUS, RAVENING, RAPACIOUS — **vo·ra·cious·ly** *adv* — **vo·ra·cious·ness** *n* — **vo·rac·i·ty** \-ˈra-sə-tē\ *n*

**vor·tex** \ˈvȯr-ˌteks\ *n, pl* **vor·ti·ces** \ˈvȯr-tə-ˌsēz\ *also* **vor·tex·es** \ˈvȯr-ˌtek-səz\ : WHIRLPOOL; *also* : something resembling a whirlpool

**vo·ta·ry** \ˈvō-tə-rē\ *n, pl* **-ries** 1 : ENTHUSIAST, DEVOTEE; *also* : a devoted adherent or admirer 2 : a devout or zealous worshiper

¹**vote** \ˈvōt\ *n* [ME (Sc), fr. L *votum* vow, wish, fr. *vovēre* to vow] 1 : a choice or opinion of a person or body of persons expressed usu. by a ballot, spoken word, or raised hand; *also* : the ballot, word, or gesture used to express a choice or opinion 2 : the decision reached by voting 3 : the right of suffrage 4 : a group of voters with some common characteristics ⟨the big city ~⟩ — **vote·less** *adj*

²**vote** *vb* **vot·ed; vot·ing** 1 : to cast a vote 2 : to elect, decide, pass, defeat, grant, or make legal by a vote 3 : to declare by general agreement 4 : to offer as a suggestion : PROPOSE 5 : to cause to vote esp. in a given way — **vot·er** *n*

**vo·tive** \ˈvō-tiv\ *adj* : consisting of or expressing a vow, wish, or desire

**vou** *abbr* voucher

**vouch** \ˈvau̇ch\ *vb* 1 : PROVE, SUBSTANTIATE 2 : to verify by examining documentary evidence 3 : to give a guarantee 4 : to supply supporting evidence or testimony; *also* : to give personal assurance

**vouch·er** \ˈvau̇-chər\ *n* 1 : an act of vouching 2 : one that vouches for another 3 : a documentary record of a business transaction 4 : a written affidavit or authorization 5 : a form indicating a credit against future purchases or expenditures

**vouch·safe** \vau̇ch-ˈsāf\ *vb* **vouch·**

**safed; vouch·saf·ing** : to grant or give as or as if a privilege or a special favor

¹**vow** \ˈvau̇\ *n* : a solemn promise or statement; *esp* : one by which a person is bound to an act, service, or condition ⟨marriage ~s⟩

²**vow** *vb* 1 : to make a vow or as a vow 2 : to bind or commit by a vow — **vow·er** *n*

**vow·el** \ˈvau̇(-ə)l\ *n* 1 : a speech sound produced without obstruction or friction in the mouth 2 : a letter representing such a sound

**vox po·pu·li** \ˈväks-ˈpä-pyə-ˌlī\ *n* [L, voice of the people] : popular sentiment

¹**voy·age** \ˈvȯi-ij\ *n* [ME, *viage, veyage*, fr. AF *veiage*, fr. LL *viaticum*, fr. L, traveling money, fr. neut. of *viaticus* of a journey, fr. *via* way] : a journey esp. by water from one place or country to another

²**voyage** *vb* **voy·aged; voy·ag·ing** : to take or make a voyage — **voy·ag·er** *n*

**voya·geur** \ˌvȯi-ə-ˈzhər, ˌvwä-yä-\ *n* [CanF] : a person employed by a fur company to transport goods to and from remote stations esp. in the Canadian Northwest

**voy·eur** \vwä-ˈyər, vȯi-ˈər\ *n* 1 : one who obtains sexual pleasure from viewing esp. covertly the nudity or sexual activity of others 2 : an observer of the sordid — **voy·eur·ism** \-ˌi-zəm\ *n* — **voy·eur·is·tic** \ˌvwä-(ˌ)yər-ˈis-tik, ˌvȯi-ər-\ *adj*

**VP** *abbr* 1 verb phrase 2 vice president

**vs** *abbr* 1 verse 2 versus

**vss** *abbr* 1 verses 2 versions

**V/STOL** *abbr* vertical or short takeoff and landing

**Vt** *or* **VT** *abbr* Vermont

**VTOL** *abbr* vertical takeoff and landing

**VTR** *abbr* videotape recorder

**vul·ca·nize** \ˈvəl-kə-ˌnīz\ *vb* **-nized; -niz·ing** : to treat rubber or rubberlike material chemically to give useful properties (as elasticity and strength)

**Vulg** *abbr* Vulgate

**vul·gar** \ˈvəl-gər\ *adj* [ME, fr. L *vulgaris* of the mob, vulgar, fr. *vulgus* mob, common people] 1 : VERNACULAR ⟨the ~ tongue⟩ 2 : of or relating to the common people : GENERAL, COMMON 3 : lacking cultivation or refinement : BOORISH; *also* : offensive to good taste or refined feelings ⟨~ language⟩ ♦ *Synonyms* GROSS, OBSCENE, RIBALD, DIRTY, INDECENT, PROFANE — **vul·gar·ly** *adv*

**vul·gar·i·an** \ˌvəl-ˈger-ē-ən\ *n* : a vulgar person

**vul·gar·ism** \ˈvəl-gə-ˌri-zəm\ *n* 1 : VULGARITY 2 : a word or expression originated or used chiefly by illiterate persons 3 : a coarse expression : OBSCENITY

**vul·gar·i·ty** \ˌvəl-ˈga-rə-tē\ *n, pl* **-ties** 1 : something vulgar 2 : the quality or state of being vulgar

**vul·gar·ize** \ˈvəl-gə-ˌrīz\ *vb* **-ized; -iz·ing** : to make vulgar — **vul·gar·i·za·tion** \ˌvəl-gə-rə-ˈzā-shən\ *n* — **vul·gar·iz·er** \ˈvəl-gə-ˌrī-zər\ *n*

**Vul·gate** \ˈvəl-ˌgāt\ *n* [ML *vulgata*, fr. LL *vulgata editio* edition in general circulationl ] : a Latin version of the Bible used by the Roman Catholic Church

**vul·ner·a·ble** \'vəl-nə-rə-bəl\ *adj* **1** : capable of being wounded : susceptible to wounds **2** : open to attack **3** : liable to increased penalties in contract bridge — **vul·ner·a·bil·i·ty** \ˌvəl-nə-rə-'bi-lə-tē\ *n* — **vul·ner·a·bly** \'vəl-nə-rə-ble\ *adv*

**vul·pine** \'vəl-ˌpīn\ *adj* : of, relating to, or resembling a fox esp. in cunning ⟨~ charms⟩

**vul·ture** \'vəl-chər\ *n* **1** : any of various large birds (as a turkey vulture) related to the hawks, eagles, and falcons but having weaker claws and the head usu. naked and living chiefly on carrion **2** : a rapacious person

**vul·va** \'vəl-və\ *n, pl* **vul·vae** \-ˌvē\ [ME, fr. ML, fr. L *volva, vulva* womb, female genitals] : the external parts of the female genital organs — **vul·val** \'vəl-vəl\ *or* **vul·var** \-vər, -ˌvär\ *adj*

**vv** *abbr* **1** verses **2** vice versa

**VX** \ˌvē-'eks\ *n* : an extremely toxic chemical weapon

**vying** *pres part of* VIE

**¹w** \'də-bəl-(ˌ)yü\ *n, pl* **w's** *or* **ws** *often cap* : the 23d letter of the English alphabet

**²w** *abbr, often cap* **1** water **2** watt **3** week **4** weight **5** west; western **6** wide; width **7** wife **8** with

**W** *symbol* [G *Wolfram*] tungsten

**WA** *abbr* **1** Washington **2** Western Australia

**wacky** \'wa-kē\ *adj* **wack·i·er; -est** : ECCENTRIC, CRAZY

**¹wad** \'wäd\ *n* **1** : a little mass, bundle, or tuft ⟨~s of clay⟩ **2** : a soft mass of usu. light fibrous material **3** : a pliable plug (as of felt) used to retain a powder charge (as in a cartridge) **4** : a considerable amount (as of money) **5** : a roll of paper money

**²wad** *vb* **wad·ded; wad·ding 1** : to push a wad into ⟨~ a gun⟩ **2** : to form into a wad **3** : to hold in by a wad ⟨~ a bullet in a gun⟩ **4** : to stuff or line with a wad : PAD

**wad·ding** \'wä-diŋ\ *n* **1** : WADS; *also* : material for making wads **2** : a soft mass or sheet of short loose fibers used for stuffing or padding

**wad·dle** \'wä-dᵊl\ *vb* **wad·dled; wad·dling** : to walk with short steps swaying from side to side like a duck — **waddle** *n*

**wade** \'wäd\ *vb* **wad·ed; wad·ing 1** : to step in or through a medium (as water) more resistant than air **2** : to move or go with difficulty or labor and often with determination ⟨~ through a dull book⟩ — **wad·able** *or* **wade·able** \'wä-də-bəl\ *adj* — **wade** *n*

**wad·er** \'wä-dər\ *n* **1** : one that wades **2** : SHOREBIRD; *also* : WADING BIRD **3** *pl* : a waterproof garment consisting of pants with attached boots for wading

**wa·di** \'wä-dē\ *n* [Ar *wādī*] : a streambed of southwest Asia and northern Africa that is dry except in the rainy season

**wading bird** *n* : any of an order of long-legged birds (as sandpipers, cranes, or herons) that wade in water in search of food

**wa·fer** \'wä-fər\ *n* **1** : a thin crisp cake or cracker **2** : a thin round piece of unleavened bread used in the Eucharist **3** : something (as a piece of candy) that resembles a wafer

**¹waf·fle** \'wä-fəl\ *n* : a soft but crisped cake of batter cooked in a special hinged metal utensil (**waffle iron**)

**²waffle** *vb* **waf·fled; waf·fling** \-f(ə)liŋ\ : to speak or write in a vague or evasive manner ⟨*waffled* on important issues⟩

**¹waft** \'wäft, 'waft\ *vb* : to cause to move or go lightly by or as if by the impulse of wind or waves

**²waft** *n* **1** : a slight breeze : PUFF **2** : the act of waving

**¹wag** \'wag\ *vb* **wagged; wag·ging 1** : to sway or swing shortly from side to side or to-and-fro ⟨the dog *wagged* his tail⟩ **2** : to move in chatter or gossip ⟨scandal caused tongues to ~⟩

**²wag** *n* : an act of wagging : a wagging movement

**³wag** *n* : WIT, JOKER

**¹wage** \'wāj\ *n* **1** : payment for labor or services usu. according to contract **2** *pl* : RECOMPENSE, REWARD

**²wage** *vb* **waged; wag·ing 1** : to engage in : CARRY ON ⟨~ a war⟩ **2** : to be in process of being waged

**¹wa·ger** \'wā-jər\ *n* **1** : BET, STAKE **2** : something on which bets are laid : GAMBLE

**²wager** *vb* : BET — **wa·ger·er** *n*

**wag·gery** \'wa-gə-rē\ *n, pl* **-ger·ies 1** : mischievous merriment : PLEASANTRY **2** : JEST, TRICK

**wag·gish** \'wa-gish\ *adj* **1** : resembling or characteristic of a wag : MISCHIEVOUS **2** : SPORTIVE, HUMOROUS

**wag·gle** \'wa-gəl\ *vb* **wag·gled; wag·gling** : to move backward and forward or from side to side : WAG — **waggle** *n*

**wag·gon** *chiefly Brit var of* WAGON

**wag·on** \'wa-gən\ *n* **1** : a 4-wheeled vehicle; *esp* : one drawn by animals and used for freight or merchandise **2** : PADDY WAGON **3** : a child's 4-wheeled cart **4** : STATION WAGON

**wag·on·er** \'wa-gə-nər\ *n* : the driver of a wagon

**wag·on·ette** \ˌwa-gə-ˈnet\ *n* : a light wagon with two facing seats along the sides behind a cross seat in front

**wa·gon–lit** \vä-gōⁿ-ˈlēˌ\ *n, pl* **wagons–lits** *or* **wagon–lits** \*same or* -ˈlēz\ [F, fr. *wagon* railroad car + *lit* bed] : a railroad sleeping car

**wagon train** *n* : a column of wagons traveling overland

**wag·tail** \ˈwag-ˌtāl\ *n* : any of various slender-bodied mostly Old World birds with a long tail that jerks up and down

**wa·hi·ne** \wä-ˈhē-nē, -ˈnä\ *n* 1 : a Polynesian woman 2 : a female surfer

**wa·hoo** \ˈwä-ˌhü\ *n, pl* **wahoos** : a large vigorous food and sport fish related to the mackerel and found in warm seas

**waif** \ˈwāf\ *n* 1 : something found without an owner and esp. by chance 2 : a stray person or animal; *esp* : a homeless child

**wail** \ˈwāl\ *vb* 1 : LAMENT, WEEP 2 : to make a sound suggestive of a mournful cry 3 : COMPLAIN — **wail** *n*

**wail·ful** \-fəl\ *adj* : SORROWFUL, MOURNFUL ♦ **Synonyms** MELANCHOLY, DOLEFUL, LUGUBRIOUS, LAMENTABLE, PLAINTIVE, WOEFUL — **wail·ful·ly** *adv*

**wain** \ˈwān\ *n* : a usu. large heavy farm wagon

**wain·scot** \ˈwän-skət, -ˌskōt, -ˌskät\ *n* 1 : a usu. paneled wooden lining of an interior wall of a room 2 : the lower part of an interior wall when finished differently from the rest — **wainscot** *vb*

**wain·scot·ing** *or* **wain·scot·ting** \-ˌskō-tiŋ, -ˌskä-, -skə-\ *n* : material for a wainscot; *also* : WAINSCOT

**waist** \ˈwāst\ *n* 1 : the narrowed part of the body between the chest and hips 2 : a part resembling the human waist esp. in narrowness or central position ⟨the ~ of a ship⟩ 3 : a garment or part of a garment (as a blouse or bodice) for the upper part of the body

**waist·band** \-ˌband\ *n* : a band (as on pants or a skirt) that fits around the waist

**waist·coat** \ˈwes-kət, ˈwāst-ˌkōt\ *n, chiefly Brit* : VEST 1

**waist·line** \ˈwāst-ˌlīn\ *n* 1 : a line around the waist at its narrowest part; *also* : the length of this 2 : the line at which the bodice and skirt of a dress meet

**¹wait** \ˈwāt\ *vb* 1 : to remain inactive in readiness or expectation : AWAIT ⟨~ for orders⟩ 2 : to delay serving (a meal) 3 : to act as attendant or servant ⟨~ on customers⟩ 4 : to attend as a waiter : SERVE ⟨~ tables⟩ ⟨~ at a banquet⟩ 5 : to be ready ⟨a letter ~ing for you⟩

**²wait** *n* 1 : a position of concealment usu. with intent to attack or surprise ⟨lie in ~⟩ 2 : an act or period of waiting

**wait·er** \ˈwā-tər\ *n* 1 : one that waits on another; *esp* : a person who waits tables 2 : TRAY

**waiting game** *n* : a strategy in which one or more participants withhold action in the hope of an opportunity for more effective action later

**waiting room** *n* : a room (as at a doctor's office) for the use of persons who are waiting

**wait·per·son** \ˈwāt-ˌpər-sən\ *n* : a waiter or waitress

**wait·ress** \ˈwā-trəs\ *n* : a woman who waits tables

**waive** \ˈwāv\ *vb* **waived; waiv·ing** [ME *weiven* to decline, reject, give up, fr. AF *waiver, gaiver*, fr. *waif* lost, stray] 1 : to give up claim to ⟨*waived* his right to a trial⟩ 2 : POSTPONE

**waiv·er** \ˈwā-vər\ *n* : the act of waiving right, claim, or privilege; *also* : a document containing a declaration of such an act

**¹wake** \ˈwāk\ *vb* **woke** \ˈwōk\ *also* **waked** \ˈwākt\; **wo·ken** \ˈwō-kən\ *also* **waked** *or* **woke; wak·ing** 1 : to be or remain awake; *esp* : to keep watch (as over a corpse) 2 : AWAKE, AWAKEN ⟨the baby *woke* up early⟩

**²wake** *n* 1 : the state of being awake 2 : a watch held over the body of a dead person prior to burial

**³wake** *n* : the track left by a ship in the water; *also* : a track left behind

**wake·board** \ˈwāk-ˌbórd\ *n* : a short board with foot bindings on which a rider is towed by a motorboat across its wake — **wake·board·er** *n* — **wake·board·ing** *n*

**wake·ful** \ˈwāk-fəl\ *adj* : not sleeping or able to sleep : SLEEPLESS, ALERT — **wake·ful·ness** *n*

**wak·en** \ˈwā-kən\ *vb* : WAKE

**wake-rob·in** \ˈwāk-ˌrä-bən\ *n* : TRILLIUM

**wak·ing** \ˈwā-kiŋ\ *adj* : passed in a conscious or alert state ⟨every ~ hour⟩

**wale** \ˈwāl\ *n* : a ridge esp. on cloth; *also* : the texture esp. of a fabric

**¹walk** \ˈwók\ *vb* [partly fr. ME *walken*, fr. OE *wealcan* to roll, toss and partly fr. ME *walkien*, fr. OE *wealcian* to roll up, muffle up] 1 : to move or cause to move on foot usu. at a natural unhurried gait ⟨~ to town⟩ ⟨~ a horse⟩ 2 : to pass over, through, or along by walking ⟨~ the streets⟩ 3 : to perform or accomplish by walking ⟨~ guard⟩ 4 : to follow a course of action or way of life ⟨~ humbly in the sight of God⟩ 5 : WALK OUT 6 : to receive a base on balls; *also* : to give a base on balls to — **walk·er** *n*

**²walk** *n* 1 : a going on foot ⟨go for a ~⟩ 2 : a place, path, or course for walking 3 : distance to be walked ⟨a quarter-mile ~ from here⟩ 4 : manner of living 5 : CONDUCT, BEHAVIOR ⟨social or economic status ⟨various ~s of life⟩ 6 : manner of walking : GAIT; *esp* : a slow 4-beat gait of a horse 7 : BASE ON BALLS

**walk·away** \ˈwó-kə-ˌwā\ *n* : an easily won contest

**walk·ie-talk·ie** \ˌwó-kē-ˈtó-kē\ *n* : a small portable radio transmitting and receiving set

**¹walk-in** \ˈwók-ˌin\ *adj* : large enough to be walked into ⟨a ~ refrigerator⟩

**²walk-in** *n* 1 : an easy election victory 2 : one that walks in

**walking papers** *n pl* : DISMISSAL, DISCHARGE

**walk·ing stick** *n* **1** : a stick used in walking **2** : STICK INSECT; *esp* : one of the U.S. and Canada

**walk–on** \'wôk-,ón, -,än\ *n* : a small part in a dramatic production

**walk·out** \-,aút\ *n* **1** : a labor strike **2** : the action of leaving a meeting or organization as an expression of disapproval

**walk out** *vb* **1** : to leave suddenly often as an expression of disapproval **2** : to go on strike

**walk·over** \-,ō-vər\ *n* : a one-sided contest : an easy victory

**walk–up** \'wôk-,əp\ *n* : a building or apartment house without an elevator — **walk–up** *adj*

**walk·way** \-,wā\ *n* : a passage for walking

¹**wall** \'wól\ *n* [ME, fr. OE *weall*, fr. L *vallum* rampart, fr. *vallus* stake, palisade] **1** : a structure (as of stone or brick) intended for defense or security or for enclosing something **2** : one of the upright enclosing parts of a building or room **3** : the inside surface of a cavity or container ⟨the ~ of a boiler⟩ **4** : something like a wall in appearance, function, or effect ⟨a tariff ~⟩ — **walled** \'wóld\ *adj*

²**wall** *vb* **1** : to provide, separate, or surround with or as if with a wall ⟨~ in a garden⟩ **2** : to close (an opening) with or as if with a wall ⟨~ up a door⟩

**wal·la·by** \'wä-lə-bē\ *n, pl* **wallabies** *also* **wallaby** : any of various small or medium-sized kangaroos

**wall·board** \'wól-,bórd\ *n* : a structural material (as of wood pulp or plaster) made in large sheets and used for sheathing interior walls and ceilings

**wal·let** \'wä-lət\ *n* **1** : a bag or sack for carrying things on a journey **2** : a pocketbook with compartments (as for personal papers and usu. unfolded money) : BILLFOLD

**wall·eye** \'wól-,ī\ *n* **1** : an eye with a whitish iris or an opaque white cornea **2** : a large vigorous No. American food and sport fish related to the perches — **wall·eyed** \-,īd\ *adj*

**wall·flow·er** \'wól-,flaú(-ə)r\ *n* **1** : any of several Old World herbs related to the mustards; *esp* : one with showy fragrant flowers **2** : a person who usu. from shyness or unpopularity remains alone (as at a dance)

**Wal·loon** \wä-'lün\ *n* : a member of a people of southern and southeastern Belgium and adjacent parts of France — **Walloon** *adj*

¹**wal·lop** \'wä-ləp\ *vb* **1** : to beat soundly : TROUNCE **2** : to hit hard : SOCK ♦ *Synonyms* BATTER, BEAT, LAMBASTE, POUND, PUMMEL, THRASH

²**wallop** *n* **1** : a powerful blow or impact **2** : the ability to hit hard **3** : emotional, sensory, or psychological force : IMPACT ⟨a story with a ~⟩

**wal·lop·ing** \'wä-lə-piŋ\ *adj* **1** : LARGE, WHOPPING ⟨a ~ storm⟩ **2** : exceptionally fine or impressive ⟨a ~ fun party⟩

¹**wal·low** \'wä-lō\ *vb* **1** : to roll oneself about sluggishly in or as if in deep mud ⟨hogs ~ing in the mire⟩ **2** : to indulge

oneself excessively ⟨~ in luxury⟩ **3** : to become or remain helpless ⟨~ in ignorance⟩ ♦ *Synonyms* BASK, INDULGE, LUXURIATE, REVEL, WELTER

²**wallow** *n* : a muddy or dust-filled area where animals wallow

**wall·pa·per** \'wól-,pā-pər\ *n* : decorative paper for the walls of a room — **wallpaper** *vb*

**wall–to–wall** *adj* **1** : covering the entire floor ⟨*wall-to-wall* carpeting⟩ **2** : covering or filling one entire space or time ⟨crowds of *wall-to-wall* people⟩

**wal·nut** \'wól-(,)nət\ *n* [ME *walnot*, fr. OE *wealhhnutu*, lit., foreign nut, fr. *Wealh* Welshman, foreigner + *hnutu* nut] **1** : a nut with a furrowed usu. rough shell and an adherent husk from any of a genus of trees related to the hickories; *esp* : the large edible nut of a Eurasian tree **2** : a tree that bears walnuts **3** : the usu. reddish to dark brown wood of a walnut used esp. in cabinetwork and veneers

**wal·rus** \'wól-rəs, 'wäl-\ *n, pl* **walrus** *or* **wal·rus·es** : a large mammal of arctic waters that is related to the seals and has long ivory tusks

¹**waltz** \'wólts\ *n* [G *Walzer*, fr. *walzen* to roll, dance] **1** : a gliding dance done to music having three beats to the measure **2** : music for or suitable for waltzing

²**waltz** *vb* **1** : to dance a waltz **2** : to move or advance easily, successfully, or conspicuously ⟨he ~ed off with the championship⟩ — **waltz·er** *n*

**wam·ble** \'wäm-bəl\ *vb* **wam·bled**; **wam·bling** : to progress unsteadily or with a lurching shambling gait

**Wam·pa·no·ag** \,wäm-pə-'nō-(,)ag; ,wóm-\ *n, pl* **Wampanoag** *or* **Wampanoags** [Narragansett, lit., easterners] : a member of an American Indian people of parts of Rhode Island and Massachusetts

**wam·pum** \'wäm-pəm\ *n* [short for *wampumpeag*, fr. Massachuset (an Algonquian Indian language) *wampompeag*, fr. *wampan* white + *api* string + -*ag*, pl. suffix] **1** : beads made of shells strung in strands, belts, or sashes and used by No. American Indians as money and ornaments **2** *slang* : MONEY

**wan** \'wän\ *adj* **wan·ner**; **wan·nest 1** : SICKLY, PALLID; *also* : FEEBLE **2** : DIM, FAINT **3** : LANGUID ⟨a ~ smile⟩ ♦ *Synonyms* ASHEN, BLANCHED, DOUGHY, LIVID, PALE, WAXEN **wan·ly** *adv* — **wan·ness** *n*

**wand** \'wänd\ *n* **1** : a slender staff carried in a procession **2** : the staff of a fairy, diviner, or magician

**wan·der** \'wän-dər\ *vb* **1** : to move about aimlessly or without a fixed course or goal : RAMBLE **2** : to go astray in conduct or thought; *esp* : to become delirious ♦ *Synonyms* GAD, GALLIVANT, MEANDER, RANGE, ROAM, ROVE — **wan·der·er** *n*

**wandering Jew** *n* : either of two trailing or creeping plants cultivated for their showy and often white-striped foliage

**wan·der·lust** \'wän-dər-,ləst\ *n* : strong longing for or impulse toward wandering

**¹wane** \'wān\ *vb* **waned; wan·ing 1** : to grow gradually smaller or less ⟨the full moon ~s to new⟩ ⟨his strength *waned*⟩ **2** : to lose power, prosperity, or influence **3** : to draw near an end ⟨summer is *waning*⟩ ◆ **Synonyms** ABATE, EBB, MODERATE, RELENT, SLACKEN, SUBSIDE

**²wane** *n* : a waning (as in size or power); *also* : a period in which something is waning

**wan·gle** \'waŋ-gəl\ *vb* **wan·gled; wangling 1** : to obtain by sly or devious means; *also* : to use trickery or questionable means to achieve an end **2** : MANIPULATE; *also* : FINAGLE

**wan·na·be** *also* **wan·na·bee** \'wä-nə-‚bē\ *n* : a person who wants or aspires to be someone or something else or who tries to look or act like someone else

**¹want** \'wȯnt, 'wänt\ *vb* **1** : to fail to possess : LACK ⟨they ~ the necessities of life⟩ **2** : to feel or suffer the need of **3** : NEED, REQUIRE ⟨the house ~s painting⟩ **4** : to desire earnestly : WISH

**²want** *n* **1** : a lack of a required or usual amount : SHORTAGE **2** : dire need : DESTITUTION **3** : something wanted : DESIRE **4** : personal defect : FAULT

**¹want·ing** \'wȯn-tiŋ, 'wän-\ *adj* **1** : not present or in evidence : ABSENT **2** : falling below standards or expectations **3** : lacking in ability or capacity : DEFICIENT ⟨~ in common sense⟩

**²wanting** *prep* **1** : LESS, MINUS ⟨a month ~ two days⟩ **2** : WITHOUT ⟨a book ~ a cover⟩

**¹wan·ton** \'wȯn-tᵊn, 'wän-\ *adj* [ME, undisciplined, fr. *wan-* deficient, wrong + *towen,* pp. of *teen* to draw, train, discipline] **1** : UNCHASTE, LEWD, LUSTFUL; *also* : SENSUAL **2** : having no regard for justice or for other persons' feelings, rights, or safety : MERCILESS, INHUMANE ⟨~ cruelty⟩ **3** : having no just cause ⟨a ~ attack⟩ — **wan·ton·ly** *adv* — **wanton·ness** *n*

**²wanton** *n* : a wanton individual; *esp* : a lewd or immoral person

**³wanton** *vb* **1** : to be wanton : act wantonly **2** : to pass or waste wantonly

**wa·pi·ti** \'wä-pə-tē\ *n, pl* **wapiti** *or* **wapitis** : ELK 2

**¹war** \'wȯr\ *n* **1** : a state or period of usu. open and declared armed fighting between states or nations **2** : the art or science of warfare **3** : a state of hostility, conflict, or antagonism **4** : a struggle between opposing forces or for a particular end ⟨~ against disease⟩ — **war·less** \-ləs\ *adj*

**²war** *vb* **warred; war·ring** : to engage in warfare : be in conflict

**³war** *abbr* warrant

**¹war·ble** \'wȯr-bəl\ *n* **1** : a melodious succession of low pleasing sounds **2** : a musical trill

**²warble** *vb* **war·bled; war·bling 1** : to sing or utter in a trilling manner or with variations **2** : to express by or as if by warbling

**³warble** *n* : a swelling under the skin esp. of the back of cattle, horses, and wild mammals caused by the maggot of a fly (**warble fly**); *also* : its maggot

**war·bler** \'wȯr-blər\ *n* **1** : SONGSTER **2** : any of various small slender-billed chiefly Old World songbirds related to the thrushes and noted for their singing **3** : any of numerous small bright-colored insect-eating American birds with a usu. weak and unmusical song

**war·bon·net** \'wȯr-‚bä-nət\ *n* : a feathered American Indian ceremonial headdress

**war crime** *n* : a crime (as genocide) committed during or in connection with war

**war cry** *n* **1** : a cry used by fighters in war **2** : a slogan used esp. to rally people to a cause

**¹ward** \'wȯrd\ *n* **1** : a guarding or being under guard or guardianship; *esp* : CUSTODY **2** : a body of guards **3** : a division of a prison **4** : a division in a hospital **5** : a division of a city for electoral or administrative purposes **6** : a person (as a child) under the protection of a guardian or a law court **7** : a person or body of persons under the protection or tutelage of a government **8** : a means of defense : PROTECTION

**²ward** *vb* : to turn aside : DEFLECT — usu. used with *off* ⟨~ off a blow⟩

**¹-ward** *also* **-wards** *adj suffix* **1** : that moves, tends, faces, or is directed toward ⟨wind*ward*⟩ **2** : that occurs or is situated in the direction of ⟨sea*ward*⟩

**²-ward** *or* **-wards** *adv suffix* **1** : in a (specified) direction ⟨up*wards*⟩ ⟨after*ward*⟩ **2** : toward a (specified) point, position, or area ⟨sky*ward*⟩

**war dance** *n* : a dance performed (as by American Indians) before going to war or in celebration of victory

**war·den** \'wȯr-dᵊn\ *n* **1** : GUARDIAN, KEEPER **2** : the governor of a town, district, or fortress **3** : an official charged with special supervisory or enforcement duties ⟨game ~⟩ ⟨air raid ~⟩ **4** : an official in charge of the operation of a prison **5** : one of two ranking lay officers of an Episcopal parish **6** : any of various British college officials

**ward·er** \'wȯr-dər\ *n* : WATCHMAN, WARDEN

**ward heel·er** \-‚hē-lər\ *n* : a local worker for a political boss

**ward·robe** \'wȯr-‚drōb\ *n* [ME *warderobe,* fr. AF *warderobe, garderobe,* fr. *warder, garder* to guard + *robe* robe] **1** : a room or closet where clothes are kept; *also* : CLOTHESPRESS **2** : a collection of wearing apparel ⟨his summer ~⟩

**ward·room** \-‚drüm, -‚drúm\ *n* : the dining area for officers aboard a warship

**ward·ship** \'wȯrd-‚ship\ *n* **1** : GUARDIANSHIP **2** : the state of being under care of a guardian

**ware** \'wer\ *n* **1** : manufactured articles or products of art or craft : GOODS ⟨glass*ware*⟩ **2** : an article of merchandise ⟨a peddler hawking his ~s⟩ **3** : items (as dishes) of fired clay : POTTERY

**ware·house** \-‚haùs\ *n* : a place for the storage of merchandise or commodities

: STOREHOUSE — **warehouse** *vb*
**ware·house·man** \-mən\ *n* — **ware·hous·er** \-,haů-zər, -sər\ *n*
**ware·room** \'weɪ-,rüm, -,rům\ *n* : a room in which goods are exhibited for sale
**war·fare** \'wȯr-,fer\ *n* 1 : military operations between enemies : WAR; *also* : an activity undertaken by one country to weaken or destroy another ⟨economic ~⟩ 2 : STRUGGLE, CONFLICT
**war·fa·rin** \'wȯr-fə-rən\ *n* : an anticoagulant compound used as a rodent poison and in medicine
**war·head** \'wȯr-,hed\ *n* : the section of a missile containing the charge
**war·horse** \-,hȯrs\ *n* 1 : a horse for use in war 2 : a veteran soldier or public person (as a politician) 3 : a musical composition that is often performed
**war·like** \-,līk\ *adj* 1 : fond of war ⟨~ peoples⟩ 2 : of, relating to, or useful in war : MILITARY, MARTIAL ⟨~ supplies⟩ 3 : befitting or characteristic of war or of soldiers ⟨~ attitudes⟩
**war·lock** \-,läk\ *n* [ME *warloghe*, fr. OE *wǣrloga* one that breaks faith, the Devil, fr. *wǣr* faith, troth + *-loga* (fr. *lēogan* to lie)] : SORCERER, WIZARD
**war·lord** \-,lȯrd\ *n* 1 : a high military leader 2 : a military commander exercising local civil power by force ⟨former Chinese ~s⟩
¹**warm** \'wȯrm\ *adj* 1 : having or giving out heat to a moderate or adequate degree ⟨~ milk⟩ ⟨a ~ stove⟩ 2 : serving to retain heat ⟨~ clothes⟩ 3 : feeling or inducing sensations of heat ⟨~ from exercise⟩ ⟨a ~ climb⟩ 4 : showing or marked by strong feeling : ARDENT ⟨~ support⟩ 5 : marked by tense excitement or hot anger ⟨a ~ campaign⟩ 6 : giving a pleasant impression of warmth, cheerfulness, or friendliness ⟨a ~ colors⟩ ⟨a ~ tone of voice⟩ 7 : marked by or tending toward injury, distress, or pain ⟨made things ~ for the enemy⟩ 8 : newly made : FRESH ⟨a ~ scent⟩ 9 : near to a goal ⟨getting ~ in a search⟩ — **warm·ly** *adv*
²**warm** *vb* 1 : to make or become warm 2 : to give a feeling of warmth or vitality to 3 : to experience feelings of affection or pleasure ⟨she ~ed to her guest⟩ 4 : to reheat for eating ⟨~ed over the roast⟩ 5 : to make ready for operation or performance by preliminary exercise or operation ⟨~ up the motor⟩ 6 : to become increasingly ardent, interested, or competent ⟨the speaker ~ed to his topic⟩ — **warm·er** *n*
**warm–blood·ed** \-'blə-dəd\ *adj* : able to maintain a relatively high and constant body temperature relatively independent of that of the surroundings
**warmed–over** \'wȯrmd-'ō-vər\ *adj* 1 : REHEATED ⟨~ cabbage⟩ 2 : not fresh or new ⟨~ ideas⟩
**warm front** *n* : an advancing edge of a warm air mass
**warm–heart·ed** \'wȯrm-'här-təd\ *adj* : marked by warmth of feeling : CORDIAL — **warm·heart·ed·ness** *n*
**warming pan** *n* : a long-handled covered pan filled with live coals and formerly used to warm a bed

**war·mon·ger** \'wȯr-,məŋ-gər, -,mäŋ-\ *n* : one who urges or attempts to stir up war — **war·mon·ger·ing** \-g(ə-)riŋ\ *n*
**warmth** \'wȯrmth\ *n* 1 : the quality or state of being warm 2 : ZEAL, ARDOR, FERVOR
**warm up** *vb* : to engage in exercise or practice esp. before entering a game or contest — **warm–up** \'wȯrm-,əp\ *n*
**warn** \'wȯrn\ *vb* 1 : to put on guard : CAUTION; *also* : ADMONISH, COUNSEL 2 : to notify esp. in advance : INFORM 3 : to order to go or keep away
¹**warn·ing** \'wȯr-niŋ\ *n* 1 : the act of warning : the state of being warned 2 : something that warns or serves to warn ⟨a tornado ~⟩
²**warning** *adj* : serving as an alarm, signal, summons, or admonition ⟨a ~ bell⟩ — **warn·ing·ly** *adv*
¹**warp** \'wȯrp\ *n* 1 : the lengthwise threads on a loom or in a woven fabric 2 : a twist out of a true plane or straight line ⟨a ~ in a board⟩
²**warp** *vb* [ME, fr. OE *weorpan* to throw] 1 : to turn or twist out of shape; *also* : to become so twisted 2 : to lead astray : PERVERT; *also* : FALSIFY, DISTORT
**war paint** *n* : paint put on the face and body by American Indians as a sign of going to war
**war·path** \'wȯr-,path, -,päth\ *n* : the course taken by a party of American Indians going on a hostile expedition — **on the warpath** : ready to fight or argue
**war·plane** \-,plān\ *n* : a military airplane; *esp* : one armed for combat
**warp speed** *n* : the highest possible speed
¹**war·rant** \'wȯr-ənt, 'wär-\ *n* 1 : AUTHORIZATION; *also* : JUSTIFICATION, GROUND 2 : evidence (as a document) of authorization; *esp* : a legal writ authorizing an officer to take action (as in making an arrest, seizure, or search) 3 : a certificate of appointment issued to an officer of lower rank than a commissioned officer
²**warrant** *vb* 1 : to guarantee security or immunity to : SECURE 2 : to declare or maintain positively ⟨I ~ this is so⟩ 3 : to assure (a person) of the truth of what is said 4 : to guarantee to be as it appears or as it is represented ⟨~ goods as of the first quality⟩ 5 : SANCTION, AUTHORIZE 6 : to give proof of : ATTEST; *also* : GUARANTEE 7 : JUSTIFY ⟨his need ~s the expenditure⟩
**warrant officer** *n* 1 : an officer in the armed forces ranking next below a commissioned officer 2 : a commissioned officer ranking below an ensign in the navy or coast guard and below a second lieutenant in the marine corps
**war·ran·ty** \'wȯr-ən-tē, 'wär-\ *n, pl* **-ties** : an expressed or implied statement that some situation or thing is as it appears to be or is represented to be; *esp* : a usu. written guarantee of the integrity of a product and of the maker's responsibility for the repair or replacement of defective parts

**war·ren** \'wȯr-ən, 'wär-\ *n* **1** : an area where rabbits breed; *also* : a structure where rabbits are bred or kept **2** : a crowded tenement or district

**war·rior** \'wȯr-yər; 'wȯr-ē-ər, 'wär-\ *n* : a man engaged or experienced in warfare

**war·ship** \'wȯr-,ship\ *n* : a naval vessel

**wart** \'wȯrt\ *n* **1** : a small usu. horny projecting growth on the skin; *esp* : one caused by a virus **2** : a protuberance resembling a wart (as on a plant) — **warty** *adj*

**wart·hog** \'wȯrt-,hȯg, -,häg\ *n* : a wild African hog that has large tusks and in the male two pairs of rough warty protuberances below the eyes

**war·time** \'wȯr-,tīm\ *n* : a period during which a war is in progress

**wary** \'wer-ē\ *adj* **war·i·er; -est** : very cautious; *esp* : careful in guarding against danger or deception — **war·i·ly** \'wer-ə-lē\ *adv* — **war·i·ness** \'wer-ē-nəs\ *n*

**was** *past 1st & 3d sing of* BE

**wa·sa·bi** \'wä-sə-bē; wä-'sä-\ *n* [Jp] : a condiment prepared from the ground greenish root of an Asian herb and similar in flavor and use to horseradish; *also* : the herb or its root

**¹wash** \'wȯsh, 'wäsh\ *vb* **1** : to clean with water and usu. soap or detergent ⟨∼ clothes⟩ ⟨∼ your hands⟩ **2** : to wet thoroughly : DRENCH **3** : to flow along the border of ⟨waves ∼ the shore⟩ **4** : to pour or flow in a stream or current **5** : to move or remove by or as if by the action of water **6** : to cover or daub lightly with a liquid (as whitewash) **7** : to run water over (as gravel or ore) in order to separate valuable matter from refuse ⟨∼ sand for gold⟩ **8** : to undergo laundering ⟨a dress that doesn't ∼ well⟩ **9** : to stand a test ⟨that story will not ∼⟩ **10** : to be worn away by water

**²wash** *n* **1** : the act or process or an instance of washing or being washed **2** : articles to be washed or being washed **3** : a thin coat of paint (as watercolor) **4** : the flow or action of a mass of water (as a wave) **5** : worthless esp. liquid waste : REFUSE, SWILL **6** : erosion by waves (as of the sea) **7** : a disturbance in a fluid (as water or the air) caused by the passage of a wing or propeller **8** *West* : the dry bed of a stream

**³wash** *adj* : WASHABLE

**Wash** *abbr* Washington

**wash·able** \'wȯ-shə-bəl, 'wä-\ *adj* : capable of being washed without damage — **wash·abil·i·ty** \,wȯ-shə-'bi-lə-tē, ,wä-\ *n*

**wash–and–wear** *adj* : of, relating to, or being a fabric or garment that needs little or no ironing after washing

**wash·ba·sin** \'wȯsh-,bā-sᵊn, 'wäsh-\ *n* : WASHBOWL

**wash·board** \-,bȯrd\ *n* : a grooved board to scrub clothes on

**wash·bowl** \-,bōl\ *n* : a large bowl for water for washing hands and face

**wash·cloth** \-,klȯth\ *n* : a cloth used for washing one's face and body

**washed–out** \'wȯsht-'aut, 'wäsht-\ *adj* **1**
: faded in color **2** : EXHAUSTED ⟨felt ∼ after working all night⟩

**washed–up** \-'əp\ *adj* : no longer successful, popular, skillful, or needed

**wash·er** \'wȯ-shər, 'wä-\ *n* **1** : a ring or perforated plate used around a bolt or screw to ensure tightness or relieve friction **2** : one that washes; *esp* : a machine for washing

**wash·er·wom·an** \-,wu̇-mən\ *n* : a woman whose occupation is washing clothes

**wash·ing** \'wȯ-shiŋ, 'wä-\ *n* **1** : material obtained by washing **2** : articles washed or to be washed

**washing soda** *n* : SODIUM CARBONATE

**Wash·ing·ton's Birthday** \'wȯ-shiŋ-tənz-, 'wä-\ *n* : the 3d Monday in February observed as a legal holiday

**wash·out** \'wȯsh-,aut, 'wäsh-\ *n* **1** : the washing away of earth (as from a road); *also* : a place where earth is washed away **2** : a complete failure

**wash·room** \-,rüm, -,rum\ *n* : BATHROOM

**wash·stand** \-,stand\ *n* **1** : a stand holding articles needed for washing face and hands **2** : LAVATORY 1

**wash·tub** \-,təb\ *n* : a tub for washing or soaking clothes

**wash·wom·an** \'wȯsh-,wu̇-mən, 'wäsh-\ *n* : WASHERWOMAN

**washy** \'wȯ-shē, 'wä-\ *adj* **wash·i·er; -est** **1** : WEAK, WATERY **2** : PALLID ⟨a ∼ yellow⟩ **3** : lacking in vigor, individuality, or definiteness

**wasp** \'wäsp, 'wȯsp\ *n* : any of numerous social or solitary winged insects related to the bees and ants with biting mouthparts and in females and workers an often formidable sting

**WASP** *or* **Wasp** *n* [*w*hite *A*nglo-*S*axon *P*rotestant] : an American of northern European and esp. British ancestry and of Protestant background

**wasp·ish** \'wäs-pish, 'wȯs-\ *adj* **1** : SNAPPISH, IRRITABLE ⟨a ∼ temper⟩ **2** : resembling a wasp in form; *esp* : slightly built ♦ **Synonyms** FRACTIOUS, FRETFUL, HUFFY, PEEVISH, PETULANT, QUERULOUS

**wasp waist** *n* : a very slender waist

**¹was·sail** \'wä-səl, wä-'säl\ *n* [ME *wæs hæil, washayl,* fr. ON *ves heill* be well] **1** : an early English toast to someone's health **2** : a hot drink made with wine, beer, or cider, spices, sugar, and usu. baked apples and traditionally served at Christmas **3** : riotous drinking : REVELRY

**²wassail** *vb* **1** : CAROUSE **2** : to drink to the health of — **was·sail·er** *n*

**Was·ser·mann test** \'wä-sər-mən-, 'vä-\ *n* : a blood test for the detection of syphilis

**wast·age** \'wā-stij\ *n* : WASTE 3

**¹waste** \'wāst\ *n* **1** : a sparsely settled or barren region : DESERT; *also* : uncultivated land **2** : the act or an instance of wasting : the state of being wasted **3** : gradual loss or decrease by use, wear, or decay **4** : material left over, rejected, or thrown away; *also* : an unwanted byproduct of a manufacturing or chemical process **5** : refuse (as garbage) that accumulates about habitations **6** : material (as feces) produced but not used by a living organism — **waste·ful** \-fəl\ *adj* — **waste·ful·ly** *adv* — **waste·ful·ness** *n*

²**waste** *vb* **wast·ed; wast·ing 1** : DEVASTATE **2** : to wear away or diminish gradually : CONSUME **3** : to spend or use carelessly or uselessly : SQUANDER **4** : to lose or cause to lose weight, strength, or energy ⟨*wasting* away from fever⟩ **5** : to become diminished in bulk or substance : DWINDLE ♦ **Synonyms** DEPREDATE, DESOLATE, DESPOIL, RAVAGE, SPOIL, STRIP — **wast·er** *n*

³**waste** *adj* **1** : being wild and uninhabited : BARREN, DESOLATE; *also* : UNCULTIVATED **2** : being in a ruined condition **3** : discarded as worthless after being used ⟨~ water⟩ **4** : excreted from or stored in inert form in a living organism as a byproduct of vital activity ⟨~ matter from birds⟩

**waste·bas·ket** \'wāst-ˌbas-kət\ *n* : a receptacle for refuse

**waste·land** \-ˌland, -lənd\ *n* : land that is barren or unfit for cultivation

**waste·pa·per** \-'pā-pər\ *n* : paper thrown away as used, not needed, or not fit for use

**wast·rel** \'wā-strəl\ *n* : a person who wastes resources : SPENDTHRIFT

¹**watch** \'wäch, 'wȯch\ *vb* **1** : to be or stay awake intentionally : keep vigil ⟨~ed by the patient's bedside⟩ ⟨~ and pray⟩ **2** : to be on the lookout for danger : be on one's guard **3** : to keep guard ⟨~ outside the door⟩ **4** : OBSERVE ⟨~ a game⟩ **5** : to keep in view so as to prevent harm or warn of danger ⟨~ a brush fire carefully⟩ **6** : to keep oneself informed about ⟨~ his progress⟩ **7** : to lie in wait for esp. so as to take advantage of ⟨~ed her opportunity⟩ — **watch·er** *n*

²**watch** *n* **1** : the act of keeping awake to guard, protect, or attend; *also* : a state of alert and continuous attention **2** : a public weather alert ⟨a winter storm ~⟩ **3** : close observation **4** : LOOKOUT, WATCHMAN, GUARD **5** : a period during which a part of a ship's crew is on duty; *also* : the part of a crew on duty during a watch **6** : a portable timepiece carried on the person

**watch·band** \'wäch-ˌband, 'wȯch-\ *n* : the bracelet or strap of a wristwatch

**watch·dog** \-ˌdȯg\ *n* **1** : a dog kept to guard property **2** : one that guards or protects

**watch·ful** \-fəl\ *adj* : steadily attentive and alert esp. to danger : VIGILANT — **watch·ful·ly** *adv* — **watch·ful·ness** *n*

**watch·mak·er** \-ˌmā-kər\ *n* : a person who makes or repairs watches — **watch·mak·ing** \-ˌmā-kiŋ\ *n*

**watch·man** \-mən\ *n* : a person assigned to watch : GUARD

**watch night** *n* : a devotional service lasting until after midnight esp. on New Year's Eve

**watch·tow·er** \'wäch-ˌtaů(-ə)r, 'wȯch-\ *n* : a tower for a lookout

**watch·word** \-ˌwərd\ *n* **1** : a secret word used as a signal or sign of recognition **2** : a word or motto used as a slogan or rallying cry

¹**wa·ter** \'wȯ-tər, 'wä-\ *n* **1** : the liquid that descends as rain and forms rivers, lakes, and seas **2** : a natural mineral water — usu. used in pl. **3** *pl* : the water occupying or flowing in a particular bed; *also* : a band of seawater bordering on and under the control of a country **4** : any of various liquids containing or resembling water; *esp* : a watery fluid (as tears, urine, or sap) formed or circulating in a living organism **5** : a specified degree of thoroughness or completeness ⟨a scoundrel of the first ~⟩

²**water** *vb* **1** : to supply with or get or take water ⟨~ horses⟩ ⟨the ship ~ed at each port⟩ **2** : to treat (as cloth) so as to give a lustrous appearance in wavy lines **3** : to dilute by or as if by adding water to **4** : to form or secrete water or watery matter ⟨her eyes ~ed⟩ ⟨my mouth ~ed⟩

**water bed** *n* : a bed whose mattress is a watertight bag filled with water

**wa·ter·borne** \-ˌbȯrn\ *adj* : supported, carried, or transmitted by water

**water buffalo** *n* : a common oxlike often domesticated Asian bovine

**water chestnut** *n* : a whitish crunchy vegetable used esp. in Chinese cooking that is the peeled tuber of a widely cultivated Asian sedge; *also* : the tuber or the sedge itself

**water closet** *n* : a compartment or room with a toilet bowl : BATHROOM; *also* : a toilet bowl along with its accessories

**wa·ter·col·or** \'wȯ-tər-ˌkə-lər, 'wä-\ *n* **1** : a paint whose liquid part is water **2** : the art of painting with watercolors **3** : a picture made with watercolors

**wa·ter·course** \-ˌkȯrs\ *n* : a stream of water; *also* : the bed of a stream

**wa·ter·craft** \-ˌkraft\ *n* : a craft for water transport : SHIP, BOAT

**wa·ter·cress** \-ˌkres\ *n* : an aquatic perennial Eurasian cress that is naturalized in the U.S. and has edible leaves used esp. in salads

**wa·ter·fall** \-ˌfȯl\ *n* : a very steep descent of the water of a stream

**wa·ter·fowl** \'wȯ-tər-ˌfaů(-ə)l, 'wä-\ *n, pl* **-fowl** *also* **-fowls** : a bird that frequents water; *esp* : a swimming bird (as a duck) hunted as game

**wa·ter·front** \-ˌfrənt\ *n* : land or a section of a town fronting or abutting on a body of water

**water gap** *n* : a pass in a mountain ridge through which a stream runs

**water glass** *n* : a drinking glass

**water hyacinth** *n* : a showy floating aquatic plant of tropical America that often clogs waterways (as in the southern U.S.)

**watering hole** *n* : a place (as a bar) where people gather socially

**watering place** *n* : a resort that features mineral springs or bathing

**water lily** *n* : any of various aquatic plants

with floating roundish leaves and showy solitary flowers

**wa·ter·line** \'wȯ-tər-ˌlīn, 'wä-\ *n* : a line that marks the level of the surface of water on something (as a ship or the shore)

**wa·ter·logged** \-ˌlȯgd, -ˌlägd\ *adj* : so filled or soaked with water as to be heavy or unmanageable ⟨a ~ boat⟩

**wa·ter·loo** \ˌwȯ-tər-'lü, ˌwä-\ *n, pl* **-loos** [*Waterloo*, Belgium, scene of Napoleon's defeat in 1815] : a decisive or final defeat or setback

¹**wa·ter·mark** \'wȯ-tər-ˌmärk, 'wä-\ *n* **1** : a mark indicating height to which water has risen **2** : a marking in paper visible when the paper is held up to the light

²**watermark** *vb* : to mark (paper) with a watermark

**wa·ter·mel·on** \-ˌme-lən\ *n* : a large roundish or oblong fruit with sweet juicy usu. red pulp; *also* : a widely grown African vine related to the squashes that produces watermelons

**water moccasin** *n* : a venomous pit viper chiefly of the southeastern U.S. that is related to the copperhead

**water ou·zel** \-'ü-zəl\ *n* : DIPPER 1

**water park** *n* : an amusement park with a pool and wetted slides

**water pill** *n* : DIURETIC

**water pipe** *n* : a pipe for smoking that has a long flexible tube whereby the smoke is cooled by passing through water

**water pistol** *n* : a toy pistol for squirting a jet of liquid

**water polo** *n* : a team game played in a swimming pool with a ball resembling a soccer ball

**wa·ter·pow·er** \'wȯ-tər-ˌpaú-(ə)r, 'wä-\ *n* : the power of moving water used to run machinery

¹**wa·ter·proof** \'wȯ-tər-ˌprüf, 'wä-\ *adj* : not letting water through; *esp* : covered or treated with a material to prevent permeation by water — **wa·ter·proof·ing** *n*

²**waterproof** *n* **1** : a waterproof fabric **2** *chiefly Brit* : RAINCOAT

³**waterproof** *vb* : to make waterproof

**wa·ter–re·pel·lent** \ˌwȯ-tər-ri-'pe-lənt, ˌwä-\ *adj* : treated with a finish that is resistant to water penetration

**wa·ter–re·sis·tant** \-ri-'zis-tənt\ *adj* : WATER-REPELLENT

**wa·ter·shed** \'wȯ-tər-ˌshed, 'wä-\ *n* **1** : a dividing ridge between two drainage areas **2** : the region or area drained by a particular body of water

**wa·ter·side** \-ˌsīd\ *n* : the land bordering a body of water

**water ski** *n* : a ski used on water when the wearer is towed — **wa·ter–ski** *vb* — **wa·ter–ski·er** \-ˌskē-ər\ *n*

**water snake** *n* : any of various snakes found in or near freshwater and feeding largely on aquatic animals

**wa·ter·spout** \'wȯ-tər-ˌspaút, 'wä-\ *n* **1** : a pipe for carrying water from a roof **2** : a funnel-shaped cloud extending from a cloud down to a spray torn up by whirling winds from an ocean or lake

**water strider** *n* : any of various long-legged bugs that move about swiftly on the surface of water

**water table** *n* : the upper limit of the portion of the ground wholly saturated with water

**wa·ter·tight** \ˌwȯ-tər-'tīt, ˌwä-\ *adj* **1** : constructed so as to keep water out **2** : allowing no possibility for doubt or uncertainty ⟨a ~ case against the accused⟩

**wa·ter·way** \'wȯ-tər-ˌwä, 'wä-\ *n* : a navigable body of water

**wa·ter·wheel** \-ˌhwēl, -ˌwēl\ *n* : a wheel made to turn by water flowing against it

**water wings** *n pl* : an air-filled device to give support to a person's body esp. when learning to swim

**wa·ter·works** \'wȯ-tər-ˌwərks, 'wä-\ *n pl* : a system for supplying water (as to a city)

**wa·tery** \'wȯ-tə-rē, 'wä-\ *adj* **1** : containing, full of, or giving out water ⟨~ clouds⟩ **2** : being like water : THIN, WEAK ⟨~ lemonade⟩; *also* : being soft and soggy ⟨~ turnips⟩

**WATS** \'wäts\ *abbr* Wide-Area Telecommunications Service

**watt** \'wät\ *n* [James *Watt* †1819 Scottish engineer and inventor] : the metric unit of power equal to the work done at the rate of one joule per second or to the power produced by a current of one ampere across a potential difference of one volt

**watt·age** \'wä-tij\ *n* : amount of power expressed in watts

**wat·tle** \'wä-t°l\ *n* **1** : a framework of rods with flexible branches or reeds interlaced used esp. formerly in building; *also* : material for this framework **2** : a naked fleshy process hanging usu. from the head or neck (as of a bird) — **wat·tled** \-t°ld\ *adj*

**W Aust** *abbr* Western Australia

¹**wave** \'wāv\ *vb* **waved; wav·ing** **1** : FLUTTER ⟨flags *waving* in the breeze⟩ **2** : to motion with the hands or with something held in them in signal or salute **3** : to become moved or brandished to-and-fro; *also* : BRANDISH, FLOURISH ⟨~ a sword⟩ **4** : to move before the wind with a wavelike motion ⟨fields of *waving* grain⟩ **5** : to curve up and down like a wave : UNDULATE

²**wave** *n* **1** : a moving ridge or swell on the surface of water **2** : a wavelike formation or shape ⟨a ~ in the hair⟩ **3** : the action or process of making wavy or curly **4** : a waving motion; *esp* : a signal made by waving something **5** : FLOW, GUSH ⟨a ~ of anger swept over her⟩ **6** : a peak of activity ⟨a ~ of selling⟩ **7** : a disturbance that transfers energy progressively from point to point in a medium ⟨light travels in ~s⟩ ⟨a sound ~⟩ **8** : a period of hot or cold weather — **wave·like** *adj*

**wave·length** \'wāv-ˌleŋth\ *n* **1** : the distance in the line of advance of a wave from any one point (as a crest) to the next corresponding point **2** : a line of thought that reveals a common understanding

**wave·let** \-lət\ *n* : a little wave : RIPPLE

**wa·ver** \'wā-vǝr\ *vb* **1** : to fluctuate in opinion, allegiance, or direction **2** : REEL, TOTTER; *also* : QUIVER, FLICKER ⟨~*ing* flames⟩ **3** : FALTER **4** : to give an unsteady sound : QUAVER ♦ *Synonyms* FALTER, HESITATE, SHILLY-SHALLY, VACILLATE — **waver** *n* — **wa·ver·er** *n* — **wa·ver·ing·ly** *adv*

**wavy** \'wā-vē\ *adj* **wav·i·er; -est** : having waves : moving in waves

**¹wax** \'waks\ *n* **1** : a yellowish plastic substance secreted by bees for constructing the honeycomb **2** : any of various substances like beeswax

**²wax** *vb* : to treat or rub with wax — **wax·er** *n*

**³wax** *vb* **1** : to increase in size, numbers, strength, volume, or duration **2** : to increase in apparent size ⟨the moon ~es toward the full⟩ **3** : to take on a quality or state : BECOME ⟨~ed indignant⟩ ⟨the party ~ed merry⟩

**wax bean** *n* : a kidney bean with pods that turn creamy yellow to bright yellow when mature enough to use as snap beans

**wax·en** \'wak-sǝn\ *adj* **1** : made of or covered with wax **2** : resembling wax (as in color or consistency)

**wax museum** *n* : a place where wax effigies are exhibited

**wax myrtle** *n* : any of a genus of shrubs or trees with aromatic leaves; *esp* : an evergreen shrub or small tree of the eastern U.S. that produces small hard berries with a thick coating of bluish-white wax used for candles

**wax·wing** \'waks-ˌwiŋ\ *n* : any of a genus of chiefly brown to gray singing birds with a showy crest and red waxy material on the tips of some wing feathers

**wax·work** \-ˌwǝrk\ *n* **1** : an effigy usu. of a person in wax **2** *pl* : an exhibition of wax figures

**waxy** \'wak-sē\ *adj* **wax·i·er; -est** **1** : made of or full of wax **2** : WAXEN 2

**¹way** \'wā\ *n* **1** : a thoroughfare for travel or passage : ROAD, PATH, STREET **2** : ROUTE ⟨knew the ~ home⟩ **3** : a course of action ⟨chose the easy ~⟩; *also* : opportunity, capability, or fact of doing as one pleases ⟨always had your own ~⟩ **4** : a possible course : POSSIBILITY ⟨no two ~s about it⟩ **5** : METHOD, MODE ⟨this ~ of thinking⟩ ⟨a new ~ of painting⟩ **6** : FEATURE, RESPECT ⟨a good worker in many ~s⟩ **7** : the usual or characteristic state of affairs ⟨as is the ~ with old people⟩; *also* : individual characteristic or peculiarity ⟨used to her ~s⟩ **8** : DISTANCE ⟨a short ~ from here⟩ ⟨a long ~ from success⟩ **9** : progress along a course ⟨working my ~ through college⟩ **10** : something having direction : LOCALITY ⟨out our ~⟩ **11** : STATE, CONDITION ⟨the ~ things are⟩ **12** *pl* : an inclined structure upon which a ship is built or is supported in launching **13** : CATEGORY, KIND ⟨get what you need in the ~ of supplies⟩ **14** : motion or speed of a boat through the water — **by the way** : by way of interjection or digression

— **by way of 1** : for the purpose of ⟨*by way of* illustration⟩ **2** : by the route through : VIA — **out of the way 1** : WRONG, IMPROPER **2** : SECLUDED, REMOTE

**way·bill** \'wā-ˌbil\ *n* : a paper that accompanies a freight shipment and gives details of goods, route, and charges

**way·far·er** \'wā-ˌfer-ǝr\ *n* : a traveler esp. on foot — **way·far·ing** \-ˌfer-iŋ\ *adj*

**way·lay** \'wā-ˌlā\ *vb* **-laid** \-ˌlād\; **-lay·ing** : to lie in wait for or attack from ambush

**way–out** \'wā-'aut\ *adj* : FAR-OUT

**-ways** *adv suffix* : in (such) a way, course, direction, or manner ⟨sideways⟩

**ways and means** *n pl* : methods and resources esp. for raising revenues needed by a state; *also* : a legislative committee concerned with this function

**way·side** \'wā-ˌsīd\ *n* : the side of or land adjacent to a road or path

**way station** *n* : an intermediate station on a line of travel (as a railroad)

**way·ward** \'wā-wǝrd\ *adj* [ME, short for *awayward* turned away, fr. *away*, adv. + *-ward* directed toward] **1** : following one's own capricious or wanton inclinations ⟨~ children⟩ **2** : UNPREDICTABLE, IRREGULAR ⟨a ~ act⟩

**WBC** *abbr* white blood cells

**WC** *abbr* **1** water closet **2** without charge

**WCTU** *abbr* Women's Christian Temperance Union

**we** \'wē\ *pron* **1** — used of a group that includes the speaker or writer **2** — used for the singular *I* by a monarch, editor, or writer

**weak** \'wēk\ *adj* **1** : lacking strength or vigor : FEEBLE **2** : not able to sustain or resist much weight, pressure, or strain **3** : deficient in vigor of mind or character; *also* : resulting from or indicative of such deficiency ⟨a ~ policy⟩ ⟨a ~ will⟩ **4** : not supported by truth or logic ⟨a ~ argument⟩ **5** : lacking skill or proficiency; *also* : indicative of a lack of skill or aptitude **6** : lacking vigor of expression or effect **7** : of less than usual strength ⟨~ tea⟩ **8** : not having or exerting authority ⟨~ government⟩; *also* : INEFFECTIVE, IMPOTENT ⟨~ measures to control crime⟩ **9** : of, relating to, or constituting a verb or verb conjugation that forms the past tense and past participle by adding *-ed* or *-d* or *-t* — **weak·ly** *adv*

**weak·en** \'wē-kǝn\ *vb* : to make or become weak ⟨bodies ~ed by hunger⟩ ♦ *Synonyms* ENFEEBLE, DEBILITATE, UNDERMINE, SAP, CRIPPLE, DISABLE

**weak·fish** \'wēk-ˌfish\ *n* [obs. D *weekvis*, fr. D *week* soft + *vis* fish] : a common marine fish of the Atlantic coast of the U.S. caught for food and sport; *also* : any of several related food fishes

**weak force** *n* : the physical force responsible for particle decay processes in radioactivity

**weak–kneed** \'wēk-ˈnēd\ *adj* : lacking willpower or resolution ⟨~ appeasers⟩

**weak·ling** \'wē-kliŋ\ *n* : a person who is physically, mentally, or morally weak

**weak·ly** \'wē-klē\ *adj* : FEEBLE, WEAK

**weak·ness** \'wēk-nəs\ *n* **1** : the quality or state of being weak; *also* : an instance or period of being weak ⟨in a moment of ∼ he agreed to go⟩ **2** : FAULT, DEFECT **3** : an object of special desire or fondness ⟨chocolate is her ∼⟩

**¹weal** \'wēl\ *n* : WELL-BEING, PROSPERITY

**²weal** *n* : WELT

**weald** \'wēld\ *n* [The *Weald,* wooded district in England, fr. ME *Weeld,* fr. OE *weald* forest] **1** : FOREST **2** : WOLD

**wealth** \'welth\ *n* [ME *welthe* welfare, prosperity, fr. *wele* weal] **1** : abundance of possessions or resources : AFFLUENCE, RICHES **2** : abundant supply : PROFUSION ⟨a ∼ of detail⟩ **3** : all property that has a money or an exchange value; *also* : all objects or resources that have economic value ◆ *Synonyms* FORTUNE, PROPERTY, SUBSTANCE, WORTH

**wealthy** \'wel-thē\ *adj* **wealth·i·er; -est** : having wealth : RICH

**wean** \'wēn\ *vb* **1** : to accustom (a young mammal) to take food by means other than nursing **2** : to free from a source of dependence; *also* : to free from a usu. unwholesome habit or interest

**weap·on** \'we-pən\ *n* **1** : something (as a gun, knife, or club) used to injure, defeat, or destroy **2** : a means of contending against another ⟨a ∼ against cancer⟩ — **weap·on·less** \-ləs\ *adj*

**weap·on·ry** \-rē\ *n* : WEAPONS

**¹wear** \'wear\ *vb* **wore** \'wȯr\; **worn** \'wȯrn\; **wear·ing** **1** : to use as an article of clothing or adornment ⟨∼ a coat⟩ ⟨∼s earrings⟩; *also* : to carry on the person ⟨∼ a gun⟩ **2** : EXHIBIT, PRESENT ⟨∼ a smile⟩ **3** : to impair, diminish, or decay by use or by scraping or rubbing ⟨clothes *worn* to shreds⟩; *also* : to produce gradually by friction, rubbing, or wasting away ⟨∼ a hole in the rug⟩ **4** : to exhaust or lessen the strength of : WEARY, FATIGUE ⟨*worn* by care and toil⟩ **5** : to endure use : last under use or the passage of time ⟨this cloth ∼s well⟩ **6** : to diminish or fail with the passage of time ⟨the day ∼s on⟩ ⟨the effect of the drug *wore* off⟩ **7** : to grow or become by attrition, use, or age ⟨the coin was *worn* thin⟩ — **wear·able** \'wer-ə-bəl\ *adj* — **wear·er** *n*

**²wear** *n* **1** : the act of wearing : the state of being worn ⟨clothes for everyday ∼⟩ **2** : clothing usu. of a particular kind or for a special occasion or use ⟨children's ∼⟩ **3** : wearing or lasting quality ⟨the coat still has lots of ∼ in it⟩ **4** : the result of wearing or use : impairment due to use ⟨the suit shows ∼⟩

**wear and tear** *n* : the loss, injury, or stress to which something is subjected in the course of use; *esp* : normal depreciation

**wear down** *vb* : to weary and overcome by persistent resistance or pressure

**wea·ri·some** \'wir-ē-səm\ *adj* : causing weariness : TIRESOME — **wea·ri·some·ly** *adv* — **wea·ri·some·ness** *n*

**wear out** *vb* **1** : TIRE **2** : to make or become useless by wear

**¹wea·ry** \'wir-ē\ *adj* **wea·ri·er; -est** **1** : worn out in strength, energy, or freshness **2** : expressing or characteristic of weariness ⟨a ∼ sigh⟩ **3** : having one's patience, tolerance, or pleasure exhausted ⟨∼ of war⟩ — **wea·ri·ly** \'wir-ə-lē\ *adv* — **wea·ri·ness** \-ē-nəs\ *n*

**²weary** *vb* **wea·ried; wea·ry·ing** : to become or make weary : TIRE

**wea·sel** \'wē-zəl\ *n, pl* **weasels** : any of various small slender flesh-eating mammals related to the minks — **wea·sel·ly** *also* **wea·sely** \'wēz-lē, 'wē-zə-lē\ *adj*

**²weasel** *vb* **wea·seled; wea·sel·ing** **1** : to use weasel words : EQUIVOCATE **2** : to escape from or evade a situation or obligation — often used with *out*

**weasel word** *n* [fr. the weasel's reputed habit of sucking the contents out of an egg while leaving the shell intact] : a word used to avoid a direct or forthright statement or position

**¹weath·er** \'we-thər\ *n* **1** : the state of the atmosphere with respect to heat or cold, wetness or dryness, calm or storm, clearness or cloudiness **2** : a particular and esp. a disagreeable atmospheric state : RAIN, STORM

**²weather** *vb* **1** : to expose to or endure the action of weather; *also* : to alter (as in color or texture) by such exposure **2** : to bear up against successfully ⟨∼ a storm⟩ ⟨∼ troubles⟩

**³weather** *adj* : WINDWARD

**weath·er-beat·en** \'we-thər-ˌbē-t³n\ *adj* : worn or damaged by exposure to the weather; *also* : toughened or tanned by the weather ⟨∼ face⟩

**weath·er·cock** \-ˌkäk\ *n* : a weather vane shaped like a rooster

**weath·er·ing** \'we-thə-riŋ\ *n* : the action of the weather in altering the color, texture, composition, or form of exposed objects; *also* : alteration thus effected

**weath·er·ize** \'we-thə-ˌrīz\ *vb* **-ized; -iz·ing** : to make (as a house) better protected against winter weather (as by adding insulation)

**weath·er·man** \-ˌman\ *n* : one who reports and forecasts the weather : METEOROLOGIST

**weath·er·per·son** \-ˌpər-sən\ *n* : a person who reports and forecasts the weather : METEOROLOGIST

**weath·er·proof** \'we-thər-ˌprüf\ *adj* : able to withstand exposure to weather — **weatherproof** *vb*

**weath·er·strip·ping** \'we-thər-ˌstri-piŋ\ *n* : material used to seal a door or window at the edges — **weath·er–strip** *vb* — **weather strip** *n*

**weather vane** *n* : VANE 1

**weath·er·worn** \'we-thər-ˌwȯrn\ *adj* : worn by exposure to the weather

**¹weave** \'wēv\ *vb* **wove** \'wōv\ *or* **weaved; wo·ven** \'wō-vən\ *or* **weaved; weav·ing** **1** : to form by interlacing strands of material; *esp* : to make on a loom by interlacing warp and filling threads ⟨∼ cloth⟩ **2** : to interlace (as threads) into a fabric and esp. cloth **3** : SPIN 2 **4** : to make as if by weaving together parts **5** : to insert as a part : work in **6** : to move in a winding or zigzag course esp. to avoid obstacles ⟨we *wove* our way through the crowd⟩ — **weav·er** *n*

²**weave** *n* : something woven; *also* : a pattern or method of weaving ⟨a loose ~⟩

¹**web** \'web\ *n* **1** : a fabric on a loom or coming from a loom **2** : COBWEB; *also* : SNARE, ENTANGLEMENT ⟨caught in a ~ of deceit⟩ **3** : an animal or plant membrane; *esp* : one uniting the toes (as in many birds) **4** : NETWORK ⟨a ~ of highways⟩ **5** : the series of barbs on each side of the shaft of a feather **6** : WORLD WIDE WEB — **webbed** \'webd\ *adj*

²**web** *vb* **webbed; web·bing 1** : to make a web **2** : to cover or provide with webs or a network **3** : ENTANGLE, ENSNARE

**web·bing** \'we-biŋ\ *n* : a strong closely woven tape designed for bearing weight and used esp. for straps, harness, or upholstery

**web·cam** \'web-ˌkam\ *n* : a camera used in transmitting live images over the World Wide Web

**web·cast** \'web-ˌkast\ *n* : a transmission of sound and images via the World Wide Web — **webcast** *vb*

**web–foot·ed** \'web 'fù təd\ *adj* : having webbed feet

**web·log** \'web-ˌlog, -ˌläg\ *n* : BLOG

**web·mas·ter** \'web-ˌmas-tər\ *n, often cap* : a person responsible for the creation or maintenance of a website

**web·site** *or* **Web site** \'web-ˌsīt\ *n* : a group of World Wide Web pages made available online (as by an individual or business)

**wed** \'wed\ *vb* **wed·ded** *also* **wed; wed·ding 1** : to take, give, enter into, or join in marriage : MARRY **2** : to unite firmly

**Wed** *abbr* Wednesday

**wed·ding** \'we-diŋ\ *n* **1** : a marriage ceremony usu. with accompanying festivities : NUPTIALS **2** : a joining in close association **3** : a wedding anniversary or its celebration

¹**wedge** \'wej\ *n* **1** : a piece of wood or metal that tapers to a thin edge and is used to split logs or rocks or to raise heavy weights **2** : something (as an action or policy) that serves to open up a way for a breach, change, or intrusion **3** : a wedge-shaped object or part ⟨a ~ of pie⟩

²**wedge** *vb* **wedged; wedg·ing 1** : to hold firm by or as if by driving in a wedge **2** : to force (something) into a narrow space

**wed·lock** \'wed-ˌläk\ *n* [ME *wedlok*, fr. OE *wedlāc* marriage bond, fr. *wedd* pledge + *-lāc*, suffix denoting activity] : the state of being married : MARRIAGE, MATRIMONY

**Wednes·day** \'wenz-(ˌ)dā, -dē\ *n* [ME, fr. OE *wōdnesdæg*, lit., day of Woden (supreme god of the pagan Anglo-Saxons)] : the 4th day of the week

**wee** \'wē\ *adj* [ME (Sc) *we*, fr. *we*, n., little bit, fr. OE *wǣge* weight] **1** : very small : TINY **2** : very early ⟨~ hours of the morning⟩

¹**weed** \'wēd\ *n* **1** : a plant that tends to grow thickly where it is not wanted and to choke out more desirable plants **2** : MARIJUANA

²**weed** *vb* **1** : to clear of or remove weeds or something harmful, inferior, or superfluous ⟨~ a garden⟩ **2** : to get rid of ⟨~ out the troublemakers⟩ — **weed·er** *n*

³**weed** *n* : mourning clothes — usu. used in pl. ⟨widow's ~s⟩

**weedy** \'wē-dē\ *adj* **1** : full of weeds **2** : resembling a weed esp. in vigor of growth or spread **3** : noticeably lean and scrawny : LANKY ⟨a ~ little man⟩

**week** \'wēk\ *n* **1** : seven successive days; *esp* : a calendar period of seven days beginning with Sunday and ending with Saturday **2** : the working or school days of the calendar week

**week·day** \'wēk-ˌdā\ *n* : a day of the week except Sunday or sometimes except Saturday and Sunday

¹**week·end** \-ˌend\ *n* : the period between the close of one working or business or school week and the beginning of the next

²**weekend** *vb* : to spend the weekend

¹**week·ly** \'wē-klē\ *adj* **1** : occurring, appearing, or done every week **2** : computed in terms of one week ⟨~ rental rates⟩ — **weekly** *adv*

²**weekly** *n, pl* **weeklies** : a weekly publication

**ween** \'wēn\ *vb, archaic* : SUPPOSE 3

**wee·ny** \'wē-nē\ *also* **ween·sy** \'wēn-sē\ *adj* : exceptionally small

**weep** \'wēp\ *vb* **wept** \'wept\; **weep·ing 1** : to express emotion and esp. sorrow by shedding tears : BEWAIL, CRY **2** : to give off fluid slowly : OOZE — **weep·er** *n*

**weeping** *adj* **1** : TEARFUL ⟨~ gratitude⟩ **2** : having slender drooping branches

**weeping willow** *n* : a willow with slender drooping branches

**weepy** \'wē-pē\ *adj* : inclined to weep

**wee·vil** \'wē-vəl\ *n* : any of a large group of beetles having a long head usu. curved into a snout and including many whose larvae are destructive plant-feeding pests — **wee·vily** *or* **wee·vil·ly** \'wē-və-lē\ *adj*

**weft** \'weft\ *n* **1** : a filling thread or yarn in weaving **2** : WEB, FABRIC; *also* : something woven

¹**weigh** \'wā\ *vb* [ME *weyen*, fr. OE *wegan* to move, carry, weigh] **1** : to find the heaviness of **2** : to have weight or a specified weight **3** : to consider carefully : PONDER **4** : to merit consideration as important : COUNT ⟨evidence ~ing against him⟩ **5** : to raise before sailing ⟨~ anchor⟩ **6** : to press down with or as if with a heavy weight

²**weigh** *n* [alter. of *way*] : WAY — used in the phrase *under way*

¹**weight** \'wāt\ *n* **1** : the amount that something weighs; *also* : the standard amount that something should weigh **2** : a quantity or object weighing a usu. specified amount **3** : a unit (as a pound or kilogram) of weight or mass; *also* : a system of such units **4** : a heavy object for holding or pressing something down;

# U.S. WEIGHTS AND MEASURES

## LENGTH

| UNIT | SYMBOL | U.S. EQUIVALENT | METRIC EQUIVALENT |
|------|--------|-----------------|-------------------|
| mile | mi | 5280 feet, 1760 yards | 1.609 kilometers |
| rod | rd | 5.50 yards, 16.5 feet | 5.029 meters |
| yard | yd | 3 feet, 36 inches | 0.9144 meter |
| foot | ft $or$ ' | 12 inches, 0.333 yard | 30.48 centimeters |
| inch | in $or$ " | 0.083 foot, 0.028 yard | 2.54 centimeters |

## AREA

| UNIT | SYMBOL | U.S. EQUIVALENT | METRIC EQUIVALENT |
|------|--------|-----------------|-------------------|
| square mile | sq mi $or$ mi$^2$ | 640 acres | 2.590 square kilometers |
| acre | ac | 4840 square yards, 43,560 square feet | 4047 square meters |
| square rod | sq rd $or$ rd$^2$ | 30.25 square yards | 25.293 square meters |
| square yard | sq yd $or$ yd$^2$ | 9 square feet | 0.836 square meter |
| square foot | sq ft $or$ ft$^2$ | 144 square inches | 0.093 square meter |
| square inch | sq in $or$ in$^2$ | 0.0069 square foot | 6.452 square centimeter |

## VOLUME

| UNIT | SYMBOL | U.S. EQUIVALENT | METRIC EQUIVALENT |
|------|--------|-----------------|-------------------|
| cubic yard | cu yd $or$ yd$^3$ | 27 cubic feet | 0.765 cubic meter |
| cubic foot | cu ft $or$ ft$^3$ | 1728 cubic inches | 0.028 cubic meter |
| cubic inch | cu in $or$ in$^3$ | 0.00058 cubic foot | 16.387 cubic centimeters |

## WEIGHT—AVOIRDUPOIS

| UNIT | SYMBOL | U.S. EQUIVALENT | METRIC EQUIVALENT |
|------|--------|-----------------|-------------------|
| ton | | | |
|   short ton | | 2000 pounds | 0.907 metric ton |
|   long ton | | 2240 pounds | 1.016 metric tons |
| hundredweight | cwt | | |
|   short hundredweight | | 100 pounds | 45.359 kilograms |
|   long hundredweight | | 112 pounds | 50.802 kilograms |
| pound | lb $also$ # | 16 ounces | 0.454 kilogram |
| ounce | oz | 16 drams, 437.5 grains | 28.350 grams |
| dram | dr | 27.344 grains | 1.772 grams |
| grain | gr | 0.037 dram | 0.0648 gram |

## CAPACITY

| UNIT | SYMBOL | U.S. EQUIVALENT | METRIC EQUIVALENT |
|------|--------|-----------------|-------------------|
| | | *LIQUID MEASURE* | |
| gallon | gal | 4 quarts | 3.785 liters |
| quart | qt | 2 pints | 0.946 liter |
| pint | pt | 4 gills | 473.176 milliliters |
| gill | gi | 4 fluid ounces | 118.294 milliliters |
| fluid ounce | fl oz $or$ f℥ | 8 fluid drams | 29.573 milliliters |
| fluid dram | fl dr $or$ fℨ | 60 minims | 3.697 milliliters |
| minim | min $or$ ♍ | ⅟₆₀ fluid dram | 0.061610 milliliter |
| | | *DRY MEASURE* | |
| bushel | bu | 4 pecks | 35.239 liters |
| peck | pk | 8 quarts | 8.810 liters |
| quart | qt | 2 pints | 1.101 liters |
| pint | pt | ½ quart | 0.551 liter |

*also* : a heavy object for throwing or lifting in an athletic contest **5** : a mental or emotional burden **6** : IMPORTANCE; *also* : INFLUENCE ⟨threw his ~ around⟩ **7** : overpowering force **8** : relative thickness (as of a textile) ⟨summer-*weight* clothes⟩ ◆ *Synonyms* SIGNIFICANCE, MOMENT, CONSEQUENCE, IMPORT, AUTHORITY, PRESTIGE, CREDIT

²**weight** *vb* **1** : to oppress with a burden ⟨~ed down with cares⟩ **2** : to load with or as if with a weight

**weight·less** \'wāt-ləs\ *adj* : having little weight : lacking apparent gravitational pull ⟨a ~ environment⟩ — **weight·less·ly** *adv* — **weight·less·ness** *n*

**weighty** \'wā-tē\ *adj* **weight·i·er; -est 1** : of much importance or consequence ⟨MOMENTOUS, SERIOUS ⟨~ problems⟩ **2** : SOLEMN ⟨a ~ manner⟩ **3** : HEAVY **4** : POWERFUL, TELLING ⟨~ arguments⟩

**weiner** *var of* WIENER

**weir** \'wer, 'wir\ *n* **1** : a fence set in a waterway for catching fish **2** : a dam in a stream to raise the water level or divert its flow

**weird** \'wird\ *adj* [ME *wird, werd* fate, destiny, fr. OE *wyrd*] **1** : MAGICAL **2** : ODD, UNUSUAL ⟨~ noises⟩ ◆ *Synonyms* EERIE, UNCANNY, SPOOKY — **weird·ly** *adv* — **weird·ness** *n*

**weirdo** \'wir-(ˌ)dō\ *n, pl* **weird·os** : a person who is extraordinarily strange or eccentric

**Welch** *var of* WELSH

¹**wel·come** \'wel-kəm\ *vb* **wel·comed; wel·com·ing 1** : to greet cordially or courteously **2** : to accept, meet, or face with pleasure ⟨he ~s criticism⟩

²**welcome** *adj* **1** : received gladly into one's presence ⟨a ~ visitor⟩ **2** : giving pleasure : PLEASING ⟨~ news⟩ **3** : willingly permitted or admitted ⟨all are ~ to use the books⟩ **4** — used in the phrase "You're welcome" as a reply to an expression of thanks

³**welcome** *n* **1** : a cordial greeting or reception **2** : the state of being welcome ⟨overstayed their ~⟩

¹**weld** \'weld\ *vb* **1** : to unite (metal or plastic parts) either by heating and allowing the parts to flow together or by hammering or pressing together **2** : to unite closely or intimately ⟨~ed together in friendship⟩ — **weld·er** *n*

²**weld** *n* **1** : a welded joint **2** : union by welding

**wel·fare** \'wel-ˌfer\ *n* **1** : the state of doing well esp. in respect to happiness, well-being, or prosperity **2** : aid in the form of money or necessities for those in need; *also* : the agency through which the aid is given

**welfare state** *n* : a nation or state that assumes primary responsibility for the individual and social welfare of its citizens

**wel·kin** \'wel-kən\ *n* : SKY; *also* : AIR

¹**well** \'wel\ *n* **1** : a spring with its pool : FOUNTAIN; *also* : a source of supply ⟨a ~ of information⟩ **2** : a hole sunk in the earth to obtain a natural deposit (as of

water, oil, or gas) **3** : an open space (as for a staircase) extending vertically through floors of a structure **4** : something suggesting a well

²**well** *vb* : to rise up and flow out

³**well** *adv* **bet·ter** \'be-tər\; **best** \'best\ **1** : in a good or proper manner : RIGHTLY; *also* : EXCELLENTLY, SKILLFULLY **2** : SATISFACTORILY, FORTUNATELY ⟨the party turned out ~⟩ **3** : ABUNDANTLY ⟨eat ~⟩ **4** : with reason or courtesy : PROPERLY ⟨I cannot ~ refuse⟩ **5** : COMPLETELY, FULLY, QUITE ⟨~ worth the price⟩ ⟨*well*-hidden⟩ **6** : INTIMATELY, CLOSELY ⟨I know him ~⟩ **7** : CONSIDERABLY, FAR ⟨~ over a million⟩ ⟨~ ahead⟩ **8** : without trouble or difficulty ⟨we could ~ have gone⟩ **9** : EXACTLY, DEFINITELY ⟨remember it ~⟩

⁴**well** *adj* **1** : PROSPEROUS; *also* : being in satisfactory condition or circumstances **2** : SATISFACTORY, PLEASING ⟨all is ~⟩ **3** : ADVISABLE, DESIRABLE ⟨it is not ~ to anger him⟩ **4** : free or recovered from ill health : HEALTHY **5** : FORTUNATE ⟨it is ~ that this has happened⟩

**well ad·just·ed** \ˌwel-ə-'jəs-təd\ *adj* : WELL-BALANCED 2

**well-ad·vised** \-əd-'vīzd\ *adj* **1** : PRUDENT ⟨~ restraint⟩ **2** : resulting from, based on, or showing careful deliberation or wise counsel ⟨~ plans⟩

**well-ap·point·ed** \-ə-'pȯin-təd\ *adj* : properly fitted out ⟨a ~ house⟩

**well-ba·lanced** \'wel-'ba-lənst\ *adj* **1** : nicely or evenly balanced or arranged ⟨a ~ meal⟩ **2** : emotionally or psychologically untroubled

**well-be·ing** \-'bē-iŋ\ *n* : the state of being happy, healthy, or prosperous

**well-born** \-'bȯrn\ *adj* : born of noble or wealthy lineage

**well-bred** \-'bred\ *adj* : having or indicating good breeding : REFINED

**well-de·fined** \-di-'fīnd\ *adj* : having clearly distinguishable limits or boundaries

**well-dis·posed** \-di-'spōzd\ *adj* : disposed to be friendly, favorable, or sympathetic ⟨~ to the idea⟩

**well-done** \'wel-'dən\ *adj* **1** : rightly or properly performed **2** : cooked thoroughly

**well-en·dowed** \ˌwel-in-'daud\ *adj* **1** : having plenty of money or property **2** : having large breasts **3** : having a large penis

**well-fa·vored** \-'fā-vərd\ *adj* : GOOD-LOOKING, HANDSOME ⟨a ~ face⟩

**well-fixed** \-'fikst\ *adj* : WELL-HEELED

**well-found·ed** \-'faun-dəd\ *adj* : based on good reasons

**well-groomed** \-'grümd, -'grumd\ *adj* : neatly dressed or cared for

**well-ground·ed** \-'graun-dəd\ *adj* **1** : having a firm foundation **2** : WELL-FOUNDED

**well·head** \-ˌhed\ *n* **1** : the source of a spring or a stream **2** : principal source **3** : the top of or a structure built over a well

**well–heeled** \-'hēld\ *adj* : financially well-off

**well–known** \-'nōn\ *adj* : fully or widely known

**well–mean·ing** \-'mē-niŋ\ *adj* : having or based on good intentions

**well·ness** \-nəs\ *n* : good health esp. as an actively sought goal ⟨~ clinics⟩ ⟨life-styles that promote ~⟩

**well–nigh** \-'nī\ *adv* : ALMOST, NEARLY ⟨~ impossible⟩

**well–off** \-'óf\ *adj* : being in good condition or circumstances; *esp* : WELL-TO-DO

**well–or·dered** \-'ór-dərd\ *adj* : having an orderly procedure or arrangement

**well–placed** \-'plāst\ *adj* : appropriately or advantageously directed or positioned

**well–read** \-'red\ *adj* : well informed through reading

**well–round·ed** \-'raùn-dəd\ *adj* 1 : broadly trained, educated, and experienced 2 : COMPREHENSIVE ⟨a ~ program of activities⟩

**well–spo·ken** \'wel-'spō-kən\ *adj* 1 : speaking well and esp. courteously 2 : spoken with propriety ⟨~ words⟩

**well·spring** \-,spriŋ\ *n* : a source of continuous supply ⟨a ~ of information⟩

**well–timed** \-'tīmd\ *adj* : TIMELY ⟨a ~ announcement⟩

**well–to–do** \,wel-tə-'dü\ *adj* : having more than adequate financial resources : PROSPEROUS

**well–turned** \'wel-'tərnd\ *adj* 1 : pleasingly shaped ⟨a ~ ankle⟩ 2 : pleasingly expressed ⟨a ~ phrase⟩

**well–wish·er** \'wel-,wi-shər\ *n* : an admiring supporter or fan — **well–wish·ing** *adj or n*

**welsh** \'welsh, 'welch\ *vb* 1 : to avoid payment 2 : to break one's word ⟨~ed on his promises⟩

**Welsh** \'welsh\ *also* **Welch** \'welch\ *n* [ME *walisch, welisch,* adj., Welsh, fr. OE *wælisc* foreign, British, Welsh, fr. *Wealh* foreigner, Briton, Welshman] 1 **Welsh** *pl* : the people of Wales 2 : the Celtic language of Wales — **Welsh** *adj* — **Welsh-man** \-mən\ *n*

**Welsh cor·gi** \-'kór-gē\ *n* [W *corgi,* fr. *cor* dwarf + *ci* dog] : a short-legged long-backed dog with foxy head of either of two breeds of Welsh origin

**Welsh rabbit** *n* : melted often seasoned cheese served over toast or crackers

**Welsh rare·bit** \-'rer-bət\ *n* : WELSH RABBIT

¹**welt** \'welt\ *n* 1 : the narrow strip of leather between a shoe upper and sole to which other parts are stitched 2 : a doubled edge, strip, insert, or seam for ornament or reinforcement 3 : a ridge or lump raised on the skin usu. by a blow; *also* : a heavy blow

²**welt** *vb* 1 : to furnish (as a shoe) with a welt 2 : to hit hard

¹**wel·ter** \'wel-tər\ *vb* 1 : WRITHE, TOSS; *also* : WALLOW 2 : to rise and fall or toss about in or with waves 3 : to become deeply sunk, soaked, or involved 4 : to be in turmoil

²**welter** *n* 1 : TURMOIL 2 : a chaotic mass or jumble ⟨a ~ of data⟩

**wel·ter·weight** \'wel-tər-,wāt\ *n* : a boxer weighing more than 135 but not over 147 pounds

**wen** \'wen\ *n* : an abnormal growth or a cyst protruding from a surface esp. of the skin

**wench** \'wench\ *n* [ME *wenche,* short for *wenchel* child, fr. OE *wencel*] 1 : a young woman 2 : a female servant

**wend** \'wend\ *vb* : to direct one's course : proceed on (one's way)

**went** *past of* GO

**wept** *past and past part of* WEEP

**were** *past 2d sing, past pl, or past subjunctive of* BE

**were·wolf** \'wer-,wùlf, 'wir-, 'wər-\ *n, pl* **were·wolves** \-,wùlvz\ [ME, fr. OE *wer-wulf,* fr. *wer* man + *wulf* wolf] : a person who in stories is transformed into a wolf or is capable of assuming a wolf's form

**wes·kit** \'wes-kət\ *n* : VEST 1

¹**west** \'west\ *adv* : to or toward the west

²**west** *adj* 1 : situated toward or at the west 2 : coming from the west

³**west** *n* 1 : the general direction of sunset 2 : the compass point directly opposite to east 3 *cap* : regions or countries west of a specified or implied point 4 *cap* : Europe and the Americas — **west·er·ly** \'wes-tər-lē\ *adv or adj* — **west·ward** *adv or adj* — **west·wards** *adv*

¹**west·ern** \'wes-tərn\ *adj* 1 : lying toward or coming from the west 2 *cap* : of, relating to, or characteristic of a region conventionally designated West 3 *cap* : of or relating to the Roman Catholic or Protestant segment of Christianity — **West·ern·er** *n*

²**western** *n, often cap* : a novel, story, film, or radio or television show about life in the western U.S. during the latter half of the 19th century

**west·ern·ize** \'wes-tər-,nīz\ *vb* **-ized; -iz·ing** : to give western characteristics to ⟨wanted to ~ the country⟩ — **west·ern·i·za·tion** \,wes-tər-nə-'zā-shən\ *n*

**West Nile virus** \-'nī(-ə)l-\ *n* [*West Nile* province of Uganda] : a virus that is transmitted to humans by mosquitoes and causes an illness marked by fever, headache, muscle ache, and sometimes encephalitis or meningitis; *also* : this illness

¹**wet** \'wet\ *adj* **wet·ter; wet·test** 1 : consisting of or covered or soaked with liquid (as water) 2 : RAINY ⟨~ days⟩ 3 : not dry ⟨~ paint⟩ 4 : permitting or advocating the manufacture and sale of alcoholic beverages ⟨a ~ town⟩ ⟨a ~ candidate⟩ ♦ **Synonyms** DAMP, DANK, MOIST, HUMID — **wet·ly** *adv* — **wet·ness** *n*

²**wet** *n* 1 : WATER; *also* : WETNESS, MOISTURE 2 : rainy weather : RAIN 3 : an advocate of a wet liquor policy

³**wet** *vb* **wet** *or* **wet·ted; wet·ting** : to make or become wet

**wet blanket** *n* : one that quenches or dampens enthusiasm or pleasure

**weth·er** \'we-thər\ *n* : a castrated male sheep or goat

**wet·land** \'wet-,land, -lənd\ *n* : land or areas (as swamps) containing much soil moisture — usu. used in pl.

**wet nurse** *n* : a woman who cares for and suckles children not her own

**wet suit** *n* : a rubber suit for swimmers that acts to retain body heat by keeping a layer of water against the body as insulation

**wh** *abbr* **1** which **2** white

¹**whack** \'hwak\ *vb* **1** : to strike with a smart or resounding blow **2** : to cut with or as if with a whack

²**whack** *n* **1** : a smart or resounding blow; *also* : the sound of such a blow **2** : POR-TION, SHARE ⟨must each pay our ∼⟩ **3** : CONDITION, STATE ⟨the machine is out of ∼⟩ **4** : an opportunity or attempt to do something : CHANCE **5** : a single action or occasion ⟨made three pies at a ∼⟩

¹**whale** \'hwāl\ *n*, *pl* **whales 1** *or pl* **whale** : CETACEAN; *esp* : one (as a sperm whale or killer whale) of large size **2** : a person or thing impressive in size or quality ⟨a ∼ of a story⟩

²**whale** *vb* **whaled; whal·ing** : to fish or hunt for whales

³**whale** *vb* **whaled; whal·ing 1** : THRASH **2** : to strike or hit vigorously

**whale·boat** \-,bōt\ *n* : a long narrow rowboat originally used by whalers

**whale·bone** \-,bōn\ *n* : BALEEN

**whal·er** \'hwā-lər\ *n* **1** : a person or ship that hunts whales **2** : WHALEBOAT

**whale shark** *n* : a shark of warm waters that is the largest known fish

**wham·my** \'hwa-mē\ *n*, *pl* **wham·mies** : JINX, HEX ⟨put the ∼ on him⟩

**wharf** \'hwȯrf\ *n*, *pl* **wharves** \'hwȯrvz\ *also* **wharfs** : a structure alongside which ships lie to load and unload

¹**what** \'hwät, 'hwət\ *pron* **1** — used to inquire about the identity or nature of a being, an object, or some matter or situation ⟨∼ is he, a salesman⟩ ⟨∼'s that⟩ ⟨∼ happened⟩ **2** : that which ⟨I know ∼ you want⟩ **3** : WHATEVER 1 ⟨take ∼ you want⟩

²**what** *adv* **1** : in what respect : HOW ⟨∼ does he care⟩ **2** — used with *with* to introduce a prepositional phrase that expresses cause ⟨kept busy ∼ with school and work⟩

³**what** *adj* **1** — used to inquire about the identity or nature of a person, object, or matter ⟨∼ books do you read⟩ **2** : how remarkable or surprising ⟨∼ an idea⟩ **3** : WHATEVER

¹**what·ev·er** \hwät-'e-vər, hwət-\ *pron* **1** : anything or everything that ⟨does ∼ he wants to⟩ **2** : no matter what ⟨∼ you do, don't cheat⟩ **3** : WHAT 1 — used as an intensive ⟨∼ do you mean⟩

²**whatever** *adj* : of any kind at all ⟨no food ∼⟩

³**whatever** *adv* : in any case : whatever the case may be — often used to suggest the unimportance of an issue or choice ⟨see a movie, watch TV,—∼⟩

¹**what·not** \'hwät-,nät, 'hwət-\ *pron* : any of various other things that might also be mentioned ⟨needles, pins, and ∼⟩

²**whatnot** *n* : a light open set of shelves for small ornaments

**what·so·ev·er** \,hwät-sō-'e-vər, ,hwət-\ *pron or adj* : WHATEVER

**wheal** \'hwēl\ *n* : a rapidly formed flat slightly raised itching or burning patch on the skin; *also* : WELT

**wheat** \'hwēt\ *n* : a cereal grain that yields a fine white flour used chiefly in breads, baked goods, and pastas; *also* : any of several widely grown grasses yielding wheat — **wheat·en** *adj*

**wheat germ** *n* : the vitamin-rich wheat embryo separated in milling

**whee·dle** \'hwē-dᵊl\ *vb* **whee·dled; whee·dling 1** : to entice by flattery **2** : to gain or get by wheedling

¹**wheel** \'hwēl\ *n* **1** : a disk or circular frame that turns on a central axis **2** : a device whose main part is a wheel **3** : something resembling a wheel in shape or motion **4** : a curving or circular movement **5** : machinery that imparts motion : moving power ⟨the ∼s of government⟩ **6** : a person of importance **7** *pl, slang* : AUTOMOBILE — **wheeled** \'hwēld\ *adj* — **wheel·less** *adj*

²**wheel** *vb* **1** : ROTATE, REVOLVE **2** : to change direction as if turning on a pivot **3** : to convey or move on wheels or in a vehicle

**wheel·bar·row** \-,ber-ō\ *n* : a vehicle with handles and usu. one wheel for carrying small loads

**wheel·base** \-,bās\ *n* : the distance in inches between the front and rear axles of an automotive vehicle

**wheel·chair** \-,cher\ *n* : a chair mounted on wheels esp. for the use of disabled persons

**wheel·er** \'hwē-lər\ *n* **1** : one that wheels **2** : WHEELHORSE **3** : something that has wheels — used in combination ⟨a side-*wheeler*⟩

**wheel·er–deal·er** \,hwē-lər-'dē-lər\ *n* : a shrewd operator esp. in business or politics

**wheel·horse** \'hwēl-,hȯrs\ *n* **1** : a horse in a position nearest the front wheels of a wagon **2** : a steady and effective worker esp. in a political body

**wheel·house** \-,haús\ *n* : PILOTHOUSE

**wheel–thrown** \'hwel-,thron\ *adj* : made on a potter's wheel

**wheel·wright** \-,rīt\ *n* : a maker and repairer of wheels and wheeled vehicles

¹**wheeze** \'hwēz\ *vb* **wheezed; wheez·ing** : to breathe with difficulty usu. with a whistling sound

²**wheeze** *n* **1** : a sound of wheezing ⟨the ∼ of an engine⟩ **2** : an often repeated and well-known joke **3** : a trite saying

**wheezy** \'hwē-zē\ *adj* **wheez·i·er; -est 1** : inclined to wheeze **2** : having a wheezing sound — **wheez·i·ly** \-zə-lē\ *adv* — **wheez·i·ness** \-zē-nəs\ *n*

**whelk** \'hwelk\ *n* : a large sea snail; *esp* : one much used as food in Europe

**whelm** \'hwelm\ *vb* : to overcome or engulf completely : OVERWHELM

**¹whelp** \'hwelp\ *n* : any of the young of various carnivorous mammals (as a dog)

**²whelp** *vb* : to give birth to (whelps); *also* : bring forth young

**¹when** \'hwen\ *adv* **1** : at what time ⟨~ will you return⟩ **2** : at or during which time ⟨a time ~ things were better⟩

**²when** *conj* **1** : at or during the time that ⟨leave ~ I do⟩ **2** : every time that ⟨they all clapped ~ he sang⟩ **3** : in the event that : IF ⟨disqualified ~ you cheat⟩ **4** : ALTHOUGH ⟨quit politics ~ he might have had a great career in it⟩

**³when** *pron* : what or which time ⟨since ~ have you been the boss⟩

**⁴when** *n* : the time of a happening

**whence** \'hwens\ *adv or conj* : from what place, source, or cause

**when·ev·er** \hwe-'ne-vər, hwə-\ *conj or adv* : at whatever time

**when·so·ev·er** \'hwen-sō-,e-vər\ *conj* : at any or every time that

**¹where** \'hwer\ *adv* **1** : at, in, or to what place ⟨~ is it⟩ ⟨~ will we go⟩ **2** : at, in, or to what situation, position, direction, circumstances, or respect ⟨~ does this road lead⟩

**²where** *conj* **1** : at, in, or to what place ⟨knows ~ the house is⟩ **2** : at, in, or to what situation, position, direction, circumstances, or respect ⟨shows ~ the road leads⟩ **3** : WHEREVER ⟨goes ~ she likes⟩ **4** : at, in, or to which place ⟨the town ~ we live⟩ **5** : at, in, or to the place at, in, or to which ⟨stay ~ you are⟩ **6** : in a case, situation, or respect in which ⟨outstanding ~ endurance is called for⟩

**³where** *n* : PLACE, LOCATION ⟨the ~ and how of the accident⟩

**¹where·abouts** \-ə-,bauts\ *also* **where·about** \-,baut\ *adv* : about where : near what place ⟨~ does he live⟩

**²whereabouts** *n sing or pl* : the place where a person or thing is ⟨his present ~ are unknown⟩

**where·as** \hwer-'az\ *conj* **1** : while on the contrary; *also* : ALTHOUGH **2** : in view of the fact that : SINCE

**where·at** \-'at\ *conj* **1** : at or toward which **2** : in consequence of which : WHEREUPON

**where·by** \-'bī\ *conj* : by, through, or in accordance with which ⟨the means ~ we achieved our goals⟩

**¹where·fore** \'hwer-,fòr\ *adv* **1** : for what reason or purpose : WHY **2** : THEREFORE

**²wherefore** *n* : an answer or statement giving an explanation : REASON

**¹where·in** \hwer-'in\ *adv* : in what : in what respect ⟨~ was I wrong⟩

**²wherein** *conj* **1** : in which : WHERE ⟨the city ~ we live⟩ **2** : during which **3** : in what way : HOW ⟨showed me ~ I was wrong⟩

**where·of** \-'ov, -'äv\ *conj* **1** : of what ⟨knows ~ he speaks⟩ **2** : of which or whom ⟨books ~ the best are lost⟩

**where·on** \-'òn, -'än\ *conj* : on which ⟨the base ~ it rests⟩

**where·so·ev·er** \'hwer-sō-,e-vər\ *conj* : WHEREVER

**where·to** \'hwer-,tü\ *conj* : to which

**where·up·on** \'hwer-ə-,pòn, -,pän\ *conj* **1** : on which **2** : closely following and in consequence of which

**¹wher·ev·er** \hwer-'e-vər\ *adv* : where in the world ⟨~ did he get that tie⟩

**²wherever** *conj* **1** : at, in, or to whatever place ⟨thrives ~ he goes⟩ **2** : in any circumstance in which

**where·with** \'hwer-,with, -,with\ *conj* : with or by means of which ⟨lack the tools ~ to repair the damage⟩

**where·with·al** \'hwer-wi-,thòl, -,thòl\ *n* : MEANS, RESOURCES; *esp* : MONEY

**wher·ry** \'hwer-ē\ *n, pl* **wherries** : a long light rowboat sharp at both ends

**whet** \'hwet\ *vb* **whet·ted; whet·ting** **1** : to sharpen by rubbing on or with something abrasive (as a whetstone) **2** : to make keen : STIMULATE ⟨~ the appetite⟩

**wheth·er** \'hwe-thər\ *conj* **1** : if it is or was true that ⟨ask ~ he is going⟩ **2** : if it is or was better ⟨uncertain ~ to go or stay⟩ **3** : whichever is or was the case, namely that ⟨~ we succeed or fail, we must try⟩ **4** : EITHER ⟨turned out well ~ by accident or design⟩

**whet·stone** \'hwet-,stōn\ *n* : a stone for sharpening blades

**whey** \'hwā\ *n* : the watery part of milk that separates after the milk sours and thickens

**¹which** \'hwich\ *adj* **1** : being what one or ones out of a group ⟨~ shirt should I wear⟩ **2** : WHICHEVER

**²which** *pron* **1** : which one or ones ⟨~ is yours⟩ ⟨~ are his⟩ ⟨it's in May or June, I'm not sure ~⟩ **2** : WHICHEVER ⟨we have all kinds; take ~ you like⟩ **3** — used to introduce a relative clause and to serve as a substitute therein for the noun modified by the clause ⟨the money ~ is coming to me⟩

**¹which·ev·er** \hwich-'e-vər\ *adj* : no matter which ⟨~ way you go⟩

**²whichever** *pron* : whatever one or ones

**which·so·ev·er** \,hwich-sō-'e-vər\ *pron or adj, archaic* : WHICHEVER

**whick·er** \'hwi-kər\ *vb* : NEIGH, WHINNY — **whicker** *n*

**¹whiff** \'hwif\ *n* **1** : a quick puff or slight gust (as of air) **2** : an inhalation of odor, gas, or smoke **3** : a slight trace ⟨a ~ of scandal⟩ **4** : STRIKEOUT

**²whiff** *vb* **1** : to expel, puff out, or blow away in or as if in whiffs **2** : to inhale an odor **3** : STRIKE OUT 3

**Whig** \'hwig\ *n* [short for *Whiggamore*, member of a Scottish group that marched to Edinburgh in 1648 to oppose the court party] **1** : a member or supporter of a British political group of the late 17th through early 19th centuries seeking to limit royal authority and increase parliamentary power **2** : an American favoring independence from Great Britain during the American Revolution **3** : a member or supporter of an American political party formed about 1834 to oppose the Democrats

**¹while** \'hwī(-ə)l\ n 1 : a period of time ⟨stay a ~⟩ 2 : the time and effort used : TROUBLE ⟨worth your ~⟩

**²while** conj 1 : during the time that ⟨she called ~ you were out⟩ 2 : AS LONG AS ⟨~ there's life there's hope⟩ 3 : ALTHOUGH ⟨~ he's respected, he's not liked⟩

**³while** vb whiled; whil·ing : to cause to pass esp. pleasantly ⟨~ away an hour⟩

**¹whi·lom** \'hwī-ləm\ adv [ME, lit., at times, fr. OE hwīlum, dat. pl. of hwīl time, while] archaic : FORMERLY

**²whilom** adj : FORMER ⟨his ~ friends⟩

**whilst** \'hwilst\ conj, chiefly Brit : WHILE

**whim** \'hwim\ n : a sudden wish, desire, or change of mind

**whim·per** \'hwim-pər\ vb : to make a low whining plaintive or broken sound — **whimper** n

**whim·si·cal** \'hwim-zi-kəl\ adj 1 : full of whims : CAPRICIOUS 2 : resulting from or characterized by whim or caprice : ERRATIC ⟨~ notions⟩ — **whim·si·cal·i·ty** \ˌhwim-zə-'ka-lə-tē\ n — **whim·si·cal·ly** \'hwim-zi-k(ə-)lē\ adv

**whim·sy** also **whim·sey** \'hwim-zē\ n, pl **whimsies** also **whimseys** 1 : WHIM, CAPRICE 2 : a fanciful or fantastic device, object, or creation esp. in writing or art ⟨decorative ~⟩

**whine** \'hwīn\ vb whined; whin·ing [ME, fr. OE hwīnan to whiz] 1 : to utter a usu. high-pitched plaintive or distressed cry; also : to make a sound similar to such a cry 2 : to complain with or as if with a whine — **whine** n — **whin·er** n — **whiny** also **whin·ey** \'hwī-nē\ adj

**¹whin·ny** \'hwi-nē\ vb whin·nied; whin·ny·ing : to neigh usu. in a low or gentle manner

**²whinny** n, pl **whinnies** : NEIGH

**¹whip** \'hwip\ vb whipped; whip·ping 1 : to move, snatch, or jerk quickly or forcefully ⟨~ out a gun⟩ 2 : to strike with a slender lithe implement (as a lash) esp. as a punishment; also : SPANK 3 : to drive or urge on by or as if by using a whip 4 : to bind or wrap (as a rope or rod) with cord in order to protect and strengthen; also : to wind or wrap around something 5 : DEFEAT 6 : to stir up : INCITE ⟨~ up enthusiasm⟩ 7 : to produce in a hurry ⟨~ up a meal⟩ 8 : to beat (as eggs or cream) into a froth 9 : to proceed nimbly or briskly; also : to flap about forcefully ⟨flags whipping in the wind⟩ — **whip·per** n — **whip into shape** : to bring forcefully to a desired state or condition

**²whip** n 1 : a flexible instrument used for whipping 2 : a stroke or cut with or as if with a whip 3 : a dessert made by whipping a portion of the ingredients ⟨prune ~⟩ 4 : a person who handles a whip 5 : a member of a legislative body appointed by a party to enforce party discipline 6 : a whipping or thrashing motion

**whip·cord** \-ˌkȯrd\ n 1 : a thin tough

braided cord 2 : a strong cloth with fine diagonal cords or ribs

**whip hand** n : positive control : ADVANTAGE

**whip·lash** \'hwip-ˌlash\ n 1 : the lash of a whip 2 : injury resulting from a sudden sharp movement of the neck and head (as of a person in a vehicle that is struck from the rear)

**whip·per·snap·per** \'hwi-pər-ˌsna-pər\ n : a small, insignificant, or presumptuous person

**whip·pet** \'hwi-pət\ n : any of a breed of small swift slender dogs that are used for racing

**whipping boy** n : SCAPEGOAT

**whip-poor-will** \'hwi-pər-ˌwil\ n : an American insect-eating bird with dull variegated plumage whose call at nightfall and just before dawn is suggestive of its name

**whip·saw** \'hwip-ˌsȯ\ vb : to beset with two or more adverse conditions or situations at once

**¹whir** also **whirr** \'hwər\ vb whirred; whir·ring : to move, fly, or revolve with a whir

**²whir** also **whirr** n : a continuous fluttering or vibratory sound made by something in rapid motion

**¹whirl** \'hwərl\ vb 1 : to move or drive in a circle or curve esp. with force or speed 2 : to turn or cause to turn rapidly in circles 3 : to turn abruptly : WHEEL 4 : to move or go quickly 5 : to become dizzy or giddy : REEL

**²whirl** n 1 : a rapid rotating or circling movement; also : something whirling 2 : COMMOTION, BUSTLE ⟨the social ~⟩ 3 : a state of mental confusion 4 : TRY ⟨gave it a ~⟩

**whirl·i·gig** \'hwər-li-ˌgig\ n [ME whirlegigg, fr. whirlen to whirl + gigg top] 1 : a child's toy having a whirling motion 2 : something that continuously whirls or changes

**whirl·pool** \'hwərl-ˌpül\ n : water moving rapidly in a circle so as to produce a depression in the center into which floating objects may be drawn

**whirl·wind** \-ˌwind\ n 1 : a small whirling windstorm 2 : a confused rush 3 : a violent or destructive force

**whirly·bird** \'hwər-lē-ˌbərd\ n : HELICOPTER

**¹whish** \'hwish\ vb : to move with a whish or swishing sound

**²whish** n : a rushing sound : SWISH

**¹whisk** \'hwisk\ n 1 : a quick light sweeping or brushing motion 2 : a usu. wire kitchen implement for beating food by hand 3 : WHISK BROOM

**²whisk** vb 1 : to move nimbly and quickly 2 : to move or convey briskly ⟨~ed the children off to bed⟩ 3 : to beat or whip lightly ⟨~ eggs⟩ 4 : to brush or wipe off lightly ⟨~ a coat⟩

**whisk broom** n : a small broom with a short handle used esp. as a clothes brush

**whis·ker** \'hwis-kər\ n 1 : one hair of the beard 2 pl : the part of the beard that grows on the sides of the face or on the chin 3 : one of the long bristles or hairs growing near the mouth of an animal (as a cat or mouse) — **whis·kered** \-kərd\ *adj*

**whis·key** *or* **whis·ky** \ʰhwis-kē\ *n, pl* **whiskeys** *or* **whiskies** [Ir *uisce beatha* & ScGael *uisge beatha*, lit., water of life] : a liquor distilled from fermented wort (as that obtained from rye, corn, or barley mash)

¹**whis·per** \ʰhwis-pər\ *vb* **1** : to speak very low or under the breath; *also* : to tell or utter by whispering ⟨∼ a secret⟩ **2** : to make a low rustling sound — **whis·per·er** \-pər-ər\ *n*

²**whisper** *n* **1** : something communicated by or as if by whispering : HINT, RUMOR **2** : an act or instance of whispering

**whist** \ʰhwist\ *n* : a card game played by four players in two partnerships with a deck of 52 cards

¹**whis·tle** \ʰhwi-səl\ *n* **1** : a device by which a shrill sound is produced ⟨steam ∼⟩ ⟨tin ∼⟩ **2** : a shrill clear sound made by forcing breath out or air in through the puckered lips **3** : the sound or signal produced by a whistle or as if by whistling **4** : the shrill clear note of an animal (as a bird)

²**whistle** *vb* **whis·tled**; **whis·tling** **1** : to utter a shrill clear sound by blowing or drawing air through the puckered lips **2** : to utter a shrill note or call resembling a whistle **3** : to make a shrill clear sound esp. by rapid movements ⟨the wind *whistled*⟩ **4** : to blow or sound a whistle **5** : to signal or call by a whistle **6** : to produce, utter, or express by whistling ⟨∼ a tune⟩ — **whis·tler** *n*

**whis·tle-blow·er** \ʰhwi-səl-ˌblō-ər\ *n* : IN-FORMER

**whis·tle-stop** \-ˌstäp\ *n* : a brief personal appearance by a political candidate orig. on the rear platform of a touring train

**whit** \ʰhwit\ *n* [prob. alter. of ME *wiht*, *wight* creature, thing, fr. OE *wiht*] : the smallest part or particle : BIT

¹**white** \ʰhwit\ *adj* **whit·er**; **whit·est** **1** : free from color **2** : of the color of new snow or milk; *esp* : of the color white **3** : light or pallid in color ⟨lips ∼ with fear⟩ **4** : SILVERY; *also* : made of silver **5** : of, relating to, or being a member of a group or race characterized by light-colored skin **6** : free from spot or blemish : PURE, INNOCENT **7** : BLANK 2 ⟨∼ space in printed matter⟩ **8** : not intended to cause harm ⟨a ∼ lie⟩ **9** : wearing white ⟨∼ friars⟩ **10** : marked by snow ⟨∼ Christmas⟩ **11** : consisting of a wide range of frequencies ⟨∼ light⟩ — **white-ness** \-nəs\ *n* — **whit·ish** \ʰhwī-tish\ *adj*

²**white** *n* **1** : the color of maximal lightness that characterizes objects which both reflect and transmit light : the opposite of black **2** : a white or light-colored part or thing ⟨the ∼ of an egg⟩; *also, pl* : white garments **3** : the light-colored pieces in a 2-player board game; *also* : the person by whom these are played **4** : one that is or approaches the color white **5** : a person of a light-skinned race

**white ant** *n* : TERMITE

**white blood cell** *n* : any of the colorless blood cells (as lymphocytes) that do not contain hemoglobin but do have a nucleus

**white—bread** \ʰhwit-ˈbred\ *adj* : being, typical of, or having qualities (as blandness) associated with the white middle class ⟨∼ values⟩

**white·cap** \ʰhwit-ˌkap\ *n* : a wave crest breaking into white foam

**white chocolate** *n* : a whitish confection chiefly of cocoa butter, milk, and sugar

**white—col·lar** \ʰhwit-ˈkä-lər\ *adj* : of, relating to, or constituting the class of salaried workers whose duties do not require the wearing of work clothes or protective clothing ⟨∼ jobs⟩

**white dwarf** *n* : a small very dense whitish star of low luminosity

**white elephant** *n* **1** : an Indian elephant of a pale color that is sometimes venerated in India, Sri Lanka, Thailand, and Myanmar **2** : something requiring much care and expense and giving little profit or enjoyment

**white feather** *n* [fr. the superstition that a white feather in the plumage of a gamecock is a mark of a poor fighter] : a mark or symbol of cowardice

**white·fish** \ʰhwit-ˌfish\ *n* : any of various freshwater food fishes related to the salmons and trouts

**white flag** *n* : a flag of pure white used to signify truce or surrender

**white gold** *n* : a pale alloy of gold resembling platinum in appearance

**white goods** *n pl* : white fabrics or articles (as sheets or towels) typically made of cotton or linen

**White·hall** \ʰhwit-ˌhȯl\ *n* : the British government

**white hat** *n* **1** : an admirable and honorable person **2** : a mark or symbol of goodness

**white·head** \-ˌhed\ *n* : a small whitish lump in the skin due to retention of secretion in an oil gland duct

**white heat** *n* : a temperature higher than red heat at which a body becomes brightly incandescent

**white—hot** *adj* **1** : being at or radiating white heat **2** : FERVID ⟨∼ enthusiasm⟩

**White House** \-ˌhaús\ *n* **1** : a residence of the president of the U.S. **2** : the executive department of the U.S. government

**white lead** *n* : a heavy white poisonous carbonate of lead used esp. formerly as a pigment in exterior paints

**white matter** *n* : whitish nerve tissue esp. of the brain and spinal cord that consists largely of neuron processes enclosed in a fatty material and that typically lies under the cortical gray matter

**whit·en** \ʰhwi-tᵊn\ *vb* : to make or become white ♦ **Synonyms** BLANCH, BLEACH — **whit·en·er** *n*

**white oak** *n* : any of various oaks with acorns that take one year to mature; *also* : its hard durable wood

**white pepper** *n* : a spice that consists of the berry of a pepper plant ground after removal of its black husk

**white pine** *n* : a tall-growing pine of eastern No. America with needles in clusters of five; *also* : its wood

**white sale** *n* : a sale on white goods

**white shark** *n* : GREAT WHITE SHARK

**white slave** *n* : a woman or girl held unwillingly for purposes of prostitution — **white slavery** *n*

**white·tail** \'hwit-ˌtāl\ *n* : WHITE-TAILED DEER

**white–tailed deer** *n* : a No. American deer with a rather long tail white on the underside and the males of which have forward-arching antlers

**white–tie** \-ˌtī\ *adj* : characterized by or requiring formal evening clothes consisting of usu. white tie and tailcoat for men and a formal gown for women

**white·wall** \'hwit-ˌwȯl\ *n* : an automobile tire having a white band on the sidewall

¹**white·wash** \-ˌwȯsh, -ˌwäsh\ *vb* 1 : to whiten with whitewash 2 : to clear of a charge of wrongdoing by offering excuses, hiding facts, or conducting a perfunctory investigation 3 : SHUT OUT 2

²**whitewash** *n* 1 : a liquid mixture (as of lime and water) for whitening a surface 2 : a clearing of wrongdoing by whitewashing

**white water** *n* : frothy water (as in breakers, rapids, or falls)

**white·wood** \-ˌwu̇d\ *n* : any of various trees and esp. a tulip tree having light-colored wood; *also* : such wood

¹**whith·er** \'hwi-thər\ *adv* 1 : to what place 2 : to what situation, position, degree, or end 〈~ will this drive him〉

²**whither** *conj* 1 : to the place at, in, or to which; *also* : to which place 2 : to whatever place

**whith·er·so·ev·er** \ˌhwi-thər-sō-'e-vər\ *conj* : to whatever place

¹**whit·ing** \'hwī-tiŋ\ *n, pl* **whiting** *also* **whit·ings** : any of several usu. light or silvery food fishes (as a hake) found mostly near seacoasts

²**whiting** *n* : calcium carbonate in powdered form used esp. as a pigment and in putty

**whit·low** \'hwit-ˌlō\ *n* : a deep inflammation of a finger or toe with pus formation

**Whit·sun·day** \'hwit-'sən-dē, -sən-ˌdā\ *n* [ME *Whitsonday*, fr. OE *hwīta sunnandæg*, lit., white Sunday; prob. fr. the custom of wearing white robes by those newly baptized at this season] : PENTECOST

**whit·tle** \'hwi-tᵊl\ *vb* **whit·tled; whit·tling** 1 : to pare or cut off chips from the surface of (wood) with a knife; *also* : to cut or shape by such paring 2 : to reduce as if by paring down 〈~ down expenses〉

¹**whiz** *or* **whizz** \'hwiz\ *vb* **whizzed; whiz·zing** : to hum, whir, or hiss like a speeding object (as an arrow or ball) passing through air

²**whiz** *or* **whizz** *n, pl* **whiz·zes** : a hissing, buzzing, or whizzing sound

³**whiz** *n, pl* **whiz·zes** : WIZARD 2

**who** \'hü\ *pron* 1 : what or which person or persons 〈~ did it〉 〈~ is he〉 〈~ are they〉 2 : the person or persons that 〈knows ~ did it〉 3 — used to introduce a relative clause and to serve as a substitute therein for the substantive modified by the clause 〈the person ~ lives there is rich〉

**WHO** *abbr* World Health Organization

**whoa** \'wō, 'hwō, 'hō\ *vb imper* 1 — a command to an animal to stand still 2 : cease or slow a course of action or a line of thought

**who·dun·it** *also* **who·dun·nit** \hü-'də-nət\ *n* : a detective or mystery story

**who·ev·er** \hü-'e-vər\ *pron* : whatever person : no matter who

¹**whole** \'hōl\ *adj* [ME *hool* healthy, unhurt, entire, fr. OE *hāl*] 1 : being in healthy or sound condition : free from defect or damage 2 : having all its proper parts or elements 〈~ milk〉 3 : constituting the total sum of : ENTIRE 〈owns the ~ island〉 4 : each or all of the 〈the ~ family〉 5 : not scattered or divided : CONCENTRATED 〈gave me his ~ attention〉 6 : seemingly complete or total 〈the ~ idea is to help, not hinder〉 ♦ *Synonyms* PERFECT, INTACT, SOUND — **whole·ness** *n*

²**whole** *n* 1 : a complete amount or sum 2 : something whole or entire — **on the whole** 1 : in view of all the circumstances or conditions 2 : in general

³**whole** *adv* : COMPLETELY, WHOLLY, ENTIRELY 〈a ~ new term〉

**whole food** *n* : a food eaten in its natural state with little or no artificial additives

**whole·heart·ed** \'hōl-'här-təd\ *adj* : undivided in purpose, enthusiasm, will, or commitment

**whole hog** *adv* : to the fullest extent : COMPLETELY 〈accepted the proposals *whole hog*〉

**whole note** *n* : a musical note equal to one measure of four beats

**whole number** *n* : any of the set of nonnegative integers; *also* : INTEGER

¹**whole·sale** \'hōl-ˌsāl\ *n* : the sale of goods in quantity usu. for resale by a retail merchant

²**wholesale** *adj* 1 : performed on a large scale without discrimination 〈~ slaughter〉 2 : of, relating to, or engaged in wholesaling — **wholesale** *adv*

³**wholesale** *vb* **whole·saled; whole·sal·ing** : to sell at wholesale — **whole·sal·er** *n*

**whole·some** \'hōl-səm\ *adj* 1 : promoting mental, spiritual, or bodily health or well-being 〈a ~ environment〉 2 : sound in body, mind, or morals : HEALTHY 3 : PRUDENT 〈~ respect for the law〉 — **whole·some·ness** *n*

**whole step** *n* : a musical interval comprising two half steps (as C–D or F♯–G♯)

**whole wheat** *adj* : made of ground entire wheat kernels

**whol·ly** \'hōl-lē\ *adv* 1 : COMPLETELY, TOTALLY 2 : SOLELY, EXCLUSIVELY

**whom** \'hüm\ *pron, objective case of* WHO

**whom·ev·er** \hü-'me-vər\ *pron, objective case of* WHOEVER

**whom·so·ev·er** \ˌhüm-sō-'e-vər\ *pron, objective case of* WHOSOEVER

¹**whoop** \'hwüp, 'hwu̇p, 'hüp, 'hu̇p\ *vb* **1**
: to shout or call loudly and vigorously **2**
: to make the characteristic whoop of
whooping cough **3** : to go or pass with a
loud noise **4** : to utter or express with a
whoop; *also* : to urge, drive, or cheer with
a whoop

²**whoop** *n* **1** : a whooping sound or utterance : SHOUT, HOOT **2** : a crowing intake
of breath after a fit of coughing in
whooping cough

¹**whoop·ee** \'hwu̇-(,)pē, 'hwü-\ *interj* —
used to express exuberance

²**whoopee** *n* **1** : boisterous fun **2** : sexual
play — usu. used with *make*

**whooping cough** *n* : an infectious bacterial disease esp. of children marked by
convulsive coughing fits often followed
by a shrill gasping intake of breath

**whooping crane** *n* : a large white nearly
extinct No. American crane noted for its
loud whooping call

**whoop·la** \'hwüp-,lä, 'hwu̇p-\ *n* **1**
: HOOPLA **2** : boisterous merrymaking

**whop·per** \'hwä-pər\ *n* : something unusually large or extreme of its kind; *esp*
: a monstrous lie

**whop·ping** \'hwä-piŋ\ *adj* : extremely
large ⟨a ∼ increase⟩

**whore** \'hȯr\ *n* : PROSTITUTE

**whorl** \'hwȯrl, 'hwərl\ *n* **1** : a group of
parts (as leaves or petals) encircling an
axis and esp. a plant stem **2** : something
that whirls or coils around a center
: COIL, SPIRAL **3** : one of the turns of a
snail shell

**whorled** \'hwȯrld, 'hwərld\ *adj* : having
or arranged in whorls

¹**whose** \'hüz\ *adj* : of or relating to whom
or which esp. as possessor or possessors,
agent or agents, or object or objects of an
action ⟨asked ∼ bag it was⟩

²**whose** *pron* : whose one or ones ⟨∼ is
this car⟩ ⟨∼ are those books⟩

**who·so** \'hü-,sō\ *pron* : WHOEVER

**who·so·ev·er** \,hü-sō-'e-vər\ *pron* : WHO-
EVER

**whs** *or* **whse** *abbr* warehouse

**whsle** *abbr* wholesale

¹**why** \'hwī\ *adv* : for what reason, cause,
or purpose ⟨∼ did you do it⟩

²**why** *conj* **1** : the cause, reason, or purpose for which ⟨that is ∼ you did it⟩ **2**
: for which : on account of which ⟨knows
the reason ∼ you did it⟩

³**why** *n, pl* **whys** : REASON, CAUSE ⟨the ∼s
of racial prejudice⟩

⁴**why** \'wī, 'hwī\ *interj* — used to express
surprise, hesitation, approval, disapproval, or impatience ⟨∼, here's what I was
looking for⟩

**WI** *abbr* **1** West Indies **2** Wisconsin

**WIA** *abbr* wounded in action

**Wic·ca** \'wi-kə\ *n* [prob. fr. OE *wicca* wiz-
ard] : a religion that affirms the existence
of supernatural power (as magic) and of
deities who inhere in nature and that ritually observes seasonal and life cycles

**wick** \'wik\ *n* : a loosely bound bundle of
soft fibers that draws up oil, tallow, or
wax to be burned in a candle, oil lamp, or
stove

**wick·ed** \'wi-kəd\ *adj* **1** : morally bad
: EVIL, SINFUL **2** : FIERCE, VICIOUS **3**
: ROUGISH ⟨a ∼ glance⟩ **4** : REPUG-
NANT, VILE ⟨a ∼ odor⟩ **5** : HARMFUL,
DANGEROUS ⟨a ∼ attack⟩ **6** : impres-
sively excellent ⟨throws a ∼ fastball⟩ —
**wick·ed·ly** *adv* — **wick·ed·ness** *n*

**wick·er** \'wi-kər\ *n* **1** : a small pliant
branch (as an osier or a withe) **2** : WICK-
ERWORK — **wicker** *adj*

**wick·er·work** \-,wərk\ *n* : work made of
osiers, twigs, or rods : BASKETRY

**wick·et** \'wi-kət\ *n* **1** : a small gate or
door; *esp* : one forming a part of or
placed near a larger one **2** : a window-
like opening usu. with a grille or grate (as
at a ticket office) **3** : a set of three upright rods topped by two crosspieces
bowled at in cricket **4** : an arch or hoop
in croquet

**wick·i·up** \'wi-kē-,əp\ *n* : a hut used by
nomadic Indians of the western and
southwestern U.S. with a usu. oval base
and a rough frame covered with reed
mats, grass, or brushwood

**wid** *abbr* widow, widower

¹**wide** \'wīd\ *adj* **wider; wid·est 1** : covering a vast area **2** : measured across or at
right angles to the length **3** : not narrow
: BROAD; *also* : ROOMY **4** : opened to full
width ⟨eyes ∼ with wonder⟩ **5** : not limited : EXTENSIVE ⟨∼ experience⟩ **6** : far
from the goal, mark, or truth ⟨was ∼ of
the truth⟩ — **wide·ly** *adv*

²**wide** *adv* **wid·er; wid·est 1** : over a great
distance or extent : WIDELY ⟨searched
far and ∼⟩ **2** : over a specified distance,
area, or extent **3** : so as to leave a wide
space between ⟨∼ apart⟩ **4** : so as to
clear by a considerable distance ⟨ran ∼
around left end⟩ **5** : COMPLETELY, FUL-
LY ⟨opened her eyes ∼⟩

**wide area network** *n* : a computer network (as the Internet) over a large area
(as a country or the globe) for sharing
resources or exchanging data

**wide–awake** \,wīd-ə-'wāk\ *adj* : fully
awake; *also* : KNOWING, ALERT

**wide–body** \'wīd-,bä-dē\ *n* : a large jet
aircraft having a wide cabin

**wide–eyed** \'wīd-'īd\ *adj* **1** : having the
eyes wide open esp. with wonder or astonishment **2** : NAIVE ⟨∼ innocence⟩

**wide·mouthed** \-'mau̇thd, -'mau̇tht\ *adj*
**1** : having one's mouth opened wide (as
in awe) **2** : having a wide mouth ⟨∼
jars⟩

**wid·en** \'wī-d³n\ *vb* : to increase in width,
scope, or extent

**wide·spread** \'wīd-'spred\ *adj* **1** : widely
scattered or prevalent **2** : widely extended or spread out ⟨∼ wings⟩

**widgeon** *var of* WIGEON

¹**wid·ow** \'wi-dō\ *n* : a woman who has lost
her husband by death and has not married again — **wid·ow·hood** *n*

²**widow** *vb* : to cause to become a widow
or widower

**wid·ow·er** \'wi-də-wər\ *n* : a man who has
lost his wife by death and has not married
again

**width** \'width\ *n* **1** : a distance from side

to side : the measurement taken at right angles to the length : BREADTH **2** : largeness of extent or scope; *also* : FULLNESS **3** : a measured and cut piece of material ⟨a ~ of calico⟩

**wield** \'wēld\ *vb* **1** : to use or handle esp. effectively ⟨~ a broom⟩ **2** : to exert authority by means of : EMPLOY ⟨~ influence⟩ — **wield·er** *n*

**wic·ner** *also* **wei·ner** \'wē-nər\ *n* [short for *wienerwurst*, fr. G, lit., Vienna sausage] : FRANKFURTER

**wife** \'wīf\ *n, pl* **wives** \'wīvz\ **1** *dial* : WOMAN **2** : a woman acting in a specified capacity — used in combination ⟨fish*wife*⟩ **3** : a female partner in a marriage — **wife·hood** *n* — **wife·less** *adj* — **wife·ly** *adj*

**wig** \'wig\ *n* [short for *periwig*, modif. of MF *perruque*, fr. It *parrucca, perrucca* hair, wig] : a manufactured covering of natural or synthetic hair for the head; *also* : TOUPEE

**wi·geon** *or* **wid·geon** \'wi-jən\ *n, pl* **wigeon** *or* **wigeons** *or* **widgeon** *or* **widgeons** : any of several medium-sized freshwater ducks

**wig·gle** \'wi-gəl\ *vb* **wig·gled; wig·gling 1** : to move to and fro with quick jerky or shaking movements : JIGGLE ⟨*wiggled* his toes⟩ **2** : WRIGGLE — **wiggle** *n*

**wig·gler** \'wi-glər, -gə-lər\ *n* **1** : a larva or pupa of a mosquito **2** : one that wiggles

**wig·gly** \'wi-glē, -gə-lē\ *adj* **1** : tending to wiggle ⟨a ~ worm⟩ **2** : WAVY ⟨~ lines⟩

**wight** \'wīt\ *n* : a living being : CREATURE

**wig·let** \'wi-glət\ *n* : a small wig used esp. to enhance a hairstyle

**¹wig·wag** \'wig-,wag\ *vb* **1** : to signal by or as if by a flag or light waved according to a code **2** : to make or cause to make a signal (as with the hand or arm)

**²wigwag** *n* : the art or practice of wigwagging

**wig·wam** \'wig-,wäm\ *n* : a hut of the Indians of the eastern U.S. having typically an arched framework of poles overlaid with bark, rush mats, or hides

**¹wild** \'wī(-ə)ld\ *adj* **1** : living in a state of nature and not ordinarily tamed ⟨~ ducks⟩ **2** : growing or produced without human aid or care ⟨~ honey⟩ ⟨~ plants⟩ **3** : WASTE, DESOLATE ⟨~ country⟩ **4** : UNCONTROLLED, UNRESTRAINED, UNRULY ⟨a ~ passions⟩ ⟨a ~ young stallion⟩ **5** : TURBULENT, STORMY ⟨a ~ night⟩ **6** : EXTRAVAGANT, FANTASTIC, CRAZY ⟨~ ideas⟩ **7** : indicative of strong passion, desire, or emotion ⟨a ~ stare⟩ **8** : UNCIVILIZED, SAVAGE **9** : deviating from the natural or expected course : ERRATIC ⟨a ~ throw⟩ **10** : able to represent any playing card designated by the holder ⟨deuces ~⟩ — **wild·ly** *adv* — **wild·ness** *n*

**²wild** *adv* **1** : WILDLY **2** : without regulation or control ⟨running ~⟩

**³wild** *n* **1** : WILDERNESS **2** : a natural or undomesticated state or existence

**wild boar** *n* : an Old World wild hog from which most domestic swine have been derived

**wild card** *n* **1** : an unknown or unpredictable factor **2** : one picked to fill a leftover play-off or tournament position **3** *usu* **wild-card** : a symbol (as ? or *) used in a keyword search to represent the presence of unspecified characters

**wild carrot** *n* : QUEEN ANNE'S LACE

**¹wild·cat** \'wī(-ə)ld-,kat\ *n, pl* **wildcats 1** : any of various small or medium-sized cats (as a lynx or ocelot) **2** : a quick-tempered hard-fighting person

**²wildcat** *adj* **1** : not sound or safe ⟨~ schemes⟩ **2** : initiated by a group of workers without formal union approval ⟨~ strike⟩

**³wildcat** *vb* **wild·cat·ted; wild·cat·ting** : to drill an oil or gas well in a region not known to be productive

**wil·de·beest** \'wil-də-,bēst\ *n, pl* **wildebeests** *also* **wildebeest** [Afrikaans *wildebees*, fr. *wilde* wild + *bees* ox] : either of two large African antelopes with an ox-like head and horns and a horselike mane and tail

**wil·der·ness** \'wil-dər-nəs\ *n* [ME, fr. *wildern* wild, fr. OE *wilddēoren* of wild beasts] : an uncultivated and uninhabited region

**wild·fire** \'wī(-ə)ld-,fī(-ə)r\ *n* : an uncontrollable fire — **like wildfire** : very rapidly

**wild·flow·er** \-,flau(-ə)r\ *n* : the flower of a wild or uncultivated plant or the plant bearing it

**wild·fowl** \-,fau(-ə)l\ *n* : a bird and esp. a waterfowl hunted as game

**wild–goose chase** *n* : the pursuit of something unattainable

**wild·life** \'wī(-ə)ld-,līf\ *n* : nonhuman living things and esp. wild animals living in their natural environment

**wild oat** *n* **1** : any of several Old World wild grasses **2** *pl* : offenses and indiscretions attributed to youthful exuberance — usu. used in the phrase *sow one's wild oats*

**wild rice** *n* : a No. American aquatic grass; *also* : its edible seed

**wild type** *n* : a gene or trait that is typical of a natural population of organisms in contrast to that of mutant forms; *also* : an organism with such a gene or trait

**wild·wood** \'wī(-ə)ld-,wud\ *n* : a wood unaltered or unfrequented by humans

**¹wile** \'wī(-ə)l\ *n* **1** : a trick or stratagem intended to ensnare or deceive; *also* : a playful trick **2** : TRICKERY, GUILE

**²wile** *vb* **wiled; wil·ing** : LURE, ENTICE

**¹will** \'wil\ *vb, past* **would** \'wud\ *pres sing & pl* **will 1** : WISH, DESIRE ⟨call it what you ~⟩ **2** — used as an auxiliary verb to express (1) desire, willingness, or in negative constructions refusal ⟨~ you have another⟩ ⟨he *won't* do it⟩, (2) customary or habitual action ⟨~ get angry over nothing⟩, (3) simple futurity ⟨tomorrow we ~ go shopping⟩, (4) capability or sufficiency ⟨the back seat ~ hold three⟩, (5) determination or willfulness ⟨I ~ go despite them⟩, (6) probability ⟨that ~ be the mailman⟩, (7) inevitability ⟨accidents

~ happen⟩, or (8) a command ⟨you ~ do as I say⟩

²**will** *n* **1** : wish or desire often combined with determination ⟨the ~ to win⟩ **2** : something desired; *esp* : a choice or determination of one having authority or power **3** : the act, process, or experience of willing : VOLITION, **4** : the mental powers manifested as wishing, choosing, desiring, or intending **5** : a disposition to act according to principles or ends **6** : power of controlling one's own actions or emotions ⟨a leader of iron ~⟩ **7** : a legal document in which a person declares to whom his or her possessions are to go after death

³**will** *vb* **1** : to dispose of by or as if by a will : BEQUEATH **2** : to determine by an act of choice; *also* : DECREE, ORDAIN **3** : INTEND, PURPOSE; *also* : CHOOSE

**will·ful** *or* **wil·ful** \'wil-fəl\ *adj* **1** : governed by will without regard to reason : OBSTINATE **2** : INTENTIONAL ⟨~ murder⟩ — **will·ful·ly** *adv*

**wil·lies** \'wi-lēz\ *n pl* : a fit of nervousness : JITTERS — used with *the*

**will·ing** \'wi-liŋ\ *adj* **1** : inclined or favorably disposed in mind : READY ⟨~ to go⟩ **2** : prompt to act or respond ⟨~ workers⟩ **3** : done, borne, or accepted voluntarily or without reluctance **4** : of or relating to the will : VOLITIONAL — **will·ing·ly** *adv* — **will·ing·ness** *n*

**wil·li·waw** \'wi-lē-ˌwȯ\ *n* : a sudden violent gust of cold land air common along mountainous coasts of high latitudes

**will-o'-the-wisp** \ˌwil-ə-thə-'wisp\ *n* **1** : a light that appears at night over marshy grounds **2** : a misleading or elusive goal or hope

**wil·low** \'wi-lō\ *n* **1** : any of a genus of quick-growing shrubs and trees with tough pliable shoots **2** : an object made of willow wood

**wil·low·ware** \-ˌwer\ *n* : dinnerware that is usu. blue and white and that is decorated with a story-telling design featuring a large willow tree by a little bridge

**wil·lowy** \'wi-lə-wē\ *adj* : PLIANT; *also* : gracefully tall and slender

**will·pow·er** \'wil-ˌpau̇-(ə)r\ *n* : energetic determination : RESOLUTENESS

**wil·ly-nil·ly** \ˌwil-ē-'ni-lē\ *adv or adj* [alter. of *will I nill I* or *will ye nill ye* or *will he nill he; nill* fr. archaic *nill* to be unwilling, fr. ME *nilen,* fr. OE *nyllan,* fr. *ne* not + *wyllan* to wish] : without regard for one's choice : by compulsion ⟨they rushed us along ~⟩

¹**wilt** \'wilt\ *vb* **1** : to lose or cause to lose freshness and become limp esp. from lack of water : DROOP ⟨the roses were ~ing⟩ **2** : to grow weak or faint : LANGUISH

²**wilt** *n* : any of various plant disorders marked by wilting and often shriveling

**wily** \'wī-lē\ *adj* **wil·i·er; -est** : full of guile : TRICKY — **wil·i·ness** \-lē-nəs\ *n*

**wimp** \'wimp\ *n* : a weak, cowardly, or ineffectual person — **wimpy** \'wim-pē\ *adj*

¹**wim·ple** \'wim-pəl\ *n* : a cloth covering worn over the head and around the neck and chin by women esp. in the late medieval period and by some nuns

²**wimple** *vb* **wim·pled; wim·pling 1** : to cover with or as if with a wimple **2** : to ripple or cause to ripple

¹**win** \'win\ *vb* **won** \'wən\; **win·ning** [ME *winnen,* fr. OE *winnan* to struggle] **1** : to get possession of esp. by effort : GAIN; *also* : to obtain by work : EARN **2** : to gain in or as if in battle or contest; *also* : to be the victor in ⟨*won* the war⟩ **3** : to solicit and gain the favor of; *esp* : to induce to accept oneself in marriage

²**win** *n* : VICTORY; *esp* : 1st place at the finish (as of a horse race)

**wince** \'wins\ *vb* **winced; winc·ing** : to shrink back involuntarily (as from pain) : FLINCH — **wince** *n*

**winch** \'winch\ *n* : a machine that has a drum on which is wound a rope or cable for hauling or hoisting — **winch** *vb*

¹**wind** \'wind\ *n* **1** : a movement of the air **2** : a prevailing force or influence : TENDENCY, TREND **3** : BREATH ⟨he had the ~ knocked out of him⟩ **4** : gas produced in the stomach or intestines **5** : something insubstantial; *esp* : idle words **6** : air carrying a scent (as of game) **7** : INTIMATION ⟨they got ~ of our plans⟩ **8** : WIND INSTRUMENTS; *also, pl* : players of wind instruments

²**wind** *vb* **1** : to get a scent of ⟨the dogs ~ed the game⟩ **2** : to cause to be out of breath ⟨he was ~ed from the climb⟩ **3** : to allow (as a horse) to rest so as to recover breath

³**wind** \'wind, 'wind\ *vb* **wind·ed** \'win-dəd, 'win-\ *or* **wound** \'wau̇nd\; **wind·ing** : to sound by blowing ⟨~ a horn⟩

⁴**wind** \'wind\ *vb* **wound** \'wau̇nd\ *also* **wind·ed; wind·ing 1** : ENTANGLE, INVOLVE **2** : to introduce stealthily : INSINUATE **3** : to encircle or cover with something pliable : WRAP, COIL, TWINE ⟨~ a bobbin⟩ **4** : to hoist or haul by a rope or chain and a winch **5** : to tighten the spring of; *also* : CRANK **6** : to raise to a high level (as of excitement) **7** : to cause to move in a curving line or path **8** : to have a curving course or shape ⟨a river ~ing through the valley⟩ **9** : to move or lie so as to encircle

⁵**wind** \'wind\ *n* : COIL, TURN

**wind·age** \'win-dij\ *n* : the influence of the wind in deflecting the course of a projectile through the air; *also* : the amount of such deflection

**wind·bag** \'wind-ˌbag\ *n* : an overly talkative person

**wind·blown** \-ˌblōn\ *adj* : blown by the wind; *also* : having the appearance of being blown by the wind ⟨~ hair⟩

**wind·break** \-ˌbrāk\ *n* : a growth of trees or shrubs serving to break the force of the wind; *also* : a shelter from the wind

**wind·burned** \-ˌbərnd\ *adj* : irritated and inflamed by exposure to the wind — **wind·burn** \-ˌbərn\ *n*

**wind·chill** \-ˌchil\ *n* : a still-air temperature that would have the same cooling effect on exposed human skin as a given combination of temperature and wind speed

**windchill factor** *n* : WINDCHILL

**wind down** *vb* **1** : to draw toward an end **2** : RELAX, UNWIND

**wind·er** \'wīn-dər\ *n* : one that winds

**wind·fall** \'wind-ˌfȯl\ *n* **1** : something (as a tree or fruit) blown down by the wind **2** : an unexpected or sudden gift, gain, or advantage ⟨a ～ from the lottery⟩

**wind·flow·er** \-ˌflau̇-(ə)r\ *n* : ANEMONE

¹**wind·ing** \'wīn-diŋ\ *n* : material (as wire) wound or coiled about an object

²**winding** *adj* **1** : having a pronounced curve or spiral ⟨～ stairs⟩ **2** : having a course that winds ⟨a ～ road⟩

**wind·ing–sheet** \-ˌshēt\ *n* : SHROUD

**wind instrument** *n* : a musical instrument (as a flute or horn) sounded by wind and esp. by the breath

**wind·jam·mer** \'wind-ˌja-mər\ *n* : a sailing ship; *also* : one of its crew

**wind·lass** \'wind-ləs\ *n* [ME *wyndlas*, alter. of *wyndase*, fr. OF *guindas, windas*, fr. ON *vindāss*, fr. *vinda* to wind + *āss* pole] : a winch used esp. on ships for hoisting or hauling

**wind·mill** \'wind-ˌmil\ *n* : a mill or machine worked by the wind turning sails or vanes that radiate from a central shaft

**win·dow** \'win-dō\ *n* [ME *windowe*, fr. ON *vindauga*, fr. *vindr* wind + *auga* eye] **1** : an opening in the wall of a building to let in light and air; *also* : the framework with fittings that closes such an opening **2** : WINDOWPANE **3** : an opening resembling or suggesting that of a window in a building **4** : an interval of time during which certain conditions or an opportunity exists **5** : a rectangular box appearing on a computer screen on which information (as files or program output) is displayed — **win·dow·less** *adj*

**window box** *n* : a box for growing plants in or by a window

**window dressing** *n* **1** : display of merchandise in a store window **2** : a showing made to create a deceptively favorable impression

**win·dow·pane** \'win-dō-ˌpān\ *n* : a pane in a window

**win·dow–shop** \-ˌshäp\ *vb* : to look at the displays in store windows without going inside the stores to make purchases — **win·dow–shop·per** *n*

**win·dow·sill** \-ˌsil\ *n* : the horizontal member at the bottom of a window

**wind·pipe** \'wind-ˌpīp\ *n* : TRACHEA

**wind·proof** \-'prüf\ *adj* : impervious to wind ⟨a ～ jacket⟩

**wind·row** \'wind-ˌrō\ *n* **1** : hay raked up into a row to dry **2** : a row of something (as dry leaves) swept up by or as if by the wind

**wind shear** *n* : a radical shift in wind speed and direction that occurs over a very short distance

**wind·shield** \'wind-ˌshēld\ *n* : a transparent screen (as of glass) in front of the occupants of a vehicle

**wind sock** *n* : an open-ended truncated cloth cone mounted in an elevated position to indicate wind direction

**wind·storm** \-ˌstȯrm\ *n* : a storm with high wind and little or no rain

**wind·surf·ing** \-ˌsər-fiŋ\ *n* : the sport or activity of riding a sailboard — **wind·surf** \-ˌsərf\ *vb* — **wind·surf·er** *n*

**wind·swept** \'wind-ˌswept\ *adj* : swept by or as if by wind ⟨～ plains⟩

**wind tunnel** *n* : an enclosed passage through which air is blown to investigate air flow around an object

**wind–up** \'wīn-ˌdəp\ *n* **1** : CONCLUSION, FINISH **2** : a series of regular and distinctive motions made by a pitcher preliminary to delivering a pitch

**wind up** *vb* **1** : to bring or come to a conclusion : END ⟨*wind up* the meeting⟩ **2** : to put in order for the purpose of bringing to an end **3** : to arrive in a place, situation, or condition at the end or as a result of a course of action ⟨*wound up* as paupers⟩ **4** : to make a pitching windup

¹**wind·ward** \'win-dwərd\ *n* : the side or direction from which the wind is blowing

²**windward** *adj* : being in or facing the direction from which the wind is blowing

**windy** \'win-dē\ *adj* **wind·i·er**; **-est 1** : having wind : exposed to winds ⟨a ～ day⟩ ⟨a ～ prairie⟩ **2** : STORMY **3** : FLATULENT **4** : indulging in or characterized by useless talk : VERBOSE

¹**wine** \'wīn\ *n* [ME *win*, fr. OE *wīn*, ultim. fr. L *vinum*] **1** : fermented grape juice used as a beverage **2** : the usu. fermented juice of a plant product (as fruit) used as a beverage ⟨rice ～⟩

²**wine** *vb* **wined**; **win·ing** : to treat to or drink wine

**wine cellar** *n* : a room for storing wines; *also* : a stock of wines

**wine-grow·er** \-ˌgrō-ər\ *n* : one that cultivates a vineyard and makes wine

**wine·press** \-ˌpres\ *n* : a vat in which juice is pressed from grapes

**win·ery** \'wī-nə-rē, 'win-rē\ *n, pl* **-eries** : a wine-making establishment

¹**wing** \'win\ *n* **1** : one of the movable feathered or membranous paired appendages by means of which a bird, bat, or insect flies **2** : something suggesting a wing; *esp* : an airfoil that develops the lift which supports an aircraft in flight **3** : a plant or animal appendage or part likened to a wing **4** : a turned-back or extended edge on an article of clothing **5** : a means of flight or rapid progress **6** : the act or manner of flying : FLIGHT **7** *pl* : the area at the side of the stage out of sight **8** : one of the positions or players on either side of a center position or line **9** : either of two opposing groups within an organization : FACTION **10** : a unit in military aviation consisting of two or more squadrons — **wing·less** *adj* — **wing·like** \-ˌlīk\ *adj* — **on the wing** : in flight : FLYING — **under one's wing** : in one's charge or care

²**wing** *vb* **1** : to fit with wings; *also* : to enable to fly easily **2** : to pass through in flight : FLY ⟨～ the air⟩ ⟨swallows ～*ing* southward⟩ **3** : to let fly : DISPATCH **4**

: to wound in the wing ⟨~ a bird⟩; *also*
: to wound without killing 5 : to perform without preparation : IMPROVISE ⟨~*ing* it⟩

**wing·ding** \'wiŋ-ˌdiŋ\ *n* : a wild, lively, or lavish party

**winged** \'wiŋd, 'wiŋ-əd, *in compounds* 'wind\ *adj* 1 : having wings esp. of a specified character 2 : soaring with or as if with wings : ELEVATED 3 : SWIFT, RAPID

**wing nut** *n* : a nut with winglike extensions that can be gripped with the thumb and finger

**wing·span** \'wiŋ-ˌspan\ *n* : the distance between the tips of a pair of wings

**wing·spread** \-ˌspred\ *n* : the spread of the wings; *esp* : the distance between the tips of the fully extended wings of a winged animal

¹**wink** \'wiŋk\ *vb* 1 : to close and open one eye quickly as a signal or hint 2 : to close and open the eyes quickly : BLINK 3 : to avoid seeing or noticing something ⟨~ at a traffic violation⟩ 4 : TWINKLE, FLICKER — **wink·er** \'wiŋ-kər\ *n*

²**wink** *n* 1 : a brief period of sleep : NAP 2 : an act of winking; *esp* : a hint or sign given by winking 3 : INSTANT ⟨dries in a ~⟩

**win·ner** \'wi-nər\ *n* : one that wins

¹**win·ning** \'wi-niŋ\ *n* 1 : VICTORY 2 : something won; *esp* : money won at gambling ⟨large ~s⟩

²**winning** *adj* 1 : successful esp. in competition 2 : ATTRACTIVE, CHARMING

**win·now** \'wi-nō\ *vb* 1 : to remove (as chaff) by a current of air; *also* : to free (as grain) from waste in this manner 2 : to sort or separate as if by winnowing

**wino** \'wī-nō\ *n, pl* **win·os** : one who is addicted to drinking wine

**win·some** \'win-səm\ *adj* [ME *winsum,* fr. OE *wynsum,* fr. *wynn* joy] 1 : generally pleasing and engaging ⟨a ~ smile⟩ 2 : CHEERFUL, GAY — **win·some·ly** *adv* — **win·some·ness** *n*

¹**win·ter** \'win-tər\ *n* : the season of the year in any region in which the noonday sun shines most obliquely : the coldest period of the year

²**winter** *vb* 1 : to pass the winter ⟨~*ed* in Florida⟩ 2 : to feed or find food during the winter ⟨~*ed* on hay⟩

³**winter** *adj* : sown in autumn for harvesting in the following spring or summer ⟨~ wheat⟩

**win·ter·green** \'win-tər-ˌgrēn\ *n* 1 : a low evergreen plant of the heath family with white bell-shaped flowers and spicy red berries 2 : an aromatic oil or its flavor from the wintergreen

**win·ter·ize** \'win-tə-ˌrīz\ *vb* **-ized; -iz·ing** : to make ready for winter

**win·ter–kill** \'win-tər-ˌkil\ *vb* : to kill or die by exposure to winter weather

**winter squash** *n* : any of various hard-shelled squashes that keep well in storage

**win·ter·tide** \-ˌtīd\ *n* : WINTER

**win·ter·time** \-ˌtīm\ *n* : WINTER

**win·try** \'win-trē\ *also* **win·tery** \'win-tə-rē\ *adj* **win·tri·er; -est** 1 : of, relating to, or characteristic of winter ⟨~ weather⟩ 2 : CHILLING, CHEERLESS ⟨a ~ welcome⟩

¹**wipe** \'wīp\ *vb* **wiped; wip·ing** 1 : to clean or dry by rubbing ⟨~ dishes⟩ 2 : to remove by or as if by rubbing ⟨~ away tears⟩ 3 : to erase completely : OBLITERATE 4 : to pass or draw over a surface ⟨*wiped* his hand across his face⟩ — **wip·er** *n*

²**wipe** *n* 1 : an act or instance of wiping; *also* : BLOW, STRIKE, SWIPE 2 : something used for wiping ⟨disposable ~s⟩

**wipe out** *vb* : to destroy completely

¹**wire** \'wī(-ə)r\ *n* 1 : metal in the form of a thread or slender rod; *also* : a thread or rod of metal 2 : hidden or secret influences controlling the action of a person or organization — usu. used in pl. ⟨pull ~s⟩ 3 : a line of wire for conducting electric current 4 : a telegraph or telephone wire or system 5 : TELEGRAM, CABLEGRAM 6 : the finish line of a race

²**wire** *vb* **wired; wir·ing** 1 : to provide or equip with wire ⟨~ a house⟩ 2 : to bind, string, or mount with wire 3 : to send or send word to by telegraph

**wired** *adj* 1 : furnished with wires 2 : connected to the Internet 3 : feverishly excited ⟨~ fans⟩

**wire·hair** \'wī(-ə)r-ˌher\ *n* : a wirehaired dog or cat

**wire·haired** \-'herd\ *adj* : having a stiff wiry outer coat of hair

¹**wire·less** \-ləs\ *adj* 1 : having no wire or wires 2 : RADIO 3 : of or relating to data communications using radio waves

²**wireless** *n* 1 : telecommunication involving signals transmitted by radio waves; *also* : the technology used in radio telecommunication 2 *chiefly Brit* : RADIO

**wire–pull·er** \-ˌpu̇-lər\ *n* : one who uses secret or underhanded means to influence the acts of a person or organization — **wire–pull·ing** *n*

**wire service** *n* : a news agency that sends out syndicated news copy to subscribers by wire or satellite

**wire·tap** \-ˌtap\ *n* : the act or an instance of tapping a telephone or telegraph wire to get information; *also* : an electrical connection used for such tapping — **wiretap** *vb* — **wire·tap·per** \-ˌta-pər\ *n*

**wire·worm** \-ˌwərm\ *n* : any of various slender hard-coated beetle larvae esp. destructive to plant roots

**wir·ing** \'wī(-ə)r-iŋ\ *n* : a system of wires

**wiry** \'wī(-ə)r-ē\ *adj* **wir·i·er** \'wī-rē-ər\; **-est** 1 : made of or resembling wire 2 : slender yet strong and sinewy ⟨~ arms⟩ — **wir·i·ness** \'wī-rē-nəs\ *n*

**Wis** *or* **Wisc** *abbr* Wisconsin

**Wisd** *abbr* Wisdom

**wis·dom** \'wiz-dəm\ *n* [ME, fr. OE *wīsdom,* fr. *wīs* wise] 1 : accumulated philosophic or scientific learning : KNOWLEDGE; *also* : INSIGHT 2 : good sense : JUDGMENT 3 : a wise attitude or course of action

**Wisdom** *n* — see BIBLE table

**Wisdom of Sol·o·mon** \-'sä-lə-mən\ — see BIBLE table

**wisdom tooth** *n* : the last tooth of the full set on each side of the upper and lower jaws of humans

¹**wise** \'wīz\ *n* : WAY, MANNER, FASHION ⟨in no ~⟩ ⟨in this ~⟩

²**wise** *adj* **wis·er; wis·est** **1** : having wisdom : SAGE **2** : having or showing good sense or good judgment **3** : aware of what is going on : KNOWING ⟨got ~ to his secrets⟩; *also* : CRAFTY, SHREWD **4** : possessing inside information **5** : INSOLENT, FRESH ⟨a ~ retort⟩ — **wise·ly** *adv*

**-wise** \-ˌwīz\ *adv comb form* : in the manner or direction of ⟨slant*wise*⟩

**wise·acre** \'wīz-ˌā-kər\ *n* [MD *wijssegger* soothsayer] : SMART ALECK

¹**wise·crack** \'wīz-ˌkrak\ *n* : a clever, smart, or flippant remark

²**wisecrack** *vb* : to make a wisecrack

**wise guy** *n* : SMART ALECK

¹**wish** \'wish\ *vb* **1** : to have a desire : long for ⟨~ you were here⟩ ⟨~ for a puppy⟩ **2** : to form or express a wish concerning ⟨~ed him a happy birthday⟩ **3** : BID ⟨he ~ed me good morning⟩ **4** : to request by expressing a desire ⟨I ~ you to go now⟩

²**wish** *n* **1** : an act or instance of wishing or desire : WANT; *also* : GOAL **2** : an expressed will or desire

**wish·bone** \-ˌbōn\ *n* : a forked bone in front of the breastbone in most birds

**wish·ful** \'wish-fəl\ *adj* **1** : expressive of a wish; *also* : having a wish **2** : according with wishes rather than fact ⟨~ thinking⟩

**wishy–washy** \'wi-shē-ˌwȯ-shē, -ˌwä-\ *adj* : WEAK, INSIPID; *also* : morally feeble

**wisp** \'wisp\ *n* **1** : a small handful (as of hay or straw) **2** : a thin strand, strip, or fragment ⟨a ~ of hair⟩; *also* : a thready streak ⟨a ~ of smoke⟩ **3** : something frail, slight, or fleeting ⟨a ~ of a smile⟩ — **wispy** *adj*

**wis·te·ria** \wis-'tir-ē-ə\ *also* **wis·tar·ia** \-'tir-ē-ə *also* -'ter-\ *n* : any of a genus of chiefly Asian mostly woody vines related to the peas and widely grown for their long showy clusters of blue, white, purple, or rose flowers

**wist·ful** \'wist-fəl\ *adj* : feeling or showing a timid desire ⟨~ memories⟩ — **wist·ful·ly** *adv* — **wist·ful·ness** *n*

**wit** \'wit\ *n* **1** : reasoning power : INTELLIGENCE **2** : mental soundness : SANITY — usu. used in pl. **3** : RESOURCEFULNESS, INGENUITY; *esp* : quickness and cleverness in handling words and ideas **4** : a talent for making clever remarks; *also* : a person noted for making witty remarks — **wit·ted** \'wi-təd\ *adj* — **at one's wit's end** : at a loss for a means of solving a problem

¹**witch** \'wich\ *n* **1** : a person believed to have magic power; *esp* : SORCERESS **2** : an ugly old woman : HAG **3** : a charming or alluring girl or woman

²**witch** *vb* : BEWITCH

**witch·craft** \'wich-ˌkraft\ *n* : the power or practices of a witch : SORCERY

**witch doctor** *n* : a person in a primitive society who uses magic to treat sickness and to fight off evil spirits

**witch·ery** \'wi-chə-rē\ *n, pl* **-er·ies** **1** : SORCERY **2** : FASCINATION, CHARM

**witch·grass** \'wich-ˌgras\ *n* : any of several grasses that are weeds in cultivated areas

**witch ha·zel** \'wich-ˌhā-zəl\ *n* **1** : a shrub of eastern No. America bearing small yellow flowers in the fall **2** : a soothing alcoholic lotion made from witch hazel bark

**witch–hunt** \'wich-ˌhənt\ *n* **1** : a searching out and persecution of persons accused of witchcraft **2** : the searching out and deliberate harassment esp. of political opponents

**witch·ing** \'wi-chiŋ\ *adj* : of, relating to, or suitable for sorcery or supernatural occurrences

**with** \'with, 'with\ *prep* **1** : AGAINST ⟨a fight ~ his brother⟩ **2** : FROM ⟨parting ~ friends⟩ **3** : in mutual relation to ⟨talk ~ a friend⟩ **4** : in the company of ⟨went there ~ her⟩ **5** : AS REGARDS, TOWARD ⟨is patient ~ children⟩ **6** : compared to ⟨on equal terms ~ another⟩ **7** : in support of ⟨I'm ~ you all the way⟩ **8** : in the presence of : CONTAINING ⟨tea ~ sugar⟩ **9** : in the opinion of : as judged by ⟨their arguments had weight ~ her⟩ **10** : BECAUSE OF, THROUGH ⟨pale ~ anger⟩; *also* : by means of ⟨hit him ~ a club⟩ **11** : in a manner indicating ⟨work ~ a will⟩ **12** : GIVEN, GRANTED ⟨~ your permission I'll leave⟩ **13** : HAVING ⟨came ~ good news⟩ ⟨stood there ~ his mouth open⟩ **14** : characterized by ⟨boys ~ good morals⟩ **15** : at the time of : right after ⟨~ that we left⟩ **16** : DESPITE ⟨~ all her cleverness, she failed⟩ **17** : in the direction of ⟨swim ~ the tide⟩

**with·al** \wi-'thȯl, -'thȧl\ *adv* **1** : together with this : BESIDES **2** : on the other hand : NEVERTHELESS

**with·draw** \with-'drȯ, with-\ *vb* **-drew** \-'drü\; **-drawn** \-'drȯn\; **-draw·ing** \-'drȯ-iŋ\ **1** : to take back or away : REMOVE **2** : to call back (as from consideration); *also* : RETRACT **3** : to go away : RETREAT, LEAVE **4** : to terminate one's participation in or use of something

**with·draw·al** \-'drȯ-əl\ *n* **1** : an act or instance of withdrawing **2** : the discontinuance of the use or administration of a drug and esp. an addicting drug; *also* : the period following such discontinuance marked by often painful physiological and psychological symptoms **3** : a pathological retreat from the real world (as in some schizophrenic states)

**with·drawn** \with-'drȯn\ *adj* **1** : ISOLATED, SECLUDED **2** : socially detached and unresponsive ⟨became depressed and ~⟩

**withe** \'with\ *n* : a slender flexible twig or branch

**with·er** \'wi-thər\ *vb* **1** : to shrivel from or as if from loss of bodily moisture and esp. sap **2** : to lose or cause to lose vitality, force, or freshness ⟨their enthusiasm ~ed⟩ **3** : to cause to feel shriveled ⟨~ed him with a glance⟩

**with·ers** \'wi-thərz\ *n pl* : the ridge between the shoulder bones of a horse; *also* : the corresponding part in other 4-footed animals

**with·hold** \with-'hōld, with-\ *vb* **-held** \-'held\; **-hold·ing 1** : to hold back : RESTRAIN; *also* : RETAIN **2** : to refrain from granting, giving, or allowing ⟨∼ permission⟩ ⟨∼ names⟩

**withholding tax** *n* : a tax on income withheld at the source

**¹with·in** \wi-'thin, -'thin-\ *adv* **1** : in or into the interior : INSIDE **2** : inside oneself : INWARDLY

**²within** *prep* **1** : inside the limits or influence of ⟨∼ call⟩ **2** : in the limits or compass of ⟨∼ a mile⟩ **3** : in or to the inner part of ⟨∼ the room⟩

**with–it** \'wi-thət, -thət\ *adj* : socially or culturally up-to-date

**¹with·out** \wi-'thaut, -'thaut\ *prep* **1** : OUTSIDE **2** : LACKING ⟨∼ hope⟩; *also* : not accompanied by or showing ⟨spoke ∼ thinking⟩

**²without** *adv* **1** : on the outside : EXTERNALLY **2** : with something lacking or absent ⟨has learned to do ∼⟩

**with·stand** \with-'stand, with-\ *vb* **-stood** \-'stud\; **-stand·ing** : to stand against : RESIST; *esp* : to oppose (as an attack) successfully

**wit·less** \'wit-ləs\ *adj* : lacking wit or understanding : FOOLISH — **wit·less·ly** *adv* — **wit·less·ness** *n*

**¹wit·ness** \'wit-nəs\ *n* [ME *witnesse*, fr. OE *witnes* knowledge, testimony, witness, fr. *wit* mind, intelligence] **1** : TESTIMONY ⟨bear ∼ to the fact⟩ **2** : one that gives evidence; *esp* : one who testifies in a cause or before a court **3** : one present at a transaction so as to be able to testify that it has taken place **4** : one who has personal knowledge or experience of something **5** : something serving as evidence or proof : SIGN

**²witness** *vb* **1** : to bear witness : TESTIFY **2** : to act as legal witness of **3** : to furnish proof of : BETOKEN **4** : to be a witness of **5** : to be the scene of ⟨this region has ∼ed many wars⟩

**wit·ti·cism** \'wi-tə-ˌsi-zəm\ *n* : a witty saying or phrase

**wit·ting** \'wi-tiŋ\ *adj* : done knowingly : INTENTIONAL — **wit·ting·ly** *adv*

**wit·ty** \'wi-tē\ *adj* **wit·ti·er; -est** : marked by or full of wit : AMUSING ⟨a ∼ writer⟩ ⟨a ∼ remark⟩ ♦ *Synonyms* HUMOROUS, FACETIOUS, JOCULAR, JOCOSE — **wit·ti·ly** \-tə-lē\ *adv* — **wit·ti·ness** \-tē-nəs\ *n*

**wive** \'wīv\ *vb* **wived; wiv·ing** : to take a wife

**wives** *pl of* WIFE

**wiz·ard** \'wi-zərd\ *n* [ME *wysard*, fr. *wys* wise man, fr. *wys* wise] **1** : MAGICIAN, SORCERER **2** : a very clever or skillful person ⟨a ∼ at chess⟩

**wiz·ard·ry** \'wi-zər-drē\ *n, pl* **-ries 1** : magic skill : SORCERY **2** : great skill or cleverness in an activity

**wiz·en** \'wi-zⁿn, 'wē-\ *vb* : to become or cause to become dry, shrunken, or wrinkled ⟨a face ∼ed by age⟩

**wk** *abbr* **1** week **2** work

**WL** *abbr* wavelength

**wmk** *abbr* watermark

**WNW** *abbr* west-northwest

**WO** *abbr* warrant officer

**w/o** *abbr* without

**woad** \'wōd\ *n* : a European herb related to the mustards; *also* : a blue dyestuff made from its leaves

**wob·ble** \'wä-bəl\ *vb* **wob·bled; wob·bling 1** : to move or cause to move with an irregular rocking or side-to-side motion **2** : TREMBLE, QUAVER **3** : WAVER, VACILLATE — **wobble** *n* — **wob·bly** \-bə-lē\ *adj*

**woe** \'wō\ *n* **1** : deep suffering from misfortune, affliction, or grief **2** : TROUBLE, MISFORTUNE ⟨economic ∼s⟩

**woe·be·gone** \'wō-bi-ˌgòn\ *adj* : exhibiting woe, sorrow, or misery ⟨∼ faces⟩; *also* : being in a sorry condition

**woe·ful** *also* **wo·ful** \'wō-fəl\ *adj* **1** : full of woe : AFFLICTED **2** : involving, bringing, or relating to woe ⟨∼ stories⟩ **3** : DEPLORABLE ⟨∼ test scores⟩ — **woe·ful·ly** *adv*

**wok** \'wäk\ *n* [Chin (Guangzhou & Hong Kong dial.) *wohk*] : a bowl-shaped cooking utensil used esp. in stir-frying

**woke** *past and past part of* WAKE

**woken** *past part of* WAKE

**wold** \'wōld\ *n* : an upland plain or stretch of rolling land without woods

**¹wolf** \'wulf\ *n, pl* **wolves** \'wulvz\ **1** : any of several large erect-eared bushy-tailed doglike predatory mammals that live and hunt in packs; *esp* : GRAY WOLF **2** : a fierce or destructive person — **wolf·ish** *adj* — **wolf in sheep's clothing** : one who hides a hostile intention with a friendly manner

**²wolf** *vb* : to eat greedily : DEVOUR

**wolf·hound** \-ˌhaund\ *n* : any of several large dogs orig. used in hunting wolves

**wol·fram** \'wul-frəm\ *n* : TUNGSTEN

**wol·ver·ine** \ˌwul-və-'rēn\ *n, pl* **wolverines** *also* **wolverine** : a dark shaggy-coated flesh-eating mammal of northern forests and associated tundra that is related to the weasels

**wom·an** \'wu-mən\ *n, pl* **wom·en** \'wi-mən\ [ME, fr. OE *wīfman*, fr. *wīf* woman, wife + *man* human being, man] **1** : an adult female person **2** : WOMANKIND **3** : feminine nature : WOMANLINESS **4** : a female servant or attendant

**wom·an·hood** \'wu-mən-ˌhud\ *n* **1** : the state of being a woman : the distinguishing qualities of a woman or of womankind **2** : WOMEN, WOMANKIND

**wom·an·ish** \'wu-mə-nish\ *adj* **1** : associated with or characteristic of women rather than men **2** : suggestive of a weak character : EFFEMINATE ⟨a ∼ voice⟩

**wom·an·ize** \'wu-mə-ˌnīz\ *vb* : to pursue casual sexual relationships with numerous women — **wom·an·iz·er** *n*

**wom·an·kind** \'wu-mən-ˌkīnd\ *n* : the females of the human race : WOMEN

**wom·an·like** \-ˌlīk\ *adj* : WOMANLY

**wom·an·ly** \-lē\ *adj* : having qualities characteristic of a woman — **wom·an·li·ness** \-lē-nəs\ *n*

**woman suffrage** *n* : possession and exercise of suffrage by women

**womb** \'wüm\ *n* **1** : UTERUS **2** : a place where something is generated

**wom·bat** \'wäm-,bat\ *n* : any of several stocky burrowing Australian marsupials that resemble small bears

**wom·en·folk** \'wi-mən-,fōk\ *also* **wom·en·folks** \-,fōks\ *n pl* : WOMEN

**¹won** \'wən\ *past and past part of* WIN

**²won** \'wän\ *n, pl* won — see MONEY table

**¹won·der** \'wən-dər\ *n* **1** : a cause of astonishment or surprise : MARVEL; *also* : MIRACLE **2** : the quality of exciting wonder ⟨the charm and ~ of the scene⟩ **3** : a feeling (as of awed astonishment or uncertainty) aroused by something extraordinary or affecting

**²wonder** *vb* **1** : to feel surprise or amazement **2** : to feel curiosity or doubt ⟨~ about the future⟩

**wonder drug** *n* : MIRACLE DRUG

**won·der·ful** \'wən-dər-fəl\ *adj* **1** : exciting wonder : MARVELOUS, ASTONISHING **2** : unusually good : ADMIRABLE ⟨did a ~ job⟩ — **won·der·ful·ly** \-f(ə-)lē\ *adv* — **won·der·ful·ness** *n*

**won·der·land** \-,land, -lənd\ *n* **1** : an imaginary place of delicate beauty or magical charm **2** : a place that excites admiration or wonder ⟨a scenic ~⟩

**won·der·ment** \-mənt\ *n* **1** : ASTONISHMENT, SURPRISE **2** : a cause of or occasion for wonder **3** : curiosity about something

**won·drous** \'wən-drəs\ *adj* : WONDERFUL, MARVELOUS ⟨a ~ feat⟩ — **won·drous·ly** *adv* — **won·drous·ness** *n*

**wonk** \'wäŋk, 'wóŋk\ *n* : one who works in a specialized usu. intellectual field ⟨computer ~s⟩

**¹wont** \'wónt, 'wōnt\ *adj* [ME *woned, wont,* fr. pp. of *wonen* to dwell, be used to, fr. OE *wunian*] **1** : ACCUSTOMED, USED ⟨as we are ~ to do⟩ **2** : INCLINED, APT

**²wont** *n* : CUSTOM, USAGE, HABIT ⟨according to her ~⟩

**won't** \'wōnt\ : will not

**wont·ed** \'wón-təd, 'wōn-\ *adj* : ACCUSTOMED, CUSTOMARY ⟨his ~ courtesy⟩

**woo** \'wü\ *vb* **1** : to try to gain the love of : COURT **2** : SOLICIT, ENTREAT **3** : to try to gain or bring about ⟨~ public favor⟩ — **woo·er** *n*

**¹wood** \'wúd\ *n* **1** : a dense growth of trees usu. larger than a grove and smaller than a forest — often used in pl. **2** : a hard fibrous substance that is basically xylem and forms the bulk of trees and shrubs beneath the bark; *also* : this material fit or prepared for some use (as burning or building) **3** : something made of wood

**²wood** *adj* **1** : WOODEN **2** : suitable for holding, cutting, or working with wood **3** *or* **woods** \'wúdz\ : living or growing in woods

**³wood** *vb* **1** : to supply or load with wood esp. for fuel **2** : to cover with a growth of trees

**wood alcohol** *n* : METHANOL

**wood·bine** \'wúd-,bīn\ *n* : any of several honeysuckles; *also* : VIRGINIA CREEPER

**wood·block** \-,bläk\ *n* : WOODCUT

**wood·chop·per** \-,chä-pər\ *n* : one engaged esp. in chopping down trees

**wood·chuck** \-,chək\ *n* : a thickset grizzled marmot of Alaska, Canada, and the northeastern U.S.

**wood·cock** \'wúd-,käk\ *n, pl* **woodcocks** : a brown eastern No. American game bird with a short neck and long bill that is related to the snipe; *also* : a related and similar Old World bird

**wood·craft** \-,kraft\ *n* **1** : skill and practice in matters relating to the woods and esp. in how to take care of oneself in them **2** : skill in shaping or constructing articles from wood

**wood·cut** \-,kət\ *n* **1** : a relief printing surface engraved on a block of wood **2** : a print from a woodcut

**wood·cut·ter** \-,kə-tər\ *n* : a person who cuts wood

**wood duck** *n* : a showy crested American duck of which the male has iridescent multicolored plumage

**wood·ed** \'wú-dəd\ *adj* : covered with woods or trees ⟨~ slopes⟩

**wood·en** \'wú-dᵊn\ *adj* **1** : made of wood **2** : lacking flexibility : awkwardly stiff ⟨~ acting⟩ — **wood·en·ly** *adv* — **wood·en·ness** *n*

**wood·en·ware** \'wú-dᵊn-,wer\ *n* : articles made of wood for domestic use

**wood·land** \'wúd-lənd, -,land\ *n* : land covered with trees : FOREST — **woodland** *adj*

**wood·lot** \'wúd-,lät\ *n* : a restricted area of woodland usu. privately kept to meet fuel and timber needs

**wood louse** *n* : any of various small flat crustaceans that live esp. in ground litter and under stones and bark

**wood·man** \'wúd-mən\ *n* : WOODSMAN

**wood·note** \-,nōt\ *n* : verbal expression that is natural and artless

**wood nymph** *n* : a nymph living in the woods

**wood·peck·er** \'wúd-,pe-kər\ *n* : any of numerous usu. brightly marked climbing birds with stiff spiny tail feathers and a chisellike bill used to drill into trees for insects

**wood·pile** \-,pī(-ə)l\ *n* : a pile of wood and esp. firewood

**wood rat** *n* : PACK RAT

**wood·shed** \-,shed\ *n* : a shed for storing wood and esp. firewood

**woods·man** \'wúdz-mən\ *n* : a person who frequents or works in the woods; *esp* : one skilled in woodcraft

**woodsy** \'wúd-zē\ *adj* **woods·i·er; -est** : relating to or suggestive of woods ⟨a ~ odor⟩

**wood·wind** \'wúd-,wind\ *n* : one of a group of wind instruments including flutes, clarinets, oboes, bassoons, and sometimes saxophones

**wood·work** \-,wərk\ *n* : work made of wood; *esp* : interior fittings (as moldings or stairways) of wood

**woody** \'wu̇-dē\ *adj* **wood·i·er; -est** **1** : abounding or overgrown with woods ⟨a ~ trail⟩ **2** : of or containing wood or wood fibers ⟨~ plants⟩ **3** : characteristic or suggestive of wood ⟨a ~ flavor⟩ — **wood·i·ness** \'wu̇-dē-nəs\ *n*

**woof** \'wu̇f\ *n* [alter. of ME *oof*, fr. OE *ōwef*, fr. *ō-* (fr. *on* on) + *wefan* to weave] **1** : WEFT 1 **2** : a woven fabric; *also* : its texture

**woof·er** \'wu̇-fər\ *n* : a loudspeaker that reproduces sounds of low pitch

**wool** \'wu̇l\ *n* **1** : the soft wavy or curly hair of some mammals and esp. the domestic sheep; *also* : something (as a textile or garment) made of wool **2** : material that resembles a mass of wool — **wooled** \'wu̇ld\ *adj*

**¹wool·en** *or* **wool·len** \'wu̇-lən\ *adj* **1** : made of wool **2** : of or relating to the manufacture or sale of woolen products ⟨~ mills⟩

**²woolen** *or* **woollen** *n* **1** : a fabric made of wool **2** : garments of woolen fabric — usu. used in pl.

**wool·gath·er·ing** \-ˌga-thə-riŋ\ *n* : idle daydreaming

**¹wool·ly** *also* **wooly** \'wu̇-lē\ *adj* **wool·li·er; -est** **1** : of, relating to, or bearing wool **2** : consisting of or resembling wool **3** : mentally confused ⟨~ thinking⟩ **4** : marked by a lack of order or restraint ⟨the wild and ~ West⟩

**²wool·ly** *also* **wool·ie** *or* **wooly** \'wu̇-lē\ *n, pl* **wool·lies** : a garment made from wool; *esp* : underclothing of knitted wool — usu. used in pl.

**woolly adel·gid** \-ə-'del-jəd\ *n* : either of two aphids accidentally introduced into No. America where they are serious pests of firs and hemlocks

**woolly bear** *n* : any of numerous very hairy moth caterpillars

**woolly mammoth** *n* : a heavy-coated mammoth formerly inhabiting colder parts of the northern hemisphere

**woo·zy** \'wü-zē\ *adj* **woo·zi·er; -est** **1** : BEFUDDLED **2** : somewhat dizzy, nauseated, or weak ⟨~ from fatigue⟩ **3** : somewhat indistinct or unfocused : FUZZY — **woo·zi·ness** \'wü-zē-nəs\ *n*

**¹word** \'wərd\ *n* **1** : something that is said; *esp* : a brief remark **2** : a speech sound or series of speech sounds that communicates a meaning; *also* : a graphic representation of such a sound or series of sounds **3** : ORDER, COMMAND **4** *often cap* : the 2d person of the Trinity; *also* : GOSPEL **5** : NEWS, INFORMATION **6** : PROMISE **7** *pl* : QUARREL, DISPUTE **8** : a verbal signal : PASSWORD — **word·less** *adj*

**²word** *vb* : to express in words : PHRASE

**word-age** \'wər-dij\ *n* **1** : WORDS **2** : number of words **3** : WORDING

**word·book** \'wərd-ˌbu̇k\ *n* : VOCABULARY, DICTIONARY

**word·ing** \'wər-diŋ\ *n* : verbal expression : PHRASEOLOGY

**word of mouth** : oral communication

**word·play** \'wərd-ˌplā\ *n* : playful use of words

**word processing** *n* : the production of typewritten documents with automated and usu. computerized text-editing equipment — **word process** *vb*

**word processor** *n* : a keyboard-operated terminal for use in word processing; *also* : software to perform word processing

**wordy** \'wər-dē\ *adj* **word·i·er; -est** : using or having too many words ⟨~ sentences⟩ ♦ *Synonyms* PROLIX, DIFFUSE, REDUNDANT — **word·i·ness** \-dē-nəs\ *n*

**wore** *past of* WEAR

**¹work** \'wərk\ *n* **1** : TOIL, LABOR; *also* : EMPLOYMENT ⟨out of ~⟩ **2** : TASK, JOB ⟨have ~ to do⟩ **3** : the energy used when a force is applied over a given distance **4** : DEED, ACHIEVEMENT **5** : a fortified structure **6** *pl* : engineering structures **7** *pl* : a place where industrial labor is done : PLANT, FACTORY **8** *pl* : the moving parts of a mechanism **9** : something produced by mental effort or physical labor; *esp* : an artistic production (as a book or needlework) **10** : WORKMANSHIP ⟨careless ~⟩ **11** : material in the process of manufacture **12** *pl* : everything possessed, available, or belonging ⟨the whole ~s went overboard⟩; *also* : drastic treatment ⟨gave him the ~s⟩ ♦ *Synonyms* OCCUPATION, EMPLOYMENT, BUSINESS, PURSUIT, CALLING — **in the works** : in process of preparation

**²work** *adj* **1** : used for work ⟨~ elephants⟩ **2** : suitable or styled for wear while working ⟨~ clothes⟩

**³work** *vb* **worked** \'wərkt\ *or* **wrought** \'rȯt\; **work·ing** **1** : to bring to pass : EFFECT **2** : to fashion or create a useful or desired product through labor or exertion **3** : to prepare for use (as by kneading) **4** : to bring into a desired form by a manufacturing process ⟨~ cold steel⟩ **5** : to set or keep in operation : OPERATE ⟨a pump ~ed by hand⟩ **6** : to solve by reasoning or calculation ⟨~ out a problem⟩ **7** : to cause to toil or labor ⟨~ed the men hard⟩; *also* : to make use of ⟨~ a mine⟩ **8** : to pay for with labor or service ⟨~ off a debt⟩ **9** : to bring or get into some position or condition by stages ⟨the stream ~ed itself clear⟩ ⟨the knot ~ed loose⟩ **10** : CONTRIVE, ARRANGE ⟨~ it so you can leave early⟩ **11** : to practice trickery or cajolery on ⟨~ed the management for a free ticket⟩ **12** : EXCITE, PROVOKE ⟨~ed himself into a rage⟩ **13** : to exert oneself physically or mentally; *esp* : to perform work regularly for wages **14** : to function according to plan or design **15** : to produce a desired effect : SUCCEED ⟨the plan ~ed⟩ **16** : to make way slowly and with difficulty ⟨he ~ed forward through the crowd⟩ **17** : to permit of being worked ⟨this wood ~s easily⟩ **18** : to be in restless motion; *also* : FERMENT 1 — **work on** **1** : AFFECT **2** : to try to influence or persuade — **work upon** : to have effect upon : operate on : INFLUENCE

**work·able** \'wər-kə-bəl\ *adj* **1** : capable of being worked ⟨~ clay⟩ **2** : PRACTICABLE, FEASIBLE — **work·able·ness** *n*

**work·a·day** \'wər-kə-ˌdā\ *adj* **1** : relating to or suited for working days **2** : PROSAIC, ORDINARY ⟨~ chores⟩

**work·a·hol·ic** \ˌwər-kə-'hȯ-lik, -'hä-\ *n* : a compulsive worker

**work·bench** \-ˌbench\ *n* : a bench on which work esp. of mechanics, machinists, and carpenters is performed

**work·book** \-ˌbu̇k\ *n* **1** : a worker's manual **2** : a student's book of problems to be answered directly on the pages

**work·day** \'wərk-ˌdā\ *n* **1** : a day on which work is done as distinguished from a day off **2** : the period of time in a day when work is performed

**work·er** \'wər-kər\ *n* **1** : one that works; *esp* : a person who works for wages **2** : any of the sexually undeveloped individuals or a colony of social insects (as bees, ants, or termites) that perform the work of the community

**workers' compensation** *n* : a system of insurance that reimburses an employer for damages paid to an employee who was injured while working

**work ethic** *n* : belief in work as a moral good

**work farm** *n* : a farm on which persons guilty of minor law violations are confined

**work·horse** \'wərk-ˌhȯrs\ *n* **1** : a horse used for hard work **2** : a person who does most of the work of a group task **3** : something that is useful, durable, or dependable

**work·house** \-ˌhau̇s\ *n* **1** *Brit* : POOR-HOUSE **2** : a house of correction for persons guilty of minor law violations

**¹work·ing** \'wər-kiŋ\ *n* **1** : manner of functioning — usu. used in pl. **2** *pl* : an excavation used in mining or tunneling

**²working** *adj* **1** : engaged in work ⟨a ~ journalist⟩ **2** : adequate to allow work to be done ⟨a ~ majority⟩ ⟨a ~ knowledge of French⟩ **3** : adopted or assumed to help further work or activity ⟨a ~ draft⟩ **4** : spent at work ⟨~ life⟩

**work·ing·man** \'wər-kiŋ-ˌman\ *n* : WORKER 1

**work·man** \'wərk-mən\ *n* **1** : WORKER 1 **2** : ARTISAN, CRAFTSMAN

**work·man·like** \-ˌlīk\ *adj* : worthy of a good workman : SKILLFUL

**work·man·ship** \-ˌship\ *n* : the art or skill of a workman : CRAFTSMANSHIP; *also* : the quality of a piece of work ⟨a vase of exquisite ~⟩

**work·out** \'wərk-ˌau̇t\ *n* **1** : a practice or exercise to test or improve one's fitness, ability, or performance **2** : a test or trial to determine ability or capacity or suitability

**work out** *vb* **1** : to bring about esp. by resolving difficulties **2** : DEVELOP, ELABORATE **3** : to prove effective, practicable, or suitable ⟨our plan didn't *work out*⟩ **4** : to amount to a total or calculated figure — used with *at* **5** : to engage in a workout

**work·place** \'wərk-ˌplās\ *n* : a place (as an office) where work is done

**work·room** \'wərk-ˌrüm, -ˌru̇m\ *n* : a room used for work

**work·shop** \-ˌshäp\ *n* **1** : a shop where manufacturing or handicrafts are carried on **2** : a seminar emphasizing exchange of ideas and practical methods

**work·sta·tion** \-ˌstā-shən\ *n* : an area with equipment for the performance of a specialized task; *also* : a personal computer usu. connected to a computer network

**world** \'wərld\ *n* [ME, fr. OE *woruld* human existence, this world, age, fr. a prehistoric compound whose first constituent is represented by OE *wer* man and whose second constituent is akin to OE *eald* old] **1** : the earth with its inhabitants and all things upon it **2** : people in general : MANKIND **3** : human affairs ⟨withdraw from the ~⟩ **4** : UNIVERSE, CREATION **5** : a state of existence : scene of life and action ⟨the ~ of the future⟩ **6** : a distinctive class of persons or their sphere of interest ⟨the musical ~⟩ **7** : a part or section of the earth or its inhabitants by itself **8** : a great number or quantity ⟨a ~ of troubles⟩ **9** : a celestial body

**world–beat·er** \-ˌbē-tər\ *n* : one that excels all others of its kind : CHAMPION

**world–class** *adj* : of the highest caliber in the world ⟨a ~ athlete⟩

**world·ling** \-liŋ\ *n* : a person absorbed in the concerns of the present world

**world·ly** \-lē\ *adj* **1** : of, relating to, or devoted to this world and its pursuits rather than to religion or spiritual affairs ⟨~ pleasures⟩ **2** : WORLDLY-WISE, SOPHISTICATED — **world·li·ness** \-lē-nəs\ *n*

**world·ly–wise** \-ˌwīz\ *adj* : possessing a practical and often shrewd understanding of human affairs

**world·wide** \'world-'wīd\ *adj* : extended throughout the entire world ⟨attracted ~ attention⟩ — **worldwide** *adv*

**World Wide Web** *n* : a part of the Internet usu. accessed through a browser and containing files connected by hyperlinks

**¹worm** \'wərm\ *n* **1** : any of various small long usu. naked and soft-bodied round or flat invertebrate animals (as an earthworm, nematode, tapeworm, or maggot) **2** : a human being who is an object of contempt, loathing, or pity : WRETCH **3** : something that inwardly torments or devours **4** *pl* : infestation with or disease caused by parasitic worms **5** : a spiral or wormlike thing (as the thread of a screw) — **worm·like** \-ˌlīk\ *adj* — **wormy** *adj*

**²worm** *vb* **1** : to move or cause to move or proceed slowly and deviously **2** : to insinuate or introduce (oneself) by devious or subtle means **3** : to obtain or extract by artful or insidious pleading, asking, or persuading ⟨~ed the truth out of him⟩ **4** : to treat (an animal) with a drug to destroy or expel parasitic worms

**worm–eat·en** \'wərm-ˌē-t°n\ *adj* : eaten or burrowed by worms

**worm gear** *n* : a mechanical linkage consisting of a short rotating screw whose threads mesh with the teeth of a gear wheel

**worm·hole** \'wərm-ˌhōl\ *n* : a hole or passage burrowed by a worm

**worm·wood** \-ˌwu̇d\ *n* 1 : any of a genus of aromatic woody plants (as a sagebrush); *esp* : one of Europe used in absinthe 2 : something bitter or grievous : BITTERNESS

**worn** *past part of* WEAR

**worn–out** \'wōrn-'au̇t\ *adj* : exhausted or used up by or as if by wear

**wor·ri·some** \'wər-ē-səm\ *adj* 1 : causing distress or worry ⟨~ news⟩ 2 : inclined to worry or fret ⟨a ~ mother⟩

¹**wor·ry** \'wər-ē\ *vb* **wor·ried; wor·ry·ing** 1 : to shake and mangle with the teeth ⟨a terrier ~*ing* a rat⟩ 2 : to make anxious or upset ⟨her poor health *worries* me⟩ 3 : to feel or express great care or anxiety : FRET ⟨~*ing* about his health⟩ — **wor·ri·er** *n*

²**worry** *n, pl* **worries** 1 : ANXIETY 2 : a cause of anxiety : TROUBLE

**wor·ry·wart** \'wər-ē-ˌwȯrt\ *n* : one who is inclined to worry unduly

¹**worse** \'wərs\ *adj, comparative of* BAD *or of* ILL 1 : bad or evil in a greater degree : less good 2 : more unfavorable, unpleasant, or painful; *also* : SICKER

²**worse** *n* 1 : one that is worse 2 : a greater degree of ill or badness ⟨a turn for the ~⟩

³**worse** *adv, comparative of* BAD *or of* ILL : in a worse manner : to a worse extent or degree ⟨you drive ~ than he does⟩

**wors·en** \'wər-sᵊn\ *vb* : to make or become worse ⟨the rash ~*ed*⟩

¹**wor·ship** \'wər-shəp\ *n* [ME *worshipe*, worthiness, respect, reverence paid to a divine being, fr. OE *weorthscipe* worthiness, respect, fr. *weorth* worthy, worth + -*scipe* -ship, suffix denoting quality or condition] 1 *chiefly Brit* : a person of importance — used as a title for officials 2 : reverence toward a divine being or supernatural power; *also* : the expression of such reverence 3 : extravagant respect or admiration for or devotion to ⟨~ of the dollar⟩

²**worship** *vb* **-shipped** *also* **-shiped; -shipp·ing** *also* **-ship·ing** 1 : to honor or reverence as a divine being or supernatural power 2 : IDOLIZE ⟨~*s* his brother⟩ 3 : to perform or take part in worship — **wor·ship·er** *or* **wor·ship·per** *n*

**wor·ship·ful** \'wər-shəp-fəl\ *adj* 1 *archaic* : NOTABLE, DISTINGUISHED 2 *chiefly Brit* — used as a title for various persons or groups of rank or distinction 3 : VENERATING, WORSHIPING ⟨~ fans⟩

¹**worst** \'wərst\ *adj, superlative of* BAD *or of* ILL 1 : most bad, evil, ill, or corrupt ⟨the ~ criminals⟩ 2 : most unfavorable, unpleasant, or painful ⟨the ~ scenario⟩; *also* : most unsuitable, faulty, or unattractive ⟨the ~ students⟩

²**worst** *adv, superlative of* ILL *or of* BAD *or* BADLY 1 : to the extreme degree of badness or inferiority ⟨the ~ dressed person⟩ : in the worst manner 2 : MOST ⟨those who need help ~⟩

³**worst** *n* : one that is worst

⁴**worst** *vb* : DEFEAT

**wor·sted** \'wu̇s-təd, 'wər-stəd\ *n* [ME, fr. *Worsted* (now *Worstead*), England] : a smooth compact yarn from long wool fibers; *also* : a fabric made from such yarn

**wort** \'wərt, 'wȯrt\ *n* : a sweet liquid drained from mash and fermented to form beer and whiskey

**worth** \'wərth\ *n* 1 : monetary value; *also* : the equivalent of a specified amount or figure ⟨$5 ~ of gas⟩ 2 : the value of something measured by its qualities 3 : MERIT, EXCELLENCE

**worth** *prep* 1 : equal in value to; *also* : having possessions or income equal to 2 : deserving of ⟨well ~ the effort⟩

**worth·less** \'wərth-ləs\ *adj* 1 : lacking worth : VALUELESS; *also* : USELESS 2 : LOW, DESPICABLE ⟨a ~ coward⟩ — **worth·less·ness** *n*

**worth·while** \'wərth-'hwī(-ə)l\ *adj* : being worth the time or effort spent

**wor·thy** \'wər-thē\ *adj* **wor·thi·er; -est** 1 : having worth or value : ESTIMABLE ⟨a ~ cause⟩ 2 : HONORABLE, MERITORIOUS ⟨my ~ opponent⟩ 3 : having sufficient worth ⟨~ of the honor⟩ — **wor·thi·ly** \'wər-thə-lē\ *adv* — **wor·thi·ness** \-thē-nəs\ *n*

**worthy** *n, pl* **worthies** : a worthy person

**would** \'wu̇d\ *past of* WILL 1 *archaic* : wish for : WANT 2 : strongly desire : WISH ⟨I ~ I were young again⟩ 3 — used as an auxiliary to express (1) preference ⟨~ rather run than fight⟩, (2) wish, desire, or intent ⟨those who ~ forbid gambling⟩, (3) habitual action ⟨we ~ meet often for lunch⟩, (4) a contingency or possibility ⟨if he were coming, he ~ be here by now⟩, (5) probability ⟨~ have won if he hadn't tripped⟩, or (6) a request ⟨~ you help us⟩ 4 : COULD 5 : SHOULD

**would–be** \'wu̇d-'bē\ *adj* : desiring or pretending to be ⟨a ~ artist⟩

¹**wound** \'wu̇nd\ *n* 1 : an injury involving cutting or breaking of bodily tissue (as by violence, accident, or surgery) 2 : an injury or hurt to feelings or reputation

²**wound** *vb* : to inflict a wound to or in

³**wound** \'wau̇nd\ *past and past part of* WIND

**wove** *past of* WEAVE

**woven** *past part of* WEAVE

**wow** \'wau̇\ *n* : a striking success : HIT

²**wow** *vb* : to arouse enthusiastic approval ⟨~*ed* the critics⟩

**WP** *abbr* word processing; word processor

**WPM** *abbr* words per minute

**wpn** *abbr* weapon

**wrack** \'rak\ *n* [ME, fr. OE *wræc* misery, punishment, something driven by the sea] : violent or total destruction

**wraith** \'rāth\ *n, pl* **wraiths** \'rāths, 'rāt͟hz\ 1 : GHOST, SPECTER 2 : an insubstantial appearance : SHADOW

¹**wran·gle** \'raŋ-gəl\ *vb* **wran·gled; wran·gling** 1 : to quarrel angrily or peevishly : BICKER 2 : ARGUE ⟨they *wrangled* about money⟩ 3 : to obtain by persistent arguing 4 : to herd and care for (livestock) on the range — **wran·gler** *n*

²**wrangle** *n* : an angry, noisy, or prolonged dispute; *also* : CONTROVERSY

¹**wrap** \'rap\ *vb* **wrapped; wrap·ping** 1 : to cover esp. by winding or folding 2 : to envelop and secure for transportation or storage 3 : to enclose wholly : ENFOLD 4 : to coil, fold, draw, or twine about something 5 : SURROUND, ENVELOP ⟨*wrapped* in mystery⟩ 6 : INVOLVE, ENGROSS ⟨*wrapped* up in a hobby⟩ 7 : to complete filming or recording

²**wrap** *n* 1 : WRAPPER, WRAPPING 2 : an article of clothing that may be wrapped around a person 3 *pl* : SECRECY ⟨kept under ~*s*⟩ 4 : completion of filming or recording 5 : a thin piece of bread that is rolled around a filling

**wrap·around** \'ra-pə-,raund\ *n* : a garment (as a dress) adjusted to the figure by wrapping around

**wrap·per** \'ra-pər\ *n* 1 : that in which something is wrapped 2 : one that wraps 3 : an article of clothing worn wrapped around the body

**wrap·ping** \'ra-piŋ\ *n* : something used to wrap an object : WRAPPER

**wrap–up** \'rap-,əp\ *n* : SUMMARY

**wrap up** *vb* 1 : SUMMARIZE, SUM UP 2 : to bring to a usu. successful conclusion

**wrasse** \'ras\ *n* : any of a large family of usu. brightly colored marine fishes including many food fishes

**wrath** \'rath\ *n* 1 : violent anger : RAGE 2 : divine punishment ♦ *Synonyms* INDIGNATION, IRE, FURY, ANGER

**wrath·ful** \-fəl\ *adj* 1 : filled with wrath : very angry 2 : showing, marked by, or arising from anger ⟨a ~ assault⟩ — **wrath·ful·ly** *adv* — **wrath·ful·ness** *n*

**wreak** \'rēk\ *vb* **wreaken,** fr. OE *wrecan* to drive, punish, avenge] 1 : to exact as a punishment : INFLICT ⟨~ vengeance on an enemy⟩ 2 : to give free scope or rein to ⟨~*ed* his wrath⟩ 3 : BRING ABOUT, CAUSE ⟨~ havoc⟩

**wreath** \'rēth\ *n, pl* **wreaths** \'rēthz, 'rēths\ : a circular band of flowers or leaves usu. for decoration; *also* : something having a circular or coiling form ⟨a ~ of smoke⟩

**wreathe** \'rēth\ *vb* **wreathed; wreathing** 1 : to shape or take on the shape of a wreath 2 : to crown, decorate, or cover with or as if with a wreath ⟨a face *wreathed* in smiles⟩

¹**wreck** \'rek\ *n* 1 : something (as goods) cast up on the land by the sea after a shipwreck 2 : SHIPWRECK 3 : a destructive crash ⟨a car ~⟩ 4 : the action of breaking up or destroying something 5 : broken remains (as of a vehicle after a crash) 6 : something disabled or in a state of ruin; *also* : an individual broken in health or strength, or spirits ⟨he's a nervous ~⟩

²**wreck** *vb* 1 : SHIPWRECK 2 : to ruin or damage by breaking up ⟨~*ed* his marriage⟩ : involve in disaster or ruin

**wreck·age** \'re-kij\ *n* 1 : the act of wrecking : the state of being wrecked : RUIN 2 : the remains of a wreck

**wreck·er** \'re-kər\ *n* 1 : one that searches

for or works upon the wrecks of ships 2 : TOW TRUCK 3 : one that wrecks; *esp* : one whose work is the demolition of buildings

**wren** \'ren\ *n* : any of a family of small mostly brown singing birds with short wings and often a tail that points upward

¹**wrench** \'rench\ *vb* 1 : to move with a violent twist 2 : to pull, strain, or tighten with violent twisting or force 3 : to injure or disable by a violent twisting or straining ⟨~*ed* her back⟩ 4 : to snatch forcibly : WREST

²**wrench** *n* 1 : a forcible twisting; *also* : an injury (as to one's ankle) by twisting 2 : a tool for holding, twisting, or turning (as nuts or bolts)

¹**wrest** \'rest\ *vb* 1 : to pull or move by a forcible twisting movement 2 : to gain with difficulty by or as if by force or violence ⟨~ control of the government from the dictator⟩

²**wrest** *n* : a forcible twist : WRENCH

¹**wres·tle** \'re-səl, 'ra-\ *vb* **wres·tled; wres·tling** 1 : to grapple with and try to throw down an opponent 2 : to compete against in wrestling 3 : to struggle for control (as of something difficult) ⟨~ with a problem⟩ — **wres·tler** \'res-lər, 'ras-\ *n*

²**wrestle** *n* : the action or an instance of wrestling : STRUGGLE

**wres·tling** \'res-liŋ\ *n* : the sport in which two opponents wrestle each other

**wretch** \'rech\ *n* [ME *wrecche*, fr. OE *wrecca* outcast, exile] 1 : a miserable unhappy person 2 : a base, despicable, or vile person

**wretch·ed** \'re-chəd\ *adj* 1 : deeply afflicted, dejected, or distressed : MISERABLE 2 : WOEFUL, GRIEVOUS ⟨a ~ accident⟩ 3 : DESPICABLE ⟨a ~ trick⟩ 4 : poor in quality or ability : INFERIOR ⟨~ workmanship⟩ — **wretch·ed·ly** *adv* — **wretch·ed·ness** *n*

**wrig·gle** \'ri-gəl\ *vb* **wrig·gled; wrig·gling** 1 : to twist or move to and fro like a worm : SQUIRM ⟨*wriggled* in his chair⟩ ⟨~ your toes⟩; *also* : to move along by twisting and turning ⟨a snake *wriggled* along the path⟩ 2 : to extricate oneself as if by wriggling ⟨~ out of difficulty⟩ — **wriggle** *n*

**wrig·gler** *n* 1 : one that wriggles 2 : WIGGLER 1

**wring** \'riŋ\ *vb* **wrung** \'rəŋ\; **wring·ing** \'riŋ-iŋ\ 1 : to squeeze or twist esp. so as to make dry or to extract moisture or liquid ⟨~ wet clothes⟩ 2 : to get by or as if by twisting or pressing ⟨~ the truth out of him⟩ 3 : to twist so as to strain or sprain : CONTORT ⟨~ his neck⟩ 4 : to twist together as a sign of anguish ⟨*wrung* her hands⟩ 5 : to affect painfully as if by wringing : TORMENT ⟨her plight *wrung* my heart⟩

**wring·er** \'riŋ-ər\ *n* : one that wrings; *esp* : a device for squeezing out liquid or moisture ⟨clothes ~⟩

¹**wrin·kle** \'riŋ-kəl\ *n* 1 : a crease or small fold on a smooth surface (as in the skin

or in cloth) **2** : a clever or new method, trick, or idea — **wrin·kly** \-k(ə-)lē\ adj

²**wrinkle** vb **wrin·kled; wrin·kling** : to develop or cause to develop wrinkles

**wrist** \'rist\ n : the joint or region between the hand and the arm; also : a corresponding part in a lower animal

**wrist·band** \-ˌband\ n : a band or the part of a sleeve encircling the wrist

**wrist·let** \-lət\ n : WRISTBAND; esp : a close-fitting knitted band attached to the top of a glove or the end of a sleeve

**wrist·watch** \-ˌwäch\ n : a small watch attached to a bracelet or strap to fasten about the wrist

**writ** \'rit\ n **1** : something written **2** : a written legal order signed by a court officer

**writ·able** \'rī-tə-bəl\ adj : being an electronic storage medium on which it is possible to introduce new data ⟨a ~ DVD⟩

**write** \'rīt\ vb **wrote** \'rōt\; **writ·ten** \'ri-t⁵n\ also **writ** \'rit\; **writ·ing** \'rī-tiŋ\ [ME, fr. OE *wrītan* to scratch, draw, inscribe] **1** : to form characters, letters, or words on a surface ⟨learn to read and ~⟩ **2** : to form the letters or the words of ⟨~ your name⟩ ⟨~ a check⟩ **3** : to put down on paper : express in writing **4** : to make up and set down for others to read ⟨~ a book⟩ ⟨~ music⟩ **5** : to write a letter to **6** : to communicate by letter : CORRESPOND

**write-in** \'rīt-ˌin\ n : a vote cast by writing in the name of a candidate; also : a candidate whose name is written in

**write in** vb : to insert (a name not listed on a ballot) in an appropriate space; also : to cast (a vote) in this manner

**write off** vb : to eliminate (an asset) from a bookkeeping record : enter as a loss or expense

**writ·er** \'rī-tər\ n : one that writes esp. as a business or occupation : AUTHOR

**writer's cramp** n : a painful spasmodic contraction of muscles of the hand or fingers brought on by excessive writing

**write-up** \'rīt-ˌəp\ n : a written account (as in a newspaper); esp : a flattering article

**writhe** \'rīth\ vb **writhed; writh·ing 1** : to twist and turn this way and that ⟨~ in pain⟩ **2** : to suffer with shame or confusion

**writing** n **1** : the act of one that writes; also : HANDWRITING **2** : something that is written or printed **3** : a style or form of composition **4** : the occupation of a writer

**Writings** \'rī-tiŋz\ n pl : the third part of the Jewish scriptures

**wrnt** abbr warrant

¹**wrong** \'ròŋ\ n **1** : an injurious, unfair, or unjust act **2** : a violation of the legal rights of another person **3** : something that is wrong : wrong principles, practices, or conduct ⟨know right from ~⟩ **4** : the state, position, or fact of being wrong ⟨was in the ~⟩

²**wrong** adj **wrong·er** \'ròŋ-ər\; **wrong·est** \'ròŋ-əst\ **1** : SINFUL, IMMORAL **2** : not right according to a standard or code : IMPROPER **3** : INCORRECT ⟨a ~ solution⟩ **4** : UNSATISFACTORY **5** : UNSUITABLE, INAPPROPRIATE **6** : constituting a surface that is considered the back, bottom, inside, or reverse of something ⟨iron only on the ~ side of the fabric⟩ ♦ *Synonyms* FALSE, ERRONEOUS, INCORRECT, INACCURATE, UNTRUE — **wrong·ly** adv

³**wrong** adv **1** : INCORRECTLY **2** : in a wrong direction, manner, or relation

⁴**wrong** vb **wronged; wrong·ing** \'ròŋ-iŋ\ **1** : to do wrong to : INJURE, HARM **2** : to treat unjustly : DISHONOR, MALIGN ♦ *Synonyms* OPPRESS, PERSECUTE, AGGRIEVE

**wrong·do·er** \'ròŋ-ˌdü-ər\ n : a person who does wrong and esp. moral wrong — **wrong·do·ing** \-ˌdü-iŋ\ n

**wrong·ful** \'ròŋ-fəl\ adj **1** : WRONG, UNJUST **2** : UNLAWFUL ⟨~ conduct⟩ — **wrong·ful·ly** adv — **wrong·ful·ness** n

**wrong·head·ed** \-'he-dəd\ adj : stubborn in clinging to wrong opinion or principles — **wrong·head·ed·ly** adv — **wrong·head·ed·ness** n

**wrote** past of WRITE

**wroth** \'ròth, 'rōth\ adj : filled with wrath : ANGRY

**wrought** \'ròt\ adj [ME, fr. pp. of *worken* to work] **1** : FASHIONED, FORMED ⟨carefully ~ essays⟩ **2** : ORNAMENTED **3** : beaten into shape by tools : HAMMERED ⟨~ metals⟩ **4** : deeply stirred : EXCITED ⟨gets easily ~ up⟩

**wrung** past and past part of WRING

**wry** \'rī\ adj **wry·er** \'rī-ər\; **wry·est** \'rī-əst\ **1** : having a bent or twisted shape ⟨a ~ smile⟩; also : turned abnormally to one side : CONTORTED ⟨a ~ neck⟩ **2** : cleverly and often ironically humorous — **wry·ly** adv — **wry·ness** n

**wry·neck** \'rī-ˌnek\ n **1** : either of two Old World woodpeckers that differ from typical woodpeckers in having a peculiar manner of twisting the head and neck **2** : an abnormal twisting of the neck and head to one side caused by muscle spasms

**WSW** abbr west-southwest

**wt** abbr weight

**wurst** \'wərst, 'wu̇rst\ n : SAUSAGE

**wu·shu** \'wü-'shü\ n [Chin (Beijing) *wǔshù*, fr. *wǔ* martial + *shù* art] : Chinese martial arts

**wuss** \'wu̇s\ n : WIMP — **wussy** \'wu̇-sē\ adj

**WV** or **W Va** abbr West Virginia

**WW** abbr World War

**w/w** abbr wall-to-wall

**WY** or **Wyo** abbr Wyoming

**WYS·I·WYG** \'wi-zē-ˌwig\ adj [what you see is what you get] : of, relating to, or being a computer display that shows a document exactly as it will appear when printed out

**¹x** \'eks\ *n, pl* **x's** *or* **xs** \'ek-səz\ *often cap*
**1** : the 24th letter of the English alphabet
**2** : an unknown quantity
**²x** *vb* **x-ed** *also* **x'd** *or* **xed** \'ekst\; **x-ing** *or*
**x'ing** \'ek-siŋ\ : to cancel or obliterate
with a series of *x*'s — usu. used with *out*
**³x** *abbr* **1** ex **2** experimental **3** extra
**⁴x** *symbol* **1** times ⟨3 x 2 is 6⟩ **2** by ⟨a 3 x
5 index card⟩ **3** *often cap* power of magnification
**Xan·a·du** \'za-nə-,dü, -,dyü\ *n* [fr. *Xanadu*,
locality in *Kubla Khan* (1798), poem by
Eng. poet Samuel Taylor Coleridge †1834]
: an idyllic, exotic, or luxurious place
**Xan·thip·pe** \zan-'thi-pē, -'ti-\ *or* **Xan·tip·pe** \-'ti-pē\ *n* [Gk *Xanthippē*, shrewish
wife of Socrates] : an ill-tempered woman
**x–ax·is** \'eks-,ak-səs\ *n* : the axis of a graph
or of a system of coordinates in a plane
parallel to which abscissas are measured
**X–C** *abbr* cross-country
**X chromosome** *n* : a sex chromosome
that usu. occurs paired in each female
cell and single in each male cell in organisms (as humans) in which the male normally has two unlike sex chromosomes
**Xe** *symbol* xenon
**xe·non** \'zē-,nän, 'ze-\ *n* [Gk, neut. of *xenos*
strange] : a heavy gaseous chemical element occurring in minute quantities in air
**xe·no·pho·bia** \,ze-nə-'fō-bē-ə, ,zē-\ *n*
: fear and hatred of strangers or foreigners or of what is strange or foreign — **xe·no·phobe** \'ze-nə-,fōb, 'zē-\ *n* — **xe·no·pho·bic** \,ze-nə-'fō-bik, ,zē-\ *adj*
**xe·ric** \'zir-ik, 'zer-\ *adj* : characterized by
or requiring only a small amount of
moisture ⟨a ∼ habitat⟩
**xeri·scape** \'zir-ə-,skāp, 'zer-\ *n, often
cap* : a landscaping method utilizing water-conserving techniques
**xe·rog·ra·phy** \zə-'rä-grə-fē\ *n* : a process
for copying printed matter by the action
of light on an electrically charged surface

in which the latent image is developed
with a powder — **xe·ro·graph·ic** \,zir-ə-'gra-fik\ *adj*
**xe·ro·phyte** \'zir-ə-,fīt\ *n* : a plant adapted for growth with a limited water supply
— **xe·ro·phyt·ic** \,zir-ə-'fi-tik\ *adj*
**xi** \'zī, 'ksī\ *n* : the 14th letter of the Greek
alphabet — Ξ or ξ
**XL** *abbr* **1** extra large **2** extra long
**Xmas** \'kris-məs *also* 'eks-məs\ *n* [*X* (symbol for *Christ*, fr. the Gk letter chi (X),
initial of *Christos* Christ) + *mas* (in
*Christmas*)] : CHRISTMAS
**XML** \,eks-(,)em-'el\ *n* : a markup language that indicates the structural type
of data
**XO** *abbr* executive officer
**x–ra·di·a·tion** \,eks-,rā-dē-'ā-shən\ *n, often cap* **1** : exposure to X-rays **2** : radiation consisting of X-rays
**x–ray** \'eks-,rā\ *vb, often cap* : to examine,
treat, or photograph with X-rays
**X–ray** \'eks-,rā\ *n* **1** : a radiation with an
extremely short wavelength of less than
100 angstroms that is able to penetrate
through various thicknesses of solids and
to act on photographic film **2** : a photograph taken with X-rays — **X–ray** *adj*
**XS** *abbr* extra small
**xu** \'sü\ *n, pl* **xu** — see *dong* at MONEY
table
**xy·lem** \'zī-ləm, -,lem\ *n* : a woody tissue
of vascular plants that transports water
and dissolved materials upward, functions in support and storage, and lies central to the phloem
**xy·lo·phone** \'zī-lə-,fōn\ *n* [Gk *xylon*
wood + *phōnē* voice, sound] : a musical
instrument consisting of a series of wooden bars graduated in length to produce
the musical scale, supported on belts of
straw or felt, and sounded by striking
with two small wooden hammers — **xy·lo·phon·ist** \-,fō-nist\ *n*

**¹y** \'wī\ *n, pl* **y's** *or* **ys** \'wīz\ *often cap* : the
25th letter of the English alphabet
**²y** *abbr* **1** yard **2** year
**¹Y** \'wī\ *n* : YMCA, YWCA
**²Y** *symbol* yttrium
**¹-y** *also* **-ey** \ē\ *adj suffix* **1** : characterized
by : full of ⟨dirty⟩ ⟨clayey⟩ **2** : having the
character of : composed of ⟨icy⟩ **3** : like
: like that of ⟨homey⟩ ⟨wintry⟩ ⟨stagy⟩ **4**
: tending or inclined to ⟨sleepy⟩ ⟨chatty⟩
**5** : giving occasion for (specified) action
⟨teary⟩ **6** : performing (specified) action
⟨curly⟩

**²-y** \ē\ *n suffix, pl* **-ies** **1** : state : condition
: quality ⟨beggary⟩ **2** : activity, place of
business, or goods dealt with ⟨laundry⟩ **3**
: whole body or group ⟨soldiery⟩
**³-y** *n suffix, pl* **-ies** : instance of a (specified) action ⟨entreaty⟩ ⟨inquiry⟩
**YA** *abbr* young adult
**¹yacht** \'yät\ *n* [obs. D *jaght*, fr. Middle
Low German *jacht*, short for *jachtschip*,
lit., hunting ship] : a usu. large recreational watercraft
**²yacht** *vb* : to race or cruise in a yacht

**yacht·ing** \'yä-tiŋ\ *n* : the sport of racing or cruising in a yacht

**yachts·man** \'yäts-mən\ *n* : a person who owns or sails a yacht

**ya·hoo** \'yä-hü, 'yä-\ *n, pl* **yahoos** [fr. *Yahoo*, one of a race of brutes having the form of men in Jonathan Swift's *Gulliver's Travels*] : a boorish, crass, or stupid person

**Yah·weh** \'yä-,wä\ *also* **Yah·veh** \-,vä\ *n* : GOD 1 — used esp. by the Hebrews

¹**yak** \'yak\ *n, pl* **yaks** *also* **yak** : a large long-haired wild or domesticated ox of Tibet and adjacent Asian uplands

²**yak** *also* **yack** \'yak\ *n* : persistent or voluble talk — **yak** *also* **yack** *vb*

**yam** \'yam\ *n* 1 : the edible starchy root of various twining plants used as a staple food in tropical areas; *also* : a plant that produces yams 2 : a usu. deep orange sweet potato

**yam·mer** \'ya-mər\ *vb* [ME *yameren*, alter. of *yomeren* to murmur, be sad, fr. OE *gēomrian*] 1 : WHIMPER 2 : CHATTER — **yammer** *n*

¹**yank** \'yaŋk\ *vb* : to pull with a quick vigorous movement

²**yank** *n* : a strong sudden pull : JERK

**Yank** \'yaŋk\ *n* : YANKEE

**Yan·kee** \'yaŋ-kē\ *n* 1 : a native or inhabitant of New England; *also* : a native or inhabitant of the northern U.S. 2 : AMERICAN 2

**yan·qui** \'yäŋ-kē\ *n, often cap* [Sp] : a citizen of the U.S. as distinguished from a Latin American

¹**yap** \'yap\ *vb* **yapped; yap·ping** 1 : BARK, YELP 2 : GAB

²**yap** *n* 1 : a quick sharp bark 2 : CHATTER

¹**yard** \'yärd\ *n* [ME, fr. OE *geard* enclosure, yard] 1 : a small enclosed area open to the sky and adjacent to a building 2 : the grounds of a building 3 : the grounds surrounding a house usu. covered with grass 4 : an enclosure for livestock 5 : an area set aside for a particular business or activity 6 : a system of railroad tracks for storing cars and making up trains

²**yard** *n* [ME *yarde*, fr. OE *gierd* twig, measure, yard] 1 — see WEIGHT table 2 : a long spar tapered toward the ends that supports and spreads the head of a sail — **the whole nine yards** : all of a set of circumstances, conditions, or details

**yard·age** \'yär-dij\ *n* : an aggregate number of yards; *also* : the length, extent, or volume of something as measured in yards

**yard·arm** \'yärd-,ärm\ *n* : either end of the yard of a square-rigged ship

**yard·man** \-mən, -,man\ *n* : a person employed in or about a yard

**yard·mas·ter** \-,mas-tər\ *n* : the person in charge of a railroad yard

**yard·stick** \-,stik\ *n* 1 : a graduated measuring stick three feet long 2 : a standard for making a critical judgment : CRITERION ♦ **Synonyms** GAUGE, TOUCHSTONE, BENCHMARK, MEASURE

**yar·mul·ke** \'yä-mə-kə, 'yär-, -məl-\ *n* [Yiddish *yarmlke*] : a skullcap worn esp. by Jewish males in the synagogue and the home

**yarn** \'yärn\ *n* 1 : a continuous often plied strand composed of fibers or filaments and used in weaving and knitting to form cloth 2 : STORY; *esp* : a tall tale

**yar·row** \'ya-rō\ *n* : a strong-scented herb related to the daisies that has white or pink flowers in flat clusters

**yaw** \'yȯ\ *vb* : to deviate erratically from a course ⟨the ship ⁓ed in the heavy seas⟩ — **yaw** *n*

**yawl** \'yȯl\ *n* : a 2-masted sailboat with the shorter mast aft of the rudder

¹**yawn** \'yȯn\ *vb* : to open wide; *esp* : to open the mouth wide and take a deep breath usu. as an involuntary reaction to fatigue or boredom — **yawn·er** *n*

²**yawn** *n* : the act of yawning

**yawp** *or* **yaup** \'yȯp\ *vb* 1 : to make a raucous noise : SQUAWK 2 : CLAMOR, COMPLAIN — **yawp·er** *n*

**yaws** \'yȯz\ *n pl* : a contagious tropical disease caused by a spirochete closely resembling the causative agent of syphilis and marked by skin lesions

**y-ax·is** \'wī-,ak-səs\ *n* : the axis of a graph or of a system of coordinates in a plane parallel to which the ordinates are measured

**Yb** *symbol* ytterbium

**YB** *abbr* yearbook

**Y chromosome** *n* : a sex chromosome that is characteristic of male cells in organisms (as humans) in which the male typically has two unlike sex chromosomes

**yd** *abbr* yard

¹**ye** \'yē\ *pron* : YOU 1

²**ye** \yē, yə, *originally same as* THE\ *definite article, archaic* : THE — used by early printers to represent the manuscript word þe (the)

¹**yea** \'yā\ *adv* 1 : YES — used in oral voting 2 : INDEED, TRULY

²**yea** *n* : an affirmative vote; *also* : a person casting such a vote

**yeah** \'yeə, 'yaə\ *adv* : YES

**year** \'yir\ *n* 1 : the period of about 365¼ solar days required for one revolution of the earth around the sun; *also* : the time in which a planet completes a revolution about the sun 2 : a cycle of 365 or 366 days beginning with January 1; *also* : a calendar year specified usu. by a number 3 *pl* : a time of special significance ⟨their glory ⁓s⟩ 4 *pl* : AGE ⟨advanced in ⁓s⟩ 5 : a period of time other than a calendar year ⟨the school ⁓⟩

**year·book** \-,bu̇k\ *n* 1 : a book published annually esp. as a report 2 : a school publication recording the history and activities of a graduating class

**year·ling** \'yir-liŋ, 'yər-lən\ *n* 1 : one that is a year old 2 : a racehorse between January of the year after the year in which it was born and the next January

**year·long** \'yir-'lȯŋ\ *adj* : lasting through a year

¹**year·ly** \'yir-lē\ *adj* : ANNUAL

²**yearly** *adv* : every year

**yearn** \'yərn\ *vb* 1 : to feel a longing or

craving ⟨~*ing* for freedom⟩  **2** : to feel tenderness or compassion  ♦ **Synonyms** LONG, PINE, HANKER, HUNGER, THIRST

**yearn·ing** *n* : a tender or urgent longing

**year–round** \'yir-'raûnd\ *adj* : effective, employed, or operating for the full year : not seasonal ⟨a ~ resort⟩

**yeast** \'yēst\ *n*  **1** : a surface froth or a sediment in sugary liquids (as fruit juices) that consists largely of cells of a tiny fungus and is used in making alcoholic liquors and as a leaven in baking  **2** : a commercial product containing yeast fungi in a moist or dry medium  **3** : a minute one-celled fungus present and functionally active in yeast that reproduces by budding; *also* : any of several similar fungi  **4** *archaic* : the foam of waves : SPUME  **5** : something that causes ferment or activity

**yeast infection** *n* : infection of the vagina with an excess growth of a normally present fungus that resembles a yeast

**yeasty** \'yē-stē\ *adj* **yeast·i·er; -est**  **1** : of, relating to, or resembling yeast  **2** : UNSETTLED  **3** : full of vitality ⟨~ youths⟩; *also* : FRIVOLOUS

**yegg** \'yeg\ *n* : one that breaks open safes to steal; *also* : ROBBER

¹**yell** \'yel\ *vb* : to utter a loud cry or scream : SHOUT — **yell·er** *n*

²**yell** *n*  **1** : SHOUT  **2** : a cheer used esp. to encourage an athletic team (as at a college)

¹**yel·low** \'ye-lō\ *adj*  **1** : of the color yellow  **2** : having a yellow complexion or skin  **3** : SENSATIONAL ⟨~ journalism⟩  **4** : COWARDLY ⟨was too ~ to fight⟩ — **yel·low·ish** \'ye-lə-wish\ *adj*

²**yellow** *n*  **1** : a color between green and orange in the spectrum : the color of ripe lemons or sunflowers  **2** : something yellow; *esp* : the yolk of an egg  **3** *pl* : any of several plant diseases marked by stunted growth and yellowing of foliage

³**yellow** *vb* : to make or turn yellow

**yellow birch** *n* : a No. American birch with thin lustrous gray or yellow bark; *also* : its strong hard wood

**yellow fever** *n* : an acute infectious viral disease marked by prostration, jaundice, fever, and often hemorrhage and transmitted by a mosquito

**yellow jack** *n* : YELLOW FEVER

**yellow jacket** *n* : any of various small social wasps having the body barred with bright yellow

**yel·low·tail** \'ye-lō-,tāl\ *n* : any of various fishes with a yellow or yellowish tail including several valuable food fishes

**yelp** \'yelp\ *vb* [ME, to boast, cry out, fr. OE *gielpan* to boast, exult] : to utter a sharp quick shrill cry — **yelp** *n*

**Ye·me·ni** \'ye-mə-nē\ *n* : YEMENITE — **Yemeni** *adj*

**Ye·men·ite** \'ye-mə-,nīt\ *n* : a native or inhabitant of Yemen — **Yemenite** *adj*

¹**yen** \'yen\ *n, pl* **yen** — see MONEY table

²**yen** *n* [obs. E argot *yen-yen* craving for opium, fr. Chin (Guangdong dial.) *yīn-yáhn*, fr. *yīn* opium + *yáhn* craving] : a strong desire : LONGING ⟨a ~ to travel⟩

**yeo·man** \'yō-mən\ *n*  **1** : an attendant or officer in a royal or noble household  **2**

: a naval petty officer who performs clerical duties  **3** : a person who owns and cultivates a small farm; *esp* : one of a class of English freeholders below the gentry — **yeo·man·ly** \-lē\ *adj*

**yeo·man·ry** \-rē\ *n* : the body of yeomen and esp. of small landed proprietors

**-yer** — see -ER

¹**yes** \'yes\ *adv* — used as a function word esp. to express assent or agreement or to introduce a more emphatic or explicit phrase

²**yes** *n* : an affirmative reply

**ye·shi·va** *also* **ye·shi·vah** \yə-'shē-və\ *n, pl* **yeshivas** *or* **ye·shi·voth** \-,shē-'vōt, -'vōth\ : a Jewish school esp. for religious instruction

**yes–man** \'yes-,man\ *n* : a person who endorses uncritically every opinion or proposal of a superior

¹**yes·ter·day** \'yes-tər-dē, -,dā\ *adv*  **1** : on the day preceding today  **2** : only a short time ago

²**yesterday** *n*  **1** : the day last past  **2** : time not long past

**yes·ter·year** \'yes-tər-,yir\ *n*  **1** : last year  **2** : the recent past

¹**yet** \'yet\ *adv*  **1** : in addition : BESIDES; *also* : EVEN  **6  2** : up to now; *also* : STILL  **3** : so soon as now ⟨not time to go ~⟩.  **4** : EVENTUALLY  **5** : NEVERTHELESS, HOWEVER

²**yet** *conj* : but nevertheless : BUT

**ye·ti** \'ye-tē, 'yā-\ *n* : ABOMINABLE SNOWMAN

**yew** \'yü\ *n*  **1** : any of a genus of evergreen trees and shrubs with dark stiff poisonous needles and fleshy fruits  **2** : the wood of a yew; *esp* : that of an Old World yew

**Yid·dish** \'yi-dish\ *n* [Yiddish *yidish*, short for *yidish daytsh*, lit., Jewish German] : a language derived from medieval German and spoken by Jews esp. of eastern European origin — **Yiddish** *adj*

¹**yield** \'yēld\ *vb*  **1** : to give as fitting, owed, or required  **2** : GIVE UP; *esp* : to give up possession of on claim or demand  **3** : to bear as a natural product  **4** : PRODUCE, SUPPLY  **5** : to bring in : RETURN  **6** : to give way (as to force or influence)  **7** : to give place  ♦ **Synonyms** RELINQUISH, CEDE, WAIVE, SURRENDER

²**yield** *n* : something yielded; *esp* : the amount or quantity produced or returned

**yield·ing** \'yēl-diŋ\ *adj*  **1** : not rigid or stiff : FLEXIBLE  **2** : SUBMISSIVE, COMPLIANT

**yikes** \'yīks\ *interj* — used to express fear or astonishment

**yip** \'yip\ *vb* **yipped; yip·ping** : YAP

**YK** *abbr* Yukon Territory

**YMCA** \,wī-,em-(,)sē-'ā\ *n* : Young Men's Christian Association

**YMHA** \,wī-,em-,āch-'ā\ *n* : Young Men's Hebrew Association

**yo** \'yō\ *interj* — used to call attention, indicate attentiveness, or express affirmation

**YOB** *abbr* year of birth

**yo·del** \'yō-dᵊl\ *vb* **yo·deled** *or* **yo·delled; yo·del·ing** *or* **yo·del·ling** : to sing by suddenly changing from chest voice to falsetto and back; *also* : to shout or call in this manner — **yodel** *n* — **yo·del·er** *n*

**yo·ga** \'yō-gə\ n [Skt, lit., yoking, fr. *yunakti* he yokes] **1** cap : a Hindu theistic philosophy teaching the suppression of all activity of body, mind, and will in order that the self may realize its distinction from them and attain liberation **2** : a system of exercises for attaining bodily or mental control and well-being — **yo·gic** \-gik\ adj, often cap

**yo·gi** \'yō-gē\ also **yo·gin** \-gən, -ˌgin\ n **1** : a person who practices yoga **2** cap : an adherent of Yoga philosophy

**yo·gurt** also **yo·ghurt** \'yō-gərt\ n [Turk *yoğurt*] : a soured slightly acid often flavored semisolid food made of milk and milk solids to which cultures of bacteria have been added

**¹yoke** \'yōk\ n, pl **yokes 1** : a wooden bar or frame by which two draft animals (as oxen) are coupled at the heads or necks for working together; also : a frame fitted to a person's shoulders to carry a load in two equal portions **2** : a clamp that embraces two parts to hold or unite them in position **3** pl usu **yoke** : two animals yoked together **4** : SERVITUDE, BONDAGE **5** : TIE, LINK ⟨the ~ of matrimony⟩ **6** : a fitted or shaped piece esp. at the shoulder of a garment ♦ **Synonyms** COUPLE, PAIR, BRACE

**²yoke** vb **yoked; yok·ing 1** : to put a yoke on : couple with a yoke **2** : to attach a draft animal to ⟨~ a plow⟩ **3** : JOIN; esp : MARRY

**yo·kel** \'yō-kəl\ n : a naive or gullible country person

**yolk** \'yōk\ n **1** : the yellow rounded inner mass of the egg of a bird or reptile **2** : the stored food material of an egg that supplies nutrients (as proteins and cholesterol) to the developing embryo — **yolked** \'yōkt\ adj

**Yom Kip·pur** \ˌyōm-ki-ˈpu̇r, ˌyäm-, -ˈkipər\ n [Heb *yōm kippūr*, lit., day of atonement] : a Jewish holiday observed in September or October with fasting and prayer as a day of atonement

**¹yon** \'yän\ adj : YONDER

**²yon** adv **1** : YONDER **2** : THITHER ⟨ran hither and ~⟩

**¹yon·der** \'yän-dər\ adv : at or to that place

**²yonder** adj **1** : more distant ⟨the ~ side of the river⟩ **2** : being at a distance within view ⟨~ hills⟩

**yore** \'yȯr\ n [ME, fr. *yore*, adv., long ago, fr. OE *geāra*, fr. *gēar* year] : time long past ⟨in days of ~⟩

**York·ie** \'yȯr-kē\ n : YORKSHIRE TERRIER

**York·shire terrier** \'yȯrk-ˌshir-, -shər-\ n : any of a breed of compact toy terriers with long straight silky hair

**you** \'yü\ pron **1** : the person or persons addressed ⟨~ are a nice person⟩ ⟨~ are nice people⟩ **2** : ONE 2 ⟨~ turn this knob to open it⟩

**¹young** \'yəŋ\ adj **youn·ger** \'yəŋ-gər\; **youn·gest** \'yəŋ-gəst\ **1** : being in the first or an early stage of life, growth, or development **2** : having little experience **3** : recently come into being **4** : YOUTHFUL **5** cap : belonging to or representing a new or revived usu. political group or movement — **young·ish** \'yəŋ-ish\ adj

**²young** n, pl **young** : young persons; also : young animals

**young·ling** \'yəŋ-liŋ\ n : one that is young — **youngling** adj

**young·ster** \-stər\ n **1** : a young person **2** : CHILD

**your** \'yu̇r, 'yȯr, yər\ adj : of or relating to you or yourself

**yours** \'yu̇rz, 'yȯrz\ pron : one or the ones belonging to you

**your·self** \yər-ˈself\ pron, pl **yourselves** \-ˈselvz\ : YOU — used reflexively, for emphasis, or in absolute constructions ⟨you'll hurt ~⟩ ⟨do it ~⟩

**youth** \'yüth\ n, pl **youths** \'yüthz, 'yüths\ **1** : the period of life between childhood and maturity **2** : a young man; also : young persons **3** : YOUTHFULNESS

**youth·ful** \'yüth-fəl\ adj **1** : of, relating to, or appropriate to youth **2** : being young and not yet mature **3** : FRESH, VIGOROUS ⟨~ fervor⟩ — **youth·ful·ly** adv — **youth·ful·ness** n

**youth hostel** n : HOSTEL 2

**yowl** \'yau̇(-ə)l\ vb : to utter a loud long mournful cry : WAIL — **yowl** n

**yo–yo** \'yō-(ˌ)yō\ n, pl **yo-yos** [prob. fr. Ilocano (a Philippine language) *yóyó*] : a thick grooved double disk with a string attached to its center that is made to fall and rise to the hand by unwinding and rewinding on the string — **yo-yo** vb

**yr** abbr **1** year **2** your

**yrbk** abbr yearbook

**YT** abbr Yukon Territory

**yt·ter·bi·um** \i-ˈtər-bē-əm\ n : a rare metallic chemical element

**yt·tri·um** \'i-trē-əm\ n : a rare metallic chemical element

**yu·an** \'yü-ən, yü-ˈän\ n, pl **yuan 1** — see MONEY table **2** : the dollar of the Republic of China (Taiwan)

**yuc·ca** \'yə-kə\ n : any of a genus of plants related to the agaves that grow esp. in warm dry regions and bear large clusters of white cup-shaped flowers atop a long stiff stalk

**yuck** also **yuk** \'yək\ interj — used to express rejection or disgust

**yule** \'yül\ n, often cap : CHRISTMAS

**Yule log** n : a large log formerly put on the hearth on Christmas Eve as the foundation of the fire

**yule·tide** \'yül-ˌtīd\ n, often cap : CHRISTMASTIDE

**yum·my** \'yə-mē\ adj **yum·mi·er; -est** : highly attractive or pleasing

**yup·pie** \'yə-pē\ n [prob. fr. *young urban professional* + *-ie* (as in hippie)] : a young college-educated adult employed in a well-paying profession and living and working in or near a large city — **yup·pie·dom** \-dəm\ n

**yurt** \'yu̇rt\ n : a light round tent of skins or felt stretched over a lattice framework used by pastoral peoples of inner Asia

**YWCA** \ˌwī-ˌdə-bəl-yü-(ˌ)sē-ˈā\ n : Young Women's Christian Association

**YWHA** \-ˌāch-ˈā\ n : Young Women's Hebrew Association

**¹z** \'zē\ *n, pl* **z's** *or* **zs** \'zēz\ *often cap* : the 26th letter of the English alphabet

**²z** *abbr* **1** zero **2** zone

**Z** *symbol* atomic number

**Zach** *abbr* Zacharias

**Zach·a·ri·as** \,za-kə-'rī-əs\ *n* : ZECHARIAH

**¹za·ny** \'zā-nē\ *n, pl* **zanies** [It *zanni*, a traditional masked clown, fr. It dial. *Zanni*, nickname for It *Giovanni* John] **1** : CLOWN, BUFFOON **2** : a silly or foolish person

**²zany** *adj* **za·ni·er; -est 1** : characteristic of a zany **2** : CRAZY, FOOLISH ⟨a ∼ movie⟩ — **za·ni·ly** \'zā-nə-lē\ *adv* — **za·ni·ness** \'zā-nē-nəs\ *n*

**zap** \'zap\ *vb* **zapped; zap·ping 1** : DESTROY, KILL **2** : to heat or cook in a microwave oven ⟨*zapped* the soup⟩

**zeal** \'zēl\ *n* : eager and ardent interest in the pursuit of something : FERVOR
♦ *Synonyms* ENTHUSIASM, PASSION, ARDOR

**zeal·ot** \'ze-lət\ *n* : a zealous person; *esp* : a fanatical partisan ⟨a religious ∼⟩
♦ *Synonyms* ENTHUSIAST, BIGOT

**zeal·ous** \'ze-ləs\ *adj* : filled with, characterized by, or due to zeal — **zeal·ous·ly** *adv* — **zeal·ous·ness** *n*

**ze·bra** \'zē-brə\ *n, pl* **zebras** *also* **zebra** : any of several African mammals related to the horse but conspicuously striped with black or dark brown and white or buff

**zebra mussel** *n* : a freshwater Eurasian mollusk introduced into U.S. waterways where it colonizes and clogs water intake pipes

**ze·bu** \'zē-bü, -byü\ *n* : any of various breeds of domestic oxen developed in India that have a large fleshy hump over the shoulders, a dewlap, drooping ears, and marked resistance to heat and to insect attack

**Zech** *abbr* Zechariah

**Zech·a·ri·ah** \,ze-kə-'rī-ə\ *n* — see BIBLE table

**zed** \'zed\ *n, chiefly Brit* : the letter z

**zeit·geist** \'tsīt-,gīst, 'zīt-\ *n* [G, fr. *Zeit* time + *Geist* spirit] : the general intellectual, moral, and cultural state of an era

**Zen** \'zen\ *n* : a Japanese Buddhist sect that teaches self-discipline, meditation, and attainment of enlightenment through direct intuitive insight

**ze·na·na** \zə-'nä-nə\ *n* : HAREM

**ze·nith** \'zē-nəth\ *n* **1** : the point in the heavens directly overhead **2** : the highest point : ACME ⟨the ∼ of her career⟩
♦ *Synonyms* CULMINATION, PINNACLE, APEX

**ze·o·lite** \'zē-ə-,līt\ *n* : any of various feldsparlike silicates used esp. as water softeners

**Zeph** *abbr* Zephaniah

**Zeph·a·ni·ah** \,ze-fə-'nī-ə\ *n* — see BIBLE table

**zeph·yr** \'ze-fər\ *n* : a breeze from the west; *also* : a gentle breeze

**zep·pe·lin** \'ze-plən, -pə-lən\ *n* [Count Ferdinand von *Zeppelin* †1917 Ger. airship manufacturer] : a cylindrical rigid blimplike airship

**¹ze·ro** \'zē-rō, 'zir-ō\ *n, pl* **zeros** *also* **zeroes** [ultim. fr. Ar *ṣifr*] **1** : the numerical symbol 0 **2** : the number represented by the symbol 0 **3** : the point at which the graduated degrees or measurements on a scale (as of a thermometer) begin **4** : the lowest point

**²zero** *adj* **1** : of, relating to, or being a zero **2** : having no magnitude or quantity **3** : ABSENT, LACKING; *esp* : having no modified inflectional form

**³zero** *vb* : to adjust the sights of a firearm to hit the point aimed at — usu. used with *in*

**zero hour** *n* : the time at which an event (as a military operation) is scheduled to begin

**zest** \'zest\ *n* **1** : a quality of enhancing enjoyment : PIQUANCY **2** : keen enjoyment : GUSTO ⟨a ∼ for life⟩ — **zest·ful** \-fəl\ *adj* — **zest·ful·ly** *adv* — **zest·ful·ness** *n* — **zesty** \'zes-tē\ *adj*

**ze·ta** \'zā-tə, 'zē-\ *n* : the 6th letter of the Greek alphabet — Z or ζ

**zi·do·vu·dine** \zī-'dō-vyü-,dēn\ *n* : AZT

**¹zig·zag** \'zig-,zag\ *n* : one of a series of short sharp turns, angles, or alterations in a course; *also* : something marked by such a series

**²zigzag** *adv* : in or by a zigzag path

**³zigzag** *adj* : having short sharp turns or angles

**⁴zigzag** *vb* **zig·zagged; zig·zag·ging** : to form into or proceed along a zigzag

**zil·lion** \'zil-yən\ *n* : a large indeterminate number

**zinc** \'ziŋk\ *n* : a bluish-white metallic chemical element that is commonly found in minerals and is used esp. in alloys and as a protective coating for iron and steel

**zinc oxide** *n* : a white solid used esp. as a pigment, in compounding rubber, and in ointments and sunblocks

**zine** \'zēn\ *n* : a noncommercial publication usu. devoted to specialized subject matter

**zin·fan·del** \'zin-fən-,del\ *n, often cap* : a dry red table wine made chiefly in California

**zing** \'ziŋ\ *n* **1** : a shrill humming noise **2** : VITALITY **4** — **zing** *vb*

**zing·er** \'ziŋ-ər\ *n* : a pointed witty remark or retort

**zin·nia** \'zi-nē-ə, 'zēn-yə\ *n* : any of a genus of tropical American herbs or low shrubs related to the daisies and widely grown for their showy long-lasting flowers

**Zi·on** \'zī-ən\ n 1 : the Jewish people 2 : the Jewish homeland as a symbol of Judaism or of Jewish national aspiration 3 : HEAVEN 4 : UTOPIA

**Zi·on·ism** \'zī-ə-ˌni-zəm\ n : an international movement orig. for the establishment of a Jewish national or religious community in Palestine and later for the support of modern Israel — **Zi·on·ist** \-nist\ adj or n

¹**zip** \'zip\ vb **zipped; zip·ping** : to move, act, or function with speed or vigor

²**zip** n 1 : a sudden sharp hissing sound 2 : ENERGY, VIM ⟨the performance lacked ∼⟩

³**zip** n : NOTHING, ZERO ⟨the score was 27 to ∼⟩

⁴**zip** vb **zipped; zip·ping** : to close or open with a zipper

**zip code** n, often cap Z&IP [zone improvement plan] : a number that identifies each postal delivery area in the U.S.

**zip line** n : a cable suspended usu. over an incline to which a rider is harnessed

**zip·per** \'zi-pər\ n : a fastener consisting of two rows of metal or plastic teeth on strips of tape and a sliding piece that closes an opening by drawing the teeth together

**zip·py** \'zi-pē\ adj **zip·pi·er; -est** 1 : very speedy ⟨a ∼ car⟩ 2 : strikingly appealing ⟨∼ clothes⟩

**zir·con** \'zər-ˌkän\ n : a zirconium-containing mineral transparent varieties of which are used as gems

**zir·co·ni·um** \ˌzər-'kō-nē-əm\ n : a gray corrosion-resistant metallic chemical element used esp. in alloys and ceramics

**zit** \'zit\ n : PIMPLE

**zith·er** \'zi-thər, -thər\ n : a musical instrument having 30 to 40 strings played with plectrum and fingers

**zi·ti** \'zē-tē\ n, pl **ziti** [It] : medium-size tubular pasta

**zlo·ty** \'zlȯ-tē\ n, pl **zlo·tys** \-tēz\ or **zloty** — see MONEY table

**Zn** symbol zinc

**zo·di·ac** \'zō-dē-ˌak\ n [ME, fr. AF, fr. L zodiacus, fr. Gk zōidiakos, fr. zōidion carved figure, sign of the zodiac, fr. dim. of zōion living being, figure] 1 : an imaginary belt in the heavens that encompasses the paths of most of the planets and that is divided into 12 constellations or signs 2 : a figure representing the signs of the zodiac and their symbols — **zo·di·a·cal** \zō-'dī-ə-kəl\ adj

**zom·bie** also **zom·bi** \'zäm-bē\ n : a person who is believed to have died and been brought back to life without speech or free will

**zon·al** \'zō-nᵊl\ adj : of, relating to, or having the form of a zone — **zon·al·ly** adv

¹**zone** \'zōn\ n [ME, fr. AF, fr. L zona belt, zone, fr. Gk zōnē] 1 : any of five great divisions of the earth's surface made according to latitude and temperature including the torrid zone, two temperate zones, and two frigid zones 2 : something that forms an encircling band ⟨a ∼ of tissue⟩ 3 : a region or area set off as distinct from surrounding parts ⟨business ∼⟩ ⟨postal ∼⟩

²**zone** vb **zoned; zon·ing** 1 : ENCIRCLE 2 : to arrange in or mark off into zones; esp : to divide (as a city) into sections reserved for different purposes

**zonked** \'zäŋkt\ adj : being or acting as if under the influence of alcohol or a drug : HIGH

**zoo** \'zü\ n, pl **zoos** : a park where wild animals are kept for exhibition

**zoo·ge·og·ra·phy** \ˌzō-ə-jē-'ä-grə-fē\ n : a branch of biogeography concerned with the geographical distribution of animals — **zoo·ge·og·ra·pher** \-fər\ n — **zoo·geo·graph·ic** \-ˌjē-ə-'gra-fik\ also **zoo·geo·graph·i·cal** \-fi-kəl\ adj

**zoo·keep·er** \'zü-ˌkē-pər\ n : a person who cares for animals in a zoo

**zool** abbr zoological; zoology

**zoological garden** n : ZOO

**zo·ol·o·gy** \zō-'ä-lə-jē\ n : a branch of biology that deals with the classification and the properties and vital phenomena of animals — **zo·o·log·i·cal** \ˌzō-ə-'lä-ji-kəl\ adj — **zo·ol·o·gist** \zō-'ä-lə-jist\ n

**zoom** \'züm\ vb 1 : to move with a loud hum or buzz 2 : to gain altitude quickly 3 : to focus a camera or microscope using a special lens that permits the apparent distance of the object to be varied — **zoom** n

**zoom lens** n : a camera lens in which the image size can be varied continuously while the image remains in focus

**zoo·mor·phic** \ˌzō-ə-'mȯr-fik\ adj 1 : having the form of an animal 2 : of, relating to, or being the representation of a deity in the form or with the attributes of an animal

**zoo·plank·ton** \ˌzō-ə-'plaŋk-tən, -ˌtän\ n : plankton composed of animals

**zoo·spore** \'zō-ə-ˌspȯr\ n : a motile spore

**zoot suit** \'züt-\ n : a flashy suit of extreme cut typically consisting of a thigh-length jacket with wide padded shoulders and pants that are wide at the top and narrow at the bottom — **zoot-suit·er** \-ˌsü-tər\ n

**Zo·ro·as·tri·an·ism** \ˌzȯr-ə-'was-trē-ə-ˌni-zəm\ n : a religion founded by the Persian prophet Zoroaster — **Zo·ro·as·tri·an** \-trē-ən\ adj or n

**zounds** \'zaündz\ interj [euphemism for God's wounds] — used as a mild oath

**zoy·sia** \'zȯi-shə, -zhə, -sē-ə, -zē-ə\ n : any of a genus of creeping perennial grasses having fine wiry leaves and including some used as lawn grasses

**ZPG** abbr zero population growth

**Zr** symbol zirconium

**zuc·chet·to** \zü-'ke-tō, tsü-\ n, pl **-tos** [It] : a small round skullcap worn by Roman Catholic ecclesiastics

**zuc·chi·ni** \zü-'kē-nē\ n, pl **-ni** or **-nis** [It] : a smooth usu. dark green summer squash; also : a plant that bears zucchini

**Zu·lu** \'zü-ˌlü\ n, pl **Zulu** or **Zulus** : a member of a Bantu-speaking people of

South Africa; *also* : the Bantu language of the Zulus

**Zu·ni** \'rü-nē\ *or* **Zu·ñi** \-nyē\ *n, pl* **Zuni** *or* **Zunis** *or* **Zuñi** *or* **Zuñis** : a member of an American Indian people of western New Mexico; *also* : the language of the Zuni people

**zwie·back** \'swē-,bak, 'swī-, 'zwē-, 'zwī-, -,bäk\ *n* [G, lit., twice baked, fr. *zwie-* twice + *backen* to bake] : a usu. sweetened bread that is baked and then sliced and toasted until dry and crisp

**Zwing·li·an** \'zwiŋ-glē-ən, 'swiŋ-, -lē-; 'tsfiŋ-lē-\ *adj* : of or relating to the Swiss religious reformer Ulrich Zwingli or his teachings — **Zwinglian** *n*

**zy·de·co** \'zī-də-,kō\ *n* : popular music of southern Louisiana that combines tunes of French origin with elements of Caribbean music and the blues

**zy·gote** \'zī-,gōt\ *n* : a cell formed by the union of two sexual cells; *also* : the developing individual produced from such a cell — **zy·got·ic** \zī-'gä-tik\ *adj*

# Foreign Words & Phrases

# Biographical Names

# Geographical Names

# FOREIGN WORDS & PHRASES

These words and phrases occur frequently enough in English context to be included in a general English dictionary, but they merit a special section because they have not become a part of the English vocabulary.

**ab·eunt stu·dia in mo·res** \'ä-be-ˌu̇nt-'stü-dē-ˌä-ˌin-'mō-ˌräs\ [L] : practices zealously pursued pass into habits

**à bien·tôt** \ä-bya<sup>n</sup>-'to\ [F] : so long

**ab in·cu·na·bu·lis** \ˌäb-ˌin-ku̇-'nä-bu̇-ˌlēs\ [L] : from the cradle : from infancy

**a bon chat, bon rat** \ä-bō<sup>n</sup>-'shä bō<sup>n</sup>-'rä\ [F] : to a good cat, a good rat : retaliation in kind

**à bouche ou·verte** \ä-bü-shü-vert\ [F] : with open mouth : eagerly : uncritically

**ab ovo us·que ad ma·la** \ˌäb-'ō-vō-ˌu̇s-kwe-ˌäd-'mä-lä\ [L] : from egg to apples : from soup to nuts : from beginning to end

**à bras ou·verts** \ä-brä-zü-ver\ [F] : with open arms : cordially

**ab·sit in·vi·dia** \'äb-ˌsit-in-'wi-dē-ˌä\ [L] : let there be no envy or ill will

**ab uno dis·ce om·nes** \ˌäb-'ü-nō-ˌdis-ke-'ōm-ˌnäs\ [L] : from one learn to know all

**ab ur·be con·di·ta** \ˌäb-'u̇r-be-'kōn-di-ˌtä\ [L] : from the founding of the city (Rome, founded 753 B.C.) — used by the Romans in reckoning dates

**ab·usus non tol·lit usum** \'ä-ˌbü-su̇s-ˌnōn-ˌtō-lit-'ü-sùm\ [L] : abuse does not take away use, i.e., is not an argument against proper use

**à compte** \ä-'kō<sup>n</sup>t\ [F] : on account

**à coup sûr** \ä-kü-su̇er\ [F] : with sure stroke : surely

**acte gra·tuit** \äk-tə-grä-tw<sup>y</sup>ē\ [F] : gratuitous impulsive act

**ad ar·bi·tri·um** \ˌad-är-'bi-trē-u̇m\ [L] : at will : arbitrarily

**ad as·tra per as·pe·ra** \ˌad-'as-trə-ˌpər-'as-pə-rä\ [L] : to the stars by hard ways — motto of Kansas

**ad ex·tre·mum** \ˌäd-ck-'strä-ˌmu̇m, ˌad-ik-'strē-məm\ [L] : to the extreme : at last

**ad ma·jo·rem Dei glo·ri·am** \ˌäd-mä-'yòr-ˌem-'dē-ˌē-'glòr-ē-ˌäm\ [L] : to the greater glory of God — motto of the Society of Jesus

**ad pa·tres** \ˌäd-'pä-ˌträs\ [L] : (gathered) to his fathers : deceased

**ad re·fe·ren·dum** \ˌäd-ˌre-fe-'ren-du̇m\ [L] : for reference : for further consideration by one having the authority to make a final decision

**à droite** \ä-drwät\ [F] : to or on the right hand

**ad utrum·que pa·ra·tus** \ˌäd-ù-'trùm-kwe-pä-'rä-tús\ [L] : prepared for either (event)

**ad vi·vum** \ˌäd-'wē-ˌwu̇m\ [L] : to the life.

**ae·gri som·nia** \ˌī-grē-'sòm-nē-ˌä\ [L] : a sick man's dreams

**ae·quam ser·va·re men·tem** \'ī-ˌkwäm-ˌser-ˌwä-rä-'men-ˌtem\ [L] : to preserve a calm mind

**ae·quo ani·mo** \ˌī-kwō-'ä-ni-ˌmō\ [L] : with even mind : calmly

**à gauche** \ä-gōsh\ [F] : to or on the left hand

**age quod agis** \'ä-ge-ˌkwòd-'ä-ˌgis\ [L] : do what you are doing : to the business at hand

**à grands frais** \ä-grä<sup>n</sup>-fre\ [F] : at great expense

**à huis clos** \ä-wē-klō\ [F] : with closed doors : behind closed doors

**aide-toi, le ciel t'ai·dera** \ed-twä lə-'syel-te-drä\ [F] : help yourself (and) heaven will help you

**aî·né** \e-nä\ [F] : elder : senior (masc.)

**aî·née** \e-nä\ [F] : elder : senior (fem.)

**à l'aban·don** \ä-lä-bä<sup>n</sup>-dō<sup>n</sup>\ [F] : carelessly : in disorder

**à la belle étoile** \ä-lä-bel-ā-twäl\ [F] : under the beautiful star : in the open air at night

**à la bonne heure** \a-lä-bò-nœr\ [F] : at a good time : well and good : all right

**à la fran·çaise** \ä-lä-frä<sup>n</sup>-sez\ [F] : in the French manner

**à l'amé·ri·caine** \ä-lä-mä-rē-ken\ [F] : in the American manner : of the American kind

**à l'an·glaise** \ä-lä<sup>n</sup>-glez\ [F] : in the English manner

**à la page** \ä-lä-päzh\ [F] : at the page : up-to-the-minute

**à la russe** \ä-lä-rues\ [F] : in the Russian manner

**alea jac·ta est** \'ä-lē-ˌä-ˌyäk-tä-'est\ [L] : the die is cast

**à l'im·pro·viste** \ä-la<sup>n</sup>-prò-vēst\ [F] : unexpectedly

**alis vo·lat pro·pri·is** \'ä-ˌlēs-'wò-ˌlät-'prō-prē-ˌēs\ [L] : she flies with her own wings — motto of Oregon

**al·ki** \'al-ˌkī, -kē\ [Chinook Jargon] : by and by — motto of Washington

**alo·ha oe** \ä-ˌlō-hä-'ói, -'ō-ē\ [Hawaiian] : love to you : greetings : farewell

**al·ter idem** \ˌòl-tər-'ī-ˌdem, ˌäl-ter-'ē-\ [L] : second self

**à mer·veille** \ä-mer-vā\ [F] : marvelously : wonderfully

**ami·cus hu·ma·ni ge·ne·ris** \ä-'mē-kús-hü-,mä-nē-'ge-ne-ris\ [L] : friend of the human race

**ami·cus us·que ad aras** \-,ùs-kwe-,äd-'är-,äs\ [L] : a friend as far as to the altars, i.e., except in what is contrary to one's religion; *also* : a friend to the last extremity

**ami de cour** \ä-,mē-dǝ-'kúr\ [F] : court friend : insincere friend

**amor pa·tri·ae** \'ä-,mòr-'pä-trē-,ī\ [L] : love of one's country

**amor vin·cit om·nia** \'ä-,mòr-,wiŋ-kit-'òm-nē-ä\ [L] : love conquers all things

**an·guis in her·ba** \,äŋ-gwis-in-'her-,bä\ [L] : snake in the grass

**ani·mal bi·pes im·plu·me** \'ä-ni-,mäl-,bi-,pās-im-'plü-me\ [L] : two-legged animal without feathers (i.e., the human race)

**ani·mis opi·bus·que pa·ra·ti** \'ä-ni-,mēs-,ó-pi-'bús-kwe-pä-'rä-tē\ [L] : prepared in mind and resources — one of the mottoes of South Carolina

**an·no ae·ta·tis su·ae** \'ä-nō-ī-,tä-tis-'sü-,ī\ [L] : in the (specified) year of his (or her) age

**an·no mun·di** \,ä-nō-'mún-dē\ [L] : in the year of the world — used in reckoning dates from the supposed period of the creation of the world, esp. as fixed by James Ussher at 4004 B.C. or by the Jews at 3761 B.C.

**an·no ur·bis con·di·tae** \,ä-nō-,úr-bis-'kòn-di-,tī\ [L] : in the year of the founded city : in the year that the city was founded (Rome, founded 753 B.C.)

**an·nu·it coep·tis** \'ä-nü-,it-'kòip-,tēs\ [L] : He (God) has approved our beginnings — motto on the reverse of the Great Seal of the United States

**à peu près** \ä-pœ-pre\ [F] : nearly : approximately

**à pied** \ä-pyā\ [F] : on foot

**à point** \ä-pwä<sup>n</sup>\ [F] : at the right time

**après moi le dé·luge** \ä-prĕ-mwä-lǝ-dä-luezh\ *or* **après nous le déluge** \ä-prenü-\ [F] : after me the deluge — attributed to Louis XV

**à pro·pos de rien** \-ryä<sup>n</sup>\ [F] : apropos of nothing

**aqua et ig·ni in·ter·dic·tus** \,ä-kwä-et-'ig-nē-,in-ter-'dik-tús\ [L] : forbidden to be furnished with water and fire : outlawed

**Ar·ca·des am·bo** \'är-kä-,des-'äm-bō\ [L] : both Arcadians : two persons of like occupations or tastes; *also* : two rascals

**ar·rec·tis au·ri·bus** \ä-'rek-,tēs-'aù-ri-,bús\ [L] : with ears pricked up : attentively

**ar·ri·ve·der·ci** \,är-ē-vä-'der-chē\ [It] : till we meet again : farewell

**ars lon·ga, vi·ta bre·vis** \ärs-'lòŋ-,gä ,wē-,tä-'bre-wis\ [L] : art is long, life is short

: human life span limits all that might be accomplished

**as–sa·laam alai·kum** \,ǝs-sǝ-'läm-ǝ-'līkúm\ [Ar *as-salāmu 'alaykum*] : peace to you — used as a traditional greeting among Muslims

**a ter·go** \ä-'ter-(,)gō\ [L] : from behind

**à tort et à tra·vers** \ä-tòr-ä-ä-trä-ver\ [F] : wrong and crosswise : at random : without rhyme or reason

**au bout de son la·tin** \ō-büd-sō<sup>n</sup>-lä-ta<sup>n</sup>, -bü-dǝ-\ [F] : at the end of one's Latin : at the end of one's mental resources

**au con·traire** \ō-kō<sup>n</sup>-trer\ [F] : on the contrary

**au·de·mus ju·ra nos·tra de·fen·de·re** \aù-'dā-mùs-,yùr-ä-'nó-strä-dā-'fen-de-rä\ [L] : we dare defend our rights — motto of Alabama

**au·den·tes for·tu·na ju·vat** \aù-'den-,tās-fòr-,tü-nä-'yù-,wät\ [L] : fortune favors the bold

**au·di al·te·ram par·tem** \'aù-,dē-,äl-te-,räm-'pär-,tem\ [L] : hear the other side

**au fait** \ō-fet, -fe\ [F] : to the point : fully competent : fully informed : socially correct

**au fond** \ō-fō<sup>n</sup>\ [F] : at bottom : fundamentally

**au grand sé·rieux** \ō-grä<sup>n</sup>-sä-ryœ\ [F] : in all seriousness

**au mieux** \ō-myœ\ [F] : on the best terms : on intimate terms

**au pays des aveugles les borgnes sont rois** \ō-pā-ē-dä-zä-vœgl<sup>y</sup>-lā-bòrn<sup>y</sup>-ǝ-sō<sup>n</sup>-rwä\ [F] : in the country of the blind the one-eyed men are kings

**au·rea me·di·o·cri·tas** \'aù-re-ä-,me-dē-'ò-kri-,täs\ [L] : the golden mean

**au reste** \ō-rest\ [F] : for the rest : besides

**au sé·rieux** \ō-sä-ryœ\ [F] : seriously

**aus·si·tôt dit, aus·si·tôt fait** \ō-sē-tō-dē ō-sē-tō-fe\ [F] : no sooner said than done

**aut Cae·sar aut ni·hil** \aùt-'kī-sär-,aùt-'ni-,hil\ [L] : either a Caesar or nothing

**au·tres temps, au·tres mœurs** \ō-trǝ-tä<sup>n</sup> ō-trǝ-mœrs\ [F] : other times, other customs

**aut vin·ce·re aut mo·ri** \aùt-'wiŋ-ke-rä-,aùt-'mó-,rē\ [L] : either to conquer or to die

**aux armes** \ō-zärm\ [F] : to arms

**avant la lettre** \ä-vä<sup>n</sup>-lä-letr<sup>9</sup>\ [F] : before the letter : before a (specified) name or entity existed

**ave at·que va·le** \'ä-,wā-,ät-kwe-'wä-,lā\ [L] : hail and farewell

**à vo·tre san·té** \ä-vòt-sä<sup>n</sup>-tä, -vò-trǝ-\ [F] : to your health — used as a toast

**ax·is mun·di** \'ak-sǝs-'mùn-dē\ [L] : turning point of the world : line through the earth's center around which the universe revolves

**bel·la fi·gu·ra** \'bel-lǝ-fē-'gü-rä\ [It] : fine appearance or impression

**bel·lum om·ni·um con·tra om·nes** \'belúm·'tóm·nē·ùm·ˌkon·trä·'tóm·ˌnās\ [L] : war of all against all

**bien en·ten·du** \byaⁿ-ˌnäⁿ-täⁿ-dᵫ\ [F] : well understood : of course

**bien–pen·sant** \byaⁿ-päⁿ-säⁿ\ [F] : right-minded : one who holds orthodox views

**bis dat qui ci·to dat** \'bis-ˌdät-kwē-'ki-tō-ˌdät\ [L] : he gives twice who gives promptly

**bon ap·pé·tit** \bô-nä-pä-tē\ [F] : good appetite : enjoy your meal

**bon gré, mal gré** \'bôⁿ-ˌgrä 'mäl-ˌgrä\ [F] : whether with good grace or bad : willy-nilly

**bon·jour** \bôⁿ-zhür\ [F] : good day : good morning

**bonne foi** \bôn-fwä\ [F] : good faith

**bon·soir** \bôⁿ-swär\ [F] : good evening

**bru·tum ful·men** \brü-tùm-'fül-men\ [L] : insensible thunderbolt : a futile threat or display of force

**ca·dit quaes·tio** \ˌkä-dit-'kwī-stē-ˌō\ [L] : the question drops : the argument collapses

**carte d'iden·ti·té** \kärt-de-däⁿ-tē-tä\ [F] : identity card

**cau·sa si·ne qua non** \'kaù-ˌsä-ˌsi-nä-kwä-'nōn\ [L] : an indispensable cause or condition

**ça va sans dire** \sä-vä-säⁿ-dir\ [F] : it goes without saying

**ca·ve ca·nem** \ˌkä-wā-'kä-ˌnem\ [L] : beware the dog

**ce·dant ar·ma to·gae** \'kā-ˌdänt-ˌär-mə-'tō-ˌgī\ [L] : let arms yield to the toga : let military power give way to civil power — motto of Wyoming

**ce n'est que le pre·mier pas qui coûte** \snek-lə-prə-myā pä-kē-küt\ [F] : it is only the first step that costs

**c'est–à–dire** \se-tä-dir\ [F] : that is to say : namely

**c'est au·tre chose** \se-tōt-shōz, -to-trə-\ [F] : that's a different thing

**c'est la guerre** \se-lä-ger\ [F] : that's war : it cannot be helped

**c'est la vie** \se-lä-vē\ [F] : that's life : that's how things happen

**c'est plus qu'un crime, c'est une faute** \se-plu-koⁿ krēm se-tᵫn-fōt\ [F] : it is worse than a crime, it is a blunder

**ce·te·ra de·sunt** \ˌkā-te-rä-'dā-ˌsùnt\ [L] : the rest is missing

**cha·cun à son goût** \shä-kœⁿ-nä-sōⁿ-gü\ [F] : everyone to his taste

**châ·teau en Es·pagne** \shä-tō-äⁿ-nes-pän'\ [F] : castle in Spain : a visionary project

**cher·chez la femme** \sher-shā-lä-fäm\ [F] : look for the woman

**che sa·rà, sa·rà** \ˌkā-sä-ˌrä sä-'rä\ [It] : what will be, will be

**che·val de ba·taille** \shə-väl-də-bä-tä'\ [F] : warhorse : argument constantly relied on : favorite subject

**oo·gi·to, er·go sum** \'kō-gi-ˌtō 'er-gō-'sùm\ [L] : I think, therefore I exist

**co·mé·die hu·maine** \kò-mā-dē-ᵫ-men\ [F] : human comedy : the whole variety of human life

**comme ci, comme ça** \kóm-sē kóm-sä\ [F] : so-so

**com·pa·gnon de voy·age** \kōⁿ-pä-nyōⁿ-də-vwä-yäzh\ [F] : traveling companion

**compte ren·du** \kōⁿt-räⁿ-dᵫ\ [F] : report (as of proceedings in an investigation)

**con·cor·dia dis·cors** \kòn-'kòr-dē-ä-'dis-ˌkòrs\ [L] : discordant harmony

**con·fes·sio fi·dei** \kòn-'fe-sē-ō-'fi-dē-ˌē\ [L] : confession of faith

**cor·rup·tio op·ti·mi pes·si·ma** \kò-'rùp-tē-ˌō-'äp-ti-ˌmē-'pe-si-ˌmä\ [L] : the corruption of the best is the worst of all

**coup de maî·tre** \küd-metrᵉ, kü-də-\ [F] : masterstroke

**coup d'es·sai** \kü-dä-se\ [F] : experiment : trial

**coûte que coûte** \küt-kə-küt\ [F] : cost what it may

**cre·do quia ab·sur·dum est** \ˌkrā-dō-'kwē-ä-äp-ˌsùr-dùm-'est\ [L] : I believe it because it is absurd

**cres·cit eun·do** \ˌkres-kit-'eùn-dō\ [L] : it grows as it goes — motto of New Mexico

**crise de nerfs** or **crise des nerfs** \krēz-də-ner\ [F] : crisis of nerves : nervous collapse : hysterical fit

**cuj·us re·gio, ej·us re·li·gio** \ˌkü-yùs-'re-gē-ˌō ˌe-yùs-re-'li-gē-ˌō\ [L] : whose region, his or her religion : subjects are to accept the religion of their ruler

**cum gra·no sa·lis** \ˌkùm-ˌgrä-nō 'sä-lis\ [L] : with a grain of salt

**cus·tos mo·rum** \ˌkùs-tōs-'mòr-ùm\ [L] : guardian of manners or morals : censor

**d'ac·cord** \dä-kòr\ [F] : in accord : agreed

**dame d'hon·neur** \däm-dò-nœr\ [F] : lady-in-waiting

**dam·nant quod non in·tel·li·gunt** \'däm-ˌnänt-ˌkwòd-ˌnōn-in-'te-li-ˌgùnt\ [L] : they condemn what they do not understand

**de bonne grâce** \də-bòn-gräs\ [F] : with good grace : willingly

**de gus·ti·bus non est dis·pu·tan·dum** \dä-'gùs-tə-ˌbùs-ˌnōn-ˌest dis-pù-'tän-ˌdùm\ [L] : there is no disputing about tastes

**Dei gra·tia** \ˌde-ˌē-'grä-tē-ˌä\ [L] : by the grace of God

**de in·te·gro** \dä-'in-te-ˌgrō\ [L] : anew : afresh

**de·len·da est Car·tha·go** \dā-'len-dä-ˌest-kär-'tä-gō\ [L] : Carthage must be destroyed

**de mal en pis** \də-mä-läⁿ-pē\ [F] : from bad to worse

**de mi·ni·mis non cu·rat lex** \dā-'mi-ni-ˌmēs-ˌnōn-ˌkü-ˌrät-'leks\ [L] : the law takes no account of trifles

**de mor·tu·is nil ni·si bo·num** \dā-'mòr-tù-,ēs-,nēl-,nĭ-sē-'bò-,núm\ [L] : of the dead (say) nothing but good

**de nos jours** \də-nō-zhür\ [F] : of our time : contemporary — used postpositively esp. after a proper name

**Deo fa·ven·te** \,dā-ō-fä-'ven-tā\ [L] : with God's favor

**Deo gra·ti·as** \,dā-ō-'grä-tē-,äs\ [L] : thanks (be) to God

**de pro·fun·dis** \,dā-prō-'fún-dēs\ [L] : out of the depths

**de·si·pe·re in lo·co** \dā-'si-pe-rā-in-'lò-kō\ [L] : to indulge in trifling at the proper time

**de te fa·bu·la nar·ra·tur** \,dā-,tā-,fä-bù-lä-nä-'rä-,túr\ [L] : the story applies to you

**De·us ab·scon·di·tus** \,dā-ùs-,äp-'skòn-di-,tùs\ [L] : hidden God : God unknowable by the human mind

**De·us vult** \,dā-ùs-'wúlt\ [L] : God wills it — rallying cry of the First Crusade

**di·es fau·stus** \,dē-,äs-'faù-stùs\ [L] : lucky day

**dies in·fau·stus** \-'in-,faù-stùs\ [L] : unlucky day

**dies irae** \-'ē-,rī, -,rā\ [L] : day of wrath — used of the Judgment Day

**Dieu et mon droit** \dyœ-ā-móⁿ-drwä\ [F] : God and my right — motto on the British royal arms

**Dieu vous garde** \dyœ-vü-gärd\ [F] : God keep you

**di·ri·go** \'dē-ri-,gō\ [L] : I direct — motto of Maine

**dis ali·ter vi·sum** \,dēs-,ä-li-ter-'wē-,sùm\ [L] : the Gods decreed otherwise

**di·tat De·us** \,dē-,tät-'dā-,ùs\ [L] : God enriches — motto of Arizona

**di·vi·de et im·pe·ra** \'dē-wi-,de-,et-'im-pe-,rä\ [L] : divide and rule

**do·cen·do dis·ci·mus** \dò-,ken-dō-'dis-ki-,mùs\ [L] : we learn by teaching

**Do·mi·ne, di·ri·ge nos** \'dò-mi-,ne 'dē-ri-ge-'nōs\ [L] : Lord, direct us — motto of the City of London

**Do·mi·nus vo·bis·cum** \,dò-mi-,nús-wō-'bēs-,kúm\ [L] : the Lord be with you

**dul·ce et de·co·rum est pro pa·tria mo·ri** \,dùl-,ke-et-de-'kòr-ùm-,est-prō-,pä-trē-,ä-'mò-,rē\ [L] : it is sweet and seemly to die for one's country

**dum spi·ro, spe·ro** \dùm-'spē-rō 'spä-rō\ [L] : while I breathe, I hope — one of the mottoes of South Carolina

**dum vi·vi·mus vi·va·mus** \dùm-'wē-wē-,mùs-wē-'wä-mùs\ [L] : while we live, let us live

**d'un cer·tain âge** \dœⁿ-ser-te-näzh\ [F] : of a certain age : no longer young

**dux fe·mi·na fac·ti** \,dúks-,fā-mi-nä-'fäk-,tē\ [L] : a woman was leader of the exploit

**ec·ce sig·num** \,e-ke-'sig-,núm\ [L] : behold the sign : look at the proof

**e con·tra·rio** \,ā-kòn-'trär-ē-,ō\ [L] : on the contrary

**écra·sez l'in·fâme** \ā-krä-zä-laⁿ-'fäm\ [F] : crush the infamous thing

**eheu fu·ga·ces la·bun·tur an·ni** \,ā-,heú-fù-'gä,kās-lä-'bún-,tùr-'ä-,nē\ [L] : alas! the fleeting years glide on

**ein' fes·te Burg ist un·ser Gott** \in-,fes-tə-'bùrk-ist-,ùn-zər-'gót\ [G] : a mighty fortress is our God

**em·bar·ras de choix** \äⁿ-bä-rä-də-shwä\ or **embarras du choix** \-dœ-shwä\ [F] : embarrassing variety of choice

**em·bar·ras de ri·chesses** or **embarras de ri·chesse** \äⁿ-bä-räd-rē-shes, -rä-də-\ [F] : embarrassing surplus of riches : confusing abundance

**en ami** \äⁿ-nä-mē\ [F] : as a friend

**en ef·fet** \äⁿ-nä-fe\ [F] : in fact : indeed

**en fa·mille** \äⁿ-fä-mē\ [F] : in or with one's family : at home : informally

**en·fant ché·ri** \äⁿ-fäⁿ-shä-rē\ [F] : loved or pampered child : one that is highly favored

**en·fant gâ·té** \äⁿ-fäⁿ-gä-tā\ [F] : spoiled child

**en·fants per·dus** \äⁿ-fäⁿ-per-dœ\ [F] : lost children : soldiers sent to a dangerous post

**en·fin** \äⁿ-faⁿ\ [F] : in conclusion : in a word

**en gar·çon** \äⁿ-gär-sōⁿ\ [F] : as or like a bachelor

**en garde** \äⁿ-gärd\ [F] : on guard

**en plein air** \äⁿ-ple-ner\ [F] : in the open air

**en plein jour** \äⁿ-plaⁿ-zhür\ [F] : in broad day

**en règle** \äⁿ-reglᵃ\ [F] : in order : in due form

**en re·tard** \äⁿr-(ə-)tär\ [F] : behind time : late

**en re·traite** \äⁿr-(ə-)tret\ [F] : in retreat : in retirement

**en re·vanche** \äⁿr-(ə-)väⁿsh\ [F] : in return : in compensation

**en·se pe·tit pla·ci·dam sub li·ber·ta·te qui·e·tem** \,en-se-,pe-tit-'plä-ki-,däm-,sùb-,lē-ber-,tä-te-kwē-'ä-,tem\ [L] : with the sword she seeks calm repose under liberty : by the sword we seek peace, but peace only under liberty — motto of Massachusetts

**eo ip·so** \ā-ō-'ip-(,)sō\ [L] : by that itself : by that fact alone

**épa·ter le bour·geois** \ā-pä-tä-lə-bür-zhwä\ or **épater les bour·geois** \-lā-bür-\ [F] : to shock the middle classes

**e plu·ri·bus unum** \,ē-,plùr-ə-bəs-'(y)ü-nəm, ,ä-,plùr-i-bùs-'ü-núm\ [L] : one out of many — used on the Great Seal of the U.S. and on several U.S. coins

**ep·pur si muo·ve** \āp-,pür-sē-'mwò-vā\ [It] : and yet it does move — attributed to Galileo after recanting his assertion of the earth's motion

**Erin go bragh** \ˌer-ən-gə-'brȯ, -gō-'brä\ [Ir go brách or go bráth, lit., till doomsday] : Ireland forever

**er·ra·re hu·ma·num est** \e-'rär-ä-hü-ˌmä-nùm-'est\ [L] : to err is human

**es·prit de l'es·ca·lier** \es-prēd-les-kä-lyä\ or **es·prit d'es·ca·lier** \-prē-des-\ [F] : wit of the staircase : repartee thought of only too late

**es·se quam vi·de·ri** \'e-sā-ˌkwäm-wi-'dā-rē\ [L] : to be rather than to seem — motto of North Carolina

**est mo·dus in re·bus** \est-'mō-ˌdùs-in-'rä-ˌbùs\ [L] : there is a proper measure in things, i.e., the golden mean should always be observed

**es·to per·pe·tua** \'es-ˌtō-per-'pe-tù-ˌä\ [L] : may she endure forever — motto of Idaho

**et hoc ge·nus om·ne** \et-ˌhōk-ˌge-nùs-'ȯm-ne\ or **et id genus omne** \et-ˌid-\ [L] : and everything of this kind

**et sic de si·mi·li·bus** \et-ˌsēk-dä-si-'mi-li-bùs\ [L] : and so of like things

**et tu Bru·te** \et-'tü-'brü-te\ [L] : thou too, Brutus — exclamation attributed to Julius Caesar on seeing his friend Brutus among his assassins

**eu·re·ka** \yù-'rē-kä\ [Gk] : I have found it — motto of California

**Ewig–Weib·li·che** \ˌā-vik-'vīp-li-kə\ [G] : eternal feminine

**ex·al·té** \eg-zäl-tā\ [F] : emotionally excited or elated : fanatic

**ex ani·mo** \eks-'ä-ni-ˌmō\ [L] : from the heart : sincerely

**ex·cel·si·or** \ik-'sel-sē-ər, eks-'kel-sē-ˌȯr\ [L] : still higher — motto of New York

**ex·cep·tio pro·bat re·gu·lam de re·bus non ex·cep·tis** \eks-'kep-tē-ˌō-ˌprō-bät-'rä-gù-ˌläm-dä-'rä-ˌbùs-ˌnōn-eks-'kep-ˌtēs\ [L] : an exception establishes the rule as to things not excepted

**ex·cep·tis ex·ci·pi·en·dis** \eks-'kep-ˌtēs-eks-ˌki-pē-'en-ˌdēs\ [L] : with the proper or necessary exceptions

**ex·i·tus ac·ta pro·bat** \'ek-sī-ˌtùs-ˌäk-tä-'prȯ-ˌbät\ [L] : the outcome justifies the deed

**ex li·bris** \eks-'le-bris\ [L] : from the books of — used on bookplates

**ex me·ro mo·tu** \eks-ˌmer-ō-'mō-tü\ [L] : out of mere impulse : of one's own accord

**ex ne·ces·si·ta·te rei** \eks-ne-ˌke-si-'tä-te-'ra(-ˌē)\ [L] : from the necessity of the case

**ex ni·hi·lo ni·hil fit** \eks-'ni-hi-ˌlō-ˌni-ˌhil-'fit\ [L] : from nothing nothing is produced

**ex pe·de Her·cu·lem** \eks-ˌpe-de-'her-kù-ˌlem\ [L] : from the foot (we may judge of the size) Hercules : from a part we may judge of the whole

**ex·per·to cre·de** \eks-ˌper-tō-'krä-de\ or

**experto cre·di·te** \-'krä-di-ˌte\ [L] : believe one who has had experience

**ex un·gue le·o·nem** \eks-'ùn-gwe-le-'ō-ˌnem\ [L] : from the claw (we may judge of) the lion : from a part we may judge of the whole

**ex vi ter·mi·ni** \eks-ˌwē-'ter-mə-ˌnē\ [L] : from the force of the term

**fa·ci·le prin·ceps** \ˌfä-ki-le-'prin-ˌkeps\ [L] : easily first

**fa·ci·lis de·scen·sus Aver·no** \'fä-ki-ˌlis-dā-ˌskän-ˌsùs-ä-'wer-nō\ or **facilis descensus Aver·ni** \-(ˌ)nē\ [L] : the descent to Avernus is easy : the road to evil is easy

**fa·çon de par·ler** \fä-sōⁿ-də-pär-lā\ [F] : manner of speaking : figurative or conventional expression

**fas est et ab ho·ste do·ce·ri** \fäs-'est-et-äb-'hȯ-ste-dō-'kä-(ˌ)rē\ [L] : it is right to learn even from an enemy

**Fa·ta vi·am in·ve·ni·ent** \ˌfä-tä-'wē-ˌäm-in-'we-nē-ˌent\ [L] : the Fates will find a way

**fat·ti mas·chii, pa·ro·le fe·mi·ne** \ˌfät-tē-'mäs-ˌkē-pä-ˌro-la-'fä-mē-ˌnä\ [It] : deeds are males, words are females : deeds are more effective than words — motto of Maryland, where it is generally interpreted as meaning "manly deeds, womanly words"

**taux·bon·homme** \fō-bȯ-nȯm\ [F] : pretended good fellow

**faux–naïf** \fō-nä-ēf\ [F] : spuriously or affectedly childlike : artfully simple

**fe·lix cul·pa** \ˌfä-liks-'kùl-pä\ [L] : fortunate fault — used esp. of original sin in relation to the consequent coming of Christ

**femme de cham·bre** \fäm-də-shä"br°\ [F] : chambermaid : lady's maid

**fe·sti·na len·te** \fe-ˌstē-nä-'len-ˌtä\ [L] : make haste slowly

**feux d'ar·ti·fice** \fœ-där-tē-fēs\ [F] : fireworks : display of wit

**fi·at ju·sti·tia, ru·at cae·lum** \ˌfē-ät-yùs-'ti-tē-ä-ˌrù-ˌät-'kī-ˌlùm\ [L] : let justice be done though the heavens fall

**fi·at lux** \ˌfē-ät-'lùks\ [L] : let there be light

**Fi·dei De·fen·sor** \ˌfi-de-ˌē-dā-'fän-ˌsȯr\ [L] : Defender of the Faith — a title of the sovereigns of England

**fille de cham·bre** \fē-də-shä"br°\ [F] : lady's maid

**fille d'hon·neur** \fē-dȯ-nœr\ [F] : maid of honor

**fi·nem re·spi·ce** \ˌfē-ˌnem-'rä-spi-ˌke\ [L] : consider the end

**fi·nis co·ro·nat opus** \ˌfē-nis-kȯ-ˌrō-ˌnät-'ō-ˌpùs\ [L] : the end crowns the work

**flo·re·at** \'flō-re-ˌät\ [L] : may (he, she, or it) flourish — usu. followed by a name

**fluc·tu·at nec mer·gi·tur** \'flùk-tù-ˌät-ˌnek-'mer-gi-ˌtùr\ [L] : it is tossed by the waves but does not sink — motto of Paris

**fo·lie de gran·deur** or **fo·lie des gran·deurs** \fȯ-lē-də-grä<sup>n</sup>-dœr\ [F] : delusion of greatness : megalomania

**force de frappe** \fȯrs-də-fräp\ [F] : a force equipped to deal a retaliatory blow

**fors·an et haec olim me·mi·nis·se ju·va·bit** \ˈfȯr-ˌsän-ˌet-ˈhīk-ˌō-lim-ˌme-mi-ˈni-se-yu̇-ˈwä-bit\ [L] : perhaps this too will be a pleasure to look back on one day

**for·tes for·tu·na ju·vat** \ˈfȯr-ˌtās-fȯr-ˌtü-nä-ˈyu̇-ˌwät\ [L] : fortune favors the brave

**fron·ti nul·la fi·des** \ˈfrȯn-ˌtē-ˌnu̇-lä-ˈfi-ˌdās\ [L] : no reliance can be placed on appearance

**fu·it Ili·um** \ˈfu̇-it-ˈi-lē-u̇m\ [L] : Troy has been (i.e., is no more)

**fu·ror lo·quen·di** \ˌfu̇r-ˌȯr-lȯ-ˈkwen-(ˌ)dē\ [L] : rage for speaking

**furor po·e·ti·cus** \-ˌpȯ-ˈā-ti-ku̇s\ [L] : poetic frenzy

**furor scri·ben·di** \-skrē-ˈben-(ˌ)dē\ [L] : rage for writing

**Gal·li·ce** \ˈgä-li-ˌke\ [L] : in French : after the French manner

**gar·çon d'hon·neur** \gär-sō<sup>n</sup>-dȯ-nœr\ [F] : bridegroom's attendant

**garde du corps** \gärd-du̇-kȯr\ [F] : bodyguard

**gar·dez la foi** \gär-dā-lä-fwä\ [F] : keep faith

**gau·de·a·mus igi·tur** \ˌgau̇-dē-ˈä-mu̇s-ˈi-gi-ˌtu̇r\ [L] : let us then be merry

**gens d'é·glise** \zhä<sup>n</sup>-dā-glēz\ [F] : church people : clergy

**gens de guerre** \zhä<sup>n</sup>-də-ger\ [F] : military people : soldiery

**gens du monde** \zhä<sup>n</sup>-du̇-mō<sup>n</sup>d\ [F] : people of the world : fashionable people

**gno·thi se·au·ton** \ˈgnō-thē-ˌse-au̇-ˈtȯn\ [Gk] : know thyself

**goût de ter·roir** \gü-də-te-rwär\ [F] : taste of the earth

**grand monde** \grä<sup>n</sup>-mō<sup>n</sup>d\ [F] : great world : high society

**gros·so mo·do** \ˈgrȯs-(ˌ)sō-ˈmō-(ˌ)dō\ [It] : roughly

**guerre à ou·trance** \ger-ä-ü-trä<sup>n</sup>s\ [F] : war to the uttermost

**gu·ten Tag** \ˌgü-tən-ˈtäk\ [G] : good day

**has·ta la vis·ta** \ˌäs-tə-lä-ˈvēs-tə\ [Sp] : good-bye

**haute vul·ga·ri·sa·tion** \ōt-vu̇l-gä-rē-zä-syō<sup>n</sup>\ [F] : high popularization : effective presentation of a difficult subject to a general audience

**hic et nunc** \ˈhēk-et-ˈnu̇ŋk\ [L] : here and now

**hic et ubi·que** \ˌhēk-et-u̇-ˈbē-kwe\ [L] : here and everywhere

**hic ja·cet** \ˈhik-ˈjä-sət, ˈhēk-ˈyä-ket\ [L] : here lies — used preceding a name on a tombstone

**hinc il·lae la·cri·mae** \ˌhiŋk-ˌi-ˌlī-ˈlä-kri-ˌmī\ [L] : hence those tears

**hoc age** \ˈhōk-ˈä-ge\ [L] : do this : apply yourself to what you are about

**homme d'af·faires** \ȯm-dä-fer\ [F] : man of business : business agent

**homme d'es·prit** \ȯm-des-prē\ [F] : man of wit

**homme moyen sen·suel** \ȯm-mwä-ya<sup>n</sup>-sä<sup>n</sup>-swᵉel\ [F] : the average nonintellectual man

**ho·mo sum: hu·ma·ni nil a me ali·e·num pu·to** \ˈhō-mō-ˌsu̇m hü-ˌmä-nē-ˈnēl-ä-ˌmä-ˌä-lē-ˈä-nu̇m-ˈpu̇-tō\ [L] : I am a human being: I regard nothing of human concern as foreign to my interests

**ho·ni soit qui mal y pense** \ȯ-nē-swä-kē-mäl-ē-pä<sup>n</sup>s\ [F] : shamed be he who thinks evil of it — motto of the Order of the Garter

**hu·ma·num est er·ra·re** \hü-ˌmä-nu̇m-ˌest-e-ˈrär-ä\ [L] : to err is human

**ich dien** \ik-ˈdēn\ [G] : I serve — motto of the Prince of Wales

**ici on parle fran·çais** \ē-sē-ō<sup>n</sup>-pärl-frä<sup>n</sup>-se\ [F] : French is spoken here

**idées re·çues** \ē-dār-(ə-)su̇e\ [F] : received ideas : conventional opinions

**id est** \id-ˈest\ [L] : that is

**ig·no·ran·tia ju·ris ne·mi·nem ex·cu·sat** \ˌig-nȯ-ˌrän-tē-ä-ˈyu̇r-is-ˈnä-mi-ˌnem-eks-ˈkü-ˌsät\ [L] : ignorance of the law excuses no one

**ig·no·tum per ig·no·ti·us** \ig-ˈnō-tu̇m-ˌper-ig-ˈnō-tē-ˌu̇s\ [L] : (explaining) the unknown by means of the more unknown

**il faut cul·ti·ver no·tre jar·din** \ēl-fō-ku̇l-tē-vā-nȯt-zhär-da<sup>n</sup>, -nȯ-trə-zhär-\ [F] : we must cultivate our garden : we must tend to our own affairs

**in ae·ter·num** \ˌin-ī-ˈter-ˌnu̇m\ [L] : forever

**in du·bio** \in-ˈdu̇-bē-ˌō\ [L] : in doubt : undetermined

**in fu·tu·ro** \ˌin-fu̇-ˈtu̇r-ō\ [L] : in the future

**in hoc sig·no vin·ces** \in-hōk-ˈsig-nō-ˈwin-ˌkās\ [L] : by this sign (the Cross) you will conquer

**in li·mi·ne** \in-ˈlē-mi-ˌne\ [L] : on the threshold : at the beginning

**in om·nia pa·ra·tus** \in-ˈȯm-nē-ä-pä-ˈrä-ˌtu̇s\ [L] : ready for all things

**in par·ti·bus in·fi·de·li·um** \in-ˈpär-ti-ˌbu̇s-ˌin-fi-ˈdä-lē-ˌu̇m\ [L] : in the regions of the infidels — used of a titular bishop having no diocesan jurisdiction, usu. in non-Christian countries

**in prae·sen·ti** \ˌin-prī-ˈsen-ˌtē\ [L] : at the present time

**in sae·cu·la sae·cu·lo·rum** \in-ˈsī-ku̇-ˌlä-ˌsī-ku̇-ˈlȯr-u̇m, -ˈsä-ku̇-ˌlä-ˌsä-\ [L] : for ages of ages : forever and ever

**in·shal·lah** \ˌin-shä-ˈlä\ [Ar in shā' Allāh] : if Allah wills : God willing

**in·te·ger vi·tae sce·le·ris·que pu·rus** \,in-te-,ger-'we-,ti-,ske-le-'is-kwe-'pü rüs\ [L] : upright of life and free from wickedness

**in·ter nos** \,in-ter-'nōs\ [L] : between ourselves

**in·tra mu·ros** \,in-trä-'mü-,rōs\ [L] : within the walls

**in utrum·que pa·ra·tus** \,in-ü-'trùm-kwe-pä-'rä-,tùs\ [L] : prepared for either (event)

**in·ve·nit** \in-'wā-nit\ [L] : he or she devised it

**in vi·no ve·ri·tas** \in-wē-nō-'wā-ri-,tās\ [L] : there is truth in wine

**ip·sis·si·ma ver·ba** \ip-'si si-,mä-'wer-,bä\ [L] : the very words

**ira fu·ror bre·vis est** \,ē-rä-'für-,ôr-'bre-wis-,est\ [L] : anger is a brief madness

**j'ac·cuse** \zhä-kuez\ [F] : I accuse : bitter denunciation

**jac·ta alea est** \'yäk-,tä-,ä-lē-,ä-'est\ [L] : the die is cast

**j'adoube** \zhä-düb\ [F] : I adjust — used in chess when touching a piece without intending to move it

**ja·nu·is clau·sis** \,yä-nù-,ēs-'klaù-,sēs\ [L] : behind closed doors

**je main·tien·drai** \zhə-man-tyä^n-,drā\ [F] : I will maintain — motto of the Netherlands

**jeu de mots** \zhœd-mō, zhœ-də-\ [F] : play on words : pun

**Jo·an·nes est no·men eius** \yō-'ä-näs-est-,nō-men-'ā-yùs\ [L] : John is his name — motto of Puerto Rico

**jour·nal in·time** \zhür-näl-a^n-tēm\ [F] : intimate journal : private diary

**jus di·vi·num** \,yüs-di-'wē-,nùm\ [L] : divine law

**jus·ti·tia om·ni·bus** \,yùs-,ti-tē-,ä-'ōm-ni-,bùs\ [L] : justice for all — motto of the District of Columbia

**j'y suis, j'y reste** \zhē-swᵉē zhē-rest\ [F] : here I am, here I remain

**Kin·der, Kir·che, Küche** \'kin-dər 'kir-kə 'kœ-kə\ [G] : children, church, kitchen

**la belle dame sans mer·ci** \lä-bel-däm-sä^n-mer-sē\ [F] : the beautiful lady without mercy

**la·bo·ra·re est ora·re** \'lä-bō-,rär-ā-,est-'ō-,rär-ä\ [L] : to work is to pray

**la·bor om·nia vin·cit** \'lä-,bôr-,ôm-nē-,ä-'win-kit\ [L] : labor conquers all things — motto of Oklahoma

**la·cri·mae re·rum** \,lä-kri-,mī-'ra-,rùm\ [L] : tears for things : pity for misfortune; *also* : tears in things : tragedy of life

**lais·sez–al·ler** *or* **lais·ser–al·ler** \le-sā-ä-lā\ [F] : letting go : lack of restraint

**lap·sus ca·la·mi** \,läp-sùs-'kä-lä-,mē\ [L] : slip of the pen

**lap·sus lin·guae** \,-'liŋ-,gwī\ [L] : slip of the tongue

**la reine le veut** \lä-ren-lə-vœ\ [F] : the queen wills it

**la·scia·te ogni spe·ran·za, voi ch'en·tra·te** \läsh-'shä-tä-,ō-nᵉspä-'rän-tsä ,vō-ē-kän-'trä-tä\ [It] : abandon all hope, ye who enter

**lau·da·tor tem·po·ris ac·ti** \laù-'dä-,tôr-,tem-pó-ris-'äk-,tē\ [L] : one who praises past times

**laus Deo** \laùs-'dā-ō\ [L] : praise (be) to God

**Le·bens·welt** \'lā-bəns-,velt\ [G] : life world : world of lived experience

**le cœur a ses rai·sons que la rai·son ne con·naît point** \lə-kœr-ä-sā-re-zō^n-lä re-zō^n-kó-ne-pwa^n\ [F] : the heart has its reasons that reason knows nothing of

**le roi est mort, vive le roi** \lə-rwä-e-mór vēv-lə-rwä\ [F] : the king is dead, long live the king

**le roi le veut** \lə-rwä-lə-vœ\ [F] : the king wills it

**le style, c'est l'homme** \lə-stēl se-lóm\ [F] : the style is the man

**l'état, c'est moi** \lä-tä se-mwä\ [F] : the state, it is I

**l'étoile du nord** \lā-twäl-due-nór\ [F] : the star of the north — motto of Minnesota

**Lie·der·kranz** \'lē-dər-,kränts\ [G] : wreath of songs : German singing society

**lit·tera scrip·ta ma·net** \'li-te-,rä-,skrip-tä-'mä-net\ [L] : the written letter abides

**lo·cus in quo** \,lō-kùs-in-'kwō\ [L] : place in which

**l'union fait la force** \lue-nyō^n-fe-lä-fórs\ [F] : union makes strength — motto of Belgium

**lu·sus na·tu·rae** \,lü-sùs-nä-'tùr-ē, -'tùr-,ī\ [L] : freak of nature

**ma foi** \mä-fwä\ [F] : my faith! : indeed

**mag·na est ve·ri·tas et prae·va·le·bit** \,mag-nä-,est-'wä-ri-,tās-et-,prē-wä-'lā-bit\ [L] : truth is mighty and will prevail

**ma·ha·lo** \'mä-hä-lō\ [Hawaiian] : thank you

**ma·lade ima·gi·naire** \mä-läd-ē-mä-zhē-ner\ [F] : imaginary invalid : hypochondriac

**mal de siècle** \mäl-də-syekl^ᵃ\ [F] : illness from worldly concerns : world-weariness

**ma·lis avi·bus** \,mä-,lēs-'ä-wi-,bùs\ [L] : under evil auspices

**man spricht Deutsch** \män-shprikt-'dòich\ [G] : German spoken

**ma·riage de con·ve·nance** \mä-ryäzh-də-kō^n-v-nä^ns\ [F] : marriage of convenience

**ma·ri com·plai·sant** \mä-rē-kō^n-ple-zä^n\ [F] : complaisant husband : cuckold who accepts his wife's infidelity

**mau·vaise honte** \mō-vez-ō^nt\ [F] : bad shame : bashfulness

**mau·vais quart d'heure** \mō-ve-kär-dœr\ [F] : bad quarter hour : an uncomfortable though brief experience

**me·dio tu·tis·si·mus ibis** \'me-dē-,ō-tü-ti·si·mùs·'ē·bis\ [L] : you will go most safely by the middle course

me ju·di·ce \mā-'yü-di-ke\ [L] : I being judge : in my judgment

mens sa·na in cor·po·re sa·no \māns-'sä-nä-in-,kȯr-pȯ-re-'sä-nō\ [L] : a sound mind in a sound body

me·um et tu·um \,mē-əm-,et-'tü-əm, ,me-ùm-,et-'tü-ùm\ [L] : mine and thine : distinction of private property

mi·ra·bi·le vi·su \mē-,rä-bi-lā-'wē-sü\ [L] : wonderful to behold

mi·ra·bil·ia \,mir-ə-'bi-lē-,ä\ [L] : wonders : miracles

mœurs \mœr(s)\ [F] : mores : attitudes, customs, and manners of a society

mo·le ru·it sua \'mō-le-'rü-it,sü-ä\ [L] : it collapses from its own bigness

monde \mōⁿd\ [F] : world : fashionable world : society

mon·ta·ni sem·per li·be·ri \mȯn-'tä-nē-,sem-per-'lē-be-,rē\ [L] : mountaineers are always free — motto of West Virginia

mo·nu·men·tum ae·re per·en·ni·us \,mō-nü-'men-tùm-,ī-re-pe-'re-nē-ùs\ [L] : a monument more lasting than bronze — used of an immortal work of art or literature

mo·re suo \,mȯr-ā-'sü-ō\ [L] : in his (or her) own manner

mo·ri·tu·ri te sa·lu·ta·mus \,mȯr-i-'tùr-ē-,tā-,sä-lü-'tä-mùs\ or morituri te sa·lu·tant \-'sä-lü-,tänt\ [L] : we (or those) who are about to die salute thee

mul·tum in par·vo \,mùl-tùm-in-'pär-vō, -'pär-wō\ [L] : much in little

mu·ta·to no·mi·ne de te fa·bu·la nar·ra·tur \mù-,tä-tō-'nō-mi-ne-,dā-,tā-'fä-bù-lä-nä-'rä-,túr\ [L] : with the name changed the story applies to you

mys·te·ri·um tre·men·dum \mi-'ster-ē-,ùm-tre-'men-dùm\ [L] : overwhelming mystery

na·tu·ram ex·pel·las fur·ca, ta·men us·que re·cur·ret \nä-'tü-,räm-ek-,spe-läs-'fùr-,kä ,tä-men-'ùs-kwe-re-'kùr-et\ [L] : you may drive nature out with a pitchfork, but she will keep coming back

na·tu·ra non fa·cit sal·tum \nä-'tü-rä-,nōn-,fä-kit-'säl,tùm\ [L] : nature makes no leap

ne ce·de ma·lis \nä-,kā-de-'mä-,lēs\ [L] : yield not to misfortunes

ne·mo me im·pu·ne la·ces·sit \'nä-mō-'mā-im,-pü-nä-lä-'ke-sit\ [L] : no one attacks me with impunity — motto of Scotland and of the Order of the Thistle

ne quid ni·mis \,nä-,kwid-'ni-mis\ [L] : not anything in excess

n'est–ce pas? \nes-pä\ [F] : isn't it so?

nicht wahr? \nikt-'vär\ [G] : not true? : isn't it so?

nil ad·mi·ra·ri \'nēl-,äd-mi-'rär-ē\ [L] : to be excited by nothing : equanimity

nil de·spe·ran·dum \'nēl,dā-spā-'rän-dúm\ [L] : never despair

nil si·ne nu·mi·ne \'nēl-,si-nä-'nü-mi-ne\ [L] : nothing without the divine will — motto of Colorado

n'im·porte \naⁿ-'pȯrt\ [F] : it's no matter

no·lens vo·lens \,nō-,lenz-'vō-,lenz\ [L] : unwilling (or) willing : willy-nilly

non om·nia pos·su·mus om·nes \nōn-'ȯm-nē-ä-,pȯ-sù-mùs-'ȯm-,näs\ [L] : we can't all (do) all things

non sans droict \nōⁿ-säⁿ-drwä\ [OF] : not without right — motto on Shakespeare's coat of arms

non sum qua·lis eram \,nōn-,sùm-,kwä-lis-'er-,äm\ [L] : I am not what I used to be

nos·ce te ip·sum \,nȯs-ke-,tā-'ip-,sùm\ [L] : know thyself

nos·tal·gie de la boue \nȯs-täl-zhēd-lä-bü, -zhē-də-\ [F] : yearning for the mud : attraction to what is unworthy, crude, or degrading

nous avons chan·gé tout ce·la \nü-zä-vōⁿ-shäⁿ-zhā-,tü-sə-lä\ [F] : we have changed all that

nous ver·rons ce que nous ver·rons \nü-ve-rōⁿs-kə-nü-ve-rōⁿ, -rōⁿ-sə-kə-\ [F] : we shall see what we shall see

no·vus ho·mo \,nō-wùs-'hȯ-mō\ [L] : new man : man newly ennobled : upstart

novus or·do se·clo·rum \-'ȯr-,dō-sā-'klȯr-úm\ [L] : a new cycle of the ages — motto on the reverse of the Great Seal of the United States

nu·gae \'nü-,gī\ [L] : trifles

nuit blanche \nwē-blänⁿsh\ [F] : white night : a sleepless night

nyet \'nyet\ [Russ] : no

ob·iit \'ȯ-bē-,it\ [L] : he or she died

ob·scu·rum per ob·scu·ri·us \ȯb-'skyùr-ùm-,per-ȯb-'skyùr-ē-ùs\ [L] : (explaining) the obscure by means of the more obscure

ode·rint dum me·tu·ant \'ō-de-,rint-,dùm-me-tú-,änt\ [L] : let them hate, so long as they fear

odi et amo \'ō-,dē-et-'ä-(,)mō\ [L] : I hate and I love

omer·tà \ȯ-'mer-tä\ [It] : conspiracy of silence

om·ne ig·no·tum pro mag·ni·fi·co \,ȯm-ne-ig-'nō-,tùm-prō-mäg-'ni-fi-,kō\ [L] : everything unknown (is taken) as grand : the unknown tends to be exaggerated in importance or difficulty

om·nia mu·tan·tur, nos et mu·ta·mur in il·lis \,ȯm-nē-ä-mü-'tän-,túr ,nȯs-et-mü-,tä-mùr-in-'i-,lēs\ [L] : all things are changing, and we are changing with them

om·nia vin·cit amor \'ȯm-nē-ä-'wiⁿ-kit-'ä-,mȯr\ [L] : love conquers all

onus pro·ban·di \ō-nùs-prō-'ban-,dī, -dē\ [L] : burden of proof

ora pro no·bis \ō-rä-prō-'nō-,bēs\ [L] : pray for us

**ore ro·tun·do** \ˌōr-ē-rō-'tən-dō\ [L] : with round mouth : eloquently

**oro y pla·ta** \ˌōr-o-e-'plä-tə\ [Sp] : gold and silver — motto of Montana

**o tem·po·ra! o mo·res!** \ō-'tem-pò-rä ō-'mō-ˌräs\ [L] : oh the times! oh the manners!

**oti·um cum dig·ni·ta·te** \'ō-tē-ˌùm-kùm-ˌdig-ni-'tä-te\ [L] : leisure with dignity

**où sont les neiges d'an·tan?** \ü-sōⁿ-lä-nezh-däⁿ-täⁿ\ [F] : where are the snows of yesteryear?

**outre—mer** \ütrᵒ-'mer\ [F] : overseas : distant lands

**pal·li·da Mors** \ˌpä-li-dä-'mōrz\ [L] : pale Death

**pa·nem et cir·cen·ses** \'pä-ˌnem-et-kir-'kän-ˌsäs\ [L] : bread and circuses : provision of the means of life and recreation by government to appease discontent

**pan·ta rhei** \ˌpän-ˌtä-'rā\ [Gk] : all things are in flux

**par avance** \pär-ä-väⁿs\ [F] : in advance : by anticipation

**par avion** \pär-ä-vyoⁿ\ [F] : by airplane — used on airmail

**par ex·em·ple** \pär-äg-zäⁿplᵃ\ [F] : for example

**pars pro to·to** \'pärs-(ˌ)prō-'tō-(ˌ)tō\ [L] : part (taken) for the whole

**par·tu·ri·unt mon·tes, nas·ce·tur ri·di·cu·lus mus** \pär-'tùr-ē-ˌùnt-'mòn-ˌtäs näs-'kä-ˌtùr-ri-ˌdi-kù-lùs-'mūs\ [L] : the mountains are in labor, and a ridiculous mouse will be brought forth

**pa·ter pa·tri·ae** \'pä-ˌter-'pä-trē-ˌī\ [L] : father of his country

**pau·cis ver·bis** \ˌpaù-kēs-'wer-bēs\ [L] : in a few words

**pax vo·bis·cum** \ˌpäks-vō-'bēs-ˌkùm\ [L] : peace (be) with you

**peine forte et dure** \pen-fòr-tā-dʉer\ [F] : strong and hard punishment : torture

**per an·gus·ta ad au·gus·ta** \per-'än-ˌgùs-tä-äd-'aù-ˌgùs-tä\ [L] : through difficulties to honors

**per·fide Al·bion** \per-fēd-äl-byōⁿ\ [F] : perfidious Albion (England)

**peu à peu** \pœ-ä-pœ\ [F] : little by little

**peu de chose** \pœd-shōz, pœ-də-\ [F] : a trifle

**pinx·it** \'piŋk-sit\ [L] : he or she painted it

**place aux dames** \pläs-ō-däm\ [F] : (make) room for the ladies

**ple·no ju·re** \ˌplä-no-'yùr-e\ [L] : with full right

**plus ça change, plus c'est la même chose** \plue-sä-shäⁿzh plue-se-lä-mem-shōz\ [F] : the more that changes, the more it's the same thing — often shortened to *plus ça change*

**plus roy·a·liste que le roi** \plue-rwä-yä-lēst-kəl-rwä\ [F] : more royalist than the king

**po·cas pa·la·bras** \ˌpō-käs-pä-'lä-vräs\ [Sp] : few words

**po·eta nas·ci·tur, non fit** \po-ˌä-tä-'näs-ki-ˌtùr nōn-'fit\ [L] : a poet is born, not made

**po·ète mau·dit** \pò-et-mo-dē\ [F] : accursed poet : a writer dogged by misfortune and lack of recognition

**pol·li·ce ver·so** \ˌpò-li-ke-'wer-sō\ [L] : with thumb turned : with a gesture or expression of condemnation

**post hoc, er·go prop·ter hoc** \'post-ˌhōk ˌer-gō-'pròp-ter-ˌhōk\ [L] : after this, therefore on account of it (a fallacy of argument)

**post ob·itum** \ˌpost-'ò-bi-ˌtúm\ [L] : after death

**pour en·cou·ra·ger les autres** \pür-äⁿ-kü-rä-zhä-la-zōtrᵉ\ [F] : in order to encourage the others — said ironically of an action (as an execution) carried out in order to compel others to obey

**pri·mum non no·ce·re** \ˌprē-mùm-ˌnōn-nō-'kä-rä\ [L] : the first thing (is) to do no harm

**pro bo·no pu·bli·co** \ˌprō-ˌbò-nō-'pü-bli-ˌkō\ [L] : for the public good

**pro hac vi·ce** \ˌprō-ˌhäk-'wi-ke\ [L] : for this occasion

**pro pa·tria** \ˌprō-'pä-trē-ˌä\ [L] : for one's country

**pro re·ge, le·ge, et gre·ge** \ˌprō-'rä-ˌge 'lä-ˌge et-'gre-ˌge\ [L] : for the king, the law, and the people

**pro re na·ta** \ˌprō-ˌrä-'nä-tä\ [L] : for an occasion that has arisen : as needed — used in medical prescriptions

**quand même** \käⁿ-mem\ [F] : even so : all the same

**quan·tum mu·ta·tus ab il·lo** \ˌkwän-tùm-mü-'tä-tùs-äb-'i-lō\ [L] : how changed from what he once was

**quan·tum suf·fi·cit** \ˌkwän-təm-'sə-fə-kit\ [L] : as much as suffices : a sufficient quantity — used chiefly in medical prescriptions

**¿quién sa·be?** \kyän-'sä-vä\ [Sp] : who knows?

**qui fa·cit per ali·um fa·cit per se** \ˌkwē-ˌfä-kit-ˌper-'ä-lē-ˌùm-ˌfä-kit-ˌper-'sä\ [L] : he who does (something) through another does it through himself

**quis cus·to·di·et ip·sos cus·to·des?** \ˌkwis-kùs-'tō-dē-ˌet-ip-ˌsōs-kùs-'tō-däs\ [L] : who will keep the keepers themselves?

**qui s'ex·cuse s'ac·cuse** \kē-'sek-ˌskuez-'sä-ˌkuez\ [F] : he who excuses himself accuses himself

**quis se·pa·ra·bit?** \ˌkwis-ˌsä-pə-'rä-bit\ [L] : who shall separate (us)? — motto of the Order of St. Patrick

**qui trans·tu·lit sus·ti·net** \kwē-'träns-tù-ˌlit-'sùs-ti-ˌnet\ [L] : He who transplanted sustains (us) — motto of Connecticut

**qui va là?** \kē-vä-lä\ [F] : who goes there?

**quo·ad hoc** \ˌkwō-ˌäd-'hōk\ [L] : as far as this : to this extent

**quod erat de·mon·stran·dum** \ˌkwäd-ˈer-ˌät-ˌde-mən-ˈstran-dəm, -ˌdā-ˌmòn-ˈsträn-ˌdùm\ [L] : which was to be proved

**quod erat fa·ci·en·dum** \-ˌfä-kē-ˈen-ˌdùm\ [L] : which was to be done

**quod sem·per, quod ubi·que, quod ab om·ni·bus** \kwòd-ˈsem-ˌper kwòd-ˈù-bi-ˌkwä ˌkwòd-ab-ˈòm-ni-ˌbùs, -ˌkwòd-ù-ˈbē-(ˌ)kwä-\ [L] : what (has been held) always, everywhere, by everybody

**quod vi·de** \kwòd-ˈwi-ˌde\ [L] : which see

**quo·rum pars mag·na fui** \ˈkwòr-ùm-ˌpärs-ˌmäg-nä-ˈfü-ē\ [L] : in which I played a great part

**quos de·us vult per·de·re pri·us de·men·tat** \kwòs-ˈdā-ùs-ˌwùlt-ˈper-de-ˌrä-ˌpri-ùs-dä-ˈmen-ˌtät\ [L] : those whom a god wishes to destroy he first drives mad

**quot ho·mi·nes, tot sen·ten·ti·ae** \kwòt-ˈhò-mi-ˌnäs ˌtòt-sen-ˈten-tē-ˌī\ [L] : there are as many opinions as there are men

**quo va·dis?** \kwō-ˈwä-dis, -ˈvä-dəs\ [L] : whither are you going?

**rai·son d'état** \re-zōⁿ-dā-tä\ [F] : reason of state

**reg·nat po·pu·lus** \ˌreg-ˌnät-ˈpò-pù-ˌlùs\ [L] : the people rule — motto of Arkansas

**re in·fec·ta** \ˌrä-in-ˈfek-ˌtä\ [L] : the business being unfinished : without accomplishing one's purpose

**re·li·gio lo·ci** \re-ˈli-gē-ˌō-ˈlò-ˌkē\ [L] : religious sanctity of a place

**rem acu te·ti·gis·ti** \rem-ˈä-ˌkü-ˌte-ti-ˈgis-tē\ [L] : you have touched the point with a needle : you have hit the nail on the head

**ré·pon·dez s'il vous plaît** \rā-pōⁿ-dā-sēl-vü-ple\ [F] : reply, if you please

**re·qui·es·cat in pa·ce** \ˌre-kwē-ˈes-ˌkät-in-ˈpä-ˌke, ˌrā-kwē-ˈes-ˌkät-in-ˈpä-ˌchä\ [L] : may he or she rest in peace — used on tombstones

**re·spi·ce fi·nem** \ˌrä-spi-ˌke-ˈfē-ˌnem\ [L] : look to the end : consider the outcome

**re·sur·gam** \re-ˈsùr-ˌgäm\ [L] : I shall rise again

**re·te·nue** \rət-nœ\ [F] : self-restraint : reserve

**re·ve·nons à nos mou·tons** \rəv-nōⁿ-ä-nō-mü-tōⁿ\ [F] : let us return to our sheep : let us get back to the subject

**ruse de guerre** \rœz-də-ger\ [F] : war stratagem

**rus in ur·be** \ˌrüs-in-ˈùr-ˌbe\ [L] : country in the city

**sae·va in·dig·na·tio** \ˌsī-wä-ˌin-dig-ˈnä-tē-ō\ [L] : fierce indignation

**salle à man·ger** \säl-ä-mäⁿ-zhä\ [F] : dining room

**sa·lus po·pu·li su·pre·ma lex es·to** \ˌsä-ˌlùs-ˈpò-pù-ˌlē-sù-ˌprä-mä-ˌleks-ˈes-tō\ [L] : let the welfare of the people be the supreme law — motto of Missouri

**sanc·ta sim·pli·ci·tas** \ˌsäŋk-tä-sim-ˈpli-ki-ˌtäs\ [L] : holy simplicity — often used

ironically in reference to another's naïveté

**sans doute** \säⁿ-düt\ [F] : without doubt

**sans gêne** \säⁿ-zhen\ [F] : without embarrassment or constraint

**sans peur et sans re·proche** \säⁿ-pœr-ä-säⁿ-rə-ˈprósh\ [F] : without fear and without reproach

**sans sou·ci** \säⁿ-sü-sē\ [F] : without worry

**sa·yo·na·ra** \ˌsī-ə-ˈnär-ə, ˌsä-yə-\ [Jp] : good-bye

**sculp·sit** \ˈskəlp-sət, ˈskùlp-sit\ [L] : he or she carved it

**scu·to bo·nae vo·lun·ta·tis tu·ae co·ro·nas·ti nos** \ˈskü-ˌtō-ˈbò-ˌnī-vò-lùn-ˌtä-tis-ˈtù-ˌī-ˈkòr-ò-ˌnäs-tē-ˈnòs\ [L] : Thou hast crowned us with the shield of Thy good will — a motto on the Great Seal of Maryland

**se·cun·dum ar·tem** \se-ˌkùn-dùm-ˈär-ˌtem\ [L] : according to the art : according to the accepted practice of a profession or trade

**secundum na·tu·ram** \-nä-ˈtü-ˌräm\ [L] : according to nature : naturally

**se de·fen·den·do** \ˈsä-ˌdā-ˌfen-ˈden-dō\ [L] : in self-defense

**se ha·bla es·pa·ñol** \sä-ˌäv-lä-ˌäs-pä-ˈnyól\ [Sp] : Spanish spoken

**sem·per ea·dem** \ˌsem-ˌper-ˈe-ä-ˌdem\ [L] : always the same (fem.) — motto of Queen Elizabeth I

**sem·per fi·de·lis** \ˌsem-pər-fə-ˈdā-ləs\ [L] : always faithful — motto of the U.S. Marine Corps

**sem·per idem** \ˌsem-ˌper-ˈē-ˌdem\ [L] : always the same (masc.)

**sem·per pa·ra·tus** \ˌsem-pər-pə-ˈrä-təs\ [L] : always prepared — motto of the U.S. Coast Guard

**se non è ve·ro, è ben tro·va·to** \sä-ˌnōn-e-ˈvä-rō e-ˌben-trō-ˈvä-tō\ [It] : even if it is not true, it is well conceived

**sha·lom alei·chem** \ˌshò-ləm-ə-ˈlä-kəm, ˌshō-, -kəm\ [Heb *shālōm 'alēkhem*] : peace to you — used as a traditional Jewish greeting

**sic itur ad as·tra** \sēk-ˈi-ˌtúr-ˌäd-ˈäs-trə\ [L] : thus one goes to the stars : such is the way to immortality

**sic sem·per ty·ran·nis** \ˌsik-ˌsem-pər-tə-ˈra-nəs\ [L] : thus ever to tyrants — motto of Virginia

**sic trans·it glo·ria mun·di** \sēk-ˈträn-sit-ˌglòr-ē-ä-ˈmùn-dē\ [L] : so passes away the glory of the world

**si jeu·nesse sa·vait, si vieil·lesse pou·vait!** \sē-ˈzhœ-nes-ˌsä-ve sē-ˈvye-yes-ˈpü-ve\ [F] : if youth only knew, if age only could!

**si·lent le·ges in·ter ar·ma** \ˌsi-ˌlent-ˈlä-gäs-ˌin-ter-ˈär-mä\ [L] : the laws are silent in the midst of arms (i.e., in time of war)

**s'il vous plaît** \sēl-vü-ple\ [F] : if you please

**si·mi·lia si·mi·li·bus cu·ran·tur** \si-ˈmi-lē-ä-si-ˈmi-li-bùs-kü-ˈrän-tùr\ [L] : like is cured by like

**si·mi·lis si·mi·li gau·det** \ˈsi-mi-lis-ˈsi-mi-lē-ˈgaù-det\ [L] : like takes pleasure in like

**si mo·nu·men·tum re·qui·ris, cir·cum·spi·ce** \sē-ˌmó-nù-ˌmen-túm-re-ˈkwē-ris kir-ˈkúm-spi-ke\ [L] : if you seek his monument, look around — epitaph of Sir Christopher Wren in St. Paul's, London, of which he was architect

**sim·pliste** \saⁿ-plēst\ [F] : simplistic : overly simple or naïve

**si quae·ris pen·in·su·lam amoe·nam, cir·cum·spi·ce** \sē-ˈkwī-ris-pā-ˈnin-sə-ˌläm-ä-ˈmói-ˌnäm kir-ˈkúm-spi-ke\ [L] : if you seek a beautiful peninsula, look around — motto of Michigan

**sis·te vi·a·tor** \ˌsis-te-wē-ˈä-ˌtòr\ [L] : stop, traveler — used on Roman roadside tombs

**si vis pa·cem, pa·ra bel·lum** \sē-ˈwēs-ˈpä-ˌkem ˈpä-rä-ˈbe-ˌlùm\ [L] : if you wish peace, prepare for war

**sol·vi·tur am·bu·lan·do** \ˈsòl-wi-ˌtùr-ˌäm-bù-ˈlän-dò\ [L] : it is solved by walking : the problem is solved by a practical experiment

**spo·lia opi·ma** \ˌspò-lē-ä-ò-ˈpē-mä\ [L] : rich spoils : the arms taken by the victorious from the vanquished general

**sta·tus quo an·te bel·lum** \ˈstä-tùs-kwò-ˌän-te-ˈbe-lùm\ [L] : the state existing before the war

**sua·vi·ter in mo·do, for·ti·ter in re** \ˈswä-wi-ˌter-in-ˈmò-dò ˈfór-ti-ˌter-in-ˈrā\ [L] : gently in manner, strongly in deed

**sub ver·bo** \sùb-ˈwer-bò, ˌsəb-ˈvər-bò\ or **sub vo·ce** \ˈsùb-ˈwò-ke, ˌsəb-ˈvò-sē\ [L] : under the word — introducing a cross-reference in a dictionary or index

**sunt la·cri·mae re·rum** \sùnt-ˌlä-kri-ˌmī-ˈrä-rùm\ [L] : there are tears for things : tears attend trials

**suo ju·re** \ˌsù-ò-ˈyùr-e\ [L] : in his or her own right

**suo lo·co** \-ˈló-kò\ [L] : in its proper place

**suo Mar·te** \-ˈmär-te\ [L] : by one's own exertions

**su·um cui·que** \ˌsù-ùm-ˈkwi-kwe\ [L] : to each his own

**tant mieux** \täⁿ-myœ\ [F] : so much the better

**tant pis** \-pē\ [F] : so much the worse : too bad

**tem·po·ra mu·tan·tur, nos et mu·ta·mur in il·lis** \ˌtem-pò-rä-mü-ˈtän-ˌtùr ˌnòs-et-mü-ˌtä-mùr-in-ˈi-ˌlēs\ [L] : the times are changing, and we are changing with them

**tem·pus edax re·rum** \ˈtem-pús-ˌe-ˌdäks-ˈrä-rùm\ [L] : time, that devours all things

**tem·pus fu·git** \ˌtem-pəs-ˈfyü-jət, ˌtem-pús-ˈfü-git\ [L] : time flies

**ti·meo Da·na·os et do·na fe·ren·tes** \ˌti-mē-ˌō-ˈdä-nä-ˌōs-ˌet-ˌdò-nä-fe-ˈren-ˌtäs\ [L] : I fear the Greeks even when they bring gifts

**to·ti·dem ver·bis** \ˌtò-ti-ˌdem-ˈwer-ˌbēs\ [L] : in so many words

**to·tis vi·ri·bus** \ˌtō-ˌtēs-ˈwē-ri-ˌbùs\ [L] : with all one's might

**to·to cae·lo** \ˌtò-tò-ˈkī-lò\ or **toto coe·lo** \-ˈkói-lò\ [L] : by the whole extent of the heavens : diametrically

**tou·jours per·drix** \tü-zhür-per-drē\ [L] : always partridge : too much of a good thing

**tour d'ho·ri·zon** \tür-dó-rē-zòⁿ\ [F] : circuit of the horizon : general survey

**tous frais faits** \tü-fre-fe\ [F] : all expenses defrayed

**tout à fait** \tü-tä-fe\ [F] : altogether : quite

**tout au con·traire** \tü-tò-kòⁿ-trer\ [F] : quite the contrary

**tout à vous** \tü-tä-vü\ [F] : wholly yours : at your service

**tout bien ou rien** \tü-ˈbyaⁿ-nü-ˈryaⁿ\ [F] : everything well (done) or nothing (attempted)

**tout com·pren·dre c'est tout par·don·ner** \ˈtü-kòⁿ-präⁿ-drə-se-ˈtü-pär-dó-nä\ [F] : to understand all is to forgive all

**tout court** \tü-kür\ [F] : quite short : and nothing else : simply : just; also : brusquely

**tout de même** \tüt-mem\ [F] : all the same : nevertheless

**tout de suite** \tüt-swᵉēt\ [F] : immediately; also : all at once : consecutively

**tout en·sem·ble** \tü-täⁿ-sänblᵊ\ [F] : all together : general effect

**tout est per·du fors l'hon·neur** \tü-te-per-dᵉ-fór-ló-nœr\ or **tout est perdu hors l'honneur** \-dᵉ-ór-\ [F] : all is lost save honor

**tout le monde** \tü-lə-mòⁿd\ [F] : all the world : everybody

**tra·hi·son des clercs** \trä-ē-zòⁿ-dä-klerk\ [F] : treason of the intellectuals

**tranche de vie** \träⁿsh-də-ˈvē\ [F] : slice of life

**trist·esse** \trē-stes\ [F] : melancholy

**tu·e·bor** \tü-ˈā-ˌbòr\ [L] : I will defend — a motto on the Great Seal of Michigan

**ua mau ke ea o ka ai·na i ka po·no** \ˌù-ä-ˈmä-ù-kā-ˈä-ä-ò-kä-ˈä-ē-nä-ˌē-kä-ˈpò-nò\ [Hawaiian] : the life of the land is perpetuated in righteousness — motto of Hawaii

**über al·les** \ˌᵫe-ber-ˈä-les\ [G] : above everything else

**Über·mensch** \ˈᵫe-bər-ˌmench\ [G] : superman

**ul·ti·ma ra·tio re·gum** \ˈùl-ti-mä-ˌrä-tē-ò-ˈrä-gùm\ [L] : the final argument of kings, i.e., war

**und so wei·ter** \ùnt-zō-ˈvī-tər\ [G] : and so on

**u·no an·i·mo** \ˌü-nō-ˈä-ni-ˌmō\ [L] : with one mind : unanimously

**ur·bi et or·bi** \ˌùr-bē-ˌet-ˈòr-bē\ [L] : to the city (Rome) and the world : to everyone

**uti·le dul·ci** \ˌü-ti-le-ˈdùl-ˌkē\ [L] : the useful with the agreeable

**ut in·fra** \ùt-ˈin-frä\ [L] : as below

**ut su·pra** \ùt-ˈsü-prä\ [L] : as above

**va·de re·tro me, Sa·ta·na** \ˌwä-de-ˈrä-trō-ˌmä ˈsä-tä-ˌnä\ [L] : get thee behind me, Satan

**vae vic·tis** \wī-ˈwik-ˌtēs\ [L] : woe to the vanquished

**va·ri·um et mu·ta·bi·le sem·per fe·mi·na** \ˌwär-ē-ùm-ˌet-ˌmü-ˈtä-bi-le-ˌsem-per-ˈfä-mi-nä\ [L] : woman is ever a fickle and changeable thing

**ve·di Na·po·li e poi mo·ri** \ˌvä-dē-ˈnä-pō-lē-ä-ˌpò-ē-ˈmò-rē\ [It] : see Naples and then die

**ve·ni, vi·di, vi·ci** \ˌwä-nē ˌwē-dē ˈwē-kē, ˌvā-nē ˌvē-dē ˈvē-chē\ [L] : I came, I saw, I conquered

**ven·tre à terre** \vänⁿ-trä-ter\ [F] : belly to the ground : at very great speed

**ver·ba·tim ac lit·te·ra·tim** \wer-ˈbä-tim-ˌäk-ˌli-te-ˈrä-tim\ [L] : word for word and letter for letter

**ver·bum sat sa·pi·en·ti est** \ˌwer-bùm-ˈsät-ˌsä-pē-ˈen-tē-ˌest\ [L] : a word to the wise is sufficient

**via cru·cis** \wē-ä-ˈkrü-sis\ [L] : Way of the Cross : path of suffering

**vieux jeu** \vyœ-zhœ\ [F] : old game : old hat

**vin·cit om·nia ve·ri·tas** \ˌwiŋ-kit-ˈòm-nē-ä-ˈwā-ri-ˌtäs\ [L] : truth conquers all things

**vin·cu·lum ma·tri·mo·nii** \ˌwiŋ-kù-lùm-ˌmä-tri-ˈmō-nē-ˌē\ [L] : bond of marriage

**vin du pays** \vanⁿ-dœ-pä-ē\ or **vin de pays** \vanⁿ-də-\ [F] : wine of the locality

**vir·gi·ni·bus pu·e·ris·que** \wir-ˈgi-ni-bùs-ˌpù-e-ˈrēs-kwe\ [L] : for girls and boys

**vir·go in·tac·ta** \ˈvir-ˌgō-in-ˈtäk-tä\ [L] : untouched virgin

**vir·tu·te et ar·mis** \wir-ˈtü-te-ˌet-ˈär-mēs\ [L] : by valor and arms — motto of Mississippi

**vis me·di·ca·trix na·tu·rae** \ˈwēs-ˌme-di-ˈkä-triks-nä-ˈtü-ˌrī\ [L] : the healing power of nature

**vive la dif·fé·rence** \vēv-lä-dē-fä-räⁿs\ [F] : long live the difference (between the sexes)

**vive la reine** \vēv-lä-ren\ [F] : long live the queen

**vive le roi** \vēv-lə-rwä\ [F] : long live the king

**vogue la ga·lère** \vòg-lä-gä-ler\ [F] : let the galley be kept rowing : keep on, whatever may happen

**voi·là tout** \vwä-lä-tü\ [F] : that's all

**vox et prae·te·rea ni·hil** \ˈwòks-et-prī-ˈter-e-ä-ˈni-ˌhil\ [L] : voice and nothing more

**vox po·pu·li vox Dei** \wòks-ˈpó-pù-ˌlē-ˌwòks-ˈdā-ē\ [L] : the voice of the people is the voice of God

**Wan·der·jahr** \ˈvän-dər-ˌyär\ [G] : year of wandering

**wie geht's?** \vē-ˈgäts\ [G] : how goes it? : how is it going? — used as a greeting

**wun·der·bar** \ˈvùn-dər-ˌbär\ [G] : wonderful

# BIOGRAPHICAL NAMES

This section gives basic information on many notable figures from contemporary culture, history, legend, mythology, and biblical tradition. Figures from the Bible, myth, and legend are clearly identified as such.

In cases where individuals have alternate names, they are entered under the name by which they are best known. Names are generally alphabetized by the main element of the surname, without regard for connectives such as *da, de, van,* or *von* (as **Gama**... Vasco da). Names appearing in the entry in italics are original names, maiden names, or nicknames.

The first dates given in the entry are birth/death dates; other dates refer to terms in office, reigns, achievements, or honors. Abbreviations used here are listed in the front section Abbreviations in This Work.

---

**Aar·on** \'er-ən\ brother of Moses and 1st high priest of the Hebrews in the Bible

**Aaron** Hank 1934– *Henry Louis Aaron* Amer. baseball player

**Abel** \'ā-bəl\ son of Adam and Eve and brother of Cain in the Bible

**Abra·ham** \'ā-brə-,ham\ patriarch and founder of the Hebrew people in the Bible; also revered by Muslims

**Achil·les** \ə-'ki-lēz\ hero of the Trojan War in Greek mythology

**Ad·am** \'a-dəm\ the 1st man in biblical tradition

**Ad·ams** \'a-dəmz\ Abigail 1744–1818 née *Smith* Amer. writer; wife of John Adams

**Adams** Ansel Easton 1902–1984 Amer. photographer

**Adams** John 1735–1826 2d pres. of the U.S. (1797–1801)

**Adams** John Quin·cy \'kwin-zē, -sē\ 1767–1848 6th pres. of the U.S. (1825–29); son of John and Abigail Adams

**Adams** Samuel 1722–1803 patriot in the Amer. Revolution

**Ad·dams** \'a-dəmz\ Jane 1860–1935 Amer. social worker; Nobel Prize winner (1931)

**Ado·nis** \ə-'dä-nəs, -'do-\ youth in Greek mythology loved by Aphrodite

**Ae·ne·as** \i-'nē-əs\ Trojan hero in Greek and Roman mythology

**Ae·o·lus** \'ē-ə-ləs\ god of the winds in Greek mythology

**Aes·chy·lus** \'es-kə-ləs, 'ēs-\ 525–456 B.C. Greek dramatist

**Aes·cu·la·pi·us** \,es-k(y)ə-'lā-pē-əs\ god of medicine in Roman mythology — compare ASCLEPIUS

**Ae·sop** \'ē-,säp, -səp\ legendary Greek writer of fables

**Ag·a·mem·non** \,a-gə-'mem-,nän, -nən\ leader of the Greeks during the Trojan War in Greek mythology

**Ag·nes** \'ag-nəs\ Saint *died* 304 A.D. Christian martyr

**Ahab** \'ā-,hab\ king of Israel in the 9th cent. B.C. and husband of Jezebel

**Ajax** \'ā-,jaks\ hero in Greek mythology who kills himself because the armor of Achilles is awarded to Odysseus during the Trojan War

**Alad·din** \ə-'la-dən\ youth in the *Arabian Nights' Entertainments* who acquires a magic lamp

**Al·bee** \'ol-(,)bē, 'al-\ Edward Franklin 1928– Amer. dramatist

**Al·bright** \'ol-,brīt\ Madeleine 1937– née *Korbel* Amer. (Czech-born) diplomat; U.S. secretary of state (1997–2001)

**Al·cott** \'ol-kət, 'al-, -,kät\ Louisa May 1832–1888 Amer. author

**Al·ex·an·der** \,a-lig-'zan-dər, ,e-\ name of eight popes: esp. **VI** 1431–1503 (pope 1492–1503)

**Alexander the Great** 356–323 B.C. *Alexander III* king of Macedonia (336–323)

**Al·fred** \'al-frəd, -fərd\ 849–899 *Alfred the Great* king of the West Saxons (871–899)

**Ali** \ä-'lē\ Muhammad 1942– orig. *Cassius Clay* Amer. boxer

**Ali Ba·ba** \,a-lē-'bä-bə, ,ä-lē-\ woodcutter in the *Arabian Nights' Entertainments* who enters the cave of the Forty Thieves by using the password *Sesame*

**Al·len** \'a-lən\ Ethan 1738–1789 Amer. Revolutionary soldier

**Al·va·rez** \'al-və-,rez\ Luis 1911–1988 Amer. physicist

**Amerigo Vespucci** — see VESPUCCI

**Am·herst** \'a-(,)mərst\ Jeffery 1717–1797 Baron *Amherst* Brit. general in America

**Amund·sen** \'ä-mən-sən\ Roald 1872–1928 Norwegian explorer

**An·a·ni·as** \,a-nə-'nī-əs\ early Christian in the Bible struck dead for lying

**An·der·sen** \'an-dər-sən\ Hans Christian 1805–1875 Danish writer of fairy tales

**An·der·son** \'an-dər-sən\ Marian 1897–1993 Amer. contralto

**An·ge·lou** \'an-jə-(,)lō, *commonly* -,lü\ Maya 1928–2014 orig. *Marguerite Johnson* Amer. author

**Anne** \'an\ 1665–1714 queen of Great Britain (1702–14)

**An·tho·ny** \'an(t)-thə-nē\ Susan Brownell 1820–1906 Amer. suffragist

**An·tig·o·ne** \an-'ti-gə-(,)nē\ daughter of Oedipus and Jocasta in Greek mythology

**An·to·ny** \'an-tə-nē\ Mark *ca* 82–30 B.C. *Marc Antony; Marcus An·to·ni·us* \an-'tō-nē-əs\ Roman general and triumvir (43–30)

**Aph·ro·di·te** \,a-frə-'dī-tē\ goddess of love and beauty in Greek mythology — compare VENUS

**Apol·lo** \ə-'pä-(,)lō\ god of sunlight, prophecy, music, and poetry in Greek and Roman mythology

**Ap·ple·seed** \'ap-əl-,sēd\ Johnny 1774–1845 orig. *John Chapman* Amer. pioneer

**Aqui·nas** \ə-'kwī-nəs\ Saint Thomas 1224/25–1274 Ital. theologian

**Ar·chi·me·des** \,är-kə-'mē-dēz\ *ca* 287–212 B.C. Greek mathematician and inventor

**Ares** \'a-(,)rēz, 'er-(,)ēz\ god of war in Greek mythology — compare MARS

**Ar·is·toph·a·nes** \,a-rə-'stä-fə-,nēz\ *ca* 450–*ca* 388 B.C. Greek playwright

**Ar·is·tot·le** \'a-rə-,stä-t°l\ 384–322 B.C. Greek philosopher

**Arm·strong** \'ärm-,strȯŋ\ Lance 1971– Amer. cyclist

**Armstrong** Louis 1901–1971 *Satch·mo* \'sach-,mō\ Amer. jazz musician

**Armstrong** Neil Alden 1930–2012 Amer. astronaut; 1st man on the moon (1969)

**Ar·nold** \'är-n°ld\ Benedict 1741–1801 Amer. Revolutionary general and traitor

**Ar·te·mis** \'är-tə-məs\ goddess of the moon, wild animals, and hunting in Greek mythology — compare DIANA

**Ar·thur** \'är-thər\ legendary king of the Britons whose story is based on traditions of a 6th-century military leader — **Ar·thu·ri·an** \är-'thür-ē-ən, -'thyür-\ *adj*

**Arthur** Chester Alan 1829–1886 21st pres. of the U.S. (1881–85)

**As·cle·pi·us** \ə-'sklē-pē-əs\ god of medicine in Greek mythology — compare AESCULAPIUS

**Astaire** \ə-'ster\ Fred 1899–1987 orig. *Frederick Austerlitz* Amer. dancer and actor

**As·tor** \'as-tər\ John Jacob 1763–1848 Amer. (Ger.-born) fur trader and capitalist

**Athe·na** \ə-'thē-nə\ *or* **Athe·ne** \-nē\ goddess of wisdom in Greek mythology — compare MINERVA

**At·las** \'at-ləs\ Titan in Greek mythology forced to bear the heavens on his shoulders

**At·ti·la** \'a-tə-lə, ə-'ti-lə\ 406?–453 A.D. king of the Huns

**At·tucks** \'a-təks\ Crispus 1723?–1770 Amer. patriot

**At·wood** \'at-,wůd\ Margaret 1939– Canad. author

**Au·den** \'ȯ-d°n\ Wystan Hugh 1907–1973 Amer. (Eng.-born) poet

**Au·du·bon** \'ȯ-də-bən, -,bän\ John James 1785–1851 Amer. (Haitian-born) artist and naturalist

**Au·gus·tine** \'ȯ-gə-,stēn; ȯ-'gəs-tən, ə-\ Saint 354–430 A.D. church father; bishop of Hippo (396–430)

**Au·gus·tus** \ȯ-'gəs-təs, ə-\ *or* **Caesar Augustus** *or* **Oc·ta·vi·an** \äk-'tā-vē-ən\ 63 B.C.–14 A.D. 1st Roman emperor (27 B.C.–14 A.D.)

**Aus·ten** \'ȯs-tən, 'äs-\ Jane 1775–1817 Eng. author

**Bab·bage** \'ba-bij\ Charles 1791–1871 Eng. mathematician and inventor

**Bac·chus** \'ba-kəs, 'bä-\ — see DIONYSUS

**Bach** \'bäk, 'bäk\ Johann Sebastian 1685–1750 Ger. composer

**Ba·con** \'bā-kən\ Francis 1561–1626 Eng. philosopher and author

**Ba·den-Pow·ell** \'bā-d°n-'pō-əl\ Robert Stephenson Smyth 1857–1941 Baron *Baden-Powell* Brit. general and founder of Boy Scout movement

**Baf·fin** \'ba-fən\ William *ca* 1584–1622 Eng. navigator

**Bal·an·chine** \,ba-lən-'shēn\ George 1904–1983 orig. *Georgy Melitonovich Balanchivadze* Amer. (Russ.-born) choreographer

**Bal·boa** \bal-'bō-ə\ Vasco Núñez de 1475–1519 Span. explorer

**Bal·zac** \'bȯl-,zak, 'bal-\ Honoré de 1799–1850 French author

**Ba·rab·bas** \bə-'ra-bəs\ prisoner in the Bible released in preference to Jesus at the demand of the multitude

**Bar·num** \'bär-nəm\ P. T. 1810–1891 *Phineas Taylor Barnum* Amer. showman

**Bar·rie** \'ba-rē\ Sir James Matthew 1860–1937 Scot. author

**Bar·thol·di** \bär-'täl-dē, -'tȯl-, -'thäl-, -'thȯl-\ Frédéric-Auguste 1834–1904 French sculptor of the Statue of Liberty

**Bar·tók** \'bär-,täk\ Béla 1881–1945 Hung. composer

**Bar·ton** \'bär-t°n\ Clara 1821–1912 founder of American Red Cross

**Beau·re·gard** \'bȯr-ə-,gärd\ Pierre Gustave Toutant 1818–1893 Amer. Confederate general

**Beck·et** \'be-kət\ Saint Thomas *ca* 1118–1170 *Thomas à Becket* archbishop of Canterbury (1162–70)

**Beck·ett** \'be-kət\ Samuel 1906–1989 Irish playwright in France; Nobel Prize winner (1969)

**Bee·tho·ven** \'bā-,tō-vən\ Ludwig van 1770–1827 Ger. composer

**Bell** \'bel\ Alexander Graham 1847–1922 Amer. (Scot.-born) inventor of the telephone

**Bel·low** \'be-(,)lō\ Saul 1915–2005 Amer. (Canad.-born) author

**Ben·e·dict** \'be-nə-,dikt\ name of 16 popes: esp. **XIV** 1675–1758 (pope 1740–58); **XV** 1854–1922 (pope 1914–22); **XVI** 1927– (pope 2005–13)

**Be·nét** \bə-'nā\ Stephen Vincent 1898–1943 Amer. author

**Ben·ja·min** \'ben-jə-mən\ youngest son of Jacob and ancestor of one of the 12 tribes of Israel in the Bible

**Ben·ton** \'ben-tᵊn\ Thomas Hart 1889–1975 Amer. painter

**Be·o·wulf** \'bā-ə-,wulf\ legendary warrior and hero of the Old Eng. poem *Beowulf*

**Berg·man** \'bərg-mən\ Ingmar 1918–2007 Swed. film director

**Be·ring** \'bir-in, 'ber-\ Vitus 1681–1741 Danish navigator and explorer for Russia

**Ber·lin** \(,)bər-'lin\ Irving 1888–1989 Amer. (Russ.-born) composer

**Ber·ners-Lee** \'bər-nərz-'lē\ Sir Timothy John 1955– Brit. inventor

**Ber·ni·ni** \ber-'nē-nē\ Gian Lorenzo 1598–1680 Ital. sculptor, architect, and painter

**Bern·stein** \'bərn-,stīn, -,stēn\ Leonard 1918–1990 Amer. conductor and composer

**Bes·se·mer** \'be-sə-mər\ Sir Henry 1813–1898 Eng. engineer and inventor

**Bi·den** \'bī-dᵊn\ Joseph Robinette, Jr. 1942– vice pres. of the U.S. (2009– )

**Bish·op** \'bi-shəp\ Elizabeth 1911–1979 Amer. poet

**Bi·zet** \bē-'zā\ Georges 1838–1875 French composer

**Black Hawk** \'blak-,hok\ 1767–1838 Amer. Indian chief

**Black·well** \'blak-,wel, -wəl\ Elizabeth 1821–1910 Amer. (Eng.-born) physician

**Blair** \'bler\ Tony 1953– *Anthony Charles Lynton Blair* Brit. prime minister (1997–2007)

**Blake** \'blāk\ William 1757–1827 Eng. poet and artist

**Bloom·er** \'blü-mər\ Amelia 1818–1894 née *Jenks* Amer. social reformer

**Boc·cac·cio** \bō-'kä-ch(ē-,)ō\ Giovanni 1313–1375 Ital. author

**Bohr** \'bor\ Niels 1885–1962 Danish physicist; Nobel Prize winner (1922)

**Bo·leyn** \bu-'lin, -'len\ Anne 1507?–1536 2d wife of Henry VIII and mother of Elizabeth I of England

**Bo·li·var** \bə-'lē-,vär; 'bä-lə-,vär, -vər\ Simón \sē-,mōn, ,sī-mən\ 1783–1830 South Amer. liberator

**Bon·i·face** \'bä-nə-fəs, -,fās\ name of 9 popes: esp. **VIII** *ca* 1235 (or 1240)–1303 (pope 1294–1303)

**Boone** \'bün\ Daniel 1734–1820 Amer. pioneer

**Booth** \'büth\ John Wilkes 1838–1865 Amer. actor; assassin of Abraham Lincoln

**Bo·re·as** \'bor-ē-əs\ god of the north wind in Greek mythology

**Bosch** \'bäsh, 'bosh\ Hieronymus *ca* 1450–*ca* 1516 Dutch painter

**Bot·ti·cel·li** \,bä-tə-'che-lē\ Sandro 1445–1510 Ital. painter

**Bow·ie** \'bü-ē, 'bō-\ Jim 1796–1836 *James Bowie* Amer. hero of the Texas revolution

**Boyle** \'boi(-ə)l\ Robert 1627–1691 Eng. physicist and chemist

**Brad·bury** \'brad-,ber-ē, -b(ə-)rē\ Ray Douglas 1920–2012 Amer. author

**Brad·dock** \'bra-dək\ Edward 1695–1755 Brit. general in America

**Brad·ford** \'brad-fərd\ William 1590–1657 Pilgrim leader

**Brad·street** \'brad-,strēt\ Anne *ca* 1612–1672 Amer. poet

**Bra·dy** \'brā-dē\ Mathew B. 1823?–1896 Amer. photographer

**Brahe** \'brä, 'brä-hē, -hə\ Tycho 1546–1601 Danish astronomer

**Brah·ma** \'brä-mə\ creator god of the Hindu sacred triad — compare SHIVA, VISHNU

**Brahms** \'brämz\ Johannes 1833–1897 Ger. composer

**Braille** \'brāl, 'brī\ Louis 1809–1852 French blind teacher of the blind

**Bran·deis** \'bran-,dīs, -,dīz\ Louis Dembitz 1856–1941 Amer. jurist

**Brant** \'brant\ Joseph 1742–1807 *Thayendanegea* Mohawk Indian chief

**Brant** Mary 1736?–1796 *Molly Brant* Mohawk Indian leader; sister of Joseph Brant

**Braun** \'braun\ Wernher von 1912–1977 Amer. (Ger.-born) rocket engineer

**Brezh·nev** \'brezh-,nef\ Leonid Ilich 1906–1982 Soviet leader of the Communist Party (1964–82); pres. of the U.S.S.R. (1960–64; 1977–82)

**Brit·ten** \'bri-tᵊn\ Edward Benjamin 1913–1976 *Baron Britten of Aldeburgh* Eng. composer

**Bron·të** \'brän-të, -(,)tā\ family of Eng. writers: Charlotte 1816–1855 and her sisters Emily 1818–1848 and Anne 1820–1849

**Brooks** \'bruks\ Gwendolyn Elizabeth 1917–2000 Amer. poet

**Brown** \'braun\ John 1800–1859 Amer. abolitionist

**Brown** James Gordon 1951– Brit. prime minister (2007–10)

**Brow·ning** \'brau-nin\ Elizabeth Barrett 1806–1861 Eng. poet

**Browning** Robert 1812–1889 Eng. poet; husband of the preceding

**Brue·ghel** \'brü-gəl, 'broi-\ Pieter *ca*

1525–1569 known as *Pieter Brughel the Elder* Flemish painter

**Bru·tus** \'brü-təs\ Marcus Junius 85–42 B.C. Roman politician; one of Julius Caesar's assassins

**Bry·an** \'brī-ən\ William Jennings 1860–1925 Amer. lawyer and politician

**Bu·chan·an** \byü-'ka-nən, bə-\ James 1791–1868 15th pres. of the U.S. (1857–61)

**Buck** \'bək\ Pearl S. 1892–1973 née *Sydenstricker* Amer. author; Nobel Prize winner (1938)

**Bud·dha** \'bü-də, 'bù-\ ca 563–ca 483 B.C. orig. *Siddhartha Gautama* Indian founder of Buddhism

**Buffalo Bill** — see W. F. CODY

**Bun·yan** \'bən-yən\ John 1628–1688 Eng. preacher and author

**Bunyan** Paul — see PAUL BUNYAN

**Bur·bank** \'bər-,baŋk\ Luther 1849–1926 Amer. horticulturist

**Bur·goyne** \(,)bər-'göin, 'bər-,\ John 1722–1792 Brit. general in America

**Burns** \'bərnz\ Robert 1759–1796 Scot. poet

**Burn·side** \'bərn-,sīd\ Ambrose Everett 1824–1881 Amer. general

**Burr** \'bər\ Aaron 1756–1836 vice pres. of the U.S. (1801–5)

**Bush** \'bùsh\ George (Herbert Walker) 1924– 41st pres. of the U.S. (1989–93)

**Bush** George W. 1946– *George Walker Bush* 43rd pres. of the U.S. (2001–09); son of the preceding

**By·ron** \'bī-rən\ Lord 1788–1824 *George Gordon Byron*, 6th Baron *Byron* Eng. poet

**Cab·ot** \'ka-bət\ John ca 1450–ca 1499 orig. *Giovanni Ca·bo·to* \kä-'bō-tō\ Ital. navigator; explorer for England

**Cabot** Sebastian 1476?–1557 Eng. navigator; son of J. Cabot

**Ca·bri·ni** \kə-'brē-nē\ Saint Frances Xavier 1850–1917 *Mother Cabrini* 1st Amer. (Ital.-born) saint (1946)

**Cae·sar** \'sē-zər\ (Gaius) Julius 100?–44 B.C. Roman general, political leader, and writer

**Cain** \'kān\ son of Adam and Eve and brother of Abel in the Bible

**Calamity Jane** \kə-'la-mə-tē-\ 1852?–1903 *Martha Jane Burk* \'bərk\ née *Cannary* \'ka-nə-rē\ Amer. frontier figure

**Cal·houn** \kal-'hün\ John Caldwell 1782–1850 vice pres. of the U.S. (1825–32)

**Ca·lig·u·la** \kə-'li-gyə-lə\ 12–41 A.D. Roman emperor (37–41)

**Cal·li·ope** \kə-'lī-ə-(,)pē\ muse of heroic poetry in Greek mythology

**Cal·vert** \'kal-vərt\ George 1580?–1632 Baron *Baltimore* Eng. colonist in America

**Cal·vin** \'kal-vən\ John 1509–1564 *Jean Calvin* or *Cau·vin* \kō-'vaⁿ\ French theologian and reformer

**Ca·mus** \kä-'mue\ Albert 1913–1960 French author; Nobel Prize winner (1957)

**Ca·nute** \kə-'nüt, -'nyüt\ *died* 1035 *Canute the Great* Danish king of England (1016–35); of Denmark (1018–35); of Norway (1028–35)

**Ca·ra·vag·gio** \,ka-rə-'vä-j(ē-)ō\ Michelangelo da 1571–1610 orig. *Michelangelo Merisi* Ital. painter

**Car·ne·gie** \kär-'ne-gē, 'kär-nə-gē\ Andrew 1835–1919 Amer. (Scot.-born) industrialist and philanthropist

**Car·roll** \'ka-rəl\ Lewis 1832–1898 pseud. of *Charles Lutwidge Dodgson* Eng. author and mathematician

**Car·son** \'kär-sⁿ\ Kit 1809–1868 *Christopher Carson* Amer. frontiersman and guide

**Carson** Rachel Louise 1907–1964 Amer. scientist and writer

**Car·ter** \'kär-tər\ Jimmy 1924– orig. *James Earl Carter, Jr.* 39th pres. of the U.S. (1977–81); Nobel Prize winner (2002)

**Car·tier** \kär-'tyā, 'kär-tē-,ā\ Jacques 1491–1557 French explorer

**Ca·ru·so** \kə-'rü-(,)sō, -(,)zō\ En·ri·co \en-'rē-kō\ 1873–1921 Ital. tenor

**Car·ver** \'kär-vər\ George Washington 1861?–1943 Amer. agricultural chemist and agronomist

**Ca·sa·no·va** \,ka-zə-'nō-və, ,ka-sə-\ Giovanni Giacomo 1725–1798 Ital. adventurer

**Cas·san·dra** \kə-'san-drə, -'sän-\ daughter of Priam in Greek mythology who is endowed with the gift of prophecy but fated never to be believed

**Cas·satt** \kə-'sat\ Mary 1845–1926 Amer. painter

**Cas·tro** \'käs-(,)trō\ (Ruz) \'rüs\ Fidel 1926– Cuban leader (1959–2008)

**Cath·er** \'ka-thər\ Willa 1873–1947 Amer. author

**Cath·er·ine** \'ka-th(ə-)rən\ name of 1st, 5th, and 6th wives of Henry VIII of England: Catherine of Aragon 1485–1536; Catherine Howard 1520?–1542; Catherine Parr 1512–1548

**Catherine I** 1684–1727 wife of Peter the Great; empress of Russia (1725–27)

**Catherine II** 1729–1796 *Catherine the Great* empress of Russia (1762–96)

**Catherine de Mé·di·cis** \-də-,mā-dē-'sēs, -'me-də-(,)chē\ 1519–1589 Ital. *Ca·te·ri·na de' Me·di·ci* \,kä-tā-'rē-nä-dā-'me-dē-(,)chē\ queen consort of Henry II of France (1547–59) and regent of France (1560–74)

**Cav·en·dish** \'ka-vən-(,)dish\ Henry 1731–1810 Eng. scientist

**Ce·ci·lia** \sə-'sēl-yə, -'sil-\ Saint *fl.* 3d cent. A.D. Christian martyr; patron saint of music

**Ce·res** \'sir-(,)ēz\ goddess of agriculture

in Roman mythology — compare DEME-TER

**Cer·van·tes** \sər-'van-ˌtēz, -'vän-ˌtās\ Miguel de 1547–1616 Span. author

**Cé·zanne** \sā-'zan\ Paul 1839–1906 French painter

**Cha·gall** \shə 'gäl, -'gal\ Marc 1887–1985 Russ. painter in France

**Cham·plain** \ˌsham-'plān, shäⁿ-'plaⁿ\ Samuel de 1567–1635 French explorer in America

**Chap·lin** \'cha-plən\ Charlie 1889–1977 Sir *Charles Spencer Chaplin* Brit. actor and producer

**Chapman** \'chap-mən\ John — see Johnny APPLESEED

**Char·le·magne** \'shär-lə-ˌmän\ 742–814 A.D. *Charles the Great* or *Charles I* Frankish king (768–814); Holy Roman emperor (800–814)

**Charles** \'chär(-ə)lz\ name of 10 kings of France: esp. **II** 823–877 A.D. *Charles the Bald* (r. 840–77); Holy Roman emperor (875–77); **IV** 1294–1328 *Charles the Fair* (r. 1322–28); **V** 1337–1380 *Charles the Wise* (r. 1364–80); **VI** 1368–1422 *Charles the Mad* (or the *Beloved*) (r. 1380–1422); **VII** 1403–1461 *Charles the Well-Served* or *the Victorious* (r. 1422–61); **IX** 1550–1574 (r. 1560–74); **X** 1757–1836 (r. 1824–30)

**Charles** name of 2 kings of Great Britain: **I** 1600–1649 (r. 1625–49); **II** 1630–1685 (r. 1660–85); son of Charles I

**Charles V** 1500–1558 Holy Roman emperor (1519–56); king of Spain as *Charles I* (1516–56)

**Charles Edward Stuart** — see Charles Edward STUART

**Charles Mar·tel** \-mär-'tel\ ca 688–741 A.D. Frankish ruler (719–41); grandfather of Charlemagne

**Cha·ryb·dis** \kə-'rib-dəs\ whirlpool off the coast of Sicily personified in Greek mythology as a female monster

**Chau·cer** \'chȯ-sər\ Geoffrey ca 1342–1400 Eng. poet

**Cha·vez** \'chä-vəs, -ˌvez\ Cesar Estrada 1927–1993 Amer. labor leader

**Che·khov** \'che-ˌkȯf, -ˌkȯv\ Anton Pavlovich 1860–1904 Russ. author

**Che·ney** \'chē-nē, *commonly* 'chā-\ Richard Bruce 1941–   vice pres. of the U.S. (2001–2009)

**Cheops** — see KHUFU

**Ches·ter·ton** \'ches-tər-tən\ G. K. 1874–1936 *Gilbert Keith Chesterton* Eng. author

**Chiang Kai-shek** \jē-'äŋ-'kī-'shek, 'chaŋ-\ 1887–1975 Chinese general and politician; president of China (1948–1949; Taiwan, 1950–1975)

**Cho·pin** \'shō-ˌpan, -ˌpaⁿ\ Frédéric François 1810–1849 Polish composer

**Chou En–lai** or **Zhou Enlai** \'jō-'en-'lī\ 1898–1976 Chinese Communist politician; premier (1949–76)

**Chré·tien** \krā-'tyaⁿ\ Jean 1934– Canad. prime minister (1993–2003)

**Christ** Jesus — see JESUS

**Chris·tie** \'kris-tē\ Dame Agatha 1890–1976 née *Miller* Eng. author

**Chur·chill** \'chər-ˌchil, 'chərch-ˌhil\ Sir Winston Leonard Spencer 1874–1965 Brit. prime minister (1940–45; 1951–55) Nobel Prize winner (1953)

**Cic·ero** \'si-sə-ˌrō\ Marcus Tullius 106–43 B.C. Roman statesman, orator, and author

**Clark** \'klärk\ George Rogers 1752–1818 Amer. soldier and frontiersman

**Clark** William 1770–1838 Amer. explorer (with Meriwether Lewis)

**Clay** \'klā\ Henry 1777–1852 Amer. politician and orator

**Clem·ens** \'kle-mənz\ Samuel Langhorne — see Mark TWAIN

**Cle·o·pa·tra** \ˌklē-ə-'pa-trə, -'pä-\ 69–30 B.C. queen of Egypt (51–30)

**Cleve·land** \'klēv-lənd\ (Stephen) Grover 1837–1908 22nd and 24th pres. of the U.S. (1885–89; 1893–97)

**Clin·ton** \'klin-tᵊn\ Hillary Rodham née *Rodham* 1947–   Amer. politician; U.S. secretary of state (2009–13); wife of W.J. Clinton

**Clinton** William Jefferson 1946– *Bill Clinton* 42nd pres. of the U.S. (1993–2001)

**Cly·tem·nes·tra** \ˌklī-təm-'nes-trə\ wife of Agamemnon in Greek mythology

**Cobb** \'käb\ Ty 1886–1961 *Tyrus Raymond Cobb* Amer. baseball player

**Co·chise** \kō-'chēs\ 1812?–1874 Apache Indian chief

**Co·dy** \'kō-dē\ William Frederick 1846–1917 *Buffalo Bill* Amer. hunter, guide, and showman

**Co·han** \'kō-ˌhan\ George Michael 1878–1942 Amer. composer

**Cole·ridge** \'kōl-rij, 'kō-lə-rij\ Samuel Taylor 1772–1834 Eng. poet

**Co·lette** \kō-'let\ 1873–1954 orig. *Sidonie-Gabrielle Colette* French author

**Co·lum·bus** \kə-'ləm-bəs\ Christopher 1451–1506 Ital. navigator and explorer for Spain

**Con·fu·cius** \kən-'fyü-shəs\ 551–479 B.C. Chinese philosopher

**Con·rad** \'kän-ˌrad\ Joseph 1857–1924 Brit. (Polish-born) author

**Con·sta·ble** \'kən(t)-stə-bəl, 'kän(t)-\ John 1776–1837 Eng. painter

**Con·stan·tine I** \'kän(t)-stən-ˌtēn, -ˌtīn\ *after* 280–337 A.D. *Constantine the Great* Roman emperor (306–37)

**Cook** \'kuk\ Captain James 1728–1779 Eng. navigator

**Coo·lidge** \'kü-lij\ (John) Calvin 1872–1933 30th pres. of the U.S. (1923–29)

**Coo·per** \'kü-pər, 'kü-\ James Fenimore 1789–1851 Amer. author

**Co·per·ni·cus** \kō-'pər-ni-kəs\ Nicolaus 1473–1543 Polish astronomer

**Cop·land** \'kō-plənd\ Aaron 1900–1990 Amer. composer

**Cop·ley** \'kä-plē\ John Singleton 1738–1815 Amer. painter

**Corn·wal·lis** \kȯrn-'wä-ləs\ Charles 1738–1805 1st Marquess *Cornwallis* Brit. general in America

**Co·ro·na·do** \ˌkȯr-ə-'nä-(ˌ)dō, ˌkär-\ Francisco Vásquez de *ca* 1510–1554 Span. explorer of southwestern U.S.

**Cor·tés** \kȯr-'tez, 'kȯr-,\ Hernán *or* Hernando 1485–1547 Span. conqueror of Mexico

**Cous·teau** \kü-'stō\ Jacques-Yves 1910–1997 French marine explorer

**Crane** \'krān\ Stephen 1871–1900 Amer. author

**Crazy Horse** \'krā-zē-ˌhȯrs\ 1842?–1877 *Ta-sunko-witko* Sioux Indian chief

**Crock·ett** \'krä-kət\ Davy 1786–1836 *David Crockett* Amer. frontiersman

**Crom·well** \'kräm-ˌwel, 'krəm-, -wəl\ Oliver 1599–1658 Eng. general; lord protector of England (1653–58)

**Cro·nus** \'krō-nəs, 'krä-\ Titan in Greek mythology overthrown by his son Zeus

**Cum·mings** \'kə-minz\ Edward Estlin 1894–1962 known as *e. e. cummings* Amer. poet

**Cu·pid** \'kyü-pəd\ god of love in Roman mythology — compare EROS

**Cu·rie** \kyu̇-'rē, 'kyu̇r-(ˌ)ē\ Marie 1867–1934 née *Sklo-dow-ska* \sklə-'dȯf-skə\ French (Polish-born) chemist; Nobel Prize winner (1903, 1911)

**Curie** Pierre 1859–1906 French chemist; husband of M. Curie; Nobel Prize winner (1903)

**Cus·ter** \'kəs-tər\ George Armstrong 1839–1876 Amer. general

**Cy·ra·no de Ber·ge·rac** \'sir-ə-ˌnō-də-'berzhə-ˌrak\ Savinien 1619–1655 French playwright

**Cy·rus II** \'sī-rəs\ *ca* 585–*ca* 529 B.C. *Cyrus the Great* king of Persia (*ca* 550–529)

**Dae·da·lus** \'de-də-ləs, 'dē-\ builder in Greek mythology of the Cretan labyrinth and inventor of wings by which he and his son Icarus escape imprisonment

**Da·lí** \'dä-lē, *by himself* dä-'lē\ Salvador 1904–1989 Span. painter

**Dal·ton** \'dȯl-tᵊn\ John 1766–1844 Eng. chemist and physicist

**Dan·iel** \'dan-yəl\ prophet in the Bible who is held captive in Babylon and delivered from a den of lions

**Dan·te** \'dän-(ˌ)tā, 'dan-, -(ˌ)tē\ 1265–1321 *Dante Ali·ghie·ri* \ˌa-lə-'gyer-ē\ Ital. poet

**Da·ri·us I** \də-'rī-əs\ 550–486 B.C. *Darius the Great* king of Persia (522–486)

**Dar·row** \'da-(ˌ)rō\ Clarence Seward 1857–1938 Amer. lawyer

**Dar·win** \'där-wən\ Charles Robert 1809–1882 Eng. naturalist

**Da·vid** \'dā-vəd\ a youth in the Bible who slays Goliath and succeeds Saul as king of Israel

**Da·vis** \'dā-vəs\ Jefferson 1808–1889 pres. of the Confederate States of America (1861–65)

**Davis** Miles 1926–1991 Amer. jazz musician

**Debs** \'debz\ Eugene Victor 1855–1926 Amer. socialist and labor organizer

**De·bus·sy** \ˌde-byü-'sē, ˌdā-\ Claude 1862–1918 French composer

**De·ca·tur** \di-'kā-tər\ Stephen 1779–1820 Amer. naval officer

**De·foe** \di-'fō\ Daniel 1660–1731 Eng. author

**De·gas** \də-'gä\ Edgar 1834–1917 French painter

**de Gaulle** \di-'gōl, -'gȯl\ Charles 1890–1970 French general; pres. of Fifth Republic (1958–69)

**De·li·lah** \di-'lī-lə\ mistress and betrayer of Samson in the Bible

**De·me·ter** \di-'mē-tər\ goddess of agriculture in Greek mythology — compare CERES

**de Mille** \də-'mil\ Agnes 1905–1993 Amer. dancer and choreographer

**De·mos·the·nes** \di-'mäs-thə-ˌnēz\ 384–322 B.C. Athenian orator and statesman

**Demp·sey** \'dem(p)-sē\ Jack 1895–1983 orig. *William Harrison Dempsey* Amer. boxer

**Des·cartes** \dā-'kärt\ René 1596–1650 French mathematician and philosopher

**de So·to** \thä-'sō-(ˌ)tō, di-\ Hernando *ca* 1496–1542 Span. explorer

**Dew·ey** \'dü-ē, 'dyü-\ George 1837–1917 Amer. admiral

**Dewey** John 1859–1952 Amer. philosopher and educator

**Di·ana** \dī-'a-nə\ ancient Ital. goddess of the forest and of childbirth who was identified with Artemis by the Romans

**Dick·ens** \'di-kənz\ Charles 1812–1870 pseud. *Boz* \'bäz, 'bōz\ Eng. author

**Dick·in·son** \'di-kən-sən\ Emily Elizabeth 1830–1886 Amer. poet

**Di·do** \'dī-(ˌ)dō\ legendary queen of Carthage who falls in love with Aeneas and kills herself when he leaves her

**Di·Mag·gio** \də-'mä-zhē-(ˌ)ō, -'ma-jē-(ˌ)ō\ Joe 1914–1999 *Joseph Paul DiMaggio* Amer. baseball player

**Di·o·ny·sus** \ˌdī-ə-'nī-səs, -'nē-\ god of wine and ecstasy in classical mythology

**Dis·ney** \'diz-nē\ Walt 1901–1966 *Walter Elias Disney* Amer. film producer and cartoonist

**Dis·rae·li** \diz-'rā-lē\ Benjamin 1804–1881 Earl of *Beaconsfield* Brit. prime minister (1868; 1874–80)

**Dix** \'diks\ Dorothea Lynde 1802–1887 Amer. social reformer

**Dodg·son** \'däd-sən, 'däj-\ Charles Lutwidge — see Lewis CARROLL

**Donne** \'dən\ John 1572–1631 Eng. poet and clergyman

**Don Qui·xote** \,dän-kē-'(h)ō-tē, ,dän-\ hero of Cervantes' *Don Quixote*

**Dos·to·yev·sky** \,däs-tə-'yef-skē, -'yev-\ Fyodor Mikhaylovich 1821–1881 Russ. novelist

**Doug·las** \'də-gləs\ Stephen Arnold 1813–1861 Amer. politician

**Doug·lass** \'də-gləs\ Frederick 1817–1895 Amer. abolitionist

**Doyle** \'dȯi(-ə)l\ Sir Arthur Conan 1859–1930 Brit. physician and author

**Drake** \'drāk\ Sir Francis *ca* 1540–1596 Eng. navigator, explorer, and admiral

**Drei·ser** \'drī-sər, -zər\ Theodore 1871–1945 Amer. author

**Du·Bois** \dü-'bȯis, dyü-\ William Edward Burghardt 1868–1963 Amer. educator and writer

**Du·mas** \dü-'mä, dyü-\ Alexandre 1802–1870 *Dumas père* \'per\ French author

**Dun·can** \'dən-kən\ Isadora 1877–1927 Amer. dancer

**Dü·rer** \'dür-ər, 'dyùr-, 'dùer-\ Albrecht 1471–1528 Ger. painter and engraver

**Dy·lan** \'di-lən\ Bob 1941– orig. *Robert Allen Zimmerman* Amer. singer and songwriter

**Ea·kins** \'ā-kənz\ Thomas 1844–1916 Amer. artist

**Ear·hart** \'er-,härt, 'ir-\ Amelia 1897–1937 Amer. aviator

**Earp** \'ərp\ Wyatt 1848–1929 Amer. frontiersman and lawman

**Ed·dy** \'e-dē\ Mary Baker 1821–1910 Amer. founder of Christian Science

**Ed·i·son** \'e-də-sən\ Thomas Alva 1847–1931 Amer. inventor

**Ed·ward** \'ed-wərd\ name of 8 post-Norman kings of England: **I** 1239–1307 *Edward Longshanks* (r. 1272–1307); **II** 1284–1327 (r. 1307–27); **III** 1312–1377 (r. 1327–77); **IV** 1442–1483 (r. 1461–70; 1471–83); **V** 1470–1483 (r. 1483); **VI** 1537–1553 (r. 1547–53); son of Henry VIII and Jane Seymour; **VII** 1841–1910 (r. 1901–10); son of Queen Victoria; **VIII** 1894–1972 (r. 1936; abdicated) *Duke of Windsor*; son of George V

**Ein·stein** \'īn-,stīn\ Albert 1879–1955 Amer. (Ger.-born) physicist; Nobel Prize winner (1921)

**Ei·sen·how·er** \'ī-z°n-,haù(-ə)r\ Dwight David 1890–1969 Amer. general; 34th pres. of the U.S. (1953–61)

**Elec·tra** \i-'lek-trə\ sister of Orestes in Greek mythology who aids him in avenging their father's murder

**Eli·jah** \i-'lī-jə\ Hebrew prophet of the 9th cent. B.C.

**El·i·on** \'e-lē-ən\ Gertrude Belle 1918–1999 Amer. pharmacologist; Nobel Prize winner (1988)

**El·i·ot** \'e-lē-ət, 'el-yət\ George 1819–1880 pseud. of *Mary Ann Evans* Eng. author

**Eliot** T. S. 1888–1965 *Thomas Stearns Eliot* Brit. (Amer.-born) poet; Nobel Prize winner (1948)

**Eliz·a·beth I** \i-'li-zə-bəth\ 1533–1603 queen of England (1558–1603); daughter of Henry VIII and Anne Boleyn

**Elizabeth II** 1926– queen of the United Kingdom (1952– ); daughter of George VI

**El·ling·ton** \'e-liŋ-tən\ Duke 1899–1974 *Edward Kennedy Ellington* Amer. bandleader and composer

**Em·er·son** \'e-mər-sən\ Ralph Waldo 1803–1882 Amer. essayist and poet

**En·dym·i·on** \en-'di-mē-ən\ beautiful youth in Greek mythology loved by the goddess of the moon

**Ep·i·cu·rus** \,e-pi-'kyùr-əs\ 341–270 B.C. Greek philosopher

**Er·ik the Red** \'er-ik\ *fl.* 10th cent. orig. *Erik Thorvaldson* Norwegian explorer; father of Leif Eriksson

**Eriksson** Leif — see LEIF ERIKSSON

**Eros** \'er-,äs, 'ir-\ god of love in Greek mythology — compare CUPID

**Esau** \'ē-(,)sȯ\ son of Isaac and Rebekah and elder twin brother of Jacob in the Bible

**Es·ther** \'es-tər\ Hebrew woman in the Bible who as the queen of Persia delivers her people from destruction

**Eu·clid** \'yü-kləd\ *fl. ca.* 300 B.C. Greek mathematician

**Eu·rip·i·des** \yù-'ri-pə-,dēz\ *ca* 484–406 B.C. Greek playwright

**Eu·ro·pa** \yù-'rō-pə\ princess in Greek mythology who was carried off by Zeus disguised as a white bull

**Eu·ryd·i·ce** \yù-'ri-də-(,)sē\ wife of Orpheus in Greek mythology

**Eve** \'ēv\ the 1st woman in biblical tradition; wife of Adam

**Eze·kiel** \i-'zē-kyəl, -kē-əl\ Hebrew prophet of the 6th cent. B.C.

**Fahr·en·heit** \'fa-rən-,hīt, 'fär-ən-\ Daniel Gabriel 1686–1736 Ger. physicist

**Far·a·day** \'fa-rə-,dā, -dē\ Michael 1791–1867 Eng. chemist and physicist

**Far·ra·gut** \'fa-rə-gət\ David Glasgow 1801–1870 Amer. admiral

**Faulk·ner** \'fȯk-nər\ William 1897–1962 Amer. author; Nobel Prize winner (1949)

**Faust** \'faùst\ *or* **Fau·stus** \'faù-stəs, 'fȯ-\ magician in Ger. legend who sells his soul to the devil for knowledge and power

**Fawkes** \'fȯks\ Guy 1570–1606 Eng. conspirator

**Fel·li·ni** \fə-'lē-nē\ Federico 1920–1993 Ital. film director

**Fer·di·nand** \'fər-də-,nand\ **V** of Castile *or* **II** of Aragon 1452–1516 *Ferdinand the Catholic* king of Castile (1474–1504), of Aragon (1479–1516), of Naples (1504–16); husband of Isabella I

**Fer·mi** \\'fer-(,)mē\\ Enrico 1901–1954 Amer. (Ital.-born) physicist; Nobel Prize winner (1938)

**Field·ing** \\'fēl-diŋ\\ Henry 1707–1754 Eng. author

**Fill·more** \\'fil-,mòr\\ Millard 1800–1874 13th pres. of the U.S. (1850–53)

**Fitz·ger·ald** \\fits-'jer-əld\\ Ella 1917–1996 Amer. singer

**Fitzgerald** F. Scott 1896–1940 *Francis Scott Key Fitzgerald* Amer. author

**Flem·ing** \\'fle-miŋ\\ Sir Alexander 1881–1955 Brit. bacteriologist; Nobel Prize winner (1945)

**Flying Dutchman** legendary Dutch mariner condemned to sail the seas until Judgment Day

**Ford** \\'fòrd\\ Gerald Rudolph 1913–2007 38th pres. of the U.S. (1974–77)

**Ford** Henry 1863–1947 Amer. automobile manufacturer

**Fos·sey** \\'fò-sē, 'fä-\\ Dian 1932–1985 Amer. zoologist

**Fos·ter** \\'fòs-tər, 'fäs-\\ Stephen Collins 1826–1864 Amer. songwriter

**Fran·cis** \\'fran(t)-səs\\ 1936– pope (2013– )

**Francis of As·si·si** \\-əv-ə-'si-sē, -'sē-\\ Saint 1181/1182–1226 Ital. friar; founder of Franciscan order

**Fran·co** \\'fräŋ-(,)kō, 'fraŋ-\\ Francisco 1892–1975 Span. general, dictator, and head of Span. state (1936–75)

**Frank** \\'fraŋk, 'fräŋk\\ Anne 1929–1945 Ger.-born diarist during the Holocaust

**Frank·lin** \\'fraŋ-klən\\ Benjamin 1706–1790 Amer. patriot, author, and inventor

**Fred·er·ick I** \\'fre-d(ə-)rik\\ *ca* 1123–1190 *Frederick Barbarossa* Holy Roman emperor (1152–90)

**Frederick II** 1712–1786 *Frederick the Great* king of Prussia (1740–86)

**Fré·mont** \\'frē-,mänt\\ John Charles 1813–1890 Amer. general and explorer

**French** \\'french\\ Daniel Chester 1850–1931 Amer. sculptor

**Freud** \\'fròid\\ Sigmund 1856–1939 Austrian neurologist; founder of psychoanalysis

**Fried·man** \\'frēd-mən\\ Milton 1912–2006 Amer. economist

**Frig·ga** \\'fri-gə\\ wife of Odin and goddess of married love and the hearth in Norse mythology

**Frost** \\'fròst\\ Robert Lee 1874–1963 Amer. poet

**Ful·ler** \\'fù-lər\\ (Richard) Buckminster 1895–1983 Amer. engineer and architect

**Fuller** (Sarah) Margaret 1810–1850 Amer. author and reformer

**Ful·ton** \\'fùl-tᵊn\\ Robert 1765–1815 Amer. inventor

**Ga·bri·el** \\'gā-brē-əl\\ archangel named in Hebrew tradition — compare MICHAEL, RAPHAEL, URIEL

**Ga·ga·rin** \\gə-'gär-ən\\ Yury Alekseyevich 1934–1968 Russ. astronaut; 1st man in space (1961)

**Gage** \\'gāj\\ Thomas 1721–1787 Brit. general in America

**Gal·a·had** \\'ga-lə-,had\\ knight of the Round Table in medieval legend who finds the Holy Grail

**Gal·a·tea** \\,ga-lə-'tē-ə\\ female figure sculpted by Pygmalion in Greek mythology and given life by Aphrodite in answer to the sculptor's prayer

**Ga·len** \\'gā-lən\\ 129–*ca* 216 A.D. Greek physician and writer

**Ga·li·leo** \\,ga-lə-'lē-(,)ō, -'lā-\\ 1564–1642 *Galileo Galilei* Ital. astronomer and physicist

**Gall** \\'gòl\\ 1840?–1894 Sioux Indian leader

**Ga·ma** \\'ga-mə, 'gä-\\ Vasco da *ca* 1460–1524 Portuguese navigator and explorer

**Gan·dhi** \\'gän-dē, 'gan-\\ Indira 1917–1984 Indian prime minister (1966–77; 1980–84); daughter of Jawaharlal Nehru

**Gandhi** Mohandas Karamchand 1869–1948 *Ma·hat·ma* \\mə-'hät-mə, -'hat-\\ *Gandi* Indian leader

**Gar·cía Már·quez** \\gär-'sē-ə-'mär-,kās\\ Gabriel 1928–2014 Colombian author; Nobel Prize winner (1982)

**Gar·field** \\'gär-,fēld\\ James Abram 1831–1881 20th pres. of the U.S. (1881)

**Gar·i·bal·di** \\,ga-rə-'bòl-dē\\ Giuseppe 1807–1882 Ital. patriot

**Gar·ri·son** \\'ga-rə-sən\\ William Lloyd 1805–1879 Amer. abolitionist

**Gates** \\'gāts\\ Bill 1955– *William Henry Gates III* Amer. computer software manufacturer

**Gau·guin** \\gō-'gaⁿ\\ Paul 1848–1903 French painter

**Geh·rig** \\'ger-ig\\ Lou 1903–1941 *Henry Louis Gehrig* Amer. baseball player

**Gehry** \\'ger-ē\\ Frank Owen 1929– orig. *Ephraim Owen Goldberg* Amer. (Canad.-born) architect

**Gei·sel** \\'gī-zəl\\ Theodor Seuss 1904–1991 pseud. *Dr. Seuss* \\'süs\\ Amer. author and illustrator

**Gen·ghis Khan** \\,jeŋ-gəs-'kän, ,geŋ-\\ *ca* 1162–1227 Mongol conqueror

**George** \\'jòrj\\ name of 6 kings of Great Britain: **I** 1660–1727 (r. 1714–27); **II** 1683–1760 (r. 1727–60); **III** 1738–1820 (r. 1760–1820); **IV** 1762–1830 (r. 1820–30); **V** 1865–1936 (r. 1910–36); **VI** 1895–1952 (r. 1936–52); father of Elizabeth II

**Ge·ron·i·mo** \\jə-'rä-nə-,mō\\ 1829–1909 Apache Indian leader

**Gersh·win** \\'gərsh-wən\\ George 1898–1937 Amer. composer

**Gil·bert** \\'gil-bərt\\ Sir William Schwenck 1836–1911 Eng. librettist and poet; collaborator with Sir Arthur Sullivan

**Gins·burg** \\'ginz-,bərg\\ Ruth Bader 1933– Amer. jurist

**Glad·stone** \\'glad-,stōn, *chiefly Brit* -stən\\

William Ewart 1809–1898 Brit. prime minister (1868–74; 1880–85; 1886; 1892–94)

**Glenn** \'glen\ John Herschel 1921– Amer. astronaut and politician; 1st Amer. to orbit the earth (1962)

**Go·di·va** \gə-'dī-və\ an Eng. gentlewoman who in legend rode naked through Coventry to save its citizens from a tax

**Goe·thals** \'gō-thəlz\ George Washington 1858–1928 Amer. engineer who directed the building of the Panama Canal

**Goe·the** \'gə(r)-tə, 'gœ-tə\ Johann Wolfgang von 1749 1832 Ger. author

**Gogh, van** \van-'gō, -'gäk\ Vincent Willem 1853–1890 Dutch painter

**Gol·ding** \'gōl-diŋ\ William Gerald 1911–1993 Eng. author; Nobel Prize winner (1983)

**Go·li·ath** \gə-'lī-əth\ Philistine giant who is killed by David in the Bible

**Gom·pers** \'gäm-pərz\ Samuel 1850–1924 Amer. (Brit.-born) labor leader

**Goo·dall** \'gù-(,)dól, (,)däl\ Jane 1934– Brit. zoologist

**Good·year** \'gùd-,yir\ Charles 1800–1860 Amer. inventor

**Gor·ba·chev** \,gòr-bə-'chóf, -'chef\ Mikhail Sergeyevich 1931– Soviet leader of Communist party (1985–91); pres. of U.S.S.R. (1990–91); Nobel Prize winner (1990)

**Gore** \'gór\ Albert, Jr. 1948– vice pres. of the U.S. (1993–2001); Nobel Prize winner (2007)

**Gor·gas** \'gòr-gəs\ William Crawford 1854–1920 Amer. army surgeon

**Go·ya (y Lu·cien·tes)** \'gòi-ə-,(,)lü-sē-'en-,täs\ Francisco José de 1746–1828 Span. painter

**Gra·ham** \'grā-əm, 'gra(-ə)m\ Martha 1893–1991 Amer. dancer and choreographer

**Grant** \'grant\ Ulysses S. 1822–1885 orig. Hiram Ulysses Grant Amer. general; 18th pres. of the U.S. (1869–77)

**Gre·co, El** \el-'gre-(,)kō\ 1541–1614 Doménikos Theotokópoulos Span. (Cretan-born) painter

**Gree·ley** \'grē-lē\ Horace 1811–1872 Amer. journalist and politician

**Greene** \'grēn\ (Henry) Graham 1904–1991 Brit. author

**Greene** Nathanael 1742–1786 Amer. Revolutionary general

**Greg·o·ry** \'gre-g(ə-)rē\ name of 16 popes: esp. **I** Saint ca 540–604 A.D. Gregory the Great (pope 590–604); **VII** Saint ca 1020–1085 (pope 1073–85); **XIII** 1502–1585 (pope 1572–85)

**Grey** \'grā\ Lady Jane 1537–1554 queen of England for 9 days (1553)

**Grey** Zane 1872–1939 Amer. author

**Grieg** \'grēg\ Edward Hagerup 1843–1907 Norwegian composer

**Grimm** \'grim\ Jacob 1785–1863 and his brother Wilhelm 1786 1859 Ger. philologists and folklorists

**Gro·pi·us** \'grō-pē-əs\ Walter 1883–1969 Amer. (Ger.-born) architect

**Gue·va·ra** \ge-'vär-ə, gā-\ Che 1928–1967 orig. Ernesto Cuban (Arg.-born) revolutionary

**Guin·e·vere** \'gwi-nə-,vir\ legendary wife of King Arthur and lover of Lancelot

**Gu·ten·berg** \'gü-t°n-,bərg\ Johannes ca 1400–1468 Ger. inventor of printing method from movable type

**Ha·des** \'hā-(,)dēz\ — see PLUTO

**Ha·dri·an** \'hā-drē-ən\ 76–138 A.D. Roman emperor (117–138)

**Hai·le Se·las·sie** \'hī-lē-sə-'la-sē, -'lä-\ 1892–1975 emperor of Ethiopia (1930–36; 1941–74)

**Hale** \'hāl\ Edward Everett 1822–1909 Amer. minister and author

**Hale** Nathan 1755–1776 Amer. Revolutionary hero

**Hal·ley** \'ha-lē\ Edmond or Edmund 1656–1742 Eng. astronomer and mathematician

**Hal·sey** \'hól-sē, -zē\ William Frederick 1882–1959 Amer. admiral

**Ham·il·ton** \'ha-məl-tən\ Alexander 1755–1804 Amer. political leader

**Ham·mu·ra·bi** \,ha-mə-'rä-bē\ died ca 1750 B.C. king of Babylon (ca 1792–50)

**Han·cock** \'han-,käk\ John 1737–1793 Amer. Revolutionary patriot

**Han·del** \'han-d°l\ George Frideric 1685–1759 Brit. (Ger.-born) composer

**Han·dy** \'han-dē\ W. C. 1873–1958 William Christopher Handy Amer. blues musician and composer

**Han·ni·bal** \'ha-nə-bəl\ 247–183? B.C. Carthaginian general

**Har·ding** \'här-diŋ\ Warren Gamaliel 1865–1923 29th pres. of the U.S. (1921–23)

**Har·dy** \'här-dē\ Thomas 1840–1928 Eng. author

**Har·per** \'här-pər\ Stephen 1959– Canad. prime minister (2006– )

**Har·ri·son** \'ha-rə-sən\ Benjamin 1833–1901 23rd pres. of the U.S. (1889–93); grandson of W. H. Harrison

**Harrison** William Henry 1773–1841 Amer. general; 9th pres. of the U.S. (1841)

**Harte** \'härt\ Bret 1836–1902 orig. Francis Brett Harte Amer. author

**Har·vey** \'här-vē\ William 1578–1657 Eng. physician and anatomist

**Haw·king** \'hò-kiŋ\ Stephen William 1942– Brit. physicist

**Haw·thorne** \'hò-,thórn\ Nathaniel 1804–1864 Amer. author

**Haydn** \'hī-d°n\ Franz Joseph 1732–1809 Austrian composer

**Hayes** \'hāz\ Rutherford Birchard 1822–1893 19th pres. of the U.S. (1877–81)

**Hearst** \\'hərst\\ William Randolph 1863–1951 Amer. newspaper publisher

**Hec·tor** \\'hek-tər\\ son of Priam and Hecuba; Trojan hero slain by Achilles in Greek mythology

**Hec·u·ba** \\'he-kyə-bə\\ wife of Priam in Greek mythology

**He·gel** \\'hā-gəl\\ Georg Wilhelm Friedrich 1770–1831 Ger. philosopher

**Hei·sen·berg** \\'hī-zᵊn-bərg, -ˌberk\\ Werner Karl 1901–1976 Ger. physicist

**Hel·en of Troy** \\ˌhe-lən-əv-'trȯi\\ wife of Menelaus whose abduction by Paris in Greek mythology causes the Trojan War

**He·li·os** \\'hē-lē-əs, -ˌ(ˌ)ōs\\ god of the sun in Greek mythology — compare SOL

**Hem·ing·way** \\'he-miŋ-ˌwā\\ Ernest Miller 1899–1961 Amer. author; Nobel Prize winner (1954)

**Hen·ry** \\'hen-rē\\ name of 8 kings of England: I 1068–1135 (r. 1100–35); II 1133–1189 (r. 1154–89); III 1207–1272 (r. 1216–72); IV 1366–1413 (r. 1399–1413); V 1387–1422 (r. 1413–22); VI 1421–1471 (r. 1422–61; 1470–71); VII 1457–1509 (r. 1485–1509); VIII 1491–1547 (r. 1509–47)

**Henry** name of 4 kings of France: I ca 1008–1060 (r. 1031–60); II 1519–1559 (r. 1547–59); III 1551–1589 (r. 1574–89); IV 1553–1610 *Henry of Navarre* (r. 1589–1610)

**Henry O.** 1862–1910 pseud. of *William Sydney Porter* Amer. author

**Henry Patrick** 1736–1799 Amer. patriot and orator

**Hen·son** \\'hen(t)-sən\\ Matthew Alexander 1866–1955 Amer. arctic explorer

**He·phaes·tus** \\hi-'fes-təs, -'fēs-\\ god of fire and metalworking in Greek mythology — compare VULCAN

**He·ra** \\'hir-ə, 'he-rə, 'her-ə\\ sister and wife of Zeus and goddess of women and marriage in Greek mythology — compare JUNO

**Her·cu·les** \\'hər-kyə-ˌlēz\\ *or* **Her·a·cles** \\'her-ə-ˌklēz-, 'he-rə-\\ hero in Greek mythology noted for his strength

**Her·mes** \\'hər-(ˌ)mēz\\ god of commerce, eloquence, invention, travel, and theft who serves as herald and messenger of the other gods in Greek mythology — compare MERCURY

**Her·od** \\'her-əd\\ 73–4 B.C. *Herod the Great* Roman king of Judea (37–4)

**Herod An·ti·pas** \\'an-tə-pəs, -ˌpas\\ 21 B.C.–39 A.D. Roman governor of Galilee (4 B.C.–39 A.D.); son of Herod the Great

**Her·schel** \\'hər-shəl\\ Sir William 1738–1822 Eng. astronomer

**Hes·se** \\'he-sə\\ Hermann 1877–1962 Ger. author; Nobel Prize winner (1946)

**Hey·er·dahl** \\'hā-ər-ˌdäl\\ Thor 1914–2002 Norwegian explorer and author

**Hi·a·wa·tha** \\ˌhī-ə-'wȯ-thə, ˌhē-ə-, -'wä-\\ legendary Iroquois Indian chief

**Hick·ok** \\'hi-ˌkäk\\ Wild Bill 1837–1876

orig. *James Butler Hickok* Amer. frontiersman and U.S. marshal

**Hi·dal·go (y Cos·ti·lla)** \\ē-'thäl-gō-ē-kò-'stē-yä\\ Miguel 1753–1811 Mex. priest and revolutionary leader

**Hil·ton** \\'hil-tᵊn\\ James 1900–1954 Eng. novelist

**Hip·poc·ra·tes** \\hi-'pä-krə-ˌtēz\\ *ca* 460–*ca* 377 B.C. Greek physician

**Hi·ro·hi·to** \\ˌhir-ō-'hē-(ˌ)tō\\ 1901–1989 emperor of Japan (1926–89)

**Hitch·cock** \\'hich-ˌkäk\\ Sir Alfred Joseph 1899–1980 Eng. film director

**Hit·ler** \\'hit-lər\\ Adolf 1889–1945 Ger. (Austrian-born) chancellor and dictator (1933–45)

**Hodg·kin** \\'häj-kin\\ Dorothy Mary 1910–1994 née *Crowfoot* Brit. physicist; Nobel Prize winner (1964)

**Hol·i·day** \\'hä-lə-ˌdā\\ Billie 1915–1959 orig. *Eleanora Fagan* Amer. jazz singer

**Holmes** \\'hōmz, 'hōlmz\\ Oliver Wendell 1809–1894 Amer. physician and author

**Holmes** Oliver Wendell, Jr. 1841–1935 Amer. jurist; son of the preceding

**Ho·mer** \\'hō-mər\\ *fl.* 9th *or* 8th cent. B.C. Greek epic poet

**Homer** Winslow 1836–1910 Amer. painter

**Hooke** \\'hùk\\ Robert 1635–1703 Eng. scientist

**Hook·er** \\'hù-kər\\ Thomas 1586?–1647 Eng. colonist; a founder of Connecticut

**Hoo·ver** \\'hü-vər\\ Herbert Clark 1874–1964 31st pres. of the U.S. (1929–33)

**Hoover** John Edgar 1895–1972 Amer. director of the Federal Bureau of Investigation (1924–72)

**Hop·per** \\'hä-pər\\ Edward 1882–1967 Amer. painter

**Hopper** Grace 1906–1992 née *Murray* Amer. admiral, mathematician, and computer scientist

**Hou·di·ni** \\hü-'dē-nē\\ Harry 1874–1926 orig. *Erik Weisz* Amer. magician

**Hous·ton** \\'hyü-stən, 'yü-\\ Sam 1793–1863 *Samuel Houston* Amer. politician; pres. of the Republic of Texas (1836–38; 1841–44)

**Howe** \\'haù\\ Elias 1819–1867 Amer. inventor

**Howe** Julia 1819–1910 née *Ward* Amer. suffragist and reformer

**Hub·ble** \\'hə-bəl\\ Edwin Powell 1889–1953 Amer. astronomer

**Hud·son** \\'həd-sən\\ Henry *ca* 1565–1611 Eng. explorer

**Hughes** \\'hyüz\\ Charles Evans 1862–1948 Amer. jurist; chief justice U.S. Supreme Court (1930–1941)

**Hughes** (James) Langston 1902–1967 Amer. author

**Hugo** \\'hyü-(ˌ)gō, 'yü-\\ Victor 1802–1885 French author

**Hus·sein I** \\hü-'sān\\ 1935–1999 king of Jordan (1952–99)

**Hussein** Saddam 1937–2006 pres. of Iraq (1979–2003)

**Hutch·in·son** \'hə-chə(n)-sən\ Anne 1591–1643 née *Marbury* Eng. colonist and religious leader in America

**Hutchinson** Thomas 1711–1780 Amer. colonial administrator

**Hux·ley** \'həks-lē\ Aldous Leonard 1894–1963 Eng. author

**Hy·men** \'hī-mən\ god of marriage in Greek mythology

**Ib·sen** \'ib-sən, 'ip-\ Henrik 1828–1906 Norwegian playwright

**Ic·a·rus** \'i-kə-rəs\ son of Daedalus who in Greek mythology falls into the sea when the wax of his artificial wings melts as he flies too near the sun

**Ig·na·tius** \ig-'nā-sh(ē-)əs\ Saint 1491–1556 *Ignatius of Loyola* Span. priest; founder of Society of Jesus (Jesuits)

**In·no·cent** \'i-nə-sənt\ name of 13 popes: esp. **III** 1160/61–1216 (pope 1198–1216); **IV** *died* 1254 (pope 1243–54)

**Ir·ving** \'ər-viŋ\ Washington 1783–1859 Amer. author

**Isaac** \'ī-zik, -zək\ son of Abraham and father of Jacob in the Bible

**Is·a·bel·la I** \ˌi-zə-'be-lə\ 1451–1504 queen of Castile (1474–1504) and of Aragon (1479–1504); wife of Ferdinand V

**Isa·iah** \ī-'zā-ə, *chiefly Brit* -'zī-\ Hebrew prophet of the 8th cent. B.C.

**Ish·ma·el** \'ish-(ˌ)mā-əl, -mē-\ outcast son of Abraham and Hagar in the Bible

**Ives** \'īvz\ Charles Edward 1874–1954 Amer. composer

**Jack·son** \'jak-sən\ Andrew 1767–1845 Amer. general; 7th pres. of the U.S. (1829–37)

**Jackson** Thomas Jonathan 1824–1863 *Stonewall Jackson* Amer. Confederate general

**Ja·cob** \'jā-kəb\ son of Isaac and Rebekah and younger twin brother of Esau in the Bible

**James** \'jāmz\ one of the 12 apostles in the Bible

**James** *the Less* one of the 12 apostles in the Bible

**James** name of 2 kings of Great Britain: **I** 1566–1625 (r. 1603–25); king of Scotland as *James VI* (r. 1567–1625); **II** 1633–1701 (r. 1685–88)

**James** Henry 1843–1916 Brit. (Amer.-born) author

**Ja·nus** \'jā-nəs\ god of gates and doors and of all beginnings in Roman mythology and that is pictured with two opposite faces

**Ja·son** \'jā-sᵊn\ hero in Greek mythology noted for his successful quest of the Golden Fleece

**Jay** \'jā\ John 1745–1829 Amer. jurist and statesman; 1st chief justice of the U.S. Supreme Court (1789–95)

**Jef·fer·son** \'je-fər-sən\ Thomas 1743–1826 3d pres. of the U.S. (1801–09)

**Jer·e·mi·ah** \ˌjer-ə-'mī-ə\ Hebrew prophet of the 7th–6th cent. B.C.

**Je·sus** \'jē-zəs, -zəz\ or **Jesus Christ** *ca* 6 B.C.–*ca* 30 A.D. source of the Christian religion and Savior in the Christian faith

**Jez·e·bel** \'je-zə-ˌbel\ queen of Israel and wife of Ahab who is noted for her wickedness in the Bible

**Joan of Arc** \ˌjōn-əv-'ärk\ Saint *ca* 1412–1431 *the Maid of Orléans* French national heroine

**Job** \'jōb\ man in the Bible who has many sufferings but keeps his faith

**Jobs** \'jäbz\ Steven Paul 1955–2011 Amer. computer entrepreneur

**Jo·cas·ta** \jo-'kas-tə\ queen of Thebes in Greek mythology who unknowingly marries her son Oedipus

**John** \'jän\ one of the 12 apostles believed to be the author of the 4th Gospel, three Epistles, and the Book of Revelation

**John** name of 21 popes: esp. **XXIII** 1881–1963 (pope 1958–63)

**John** 1167–1216 *John Lackland* king of England (1199–1216)

**John Paul** \'pȯl\ name of 2 popes: esp. **II** 1920–2005 (pope 1978–2005)

**John·son** \'jän(t)-sən\ Andrew 1808–1875 17th pres. of the U.S. (1865–69)

**Johnson** Lyndon Baines 1908–1973 36th pres. of the U.S. (1963–69)

**Johnson** Samuel 1709–1784 *Dr. Johnson* Eng. lexicographer and author

**John the Baptist** Saint, 1st cent. A.D. prophet and baptizer of Jesus in the Bible

**Jol·liet** *or* **Jo·liet** \zhȯl-'yā\ Louis 1645–1700 French-Canad. explorer

**Jo·nah** \'jō-nə\ Hebrew prophet who in the Bible spends three days in the belly of a great fish

**Jones** \'jōnz\ John Paul 1747–1792 Amer. (Scot.-born) naval officer

**Jop·lin** \'jä-plən\ Scott 1868–1917 Amer. pianist and composer

**Jor·dan** \'jȯr-dᵊn\ Michael 1963– Amer. basketball player

**Jo·seph** \'jō-zəf\ son of Jacob in the Bible who rises to high office in Egypt after being sold into slavery by his brothers

**Joseph** Chief *ca* 1840–1904 Nez Percé Indian chief

**Joseph** Saint, husband of Mary, the mother of Jesus, in the Bible

**Josh·ua** \'jä-sh(ə-)wə\ Hebrew leader in the Bible who succeeds Moses during the settlement of the Israelites in Canaan

**Joyce** \'jȯis\ James Augustine 1882–1941 Irish author

**Juan Car·los** \'(h)wän-'kär-ˌlōs\ 1938– king of Spain (1975–2014)

**Juá·rez** \'(h)wär-əs\ Benito Pablo 1806–1872 president of Mexico (1861–65; 1867–72)

**Ju·dah** \'jü-də\ son of Jacob and ancestor of one of the 12 tribes of Israel in the Bible

**Ju·das** \'jü-dəs\ *or* **Judas Is·car·i·ot** \-is-'ka-rē-ət\ one of the 12 apostles and the betrayer of Jesus in the Bible

**Jung** \'yu̇ŋ\ Carl Gustav 1875–1961 Swiss psychologist

**Ju·no** \'jü-(,)nō\ queen of heaven, wife of Jupiter, and goddess of light, birth, women, and marriage in Roman mythology — compare HERA

**Ju·pi·ter** \'jü-pə-tər\ chief god and god of light, of the sky and weather, and of the state in Roman mythology — compare ZEUS

**Kaf·ka** \'käf-kə, 'kaf-\ Franz 1883–1924 Czech author

**Kalb** \'kälp, 'kalb\ Johann 1721–1780 Baron *de Kalb* \di-'kalb\ Ger. general in Amer. Revolutionary army

**Ka·me·ha·me·ha I** \kə-,mā-ə-'mā-(,)hä\ 1758?–1819 orig. *Paiea* Hawaiian king (1795–1819)

**Kant** \'kant, 'känt\ Immanuel 1724–1804 Ger. philosopher

**Keats** \'kēts\ John 1795–1821 Eng. poet

**Kel·ler** \'ke-lər\ Helen Adams 1880–1968 Amer. deaf and blind lecturer and author

**Kel·vin** \'kel-vən\ 1st Baron 1824–1907 *William Thomson* Brit. mathematician and physicist

**Ken·ne·dy** \'ke-nə-dē\ John Fitzgerald 1917–1963 35th pres. of the U.S. (1961–63)

**Kennedy** Robert Francis 1925–1968 attorney general of the U.S. (1961–64); brother of the preceding

**Ke·o·kuk** \'kē-ə-,kək\ 1780?–1848 Amer. Indian chief

**Kep·ler** \'ke-plər\ Johannes 1571–1630 Ger. astronomer

**Key** \'kē\ Francis Scott 1779–1843 Amer. lawyer; author of "The Star-Spangled Banner"

**Keynes** \'kānz\ John Maynard 1883–1946 Eng. economist

**Khayyám** Omar — see OMAR KHAYYÁM

**Khru·shchev** \'krüsh-'chȯf, -'chȯv\ Nikita Sergeyevich 1894–1971 premier of U.S.S.R. (1958–64)

**Khu·fu** \'kü-(,)fü\ *or Greek* **Che·ops** \'kē-,äps\ *fl.* 25th cent. B.C. king of Egypt and pyramid builder

**Kidd** \'kid\ William *ca* 1645–1701 *Captain Kidd* Scot. pirate

**Kier·ke·gaard** \'kir-kə-,gär(d), -,gȯr\ Søren 1813–1855 Danish philosopher

**King** \'kiŋ\ Billie Jean 1943–    Amer. tennis player

**King** Martin Luther, Jr. 1929–1968 Amer. minister and civil rights leader; Nobel Prize winner (1964)

**Kip·ling** \'kip-liŋ\ Rudyard 1865–1936 Eng. author; Nobel Prize winner (1907)

**Kis·sin·ger** \'ki-sⁿn-jər\ Henry Alfred

1923–    Amer. (Ger.-born) government official; U.S. secretary of state (1973–77); Nobel Prize winner (1973)

**Knox** \'näks\ John *ca* 1514–1572 Scot. religious reformer

**Koch** \'kȯk, 'kȯk̲, 'kōk, 'kōk̲\ Robert 1843–1910 Ger. bacteriologist; Nobel Prize winner (1905)

**Koś·ciusz·ko** \kȯsh-'chu̇sh-(,)kō, ,kä-sē-'əs-,kō\ Tadeusz 1746–1817 Polish patriot and general in Amer. Revolutionary army

**Krish·na** \'krish-nə, 'krēsh-\ god worshipped in later Hinduism

**Ku·blai Khan** \'kü-,blə-'kän, -,blī-\ 1215–1294 Mongol leader; grandson of Genghis Khan

**La·fa·yette** \,lä-fē-'et, ,la-\ Marquis de 1757–1834 French general in Amer. Revolutionary army

**La·ius** \'lā-əs, 'lī-əs\ king of Thebes who in Greek mythology is killed by his son Oedipus

**Lan·ce·lot** \'lan(t)-sə-,lät, 'län(t)-, -s(ə-)lət\ legendary knight of the Round Table and lover of Queen Guinevere

**Lange** \'laŋ\ Dorothea 1895–1965 Amer. photographer

**Lao·tzu** \'lau̇d-'zə\ *fl.* 6th cent. B.C. Chinese philosopher

**La Salle** \lə-'sal\ Sieur de 1643–1687 *René-Robert Cavelier* French explorer

**La·voi·sier** \ləv-'wä-zē-,ā\ Antoine-Laurent 1743–1794 French chemist

**Law·rence** \'lȯr-ən(t)s, 'lär-\ D. H. 1885–1930 *David Herbert Lawrence* Eng. author

**Lawrence** Thomas Edward 1888–1935 *Lawrence of Arabia* Brit. soldier and author

**Laz·a·rus** \'laz-rəs, 'la-zə-\ brother of Mary and Martha who in the Bible is raised by Jesus from the dead

**Lazarus** beggar in the biblical parable of the rich man and the beggar

**Le·da** \'lē-də\ Spartan princess in Greek mythology who is courted by Zeus in the form of a swan

**Lee** \'lē\ Ann 1736–1784 Eng. mystic; founder of Shaker society in the U.S.

**Lee** Robert Edward 1807–1870 Amer. Confederate general

**Leeu·wen·hoek** \'lā-vən-,hu̇k\ Antonie van 1632–1723 Dutch naturalist

**Leib·niz** \'līb-nəts\ Gottfried Wilhelm 1646–1716 Ger. philosopher and mathematician

**Leif Er·iks·son** *or* **Er·ics·son** \,lāv-'er-ik-sən, ,lēf-\ *fl.* 1000 Norwegian explorer; son of Erik the Red

**Le·nin** \'le-nən\ 1870–1924 orig. *Vladimir Ilyich Ulyanov* \ül-'yän-əf, -,ȯf, -,ȯv\ Russ. Communist leader

**Leo** \'lē-(,)ō\ name of 13 popes: esp. **I** Saint *died* 461 A.D. *Leo the Great* (pope 440–61); **III** Saint *died* 816 (pope 795–816); **XIII** 1810–1903 (pope 1878–1903)

**Le·o·nar·do da Vin·ci** \ˌlē-ə-'när-(ˌ)dō-də 'vin-chē, ˌlā-, -'vēn-\ 1452–1519 Ital. painter, sculptor, architect, and engineer

**Lew·is** \'lü-əs\ C. S. 1898–1963 *Clive Staples Lewis* Brit. author

**Lewis** John Llewellyn 1880–1969 Amer. labor leader

**Lewis** Meriwether 1774–1809 Amer. explorer (with William Clark)

**Lewis** Sinclair 1885–1951 Amer. author; Nobel Prize winner (1930)

**Lin·coln** \'liŋ-kən\ Abraham 1809–1865 16th pres. of the U.S. (1861–65)

**Lind·bergh** \'lin(d)-ˌbərg\ Charles Augustus 1902–1974 Amer. aviator

**Lin·nae·us** \lə-'nē-əs, -'nā-\ Carolus 1707–1778 *Carl von Linné* Swedish botanist

**Lis·ter** \'lis-tər\ Joseph 1827–1912 Eng. surgeon and medical scientist

**Liszt** \'list\ Franz 1811–1886 Hungarian pianist and composer

**Liv·ing·stone** \'li-viŋ-stən\ David 1813–1873 Scot. missionary in Africa

**Locke** \'läk\ John 1632–1704 Eng. philosopher

**Lon·don** \'lən-dən\ Jack 1876–1916 *John Griffith London* Amer. author

**Long·fel·low** \'lȯŋ-ˌfe-(ˌ)lō\ Henry Wadsworth 1807–1882 Amer. poet

**Lou·is** \'lü-ē, lü-'ē\ name of 18 kings of France: esp. **IX** Saint 1214–1270 (r. 1226–70); **XI** 1423–1483 (r. 1461–83); **XII** 1462–1515 (r. 1498–1515); **XIII** 1601–1643 (r. 1610–43); **XIV** 1638–1715 (r. 1643–1715); **XV** 1710–1774 (r. 1715–74); **XVI** 1754–1793 (r. 1774–92; guillotined); **XVII** 1785–1795 (r. in name 1793–95); **XVIII** 1755–1824 (r. 1814–15; 1815–24)

**Lou·is** \'lü-əs\ Joe 1914–1981 orig. *Joseph Louis Barrow* Amer. boxer

**Low** \'lō\ Juliette 1860–1927 née *Gordon* Amer. founder of the Girl Scouts

**Low·ell** \'lō-əl\ Amy 1874–1925 Amer. poet

**Lowell** James Russell 1819–1891 Amer. author

**Luke** \'lük\ physician and companion of the apostle Paul believed to be the author of the 3d Gospel and the Book of Acts

**Lu·ther** \'lü-thər\ Martin 1483–1546 Ger. Reformation leader

**Ly·on** \'lī-ən\ Mary 1797–1849 Amer. educator

**Mac·Ar·thur** \mə-'kär-thər\ Douglas 1880–1964 Amer. general

**Mac·don·ald** \mək-'dä-nʰld\ Sir John Alexander 1815–1891 first prime minister of Canada (1867–1873; 1878–1891)

**Ma·chi·a·vel·li** \ˌma-kē-ə-'ve-lē\ Niccolò 1469–1527 Ital. political philosopher

**Mad·i·son** \'ma-də-sən\ James 1751–1836 4th pres. of the U.S. (1809–17)

**Ma·gel·lan** \mə-'je-lən, *chiefly Brit* -'ge-\ Ferdinand *ca* 1480–1521 Portuguese navigator and explorer

**Mah·ler** \'mä-lər\ Gustav 1860–1911 Austrian composer

**Mal·colm X** \'mal-kəm-'eks\ *Malcolm Little* 1925–1965 Amer. civil rights leader

**Man·dela** \man-'de-lə\ Nelson Rolihlahla 1918–2013 pres. of South Africa (1994–99); Nobel Prize winner (1993)

**Ma·net** \ma-'nā, mä-\ Édouard 1832–1883 French painter

**Mann** \'man\ Horace 1796–1859 Amer. educator

**Mao Tse-tung** *or* **Mao Zedong** \'maȯ-(ˀ)(d)zə-'dùn, -(ˀ)tsə-\ 1893–1976 leader of People's Republic of China (1949–76)

**Mar·co·ni** \mär-'kō-nē\ Guglielmo 1874–1937 Ital. physicist and inventor; Nobel Prize winner (1909)

**Marco Polo** — see POLO

**Ma·rie An·toi·nette** \ˌan-twə-'net, -tə-\ 1755–1793 wife of Louis XVI of France

**Mar·i·on** \'mer-ē-ən\ Francis 1732?–1795 *the Swamp Fox* Amer. commander in Revolution

**Mark** \'märk\ evangelist believed to be the author of the 2d Gospel

**Mark Antony** — see ANTONY

**Mar·quette** \mär-'ket\ Jacques 1637–1675 *Père Marquette* French-born Jesuit missionary and explorer in America

**Mars** \'märz\ god of war in Roman mythology — compare ARES

**Mar·shall** \'mär-shəl\ George Catlett 1880–1959 Amer. general and diplomat; Nobel Prize winner (1953)

**Marshall** John 1755–1835 Amer. jurist; chief justice of the U.S. Supreme Court (1801–35)

**Marshall** Thurgood 1908–1993 Amer. jurist

**Mar·tha** \'mär-thə\ sister of Lazarus and Mary and friend of Jesus in the Bible

**Mar·tin** \'mär-tʰn, mär-'taⁿ\ Saint 316–397 *Martin of Tours* \-'tùr\ patron saint of France

**Mar·tin** \'mär-tʰn\ Paul (Edgar Phillipe) 1938– Canad. prime minister (2003–06)

**Marx** \'märks\ Karl 1818–1883 Ger. political philosopher and socialist

**Mary** \'mer-ē, 'ma-rē, 'mā-rē\ *Saint Mary*; *Virgin Mary* mother of Jesus

**Mary** sister of Lazarus and Martha in the Bible

**Mary I** 1516–1558 *Mary Tudor*; *Bloody Mary* queen of England (1553–58)

**Mary II** 1662–1694 joint Brit. sovereign with William III (1689–94)

**Mary Mag·da·lene** \'mag-də-lən, -ˌlēn\ woman in the Bible who sees the risen Christ

**Mary, Queen of Scots** 1542–1587 *Mary Stuart* queen of Scotland (1542–67)

**Mas·sa·soit** \ˌma-sə-'sȯit\ *died* 1661 Amer. Indian chief

**Math·er** \'ma-thər, -thər\ Cotton 1663–1728 Amer. religious leader and author

**Mather** Increase 1639–1723 Amer. minister and author; father of Cotton Mather

**Ma·tisse** \ma-'tēs, mə-\ Henri 1869–1954 French painter

**Mat·thew** \'ma-(ˌ)thyü\ apostle believed to be the author of the 1st Gospel

**Mau·pas·sant** \ˌmō-pə-'säⁿ\ Guy de 1850–1893 French author

**Max·well** \'maks-ˌwel, -ˌwəl\ James Clerk 1831–1879 Scot. physicist

**Mays** \'māz\ Willie Howard 1931– Amer. baseball player

**Mc·Au·liffe** \mə-'kȯl-əf\ Christa 1948–1986 Amer. teacher; 1st private citizen in space (1986)

**Mc·Car·thy** \mə-'kär-thē\ Joseph Raymond 1908–1957 Amer. politician

**Mc·Clel·lan** \mə-'kle-lən\ George Brinton 1826–1885 Amer. general

**Mc·Clin·tock** \mə-'klin-tək\ Barbara 1902–1992 Amer. botanist; Nobel Prize winner (1983)

**Mc·Cor·mick** \mə-'kȯr-mik\ Cyrus Hall 1809–1884 Amer. inventor

**Mc·Kin·ley** \mə-'kin-lē\ William 1843–1901 25th pres. of the U.S. (1897–1901)

**Mead** \'mēd\ Margaret 1901–1978 Amer. anthropologist

**Meade** \'mēd\ George Gordon 1815–1872 Amer. Civil War general

**Mea·ny** \'mē-nē\ George 1894–1980 Amer. labor leader

**Me·dea** \mə-'dē-ə\ woman with magic powers in Greek mythology who helps Jason to win the Golden Fleece and who kills her children when he leaves her

**Medici** Catherine de' — see CATHERINE DE MÉDICIS

**Me·di·ci** \'me-də-chē\ Lorenzo de' 1449–1492 *Lorenzo the Magnificent* Florentine statesman, ruler, and patron of the arts

**Me·du·sa** \mi-'dü-sə, -'dyü-, -zə\ Gorgon in Greek mythology slain by Perseus

**Me·ir** \mā-'ir\ Golda 1898–1978 prime minister of Israel (1969–74)

**Mel·ville** \'mel-ˌvil\ Herman 1819–1891 Amer. author

**Men·del** \'men-dᵊl\ Gregor Johann 1822–1884 Austrian botanist

**Men·dels·sohn** (**–Bar·thol·dy**) \'mend-ᵊl-sən(-ˌbär-'tōl-dē, -'thȯl-)\ Felix 1809–1847 Ger. composer

**Men·e·la·us** \ˌme-nə-'lā-əs\ king of Sparta, brother of Agamemnon, and husband of Helen of Troy in Greek mythology

**Meph·is·toph·e·les** \ˌme-fə-'stä-fə-ˌlēz\ chief devil in the Faust legend

**Mer·ca·tor** \(ˌ)mər-'kā-tər\ Gerardus 1512–1594 orig. *Gerhard Kremer* Flemish cartographer

**Mer·cu·ry** \'mər-kyə-rē, -k(ə-)rē\ god of commerce, eloquence, travel, and theft who serves as messenger of the other gods in Roman mythology — compare HERMES

**Mer·lin** \'mər-lən\ prophet and magician in the legend of King Arthur

**Met·a·com** \'me-tə-ˌkäm\ *or* King Philip *ca* 1638–1676 *Met·a·com·et* \ˌme-tə-'käm-ət\ Amer. Indian chief; son of Massasoit

**Mi·chael** \'mī-kəl\ archangel named in Hebrew tradition — compare GABRIEL, RAPHAEL, URIEL

**Mi·chel·an·ge·lo** \ˌmī-kə-'lan-jə-ˌlō, ˌmi-, ˌmē-kə-'län-\ 1475–1564 Ital. sculptor, painter, architect, and poet

**Mi·das** \'mī-dəs\ legendary king having the power to turn everything he touched into gold

**Mil·lay** \mi-'lā\ Edna St. Vincent 1892–1950 Amer. poet

**Mil·ler** \'mi-lər\ Arthur 1915–2005 Amer. playwright

**Milne** \'mil(n)\ A. A. 1882–1956 *Alan Alexander Milne* Eng. author

**Mil·ton** \'mil-tᵊn\ John 1608–1674 Eng. poet

**Mi·ner·va** \mə-'nər-və\ goddess of wisdom in Roman mythology — compare ATHENA

**Mi·no·taur** \'mi-nə-ˌtȯr, 'mī-\ monster in Greek mythology shaped half like a man and half like a bull

**Min·u·it** \'min-yə-wət\ Peter *ca* 1580–1638 Dutch colonial administrator in America

**Mitch·ell** \'mi-chəl\ Maria 1818–1889 Amer. astronomer

**Mo·lière** \mōl-'yer, mōl-'yer\ 1622–1673 orig. *Jean-Baptiste Poquelin* French actor and playwright

**Mo·net** \mō-'nā\ Claude 1840–1926 French painter

**Mon·roe** \mən-'rō\ James 1758–1831 5th pres. of the U.S. (1817–25)

**Mont·calm** \mänt-'kälm-, -'käm-\ Marquis de 1712–1759 *Louis-Joseph de Montcalm-Grozon* French field marshal in Canada

**Mon·tes·so·ri** \ˌmän-tə-'sȯr-ē\ Maria 1870–1952 Ital. educator

**Mon·te·ver·di** \ˌmän-tə-'ver-dē, -'vər-\ Claudio 1567–1643 Ital. composer

**Mon·te·zu·ma II** \ˌmän-tə-'zü-mə\ 1466–1520 last Aztec emperor of Mexico (1502–20)

**Moore** \'mȯr, 'mùr\ Marianne 1887–1972 Amer. poet

**More** \'mȯr\ Sir Thomas 1478–1535 *Saint Thomas More* Eng. public official and author

**Mor·gan** \'mȯr-gən\ J. P. 1837–1913 *John Pierpont Morgan* Amer. financier

**Mor·ri·son** \'mȯr-ə-sən, 'mär-\ Toni 1931– orig. *Chloe Anthony Wofford* Amer. author; Nobel Prize winner (1993)

**Morse** \'mȯrs\ Samuel Finley Breese 1791–1872 Amer. artist and inventor

**Mo·ses** \'mō-zəz\ Hebrew prophet and lawgiver in the Bible

**Moses** Grandma 1860–1961 *Anna Mary Moses* née *Robertson* Amer. painter

**Mott** \'mät\ Lucretia 1793 1880 Amer. reformer

**Mo·zart** \'mōt-,särt\ Wolfgang Amadeus 1756–1791 Austrian composer

**Mu·ham·mad** \mō-'ha-məd, -'hä-\ *ca* 570–632 A.D. Arab prophet and founder of Islam

**Mun·ro** \(,)mən-'rō\ Alice 1931– née *Laidlaw* Canadian writer; Nobel Prize Winner (2013)

**Mur·row** \'mər-(,)ō, 'mə-(,)rō\ Edward Roscoe 1908–1965 Amer. journalist

**Mus·so·li·ni** \,mü-sə-'lē-nē, ,mú-\ Be·ni·to \bə-'nēt-ō\ 1883–1945 *Il Duce* \ēl-'dü-chā\ Ital. fascist premier (1922–43)

**Na·bo·kov** \nə-'bò-kəf\ Vladimir 1899–1977 Amer. (Russ.-born) author

**Na·po·leon I** \nə-'pōl-yən, 'pō-lē-ən\ *or* **Napoleon Bo·na·parte** \'bō-nə-,pärt\ 1769–1821 French general and emperor of the French (1804–15)

**Nar·cis·sus** \när-'si-səs\ beautiful youth in Greek mythology who pines away for love of his own reflection and is then turned into the narcissus flower

**Nash** \'nash\ Ogden 1902–1971 Amer. poet

**Na·tion** \'nā-shən\ Car·ry \'kar-ē\ Amelia 1846–1911 née *Moore* Amer. temperance agitator

**Nav·ra·ti·lo·va** \,nav-rə-tə-'lō-və\ Martina 1956–    Amer. (Czech-born) tennis player

**Neb·u·cha·drez·zar II** \,ne-byə-kə-'dre-zər, -bə-\ *or* **Neb·u·chad·nez·zar** \-kəd-'ne-\ *ca* 630–*ca* 561 B.C. Chaldean king of Babylon (605–562)

**Neh·ru** \'ner-(,)ü, 'nā-(,)rü\ Ja·wa·har·lal \jə-'wä-hər-,läl\ 1889–1964 1st prime minister of Republic of India (1947–64)

**Nel·son** \'nel-sən\ Horatio 1758–1805 Viscount *Nelson* Brit. admiral

**Nem·e·sis** \'ne-mə-səs\ goddess of reward and punishment in Greek mythology

**Nep·tune** \'nep-,tün, -,tyün\ god of the sea in Roman mythology — compare POSEIDON

**Ne·ro** \'nē-(,)rō, 'nir-(,)o\ 37–68 A.D. Roman emperor (54 68)

**Ne·ru·da** \nā-'rü-də, -(,)thä\ Pablo 1904–1973 orig. *Neftalí Ricardo Reyes Basoalto* Chilean poet

**Nev·el·son** \'ne-vəl-sən\ Louise 1900?–1988 Amer. sculptor

**New·ton** \'nü-t°n, 'nyü-\ Sir Isaac 1642–1727 Eng. mathematician and physicist

**Nich·o·las** \'ni-k(ə-)ləs\ Saint *fl.* 4th cent. A.D. Christian bishop

**Nicholas I** 1796–1855 czar of Russia (1825–55)

**Nicholas II** 1868–1918 last czar of Russia (1894–1917)

**Nietz·sche** \'nē-chə, -chē\ Friedrich Wilhelm 1844–1900 Ger. philosopher

**Night·in·gale** \'nī-t°n-,gäl, -tin-\ Florence 1820–1910 *Lady of the Lamp* Eng. nurse and philanthropist

**Ni·ke** \'nī-kē\ goddess of victory in Greek mythology

**Ni·o·be** \'nī-ə-bē\ bereaved mother in Greek mythology who while weeping for her slain children is turned into a stone from which her tears continue to flow

**Nix·on** \'nik-sən\ Richard Milhous 1913–1994 37th pres. of the U.S. (1969–74)

**No·ah** \'nō-ə\ biblical builder of the ark in which he, his family, and living creatures of every kind survive the biblical Flood

**No·bel** \nō-'bel\ Alfred Bernhard 1833–1896 Swedish manufacturer, inventor, and philanthropist

**Oak·ley** \'ōk-lē\ Annie 1860–1926 orig. *Phoebe Anne Oakley Moses* Amer. sharpshooter

**Oba·ma** \ō-'bä-mə\ **Ba·rack** \bə-'räk\ Hussein, Jr. 1961–    44th pres. of the U.S. (2009–   ); Nobel Prize winner (2009)

**Oce·anus** \ō-'sē-ə-nəs\ Titan who rules over a great river encircling the earth in Greek mythology

**O'·Con·nor** \ō-'kä-nər\ (Mary) Flannery 1925–1964 Amer. author

**O'Connor** Sandra Day 1930–    Amer. jurist

**Odin** \'ō-d°n\ *or* **Wo·den** \'wō-d°n\ chief god, god of war, and patron of heroes in Norse mythology

**Odys·seus** \ō-'di-sē-əs, -'dis-yəs, -'di-shəs, -'di-,shüs\ *or* **Ulys·ses** \yü-'li-(,)sēz\ king of Ithaca and hero in Greek mythology

**Oe·di·pus** \'e-də-pəs, 'ē-\ son of Laius and Jocasta who in Greek mythology kills his father and marries his mother not knowing their identity

**Ogle·thorpe** \'ō-gəl-,thòrp\ James Edward 1696–1785 Eng. general and founder of Georgia

**O'·Keeffe** \ō-'kēf\ Georgia 1887–1986 Amer. painter

**Olaf V** \'ō-ləf, -,läf, -,laf; 'ü-,läf\ 1903–1991 king of Norway (1957–91)

**Omar Khay·yám** \,ō-,mär-,kī-'yäm, ,ō-mər-, -'yam\ 1048–1131 Persian poet and astronomer

**O'·Neill** \ō-'nēl\ Eugene Gladstone 1888–1953 Amer. playwright; Nobel Prize winner (1936)

**Or·pheus** \'òr-,fyüs, -fē-əs\ poet and musician in Greek mythology

**Or·well** \'òr-,wel, -wəl\ George 1903–1950 pseud. of *Eric Arthur Blair* Eng. author

**Osce·o·la** \,ä-sē-'ō-lə, ,ō-\ *ca* 1804–1838 Seminole Indian chief

**Otis** \'ō-təs\ James 1725–1783 Amer. Revolutionary patriot

**Ov·id** \'ä-vəd\ 43 B.C.–17 A.D.? Roman poet

**Ow·en** \'ō-ən\ Robert 1771–1858 Welsh social reformer

**Ow·ens** \'ō-ənz\ Jesse 1913–1980 orig. *James Cleveland Owens* Amer. track-and-field athlete

**Paine** \'pān\ Thomas 1737–1809 Amer. (Eng.-born) political philosopher and author

**Pan** \'pan\ god of pastures, flocks, and shepherds in Greek mythology who is usu. represented as having the legs, ears, and horns of a goat

**Pan·do·ra** \pan-'dȯr-ə\ woman in Greek mythology who out of curiosity opens a box and lets loose all of the evils that trouble humans

**Pank·hurst** \'paŋk-ˌhərst\ Emmeline 1858–1928 née *Goulden* Eng. suffragist

**Par·is** \'pa-rəs\ son of Priam whose abduction of Helen of Troy in Greek mythology leads to the Trojan War

**Park·man** \'pärk-mən\ Francis 1823–1893 Amer. historian

**Parks** \'pärks\ Rosa 1913–2005 née *McCauley* Amer. civil rights activist

**Pas·cal** \pa-'skal, päs-'käl\ Blaise 1623–1662 French mathematician and philosopher

**Pas·ter·nak** \'pas-tər-ˌnak\ Boris Leonidovich 1890–1960 Russ. author; Nobel Prize winner (1958)

**Pas·teur** \pas-'tər\ Louis 1822–1895 French chemist and microbiologist

**Pat·rick** \'pa-trik\ Saint *fl.* 5th cent. A.D. apostle and patron saint of Ireland

**Pat·ton** \'pa-tᵊn\ George Smith 1885–1945 Amer. general

**Paul** \'pȯl\ Saint *died ca.* 67 A.D. Christian missionary and author of several New Testament epistles

**Paul** name of 6 popes: esp. **III** 1468–1549 (pope 1534–49); **V** 1552–1621 (pope 1605–21); **VI** 1897–1978 (pope 1963–78)

**Paul Bun·yan** \'bən-yən\ giant lumberjack in Amer. folklore

**Pau·ling** \'pȯ-liŋ\ Linus Carl 1901–1994 Amer. chemist; Nobel Prize winner (1954, 1962)

**Pav·lov** \'päv-ˌlȯf, 'pav-, -ˌlȯv\ Ivan Petrovich 1849–1936 Russ. physiologist; Nobel Prize winner (1904)

**Pav·lo·va** \'pav-lə-və, pav-'lō-\ Anna 1881–1931 Russ. ballerina

**Pea·ry** \'pir-ē\ Robert Edwin 1856–1920 Amer. arctic explorer

**Peg·a·sus** \'pe-gə-səs\ winged horse in Greek mythology

**Pei** \'pā\ Ieoh Ming 1917– Amer. (Chinese-born) architect

**Penn** \'pen\ William 1644–1718 Eng. Quaker leader and founder of Pennsylvania

**Per·i·cles** \'per-ə-ˌklēz\ *ca* 495–429 B.C. Athenian political leader

**Per·ry** \'per-ē\ Matthew Calbraith 1794–1858 Amer. commodore

**Perry** Oliver Hazard 1785–1819 Amer. naval officer; brother of the preceding

**Per·seph·o·ne** \pər-'se-fə-nē\ daughter of Zeus and Demeter who in Greek mythology is abducted by Pluto to rule with him over the underworld

**Per·shing** \'pər-shiŋ, -zhiŋ\ John Joseph 1860–1948 Amer. general

**Pe·ter** \'pē-tər\ Saint *died ca.* 64 A.D. orig. *Si·mon* \'sī-mən-\ one of the 12 apostles in the Bible

**Peter I** 1672–1725 *Peter the Great* czar of Russia (1682–1725)

**Phil·ip** \'fi-ləp\ Saint, one of the 12 apostles in the Bible

**Philip King** — see METACOM

**Philip** name of 6 kings of France: esp. **II** *or* **Philip Augustus** 1165–1223 (r. 1179–1223); **IV** 1268–1314 *Philip the Fair* (r. 1285–1314); **VI** 1293–1350 (r. 1328–50)

**Philip** name of 5 kings of Spain: esp. **II** 1527–1598 (r. 1556–98); **V** 1683–1746 (r. 1700–46)

**Philip II** 382–336 B.C. king of Macedon (359–336); father of Alexander the Great

**Pi·cas·so** \pi-'kä-(ˌ)sō, -'ka-\ Pablo 1881–1973 Span. painter and sculptor in France

**Pic·card** \pi-'kär, -'kärd\ Auguste 1884–1962 and his son Jacques 1922–2008 Swiss scientists and developers of the bathyscaphe

**Pick·ett** \'pi-kət\ George Edward 1825–1875 Amer. Confederate general

**Pierce** \'pirs\ Franklin 1804–1869 14th pres. of the U.S. (1853–57)

**Pi·late** \'pī-lət\ Pon·tius \'pän-chəs, 'pən-chəs\ *died after* 36 A.D. Roman governor of Judea (26–36)

**Pin·ker·ton** \'piŋ-kər-tᵊn\ Allan 1819–1884 Amer. (Scot.-born) detective

**Pis·sar·ro** \pə-'sär-(ˌ)ō\ Camille 1830–1903 French (West Indian-born) painter

**Pitt** \'pit\ William 1759–1806 *the Younger Pitt* Eng. prime minister (1783–1801; 1804–6)

**Pi·us** \'pī-əs\ name of 12 popes: esp. **VII** 1742–1823 (pope 1800–23); **IX** 1792–1878 (pope 1846–78); **X** Saint 1835–1914 (pope 1903–14); **XI** 1857–1939 (pope 1922–39); **XII** 1876–1958 (pope 1939–58)

**Pi·zar·ro** \pə-'zär-(ˌ)ō\ Francisco *ca* 1475–1541 Span. conqueror of Peru

**Planck** \'pläŋk\ Max Karl Ernst Ludwig 1858–1947 Ger. physicist

**Pla·to** \'plā-(ˌ)tō\ *ca* 428–348 (*or* 347) B.C. Greek philosopher

**Plu·to** \'plü-(ˌ)tō\ god of the underworld in Greek mythology

**Po·ca·hon·tas** \ˌpō-kə-'hän-təs\ *ca* 1595–1617 Amer. Indian friend of the colonists at Jamestown; daughter of Powhatan

**Poe** \'pō\ Edgar Allan 1809–1849 Amer. author

**Polk** \'pōk\ James Knox 1795–1849 11th pres. of the U.S. (1845–49)

**Pol·lock** \'pä-lək\ (Paul) Jackson 1912–1956 Amer. painter

**Po·lo** \'pō-(,)lō\ Marco ca 1254–1324 Venetian merchant and traveler

**Poly·phe·mus** \,pä-lə-'fē-məs\ a one-eyed creature in Greek mythology that is blinded by Odysseus

**Ponce de Le·ón** \,pän(t)-sə-,dā-lē-'ōn, ,pänts-də-, -'lē-ən\ Juan 1460–1521 Span. explorer

**Pon·ti·ac** \'pän-tē-,ak\ ca 1720–1769 Ottawa Indian chief

**Por·ter** \'pȯr-tər\ Cole Albert 1891–1964 Amer. composer

**Porter** Katherine Anne 1890–1980 Amer. author

**Porter** William Sydney — see O. HENRY

**Po·sei·don** \pə-'sī-dᵊn\ god of the sea in Greek mythology — compare NEPTUNE

**Pot·ter** \'pä-tər\ (Helen) Beatrix 1866–1943 Brit. author and illustrator

**Pound** \'paúnd\ Ezra Loomis 1885–1972 Amer. poet

**Pound·mak·er** \'paúnd-,mā-kər\ 1826–1886 Cree Indian chief

**Pow·ell** \'paú(-ə)l\ Colin Luther 1937–       Amer. general; U.S. secretary of state (2001–05)

**Pow·ha·tan** \,paú-ə-'tan, paú-'ha-tᵊn\ 1550?–1618 Amer. Indian chief of a confederacy of Algonquian-speaking tribes; father of Pocahontas

**Pres·ley** \'pres-lē, 'prez-\ Elvis Aaron 1935–1977 Amer. popular singer

**Pri·am** \'prī-əm, -,am\ king of Troy during the Trojan War in Greek mythology

**Price** \'prīs\ (Mary) Leontyne 1927–       Amer. soprano

**Pro·me·theus** \prə-'mē-thē-əs, -,thyüs\ Titan in Greek mythology who is punished by Zeus for stealing fire from heaven and giving it to humans

**Pro·teus** \'prō-tyüs, -tē-əs\ sea god in Greek mythology who is capable of assuming different forms

**Proust** \'prüst\ Marcel 1871–1922 French novelist

**Ptol·e·my** \'tä-lə-mē\ fl. 2d cent. A.D. Greco-Egyptian astronomer, geographer, and mathematician in Alexandria

**Puc·ci·ni** \pü-'chē-nē\ Giacomo 1858–1924 Ital. composer

**Pu·las·ki** \pə-'las-kē, pyü-\ Kazimierz 1747–1779 Polish soldier in Amer. Revolutionary army

**Pu·lit·zer** \'pú-lət-sər (family's pron), 'pyü-\ Joseph 1847–1911 Amer. (Hungarian-born) journalist

**Pu·tin** \'pü-tin\ Vladimir Vladimirovich 1952–       pres. of Russia (2000–08; 2012–   )

**Pyg·ma·lion** \pig-'māl-yən, -'mā-lē-ən\ sculptor in Greek mythology who creates Galatea

**Py·thag·o·ras** \pə-'tha-gə-rəs, pī-\ ca 580–ca 500 B.C. Greek philosopher and mathematician

**Ra** \'rä\ god of the sun and chief deity of ancient Egypt

**Ra·leigh** or **Ra·legh** \'rȯ-lē, 'rä- also 'ra-\ Sir Walter 1554?–1618 Eng. navigator and writer

**Ram·ses** \'ram-,sēz\ or **Ram·e·ses** \'ra-mə-,sēz\ name of 12 kings of Egypt: esp. **II** (r. 1279–1213 B.C.); **III** (r. 1187–1156 B.C.)

**Ran·dolph** \'ran-,dälf\ Asa Philip 1889–1979 Amer. labor and civil rights leader

**Ra·pha·el** \'ra-fē-əl, 'rä-, -,el\ archangel named in Hebrew tradition — compare GABRIEL, MICHAEL, URIEL

**Ra·pha·el** \'ra-fē-əl, 'rä-, 'rä-\ 1483–1520 orig. Raffaello Sanzio or Santi Ital. painter

**Ras·pu·tin** \ra-'spyü-tᵊn, -'spü-, 'spü-\ Grigory Yefimovich 1872–1916 Russ. mystic

**Ra·vel** \rə-'vel, ra-\ Joseph Maurice 1875–1937 French composer

**Rea·gan** \'rā-gən\ Ronald Wilson 1911–2004 40th pres. of the U.S. (1981–89)

**Re·bek·ah** \ri-'be-kə\ wife of Isaac and mother of Jacob in the Bible

**Red Cloud** \'red-,klaúd\ 1822–1909 Sioux Indian chief

**Red Jack·et** \'red-'ja-kət\ 1758?–1830 Sago·ye·wa·tha \sä-,goi-(y)ə-'wä-thə\ Seneca Indian chief

**Reed** \'rēd\ Walter 1851–1902 Amer. army surgeon

**Rehn·quist** \'ren-,kwist, 'ren-kwəst\ William Hubbs 1924–2005 Amer. jurist; chief justice of the U.S. Supreme Court (1986–2005)

**Rem·brandt** \'rem-,brant also -,bränt\ 1606–1669 Rembrandt (Harmenszoon) van Rijn Dutch painter

**Rem·ing·ton** \'re-miŋ-tən\ Frederic 1861–1909 Amer. painter and sculptor

**Re·mus** \'rē-məs\ son of Mars who in Roman mythology is killed by his twin brother Romulus

**Re·noir** \'ren-,wär, rən-'\ (Pierre-) Auguste 1841–1919 French painter

**Re·vere** \ri-'vir\ Paul 1735–1818 Amer. patriot and silversmith

**Rich·ard** \'ri-chərd\ name of 3 kings of England: **I** 1157–1199 Richard the Lion-Hearted (r. 1189–99); **II** 1367–1400 (r. 1377–99); **III** 1452–1485 (r. 1483–85)

**Ride** \'rīd\ Sally Kristen 1951–2012 Amer. astronaut; 1st Amer. woman in space (1983)

**Rob·erts** \'rä-bərts\ John Glover Jr. 1995–       Amer. jurist; chief justice of the U.S. Supreme Court (2005–   )

**Rob·in Good·fel·low** \'rä-bən-'gúd-,fe-(,)lō\ mischievous elf in Eng. folklore

**Robin Hood** \ˌhu̇d\ legendary Eng. outlaw who gave to the poor what he stole from the rich

**Rob·in·son** \ˈrä-bən-sən\ Edwin Arlington 1869–1935 Amer. poet

**Robinson** Jackie 1919–1972 *Jack Roosevelt Robinson* Amer. baseball player

**Rob·in·son Cru·soe** \ˈrä-bə(n)-sən-ˈkrü-(ˌ)sō\ shipwrecked sailor in Daniel Defoe's *Robinson Crusoe* who lives for many years on a desert island

**Ro·cham·beau** \ˌrō-ˌsham-ˈbō\ Comte de 1725–1807 French general in Amer. Revolution

**Rocke·fel·ler** \ˈrä-ki-ˌfe-lər\ John Davison 1839–1937 and his son John Davison, Jr. 1874–1960 Amer. oil magnates and philanthropists

**Ro·din** \rō-ˈdaⁿ(n)\ François-Auguste-René 1840–1917 French sculptor

**Ro·ma·nov** \rō-ˈmä-nəf, ˈrō-mə-ˌnäf\ Michael 1596–1645 1st czar (1613–45) of Russ. Romanov dynasty (1613–1917)

**Rom·u·lus** \ˈräm-yə-ləs\ son of Mars in Roman mythology who is the twin brother of Remus and the founder of Rome

**Rönt·gen** *or* **Roent·gen** \ˈrent-gən, ˈrənt-, -jən\ Wilhelm Conrad 1845–1923 Ger. physicist; Nobel Prize winner (1901)

**Roo·se·velt** \ˈrō-zə-vəlt, -ˌvelt\ (Anna) Eleanor 1884–1962 Amer. lecturer and writer; wife of F. D. Roosevelt

**Roosevelt** Franklin Delano 1882–1945 32nd pres. of the U.S. (1933–45)

**Roosevelt** Theodore 1858–1919 26th pres. of the U.S. (1901–09); Nobel Prize winner (1906)

**Ross** \ˈrȯs\ Betsy 1752–1836 née *Griscom* reputed maker of 1st Amer. flag

**Ros·si·ni** \rȯ-ˈsē-nē, rə-\ Gioacchino Antonio 1792–1868 Ital. composer

**Roth** \ˈrȯth\ Philip Milton 1933– Amer. author

**Rous·seau** \rü-ˈsō, ˈrü-ˌ\ Jean-Jacques 1712–1778 French (Swiss-born) philosopher and writer

**Row·ling** \ˈrō-liŋ\ J. K. 1965– *Joanne Kathleen Rowling* Brit. author

**Ru·bens** \ˈrü-bənz\ Peter Paul 1577–1640 Flemish painter

**Ru·dolph** \ˈrü-ˌdȯlf, -ˌdälf\ Wilma Glodean 1940–1994 Amer. athlete

**Rus·sell** \ˈrə-səl\ Bertrand Arthur William 1872–1970 3d Earl *Russell* Eng. mathematician and philosopher; Nobel Prize winner (1950)

**Ruth** \ˈrüth\ woman in the Bible who was one of the ancestors of King David

**Ruth** Babe 1895–1948 *George Herman Ruth* Amer. baseball player

**Ruth·er·ford** \ˈrə-thə(r)-fərd, -thə(r)-\ Ernest 1871–1937 Baron *Rutherford* Brit. physicist; Nobel Prize winner (1908)

**Sa·bin** \ˈsā-bin\ Albert Bruce 1906–1993 Amer. (Polish-born) physician and microbiologist

**Sac·a·ga·wea** \ˌsa-kə-jə-ˈwē-ə\ 1786?–1812 Shoshone Indian guide to Lewis and Clark

**Sa·dat** \sə-ˈdat, -ˈdät\ Anwar el- 1918–1981 pres. of Egypt (1970–81); Nobel Prize winner (1978)

**Sa·gan** \ˈsā-gən\ Carl Edward 1934–1996 Amer. astronomer and science writer

**Saint Nicholas** — see Saint NICHOLAS, SANTA CLAUS

**Sal·a·din** \ˈsa-lə-ˌdēn, -dən\ 1137 (or 1138)–1193 Kurdish general; sultan of Egypt and Syria

**Sal·in·ger** \ˈsa-lən-jər\ J. D. 1919–2010 *Jerome David Salinger* Amer. author

**Salk** \ˈsȯ(l)k\ Jonas Edward 1914–1995 Amer. physician and medical researcher

**Sa·lo·me** \sə-ˈlō-mē, ˈsa-lə-(ˌ)mā\ niece of Herod Antipas who in the Bible is given the head of John the Baptist as a reward for her dancing

**Sa·mo·set** \ˈsa-mə-ˌset, sə-ˈmä-sət\ *died ca.* 1653 Amer. Indian leader

**Sam·son** \ˈsam(p)-sən\ powerful Hebrew hero in the Bible who fights against the Philistines but is betrayed by Delilah

**Sam·u·el** \ˈsam-yə-wəl, -yəl\ Hebrew judge in the Bible who appoints Saul and then David king

**Sand·burg** \ˈsan(d)-ˌbərg\ Carl 1878–1967 Amer. author

**Sang·er** \ˈsaŋ-ər\ Margaret 1883–1966 née *Higgins* Amer. birth-control activist

**San·ta Claus** \ˈsan-tə-ˌklȯz\ plump white-bearded and red-suited old man in modern folklore who delivers presents to good children at Christmastime

**Sap·pho** \ˈsa-(ˌ)fō\ *fl. ca* 610–*ca* 580 B.C. Greek poet

**Sa·rah** \ˈser-ə, ˈsä-rə\ wife of Abraham and mother of Isaac in the Bible

**Sar·gent** \ˈsär-jənt\ John Singer 1856–1925 Amer. painter

**Sar·tre** \ˈsärtrᵊ\ Jean-Paul 1905–1980 French philosopher and author

**Sat·urn** \ˈsa-tərn\ god of agriculture in Roman mythology

**Saul** \ˈsȯl, ˈsäl\ 1st king of Israel in the Bible

**Saul** *or* **Saul of Tarsus** the apostle Paul in the Bible

**Sche·her·a·zade** \shə-ˌher-ə-ˈzäd\ fictional wife of a sultan and narrator of the tales in the *Arabian Nights' Entertainments*

**Schin·dler** \ˈshind-lər\ Oskar 1908–1974 Ger. humanitarian during the Holocaust

**Schoen·berg** \ˈshə(r)n-ˌbərg, ˈshœn-ˌberk\ Arnold Franz Walter 1874–1951 Amer. (Austrian-born) composer

**Schu·bert** \ˈshü-bərt, -ˌbert\ Franz Peter 1797–1828 Austrian composer

**Schu·mann** \ˈshü-ˌmän, -mən\ Clara 1819–1896 née *Wieck* \ˈvēk\ Ger. pianist; wife of R. Schumann

**Schumann** Robert Alexander 1810–1856 Ger. composer

**Schweit·zer** \\'shwɪt-sər, 'shvɪt-, 'swɪt-\\ Albert 1875–1965 French theologian, philosopher, physician, and music scholar; Nobel Prize winner (1952)

**Scott** \\'skät\\ Dred \\'dred\\ 1795?–1858 Amer. slave

**Scott** Robert Falcon 1868–1912 Brit. polar explorer

**Scott** Sir Walter 1771–1832 Scot. author

**Scott** Winfield 1786–1866 Amer. general

**Scyl·la** \\'si-lə\\ nymph in Greek mythology who is changed into a monster and inhabits a cave opposite the whirlpool Charybdis off the coast of Sicily

**Se·at·tle** \\sē-'a-t⁵l\\ 1786?–1866 Amer. Indian chief

**Se·le·ne** \\sə-'lē-nē\\ goddess of the moon in classical mythology

**Se·quoy·ah** or **Se·quoia** \\si-'kwòi-ə\\ ca 1760–1843 George Guess Cherokee Indian scholar

**Ser·ra** \\'ser-ə\\ Junípero 1713–1784 Span. missionary in Mexico and California

**Se·ton** \\'sē-t⁵n\\ Saint Elizabeth Ann 1774–1821 Mother Seton née Bayley Amer. religious leader

**Seu·rat** \\sə-'rä\\ Georges 1859–1891 French painter

**Seuss** Dr. — see GEISEL, THEODOR SEUSS

**Sew·ard** \\'sü-ərd, 'sùrd\\ William Henry 1801–1872 Amer. politician; U.S. secretary of state (1861–69)

**Shack·le·ton** \\'sha-kəl-tən\\ Sir Ernest Henry 1874–1922 Brit. polar explorer

**Shake·speare** \\'shāk-ˌspir\\ William 1564–1616 Eng. playwright and poet

**Shaw** \\'shò\\ George Bernard 1856–1950 Brit. playwright; Nobel Prize winner (1925)

**Shaw** Robert Gould 1837–1863 Amer. soldier

**Shel·ley** \\'she-lē\\ Mary Wollstonecraft 1797–1851 née Godwin Eng. author; wife of P. B. Shelley

**Shelley** Percy Bysshe \\'bish\\ 1792–1822 Eng. poet

**Shep·ard** \\'she-pərd\\ Alan Bartlett, Jr. 1923–1998 Amer. astronaut; 1st Amer. in space (1961)

**Sher·i·dan** \\'sher-ə-dən\\ Philip Henry 1831–1888 Amer. general

**Sher·lock Holmes** \\'shər-ˌläk-'hōmz, -'hōlmz\\ detective in stories by Sir Arthur Conan Doyle

**Sher·man** \\'shər-mən\\ John 1823–1900 Amer. statesman; brother of W. T. Sherman

**Sherman** William Tecumseh 1820–1891 Amer. general

**Shi·va** \\'shi-və, 'shē-\\ or **Si·va** \\'si-və, 'shi-, -ˌsē-, 'shē-\\ god of destruction and regeneration in the Hindu sacred triad — compare BRAHMA, VISHNU

**Sieg·fried** \\'sig-ˌfrēd, 'sēg-\\ hero in Germanic legend who kills a dragon guarding a gold hoard

**Si·mon** \\'sī-mən\\ or **Simon the Zealot** one of the 12 apostles in the Bible

**Si·na·tra** \\sə-'nä-trə\\ Frank 1915–1998 Francis Albert Sinatra Amer. singer and actor

**Sind·bad the Sailor** \\'sin-ˌbad\\ citizen of Baghdad whose adventures are narrated in the Arabian Nights' Entertainments

**Sis·y·phus** \\'si-sə-fəs\\ king of Corinth who in Greek mythology is condemned to roll a heavy stone up a hill in Hades only to have it roll down again as it nears the top

**Sit·ting Bull** \\ˌsi-tiŋ-'bùl\\ ca 1831–1890 Sioux Indian chief

**Siva** — see SHIVA

**Smith** \\'smith\\ Adam 1723–1790 Scot. economist

**Smith** Bessie 1894?–1937 Amer. blues singer

**Smith** John ca 1580–1631 Eng. colonist in America

**Smith** Joseph 1805–1844 Amer. founder of the Mormon Church

**Soc·ra·tes** \\'sä-krə-ˌtēz\\ ca 470–399 B.C. Greek philosopher

**Sol** \\'säl\\ god of the sun in Roman mythology — see HELIOS

**Sol·o·mon** \\'sä-lə-mən\\ 10th-century B.C. king of Israel noted for his wisdom

**Sond·heim** \\'sänd-ˌ()hīm\\ Stephen Joshua 1930– Amer. composer and songwriter

**Soph·o·cles** \\'sä-fə-ˌklēz\\ ca 496–406 B.C. Greek playwright

**Sou·sa** \\'sü-zə, 'sü-sə\\ John Philip 1854–1932 Amer. bandmaster and composer

**Spar·ta·cus** \\'spär-tə-kəs\\ died 71 B.C. Roman slave and gladiator

**Sphinx** \\'sfiŋ(k)s\\ monster in Greek mythology having a lion's body, wings, and the head and bust of a woman

**Spiel·berg** \\'spēl-ˌbərg\\ Steven 1947– Amer. filmmaker

**Spi·no·za** \\spi-'nō-zə\\ Benedict de 1632–1677 Hebrew Baruch Spinoza Dutch philosopher

**Squan·to** \\'skwän-tō\\ died 1622 Amer. Indian friend of the Pilgrims

**Sta·lin** \\'stä-lən, 'sta-, -ˌlēn\\ Joseph 1879–1953 Soviet Communist party leader (1922–53), premier (1941–53), and dictator

**Stan·dish** \\'stan-dish\\ Myles or Miles 1584?–1656 Amer. colonist

**Stan·ley** \\'stan-lē\\ Sir Henry Morton 1841–1904 Brit. explorer in Africa

**Stan·ton** \\'stan-t⁵n\\ Elizabeth Cady 1815–1902 Amer. suffragist

**Stein** \\'stīn\\ Gertrude 1874–1946 Amer. author

**Stein·beck** \\'stīn-ˌbek\\ John Ernst 1902–

1968 Amer. author; Nobel Prize winner (1962)

**Steu·ben** \'stü-bən, 'styü-, 'shtȯi-\ Friedrich Wilhelm von 1730–1794 Prussian⸗born general in Amer. Revolution

**Ste·vens** \'stē-vənz\ Wallace 1879–1955 Amer. poet

**Ste·ven·son** \'stē-vən-sən\ Adlai Ewing 1900–1965 Amer. politician

**Stevenson** Robert Louis 1850–1894 Scot. author

**Sto·ker** \'stō-kər\ Bram 1847–1912 *Abraham Stoker* Irish author

**Stowe** \'stō\ Harriet Beecher 1811–1896 Amer. author

**Stra·di·va·ri** \ˌstra-də-'vär-ē, -'ver-\ Antonio 1644?–1737 Ital. violin maker

**Strauss** \'shtraùs, 'straùs\ Johann 1804–1849 and his sons Johann, Jr. 1825–1899 and Josef 1827–1870 Austrian composers

**Strauss** Richard 1864–1949 Ger. composer

**Stra·vin·sky** \strə-'vin(t)-skē\ Igor 1882–1971 Amer. (Russ.-born) composer

**Stu·art** \'stü-ərt, 'styü-; 'st(y)ùrt\ Charles Edward 1720–1788 *the Young Pretender; Bonnie Prince Charlie* claimant to the Brit. throne

**Stuart** Gilbert Charles 1755–1828 Amer. painter

**Stuart** Jeb 1833–1864 *James Ewell Brown Stuart* Amer. Confederate general

**Stuy·ve·sant** \'stī-və-sənt\ Peter *ca* 1610–1672 Dutch colonial administrator in America

**Sul·li·van** \'sə-lə-vən\ Sir Arthur Seymour 1842–1900 Eng. composer; collaborator with Sir William Gilbert

**Sullivan** Louis Henri 1856–1924 Amer. architect

**Sum·ner** \'səm-nər\ Charles 1811–1874 Amer. politician

**Sun Yat–sen** \'sùn-'yät-'sen\ 1866–1925 Chinese statesman

**Sut·ter** \'sə-tər, 'sü-\ John Augustus 1803–1880 Amer. (Ger.-born) pioneer in California

**Swift** \'swift\ Jonathan 1667–1745 Eng. (Irish-born) author

**Synge** \'siŋ\ John Millington 1871–1909 Irish playwright

**Taft** \'taft\ William Howard 1857–1930 27th pres. of the U.S. (1909–13); chief justice of the U.S. Supreme Court (1921–30)

**Ta·gore** \tə-'gȯr\ Ra·bin·dra·nath \rə-'bin-drə-ˌnät\ 1861–1941 Indian poet; Nobel Prize winner (1913)

**Tall·chief** \'tȯl-ˌchēf\ Maria 1925–2013 Amer. dancer

**Tan** \'tan\ Amy 1952– Amer. author

**Ta·ney** \'tȯ-nē\ Roger Brooke 1777–1864 Amer. jurist; chief justice of the U.S. Supreme Court (1836–64)

**Tan·ta·lus** \'tan-tə-ləs\ king in Greek mythology who is condemned to stand up to his chin in a pool of water in Hades and beneath fruit-laden boughs only to have the water or fruit go out of reach at each attempt to drink or eat

**Tay·lor** \'tā-lər\ Zachary 1784–1850 Amer. general; 12th pres. of the U.S. (1849–50)

**Tchai·kov·sky** \chī-'kȯf-skē, chə-, -'kȯv-\ Pyotr Ilich 1840–1893 Russ. composer

**Te·cum·seh** \tə-'kəm(p)-sə, -sē\ 1768–1813 Shawnee Indian chief

**Tek·a·kwitha** \ˌte-kə-'kwi-thə\ Kateri 1656–1680 *Lily of the Mohawks* canonized Mohawk Indian religious

**Ten·ny·son** \'te-nə-sən\ Alfred 1809–1892 Baron *Tennyson* known as *Alfred, Lord Tennyson* Eng. poet

**Te·re·sa** \tə-'rā-zə, -'rē-sə\ Mother 1910–1997 beatified Albanian religious in India; Nobel Prize winner (1979)

**Teresa of Ávi·la** \'ä-vi-lə\ Saint 1515–1582 Span. nun and mystic

**Tes·la** \'tes-lə\ Nikola 1856–1943 Amer. (Croatian-born) electrical engineer and inventor

**Thatch·er** \'tha-chər\ Margaret Hilda 1925–2013 Baroness *Thatcher of Kesteven* née *Roberts* Brit. prime minister (1979–90)

**The·seus** \'thē-ˌsüs, -sē-əs\ hero in Greek mythology who kills the Minotaur and conquers the Amazons

**Thom·as** \'tä-məs\ apostle in the Bible who demanded proof of Jesus' resurrection

**Thomas à Becket** — see Saint Thomas BECKET

**Thomas Aquinas** Saint — see AQUINAS

**Thor** \'thȯr\ god of thunder, weather, and crops in Norse mythology

**Tho·reau** \thə-'rō, thȯ-\ Henry David 1817–1862 Amer. author

**Thorpe** \'thȯrp\ Jim 1888–1953 *James Francis Thorpe* Amer. athlete

**Thur·ber** \'thər-bər\ James Grover 1894–1961 Amer. author

**Ti·be·ri·us** \tī-'bir-ē-əs\ 42 B.C.–37 A.D. Roman emperor (14–37)

**Ti·tian** \'ti-shən\ *ca* 1488–1576 orig. *Tiziano Vecellio* Ital. painter

**Tocque·ville** \'tōk-ˌvil, 'tȯk-, 'täk-, -ˌvēl, -vəl\ Alexis de 1805–1859 French politician and author

**Tol·kien** \'tȯl-ˌkēn\ J. R. R. 1892–1973 *John Ronald Reuel Tolkien* Brit. author

**Tol·stoy** \tȯl-'stȯi, tōl-', täl-', 'tȯl-, 'tōl-, 'täl-\ Leo 1828–1910 Count *Lev Nikolayevich Tolstoy* Russ. author

**Tou·louse–Lau·trec** \ˌtü-ˌlüz-lō-'trek\ Henri de 1864–1901 French painter

**Tri·ton** \'trī-tᵊn\ sea god in Greek mythology who is half man and half fish

**Trots·ky** \'trät-skē\ Leon 1879–1940 orig. *Lev Davidovich Bronstein* Russ. Communist leader

**Tru·deau** \'trü-(ˌ)dō, trü-'\ Pierre Elliott

**Tru·man** \\'trü-mən\\ Harry S. 1884–1972 33rd pres. of the U.S. (1945–53)

**Truth** \\'trüth\\ Sojourner 1797?–1883 Amer. abolitionist

**Tub·man** \\'təb-mən\\ Harriet *ca* 1820–1913 Amer. abolitionist

**Tu·ring** \\'túr-iŋ\\ Alan Mathison 1912–1954 Eng. mathematician and logician

**Tur·ner** \\'tər-nər\\ Joseph Mallord William 1775–1851 Eng. painter

**Tut·ankh·a·men** \\,tü-,taŋ-'kä-mən, -,tän-\\ originally *Tut·ankh·a·ten* \\-'kä-tᵊn\\ *ca* 1370–1352 B.C. king of Egypt (1361–1352 B.C.)

**Twain** \\'twän\\ Mark 1835–1910 pseud. of *Samuel Langhorne Clem·ens* \\'klem-ənz\\ Amer. author

**Tweed** \\'twēd\\ William Marcy 1823–1878 *Boss Tweed* Amer. politician

**Ty·ler** \\'tī-lər\\ John 1790–1862 10th pres. of the U.S. (1841–45)

**Ulysses** — see ODYSSEUS

**Up·dike** \\'əp-,dīk\\ John 1932–2009 Amer. author

**Ura·nus** \\'yúr-ə-nəs, yù-'rā-\\ the sky personified as a god and father of the Titans in Greek mythology

**Ur·ban** \\'ər-bən\\ name of eight popes: esp. **II** *ca* 1035–1099 (pope 1088–99)

**Uri·el** \\'yúr-ē-əl\\ archangel named in Hebrew tradition — compare GABRIEL, MICHAEL, RAPHAEL

**Val·en·tine** \\'va-lən-,tīn\\ Saint, 3d cent. Christian martyr

**Van Bu·ren** \\van-'byúr-ən, vən-\\ Martin 1782–1862 8th pres. of the U.S. (1837–41)

**Van Dyck** *or* **Van·dyke** \\van-'dīk, vən-\\ Sir Anthony 1599–1641 Flemish painter

**van Gogh** Vincent — see GOGH, VAN

**Ve·láz·quez** \\və-'las-kəs, -'läs-, -kwiz, -(,)käs\\ Diego 1599–1660 Span. painter

**Ve·nus** \\'vē-nəs\\ goddess of love and beauty in Roman mythology — compare APHRODITE

**Ver·di** \\'ver-dē\\ Giuseppe 1813–1901 Ital. composer

**Ver·meer** \\vər-'mer, -'mir\\ Jan *or* Johannes 1632–1675 Dutch painter

**Verne** \\'vərn, 'vern\\ Jules \\'jülz\\ 1828–1905 French author

**Ves·puc·ci** \\ve-'spü-chē, -'spyü-\\ Amerigo \\ə-'fner-i-,gō\\ 1454–1512 Latin *Americus Ves·pu·cius* \\ə-'mer-ə-kəs-,ves-'pyüsh(ē-)əs\\ Ital. navigator for Spain and namesake of America

**Vic·to·ria** \\vik-'tòr-ē-ə\\ 1819–1901 *Alexandrina Victoria* queen of the United Kingdom (1837–1901)

**Vinci, da** Leonardo — see LEONARDO DA VINCI

**Vir·gil** *also* **Ver·gil** \\'vər-jəl\\ 70–19 B.C. Roman poet

**Vish·nu** \\'vish-(,)nü\\ god of preservation

**Vi·val·di** \\vi-'väl-de, -'vòl-\\ Antonio Lucio 1678–1741 Ital. composer

**Vol·ta** \\vòl-'tar, väl-, vòl-, -'ter\\ Alessandro 1745–1827 Ital. physicist

**Vol·taire** \\vòl-'tar, väl-, vòl-, -'ter\\ 1694–1778 orig. *François-Marie Arouet* French author

**Vul·can** \\'vəl-kən\\ god of fire and metalworking in Roman mythology — compare HEPHAESTUS

**Wag·ner** \\'väg-nər\\ Ri·chard \\'ri-,kärt, -,kärt\\ 1813–1883 Ger. composer

**Walk·er** \\'wò-kər\\ Alice Malsenior 1944– Amer. writer

**Wal·lace** \\'wä-ləs\\ Alfred Russel 1823–1913 Eng. naturalist

**Wal·len·berg** \\'wä-lən-,bərg\\ Raoul 1912–1947? Swedish diplomat and hero of the Holocaust

**War·hol** \\'wär-,hòl, -,hōl\\ Andy 1928–1987 orig. *Andrew Warhola* Amer. artist and filmmaker

**War·ren** \\'wòr-ən, 'wär-\\ Earl 1891–1974 Amer. jurist; chief justice of the U.S. Supreme Court (1953–69)

**Wash·ing·ton** \\'wò-shiŋ-tən, 'wä-\\ Booker Tal·ia·ferro \\'tä-lə-vər\\ 1856–1915 Amer. educator

**Washington** George 1732–1799 Amer. general; 1st pres. of the U.S. (1789–97)

**Watt** \\'wät\\ James 1736–1819 Scot. inventor

**Wayne** \\'wän\\ Anthony 1745–1796 *Mad Anthony* Amer. general

**Web·ster** \\'web-stər\\ Daniel 1782–1852 Amer. politician

**Webster** Noah 1758–1843 Amer. lexicographer

**Wel·ling·ton** \\'we-liŋ-tən\\ Duke of 1769–1852 *Arthur Wellesley; the Iron Duke* Brit. general and statesman

**Wells** \\'welz\\ H. G. 1866–1946 *Herbert George Wells* Eng. author and historian

**Wel·ty** \\'wel-tē\\ Eudora 1909–2001 Amer. author

**Wes·ley** \\'wes-lē, 'wez-\\ John 1703–1791 Eng. founder of Methodism

**Wes·ting·house** \\'wes-tiŋ-,haús\\ George 1846–1914 Amer. inventor and industrialist

**Whar·ton** \\'hwòr-tᵊn, 'wòr-\\ Edith 1862–1937 née *Jones* Amer. author

**Whis·tler** \\'hwis-lər, 'wis-\\ James (Abbott) McNeill 1834–1903 Amer. artist

**Whit·man** \\'hwit-mən, 'wit-\\ Walt 1819–1892 Amer. poet

**Whit·ney** \\'hwit-nē, 'wit-\\ Eli 1765–1825 Amer. inventor

**Whit·ti·er** \\'hwit-ē-ər, 'wit-\\ John Greenleaf 1807–1892 Amer. poet

**Wie·sel** \\vē-'zel, wē-\\ Elie 1928– Amer. (Romanian-born) author; Nobel Prize winner (1986)

**Wilde** \\'wī(-ə)ld\\ Oscar 1854–1900 Irish author

**Wil·der** \\'wī(-ə)l-dər\\ Thornton Niven 1897–1975 Amer. author

**Wil·liam** \\'wil-yəm\\ name of 4 kings of England: **I** *ca* 1028–1087 *William the Conqueror* (r. 1066–87); **II** *ca* 1056–1100 *William Rufus* \\'rü-fəs\\ (r. 1087–1100); **III** 1650–1702 (r. 1689–1702); **IV** 1765–1837 (r. 1830–37)

**Wil·liam Tell** \\,wil-yəm-'tel\\ legendary Swiss patriot commanded to shoot an apple off his son's head

**Wil·liams** \\'wil-yəmz\\ Roger 1603?–1683 Eng. colonist

**Williams** Ted 1918–2002 *Theodore Samuel Williams* Amer. baseball player

**Williams** Tennessee 1911–1983 orig. *Thomas Lanier Williams* Amer. playwright

**Williams** Venus 1980–      and her sister Serena 1981–      Amer. tennis players

**Wil·son** \\'wil-sən\\ August 1945–2005 orig. *Frederick August Kittel* Amer. playwright

**Wilson** Edward Osborne 1929–      Amer. biologist

**Wilson** (Thomas) Woodrow 1856–1924 28th pres. of the U.S. (1913–21); Nobel Prize winner (1919)

**Win·throp** \\'win(t)-thrəp\\ John 1588–1649 1st governor of Massachusetts Bay Colony

**Witt·gen·stein** \\'vit-gən-,shtīn, -,stīn\\ Ludwig Josef Johan 1889–1951 Eng. (Austrian-born) philosopher

**Woden** — see ODIN

**Woll·stone·craft** \\'wùl-stən-,kraft\\ Mary 1759–1797 Eng. feminist and writer

**Woods** \\'wùdz\\ Tiger 1975–      *Eldrick Woods* Amer. golfer

**Woolf** \\'wùlf\\ Virginia 1882–1941 Eng. author

**Words·worth** \\'wərdz-(,)wərth\\ William 1770–1850 Eng. poet

**Wo·vo·ka** \\wō-'vō-kə\\ 1858?–1932 *Jack Wilson* Paiute Indian mystic

**Wren** \\'ren\\ Sir Christopher 1632–1723 Eng. architect

**Wright** \\'rīt\\ Frank Lloyd 1867–1959 Amer. architect

**Wright** Orville 1871–1948 and his brother Wilbur 1867–1912 Amer. pioneers in aviation

**Wright** Richard 1908–1960 Amer. author

**Wy·eth** \\'wī-əth\\ Andrew Newell 1917–2009 Amer. painter

**Xi Jin·ping** \\'shē-'jin-'piŋ\\ 1953–      general secretary of Chinese Communist Party (2012–   ); president of China (2013–   )

**Yeats** \\'yāts\\ William Butler 1865–1939 Irish author

**Yel·tsin** \\'yelt-sən, 'yel-sin\\ Boris Nikolayevich 1931–2007 pres. of Russia (1990–99)

**York** \\'yòrk\\ Alvin Cullum 1887–1964 Amer. hero in World War I

**Young** \\'yəŋ\\ Brig·ham \\'brig-əm\\ 1801–1877 Amer. Mormon leader

**Za·har·i·as** \\zə-'ha-rē-əs\\ Babe Didrikson 1914–1956 *Mildred Ella Zaharias* née *Didrikson* Amer. athlete

**Za·pa·ta** \\sä-'pä-tä\\ Emiliano 1879–1919 Mex. revolutionary

**Zech·a·ri·ah** \\,ze-kə-'rī-ə\\ Hebrew prophet of the 6th cent. B.C.

**Zeng·er** \\'zeŋ-gər, -ər\\ John Peter 1697–1746 Amer. (Ger.-born) journalist and printer

**Zeph·y·rus** \\'ze-fə-rəs\\ god of the west wind in Greek mythology

**Zeus** \\'züs\\ chief god and ruler of the sky and weather in Greek mythology — compare JUPITER

# GEOGRAPHICAL NAMES

This section gives basic information about the world's countries, regions, cities, and major physical features. The latest population figures are given for nations, cities, and some regions. For many of these entries, derived nouns and adjectives are also listed (as **Ice-land . . . Icelander . . . n**). Other derived words not shown here have been separately entered in the main A-Z section, because of the presence of additional senses (as **Chinese**).

Abbreviations used here are listed in the front section Abbreviations in This Work. The capital letters N, E, S, and W, used singly or in combination and without a period, indicate direction. For example, "N India" means "northern India." Where direction is a part of the name, the word is spelled out.

The symbol ✳ denotes a capital. Sizes are given in conventional U.S. units, with metric equivalents following.

---

**Ab·er·deen** \,a-bər-'dēn\ city NE Scotland; *pop* 223,000 — **Ab·er·do·ni·an** \,a-bər-'dō-nē-ən\ *adj or n*

**Ab·i·djan** \,ä-bē-'jän, ,a-bi-\ city, seat of government of Cote d'Ivoire; *pop* 1,934,342

**Ab·i·lene** \'a-bə-,lēn\ city NW *cen* Texas; *pop* 117,063

**Abu Dha·bi** \,ä-bü-'dä-bē, -'thä-\ city, ✳ of United Arab Emirates; *pop* 2,394,000

**Abu·ja** \ä-'bü-jä\ city *cen* Nigeria; its ✳; *pop* 1,144,000

**Ab·ys·sin·ia** \,a-bə-'si-nē-ə, -nyə\ — see ETHIOPIA — **Ab·ys·sin·i·an** \-ne-ən, -nyən\ *adj or n*

**Aca·dia** \ə-'kā-dē-ə\ *or French* **Aca·die** \à-kà-'dē\ NOVA SCOTIA — an early name — **Aca·di·an** \-ē-ən\ *adj or n*

**Aca·pul·co** \,ä-kə-'pül-(,)kō, ,a-\ city & port S Mexico on the Pacific; *pop* 789,971

**Ac·cra** \'ä-krə, 'a-; ə-'krä\ city & port, ✳ of Ghana; *pop* 1,849,000

**Acon·ca·gua** \,ä-kōn-'kä-gwä\ mountain 22,834 ft. (6960 m.) W Argentina; highest in the Andes & in Western Hemisphere

**Ad·dis Aba·ba** \'ä-dis-'ä-bä-,bä, ,a-dəs-'a-bə-bə\ city, ✳ of Ethiopia; *pop* 2,740,000

**Ad·e·laide** \'a-də-,lād\ city S Australia, ✳ of South Australia; *pop* 1,103,979

**Aden** \'ä-d⁰n, 'ā-\ city & port S Yemen; *pop* 240,370

**Aden, Gulf of** arm of Indian Ocean between Yemen (Arabia) & Somalia (Africa)

**Ad·i·ron·dack** \,a-də-'rän-,dak\ mountains NE New York; highest Mount Marcy 5344 ft. (1629 m.)

**Admiralty** \'ad-m(ə-)rəl-tē\ **1** island SE Alaska **2** islands W Pacific N of New Guinea; part of Papua New Guinea

**Adri·at·ic Sea** \,ä-drē-'a-tik, ,a-\ arm of Mediterranean between Italy & Balkan Peninsula

**Ae·ge·an Sea** \i-'jē-ən\ arm of Mediterranean between Asia Minor & Greece

**Af·ghan·i·stan** \af-'ga-nə-,stan, -'gä-nə ,stän\ country W Asia E of Iran; ✳, Kabul; *pop* 22,576,000

**Af·ri·ca** \'a-fri-kə\ continent S of the Mediterranean

**Agana** — see HAGÁTÑA

**Agra** \'ä-grə, 'ə-\ city N India SSE of Delhi; *pop* 1,585,704

**Aguas·ca·lien·tes** \,ä-gwäs-,käl-'yen-,täs\ city *cen* Mexico NE of Guadalajara; *pop* 797,010

**Agul·has, Cape** \ə-'gə-ləs\ cape Republic of South Africa; most southerly point of Africa, at 34° 52′ S latitude

**Ahag·gar** \ə-'hä-gər, ,ä-hə-'gär\ mountains S Algeria in W *cen* Sahara

**Ah·mad·abad** \'ä-mə-də-,bäd, -,bad\ city W India N of Bombay; *pop* 5,577,940

**Ak·ron** \'a-krən\ city NE Ohio; *pop* 199,110

**Al·a·bama** \,a-lə-'ba-mə\ state SE U.S.; ✳, Montgomery; *pop* 4,779,736 — **Al·a·bam·i·an** \-'ba-mē-ən\ *or* **Al·a·bam·an** \-'ba-mən\ *adj or n*

**Alas·ka** \ə-'las-kə\ **1** peninsula SW Alaska SW of Cook Inlet **2** state of U.S. in NW North America; ✳, Juneau; *pop* 710,231 **3** mountain range S Alaska extending from Alaska Peninsula to Yukon boundary — **Alas·kan** \-kən\ *adj or n*

**Alaska, Gulf of** inlet of Pacific off S Alaska between Alaska Peninsula on W & Alexander Archipelago on E

**Al·ba·nia** \al-'bā-nē-ə, -nyə\ country S Europe in Balkan Peninsula on Adriatic; ✳, Tirane; *pop* 3,823,000

**Al·ba·ny** \'òl-bə-nē\ city, ✳ of New York; *pop* 97,856

**Albemarle Sound** \'al-bə-,märl\ inlet of the Atlantic in NE North Carolina

**Albert, Lake** \'al-bərt\ lake E Africa between Uganda & Democratic Republic of the Congo in course of the Nile

**Al·ber·ta** \al-'bər-tə\ province W Canada;

✳, Edmonton; *pop* 3,290,350 — **Al·ber·tan** \-'bər-t³n\ *adj or n*

**Al·bu·quer·que** \'al-bə-ˌkər-kē\ city *cen* New Mexico; *pop* 545,852

**Al·ca·traz** \'al-kə-ˌtraz\ island California in San Francisco Bay

**Al·da·bra** \äl-'dä-brə\ island NW Indian Ocean N of Madagascar; belongs to Seychelles

**Alep·po** \ə-'le-(ˌ)pō\ city N Syria; *pop* 1,445,000

**Aleu·tian** \ə-'lü-shən\ islands SW Alaska extending 1700 mi. (2735 km.) W from Alaska Peninsula

**Al·ex·an·der** \ˌal-ig-'zan-dər, ˌel-\ archipelago SE Alaska

**Al·ex·an·dria** \ˌa-lig-'zan-drē-ə, ˌe-\ **1** city N Virginia S of District of Columbia; *pop* 139,966 **2** city N Egypt on the Mediterranean; *pop* 4,123,869 — **Al·ex·an·dri·an** \-drē-ən\ *adj or n*

**Al·ge·ria** \al-'jir-ē-ə\ country NW Africa on Mediterranean; ✳, Algiers; *pop* 34,200,000 — **Al·ge·ri·an** \-ē-ən\ *adj or n*

**Al·giers** \al-'jirz\ city, ✳ of Algeria; *pop* 2,364,230 — **Al·ge·rine** \ˌal-jə-'rēn\ *adj or n*

**Al·lah·a·bad** \'ä-lə-hä-ˌbäd, 'a-lə-hə-ˌbad\ city N India on the Ganges; *pop* 1,212,395

**Al·le·ghe·ny** \ˌa-lə-'gā-nē\ **1** river 325 mi. (523 km.) long W Pennsylvania & SW New York **2** mountains of Appalachian system E U.S. in Pennsylvania, Maryland, Virginia, & West Virginia

**Al·len·town** \'a-lən-ˌtaún\ city E Pennsylvania; *pop* 118,032

**Al·ma·ty** \äl-'mä-tē\ *or* **Al·ma–Ata** \ˌäl-ˈmä-ə-ˈtä; ˌal-mə-ˈä-tə, -ə-ˈtä\ city, former ✳ of Kazakhstan; *pop* 1,365,632

**Alps** \'alps\ mountain system *cen* Europe — see MONT BLANC

**Al·tai** *or* **Al·tay** \ˌal-'tī\ mountain system *cen* Asia between Mongolia & W China & between Kazakhstan & Russia

**Ama·ga·sa·ki** \ˌä-mä-gä-'sä-kē\ city Japan in W *cen* Honshu; *pop* 453,748

**Am·a·ril·lo** \ˌa-mə-'ri-(ˌ)lō, -lə\ city NW Texas; *pop* 190,695

**Am·a·zon** \'a-mə-ˌzän, -zən\ river 3900 mi. (6436 km.) long N South America flowing from Peruvian Andes into Atlantic in N Brazil

**Amer·i·ca** \ə-'mer-ə-kə, -'me-rə-\ **1** either continent (**North America** or **South America**) of Western Hemisphere **2** *or* **the Amer·i·cas** \-kəz\ lands of Western Hemisphere including North, Central, & South America & West Indies **3** UNITED STATES OF AMERICA — **American** *adj or n*

**American Falls** — see NIAGARA FALLS

**American Samoa** *or* **Eastern Samoa** islands SW *cen* Pacific; U.S. territory; ✳, Pago Pago (on Tutuila Island); *pop* 55,519

**Am·man** \ä-'män, a-, -'man\ city, ✳ of Jordan; *pop* 627,505

**Am·ster·dam** \'am(p)-stər-ˌdam, 'äm(p)-stər-ˌdäm\ city, official ✳ of the Netherlands; *pop* 810,767

**Amur** \ä-'múr\ river 1780 mi. (2784 km.) long E Asia flowing into the Pacific & forming part of boundary between China & Russia

**An·a·heim** \'a-nə-ˌhīm\ city SW California E of Long Beach; *pop* 336,265

**An·a·to·lia** \ˌa-nə-'tō-lē-ə, -'tōl-yə\ — see ASIA MINOR — **An·a·to·li·an** \-'tō-lē-ən, -'tōl-yən\ *adj or n*

**An·chor·age** \'aŋ-k(ə-)rij\ city S *cen* Alaska; *pop* 291,826

**An·da·man** \'an-də-mən, -ˌman\ **1** islands India in Bay of Bengal S of Myanmar & N of Nicobar Islands **2** sea, arm of Bay of Bengal S of Myanmar — **An·da·man·ese** \ˌan-də-mə-'nēz, -'nēs\ *adj or n*

**An·des** \'an-(ˌ)dēz\ mountain system W South America extending from Panama to Tierra del Fuego — see ACONCAGUA — **An·de·an** \'an-(ˌ)dē-ən, an-'\ *adj* — **An·dine** \'an-ˌdēn, -ˌdīn\ *adj*

**An·dor·ra** \an-'dór-ə, -'där-ə\ country SW Europe in E Pyrenees between France & Spain; ✳, Andorra la Vella; *pop* 76,100 — **An·dor·ran** \-ən\ *adj or n*

**Andorra la Vel·la** \-lä-'vel-yä\ town, ✳ of Andorra; *pop* 21,513

**An·dros** \'an-drəs\ island, largest of Bahamas

**An·gel Falls** \'än-jəl\ waterfall 3212 ft. (979 m.) SE Venezuela; world's highest waterfall

**Ang·kor** \'aŋ-ˌkór\ ruins of ancient city NW Cambodia

**An·gle·sey** \'aŋ-gəl-sē\ island NW Wales

**An·go·la** \aŋ-'gō-lə, an-\ country SW Africa S of mouth of Congo River; ✳, Luanda; *pop* 24,383,000 — **An·go·lan** \-lən\ *adj or n*

**An·i·ak·chak Crater** \ˌa-nē-'ak-ˌchak\ volcanic crater SW Alaska on Alaska Peninsula; 6 mi. (10 km.) in diameter

**An·ka·ra** \'aŋ-kə-rə, 'äŋ-\ city, ✳ of Turkey in N *cen* Anatolia; *pop* 4,609,000

**An·nap·o·lis** \ə-'na-pə-lis\ city, ✳ of Maryland; *pop* 38,394

**Ann Ar·bor** \(ˌ)an-'är-bər\ city SE Michigan; *pop* 113,934

**An·shan** \'än-'shän\ city NE China; *pop* 1,203,986

**An·ta·nan·a·ri·vo** \ˌän-tä-ˌnä-nä-'rē-(ˌ)vō\ city, ✳ of Madagascar; *pop* 958,929

**Ant·arc·ti·ca** \ant-'ärk-ti-kə, -'är-ti-\ body of land around the South Pole; plateau covered by great ice cap

**An·ti·gua** \an-'tē-gə, -gwə\ island West Indies in the Leewards; with Barbuda forms independent **Antigua and Barbuda**; ✳, Saint John's; *pop* 83,700

**An·til·les** \an-'ti-lēz\ the West Indies except for the Bahamas — see GREATER ANTILLES, LESSER ANTILLES — **An·til·le·an** \-lē-ən\ adj

**An·trim** \'an-trəm\ district E Northern Ireland; pop 54,000

**Ant·werp** \'ant-ˌwərp, 'an-ˌtwərp\ city N Belgium; pop 509,200

**Aomen** — see MACAO

**Aoraki** — see COOK, MOUNT

**Ap·en·nines** \'a-pə-ˌnīnz\ mountain chain Italy extending length of the peninsula; highest peak Monte Corno (NE of Rome) 9560 ft. (2897 m.) — **Ap·en·nine** \'a-pə-ˌnīn\ adj

**Apia** \ä-'pē-ä\ town, ✴ of Samoa; pop 36,735

**Apo, Mount** \'ä-(ˌ)pō\ volcano Philippines in SE Mindanao 9692 ft. (2954 m.); highest peak in the Philippines

**Ap·pa·la·chia** \ˌa-pə-'lā-chə, -'la-chə, -'lā-shə\ region E U.S. including Appalachian Mountains from S cen New York to cen Alabama

**Ap·pa·la·chian Mountains** \ˌa-pə-'lā-ch(e-)ən, -sh(ē-)ən\ mountain system E North America extending from S Quebec to cen Alabama — see MITCHELL, MOUNT

**Aqa·ba, Gulf of** \'ä-kä-bə\ arm of Red Sea E of Sinai Peninsula

**Aquid·neck** \ə-'kwid-ˌnek\ or **Rhode** island SE Rhode Island in Narragansett Bay

**Ara·bia** \ə-'rā-bē-ə\ peninsula of SW Asia including Saudi Arabia, Yemen, Oman, & Persian Gulf States

**Ara·bi·an Sea** \ə-'rā-bē-ən\ NW section of Indian Ocean between Arabia & India

**Ara·fu·ra** \ˌä-rä-'fü-rä\ sea between N Australia & W New Guinea

**Ar·al Sea** \'a-rəl\ formerly **Lake Aral** formerly large lake W Asia which has shrunk into sections some of which are now entirely in Kazakhstan and others between Kazakhstan & Uzbekistan

**Ar·a·rat** \'a-rə-ˌrat\ mountain 16,946 ft. (5165 m.) E Turkey near border of Iran

**Arc·tic** \'ärk-tik, 'är-tik\ 1 ocean N of Arctic Circle 2 Arctic regions 3 archipelago N Canada in Nunavut & Northwest Territories

**Ar·da·bil** or **Ar·de·bil** \ˌär-də-'bēl\ city NW Iran; pop 418,000

**Ards** \'ärdz\ district E Northern Ireland; pop 78,000

**Are·ci·bo** \ˌä-rä-'sē-(ˌ)bō\ city & port N Puerto Rico; pop 96,440

**Ar·gen·ti·na** \ˌär-jən-'tē-nə\ country S South America between the Andes & the Atlantic; ✴, Buenos Aires; pop 40,117,000 — **Ar·gen·tine** \'är-jən-ˌtīn, -ˌtēn\ adj or n or **Ar·gen·tin·ean** or **Ar·gen·tin·i·an** \ˌär-jən-'ti-nē-ən\ adj or n

**Ar·gos** \'är-ˌgos, -gəs\ ancient Greek city-state S Greece

**Ar·i·zo·na** \ˌa-rə-'zō-nə\ state SW U.S.; ✴,

Phoenix; pop 6,392,017 — **Ar·i·zo·nan** \-nən\ or **Ar·i·zo·nian** \-nē-ən, -nyən\ adj or n

**Ar·kan·sas** \'är-kən-ˌsò\ 1 river 1450 mi. (2334 km.) long SW cen U.S. flowing SE into the Mississippi 2 state S cen U.S.; ✴, Little Rock; pop 2,915,918 — **Ar·kan·san** \är-'kan-zən\ adj or n

**Ar·ling·ton** \'är-liŋ tən\ city N Texas; pop 365,438

**Ar·magh** \är-'mä, 'är-ˌ\ 1 district S Northern Ireland; pop 119,900 2 town cen Armagh district; pop 14,265

**Ar·me·nia** \är-'mē-nē-ə, -nyə\ 1 region W Asia in mountainous area SE of Black Sea & SW of Caspian Sea divided between Iran, Turkey, & Armenia (country) 2 country W Asia; ✴, Yerevan; pop 3,018,854

**Arn·hem Land** \'är-nəm\ region N Australia on N coast of Northern Territory

**Ar·no** \'är-(ˌ)nō\ river 150 mi. (241 km.) long cen Italy flowing through Florence

**Aru·ba** \ə-'rü-bə\ Dutch island in Caribbean Sea off coast of NW Venezuela; pop 101,484

**Ar·va·da** \är-'va-də\ city N cen Colorado NW of Denver; pop 106,433

**Ash·ga·bat** \'äsh-gə-ˌbät\ or **Ashkh·a·bad** \'äsh-kə-ˌbad, -ˌbäd\ city, ✴ of Turkmenistan; pop 412,200

**Asia** \'ā-zhə, -shə\ continent of Eastern Hemisphere N of the Equator — see EURASIA

**Asia Mi·nor** \-'mī-nər\ or **An·a·to·lia** \ˌa-nə-'tō-lē-ə, -'tōl-yə\ peninsula in modern Turkey between Black Sea on N & the Mediterranean on S

**As·ma·ra** \az-'mä-rə, -'ma-rə\ city, ✴ of Eritrea; pop 342,706

**As·syr·ia** \ə-'sir-ē-ə\ ancient empire W Asia extending along the middle Tigris & over foothills to the E — **As·syr·i·an** \-ən\ adj or n

**As·ta·na** \ä-stä-'nä\ city, ✴ of Kazakhstan; pop 814,400

**Asun·ción** \ä-sün-'syōn\ city, ✴ of Paraguay; pop 502,426

**As·wân** \ä-'swän, ä-\ city S Egypt on the Nile near site of **Aswân High Dam**; pop 265,500

**Ata·ca·ma** \ˌä-tä-'kä-mä\ desert N Chile

**Atchaf·a·laya** \(ə-)ˌcha-fə-'lī-ə\ river 225 mi. (362 km.) long S Louisiana flowing S into Gulf of Mexico

**Ath·a·bas·ca** \ˌa-thə-'bas-kə, ˌä-\ river 765 mi. (1231 km.) long NE Alberta flowing into **Lake Athabasca** on Alberta-Saskatchewan border

**Ath·ens** \'a-thənz\ 1 city NE Georgia; pop 115,452 2 city, ✴ of Greece; pop 664,046 — **Athe·nian** \ə-'thē-nē-ən, -nyən\ adj or n

**At·lan·ta** \ət-'lan-tə, at-\ city, ✴ of Georgia; pop 420,003

**At·lan·tic** \ət-'lan-tik, at-\ ocean separating North America & South America from Europe & Africa; often divided into **North Atlantic** and **South Atlantic** — **Atlantic** *adj*

**At·las** \\'at-ləs\\ mountains NW Africa extending from SW Morocco to N Tunisia

**At·ti·ca** \\'a-ti-kə\\ ancient state E Greece; chief city Athens — **At·tic** \\'at-ik\\ *adj*

**Auck·land** \\'o-klənd\\ city N New Zealand on NW North Island; *pop* 404,658

**Au·gus·ta** \\o-'gəs-tə, ə-\\ **1** city E Georgia; *pop* 195,844 **2** city, ✳ of Maine; *pop* 19,136

**Au·ro·ra** \\ə-'ror-ə, o-\\ **1** city NE *cen* Colorado; *pop* 325,078 **2** city NE Illinois; *pop* 197,899

**Auschwitz** — see OSWIECIM

**Aus·tin** \\'os-tən, 'äs-\\ city, ✳ of Texas; *pop* 790,390

**Aus·tral·asia** \\,os-trə-'lā-zhə, ,äs-, -'lā-shə\\ Australia, Tasmania, New Zealand, & Melanesia — **Aus·tral·asian** \\-zhən, -shən\\ *adj or n*

**Aus·tra·lia** \\o-'sträl-yə, ä-, ə-\\ **1** continent of Eastern Hemisphere SE of Asia **2** country including continent of Australia & island of Tasmania; ✳, Canberra; *pop* 21,508,000 — **Aus·tra·lian** \\-yən\\ *adj or n*

**Australian Alps** mountain range SE Australia in E Victoria & SE New South Wales; part of Great Dividing Range

**Australian Capital Territory** district SE Australia including two areas, one containing Canberra (✳ of Australia) & the other on Jervis Bay (inlet of the South Pacific); surrounded by New South Wales

**Aus·tria** \\'os-trē-ə, 'äs-\\ country *cen* Europe; ✳, Vienna; *pop* 8,402,000 — **Aus·tri·an** \\-ən\\ *adj or n*

**Aus·tria–Hun·ga·ry** \\-'hən-gə-rē\\ country 1867–1918 *cen* Europe including Bohemia, Moravia, Transylvania, Galicia, and what are now Austria, Hungary, Slovenia, Croatia, & part of NE Italy — **Aus·tro-Hun·gar·i·an** \\'os-(,)trō-,hən-'ger-ē-ən, ,äs-\\ *adj or n*

**Aus·tro·ne·sia** \\,os-trə-'nē-zhə, ,äs-, -'nē-shə\\ **1** islands of the South Pacific **2** area extending from Madagascar through Malay Peninsula & Malay Archipelago to Hawaii & Easter Island — **Aus·tro·ne·sian** \\-zhən, -shən\\ *adj or n*

**Avon** \\'ā-vən, 'a-\\ river 96 mi. (154 km.) long *cen* England flowing WSW into the Severn

**Ayers Rock** — see ULURU

**Ayles·bury** \\'ālz-b(ə-)rē\\ town SE *cen* England; *pop* 41,288

**Ayr** \\'er\\ *or* **Ayr·shire** \\-,shir, -shər\\ former county SW Scotland

**Azer·bai·jan** \\,a-zər-,bī-'jän, ,ä-\\ country W Asia & SE Europe bordering on Caspian Sea; ✳, Baku; *pop* 9,477,000 — **Azer·bai·ja·ni** \\,a-zər-,bī-'jä-nē, ,ä-\\ *adj or n*

**Azores** \\'ā-,zorz, ə-'\\ islands Portugal in North Atlantic lying 800 mi. (1287 km.) W of Portuguese coast; *pop* 246,800 — **Azor·e·an** \\ā-'zor-ē-ən, ə-\\ *adj or n*

**Bab·y·lon** \\'ba-bə-lən, -,län\\ ancient city, ✳ of Babylonia; site 55 mi. (89 km.) S of Baghdad near the Euphrates — **Bab·y·lo·nian** \\,ba-bə-'lō-nyən, -nē-ən\\ *adj or n*

**Bab·y·lo·nia** \\,ba-bə-'lō-nyə, -nē-ə\\ ancient country W Asia in valley of lower Euphrates and Tigris rivers

**Bac·tria** \\'bak-trē-ə\\ ancient country W Asia in present NE Afghanistan — **Bac·tri·an** \\'bak-trē-ən\\ *adj or n*

**Bad·lands** barren region SW South Dakota & NW Nebraska

**Baf·fin** \\'ba-fən\\ **1** bay of the Atlantic between W Greenland & E Baffin Island **2** island NE Canada in Arctic Archipelago N of Hudson Strait

**Bagh·dad** \\'bag-,dad, ,bäg-'däd\\ city, ✳ of Iraq on the Tigris; *pop* (est.) 3,841,000

**Ba·guio** \\,bä-gē-'ō\\ city, former summer ✳ of the Philippines in NW *cen* Luzon; *pop* 318,676

**Ba·ha·mas** \\bə-'hä-məz\\ islands in N Atlantic SE of Florida; ✳, Nassau; *pop* 367,000 — **Ba·ha·mi·an** \\bə-'hä-mē-ən, -'hä-\\ *or* **Ba·ha·man** \\-'hä-mən, -'hä-mən\\ *adj or n*

**Bahia** — see SALVADOR

**Bah·rain** \\bä-'rān\\ islands in Persian Gulf off coast of Arabia; country; ✳, Manama; *pop* 651,000 — **Bah·raini** \\-'rä-nē\\ *adj or n*

**Bai·kal, Lake** *or* **Lake Bay·kal** \\bī-'käl, -'kal\\ lake Russia, in mountains N of Mongolia

**Ba·ja California** \\'bä-(,)hä\\ peninsula NW Mexico W of Gulf of California

**Ba·kers·field** \\'bā-kərz-,fēld\\ city S California; *pop* 347,483

**Ba·ku** \\bä-'kü\\ city, ✳ of Azerbaijan on W coast of Caspian Sea; area *pop* 2,046,000

**Bal·a·ton** \\'ba-lə-,tän, 'bo-lò-,tōn\\ lake W Hungary

**Bal·boa Heights** \\(,)bal-'bō-ə\\ town Panama; formerly the center of administration for Canal Zone

**Bal·e·ar·ic Islands** \\,ba-lē-'a-rik\\ islands E Spain in the W Mediterranean

**Ba·li** \\'bä-lē, 'ba-\\ island Indonesia off E end of Java; *pop* 3,891,000 — **Ba·li·nese** \\,bäl-i-nēz, ,bal-, -'nēs\\ *adj or n*

**Bal·kans** \\'bol-kənz\\ **1** *or* **Balkan Mountains** mountains N Bulgaria extending from Serbia border to Black Sea; highest 7793 ft. (2375 m.) **2** *or* **Balkan Peninsula** peninsula SE Europe between Adriatic & Ionian seas on the W & Aegean & Black seas on the E **3** *or* **Balkan States** countries occupying the Balkan Peninsula: Slovenia, Croatia, Bosnia and Herzegovina, Macedonia, Kosovo, Serbia,

Montenegro, Romania, Bulgaria, Albania, Greece, Turkey (in Europe)

**Bal·ly·me·na** \ˌba-lē-ˈmē-nə\ district NE *cen* Northern Ireland; *pop* 64,000

**Bal·ly·mon·ey** \ˌba-lē-ˈmə-nē\ district N *cen* Northern Ireland; *pop* 31,000

**Bal·tic Sea** \ˈbȯl-tik\ arm of the Atlantic N Europe E of Scandinavian Peninsula

**Bal·ti·more** \ˈbȯl-tə-ˌmȯr, -mər\ city N *cen* Maryland; *pop* 620,961

**Ba·ma·ko** \ˈbä-mä-ˌkō\ city, ✻ of Mali on the Niger; *pop* 1,016,000

**Ban·bridge** \ban-ˈbrij\ district SE *cen* Northern Ireland; *pop* 48,000

**Ban·dar Se·ri Be·ga·wan** \ˌhan-dar-ˌser-ē-bə-ˈgä-wän\ town, ✻ of Brunei; *pop* 27,285

**Ban·dung** \ˈbän-ˌdu̇ŋ\ city Indonesia in W Java SE of Jakarta; *pop* 2,394,873

**Ban·ga·lore** \ˈbaŋ-gə-ˌlȯr\ city S India W of Madras; *pop* 8,482,000

**Bang·kok** \ˈbaŋ-ˌkäk, baŋ-ˈ\ city, ✻ of Thailand; *pop* 6,160,000

**Ban·gla·desh** \ˌbäŋ-glə-ˈdesh, ˌbaŋ-, ˌbəŋ-, -ˈdash\ country S Asia E of India; ✻, Dhaka; *pop* 149,772,000 — see EAST PAKISTAN — **Ban·gla·deshi** \-ˈde-shē, -ˈdä-\ *adj or n*

**Ban·gor** \ˈbaŋ-ˌgȯr, ˈhaŋ-gȯr\ town E Northern Ireland; *pop* 46,585

**Ban·gui** \bäŋ-ˈgē\ city, ✻ of Central African Republic; *pop* 532,000

**Ban·jul** \ˈbän-ˌjül\ *formerly* **Bath·urst** \ˈbath-(ˌ)ərst\ city & port, ✻ of Gambia; *pop* 44,188

**Bao·tou** *or* **Pao–t'ou** \ˈbau̇-ˈtō\ city N China; *pop* 1,999,000

**Bar·ba·dos** \bär-ˈbā-(ˌ)dōs, -dəs, -(ˌ)dōz\ island West Indies in Lesser Antilles E of Windward Islands; country, ✻, Bridgetown; *pop* 277,821 — **Bar·ba·di·an** \-ˈbä-dē-ən\ *adj or n*

**Bar·bu·da** \bär-ˈbü-də\ island West Indies; part of independent Antigua and Barbuda; *pop* 1600

**Bar·ce·lo·na** \ˌbär-sə-ˈlō-nə\ city NE Spain on the Mediterranean; chief city of Catalonia; *pop* 1,611,013

**Bar·king and Dag·en·ham** \ˈbär-kiŋ-ən(d)-ˈda-gə-nəm\ borough of E Greater London, England; *pop* 186,000

**Bar·na·ul** \ˌbär-nə-ˈül\ city S Russia; *pop* 612,000

**Bar·net** \ˈbär-nət\ borough of N Greater London, England; *pop* 356,000

**Bar·ran·qui·lla** \ˌbär-än-ˈkē-yä\ city N Colombia; *pop* 1,142,000

**Barren Grounds** treeless plains N Canada W of Hudson Bay

**Bar·row, Point** \ˈber-(ˌ)rō\ most northerly point of Alaska & of U.S. at about 71°25′ N latitude

**Ba·si·lan** \bä-ˈsē-ˌlän\ island S Philippines SW of Mindanao

**Bas·il·don** \ˈba-zəl-dən\ town SE England; *pop* 157,500

**Bass** \ˈbas\ strait separating Tasmania & continent of Australia

**Basse·terre** \bas-ˈter, bäs-\ seaport Saint Kitts, ✻ of Saint Kitts and Nevis; *pop* 14,725

**Basutoland** — see LESOTHO

**Bathurst** — see BANJUL

**Bat·on Rouge** \ˌba-tᵊn-ˈrüzh\ city, ✻ of Louisiana; *pop* 229,493

**Ba·var·ia** \bə-ˈver-ē-ə\ *or German* **Bay·ern** \ˈbī-ərn\ state SE Germany bordering on Czech Republic & Austria; *pop* 12,397,614 — **Ba·var·i·an** \bə-ˈver-ē-ən, -ˈvar-\ *adj or n*

**Ba·ya·mon** \ˌbī-ä-ˈmōn\ city NE *cen* Puerto Rico; *pop* 208,116

**Beau·fort** \ˈbō-fərt\ sea consisting of part of Arctic Ocean NE of Alaska & NW of Canada

**Beau·mont** \ˈbō-ˌmänt, bō-ˈ\ city SE Texas; *pop* 118,296

**Bech·u·a·na·land** \ˌbech-ˈwä-nə-ˌland, ˌbe-chə-\ **1** region S Africa N of Orange River **2** — see BOTSWANA — **Bech·u·a·na** \ˌbech-ˈwä nə, ˌbe-chə-\ *adj or n*

**Bed·ford·shire** \ˈbed-fərd-ˌshir, -shər\ *or* **Bedford** county SE England

**Bedloe's** — see LIBERTY

**Bei·jing** \ˈbā-ˈjiŋ\ *or* **Pe·king** \ˈpē-ˈkiŋ, ˈpā-\ city, ✻ of China; *pop* 10,819,407

**Bei·rut** \bā-ˈrüt\ city, ✻ of Lebanon; urban area *pop* 1,100,000

**Be·la·rus** \ˌbē-lə-ˈrüs, ˌbye-lə-\ country *cen* Europe; ✻, Minsk; *pop* 9,503,807 — **Be·la·ru·si·an** \-ˈrü-sē-ən, -ˈrə-shən\ *or* **Be·la·rus·sian** \-ˈrə-shən\ *adj or n*

**Belau** — see PALAU

**Be·lém** \bə-ˈlem\ city N Brazil; *pop* 1,393,399

**Bel·fast** \ˈbel-ˌfast, bel-ˈ\ city, ✻ of Northern Ireland; *pop* 281,000

**Bel·gium** \ˈbel-jəm\ *or French* **Bel·gique** \bel-ˈzhēk\ *or Flemish* **Bel·gië** \ˈbel-kē-ə\ country W Europe; ✻, Brussels; *pop* 11,125,500 — **Bel·gian** \ˈbel-jən\ *adj or n*

**Bel·grade** \ˈbel-ˌgräd, -ˌgräd, -ˌgrad, bel-ˈ\ *or* **Beo·grad** \bā-ˈō-ˌgräd\ city, ✻ of Serbia on the Danube; *pop* 1,120,000

**Be·lize** \bə-ˈlēz\ *formerly* **British Honduras** country Central America on the Caribbean; ✻, Belmopan; *pop* 324,500 — **Be·liz·ean** *adj or n*

**Belize City** seaport E Belize; *pop* 55,400

**Belle·vue** \ˈbel-ˌvyü\ city W Washington E of Seattle; *pop* 122,363

**Bel·mo·pan** \ˌbel-mō-ˈpän\ city, ✻ of Belize; *pop* 13,800

**Be·lo Ho·ri·zon·te** \ˈbā-lō-ˌȯr-ē-ˈzȯn-tē\ city E Brazil N of Rio de Janeiro; *pop* 2,375,151

**Be·lo·rus·sia** \ˌbe-lō-ˈrə-shə, ˌbye-lō-\ *or* **Bye·lo·rus·sia** \bē-ˌe-lō-, ˌbye-lō-\ former republic of U.S.S.R.; became independent Belarus in 1991 — **Belo·rus·sian** \ˌbe-lō-ˈrə-shən, ˌbye-\ *adj or n*

**Ben·gal** \ben-ˈgȯl, beŋ-, -ˈgäl\ region S

Asia including delta of Ganges & Brahmaputra rivers; divided between Bangladesh & India — **Ben·gal·ese** \ˌben-gə-ˈlēz, ˌben-, -ˈlēs\ *adj or n*

**Bengal, Bay of** arm of Indian Ocean between India & Myanmar

**Be·nin** \bə-ˈnēn, -ˈnin; ˈbe-nin\ *formerly* **Da·ho·mey** \də-ˈhō-mē\ country W Africa on Gulf of Guinea; *, Porto-Novo; pop 9,984,000 — **Ben·i·nese** \bə-ˌni-ˈnēz, -ˌnē-, -ˈnēs; ˌbe-ni-ˈnēz, -ˈnēs\ *adj or n*

**Ben Nev·is** \ben-ˈne-vəs\ mountain 4406 ft. (1343 m.) W Scotland in the Grampians; highest in Great Britain

**Beograd** — see BELGRADE

**Ber·gen** \ˈbər-gən, ˈber-\ city & port SW Norway; *pop* 271,949

**Be·ring** \ˈbir-iŋ, ˈber-\ **1** sea, arm of the North Pacific between Alaska & NE Siberia **2** strait at narrowest point 53 mi. (85 km.) wide between North America (Alaska) and Asia (Russia)

**Berke·ley** \ˈbər-klē\ city W California on San Francisco Bay N of Oakland; *pop* 112,580

**Berk·shire** \ˈbərk-ˌshir, -shər\ hills W Massachusetts; highest point Mount Greylock 3491 ft. (1064 m.)

**Ber·lin** \(ˌ)bər-ˈlin, *G* ber-ˈlēn\ city, * of Germany; divided 1945–90 into **East Berlin** (* of East Germany) & **West Berlin** (city of West Germany lying within East Germany); *pop* 3,292,365 — **Ber·lin·er** \(ˌ)bər-ˈli-nər\ *n*

**Ber·mu·da** \(ˌ)bər-ˈmyü-də\ islands W Atlantic ESE of Cape Hatteras; a British colony; *, Hamilton; *pop* 71,000 — **Ber·mu·dan** \-dᵊn\ *or* **Ber·mu·di·an** \-dē-ən\ *adj or n*

**Bern** \ˈbərn, ˈbern\ city, * of Switzerland; *pop* 128,848 — **Ber·nese** \(ˌ)bər-ˈnēz, -ˈnēs\ *adj or n*

**Bes·sa·ra·bia** \ˌbe-sə-ˈrā-bē-ə\ region SE Europe now chiefly in Moldova — **Bes·sa·ra·bi·an** \-bē-ən\ *adj or n*

**Beth·le·hem** \ˈbeth-li-ˌhem, -lē-həm, -lē-əm\ town of ancient Palestine in Judaea; the present-day town is SW of Jerusalem in the West Bank; *pop* 30,200

**Bev·er·ly Hills** \ˈbe-vər-lē\ city SW California within Los Angeles; *pop* 34,109

**Bex·ley** \ˈbek-slē\ borough of E Greater London, England; *pop* 211,200

**Bho·pal** \bō-ˈpäl\ city N *cen* India; *pop* 1,886,100

**Bhu·tan** \bü-ˈtän, -ˈtan\ country S Asia in the Himalayas on NE border of India; *, Thimphu; *pop* 753,000 — **Bhu·ta·nese** \ˌbü-tə-ˈnēz, -ˈnēs\ *adj or n*

**Bi·ki·ni** \bi-ˈkē-nē\ atoll W Pacific in Marshall Islands

**Bil·lings** \ˈbi-liŋz\ city S *cen* Montana; largest in state; *pop* 104,170

**Bi·loxi** \bə-ˈlək-sē, -ˈläk-\ city & port SE Mississippi on Gulf of Mexico; *pop* 44,054

**Bi·o·ko** \bē-ˈō-(ˌ)kō\ *formerly* **Fer·nan·do**

**Póo** \fer-ˈnän-(ˌ)dō-ˈpō\ island portion of Equatorial Guinea in Gulf of Guinea

**Bir·ken·head** \ˈbər-kən-ˌhed, ˌbər-kən-ˈ\ borough NW England on the Mersey opposite Liverpool; *pop* 123,907

**Bir·ming·ham** \ˈbər-miŋ-ˌham\ **1** city N *cen* Alabama; *pop* 212,237 **2** city W *cen* England; *pop* 1,086,000

**Bis·cay, Bay of** \ˈbis-ˌkā, -kē\ inlet of the Atlantic between W coast of France & N coast of Spain

**Bish·kek** \bish-ˈkek\ *formerly 1926–91* **Frun·ze** \ˈfrün-zi\ city, * of Kyrgyzstan; *pop* 794,000

**Bis·marck** \ˈbiz-ˌmärk\ **1** city, * of North Dakota; *pop* 61,272 **2** archipelago W Pacific N of E end of New Guinea

**Bis·sau** \bi-ˈsaù\ city, * of Guinea-Bissau; *pop* 386,500

**Bi·thyn·ia** \bə-ˈthi-nē-ə\ ancient country NW Asia Minor bordering on Sea of Marmara and Black Sea — **Bi·thyn·i·an** \-nē-ən\ *adj or n*

**Bit·ter·root** \ˈbi-tə(r)-ˌrüt, -ˌrùt\ range of the Rockies along Idaho–Montana boundary

**Black·burn** \ˈblak-(ˌ)bərn\ town NW England; *pop* 132,800

**Black Forest** forested mountain region Germany along E bank of the upper Rhine

**Black Hills** mountains W South Dakota & NE Wyoming

**Black·pool** \ˈblak-ˌpül\ town NW England on Irish Sea; *pop* 144,500

**Black Sea** sea between Europe & Asia connected with Aegean Sea through the Bosporus, Sea of Marmara, & Dardanelles

**Blanc, Mont** — see MONT BLANC

**Blan·tyre** \ˈblan-ˌtī(-ə)r\ city S Malawi; *pop* 661,000

**Bloem·fon·tein** \ˈblüm-fən-ˌtān, -ˌfän-\ city Republic of South Africa, judicial * of the country; *pop* 149,836

**Blue Ridge** E range of the Applachians E U.S. extending from S Pennsylvania to N Georgia

**Bodh Gaya** \ˈbōd-ˈgī-ä\ village NE India; one of the holiest sites of Buddhism

**Boe·o·tia** \bē-ˈō-sh(ē-)ə\ ancient state E *cen* Greece NW of Attica; chief ancient city, Thebes — **Boe·o·tian** \bē-ˈō-shən\ *adj or n*

**Bo·go·tá** \ˌbō-gō-ˈtä, -ˈtò, ˈbō-gə-ˌ\ city, * of Colombia; *pop* 6,850,500

**Bo Hai** *or* **Po Hai** \ˈbō-ˈhī\ *or* **Gulf of Chih·li** \ˈchē-ˈlē, ˈjir-\ arm of Yellow Sea NE China

**Bo·he·mia** \bō-ˈhē-mē-ə\ region W Czech Republic; chief city, Prague

**Bo·hol** \bō-ˈhòl\ island S *cen* Philippines

**Boi·se** \ˈbòi-sē, -zē\ city, * of Idaho; *pop* 205,761

**Bo·liv·ia** \bə-ˈli-vē-ə\ country W *cen* South America; administrative *, La Paz;

constitutional ✳, Sucre; *pop* 10,044,000 — **Bo·liv·i·an** \-vē-ən\ *adj or n*

**Bo·lo·gna** \bō-'lō-nyä\ city N Italy; *pop* 371,000

**Bol·ton** \'bōl-tᵊn\ town NW England; *pop* 253,300

**Bom·bay** \bäm-'bā\ *or* **Mum·bai** \'məm-,bī\ city & port W India; area *pop* 12,442,373

**Bonn** \'bän, 'bȯn\ city Germany on the Rhine SSE of Cologne, formerly (1949–99) ✳ of West Germany; *pop* 305,765

**Boo·thia** \'bü-thē-ə\ peninsula N Canada W of Baffin Island; its N tip is most northerly point in mainland North America

**Bor·ders** \'bȯr-dərz\ former administrative region SE Scotland

**Bor·neo** \'bȯr-nē-,ō\ island Malay Archipelago SW of the Philippines; divided between Brunei, Indonesia, and Malaysia

**Bos·nia** \'bäz-nē-ə, 'bȯz-\ region S Europe; with Herzegovina forms independent **Bosnia and Her·ze·go·vi·na** \,hert-sə-gō-'vē-nə, ,hərt-, -'gō-və nə\, ✳, Sarajevo; *pop* 3,832,000 — **Bos·ni·an** \-nē-ən\ *adj or n*

**Bos·po·rus** \'bäs-p(ə-)rəs\ strait 18 mi. (29 km.) long between Turkey in Europe & Turkey in Asia connecting Sea of Marmara & Black Sea

**Bos·ton** \'bȯs-tən\ city, ✳ of Massachusetts; *pop* 617,594 — **Bos·to·nian** \bȯ-'stō-nē-ən, -nyən\ *adj or n*

**Bot·a·ny Bay** \'bä-tə-nē\ inlet of South Pacific SE Australia in New South Wales S of Sydney

**Both·nia, Gulf of** \'bäth-nē-ə\ arm of Baltic Sea between Sweden & Finland

**Bo·tswa·na** \bät-'swä-nə\ *formerly* **Bech·u·a·na·land** \,bech-'wä-nə-land\ country S Africa; ✳, Gaborone; *pop* 2,032,000

**Boul·der** \'bōl-dər\ city N *cen* Colorado; *pop* 97,385

**Boulder Dam** — see HOOVER DAM

**Bourne·mouth** \'bȯrn-məth, 'bürn-\ town S England on English Channel; *pop* 154,400

**Brad·ford** \'brad-fərd\ city N England; *pop* 350,000

**Brah·ma·pu·tra** \,brä-mə-'pü trə\ river about 1800 mi. (2900 km.) long S Asia flowing from the Himalayas in Tibet to Ganges Delta

**Bra·sí·lia** \brə-'zil-yə\ city, ✳ of Brazil; *pop* 2,570,160

**Bra·ti·sla·va** \,bra-tə-'slä-və, ,brä-\ city on the Danube; ✳ of Slovakia; *pop* 411,000

**Bra·zil** \brə-'zil\ country E & *cen* South America; ✳, Brasília; *pop* 190,733,000 — **Bra·zil·ian** \brə-'zil-yən\ *adj or n*

**Braz·za·ville** \'bra-zə-,vil, 'brä-zə-,vēl\ city, ✳ of Republic of the Congo on W bank of lower Congo River; *pop* 1,373,000

**Bre·men** \'bre-mən, 'brä-\ city & port NW Germany; *pop* 542,707

**Bren·ner** \'bre-nər\ pass 4495 ft. (1370 m.) high in the Alps between Austria & Italy

**Brent** \'brent\ borough of W Greater London, England; *pop* 311,200

**Bret·on, Cape** \kāp-'bre-tᵊn, kə-'bre-, -'bri-\ cape Canada; most easterly point of Cape Breton Island & of Nova Scotia

**Bridge·port** \'brij-,pȯrt\ city SW Connecticut on Long Island Sound; *pop* 144,229

**Bridge·town** \'brij-,taún\ city, ✳ of Barbados; *pop* 5996

**Brigh·ton** \'brī-tᵊn\ town S England on English Channel; *pop* 133,400

**Bris·bane** \'briz-bən, -,bān\ city & port E Australia, ✳ of Queensland; *pop* 1,874,427

**Bris·tol** \'bris-tᵊl\ **1** city & port SW England; *pop* 536,000 **2** channel between S Wales & SW England

**Brit·ain** \'bri-tᵊn\ **1** the island of Great Britain **2** UNITED KINGDOM

**British Columbia** province W Canada on Pacific coast; ✳, Victoria; *pop* 4,113,487

**British Commonwealth** — see COMMONWEALTH, THE

**British Empire** former empire consisting of Great Britain & the British dominions & dependencies

**British Guiana** — see GUYANA

**British Honduras** — see BELIZE

**British India** the part of India formerly under direct British administration

**British Indian Ocean Territory** British colony in Indian Ocean consisting of Chagos Archipelago

**British Isles** island group W Europe consisting of Great Britain, Ireland, & nearby islands

**British Virgin Islands** E islands of Virgin Islands; a British possession; *pop* 14,786

**British West Indies** islands of the West Indies including Jamaica, Trinidad and Tobago, & the Bahama & Cayman islands, Windward Islands, Leeward Islands, & British Virgin Islands •

**Brit·ta·ny** \'bri-tə-nē\ region NW France SW of Normandy

**Brom·ley** \'bräm-lē\ borough of SE Greater London, England; *pop* 309,000

**Bronx** \'bräŋks\ *or* **The Bronx** borough of New York City NE of Manhattan; *pop* 1,385,108

**Brook·lyn** \'brúk-lən\ borough of New York City at SW end of Long Island; *pop* 2,504,700

**Brooks Range** \'brúks\ mountains N Alaska

**Browns·ville** \'braúnz-,vil, -vəl\ city S Texas on the Rio Grande; *pop* 175,023

**Bru·nei** \brü-'nī, 'brü-,nī\ country NE Borneo; ✳, Bandar Seri Begawan; *pop* 406,200 — **Bru·nei·an** \brü-'nī-ən\ *adj or n*

**Brus·sels** \'brə-səlz\ city, ✻ of Belgium; *pop* 163,000

**Bu·cha·rest** \'bü-kə-,rest, 'byü-\ city, ✻ of Romania; *pop* 1,926,000

**Buck·ing·ham·shire** \'bə-kiŋ-əm-,shir\ *or* **Buckingham** county SE *cen* England

**Bu·da·pest** \'bü-də-,pest\ city, ✻ of Hungary; *pop* 1,729,040

**Bue·nos Ai·res** \,bwä-nōs-'ī-rās\ *Sp* \,bwä-nōs-'ī-rās\ city, ✻ of Argentina; *pop* 2,960,976

**Buf·fa·lo** \'bə-fə-,lō\ city W New York on Lake Erie; *pop* 261,310

**Bu·jum·bu·ra** \,bü-jəm-'bür-ə\ city, ✻ of Burundi; *pop* 497,166

**Bu·ko·vi·na** \,bü-kō-'vē-nə\ region E *cen* Europe in foothills of E Carpathians

**Bul·gar·ia** \,bəl-'ger-ē-ə, bul-\ country SE Europe on Black Sea; ✻, Sofia; *pop* 7,246,000 — **Bul·gar·i·an** \,bəl-'ger-ē-ən, bul-\ *adj or n*

**Bull Run** \'bul-'rən\ stream NE Virginia

**Bun·ker Hill** \'bəŋ-kər\ height in Boston, Massachusetts

**Bur·bank** \'bər-,baŋk\ city SW California; *pop* 103,340

**Bur·gun·dy** \'bər-gən-dē\ region E France — **Bur·gun·di·an** \(,)bər-'gən-dē-ən\ *adj or n*

**Bur·ki·na Fa·so** \bür-'kē-nə-'fä-sō, bər-\ *formerly* **Upper Vol·ta** \'vōl-tə, 'vȯl-\ country W Africa N of Cote d'Ivoire, Ghana, & Togo; ✻, Ouagadougou; *pop* 14,017,000

**Bur·ling·ton** \'bər-liŋ-tən\ city NW Vermont; largest in state; *pop* 42,417

**Bur·ma** \'bər-mə\ — see MYANMAR — **Bur·mese** \,bər-'mēz, -'mēs\ *adj or n*

**Bu·run·di** \bü-'rün-dē, -'rün-\ country E *cen* Africa; ✻, Bujumbura; *pop* 8,300,000 — **Bu·run·di·an** \-dē-ən\ *adj or n*

**Busan** — see PUSAN

**Bute** \'byüt\ island SW Scotland in Firth of Clyde

**Butte** \'byüt\ city SW Montana; county *pop* 32,996

**Byelorussia** — see BELORUSSIA

**By·zan·tine Empire** \'bi-zⁿn-,tēn, 'bī-, -,tīn; bə-'zan-,tēn, -tīn, bī-\ empire of SE & S Europe and W Asia from 4th to 15th century

**By·zan·ti·um** \bə-'zan-sh(ē-)əm, -'zant-ē-əm\ ancient city on site of modern Istanbul

**Cabo Verde** — see CAPE VERDE

**Caer·nar·von** \kär-'när-vən, kə(r)-\ town & seaport NW Wales; *pop* 9506

**Ca·guas** \'kä-,gwäs\ town E *cen* Puerto Rico; *pop* 142,893

**Cai·ro** \'kī-(,)rō\ city, ✻ of Egypt; *pop* 7,787,000 — **Cai·rene** \kī-'rēn\ *adj or n*

**Ca·la·bria** \kə-'lä-brē-ə, -'lä-\ district of ancient Italy consisting of area forming heel of Italian Peninsula — **Ca·la·bri·an** \kə-'lä-brē-ən, -'lä-\ *adj or n*

**Cal·cut·ta** \kal-'kə-tə\ *or* **Kol·ka·ta** \kōl-'kä-tä\ city E India on Hugli River; *pop* 4,496,694 — **Cal·cut·tan** \-'kə-tⁿn\ *adj or n*

**Cal·e·do·nia** \,ka-lə-'dō-nyə, -nē-ə\ — see SCOTLAND — **Cal·e·do·nian** \-nyən, -nē-ən\ *adj or n*

**Cal·ga·ry** \'kal-gə-rē\ city SW Alberta, Canada; *pop* 1,096,833

**Ca·li** \'kä-lē\ city W Colombia; *pop* 2,326,500

**Cal·i·for·nia** \,ka-lə-'fȯr-nyə\ state SW U.S.; ✻, Sacramento; *pop* 37,253,956 — **Cal·i·for·nian** \-nyən\ *adj or n*

**California, Gulf of** arm of the Pacific NW Mexico

**Cal·va·ry** \'kal-v(ə-)rē\ place outside ancient Jerusalem where Jesus was crucified

**Cambay, Gulf of** — see KHAMBHAT (Gulf of)

**Cam·bo·dia** \kam-'bō-dē-ə\ *or* **Kam·pu·chea** \,kam-pu-'chē-ə\ country SE Asia in S Indochina; ✻, Phnom Penh; *pop* 13,396,000 — **Cam·bo·di·an** \kam-'bō-dē-ən\ *adj or n*

**Cam·bria** \'kam-brē-ə\ WALES — an old name

**Cam·bridge** \'kām-brij\ **1** city E Massachusetts W of Boston; *pop* 105,162 **2** city E England; *pop* 92,772

**Cam·bridge·shire** \'kām-brij-,shir, -shər\ *or* **Cambridge** county E England

**Cam·den** \'kam-dən\ borough of N Greater London, England; *pop* 220,000

**Cam·er·oon** *or French* **Cam·er·oun** \,ka-mə-'rün\ country W Africa; ✻, Yaoundé; *pop* 17,464,000 — **Cam·er·oo·nian** \-'rü-nē-ən, -rü-nyən\ *adj or n*

**Ca·mi·guin** \,kä-mē-'gēn\ island Philippines, off N coast of Mindanao

**Ca·naan** \'kā-nən\ the part of ancient Palestine between Jordan River & Mediterranean Sea; sometimes used to refer to all of ancient Palestine — **Ca·naan·ite** \'kā-nə-,nīt\ *adj or n*

**Can·a·da** \'ka-nə-də\ country N North America; ✻, Ottawa; *pop* 33,476,688 — **Ca·na·di·an** \kə-'nā-dē-ən\ *adj or n*

**Canadian Falls** — see NIAGARA FALLS

**Canadian Shield** *or* **Lau·ren·tian Pla·teau** \lȯ-'ren(t)-shən\ plateau region E Canada & NE U.S. extending from Mackenzie River basin E to Davis Strait & S to S Quebec, S *cen* Ontario, NE Minnesota, N Wisconsin, NW Michigan, and NE New York including the Adirondacks

**Canal Zone** *or* **Panama Canal Zone** strip of territory Panama leased to U.S. (until 1979) for Panama Canal

**Ca·nary** \kə-'ner-ē\ islands Spain in the Atlantic off NW coast of Africa; *pop* 2,118,679

**Ca·nav·er·al, Cape** \kə-'nav-rəl, -'na-və-\ *or 1963–73* **Cape Ken·ne·dy** \-'ken-ə-dē\

cape E Florida in the Atlantic on **Canav·eral Peninsula** E of Indian River

**Can·ber·ra** \'kan-h(ə-)rə, -,ber-ə\ city, ✳ of Australia in Australian Capital Territory; *pop* 355,596

**Cannes** \'kan, 'kän\ port SE France; *pop* 73,671

**Can·ter·bury** \'kan-tə(r)-,ber-ē, -b(ə-)rē\ city SE England; *pop* 34,404

**Canton** — see GUANGZHOU

**Cape Bret·on Island** \'kap-'bret-°n, kə-'bre-, -'bri-\ island NE Nova Scotia

**Cape Coral** city SW Florida; *pop* 154,305

**Cape Horn** — see HORN, CAPE

**Cape of Good Hope** — see GOOD HOPE, CAPE OF

**Cape Province** *or* **Cape of Good Hope** *or before 1910* **Cape Colony** former province S Republic of South Africa

**Cape Town** \'kāp-,taùn\ city, legislative ✳ of Republic of South Africa and formerly ✳ of Cape Province; *pop* 3,740,026

**Cape Verde** \'vərd\ *or* **Ca·bo Ver·de** \,kä-bü-'ver-də\ islands in the North Atlantic off W Africa; country; ✳, Praia; *pop* 491,875 — **Cape Verd·ean** \'vər-dē-ən\ *adj or n*

**Cape York Peninsula** \'yórk\ peninsula NE Australia in N Queensland

**Ca·pri** \kə-'prē, kə-; 'kä-(,)prē, 'ka-\ island Italy S of Bay of Naples; *pop* 7270

**Ca·ra·cas** \kə-'rä-käs\ city, ✳ of Venezuela; *pop* 1,836,000

**Car·diff** \'kar-dif\ city, ✳ of Wales; *pop* 335,000

**Ca·rib·be·an Sea** \,ka-rə-'bē-ən, kə-'ri-bē-\ arm of the Atlantic; on N & E are the West Indies, on S is South America, & on W is Central America — **Caribbean** *adj*

**Car·lisle** \kär-'lī(-ə)l, kər-, 'kär-,\ city NW England; *pop* 99,800

**Carls·bad Caverns** \'kär(-ə)lz-,bad\ series of caves SE New Mexico

**Car·mar·then** \kär-'mär-thən, kə(r)-\ port S Wales; *pop* 54,800

**Car·o·li·na** \,ka-rə-'lī-nə\ English colony on E coast of North America founded 1663 & divided 1729 into North Carolina & South Carolina (the **Carolinas**) — **Car·o·lin·i·an** \,ka-rə-'li-nē-ən, -nyən\ *adj or n*

**Ca·ro·li·na** \,kä-rō-'lē-nä\ city NE Puerto Rico; *pop* 176,762

**Car·o·line** \'ka-rə-,līn, -lən\ islands W Pacific E of S Philippines; comprising Palau & the Federated States of Micronesia

**Car·pa·thi·an** \kär-'pā-thē-ən\ mountains E cen Europe along boundary between Slovakia & Poland & in N & cen Romania; highest Gerlachovsky 8711 ft. (2655 m.)

**Car·pen·tar·ia, Gulf of** \,kär-pən-'ter-ē-ə\ inlet of Arafura Sea N of Australia

**Car·rick·fer·gus** \,ka-rik-'fər-gəs\ district E Northern Ireland; *pop* 39,000

**Car·roll·ton** \'ka-rəl-rən\ city N Texas; *pop* 119,097

**Car·son City** \'kär-s°n\ city, ✳ of Nevada; *pop* 55,274

**Car·thage** \'kär-thij\ ancient city N Africa NE of modern Tunis; ✳ of an empire that once included much of NW Africa, E Spain, & Sicily — **Car·tha·gin·ian** \,kär-thə-'ji-nyən, -nē-ən\ *adj or n*

**Ca·sa·blan·ca** \,ka-sə-'blaŋ-kə, ,kä-sə-'bläŋ-, -zə-\ city W Morocco on the Atlantic; *pop* 3,102,000

**Cas·cade Range** \(,)kas-'kād\ mountains NW U.S. in Washington, Oregon, & N California — see RAINIER, MOUNT

**Cas·per** \'kas-pər\ city cen Wyoming; *pop* 55,316

**Cas·pi·an Sea** \'kas-pē-ən\ salt lake between Europe and Asia about 90 ft. (27 m.) below sea level

**Cas·tile** \ka-'stēl\ *or in full* **Cas·ti·lla** \kä-'stēl-yä, 'stē-yä\ region & ancient kingdom cen & N Spain

**Cast·le·reagh** \'ka-səl-(,)rā\ district E Northern Ireland; *pop* 67,000

**Cas·tries** \'kas-,trēz, -,trēs\ seaport, ✳ of Saint Lucia; *pop* 11,900

**Cat·a·lo·nia** \,ka-tə-'lō-nyə, -nē-ə\ region NE Spain bordering on France & the Mediterranean; chief city, Barcelona; *pop* 7,519,843 — **Cat·a·lo·nian** \-'ō-nyən, -nē-ən\ *adj or n*

**Ca·thay** \ka-'thā\ an old name for China

**Cats·kill** \'kat-,skil\ mountains in Appalachian system SE New York W of the Hudson

**Cau·ca·sus** \'kó-kə-səs\ mountain system SE Europe between Black & Caspian seas in Russia, Georgia, Azerbaijan, & Armenia

**Cay·enne** \kī-'en, kā-\ city, ✳ of French Guiana; *pop* 37,097

**Cay·man** \(,)kā-'man, *attributively* 'kā-mən\ islands West Indies NW of Jamaica; a British colony; *pop* 56,700

**Ce·bu** \sā-'bü\ island E cen Philippines

**Ce·dar Rapids** \'sē-dər\ city E Iowa; *pop* 126,326

**Cel·tic Sea** \'kel-tik, 'sel-\ inlet of the Atlantic in British Isles SE of Ireland, SW of Wales, & W of SW England

**Central African Republic** country N cen Africa; ✳, Bangui; *pop* 2,998,000

**Central America** narrow portion of North America from S border of Mexico to South America — **Central American** *adj or n*

**Central Valley** valley of Sacramento & San Joaquin rivers in California between Sierra Nevada & Coast Ranges

**Cey·lon** \si-'län, sā-\ **1** island in Indian Ocean off S India **2** — see SRI LANKA — **Cey·lon·ese** \,sā-lə-'nēz, ,sē-, ,se-, -'nēs\ *adj or n*

**Chad** \'chad\ country N cen Africa; ✳,

N'Djamena; *pop* 9,253,000 — **Chad·ian** \\'cha-dē-ən\\ *adj or n*

**Chad, Lake** shallow lake N *cen* Africa at junction of boundaries of Chad, Niger, & Nigeria

**Cha·gos Archipelago** \\'chä-gəs\\ island group *cen* Indian Ocean; forms British Indian Ocean Territory — see DIEGO GARCIA

**Chal·dea** \\kal-'dē-ə\\ ancient region SW Asia on Euphrates River & Persian Gulf — **Chal·de·an** \\-'dē-ən\\ *adj or n* — **Chal·dee** \\'kal-ˌdē\\ *n*

**Cham·pagne** \\sham-'pān\\ region NE France

**Cham·plain, Lake** \\sham-'plān\\ lake between New York & Vermont extending N into Quebec

**Chan·di·garh** \\'chən-dē-gər\\ city N India N of Delhi; *pop* 809,000

**Chan·dler** \\'chan(d)-lər\\ city SW *cen* Arizona; *pop* 236,123

**Chang** \\'chäŋ\\ *or traditionally* **Yang·tze** \\'yaŋ-'sē, 'yaŋ(k)t-'sē; 'yäŋ-'tsə\\ river 3434 mi. (5525 km.) long *cen* China flowing into East China Sea

**Chang·chun** \\'chäŋ-'chùn\\ city NE China; *pop* 3,802,000

**Chang·sha** \\'chäŋ-'shä\\ city SE *cen* China; *pop* 3,094,000

**Channel** islands in English Channel including Jersey, Guernsey, & Alderney & belonging to United Kingdom; *pop* 135,694

**Charles** \\'chär(-ə)lz\\ river 47 mi. (76 km.) long E Massachusetts flowing into Boston harbor

**Charles, Cape** cape E Virginia N of entrance to Chesapeake Bay

**Charles·ton** \\'chär(-ə)l-stən\\ **1** seaport SE South Carolina; *pop* 120,083 **2** city, ✳ of West Virginia; *pop* 51,400

**Char·lotte** \\'shär-lət\\ city S North Carolina; *pop* 731,424

**Charlotte Ama·lie** \\ə-'mäl-yə, 'a-mə-lē\\ city, ✳ of Virgin Islands of the U.S.; on island of Saint Thomas; *pop* 11,004

**Char·lottes·ville** \\'shär-ləts-ˌvil, -vəl\\ city *cen* Virginia; *pop* 43,475

**Char·lotte·town** \\'shär-lət-ˌtaùn\\ city, ✳ of Prince Edward Island, Canada; *pop* 32,174

**Chat·ta·noo·ga** \\ˌcha-tə-'nü-gə\\ city SE Tennessee; *pop* 167,674

**Chech·nya** \\chech-'nyä, 'chech-nyə\\ republic of SE Russia in Europe; ✳, Grozny

**Chelms·ford** \\'chemz-fərd\\ town SE England; *pop* 150,000

**Che·lya·binsk** \\chel-'yä-bən(t)sk\\ city W Russia; *pop* 1,130,000

**Cheng·chou** — see ZHENGZHOU

**Cheng·du** *or* **Ch'eng·tu** \\'chəŋ-'dü\\ city SW *cen* China; *pop* 7,416,000

**Chennai** — see MADRAS

**Cher·no·byl** \\chər-'nō-bəl, (ˌ)cher-\\ site N Ukraine of town abandoned after 1986 nuclear accident

**Ches·a·peake** \\'che-sə-ˌpēk, 'ches-ˌpēk\\ city SE Virginia; *pop* 222,209

**Chesapeake Bay** inlet of the Atlantic in Virginia & Maryland

**Chesh·ire** \\'che-shər, -ˌshir\\ *or* **Ches·ter** \\'ches-tər\\ former county W England bordering on Wales

**Chester** \\'ches-tər\\ city NW England; *pop* 58,436

**Chev·i·ot** \\'che-vē-ət, 'che-\\ hills along English–Scottish border

**Chey·enne** \\shī-'an, -'en\\ city, ✳ of Wyoming; *pop* 59,466

**Chi·ba** \\'chē-bä\\ city E Japan in Honshu on Tokyo Bay E of Tokyo; *pop* 961,749

**Chi·ca·go** \\shə-'kä-(ˌ)gō, -'kó-, -gə\\ city & port NE Illinois on Lake Michigan; *pop* 2,695,598 — **Chi·ca·go·an** \\-'kä-gō-ən, -'kó-\\ *n*

**Chi·chén It·zá** \\chē-ˌchen-ēt-'sä, -'ēt-sə\\ ruined Mayan city SE Mexico in Yucatán Peninsula

**Chich·es·ter** \\'chi-chəs-tər\\ city S England; *pop* 24,189

**Ch'i–ch'i–ha–erh** — see QIQIHAR

**Chihli, Gulf of** — see BO HAI

**Chi·le** \\'chi-lē, 'chē-(ˌ)lā\\ country SW South America; ✳, Santiago; *pop* 16,341,929 — **Chil·ean** \\'chi-lē-ən, chə-'lā-ən\\ *adj or n*

**Chim·bo·ra·zo** \\ˌchēm-bō-'rä-(ˌ)zō\\ mountain 20,561 ft. (6267 m.) W *cen* Ecuador

**Chi·na** \\'chī-nə\\ **1** country E Asia; ✳, Beijing; *pop* 1,335,000,000 — see TAIWAN **2** sea section of the W Pacific; divided into East China & South China seas

**Chin–chou** *or* **Chinchow** — see JINZHOU

**Chi·şi·nău** \\ˌkē-shē-'naù\\ *or* **Ki·shi·nev** \\ˌki-shi-'nyóf; 'ki-shə-ˌnef, -ˌnev\\ city *cen* Moldova; its ✳; *pop* 669,000

**Chit·ta·gong** \\'chi-tə-ˌgäŋ, -ˌgóŋ\\ city SE Bangladesh on Bay of Bengal; *pop* 7,616,000

**Chong·qing** *or* **Ch'ung–ch'ing** \\'chùŋ-'chiŋ\\ *or* **Chung·king** \\'chùŋ-'kiŋ\\ city SW *cen* China; *pop* 6,861,000

**Christ·church** \\'krīs(t)-ˌchərch\\ city New Zealand on E coast of South Island; urban area *pop* 341,469

**Christ·mas** \\'kris-məs\\ island E Indian Ocean SW of Java; governed by Australia; *pop* 1000

**Chu·la Vis·ta** \\ˌchü-lə-'vis-tə\\ city SW California S of San Diego; *pop* 243,916

**Chuuk** \\'chùk\\ *or* **Truk** \\'trək, 'trùk\\ islands *cen* Carolines, part of Federated States of Micronesia; *pop* 53,300

**Cin·cin·na·ti** \\ˌsin(t)-sə-'na-tē, -'na-tə\\ city SW Ohio; *pop* 296,943

**Ci·u·dad Juá·rez** \\syü-'thäth-'hwär-es, 'wär-; ˌsē-ù-'dad-\\ city Mexico on Texas border; *pop* 1,332,131

**Ciudad Trujillo** — see SANTO DOMINGO

**Clarks·ville** \'klärks-ˌvil, -vəl\ city N Tennessee NW of Nashville; *pop* 132,929

**Clear·wa·ter** \'klir-ˌwȯ tər, -ˌwä-\ city W Florida NW of St. Petersburg; *pop* 107,685

**Cleve·land** \'klēv-lənd\ city & port NE Ohio on Lake Erie; *pop* 396,815

**Clyde** \'klīd\ river 106 mi. (171 km.) long SW Scotland flowing into **Firth of Clyde** (estuary)

**Coast Mountains** mountain range W British Columbia, Canada; the N continuation of Cascade Range

**Coast Ranges** chain of mountain ranges W North America extending along Pacific coast W of Sierra Nevada & Cascade Range & through Vancouver Island into S Alaska to Kenai Peninsula & Kodiak Island

**Cod, Cape** \-'käd\ peninsula SE Massachusetts

**Coim·ba·tore** \ˌkȯim-bə-'tȯr\ city S India; *pop* 1,050,721

**Cole·raine** \kōl-'rān, 'kōl-ˌ\ 1 district N Northern Ireland; *pop* 59,000 2 port in Coleraine district

**Co·logne** \kə-'lōn\ city W Germany on the Rhine; *pop* 1,005,775

**Co·lom·bia** \kə-'ləm-bē-ə\ country NW South America; ✳, Bogotá; *pop* 41,468,000 — **Co·lom·bi·an** \-bē-ən\ *adj or n*

**Co·lom·bo** \kə-'ləm-(ˌ)bō\ city, ✳ of Sri Lanka; *pop* 647,100

**Col·o·ra·do** \ˌkä-lə-'ra-(ˌ)dō\ 1 river 1450 mi. (2334 km.) long SW U.S. & NW Mexico flowing from N Colorado into Gulf of California 2 desert SE California 3 plateau region SW U.S. W of Rocky Mountains 4 state W U.S.; ✳, Denver; *pop* 5,029,196 — **Col·o·rad·an** \-'ra-dᵊn, -'rä-\ *or* **Co·lo·ra·do·an** \-'ra-dō-ən, -'rä-\ *adj or n*

**Colorado Springs** city *cen* Colorado E of Pikes Peak; *pop* 416,427

**Co·lum·bia** \kə-'ləm-bē-ə\ 1 river 1214 mi. (1953 km.) long SW Canada & NW U.S. flowing S & W from SE British Columbia into the Pacific 2 plateau in Columbia River basin in E Washington, E Oregon, & SW Idaho 3 city, ✳ of South Carolina; *pop* 129,272

**Co·lum·bus** \kə-'ləm-bəs\ 1 city W Georgia; *pop* 189,885 2 city, ✳ of Ohio; *pop* 787,033

**Com·mon·wealth, the** \'käm-ən-ˌwel(t)\ th\ *or* **Commonwealth of Nations** *formerly* **British Commonwealth** the United Kingdom & most of the countries formerly dependent on it

**Com·o·ros** \'kä-mə-ˌrōz\ islands off SE Africa NW of Madagascar; country (except for Mayotte Island); ✳, Moroni; *pop* 752,000

**Con·a·kry** \'kä-nə-krē\ city, ✳ of Guinea; *pop* 1,668,000

**Con·cord** \'kän-ˌkȯrd, 'käŋ\ 1 city W California; *pop* 122,067 2 town E Massachusetts NW of Boston; *pop* 17,668 3 city, ✳ of New Hampshire; *pop* 42,695

**Con·go** \'käŋ-(ˌ)gō\ 1 *or* **Zaire** \zä-'ir\ river over 2700 mi. (4344 km.) long W Africa flowing into the Atlantic 2 *officially* **Democratic Republic of the Congo** *formerly* *1971–97* **Zaire** country *cen* Africa consisting of most of Congo River basin E of lower Congo River; ✳, Kinshasa; *pop* 67,800,000 3 *or officially* **Republic of the Congo** country W *cen* Africa W of lower Congo River; ✳, Brazzaville; *pop* 3,697,000 — **Con·go·lese** \ˌkäŋ-gə-'lēz, -'lēs\ *adj or n*

**Con·nooht** \'kä-ˌnȯt\ province W Ireland; *pop* 464,296

**Con·nect·i·cut** \kə-'ne-ti-kət\ 1 river 407 mi. (655 km.) long NE U.S. flowing S from N New Hampshire into Long Island Sound 2 state NE U.S.; ✳, Hartford; *pop* 3,574,097

**Constantinople** — see ISTANBUL

**Continental Divide** line of highest points of land separating the waters flowing W from those flowing N or E and extending SSE from NW Canada across W U.S. through Mexico & Central America to South America where it joins the Andes Mountains

**Cook** \'kuk\ 1 inlet of the Pacific S Alaska W of Kenai Peninsula 2 islands South Pacific SW of Society Islands belonging to New Zealand; *pop* 19,600 3 strait New Zealand between North Island & South Island

**Cook, Mount** *or* **Ao·ra·ki** \au̇-'rä-kē\ mountain 12,349 ft. (3764 m.) New Zealand in W *cen* South Island in Southern Alps; highest in New Zealand

**Cooks·town** \'kuks-ˌtau̇n\ district *cen* Northern Ireland; *pop* 37,000

**Co·pen·ha·gen** \ˌkō-pən-'hā-gən, -'hä-\ city, ✳ of Denmark; *pop* 579,513

**Cor·al Sea** \'kȯr-əl, 'kär-\ arm of the W Pacific NE of Australia

**Coral Springs** city SE Florida; *pop* 121,096

**Cór·do·ba** \'kȯr-də-bə, 'kȯr-thō-ˌvä\ city N *cen* Argentina; *pop* 1,293,000

**Cor·inth** \'kȯr-ən(t)th, 'kär-\ 1 region of ancient Greece 2 ancient city; site SW of present city of Corinth — **Co·rin·thi·an** \kə-'rin(t)-thē-ən\ *adj or n*

**Corinth, Gulf of** inlet of Ionian Sea *cen* Greece N of the Peloponnese

**Cork** \'kȯrk\ city S Ireland; *pop* 198,582

**Corn·wall** \'kȯrn-ˌwȯl, -wəl\ *or* *1974–2009* **Cornwall and Isles of Scilly** \'si-lē\ former county SW England

**Co·ro·na** \kə-'rō-nə\ city SW California E of Los Angeles; *pop* 152,374

**Cor·pus Chris·ti** \ˌkȯr-pəs-'kris-tē\ city & port S Texas; *pop* 305,215

**Cor·reg·i·dor** \kə-'re-gə-ˌdȯr\ island Philippines at entrance to Manila Bay

**Cor·si·ca** \'kȯr-si-kə\ island France in the Mediterranean N of Sardinia; *pop* 309,693 — **Cor·si·can** \'kȯr-si-kən\ *adj or n*

**Cos·ta Me·sa** \ˌkōs-tə-'mā-sə\ city SW California; *pop* 109,960

**Costa Ri·ca** \'rē-kə\ country Central America between Nicaragua & Panama; ✳, San José; *pop* 4,301,712 — **Cos·ta Ri·can** \-kən\ *adj or n*

**Côte d'Ivoire** \ˌkōt-dē-'vwär\ *or English* **Ivory Coast** country W Africa on Gulf of Guinea; official ✳, Yamoussoukro; seat of government, Abidjan; *pop* 22,650,000

**Cots·wold** \'kät-ˌswōld, -swəld\ hills SW *cen* England

**Cov·en·try** \'kə-vən-trē\ city *cen* England; *pop* 326,000

**Craig·av·on** \krā-'ga-vən\ district *cen* Northern Ireland; *pop* 93,000

**Cra·ter** \'krā-tər\ lake 1932 ft. (589 m.) deep SW Oregon in Cascade Range

**Crete** \'krēt\ island Greece in E Mediterranean; *pop* 623,065 — **Cre·tan** \'krē-t°n\ *adj or n*

**Cri·mea** \krī-'mē-ə, krə-\ peninsula SE Europe extending into Black Sea — **Cri·me·an** \krī-'mē-ən, krə-\ *adj*

**Cro·atia** \krō-'ā-sh(ē-)ə\ country SE Europe; ✳, Zagreb; *pop* 4,288,000 — **Croat** \'krō-ˌat\ *n*

**Croy·don** \'krȯi-d°n\ borough of S Greater London, England; *pop* 363,000

**Cu·ba** \'kyü-bə, 'kü-vä\ island in the West Indies; country; ✳, Havana; *pop* 11,167,000 — **Cu·ban** \'kyü-bən\ *adj or n*

**Cum·ber·land** \'kəm-bər-lənd\ river 687 mi. (1106 km.) long S Kentucky & N Tennessee

**Cumberland Gap** pass through Cumberland Plateau NE Tennessee

**Cumberland Plateau** mountain region E U.S.; part of S Appalachian Mountains extending from S West Virginia to NE Alabama

**Cum·bria** \'kəm-brē-ə\ county NW England; *pop* 499,858

**Cum·bri·an** \'kəm-brē-ən\ mountains NW England chiefly in Cumbria county

**Cu·par** \'kü-pər\ town E Scotland; *pop* 6642

**Cu·ri·ti·ba** \ˌkúr-ə-'tē-bə\ city S Brazil SW of São Paulo; *pop* 1,751,907

**Cush** \'kəsh, 'kúsh\ ancient country NE Africa in upper Nile valley S of Egypt — **Cush·ite** \'kə-ˌshīt, 'kú-\ *n* — **Cush·it·ic** \kə-'shi-tik, kú-\ *adj*

**Cuz·co** \'küs-(ˌ)kō\ city S *cen* Peru; *pop* 348,935

**Cymru** — see WALES

**Cy·prus** \'sī-prəs\ island E Mediterranean S of Turkey; country; ✳, Nicosia; *pop* 1,100,000 — **Cyp·ri·ot** \'si-prē-ə, -ˌät\ *or* **Cyp·ri·ote** \-ˌōt, -ət\ *adj or n*

**Cy·re·na·ica** \ˌsir-ə-'nā-ə-kə, ˌsī-rə-\ ancient region N Africa on coast W of Egypt — **Cy·re·na·i·can** \-'nā-ə-kən\ *adj or n*

**Czecho·slo·va·kia** \ˌche-kə-slō-'vä-kē-ə, -slə-, -'va-\ former country *cen* Europe divided into the independent states of the Czech Republic & Slovakia — **Czecho·slo·vak** \-'slō-ˌväk, -ˌvak\ *adj or n* — **Czecho·slo·va·ki·an** \-slō-'vä-kē-ən, -slə-, -'va-\ *adj or n*

**Czech Republic** country *cen* Europe; ✳, Prague; *pop* 10,332,000

**Daegu** — see TAEGU

**Daejeon** — see TAEJON

**Dahomey** — see BENIN

**Dairen** — see DALIAN

**Da·kar** \'da-ˌkär, dä-'kär\ city, ✳ of Senegal; *pop* 2,200,000

**Da·ko·ta** 1 *or* **James** river 710 mi. (1143 km.) long North Dakota & South Dakota flowing S into the Missouri **2** territory 1861–89 NW U.S. divided 1889 into states of North Dakota & South Dakota (the **Dakotas** \-təz\ )

**Da·lian** *or* **Ta·lien** \'dä-'lyen\ *or* **Lü·da** *or* **Lü–ta** \'lü-'dä\ *or* **Dai·ren** \'dī-'ren\ city NE China; *pop* 3,995,000

**Dal·las** \'da-ləs, -lis\ city NE Texas; *pop* 1,197,816

**Dal·ma·tia** \dal-'mā-sh(ē-)ə\ region W Balkan Peninsula on the Adriatic — **Dal·ma·tian** \-shən\ *adj or n*

**Da·ly City** \'dä-lē\ city W California S of San Francisco; *pop* 101,123

**Da·mas·cus** \də-'mas-kəs\ city, ✳ of Syria; *pop* 1,451,000

**Dan·ube** \'dan-(ˌ)yüb\ river 1771 mi. (2850 km.) long S Europe flowing from SW Germany into Black Sea — **Da·nu·bi·an** \də-'nü-bē-ən, da-, -'nyü-\ *adj*

**Dar·da·nelles** \ˌdär-də-'nelz\ *or* **Hel·les·pont** \'he-lə-ˌspänt\ strait NW Turkey connecting Sea of Marmara & the Aegean

**Dar es Sa·laam** \ˌdär-ˌe(s)-sə-'läm\ city, historic ✳ of Tanzania; *pop* 4,365,000

**Dar·ling** \'där-liŋ\ river about 1700 mi. (2735 km.) long SE Australia in Queensland & New South Wales flowing SW into the Murray

**Dar·win** \'där-wən\ city Australia, ✳ of Northern Territory; *pop* 103,016

**Da·vao** \'dä-ˌvaú, dä-'vaú\ city S Philippines in E Mindanao on Davao Gulf; *pop* 1,313,000

**Dav·en·port** \'da-vən-ˌpȯrt\ city E Iowa; *pop* 99,685

**Da·vis** \'dä-vəs\ strait between SW Greenland & E Baffin Island connecting Baffin Bay & the Atlantic

**Day·ton** \'dā-t°n\ city SW Ohio; *pop* 141,527

**Dead Sea** salt lake between Israel & Jordan; 1312 ft. (400 m.) below sea level

**Death Valley** dry valley E California & S

Nevada containing lowest point in U.S. (282 ft. *or* 86 m. below sea level)

**Deccan** \'de kən, -ˌkan\ plateau region S India

**Del·a·ware** \'de-lə-ˌwer, -wər\ **1** river 296 mi. (476 km.) long E U.S. flowing S from S New York into Delaware Bay **2** state E U.S.; *, Dover; *pop* 897,934 — **Del·a·war·ean** *or* **Del·a·war·ian** \de-lə-'wer-ē-ən\ *adj or n*

**Delaware Bay** inlet of the Atlantic between SW New Jersey & E Delaware

**Del·hi** \'de-lē\ city N India; *pop* 11,034,555 — see NEW DELHI

**De·los** \'dē-ˌläs\ island Greece — **De·lian** \'dē-lē-ən, 'dēl-yən\ *adj or n*

**Del·phi** \'del-ˌfī\ ancient town *cen* Greece on S slope of Mt. Parnassus

**Democratic Republic of the Congo** — see CONGO 2

**Denali** — see MCKINLEY, MOUNT

**Den·mark** \'den-ˌmärk\ country N Europe occupying most of Jutland & neighboring islands; *, Copenhagen; *pop* 5,604,000

**Den·ver** \'den-vər\ city, * of Colorado; *pop* 600,158

**Der·by** \'där-bē\ city N *cen* England; *pop* 214,000

**Der·by·shire** \'där-bē-ˌshir, -shər\ *or* **Derby** county N *cen* England

**Der·ry** \'der-ē\ *or* **Lon·don·der·ry** \ˌlon-dən-'der-ē\ city & port NW Northern Ireland; *pop* 83,000

**Des Moines** \di-'moin\ city, * of Iowa; *pop* 203,433

**De·troit** \di-'troit\ **1** river 31 mi. (50 km.) long between SE Michigan & Ontario connecting Lake Saint Clair & Lake Erie **2** city SE Michigan; *pop* 713,777

**Dev·on** \'de-vən\ *or* **De·von·shire** \'de-vən-ˌshir, -shər\ county SW England

**Dha·ka** \'dä-kə\ city, * of Bangladesh; *pop* 7,033,000

**Die·go Gar·cia** \dē-ˌā-gō-'gär-'sē-ə\ island in Indian Ocean; chief island of Chagos Archipelago

**Di·li** *also* **Dil·li** \'di-le\ city & port N Timor, * of East Timor; *pop* 193,000

**Di·nar·ic Alps** \də-'na-rik\ range of the E Alps in W Slovenia, W Croatia, Bosnia and Herzegovina, & Montenegro

**District of Co·lum·bia** \kə-'ləm-bē-ə\ federal district E U.S. coextensive with city of Washington; *pop* 601,723

**Djakarta** — see JAKARTA

**Dji·bou·ti** \jə-'bü-tē\ **1** country E Africa on Gulf of Aden; *pop* 818,000 **2** city, its *; *pop* 339,500

**Dni·pro·pe·trovs'k** *or* **Dne·pro·pe·trovsk** \də-ˌnye-prə-pə-'trófsk\ city E *cen* Ukraine; *pop* 996,500

**Dodge City** \'däj\ city S Kansas on Arkansas River; *pop* 27,340

**Do·do·ma** \dō-'dō-(ˌ)mä\ city, legislative * of Tanzania; *pop* 312,500

**Do·ha** \'dō-(ˌ)hä\ city & port, * of Qatar on Persian Gulf; *pop* 521,000

**Dom·i·ni·ca** \ˌdä-mə-'nē-kə\ island West Indies in the Leeward Islands, country, *, Roseau; *pop* 71,300

**Do·min·i·can Republic** \də-'mi-ni-kən\ country West Indies in E Hispaniola; *, Santo Domingo; *pop* 9,445,000 — **Dominican** *adj or n*

**Don** \'dän\ river 1224 mi. (1969 km.) long SW Russia

**Do·nets'k** \də-'nyetsk\ city E Ukraine; *pop* 952,500

**Dor·ches·ter** \'dòr-chəs-tər, -ˌches-\ town S England; *pop* 14,049

**Dor·set** \'dòr-sət\ *or* **Dor·set·shire** \-ˌshir, -shər\ county S England on English Channel

**Dort·mund** \'dòrt-ˌmùnt, -mənd\ city W Germany in the Ruhr; *pop* 571,143

**Dou·a·la** \dü-'ä-lä\ seaport W Cameroon; *pop* 1,900,000

**Dou·ro** \'dòr-(ˌ)ü\ *or Spanish* **Due·ro** \'dwe(ə)r-ō\ river 556 mi. (895 km.) long N Spain & N Portugal flowing into the Atlantic

**Do·ver** \'dō-vər\ city, * of Delaware; *pop* 36,047

**Dover, Strait of** channel between SE England & N France; the most easterly part of English Channel

**Down** \'daùn\ district SE Northern Ireland; *pop* 67,000

**Dow·ney** \'daù-nē\ city SW California SE of Los Angeles; *pop* 111,772

**Down·pat·rick** \daùn-'pa-trik\ town E Northern Ireland; *pop* 8245

**Dra·kens·berg** \'drä-kənz-ˌbərg\ mountain range E Republic of South Africa & Lesotho; highest peak Thabana Ntlenyana 11,425 ft. (3482 m.)

**Dres·den** \'drez-dən\ city E Germany; *pop* 512,354

**Dub·lin** \'də-blən\ city, * of Ireland; *pop* 527,612

**Dud·ley** \'dəd-lē\ town W *cen* England; *pop* 300,000

**Duis·burg** \'dü-əs-ˌbərg, 'düz-ˌ, 'dyüz-ˌ\ city W Germany at junction of Rhine & Ruhr rivers; *pop* 488,468

**Du·luth** \də-'lüth\ city & port NE Minnesota at W end of Lake Superior; *pop* 86,265

**Dum·fries** \ˌdəm-'frēs, -'frēz\ burgh S Scotland; *pop* 32,084

**Dumfries and Gal·lo·way** \'ga-lə-ˌwā\ administrative subdivision of S Scotland

**Dun·dee** \ˌdən-'dē\ city E Scotland; *pop* 147,000

**Dun·gan·non** \ˌdən-'ga-nən\ district W Northern Ireland; *pop* 53,000

**Dur·ban** \'dər-bən\ city and seaport E Republic of South Africa; *pop* 736,852

**Dur·ham** \'dər-əm, 'də-rəm, 'dùr-əm\ city N *cen* North Carolina; *pop* 228,330

**Du·shan·be** \dü-'sham-bə, dyü-, -'shäm-,

'dyü-; ˌdyü-shäm-'bā\ city, ✳ of Tajikistan; *pop* 749,500

Düs·sel·dorf \'dü-səl-ˌdórf, 'dyü-, 'dœ-\ city W Germany on the Rhine; *pop* 586,291

Ea·ling \'ē-liŋ\ borough of W Greater London, England; *pop* 338,000

East An·glia \'aŋ-glē-ə\ region E England; *pop* 1,366,300

East China Sea — see CHINA

Eas·ter \'ē-stər\ island Chile SE Pacific about 2000 mi. (3200 km.) W of Chilean coast

Eastern Cape province SE Republic of South Africa; *pop* 6,562,053

Eastern Desert desert E Egypt between the Nile & the Red Sea

Eastern Ghats \'gäts, 'góts, 'gəts\ chain of low mountains SE India along coast

Eastern Hemisphere the half of the earth E of the Atlantic Ocean including Europe, Asia, Australia, and Africa

Eastern Roman Empire the Byzantine Empire from 395 to 474

Eastern Samoa — see AMERICAN SAMOA

East Germany — see GERMANY

East Indies the Malay Archipelago — East Indian *adj or n*

East London city S Republic of South Africa; *pop* 296,000

East Pakistan the former E division of Pakistan consisting of E portion of Bengal; now Bangladesh

East River strait SE New York connecting upper New York Bay & Long Island Sound and separating Manhattan & Long Island

East Sea — see JAPAN, SEA OF

East Sus·sex \'sə-siks\ county SE England; *pop* 526,671

East Timor *or* Ti·mor–Les·te \'tē-mór-'lesh-ˌtā\ country SE Asia on E Timor; ✳, Dili; *pop* 1,066,000

Ebro \'ā-(ˌ)brō\ river 565 mi. (909 km.) long NE Spain flowing into the Mediterranean

Ec·ua·dor \'e-kwə-ˌdór, ˌe-kwä-'thór\ country W South America; ✳, Quito; *pop* 14,483,000 — Ec·ua·dor·an \'e-kwə-'dór-ən\ *or* Ec·ua·dor·ean *or* Ec·ua·dor·ian \-ē-ən\ *adj or n*

Ed·in·burgh \'e-dᵊn-ˌbər-ə\ city, ✳ of Scotland; *pop* 459,000

Ed·mon·ton \'ed-mən-tən\ city, ✳ of Alberta, Canada; *pop* 812,201

Edom \'ē-dəm\ ancient country SW Asia S of Judaea & Dead Sea — Edom·ite \'ēd-ə-ˌmīt\ *n*

Egypt \'ē-jipt\ country NE Africa & Sinai Peninsula of SW Asia bordering on Mediterranean & Red seas; ✳, Cairo; *pop* 72,798,000

Eire — see IRELAND

Elam \'ē-ləm\ ancient country SW Asia at head of Persian Gulf E of Babylonia — Elam·ite \'ē-lə-ˌmīt\ *n*

Elbe \'el-bə, 'elb\ river 720 mi. (1159 km.) long N Czech Republic & NE Germany flowing NW into North Sea

El·bert, Mount \'el-bərt\ mountain 14,433 ft. (4399 m.) W *cen* Colorado; highest in Colorado & the Rocky Mountains

El·brus, Mount \el-'brüz, -'brüs\ mountain 18,510 ft. (5642 m.) Russia; highest in the Caucasus & in Europe

El·burz \el-'búrz\ mountains N Iran

Eliz·a·beth \i-'li-zə-bəth\ city NE New Jersey; *pop* 124,969

Elles·mere \'elz-ˌmir\ island N Canada in Nunavut

Ellice — see TUVALU

El·lis Island \'e-ləs\ island SE New York S of Manhattan; served as immigration station 1892–1954

El Mon·te \el-'män-tē\ city SW California E of Los Angeles; *pop* 113,475

El Paso \el-'pa-(ˌ)sō\ city W Texas on Rio Grande; *pop* 649,121

El Sal·va·dor \el-'sal-və-ˌdór, -ˌsal-və-'; ˌel-ˌsäl-vä-'thór\ country Central America bordering on the Pacific; ✳, San Salvador; *pop* 5,744,113

Ely, Isle of \'ē-lē\ area of high ground amid marshes in East Anglia, England

En·field \'en-ˌfēld\ borough of N Greater London, England; *pop* 312,000

En·gland \'iŋ-glənd, 'iŋ-lənd\ country S Great Britain; a division of United Kingdom; ✳, London; *pop* 53,012,456

English Channel arm of the Atlantic between S England & N France

En·nis·kil·len \ˌe-nə-'ski-lən\ town SW Northern Ireland in Fermanagh district

Ephra·im \'ē-frē-əm\ 1 hilly region N Jordan E of Jordan River 2 — see ISRAEL — Ephra·im·ite \'ē-frē-ə-ˌmīt\ *n*

Equatorial Guinea *formerly* Spanish Guinea country W Africa including Mbini & Bioko; ✳, Malabo; *pop* 722,000

Erie \'ir-ē\ 1 city & port NW Pennsylvania; *pop* 101,786 2 canal New York between Hudson River at Albany & Lake Erie at Buffalo; now superseded by New York State Barge Canal

Erie, Lake lake E *cen* North America in U.S. & Canada; one of the Great Lakes

Er·in \'er-ən\ poetic name of Ireland

Er·i·trea \ˌer-ə-'trē-ə, -'trā-\ country NE Africa; ✳, Asmara; *pop* 4,252,000 — Er·i·tre·an \-ən\ *adj or n*

Es·con·di·do \ˌes-kən-'dē-(ˌ)dō\ city SW California N of San Diego; *pop* 143,911

Es·fa·han \ˌes-fə-'hän, -'han\ *or* Is·fa·han \ˌis-\ city W *cen* Iran; *pop* 1,756,126

Española — see HISPANIOLA

Es·sen \'e-sᵊn\ city W Germany in the Ruhr; *pop* 566,201

Es·sex \'e-siks\ county SE England on North Sea; *pop* 1,393,587

**Es·to·nia** \e-'stō-nē-ə, -nyə\ country E
Europe on Baltic Sea; ✱, Tallinn; *pop*
1,294,000 — **Es·to·nian** \ɔ-'stō nē-ən,
-nyən\ *adj or n*

**Ethi·o·pia** \ˌē-thē-'ō-pē-ə\ *historically* **Ab-
ys·sin·ia** \ˌa-bə-'si-nē-ə, -nyə\ country E
Africa; ✱, Addis Ababa; *pop* 73,835,000
— **Ethi·o·pi·an** \-pē-ən\ *adj or n*

**Et·na, Mount** \'et-nə\ volcano 10,902 ft.
(3323 m.) Italy in NE Sicily

**Eto·bi·coke** \e-'tō-bi-ˌkō\ former city
Canada in SE Ontario; now part of Toronto

**Etru·ria** \i-'trür-ē-ə\ ancient country *cen*
peninsula of Italy

**Eu·gene** \yü-'jēn\ city W Oregon; *pop*
156,185

**Eu·phra·tes** \yü-'frā-(ˌ)tēz\ river 1700 mi.
(2736 km.) long SW Asia flowing from E
Turkey & uniting with the Tigris to form
the Shatt al Arab

**Eur·asia** \yü-'rā-zhə, -shə\ landmass consisting of Europe & Asia — **Eur·asian**
\-zhən, -shən\ *adj or n*

**Eu·rope** \'yur-əp\ continent of the Eastern Hemisphere between Asia & the Atlantic

**European Union** economic, scientific, &
political organization consisting of Belgium, France, Italy, Luxembourg, Netherlands, Germany, Denmark, Greece,
Ireland, United Kingdom, Spain, Portugal, Austria, Finland, Sweden, Cyprus,
Czech Republic, Estonia, Hungary, Latvia, Lithuania, Malta, Poland, Slovakia,
Slovenia, Bulgaria, Romania, & Croatia

**Ev·ans·ville** \'e-vənz-ˌvil\ city SW Indiana; *pop* 117,429

**Ev·er·est, Mount** \'ev-rəst, 'e-və-\ moun-
tain 29,035 ft. (8850 m.) S Asia in the
Himalayas on border between Nepal &
Tibet; highest in the world

**Ev·er·glades** \'e-vər-ˌglādz\ swamp region S Florida now partly drained

**Ex·e·ter** \'ek-sə-tər\ city SW England;
*pop* 101,100

**Faer·oe** *or* **Far·oe** \'fer-(ˌ)ō\ islands NE
Atlantic NW of the Shetlands belonging
to Denmark; *pop* 48,250 — **Faer·o·ese**
\ˌfar-ə-'wēz, ˌfer-, -'wēs\ *adj or n*

**Fair·banks** \'fer-ˌbaŋks\ city E *cen* Alaska; *pop* 31,535

**Fai·sa·la·bad** \ˌfī-ˌsä-lə-'bäd, -ˌsä-lə-'bad\
*formerly* **Ly·all·pur** \lē-ˌäl-'púr\ city NE
Pakistan W of Lahore; *pop* 2,008,861

**Falk·land Islands** \'fȯ-klənd, 'fȯl-\ *or*
*Spanish* **Is·las Mal·vi·nas** \ˌēs-läs-mäl-
'vē-näs\ island group SW Atlantic E of S
end of Argentina; a British colony; ✱,
Stanley; *pop* 2700

**Far East** the countries of E Asia & the
Malay Archipelago — usually thought to
consist of the Asian countries bordering
on the Pacific but sometimes including
also India, Sri Lanka, Bangladesh, Tibet,
& Myanmar — **Far Eastern** *adj*

**Far·go** \'fär-(ˌ)gō\ city E North Dakota;
largest in state; *pop* 105,549

**Faroe** — see FAEROE

**Fay·ette·ville** \'fā-ət-ˌvil, -vəl\ city SE *cen*
North Carolina; *pop* 200,564

**Fear, Cape** \'fir\ cape SE North Carolina

**Fer·man·agh** \fər-'ma-nə\ district SW
Northern Ireland; *pop* 62,000

**Fornando Póo** — see BIOKO

**Fes** \'fes\ city N *cen* Morocco; *pop*
947,000

**Fife** \'fīf\ administrative subdivision of E
Scotland; *pop* 365,198

**Fi·ji** \'fē-(ˌ)jē\ islands SW Pacific; country; ✱, Suva; *pop* 837,000 — **Fi·ji·an** \'fē-
(ˌ)jē-ən, fi-'\ *adj or n*

**Fin·land** \'tin-lənd\ country NE Europe;
✱, Helsinki; *pop* 5,453,000 — **Fin·land·er**
*n*

**Flan·ders** \'flan-dərz\ **1** region W Belgium & N France on North Sea **2** semiautonomous region W Belgium; *pop*
6,396,000

**Flat·tery, Cape** \'fla-tə-rē\ cape NW
Washington at entrance to Strait of Juan
de Fuca

**Flint** \'flint\ city SE Michigan; *pop*
102,434

**Flor·ence** \'flȯr-ən(t)s, 'flär-\ *or Italian*
**Fi·ren·ze** \fē-'rent-sā\ city *cen* Italy; *pop*
358,079 — **Flor·en·tine** \'flȯr-ən-ˌtēn,
'flär-, -ˌtīn\ *adj or n*

**Flor·i·da** \'flȯr-ə-də, 'flär-\ state SE U.S.;
✱, Tallahassee; *pop* 18,801,310 — **Flo-
rid·i·an** \flə-'ri-dē-ən\ *or* **Flor·i·dan**
\'flȯr-ə-dən, 'flär-\ *adj or n*

**Florida, Straits of** channel between Flor-
ida Keys on NW & Cuba & Bahamas on
S & E connecting Gulf of Mexico & the
Atlantic

**Florida Keys** chain of islands off S tip of
Florida

**Foochow** — see FUZHOU

**For·a·ker, Mount** \'fȯr-i-kər, 'fär-\ mountain 17,400 ft. (5304 m.) S *cen* Alaska in
Alaska Range

**For·mo·sa** \fȯr-'mō-sə, fər-, -zə\ — see
TAIWAN — **For·mo·san** \fȯr-'mō-sⁿn,
fər-, -zⁿn\ *adj or n*

**For·ta·le·za** \ˌfȯr-tə-'lā-zə\ city & port
NE Brazil on the Atlantic; *pop* 2,452,185

**Fort Col·lins** \'kä-lənz\ city N Colorado;
*pop* 143,986

**Fort–de–France** \ˌfȯr-də-'frä°s\ city
West Indies, ✱ of Martinique on W coast;
*pop* 87,216

**Forth** \'fȯrth\ river 116 mi. (187 km.) long
S *cen* Scotland flowing E into North Sea
through **Firth of Forth**

**Fort Knox** \'näks\ military reservation N
*cen* Kentucky SSW of Louisville; location of U.S. Gold Bullion Depository

**Fort Lau·der·dale** \'lȯ-dər-ˌdāl\ city SE
Florida; *pop* 165,521

**Fort Wayne** \'wān\ city NE Indiana; *pop*
253,691

**Fort Worth** \'wərth\ city NE Texas; *pop* 741,206

**Fox** \'fäks\ islands SW Alaska in the E Aleutians

**Foxe Basin** \'fäks\ inlet of the Atlantic N Canada in E Nunavut W of Baffin Island

**France** \'fran(t)s, 'frä⁽ⁿ⁾s\ country W Europe between the English Channel & the Mediterranean; ✻, Paris; *pop* 64,613,000

**Frank·fort** \'frank-fərt\ city, ✻ of Kentucky; *pop* 25,527

**Frank·furt** \'frank-fərt, 'fränk-₁fûrt\ *or in full* **Frankfurt am Main** \₁-¸äm-'mīn\ city W Germany on Main River; *pop* 667,925

**Frank·lin** \'fran-klən\ former district N Canada in Northwest Territories including Arctic Archipelago & Boothia & Melville peninsulas

**Fra·ser** \'frā-zər, -zhər\ river 850 mi. (1368 km.) long Canada in S *cen* British Columbia flowing into the Pacific

**Fred·er·ic·ton** \'fre-drik-tən, 'fre-də-rik-\ city, ✻ of New Brunswick, Canada; *pop* 50,535

**Free State** *formerly* **Or·ange Free State** \'ȯr-inj, 'är-, -ənj\ province E *cen* Republic of South Africa; *pop* 2,745,590

**Free·town** \'frē-₁taún\ city, ✻ of Sierra Leone; *pop* 178,600

**Fre·mont** \'frē-₁mänt\ city W California; *pop* 214,089

**French Guiana** country N South America on the Atlantic; an overseas division of France; ✻, Cayenne; *pop* 239,849

**French Indochina** — see INDOCHINA

**Fres·no** \'frez-(₁)nō\ city S *cen* California SE of San Francisco; *pop* 494,665

**Frunze** — see BISHKEK

**Fu·ji, Mount** \'fü-jē\ *or* **Fu·ji·ya·ma** \₁fü-jē-'yä-mä\ mountain 12,388 ft. (3776 m.) Japan in S *cen* Honshu; highest in Japan

**Fu·ku·o·ka** \₁fü-kü-'ō-kä\ city Japan in N Kyushu; *pop* 1,463,743

**Ful·ler·ton** \'fú-lər-tən\ city SW California; *pop* 135,161

**Fu·na·fu·ti** \₁fü-nä-'fü-tē\ city, ✻ of Tuvalu; *pop* 1328

**Fun·dy, Bay of** \'fən-dē\ inlet of the Atlantic SE Canada between New Brunswick & Nova Scotia

**Fu·shun** \'fü-'shùn\ city NE China E of Shenyang; *pop* 1,319,000

**Fu·zhou** \'fü-'jō\ *or* **Foo·chow** \'fü-'jō, -'chaú\ city & port SE China; *pop* 2,873,000

**Ga·bon** \gä-'bōⁿ\ country W Africa on the Equator; ✻, Libreville; *pop* 1,600,000 — **Gab·o·nese** \₁ga-bə-'nēz, -'nēs\ *adj or n*

**Ga·bo·rone** \₁gä-bō-'rō-(₁)nä, ₁kä-\ city, ✻ of Botswana; *pop* 229,500

**Gads·den Purchase** \'gadz-dən\ area of land S of Gila River in present Arizona & New Mexico purchased 1853 by the U.S. from Mexico

**Ga·la·pa·gos Islands** \gə-'lä-pə-gəs, -'la-, -gōs\ island group Ecuador in the Pacific 600 mi. (965 km.) W of South America; *pop* 25,000

**Ga·la·tia** \gə-'lā-sh(ē-)ə\ ancient country *cen* Asia Minor in region around modern Ankara, Turkey — **Ga·la·tian** \-shən\ *adj or n*

**Ga·li·cia** \gə-'li-sh(ē-)ə\ **1** region E *cen* Europe now divided between Poland & Ukraine **2** region NW Spain on the Atlantic — **Ga·li·cian** \-'li-shən\ *adj or n*

**Gal·i·lee** \'ga-lə-₁lē\ hilly region N Israel — **Gal·i·le·an** \₁ga-lə-'lē-ən\ *adj or n*

**Galilee, Sea of** *or modern* **Lake Ti·be·ri·as** \tī-'bir-ē-əs\ lake N Israel on Syrian border; crossed by Jordan River

**Gal·lo·way** \'ga-lə-₁wā\ former administrative district of SW Scotland — see DUMFRIES AND GALLOWAY

**Gam·bia** \'gam-bē-ə, 'gäm-\ country W Africa; ✻, Banjul; *pop* 1,882,000 — **Gam·bi·an** \-bē-ən\ *adj or n*

**Gan·ges** \'gan-₁jēz\ river 1550 mi. (2494 km.) long N India flowing from the Himalayas SE & E to unite with the Brahmaputra and empty into Bay of Bengal through a vast delta — **Gan·get·ic** \gan-'je-tik\ *adj*

**Gao·xiong** \'gaú-'shyùn\ *or* **Kao–hsiung** \'kaú-'shyùn, 'gaú-\ city & port SW Taiwan; *pop* 2,780,000

**Garden Grove** city SW California; *pop* 170,883

**Gar·land** \'gär-lənd\ city NE Texas NNE of Dallas; *pop* 226,876

**Ga·ronne** \gə-'rän, gä-'rȯn\ river 355 mi. (571 km.) long SE France flowing NW

**Gary** \'ger-ē\ city NW Indiana on Lake Michigan; *pop* 80,294

**Gas·co·ny** \'gas-kə-nē\ region SW France — **Gas·con** \'gas-kən\ *adj or n*

**Gas·pé** \ga-'spā, 'ga-₁\ peninsula SE Quebec E of mouth of the Saint Lawrence — **Gas·pe·sian** \ga-'spē-zhən\ *adj or n*

**Gaul** \'gȯl\ *or Latin* **Gal·lia** \'ga-lē-ə\ ancient country W Europe chiefly consisting of region occupied by modern France & Belgium

**Gau·teng** \'gaú-₁teŋ\ province *cen* NE Republic of South Africa; *pop* 12,272,000

**Ga·za Strip** \'gä-zə, 'ga-\ district NE Sinai Peninsula on the Mediterranean

**Ge·ne·va** \jə-'nē-və\ city SW Switzerland on Lake Geneva; *pop* 187,000 — **Ge·ne·van** \-vən\ *adj or n* — **Gen·e·vese** \₁je-nə-'vēz, -'vēs\ *adj or n*

**Geneva, Lake** lake on border between SW Switzerland & E France

**Gen·oa** \'je-nō-ə\ *or Italian* **Ge·no·va** \'je-nō-(₁)vä\ city & port NW Italy; *pop* 586,180 — **Gen·o·ese** \₁je-nō-'ēz, -'ēs\ *or* **Gen·o·vese** \-nə-'vēz, -'vēs\ *adj or n*

**George·town** \'jȯrj-₁taún\ **1** a W section of Washington, District of Columbia **2** city & port, ✻ of Guyana; *pop* 162,000

**Geor·gia** \'jȯr-jə\ **1** state SE U.S.; ✻, Atlanta; *pop* 9,687,653  **2** *or* **Republic of Georgia** country SW Asia on Black Sea S of Caucasus Mountains; ✱, Tbilisi; *pop* 4,630,000 — **Geor·gian** \'jòr-jən\ *adj or n*

**Georgia, Strait of** channel Canada & U.S. between Vancouver Island & main part of British Columbia NW of Puget Sound

**Georgian Bay** inlet of Lake Huron in S Ontario

**Ger·man·town** \'jər-mən-ˌtaún\ a NW section of Philadelphia, Pennsylvania

**Ger·ma·ny** \'jər-mə-nē\ country cen Europe bordering on North & Baltic seas; ✱, Berlin; divided 1946–90 into two independent states: the **Federal Republic of Germany** (West Germany; ✱, Bonn) & the **German Democratic Republic** (East Germany; ✱, East Berlin); *pop* 80,219,695

**Get·tys·burg** \'ge-tēz-ˌbərg\ town S Pennsylvania; *pop* 7620

**Gha·na** \'gä-nə, 'ga-\ *formerly* **Gold Coast** country W Africa on Gulf of Guinea; ✱, Accra, *pop* 24,659,000 — **Gha·na·ian** \gä-'nä-ən, ga-, -'nī-ən\ *or* **Gha·ni·an** \'gä-nē-ən, 'ga-, -nyən\ *adj or n*

**Ghats** \'gòts\ two mountain chains S India consisting of **Eastern Ghats** & **Western Ghats**

**Ghent** \'gent\ city NW cen Belgium; *pop* 250,000

**Gi·bral·tar** \jə-'bròl-tər\ British colony on S coast of Spain including Rock of Gibraltar; *pop* 31,000

**Gibraltar, Rock of** cape on S coast of Spain in Gibraltar at E end of Strait of Gibraltar; highest point 1396 ft. (426 m.)

**Gibraltar, Strait of** passage between Europe & Africa connecting the Atlantic & the Mediterranean

**Gi·la** \'hē-lə\ river 630 mi. (1014 km.) long SW New Mexico and S Arizona flowing W into the Colorado

**Gil·bert** \'gil-bərt\ town SW cen Arizona; *pop* 208,453

**Gilbert and El·lice Islands** \'e-lis\ island group N Pacific; divided into Kiribati and Tuvalu

**Gil·e·ad** \'gi-lē-əd\ mountain region of NE ancient Palestine E of Jordan River; now in NW Jordan — **Gil·e·ad·ite** \-lē-ə-ˌdīt\ *n*

**Gi·za** \'gē-zə\ city N Egypt on the Nile SW of Cairo; *pop* 2,865,000

**Gla·cier Bay** \'glā-shər\ inlet SE Alaska at S end of Saint Elias Range

**Glas·gow** \'glas-(ˌ)kō, 'glas-(ˌ)gō, 'glaz-(ˌ)gō\ city S cen Scotland on the Clyde; *pop* 586,000 — **Glas·we·gian** \glä-'swē-jən, glaz-\ *adj or n*

**Glen·dale** \'glen-ˌdāl\ **1** city cen Arizona NW of Phoenix; *pop* 226,721  **2** city S California NE of Los Angeles; *pop* 191,719

**Glouces·ter** \'gläs-tər, 'glòs-\ town SW cen England; *pop* 91,800

**Glouces·ter·shire** \'glän-tər-ˌshir, -shər, 'glòs-\ *or* **Gloucester** county SW cen England; *pop* 596,984

**Goa** \'gō-ə\ state W India on Malabar coast; *pop* 1,458,545

**Goat Island** island W New York in Niagara River — see NIAGARA FALLS

**Go·bi** \'gō-(ˌ)bē\ desert E cen Asia in Mongolia & N China

**Godthab** — see NUUK

**Godwin Austen** — see K2

**Go·lan Heights** \'gō-ˌlän, -lən\ hilly region NE of Sea of Galilee

**Gol·con·da** \gäl-'kän-də\ ruined city cen India W of Hyderabad

**Gold Coast 1** — see GHANA  **2** coast region W Africa on N shore of Gulf of Guinea E of Côte d'Ivoire

**Golden Gate** strait W California connecting San Francisco Bay with Pacific Ocean

**Good Hope, Cape of** \gùd-'hōp\ cape S Republic of South Africa on SW coast of Western Cape province

**Gorki** — see NIZHNIY NOVGOROD

**Gö·te·borg** \yœ-tə-'bór-ē\ city & port SW Sweden; *pop* 538,000

**Gram·pi·an** \'gram-pē-ən\ hills N cen Scotland

**Grand Banks** shallow area in the W North Atlantic SE of Newfoundland

**Grand Canyon** gorge of Colorado River NW Arizona

**Grand Canyon of the Snake** — see HELLS CANYON

**Grande, Rio** — see RIO GRANDE

**Grand Prairie** city NE cen Texas W of Dallas; *pop* 175,396

**Grand Rapids** city SW Michigan; *pop* 188,040

**Graz** \'gräts\ city S Austria; *pop* 253,000

**Great Australian Bight** wide bay on S coast of Australia

**Great Barrier Reef** coral reef Australia off NE coast of Queensland

**Great Basin** region W U.S. between Sierra Nevada & Wasatch Range including most of Nevada & parts of California, Idaho, Utah, Wyoming, & Oregon; has no drainage to ocean

**Great Bear** lake Canada in Northwest Territories draining through Great Bear River into Mackenzie River

**Great Brit·ain** \'bri-t²n\ **1** island W Europe NW of France consisting of England, Scotland, & Wales; *pop* 61,371,000  **2** UNITED KINGDOM

**Great Dividing Range** mountain system E Australia extending S from Cape York Peninsula into Tasmania — see KOSCIUSKO, MOUNT

**Greater Antilles** group of islands of the West Indies including Cuba, Hispaniola,

Jamaica, & Puerto Rico — see LESSER ANTILLES

**Greater London** metropolitan county SE England consisting of City of London & 32 surrounding boroughs

**Greater Manchester** metropolitan county NW England including city of Manchester

**Greater Sudbury** — see SUDBURY, GREATER

**Great Lakes** chain of five lakes (Superior, Michigan, Huron, Erie, & Ontario) *cen* North America in U.S. & Canada

**Great Plains** elevated plains region W *cen* U.S. & W Canada E of the Rockies; extending from S Texas to NE British Columbia & NW Alberta

**Great Rift Valley** basin SW Asia & E Africa extending with several breaks from valley of the Jordan S to *cen* Mozambique

**Great Salt Lake** lake N Utah having salty water & no outlet

**Great Slave Lake** lake NW Canada in S Northwest Territories drained by Mackenzie River

**Great Smoky** mountains between N North Carolina & E Tennessee

**Greece** \'grēs\ country S Europe at S end of Balkan Peninsula; ✻, Athens; *pop* 10,816,286

**Green** \'grēn\ **1** mountains E North America in the Appalachians extending from S Quebec S through Vermont into W Massachusetts **2** river 730 mi. (1175 km.) long W U.S. flowing from W Wyoming S into the Colorado in SE Utah

**Green Bay 1** inlet of NW Lake Michigan 120 mi. (193 km.) long in NW Michigan & NE Wisconsin **2** city NE Wisconsin on Green Bay; *pop* 104,057

**Green·land** \'grēn-lənd, -ˌland\ island in the North Atlantic off NE North America belonging to Denmark; ✻, Nuuk; *pop* 56,300

**Greens·boro** \'grēnz-ˌbər-ō\ city N *cen* North Carolina; *pop* 296,666

**Green·wich** \'gre-nich, 'grēn-ˌwich, 'grin-ˌwich\ borough of SE Greater London, England; *pop* 200,800

**Green·wich Village** \'gre-nich\ section of New York City in W Manhattan

**Gre·na·da** \grə-'nā-də\ island West Indies in S Windward Islands; independent country; ✻, Saint George's; *pop* 102,632

**Gren·a·dines** \ˌgre-nə-'dēnz, 'gre-nə-ˌ\ islands West Indies in *cen* Windward Islands; N islands part of Saint Vincent and the Grenadines; S islands dependency of Grenada

**Groz·ny** \'gróz-nē, 'grāz-\ city S Russia in Europe; ✻ of Chechnya; *pop* 272,000

**Gua·da·la·ja·ra** \ˌgwä-də-lə-'här-ə, ˌgwä-thä-lä-'hä-rä\ city W *cen* Mexico; *pop* 1,495,189

**Gua·dal·ca·nal** \ˌgwä-dᵊl-kə-'nal, ˌgwä-

də-kə-\ island W Pacific in the SE Solomons; *pop* 93,600

**Gua·dal·qui·vir** \ˌgwä-dᵊl-ki-'vir, -'kwi-vər\ river 408 mi. (656 km.) long S Spain flowing into the Atlantic

**Gua·de·loupe** \ˌgwä-də-ˌlüp\ two islands separated by a narrow channel in West Indies in *cen* Leeward Islands; an overseas division of France; *pop* 403,400

**Gua·lla·ti·ri** \ˌgwä-yə-'tir-ē, ˌgwī-ə-\ volcano 19,882 ft. (6060 m.) high N Chile

**Guam** \'gwäm\ island W Pacific in S Marianas belonging to U.S.; ✻, Hagåtña; *pop* 159,400 — **Gua·ma·ni·an** \gwä-'mä-nē-ən\ *adj or n*

**Gua·na·ba·ra Bay** \ˌgwä-nä-'bär-ə\ inlet of the Atlantic SE Brazil on which city of Rio de Janeiro is located

**Guang·dong** \'gwäŋ-'duŋ\ *or* **Kwang·tung** \'gwäŋ-'duŋ, 'kwäŋ-, -'tuŋ\ province SE China bordering on South China Sea & Gulf of Tonkin; ✻, Guangzhou; *pop* 104,320,459

**Guang·zhou** \'gwäŋ-'jō\ *or* **Can·ton** \'kan-ˌtän, kan-'\ city & port SE China; *pop* 11,000,000

**Guan·tá·na·mo Bay** \gwän-'tä-nä-ˌmō\ inlet of the Caribbean in SE Cuba; site of U.S. naval station

**Gua·te·ma·la** \ˌgwä-tə-'mä-lə, -tä-'mä-lä\ **1** country Central America; *pop* 15,073,000 **2** *or* **Guatemala City** city, its ✻; *pop* 942,000 — **Gua·te·ma·lan** \-'mä-lən\ *adj or n*

**Gua·ya·quil** \ˌgwī-ə-'kēl, -'kil\ city & port W Ecuador; *pop* 2,285,000

**Guay·na·bo** \gwī-'nä-(ˌ)bō, -(ˌ)vō\ city NE *cen* Puerto Rico; *pop* 97,924

**Guern·sey** \'gərn-zē\ — see CHANNEL

**Gui·a·na** \gē-'a-nə, -'ä-nə; gī-'a-nə\ region N South America on the Atlantic; includes Guyana, French Guiana, Suriname, & nearby parts of Brazil & Venezuela — **Gui·a·nan** \-nən\ *adj or n*

**Guin·ea** \'gi-nē\ **1** region W Africa on the Atlantic extending along coast from Gambia to Angola **2** country W Africa N of Sierra Leone & Liberia; ✻, Conakry; *pop* 10,629,000 — **Guin·ean** \'gi-nē-ən\ *adj or n*

**Guinea, Gulf of** arm of the Atlantic W *cen* Africa

**Guin·ea–Bis·sau** \ˌgi-nē-bi-'saú\ country W Africa; ✻, Bissau; *pop* 1,521,000

**Gui·yang** \'gwā-'yäŋ\ *or* **Kuei·yang** \'gwā-'yäŋ\ city S China; *pop* 2,750,000

**Gulf States** states of U.S. bordering on Gulf of Mexico: Florida, Alabama, Mississippi, Louisiana, and Texas

**Gulf Stream** warm current of the Atlantic Ocean flowing from Gulf of Mexico NE along coast of U.S. to Nantucket Island and from there eastward

**Guy·ana** \gī-'an-ə\ *formerly* **British Guiana** country N South America on the

Atlantic; ✻, Georgetown; *pop* 748,000 —
Guy·a·ne·se \ˌgī-ə-ˈnēz, -ˈnēs\ *adj or n*

**Gwangju** — see KWANGJU

**Gwent** \ˈgwent\ former county SE Wales

**Gwyn·edd** \ˈgwi-neth\ former county
NW Wales

**Hack·ney** \ˈhak-nē\ borough of N Greater London, England; *pop* 246,000

**Ha·gât·ña** \hə-ˈgät-nyə\ *formerly* **Aga·na**
\ä-ˈgä-nyä\ town, ✻ of Guam; *pop* 1051

**Hague, The** \thə-ˈhāg\ city, seat of government of Netherlands; *pop* 825,018

**Hai·kou** \ˈhī-ˈkō\ city & port SE China;
*pop* 1,517,000

**Hai·phong** \ˈhī-ˈfȯŋ, ˈfäŋ\ city & port N
Vietnam; *pop* 808,000

**Hai·ti** \ˈhā-tē\ country West Indies in W
Hispaniola; ✻, Port-au-Prince; *pop*
9,923,000 — **Hai·tian** \ˈhā-shən\ *adj or n*

**Ha·le·a·ka·la Crater** \ˌhä-lā-ˌä-kä-ˈlä\ crater over 2500 ft. (762 m.) deep Hawaii in
E Maui

**Hal·i·fax** \ˈha-lə-ˌfaks\ municipality &
port, ✻ of Nova Scotia, Canada; *pop*
390,096

**Ham·burg** \ˈham-ˌbərg; ˈhäm-ˌbu̇rg,
-ˌbu̇rk\ city N Germany on the Elbe; *pop*
1,706,696 — **Ham·burg·er** \-ˌbər-gər,
-ˌbu̇r-\ *n*

**Ham·hung** *or* **Ham·heung** \ˈhäm-ˌhu̇ŋ\
city E cen North Korea; *pop* 704,000

**Ham·il·ton** \ˈha-məl-tən\ **1** town, ✻ of
Bermuda; *pop* 1010 **2** city & port, S Ontario, Canada on Lake Ontario; *pop*
519,949

**Ham·mer·smith and Ful·ham** \ˈha-mər-
ˌsmith-ənd-ˈfu̇l-əm\ borough of SW
Greater London, England; *pop* 182,000

**Hamp·shire** \ˈhamp-ˌshir, -shər\ county
S England on English Channel

**Hamp·ton** \ˈhamp-tən\ city SE Virginia;
*pop* 137,436

**Hampton Roads** channel SE Virginia
through which James River flows into
Chesapeake Bay

**Hang·zhou** \ˈhäŋ-ˈjō\ *or* **Hang·chow**
\ˈhaŋ-ˈchau̇, ˈhäŋ-ˈjō\ *or* **Hang–chou**
\-ˈjō\ city E China; *pop* 5,700,000

**Han·ni·bal** \ˈha-nə-bəl\ city NE Missouri
on the Mississippi River; *pop* 17,916

**Han·no·ver** *or* **Han·o·ver** \ˈha-ˌno-vər,
-nə-vər, *G* hä-ˈnō-fər\ city N cen Germany; *pop* 506,416

**Ha·noi** \ha-ˈnȯi, hə-, hä-\ city, ✻ of Vietnam; *pop* 2,481,000

**Hao·ra** \ˈhau̇-rə\ city E India on Hugli
River opposite Calcutta; *pop* 1,077,000

**Ha·ra·re** \hə-ˈrä-(ˌ)rā\ *formerly* **Salisbury** \ˈsȯlz-ˌber-ē, -b(ə-)rē\ city, ✻ of
Zimbabwe; *pop* 1,485,000

**Har·bin** \ˈhär-bən, här-ˈbin\ *or* **Ha–erh-
pin** \ˈhä-ˈər-ˈbin\ city NE China; *pop*
5,237,000

**Har·in·gey** \ˈha-riŋ-ˌgā\ borough of N
Greater London, England; *pop* 255,000

**Har·lem** \ˈhär-ləm\ section of New York
City in N Manhattan

**Har·ris·burg** \ˈha-rəs-ˌbərg\ city, ✻ of
Pennsylvania; *pop* 49,528

**Har·row** \ˈha-(ˌ)rō\ borough of NW
Greater London, England; *pop* 239,000

**Hart·ford** \ˈhärt-fərd\ city, ✻ of Connecticut; *pop* 124,775

**Hat·ter·as, Cape** \ˈha-tə-rəs\ cape North
Carolina on **Hatteras Island**

**Ha·vana** \hə-ˈva-nə\ city, ✻ of Cuba; *pop*
2,106,000

**Hav·ant** \ˈha-vənt\ town S England; *pop*
117,400

**Ha·ver·ing** \ˈhāv-riŋ, ˈhā-və-riŋ\ borough
of NE Greater London, England; *pop*
237,000

**Ha·waii** \hə-ˈwä-yē, -ˈwä-ē\ **1** *or* **Ha·wai-
ian Islands** *formerly* **Sand·wich Islands** \ˌsan-(d)wich-\ group of islands
cen Pacific belonging to U.S. **2** island,
largest of the group **3** state of U.S., ✻,
Honolulu; *pop* 1,360,301

**Hay·ward** \ˈhā-wərd\ city W California
SE of Oakland; *pop* 144,186

**Heb·ri·des** \ˈhe-brə-ˌdēz\ islands W Scotland in the North Atlantic consisting of
**Outer Hebrides** (to W) and **Inner Hebrides** (to E); *pop* 30,660 — **Heb·ri·de·an**
\ˌhe-brə-ˈdē-ən\ *adj or n*

**Hel·e·na** \ˈhe-lə-nə\ city, ✻ of Montana;
*pop* 28,190

**Hellespont** — see DARDANELLES

**Hells Canyon** \ˈhelz\ canyon of Snake
River on Idaho–Oregon boundary

**Hel·sin·ki** \ˈhel-ˌsiŋ-ke, hel-ˈ\ city, ✻ of
Finland; *pop* 612,664

**Hen·der·son** \ˈhen-dər-sən\ city S Nevada; *pop* 257,729

**Hen·ry, Cape** \ˈhen-rē\ cape E Virginia S
of entrance to Chesapeake Bay

**Here·ford and Worces·ter** \ˈher-ə-fərd-
ən-ˈwu̇s-tər\ former county W England

**Hert·ford·shire** \ˈhär-fərd-ˌshir, ˈhärt-
-shər\ *or* **Hertford** county SE England

**Her·ze·go·vi·na** \ˌhert-sə-gō-ˈvē-nə,
ˌhert-, -ˈgō-və-nə\ *or Serb* **Her·ce·go·vi-
na** \ˌkert-sə-gō-vē-nō\ region S Europe;
with Bosnia to the N forms Bosnia and
Herzegovina — **Her·ze·go·vi·ni·an**
\ˌhert-sə-gō-ˈvē-nē-ən, ˌhȯrt-, -nyən\ *n*

**Hi·a·le·ah** \ˌhī-ə-ˈlē-ə\ city SE Florida;
*pop* 224,669

**Hi·ber·nia** \hī-ˈbər-nē-ə\ — see IRELAND
— **Hi·ber·ni·an** \-ən\ *adj or n*

**Hi·ga·shi·Ōsa·ka** \hē-ˌgä-shē-ˈō-sä-kä\
city Japan in S Honshu E of Osaka; *pop*
509,533

**High·land** \ˈhī-lənd\ administrative subdivision of NW Scotland; *pop* 232,132

**High·lands** \ˈhī-ləndz\ the mountainous
N part of Scotland lying N & W of the
Lowlands

**High Plains** the Great Plains esp. from
Nebraska southward

**Hil·ling·don** \\'hi-liŋ-dən\\ borough of W Greater London, England; *pop* 274,000

**Hi·ma·la·yas, the** \\,hi-mə-'lā-əz\\ *or the* **Himalaya** mountain system S Asia on border between India & Tibet and in Kashmir, Nepal, & Bhutan — see EVEREST, MOUNT — **Hi·ma·la·yan** \\,him-ə-'lā-ən, hə-'mäl-(ə-)yən\\ *adj*

**Hin·du Kush** \\'hin-(,)dü-'kush, -'kəsh\\ mountain range *cen* Asia SW of the Pamirs on border of Kashmir and in Afghanistan

**Hin·du·stan** \\,hin-(,)dü-'stan, -də-, -'stän\\ **1** a name for N India **2** the subcontinent of India **3** the country of India

**Hi·ro·shi·ma** \\,hir-ə-'shē-mə, hə-'rō-shə-mə\\ city Japan in SW Honshu on Inland Sea; *pop* 1,173,843

**His·pa·ni·o·la** \\,his-pə-'nyō-lə\\ *or Spanish* **Es·pa·ño·la** \\,es-pä-'nyō-lä\\ island West Indies in Greater Antilles; divided between Haiti on W & Dominican Republic on E

**Ho·bart** \\'hō-bərt\\ city Australia, ✳ of Tasmania; *pop* 170,975

**Ho Chi Minh City** \\,hō-,chē-'min\\ *formerly* **Sai·gon** \\sī-'gän, 'sī-\\ city S Vietnam; *pop* 5,950,000

**Hoh·hot** \\'hō-'hōt\\ *or* **Hu·he·hot** \\'hü-(,)hä-'hōt\\ city N China, ✳ of Inner Mongolia; *pop* 1,497,000

**Hok·kai·do** \\hō-'kī-(,)dō\\ island N Japan N of Honshu; *pop* 5,506,419

**Hol·land** \\'hä-lənd\\ **1** county of Holy Roman Empire bordering on North Sea & consisting of area now forming part of W Netherlands **2** — see NETHERLANDS — **Hol·land·er** \\-lən-dər\\ *n*

**Hol·ly·wood** \\'hä-lē-,wud\\ **1** section of Los Angeles, California, NW of downtown district **2** city SE Florida; *pop* 140,768

**Holy Roman Empire** empire consisting mainly of German & Italian territories & existing from 9th or 10th century to 1806

**Hon·du·ras** \\hän-'dur-əs, -'dyur-; ón-'dü-räs\\ country Central America; ✳, Tegucigalpa; *pop* 8,100,000 — **Hon·du·ran** \\-ən\\ *adj or n*

**Hong Kong** \\'häŋ-,käŋ, -'käŋ\\ *or Chinese* **Xiang·gang** \\'shyäŋ-'gäŋ\\ special administrative region China on SE coast including Hong Kong Island & Jiulong Peninsula; chief city Victoria; *pop* 7,072,000

**Ho·ni·a·ra** \\,hō-nē-'är-ə\\ town, ✳ of Solomon Islands; *pop* 49,107

**Ho·no·lu·lu** \\,hä-nə-'lü-(,)lü, ,hō-nə-\\ city, ✳ of Hawaii on Oahu; *pop* 337,256

**Hon·shu** \\'hän-(,)shü, 'hón-\\ island Japan; largest of the four chief islands; *pop* 100,254,208

**Hood, Mount** \\'hud\\ mountain 11,235 ft. (3424 m.) NW Oregon in Cascade Range

**Hoo·ver Dam** \\'hü-vər\\ *or* **Boul·der Dam** \\'bōl-dər\\ dam 726 ft. (221 m.) high in Colorado River between Arizona & Nevada — see MEAD, LAKE

**Hor·muz, Strait of** \\'(h)ór-,məz, (h)ór-'müz\\ strait connecting Persian Gulf & Gulf of Oman

**Horn, Cape** \\'hórn\\ cape S Chile on an island in Tierra del Fuego; the most southerly point of South America at 56° S latitude

**Horn of Africa** the easternmost projection of Africa; variously used to refer to Somalia, SE or all of Ethiopia, often Djibouti, & sometimes Eritrea, Sudan, & Kenya

**Horseshoe Falls** — see NIAGARA FALLS

**Houns·low** \\'haunz-,lō\\ borough of SW Greater London, England; *pop* 254,000

**Hous·ton** \\'hyüs-tən, 'yüs-\\ city SE Texas; *pop* 2,096,798

**Hsi·an** — see XI'AN

**Huang** *or* **Hwang** \\'hwäŋ\\ *or* **Yellow** river about 3396 mi. (5464 km.) long N China flowing into Bo Hai

**Hud·ders·field** \\'hə-dərz-,fēld\\ town N England NE of Manchester; *pop* 123,888

**Hud·son** \\'həd-sən\\ **1** river 306 mi. (492 km.) long E New York flowing S **2** bay, inlet of the Atlantic in N Canada **3** strait NE Canada connecting Hudson Bay & the Atlantic

**Hu·gli** *or* **Hoo·ghly** \\'hü-glē\\ river 120 mi. (193 km.) long E India flowing S into Bay of Bengal

**Huhehot** — see HOHHOT

**Hull** \\'həl\\ *or* **Kings·ton upon Hull** \\'kiŋ-stən\\ city & port N England; *pop* 284,000

**Hun·ga·ry** \\'həŋ-gə-rē\\ country *cen* Europe; ✳, Budapest; *pop* 9,937,628

**Hunt·ing·ton Beach** \\'hən-tiŋ-tən\\ city SW California; *pop* 189,992

**Hunts·ville** \\'hənts-,vil, -vəl\\ city N Alabama; *pop* 180,105

**Hu·ron, Lake** \\'hyur-,än, 'yur-\\ lake E *cen* North America in U.S. & Canada; one of the Great Lakes

**Hy·der·abad** \\'hī-d(ə-)rə-,bad, -,bäd\\ **1** city S *cen* India; *pop* 7,204,000 **2** city SE Pakistan on the Indus; *pop* 1,166,894

**Iba·dan** \\i-'bä-d^n, -'ba-\\ city SW Nigeria; *pop* 2,600,000

**Ibe·ri·an** \\ī-'bir-ē-ən\\ peninsula SW Europe occupied by Spain & Portugal

**Ice·land** \\'īs-lənd, 'īs-,land\\ island SE of Greenland between Arctic & Atlantic oceans; country; ✳, Reykjavik; *pop* 315,000 — **Ice·land·er** \\'īs-,lan-dər, 'īs-lən-\\ *n*

**Ida·ho** \\'ī-də-,hō\\ state NW U.S.; ✳, Boise; *pop* 1,567,582 — **Ida·ho·an** \\,ī-də-'hō-ən\\ *adj or n*

**Igua·çú** *or* **Igua·zú** \\,ē-gwə-'sü\\ river 745 mi. (1199 km.) long S Brazil flowing W

**IJs·sel** *or* **Ijs·sel** \\'ī-səl, 'ā-\\ river 70 mi. (113 km.) long E Netherlands flowing out of Rhine N into IJsselmeer

**IJs·sel·meer** \\'ī-səl-,mer, 'ā-\\ *or* **Lake Ijs-**

**sel** freshwater lake N Netherlands separated from North Sea by a dike; part of former Zuider Zee (inlet of North Sea)

**Ilium** — see TROY

**Il·li·nois** \,i-lə-'nȯi\ state N *cen* U.S.; *, Springfield; *pop* 12,830,632 — **Il·li·nois·an** \,i-lə-'nȯi-ən\ *adj or n*

**Il·lyr·i·a** \i-'lir-ē-ə\ ancient country S Europe and Balkan Peninsula on the Adriatic — **Il·lyr·i·an** \-ē-ən\ *adj or n*

**Im·pe·ri·al Valley** \im-'pir-ē-əl\ valley SE corner of California & partly in NE Baja California, Mexico

**In·chon** *or* **In·cheon** \'in-,chən\ city South Korea on Yellow Sea; *pop* 2,650,000

**In·de·pen·dence** \,in-də-'pen-dən(t)s\ city W Missouri E of Kansas City; *pop* 116,830

**In·dia** \'in-dē-ə\ **1** subcontinent S Asia S of the Himalayas between Bay of Bengal & Arabian Sea **2** country consisting of major portion of the subcontinent; *, New Delhi; *pop* 1,210,855,000 **3** *or* **Indian Empire** before 1947 those parts of the subcontinent of India under British rule or protection

**In·di·an** \'in-dē-ən\ ocean E of Africa, S of Asia, W of Australia, & N of Antarctica

**In·di·ana** \,in-dē-'a-nə\ state E *cen* U.S.; *, Indianapolis; *pop* 6,483,802 — **In·di·an·an** \-'a-nən\ *or* **In·di·an·i·an** \-'a-nē-ən\ *adj or n*

**In·di·a·nap·o·lis** \,in-dē-ə-'na-pə-lis\ city, * of Indiana; *pop* 820,445

**Indian River** lagoon 165 mi. (266 km.) long E Florida between main part of the state & coastal islands

**Indian Territory** former territory S U.S. in present state of Oklahoma

**In·dies** \'in-(,)dēz\ **1** EAST INDIES **2** WEST INDIES

**In·do·chi·na** \,in-(,)dō-'chī-nə\ **1** peninsula SE Asia including Myanmar, Malay Peninsula, Thailand, Cambodia, Laos, & Vietnam **2** *or* **French Indochina** former country SE Asia consisting of area now forming Cambodia, Laos, & Vietnam — **In·do–Chi·nese** \-chī-'nēz, -'nēs\ *adj or n*

**In·do·ne·sia** \,in-də-'nē-zhə, -shə\ country SE Asia in Malay Archipelago consisting of Sumatra, Java, S & E Borneo, Sulawesi, W New Guinea, & many smaller islands; *, Jakarta; *pop* 237,641,000 — **In·do·ne·sian** \-zhən, -shən\ *adj or n*

**In·dore** \in-'dȯr\ city W *cen* India; *pop* 2,067,000

**In·dus** \'in-dəs\ river 1800 mi. (2897 km.) long S Asia flowing from Tibet NW & SSW through Pakistan into Arabian Sea

**In·gle·wood** \'iŋ-gəl-,wu̇d\ city SW California; *pop* 109,673

**In·land Sea** \'in-,land, -lənd\ inlet of the Pacific in SW Japan between Honshu on N and Shikoku and Kyushu on S

**Inner Hebrides** — see HEBRIDES

**Inner Mon·go·lia** \män-'gōl-yə, maŋ-, -'go-le-ə\ *or* **Nei Mong·gol** \'nā-'män-,gōl, -'maŋ-\ region N China; *pop* 24,706,291

**Inside Passage** protected shipping route between Puget Sound, Washington, & the lower part of Alaska

**In·ver·ness** \,in-vər-'nes\ town NW Scotland; *pop* 48,000

**Io·ni·an** \ī-'ō-nē-ən\ sea, arm of the Mediterranean between SE Italy & W Greece

**Io To** — see IWO JIMA

**Io·wa** \'ī-ə-wə\ state N *cen* U.S.; *, Des Moines; *pop* 3,046,355 — **Io·wan** \-wən\ *adj or n*

**Ips·wich** \'ip-(,)swich\ town SE England; *pop* 145,000

**Iqa·lu·it** \ē-'ka-lü-ət\ town Canada, * of Nunavut on Baffin Island; *pop* 6699

**Iran** \i-'rän, -'ran\ *formerly by outsiders* **Per·sia** \'pər-zhə\ country SW Asia; *, Tehran; *pop* 75,150,000 — **Irani** \i-'rä-nē, -'ra-\ *adj or n* — **Ira·nian** \i-'rä-nē-ən, -'ran-ē-, -'rän-ē-\ *adj or n*

**Iraq** \i-'räk, -'rak\ country SW Asia in Mesopotamia; *, Baghdad; *pop* (est.) 34,500,000 — **Iraqi** \-'räk-ē, -'rak-\ *adj or n*

**Ire·land** \'ī(-ə)r-lənd\ **1** *or Latin* **Hi·ber·nia** \hī-'bər-nē-ə\ island W Europe in the North Atlantic; one of the British Isles **2** *or* **Eire** \'er-ə\ country occupying major portion of Ireland (island); *, Dublin; *pop* 4,588,000

**Irish Sea** arm of the North Atlantic between Great Britain & Ireland

**Ir·kutsk** \ir-'kütsk, ,ər-\ city S Russia near Lake Baikal; *pop* 587,500

**Ir·ra·wad·dy** \,ir-ə-'wä-dē\ river 1300 mi. (2092 km.) long Myanmar flowing S into Bay of Bengal

**Ir·tysh** \ir-'tish, ,ər-\ river over 2600 mi. (4180 km.) long *cen* Asia flowing NW & N from Altay Mountains in China, through Kazakhstan, & into W *cen* Russia

**Ir·vine** \'ər-,vīn\ city SW California; *pop* 212,375

**Ir·ving** \'ər-viŋ\ city NE Texas NW of Dallas; *pop* 216,290

**Is·fa·han** — see ESFAHAN

**Is·lam·abad** \is-'lä-mə-,bäd, iz-, -'la-mə-,bad\ city, * of Pakistan; *pop* 529,180

**Islas Malvinas** — see FALKLAND ISLANDS

**Isle of Man** — see MAN, ISLE OF

**Isle of Wight** \'wīt\ island England in English Channel

**Isle Roy·ale** \ī-(,)l-'rȯi(-ə)l\ island Michigan in Lake Superior

**Isles of Scilly 1** — see CORNWALL AND ISLES OF SCILLY **2** — see SCILLY

**Is·ling·ton** \'iz-liŋ-tən\ borough of N Greater London, England; *pop* 206,000

**Is·pa·han** — see ESFAHAN

**Is·ra·el** \'iz-rē(-ə)l, -(,)rā(-ə)l\ **1** kingdom in ancient Palestine consisting of lands occupied by the Hebrew people **2** *or* **Ephra·im** \'ē-frē-əm\ the N part of the Hebrew kingdom after about 933 B.C. **3** country SW Asia; ✳, Jerusalem; *pop* 7,412,000 — **Is·rae·li** \iz-'rā-lē\ *adj or n*

**Is·tan·bul** \,is-tən-'bül, -,tan-, -,tän-, -,bül, 'is-tən-,\ *or with m for n formerly* **Con·stan·ti·no·ple** \,kän-,stan-tə-'nō-pəl\ city NW Turkey on the Bosporus & Sea of Marmara; *pop* 12,500,000

**Is·tria** \'is-trē-ə\ peninsula in Croatia & Slovenia extending into the N Adriatic — **Is·tri·an** \-trē-ən\ *adj or n*

**It·a·ly** \'i-tə-lē\ country S Europe including a boot-shaped peninsula & the islands of Sicily & Sardinia; ✳, Rome; *pop* 59,434,000

**Itas·ca, Lake** \ī-'tas-kə\ lake NW *cen* Minnesota; source of the Mississippi

**Ivory Coast** — *see* COTE D'IVOIRE — **Ivor·i·an** \(,)ī-'vòr-ē-ən\ *adj or n* — **Ivory Coast·er** \'kō-stər\ *n*

**Iwo Ji·ma** \,ē-(,)wō-'jē-mə\ *or* **Io To** \-(,)ō-'tō\ island Japan in W Pacific SSE of Tokyo

**Izhevsk** \ē-,zhefsk\ *or 1985–87* **Usti·nov** \'üs-ti-,nòf, -,nòv\ city W Russia; *pop* 628,000

**Iz·mir** \iz-'mir\ *formerly* **Smyr·na** \'smər-nə\ city W Turkey; *pop* 1,757,414

**Jack·son** \'jak-sən\ city, ✳ of Mississippi; *pop* 173,514

**Jack·son·ville** \'jak-sən-,vil\ city NE Florida; *pop* 821,784

**Jai·pur** \'jī-,pùr\ city NW India; *pop* 3,046,000

**Ja·kar·ta** *also* **Dja·kar·ta** \jə-'kär-tə\ city, ✳ of Indonesia in NW Java; *pop* 9,608,000

**Ja·mai·ca** \jə-'mā-kə\ island West Indies in Greater Antilles; country; ✳, Kingston; *pop* 2,698,000 — **Ja·mai·can** \-kən\ *adj or n*

**James** \'jāmz\ **1** — *see* DAKOTA **2** river 340 mi. (547 km.) long Virginia flowing E into Chesapeake Bay

**James Bay** the S extension of Hudson Bay between NE Ontario & W Quebec

**James·town** \'jāmz-,taùn\ ruined village E Virginia on James River; first permanent English settlement in America (1607)

**Jam·shed·pur** \'jäm-,shed-,pùr\ city E India; *pop* 570,349

**Ja·pan** \jə-'pan, ja-\ country E Asia consisting of Honshu, Hokkaido, Shikoku, & other islands in the W Pacific; ✳, Tokyo; *pop* 128,057,000

**Japan, Sea of** *also* **East Sea** arm of the Pacific between Japan & Korea

**Ja·va** \'jä-və, 'ja-\ island Indonesia SW of Borneo; chief city, Jakarta; *pop* 107,581,306 — **Ja·va·nese** \,ja-və-'nēz, ,jä-, -'nēs\ *n*

**Jef·fer·son City** \'je-fər-sən\ city, ✳ of Missouri; *pop* 43,079

**Jer·sey** \'jər-zē\ — *see* CHANNEL

**Jersey City** city NE New Jersey on Hudson River; *pop* 247,597

**Je·ru·sa·lem** \jə-'rü-s(ə-)ləm, -'rü-z(ə-)ləm\ city NW of Dead Sea, ✳ of Israel; *pop* 765,000

**Jid·da** *or* **Jid·dah** \'ji-də\ *or* **Jed·da** *or* **Jed·dah** \'je-də\ city W Saudi Arabia on Red Sea; *pop* 561,104

**Ji·lin** \'jē-'lin\ *or* **Ki·rin** \'kē-'rin\ city NE China; *pop* 1,470,000

**Ji·nan** *or* **Tsi·nan** \'jē-'nän\ city E China; *pop* 3,932,000

**Jin·zhou** *or* **Chin–chou** *or* **Chin·chow** \'jin-'jō\ city NE China; *pop* 946,000

**Jiu·long** \'jü-'lòŋ\ *or* **Kow·loon** \'kaù-'lün\ **1** peninsula SE China in Hong Kong opposite Hong Kong Island **2** city on Jiulong Peninsula; *pop* 1,975,265

**Jo·han·nes·burg** \jō-'hä-nəs-,bərg, -'ha-\ city NE Republic of South Africa; *pop* 4,434,827

**Jo·li·et** \,jō-lē-'et\ city NE Illinois; *pop* 147,433

**Jor·dan** \'jòr-d²n\ **1** river 200 mi. (322 km.) long Israel & Jordan flowing S from Syria into Dead Sea **2** country SW Asia in NW Arabia; ✳, Amman; *pop* 6,350,000 — **Jor·da·ni·an** \jòr-'dā-nē-ən\ *adj or n*

**Juan de Fu·ca, Strait of** \,wän-də-'fyü-kə, ,hwän-\ strait 100 mi. (161 km.) long between Vancouver Island, British Columbia, & Olympic Peninsula, Washington

**Ju·ba** \'jü-bə, -,bä\ town, ✳ of South Sudan

**Ju·daea** *or* **Ju·dea** \jü-'dē-ə, -'dā-\ region of ancient Palestine forming its S division under Persian, Greek, & Roman rule — **Ju·dae·an** *or* **Ju·dean** \-ən\ *adj or n*

**Ju·neau** \'jü-(,)nō, jü-'\ city, ✳ of Alaska; *pop* 31,275

**Ju·ra** \'jùr-ə\ mountain range extending along boundary between France & Switzerland N of Lake of Geneva

**Jut·land** \'jət-lənd\ **1** peninsula N Europe extending into North Sea and consisting of main part of Denmark & N portion of Germany **2** the main part of Denmark

**Ka·bul** \'kä-bəl, -,bül; kə-'bül\ city, ✳ of Afghanistan; *pop* 1,424,000

**Ka Lae** \kä-'lä-ä\ *or* **South Cape** *or* **South Point** most southerly point of Hawaii & of U.S.

**Kal·a·ha·ri** \,ka-lə-'här-ē, ,kä-\ desert region S Africa N of Orange River in S Botswana & NW Republic of South Africa

**Kalgan** — *see* ZHANGJIAKOU

**Ka·li·man·tan** \,ka-lə-'man-,tan, ,kä-lē-'män-,tän\ **1** BORNEO — its Indonesian name **2** the S & E portion of Borneo belonging to Indonesia

**Ka·li·nin·grad** \kə-'lē-nən-ˌgrad, -nyən-, -ˌgrät\ *formerly* **Kö·nigs·berg** \'kä-nigz-ˌbərg\ city & port W Russia; *pop* 431,500

**Kam·chat·ka** \kam-'chat-kə, -'chät-\ peninsula 750 mi. (1207 km.) long E Russia

**Kam·pa·la** \käm-'pä-lä, kam-\ city, ✳ of Uganda; *pop* 1,516,000

**Kampuchea** — see CAMBODIA

**Kan·da·har** \'kän-də-ˌhär\ city SE Afghanistan; *pop* 130,200

**Ka·no** \'kä-(ˌ)nō\ city N *cen* Nigeria; *pop* 3,000,000

**Kan·pur** \'kän-ˌpúr\ city N India on the Ganges; *pop* 2,900,000

**Kan·sas** \'kan-zəs\ state W *cen* U.S.; ✳, Topeka; *pop* 2,853,118 — **Kan·san** \'kan-zən\ *adj or n*

**Kansas City 1** city NE Kansas bordering on Kansas City, Missouri; *pop* 145,786 **2** city W Missouri; *pop* 459,787

**Kao–hsiung** — see GAOXIONG

**Ka·ra·chi** \kə-'rä-chē\ city S Pakistan on Arabian Sea; *pop* 12,100,000

**Ka·ra·gan·da** \ˌkär-ə-'gän-də\ *or* **Qa·ra·ghan·dy** \-dē\ city *cen* Kazakhstan *pop* 460,000

**Kar·a·ko·ram Pass** \ˌkär-ə-'kòr-əm\ mountain pass NE Kashmir in **Karakoram Range** (system connecting the Himalayas with the Pamirs)

**Ka·re·lia** \kə-'rēl-ē-ə, -'rēl-yə\ region NE Europe in Finland & Russia; *pop* 643,548 — **Ka·re·lian** \kə-'rē-lē-ən, -'rēl-yən\ *adj or n*

**Ka·roo** *or* **Kar·roo** \kə-'rü\ plateau region W Republic of South Africa W of Drakensberg Mountains

**Kash·mir** \'kash-ˌmir, 'kazh-, kash-', kazh-'\ disputed territory N subcontinent of India; claimed by India & Pakistan — **Kash·miri** \kash-'mi(ə)r-ē, kazh-\ *adj or n*

**Ka·thi·a·war** \ˌkä-tē-ə-'wär\ peninsula W India N of Gulf of Khambhat

**Kath·man·du** *or* **Kat·man·du** \ˌkat-ˌman-'dü, ˌkät-ˌmän-\ city, ✳ of Nepal; *pop* 1,003,000

**Kat·mai, Mount** \'kat-ˌmī\ volcano 6715 ft. (2047 m.) S Alaska on Alaska Peninsula

**Kat·te·gat** \'ka-ti-ˌgat\ arm of North Sea between Sweden & E coast of Jutland Peninsula of Denmark

**Kau·ai** \kä-'wä-ē\ island Hawaii NW of Oahu; *pop* 67,091

**Kau·nas** \'kaú-nəs, -ˌnäs\ city *cen* Lithuania; *pop* 315,993

**Ka·wa·sa·ki** \ˌkä-wä-'sä-kē\ city Japan in E Honshu S of Tokyo; *pop* 1,425,512

**Ka·zakh·stan** *also* **Ka·zak·stan** \ˌkä-(ˌ)zak-'stan\ country NW *cen* Asia; ✳, Astana; *pop* 16,010,000 — **Ka·zakh** *also* **Ka·zak** \kə-'zak, -'zäk\ *n*

**Ka·zan** \kə-'zan\ city W Russia; *pop* 1,144,000

**Kee·wa·tin** \kē-'wä-tᵊn, -'wä-\ former district N Canada in E Northwest Territories NW of Hudson Bay; area now part of Nunavut

**Ke·me·ro·vo** \'kye-mə-rə-və\ city S *cen* Russia; *pop* 533,000

**Ke·nai** \'kē-ˌnī\ peninsula S Alaska E of Cook Inlet

**Kennedy, Cape** — see CANAVERAL, CAPE

**Ken·sing·ton and Chel·sea** \'ken-ziŋ-tən-ənd-'chel-sē, 'ken(t)-siŋ\ borough of W Greater London, England; *pop* 158,500

**Kent** \'kent\ county SE England; *pop* 1,463,740 — **Kent·ish** \'ken-tish\ *adj*

**Ken·tucky** \kən-'tə-kē\ state E *cen* U.S.; ✳, Frankfort; *pop* 4,339,367 — **Ken·tuck·i·an** \-kē-ən\ *adj or n*

**Ken·ya** \'ke-nyə, 'kē-\ **1** mountain 17,058 ft. (5199 m.) *cen* Kenya **2** country E Africa S of Ethiopia; ✳, Nairobi; *pop* 38,610,000 — **Ken·yan** \-nyən\ *adj or n*

**Key West** \'west\ city SW Florida on Key West (Island); *pop* 24,649

**Kha·ba·rovsk** \kə-'bär-əfsk, kə-\ city SE Russia; *pop* 577,500

**Kham·bhat, Gulf of** \'kəm-bət\ *or* **Gulf of Cam·bay** \kam-'bā\ inlet of Arabian Sea in India N of Bombay

**Khar·kiv** \'kär-kəf, 'kär-\ *or* **Khar·kov** \'kär-ˌkóf, 'kär-, -ˌkòv, -kəf\ city NE Ukraine; *pop* 1,446,000

**Khar·toum** \kär-'tüm\ city, ✳ of Sudan; *pop* 1,950,000

**Khy·ber** \'kī-bər\ pass 33 mi. (53 km.) long on border between Afghanistan & Pakistan

**Ki·bo** \'kē-(ˌ)bo\ mountain peak 19,340 ft. (5895 m.) NE Tanzania; highest peak of Kilimanjaro & highest point in Africa

**Kiel** \'kēl\ — see NORD-OSTSEE

**Ki·ev** \'kē-ˌef, -ˌev, -if\ *or Ukrainian* **Kyiv** \'kyē-ü\ city, ✳ of Ukraine; *pop* 2,800,000

**Ki·ga·li** \kē-'gä-lē\ city, ✳ of Rwanda; *pop* 859,000

**Ki·lau·ea** \ˌkē-ˌlä-'wä-ä\ volcanic crater Hawaii on Hawaii Island on E slope of Mauna Loa

**Kil·i·man·ja·ro** \ˌki-lə-mən-'jär-(ˌ)ō, -'ja-(ˌ)rō\ mountain NE Tanzania; highest in Africa — see KIBO

**Kil·lar·ney, Lakes of** \ki-'lär-nē\ three lakes SW Ireland

**Kings·ton** \'kiŋ-stən\ city & port, ✳ of Jamaica; *pop* 103,771

**Kingston upon Hull** — see HULL

**Kingston upon Thames** borough of SW Greater London, England; *pop* 160,000

**Kings·town** \'kiŋz-ˌtaún\ seaport, ✳ of Saint Vincent and the Grenadines; *pop* 12,900

**Kin·sha·sa** \kin-'shä-sə\ city, ✳ of Democratic Republic of the Congo; *pop* 3,804,000

**Ki·ri·bati** \\'kir-ə-,bas\ island group W Pacific; country; \*, Tarawa; *pop* 103,000

**Kirin** — see JILIN

**Kirk·wall** \\'kər-,kwôl\ town and port N Scotland, \* of Orkney Islands; *pop* 5947

**Kishinev** — see CHIŞINĂU

**Ki·ta·kyu·shu** \kē-,tä-'kyü-(,)shü\ city Japan in N Kyushu; *pop* 976,846

**Kitch·e·ner** \\'kich-nər, 'ki-chə-\ city SE Ontario, Canada; *pop* 219,153

**Kit·ty Hawk** \\'kit-ē-,hôk\ town E North Carolina; *pop* 3272

**Klon·dike** \\'klän-,dīk\ region NW Canada in *cen* Yukon in valley of Klondike River

**Knox·ville** \\'näks-,vil, -vəl\ city E Tennessee; *pop* 178,874

**Ko·be** \\'kō-bē, -,bā\ city Japan in S Honshu; *pop* 1,544,200

**Ko·di·ak** \\'kō-dē-,ak\ island S Alaska E of Alaska Peninsula

**Ko·la** \\'kō-lə\ peninsula NW Russia bordering on Finland

**Ko·rea** \kə-'rē-ə\ peninsula E Asia between Yellow Sea & East Sea (Sea of Japan); divided 1948 into independent countries of North Korea & South Korea — **Ko·re·an** \kə-'rē-ən\ *adj or n*

**Ko·ror** \'kôr-,ôr\ town, former \* of Palau; *pop* 13,303

**Kos·ci·us·ko, Mount** \,kä-zē-'əs-(,)kō, ,kä-sē-\ mountain 7310 ft. (2228 m.) SE Australia in SE New South Wales; highest in Great Dividing Range & in Australia

**Ko·so·vo** \'kô-sô-,vō, 'kä-\ country S Europe in the Balkans; *pop* 1,757,000

**Kowloon** — see JIULONG

**Krak·a·tau** \,kra-kə-'taú\ *or* **Krak·a·toa** \-'tō-ə\ island & volcano Indonesia between Sumatra & Java

**Kra·kow** \'krä-,kaú, 'kra-, 'krä-, -(,)kō, *Pol* 'krä-,küf\ city S Poland; *pop* 758,000

**Kras·no·dar** \,kräs-nə-'där\ city SW Russia; *pop* 745,000

**Kras·no·yarsk** \,kräs-nə-'yärsk\ city S *cen* Russia; *pop* 973,850

**Kry·vyy Rih** \kri-'vē-'rik\ *or* **Kri·voy Rog** \,kri-,vôi-'rôg, -'rôk\ city SE *cen* Ukraine; *pop* 675,000

**K2** \,kä-'tü\ *or* **God·win Aus·ten** \,gä-dwən-'ôs-tən, ,gô-, -'äs-\ mountain 28,250 ft. (8611 m.) N Kashmir in Karakoram Range; second highest in the world

**Kua·la Lum·pur** \,kwä-lə-'lùm-,pùr, -'ləm-, -,lùm-'\ city, \* of Malaysia; *pop* 1,145,075

**Kuei–yang** — see GUIYANG

**Kun·lun** \'kün-'lün\ mountain system W China extending E from the Pamirs; highest peak Muztag 25,340 ft. (7724 m.)

**Kun·ming** \'kùn-'miŋ\ city S China; *pop* 3,567,000

**Kur·di·stan** \,kùr-də-'stan, ,kər-, -'stän; 'kər-də-,\ region SW Asia chiefly in E Turkey, NW Iran, & N Iraq — **Kurd**

\'kùrd, 'kərd\ *n* — **Kurd·ish** \'kùr-dish, 'kər-\ *adj*

**Ku·ril** *or* **Ku·rile** \'kyùr-,ēl, 'kùr-; kyù-'rēl, kù-\ islands Russia in W Pacific between Kamchatka Peninsula & Hokkaido Island

**Ku·wait** \kù-'wät\ **1** country SW Asia in Arabia at head of Persian Gulf; *pop* 3,986,000 **2** city, its \*; *pop* 28,859 — **Ku·waiti** \-'wä-tē\ *adj or n*

**Kuybyshev** — see SAMARA

**Kuz·netsk Basin** \kùz-'netsk\ *or* **Kuz·bas** *or* **Kuz·bass** \'kùz-,bas\ basin S *cen* Russia

**Kwa·ja·lein** \'kwä-jə-lən, -,lān\ island W Pacific in Marshall Islands

**Kwang·ju** *or* **Gwang·ju** \'gwäŋ-(,)jü\ city SW South Korea; *pop* 1,472,000

**Kwa·Zu·lu–Na·tal** \kwä-'zü-(,)lü-nə-'täl\ province E Republic of South Africa; *pop* 10,267,300

**Kyo·to** \kē-'ōt-ō\ city Japan in W *cen* Honshu; *pop* 1,474,015

**Kyr·gyz·stan** \,kir-gi-'stan, -'stän\ country W *cen* Asia; \*, Bishkek; *pop* 5,234,000

**Kyu·shu** \'kyü-(,)shü\ island Japan S of W end of Honshu; *pop* 13,445,561

**Lab·ra·dor** \'la-brə-,dòr\ **1** peninsula E Canada between Hudson Bay & the Atlantic divided between the provinces of Quebec & Newfoundland and Labrador **2** the part of the peninsula belonging to the province of Newfoundland and Labrador — **Lab·ra·dor·ean** *or* **Lab·ra·dor·ian** \,la-brə-'dòr-ē-ən\ *adj or n*

**Lac·ca·dive** \'la-kə-,dēv, -,dīv, -div\ islands India in Arabian Sea N of Maldive Islands

**La·co·nia** \lə-'kō-nē-ə, -nyə\ ancient country S Greece in SE Peloponnese; \*, Sparta — **La·co·nian** \-nē-ən, -nyən\ *adj or n*

**La·fay·ette** \,la-fē-'et, ,lä-\ city S Louisiana; *pop* 120,623

**La·gos** \'lä-,gäs, -,gōs\ city, former \* (1960–91) of Nigeria; *area pop* 9,114,000

**La·hore** \lə-'hòr\ city E Pakistan; *pop* 5,143,495

**Lake District** region NW England containing many lakes & mountains

**Lake·hurst** \'läk-(,)hərst\ borough E New Jersey; *pop* 2654

**Lake·wood** \'läk-,wùd\ city *cen* Colorado; *pop* 142,980

**Lam·beth** \'lam-bəth, -,beth\ borough of S Greater London, England; *pop* 303,000

**La·nai** \lə-'nī, lä-\ island Hawaii W of Maui

**Lan·ca·shire** \'laŋ-kə-,shir, -shər\ *or* **Lan·cas·ter** \'laŋ-kəs-tər\ county NW England — **Lan·cas·tri·an** \laŋ-'kas-trē-ən, lan-\ *adj or n*

**Lan·cas·ter** \'laŋ-kəs-tər, 'lan-,kas-tər\ city NW England; *pop* 125,600

**Land's End** \'landz-'end\ cape SW England; most westerly point of England

**Lan·sing** \'lan-siŋ\ city, ✻ of Michigan; *pop* 114,297

**Lan·zhou** *or* **Lan–chou** \'län-'jō\ city W China; *pop* 2,533,000

**Laos** \'laùs, 'lä-(,)ōs, 'lā-,äs\ country SE Asia in Indochina NE of Thailand; ✻, Vientiane; *pop* 6,514,000 — **Lao·tian** \lā-'ō-shən, 'laù-shən\ *adj or n*

**La Paz** \lä-'päz, -'päs\ city, administrative ✻ of Bolivia; *pop* 762,000

**Lap·land** \'lap-,land, -lənd\ region N Europe above the Arctic Circle in N Norway, N Sweden, N Finland, & Kola Peninsula of Russia — **Lap·land·er** \-,lan-dər, -lən-\ *n*

**La·re·do** \lə-'rā-(,)dō\ city S Texas on the Rio Grande; *pop* 236,091

**Larne** \'lärn\ district NE Northern Ireland; *pop* 32,000

**Las·sen Peak** \'la-sᵊn\ volcano 10,457 ft. (3187 m.) N California at S end of Cascade Range

**Las Ve·gas** \läs-'vā-gəs\ city SE Nevada; *pop* 583,756

**Latin America 1** Spanish America and Brazil **2** all of the Americas S of the U.S. — **Latin–American** *adj* — **Latin American** *n*

**Latin Quarter** section of Paris, France S of the Seine

**Lat·via** \'lat-vē-ə\ country E Europe on Baltic Sea; ✻, Riga; *pop* 2,070,000

**Lau·ren·tian Mountains** \lò-'ren(t)-shən\ hills E Canada in S Quebec N of the Saint Lawrence on S edge of Canadian Shield

**Laurentian Plateau** — see CANADIAN SHIELD

**La·val** \lə-'val\ city S Quebec NW of Montreal; *pop* 401,553

**Law·rence** \'lòr-ən(t)s, 'lär-\ **1** city NE Kansas *pop* 87,643 **2** city NE corner of Massachusetts; *pop* 76,377

**League of Nations** political organization established at the end of World War I; replaced by United Nations 1946

**Leb·a·non** \'le-bə-nən\ **1** mountains Lebanon (country) running parallel to coast **2** country SW Asia on the Mediterranean; ✻, Beirut; *pop* 4,100,000 — **Leb·a·nese** \,le-bə-'nēz, -'nēs\ *adj or n*

**Leeds** \'lēdz\ city N England; *pop* 475,000

**Lee·ward Islands** \'lē-wərd, 'lü-ərd\ **1** islands Hawaii extending WNW from main islands of the group **2** islands South Pacific in W Society Islands **3** islands West Indies in N Lesser Antilles extending from Virgin Islands (on N) to Dominica (on S)

**Le Ha·vre** \lə-'hävrᵊ, -'häv\ city N France on English Channel; *pop* 175,497

**Leh·man Caves** \'lē-mən\ limestone caverns E Nevada

**Leices·ter** \'les-tər\ city *cen* England ENE of Birmingham; *pop* 444,000

**Leices·ter·shire** \'les-tər-,shir, -shər\ *or* **Leicester** county *cen* England

**Lein·ster** \'len(t)-star\ province E Ireland; *pop* 2,504,814

**Leip·zig** \'līp-sig, -sik\ city E Germany; *pop* 502,979

**Le·na** \'lē-nə, 'lā-\ river about 2700 mi. (4345 km.) long E Russia, flowing NE & N from mountains W of Lake Baikal into Arctic Ocean

**Leningrad** — see SAINT PETERSBURG

**Le·ón** \lā-'ōn\ city *cen* Mexico; *pop* 1,436,000

**Ler·wick** \'lər (,)wik, 'ler-\ town and port N Scotland in the Shetlands; *pop* 7223

**Le·so·tho** \lə-'sō-(,)tō, -'sü-(,)tü\ *formerly* **Ba·su·to·land** \bə-'sü-tō-,land\ country S Africa surrounded by Republic of South Africa; ✻, Maseru; *pop* 1,877,000

**Lesser Antilles** islands in the West Indies including Virgin Islands, Leeward Islands, & Windward Islands, Barbados, Trinidad, Tobago, & islands in the S Caribbean N of Venezuela — see GREATER ANTILLES

**Le·vant** \lə-'vant\ the countries bordering on the E Mediterranean — **Lev·an·tine** \'lev-ən-,tīn, -,tēn, lə-'van-\ *adj or n*

**Lew·es** \'lü-əs\ town S England

**Lew·i·sham** \'lü-ə-shəm\ borough of SE Greater London, England; *pop* 276,000

**Lew·is with Har·ris** \'lü-əs-with-'ha-rəs, -with-\ island NW Scotland in Outer Hebrides

**Lex·ing·ton** \'lek-siŋ-tən\ **1** city NE *cen* Kentucky; area *pop* 295,803 **2** town NE Massachusetts; *pop* 31,394

**Ley·te** \'lā-tē\ island Philippines S of Samar

**Lha·sa** \'lä-sə, 'la-\ city SW China, ✻ of Tibet; *pop* 199,000

**Li·be·ria** \lī-'bir-ē-ə\ country W Africa on the North Atlantic; ✻, Monrovia; *pop* 3,477,000 — **Li·be·ri·an** \-ē-ən\ *adj or n*

**Lib·er·ty** \'li-bər-tē\ *formerly* **Bed·loe's** \'bed-,lōz\ island SE New York; site of the Statue of Liberty

**Li·bre·ville** \'lē-brə-,vil, -,vēl\ city, ✻ of Gabon; *pop* 419,596

**Lib·ya** \'li-bē-ə\ country N Africa on the Mediterranean W of Egypt; ✻, Tripoli; *pop* 5,658,000 — **Lib·y·an** \'li-bē-ən\ *adj or n*

**Libyan** desert N Africa W of the Nile in Libya, Egypt, & Sudan

**Liech·ten·stein** \'lik-tən-,stīn, 'lik-tən-,shtīn\ country W Europe between Austria & Switzerland; ✻, Vaduz; *pop* 36,000 — **Liech·ten·stein·er** \-,stī-nər, -,shtī-\ *n*

**Lif·fey** \'li-fē\ river 50 mi. (80 km.) long E Ireland

**Li·gu·ria** \lə-'gyùr-ē-ə\ region NW Italy on Ligurian Sea — **Li·gu·ri·an** \-ē-ən\ *adj or n*

**Ligurian Sea** arm of the Mediterranean N of Corsica

**Li·lon·gwe** \li-ˈlȯn-(ˌ)gwä\ city, ✴ of Malawi; *pop* 674,448

**Li·ma** \ˈlē-mə\ city, ✴ of Peru; *pop* 8,039,000

**Lim·a·vady** \ˌli-mə-ˈva-dē\ district NW Northern Ireland; *pop* 34,000

**Lim·po·po** \lim-ˈpō-(ˌ)pō\ river 1000 mi. (1609 km.) long Africa flowing from Republic of South Africa into Indian Ocean in Mozambique

**Lin·coln** \ˈliŋ-kən\ **1** city, ✴ of Nebraska; *pop* 258,379 **2** city E England; *pop* 81,900

**Lin·coln·shire** \ˈliŋ-kən-ˌshir, -shər\ *or* **Lincoln** county E England

**Line** \ˈlīn\ islands Kiribati S of Hawaii; *pop* 4782

**Lis·bon** \ˈliz-bən\ *or Portuguese* **Lis·boa** \lēzh-ˈvȯ-ə\ city, ✴ of Portugal; *pop* 547,733

**Lis·burn** \ˈliz-(ˌ)bərn\ district E Northern Ireland; *pop* 120,000

**Lith·u·a·nia** \ˌli-thə-ˈwā-nē-ə, ˌli-thyə-, -nyə\ country E Europe; ✴, Vilnius; *pop* 3,043,000

**Lit·tle Rock** \ˈli-t³l-ˌräk\ city, ✴ of Arkansas; *pop* 193,524

**Liv·er·pool** \ˈli-vər-ˌpül\ city NW England; *pop* 552,000

**Li·vo·nia** \lə-ˈvō-nē-ə, -nyə\ city SE Michigan; *pop* 96,942

**Lju·blja·na** \lē-ˌü-blē-ˈä-nə\ city, ✴ of Slovenia; *pop* 272,000

**Lla·no Es·ta·ca·do** \ˈla-(ˌ)nō-ˌes-tə-ˈkä-(ˌ)dō, ˈlä-, ˈyä-\ *or* **Staked Plain** \ˈstāk(t)-\ plateau region SE New Mexico & NW Texas

**Lo·bam·ba** \lō-ˈbäm-bə\ town, legislative ✴ of Swaziland; *pop* (est.) 10,000

**Lodz** \ˈlüj, ˈlädz\ city *cen* Poland WSW of Warsaw; *pop* 729,000

**Lo·fo·ten** \ˈlō-ˌfō-t³n\ islands NW Norway

**Lo·gan, Mount** \ˈlō-gən\ mountain 19,551 ft. (5959 m.) NW Canada in Saint Elias Range; highest in Canada & second highest in North America

**Loire** \lə-ˈwär, ˈlwär\ river 634 mi. (1020 km.) long *cen* France flowing NW & W into Bay of Biscay

**Lo·mé** \lō-ˈmā\ city, ✴ of Togo; *pop* 838,500

**Lo·mond, Loch** \ˈlō-mənd\ lake S *cen* Scotland

**Lon·don** \ˈlən-dən\ **1** city SE Ontario, Canada; *pop* 366,151 **2** city, ✴ of England & of United Kingdom on the Thames; consists of **City of London** & **Greater London** metropolitan county; *pop* 8,174,000 — **Lon·don·er** \-də-nər\ *n*

**Londonderry** — see DERRY

**Long Beach** city SW California S of Los Angeles; *pop* 462,257

**Long Island** island 118 mi. (190 km.) long SE New York S of Connecticut

**Long Island Sound** inlet of the Atlantic between Connecticut & Long Island, New York

**Lon·gueuil** \lȯn-ˈgāl\ city Canada in S Quebec E of Montreal; *pop* 231,409

**Lor·raine** \lə-ˈrān, lȯ-\ region NE France

**Los An·ge·les** \lȯs-ˈan-jə-ləs\ city SW California; *pop* 3,792,621

**Lou·ise, Lake** \lü-ˈēz\ lake SW Alberta, Canada

**Lou·i·si·ana** \lù-ˌē-zē-ˈa-nə, ˌlü-ə-zē-, ˌlü-zē-\ state S U.S.; ✴, Baton Rouge; *pop* 4,533,372 — **Lou·i·si·an·ian** \-ˈa-nē-ən, -ˈa-nyən\ *or* **Lou·i·si·an·an** \-ˈa-nən\ *adj or n*

**Louisiana Purchase** area W *cen* U.S. between Rocky Mountains & the Mississippi purchased 1803 from France

**Lou·is·ville** \ˈlü-i-ˌvil, -vəl\ city N Kentucky on the Ohio River; *pop* 597,337

**Low Countries** region W Europe consisting of modern Belgium, Luxembourg, & the Netherlands

**Low·ell** \ˈlō-əl\ city NE Massachusetts NW of Boston; *pop* 106,519

**Lower 48** the continental states of the U.S. excluding Alaska

**Low·lands** \ˈlō-ləndz, -ˌlandz\ the *cen* & E part of Scotland

**Lu·an·da** \lü-ˈän-də\ city, ✴ of Angola; *pop* 2,600,000

**Lub·bock** \ˈlə-bək\ city NW Texas; *pop* 229,573

**Lu·bum·ba·shi** \ˌlü-büm-ˈbä-shē\ city SE Democratic Republic of the Congo; *pop* 739,000

**Luck·now** \ˈlək-ˌnau̇\ city N India ESE of Delhi; *pop* 2,817,105

**Lüda** *or* **Lü·ta** — see DALIAN

**Lu·ray Caverns** \ˈlü-ˌrā, lü-ˈ\ series of caves N Virginia

**Lu·sa·ka** \lü-ˈsä-kä\ city, ✴ of Zambia; *pop* 1,747,000

**Lü·shun** \ˈlü-ˈshün, ˈlu̇e-\ *or* **Port Ar·thur** \-ˈär-thər\ seaport NE China; part of Dalian

**Lu·ton** \ˈlü-t³n\ town SE *cen* England; *pop* 211,000

**Lux·em·bourg** *or* **Lux·em·burg** \ˈlək-səm-ˌbərg, ˈlu̇k-səm-ˌbu̇rk\ **1** country W Europe bordered by Belgium, France, & Germany; *pop* 512,000 **2** city, its ✴; *pop* 95,000 — **Lux·em·bourg·er** \-ˌbər-gər, -ˌbu̇r-\ *n* — **Lux·em·bourg·ian** \ˌlək-səm-ˈbər-gē-ən, ˌlu̇k-səm-ˈbu̇r-\ *adj*

**Lu·zon** \lü-ˈzän\ island N Philippines; *pop* 42,784,360

**L'viv** \lə-ˈvē-ü, -ˈvēf\ *or* **L'vov** \lə-ˈvȯf, -ˈvȯv\ *or Polish* **Lwów** \lə-ˈvüf, -ˈvüv\ city W Ukraine; *pop* 729,400

**Lyallpur** — see FAISALABAD

**Lyd·ia** \ˈli-dē-ə\ ancient country W Asia Minor on the Aegean — **Lyd·i·an** \-ē-ən\ *adj or n*

**Lyon** \lē-ˈōⁿ, ˈlī-ənz\ *or* **Lyons** \lē-ˈōⁿ, ˈlī-ənz\ city SE *cen* France; *pop* 505,094

**Ma·cao** *or Portuguese* **Ma·cau** \mə-ˈkau̇\ *or Chinese* **Ao·men** \ˈau̇-ˈmən\ **1** special administrative region on coast of SE

China W of Hong Kong; *pop* 553,000 **2** city, its ✳; *pop* 469,000 — **Mac·a·nese** \ˌmä-kə-ˈnēz, -ˈnēs\ *n*

**Mac·e·do·nia** \ˌma-sə-ˈdō-nē-ə, -nyə\ **1** region S Europe in Balkan Peninsula in NE Greece, the former Yugoslav section & now independent country of Macedonia, & SW Bulgaria including territory of ancient kingdom of Macedonia (**Mac·e·don** \ˈmas-ə-dən, -ə-ˌdän\ ) **2** country S *cen* Balkan Peninsula; ✳, Skopje; a former republic of Yugoslavia; *pop* 2,063,000 — **Mac·e·do·nian** \ˌmas-ə-ˈdō-nyən, -nē-ən\ *adj or n*

**Mac·gil·li·cud·dy's Reeks** \mə-ˈgi-lə-ˌkə-dēz-ˈrēks\ mountains SW Ireland; highest Carrantuohill 3414 ft. (1041 m.)

**Ma·chu Pic·chu** \ˌmä-(ˌ)chü-ˈpē-(ˌ)chü, -ˈpēk-\ site SE Peru of ancient Inca city

**Mac·ken·zie** \mə-ˈken-zē\ river 1120 mi. (1802 km.) long NW Canada flowing from Great Slave Lake NW into Beaufort Sea

**Mack·i·nac, Straits of** \ˈma-kə-ˌnò, -ˌnak\ channel N Michigan connecting Lake Huron & Lake Michigan

**Ma·con** \ˈmä-kən\ city *cen* Georgia; *pop* 91,351

**Mad·a·gas·car** \ˌma-də-ˈgas-kər, -ˌkär\ *formerly* **Mal·a·gasy Re·public** \ˌma-lə-ˈga-sē\ island country W Indian Ocean off SE Africa; ✳, Antananarivo; *pop* 21,842,000 — **Mad·a·gas·can** \ˌma-də-ˈgas-kən\ *adj or n*

**Ma·dei·ra** \mə-ˈdir-ə, -ˈder-ə\ **1** river 2013 mi. (3239 km.) long W Brazil flowing NE into the Amazon **2** islands Portugal in the North Atlantic N of the Canary Islands; *pop* 261,313 **3** island: chief of the Madeira group — **Ma·dei·ran** \-ˈdir-ən, -ˈder-\ *adj or n*

**Ma·di·nat ash Sha'b** \mə-ˌdē-,nə-tash-ˈshäb\ city S Yemen

**Mad·i·son** \ˈma-də-sən\ city, ✳ of Wisconsin; *pop* 233,209

**Ma·dras** \mə-ˈdras, -ˈdräs\ *or* **Chen·nai** \ˈche-,nī\ city SE India; *pop* 4,646,732

**Ma·drid** \mə-ˈdrid\ city, ✳ of Spain; *pop* 3,198,645

**Ma·du·rai** \ˌmä-də-ˈrī\ city S India; *pop* 1,241,000

**Mag·da·len Islands** \ˈmag-də-lən\ *or F* **Îles de la Ma·de·leine** \ˌēl-də-lä-mäd-ˈlen, -mä-də-ˈlen\ islands Canada in Gulf of Saint Lawrence between Newfoundland & Prince Edward Island

**Ma·gel·lan, Strait of** \mə-ˈje-lən, *chiefly Brit* -ˈge-\ strait at S end of South America between mainland & Tierra del Fuego

**Magh·er·a·felt** \ˈmär-ə-,felt, ˈma-kə-rə-,felt\ district *cen* Northern Ireland; *pop* 45,000

**Maid·stone** \ˈmād-stən, -ˌstōn\ town SE England; *pop* 108,000

**Main** \ˈmīn, ˈmän\ river 325 mi. (523 km.)

long S *cen* Germany flowing W into the Rhine

**Maine** \ˈmān\ state NE U.S.; ✳, Augusta; *pop* 1,328,361 — **Main·er** \ˈmā-nər\ *n*

**Ma·jor·ca** \mä-ˈjór-kə, mə-, -ˈyór-\ *or Spanish* **Ma·llor·ca** \mä-ˈyòr-kä\ island Spain in W Mediterranean — **Ma·jor·can** \-ˈjór-kən, -ˈyór\ *adj or n*

**Ma·ju·ro** \mə-ˈjúr-(ˌ)ō\ atoll that contains ✳ of Marshall Islands; *pop* 23,700

**Mal·a·bar Coast** \ˈma-lə-,bär\ region SW India on Arabian Sea

**Ma·la·bo** \mä-ˈlä-(ˌ)bō\ city, ✳ of Equatorial Guinea; *pop* 134,400

**Ma·lac·ca, Strait of** \mə-ˈla-kə, -ˈlä-\ channel between S Malay Peninsula & island of Sumatra

**Ma·la·wi** \mə-ˈlä-wē\ *formerly* **Ny·asa·land** \nī-ˈa-sə-,land, nē-\ country SE Africa on Lake Nyasa; ✳, Lilongwe; *pop* 13,077,000 — **Ma·la·wi·an** \-ən\ *adj or n*

**Ma·lay** \mə-ˈlā, ˈmā-(ˌ)lā\ **1** archipelago SE Asia including Sumatra, Java, Borneo, Sulawesi, Moluccas, & Timor; usu. thought to include the Philippines & sometimes New Guinea **2** peninsula SE Asia divided between Thailand & Malaysia (country)

**Ma·laya** \mə-ˈlā-ə, mä-\ **1** the Malay Peninsula **2** former country SE Asia on Malay Peninsula; now part of Malaysia

**Ma·lay·sia** \mə-ˈlā-zh(ē-)ə, -sh(ē-)ə\ **1** the Malay Archipelago **2** the Malay Peninsula & Malay Archipelago **3** country SE Asia; ✳, Kuala Lumpur; *pop* 27,566,000 — **Ma·lay·sian** \-ˈlā zhən, shən\ *adj or n*

**Mal·dives** \ˈmòl-,dēvz, -,dīvz\ islands in Indian Ocean SW of Sri Lanka; country; ✳, Male Atoll; *pop* 299,000 — **Mal·div·i·an** \mòl-ˈdi-vē-ən, mal-\ *adj or n*

**Ma·le** \ˈmä-lē\ atoll containing national ✳ of Maldives; *pop* 103,693

**Ma·li** \ˈmä-lē, ˈma-\ country W Africa; ✳, Bamako; *pop* 14,500,000 — **Ma·li·an** \-lē-ən\ *adj or n*

**Mal·ta** \ˈmòl-tə\ islands in the Mediterranean S of Sicily; country since 1964; ✳, Valletta; *pop* 417,000 — **Mal·tese** \mòl-ˈtēz, -ˈtēs\ *adj or n*

**Malvinas, Islas** — *see* FALKLAND ISLANDS

**Mam·moth Cave** \ˈma-məth\ limestone caverns SW *cen* Kentucky

**Man, Isle of** \ˈman\ island British Isles in Irish Sea; has own legislature & laws; *pop* 60,496

**Ma·na·gua** \mä-ˈnä-gwä\ city, ✳ of Nicaragua; *pop* 1,007,000

**Ma·na·ma** \mə-ˈna-mə\ city, ✳ of Bahrain; *pop* 143,045

**Man·ches·ter** \ˈman-,ches-tər, -chəs-tər\ **1** city S *cen* New Hampshire; *pop* 109,565 **2** city NW England; *pop* 503,000

**Man·chu·ria** \man-ˈchùr-ē-ə\ region NE

China S of the Amur — **Man·chu·ri·an** \-ē-ən\ *adj or n*

**Man·hat·tan** \man-'ha-t°n, mən-\ **1** island SE New York in New York City **2** borough of New York City consisting chiefly of Manhattan Island; *pop* 1,585,873

**Ma·nila** \mə-'ni-lə\ city, ✳ of Philippines in W Luzon; *pop* 1,661,000

**Man·i·to·ba** \ˌma-nə-'tō-bə\ province *cen* Canada; ✳, Winnipeg; *pop* 1,208,268 — **Man·i·to·ban** \-bən\ *adj or n*

**Man·i·tou·lin** \ˌma-nə-'tü-lən\ island 80 mi. (129 km.) long S Ontario in Lake Huron

**Ma·pu·to** \mä-'pü-(ˌ)tō, -(ˌ)tü\ city, ✳ of Mozambique; *pop* 1,094,628

**Mar·a·cai·bo** \ˌma-rə-'kī-(ˌ)bō, ˌmär-\ city NW Venezuela; *pop* 1,207,513

**Maracaibo, Lake** extension of a gulf of the Caribbean NW Venezuela

**Mar·a·thon** \'ma-rə-ˌthän\ plain E Greece NE of Athens

**Mar·i·ana** \ˌmer-ē-'a-nə\ islands W Pacific N of Caroline Islands; comprise Commonwealth of Northern Mariana Islands & Guam

**Mariana Trench** ocean trench W Pacific extending from SE of Guam to NW of Mariana Islands; deepest in world

**Ma·rin·du·que** \ˌma-rən-'dü-(ˌ)kā, ˌmär-ēn-\ island *cen* Philippines; *pop* 173,715

**Maritime Provinces** the Canadian provinces of New Brunswick, Nova Scotia, & Prince Edward Island & formerly thought by some to include Newfoundland and Labrador

**Ma·ri·u·pol** \ˌma-rē-'ü-ˌpól, -pəl\ *or* 1949–89 **Zhda·nov** \zhə-'dä-nəf\ city E Ukraine; *pop* 461,000

**Mar·ma·ra, Sea of** \'mär-mə-rə\ sea NW Turkey connected with Black Sea by the Bosporus & with Aegean Sea by the Dardanelles

**Marne** \'märn\ river 325 mi. (523 km.) long NE France flowing W into the Seine

**Mar·que·sas** \mär-'kā-zəz, -zəs, -səz, -səs\ islands South Pacific; belonging to France; *pop* 7358 — **Mar·que·san** \-zən, -sən\ *adj or n*

**Mar·ra·kech** \ˌma-rə-'kesh, 'ma-rə-ˌ, mə-'rä-kish\ city *cen* Morocco; *pop* 823,154

**Mar·seille** \mär-'sä\ *or* **Mar·seilles** \mär-'sä, -'sālz\ city SE France; *pop* 850,726

**Mar·shall Islands** \'mär-shəl\ islands W Pacific E of the Carolines; republic, in association with U.S.; Majuro; *pop* 53,200

**Mar·tha's Vineyard** \'mär-thəz\ island SE Massachusetts off SW coast of Cape Cod WNW of Nantucket

**Mar·ti·nique** \ˌmär-tə-'nēk\ island West Indies in the Windward Islands; an overseas division of France; ✳, Fort-de-France; *pop* 394,173

**Mary·land** \'mer-ə-lənd\ state E U.S.; ✳, Annapolis; *pop* 5,773,552 — **Mary·land·er** \-lən-dər, -ˌlan-\ *n*

**Mas·ba·te** \mäz-'bä-tē, mäs-\ island *cen* Philippines

**Mas·e·ru** \'ma-sə-ˌrü, -zə-\ city, ✳ of Lesotho; *pop* 227,880

**Mash·had** \mə-'shad\ city NE Iran; *pop* 2,749,374

**Ma·son–Dix·on Line** \'mä-s°n-'dik-sən\ boundary between Maryland & Pennsylvania; often considered the boundary between N & S states

**Masqat** — see MUSCAT

**Mas·sa·chu·setts** \ˌma-sə-'chü-səts, -zəts\ state NE U.S.; ✳, Boston; *pop* 6,547,629

**Mat·a·be·le·land** \ˌma-tə-'bē-lē-ˌland, ˌmä-tä-'bä-lä-\ region SW Zimbabwe

**Mat·lock** \'mat-ˌläk\ town N England; *pop* 20,610

**Mat·ter·horn** \'ma-tər-ˌhórn, 'mä-\ mountain 14,691 ft. (4478 m.) on border between Switzerland & Italy

**Maui** \'maù-ē\ island Hawaii NW of Hawaii Island; *pop* 154,834

**Mau·na Kea** \ˌmaù-nä-'kä-ä, ˌmó-\ extinct volcano 13,796 ft. (4205 m.) Hawaii in N *cen* Hawaii Island

**Mau·na Loa** \-'lō-ə\ volcano 13,680 ft. (4170 m.) Hawaii in S *cen* Hawaii Island

**Mau·re·ta·nia** *or* **Mau·ri·ta·nia** \ˌmór-ə-'tā-nē-ə, ˌmär-, -nyə\ ancient country NW Africa in modern Morocco & W Algeria — **Mau·re·ta·ni·an** *or* **Mau·ri·ta·ni·an** \-nē-ən, -nyən\ *adj or n*

**Mauritania** country NW Africa on the Atlantic N of Senegal River; ✳, Nouakchott; *pop* 3,537,000 — **Mauritanian** *adj or n*

**Mau·ri·tius** \mó-'ri-sh(ē-)əs\ island in Indian Ocean E of Madagascar; country; ✳, Port Louis; *pop* 1,237,091 — **Mau·ri·tian** \-'ri-shən\ *adj or n*

**May, Cape** \'mā\ cape S New Jersey at entrance to Delaware Bay

**Ma·yon, Mount** \mä-'yón\ volcano 8077 ft. (2462 m.) Philippines in SE Luzon

**Ma·yotte** \mä-'yät, -'yót\ island Comoros group; French dependency; *pop* 213,000 — see COMOROS

**Ma·za·ma, Mount** \mə-'zäm-ə\ prehistoric mountain SW Oregon the collapse of whose top formed Crater Lake

**Mba·bane** \ˌəm-bä-'bä-nä\ city, ✳ of Swaziland; *pop* 57,992

**Mbi·ni** \em-'bē-nē\ *formerly* **Río Mu·ni** \ˌrē-ō-'mü-nē\ mainland portion of Equatorial Guinea; *pop* 750,000

**Mc·Al·len** \mə-'ka-lən\ city S Texas; *pop* 129,877

**Mc·Kin·ley, Mount** \mə-'kin-lē\ *or* **De·na·li** \də-'nä-lē\ mountain 20,320 ft. (6194 m.) S *cen* Alaska in Alaska Range; highest in U.S. & North America

**Mead, Lake** \'mēd\ reservoir NW Arizona

& SE Nevada formed by Hoover Dam in Colorado River

**Mec·ca** \'me-kə\ city W Saudi Arabia; contains Islam's Great Mosque; *pop* 1,294,106

**Me·dan** \mā-'dän\ city Indonesia, in N Sumatra; *pop* 2,097,610

**Me·de·llín** \,me-də-'lēn, ,mā-thā-'yēn\ city NW Colombia; *pop* 2,400,000

**Me·di·na** \mə-'di-nə\ city W Saudi Arabia; *pop* 1,100,000

**Med·i·ter·ra·nean** \,me-də-tə-'rā-nē-ən, -nyən\ sea 2300 mi. (3700 km.) long between Europe & Africa connecting with the Atlantic through Strait of Gibraltar

**Me·kong** \'mā-'koŋ, -'käŋ; 'mā-\ river 2600 mi (4184 km.) long SE Asia flowing from E Tibet S & SE into South China Sea in S Vietnam

**Mel·a·ne·sia** \,me-lə-'nē-zhə, -shə\ islands of the Pacific NE of Australia & S of Micronesia including Bismarck, the Solomons, Vanuatu, New Caledonia, & the Fijis

**Mel·bourne** \'mel-bərn\ city SE Australia, ✻ of Victoria; metropolitan area *pop* 3,708,000

**Mel·e·ke·ok** \'me-lə-,kā-,ók\ town, ✻ of Palau

**Melos** — see MÍLOS

**Mel·ville** \'mel-,vil\ 1 island N Canada, split between Northwest Territories & Nunavut 2 peninsula Canada in Nunavut

**Mem·phis** \'mem(p)-fəs\ 1 city SW Tennessee; *pop* 646,889 2 ancient city N Egypt S of modern Cairo

**Mem·phre·ma·gog, Lake** \,mem(p)-fri-'mā-,gäg\ lake on border between Canada (Quebec) & United States (Vermont)

**Men·do·ci·no, Cape** \,men-də-'sē-(,)nō\ cape NW California

**Mer·cia** \'mər-sh(ē-)ə\ ancient Anglo-Saxon kingdom *cen* England — **Mer·cian** \'mər-shən\ *adj or n*

**Mer·sey** \'mər-zē\ river 70 mi. (113 km.) long NW England flowing NW & W into Irish Sea

**Mer·sey·side** \'mər-zē-,sīd\ metropolitan county NW England; includes Liverpool

**Mer·ton** \'mər-t³n\ borough of SW Greater London, England; *pop* 200,000

**Me·sa** \'mā-sə\ city S *cen* Arizona; *pop* 439,041

**Me·sa·bi Range** \mə-'sä-bē\ region NE Minnesota that contains iron ore

**Mes·o·po·ta·mia** \,mc-s(ə-)pə-'tā-mē-ə, -myə\ 1 region SW Asia between Euphrates & Tigris rivers 2 the entire Tigris–Euphrates valley — **Mes·o·po·ta·mian** \-mē-ən, -myən\ *adj or n*

**Mes·quite** \mə-'skēt, me-\ city NE Texas E of Dallas; *pop* 139,824

**Meuse** \'myüz, 'mə(r)z, 'mœz\ river 580 mi. (933 km.) long W Europe flowing from NE France into North Sea in the Netherlands

**Mex·i·co** \'mek-si-,kō\ 1 country S North America; *pop* 112,337,000 2 *or* **Mexico City** city, its ✻; *pop* 8,851,000 — **Mex·i·can** \'mek-si-kən\ *adj or n*

**Mexico, Gulf of** inlet of the Atlantic SE North America

**Mi·ami** \mī-'a-mē\ city & port SE Florida; *pop* 399,457

**Miami Beach** city SE Florida; *pop* 87,779

**Mich·i·gan** \'mi-shi-gən\ state N *cen* U.S.; ✻, Lansing; *pop* 9,883,640 — **Mich·i·gan·der** \,mi-shi-'gan-dər\ *n* — **Mich·i·ga·ni·an** \,mi-shə-'gä-nē-ən, -'ga-\ *n* — **Mich·i·gan·ite** \'mi-shi-gə-,nīt\ *n*

**Michigan, Lake** lake N *cen* U.S.; one of the Great Lakes

**Mi·cro·ne·sia** \,mī-krə-'nē-zhə, -shə\ islands of the W Pacific E of the Philippines & N of Melanesia including Caroline, Kiribati, Mariana, & Marshall groups — **Mi·cro·ne·sian** \-zhən, -shən\ *adj or n*

**Micronesia, Federated States of** islands W Pacific in the Carolines; country in association with U.S.; ✻, Palikir; *pop* 103,000

**Middle East** the countries of SW Asia & N Africa — usually thought to include the countries extending from Libya on the W to Afghanistan on the E — **Middle Eastern** *adj*

**Mid·dles·brough** \'mi-d³lz-brə\ town N England; *pop* 175,000

**Middle West** — see MIDWEST

**Mid Gla·mor·gan** \'mid-glə-'mór-gən\ former county SE Wales

**Mid·i·an** \'mi-dē-ən\ ancient region NW Arabia E of Gulf of Aqaba — **Mid·i·an·ite** \-ē-ə-,nīt\ *n*

**Mid·lands** \'mid-ləndz\ the *cen* counties of England

**Mid·way** \'mid-,wā\ islands *cen* Pacific 1300 mi. (2092 km.) WNW of Honolulu belonging to U.S.

**Mid·west** \'mid-'west\ *or* **Middle West** region N *cen* U.S. including area around Great Lakes & in upper Mississippi valley from Ohio on the E to North Dakota, South Dakota, Nebraska, & Kansas on the W — **Mid·west·ern** \,mid-'wes-tərn\ *or* **Middle Western** *adj* — **Mid·west·ern·er** \,mid-'wes-tə(r)-nər\ *or* **Middle Westerner** *n*

**Mi·lan** \mə-'lan, -'län\ *or Italian* **Mi·la·no** \mē-'lä-(,)nō\ city NW Italy; *pop* 1,242,123 — **Mil·a·nese** \,mi-lə-'nēz, -'nēs\ *adj or n*

**Mí·los** *or* **Me·los** \'mē-,lós\ island Greece

**Mil·wau·kee** \mil-'wó-kē\ city SE Wisconsin on Lake Michigan; *pop* 594,833

**Mi·nas Basin** \'mī-nəs\ bay *cen* Nova Scotia; NE extension of Bay of Fundy

**Min·da·nao** \,min-də-'nä-,ō, -'nau̇\ island S Philippines; *pop* 13,966,000

**Min·do·ro** \min-'dór-(,)ō\ island *cen* Philippines; *pop* 473,940

**Min·ne·ap·o·lis** \\ˌmi-nē-'a-pə-lis\ city SE Minnesota; *pop* 383,578

**Min·ne·so·ta** \ˌmi-nə-'sō-tə\ state N *cen* U.S.; ✳, Saint Paul; *pop* 5,303,925 — **Min·ne·so·tan** \-'sō-t°n\ *adj or n*

**Mi·nor·ca** \mə-'nòr-kə\ island Spain in W Mediterranean — **Mi·nor·can** \mə-'nòr-kən\ *adj or n*

**Minsk** \'min(t)sk\ city, ✳ of Belarus; *pop* 1,836,808

**Mis·sis·sau·ga** \ˌmi-sə-'sò-gə\ city Canada in S Ontario; *pop* 713,443

**Mis·sis·sip·pi** \ˌmi-sə-'si-pē\ **1** river 2340 mi. (3765 km.) long *cen* U.S. flowing into Gulf of Mexico — see ITASCA, LAKE **2** state S U.S.; ✳, Jackson; *pop* 2,967,297

**Mis·sou·ri** \mə-'zùr-ē\ **1** river 2466 mi. (3968 km.) long W U.S. flowing from SW Montana to the Mississippi in E Missouri (state) **2** state *cen* U.S.; ✳, Jefferson City; *pop* 5,988,927 — **Mis·sou·ri·an** \-'zùr-ē-ən\ *adj or n*

**Mitch·ell, Mount** \'mi-chəl\ mountain 6684 ft. (2037 m.) W North Carolina in the Appalachians; highest in U.S. E of the Mississippi

**Mo·bile** \mō-'bēl, 'mō-ˌbēl\ city SW Alabama on **Mobile Bay** (inlet of Gulf of Mexico); *pop* 195,111

**Mo·des·to** \mə-'des-(ˌ)tō\ city *cen* California; *pop* 201,165

**Mog·a·di·shu** \ˌmä-gə-'di-(ˌ)shü, ˌmō-, -'dē-\ *or* **Mog·a·di·scio** \-(ˌ)shō\ city, ✳ of Somalia; *pop* 349,245

**Mo·hawk** \'mō-ˌhòk\ river E *cen* New York flowing into the Hudson

**Mo·hen·jo Da·ro** \mō-'hen-(ˌ)jō-'där-(ˌ)ō\ prehistoric city in valley of the Indus NE of modern Karachi, Pakistan

**Mo·ja·ve** *or* **Mo·ha·ve** \mə-'hä-vē, mō-\ desert S California SE of S end of Sierra Nevada

**Mol·da·via** \mäl-'dā-vē-ə, -vyə\ region E Europe in NE Romania & Moldova — **Mol·da·vian** \-vē-ən, -vyən\ *adj or n*

**Mol·do·va** \mäl-'dō-və, mòl-\ country E Europe in E Moldavia region; ✳, Chişinău; *pop* 3,785,000 — **Mol·do·van** \-vən\ *adj or n*

**Mol·o·kai** \ˌmä-lə-'kī, ˌmō-lō-'kä-ē\ island Hawaii ESE of Oahu

**Mo·luc·cas** \mə-'lə-kəz\ islands Indonesia E of Sulawesi; *pop* 2,300,000 — **Mo·luc·ca** \mə-'lə-kə\ *adj* — **Mo·luc·can** \-kən\ *adj or n*

**Mom·ba·sa** city & port S Kenya; *pop* 926,000

**Mo·na·co** \'mä-nə-ˌkō\ country W Europe on Mediterranean coast of France; ✳, Monaco; *pop* 31,100 — **Mo·na·can** \'mä-nə-kən, mə-'nä-kən\ *adj or n* — **Mon·e·gasque** \ˌmä-ni-'gask\ *n*

**Mon·go·lia** \män-'gōl-yə, mäŋ-, -'gō-lē-ə\ **1** region E Asia E of Altay Mountains; includes Gobi Desert **2** country E Asia consisting of major portion of Mongolia region; ✳, Ulaanbaatar; *pop* 2,701,000

**Mo·non·ga·he·la** \mə-ˌnän-gə-'hē-lə, -ˌnäŋ-gə-, -'hä-lə\ river N West Virginia & SW Pennsylvania

**Mon·ro·via** \(ˌ)mən-'rō-vē-ə\ city, ✳ of Liberia; *pop* 1,016,500

**Mon·ta·na** \män-'ta-nə\ state NW U.S.; ✳, Helena; *pop* 989,415 — **Mon·tan·an** \-nən\ *adj or n*

**Mont Blanc** \ˌmōⁿ-'bläⁿ\ mountain 15,771 ft. (4807 m.) SE France on Italian border; highest in the Alps

**Mon·te·go Bay** \män-'tē-(ˌ)gō\ city & port NW Jamaica on **Montego Bay** (inlet of the Caribbean); *pop* 110,115

**Mon·te·ne·gro** \ˌmän-tə-'nē-(ˌ)grō, -'nä-, -'ne-\ country S Europe on the Adriatic Sea; ✳, Podgorica; *pop* 620,029

**Mon·ter·rey** \ˌmän-tə-'rā\ city NE Mexico; *pop* 1,135,550

**Mon·te·vi·deo** \ˌmän-tə-və-'dā-(ˌ)ō, -'vi-dē-ˌō, ˌmón-tä-vē-'thä-ō\ city, ✳ of Uruguay; *pop* 1,312,000

**Mont·gom·ery** \(ˌ)mən(t)-'gə-mə-rē, män(t)-, -'gä-; -'gəm-rē, -'gäm-\ city, ✳ of Alabama; *pop* 205,764

**Mont·pe·lier** \mänt-'pēl-yər, -'pil-\ city, ✳ of Vermont; *pop* 7855

**Mon·tre·al** \ˌmän-trē-'òl, ˌmən-\ city S Quebec, Canada on **Montreal Island** in the Saint Lawrence; *pop* 1,649,519

**Mont·ser·rat** \ˌmän(t)-sə-'rat\ island British West Indies in the Leeward Islands; *pop* 4922

**Mo·ra·via** \mə-'rä-vē-ə\ region E Czech Republic — **Mo·ra·vi·an** \mə-'rä-vē-ən\ *adj or n*

**Mo·re·no Valley** \mə-'rē-(ˌ)nō\ city S California; *pop* 193,365

**Mo·roc·co** \mə-'rä-(ˌ)kō\ country NW Africa; ✳, Rabat; *pop* 31,900,000 — **Mo·roc·can** \-kən\ *adj or n*

**Mo·ro·ni** \mò-'rō-nē\ city, ✳ of Comoros; *pop* 41,500

**Mos·cow** \'mäs-(ˌ)kō, -ˌkaù\ *or Russian* **Mos·kva** \mäsk-'vä\ city, ✳ of Russia; *pop* 11,563,000

**Mo·selle** \mō-'zel\ river about 340 mi. (545 km.) long E France & W Germany

**Moyle** \'mòi(-ə)l\ district N Northern Ireland; *pop* 17,000

**Mo·zam·bique** \ˌmō-zəm-'bēk\ **1** channel SE Africa between Mozambique (country) & Madagascar **2** country SE Africa; ✳, Maputo; *pop* 20,252,000 — **Mo·zam·bi·can** \ˌmō-zəm-'bē-kən\ *adj or n*

**Mpu·ma·lan·ga** \əm-ˌpü-mä-'läŋ-gä\ province NE Republic of South Africa; *pop* 4,040,000

**Mukden** — see SHENYANG

**Mul·tan** \mùl-'tän\ city NE Pakistan SW of Lahore; *pop* 1,197,384

**Mumbai** — see BOMBAY

**Mu·nich** \'myü-nik\ *or German* **Mün-**

chen \'mœn-kən\ city S Germany in Bavaria; *pop* 1,348,335

Mun·ster \'mən(t)-stər\ province S Ireland; *pop* 1,246,000

Mur·cia \'mər-sh(ē-)ə\ region & ancient kingdom SE Spain

Mur·ray \'mər-ē, 'mə-rē\ river over 1560 mi. (2510 km.) long SE Australia flowing W from E Victoria into Indian Ocean in South Australia

Mur·rum·bidg·ee \,mər-əm-'bi-jē, ,mə-rəm-\ river almost 1000 mi. (1609 km.) long SE Australia in New South Wales flowing W into the Murray

Mus·cat \'məs-,kät, -,kat, -kət\ *or* Mas·qat \'məs-,kät\ town E Arabia; * of Oman *pop* 24, 893

Muz·tag \'müs-täg, məz-\ mountain 25,340 ft. (7724 m.) W China; highest in Kunlun Mountains

Myan·mar \'myän-,mär\ *or unofficially* Bur·ma \'bər-mə\ country SE Asia; *, Nay Pyi Taw; *pop* 51,419,000

My·ce·nae \mī-'sē-(,)nē\ ancient city S Greece in NE Peloponnese

Myr·tle Beach \'mər-t°l\ city E South Carolina on the Atlantic; *pop* 27,109

My·sore \mī-'sòr\ city S India; *pop* 991,000

Nab·a·taea *or* Nab·a·tea \,na-bə-'tē-ə\ ancient Arab kingdom SE of Palestine — Nab·a·tae·an *or* Nab·a·te·an \-'tē-ən\ *adj or n*

Na·go·ya \nə-'gòi-ə, 'nä-gò-(,)yä\ city Japan in S *cen* Honshu; *pop* 2,263,894

Nag·pur \'näg-,pùr\ city E *cen* India; *pop* 2,452,000

Nai·ro·bi \nī-'rō-bē\ city, * of Kenya; *pop* 3,133,518

Na·mib·ia \nə-'mi-bē-ə\ *formerly* South-West Africa country SW Africa on the Atlantic; *, Windhoek; *pop* 2,113,000 — Na·mib·ian \-bē-ən, -byən\ *adj or n*

Nan·chang \'nän-'chäŋ\ city SE China; *pop* 2,291,000

Nan·jing \'nän-'jiŋ\ *or* Nan·king \'nan-'kiŋ, 'nän-\ city E China; *pop* 6,496,000

Nan·tuck·et \nan-'tə-kət\ island SE Massachusetts S of Cape Cod; *pop* 7446

Na·per·ville \'nä-pər-,vil\ city NE Illinois W of Chicago; *pop* 141,853

Na·ples \'nā-pəlz\ *or Italian* Na·po·li \'nä-pō-lē\ *ancient* Ne·ap·o·lis \nē-'a-pə-ləs\ city S Italy on Bay of Naples; *pop* 962,003 — Ne·a·pol·i·tan \,nē-ə-'päl-ə-tən\ *adj or n*

Nar·ra·gan·sett Bay \,na-rə-'gan(t)-sət\ inlet of the Atlantic S Rhode Island

Nash·ville \'nash-,vil, -vəl\ city, * of Tennessee; *pop* 601,222

Nas·sau \'na-,sò\ city, * of Bahamas on New Providence Island; *pop* 246,329

Na·tal \nə-'tal, -'täl\ former province E Republic of South Africa

Na·u·ru \nä-'ü-(,)rü\ island W South Pacific; country; *, Yaren; *pop* 10,065 —
Na·u·ru·an \-'ü-rə-wən\ *adj or n*

Nay Pyi Taw *or* Nay·pyi·daw \'nē-pyē-,dò\ site of * of Myanmar

Naz·a·reth \'na-zə-rəth\ town of ancient Palestine in *cen* Galilee; now a city of N Israel; *pop* 72,000

N'Dja·me·na \an-jä-'mä-nä, -'mē-\ city, * of Chad; *pop* 951,000

Neagh, Lough \,läk-'nā\ lake Northern Ireland; largest in British Isles

Near East the countries of NE Africa & SW Asia — Near Eastern *adj*

Ne·bras·ka \nə-'bras-kə\ state *cen* U.S.; *, Lincoln; *pop* 1,826,341 — Ne·bras·kan \-kən\ *adj or n*

Neg·ev \'ne-,gev\ desert region S Israel

Ne·gro \'nā-(,)grō, 'ne-\ river 1400 mi. (2253 km.) long in E Colombia & N Brazil flowing into the Amazon

Ne·gros \'nā-(,)grōs, 'ne-\ island *cen* Philippines

Nei Monggol — see INNER MONGOLIA

Ne·pal \nə-'pól, nä-\ country Asia on NE border of India in the Himalayas; *, Kathmandu; *pop* 26,495,000 — Nep·a·lese \,ne-pə-'lēz, -'lēs\ *adj or n* — Ne·pali \nə-'pól-ē, -'päl-, -'pal-\ *adj or n*

Ness, Loch \'nes\ lake NW Scotland

Neth·er·lands \'ne-thər-ləndz\ 1 *or Dutch* Ne·der·land \'näd-ər-,länt\ *also* Holland country NW Europe on North Sea; *, Amsterdam; seat of the government, The Hague; *pop* 16,829,000 2 LOW COUNTRIES — an historical usage — Neth·er·land \'ne-thər-lənd\ *adj* — Neth·er·land·er \-,lan-dər, -lən-\ *n* — Neth·er·land·ish \-,lan-dish, -lən-\ *adj*

Netherlands Antilles islands of the West Indies, formerly an overseas territory of the Netherlands; *, Willemstad

Ne·va \'nē-və, 'nä-, nye-'vä\ river 40 mi. (64 km.) long W Russia; flows through Saint Petersburg

Ne·vada \nə-'va-də\ state W U.S.; *, Carson City; *pop* 2,700,551 — Ne·vad·an \-'va-d°n, -'vä-\ *or* Ne·vad·i·an \-'va-dē-ən, -'vä-\ *adj or n*

Ne·vis \'nē-vəs\ island West Indies in the Leeward Islands — see SAINT KITTS

New Amsterdam town founded 1625 on island of Manhattan by the Dutch; renamed New York 1664 by the British

New·ark \'nü-ərk, 'nyü-\ city NE New Jersey; *pop* 277,140

New Britain island W Pacific in Bismarck group; *pop* 263,500

New Bruns·wick \-'brənz-(,)wik\ province SE Canada; *, Fredericton; *pop* 751,171

New Caledonia island SW Pacific SW of Vanuatu; an overseas department of France; *, Nouméa; *pop* 245,600

New·cas·tle \'nü-,ka-səl, 'nyü-\ city SE Australia in E New South Wales; metropolitan area *pop* 308,308

**Newcastle** *or* **Newcastle upon Tyne** \'tīn\ city N England; *pop* 268,000

**New Delhi** city, ✳ of India S of Delhi; *pop* 294,783

**New England** section of NE U.S. consisting of states of Maine, New Hampshire, Vermont, Massachusetts, Rhode Island, & Connecticut — **New En·gland·er** \'in-glən-dər\ *n*

**New·found·land** \'nü-fən(d)-lənd, 'nyü-, -ˌlend; ˌnü-fən(d)-'land, ˌnyü-\ island Canada in the Atlantic — **New·found·land·er** \-lən-dər, -ˌlan-\ *n*

**Newfoundland and Labrador** province E Canada consisting of Newfoundland Island and Labrador; ✳, Saint John's; *pop* 514,536

**New France** the possessions of France in North America before 1763

**New Guinea 1** island W Pacific N of E Australia; divided between West Papua, Indonesia & independent Papua New Guinea **2** the NE portion of the island of New Guinea together with some nearby islands; now part of Papua New Guinea — **New Guinean** *adj or n*

**New·ham** \'nü-əm, 'nyü-\ borough of E Greater London, England; *pop* 308,000

**New Hamp·shire** \'hamp-shər, -ˌshir\ state NE U.S.; ✳, Concord; *pop* 1,316,470 — **New Hamp·shire·man** \-mən\ *n* — **New Hamp·shir·ite** \-ˌīt\ *n*

**New Ha·ven** \'hā-vən\ city S Connecticut; *pop* 129,779

**New Hebrides** — see VANUATU

**New Jersey** state E U.S.; ✳, Trenton; *pop* 8,791,894 — **New Jer·sey·an** \-ən\ *n* — **New Jer·sey·ite** \-ˌīt\ *n*

**New Mex·i·co** \'mek-si-ˌkō\ state SW U.S.; ✳, Santa Fe; *pop* 2,059,179 — **New Mex·i·can** \-si-kən\ *adj or n*

**New Neth·er·land** \'ne-thər-lənd\ former Dutch colony (1613–64) North America along Hudson & lower Delaware rivers

**New Or·leans** \'òr-lē-ənz, 'òr-lənz, 'òrlyənz, (ˌ)òr-'lēnz\ city SE Louisiana; *pop* 343,829

**New·port** \'nü-ˌpōrt, 'nyü-, -ˌpôrt\ **1** town S England in Isle of Wight; *pop* 25,000 **2** city SE Wales; *pop* 128,000

**Newport News** \'nü-ˌpòrt-'nüz, 'nyü-ˌpòrt-'nyüz, -pərt-\ city SE Virginia; *pop* 180,719

**New Providence** island NW *cen* Bahamas; chief town, Nassau; *pop* 247,500

**New·ry and Mourne** \'n(y)ü-rē-ən(d)-'mòrn\ district S Northern Ireland; *pop* 99,000

**New South Wales** state SE Australia; ✳, Sydney; *pop* 6,917,658

**New Spain** former Spanish possessions in North America, Central America, West Indies, & the Philippines

**New Sweden** former Swedish colony (1638–55) North America on W bank of Delaware River

**New·town·ab·bey** \ˌnü-t°n-'a-bē, ˌnyü-\ district E Northern Ireland; *pop* 85,000

**Newtown Saint Bos·wells** \ˌnü-ˌtaùnsənt-'bäz-wəlz, 'nyü-, -sänt-\ village S Scotland

**New World** the Western Hemisphere including North America and South America

**New York 1** state NE U.S.; ✳, Albany; *pop* 19,378,102 **2** *or* **New York City** city SE New York (state); *pop* 8,175,133 — **New York·er** \'yòr-kər\ *n*

**New York State Barge Canal** — see ERIE

**New Zea·land** \'zē-lənd\ country SW Pacific ESE of Australia; ✳, Wellington; *pop* 4,242,000 — **New Zea·land·er** \-lən-dər\ *n*

**Ni·ag·a·ra Falls** \(ˌ)nī-'a-g(ə-)rə\ falls New York & Ontario in **Niagara River** (flowing N from Lake Erie into Lake Ontario); divided by Goat Island into Horseshoe Falls, or Canadian Falls (158 ft. or 48 m. high) & American Falls (167 ft. or 51 m. high)

**Nia·mey** \nē-'ä-(ˌ)mā, nyä-'mā\ city, ✳ of Niger; *pop* 1,026,848

**Ni·caea** \nī-'sē-ə\ *or* **Nice** \'nīs\ ancient city W Bithynia; site at modern village in NW Turkey — **Ni·cae·an** \nī-'sē-ən\ *adj or n* — **Ni·cene** \'nī-ˌsēn, nī-'sēn\ *adj*

**Ni·ca·ra·gua** \ˌni-kə-'rä-gwə, ˌnē-kä-'rä-gwä\ **1** lake about 100 mi. (160 km.) long S Nicaragua **2** country Central America; ✳, Managua; *pop* 5,142,000 — **Ni·ca·ra·guan** \-'rä-gwən\ *adj or n*

**Nice** \'nēs\ city & port SE France on the Mediterranean; *pop* 343,304

**Nic·o·bar** \'ni-kə-ˌbär\ islands India in Bay of Bengal S of the Andamans; *pop* 14,563

**Nic·o·sia** \ˌni-kə-'sē-ə\ city, ✳ of Cyprus; *pop* 55,014

**Ni·ger** \'nī-jər, nē-'zher\ **1** river 2600 mi. (4184 km.) long W Africa flowing into Gulf of Guinea **2** country W Africa N of Nigeria; ✳, Niamey; *pop* 17,139,000 — **Ni·ger·ien** \ˌnī-ˌjir-ē-'en, nē-'zher-ē-ən\ *adj or n* — **Ni·ger·ois** \ˌnē-zhər-'wä, -zher-\ *n*

**Ni·ge·ria** \nī-'jir-ē-ə\ country W Africa on Gulf of Guinea; ✳, Abuja; *pop* 140,432,000 — **Ni·ge·ri·an** \-ē-ən\ *adj or n*

**Nii·hau** \'nē-ˌhaù\ island Hawaii WSW of Kauai

**Nile** \'nī(-ə)l\ river 4160 mi. (6693 km.) long E Africa flowing from Lake Victoria in Uganda N into the Mediterranean in Egypt

**Nil·gi·ri** \'nil-gə-rē\ hills S India

**Nin·e·veh** \'ni-nə-və\ ancient city, ✳ of Assyria; ruins in Iraq on the Tigris

**Nip·i·gon, Lake** \'ni-pə-ˌgän\ lake Canada in W Ontario N of Lake Superior

**Nizh·niy Nov·go·rod** \'nizh-nē-'näv-gə-

,räd, -ˈnȯv-gə-rət\ *formerly 1932–89* **Gor-ki** \ˈgȯr-kē\ city W Russia; *pop* 1,250,600

**Nord Ost·see** \ˈnȯrt-ˈȯst-ˈzā\ *or* **Kiel** \ˈkēl\ canal 61 mi. (98 km.) long N Germany across base of Jutland Peninsula connecting Baltic Sea & North Sea

**Nor·folk** \ˈnȯr-fək\ city & port SE Virginia; *pop* 242,803

**Nor·man·dy** \ˈnȯr-mən-dē\ region NW France NE of Brittany

**North 1** river estuary of the Hudson between NE New Jersey & SE New York **2** sea, arm of the Atlantic E of Great Britain **3** island N New Zealand; *pop* 3,237,048

**North·al·ler·ton** \nȯr-ˈtha-lər-tən\ town N England; *pop* 9556

**North America** continent of Western Hemisphere NW of South America & N of the Equator — **North American** *adj or n*

**North·amp·ton** \nȯr-ˈtham(p)-tən, nȯrth-ˈham(p)-\ town *cen* England; *pop* 215,000

**North·amp·ton·shire** \-ˌshir, -shər\ *or* **Northampton** county *cen* England

**North Cape** cape New Zealand at N end of North Island

**North Car·o·li·na** \ˌker(-ə)-ˈlī-nə, ˌka-rə-\ state E U.S.; ✳, Raleigh; *pop* 9,535,483 — **North Car·o·lin·i·an** \-ˈli-nē-ən, -ˈli-nyən\ *adj or n*

**North Da·ko·ta** \də-ˈkō-tə\ state N U.S.; ✳, Bismarck; *pop* 672,591 — **North Da·ko·tan** \-ˈkō-tᵊn\ *adj or n*

**North Down** district E Northern Ireland; *pop* 79,000

**Northern Cape** province W Republic of South Africa; *pop* 1,145,861

**Northern Cook** islands S *cen* Pacific N of Cook Islands

**Northern Hemisphere** the half of the earth that lies N of the Equator

**Northern Ireland** region N Ireland comprising 26 districts of Ulster; a division of United Kingdom; ✳, Belfast; *pop* 1,810,900

**Northern Mar·i·ana Islands** \ˌmer-ē-ˈa-nə\ islands W Pacific; commonwealth in association with U.S.; seat of the government on Saipan; *pop* 53,900

**Northern Rhodesia** — see ZAMBIA

**Northern Territory** territory N & *cen* Australia; ✳, Darwin; *pop* 211,945

**North Korea** *or* **Democratic People's Republic of Korea** country N half of Korean Peninsula in E Asia; ✳, Pyongyang; *pop* 24,700,000

**North Las Vegas** city SE Nevada; *pop* 216,061

**North Slope** region N Alaska between Brooks Range & Arctic Ocean

**North·um·ber·land** \nȯr-ˈthəm-bər-lənd\ county N England

**North·um·bria** \nȯr-ˈthəm-brē-ə\ ancient country Great Britain in what is now N England and S Scotland — **North·um·bri·an** \-brē-ən\ *adj or n*

**North Vietnam** — see VIETNAM

**North West** province N Republic of South Africa; *pop* 3,509,953

**Northwest Passage** sea passage between the Atlantic and the Pacific along the N coast of North America

**Northwest Territories** territory NW Canada consisting of the area of the mainland north of 60° between Yukon (territory) & Nunavut; ✳, Yellowknife; *pop* 41,462

**North York** former city Canada in SE Ontario; now part of Toronto

**North Yorkshire** county N England

**Nor·walk** \ˈnȯr-ˌwȯk\ city SW California SE of Los Angeles; *pop* 105,549

**Nor·way** \ˈnȯr-ˌwā\ country N Europe in Scandinavia; ✳, Oslo; *pop* 5,156,000

**Nor·wich** \ˈnȯr-(ˌ)wich\ city E England; *pop* 187,000

**Not·ting·ham** \ˈnä-tiŋ-əm\ city N *cen* England; *pop* 289,000

**Not·ting·ham·shire** \ˈnä-tiŋ-əm-ˌshir, -shər\ *or* **Nottingham** county N *cen* England; *pop* 692,000

**Nouak·chott** \nü-ˈäk-ˌshät\ city, ✳ of Mauritania; *pop* 958,399

**Nou·méa** \nü-ˈmā-ə\ city, ✳ of New Caledonia; *pop* 76,293

**No·va Sco·tia** \ˌnō-və-ˈskō-shə\ province SE Canada; ✳, Halifax; *pop* 921,727 — **No·va Sco·tian** \-shən\ *adj or n*

**No·vo·kuz·netsk** \ˌnō-(ˌ)vō-kůz-ˈnetsk, ˌnȯ-vō-kůz-ˈnyetsk\ city S Russia in Asia; *pop* 548,000

**No·vo·si·birsk** \ˌnō-(ˌ)vō-sə-ˈbirsk, ˌnȯ-və-\ city S Russia in Asia; *pop* 1,474,000

**Nu·bia** \ˈnü-bē-ə, ˈnyü-\ region NE Africa in Nile valley in S Egypt & N Sudan — **Nu·bi·an** \ˈnü-bē-ən, ˈnyü-\ *adj or n*

**Nu·ku·a·lo·fa** \ˌnü-kü-ä-ˈlō-fä\ seaport, ✳ of Tonga; *pop* 24,000

**Nu·mid·ia** \nü-ˈmi-dē-ə, nyü-\ ancient country N Africa E of Mauretania in modern Algeria — **Nu·mid·i·an** \-dē-ən\ *adj or n*

**Nu·na·vut** \ˈnü-nə-ˌvüt\ semiautonomous territory NE Canada; ✳, Iqaluit; *pop* 31,906

**Nu·rem·berg** \ˈnůr-əm-ˌbərg, ˈnyůr-\ *or German* **Nürn·berg** \ˈnůrn-ˌberk\ city S Germany; *pop* 486,314

**Nuuk** \ˈnük\ *or Danish* **Godt·håb** \ˈgȯt-ˌhȯp\ town, ✳ of Greenland on SW coast; *pop* 15,000

**Ny·asa, Lake** \nī-ˈas-ə, nē-\ lake SE Africa in Malawi, Mozambique, & Tanzania

**Nyasaland** — see MALAWI

**Oa·hu** \ō-ˈä-(ˌ)hü\ island Hawaii; site of Honolulu

**Oak·land** \ˈō-klənd\ city W California on San Francisco Bay E of San Francisco; *pop* 390,724

**Ob'** \'äb, 'ôb\ river over 2250 mi. (3620 km.) long W Russia in Asia flowing NW & N into Arctic Ocean

**Oce·a·nia** \ˌō-shē-'a-nē-ə, -'ä-\ lands of the *cen* & S Pacific: Micronesia, Melanesia, Polynesia including New Zealand, & by some thought to include Australia & Malay Archipelago

**Ocean·side** \'ō-shən-ˌsīd\ city SW California NNW of San Diego; *pop* 167,086

**Oder** \'ō-dər\ *or* **Odra** \'ō-drä\ river about 565 mi. (909 km.) long *cen* Europe flowing from Silesia NW into Baltic Sea; forms part of boundary between Poland & Germany

**Odes·sa** \ō-'de-sə\ city & port S Ukraine on Black Sea; *pop* 1,012,500

**Ohio** \ō-'hī-(ˌ)ō, ə-, -ə\ **1** river about 981 mi. (1578 km.) long E U.S. flowing from W Pennsylvania into the Mississippi **2** state E *cen* U.S.; *, Columbus; *pop* 11,536,504 — **Ohio·an** \-'hī-ō-ən\ *adj or n*

**Oka·ya·ma** \ˌō-kä-'yä-mä\ city Japan in W Honshu on Inland Sea; *pop* 709,584

**Okee·cho·bee, Lake** \ˌō-kə-'chō-bē\ lake S *cen* Florida

**Oke·fe·no·kee** \ˌō-kə-fə-'nō-kē, ˌō-kē-\ swamp SE Georgia & NE Florida

**Okhotsk, Sea of** \ō-'kätsk, ə-'kötsk\ inlet of the North Pacific E Russia in Asia

**Oki·na·wa** \ˌō-kə-'nä-wə, -'naù-ə\ **1** islands Japan in *cen* Ryukyus **2** island, chief of group — **Oki·na·wan** \-'nä-wən, -'naù-ən\ *adj or n*

**Okla·ho·ma** \ˌō-klə-'hō-mə\ state S *cen* U.S.; *, Oklahoma City; *pop* 3,751,351 — **Okla·ho·man** \-mən\ *adj or n*

**Oklahoma City** city, * of Oklahoma; *pop* 579,999

**Old·ham** \'ōl-dəm\ city NW England; *pop* 97,000

**Old Point Comfort** cape SE Virginia N of entrance to Hampton Roads

**Ol·du·vai Gorge** \'ōl-də-ˌvī\ canyon N Tanzania SE of Serengeti Plain; site of fossil beds

**Old World** the half of the earth to the E of the Atlantic Ocean including Europe, Asia, and Africa & esp. the continent of Europe

**Olym·pia** \ə-'lim-pē-ə, ō-\ **1** city, * of Washington; *pop* 46,478 **2** plain S Greece in NW Peloponnese

**Olym·pic** \-pik\ mountains NW Washington on Olympic Peninsula; highest Mt. Olympus 7965 ft. (2428 m.)

**Olym·pus** \ə-'lim-pəs, ō-\ mountains NE Greece

**Omagh** \'ō-mə, -(ˌ)mä\ **1** district W Northern Ireland; *pop* 51,000 **2** town in Omagh district; *pop* 19,000

**Oma·ha** \'ō-mə-ˌhö, -ˌhä\ **1** beach NW France in Normandy **2** city E Nebraska on Missouri River; *pop* 408,958

**Oman** \ō-'män, -'man\ country SW Asia in SE Arabia; *, Muscat; *pop* 2,773,479 — **Omani** \ō-'mä-nē, -'ma-\ *adj or n*

**Oman, Gulf of** arm of Arabian Sea between Oman & SE Iran

**Omsk** \'ōm(p)sk, 'äm(p)sk\ city SW Russia in Asia; *pop* 1,154,000

**On·tar·io** \än-'ter-ē-ˌō\ **1** city SW California; *pop* 163,924 **2** province E Canada; *, Toronto; *pop* 12,851,821 — **On·tar·i·an** \-ē-ən\ *adj or n*

**Ontario, Lake** lake E *cen* North America in U.S. & Canada; one of the Great Lakes

**Oran** \ō-'rän\ city & port NW Algeria; *pop* 803,329

**Or·ange** \'är-inj, 'är-(-ə)nj, 'ör-inj, 'ör-(-ə)nj\ **1** city SW California; *pop* 136,416 **2** river 1300 mi. (2092 km.) long S Africa flowing W from Drakensberg Mountains into the Atlantic

**Orange Free State** — see FREE STATE

**Or·e·gon** \'ör-i-gən, 'är-\ state NW U.S.; *, Salem; *pop* 3,831,074 — **Or·e·go·nian** \ˌör-i-'gō-nē-ən, ˌär-, -nyən\ *adj or n*

**Oregon Trail** pioneer route to the NW U.S. about 2000 mi. (3220 km.) long from Missouri to Washington

**Ori·no·co** \ˌör-ə-'nō-(ˌ)kō\ river 1336 mi. (2150 km.) long Venezuela flowing into the Atlantic

**Ork·ney** \'örk-nē\ islands N Scotland; *pop* 19,570

**Or·lan·do** \ör-'lan-(ˌ)dō\ city *cen* Florida; *pop* 238,300

**Osa·ka** \ō-'sä-kä, 'ō-sä-ˌkä\ city Japan in S Honshu; *pop* 2,665,314

**Osh·a·wa** \'ä-shə-wə, -ˌwä, -ˌwö\ city SE Ontario, Canada on Lake Ontario ENE of Toronto; *pop* 149,607

**Os·lo** \'äz-(ˌ)lō, 'äs-\ city, * of Norway; *pop* 636,000

**Oś·wię·cim** \ˌösh-'fyen-chēm\ *or German* **Ausch·witz** \'aùsh-ˌvits\ town S Poland W of Krakow; *pop* 45,282

**Ot·ta·wa** \'ä-tə-wə, -ˌwä, -ˌwö\ **1** river 696 mi. (1120 km.) E Canada in SE Ontario & S Quebec flowing E into the Saint Lawrence **2** city, * of Canada in SE Ontario on Ottawa River; *pop* 883,391

**Ot·to·man Empire** \'ä-tə-mən\ former Turkish sultanate in SE Europe, W Asia, & N Africa

**Oua·ga·dou·gou** \ˌwä-gä-'dü-(ˌ)gü\ city, * of Burkina Faso; *pop* 1,475,223

**Outer Hebrides** — see HEBRIDES

**Over·land Park** \'ō-vər-lənd\ city NE Kansas; *pop* 173,372

**Ox·ford** \'äks-fərd\ city *cen* England; *pop* 160,000

**Ox·ford·shire** \'äks-fərd-ˌshir, -shər\ *or* **Oxford** county *cen* England

**Ox·nard** \'äks-ˌnärd\ city SW California; *pop* 197,899

**Ozark Plateau** \'ō-ˌzärk\ *or* **Ozark Mountains** eroded plateau N Arkansas, S Missouri, & NE Oklahoma with E extension into S Illinois

**Pa·cif·ic** \pə-'si-fik\ ocean extending from Arctic Circle to the Equator (**North Pacific**) and from the Equator to the Antarctic regions (**South Pacific**) & from W North America & W South America to E Asia & Australia — **Pacific** adj

**Pacific Islands, Trust Territory of the** grouping of islands in W Pacific formerly under U.S. administration: the Carolines & the Marshalls

**Pacific Rim** the countries bordering on or located in the Pacific Ocean — used esp. of Asian countries on the Pacific

**Pa·dang** \'pä-,däŋ\ city Indonesia in W Sumatra; pop 834,000

**Pa·dre** \'pä-drē, -drā\ island 113 mi. (182 km.) long S Texas in Gulf of Mexico

**Pa·go Pa·go** \pä-(,)gō-'pä-(,)gō, ,päŋ-(,)ō-'päŋ-(,)ō\ town, * of American Samoa on Tutuila Island; pop 3656

**Painted Desert** region N cen Arizona

**Pak·i·stan** \'pa-ki-,stan, ,pä-ki-'stän\ country S Asia NW of India; *, Islamabad; pop 193,240,000 — see EAST PAKISTAN — **Pak·i·stani** \,pa-ki-'sta-nē, ,pä-ki-'stä-\ adj or n

**Pa·lau** \pə-'laú\ or **Be·lau** \bə-\ island group W Pacific in the W Carolines; country in association with U.S.; *, Melekeok; pop 17,501 — **Pa·lau·an** \pə-'laú-ən\ n

**Pa·la·wan** \pə-'lä-wən, -,wän\ island W Philippines between South China & Sulu seas; pop 528,287

**Pa·lem·bang** \,pä-ləm-'bäŋ\ city Indonesia in SE Sumatra; pop 1,455,000

**Pa·ler·mo** \pə-'lər-(,)mō, pä-'ler-\ city Italy, * of Sicily; pop 657,561

**Pal·es·tine** \'pa-lə-,stīn\ region SW Asia dating back to ancient times with unofficial, disputed, & fluctuating boundaries, but extending from E coast of Mediterranean Sea up to or beyond Jordan River — **Pal·es·tin·ian** \,pa-lə-'sti-nē-ən, -nyən\ adj or n

**Pa·li·kir** \,pä-lē-'kir\ town, * of Federated States of Micronesia on Pohnpei Island; pop 6227

**Pal·i·sades** \,pa-lə-'sādz\ line of high cliffs 15 mi. (24 km.) long on W bank of the Hudson in SE New York & NE New Jersey

**Palm·dale** \'päm-,dāl, 'pälm-\ city SW California NE of Los Angeles; pop 152,750

**Pa·mirs** \pə-'mirz\ elevated mountainous region cen Asia in E Tajikistan & on borders of China, India, Pakistan, & Afghanistan; many peaks over 20,000 ft. (6096 m.)

**Pam·li·co Sound** \'pam-li-,kō\ inlet of the North Atlantic E North Carolina between main part of the state & offshore islands

**Pam·pa** \'pam-pə\ city NW Texas; pop 17,994

**Pan·a·ma** \'pan-ə-,mä, -,mò; ,pan-ə-'mä, -'mò\ **1** country S Central America; pop 3,406,000 **2** or **Panama City** city, its * on the Pacific; pop 411,549 **3** canal 40 mi. (64 km.) long Panama connecting Atlantic & Pacific oceans — **Pan·a·ma·ni·an** \,pan-ə-'mä-nē-ən\ adj or n

**Panama, Isthmus of** formerly **Isthmus of Dar·i·en** \,der-ē-'en\ strip of land cen Panama connecting North America & South America

**Panama Canal Zone** — see CANAL ZONE

**Pa·nay** \pə-'nī\ island cen Philippines in the Visayas

**Pan·gaea** \pan-'jē-ə\ land area believed to have once connected the landmasses of the Southern Hemisphere with those of the Northern Hemisphere

**Pan·mun·jom** or **Pan·mun·jeom** \,pän-,mùn-'jòm\ village on North Korea–South Korea border

**Pao·t'ou** — see BAOTOU

**Pap·ua, Territory of** \'pa-pyù-wə, 'pä-pù-wə\ former British territory consisting of SE New Guinea & offshore islands; now part of Papua New Guinea

**Papua New Guinea** country SW Pacific; *, Port Moresby; pop 7,275,000

**Par·a·guay** \'pa-rə-,gwī, -,gwä\ **1** river 1584 mi. (2549 km.) long cen South America flowing from Brazil S into the Paraná in Paraguay **2** country cen South America; *, Asunción; pop 6,600,000 — **Par·a·guay·an** \,pa-rə-'gwī-ən, -'gwä-\ adj or n

**Par·a·mar·i·bo** \,pa-rə-'ma-rə-,bō\ city, * of Suriname; pop 240,924

**Pa·ra·ná** \,pär-ə-'nä\ river about 2500 mi. (4022 km.) long cen South America flowing S from Brazil into Argentina

**Pa·ri·cu·tin** \,pä-,rē-kü-'tēn\ volcano Mexico on site of a former village

**Par·is** \'pa-rəs\ city, * of France; pop 2,243,833 — **Pa·ri·sian** \pə-'ri-zhən, -'rē-\ adj or n

**Par·nas·sus** \pär-'na-səs\ mountain cen Greece

**Par·os** \'pär-,òs\ island Greece — **Par·i·an** \'par-ē-ən, 'per-\ adj

**Par·ra·mat·ta** \,pa-rə-'ma-tə\ city SE Australia in New South Wales; pop 166,858

**Par·thia** \'pär-thē-ə\ ancient country SW Asia in NE modern Iran — **Par·thi·an** \-thē-ən\ adj or n

**Pas·a·de·na** \,pa-sə-'dē-nə\ **1** city SW California E of Glendale; pop 137,122 **2** city SE Texas; pop 149,043

**Pat·a·go·nia** \,pa-tə-'gō-nyə, -nē-ə\ region South America S of about 40° S latitude in S Argentina & S tip of Chile; sometimes thought to include Tierra del Fuego — **Pat·a·go·nian** \-nyən, -nē-ən\ adj or n

**Pat·er·son** \\'pa-tər-sən\\ city NE New Jersey; *pop* 146,199

**Pat·mos** \\'pat-məs\\ island Greece SSW of Samos

**Pat·na** \\'pət-nə\\ city NE India on the Ganges; *pop* 1,866,500

**Pearl Harbor** inlet Hawaii on S coast of Oahu W of Honolulu

**Peking** — see BEIJING

**Pe·li·on** \\'pē-lē-ən\\ mountain 5089 ft. (1551 m.) NE Greece

**Pel·o·pon·nese** \\'pe-lə-pə-,nēz, -,nēs\ *or* **Pel·o·pon·ni·sos** \,pe-lə-pə-'nē-səs\ peninsula forming S part of mainland of Greece

**Pem·broke Pines** \\'pem-,brōk\\ city SE Florida; *pop* 154,750

**Pen·nine Chain** \\'pe-,nīn\\ mountains N England; highest Cross Fell 2930 ft. (893 m.)

**Penn·syl·va·nia** \,pen(t)-səl-'vā-nyə, -nē-ə\ state E U.S.; ✳, Harrisburg; *pop* 12,702,379

**Pe·o·ria** \pē-'ȯr-ē-ə\ **1** town SW central Arizona; *pop* 154,065 **2** city N *cen* Illinois; *pop* 115,007

**Per·ga·mum** \\'pər-gə-məm\ *or* **Per·ga·mus** \-məs\ ancient Greek kingdom including most of Asia Minor

**Perm** \\'pərm, 'perm\\ city E Russia in Europe; *pop* 991,300

**Pernambuco** — see RECIFE

**Persia** — see IRAN

**Per·sian Gulf** \\'pər-zhən\\ arm of Arabian Sea between Iran & Arabia

**Perth** \\'pərth\\ city, ✳ of Western Australia; area *pop* 1,728,867

**Pe·ru** \pə-'rü, pā-\ country W South America; ✳, Lima; *pop* 27,412,000 — **Pe·ru·vi·an** \-'rü-vē-ən\ *adj or n*

**Pe·tra** \\'pē-trə, 'pe-\\ ancient city NW Arabia; site in SW Jordan

**Petrograd** — see SAINT PETERSBURG

**Phil·a·del·phia** \,fi-lə-'del-fyə, -fē-ə\ city SE Pennsylvania; *pop* 1,526,006 — **Phil·a·del·phian** \-fyən, -fē-ən\ *adj or n*

**Phil·ip·pines** \,fi-lə-'pēnz, 'fi-lə-,pēnz\ island group approximately 500 mi. (805 km.) off SE coast of Asia; country; ✳, Manila; *pop* 92,338,000 — **Phil·ip·pine** \,fi-lə-'pēn, 'fi-lə-,\ *adj*

**Phnom Penh** \(pə-)'näm-'pen, (pə-)'nöm-\ city, ✳ of Cambodia; *pop* 1,200,000

**Phoe·ni·cia** \fi-'ni-sh(ē-)ə, -'nē-\ ancient country SW Asia on the Mediterranean in modern Syria & Lebanon

**Phoe·nix** \\'fē-niks\\ city, ✳ of Arizona; *pop* 1,445,632

**Phry·gia** \\'fri-j(ē-)ə\\ ancient country W *cen* Asia Minor

**Pic·ar·dy** \\'pi-kər-dē\ *or F* **Pi·car·die** \pē-kär-'dē\ region & former province N France bordering on English Channel N of Normandy — **Pi·card** \\'pi-,kärd, -kərd\ *adj or n*

**Pied·mont** \\'pēd-,mänt\\ plateau region E

U.S. E of the Appalachians between SE New York & NE Alabama

**Pierre** \\'pir\\ city, ✳ of South Dakota; *pop* 13,646

**Pie·ter·mar·itz·burg** \,pē-tər-'ma-rəts-,bərg\ city E Republic of South Africa; *pop* 475,000

**Pigs, Bay of** \\'pigz\ *or* **Ba·hía de Co·chi·nos** \bä-'ē-ä-thä-kō-'chē-nōs\ bay W Cuba on S coast

**Pikes Peak** \\'piks\\ mountain 14,110 ft. (4301 m.) E *cen* Colorado in a range of the Rockies

**Pin·dus** \\'pin-dəs\\ mountains W Greece; highest point 8136 ft. (2480 m.)

**Pi·sa** \\'pē-zə, *It* -sä\\ city W *cen* Italy W of Florence; *pop* 85,900

**Pit·cairn** \\'pit-,kern\\ island South Pacific; a British colony; *pop* 62

**Pitts·burgh** \\'pits-,bərg\\ city SW Pennsylvania; *pop* 305,704

**Plac·id, Lake** \\'pla-səd\\ lake NE New York

**Pla·no** \\'plā-(,)nō\\ city NE Texas N of Dallas; *pop* 259,841

**Plov·div** \\'plȯv-,dif, -,div\\ city S Bulgaria; *pop* 335,000

**Plym·outh** \\'pli-məth\\ **1** town SE Massachusetts; *pop* 56,468 **2** city & port SW England; *pop* 235,000

**Po** \\'pō\\ river 405 mi. (652 km.) N Italy flowing into the Adriatic

**Pod·go·ri·ca** \\'pȯd-,gȯr-ēt-sä\\ city ✳ of Montenegro; *pop* 150,977

**Po Hai** — see BO HAI

**Pohn·pei** \\'pōn-,pā\\ island W Pacific in the E Carolines; part of Federated States of Micronesia

**Po·land** \\'pō-lənd\\ country *cen* Europe on Baltic Sea; ✳, Warsaw; *pop* 38,512,000 — **Pole** \\'pōl\\ *n*

**Pol·y·ne·sia** \,pä-lə-'nē-zhə, -shə\ islands of the *cen* & S Pacific including Hawaii, the Line, Tonga, Cook, & Samoa islands, & often New Zealand among others

**Pom·er·a·nia** \,pä-mə-'rā-nē-ə, -nyə\ region N Europe on Baltic Sea; formerly in Germany, now mostly in Poland

**Po·mo·na** \pə-'mō-nə\ city SW California E of Los Angeles; *pop* 149,058

**Pom·peii** \päm-'pā, -'pā,ē\ ancient city S Italy SE of Naples destroyed 79 A.D. by eruption of Vesuvius — **Pom·pe·ian** \-'pā-ən\ *adj or n*

**Pon·ce** \\'pȯn(t)-(,)sä\\ city S Puerto Rico; *pop* 166,327

**Pon·do·land** \\'pän-(,)dō-,land\\ region S Republic of South Africa

**Pon·ta Del·ga·da** \,pȯn-tə-del-'gä-də\ city & port Portugal, largest in the Azores; *pop* 41,000

**Pont·char·train, Lake** \\'pänt-shər-,trān, ,pänt-shər-'\\ lake SE Louisiana E of the Mississippi & N of New Orleans

**Pon·tus** \\'pän-təs\\ ancient country NE Asia Minor — **Pon·tic** \\'pänt-ik\\ *adj or n*

**Poole** \\'pül\ town S England on English Channel; *pop* 155,000

**Po·po·ca·te·petl** \\,pō-pə-'ka-tə-,pe-t''l, -,ka-tə-'\ volcano 17,887 ft. (5452 m.) SE *cen* Mexico

**Port Arthur** — see LÜSHUN

**Port—au—Prince** \\,pòrt-ō-'prin(t)s, ,pòr-(t)ō-'pra°s\ city, * of Haiti; *pop* 875,978

**Port Jack·son** \\'jak-sən\ inlet of South Pacific SE Australia in New South Wales; harbor of Sydney

**Port·land** \\'pòrt-lənd\ 1 city SW Maine; largest in state; *pop* 66,194 2 city NW Oregon; *pop* 583,776

**Port Lou·is** \\'lü-əs, 'lü-ē\ city, * of Mauritius; *pop* 146,876

**Port Mores·by** \\'mòrz-bē\ city, * of Papua New Guinea; *pop* 341,000

**Por·to** \\'pòr-(,)tü\ city & port NW Portugal; *pop* 327,368

**Por·to Ale·gre** \\'pòr-(,)tü-ä-'lä-grē\ city & port S Brazil; *pop* 1,409,351

**Port of Spain** city NW Trinidad, * of Trinidad and Tobago; *pop* 37,074

**Por·to-No·vo** \\,pòr-to-'no-(,)vo\ city, * of Benin; *pop* 263,600

**Port Phil·lip Bay** \\'fi-ləp\ inlet of South Pacific SE Australia in Victoria; harbor of Melbourne

**Port Said** \\sä-'ēd, 'sīd\ city & port NE Egypt on the Mediterranean at N end of the Suez Canal; *pop* 571,000

**Ports·mouth** \\'pòrts-məth\ 1 city SE Virginia; *pop* 95,535 2 city S England; *pop* 238,000

**Por·tu·gal** \\'pòr-chi-gəl, ,pür-tü-'gäl\ country SW Europe; *, Lisbon; *pop* 10,562,178

**Portuguese India** former Portuguese possession on W coast of India; became part of India 1962

**Port—Vi·la** \\'vē-lə\ or **Vila** city, * of Vanuatu; *pop* 44,040

**Po·to·mac** \\pə-'tō-mək, -mik\ river 287 mi. (462 km.) long flowing from West Virginia into Chesapeake Bay and forming boundary between Maryland & Virginia

**Pough·keep·sie** \\pə-'kip-sē, pō-\ city & river port SE New York on the Hudson; *pop* 32,736

**Po·wys** \\'pō-əs\ administrative subdivision E *cen* Wales; *pop* 132,976

**Prague** \\'präg\ or Czech **Pra·ha** \\'prä-(,)hä\ city, * of Czech Republic; *pop* 1,169,106

**Praia** \\'prī-ə\ town, * of Cape Verde; *pop* 132,000

**Prairie Provinces** the Canadian provinces of Alberta, Manitoba, & Saskatchewan

**Pres·ton** \\'pres-tən\ town NW England; *pop* 98,000

**Pre·to·ria** \\pri-'tòr-ē-ə\ city Republic of South Africa in the municipality of Tshwa-

ne, administrative * of the country; *pop* 742,000

**Prib·i·lof** \\'pri-bə-,lòf\ islands Alaska in Bering Sea

**Prince Ed·ward Island** \\'ed-wərd\ island SE Canada in Gulf of Saint Lawrence; a province; *, Charlottetown; *pop* 140,204

**Prince Ru·pert's Land** \\'rü-pərts\ historical region N & W Canada consisting of drainage basin of Hudson Bay

**Prince·ton** \\'prin(t)-stən\ borough W *cen* New Jersey; *pop* 12,307

**Prín·ci·pe** \\'prin(t)-si-pē\ island W Africa in Gulf of Guinea; *pop* 7450 — see SÃO TOMÉ AND PRÍNCIPE

**Pro·vence** \\prə-'vän(t)s, prō-'vä''s\ region SE France on the Mediterranean

**Prov·i·dence** \\'prä-və-dən(t)s, -,den(t)s\ city, * of Rhode Island; *pop* 178,042

**Pro·vo** \\'prō-(,)vō\ city N *cen* Utah; *pop* 112,488

**Prud·hoe Bay** \\'prü-(,)dō, 'prə-\ inlet of Beaufort Sea N Alaska

**Prus·sia** \\'prə-shə\ former kingdom, & later, state Germany — **Prus·sian** \\'prə-shən\ *adj or n*

**Pueb·lo** \\'pwe-,blō\ city SE *cen* Colorado SSE of Colorado Springs; *pop* 106,595

**Puer·to Ri·co** \\,pòr-tə-'rē-(,)kō, ,pwer-tō-\ island West Indies E of Hispaniola; a self-governing commonwealth associated with U.S.; *, San Juan; *pop* 3,725,789 — **Puer·to Ri·can** \\'rē-kən\ *adj or n*

**Pu·get Sound** \\'pyü-jət\ arm of the North Pacific W Washington

**Pu·ne** \\'pü-nə\ city W India, ESE of Bombay; *pop* 5,057,709

**Pun·jab** \\pən-'jäb, -'jab, 'pən-,\ region in Pakistan & NW India in valley of the Indus

**Pu·san** \\'pü-,sän, 'bü-\ or **Bu·san** \\'bü-\ city SE South Korea; *pop* 3,403,000

**Pyong·yang** or **Pyeong·yang** \\'pyòn-'yaṅ, 'pyəṅ-, -'yäṅ\ city, * of North Korea; *pop* 2,581,076

**Pyr·e·nees** \\'pir-ə-,nēz\ mountains on French–Spanish border extending from Bay of Biscay to the Mediterranean

**Qaraghandy** — see KARAGANDA

**Qa·tar** \\'kä-tər, 'gä-, 'gə-; kə-'tär\ country E Arabia on peninsula extending into Persian Gulf; *, Doha; *pop* 1,699,000 — **Qa·tari** \\kə-'tär-ē, gə-\ *adj or n*

**Qing·dao** \\'chiŋ-'daů\ or **Tsing·tao** \\'chiŋ-'daů, '(t)siŋ-'daů\ city & port E China; *pop* 3,719,000

**Qi·qi·har** \\'chē-'chē-'här\ or **Ch'i·ch'i·ha·erh** \\'chē-'chē-'hä-'ər\ city NE China; *pop* 1,315,000

**Que·bec** \\kwi-'bek, ki-\ or *French* **Qué·bec** \\kā-'bek\ 1 province E Canada; *pop* 7,903,001 2 city, its *, on the Saint Lawrence; *pop* 516,622

**Queens** \\'kwēnz\ borough of New York City on Long Island E of Brooklyn; *pop* 2,230,722

**Queens·land** \'kwēnz-ˌland, -lənd\ state NE Australia; \*, Brisbane; *pop* 4,332,739 — **Queens·land·er** \-ˌlan-dər, -ˌlən-\ *n*

**Que·zon City** \'kā-ˌsòn\ city Philippines in Luzon; formerly \* of the country; *pop* 2,761,720

**Qui·to** \'kē-(ˌ)tō\ city, \* of Ecuador; *pop* 1,607,734

**Ra·bat** \rə-'bät\ city, \* of Morocco; *pop* 621,480

**Rai·nier, Mount** \rə-'nir, rā-\ mountain 14,410 ft. (4392 m.) W *cen* Washington; highest in Cascade Range

**Raj·pu·ta·na** \ˌräj-pə-'tä-nə\ *or* **Ra·ja·sthan** \'räj-ə-ˌstän\ region NW India S of Punjab

**Ra·leigh** \'rò-lē, 'rä-lē\ city, \* of North Carolina; *pop* 403,892

**Ran·cho Cu·ca·mon·ga** \'ran-(ˌ)chō-ˌkü-kə-'məŋ-gə, ˌrän-, -'mäŋ-\ city SW California; *pop* 165,269

**Rand·wick** \'ran-(ˌ)dwik\ municipality SE Australia in E New South Wales; *pop* 128,989

**Rangoon** — see YANGON

**Ra·wal·pin·di** \ˌrä-wəl-'pin-dē, ˌraùl-, ˌròl-\ city NE Pakistan NNW of Lahore; *pop* 1,409,768

**Read·ing** \'re-diŋ\ town S England; *pop* 219,000

**Re·ci·fe** \ri-'sē-fē\ *formerly* **Per·nam·bu·co** \ˌpər-nəm-'bü-(ˌ)kō, -'byü-\ city NE Brazil; *pop* 1,537,704

**Red** \'red\ **1** river 1018 mi. (1638 km.) long flowing E on Oklahoma–Texas boundary and into the Atchafalaya & the Mississippi in Louisiana **2** sea between Arabia & NE Africa

**Red·bridge** \'red-(ˌ)brij\ borough of NE Greater London, England; *pop* 279,000

**Re·gi·na** \ri-'jī-nə\ city, \* of Saskatchewan, Canada; *pop* 193,100

**Re·no** \'rē-(ˌ)nō\ city NW Nevada; *pop* 225,221

**Republic of the Congo** — see CONGO 3

**Ré·union** \rē-'yü-nyən, ˌrā-ʉ-'nyōⁿ\ island W Indian Ocean; an overseas division of France; \*, Saint-Denis; *pop* 834,000

**Reyk·ja·vik** \'rā-kyə-ˌvik, -ˌvēk\ city, \* of Iceland; *pop* 117,976

**Rhine** \'rīn\ river 820 mi. (1320 km.) long W Europe flowing from SE Switzerland to North Sea in the Netherlands — **Rhen·ish** \'re-nish, 'rē-\ *adj*

**Rhine·land** \'rīn-ˌland, -lənd\ *or German* **Rhein·land** \'rīn-ˌlänt\ the part of Germany W of the Rhine — **Rhine·land·er** \'rīn-ˌlan-dər, -lən-\ *n*

**Rhode Is·land** \ˌrōd-'ī-lənd\ **1** *or officially* **Rhode Island and Providence Plantations** state NE U.S.; \*, Providence; *pop* 1,052,567 **2** — see AQUIDNECK — **Rhode Is·land·er** \-lən-dər\ *n*

**Rhodes** \'rōdz\ island Greece in the SE Aegean

**Rho·de·sia** \rō-'dē-zh(ē-)ə\ — see ZIMBABWE — **Rho·de·sian** \-zh(ē-)ən\ *adj or n*

**Rhone** *or French* **Rhône** \'rōn\ river 505 mi. (813 km.) long Switzerland & SE France

**Rich·mond** \'rich-mənd\ **1** — see STATEN ISLAND **2** city, \* of Virginia; *pop* 204,214

**Richmond upon Thames** borough of SW Greater London, England; *pop* 187,000

**Ri·ga** \'rē-gə\ city, \* of Latvia; *pop* 658,640

**Rio de Ja·nei·ro** \'rē-(ˌ)ō-dā-zhə-'ner-(ˌ)ō, -dē-\ city SE Brazil on Guanabara Bay; *pop* 6,320,446

**Rio Grande** \ˌrē-(ˌ)ō-'grand, -'gran-dē\ *or Mexican* **Rio Bra·vo** \ˌrē-(ˌ)ō-'brä-(ˌ)vō\ river 1885 mi. (3034 km.) long SW U.S., forming part of U.S.–Mexico boundary, and flowing into Gulf of Mexico

**Río Muni** — see MBINI

**Riv·er·side** \'ri-vər-ˌsīd\ city S California; *pop* 303,871

**Riv·i·era** \ˌri-vē-'er-ə\ coast region SE France & NW Italy

**Ri·yadh** \rē-'yäd\ city, \* of Saudi Arabia; *pop* 4,700,000

**Ro·a·noke** \'rō-(ə-)ˌnōk\ city W Virginia; *pop* 97,032

**Roanoke Island** island North Carolina S of entrance to Albemarle Sound

**Rob·son, Mount** \'räb-sən\ mountain 12,972 ft. (3954 m.) W Canada in E British Columbia; highest in the Canadian Rockies

**Roch·es·ter** \'rä-chəs-tər, -ˌches-tər\ city N New York; *pop* 210,565

**Rock·ford** \'räk-fərd\ city N Illinois; *pop* 152,871

**Rocky Mountains** *or* **Rock·ies** \'rä-kēz\ mountains W North America extending SE from N Alaska to *cen* New Mexico

**Roman Empire** the empire of ancient Rome

**Ro·ma·nia** \rù-'mā-nē-ə, rō-, -nyə\ *or* **Ru·ma·nia** \rù-\ country SE Europe on Black Sea; \*, Bucharest; *pop* 20,122,000

**Rom·blon** \räm-'blōn\ island group *cen* Philippines

**Rome** \'rōm\ *or Italian* **Ro·ma** \'rō-mä\ city, \* of Italy; *pop* 2,617,175

**Ro·sa·rio** \rō-'zär-ē-ˌō, -'sär-\ city E *cen* Argentina on the Paraná; *pop* 1,236,000

**Ro·seau** \rō-'zō\ seaport, \* of Dominica; *pop* 14,725

**Ros·tov–on–Don** \rə-'stóf-ˌän-'dän, -'stóv, -ˌòn-\ city S Russia in Europe; *pop* 1,090,000

**Ros·well** \'räz-ˌwel, -wəl\ city SE New Mexico; *pop* 48,366

**Ro·ta** \'rō-tə\ island W Pacific in the Marianas

**Rot·ter·dam** \'rä-tər-ˌdam, -ˌdäm\ city & port SW Netherlands; *pop* 618,357

**Ru·an·da–Urun·di** \rü-ˌän-dä-ü-'rün-dē\

former trust territory E *cen* Africa bordering on Lake Tanganyika; now divided into Burundi & Rwanda

**Rudolf, Lake** — see TURKANA, LAKE

**Ruhr** \'rür\ **1** river 146 mi. (235 km.) long W Germany flowing NW & W to the Rhine **2** industrial district W Germany E of the Rhine in valley of Ruhr River

**Rumania** — see ROMANIA

**Rupert's Land** PRINCE RUPERT'S LAND

**Rush·more, Mount** \'rəsh-,mȯr\ mountain 5600 ft. (1707 m.) W South Dakota in Black Hills

**Rus·sia** \'rə-shə\ **1** former empire largely having the same boundaries as U.S.S.R. **2** UNION OF SOVIET SOCIALIST REPUBLICS **3** country E Europe & N Asia; *, Moscow; *pop* 143,300,000

**Ru·the·nia** \rü-'thē-nyə, -nē-ə\ region W Ukraine W of the N Carpathians — **Ru·the·nian** \-'thē-nyən, -nē-ən\ *adj or n*

**Ru·wen·zo·ri** \,rü-ən-'zȯr-ē\ mountain group E *cen* Africa between Uganda & Democratic Republic of the Congo; highest Mount Margherita 16,763 ft. (5109 m.)

**Rwan·da** *formerly* **Ru·an·da** \rü-'än-də\ country E *cen* Africa; *, Kigali; *pop* 10,516,000 — **Rwan·dan** \-dən\ *adj or n*

**Ryu·kyu** \rē-'yü-(,)kyü, -(,)kü\ islands Japan extending in an arc from S Japan, to N tip of Taiwan; *pop* 1,222,458 — **Ryu·kyu·an** \-,kyü-ən, -,kü-\ *adj or n*

**Saar** \'sär, 'zär\ **1** river about 150 mi. (241 km.) long Europe flowing from E France to W Germany **2** *or* **Saar·land** \'sär-,land, 'zär-\ region W Europe in valley of Saar River between France & Germany

**Sac·ra·men·to** \,sa-krə-'men-(,)tō\ **1** river 382 mi. (615 km.) long N California flowing S into Suisun Bay **2** city, * of California; *pop* 466,488

**Sag·ue·nay** \'sa-gə-,nā, ,sa-gə-'\ **1** river 105 mi. (169 km.) long Canada in S Quebec flowing E into the Saint Lawrence **2** city Canada in S Quebec; *pop* 144,746

**Sa·ha·ra** \sə-'her-ə, -'här-\ desert region N Africa extending from Atlantic coast to Red Sea — **Sa·ha·ran** \-ən\ *adj*

**Sa·hel** \'sa-hil, sə-'hil\ the S fringe of the Sahara

**Saigon** — see HO CHI MINH CITY

**Saint Al·bans** \'ȯl-bənz\ city SE England; *pop* 82,000

**Saint Cath·a·rines** \'ka-th(ə-)rənz\ city Canada in SE Ontario; *pop* 131,400

**Saint Christopher** — see SAINT KITTS

**Saint Clair, Lake** \'kler\ lake SE Michigan & SE Ontario connected by **Saint Clair River** (40 mi. or 64 km. long) with Lake Huron & draining by Detroit River into Lake Erie

**Saint Croix** \sänt-'krȯi, sənt-\ **1** river 129 mi. (208 km.) long Canada & U.S. on border between New Brunswick & Maine **2** island West Indies; largest of Virgin Islands of the U.S.; *pop* 50,601

**Saint Eli·as, Mount** \i-'lī-əs\ mountain 18,008 ft. (5489 m.) on Alaska–Canada boundary in **Saint Elias Range**

**Saint George's** \'jȯr-jəz\ town, * of Grenada; *pop* 4000

**Saint George's Channel** channel British Isles between SW Wales & Ireland

**Saint Gott·hard** \sänt-'gä-tərd, sənt-, 'gät-hərd\ pass S *cen* Switzerland in Saint Gotthard Range of the Alps

**Saint He·le·na** \,sänt-ə-'lē-nə, ,sänt-hə-'lē-\ island South Atlantic; a British colony; *pop* 4100

**Saint Hel·ens, Mount** \sänt-'he-lənz, sənt-\ volcano S Washington

**Saint John** \sänt-'jän, sənt-\ city & port Canada in New Brunswick; *pop* 70,063

**Saint John's** \sänt-'jänz, sənt-\ **1** city, * of Antigua and Barbuda; *pop* 23,000 **2** city, * of Newfoundland and Labrador, Canada; *pop* 106,172

**Saint Kitts** \'kits\ *or* **Saint Chris·to·pher** \'kris-tə-fər\ island West Indies in the Leeward Islands; with Nevis forms independent **Saint Kitts and Nevis**; *, Basseterre (on Saint Kitts); *pop* 51,000

**Saint Law·rence** \sänt-'lȯr-ən(t)s, sənt-, -'lär-\ **1** river 760 mi. (1223 km.) long E Canada in Ontario & Quebec bordering on U.S. in New York and flowing from Lake Ontario NE into the **Gulf of Saint Lawrence** (inlet of the Atlantic) **2** seaway Canada & U.S. in and along the Saint Lawrence between Lake Ontario & Montreal

**Saint Lou·is** \sänt-'lü-əs, sənt-\ city E Missouri on the Mississippi; *pop* 319,294

**Saint Lu·cia** \sänt-'lü-shə, sənt-\ island West Indies in the Windwards S of Martinique; country; *, Castries; *pop* 166,500

**Saint Mo·ritz** \sänt-mə-'rits, ,sän-mə-\ *or* **G Sankt Mo·ritz** \zäŋkt-mə-'rits\ town E Switzerland; *pop* 5900

**Saint Paul** \'pȯl\ city, * of Minnesota; *pop* 285,068

**Saint Pe·ters·burg** \'pē-tərz-,bərg\ **1** city W Florida; *pop* 244,769 **2** *or* *1914–24* **Pet·ro·grad** \'pe-trə-,grad, -,grät\ *or* *1924–91* **Le·nin·grad** \'le-nən-,grad, -,grät\ city W Russia in Europe; *pop* 4,864,500

**Saint Thom·as** \'tä-məs\ island West Indies, one of Virgin Islands of the U.S.; chief town, Charlotte Amalie

**Saint Vin·cent** \sänt-'vin(t)-sənt, sənt-\ island West Indies in the *cen* Windward Islands; with N Grenadines forms independent **Saint Vincent and the Grenadines**; *, Kingstown (on Saint Vincent); *pop* 110,000

**Sai·pan** \sī-'pan, -'pän, 'sī-,\ island W Pacific in S *cen* Marianas; *pop* 48,220

**Sa·kai** \(,)sä-'kī\ city Japan in S Honshu; *pop* 841,966

**Sa·kha·lin** \'sä-kə-ˌlēn, -lən; ˌsä-kä-'lēn\ island SE Russia in W Pacific N of Hokkaido, Japan

**Sal·a·mis** \'sa-lə-məs\ ancient city Cyprus on E coast

**Sa·lem** \'sā-ləm\ city, ✲ of Oregon; *pop* 154,637

**Sa·li·nas** \sə-'lē-nəs\ city W California; *pop* 150,441

**Salisbury** — see HARARE

**Salisbury Plain** plateau S England; site of Stonehenge

**Salop** — see SHROPSHIRE

**Salt Lake City** city, ✲ of Utah; *pop* 186,440

**Sal·ton Sea** \'sȯl-tⁿn\ saline lake about 235 ft. (72 m.) below sea level SE California; formed by diversion of water from Colorado River

**Sal·va·dor** \ˌsal-və-ˌdȯr, ˌsal-və-'\ *or* **Bahia** \bä-'ē-ə\ city NE Brazil on the Atlantic; *pop* 2,675,656 — **Sal·va·dor·an** \ˌsal-və-'dȯr-ən\ *or* **Sal·va·dor·ean** *or* **Sal·va·dor·ian** \-ē-ən\ *adj or n*

**Sal·ween** \sal-'wēn\ river about 1500 mi. (2415 km.) long SE Asia flowing from Tibet S into Bay of Bengal in Myanmar

**Sa·mar** \'sä-ˌmär\ island *cen* Philippines

**Sa·ma·ra** \sə-'mär-ə\ *or 1935–91* **Kuy·by·shev** \'kwē-bə-ˌshef, 'kü-ē-bə-, -ˌshev\ city W Russia, on the Volga; *pop* 1,165,000

**Sa·mar·ia** \sə-'mer-ē-ə\ district of ancient Palestine W of the Jordan between Galilee & Judaea

**Sam·ar·qand** *or* **Sam·ar·kand** \'sa-mərˌkand\ city E Uzbekistan; *pop* 370,500

**Sam·ni·um** \'sam-nē-əm\ ancient country S *cen* Italy — **Sam·nite** \'sam-ˌnīt\ *adj or n*

**Sa·moa** \sə-'mō-ə\ **1** islands SW *cen* Pacific N of Tonga; divided at longitude 171° W into American Samoa (or Eastern Samoa) & independent Samoa **2** *formerly* **Western Samoa** islands Samoa W of 171° W; country; ✲ Apia; *pop* 187,800 — **Sa·mo·an** \sə-'mō-ən\ *adj or n*

**Sa·mos** \'sā-ˌmäs, 'sä-ˌmös\ island Greece in the Aegean off coast of Turkey

**San·aa** *or* **Sana** \sa-'nä, 'sa-ˌnä\ city SW Arabia, ✲ of Yemen; *pop* 1,700,000

**San An·dre·as Fault** \ˌsan-an-'drā-əs\ zone of faults in California extending from N coast toward head of Gulf of California

**San An·to·nio** \ˌsan-ən-'tō-nē-ˌō\ city S Texas; *pop* 1,327,407

**San Ber·nar·di·no** \ˌsan-ˌbər-nə(r)-'dē-(ˌ)nō\ city S California; *pop* 209,924

**San Di·ego** \ˌsan-dē-'ā-(ˌ)gō\ coastal city SW California; *pop* 1,307,402

**San·i·bel Island** \'sa-nə-bəl, -ˌbel\ island SW Florida

**Sand·wich** \'san(d)-(ˌ)wich\ town SE England; *pop* 4227

**Sandwich Islands** — see HAWAII

**San Fran·cis·co** \ˌsan-frən-'sis-(ˌ)kō\ city W California on San Francisco Bay & Pacific Ocean; *pop* 805,235

**San Joa·quin** \ˌsan-wä-'kēn, -wȯ-\ river 350 mi. (563 km.) long *cen* California flowing NW into the Sacramento

**San Jo·se** \ˌsan-(h)ō-'zā\ city W California SE of San Francisco; *pop* 945,942

**San Jo·sé** \ˌsän-hō-'sā, ˌsan-(h)ō-'zā\ city, ✲ of Costa Rica; *pop* 330,529

**San Juan** \san-'wän, ˌsän-'hwän\ city, ✲ of Puerto Rico; *pop* 395,326

**San Ma·ri·no** \ˌsan-mə-'rē-(ˌ)nō\ **1** small country S Europe surrounded by Italy ENE of Florence near Adriatic Sea; *pop* 32,500 **2** town, its ✲; *pop* 4100 — **Sam·mar·i·nese** \ˌsa(m)-ˌma-rə-'nēz, -'nēs\ *n* — **San Mari·nese** \ˌsan-ˌma-\ *adj or n*

**San Pe·dro Su·la** \ˌsän-'pā-(ˌ)thrō-'sü-lä\ city NW Honduras; *pop* 300,400

**San Sal·va·dor** \san-'sal-və-ˌdȯr, ˌsän-'säl-vä-ˌthȯr\ **1** island *cen* Bahamas **2** city, ✲ of El Salvador; *pop* 316,090

**San·ta Ana** \ˌsan-tə-'a-nə, ˌsän-tä-'ä-nä\ city SW California ESE of Long Beach; *pop* 324,528

**San·ta Bar·ba·ra** \'bär-b(ə-)rə\ *or* **Channel Islands** California off SW coast in the North Pacific

**Santa Clara** \'kler-ə\ city W California NW of San Jose; *pop* 116,468

**Santa Cla·ri·ta** \klə-'rē-tə\ city S California N of Los Angeles; *pop* 176,320

**San·ta Fe** \ˌsan-tə-'fā\ city, ✲ of New Mexico; *pop* 67,947

**Santa Fe Trail** pioneer route to the SW U.S. about 1200 mi. (1900 km.) long used esp. 1821–80 from vicinity of Kansas City, Missouri, to Santa Fe, New Mexico

**San·ta Ro·sa** \ˌsan-tə-'rō-zə\ city W California N of San Francisco; *pop* 167,815

**San·ti·a·go** \ˌsan-tē-'ä-(ˌ)gō, ˌsän-\ city, ✲ of Chile; metropolitan area *pop* 4,668,500

**San·to Do·min·go** \ˌsan-tə-də-'miŋ-(ˌ)gō\ *formerly* **Tru·ji·llo** \trü-'hē-(ˌ)yō\ city, ✲ of Dominican Republic; *pop* 1,971,000

**São Pau·lo** \saúⁿ-'paú-(ˌ)lü, -(ˌ)lō\ city SE Brazil; *pop* 11,253,503

**São To·mé** \ˌsaú-tə-'mā\ town, ✲ of São Tomé and Príncipe; *pop* 43,420

**São Tomé and Príncipe** country W Africa; ✲ São Tomé; *pop* 192,000

**Sap·po·ro** \ˌsä-pō-ˌrō; sä-'pȯr-(ˌ)ō\ city Japan on W Hokkaido; *pop* 1,913,545

**Sa·ra·je·vo** \ˌsa-rə-'yä-(ˌ)vō, ˌsär-ə-\ city SE *cen* Bosnia and Herzegovina, its ✲; *pop* 330,500

**Sa·ra·tov** \sə-'rä-təf\ city W Russia, on the Volga; *pop* 838,000

**Sar·din·ia** \sär-'di-nē-ə, -'di-nyə\ island Italy in the Mediterranean S of Corsica; *pop* 1,639,362 — **Sar·din·ian** \sär-'di-nē-ən, -'din-yən\ *adj or n*

**Sar·gas·so Sea** \sär-'ga-(ˌ)sō\ area of nearly still water in the North Atlantic lying chiefly between 20° & 35° N latitude & 30° & 70° W longitude

**Sas·katch·e·wan** \sə-'ska-chə-wən, sa-, -,wän\ province W Canada; ✻, Regina; *pop* 1,033,381

**Sas·ka·toon** \,sas-kə-'tün\ city *cen* Saskatchewan, Canada; *pop* 222,189

**Sau·di Ara·bia** \'saú-dē, 'só-dē, sä-'ü-dē\ country SW Asia occupying largest part of Arabian Peninsula; ✻, Riyadh; *pop* 27,000,000 — **Saudi** *adj or n* — **Saudi Arabian** *adj or n*

**Sault Sainte Ma·rie Canals** \'sü-(,)sänt-mə-'rē\ *or* **Soo Canals** \,sü\ three ship canals, two in U.S. (Michigan) & one in Canada (Ontario), at rapids in river connecting Lake Superior & Lake Huron

**Sa·vaii** \sə-'vī-,ē\ island, largest in independent Samoa

**Sa·van·nah** \sə-'va-nə\ city & port E Georgia; *pop* 136,286

**Sa·voy** \sə-'vói\ *or French* **Sa·voie** \sä-'vwä\ region SE France SW of Switzerland bordering on Italy — **Sa·voy·ard** \sə-'vói-,ärd, ,sa-,vói-'ärd, ,sa-,vwä-'yär(d)\ *adj or n*

**Sca·fell Pike** \,skó-'fel\ mountain 3210 ft. (978 m.) NW England; highest in Cumbrian Mountains & in England

**Scan·di·na·via** \,skan-də-'nā-vē-ə, -vyə\ 1 peninsula N Europe occupied by Norway & Sweden 2 Denmark, Norway, Sweden, & as used by some also Iceland & Finland — **Scan·di·na·vian** \,skan-də-'nā-vē-ən, -vyən\ *adj or n*

**Scar·bor·ough** \'skär-,hər-ō\ former city Canada in SE Ontario; now part of Toronto

**Schel·de** \'skel-də\ *or* **Scheldt** \'skelt\ river 270 mi. (434 km.) long W Europe flowing from N France through Belgium into North Sea in Netherlands

**Schuyl·kill** \'skü-k°l, 'skül-,kil\ river 131 mi. (211 km.) long SE Pennsylvania flowing SE into the Delaware River at Philadelphia

**Scil·ly, Isles of** \'si-lē\ island group SW England off Land's End; *pop* 2900

**Sco·tia** \'skō-shə\ SCOTLAND — the Medieval Latin name

**Scot·land** \'skät-lənd\ *or Latin* **Cal·e·do·nia** \,ka-lə-'dō-nyə, -nē-ə\ country N Great Britain; a division of United Kingdom; ✻, Edinburgh; *pop* 5,295,000

**Scotts·dale** \'skäts-,dāl\ city SW *cen* Arizona E of Phoenix; *pop* 217,385

**Scyth·ia** \'si-thē-ə, -thē\ ancient area of Europe & Asia N & NE of Black Sea & E of Aral Sea — **Scyth·i·an** \'si-thē-ən, -thē-\ *adj or n*

**Se·at·tle** \sē-'a-t°l\ city & port W Washington; *pop* 608,660

**Seine** \'sān, 'sen\ river 480 mi. (772 km.) long N France flowing NW into English Channel

**Sel·kirk** \'sel-,kərk\ range of the Rocky Mountains SE British Columbia, Canada, highest peak, 11,555 ft. (3522 m.)

**Se·ma·rang** \sə-'mär-,äŋ\ city Indonesia in *cen* Java; *pop* 1,556,000

**Sen·dai** \(,)sen-'dī\ city Japan in NE Honshu; *pop* 1,045,986

**Sen·e·ca Falls** \'se-ni-kə\ village W *cen* New York; *pop* 6681

**Sen·e·gal** \,se-ni-'gól, -'gäl, 'se-ni-,\ 1 river 1015 mi. (1633 km.) long W Africa flowing W into the North Atlantic 2 country W Africa; ✻, Dakar; *pop* 13,509,000 — **Sen·e·ga·lese** \,se-ni-gə-'lēz, -'lēs\ *adj or n*

**Seoul** \'sōl\ city, ✻ of South Korea; *pop* 9,750,000

**Ser·bia** \'sər-bē-ə\ country S Europe in the Balkans; ✻ Belgrade; *pop* 7,150,000

**Serbia and Montenegro** *or 1992–2003* **Yugoslavia** former country S Europe on Balkan Peninsula

**Ser·en·ge·ti Plain** \,ser-ən-'ge-tē\ area N Tanzania

**Seven Hills** the seven hills upon and about which was built the city of Rome, Italy

**Sev·ern** \'se-vərn\ river 210 mi. (338 km.) long Wales & England flowing from E *cen* Wales into Bristol Channel

**Se·ville** \sə-'vil\ *or Spanish* **Se·vi·lla** \sā-'vē-(,)yä\ city SW Spain; *pop* 700,169

**Sew·ard Peninsula** \'sü-ərd\ peninsula 180 mi. (290 km.) long W Alaska projecting into Bering Sea

**Sey·chelles** \sā-'shel(z)\ islands W Indian Ocean NE of Madagascar; country; ✻, Victoria; *pop* 90,900 — **Sey·chel·lois** \,sā-shəl-'wä, -,shel-\ *n*

**Shang·hai** \shaŋ-'hī\ city & port E China; *pop* 12,693,000

**Shan·non** \'sha-nən\ river 230 mi. (370 km.) long W Ireland flowing S & W into the North Atlantic

**Shar·on, Plain of** \'sher-ən\ region Israel on the coast

**Shas·ta, Mount** \'shas-tə\ mountain 14,162 ft. (4316 m.) N California in Cascade Range

**Shatt al Ar·ab** \,shat-al-'a-rəb\ river 120 mi. (193 km.) long SE Iraq formed by flowing together of Euphrates & Tigris rivers and flowing SE into Persian Gulf

**Shef·field** \'she-,fēld\ city N England; *pop* 518,000

**Shen·an·do·ah** \,she-nən-'dō-ə, ,sha-nə-'dō-ə\ valley Virginia between the Allegheny & Blue Ridge mountains

**Shen·yang** \'shən-'yäŋ\ *or traditionally* **Muk·den** \'mük-dən, 'mək-; mük-'den\ city NE China; chief city of Manchuria; *pop* 5,987,000

**Sher·brooke** \'shər-,brúk\ city Quebec, Canada E of Montreal; *pop* 154,601

**Sher·wood Forest** \'shər-,wúd\ ancient royal forest *cen* England

**Shet·land** \'shet-lənd\ islands N Scotland NE of the Orkneys; *pop* 21,960

**Shi·jia·zhuang** *or* **Shih–chia–chuang** \'shir-'jyä-'jwäŋ, 'shē-\ city NE China; *pop* 2,802,500

**Shi·ko·ku** \shē-'kō-(,)kü\ island S Japan E of Kyushu; *pop* 4,154,039

**Shi·raz** \shi-'räz, -'raz\ city SW *cen* Iran; *pop* 1,460,665

**Shreve·port** \'shrēv-,pórt\ city NW Louisiana on Red River; *pop* 199,311

**Shrews·bury** \'sh(r)üz-,ber-ē, -b(ə-)rē\ town W England; *pop* 31,640

**Shrop·shire** \'shräp-shər, -,shir\ *or 1974– 80* **Sal·op** \'sal-əp\ county W England bordering on Wales; *pop* 306,000

**Shu·ma·gin** \'shü-mə-gən\ islands SW Alaska S of Alaska Peninsula

**Siam** — see THAILAND

**Siam, Gulf of** — see THAILAND, GULF OF

**Si·be·ria** \sī-'bir-ē-ə\ region N Asia in Russia between the Urals & the North Pacific — **Si·be·ri·an** \-ən\ *adj or n*

**Sic·i·ly** \'si-s(ə-)lē\ *or Italian* **Si·ci·lia** \sē-'chēl-yä\ island S Italy SW of toe of peninsula of Italy; ✽, Palermo; *pop* 5,002,904 — **Si·cil·ian** \sə-'sil-yən\ *adj or n*

**Si·er·ra Le·one** \sē-,er-ə-lē-'ōn, ,sir-ə-, -lē-'ō-nē\ country W Africa on the North Atlantic; ✽, Freetown; *pop* 4,491,000 — **Si·er·ra Le·on·ean** \-'ō-nē-ən\ *adj or n*

**Si·er·ra Ma·dre** \sē-,er-ə-'mä-drä, 'syer-ä-'mä-thrä\ mountain system Mexico including **Sierra Madre Oc·ci·den·tal** \,äk-sə-,den-'täl, ,ók-sē-,then-'täl\ range W of the *cen* plateau, **Sierra Madre Ori·en·tal** \,ór-ē-,en-'täl\ range E of the plateau, & **Sierra Madre del Sur** \'sùr, 'sür\ range to the S

**Sierra Ne·va·da** \nə-'va-də, -'vä-\ 1 mountain range E California & W Nevada — see WHITNEY, MOUNT 2 mountain range S Spain

**Sik·kim** \'si-kəm, -,kim\ former country SE Asia on S slope of the Himalayas between Nepal & Bhutan; state of India since 1975; *pop* 610,577

**Si·le·sia** \sī-'lē-zh(ē-)ə, sə-, -sh(ē-)ə\ region E *cen* Europe in valley of the upper Oder; formerly chiefly in Germany now chiefly in E Czech Republic & SW Poland — **Si·le·sian** \-zh(ē-)ən, -sh(ē-)ən\ *adj or n*

**Silk Road** *or* **Silk Route** ancient trade route that extended from China to the Mediterranean

**Sim·coe, Lake** \'sim-(,)kō\ lake Canada in SE Ontario

**Si·mi Valley** \sē-'mē\ city SW California W of Los Angeles; *pop* 124,237

**Sim·plon Pass** \'sim-,plän\ mountain pass 6590 ft. (2009 m.) between Switzerland & Italy

**Si·nai** \'sī-,nī\ 1 mountain on Sinai Peninsula where according to the Bible the Law was given to Moses 2 peninsula extension of continent of Asia NE Egypt between Red Sea & the Mediterranean

**Sin·ga·pore** \'siŋ-ə-,pòr\ 1 island off S end of Malay Peninsula; country; *pop* 5,077,000 2 city, its ✽; *pop* 206,500 — **Sin·ga·por·ean** \,siŋ-ə-'pór-ē-ən\ *adj or n*

**Sinkiang Uighur** — see XINJIANG UYGUR

**Sioux Falls** \'sü\ city SE South Dakota; largest in state; *pop* 153,888

**Skag·ge·rak** \'ska-gə-,rak\ arm of North Sea between S Norway & N Denmark

**Skop·je** \'skò-pye, -pyə\ city, ✽ of independent Macedonia; *pop* 487,000

**Sla·vo·nia** \slə-'vō-nē-ə, -nyə\ region E Croatia; *pop* 78,000 — **Sla·vo·ni·an** \-nē-ən, -nyən\ *adj or n*

**Slo·va·kia** \slō-'vä-kē-ə, -'va-\ country *cen* Europe; ✽, Bratislava; *pop* 5,397,036

**Slo·ve·nia** \slō-'vē-nē-ə, -nyə\ country S Europe; ✽, Ljubljana; *pop* 2,050,000

**Smyrna** — see IZMIR

**Snake** \'snāk\ river NW U.S. flowing from NW Wyoming into the Columbia in SE Washington

**Snow·don** \'snō-dᵊn\ massif 3560 ft. (1085 m.) in **Snow·do·nia** \snō-'dō-nē-ə, -nyə\ (mountainous district) NW Wales; highest point in Wales

**So·ci·e·ty** \sə-'sī-ə-tē\ islands South Pacific; belonging to France; chief island, Tahiti; *pop* 162,573

**So·fia** \'sō-fē-ə, 'sò-, sō-'\ city, ✽ of Bulgaria; *pop* 1,291,600

**So·ho** \'sō-,hō\ district of *cen* London, England

**So·li·hull** \,sō-li-'həl\ city *cen* England; *pop* 123,000

**Sol·o·mon** \'sä-lə-mən\ 1 islands W Pacific E of New Guinea divided between Papua New Guinea & independent Solomon Islands 2 sea, arm of Coral Sea W of the Solomons

**Solomon Islands** country, SW Pacific E of New Guinea; ✽, Honiara (on Guadalcanal); *pop* 516,000

**So·ma·lia** \sō-'mä-lē-ə, sə-, -'mäl-yə\ country E Africa on Gulf of Aden & Indian Ocean; ✽, Mogadishu; *pop* 10,250,000 — **So·ma·li·an** \-'mä-lē-ən, -'mäl-yən\ *adj or n*

**So·ma·li·land** \sō-'mä-lē-,land, sə-\ historical region E Africa consisting of Somalia, Djibouti, & part of E Ethiopia — **So·ma·li** \sō-'mä-lē, sə-\ *n*

**Som·er·set** \'sə-mər-,set, -sət\ *or* **Som·er·set·shire** \-,shir, -shər\ county SW England

**So·nor·an** \sə-'nór-ən\ *or* **So·no·ra** \sə-'nòr-ə\ desert SW U.S. & NW Mexico

**Soo Canals** — see SAULT SAINTE MARIE CANALS

**South** island S New Zealand; *pop* 906,756

**South Africa, Republic of** *formerly* **Union of South Africa** country S Africa; administrative ✽, Pretoria; legislative

✻, Cape Town; judicial ✻, Bloemfontein; *pop* 51,771,000 — **South African** *adj or n*

**South America** continent of Western Hemisphere SE of North America and chiefly S of the Equator — **South American** *adj or n*

**South-amp-ton** \saů-'tham(p)-tǝn, saůth-'ham(p)-\ city S England; *pop* 254,000

**South Australia** state S Australia; ✻, Adelaide; *pop* 1,596,572 — **South Australian** *adj or n*

**South Bend** \'bend\ city N Indiana; *pop* 101,168

**South Cape** *or* **South Point** — see KA LAE

**South Car-o-li-na** \,ker(-ǝ)-'lī-nǝ, ,ka-rǝ-\ state SE U.S.; ✻, Columbia; *pop* 4,625,364 — **South Car-o-lin-i-an** \-'li-nē-ǝn, -'li-nyǝn\ *adj or n*

**South China Sea** — see CHINA

**South Da-ko-ta** \dǝ-'kō-tǝ\ state NW *cen* U.S.; ✻, Pierre; *pop* 814,180 — **South Da-ko-tan** \-'kō-tᵊn\ *adj or n*

**South-end-on—Sea** \saů-,thend-,ȯn-'sē, -,än-\ seaside resort SE England E of London; *pop* 176,000

**Southern Alps** mountain range New Zealand in W South Island extending almost the length of the island

**Southern Hemisphere** the half of the earth that lies S of the Equator

**South Georgia** island S Atlantic E of Tierra del Fuego; administered by United Kingdom

**South Korea** *or* **Republic of Korea** country S half of Korean Peninsula in E Asia; ✻, Seoul; *pop* 48,400,000

**South Seas** the areas of the Atlantic, Indian, & Pacific oceans in the Southern Hemisphere

**South Shields** \'shēldz\ seaport N England; *pop* 75,000

**South Sudan** country E Africa formed 2011 from the S part of Sudan; ✻, Juba; *pop* 8,260,500

**South Vietnam** — see VIETNAM

**South-wark** \'sǝ-thǝrk, 'saůth-wǝrk\ borough of S Greater London, England; *pop* 288,000

**South—West Africa** — see NAMIBIA

**South Yorkshire** metropolitan county N England; *pop* 1,343,600

**Soviet Central Asia** portion of *cen* & SW Asia formerly belonging to U.S.S.R. and including the former soviet socialist republics of present-day Kyrgyzstan, Tajikistan, Turkmenistan, Uzbekistan & by some thought also to include Kazakhstan

**Soviet Union** — see UNION OF SOVIET SOCIALIST REPUBLICS

**So-we-to** \sō-'wā-tō, -'we-, -tü\ residential area NE Republic of South Africa adjoining SW Johannesburg

**Spain** \'spān\ country SW Europe on Iberian Peninsula; ✻, Madrid; *pop* 46,816,000

**Spanish America** 1 the Spanish-speaking countries of America 2 the parts of America settled and formerly governed by the Spanish

**Spanish Guinea** — see EQUATORIAL GUINEA

**Spanish Sahara** — see WESTERN SAHARA

**Spar-ta** \'spär-tǝ\ ancient city S Greece in Peloponnese; ✻ of Laconia

**Spo-kane** \spō-'kan\ city E Washington; *pop* 208,916

**Spring-field** \'spriŋ-,fēld\ 1 city, ✻ of Illinois, *pop* 116,250 2 city SW Massachusetts; *pop* 153,060 3 city SW Missouri; *pop* 159,498

**Sri Lan-ka** \(,)srē-'läŋ-kǝ, (,)shrē-, -'laŋ-\ *formerly* **Cey-lon** \si-'län, sā-\ country having the same boundaries as island of Ceylon; ✻, Colombo; *pop* 20,300,000 — **Sri Lan-kan** \-'läŋ-kǝn, -'laŋ-\ *adj or n*

**Sri-na-gar** \srē-'nǝ-gǝr\ city N India; *pop* 1,222,500

**Staf-ford** \'sta-fǝrd\ town W *cen* England; *pop* 68,000

**Staf-ford-shire** \'sta-fǝrd-,shir, -shǝr\ *or* **Stafford** county W *cen* England

**Staked Plain** — see LLANO ESTACADO

**Stam-ford** \'stam-fǝrd\ city SW Connecticut; *pop* 122,643

**Stan-ley** \'stan-lē\ town, ✻ of Falkland Islands; *pop* 1559

**Stat-en Island** \'sta-tᵊn\ 1 island SE New York SW of mouth of the Hudson 2 *formerly* **Rich-mond** \'rich-mǝnd\ borough of New York City including Staten Island; *pop* 468,730

**Ster-ling Heights** \'stǝr-liŋ\ city SE Michigan; *pop* 129,699

**Stir-ling** \'stǝr-liŋ\ town *cen* Scotland; *pop* 36,000

**Stock-holm** \'stäk-,hō(l)m\ city, ✻ of Sweden; *pop* 758,148

**Stock-port** \'stäk-,pȯrt\ town NW England; *pop* 106,000

**Stock-ton** \'stäk-tǝn\ city *cen* California; *pop* 291,707

**Stoke—on—Trent** \'stōk-,än-'trent, -,ȯn-\ city *cen* England; *pop* 271,000

**Stone-henge** \'stōn-,henj, (,)stōn-'\ prehistoric assemblage of megaliths S England in Wiltshire on Salisbury Plain

**Stone Mountain** mountain 1686 ft. (514 m.) NW Georgia E of Atlanta

**Stor-no-way** \'stȯr-nǝ-,wā\ seaport NW Scotland; chief town of Lewis with Harris Island; *pop* 8660

**Stra-bane** \strǝ-'ban\ district W Northern Ireland; *pop* 39,843

**Strath-clyde** \strath-'klīd\ former region SW Scotland; included Glasgow

**Strom-bo-li** \'sträm-bō-(,)lē\ volcano 2500 ft. (758 m.) Italy on **Stromboli Island** in Tyrrhenian Sea

**Stutt-gart** \'shtůt-,gärt, 'stůt-, 'stǝt-\ city SW Germany; *pop* 585,890

# Geographical Names

**Styx** \'stiks\ chief river of the underworld in Greek mythology

**Süchow** — see XUZHOU

**Su·cre** \'sü-(ˌ)krā\ city, constitutional ✳ of Bolivia; *pop* 244,000

**Su·dan** \sü-'dan, -'dän\ **1** region N Africa S of the Sahara between the Atlantic & the upper Nile **2** country NE Africa S of Egypt; ✳, Khartoum; *pop* 30,900,000 — **Su·da·nese** \ˌsü-də-'nēz, -'nēs\ *adj or n*

**Sud·bury, Greater** \'səd-ˌber-ē, -b(ə-)rē\ city SE Ontario, Canada; *pop* 160,274

**Su·ez, Gulf of** \sü-'ez, 'sü-ˌez\ arm of Red Sea

**Suez, Isthmus of** isthmus NE Egypt between Mediterranean & Red seas connecting Africa & Asia

**Suez Canal** canal 100 mi. (161 km.) long NE Egypt across the Isthmus of Suez

**Suf·folk** \'səf-ək\ county E England on North Sea; *pop* 728,163

**Sui·sun Bay** \sə-'sün\ inlet of San Francisco Bay, W *cen* California

**Su·la·we·si** \ˌsü-lä-'wä-sē\ island Indonesia E of Borneo; *pop* 12,520,711

**Su·lu** \'sü-(ˌ)lü\ **1** archipelago SW Philippines SW of Mindanao **2** sea W Philippines

**Su·ma·tra** \sù-'mä-trə\ island W Indonesia S of Malay Peninsula — **Su·ma·tran** \-trən\ *adj or n*

**Su·mer** \'sü-mər\ the S division of ancient Babylonia — **Su·me·ri·an** \sü-'mer-ē-ən, -'mir-\ *adj or n*

**Sun·belt** \'sən-ˌbelt\ region S & SW U.S.

**Sun·da** \'sün-də, 'sən-\ strait between Java & Sumatra

**Sun·der·land** \'sən-dər-lənd\ seaport N England; *pop* 174,000

**Sun·ny·vale** \'sə-nē-ˌvāl\ city W California; *pop* 140,081

**Sun Valley** resort center *cen* Idaho

**Su·pe·ri·or, Lake** \sù-'pir-ē-ər\ lake E *cen* North America in U.S. & Canada; largest of the Great Lakes

**Su·ra·ba·ya** \ˌsùr-ə-'bī-ə\ city Indonesia in NE Java; *pop* 2,765,000

**Su·ri·na·me** \ˌsùr-ə-'nä-mə\ country N South America between Guyana & French Guiana; ✳, Paramaribo; *pop* 542,000 — **Su·ri·nam·er** \'sùr-ə-ˌnä-mər, ˌsùr-ə-'nä-\ *n* — **Su·ri·nam·ese** \ˌsùr-ə-nə-'mēz, -'mēs\ *adj or n*

**Sur·rey** \'sər-ē, 'sə-rē\ city Canada in SW British Columbia; *pop* 468,251

**Sut·ton** \'sə-tᵊn\ borough of S Greater London, England; *pop* 190,000

**Su·va** \'sü-və\ city & port, ✳ of Fiji on Viti Levu Island; *pop* 86,178

**Su·wan·nee** \sə-'wä-nē, 'swä-\ river 250 mi. (400 km.) long SE U.S. flowing SW into Gulf of Mexico

**Sverdlovsk** — see YEKATERINBURG

**Swan·sea** \'swän-zē\ city & port SE Wales; *pop* 179,000

**Swa·zi·land** \'swä-zē-ˌland\ country SE Africa between Republic of South Africa & Mozambique; ✳, Mbabane; *pop* 1,018,000 — **Swa·zi** \'swä-zē\ *adj or n*

**Swe·den** \'swē-dᵊn\ country N Europe on Scandinavia (peninsula) bordering on Baltic Sea; ✳, Stockholm; *pop* 8,016,000

**Swit·zer·land** \'swit-sər-lənd\ country W Europe in the Alps; ✳, Bern; *pop* 7,800,000

**Syd·ney** \'sid-nē\ city SE Australia, ✳ of New South Wales; *pop* 3,908,642

**Syr·a·cuse** \'sir-ə-ˌkyüs, -ˌkyüz\ city *cen* New York; *pop* 145,170

**Syr·ia** \'sir-ē-ə\ **1** ancient region SW Asia bordering on the Mediterranean **2** country S of Turkey; ✳, Damascus; *pop* 17,952,000 — **Syr·i·an** \'sir-ē-ən\ *adj or n*

**Syrian Desert** desert region between Mediterranean coast & the Euphrates in N Saudi Arabia, SE Syria, W Iraq, & NE Jordan

**Table Bay** harbor of Cape Town, Republic of South Africa

**Ta·briz** \tə-'brēz\ city NW Iran; *pop* 1,494,998

**Ta·co·ma** \tə-'kō-mə\ city & port W Washington S of Seattle; *pop* 198,397

**Tae·gu** \'tā-gü, 'dā-\ *or* **Dae·gu** \'dā-\ city SE South Korea; *pop* 2,444,000

**Tae·jon** \'tā-jon, 'dā-\ *or* **Dae·jeon** \'dā-\ city *cen* South Korea NW of Taegu; *pop* 1,495,000

**Ta·gus** \'tā-gəs\ *or Spanish* **Ta·jo** \'tä-(ˌ)hō\ *or Portuguese* **Te·jo** \'tā-(ˌ)zhü\ river 626 mi. (1007 km.) long Spain & Portugal flowing W into the North Atlantic

**Ta·hi·ti** \tə-'hē-tē\ island South Pacific in Society Islands; *pop* 131,309

**Tai·bei** \'tī-'bā\ *or* **Tai·pei** \'tī-'pā, -'bā\ city, ✳ of (Nationalist) China in N Taiwan; *pop* 2,700,000

**T'ai·nan** \'tī-'nän\ city SW Taiwan; *pop* 1,883,000

**Tai·wan** \'tī-'wän\ *formerly* **For·mo·sa** \fòr-'mō-sə, fər-, -zə\ **1** island China off SE coast of mainland; seat of government of (Nationalist) Republic of China; ✳, Taibei; *pop* 23,340,000 **2** strait between Taiwan & mainland of China connecting East China & South China seas — **Tai·wan·ese** \ˌtī-wə-'nēz, -'nēs\ *adj or n*

**Tai·yuan** \'tī-'ywen, -'ywän\ city N China; *pop* 3,290,500

**Tai·zhong** \'tī-'jùŋ\ *or* **Tai·chung** \'tī-'chùŋ\ city W Taiwan; *pop* 1,004,400

**Ta·jik·i·stan** \tä-ˌji-ki-'stan, tə-, -ˌjē-, -'stän\ country W *cen* Asia bordering on China & Afghanistan; ✳, Dushanbe; *pop* 7,564,500

**Ta·kli·ma·kan** *or* **Ta·kla Ma·kan** \ˌtä-klə-mə-'kän\ desert W China

**Ta·lien** — see DALIAN

**Tal·la·has·see** \ˌta-lə-'ha-sē\ city, ✳ of Florida; *pop* 181,376

**Tal·linn** \'ta-lən, 'tä-\ city, ✳ of Estonia; *pop* 405,000

**Tam·pa** \'tam-pə\ city W Florida on **Tampa Bay** (inlet of Gulf of Mexico); *pop* 335,709

**Tan·gan·yi·ka** \,tan-gə-'nyē-kə, ,taŋ-gə-, -'nē-\ former country E Africa S of Kenya; now part of Tanzania

**Tanganyika, Lake** lake E Africa between Tanzania & Democratic Republic of the Congo

**Tang·shan** \'däŋ-'shän, 'täŋ-\ city NE China; *pop* 2,750,000

**Tan·za·nia** \,tan-zə-'nē-ə, ,tän-\ country E Africa on Indian Ocean, including Zanzibar; legislative ✳, Dodoma; historic ✳, Dar es Salaam; *pop* 44,929,000 — **Tan·za·ni·an** \-'nē-ən\ *adj or n*

**Ta·ra·wa** \tə-'rä-wə, 'ta-rə-,wä\ island *cen* Pacific, contains ✳ of Kiribati; *pop* 41,194

**Tar·ry·town** \'ta-rē-,taùn\ village SE New York; *pop* 11,277

**Tar·sus** \'tär-səs\ ancient city of S Asia Minor; now a city in S Turkey

**Tash·kent** \tash-'kent, täsh-\ city, ✳ of Uzbekistan; *pop* 2,200,000

**Tas·ma·nia** \taz-'mā-nē-ə, -nyə\ *or earlier* **Van Die·men's Land** \van-'dē-mənz\ island SE Australia S of Victoria; a state; ✳, Hobart; *pop* 495,354 — **Tas·ma·nian** \taz-'mā-nē-ən, -nyən\ *adj or n*

**Tas·man Sea** \'taz-mən\ the part of the South Pacific between SE Australia & New Zealand

**Ta·try** \'tä-trē\ *or* **Ta·tra** \'tä-trə\ mountains N Slovakia & S Poland in *cen* Carpathian Mountains

**Taun·ton** \'tòn-tᵊn, 'tän-\ town SW England; *pop* 60,000

**Tbi·li·si** \tə-bə-lə-sē, tə-bə-'lē-sē\ *or* **Tiflis** \'ti-fləs, tə-'flēs\ city, ✳ of Republic of Georgia; *pop* 1,106,500

**Te·gu·ci·gal·pa** \tə-,gü-sə-'gal-pə, tä-,gü-sē-'gäl-pä\ city, ✳ of Honduras; *pop* 879,000

**Teh·ran** \,tā-(ə-)'ran, te-'ran, -'rän\ city, ✳ of Iran; at foot of S slope of Elburz Mountains; *pop* 8,154,051

**Tel Aviv** \,tel-ə-'vēv\ *or officially* **Tel Aviv–Ya·fo** \-'yä-fō\ city W Israel on the Mediterranean; *pop* 410,000

**Tem·pe** \tem-'pē\ city S *cen* Arizona; *pop* 161,719

**Ten·nes·see** \,te-nə-'sē, 'te-nə-,\ 1 river 652 mi. (1049 km.) long in Tennessee, N Alabama, & W Kentucky 2 state E *cen* U.S.; ✳, Nashville; *pop* 6,346,105 — **Ten·nes·se·an** *or* **Ten·nes·see·an** \,te-nə-'sē-ən\ *adj or n*

**Te·noch·ti·tlan** \tā-,nòch-tēt-'län\ ancient name of Mexico City

**Tex·as** \'tek-səs, -siz\ state S U.S.; ✳, Austin; *pop* 25,145,561 — **Tex·an** \-sən\ *adj or n*

**Texas Panhandle** the NW projection of land in Texas

**Thai·land** \'tī-,land, -lənd\ *formerly* **Si·am** \sī-'am\ country SE Asia on Gulf of Thailand; ✳, Bangkok; *pop* 65,982,000 — **Thai·land·er** \-,lan-dər, -lən-\ *n*

**Thailand, Gulf of** *formerly* **Gulf of Siam** arm of South China Sea between Indochina & Malay Peninsula

**Thames** \'temz\ river over 200 mi. (322 km.) long S England flowing E from the Cotswolds into the North Sea

**Thar** \'tär\ desert E Pakistan & NW India (country) E of Indus River

**Thebes** \'thēbz\ 1 *or* **The·bae** \'thē-(,)bē\ ancient city S Egypt on the Nile 2 ancient city E Greece NNW of Athens — **The·ban** \'thē-bən\ *adj or n*

**Thes·sa·lo·ní·ki** \,the-sä-lō-'nē-kē\ city N Greece; *pop* 325,000

**Thim·phu** \tim-'pü\ city, ✳ of Bhutan; *pop* 79,185

**Thi·ru·van·an·tha·pur·am** \,tir-ü-və-,nan-tə-'pùr-əm\ city S India; *pop* 744,700

**Thousand Islands** island group Canada & U.S. in the Saint Lawrence River in Ontario & New York

**Thousand Oaks** city SW California W of Los Angeles; *pop* 126,683

**Thrace** \'thrās\ *or ancient* **Thra·cia** \'thrā-sh(ē-)ə\·region SE Europe in Balkan Peninsula N of the Aegean now divided between Greece & Turkey; in ancient times extended N to the Danube — **Thra·cian** \'thrā-shən\ *adj or n*

**Thunder Bay** city SW Ontario, Canada on Lake Superior; *pop* 108,359

**Tian·jin** \'tyän-'jin\ *or* **Tien·tsin** \'tyen-'tsin, 'tin-\ city NE China SE of Beijing; *pop* 10,190,000

**Tian Shan** *or* **Tien Shan** \'tyen-'shän, -'shan\ mountain system *cen* Asia extending NE from Pamirs

**Ti·ber** \'tī-bər\ *or Italian* **Te·ve·re** \'tā-vā-rā\ river 252 mi. (405 km.) long *cen* Italy flowing through Rome into Tyrrhenian Sea

**Tiberias, Lake** — see GALILEE, SEA OF

**Ti·bes·ti** \tə-'bes-tē\ mountains N *cen* Africa in *cen* Sahara in NW Chad; highest 11,204 ft. (3415 m.)

**Ti·bet** \tə-'bet\ *or* **Xi·zang** \'shēd-'zäŋ\ region SW China on high plateau at average altitude 16,000 ft. (4877 m.) N of the Himalayas; ✳, Lhasa; *pop* 3,002,165

**Tier·ra del Fue·go** \tē-'er-ə-(,)del-fü-'ā-(,)gō, 'tyer-ä-(,)thel-'fwä-gō\ 1 island group off S South America 2 chief island of the group; divided between Argentina & Chile

**Tiflis** — see TBILISI

**Ti·gris** \'tī-grəs\ river 1180 mi. (1899 km.) long Turkey & Iraq flowing SSE and uniting with the Euphrates to form the Shatt al Arab

**Ti·jua·na** \tē-ə-'wä-nə, tē-'hwä-nä\ city NW Mexico on the U.S. border; *pop* 1,559,683

**Tim·buk·tu** \,tim-'bək-'tü, tim-'bək-(,)tü\ *or* **Tom·bouc·tou** \tōⁿ-bük-'tü\ town Mali near Niger River; *pop* 31,925

**Ti·mor** \'tē-,mȯr, tē-'\ island S Malay Archipelago SE of Sulawesi; W half part of Indonesia, E half independent East Timor

**Timor–Leste** — see EAST TIMOR

**Ti·ra·ne** *or* **Ti·ra·na** \ti-'rä-nə, tē-\ city, * of Albania; *pop* 418,495

**Ti·rol** *or* **Ty·rol** \tə-'rōl\ *or Italian* **Ti·ro·lo** \tē-'rȯ-(,)lō\ region in E Alps in W Austria & NE Italy — **Ti·ro·le·an** \tə-'rō-lē-ən, tī-\ *or* **Tir·o·lese** \,tir-ə-'lēz, ,tī-rə-, -'lēs\ *adj or n*

**Ti·ti·ca·ca, Lake** \,ti-ti-'kä-kä, ,tē-tē-\ lake on Bolivia–Peru boundary at altitude of 12,500 ft. (3810 m.)

**To·ba·go** \tə-'bā-(,)gō\ island West Indies NE of Trinidad; part of independent Trinidad and Tobago; *pop* 60,874 — **To·ba·go·ni·an** \,tō-bə-'gō-nē-ən, -nyən\ *n*

**To·go** \'tō-(,)gō\ country W Africa on Gulf of Guinea; *, Lomé; *pop* 6,191,000 — **To·go·lese** \,tō-gə-'lēz, -'lēs\ *adj or n*

**To·kyo** \'tō-kē-,ō, -,kyō\ city, * of Japan in SE Honshu on Tokyo Bay; *pop* 8,945,695 — **To·kyo·ite** \-kē-(,)ō-,īt\ *n*

**To·le·do** \tə-'lē-(,)dō, -'lē-də\ city NW Ohio; *pop* 287,208

**Tol'·yat·ti** \tȯl-'yä-tē\ city W Russia; NW of Samara; *pop* 720,000

**Ton·ga** \'täŋ-gə, 'täŋ-ə, 'tȯŋ-ä\ islands SW Pacific E of Fiji Islands; country; *, Nukualofa; *pop* 103,300 — **Ton·gan** \-(g)ən\ *adj or n*

**Ton·kin, Gulf of** \'täŋ-kən\ arm of South China Sea E of N Vietnam

**To·pe·ka** \tə-'pē-kə\ city, * of Kansas; *pop* 127,473

**Tor·bay** \(,)tȯr-'bā\ district SW England; *pop* 131,000

**To·ron·to** \tə-'rän-(,)tō, -'rän-tə\ city, * of Ontario, Canada; *pop* 2,615,060

**Tor·rance** \'tȯr-ən(t)s, 'tär-\ city SW California; *pop* 145,438

**Tor·res** \'tȯr-əs\ strait between New Guinea & Cape York Peninsula, Australia

**Tou·louse** \tü-'lüz\ city SW France; *pop* 441,802

**Tower Hamlets** borough of E Greater London, England; *pop* 254,000

**Trans·vaal** \tran(t)s-'väl, tranz-\ former province NE Republic of South Africa

**Tran·syl·va·nia** \,tran(t)-səl-'vä-nyə, -nē-ə\ region W Romania — **Tran·syl·va·nian** \-nyən, -nē-ən\ *adj or n*

**Transylvanian Alps** a S extension of Carpathian Mountains in *cen* Romania

**Tren·ton** \'tren-t°n\ city, * of New Jersey; *pop* 84,913

**Trin·i·dad** \'tri-nə-,dad\ island West Indies off NE coast of Venezuela; with Tobago forms the independent country of Trinidad and Tobago; *, Port of Spain;

*pop* 1,328,000 — **Trin·i·da·di·an** \,tri-nə-'dä-dē-ən, -'da-\ *adj or n*

**Trip·o·li** \'tri-pə-lē\ **1** city & port NW Lebanon; *pop* 127,611 **2** city & port, * of Libya; *pop* 591,062

**Tris·tan da Cu·nha** \,tris-tən-də-'kü-nə, -nyə\ island South Atlantic, chief of the Tristan da Cunha Islands (part of British colony of Saint Helena); *pop* 274

**Tro·bri·and** \'trō-brē-,änd, -,and\ islands SW Pacific in Solomon Sea belonging to Papua New Guinea

**Trond·heim** \'trän-,hām\ city & port *cen* Norway; *pop* 182,035

**Trow·bridge** \'trō-(,)brij\ town S England; *pop* 39,000

**Troy** \'trȯi\ *or* **Il·i·um** \'i-lē-əm\ *or* **Tro·ja** \'trō-jə, -yə\ ancient city NW Asia Minor SW of the Dardanelles

**Truk** — see CHUUK

**Tru·ro** \'trür-(,)ō\ city SW England; *pop* 20,000

**Tshwa·ne** \'chwä-nā\ municipality Republic of South Africa which includes city of Pretoria; *pop* 2,921,488

**Tsinan** — see JINAN

**Tsingtao** — see QINGDAO

**Tuc·son** \'tü-,sän\ city SE Arizona; *pop* 520,116

**Tu·la** \'tü-lä\ city W Russia S of Moscow; *pop* 501,000

**Tul·sa** \'təl-sə\ city NE Oklahoma; *pop* 391,906

**Tu·nis** \'tü-nəs, 'tyü-\ city, * of Tunisia; *pop* 674,100

**Tu·ni·sia** \tü-'nē-zh(ē-)ə, tyü-, -'ni-\ country N Africa on the Mediterranean E of Algeria; *, Tunis; *pop* 10,983,000 — **Tu·ni·sian** \-zh(ē-)ən\ *adj or n*

**Tu·rin** \'tür-ən, 'tyür-\ city NW Italy on the Po; *pop* 872,367

**Tur·ka·na, Lake** \tər-'ka-nə\ *or* **Lake Ru·dolf** \'rü-,dȯlf, -,dälf\ lake N Kenya in Great Rift Valley

**Tur·key** \'tər-kē\ country W Asia & SE Europe between Mediterranean & Black seas; *, Ankara; *pop* 73,085,000 — **Turk** \'tərk\ *n*

**Turk·men·i·stan** \(,)tərk-,me-nə-'stan, -'stän\ country *cen* Asia; *, Ashkhabad; *pop* 5,479,000 — **Turk·me·ni·an** \tərk-'mē-nē-ən\ *adj*

**Turks and Cai·cos** \'tərks-ənd-'kā-kəs, -,kōs\ two groups of islands West Indies at SE end of the Bahamas; a British colony; *pop* 31,458

**Tu·tu·i·la** \,tü-tü-'wē-lä\ island South Pacific, chief of American Samoa group

**Tu·va·lu** \tü-'vä-(,)lü, -'vär-(,)ü\ *formerly* **El·lice** \'e-lis\ islands W Pacific N of Fiji; country; *, Funafuti; *pop* 11,000 — see GILBERT AND ELLICE ISLANDS

**Tyne and Wear** \'tīn-ənd-'wir\ metropolitan county N England; *pop* 1,105,000

**Tyre** \'tī(-ə)r\ ancient city, * of Phoenicia; now a town of S Lebanon — **Tyr·i·an** \'tir-ē-ən\ adj or n

**Tyrol** — see TIROL — **Ty·ro·le·an** \tə-'rō-lē-ən, tī-\ adj or n — **Ty·ro·lese** \,tir-ə-'lēz, ,tī-rə-, -'lēs\ adj or n

**Tyr·rhe·ni·an Sea** \tə-'rē-nē-ən\ the part of the Mediterranean SW of Italy, N of Sicily, & E of Sardinia & Corsica

**Ufa** \ü-'fä\ city W Russia NE of Samara; pop 1,062,000

**Ugan·da** \ü-'gän-də, yü-, -'gan-\ country E Africa N of Lake Victoria; ✳, Kampala; pop 34,857,000 — **Ugan·dan** \-dən\ adj or n

**Ukraine** \yü-'krān, 'yü-,\ country E Europe on N coast of Black Sea; ✳, Kiev; pop 45,500,000 — **Ukrai·ni·an** \yü-'krā-nē-ən\ adj or n

**Ulaan·baa·tar** or **Ulan Ba·tor** \,ü-,län-'bä-,tȯr\ city, ✳ of Mongolia; pop 1,088,000

**Ul·san** \'ül-'sän\ city SE South Korea; pop 1,130,500

**Ul·ster** \'əl-stər\ **1** region N Ireland (island) consisting of Northern Ireland & N Ireland (country) **2** province N Ireland (country); pop 295,000 **3** NORTHERN IRELAND

**Ulu·ru** \ü-'lü-rü\ or **Ayers Rock** \'erz\ outcrop cen Australia in SW Northern Territory

**Um·bria** \'əm-brē-ə\ region cen Italy in the Apennines; pop 884,268

**Un·ga·va** \,ən-'ga-və\ **1** bay, inlet of Hudson Strait NE Canada **2** peninsula region NE Canada in N Quebec

**Union of South Africa** — see SOUTH AFRICA, REPUBLIC OF

**Union of Soviet Socialist Republics** or **U.S.S.R.** or **Soviet Union** country 1922–91 E Europe & N Asia; former union of 15 republics comprising present-day countries of Armenia, Azerbaijan, Belarus, Estonia, Georgia, Kazakhstan, Krygyzstan, Latvia, Lithuania, Moldova, Russia, Tajikistan, Turkmenistan, Ukraine, & Uzbekistan

**United Arab Emir·ates** \'e-mə-rəts, -,rāts\ country E Arabia on Persian Gulf; composed of seven emirates; ✳, Abu Dhabi; pop 4,105,000

**United Kingdom** or in full **United Kingdom of Great Britain and Northern Ireland** country W Europe in British Isles consisting of England, Scotland, Wales, Northern Ireland, Channel Islands, & Isle of Man; ✳, London; pop 63,182,000

**United Nations** political organization established in 1945 with headquarters in international territory in New York City

**United States of America** or **United States** country North America bordering on Atlantic, Pacific, & Arctic oceans & including Hawaii; ✳, Washington; pop 308,745,538

**Upper Volta** — see BURKINA FASO

**Upper Vol·tan** \'väl-t³n, 'vōl-, 'vȯl-\ adj or n

**Ural** \'yu̇r-əl\ **1** mountains Russia & Kazakhstan extending about 1640 mi. (2640 km.); usually thought of as dividing line between Europe & Asia; highest about 6214 ft. (1894 m.) **2** river over 1500 mi. (2414 km.) long Russia & Kazakhstan flowing from S end of Ural Mountains into Caspian Sea

**Uru·guay** \'u̇r-ə-,gwī, 'yu̇r-\ **1** river about 1000 mi. (1609 km.) long SE South America **2** country SE South America; ✳, Montevideo; pop 3,286,314 — **Uru·guay·an** \,u̇r-ə-'gwī-ən, ,yu̇r-\ adj or n

**Ürüm·qi** \'ue-'ru̇m-'chē\ or **Urum·chi** \ü-'ru̇m-chē, ,u̇r-əm-'\ city NW China; pop 2,941,000

**Us·pa·lla·ta** \,üs-pä-'yä-tä, -'zhä-\ mountain pass S South America in the Andes between Argentina & Chile

**Ustinov** — see IZHEVSK

**Utah** \'yü-,tȯ, -,tä\ state W U.S.; ✳, Salt Lake City; pop 2,763,885 — **Utah·an** \-,tȯ(-ə)n, -,tä(-ə)n\ adj or n — **Utahn** \-,tȯ(-ə)n, -,tä(-ə)n\ n

**Uz·bek·i·stan** \(,)u̇z-,be-ki-'stan, ,əz-, -'stän\ country W cen Asia between Aral Sea & Afghanistan; ✳, Tashkent; pop 30,000,000

**Va·duz** \vä-'düts\ town, ✳ of Liechtenstein; pop 5400

**Val·dez** \val-'dēz\ city & port S Alaska; pop 4949

**Va·len·cia** \və-'len(t)-sh(ē-)ə, -sē-ə\ **1** region & ancient kingdom E Spain **2** city, its ✳, on the Mediterranean; pop 792,000

**Val·le·jo** \və-'lā-(,)ō\ city W California; pop 115,942

**Valley Forge** locality SE Pennsylvania

**Val·let·ta** \və-'le-tə\ city, ✳ of Malta; pop 5760

**Van·cou·ver** \van-'kü-vər\ **1** city SW Washington on Columbia River opposite Portland, Oregon; pop 161,791 **2** island W Canada in SW British Columbia **3** city & port SW British Columbia, Canada; pop 603,502

**Van Diemen's Land** — see TASMANIA

**Van·u·atu** \,van-,wä-'tü, ,vän-\ formerly **New Heb·ri·des** \'he-brə-,dēz\ islands SW Pacific W of Fiji; country; ✳, Port-Vila; pop 234,000

**Va·ra·na·si** \və-'rä-nə-sē\ city N India; pop 1,432,280

**Vat·i·can City** \'va-ti-kən\ independent state within Rome, Italy; pop 800

**Ven·e·zu·e·la** \,ve-nə-'zwā-lə, -zə-'wā-; ,bā-nā-'swä-lä\ country N South America; ✳, Caracas; pop 29,000,000 — **Ven·e·zu·e·lan** \-lən\ adj or n

**Ven·ice** \'ve-nəs\ or Italian **Ve·ne·zia** \ve-'net-sē-ä\ city N Italy on islands in Lagoon of Venice; *pop* 261,362 — **Ve·ne·tian** \və-'nē-shən\ *adj or n*

**Ven·tu·ra** \ven-'tur-ə, -'tyur-\ city & port SW California; *pop* 106,433

**Ve·ra·cruz** \ˌver-ə-'krüz, -'krüs\ city E Mexico; *pop* 552,156

**Ver·mont** \vər-'mänt\ state NE U.S.; ✳, Montpelier; *pop* 625,741 — **Ver·mont·er** \-'mänt-ər\ *n*

**Ve·ro·na** \ve-'rō-nä\ city N Italy W of Venice; *pop* 252,520

**Ver·sailles** \(ˌ)vər-'sī, ver-\ city N France, WSW suburb of Paris; *pop* 86,110

**Ve·su·vi·us** \və-'sü-vē-əs\ volcano about 4190 ft. (1277 m.) S Italy near Bay of Naples

**Vicks·burg** \'viks-ˌbərg\ city W Mississippi; *pop* 23,856

**Vic·to·ria** \vik-'tȯr-ē-ə\ **1** city, ✳ of British Columbia, Canada on Vancouver Island; *pop* 80,017 **2** island N Canada in Arctic Archipelago **3** state SE Australia, ✳, Melbourne; *pop* 5,354,042 **4** city & port, Hong Kong; *pop* 1,035,000 **5** seaport, ✳ of Seychelles; *pop* 26,000 — **Vic·to·ri·an** \vik-'tȯr-ē-ən\ *adj or n*

**Victoria, Lake** lake E Africa in Tanzania, Kenya, & Uganda

**Victoria Falls** waterfall 355 ft. (108 m.) S Africa in the Zambezi on border between Zambia & Zimbabwe

**Vi·en·na** \vē-'e-nə\ *or German* **Wien** \'vēn\ city, ✳ of Austria on the Danube; *pop* 1,700,000 — **Vi·en·nese** \ˌvē-ə-'nēz, -'nēs\ *adj or n*

**Vien·tiane** \(ˌ)vyen-'tyän\ city, ✳ of Laos; *pop* 200,000

**Vie·ques** \vē-'ā-käs\ island Puerto Rico off E end of main island; *pop* 9301

**Viet·nam** \vē-'et-'näm, vyet-, ˌvē-ət-, vēt-, -'näm\ country SE Asia in Indochina; ✳, Hanoi; *pop* 85,847,000 ; divided 1954–75 into the independent states of **North Vietnam** (✳, Hanoi) & **South Vietnam** (✳, Saigon) — **Viet·nam·ese** \vē-ˌet-nə-'mēz, ˌvyet-, ˌvē-ət-, ˌvēt-, -na-, -nä-, -'mēs\ *adj or n*

**Vila** — see PORT-VILA

**Vi·la No·va de Ga·ia** \'vē-lə-'nȯ-və-dē-'gī-ə\ city NW Portugal; *pop* 302,295

**Vil·ni·us** \'vil-nē-əs\ city, ✳ of Lithuania; *pop* 524,000

**Vin·land** \'vin-lənd\ a portion of the coast of North America visited & so called by Norse voyagers about 1000 A.D.; thought to be located along the North Atlantic in what is now E or NE Canada

**Vir·gin·ia** \vər-'ji-nyə, -'ji-nē-ə\ state E U.S.; ✳, Richmond; *pop* 8,001,024 — **Vir·gin·ian** \-nyən, -nē-ən\ *adj or n*

**Virginia Beach** city SE Virginia; *pop* 437,994

**Virginia City** locality W Nevada; *pop* 855

**Virgin Islands** island group West Indies E of Puerto Rico — see BRITISH VIRGIN ISLANDS, VIRGIN ISLANDS OF THE UNITED STATES

**Virgin Islands of the United States** the W islands of the Virgin Islands; U.S. territory; ✳, Charlotte Amalie (on Saint Thomas); *pop* 106,405

**Vi·sa·yan** \və-'sī-ən\ islands *cen* Philippines

**Vish·a·kha·pat·nam** \vi-ˌshä-kə-'pət-nəm\ *or* **Vis·a·kha·pat·nam** \vi-ˌsä-\ city E India; *pop* 1,728,128

**Vis·tu·la** \'vis-chə-lə, 'vish-chə-, 'vis-tə-\ river over 660 mi. (1062 km.) long Poland flowing N from the Carpathians

**Vi·ti Le·vu** \ˌvē-tē-'le-(ˌ)vü\ island SW Pacific; largest of the Fiji group

**Vlad·i·vos·tok** \ˌvla-də-və-'stäk, -'väs-ˌtäk\ city & port SE Russia on an inlet of Sea of Japan; *pop* 592,000

**Vol·ga** \'väl-gə, 'vȯl-, 'vōl-\ river about 2300 mi. (3700 km.) long W Russia; longest river in Europe

**Vol·go·grad** \'väl-gə-ˌgrad, 'vȯl-, 'vōl-, -ˌgrät\ city S Russia in Europe, on the Volga; *pop* 1,021,000

**Vol·ta** \'väl-tə, 'vȯl-, 'vōl-\ river about 300 mi. (485 km.) long Ghana flowing from **Lake Volta** (reservoir) into Gulf of Guinea

**Vo·ro·nezh** \və-'rȯ-nish\ city S *cen* Russia in Europe; *pop* 932,500

**Vosges** \'vōzh\ mountains NE France on W side of Rhine valley

**Wa·co** \'wā-(ˌ)kō\ city *cen* Texas; *pop* 124,805

**Wad·den·zee** \ˌvä-dᵊn-'zā\ inlet of the North Sea N Netherlands

**Wake** \'wāk\ island North Pacific N of Marshall Islands; U.S. territory

**Wake·field** \'wāk-ˌfēld\ city N England; *pop* 99,000

**Wa·la·chia** *or* **Wal·la·chia** \wä-'lā-kē-ə\ region S Romania between Transylvanian Alps & the Danube

**Wales** \'wālz\ *or Welsh* **Cym·ru** \'kəm-ˌrē\ principality SW Great Britain; a division of United Kingdom; ✳, Cardiff; *pop* 3,063,456

**Wal·lo·nia** \wä-'lō-nē-ə\ semiautonomous region S Belgium; *pop* 3,600,000

**Wal·sall** \'wȯl-ˌsȯl, -səl\ town W *cen* England; *pop* 68,000

**Wal·tham Forest** \'wȯl-thəm\ borough of NE Greater London, England; *pop* 258,000

**Wal·vis Bay** \'wȯl-vəs\ town & port W Namibia on Walvis Bay (inlet of the Atlantic); formerly administered by Republic of South Africa; *pop* 61,700

**Wands·worth** \'wän(d)z-(ˌ)wərth\ borough of SW Greater London, England; *pop* 307,000

**War·ren** \'wȯr-ən, 'wär-\ city SE Michigan; *pop* 134,056

**War·saw** \'wȯr-ˌsȯ\ *or Polish* **War·sza·wa**

\vär-'shä-vä\ city, ✳ of Poland; *pop* 1,700,000

**War·wick** \'wär-ik\ town *cen* England; *pop* 31,000

**War·wick·shire** \'wär-ik-,shir, -shər\ *or* **Warwick** county *cen* England

**Wa·satch** \'wȯ-,sach\ range of the Rockies SE Idaho & N *cen* Utah; highest Mount Timpanogos 12,008 ft. (3660 m ) in Utah

**Wash·ing·ton:** \'wȯ-shiŋ-tən, 'wä-\ **1** state NW U.S.; ✳, Olympia; *pop* 6,724,540 **2** city, ✳ of U.S.; having the same boundaries as District of Columbia; *pop* 601,723 — **Wash·ing·to·nian** \,wȯ-shiŋ-'tō-nē-ən, ,wä-, -nyən\ *adj or n*

**Washington, Mount** mountain 6288 ft. (1916 m.) N New Hampshire; highest in White Mountains

**Wa·ter·bury** \'wȯ-tə(r)-,ber-ē, 'wä-\ city W *cen* Connecticut; *pop* 110,366

**Wei·mar Republic** \'vī-,mär, 'wī-\ the German republic 1919–33

**Wel·land** \'we-lənd\ canal 27 mi. (44 km.) long SE Ontario connecting Lake Erie & Lake Ontario

**Wel·ling·ton** \'we-liŋ-tən\ city, ✳ of New Zealand; *pop* 179,466

**Wes·sex** \'we-siks\ ancient kingdom S England

**West Bank** area Middle East W of Jordan River; occupied by Israel since 1967 with parts having been transferred to Palestinian administration since 1993

**West Brom·wich** \'brä-mich\ town W *cen* England; *pop* 73,000

**West Co·vi·na** \kō-'vē-nə\ city SW California; *pop* 106,098

**Western Australia** state W Australia; ✳, Perth; *pop* 2,239,170 — **Western Australian** *adj or n*

**Western Cape** province SW Republic of South Africa; *pop* 5,822,734

**Western Ghats** — see GHATS

**Western Hemisphere** the half of the earth lying W of the Atlantic Ocean & comprising North America, South America, & surrounding waters

**Western Isles** former administrative area of W Scotland consisting of the Outer Hebrides

**Western Sahara** *formerly* **Spanish Sahara** territory NW Africa; occupied by Morocco; *pop* 522,000

**Western Samoa** — see SAMOA

**West Germany** — see GERMANY

**West Indies** islands lying between SE North America & N South America & consisting of the Greater Antilles, Lesser Antilles, & Bahamas — **West Indian** *adj or n*

**West Midlands** metropolitan county W *cen* England; includes Birmingham

**West·min·ster** \'wes(t)-,min(t)-stər\ city N *cen* Colorado NW of Denver; *pop* 106,114

**West Pakistan** the former W division of Pakistan now having the same boundaries as Pakistan

**West·pha·lia** \west-'fāl-yə, -'fā-lē-ə\ region W Germany E of the Rhine — **West·pha·lian** \west-'fāl-yən, -'fā-lē-ən\ *adj or n*

**West Point** site SE New York of United States Military Academy on W bank of Hudson River N of New York City

**West Quod·dy Head** \'kwä-dē\ cape; most easterly point of Maine & of the Lower 48

**West Sus·sex** \'sə-siks\ county SE England; *pop* 806,892

**West Valley City** city N Utah S of Salt Lake City; *pop* 129,480

**West Virginia** state E U.S.; ✳, Charleston; *pop* 1,852,994 — **West Virginian** *adj or n*

**West York·shire** metropolitan county NW England; includes Wakefield

**White** sea NW Russia in Europe

**White·horse** \'hwīt-,hȯrs, 'wīt-\ city, ✳ of Yukon, Canada; *pop* 23,276

**White Mountains** mountains N New Hampshire in the Appalachians — see WASHINGTON, MOUNT

**Whit·ney, Mount** \'hwit-nē, 'wit-\ mountain 14,495 ft. (4418 m.) SE *cen* California in Sierra Nevada; highest in U.S. outside of Alaska

**Wich·i·ta** \'wi-chə-,tȯ\ city S Kansas; *pop* 382,368

**Wichita Falls** city N Texas; *pop* 104,553

**Wien** — see VIENNA

**Wight, Isle of** — see ISLE OF WIGHT

**Wil·lem·stad** \'vi-ləm-,stät\ city, formerly ✳ of Netherlands Antilles; *pop* 93,600

**Wil·liams·burg** \'wil-yəmz-,bərg\ city SE Virginia; *pop* 14,068

**Wil·ming·ton** \'wil-miŋ tən\ city N Delaware; largest in state; *pop* 70,851

**Wilt·shire** \'wilt-,shir, -shər\ county S England; *pop* 470,981

**Win·ches·ter** \'win-,ches-tər, -chəs-tər\ city S England; *pop* 45,000

**Win·der·mere** \'win-də(r)-,mir\ lake NW England in Lake District

**Wind·hoek** \'vint-,hùk\ city, ✳ of Namibia; *pop* 233,529

**Wind·sor** \'win-zər\ city S Ontario, Canada on Detroit River; *pop* 210,891

**Wind·ward Islands** \'wind-wərd\ islands West Indies in the S Lesser Antilles extending S from Martinique but not including Barbados, Tobago, or Trinidad

**Win·ni·peg** \'wi-nə-,peg\ city, ✳ of Manitoba, Canada; *pop* 663,617

**Winnipeg, Lake** lake S *cen* Manitoba, Canada

**Win·ni·pe·sau·kee, Lake** \,wi-nə-pə-'sȯ-kē\ lake *cen* New Hampshire

**Win·ston–Sa·lem** \,win(t)-stən-'sā-ləm\ city N *cen* North Carolina; *pop* 229,617

**Wis·con·sin** \wi-'skän(t)-sən\ state N cen U.S.; ✳, Madison; pop 5,686,986 — **Wis·con·sin·ite** \-sə-,nīt\ n

**Wit·wa·ters·rand** \'wit-,wò-tərz-,rand, -,wä-, -,ränd, -,ränt\ ridge of gold-bearing rock NE Republic of South Africa

**Wol·lon·gong** \'wü-lən-,gäŋ, -,gòŋ\ city SE Australia in E New South Wales S of Sydney; pop 245,942

**Wol·ver·hamp·ton** \,wùl-vər-'ham(p)-tən\ town W cen England NW of Birmingham; pop 210,000

**Worces·ter** \'wùs-tər\ city E cen Massachusetts; pop 181,045

**Wran·gell, Mount** \'raŋ-gəl\ volcano 14,163 ft. (4317 m.) S Alaska in **Wrangell Mountains**

**Wro·claw** \'vròt-,swäf, -,släv\ city SW Poland in Silesia; pop 630,500

**Wu·han** \'wü-'hän\ city E cen China; pop 8,663,500

**Wu·xi** or **Wu–hsi** \'wü-'shē\ city E China; pop 3,151,000

**Wy·o·ming** \wī-'ō-miŋ\ state NW U.S.; ✳, Cheyenne; pop 563,626 — **Wy·o·ming·ite** \-miŋ-,īt\ n

**Xi'·an** or **Hsi–an** \'shē-'än\ city E cen China; pop 5,853,500

**Xianggang** — see HONG KONG

**Xin·jiang Uy·gur** or **Sin·kiang Ui·ghur** \'shin-'jyäŋ-'wē-gər\ region W China between the Kunlun & Altai mountains; pop 21,815,815

**Xizang** — see TIBET

**Xu·zhou** \'shü-'jō\ or **Sü·chow** \'shü-'jō, 'sü-\ city E China; pop 2,634,500

**Yak·i·ma** \'ya-kə-,mò\ city S cen Washington; pop 91,067

**Ya·lu** \'yä-(,)lü\ river 500 mi. (804 km.) long SE Manchuria & North Korea

**Ya·mous·sou·kro** \,yä-mə-'sü-krō\ town, official ✳ of Cote d'Ivoire; pop 207,412

**Yan·gon** \,yän-'gòn\ formerly **Ran·goon** \ran-'gün, raŋ-\ city, former ✳ of Myanmar; pop 4,477,600

**Yangtze** — see CHANG

**Yaoun·dé** \yaün-'dā\ city, ✳ of Cameroon; pop 1,817,524

**Yap** \'yap, 'yäp\ island W Pacific in the W Carolines; pop 11,377

**Ya·ren** \'yä-,rən\ district containing ✳ of Nauru; pop 747

**Ya·ro·slavl** \,yär-ə-'slä-v°l\ city cen Russia in Europe, NE of Moscow; pop 591,486

**Yaz·oo** \ya-'zü, 'ya-(,)zü\ river W cen Mississippi

**Ye·ka·te·rin·burg** \yi-'ka-tə-rən-,bərg, yi-,kä-ti-rēm-'bùrk\ formerly **Sverd·lovsk** \sverd-'lòfsk\ city N Russia, in cen Ural Mountains; pop 1,350,000

**Yellow 1** — see HUANG **2** sea, section of East China Sea between N China, North Korea, & South Korea

**Yel·low·knife** \'ye-lō-,nīf\ town, ✳ of Northwest Territories, Canada; pop 19,234

**Ye·men** \'ye-mən\ country S Arabia bordering on Red Sea & Gulf of Aden; ✳, Sanaa; pop 24,500,000 — **Ye·me·ni** \'ye-mə-nē\ adj or n — **Ye·men·ite** \-mə-,nīt\ adj or n

**Ye·ni·sey** or **Ye·ni·sei** \,yi-ni-'sā\ river over 2500 mi. (4022 km.) long cen Russia, flowing N into Arctic Ocean

**Ye·re·van** \,yer-ə-'vän\ city, ✳ of Armenia; pop 1,100,000

**Yo·ko·ha·ma** \,yō-kō-'hä-mä\ city Japan in SE Honshu on Tokyo Bay S of Tokyo; pop 3,688,773

**Yon·kers** \'yäŋ-kərz\ city SE New York N of New York City; pop 195,976

**York** \'yòrk\ city N England; pop 153,000

**York, Cape** cape NE Australia in Queensland at N tip of Cape York Peninsula

**York·shire** \-,shir, -shər\ former county N England

**Yo·sem·i·te Falls** \yō-'se-mə-tē\ waterfall E California in Yosemite Valley; includes two falls, the upper 1430 ft. (436 m.) & the lower 320 ft. (98 m.)

**Youngs·town** \'yəŋz-,taùn\ city NE Ohio; pop 66,982

**Yu·ca·tán** \,yü-kə-'tan, -kä-'tän\ peninsula SE Mexico & N Central America including Belize & N Guatemala

**Yu·go·sla·via** \,yü-gō-'slä-vē-ə, ,yü-gə-\ **1** former country S Europe including Serbia, Montenegro, Slovenia, Croatia, Bosnia and Herzegovina, & Macedonia; ✳, Belgrade **2** — see SERBIA AND MONTENEGRO — **Yu·go·slav** \,yü-gō-'släv, -'slav; 'yü-gō-,\ or **Yu·go·sla·vi·an** \,yü-gō-'slä-vē-ən, -gə-\ adj or n

**Yu·kon** \'yü-,kän\ **1** river 1979 mi. (3185 km.) long NW Canada & Alaska flowing into Bering Sea **2** or formerly **Yukon Territory** territory NW Canada; ✳, Whitehorse; pop 33,897

**Yu·ma** \'yü-mə\ city SW corner of Arizona on the Colorado; pop 93,064

**Za·greb** \'zä-,greb\ city, ✳ of Croatia; pop 687,000

**Zaire** \zä-'ir\ **1** river in Africa — see CONGO 1 **2** country in Africa — see CONGO 2 — **Zair·ean** or **Zair·ian** \zä-'ir-ē-ən\ adj or n

**Zam·be·zi** or **Zam·be·si** \zam-'bē-zē, zäm-'bä-zē\ river about 1700 mi. (2735 km.) long SE Africa flowing from NW Zambia into Mozambique Channel

**Zam·bia** \'zam-bē-ə\ formerly **Northern Rhodesia** country S Africa N of the Zambezi; ✳, Lusaka; pop 13,200,000 — **Zam·bi·an** \'zam-bē-ən\ adj or n

**Zan·zi·bar** \'zan-zə-,bär\ island Tanzania off NE Tanganyika coast; united 1964 with Tanganyika forming Tanzania

**Za·po·rizh·zhya** or **Za·po·ro·zh'ye** \,zä-pə-'rēzh-zhyə\ city SE Ukraine; *pop* 815,000

**Zhang·jia·kou** \'jäŋ-'jyä-'kō\ *or* **Kal·gan** \'kal-'gan\ city NE China NW of Beijing; *pop* 925,000

**Zhdanov** — see MARIUPOL

**Zheng·zhou** *or* **Cheng–chou** \'jən-'jō\ city NE *cen* China; *pop* 3,965,500

**Zim·ba·bwe** \zim-'bä-bwe, -(ₗ)bwä\ *for-merly* **Rhodesia** country S Africa S of Zambezi River; ✳, Harare; *pop* 13,061,000 — **Zim·ba·bwe·an** \-ən\ *adj or n*

**Zui·der Zee** \ₗzī-dər-'zā, -'zē\ — see IJS-SELMEER

**Zu·lu·land** \'zü-(ₗ)lü-ₗland\ territory E Republic of South Africa on Indian Ocean

**Zu·rich** \'zúr-ik\ city N Switzerland; *pop* 363,300